The Timber Press Dictionary of Plant Names

The Timber Press
Dictionary
of Plant Names

Walter Erhardt
Erich Götz
Nils Bödeker
Siegmund Seybold
Edited by Allen Coombes

Timber Press
Portland | London

The Haseltine Building
133 s.w. Second Avenue, Suite 450
Portland, Oregon 97204-3527
www.timberpress.com

2 The Quadrant
135 Salusbury Road
London NW6 6RJ
www.timberpress.co.uk

ISBN-13: 978-1-60469-115-3

All maps prepared by Helmuth Flubacher, Waiblingen, Germany
in accordance with authors' drafts or noted sources.
Designed by Dick Malt
Printed in the United States of America

Catalogue records for this book are also available from the Library of
Congress and the British Library.

Contents

6

Foreword

The Timber Press Dictionary of Plant Names makes the wealth of knowledge contained in the 18th edition of the *Zander Handwörterbuch der Pflanzennamen* more accessible to English-speaking readers. Changes include some minor amendments to the introduction and the addition of a considerable number of English common names used in English-speaking countries, primarily the United States of America and Great Britain.

The bulk of the text remains unchanged, except for a few small corrections. Although at times the temptation to start moving names around was strong, it was resisted and I fully sympathise with the feelings on this matter expressed by the authors in the foreword to the 18th edition. A publication such as this is the better for being on the conservative side. While opinions can be expressed one year and contradicted the next, there needs to be some stability in a book that will remain in use for many years.

That said, it must be understood that changes need to be accepted at some time and there is no need to retain an old name just because it is familiar to us. The quotation from Peter Yeo that states "… classifications are never right or wrong …" is a sharp contradiction to those who say there is only one correct name for a plant. In fact, the correct name is often a matter of opinion. The example of the *Magnoliaceae* cited in the previous foreword shows this perfectly, as well as demonstrating how quickly things are moving. When the foreword was written in 2008, the online World Checklist of Selected Plant Families listed three genera (reduced from seven in the 2006 printed version) but it now lists only two (*Liriodendron* and *Magnolia*). On the other hand, the Flora of China (online version) lists 13 genera in the family *Magnoliaceae*, having added two new ones. An example of two divergent opinions, both, in their own view, correct.

At least there are no such complications with common names. Or are there? In fact common names are a great deal more complicated and confusing than scientific names. Although there may be more than one correct (depending on opinion) scientific name for a plant, at least an authoritative publication can only use one of these. A quick glance at this publication will show that there are often several common names for each plant. While sometimes this is simply a case of each language having its own common name for a plant there are also occasions when one plant can have many different common names in a single language, any one of which can also be used, correctly, for a completely different plant. There is a current trend for inventing new common names in the belief that these are needed. Not only does this compound the complications, these names are often meaningless, mere translations of the scientific name. All the names added for this edition are already in use, no new names have been invented.

Any problems with confusing common names are not new. In 1876, the botanist, author and horticulturist Thomas Meehan wrote:

"We have a suspicion that 'common' names made all that great trouble at the tower of Babel."

Allen Coombes
Puebla, Mexico
November 2009

I About the Authors

1 Who was the originator of the *Dictionary of Plant Names*?

Prof. Dr. Robert Zander

Born 26.07.1892 Magdeburg, died 8.05.1969 Berlin

Editor of the following editions of the *Zander Handwörterbuch der Pflanzennamen*: 1st ed. (1927), with supplement 1928; 2nd ed. (1932); 3rd ed. (1936); 4th ed. (1938); 5th ed. (1938); 6th ed. (1940); 7th ed. (1954); 8th ed. (1955); 9th ed. (1964).

Robert Zander led a rich life that was devoted to botany and horticulture. His work is reflected most conspicuously in his numerous publications and in the establishment of the German Horticultural Library, with 35,000 volumes it is one of the most extensive horticultural libraries in the world. In his final working years, Robert Zander concentrated on recording the contents of horticultural journals. His index cards from the time bear witness to a laborious task, the results of which still benefit specialists working in the horticultural field today.

The diversity of Robert Zander's work is evident in the list of his most important publications. For years, he had a formative influence on a number of journals as an editor, including the renowned *Gartenflora*, whose publication had to be discontinued during the Second World War. However, Zander's most influential publication was the *Zander Handwörterbuch der Pflanzennamen*, which has been revised and edited by Allen Coombes to produce *The Timber Press Dictionary of Plant Names*. Zander had the stimulus for the original work in 1926, when the Imperial German Horticultural Union summoned him to Berlin to produce a dictionary of plant names as the basis for a standardized naming of plants used in horticulture. The first edition was published in 1927, with a supplement in 1928.

The *Zander Handwörterbuch der Pflanzennamen* became an indispensable reference work for horticulturists, foresters, pharmacists and many botanists, i. e., all those wishing to find the correct name of a plant quickly and reliably, whether used commercially or otherwise. *The Timber Press Dictionary of Plant Names* fulfils these same goals for an international readership. Robert Zander's work on horticultural nomenclature led to his joining the International Commission for the Nomenclature of Cultivated Plants, for which he served as Secretary at the 12th International Horticultural Congress in Berlin. He was an active member of the German Study Group for Horticultural Nomenclature right up to his death.

During his life, in particular as head of the horticultural library that today is affiliated to the Library of the Technical University of Berlin, he let countless people partake in his great knowledge, including his unique grasp of the literature, stimulating them and giving them every possible assistance in their scientific work. His extensive index system, comprising some 216,000 index cards on horticultural literature and including the personal details of many gardeners, can now be viewed on the Internet at http://zander.ub.tu-berlin.de/.

List of most important publications:
- *Beitrag zur Kenntnis der tertiären Hölzer des Geiseltals.* Doctoral dissertation, in *Braunkohle* Vol. XXII, No. 2, 1923.
- *Führer durch den Botanischen Garten der Universität Halle/Saale,* 1925.
- *Handwörterbuch der Pflanzennamen und ihrer Erklärungen.* Gärtnerische Verlagsgesellschaft Berlin, Berlin. From the 7th ed. on: Verlag Eugen Ulmer, Stuttgart.
- *Wunder der Blüten,* in *Weg zum Wissen* Vol. 76, 1927.
- *Schmarotzende Pflanzen,* 1930.
- *Zanders grosses Gartenlexikon,* 1934.
- *Wörterbuch der gärtnerischen Fachausdrücke in vier Sprachen,* 1938.
- *Fachwörterbuch der Konservenindustrie in acht Sprachen,* 1939.
- *Die Kunst des Pflanzenbeschreibens,* 1947.
- *Deutsch-Botanisches Wörterbuch,* 1940, 2nd ed. *Kleines Botanisches Fremdwörterbuch,* 1947.
- *Die Pflanze im Liebesleben der Völker,* 1951.
- *Geschichte des Gärtnertums,* 1952.
- Contribution to *Leitfaden für den gärtnerischen Berufsschulunterricht,* 1929.
- Contribution to *Kluges Alphabet,* 1934/35.
- In collaboration with Dr. CLARA TESCHNER, *Der Rosengarten, eine geschichtliche Studie durch zwei Jahrtausende,* 1939.
- *Geschichte des Obstbaues,* in *Trenkles Lehrbuch des Obstbaus,* 1942, and also subsequent editions.

2 Who has revised the work?

Dr. h. c. Fritz Joseph Encke
Born 1.08.1904, Cologne; died 4.03.2002, Greifenstein (Hesse)

Co-editor of the following editions of the *Zander Handwörterbuch der Pflanzennamen*: 9th ed. (1964); 10th ed. (1972); 11th ed. (1979); 12th ed. (1980); 13th ed. (1984); 14th ed. (1993); 15th ed. (1994).

In the 1920s, Fritz Joseph Encke worked as a horticulturist in German and American nurseries, and from 1929 in the Palmengarten in Frankfurt, where he was to serve as director from 1945 to 1968. The continued existence of the Palmengarten following the Second World War and the later establishment of the important plant collection there were due to his considerable personal efforts. In 1968, he was awarded an honorary doctorate, and he also holds the Order of the Federal Republic of Germany, 1st Class. It is clear from his extensive literary oeuvre that he is committed to imparting horticultural and botanical knowledge to specialists and plant enthusiasts. He keeps abreast of developments in botany and has had a crucial influence on the *Zander Handwörterbuch der Pflanzennamen* in the years after Robert Zander. His abundant knowledge and dedicated working method have made it possible to include the home territories of all the plant species included in this *Dictionary*.

List of most important publications:
- *Pflanzen für Zimmer und Balkon,* 1st ed. 1952 until 8th ed. 1964; 9th ed. 1973 until 13th ed. 1987, entitled *Zimmerpflanzen.*
- *Sommerblumen,* 1961.

- *Die schönsten Kalt- und Warmhauspflanzen*, 1968; 2nd ed. 1987, entitled *Kalt- und Warm-hauspflanzen.*
- *Zwergsteingärten*, 1978.
- *Kletterpflanzen für Haus und Garten*, 1980.
- *Kübelpflanzen*, 1982.

Dr. Arno Fritz Günther Buchheim

Born 26.10.1924, Döbeln, died 20.01.2007, Mentor, Ohio, USA

Co-editor of the following editions of the *Zander Handwörterbuch der Pflanzennamen*: 9th ed. (1964); 10th ed. (1972); 11th ed. (1979); 12th ed. (1980); 13th ed. (1984); 14th ed. (1993); 15th ed. (1994).

Arno Fritz Günther Buchheim was a botanist, bibliographer and librarian. He worked for a time at the Botanical Museum Berlin-Dahlem, and from 1963 to 1981 he was at the Hunt Institute for Botanical Documentation in Pittsburgh, Pennsylvania. In 1985, he moved to the John Carter Brown Library, Providence, Rhode Island, where he worked until his retirement in 1993. His main areas of work were the taxonomy and nomenclature of central European cultivated plants and the bibliography of botanical literature from 1730 to 1840.

List of most important publications:
- Contributor to the *Syllabus der Pflanzenfamilien*, 12th ed., 1968.
- Co-editor of the *Botanico-Periodicum-Huntianum*, 1968.

Prof. Dr. Siegmund Gerhard Seybold

Born 5.09.1939, Stuttgart

Co-editor of the following editions of the *Zander Handwörterbuch der Pflanzennamen*: 10th ed. (1972); 11th ed. (1979); 12th ed. (1980); 13th ed. (1984); 14th ed. (1993); 15th ed. (1994); 16th ed. (2000); 17th ed. (2002), 18th ed. (2008).

Siegmund Seybold is a botanist. He worked at the State Museum of Natural History in Stuttgart, and is an Honorary Professor at the University of Stuttgart. His work focused on the flora of the German federal state of Baden-Württemberg.

As has been the case in the past, in future editions he will continue to be responsible for updating the translations of species designations, as well as maintaining the list of authors' names, including the short biographies.

List of most important publications:
- Co-editor of *Die Farn- und Blütenpflanzen Baden-Württembergs* in eight volumes, 1990 to 1998.
- Contributor to SCHMEIL and FITSCHEN, *Flora von Deutschland und angrenzender Gebiete*, from the 89th ed., 1993. From the 93rd ed., 2006 sole contributor; issuer of this work on CD-ROM, 2001.
- *Die wissenschaftlichen Namen der Pflanzen und was sie bedeuten*, 2002, 2nd ed., 2005.
- Contribution to the *Index Holmiensis*, from 1988.

3   Who are the current authors of the work?

Walter Erhardt

Born 19.02.1952, Kulmbach

Co-editor of the 16th (2000) and 17th (2002) editions of the *Zander Handwörterbuch der Pflanzennamen*, 18th ed. (2008).

Walter Erhardt is a teacher and media and information consultant to the German administrative district of Kulmbach, as well as being the head of the media centre there. As a horticultural writer, he has written numerous books and articles. His intensive occupation with plants and his literary work led to the establishment of an extensive botanical library, which amongst other things contains nearly all the international registers of cultivars. He compiled the data for the publication of the *Zander Handwörterbuch der Pflanzennamen* and verified their nomenclatural accuracy. Additionally, he attempted to solve contentious nomenclatural issues by consulting specialists both in Germany and abroad. German plant names represent for him another important field.

List of most important publications:

- *Hemerocallis* (day-lilies), 1988; translation into English, 1992.
- *Pflanzen-Einkaufsführer*, 1990; published in several languages from the 2nd ed. on, entitled *PPP-Index*: 2nd ed. 1995; 3rd ed. 1997; 4th ed. 2000, with the title *Pflanze gesucht?*.
- *Schöne Usambaraveilchen und andere Gesnerien*, 1993.
- *Narzissen, Narcissi, Daffodils*, 1993.
- Contribution to the book *35.000 plantes* (published by the Société Nationale d'Horticulture de France), 1997.
- *Namensliste der Koniferen – List of Conifer Names*, 2005.

Dr. Erich Götz

Born 12.12.1940, Munich

Co-editor of the 16th (2000) and 17th (2002) editions of the *Zander Handwörterbuch der Pflanzennamen*, 18th ed. (2008).

Erich Götz was an unsalaried lecturer at the University of Hohenheim. He taught and researched there at the Institute of Botany, where he was also in charge of a very extensive plant collection. He is considered to be an excellent systematist.

His areas of work include the garden perennial shrubs, cacti, European trees and shrubs, and central European wild plants. In particular, he has researched the entries concerning the origin and use of both hitherto and newly included species.

List of most important publications:

- *Die Gehölze der Mittelmeerländer*, 1975.
- With H. Knodel: *Erkenntnisgewinnung in der Biologie*, 1980.
- With G. Gröner: *Kakteen*, 7th ed., 2000.
- Additionally, a series of book contributions.

Nils Bödeker
Born 22.05.1966, Mettmann

Co-editor of the 16th (2000) and 17th (2002) editions of the *Zander Handwörterbuch der Pflanzennamen*, 18th ed. (2008).

Following his studies in landscape husbandry, Nils Bödeker dedicated himself to software development in this specialist field. The main focus of his work has been the development of user-friendly software programs for the end user. On the basis of his well-structured database, it has been possible to compile, process and supplement the data in the *Zander Handwörterbuch der Pflanzennamen* using digital means.

List of most important publications:
– *PLANTUS*, 2nd edition, 1999 in collaboration with PETER KIERMEIER.
– *PLANTUS-SÜD (CD-ROM)*, 2000, in collaboration with CHRISTOPH WIESCHUS.

Additional publications on the topic of databases, in various specialist horticultural journals.

Prof. Dr. Siegmund Gerhard Seybold
see above

Allen Coombes
Born 07.12.1951, Syon Park

Allen Coombes is a botanist who worked for the Sir Harold Hillier Gardens in Hampshire for many years and is now Coordinator of Scientific Collections at the University Botanic Garden in Puebla, Mexico. He has been a member of Hortax, the Horticultural Taxonomy Group, for several years and he is also a member of the International Dendrology Society's Scientific and Education Committee, the IUCN/SSC Global Tree Specialist Group and was President of the International Oak Society 2006-2009. He is the author of the bestselling *Dictionary of Plant Names* published by Timber Press in the U.S.A. as well as several books and other publications on woody plants.

II An introduction to botanical nomenclature

1 How are botanical names formed?

It should be remembered that plant names are merely a means of designation. Like other words, they have been subject to changes in meaning. The first flower to be designated *Chrysanthemum* was evidently yellow-flowered (*chrysos* = gold, *anthemon* = flower). Later, this word became the generic name. Subject to many exceptions, it can be said that plant names tend to refer to:

- The qualities of the plant, or parts of it, e. g. *Adiántum* = cannot be moistened (*a* = not, *diainein* = to moisten), *tuberósus* = bulbous (*tuber* = tuber or bulb).
- The home territory of the plant, e. g. *Castánea* = the plant from Kastana in Thessalia, *bogorènsis* = from Buitenzorg in Java (Buitenzorg is a Dutch name which means "without worry" or "beyond worry"; the Javanese name for the settlement is Bogor).
- The similarity to another plant, to animals or to certain objects: *Bellis* – *Bellidiástrum* (*-ástrum* indicates the similarity), *Artemísia* – *artemisiifólius* (*artemisia*-leaved).
- Important people, such as saints or scientists, after whom the plant is named: *Robínia* (after the gardener ROBIN, who imported the plant around 1600), *engleriánus* (after the botanist ENGLER), *Dianthus* (literally "flower of the Gods"), *mariae* (dedicated to the Virgin Mary).
- The use of the plant: *Aristolóchia* (= the best for giving birth), *torminális* (= for the alleviation of colic), etc.

The *generic names* make up the noun and have a particular gender: masculine (-m-), feminine (-f-) or neuter (-n-). There are, however, so many exceptions to the rules for determining the gender that we have decided to specify the gender of each generic name in the alphabetical list, rather than itemizing the rules here with all their exceptions. Trees are usually feminine, even if they often end in *-us*, hence *Táxus* (-f-), *Búxus* (-f-), but *Ácer* and *Brosimum*, amongst others, are exceptions to the rule. The *specific epithets* (colloquially referred to as "species names", although this designation is incorrect, since the name of a species is made up of the combination of a generic name with a specific epithet) are mostly adjectives, the endings of which are modified according to the gender of the genus with which they are associated.

The modification of gender in the following order (from left to right) is:

male	female	neuter
-us	*-a*	*-um*
-er	*-a*	*-um*
-er	*-is*	*-e*
-is	*-is*	*-e*
-or	*-or*	*-us*

Additionally, there are endings that are the same for all three genders:

- All main words in the first case (nominative). This is especially the case if a generic name is used as the specific epithet for another genus; in this case, it remains unchanged. For example, to TOURNEFORT's genus *Cichórium* (-n-) are added the species that BAUHIN lists as the independent genus *Endívia* (-f-) and HERMANN as *Ìntybus* (-m-). The resultant name is therefore *Cichórium endívia* (not *C. endivium*), and *Cichórium íntybus* (not *C. intybum*). A similar situation exists for *Schínus molle* (not *mollis*), since *Mólle* was for TOURNEFORT and LINNAEUS a generic name.
- Proper names, too, remain unchanged in generic names in the second case (genitive), singular and plural, e.g. *éngleri*. On the other hand, names such as *englieriánus, dielsiánus* or other adjectives named after persons are regularly formed with -us, -a or -um.
- Specific epithets consisting of two words also remain unchanged, e.g. *agnus-castus*.
- All specific epithets of foreign languages that do not have Latin endings, e.g., *mono* in the case of *Ácer móno*.
- Specific epithets that consist of two words, e.g. *agnus-castus*.
- The epithets of subspecies (subsp. ...), varieties (var. ...), forms (fo. ...), etc. have, when they are adjectives, the same gender as the generic name, e.g.: *Andrósace cárnea* subsp. *brigantíaca, Cápsicum baccatum* var. *péndulum, Hydrangea macrophýlla* fo. *coerúlea*. This also applies if the specific epithet for the species is a former generic name and had a different gender from that of the generic name, e.g. *Dáphne* (-f-) *mezéreum* var. *álba*.

2   How are botanical names pronounced?

Botanical Latin is principally a written language, but there are occasions when Latin words – particularly plant names – have to be spoken, and this may cause quite unnecessary anxiety or criticism. Latin is spoken by different people in so many different ways that the English-speaking world has tended to adopt a relaxed attitude to the whole issue. There are no hard and fast rules of pronunciation or accentuation: the important thing is to be able to understand, and to be understood. Latin speakers tend to apply the rules of pronunciation which apply to their own mother-tongue: hence Italians, Spanish, French and Germans all have their idiosyncrasies that sound strange to our ears when they speak Latin. Church Latin offers further rules and complications. Additionally, within the English-speaking world, there is a division between traditional pronunciation and the academic pronunciation which is taught in the classics faculties of our universities. In practice, the everyday pronunciation of plant names tends more towards the traditional pronunciation than the academic, but it cannot be emphasized too strongly that there are no rules for pronouncing botanical Latin – speakers should concentrate instead upon making themselves understood.

That said, there are a number of generally accepted conventions which help to ensure that people do not have problems when they pronounce botanical names. One is that, with the exception of varietal names, all scientific plant names should be pronounced consistently; there is, in fact, a high degree of unanimity on the correct pronunciation of words derived from ancient languages. But the convention on pronunciation is full of exceptions, largely because nearly 80 percent of generic names and 30 percent of specific epithets are derived from languages other than Latin and Greek – often from proper names. Different nationalities pronounce letters in different ways. For example, generic names such as *Choisya, Decaisnea, Deschampsia, Duchesnea, Lejeunia* and *Michauxia* are all derived from French surnames, and will be pronounced differently by native French speakers than English speakers. Likewise, Germans will tend to pronounce such names as *Deutzia*, *Fuchsia*, *Heuchera* and *Weigela* according to the rules of German pronunciation, while botanists from the Slavonic world can be expected to pronounce such epithets as *przewalskii*, *warscewiczii* and *warshenewskiana* in ways that seem strange to the rest of us. They have the same problem with English names: it is sometimes difficult for them to know how we pronounce such names as *Forsythia*, *Cattleya*, *Downingia* and *Humea*. And there is a further problem, which is that, of all European languages, English is the least phonetic, so that it becomes difficult even for a native English speaker to know how to pronounce such names as *Leycestria*, *Mahonia* and *Menziesia*. Botanists in such countries as Germany and Austria have for many years tried to impose a uniform formula for the pronunciation of all botanical Latin. The English-speaking world is much more pragmatic, and insists that there can be no correct system of pronunciation. There is much to be said in favour of uniformity, but the worlds of botany and horticulture have a long way to go before any rules of pronunciation are universally accepted in principle, let alone practised in everyday usage.

All pronunciation is governed by three variables: the length of the vowels, the actual sound of a spoken letter and the incidence of stress. In order to make it easier to recognize whether a vowel is pronounced short or long (this is also important for the rules of accentuation – see below), we use two different accent marks in this Section (but not in the rest of the book!). The acute accent (á) indicates a short vowel, and the grave (à) a long vowel. Pronunciation is therefore as follows:

short and stressed:	long and stressed:
á like *a* in marigold	à like *a* in grass
é like *e* in cress	è like *a* in hay
í like *i* in chicory	ì like *ee* in seed
ó like *o* in hops	ò like *o* in crocus
ú like *u* in bush	ù like *oo* in bloom

Guidelines for vowels

- All vowels are pronounced separately, e. g. "del-to-id-es" (= *deltoides*), not "del-toi-des". Purists sometimes place a diacritic mark (a dieresis or umlaut) over the second vowel, to make this distinction: hence *Aizoön*, *Aloë* and, of course, *deltoïdes*. In daily horticultural use, however, there is no objection to colloquial pronunciations: thus, *Cotoneaster* is generally pronounced "co-to-ne-a-ster" by botanists, but not infrequently "co-to-nee-ster" by gardeners. And, since German vowels with umlauts, ä, ö and ü, are often transcribed in ordinary German writing as ae, oe and ue, they are treated as one vowel, not two, when they occur in this volume.
- *I* is pronounced like ee in "seed" at the beginning of a word, never like j or y: thus *ionánthus* (= violet-like flowers) is "ee-o-nan-thus", not "jonánthus" or "yonánthus". It is worth noting here that all languages except English invariably pronounce the long *i* as ee: thus, we often refer to *Víola* as "V-eye-ola", and the ending attached to a specific epithet is usually pronounced "i-eye" by English speakers (but no one else). Likewise, the dipthong *-ae* is usually pronounced ee (as in seed), e. g. *graecus* ("greek-us"), but as "eye" when it occurs after *i* at the end of a specific epithet, e. g. *banksiae* ("banks-i-eye").
- *Y* is pronounced like y in yacht at the beginning of a word, or when it is between two vowels (*delavayi*). Otherwise, it is pronounced like a short í (see above) as in *scotophýllus*

(sko-to-fill-us) (= dark-leaved), or like "eye", as in *scotóphyllus,* pronounced sko-to-fye-lus (= growing in shade).

Guidelines for consonants

English speakers pronounce Latin consonants as if they were English. Thus:

- *C* is normally hard before a, o and u ("cat", "cot", "cut") and soft before e, i and y ("cell", "city", "cyst"). The same is true of *g,* which is normally hard before a, o and u ("gate", "got", "gut") and soft before e, i and y ("gem", "gin", "gyre"). These conventions do not apply to native speakers of other languages. The hard *c* is pronounced ts by Slavs, while the soft *c* is pronounced ts by Germans, ch by Italians and th by Spaniards.
- *Ch* has a hard pronunciation in German and Italian, but soft in English and Spanish.
- *Ti* is pronounced "ti", not "tsi": *lutetianus* (= Parisian) is pronounced "lu-te-ti-a-nus", not "lu-tet-si-a-nus". Italian speakers, however, pronounce *ti* as "tsi". And there are many similar anomalies which one hears, and learns to recognize. For example, some Italians pronounce *gu* (e. g., *guineénsis*) as gw, some Spaniards pronounce *qu* (e. g., *Quércus*) as a k, and some Germans pronounce *Scílla* as "stsil-la" (giving it a hard German s, and enunciating every consonant separately). Italians, on the other hand, pronounce it like the girl's name "Sheila".

Germans, in particular, tend to use different stresses and vowel lengths, and insist that their usage is correct. Thus, they refer to *Erìca, balsàmina, fólius, Gladíolus, róseus, glòssa* and *túba.*

They point out that a different pronunciation may change the meaning of a word and cite many examples: *àpis* = bull, *ápis* = bee; *làbrum* = tub, basin, *lábrum* = lip; *làtus* = wide, *látus* = side; *òs* = face, *ós* = bone. They insist that *pòpulus* is a poplar, but *pópulus* is the people. Nevertheless, English speakers invariably refer to the tree as *Pópulus.* German authorities point out that transferring the accent to another syllable may result in a different meaning: e. g., *bíos* = life, *biós* = bow / arch. And they point out that these differences exist in English (e. g., contént/cóntent). But stress is less of a problem for English and American speakers of Latin. Ultimately, anglophones insist that Latin is a written language, and that the principal aim when speaking it should be to ensure that the audience recognizes the name of the plant in question: too many rules of pronunciation dissuade people from trying to use it at all.

Part of the problem, in the English-speaking world, is the difference between the traditional pronunciation of Latin, and the academic pronunciation set out by such writers as Allen, W. S., *Vox Latina* (London, 1978). Academics pronounce *v* as w, *oe* as oi, *ei* as ay, and *ch* as k. Moreover, *c* and *g* are always hard, so that Cicero is pronounced "Kikero". Some botanists and horticulturists in the English-speaking world adopt some elements of the academic pronunciation for some words or on some occasions. But the traditional pronunciation prevails in almost every English-speaking country, institute and organization.

The same is true of accentuation: in English, there are no rules. As a general guide, however, the stress should be put on the penultimate syllable. If the word has more than two syllables, and the penultimate syllable contains a short vowel, then the accent is shifted back to the previous syllable. How does one discover whether that penultimate syllable is short or long? Here, English speakers again part company with the foreign authorities. The English generally apply the traditions of English pronunciation, and then put the stress where it would be in English. Thus, the German authorities argue that *Sempervivum* should be pronounced "sem-per-vì-vum" (since the *i* in *vìvum* [= living] is long), but *sempervirens* should be pronounced "sem-pèr-vi-rens" (since the *i* in *vìrens* (= greening) is short). The English tend to put the stress in *Sempervivum* upon the penultimate *i*, because they pronounce it "sem-per-vee-vum" or "sem-per-vye-vum" (i.e. with a long English vowel). But they invariably refer not to "sem-pèr-vi-rens", but to "sem-per-vì-rens" for exactly the same reason, i.e. because they put a long vowel on the penultimate syllable and refer to "sem-per-veer-ens" or "sem-per-vye-rens".

The classical authorities sometimes look to the original Greek to determine where the stress should lie. Thus, they distinguish a short e (ε = epsilon) from a long e (η = eta), and a short o (o= omicron) and long o (ω = omega), and maintain that knowing the original Greek word helps us to decide where to put the stress. However, they are the first to point out that such rules have many exceptions (not least because a long vowel may become a short one when a noun is declined or a verb is conjugated). Likewise, the Latin verb *compònere* means to compose or assemble, but the word *compósitus* that is derived from it has a short o. It follows that that knowing where to put the stress within a word depends upon a detailed knowledge of Latin and Greek vocabulary. Professor WILLIAM STEARN sums up the best approach in his *Botanical Latin* (4th edition, 1992): "Whichever system is adopted, the word will sound best and be least objectionable to scholars if a distinction is made between long and short vowels and the stress put in the right place according to classical Latin procedure." For practical purposes, therefore, the most reliable solution is to become familiar with the usual accentuation, so that speakers have a better chance of making themselves understood.

3 How is the plant kingdom classified?

The order of rank as internationally laid down in Articles 1–5 of the ICBN serves as the basis for the classification of the plant kingdom, and is as follows:

Regnum*		Kingdom
Subregnum*		Subkingdom
Divisio, Phylum	(ending -phyta)**	Division, Phylum
Subdivisio	(ending -phytina)	Subdivision
Classis	(ending -opsida)	Class
Subclassis	(ending -idae)	Subclass
Ordo	(ending -ales)	Order
Subordo*	(ending -ineae)	Suborder
Familia	(ending -aceae)***	Family
Subfamilia	(ending -oideae)	Subfamily
Tribus*	(ending -eae)	Tribe
Subtribus*	(ending -inae)	Subtribe
Genus		Genus
Subgenus*		Subgenus
Sectio*		Section
Subsectio*		Subsection

Series*		Series
Subseries*		Subseries
Spezies		Species
Subspezies	(abbreviated to subsp.)	Subspecies
Varietas	(abbreviated to var.)	Variety
Subvarietas*	(abbreviated to subvar.)	Subvariety
Forma	(abbreviated to fo.)	Form
Subforma*	(abbreviated to subfo.)	Subform

The × symbol stands for hybrids; an example is *Dactylorhiza × aschersoniana (= D. incarnata × D. majalis)*. Here, the parent plants are given in alphabetical order, "species name × species name". Hybrids between two species are called nothospecies (abb. = nothosp.) If the parents are not pure species, but instead subspecies or varieties, the resulting hybrids are called nothosubspecies (abb. = nothosubsp.) or nothovarieties (abb. = nothovar.), e. g., for the example above, *Dactylorhiza × aschersoniana* nothovar. *uliginosa (= D. incarnata* subsp. *pulchella* var. *serotina × D. majalis* subsp. *brevifolia)*.

The Pale Petticoat Daffodil, *Narcissus bulbocodium* subsp. *bulbocodium* var. *pallidus*, is given below as an example of how a plant is classified.

Divisio	*Spermatophyta*	Seed plants
Subdivisio	*Magnoliophytina*	
(Angiospermae)	Angiosperms	
Classis	*Liliopsida*	
(Monocotyledoneae)	Monocotyledons	
Subclassis	*Liliidae*	Liliaceous plants
Ordo	*Asparagales*	Asparagus-like plants
Familia	*Amaryllidaceae*	Amaryllis plants
Genus	*Narcissus*	Narcissi
Spezies	*bulbocodium*	Petticoat Daffodil
Subspezies	subsp. *bulbocodium*	Petticoat Daffodil
Varietas	var. *pallidus*	Pale Petticoat Daffodil
Cultivar	'Kenellis'	Cultivar 'Kenellis'

4   How are vernacular names formed?

Names of species often come from Greek or Latin, or are at least latinized. In addition to the generic name and specific epithet, cultivar names may contain a name in any language; even "fancy names" are possible. Vernacular names, on the other hand, are the names of a particular plant in the respective language of the country. The principles that we follow are in accordance with the article *Die Schreibweise deutscher Pflanzennamen* ("The Spelling

---

*   Not relevant for the explanations in this volume.

**   The endings from divisio to subordo are recommended, but not prescribed endings.

*** Permitted exceptions are regulated by Article 18.5 of the ICBN (see page 53)

*   An example of changing classification: in the "World Checklist of Selected Plants" (http://www.kew.org/wcsp/home.do), the *Amaryllidaceae* are classified with the Alliaceae.

of German Plant Names") by Agnes Pahler and Karlheinz Rücker in the journal *Gartenpraxis*, issue No. 12/2001. These principles are followed firstly in the plant identification book *Exkursionsflora von Deutschland* by ROTHMALER, and for ornamental plants in the *Zander Handwörterbuch der Pflanzennamen* from the year 2000.

The written form of the German plant names is governed by German spelling conventions. Here, the Duden language usage reference determines that the use of hyphens is acceptable, as long as this requirement exists in specialist nomenclature. The German Tree Nurseries Association (Bund deutscher Baumschulen, BdB), too, has formally decided on the insertion of a hyphen between the modifier and the root word. The following rules apply:

1. A hyphen separates the modifier and the root word if the latter denotes a taxon, usually a genus (e. g. "Korea-Tanne", literally "Korea Fir", or "Schnitt-Lauch", or Chives). Both the genus *Abies* and the species *Abies koreana* denote a taxon. In this case, the German name, "Tanne", denotes the genus, while the name "Korea-Tanne" denotes the species.

2. A hyphen does not separate the modifier and the root word if the latter refers to an "invalid" taxon (e. g. "Sicheltanne" (Japanese Cedar) = *Cryptomeria* or "Stockrose" (Hollyhock) = *Alcea*). In contrast to the example above, the "Sicheltanne" is not a fir (*Abies*), but an independent genus, while the "Stockrose", similarly, is not a rose. On the other hand, there exist a Japanese and a Chinese Cedar (*Cryptomeria japonica* var. *japonica* and *Cryptomeria japonica* var. *sinensis*, respectively).

3. If the root word relates not to a taxon, but to a growth form or a part of a plant, a hyphen does not separate it and the modifier (e. g. "Wurmfarn" (Buckler Fern, Wood Fern) = *Dryopteris* or "Dreiblatt" (Trinity Flower) = *Trillium*). Such designations of growth forms or plant parts include "Baum", "Farn", "Dorn", "Moos", "Wurz", "Sporn", "Kraut", "Gras", "Blatt", "Beere", "Blume" and "Zwiebel" (tree, fern, thorn, moss, root, spur, herb, grass, leaf, berry, flower and bulb, respectively).

4. If the root word bears no relation to the plant at all, a hyphen does not separate it and the modifier (e. g. "Löwenzahn" (Dandelion, Hawkbit) = *Taraxacum, Leontodon* or "Silberkerze" (Bugbane) = *Cimicfuga*).

5. If the modifier and root word are in any case separate words, no hyphen is inserted between them (e. g. "Griechische Tanne" (Grecian Fir) = *Abies cephalonica*, or "Schwarzer Nachtsschatten" (Black Nightshade) = *Solanum nigrum*).

The root word should generally not contain a hyphen, unless meaningless combinations of terms would otherwise occur (e. g. "Hängeblut-Buche" instead of "Hänge-Blut-Buche" (Purple-Leaved Weeping Beech) = *Fagus sylvatica* "Purpurea Pendula"). Cases of doubt arise in the case of such terms that were originally written together in a vernacular form – here, it is up to the author to decide on the valid name (e. g. "Pfeffer-Minze/Pfefferminze" = Peppermint). Since the root word "Knob" does not exist in German, the only exception is the word "Knoblauch" = Garlic, which should always be written without a hyphen.

Since some genera contain several plant groups, there can be some doubt as to which species are to be assigned to which German names. An example is the genus *Prunus*, with German names such as Pflaume (Plum), Kirsche (Cherry), Pfirsich (Peach), Mandel (Almond) and Aprikose (Apricot). In unclear cases, it is permissible to use one of these terms, which will nevertheless be considered correct.

For combinations of scientific names and German terms, German spelling conventions apply. All elements of the name are then connected by hyphens, e. g. *Rosa-rugosa*-Sorten (*Rosa rugosa* varieties) or *Rosa-×-richardii*-Hybride (*Rosa × richardii* German "Hybride").

In English, written forms can vary greatly from one source to another. The names can be written in upper or lower case, and with or without a hyphen. Since the English vernacular names have been taken from a wide range of different sources, in this book we thought it best to include them in a standardized form. We have therefore decided to list them in upper case without a hyphen.

5   What governs the International Code of Botanical Nomenclature (ICBN)?

The naming of both wild and cultivated plants with scientific names (i. e., botanical names in Latin) is regulated by the "International Code of Botanical Nomenclature" (Vienna Code) of 2006 (abbreviated to ICBN). Foreign translations should always, if possible, be used in conjunction with the original English version.

The naming of agricultural, forestry and horticultural plants is regulated by the "International Code of Nomenclature for Cultivated Plants" (ICNCP) of 2004, published by PIERS TREHANE. This dictionary contains only an easily readable summary of the ICBN and the ICNCP. For a more detailed study of the material, reference to the original literature remains essential.

Botany requires a precise and simple system of nomenclature that botanists of all countries can use. On the one hand, it must deal with the terms that denote taxonomic groups or units, and on the other with the scientific plant names that are applied to the individual taxonomic groups of plants. Hence, this Code governs the correct naming and its recognition, also independent of the priority rule. Here, it is not absolute grammatical correctness that counts, or the regularity or melodious sound of the names and their more or less common usage. The Code dictates that the only proper reasons for changing a name are either a more profound knowledge of the facts resulting from adequate taxonomic research, or the necessity of giving up a nomenclature that is contrary to the rules.

Nevertheless, the priority rule is expressly emphasized in the Principles, stating that, as a rule, the oldest publication determines the nomenclature of a taxonomic group. Since, in the past, this often led to renaming, when a once-established generic name suddenly became invalid owing to another name turning up in an older publication, it was decided that commonly used names should become *nomina conservanda* (protected names; singular: *nomen conservandum*). Although this provisionally applied only to generic names, since 1994 this regulation can also be applied to specific epithets. Hence, if we follow more recent research and accept that *Lychnis* and *Silene* are one and the same genus, both genera have the same "priority" because they are of the same age. However, since both genera were already combined under *Lychnis* in 1771, *Lychnis* would now be the valid name. On the other hand, since there are far more species to be ascribed to *Silene*, it was decided to keep things as simple as possible and rename the species of *Lychnis* instead. *Silene*, then, became a *nomen conservandum*. Nevertheless, *Lychnis*, too, is still valid, if both genera are recognized as separate.

The taxonomic groups from *Regnum* to *Subforma* have been explained in an example in the previous section; in addition, there are the taxonomic groups of the hybrid names. These are denoted by the prefix *Notho-*, e. g. *Nothogenus* for the genus and *Nothospecies* for the species. The ranks are the same as for genus and species, and serve merely to denote the hybrid character.

A generic name may not consist of two words. The name of a species, on the other hand, always consists of two words: the generic name and the specific epithet. If the latter also consists of two words, they are joined by a hyphen (e. g. *Euphorbia caput-medusae*). Moreover, the specific epithet may not repeat the generic name. The gender of the name of the species depends on the genus; for example, trees, as a rule, are feminine (*Fagus sylvatica*).

In Latin, the endings for the gender are *-us* for the masculine form, in addition to other combinations with *-codon, -myces, -odon, -pogon* or *-stemon*. Feminine designations are those ending in *-a, -achne, -chlamys, -daphne, -mecon* or *-osma*. Finally, neuter designations end in *-um, -ceras, -dendron, -nema, -stigma* or *-stoma*. That the choice of the correct gender alone is a science in itself is demonstrated by the fact that endings derived from Greek such as *-anthus* (from *-anthos*) and *-chilus* (from *-chilos*) ought to be neuter, but are treated as masculine, in accordance with botanical nomenclature.

In botanical designations, there is often mention of "Latin" plant names, although the epithets are by no means always of Latin origin. Even letters that are foreign to Latin, such as w and y, or k, which is only seldom used, may be present in a generic name or specific epithet. The German umlauts ä, ö and ü are replaced by ae, oe and ue, respectively, while national peculiarities such as the French è, é or ê, or the Spanish ñ, are also prohibited. Hence, this is another reason why we completely eschew the accent marks that were used up to the 15th edition of the *Zander Handwörterbuch der Pflanzennamen*, even the one permitted exception, the spoken ë as in *Aloë*.

A specific epithet is valid only once it has been published, featuring the name of the circumscribing author. We follow the now international practice of using the abbreviations of the standard reference BRUMMITT AND POWELL (1992): *Authors of Plant Names*. You will also find these abbreviations in the chapter XII "Authors of plant names", beginning on page 860. Epithets which are without an author, but which are nevertheless in horticultural usage, are generally assigned the additional name hort. (= hortulanorum); see also page 37. Parentheses are not used in conjunction with an author citation, unless an author changes the rank or genus of a specific epithet. The name of the original author must then be retained. Hence, *Achillea ageratifolia* var. *serbica* (NYMAN) HEIMERL indicates that Nyman first published the epithet *serbica* for this taxon (in this case as a species, *A. serbica* NYMAN), but Heimerl transferred it to a variety of *Achillea ageratifolia*.

As a rule, when plants are renamed, this means that new findings have come to light, and have been considered. In particular, scanning electron microscopy or molecular studies of genes – possible only in recent times – are among those factors which make it necessary to reassign a plant to another genus. However, the Code expressly forbids renaming merely because another specific epithet is more commonly used, or sounds better. Whenever a new plant is named, a description in Latin must accompany it and a herbarium sheet must be completed. Alternatively, specimens or drawings can be prepared. Such a specimen, which at the same time is described, prepared and/or drawn by the author, is called the "holotype" of a species.

In the appendix of the Code, there are also references to the use of hybrid names. An intergeneric hybrid is termed a nothogenus and is characterized by the hybrid sign × (× *Solidaster* = *Aster* × *Solidago*). By the same token, interspecific hybrids are termed nothospecies and are characterized by the same sign, which now, however, comes before the specific epithet (*Dactylorhiza* × *carnea* = *D. incarnata* × *D. maculata*). In naming the parent plants, it is not necessary to list "father" and "mother" in a particular order; they are simply listed alphabetically.

Article 18.5 of the ICBN deserves special mention. It dictates that family names do not necessarily have to end in -ceae. Already valid names may be retained, such as the following: Compositae (Asteraceae; Typus Aster L.); Cruciferae (Brassicaceae; Typus Brassica L.); Gramineae (Poaceae; Typus Poa L.); Guttiferae (Clusiaceae; Typus Clusia L.); Labiatae (Lamiaceae; Typus Lamium L.); Leguminosae (Fabaceae; Typus Faba MILL.); Palmae (Arecaceae; Typus Areca L.); Umbelliferae (Apiaceae; Typus Apium L.).

III Cultivars

1 What principles apply for cultivar names?

In contrast to scientific nomenclature, simplified or abbreviated names are often used in horticultural practice. The following principles should help clarify the differences between both nomenclatural forms and also the naming of cultivars in horticultural practice.

1. A cultivar is sufficiently denoted by genus, species and cultivar name. The additional names subspecies (subsp.) or variety (var.) may be omitted when a definite cultivar name is present; autonyms should be avoided. By contrast, cultivar names such as 'Alba', 'Rubra' and the like are ambiguous, since these names have been used for subspecies and varieties of a species that are often different; here, it is necessary to give the name of the subspecies. Whereas, in *Heliopsis helianthoides* var. *scabra*, it is not strictly necessary to name the variety, since there are no cultivars of the var. *helianthoides*, this is necessary in the case of *Astilbe chinensis* var. *taquetii* if the respective cultivars are not to be lumped together with those of var. *chinensis*.
2. This distinction between selections and hybrids is no longer reflected in the naming of a cultivar; the root word -Hybride should be given up. *Iris* Sibirica-Hybride 'Caesar's Brother' therefore becomes *Iris sibirica* 'Caesar's Brother'.

It is not necessary to classify a cultivar through the classification of a group. This classification is helpful for presenting characteristics clearly, and in catalogues this additional name is usually an advantage. Although the group designation in parentheses may also come before the cultivar name, e. g. *Acer palmatum* (Dissectum Group) 'Ornatum', it is recommended that the group designation follow the cultivar name (see ICNCP Art. 4). The internationally standard abbreviations given in Section 4 of this chapter are also helpful.

2 Rules on cultivar names

Cultivars showing similar characteristics may be combined to form a Group. Depending on the goal of breeding, different features can be used as a group designation, e.g. frost resistance, and also morphological features. It is of little consequence whether the individual plants differ only slightly in form and colour, such as the above named individuals of the *Delphinium* Astolat Group, or more markedly, e.g. in flower form and colour, such as in *Anemone coronaria* St. Brigid Group. The use of a Group name can give useful information on the characteristics of a cultivar. For example *Delphinium* 'Jubelruf' (Elatum Group) is a vegetatively propagated cultivar that has higher air and soil moisture requirements than, for example, *Delphinium* Astolat Group (Pacific Group). Some examples of Group names in a selection of genera are given in the list starting on page 24.

Renaming of plant species can lead to new groupings. As an example, owing to its close relationship with another taxon, *Rhododendron repens* BALF. f. et FORREST was renamed *Rhododendron forrestii* (BALF. f. et FORREST) COWAN et DAVIDIAN. *Rhododendron repens*

BALF. f. et FORREST is hence a synonym for the now accepted name *R. forrestii* (BALF. f. et FORREST) COWAN et DAVIDIAN. Through combination to form a group, cultivars with the characteristics of *R. repens* are formally distinguished from other groups and cultivars. The correct name of this plant group is now *Rhododendron forrestii* subsp. *forrestii* Repens Group. The correct scientific name of a cultivar of this group would hence be *R. forrestii* subsp. *forrestii* (Repens Group) 'Seinghku', since according to the ICNCP, group designations may come before or after the cultivar name. To avoid using a very long name, it is equally correct to call this cultivar *R. forrestii* 'Seinghku'.

Many gardeners do not always adopt scientific renaming. This is understandable, since otherwise it would be necessary to print new labels and catalogues. Comprehensive synonym listings in this book and knowledge of a few basic principles help clarify the differences between the two nomenclatural forms.

The term "strain", used for lilies in particular, has been superseded by the term "group". Whereas the former convention was *Lilium* 'Bellingham Strain' or Bellingham-Hybriden, the correct designation is now *L.* Bellingham Group.

The term "series", abbreviated to Ser. (from the English word *series*), is used to name individuals of a cross with uniform characteristics, but different flower colours. The term is mainly used for annuals. For example, a typical feature of all cultivars of the Kablouna series (Kablouna Ser.) of *Calendula officinalis* is that of double flowers with divided or incised petals, but there are golden-yellow flowers ('Kablouna Goldgelb'), orange flowers ('Kablouna Orange') or golden-yellow flowers with a black centre ('Kablouna Goldgelb mit schwarzer Mitte'). Hence, as an example, a series is correctly designated *Calendula officinalis* Kablouna Ser., while a cultivar of this series is named 'Kablouna Goldgelb'. It should also be noted that the name of a series is not enclosed within single quotation marks (Kablouna Ser.), but the name of a cultivar is ('Kablouna Goldgelb').

The designation "grex" is used only for the classification of cultivated orchids. Individuals of a generation that correspond to a particular cross combination – independently of whether the cross has been made once, or more than once by different breeders – are all given the same grex designation. For example, the offspring of the cross *Phalaenopsis stuartiana* × *P. lueddemanniana* are denoted by the grex Hermione. A cultivar of this grex is therefore *Phalaenopsis* Hermione 'Sachsen Anhalt'. The term "grex" is not normally used as part of a plant name. Instead, the name of the grex follows the name of the genus and is always written with a capital initial. If there is a cultivar epithet (many orchids are distributed as a grex) it follows the grex name.

3 What governs the International Code of the Nomenclature of Cultivated Plants (ICNCP)?

The International Code of the Nomenclature of Cultivated Plants of 1995 was revised in 2004, and governs the written form of cultivar names. As an example of the rules of the ICNCP, various terms used in cultivar names, such as "sort", "selection" and "hybrid" are no longer allowed. Often the term 'hybrid' was used to designate what is in effect a cultivar or a Group.

Cultivars are plants that have been selected for various characteristics and maintained in cultivation in a way that retains those characters. They can be selected from cultivated or wild plants, or from the products of hybridization. Nevertheless, the particular characteristics of such a selection must be maintained over generations. To date, in contrast to wild plants, it has not been an official requirement to deposit a voucher specimen of cultivated plants in order to clarify later ambiguities on the basis of this herbarium specimen or preparations, yet such a procedure ought to be promoted. The principle of priority of publication applies to both cultivated and wild plants. Since, for example, *Cimicifuga simplex* 'Armleuchter' was bred by Karl Foerster, the name 'White Pearl' should be given up or considered a synonym.

A distinction must be made between cultivar names and trademarks. Since the latter are, however, the property of horticulturalists or jurists, they cannot be used universally, and hence are also not considered cultivar epithets. The Code makes just as little advocacy for the practice of substituting trade names for cultivar names. By contrast, there is no regulation that governs the written form of cultivar epithets. These can be taken from any language, or even from jargon, and may contain any special national characters. Thus, in contrast to the ICBN, the ICNCP has far more to recommend in terms of binding character.

It is binding that a variety may not be designated a cultivar. The term is used for clones, graft-chimeras, lines that have resulted from inbreeding, F1 hybrids and genetically modified plants. Since seed-raised individuals frequently vary, the terms "selection" or "group" in cultivar epithets may also be used in this context. In contrast to cultivar names, however, the name of a group is not written in single quotation marks (e.g. *Delphinium* 'Finsteraarhorn', in contrast to *D.* Black Knight Group). The abbreviation "Grp." is also governed by the Code, since it can be understood internationally (for group, *Gruppe*, *groupe*).

The full name of a cultivar consists of the recognized taxonomic name in Latin form (e.g. *Iris sibirica*), followed by the cultivar epithet. This must start with an initial capital letter and be enclosed in single quotation marks (e.g. *I. sibirica* 'Caesar's Brother'). Double quotation marks ("...") or the abbreviation cv. are not permitted. A further regulation states that new cultivar epithets may not be Latin words, and since 1996 they should not contain more than 30 letters or characters. In contrast to botanical names, cultivar epithets may not be printed in italics.

When a publication is issued in a foreign language, the cultivar epithet may not be translated if the same alphabet as the language of the original publication is used. Otherwise, however, a transliteration is permitted (e.g. from Chinese). Abbreviations are prohibited (e.g. 'Mount Helena', and not 'Mt. Helena'); only titles and forms of address are permitted (Mr, Ms, Dr, Prof – now without full stops, in accordance with international custom). The hybrid sign may not be used (i.e. never *Iris* × 'Caesar's Brother'). It is not necessary to include the circumscribing author. The breeder may be listed, but this in no way forms part of a cultivar epithet.

4 Which cultivars are classified?

Acer palmatum

(P)	Group 1: Palmatum		(L)	Group 4: Linearilobum
(A)	Group 2: Amoenum		(B)	Group 6: Dwarf, bonsai and penjing
(M)	Group 3: Matsumarae		(O)	Group 7: Others
(D)	Group 4: Dissectum			

Example: *Acer palmatum* 'Autumn Glory' (A) is a member of the Amoenum group.

Source: GELDEREN, D. M. VAN, JONG, P. C. DE, OTERDAM, H. J. (1994)

Acer pseudoplatanus

(1) Group 1: Leaves 5-lobed, green (4) Group 4: Leaves 3-lobed

(2) Group 2: Leaves 5-lobed, red or variegated (5) Group 5: Leaves triangular

(3) Group 3: Leaves 5-lobed, green with purple undersides (6) Group 6: Leaves with aberrant forms

Example: *Acer pseudoplatanus* 'Prinz Handjéry' (2) has 5-lobed leaves and is variegated.

Source: GELDEREN, D. M. VAN, JONG, P. C. DE, OTERDAM, H. J. (1994)

Actinidia

(sp) Self-pollinating

Example: *Actinidia* 'Jenny' (sp) is self-pollinating.

Source: PHILIP, C., LORD, T. (2006)

Agapanthus

(F) Funnel group (Tu) Tubular group

(S) Salver group (V) Variegated

(Tr) Trumpet group

Example: *Agapanthus* 'Black Beauty' (Tr) has trumpet-shaped flowers.

Source: SNOJEIJER, W. (2004)

Anemone

(AD) Autumn Double group (AS) Autumn Single group

(AE) Autumn Elegans group

Example: *Anemone* 'Septemberglanz' (AE) is autumn-flowering and has semi-double flowers.

Source: HOP, M.E.C.M. (2001)

Begonia

(C) Reed-like group (S) Semperflorens group

(Cl) Trailing/scandent group (Sh) Shrub-like group

(R) Rex-Cultorum group (T) Tuberous group

(Rh) Rhizomatous group (Th) Thick-stemmed group

Example: *Begonia* 'Tahiti' (T) is a Tuberous Begonia.

Source: PHILIP, C., LORD, T. (2006), in part

Calceolaria

(F)	Fructohybrida group	(HG)	Grandiflora subgroup
(H)	Herbeohybrida group	(HM)	Multiflora subgroup

Example: *Calceolaria* 'Bunter Bikini' (HM) is a member of the Herbeohybrida group, Multiflora subgroup.

Catharanthus roseus

(A)	Albus group	(R)	Roseus group
(O)	Ocellatus group		

Example: *Catharanthus roseus* 'Apricot Delight' (R) has delicate apricot-coloured flowers with a raspberry-coloured bud.

Source: BERGEN, M. VAN, SNOEIJER, W. (1996)

Celosia argentea

(Ch)	Childsii group	(P)	Plumosus group (Plume Flower)
(Cr)	Cristata group (Cockscomb)	(S)	Spicata group

Example: *Celosia argentea* 'New Look' (P) is a 'Plume Flower'.

Chrysanthemum

(1)	Indoor Large (Exhibition)	(17)	October-flowering Single
(2)	Indoor Medium (Exhibition)	(18)	October-flowering Pompon
(3)	Indoor Incurved	(19)	October-flowering Spray
(4)	Indoor Reflexed	(20)	Any other October-flowering Type
(5)	Indoor Intermediate	(22)	Charm
(6)	Indoor Anemone	(23)	Early-flowering Outdoor Incurved
(7)	Indoor Single	(24)	Early-flowering Outdoor Reflexed
(8)	Indoor True Pompon and Semi-Pompon	(25)	Early-flowering Outdoor Intermediate
(9)	Indoor Spray	(26)	Early-flowering Outdoor Anemone
(10)	Indoor Spider, Quill and Spoon	(27)	Early-flowering Outdoor Single
(11)	Any other Indoor Type	(28)	Early-flowering Outdoor Pompon
(12)	Indoor Charm and Cascade	(29)	Early-flowering Outdoor Spray
(13)	October-flowering Incurved	(30)	Any other Early-flowering Outdoor Type
(14)	October-flowering Reflexed	(K)	Korean Type
(15)	October-flowered Intermediate	(Rub)	Rubellum Type
(16)	October-flowering Large		

Example: *Chrysanthemum* 'Harvey' (29-KP) is an early-flowering Field Chrysanthemum of the Korean type.

Source: PHILIP, C., LORD, T. (2006)

Clematis

(A)	Atragene group	(LL)	Late Large-flowered group
(Ar)	Armandii group	(M)	Montana group
(C)	Cirrhosa group	(T)	Tangutica group
(EL)	Early Large-flowered group	(Te)	Texensis group
(Fl)	Flammula group	(V)	Viorna group
(Fo)	Forsteri group	(Vi)	Vitalba group
(H)	Heracleifolia group	(Vt)	Viticella group
(I)	Integrifolia group	(d)	Double

Example: *Clematis* 'Duchess of Edinburgh' (EL-d) is an early-flowering plant and has large, double flowers (formerly Patens group).

Source: MATTHEWS, V. (2002). N.B.: PHILIP, C., LORD, T. (2006) uses a different classification; we use the "International Clematis Register".

Dahlia

(1)	Single (Sin.)	(8)	Cactus (C)
(2)	Anemone-flowered (Anem.)	(9)	Semi-cactus (S-c)
(3)	Collerette (Coll.)	(10)	Miscellaneous (Misc.)
(4)	Water Lily (WL)	(11)	Fimbriated
(5)	Decorative (D)	(12)	Single Orchid
(6)	Ball (Ba.)	(13)	Double Orchid
(7)	Pompon (Pom.)		

The above classes are supplemented by the following letters:

(-a)	Giant	(-d)	Small
(-b)	Large	(-e)	Miniature
(-c)	Medium		

Example: *Dahlia* 'Cream Beauty' (4-d) is a small-flowered Starfish Dahlia.

Source: The International Dahlia Register

Delphinium

(B)	Belladonna group	(P)	Pacific group
(E)	Elatum group		

Example: *Delphinium* Black Knight Group (P) is a member of the Pacific group.

Dianthus

(B)	Border Carnations	(Pf)	Perpetual-flowering Carnations
(M)	Malmaison Carnations	(Pa)	Annual Pink
(P)	Pink		

Example: *Dianthus* 'Princess of Wales' (M) is a Malmaison Carnation.

Source: The International Dianthus Register and Checklist

Gladiolus

(100)	Miniature	(400)	Large
(200)	Small	(500)	Giant
(300)	Medium		

The flower size is supplemented by a colour code, as follows:

Colour	Pale	Light	Medium	Dark	Other
White	00				
Green		02	04		
Yellow	10	12	14	16	
Orange	20	22	24	26	
Colour	Pale	Light	Medium	Dark	Other
Salmon-pink	30	32	34	36	
Pink	40	42	44	46	
Red	50	52	54	56	58
Rosé	60	62	64	66	68
Lavender	70	72	74	76	78
Violet	80	82	84	86	88
"Smoky"	90	92	94	96	98

Example: *Gladiolus* 'Oscar' (556) is giant-flowering and dark red.

Source: North American Gladiolus Council

The RHS, by contrast, uses the following classification:

(B)	Butterfly group	(Min)	Miniature-flowering group
(E)	Exotic group	(N)	Nanus group
(G)	Giant-flowering group	(P)	Primulinus group
(L)	Large-flowering group	(S)	Small-flowering group
(M)	Medium-size-flowering group	(Tub)	Tubergenii group

Source: PHILIP, C., LORD, T. (2006)

Hydrangea

(B)	Guelder Rose Hydrangeas	(S)	Velvet Hydrangeas
(R)	Paniculate Hydrangeas	(St)	Shrub Hydrangeas

The Hydrangea *H. macrophylla* is additionally subdivided into:

(H)	Spherical inflorescences (Hortensia type)	(L)	Dish-shaped inflorescences (Lacecup Type)

Example: *Hydrangea* 'Blaumeise' (L) is a member of the Lacecup group.

Source: BÄRTELS, A. (2001)

Iris

(AB)	Arilbred group	(MTB)	Miniature Tall Bearded
(AR)	Aril group	(OB)	Oncobred
(BB)	Border Bearded	(OG)	Oncoregelia
(CA)	Californian Hybrid	(OGB)	Oncoregeliabred
(CS)	Calsib Hybrid	(OH)	Oncocyclus Hybrid
(Dut)	Dutch Hybrid	(SS)	Sino-Sibiricas
(IB)	Intermedia Bearded	(SDB)	Standard Dwarf Bearded
(LA)	Louisiana Hybrid	(TB)	Tall Bearded
(MDB)	Miniature Dwarf Bearded		

Further hybrids are listed under *Iris ensata* (formerly *I.* Kaempferi hybrids), *I. sibirica* and *I. spuria*.

Example: *Iris* 'Gingerbread Man' (SDB) is a member of the Standard Dwarf Bearded (formerly Barbata Nana group).

Source: Iris Check List (The American Iris Society 2001)

Lilium

(I)   Early-flowering Asiatic hybrids
   (a) Cultivars with erect flowers
   (b) Cultivars with horizontal flowers
   (c) Cultivars with pendent flowers
(II)   Hybrids of the Martagon type
(III)   Hybrids of the Candidum type
(IV)   Hybrids of American species
(V)   Hybrids of the Longiflorum type
(VI)   Hybrid trumpet lilies
   (a) Cultivars with trumpet-shaped flowers
   (b) Cultivars with cup-shaped flowers
   (c) Cultivars with flat flowers
   (d) Cultivars with reflexed petals

(VII)   Hybrids of oriental species
      (a) Cultivars with trumpet-shaped flowers
      (b) Cultivars with cup-shaped flowers
      (c) Cultivars with flat flowers
      (d) Cultivars with reflexed petals

(VIII)   All hybrids that do not belong in one of the other divisions

(IX)   All species and their varieties and forms

Example: *Lilium* 'Black Beauty' (VIId) is an oriental hybrid with reflexed petals.

Source: The International Lily Register (2007)

Meconopsis

(FB)	Fertile Blue Group	(Sp)	Species
(GS)	George Sherriff Group	(St)	Other sterile clonal cultivars /plants so distinctive they did not need, or could not readily be place in a group
(IB)	Infertile Blue Group		

Example: *Meconopsis* 'Barney's Blue' (GS) is a member of the George Sherriff group

Source: Meconopsis Group (www.meconopsis.org)

Narcissus

(1)	Trumpet	(8)	Tazetta
(2)	Large-cupped	(9)	Poeticus
(3)	Small-cupped	(10)	Bulbocodium
(4)	Double	(11a)	Split-corona Narcissi (Collar)
(5)	Triandrus	(11b)	Split-corona Narcissi (Papillon)
(6)	Cyclamineus	(12)	Miscellaneous
(7)	Jonquilla and Apodanthus	(13)	Species

There is also a colour code which describes the colour of the perianth and corona:

(G)	Green	(O)	Orange
(R)	Red	(W)	White
(P)	Pink	(Y)	Yellow

Example: *Narcissus* 'Moyle' (9 W-GYO) is a white-flowering Poeticus Narcissus with a yellow corona, green throat and orange-coloured margin.

Source: The Royal Horticultural Society: The International Daffodil Register and Classified List 1998

Nymphaea

(H)	Hardy	(D)	Day-flowering
(T)	Tropical	(N)	Night-flowering

Example: *Nymphaea* 'Saint Louis' (T/D) is a tropical, day-flowering Water Lily.

Source: PHILIP, C., LORD, T. (2006)

Paeonia

Shrub Peonies that can be assigned to a species are found under the following: *P. lactiflora, P. officinalis* and *P. peregrina*. Shrub peonies with different parents belong to the Hybrid Peonies.

(H)	Hybrid Peonies	(L)	Lutea group
(I)	Intersectional group (Itoh-Group)	(S)	Suffruticosa group

Example: *Paeonia* 'Luxuriant' (I) is an intersectional cultivar (Itoh-Hybride).

Source: Carsten Burkhard's Web Projekt Paeonia (www.paeon.de) – simplified

Pelargonium

(A)	Angel group	(Min)	Miniature group
(C)	Coloured foliage group	(MinI)	Miniature Ivy-leaved group
(Dec)	Decorative group	(R)	Regal group
(Dw)	Dwarf group	(Sc)	Scented group
(DwI)	Dwarf Ivy-leaved group	(U)	Unique group
(Fr)	Frutetorum group	(Z)	Zonal group
(I)	Ivy-leaved group		

In combination with these groups, the following information on flower form can be included:

(Ca)	Cactus	(St)	Stellar
(-d)	Double	(T)	Tulip

Example: *Pelargonium* 'Wallis Friesdorf' (Dw/Ca-d) is a dwarf cultivar with cactus-flowered, double flowers.

Source: PHILIP, C., LORD, T. (2006)

Primula

(Ag)	Auganthus	(Ma)	Malvaceae
(Al)	Aleuritia	(Mi)	Minutissimae
(Am)	Amethystinae	(Mo)	Monocarpicae
(Ar)	Armerina	(Mu)	Muscarioides
(Au)	Auricula	(Ob)	Obconicolesteri
(A)	Alpine Auricula	(Or)	Oreophlomis
(B)	Border Auricula	(Pa)	Parryi
(S)	Show Auricula	(Pe)	Petiolares
(St)	Striped Auricula	(Pf)	Proliferae
(Bu)	Bullatae	(Pi)	Pinnatae
(Ca)	Capitatae	(Pr)	Primula
(Cf)	Cordifoliae	(Poly)	Polyanthus
(Ch)	Chartaceae	(Prim)	Primrose
(Co)	Cortusoides	(Pu)	Pulchellae
(Cr)	Carolinella	(Py)	Pycnoloba

(Cu)	Cuneifoliae	(R)	Reinii
(Cy)	Crystallophlomis	(Si)	Sikkimenses
(Da)	Davidii	(So)	Soldanelloides
(De)	Denticulatae	(Sp)	Sphondylia
(Dr)	Dryadifoliae	(Sr)	Sredinskya
(F)	Fedtschenkoanae	(Su)	Suffrutescens
(G)	Glabrae	(Y)	Yunnanenses

Example: *Primula* 'Roberto' (Au/S) is a Show Auricula.

Source: RICHARDS, J. (2002)

Rhododendron

The international *Rhododendron*-Register classifies rhododendrons into four main groups:

(A)	Azaleas	(R)	Rhododendron
(AZ)	Azaleodendron	(V)	Virea-Rhododendron

The following subcategories also apply:

-d	Deciduous Azaleas	-e	Elepidote Rhododendron
-ev	Evergreen Azaleas	-e/l	Cross Elepidote × Lepidote
-s	Semi-evergreen Azaleas	-l	Lepidote Rhododendron

The RHS also classifies the following to the Azaleas:

(G)	Ghent Azaleas	(M)	Mollis Azaleas
(K)	Knap-Hill Azaleas	(O)	(Occidentalis Azaleas)

Example: *Rhododendron* 'Glowing Embers' (A, K) is a Knap-Hill Azalea.

Source: The International Rhododendron Register and Checklist (2004)

Rosa

(A)	"Ancient European Roses"	(C1)	Ground Cover
(A1)	Alba	(C2)	English
(A2)	Damask	(C3)	Floribunda or Cluster-flowered
(A3)	Gallica	(C4)	Climbing (in combination)
(A4)	Moss (in combination)	(C5)	Miniature
(A5)	Centifolia	(C6)	Hybrid Musk
(B)	"Roses with the Influence of Chinese Roses"	(C7)	Polyantha
(B1)	Bourbon	(C8)	Rambler
(B2)	China	(C9)	Rugosa
(B3)	Damask Portland	(C10)	Shrub
(B4)	Hybrid Perpetual	(C11)	Outdoor Cut Roses
(B5)	Tea	(D)	Wild Roses/Species
(C)	"Modern Roses"		

Example: *Rosa* 'The Fairy' (C7) is a Polyantha Rose.

Source: SCHULTHEIS, H., URBAN, H. U. K. (2006)

Saxifraga

(1)	Ciliatae	(9)	Xanthizoon
(2)	Cymbalaria	(10)	Trachyphyllum
(3)	Merkianae	(11)	Gymnopera
(4)	Micranthes	(12)	Cotylea
(5)	Irregulares	(13)	Odontophyllae
(6)	Heterisia	(14)	Mesogyne
(7)	Porphyrion	(15)	Saxifraga
(8)	Ligulatae		

Example: *Saxifraga* 'Hi-Ace' (15) is a member of the section Saxifraga.

Source: GORNALL, R.J. (1987)

Silene banksia

(C)	Coronata group	(S)	Senno group
(H)	Haageana group		

Example: *Silene banksia* 'Haageana' (H) is a member of the Haageana group.

Tulipa

(1)	Single early group	(9)	Rembrandt group
(2)	Double early group	(10)	Parrot group
(3)	Triumph group	(11)	Double late group
(4)	Darwin hybrid group	(12)	Kaufmanniana group
(5)	Single late group	(13)	Fosteriana group
(6)	Lily-flowered group	(14)	Greigii group
(7)	Fringed group	(15)	Miscellaneous
(8)	Viridiflora group		

Example: *Tulipa* 'Daydream' (4) is a Darwin hybrid.

Source: Classified List and International Register of Tulip Names (1996)

Viola			
(A)	Section Violets	(B)	Section Melanium
(A1)	Single Violets	(B1)	Pansies
	(a) Heirloom Sweet Violets		(a) Early Pansies
	(b) Governor Herrick Type		(b) Fancy Pansies
	(c) Cultivars and Hybrids of *V. sororia*		(c) Show Pansies
	(d) Miscellaneous Violet Cultivars		(d) Bedding Pansies
(A2)	Semi-double Violets	(B2)	Violas
(A3)	Double Violets		(a) Bedding Violas
(A4)	Parma Violets		(b) Exhibition Violas
		(B3)	Violettas
		(B4)	Cornuta Hybrids

Example: *Viola* 'Rebecca' (B3) is a Violetta hybrid.

Source: The American Violet Society – Class of the cultivated forms of the genus *Viola* (www.americanvioletsociety.org/registry)

Other possible designations			
(f)	Female	(sd)	Semi-double
(m)	Male	(d)	Double
(v)	Variegated		

Example: *Salix caprea* 'Pendula' (f) = *Salix caprea* 'Weeping Sally'

Salix caprea 'Pendula' (m) = *Salix caprea* 'Kilmarnock'

IV How to use the book

1 How is the alphabetical list structured?

- In Section IX, the scientific plant names are ordered alphabetically, according to their generic names. The correct names are printed in bold type, references to other names in ordinary type.
- The names of species within the genera are also ordered alphabetically, the correct names emphasized by the use of bold face. Synonyms are printed in light face; the symbol "=" indicates the valid plant names.
- In contrast to previous editions, synonyms are no longer given in parentheses after the names of species.
- In the case of species hybrids, which are denoted by an epithet in Latin form preceded by a multiplication sign (×), the names of the parent species are then given in alphabetical order, e. g. *Begonia × duchartrei* (*B. echinosepala × B. scharffiana*).
- Authors' names are given according to the valid spelling in BRUMMIT, *Authors of Plant Names*. In practice, these can often be dispensed with if the correct name of the species is used. Nevertheless, it should be ascertained whether the same name with a different author constitutes a synonym, e. g. *Dipsacus fullonum* (L.) is now the valid name for *D. sylvestris* HUDS., while *D. fullonum* (auct. non L.) has become a synonym for *D. sativus* (L.) HONCK.
- Only the most commonly used English, French and German plant names have been included. These may be found in the alphabetical list of vernacular names in Section X.
- In addition to the author, the gender of the generic name (-m-, -f- or -n-) and the plant family are given in the header for each genus.
- Degrees of winter hardiness are based on the climate of central Europe – especially that of Germany and areas with a similar climate – and also on the equivalent climatic zones of the USA.

2 How are the winter hardiness zones classified?

The winter hardiness zone (Z1 to Z10) gives an indication of the minimum temperature that a particular species can survive without suffering severe damage. As an example: the winter hardiness zone Z6 indicates that, in this zone, plant species of the winter hardiness zone Z6 or below, down to Z1, can survive average winters outdoors, while plants of the winter hardiness zone Z7 or above would suffer severe damage or freeze. Soil and microclimate can influence winter hardiness to some degree.

An indication of the winter hardiness zone is very helpful for woody plants that are fully exposed to the climate. It is less reliable for perennial herbs, and of only limited value for bulbous plants. For annuals, an indication of winter hardiness has little meaning, since dry seeds are mostly completely insensitive to cold.

3   What symbols are used?

The symbols and abbreviations used in Section IX are nearly all taken from the German Industrial Standards Sheet DIN 11 530. This standard was laid down by the Horticultural Nomenclature Committee of the Central Federation of German Vegetable and Fruit-growers and Horticulturists (Gartenbau-Nomenklatur-Ausschuss im Zentralverband des Deutschen Gemüse-, Obst- und Gartenbaus e. V.) in collaboration with the German Tree Nurseries Association (Bund deutscher Baumschulen, BdB). They include all the most important symbols and abbreviations used in the catalogues and brochures of market gardens, tree-nurseries and seedsmen, as well as other horticultural publications. It is intended to set up a system of information with common symbols which will ensure that plants are correctly treated at all stages.

The Standards Sheet DIN 11 530 should be consulted by anyone concerned with the compilation of catalogues, brochures and pricelists, and by any horticultural writer who intends to use symbols in a technical document. The Standards Sheet DIN 11 530 is obtainable from the company Beuth-Vertrieb GmbH.

Symbols used in this dictionary are listed on page 58.

4   What abbreviations and technical terms are used?

agg. (aggregate): An informal designation for a group of allied species.

alt. (alternus): A name that can be used as an alternative: e. g., in the case of *Asteraceae* alt.: *Compositae*, either family name may be used.

auct. non (auctorum non): A reference to other authors, who are not the actual authors of the name. This denotes the incorrect use of a name, the "auct." case. This refers to situations in which one or more authors have used a name incorrectly.

Autonym (a name that arises by itself): If, within a species, a distinct taxon is recognized and a distinct name for it is published (e. g., *Campanula latifolia* L. var. *macrantha* FISCH. ex FISCH.), an autonym automatically arises, i. e. independently of the naming (in this case, *Campanula latifolia* L. var. *latifolia*). The autonym repeats the specific epithet and contains the nomenclatural type expressed in the name of the species, but has no author.

comb. nov. (combinatio nova): Used for new combinations of taxonomic designations.

emend. (emendavit): Changed by: e. g. the description *Adonis autumnalis* L. was changed by WILLIAM HUDSON so the citation becomes *Adonis autumnalis* L. emend. HUDS.

Epithet: The second word in the name of a species, or the last word in infraspecific names: e. g. *campestre* is the specific epithet of *Acer campestre*; *Acer* itself is the generic name. Together, the generic name and specific epithet make up the name of a species. In infraspecific names, a second epithet is added at the end: e. g. *leiocarpum* is the infraspecific epithet of *Acer campestre* subsp. *leiocarpum*.

et (and ...): In some books, "&" is used in place of "et" (e. g. as in HUMB., BONPL. & KUNTH).

ex (from ...): The name of the author before "ex" is the person who first suggested but did not validly publish the name. The person after the "ex" is the one who validly published the name.

f. (filius): The son. Used in some cases to distinguish between two related authors (father and son), whereby the abbreviation denotes only the son: e. g., "L." for LINNAEUS and "L. f." for LINNAEUS filius. Also used for Reichenbach (RCHB. f.), Hooker (HOOK. f.) and other authors.

fam. (familia): Rank: family.

fo. (forma): Rank: form. Often denoted only by quotation marks: e.g. "fo. Alba" corresponds to 'Alba'.

-f- (femininum): Female gender, characterized in Latin by the ending -*a*.

Group: This is sometimes used by English language writers to indicate a group of allied species: technically speaking, this corresponds to "aggregate". In this volume, however, the term is mainly used to distinguish between horticultural groups, e.g. *Delphinium* Belladonna Group and *Delphinum* Elatum Group.

Homonym (a name that has the same form or sound as another, but a different meaning): All the more recent homonyms are illegitimate and therefore cannot be used as names. The oldest homonym is legitimate if the name otherwise corresponds to the rules. Only validly published names are considered under the homonym rule. Also considered as homonyms are infraspecific names of different ranks with the same, but heterotypical, epithet.

hort. (hortulanorum): This is used instead of the name of an author. It indicates a horticultural designation for a taxon without reference to an author: the name has not been validly published. In English, the term is often equated with "... of gardens". This may mean that a plant appears in the trade under an incorrect name, e.g. the true *Passiflora antioquiensis* (H. KARST) is hardly ever supplied; *P.* × *exoniensis* (L.H. BAILEY) usually takes its place. Hence, "*P. antioquiensis* of gardens" is designated *P. antioquiensis* hort.

in (in...): Published in the work of the following author (the "in-author"), who, according to the new nomenclatural rules, no longer attaches to the author citation. The "in" appears between the author of the name and the author of the work.

incl. (incluso): Including (a synonym).

Infraspecific: An infraspecific taxon is one that is ordered within a species, i.e. below it in rank. Here, a distinction is mainly made between subspecies (subsp.), variety (var.) and form (fo.). *Ballota nigra* subsp. *meridionalis* is an infraspecific name, while *meridionalis* is an infraspecific epithet.

-m- (maskulinum): Male gender, characterized in Latin by the ending -*us*.

mult. (multorum): ... of many: e.g. "auct. mult. non ..." means in the sense of many authors, but not in the sense of the author of the name.

-n- (neutrum): Neuter gender, characterized in Latin by the ending -*um*.

nec (also not): Appears in connection with non-citations, where further homonyms are mentioned.

nom. cons. (nomen conservandum): A conserved name (according to the ICBN).

nom. illeg. (nomen illegitimum): An illegitimate name (usually a more recent homonym or a superfluous name that threatens to supersede a legitimate name already in existence).

nom. nud. (nomen nudum): A "naked name", without the nomenclaturally required description.

nom. rej. (nomen rejiciendum): A name to be rejected (according to the ICBN). Also applies to all names that are based on these combinations. In the case of taxonomic synonyms, the rejection applies only if both names are judged not to be different.

nom. superfl. (nomen superfluum): A superfluous name exists when an author, in publishing a name, cites an already existing (and, according to the rules, legitimate), older name or its nomenclatural type. All combinations that are based on this older name, i.e. those with the same nomenclatural type, are considered to be cited as well.

non (not): Negation, appearing in connection with auct. cases and homonyms. The name before the "non" is the more recent (as a rule illegitimate) homonym; the name after the "non" is the older homonym).

notho- (hybrid): The hybrid nature is designated by the use of the multiplication sign × or by the addition of the prefix "notho-" to the taxonomic rank (e. g. *nothosubsp., nothovar.*).

p.p. (pro parte): In part, i. e. in the case of names that relate to two or more taxa – either in names whose nomenclatural type has not yet been established, or which have been used in the past for more than one taxon. However, a "p.p." designation is also used in connection with taxonomic names that have been used by certain authors in a broader definition than in the current classification.

s.l. (sensu lato): "In a broad sense", i. e. the broad limits of a taxon (of any rank). Not – as in some floras – to be understood as an alternative designation for a species group or aggregate.

s.str. (sensu stricto): "In a narrow sense": a taxon (of any rank) in a taxonomically narrow definition.

sensu (in the sense of...): According to the taxonomic interpretation or definition of a (subsequently named) author or his/her work.

sp. (species): Rank: species.

stat. nov. (Status novus): Change in rank (at this level).

subsp. (subspecies): Rank: subspecies.

Syn. (synonym): A synonym is a name that is not validly published, or one that is illegitimate or incorrect (the oldest), or one that is not accepted because of the systematic level or value that it expresses.

Tautonym: A name that is not permitted in botanical nomenclature, one in which the specific epithet repeats the generic name. For example, if *Acer negundo* L. is placed into the separate genus *Negundo*, the species name may not be renamed to give the tautonym *Negundo negundo* L.; in this case, the species is called *Negundo aceroides* MOENCH.

var. (varietas): Rank: variety.

vel (also, but also): Appears when a taxonomic name is used in the sense of several authors, e. g. *Philadelphus satsumanus* sensu KOCH vel REHDER.

V The Zander Information System

1 What supplementary volumes are there?

A database has been generated containing around 140,000 generic, species and cultivar names. Thanks to numerous additions, this has now grown to include over a million plant names. *The Timber Press Dictionary of Plant Names* contains some 20,000 valid names and 10,000 synonyms. However, far more have been incorporated in the database, and are now available online.

To date, the following supplementary volumes have also been made available:

SEYBOLD, S.: *Die wissenschaftlichen Namen der Pflanzen und was sie bedeuten.* More than 8500 scientific species designations – the specific epithets – the scientific plant names were translated into German, and, in part, explained. Stress marks indicate the correct pronunciation of the specific epithets. All the species, subspecies and varieties that are listed in *The Timber Press Dictionary of Plant Names* have been included.

ERHARDT, W.: *List of Conifer Names.* This book provides an overview of the names of all the conifer genera, species and cultivars, whereby the latter in particular are absent from *The Timber Press Dictionary of Plant Names.* In addition to the correct designations for conifers, the book includes their synonyms and trade names, and also their vernacular names in German and English.

2 The *Große Zander-Enzyklopädie der Pflanzennamen*

The *Große Zander-Enzyklopädie der Pflanzennamen* (available from Ulmer-Verlag) includes the following information:

ICBN and ICNCP are cited in detail.

The profiles of the genera describe the leaves, inflorescences, flowers, fruits and particular distinguishing features.

Additional genera and species.

Cultivars that, according to the *PPP Index*, are often to be found in the trade.

Numerous illustrations of nearly all the genera are included.

The details of the authors include brief biographies.

VI Abbreviations of home territories

Distribution entries

As far as possible, the distribution entries have been standardized. Eight major regions are distinguished world-wide. These are clearly demarcated in the world maps on pages 918–920.

N-Am.	= North America, including USA, Canada, and Greenland
Lat.-Am.	= Latin America, from Mexico to Tierra del Fuego
Eur.	= Europe and northern Africa
NE-As.	= Northern and eastern Asia
M.-East	= Middle East
Afr.	= Africa south of the Sahara
trop. As.	= Tropical Asia, from western and Southeast Asia to the South Sea islands
Austr. NZ	= Australia and New Zealand

These major regions are, in turn, subdivided into smaller regions. In some cases, the demarcation corresponds to the political borders of a country. These regions are shown underlined in the overview. Down to this level, we have attempted to list the distribution entries as completely as possible.

In the case of species with small geographic distributions, the names of federal states, provinces, or smaller countries are given. The geographic distributions of endemic species occurring over very restricted areas have been designated by correspondingly small-scale geographic entries.

To give the distributions of plants in terms of the political boundaries of countries, states, and provinces often gives a wrong impression of their true geographic distributions. For instance, plant species of the European Alps can occur in all six countries of the region. In such cases, the entry for area has been further restricted in geographic terms, e.g., by Alp. Pyr. (Alps and Pyrenees). Such entries may be expected in the case of alpine and coastal species in particular.

Overview of geographic distributions

We have used the official abbreviations of the federal states of Canada and the USA on the one hand and the internationally customary abbreviations for European countries on the other. Additional abbreviations have had to be introduced for nine larger European regions (see Europe map on page 920). All abbreviations and geographic designations used are contained in the following overview.

N-Am.		North America
Greenl.		Greenland
Alaska		Alaska
Can.		Canada
Can:W		Western Canada
	B. C.	British Columbia
	Alta.	Alberta
	Sask.	Saskatchewan
	Yukon	Yukon
	Mackenzie	District of Mackenzie
Can:E		Eastern Canada
	Man.	Manitoba
	Keewatin	District of Keewatin
	Ont.	Ontario
	Que.	Quebec
	Labrador	Labrador
	Nfld.	Newfoundland *(incl. St. Pierre and Miquelon Island)*
	N. B.	New Brunswick
	P. E. I.	Prince Edward Island
	N. S.	Nova Scotia
USA:NW		USA: Northwest
	Wash.	Washington
	Oreg.	Oregon
USA:Calif.		USA: California
	Calif.	California
USA:Rocky Mts		USA: Rocky Mountains
	Mont.	Montana
	Idaho	Idaho
	Wyo.	Wyoming
	Nev.	Nevada
	Utah	Utah
	Colo.	Colorado
USA:SW		USA: Southwest
	Ariz.	Arizona
	N.Mex.	New Mexico
USA:NC		USA: Northern prairie states
	N.Dak.	North Dakota
	S.Dak.	South Dakota
	Nebr.	Nebraska

	Kans.	Kansas
USA:SC		USA: Southern prairie states
	Okla.	Oklahoma
	Tex	Texas
USA:NE		USA: Northeast
	Maine	Maine
	Vt.	Vermont
	N. H.	New Hampshire
	Mass.	Massachusetts
	R. I.	Rhode Island
	Conn.	Connecticut
	N. Y.	New York
	N. J.	New Jersey
	Pa.	Pennsylvania
	Del.	Delaware
	Md.	Maryland
	Va.	Virginia
	W. Va	West Virginia
	Ky.	Kentucky
USA:NEC		USA: Northeast-Central
	Minn.	Minnesota
	Wis.	Wisconsin
	Mich.	Michigan
	Ohio	Ohio
	Indiana	Indiana
	Ill.	Illinois
	Iowa	Iowa
	Mo.	Missouri
USA:SE		USA: Southeast
	Ark.	Arkansas
	La.	Louisiana
	Miss.	Mississippi
	Tenn.	Tennessee
	Ala.	Alabama
	Ga.	Georgia
	N. C.	North Carolina
	S. C.	South Carolina
USA:Fla.		USA: Florida
	Fla.	Florida

Lat.-Am.			Latin America
Mex.			Mexico
C-Am.			Central America
	Belize		Belize
	Guat.		Guatemala
	Hond.		Honduras
	El Salv.		El Salvador
	Nicar.		Nicaragua
	Costa Rica		Costa Rica
	Panama		Panama
W.Ind.			West Indies
	Cuba		Cuba
	Hispaniola		Hispaniola *(Haiti and Dominican Republic)*
	Jamaica		Jamaica
	Puerto Rico		Puerto Rico
	Bahamas		Bahamas
	Lesser Antilles		Lesser Antilles
Venez.			Venezuela
Col.			Colombia
Ecuad.			Ecuador
Galapagos			Galapagos Islands
Peru			Peru
Bol.			Bolivia
Chile			Chile
Arg.			Argentina
	Patag.		Patagonia
Falkland			Falkland Islands
Urug.			Uruguay
Parag.			Paraguay
Braz.			Brazil
Amaz.			Amazon Region
	Gran Chaco		Gran Chaco
	Rio Grande do Su		Rio Grande do Sul
	Braz.:W		West Brazil *(Planalto Brasileiro incl. all remaining federal states)*
Guianas			Guianas
	Guyana		Guyana
	Surinam		Surinam
	French Guiana		French Guiana

Eur.		Europe and North Africa
Sc		Scandinavia
	DK	Denmark
	Ice	Iceland
	Norw.	Norway
	Swed	Sweden
	FIN	Finland
BrI		British Isles
	GB	Great Britain
	IRL	Ireland
Ib		Iberian Peninsula
	P	Portugal *(excluding. the Azores and Madeira)*
	Sp	Spain *(incl. the Balearics, but excluding the Canary Islands)*
Fr		France and Benelux countries
	F	France *(excluding Corsica)*
	NL	The Netherlands
	B	Belgium *(incl. Luxembourg)*
Ital.-P		Italian Peninsula
	I	Italy
	Cors.	Corsica
	Sard.	Sardinia
	Sic.	Sicily *(incl. Malta)*
C-Eur.		Central Europe
	G	Germany
	Sw	Switzerland
	A	Austria
EC-Eur.		Eastern Central Europe
	H	Hungary
	Slova.	Slovakia
	CZ	Czech Republic
	PL	Poland
Ba		Balkan Peninsula
	Slove.	Slovenia
	Croatia	Croatia
	Bosn.	Bosnia and Herzegovina
	YU	Yugoslavia *(Serbia, Montenegro)*
	Maced.	Macedonia
	AL	Albania
	GR	Greece

		Crete	Crete
		BG	Bulgaria
		Eur.TR	European Turkey
E-Eur.			Eastern Europe
		Balt.	Baltic States *(Lithuania, Latvia, Estonia, Kaliningrad)*
		RUS.	European Russia *(Belorussia (BY), Ukraine (UA), Moldavia (MO), and Crimea)*
		RO	Romania
N-Afr.			N. Africa
		Moroc.	Morocco
		Alger.	Algeria
		Tun.	Tunisia
		Libya	Libya
		Egypt	Egypt
Macaron.			Macaronesia
		Azor.	Azores
		Canar.	Canary Islands
		Madeira	Madeira

NE-As.		**Northern and eastern Asia**

		Sib.	Siberia
		W-Sib.	Western Siberia *(west of the Yenisei)*
		E-Sib.	Eastern Siberia
		Kamchat.	Kamchatka
		Sakhal.	Sakhalin
C-As.			Central Asia
		Kazakh.	Kazakhstan
		Turkm.	Turkmenistan
		Uzbek.	Uzbekistan
		Kirgi.	Kirgizia
		Tajik.	Tajikistan
Mong.			Mongolia
China			China
		Tibet	Tibet
		Manch.	Manchuria
		Sinkiang	Sinkiang
		Sichuan	Szechwan
		Yunnan	Yunnan
		China:S	Southern China *(south of the Qin-lin)*
		China:N	Northern China *(north of the Qin-lin)*

	Hainan	Hainan
Taiwan		Taiwan
Korea		Korea
Jap.		Japan

M-East		**Middle East**
TR		Turkey (except. Europ. Turkey)
Cauc.		Caucasus Region (states)
	Georg.	Georgia
	Armen.	Armenia
	Azerb.	Azerbaijan
Levant		Levant
	Syr.	Syria
	Lebanon	Lebanon
	Palest.	Israel, Jordan
	Cyprus	Cyprus
Iraq		Iraq
Iran		Iran
Afgh.		Afghanistan
Arab.		Arabia (with Kuwait, Arab Emirates, Oman)
Yemen		Yemen
Socotra		Socotra

Afr.		**Africa**
Cap Ver		Cape Verde
W-Sah.		Western Sahara
	Maur.	Mauritania
	Seneg.	Senegal (incl. Gambia)
	Mali	Mali
	Burkina Faso	Burkina Faso
	Niger	Niger
	Chad	Chad
Sudan		Sudan
	Sudan	Sudan
W-Afr.		West Africa
	Guinea Bis.	Guinea-Bissau
	Guinea	Guinea
	Sierra Leone	Sierra Leone
	Liberia	Liberia
	Ivory Coast	Ivory Coast

	Ghana	Ghana
	Togo	Togo
	Benin	Benin
	Nigeria	Nigeria
C-Afr.		Central Africa
	Cameroon	Cameroon
	Sao Tome	Sao Tome and Principe
	Equat. Guinea	Equatorial Guinea
	Gabon	Gabon
	Congo	Congo
	DRC	DR Congo
	CAfr. Rep.	Central African Republic
	Eth.	Ethiopia, Eritraea
E-Afr.		East Africa
	Djibouti	Djibouti
	Somalia	Somalia
	Kenya	Kenya
	Uganda	Uganda
	Rwanda	Rwanda
	Burundi	Burundi
	Tanzania	Tanzania
trop. Afr		Tropical Africa
	Angola	Angola
	Namibia	Namibia
	Zambia	Zambia
	Botswana	Botswana
	Zimbabwe	Zimbabwe
	Malawi	Malawi
	Mozamb.	Mozambique
S-Afr.		South Africa *(with Lesotho and Swaziland)*
		Cape
Madag.		Madagascar *(incl. Comoro Islands*
Seych.		Seychelles
Mascarene Is.		Mascarene Is.
St. Helena		St. Helena
Ascension		Ascension

trop. As.		Tropical Asia
Indian sub.-C		Indian Sub-Continent
	Pakist.	Pakistan
	Ind.	India
	Nepal	Nepal
	Bhutan	Bhutan
	Bangladesh	Bangladesh
	Sri Lanka	Sri Lanka
Indochina		Indochina
	Burma	Burma
	Thailand	Thailand
	Laos	Laos
	Cambodia	Cambodia
	Vietnam	Vietnam
Malay. Arch.		Malay Archipelago
	Malay. Pen.	Malay Peninsula (Malacca)
	Sumat.	Sumatra
	Java	Java
	Kalimantan	Kalimantan (Borneo)
	Sulawesi	Sulawesi (Celebes)
	Lesser Sunda	Lesser Sunda
	Is.	Islands
	Molucca	Moluccas
Phil.		Philippines
N.Guinea		New Guinea
Solom.		Solomon Islands
Vanuatu		Vanuatu *(New Hebrides)*
N.Caled		New Caledonia
Fiji		Fiji
Hawaii		Hawaiian Islands
Polyn.		Polynesia *(exept Hawaii)*
Micron.		Micronesia

Austr., NZ		Australia, New Zealand
Austr.		Australia
	W-Austr.	Western Australia
	S-Austr.	South Australia
	N.Terr.	Northern Territory
	Queensl.	Queensland
	N.S.Wales	New South Wales *(with Australian Capital Territory)*
	Victoria	Victoria
	Tasman.	Tasmania
NZ		New Zealand
	NZ:N	North Island
	NZ:S	South Island
	Norfolk	Norfolk Island

Other abbreviations	
N	North
S	South
E	East
W	West
C	Central
M	Mid-
Alp.	Alps
Pyr.	Pyrenees
Carp. Mts.	Carpathian Mts.
Apenn.	Apennines
Balkan Mts.	Balkan Mts.
Altai Mts.	Altai Mts.
Him.	Himalayas
And.	Andes
mts.	Mountains
nat. in	naturalized
orig.?	native home unknown
cult.	horticultural origin
cosmopl.	Cosmopolitan (all eight major regions)
+	Distribution incomplete
*	all regions
(e.g. Eur.*)	
exc.	except

VII Systematic overview of the vascular plants

An overview of the various plant classification systems may be found in Brummit (1992), beginning with Bentham & Hooker (1862–1883), "Genera Plantarum" and ending with Cronquist (1988), "The Evolution and Classification of Flowering Plants". Basically, this dictionary follows the latter work; however, in the case of the Liliopsida (Monocotyledoneae) we take account of Dahlgren, Clifford & Yeo (1985), "The Families of Monocotyledons". Hence, the classification system in this volume largely corresponds to the classification of Brummit (1992), "Vascular Plant Families and Genera", cited above. The spelling of the generic names in particular follows this book strictly.

1. DIVISIO: PTERIDOPHYTA
   1. Classis: Psilotopsida
      1. Ordo: Psilotales
         Psilotaceae
   2. Classis: Lycopodiopsida
      1. Ordo: Isoetales
         Isoetaceae
      2. Ordo: Lycopodiales
         Lycopodiaceae
      3. Ordo: Selaginellales
         Selaginellaceae
   3. Classis: Equisetopsida
      1. Ordo: Equisetales
         Equisetaceae
   4. Classis: Pteridopsida (Filices)
      1. Ordo: Ophioglossales
         Ophioglossaceae
      2. Ordo: Marattiales
         Marattiaceae
      3. Ordo: Osmundales
         Osmundaceae
      4. Ordo: Pteridales
         Actiniopteridaceae, Adiantaceae, Aspleniaceae, Blechnaceae,
         Cheiropleuriaceae, Cyatheaceae, Davalliaceae, Dennstaedtiaceae, Dicksoniaceae,
         Dipteridaceae, Dryopteridaceae, Gleicheniaceae, Grammititdaceae,
         Hymenophyllaceae, Hymenophyllopsidaceae, Lomariopsidaceae,
         Lophosoriaceae, Loxsomataceae, Matoniaceae, Metaxyaceae,
         Monachosoraceae, Nephrolepidaceae, Oleandraceae, Parkeriaceae,
         Plagiogyriaceae, Platyzomataceae, Polypodiaceae, Pteridaceae, Schizaeaceae,
         Stromatopteridaceae, Thelypteridaceae, Vittariaceae, Woodisiaceae
      5. Ordo: Marsileales
         Marsileaceae

6. Ordo: Salviniales
Azollaceae, Salviniaceae

2. DIVISIO: SPERMATOPHYTA
ɪ. SUBDIVISIO: CONIFEROPHYTINA
  ɪ. Classis: Ginkgoopsida
    ɪ. Ordo: Ginkgoales
    Ginkgoaceae*
  2. Classis: Pinopsida (Coniferae)
    ɪ. Ordo: Pinales
    Araucariaceae*, Cephalotaxaceae*, Cupressaceae, Phyllocladaceae,
    Pinaceae*, Podocarpaceae, Sciadopityaceae, Taxodiaceae*
    2. Ordo: Taxales
    Taxaceae*
2. SUBDIVISIO: CYCADOPHYTINA
  ɪ. Classis: Cycadopsida
    ɪ. Ordo: Cycadales
    Boweniaceae, Cycadaceae, Stangeriaceae, Zamiaceae
  2. Classis: Gnetopsida
    ɪ. Ordo: Gnetales
    Ephedraceae*, Gnetaceae*, Welwitschiaceae*
3. SUBDIVISIO: MAGNOLIOPHYTINA (ANGIOSPERMAE)
  ɪ. Classis: Magnoliopsida (Dicotyledoneae)
    ɪ. Subclassis: Magnoliidae
      ɪ. Ordo: Magnoliales
      Annonaceae*, Austrobaileyaceae*, Canellaceae*, Degeneriaceae*,
      Eupomatiaceae*, Himantandraceae*, Lactoridaceae*, Magnoliaceae*,
      Myristicaceae*, Winteraceae*
      2. Ordo: Laurales
      Amborellaceae*, Calycanthaceae*, Gomortegaceae*, Hernandiaceae*,
      Idiospermaceae, Lauraceae*, Monimiaceae*, Trimeniaceae*
      3. Ordo: Piperales
      Chloranthaceae*, Piperaceae*, Saururaceae*
      4. Ordo: Aristolochiales
      Aristolochiaceae*
      5. Ordo: Illiciales
      Illiciaceae*, Schisandraceae*
      6. Ordo: Nymphaeales
      Cabombaceae*, Ceratophyllaceae*, Nymphaeaceae*
      7. Ordo: Nelumbonales
      Nelumbonaceae*
      8. Ordo: Ranunculales
      Berberidaceae*, Circaeasteraceae*, Glaucidiaceae, Lardizabalaceae*,
      Menispermaceae*, Ranunculaceae*, Sargentodoxaceae*
      9. Ordo: Papaverales
      Fumariaceae*, Papaveraceae*
    2. Subclassis: Hamamelididae
      ɪ. Ordo: Trochodendrales
      Tetracentraceae*, Trochodendraceae*

2. **Ordo: Hamamelidales**
   Cercidiphyllaceae*, Eupteleaceae*, Hamamelidaceae*, Myrothamnaceae*, Platanaceae*
3. **Ordo: Daphniphyllales**
   Daphniphyllaceae*
4. **Ordo: Didymelales**
   Didymelaceae
5. **Ordo: Eucommiales**
   Eucommiaceae*
6. **Ordo: Urticales**
   Barbeyaceae*, Cannabaceae*, Cecropiaceae, Moraceae*, Ulmaceae*, Urticaceae*
7. **Ordo: Leitneriales**
   Leitneriaceae*
8. **Ordo: Juglandales**
   Juglandaceae*, Rhoipteleaceae*
9. **Ordo: Myricales**
   Myricaceae*
10. **Ordo: Fagales**
    Balanopaceae*, Betulaceae*, *Corylaceae* see Betulaceae*, Fagaceae*, Ticodendraceae
11. **Ordo: Casuarinales**
    Casuarinaceae*

3. **Subclassis: Caryophyllidae**
   1. **Ordo: Caryophyllales**
      Achatocarpaceae*, Agdestidaceae, Aizoaceae*, Amaranthaceae*, Barbeuiaceae, Basellaceae*, Cactaceae*, Caryophyllaceae*, Chenopodiaceae*, Didiereaceae*, Gisekiaceae, Halophytaceae, Hectorellaceae, Illecebraceae*, Molluginaceae*, Nyctaginaceae*, Phytolaccaceae*, Portulacaceae*, Stegnospermataceae
   2. **Ordo: Polygonales**
      Polygonaceae*
   3. **Ordo: Plumbaginales**
      Plumbaginaceae*

4. **Subclassis: Dilleniidae**
   1. **Ordo: Dilleniales**
      Dilleniaceae*, Paeoniaceae*
   2. **Ordo: Theales**
      Actinidiaceae*, Asteropeiaceae, Caryocaraceae*, Clusiaceae*, Diegodendraceae, Dipterocarpaceae*, Elatinaceae*, *Guttiferae see Clusiaceae*, Marcgraviaceae*, Medusagynaceae*, Nepenthaceae*, Ochnaceae*, Oncothecaceae, Paracryphiaceae, Pellicieraceae, Pentaphylacaceae*, Quiinaceae *, Sarcolaenaceae*, Scytopetalaceae*, Sphaerosepalaceae, Strasburgeriaceae *, Tetrameristaceae, Theaceae*
   3. **Ordo: Malvales**
      Bombacaceae*, Elaeocarpaceae*, Malvaceae*, Sterculiaceae*, Tiliaceae*
   4. **Ordo: Lecythidales**
      Lecythidaceae*

5. **Ordo: Sarraceniales**
   Sarraceniaceae*
6. **Ordo: Droserales**
   Droseraceae*
7. **Ordo: Violales**
   Achariaceae*, Ancistrocladaceae*, Begoniaceae*, Bixaceae*, Caricaceae *,
   Cistaceae*, *Cochlospermaceae* see Bixaceae*, Cucurbitaceae*,
   Datiscaceae*, Dioncophyllaceae*, Flacourtiaceae*, Fouquieriaceae*,
   Frankeniaceae*, Hoplestigmataceae*, Huaceae, Lacistemataceae*,
   Loasaceae*, Malesherbiaceae*, Passifloraceae*, Peridiscaceae*,
   Plagiopteraceae, Scyphostegiaceae*, Stachyuraceae*, Tamaricaceae*,
   Turneraceae*, Violaceae *
8. **Ordo: Salicales**
   Salicaceae*
9. **Ordo: Capparales**
   Brassicaceae*, Capparaceae*, *Cruciferae see Brassicaceae*, Moringaceae*,
   Resedaceae*, Tovariaceae*
10. **Ordo: Batales**
    Bataceae*, Gyrostemonaceae*
11. **Ordo: Ericales**
    Clethraceae*, Cyrillaceae*, Empetraceae*, Epacridaceae*, Ericaceae*,
    Grubbiaceae*, Monotropaceae*, Pyrolaceae*
12. **Ordo: Diapensiales**
    Diapensiaceae*
13. **Ordo: Ebenales**
    Ebenaceae*, Lissocarpaceae*, Sapotaceae*, Styracaceae*, Symplocaceae*
14. **Ordo: Primulales**
    Myrsinaceae*, Primulaceae*, Theophrastaceae*

5. **Subclassis: Rosidae**
   1. **Ordo: Rosales**
      Chrysobalanaceae*, Crossosomataceae*, Neuradaceae*,
      Rhabdodendraceae, Rosaceae*, Stylobasiaceae, Surianaceae*
   2. **Ordo: Fabales**
      Caesalpiniaceae*, Fabaceae*, Mimosaceae*, *Papilionaceae see Fabaceae*
   3. **Ordo: Proteales**
      Proteaceae*
   4. **Ordo: Elaeagnales**
      Elaeagnaceae*
   5. **Ordo: Podostemales**
      Podostemaceae*
   6. **Ordo: Haloragales**
      Gunneraceae*, Haloragaceae*
   7. **Ordo: Myrtales**
      Alzateaceae, Combretaceae*, Crypteroniaceae*, Lythraceae*,
      Melastomataceae*, Myrtaceae*, Oliniaceae*, Onagraceae*, Penaeaceae*,
      Punicaceae *, Rhynchocalycaceae, Sonneratiaceae*, Thymelaeaceae*,
      Trapaceae*
   8. **Ordo: Rhizophorales**
      Anisophylleaceae, Rhizophoraceae*

9. **Ordo: Cornales**
Alangiaceae*, Aralidiaceae, Aucubaceae, Cornaceae*, Garryaceae*, Griseliniaceae, Helwingiaceae, Melanophyllaceae, Nyssaceae*, Torricelliaceae

10. **Ordo: Santalales**
Dipentodontaceae*, Eremolepidaceae, Loranthaceae*, Medusandraceae*, Misodendraceae*, Olacaceae*, Opiliaceae*, Santalaceae*, Viscaceae

11. **Ordo: Balanophorales**
Balanophoraceae*, Cynomoriaceae*

12. **Ordo: Rafflesiales**
Hydnoraceae*, Mitrastemonaceae*, Rafflesiaceae*

13. **Ordo: Celastrales**
Aextoxicaceae*, Aquifoliaceae*, Canotiaceae, Cardiopteridaceae*, Celastraceae*, Corynocarpaceae*, Dichapetalaceae*, Geissolomataceae*, Goupiaceae, Hippocrateaceae*, Icacinaceae*, Lophopyxidaceae, Phelliniaceae, Salvadoraceae*, Sphenostemonaceae, Stackhousiaceae*, Tepuianthaceae

14. **Ordo: Euphorbiales**
Buxaceae*, Euphorbiaceae*, Pandaceae*, Simmondsiaceae

15. **Ordo: Rhamnales**
Leeaceae*, Rhamnaceae*, Vitaceae*

16. **Ordo: Polygalales**
Emblingiaceae, Euphroniaceae, Krameriaceae*, Malpighiaceae*, Polygalaceae*, Tremandraceae*, Trigoniaceae*, Vochysiaceae*, Xanthophyllaceae

17. **Ordo: Sapindales**
Aceraceae*, Akaniaceae*, Anacardiaceae*, Balanitaceae*, Bretschneideraceae*, Burseraceae*, Cneoraceae*, Connaraceae*, Coriariaceae*, Hippocastanaceae*, Irvingiaceae*, Julianiaceae*, Meliaceae*, Melianthaceae*, *Meliosmaceae see Sabiaceae*, Physenaceae, Podoonaceae, Ptaeroxylaceae, Rutaceae*, Sabiaceae*, Sapindaceae*, Simaroubaceae*, Staphyleaceae*, Zygophyllaceae*

18. **Ordo: Geraniales**
Balsaminaceae*, Ctenolophonaceae, Erythroxylaceae*, Geraniaceae*, Humiriaceae*, Ixonanthaceae*, Lepidobotryaceae*, Limnanthaceae*, Linaceae*, Oxalidaceae*, Tropaeolaceae*

19. **Ordo: Apiales**
Apiaceae*, Araliaceae*, *Umbelliferae see Apiaceae*

20. **Ordo: Saxifragales**
Cephalotaceae*, Crassulaceae*, Eremosynaceae, Greyiaceae*, Grossulariaceae*, Parnassiaceae*, Penthoraceae*, Saxifragaceae*, Vahliaceae

21. **Ordo: Cunoniales**
Brunelliaceae*, Bruniaceae*, Cunoniaceae*, Davidsoniaceae, Eucryphiaceae*

22. **Ordo: Hydrangeales**
Alseuosmiaceae, Columelliaceae*, Escalloniaceae*, Hydrangeaceae*, Montiniaceae*, Pterostemonaceae*

23. **Ordo: Pittosporales**
    Byblidaceae*, Pittosporaceae*, Roridulaceae*
6. **Subclassis: Asteridae**
    1. **Ordo: Gentianales**
       Apocynaceae*, Asclepiadaceae*, Dialypetalanthaceae*, Gentianaceae*,
       Loganiaceae*, Retziaceae, Saccifoliaceae
    2. **Ordo: Solanales**
       Boraginaceae*, Cobaeaceae, Convolvulaceae*, Cuscutaceae*,
       Duckeodendraceae, Goetzeaceae, Hydrophyllaceae*, Menyanthaceae*,
       Nolanaceae*, Polemoniaceae*, Solanaceae*
    3. **Ordo: Lamiales**
       Avicenniaceae*, Cyclocheilaceae, *Labiatae see Lamiaceae*, Lamiaceae*,
       Lennoaceae*, Nesogenaceae, Phrymaceae*, Stilbaceae*,
       Tetrachondraceae, Verbenaceae*
    4. **Ordo: Callitrichales**
       Callitrichaceae*, Hippuridaceae*, Hydrostachyaceae*
    5. **Ordo: Plantaginales**
       Plantaginaceae*
    6. **Ordo: Scrophulariales**
       Acanthaceae*, Bignoniaceae*, Buddlejaceae*, Gesneriaceae*,
       Globulariceae*, Lentibulariaceae*, Mendonciaceae, Myoporaceae*,
       Oleaceae*, Orobanchaceae*, Pedaliaceae*, Scrophulariaceae*
    7. **Ordo: Campanulales**
       Brunoniaceae*, Campanulaceae*, Donatiaceae*, Goodeniaceae*,
       Pentphragmataceae*, Sphenocleaceae*, Stylidiaceae*
    8. **Ordo: Rubiales**
       Rubiaceae*, Theligonaceae*
    9. **Ordo: Dipsacales**
       Adoxaceae*, Caprifoliaceae*, Carlemanniaceae, Dipsacaceae*,
       Morinaceae, Triplostegiaceae, Valerianaceae*
    10. **Ordo: Calycerales**
        Calyceraceae*
    11. **Ordo: Asterales**
        Asteraceae*, *Compositae see Asteraceae*
2. **Classis: Liliopsida (Monocotyledoneae)**
    1. **Subclassis: Alismatidae**
       1. **Ordo: Alismatales**
          Alismataceae*, Butomaceae*, Limnocharitaceae
       2. **Ordo: Hydrocharitales**
          Hydrocharitaceae*
       3. **Ordo: Najadales**
          Aponogetonaceae*, Cymodoceaceae*, Juncaginaceae*, Lilaeaceae*,
          Najadaceae*, Posidoniaceae*, Potamogetonaceae*, Ruppiaceae*,
          Scheuchzeriaceae*, Zannichelliaceae*, Zosteraceae*
       4. **Ordo: Triuridales**
          Triuridaceae*
    2. **Subclassis: Arecidae**
       1. **Ordo: Arecales**
          Arecaceae*, *Palmae see Arecaceae*

2. **Ordo: Cyclanthales**
   Cyclanthaceae*
3. **Ordo: Pandanales**
   Pandanaceae*
4. **Ordo: Arales**
   Acoraceae, Araceae*, Lemnaceae*
3. **Subclassis: Commelinidae**
   1. **Ordo: Commelinales**
      Commelinaceae*, Mayacaceae*, Rapateaceae*, Xyridaceae*
   2. **Ordo: Eriocaulales**
      Eriocaulaceae*
   3. **Ordo: Restionales**
      Anarthricaceae, Centrolepidaceae*, Ecdeiocoleaceae, Flagellariaceae*,
      Joinvilleaceae, Restionaceae*
   4. **Ordo: Juncales**
      Juncaceae*, Thurniaceae*
   5. **Ordo: Cyperales**
      Cyperaceae*
   6. **Ordo: Poales**
      Gramineae see Poaceae, Poaceae*
   7. **Ordo: Hydatellales**
      Hydatellaceae
   8. **Ordo: Typhales**
      Sparganiaceae*, Typhaceae*
4. **Subclassis: Zingiberidae**
   1. **Ordo: Bromeliales**
      Bromeliaceae*
   2. **Ordo: Zingiberales**
      Cannaceae*, Costaceae, Heliconiaceae, Lowiaceae*, Marantaceae*,
      Musaceae*, Strelitziaceae*, Zingiberaceae*
5. **Subclassis: Liliidae**
   1. **Ordo: Liliales**
      Alstroemeriaceae*, Colchicaceae*, Iridaceae*, Liliaceae*
   2. **Ordo: Dioscoreales**
      Dioscoreaceae*, Petermanniaceae*, Rhipogonaceae, Smilacaceae*,
      Stemonaceae*, Taccaceae*, Trichopodaceae*, Trilliaceae*
   3. **Ordo: Melanthiales**
      Melanthiaceae*
   4. **Ordo: Pontederiales**
      Pontederiaceae*
   5. **Ordo: Philydrales**
      Philydraceae*
   6. **Ordo: Haemodorales**
      Haemodoraceae*
   7. **Ordo: Velloziales**
      Velloziaceae*

8. Ordo: Asparagales
Agavaceae*, Alliaceae*, Aloeaceae, Amaryllidaceae*, Anthericaceae,
Aphyllanthaceae, Asparagaceae*, Asphodelaceae, Asteliaceae,
Blandfordiaceae, Calectasiaceae, Convallariaceae, Cyanastraceae*,
Dasypogonceae, Doryanthaceae, Dracaenaceae*, Eriospermaceae,
Hanguanaceae, Hemerocallidaceae, Herreriaceae, Hostaceae,
Hyacinthaceae, Hypoxidceae*, Ixioliriaceae, Lomandraceae,
Philesiaceae*, Phormiaceae, Ruscceae*, Tecophilaeaceae*,
Xanthorrhoeaceae*

9. Ordo: Orchidales
Orchidaceae*

10. Ordo: Burmanniales
Burmanniaceae*, Corsiaceae*, Geosiridaceae*

VIII Key to alphabetical overview

Acer[1] L.[2] –n–[3] Aceraceae[4] · 124 spp[5] · E: Maple[6], F: Erable[7], G: Ahorn[8]
– **campestre**[9] L.[10]
some cultivars

-     subsp. **campestre**[11] · E: Field Maple[12], Hedge Maple; F:Erable champêtre[13]; G: Feld-Ahorn[14] · ♄ ♄[15] d Z 5[16] ⚕ V[17] Ⓝ[18]; Eur. *, Kauk., TR, N-Iran, Maroc., Alger.[19];
-     var. *hebecarpum*[20] DC. =[21] Acer campestre subsp. campestre
-     subsp. **leiocarpum**[22] Pax · G: Kahlfrüchtiger Feld-Ahorn

1 genus	12 English name
2 author of genus	13 French name
3 Latin gender	14 German name
4 family	15 type of plant
5 number of species	16 winter hardiness zone
6 English name for genus	17 flowering time (month in Roman numerals)
7 French name for genus	18 additional details
8 German name for genus	19 distribution
9 species	20 synonym (italics)
10 author of species	21 cross reference to correct name
11 autonym	22 subspecies (or variety) of the species (indented)

Symbols

☉	Annual plant		▭	Window-box
☉	Biennial plant		∧	Winter protection
♃	Perennial		⚕	Medicinal plant
♄	Sub-shrub		☠	Toxic plant
♄	Shrub		⊗	Fruit decoration
♄	Tree		Ⓝ	Useful plant
ψ	Succulents		✂	Cut flowers for floristry purpose
d	Deciduous		I-XII	Flowering time: month(s) in
s	Semi-evergreen			Roman numerals
e	Evergreen		D	Scent
×	Hybrid		▽	Protected according to the terms
+	Graft-chimaera			of Federal Nature Conservation
≶	Hanging plant			law of 1st Febuary 2001.
≶	Climbing plant		*	Protected species according to
⤳	Creeping plant			the Convention on International
∫	Liane			Trade in Endangered Species of
╠	Border			Wild Fauna and Flora [CITES]
⌒	Cushion plant			(cf. European Community
△	Rockery			Ordinance No. 338/97,
∼	Riparian and marsh plant			Supplements A and B, of
≈	Aquatic plant			9th December 1996, amended
Z1–Z10	Z1–Z10 Winter hardiness zones			18th December 2000)[†].
	(see page 35)			
Ⓦ	Hothouse			
Ⓚ	Cold house, winter house			
Ⓐ	Alpine house			

† Anyone wishing to import or otherwise introduce plants from a foreign country or overseas should first ascertain whether they may be collected or imported according to the terms of CITES.

IX Alphabetical overview of genera and species

Abelia R. Br. -f- *Caprifoliaceae* · 40 spp. ·
E:Abelia; F:Abélia; G:Abelien
- **chinensis** R. Br. · E:Chinese Abelia;
G:China-Abelie · ♄ d Z8 ⓚ VII-IX; China
- **engleriana** (Graebn.) Rehder · E:Engler's
Abelia; G:Englers Abelie· ♄ d Z8 ⓚ
VI-VII; China
- **floribunda** (Mart. & Galeotti) Decne. ·
E:Mexican Abelia; G:Reichblütige Abelie
· ♄ e Z8 ⓚ V-VI; Mex.
- **graebneriana** Rehder · E:Graebner's
Abelia; G:Graebners Abelie · ♄ d Z8 ⓚ
VII; C-China
- × **grandiflora** (Rovelli ex André) Rehder
(*A. chinensis* × *A. uniflora*) · E:Glossy
Abelia; G:Großblütige Abelie · ♄ s Z8 ⓚ
∧ VII-X; cult.
- *longituba* Rehder = Abelia schumannii
- **mosanensis** T.H. Chung ex Nakai ·
G:Koreanische Abelie · ♄ Z8 ⓚ V-VI;
Korea
- *rupestris* hort. Späth = Abelia × grandiflora
- var. *grandiflora* André = Abelia ×
grandiflora
- *rupestris* Lindl. = Abelia chinensis
- **schumannii** (Graebn.) Rehder ·
E:Schumann's Abelia; G:Schumanns
Abelie · ♄ s Z8 ⓚ ∧ VI-IX; W-China
- **spathulata** Siebold & Zucc. · ♄ d Z8 ⓚ
V; Jap.
- **triflora** R. Br. ex Wall. · G:Dreiblütige
Abelie · ♄ d Z8 ⓚ VI-VII; NW-Him.
- **uniflora** R. Br. ex Wall. · G:Einblütige
Abelia · ♄ e Z8 ⓚ VI-IX; E-China
- **zanderi** (Graebn.) Rehder · G:Zanders
Abelie · ♄ d Z8 ⓚ VII-VIII; China

Abeliophyllum Nakai -n- *Oleaceae* · 1 sp. ·
E:White Forsythia; F:Forsythia blanc;
G:Schneeforsythie
- **distichum** Nakai · E:White Forsythia;
G:Schneeforsythie · ♄ d Z7 ∧ V; C-Korea

Abelmoschus Medik. -m- *Malvaceae* ·
20 spp. · F:Gombo, Okra; G:Bisameibisch
- **esculentus** (L.) Moench · E:Gumbo,
Lady's Fingers, Okra; G:Essbarer
Bisameibisch, Okra · ⊙ Z9 ⓜ VII-VIII ⓝ;
Ind., NE-Afr., nat. in Trop.

- **manihot** (L.) Medik. · E:Manioc
Hibiscus; G:Maniok-Bisameibisch · ⊙ ⊙
⁴ Z9 ⓚ VII-IX ⓝ; trop. As., nat. in Trop.
- **moschatus** Medik. · E:Musk Mallow;
G:Moschus-Bisameibisch · ⊙ ⊙ Z9 ⓚ
VII-VIII ⚥ ⓝ; Ind., nat. in Trop.

Aberia Hochst. = Dovyalis
- *caffra* Hook. f. & Harv. = Dovyalis caffra
- *gardneri* Clos = Dovyalis hebecarpa

Abies Mill. -f- *Pinaceae* · 48 spp. · E:Fir,
Silver Fir; F:Sapin; G:Tanne
- **alba** Mill. · E:European Silver Fir; G:Weiß-
Tanne · ♄ Z4 V-VI ⓝ; Eur.* exc. BrI, Sc
- **amabilis** (Douglas ex Loudon) Douglas
ex J. Forbes · E:Pacific Silver Fir, Red
Silver Fir; G:Purpur-Tanne · ♄ e Z6 ⓝ;
SE-Alaska, B.C., Wash., Oreg., N-Calif.
- **balsamea** (L.) Mill. · E:Balsam Fir;
G:Gewöhnliche Balsam-Tanne · ♄ e D Z2
⚥ ⓝ; Can., USA: NE, NCE
- **borisii-regis** Mattf. · E:King Boris Fir;
G:Bulgarische Tanne, König-Boris-Tanne
· ♄ e Z6; GR, S-BG
- *bornmuelleriana* Mattf. = Abies nordmanniana subsp. equi-trojani
- *brachyphylla* Maxim. = Abies homolepis
var. homolepis
- **bracteata** (D. Don) A. Poit. · E:Bristlecone
Fir, Santa Lucia Fir; G:Grannen-Tanne,
Santa-Lucia-Tanne · ♄ e Z8; SW-Calif.
- *candicans* Fisch. ex Henkel & W. Hochst.
= Abies nordmanniana subsp. nordmanniana
- **cephalonica** Loudon · E:Grecian Fir,
Greek Fir; G:Griechische Tanne · ♄ e Z6
ⓝ
- var. *apollinis* (Link) Beissn. = Abies
cephalonica
- var. *graeca* (Fraas) T.S. Liu = Abies
nordmanniana subsp. equi-trojani
- **chensiensis** Tiegh. · G:Gewöhnliche
Shensi-Tanne · ♄ e Z6; China: Shaanxi,
Hubei, Yunnan
- **cilicica** (Antoine & Kotschy) Carrière ·
E:Cilician Fir; G:Gewöhnliche Cilicische
Tanne · ♄ e Z6; TR, N-Syr.
- **concolor** (Gordon) Lindl. ex Hildebr. ·

E:Colorado Fir, White Fir; G:Colorado-Tanne · ♄ e Z5 V Ⓝ; USA: Oreg., Calif., Rocky Mts., SW; Mex.: Baja Calif., Sonora

– **Lowiana Group** · E:Low's Fir, Pacific White Fir, Sierra White Fir; G:Pazifische Weiß-Tanne, Sierra-Tanne · ♄ e Z4; USA: Oreg., Calif.

– **delavayi** Franch. · E:Delavay's Fir; G:Delavays Tanne

– var. **delavayi** · G:Yunnan-Tanne · ♄ e Z7; SW-China, NE-Ind., N-Burma

– var. *fabri* (Mast.) D.R. Hunt = Abies fabri

– var. *faxoniana* (Rehder & E.H. Wilson) A.B. Jacks. = Abies fargesii var. faxoniana

– var. *forrestii* (Coltm.- Rog.) A.B. Jacks. = Abies forrestii

– var. *smithii* (Viguié & Gaussen) T.S. Liu = Abies forrestii

– *equi-trojani* (Asch. & Sint. ex Boiss.) Mattf. = Abies nordmanniana subsp. equi-trojani

– *excelsa* (Lam.) Poir. = Picea abies var. abies

– **fabri** (Mast.) Craib · E:Faber's Fir; G:Fabers Tanne · ♄ e Z6; China: Yunnan

– **fargesii** Franch. · E:Farges' Fir; G:Farges' Tanne

– var. **fargesii** · G:Gewöhnliche Farges' Tanne · ♄ e Z7; C-China

– var. **faxoniana** (Rehder & E.H. Wilson) T.S. Liu · G:Sichuan-Tanne · ♄ e Z7; W-China: Sichuan

– var. **sutchuensis** Franch. · G:Gansu-Tanne · ♄ e Z7; W-China

– **firma** Siebold & Zucc. · E:Japanese Fir, Momi Fir; G:Momi-Tanne · ♄ e Z6; Jap.

– **forrestii** Coltm.- Rog. · G:Gewöhnliche Forrest-Tanne · ♄ e Z7; SW-China

– **fraseri** (Pursh) Poir. · E:Fraser Fir, Southern Balsam Fir; G:Frasers Tanne · ♄ e Z5 Ⓝ; USA: Va., W.Va., Tenn., N.C.

– **grandis** (Douglas ex D. Don) Lindl. · E:Giant Fir, Grand Fir; G:Küsten-Tanne, Riesen-Tanne · ♄ e Z6 V Ⓝ; B.C., USA: NW, Rocky Mts., N-Calif.

– **holophylla** Maxim. · E:Manchurian Fir, Needle Fir; G:Mandschurische Tanne, Nadel-Tanne · ♄ e Z6; Korea, Manch.

– **homolepis** Siebold & Zucc. · E:Nikko Fir; G:Nikko-Tanne

– var. **homolepis** · G:Gewöhnliche Nikko-Tanne · ♄ e Z5 Ⓝ; Jap.

– var. **umbellata** (Mayr) E.H. Wilson · G:Schirmförmige Nikko-Tanne · ♄ e Z5; Honshu

– × **insignis** Carrière ex Bailly (A.

nordmanniana × A. pinsapo) · G:Prächtige Hybrid-Tanne · ♄ e Z6; cult.

– **kawakamii** (Hayata) T. Itô · E:Formosan Fir, Taiwan Fir; G:Formosa-Tanne · ♄ e Z7; Taiwan

– **koreana** E.H. Wilson · E:Korean Fir; G:Korea-Tanne · ♄ e ⚘ Z5; Korea

– **lasiocarpa** (Hook.) Nutt. · E:Subalpine Fir; G:Gewöhnliche Felsengebirgs-Tanne · ♄ e Z4 Ⓝ; Alaska, Can.: W; USA: NW, Rocky Mts., SW

– *lowiana* (Gordon) A. Murray bis = Abies concolor Lowiana Group

– **magnifica** A. Murray bis · E:California Red Fir, Red Fir; G:Kalifornische Rot-Tanne · ♄ e Z6 Ⓝ; USA: Oreg., Calif., Nev.

– **mariesii** Mast. · E:Maries' Fir; G:Aomori-Tanne, Maries' Tanne · ♄ e Z6; Jap.

– **nobilis** (Douglas ex D. Don) Lindl. = Abies procera

– *nobilis* A. Dietr. = Abies alba

– var. *magnifica* (A. Murray bis) Kellogg = Abies magnifica

– **nordmanniana** (Steven) Spach · E:Caucasian Fir, Christmas Tree; G:Nordmanns-Tanne

– subsp. **equi-trojani** (Asch. & Sint. ex Boiss.) Coode & Cullen · E:Bornmueller's Fir; G:Troja-Tanne, Türkische Tanne · ♄ e Z4; NW-TR

– subsp. **nordmanniana** · E:Caucasian Fir, Christmas Tree; G:Gewöhnliche Nordmanns-Tanne · ♄ e Z5 V Ⓝ; Cauc., TR

– **numidica** de Lannoy ex Carrière · E:Algerian Fir; G:Algier-Tanne, Numidische Tanne · ♄ e Z6; NE-Alger.

– *pectinata* (Lam.) Lam. & DC. = Abies alba

– *pichta* Forbes = Abies sibirica

– **pindrow** (Lamb.) Royle · E:West Himalayan Fir; G:Gewöhnliche Pindrow-Tanne · ♄ e Z8 Ⓝ; Him.: Afgh., Kashmir, NW-Ind., W-Nepal

– **pinsapo** Boiss. · E:Spanish Fir; G:Gewöhnliche Spanische Tanne · ♄ e Z6 Ⓝ; S-Sp., N-Moroc.

– **procera** Rehder · E:Christmas Tree, Noble Fir; G:Edel-Tanne, Edle Tanne · ♄ e Z6 Ⓝ; USA: Wash., Oreg., N-Calif.

– **recurvata** Mast. · E:Min Fir; G:Gewöhnliche Min-Tanne · ♄ e Z5; W-China: Sichuan

– **sachalinensis** (Honda) W.G. Schmid · E:Sakhalin Fir; G:Gewöhnliche Sachalin-Tanne · ♄ e Z4 Ⓝ; N-Jap., Sakhal.

– **sibirica** Ledeb. · E:Siberian Fir;

G:Sibirische Tanne · ♄ e Z4 Ⓝ; Eur.:
Russ.; N-As., C-As., Mong., nat. in Sc
– **spectabilis** (D. Don) Spach ·
E:Himalayan Fir; G:Himalaya-Tanne · ♄
e Z8 Ⓝ; Him.: Afgh., Kashmir, NW-Ind.,
Nepal, Bhutan
– **squamata** Mast. · E:Flaky Fir; G:Schup-
penrindige Tanne · ♄ e Z6; SW-China:
Sichuan
– *subalpina* Engelm. = Abies lasiocarpa
– **veitchii** Lindl. · E:Veitch Fir, Veitch's
Silver Fir; G:Veitchs Tanne
– var. *sachalinensis* F. Schmidt = Abies
sachalinensis
– var. **veitchii** · E:Veitch Fir, Veitch's Silver
Fir; G:Veitchs Tanne · ♄ e Z5; C-Jap.
– *venusta* (Douglas ex Hook.) K. Koch =
Abies bracteata
– × **vilmorinii** Mast. (*A. cephalonica* × *A.
pinsapo*) · E:Vilmorin's Fir; G:Vilmorins
Tanne · ♄ e Z6; cult.
– *webbiana* (Wall. ex D. Don) Lindl. = Abies
spectabilis

Abobra Naudin -f- *Cucurbitaceae* · 1 sp.
– **tenuifolia** (Gillies) Cogn. · ⌐ ⚥ ⚭ ⚑ ∧;
Arg., Urug.
– *viridiflora* Naudin = Abobra tenuifolia

Abroma Jacq. -n- *Sterculiaceae* · 2 spp.
– **augustum** (L.) L. f. · E:Devil's Cotton · ♄
e ⚑ ⚜ Ⓝ; SE-As, N-Austr.

Abromeitiella Mez = Deuterocohnia
– *brevifolia* (Griseb.) A. Cast. = Deuterocohnia brevifolia
– *chlorantha* (Speg.) Mez = Deuterocohnia
brevifolia
– *lorentziana* (Mez) A. Cast. = Deuterocohnia lorentziana

Abronia Juss. -f- *Nyctaginaceae* · c. 35 spp. ·
E:Sand Verbena; F:Verveine des sables;
G:Sandverbene
– **umbellata** Lam. · E:Pink Sand Verbena;
G:Rosafarbene Sandverbene · ⊙ ⌐ D Z8
⚑ VII-X; B.C.; USA: Wash., Oreg., Calif.;
Mex.: Baja Calif.

Abrus Adans. -m- *Fabaceae* · 17 spp. · F:Pois
à chapelet; G:Paternostererbse
– **precatorius** L. · E:Crab's Eye Vine, Indian
Liquorice, Rosary Pea; G:Paternostererbse
· ♄ ⚥ ⚑ ⚢ ⚜ Ⓝ; Trop., nat. in S-Fla.

Abutilon Mill. -n- *Malvaceae* · 150-200 spp. ·
E:Flowering Maple, Indian Mallow;
F:Abutilon, Lanterne chinoise; G:Sam-
metmalve, Samtpappel, Schönmalve
– **darwinii** Hook. f. · G:Darwins Samtpappel · ♄ Z8 ⚑; Braz.
– *globosum* hort. = Abutilon × hybridum
– × **hybridum** hort. (*A. darwinii* × *A.
pictum*) · E:Chinese Lantern; G:Chinalat-
erne · ♄ Z8 ⚑; cult. in many forms
– **indicum** (L.) Sweet · E:Indian Mallow;
G:Indische Samtpappel · ⊙ ⊙ ⌐ Z10 ⚑
⚥ Ⓝ; trop. Afr., trop. As., nat. in Fla.,
W-Ind., trop. S-Am.
– **insigne** Planch. · ♄ Z9 ⚑; Col., Venez.
– **megapotamicum** (Spreng.) A.
St.-Hil. & Naudin · E:Trailing Abutilon;
G:Kriechende Samtpappel · ♄ e ⚥ Z8 ⚑
I-XII; Braz.
– **ochsenii** (Phil.) Phil. · G:Chile-Samtpap-
pel · ♄ e Z8 ⚑; Chile
– **pictum** (Gillies ex Hook. & Arn.) Walp. ·
E:Painted Indian Mallow; G:Bunte
Samtpappel · ♄ ♄ Z9 ⚑ VIII-XI; Braz.,
nat. in C-Am., s S-Am.
– **sellowianum** (Klotzsch) Regel · G:Sel-
lows Samtpappel · ♄ ⚑
– *striatum* G.F. Dicks. ex Lindl. = Abutilon
pictum
– × **suntense** C.D. Brickell (*A. ochsenii* × *A.
vitifolium*) · G:Purpur-Samtpappel · ♄ e
⚑; cult.
– **theophrasti** Medik. · E:Butter-Print,
China Jute, Velvet Leaf; G:Chinesische
Samtpappel · ⊙ Z4 VII-VIII Ⓝ; Ind., China,
nat. in Eur.: Ib, F Ital-P, H, Ba, EC-Eur.;
TR, Cauc., C-As., N-Afr., USA, Austr.
– **venosum** Lem. · G:Geaderte Samtpappel · ♄ Z9 ⚑ VIII-XI; ? Braz.
– *vexillarium* E. Morren = Abutilon
megapotamicum
– **vitifolium** (Cav.) C. Presl · G:Kurzlebige
Samtpappel · ♄ e Z8 ⚑ V-VI; Chile

Acacia Mill. -f- *Mimosaceae* · c. 1200 spp. ·
E:Mimosa, Wattle; F:Acacia, Mimosa;
G:Mimose der Gärtner, Akazie
– **acinacea** Lindl. · E:Gold-dust Wattle;
G:Goldstaub-Akazie · ♄ e Z9 ⚑; Austr.:
N.S.Wales, Victoria, S-Austr.
– **aculeatissima** J.F. Macbr. · E:Creeping
Wattle, Thin-leaf Wattle; G:Schmalblät-
trige Akazie · ♄ e Z9 ⚑ I-XII; Austr.:
N.S.Wales, Victoria
– **acuminata** Benth. · E:Raspberry Acacia;

G:Himbeer-Akazie · ħ Z9 ⓐ; Austr.:
W-Austr.
– **adunca** A. Cunn. ex G. Don ·
E:Wallangarra Wattle; G:Wallangarra-
Akazie · ħ ħ e Z9 ⓐ; Austr.: N.S.Wales
– **alata** R. Br. · E:Winged Wattle;
G:Geflügelte Akazie
– var. **alata** · ħ e Z8 ⓐ; W-Austr.
– var. **platyptera** (Lindl.) Meisn. · G:Breit-
geflügelte Akazie · ħ e Z8 ⓐ III-V;
W-Austr.
– **aneura** F. Muell. · G:Mulga-Akazie;
E:Mulga · ħ ħ e Z9 ⓐ; Austr.: Queensl.,
N.S.Wales, S-Austr., W-Austr., N.Terr.
– *arabica* (Lam.) Willd. = Acacia nilotica
– *argyrophylla* Hook. ex F. Muell. = Acacia
brachybotrya
– **auriculiformis** A. Cunn. ex Benth. ·
E:Black Wattle; G:Ohrförmige Akazie · ħ
e Z9 ⓐ ⓝ; N.Guinea
– **baileyana** F. Muell. · E:Bailey Acacia,
Cootamundra Wattle; G:Baileys Akazie ·
ħ ħ e Z8 ⓐ III-IV ⓝ; Austr.: N.S.Wales
– **brachybotrya** Benth. · E:Grey Mulga;
G:Graue Mulga-Akazie · ħ Z9 ⓐ; S-Austr.
– **buxifolia** A. Cunn. · E:Box Leaf Wattle;
G:Buchsblättrige Akazie · ħ e Z9 ⓐ;
Austr.: Queensl., N.S.Wales, Victoria
– **caffra** (Thunb.) Willd. · E:Common
Hookthorn; G:Knorrige Akazie · ħ Z9 ⓐ;
trop. Afr, S-Afr.
– **calamifolia** Sweet ex Lindl. · E:Broom
Wattle; G:Besen-Akazie · ħ e Z9 ⓐ III-IV;
Austr.: N.S.Wales, Victoria
– **cardiophylla** A. Cunn. ex Benth. ·
E:Wyalong Wattle; G:Herzblättrige
Akazie · ħ ħ Z9 ⓐ; Austr.: N.S.Wales
– **catechu** (L. f.) Willd. · E:Cachou Acacia;
G:Cachou-Akazie · ħ d Z9 ⓐ ⚥ ⓝ; Eth.,
Sambia, Pakist., Ind., Burma, Thail.,
Sumat., Java
– **caven** (Molina) Molina · E:Roman-
cassie · ħ d Z9 ⓐ; Chile, Arg.
– **cornigera** (L.) Willd. · E:Bull Horn
Acacia; G:Stierhorn-Akazie · ħ ħ d Z9 ⓜ
III; Mex., C-Am., nat. in W.Ind., S-Fla.
– **cultriformis** A. Cunn. ex G. Don · E:Knife
Leaf Wattle; G:Messerblatt-Akazie ·
ħ e Z8-9 ⓐ III-IV; Austr.: Queensl.,
N.S.Wales
– **cyanophylla** Lindl. · E:Orange Wattle · ħ
e Z9 ⓐ II-IV ⓝ; Austr.: W-Austr., nat. in
S-Eur., N-Afr.
– **cyclops** A. Cunn. ex G. Don · E:Coastal
Wattle, Rooikrans; G:Küsten-Akazie · ħ e

Z9 ⓐ ⓝ; Austr.: W-Austr., nat. in C-P
– **dealbata** Link · E:Mimosa, Silver Wattle ·
ħ e Z8 ⓐ I-IV ⓝ; Austr.: Queensl.,
N.S.Wales, Victoria, Tasman., nat. in
S-Eur.
– **decora** Rchb. · E:Showy Wattle, Western
Silver Wattle; G:Prächtige Akazie · ħ ħ
e Z9 ⓐ; Austr.: Queensl., N.S.Wales,
Victoria
– **decurrens** (J.C. Wendl.) Willd. · E:Early
Black Wattle, Green Wattle; G:Frühe
Schwarzholz-Akazie · ħ e Z7-8 I-IV ⓝ;
Austr.: N.S.Wales, nat. in S-Austr., Vict.,
Tasman.
– var. *dealbata* (Link) F. Muell. = Acacia
dealbata
– var. *mollis* Lindl. = Acacia mearnsii
– **drummondii** Lindl. · E:Drummond's
Wattle; G:Drummonds Akazie · ħ e Z9 ⓐ
⛉ III-IV; W-Austr.
– **dunnii** (Maiden) Turrill · E:Elephant Ear
Wattle; G:Elefantenohr-Akazie · ħ ħ e Z9
ⓐ; N-Austr.
– **eburnea** Willd. · ħ Z9 ⓐ; Arab., Ind., Sri
Lanka
– **extensa** Lindl. · E:Wiry Wattle; G:Borstige
Akazie · ħ e Z9 ⓐ; Austr.: W-Austr.
– **farnesiana** (L.) Willd. · E:Scented
Wattle, Sweet Acacia; G:Antillen-Akazie
· ħ ħ e Z8 ⓐ II-IV ⚥ ⓝ; USA: Tex., SW,
S-Calif., Fla.; Mex., W.Ind., S-Am., nat. in
USA: SE; sp.
– **fimbriata** A. Cunn. ex G. Don · E:Fringed
Wattle; G:Gefranste Akazie · ħ ħ e Z9 ⓐ;
Austr.: Queensl., N.S.Wales
– **floribunda** (Vent.) Willd. · E:Sally Wattle, White Sallow; G:Blassgelbe Akazie ·
ħ ħ Z9 ⓐ III
– **glaucoptera** Benth. · E:Clay Wattle, Flat
Wattle; G:Lehm-Akazie · ħ ħ e Z9 ⓐ;
W-Austr.
– **hakeoides** A. Cunn. ex Benth. · E:Hakea-
leaf Wattle, Western Black Wattle;
G:Westliche Schwarzholz-Akazie · ħ ħ
e Z9 ⓐ; Austr.: Queensl., N.S.Wales,
Victoria, S-Austr., W-Austr.
– **hemiteles** Benth. · E:Tan Wattle;
G:Braune Akazie · ħ e Z9 ⓐ; Austr.
– *horrida* hort. non Willd. = Acacia karroo
– **karroo** Hayne · E:Sweet Thorn;
G:Karroo-Akazie · ħ ħ d Z8 ⓐ ⓝ; S-Afr.,
nat. in SW-Eur., N-Afr.
– **kirkii** Oliv. · G:Kirks Akazie · ħ Z9 ⓜ ⓝ;
W-Sah, Tanzania, trop-Afr.
– **latifolia** Benth. · E:Broadleaf Acacia;

G:Breitblättrige Akazie · ♄ e Z9 ⌂;
NE-Austr.
- *lebbeck* Willd. = Albizia lebbeck
- **ligulata** A. Cunn. ex Benth. · E:Dune
Wattle, Sandhill Wattle; G:Dünen-Akazie
· ♄ ♄ e Z9 ⌂; Austr.
- **longifolia** (Andrews) Willd. · E:Sydney
Golden Wattle; G:Sydney Gold-Akazie · ♄
♄ e Z8 ⌂; E-Austr.
- var. *floribunda* (Vent.) F. Muell. = Acacia
floribunda
- **mearnsii** De Wild. · E:Black Wattle;
G:Gerber-Akazie · ♄ e Z9 ⌂ I-IV Ⓝ;
Austr.: Queensl., N.S.Wales, Victoria,
Tasman., nat. in P, sp., I
- **melanoxylon** R. Br. · E:Black Wood
Acacia, Blackwood; G:Schwarzholz-
Akazie · ♄ e Z8 ⌂ III-IV Ⓝ; Austr.:
Queensl., N.S.Wales, Victoria, Tasman.,
nat. in SW-Eur., N-Afr.
- *mollissima* auct. non Willd. = Acacia
mearnsii
- **nilotica** (L.) Willd. ex Delile · E:Babul,
Gum Arabic Tree; G:Ägyptischer
Schotendorn · ♄ Z9 ⌂ ⚘ Ⓝ; trop. Afr.,
S-Afr., nat. in Ind.
- **omalophylla** A. Cunn. ex Benth. ·
E:Fragrant Mimosa; G:Australisches
Veilchenholz · ♄ e Z9 ⌂ Ⓝ; Austr.
- **paradoxa** DC. · E:Hedge Wattle,
Kangaroo Thorn; G:Känguru-Akazie · ♄
Z8-9 ⌂ ⛉ III-IV Ⓝ
- **podalyriifolia** A. Cunn. ex G. Don ·
E:Pearl Acacia, Queensland Silver
Wattle; G:Queensland-Akazie · ♄ ♄ e Z8
⌂ XII-III; Austr.: Queensl., N.S.Wales
- **polyacantha** Willd. · E:Catechu Tree;
G:Vielstachlige Akazie · ♄ Z9 ⌂ Ⓝ; trop.
Afr., Sri Lanka, Burma
- **pubescens** (Vent.) R. Br. · E:Downy
Wattle; G:Flaumige Akazie · ♄ ♄ e Z9 ⌂;
Austr.
- **pulchella** R. Br. · E:Prickly Moses;
G:Mosesdorn · ♄ Z8 ⌂ ⛉ IV-V; Austr.:
W-Austr.
- **pycnantha** Benth. · E:Golden Wattle;
G:Gold-Akazie · ♄ ♄ e Z8 ⌂ III-IV Ⓝ;
Austr.: N.S.Wales, Victoria, S-Austr., nat.
in S-P, I
- **retinodes** Schltdl. · E:Water Wattle,
Wirilda; G:Wasser-Akazie · ♄ ♄ e D Z9 ⌂
II-IX; Austr.: Victoria, S-Austr., Tasman.,
nat. in S-Eur.
- **riceana** Hensl. · E:Rice's Wattle; G:Rices
Akazie · ♄ ♄ e Z8 ⌂ III-IV; Tasman.

- **rigens** A. Cunn. ex G. Don · E:Nealie,
Needle-bush Wattle; G:Nadelkissen-
Akazie · ♄ e Z9 ⌂; Austr.: N.S.Wales,
Victoria, S-Austr.
- **saligna** (Labill.) H.L. Wendl. · E:Blue
Leaf Wattle; G:Blaublättrige Akazie · ♄ ♄
e Z9 ⌂; W-Austr.
- **senegal** (L.) Willd. · E:Gum Arabic Tree,
Sudan Gum Arabic; G:Gummi-Akazie,
Gummi-Arabicumbaum · ♄ ♄ d Z9 ⌂ ⚘
Ⓝ; W.Sudan, Nigeria, Arab.
- **seyal** Delile · E:Thirty Thorn, Whistling
Tree; G:Seyal Gummi-Akazie · ♄ d Z9 ⌂
Ⓝ; trop. Afr, Egypt
- *spadicigera* Schltdl. & Cham. = Acacia
cornigera
- **spectabilis** A. Cunn. ex Benth. · E:Glory
Wattle, Mudgee; G:Ruhmes-Akazie · ♄ ♄
e Z9 ⌂; Austr.: Queensl., N.S.Wales
- **sphaerocephala** Schltdl. & Cham. ·
E:Bee Wattle; G:Ameisen-Akazie · ♄ ♄ Z9
⌂; Mex.
- **stenophylla** A. Cunn. ex Benth. ·
E:Shoestring Acacia; G:Schnürsenkel-
Akazie · ♄ e Z9 ⌂; Austr.
- **suaveolens** (Sm.) Willd. · E:Sweet
Scented Wattle; G:Duft-Akazie · ♄ e Z9
⌂ III-VIII; Austr.: Queensl., N.S.Wales,
Victoria, Tasman.
- **subulata** Bonpl. · E:Awl-leaf Wattle;
G:Ahlenblättrige Akazie · ♄ e Z8 ⌂;
SE-Austr.
- *suma* (Roxb.) Kurz = Acacia polyacantha
- *tenuifolia* F. Muell. non L. = Acacia
aculeatissima
- **terminalis** (Salisb.) J.F. Macbr. ·
E:Sunshine Wattle; G:Sonnenschein-
Akazie · ♄ ♄ e Z9 ⌂; Austr.: N.S.Wales,
Victoria, Tasman.
- **tortilis** (Forssk.) Hayne · E:Umbrella
Thorn; G:Drehfrüchtige Akazie · ♄ ♄ Z9
⌂ Ⓝ; N-Afr., Arab.
- **ulicifolia** (Salisb.) Court · E:Juniper Wat-
tle; G:Stechginsterblättrige Akazie · ♄ e
Z9 ⌂ III-IV; Austr.: Queensl., N.S.Wales,
Victoria, Tasman.
- *verek* Guill. & Perr. = Acacia senegal
- **verniciflua** A. Cunn. · E:Varnish Wattle;
G:Firnis-Akazie · ♄ ♄ e Z8 ⌂; Austr.:
Queensl., N.S.Wales, Victoria, S-Austr.,
Tasman.
- **verticillata** (L'Hér.) Willd. · E:Prickly
Moses; G:Quil-Akazie · ♄ e Z8 ⌂ III-IV;
Austr.: N.S.Wales, S-Austr., Tasman.,
Victoria

– **victoriae** Benth. · E:Bramble Wattle; G:Brombeer-Akazie · ♄ ♄ e Z9 ⓐ; E-Austr.
– **villosa** (Sw.) Willd. · G:Dornenlose Akazie · ♄ Z9 ⓐ; W.Ind.
– **williamsonii** Court · E:Whirakee Wattle; G:Whiraki-Akazie · ♄ ♄ e Z9 ⓐ; Austr.

Acaena Mutis ex L. -f- *Rosaceae* · 100-150 spp. · E:New Zealand Bur; F:Acaena; G:Stachelnüsschen
– **adscendens** Vahl · ⳨ Z6; Magellan region, Antarctic Is., Macquarie Is.
– *affinis* Hook. f. = Acaena adscendens
– **anserinifolia** (J.R. Forst. & G. Forst.) Druce · E:Bidgee Widgee · ♄ ⤳ Z6; NZ, nat. in BrI
– **argentea** Ruiz & Pav. · G:Silber-Stachelnüsschen · ⳨ ⤳ Z6; Peru, Chile
– **buchananii** Hook. f. · G:Blaugrünes Stachelnüsschen · ⳨ ⤳ Z6; NZ
– **caesiiglauca** (Bitter) Bergmans · G:Graublaues Stachelnüsschen · ⳨ ⤳ Z6; NZ
– *glauca* hort. = Acaena caesiiglauca
– *glaucophylla* Bitter = Acaena magellanica
– **lucida** Vahl · ⳨ ⤳ Z5-6; Chile, W-Arg., Falkland Is.
– **magellanica** (Lam.) Vahl · G:Magellanen-Stachelnüsschen · ⳨ ⤳ Z6; Patag., S-Chile
– **microphylla** Hook. f. · E:New Zealand Burr; G:Braunblättriges Stachelnüsschen · ⳨ ⤳ Z6; NZ
– **novae-zelandiae** Kirk · E:Biddy Biddy, Piripiri; G:Piripiri-Stachelnüsschen · ⳨ ⤳ Z6; NZ
– **pinnatifida** Ruiz & Pav. · E:Argentinian Biddy Biddy; G:Schwarzes Stachelnüsschen · ⳨ Z6; Chile, Patag.
– *sanguisorbae* (L. f.) Vahl = Acaena anserinifolia
– **splendens** Hook. & Arn. · ⳨ ◠ Z6; Chile, Patag.

Acalypha L. -f- *Euphorbiaceae* · 457 spp. · E:Cat's Tail, Copperleaf; F:Queue-de-chat; G:Katzenschwanz, Nesselblatt
– **amentacea** Roxb. · E:Catch Me If You Can, Copper Leaf; G:Kupferblatt · Borneo (Sabah), Philippines, Sulawesi, Maluku, Caroline Is.
– subsp. **wilkesiana** (Müll. Arg.) Fosberg · E:Beefsteak Plant, Jacob's Coat; G:Buntlaubiges Kupferblatt · ♄ e Z10 ⓜ; N.Guinea
– **chamedrifolia** (Lam.) Müll. Arg. · ♄ ⚡

– ⤳ Z10 ⓜ III-IX; Hispaniola
– *godseffiana* Mast. = Acalypha amentacea subsp. wilkesiana
– *hispaniolae* Urb. = Acalypha chamedrifolia
– **hispida** Burm. f. · E:Red Hot Cat's Tail; G:Roter Katzenschwanz · ♄ e Z10 ⓜ ⛉ I-X ⚘; ? Malay. Arch., cult. Trop., nat. in Trop.
– **indica** L. · E:Indian Acalypha; G:Indisches Kupferblatt · ⊙ Z10 ⓜ VII-VIII ⚘; trop. Afr., trop. As.
– **integrifolia** Willd.
– subsp. **integrifolia** · ♄ Z10 ⓜ; trop. Afr., trop. As.
– var. *colorata* (Poir.) Pax & K. Hoffm. = Acalypha integrifolia subsp. integrifolia
– *pendula* hort. = Acalypha chamedrifolia
– **virginica** L. · E:Virginia Acalypha; G:Virginisches Kupferblatt · ⊙ V-VIII; USA: NE, NCE, SC, SE, Fla, nat. in I, Sw, A
– *wilkesiana* Müll. Arg. = Acalypha amentacea subsp. wilkesiana

Acampe Lindl. -f- *Orchidaceae* · 7 spp.
– **rigida** (Buch.-Ham. ex Sm.) P.F. Hunt · ⳨ Z10 ⓜ VII-X ▽ ✳; E-Afr., trop. As.

Acanthephippium Blume -n- *Orchidaceae* · 12 spp.
– **bicolor** Lindl. · ⳨ Z10 ⓜ V-VI ▽ ✳; Sri Lanka
– **javanicum** Blume · ⳨ Z10 ⓜ III-IV ▽ ✳; Malay. Pen., Sumat., Java, Kalimantan

Acanthocalycium Backeb. -n- *Cactaceae* · 5 spp.
– *formosum* (Pfeiff.) Backeb. = Trichocereus formosus
– *hyalacanthum* (Speg.) Backeb. = Trichocereus huascha
– **klimpelianum** (Weidlich & Werderm.) Backeb. · ⳋ Z9 ⓐ; Arg.
– *peitscherianum* Backeb. = Acanthocalycium spiniflorum var. spiniflorum
– **spiniflorum** (K. Schum.) Backeb.
– var. *klimpelianum* (Weidlich & Werderm.) = Acanthocalycium klimpelianum
– var. **spiniflorum** · ⳋ Z9 ⓐ ▽ ✳; Arg.
– *violaceum* (Werderm.) Backeb. = Acanthocalycium spiniflorum

Acantholimon Boiss. -n- *Plumbaginaceae* · 120-170 spp. · E:Prickly Thrift; F:Acantholimon; G:Igelpolster
– *albanicum* hort. = Acantholimon ulicinum

– *androsaceum* (Jaub. & Spach) Boiss. =
Acantholimon ulicinum
– **avenaceum** Bunge · ħ e Z3; C-As
– **bracteatum** (Girard) Boiss. · ħ e Z3;
Cauc., Iran
– **caryophyllaceum** Boiss. · ħ e Z3; TR,
N-Iraq, Cauk., Iran
– *echinus* Boiss. = Acantholimon ulicinum
– **glumaceum** (Jaub. & Spach) Boiss. · ħ e
⌂ △ Z3 VII-VIII; TR, Cauc., N-Iran
– **hohenackeri** (Jaub. & Spach) Boiss. · ħ e
Z3; Cauc., Iran
– **kotschyi** (Jaub. & Spach) Boiss. · ħ e ⌂
△ Z3 VII-VIII; Syr.
– **libanoticum** (Fenzl) Boiss. · ħ e ⌂ △ Z3
VII-VIII; Lebanon
– **olivieri** (Jaub. & Spach) Boiss. · ħ e ⌂ △
Z3 VII-VIII; TR: Cilician Taurus
– **ulicinum** (Willd. ex Schult.) Boiss. · ħ e
⌂ △ Z3 VII-VIII; Eur.: Ba; TR, Lebanon
– **venustum** Boiss.

Acanthopanax (Decne. & Planch.) Witte =
Eleutherococcus
– *pentaphyllus* (Siebold & Zucc.) Marchal =
Eleutherococcus sieboldianus
– *ricinifolius* (Siebold & Zucc.) Seem. =
Kalopanax septemlobus
– *senticosus* (Rupr. & Maxim.) Harms =
Eleutherococcus senticosus
– *sieboldianus* Makino = Eleutherococcus
sieboldianus
– *spinosus* hort. non (L. f.) Miq. =
Eleutherococcus sieboldianus

Acanthophoenix H. Wendl. -f- *Arecaceae* ·
1 sp. · E:Barbel Palm; F:Palmier épineux;
G:Bartelpalme
– *crinita* (Bory) H. Wendl. = Acanthophoenix rubra
– **rubra** (Bory) H. Wendl. · E:Barbel Palm;
G:Bartelpalme · ħ e Z10 ⓦ; Maskarene Is

Acanthorrhiza H. Wendl. = Cryosophila
– *aculeata* (Liebm. ex Mart.) H. Wendl. =
Cryosophila nana
– *warscewiczii* H. Wendl. = Cryosophila
warscewiczii

Acanthosicyos Welw. ex Hook. f. -m-
Cucurbitaceae · 2 spp. · G:Naraspflanze
– **horridus** Welw. ex Hook. f. · E:Butterpips,
Nara; G:Narakürbis, Naraspflanze · ⍭
Z10 ⓚ ⓝ; Angola, Namibia

Acanthostachys Klotzsch -f- *Bromeliaceae* ·
2 spp. · E:Prickly Ear; F:Acantostachys;
G:Stachelähre
– **strobilacea** (Schult. & Schult. f.)
Klotzsch · E:Prickly Ear; G:Stachelähre ·
⍭ ⌇ Z10 ⓦ; Braz., Parag., Arg.

Acanthus L. -m- *Acanthaceae* · 30 spp. ·
E:Bear's Breeches; F:Acanthe; G:Akan-
thus, Bärenklau
– *balcanicus* Heywood & Richardson =
Acanthus hungaricus
– *caroli-alexandri* Hausskn. = Acanthus
spinosus
– **dioscoridis** L.
– var. **dioscoridis** · ⍭ Z8; TR, Iraq, Iran
– var. **perringii** (Siehe) E. Hossain · ⍭ △
Z8 ⋀ VI-VII; TR; mts.
– **hungaricus** (Borbás) Baen. ·
E:Hungarian Bear's Breeches; F:Acanthe
de Hongrie; G:Ungarischer Akanthus · ⍭
⋉ Z6 VI-VIII; Eur.: Ba, SW-RO
– **ilicifolius** L. · ħ ⌇ Z8 ⓦ; SE-Afr., Ind.,
Sri Lanka, Malay. Arch., Phil., Austr.,
Polyn.; coasts
– *longifolius* Host non Poir. = Acanthus
hungaricus
– **mollis** L. · E:Bear's Breeches; F:Acanthe
molle; G:Pracht-Akanthus · ⍭ Z6 VII-VIII
⍦ ; Eur.: Ib, Fr, Ital-P, Croatia, Maced.
– **montanus** (Nees) T. Anderson ·
E:Mountain Thistle; G:Gebirgs-Akanthus
· ħ Z10 ⓦ IX-II; W-Afr.
– *perringii* Siehe = Acanthus dioscoridis
var. perringii
– *spinosissimus* Desf. = Acanthus spinosus
– **spinosus** L. · E:Spiny Bear's Breeches;
F:Acanthe épineuse; G:Stachliger
Akanthus · ⍭ △ Z6 VII-VIII; Eur.: S-I, Ba;
TR, Alger.

Acca O. Berg -f- *Myrtaceae* · 3 spp. · G:Feijoa
– **sellowiana** (O. Berg) Burret ·
E:Pineapple Guava; G:Feijoa · ħ e Z8 ⓦ
ⓝ; S-Braz., Parag., Urug., N-Arg.

Acer L. -n- *Aceraceae* · 111 sp. · E:Maple;
F:Erable; G:Ahorn
– **acuminatum** Wall. ex D. Don · ħ d Z6;
N-Indien, Nepal, Sikkim, SE-Tibet
– **argutum** Maxim. · E:Pointed-leaf Maple;
G:Feinzähniger Ahorn · ħ ħ d Z6 IV-V;
Japan
– **buergerianum** Miq.
– subsp. **buergerianum** · E:Three-toothed

Maple, Trident Maple; G:Dreizähniger Ahorn · ♄ d Z6; Jap., Taiwan, E-China
- var. *trinerve* (Siesm.) Rehder = Acer buergerianum subsp. buergerianum
- *californicum* (Torr. & A. Gray) D. Dietr. = Acer negundo subsp. californicum
- **campestre** L.
- subsp. **campestre** · E:Field Maple, Hedge Maple; F:Erable champêtre; G:Feld-Ahorn · ♄ ♄ d Z5 V ⚘ Ⓝ; Eur.*, Cauc., TR, N-Iran, Moroc., Alger.
- var. *hebecarpum* DC. = Acer campestre subsp. campestre
- **capillipes** Maxim. · E:Red Snake Bark Maple; F:Erable oriental rouge; G:Roter Schlangenhaut-Ahorn · ♄ d Z6 V; Jap.
- **cappadocicum** Gled.
- subsp. **cappadocicum** · E:Caucasian Maple; F:Erable de Colchide; G:Kolchischer Ahorn · ♄ d Z6 V-VI; TR, Cauc., N-Iran, W-Him., W-China
- subsp. **lobelii** (Ten.) E. Murray · E:Lobel's Maple; F:Erable de Lobel; G:Italienischer Ahorn · ♄ Z6 V; I (Neapel)
- var. *indicum* (Pax) Rehder = Acer cappadocicum subsp. cappadocicum
- **carpinifolium** Siebold & Zucc. · E:Hornbeam Maple; F:Erable à feuilles de charme; G:Hainbuchen-Ahorn · ♄ ♄ d Z6 V; Jap.
- **caudatifolium** Hayata · E:Kawakami Maple; G:Kawakami-Ahorn · ♄ d Z8 Ⓚ; Taiwan
- *caudatum* Nicholls non Wall. ex Rehder = Acer acuminatum
- **circinatum** Pursh · E:Vine Maple; F:Erable à feuilles de vigne; G:Wein-Ahorn · ♄ ♄ d Z5 IV-V Ⓝ; Alaska, USA: Wash., Oreg., N-Calif.
- **cissifolium** (Siebold & Zucc.) K. Koch · E:Vine-Leafed Maple; G:Cissusblättriger Ahorn · ♄ d Z6 V; Jap.
- subsp. *henryi* (Pax) E. Murray = Acer henryi
- × **conspicuum** van Gelderen & Oterdoom (*A. davidii* × *A. pensylvanicum*) · ♄ ♄ d Z6; cult.
- **crataegifolium** Siebold & Zucc. · E:Hawthorn Maple; G:Weißdornblättriger Ahorn · ♄ ♄ d Z6 V; Jap.
- *creticum* L. = Acer sempervirens
- *dasycarpum* Ehrh. = Acer saccharinum
- **davidii** Franch.
- subsp. **davidii** · E:Père David's Maple, Snakebark Maple; F:Erable de David;

G:Davids-Ahorn · ♄ d Z6 V; China: Hubei, Yunnan, Sichuan
- subsp. **grosseri** (Pax) P.C. De Jong · F:Erable de Grosser; G:Grossers Ahorn · ♄ ♄ d Z6 IV-V; C-China
- **diabolicum** Blume ex K. Koch · E:Devil's Maple; G:Hornfrucht-Ahorn · ♄ d Z5 IV-V; Jap.
- × **dieckii** (Pax) Pax (*A. cappadocicum subsp. lobelii* × *A. platanoides*) · G:Diecks Ahorn · ♄ d Z5; Naturhybride
- *forrestii* Diels = Acer pectinatum subsp. forrestii
- *ginnala* Maxim. = Acer tataricum subsp. ginnala
- subsp. *semenowii* (Regel & Herder) Pax = Acer tataricum subsp. semenowii
- **glabrum** Torr. · E:Rocky Mountain Maple; G:Rocky-Mountain-Ahorn
- subsp. **douglasii** (Hook.) Wesm. · E:Douglas Maple; G:Roter Rocky-Mountain-Ahorn · ♄ ♄ d Z5 V; Alaska, Can.: W; USA: NW, Rocky Mts.
- subsp. **glabrum** · E:Rocky Mountain Maple; G:Kahler Rocky-Mountain-Ahorn · ♄ ♄ d Z6 V; N-USA, Can.: Rocky Mts.
- **griseum** (Franch.) Pax · E:Paperbark Maple; F:Erable à écorce de bouleau; G:Zimt-Ahorn · ♄ d Z6 V; W-China
- *grosseri* Pax = Acer davidii subsp. grosseri
- var. *hersii* (Rehder) E. Murray = Acer davidii subsp. grosseri
- **heldreichii** Orph. ex Boiss.
- subsp. **heldreichii** · E:Greek Maple; G:Griechischer Ahorn · ♄ d Z6 V Ⓝ; Eur.: Ba; mts.
- subsp. **trautvetteri** (Medw.) E. Murray · E:Red Bud Maple; F:Erable de Trautvetter; G:Kaukasischer Ahorn · ♄ d Z6 V; N-TR, W-Cauc.
- **henryi** Pax · E:Henry's Maple; G:Henrys Ahorn · ♄ d Z6 V; C-China: Hupeh, Sichuan
- *hersii* Rehder = Acer davidii subsp. grosseri
- × **hybridum** Bosc (*A. opalus* × *A. pseudoplatanus*) · G:Hybrid-Ahorn · ♄ d Z6
- **hyrcanum** Fisch. & C.A. Mey. · G:Grüner Balkan-Ahorn · ♄ d Z5 IV-V; Eur.: Ba
- *insigne* Boiss. & Buhse = Acer velutinum var. velutinum
- *insigne* G. Nicholson = Acer heldreichii subsp. trautvetteri
- *italum* Lauth = Acer opalus subsp. opalus
- **japonicum** Thunb. · E:Full Moon Maple,

Japanese Maple; F:Erable du Japon;
G:Japanischer Ahorn · ħ ħ d Z5 V; Jap.
- *kawakamii* Koidz. = Acer caudatifolium
- *laetum* C.A. Mey. non Schwer. = Acer
  cappadocicum subsp. cappadocicum
- *lobelii* Ten. = Acer cappadocicum subsp.
  lobelii
- **macrophyllum** Pursh · E:Big Leaf Maple,
  Oregon Maple; G:Oregon-Ahorn · ħ d Z7
  V Ⓝ; SE-Alaska, B.C., Wash., Oreg., Calif.
- **mandshuricum** Maxim. · E:Manchurian
  Maple; G:Mandschurischer Ahorn · ħ ħ d
  Z6 V; Manch., Amur, Korea
- **maximowiczianum** Miq. · E:Nikko
  Maple; G:Nikko-Ahorn · ħ d Z6 V; Jap.,
  C-China
- *maximowiczii* Pax = Acer pectinatum
  subsp. maximowiczii
- **miyabei** Maxim. · E:Miyabe's Maple;
  F:Erable de Miyabe; G:Miyabes Ahorn · ħ
  d Z5 V; Jap.
- **mono** Maxim.
- subsp. **mono** var. **mayrii** (Schwer.)
  Nakai · ħ d Z7 IV-V; Jap.
- subsp. **mono** var. **mono** · E:Painted
  Maple; G:Nippon-Ahorn · ħ d Z6 IV-V;
  Amur, China, Manch., Korea, Jap., Sakhal.
- subsp. **okamotoanum** (Nakai) P.C. De
  Jong · ħ d Z6; Korea
- **monspessulanum** L. · E:Montpelier
  Maple; F:Erable de Montpellier;
  G:Felsen-Ahorn, Französischer Ahorn ·
  ħ d Z5 IV Ⓝ; Eur.: Ib, Fr, Ital-P, Ba, RO,
  C-Eur.; TR, Syr., NW-Afr.
- *montanum* Aiton = Acer spicatum
- *morrisonense* Hayata = Acer caudatifolium
- **negundo** L. · E:Ash Leafed Maple;
  G:Eschen-Ahorn
- **some cultivars**
- subsp. **californicum** (Torr. & A. Gray)
  Wesm. · E:Californian Box Elder;
  G:Kalifornischer Eschen-Ahorn · ħ d Z3
  IV; Calif.
- subsp. **negundo** L. · E:Common Box
  Elder; F:Erable à feuilles de frêne;
  G:Gewöhnlicher Eschen-Ahorn · ħ d Z2
  IV Ⓝ; USA: NEC, NC, Mont., Colo., nat.
  in Can.: E; USA: NW, Eur.
- *nigrum* F. Michx. = Acer saccharum
  subsp. nigrum
- *nikoense* (Maxim.) Miq. = Acer maximowiczianum
- *obtusatum* Waldst. & Kit. ex Willd. = Acer
  opalus subsp. obtusatum
- *okamotoanum* Nakai = Acer mono subsp.
  okamotoanum
- **oliverianum** Pax · ħ d Z6 IV-V; China:
  Yunnan, Hupeh, Taiwan
- **opalus** Mill. · E:Italian Maple; G:Früh-
  lings-Ahorn, Schneeballblättriger Ahorn
- subsp. **obtusatum** (Willd.) Gams ·
  E:Bosnian Maple; G:Bosnischer Ahorn · ħ
  d Z6 IV Ⓝ; Eur.: Ital-P, Ba; Alger.
- subsp. **opalus** · ħ d Z6 IV-V; Eur.: Ib, Fr,
  Ital-P, C-Eur.
- var. **tomentosum** (Tausch) Rehder Z6; I
  (Naples)
- var. *hyrcanum* (Fisch. & C.A. Mey.)
  Rehder = Acer hyrcanum
- *opulifolium* Vill. = Acer opalus subsp.
  opalus
- *orientale* auct. non L. = Acer sempervirens
- **palmatum** Thunb. ex E. Murray ·
  G:Fächer-Ahorn; E:Japanese Maple
- **many cultivars, see Section III**
- subsp. **amoenum** (Carrière) H. Hara · ħ
  ħ Z5 V; Jap., Korea
- subsp. **palmatum** · F:Erable japonais · ħ
  d Z6 VI; cult.
- var. *coreanum* Nakai = Acer palmatum
  subsp. amoenum
- var. *heptalobum* Rehder = Acer palmatum
  subsp. amoenum
- **pectinatum** Wall.
- subsp. **forrestii** (Diels) E. Murray ·
  E:Forrest's Maple; G:Forrests Ahorn · ħ d
  Z6; SW-China
- subsp. **maximowiczii** (Pax) E. Murray
  Z6; C-China
- subsp. **pectinatum** · ħ Z6; Him.
- **pensylvanicum** L. · E:Moosewood,
  Snakebark Maple; F:Erable jaspé;
  G:Streifen-Ahorn · ħ d Z6 VI; Can.: E;
  USA: NE, NCE, SE
- *pictum* Thunb. ex E. Murray = Acer mono
  subsp. mono var. mono
- **platanoides** L. · E:Norway Maple;
  G:Spitz-Ahorn
- subsp. **platanoides** · F:Erable plane;
  G:Gewöhnlicher Spitz-Ahorn · ħ d Z4
  IV-V Ⓝ; Eur.* exc. BrI, Cauc.
- *polymorphum* Siebold & Zucc. = Acer
  palmatum subsp. palmatum
- **pseudoplatanus** L. · E:Sycamore;
  F:Erable sycomore; G:Berg-Ahorn · ħ d
  Z4 V Ⓝ; Eur.* exc. BrI, Sc; TR, Cauc.
- **some cultivars siehe Kapitel III**
- **rubrum** L. · E:Red Maple, Scarlet Maple;
  G:Rot-Ahorn
- var. **rubrum** · F:Erable rouge;

G:Gewöhnlicher Rot-Ahorn · ♄ d Z4 III-IV Ⓝ; Can.: E; USA: NE, NCE, NC, SC, SE, Fla.
– var. **trilobum** Torr. & A. Gray ex K. Koch · G:Dreifingriger Rot-Ahorn · Z4; USA: NE, SE, Fla.
– **rufinerve** Siebold & Zucc. · E:Red-veined Maple; F:Erable rufinerve; G:Rotnerviger Ahorn · ♄ d Z6 V; Jap.
– **saccharinum** L. · E:Silver Maple; F:Erable argenté; G:Silber-Ahorn · ♄ d Z5 III-IV Ⓝ; Can.: E; USA: NE, NCE, NC, Okla., SE, Fla.
– **saccharum** Marshall
– subsp. **nigrum** (F. Michx.) Desmarais · E:Black Sugar Maple; G:Schwarzer Zucker-Ahorn · ♄ d Z5 IV; E-Can.; USA: NE, NEC
– subsp. **saccharum** · E:Common Sugar Maple; F:Erable à sucre; G:Gewöhnlicher Zucker-Ahorn · ♄ d Z3 IV Ⓝ; Can.: E; USA: NE, NCE, SE, SC
– *semenovii* Regel & Herder = Acer tataricum subsp. semenovii
– **sempervirens** L. · E:Cretan Maple; G:Kretischer Ahorn · ♄ ♄ e Z8 ⓚ; Eur.: GR, Crete; TR
– *septemlobum* Thunb. ex Murray = Acer palmatum subsp. palmatum
– **shirasawanum** L. · F:Erable du Japon; G:Breitfingriger Shirasawa-Ahorn · ♄ d Z6; Jap.
– **sieboldianum** Miq. · E:Siebold's Maple; F:Erable de Siebold; G:Siebolds Ahorn · ♄ ♄ d Z5 V; Jap.
– **spicatum** Lam. · E:Mountain Maple; G:Vermont-Ahorn · ♄ ♄ d Z2 V-VI; Can.: E, Sask.; USA: NE, NCE, SE
– *striatum* Du Roi = Acer pensylvanicum
– **tataricum** L.
– subsp. **ginnala** (Maxim.) Wesm. · E:Amur Maple; F:Erable du fleuve Amour; G:Feuer-Ahorn · ♄ d Z4 V Ⓝ; E-Sib., Mong., China, Manch., Korea, Jap.
– subsp. **semenovii** (Regel & Herder) Pax · ♄ ♄ d Z4 V; C-As., Iran, Afgh.
– subsp. **tataricum** · E:Tatarian Maple; F:Erable de Tartarie; G:Tataren-Ahorn · ♄ ♄ d Z4 V Ⓝ; Eur.: A, EC-Eur., Ba, E-Eur.; TR, Cauc., N-Iran
– **tegmentosum** Maxim. · G:Amur-Ahorn · ♄ d Z5 V; Amur, Manch., Korea
– *trautvetteri* Medw. = Acer heldreichii subsp. trautvetteri
– *trifidum* Hook. ex Arn. non Thunb. = Acer buergerianum subsp. buergerianum

– **triflorum** Kom. · E:Rough Barked Maple, Three-flowered Maple; F:Erable à trois fleurs; G:Dreiblütiger Ahorn · ♄ d Z6 V; Korea, NE-China
– **truncatum** Bunge · E:Purpleblow Maple, Shantung Maple · ♄ ♄ d Z5 V Ⓝ; N-China
– subsp. *mono* (Maxim.) E. Murray = Acer mono subsp. mono var. mono
– **velutinum** Boiss. · G:Samt-Ahorn; E:Velvet Maple
– var. **glabrescens** (Boiss. & Buhse) Rehder · ♄ d Z6
– var. **vanvolxemii** (Mast.) Rehder · ♄ d Z5 V; E--Cauc.
– var. **velutinum** · ♄ d Z5; Cauc., N-Iran; mts.
– × **zoeschense** Pax (*A. campestre × A. cappadocicum* subsp. *lobelii*) · E:Zoeschen Maple; F:Erable de Zoeschen; G:Zöschener Ahorn · ♄ d Z6 IV; cult.

Aceras R. Br. = Orchis
– *anthropophorum* (L.) R. Br. = Orchis anthropophora

Aceriphyllum Engl. = Mukdenia
– *rossii* (Oliv.) Engl. = Mukdenia rossii

Acetosa Mill. = Rumex
– *alpina* (L.) Moench = Rumex alpinus
– *scutata* (L.) Mill. = Rumex scutatus

Achillea L. -f- *Asteraceae* · 85 spp. · E:Milfoil, Yarrow; F:Achillée; G:Garbe, Schafgarbe
– **abrotanoides** (Vis.) Vis. · ⵣ Z6 VI-VIII; Eur.: Ba; mts.
– **aegyptiaca** L. · G:Griechische Schafgarbe
– var. **taygetea** (Boiss. & Heldr.) Halácsy · F:Achillée de Grèce; G:Griechische Edel-Schafgarbe · ⵣ; GR
– **ageratifolia** (Sibth. & Sm.) Boiss.
– subsp. **ageratifolia** · E:Greek Yarrow; F:Achillée à feuilles d'agérate; G:Agera-tumblättrige Schafgarbe · ⵣ △ △ Z3 VI-VII; Eur.: Ba; mts.
– subsp. **aizoon** (Griseb.) Heimerl · G:Immergrüne Schafgarbe · Z3; Eur.: Ba
– subsp. **serbica** (Nyman) Heimerl · F:Achillée de Serbie; G:Serbische Schafgarbe · ⵣ △ △ Z3 V-VI
– **ageratum** L. · E:Sweet Nancy; G:Süße Schafgarbe · ⵣ Z7; Eur.: Ib, Fr, Ital-P, ? Croatia, ? GR +
– *aizoon* (Griseb.) Halácsy = Achillea

ageratifolia subsp. aizoon
- **aspleniifolia** Vent. · G:Farn-Schafgarbe · ♃ V-VII; Eur.: A, H, CZ, PL, Bosn., Serb., RO, S-Russ.
- **atrata** L. · E:Dark-stemmed Sneezewort; G:Schwarzrandige Schafgarbe · ♃ Z6 VII-IX ▽; Eur.: F, I, Sw, G, A, Slove.; Alp.
- **canescens** Formánek · ♃ △ VI; Montenegro, AL, GR
- **chrysocoma** Friv. · F:Achillée à cheveux dorés · ♃ ⤳ △ Z6 VI-VIII; Maced., AL, TR
- **clavennae** L. · E:Silvery Milfoil; G:Bittere Schafgarbe, Steinraute, Weißer Speik · ♃ Z3 VII-IX ▽; Eur.: C-Eur., E-Alp., S-Alp., I, ? Ba, RO
- **clusiana** Tausch · G:Ostalpen-Schafgarbe · ♃ Z6 VII-VIII; Eur.: A, Ba, ? RO; mts.
- **clypeolata** Sibth. & Sm. non hort. · G:Goldquirl-Garbe · ♃ Z6 VI-VII; Eur.: Ba.
- **collina** Becker ex Rchb. · G:Hügel-Schafgarbe · ♃ Z6 VI-XI; Eur.: C-Eur., Ital-P, EC-Eur., Ba, RO
- **crithmifolia** Waldst. & Kit. · G:Meerfenchelblättrige Schafgarbe · ♃ V-VII; Eur.: EC-Eur., Ba, RO; mts.
- *decolorans* Schrad. = Achillea ageratum
- **distans** Waldst. & Kit. ex Willd. · E:Tall Yarrow; G:Zahnblatt-Schafgarbe · ♃ Z6 VII-IX; Eur.: Fr, C-Eur., Ital-P, EC-Eur., Ba, RO, W-Russ.; Alp., Carp., BG
- **erba-rotta** All.
- subsp. **ambigua** (Heimerl) I. Richardson Z6; Eur.: W-Alp., Apenn.
- subsp. **erba-rotta** · E:Simple-leaved Milfoil · ♃ Z6; Eur.: F, I, Sw, A, ; SW-Alp.
- subsp. **moschata** (Wulfen) I. Richardson · E:Musk Milfoil; G:Bisam-Schafgarbe, Moschus-Schafgarbe · ♃ △ Z6 VI-IX; Eur.: F, I, Sw, A; Alp.
- subsp. **rupestris** (Porta) I. Richardson · ♃ △ Z6 V-VI; I: Apenn.
- *eupatorium* M. Bieb. = Achillea filipendulina
- **filipendulina** Lam. · E:Fernleaf Yarrow; F:Achillée jaune; G:Gold-Garbe · ♃ ⋊ Z3 VII-IX; TR, Cauc., Iran, Afgh., C-As.
- **grandifolia** Friv. · ♃ Z6 VI; Eur.: Ba
- **holosericea** Sibth. & Sm. · ♃ △ Z6 V-VIII; Eur.: Ba
- × **jaborneggii** Halácsy (A. clavennae × A. erba-rotta) · ♃ △ Z6 VI-VIII; cult.
- × **kellereri** Sünd. (A. clypeolata × A. ptarmica) · ♃ △ Z6 VI-VIII; cult.
- × **kolbiana** Sünd. (A. clavennae × A. umbellata) · ♃ △ Z6 VI-VIII; cult.

- × **lewisii** Ingw. (A. clavennae × A. clypeolata) · ♃ Z5; cult.
- **ligustica** All. · E:Southern Yarrow; G:Mediterrane Schafgarbe · ♃ Z6; Eur.: Ib, Fr, Ital-P, Ba; Moroc., Alger., Tun.
- **lingulata** Waldst. & Kit. · ♃ △ Z6 VI-VII; Eur.: Ba, RO, W-Russ.; Carp., Balkan
- **macrophylla** L. · E:Large-leaved Sneezewort; G:Großblättrige Schafgarbe · ♃ VII-IX; Eur.: F, I, Sw, G, A; Alp., N-Apenn., nat. in EC-Eur.
- **millefolium** L. · G:Wiesen-Schafgarbe
- subsp. **millefolium** · E:Common Yarrow; F:Achillée millefeuille; G:Gewöhnliche Wiesen-Schafgarbe · ♃ ⋊ Z2 X ☿ Ⓝ; Eur.*, TR, Cauc., Iran, Him., W-Sib., Amur, C-As., nat. in N-Am., Austr., NZ
- *mongolica* Fisch. = Achillea sibirica
- *moschata* Wulfen = Achillea erba-rotta subsp. moschata
- **nana** L. · E:Dwarf Milfoil; G:Zwerg-Schafgarbe · ♃ Z6 VII-VIII; Eur.: I, F, Sw; Alp., Apenn.
- **nobilis** L. · ♃ Z6 VI-X; Eur.* exc. BrI, Sc; TR, Cauc.
- × **obristii** Sünd. (A. erba-rotta subsp. rupestris × A. umbellata) · ♃; cult.
- **oxyloba** (DC.) Sch. Bip. · E:Alpine Sneezewort; G:Dolomiten-Schafgarbe · ♃ Z6 VII-IX; Eur.: I, A, RO, W-Russ.; SE-Alp., Apenn., Carp.
- **pannonica** Scheele · G:Ungarische Schafgarbe · ♃ VI-VIII; Eur.: G, A, EC-Eur., Ba, E-Eur.
- **pratensis** Saukel & Länger · G:Rasige Schafgarbe · ♃ V-XI; Eur.: G, A +
- **ptarmica** L. · E:Sneezewort; G:Sumpf-Schafgarbe · ♃ ⌢ ⋊ Z5 VII-IX Ⓝ; Eur.*, nat. in N-Am.
- subsp. **pyrenaica** (Sibth. ex Godr.) Heimerl = Achillea pyrenaica
- **pyrenaica** Sibth. ex Godr. · E:Pyrenean Sneezewort · ♃ Z6 VII-IX; Eur.: sp.(Pyr.), F
- **roseoalba** Ehrend. · G:Blassrote Schafgarbe · ♃ VII-IX; Eur.: I, Sw, G, A, Slove.
- *rupestris* Porta = Achillea erba-rotta subsp. rupestris
- **salicifolia** Besser · G:Weidenblättrige Schafgarbe · ♃ VII-IX; Eur.: G, PL, E-Eur.; Cauc., Sib., C-As., nat. in FIN
- *serbica* Nyman = Achillea ageratifolia subsp. serbica
- **setacea** Waldst. & Kit. · G:Feinblättrige Schafgarbe · ♃ V-VI; Eur.: Ital-P, C-Eur.,

EC-Eur., Ba, ? Ib; TR, Cauc., Iran
- **sibirica** Ledeb. · ⅃ ⁓ ✕ Z6 VII-IX;
Alaska, Can., Kamchat., E-Sib., Sakhal.,
Jap., Korea, Manch., China
- **stricta** (Koch) Schleich. ex Gremli ·
G:Straffe Schafgarbe · ⅃ VII-VIII; Eur.:
I, C-Eur., EC-Eur., W-Ba, RO, W-Russ.;
Alp., Apenn., Carp.
- *taygetea* Boiss. & Heldr. = Achillea
aegyptiaca var. taygetea
- ✕ **taygetea** hort. (*A. clypeolata* × *A.
millefolium*) · ⅃ Z6 VI-VII; cult.
- **tomentosa** L. · E:Woolly Yarrow;
F:Achillée laineuse, Petite achillée d'or;
G:Gelbe Schafgarbe · ⅃ △ Z3 V-VII;
Eur.: sp., F, I, Sw
- **umbellata** Sibth. & Sm. · ⅃ △ Z6 VI-VIII;
GR
- **Cultivars:**
- **many cultivars**

Achimenes Pers. -f- *Gesneriaceae* ·
25 spp. · E:Hot Water Plant; F:Achimène;
G:Schiefteller
- **candida** Lindl. · G:Weißer Schiefteller ·
⅃ Z10 🌢 VI-VIII; C-Am.
- *coccinea* (Scop.) Pers. = Achimenes erecta
- **dulcis** C.V. Morton · ⅃ Z10 🌢 VII-IX; Mex.
- *ehrenbergii* (Hanst.) H.E. Moore =
Eucodonia verticillata
- **erecta** (Lam.) H.P. Fuchs · G:Aufrechter
Schiefteller · ⅃ Z10 🌢 VII-IX; Mex.,
C-Am., Jamaica, Col.
- *erinoides* DC. = Koellikeria erinoides
- **flava** C.V. Morton · G:Gelber Schiefteller · ⅃ Z10 🌢 VII-VIII; Mex.
- **glabrata** (Zucc.) Fritsch · ⅃ Z10 🌢
VI-VIII; Mex.
- *gloxiniiflora* (Scheidw.) Forkel & Lem. =
Achimenes glabrata
- **grandiflora** (Schiede) DC. · G:Groß-
blütiger Schiefteller · ⅃ Z10 🌢 🗍 VII-IX;
Mex., C-Am.
- **heterophylla** (Mart.) DC. · ⅃ Z10 🌢 🗍
VII-IX; Mex., Guat.
- *ignescens* Lem. = Achimenes heterophylla
- *lanata* (Planch. & Lindl. ex Lem.) Hanst.
= Eucodonia verticillata
- **longiflora** (Sessé & Moç.) DC. · ⅃ Z10 🌢
🗍 VII-IX; C-Am.
- **mexicana** (Seem.) Benth. & Hook. f. ex
Fritsch · G:Mexikanischer Schiefteller · ⅃
Z10 🌢 🗍 VII-IX; Mex.
- **misera** Lindl. · ⅃ Z10 🌢 VII-IX; Mex.,
Guat., Hond.

- **patens** Benth. · ⅃ Z10 🌢 🗍 VII-IX; Mex.
- **pedunculata** Benth. · ⅃ Z10 🌢 🗍 VII-IX;
Mex., C Am., Col., Venez.
- *pulchella* (L'Hér.) Hitchc. = Achimenes
erecta
- *rosea* Lindl. = Achimenes erecta
- **skinneri** Lindl. · ⅃ Z10 🌢 🗍 VII-IX;
Mex., Guat.
- *tubiflora* (Hook.) Britton = Sinningia
tubiflora
- **warszewicziana** (Regel) H.E. Moore ·
⅃ Z10 🌢 VII-IX; Mex., Guat., Hond., El
Salv.
- **Cultivars:**
- **many cultivars**

Achlys DC. -f- *Berberidaceae* · 2 spp. ·
E:Vanilla Leaf; G:Vanilleblatt
- **triphylla** (Sm.) DC. · G:Vanilleblatt;
E:Vanilla Leaf · ⅃ VII-VIII; B.C., Wash.,
Oreg., Calif.

Achnatherum P. Beauv. = Stipa
- *calamagrostis* (L.) P. Beauv. = Stipa
calamagrostis

Achras L. = Manilkara
- *caimito* Ruiz & Pav. = Pouteria caimito
- *lucuma* Ruiz & Pav. = Pouteria lucuma
- *zapota* L. = Manilkara zapota

Achyranthes L. -f- *Amaranthaceae* · 6 spp. ·
E:Devil's Horsewhip; F:Achyranthes;
G:Spreublume
- **aspera** L. · ⊙ ⅃ Z8; Trop., nat. in sp., Sic.
- *lindenii* (Van Houtte) hort. = Iresine
lindenii
- *verschaffeltii* Lem. = Iresine herbstii

Acianthera Scheidw. -f- *Orchidaceae* ·
179 spp.
- **pectinata** (Lindl.) Pridgeon & M.W.
Chase · ⅃ Z10 🌢 V-VII ▽ ✳; Braz.
- **saurocephala** (Lodd.) Pridgeon & M.W.
Chase · ⅃ Z10 🌢 ▽ ✳; Braz.

Acicarpha Juss. -f- *Calyceraceae* · 5 spp.
- **tribuloides** Juss. · ⊙; S-Am.

Acidanthera Hochst. = Gladiolus
- *bicolor* Hochst. = Gladiolus murielae
- var. *murielae* R.H. Perry = Gladiolus
murielae

Acineta Lindl. -f- *Orchidaceae* · 18 spp.

– **barkeri** (Bateman) Lindl. · ⁴ Z10 ⓜ
IX-XI ▽ ✳; Mex.
– **chrysantha** (C. Morren) Lindl. &
Paxton · ⁴ Z10 ⓜ IX-X ▽ ✳; Costa Rica,
Panama, Col.
– **densa** Lindl.
– **superba** (Kunth) Rchb. f. · ⁴ Z10 ⓜ
III-VI ▽ ✳; Ecuad., Col., Venez.

Acinos Mill. -m- *Lamiaceae* · 10 spp. ·
E:Calamint; F:Calament; G:Steinquendel
– **alpinus** (L.) Moench · E:Alpine Calamint;
F:Calament des Alpes; G:Alpen-
Steinquendel · ⁴ △ Z5 VII-IX; Eur.* exc.
BrI, Sc; TR, NW-Afr.
– **arvensis** (Lam.) Dandy · G:Feld-
Steinquendel; E:Mother of Thyme · ☉ ☉
Z7 VI-IX ⚲ ; Eur.*, TR, Cauc., N-Iran
– *thymoides* Moench = Acinos arvensis

Aciphylla J.R. Forst. & G. Forst.
-f- *Apiaceae* · 40 spp. · E:Speargrass;
F:Aciphylla; G:Speergras
– **aurea** W.R.B. Oliv. · E:Golden Spaniard;
G:Goldenes Speergras · ⅃ e Z7 ⓐ; NZ
– **squarrosa** J.R. Forst. & G. Forst. ·
E:Bayonet Plant, Speargrass; G:Sperriges
Speergras · ⁴ Z5 VIII; NZ

Acmella Rich. ex Pers. -f- *Asteraceae* ·
E:Para Cress; F:Cresson de Para; 30 spp. ·
G:Parakresse
– **oleracea** (L.) R.K. Jansen · E:Para Cress,
Toothache Plant; G:Parakresse · ⁴ ⓐ ⚲
Ⓝ; cult. in W.Ind., Braz., Ind.

Acnistus Schott -m- *Solanaceae* · 1 sp.
– **arborescens** (L.) Schltdl. ·
E:Hollowheart · ℏ ⓐ; Mex.
– *australis* (Griseb.) Griseb. = Iochroma
australe

Acoelorrhaphe H. Wendl. -f- *Arecaceae* ·
1 sp. · E:Everglades Palm, Paurotis Palm,
Silver Saw Palm; G:Evergladespalme
– **wrightii** (Griseb. & H. Wendl.) H.
Wendl. ex Becc. · E:Everglades Palm,
Paurotis Palm, Silver Saw Palm;
G:Evergladespalme · ℏ e Z10 ⓜ; S-Fla.,
Mex., Guat., Hond., Cuba, Bahamas

Acokanthera G. Don -f- *Apocynaceae* ·
5 spp. · E:Poison Bush, Poison Tree;
F:Acokanthéra; G:Schöngift
– **oblongifolia** (Hochst.) Codd · E:African

Wintersweet; G:Afrikanisches Schöngift ·
ℏ e D Z10 ⓜ II-IV ⚘; S-Afr.: Cape, Natal
– **oppositifolia** (Lam.) Codd · E:Bushman's
Poison; G:Buschmanns Schöngift · ℏ e D
Z10 ⓐ II-IV ⚘; E-Afr., S-Afr.
– *ouabaio* Boiss. = Acokanthera oppositifolia
– **schimperi** (A. DC.) Schweinf. · E:Arrow
Poison Tree; G:Pfeilspitzen-Schöngift · ℏ
e Z10 ⓐ II-IV ⚲ ⚘; E-Afr., SW-Arab.
– *spectabilis* (Sond.) Hook. f. = Acokanthera oblongifolia
– *venenata* auct. non (Thunb.) G. Don =
Acokanthera oppositifolia

Aconitum L. -n- *Ranunculaceae* · c. 100 (or
300-350) spp. · E:Monk's Hood; F:Aconit;
G:Eisenhut, Wolfshut
– **anthora** L. · E:Pale Aconite, Yellow
Monkshood; G:Blassgelber Eisenhut,
Giftheil · ⁴ Z7 VIII ⚘ ▽; Eur.* exc. BrI,
Sc; TR, Cauc., W-Sib., E-Sib., C-As.
– × *arendsii* hort. = Aconitum carmichaelii
var. carmichaelii
– × *bicolor* Schult. = Aconitum × cammarum
– × **cammarum** L. (*A. napellus × A.*
variegatum) · G:Garten-Eisenhut · ⁴ ⋉ Z3
VII-VIII ⚘; Eur.: Sc
– **some cultivars**
– **carmichaelii** Debeaux
– var. *arendsii* hort. = Aconitum carmichaelii var. carmichaelii
– var. **carmichaelii** · E:Aconite,
Carmichael's Monk's Hood; F:Aconit
d'automne; G:Chinesischer Eisenhut · ⁴
Z3 ⚲ ⚘ ▽; C-China, W-China
– var. *wilsonii* (Stapf ex Mottet) Munz =
Aconitum carmichaelii var. carmichaelii
– **degenii** Gáyer
– subsp. **degenii** · G:Degens Eisenhut · ⁴
⚘ ▽; RO, Russ.; mts.
– subsp. **paniculatum** (Arcang.) Mucher ·
G:Rispen-Eisenhut · ⁴ VII-IX ⚘ ▽; Eur.:
F, I, C-Eur., Slove., Bosn., Montenegro;
mts.
– *fischeri* F.B. Forbes & Hemsl. = Aconitum
carmichaelii var. carmichaelii
– **hemsleyanum** E. Pritz. · ⁴ ⚲ Z4 VII-IX
⚘ ▽; C-China
– **henryi** E. Pritz. · G:Heinrich-Eisenhut · ⁴
Z4 VII-VIII ⚘ ▽; W-China
– × *intermedium* DC. = Aconitum × cammarum
– **lycoctonum** L.
– subsp. **lycoctonum** · E:Wolf's Bane;
G:Wolfs-Eisenhut · ⁴ Z3 VI ⚘; Eur.: Sc,

E-Eur.
- subsp. **moldavicum** (Hacq.) Jalas · G:Moldau-Eisenhut · ♃ Z3 ▽; Eur.: PL, EC-Eur., RO, W-Russ.
- subsp. **neapolitanum** (Ten.) Nyman · F:Aconit des Pyrénées; G:Hahnenfuß-blättriger Eisenhut · ♃ Z3 VI-VIII ☠ ▽; S-Eur., C-Eur., Moroc.; mts.
- subsp. **vulparia** (Rchb. ex Spreng.) Nyman · E:Monkshood; F:Aconit tue-loup; G:Fuchs-Eisenhut · ♃ Z3 VI-VIII ☠ ▽; Eur.: F, NL, C-Eur., EC-Eur., RO, I, W-Ba
- *moldavicum* Hacq. = Aconitum lycoctonum subsp. moldavicum
- **napellus** L. · E:Friar's Cap, Garden Monkshood; G:Blauer Eisenhut
- subsp. *hians* = Aconitum plicatum
- subsp. **napellus** · F:Aconit blanc; G:Gewöhnlicher Blauer Eisenhut · ♃ Z6 VI-VIII ⚕ ☠ ▽; Eur.*
- subsp. **pyramidale** (Mill.) Rouy & Foucaud · G:Pyramiden-Eisenhut · ♃ Z6 VII-VIII ☠ ▽; Eur.: C-Eur., S-Alp.
- subsp. *tauricum* (Wulfen) Gáyer = Aconitum tauricum
- **orientale** Mill. · ♃ Z6 ☠ ▽; TR, Cauc., Iran
- *paniculatum* auct. non Lam. = Aconitum degenii subsp. paniculatum
- *paniculatum* Lam. = Aconitum × cammarum
- **plicatum** Köhler ex Rchb. · G:Klaffender Eisenhut · ♃ ☠ ▽; G, A, CZ
- *pyramidale* Mill. = Aconitum napellus subsp. pyramidale
- *pyrenaicum* L. p.p. = Aconitum lycoctonum subsp. neapolitanum
- *ranunculifolium* Rchb. = Aconitum lycoctonum subsp. neapolitanum
- *rostratum* Bernh. = Aconitum variegatum
- *septentrionale* Koelle = Aconitum lycoctonum subsp. lycoctonum
- × *stoerkianum* Rchb. = Aconitum × cammarum
- **tauricum** Wulfen · G:Tauern-Eisenhut · ♃ Z6; Eur.: E-Alp., Carp.
- **variegatum** L. · E: Variegated Monk's Hood; G:Gewöhnlicher Bunter Eisenhut · ♃ Z6 VII-VIII ☠ ▽; Eur.* exc. BrI, Sc; Cauc.; mts.
- **volubile** Pall. ex Koelle · G:Windender Eisenhut · ♃ ≹ Z2 VII-VIII ☠ ▽; Jap., Korea, Manch., E-Sib.
- *vulparia* Rchb. ex Spreng. = Aconitum lycoctonum subsp. vulparia
- *wilsonii* Stapf ex Mottet = Aconitum carmichaelii var. carmichaelii
- **Cultivars:**
- **some cultivars**

Aconogonon (Meisn.) Rchb. -n- *Polygonaceae* · c. 30 spp. · F:Renouée des montagnes; G:Bergknöterich
- **alpinum** (All.) Schur · E:Alpine Knotweed; G:Alpen-Bergknöterich · ♃ Z5 VII-IX; Eur.: Ib, Fr, Ital-P, C-Eur., Ba, EC-Eur.; TR, Cauc., N-Iran, Him., W-Sib., E-Sib, Amur, C-As., Mong., nat. in BrI, Sc
- **campanulatum** (Hook. f.) H. Hara · ♃ Z8; Him.
- **lichiangense** (W.W. Sm.) Soják · ♃ Z5 VIII-X; W-Him.
- **polystachyum** (Wall. ex Meisn.) Small · E:Himalayan Knotweed; F:Renouée de l'Himalaya; G:Himalaya-Bergknöterich, Vielähriger Bergknöterich · ♃ D Z6 X; Him., nat. in BrI, Sc, C-Eur., Fr
- **sericeum** (Pall.) H. Hara · ♃ Z5 V-VI; Sib.
- **weyrichii** (F. Schmidt ex Maxim.) H. Hara · E:Weyrich's Knotweed; F:Renouée de Weyrich; G:Weyrichs Bergknöterich · ♃ Z5 VII-VIII; Sakhal., Kurilen

Acorus L. -m- *Acoraceae* · 2 spp. · E:Sweet Flags; F:Acore; G:Kalmus
- **calamus** L.
- var. **calamus** · E:Calamus, Flag Root, Sweet Myrtle; F:Acore odorant; G:Gewöhnlicher Kalmus · ♃ ~ Z3 VI-VII ⚕ ☠ Ⓝ; Him., Ind., Sri Lanka, E-As., nat. in Eur., W-As., N-Am.
- **gramineus** Sol. · E:Japanese Sweet Flag; F:Acore à feuilles de graminée; G:Lakritz-Kalmus, Zwerg-Kalmus · ♃ ~ Z7 Ⓐ ∧ ⚕ ; Ind., Thail., China, Jap.
- var. *pusillus* (Siebold) Engl. = Acorus gramineus
- *pusillus* Siebold = Acorus gramineus

Acroceras Stapf -n- *Poaceae* · c. 20 spp.
- **macrum** Stapf · ♃ Ⓝ; S-Afr., E-Afr.

Acroclinium A. Gray -n- *Asteraceae* · 3 spp. · E:Paper Daisy; F:Acroclinium; G:Papierblümchen
- **roseum** Hook. · E:Pink Paper Daisy, Rosy Sunray; G:Rosa Papierblümchen · ⊙ ✂ Z9 VII-IX; Austr.

Acrocomia Mart. -f- *Arecaceae* · 2 spp. ·

E:Gru Gru Palm; F:Acrocomia; G:Schopf-
palme
- **aculeata** (Jacq.) Lodd. ex Mart. · E:Gru
Gru Nut, Mucaja; G:Coyoli-Palme · ♄ e
Z10 ⓜ ⓝ; Mex., C-Am., W.Ind., trop.
S-Am.
- *totai* Mart. = Acrocomia aculeata
- *vinifera* Oerst. = Acrocomia aculeata

Acrodon N.E. Br. -m- *Aizoaceae* · 4 spp.
- **bellidiflorus** (L.) N.E. Br. · ⑵ ⍦ ⓜ; Cape

Acroptilon Cass. -n- *Asteraceae* · 1 sp. ·
E:Russian Knapweed; G:Federblume
- **repens** (L.) DC. · G:Federblume · ⑵
VII-IX; Eur.: Russ.; TR, Iraq, Cauc., Iran,
Afgh., C-As., Mong., nat. in N-Am.

Acrostichum L. -n- *Pteridaceae* · 3 spp. ·
E:Leather Fern; F:Acrostic; G:Mangrove-
farn
- **aureum** L. · E:Golden Leather Fern;
G:Goldener Mangrovefarn · ⑵ ⌣ ≈
Z10 ⓜ; Trop.; coasts
- *latifolium* Sw. = Elaphoglossum
latifolium
- *villosum* Sw. = Elaphoglossum villosum

Actaea L. -f- *Ranunculaceae* · 8 spp. ·
E:Baneberry; F:Herbe de St-Christophe;
G:Christophskraut
- **alba** (L.) Mill. · E:White Baneberry;
F:Actée blanche; G:Weißfrüchtiges
Christophskraut · ⑵ ⚘ Z3 V-VI ⚕; Can.:
W; USA: NE, NEC, SE, Fla., Nebr., Kans.,
Okla.
- *pachypoda* Elliott = Actaea alba
- **rubra** (Aiton) Willd. · E:Red Baneberry;
F:Actée rouge; G:Rotfrüchtiges Chris-
tophskraut · ⑵ ⚘ Z3 V-VI ⚕; Alaska,
Can., USA: NE, NCE, NC, Rocky Mts.,
NW, SW, Calif.
- **spicata** L. · E:Baneberry; F:Actée en épis;
G:Schwarzfrüchtiges Christophskraut
· ⑵ ⚘ Z5 V-VI ⚕; Eur.*, Cauc., W-Sib.
(Altai)
- var. *alba* L. = Actaea alba

Actinea A. Juss. = Hymenoxys
- *acaulis* (Pursh) Spreng. = Hymenoxys
acaulis
- *grandiflora* (Torr. & A. Gray ex A. Gray)
Kuntze = Hymenoxys grandiflora
- *herbacea* (Greene) B.L. Rob. =
Hymenoxys acaulis

Actinella Pers. = Hymenoxys
- *grandiflora* Torr. & A. Gray ex A. Gray =
Hymenoxys grandiflora
- *linearifolia* (Hook.) Torr. & A. Gray =
Hymenoxys linearifolia
- *scaposa* Nutt. = Hymenoxys scaposa

Actinidia Lindl. -f- *Actinidiaceae* · 40+ spp. ·
E:Kiwi Fruit; F:Actinidia, Kiwi; G:Kiwi-
pflanze, Strahlengriffel
- **arguta** (Siebold & Zucc.) Planch. ex Miq. ·
E:Tara Vine, Yang-Tao; F:Actinidier;
G:Scharfzähniger Strahlengriffel · ♄ d ⚥
D Z5 VI ⓝ; China, Korea, Jap.
- **callosa** Lindl.
- var. **callosa** Z7
- var. **henryi** Maxim. · ♄ d Z6; C-China,
W-China
- *chinensis* hort. non Planch. = Actinidia
deliciosa
- **coriacea** (Finet & Gagnep.) Dunn · ⑂ d ⚥
Z6 V-VI; W-China
- **deliciosa** (A. Chev.) C.F. Liang & A.R.
Ferguson · E:Chinese Gooseberry, Kiwi
Fruit; F:Kiwi de Chine; G:Chinesische
Stachelbeere, Kiwifrucht · ♄ ⚐ d ⚥ Z6 V-VI
ⓝ; China, Taiwan
- **some cultivars siehe Kapitel III**
- **kolomikta** (Rupr. & Maxim.) Maxim. ·
F:Kiwi d'ornement; G:Kolomikta-
Strahlengriffel · ♄ d ⚥ D Z5 V ⓝ; Jap.,
Korea, China
- **melanandra** Franch. · ♄ d ⚥ Z6 VI-VII ⓝ;
China
- **polygama** (Siebold & Zucc.) Planch. ex
Maxim. · E:Silver Vine; G:Silberrebe · ♄
d ⚥ D Z4 VI-VII ⓝ; Jap., Korea, Sakhal.,
Manch., W-China
- **purpurea** Rehder · G:Purpur-Strahlen-
griffel · ♄ d ⚥ Z8 ∧ VI-VII; W-China

Actiniopteris Link -f- *Actiniopteridaceae* ·
4 spp. · F:Actinioptéris; G:Strahlenfarn
- **australis** (L. f.) Link · ⑵ Z10 ⓜ; E-Afr.,
S-Afr., Arab., Ind.

Actinomeris Nutt. = Verbesina
- *squarrosa* Nutt. = Verbesina alternifolia

Actinophloeus (Becc.) Becc. = Ptychosperma
- *macarthurii* (H. Wendl. ex H.J. Veitch)
Becc. ex Raderm. = Ptychosperma
macarthurii

Ada Lindl. -f- *Orchidaceae* · 16 spp.

– **aurantiaca** Lindl. · ⚥ Z9 ⓚ II-III ▽ ✳;
Ecuad., Col., Venez.

× **Adaglossum** hort. -n- *Orchidaceae* (*Ada* ×
Odontoglossum)

× **Adamara** hort. -f- *Orchidaceae*
(*Brassavola* × *Cattleya* × *Epidendrum* ×
Laelia)

Adamsia Willd. = Puschkinia
– *scilloides* (Adams) Willd. = Puschkinia
  scilloides var. scilloides

Adansonia L. -f- *Bombacaceae* · 8-10 spp. ·
E:Monkey-bread Tree; F:Baobab;
G:Affenbrotbaum, Baobab
– **digitata** L. · G:Affenbrotbaum;
E:Baobab · ♄ d Z10 ⓚ Ⓝ; trop. Afr.,
Madag.

Adelia P. Browne = Forestiera
– *acuminata* Michx. = Forestiera acuminata

Adelocaryum Brand = Lindelofia
– *anchusoides* (Lindl.) Brand = Lindelofia
  anchusoides
– *coelestinum* (Lindl.) Brand = Cynoglossum coelestinum

Adenandra Willd. -f- *Rutaceae* · 18 spp.
– **fragrans** (Sims) Roem. & Schult. ·
E:Breath of Heaven; G:Himmelsduft · ♄ e
D Z9 ⓚ III-IV Ⓝ; Cape

Adenanthera L. -f- *Mimosaceae* · 8-15 spp. ·
E:Coral Wood, Redwood; F:Adénanthéra;
G:Drüsenbaum
– **pavonina** L. · E:Bead Tree, Coralwood,
Peacock Flower Fence, Red Sandalwood
Tree; G:Indischer Drüsenbaum, Roter
Sandelholzbaum · ♄ e ⚭ Z10 ⓚ Ⓝ;
Him., Ind., Sri Lanka, Malay. Arch., Phil.,
China; cult. Trop.

Adenia Forssk. -f- *Passifloraceae* · 94 spp.
– **pechuelii** (Engl.) Harms · ♄ Ⴘ Z9 ⓚ;
Namibia

Adenium Roem. & Schult. -n-
Apocynaceae · 1 sp. · E:Desert Rose, Mock
Azalea; F:Lis des impalas, Rose du désert;
G:Wüstenrose
– *arabicum* Balf. f. = Adenium obesum
– *namaquanum* Wyley ex Harv. =

Pachypodium namaquanum
– **obesum** (Forssk.) Roem. & Schult. ·
E:Desert Rose, Mock Azalea; G:Gewöhn-
liche Wüstenrose · ♄ Ⴘ d Z10 Ⓦ ✺;
trop-Afr., S-Afr.

Adenocarpus DC. -m- *Fabaceae* · 15 spp. ·
F:Adénocarpe; G:Drüsenginster
– **complicatus** (L.) J. Gay · ♄ d Z9 ⓚ
V-VII; Eur.: Ib, Fr, Ital-P, Ba; TR, Syr.,
Moroc., Alger.
– **decorticans** Boiss. · ♄ d Z8 ⓚ V-VI;
Eur.: sp.; Moroc., Alger.
– **foliolosus** (Aiton) DC. · E:Canary Island
Flatpod · ♄ e Z8 ⓚ V-VI; Canar.
– *intermedius* DC. = Adenocarpus complicatus

Adenophora Fisch. -f- *Campanulaceae* ·
c. 40 spp. · E:Ladybells; F:Adénophore;
G:Schellenblume
– **bulleyana** Diels · G:Bulleys Schellenblume · ⚥ Z3 VII-VIII; W-China
– **confusa** Nannf. · G:Verkannte Schellenblume · ⚥ Z3 VI-VII; W-China
– **coronopifolia** Fisch. · G:Krähenfußblät-
trige Schellenblume · ⚥ Z6 VII-VIII;
E-Sib., Amur, Mong., N-China
– **divaricata** Franch. & Sav. · G:Sperrige
Schellenblume · ⚥; NE-China, Korea, Jap.
– *farreri* hort. = Adenophora confusa
– *himalayana* Feer = Adenophora coronopifolia
– **liliifolia** (L.) Ledeb. ex A. DC. · G:Lilien-
blättrige Schellenblume, Sibirische
Schellenblume · ⚥ Z2 VII-VIII ▽; Eur.:
C-Eur., EC-Eur., I, Ba, E-Eur.; W-Sib.,
C-As.
– **megalantha** Diels · G:Großblütige
Schellenblume · ⚥ Z6 VII-VIII; C-China.
– **ornata** Diels · G:Schmuck-Schellen-
blume · ⚥ Z6 VII-VIII; W-China
– **palustris** Kom. · G:Sumpf-Schellen-
blume · ⚥ Z6 VII-VIII; China, Jap.
– **potaninii** Korsh. · E:Bush Ladybell;
G:Potanins Schellenblume · ⚥ Z3 VII-VIII;
W-China
– **tashiroi** (Makino & Nakai) Makino &
Nakai · ⚥ Z7 VII-VIII; Jap.
– **triphylla** (Thunb.) A. DC. · E:Giant Bellflower; G:Dreiblättrige Schellenblume ·
⚥ Z7 VII-VIII; E-Sib., China, Jap., Taiwan
– *verticillata* (Pall.) Fisch. = Adenophora
triphylla

Adenostoma Hook. & Arn. -n- *Rosaceae* ·
2 spp. · E:Ribbonwood; F:Adénostome;
G:Scheinheide
– **fasciculatum** Hook. & Arn. · E:Common
Chamise; G:Strauchige Scheinheide · ♄ e
Z8 ⓧ V-VI; Calif., Baja Calif.
– **sparsifolium** Torr. · E:Greasewood, Red-
shank, Ribbonwood; G:Lockerblättrige
Scheinheide · ♄ e Z8 ⓧ V-VI; S-Calif.,
Baja Calif.

Adenostyles Cass. -f- *Asteraceae* · 4 spp. ·
F:Adénostyle; G:Alpendost
– **alliariae** (Gouan) A. Kern. ·
E:Adenostyles; G:Grauer Alpendost · ⚃ △
Z6 VII-VIII; Eur.* exc. BrI, Sc ; mts.
– *alpina* (L.) Bluff & Fingerh. = Adenostyles
alliariae
– **glabra** (Mill.) DC. · G:Kahler Alpendost ·
⚃ △ Z6 VII-VIII; Eur.: C-Eur., F, Cors, I,
Slove., Croatia; Alp., Apenn., Jura, Cors
– **leucophylla** (Willd.) Rchb. · G:Filziger
Alpendost · ⚃ Z6 VII-VIII; Eur.: I, F, Sw,
A; Alp.

Adesmia DC. -f- *Fabaceae* · c. 230 spp.
– **boronioides** Hook. f. · ♄ ⓧ V; Chile

Adhatoda Mill. = Justicia
– *cydoniifolia* Nees = Justicia cydoniifolia

Adiantopsis Fée -f- *Adiantaceae* · 14 spp.
– **pedata** (Hook.) T. Moore · ⚃ Z10 ⓦ;
Jamaica, Cuba
– **radiata** (L.) Fée · ⚃ Z10 ⓦ; Mex.,
W-Ind., trop. S-Am.

Adiantum L. -n- *Adiantaceae* · 220 spp. ·
E:Maidenhair Fern; F:Capillaire;
G:Frauenhaarfarn
– **aethiopicum** L. · E:Common Maidenhair
Fern; G:Buschiger Frauenhaarfarn · ⚃ Z9
ⓦ; trop. Afr., trop. As., Austr., NZ, S-Afr.
– *assimile* Sw. = Adiantum aethiopicum
– **bessoniae** Jenman · ⚃ ⓦ; W.Ind.
– **capillus-veneris** L. · E:Maidenhair Fern,
Southern Maidenhair, Venus Maidenhair;
G:Gewöhnlicher Frauenhaarfarn,
Venushaar · ⚃ Z8 ⓧ ⓐ VI-IX ♊ ; Eur.:
Ib., BrI, F, Ital-P, Sw, Ba, Crim; Can.:
B.C.; USA*; Trop., nat. in B, H
– **caudatum** L. · E:Trailing Maidenhair
Fern; G:Ausläufertreibender Frauenhaarfarn · ⚃ ♊ ⤳ Z10 ⓦ; trop. Afr., trop. As.
– *ciliatum* Blume = Adiantum caudatum

– **concinnum** Humb. & Bonpl. ex Willd. ·
E:Brittle Maidenhair; G:Zerbrechlicher
Frauenhaarfarn · ⚃ Z9 ⓐ; Mex., W.Ind.,
Venez., Braz., Peru, nat. in Sri Lanka
– **curvatum** Kaulf. · ⚃ Z10 ⓦ; Braz.
– *decorum* T. Moore = Adiantum raddianum
– **diaphanum** Blume · E:Filmy Maidenhair
Fern; G:Zarter Frauenhaarfarn · ⚃ Z9 ⓦ;
trop. As., E-Austr., NZ, Pacific Is., nat. in
Sri Lanka
– **dolabriforme** Hook. · ⚃ Z10 ⓦ; Panama,
Braz.
– **edgeworthii** Hook. · ⚃ ♊ ⤳ Z10 ⓦ;
Him., China
– **feei** T. Moore ex Fée · ⚃ Z10 ⓦ; Mex.,
Guat.
– **formosum** R. Br. · E:Australian
Maidenhair Fern, Giant Maidenhair Fern;
G:Australischer Frauenhaarfarn · ⚃ Z9
ⓦ; Austr., NZ, nat. in Sri Lanka
– *fragrans* L. f. = Cheilanthes pteridioides
– **fulvum** Raoul · ⚃ Z10 ⓧ; Austr., NZ,
Polyn.
– **hispidulum** Sw. · E:Rosy Maidenhair,
Rough Maidenhair; G:Rauer Frauenhaarfarn · ⚃ Z10 ⓧ; trop. Afr., trop. As.,
Austr., NZ
– *lunulatum* Burm. f. = Adiantum philip-
pense
– **macrophyllum** Sw. · E:Largeleaf
Maidenhair · ⚃ Z10 ⓦ; C-Am., W.Ind.,
Galapagos, Bol., Braz.
– *monosoratum* Willd. = Adiantum
pulverulentum
– **pedatum** L.
– var. **aleuticum** Rupr. · E:Aleutian
Maidenhair; G:Krauser Pfauenradfarn · ⚃
Z5; Alaska, Can., USA: NW, Calif., Rocky
Mts., Ariz., NE; Mex.(Chihuahua)
– var. **pedatum** · E:American Maidenhair,
Five Finger Fern; F:Capillaire pédalée,
Fougère fer-à-cheval; G:Amerikanischer
Frauenhaarfarn, Pfauenradfarn · ⚃ Z5;
Can.: E; USA: NE, NCE, NC, SC, SE; ,
NW, Rocky Mts., Calif., Ariz., NO; Mex.:
Chihuahua
– **peruvianum** Klotzsch · E:Silver Dollar
Maidenhair; G:Silberdollar-Frauenhaar-
farn · ⚃ Z10 ⓦ; Ecuad., Peru, Bol.
– **philippense** L. · E:Walking Maidenhair
Fern, Wild Tea-Leaves; G:Kriechender
Frauenhaarfarn · ⚃ Z10 ⓦ; trop. Afr.,
trop. As.
– **platyphyllum** Sw. · ⚃ Z10 ⓦ; C-Am.,

Ecuad., Peru, Bol., Braz.
- **polyphyllum** Willd. · ⃒ Z10 ⓦ; Col,
Venez., Trinidad
- **princeps** T. Moore · ⃒ Z10 ⓦ; C-Am., Col.
- **pulverulentum** L. · E:Glossy Maidenhair ·
⃒ Z10 ⓦ; Mex., C-Am., trop. S-Am., nat.
in Sri Lanka
- **raddianum** C. Presl · E:Delta Maidenhair
Fern; G:Dreieckiger Frauenhaarfarn · ⃒
⋈ Z10 ⓦ ⓤ; C-Am., trop. S-Am., nat. in
Azor., Sri Lanka
- **reniforme** L. · G:Talerfarn · ⃒ Z9 ⓚ;
Canar., Madeira
- *rhomboideum* Schkuhr = Adiantum
trapeziforme
- **rubellum** T. Moore · ⃒ Z10 ⓦ; Bol.
- *seemannii* Hook. = Adiantum platyphyllum
- **tenerum** Sw. · E:Brittle Maidenhair
Fern, Fan Maidenhair; G:Fächer-
Frauenhaarfarn · ⃒ Z9 ⓦ ⓤ; USA: Fla.;
Mex., W.Ind., C-Am., trop. S-Am.
- **tetraphyllum** Humb. & Bonpl. ex Willd. ·
E:Four Leaf Maidenhair; G:Vierblättriger
Frauenhaarfarn · ⃒ Z10 ⓦ; trop. Am.,
W-Afr.
- **trapeziforme** L. · E:Diamond Maidenhair
Fern; G:Diamant-Frauenhaarfarn · ⃒ Z10
ⓦ; Mex., W-Ind., Venez., Braz., nat. in
Sri Lanka
- **venustum** G. Don · E:Evergreen
Maidenhair Fern; F:Capillaire cheveux de
Vénus; G:Immergrüner Frauenhaarfarn ·
⃒ Z8 ∧; Him.
- **williamsii** T. Moore · ⃒ Z10 ⓚ; Peru

Adina Salisb. -f- *Rubiaceae* · 3 spp.
- *cordifolia* (Roxb.) Benth. & Hook. f. ex
B.D. Jacks. = Haldina cordifolia

× **Adioda** hort. -f- *Orchidaceae* (*Ada* ×
Cochlioda)

Adlumia Raf. ex DC. -f- *Fumariaceae* ·
1 sp. · G:Doppelkappe
- *cirrhosa* Raf. = Adlumia fungosa
- **fungosa** (Aiton) Greene ex Britton,
Sterns & Poggenb. · E:Allegheny Vine,
Climbing Fumitory, Mountain Fringe;
G:Doppelkappe · ☉ ⚥ Z6 VII-X; Can.: E;
USA: NE, NCE, N.C., Tenn

Adonidia Becc. -f- *Arecaceae* · 1 sp. ·
G:Manilapalme; E:Manila Palm
- **merrillii** (Becc.) Becc. · E:Christmas
Palm, Manila Palm; G:Manilapalme · ♄ e

Z10 ⓦ; Phil.

Adonis L. -f- *Ranunculaceae* · 26 spp. ·
E:Pheasant's Eye; F:Adonide; G:Adonis-
röschen, Teufelsauge
- **aestivalis** L. · E:Summer Adonis,
Summer Pheasant's Eye; G:Sommer-
Adonisröschen · ☉ ⫽ Z6 V-VIII ⚥ ✿;
Eur.* exc. BrI, Sc; TR, Levant, Iraq,
Cauc., Iran, Afgh., Pakist., C-As., W-Sib.,
NW-Afr., Libya
- **aleppica** Boiss. · ☉ ⫽ Z7 IV-VI ✿; TR,
Syr., N-Iraq
- **amurensis** Regel & Radde · E:Amur
Pheasant's Eye; F:Adonis de l'Amour;
G:Amur-Adonisröschen · ⃒ △ Z3 II-IV
✿; Amur, Manch., Korea, Jap. Sakhal.
- **annua** L. · E:Pheasant's Eye; G:Herbst-
Adonisröschen · ☉ ⫽ Z3 VI-VIII ✿;
Eur.: Ib, Fr, Ital-P, Sw, Ba; TR, Levant,
NW-Afr., nat. in BrI
- *autumnalis* L. = Adonis annua
- *dahurica* Ledeb. ex Rchb. = Adonis
amurensis
- *davurica* hort. = Adonis amurensis
- **flammea** Jacq. · G:Flammen-Adonis-
röschen · ☉ ⫽ Z3 V-VII ✿; Eur.* exc. BrI,
Sc; TR, Syr., Cauc., Iran
- **pyrenaica** DC. · G:Pyrenäen-Adonis-
röschen · ⃒ △ Z6 VI-VII ✿; Eur.: sp.,
F; Cordillera Cantábrica, Pyr., Alp.
Maritimes
- **vernalis** L. · E:Spring Adonis, Yellow
Pheasant's Eye; F:Adonis de printemps;
G:Frühlings-Adonisröschen · ⃒ △ Z3 IV-V
⚥ ✿ ▽ ✼; Eur.* exc. BrI; Cauc., W-Sib.,
E-Sib.

Adoxa L. -f- *Adoxaceae* · 4 spp. ·
E:Muskroot; F:Adoxa; G:Moschuskraut
- **moschatellina** L. · E:Muskroot, Town
Hall Clock; G:Moschuskraut · ⃒ III-V;
Eur.*, Cauc., W-Sib., E-Sib., Amur, C-As.,
W-Him., China, Manch., Jap., Alaska,
Can., USA: NE, NCE, NC, Rocky Mts.

Adromischus Lem. -m- *Crassulaceae* ·
28 spp. · F:Adromischus; G:Kurzstiel
- *clavifolius* (Haw.) Lem. = Adromischus
cristatus var. clavifolius
- **cooperi** (Baker) A. Berger · E:Plover Eggs;
G:Kiebitzei-Kurzstiel · ⃒ ⵌ Z9 ⓚ; Cape
- **cristatus** (Haw.) Lem. · G:Kamm-
Kurzstiel
- var. **clavifolius** (Haw.) Toelken · ⃒ Z9

ⓐ; S-Afr. (Cape Prov.)
- var. **cristatus** · ♃ Ψ Z9 ⓐ; Cape
- *festivus* C.A. Sm. = Adromischus cooperi
- **hemisphaericus** (L.) Lem. · G:Rundblättriger Kurzstiel · ♃ Ψ Z9 ⓐ; Cape, Namibia
- **maculatus** hort. non (Salm-Dyck) Lem. · E:Calico Hearts; G:Gefleckter Kurzstiel · ♃ Ψ Z9 ⓐ; Cape
- **mammillaris** (L. f.) Lem. · G:Warzen-Kurzstiel · ♃ Ψ Z9 ⓐ; Cape, Namibia
- **marianiae** (Marloth) A. Berger
- var. **marianiae** · ♃ Ψ Z9 ⓐ; Cape
- **rhombifolius** (Haw.) Lem. · G:Rautenblättriger Kurzstiel · ♄ Ψ e Z9 ⓐ; Cape
- var. *bakeri* Poelln. = Adromischus sphenophyllus
- *rotundifolius* (Haw.) C.A. Sm. = Adromischus hemisphaericus
- **sphenophyllus** C.A. Sm. · G:Keilblättriger Kurzstiel · Ψ Z9 ⓐ; Cape
- **trigynus** (Burch.) Poelln. · G:Dreigriffliger Kurzstiel · ♃ Ψ Z9 ⓐ; S-Afr., Namibia
- **umbraticola** C.A. Sm. · ♃ Ψ Z9 ⓐ; Cape
- *vanderheydenii* hort. ex A. Berger = Adromischus cristatus var. clavifolius

Aechmea Ruiz & Pav. -f- *Bromeliaceae* · 253 spp. · E:Livingvase; F:Aechméa; G:Lanzenrosette
- **aquilega** (Salisb.) Griseb. · ♃ Z10 ⓦ; Costa Rica, Venez., Trinidad, Braz.
- *bernoulliana* Wittm. = Aechmea mexicana
- **bicolor** L.B. Sm. · ♃ Z9 ⓐ; Braz.: Bahia
- **bracteata** (Sw.) Griseb. · ♃ Z9 ⓦ; C-Am., Col.
- **bromeliifolia** (Rudge) Baker · ♃ Z9 ⓦ; C-Am., S-Am.
- *caerulescens* (Regel) Baker = Aechmea lueddemanniana
- **calyculata** (E. Morren) Baker · ♃ Z9 ⓦ; Braz., Arg.
- **candida** E. Morren ex Baker · ♃ Z10 ⓦ; Braz.
- **caudata** Lindm. · ♃ Z10 ⓦ; Braz.
- **chantinii** (Carrière) Baker · ♃ Z10 ⓦ; Col., N-Peru, Braz.: Amazon.
- **coelestis** (K. Koch) E. Morren · ♃ Z10 ⓦ; Braz.
- **comata** (Gaudin) Baker · ♃ Z9 ⓦ; Braz.
- var. *mackoyana* (Mez) L.B. Sm. = Aechmea comata
- *crocophylla* (E. Morren) Baker = Aechmea pectinata
- **cylindrata** Lindm. · ♃ Z10 ⓦ; Braz.

- **dealbata** E. Morren ex Baker · ♃ Z10 ⓦ; Braz.
- **distichantha** Lem.
- var. **distichantha** · ♃ Z9 ⓦ; Braz., Urug., Parag., Bol., Arg.
- var. **glaziovii** (Baker) L.B. Sm. · ♃ Z9 ⓦ; Braz.
- **farinosa** (Regel) L.B. Sm.
- var. **conglomerata** (Baker) L.B. Sm. · ♃ Z10 ⓦ; Braz.
- var. **farinosa** · ♃ Z10 ⓦ; Braz.
- **fasciata** (Lindl.) Baker · E:Urn Plant, Vase Plant; G:Silbervase · ♃ Z9 ⓦ VII-IX; Braz.
- **fendleri** André · ♃ Z9 ⓦ; Venez.
- **filicaulis** (Griseb.) Mez · ♃ Z9 ⓦ; Venez.
- **fosteriana** L.B. Sm. · ♃ Z10 ⓦ; Braz.
- **fulgens** Brongn.
- var. **discolor** (C. Morren) Brongn. ex Baker Z9 ⓦ; Braz.
- var. **fulgens** · ♃ Z9 ⓦ; Braz.
- *galeottii* Baker = Aechmea lueddemanniana
- **gamosepala** Wittm. · ♃ Z10 ⓦ; Braz.
- *glaziovii* Baker = Aechmea distichantha var. glaziovii
- *glomerata* (Beer) Mez = Aechmea farinosa var. conglomerata
- var. *farinosa* (Regel) Mez = Aechmea farinosa var. farinosa
- **gracilis** Lindm. · ♃ Z10 ⓦ; Braz.
- *hystrix* E. Morren = Aechmea ornata
- **kertesziae** Reitz · ♃ Z10 ⓦ; Braz.
- *lalindei* Linden & Rodigas = Aechmea mariae-reginae
- *legrelliana* (Baker) Baker = Aechmea recurvata
- *lindenii* (E. Morren) Baker = Aechmea comata
- var. *mackoyana* Mez = Aechmea comata
- **lingulata** (L.) Baker · E:West Indian Livingvase · ♃ Z10 ⓦ; Lesser Antilles, Trinidad, Venez., Braz.
- **longifolia** (Rudge) L.B. Sm. & M.A. Spencer · ♃ Z10 ⓦ; Col., Peru, Bol., Braz.
- **lueddemanniana** (K. Koch) Mez · ♃ Z10 ⓦ; S-Mex., Guat., Belize
- **magdalenae** (André) André ex Baker · ♃ Z10 ⓦ ⓝ; Mex., C-Am., Col., Ecuad., Venez.
- **mariae-reginae** H. Wendl. · ♃ Z10 ⓦ; Costa Rica, Col.
- *marmorata* (Lem.) Mez = Quesnelia marmorata
- **melinonii** Hook. · ♃ Z10 ⓦ; Braz.:

Amazon.; Guyana
- **mertensii** (G. Mey.) Schult. f. · ⧫ Z9
  ⟨⟩; Col., Ecuad., Peru. Venez., Guyan.,
  Trinidad, Venez.
- **mexicana** Baker · ⧫ Z9 ⟨⟩; Mex., Guat.,
  Costa Rica, Ecuad.
- **miniata** (Beer) Baker · ⧫ Z9 ⟨⟩; Braz.
- **nidularioides** L.B. Sm. · ⧫ Z10 ⟨⟩;
  S-Col., N-Peru
- **nudicaulis** (L.) Griseb. · E:Naked Stem
  Livingvase · ⧫ Z10 ⟨⟩; Mex., C-Am.,
  W.Ind., Ecuad., Venez., Braz.
- **orlandiana** L.B. Sm. · ⧫ Z10 ⟨⟩; Braz.
- **ornata** Baker · ⧫ Z10 ⟨⟩; Braz.
- **pectinata** Baker · ⧫ Z10 ⟨⟩; Braz.
- **penduliflora** André · ⧫ Z10 ⟨⟩; C-Am.,
  trop. S-Am.
- **pineliana** (Brongn. ex Planch.) Baker · ⧫
  Z10 ⟨⟩; Braz.
- **pubescens** Baker · ⧫ Z10 ⟨⟩; C-Am., Col.
- **purpureorosea** (Hook.) Wawra · ⧫ Z9
  ⟨⟩; Braz.
- **racinae** L.B. Sm. · ⧫ Z10 ⟨⟩; Braz.
- **ramosa** Mart. ex Schult. f. · ⧫ Z10 ⟨⟩;
  Braz.
- **recurvata** (Klotzsch) L.B. Sm. · ⧫ Z9 ⟨⟩;
  Braz., Urug.
- **saxicola** L.B. Sm. · ⧫ Z10 ⟨⟩; E-Braz.
- *schiedeana* Schltdl. = Aechmea bracteata
- *schultesiana* Mez = Aechmea penduliflora
- **spectabilis** Brongn. ex Houllet · ⧫ Z10
  ⟨⟩; Col., Venez.
- **sphaerocephala** Baker · ⧫ Z10 ⟨⟩; Braz.
- *suaveolens* Knowles & Westc. = Aechmea
  purpureorosea
- **tessmannii** Harms · ⧫ Z10 ⟨⟩; Col., Peru
- **tillandsioides** (Mart. ex Schult. f.)
  Baker · ⧫ Z10 ⟨⟩; Mex., C-Am., Col.
  Venez., Guyana, Braz.
- **vallerandii** (Carrière) Erhardt, Götz &
  Seybold · ⧫ Z10 ⟨⟩; Braz., Peru, Bol.
- **victoriana** L.B. Sm. · ⧫ Z10 ⟨⟩; Braz.
- **warasii** E. Pereira · ⧫ Z10 ⟨⟩; Braz.:
  Espírito Santo
- **weilbachii** Didr. · ⧫ Z10 ⟨⟩; Braz.
- var. *leodiensis* André = Aechmea
  weilbachii
- **zebrina** L.B. Sm. · ⧫ Z10 ⟨⟩; S-Col.,
  N-Ecuad.

Aegilops L. -f- *Poaceae* · 21-25 spp. ·
E:Goatgrass; F:Egylops; G:Walch
- **cylindrica** Host · E:Jointed Goatgrass;
  G:Walzenförmiger Walch · ⊙ Z9 V-VII;
  Eur.: EC-Eur., Ba, E-Eur.; TR, Cauc.,

C-As., nat. in F, I
- **geniculata** Roth · E:Ovate Goatgrass;
  G:Zylindrischer Walch · ⊙ ✕ Z9 VI-VIII;
  Eur.: Ib, Fr, Ital-P, Ba, RO, Crim; TR,
  SW-As., N-Afr.
- **neglecta** Req. ex Bertol. · G:Übersehener
  Walch · ⊙ Z9; Eur.: Ib, Fr, Ital-P, Ba, RO,
  Crim; TR, Cauc., Iran
- **triuncialis** L. · E:Barbed Goatgrass;
  G:Langgranniger Walch · ⊙ Z9 VI-VIII ⟨N⟩;
  Eur.: Ib, Fr, Ital-P, Ba, Crim; TR, Cauc.,
  Iran, C-As., N-Afr.
- **ventricosa** Tausch · G:Bauchiger Walch ·
  ⊙ ✕ Z9 VII-VIII ⟨N⟩; Eur.: sp., Balear.,
  Sard., I, Slove.; Egypt, NW-Afr., nat. in F

Aeginetia L. -f- *Scrophulariaceae* · 3 spp. ·
G:Indische Sommerwurz
- **indica** L. · E:Indian Broomrape;
  G:Indische Sommerwurz · ⧫ Z10 ⟨⟩
  VIII-X; Ind., Malay. Pen., Jap.

Aegle Corrêa -f- *Rutaceae* · 3 spp. · E:Bael
Tree; G:Belbaum
- **marmelos** (L.) Corrêa · E:Indian Bael · ♄
  d ⟨⟩ ♀ ⟨N⟩; Ind., Burma

Aegonychon Gray = Lithospermum
- *purpurocaeruleum* (L.) Holub = Lithospermum purpurocaeruleum

Aegopodium L. -n- *Apiaceae* · 5-7 spp. ·
E:Goutweed, Ground Elder; F:Aegopode,
Herbe-aux-goutteux; G:Geißfuß, Giersch
- **podagraria** L. · E:Bishop's Weed, Ground
  Elder; G:Geißfuß, Gewöhnlicher Giersch
  · ⧫ VI-VIII ♀ ⟨N⟩; Eur.* exc. BrI, Sc; TR,
  Cauc., W-Sib., E-Sib., C-As., nat. in BR, e
  N-Am.

Aeollanthus Mart. ex Spreng. -m-
Lamiaceae · 43 spp.
- **repens** Oliv. · ♄ e ⟨⟩ IV-V; Cameroon,
  E-Afr., Sudan

Aeonium Webb & Berthel. -n-
Crassulaceae · 36 spp.
- **arboreum** (L.) Webb & Berthel. · E:Tree
  Aeonium · ♄ ⧫ Z9 ⟨⟩ I-II; Moroc., nat. in
  S-Eur.
- **balsamiferum** Webb & Berthel. · ♄ ⧫ D
  Z9 ⟨⟩; Canar.
- **canariense** (L.) Webb & Berthel. · E:Giant
  Velvet Rose · ♄ ⧫ Z9 ⟨⟩ IV-V; Canar.
- **ciliatum** (Willd.) Webb & Berthel. · ♄ ⧫

Z9 🏛 III-IV; Canar.
- **cuneatum** Webb & Berthel. · ♄ Ψ e Z9 🏛
  IV-VI; Canar.: Teneriffa
- **decorum** (H. Christ) Webb ex Bolle · ♄ Ψ
  Z9 🏛 IV-VI; Canar.
- × *domesticum* (Praeger) A. Berger =
  Aichryson × aizoides
- *giganteum* Webb ex H. Christ = Aeonium
  canariense
- **glutinosum** (Aiton) Webb & Berthel. · ♄
  Ψ Z9 🏛 VI-VIII; Madeira
- **goochiae** Webb & Berthel. · ♄ Ψ Z9 🏛
  V-VIII; Canar.
- **haworthii** Webb & Berthel. · E:Haworth's
  Aeonium, Pin Wheel · ♄ Ψ Z9 🏛 IV-V;
  Canar.
- **hierrense** (Murray) Pit. & Proust · ♄ Ψ Z9
  🏛 IV-V; Canar.
- **holochrysum** Webb & Berthel. · ♄ Ψ Z9
  🏛 XII-III; Canar.
- **lindleyi** Webb & Berthel. · ♄ Ψ Z9 🏛
  VII-IX; Canar.
- *manriqueorum* (H. Christ) Bolle =
  Aeonium arboreum
- **nobile** Praeger · ⊙ ♄ Ψ e Z9 🏛 VI; Canar.
- **percarneum** (Murray) Pit. & Proust · ♄ Ψ
  e Z9 🏛 IV-V; Canar.
- **sedifolium** (Webb ex Bolle) Pit. &
  Proust · ♄ Ψ e Z9 🏛 V; Canar.
- **simsii** (Sweet) Stearn · ⳨ Ψ Z9 🏛 IV-V;
  Canar.
- **spathulatum** (Hornem.) Praeger · ♄ Ψ Z9
  🏛 III-V; Canar.
- *strepsicladum* Webb & Berthel. =
  Aeonium spathulatum
- **tabuliforme** (Haw.) Webb & Berthel. · ⊙
  ⳨ Ψ e Z9 🏛 VII-VIII; Canar.
- **undulatum** Webb & Berthel. · E:Saucer
  Plant · ♄ Ψ Z9 🏛 IV-V; Canar.
- **urbicum** (C. Sm. ex Hornem.) Webb &
  Berthel. · ♄ Ψ e Z9 🏛 IV-V; Canar.
- *youngianum* Webb & Berthel. = Aeonium
  undulatum

Aerangis Rchb. f. -f- *Orchidaceae* · 48 spp.
- **articulata** (Rchb. f.) Schltr. · ⳨ Z10 🌸
  III-IV ▽ ✳; Madag.
- **citrata** (Thouars) Schltr. · ⳨ Z10 🌸 II-IV
  ▽ ✳; Madag.
- **ellisii** (Rchb. f.) Schltr. · ⳨ Z10 🌸 VII-IX
  ▽ ✳; Madag.
- **hyaloides** (Rchb. f.) Schltr. · ⳨ Z10 🌸
  II-III ▽ ✳; Madag.
- **kotschyana** (Rchb. f.) Schltr. · ⳨ Z10 🌸
  IX-X ▽ ✳; E-Afr., S-Afr.

- **modesta** (Hook. f.) Schltr. · ⳨ Z10 🌸
  IV-V ▽ ✳; Madag.

× **Aeridachnis** hort. -f- *Orchidaceae*
  (*Aerides* × *Arachnis*)

Aerides Lour. -n- *Orchidaceae* · 26 spp.
- **crassifolium** C.S.P. Parish & Rchb. f. · ⳨
  Z10 🌸 V-VI ▽ ✳; Burma: Moulmein
- **crispum** Lindl. · ⳨ Z10 🌸 V-VI ▽ ✳;
  Malay.Arch.
- *cylindricum* Hook. = Papilionanthe
  vandarum
- **falcatum** Lindl. ex Paxton · ⳨ Z10 🌸
  V-VI ▽ ✳; Burma
- *larpentiae* Rchb. f. = Aerides falcatum
- **lawrenceae** Rchb. f. · ⳨ Z10 🌸 VI-VIII ▽
  ✳; Phil.
- **multiflorum** Roxb. · ⳨ Z10 🌸 VI-IX ▽
  ✳; Him., Burma, Vietn.
- **odoratum** Lour. · ⳨ Z10 🌸 VI-VII ▽ ✳;
  Ind., China, Malay. Arch., Phil.
- *vandarum* Rchb. f. = Papilionanthe
  vandarum

× **Aeridocentrum** hort. -n- *Orchidaceae*
  (*Aerides* × *Ascocentrum*)

× **Aeridofinetia** hort. -f- *Orchidaceae*
  (*Aerides* × *Neofinetia*)

× **Aeridoglossum** hort. -n- *Orchidaceae*
  (*Aerides* × *Ascoglossum*)

× **Aeridopsis** hort. -f- *Orchidaceae* (*Aerides*
  × *Phalaenopsis*)

× **Aeridostylis** A.D. Hawkes -f- *Orchidaceae*
  (*Aerides* × *Rhynchostylis*)

× **Aeridovanda** hort. -f- *Orchidaceae*
  (*Aerides* × *Vanda*)

Aerva Forssk. -f- *Amaranthaceae* · 10 spp.
- **scandens** (Roxb.) Wall. · ⳨ 🐌; Trop. Old
  World

Aesandra Pierre = Diploknema
- *butyracea* (Roxb.) Baehni = Diploknema
  butyracea

Aeschrion Vell. = Picrasma
- *excelsa* (Sw.) Kuntze = Picrasma excelsa

Aeschynanthus Jack -m- *Gesneriaceae* ·

100-140 spp. · E:Basket Plant, Blush Wort;
F:Aeschynanthus; G:Sinnblume
- **boscheanus** de Vriese · ♄ e ⚥ Z10 ⓦ
VI-VIII; Sumat.
- **evrardii** Pellegr. · ♄ e Z10 ⓦ; Vietn.:
Annam
- **hildebrandtii** Hemsl. · ♄ e ⤳ Z10 ⓦ;
Burma
- *javanicus* Hook. = Aeschynanthus
radicans
- *lamponga* Miq. = Aeschynanthus
boscheanus
- **lobbianus** Hook. · E:Lipstick Plant;
G:Lippenstift-Sinnblume · ♄ ⚥ Z10 ⓦ;
Java
- **longicaulis** Wall. · E:Zebra Basket Vine;
G:Gefleckte Sinnblume · ♄ e ⚥ Z10 ⓦ;
Thail., Malay. Pen.
- *marmoratus* T. Moore = Aeschynanthus
longicaulis
- **micranthus** C.B. Clarke · ♄ e ⚥ Z10 ⓦ
VI-VIII; Him., Burma
- **parasiticus** (Roxb.) Wall. · ♄ e ⚥ Z10 ⓦ
VII-VIII; Ind.: Khasia Hills
- **pulcher** (Blume) G. Don · E:Scarlet
Basket Vine · ⚃ Z10 ⓦ; Java
- **radicans** Jack · E:Lipstick Plant;
G:Strahlige Sinnblume · ⚃ ♄ e Z10 ⓦ;
Malay. Pen., Java
- **speciosus** Hook. · ♄ e ⚥ Z10 ⓦ VI-IX;
Malay. Pen., Java, Kalimantan
- × **splendidus** T. Moore (A. parasiticus ×
A. speciosus) · ♄ e ⚥ Z10 ⓦ; cult.
- **tricolor** Hook. · ♄ e ⚥ Z10 ⓦ V-VII;
Kalimantan

Aeschynomene L. -f- *Fabaceae* · c.
150 spp. · E:Joint Vetch; G:Schampflanze
- **americana** L. · E:American Joint Vetch,
Shyleaf; G:Amerikanische Schampflanze
· ♄ ⓦ Ⓝ; trop. Am., nat. in Malay. Arch.
- **aspera** L. · E:Sola Pith Plant; G:Raue
Schampflanze · ♄ ⌇ ⓦ Ⓝ; Ind.
- **elaphroxylon** (Guill. & Perr.) Taub. ·
E:Ambatch; G:Ambatsch · ♄ ⓦ Ⓝ; trop.
Afr.
- **indica** L. · E:Curly Indigo, Hard Sola,
Indian Joint Vetch; G:Indische Schampflanze · ☉ ⌇ ⓦ VII-IX Ⓝ; Ind.

Aesculus L. -f- *Hippocastanaceae* · 15 spp. ·
E:Horse Chestnut; F:Marronnier;
G:Rosskastanie
- *arguta* Buckley = Aesculus glabra var.
arguta

- **californica** (Spach) Nutt. · E:California
Buckeye; G:Kalifornische Rosskastanie ·
♄ ♄ d Z7; Calif.
- × **carnea** Hayne (A. hippocastanum
× A. pavia) · E:Red Horse Chestnut;
F:Marronnier rouge; G:Rote Rosskastanie · ♄ d Z4 V-VI ⚘; cult.
- **chinensis** Bunge · E:Chinese Horse
Chestnut; G:Chinesische Rosskastanie · ♄
d Z6 ⚘; N-China
- **discolor** Pursh · F:Marronnier bicolore ·
♄ ♄ Z6 V-VI ⚘
- **flava** Sol. · E:Sweet Buckeye, Yellow
Buckeye; F:Marronnier jaune; G:Gelbe
Rosskastanie · ♄ d Z6 V-VI ⚘ Ⓝ; USA:
NE, SE
- *georgiana* Sarg. = Aesculus sylvatica
- **glabra** Willd.
- var. **arguta** (Buckley) B.L. Rob. ·
G:Texas-Rosskastanie · ♄ d Z6 V ⚘;
USA: Kans., SC
- var. **glabra** · E:Ohio Buckeye;
F:Marronnier de l'Ohio; G:Ohio-
Rosskastanie · ♄ d Z6 V ⚘ Ⓝ; USA: NE,
NCE, NC, SC, SE
- var. *monticola* Sarg. = Aesculus glabra
var. glabra
- × **glaucescens** Sarg. (A. flava × A.
sylvatica) · F:Marronnier aurore · Z5;
USA: Ga.
- **hippocastanum** L. · E:Horse Chestnut;
F:Marronnier d'Inde; G:Gewöhnliche
Rosskastanie · ♄ d Z4 V ⚥ Ⓝ; Eur.: Ba;
? Cauc., N-Iran, Him., nat. in Fr, IRL,
C-Eur., EC-Eur.
- **some cultivars**
- × **hybrida** DC. (A. flava × A. pavia) ·
F:Marronnier hybride; G:Allegheny-
Rosskastanie · ♄ d Z5 V-VI; cult.
- **indica** (Wall. ex Cambess.) Hook. ·
E:Indian Horse Chestnut; F:Marronnier
de l'Himalaya; G:Indische Rosskastanie ·
♄ d Z7 VI-VII; Afgh., Him.
- *lutea* Wangenh. = Aesculus flava
- × **marylandica** J.R. Booth (A. flava × A.
glabra) · G:Maryland-Rosskastanie · ♄ d
Z5; cult.
- × **mutabilis** (Spach) Schelle (A. pavia ×
A. sylvatica) · F:Marronnier hybride · ♄ d
Z5 V-VI; cult.
- × **neglecta** Lindl. (A. flava × A. sylvatica) ·
E:Sunrise Horse Chestnut; F:Marronnier
aurore; G:Carolina-Rosskastanie · ♄ d Z5
V-VI; USA: Va., SE, Fla.
- *octandra* Marshall = Aesculus flava

– *ohioensis* (F. Michx.) DC. = Aesculus glabra var. glabra
– **parviflora** Walter · E:Bottlebrush Buckeye, Dwarf Buckeye, Shrubby Pavia; F:Pavier blanc; G:Strauch-Rosskastanie · ♄ d Z5 VII-VIII; USA: SE, Fla.
– **pavia** L. · E:Red Buckeye; F:Pavier rouge; G:Echte Pavie · ♄ ♄ d Z5 VI ⚥ ✷; USA: Va., W.Va., SC, SE, Fla.
– var. *discolor* (Pursh) Torr. & A. Gray = Aesculus discolor
– × *plantierensis* André = Aesculus × carnea
– × *rubicunda* Loisel. = Aesculus × carnea
– *splendens* Sarg. = Aesculus pavia
– **sylvatica** W. Bartram · E:Painted Buckeye; G:Georgia-Rosskastanie · ♄ ♄ d Z5; USA: SE (N.C., Tenn., Ga.)
– **turbinata** Blume · E:Japanese Horse Chestnut; F:Marronnier du Japon; G:Japanische Rosskastanie · ♄ d Z6 V-VI Ⓝ; Jap.
– × *versicolor* (Spach) Wender. = Aesculus × hybrida

Aethephyllum N.E. Br. -n- *Aizoaceae* · 1 sp.
– **pinnatifidum** (L. f.) N.E. Br. · ⊙ ⴱ ⓚ; Cape

Aethionema R. Br. -n- *Brassicaceae* · 46 spp. · E:Stone Cress; F:Aethionema; G:Steintäschel
– **armenum** Boiss. · ⴱ △ Z7 V; TR
– **cordatum** (Desf.) Boiss. · ⴱ △ Z7 ∧ V-VI; Eur.: GR; TR, Cauc.
– **coridifolium** DC. · E:Stonecress; G:Zierliches Steintäschel · ♄ △ Z6-7 V-VIII; S-TR, Lebanon
– **diastrophis** Bunge · ⴱ ♄ △ Z7 ∧ V-VI; Cauc. (Armen.)
– *graecum* Boiss. & Spruner = Aethionema saxatile
– **grandiflorum** Boiss. & Hohen. · E:Persian Stone Cress; F:Aethionema à grandes fleurs, Aethionema de Perse; G:Großblütiges Steintäschel · ♄ △ Z6-7 VI-VII; TR, N-Iraq, Cauc., Iran
– **Pulchellum Group** · ; cult.
– **iberideum** (Boiss.) Boiss. · ⴱ △ Z7 ∧ V; E-GR, TR, Cauc.
– **oppositifolium** (Pers.) Hedge · ⴱ △ Z7 ∧ IV-V; TR, Cauc., Lebanon
– *pulchellum* Boiss. & A. Huet = Aethionema grandiflorum Pulchellum Group
– **saxatile** (L.) R. Br. · E:Candy Mustard; G:Felsen-Steintäschel · ⊙ ⴱ △ IV-VI;

Eur.* exc. Sc, BrI; TR, Alger., Moroc.
– **schistosum** (Boiss. & Kotschy) Kotschy · ⴱ △ Z7 ∧ VI; TR: Cilician Taurus
– **speciosum** Boiss. & A. Huet · ⴱ △ Z7 ∧; E-TR, Iraq
– **stylosum** DC. · ⴱ △ Z7 ∧ VI; TR: Cilician Taurus, W-Syr.
– **thomasianum** J. Gay · ⴱ Z7; Eur.: F, I, ? Sw
– × *warleyense* C.K. Schneid. ex Boom = Aethionema armenum

Aethusa L. -f- *Apiaceae* · 1 sp. · E:Fool's Parsley; F:Ethuse, Petite ciguë; G:Hundspetersilie
– **cynapium** L. · G:Hundspetersilie
– subsp. **cynapium** · E:Dog Poison, Fool's Parsley; G:Acker-Hundspetersilie · ⊙ VI-X ✷; Eur.*, Cauc, N-TR, Alger., nat. in N-Am.
– subsp. **elata** (Friedlein ex Fisch.) Schübl. & G. Martens · G:Wald-Hundspetersilie

Aframomum K. Schum. -n- *Zingiberaceae* · 53 spp. · E:Melagueta Pepper; F:Malaguette, Maniguette; G:Malaguetapfeffer
– **angustifolium** (Sonn.) K. Schum. · E:Cameroon Cardamom; G:Kamerun-Kardamom · ⴱ Z10 ⓦ Ⓝ; Madag., Seych., Mauritius
– **melegueta** K. Schum. · E:Grains of Paradise, Guinea Grains ;G:Paradieskörnerpflanze · ⴱ Z10 ⓦ ⚥ Ⓝ; W-Afr.

Afrocarpus (J. Buchholz & N.E. Gray) C.N. Page -m- *Podocarpaceae* · 6 spp. · E:Yellowwood; G:Afrogelbholz
– **falcatus** (Thunb.) C.N. Page · E:Common Yellowwood, Oteniqua Yellowwood; G:Gewöhnliches Afrogelbholz · ♄ e Z10; S-Afr., Angola
– **gracilior** (Pilg.) C.N. Page · E:African Fern Pine; G:Schlankes Afrogelbholz · ♄ e Z10 ⓚ; Eth., Uganda, Kenya

Afzelia Sm. -f- *Caesalpiniaceae* · 8 (-13) spp. · E:Makola; G:Makolabaum
– **africana** Sm. ex Pers. · E:African Mahogany, Makola; G:Makolabaum · ♄ ⋊ Z10 ⓦ Ⓝ; W-Afr., C-Afr.

Aganisia Lindl. -f- *Orchidaceae* · 3 spp.
– **cyanea** (Lindl.) Rchb. f. · ⴱ Z10 ⓦ V-VI ▽ ✳; Col., Venez., Braz.

Agapanthus L'Hér. -m- *Alliaceae* · 6 spp. ·
E:African Lily; F:Agapanthe; G:Liebes-
blume, Schmucklilie
– **africanus** (L.) Hoffmanns. · E:African
Lily; G:Afrikanische Schmucklilie · ⒉ Z9
⒧ VII-VIII ⚥; Cape
– **campanulatus** F.M. Leight. · ⒉ Z8 ⒧
VII-VIII; S-Afr.
– **caulescens** Spreng. · ⒉ Z8 ⒧ VIII-IX;
S-Afr.
– *comptonii* F.M. Leight. = Agapanthus
praecox subsp. minimus
– **inapertus** P. Beauv. · ⒉ Z8 ⒧ IX-X;
S-Afr.: Transvaal
– *orientalis* F.M. Leight. = Agapanthus
praecox subsp. orientalis
– **praecox** Willd.
– subsp. **minimus** (Lindl.) F.M. Leight. Z9
⒧; S-Afr.
– subsp. **orientalis** (F.M. Leight.) F.M.
Leight. · ⒉ Z9 ⒧; S-Afr.
– subsp. **praecox** · ⒉ ⚥ Z9 ⒧ VII-VIII;
S-Afr.: Cape, Natal
– *umbellatus* L'Hér. = Agapanthus africanus
– **Cultivars:**
– **many cultivars, see Section III**

Agapetes D. Don ex G. Don -f- *Ericaceae* ·
95 spp.
– **acuminata** D. Don ex G. Don · ♄ Z9 ⒧;
Bhutan, Ind.: Khasia Hills
– **buxifolia** Nutt. · ♄ e Z9 ⒧ ♡ III-V;
Bhutan
– **rugosa** (Hook.) Sleumer · ♄ e Z9 ⒧
III-V; Ind.: Khasia Hills
– **serpens** (Wight) Sleumer · ♄ e ⚵ Z9 ⒧
I-V; Him.

Agastache Gronov. -f- *Lamiaceae* · 22 spp. ·
E:Mexican Hyssop; F:Agastache;
G:Duftnessel
– *anethiodora* Britton = Agastache
foeniculum
– *anisata* hort. = Agastache foeniculum
– **cana** (Hook.) Wooton & Standl. ·
E:Mosquito Plant; G:Moskitopflanze · ⊙
♄ Z9 VII-VIII; USA: N.Mex., Tex.
– **foeniculum** (Pursh) Kuntze · E:Anise
Hyssop; F:Hysope anisée; G:Anis-Ysop,
Duftnessel · ⒉ Z7 ⚵ ; Can., USA: NEC,
NC, Rocky Mts.
– **mexicana** (Kunth) Lint & Epling ·
E:Mexican Giant Hyssop; F:Agastache;
G:Limonen-Ysop · ⒉ Z9 VII-IX; Mex.
– **urticifolia** (Benth.) Kuntze · E:Nettle

Leaf Giant Hyssop; G:Falsche Brennnessel · ⊙ ⒉ ⚥ Z7 VIII; B.C., USA: NW,
Mont., Calif.
– **Cultivars:**
– **some cultivars**

Agathis Salisb. -f- *Araucariaceae* · 21 sp. ·
E:Kauri Pine; F:Agathis; G:Dammara-
baum, Kaurifichte
– *alba* (Rumph. ex Hassk.) Foxw. = Agathis
dammara
– **australis** (D. Don) Salisb. · E:Kauri Pine,
New Zealand Kauri; G:Neuseeländische
Kaurifichte · ♄ e Z9 ⒧ ⓝ; NZ
– **dammara** (Lamb.) Rich. & A. Rich. ·
E:Amboina Pine, East Indian Kauri;
G:Dammarabaum
– *loranthifolia* Salisb. = Agathis philippinensis
– **philippinensis** Warb. · E:Pitch Tree;
G:Harzige Kaurifichte · ♄ e Z9 ⒧ ⓝ;
Indochina, Malay. Arch., Phil.
– **robusta** (C. Moore ex F. Muell.) F.M.
Bailey · E:Queensland Kauri, Smooth
Bark Kauri; G:Queensland-Kaurifichte · ♄
e Z9 ⒧ ⓝ; Austr.: Queensl.

Agathosma Willd. -f- *Rutaceae* · 135 spp. ·
E:Buchu; G:Duftraute
– **betulina** (P.J. Bergius) Pillans · E:Round
Buchu; G:Birkenähnliche Duftraute · ♄ e
Z9 ⒧ ⚵ ; Cape
– **ciliata** (L.) Link · ♄ e Z9 ⒧ III-V; S-Afr.
– **crenulata** (L.) Pillans · E:Buchu;
G:Feinzähnige Duftraute · ♄ e Z9 ⒧ ⚵ ;
S-Afr.
– **foetidissima** (Bartl. & H.L. Wendl.)
Steud. · ♄ e Z9 ⒧ III-IV; Cape
– **hirta** (Lam.) Bartl. & H.L. Wendl. · ♄ e
Z9 ⒧ VI-VII; S-Afr.
– **imbricata** (L.) Willd. · ♄ e Z9 ⒧ VI-VII;
S-Afr.
– **lanceolata** (L.) Engl. · ♄ e Z9 ⒧ II-III;
S-Afr.: Cape, Natal
– **pulchella** (L.) Link · ♄ e Z9 ⒧ II-VI; Cape
– **serratifolia** (Curtis) Spreeth · E:Longleaf
Buchu · ♄ e Z9 ⒧ IV-V ⚵ ; Cape

Agave L. -f- *Agavaceae* · 221 sp. · E:Century
Plant, Maguey; F:Agave; G:Agave
– *albicans* Jacobi = Agave celsii var.
albicans
– **americana** L. · E:Century Plant;
G:Hundertjährige Agave · ⚘ Z9 ⒧ VII-VIII
⚵ ⓝ; Mex., nat. in Trop., Subtrop.

– *angustifolia* Haw. = Agave vivipara var. vivipara
– **applanata** K. Koch ex Jacobi · ⚲ Z9 ⚑; Mex.
– **atrovirens** Karw. ex Salm-Dyck · E:Maguey
– var. **atrovirens** · ⚲ Z9 ⚑ Ⓝ; Mex.; mts.
– var. *salmiana* (Otto ex Salm-Dyck) Trel. = Agave salmiana var. salmiana
– **attenuata** Salm-Dyck · G:Drachenbaum-Agave · ⚲ Z9 ⚑;
– *beaucarnei* Lem. = Agave kerchovei
– *besseriana* Jacobi = Agave macroacantha
– **bracteosa** S. Watson ex Engelm. · ⚲ Z9 ⚑; NE-Mex.
– *californica* Baker = Agave striata subsp. falcata
– **cantala** (Haw.) Roxb. ex Salm-Dyck · E:Cantala; G:Cantala-Agave · ⚲ Z9 ⚑ Ⓝ; ? W-Mex., nat. in SE-As.
– *caroli-schmidtii* A. Berger = Agave seemanniana
– **celsii** Hook.
– var. **albicans** (Jacobi) Gentry Z9 ⚑; Mex.
– var. **celsii** · ⚲ Z9 ⚑; Mex.
– *cernua* A. Berger = Agave attenuata
– **chiapensis** Jacobi · ♃ ⚲ Z9 ⚑; Mex.
– *coccinea* Roezl ex Jacobi = Agave atrovirens var. atrovirens
– *cornuta* hort. = Agave xylonacantha
– *cubensis* Haw. = Furcraea hexapetala
– **dasylirioides** Jacobi & C.D. Bouché · ⚲ Z8 ⚑; Guat.
– var. *dealbata* (Lem. ex Jacobi) Baker = Agave dasylirioides
– *dealbata* Lem. ex Jacobi = Agave dasylirioides
– *deweyana* Trel. = Agave vivipara var. deweyana
– *echinoides* Jacobi = Agave striata subsp. striata
– *excelsa* Jacobi = Agave vivipara var. vivipara
– *falcata* Engelm. = Agave striata subsp. falcata
– var. *espadina* A. Berger = Agave striata subsp. falcata
– *ferdinandi-regis* A. Berger = Agave victoriae-reginae
– *ferox* K. Koch = Agave salmiana var. ferox
– *filamentosa* Salm-Dyck = Agave filifera subsp. filifera
– **filifera** Salm-Dyck
– subsp. **filifera** · E:Thread Agave; G:Faden-Agave · ⚲ Z9 ⚑; Mex.

– subsp. **schidigera** (Lem.) B. Ullrich · ⚲ Z9 ⚑; Mex.
– var. *filamentosa* (Salm-Dyck) Baker = Agave filifera subsp. filifera
– *foetida* L. = Furcraea foetida
– **fourcroydes** Lem. · E:Henequen, Sisal Hemp; G:Weiber-Sisal · ⚲ Z8 ⚑ Ⓝ; Mex.: Yucatan
– **franzosinii** Baker · ⚲ Z9 ⚑; Mex.
– **funkiana** K. Koch & C.D. Bouché · G:Jamauvefaser · ⚲ Z9 ⚑ Ⓝ; Mex.
– **geminiflora** (Tagl.) Ker-Gawl. · E:Twin-flowered Agave · ⚲ Z9 ⚑; ? Mex.
– **ghiesbreghtii** Lem. ex Jacobi · ⚲ Z9 ⚑; Mex.
– *guadelajara* Trel. = Agave inaequidens
– *hexapetala* Jacq. = Furcraea hexapetala
– **horrida** Lem. ex Jacobi · ♃ ⚲ Z9 ⚑; Mex.
– **inaequidens** K. Koch · ⚲ Z8; Mex.
– *ingens* A. Berger = Agave americana
– *ixtlioides* Hook. f. = Agave vivipara var. vivipara
– **karatto** Mill. · ⚲ Z9 ⚑; W.Ind.
– **kerchovei** Lem. · ⚲ Z9 ⚑; Mex.
– *latissima* Jacobi = Agave atrovirens var. atrovirens
– **lechuguilla** Torr. · E:Lechuguilla; G:Ixtlefaser · ⚲ Z9 ⚑ Ⓝ; Tex., N-Mex.
– **lophantha** Schiede · E:Lechuguilla; G:Tula-Ixtle · ⚲ Z9 ⚑ Ⓝ; Mex.
– **lurida** Aiton · ⚲ Z9 ⚑; Mex.
– **macroacantha** Zucc. · ⚲ Z9 ⚑; Mex.
– *macroculmis* Tod. = Agave atrovirens
– **maculosa** Hook. · E:Spice Lily · ⚲ Z9 ⚑ V-VIII; S-Tex., N-Mex.
– **margaritae** Brandegee · ⚲ Z9 ⚑; Mex.: Baja Calif.
– **marmorata** Roezl · ⚲ Z9 ⚑; Mex.
– *megalacantha* Hemsl. = Agave inaequidens
– *mexicana* Lam. = Agave lurida
– **mitis** Mart.
– **obscura** Schiede ex Schltdl. · ⚲ Z9 ⚑; Mex.
– **parrasana** A. Berger · ⚲ Z9 ⚑; Mex.
– **parryi** Engelm. · E:Mescal, Parry's Agave; G:Mescal-Agave · ⚲ Z8 ⚑; Ariz., Mex.
– **polyacantha** Haw. · ⚲ Z9 ⚑; E-Mex.
– var. *xalapensis* (Roezl ex Jacobi) A.H. Gentry = Agave obscura
– **potatorum** Zucc. · ⚲ Z9 ⚑; Mex.
– var. *verschaffeltii* (Lem.) A. Berger = Agave potatorum
– *purpusorum* A. Berger = Agave ghiesbreghtii
– *roezliana* Baker = Agave ghiesbreghtii

- **salmiana** Otto ex Salm-Dyck
- var. **ferox** (K. Koch) A.H. Gentry · ⚘ Z9 ⓓ; Mex.
- var. **salmiana** · ⚘ Z9 ⓓ Ⓝ; Mex.
- **scabra** Ortega · ⚘ Z9 ⓓ; Mex.
- *schidigera* Lem. = Agave filifera subsp. schidigera
- *schnittspahnii* Jacobi = Agave applanata
- *scolymus* Karw. ex Salm-Dyck = Agave potatorum
- **seemanniana** Jacobi · ⚘ Z9 ⓓ; Guat.
- **shawii** Engelm. · E:Coastal Agave · ⚘ Z9 ⓓ; USA: S-Calif.; Mex. (Baja Calif.)
- **sisalana** Perrine · E:Sisal ; G:Sisal, Sisal-Agave · ⚘ Z9 ⓓ Ⓝ; Mex.
- **spicata** Cav. · ⚘ Z9 ⓓ; Mex.
- **striata** Zucc.
- subsp. **falcata** (Engelm.) A.H. Gentry · ⚘ Z9 ⓓ Ⓝ; Mex.
- subsp. **striata** · ⚘ Z9 ⓓ; Mex.
- **stricta** Salm-Dyck · ⚘ Z9 ⓓ; Mex.
- *univittata* Haw. = Agave lophantha
- **utahensis** Engelm.
- subsp. **utahensis** · E:Utah Agave · ⚘ Z7 ⓓ; USA: Calif., Nev.
- var. *discreta* M.E. Jones = Agave utahensis subsp. utahensis
- *vangrolae* Trel. = Agave karatto
- **variegata** Jacobi · ⚘ Z9 ⓓ IV-V; S-Tex., N-Mex.
- *vera-cruz* Mill. = Agave lurida
- *verschaffeltii* Lem. = Agave potatorum
- **victoriae-reginae** T. Moore · E:Royal Agave; G:Königs-Agave · ⚘ Z9 ⓓ ▽ ✳; Mex.
- **vilmoriniana** A. Berger · ⚃ ⚘ Z9 ⓓ; NW-Mex.
- **virginica** L. · E:False Aloe, Snake Chief Root · ⚘ Z8 ⓓ ∧ VIII-IX; USA: NE, NCE, NC, SE, Fla.
- **vivipara** L.
- var. **deweyana** (Trel.) P.I. Forst. · ⚘ Z9 Ⓝ; Mex.
- var. **letonae** (F.W. Taylor ex Trel.) P.I. Forst. · ⚘ Z9 Ⓝ; El Salv.
- var. **vivipara** · ⚘ Z9 ⓓ; Mex.
- *wislizeni* Engelm. = Agave parryi
- *xalapensis* Roezl ex Jacobi = Agave obscura
- **xylonacantha** Salm-Dyck · ⚘ Z9 ⓓ; Mex.
- *yuccaefolia* F. Delaroche = Agave spicata

Ageratina Spach -f- *Asteraceae* · c. 290 spp.
- **altissima** (L.) R.M. King & H. Rob. · E:Mist Flower, White Snakeroot;

F:Eupatoire à feuilles molles; G:Weiße Natternwurz · ⚃ Z6 VII-IX ✺; Can.: E, Sask.; USA: NE, NC, SE, Fla., SC
- **aromatica** (L.) Spach · E:Lesser Snakeroot · ⚃ Z4 VIII-X; USA: NE, Ohio, SE, Fla.
- **glechonophylla** (Less.) R.M. King & H. Rob. · ♄ Z9 ⓓ VII-X; Chile
- **riparia** (Regel) R.M. King & H. Rob. · E:Spreading Snakeroot; G:Wuchernde Natternwurz · ⚃ Z10 ⓓ IX-V; Mex., W.Ind.
- **vernalis** (Vatke & Kurtz) R.M. King & H. Rob. · ⚃ ♄ Z10 ⓓ II-III; Mex.

Ageratum L. -n- *Asteraceae* · 44 spp. · E:Flossflower; F:Agératum; G:Leberbalsam
- **conyzoides** L. · E:Mexican Ageratum, Tropical Whiteweed; G:Mexikanischer Leberbalsam · ⊙ Z9 VII-IX; C-Am., S-Am., nat. in Trop.
- **corymbosum** Zucc. · E:Flat-top Whiteweed · ♄ Z9 ⓓ VI-IX; Mex.
- **houstonianum** Mill. · E:Bluemink, Floss Flower; F:Agérate; G:Leberbalsam · ⊙ Z8 ⓓ X; Mex., Guat., Belize
- **many cultivars**
- *mexicanum* Sims = Ageratum houstonianum

Aglaia Lour. -f- *Meliaceae* · c. 120 spp. · G:Glanzbaum
- *domestica* (Corrêa) Pellegr. = Lansium domesticum
- *odorata* Lour. = Aglaia pinnata
- **pinnata** (L.) Druce · E:Chulan; G:Glanzbaum · ♄ D ⓓ ⚘ Ⓝ; SE-As., Phil.

Aglaomorpha Schott -f- *Polypodiaceae* · 14 spp.
- **coronans** (Wall.) Copel. · ⚃ Z10 ⓓ; S-Him., Indochina
- **heraclea** (Kunze) Copel. · ⚃ Z10 ⓓ; Malay.Arch., N.Guinea
- **meyeniana** Schott · ⚃ Z10 ⓓ; Phil., Taiwan

Aglaonema Schott -n- *Araceae* · 24 spp. · F:Aglaonema; G:Kolbenfaden
- **brevispathum** (Engl.) Engl. · ♄ e Z10 ⓓ; SE-As.
- f. **hospitum** (F.N. Williams) Nicolson · ♄ e ⓓ; Thail.
- **commutatum** Schott · E:Philippine Evergreen · ✺
- var. **commutatum** · ♄ e Z10 ⓓ; Phil.,

Sulawesi
- var. **elegans** (Engl.) Nicolson · ♄ Z10 ⓦ;
Phil.: Luzon
- var. **maculatum** (Hook. f.) Nicolson ·
G:Gefleckter Kolbenfaden · ♄ Z10 ⓦ;
Phil.: Luzon
- var. *robustum* (Alderw.) Nicolson =
Aglaonema commutatum var. commutatum
- **costatum** N.E. Br. · ♄ e Z10 ⓦ; Malay.
Pen.: Lankawi
- **crispum** (R. Pitcher & Manda) Nicolson ·
E:Painted Drop Tongue; G:Gezeichneter
Kolbenfaden · ♄ e Z10 ⓚ; Phil.: Luzon
- *elegans* Engl. = Aglaonema commutatum
var. elegans
- *hospitum* F.N. Williams = Aglaonema
brevispathum f. hospitum
- **marantifolium** Blume · ♄ e Z10 ⓦ;
N.Guinea, Molucca Is.
- var. *maculatum* Hook. f. = Aglaonema
commutatum var. maculatum
- var. *tricolor* hort. = Aglaonema commutatum var. commutatum
- **modestum** Schott ex Engl. · E:Chinese
Evergreen; G:Chinesischer Kolbenfaden ·
♄ e Z10 ⓦ; N-Thail., N-Laos, S-China
- **nitidum** (Jack) Kunth · E:Aglaonema
Aroid · ♄ e Z10 ⓦ; Malay. pen., Kalimantan
- *oblongifolium* Schott non (Roxb.) Kunth =
Aglaonema nitidum
- var. *curtisii* N.E. Br. = Aglaonema nitidum
- **pictum** (Roxb.) Kunth · E:Aglaonema
Aroid, Cara de Caballo; G:Punktierter
Kolbenfaden · ♄ e Z10 ⓦ; Sumat.
- *pseudobracteatum* hort. = Aglaonema
commutatum var. commutatum
- *robustum* Alderw. = Aglaonema commutatum var. commutatum
- *roebelinii* R. Pitcher & Manda =
Aglaonema crispum
- **rotundum** N.E. Br. · ♄ e Z10 ⓦ; Sumat.
- **simplex** (Blume) Blume · E:Malayan
Sword; G:Malayischer Kolbenfaden · ♄ e
Z10 ⓦ; Nicobar., S-Burma, Thail., Malay.
Arch., Phil.
- *treubii* hort. non Engl. = Aglaonema
commutatum var. commutatum

Agonis (DC.) Sweet -f- *Myrtaceae* · 12 spp. ·
E:Willow Myrtle; F:Agonis; G:Weiden-
myrte
- **flexuosa** (Willd.) Sweet · E:Sweet
Willow Myrtle, Willow Peppermint;

G:Trauer-Weidenmyrte · ♄ ♄ e ⓚ;
W-Austr.
- **parviceps** Schauer · G:Stachlige
Weidenmyrte · ♄ e ⓚ; W-Austr.

Agrimonia L. -f- *Rosaceae* · 15 spp. ·
E:Agrimony, Cocklebur; F:Aigremoine;
G:Odermennig
- **eupatoria** L. · E:Agrimony, Cocklebur;
G:Kleiner Odermennig · ⚃ VI-VIII ⚥ ;
Eur.*, TR, Iran, Levant, N-Afr.,
- *odorata* Mill. = Agrimonia repens
- **procera** Wallr. · E:Fragrant Agrimony;
G:Großer Odermennig · ⚃ VI-VIII ⚥ ; Eur.*
- **repens** L. · ⚃ ; TR, Iraq

Agropyron Gaertn. -n- *Poaceae* · 15 spp. ·
E:Dog Grass, Wheatgrass; F:Chiendent;
G:Kammquecke
- **cristatum** (L.) Gaertn.
- subsp. **cristatum** · E:Crested Wheatgrass;
G:Kammquecke · ⚃ ⓝ; Eur.: Ib, Ital-P,
C-Eur., EC-Eur., Ba, E-Eur.; TR, Cauc.,
Iran, Afgh., W-Sib., E-Sib., Amur, C-As.,
Mong., Tibet, China: Xijiang
- subsp. **sabulosum** Lavrenko · ⚃ ; Eur.:
S-Russ.
- *elongatum* = Elymus obtusiflorus
- *intermedium* (Host) P. Beauv. ex Baumg.
= Elymus hispidus subsp. hispidus
- subsp. *trichophorum* (Link) Volkart =
Elymus hispidus subsp. hispidus
- *junceiforme* (Á. Löve & D. Löve)Á.
Löve & D. Löve = Elymus farctus subsp.
boreoatlanticus
- **junceum** (Viv.) Runemark ex Melderis
- subsp. *borealiatlanticum* Simonet & Guin.
= Elymus farctus subsp. boreoatlanticus
- *pauciflorum* (Schwein.) Hitchc. non
Schur = Elymus trachycaulus
- *pungens* = Elymus athericus
- *repens* (L.) P. Beauv. = Elymus repens
- *trachycaulum* (Link) Malte ex H.F. Lewis
= Elymus trachycaulus
- *trichophorum* (Link) K. Richt. = Elymus
hispidus subsp. hispidulus

Agrostemma L. -n- *Caryophyllaceae* ·
2-4 spp. · E:Corncockle; F:Nielle;
G:Kornrade, Rade
- **githago** L. · E:Corn Cockle ; G:Gewöhn-
liche Kornrade · ☉ VI-VIII ⚘; Eur.*, TR,
Syr., Palest., Iran, C-As., W-Sib., E-Sib.,
Amur, N-China, NW-Afr., Libya, nat. in
N-Am.

– **gracilis** Boiss. · ⊙; E-GR, TR

Agrostis L. -f- *Poaceae* · 120 (- 150-
220) spp. · E:Bent Grass; F:Agrostis;
G:Straußgras
– **agrostiflora** (Beck) Rauschert · G:Zartes
Straußgras · ⌅ VII-VIII; Eur.: F, I, Sw, G,
A, Slove.; Alp., Apenn., ? Pyr.
– **alba** L.
– var. **gigantea** (Roth) G. Mey. = Agrostis
gigantea
– **alpina** Scop. · G:Alpen-Straußgras · ⌅
VII-VIII; Eur.: sp., F, I, C-Eur., EC-Eur.,
Slove., Croatia, Bosn., RO, W-Russ.; mts.
– *calamagrostis* L. = Stipa calamagrostis
– **canina** L. · E:Velvet Bent Grass;
G:Sumpf-Straußgras · ⌅ ⁓ VI-VIII ⓝ;
Eur.*, W-Sib., E-Sib., Amur, Sakhal.,
Kamchat., Mong., nat. in N-Am.
– **capillaris** L. · E:Common Bent; G:Rotes
Straußgras · ⌅ VI-VII ⓝ; Eur.*, TR, Cauc.,
N-Iran, W-Sib., E-Sib., Afgh., Pakist.,
Ind., Tun. Canar., nat. in N-Am., C-Am.,
S-Am., Greenl., S-Afr., Austr., NZ
– **castellana** Boiss. & Reut. · E: Highland
Bent Grass; G:Kastilisches Straußgras · ⌅
VI-VII; Eur.: Ib, Fr, Ital-P, Ba; TR
– *coarctata* Ehrh. ex Hoffm. = Agrostis
vinealis
– **curtisii** Kerguélen · E:Bristle Bent · ⌅
VI-VII; Eur.: BrI, F, Ib
– **gigantea** Roth · E:Black Bent, Redtop;
G:Fioringras, Riesen-Straußgras · ⌅
VI-VIII ⓝ; Eur.*, TR, Iraq, Cauc., Iran,
W-Sib., E-Sib., Afgh., Pakist., NW-Ind.,
Mong., China, Moroc., Alger., nat. in
N-Am., C-Am., S-Am., S-Afr., Austr., NZ
– *miliacea* L. = Piptatherum miliaceum
– **nebulosa** Boiss. & Reut. · E:Cloud Grass;
F:Agrostide brouillard; G:Schleier-
Straußgras · ⊙ ⌅ ⋊ Z7 VI-IX; Ib, Moroc.
– *nigra* With. = Agrostis gigantea
– *palustris* Huds. = Agrostis stolonifera
– *pulchella* hort. = Aira elegantissima
– *pusilla* Dumort. = Agrostis vinealis
– **rupestris** All. · G:Felsen-Straußgras · ⌅
VII-VIII; Eur.* exc. BrI, Sc; mts.
– **scabra** Willd. · G E:Rough Bent
Grass;:Raues Straußgras · ⌅ VI-VII;
NE-As., N-Am., Greenl., nat. in G, A
– **schleicheri** Jord. & Verl. · G:Pyrenäen-
Straußgras, Schleichers Straußgras · ⌅
VII-IX; Eur.: sp., F, I, C-Eur.; mts.
– *schraderiana* = Agrostis agrostiflora
– *setacea* Curtis = Agrostis curtisii

– **stolonifera** L. · E:Creeping Bent,
Spreading Bent; G:Gewöhnliches Weißes
Straußgras · ⌅ VI-VII ⓝ; Eur.*, TR,
Levant, Iraq, Cauc., Iran, Afgh., Pakist.,
NW-Ind., W-Sib., E-Sib., Amur, Sakhal.,
Kamchat., Tibet, Him., Mong., China,
Korea, N-Afr., nat. in Jap., N-Am., C-Am.,
S-Am., Austr., NZ
– *stricta* J.F. Gmel. = Agrostis vinealis
– **tenerrima** Trin. · ⊙ Z6 V-VI; Eur.: F, Ib;
NW-Afr.
– *tenuis* Sibth. = Agrostis capillaris
– **vinealis** Schreb. · E: Brown Bent Grass;
G:Sand-Straußgras · ⌅ VI-VIII ⓝ; Eur.*
exc. Ib, Ital-P; TR, Cauc., Iran, W-Sib.,
E-Sib., Amur, Sakhal., Kamchat., Pakist.,
Him., Mong., NE-China, NW-Afr., Greenl.
– *vulgaris* With. = Agrostis capillaris

Aichryson Webb & Berthel. -n-
Crassulaceae · 14 spp. · E:Youth-and-Old-
Age; G:Immergold
– × **aizoides** (Lam.) (*A. tortuosum* × *A.
punctatum*) · E:Youth-and-Old-Age;
G:Immergold · ♄ ⍦ e Z9 ⌂ VII; cult.
– **dichotomum** (DC.) Webb & Berthel. =
Aichryson laxum
– **laxum** (Haw.) Bramwell · ⊙ ⊙ ⍦ Z9 ⌂
V-VI; Canar., nat. in P
– *pygmaeum* (C.A. Sm. ex Link) Webb &
Berthel. = Aichryson tortuosum
– *sedifolium* Webb ex Bolle = Aeonium
sedifolium
– **tortuosum** (Aiton) Praeger · ♄ ⍦ Z9 ⌂
V-VI; Canar. (Lanzarote, Fuerteventura)

Ailanthus Desf. -f- *Simaroubaceae* · 5 spp. ·
E:Tree of Heaven; F:Ailanthe, Faux vernis
du Japon; G:Götterbaum
– **altissima** (Mill.) Swingle · ♄ d Z6 VII ⚘
⚘ ⓝ; China, nat. in N-Am., Eur.
– **giraldii** Dode · ♄ d Z6; W-China: Sichuan
– *glandulosa* Desf. = Ailanthus altissima
– *peregrina* (Buc'hoz) F.A. Barkley =
Ailanthus altissima
– **vilmoriniana** Dode · ♄ d Z6; W-China:
Sichuan, W-Hupeh

Aiphanes Willd. -f- *Arecaceae* · 24 spp. ·
E:Ruffle Palm; F:Palmier; G:Stachel-
palme
– *aculeata* Willd. = Aiphanes horrida
– **horrida** (Jacq.) Burret · ♄; Trinidad,
trop. S.-Am.

Aira L. -f- *Poaceae* · c. 10 spp. · E:Hair Grass; F:Aira; G:Haferschmiele, Schmielenhafer
- *capillaris* Host = Aira elegantissima
- **caryophyllea** L. · E:Silver Hair Grass
- subsp. **caryophyllea** · E:Silver Hair Grass; G:Nelken-Haferschmiele · ⊙ Z6 VI-VII; Eur.*, Canar., Azor., TR, Cauc., N-Iran, NW-Afr., Eth., trop. Afr., S-Afr., nat. in N-Am., S-Am., Austr., NZ
- subsp. **multiculmis** (Dumort.) Bonnier & Layens · ⊙ Z6; Eur.: Ib, F, Sw, Cors., Sic.; Alger.
- *cespitosa* L. = Deschampsia cespitosa subsp. cespitosa
- *elegans* (Willd. ex Gaudin) hort. = Aira elegantissima
- **elegantissima** Schur · E:Delicate Hair Grass; G:Haar-Haferschmiele, Zierliche Haferschmiele · ⊙ ⋈ Z6 V-VIII; Eur.: Ib, Fr, Ital-P, Ba, RO, Crim, A, Sw; TR, Syr., Cyprus, Lebanon, Cauc., Iran, Moroc., Alger., nat. in N-Am.
- *flexuosa* L. = Deschampsia flexuosa
- *multiculmis* Dumort. = Aira caryophyllea subsp. multiculmis
- **praecox** L. · E:Early Hair Grass; G:Frühe Haferschmiele · ⊙ Z6 V-VI; Eur.* exc. Ba, Ital-P; Canar., nat. in TR, N-Am.
- *pulchella* Link = Aira tenorii
- **tenorii** Guss. · ⊙ Z6 IV-V; Eur.: Ib, Ital-P, GR; NW-Afr., Libya

Ajania Poljakov -f- *Asteraceae* · 34 spp. · E:Gold-and-Silver Chrysanthemum; G:Gold-und-Silber-Chrysantheme
- **pacifica** (Nakai) K. Bremer & Humphries · E:Gold-and-Silver Chrysanthemum; G:Gold-und-Silber-Chrysantheme · 4 ⋈ X; Jap.

Ajuga L. -f- *Lamiaceae* · 66 spp. · E:Bugle; F:Bugle; G:Günsel
- **chamaepitys** (L.) Schreb. · E:Ground Pine, Yellow Bugle; G:Gelber Günsel · ⊙ ⊙ △ Z6 V-IX ⚥ ; Eur.* exc. Sc; TR, Levant, N-Iraq, Iran, C-As., NW-Afr., nat. in USA: Va.
- *crispa* hort. = Ajuga pyramidalis
- **genevensis** L. · E:Blue Bugle, Upright Bugle; G:Genfer Günsel, Heide-Günsel · 4 △ Z6 IV-VI; Eur.: Fr, Ital-P, C-Eur., EC-Eur., Ba, E-Eur.; TR, Cauc., nat. in Am.
- × **hybrida** A. Kern. (*A. genevensis* × *A.*

reptans) · G:Hybrid-Günsel · 4 Z6
- **pyramidalis** L. · E:Pyramid Bugle; G:Pyramiden-Günsel · 4 △ Z6 V-VII; Eur.*
- **reptans** L. · E:Bugle; F:Bugle rampante; G:Kriechender Günsel · 4 ⤳ △ Z6 V-VI ⚥ ; Eur.*, TR, Cauc., N-Iran, Alger., Tun., nat. in N-Am.
- **some cultivars**

Akebia Decne. -f- *Lardizabalaceae* · 5 spp. · E:Chocolate Vine; F:Akébia; G:Akebie
- *lobata* Decne. = Akebia trifoliata
- **quinata** (Houtt.) Decne. · E:Chocolate Vine, Five Leaf Akebia; F:Akébie à cinq feuilles; G:Fingerblättrige Akebie · ♇ d ⚥ Z6 IV-VI; C-China, Korea, Jap.
- **trifoliata** (Thunb.) Koidz. · E:Chocolate Vine, Three Leaf Akebia; F:Akébie à trois feuilles; G:Kleeblättrige Akebie · ♇ d ⚥ Z6 V ⚥ ; China, Jap.

Alangium Lam. -n- *Alangiaceae* · 20-30 spp. · F:Alangium; G:Alangie
- **chinense** (Lour.) Harms · G:Chinesische Alangie · ♇ d Z8 ∧; Afr., C-China, SE-As.
- **platanifolium** (Siebold & Zucc.) Harms · G:Platanenblättrige Alangie
- var. **platanifolium** · F:Alangium à feuilles de platane · ♇ ♇ d D Z9 ∧ VI-VII; Jap., Korea
- var. **trilobum** (Miq.) Ohwi · G:Kurzgelappte Alangie · ♇ d Z8 ⌂; Jap., Korea, Manch.

Albizia Durazz. -f- *Mimosaceae* · c. 150 spp. · F:Albizzia ; G:Seidenakazie
- **adianthifolia** (Schumach.) W. Wight · E:West African Albizia; G:Farnblättrige Seidenakazie · ♇ d Z9 ⌂; trop. Afr.
- **chinensis** (Osbeck) Merr. · E:Chinese Albizia; G:Chinesische Seidenakazie · ♇ d Z9 ⌳ Ⓝ; SE-As.
- *distachya* (Vent.) J.F. Macbr. = Paraserianthes lophantha subsp. lophantha
- *falcata* auct. = Paraserianthes falcataria subsp. falcata
- *falcataria* (L.) Fosberg = Paraserianthes falcataria subsp. falcata
- **julibrissin** Durazz. · E:Pink Siris, Silk Tree; F:Acacia de Constantinople, Arbre de soie; G:Schlafbaum, Seidenakazie · ♇ d Z8 ⌂ VIII-IX Ⓝ; Iran, Pakist., Him., C-China, Jap., nat. in SE-USA

– **lebbeck** (L.) Benth. · E:Siris Tree; G:Leb-
bekbaum · ♄ d Z9 ⓐ Ⓝ; Him., Ind., Sri
Lanka, Indochina, S-China, Malay. Arch.,
NE-Austr., nat. in Afr., W.Ind.
– *lophantha* (Willd.) Benth. = Paraserianthes lophantha subsp. lophantha
– *moluccana* Miq. = Paraserianthes
falcataria subsp. falcataria
– **procera** (Roxb.) Benth. ‡ E:Forest Siris,
Rain Siris, Tall Albizia · ♄ d Z9 ⓐ; Ind.,
Burma, China, Malay. Arch.
– **saman** F. Muell. · E:Rain Tree, Saman;
G:Regenbaum · ♄ Z9 ⓐ Ⓝ; Mex., C-Am.,
S-Am., nat. in W.Ind., trop. Afr., trop. As.
– *stipulata* (Roxb.) Boivin = Albizia
chinensis

Albuca L. -f- *Hyacinthaceae* · 94 spp. ·
G:Stiftblume
– **nelsonii** N.E. Br. · G:Nelsons Stiftblume ·
⧬ ⓐ VII-VIII; S-Afr.: Natal

Alcea L. -f- *Malvaceae* · 60 spp. ·
E:Hollyhook; F:Rose trémière; G:Stock-
rose
– **ficifolia** L. · E:Antwerp Hollyhook ;
G:Holländische Stockrose · ⧬ ⊙ Z3; Sib.
– **pallida** (Willd.) Waldst. & Kit. · G:Blasse
Stockrose · ⧬ ⊙ VII-IX; Eur.: A, EC-Eur.,
Ba, E-Eur.; TR, nat. in I
– **rosea** L. · E:Hollyhock; F:Rose trémière;
G:Chinesische Stockrose, Gewöhnliche
Stockrose · ⊙ ⊙ ⧬ ⚭ VI-X ⚥ Ⓝ; ? Ba, ?
SW-As., nat. in Eur.* exc. Sc, cosmop.
– **some cultivars**
– **rugosa** Alef. · G:Runzlige Stockrose · ⧬ ;
SW-Russ.
– **sulphurea** (Boiss. & Hohen.) Alef. ·
G:Schwefelgelbe Stockrose · ⧬ ; Iraq, Iran

Alchemilla L. -f- *Rosaceae* · c. 300 spp. ·
E:Lady's Mantle; F:Alchémille, Manteau
de Notre-Dame; G:Frauenmantel
– **alpina** L. · E:Alpine Lady's Mantle;
F:Alchémille des Alpes; G:Alpen-
Frauenmantel · ⧬ △ VI-VIII ⚥ ; Eur.* exc.
EC-Eur., Ba
– **conjuncta** Bab. · E:Silver Lady's Mantle;
G:Verbundener Frauenmantel · ⧬ △
VI-VIII; Eur.: F, Sw; SW-Alp., Jura, nat.
in GB
– **erythropoda** Juz. · G:Karpaten-
Frauenmantel · ⧬ VI-VIII; Eur.: EC-Eur.,
Ba, Crim; Cauc.
– **fissa** Günther & Schummel ·

G:Zerschlitzter Frauenmantel · ⧬ △
VI-VIII; Eur.: sp., F, C-Eur., CZ, PL; Pyr.,
Alp., Sudeten
– **glaucescens** Wallr. · E:Small Lady's
Mantle; G:Graugrüner Frauenmantel · ⧬
V-IX; Eur.* exc. Ib
– **hoppeana** (Rchb.) Dalla Torre ·
E:Hoppe's Lady's Mantle; F:Alchémille
de Hoppe; G:Hoppes Frauenmantel · ⧬
△ VI-VIII; Eur.: Sw, G, A; N-Alp., Jura,
SW-D
– **mollis** (Buser) Rothm. · E:Lady's Mantle;
F:Manteau de Notre-Dame; G:Weicher
Frauenmantel · ⧬ VI; Eur.: RO, W-Russ.;
N-TR, Cauc., N-Iran; mts., nat. in A
– **pentaphyllea** L. · G:Schneetälchen-
Frauenmantel · ⧬ VII-IX; Eur.: F, I, Sw, A;
Alp.
– **splendens** H. Christ ex Favrat · G:Schim-
mernder Frauenmantel · ⧬ △ VI-VIII;
Eur.: F, Sw; Alp., Jura
– **subsericea** Reut. · G:Schwachseidiger
Frauenmantel · ⧬ VII-IX; Eur.: sp., F, I,
Sw, A; mts.
– *vulgaris* auct. non L. = Alchemilla
xanthochlora
– **xanthochlora** Rothm. · G:Gelbgrüner
Frauenmantel, Gewöhnlicher Frauenmantel · ⧬ V-VIII ⚥ ; Eur.*, nat. in N-Am.

Aldrovanda L. -f- *Droseraceae* · 1 sp. ·
E:Waterwheel Plant; F:Aldrovandie;
G:Wasserfalle
– **vesiculosa** L. · E:Waterwheel Plant;
G:Wasserfalle · ⧬ ≈ VII-VIII ▽; Eur.:
F, I, G, EC-Eur., W-Ba; C-As, S-As.,
E-As., NE-Afr., Austr: N.Terr., Queensl.,
N.S.Wales

Alectryon Gaertn. -n- *Sapindaceae* · 17 spp.
– **subinereus** (A. Gray) Radlk. · ♄ e Z10
ⓐ; E-Austr.

Aletris L. -f- *Melanthiaceae* · 23 spp. ·
E:Colic Root, Star Grass; G:Sternwurzel
– **farinosa** L. · E:Ague Root, Colic
Root, Unicorn Root; G:Runzelwurzel,
Sternwurzel · ⧬ VII-VIII ⚥ ; Can.: E; USA:
NE, NCE, SE, SC, Fla.
– *punicea* Labill. = Blandfordia punicea

Aleurites J.R. Forst. & G. Forst. -f-
Euphorbiaceae · 2 spp. · E:Candlenut Tree;
F:Aleurite, Bancoulier; G:Lichtnussbaum
– *cordata* (Thunb.) R. Br. ex Steud. =

Vernicia cordata
- *fordii* Hemsl. = Vernicia fordii
- **moluccana** (L.) Willd. · E:Candlenut
Tree, Indian Walnut; G:Lichtnussbaum
· ♄ e Z10 ⓜ ⚘ Ⓝ; Malay. Arch., nat. in
Trop.
- *montana* (Lour.) E.H. Wilson = Vernicia
montana
- *triloba* J.R. Forst. & G. Forst. = Aleurites
moluccana
- *trisperma* Blanco = Reutealis trisperma

Alhagi Gagnebin -f- *Fabaceae* · 4 spp. ·
E:Camel Thorn; F:Epine de chameau;
G:Kameldorn
- *camelorum* Fisch. = Alhagi maurorum
- **maurorum** Medik. · E:Camel Thorn;
G:Kameldorn · ♄ ⓐ Ⓝ; TR, Syr., Cyprus,
Arab., N-Afr.
- *pseudalhagi* (M. Bieb.) Desv. ex B. Keller
& Shap. = Alhagi maurorum

Alibertia A. Rich. ex DC. -f- *Rubiaceae* ·
35 spp.
- **edulis** (A. Rich.) A. Rich. · E:Wild Guava;
G:Wilde Guave · ♄ e Z10 ⓜ Ⓝ; Mex.,
C-Am., W.Ind., trop. S-Am.

× **Aliceara** hort. -f- *Orchidaceae* (*Brassaia* ×
Miltonia × *Oncidium*)

Alisma L. -n- *Alismataceae* · 8 spp. ·
E:Water Plantain; F:Grenouillette,
Plantain d'eau; G:Froschlöffel
- **gramineum** Lej. · E:Ribbon Leaved
Water Plantain; G:Grasblättriger
Froschlöffel · ⁤ ~ ≈ Z6 VII-VIII;
Eur.* exc. Ib; Cauc., W-Sib., E-Sib., C-As.,
China, Moroc., Egypt, USA: NE, NCE, NC,
Rocky Mts.
- **lanceolatum** With. · E:Narrow-leaved
Water Plantain; F:Plantain d'eau
lancéolé; G:Lanzettblättriger Froschlöffel
· ⁤ ~ Z6 VI-VII; Eur.*, TR, Levant,
Cauc., Iran, C-As., Afgh., Pakist., NW-Afr.
- *loeselii* Górski = Alisma gramineum
- *natans* L. = Luronium natans
- *parnassiifolium* L. = Caldesia parnassifolia
- **plantago-aquatica** L.
- subsp. *brevipes* (Greene) Sam. = Alisma
triviale
- subsp. **orientale** (Sam.) Sam. · E:Asiatic
Water Plantain; G:Asiatischer Froschlöffel · ⁤ ~ Z6 VI-IX; E-Sib., Mong.,
Sakhal., Manch., Korea, Jap.

- subsp. **plantago-aquatica** · E:Water
Plantain; F:Fluteau, Plantain d'eau;
G:Gewöhnlicher Froschlöffel · ⁤ ≈ Z6
VII-VIII ⚘; Eur.*, TR, Levant, Cauc., Iran,
W-Sib., Afgh., Pakist.
- var. *parviflorum* (Pursh) Torr. = Alisma
subcordatum
- *ranunculoides* L. = Baldellia ranuncu-
loides
- *stenophyllum* (Asch. & Graebn.) Sam. =
Alisma lanceolatum
- **subcordatum** Raf. · E:Southern Water
Plantain; F:Plantain d'eau américain;
G:Südstaaten Froschlöffel · ⁤ ≈ Z6;
E-Can.; USA: NE, NEC, NC, SE, SC
- *subulatum* L. = Sagittaria subulata
- *tenellum* Mart. = Echinodorus tenellus
- **triviale** Pursh · E:Northern Water
Plantain; G:Amerikanischer Froschlöffel ·
⁤ ~ Z6 VI-IX; Can., USA: NE, NCE, NC,
SW, NW, Rocky Mts., Calif.; Mex.

Alkanna Tausch -f- *Boraginaceae* · c.
30 spp. · E:Alkanet; F:Orcanette;
G:Alkannawurzel
- **graeca** Boiss. & Spruner · ⁤; Eur.: Ba
- **tinctoria** (L.) Tausch · E:Dyer's Alkanet;
G:Schminkwurz · ⁤ ⓐ VI ⚘ Ⓝ;
Eur.: sp., F, Ital-P, EC-Eur., Ba, RO;
NW-Afr.

Allamanda L. -f- *Apocynaceae* · 14 spp. ·
E:Allamanda; F:Allamande; G:Allamande
- **blanchetii** A. DC. · E:Purple Allamanda;
G:Purpur-Allamande · ♄ e ⚘ Z10 ⓜ IX-X;
S-Am.
- **cathartica** L. · E:Golden Trumpet;
G:Goldtrompete · ♄ ⚘ e ⚘ Z10 ⓜ V-XI;
S-Am.
- var. *schottii* (Pohl) Raffill = Allamanda
schottii
- *grandiflora* Lam. = Allamanda cathartica
- *hendersonii* Bull. = Allamanda cathartica
- *neriifolia* Hook. = Allamanda schottii
- **nobilis** T. Moore · S-Am
- **schottii** Pohl · E:Bush Allamanda;
G:Strauch-Allamande · ♄ e ⚘ Z10 ⓜ;
trop. S-Am.
- *violacea* Gardner & Fielding = Allamanda
blanchetii

Alliaria Heist. ex Fabr. -f- *Brassicaceae* ·
2 spp. · E:Garlic Mustard; F:Alliaire;
G:Knoblauchsrauke, Lauchkraut
- **petiolata** (M. Bieb.) Cavara & Grande ·

E:Garlic Mustard, Hedge Garlic, Jack-by-the-Hedge; G:Gewöhnliche Knoblauchsrauke · ⊙ IV-VI ⚕ ; Eur.*, TR, Cyprus, Syr., Cauc., Iran, W-Sib., C-As., Afgh., Him., Pakist., NW-Afr., nat. in N-Am.

Allium L. -n- *Alliaceae* · 824 spp. · E:Garlic, Onion; F:Ail; G:Knoblauch, Lauch, Zwiebel
- **acuminatum** Hook. · E:Hooker's Onion, Taper Tip Onion; G:Kerzen-Lauch · ♃ △ Z6 V-VI; Can.: B.C.; USA: NW, Calif., Rocky Mts., Ariz.
- **aflatunense** B. Fedtsch. · G:Iran-Lauch · ♃ Z8 V; C-As.
- *albopilosum* C.H. Wright = Allium christophii
- **ampeloprasum** L. · E:Kurrat, Wild Leek; G:Acker-Knoblauch, Sommer-Lauch · ♃ Z6 ⚕ Ⓝ; Eur.: BrI, Fr, Ib, Ba, RO; TR, Syr., N-Iraq, ? Cauc., Iran, N-Afr., nat. in Va.
- var. *porrum* (L.) Gay = Allium porrum
- **angulosum** L. · G:Kantiger Lauch · ♃ Z5 VII-VIII; Eur.: H, I, C-Eur., Ba, E-Eur.; Sib.
- **atropurpureum** Waldst. & Kit. · G:Schwarzpurpurner Lauch · ♃ Z7 VI-VII; Eur.: H, Croatia, Serb., BG, RO; TR, nat. in A
- *beesianum* hort. = Allium cyaneum
- **beesianum** W.W. Sm. · G:Yunnan-Lauch · ♃ △ Z7 VI-VII; W-China
- *bulgaricum* (Janka) Prodán = Nectaroscordum siculum subsp. bulgaricum
- **caeruleum** Pall. · E:Blue Allium; F:Ail azuré; G:Blau-Lauch, Sibirischer Enzian-Lauch · ♃ ✂ Z7 VI-VII; Eur.: E-Russ.; W-Sib., C-As., China: Sinkiang
- **caesium** Schrenk · ♃ △ Z7 ▭ ∧ V-VI; C-As., Sib.
- **carinatum** L.
- subsp. **carinatum** · E:Keeled Garlic; G:Gekielter Lauch · ♃ Z7 VI-VII; Eur.* exc. BrI, N-TR, nat. in BrI
- subsp. **pulchellum** (G. Don) Bonnier & Layens · F:Ail à carène élégant; G:Schöner Lauch · ♃ Z7 VII-VIII; Eur.: F, I, C-Eur., Ba, E-Eur.; N-TR, Cauc.
- **cepa** L. · ⊙ ♃ Z5 VI-VIII ⚕ Ⓝ; cult.
- **Aggregatum Group** · E:Ever-ready Onion, Shallot; G:Schalotte · ♃ VI-VII; cult.
- **Cepa Group** · E:Onion; G:Küchen-Zwiebel, Sommer-Zwiebel · ; cult.
- **Proliferum Group** · E:Egyptian Onion, Tree Onion; G:Ägyptische Zwiebel · ♃ Ⓝ; cult.
- var. *ascalonicum* Baker = Allium cepa Aggregatum Group
- var. *proliferum* (Moench) Alef. = Allium cepa Proliferum Group
- var. *viviparum* (Metzg.) Alef. = Allium cepa Proliferum Group
- **cernuum** Roth · E:Lady's Leek, Nodding Onion, Wild Onion; F:Ail penché; G:Nickender Lauch · ♃ Z6 VI-VII Ⓝ; Can., USA* exc. Fla., Calif; Mex.
- **chinense** G. Don · E:Rakkyo; G:Chinesischer Lauch · ♃ Z7 Ⓝ; China, cult. Austr., Calif.
- **christophii** Trautv. · E:Star of Persia; F:Ail à boule étoilée; G:Sternkugel-Lauch · ♃ Z8 VI-VII; TR, Iran
- *cirrhosum* Vand. = Allium carinatum subsp. pulchellum
- *cowanii* Lindl. = Allium neapolitanum
- **crispum** Greene · E:Crinkled Onion; G:Krauser Lauch · ♃ ∧ V; Calif.
- **cyaneum** Regel · G:Enzian-Lauch · ♃ △ Z8 V-VI; W-China
- **cyathophorum** Bureau & Franch.
- var. **cyathophorum** · E:Onion; G:Becher-Lauch · ♃ Z7; China
- var. **farreri** (Stearn) Stearn · G:Farrers Becher-Lauch · ♃ Z7 VII-VIII; China: Kansu
- **ericetorum** Thore · G:Gelblichweißer Lauch · ♃ VII-VIII; Eur.* exc. Sc
- *farreri* Stearn = Allium cyathophorum var. farreri
- **fistulosum** L. · E:Japanese Bunching Onion, Welsh Onion; G:Winter-Zwiebel · ♃ Z5 VI-VIII ⚕ Ⓝ; cult.
- **flavum** L.
- subsp. **flavum** · E:Small Yellow Onion; F:Ail jaune; G:Gelber Lauch · ♃ △ Z7 VI-VII; Eur.: Fr, Ital-P, A, EC-Eur., Ba, E-Eur.
- var. *pulchellum* (G. Don) Regel = Allium carinatum subsp. pulchellum
- **giganteum** Regel · E:Giant Allium; F:Ail géant de l'Himalaya; G:Riesen-Lauch · ♃ ✂ Z7 VII-VIII; Him., C-As.
- **insubricum** Boiss. & Reut. · ♃ △ Z8 V-VI; I: Alp.
- **jesdianum** Boiss. · ♃ V; Iran, Iraq
- *kansuense* Regel = Allium sikkimense
- **karataviense** Regel · E:Turkestan Allium; F:Ail du Turkestan; G:Blauzungen-Lauch · ♃ △ Z7 IV-V; C-As.

– *kurrat* Schweinf. ex K. Krause = Allium ampeloprasum
– **moly** L. · E:Lily Leek, Moly; F:Ail doré; G:Gold-Lauch · ♃ △ Z7 V-VI; sp., SW-F
– *montanum* F.W. Schmidt = Allium senescens subsp. montanum
– *multibulbosum* Jacq. = Allium nigrum
– *murrayanum* auct. non Regel = Allium unifolium
– **narcissiflorum** Vill. · G:Narzissen-Lauch · ♃ △ Z7 V-VI; Eur.: P, F, I; N-P, SW-Alp.
– var. *insubricum* (Boiss. & Reut.) Fiori = Allium insubricum
– **neapolitanum** Cirillo · E:Daffodil Garlic, Flowering Onion; G:Neapel-Lauch · ♃ Z8 ⚘ V-VI; Eur.: Ib, Fr, Ital-P, Ba; TR, Med.
– **nigrum** L. · E:Black Garlic; G:Schwarzer Lauch, Zwiebelreicher Lauch · ♃ Z7 III-V; Eur.: Ib, Fr, Ital-P, Ba, ? Crim, ? A; TR, Syr, N-Afr
– **nutans** L. · ♃ Z5; Sib.
– **oleraceum** L. · E:Field Garlic; G:Gemüse-Lauch, Kohl-Lauch · ♃ Z5 VII-VIII; Eur.* exc. Ib; Cauc.
– **oreophilum** C.A. Mey. · F:Ail décoratif; G:Rosen-Zwerg-Lauch · ♃ △ Z7 VI-VII; Cauc., C-As.
– *ostrowskianum* Regel = Allium oreophilum
– **paradoxum** (M. Bieb.) G. Don · E:Few-flowered Leek; G:Seltsamer Lauch · ♃ △ Z7 IV-V; Cauc., N-Iran, C-As., nat. in G, EC-Eur.
– **porrum** L. · G:Winter-Lauch
– var. **porrum** · E:Leek; G:Porree · ⊙ ♃ Z6 VI-VII ⓝ; cult.
– var. **sectivum** Lueder · E:Kurrat; G:Perl-Zwiebel · Z6 ⓝ; cult.
– × *proliferum* (Moench) Schrad. ex Willd. = Allium cepa Proliferum Group
– *pulchellum* G. Don = Allium carinatum subsp. pulchellum
– *purdomii* W.W. Sm. = Allium cyaneum
– **ramosum** L. · E:Fragrant Garlic; G:Ästiger Lauch · ♃ Z7 VI ⓝ; C-As.
– **rosenbachianum** Regel · G:Pauken-schläger-Lauch · ♃ ⋉ Z7 V-VI; Afgh., Pakist.
– **roseum** L. · E:Rosy Garlic; G:Rosen-Lauch
– var. **bulbiferum** DC. · G:Steriler Rosen-Lauch · ♃ Z8
– var. **roseum** · ♃ Z8 V-VI; Eur.: Ib, Fr, Ital-P, Ba; TR, N-Afr., nat. in BrI

– **sativum** L. · E:Garlic; G:Knob-Lauch, Knoblauch
– var. **ophioscorodon** (Link) Döll · E:Rocambole, Serpent Garlic; G:Rocken-bolle, Schlangen-Knoblauch · ♃ Z7; cult.
– var. **sativum** · E:Common Garlic; G:Echter Knoblauch · ♃ Z7 VII-VIII ⚥ ⓝ; cult.
– **schoenoprasum** L.
– var. **schoenoprasum** · E:Chives; F:Ciboulette; G:Schnitt-Lauch, Schnitt-lauch · ♃ Z5 VI-VII ⓝ; Eur.*, TR, Iraq, Cauc., Iran, Pakist., W-Sib., E-Sib., Amur, Kamchat., C-As., Mong., Him., Jap. China, Alaska, Can., USA: NE, NCE, Rocky Mts.
– var. **sibiricum** (L.) Garcke · G:Alpen-Schnittlauch · ♃ Z5
– **schubertii** Zucc. · ♃ Z7 VI-VII; TR, Syr., Libya
– **scorodoprasum** L.
– subsp. **rotundum** (L.) Stearn · G:Rund-köpfiger Lauch · ♃ Z7 VI-VIII; Eur.* exc. BrI, Sc; TR, Levant, Cauc., N-Iran, Moroc., Canar.
– subsp. **scorodoprasum** · E:Giant Garlic, Sand Leek; G:Schlangen-Lauch · ♃ Z7 VI-VII; Eur.*, TR, Cauc.
– **senescens** L.
– subsp. **montanum** (Fr.) Holub · G:Berg-Lauch · ♃ Z5 VII-VIII ▽; E-Sib., Mong.
– subsp. **senescens** · E:German Garlic; G:Ausdauernder Lauch · ♃ Z5; Eur.* exc. BrI; W-Sib., E-Sib., Amur, C-As., Mong., Manch., Korea
– *senescens* Miq. non L. = Allium tuberosum subsp. siculum
– *siculum* Ucria = Nectaroscordum siculum subsp. siculum
– **sikkimense** Baker · ♃ △ Z7 VI-VII; Him., W-China
– **sphaerocephalon** L. · E:Round-headed Leek; G:Kugel-Lauch ; F:Ail à tête ronde · ♃ ⋉ Z5 VI-VII; Eur.* exc. Sc; TR, N-Afr., Cauc.
– **stipitatum** Regel · ♃ Z7 VII; C-As., Afgh., Pakist.
– **strictum** Schrad. · G:Steifer Lauch · ♃ Z4 VI-VIII; Eur.: F, I, C-Eur., EC-Eur., Russ.; W-Sib., E-Sib., Amur, Sakhal., Kamchat., C-As., Mong.
– **suaveolens** Jacq. · E:Fragrant Onion; G:Wohlriechender Lauch · ♃ VII-IX; Eur.: F, I, C-Eur., EC-Eur., Russ.
– **subhirsutum** L. · ♃ Z9 ⚘; Eur.: Ib, Fr, Ital-P, Ba + TR, N-Afr.

– *tibeticum* Rendle = Allium sikkimense
– **triquetrum** L. · E:Three-cornered Leek;
  G:Dreikantiger Lauch · ⁴ △ Z8 ⓚ ▭ ⋏
  III-V; Eur.: Ib, F, Ital-P; N-Afr., Eth., nat.
  in BrI
– **tuberosum** Rottler ex Spreng. ·
  E:Chinese Chives, Oriental Garlic;
  G:Schnitt-Knoblauch · ⁴ Z7 VIII-IX ♀ Ⓝ;
  Ind., Nepal, China, Jap.
– **unifolium** Kellogg · E:One-leaf Onion,
  Wild Onion; G:Einblättriger Lauch · ⁴
  Z8; USA: Oreg., Calif.
– *urceolatum* Regel = Allium caesium
– **ursinum** L. · E:Ramsons, Wood Garlic;
  G:Bär-Lauch · ⁴ Z5 V ♀ ; Eur.*, Cauc.
– **victorialis** L. · E:Alpine Leek; G:Aller-
  mannsharnisch · ⁴ Z6 VII-VIII ♀ ; Eur.*
  exc. BrI, Sc; mts.; Cauc., Him., W-Sib.,
  E-Sib., Amur, Sakhal., Kamchat., China,
  Korea, Jap.
– **vineale** L. · E:Crow Garlic, False Garlic;
  G:Kochs Lauch, Weinbergs-Lauch · ⁴ Z5
  VI-VII; Eur.*, TR, Cauc., nat. in E-USA
– **zebdanense** Boiss. & Noë · ⁴ △ Z8 V;
  TR, Lebanon
– **Cultivars:**
– **some cultivars**

Alloplectus Mart. -m- *Gesneriaceae* ·
  65 spp.
– **capitatus** Hook. · ♄ Z10 ⓦ; Col., Venez.
– *forgetii* Sprague = Nautilocalyx forgetii
– *lynchii* Hook. f. = Nautilocalyx lynchii
– *pallidus* Sprague = Nautilocalyx pallidus
– *sanguineus* (Pers.) Mart. = Dalbergaria
  sanguinea
– **schlimii** Planch. & Linden · ♄ Z10 ⓦ;
  Col., Venez.; And.
– **vittatus** Linden & André · ♄ Z10 ⓦ;
  E-Peru

Alniphyllum Matsum. -n- *Styracaceae* ·
  3 spp. · G:Erlenblatt
– **fortunei** (Hemsl.) Perkins · ♄ ♄ ⓚ;
  W-China. Sichuan, Fujian

Alnus Mill. -f- *Betulaceae* · 35 spp. ·
  E:Alder; F:Aulne; G:Erle
– *alnobetula* = Alnus viridis subsp. viridis
– **cordata** (Loisel.) Desf. · E:Italian Alder;
  F:Aulne de Cors; G:Herzblättrige Erle · ♄
  d Z6 III-IV Ⓝ; Eur.: Cors, S-I, nat. in sp.,
  Azor.
– *cordifolia* Ten. = Alnus cordata
– × **elliptica** Regel (*A. cordata* × *A.*

glutinosa) · ♄ d; Cors
– **firma** Siebold & Zucc. · ♄ d Z6 IV Ⓝ; Jap.
– **glutinosa** (L.) Gaertn. · E:Common
  Alder, European Alder; F:Aulne commun,
  Aulne glutineux; G:Schwarz-Erle · ♄ ♄ d
  Z3 III ♀ Ⓝ; Eur.*, Cauc., W-Sib., C-As.,
  TR, N-Iran, NW-Afr., nat. in N-Am.
– **hirsuta** (Spach) Rupr. · E:Manchurian
  Alder; G:Färber-Erle · ♄ d Z4 Ⓝ; Jap.,
  Korea, Sakhal., Kamchat., E-Sib.
– **incana** (L.) Moench
– subsp. **incana** · E:Grey Alder; F:Aulne
  blanc; G:Grau-Erle · ♄ ♄ d Z2 II-IV; Eur.*
  exc. BrI, Ib; Cauc., W-Sib., nat. in BrI, Ib,
  N-Am.
– subsp. **rugosa** (Du Roi) Clausen ·
  E:Speckled Alder; G:Runzelblättrige Erle
  · ♄ ♄ d ⌒ Z4 III-IV; Can.: E; USA: NE,
  NCE, Kans., SC, SE, Fla., nat. in C-Eur.
– **japonica** (Thunb.) Steud. · E:Japanese
  Alder; F:Aulne du Japon; G:Japanische
  Erle · ♄ d Z4 IV Ⓝ; Jap., Korea, Manch.,
  Amur
– **jorullensis** Kunth · ♄ d Z8 ⓚ Ⓝ; Mex.,
  Ecuad., Peru, Bol., Arg., Venez.
– × **koehnei** Callier (*A. incana* subsp.
  incana × *A. subcordata*) · ♄ d; orig. ?
– **maximowiczii** Callier ex C.K. Schneid. ·
  F:Aulne de Maximowicz; G:Maximowicz
  Esche · ♄ ♄ d Z6; Jap., Sakhal.
– **nitida** (Spach) Endl. · G:Himalaya-Erle ·
  ♄ d Z7 IX; Kashmir, Him., W-Nepal
– *oregana* Nutt. = Alnus rubra
– × **pubescens** Tausch (*A. glutinosa* × *A.*
  incana subsp. *incana*) · ♄ d; Eur.
– **rubra** Bong. · E:Oregon Alder, Red Alder;
  F:Aulne de l'Orégon; G:Oregon-Erle · ♄ d
  Z6 Ⓝ; Alaska, Can.: W; USA: NW, Idaho,
  Calif.
– *rubra* Desf. ex Steud. = Alnus serrulata
– *rugosa* (Du Roi) Spreng. = Alnus incana
  subsp. rugosa
– **serrulata** (Aiton) Willd. · E:Hazel Alder;
  G:Hasel-Erle · ♄ ♄ d Z5; Can.: Ont.; USA:
  NE, NCE, NC, SC, SE, Fla.
– *sinuata* (Regel) Rydb. = Alnus viridis
  subsp. sinuata
– × **spaethii** Callier (*A. japonica* × *A.*
  subcordata) · F:Aulne de Späth; G:Späths
  Erle · ♄ d; cult.
– **subcordata** C.A. Mey. · E:Caucasian
  Alder; G:Kaukasische Erle · ♄ d Z5 IV;
  Cauc., Iran
– *tinctoria* Sarg. = Alnus hirsuta
– **viridis** (Chaix) DC. · E:Green Alder;

F:Aulne vert ; G:Grün-Erle
- subsp. **sinuata** (Regel) Á. Löve & D.
Löve · E:Sitka Alder; G:Sitka-Erle · ♄ ♄ d
Z4 IV-VI; Alaska, B.C., USA: NW, Calif.
- subsp. **viridis** · ♄ ♄ d Z2 IV-VI; Eur.:
Fr, Ital-P, C-Eur., EC-Eur., Ba, E-Eur.;
W-Sib., E-Sib., Amur, N-Mong.

Alocasia (Schott) G. Don -f- *Araceae* ·
74 spp. · E:Elephant's-Ear Plant;
F:Alocasia, Oreille d'éléphant; G:Pfeil-
blatt
- × **amazonica** André (*A. lowii × A.
sanderiana*) · G:Amazonas-Pfeilblatt · ⏛
Z10 ⊚; cult.
- **cucullata** (Lour.) G. Don · E:Chinese
Taro; G:Kupfer-Pfeilblatt · ⏛ Z10 ⊚ Ⓝ;
Ind.: Bengalen; Sri Lanka, Burma
- **cuprea** (K. Koch & C.D. Bouché) K.
Koch · G:Metallisches Pfeilblatt · ⏛ Z9 ⊚;
Kalimantan
- *indica* (Roxb.) Schott = Alocasia macrorrhizos
- *korthalsii* Schott = Alocasia longiloba
- *lindenii* Rodigas = Homalomena lindenii
- **longiloba** Miq. · G:Langes Pfeilblatt · ⏛
Z10 ⊚; Kalimantan
- *lowii* Hook. f. = Alocasia longiloba
- **macrorrhizos** (L.) G. Don · E:Giant Taro;
G:Riesenblättriges Pfeilblatt · ⏛ Z10 ⊚
Ⓝ; ? Sri Lanka
- var. *variegata* (K. Koch & C.D. Bouché)
Furtado = Alocasia macrorrhizos
- *metallica* (Otto) Hook. f. = Alocasia
cucullata
- **micholitziana** Sander · E:Elephant's Ear;
G:Elefantenohr-Pfeilblatt · ⏛ Z10 ⊚;
Phil.
- **odora** (Lindl.) K. Koch · E:Asian Taro · ⏛
Z10 ⊚; NE-Ind., China, Phil.
- *plumbea* K. Koch ex Van Houtte =
Alocasia macrorrhizos
- **portei** Schott · ⏛ Z10 ⊚; Phil.
- *putzeysii* N.E. Br. = Alocasia longiloba
- **sanderiana** W. Bull · E:Kris Plant;
G:Sanders Pfeilblatt · ⏛ Z10 ⊚; Phil.:
Mindanao
- *thibautiana* Mast. = Alocasia longiloba
- **watsoniana** Mast. · ⏛ Z10 ⊚; Sumat.
- **zebrina** K. Koch & Veitch · ⏛ Z10 ⊚; Phil.

Aloe L. -f- *Aloaceae* · 446 spp. · E:Aloe;
F:Aloe; G:Aloe
- **africana** Mill. · E:Spiny Aloe · ♄ ♆ e Z9 ⊚
III-IV ⚘ ▽ ✳; S-Afr.: Cape, Transvaal

- **arborescens** Mill. · E:Candelabra Aloe,
Octopus Plant; G:Tintenfisch-Aloe · ♄
♆ Z9 ⊚ I-IV ▽ ✳; S-Afr.: Cape, Natal;
Malawi, nat. in S-Sp., S-F, P
- **aristata** Haw. · E:Lace Aloe, Torch Plant;
G:Bebänderte Aloe · ⏛ ♆ Z9 ⊚ V-VI ▽ ✳;
S-Afr.: Orange Free State, Natal
- *atrovirens* DC. = Haworthia herbacea
- *barbadensis* Mill. = Aloe vera
- **barberae** Dyer · ♄ ♆ Z9 ⊚ ▽ ✳; S-Afr.
- **brevifolia** Mill. · E:Short-leaved Aloe;
G:Kurzblättrige Aloe · ⏛ ♆ Z9 ⊚ ▽ ✳;
Cape
- **camperi** Schweinf. · ♄ ♆ Z10 ⊚ IV-VI ▽
✳; Eth.
- **ciliaris** Haw. · E:Climbing Aloe;
G:Kletter-Aloe · ♄ ♆ ⚡ Z9 ⊚ I-III ▽ ✳;
S-Afr.
- **comosa** Marloth & A. Berger · ♄ ♆ Z9 ⊚
▽ ✳; Cape
- **dichotoma** Masson · G:Drachenbaum-
Aloe, Köcherbaum · ♄ ♆ e Z9 ⊚ ▽ ✳;
Namibia, S-Afr.
- **distans** Haw. · E:Jewelled Aloe,
Kokerboom; G:Goldzahn-Aloe · ♄ ♆ Z9 ⊚
VI-VII ▽ ✳; Cape
- *disticha* L. = Gasteria disticha
- **divaricata** A. Berger · ♄ ♆ Z10 ⊚ ▽ ✳;
W-Madag.
- *eru* A. Berger = Aloe camperi
- **ferox** Mill. · E:Bitter Aloe, Cape Aloe;
G:Kap-Aloe · ♄ ♆ e Z9 ⊚ III-IV ⚘ ⚘ ▽
✳; S-Afr.
- **glauca** Mill. · ⏛ ♆ Z9 ⊚ ▽ ✳; Cape
- **grandidentata** Salm-Dyck · ♄ ♆ Z9 ⊚
VI-VII ▽ ✳; S-Afr.
- **humilis** (L.) Mill. · E:Crocodile Jaws,
Hedgehog Aloe, Spider Aloe; G:Igel-Aloe
· ⏛ ♆ Z9 ⊚ III-VII ▽ ✳; Cape
- **littoralis** Baker · ♆ Z9 ⊚ ▽ ✳; Angola,
Namibia
- **longistyla** Baker · ⏛ ♆ Z9 ⊚ ▽ ✳; Cape
- *macowanii* Baker = Aloe striatula
- **maculata** All.
- *maculata* Thunb. = Gasteria bicolor var.
bicolor
- **marlothii** A. Berger · E:Mountain Aloe ·
♄ ♆ Z9 ⊚ ▽ ✳; S-Afr.: Natal, Transvaal;
Botswana
- **mitriformis** Mill. · E:Purple Crown;
G:Bischofsmützen-Aloe · ♄ ♆ Z9 ⊚
VI-VIII ▽ ✳; Cape
- *nigricans* Haw. = Gasteria disticha
- *nitida* Salm-Dyck = Gasteria nitida var.
nitida

– *nobilis* Haw. = Aloe mitriformis
– *obliqua* (Aiton) Haw. = Gasteria bicolor var. bicolor
– *obliqua* DC. = Gasteria pulchra
– *obliqua* Jacq. = Gasteria disticha
– *perfoliata* L. = Aloe ferox
– var. *vera* L. = Aloe vera
– **perryi** Baker · E:Perry's Aloe, Socotrine Aloe; G:Sokotra-Aloe · ♄ Ψ Z10 ⚘ ⚘ Ⓝ ▽ ✳; Socotra; cult. E-Afr., Arab.
– **plicatilis** (L.) Mill. · E:Fan Aloe · ♄ ♄ Ψ e Z9 ⚘ V-VI ⚘ ▽ ✳; Cape
– × **principis** (Haw.) Stearn (*A. arborescens* × *A. ferox*) · ♄ Ψ Z9 ⚘ III-IV ▽ ✳; S-Afr.
– *prolifera* Haw. = Aloe brevifolia
– *pulchra* (Aiton) Jacq. = Gasteria pulchra
– *rubrolutea* Schinz = Aloe littoralis
– **rubroviolacea** Schweinf. · ♄ Ψ Z10 ⚘ ▽ ✳; Yemen
– × *salmdyckiana* Roem. & Schult. = Aloe × principis
– *saponaria* (Aiton) Haw. = Aloe maculata
– **spicata** Baker · ♄ Ψ e Z9 ⚘ ⚘ ▽ ✳; S-Afr.
– *spiralis* L. = Astroloba spiralis
– **striata** Haw. · E:Coral Aloe; G:Rotrandige Aloe · ⨊ Ψ Z9 ⚘ IV-V ▽ ✳; Cape, Namibia
– **striatula** Haw. · ♄ Ψ Z9 ⚘ ▽ ✳; S-Afr.
– *subcarinata* Salm-Dyck = Gasteria carinata var. carinata
– **succotrina** All. · E:Fynbos Aloe · ♄ Ψ Z9 ⚘ I-II ⚘ ▽ ✳; Cape, nat. in S-Sp., S-F
– *supralaevis* Haw. = Aloe ferox
– **tenuior** Haw. · ♄ Ψ Z9 ⚘ I-II ▽ ✳; S-Afr.
– **thraskii** Baker · E:Dune Aloe · ♄ Ψ Z9 ⚘ ▽ ✳; S-Afr.
– *umbellata* DC. = Aloe maculata
– **variegata** L. · E:Partridge Breast Aloe, Tiger Aloe; G:Tiger-Aloe · ♄ Ψ Z9 ⚘ IV-V ⚘ ▽ ✳; Botswana, Cape
– **vera** (L.) Burm. f. · E:Barbados Aloe, Bitter Aloe; G:Echte Aloe · ⨊ ♄ Ψ e Z8 ⚘ I-IV ⚘ Ⓝ ▽ ✳; NE-Afr, trop. Afr., S-Afr., Arab., Ind., nat. in Eur.: Ib, Ital-P, GR, Crete; TR
– *verrucosa* Mill. = Gasteria carinata var. verrucosa
– *virens* Haw. = Aloe humilis
– *vulgaris* Lam. = Aloe vera
– **zebrina** Baker · E:Zebra Leaf Aloe; G:Zebra-Aloe · ⨊ Z9 ⚘ ▽ ✳; Angola, Namibia, Botswana, S-Afr.: Transvaal

Aloinopsis Schwantes -f- *Aizoaceae* · 8 spp.

– *orpenii* (N.E. Br.) L. Bolus = Prepodesma orpenii

Alonsoa Ruiz & Pav. -f- *Scrophulariaceae* · 16 spp. · E:Mask Flower; F:Alonsoa; G:Maskenblume
– **acutifolia** Ruiz & Pav. · ☉ ♄ Z10 VII-IX; Peru, Bol.
– **incisifolia** Ruiz & Pav. · E:Cut-leaved Mask Flower · ⨊ ♄ Z10; Peru, Chile
– **linearis** (Jacq.) Ruiz & Pav. · E:Cut-leaved Mask Flower · ☉ ♄ Z10 VII-IX; Peru
– *linifolia* Roezl = Alonsoa linearis
– **meridionalis** (L. f.) Kuntze · ☉ ☉ ⨊ ♄ Z10 VII-IX; Mex., C-Am., S-Am.
– *myrtifolia* Roezl = Alonsoa acutifolia
– **warscewiczii** Regel · E:Mask Flower; G:Maskenblume · ☉ ♄ Z10; Peru

Alopecurus L. -m- *Poaceae* · 36 (-50) spp. · E:Foxtail Grass; F:Queue-de-renard, Vulpin; G:Fuchsschwanzgras
– **aequalis** Sobol. · E:Shortawn Foxtail; G:Rotgelbes Fuchsschwanzgras · ⨊ Z5 V-X; Eur.*, TR, Cauc., W-Sib., E-Sib., Amur, Sakhal., Kamchat., C-As.
– *agrestis* L. = Alopecurus myosuroides
– **arundinaceus** Poir. · E:Creeping Meadow Foxtail; G:Rohr-Fuchsschwanzgras · ⨊ Z5 V-VI; Eur.*, TR, N-As.
– **bulbosus** Gouan · E:Bulbous Foxtail; G:Knolliges Fuchsschwanzgras · ⨊ Z5 V-VII; Eur.: Ib, Fr, BrI, Ital-P, G, N-Ba; TR, Alger., Tun.
– **geniculatus** L. · E:Marsh Foxtail, Marsh Meadow Foxtail; G:Knick-Fuchsschwanzgras · ⨊ ～ Z5 V-X; Eur.*, Iran, Afgh., Ind., W-Sib., China, Jap., nat. in N-Am., Austr., NZ
– **lanatus** Sibth. & Sm. · ⨊ △ Z4 V; TR
– **myosuroides** Huds. · E:Black Grass; G:Acker-Fuchsschwanzgras · ☉ Z5 V-X; Eur.: Ib, Fr, Ital-P, Ba, E-Eur., nat. in Sc, C-Eur., EC-Eur., NZ
– **pratensis** L. · E:Meadow Foxtail; G:Gewöhnliches WiesenFuchsschwanzgras · ⨊ Z5 V-VII Ⓝ; Eur.*, Cauc., W-Sib., E-Sib., C-As., nat. in n N-Am.
– **rendlei** Eig · E:Rendle's Meadow Foxtail; G:Aufgeblasenes Fuchsschwanzgras · ☉ Z5 V-VI; Eur.: Ib, Fr, Ital-P, C-Eur., Ba; TR
– *utriculatus* (L.) Sm. = Alopecurus rendlei

Aloysia Juss. -f- *Verbenaceae* · 42 spp. ·
F:Citronnelle; G:Zitronenstrauch
- **chamaedryfolia** Cham. · ♄ Z8 ⓚ VII-
VIII; Braz., Arg.
- **citriodora** Palau · E:Lemon Verbena;
F:Citronnelle verveine; G:Zitronen-
strauch, Zitronenverbene · ♄ e D Z8 ⓚ
VII-IX ⚥ Ⓝ; Urug., Arg., Chile
- *triphylla* (L'Hér.) Britton = Aloysia
citriodora

Alpinia Roxb. -f- *Zingiberaceae* · 237 spp. ·
E:Ginger Lily; F:Alpinie; G:Alpinie,
Ingwerlilie
- **calcarata** (Haw.) Roscoe · E:Indian
Ginger; G:Indische Ingwerlilie · ⚅ Z10 ⓦ
IX-X; Ind.
- **galanga** (L.) Willd. · E:Galangal;
G:Siamesische Ingwerlilie · ⚅ Z10 ⓦ ⚥
Ⓝ; Ind., Sri Lanka, Malay. Arch.
- **japonica** (Thunb.) Miq. · E:Japanese
Ginger; G:Japanische Ingwerlilie · ⚅ Z10
ⓚ; China, Jap., Taiwan
- **malaccensis** (Burm. f.) Roscoe · ⚅ Z10
ⓦ III-V Ⓝ; E-Him., Burma, Malay. Arch.
- *nutans* (L.) Roscoe = Alpinia zerumbet
- **officinarum** Hance · E:Lesser Galangal;
G:Galgant · ⚅ Z10 ⓦ ⚥ Ⓝ; S-China,
Hainan
- **purpurata** (Vieill.) K. Schum. · E:Red
Ginger; G:Roter Ingwer · ♄ ✕ Z10 ⓦ;
Pacific Is.
- **rafflesiana** Wall. ex Baker · ⚅ Z10 ⓦ;
Malay. Pen.
- *sanderae* hort. Sander = Alpinia vittata
- *speciosa* (J.C. Wendl.) K. Schum. =
Alpinia zerumbet
- **vittata** W. Bull · E:Variegated Ginger;
G:Gestreifte Ingwerlilie · ♄ Z10 ⓦ;
Solom.
- **zerumbet** (Pers.) B.L. Burtt & R.M.
Sm. · E:Pink Porcelain Lily, Shell Ginger;
G:Porzellan-Ingwerlilie · ⚅ Z10 ⓦ IV-VI;
S-As., E-As.
- *zingiberina* Hook. f. = Alpinia galanga

Alsobia Hanst. -f- *Gesneriaceae* · 2 spp.
- **dianthiflora** (H.E. Moore & R.G. Wilson)
Wiehler · E:Lace Flower Vine, Lace
Flower · ⚅ Z10 ⓦ VI-IX; Mex., Costa Rica
- **punctata** (Lindl.) Hanst. · ♄ Z10 ⓦ;
Mex., Guat.

Alsomitra (Blume) M. Roem. -f-
Cucurbitaceae · 2 spp.

- **macrocarpa** (Blume) M. Roem. · ⚴ Z10
ⓦ; Malay. Arch.
- *sarcophylla* (Wall.) M. Roem. = Neoalsomitra sarcophylla

Alsophila R. Br. = Cyathea
- *australis* R. Br. = Cyathea australis
- *capensis* (L. f.) J. Sm. = Cyathea capensis
- *tricolor* (Colenso) R.M. Tryon = Cyathea
dealbata

Alstonia R. Br. -f- *Apocynaceae* · 42 spp.
- **congensis** Engl. · G:Bokukabambale,
Emien · ♄ e Z10 ⓦ Ⓝ; W-Afr., C-Afr.,
E-Afr.
- **constricta** F. Muell. · E:Fever Bark;
G:Bitterrinde · ♄ e Z10 ⓚ; Austr.:
Queensl., N.S.Wales
- **scholaris** (L.) R. Br. · E:Devil Tree,
Pali-mari; G:Teufelsbaum · ♄ e Z10 ⓦ ⚥
Ⓝ; Him., Ind., Sri Lanka, Malay. Arch.,
Austr.

Alstroemeria L. -f- *Alstroemeriaceae* · 50
(-70) spp. · E:Lily of the Incas, Peruvian
Lily; F:Alstroemère, Lis des Incas ;
G:Inkalilie
- *aurantiaca* D. Don = Alstroemeria aurea
- **aurea** Graham · F:Lis des Incas; G:Gold-
ene Inkalilie · ⚅ Z7 ⋀ VI-VIII; Chile
- **haemantha** Ruiz & Pav. · ⚅ Z8 ⓚ ⋀
VI-VII; Chile
- **ligtu** L. · E:St Martin's Flower; G:Inkalilie
· ⚅ Z8 ⌷ ⋀ VI-VII; Arg., Chile
- **pelegrina** L. · ⚅ Z9 ⓚ ⌷ VI-VIII; Peru,
N-Chile
- *peregrina* Ruiz & Pav. = Alstroemeria
pelegrina
- *psittacina* Lehm. = Alstroemeria pulchella
- **pulchella** L. f. · E:Parrot Lily · ⚅ Z8;
N-Braz.
- **versicolor** Ruiz & Pav. · ⚅ Z9 ⓚ ⌷
VI-VII; Chile
- **Cultivars:**
- **many cultivars**

Altamiranoa Rose = Villadia
- *ericoides* (Rose) H. Jacobsen = Villadia
imbricata
- *guatemalensis* (Rose) E. Walther =
Villadia guatemalensis

Alternanthera Forssk. -f- *Amaranthaceae* ·
80-100 (-200) spp. · E:Copperleaf,
Joseph's Coat; F:Alternanthère;

G:Papageienblatt
- *amoena* (Lem.) Voss = Alternanthera ficoidea
- **bettzickiana** (Regel) G. Nicholson · E:Calico Plant · ⧎ Z8 ⓐ; Peru
- **dentata** (Moench) Scheygr.
- **ficoidea** (L.) P. Beauv. · E:Parrot Leaf, Sanguinaria · ⧎ Ⅰ: Z8 ⓦ Ⓝ; Mex., C-Am., trop. S-Am.
- **reineckii** Briq. · ⊙ Z8; e S-Am.
- *versicolor* (Lem.) Regel = Alternanthera reineckii

Althaea L. -f- *Malvaceae* · 12 spp. · E:Marsh Mallow; F:Guimauve; G:Eibisch, Stockmalve
- **cannabina** L. · E:Armenian Mallow; G:Hanfblättriger Eibisch · ⧎ Z6 VII-IX Ⓝ; Eur.: Ib, Fr, Ital-P, Ba, EC-Eur., E-Eur.; TR, Cauc., Iran, C-As.
- **hirsuta** L. · E:Rough Marsh Mallow; G:Rauhaariger Eibisch · ⊙ VII-VIII; Eur.* exc. BrI, Sc; TR, Levant, Cauc., Iran, C-As., NW-Afr., Libya
- **officinalis** L. · E:Marsh Mallow, White Mallow; G:Echter Eibisch · ⧎ Z3 VII ⚘ Ⓝ ▽; Eur.*, TR, Syr., Palest., Cauc., Iran, Afgh., W-Sib., E-Sib., C-As., Alger., Tun., nat. in N-Am.
- *rosea* (L.) Cav. = Alcea rosea
- *rugosostellulata* Czeczott = Alcea rugosa

Altingia Noronha -f- *Hamamelidaceae* · 13 spp.
- **excelsa** Noronha · E:Rasamala; G:Kindan · ♭ ⓦ Ⓝ; Malay. Arch. , China: Yunnan

Alyogyne Alef. -f- *Malvaceae* · 4 spp. · E:Lilac Hibiscus; F:Alyogyne, Hibiscus bleu; G:Blauer Hibiscus
- **hakeifolia** (Giord.) Alef. · ♭ Z10 ⓦ; Austr.: S-Austr., W-Austr.
- **huegelii** (Endl.) Fryxell · E:Lilac Hibiscus; G:Blauer Hibiscus · ⧎ Z10 ⓐ IV-XI; Austr.: S-Austr., W-Austr.

Alysicarpus Desv. -m- *Fabaceae* · 25-30 spp.
- **vaginalis** (L.) DC. · E:White Moneywort · ⧎ ⓦ Ⓝ; Trop. Old World

Alyssoides Mill. -f- *Brassicaceae* · 3 spp. · F:Faux-alysson, Vésicaire; G:Blasenschötchen
- **utriculata** (L.) Medik. · E:Bladderpods; G:Blasenschötchen · ⧎ △ Z7 IV-VI; Eur.:

F, I, Ba, RO; TR, nat. in D

Alyssum L. -n- *Brassicaceae* · 168 spp. · E:Alison, Madwort; F:Alysson, Corbeille d'or; G:Steinkraut
- **alpestre** L. · G:Alpen-Steinkraut · ⧎ ⤳ △ Z6 VI-VII; Eur.: F, I, Ch; Alp.
- **alyssoides** (L.) L. · E:Small Alison; G:Kelch-Steinkraut · ⊙ Z6 IV-IX; Eur.* exc. BrI, Sc; Moroc.
- *arduini* Fritsch = Aurinia saxatilis
- **argenteum** All. · G:Silbergraues Steinkraut · ♭ △ Z6 VII-VIII; Eur.: I; SW-Alp.
- *argenteum* hort. = Alyssum murale
- **desertorum** Stapf · E:Desert Madwort; G:Steppen-Steinkraut · ⊙ Z6 IV-V; Eur.: A, EC-Eur., Ba, E-Eur.; TR, Levant, Cauc., Iran, W-Sib., E-Sib., C-As., Him., Mong., Egypt
- **diffusum** Ten. · G:Lockeres Steinkraut · ⧎ ⤳ △ Z6 IV-VI; Eur.: sp., F, I, ? GR; mts.
- *maritimum* (L.) Lam. = Lobularia maritima var. maritima
- **markgrafii** O.E. Schulz · G:Holziges Steinkraut · ⧎ △ Z7 ⋀ V-VI; Eur.: W-Ba
- **moellendorfianum** Asch. ex Beck · G:Kroatisches Steinkraut · ⧎ △ Z6 VI-VII; Eur.: Bosn.
- **montanum** L. · E:Mountain Alison; F:Alysse des montagnes; G:Gewöhnliches Berg-Steinkraut · ⧎ ⤳ △ D Z6 III-VI ▽; Eur.* exc. BrI, Sc
- **murale** Waldst. & Kit. · E:Yellow Tuft; F:Alysse des murailles; G:Mauer-Steinkraut, Silbriges Steinkraut · ⧎ △ Z5 V-VI; Eur.: Ba, EC-Eur.; TR, Syr., Lebanon, Cauc., Iran, nat. in G, A
- **ovirense** A. Kern. · G:Karawanken-Steinkraut · ⧎ ⤳ △ Z6 VI; Eur.: I, A, Slove., Bosn., Montenegro; mts.
- **repens** Baumg. · G:Kriechendes Steinkraut · ⧎ △ Z5 IV-VI; Eur.: A, Ba, RO, Crim; Cauc., Syr., N-Iran, C-As.
- **rostratum** Steven · ⊙ Z8 V-VI; Eur.: W-Ba, RO, Russ.; N-TR, Cauc.
- *rupestre* Ten. = Aurinia rupestris
- *saxatile* L. = Aurinia saxatilis
- **serpyllifolium** Desf. · G:Obir-Steinkraut · ⧎ △ Z7 VI; Eur.: Ib, F; NW-Afr.
- **spinosum** L. · E:Spiny Alison; G:Dorn-Steinkraut · ♭ △ Z8 ⓐ ⋀ V-VI; Eur.: sp., F; Moroc., Alger.
- *transsylvanicum* Schur = Alyssum repens
- **wulfenianum** Bernh. · G:Wulfens

Steinkraut · ⏀ ⤳ △ Z7 V-VIII; Eur.: I, A, Bosn., Montenegro, Maced.; SE-Alp.

Amaranthus L. -m- *Amaranthaceae* · 60 spp. · E:Amaranth, Pigweed; F:Amaranthe; G:Fuchsschwanz
– **albus** L. · E:Tumbleweed, White Pigweed; G:Weißer Fuchsschwanz · ⊙ Z5 VII-X; s N-Am., C-Am, nat. in Eur.* exc. BrI, Sc; Cauc., W-Sib., Amur, C-As., TR, N-Afr
– **blitoides** S. Watson · E:Mat Amaranth, Prostrate Pigweed; G:Westamerikanischer Fuchsschwanz · ⊙ Z5 VII-IX; s N-Am., C-Am., nat. in Eur.* exc. BrI, Sc
– **blitum** L. · ⊙
– subsp. **blitum** · E:Purple Amaranth; G:Aufsteigender Fuchsschwanz · ⊙ Z5 VII-IX; Eur., As, Afr.
– subsp. **emarginatus** (Moq. ex Uline & W.L. Bray) Carretero et al. · G:Ausgerandeter Fuchssschwanz, Ufer-Fuchsschwanz · ⊙ Z5 VI-X; Trop.
– **bouchonii** Thell. · E:Indehiscent Amaranth; G:Bouchons Fuchsschwanz · ⊙ Z5 VI-X; ? S-USA, nat. in F, C-Eur.
– **caudatus** L. · E:Love Lies Bleeding; F:Amarante queue-de-renard; G:Garten-Fuchsschwanz · ⊙ Z5 VII-X Ⓝ; S-Am., nat. in Cauc., C-As., Iran, TR, S-Eur., ? Eth., ? Tibet
– subsp. *mantegazzianus* (Pass.) Hanelt = Amaranthus mantegazzianus
– *chlorostachys* Willd. = Amaranthus hybridus
– **crispus** (Lesp. & Thévenau) N. Terracc. · E:Crispleaf Amaranth; G:Krauser Fuchsschwanz · ⊙ Z5 VII-IX; Arg., nat. in Eur.: I, A, EC-Eur., Ba, RO
– **cruentus** L. · E:Red Amaranth; G:Rispiger Fuchsschwanz · ⊙ Z5 VIII-IX Ⓝ; ? S-Mex., ? Guat., nat. in S-Eur.
– **deflexus** L. · E:Perennial Pigweed; G:Liegender Fuchsschwanz · ⏀ Z5 VI-X; n S-Am., nat. in Eur.* exc. BrI, Sc., Cauc., C-As.
– **dubius** Mart. ex Thell. · E:Largefruit Amaranth · ⊙ Z5 Ⓝ; trop. Am.
– *emarginatus* Salzm. ex Uline & W.L. Bray = Amaranthus blitoides
– *gangeticus* L. = Amaranthus tricolor
– **graecizans** L. · E:Mediterranean Amaranth; G:Wilder Fuchsschwanz · ⊙ Z5 VII-IX; Eur.: Ib, Fr, Ital-P, Ba, A, Crim; TR, Levant, Cauc., C-As., N-Afr., nat. in

G, Sw, H, RO
– **hybridus** L. · E:Purple Amaranth; F:Amarante queue-de -renard; G:Ausgebreiteter Fuchsschwanz · ⊙ Z5 VII-X Ⓝ; trop. Am., nat. in N-Am., Eur., As.
– subsp. *cruentus* (L.) Thell. = Amaranthus cruentus
– subsp. *hypochondriacus* (L.) Thell. = Amaranthus hypochondriacus
– **hypochondriacus** L. · E:Prince's Feather; G:Trauer-Fuchsschwanz · ⊙ Z5 VII-IX ⚥ Ⓝ; N-Am., nat. in Eur., China, Ind.
– *leucocarpus* S. Watson = Amaranthus hypochondriacus
– *lividus* L. = Amaranthus blitum
– **mantegazzianus** Pass. · ⊙ Z5 Ⓝ
– *melancholicus* L. = Amaranthus tricolor
– **muricatus** (Gillies ex Moq.) Hieron. · E:African Amaranth · ⏀ Z5; S-Am., nat. in Eur.: Ib, Sard., Sic., GR
– **paniculatus** L. · ⊙ Z5 Ⓝ; trop. As
– **powellii** S. Watson · E:Powell's Amaranth; G:Grünähriger Fuchsschwanz · ⊙ Z5; N-Am., S-Am., nat. in Eur.: sp., F, I, D
– **retroflexus** L. · E:Common Amaranth, Pigweed; G:Zurückgekrümmter Fuchsschwanz · ⊙ Z5 VII-IX Ⓝ; ? N-Am., nat. in cosmop.
– **standleyanus** Parodi ex Covas · G:Standleys Fuchsschwanz · ⊙ Z5 VII-X; Arg.
– **tricolor** L. · E:Chinese Spinach, Joseph's Coat; G:Surinamesischer Fuchsschwanz · ⊙ Z5 Ⓝ; trop. As.

× **Amarcrinum** Coutts -n- *Amaryllidaceae* (*Amaryllis × Crinum*)
– *howardii* Coutts = × Amarcrinum memoria-corsii
– **memoria-corsii** (Ragion.) H.E. Moore (*Amaryllis belladonna × Crinum moorei*) · ⏀ Z8 ⚘; cult.

× **Amarygia** Cif. & Giacom. -f- *Amaryllidaceae* (*Amaryllis × Brunsvigia*)
– **parkeri** (W. Watson) H.E. Moore (*Amaryllis belladonna × Brunsvigia josephinae*) · ⏀ Z9 ⚘; cult.

Amaryllis L. -f- *Amaryllidaceae* · 2 spp. · E:Belladonna Lily, Jersey Lily; F:Amaryllis; G:Belladonnenlilie
– *aulica* Ker-Gawl. = Hippeastrum aulicum
– **belladonna** L. · E:Belladonna Lily, Jersey Lily; F:Amaryllis Belle-dame;

G:Belladonnenlilie · ♃ ✂ Z8 🅚 ⮂ VIII-IX
✿; Cape
- **some cultivars**
- *bulbisperma* Burm. f. = Crinum bulbispermum

Amasonia L. f. -f- *Verbenaceae* · 8 spp.
- **calycina** Hook. f. · ♄ ♄ d Z10 🅦 XI-III;
Guyan.
- *punicea* hort. ex Hook. f. = Amasonia
calycina

Amberboa (Pers.) Less. -f- *Asteraceae* ·
6 spp. · F:Centaurée musquée; G:Amber-
körbchen, Bisampflanze
- **moschata** (L.) DC. · E:Sweet Sultan;
G:Duftende Bisampflanze · ☉ ☉ ✂ Z8
VII-IX; TR, Cauc.

Ambrosia L. -f- *Asteraceae* · 43 spp. ·
E:Ragweed; F:Ambroisie; G:Ambrosie,
Traubenkraut
- **artemisiifolia** L. · E:Annual Ragweed,
Common Ragweed; G:Beifußblättriges
Traubenkraut · ☉ VIII-X; Can., USA*,
Mex., nat. in EC-Eur., Ba
- **coronopifolia** Torr. & A. Gray ·
G:Ausdauerndes Traubenkraut · ♃ VII-X;
N-Am., nat. in Eur: sp., Fr, I, C-Eur., DK,
EC-Eur., W-Russ.
- *elatior* L. = Ambrosia artemisiifolia
- **maritima** L. · G:Strand-Ambrosie · ☉
VIII-X; Eur.: Ib, Fr, Ital-P, Ba; TR, Afr.
- *mexicana* hort. = Chenopodium botrys
- **psilostachya** DC. · E:Ragweed, Western
Ragweed; G:Stauden-Ambrosie · ♃ X;
Can.: Sask.; USA*, nat. in Eur., Cauc.,
S-Afr., Austr.
- **trifida** L. · E:Giant Ragweed; G:Dreilap-
piges Traubenkraut · ☉ VIII-X; Can.,
USA*; Mex., nat. in D

Ambulia Lam. = Limnophila
- *gratioloides* (R. Br.) Baill. = Limnophila
indica
- *heterophylla* (Roxb.) Baill. = Limnophila
heterophylla
- *sessiliflora* (Blume) Baill. = Limnophila
sessiliflora

Amelanchier Medik. -f- *Rosaceae* ·
33 spp. · E:Juneberry, Serviceberry;
F:Amélanchier; G:Felsenbirne
- **alnifolia** (Nutt.) Nutt. · E:Saskatoon
Service Berry; F:Amélanchier à feuilles

d'aulne; G:Erlenblättrige Felsenbirne · ♄
♄ d Z5 IV-V 🅦; Alaska, Can., USA: NCE,
NC, Rocky Mts., SW, NW, Calif.
- var. *florida* (Lindl.) C.K. Schneid. =
Amelanchier florida
- var. *semiintegrifolia* (Hook.) C.L. Hitchc.
= Amelanchier florida
- *alnifolia* auct. non (Nutt.) Nutt. =
Amelanchier florida
- *amabilis* Wiegand = Amelanchier
sanguinea
- **arborea** (F. Michx.) Fernald · E:Downy
Service Berry, June Berry; G:Schnee-
Felsenbirne · ♄ ♄ d Z5 III-IV 🅦; Can.: E;
USA: NE, NCE, SC, SE, Fla.
- **asiatica** (Siebold & Zucc.) Endl. ex
Walp. · G:Japanische Felsenbirne · ♄ ♄ d
Z6 V; Jap., Korea
- *botryapium* (L. f.) Borkh. = Amelanchier
canadensis
- *botryapium* DC. = Amelanchier lamarckii
- **canadensis** (L.) Medik. · E:Canadian
Service Berry, Snowy Mespilus;
G:Kanadische Felsenbirne · ♄ ♄ d Z5 IV
🅦; Can.: E; USA: NE, SE
- *canadensis* K. Koch = Amelanchier
lamarckii
- *confusa* auct. non Hyl. = Amelanchier
lamarckii
- **confusa** Hyl. · ♄ d Z5; orig. ?, nat. in
S-Swed
- **florida** Lindl. · E:Western Service Berry;
G:Blütenreiche Felsenbirne · ♄ ♄ d Z5 V;
Alaska, Can.: W; USA: NW, Idaho, Calif.
- *laevis* A.R. Clapham, Tutin & E.F. Warb. =
Amelanchier lamarckii
- **laevis** Wiegand · E:Allegheny Service
Berry; G:Kahle Felsenbirne · ♄ ♄ d Z5
IV-V 🅦; Can.: E; USA: NE, NCE, Kans.,
SE
- **lamarckii** F.G. Schroed. · E:Snowy
Mespilus; G:Kupfer-Felsenbirne · ♄ ♄ d
Z5 IV-V; Can.: E; USA: NE, NCE, nat. in
G, NL, B
- *oblongifolia* (Torr. & A. Gray) M. Roem. =
Amelanchier canadensis
- *ovalis* Borkh. non Medik. = Amelanchier
spicata
- **ovalis** Medik. · F:Amélanchier des bois;
G:Gewöhnliche Felsenbirne, Mitteleu-
ropäische Felsenbirne · ♄ d Z5 IV-V 🅦;
Eur.: Ib, Fr.Ital-P, C-Eur, EC-Eur., Ba,
RO, Crim; TR, Lebanon, N-Iraq, Cauc.,
NW-Afr.
- *oxyodon* Koehne = Amelanchier florida

– **pumila** Nutt. ex Torr. & A. Gray ·
E:Dwarf Serviceberry · ♄ d; USA: NW,
Calif., Rocky Mts., NC
– *rotundifolia* (Lam.) Dum.-Cours. =
Amelanchier ovalis
– *rotundifolia* M. Roem. = Amelanchier
sanguinea
– **sanguinea** (Pursh) DC. · E:Roundleaf
Serviceberry; F:Amélanchier sanguin;
G:Vermont-Felsenbirne · ♄ ♄ d Z5 V;
Can.: E; USA: NE, NCE, Tenn.
– **spicata** (Lam.) K. Koch · E:Garden
Shadblow; F:Amélanchier; G:Ährige
Felsenbirne, Besen-Felsenbirne · ♄ a d Z5
IV-V; Can.: E; USA: NE, NCE, N.Dak.,
nat. in N-Eur., G, A, F
– **stolonifera** Wiegand · E:Running Service
Berry; G:Ausläufertreibende Felsenbirne
· ♄ d Z5 V Ⓝ; Can.: E; USA: NE, NCE
– **utahensis** Koehne · E:Utah Service Berry;
G:Utah-Felsenbirne · ♄ ♄ d Z3 V; USA:
NW, Calif., Rocky Mts., Tex., SW; Mex. ,
Baja Calif.
– *vulgaris* Moench = Amelanchier ovalis

× **Amelasorbus** Rehder -m- *Rosaceae*
(*Amelanchier* × *Sorbus*)
– **jackii** Rehder (*Amelanchier florida* ×
Sorbus scopulina) · ♄ d Z5; USA: Idaho,
Oreg.

Amethystea L. -f- *Lamiaceae* · 1 sp. ·
G:Amethystblume
– **caerulea** L. · G:Amethystblume · ⊙ Z7;
TR, N-As., China, Mandsch., Korea,
Japan

Amherstia Wall. -f- *Caesalpiniaceae* · 1 sp. ·
F:Gloire de Birmanie; G:Tohabaum
– **nobilis** Wall. · E:Pride of Burma;
G:Tohabaum · ♄ e 🏵; Burma

Ammi L. -n- *Apiaceae* · 10 spp. · E:Bullwort;
F:Ammi; G:Knorpelmöhre
– **majus** L. · E:Bullwort, False Bishop's
Weed, Large Bullwort; G:Bischofskraut,
Große Knorpelmöhre · ⊙ Z6 VI-X 🌾 Ⓝ;
Eur.: Ib, Fr, Ital-P, Ba; TR, Cyprus, Syr.,
Iraq, Iran, N-Afr., Eth., nat. in W-Eur.,
C-Eur. N-Am., Austr., NZ
– **visnaga** (L.) Lam. · E:Pick Tooth,
Toothpick Weed; G:Zahnstocher-Ammei
· ⊙ ⊙ Z6 VII-IX 🌾 Ⓝ; Eur.: Ib, Fr, Ital-P,
Ba; TR, Cyprus, N-Iraq, Iran; Canar.,
N-Afr., nat. in N-Am., Mex., Chile, Arg.

Ammobium R. Br. ex Sims -n- *Asteraceae* ·
3 spp. · E:Winged Everlasting;
F:Immortelle de sables; G:Papierknöpf-
chen, Sandimmortelle
– **alatum** R. Br. · E:Winged Everlasting;
G:Papierknöpfchen, Sandimmortelle
· ⊙ ⁊ ⋉ Z9 VII-IX; Austr.: Queensl.,
N.S.Wales
– *grandiflorum* hort. = Ammobium alatum

Ammodaucus Coss. -m- *Apiaceae* · 1 sp.
– **leucotrichus** Coss. · ⊙ 🕮 Ⓝ; Alger.

Ammodendron Fisch. ex DC. -n- *Fabaceae* ·
3-6 spp.
– **conollyi** Bunge ex Boiss. · ♄ d 🕮; C-As.

Ammoides Adans. -f- *Apiaceae* · 2 spp.
– **pusilla** (Brot.) Breistr. · ⊙; Eur.: Ib,
Ital-P, Ba, nat. in G, Sw

Ammophila Host -f- *Poaceae* · 2-4 spp. ·
E:Beach Grass; F:Oyat; G:Helmgras,
Strandhafer
– **arenaria** (L.) Link · E:Beach Grass, Mar-
ram Grass; G:Gewöhnlicher Strandhafer,
Helm · ⁊ Z5 VI-VIII Ⓝ; Eur.*, TR, Cyprus,
Palest., N-Afr.; coasts, nat. in N-Am.
– **breviligulata** Fernald · E:American
Beach Grass; G:Amerikanischer Strand-
hafer · ⁊ Z5 VII-IX Ⓝ; Can.: E; USA: NE,
NCE; N.C.

Amomum Roxb. -n- *Zingiberaceae* ·
175 spp. · E:Cardamom; F:Cardamome;
G:Kardamom
– **aromaticum** Roxb. · E:Bengal Cardamom; G:Bengal-Kardamomn · ⁊ Z10 🏵
Ⓝ; Ind., Pakist.
– *cardamomum* L. = Elettaria cardamomum
– *cardamomum* Willd. = Amomum
compactum
– **compactum** Sol. ex Maton · E:Round
Cardamom; G:Java-Kardamom · ⁊ ⋉ Z10
🏵 Ⓝ; Malay. Arch.
– **krervanh** Pierre ex Gagnep. ·
G:Kambodja-Kardamom · ⁊ Z10 🏵 Ⓝ;
Cambodia, Thail.
– **subulatum** Roxb. · E:Indian Cardamom;
G:Nepal-Kardamom · ⁊ Z10 🏵 Ⓝ; trop.
As.
– **villosum** Lour.
– var. **xanthioides** (Wall. ex Baker)
T.L. Wu & S.J. Chen · E:Wild Siamese
Cardamom; G:Bastard-Kardamom · ⁊

Z10 ⓦ ⚥ Ⓝ; Burma, Thail.

Amorpha L. -f- *Fabaceae* · 15 spp. · E:False
Indogo; F:Amorpha, Faux-indigo;
G:Bastardindigo, Bleibusch, Scheinindigo
– **canescens** Pursh · E:Lead Plant;
G:Weißgrauer Bleibusch · ♄ d △ Z5 VI-VII
Ⓝ; Can.: E, Sask.; USA: NCE, NC, SC, SE,
N.Mex.
– **fruticosa** L. · E:False Indigo; F:Faux
indigo; G:Gewöhnlicher Bastardindigo,
Scheinindigo · ♄ d Z5 VI-VIII Ⓝ; Can.:
Man., Sask.; USA: NE, NCE, Fla., SC, SW;
Mex., nat. in C-Eur., S-Eur.
– **nana** Nutt. · E:Fragrant Indigo Bush;
G:Duft-Bleibusch · ♄ d △ Z4 VI-VII Ⓝ;
Can.: Man., Sask.; USA: NC, NCE, SW

Amorphophallus Blume ex Decne.
-m- *Araceae* · 177 spp. · E:Devil's Tongue;
F:Langue du diable; G:Titanenwurz
– **bulbifer** (Roxb.) Blume · ⴕ Z10 ⓦ;
NE-Ind.
– *campanulatus* Decne. = Amorphophallus
paeoniifolius
– **konjac** K. Koch · E:Devil's Tongue,
Umbrella Arum; G:Stinkende Titanenwurz · ⴕ Z10 ⓦ Ⓝ; cult. SE-As., E-As.
– **paeoniifolius** (Dennst.) Nicolson ·
E:Elephant Yam, Telingo Potato; G:Ele-
fantenkartoffel · ⴕ Z10 ⓦ Ⓝ; NE-Ind.,
Indochina, Phil., N.Guinea, Polyn.
– *rivieri* Durand ex Carrière = Amorphophallus konjac
– **titanum** (Becc.) Becc. ex Arcang. ·
E:Titan Arum; G:Titanenwurz · ⴕ Z10 ⓦ;
Sumat.

Ampelopsis Michx. -f- *Vitaceae* · 25 spp. ·
F:Vigne vierge G:Doldenrebe, Scheinrebe
– **aconitifolia** Bunge · E:Monkshood Vine;
F:Vigne vierge à fruits jaunes; G:Stur-
mhutblättrige Scheinrebe · ♄ d ⚥ Z6;
Mong., N-China
– **bodinieri** (H. Lév. & Vaniot) Rehder · ♄ ⌇
d ⚥ Z5; C-China
– **brevipedunculata** (Maxim.) Trautv.
– var. **brevipedunculata** · E:Blueberry
Climber; F:Vigne vierge à fruits bleus;
G:Ussuri-Scheinrebe · ♄ ⌇ d ⚥ Z5 VII-VIII;
China, Korea, Jap.
– var. *citrulloides* (Lebas) C.K. Schneid.
= Ampelopsis brevipedunculata var.
maximowiczii

– var. *elegans* L.H. Bailey = Ampelopsis
brevipedunculata var. maximowiczii
– var. **maximowiczii** (Regel) Rehder · ♄ ⌇ d
⚥ ⚹ Z5 ▱; E-China
– *hederacea* (Ehrh.) DC. = Parthenocissus
quinquefolia var. quinquefolia
– *henryana* (Hemsl.) Rehder = Parthenocissus henryana
– *heterophylla* (Thunb.) Siebold & Zucc.
= Ampelopsis brevipedunculata var.
maximowiczii
– **japonica** (Thunb.) Makino · E:Japanese
Pepper Vine; F:Vigne vierge du Japon;
G:Japanische Scheinrebe · ⌇ d ⤳ ⚹ Z7
△; Jap., N-China
– **megalophylla** (Veitch) Diels & Gilg ·
G:Riesenblättrige Scheinrebe · ⌇ d ⚥ ⚹
Z6; W-China
– **orientalis** (Lam.) Planch. · F:Vigne
vierge · ♄ ⌇ d ⚥ ⚘ ▱ △; TR, Syr.
– *quinquefolia* (L.) Michx. = Parthenocissus
quinquefolia var. quinquefolia
– *serjaniifolia* Bunge = Ampelopsis japonica
– *tricuspidata* Siebold & Zucc. = Parthenocissus tricuspidata
– *veitchii* hort. = Parthenocissus tricuspidata

Amphiblemma Naudin -n-
Melastomataceae · 13 spp.
– **cymosum** (Schrad. & J.C. Wendl.)
Naudin · ♄ ⓦ VII-VIII; W-Afr.

Amphicarpaea Elliott ex Nutt.
-f- *Fabaceae* · 3 spp. · E:Hog Peanut;
G:Doppelfrucht, Futtererdnuss
– **bracteata** (L.) Fernald · E:Hog Peanut ·
ⴕ Z7; Can.: E; USA: NE, NCE, NC, Rocky
Mts., SC, SE, Fla.

Amphicome Royle = Incarvillea
– *emodi* Lindl. = Incarvillea delavayi

Amsinckia Lehm. -f- *Boraginaceae* · c.
50 spp. · E:Fiddleneck; G:Gelbe Klette
– **calycina** (Moris) Chater · ☉ Z7; N-Am.,
S-Am., nat. in F
– **douglasiana** A. DC. · E:Douglas' Fiddleneck · ☉ Z7; N-Am.
– **intermedia** Fisch. & C.A. Mey. · E:Yellow
Burweed · ☉ Z7; N-Am.
– **lycopsoides** Lehm. · E:Tarweed Fiddleneck · ☉ Z7; N-Am., nat. in Sc, BrI, Fr
– **menziesii** (Lehm.) A. Nelson & J.F.
Macbr. · E:Menzies' Fiddleneck · ☉ Z7;
N-Am.

Amsonia Walter -f- *Apocynaceae* · 18 spp. · E:Blue Star; F:Amsonia; G:Amsonie
- *amsonia* (L.) Britton = Amsonia tabernaemontana
- **ciliata** Walter · E:Fringed Bluestar · ♃ Z7 IV-V; USA: SC, SE, Fla.
- **orientalis** Decne. · ♃ Z7 VII-IX ▽; GR, NW-TR
- **tabernaemontana** Walter · E:Eastern Bluestar; G:Gewöhnliche Texas-Amsonie · ♃ Z7 IV-V; USA: NE, NCE, Kans., SE, Okla., nat. in USA

Amyris P. Browne -f- *Rutaceae* · 31-40 spp. · E:Torchwood; F:Arbre à gomme, Bois chandelle; G:Balsamstrauch, Fackelholz
- **balsamifera** L. · E:Balsam Torchwood; G:Balsamstrauch · ♄ ♄ ⓚ Ⓝ; Fla., Mex., W.Ind., C-Am., S-Am.

Anabasis L. -f- *Chenopodiaceae* · 27 (-42) spp.
- **aphylla** L. · ♄ e ⓚ Ⓝ; Eur.: E-Russ.; Cauc., W-Iran, C-As., Him.

Anacampseros L. -f- *Portulacaceae* · 15 spp. · E:Love Plant; F:Anacampseros; G:Liebesröschen
- *albissima* Marloth = Avonia albissima
- **arachnoides** (Haw.) Sims · ♃ ψ Z10 ⓚ ▽ *; S-Afr.: Cape, Transvaal
- *arachnoides* hort. = Anacampseros rufescens
- *avasmontana* Dinter ex Poelln. = Avonia albissima
- *dinteri* Schinz = Avonia dinteri
- **filamentosa** (Haw.) Sims
- subsp. **filamentosa** · ♃ ψ Z10 ⓚ ▽ *; Cape
- subsp. **tomentosa** (A. Berger) Gerbaulet · ♃ ψ Z10 ⓚ ▽ *; Namibia
- **rufescens** (Haw.) Sweet · ♃ ψ Z10 ⓚ ▽ *; Cape
- **telephiastrum** DC. · ♃ ψ Z10 ⓚ ▽ *; Cape
- *tomentosa* A. Berger = Anacampseros filamentosa subsp. tomentosa

Anacamptis Rich. -f- *Orchidaceae* · 13 spp. · E:Pyramid Orchid; F:Anacamptis, Orchis; G:Hundswurz
- **coriophora** (L.) R.M. Bateman, Pridgeon & M.W. Chase · E:Bug Orchid; G:Stinkende Wanzen-Hundswurz · ♃ Z5 VI-VIII ▽ *; Eur.* exc. BrI, Sc; TR, N-Iraq, Cauc., Iran, C-As., NW-Afr.
- **laxiflora** (Lam.) R.M. Bateman, Pridgeon & M.W. Chase · E:Lax-flowered Orchid; G:Lockerblütige Hundswurz · ♃ Z8 ⓐ V ▽ *; Eur.: Ib, F, Ital-P, Ba ; TR, Cyprus
- **morio** (L.) R.M. Bateman, Pridgeon & M.W. Chase · E:Green Winged Orchid; G:Kleine Hundswurz, Salep-Hundswurz · ♃ Z5 IV-VI ⚕ Ⓝ ▽ *; Eur.*, TR, Cyprus, Syr., N-Iraq, Cauc., N-Iran, Moroc.
- **palustris** (Jacq.) R.M. Bateman, Pridgeon & M.W. Chase · G:Sumpf-Hundswurz
- subsp. **palustris** · G:Gewöhnliche Sumpf-Hundswurz · ♃ Z5 VI-VII ▽ *; N-Eur., C-Eur., E-Eur., TR, Iraq, Cauc., Iran, C-As.
- subsp. **elegans** (Heuff.) R.M. Bateman, Pridgeon & M.W. Chase · G:Zierliche Sumpf-Hundswurz · Z5 VI-VII ▽ *; EC-Eur., E-Eur.
- **pyramidalis** (L.) Rich. · E:Pyramidal Orchid; G:Pyramiden-Hundswurz, Spitzorchis · ♃ Z6 VI-VII ▽ *; Eur.*, TR, Cauc., Iran, NW-Afr.

Anacardium L. -n- *Anacardiaceae* · 8 spp. · E:Cashew; F:Anacardier; G:Acajubaum, Cashewnuss, Herznussbaum
- **occidentale** L. · E:Cashew; G:Acajubaum, Cashewnuss, Kaschubaum · ♄ e Z10 ⓦ ⚕ Ⓝ; ? Braz., nat. in Trop.

Anacharis Rich. = Elodea
- *densa* (Planch.) Vict. = Egeria densa
- *occidentalis* (Pursh) Vict. = Elodea nuttallii

Anacyclus L. -m- *Asteraceae* · 12 spp. · E:Anacyclus; F:Camomille du Moroc; G:Bertram, Kreisblume, Ringblume
- **clavatus** (Desf.) Pers. · G:Keulen-Bertram · ⊙ Z6 VI-VII; Eur.: Ib, Fr, Ital-P, Ba; TR, N-Afr., Canar.
- *depressus* Ball = Anacyclus pyrethrum var. depressus
- **officinarum** Hayne · E:Apothecary's Anacyclus; G:Deutscher Bertram · ⊙ Z6 ⚕ Ⓝ; cult.
- **pyrethrum** (L.) Link
- var. **depressus** (Ball) Maire · E:Mount Atlas Daisy; F:Camomille marocaine; G:Marokko-Bertram, Marokkokamille · ♃ △ Z7 ∧ V-VIII; Alger.; Atlas
- var. **pyrethrum** · E:Pellitory, Pyrethrum; G:Römischer Bertram · ⊙ ♃ Z7 ⚕ Ⓝ; Eur.: SE-Sp.; Moroc., Alger.

– **radiatus** Loisel. · E:Yellow Anacyclus;
G:Gelber Betram · ⊙ Z6 VI-VIII; Eur.: Ib,
Fr, Ital-P, Ba; Syr., N-Afr.
– *tomentosus* DC. = Anacyclus clavatus

Anagallis L. -f- *Primulaceae* · 28-30 spp. ·
E:Pimpernel; F:Mouron; G:Gauchheil
– **arvensis** L.
– var. **arvensis** · E:Scarlet Pimpernel;
G:Acker-Gauchheil · ⊙ VI-X ⚥ ⚘; Eur.*,
TR, Levant, Iraq, Arab., Cauc., Iran,
C-As., Afgh., Ind., Korea, Jap., Taiwan,
SE-China, N-Afr., Sudan, Eth., Can., USA:
NC, SC, SW, Rocky Mts., Calif., Greenl.,
S-Am., Austr., NZ
– var. *caerulea* (L.) Gouan = Anagallis
foemina
– *collina* Schousb. = Anagallis monelli
subsp. linifolia
– × **doerfleri** Ronniger (*A. arvensis × A.
foemina*) · ⊙ Z7; C-Eur., CZ, Swed
– **foemina** Mill. · E:Poor Man's Weather-
glass; G:Blauer Gauchheil · ⊙ VI-X ⚘;
Eur.*
– *grandiflora* Andrews = Anagallis monelli
subsp. linifolia
– *linifolia* L. = Anagallis monelli subsp.
linifolia
– **minima** (L.) E.H.L. Krause ·
E:Chaffweed; G:Kleinling, Zwerg-
Gauchheil · ⊙ Z7 V-IX; Eur.*, Alger, Tun.
– **monelli** L.
– subsp. **linifolia** (L.) Maire · F:Mouron · ⊙
♃ Z7; Eur.: Ib, Sic.; NW-Afr., Libya
– subsp. **monelli** · E:Blue Pimpernel · ⊙ ♃
Z7 VI-IX; Eur.: Ib, Sard., Sic.; NW-Afr.,
Libya
– **tenella** (L.) L. · E:Bog Pimpernel;
G:Zarter Gauchheil · ♃ Z7 VII-VIII ▽;
Eur.: Ib, BrI, Fr, Ital-P, C-Eur., GR;
NW-Afr.

Anagyris L. -f- *Fabaceae* · 2 spp. ·
E:Stinking Bean Trefoil; F:Anagyre, Bois
puant; G:Stinkstrauch
– **foetida** L. · E:Stinking Bean Trefoil;
G:Stinkstrauch · ♄ d Z8 ⌂ V ⚘; Eur.: Ib,
Fr, Ital-P; TR, Levant, NW-Afr., Libya

Anamirta Colebr. -f- *Menispermaceae* ·
1 sp. · E:False Myrtle; F:Faux-myrte;
G:Scheinmyrte
– *cocculus* Wight & Arn. = Anamirta
paniculata
– *flavescens* Miq. = Anamirta paniculata

– **paniculata** Colebr. · E:Levant Berry;
G:Scheinmyrte · ♄ ⚥ ⌂ ⚥ ⚘ Ⓝ; Ind., Sri
Lanka, Malay. Arch., N.Guinea

Ananas Mill. -m- *Bromeliaceae* · 8 spp. ·
E:Pineapple; F:Ananas; G:Ananas
– *ananas* (L.) H. Karst. ex Voss = Ananas
comosus
– **bracteatus** (Lindl.) Schult. f. · E:Red
Pineapple, Wild Pineapple; G:Rote
Ananas · ♃ Z10 ⌂; Braz., Parag.
– **comosus** (L.) Merr. · E:Pineapple;
G:Ananas · ♃ Z10 ⌂ ⚥ Ⓝ; cult.
– **nanus** (L.B. Sm.) L.B. Sm. · E:Miniature
Pineapple · ♃ Z10 ⌂; Braz.
– *sativus* Schult. & Schult. f. = Ananas
comosus

Ananassa Lindl. = Ananas
– *sativa* (Schult. & Schult. f.) Lindl. ex Beer
= Ananas comosus

Anaphalis DC. -f- *Asteraceae* · 60-110 spp. ·
E:Pearly Everlasting; F:Immortelle
d'argent; G:Perlkörbchen, Silberimmortelle
– **margaritacea** (L.) Benth. & Hook. f.
– var. **cinnamomea** (DC.) Herder &
Maxim. · ♃ Z3 VII-VIII; Him.
– var. **margaritacea** · E:Pearly Everlasting;
F:Immortelle d'argent; G:Großblütiges
Perlkörbchen, Silberimmortelle · ♃ Z3
VII-IX; Alaska, Can., USA: NE, NCE, NC,
Rocky Mts., SW, NW, Calif.; Jap., China,
nat. in N-Eur., D
– var. **yedoensis** (Franch. & Sav.) Ohwi ·
♃ VII-IX; Jap.
– **nepalensis** (Spreng.) Hand.-Mazz. · ♃
Z6; Him., W-China
– var. *monocephala* (DC.) Hand.-Mazz. =
Anaphalis nubigena
– **nubigena** DC. · ♃ △ Z6 VI-VII; Afgh.,
Pakist., Tibet, Yunnan
– **triplinervis** (Sims) C.B. Clarke ·
F:Immortelle de l'Himalaya · ♃ △ Z5
VII-VIII; Him.
– *yedoensis* (Franch. & Sav.) Maxim. =
Anaphalis margaritacea var. yedoensis

Anarrhinum Desf. -n- *Scrophulariaceae* · 8
(-12) spp. · G:Lochschlund; F:Anarrhinum
– **bellidifolium** (L.) Willd. · E:Anarrhinum;
G:Lochschlund · ⊙ ♃ △ Z7 VI-VII; Eur.:
P, sp., F, I, G, nat. in Sw

Anastatica L. -f- *Brassicaceae* · 1 sp. · E:Rose of Jericho; F:Rose de Jéricho; G:Rose von Jericho, Jerichorose
- **hierochuntica** L. · E:Resurrection Plant, Rose of Jericho; G:Rose von Jericho · ⊙ Z9 Ⓚ VII; Moroc., Alger., Sahara, S-Iran

Anchusa L. -f- *Boraginaceae* · c. 35 spp. · E:Alkanet; F:Buglosse; G:Ochsenzunge, Wolfsauge
- **arvensis** (L.) M. Bieb. · E:Bugloss; G:Gewöhnlicher Acker-Krummhals · ⊙ V-IX; Eur.*, N-As., Eth.
- **azurea** Mill. · E:Large Blue Alkanet; G:Italienische Ochsenzunge · ⊙ ♃ Z3 V-IX; Eur.: Ib, Fr, Ital-P, Ba, EC-Eur., E-Eur.; TR, Levant, Iraq, Arab., Cauc., Iran, C-As., Him.; N-Afr.
- **some cultivars**
- **barrelieri** (All.) Vitman · ⊙ ♃ Z3 VI-VIII; Eur.: H, Ba, E-Eur.; TR
- *caespitosa* hort. = Anchusa leptophylla subsp. incana
- **capensis** Thunb. · E:Annual Anchusa, Cape Forget-Me-Not; G:Kap-Ochsenzunge · ⊙ ⊙ Z9 VII-VIII; S-Afr.
- **cespitosa** Lam. · ♃ △ Ⓐ V-IX; Crete
- *echioides* (L.) M. Bieb. = Arnebia pulchra
- *italica* Retz. = Anchusa azurea
- **leptophylla** Roem. & Schult.
- subsp. **incana** (Ledeb.) D.F. Chamb. · ♃ △ ∧ V-X; N-TR, C-TR
- subsp. **leptophylla** · ⊙ ♃ Ⓚ; Eur.: RO, BG, Crim; TR
- **ochroleuca** M. Bieb. · G:Gelbe Ochsenzunge · ⊙ ♃ Z5 V-VII; Eur.: H, BG, E-Eur., nat. in NL, I
- **officinalis** L. · E:Alkanet; G:Gewöhnliche Ochsenzunge · ⊙ ♃ Z5 V-IX ⚕ ☠; Eur.* exc. BrI; TR
- **undulata** L. · G:Welligblättrige Ochsenzunge · ♃ VI-IX; Eur.: Ib, Fr, Ital-P, Ba; TR, Alger., Moroc.

Ancistrocactus (K. Schum.) Britton & Rose = Sclerocactus
- *crassihamatus* (F.A.C. Weber) L.D. Benson = Sclerocactus uncinatus var. crassihamatus
- *scheerii* (Salm-Dyck) Britton & Rose = Sclerocactus scheerii
- *uncinatus* (Galeotti) L.D. Benson = Sclerocactus uncinatus var. uncinatus

Andira Juss. -f- *Fabaceae* · 21 sp. · E:Andelmin, Angelim; G:Kohlbaum
- **araroba** Aguiar · E:Angelim; G:Drogen-Kohlbaum · ♄ Z10 Ⓦ ⚕ ☠; Braz.
- **inermis** (W. Wright) Kunth ex DC. · E:Cabbage Tree; G:Kohlbaum · ♄ e Z9 Ⓦ ☠ Ⓝ; S-Fla., Mex., C-Am., W.Ind., S-Am., W-Afr.

Andrachne L. -f- *Euphorbiaceae* · 43 spp. · F:Andrachné; G:Andrachne, Myrtenkraut
- **colchica** Fisch. & C.A. Mey. ex Boiss. · F:Andrachne de Colchide; G:Kolchische Andrachne · ♄ d Z6 VII-IX; Cauc.
- **phyllanthoides** (Nutt.) Müll. Arg. · ♄ d VII-IX; USA: SE, Tex.

Andromeda L. -f- *Ericaceae* · 2 spp. · E:Bog Rosemary; F:Andromède; G:Rosmarinheide
- *arborea* L. = Oxydendrum arboreum
- *catesbaei* Walter = Leucothoe axillaris
- *dealbata* W. Bartram ex Willd. = Zenobia pulverulenta var. pulverulenta
- *fontanesiana* Steud. = Leucothoe fontanesiana
- **glaucophylla** Link · E:Bog Rosemary; F:Andromède à feuilles glauques; G:Behaarte Rosmarinheide · ♄ e Z3 V-VI ☠; Greenl., Can.: E, Sask.; USA: NE, NCE
- *lucida* Lam. = Lyonia lucida
- *mariana* L. = Lyonia mariana
- **polifolia** L. · E:Common Bog Rosemary; F:Andromède à feuilles de polium; G:Kahle Rosmarinheide · ♄ e Z3 V-VIII ⚕ ☠; Eur.* exc. Ib; W-Sib., E-Sib., Amur, Sakhal., Kamchat., Jap., Mong., Alaska, Can., USA: NW; Greenl.
- *pulverulenta* W. Bartram ex Willd. = Zenobia pulverulenta var. pulverulenta
- *racemosa* L. = Leucothoe racemosa
- *racemosa* Lam. = Lyonia mariana
- *recurva* Buckland = Leucothoe recurva

Andropogon L. -m- *Poaceae* · c. 100 spp. · E:Beard Grass, Blue Stem; F:Andropogon, Barbon; G:Blauhalm, Gambagras
- *barbatus* L. = Chloris barbata
- *citratus* DC. ex Nees = Cymbopogon citratus
- *confertiflorus* Steud. = Cymbopogon nardus var. confertiflorus
- *flexuosus* Nees ex Steud. = Cymbopogon flexuosus
- **gayanus** Kunth · E:Bluestem · ♃ Ⓦ Ⓝ;

trop. Afr., nat. in Braz., Ind., Austr.: Queensl.
- **gerardii** Vitman · E:Big Bluestem; G:Gambagras, Großer Blauhalm · ⁴ Z4; N-Am.
- *martinii* Roxb. = Cymbopogon martinii
- *muricatus* Retz. = Vetiveria zizanioides
- *nardus* L. = Cymbopogon nardus var. nardus
- *polydactylon* L. = Chloris barbata
- *schoenanthus* L. = Cymbopogon schoenanthus
- *scoparius* Michx. = Schizachyrium scoparium

Androsace L. -f- *Primulaceae* · 153 spp. · E:Rock Jasmine; F:Androsace; G:Mannsschild
- **aizoon** Duby · ⁴ △ Z5 V ▽; Ind., China
- **albana** Steven · E:Alpine Rock Jasmine · ⊙ △ Z6 IV-V ▽; TR, Cauc. (Armen.), N-Iran
- **alpina** (L.) Lam. · G:Alpen-Mannsschild · ⁴ Z5 VII-VIII ▽; Eur.: F, Sw, A, I; Alp.
- **brevis** (Hegetschw.) Ces. · G:Charpentiers Mannsschild · ⁴ Z7 VI ▽; E-Alp.: Sw, I (Lago di Como)
- *brigantiaca* Jord. & Fourr. = Androsace carnea subsp. brigantiaca
- **carnea** L.
- subsp. **brigantiaca** (Jord. & Fourr.) I.K. Ferguson · ⁴ △ Z5 VI ▽; Eur.: F, I; SW-Alp.
- subsp. **carnea** · E:Pink Rock Jasmine; G:Flaumigbehaarter Mannsschild, Fleischroter Mannsschild · ⁴ △ Z5 VI-VII ▽; Eur.: sp., F, Sw, I; mts.
- subsp. **laggeri** (A. Huet) Nyman · ⁴ △ Z5 IV-VI ▽; Eur.: sp., F; C-Pyr.
- subsp. **rosea** (Jord. & Fourr.) Gremli · G:Hallers Mannsschild · ⁴ △ Z5 VI-VII ▽; E-Pyr., mts. F
- **chamaejasme** Wulfen ex Host · E:Ciliate Rock Jasmine; G:Bewimperter Mannsschild · ⁴ △ Z5 VI ▽; Eur.: F, I, C-Eur., EC-Eur.; Pyr., Alp., Carp.; Cauc., Him., E-Sib., Alaska, Can.: W
- *charpentieri* Heer = Androsace brevis
- *chumbyi* hort. ex Pax & Kunth = Androsace sarmentosa
- **ciliata** DC. · ⁴ Z6 ▽; Eur.: F, sp., C-Pyr.
- **cylindrica** DC. · E:Cylindrical Rock Jasmine · ⁴ Z6 ▽; Eur.: F, sp.; C-Pyr.
- **elongata** L. · E:Californian Rock Jasmine; G:Langgestielter Mannsschild

· ⊙ Z6 IV-V ▽; Eur.: Ib, Sic., Fr, C-Eur., EC-Eur., Ba, E-Eur.; Cauc., ? W-Sib., E-Sib., Mong., China, nat. in Norw.
- **foliosa** Duby ex Decne. · ⁴ △ Z6 V-VI ▽; NW-Him.
- **globifera** Duby · ⁴ Z4 ▽; Him.
- *halleri* L. = Androsace carnea subsp. rosea
- **hausmannii** Leyb. · G:Dolomiten-Mannsschild · ⁴ Z6 VII-VIII ▽; E-Alp.: G, A, I, W-Ba
- **hedraeantha** Griseb. · ⁴ △ Z6 V-VI ▽; Eur.: Ba; mts.
- **helvetica** (L.) All. · E:Swiss Rock Jasmine; G:Schweizer Mannsschild · ⁴ △ Z6 V-VI ▽; Eur.: F, I, Sw, G, A; Alp., ? Pyr.
- **hirtella** Dufour · ⁴ Z6 ▽; Eur. ; F, sp.; C-Pyr.
- **lactea** L. · E:Milkwhite Rock Jasmine; G:Milchweißer Mannsschild · ⁴ △ Z6 VI ▽; Eur.: Fr, C-Eur., EC-Eur., Ital-P, Slove., Croatia, Bosn., Serb., RO; mts.
- **lactiflora** Pall. · ⊙ △ Z4 V-VI ▽; Sib., Mong.
- *laggeri* A. Huet = Androsace carnea subsp. laggeri
- **lanuginosa** Wall. · E:Rock Jasmine; G:Himalaya-Mannsschild · ⁴ △ Z6 V-VI ▽; Him.
- **limprichtii** Pax & Hoffm. · ⁴ ▽; China (Sichuan, Xizang)
- **mathildae** Levier · ⁴ Z6 ▽; I: C-Apenn.
- **maxima** L. · E:Greater Rock Jasmine; G:Großer Mannsschild · ⊙ △ IV-V ▽; Eur.* exc. BrI, Sc; TR, Iraq, Levant, Cauc., Iran, C-As., W-Sib., Mong., NW-Afr., Libya
- **mucronifolia** G. Watt · ⁴ Z5 ▽; Him., Tibet, Afgh.; Kashmir
- **muscoidea** Duby · ⁴ Z5 ▽; Him., Tibet
- **obtusifolia** All. · E:Blunt-leaved Rock Jasmine; G:Stumpfblättriger Mannsschild · ⁴ △ Z4 V-VI ▽; Eur.: Fr, C-Eur., EC-Eur., Ital-P, Ba, RO; mts.
- **primuloides** Duby · ⁴ △ Z6 VI-VII ▽; W-Him.: Kashmir
- *primuloides* hort. = Androsace sarmentosa
- **pubescens** DC. · E:Hairy Rock Jasmine · ⁴ Z5 ▽; sp., F, Sw, I; C-Alp., SW-Alp., Pyren.
- **pyrenaica** Lam. · E:Pyrenean Rock Jasmine; G:Pyrenäen-Mannsschild · ⁴ Z6 ▽; F, sp.; Pyr.
- **rotundifolia** Hardw. · ⁴ Z4 ▽; Afgh.,

N-Ind., Bhutan
- var. *elegans* (Duby) R. Knuth = Androsace rotundifolia
- **sarmentosa** Wall. · F:Androsace de Chine, Androsace sarmenteuse · ⚃ △ Z3 VI-VII ▽; Him., W-China
- var. *chumbyi* Fitzh. = Androsace sarmentosa
- var. *watkinsii* Hook. f. = Androsace limprichtii
- **sempervivoides** Jacquem. ex Duby · F:Androsace naine de l'Himalaya · ⚃ △ Z5 VI-VII ▽; Kashmir, Tibet
- **septentrionalis** L. · E:Pygmy Flower, Rock Jasmine; G:Nördlicher Mannsschild · ⊙ △ Z4 IV-V ▽; Eur.: Fr, Ital-P, C-Eur., EC-Eur., Sc, EC-Eur.; Cauc., W-Sib., E-Sib., Amur, Kamchat., Mong., China: Xijiang; Alaska, Can., USA: NE, NCE, SW, Rocky Mts., NW, Calif.; Greenl.
- **strigillosa** Franch. · ⚃ △ Z7 VI ▽; Sikkim
- **vandellii** (Turra) Chiov. · G:Vandellis Mannsschild · ⚃ Z6 VII ▽; Eur.: sp., F, I, Sw, A; Sierra Nevada, Pyr., Alp.
- **villosa** L.
- var. **arachnoidea** (Schott, Nyman & Kotschy) R. Knuth · ⚃ △ Z4 VI-VII ▽; Eur.: I, SE-Eur.
- var. **villosa** · G:Zottiger Mannsschild · ⚃ Z4 VI-VII ▽; Eur.: Ib, Fr, C-Eur., Ital-P, Ba, EC-Eur.; TR, Syr., Cauc., C-As., W-Him.; mts.
- **wulfeniana** Sieber ex W.D.J. Koch · G:Wulfens Mannsschild · ⚃ Z5 VI-VII ▽; A, I; E-Alp.

Andryala L. -f- *Asteraceae* · 25 spp.
- **agardhii** Haens. ex DC. · ⚃ Z7 Ⓐ ▭ V-VII; S-Sp.: Sierra Nevada

Aneilema R. Br. -n- *Commelinaceae* · 62 spp.
- *geniculatum* (Jacq.) Woodson = Gibasis geniculata
- **zebrinum** Chiov. · ⚃ ⤳ Z10 VIII-XI; Eth.

Anemia Sw. -f- *Schizaeaceae* · 116 spp. · E:Flowering Fern; G:Blütenfarn
- **mandiocana** Raddi · ⚃ Z10 ⊛; Braz.
- **phyllitidis** (L.) Sw. · ⚃ Z10 ⊛; Mex., C-Am., W.Ind., trop. S-Am., nat. in Sri Lanka
- **rotundifolia** Schrad. · ⚃ Z10 ⊛; S-Braz.

- **tomentosa** (Savigny) Sw. · ⚃ Z10 ⊛; S-Am., Eth., S-Afr. (Natal), S-Ind.

Anemone L. -f- *Ranunculaceae* · 144 spp. · E:Anemone, Windflower; F:Anémone; G:Anemone, Windröschen
- *alpina* L. = Pulsatilla alpina subsp. alpina
- **apennina** L. · E:Blue Wood Anemone; F:Anémone des Apennins; G:Apenninen-Windröschen · ⚃ △ Z6 IV-V; Eur.: Cors, I, Sic., Croatia, YU, AL, nat. in BrI, Sc, Fr, C-Eur.
- **baicalensis** Turcz. & Ledeb. · G:Baikal-Windröschen · ⚃ ⤳ Z5 IV-V; E-Sib.
- **baldensis** Jacq. · E:Monte Baldo Anemone; G:Monte-Baldo-Windröschen, Tiroler Windröschen · ⚃ △ Z6 VII-VIII; Eur.: F, I, Sw, A, Slove., Montenegro; Alp., Montenegro
- **blanda** Schott & Kotschy · E:Windflower; F:Anémone de mars des Balkans; G:Balkan-Windröschen, Berg-Anemone · ⚃ △ Z5 III-IV; Eur.: Ba; TR, Cauc.
- some cultivars
- **canadensis** L. · E:Canada Anemone; G:Kanadisches Windröschen · ⚃ △ Z3 V; Can., USA: NE, NCE, NC, N.Mex.
- **coronaria** L. · E:Crown Anemone; G:Garten-Anemone, Kronen-Anemone · ⚃ ⋉ Z8 III-V; Eur.: Ib, Fr, Ital-P, Ba; TR, Levant, Egypt, Tun., Alger.
- many cultivars
- **cylindrica** A. Gray · E:Candle Anemone; G:Prärie-Anemone · ⚃ Z5; Can., USA: NE, NCE, NC, Rocky Mts., SW
- *dichotoma* Michx. non L. = Anemone canadensis
- × **fulgens** (DC.) J. Gay (*A. hortensis* × *A. pavonina*) · ⚃ ⋉ Z8 III-V; cult.
- *hepatica* L. = Hepatica nobilis var. nobilis
- **hortensis** L. · G:Stern-Anemone · ⚃ Z8 Ⓐ; Eur.: F, Ital-P, Ba
- **hupehensis** (Lemoine) Lemoine · G:Herbst-Anemone
- var. **hupehensis** · G:Hupeh-Herbst-Anemone · ⚃ Z6; C-China
- var. **japonica** (Thunb.) Bowles & Stearn · G:Japanische Herbst-Anemone · ⚃ ⋉ Z6 VIII-IX; Jap., S-China
- *japonica* (Thunb.) Siebold & Zucc. = Anemone hupehensis var. japonica
- var. *hupehensis* Lemoine = Anemone hupehensis var. hupehensis
- × **lesseri** H.R. Wehrh. (*A. multifida* × *A. sylvestris*) · ⚃ △ Z3 V-VI; cult.

– **leveillei** Ulbr. · ⚃ Z6; C-China
– *magellanica* hort. ex Wehrh. = Anemone multifida
– **multifida** Poir. · E:Pacific Anemone; G:Pazifisches Windröschen · ⚃ Z2 VI; Alaska, Can., USA: NE, NCE, NC, Rocky Mts., NW, SW, Calif.; s S-Am
– **narcissiflora**
– var. **narcissiflora** · E:Narcissus Anemone · ⚃ △ Z3 V-VI ✻ ▽; Eur.* exc. BrI, Sc; TR, Cauc., W-Sib. (Ural); mts.
– **nemorosa** L. · E:Wind Flower, Wood Anemone; F:Anémone des bois, Anémone Sylvie; G:Busch-Windröschen · ⚃ Z5 III-V ✻; Eur.*, TR
– **some cultivars**
– *nipponica* Merr. = Anemone hupehensis var. japonica
– **palmata** L. · ⚃ Z8 ⬡ V-VI; Eur.: Ib, F, Sard., Sic., ? GR; NW-Afr.
– *patens* L. = Pulsatilla patens
– **pavonina** Lam. · G:Pfauen-Anemone · ⚃ Z8 V-VI; Eur.: N-Sp.; mts.
– :*pennsylvanica* L. = Anemone canadensis
– **polyanthes** D. Don · G:Vielblütiges Windröschen · ⚃ △ Z6 VI; Pakist., Him.
– **ranunculoides** L. · E:Yellow Anemone; G:Gewöhnliches Gelbes Windröschen · ⚃ Z4 IV-V ✻; Eur.* exc. BrI; TR, Cauc., ? Tibet
– **rivularis** Buch.-Ham. ex DC. · F:Anémone des rives; G:Gewöhnliches Bach-Windröschen · ⚃ Z7 V-VI; Ind., SW-China
– **rupicola** Cambess. · E:Rock Windflower; G:Felsen-Windröschen · ⚃ △ Z6 VII-VIII; Afgh., Him., SW-China
– :*slavica* G. Reuss = Pulsatilla halleri subsp. slavica
– :*stellata* Lam. = Anemone hortensis
– **sylvestris** L. · E:Snowdrop Windflower, Windflower; F:Anémone des forêts printanière; G:Großes Windröschen · ⚃ Z4 IV-VI ✻ ▽; Eur.* exc. BrI; Cauc., W-Sib., E-Sib., Amur, ? Kamchat., C-As., Mong., ? Manch.
– **tetrasepala** Royle · G:Himalaya-Windröschen · ⚃ Z6; W-Him.: Afgh., NW-Ind.
– **tomentosa** (Maxim.) C. Pei · G:Filzblättrige Herbst-Anemone · ⚃ Z3 VIII-IX; N-China
– :*transsylvanica* (Fuss) Heuff. = Hepatica transsilvanica
– **trifolia** L. · G:Dreiblättriges Windröschen · ⚃ Z6 V; Eur.: Ib, F, I, A, H

– :*vernalis* L. = Pulsatilla vernalis
– **virginiana** L. · G:Virginia-Anemone, Virginisches Windröschen · ⚃ Z4; Can., USA: NE, NCE, NC, SE
– **vitifolia** Buch.-Ham. ex DC. · G:Weinblättriges Windröschen · ⚃ Z7 VIII-X; Afgh., Him., W-China, Burma

Anemonella Spach -f- :*Ranunculaceae* · I sp. · E:Rue Anemone; F:Anémonelle ; G:Rautenanemone
– **thalictroides** (L.) Spach · E:Rue-Anemone; G:Rauten:anemone · ⚃ Z4 IV-V; Ont., USA: NE, NCE, Okla., SE, Fla.

Anemonopsis Siebold & Zucc. -f- :*Ranunculaceae* · I sp. · E:False Anemone; F:Fausse-anémone; G:Scheinanemone
– **macrophylla** Siebold & Zucc. · E:False Anemone; G:Scheinanemone · ⚃ Z4 VIII; Jap.; mts.

Anemopaegma Mart. ex Meisn. -n- :*Bignoniaceae* · 43 spp.
– **chamberlaynii** (Sims) Bureau & K. Schum. · E:Yellow Trumpet Vine · ♄ e ⚡ Z10 ⬡ IX; Braz.

Anemopsis Hook. & Arn. -f- :*Saururaceae* · I sp. · E:Yerba Mansa; F:Queue-de-lézard; G:Eidechsenschwanz
– **californica** (Nutt.) Hook. & Arn. · E:American Swamp Root, Lizard's Tail, Yerba Mansa; G:Eidechsenschwanz · ⚃ ⌢ Z8 ⬡ VII-VIII; USA: Oreg., Calif., Rocky Mts., SW, SC, Kans. ; Mex.

Anethum L. -n- :*Apiaceae* · I (-2) spp. · G:Dill; E:Dill; F:Aneth
– **graveolens** L.
– var. **graveolens** · G:Acker-Dill · ⊙ Z8 VII-IX; SW-As, Ind., ? N-Afr, nat. in Eur.* exc. BrI, Sc; N-Am.
– var. **hortorum** Alef. · G:Garten-Dill · ⊙ Z8 VII-VIII ⚥ Ⓝ; cult.
– :*sowa* hort. = Anethum graveolens var. hortorum

Angelica L. -f- :*Apiaceae* · c. 110 spp. · E:Archangel; F:Angélique; G:Engelwurz
– **archangelica** L. · G:Arznei-Engelwurz
– subsp. **archangelica** · E:Archangel, Garden Angelica; G:Echte Arznei-Engelwurz · ⚃ Z4 VI-VIII ⚥ ; Eur.: Sc, NL, C-Eur., EC-Eur., E-Eur.; Cauc., W-Sib., nat. in

BrI, F, Ital-P, Ba
- var. *sativa* (Mill.) Rikli = Angelica archangelica subsp. archangelica
- **palustris** (Besser) Hoffm. · G:Sumpf-Engelwurz · ⊙ VII-VIII ▽; Eur.: C-Eur., EC-Eur., Serb., Montenegro, E-Eur.; W-Sib., E-Sib., C-As.
- **pyrenaea** (L.) Spreng. · G:Pyrenäen-Engelwurz · ⊙ VI-IX; Eur.: sp., F; NW-Sp., Vosges
- **sylvestris** L. · E:Wild Angelica; G:Gewöhnliche Wald-Engelwurz · ⧫ Z7 VII-IX ⚥ Ⓝ; Eur.*; TR, Cauc., W-Sib., E-Sib.

Angelonia Bonpl. -f- :Scrophulariaceae · 25 spp.
- **angustifolia** Benth. · E:Narrowleaf Angelon · ⧫ Z9 Ⓜ VII-X; Mex., C-Am., trop. S-Am.
- **cornigera** Hook. · ⊙ Z9 Ⓜ VII-VIII; Braz.
- **gardneri** Hook. · ⧫ ♄ e Z9 Ⓜ VII-VIII; Braz.
- **salicariifolia** Humb. & Bonpl. · E:Willowleaf Angelon · ⧫ Z9 Ⓜ VII-X; W.Ind., trop. S-Am.

Angiopteris Hoffm. -f- Marattiaceae · 146 spp. · E:Turnip Fern; F:Fougère arborescente; G:Bootfarn
- **evecta** (G. Forst.) Hoffm. · E:Giant Fern, King Fern, Turnip Fern; G:Bootfarn · ⧫ Z10 Ⓜ; Madag., Ind., Sri Lanka, Jap., N-Austr., Polyn.

Angophora Cav. -f- Myrtaceae · 13 spp. · E:Gum Myrtle; G:Gummimyrte
- **floribunda** (Sm.) Sweet · E:Rough-barked Apple · ♄ e Z9 Ⓚ; Austr.: Queensl., N.S.Wales, Victoria

Angostura Roem. & Schult. -f- Rutaceae · 30 spp.
- **trifoliata** (Willd.) T.S. Elias · E:Angostura; G:Angostura · ♄ e Ⓜ ⚥; Col.

Angraecum Bory -n- Orchidaceae · 222 spp.
- *articulatum* Rchb. f. = Aerangis articulata
- *citratum* Thouars = Aerangis citrata
- **eburneum** Bory
- subsp. **eburneum** · ⧫ Z10 Ⓜ XI-I ▽ ✳; Maskarene Is.
- subsp. **superbum** (Thouars) H. Perrier · ♄ Z10 Ⓜ XI-I ▽ ✳; Madag.

- **eichlerianum** Kraenzl. · ♄ Z10 Ⓜ IX ▽ ✳; Cameroon, Nigeria, Gabon, Zaire, Angola
- *ellisii* Rchb. f. = Aerangis ellisii
- *falcatum* (Thunb.) Lindl. = Neofinetia falcata
- *hyaloides* Rchb. f. = Aerangis hyaloides
- *kotschyanum* Rchb. f. = Aerangis kotschyana
- *kotschyi* Rchb. f. = Aerangis kotschyana
- *modestum* Hook. f. = Aerangis modesta
- **sesquipedale** Thouars · E:Comet Orchid, Star of Bethlehem Orchid; G:Kometen-orchidee · ♄ Z10 Ⓜ XII-II ▽ ✳; Madag.
- *superbum* Thouars = Angraecum eburneum subsp. superbum

Anguloa Ruiz & Pav. -f- Orchidaceae · 11 sp. · E:Cradle Orchid, Tulip Orchid; F:Anguloa; G:Nussmaul, Tulpenorchidee
- **brevilabris** Rolfe · ⧫ Z10 Ⓜ VI ▽ ✳; Col.
- **cliftonii** Rolfe · ⧫ Z10 Ⓜ ▽ ✳; Col.
- **clowesii** Lindl. · ⧫ Z10 Ⓜ V-VII ▽ ✳; Col., Venez.
- × **ruckeri** Lindl. (A. clowesii × A. hohenlohii) · ⧫ Z10 Ⓜ V-VI ▽ ✳; Col.
- **uniflora** Ruiz & Pav. · ⧫ Z10 Ⓜ V-VII ▽ ✳; Col., Ecuad., Peru, Venez.
- *virginalis* Lindl. = Anguloa uniflora

× **Angulocaste** hort. -f- Orchidaceae (Anguloa × Lycaste)

Anhalonium Lem. = Ariocarpus
- *fissuratum* (Engelm.) Engelm. = Ariocarpus fissuratus var. fissuratus
- *furfuraceum* (S. Watson) J.M. Coult. = Ariocarpus retusus
- *kotschoubeanum* Lem. = Ariocarpus kotschoubeyanus
- *lewinii* Henn. = Lophophora williamsii var. lutea
- *trigonum* F.A.C. Weber = Ariocarpus trigonus
- *williamsii* (Lem. ex Salm-Dyck) Rümpler = Lophophora williamsii var. williamsii

Anigozanthos Labill. -m- Haemodoraceae · 11 sp. · E:Kangaroo Paw; F:Fleur-de-kangourou; G:Kängurublume, Kängurup-fote, Spaltlilie
- **flavidus** DC. · E:Tall Kangaroo Paw; G:Große Kängurupfote · ⧫ Z9 Ⓚ V-VI; W-Austr.
- **gabrielae** Domin · E:Dwarf Kangaroo

Paw · ♃ Z9 Ⓚ V-VI; W-Austr.
- *grandiflorus* Salisb. = Anigozanthos flavidus
- **humilis** Lindl. · E:Common Cats Paw; G:Horstbildende Kängurupfote · ♃ Z9 Ⓚ V-VI; W-Austr.
- **manglesii** D. Don · E:Red and Green Kangaroo Paw; G:Riemenblättrige Kängurupfote · ♃ Z9 Ⓚ V-VI; W-Austr.
- **pulcherrimus** Hook. · E:Yellow Kangaroo Paw; G:Gelbe Kängurupfote · ♃ Z9 Ⓚ V-VI; W-Austr.
- **rufus** Labill. · E:Red Kangaroo Paw; G:Rote Kängurupfote · ♃ Z9 Ⓚ V-VI; W-Austr.
- **viridis** Lindl. · E:Green Kangaroo Paw; G:Grüne Kängurupfote · ♃ Z9 Ⓚ V-VI; W-Austr.

Anisantha K. Koch = Bromus
- *sterilis* (L.) Nevski = Bromus sterilis
- *tectorum* (L.) Nevski = Bromus tectorum

Anisodontea C. Presl -f- *Malvaceae* · 19 spp.
- **capensis** (L.) D.M. Bates · E:Cape African Queen · ♄ e Z9 Ⓚ VI-IX; S-Afr.
- **scabrosa** (L.) D.M. Bates · E:Pink Mallow · ♄ e Z9 Ⓚ; Cape

Annona L. -f- *Annonaceae* · 137 spp. · E:Custard Apple; F:Anone, Cachiman, Chérimolier, Corossol; G:Anone, Vanilleapfel, Zimtapfel
- **cherimola** Mill. · E:Cherimoya, Custard Apple; G:Rahmapfel · ♄ d Z9 Ⓦ Ⓝ; Ecuad., Peru, nat. in Trop., Subtrop.
- **diversifolia** Saff. · ♄ Z9 Ⓚ Ⓝ; S-Mex., C-Am., nat. in Fla.
- **glabra** L. · G:Wasserapfel; E:Pondapple · ♄ e Z9 Ⓦ Ⓝ; USA: S-Fla.; trop. Am., W-Afr.
- **montana** Macfad. · E: Mountain Soursop; G:Schleimapfel · ♄ Z9 Ⓦ Ⓝ; C-Am., W.Ind.
- **muricata** L. · E:Prickly Custard Apple, Sour Sop; G:Sauersack, Stachliger Rahmapfel · ♄ e Z9 Ⓦ Ⓝ; S-Mex., C-Am., W.Ind., trop. S-Am.
- **purpurea** Moq. & Sessé ex Dunal · ♄ Z9 Ⓦ Ⓝ; S-Mex., C-Am., W.Ind.
- **reticulata** L. · E:Bullock's Heart, Custard Apple; G:Netzapfel, Ochsenherz · ♄ d Z9 Ⓦ Ⓝ; Mex., W.Ind.
- **squamosa** L. · E:Custard Apple, Sweet Sop; G:Süßsack, Zimtapfel · ♄ s Z9 Ⓦ ⚕ Ⓝ; C-Am., W.Ind., nat. in Fla.
- *triloba* L. = Asimina triloba

Anoda Cav. -f- *Malvaceae* · 23 spp.
- **cristata** (L.) Schltdl. · E:Crested Anoda · ⊙ ♃ Z9; SW-USA, Mex., W.Ind., trop. S-Am.
- **wrightii** A. Gray · E:Lanceleaf Anoda · ⊙ Z9; USA: N.Mex., S-Ariz.; Mex.

Anoectochilus Blume -m- *Orchidaceae* · 48 spp.
- *regalis* Blume = Anoectochilus setaceus
- **setaceus** Blume · ♃ Z10 Ⓦ IV-VI ▽ ✱; Sri Lanka
- **sikkimensis** King & Pantl. · ♃ Z10 Ⓦ ▽ ✱; Ind.: Sikkim

× **Anoectomaria** Rolfe -f- *Orchidaceae* (*Anoectochilus* × *Ludisia*)

Anogeissus (DC.) Wall. -m- *Combretaceae* · 8 spp.
- **latifolia** (Roxb. ex DC.) Wall. ex Bedd. · E:Gum Ghatti; G:Knopfbaum · ♄ d Ⓦ Ⓝ; Ind., Sri Lanka

Anogramma Link -f- *Adiantaceae* · 7 spp. · E:Jersey Fern; F:Anogramma; G:Nacktfarn
- **leptophylla** (L.) Link · E:Jersey Fern; G:Dünner Nacktfarn · ♃ Z9 Ⓚ III-IV; Eur.: Ib, Fr, Sw, Ital-P, Ba, Crim; TR, Levant, Cauc., Ind., Austr., NW-Afr., Libya, S-Afr., N-Am
- *schizophylla* (Baker ex Jenman) Diels = Pityrogramma schizophylla

Anomatheca Ker-Gawl. -f- *Iridaceae* · 6 spp.
- **grandiflora** Baker · ♃ Ⓚ IV-V; S-Afr.
- **laxa** (Thunb.) Goldblatt · ♃ Ⓚ IV-VI; S-Afr.
- **verrucosa** (Vogel) Goldblatt · ♃ Ⓚ IV-V; Cape

Anredera Juss. -f- *Basellaceae* · 9 spp. · E:Madeira Vine; F:Vigne de Madeire; G:Resedenwein
- **baselloides** (Humb., Bonpl. & Kunth) Baill. · ♃ ≹
- *baselloides* hort. = Anredera cordifolia
- **cordifolia** (Ten.) Steenis · E:Madeira Vine; G:Resedenwein · ♃ ≹ Z9 Ⓚ Ⓝ;

Parag., S-Braz., N-Arg., nat. in Ib, F, Malta

Ansellia Lindl. -f- *Orchidaceae* · 1 sp.
– **africana** Lindl. · ♭ Z9 ⓜ XII-I ▽ ✳;
W-Afr.
– *gigantea* Rchb. f. = Ansellia africana
– var. *nilotica* N.E. Br. = Ansellia africana

× **Ansidium** hort. -n- *Orchidaceae* (*Ansellia*
× *Cymbidium*)

Antelaea Gaertn. = Azadirachta
– *azadirachta* (L.) Adelb. = Azadirachta
indica subsp. indica

Antennaria Gaertn. -f- *Asteraceae* · c.
70 spp. · E:Cat's Ears, Pussy-Toes; F:Pied-
de-chat; G:Katzenpfötchen
– **alpina** (L.) Gaertn. · E:Alpine Pussytoes;
G:Alpen-Katzenpfötchen · ⁴ ⤳ △ Z2
VII-VIII; Eur.: Sc, N-Russ.
– *candida* Greene = Antennaria dioica var.
borealis
– **carpatica** (Wahlenb.) Bluff & Fingerh. ·
G:Karpaten-Katzenpfötchen · ⁴ Z2 VI-
VIII; Eur.: Ib, Fr, C-Eur., Ital-P, EC-Eur.,
RO, W-Russ.; Pyr., Alp., Carp.
– *cinnamomea* DC. = Anaphalis margaritacea var. cinnamomea
– **dioica** (L.) Gaertn.
– var. **borealis** E.G. Camus · G:Filziges
Katzenpfötchen · ⁴ ⤳ △ Z5 V-VI;
subarct. Zone
– var. **dioica** · E:Cat's Foot; F:Patte de
chat, Pied de chat; G:Gewöhnliches
Katzenpfötchen · ⁴ ⤳ Z5 VI-VI ⚥ Ⓝ ▽;
Eur.*, Cauc., TR, Sib., Mong., Amur,
N-Jap., Sakhal.
– *margaritacea* R. Br. = Anaphalis margaritacea var. margaritacea
– **neglecta** Greene
– var. **attenuata** (Fernald) Cronquist · ⁴
⤳ △ V-VI; Alaska, Can., USA: NE, NCE,
NW, SW; Mex.
– var. **neglecta** · E:Field Pussytoes;
G:Feld-Katzenpfötchen · ⁴; Alaska, Can.:
W; USA: NE, NCE, NC, SW, Rocky Mts.,
Calif.
– **neodioica** Greene · E:Lesser Cat's Foot;
G:Kanadisches Katzenpfötchen · ⁴ Z2;
Can.
– **parvifolia** Nutt. · E:Little Leaf Pussytoes;
F:Camomille à petites fleurs; G:Kleinblät-
triges Katzenpfötchen · ⁴ ⤳ △ Z3 V-VI;

Alaska, Can., USA: NCE, NC, SW, Rocky
Mts., NW; Mex.
– **plantaginifolia** (L.) Hook. · E:Woman's
Tobacco; G:Wegerichblättriges
Katzenpfötchen · ⁴ ⤳ △ Z3 V-VI; Can.:
E; USA: NE, NCE, SC, SE
– *rupicola* Fernald = Antennaria neglecta
var. attenuata
– *tomentosa* G. Nicholson = Antennaria
dioica var. borealis

Anthemis L. -f- *Asteraceae* · 100-200 spp. ·
E:Chamomile, Dog Daisy, Dog Fennel;
F:Camomille; G:Färberkamille,
Hundskamille
– **altissima** L. · G:Höchste Hundskamille ·
⊙ Z6 VII-VIII Ⓝ; Eur.: Ib, Fr, Ital-P, Ba,
Crim; TR, Cauc., C-As., nat. in C-Eur.
– **arvensis** L. · E:Corn Chamomile;
G:Acker-Hundskamille · ⊙ ⊙ V-X; Eur.*,
TR, Cauc., Iran, nat. in N-Am., S-Am.,
Austr., NZ
– **austriaca** Jacq. · E:Austrian Chamomile;
G:Österreichische Hundskamille · ⊙ ⊙
VII-VIII; Eur.: A, I, EC-Eur., Ba, E-Eur.;
TR, Cauc.
– **carpatica** Waldst. & Kit. ex Willd. ·
E:Carpathian Dog Daisy; G:Karpaten-
Hundskamille · ⁴ △ VII-VIII; Eur.: Ib,
Ital-P, C-Eur., Ba, PL, E-Eur.; NW-TR;
mts.
– **cinerea** Pančić · ⁴ △ Z7 ⋏ VI-VIII; Eur.:
E-Pyr., Serb., Maced., AL, BG
– *cota* auct. = Anthemis altissima
– **cotula** L. · E:Mayweed, Stinking Chamomile; G:Stinkende Hundskamille · ⊙ Z5
VI-X ⚥ Ⓝ; Eur.*, TR, Levant, Cauc., Iraq,
Iran, N-Afr., Eth., nat. in N-Am., S-Am.,
Austr., NZ
– **cretica** L. · E:Mountain Dog Daisy · ⁴ △
Z6 VI-VII; Eur.: ? sp., F, I, Ba, RO; TR,
Lebanon, Cauc.
– **haussknechtii** Boiss. & Reut. · ⁴ △ Z7
VI-VII; S-TR, Syr., Iraq, Iran
– **marschalliana** Willd. · F:Camomille
argentée; G:Anatolische Hundskamille ·
⁴ △ Z7 ⋏ V-VII; TR mts., Cauc.
– *montana* L. = Anthemis cretica
– *nobilis* L. = Chamaemelum nobile
– *orientalis* (L.) Degen = Anthemis
pectinata
– subsp. *montana* Hayek = Anthemis
cretica
– **pectinata** (Bory & Chaub.) Boiss. &
Reut. · ⁴; GR, eur. TR

– *pyrethrum* L. = Anacyclus pyrethrum var. pyrethrum
– *rudolfiana* Adams = Anthemis marschalliana
– **ruthenica** M. Bieb. · G:Ruthenische Hundskamille · ☉ V-VIII; Eur.: C-Eur., EC-Eur., Ba, E-Eur; Cauc..
– **sancti-johannis** Stoj. & Turrill · E:Roman Chamomile; G:Bulgarische Hundskamille · ⅄ Z7 ∧ VI-VIII; Eur.: I, Ba, nat. in A
– **segetalis** Ten. · ☉; Eur.: I, Ba, nat. in A
– **tinctoria** L. · E:Dyer's Chamomile, Yellow Chamomile; F:Camomille des teinturiers; G:Färber-Hundskamille · ⅄ ✂ Z6 VI-IX; Eur.* exc. BrI, Ib; TR, Syr., Cauc., Iran, nat. in BrI
– **some cultivars**
– **triumfettii** (L.) DC. · G:Trionfettis Hundskamille · ⅄ Z7 VII-VIII; Eur.: Ib, Fr, Ital-P, Ba, Sw, RO; TR, Cauc.

Anthericum L. -n- *Anthericaceae* · 7 spp. · E:Spider Plant; F:Phalangère; G:Graslilie, Zaunlilie
– *bichetii* Karrer = Chlorophytum laxum
– **liliago** L. · E:St Bernard's Lily; F:Phalangère faux-lis;G:Astlose Graslilie · ⅄ Z7 V-VI ▽; Eur.* exc. BrI; TR
– **ramosum** L. · E:Branched St Bernard's Lily; F:Phalangère rameuse; G:Ästige Graslilie · ⅄ Z7 VI-VIII ▽; Eur.* exc. BrI; Cauc.

Antholyza L. = Babiana
– *aethiopica* L. = Chasmanthe aethiopica
– *caffra* Ker-Gawl. ex Baker = Tritoniopsis caffra
– *cunonia* L. = Gladiolus cunonius
– *paniculata* Klatt = Crocosmia paniculata

Anthoxanthum L. -n- *Poaceae* · 15-20 spp. · E:Vernal Grass; F:Flouve; G:Ruchgras
– **alpinum** Á. Löve & D. Löve · G:Alpen-Ruchgras, Japanisches Ruchgras · ⅄ V-VII; Eur.: N, mts.; TR, Cauc., Iran, W-Sib., E-Sib., C-As., Mong., ? N-Am.
– **aristatum** Boiss. · E:Annual Vernal Grass, Small Sweet Vernal Grass; G:Grannen-Ruchgras · ☉ Z7 V-VII; Eur.: Ib, Fr, Ital-P, Ba; Canar., Madeira, nat. in BrI, G, DK, PL, Balt., N-Am.
– *nipponicum* Honda = Anthoxanthum alpinum
– **odoratum** L. · E:Scented Vernal Grass; F:Flouve odorante; G:Gewöhnliches Ruchgras · ⅄ D V-VI ⚘ Ⓝ; Eur.*, TR, Cauc., W-Sib., E-Sib., C-As., NW-Afr., Greenl., nat. in N-Am., Austr., Tasman.

Anthriscus Pers. -m- *Apiaceae* · 12 spp. · E:Chervil; F:Cerfeuil; G:Kerbel
– **caucalis** M. Bieb. · E:Bur Chervil; G:Hunds-Kerbel · ☉ Z7 V-VI; Eur.*, TR, Syr., Cyprus, Cauc., NW-Afr., nat. in N-Am., NZ
– **cerefolium** (L.) Hoffm.
– var. **cerefolium** · E:Garden Chervil; G:Echter Garten-Kerbel · ☉ Z7 V-VIII ⚘ Ⓝ; cult.
– var. *sativus* (Lam.) Endl. = Anthriscus cerefolium var. cerefolium
– var. **trichocarpa** · G:Wilder Garten-Kerbel · ☉ Z7 VI; Eur., TR, N-Iraq, Cauc., Iran, C-As., NW-Afr., Libya
– **nitida** (Wahlenb.) Hazsl. · G:Glanz-Kerbel · ⅄ Z7 VI-VIII; Eur.: Fr, Ital-P, C-Eur., EC-Eur., Ba; mts.
– **sylvestris** (L.) Hoffm. · E:Cow Parsley, Queen Anne's Lace; G:Gewöhnlicher Wiesen-Kerbel · ⅄ V-VII Ⓝ; Eur.*, Cauc., Sib., N-Afr., Eth.,, nat. in N-Am.
– *trichospermus* Spreng. non Pers. = Anthriscus cerefolium var. trichocarpa

Anthurium Schott -n- *Araceae* · 744 spp. · E:Flamingo Flower, Tail Flower; F:Anthurium; G:Flamingoblume, Schwanzblume, Schweifblume
– **acaule** (Jacq.) Schott · ⅄ Z10 ⌂; W.Ind.
– **andraeanum** Linden ex André · E:Flamingo Flower; G:Große Flamingoblume · ⅄ Z10 ⌂; Col.
– **bakeri** Hook. f. · ⅄ ⚭ Z10 ⌂; C-Am., Col.
– **bellum** Schott · ♄ Z10 ⌂; Braz.
– **bogotense** Schott · ♄ Z10 ⌂; Col.
– × *carneum* L. Linden & Rodigas = Anthurium × ferrierense
– **clavigerum** Poepp. · ♄ ⚘ Z10 ⌂; Col.
– **corrugatum** Sodiro · ♄ Z10 ⌂; Col., Ecuad.
– **crassinervium** (Jacq.) Schott · ⅄ Z10 ⌂; Venez.
– **crystallinum** Linden & André · E:Crystal Anthurium; G:Kristall-Schweifblume · ⅄ D Z10 ⌂; Panama, Col., Ecuad., Peru
– × *cultorum* Birdsey = Anthurium × ferrierense
– **digitatum** (Jacq.) G. Don · ♄ Z10 ⌂; Venez.

– **dolichostachyum** Sodiro · ♄ Z10 ⊛;
Braz.
– *ellipticum* K. Koch & C.D. Bouché =
Anthurium crassinervium
– *erythrocarpum* Sodiro = Anthurium
dolichostachyum
– × **ferrierense** Mast. & T. Moore (*A.
andraeanum* × *A. nymphaeifolium*) · ⑭
Z10 ⊛; cult.
– *fissum* K. Koch ex Regel = Anthurium
palmatum
– **forgetii** N.E. Br. · ♄ D Z10 ⊛; Col.
– **galeottii** K. Koch · ⑭ Z10 ⊛; S-Braz.
– **harrisii** (Graham) G. Don · ♄ Z10 ⊛;
Braz.
– **hookeri** Kunth · ♄ Z10 ⊛; Lesser
Antilles, Trinidad, Surinam
– × *hortulanum* Birdsey = Anthurium
scherzerianum
– **insigne** Mast. · ♄ ⚡ Z10 ⊛; Col., Ecuad.
– *kalbreyeri* Mast. = Anthurium clavigerum
– **leuconeurum** Lem. · ♄ Z10 ⊛; Mex.
– **macrolobum** W. Bull (*A. leuconeurum* ×
A. pedatoradiatum) · ♄ Z10 ⊛; Braz.
– **magnificum** Linden · ♄ Z10 ⊛; Col.
– **nymphaeifolium** K. Koch & C.D.
Bouché · ♄ Z10 ⊛; Venez., Col.
– **obtusum** (Engl.) Grayum · ♄ Z10 ⊛;
Braz.
– *ornatum* Schott = Anthurium nymphaeifolium
– **palmatum** (L.) G. Don · ♄ Z10 ⊛; W.Ind.
– *papillosum* Markgr. = Anthurium corrugatum
– **paraguayense** Engl. · ⑭ Z10 ⊛; Parag.
– **pedatoradiatum** Schott · ♄ Z10 ⊛; Mex.
– **radicans** K. Koch & Haage · ♄ ⚡ Z10 ⊛;
? S-Braz.
– **regale** Linden · ♄ Z10 ⊛; Peru
– **scandens** (Aubl.) Engl. · E:Pearl
Laceleaf · ♄ ⚡ ⊗ Z10 ⊛; S-Mex., C-Am.,
W.Ind., trop. S-Am.
– **scherzerianum** Schott · G:Kleine
Flamingoblume · ♄ Z10 ⊛ ✿; Guat.,
Costa Rica
– **signatum** K. Koch & L. Mathieu · ♄ Z10
⊛; Venez.
– **subsignatum** Schott · ♄ Z10 ⊛; Costa
Rica
– **veitchii** Mast. · ♄ Z10 ⊛; Col.
– **warocqueanum** T. Moore · ♄ Z10 ⊛;
Col.
– **wendlingeri** G.M. Barroso · ⑭ ⚡ ⊗ Z10
⊛; Costa Rica

Anthyllis L. -f- *Fabaceae* · c. 25 spp. ·
E:Kidney Vetch; F:Anthyllis; G:Wundklee
– **barba-jovis** L. · E:Jupiter's Beard · ♄ e Z8
⌂ III-V; Eur.: Ib, Fr, Ital-P, Ba
– **hermanniae** L. · ♄ ♄ e △ Z6-7 V-VI; Eur.:
Ib, Ital-P, Ba; TR
– **montana** L.
– subsp. **jacquinii** (A. Kern.) Hayek ·
G:Jacquins Wundklee · ⑭ Z7 VI; Eur.:
E-Alp., mts. Ba
– subsp. **montana** · G:Berg-Wundklee · ⑭
△ Z7 VI-VIII; Eur.: F, Ital-P, Ba, C-Eur.,
Alp., Apenn.
– **vulneraria** L. · E:Kidney Vetch, Ladies'
Fingers; G:Gewöhnlicher Wundklee ·
⑭ Z7 V-VI ⚡ Ⓝ; Eur.*, TR, Syr., Palest.,
N-Afr., Eth.
– **webbiana** Hook. · ⑭ ⌂; Madeira

Antiaris Lesch. -f- *Moraceae* · 6 spp. ·
E:Upas Tree; F:Arbre à upas; G:Upas-
baum
– **toxicaria** (Pers.) Lesch. · E:Upas Tree;
G:Upasbaum · ♄ d Z10 ⊛ ✿ Ⓝ; trop.
Afr., Ind., Sri Lanka, Malay. Arch., Phil.,
Fiji

Antidesma L. -n- *Euphorbiaceae* · 154 spp.
– **bunius** (L.) Spreng. · E:Bignay, Chinese
Laurel; G:Salamanderbaum · ♄ e Z10
⊛ Ⓝ; Him., Ind., Sri Lanka, SW-China,
Malay. Arch., Phil., Austr.: Queensl.

Antigonon Endl. -n- *Polygonaceae* · 3 spp. ·
E:Coral Vine; F:Liane corail; G:Mexikani-
scher Knöterich, Korallenwein
– **leptopus** Hook. & Arn. · E:Chain of
Love, Coral Vine, Mexican Creeper;
G:Dünnstieliger Korallenwein · ♄ ⚡ Z10
⊛ VII-VIII; W-Mex.

Antirrhinum L. -n- *Scrophulariaceae* ·
42 spp. · E:Snapdragon; F:Gueule-de-
loup, Muflier; G:Löwenmaul
– *bellidifolium* L. = Anarrhinum bellidifolium
– **braun-blanquetii** Rothm. · ⑭ Z8 ⌂;
Eur.: N-P, N-Sp.
– **hispanicum** Chav. · ⑭ △ Z7 ∧ VII-IX;
SE-Sp., Moroc.
– **latifolium** Mill. · E:Large Snapdragon;
G:Breitblättriges Löwenmaul · ⑭ Z7;
Eur.: I, F, NE-Ital-P
– **majus** L.
– **many cultivars**

– subsp. **majus** · E:Snapdragon; F:Gueule-
de-loup, Muflier; G:Garten-Löwenmaul,
Großes Löwenmaul · ☉ ⏚ ✕ Z7 VI-IX ⚥ ;
Eur.: Ib, F„ nat. in Eur.
– **molle** L. · ⏚ △ Z7 ⌂ ∧ VII-IX; Eur.: N-P,
N-Sp.

Anubias Schott -f- *Araceae* · 8 spp.
– **afzelii** Schott · ⏚ ⏦ Z10 ⓦ; W-Afr.
– **barteri** Schott
  – var. **barteri** · ⏚ Z10 ⓦ; W-Afr.,
  Cameroon, Gabun
  – var. **glabra** N.E. Br. · ⏚ ⏦ Z10 ⓦ;
  S-Nigeria, Cameroon, Gabon
  – var. **nana** (Engl.) Crusio · ⏚ ⏦ Z10 ⓦ;
  Cameroon
– *congensis* N.E. Br. = Anubias heterophylla
– **heterophylla** Engl. · ⏚ ⏦ Z10 ⓦ; trop.
  Afr.
– *lanceolata* hort. = Anubias afzelii
– *lanceolata* N.E. Br. = Anubias barteri var.
  glabra
– *nana* Engl. = Anubias barteri var. nana

Apera Adans. -f- *Poaceae* · 3 spp. · E:Silky
Bent; G:Windhalm
– **interrupta** (L.) P. Beauv. · E:Dense Silky
Bent; G:Unterbrochener Windhalm · ☉
Z6 VI-VII; Eur.*, TR, Cauc., Iran, Afgh.,
Pakist., C-As., NW-Afr.
– **spica-venti** (L.) P. Beauv. · E:Loose Silky
Bent; G:Gewöhnlicher Windhalm · ☉ Z6
VI-VII; Eur.*, W-Sib.

Aphananthe Planch. -f- *Ulmaceae* · 5 spp.
– **aspera** (Blume) Planch. · ⏛ ⏚ d Z7 IV-V;
Jap., Korea, E-China

Aphanes L. -f- *Rosaceae* · 20 spp. ·
E:Parsley Piert; F:Alchémille des champs;
G:Ackerfrauenmantel, Sinau
– **arvensis** L. · E:Breakstone, Parsley Piert;
G:Gewöhnlicher Ackerfrauenmantel · ☉
V-IX ⚥ ; Eur.*, TR, Levant, Cauc., N-Iran,
Madeira, NW-Afr., nat. in N-Am., Austr.
– **inexspectata** W. Lippert · G:Kleinfrüchti-
ger Ackerfrauenmantel · ☉ V-IX; Eur.*
exc. Ital-P, Ba
– *microcarpa* auct. non (Boiss. & Reut.)
Rothm. = Aphanes inexspectata

Aphelandra R. Br. -f- *Acanthaceae* ·
175 spp. · E:Saffron Spike; F:Aphélandra;
G:Glanzkölbchen
– *atrovirens* N.E. Br. = Aphelandra

bahiensis
– **aurantiaca** (Scheidw.) Lindl.
  – var. **aurantiaca** · ⏚ e Z10 ⓦ; Mex.,
  C-Am., trop. S-Am.
  – var. **nitens** (Hook. f.) Wassh. · ⏚ e Z10 ⓦ
  IV-V; Col., Ecuad., Peru
  – var. **roezlii** Van Houtte
– **bahiensis** (Nees) Wassh. · ⏚ Z10 ⓦ;
  Braz.: Bahia
– **blanchetiana** (Nees) Hook. f. · ⏚ e Z10
  ⓦ VII-VIII; Braz.: Bahia
– **chamissoniana** Nees · ⏚ e Z10 ⓦ IX-X;
  S-Braz.
– *fascinator* Linden & André = Aphelandra
  aurantiaca var. aurantiaca
– **flava** Nees · ⏚ e Z10 ⓦ IX-X; Col.
– *fuscopunctata* Markgr. = Aphelandra flava
– *leopoldii* (Van Houtte) Lowe = Aphelandra squarrosa
– **liboniana** Linden ex Hook. f. · ⏚ e Z10 ⓦ
  IV-VI; Braz.
– *maculata* (Tafalla ex Nees) Voss =
  Stenandrium lindenii
– *nitens* Hook. f. = Aphelandra aurantiaca
  var. aurantiaca
– *punctata* hort. = Aphelandra aurantiaca
  var. aurantiaca
– *punctata* W. Bull = Aphelandra chamissoniana
– **sinclairiana** Nees · G:Rotes Glanzkölbchen · ⏚ e Z10 ⓦ IV-IX; Costa Rica,
  Panama
– **squarrosa** Nees · E:Saffron Spike, Zebra
  Plant; G:Glanzkölbchen · ⏚ e Z10 ⓦ ⏁
  VI-X; SE-Braz.
– **tetragona** (Vahl) Nees · G:Sparriges
  Glanzkölbchen · ⏚ e Z10 ⓦ VI-X; Venez.

Aphyllanthes L. -f- *Aphyllanthaceae* · 1 sp. ·
F:Aphyllanthe; G:Binsenlilie
– **monspeliensis** L. · G:Binsenlilie · ⏚ Z8
⌂; Eur.: , Ib, Fr, Ital-P; Moroc.

Apicra Willd. = Haworthia
– *deltoidea* (Hook. f.) Baker = Astroloba
  congesta
– *foliolosa* (Haw.) Willd. = Astroloba
  foliolosa
– *pentagona* (Aiton) Willd. = Astroloba
  spiralis
– *rubriflora* L. Bolus = Poellnitzia rubriflora
– *spiralis* (L.) Baker = Astroloba spiralis

Apios Fabr. -f- *Fabaceae* · 10 spp. · E:Potato
Bean; F:Glycine tubéreuse; G:Erdbirne

– **americana** Medik. · E:Earthnut, Potato Bean; G:Amerikanische Erdbirne · ⭸ ⚥ D Z3 VII-IX Ⓝ; Can.: E; USA: NE, NCE, NC, Colo., SC, SE, Fla., nat. in I, F
– *tuberosa* Moench = Apios americana

Apium L. -n- *Apiaceae* · 20-30 spp. · E:Marshwort; F:Céleri; G:Sellerie
– **graveolens** L. · E:Celery; G:Echter Sellerie
– var. **dulce** (Mill.) Pers. · E:Celery; G:Bleich-Sellerie, Stiel-Sellerie · ⊙ Ⓝ; cult.
– var. **graveolens** · E:Wild Celery; G:Sumpf-Sellerie, Wilder Sellerie · ⊙ ⭸ ⌇ VII-IX ⚥ ; Eur.*, Cauc., TR, Levant, Iraq, Cauc., N-Iran, W-Him., Pakist., Canar., Madeira, N-Afr.
– var. **rapaceum** (Mill.) Gaudin · E:Celeriac, Turnip-rooted Celery; G:Knollen-Sellerie, Wurzel-Sellerie · Ⓝ; cult.
– var. **secalinum** Alef. · E:Chinese Celery; G:Schnitt-Sellerie · Ⓝ; cult.
– **inundatum** (L.) Rchb. f. · E:Lesser Marshwort; G:Flutender Sellerie · ⭸ VI-VII ▽; Eur.: Ib, Fr, BrI, I, G, Sc, PL
– **nodiflorum** (L.) Lag. · E:Fool's Water Cress; G:Knotenblütiger Sellerie · ⭸ VII-IX; Eur.: Ib, Fr, Ital-P, Ba, BrI, C-Eur., ? RO; TR, Iran, SW-As., C-As., N-Afr., nat. in N-Am., S-Am.
– **repens** (Jacq.) Lag. · E:Creeping Marshwort; G:Kriechender Sellerie · ⭸ VII-IX ▽; Eur.: Fr, C-Eur., EC-Eur., Russ., Ib, Ital-P, Sc

Aploleia Raf. = Callisia
– *monandra* (Sw.) H.E. Moore = Callisia monandra
– *multiflora* (M. Martens & Galeotti) H.E. Moore = Callisia multiflora

Apocynum L. -n- *Apocynaceae* · 4 spp. · E:Dogbane; F:Apocyn; G:Hundsgift
– **androsaemifolium** L. · E:Spreading Dogbane; G:Gewöhnliches Hundsgift · ⭸ Z4 VII-IX ⚘; Alaska, Can., USA* ; Mex.
– **cannabinum** L. · E:American Hemp; G:Amerikanisches Hundsgift · ⭸ Z4 VII-IX ⚥ ⚘
– *venetum* A. DC. = Apocynum cannabinum
– **venetum** L. · ⭸ Z8 VI-VII ⚘ Ⓝ; Eur.: I, Ba, ? RO; TR, Cauc., Iran; coasts

Apollonias Nees -f- *Lauraceae* · 2 spp.
– **barbujana** (Cav.) Bornm. · ♄ d Ⓚ; Canar.
– *canariensis* Nees = Apollonias barbujana

Aponogeton L. f. -m- *Aponogetonaceae* · 52 spp. · E:Pondweed; F:Aponogeton; G:Wasserähre
– **bernierianus** (Decne.) Hook. f. · G:Berniers Wasserähre · ⭸ ≈ Z9 Ⓦ; E-Madag.
– **boivinianus** Baill. ex Jum. · G:Boivins Wasserähre · ⭸ ≈ Z10 Ⓦ IX-II; N-Madag.
– **crispus** Thunb. · G:Krause Wasserähre · ⭸ ≈ Z10 Ⓦ; Sri Lanka
– **desertorum** Zeyh. ex Spreng. · G:Ostafrikansiche Wasserähre · ⭸ ⌇ Z9 Ⓦ; E-Afr., S-Afr.
– **distachyos** L. f. · E:Cape Pondweed, Water Hawthorn; G:Kap-Wasserähre · ⭸ ≈ D Z9 Ⓚ; Cape, nat. in S-Austr., NZ, w. S-Am., W-Eur.
– **elongatus** F. Muell. ex Benth. · G:Langblättrige Wasserähre · ⭸ ≈ Z10 Ⓦ; N-Austr., E-Austr.
– *fenestralis* (Poir.) Hook. f. = Aponogeton madagascariensis
– *henkelianus* Falkenb. & Baum = Aponogeton madagascariensis
– *kraussianus* Hochst. = Aponogeton desertorum
– *leptostachyus* E. Mey. = Aponogeton desertorum
– **madagascariensis** (Mirb.) H. Bruggen · E:Lace Leaf; G:Gitterpflanze, Madagaskar-Wasserähre · ⭸ ≈ Z10 Ⓦ; Madag.
– **nudiflorus** Peter · G:Nacktblütige Wasserähre · ⭸ ≈ Z9 Ⓦ; E-Afr.
– **ulvaceus** Baker · G:Meersalatähnliche Wasserähre · ⭸ ≈ Z10 Ⓦ; Madag.
– **undulatus** Roxb. · G:Gewellte Wasserähre · ⭸ ≈ Z10 Ⓦ; SW-Ind. Sri Lanka, Malay. Arch., Austr.

Aporocactus Lem. -m- *Cactaceae* · 2 spp. · E:Rat's-Tail Cactus; F:Cactus-serpent, Queue-de-rat; G:Peitschenkaktus, Schlangenkaktus
– *conzattii* Britton & Rose = Aporocactus martianus
– **flagelliformis** (L.) Lem. · E:Rat's Tail Cactus; G:Peitschenkaktus · ⭙ ⚥ Z9 Ⓚ ▽ ✳; Mex. (Oaxaca)

– *leptophis* (DC.) Britton & Rose =
Aporocactus flagelliformis
– **martianus** (Zucc.) Britton & Rose ·
G:Schlangenkaktus · ♥ ⚜ Z8 ⓦ ▽ ✳;
Mex.: Oaxaca

× **Aporophyllum** hort. ex D.R. Hunt -n-
Cactaceae (*Aporocactus* × *Epiphyllum*)
– **Cultivars:**
– **many cultivars**

Aposeris Neck. ex Cass. -f- *Asteraceae* ·
1 sp. · F:Aposéris; G:Stinksalat
– **foetida** (L.) Less. · E:Heart-leaf Iceplant;
G:Hainsalat, Stinksalat · ⅃ △ VI-VII;
Eur.: ? sp., Fr, N-I, C-Eur., EC-Eur., Ba

Aptenia N.E. Br. -f- *Aizoaceae* · 4 spp.
– **cordifolia** (L. f.) N.E. Br. · E:Baby Sun
Rose · ♄ ♥ e Z8 ⓚ VII-IX; S-Afr., nat. in
S-Eur.

Aquilegia L. -f- *Ranunculaceae* · c.
80 spp. · E:Columbine, Granny's Bonnet;
F:Ancolie; G:Akelei
– *akitensis* Huth = Aquilegia flabellata var.
flabellata
– **alpina** L. · E:Alpine Columbine; G:Alpen-
Akelei · ⅃ △ Z5 V-VII ▽; Eur.: F, I, Sw, A;
Alp., Apenn.
– **amaliae** Heldr. ex Boiss. · ⅃ △ Z5 V ▽;
Eur.: Ba
– **atrata** W.D.J. Koch · E:Dark Columbine;
F:Ancolie; G:Schwarzviolette Akelei
noirâtre · ⅃ Z5 VI ▽; Eur.: F, I, C-Eur.,
Slove.; Alp., Apenn.
– *atropurpurea* Willd. = Aquilegia
viridiflora
– **bertolonii** Schott · ⅃ Z5 ▽; SE-F, NW-I
– **buergeriana** Siebold & Zucc. · ⅃ Z7 ▽;
Jap.
– **caerulea** James · E:Rocky Mountain
Columbine; G:Rocky-Mountain-Akelei ·
⅃ ≈ Z3 V-VI ▽; USA: Rocky Mts., N.Mex.
– **canadensis** L. · E:Meeting House, Red
Columbine; F:Ancolie du Canada; G:Rote
Akelei · ⅃ ≈ Z3 V-VI ▽; Can.: E, Sask.;
USA: NE, NCE, NC, SE, SC, Fla.
– **chrysantha** A. Gray · E:Golden Spurred
Columbine; F:Ancolie à fleur dorée;
G:Gold-Akelei · ⅃ ≈ Z3 VI-VIII ▽; USA:
Color., SW; N-Mex.
– **discolor** Levier & Leresche · ⅃ △ Z7 V
▽; N-Sp.
– **einseleana** F.W. Schultz · G:Einseles

Akelei, Kleinblütige Akelei · ⅃ △ Z5
VI-VII ▽; Eur.: I, C-Eur., Slove.; Alp.
– *elegantula* Greene = Aquilegia canadensis
– **flabellata** Siebold & Zucc.
– var. **flabellata** · E:Fan Columbine;
F:Ancolie du Japon; G:Kurilen-Akelei · ⅃
Z3 ▽; N-Jap., Sakhal.
– var. *nana* hort. = Aquilegia flabellata var.
pumila
– var. **pumila** (Huth) Kudô · G:Zwerg-
Akelei · ⅃ △ Z3 V ▽; Jap.
– **flavescens** S. Watson · E:Yellow
Columbine · ⅃ Z4 ▽; B.C., USA: NW,
Rocky Mts
– **formosa** Fisch. ex DC. · E:Western
Columbine; G:Schöne Akelei · ⅃ ≈ Z3
V-VII ▽; Alaska, Can.: B.C.; USA: NW,
Rocky Mts., Calif.
– **fragrans** Benth. · ⅃ Z7 ▽; W-Him.:
Pakist., W-Ind.
– **glandulosa** Fisch. ex Link
– var. **glandulosa** · ⅃ Z3 ▽; W-Sib., E-Sib.,
C-As., Mong., China: Sikiang
– var. **jucunda** (Fisch. & Avé-Lall.) Baker ·
⅃ △ Z3 V-VI ▽; Altai
– **grata** Malý ex Borbás · ⅃ △ Z6 V ▽;
Eur.: Bosn., Serb.
– **jonesii** Parry · E:Limestone Columbine;
G:Kalk-Akelei · ⅃ △ Z3 V ▽; Can.: Alta.;
USA: Rocky Mts.
– *jucunda* Fisch. & Avé-Lall. = Aquilegia
glandulosa var. jucunda
– **longissima** A. Gray ex S. Watson ·
E:Longspur Columbine · ⅃ ≈ D Z8 VI-VII
▽; USA: Tex., N.Mex.; Mex.
– *macrantha* Hook. & Arn. = Aquilegia
caerulea
– **micrantha** Eastw. · E:Mancos Columbine · ⅃ Z4 ▽; USA: Utah, Colo., Ariz.
– **nigricans** Baumg. · G:Dunkle Akelei ·
⅃ Z4 VI-VII ▽; Eur.: I, A, EC-Eur., Ba,
E-Eur.
– **olympica** Boiss. · ⅃ △ Z5 V ▽; Cauc.,
N-Iran
– **pyrenaica** DC. · E:Pyrenean Columbine;
G:Pyrenäen-Akelei · ⅃ △ Z5 IV-VI ▽;
Eur.: sp., F; Pyr.
– **scopulorum** Tidestr. · E:Utah Columbine
– subsp. *perplexans* Clokey = Aquilegia
scopulorum var. scopulorum
– var. **scopulorum** · ⅃ △ Z3 V-VI ▽; USA:
Wyo., Nev., Utah
– **shockleyi** Eastw. · ⅃ Z7 ▽; Calif., Nev.
– **sibirica** (L.) Lam. · ⅃ △ ≈ Z2 V-VI ▽;
W-Sib., E-Sib., C-As., Mong.

- **skinneri** Hook. · ⁴ ⋈ Z8 ∧ V-VII ▽;
  USA: N.Mex.: mts.
- **thalictrifolia** Schott & Kotschy · ⁴ △ Z7
  V-VI ▽; Eur.: N-I
- *viridiflora* Pall. · ⁴ Z3 ▽; E-Sib.,
  W-China
- **vulgaris** L.
- **many cultivars**
- var. **stellata** Schur · G:Spornlose Akelei ·
  ⁴ Z4; F, C-Eur., I, Slove.; Alp., Apenn.,
  Abruzz.
- var. **vulgaris** · E:Columbine, Granny's
  Bonnet; F:Ancolie vulgaire; G:Gewöhn-
  liche Akelei · ⁴ ⋈ Z4 V-VI ⚘ ▽; Eur.*
  exc. Sc; Canar., Madeira, Moroc., Alger.,
  nat. in Sc
- **Cultivars:**
- **many cultivars**

Arabidopsis Heynh. -f- *Brassicaceae* ·
c. 20 spp. · E:Thale Cress; F:Fausse-
arabette; G:Schmalwand
- **suecica** (Fr.) Norrl. · G:Schwedische
  Schmalwand · ☉ V-VI; Eur.: Sc, Russ., D
- **thaliana** (L.) Heynh. · E:Thale Cress;
  G:Acker-Schmalwand · ☉ IV-V; Eur.*,
  TR, Levant, Cauc., W-Sib., C-As., NW-
  Afr., Libya

Arabis L. -f- *Brassicaceae* · c. 120 spp. ·
E:Rockcress; F:Arabette, Corbeille
d'argent; G:Gänsekresse
- *albida* Steven ex Fisch. = Arabis caucasica
- **allionii** DC. · G:Sudeten-Gänsekresse ·
  ⁴ Z6 VI-VII; Eur.: Fr, Ital-P, C-Eur.,
  EC-Eur., Ba, W-Russ.; mts.
- **alpina** L. · E:Alpine Rock Cress; G:Alpen-
  Gänsekresse · ⁴ △ Z5 III-X; Eur.*, W-Sib.,
  E-Sib., Kamchat.
- subsp. *caucasica* (Willd.) Briq. = Arabis
  caucasica
- **androsacea** Fenzl · ⁴ ⌒ △ Z6 V-VI; TR
  (Cilician Taurus)
- × **arendsii** H.R. Wehrh. (*A. aubrietoides* ×
  A. caucasica) · ⁴ △ Z5 IV; cult.
- **aubrietoides** Boiss. · ⁴ △ Z6 IV; TR
  (Cilician Taurus)
- **auriculata** Lam. · G:Öhrchen-
  Gänsekresse · ☉ IV-V; Eur.* exc. BrI, Sc;
  TR, Levant, Cauc., Iran, ? Afgh., Him.,
  C-As., NW-Afr., Libya
- **bellidifolia** Crantz · G:Zwerg-
  Gänsekresse · ⁴
- subsp. **bellidifolia** · G:Gewöhnliche
  Zwerg-Gänsekresse · ⁴ VI-VIII

- subsp. **stellulata** (Bertol.) Greuter & Burdet · G:Sternhaarige Zwerg-Gänsekresse ·
  ⁴ VI-VIII; Eur.: F, I, C-Eur., W-Ba; mts.
- **blepharophylla** Hook. & Arn. · E:Rose
  Rock Cress · ⁴ △ Z7 ⌂ ∧ III-V; C-Calif.
- **bryoides** Boiss. · ⁴ ⌒ △ Z7 VI-VII; Eur.:
  Maced., AL, GR
- **caerulea** (All.) Haenke · E:Blue Arabis;
  G:Blaue Gänsekresse · ⁴ Z6 VII-VIII;
  Eur.: F, I, C-Eur., Slove.; Alp.
- **carduchorum** Boiss. · ⁴ △ Z6 VI-VII; TR,
  Cauc. (Armen.)
- **caucasica** Willd. · E:Garden Arabis,
  Snow on the Mountain, Variegated Wall
  Rock Cress; F:Arabette du Caucase;
  G:Kaukasische Gänsekresse · ⁴ △ Z4
  III-IV; Eur.: Sic., GR, Crete, BG; TR, Syr.,
  Cauc., Iran, C-As., Moroc., Alger.
- **ciliata** Clairv. · G:Doldige Gänsekresse ·
  ☉ ⁴; Eur.: Ib, Fr, C-Eur., EC-Eur., Ital-P,
  Ba, nat. in DK
- **collina** Ten. · E:Rosy Cress; G:Hügel-
  Gänsekresse, Mauer-Gänsekresse · ⁴ V;
  Eur.: Ib, F, Ital-P, Sw, Ba, nat. in B
- *corymbiflora* Vest = Arabis ciliata
- **ferdinandi-coburgii** Kellerer & Sünd. · ⁴
  △ Z7 IV-VI; Maced.
- **glabra** (L.) Bernh. · E:Tower Mustard;
  G:Kahle Gänsekresse, Turmkraut · ☉
  V-VII; Eur.*, TR, Cauc., Afgh., C-As.,
  Moroc., Alger.
- **hirsuta** (L.) Scop. · E:Hairy Rock Cress;
  G:Behaarte Gänsekresse · ☉ ⁴ V-VII;
  Eur.*, TR, Iraq, Cauc., Iran, W-Sib.,
  E-Sib., Amur, Moroc., Alger., nat. in
  China, N-Am.
- *jacquinii* Beck = Arabis soyeri subsp.
  subcoriacea
- × **kellereri** Sünd. (*A. bryoides* × *A.
  ferdinandi-coburgii*) · ⁴ Z6; cult.
- *muralis* Bertol. = Arabis collina
- *muricola* Jord. = Arabis collina
- **nemorensis** (Hoffm.) W.D.J. Koch ·
  G:Flachschotige Gänsekresse · ☉ V-VII;
  Eur.* exc. BrI, Sc
- **nova** Vill. · G:Felsen-Gänsekresse · ☉
  V-VI; Eur.: sp., I, Sw, A, Ba; Pyr., Alp.,
  Jura, Balkan
- **pauciflora** (Grimm) Garcke · G:Arm-
  blütige Gänsekresse, Wenigblütige
  Gänsekresse · ⁴ V-VII; Eur.: sp., Fr, Ital-P,
  C-Eur., EC-Eur., Slove., ? Bosn., Serb.
- **planisiliqua** (Pers.) Rich. · ☉; Eur.* exc.
  BrI, Sc
- **procurrens** Waldst. & Kit. · G:Ungarische

Gänsekresse · ⏀ △ Z5 IV-V; Eur.: Ba, RO;
mts.
– *pumila* Jacq. = Arabis bellidifolia subsp.
bellidifolia
– *rosea* DC. = Arabis collina
– **sagittata** (Bertol.) DC. · G:Pfeilblättrige
Gänsekresse · ⊙ V-VII; Eur.: Fr, Ital-P,
C-Eur., EC-Eur., Ba, E-Eur.; TR, Syr.,
N-Iran, Alger.
– **scopoliana** Boiss. · ⏀ ⌒ △ Z6 V; Eur.:
Slove., Croatia, Bosn.
– **serpillifolia** Vill. · ⊙ ⏀ Z6; Eur.: F, I, Sw,
Ba; mts.
– **soyeri** Reut. & A. Huet
– subsp. *jacquinii* (Beck) B.M.G. Jones =
Arabis soyeri subsp. subcoriacea
– subsp. **soyeri** · E:Rock Cress;
G:Glänzende Gänsekresse · ⏀ Z5 V-VIII;
Pyr.
– subsp. **subcoriacea** (Gren.) Breistr. ·
G:Sternhaar-Gänsekresse · ⏀ △ Z5 VI-VII;
Eur.: Alp., W-Carp.
– *stellulata* Desv. & Berthel. = Arabis
bellidifolia subsp. stellulata
– × **suendermannii** Kellerer ex Sünd. (*A.
ferdinandi-coburgii* × *A. procurrens*) · ⏀
⌒ △ Z6 IV-V; cult.
– **turrita** L. · E:Tower Cress; G:Turm-
Gänsekresse · ⊙ ⏀ Z6 IV-VI; Eur.* exc.
BrI, Sc; TR, Levant, Cauc., Alger.
– **vochinensis** Spreng. · G:Wocheiner
Gänsekresse · ⏀ ⤳ △ Z6 V; Eur.: I, A,
Slove.; SE-Alp.
– × **wilczekii** Sünd. (*A. bryoides* × *A.
carduchorum*) · ⏀ Z6; cult.

Arachis L. -f- Fabaceae · 22 spp. · E:Peanut;
F:Arachide, Cacahuète; G:Erdnuss
– **glabrata** Benth. · E:Rhizoma Peanut · ⏀
Z8 ⍟ Ⓝ; Braz., Arg., Bol.
– **hypogaea** L. · E:Groundnut, Monkey
Nut, Peanut; G:Erdnuss · ⊙ Z8 ▭ ♀ Ⓝ;
? Bol.

Arachniodes Blume -f- Dryopteridaceae ·
148 spp.
– **nipponica** (Rosenst.) Ohwi · ⏀ Z7 ⋀;
China, Jap.
– **standishii** (T. Moore) Ohwi · E:Upside-
down Fern · ⏀ Z7; Jap., Korea

Arachnis Blume -f- Orchidaceae · 11 sp. ·
E:Scorpion Orchid; F:Arachnanthe,
Fleur-araignée; G:Spinnenorchidee
– *lowii* (Lindl.) Rchb. f. = Dimorphorchis

lowii

Arachnites F.W. Schmidt = Ophrys

× **Arachnoglottis** hort. -f- Orchidaceae
(*Arachnis* × *Trichoglottis*)

× **Arachnopsis** hort. -f- Orchidaceae
(*Arachnis* × *Phalaenopsis*)

× **Arachnostylis** hort. -f- Orchidaceae
(*Arachnis* × *Rhynchostylis*)

Araeococcus Brongn. -m- Bromeliaceae ·
7 spp.
– **flagellifolius** Harms · ⏀ ⍟; Amazon.

Aralia L. -f- Araliaceae · 73 spp. · E:Angelica
Tree; F:Aralia; G:Angelikabaum, Aralie
– *balfouriana* Sander ex André = Polyscias
scutellaria
– **cachemirica** Decne. · ⏀ Z7 VI-VII;
Kashmir
– **californica** S. Watson · E:California
Spikenard, Elk Clover; G:Kalifornische
Aralie · ⏀ Z8 VII-VIII; USA: S-Oreg., Calif.
– *chabrieri* Van Geert = Cassine orientalis
– **chinensis** L. · E:Chinese Angelica Tree,
Chinese Angelica; F:Aralia de Chine;
G:Chinesische Aralie · ♄ d Z6 VIII-IX Ⓝ;
China
– var. *mandshurica* (Rupr. & Maxim.)
Rehder = Aralia elata var. mandshurica
– **cordata** Thunb. · E:Angelica Tree, Udo;
G:Herzförmige Aralie · ⏀ Z7 VI-VII Ⓝ;
China, Korea, Manch., Jap., Sakhal.
– *edulis* Siebold & Zucc. = Aralia cordata
– **elata** (Miq.) Seem.
– var. **elata** · E:Japanese Angelica
Tree; F:Angélique en arbre du Japon;
G:Japanische Aralie · ♄ ♄ Z5 VIII-X Ⓝ
– var. **mandshurica** (Rupr. & Maxim.) J.
Wen · G:Mandschurische Aralie
– *elegantissima* Veitch ex Mast. = Schefflera
elegantissima
– *filicifolia* C. Moore ex E. Fourn. =
Polyscias cumingiana
– *fruticosa* (L.) L.H. Bailey = Polyscias
fruticosa
– *guilfoylei* Bull. = Polyscias guilfoylei
– **hispida** Vent. · E:Bristly Sarsaparilla,
Dwarf Elder; G:Steifhaariger Angelikabaum · ♄ d Z3 VI-VII; Can.: E; USA:
NE, NCE, N.C.
– *japonica* Thunb. = Fatsia japonica

– *kerchoveana* Veitch ex P.W. Richards = Schefflera kerchoveana
– *mandshurica* Rupr. & Maxim. = Aralia elata var. mandshurica
– **nudicaulis** L. · E:American Sarsaparilla, Wild Sarsaparilla; F:Angélique à tige nue; G:Nacktstänglige Aralie · ⚁ Z4 VI-VII ⚥ ; Can., USA: NE, NCE, NC, SE, Rocky Mts., NW
– *nymphaeifolia* Hibberd = Oreopanax nymphaeifolius
– *papyrifera* Hook. = Tetrapanax papyrifer
– **racemosa** L. · E:American Spikenard, Life-of-Man; G:Amerikanische Aralie · ⚁ Z4 VII-VIII ⚥ ; Can.: E; USA: NE, NCE, NC, Rocky Mts., SW, SE, SC; Mex.
– *reticulata* Linden ex B.S. Williams = Meryta denhamii
– *schefflera* Spreng. = Schefflera digitata
– *sieboldii* K. Koch = Fatsia japonica
– **spinosa** L. · E:Devil's Walking Stick, Hercules' Club; F:Angélique épineuse; G:Herkuleskeule · ♄ ♄ d Z5 VII-VIII ⚘; USA: NE, NCE, SC, SE, Fla.
– *veitchii* Carrière = Schefflera veitchii

× **Aranda** hort. -f- *Orchidaceae* (*Arachnis × Vanda*)

× **Arandanthe** hort. -f- *Orchidaceae* (*Arachnis × Euanthe × Vanda*)

× **Aranthera** hort. -f- *Orchidaceae* (*Arachnis × Renanthera*)

Araucaria Juss. -f- *Araucariaceae* · 19 spp. · E:Monkey Puzzle; F:Araucaria; G:Araukarie, Zimmertanne
– **angustifolia** (Bertol.) Kuntze · E:Brazilian Pine, Candelabra Tree, Parana Pine; G:Kandelaber-Araukarie · ♄ e Z9 ⊛ Ⓝ; S-Braz., N-Arg. ; mts.
– **araucana** (Molina) K. Koch · E:Chile Pine, Monkey Puzzle; F:Araucaria du Chili, Bourreau des singes; G:Andentanne, Chilenische Araukarie · ♄ e Z8 ⊛ △ Ⓝ ▽ ✵; S-Chile, Patag.
– **bidwillii** Hook. · E:Bunya Bunya; G:Bunya-Bunya Baum, Queensland-Araukarie · ♄ e Z9 ⊛ Ⓝ; Austr.: SE-Queensl.
– *Braziliana* A. Rich. = Araucaria angustifolia
– **columnaris** (J.R. Forst.) Hook. · E:Cook Pine, New Caledonia Pine;

G:Neukaledonische Araukarie · ♄ e Z10 ⊛; N.Caled., Vanuatu
– *cookii* R. Br. ex Lindl. = Araucaria columnaris
– **cunninghamii** Aiton ex D. Don · E:Hoop Pine, Moreton Bay Pine; G:Neuguinea-Araukarie · ♄ e Z10 ⊛ Ⓝ; N.Guinea, Queensl.
– *excelsa* (Lamb.) R. Br. = Araucaria columnaris
– **heterophylla** (Salisb.) Franco · E:Norfolk Island Pine; G:Zimmertanne · ♄ e Z9 ⊛; Norfolk Is.
– *imbricata* Pav. = Araucaria araucana

Araujia Brot. -f- *Asclepiadaceae* · 4 spp.
– **sericifera** Brot. · E:Cruel Plant · ♄ e ⚑ Z9 ⊛ VII-IX Ⓝ; Peru, Arg, S-Braz., nat. in SW-Eur.

Arbutus L. -f- *Ericaceae* · 14 spp. · E:Manzanita, Strawberry Tree; F:Arbousier; G:Erdbeerbaum
– **andrachne** L. · E:Cyprus Strawberry Tree, Grecian Strawberry Tree; F:Arbousier; G:Östlicher Erdbeerbaum hybride de Chypre · ♄ ♄ e Z8 ⊛ III-IV; Eur.: AL, GR, Crete, Crim; TR, Levant
– × **andrachnoides** Link (*A. andrachne × A. unedo*) · E:Hybrid Strawberry Tree; F:Arbousier hybride de Chypre; G:Bastard-Erdbeerbaum · ♄ ♄ e Z8 ⊛ III-IV; Eur.: Ba
– **menziesii** Pursh · G:Madrone; E:Madrona, Madrone · ♄ e Z8 Ⓝ; B.C., USA: NW, Calif.; Mex: Baja Calif.
– **unedo** L. · E:Strawberry Tree; F:Arbousier commun; G:Westlicher Erdbeerbaum · ♄ ♄ e Z7 XI-XII ⚥ Ⓝ; Eur.: Ib, Fr, IRL, Ital-P, Ba; TR, Cyprus, Lebanon, Canar., NW-Afr.
– *uva-ursi* L. = Arctostaphylos uva-ursi

Arceuthos Antoine & Kotschy = Juniperus
– *drupacea* (Labill.) Antoine & Kotschy = Juniperus drupacea

Archangelica Wolf = Angelica
– *officinalis* (Moench) Hoffm. = Angelica archangelica subsp. archangelica
– *sativa* (Mill.) Besser = Angelica archangelica subsp. archangelica

Archontophoenix H. Wendl. & Drude -f- *Arecaceae* · 6 spp. · E:King Palm;

F:Palmier royal; G:Feuerpalme, Herrscherpalme
- **alexandrae** (F. Muell.) H. Wendl. & Drude · E:Alexandra Palm, King Palm; G:Alexandrapalme, Herrscherpalme · ♄ e Z10 ⓦ; Austr.: Queensl.
- **cunninghamiana** (H. Wendl.) H. Wendl. & Drude · E:Bangalow Palm, Piccabeen Palm; G:Feuerpalme · ♄ e Z10 ⓦ; Austr.: Queensl., N.S.Wales, S-Austr.

Arctanthemum (Tzvelev) Tzvelev -n- *Asteraceae* · 4 spp. · E:Arctic Chrysanthemum; G:Grönlandmargerite
- **arcticum** (L.) Tzvelev · E:Arctic Chrysanthemum; G:Grönlandmargerite · ♃ Z1 IX-X

Arcterica Coville = Pieris
- *nana* (Maxim.) Makino = Pieris nana

Arctium L. -n- *Asteraceae* · 10 spp. · E:Burdock; F:Bardane; G:Klette
- **lappa** L. · E:Greater Burdock; G:Große Klette · ⊙ Z3 VII-VIII ⚕; Eur.*, TR, Cauc., Iran, W-Sib., Amur, Sakhal., C-As., Him., China, Alaska, Can., USA: NE, NCE, NC, SE, NW, Calif.
- **minus** (Hill) Bernh. · E:Common Burdock, Lesser Burdock; G:Kleine Klette · ⊙ Z3 VII-VIII ⚕; Eur.*, TR, Syr., Cauc., NW-Afr., nat. in N-Am.
- **nemorosum** Lej. · E:Wood Burdock; G:Hain-Klette · ⊙ Z3 VIII; Eur.* exc. Ib
- **pubens** Bab. · ⊙ Z3 VIII; Eur.: BrI, DK, Fr, Ib, Ital-P, Sw, RO; TR, Syr., Iran, C-As., N-As., Jap.
- **tomentosum** Mill. · E:Hairy Burdock; G:Filzige Klette · ⊙ Z3 VII-VIII ⚕; Eur.* exc. BrI; TR, C-As., nat. in BrI, Can. N-USA

Arctostaphylos Adans. -f- *Ericaceae* · c. 50 spp. · E:Bearberry; F:Busserole, Raisin-d'ours; G:Bärentraube
- **alpina** (L.) Spreng. · E:Alpine Bearberry, Black Bearberry; F:Busserolle des Alpes; G:Alpen-Bärentraube · ♄ ♄ d ⇝ △ Z3 ⓐ V-VI; Eur.*, W-Sib., E-Sib., Amur, Kamchat., C-As., Alaska, Can., USA: NE; Greenl.
- **manzanita** Parry · E:Manzanita, Parry Manzanita; G:Manzanita · ♄ e Z8 ⓚ IV-V; USA: Oreg., N-Calif.
- **myrtifolia** Parry · E:Ione Manzanita · ♄ e Z8 ⓚ; Calif.
- **nevadensis** A. Gray · E:Pine-mat Manzanita; F:Busserolle · ♄ e Z3; Oregon, Calif.; Sierra Nevada
- **uva-ursi** (L.) Spreng. · E:Bearberry, Mountain Cranberry; F:Busserolle, Raisin d'ours; G:Echte Bärentraube, Immergrüne Bärentraube · ♄ ♄ e ⇝ △ Z3 III-V ⚕ ▽; Eur.*, Cauc., W-Sib., E-Sib., Amur, Alaska, Can., USA: NE, NCE, NC, Rocky Mts., SW, NW, Calif.; Greenl.

Arctotheca J.C. Wendl. -f- *Asteraceae* · 5 spp. · E:Plain Treasureflower; F:Souci du Cap; G:Kaplöwenzahn
- **calendula** (L.) Levyns · E:Cape Dandelion, Cape Weed; G:Kaplöwenzahn · ⊙ ♃ Z9 VII-X; S-Afr.

Arctotis L. -f- *Asteraceae* · c. 50 spp. · E:African Daisy; F:Arctotide; G:Bärenohr
- **acaulis** L. · G:Stängelloses Bärenohr · ⊙ ♃ Z9 VI-IX; S-Afr.
- **breviscapa** Thunb. · G:Kurzstängeliges Bärenohr · ⊙ ⊙ Z9 VII-IX; S-Afr.
- **fastuosa** Jacq. · E:Cape Daisy; G:Prächtiges Bärenohr · ⊙ Z9 ⓚ VI-IX; S-Afr.
- *scapigera* Thunb. = Arctotis acaulis
- **venusta** Norl. · E:African Daisy, Blue-Eyed African Daisy; G:Anmutiges Bärenohr · ⊙ ♃ Z8 VIII-X; S-Afr.
- **Cultivars:**
- **many cultivars**

Ardisia Sw. -f- *Myrsinaceae* · c. 250 spp. · E:Marlberry; F:Ardisia; G:Ardisie, Spitzenblume
- **crenata** Sims · E:Coralberry, Hen's Eyes, Spiceberry; G:Gewürzbeere · ♄ e ꕥ Z9 ⓦ ▽; N-Ind., China, Korea, Jap., Taiwan
- *crenulata* Lodd. = Ardisia crenata
- **crispa** (Thunb.) A. DC. · E:Japanese Holly; G:Korallenbeere · ♄ Z7
- **japonica** (Thunb.) Blume · E:Marlberry; G:Mergelbeere · ♄ e Z8 ⓚ; China, Jap.
- **malouiana** (Linden & Rodigas) Markgr. · ♄ e ⓦ; Kalimantan

Ardisiandra Hook. f. -f- *Primulaceae* · 3 spp.
- **wettsteinii** J. Wagner · ♃ ⇝ Z8 ⓚ ⓐ VI-VIII; trop. Afr.; mts.

Areca L. -f- *Arecaceae* · 48 spp. · F:Arec,

Aréquier, Noix d'Arec; G:Betelpalme
- *alba* Bory = Dictyosperma album
- *aliceae* W. Hill ex F. Muell. = Areca triandra
- *baueri* Hook. f. ex Lem. = Rhopalostylis baueri
- **catechu** L. · E:Betel Nut, Betel Palm; G:Betelnuss, Betelpalme · ♄ e Z10 ⌂ ⚕ Ⓝ; ? Phil.
- *crinita* Bory = Acanthophoenix rubra
- *rubra* Bory = Acanthophoenix rubra
- *sapida* Sol. ex G. Forst. = Rhopalostylis sapida
- **triandra** Roxb. ex Buch.-Ham. · ♄ e Z10 ⌂; Austr.
- **vestiaria** Giseke · ♄ e Z10 ⌂; Sulawesi, Molucca

Arecastrum (Drude) Becc. = Syagrus
- *romanzoffianum* (Cham.) Becc. = Syagrus romanzoffiana

Aremonia Neck. ex Nestl. -f- *Rosaceae* · 1 sp. · E:Bastard Agrimony; F:Arémonia; G:Aremonie, Nelkenwurzodermennig
- **agrimonoides** (L.) DC. · E:Bastard Agrimony; G:Nelkenwurzodermennig · ♃ V-VI; Eur.: Ital-P, C-Eur., EC-Eur., Ba, RO; TR, nat. in BrI

Arenaria L. -f- *Caryophyllaceae* · c. 160 spp. · E:Sandwort; F:Arénaire, Sabline; G:Sandkraut
- *armeriastrum* Boiss. = Arenaria armerina
- **armerina** Bory · ♃ ⇝ △ VI-VII; S-Sp., Moroc.
- **balearica** L. · E:Corsican Sandwort, Mossy Sandwort; G:Korsisches Sandkraut · ♃ △ Z7 IV-VIII; Eur.: Balear., Cors, Sard., I, nat. in BrI, F
- **biflora** L. · G:Zweiblütiges Sandkraut · ♃ VII-IX; Eur.: Ib, Fr, Ital-P, C-Eur., Ba, RO; mts.
- **ciliata** L.
- subsp. **ciliata** · E:Fringed Sandwort; G:Wimper-Sandkraut · ♃ Z1 VII-VIII; Alp., Cap., IRL
- subsp. *moehringioides* (Murr) Braun-Blanq. = Arenaria ciliata subsp. multicaulis
- subsp. **multicaulis** L. · G:Vielstängeliges Sandkraut · ♃ Z1 VII-VIII; Eur.: sp., F, I, Sw, G, A; mts. sp., Pyr., Alp., Jura
- **gothica** Fr. · G:Gothisches Sandkraut · ⊙ ⊙; Eur.: Swed, Ch
- **gracilis** Waldst. & Kit. · ♃ △ V-VI; Eur.: Croatia, Bosn., Montenegro, AL
- *graminifolia* Schrad. = Arenaria procera subsp. glabra
- **grandiflora** L. · G:Großblütiges Sandkraut · ♃ △ V-VIII; Eur.: Ib, F, Ital-P, Sw, A, Slova.; Afr. mts.
- **gypsophiloides** L. · ♃ △ VI-VII; Eur.: BG; TR, Iraq, Cauc., Iran
- **ledebouriana** Fenzl · ♃ ⇝ △ Z6 VII-VIII; TR
- **leptoclados** (Rchb.) Guss. · G:Dünnstängeliges Sandkraut · ⊙ V-IX; Eur.*, TR, Levant, Cauc., Afr.
- *lloydii* Jord. = Arenaria serpyllifolia subsp. lloydii
- **longifolia** M. Bieb. · ♃; Russ.
- **marschlinsii** W.D.J. Koch · ⊙ VII-VIII; Eur.: Pyr., Sw
- *micradenia* P.A. Smirn. = Arenaria procera subsp. glabra
- *moehringioides* Murr = Arenaria ciliata subsp. multicaulis
- **montana** L. · E:Alpine Sandwort, Large-flowered Sandwort; G:Alpen-Sandkraut · ♃ △ Z4 V-VIII; Eur.: Ib, F; Moroc.
- *multicaulis* Jacq. = Arenaria ciliata subsp. multicaulis
- **procera** Spreng.
- subsp. **glabra** (F.N. Williams) Holub · ♃ △ Z3 VI-VII
- subsp. **procera** · G:Grasblättriges Sandkraut · ♃ △ Z3 VI-VII; Eur.: A, EC-Eur., E-Eur.
- **purpurascens** Ramond ex DC. · E:Pink Sandwort; G:Rosafarbenes Sandkraut · ♃ △ Z6 VII-VIII; Eur.: sp., F; Cordillera Cantábrica, Pyr., Vercors
- **rigida** M. Bieb. · ♃ ⇝ △ VII-IX; Eur.: BG, EC-Eur.
- **rotundifolia** M. Bieb. · ♃ △ VII-VIII; Eur.: Ba, RO; TR, Cauc.
- **serpyllifolia** L.
- subsp. *leptoclados* (Rchb.) Nym. = Arenaria leptoclados
- subsp. **lloydii** (Jord.) Bonnier · G:Lloyds Sandkraut · ; Eur.: D + ; coasts
- subsp. **serpyllifolia** · E:Thyme Leaved Sandwort; G:Thymianblättriges Sandkraut · ⊙ ⊙ V-IX; Eur.*, TR, Syr., Cauc., W-Sib., C-As., China, Jap., NW-Afr., Egypt, Eth., nat. in N-Am., Austr.
- **tetraquetra** L. · ♃ ⌓ △ Z6 VII-VIII; Eur.: sp., F; mts.
- **tmolea** Boiss. · ♃ Z6; TR

Arenga Labill. ex DC. -f- *Arecaceae* ·
20 spp. · F:Palmier à sucre; G:Zucker-
palme
- **engleri** Becc. · G:Riukiu Zucker-Palme · ♄
e Z10 ⓦ; Riukiu-Is., Taiwan
- **pinnata** (Wurmb) Merr. · E:Sugar Palm;
G:Molukken-Zuckerpalme · ♄ e Z10 ⓦ
ⓝ; Malay. Arch.
- **porphyrocarpa** (Blume) H.E. Moore ·
G:Gomuti-Palme · ♄ e D Z10 ⓦ; Java
- *saccharifera* Labill. ex DC. = Arenga
pinnata

Arequipa Britton & Rose -f- *Cactaceae* ·
2 spp.
- *aurantiaca* (Vaupel) Werderm. =
Matucana aurantiaca subsp. aurantiaca
- *erectocylindrica* Rauh & Backeb. =
Arequipa hempeliana
- *haynii* (Otto ex Salm-Dyck) Krainz =
Matucana haynei subsp. haynei
- **hempeliana** (Gürke) Oehme · Ψ Z9 ⓚ ▽
✳; S-Peru, N-Chile; mts.
- **leucotricha** (Phil.) Britton & Rose · Ψ Z9
ⓚ ▽ ✳; S-Peru, N-Chile
- *myriacantha* (Vaupel) Britton & Rose =
Matucana weberbaueri
- *rettigii* (Quehl) Oehme = Arequipa
hempeliana
- *weingartiana* Backeb. = Arequipa
hempeliana

Arethusa L. -f- *Orchidaceae* · 1 sp.
- **bulbosa** L. · E:Dragon's Mouth, Swamp
Pink; G:Drachenmaul-Ochidee
- *chinensis* Rolfe = Bletilla foliosa

Aretia L. = Vitaliana
- *vitaliana* (L.) Murray = Vitaliana
primuliflora subsp. primuliflora

Argania Roem. & Schult. -f- *Sapotaceae* ·
1 sp. · E:Argantree; G:Arganbaum
- **spinosa** (L.) Skeels · E:Argantree;
G:Arganbaum · ♄ e ⓚ ⓝ; SW-Moroc.

Argemone L. -f- *Papaveraceae* · c. 28 spp. ·
E:Mexican Poppy; F:Argémone;
G:Stachelmohn
- **albiflora** Hornem. · E:White Prickly
Poppy; G:Weißer Stachelmohn · ☉ Z7;
USA: NE, SE, Fla.
- **grandiflora** Sweet · G:Großblütiger
Stachelmohn · ☉ Z8 VII-IX; Mex.
- **mexicana** L. · E:Devil's Fig, Mexican

Poppy; G:Mexikanischer Stachelmohn ·
☉ Z8 VII-IX ⚡ ⓝ; C-Am., W.Ind., nat. in
S-Eur., C-Eur.
- **ochroleuca** Sweet · E:Pale Mexican
Poppy; G:Bleicher Stachelmohn · ☉ ⚃
Z8; Mex.
- **platyceras** Link & Otto · E:Crested
Poppy, Prickly Poppy; G:Riesenblütiger
Stachelmohn · ☉ Z8 VIII-IX; Mex.
- **polyanthemos** (Fedde) G.B. Ownbey ·
E:Plains Prickly Poppy; G:Gehörnter
Stachelmohn · ☉ ⊙ Z6 VII-IX; USA:
Rocky Mts., NC, SW, Tex.

Argyranthemum Webb -n- *Asteraceae* ·
23 spp. · E:Marguerite; F:Marguerite en
arbre; G:Strauchmargerite
- **foeniculaceum** (Willd.) Webb · ♄ Z9 ⓚ
I-XII; Canar.: Teneriffa
- **frutescens** (L.) Sch. Bip. · E:Boston
Daisy, Marguerite; F:Anthémis;
G:Strauchmargerite · ♄ Z9 ⓚ I-XII;
Canar.
- **many cultivars**

Argyreia Lour. -f- *Convolvulaceae* · c.
90 spp. · E:Morning Glory; F:Liseron
arbustif; G:Silberwinde
- **nervosa** (Burm. f.) Bojer · E:Elephant
Creeper, Woolly Morning Glory;
G:Holzrose · ♄ ⚡ Z9 ⓚ VII; Ind.

Argyrocytisus (Maire) Raynaud
-m- *Fabaceae* · 1 sp. · F:Genêt argenté;
G:Silberginster
- **battandieri** (Maire) Raynaud ·
E:Moroccan Broom, Pineapple Broom;
G:Silberginster · ♄ d D Z7 V-VI; NW-Afr.

Argyroderma N.E. Br. -n- *Aizoaceae* ·
10 spp. · F:Plante-caillou; G:Silberhaut
- **testiculare** (Aiton) N.E. Br. · ⚃ Z9 ⓚ;
Cape

Aridaria N.E. Br. -f- *Aizoaceae* · 4 spp.
- **noctiflora** (L.) Schwantes · ⚃ Ψ D ⓚ
VII-VIII; Namibia

Ariocarpus Scheidw. -m- *Cactaceae* ·
6 spp. · E:Living Rock; F:Cactus;
G:Wollfruchtkaktus
- **agavoides** (Castañeda) E.F. Anderson · Ψ
Z8 ⓚ ▽ ✳; Mex.: Tamaulipas
- *denegrii* (Frič) W.T. Marshall = Obregonia denegrii

- **fissuratus** (Engelm.) K. Schum.
- var. **fissuratus** · E:Chautle Livingrock · Ψ
  Z8 ⓐ ▽ ✳; SW-Tex., Mex.: Coahuila
- var. **lloydii** (Rose) W.T. Marshall · Ψ
  Z8 ⓐ ▽ ✳; Mex.: Coahuila, Durango,
  Zacatecas
- *furfuraceus* (S. Watson) C.H. Thomps. =
  Ariocarpus retusus
- **kotschoubeyanus** (Lem.) K. Schum. · Ψ
  Z8 ⓐ ▽ ✳; Mex.: Durango, Nuevo Leon,
  San Luis Potosí
- *lloydii* Rose = Ariocarpus fissuratus var.
  lloydii
- **retusus** Scheidw. · Ψ Z8 ⓐ ▽ ✳; Mex.:
  Coahuila, San Luis Potosi, Zacatecas
- **scapharostrus** Boed. · Ψ Z9 ⓐ ▽ ✳;
  Mex.: Nuevo León
- *strobiliformis* Werderm. = Encephalocarpus strobiliformis
- **trigonus** (F.A.C. Weber) K. Schum. ·
  Ψ Z9 ⓐ ▽ ✳; Mex.: Nuevo León,
  Tamaulipas

Ariopsis Nimmo -f- *Araceae* · 2 spp.
- **peltata** Nimmo · ⏀ ⓦ II-III; Malay. Arch.

Arisaema Mart. -n- *Araceae* · 220 spp. ·
  E:Cobra Lily; F:Arisaema; G:Feuerkolben
- **candidissimum** W.W. Sm. · ⏀ Z8 ⓦ;
  W-China
- **consanguineum**
- subsp. **consanguineum** · E:Chinese
  Jack-in-the-Pulpit; G:Chinesischer
  Feuerkolben · ⏀ ⚭ Z7 ∧ V ⚥; Him.,
  SW-China
- **dracontium** (L.) Schott · E:Dragon Root;
  G:Drachen-Feuerkolben · ⏀ Z4 VI; Can.:
  E; USA: NE, NCE, SC, SE, Fla.
- **fargesii** Buchet · ⏀ ⓐ III-IV; China:
  Sichuan
- **flavum** (Forssk.) Schott · ⏀ Z7; Afgh.,
  Him., SW-China
- **griffithii** Schott · E:Yellow Cobra Lily;
  G:Gelber Feuerkolben · ⏀ Z8 ∧ III-IV;
  Him.: Nepal, Sikkim, Bhutan
- *helleborifolium* Schott = Arisaema
  tortuosum
- **heterophyllum** Blume · ⏀; Ind.
- *quinatum* (Nutt.) Schott = Arisaema
  triphyllum
- **ringens** (Thunb.) Schott · G:Japanischer
  Feuerkolben · ⏀ Z7 III-IV; Jap., S-Korea,
  E-China
- **serratum** (Thunb.) Schott · ⏀ Z8 ⓐ
  III-IV; China, Korea, Jap.

- **speciosum** (Wall.) Mart. · E:Showy
  Cobra Lily; G:Prächtiger Feuerkolben · ⏀
  Z8 ⓐ III Ⓝ; Him.: Nepal, Sikkim
- **tortuosum** (Wall.) Schott · ⏀ Z9 ⓦ V-VI
  Ⓝ; Ind.
- **triphyllum** (L.) Torr. · E:Indian Turnip,
  Jack in the Pulpit; G:Dreiblättriger
  Feuerkolben · ⏀ ⚭ Z4 III-IV ⚥ ; Can.: E;
  USA: NE, NCE, SC, SE, Fla.

Arisarum Mill. -n- *Araceae* · 3 spp. ·
  E:Mousetailplant; F:Capuchon de moine;
  G:Mäuseschwanz
- **proboscideum** (L.) Savi · ⏀ Z7 V; Eur.:
  SW-Sp., I
- **vulgare** O. Targ. Tozz. · E:Jack-in-the-
  Pulpit; G:Gewöhnlicher Feuerkolben · ⏀
  Z7 V; Eur.: Ib, Fr, Ital-P, Ba; TR, N-Afr.,
  Azor.

Aristea Aiton -f- *Iridaceae* · 55 spp. · E:Blue
  Corn Lily; F:Aristéa; G:Grannenlilie
- **africana** (L.) Hoffm. · ⏀ Z9 ⓐ IV-X;
  S-Afr.
- *cyanea* (Sol.) Aiton = Aristea africana

Aristolochia L. -f- *Aristolochiaceae* · c.
  300 spp. · E:Birthwort; F:Aristoloche;
  G:Osterluzei, Pfeifenwinde
- *altissima* Desf. = Aristolochia sempervirens
- **californica** Torr. · E:Californian Dutchman's Pipe · ♄ ∫ ⚥ Z8 ⓐ; Calif.
- **cauliflora** Ule · ♄ ⚥ ⓦ; Peru
- **clematitis** L. · E:Birthwort; G:Gewöhnli-
  che Osterluzei · ⏀ Z6 V-VII ⚥ ⚘; Eur.*
  exc. BrI, Sc; TR, Cauc., nat. in GB, .
  Norw.
- *durior* Hill = Aristolochia macrophylla
- **fimbriata** Cham. · ♄ ⚥ Z10 ⓦ V-VII;
  Braz., Parag., Arg.
- **gigantea** Mart. & Zucc. · ♄ ∫ e ⚥ Z10 ⓦ;
  Panama
- *gigas* Lindl. = Aristolochia grandiflora
- **grandiflora** Sw. · E:Pelican Flower;
  G:Großblütige Pfeifenwinde · ♄ ∫ d ⚥ Z10
  ⓦ VII-IX; W.Ind.
- **labiata** Willd. · E:Mottled Dutchman's
  Pipe · ∫ e ⚥ Z10 ⓦ IV-IX; Braz.
- *leuconeura* Linden = Aristolochia
  cauliflora
- **lindneri** A. Berger · ⊙ ⤳ ⓦ VII-VIII;
  Bol.
- **littoralis** D. Parodi · E:Calico Flower;
  G:Strand-Pfeifenwinde · ♄ e ⚥ Z9 ⓐ

IV-X; Braz.
- **macrophylla** Lam. · E:Dutchman's Pipe, Pipevine; F:Aristoloche siphon; G:Amerikanische Pfeifenwinde · ♄ ⌇ d ⚇ Z5 VI-VIII; USA: NE, SE
- **macroura** M. Gómez · ♄ ⚇ ⓜ VI-IX; Bol., Parag., Braz., Arg.
- **manshuriensis** Kom. · ♄ ⌇ d ⚇ Z7; Manch., Korea
- **moupinensis** Franch. · G:Chinesische Pfeifenwinde · ♄ d ⚇ Z5 VI; W-China
- *ornithocephala* Hook. = Aristolochia labiata
- *ringens* Link & Otto = Aristolochia labiata
- **rotunda** L. · E:Round-leaved Birthwort; G:Rundblättrige Osterluzei · ⅃ Z8 ∧ V; Eur.: Ib, Fr, Sw, Ital-P, Ba
- **sempervirens** L. · E:Long Birthwort · ♄ e ⚇ Z8 ⓜ; Eur.: Sic., GR, Cr; W-TR, Levant, Alger., nat. in F, Sard., I
- **serpentaria** L. · E:Virginia Snakeroot · ⅃ Z8 ⓜ VII ⚥ ; USA: NE, NCE, NC, SC, SE, Fla.
- *sipho* L'Hér. = Aristolochia macrophylla
- **tomentosa** Sims · E:Woolly Dutchman's Pipe; G:Filzige Pfeifenwinde · ♄ d ⚇ Z6 VI-VII; USA: SE, Kans., SC, Fla., nat. in USA: N.Y.
- **tricaudata** Lem. · ♄ ⓜ II-IX; Mex.

Aristotelia L'Hér. -f- Elaeocarpaceae · 5 spp. · E:Wineberry; F:Aristotélia; G:Weinbeere
- **chilensis** (Molina) Stuntz · E:Wineberry; G:Chile-Weinbeere · ♄ e Z8 ⓜ; Chile
- *macqui* L'Hér. = Aristotelia chilensis

× **Arizara** hort. -f- Orchidaceae (Cattleya × Epidendrum × Domingoa)

Armeria Willd. -f- Plumbaginaceae · 80-100 spp. · E:Thrift; F:Armérie, Gazon d'Espagne; G:Grasnelke
- *alliacea* (Cav.) Hoffmanns. & Link = Armeria arenaria
- **alpina** Willd. · G:Alpen-Grasnelke · ⅃ Z4 VII-VIII; Eur.: sp., F, I, A, Ba
- **arenaria** (Pers.) Schult. · E:Jersey Thrift; G:Wegerich-Grasnelke · ⅃ ∧ Z7 VI-VII ▽; Eur.: Ib, F, I, Sw, D
- *caespitosa* Boiss. = Armeria juniperifolia
- *elongata* (Hoffm.) W.D.J. Koch = Armeria maritima subsp. elongata
- **juniperifolia** (Vahl) Hoffmanns. & Link · ⅃ ∧ Z7 IV-V ▽; Eur.: sp.

- *latifolia* Willd. = Armeria pseudarmeria
- *laucheana* hort. = Armeria maritima
- **leucocephala** Salzm. ex W.D.J. Koch · ⅃ Z8 ⓚ ▽; Cors
- **maritima** (Mill.) Willd. · E:Common Thrift, Sea Thrift; G:Gewöhnliche Grasnelke
- **some cultivars**
- subsp. **maritima** · F:Gazon d'Espagne; G:Strand-Grasnelke · ⅃ ⌇ △ IX-XI ▽; Eur.: Sc, N-Russ.
- subsp. *alpina* (Willd.) P. Silva = Armeria alpina
- subsp. **elongata** (Hoffm.) Bonnier · G:Sand-Grasnelke · ⅃ VIII ▽; Eur.: BrI, Sc, Fr, C-Eur., EC-Eur., E-Eur.
- subsp. **halleri** (Wallr.) Rothm. · G:Galmei-Grasnelke · ⅃ ▽; Eur.: F, NL, G, PL
- subsp. **purpurea** (W.D.J. Koch) Á. Löve & D. Löve · G:Purpur-Grasnelke · ⅃ ▽; Eur.: S-G, ? N-I
- *plantaginea* Willd. = Armeria arenaria
- **pseudarmeria** (Murray) Mansf. · ⅃ △ Z8 VI-VIII ▽; C-P
- *pseudarmeria* auct. non (Murray) Mansf. = Armeria arenaria
- *vulgaris* Willd. = Armeria maritima subsp. maritima

× **Armodachnis** hort. -f- Orchidaceae (Arachnis × Armodorum)

Armoracia G. Gaertn., B. Mey. & Scherb. -f- Brassicaceae · 4 spp. · E:Horse Radish; F:Cran, Cranson, Raifort; G:Meerrettich
- **rusticana** G. Gaertn., B. Mey. & Scherb. · E:Horseradish; G:Gewöhnlicher Meerrettich · ⅃ Z5 V-VII ⚥ ⓝ; ? Russ., nat. in Eur., Cauc., N-Am.

Arnebia Forssk. -f- Boraginaceae · 25 spp. · F:Fleur du prophète; G:Prophetenblume
- *echioides* (L.) A. DC. = Arnebia pulchra
- *longiflora* K. Koch = Arnebia pulchra
- **pulchra** (Willd. ex Roem. & Schult.) J.R. Edm. · E:Prophet Flower · ⅃ Z7; TR, Cauc., N-Iran

Arnica L. -f- Asteraceae · 32 spp. · F:Arnica, Panacée des montagnes; G:Arnika, Wohlverleih
- **angustifolia** Vahl · ⅃ Z2; Sc, N-Russ.
- **chamissonis** Less. · E:Leafy Leopardsbane · ⅃ Z2 V-VIII ⚥ ; Alaska, Can.:

B.C.; USA: NW, Calif., Rocky Mts., SW
– *foliosa* Nutt. = Arnica chamissonis
– **lanceolata** Nutt. · E:Soft Leaved Arnica ·
⊕ VII; Can.: E; USA: NE
– *mollis* Hook. = Arnica lanceolata
– **montana** L. · E:Mountain Arnica;
G:Berg-Wohlverleih, Echte Arnika · ⊕ △
Z6 VI ☉ Ⓝ ▽; Eur.* exc. BrI
– **sachalinensis** (Regel) A. Gray · ⊕ Z2
VII-VIII; Amur, Sakhal., ? Jap.

Arnoseris Gaertn. -f- *Asteraceae* ·
1 sp. · E:Lamb's Succory; F:Arnoséris;
G:Lämmersalat
– **minima** (L.) Schweigg. & Körte ·
E:Lamb's Succory; G:Lämmersalat · ⊙
VI-IX; Eur.*, Moroc., nat. in NZ, Austr.

Aronia Medik. -f- *Rosaceae* · 2 spp. ·
E:Chokeberry; F:Aronia; G:Apfelbeere
– **arbutifolia** (L.) Pers.
– var. **arbutifolia** · E:Red Chokeberry;
F:Aronia à feuilles d'arbousier; G:Filzige
Apfelbeere · ♄ d ♋ Z5 IV-V; Can.: E;
USA: NE, NCE, SE, Fla., Tex.
– f. **leiocalyx** Rehder Z4
– var. **atropurpurea** (Britton) F. Seym. · ♄
d Z5
– *floribunda* (Lindl.) Spach = Aronia ×
prunifolia
– **melanocarpa** (Michx.) Elliott · E:Black
Chokeberry; G:Kahle Apfelbeere
– var. **elata** Rehder · G:Birnenförmige
Kahle Apfelbeere · ♄ d Z5
– var. **grandifolia** (Lindl.) C.K. Schneid. ·
G:Apfelförmige Kahle Apfelbeere · ♄ d
Z5; S-Appalachians
– var. **melanocarpa** · G:Gewöhnliche
Kahle Apfelbeere · ♄ d Z4 V-VI Ⓝ; Can.:
E; USA; NE, NCE, SE
– × **prunifolia** (C.K. Schneid.) Graebn. (*A.
arbutifolia* × *A. melanocarpa*) · E:Purple
Chokeberry; G:Pflaumenblättrige
Apfelbeere · ♄ d Z5 V-VI; Ca.: E; E-USA
– *prunifolia* (Marshall) Rehder = Aronia ×
prunifolia

Arpophyllum Lex. -n- *Orchidaceae* · 4 spp. ·
E:Bottlebrush Orchid; F:Orchidée;
G:Sichelblattorchidee
– **giganteum** Hartw. ex Lindl. · ⊕ Z10 Ⓚ
III-IV ▽ ✱; Mex., C-Am., Jamaica, Col.
– **spicatum** Lex. · ⊕ Z10 Ⓚ XII-I ▽ ✱;
Mex., C-Am.

Arracacia Bancr. -f- *Apiaceae* · 55 spp.
– **xanthorrhiza** Bancr. · E:Peruvian Carrot;
G:Arrakatscha · ⊕ Ⓝ; orig. ?, nat. in
Venez., Col., Bol., Peru

Arrhenatherum P. Beauv. -n- *Poaceae* ·
6 spp. · E:False Oat Grass; F:Avoine en
chapelet; G:Glatthafer
– *desertorum* (Less.) Potztal = Helictotrichon desertorum
– **elatius** (L.) P. Beauv. ex J. Presl & C.
Presl
– var. **bulbosum** (Willd.) Spenn. ·
E:Bulbous Oat Grass; G:Knollen-
Glatthafer, Knolliger Glatthafer · ⊕ Z6
VI-VII; Eur.: S-Eur., W-Eur.
– var. **elatius** · E:False Oat Grass;
F:Fromental élevé; G:Gewöhnlicher Glatthafer, Hoher Glatthafer · ⊕ Z6 VI-VII;
Eur.*, TR, N-Iraq, Cauc., Iran, Canar.,
Madeira, NW-Afr., nat. in N-Am.
– *parlatorei* (J. Woods) Potztal = Helictotrichon parlatorei

Arrojadoa Britton & Rose -f- *Cactaceae* ·
3 spp.
– **penicillata** (Gürke) Britton & Rose · Ψ
Z10 Ⓚ ▽ ✱; Braz.
– **polyantha** (Werderm.) D.R. Hunt =
Micranthocereus polyanthus
– **rhodantha** (Gürke) Britton & Rose · Ψ
Z10 Ⓚ ▽ ✱; Braz.

Artabotrys R. Br. -m- *Annonaceae* · c.
100 spp. · E:Tail Grape; G:Klimmtraube
– **hexapetalus** (L. f.) Bhandari ·
E:Climbing Ilang Ilang · ♄ e ☀ D Z10 Ⓦ;
S-Ind., Sri Lanka
– **uncinatus** (Lam.) Merr. = Artabotrys
hexapetalus

Artanthe Miq. = Piper
– *magnifica* Linden = Piper magnificum

Artemisia L. -f- *Asteraceae* · c. 300 spp. ·
E:Mugwort, Sage Brush, Sagewort,
Wormwood; F:Absinthe, Armoise;
G:Absinth, Beifuß, Eberraute, Wermut
– **abrotanum** L. · E:Lad's Love, Southern-
wood; F:Citronnelle aurone; G:Eberraute
· ♄ ♄ Z6 VII-X ☉ Ⓝ; orig. ?, nat. in S-Eur.,
SE-Eur., W-As., Sib.
– **absinthium** L. · E:Absinthe, Common
Wormwood; F:Armoise absinthe;
G:Absinth, Echter Wermut · ⊕ ♄ d Z6

VII-IX ♵ ⚲ Ⓝ; Eur.*, TR, Cauc., N-Iran,
W-Sib., C-As., nat. in N-Am.
- **alba** Turra · G:Kampfer-Wermut · ♃
  Z6 VII-IX; Eur.: Sp, Fr, Ital-P, Ba, RO;
  NW-Afr.
- **annua** L. · E:Sweet Wormwood · ⊙ Z8
  VIII-X ♵ ; Eur.* exc. BrI; TR, Syr., Palest.,
  Cauc., N-Iran, W-Sib., E-Sib., China,
  Korea, Jap., nat. in Can.: W; USA: NCE,
  NC, Rocky Mts., SW
- **arborescens** L. · ♄ e Z8 ⌂; Eur.: Ib,
  Ital-P, Ba; TR, N-Afr., nat. in Fr
- **armeniaca** Lam. · ♃ ⤳ △ Z5; Cauc.
  (Armen.)
- *assoana* Willk. = Artemisia caucasica
- **austriaca** Jacq. · G:Österreichischer
  Beifuß · ♃ ⤳ VII-VIII; Eur.: A, EC-Eur.,
  BG, E-Eur.; TR, Cauc., N-Iran, nat. in F, D
- **biennis** Willd. · E:Biennial Wormwood;
  G:Zweijähriger Beifuß · ⊙ VII-IX; N-As.,
  N-Am., nat. in BrI, NL, DK, S-Swed
- **campestris** L. · G:Feld-Beifuß
- subsp. **borealis** (Pall.) H.M. Hall &
  Clem. · E:Boreal Sagebrush; G:Nor-
  discher Beifuß · ♃ Z2 VII-X; Eur.:
- subsp. **campestris** · E:Field Wormwood;
  G:Gewöhnlicher Feld-Beifuß · ♃ Z2
  VIII-X; Eur.*, TR, Cauc., W-Sib., C-As.,
  NW-Afr.
- *camphorata* Vill. = Artemisia alba
- **canariensis** (Besser) Less. · ♄ Z9 ⌂;
  Canar.
- *canescens* Willd. = Artemisia armeniaca
- **caucasica** Willd. · F:Armoise du Cau-
  case · ♃ Z5; Eur.: Ba, Ib, Ital-P, E-Eur.;
  Cauc.
- **cina** O. Berg · E:Levant Wormwood;
  G:Zitwer · ♄ VII-IX ♵ ⚲; C-As.
  (S-Kazakh.)
- **dracunculus** L. · E:Estragon, Tarragon;
  F:Estragon; G:Estragon · ♃ Z3 VIII-X
  ♵ Ⓝ; Eur.: Russ.; W-Sib., E-Sib., C-As.,
  W-Him., Mong., China, Alaska, Can.,
  USA* exc. NE, SE, Fla., nat. in F, C-Eur.,
  EC-Eur., JU, RO
- **eriantha** Ten. · ♃ △ Z5 VI-VIII; Eur.: Ib,
  Fr, Ital-P, EC-Eur., Ba, RO; mts.
- **frigida** Willd. · E:Prairie Sagewort · ♃ ♄
  ♄ Z4 VII-VIII; Alaska, Can.: W, B.C.; USA:
  NW, Rocky Mts., Ariz., NC, NCE; Sib.,
  nat. in ne N-Am.
- **genipi** Weber · G:Schwarze Edelraute · ♃
  Z4 VII-VIII ♵ ; Eur.: A, G, Sw, I; Alp.
- **glacialis** L. · E:Glacier Wormwood;
  G:Gletscher-Edelraute · ♃ Z5 VII-VIII;

Eur.: F, I, Sw; SW-Alp.
- *glauca* Pall. ex Willd. = Artemisia
  dracunculus
- **gmelinii** Webb ex Stechm. · ⊙ ♄ VIII-IX;
  S-Russ., Sib., Afgh., Him.
- *gnaphalodes* Nutt. = Artemisia ludoviciana
- **laciniata** Willd. · E:Siberian Wormwood;
  G:Schlitzblättriger Beifuß · ♃ VIII-X ▽;
  Eur.: A, G, Swed (Öland), CZ, Russ.;
  W-Sib., E-Sib., C-As., Him., Mong., Amur,
  Manch.
- **lactiflora** Wall. ex DC. · E:White
  Mugwort; F:Armoise à fleurs laiteuses;
  G:Weißer China-Beifuß · ♃ ⋈ Z4 IX-X ♵ ;
  W-China
- *lanata* Willd. = Artemisia caucasica
- var. *nitida* (Bertol.) DC. = Artemisia
  nitida
- **ludoviciana** Nutt. · E:Cudweed, Western
  Mugwort, White Sagebrush; G:Weißer
  Beifuß · ♃ Z5 VII-VIII; Alaska, Can.: W;
  USA*; Mex.
- *mutellina* Vill. = Artemisia umbelliformis
- **nitida** Bertol. · G:Glänzende Edelraute ·
  ♃ △ Z5 VIII-IX; Eur.: I, A, Slove.; SE-Alp.,
  Alpi Apuane
- **nivalis** Braun-Blanq. · G:Schnee-
  Edelraute · ♃ VIII; Eur.: SW-Sw
- **pancicii** (Janka) Ronniger · G:Waldstep-
  pen-Beifuß · ♃ IX-X ▽; Eur.: A, Serb.
- *pedemontana* Balb. = Artemisia caucasica
- *petrosa* Fritsch = Artemisia eriantha
- **pontica** L. · E:Roman Wormwood;
  F:Absinthe romaine; G:Pontischer Beifuß
  · ♃ ⤳ Z4 VIII-X Ⓝ; Eur.: G, A, EC-Eur.,
  BG, E-Eur.; Cauc., W-Sib., nat. in F, I, Sw
- *procera* Willd. = Artemisia abrotanum
- *purshiana* Besser = Artemisia ludoviciana
- **rupestris** L. · G:Steppen-Beifuß · ♃ Z3
  IX-X ▽; Eur.: G, Swed, Russ; Sib., C-As.
- *sacrorum* Ledeb. = Artemisia gmelinii
- **santonica** L. · G:Salz-Beifuß · ♃ IX-X;
  Eur.: A, EC-Eur., Ba, E-Eur.
- **schmidtiana** Maxim. · E:Angel's Hair;
  F:Armoise de Schmidt; G:Kurilen-Beifuß
  · ♃ △ Z4 VIII; Jap., Sakhal.
- **scoparia** Waldst. & Kit. · E:Redstem
  Wormwood; G:Besen-Beifuß · ⊙ Z3 VIII-
  X; Eur.: C-Eur., EC-Eur., E-Eur., Ba; TR,
  Iraq, Arab., Cauc., Iran, W-Sib., E-Sib.,
  Amur, Sakhal., C-As., Afgh., Pakist.,
  NW-Ind., Mong., China, Korea, nat. in F
- **sieversiana** Ehrh. ex Willd. · G:Sievers-
  Beifuß · ⊙ ⊙ VII-IX; Eur.: Balt.; C-As.,

N-As.
- **splendens** Willd. · E:Alpine Wormwood; G:Kaukasischer Beifuß
- var. **brachyphylla** Boiss. · ♃ △ Z5 VII-VIII; TR, Cauc., Iran
- var. **splendens** · ♃ Z5 VII-VIII; Cauc., N-Iran, N-Iraq
- **stelleriana** Besser · E:Dusty Miller, Old Woman; F:Armoise des côtes d'Extrême-Orient; G:Silber-Wermut · ♃ ⤳ Z5 VII-VIII; Korea, Jap., Sakhal., Kamchat., nat. in e N-Am., N-Eur.
- **tournefortiana** Rchb. · G:Armenischer Beifuß · ⊙ VII-IX; TR, Iran, Afgh., Him., nat. in D
- **tridentata** Nutt. · E:Big Sage, Sage Brush; G:Dreizähniger Wermut · ♄ e D Z7 VIII-IX; Can.: W; USA: NW, Calif., Rocky Mts., SW, NC; Mex: Baja Calif.
- **umbelliformis** Lam. · E:Alpine Wormwood; G:Echte Edelraute · ♃ △ Z4 VII-IX Ⓝ ▽; Eur.: F, I, C-Eur.; Pyr., Alp., N-Apenn.
- **vallesiaca** All. · E:Valais Wormwood; F:Armoise du Valais; G:Walliser Wermut · ♃ △ Z7 VIII-X; Eur.: SE-F, Sw, N-I
- **verlotiorum** Lamotte · E:Verlot's Mugwort; G:Kamtschatka-Beifuß · ♃ IX-XI; Jap., Kamchat., nat. in Eur.* exc. Sc, EC-Eur.
- *villarsii* Godr. & Gren. = Artemisia eriantha
- **vulgaris** L. · E:Mugwort; G:Gewöhnlicher Beifuß · ♃ Z3 VIII-XI ⚐ Ⓝ; Eur.*, TR, Cauc., Iran, W-Sib., E-Sib., C-As., Alger., Tun., Alaska, Can., USA: NE, NCE, NC, SE

Arthrocereus A. Berger & F.M. Knuth -m-Cactaceae · 5 spp.
- **microsphaericus** (K. Schum.) A. Berger · Ψ Z9 ⓐ ▽ ✳; Braz.
- *mirabilis* (Speg.) W.T. Marshall = Setiechinopsis mirabilis
- **rondonianus** Backeb. & Voll ex Backeb. · Ψ Z9 ⓐ ▽ ✳; Braz.

Arthromeris (T. Moore) J. Sm. -f-Polypodiaceae · 22 spp.
- **wallichiana** (Spreng.) Ching · ♃ Z9 ⓦ; China, N-Ind.

Arthropodium R. Br. -n- Anthericaceae · 9 spp. · E:Rock Lily; F:Lis des rochers; G:Felsenlilie
- **candidum** Raoul · E:Star Lily; G:Gras-Felsenlilie · ♃ Z8 ⓐ V-VI; NZ
- **cirrhatum** (G. Forst.) R. Br. · E:Rienga Lily, Rock Lily; G:Funkien-Felsenlilie · ♃ Z8 ⓐ V-VI; NZ
- **milleflorum** (DC.) J.F. Macbr. · E:Pale Vanilla Lily · ♃ Z8 ⓐ V-VI; Austr.: Queensl., N.S.Wales, Victoria, S-Austr., Tasman.
- **minus** R. Br. · E:Small Vanilla Lily · ♃ Z8 ⓐ VI-VII; Austr.
- *paniculatum* (Andrews) R. Br. = Arthropodium milleflorum
- *reflexum* Colenso = Arthropodium candidum

Artocarpus J.R. Forst. & G. Forst. -m- Moraceae · c. 50 spp. · E:Breadfruit; F:Arbre à pain; G:Brotfruchtbaum
- **altilis** (Parkinson) Fosberg · E:Breadfruit; G:Brotfruchtbaum · ♄ e Z10 ⓦ Ⓝ; Molucca, N.Guinea
- *cannonii* W. Bull ex Van Houtte = Ficus aspera
- *communis* J.R. Forst. & G. Forst. = Artocarpus altilis
- **elasticus** Reinw. ex Blume · ♄ e Z10 ⓦ Ⓝ; Malay. Arch.
- **heterophyllus** Lam. · E:Jackfruit; G:Jackfruchtbaum · ♄ e Z10 ⓦ Ⓝ; Ind.
- *incisus* (Thunb.) L. f. = Artocarpus altilis
- **integer** (Thunb.) Merr. · G:Campedak; E:Taboda · ♄ e Z10 ⓦ Ⓝ; Indochina, Malay. Pen., Sumat., Kalimantan
- *integrifolius* auct. non L. f. = Artocarpus heterophyllus
- *integrifolius* L. f. = Artocarpus integer
- *jaca* Lam. = Artocarpus heterophyllus

Arum L. -n- Araceae · 27 spp. · E:Lords and Ladies; F:Arum, Gouet, G:Aronstab
- *alpinum* Schott & Kotschy = Arum cylindraceum
- *cornutum* hort. = Sauromatum venosum
- **creticum** Boiss. & Heldr. · ♃ Z7; Crete
- **cylindraceum** Gasp. · G:Dänischer Aronstab · ♃; Eur.: DK, S-Swed
- **dioscoridis** Sibth. & Sm.
- var. **dioscoridis** · ♃ Z8 ⓐ III-IV; TR
- var. *liepoldtii* (Schott) Engl. = Arum dioscoridis var. dioscoridis
- var. *luschanii* R.R. Mill = Arum dioscoridis var. dioscoridis
- var. *smithii* Engl. = Arum dioscoridis var. dioscoridis
- var. *spectabile* (Schott) Engl. = Arum

dioscoridis var. dioscoridis
- *esculentum* L. = Colocasia esculenta
- *guttatum* Wall. = Dracunculus vulgaris
- **italicum** Mill. · E:Italian Arum; F:Gouet d'Italie; G:Italienischer Aronstab · ⑴ ⚬ Z6 IV-V ✿; Eur.: Ib, Fr, BrI, Ital-P, Sw, Ba, Crim; TR, Iraq, Cauc., Canar., Madeira, NW-Afr., nat. in NL
- **maculatum** L. · E:Cuckoo Pint, Lords-and-Ladies; F:Gouet tacheté; G:Gefleckter Aronstab · ⑴ ⚬ Z6 IV-V ⚡ ✿; Eur.* exc. Sc; TR, nat. in Sc
- **orientale** M. Bieb. · ⑴ Z6 VI; Eur.: I, A, EC-Eur., Ba, RO, S-Russ.; TR, Cyprus, Cauc.
- **palaestinum** Boiss. · E:Black Calla; G:Schwarzer Aronstab · ⑴ D Z9 ⓚ III-IV; Palest.
- *petteri* Schott = Arum orientale
- **pictum** L. f. · ⑴ Z8 ⓚ ∧ IX-X; Cors, Sard., Balear.
- *sanctum* Dammer = Arum palaestinum

Aruncus L. -m- *Rosaceae* · 4 spp. · E:Buck's Beard, Goat's Beard; F:Barbe-de-bouc; G:Geißbart
- **aethusifolius** (H. Lév.) Nakai · E:Dwarf Goat's Beard; G:Kleiner Geißbart · ⑴ V-VI; Jap., Korea
- *astilboides* Maxim. = Aruncus dioicus var. astilboides
- **dioicus** (Walter) Fernald
- var. **astilboides** (Maxim.) H. Hara · ⑴ Z6 VI-VII; Jap.
- var. **dioicus** · E:Bride's Feathers, Goat's Beard; G:Wald-Geißbart · ⑴ ✂ Z7 VI-VII ✿; Eur.* exc. BrI, Sc; TR, Cauc.
- **parvulus** Kom. · ⑴ △ VI; Sib.
- **sinensis** hort. · ⑴; cult.
- *sylvestris* Kostel. = Aruncus dioicus var. dioicus
- *vulgaris* Raf. = Aruncus dioicus var. dioicus

Arundina Blume -f- *Orchidaceae* · 1 sp. · F:Orchidée-roseau; G:Schilforchidee
- **graminifolia** (D. Don) Hochr. · E:Bamboo Orchid; G:Schilforchidee · ⑴ Z10 ⓜ III-IV ▽ ❋; Him., Nepal, Indochina, Malay. Arch., nat. in Hawaii

Arundinaria Michx. -f- *Poaceae* · c. 50 spp. · E:Cane Reed
- *acuminata* Munro = Otatea acuminata
- *alpina* K. Schum. = Yushania alpina

- *anceps* Mitford = Yushania anceps
- *auricoma* Mitford = Pleioblastus auricomus
- *chino* (Franch. & Sav.) Makino = Pleioblastus chino
- *disticha* (Mitford) Pfitzer ex J. Houz. = Pleioblastus pygmaeus
- *fastuosa* (Lat.-Marl. ex Mitford) J. Houz. = Semiarundinaria fastuosa
- *fortunei* (Van Houtte) Rivière & C. Rivière = Pleioblastus variegatus 'Fortunei'
- **gigantea** (Walter) Muhl. · E:Cane Reed, Giant Reed · ℔ e Z7 ⓚ; USA: SE, Fla., SW, Ky., Va.
- *humilis* Mitford = Pleioblastus humilis
- *japonica* Siebold & Zucc. ex Steud. = Pseudosasa japonica
- *jaunsarensis* Gamble = Yushania anceps
- *marmorea* (Mitford) Makino = Chimonobambusa marmorea
- *murieliae* Gamble = Fargesia murieliae
- *nitida* Mitford = Fargesia nitida
- *palmata* (Mitford) Bean = Sasa palmata
- *pygmaea* (Miq.) Makino = Pleioblastus pygmaeus
- *ragamowskii* (Keng f.) Pfitzer = Indocalamus tessellatus
- *ramosa* Makino = Sasaella ramosa
- *simonii* (Carrière) Rivière & C. Rivière = Pleioblastus simonii
- *spathacea* (Franch.) D.C. McClint. = Fargesia spathacea
- *tessellata* (Nees) Munro = Thamnocalamus tessellatus
- *variegata* (Siebold ex Miq.) Makino = Pleioblastus variegatus
- *viridistriata* (Siebold ex André) Makino ex Nakai = Pleioblastus auricomus

Arundo L. -f- *Poaceae* · 3 spp. · E:Giant Reed; F:Canne de Provence; G:Pfahlrohr
- *arenaria* L. = Ammophila arenaria
- **donax** L. · E:Giant Reed; G:Pfahlrohr · ⑴ ∼ Z7 ⓚ ∧ ⚡ Ⓝ; cult., nat. in Eur.: Ib, F, Ital-P, Ba; USA: Ark., Tex., Calif. SW; , trop. Am.
- var. *versicolor* (Mill.) Stokes = Arundo donax

Asarina Mill. -f- *Scrophulariaceae* · 1 sp. · E:Creeping Snapdragon; F:Maurandie, Muflier grimpant; G:Felsenlöwenmaul
- *antirrhiniflora* (Humb. & Bonpl. ex Willd.) Pennell = Maurandella antirrhiniflora

– *barclaiana* (Lindl.) Pennell = Maurandya barclaiana
– *erubescens* (D. Don) Pennell = Lophospermum erubescens
– *lophospermum* (L.H. Bailey) Pennell = Lophospermum scandens
– **procumbens** Mill. · E:Creeping Snapdragon; G:Felsenlöwenmaul, Nierenblättriges Löwenmaul · ⟁ △ Z7 Ⓐ ⋀ V-IX; Eur.: NE-Sp., S-F
– *purpusii* (Brandegee) Pennell = Lophospermum purpusii
– *scandens* (Cav.) Pennell = Maurandya scandens

Asarum L. -n- *Aristolochiaceae* · c. 70 spp. · E:Asarabacca, Wild Ginger; F:Asaret; G:Haselwurz
– **canadense** L. · E:Wild Ginger G:Kanadische Haselwurz · ⟁ Z4 ;III-IV ⚥ ; Can., USA: NE, NCE, NC, SE
– **caudatum** Lindl. · E:Wild Ginger; G:Geschwänzte Haselwurz · ⟁ Z7 VII; Can.: W; USA: NW, Rocky Mts., Calif.
– **europaeum** L. · E:Asarabacca; F:Asaret d'Europe; G:Gewöhnliche Haselwurz · ⟁ Z5 III-V ⚥ ⋊; Eur.* exc. BrI, Ib; W-Sib., nat. in BrI
– **hartwegii** S. Watson · E:Hartweg's Ginger; G:Hartwegs Haselwurz · ⟁ Z7 Ⓐ ⋀; USA: Oreg., Calif.

Asclepias L. -f- *Asclepiadaceae* · 108 spp. · E:Milkweed, Sildweed; F:Asclépiade; G:Seidenpflanze
– *cornuti* Decne. = Asclepias syriaca
– **curassavica** L. · E:Bloodflower Milkweed; G:Indianer-Seidenpflanze · ☉ ♄ e Ⓐ VI-IX; Fla., W-Ind., Mex., C-Am., trop. S-Am., nat. in sp., Moroc.
– **fruticosa** L. · E:Goose Plant; G:Baumwoll-Seidenpflanze · ♄ ⚘ Z9 Ⓐ VI-VIII Ⓝ; S-Afr., nat. in S-Eur., Austr.
– **incarnata** L. · E:Swamp Milkweed; G:Inkarnat-Seidenpflanze, Rote Seidenpflanze · ⟁ Z3 VI-VIII; Can.: E; USA: NE, NCE, NC, Rocky Mts., SW, SC, SE
– **physocarpa** (E. Mey.) Schltr. · E:Swan Plant; G:Schwanen-Seidenpflanze · ♄ d Z9 Ⓐ; trop. Afr, nat. in S-Afr.
– **speciosa** Torr. · E:Showy Milkweed; G:Pracht-Seidenpflanze · ⟁ ⚘ Z2 VI-VIII; Can.: W; USA: NW, . Calif., Rocky Mts., NC, SW, Tex.
– **syriaca** L. · E:Silkweed; G:Gewöhnliche Seidenpflanze · ⟁ ⚘ ⋀ VI-VIII ⋊ Ⓝ; Can.: E, Sask.; USA: NE, NCE, NC, SC, SE, nat. in Eur.
– **tuberosa** L. · E:Butterfly Weed, Pleurisy Root; G:Knollige Seidenpflanze · ⟁ ⚘ ⋀ VI-VIII ⚥ ⋊; USA: NE, NCE, NC, SW, Rocky Mts., SC, SE, Fla.

× **Ascocenda** hort. -f- *Orchidaceae* (*Ascocentrum* × *Vanda*)

Ascocentrum Schltr. -n- *Orchidaceae* · 13 spp.
– **ampullaceum** (Lindl.) Schltr. · ♄ Z10 ⓦ V-VI ▽ ✳; Him., Burma, Thail.
– **curvifolium** (Lindl.) Schltr. · ♄ Z10 ⓦ ▽ ✳; Ind. (Assam), Nepal, Indochina
– **miniatum** (Lindl.) Schltr. · ⟁ Z10 ⓦ ▽ ✳; Him., Indochina, Java, Phil.

× **Ascofinetia** hort. -f- *Orchidaceae* (*Ascocentrum* × *Neofinetia*)

× **Ascorachnis** hort. -f- *Orchidaceae* (*Arachnis* × *Ascocentrum*)

Asimina Adans. -f- *Annonaceae* · 8 spp. · E:Pawpaw; F:Asiminier; G:Papau
– **triloba** (L.) Dunal · E:Pawpaw; G:Dreilappige Papau, Indianerbanane · ♄ ♄ d Z6 IV-V Ⓝ; Ont., USA: NE, NCE, NC, SC, SE, Fla.

Aspalathus L. -f- *Fabaceae* · 278 spp. · E:Rooibos; G:Rotbusch
– **acuminata** Lam. · ♄ e Z9 Ⓐ; S-Afr.
– **contaminata** (L.) Druce · ♄ e Z9 Ⓐ; S-Afr.
– **linearis** (Burm. f.) R. Dahlgren · E:Rooibos; G:Rooibos, Rotbusch · ♄ e Z9 Ⓐ ⚥ Ⓝ; S-Afr.

Aspalthium Medik. = Bituminaria
– *bituminosum* (L.) Fourr. = Bituminaria bituminosa

Asparagus L. -m- *Asparagaceae* · 212 spp. · E:Asparagus; F:Asperge; G:Spargel
– **acutifolius** L. · ♄ e ⚘ Z8 Ⓐ; Eur.: Ib, Fr, Ital-P, Ba; TR, N-Afr.
– **africanus** Lam. · ♄ e ⚘ Z9 Ⓐ; Namibia, S-Afr.
– **albus** L. · ♄ e ⚘ Z8 Ⓐ; Eur.: Ib, Ital-P; NW-Afr.
– **asparagoides** (L.) W. Wight · E:Bridal

Creeper, Smilax Asparagus; G:Stech-
winden-Spargel · ⁴ ⚡ ✕ Z10 ⓦ; Cape,
nat. in S-Eur.
- **cochinchinensis** (Lour.) Merr. · E:Lucid
  Asparagus; G:Chinesischer Spargel · ♄ e
  ⚡ Z7 ∧; China, Korea, Jap., Taiwan
- **declinatus** L. · E:Basket Asparagus;
  G:Krauser Spargel · ⁴ ⚡ ⚡ Z9 ⓚ; S-Afr.
- *decumbens* Jacq. = Asparagus declinatus
- **deflexus** Baker · ♄ ⚡ ⓚ; Angola
- **densiflorus** (Kunth) Jessop · E:Emerald
  Fern, Foxtail Fern; G:Zier-Spargel · ♄ e ⚡
  ✕ Z9 ⓚ ♡; S-Afr.: Natal
- **drepanophyllus** Welw. ex Baker · ♄ e ⚡
  Z9 ⓦ XII-II; trop. Afr.
- **falcatus** L. · E:Sickle Thorn Asparagus;
  G:Sicheldorn-Spargel · ♄ e ⚡ Z10 ⓦ ⓚ
  VII-VIII; Afr., S-Afr., Sri Lanka
- **filicinus** Buch.-Ham. ex D. Don · E:Fern
  Asparagus · ⁴ ✕ Z8 ∧; Him., SW-China
- **laricinus** Burch. · ♄ e Z9 ⓚ; S-Afr.,
  Botswana
- *lucidus* Lindl. = Asparagus cochinchinensis
- *madagascariensis* Baker = Asparagus
  simluans
- *medeoloides* (L. f.) Thunb. = Asparagus
  asparagoides
- *meyeri* hort. = Asparagus densiflorus
- *myersii* hort. = Asparagus densiflorus
- **officinalis** L. · E:Asparagus, Sparrow
  Grass, Wild Asparagus; G:Gemüse-
  Spargel · ⁴ ✕ Z4 V ⚡ ⓝ; Eur.*, Cauc.,
  W-Sib., nat. in N-Am.
- *plumosus* Baker = Asparagus setaceus
- **pseudoscaber** Grecescu · ⁴ ✕ Z4 IV-V;
  Eur.: Ba, RO, W-Russ.
- **racemosus** Willd. · ♄ e ⚡ Z9 ⓚ; E-Afr.,
  S-Afr., trop. As.
- **ramosissimus** Baker · ⁴ ⚡ Z9 ⓚ; Cape
- **retrofractus** L. · ♄ e ⚡ Z9 ⓚ; S-Afr.
- **scandens** Thunb. · E:Basket Asparagus;
  G:Kletternder Spargel · ⁴ ⚡ Z9 ⓚ; S-Afr.
- var. *deflexus* Baker = Asparagus ramosissimus
- **setaceus** (Kunth) Jessop · E:Asparagus
  Fern; G:Farn-Spargel, Feder-Spargel · ♄ e
  ⚡ ✕ Z9 ⓦ ♡ IX-X; S-Afr.
- **simluans** Baker · ♄ e Z9 ⓦ; Madag.
- **tenuifolius** Lam. · G:Zartblättriger
  Spargel · ⁴ ⚭ ✕ Z7 V; Eur.: Fr, Ital-P,
  C-Eur., Ba, E-Eur.; TR
- *tetragonus* Bresler = Asparagus racemosus
- **trichophyllus** Bunge · ⁴ ✕ Z6; Sib.,

N-China
- **umbellatus** Link · ♄ e ⚭ Z9 ⓚ VI-VIII;
  Canar., Madeira
- **verticillatus** L. · ♄ ⚡ ✕ Z6; Eur.: Ba,
  E-Eur.; TR, N-Iraq, Cauc., Iran, C-As.
- **virgatus** Baker · ⁴ Z9 ⓚ; S-Afr.

Aspasia Lindl. -f- *Orchidaceae* · 8 spp.
- **lunata** Lindl. · ⁴ Z10 ⓦ IV-V ▽ ✳; Braz.

Asperugo L. -f- *Boraginaceae* · 1 sp. ·
E:Madwort; F:Rapette; G:Scharfkraut,
Schlangenäuglein
- **procumbens** L. · G:Scharfkraut,
  Schlangenäuglein · ⊙ V-VIII; Eur.:
  C-Eur., Ital-P, EC-Eur., Sc, Ba, E-Eur.;
  TR, Levant, Cauc., W-Sib., E-Sib., C-As.,
  Him., NW-Afr., Libya, nat. in Ib, Fr

Asperula L. -f- *Rubiaceae* · 181 sp. ·
E:Woodruff; F:Aspérule: G:Meier, Meister
- **arcadiensis** Sims · ⁴ Z8 V-VI; S-GR
- **aristata** L. f. · G:Grannen-Meier · ⁴ Z7
  VI-VIII; Eur.: Ib, Fr, Sw, Ital-P, A, Ba, RO
- **arvensis** L. · E:Blue Woodruff; G:Acker-
  Meier · ⊙ V-VI; Eur.* exc. BrI, Sc; TR,
  Iraq, Cauc., Iran, nat. in Sc
- **cynanchica** L. · E:Squinancy Wort;
  G:Hügel-Meier · ⁴ △ Z6 VI-IX; Eur.* exc.
  Sc; Cauc.
- **gussonii** Boiss. · ⁴ △ Z7 VII-VIII; N-Sic.
- **hexaphylla** All. · E:Six-leaved Woodruff ·
  ⁴ △ VI-VII; Eur.: F, I; SW-Alp.
- **hirta** Ramond · ⁴ △ Z6 VII-X; Eur.: sp.,
  F; Pyr.
- **lilaciflora** Boiss. · E:Woodruff · ⁴ △ Z5
  VI-VII; TR
- subsp. *caespitosa* Boiss. = Asperula
  lilaciflora
- **neilreichii** Beck · G:Ostalpen-Meier ·
  ⁴ △ VI-IX; Eur.: G, A, Slova., ? RO, ?
  W-Russ; NE-Alp., Carp.
- **nitida** Sm. · ⁴ △ Z7 VII-VIII; NW-TR
  (Ulu Dagh)
- *odorata* L. = Galium odoratum
- **orientalis** Boiss. & Hohen. · F:Aspérule
  azurée · ⊙ D VI-VII; TR, Syr., Iraq, Cauc.,
  Iran, nat. in H
- **purpurea** (L.) Ehrend. · G:Purpur-Meier ·
  ⁴ VII-VIII; Eur.: Fr, Ch, A, Ba, RO
- *setosa* hort. = Asperula orientalis
- *suberosa* Guss. = Asperula gussonii
- **suberosa** Sibth. & Sm. · ⁴ △ Z7 V-VI;
  N-GR, SW-BG
- **taurina** L. · E:Southern Woodruff;

G:Turiner Meier · ♃ Z4 V-VI; Eur.: Ib, Fr, Sw, A, Ba, RO, Crim; TR, Cauc., N-Iran, nat. in BrI, G, DK
- **tinctoria** L. · E:Dyer's Woodruff; G:Färber-Meier · ♃ Z4 VI-VII; Eur.* exc. BrI, Ib; S-Ural

Asphodeline Rchb. -f- *Asphodelaceae* · 17 spp. · E:Jacob's Rod; F:Asphodéline; G:Junkerlilie
- *balansae* Baker = Asphodeline damascena
- **damascena** (Boiss.) Baker · ♃ Z8 ⌂ ∧ V; TR, Syr.
- *isthmocarpa* Baker = Asphodeline damascena
- **liburnica** (Scop.) Rchb. · ♃ Z7 ∧ VI; Eur.: S-I, Ba, ? H; TR
- **lutea** (L.) Rchb. · E:King's Spear, Yellow Asphodel; F:Bâton de Jacob; G:Junkerlilie · ♃ Z7 ∧ V-VI; Eur.: Ital-P, Ba, RO; TR, Cauc.
- **taurica** (Pall.) Kunth · ♃ Z7 ∧ IV-V; GR, TR, Cauc.
- **tenuior** (Fisch.) Ledeb. · ♃ Z8 ⌂ ∧ VI; Cauc., Iran

Asphodelus L. -m- *Asphodelaceae* · 17 spp. · E:Asphodel; F:Asphodèle; G:Affodill
- **albus** Mill. · E:White Asphodel; F:Asphodèle blanche; G:Weißer Affoldill · ♃ Z6 V-VI ✿ Ⓝ; Eur.: Ib, Fr, Sw, Ital-P, Ba; NW-Afr.
- **fistulosus** L. · E:Hollow-stemmed Asphodel; G:Röhriger Affodill · ☉ ♃ Z8 ⌂ ✿; Eur.: Ib, Fr, Ital-P, Ba; TR, Arab., Canar., N-Afr.
- *liburnicus* Scop. = Asphodeline liburnica
- *luteus* L. = Asphodeline lutea
- *tauricus* Pall. = Asphodeline taurica

Aspidistra Ker-Gawl. -f- *Convallariaceae* · 62 spp. · E:Bar-Room Plant; F:Aspidistra, Plante des concierges; G:Schildnarbe, Schusterpalme
- **elatior** Blume · E:Bar-Room Plant, Cast-iron Plant; G:Gewöhnliche Schusterpalme · ♃ Z7 II-IV; China, nat. in Jap.
- **lurida** Ker-Gawl. · ♃ Z8 ⌂ III-V; China

Aspidosperma Mart. & Zucc. -n- *Apocynaceae* · 69 spp. · E:Quebracho; G:Quebrachobaum
- **quebracho-blanco** Schltdl. · E:Kebrako, Quebracho; G:Quebrachobaum · ♄ ⌂ ♠ ✿ Ⓝ; w S-Am.

- **ramiflorum** Müll. Arg. · ♄ ✄ ⌂; Braz.

Asplenium L. -n- *Aspleniaceae* · 745 spp. · E:Spleenwort; F:Doradille; G:Streifenfarn
- *achilleifolium* (Lam.) C. Chr. = Asplenium rutifolium
- **adiantum-nigrum** L. · E:Black Spleenwort; G:Schwarzer Streifenfarn · ♃ △ Z6 VII-VIII; Eur.*, TR, Cyprus, Cauc., C-As. (Tien-schan), NW-Afr.
- **adulterinum** Milde · G:Braungrüner Streifenfarn · ♃ Z4 VII-VIII ▽; Eur.: Sc, C-Eur., EC-Eur., Ital-P, Ba, RO
- ✕ **alternifolium** Wulfen (*A. septentrionale* ✕ *A. trichomanes*)
- **nothosubp. alternifolium** (*A. septentrionale* ✕ *A. trichomanes* subsp. *trichomanes*) · G:Deutscher Streifenfarn · ♃ VII-IX; Eur. , W-TR
- *angustifolium* Michx. = Athyrium pycnocarpon
- **antiquum** Makino · ♃ Z9 ⌂; Jap., Riukiu-Is., Taiwan
- **australasicum** (J. Sm.) Hook. · E:Bird's Nest Fern, Crow's Nest; G:Nestfarn · ♃ Z10 ⌂; E-Afr., trop. As., Austr., Polyn.
- *belangeri* Bory = Asplenium thunbergii
- *belangeri* Kunze = Asplenium decorum
- *bilotii* F.W. Schultz = Asplenium obovatum subsp. lanceolatum
- **bulbiferum** G. Forst. · E:Hen-and-Chicken Fern, Mother Fern; G:Lebendgebärender Streifenfarn · ♃ Z10 ⌂; Austr., NZ, N-Ind.
- **ceterach** L. · E:Rusty Spleenwort; F:Herbe dorée; G:Milzfarn, Schriftfarn · ♃ Z7 ⌂ ∧ VI-VIII; Eur.* exc Sc; TR, Levant, Cauc., C-As., Him., N-Afr.
- **cuneifolium** Viv. · G:Serpentin-Streifenfarn · ♃ Z5 VII-VIII ▽; Eur.* exc BrI, Sc, ? Ib; TR; Cauc., S-China
- **daucifolium** Lam. · ♃ Z10 ⌂; Mascarene Is.
- **decorum** Kunze · ♃ ⌂; Sri Lanka, Indochina, Phil., Sumat., N.Guinea
- **dimorphum** Kunze · ♃ Z9 ⌂; Norfolk Is.
- *ebeneum* Aiton · Asplenium platyneuron
- **fissum** Kit. ex Willd. · G:Zerschlitzter Streifenfarn · ♃ △ Z6 VII-IX ▽; Eur.: F, I, C-Eur., Ba; mts.
- **fontanum** (L.) Bernh. · E:Smooth Rock Spleenwort; G:Jura-Streifenfarn · ♃ △ Z6 VII-IX ▽; Eur.: Ib, Fr, , Ital-P, C-Eur., Ec-Eur., Ba; Moroc.
- **foreziense** Magnier · G:Französischer

Streifenfarn · �

Streifenfarn · ♃ Z7 VI-IX ▽; Eur.: Ib, Fr, Ital-P, C-Eur., W-Ba
- *forisiense* Legrand = Asplenium foreziense
- *halleri* (Roth) DC. = Asplenium fontanum
- *lanceolatum* Huds. = Asplenium obovatum subsp. lanceolatum
- **lepidum** C. Presl · G:Zarter Streifenfarn · ♃ Z6 III-X; Eur.: Ib, Fr, A, H, Ba, RO; TR
- **longissimum** Blume · ♃ Z10 🐾; Malay. Arch.
- *lucidum* G. Forst. non Burm. = Asplenium lyallii
- **lyallii** (Hook. f.) T. Moore · ♃ Z9 🐾; Madag., S-Afr., NZ
- × **murbeckii** Dörfl. (*A. ruta-muraria* × *A. septentrionale*) · G:Schwäbischer Streifenfarn · ♃; Eur.: sp., F, GB, Sc, C-Eur., H, RO: Cauc.
- **nidus** L. · E:Bird's Nest Fern; G:Vogel-Nestfarn · ♃ Z10 🐾; E-Afr., trop. As., Austr., Polyn.
- var. *australasicum* J. Sm. = Asplenium australasicum
- *nidus-avis* hort. = Asplenium nidus
- **obovatum** Viv.
- subsp. *bilottii* (F.W. Schultz) O. Bolòs = Asplenium obovatum subsp. lanceolatum
- subsp. **lanceolatum** (Fiori) P. Silva · E:Billot's Spleenwort; G:Billots Streifenfarn · ♃ VII-IX; Eur.: Ba; TR
- subsp. **obovatum** · E:Lanceolate Spleenwort; G:Lanzettblättriger Streifenfarn · ♃ Z8 🏠 🏡 ∧; Eur.: Ba; , Canar.; TR
- **onopteris** L. · E:Irish Spleenwort; G:Spitzer Streifenfarn · ♃ Z6 V-X; Eur.: Ib, IRL, Fr, Ital-P, H, PL, Ba, RO; TR, Levant, NW-Afr., Libya
- **platyneuron** (L.) Oakes · E:Ebony Spleenwort; G:Breitnerviger Streifenfarn · ♃ Z5; Can.: E; USA: NE, NCE, NC, Colo., SC, SE, Fla.; W-Ind., n S-Am., S-Afr.
- **rhizophyllum** L. · E:Walking Fern, Walking Leaf; G:Kriechender Streifenfarn · ♃ Z6 🏠; Can.: E; USA: NE, NCE, Mo., Okla., SE
- **ruta-muraria** L. · E:Wall Rue; G:Mauer-Streifenfarn, Mauerraute · ♃ △ Z6 VII-IX; Eur.*, TR, Syr., Cauc., C-As., W-Sib., E-Sib., Amur, Moroc., Alger., Can.: E; USA: NE., NC, SE
- **rutifolium** (P.J. Bergius) Kunze · ♃ Z10 🐾; Ind., China, S-Korea, Jap., Taiwan
- **scolopendrium** L. · E:Hart's Tongue Fern, Hart's Tongue; F:Scolopendre; G:Hirschzungenfarn · ♃ Z5 ⏱ VII-VIII 🜊

▽; Eur.*, TR, Syr., Palest., Cauc., N-Iran, Jap., Canar., NW-Afr., Libya, Can., USA: NE, NCE, SE; Mex.
- some cultivars
- **seelosii** Leyb. · G:Dolomit-Streifenfarn · ♃ Z6 VII-VIII; Eur.: Ib, Fr, C-Eur., Ital-P, Ba; N-Sp., Pyr., Alp.; Moroc.
- **septentrionale** (L.) Hoffm. · E:Forked Spleenwort, Grass Fern; G:Nordischer Streifenfarn · ♃ △ Z3 VII-VIII; Eur.*, TR, Cauc., W-Sib., C-As., Him., Moroc., USA: NC, SC, SW, Rocky Mts., Calif.
- **serra** Langsd. & Fisch. · E:Creeping Spleenwort · ♃ Z9 🐾; trop. Am., trop. Afr.
- **tenerum** G. Forst. · ♃ Z10 🐾; trop. As., Polyn.
- var. *belangeri* Bory = Asplenium thunbergii
- **thunbergii** Kunze · ♃ Z10 🐾; Malaysia
- **trichomanes** L. · E:Maidenhair Spleenwort; F:Fausse-Capillaire; G:Silikatliebender Brauner Streifenfarn · ♃ △ Z2 VII-VIII; cosmop.
- **viride** Huds. · E:Green Spleenwort; G:Grüner Streifenfarn · ♃ △ Z5 VII-VIII; Eur.*, TR, Cyprus, Cauc., W-Sib., E-Sib., C-As., Him., Moroc., Alaska, Can., USA: NE, NCE, NC, Rocky Mts., NW, Calif., Greenl.
- *viviparum* (L. f.) C. Presl = Asplenium daucifolium

Asplundia Harling -f- *Cyclanthaceae* · 100 spp.
- **humilis** (Poepp. & Endl.) Harling · ♄ e Z10 🐾; Col.
- **latifolia** (Ruiz & Pav.) Harling · ♄ e Z10 🐾; W.Ind.
- **moritziana** (Klotzsch) Harling · ♄ e Z10 🏠; Col.

× **Aspoglossum** hort. -n- *Orchidaceae* (*Aspasia* × *Odontoglossum*)

Astartea DC. -f- *Myrtaceae* · 7-8 spp.
- **fascicularis** DC. · ♄ 🏠; Austr.: W-Austr.

Astelia Banks & Sol. ex R. Br. -f- *Asteliaceae* · 26 spp.
- **banksii** A. Cunn. · ♃ Z9 🏠; NZ

Aster L. -m- *Asteraceae* · 250 spp. · E:Aster, Michaelmas Daisy; F:Aster; G:Aster
- *ageratoides* Turcz. = Aster trinervius

subsp. ageratoides
- var. *ovatus* (Fr. & Sav.) Kitam. = Aster trinervius subsp. microcephalus
- **albescens** (DC.) Hand.-Mazz. · E:Shrubby Aster · ♭ △ Z6 VII-VIII; Kashmir, Him., SW-China, Burma
- × **alpellus** hort. (*A. alpinus* × *A. amellus*) · ⁴ △ Z3 VI-VII; cult.
- **alpigenus** (Torr. & A. Gray) A. Gray · E:Tundra Aster; G:Oregon-Aster
- subsp. **alpigenus** · ⁴ Z7; USA: NW, Calif., Rocky Mts.
- subsp. **andersonii** (A. Gray) M. Peck · ⁴ Z7 VII-IX; USA: NW, Calif., Nev.
- **alpinus** L. · E:Alpine Aster, Blue Alpine Daisy; F:Aster des Alpes; G:Alpen-Aster · ⁴ △ Z3 VI ▽; Eur.* exc. BrI, Sc; mts.; TR, Cauc., N-Iran, W-Sib., E-Sib., C-As., Mong., China, Alaska, Can., USA: Rocky Mts.
- **some cultivars**
- var. *dolomiticus* (Beck) Onno = Aster alpinus
- **amellus** L. · E:Italian Aster, Italian Starwort; G:Berg-Aster, Kalk-Aster · ⁴ Z5 VII-IX ▽; Eur.: Fr, Ital-P, C-Eur., EC-Eur., Ba, E-Eur.; TR, Cauc.
- **many cultivars**
- *andersonii* A. Gray = Aster alpigenus subsp. andersonii
- **asteroides** (DC.) Kuntze · ⁴ △ Z6 V-VI; Bhutan, SE-Tibet, W-China
- **azureus** Lindl. · E:Sky blue Aster · ⁴ Z5 VIII-IX; Ont., USA: NE, NCE, SC, SE
- **bellidiastrum** (L.) Scop. · E:Daisy-star Aster; G:Alpenmaßliebchen · ⁴ △ Z6 IV-VI; Eur.: Fr, Ital-P, C-Eur., EC-Eur., Ba, ? RO; mts.
- *canus* Waldst. & Kit. = Aster sedifolius subsp. canus
- *chinensis* L. = Callistephus chinensis
- **ciliolatus** Lindl. · E:Lindley's Aster; G:Lindleys Aster · ⁴ Z2 IX-X; Can.; USA: NE, NCE, NC, Rocky Mts.
- **cordifolius** L. · E:Blue Wood Aster; G:Blaue Wald-Aster
- **some cultivars**
- subsp. **cordifolius** · F:Aster à feuilles en couer · ⁴ Z3 IX-X; Can.: E; USA; NE, NCE, SE
- **diplostephioides** (DC.) C.B. Clarke · ⁴ △ Z5 V-VI; Him., SE-Tibet, W-China
- **divaricatus** L. · E:White Wood Aster; F:Aster divariqué; G:Weiße Wald-Aster · ⁴ Z4 IX-X; Can.: E; USA: NE, NCE, SE,

nat. in NL
- **dumosus** L. · E:Bushy Aster, Rice Button Aster; F:Aster nain d'automne; G:Buschige Aster, Kissen-Aster · ⁴ Z3 VIII-X; Can.: E; USA: NE, NCE, SE
- **many cultivars**
- **ericoides** L. · E:White Heath Aster; G:Erika-Aster, Myrten-Aster
- **some cultivars**
- subsp. **ericoides** · ⁴ Z3 IX-XI; Can.: W; USA: NE, NCE, NC, Rocky Mts., SW, SC, SE; Mex.
- **farreri** W.W. Sm. & Jeffrey · ⁴ △ Z4 V-VI; Tibet, W-China
- **flaccidus** Bunge · ⁴ △ Z6 V-VI; C-As., Afgh., Pakist., Him., SW-China
- × **frikartii** Silva Tar. & C.K. Schneid. (*A. amellus* × *A. thomsonii*) · E:Frikart's Aster; F:Aster de Frikart; G:Frikarts Aster · ⁴ Z4 VIII-XI; cult.
- **some cultivars**
- **himalaicus** C.B. Clarke · ⁴ △ Z6 V-VI; Nepal, Bhutan, Sikkim, Tibet, N-Ind.: Assam; Burma
- *hirsuticaulis* Lindl. ex DC. = Aster lateriflorus
- **laevis** L. · E:Smooth Aster; G:Glatte Aster, Kahle Aster · ⁴ Z4 X; Can., USA* exc. Calif., SC, nat. in Eur.
- **lanceolatus** Willd. · E:White Panicle Aster · ⁴ Z4 VIII-X; N-Am., nat. in Eur.*
- **lateriflorus** (L.) Britton · E:Farewell Summer, Starved Aster; F:Aster à fleurs latérales; G:Kattun-Aster, Verkümmerte Aster · ⁴ Z3 IX-X; Can.: E; USA: NE, NCE, SE
- *likiangensis* Franch. = Aster asteroides
- *lindleyanus* Torr. & A. Gray = Aster ciliolatus
- **linosyris** (L.) Bernh. · E:Goldilocks; F:Aster doré; G:Goldhaar-Aster · ⁴ Z4 VIII-X; Eur.*, TR, Cauc., Alger.
- *lutescens* (Lindl.) Torr. & A. Gray = Aster ptarmicoides var. lutescens
- × *luteus* hort. = × Solidaster luteus
- **macrophyllus** L. · E:Bigleaf Aster; G:Herzblättrige Aster · ⁴ Z3 VIII; Can.: E; USA: NE, NCE, SE, nat. in NL, N-G, PL
- *multiflorus* Aiton = Aster ericoides subsp. ericoides
- **novae-angliae** L. · E:New England Aster; F:Aster de Nouvelle-Angleterre; G:Neuengland-Aster, Raublatt-Aster · ⁴ ⋈ Z2 X-XI; Can., USA: NE, SE, NC, Rocky Mts., SW, nat. in C-Eur.

- **many cultivars**
- **novi-belgii** L. · E:Michaelmas Daisy;
  F:Aster à feuilles lisses; G:Glattblatt-
  Aster, Neubelgien-Aster · ⁤⁤ 24 ✕ Z2 X; Can.:
  E; USA: NE, SE, nat. in Eur.*
- **many cultivars**
- **parviceps** (E.S. Burgess) Mack. & Bush ·
  E:Smallhead Aster · 24 ✕ X-XI; USA:
  Iowa, Ill., Mo.
- **parviflorus** Nees · E:Smallflower Tans-
  yaster; G:Kleinblütige Aster · 24 VIII-X;
  Can.: E; USA: NE, NCE, nat. in C-Eur.
- **pilosus** Willd. · E:White Oldfield Aster;
  G:Weichhaarige Aster
  - var. **demotus** S.F. Blake · G:Kleinköpfige
    Aster · 24 Z5 VIII-X; Can.: Ont.; USA: NE,
    NCE, SE
  - var. **pilosus** · 24 Z5; Can.: E; USA: NE,
    NCE, NC, SE, nat. in Eur.
- **pringlei** (A. Gray) Britton · E:Pringle's
  Aster; G:Pringles Aster · 24 IX-X; Can.:
  Ont.; USA: NE, NCE, SE
- **ptarmicoides** (Nees) Torr. & A. Gray ·
  E:Prairie Goldenrod; G:Hochland-Aster
  - var. **lutescens** (Lindl.) A. Gray · G:Gelbe
    Hochland-Aster · Z3; Can.: W, Sask.;
    USA: NCE, NC
  - var. **ptarmicoides** · G:Weiße Hochland-
    Aster · 24 Z3 VIII-IX; USA: NE, NCE, NC,
    SE
- *purdomii* Hutch. = Aster flaccidus
- **pyrenaeus** Desf. ex DC. · E:Pyrenean
  Aster; F:Aster des Pyrénées; G:Pyrenäen-
  Aster · 24 Z6 VIII-IX ▽; Eur.: F; Pyr.
- × **salignus** Willd. (*A. lanceolatus* × *A.
  novi-belgii*) · G:Weidenblättrige Aster · 24
  Z2 VIII-X; Eur.: G, BrI, F, H; W-Sib., nat.
  in Eur.* exc. Ib
- **savatieri** Makino · 24 △ Z7 V-VII; Jap.
- **schreberi** Nees · E:Schreber's Aster;
  G:Schrebers Aster · 24 VII-VIII; USA: NE,
  NCE, nat. in Scotland
- **sedifolius** L.
  - subsp. **canus** (Waldst. & Kit.) Merxm. ·
    G:Graue Aster · 24 Z6 IX-X; Eur.: A,
    Slova., H, Serb., BG, RO
  - subsp. **sedifolius** · F:Aster à fleurs en
    étoile · ☉ 24 Z6 VIII-IX; Eur.* exc. BrI, Sc;
    Cauc., Sib.
- **shortii** Lindl. · E:Short's Aster; G:Shorts
  Aster · 24 Z4 IX-X; USA: NE, NCE, SE
- **sibiricus** L. · E:Arctic Aster; G:Arktische
  Aster · 24 Z3 VIII-IX ▽; Eur.: Norw.,
  Russ., W-Sib., E-Sib., Amur, Sakhal.,
  Kamchat., Alaska, Can.: W; USA: NW

- *spectabilis* Willd. = Aster novi-belgii
- **stracheyi** Hook. f. · 24 △ Z6 V-VI;
  W-Him.
- *subcoeruleus* S. Moore = Aster tongolensis
- **subintegerrimus** (Trautv.) Ostenf. &
  Resv.-Holms. = Aster sibiricus
- **tataricus** L. f. · E:Tartarian Aster;
  G:Tatarische Aster · 24 Z3 VIII-X ♀ ; Sib.,
  Mong., China, Manch., Korea, Jap.
- **thomsonii** C.B. Clarke · 24 Z7 VII-IX;
  W-Him.
- **tibeticus** Hook. f. · G:Tibet-Aster · 24 △
  Z6 V-VI; Him., Tibet
- **tongolensis** Franch. · F:Aster de
  l'Himalaya; G:Sichuan-Aster · 24 △ Z6
  V-VI; W-China
- *tradescantii* hort. = Aster pilosus var.
  demotus
- **tradescantii** L. · E:Shore Aster, Trades-
  cant's Aster; G:Tradescants Aster · 24 Z3
  VIII-X; Can.: E; USA: NE, NCE
- **trinervius** Roxb. ex D. Don
  - subsp. **ageratoides** (Turcz.) Grierson ·
    24 Z7; Him. (Nepal, Assam), N-Burma,
    SW-China, Tibet
  - subsp. **trinervius** · 24 Z7; Him.
  - subsp. **microcephalus** (Miq.) Makino · 24
    Z7; Jap.
- **tripolium** L. · E:Sea Aster; G:Strand-
  Aster · ☉ Z6 VII-IX; Eur.*, Cauc., W-Sib.,
  E-Sib., Sakhal., C-As., Mong., China,
  Korea, Jap.
- **umbellatus** Mill. · E:Parasol Whitetop,
  Umbelled Aster; G:Schirm-Aster · 24 Z3
  VIII-IX; Can.: E; USA: NE, NCE, SE
- × **versicolor** Willd. (*A. laevis* × *A. novi-
  belgii*) · G:Bunte Glattblatt-Aster · 24 Z2
  IX-X; cult., nat. in Eur.: Fr, I, BrI, C-Eur.,
  EC-Eur., RO
- **vimineus** Lam. · E:Calico Aster · 24 Z3
  VIII-X; Can.: E; USA: NE, NCE, SC, SE
- **yunnanensis** Franch. · E:Calico Aster · 24
  △ Z5 V-VI; W-China

× *Asterago* Everett = × Solidaster
- *lutea* Everett = × Solidaster luteus

Asteranthera Hanst. -f- *Gesneriaceae* · 1 sp. ·
- **ovata** (Cav.) Hanst. · E:Estrellita · ♄ e ⚥
  Z9 ⌂ XII-V; S-Chile

Asteriscus Mill. -m- *Asteraceae* · 3 spp. ·
F:Astérolide; G:Sternauge
- **aquaticus** (L.) Less. · G:Gewöhnliches
  Sternauge · ☉ Z7; Eur.: Ib, Fr, Ital-P, Ba;

TR, N-Afr.
- **maritimus** (L.) Less. · ⁴ Z8 ⓚ VIII-IX;
Eur.: Ib, F, Ital-P, GR, Canar.; N-Afr.
- **pygmaeus** Coss. & Kralik · ☉ Z7; N-Afr.,
Iran, Pakist.
- *sericeus* (L. f.) DC. = Nauplius sericeus
- **spinosus** (L.) Cass. · ☉ ⊙ Z7; Eur.: Ib,
F, Ital-P, Ba, Crim; TR, Cyprus, Levant,
N-Afr., Canar.

Astilbe Buch.-Ham. ex G. Don -f-
Saxifragaceae · 12 spp. · E:False Buck's
Beard; F:Astilbe; G:Astilbe, Prachtspiere
- × **arendsii** Arends (*A. astilboides × A.*
chinensis var. davidii × A. thunbergii × A.
yakushimana) · G:Garten-Astilbe · ⁴ Z6;
cult.
- **many cultivars**
- **astilboides** (Maxim.) Lemoine · ⁴ Z6
VII; Jap.
- **chinensis** (Maxim.) Franch. & Sav.
- var. **chinensis** · E:Chinese Astilbe;
F:Astilbe naine; G:China-Astilbe · ⁴ Z5
VII; Amur, N-China, Korea
- var. **davidii** Franch. · G:Hohe China-
Astilbe · ⁴ VII; Amur, N-China, Manch.,
Korea, Jap.
- var. **pumila** Vilm. · G:Zwerg-Astilbe · ⁴
Z5 VIII-IX; Tibet
- var. **taquetii** (H. Lév.) Vilm. · G:Purpur-
Astilbe · ⁴ Z5 VII; E-China
- × **crispa** (Arends) Bergmans · ⁴ Z6; cult.
- *davidii* (Franch.) A. Henry = Astilbe
chinensis var. davidii
- **glaberrima** Nakai
- var. **glaberrima** · ⁴ Z6; Jap.: Kyushu
- var. **saxatilis** Nakai · ⁴ △ Z6 VII-VIII;
Jap.
- **grandis** Stapf ex E.H. Wilson · ⁴ VII-VIII;
NW-China, C-China
- **japonica** (C. Morren & Decne.) A. Gray ·
E:Japanese Astilbe; F:Astilbe du Japon;
G:Japanische Astilbe · ⁴ Z5 V-VI; Jap.
- **many cultivars**
- **koreana** (Kom.) Nakai · E:Korean
Astilbe; G:Koreanische Astilbe · ⁴ Z7
VII-VIII; Korea, N-China
- **rivularis** Buch.-Ham. · F:Astilbe des ruis-
seaux; G:Bach-Astilbe · ⁴ Z7 VIII; Him.
- **simplicifolia** Makino · F:Astilbe glabre;
G:Kleine Astilbe · ⁴ Z7 VII; Jap.
- **some cultivars**
- *taquetii* (H. Lév.) Koidz. = Astilbe
chinensis var. taquetii
- **thunbergii** (Siebold & Zucc.) Miq. ·

E:Thunberg's Astilbe · ⁴ Z7 VII-VIII; Jap.

Astilboides (Hemsl.) Engl. -f-
Saxifragaceae · 1 sp. · G:Tafelblatt
- **tabularis** (Hemsl.) Engl. · G:Tafelblatt ·
⁴ ⌇ Z7 VI; Manch., N-Korea

Astragalus L. -m- *Fabaceae* · c. 2000 spp. ·
E:Milk Vetch; F:Astragale, Réglisse
sauvage; G:Berglinse, Stragel, Tragant
- **alopecuroides** L. · G:Fuchsschwanz-
Tragant · ⁴ Z6; sp., S-F
- **alpinus** L. · E:Alpine Milk Vetch;
G:Alpen-Tragant · ⁴ Z5 VI-VIII; Eur.*,
Cauc., W-Sib., E-Sib., Amur, Kamchat.,
C-As; N-Am.
- **angustifolius** Lam. · F:Astragale à
feuilles étroites · ♄ △ Z8 ⓚ VII-VIII; Eur.:
Ba; TR, Cauc.
- **arenarius** L. · G:Sand-Tragant · ⁴ VI-VII
▽; Eur.: G, Swed, EC-Eur., E-Eur.
- **asper** Jacq. · G:Rau-Tragant · ⁴ V-VI;
Eur.: A, EC-Eur., BG, E-Eur.; Cauc.
- **australis** (L.) Lam. · E:Southern Milk
Vetch; G:Südlicher Tragant · ⁴ V-VI;
Eur.* exc. BrI, Sc; mts.; W-Sib., E-Sib.,
Mong.
- **austriacus** L. · E:Austrian Milk Vetch;
G:Österreichischer Tragant · ⁴ VI-VIII;
Eur.* exc. BrI, Sc
- **boeticus** L. · ⁴ Z8 V-VII ⓝ; Eur.: Ib, Fr,
Ital-P, Ba; Levant, Sinai, Iran, N-Afr.,
Macaron.
- **centralpinus** Braun-Blanq. · ⁴ Z6 VII-
VIII ▽; Eur.: F, I, BG; SW-Alp., Rodope
mts.
- **cicer** L. · E:Chick Pea Milk Vetch, Wild
Lentil; G:Kicher-Tragant · ⁴ VI-VIII ⓝ;
Eur.* exc. BrI, Sc; TR, Cauc.
- **danicus** Retz. · E:Purple Milk Vetch;
G:Dänischer Tragant · ⁴ △ Z5 V-VI; Eur.*
exc. Ib, Ba; Cauc., W-Sib., C-As.,
Mong.
- **depressus** L. · E:Sprawling Milk Vetch;
G:Niederliegender Tragant · ⁴ △ Z6
V-VI; Eur.: Ib, Fr, Ital-P, Ba, RO, Sw; TR,
Moroc., Alger.
- **exscapus** L. · E:Stemless Milk Vetch;
G:Stängelloser Tragant · ⁴ △ Z5 V-VI;
Eur.: F, I, C-Eur., EC-Eur., Ba, RO
- **frigidus** (L.) A. Gray · E:Pallid Milk
Vetch; G:Gletscher-Tragant · ⁴ Z5
VII-VIII; Eur.: Fr, Ital-P, C-Eur., EC-Eur.,
Sc, E-Eur.; N, mts.; W-Sib., E-Sib., Amur,
Kamchat.

– **glycyphyllos** L. · E:Wild Liquorice;
  G:Bärenschote, Süßer Tragant · ⚄ Z3
  VI-IX Ⓝ; Eur.*, N-TR, Cauc., W-Sib.
– **gummifer** Labill. · E:Gum Tragacanth;
  G:Gummi-Tragant · ♄ ⓐ ⚥ Ⓝ; TR,
  Lebanon
– **hypoglottis** L. · E:Purple Vetch;
  G:Purpur-Tragant · ⚄ VI-VII; Eur.: sp., F,
  I, Ba
– **leontinus** Wulfen · E:Tyrolean Milk
  Vetch; G:Tiroler Tragant · ⚄ Z5 VI-VII;
  Eur.: F, I, Ch, A, Croatia, Bosn.; Alp.,
  NW-Ba
– **microcephalus** Willd. · ♄ ⓐ ⚥ ; Cauc.,
  TR
– **monspessulanus** L. · E:Montpelier Milk
  Vetch; G:Französischer Tragant · ⚄ △ Z6
  V-VI; Eur.: Ib, Fr, Sw, Ital-P, Ba, E-Eur.;
  NW-Afr.
– **norvegicus** Weber · E:Norwegian Milk
  Vetch; G:Norwegischer Tragant · ⚄
  VII-VIII; Eur.: A, Slova., Sc, Russ., ? RO;
  N, E-Alp., Carp.
– **onobrychis** L. · G:Esparsetten-Tragant ·
  ⚄ Z5 VI-VII; Eur.* exc. BrI, Sc; TR, Cauc.,
  W-Sib., C-As., Alger.
– **penduliflorus** Lam. · E:Mountain Lentil;
  G:Alpen-Blasenschote, Hängeblütiger
  Tragant · ⚄ Z5 VII-VIII; Eur.* exc. BrI;
  S-Swed, Pyr., Alp., Carp.
– *purpureus* Lam. = Astragalus hypoglottis
– **sempervirens** Lam. · E:Mountain
  Tragacanth; G:Dorniger Tragant · ♄ △ Z5
  V-VIII; Eur.: sp., F, I, Sw, GR
– *sericeus* Lam. = Oxytropis halleri
– **sulcatus** L. · G:Ungarischer Tragant · ⚄
  V-VII; Eur.: A, EC-Eur., E-Eur.; W-Sib.,
  E-Sib., C-As.
– **tragacantha** L. · ♄ ⓐ VI-VII; Eur.: Ib, F,
  Cors, Sard.
– **vesicarius** L. · E:Inflated Milk Vetch;
  G:Blasen-Tragant · ⚄ V-VIII; Eur.: Ib, Fr,
  Ital-P, Ba, A, EC-Eur., E-Eur.

Astrantia L. -f- *Apiaceae* · 10 spp. ·
  E:Masterwort; F:Astrance, radiaire;
  G:Sterndolde
– **bavarica** F.W. Schultz · E:Bavarian
  Masterwort; G:Bayerische Sterndolde · ⚄
  △ Z6 VI-VIII; Eur.: I, G, A, Slove.; E-Alp.
– **carniolica** Wulfen · G:Krainer Sterndolde · ⚄ △ Z6 VII-VIII; Eur.: I, A, Slove.;
  SE-Alp.
– *heterophylla* Willd. = Astrantia maxima
– **major** L.

– **many cultivars**
– subsp. **carinthiaca** Arcang. · G:Kärntner
  Sterndolde · ⚄ Z6; Eur.: sp., F, I, Ba; mts.
– subsp. **involucrata** (W.D.J. Koch) Ces. ·
  ⚄ Z6; Eur.: C-Eur.
– subsp. **major** · E:Greater Masterwort;
  F:Grande Astrance; G:Große Sterndolde ·
  ⚄ ✕ Z6 VI-VIII; Eur.* exc. BrI, Sc, nat. in
  BrI, Sc
– **maxima** Pall. · F:Astrance à feuilles
  d'hellébore · ⚄ ✕ Z6 VI-VIII; Cauc., TR
– **minor** L. · E:Lesser Masterwort; G:Kleine
  Sterndolde · ⚄ △ Z6 VII-VIII; Eur.: sp., F,
  Sw, I; Pyr., SW-Alp., N-Apenn.
– *rubra* hort. = Astrantia major subsp.
  major

Astridia Dinter -f- *Aizoaceae* · 12 spp.
– *dinteri* L. Bolus = Astridia velutina
– **velutina** Dinter · ⚄ ♀ Z9 ⓐ; Namibia

Astrocaryum G. Mey. -n- *Arecaceae* ·
  36 spp. · F:Palmier; G:Sternnusspalme
– **aculeatum** G. Mey. · E:Tucuma · ♄ e ⓦ
  Ⓝ; Braz.
– **jauari** Mart. · ♄ e ⓦ Ⓝ; Braz.
– **mexicanum** Liebm. ex Mart. · ♄ e ⓦ;
  Mex., Guat. Hond.
– **murumuru** Mart. · ♄ e ⓦ Ⓝ; Braz.
– *tucuma* Mart. = Astrocaryum aculeatum
– **vulgare** Mart. · ♄ e ⓦ Ⓝ; Braz.

Astroloba Uitewaal -f- *Aloaceae* · 6 spp.
– **congesta** (Salm-Dyck) Uitewaal
– **corrugata** N.L. Meyer & Gideon F. Sm.
– *deltoidea* (Hook. f.) Uitewaal = Astroloba
  congesta
– **foliolosa** (Haw.) Uitewaal
– *muricata* L.E. Groen = Astroloba corrugata
– **spiralis** (L.) Uitewaal · ⚄ ♀ Z9 ⓐ; Cape
– subsp. *foliolosa* (Haw.) L.E. Groen =
  Astroloba foliolosa

Astronium Jacq. -n- *Anacardiaceae* ·
  15 spp. · G:Urundayholz
– **balansae** Engl. · E:Urunday; G:Urunday-
  holz · ♄ Ⓝ; N-Arg., Parag.

Astrophytum Lem. -n- *Cactaceae* · 6 spp. ·
  F:Bonnet d'évêque, Cactus étoilé;
  G:Bischofsmütze, Sternkaktus
– **asterias** (Zucc.) Lem. · E:Sand Dollar,
  Silver Dollar Cactus; G:Seeigel-Sternkak-
  tus · ♀ Z9 ⓐ VI-VIII ▽ ✳; S-Tex., N-Mex.

– **capricorne** (A. Dietr.) Britton & Rose ·
E:Goat's Horn Cactus; G:Bockshorn-
Kaktus · ⵁ Z9 ⊡ ▽ ✳; N-Mex.
– **myriostigma** Lem. · E:Bishop's Cap
Cactus, Bishop's Hood; G:Bischofsmütze ·
ⵁ Z9 ⊡ ▽ ✳; NE-Mex.
– **ornatum** (DC.) F.A.C. Weber · E:Bishop's
Hat, Ornamental Monk's Hood, Star
Cactus; G:Mönchskappe · ⵁ Z9 ⊡ ▽ ✳;
E-Mex.
– **senile** Frič · ⵁ Z9 ⊡; Mex.

Asyneuma Griseb. & Schenk -n-
Campanulaceae · c. 50 spp. · F:Asyneuma;
G:Traubenrapunzel
– **canescens** (Waldst. & Kit.) Griseb. &
Schenk · G:Graue Traubenrapunzel · ⵀ
Z5 VII-VIII; Eur.: EC-Eur., Ba, E-Eur.
– **michauxioides** (Boiss.) Damboldt · ⊙ Z5
VI-VII; TR

Asystasia Blume -f- *Acanthaceae* · c.
70 spp.
– **scandens** (Lindl.) Hook. · ♄ ⊛ VII-VIII;
W-Afr.: Guinea, Sierra Leone, Liberia

Ataenidia Gagnep. -f- *Marantaceae* · 1 sp.
– **conferta** (Benth.) Milne-Redh. · ⵀ Z10
⊛; C-Afr., Angola

Athamanta L. -f- *Apiaceae* · 5-6 spp. ·
E:Athamanta; F:Athamante; G:Augen-
wurz
– **cretensis** L. · E:Candy Carrot; G:Zottige
Augenwurz · ⊙ ⵀ Z6 V-VIII; Eur.: Ib, Fr,
Ital-P, Ba, C-Eur.
– *haynaldii* Borbás & R. Uechtr. =
Athamanta turbith subsp. haynaldii
– *matthioli* Wulfen = Athamanta turbith
subsp. turbith
– *rupestris* Rchb. = Athamanta turbith
subsp. turbith
– **turbith** (L.) Brot.
– subsp. **haynaldii** (Borbás & R. Uechtr.)
Tutin · ⵀ △ Z6 VI-VII; Eur.: A, Slove.,
Croatia, Bosn., YU, AL
– subsp. **turbith** · ⵀ Z6; Eur.: I, Slove.,

Athanasia L. -f- *Asteraceae* · 40 spp.
– **crithmifolia** (L.) L. · ♄ Z9 ⊡ VI-VIII;
S-Afr.
– **parviflora** Murr · ♄ Z9 ⊡; S-Afr.

Athrotaxis D. Don -f- *Taxodiaceae* · 3 spp. ·
G:Schuppenfichte

Athyrium Roth -n- *Woodsiaceae* · 200 spp. ·
E:Lady Fern; F:Fougère femelle;
G:Frauenfarn
– *acrostichoides* (Sw.) Diels = Diplazium
acrostichoides
– *alpestre* (Hoppe) Rylands = Athyrium
distentifolium
– *australe* (R. Br.) C. Presl = Diplazium
australe
– **distentifolium** Tausch ex Opiz · E:Alpine
Lady Fern; G:Gebirgs-Frauenfarn · ⵀ Z5
VII-VIII; Eur.*, TR, Cauc., N-Iran, W-Sib.,
E-Sib., Sakhal., Kamchat., Jap., Alaska,
Can., USA: NW, Rocky Mts., Calif;
Greenl.
– **filix-femina** (L.) Roth · E:Lady Fern,
Southern Lady Fern; F:Fougère femelle;
G:Wald-Frauenfarn · ⵀ Z2 VII-VIII; Eur.*,
TR, Cauc., N-Iran, W-Sib., E-Sib., Amur,
Sakhal., Kamchat., Him., Ind., China,
Jap., NW-Afr., Can., USA*, Mex. S-Am.
(And.)
– **many cultivars**
– *goeringianum* (Kunze) T.V. Moore =
Athyrium niponicum
– **niponicum** (Mett.) Hance · E:Japanese
Painted Fern · ⵀ Z4; China, Manch.,
Korea, Jap., Taiwan
– **pycnocarpon** (Spreng.) Tidestr. ·
E:Glade Fern, Silvery Spleenwort;
G:Silberner Frauenfarn · ⵀ ⌒ Z7; Can.:
E; USA: NE, NCE, SE
– *rhaeticum* (L.) Roth = Athyrium distentifolium
– *thelypteroides* (Michx.) Desv. = Diplazium
acrostichoides
– *umbrosum* (Aiton) C. Presl = Diplazium
australe
– **vidalii** (Franch. & Sav.) Nakai · ⵀ Z7;
Jap., Korea, Taiwan

Atragene L. = Clematis
– *alpina* L. = Clematis alpina
– *macropetala* (Ledeb.) Ledeb. = Clematis
macropetala
– *speciosa* Weinm. = Clematis sibirica

Atraphaxis L. -f- *Polygonaceae* · 25 spp. ·
G:Bocksknöterich
– **frutescens** (L.) K. Koch · G:Strauchiger
Bocksknöterich · ♄ d Z6; Eur.: Russ.,
W-As., C-As.
– *lanceolata* (M. Bieb.) Meisn. = Atraphaxis
frutescens
– **muschketowii** Krasn. · ♄ d △ ⊛ Z5 V-VI;

C-As (Tien-schan)
- **spinosa** L. · G:Dorniger Bocksknöterich ·
ħ d △ ⊛ Z7 VIII; Eur.: E-Russ.; TR, Iran,
SW-As.

Atriplex L. -f- *Chenopodiaceae* · > 200 spp. ·
E:Orache, Saltbush; F:Arroche; G:Melde
- **calotheca** (Rafn) Fr. · G:Pfeilblättrige
Melde · ⊙ VI-IX; Eur.: Sc, G, PL, Russ.;
coasts
- **glabriuscula** Edmondston ·
E:Babington's Orache; G:Kahle Melde · ⊙
VI-IX; Eur.* exc. Ital-P, ? Ib; coasts
- **halimus** L. · E:Tree Purslane · ħ s Z8 ⓚ
VII-IX; Eur.; Ib, Ital-P, F, GR, Crete; TR,
Levant, N-Afr.
- *hastata* L. = Atriplex prostrata
- **hortensis** L. · E:Garden Orache;
F:Arroche rouge des jardins; G:Garten-
Melde, Spanischer Salat · ⊙ Z6 VII-IX ⚥
Ⓝ; C-As., nat. in Eur.* exc. BrI, Sc
- **laciniata** L. · E:Frosted orache;
G:Gelappte Melde · ⊙ VII-IX; Eur.: Sc,
B, Fr, sp., D; Cauc., Iran, W-Sib., C-As.,
Mong., China: Sinkiang; Him.
- *latifolia* Wahlenb. = Atriplex prostrata
- **littoralis** L. · E:Grass-leaved Orache;
G:Strand-Melde · ⊙ VII-IX; Eur.* ; Syr.
Lebanon, Cauc., Iran, W-Sib., Amur,
C-As., Egypt, NW-Afr., coasts, saline
habitats
- **longipes** Drejer · E:Long-stalked Orache;
G:Langstielige Melde · ⊙ VII-IX; Eur.:
BrI, Sc, PL, N-Russ.
- **micrantha** Ledeb. · G:Verschiedensamige
Melde · ⊙ VII-IX; Eur.: Russ.; Cauc.,
W-Sib., C-As, nat. in sp., G, PL
- *nitens* Schkur. = Atriplex sagittata
- **oblongifolia** Waldst. & Kit. · G:Langblät-
trige Melde · ⊙ VII-IX; Eur.* exc. BrI, Ib;
TR, Cauc., C-As., nat. in F
- **patula** L. · E:Common Orache; G:Sprei-
zende Melde · ⊙ X; Eur.*, Cauc., TR,
Cyprus, Syr., W-Sib., E-Sib., C-As.,
N-Afr., Alaska, Can., USA*, Greenl.
- **pedunculata** L. · E:Pedunculate Sea
Purslane; G:Stielfrüchtige Salzmelde · ⊙
VII-X; Eur.* exc. Ib, Ital-P
- **portulacoides** L. · E:Sea Purslane;
G:Strand-Salzmelde · ⌣ d VII-IX; Eur.*
exc. EC-Eur., E-Eur.; TR, Levant, Cauc.,
Iran, W-Sib., C-As., China: Sinkiang;
Mong., N-Afr.
- **prostrata** Boucher ex DC. · E:Spear-
leaved Orache; G:Spieß-Melde,

Spießblättrige Melde · ⊙ VII-IX; Eur.*,
TR, Levant, NW-Afr., Egypt
- **rosea** L. · G:Rosen-Melde · ⊙ VII-IX;
Eur.* exc. BrI, Sc; TR
- *sabulosa* Rouy = Atriplex laciniata
- **sagittata** Borkh. · G:Glanz-Melde · ⊙
VII-IX; Eur.: Ital-P, C-Eur., EC-Eur., Ba,
E-Eur; TR, W-Sib., C-As., nat. in F
- **tatarica** L. · G:Tataren-Melde · ⊙ VII-IX;
Eur.* exc. BrI, Sc; TR, Cyprus, Cauc.,
Iran, W-Sib., C-As., Mong., China:
Sinkiang; Tibet, Him., NW-Afr., Egypt
- *triangularis* Willd. = Atriplex prostrata

Atropa L. -f- *Solanaceae* · 4 spp. · E:Deadly
Nightshade; F:Atropa, Belladonne;
G:Belladonna, Tollkirsche
- **acuminata** Royle ex Lindl. · ⌣ Z7 ⚘;
Ind.
- **bella-donna** L. · E:Deadly Nightshade;
G:Belladonna, Echte Tollkirsche · ⌣ Z7
VI-VII ⚥ ⚘; Eur.* exc. Sc; TR, Cauc.,
N-Iran, NW-Afr., nat. in Sc
- *rhomboidea* Gillies & Hook. = Salpichroa
origanifolia

Attalea Kunth -f- *Arecaceae* · 67 spp. ·
E:Bissaba Palm; F:Palmier piassaba;
G:Pindrowpalme, Pissavepalme
- **cohune** Mart. · ħ e Z10 ⓦ Ⓝ; Mex.,
C-Am.
- *excelsa* Mart. ex Spreng. = Attalea
phalerata
- **funifera** Mart. · E:Bahia Piassaba Palm ·
ħ e Z10 ⓦ Ⓝ; Braz.: Bahia, Espirito
Santo
- **phalerata** Mart. ex Spreng. · ħ e Z10 ⓦ
Ⓝ; Braz.
- **speciosa** Mart. · E:Babussu Palm;
G:Babussupalme · ħ e Z10 ⓦ Ⓝ;
Amazon.
- **spectabilis** Mart. · ħ e Z10 ⓦ Ⓝ; Braz.

Aubrieta Adans. -f- *Brassicaceae* · 12 spp. ·
E:Aubrietia; F:Aubriète; G:Blaukissen
- **columnae** Guss. · ⌣ ⤳ △ Z6 IV-V; Eur.:
I, Ba, RO
- **deltoidea** (L.) DC. · E:Aubretia;
G:Griechisches Blaukissen · ⌣ ⤳ △ Z6
IV-V; Eur.: Sic., Ba; TR, nat. in BrI, F, sp.
- *graeca* Griseb. = Aubrieta deltoidea
- **Cultivars:**
- **many cultivars**

Aucoumea Pierre -f- *Burseraceae* · 2 spp.

– **klaineana** Pierre · ♄ � ⓝ; W-Afr.

Aucuba Thunb. -f- *Aucubaceae* · 10 spp. ·
E:Spotted Laurel; F:Aucuba; G:Aukube
– **japonica** Thunb.
– **some cultivars**
– var. **japonica** · E:Aucuba, Spotted Laurel;
F:Aucuba du Japon; G:Japanische
Aukube · ♄ e ⚬ Z8 ⓐ III-IV ⚘; S-Jap.,
China, Taiwan

Aulax P.J. Bergius -f- *Proteaceae* · 3 spp. ·
E:Featherbush
– **umbellata** (Thunb.) R. Br. · E:Broad-
leaved Featherbush · ♄ e ⋈ ⓐ; S-Afr.

Aurinia Desv. -f- *Brassicaceae* · 11 sp. ·
E:Rock Madwort; F:Cresson des pierres;
G:Steinkresse
– **petraea** (Ard.) Schur · G:Friauler
Steinkresse · ⧫ Z7 IV-VI; Eur.: I, Ba, RO,
nat. in F, C-Eur.
– **rupestris** (Ten.) Cullen & T.R. Dudley ·
⧫ Z7; Eur.: I, Ba; TR
– **saxatilis** (L.) Desv. · E:Golden Alyssum,
Golden Tuft; F:Alysse des rochers,
Corbeille d'or; G:Felsen-Steinkresse · ⧫ ♄
⫪ △ Z6 IV-V; Eur.: Ital-P, C-Eur., EC-Eur.,
Ba, E-Eur.; TR, nat. in F
– **many cultivars**

Austrocactus Britton & Rose -m-
Cactaceae · 5 spp.
– **patagonicus** (F.A.C. Weber) Hosseus ex
Backeb. · ⵣ Z8 ⓐ ▽ ⚘; S-Arg., S-Chile
– **spiniflorus** (Phil.) F. Ritter · ⵣ Z8 ⓐ ▽
⚘; Chile

Austrocedrus Florin & Boutelje -m-
Cupressaceae · 1 sp. · E:Chilean Cedar;
F:Cèdre du Chili; G:Chilezeder
– **chilensis** (D. Don) Pic.Serm. & Bizzarri ·
E:Chilean Cedar, Chilean Incense Cedar;
G:Chilezeder · ♄ e Z8 ⓐ; Chile, W-Arg.

Austrocephalocereus Backeb. -m-
Cactaceae · 2-7 spp.
– **dybowskii** (Rol.-Goss.) Backeb. · ⵣ Z9 ⓐ
▽ ⚘; E-Braz.: Bahia
– *fluminensis* (Miq.) Buxb. = Coleocephalocereus fluminensis
– **lehmannianus** (Werderm.) Backeb. · ⵣ
Z9 ⓐ ▽ ⚘; Braz.
– **purpureus** (Gürke) Backeb. · ⵣ Z9 ⓐ ▽
⚘; Braz.

Avena L. -f- *Poaceae* · 25 spp. · E:Oat;
F:Avoine; G:Hafer
– **abyssinica** Hochst. · ⊙ Z5 ⓝ; Eth.
– **barbata** Pott ex Link · E:Slender Oat;
G:Bart-Hafer · ⊙ Z5 V-VI; Eur.: Ib, Fr,
Ital-P, Ba, RO, Crim; TR, Cauc., Iraq,
Iran, C-As., N-Afr., nat. in A, N-Am.,
S-Am.
– **byzantina** K. Koch · E:Common Red
Oats; G:Mittelmeer-Hafer · ⊙ Z5 ⓝ; cult.
TR, W-Iran, W-Pakist., NW-Afr.
– *desertorum* Less. = Helictotrichon
desertorum
– *elatior* L. = Arrhenatherum elatius var.
elatius
– **fatua** L. · E:Wild Oats; G:Flug-Hafer · ⊙
⋈ Z5 VI-VIII; Eur.*, TR, Iraq, Lebanon,
Syr., Palest., Arab., Cauc., W-Sib., E-Sib.,
Amur, Sakhal., C-As., Afgh., Pakist., Ind.,
Tibet, Mong., nat. in China, Jap., Phil.,
S-Afr., N-Am., Mex., Austr., NZ
– *flavescens* L. = Trisetum flavescens
– **nuda** L. · E:Naked Oat; G:Sand-Hafer · ⊙
Z5 VI-VIII; cult.
– subsp. *strigosa* (Schreb.) Mansf. = Avena
strigosa
– *parlatorei* J. Woods = Helictotrichon
parlatorei
– *planiculmis* Schrad. = Helictotrichon
planiculme
– **sativa** L. · E:Oats; G:Saat-Hafer · ⊙ Z5
VI-VII ⚥ ⓝ; orig. ?; cult.
– *sempervirens* Vill. = Helictotrichon
sempervirens
– **sterilis** L. · E:Animated Oat; G:Tauber
Hafer · ⊙ ⋈ Z5 VII-VIII; Eur.: Ib, Fr,
Ital-P, Ba, E-Eur.; TR, Iraq, Syr., Israel,
Arab., Cauc., Iran, Afgh., N-Afr., nat. in
BrI, EC-Eur.
– *strigosa* Schreb. = Avena nuda

Avenastrum Opiz = Helictotrichon
– *desertorum* (Less.) Podp. = Helictotrichon
desertorum
– *parlatorei* (J. Woods ex Dalla Torre) Beck
= Helictotrichon parlatorei
– *planiculme* (Schrad.) Jess. = Helictotrichon planiculme
– *pratense* (L.) Pilg. = Helictotrichon
pratense
– *pubescens* (Huds.) Jess. = Helictotrichon
pubescens

Avenella Parl. = Deschampsia
– *flexuosa* (L.) Drejer = Deschampsia

flexuosa
– subsp. *montana* (L.) Á. Löve & D. Löve =
Deschampsia flexuosa

Avenochloa Holub = Helictotrichon
– *planiculmis* (Schrad.) Holub = Helictotrichon planiculme
– *pratensis* (L.) Holub = Helictotrichon
pratense
– *pubescens* (Huds.) Holub = Helictotrichon
pubescens

Avenula (Dumort.) Dumort. = Helictotrichon
– *planiculmis* (Schrad.) W. Sauer & Chmel.
= Helictotrichon planiculme
– *pratensis* (L.) Dumort. = Helictotrichon
pratense
– *pubescens* (Huds.) Dumort. = Helictotrichon pubescens
– *versicolor* (Vill.) M. Laínz = Helictotrichon versicolor

Averrhoa L. -f- *Oxalidaceae* · 2 spp. ·
E:Cucumber Tree; F:Arbre à concombres,
Carambolier; G:Baumstachelbeere,
Gurkenbaum
– **bilimbi** L. · E:Bilimbi; G:Gurkenbaum · ♄
e Z10 ⓦ Ⓝ; orig. ?, nat. in Trop.
– **carambola** L. · E:Carambola, Star Fruit;
G:Karambole, Sternfrucht · ♄ e Z10 ⓦ Ⓝ;
Malay. Pen., nat. in Trop.

Avonia (E. Mey. ex Fenzl) G.D. Rowley
-f- *Portulacaceae* · 12 spp.
– **albissima** (Marloth) G.D. Rowley · ⟃ Ψ
Z10 ⓚ ▽ ✳; Cape, Namibia
– **dinteri** (Schinz) G.D. Rowley · ⟃ Ψ Z10
ⓚ ▽ ✳; Namibia
– **papyracea** (E. Mey. ex Fenzl) G.D.
Rowley
– subsp. **papyraceae** · ⟃ Ψ Z10 ⓚ ▽ ✳;
Cape, Namibia
– **quinaria** (E. Mey. ex Fenzl) G.D. Rowley
– subsp. **alstonii** (Schönland) G.D.
Rowley · ⟃ Ψ Z10 ⓚ ▽ ✳; Cape, Namibia
– subsp. **quinara** · ⟃ Ψ Z10 ⓚ ▽ ✳; Cape,
Namibia

Axonopus P. Beauv. -m- *Poaceae* · c. 35
(-110) spp.
– **compressus** (Sw.) P. Beauv. ·
E:Broadleaf Carpetgrass · ⟃ ⓦ Ⓝ;
C-Am., W.Ind.

Ayapana Spach -f- *Asteraceae* · 15 spp.
– **triplinervis** (Vahl) R.M. King & H. Rob. ·
E:Triplinerved Eupatorium; G:Dreinerv-
iger Wasserdost · ♄ ⓦ Ⓝ; trop. Am., nat.
in Mauritius, Ind., Java

Aylostera Speg. = Rebutia
– *deminuta* (F.A.C. Weber) Backeb. =
Rebutia deminuta
– *fiebrigii* (Gürke) Backeb. = Rebutia
fiebrigii
– *kupperiana* (Boed.) Backeb. = Rebutia
kupperiana
– *pseudodeminuta* (Backeb.) Backeb. =
Rebutia pseudodeminuta
– *spegazziniana* (Backeb.) Backeb. =
Rebutia spegazziniana
– *steinmannii* (Solms) Backeb. = Rebutia
steinmannii var. steinmannii

Azadirachta A. Juss. -f- *Meliaceae* · 3 spp. ·
E:Neem Tree; G:Nimbaum
– **indica**
– subsp. **indica** · E:Margosa, Neem Tree;
F:Margosier; G:Indischer Flieder,
Gewöhnlicher Burma-Nimbaum · ♄ Z10
ⓦ ✦ Ⓝ; Ind., Sri Lanka, Burma, Malay.
Arch., nat. in E-Afr., S-Arab., Iran

Azalea L. = Rhododendron
– *albrechtii* (Maxim.) Kuntze = Rhododendron albrechtii
– *amoena* Lindl. = Rhododendron
kiusianum
– *atlantica* Ashe = Rhododendron atlanticum
– *calendulacea* Michx. = Rhododendron
calendulaceum
– *californica* Torr. & A. Gray ex Durand =
Rhododendron occidentale
– *canadensis* (L.) Kuntze = Rhododendron
canadense
– *fragrans* Raf. = Rhododendron arborescens
– *indica* L. non hort. = Rhododendron
indicum
– *japonica* A. Gray = Rhododendron molle
subsp. japonicum
– *macrantha* Bunge = Rhododendron
indicum
– *mollis* Blume = Rhododendron molle
subsp. molle
– *mucronata* Blume = Rhododendron
mucronatum
– *occidentalis* Torr. & A. Gray =

Rhododendron occidentale
- *parvifolia* (Adams) Kuntze = Rhododendron lapponicum
- *periclymenoides* Michx. = Rhododendron periclymenoides
- *pontica* L. = Rhododendron luteum
- *procumbens* L. = Loiseleuria procumbens
- *rosea* Loisel. = Rhododendron prinophyllum
- *schlippenbachii* (Maxim.) Kuntze = Rhododendron schlippenbachii
- *sinensis* Lodd. = Rhododendron molle subsp. molle
- *vaseyi* (A. Gray) Rehder = Rhododendron vaseyi
- *viscosa* L. = Rhododendron viscosum

Azara Ruiz & Pav. -f- *Flacourtiaceae* · 10 spp. · G:Azarabaum
- **dentata** Ruiz & Pav. · ♄ e Z8 ⓚ; Chile
- **lanceolata** Hook. f. · E:Lanceolate Azara; G:Schmalblättriger Azarabaum · ♄ ♄ e Z8 ⓚ; Chile, Arg.
- **microphylla** Hook. f. · E:Boxleaf Azara; G:Buchsblättriger Azarabaum · ♄ e D Z8 ⓚ II-III; Chile
- **serrata** Ruiz & Pav. · ♄ e ⓚ III-V; Chile

Azolla Lam. -f- *Azollaceae* · 7 spp. · E:Water Fern; F:Fougère aquatique; G:Algenfarn
- **caroliniana** Willd. · E:Fairy Moss, Lesser Water Fern; F:Fougère aquatique, Mousse des fées; G:Moskito-Algenfarn · ⁴ ≈ Z7; USA: NE, NCE, SE, Fla.; Mex., W.Ind., C-Am., nat. in Eur.* exc. BrI, Sc
- **filiculoides** Lam. · E:Large Mosquito Fern; G:Feenmoos, Großer Algenfarn · ⁴ ≈ Z7 VIII-X; Alaska, USA: NW, Calif; Mex., C-Am., S-Am., nat. in Eur.* exc. BrI, Sc
- **mexicana** C. Presl · E:Mexican Mosquito Fern; G:Gefiederter Algenfarn, Kleiner Algenfarn · ⁴ ≈ Z8 ⓚ VI-VII; N-Am., C-Am., nat. in Fr, Ital-P, G, EC-Eur., Ba, EC-Eur.
- **pinnata** R. Br. · ⁴ ≈ ⓚ Ⓝ; China, cult. China, Jap., Calif. etc.

Azorella Lam. -f- *Apiaceae* · 70 spp. · G:Andenpolster
- **pedunculata** (Spreng.) Mathias & Constance · ⁴ Z8 ⓚ; Ecuad.
- **trifurcata** (Gaertn.) Pers. · F:Coussin des Andes; G:Andenpolster · ⁴ △ Z8 ∧ VI-VII; Chile, Arg.

Azorina Feer -f- *Campanulaceae* · 1 sp.
- **vidalii** (H.C. Watson) Feer · ♄ Z9 ⓚ VII-VIII ▽; Azor.

Aztekium Boed. -n- *Cactaceae* · 2 spp.
- **ritteri** (Boed.) Boed. · ⁴ Z8 ⓚ ▽ ✳; Mex.: Nuevo León

Azureocereus Akers & H. Johnson = Browningia
- *hertlingianus* (Backeb.) Rauh = Browningia hertlingiana
- *nobilis* Akers & H. Johnson = Browningia hertlingiana
- *viridis* Rauh & Backeb. = Browningia viridis

Babiana Ker-Gawl. ex Sims -f- *Iridaceae* · 64 spp. · E:Baboon Flower; F:Fleur des babouins; G:Pavianblume
- **stricta** (Aiton) Ker-Gawl. · E:Baboon Flower; G:Gerippte Pavianblume · ⁴ Z9 ⓚ III-IV; Cape

Baccaurea Lour. -f- *Euphorbiaceae* · 56 spp.
- **dulcis** (Jacq.) Müll. Arg. · ♄ ⓦ Ⓝ; Malay. Arch.
- **motleyana** (Müll. Arg.) Müll. Arg. · ♄ ⓦ Ⓝ; Malay. Pen., Sumat., Java, Kalimantan
- **ramiflora** Lour. · ♄ e ⓦ Ⓝ; Ind., China, Malay. Arch.
- *sapida* (Roxb.) Müll. Arg. = Baccaurea ramiflora

Baccharis L. -f- *Asteraceae* · c. 400 spp. · E:Tree Groundsel; F:Baccharis; G:Kreuzstrauch
- **genistelloides** Pers. · ♄ d D ⓚ XI-I; S-Am.
- **halimifolia** L. · E:Eastern Baccharis, Groundsel Tree; G:Kreuzstrauch · ♄ d ⊗ Z7 VIII-X; USA: NE, SE, Fla., SC; Mex., C-Am., W.Ind., nat. in W-F u. NW-Sp.
- **magellanica** (Lam.) Pers. · ⁴ d Z8 ⓚ; S-Chile, S-Arg., Falkland

Bacopa Aubl. -f- *Scrophulariaceae* · 56 spp. · E:Water Hyssop; F:Bacopa; G:Fettblatt, Wasserysop
- *amplexicaulis* (Pursh) Wettst. = Bacopa caroliniana
- **caroliniana** (Walter) B.L. Rob. · E:Blue Water Hyssop; G:Carolina-Fettblatt, Großblättriges Fettblatt · ⁴ ⌇ ≈ Z8

ⓜ; USA: Va, SE, Tex., Fla.
- **monnieri** (L.) Pennell · E:Baby Tears,
Water Hyssops; G:Kleines Fettblatt,
Wasserysop · ♃ ⌇ ≈ Z8 ⓜ ⚥ ; USA:
NE, SE, Fla., Tex.; Mex., C-Am., trop.
S-Am., Phil., Malay. Pen., Iraq, nat. in Ib

Bactris Jacq. ex Scop. -f- *Arecaceae* ·
76 spp. · E:Spiny-Club Palm; F:Péjibaie;
G:Pfirsichpalme
- **gasipaes** Kunth · E:Peach Palm;
G:Pfirsichpalme · ♄ e ⓜ Ⓝ; C-Am., trop.
S-Am.

Baeckea L. -f- *Myrtaceae* · c. 70 spp.
- **virgata** (J.R. Forst. & G. Forst.)
Andrews · E:Twiggy Heath Myrtle ·
♄ ♄ Z9 ⓚ VIII-X; Austr.: North Terr.,
Queensl., N.S.Wales, Victoria

Baeothryon A. Dietr. = Trichophorum
- *alpinum* (L.) T.V. Egorova = Trichophorum alpinum

Baeria Fisch. & C.A. Mey. = Lasthenia
- *coronaria* (Nutt.) A. Gray = Lasthenia
coronaria
- *gracilis* (DC.) A. Gray = Lasthenia
californica

Bahia Lag. -f- *Asteraceae* · 12-15 spp.
- **dissecta** (A. Gray) Nutt. · E:Ragleaf
Bahia · ⊙ ♃ Z9; USA: SW, Mex.

Baillonella Pierre -f- *Sapotaceae* · 1 sp. ·
E:Djave; G:Njabi
- **toxisperma** Pierre · E:Djave; G:Afri-
kanischer Birnbaum, Njabi · ♄ ⓜ Ⓝ;
Nigeria, Cameroon, Gabun, Congo

Balanites Delile -f- *Balanitaceae* · 9
(25) spp. · F:Balanites; G:Zachunbaum,
Zahnbaum;
- **aegyptiaca** (L.) Delile · E:Desert Date;
G:Zachunbaum · ♄ ♄ Ⓝ; Palest., Arab., n
trop. Afr., Eth.

Balantium Kaulf. = Culcita
- *culcita* (L'Hér.) Kaulf. = Culcita macrocarpa

Baldellia Parl. -f- *Alismataceae* · 2 spp. ·
E:Lesser Water Plantain; G:Igelschlauch
- **ranunculoides** (L.) Parl. · E:Lesser
Water Plantain; F:Fluteau d'eau fausse;

G:Gewöhnlicher Igelschlauch renoncule ·
♃ ⌇ ≈ Z7 ⓚ VII-X; Eur.*, ? TR,
NW-Afr.

Baldingera G. Gaertn., B. Mey. & Scherb. =
Phalaris
- *arundinacea* (L.) Dumort. = Phalaris
arundinacea

Ballota L. -f- *Lamiaceae* · 35 spp. ·
E:Horehound; F:Ballote; G:Gottvergess,
Schwarznessel
- **nigra** L. · E:Black Horehound;
G:Langzähnige Schwarznessel · ♃ Z6
VI-IX ⚥ ; Eur.*, TR, Levant, Iraq, Cauc.,
Iran, NW-Afr.
- **pseudodictamnus** (L.) Benth. · E:Greek
Horehound; G:Kreta-Nessel · ♃ △ Z8 ⓐ
∧ VII-VIII; Eur.: GR, Crete; TR, Libya,
nat. in I, Sic.

Balsamina Mill. = Impatiens
- *hortensis* N.H.F. Desp. = Impatiens
balsamina

Balsamita Mill. = Tanacetum
- *vulgaris* Willd. = Tanacetum balsamita

Bambusa Schreb. -f- *Poaceae* · 120 spp. ·
E:Bamboo; G:Bambus
- *apus* Schult. f. = Gigantochloa apus
- *arundinacea* (Retz.) Willd. = Bambusa
bambos
- *aspera* Schult. f. = Dendrocalamus asper
- *aurea* Carrière = Phyllostachys aurea
- **bambos** (L.) Voss · E:Spiny Bamboo,
Thorny Bamboo; G:Dorn-Bambus · ♄ e ⓜ
⚥ Ⓝ; Ind.
- *fastuosa* Lat.-Marl. ex Mitford = Semiarundinaria fastuosa
- *flexuosa* Carrière non Munro = Phyllostachys flexuosa
- *glaucescens* (Willd.) Holttum = Bambusa
multiplex
- *kumasasa* Zoll. ex Steud. = Shibataea
kumasasa
- *marmorea* Mitford = Chimonobambusa
marmorea
- *metake* Vilm. = Pseudosasa japonica
- **multiplex** (Lour.) Raeusch. · E:Hedge
Bamboo; G:Hecken-Bambus · ♄ e Z9 ⓚ;
China
- *nigra* Lodd. ex Lindl. = Phyllostachys
nigra
- *palmata* Burb. = Sasa palmata

– *ramosa* Makino = Sasaella ramosa
– *stricta* (Roxb.) Roxb. = Dendrocalamus
strictus
– *tessellata* Munro = Indocalamus tessellatus
– **tulda** Roxb. · ♄ e ⓦ Ⓝ; Ind., Burma,
Tahiti
– **tuldoides** Munro · E:Puntingpole
Bamboo · ⓦ; trop. S-Am.
– *ventricosa* McClure = Bambusa tuldoides
– *verticillata* Willd. = Gigantochloa levis
– *viridiglaucescens* Carrière = Phyllostachys
viridiglaucescens
– **vulgaris** Schrad. ex J.C. Wendl. ·
E:Common Bamboo; G:Gewöhnlicher
Bambus · ♄ e Z10 ⓦ Ⓝ; cult., nat. in
Trop.

Banisteriopsis C.B. Rob. ex Small -f-
Malpighiaceae · 92 spp.
– **caapi** (Spruce ex Griseb.) C.V. Morton ·
E:Ayahuasca · ♄ ⌇ ⚥ ⓦ ⚘ ✕ Ⓝ;
Amazon., Col., Ecuad., Peru

Banksia L. f. -f- *Proteaceae* · 73 spp. ·
E:Banksia; F:Banksia; G:Banksie
– **aemula** R. Br. · E:Wallum Banksia · ♄ ♄ e
Z9 ⓐ; E-Austr.
– **attenuata** R. Br. · E:Slender Banksia;
G:Zarte Banksie · ♄ e ✕ Z9 ⓐ; Austr.
– **baxteri** R. Br. · E:Bird's Nest Banksia;
G:Vogelnest-Banksie · ♄ e ✕ Z9 ⓐ;
W-Austr.
– **coccinea** R. Br. · E:Scarlet Banksia;
G:Scharlachrote Banksie · ♄ e ✕ Z9 ⓐ;
W-Austr.
– *collina* R. Br. = Banksia spinulosa var.
collina
– **ericifolia** L. f. · E:Heath-leaved Banksia
– **grandis** Willd. · E:Bull Banksia; G:Stier-
Banksie · ♄ e ✕ Z9 ⓐ; W-Austr.
– **hookeriana** Meisn. · E:Hooker's Banksia;
G:Hookers Banksie · ♄ e ✕ Z9 ⓐ; Austr.
– **integrifolia** L. f. · E:Coast Banksia;
G:Küsten-Banksie · ♄ e ✕ Z9 ⓐ; Austr.:
Queensl., N.S.Wales, Victoria
– *littoralis* Lindl. = Banksia grandis
– *marcescens* Bonpl. = Banksia marginata
– *marcescens* R. Br. = Banksia praemorsa
– **marginata** Cav. · E:Silver Banksia;
G:Silber-Banksie · ♄ e Z9 ⓐ; Austr.:
N.S.Wales, Victoria, S-Austr., Tasman.
– **menziesii** R. Br. · E:Firewood Banksia;
G:Feuerholz-Banksie · ♄ e ✕ Z9 ⓐ;
Austr.

– **nutans** R. Br. · E:Nodding Banksia;
G:Nickende Banksie · ♄ e ✕ Z9 ⓐ;
W-Austr.
– **occidentalis** R. Br. · E:Red Swamp
Banksia, Waterbush; G:Sumpf-Banksie ·
♄ e ✕ Z8 ⓐ; Austr.
– **paludosa** R. Br. · E:Swamp Banksia · ♄ e
Z9 ⓐ; Austr.: N.S.Wales
– **praemorsa** Andrews · E:Cut-leaf
Banksia · ♄ e ✕ Z8 ⓐ; Austr.
– **prionotes** Lindl. · E:Acorn Banksia,
Orange Banksia; G:Eichel-Banksie · ♄ e ✕
Z8 ⓐ; W-Austr.
– **sceptrum** Meisn. · E:Sceptre Banksia · ♄
e ✕ Z9 ⓐ; W-Austr.
– **speciosa** R. Br. · E:Showy Banksia;
G:Prächtige Banksie · ♄ e Z8 ⓐ; W-Austr.
– **spinulosa** Sm. · E:Hairpin Banksia · ♄
e Z9 ⓐ; Austr. (Queensl., N.S.Wales,
Victoria)
– var. **collina** (R. Br.) A.S. George · ♄ e Z9
ⓐ; Austr.: Queensl., N.S.Wales, Victoria
– var. **spinulosa** Sm.
– **verticillata** R. Br. · E:Granite Banksia · ♄
e Z9 ⓐ; W-Austr.

Baphia Afzel. ex Lodd. -f- *Fabaceae* ·
45 spp. · E:Camwood; G:Camholz
– **nitida** Afzel. ex Lodd. · E:Barwood,
Camwood; G:Camholz, Gabanholz · ♄ ♄
Z9 ⓦ Ⓝ; W-Afr.

Baptisia Vent. -f- *Fabaceae* · 17 spp. ·
E:False Indigo; F:Lupin indigo, Podalyre;
G:Färberhülsen, Indigolupine
– **alba** (L.) Vent.
– var. **macrophylla** (Larisey) Isely ·
E:White False Indigo; G:Weiße Färber-
hülse · ⚃ VI-VII; Ont., USA: NE, NCE,
Kans., SC, SE, Fla.
– **australis** (L.) R. Br. · E:Blue False Indigo;
F:Lupin indigo; G:Blaue Färberhülse,
Indigolupine · ⚃ VII-VIII; USA: NE, NCE,
SE
– **tinctoria** (L.) Vent. · E:Horsefly Weed;
G:Gelbe Färberhülse · ⚃ VII-VIII ⚘ ✕;
Ont., USA: NE, NCE, SE, Fla.

Barbacenia Vand. -f- *Velloziaceae* · 104 spp.
– *elegans* (Oliv. ex Hook. f.) Pax = Talbotia
elegans

Barbarea R. Br. -f- *Brassicaceae* · 20
(12) spp. · E:Barbara's Herb, Winter
Cress; F:Barbarée, Herbe de Ste-Barbe;

G:Barbarakraut, Barbenkraut
- **intermedia** Boreau · E:Medium-flowered
  Winter Cress; G:Mittleres Barbarakraut
  · ⊙ Z6 IV-V; Eur.: Ib, Fr, Ital-P, Ba; TR,
  Moroc., Alger., nat. in BrI, DK, PL
- **stricta** Andrz. · E:Small-flowered Winter
  Cress; G:Steifes Barbarakraut · ⊙ Z6
  IV-VI; Eur.* exc. Ib, Fr; Cauc., W-Sib.,
  E-Sib., C-As., nat. in Fr
- **verna** (Mill.) Asch. · E:American Cress,
  Land Cress; G:Frühlings-Barbarakraut ·
  ⊙ ⊙ Z6 IV-VI Ⓝ; Eur.: Ib, Fr, Ital-P, Crim;
  TR, nat. in BrI, DK, C-Eur., W-Russ.,
  N-Am., S-Afr., Austr., NZ, Jap.
- **vulgaris** R. Br. · E:Bittercress, Winter
  Cress, Yellow Rocket; G:Gewöhnliches
  Barbarakraut · ⊙ 4 Z6 V-VII Ⓝ; Eur.*,
  TR, Levant, Cauc., Iran, Him., W-Sib.,
  E-Sib., Mong., Tibet, China: Sinkiang,
  Tun., Alger., nat. in S-Afr., N-Am., Austr.,
  NZ

× **Bardendrum** hort. -n- Orchidaceae
  (*Barkeria* × *Epidendrum*)

Barkeria Knowles & Westc. -f-
  Orchidaceae · 15 spp.
- **skinneri** (Bateman ex Lindl.) Paxton · 4
  Z10 Ⓜ IX-I ▽ ✳; Guat.
- **spectabilis** Bateman ex Lindl. · 4 Z10 Ⓜ
  XI-XII ▽ ✳; S-Mex., Guat., El Salv.
- **uniflora** (Lex.) Dressler & Halb. · 4 Z10
  Ⓜ III ▽ ✳; Mex.

Barleria L. -f- *Acanthaceae* · 230-250 spp. ·
  E:Barleria; F:Barléria; G:Barlerie
- **cristata** L. · E:Phillippine Violet; G:Phil-
  ippinenveilchen · ♄ e Z10 Ⓜ VI-VIII; Ind.,
  Burma
- **obtusa** Nees · ♄ e Z10 Ⓚ; S-Afr.
- **prionitis** L. · E:Porcupine Flower;
  G:Stachelschweinblume · ♄ e Z10 Ⓜ
  VI-VIII; trop. As.

Barnadesia Mutis ex L. f. -f- *Asteraceae* ·
  23 spp.
- **rosea** Lindl. · ♄ Z9 Ⓚ V-VI; E-Braz.,
  C-Braz.

Barosma Willd. = Agathosma
- *betulina* (P.J. Bergius) Bartl. & H.L.
  Wendl. = Agathosma betulina
- *crenulata* (L.) Hook. = Agathosma
  crenulata
- *foetidissima* Bartl. & H.L. Wendl. =

Agathosma foetidissima
- *lanceolata* (Thunb.) Sond. = Agathosma
  lanceolata
- *pulchella* (L.) Bartl. & H.L. Wendl. =
  Agathosma pulchella
- *serratifolia* (Curtis) Willd. = Agathosma
  serratifolia

Barringtonia J.R. Forst. & G. Forst. -f-
  Lecythidaceae · 39 spp.
- **asiatica** (L.) Kurz · E:Sea Putat · ♄ e D
  Z10 Ⓜ; Madag., Malay. Pen., Austr.:
  Queensl.; Pacific Is.
- **racemosa** (L.) Roxb. · ♄ e Z10 Ⓜ Ⓝ;
  Malay. Arch., Pacific Is.

Bartlettina R.M. King & H. Rob. -f-
  Asteraceae · 23 (-37) spp.
- **sordida** (Less.) R.M. King & H. Rob. ·
  G:Mexikanischer Dost · ♄ ♄ D Z10 Ⓜ
  II-IV; Mex.

Bartonia Muhl. ex Willd. -f- Gentianaceae ·
  3-4 spp.
- *ornata* Nutt. = Mentzelia decapetala
- **virginica** (L.) Britton, Sterns &
  Poggenb. · E:Yellow Screwstem · 4; USA:
  NC, SC

Bartschella Britton & Rose = Mammillaria
- *schumannii* (Hildm.) Britton & Rose =
  Mammillaria schumannii

Bartsia L. -f- Scrophulariaceae · 49
  (-60) spp. · E:Bartsia; F:Bartsie; G:Alpen-
  helm, Bartisie
- **alpina** L. · E:Alpine Bartsia, Velvet Bells;
  G:Europäischer Alpenhelm · 4 Z5 VI-VIII;
  Eur.*, Can.: W; Greenl.

Basella L. -f- Basellaceae · 5 spp. ·
  E:Malabar Nightshade; F:Baselle,
  Epinard de Malabar; G:Indischer Spinat,
  Baselle
- **alba** L. · E:Indian Spinach, Malabar
  Nightshade; G:Indischer Spinat,
  Malabarspinat · ⊙ ♉ ⌇ ⌇ ⌀ Z10 Ⓜ Ⓝ; ?
  SE-As., ? Afr., nat. in Trop.
- *rubra* L. = Basella alba
- *tuberosa* (Caldas) Kunth = Ullucus
  tuberosus

Bashania Keng f. & T.P. Yi -f- Poaceae ·
  8 spp.

Bassia All. -f- *Chenopodiaceae* · 21-26 spp. ·
E:Smotherweed, Summer Cypress;
F:Bassia; G:Besenkraut, Dornmelde,
Radmelde, Sommerzypresse
– **hirsuta** (L.) Asch. · E:Hairy Smother-
weed; G:Rauhaarige Dornmelde · ⊙ Z6
VIII-IX; Eur.: Fr, Ital-P, C-Eur., Sc, Ba,
E-Eur.; Cyprus, Cauc., W-Sib., C-As.,
Mong. ; ..., nat. in N-Am.
– **hyssopifolia** (Pall.) Kuntze · E:Five-
Horn Smotherweed; G:Ysopblättrige
Dornmelde · ⊙ Z6 VIII; Eur.: Ib., Russ.;
Syr., Cauc., Iran, C-As., Sib., Mong,
China: Sinkiang, nat. in F
– **laniflora** (S.G. Gmel.) A.J. Scott ·
G:Sand-Radmelde · ⊙ Z6 VII-IX; Eur.*
exc. BrI, Sc; Cauc., W-Sib., E-Sib., C-As.,
Mong.
– **prostrata** (L.) A.J. Scott · E:Forage
Kochia; G:Halbstrauch-Radmelde · ⅄
Z6 VII-IX; Eur.* exc. BrI, Sc; TR, Cauc.,
Iran, W-Sib., E-Sib. , C-As., Him., Tibet,
Mong., China: Sinkiang, Manch., N-Afr.
– **scoparia** (L.) A.J. Scott · ⊙; W-Sib,
E-Sib., Mong., Manch., China, nat. in
C-Eur., GB, B, NL
– subsp. **densiflora** · G:Dichtblütige Besen-
Radmelde, Sommerzypresse · Z6
– subsp. **scoparia** · E:Belvedere, Burning
Bush, Summer Cypress; F:Ansérine
belvédère; G:Besen-Radmelde · ⊙ Ⅼ Z6
VII-IX Ⓝ; Russ., TR, Cyprus, Cauc., Iran,
Ind., W-Sib., Amur, C-As., Him., China,
Jap., Taiwan, nat. in Eur.* exc. BrI, Sc

× **Bateostylis** hort. -f- *Orchidaceae*
(*Batemannia × Otostylis*)

Batrachium (DC.) Gray = Ranunculus
– *aquatile* (L.) Dumort. = Ranunculus
aquatilis

Bauera Banks ex Andrews -f- *Cunoniaceae* ·
3 spp. · E:River Rose; G:Flussrose
– **rubioides** Andrews · E:River Rose;
G:Flussrose · ♄ e Z9 ⊛ II-V; Austr.:
N.S.Wales, Queensl., S-Austr., Tasman.

Bauhinia L. -f- *Caesalpiniaceae* ·
250-300 spp. · E:Mountain Ebony;
F:Bauhinia; G:Bauhinie
– **acuminata** L. · E:Mountain Orchid;
G:Berg-Bauhinie · ♄ e Z9 ⊛ V-IX; Ind.,
China, Malay. Pen.
– **esculenta** Burch. · E:Marama Bean;

G:Maramabohne · ⅄ Z9 ⊛ Ⓝ; trop-Afr.,
S-Afr.
– **forficata** Link · E:Cow's Foot · ♄ ♄ e Z9
⊛; S-Am.
– **galpinii** N.E. Br. · E:Red Butterfly Tree;
G:Rote Bauhinie · ♄ Ⅼ s ⚥ Z9 ⊛; S-Afr.,
trop. Afr.
– **monandra** Kurz · E:Napoleon's Plume · ♄
♄ e Z9 ⊛; Guyana, nat. in W.Ind.
– **purpurea** L. · E:Butterfly Tree;
G:Schmetterlings-Bauhinie · ♄ ♄ d Z9 ⊛
Ⓝ; Ind., China
– **racemosa** Lam. · ♄ e ⚥ Z9 ⊛ IV-IX;
NE-Ind.
– **tomentosa** L. · E:St Thomas Tree · ♄ e Z9
⊛; Ind., China
– **variegata** L. · E:Mountain Ebony, Orchid
Tree; G:Bunte Bauhinie · ♄ e Z9 ⊛ I-IV;
Ind., China
– **yunnanensis** Franch. · ♄ e ⚥ Z9 ⊛;
Yunnan

Beaucarnea Lem. -f- *Nolinaceae* · 9 spp. ·
F:Arbre-bouteille, Pied-d'éléphant;
G:Klumpstamm
– *glauca* (Lem.) Hereman = Beaucarnea
stricta
– **gracilis** Lem. · G:Schlanker Klumpstamm · ♄ ⅄ e Z10 ⊛; Mex.
– *longifolia* (Schult. & Schult. f.) Baker =
Nolina longifolia
– *oedipus* Rose = Beaucarnea gracilis
– **recurvata** Lem. · E:Elephant's Foot, Pony
Tail; G:Ponyschwanz-Klumpstamm · ♄ ⅄
Z10 ⊛; Mex.
– **stricta** Lem. · G:Kork-Klumpstamm · ♄ ⅄
d Z10 ⊛; Mex. (Puebla, Oaxaca)
– *tuberculata* (Lem.) Roezl = Beaucarnea
recurvata

Beaufortia R. Br. -f- *Myrtaceae* · 17-18 spp. ·
E:Bottlebrush; F:Beaufortia; G:Flaschen-
bürste
– **decussata** R. Br. · E:Gravel Bottlebrush ·
♄ Z9 ⊛ IV-V; W-Austr.
– **orbifolia** F. Muell. · E:Ravensthorpe
Bottlebrush · ♄ Z9 ⊛; Austr.: W-Austr.
– **purpurea** Lindl. · ♄ Z9 ⊛ VI-VIII;
W-Austr.
– **schaueri** L. Preiss · E:Pink Bottlebrush ·
♄ Z9 ⊛; W-Austr.
– **sparsa** R. Br. · E:Swamp Bottlebrush · ♄
Z9 ⊛ VI-VIII; W-Austr.

Beaumontia Wall. -f- *Apocynaceae* · 9 spp. ·

E:Herald's Trumpet; F:Beaumontia;
G:Heroldstrompete
– **grandiflora** (Roxb.) Wall. · E:Easter Lily
Vine, Herald's Trumpet; G:Großblütige
Heroldstrompete · ♄ e ⚥ D Z10 ⓦ XII-III;
E-Him.

Beckmannia Host -f- *Poaceae* · 2 spp. ·
E:Slough Grass; F:Beckmannia; G:Doppe-
lährengras, Fischgras, Raupenähre
– **eruciformis** (L.) Host · E:European
Slough Grass; G:Europäisches Dop-
pelährengras, Fischgras · ☉ ⚃ ⓝ; Eur.: I,
EC-Eur., Ba, E-Eur.; TR, Cauc., NW-Iran,
W-Sib., C-As., E-As., nat. in G, N-Am.
– **syzigachne** (Steud.) Fernald ·
E:American Slough Grass; G:Amerika-
nisches Doppelährengras · ☉ VI-VIII ⓝ;
C-As, S-Sib., nat. in Alaska, Can., USA:
NE, NCE, NC, Rocky Mts., SW, Calif.

Begonia L. -f- *Begoniaceae* · c. 900
(-1400) spp. · E:Begonia; F:Bégonia;
G:Begonie, Schiefblatt
– **acetosa** Vell. · ⚃ Z10 ⓦ III-V; Braz.
– *acida* Mart. ex A. DC. = Begonia subacida
– **acida** Vell. · ⚃ Z10 ⓦ; Braz.
– **aconitifolia** A. DC. · ♄ Z10 ⓦ; Braz.
– *acuminata* Dryand. = Begonia acutifolia
– **acutifolia** Jacq. · G:Ilexblättrige Begonie;
E:Holly-leaf Begonia · ⚃ Z10 ⓦ; Jamaica
– **albopicta** W. Bull · E:Guinea-wing
Begonia; G:Weißgefleckte Begonie · ♄
Z10 ⓦ; Braz.
– *angularis* Raddi = Begonia stipulacea
– *argyrostigma* Fisch. ex Link & Otto =
Begonia maculata
– **barbata** Wall. · ⚃ Z10 ⓦ; Ind., Burma
– **baumannii** Lemoine · ⚃ Z10 ⓚ; Bol.
– **bipinnatifida** J.J. Sm. · ♄ Z10 ⓦ;
N.Guinea
– **bogneri** Ziesenh. · ⚃ Z10 ⓦ VIII-IX;
Madag. (Presquelle de Masoala)
– **boliviensis** A. DC. · ⚃ Z10 ⓚ; Braz., Bol.
– **bowerae** Ziesenh. · E:Eyelash Begonia;
G:Wimpern-Begonie · ⚃ Z10 ⓦ; Mex.
– *bowringiana* hort. = Begonia cathayana
– **bradei** Irmsch. · ⚃ ♄ ♄ Z10 ⓦ; Braz.,
Cameroon
– **brevirimosa** Irmsch.
– subsp. **exotica** Tebbitt · ⚃ Z10 ⓦ;
N.Guinea
– **carolineifolia** Regel · ⚃ Z10 ⓦ; Mex.,
Guat.
– **cathayana** Hemsl. · ⚃ Z10 ⓦ; China

– **cinnabarina** Hook. · ⚃ Z10 ⓦ; Bol.
– **coccinea** Hook. · E:Angelwing Begonia,
Scarlet Begonia; G:Engelsflügel-Begonie ·
⚃ Z10 ⓦ; Braz.
– **compta** W. Bull · ♄ Z10 ⓦ; Braz.
– **conchifolia** A. Dietr. · ♄ Z10 ⓦ; Hond.,
Costa Rica, Panama
– **concinna** Schott · ⚃ Z10 ⓦ; Braz.
– **convolvulacea** A. DC. · E:Morning Glory
Begonia · ⚃ ⚥ Z10 ⓦ; Braz.
– × **corallina** Carrière (*B. coccinea* × *B.
teuscheri*) · ♄ Z10 ⓦ; Braz.
– **coriacea** A. DC. · ⚃ Z10 ⓦ III-V; Bol.
– × **credneri** Haage & E. Schmidt (*B.
metallica* × *B. scharffii*) · ♄ Z10 ⓚ; cult.
– **crispula** Brade · ⚃ Z10 ⓦ; Braz.
– **cubensis** Hassk. · E:Cuban Holly;
G:Kuba-Begonie · ⚃ Z10 ⓦ; W.Ind.
– **cucullata** Willd. · G:Sukkulente Begonie;
E:Fibrous Rooted Begonia
– var. **cucullata** · ⚃ Z10; Braz.
– var. **hookeri** (A. DC.) L.B. Sm. & B.G.
Schub. · ⚃ Z10 ⓦ; Braz.
– **cyathophora** Poepp. & Endl. · ⚃ Z10 ⓦ;
Mex.
– *daedalea* Lem. = Begonia strigillosa
– **davisii** Veitch ex Hook. f. · ⚃ Z10 ⓚ;
Peru
– **decora** Stapf · E:Hairy Begonia;
G:Haarige Begonie · ⚃ ↝ Z10 ⓦ;
Malay. Pen.
– **deliciosa** Linden ex Fotsch · ⚃ Z10 ⓦ;
Kalimantan
– **diadema** Linden ex Rodigas · ⚃ Z10 ⓦ;
Kalimantan
– **dichotoma** Jacq. · E:Kidney Begonia;
G:Gabelige Begonie · ⚃ Z10 ⓦ; Venez.
– **dichroa** Sprague · ⚃ Z10 ⓦ; Braz.
– **dietrichiana** Irmsch. · ♄ Z10 ⓦ XII-III;
Braz.
– **dipetala** Graham · ⚃ Z10 ⓦ; Ind.
– *discolor* Aiton = Begonia grandis subsp.
grandis
– **dregei** Otto & A. Dietr. · E:Maple-leaf
Begonia; G:Ahornblättrige Begonie · ⚃
Z10 ⓚ; Cape
– × **duchartrei** Bruant ex André (*B.
echinosepala* × *B. scharffii*) · ♄ Z10 ⓦ;
cult.
– **echinosepala** Regel · ⚃ Z10 ⓦ; Braz.
– **egregia** N.E. Br. · ⚃ Z10 ⓦ; Braz.
– **eminii** Warb. · ⚃ Z10 ⓦ; E-Afr.
– **epipsila** Brade · ⚃ Z10 ⓦ; Braz.
– × **erythrophylla** Neumann (*B.
hydrocotylifolia* × *B. manicata*) ·

E:Beafsteak Begonia, Kidney Begonia; G:Kidney-Begonie · ♃ Z10 Ⓦ; cult.
- *evansiana* Andrews = Begonia grandis subsp. evansiana
- *exotica* hort. = Begonia brevirimosa subsp. exotica
- **fagifolia** Fisch. · ♃ ⌇ Z10 Ⓦ; Braz.
- *faureana* Linden ex Garnier = Begonia aconitifolia
- × *feastii* hort. ex L.H. Bailey = Begonia × erythrophylla
- **fernando-costae** Irmsch. · ♃ Z10 Ⓦ; Braz.
- **ficifolia** Irmsch. · ♃ Z10 Ⓦ; Nigeria
- **foliosa** Kunth · E:Fern-leaved Begonia; G:Farnblättrige Begonie · ħ Z10 Ⓦ; Col., Venez.
- var. *fuchsifoliosa* (A. Chev.) hort. = Begonia × fuchsifoliosa
- var. *miniata* (Planch.) L.B. Sm. & Hook. = Begonia fuchsioides
- **franconis** Liebm. · ⊙ Z10 Ⓦ; S-Mex., Guat.
- **froebelii** A. DC. · ♃ Z10 Ⓚ; Ecuad.
- **fruticosa** (Klotzsch) A. DC. · ♄ Z10 Ⓦ; Braz.
- × **fuchsifoliosa** Chevall. (*B. foliosa* × *B. fuchsioides*) · ♄ Z10 Ⓦ; cult.
- **fuchsioides** Hook. · E:Corazon de Jesus, Fuchsia Begonia; G:Fuchsien-Begonie · ♄ e Z10 Ⓦ; Venez.
- **fulvosetulosa** Brade · ♃ Z10 Ⓦ; Braz.
- × **fuscomaculata** Lange (*B. heracleifolia* × *B. strigillosa*) · ♃ Z10 Ⓦ; cult.
- **glabra** Aubl. · ♃ ♄ ħ ⌇ ⌇ Z10 Ⓦ; Mex., C-Am., W.Ind., trop. S-Am.
- *glaucophylla* Hook. f. = Begonia radicans
- **goegoensis** N.E. Br. · E:Fire-king Begonia; G:Feuer-Begonie · ♃ Z10 Ⓦ; Sumat.
- **gracilis** Kunth · E:Hollyhock Begonia; G:Stockrosen-Begonie · ♃ Z10 Ⓦ; Mex., Guat.
- **grandis** Dryand.
- subsp. **evansiana** (Andrews) Irmsch. · E:Evans Begonia; G:Japan-Begonie · ♃ Z8 Ⓦ Ⓚ ∧; China
- subsp. **grandis** · E:Hardy Begonia; G:Winterharte Begonie · ♃ Z8 Ⓚ; Jap., C-China, SE-As.
- *haageana* S. Watson = Begonia scharffiana
- **hatacoa** Buch.-Ham. · ♃ Z10 Ⓦ; Him.
- **heracleifolia** Schltdl. & Cham. · E:Star-leaf Begonia · ♃ Z10 Ⓦ; Mex., Guat., Belize
- **herbacea** Vell. · ♃ Z10 Ⓦ; Braz.
- **hirtella** Link · E:Bearded Begonia; G:Bärtige Begonie · ⊙ Z10 Ⓦ Ⓚ; Braz., Peru
- **hispida** Schott
- var. **cucullifera** Irmsch. · ♃ Z10 Ⓦ; Braz.
- var. **hispida** · ♃ Z10 Ⓦ; Braz.
- **humilis** Dryand.
- var. **humilis** · ♃ Z10 Ⓦ Ⓚ; trop. S-Am.
- var. **porteriana** (Fisch., C.A. Mey. & Avé-Lall.) A. DC. · ⊙ Z10 Ⓦ Ⓚ; Mex., W.Ind., C-Am., S-Am.
- **hydrocotylifolia** Otto ex Hook. · E:Pennywort Begonia · ♃ Z10 Ⓦ; Mex.
- **imperialis** Lem.
- var. **imperialis** · ♃ ⟿ Z10 Ⓦ; Mex.
- var. **smaragdina** Lem. ex A. DC. · ♃ Z10 Ⓦ; Mex.
- *incana* Lindl. = Begonia peltata
- **incarnata** Link & Otto · ♃ Z10 Ⓦ; Mex.
- **involucrata** Liebm. · ♃ Z10 Ⓦ; C-Am.
- **isoptera** Dryand. ex Sm. · ♃ Z10 Ⓦ; Java
- **kellermannii** C. DC. · ħ Z10 Ⓦ; Guat.
- *laciniata* Roxb. = Begonia palmata
- × **langeana** Fotsch · ♃ Z10 Ⓦ; cult.
- **leptotricha** C. DC. · E:Woolly Bear · ♃ Z9 Ⓦ; Parag.
- *liebmannii* A. DC. = Begonia ludicra
- *limmingheana* C. Morren = Begonia radicans
- **lindleyana** Walp. · ♃ Z10 Ⓦ; S-Mex., C-Am., Col.
- **listada** L.B. Sm. & Wassh. · ♃ Z10 Ⓦ; Parag.
- **lubbersii** E. Morren · ♃ Z10 Ⓦ; Braz.
- **ludicra** A. DC. · ♃ Z10 Ⓦ; C-Am.
- **ludwigii** Irmsch. · ♃ Z10 Ⓦ; Ecuad.
- **luxurians** Scheidw. · E:Palm-leaf Begonia; G:Palmblättrige Begonie · ♃ Z10 Ⓦ; Braz.
- *lynchiana* Hook. f. = Begonia cyathophora
- *macrocarpa* Warb. = Begonia bradei
- **maculata** Raddi · ♄ e Z10 Ⓦ; Braz.
- **malabarica** Lam. · ♃ Z10 Ⓦ; Ind., Sri Lanka
- **manicata** Brongn. ex Cels · ♃ Z10 Ⓚ; Mex., Guat.
- **mannii** Hook. f. · ♃ Z10 Ⓦ; Zaire
- × **margaritae** hort. ex Fotsch (*B. echinosepala* × *B. metallica*) · ♃ Z10 Ⓦ; cult.
- **martiana** Link & Otto · ♃ Z10 Ⓦ; Mex.
- **masoniana** Irmsch. · E:Iron-cross Begonia; G:Ordens-Begonie · ♃ Z10 Ⓦ;

N.Guinea
- **mazae** Ziesenh. · ⁊ Z10 ⓜ XII-V; Mex.
- **metachroa** Fotsch · ⁊ Z10 ⓜ; orig. ?
- **metallica** W.G. Sm. · E:Metallic-leaf Begonia; G:Metallische Begonie · ⁊ Z10 ⓚ; Braz.
- **mexicana** H. Karst. · ⁊ ⤳ Z10 ⓜ; Mex.
- **micranthera** Griseb. · ⁊ Z10 ⓚ; Bol., Arg.
- *miniata* Planch. = Begonia fuchsioides
- **minor** Jacq. · ⁊ ♄ ⚡ Z10 ⓜ; C-Afr.: Sao Tomé
- **mollicaulis** Irmsch. · ☉ Z10 ⓜ; Braz.
- **natalensis** Hook. · G:Natal-Begonie · ⁊ Z10 ⓚ XII-III; S-Afr.: Natal
- **nelumbiifolia** Cham. & Schltdl. · E:Lilypad Begonia; G:Lotosblättrige Begonie · ⁊ Z10 ⓜ; C-Am., Col.
- **octopetala** L'Hér. · ⁊ Z10 ⓚ; Peru
- **odorata** Willd. · ♄ D Z10 ⓜ; W.Ind.
- **olbia** Kerch. · E:Maple-leaf Begonia · ⁊ Z10 ⓜ; Braz.
- **organensis** Brade · ♄ Z10 ⓜ; Braz.: Rio de Janeiro
- **palmata** D. Don · ⁊ Z10 ⓜ; Ind., Burma, S-China
- *palmifolia* hort. = Begonia vitifolia
- **partita** Irmsch. · ♄ Z10 ⓜ; S-Afr.
- *parva* Sprague non Merr. = Begonia mannii
- **paulensis** A. DC. · ⁊ Z10 ⓜ; Braz.
- **pearcei** Hook. f. · ⁊ Z10 ⓚ; Bol.
- **peltata** Schott ex A. DC. · E:Lily-pad Begonia; G:Seerosenblättrige Begonie · ⁊ ♄ ⤳ Z10 ⓜ; Mex.
- **peponifolia** Vis. ex A. DC. · ⁊ Z10 ⓜ; ? Mex.
- × **phyllomaniaca** Mart. (*B. incarnata* × *B. manicata*) · E:Crazy-leaf Begonia · ⁊ Z10 ⓜ; cult.
- × *pictavensis* Bruant ex André = Begonia × credneri
- *plagioneura* Milne-Redh. = Begonia cubensis
- **platanifolia** Schott · ♄ Z10 ⓜ; Braz.
- *poggei* Warb. = Begonia eminii
- **polygonoides** Hook. f. · ⁊ ⚡ Z10 ⓜ; W-Afr., C-Afr.
- **popenoei** Standl. · ⁊ Z10 ⓜ; Hond.
- **prismatocarpa** Hook. f. · ⁊ ⚡ Z10 ⓜ; Ivory Coast, Cameroon, Fernando Póo
- × **pseudophyllomaniaca** Lange (*B. heracleifolia* × *B. incarnata*) · ⁊ Z10 ⓜ; cult.
- **pulchella** Raddi · ⁊ Z10 ⓜ; Braz.

- *quadrilocularis* Brade = Begonia egregia
- **radicans** Vell. · E:Shrimp Begonia; G:Garnelen-Begonie · ♄ ⚡ ⚭ Z10 ⓜ III-V; Braz.
- **rajah** Ridl. · ⁊ Z10 ⓜ; Malay.Arch.
- **ramentacea** Paxton · ⁊ Z10 ⓜ; Braz.
- *reniformis* Hook. = Begonia vitifolia
- **rex** Putz. · E:King Begonia, Rex Begonia; G:Königs-Begonie · ⁊ Z10 ⓜ; InG: Assam
- **rhizocarpa** Fisch. ex A. DC. · ⁊ Z10 ⓜ III-V; Braz.
- **rhizocaulis** A. DC. · ⁊ Z10 ⓜ; C-Am.
- *richardsiana* T. Moore = Begonia suffruticosa
- *richardsoniana* Houllet = Begonia suffruticosa
- × **ricinifolia** A. Dietr. (*B. heracleifolia* × *B. peponifolia*) · E:Castor Oil Begonia; G:Rizinusblättrige Begonie · ⁊ Z10 ⓜ; cult.
- *roezlii* hort. Benary ex Lynch non Regel = Begonia cyathophora
- × *rubella* Buch.-Ham. ex D. Don = Begonia × fuscomaculata
- × *rubellina* L.H. Bailey = Begonia × fuscomaculata
- *rubra* hort. non Bl. = Begonia coccinea
- *rubrovenia* Planch. = Begonia hatacoa
- **sanguinea** Raddi · ♄ Z10 ⓜ; Braz.
- **scabrida** A. DC. · ⁊ Z10 ⓜ; Venez.
- **scharffiana** Regel · E:Elephant's Ear Begonia; G:Elefantenohr-Begonie · ♄ Z10 ⓚ; Braz.
- *scharffii* Hook. f. = Begonia scharffiana
- **schmidtiana** Regel · ⁊ Z10 ⓜ; Braz.
- *schmidtii* Haage & E. Schmidt = Begonia schmidtiana
- **schulziana** Urb. & Ekman · ⁊ ⤳ Z10 ⓜ; Haiti
- *semperflorens* Link & Otto = Begonia cucullata var. hookeri
- **serratipetala** Irmsch. · ⁊ Z10 ⓜ; N.Guinea
- *similis* Brade = Begonia pulchella
- *sinensis* A. DC. = Begonia grandis subsp. evansiana
- **socotrana** Hook. f. · ⁊ Z10 ⓜ; Socotra
- *spraguei* J.G.C. Weber = Begonia mannii
- **squamulosa** Hook. f. · ⁊ ⚡ Z10 ⓜ; Nigeria, C-Afr.
- **stipulacea** Willd. · ♄ Z10 ⓜ; Braz.
- **strigillosa** A. Dietr. · ⁊ Z10 ⓜ; Guat., Costa Rica
- *suaveolens* Lodd. = Begonia odorata
- **subacida** Irmsch. · ⁊ Z10 ⓜ; Braz.

– *subvillosa* hort. = Begonia mollicaulis
– **suffruticosa** Meisn. · 4 Z10 ⍟; S-Afr.:
Natal
– **sulcata** Scheidw. · ♄ Z10 ⍟; Col.
– **sutherlandii** Hook. f. · 4 Z9 ⍟; S-Afr.:
Natal
– × **thurstonii** hort. ex Kennedy (*B. metallica* × *B. peponifolia*) · 4 Z10 ⍟; cult.
– **tomentosa** Schott · ♄ Z10 ⍟; Braz.
– **ulmifolia** Willd. · E:Elm-leaf Begonia;
G:Ulmenblättrige Begonie · ♄ Z10 ⍟;
Venez.
– **undulata** Schott · ♄ Z10 ⍟; Braz.
– **veitchii** Hook. f. · 4 Z10 ⍟; Peru
– **venosa** Skan ex Hook. f. · 4 Z10 ⍟;
Braz.
– × **verschaffeltii** Regel (*B. carolineifolia* × *B. manicata*) · 4 Z10 ⍟; cult.
– **vitifolia** Schott · 4 Z10 ⍟; Braz.
– **wallichiana** Steud. · ⊙ Z10 ⍟; Ind.
– × **weltoniensis** hort. ex André (*B. dregei* × *B. sutherlandii*) · 4 Z10 ⍟; cult.
– **xanthina** Hook. · 4 Z10 ⍟; Bhutan
– *zebrina* hort. = Begonia stipulacea
– **Cultivars:**
– **many cultivars, see Section III**

Bejaria Mutis ex L. -f- *Ericaceae* ·
15-30 spp. · G:Andenrose; F:Rose des
Andes
– **coarctata** Humb. & Bonpl. · ♄ e Z10 ⍟;
Peru

Belamcanda Adans. -f- *Iridaceae* · 2 spp. ·
E:Leopard Lily; F:Fleur-léopard, Iris tigré;
G:Leopardenblume, Pantherblume
– **chinensis** (L.) DC. · E:Blackberry Lily,
Leopard Lily; G:Leopardenblume · 4 ⌖
Z8 ⍟ VII-VIII ⚥ ; N-Ind., China, Jap.,
Taiwan, nat. in USA

Bellevalia Lapeyr. -f- *Hyacinthaceae* ·
62 spp.
– **romana** (L.) Rchb. · E:Roman Hyacinth;
G:Römische Hyazinthe · 4 Z7 ⌂ △ IV-V;
Eur.: F, Ital-P, Ba

Bellidiastrum Cass. = Aster
– *michelii* Cass. = Aster bellidiastrum

Bellis L. -f- *Asteraceae* · 7 spp. · E:Daisy;
F:Pâquerette; G:Gänseblümchen,
Maßliebchen
– **annua** L. · E:Annual Daisy; G:Einjähriges

Gänseblümchen · ⊙ ; Eur.: Ib, Fr, Ital-P,
Ba; TR, NW-Afr., Macaron.
– **perennis** L. · E:Daisy, English Daisy;
F:Pâquerette; G:Gänseblümchen, Maßliebchen · 4 Z4 I-VI ⚥ ; Eur.*, TR, Syr.,
Palest., nat. in N-Am., Chile, NZ
– **some cultivars**
– **rotundifolia** (Desf.) Boiss. & Reut. · 4 △
Z9 ⌂ III-V; SW-Sp., Moroc., Alger.
– **sylvestris** Cirillo · 4 Z7; Eur.: Ib, Fr, Ital-P, Ba; TR, Cyprus, Syr., Palest., Moroc.,
Alger., Tun., Libya
– var. *rotundifolia* (Desf.) Batt. = Bellis
rotundifolia

Bellium L. -n- *Asteraceae* · 4 spp. · F:Faussepâquerette; G:Scheingänseblümchen,
Zwergmaßliebchen
– **bellidioides** L. · 4 △ Z8 △ V-VI; Cors,
Sard., Balear.
– **minutum** (L.) L. · E:Little Mary;
G:Zwergmaßliebchen · ⊙ △ Z8 V-VIII;
Eur.: Sic., GR, Crete

Beloperone Nees = Justicia
– *guttata* Brandegee = Justicia brandeegeana

Bencomia Webb & Berthel. -f- *Rosaceae* ·
5 spp.
– **caudata** (Aiton) Webb & Berthel. · ♄ e
Z9 ⍟; Canar.

Benincasa Savi -f- *Cucurbitaceae* · 1 sp. ·
E:Wax Gourd; F:Courge céreuse;
G:Wachskürbis
– **hispida** (Thunb. ex Murray) Cogn. ·
E:Wax Gourd; G:Wachs-Kürbis · ⊙ ⚥ ⌀
Z10 ⍟ ⚥ ⍟; cult.

Bensoniella C.V. Morton -f- *Saxifragaceae* ·
1 sp. · G:Bensonie
– **oregona** (Abrams & Bacig.) C.V. Morton · E:Oregon Bensoniella; G:Bensonie ·
4 Z6; USA: SW-Oreg., NW-Calif.

Benthamidia Spach = Cornus
– *fragifera* Lindl. = Cornus capitata

Bentinckia Berry ex Roxb. -f- *Arecaceae* ·
2 spp. · E:Bentinck's Palm; G:Bentinckpalme
– **nicobarica** (Kurz) Becc. · G:Nikobarenpalme · ♄ e ⍟; Nikobar. Is.

Benzoin Nees = Lindera
– *aestivale* Nees = Lindera benzoin
– *praecox* Siebold & Zucc. = Lindera praecox

Berardia Vill. -f- *Asteraceae* · 1 sp.
– **subacaulis** Vill. · ⟁ △ ∧ VII-VIII; Eur.: F, I; SW-Alp.

Berberidopsis Hook. f. -f- *Flacourtiaceae* · 2 spp. · E:Coral Plant; G:Korallenstrauch
– **corallina** Hook. f. · E:Coral Plant; G:Chilenischer Korallenstrauch · ♄ e ⚡ Z8 ⓚ VII-IX; Chile

Berberis L. -f- *Berberidaceae* · c. 450 spp. · E:Barberry; F:Berbéris, Epine-vinette; G:Berberitze, Sauerdorn
– **actinacantha** Mart. ex Roem. & Schult. · ♄ d △ Z7 ∧; Chile
– **aggregata** C.K. Schneid.
– var. **aggregata** · G:Knäuelfrüchtige Berberitze · ♄ d Z5; China: Sichuan, Gansu
– var. *prattii* (C.K. Schneid.) C.K. Schneid. = Berberis prattii
– var. **recurvata** (C.K. Schneid.) C.K. Schneid. · ♄ d Z6; W-China
– **amurensis** Rupr.
– var. **amurensis** Rupr. · G:Amur-Berberitze · ♄ d Z5 V; Amur, China, Manch., Korea, Jap.
– var. **japonica** (Regel) Rehder · ♄ d Z6; Jap.
– **angulosa** Wall. ex Hook. f. & Thomson · G:Kantige Berberitze · ♄ d △ Z6 V; Nepal, Bhutan, Sikkim
– **aristata** DC. · E:Chitra; G:Begrannte Berberitze · ♄ d ⚘ Z6 V Ⓝ; N-Ind., Nepal, Bhutan
– **atrocarpa** C.K. Schneid. · G:Schwarzfrüchtige Berberitze · ♄ e Z6 V-VI; W-China
– *bealei* Fortune = Mahonia bealei
– **beaniana** C.K. Schneid. · ♄ d Z6 VI; W-China
– **bergmanniae** C.K. Schneid. · G:Bergmanns Berberitze · ♄ e Z6 V-VI ⚘; W-China
– **brachypoda** Maxim. · ♄ d ⚘ Z5 V; NW-China
– **bretschneideri** Rehder · ♄ d Z5 V; Jap.
– *brevipaniculata* hort. non Schneid. = Berberis aggregata var. aggregata
– **buxifolia** Lam. ex Poir. · E:Magellan Barberry; F:Berbéris à feuilles de buis; G:Buchsblättrige Berberitze · ♄ e ⚡ Z7 V; Chile
– **calliantha** Mulligan · G:Schönblühende Berberitze · ♄ e ⚡ Z7 ∧ V; SE-Tibet
– **canadensis** Mill. · E:Allegheny Barberry, Bush Pepper; G:Kanadische Berberitze · ♄ d ⚘ Z5 V-VI Ⓝ; USA: NE, SE, NCE
– **candidula** (C.K. Schneid.) C.K. Schneid. · G:Schneeige Berberitze · ♄ e △ Z6 V; C-China
– × **carminea** Ahrendt (*B. aggregata* × *B. wilsoniae* var. *parvifolia*) · ♄ d Z6; cult.
– **caroli** C.K. Schneid. · ♄; S-Mong.
– × *chenaultii* Ahrendt = Berberis × hybrido-gagnepainii 'Chenault'
– **chillanensis** (C.K. Schneid.) Sprague
– var. **chillanensis** · ♄ e Z7 ∧ IV-V; Peru, Chile
– var. **hirsutipes** Sprague · ♄ e Z7; Chile, Arg.; Anden
– **chinensis** hort. Paris ex Poir. · ♄ d Z6 V; Cauc.
– *chitria* Buch.-Ham. ex Lindl. = Berberis aristata
– **circumserrata** (C.K. Schneid.) C.K. Schneid. · ♄ d Z5 V; NW-China
– **concinna** Hook. f. · ♄ d △ ⚘ Z6 V; Nepal, Sikkim
– **darwinii** Hook. · E:Darwin Barberry; F:Epine-vinette de Darwin; G:Darwins Berberitze · ♄ e △ Z7 ∧ IV-V; Arg., Chile
– **diaphana** Maxim. · G:Durchsichtige Berberitze · ♄ d Z6 V; China: Kansu
– **dictyophylla** Franch.
– var. **approximata** (Sprague) Rehder · ♄ d ⚘ Z6 V; W-China
– var. **dictyophylla** · G:Netzblättrige Berberitze · ♄ d Z6; Yunnan
– var. **epruinosa** C.K. Schneid. · ♄ d △ Z6 V; China: Yunnan
– **dielsiana** Fedde · G:Diels Berberitze · ♄ d ⚘ Z5 V; China: Sichuan
– *dulcis* Sweet = Berberis buxifolia
– **edgeworthiana** C.K. Schneid. · ♄ d Z6; NW-Him.
– **empetrifolia** Lam. ex Poir. · G:Krähenbeerenblättrige Berberitze · ♄ e △ Z6 V; Chile
– *fortunei* Lindl. = Mahonia fortunei
– **francisci-ferdinandi** C.K. Schneid. · G:Franz-Ferdinand-Berberitze · ♄ d ⚘ Z6 V; W-China
– × **frikartii** C.K. Schneid. (*B. candidula* × *B. verruculosa*) · G:Frikarts Berberitze · ♄

e △ Z6; cult.
- **gagnepainii** C.K. Schneid.
- var. **gagnepainii** · G:Gagnepains Berberitze · ♄ e Z6; W-China
- var. **lanceifolia** Ahrendt · ♄ e Z5 V-VI; China: Hupeh
- **gilgiana** Fedde · ♄ d Z5; N-China, C-China: Shaanxi
- **giraldii** Hesse · ♄ d ⊛ Z6 VI; China
- **henryana** C.K. Schneid. · ♄ d Z5; C-China: W-Hubei, Sichuan, Shaanxi
- **heteropoda** Schrenk ex Fisch. & C.A. Mey. · ♄ d ⊛ Z7 V; C-As., Mong., China: Sinkiang
- **hookeri** Lem. · G:Hookers Berberitze
- var. **hookeri** · ♄ e Z6 V-VI; Nepal, Bhutan, Ind.: Sikkim, Assam; China
- var. **viridis** C.K. Schneid. · ♄ e Z6 V; Him.
- × **hybrido-gagnepainii** Ahrendt (*B. gagnepainii* × *B. verruculosa*) · ♄ e Z6 V-VI; cult.
- 'Chenault'
- **hypokerina** Airy Shaw · E:Silver Holly; G:Silberne Berberitze · ♄ e △ Z8 ⌂ ⋀; N-Burma
- **ilicifolia** G. Forst. · ♄ e Z8 ⌂; S-Chile
- *ilicifolia* hort. ex Zabel = × Mahoberberis neubertii
- × **interposita** Ahrendt (*B. hookeri* var. *viridis* × *B. verruculosa*) · ♄ d Z7; cult.
- **jamesiana** Forrest & W.W. Sm. · ♄ d Z6 VI; China: NW-Yunnan
- *japonica* Thunb. = Mahonia japonica
- var. *bealei* (Fortune) Skeels = Mahonia bealei
- **julianae** C.K. Schneid. · E:Wintergreen Barberry; F:Epine-vinette de Juliana; G:Julianes Berberitze · ♄ e Z6 V-VI; China: Hupeh
- **kawakamii** Hayata · G:Taiwan-Berberitze · ♄ e Z6; Taiwan
- **koreana** Palib. · G:Koreanische Berberitze · ♄ d ⊛ Z5 V; Korea
- **lempergiana** Ahrendt · ♄ e Z5 V; China
- **linearifolia** Phil. · G:Linearblättrige Berberitze · ♄ e Z7 ⋀ V-VI; Chile
- × **lologensis** Sandwith (*B. darwinii* × *B. linearifolia*) · G:Lolog-Berberitze · ♄ e Z7 ⋀ VI; Arg.
- **lycium** Royle · E:Indian Lycium, Lycium; G:Himalaya-Berberitze · ♄ d Z6 V-VI; Him.: Kashmir, NW-Ind., Nepal
- × **macracantha** Schrad. (*B. aristata* × *B. vulgaris*) · ♄ d; cult.
- **manipurana** Ahrendt · ♄ e Z6 V; Ind.

(Assam, Manipur)
- × **mentorensis** L.M. Ames (*B. julianae* × *B. thunbergii*) · ♄ e Z6; cult.
- **mitifolia** Stapf · ♄ d Z6; China
- **morrisonensis** Hayata · E:Mount Morrison Berberis; G:Mount-Morrison-Berberitze · ♄ d △ ⊛ Z6 V; Taiwan
- *nervosa* Pursh = Mahonia nervosa
- × **notabilis** C.K. Schneid. (*B. heteropoda* × *B. vulgaris*) · ♄ d; cult.
- **oblonga** (Regel) C.K. Schneid. · ♄ d ⊛ Z6; C-As.
- **orthobotrys** Aitch. · ♄ d; Afgh., Pakist., NW-Ind., W-China
- × **ottawensis** C.K. Schneid. (*B. thunbergii* × *B. vulgaris*) · ♄ d ⊛ Z5 V; cult.
- **parvifolia** Sprague · ♄ d △ VI; W-China
- *pinnata* Lag. = Mahonia pinnata
- **poiretii** C.K. Schneid. · G:Poirets Berberitze · ♄ d Z5; NE-China, Mong., E-Sib., Korea
- **prattii** C.K. Schneid. · ♄ △ ⊛ Z5 V-VI; W-China
- **pruinosa** Franch. · G:Bereifte Berberitze · ♄ e Z7 IV-V; Yunnan
- **replicata** W.W. Sm. · ♄ e Z5 V; Yunnan
- × **rubrostilla** Chitt. (*B. aggregata* × *B. wilsoniae* var. *parvifolia*) · ♄ d ⊛ Z6 VI; cult.
- **sargentiana** C.K. Schneid. · E:Sargent's Barberry; G:Sargents Berberitze · ♄ e Z6 V-VI; C-China
- **sibirica** Pall. · G:Sibirische Berberitze · ♄ d △ V; Sib.
- **sieboldii** Miq. · G:Siebolds Berberitze · ♄ d △ ⊛ Z5 V; Jap.
- *sinensis* Desf. = Berberis chinensis
- × **stenophylla** Lindl. (*B. darwinii* × *B. empetrifolia*) · E:Rosemary Barberry; G:Schmalblättrige Berberitze · ♄ e Z7 ⋀ V; cult.
- **some cultivars**
- **thunbergii** DC. · E:Japanese Barberry, Purple Leaf Barberry; F:Epine-vinette de Thunberg; G:Thunbergs Berberitze · ♄ d ⊩ ⊛ Z4 V; Jap.
- **many cultivars**
- **tischleri** C.K. Schneid. · ♄ d V; W-China
- **veitchii** C.K. Schneid. · G:Veitchs Berberitze · ♄ e Z6 V; China (W-Hubei)
- **vernae** C.K. Schneid. · G:Vernas Berberitze · ♄ d ⊛ Z6 V; NW-China
- **verruculosa** Hemsl. & E.H. Wilson · E:Warty Barberry; F:Epine-vinette verruqueuse; G:Warzige Berberitze · ♄ e

△ Z5 V-VI; China: Kansu
- **virescens** Hook. f. & Thomson · ♂ d Z6 V-VI; Ind.: Sikkim
- **vulgaris** L. · E:Common Barberry; G:Gewöhnliche Berberitze, Sauerdorn · ♂ d Z3 IV-V ⚘ Ⓝ; Eur.* exc. BrI, Sc; TR, Cauc., nat. in BrI, Sc, E-Can., USA
- var. *amurensis* (Rupr.) Regel = Berberis amurensis var. amurensis
- *wallichiana* Hook. f. non DC. = Berberis hookeri var. hookeri
- **wilsoniae** Hemsl. & E.H. Wilson · E:Wilson's Barberry; G:Wilsons Berberitze
- var. **stapfiana** (C.K. Schneid.) C.K. Schneid. · ♂ d Z6 V; W-China
- var. **subcaulialata** (C.K. Schneid.) C.K. Schneid. · F:Epine-vinette de Wilson · ♂ d ⚘ △ ⚘ Z6 VI-VII; W-Sichuan
- var. **wilsoniae** · ♂ d △ ⚘ Z6 V-VI; W-Sichuan
- **yunnanensis** Franch. · G:Yunnan-Berberitze · ♂ d Z6; W-China

Berchemia Neck. ex DC. -f- *Rhamnaceae* · 12 (31) spp. · G:Berchemie
- **giraldiana** C.K. Schneid. · G:Giralds Berchemie · ♂ d ⚘ Z6 V-VI; China: Hupeh, Yunnan
- **racemosa** Siebold & Zucc. · G:Japanische Berchemie · ♂ d ⚘ Z6 VIII-IX; Jap., Taiwan
- **scandens** (Hill) K. Koch · E:Black Jack, Supple Jack; G:Amerikanische Berchemie · ♂ d ⚘ Z7 ∧ VI; USA: Va., NCE, SE, Fla., Tex.
- *volubilis* (L. f.) DC. = Berchemia scandens

Bergenia Moench -f- *Saxifragaceae* · 8 spp. · E:Elephant Ears; F:Bergenia, Plante-du-savetier; G:Bergenie
- **ciliata** (Haw.) Sternb. · F:Bergenia cilié; G:Kaschmir-Bergenie · ⚘ Z7; Him.
- f. **ligulata** (Wall.) Engl. · ⚘ △ ∧ III-IV; Afgh., Pakist.
- **cordifolia** (Haw.) Sternb. · E:Heart-leaf Bergenia; F:Plante des savetiers; G:Altai-Bergenie · ⚘ △ Z3 IV-V; Altai, Mong.
- **crassifolia** (L.) Fritsch · E:Winter-blooming Bergenia; G:Dickblatt-Bergenie
- var. **crassifolia** · E:Siberian Tea; F:Bergenia à feuilles épaisses · ⚘ △ Z3 IV-V Ⓝ; Sib., Mong., nat. in A, F
- var. *orbicularis* (Regel) hort. = Bergenia × schmidtii

- var. **pacifica** (Kom.) Nekr. · ⚘ △ Z3 IV-V; Amur
- *ligulata* Engl. = Bergenia ciliata f. ligulata
- var. *ciliata* (Royle) Engl. = Bergenia ciliata
- *ornata* Stein ex Guill. = Bergenia × schmidtii
- *pacifica* (Kom.) Kom. = Bergenia crassifolia var. pacifica
- **purpurascens** (Hook. f. & Thomson) Engl. · ⚘ △ Z4 V-VI; W-China, N-Burma
- × **schmidtii** (Regel) Silva Tar. (*B. ciliata* × *B. crassifolia*) · ⚘ △ Z5 III-V; cult.
- × **smithii** Engl. & Irmsch. (*B. cordifolia* × *B. purpurascens*) · ⚘ △ Z3 IV-V; cult.
- **stracheyi** (Hook. f. & Thomson) Engl. · G:Himalaya-Bergenie · ⚘ △ Z6 III; E-Afgh., Pakist., Kashmir, Nepal, W-Tibet
- var. *schmidtii* (Regel) H.R. Wehrh. = Bergenia × schmidtii
- *yunnanensis* hort. = Bergenia purpurascens
- **Cultivars:**
- **many cultivars**

Bergeranthus Schwantes -m- *Aizoaceae* · 5 spp.
- **multiceps** (Salm-Dyck) Schwantes · ⚘ ⚘ Z9 ⊞; Cape
- **scapiger** (Haw.) N.E. Br. · ⚘ ⚘ Z9 ⊞; Cape
- **vespertinus** (A. Berger) Schwantes · ⚘ ⚘ Z9 ⊞; Cape

Bergerocactus Britton & Rose -m- *Cactaceae* · 1 sp.
- **emoryi** (Engelm.) Britton & Rose · E:Golden Snake Cactus · ⚘ Z9 ⊞ ▽ ✳; Calif., Baja Calif.

Berkheya Ehrh. -f- *Asteraceae* · 75 spp.
- **macrocephala** J.M. Wood · ⚘ Z8 ⊞ VII-VIII; S-Afr.

Berlandiera DC. -f- *Asteraceae* · 4 spp. · G:Schokoladenblume
- **lyrata** Benth. · E:Lyre-leaf Greeneyes; G:Schokoladenblume · ⚘; USA: NC, SW, Tex., SE

Berteroa DC. -f- *Brassicaceae* · 5 spp. · E:Hoary Alison; F:Bertéroa; G:Graukresse
- **incana** (L.) DC. · E:Hoary Alison, Hoary False Madwort; G:Gewöhnliche

Graukresse · ⊙ ⊚ Z7 X; Eur.: C-Eur.,
EC-Eur., DK, Ba.E-Eur.; Cauc., W-Sib.,
E-Sib., C-As., nat. in BrI, Sc, Fr, Ib, N-Am.

Bertholletia Bonpl. -f- *Lecythidaceae* ·
1 sp. · E:Brazil Nut; F:Noix de Para;
G:Paranuss
– **excelsa** Bonpl. · E:Brazil Nut; G:Paranuss
· ♄ e Z10 ⓦ Ⓝ; Amazon.

Bertolonia Raddi -f- *Melastomataceae* · 14
(8) spp. · F:Bertolonia; G:Bertolonie
– *guttata* Hook. f. = Gravesia guttata
– *hirsuta* Benth. = Triolena hirsuta
– **maculata** Mart. ex DC. · ♃ Z10 ⓦ;
NE-Braz.
– **marmorata** Naudin · ♃ Z10 ⓦ; N-Braz.
– *pubescens* hort. = Triolena pustulata

× **Bertonerila** hort. -f- *Melastomataceae*
(*Bertolonia* × *Sonerila*)
– **houtteana** hort. (*Bertolonia guttata* ×
Sonerila margaritacea) · ♃ ⓦ; cult.

Berula Besser & W.D.J. Koch -f- *Apiaceae* ·
1 (-2) spp. · F:Bérula; G:Berle, Merk
– **erecta** (Huds.) Coville · E:Lesser Water
Parsnip; G:Berle, Schmalblättriger Merk
· ♃ VII-IX ⚘; Eur.*, Cauc., Iran, Afgh.,
N-As., C-As., N-Am., nat. in N-Am., Mex.,
Austr.

Beschorneria Kunth -f- *Agavaceae* · 8 spp.
– *bracteata* Jacobi ex Baker = Beschorneria
yuccoides subsp. dekosteriana
– *dekosteriana* K. Koch = Beschorneria
yuccoides subsp. dekosteriana
– *multiflora* K. Koch = Furcraea parmentieri
– *pubescens* A. Berger = Beschorneria
wrightii
– **tubiflora** (Kunth & C.D. Bouché) Kunth ·
♃ Ψ Z9 ⓐ; Mex.
– **wrightii** Hook. f. · ♃ Ψ Z9 ⓐ; Mex.
– **yuccoides** K. Koch
– subsp. **decosteriana** (K. Koch) García-
Mend. · ♃ Ψ Z9 ⓐ; Mex.
– subsp. **yuccoides** · ♃ Ψ Z9 ⓐ; Mex.

Bessera Schult. f. -f- *Alliaceae* · 3 spp. ·
E:Coral Drops; F:Bessera; G:Korallen-
tröpfchen
– **elegans** Schult. f. · E:Coral Drops;
G:Korallentröpfchen · ♃ Z9 ⓐ VII-IX;
Mex.

Beta L. -f- *Chenopodiaceae* · 6 (-12) spp. ·
E:Beet; F:Betterave, Poirée; G:Bete, Rübe
– **trigyna** Waldst. & Kit. · E:Caucasian
Beet; G:Dreiweibige Runkelrübe · ♃ Z5
VII-VIII; Eur.: Ba, E-Eur.; TR, Cauc., Iran,
nat. in BrI, F
– **vulgaris** L.
– subsp. **cicla** (L.) W.D.J. Koch · G:Man-
gold · ⊙ Z5
– var. **cicla** · E:Foliage Beet, Leaf Beet;
G:Blatt-Mangold, Schnitt-Mangold · ;
cult.
– var. **flavescens** DC. · E:Swiss Chard;
G:Römische Bete, Stiel-Mangold · ; cult.
– subsp. **maritima** (L.) Arcang. · E:Sea
Beet; G:See-Mangold, Wild-Bete · ♃ ;
Eur.: Ib, Ital-P, Ba; TR, Cyprus, Levant,
N-Afr., Canar., Azor., Iran, Iraq, NW-Ind.;
coasts
– subsp. **vulgaris** · G:Bete · ⊙ ⊚ Z5
– var. **alba** DC. · G:Weiße Bete, Weiße
Rübe · ; cult.
– var. **altissima** Döll · E:Sugar Beet;
G:Zucker-Rübe · ; cult.
– var. **lutea** DC. · E:Yellow Beet; G:Gelbe
Bete, Gelbe Rübe · ; cult.
– var. **rapacea** K. Koch · E:Field Beet;
G:Futter-Rübe, Runkel-Rübe · cult.
– var. *rubra* Moq. = Beta vulgaris subsp.
vulgaris var. vulgaris
– var. **vulgaris** · E:Beetroot, Mangel
Wurzel, Mangold, Root Beet; G:Rote
Bete, Rote Rübe · ⊙ VII-IX; Eur.* exc.
EC-Eur., E-Eur.; TR, Levant, N-Arab.,
Canar., Madeira, N-Afr.

Betonica L. = Stachys
– *alopecuros* L. = Stachys alopecuros
– *grandiflora* Steven ex Willd. = Stachys
macrantha
– *macrantha* K. Koch = Stachys macrantha
– *nivea* (Labill.) Steven = Stachys discolor
– *officinalis* L. = Stachys officinalis

Betula L. -f- *Betulaceae* · 101 sp. · E:Birch;
F:Bouleau; G:Birke
– **albosinensis** Burkill · E:Chinese Red
Birch; F:Bouleau à écorce rouge;
G:Chinesische Birke, Kupfer-Birke · ♄ d
Z7; Sichuan
– var. *septentrionalis* C.K. Schneid. = Betula
utilis var. utilis
– **alleghaniensis** Britton · E:Yellow Birch;
G:Gelb-Birke · ♄ d Z3 Ⓝ; Can.: E; USA;
NE, NCE, SE

– **alnoides** Buch.-Ham. ex D. Don ·
G:Erlenblättrige Birke · ℏ d Z8 ∧; Him.,
NE-Ind., SW-China: Sichuan, Yunnan
– *alnus* L. = Alnus incana subsp. incana
– var. *glutinosa* L. = Alnus glutinosa
– var. *incana* L. = Alnus incana subsp.
incana
– × **caerulea** Blanch. (*B. cordifolia* × *B.
populifolia*) · E:Blue Birch; G:Blaue Birke
· ℏ d Z4; Can., NE-USA
– *caerulea-grandis* Blanch. = Betula ×
caerulea
– *carpatica* Waldst. & Kit. ex Willd. =
Betula pubescens var. glabrata
– *celtiberica* Rothm. & Vasc. = Betula
pubescens var. pubescens
– **chinensis** Maxim. · G:Chinesische
Strauch-Birke · ℏ ℏ d Z5; Korea, N-China,
? Jap.
– **corylifolia** Regel & Maxim. ex Regel ·
G:Haselblättrige Birke · ℏ d Z5; Jap.
– **costata** Trautv. · E:Costata Birch;
G:Gerippte Birke · ℏ d Z5; Amur, Manch.
– **davurica** Pall. · E:Asian Black Birch;
G:Dahurische Birke · ℏ d Z5 Ⓝ; Amur,
Manch., Korea, Jap.
– **divaricata** Ledeb. · G:Sibirische Strauch-
Birke · ℏ d Z3; E-Sib., Amur, Kamchat.,
N-Manch.
– **ermanii** Cham.
– var. **ermanii** · E:Erman's Birch, Russian
Rock Birch; F:Bouleau du Japon;
G:Ermans Birke, Gold-Birke · ℏ d Z5 Ⓝ;
Jap., Korea, Sakhal., Kamchat.
– var. *subcordata* (Regel) Koidz. = Betula
ermanii var. ermanii
– *glandulifera* (Regel) B.T. Butler = Betula
pumila
– **grossa** Siebold & Zucc. · E:Japanese
Cherry Birch; G:Grossers Birke,
Zierkirschen-Birke · ℏ d Z5; Japan
– **humilis** Schrank · G:Strauch-Birke · ℏ d
Z3 IV-V; Eur.: C-Eur., PL, E-Eur.; W-Sib.,
E-Sib., Mong.
– *jacquemontii* Spach = Betula utilis var.
jacquemontii
– **kamtschatica** (Regel) C.-A. Jansson ·
G:Kamtschatka-Birke · ℏ d Z5; Jap.,
Kamchat., NE-As.
– **kenaica** W.H. Evans · E:Kenai Birch;
G:Yukon-Birke · ℏ d Z2; Alaska, Can:
Yukon
– × **koehnei** C.K. Schneid. (*B. papyrifera* ×
B. pendula) · ℏ d Z4; cult.
– **lenta** L. · E:Sweet Birch; G:Gewöhnliche

Zucker-Birke · ℏ d Z4 Ⓝ; Can.: E; USA:
NE, SE
– **luminifera** H.J.P. Winkl. · ℏ d Z7; China:
Sichuan, W-Hupeh
– *lutea* F. Michx. = Betula alleghaniensis
– *mandshurica* (Regel) Nakai = Betula
platyphylla var. platyphylla
– var. *japonica* (Miq.) Rehder = Betula
kamtschatica
– **maximowicziana** Regel · E:Monarch
Birch; F:Bouleau monarque; G:Linden-
blättrige Birke · ℏ d Z6; Jap., S-Kurilen
– **medwediewii** Regel · E:Transcaucasian
Birch; G:Transkaukasische Birke · ℏ ℏ d
Z6; Cauc.
– **nana** L. · E:Dwarf Birch; F:Bouleau
nain; G:Zwerg-Birke · ℏ d Z1 IV-VI ▽;
Eur.: Fr, BrI, C-Eur., EC-Eur., Sc, E-Eur.;
W-Sib., E-Sib.
– **nigra** L. · E:Black Birch, Red Birch, River
Birch; F:Bouleau noir; G:Schwarz-Birke ·
ℏ d Z5 Ⓝ; USA: NE, NCE, SE, SC, Fla.
– *papyracea* Aiton = Betula papyrifera var.
papyrifera
– **papyrifera** Marshall · E:Canoe Birch,
Paper Birch, White Birch; F:Bouleau à
papier; G:Papier-Birke
– var. **cordifolia** (Regel) Fernald ·
E:Mountain Paper; G:Herzblättrige
Papier-Birke · ℏ ℏ d Z1; E-Can.; USA: NE,
N.C., Minn.
– var. *kenaica* (W.H. Evans) A. Henry =
Betula kenaica
– var. **papyrifera** · E:Paper Birch;
G:Gewöhnliche Papier-Birke · ℏ d Z4 Ⓝ;
Alaska, Can., USA: NE, N.C., NCE, NC,
Rocky Mts., NW
– **pendula** Roth · E:European White Birch,
Silver Birch; F:Bouleau blanc, Bouleau
verruqueux; G:Hänge-Birke, Sand-Birke,
Warzen-Birke · ℏ d Z2 IV-V ⚥ Ⓝ; Eur.*,
W-Sib., TR, N-Iraq, Cauc., N-Iran, Moroc.
– **platyphylla** Sukaczev · E:Asian White
Birch
– var. *japonica* (Miq.) H. Hara = Betula
kamtschatica
– var. *kamtschatica* (Regel) H. Hara =
Betula kamtschatica
– var. **platyphylla** · E:Japanese White
Birch; G:Mandschurische Birke · ℏ d Z5
Ⓝ; Korea, Manch., N-China
– var. *szechuanica* (C.K. Schneid.) Rehder =
Betula szechuanica
– **populifolia** Marshall · E:Grey Birch;
G:Grau-Birke, Pappelblättrige Birke · ℏ d

Z5; Can.: E; USA: NE, NCE
- **potaninii** Batalin · ♄ d Z4; W-China
- **pubescens** Ehrh. · G:Moor-Birke
- subsp. *carpatica* (Waldst. & Kit. ex
 Willd.) Asch. & Graebn. = Betula
 pubescens var. glabrata
- subsp. *tortuosa* (Ledeb.) Nyman = Betula
 pubescens var. pumila
- var. **glabrata** Wahlenb. · G:Karpaten-
 Birke · ♄ ♄ d Z1 IV-V; N-Eur. , Pyr. Carp.
- var. **pubescens** · E:Downy Birch, White
 Birch; F:Bouleau pubescent; G:Gewöhn-
 liche Moor-Birke · ♄ ♄ d Z1 IV-V ⚘ Ⓝ;
 Eur.*, Cauc., W-Sib., E-Sib.
- var. **pumila** (L.) Govaerts · G:Zwerg-
 Moor-Birke · ♄ ♄ d Z1; Sc, N-Russ.,
 W-Sib., Greenl.
- **pumila** L. · E:American Dwarf Birch;
 G:Amerikanische Strauch-Birke, Kleine
 Birke · ♄ d Z3; Can.; USA: NE, NCE,
 N.Dak., Mont.
- subsp. *glandulifera* (Regel) A. Löve & D.
 Löve = Betula pumila
- **raddeana** Trautv. · G:Kaukasische
 Strauch-Birke · ♄ ♄ d Z5; Cauc.
- **schmidtii** Regel · G:Schmidts Birke · ♄ d
 Z5 Ⓝ; Jap., Korea, Manch., Amur
- **szechuanica** (C.K. Schneid.) C.-A. Jansson · E:Sichuan Birch; G:Sichuan-Birke
 · ♄ d Z6; W-China: Sichuan, Yunnan,
 Sikang
- **tianschanica** Rupr. · ♄ ♄ d; China
- **turkestanica** Litv. · G:Turkestan-Birke · ♄
 d; C-As.
- **utilis** D. Don · E:Himalayan Birch;
 F:Bouleau de l'Himalaya; G:Himalaya-
 Birke
- var. **jacquemontii** (Spach) H.J.P.
 Winkl. · E:Jacquemont's Birch, White
 Barked Himalayan Birch; G:Weiße
 Himalaya-Birke · ♄ d Z7; W-Him.
- var. **prattii** Burkill · ♄ d Z6; W-China
- var. **utilis** · G:Gewöhnliche Himalaya-
 Birke · ♄ d Z7; Him.
- *verrucosa* Ehrh. = Betula pendula
- *viridis* Chaix = Alnus viridis subsp. viridis
- *wilsonii* Bean = Betula potaninii

Bidens L. -f- *Asteraceae* · c. 240 spp. ·
E:Beggarticks, Bur Marigold; F:Bident;
G:Zweizahn
- **bipinnata** L. · E:Spanish Needles;
 G:Fiederblättriger Zweizahn · ⊙ Z3 VII-X;
 USA* exc. Calif., NW, nat. in F, I, Sw,
 Slove.

- **cernua** L. · E:Nodding Bur Marigold;
 G:Nickender Zweizahn · ⊙ VIII-X; Eur.*,
 TR, Cauc., N-As., N-Am.
- **connata** Muhl. ex Willd. · E:London
 Bur Marigold; G:Verwachsenblättriger
 Zweizahn · ⊙ Z3 VIII-X; Can.: E; USA:
 NE, NCE, Kans., nat. in Fr, Sw, G, PL
- *dahlioides* hort. = Cosmos atrosanguineus
- *diversifolia* (Otto) Sch. Bip. = Cosmos
 diversifolius
- **ferulifolia** (Jacq.) DC. · E:Apache Beg-
 garticks; F:Bident; G:Fenchelblättriger
 Zweizahn · ⊙ ⊙ Z8 VIII; S-Ariz., Mex.
- **frondosa** L. · E:Devil's Beggarticks;
 G:Schwarzfrüchtiger Zweizahn · ⊙
 VIII-IX; N-Am., nat. in Eur.* exc. Sk
- **radiata** Thuill. · G:Strahliger Zweizahn ·
 ⊙ VIII-X; Eur.: Fr, C-Eur., EC-Eur.,
 E-Eur., Sc; C-As., NE-As.
- **subalternans** DC. · G:Rio-Grande-
 Zweizahn · ⊙ VII-X; Bol., Braz., Urug.,
 Arg., nat. in sp., F, Sw
- **tripartita** L. · E:Marigold Burr, Trifid Bur
 Marigold; G:Dreiteiliger Zweizahn · ⊙ Z6
 VII-IX ⚘ ; Eur.*, TR, W-As. , N-Afr., N-Am.
- **triplinervia** Kunth · G:Dreinerviger
 Zweizahn
- var. **macrantha** (Wedd.) Sherff · ⊙ ♃ Z9
 VII; Mex., C-Am., S-Am.
- var. **triplinervia** · ♃ Z9; Mex., C-Am.,
 S-Am.

Biebersteinia Stephan -f- *Geraniaceae* ·
5 spp.
- **orphanidis** Boiss. · ♃ △ Z8 ⌂ ∧ V-VI;
 S-GR, TR

Bifora Hoffm. -f- *Apiaceae* · 3 spp. ·
E:Bishop; G:Hohlsame
- **radians** M. Bieb. · E:Wild Bishop;
 G:Strahlen-Hohlsame · ⊙ V-VIII; Eur.:
 Ib, Fr, Ital-P, Ba, G, EC-Eur., E-Eur.; TR,
 Cauc., Iran
- **testiculata** (L.) Spreng. · E:European
 Bishop; G:Warziger Hohlsame · ⊙; Eur.:
 Ib, Fr, Ital-P, Ba; TR, Syr., Iraq, Cauc.,
 Iran, C-As., nat. in G, Sw

Bifrenaria Lindl. -f- *Orchidaceae* · 21 sp.
- **atropurpurea** (Lodd.) Lindl. · ♃ Z10 ✤
 VI-VII ▽ ✳; Braz.
- **aureofulva** (Hook.) Lindl. · ♃ Z10 ✤ X
 ▽ ✳; Braz.
- **harrisoniae** (Hook.) Rchb. f. · ♃ Z10 ✤
 III-V ▽ ✳; Braz.

– **inodora** Lindl. · ⁴ Z10 ⓜ VII ▽ ✳; Braz.
– **tetragona** (Lindl.) Schltr. · ⁴ Z10 ⓜ
  VI-VII ▽ ✳; S-Braz.
– **tyrianthina** (Lodd. ex Loudon) Rchb. f. ·
  ⁴ Z10 ⓜ V-VII ▽ ✳; Braz.

Bignonia L. -f- *Bignoniaceae* · 1 sp. ·
  E:Trumpet Vine; F:Bignone; G:Kreuz-
  rebe, Trompetenwein
– *australis* Aiton = Pandorea pandorana
– **capreolata** L. · E:Cross Vine, Quar-
  tervine, Trumpet Vine; G:Kreuzrebe,
  Trompetenwein · ♄ e ⚡ Z8 ⓐ V-VI; USA:
  NE, NCE, SE, SC, Fla.
– *chamberlaynii* Sims = Anemopaegma
  chamberlaynii
– *chinensis* Lam. = Campsis grandiflora
– *grandiflora* Thunb. = Campsis grandiflora
– *pandorana* Andrews = Pandorea
  pandorana
– *radicans* L. = Campsis radicans
– *speciosa* Graham = Clytostoma callistegioides
– *tweediana* Lindl. = Macfadyena unguis-
  cati
– *unguis-cati* L. = Macfadyena unguis-cati
– *venusta* Ker-Gawl. = Pyrostegia venusta

Bilderdykia Dumort. = Fallopia
– *aubertii* (L. Henry) Moldenke = Fallopia
  baldschuanica
– *baldschuanica* (Regel) D.A. Webb =
  Fallopia baldschuanica
– *convolvulus* (L.) Dumort. = Fallopia
  convolvulus

Billardiera Sm. -f- *Pittosporaceae* · 8 spp. ·
  E:Apple Berry
– **longiflora** Labill. · E:Apple Berry,
  Blueberry · ♄ e ⚡ ⚡ ⊘ Z8 ⓐ VII; Tasman.
– **scandens** Sm. · ♄ e ⚡ ⚡ ⊘ Z8 ⓐ VI-IX;
  Austr.: Queensl., N.S.Wales, Victoria,
  S-Austr., Tasman.

Billbergia Thunb. -f- *Bromeliaceae* ·
  66 spp. · E:Billbergia; F:Billbergia;
  G:Zimmerhafer
– *amabilis* Beer = Billbergia vittata
– **amoena** (Lodd.) Lindl. · ⁴ Z10 ⓜ;
  E-Braz.
– *baraquiniana* Lem. = Billbergia decora
– **Braziliensis** L.B. Sm. · ⁴ Z10 ⓜ; Braz.
– *burchellii* Baker = Billbergia distachia
– **chlorosticta** Saunders · ⁴ Z10 ⓜ;
  NE-Braz.

– **decora** Poepp. & Endl. · ⁴ Z10 ⓜ; Peru,
  Bol., NW-Braz.
– **distachia** (Vell.) Mez · ⁴ Z10 ⓜ; Braz.
– **euphemiae** E. Morren · ⁴ Z10 ⓜ;
  S-Braz.
– *fasciata* Lindl. = Aechmea fasciata
– *granulosa* Brongn. = Billbergia rosea
– **horrida** Regel · ⁴ Z10 ⓜ; Braz.
– **iridifolia** (Nees & Mart.) Lindl. · ⁴ Z10
  ⓜ; E-Braz., N-Braz.
– *leopoldii* (Verschaff. ex Lem.) Linden ex
  Houllet = Billbergia Braziliensis
– *leopoldii* K. Koch = Billbergia vittata
– *liboniana* De Jonghe = Quesnelia
  liboniana
– **lietzei** E. Morren · ⁴ Z10 ⓜ; Braz.
– **macrocalyx** Hook. · ⁴ Z10 ⓜ; Braz.
– **magnifica** Mez · ⁴ Z10 ⓜ; Braz.
– **meyeri** Mez · ⁴ Z10 ⓜ; Braz.
– *moreliana* Brongn. = Billbergia vittata
– **morelii** Brongn. · ⁴ Z10 ⓜ; Braz.
– **nutans** H. Wendl. ex Regel · E:Friendship
  Plant, Queen's Tears; G:Zimmerhafer · ⁴
  Z9 ⓜ ⓐ; S-Braz., Parag., Urug., N-Arg.
– **porteana** Brongn. ex Beer · ⁴ Z10 ⓜ;
  Braz.
– **pyramidalis** (Sims) Lindl. · ⁴ Z10 ⓜ;
  E-Braz.
– *rhodocyanea* Lem. = Aechmea fasciata
– **rosea** Beer · ⁴ Z10 ⓜ; Venez
– **sanderiana** E. Morren · ⁴ Z10 ⓜ; Braz.
– *saundersii* W. Bull ex Dombrain =
  Billbergia chlorosticta
– *speciosa* Thunb. = Billbergia amoena
– *thyrsoidea* Mart. ex Schult. = Billbergia
  pyramidalis
– *venezuelana* Mez = Billbergia rosea
– **viridiflora** H. Wendl. · ⁴ Z10 ⓜ; Guat.,
  Hond.
– **vittata** Brongn. ex Morel · ⁴ Z10 ⓜ;
  Braz., Parag., N-Arg.
– *zebrina* (Herb.) Lindl. · ⁴ Z10 ⓜ;
  E-Braz., Parag., N-Arg.

Biophytum DC. -n- *Oxalidaceae* ·
  50-75 spp. · F:Sensitive; G:Sinnklee
– **proliferum** (Arn.) Wight ex Edgew. &
  Hook. f. · G:Lebendgebärender Sinnklee ·
  ⁴ Z10 ⓜ; Sri Lanka
– **sensitivum** (L.) DC. · ⁴ Z10 ⓜ; trop.
  Afr., trop. As.

Biscutella L. -f- *Brassicaceae* · 40 spp. ·
  F:Lunetière; G:Brillenschötchen
– **auriculata** L. · ⊙ Z8; Ib, Fr

- **cichoriifolia** Loisel. · E:Chicory-leaved
Buckler Mustard; G:Wegwartenblättriges
Brillenschötchen · ☉ Z8 VI; Eur.: sp., F,
Sw, I, W-Ba
- **didyma** L. · ☉ Z8; Eur.: Ital-P, Ba; TR,
Syr., Iraq, Iran
- **laevigata** L. · E:Buckler Mustard;
G:Glattes Brillenschötchen · ⌃ △ Z6 V-VI
▽; Eur.: Ib, Fr, Ital-P, C-Eur., EC-Eur.,
Ba, RO

Bistorta (L.) Adans. -f- *Polygonaceae* · c.
25 spp. · F:Bistorte, Polygonum bistorte;
G:Wiesenknöterich
- **affinis** (D. Don) Greene · F:Renouée en
tapis; G:Teppich-Wiesenknöterich · ⌃
⤳ Z3 VIII-IX; Nepal
- **amplexicaulis** (D. Don) Greene ·
E:Mountain Fleece; G:Kerzen-
Wiesenknöterich · ⌃ Z5 VI-X; Him., nat.
in BrI
- **some cultivars**
- **macrophylla** (D. Don) Soják · G:Groß-
blättriger Wiesenknöterich · ⌃ Z5 VII-IX;
Him., W-China
- **officinalis** Delarbre
- subsp. **carnea** (K. Koch) Wissk. · ⌃ △ ✕
Z4 V-VII; Him.
- subsp. **officinalis** · E:Adderwort,
Meadow Bistort; F:Renouée bistorte;
G:Schlangen-Wiesenknöterich · ⌃ Z4
V-VIII ⚥; Eur.* exc. Sc; TR, Cauc., Iran,
W-Sib., E-Sib., Amur, Sakhal., Kamchat.,
China, Korea, Jap., Moroc., Alaska, Can.:
Yukon, nat. in Sc
- **tenuicaulis** (Bisset & S. Moore) Petrov ·
E:Knotweed; G:Dünnstängeliger
Wiesenknöterich · ⌃ ⤳ △ Z6 IV-VI; Jap.
- **vacciniifolia** (Wall. ex Meisn.) Greene ·
G:Heidelbeerstrauchiger Wiesenknö-
terich · ♄ ⤳ △ Z7 ⊡ ⋀ VIII-IX; Him.
- **vivipara** (L.) Delarbre · E:Alpine Bistort,
Serpent Grass; G:Knöllchen-Wiesenknö-
terich · ⌃ △ Z3 V-VIII; Eur.*, Cauc.,
W-Sib., E-Sib., Amur, Sakhal., C-As.,
Mong., Him., China, Jap., Alaska, Can.,
USA: NE, NCE, NC, SW, Rocky Mts., NW;
Greenl.

Bituminaria Heist. ex Fabr. -f- *Fabaceae* ·
2 spp. · E:Triphyllon; G:Asphaltklee
- **bituminosa** (L.) C.H. Stirt. · E:Pitch
Trefoil, Triphyllon; G:Asphaltklee · ⌃
⊡ Ⓝ; Eur.: Ib, Fr, Ital-P, Ba, Crim; TR,
Levant, Sinai, Cauc., NW-Afr., Libya

Bixa L. -f- *Bixaceae* · 5 spp. · E:Annatto,
Lipstick Tree; F:Rocouyer; G:Anattost-
rauch, Orleanstrauch
- **orellana** L. · E:Annatto, Lipstick Tree;
G:Anattostrauch, Orleanstrauch · ♄ ♄ e
Z10 ⓖ ⚥ Ⓝ; Mex., C-Am., W.Ind, trop.
S-Am., nat. in trop. Afr., trop. As., Austr.:
Queensl.

Blackstonia Huds. -f- *Gentianaceae* ·
4-6 spp. · E:Yellow Wort; F:Centaurée
jaune ; G:Bitterling
- **acuminata** (W.D.J. Koch & Ziz) Domin ·
G:Später Bitterling · ☉ VIII-IX; C-Eur.,
S-Eur., TR, Levant, Moroc.
- **perfoliata** (L.) Huds. · E:Yellow Wort;
G:Durchwachsener Bitterling · ☉ VI-VIII;
Eur.: Ba, Fr, BrI, Ital-P, EC-Eur., Ib,
C-Eur., Crim; TR, Levant, Iraq, Cauc.,
NW-Afr.

Blandfordia Sm. -f- *Blandfordiaceae* ·
4 spp. · E:Christmas Bells; F:Blandfordia;
G:Lilientrichter, Weihnachtsglöckchen
- **cunninghamii** Lindl. · E:Christmas
Bells; G:Weihnachtsglöckchen · ⌃ Z9 ⓖ;
Austr.: N.S.Wales
- *grandiflora* auct. = Blandfordia cunninghamii
- **grandiflora** R. Br. · E:Large Christmas
Bells · ⌃ Z9 ⓑ VII-VIII; Austr.: Queensl.,
N.S.Wales
- *marginata* Herb. = Blandfordia punicea
- **nobilis** Sm. · ⌃ Z9 ⓑ VII; Austr.:
N.S.Wales
- **punicea** (Labill.) Sweet · E:Tasmanian
Christmas Bell; G:Tasmanisches
Weihnachtsglöckchen · ⌃ Z9 ⓑ; Tasman.

Blechnum L. -n- *Blechnaceae* · 191 sp. ·
E:Hard Fern; F:Blechnum; G:Rippenfarn
- **auriculatum** Cav. · ⌃ Z9 ⓑ; S-Am.; mts.
- **australe** L. · ⌃ Z9 ⓑ; S-Afr.
- **Braziliense** Desv. · ⌃ Z9 ⓑ; Guat., Col.,
Peru, Bol., Braz., Parag., Urug., Arg.
- **fraxineum** Willd. · ⌃ Z10 ⓖ; trop.
N-Am, trop. S-Am.
- **gibbum** (Labill.) Mett. · E:Miniature Tree
Fern · ⌃ Z9 ⓖ; N.Caled., Vanuatu
- **moorei** C. Chr. · ⌃ Z9 ⓖ; N.Caled.
- **occidentale** L. · E:Hammock Fern;
G:Östlicher Rippenfarn · ⌃ Z9 ⓖ;
W.Ind., trop. Am., Chile, Pacific Is., nat.
in Sri Lanka
- **penna-marina** (Poir.) Kuhn · F:Blechne

de la Terre de Feu; G:Seefeder · ⌐ △
Z8 ⌂ ∧; Austr.: N.S.Wales, Victoria,
Tasman.; NZ, s. S-Am.
- **spicant** (L.) Roth · E:Deer Fern, Hard
Fern; F:Blechne en épi; G:Gewöhnlicher
Rippenfarn · ⌐ △ Z5 VII-IX; Eur.*, TR,
Cauc., N-Iran, Levant, Jap., NW-Afr.,
Libya, Alaska, , Can.: W; USA: NW, Calif.
- **tabulare** (Thunb.) Kuhn · ⌐ Z8 ⌂ ∧;
W.Ind., Falkland Is., S-Afr., Madag.,
Austr., NZ

Bletia Ruiz & Pav. -f- *Orchidaceae* · 35 spp.
- **campanulata** Lex. · ⌐ Z10 ⌂ V-VIII ▽
✳; Mex.
- **catenulata** Ruiz & Pav. · ⌐ Z10 ⌂ V-VII
▽ ✳; Ecuad., Peru, Bol., Braz.
- **purpurea** (Lam.) DC. · E:Pinepink · ⌐
Z10 ⌂ V-VII ▽ ✳; Fla., C-Am., W.Ind.,
Col. Venez.
- *sanguinea* Poepp. & Endl. = Bletia
catenulata
- *verecunda* R. Br. = Bletia purpurea

Bletilla Rchb. f. -f- *Orchidaceae* · 5 spp. ·
E:Chinese Ground Orchid; F:Jacinthe
blétille; G:Chinaorchidee
- **foliosa** (King & Pantl.) T. Tang & F.T.
Wang · G:Chinaorchidee · ⌐ ⌂ VI ▽ ✳;
China: Yunnan
- *gebinae* (Lindl.) Rchb. f. = Bletilla striata
- *hyacinthina* (Sm.) Rchb. f. = Bletilla
striata
- **striata** (Thunb.) Rchb. f. · E:Chinese
Ground Orchid; G:Gestreifte Chinaorchidee · ⌐ ⌂ ⌂ ∧ V-VI ⚘ ▽ ✳;
China, E-Tibet, Jap., Okinawa

Blighia K.D. Koenig -f- *Sapindaceae* · 4 spp. ·
E:Akee; F:Akee; G:Akee, Akipflaume
- **sapida** K.D. Koenig · G:Akipflaume;
E:Akee · ♄ e Z9 ⌂ Ⓝ; W-Afr., Cameroon,
nat. in Trop., Subtrop., S-Fla.

× **Bloomara** hort. -f- *Orchidaceae*
(*Broughtonia* × *Laeliopsis* × *Tetramicra*)

Bloomeria Kellogg -f- *Alliaceae* · 3 spp. ·
E:Goldenstars; F:Bloomeria; G:Goldstern
- **crocea** (Torr.) Coville · E:Common
Goldenstars; G:Goldstern · ⌐ Z8 ⌂ VII;
S-Calif.

Blossfeldia Werderm. -f- *Cactaceae* · 1 sp.
- *atrovirens* F. Ritter = Blossfeldia

liliputana
- *campaniflora* Backeb. = Blossfeldia
liliputana
- *fechseri* Backeb. = Blossfeldia liliputana
- **liliputana** Werderm. · ⅄ Z9 ⌂ VII ▽ ✳;
Arg.: Catamarca, Salta, Jujuy, La Rioja;
Bol.: Tarija, Chuquisaca
- *minima* F. Ritter = Blossfeldia liliputana
- *pedicellata* F. Ritter = Blossfeldia
liliputana

Blumea DC. -f- *Asteraceae* · c. 100 spp.
- **balsamifera** (L.) DC. · E:Buffalo Ear
; G:Büffelohr · ⌐ ⌂ Ⓝ; Him., Ind.,
S-China, Taiwan, Burma, Malay. Arch.,
Phil.

Blumenbachia Schrad. -f- *Loasaceae* ·
6 spp.
- **hieronymii** Urb. · ⊙; Arg.
- **insignis** Schrad. · ⊙ VII-VIII; Braz., Arg.
- *lateritia* (Hook.) Griseb. = Caiophora
lateritia

Blysmus Panz. ex Schult. -m- *Cyperaceae* ·
3 spp. · E:Bulrush, Flat Sedge;
G:Quellbinse, Quellried
- **compressus** (L.) Panz. ex Link ·
E:Flat Sedge; G:Zusammengedrücktes
Quellried · ⌐ VI-VII; Eur.* exc. Ib; TR,
Cauc., Iran, C-As., Him., China: Sinkiang,
Moroc.
- **rufus** (Huds.) Link · E:Red Bulrush,
Saltmarsh Flat Sedge; G:Rotbraunes
Quellried · ⌐ V-VII; Eur.: BrI, Sc, G, PL,
Russ.; W-Sib., E-Sib., C-As. , Mong.,
China: Sinkiang

Bocconia L. -f- *Papaveraceae* · 9 spp. ·
E:Tree Celandine; F:Bocconia; G:Baum-
mohn
- *cordata* Willd. = Macleaya cordata var.
cordata
- **frutescens** L. · E:Tree Celandine;
G:Baummohn · ♄ ♄ Z9 ⌂ X; Mex., Costa
Rica, W.Ind.

Boea Comm. ex Lam. -f- *Gesneriaceae* ·
17 spp.
- **hygroscopica** F. Muell. · E:Rock Violet ·
⌐ e Z10 ⌂; Austr.: Queensl.

Boehmeria Jacq. -f- *Urticaceae* ·
50-100 spp. · E:False Nettle; F:Ortie de
Chine; G:Chinagras, Ramie

- *argentea* hort. = Myriocarpa stipitata
- **biloba** Wedd. · ♃ Z7 Ⓚ; Jap.
- **nivea** (L.) Gaudich.
- var. **nivea** · E:China Grass, Chinese Silk Plant, Rami; G:Ramie · ♃ Z7 Ⓝ; China, Malay. Arch., Indochina, Jap.
- var. **tenacissima** (Gaudich.) Miq. · ♃ e Z7 Ⓝ; Malay. Arch.

Boenninghausenia Rchb. ex Meisn. -f- *Rutaceae* · 1 sp.
- **albiflora** (Hook.) Rchb. ex Meisn. · ♄ Z8 Ⓚ; Ind.: Assam, China, Jap.

Boesenbergia Kuntze -f- *Zingiberaceae* · 61 sp.
- **ornata** (N.E. Br.) R.M. Sm. · ♃ Z10 Ⓦ; Kalimantan
- **rotunda** (L.) Mansf. · E:Chinese Keys, Galingale, Tropical Crocus; G:Tropenkrokus · ♃ Z10 Ⓦ V Ⓝ; Ind., Sri Lanka, Java

Boisduvalia Spach -f- *Onagraceae* · 6 spp.
- **densiflora** (Lindl.) S. Watson · ⊙ Z8; Can.: B.C.; USA: NW, Calif., Rocky Mts.

Bolbitis Schott -f- *Lomariopsidaceae* · 69 spp. · F:Fougère aquatique; G:Wasserfarn
- **heteroclita** (C. Presl) Ching · G:Geschwänzter Wasserfarn · ♃ Z10 Ⓦ; trop. SE-As.

Bolboschoenus (Asch.) Palla -m- *Cyperaceae* · 12 spp. · E:Sea Club Rush; G:Strandsimse
- **maritimus** (L.) Palla · E:Sea Club Rush; F:Scirpe maritime; G:Gewöhnliche Strandsimse · ♃ Z6 VI-VIII; Eur.*, cosmop.

Bolivicereus Cárdenas = Borzicactus
- *samaipatanus* Cárdenas = Borzicactus samaipatanus

Bollea Rchb. f. -f- *Orchidaceae* · 11 sp.
- **coelestis** Rchb. f. · ♃ Z10 Ⓦ VII-VIII ▽ *; Col.
- **lalindei** (Linden) Rchb. f. · ♃ Z10 Ⓦ VII-VIII ▽ *; Col.

Boltonia L'Hér. -f- *Asteraceae* · 5 spp. · E:Doll's Daisy, False Chamomile; F:Boltonia, Fausse-camomille; G:Boltonie, Scheinkamille
- **asteroides** (L.) L'Hér. · E:False Chamomile, White Doll's Daisy; G:Scheinkamille
- var. **asteroides** · F:Aster étoilé · ♃; USA: NE, SE, Fla.
- var. **latisquama** (A. Gray) Cronquist · ♃ VIII-IX; USA: Mo., Kans., Okla., Ark.
- *latisquama* A. Gray = Boltonia asteroides var. latisquama

Bolusanthus Harms -m- *Fabaceae* · 1 sp. · E:Elephantwood; F:Glycine en arbre; G:Elefantenholz
- **speciosus** (Bolus) Harms · ♄ e Z9 Ⓚ; S-Afr., Zimb., Mozamb., Angola

Bomarea Mirb. -f- *Alstroemeriaceae* · 156 spp.
- *caldasii* (Kunth) Asch. & Graebn. = Bomarea multiflora
- **carderi** Mast. · ♃ ≹ Z9 Ⓚ VI-VIII; Col.
- **edulis** (Tussac) Herb. · ♃ ≹ Z9 Ⓚ VI-VIII; Mex., C-Am., W.Ind., trop. S-Am.
- **multiflora** (L. f.) Mirb. · ♃ ≹ Z9 Ⓚ VI-VIII; Col., Ecuad.
- **patacoensis** Herb. · ♃ ≹ Z9 Ⓚ VI-VIII; Col., Ecuad.
- **salsilla** (L.) Herb. · ♃ ≹ Z9 Ⓚ VI-VIII; Chile

Bombax L. -n- *Bombacaceae* · c. 20 spp. · E:Silk-Cotton Tree; F:Fromager, Kapokier; G:Baumwollbaum, Seidenwollbaum
- **ceiba** L. · E:Bombax, Red Silk-Cotton Tree; G:Roter Seidenwollbaum · ♄ Ψ d Z10 Ⓦ Ⓝ; trop. As., N.Guinea, N-Austr.
- *ellipticum* Humb., Bonpl. & Kunth = Pseudobombax ellipticum
- *malabaricum* DC. = Bombax ceiba

Bonapartea Haw. = Agave
- *juncea* Willd. = Agave geminiflora

Bonatea Willd. -f- *Orchidaceae* · 17 spp.
- **speciosa** (L. f.) Willd. · ♃ Z9 Ⓚ III-V ▽ *; S-Afr.

Bongardia C.A. Mey. -f- *Berberidaceae* · 1 sp.
- **chrysogonum** (L.) Griseb. · ♃ Z9 Ⓚ IV-V; TR, Syr., Iraq, Cauc., Iran, Pakist.

Borago L. -f- *Boraginaceae* · 3 spp. · E:Borage; F:Bourrache; G:Borretsch,

Gurkenkraut
- **officinalis** L. · E:Borage; G:Einjähriger
  Borretsch, Gurkenkraut · ⊙ Z7 VI-VII ⚘
  Ⓝ; Eur.: Ib, Fr, Ital-P, Ba; Cyprus, Syr.,
  Iran, Libya, nat. in Eur.: BrI, C-Eur.,
  EC-Eur., E-Eur.; TR
- **pygmaea** (DC.) Chater & Greuter ·
  E:Dwarf Borage; G:Ausdauernder
  Boretsch · ⧾ △ Z7 ∧ VII-X; Cors, Sard.

Borassus L. -n- *Arecaceae* · 5 spp. ·
  E:Toddy Palm; F:Palmier à vin, Rondier;
  G:Borassuspalme
- **aethiopum** Mart. · G:Delebpalme · ♄ e ⓦ
  Ⓝ; E-Afr.
- **flabellifer** L. · E:Palmyra Palm, Toddy
  Palm; G:Palmyrapalme · ♄ e ⓦ Ⓝ; Ind.,
  Sri Lanka, Burma

Boronia Sm. -f- *Rutaceae* · 95-104 spp. ·
  E:Boronia; F:Boronia; G:Korallenraute
- **alata** Sm. · E:Winged Boronia · ♄ e Z9 ⓚ
  V; W-Austr.
- **denticulata** Sm. · E:Mauve Boronia · ♄ e
  Z9 ⓚ; W-Austr.
- **heterophylla** F. Muell. · E:Red Boronia;
  G:Rote Korallenraute · ♄ e Z9 ⓚ III-IV;
  W-Austr.
- **megastigma** Nees ex Bartl. · E:Brown
  Boronia, Scented Boronia; G:Duftende
  Korallenraute · ♄ e D Z9 ⓚ III-V;
  W-Austr.
- **molloyae** J.R. Drumm. · E:Pink Boronia,
  Tall Boronia; G:Hohe Korallenraute · ♄ e
  Z9 ⓚ IV-V; W-Austr.
- **pilosa** Labill. · E:Hairy Boronia;
  G:Haarige Korallenraute · ♄ e Z9 ⓚ;
  Austr.: N.S.Wales, Vict., Tasman.,
  S-Austr.
- **pinnata** Sm. · E:Pinnate Boronia;
  G:Gefiederte Korallenraute · ♄ e Z9 ⓚ V;
  Austr.: N.S.Wales, Victoria, Tasman.

Borzicactus Riccob. -m- *Cactaceae* · c.
  10 spp.
- **acanthurus** (Vaupel) Britton & Rose · ⱷ
  Z9 ⓚ; C-Peru
- *aurantiacus* (Vaupel) Kimnach &
  Hutchison = Matucana aurantiaca subsp.
  aurantiaca
- *aureispinus* (F. Ritter) G.D. Rowley =
  Hildewintera aureispina
- *aurivillus* (K. Schum.) Britton & Rose =
  Cleistocactus icosagonus
- *doelzianus* (Backeb.) Kimnach =

Oreocereus doelzianus
- *haynei* (Otto) Kimnach = Matucana
  haynei subsp. haynei
- *hempelianus* (Gürke) Donald = Arequipa
  hempeliana
- *icosagonus* (Kunth) Britton & Rose =
  Cleistocactus icosagonus
- *leucotrichus* (Phil.) Kimnach = Arequipa
  leucotricha
- **roezlii** (Haage) W.T. Marshall · ♄ ⱷ Z9
  ⓚ ▽ ✳; N-Peru
- **samaipatanus** (Cárdenas) Kimnach · ⱷ
  Z9 ⓚ ▽ ✳; Bol.
- **sepium** (Kunth) Britton & Rose · ⱷ Z9 ⓚ
  ▽ ✳; Ecuad.

Bosea L. -f- *Amaranthaceae* · 3 spp.
- **yervamora** L. · ♄ e ♋ ⓚ; Canar.

Bossiaea Vent. -f- *Fabaceae* · c. 50 spp. ·
  E:Water Bush; F:Bossiaea; G:Wasser-
  busch
- **cinerea** R. Br. · E:Showy Parrot Pea · ♄
  Z9 ⓚ III; Austr.: N.S.Wales, Victoria,
  Tasman.
- **disticha** Lindl. · ♄ Z9 ⓚ III-V; W-Austr.
- **heterophylla** Vent. · ♄ Z9 ⓚ; Austr.:
  Queensl., N.S.Wales, Victoria
- **linophylla** R. Br. · ♄ Z9 ⓚ V-VI;
  W-Austr.

Boswellia Roxb. ex Colebr. -f- *Burseraceae* ·
  c. 20 spp. · F:Arbre-à-encens; G:Weih-
  rauchbaum
- **sacra** Flueck. · E:Frankincense · ♄ e ⓚ ⚘
  Ⓝ; Egypt, Somalia, S-Arab.

Bothriochilus Lem. -m- *Orchidaceae* ·
  3 spp.
- **macrostachyus** (Lindl.) L.O. Williams ·
  ⧾ ⓦ VIII-IX ▽ ✳; Mex., Costa Rica,
  Panama, Col.

Bothriochloa Kuntze -f- *Poaceae* · 28 spp. ·
  E:Beard Grass; G:Bartgras
- **ischaemum** (L.) Keng · E:Dogstooth
  Grass, Yellow Blue Stem Grass;
  G:Gewöhnliches Bartgras · ⧾ Z5 VII-X;
  Eur.* exc. BrI, Sc; TR, Arab., Cauc., Iran,
  Afgh., W-Sib., C-As., Him., Mong., China,
  NW-Afr., Sahara (Tibesti)

Botrychium Sw. -n- *Ophioglossaceae* ·
  61 sp. · E:Moonwort; F:Lunaire;
  G:Mondraute

- **lanceolatum** (S.G. Gmel.) Ångstr. ·
E:Lanceleaf Grapefern; G:Lanzettliche
Mondraute · ⹑ VII-VIII ▽; Eur.: I, C-Eur.,
PL, Sc, N-Russ.; N, Alp., W-Carp.; W-Sib.,
E-Sib., Amur, Sakhal., Kamchat., C-As.,
N-Am.
- **lunaria** (L.) Sw. · E:Common Moonwort,
Moonwort; G:Echte Mondraute · ⹑
V-VIII ▽; Eur.*, TR, Cauc., W-Sib.,
E-Sib., Amur, Sakhal., Kamchat., C-As.,
Him., China, Jap., Alaska, Can., USA:
NW, Rocky Mts., Calif., SW, S.Dak., NE;
Greenl
- **matricariifolium** (A. Braun ex Döll)
W.D.J. Koch · E:Daisy-leaved Grape Fern;
G:Ästige Mondraute · ⹑ VI-VII ▽; Eur.*
exc. BrI, Ib; Can.: E; USA: NE, NCE, SE
- **multifidum** (S.G. Gmel.) Rupr. ·
E:Leathery Grape Fern; G:Vielteilige
Mondraute · ⹑ VII-IX ▽; Eur.* exc. BrI,
Ib; W-Sib., W-As., Him., N-Am., Patag.,
Austr.
- **simplex** E. Hitchc. · E:Little Grapefern;
G:Einfache Mondraute · ⹑ V-VI ▽; Eur.*
exc. BrI, Ib; Can., USA: NE, NCE, NC,
Va., NW, Rocky Mts., Calif.; Greenl.
- **virginianum** (L.) Sw. · E:Rattlesnake
Fern; G:Virginische Mondraute · ⹑
VI-IX ▽; Eur.: C-Eur., EC-Eur., Slove.,
Sc, E-Eur.; W-Sib., E-Sib., Him., China,
Manch. Korea, Jap., Alaska, Can., USA *
exc. Calif.; Mex., C-Am., S-Am.

Bougainvillea Comm. ex Juss. -f-
Nyctaginaceae · 18 spp. · E:Bougainvillea;
F:Bougainvillée; G:Bougainvillee
- × **buttiana** Holttum & Standl. (*B. glabra*
× *B. peruviana*) · ♄ ↾ ⹇ Z9 ⊕ IV-VI; cult.
- **some cultivars**
- **glabra** Choisy · E:Paper Flower; G:Glatte
Bougainvillee · ♄ e ⹇ Z9 ⊕ IV-VI; Braz.
- **peruviana** Humb. & Bonpl. · G:Perua-
nische Bougainvillee · ♄ ⹇ Z9 ⊕; Col.,
Ecuad., Peru
- **spectabilis** Willd. · G:Pracht-Bougainvil-
lee · ♄ e ⹇ Z9 ⊕ IV-VI; Braz.
- **some cultivars**
- **Cultivars:**
- **many cultivars**

Boussingaultia Kunth = Anredera
- *basselloides* Kunth = Anredera basselloides
- *cordifolia* Ten. = Anredera cordifolia
- *gracilis* Miers = Anredera cordifolia
- var. *pseudobasselloides* (Hauman) L.H.

Bailey = Anredera cordifolia

Bouteloua Lag. -f- *Poaceae* · 39 spp. ·
E:Grama Grass; F:Herbe-à-moustiques;
G:Haarschotengras, Moskitogras
- **curtipendula** (Michx.) Torr. · E:Sideoats
Grass, Tall Grama; G:Hohes Haarscho-
tengras · ⹑ Z6 VII-IX ⊛; Can.: Ont.; USA:
NE, NCE, NC, Rocky Mts., SE, SC, Calif.;
SW; Mex., C-Am.
- **eriopoda** Torr. · E:Black Grama;
G:Schwarzes Haarschotengras · ⹑ ⊛;
SW-USA, N-Mex.
- **gracilis** (Kunth) Griffiths · E:Blue Grama,
Mosquito Grass; G:Haarschotengras,
Moskitogras · ⹑ Z7 VII-IX ⊛; Can.: W,
Man.; USA: NCE, Rocky Mts., Calif., SW,
Sc, SE; Mex.
- *oligostachya* (Nutt.) Torr. ex A. Gray =
Bouteloua gracilis
- *racemosa* Lag. = Bouteloua curtipendula

Bouvardia Salisb. -f- *Rubiaceae* · 37 spp. ·
E:Bouvardia; F:Bouvardie; G:Bouvardie
- **laevis** M. Martens & Galeotti · ♄ e Z9 ⊕
IV-V; Mex.
- **leiantha** Benth. · ♄ e Z9 ⊕ VII-IX; Mex.,
C-Am.
- **longiflora** (Cav.) Kunth · E:Flor de San
Juan · ♄ e Z9 ⊕ VIII-XI; Mex.
- **multiflora** (Cav.) Schult. & Schult. f. · ♄
e Z9 ⊕ VIII-IX; Mex.
- **ternifolia** (Cav.) Schltdl. · E:Firecracker
Bush · ♄ e Z9 ⊕ IV-VI; Mex.
- *triphylla* Salisb. = Bouvardia ternifolia

Bowenia Hook. -f- *Boweniaceae* · 2 spp. ·
E:Byfield Fern; F:Bowénia, Fougère-
palmier; G:Queenslandpalmfarn
- **serrulata** (W. Bull) Chamb. · E:Byfield
Fern; G:Feinzähniger Queenslandpalmfarn · ⹑ e Z10 ⊕ ▽ ✳; Austr.: Queensl.
- **spectabilis** Hook. ex Hook. f. · G:Prächti-
ger Queenslandpalmfarn · ⹑ e Z10 ⊕ ▽
✳; Austr.: Queensl.

Bowiea Harv. ex Hook. f. -f-
Hyacinthaceae · 1 sp. · E:Climbing Onion;
G:Zulukartoffel
- **volubilis** Harv. ex Hook. f. · E:Climbing
Onion; G:Zulukartoffel · ⹑ ⹌ ⹇ Z10 ⊕
⚘; Namibia, S-Afr.

Bowkeria Harv. -f- *Scrophulariaceae* ·
3-5 spp.

- **gerrardiana** Harv. ex Hiern · ♄ d Z9 ⌂
  IV-V; S-Afr.: Natal

Boykinia Nutt. -f- *Saxifragaceae* · 9 spp. ·
  E:Brookfoam
- **aconitifolia** Nutt. · E:Allegheny Brook-
  foam · ⧗ Z6 VI-VII; USA: W.Va., Va., SE
- **jamesii** (Torr.) Engl. · E:James'
  Brookfoam · ⧗ Z5 ⌂ IV-VI; Can.: W;
  USA: Rocky Mts., NC
- **rotundifolia** Parry ex A. Gray ·
  E:Roundleaf Brookfoam · ⧗ Z7 VI-VIII;
  S-Calif.

Brachiaria (Trin.) Griseb. -f- *Poaceae* · c.
  100 spp. · E:Signal Grass; G:Palisaden-
  gras, Signalgras
- **brizantha** (Hochst. ex A. Rich.) Stapf ·
  E:Palisade Grass; G:Palisadengras · ⧗
  Z10 Ⓝ; trop-Afr., S-Afr., nat. in Sri Lanka,
  Braz.
- **decumbens** Stapf · E:Signal Grass;
  G:Signalgras, Surinamgras · ⧗ Z10 ⌾ Ⓝ;
  trop. Afr.
- **deflexa** (Schumach.) C.E. Hubb. ex
  Robyns · ☉ Z10 ⌂ Ⓝ; trop., Afr., S-Afr.,
  Yemen, Madag.
- **eruciformis** (Sibth. & Sm.) Griseb. ·
  E:Sweet Signalgrass · ☉ ✕ Z10 VII-VIII;
  Eur.: sp., Ital-P, Ba; TR, Cauc., Iran,
  Pakist., C-As., Him., Egypt, Arab., nat. in
  F
- **mutica** (Forssk.) Stapf · E:Para Grass;
  G:Paragras · ☉ ⧗ Z10 ⌾ Ⓝ; W-Afr.,
  W.Sudan
- **ramosa** (L.) Stapf · ☉ ⧗ Z10 ⌾ Ⓝ; Ind.
- **ruziziensis** Germ. & C.M. Evrard ·
  E:Congo Grass, Ruzi Grass; G:Nieder-
  liegendes Palisadengras · ⧗ Z10 ⌂ Ⓝ;
  Congo, nat. in Austr.

Brachychilum (R. Br. ex Wall.) Petersen =
  Hedychium
- *horsfieldii* (R. Br. ex Wall.) Petersen =
  Hedychium horsfieldii

Brachychiton Schott & Endl. -m-
  Sterculiaceae · 31 sp. · E:Bottle Tree;
  F:Sterculier; G:Flaschenbaum
- **acerifolius** (A. Cunn. ex D. Don)
  Macarthur · E:Australian Flame Tree,
  Flame Bottle Tree; G:Flammender
  Flaschenbaum · ♄ e Z10 ⌂; Austr.:
  Queensl., N.S.Wales
- **discolor** F. Muell. · E:Lacebark · ♄ d Z10

⌂; N-Austr., Queensl., New S-Wales
- **populneus** (Schott & Endl.) R. Br. ·
  E:Kurrajong; G:Kurrajong-Flaschenbaum
  · ♄ e Z10 ⌂; Austr.: Queensl., N.S.Wales
- **rupestris** (Lindl.) K. Schum. ·
  E:Queensland Bottle Tree; G:Queens-
  land-Flaschenbaum · ♄ d Z10 ⌂; Austr.:
  Queensl.

Brachyglottis J.R. Forst. & G. Forst.
  -f- *Asteraceae* · 29 spp. · E:Ragwort;
  F:Brachyglottis; G:Jakobskraut
- **greyi** (Hook. f.) B. Nord. · ♄ ⌂ VII-VIII;
  NZ (Wellington)
- **hectoris** (Buchanan) B. Nord. · ♄ ⌂;
  S-NZ
- **laxifolia** (Buchanan) B. Nord. · ♄ ⌂
  VII-VIII; S-NZ
- **monroi** (Hook. f.) B. Nord. · ♄ ⌂; NZ
- **repanda** J.R. Forst. & G. Forst. · E:Hedge
  Ragwort, Pukapuka; G:Hecken-Jakobsk-
  raut · ♄ ♄ e ⌂; NZ
- **rotundifolia** J.R. Forst. & G. Forst. · ♄ ♄
  ⌂; NZ
- **Cultivars:**
- **some cultivars**

Brachylaena R. Br. -f- *Asteraceae* ·
  17-23 spp.
- **glabra** (L. f.) Druce · E:Malbar · ♄ ♄ Z10;
  S-Afr.

Brachypodium P. Beauv. -n- *Poaceae* ·
  17 spp. · E:False Brome; F:Brachypode;
  G:Zwenke
- **distachyon** (L.) P. Beauv. · ☉ Z5; Eur.:
  Ib, Fr, Ital-P, Ba, W-Russ., Crim; TR,
  C-As., Iran, Afgh., Azor., Canar., Cape
  Verde, N-Afr., Eth., S-Afr.
- **phoenicoides** (L.) Roem. & Schult. · ⧗
  Z5; Eur.: Ib, Ital-P, Fr, Ba; Marok., Alger.,
  Tun.
- **pinnatum** (L.) P. Beauv. · E:Tor Grass;
  F:Brachypode penné; G:Fieder-Zwenke
  · ⧗ Z5 VI-VIII Ⓝ; Eur.*, TR, Cauc., Iran,
  Cauc., W-Sib., E-Sib., C-As.; Alger.
- **rupestre** (Host) Roem. & Schult. · E:Tor
  Grass; G:Felsen-Zwenke · ⧗ Z5 VI-VIII;
  Eur.: Ib, Fr, BrI, C-Eur., CZ, Ital-P, Ba,
  RO, Crim; TR, Lebanon, Syr.
- **sylvaticum** (Huds.) P. Beauv. · E:Slender
  False Brome; G:Wald-Zwenke · ⧗ Z5
  VII-IX; Eur.*, TR, Cauc., Iran, W-Sib.,
  C-As., Him., Sri Lanka, Canar., Madeira,
  NW-Afr.

Brachyscome Cass. -f- *Asteraceae* · 66 spp. ·
E:Swan River Daisy; F:Pâquerette bleue;
G:Blaues Gänseblümchen
- **iberidifolia** Benth. · E:Swan River
Daisy; F:Brachycome à feuilles d'ibéris;
G:Blaues Gänseblümchen · ⊙ D Z8
VII-IX; Austr.: W-Austr., S-Austr.
- **melanocarpa** F. Muell. & Sond. ·
E:Black-seeded Daisy · ⁴ Z8 ⌖; Austr.
- **multifida** DC. · E:Cut-leaved Daisy · ⊙
Z8 VI-IX; Austr.: Queensl.

Brachysema R. Br. -n- *Fabaceae* · 8-15 spp. ·
E:Swan River Pea; G:Kurzfähnchen
- **celsianum** Lem. · E:Swan River Pea;
G:Australischer Erbsenstrauch, Kurzfähnchen · ♄ Z9 ⌖; W-Austr.
- *lanceolatum* Meisn. = Brachysema
celsianum

Brahea Mart. -f- *Arecaceae* · 11 sp. ·
E:Hesper Palm; F:Palmier-éventail;
G:Hesperidenpalme
- **armata** S. Watson · E:Blue Fan Palm,
Blue Palm, Mexican Blue Palm; G:Blaue
Hesperidenpalme · ♄ e Z10 ⌖; Mex.:
Baja Calif.
- **brandegeei** (Purpus) H.E. Moore ·
E:San José Hesper Palm; G:San-Jose-
Hesperidenpalme · ♄ e Z10 ⌖; S-Calif.
- **dulcis** (Kunth) Mart. · E:Rock Palm · ♄ e
Z10 ⌖; Mex., Guat.
- **edulis** H. Wendl. ex S. Watson ·
E:Guadalupe Palm; G:Essbare Hesperi-
denpalme, Guadalupepalme · ♄ e Z10 ⌖;
Mex.

× **Brapasia** hort. -f- *Orchidaceae* (*Aspasia*
× *Brassia*)

Brasenia Schreb. -f- *Cabombaceae* · 1 sp. ·
E:Water Schield; F:Brasénie; G:Schleim-
kraut, Wasserschild
- **schreberi** J.F. Gmel. · E:Water Shield;
G:Schleimkraut, Wasserschild · ⁴ ≈ ⓦ
Ⓝ; Afr., subtrop. As., E-Austr., N-Am.,
Lat.-Am.

Brasilicactus Backeb. = Notocactus
- *graessneri* (K. Schum.) Backeb. =
Notocactus graessneri
- *haselbergii* (Haage) Backeb. = Notocactus
haselbergii

Brassaia Endl. = Schefflera

- *actinophylla* Endl. = Schefflera actinophylla

Brassavola R. Br. -f- *Orchidaceae* · 20 spp.
- *ceboletta* Rchb. f. = Brassavola tuberculata
- **cucullata** (L.) R. Br. · E:Daddy Longlegs
Orchid · ⁴ Z10 ⓦ IX-XII ▽ ✳; Mex.,
Guat., Hond., El Salv., W.Ind., Venez.
- *digbyana* Lindl. = Rhyncholaelia digbyana
- **flagellaris** Barb. Rodr. · ⁴ Z10 ⓦ IV ▽
✳; Braz.
- *glauca* Lindl. = Rhyncholaelia glauca
- **nodosa** (L.) Lindl. · E:Lady-of-the-Night
Orchid · ⁴ Z10 ⓦ X-XII ▽ ✳; C-Am.,
W.Ind., Col., Venez., Surinam
- *perrinii* Lindl. = Brassavola tuberculata
- **tuberculata** Hook. · ⁴ Z10 ⓦ ▽ ✳;
E-Braz., Parag.

Brassia R. Br. -f- *Orchidaceae* · 33 spp.
- **antherotes** Rchb. f.
- var. **antherotes** · ⁴ Z10 ⓦ ▽ ✳; trop.
Am.
- var. **longissima** (Rchb. f.) Teusch. · ⁴
Z10 ⓦ VI ▽ ✳; Costa Rica
- **caudata** (L.) Lindl. · E:Cricket Orchid ·
⁴ Z10 ⓦ II-III ▽ ✳; Fla., Mex., C-Am.,
W.Ind.
- **cochleata** Knowles & Westc. · E:Spider
Orchid · ⁴ Z10 ⓦ V-VI ▽ ✳; Venez.,
Guyana, Surinam, Braz.
- **gireoudiana** Rchb. f. & Warsz. · ⁴ Z10
ⓦ V-VIII ▽ ✳; Costa Rica, Panama
- **lanceana** Lindl. · ⁴ Z10 ⓦ VIII-IX ▽ ✳;
Venez., Surinam
- *lawrenceana* Lindl. = Brassia cochleata
- **longissima**
- var. *minor* Schltr. = Brassia caudata
- **maculata** R. Br. · ⁴ Z10 ⓦ VI-VIII ▽ ✳;
W.Ind., Guat., Hond., Belize
- **verrucosa** Bateman ex Lindl. · ⁴ Z10 ⓦ
IV-VI ▽ ✳; Mex., Guat., Hond., Venez.

Brassica L. -f- *Brassicaceae* · c. 35 spp. ·
E:Cabbage; F:Chou; G:Kohl
- *alboglabra* L.H. Bailey = Brassica oleracea
var. alboglabra
- *campestris* L. = Brassica rapa subsp. rapa
- **carinata** A. Braun · E:Abyssinian Cabbage; G:Abessinischer Kohl · ⊙ Ⓝ; Eth.
- *chinensis* L. = Brassica rapa subsp.
chinensis
- **elongata** Ehrh. · E:Long-stalked Rape;
G:Langtraubiger Kohl · ⊙ VI-IX; Eur.:

A, EC-Eur., Ba, E-Eur.; TR, Iran, Cauc.,
W-Sib., C-As., Moroc., nat. in Sc, Fr,
Ital-P
- **juncea** (L.) Czern. · E:Brown Mustard,
Chinese Mustard, Indian Mustard;
G:Brauner Senf, Ruten-Kohl, Sarepta-
Senf · ⊙ Z7 VI-IX Ⓝ; W-Sib., E-Sib., C-As.,
Mong., N-China, nat. in sp., BG, RO,
Russ., TR, Cauc., Iran, Afgh., Ind.
- *kaber* (DC.) L.C. Wheeler = Sinapis
arvensis
- var. *pinnatifida* (Stokes) L.C. Wheeler =
Sinapis arvensis
- *napoBrassica* (L.) Mill. = Brassica napus
subsp. rapifera
- **napus** L.
- subsp. **napus** · E:Oilseed Rape, Rape;
G:Raps · ⊙ IV-IX; cult.
- var. **annua** L. · E:Summer Rape;
G:Sommer-Raps, Sommerrübsen · Ⓝ;
Eth.
- subsp. **rapifera** (Metzg.) Sinskaya ·
E:Swedish Turnip; G:Kohl-Rübe, Steck-
Rübe · ⊙ Ⓝ; cult.
- var. *napoBrassica* (L.) Rchb. = Brassica
napus subsp. rapifera
- **nigra** (L.) W.D.J. Koch · E:Black
Mustard; G:Schwarzer Senf, Senf-Kohl ·
⊙ VI-IX ⚥ Ⓝ; Eur.*, Cauc., TR, Moroc.,
Egypt, Sudan
- **oleracea** L. · E:Wild Cabbage; G:Kohl
- var. **acephala** DC. · E:Decorative Kale,
Flowering Cabbage; G:Zier-Kohl · Ⓝ;
cult.
- var. **alboglabra** (L.H. Bailey) Musil ·
E:Chinese Broccoli, Chinese Kale; G:Chi-
nesischer Kohl, Chinesischer Brokkoli ·
Ⓝ; C-China, S-China
- var. **botrytis** L. · E:Cauliflower;
G:Blumen-Kohl, Kopf-Brokkoli · Ⓝ
- var. **capitata** (L.) Alef. · E:Red Cabbage,
White Cabbage; G:Blaukraut, Rot-Kohl,
Weiß-Kohl, Weißkraut · Ⓝ
- var. **costata** DC. · E:Portugese Cabbage;
G:Portugiesischer Kohl, Rippen-Kohl,
Tronchuda-Kohl · Ⓝ; cult.
- var. **gemmifera** (DC.) Zenker · E:Brussels
Sprouts; G:Brüsseler Kohl, Rosen-Kohl,
Rosen-Wirsing · Ⓝ
- var. **gongylodes** L. · G:Kohlrabi;
E:Kohlrabi, Turnip Kale · Ⓝ; cult.
- var. **italica** Plenck · E:Broccoli; G:Brok-
koli, Spargel-Kohl · Ⓝ; cult.
- var. **medullosa** Thell. · E:Marrow-stem
Kale; G:Mark-Kohl, Markstamm-Kohl ·

Ⓝ; cult.
- var. **oleracea** · E:Wild Cabbage;
G:Wild-Kohl · ⊙ ♃ V-IX; Eur.*, Cauc., TR,
Moroc., Egypt, Sudan, nat. in G, Ba.
- var. **ramosa** DC. · E:Branching Cabbage; G:Stauden-Kohl, Strauch-Kohl,
Tausendkopf-Kohl · Ⓝ; cult.
- var. *rubra* L. = Brassica oleracea var.
capitata
- var. **sabauda** L. · E:Savoy Cabbage;
G:Welsch-Kohl, Wirsing · Ⓝ; cult.
- var. **sabellica** L. · E:Curlies, Kale;
G:Braun-Kohl, Feder-Kohl, Grün-Kohl ·
Ⓝ; cult.
- var. *tronchuda* L.H. Bailey = Brassica
oleracea var. costata
- var. **viridis** L. · E:Collards, Cow Cabbage;
G:Blatt-Kohl, Futter-Kohl, Kuh-Kohl · Ⓝ;
cult.
- *pekinensis* (Lour.) Rupr. = Brassica rapa
subsp. pekinensis
- **rapa** L.
- subsp. **chinensis** (L.) Hanelt · E:Chinese
White Cabbage, Pak Choi; G:China-Kohl,
Chinesischer Senf-Kohl · Ⓝ; cult.
- var. **parachinensis** (L.H. Bailey) Hanelt ·
E:Choisum; G:Choisum, Tsoi-sum · Ⓝ
- subsp. **dichotoma** (Roxb. ex Fleming)
Hanelt · E:Brown Sarson, Indian Rape;
G:Indischer Kohl · Ⓝ; cult. Ind.
- subsp. **nipposinica** (L.H. Bailey) Hanelt
- var. **chinoleifera** (Vilhoever) Kitam. ·
E:Hendergreen, Spinach Mustard;
G:Komatsuna, Senf-Spinat · Ⓝ; cult.
- subsp. **oleifera** (DC.) Metzg. · E:Winter
Turnip Rape; G:Rübsaat, Rübsen · Ⓝ;
cult.
- subsp. **pekinensis** (Lour.) Hanelt ·
E:Chinese Cabbage; G:Peking-Kohl · Ⓝ;
cult.
- subsp. **rapa** L. · E:Field Mustard, Turnip;
G:Herbst-Rübe, Stoppel-Rübe, Wasser-
Rübe, Weiße Rübe · ⊙ IV-IX Ⓝ; orig. ? ,
cult. Eur., Sib., Ind., etc., nat. in Eur.*
- subsp. **trilocularis** (Roxb.) Hanelt ·
E:Indian Colza, Yellow Sarson;
G:Indischer Rübsen · Ⓝ; cult. Ind.
- var. *perviridis* L.H. Bailey = Brassica rapa
subsp. nipposinica var. chinoleifera
- var. *silvestris* (Lam.) S.M. Briggs =
Brassica rapa subsp. oleifera
- *trilocularis* (Roxb.) Hanelt = Brassica
rapa subsp. trilocularis

× **Brassidium** hort. -n- *Orchidaceae*

(*Brassia* × *Oncidium*)

× **Brassocattleya** hort. -f- *Orchidaceae*
(*Brassavola* × *Cattleya*)

× **Brassodiacrium** hort. -n- *Orchidaceae*
(*Brassavola* × *Diacrium*)

× **Brassoepidendrum** hort. -n- *Orchidaceae*
(*Brassavola* × *Epidendrum*)

× **Brassolaelia** hort. -f- *Orchidaceae*
(*Brassavola* × *Laelia*)

× **Brassolaeliocattleya** hort. -f-
Orchidaceae (*Brassavola* × *Cattleya* ×
Laelia)

× **Brassotonia** hort. -f- *Orchidaceae*
(*Brassia* × *Broughtonia*)

× **Bratonia** hort. -f- *Orchidaceae* (*Brassia* ×
Miltonia)

Braya Sternb. & Hoppe -f- *Brassicaceae* ·
20 spp. · G:Breitschötchen, Knotenschötchen
– **alpina** Sternb. & Hoppe ·
G:Breitschötchen · ⽊ Z5 VII; Eur.: I, A;
E-Alp.

Brevipodium Á. Löve & D. Löve = Brachypodium
– *sylvaticum* (Huds.) Á. Löve & D. Löve =
Brachypodium sylvaticum

Brexia Noronha ex Thouars -f-
Escalloniaceae · 1 (-9) spp.
– **madagascariensis** (Lam.) Ker-Gawl. · ♄
e ⽔; Madag.

Breynia J.R. Forst. & G. Forst. -f-
Euphorbiaceae · c. 25 spp.
– **disticha** J.R. Forst. & G. Forst. · E:Snow
Bush; G:Schneebusch · ♄ e ⽔; Pacific Is.,
nat. in S-Fla., Trop.
– **nivosa** (W.G. Sm.) Small = Breynia
disticha

Briggsia Craib -f- *Gesneriaceae* · c. 25 spp.
– **aurantiaca** B.L. Burtt · ⽊ Z8 ⽔; S-Tibet
– **muscicola** (Diels) Craib · ⽊ Z8 ⽔ V-VI;
Bhutan, SE-Tibet, Yunnan
– *penlopii* C.E.C. Fisch. = Briggsia muscicola

Brillantaisia P. Beauv. -f- *Acanthaceae* · 9
(-40) spp.
– **lamium** (Nees) Benth. · ⽊ ⽔ IV-IX; trop.
Afr.

Brimeura Salisb. -f- *Hyacinthaceae* · 3 spp. ·
F:Brimeura, Chouard; G:Scheinhyazinthe
– **amethystina** (L.) Chouard · G:Amethyst-
Scheinhyazinthe · ⽊ Z5 IV-VI ▽; Eur.:
N-Sp., F, N-Ba; Pyr.

Briza L. -f- *Poaceae* · 10-20 spp. · E:Quaking
Grass; F:Amourette, Hochet du vent;
G:Zittergras
– **gracilis** G. Nicholson = Briza minor
– **maxima** L. · E:Greater Quaking Grass;
F:Grande brize; G:Größtes Zittergras · ☉
Z5 V-VI; Eur.: Ib, Fr, Ital-P, Ba; TR, Azor.,
nat. in BrI, E-Russ., N-Am., Jap., Austr.
– **media** L. · E:Common Quaking Grass;
F:Brize intermédiaire; G:Mittleres
Zittergras · ⽊ V-VII ⽔; Eur.*, TR, Cauc.
– **minima** hort. ex G. Nicholson = Briza
minor
– **minor** L. · E:Lesser Quaking Grass;
G:Kleines Zittergras · ☉ VI-VII; Eur.: Ib,
Fr, BrI, Ital-P, Ba; TR, Cauc., SW-As.,
Subtrop.
– *rubra* Lam. = Briza maxima

Brocchinia Schult. f. -f- *Bromeliaceae* ·
20 spp.
– **paniculata** Schult. f. · ⽊ Z9 ⽔; SE-Col.,
Venez., Braz.

Brodiaea Sm. -f- *Alliaceae* · 14 spp. ·
E:Cluster Lily; F:Brodiaea; G:Brodiee
– *bridgesii* S. Watson = Triteleia bridgesii
– *congesta* Sm. = Dichelostemma congestum
– **coronaria** (Salisb.) Engl. · E:Harvest
Cluster Lily; G:Herbst-Brodiee
– subsp. **coronaria** · ⽊ Z8 ⽔ ⬚; B.C.,
USA: NW, Calif.
– var. *mundula* Jeps. = Brodiaea elegans
subsp. elegans
– **elegans** Hoover
– subsp. **elegans** · E:Cluster Lily; G:Groß-
blütige Brodiee · ⽊ Z8 ⽔ VI; USA: Oreg.,
Calif.
– *grandiflora* hort. = Brodiaea elegans
subsp. elegans
– *grandiflora* Sm. = Brodiaea coronaria
subsp. coronaria
– *ixioides* (Aitch.) S. Watson = Triteleia

ixioides
- *laxa* (Benth.) S. Watson = Triteleia laxa
- *lutea* Lindl. = Triteleia ixioides
- *multiflora* Benth. = Dichelostemma multiflorum
- *peduncularis* (Lindl.) S. Watson = Triteleia peduncularis
- *uniflora* (Lindl.) Engl. = Ipheion uniflorum

Bromelia L. -f- *Bromeliaceae* · 57 spp. · E:Bromelia
- **agavifolia** Brongn. ex Houllet · ⁊ Z9 ⓦ; Guyan.
- *ananas* L. = Ananas comosus
- **balansae** Mez · E:Heart-of-Flame; G:Zaunbromelie · ⁊ Z9 ⓦ; Arg., Parag.
- *bicolor* Ruiz & Pav. = Fascicularia bicolor
- *comosa* L. = Ananas comosus
- *fastuosa* Lindl. = Bromelia pinguin
- *lingulata* L. = Aechmea lingulata
- **pinguin** L. · E:Pinguin, Wild Pineapple; G:Wilde Ananas · ⁊ Z9 ⓦ Ⓝ; W.Ind., Panama, Guyana, Braz.
- **serra** Griseb. · ⁊ Z9 ⓦ Ⓝ; Bol., Parag., Braz., Arg.

Bromopsis (Dumort.) Fourr. = Bromus
- *ramosa* (Huds.) Holub = Bromus ramosus

Bromus L. -m- *Poaceae* · c. 100 spp. · E:Brome; F:Brome; G:Trespe
- **arvensis** L. · G:Acker-Trespe; E:Field Brome · ⊙ ⋈ V-VIII Ⓝ; Eur.: Ib, Fr, Ital-P, Ba, E-Eur.; Cauc., nat. in Eur.: BrI, Sc, C-Eur., EC-Eur.; TR, Iran, C-As., N-Am., Arg., S-Afr., NZ
- *arvensis* Lam. = Bromus erectus subsp. erectus
- *asper* Murray = Bromus ramosus
- **benekenii** (Lange) Trimen · E:Lesser Hairy Brome; G:Benekens Trespe · ⁊ VI-VII; Eur.*, TR, Cauc., NW-Iran, Afgh., Him., Ind., W-Sib. C-As., Moroc., Alger., nat. in China
- **brachystachys** Hornung · G:Kurzährige Trespe · ⊙ VI-VII; Eur.: D extinct
- **briziformis** Fisch. & C.A. Mey. · E:Rattlesnake Brome; G:Schlangen-Trespe · ⊙ ⋈ VI-VIII; Cauc., N-Iran, C-As., nat. in Alaska, Can.
- **bromoideus** (Lej.) Crép. · G:Ardennen-Trespe · ⊙; Eur.: F, B; extinct
- **carinatus** Hook. & Arn. · E:California Brome; G:Plattährige Trespe · ⊙ ⁊ VI-XI;

N-Am., nat. in BrI, NL
- **catharticus** Vahl · E:Rescue Brome, Rescue Grass; G:Ährengrasähnliche Trespe, Pampas-Trespe · ⊙ ⊙ ⁊ ⋈ VI-IX Ⓝ; S-Am., nat. in USA: SE; S-Eur.
- **commutatus** Schrad. · E:Meadow Brome; G:Verwechselte Trespe, Wiesen-Trespe · ⊙ VI; Eur.*, Cauc.
- *cristatus* L. = Agropyron cristatum subsp. cristatum
- **danthoniae** Trin. · E:Oat Brome · ⊙ VI-VIII; TR, Cauc., Iran, C-As.
- **diandrus** Roth · E:Great Brome; G:Hohe Trespe · ⊙; Eur.: Ib, Fr, Ital-P, Ba; TR, SW-As., N-Afr., nat. in BrI, Crim
- **erectus** Huds.
- subsp. **condensatus** (Hack.) Asch. & Graebn. · G:Zusammengezogene Trespe · ⁊ V-VI; Eur.: Sw, I, Ba; S-Alp., NW-Balkan
- subsp. **erectus** · E:Upright Brome; G:Aufrechte Trespe · ⁊ V-X Ⓝ; Eur.* exc. Sc; TR, NW-Afr., nat. in Sc, N-Am.
- **grossus** Desf. ex DC. · G:Dicke Trespe · ⊙ ▽; Eur.: B
- *gussonei* Parl. = Bromus diandrus
- **hordeaceus** L.
- subsp. **divaricatus** (L.) A.R. Clapham · G:Aufrechte Strandtrespe, Spreizende Trespe · ; S-Eur. , Macaron., N-Afr.
- subsp. **hordeaceus** · E:Soft Brome; G:Weiche Trespe · ⊙ V-VIII; Eur.*, TR, Cauc., Iran, Pakist., nat. in N-Am., Baja Calif., S-Am., Jap., Austr., NZ, Hawaii
- subsp. **pseudothominii** (P.M. Sm.) H. Scholz · G:Falsche Dünen-Trespe · ; Eur.: BrI, Sc, C-Eur. +
- subsp. *thominii* Hyl. = Bromus thominii
- **inermis** Leyss. · E:Hungarian Brome, Smooth Brome; G:Unbegrannte Trespe, Wehrlose Trespe · ⁊ VI-VII Ⓝ; Eur.* exc. BrI; TR, Cauc., N-Iran, W-Sib., E-Sib., C-As., Him., Mong., Manch., nat. in BrI, Sc, Amur, N-Am., S-Am., S-Afr., Austr.
- **intermedius** Guss.
- subsp. *divaricatus* Bonnier & Layens = Bromus hordeaceus subsp. divaricatus
- **japonicus** Thunb. · E:Japanese Brome ; G:Japanische Trespe · ⊙ ⁊ V-VI; Eur.: F, I, C-Eur., EC-Eur., Ba, E-Eur.; TR, Syr., Lebanon, Cauc., C-As., N-Afr., nat. in N-Am.
- *jubatus* Ten. = Bromus sterilis
- *lanceolatus* Roth = Bromus macrostachys
- **lepidus** Holmb. · E:Slender Soft Brome;

G:Zierliche Trespe · ⊙ VI-VIII; orig. ?, nat. in BrI, Sc, Fr, D
- **macrostachys** Desf. · F:Brome à grands épillets; G:Langgrannige Trespe · ⊙ VI-VIII; Eur.: Ib, Fr, Ital-P, Ba; TR, Cauc., C-As., Him., W-Sib., nat. in N-Am.
- **madritensis** L. · E:Compact Brome; G:Madrider Trespe, Mittelmeer-Trespe · ⊙ V-VII; Eur.: Ib, Fr, Ital-P, Ba, Crim; TR, Syr., Lebanon, Iraq, Arab., Iran, SW-As., Iran, N-Afr., nat. in BrI, Sc, N-Am., S-Am., Austr.
- *molliformis* Lloyd = Bromus hordeaceus subsp. divaricatus
- *mollis* L. = Bromus hordeaceus subsp. hordeaceus
- **pannonicus** Kumm. & Sendtn. · G:Pannonische Trespe · ♃ V-X; Eur.: A, H, Slove., Croatia, Bosn., RO
- × *pseudothominii* P.M. Sm. = Bromus hordeaceus subsp. pseudothominii
- **racemosus** L. · E:Smooth Brome; G:Traubige Trespe · ♃ VI; Eur.*, TR, Cauc., Iran, Afgh.
- **ramosus** Huds. · E:Hairy Brome; G:Allseitswendige Wald-Trespe · ♃ ⋈ VII-VIII; Eur.*, TR, Cauc., N-Iran, Him., NW-Afr.
- subsp. *benekenii* (Lange) H. Lindb. = Bromus benekenii
- **rigidus** Roth · E:Stiff Brome; G:Steife Trespe · ⊙ VI-VII; Eur.: Ib, Fr, Ital-P, Ba, RO; TR, Cyprus, Cauc. W-As., N-Afr., nat. in EC-Eur.
- **rubens** L. · E:Fox Tail Brome; G:Fuchsschwanz-Trespe · ⊙ VII-VIII; Eur.: Ib, Fr, Ital-P, Ba; TR, Cauc., C-As., N-Afr., nat. in USA
- **scoparius** L. · E:Broom Brome; G:Gedrungene Trespe · ⊙; Eur.: Ib.Ital-P, Ba, Crim, E-Russ.; TR, Cauc., Iran, C-As., N-Afr.
- **secalinus** L. · E:Rye Brome; G:Roggen-Trespe · ⊙ ⋈ VI-VIII; Eur.: Ib, Fr, Ital-P, Ba, EC-Eur., E-Eur.; W-Sib., Amur, Sakhal., nat. in BrI, Sc, C-Eur., N-Am.
- subsp. *multiflorus* Schübl. & G. Martens = Bromus grossus
- **squarrosus** L. · E:Corn Brome; G:Sparrige Trespe · ⊙ V-VI; Eur.* exc. BrI, Sc; TR, Iraq, Syr., Lebanon, Cauc., Iran, Him., W-Sib., C-As., NW-Afr., C-Sahara, nat. in N-Am., Chile
- **sterilis** L. · E:Barren Brome, Poverty Brome; G:Taube Trespe · ⊙ ⋈ V-VIII; Eur.*, TR, Levant, Iraq, Cauc., Iran, C-As., NW-Afr., nat. in N-Am., S-Am., Austr., NZ
- **tectorum** L. · E:Downy Brome, Drooping Brome; G:Dach-Trespe · ⊙ ⊙ V-VI; Eur.*, TR, Levant, Arab., Cauc., Iran, Afgh., Pakist., C-As., Canar., NW-Afr., Egypt, nat. in BrI, Greenl., N-Am., C-Am., S-Am., Phil., Austr., NZ, Hawaii
- **thominii** Hardouin · E:Lesser Soft Brome; G:Dünen-Trespe · ⊙ V-VI; Eur.: BrI, Fr, Sc, G, S-Eur..; TR; coasts, nat. in N-Am.
- **transsilvanicus** Steud. · G:Siebenbürgische Trespe · ♃; Eur.: N-I, Ba, RO
- *unioloides* (Willd.) Humb., Bonpl. & Kunth = Bromus catharticus
- *willdenowii* Kunth = Bromus catharticus

Brosimum Sw. -n- *Moraceae* · 13 spp. · E:Cow Tree, Milk Tree; F:Arbre à lait; G:Kuhbaum, Milchbaum
- **alicastrum** Sw. · E:Breadnut; G:Brotnussbaum · ₺ e Z10 ⓦ Ⓝ; Mex., C-Am., W.Ind., Venez., Ecuad., Peru, Braz.
- *galactodendron* D. Don ex Sweet = Brosimum utile
- **utile** (Kunth) Pittier · E:Cowtree; G:Milchbaum · ₺ e Z10 ⓦ Ⓝ; Guyan., Braz., Peru, Venez.

Broughtonia R. Br. -f- *Orchidaceae* · 3 spp.
- **domingensis** (Lindl.) Rolfe · E:King Orchid · ♃ Z10 ⓦ IV-VI ▽ *; Bahamas, Hispaniola (Dominican. Rep.)
- **sanguinea** (Sw.) R. Br. · ♃ Z10 ⓦ V-VI ▽ *; Jamaica, Cuba

× **Broughtopsis** hort. -f- *Orchidaceae* (*Broughtonia* × *Laeliopsis*)

Broussonetia L'Hér. ex Vent. -f- *Moraceae* · 8 spp. · E:Paper Mulberry; F:Mûrier à papier; G:Papiermaulbeerbaum
- **kazinoki** Siebold · ₺ ₺ d Z7 Ⓝ; Korea, Jap.
- **papyrifera** (L.) Vent. · E:Paper Mulberry; G:Papier-Maulbeere · ₺ ₺ d Z7 V Ⓝ; Burma, China, nat. in S-Eur., USA

Browallia L. -f- *Solanaceae* · 5 spp. · E:Bush Violet; F:Browalia; G:Browallie, Veilchenbusch
- **americana** L. · E:Amethyst Flower; F:Browalle; G:Amethyst-Veilchenbusch ·

⊙ Z9 ⊕ VII-IX; trop. Am.
- *demissa* L. = Browallia americana
- *elata* L. = Browallia americana
- **grandiflora** Benth. · ⊙ Z9 ⊕ VI-IX; Peru
- *grandiflora* Graham = Browallia americana
- **speciosa** Hook. · E:Sapphire Flower; G:Saphir-Veilchenbusch · ♄ Z9 ⊕ I-XII; Col.
- **viscosa** Kunth · ⊙ Z9 VI-IX; Peru

Brownea Jacq. -f- *Caesalpiniaceae* · 12 (- 26) spp.
- **ariza** Benth. · E:Rose of Venezuela; G:Rose von Venezuela · ♄ e Z10 ⊛; Col.
- **coccinea** Jacq. · ♄ e Z10 ⊛; Venez.
- *grandiceps* hort. = Brownea coccinea
- **grandiceps** Jacq. · ♄ e Z10 ⊛; Venez.

Browningia Britton & Rose -f- *Cactaceae* · 10 spp.
- **chlorocarpa** (Kunth) W.T. Marshall · Ψ Z9 ⊕ ▽ ✳; N-Peru
- **hertlingiana** (Backeb.) Buxb. · Ψ Z9 ⊕ ▽ ✳; Peru
- **microsperma** (Werderm. & Backeb.) W.T. Marshall · Ψ Z9 ⊕ Ⓝ ▽ ✳; N-Peru
- **viridis** (Rauh & Backeb.) Buxb. · Ψ Z9 ⊕ ▽ ✳; Peru

Bruckenthalia Rchb. -f- *Ericaceae* · 1 sp. · E:Spike Heath; G:Ährenheide
- **spiculifolia** (Salisb.) Rchb. · E:Spike Heath; G:Ährenheide · ♄ e △ Z6 VI-VII; Eur.: Ba, RO; NE-TR, mts.

Brugmansia Pers. -f- *Solanaceae* · 6 spp. · E:Angel's Trumpet; F:Trompette des anges; G:Engelstrompete
- *affinis* (Saff.) Moldenke = Brugmansia aurea
- **arborea** (L.) Lagerh. · E:Angel's Trumpet; G:Baumartige Engelstrompete · ♄ e Z9 ⊕ ✿; Ecuad., Peru, Bol., N-Chile
- **aurea** Lagerh. · E:Golden Angel's Trumpet; G:Goldene Engelstrompete · ♄ e Z9 ⊕ VII-IX ✿; Col. Ecuad.; And.
- **some cultivars**
- × **candida** Pers. (*B. aurea × B. versicolor*) · E:White Angel's Trumpet; G:Weiße Engelstrompete · ♄ e D Z9 ⊕ VI-XI ✿; Ecuad.
- **some cultivars**
- × **dolichocarpa** Lagerh. (*B. suaveolens × B. versicolor*) · ♄ ✿; cult.

- × **insignis** (Barb. Rodr.) Lockwood ex E.W. Davis (*B. × dolichocarpa × B. suaveolens*) · ♄ e Z9 ⊕ VII-IX; cult.
- × *longifolia* Lagerh. = Brugmansia × dolichocarpa
- *mollis* (Saff.) Moldenke = Brugmansia versicolor
- **sanguinea** (Ruiz & Pav.) D. Don
- subsp. **sanguinea** · E:Red Angel's Trumpet; G:Rote Engelstrompete · ♄ e Z9 ⊕ I-III ✿; Col., Ecuad., Peru, N-Chile
- subsp. **vulcanicola** (A.S. Barclay) Govaerts · ♄ e Z9 ⊕ ✿; Col.
- **suaveolens** (Humb. & Bonpl. ex Willd.) Bercht. & C. Presl · E:Angel's Trumpet; G:Duftende Engelstrompete · ♄ D Z9 ⊕ VIII-X ✿; SE-Braz.
- **some cultivars**
- **versicolor** Lagerh. · ♄ ♄ e Z9 ⊕ VII-IX ✿; Ecuad. (Guyaquil)
- **some cultivars**
- *vulcanicola* (A.S. Barclay) R.E. Schult. = Brugmansia sanguinea subsp. vulcanicola
- *waymannii* Paxton = Datura metel
- **Cultivars:**
- **many cultivars**

Brunfelsia L. -f- *Solanaceae* · c. 40 spp. · E:Morning, Noon and Night; F:Brunfelsia; G:Brunfelsie
- **americana** L. · E:Lady-of-the-Night; G:Weiße Brunfelsie · ♄ e D Z10 ⊛; W.Ind.
- **latifolia** (Pohl) Benth. · E:Kiss Me Quick; G:Breitblättrige Brunfelsie · ♄ e Z10 ⊛ I-V; Braz.
- **pauciflora** (Cham. & Schltdl.) Benth.
- var. **calycina** (Benth.) J.A. Schmidt · ♄ e Z10 ⊛ I-VI; Braz.
- var. **pauciflora** · E:Yesterday, Today and Tomorrow; G:Purpurne Brunfelsie · ♄ e Z10 ⊛ ✿; Braz.
- **undulata** Sw. · ♄ e D Z10 ⊛; Jamaica
- **uniflora** (Pohl) D. Don · E:Manac, Vegetable Mercury; G:Manac-Brunfelsie · ♄ e D Z10 ⊛ I-VII ✿; Guyan., Braz., Peru

Brunia Lam. -f- *Bruniaceae* · 7 spp.
- **albiflora** E. Phillips · ♄ ⋈ D Z10 ⊕; Cape
- **laevis** Thunb. · ♄ ⋈ Z9 ⊕; S-Afr.

Brunnera Steven -f- *Boraginaceae* · 3 spp. · E:Great Forget-me-not; F:Myosotis du Caucase; G:Kaukasusvergissmeinnicht

- **macrophylla** (Adams) I.M. Johnst. ·
E:Siberian Bugloss; F:Myosotis du
Caucase; G:Großblättriges Kaukasusver-
gissmeinnicht · ⌗ Z3 IV-VI; Cauc., W-Sib.

Brunsvigia Heist. -f- *Amaryllidaceae* ·
19 spp. · E:Brunsvigia; F:Lis de Joséphine;
G:Brunsvigie
- **josephinae** (Delile) Ker-Gawl. ·
E:Josephine's Lily G:Kaiserin Josephines;
Brunsvigie · ⌗ Z9 ⓐ VIII-X; S-Afr.
- *multiflora* W.T. Aiton = Brunsvigia
orientalis
- **orientalis** (L.) Aiton ex Eckl. · ⌗ Z9 ⓐ
VIII-X; S-Afr.

Bryanthus S.G. Gmel. -m- *Ericaceae* · 1 sp. ·
G:Moosheide
- **gmelinii** D. Don · ♄ e △ Z6 VII-VIII; Jap.,
Kamchat.
- *musciformis* (Poir.) Nakai = Bryanthus
gmelinii

Bryonia L. -f- *Cucurbitaceae* · 12 spp. ·
E:Bryony; F:Bryone; G:Zaunrübe
- **alba** L. · E:Bryony; G:Schwarzfrüchtige
Zaunrübe, Weiße Zaunrübe · ⌗ ⚥ ⚭ Z6
VI-VII ⚥ ✻; Eur.: I, C-Eur., EC-Eur., Ba,
E-Eur.; TR, Cauc., N-Iran, C-As., nat. in F,
Sc
- **cretica** L. · E:Cretan Bryony; G:Kretische
Zaunrübe · ⌗ Z8 ⓐ ✻; Eur.: GR, Crete;
TR, Levant, Cauc., Iran, C-As., Egypt,
Libya
- subsp. *dioica* (Jacq.) Tutin = Bryonia
dioica
- **dioica** Jacq. · E:White Bryony;
G:Rotfrüchtige Zaunrübe, Zweihäusige
Zaunrübe · ⌗ ⚥ ⚭ Z6 VI-IX ⚥ ✻; Eur.*
exc. EC-Eur.; NW-Afr.
- *punctata* Thunb. = Zehneria scabra
- *scabra* Thunb. = Zehneria scabra

Bryophyllum Salisb. -n- *Crassulaceae* ·
c. 30 spp. · F:Bryophyllum, Kalanchoe;
G:Brutblatt
- *calycinum* Salisb. = Bryophyllum pinnatum
- **daigremontianum** (Raym.-Hamet & H.
Perrier) A. Berger · E:Devil's Backbone;
G:Brutblatt · ⍦ ⓐ; SW-Madag.
- **delagoense** (Eckl. & Zeyh.) Schinz
- **laxiflorum** (Baker) Baker · ⌗ ⍦ ⓐ I-III;
Madag.
- **manginii** (Raym.-Hamet & H. Perrier)

Nothdurft · ⌗ ⍦ ≋ ⤳ ⓐ II-III; S-Madag.
- **miniatum** (Hilsenb. & Bojer) A. Berger ·
♄ ⍦ ⓐ; Madag.
- **pinnatum** (Lam.) Oken · E:Cathedral
Bells; G:Schwiegermutterpflanze · ⌗ ⍦
ⓐ; orig. ?, nat. in Trop., Subtrop.
- **porphyrocalyx** (Baker), A. Berger · ♄ ⍦
ⓐ; C-Madag.
- **proliferum** Bowie ex Hook. · ⌗ ⍦ ⓐ;
C-Madag.
- **scandens** (H. Perrier) A. Berger · ⌗ ⍦ ≋
ⓐ; Madag.
- **schizophyllum** (Baker) A. Berger · ⌗ ⍦ ≋
ⓐ; C-Madag.
- **tubiflorum** Harv. · E:Chandelier Plant;
G:Röhrenblütiges Brutblatt · ⌗ ⍦ ⓐ;
S-Madag.
- **uniflorum** (Stapf) A. Berger · ⌗ ⍦ ⤳
ⓐ; Madag.

Buchloe Engelm. -m- *Poaceae* · 1 sp. ·
E:Buffalo Gras; F:Herbe-aux-bisons;
G:Büffelgras
- **dactyloides** (Nutt.) Engelm. · E:Buffalo
Grass; G:Büffelgras · ⌗ Z4 ⓝ; Can.: Man.;
USA: NCE, NC, SW, SC; Mex.

Buddleja L. -f- *Buddlejaceae* · c. 100 spp. ·
E:Butterfly Bush; F:Arbres-aux-papillons;
G:Schmetterlingsstrauch, Sommerflieder
- **albiflora** Hemsl. · ♄ d Z6 VII-IX;
W-China, C-China
- **alternifolia** Maxim. · E:Fountain Bud-
dleia; F:Arbre aux papillons; G:Schmal-
blättriger Sommerflieder · ♄ d D Z6 VI;
NW-China
- **asiatica** Lour. · ♄ ♄ e Z8 ⓐ; Ind., China
- **auriculata** Benth. · ♄ ♄ e Z8 ⓐ; S-Afr.
- **colvilei** Hook. f. & Thomson · ♄ d Z8 ⓐ
VI; Him.
- **crispa** Benth. · ♄ d D Z8 ⓐ VII-VIII;
Pakist., N-Ind., Nepal, Bhutan, China
- **davidii** Franch. · E:Butterfly Bush,
Summer Lilac; G:Sommerflieder
- **many cultivars**
- var. **davidii** · F:Arbre aux papillons, Lilas
d'été; G:Gewöhnlicher Sommerflieder,
Schmetterlingsstrauch · ♄ d Z6 VII-X;
China, nat. in Eur.: Fr, BrI, C-Eur., I;
Calif.
- var. **nanhoensis** (Chitt.) Rehder ·
G:Kleinblättriger Sommerflieder · Z5;
C-China
- **farreri** Balf. f. & W.W. Sm. · ♄ d Z9 ⓐ
IV-V; NW-China: Kansu

– **globosa** Hope · E:Orange Ball Tree; G:Kugel-Sommerflieder · ♄ s Z7 VII-VIII; Peru, Chile
– *hemsleyana* Koehne = Buddleja albiflora
– **indica** Lam. · E:Indoor Oak; G:Zimmer-Sommerflieder · ♄ e Z10 ⊛ ⊛; Madag.
– **japonica** Hemsl. · G:Japanischer Sommerflieder · ♄ d Z7 VII-VIII; Jap., nat. in F
– **lindleyana** Fortune · ♄ e Z8 ⊛ VII-VIII; E-China
– **madagascariensis** Lam. · ♄ e ⁂ Z9 ⊛ I-V; Madag.
– × *nanhoensis* hort. = Buddleja davidii var. nanhoensis
– **nivea** Duthie · ♄ d Z7 ⊛ ∧ VIII-IX; W-China
– × **pikei** H.R. Fletcher (*B. alternifolia* × *B. crispa*) · ♄ d Z7; cult.
– *stenostachya* Rehder & E.H. Wilson = Buddleja nivea
– *variabilis* Hemsl. = Buddleja davidii var. davidii
– × **weyeriana** Weyer (*B. davidii* × *B. globosa*) · ♄ d Z7 VII-X; cult.
– **Cultivars:**
– **some cultivars**

Bufonia L. -f- *Caryophyllaceae* · 20 spp. · F:Buffonia; G:Buffonie
– **paniculata** Dubois · G:Rispige Buffonie · ⊙ VII; Eur.: sp., F, I, Sw, GR; Lebanon, Syr.

Buglossoides Moench = Lithospermum
– *purpurocaeruleum* (L.) I.M. Johnst. = Lithospermum purpurocaeruleum

Buglossum Adans. = Anchusa
– *barrelieri* All. = Anchusa barrelieri

Bulbine Wolf -f- *Asphodelaceae* · 71 sp.
– **alooides** (L.) Willd. · ♃ ⇂ Z9 ⊛ IV; S-Afr.
– **bulbosa** (R. Br.) Haw. · E:Golden Lily · ♃ ⇂ Z9 ⊛; Austr.: Queensl., N.S.Wales, Victoria, S-Austr., Tasman.
– **frutescens** (L.) Willd. · ♄ ⇂ Z9 ⊛ III; Cape
– **mesembryanthemoides** Haw. · ♃ ⇂ Z9 ⊛; Cape
– **semibarbata** (R. Br.) Haw. · E:Leek Lily · ⊙ Z9 V-VI; Austr.

Bulbinella Kunth -f- *Asphodelaceae* · 24 spp.
– **angustifolia** (Cockayne & Laing) L.B. Moore · ♃ Z8 ⊛ ⊛ VI-VII; NZ

– **hookeri** (Hook.) Cheeseman · ♃ Z8 ⊛ ⊛ VI-VII; NZ
– **rossii** (Hook. f.) Cheeseman · ♃ Z8 ⊛ ⊛ VI-VII; NZ

Bulbinopsis Borzì = Bulbine
– *bulbosa* (R. Br.) Borzì = Bulbine bulbosa
– *semibarbata* (R. Br.) Borzì = Bulbine semibarbata

Bulbocodium L. -n- *Colchicaceae* · 2 spp. · F:Bulbocode; G:Lichtblume
– **vernum** L. · E:Spring Meadow Saffron; G:Frühlings-Lichtblume · ♃ ⊛ Z6 II-III; Eur.: Ib, F; Pyr

Bulbophyllum Thouars -n- *Orchidaceae* · 1837 spp. · G:Zwiebelblatt; F:Bulbophyllum
– **auratum** (Lindl.) Rchb. f. · ♃ Z10 ⊛ X ▽ ✳; Sumat.
– **barbigerum** Lindl. · ♃ Z10 ⊛ VI-VII ▽ ✳; W-Afr., C-Afr.
– **binnendijkii** J.J. Sm. · ♃ Z10 ⊛ X ▽ ✳; Kalimantan
– *ericssonii* Kraenzl. = Bulbophyllum binnendijkii
– **falcatum** (Lindl.) Rchb. f. · ♃ Z10 ⊛ V-VI ▽ ✳; W-Afr., C-Afr., Uganda
– **gracillimum** (Rolfe) Rolfe · ♃ Z10 ⊛ VI-X ▽ ✳; Malay. Arch., Fiji
– **imbricatum** Lindl. · ♃ Z10 ⊛ IV-V ▽ ✳; Cameroon, W-Nigeria
– *leucorhachis* (Rolfe) Schltr. = Bulbophyllum imbricatum
– **lobbii** Lindl. · ♃ Z10 ⊛ V-VI ▽ ✳; Burma, Thail., Malay. Pen., Sumat., Java, Kalimantan
– **longiflorum** Thouars · ♃ Z10 ⊛ VII ▽ ✳; trop. E-Afr., Madag., SE-As., Malay. Arch., N-Austr., Pacific Is.
– **longissimum** (Ridl.) J.J. Sm. · ♃ Z10 ⊛ XI ▽ ✳; Thail., Malay. Pen.
– **makoyanum** (Rchb. f.) Ridl. · ♃ Z10 ⊛ I-II ▽ ✳; Ind.
– **mastersianum** (Rolfe) J.J. Sm. · ♃ Z10 ⊛ I-II ▽ ✳; Kalimantan, Molucca
– **medusae** (Lindl.) Rchb. f. · ♃ Z10 ⊛ X-XII ▽ ✳; Thail., Malay. Pen., Sumat., Kalimantan, Phil.
– **ornatissimum** (Rchb. f.) J.J. Sm. · ♃ Z10 ⊛ ▽ ✳; Ind.: Assam; E-Him.
– **picturatum** (Lodd.) Rchb. f. · ♃ Z10 ⊛ V-VI ▽ ✳; Burma
– **putidum** (Teijsm. & Binn.) J.J. Sm. · ♃

Z10 ⓜ IX ▽ ✳; Vietn.: Annam
- **wendlandianum** (Kraenzl.) Dammer · ⑤
Z9 ⓜ V ▽ ✳; N-Burma

Bumelia Sw. = Sideroxylon
- *lanuginosa* (Michx.) Pers. = Sideroxylon
lanuginosum

Bunchosia Rich. ex Kunth -f-
Malpighiaceae · 55 spp.
- **costaricensis** Rose ex Pittier · ♄ ♄ e Z10
ⓜ Ⓝ; Costa Rica

Bunias L. -f- *Brassicaceae* · 6 spp. · E:Warty
Cabbage; F:Bunias, fausse-roquette;
G:Zackenschötchen
- **erucago** L. · E:Southern Warty Cabbage;
G:Flügel-Zackenschötchen · ⊙ Z7 V-VII;
Eur.: Ba, Ital-P, Fr, Ib, Sw; TR, N-Afr.,
nat. in C-Eur., EC-Eur., RO
- **orientalis** L. · E:Warty Cabbage;
G:Orientalisches Zackenschötchen · ⑤ Z7
V-VIII; Eur.: EC-Eur., Ba, E-Eur.; Cauc.,
N-Iraq, N-Iran, nat. in BrI, Sc, Fr, C-Eur.,
Ital-P

Bunium L. -n- *Apiaceae* · 48 spp. · E:Great
Pignut; F:Cumin tubéreux; G:Erdknolle,
Knollenkümmel
- **bulbocastanum** L. · E:Earth Chestnut,
Great Earthnut; G:Erdkastanie, Gewöhn-
licher Knollenkümmel · ⑤ VI-VII Ⓝ; Eur.:
BrI, Fr, Ib., Ital-P, C-Eur., Slove., nat. in
DK

Buphthalmum L. -n- *Asteraceae* · 2 spp. ·
E:Ox Eye; F:Oeil-de-bœuf; G:Ochsenauge
- *maritimum* L. = Asteriscus maritimus
- **salicifolium** L. · E:Yellow Ox-Eye;
G:Rindsauge, Weidenblättriges
Ochsenauge · ⑤ Z4 VI-VIII; Eur.: F, N-I,
C-Eur., EC-Eur., Ba
- *sericeum* L. f. = Nauplius sericeus
- *speciosissimum* Ard. = Telekia speciosissima
- *speciosum* Schreb. = Telekia speciosa

Bupleurum L. -n- *Apiaceae* · c. 150 spp. ·
E:Hare's Ear; F:Buplèvre, Oreille-de-
lièvre; G:Hasenohr
- **affine** Sadler · G:Ungarisches Hasenohr ·
⊙ VII-IX; Eur.: A, EC-Eur., Ba, E-Eur.
- **commutatum** Boiss. & Balansa · ⊙; Eur.:
H, Ba, RO, Crim; TR, W-Iran
- **falcatum** L. · E:Sickle-leaved Hare's Ear;

G:Sichelblättriges Hasenohr · ⑤ Z3 VII-IX
♀; Eur.* exc. Sc; TR, Cauc., Iran, W-Sib.,
E-Sib., Him, Manch., Korea, Jap.
- **fruticosum** L. · E:Shrubby Hare's Ear;
G:Strauchiges Hasenohr · ♄ e Z7 ⓕ
VII-IX; Eur.: Ib, F, Ital-P; Med., Alger.,
Lebanon, N-Afr., nat. in BrI, Crim
- **gerardii** All. · G:Jacqins Hasenohr,
Südliches Hasenohr · ⊙ VII-VIII; Eur.:
Ib, Fr, Ital-P, Ba, Crim; TR, Cyprus, Syr.,
Cauc., W-Iran, C-As., Libya, nat. in D
- *jacquinianum* Jord. = Bupleurum gerardii
- **lancifolium** Hornem. · ⊙; Eur.: Ib, Ital-P,
Ba; Cyprus, Syr., Palest., Iraq, W-Iran,
C-As., Egypt, Libya, Alger., nat. in A, B,
Br
- **longifolium** L. · G:Langblättriges
Hasenohr · ⑤ Z3 VII-VIII; Eur.: Fr, C-Eur.,
EC-Eur., Ba, E-Eur.; W-Sib., E-Sib., C-As.,
N-China
- **petraeum** L. · E:Rock Hare's Ear;
G:Felsen-Hasenohr · ⑤ Z6 VII-VIII; Eur.:
I, F, A, Slove.; Alp.
- **praealtum** L. · G:Simsen-Hasenohr · ⊙
VII-IX; Eur.: Ib, Fr, Ital-P, Ba, A, EC-Eur.,
RO
- **ranunculoides** L. · G:Hahnenfuß-
Hasenohr · ⑤ △ Z6 VII-VIII; Eur.: sp., F, I,
C-Eur., EC-Eur., W-Ba, RO; mts.
- **rotundifolium** L. · E:Hare's Ear, Thorow
Wax; G:Durchwachsenes Hasenohr,
Rundblättriges Hasenohr · ⊙ Z6 VI-VIII;
Eur.* exc. Sc; TR, Cauc., N-Iran, C-As.,
nat. in N-Am., Austr., NZ etc.
- **stellatum** L. · G:Sternblütiges Hasenohr ·
⑤ VII-VIII; Eur.: F, Cors, I, Sw, A; Alp.,
Cors
- **tenuissimum** L. · E:Slender Hare's Ear;
G:Salz-Hasenohr · ⊙ VIII-IX; Eur.*, TR,
Cauc., Moroc., Alger.
- **veronense** Turra · ⊙; Eur.: I, Ba

Burbidgea Hook. f. -f- *Zingiberaceae* ·
5 spp.
- **schizocheila** Hackett bis · ⑤ Z10 ⓜ
III-VI; Kalimantan

× **Burkillara** hort. -f- *Orchidaceae* (Aerides
× *Arachnis* × *Vanda*)

× **Burrageara** hort. -f- *Orchidaceae*
(*Cochlioda* × *Miltonia* × *Odontoglossum* ×
Oncidium)

Bursaria Cav. -f- *Pittosporaceae* · 3 spp. ·

G:Taschenblume
- **spinosa** Cav. · E:Christmas Bush · ♄ ♄ e Z9 ⬚; Austr.: N.S.Wales, Tasman.

Bursera Jacq. ex L. -f- *Burseraceae* · 40-80 spp. · E:Torchwood; F:Arbre à térébenthine, Gommier; G:Amerikanischer Balsam-baum, Weißgummibaum
- *delpechiana* Poiss. ex Engl. = Bursera penicillata
- **fagaroides** (Kunth) Engl. · E:Fragrant Bursera, Quauhxiotl; G:Duftender Weißgummibaum · ♄ ♄ d Z10 ⬚; Ariz., Mex., Baja Calif.
- *gummifera* L. = Bursera simaruba
- **penicillata** (Sessé & Moç. ex DC.) Engl. · E:Torchwood; G:Elemi-Weißgummibaum · ♄ d Z10 ⬚ ⓝ; Mex., trop. Am.
- **simaruba** (L.) Sarg. · E:Jobo, West Indian Birch; G:Birkenblättriger Weißgummibaum · ♄ d Z10 ⬚ ⓝ; S-Fla., Mex., C-Am., W.Ind.
- **tenuifolia** Rose · ♄ d Z10 ⬚; Mex.

Burtonia R. Br. -f- *Fabaceae* · 12 spp.
- **scabra** (Sm.) R. Br. · ♄ e Z10 ⬚; Austr.: W-Austr.

Butea Roxb. ex Willd. -f- *Fabaceae* · 4 spp. · F:Arbre-à-laque, Butéa; G:Lackbaum
- **monosperma** (Lam.) Taub. · ♄ d Z10 ⬚ ❦; Ind., Sri Lanka, Burma
- **superba** Roxb. · E:Climbing Palas, Flame of the Forest; G:Kinobaum, Lackbaum · ♄ d ⬚ ⓝ; Thail.

Butia (Becc.) Becc. -f- *Arecaceae* · 9 spp. · E:Jelly Palm; F:Palmier butia, Palmier-à-gelée; G:Geleepalme, Palasabaum
- *bonnetii* (Becc.) Becc. = Butia capitata
- **capitata** (Mart.) Becc. · E:Jelly Palm; G:Gewöhnliche Geleepalme · ♄ e Z10 ⬚; S-Braz., Urug., N-Arg.
- **eriospatha** (Mart. ex Drude) Becc. · E:Woolly Butia Palm; G:Wollige Geleepalme · ♄ e Z10 ⬚; S-Braz.
- **yatay** (Mart.) Becc. · E:Yatay Palm; G:Yatay-Geleepalme · ♄ e Z10 ⬚; Arg.

Butomus L. -m- *Butomaceae* · 1 sp. · E:Flowering Rush; F:Butome, Jonc fleuri; G:Blumenbinse
- **umbellatus** L. · E:Flowering Rush, Water Gladiolus; F:Jonc fleuri; G:Blumenbinse, Schwanenblume · ⚃ ∿ Z5 VI-VIII;

Eur.*, TR, Syr., Cauc., Iran, Afgh., Him., W-Sib., E-Sib., Amur, C-As., Mong., Him., NW-Afr., nat. in N-Am.

Butyrospermum Kotschy = Vitellaria
- *paradoxum* (C.F. Gaertn.) Hepper = Vitellaria paradoxa
- *parkii* (G. Don) Kotschy = Vitellaria paradoxa

Buxus L. -f- *Buxaceae* · c. 70 spp. · G:Buchsbaum; E:Box; F:Buis
- **balearica** Lam. · E:Balearic Box; G:Balearen-Buchsbaum · ♄ e Z8 ⬚ ✿; Eur.: S-Sp., Balear., Sard.
- *harlandii* hort. = Buxus sinica var. sinica
- **henryi** Mayr · G:Henrys Buchsbaum · ♄ e Z6 ✿; China: W-Hubei, Sichuan, Guizhou
- *japonica* Müll. Arg. = Buxus microphylla var. japonica
- **microphylla** Siebold & Zucc.
- **many cultivars**
- var. **japonica** (Müll. Arg.) Rehder & E.H. Wilson · G:Japanischer Buchsbaum · ♄ ♄ e Z6 ✿; Jap.
- var. **koreana** Nakai · G:Koreanischer Buchsbaum · ♄ e Z6 ✿; China, Korea
- var. **microphylla** (Makino) Makino · E:Japanese Boxwood, Korean Boxwood; G:Kleinblättriger Buchsbaum · ♄ e Z6 ✿; Jap.
- **sempervirens** L. · E:Boxwood, Common Box; F:Buis commun; G:Europäischer Buchsbaum, Gewöhnlicher Buchsbaum · ♄ ♄ e Z6 III-IV ❦ ✿ ⓝ ▽; Cauc. (Lazistan), nat. in RO
- **many cultivars**
- **sinica** (Rehdr & E.H. Wilson)
- var. **sinica** M. Cheng · ♄ e Z6 ✿; China

Byblis Salisb. -f- *Byblidaceae* · 6 spp. · E:Rainbow Plant; F:Byblis, Plante-arc-en-ciel; G:Regenbogenpflanze
- **gigantea** Lindl. · E:Great Rainbow Plant; G:Große Regenbogenpflanze · ⚃ Z10 ⬚; N.Guinea, W-Austr.
- **liniflora** Salisb. · E:Rainbow Plant; G:Leinblütige Regenbogenpflanze · ⚃ Z10 ⬚; N.Guinea, N-Austr.

Byrsonima Rich. ex Kunth -f- *Malpighiaceae* · 130-150 spp.
- **crassifolia** (L.) Kunth · E:Nanche · ♄ e ⬚ ⓝ; trop. Am.

Cabomba Aubl. -f- *Cabombaceae* · 5 spp. ·
E:Water Shield; F:Cabomba; G:Haarnixe
– **aquatica** Aubl. · G:Riesen-Haarnixe · ♃
≈ Z10 ⓦ; Guianas, Amazon.
– *australis* Speg. = Cabomba caroliniana
var. caroliniana
– **caroliniana** A. Gray · G:Nordamerika-
nische Haarnixe
– var. **caroliniana** · E:Carolina Water
Shield, Fish Grass; G:Carolina-Haarnixe
· ♃ ≈ Z8 ⓦ; USA: NCE, SE, Fla., Tex.,
nat. in Mass.
– var. **pulcherrima** R.M. Harper ·
G:Florida-Haarnixe · ♃ ≈ Z8 ⓦ; USA:
SE, Fla.
– **furcata** Schult. · E:Forked Fanwort ·
G:Gegabelte Haarnixe · ♃ ≈ ⓦ; Braz.
– *pulcherrima* (R.M. Harper) Fassett =
Cabomba caroliniana var. pulcherrima

Cabralea A. Juss. -f- *Meliaceae* · 1 (-6) spp. ·
– **cangerana** Saldanha · ♄ ⓚ; Braz.

Cacalia L. = Adenostyles
– *alliariae* Gouan = Adenostyles alliariae
– *coccinea* Sims = Emilia coccinea
– *glabra* Mill. = Adenostyles glabra

Caccinia Savi -f- *Boraginaceae* · 6 spp.
– *glauca* Savi = Caccinia macranthera var.
crassifolia
– **macranthera** (Banks & Sol.) Brand
– var. **crassifolia** (Vent.) Brand ·
E:Kaksinia · ♄ △ Z7 V-VI; N-Iran

Caesalpinia L. -f- *Caesalpiniaceae* · c.
150 spp. · F:Brésillet; G:Caesalpinie
– **coriaria** (Jacq.) Willd. · E:Divi Divi · ♄
Z10 ⓦ ⓝ; Mex., C-Am., W.Ind., trop.
S-Am..
– **decapetala** (Roth) Alston
– var. **decapetala** · E:Mysore Thorn;
G:Mauritiusdorn · ♄ e ⚡ Z8 ⓚ VI-VII;
Ind., Sri Lanka, China, Korea, Malay.
Arch.
– var. **japonica** (Siebold & Zucc.) H.
Ohashi Z9 ⓚ; Jap.
– **digyna** Rottler · G:Tari-Hülsen · ! Z10 ⓝ;
Afr., Ind.
– **echinata** Lam. · E:Brazil Wood; G:Per-
nambucoholz · ♄ Z10 ⓦ ⓝ; trop. Am.
– **ferrea** Mart. · E:Leopard Tree; G:Leop-
ardenbaum · ♄ d Z10 ⓦ; E-Braz.
– **gilliesii** (Wall. ex Hook.) Benth. ·
E:Bird-of-Paradise Flower, Poinciana;

G:Pardiesvogelstrauch · ♄ ♄ d Z10 ⓚ
VII-VIII; Urug., Arg., Chile
– *japonica* Siebold & Zucc. = Caesalpinia
decapetala var. japonica
– **mexicana** A. Gray · E:Mexican Holdback · ♄ ♄ e Z10 ⓦ; Mex.
– **pulcherrima** (L.) Sw. · E:Barbados Pride,
Peacock Flower; G:Stolz von Barbados,
Pfauenstrauch · ♄ ♄ d Z9 ⓚ VII; W.Ind.
– **sappan** L. · E:Sappanwood, Sepang;
G:Indisches Rotholz · ♄ ♄ d Z10 ⓦ ⓝ;
Ind., Sri Lanka, China, Indochina, Malay.
Arch.
– *sepiaria* Roxb. = Caesalpinia decapetala
var. decapetala
– **spinosa** (Molina) Kuntze · E:Spiny
Holdback; G:Taragummi · ♄ ♄ ! d ⚡ Z10
ⓦ ⓝ; w S-Am.

Caiophora C. Presl -f- *Loasaceae* · 65 spp. ·
F:Liseron brûlant; G:Brennwinde,
Fackelbrennkraut
– **contorta** (Lam.) C. Presl · ⊙ ⚡ Z9 VII-IX;
Peru, Chile
– **lateritia** (Hook.) Klotzsch · ⊙ ♃ ⚡ Z9
VII-X; Arg.

Cajanus DC. -m- *Fabaceae* · 3 spp. ·
E:Catjang Pea; F:Ambreuvade, Pois
d'angol; G:Taubenerbsenbaum
– **cajan** (L.) Millsp. · E:Catjang Pea, Pigeon
Pea, Red Gram; G:Katjangstrauch,
Taubenerbsenbaum · ♄ Z10 ⓚ ⓝ; cult.,
nat. in Trop.

Cajophora C. Presl = Caiophora

Cakile Mill. -f- *Brassicaceae* · 7 spp. · E:Sea
Rocket; F:Caquilier, Roquette de mer;
G:Meersenf
– **maritima** Scop. · E:Sea Rocket;
G:Europäischer Meersenf · ⊙ Z6 VII-X;
Eur., coasts; N-Afr., SW-As., nat. in
N-Am., Austr.

Caladium Vent. -n- *Araceae* · 13 spp. ·
E:Angel Wings, Elephant's Ear;
F:Caladium; G:Kaladie
– *argyrites* Lem. = Caladium humboldtii
– **bicolor** (Aiton) Vent. · E:Elephant's
Ear, Heart of Jesus; G:Elefantenohr,
Engelsflügel · ♃ Z10 ⓦ II-IV ❀; Ecuad.
– × *hortulanum* Birdsey = Caladium bicolor
– **humboldtii** Schott · ♃ Z10 ⓦ; Venez.,
Braz.

– **lindenii** (André) Madison · 24 Z10 Ⓦ;
Col.
– *marmoratum* L. Mathieu ex K. Koch =
Caladium bicolor
– **schomburgkii** Schott · 24 Z10 Ⓦ; Guyan.,
Braz.
– *seguine* (Jacq.) Vent. = Dieffenbachia
seguine
– *thripedestum* Lem. = Caladium bicolor

Calamagrostis Adans. -f- *Poaceae* · c.
230 spp. · E:Small Reed; F:Calamagrostis;
G:Reitgras
– × **acutiflora** (Schrad.) Rchb. (*C.
arundinacea* × *C. epigejos*) · E:Feather
Reed Grass; G:Gartensandrohr · 24 Z2-6
VI-VII; Eur.: BrI, NL, G, EC-Eur., Sc
– *arenaria* (L.) Roth = Ammophila arenaria
– **arundinacea** (L.) Roth · E:Rough Small
Reed; G:Wald-Reitgras · 24 Z7 VI-VII;
Eur.* exc. BrI; TR, Cauc., W-Sib., E-Sib.
– **brachytricha** Steud. · G:Diamant-
Reitgras · 24 Z7; C-As., E-As.
– **canescens** (Weber) Roth · E:Purple
Small Reed; G:Gewöhnliches Sumpf-
Reitgras · 24 Z7 VII-VIII; Eur.*, TR, Cauc.
– **epigejos** (L.) Roth · E:Bush Grass, Wood
Small Reed; G:Land-Reitgras · 24 Z7
VII-VIII; Eur.*, TR, N-Iran, Cauc., Afgh.,
Him., W-Sib., E-Sib., Amur, Sakhal.,
C-As., Mong., China, Korea, Jap., Taiwan
– **phragmitoides** Hartm. · G:Purpur-
Reitgras · 24 Z7 VII-VIII; Eur.: Fr, C-Eur.,
EC-Eur., Sc, Russ.; Cauc., W-Sib.
– **pseudophragmites** (Haller f.) Koeler ·
G:Ufer-Reitgras · 24 Z7 VI-VII; Eur.: Fr,
Ital-P, C-Eur., EC-Eur., Ba, E-Eur., ? sp.;
TR, Iraq, Cauc., Iran, W-Sib., E-Sib.,
Amur, C-As., Mong., China: Sinkiang;
China, Korea, Jap., Moroc., Alger.
– **pseudopurpurea** Gerstl. ex O.R. Heine ·
G:Sächsisches Reitgras · 24 Z7 VI-VII;
Eur.: D (Dresden)
– **stricta** (Timm) Köhler · E:Narrow Small
Reed; G:Moor-Reitgras · 24 ; Eur.: Sc, GB,
C-Eur., EC-Eur.; Cauc., W-Sib., C-As.,
Amur, N-Am.
– *stricta* hort. = Calamagrostis × acutiflora
– **varia** (Schrad.) Host · G:Buntes Reitgras ·
24 Z7 VII-IX; Eur.* exc. BrI
– **villosa** (Chaix) J.F. Gmel. · G:Wolliges
Reitgras · 24 Z7 VII-VIII; Eur.: Fr, I,
C-Eur., EC-Eur., Ba, RO; mts.

Calamintha Mill. -f- *Lamiaceae* · 7 spp. ·
E:Calamint; F:Calament, Menthe de
montagne; G:Bergminze
– *alpina* (L.) Lam. = Acinos alpinus
– **einseleana** F.W. Schultz · G:Einseles
Bergminze · 24 VII-IX; Eur.: A, D
(Berchtesgaden) +
– **grandiflora** (L.) Moench · E:Large-flow-
ered Calamint, Mint Savory; F:Calament
à grandes fleurs; G:Großblütige
Bergminze · 24 △ Z5 VII-VIII; Eur.: Ib, Fr,
Ital-P, Sw, A, Ba, RO, Crim; TR, Cauc.,
NW-Iran
– **menthifolia** Host · E:Wood Calamint;
G:Aufsteigende Bergminze, Wald-
Bergminze · 24 VII-IX; Eur.* ex Sc.; TR,
Lebanon, Cauc., N-Iran, Alger.
– **nepeta** (L.) Savi
– subsp. **glandulosa** (Req.) P.W. Ball ·
E:Common Calamint; G:Drüsige
Bergminze · 24 Z6 VII-IX; Eur.: Ib, Ital-P.,
Crim; TR, Cauc.
– subsp. **nepeta** · E:Lesser Calamint;
F:Menthe de montagne; G:Kleinblütige
Bergminze · 24 Z6 VII-IX ⚥ ; Eur.* exc. Sc;
TR, Cauc.
– *nepetoides* Jord. = Calamintha nepeta
subsp. nepeta
– *officinalis* Moench = Calamintha nepeta
subsp. glandulosa
– *sylvatica* Bromf. = Calamintha menthifolia

× **Calammophila** Brand -f- *Poaceae* ·
2 spp. · F:Oyat bâtard; G:Bastardstrand-
hafer (*Ammophila* × *Calamagrostis*)
– **baltica** (Flüggé ex Schrad.) Brand
(*Ammophila arenaria* × *Calamagrostis
epigejos*) · G:Baltischer Bastardstrandhafer · 24 VI-VII; Eur.; coasts

Calamus L. -m- *Arecaceae* · 374 spp. ·
E:Rattan Palm; F:Rotin; G:Spanisches
Rohr, Rotangpalme
– **asperrimus** Blume · ♄ e ⚘ Z10 Ⓦ; Java
– **caesius** Blume · E:Rattan Palm;
G:Spanisches Rohr, Stuhlrohr · ♄ e ⚘ Z10
Ⓦ Ⓝ; Malay. Pen., Kalimantan
– **ciliaris** Blume · ♄ e ⚘ Z10 Ⓦ; Sumat.,
Java
– **longisetus** Griff. · ♄ e ⚘ ⋉ Z10 Ⓦ;
Burma
– **manan** Miq. · ♄ e ⚘ Z10 Ⓦ Ⓝ; Malay.
Pen., Sumat.
– **optimus** Becc. · ♄ e ⚘ Z10 Ⓦ Ⓝ;
Kalimantan

– **rotang** L. · E:Rattan Cane; G:Rattan-
palme · ♄ e ⧗ Z10 🖐 Ⓝ; S-Ind., Sri Lanka

Calandrinia Kunth -f- *Portulacaceae* · 60
(-150) spp. · E:Calandrina; F:Calandrinia;
G:Kalandrine
– **ciliata** (Ruiz & Pav.) DC.
– var. **ciliata** · E:Fringed Red Maids · ⊙;
USA: Calif., Ariz.
– var. **menziesii** (Hook.) J.F. Macbr. ·
E:Red Maids; G:Rote Kalandrine · ⊙
VI-VII; USA: Wash., Oreg., Calif.
– **grandiflora** Lindl. · ⊙ ♃ ♄ VI-IX; Chile
– *menziesii* (Hook.) Torr. & A. Gray =
Calandrinia ciliata var. menziesii
– *speciosa* Lindl. = Calandrinia ciliata var.
menziesii
– **umbellata** (Ruiz & Pav.) DC. · E:Rock
Purslane; G:Schirm-Kalandrine · ⊙ ♃ ♄
VII-IX; Peru, Chile

Calanthe Ker-Gawl. -f- *Orchidaceae* ·
185 spp. · F:Calanthe; G:Schönorchis
– **brevicornu** Lindl. · ♃ 🖐 V-VI ▽ ✳;
Nepal, Sikkim
– **cardioglossa** Schltr. · ♃ 🖐 X-XII ▽ ✳;
Ind.: Assam; Laos, Cambodia, Thail.
– *fuerstenbergiana* Kraenzl. = Calanthe
cardioglossa
– *masuca* (D. Don) Lindl. = Calanthe
sylvatica
– *regnieri* Rchb. f. = Calanthe vestita
– **rosea** (Lindl.) Benth. & Hook. f. · ♃ Z10
🖐 X-XI ▽ ✳; Thail.
– **sylvatica** (Thouars) Lindl. · ♃ Z10 🖐 V
▽ ✳; Madag., Mauritius
– **triplicata** (Willemet) Ames · ♃ Z10 🖐
IV-V ▽ ✳; S-Ind., Sri Lanka, SE-As., Jap.,
Malay. Arch., E-Austr., Fiji
– *veratrifolia* (Willd.) R. Br. = Calanthe
triplicata
– **vestita** Lindl. · ♃ Z10 🖐 XII-III ▽ ✳;
Indochina, Malay. Pen., Kalimantan,
Sulawesi

Calathea G. Mey. -f- *Marantaceae* ·
270 spp. · F:Galanga; G:Korbmaranthe
– **aemula** Körn. · ♃ Z9 🖐; orig. ?
– **allouia** (Aubl.) Lindl. · E:Guinea
Arrowroot; G:Guinea-Korbmaranthe · ♃
Z9 🖐 Ⓝ; Hispaniola, Puerto Rico, Lesser.
Antill., Guyan.
– **argyraea** Körn. · ♃ Z9 🖐; orig. ?
– **bachemiana** E. Morren · ♃ Z9 🖐; Braz.
– *bicolor* (Ker-Gawl.) Steud. = Maranta

cristata
– **crocata** E. Morren & Joriss. · ♃ Z9 🖐
IV-V; Braz.
– **cylindrica** (Roscoe & K. Koch) K.
Schum. · ♃ Z9 🖐; Braz.
– **eximia** (K. Koch & C.D. Bouché) Körn. ex
Regel · ♃ Z9 🖐; C-Am.
– **fasciata** (Linden ex K. Koch) Regel &
Körn. · ♃ Z9; Braz.
– *insignis* hort. ex W. Bull = Calathea
lancifolia
– **lancifolia** Boom · ♃ Z9 🖐; Braz.
– **leopardina** (W. Bull) Regel · G:Leop-
arden-Korbmaranthe · ♃ Z9 🖐; Braz.
– *lietzei* E. Morren = Maranta lietzei
– **lindeniana** Wallis · ♃ Z9 🖐; NW-Braz.,
Peru
– **lutea** (Aubl.) G. Mey. · E:Cauassu;
G:Cauassuwachs · ♃ Z9 🖐 Ⓝ; C-Am.,
W.Ind., Braz.
– **majestica** H. Kenn. · ♃ Z9 🖐; Col.,
Guyan.
– **makoyana** E. Morren · E:Peacock Plant;
G:Pfauen-Korbmaranthe · ♃ Z9 🖐; Braz.
– **mediopicta** (E. Morren) Jacob-Makoy ex
E. Morren · ♃ Z9 🖐; Braz.
– **micans** (L. Mathieu) Körn. · ♃ Z9 🖐;
C-Am., trop. S-Am.
– *orbiculata* Lodd. = Calathea truncata
– **orbifolia** (Linden) H. Kenn. Z9; Braz.
– **pavonii** Körn. · ♃ Z9 🖐; Peru
– **picturata** K. Koch & Linden · ♃ Z9 🖐;
Braz.
– *princeps* (Linden) Regel = Calathea
majestica
– **roseopicta** (Linden) Regel · ♃ Z9 🖐;
Braz.
– **rotundifolia**
– var. *fasciata* (Linden ex K. Koch) Petersen
= Calathea fasciata
– **rufibarba** Fenzl · ♃ Z9 🖐; Braz.
– **truncata** (Link ex A. Dietr.) K. Schum. ·
♃ Z9 🖐; Braz.
– *tubispatha* Hook. f. = Calathea pavonii
– **undulata** (Linden & André) Linden &
André · ♃ Z9 🖐; Braz., Peru
– **variegata** (K. Koch) Linden ex Körn. · ♃
Z9 🖐; orig. ?
– **veitchiana** Veitch ex Hook. f. · ♃ Z9 🖐;
trop. S-Am.
– **warscewiczii** (L. Mathieu ex Planch.)
Planch. & Linden · ♃ Z9 🖐; Costa Rica
– *wiotiana* Jacob-Makoy ex E. Morren =
Calathea wiotii
– **wiotii** (E. Morren) Regel · ♃ Z9 🖐;

E-Braz.
- **zebrina** (Sims) Lindl. · E:Zebra Plant; G:Zebra-Korbmarante · ⹏ Z9 ⓜ; SE-Braz.

Calceolaria L. -f- *Scrophulariaceae* · 388 spp. · E:Slipperwort; F:Calcéolaire; G:Pantoffelblume
- **alba** Ruiz & Pav. · ♄ Z9 ⓐ VI-VII; Peru, Chile, Arg.
- **arachnoidea** Graham · ⹏ Z9 ⓐ; Chile
- **biflora** Lam. · ⹏ △ Z8 ⓐ ∧ V-VI; Arg., Chile
- **chelidonioides** Kunth · ⊙ Z9; Mex., Peru, N-Chile
- **crenatiflora** Cav. · E:Pocketbook Flower; G:Gekerbte Pantoffelblume · ⹏ Z8 V-VI; Chile
- *darwinii* Benth. = Calceolaria uniflora var. darwinii
- **falklandica** (S. Moore) Kraenzl. · G:Falkland-Pantoffelblume · ⹏ Z7; Falkland Is.
- **integrifolia** Murray · E:Bush Slipperwort · ♄ e Z9 ⓐ V-IX; Chile (Chiloe)
- **mexicana** Benth. · ⊙ Z9 VI-VIII; Mex., C-Am.
- **pavonii** Benth. · ♄ ⚥ Z9 ⓐ VIII-X; Peru, Bol.
- **pinnata** L. · ⊙ Z9 VI-IX; Jamaica, Braz., Peru, Bol., Chile
- **polyrrhiza** Cav. · G:Patagonische Pantoffelblume · ⹏ △ Z8 ∧ VI-VIII; Arg.: Patag.
- *rugosa* Ruiz & Pav. = Calceolaria integrifolia
- **tenella** Poepp. & Endl. · ⹏ Z8 ⓐ ∧ V-VII; Chile
- **tripartita** Ruiz & Pav. · F:Calcéolaire rugueuse 'Gold Bukett' · ⊙ Z9 V-IX; Ecuad., Peru, Chile
- **uniflora** Lam.
- var. **darwinii** (Benth.) Witasek · G:Darwins Pantoffelblume · ⹏ Z8 ⓐ; Arg.: S-Patagon., Tierra del Fuego
- var. **uniflora** · G:Einblütige Pantoffelblume · ⹏ Z8 ⓐ VI-VII; Arg.: Patag., Chile
- **Cultivars:**
- **many cultivars, see Section III**

Caldesia Parl. -f- *Alismataceae* · 4 spp. · E:Parnassus-leaved Water Plantain F:Caldesia; G:Herzlöffel
- **parnassifolia** (Bassi ex L.) Parl. · G:Herzlöffel · ⹏ ⌢ ≈ ⓐ VII-IX ▽; Eur.: F, G, EC-Eur., I, Croatia, E-Eur..; Amur,

China, Manch., Jap., Egypt, NE-Afr., Madag., trop. As., Austr.

Calendula L. -f- *Asteraceae* · 12 spp. · E:Marigold; F:Souci; G:Ringelblume
- **arvensis** L. · E:Field Marigold; G:Acker-Ringelblume · ⊙ Z6 VI-X; Eur.: Ib, Fr, Ital-P, Ba, C-Eur., H, RO, Crim, W-Russ.; TR, Cauc., Iran, Afgh., NW-Afr., Macaron.
- **officinalis** L. · E:Pot Marigold, Ruddles, Scotch Marigold; F:Souci; G:Garten-Ringelblume · ⊙ ⊙ Z6 IX-X ⚥ Ⓝ; orig. ?, nat. in sp., I, Br
- **many cultivars**

Calepina Adans. -f- *Brassicaceae* · 1 sp. · G:Wendich
- **irregularis** (Asso) Thell. · E:Ball Mustard; G:Wendich · ⊙ Z8 V-VI; Eur.: Ib, Fr, Ital-P, Ba, RO, Crim; TR, Levant, Cauc., Iran, C-As., Moroc., Alger., Libya, nat. in C-Eur.

Calibrachoa La Llave & Lex. -f- *Solanaceae* · 24 spp. · G:Zauberglöckchen
- **parviflora** (Juss.) D'Arcy & Wijsman · E:Seaside Petunia
- **Cultivars:**
- **many cultivars**

Calicotome Link -f- *Fabaceae* · 2 spp.
- **spinosa** (L.) Link · E:Thorny Broom · ♄ d Z8 ⓐ; Eur.: Ib, Fr, Ital-P

Caliphruria Herb. -f- *Amaryllidaceae* · 4 spp.
- **subedentata** Baker · ⹏ Z10 ⓜ XII; Col.

Calla L. -f- *Araceae* · 1 sp. · E:Bog Arum, Water Arum; F:Arum aquatique, Calla; G:Schlangenwurz, Sumpfkalla
- **palustris** L. · E:Bog Arum, Water Arum; F:Arum d'eau; G:Schlangenwurz · ⹏ ⌢ Z4 V-VI ⚘ ▽; Eur.: Fr, C-Eur., EC-Eur., Sc, E-Eur.; W-Sib., E-Sib., Amur, Sakhal., Kamchat., N-Jap., Alaska, Can., USA: NE, SE, nat. in BrI

Calliandra Benth. -f- *Mimosaceae* · c. 200 spp. · E:Powder Puff Tree; F:Calliandra; G:Puderquastenstrauch
- **anomala** (Kunth) J.F. Macbr. · ♄ e Z10 ⓜ; Mex.
- **calothyrsus** Meisn. · ♄ e Z10 ⓜ Ⓝ;

C-Am.
- **eriophylla** Benth. · E:Fairy Duster, Mock Mesquite; G:Mexikanischer Puderquastenstrauch · ♀ e Z10 ⓦ; USA: S-Calif., Ariz., New Mex.; N-Mex.
- **fulgens** Hook. f. · ♀ e Z10 ⓦ III; Mex.
- **gracilis** Klotzsch ex Baker · ♀ e Z10 ⓦ; C-Am.
- *houstonii* (L'Hér.) Benth. = Calliandra inermis
- **inermis** (L.) Druce · ♀ e Z10 ⓦ; Mex.
- **portoricensis** (Jacq.) Benth. · ♀ e Z10 ⓦ VI-VII; C-Am., W.Ind.
- **tweedii** Benth. · E:Cunure, Mexican Flamebush; G:Brasilianischer Puderquastenstrauch · ♀ e Z10 ⓦ; Braz.

Callianthemum C.A. Mey. -n- *Ranunculaceae* · 14 spp. · F:Callianthème; G:Jägerblume, Schmuckblume
- **anemonoides** (J. Zahlbr.) Endl. ex Heynh. · G:Anemonen-Schmuckblume · ⚃ △ Z5 IV; Eur.: A; NE-Alp.
- **coriandrifolium** Rchb. · G:Korianderblättrige Schmuckblume · ⚃ △ Z6 VI-VII; Eur.: Ib, F, Ital-P, C-Eur., EC-Eur., Bosn., RO; mts.
- **kernerianum** Freyn ex A. Kern. · ⚃ △ Z6 V-VI; Eur.: I; S-Alp.
- *rutifolium* (L.) C.A. Mey. = Callianthemum coriandrifolium
- *rutifolium* Rchb. = Callianthemum anemonoides

Callicarpa L. -f- *Verbenaceae* · c. 140 spp. · E:Beautyberry; F:Callicarpa; G:Liebesperlenstrauch, Schönfrucht
- **americana** L. · E:American Beautyberry, Mulberry; G:Amerikanische Schönfrucht · ♀ d ⚭ Z7 VI-VII; USA: NE, SE, Fla., Tex; W.Ind.
- **bodinieri** H. Lév.
- var. **bodinieri** · G:Bodiniéres Schönfrucht · ♀ d Z6; W-China, C-China
- var. **giraldii** (Hesse ex Rehder) Rehder · ♀ d ⚭ Z6 VI-VII; W-China, C-China
- **dichotoma** (Lour.) K. Koch · E:Purple Beautyberry; G:Purpur-Schönfrucht · ♀ d ⚭ Z7; Jap., Korea, China, Taiwan
- *giraldii* Hesse ex Rehder = Callicarpa bodinieri var. giraldii
- **japonica** Thunb.
- var. **angusta** Rehder · G:Chinesische Schönfrucht · ♀ d ⚭ Z7 VIII; C-China
- var. *angustifolia* Sav. = Callicarpa dichotoma
- var. **japonica** · E:Japanese Beautyberry; G:Japanische Schönfrucht · ♀ d Z7; Jap.
- **mollis** Siebold & Zucc. · ♀ d Z7; Jap., Korea
- *purpurea* Juss. = Callicarpa dichotoma
- **rubella** Lindl. · ♀ d ⚭ Z9 ⓦ; Ind.: Assam; Burma, China

Calliopsis Rchb. = Coreopsis
- *tinctoria* (Nutt.) DC. = Coreopsis tinctoria var. tinctoria

Callirhoe Nutt. -f- *Malvaceae* · 8 spp. · E:Poppy Mallow; F:Mauve-pavot; G:Mohnmalve
- **digitata** Nutt. · E:Winecup · ☉ ⚃ Z5 VII-IX; USA: Mo., Kans., Ark., Okla., Tex.
- **involucrata** (Torr. & A. Gray) A. Gray · E:Purple Poppy Mallow; G:Purpurne Mohnmalve · ☉ ⚃ Z4 VII-IX; USA: NC, Rocky Mts., SC; Mex.
- **leiocarpa** R.F. Martin · E:Tall Poppy Mallow; G:Hohe Mohnmalve · ☉ ⚃ Z6 VII-IX; USA: Tex., Okla.
- **papaver** (Cav.) A. Gray · E:Woodland Poppy Mallow; G:Wald-Mohnmalve · ☉ ⚃ Z6 VII-IX; USA: SE, Mo., Fla., Tex.
- *pedata* (Torr. & A. Gray) A. Gray = Callirhoe leiocarpa
- *verticillata* (L.) Groenland = Callirhoe involucrata

Callisia Loefl. -f- *Commelinaceae* · 20 spp. · G:Callisie, Schönpolster; F:Callisia
- *elegans* Alexander ex H.E. Moore = Callisia gentlei var. elegans
- **fragrans** (Lindl.) Woodson · E:Basket Plant; G:Duftendes Schönpolster · ⚃ Z10 ⓦ; S-Mex.
- **gentlei** Matuda
- var. **elegans** (Alexander ex H.E. Moore) D.R. Hunt · G:Zierliches Schönpolster · ⚃ ⟟ ⤳ Z10 ⓦ; N-Mex.
- *martensiana* (Kunth) C.B. Clarke = Callisia multiflora
- **monandra** (Sw.) Schult. & Schult. f. · G:Einmänniges Schönpolster · ⚃ ⟟ ⤳ Z10 ⓦ; Trop.
- **multiflora** (M. Martens & Galeotti) Standl. · G:Vielblütiges Schönpolster · ⚃ ⟟ ⤳ Z10 ⓦ; Mex., Guat.
- **navicularis** (Ortgies) D.R. Hunt · G:Kahnförmiges Schönpolster; E:Chain Plant · ⚃ ⤳ Z10 ⓚ; Mex.

dichotoma

– **repens** L. · E:Creeping Inch Plant; F:Bon
Dieu Soleil; G:Kriechendes Schönpolster
· ⁴ ⚥ ⤳ Z9 ⊛; USA: Tex.; W-Ind., trop.
Am.
– *umbellata* Lam. = Callisia monandra
– **warszewicziana** (Kunth & C.D. Bouché)
D.R. Hunt · ⁴ Z10 ⊛; Guat.

Callista Lour. = Dendrobium
– *aggregata* (Roxb.) Brieger = Dendrobium
lindleyi
– *densiflora* (Wall.) Brieger = Dendrobium
densiflorum

Callistemon R. Br. -m- *Myrtaceae* · 35 spp. ·
E:Bottle-Brush Bush; F:Callistemon,
Rince-bouteille; G:Lampenputzerstrauch,
Schönfaden, Zylinderputzer
– **brachyandrus** Lindl. · E:Prickly Bottlebrush; G:Stachliger Zylinderputzer
· ♄ e Z9 ⊛ VIII-IX; Austr.: N.S. Wales,
S-Austr., Victoria
– **citrinus** (Curtis) Stapf · E:Crimson Bottlebrush; G:Kaminroter Zylinderputzer
· ♄ ♄ e Z9 ⊛ VI-VII; Austr.: Queensl.,
N.S.Wales, Victoria
– **glaucus** (Bonpl.) Sweet · E:Albany
Bottlebrush; G:Albany Zylinderputzer · ♄
♄ e Z9 ⊛ VI-VIII; W-Austr.
– *lanceolatus* (Sm.) DC. = Callistemon
citrinus
– **linearis** DC. · E:Narrow-leaved Bottlebrush; G:Schmalblättriger Zylinderputzer
· ♄ e Z8 ⊛; Austr.: Queensl., N.S.Wales
– **macropunctatus** (Dum.-Cours.) Court ·
E:Scarlet Bottlebrush; G:Scharlachroter
Zylinderputzer · ♄ e Z9 ⊛; Austr.:
N.S.Wales, Victoria, S-Austr.
– **pachyphyllus** Cheel · E:Wallum Bottlebrush ; G:Niedriger Zylinderputzer · ♄
e Z9 ⊛; Austr.: Queensl., N.S.Wales
– **pallidus** (Bonpl.) DC. · E:Lemon
Bottlebrush; G:Zitronen-Zylinderputzer
· ♄ e Z9 ⊛; Austr.: Queensl., N.S.Wales,
Victoria, Tasman.
– **phoeniceus** Lindl. · E:Lesser Bottlebrush;
G:Purpurner Zylinderputzer · ♄ e Z9 ⊛;
W-Austr.
– **pinifolius** DC. · E:Pine-leaved Bottlebrush; G:Nadelblättriger Zylinderputzer ·
♄ e Z9 ⊛; Austr.: N.S.Wales
– **rigidus** R. Br. · E:Stiff Bottlebrush;
G:Steifer Zylinderputzer · ♄ e Z9 ⊛;
Austr.: N.S.Wales
– **salignus** (Sm.) Colville ex Sweet ·

E:Willow Bottlebrush; G:Weidenblät-
triger Zylinderputzer · ♄ ♄ e Z8 ⊛ VI-VII;
Austr.: N.S. Wales, S-Austr., Queensl.
– **sieberi** DC. · E:Alpine Bottlebrush;
G:Gelber Zylinderputzer · ♄ e Z8 ⊛;
Austr.: N.S.Wales, Victoria
– *speciosus* (Sims) Sweet = Callistemon
glaucus
– **teretifolius** F. Muell. · E:Green Bottlebrush; G:Grüner Zylinderputzer · ♄ e
Z9 ⊛; S-Austr.
– **viminalis** (Sol. ex Gaertn.) G. Don ·
E:Weeping Bottle Brush; G:Trauer-
Zylinderputzer · ♄ e Z9 ⊛ IV-V; Austr.:
N.S.Wales
– **viridiflorus** (Sims) Sweet · E:Green
Bottlebrush · ♄ e Z9 ⊛; Tasman.
– **Cultivars:**
– **some cultivars**

Callistephus Cass. -m- *Asteraceae* · 1 sp. ·
E:China Aster; F:Reine-marguerite;
G:Sommeraster
– **chinensis** (L.) Nees · E:China Aster;
F:Reine-marguerite; G:Gartenaster,
Madeleine-Aster, Sommeraster · ⊙ ✄
VII-X; China
– **many cultivars**

Callitriche L. -f- *Callitrichaceae* · 17 spp. ·
E:Water Starwort; F:Callitriche, Etoile
d'eau; G:Wasserstern
– *autumnalis* L. = Callitriche hermaphro-
ditica
– **brutia** Petagna · E:Pedunculate Water
Starwort; G:Stielfrüchtiger Wasserstern ·
⁴ ≈ V-IX; Eur.: Sc, BrI, Fr, Ib, Ital-P
– **cophocarpa** Sendtn. · G:Stumpfkantiger
Wasserstern · ⁴ ≈ V-X; Eur.* exc. Ib
– **hamulata** Kütz. ex W.D.J. Koch ·
E:Narrowleaf Water Starwort; G:Haken-
Wasserstern · ⁴ ≈ IV-VI; Eur.* exc. Ib
– **hermaphroditica** L. · E:Autumn Water
Starwort; G:Herbst-Wasserstern · ⁴ ≈
Z6 VI-IX; Eur.: BrI, Sc, NL, G, PL, E-Eur.;
W-Sib., E-Sib., Amur, Sakhal., Kamchat.,
C-As., Alaska, Can., USA* exc. SC;
Greenl., Bol.
– *intermedia* auct. non Hoffm. = Callitriche
hamulata
– subsp. *hamulata* Kütz. ex W.D.J. Koch =
Callitriche hamulata
– **obtusangula** Le Gall · E:Blunt-fruited
Water Starwort; G:Nussfrüchtiger
Wasserstern · ⁴ ≈ V-X; Eur.: Ib, Fr,

Ital-P, Ba, BrI, C-Eur.; NW-Afr.
- **palustris** L. · E:Vernal Water Starwort;
G:Sumpf-Wasserstern · ⌘ ≋ ⓚ IV-X;
Eur.*, Cauc., W-Sib., E-Sib., Amur,
Sakhal., Kamchat., C-As., Him., Jap.,
Alaska, Can.
- subsp. *hamulata* Kütz. ex W.D.J. Koch =
Callitriche hamulata
- subsp. *stagnalis* (Scop.) Schinz & Thell. =
Callitriche stagnalis
- **platycarpa** Kütz. · G:Flachfrüchtiger
Wasserstern · ⌘ ≋ V-X; Eur.: Sc, BrI,
Fr, sp., C-Eur., EC-Eur., ? RO
- **stagnalis** Scop. · E:Water Starwort;
G:Teich-Wasserstern · ⌘ ≋ ⓚ V-X;
Eur.*, TR, Cauc., Ind., C-China, NW-Afr.,
E-Afr.
- *verna* L. = Callitriche palustris
- *vernalis* Kütz. ex W.D.J. Koch = Cal-
litriche palustris

Callitris Vent. -f- *Cupressaceae* ·
15 spp. · E:Cypress-Pine; F:Pin-cyprès;
G:Schmuckzypresse, Zypressenkiefer
- *arenosa* A. Cunn. ex R.T. Baker & H.G.
Sm. = Callitris columellaris
- *articulata* (Vahl) Asch. & Graebn. =
Tetraclinis articulata
- *calcarata* A. Cunn. ex Mirb. = Callitris
endlicheri
- **columellaris** F. Muell. · E:White Cypress
Pine; G:Weiße Schmuckzypresse · ♄ e
Z10 ⓚ; W-Austr.
- *cupressiformis* D. Don ex Loudon =
Callitris rhomboidea
- **endlicheri** (Parl.) F.M. Bailey · E:Red
Cypress; G:Rote Schmuckzypresse Pine ·
♄ e Z9 ⓚ ⓝ; Austr.: Queensl., N.S.Wales,
Victoria
- *glauca* R. Br. = Callitris columellaris
- **preissii** (A. Cunn. ex Parl.) F.M. Bailey ·
E:Rottnest Island Pine; G:Harzige Schmuckzypresse · ♄ e Z10 ⓚ ⓝ; W-Austr.
- *quadrivalvis* Vent. = Tetraclinis articulata
- **rhomboidea** R. Br. ex Rich. · E:Oyster
Bay Cypress Pine, Port Jackson Pine;
G:Oyster-Bay-Schmuckzypresse · ♄ e Z9
ⓚ ⓝ; Austr.: Queensl., N.S.Wales
- *robusta* A. Cunn. ex Parl. = Callitris
preissii
- **roei** (Endl.) F. Muell. · E:Roe's Cypress
Pine; G:Leisten-Schmuckzypresse · ♄ e
Z10 ⓚ; Austr.: N.S.Wales

Callopsis Engl. -f- *Araceae* · 1 sp.

- **volkensii** Engl. · ⌘ ⓦ I-XII; Tanzania

Calluna Salisb. -f- *Ericaceae* · 1 sp. ·
E:Heather; F:Bruyère à balai, Callune;
G:Besenheide, Heidekraut
- **vulgaris** (L.) Hull · E:Ling, Scots
Heather; F:Bruyère commune, Callune;
G:Besenheide, Heidekraut · ♄ ♄ e Z6 IX-X
⚥ ⓝ; Eur.*, N-TR, Azor., Moroc., nat. in
N-Am.
- **many cultivars**

Calocarpum Pierre = Pouteria
- *sapota* (Jacq.) Merr. = Pouteria sapota

Calocedrus Kurz -f- *Cupressaceae* · 3 spp. ·
F:Cèdre à encens; G:Flusszeder, Rauchzy-
presse, Weihrauchzeder
- **decurrens** (Torr.) Florin · E:Incense
Cedar; G:Kalifornische Flusszeder · ♄ e
Z7 IV ⓝ; USA: Oreg., Calif., Nev.; Baja
Calif.

Calocephalus R. Br. -m- *Asteraceae* · 11 sp.
- *brownii* Cass. = Leucophyta brownii

Calochortus Pursh -m- *Liliaceae* · 73 spp. ·
E:Globe Tulip, Mariposa Tulip; F:Tulipe
de la Prairie; G:Mormonentulpe
- **albus** (Benth.) Douglas ex Benth. ·
E:Fairy Lantern, Globe Lily; G:Weiße
Mormonentulpe · ⌘ Z6 VI-VIII; Calif.
- **amabilis** Purdy · E:Golden Fairy Lantern;
G:Goldene Mormonentulpe · ⌘ Z6 VI-VII;
Calif.
- **caeruleus** (Kellogg) S. Watson ·
E:Beavertail Grass; G:Hellblaue Mormon-
entulpe · ⌘ Z6 VII; Calif.
- **macrocarpus** Douglas · E:Sagebrush
Mariposa Lily · ⌘ Z6 VIII; B.C., USA: NW,
Rocky Mts., Calif.; N-Mex.
- **splendens** Douglas ex Benth. ·
E:Splendid Mariposa Lily; G:Schöne
Mormonentulpe · ⌘ Z6 VIII; Calif., Baja
Calif.
- **superbus** Purdy ex J.T. Howell ·
E:Superb Mariposa Lily; G:Getüpfelte
Mormonentulpe · ⌘ Z6 VI-VII; Calif.
- **venustus** Douglas ex Benth. · E:White
Mariposa Lily; G:Schmetterlings-
Mormonentulpe · ⌘ Z6 VI-VII; Calif.
- var. *vestae* (Purdy) Wilson = Calochortus
vestae
- **vestae** (Purdy) Purdy · E:
Coast Range Mariposa Lily;

G:Mischwald-Mormonentulpe · ⍓ Z6
VI-VII; Calif.

Calodendrum Thunb. -n- *Rutaceae* · 1 sp. ·
E:Cape Chestnut; F:Châtaignier du Cap;
G:Kapkastanie
– **capense** (L. f.) Thunb. · E:Cape Chestnut; G:Kapkastanie · ♄ e Z9 ⒶL; S-Afr.

Calomeria Vent. -f- *Asteraceae* · 1 sp.
– **amaranthoides** Vent. · E:Incense Plant,
Plume Bush; G:Moschus-Federbusch · ☉
D Z9 ⒶL VI-XI; Austr.: N.S.Wales, Victoria

Calophaca Fisch. ex DC. -f- *Fabaceae* ·
5 spp. · G:Schönhülse
– **grandiflora** Regel · G:Großblütige
Schönhülse · ♄ d ⤳ Z6 VI-VII; C-As.
– **wolgarica** (L. f.) Fisch. · G:Wolga-
Schönhülse · ♄ d Z5 VI-VII; Eur.: Russ.

Calophyllum L. -n- *Clusiaceae* · 187 spp.
– *antillanum* Britton = Calophyllum
Braziliense
– **Braziliense** Cambess. · E:Dame Marie,
Santa Maria; F:Bois Marie; G:Marien-
lorbeer · ♄ e Z10 ⓌL ⚔ Ⓝ; W.Ind., Mex.,
C-Am., n S-Am.
– *calaba* Jacq. = Calophyllum Braziliense
– **inophyllum** L. · E:Alexandrian Laurel,
Indian Laurel; G:Indischer Lorbeer · ♄ e
Z10 ⓌL ⚔ Ⓝ; E-Afr., S-Ind., Sri Lanka,
Indochina, Malay. Arch., Austr.: N.Terr.,
Queensl.; Polyn.
– *jacquinii* Fawc. & Rendle = Calophyllum
Braziliense

Calopogonium Desv. -n- *Fabaceae* · 8 spp.
– **mucunoides** Desv. · E:Calopo · ⍓ ⑂ ⤳
ⓌL Ⓝ; trop. Am.

Calothamnus Labill. -m- *Myrtaceae* ·
24 spp.
– **asper** Turcz. · ♄ e Z9 ⒶL; W-Austr.
– **longissimus** F. Muell. · ♄ e Z9 ⒶL;
W-Austr.
– **quadrifidus** R. Br. · ♄ e Z9 ⒶL; W-Austr.
– **sanguineus** Labill. · ♄ e Z9 ⒶL; W-Austr.
– **villosus** R. Br. · ♄ e Z9 ⒶL; W-Austr.

Calotropis R. Br. -f- *Asclepiadaceae* ·
3 spp. · F:Calotropis, Pomme de Sodome;
G:Kielkrone
– **gigantea** (L.) Dryand. · E:Crownplant,
Giant Milkweed; G:Mudarpflanze · ♄ e

Z10 ⓌL ⚔ Ⓝ; Ind., Sri Lanka, S-China,
Burma, Malay. Arch.
– **procera** (Aiton) Dryand. · E:Apple of
Sodom, Giant Milkweed; G:Oscher-
strauch · ♄ e Z9 ⒶL ⚔ Ⓝ; W-Afr., C-Afr.,
E-Afr., Arab., Iran, Pakist., Ind.

Caltha L. -f- *Ranunculaceae* · 10 spp. ·
E:Marsh Marigold; F:Populage;
G:Dotterblume
– **leptosepala** DC. · E:White Marsh
Marigold · ⍓ ⌇ Z3 V; Alaska, Can.: W;
USA: NW, Rocky Mts., SW
– **natans** Pall. · E:Floating Marsh Marigold;
F:Populage nageant; G:Schwimmende
Dotterblume · ⍓ ⌇ ≈ Z2; N-As.,
Alaska, Can., Minn., Wisc.
– **palustris** L. · E:Kingcup, Marsh Marigold;
G:Sumpf-Dotterblume
– var. **alba** (Cambess.) Hook. f. & Thom-
son · G:Weiße Sumpf-Dotterblume · ⍓
⌇ ; Kashmir
– var. *minor* (Mill.) DC. = Caltha palustris
var. palustris
– var. **palustris** · F:Populage des marais;
G:Gewöhnliche Sumpf-Dotterblume ·
⍓ ⌇ Z3 IV-V ⚥ ⚔; Eur.*, TR, Cauc.,
W-Sib., E-Sib., Amur, Sakhal., Kamchat.,
C-As., Mong., China, Jap. , Alaska, Can.,
USA: NE, NCE, NC, SE, NW

Calvoa Hook. f. -f- *Melastomataceae* ·
18 spp.
– **orientalis** Taub. · ⍓ ⓌL; trop. Afr.
– *sessiliflora* Cogn. ex De Wild. & T.
Durand = Calvoa orientalis

Calycanthus L. -m- *Calycanthaceae* ·
6 spp. · E:Spicebush; F:Calycanthus;
G:Gewürzstrauch, Nelkenpfeffer
– **fertilis** Walter
– var. **fertilis** · E:Allspice; G:Fruchtbarer
Gewürzstrauch, Nelkenpfeffer · ♄ d Z6;
USA: NE, SE
– var. **laevigatus** (Willd.) Bean · ♄ d Z6
V-VII; USA: NE, Ohio, SE
– **floridus** L. · E:Carolina Allspice; F:Arbre
aux anémones; G:Echter Gewürzstrauch ·
♄ d D Z6 V-VII; USA: Va., W.Va., SE, Fla.
– var. *laevigatus* (Willd.) Torr. & A. Gray =
Calycanthus fertilis var. laevigatus
– *glaucus* Willd. = Calycanthus floridus
– *laevigatus* Willd. = Calycanthus fertilis
var. laevigatus
– **occidentalis** Hook. & Arn. · E:California

Allspice, Spice Bush; G:Westlicher
Gewürzstrauch · ♄ d D Z6 VI-VIII; USA:
Calif.
- *sterilis* Walter = Calycanthus floridus

Calypso Salisb. -f- *Orchidaceae* · 1 sp. ·
E:Calypso; F:Calypso; G:Kappenständel
- **bulbosa** (L.) Oakes · E:Calypso, Fairy
Slipper Orchid; G:Gewöhnlicher
Kappenständel · ⹋ Z5 IV-V ▽ ✳; Alaska,
Can., USA: NE, NCE, NC, Rocky Mts.,
SW, NW, Calif.

Calyptrogyne H. Wendl. -f- *Arecaceae* ·
9 spp.
- **ghiesbreghtiana** (Linden & H. Wendl.)
H. Wendl. · ♄ e ⊕; Mex., Guat., Hond.

Calystegia R. Br. -f- *Convolvulaceae* · c.
25 spp. · E:Bindweed; F:Liseron des haies;
G:Zaunwinde
- **dahurica** (Herb.) Sweet · ⹋ ↯ VII-VIII;
C-As.
- **hederacea** Wall. · E:Japanese False
Bindweed · ⹋ Z5 VI-IX; Jap., Korea,
N-China
- *pellita* (Ledeb.) G. Don = Calystegia
hederacea
- **pulchra** Brummitt & Heywood ·
G:Schöne Zaunwinde · ⹋ ↯ Z5 VI-X; ?
NE-As., nat. in N-Eur., C-Eur.
- **sepium** (L.) R. Br. · E:Bindweed, Granny
Pop Out Of Bed; G:Gewöhnliche Zaun-
winde · ⹋ ↯ Z4 VI-IX ↯ ⓝ; Eur.*, TR,
Levant, Cauc., Iran, W-Sib., E-Sib., Amur,
Mong., Him., China, Jap., NW-Afr.,
N-Am., S-Am., Austr., NZ
- **silvatica** (Kit.) Griseb. · E:Large
Bindweed; G:Wald-Zaunwinde · ⹋ Z7
VI-IX; Eur.: Ib, Fr, Ital-P, Ba, RO, Crim;
TR, Syr., Cauc., Iran, NW-Afr., nat. in
BrI, D
- **soldanella** (L.) R. Br. ex Roem. &
Schult. · E:Sea Bindweed; G:Strand-
Zaunwinde · ⹋ VII-VIII ▽; Eur.* exc.
EC-Eur.; TR, Syr., Sakhal., Jap., N-China,
Korea, NW-Afr., Libya, USA: NW, Calif.;
Arg., Chile SE-Austr., NZ; coasts

Camassia Lindl. -f- *Hyacinthaceae* · 6 spp. ·
E:Camass, Quamash; F:Camassia, Lis de
la prairie; G:Camassie, Prärielilie
- **cusickii** S. Watson · E:Cusick's Camass;
G:Cusicks Prärielilie · ♄ Z6 IV-V; USA:
Oreg.

- *esculenta* (Nutt.) Lindl. = Camassia
quamash subsp. quamash
- *fraseri* Torr. = Camassia scilloides
- **leichtlinii** (Baker) S. Watson ·
E:Leichtlin's Camass; G:Leichtlins
Prärielilie · ⹋ Z6; Can.: B.C., USA: NW,
Calif.
- **quamash** (Pursh) Greene
- subsp. **azurea** (A. Heller) Gould Z6;
USA: Wash.
- subsp. **quamash** · E:Quamash; G:Essbare
Prärielilie · ⹋ Z5 V-VI; Can.; W; USA:
NW, Rocky Mts., Calif.
- **scilloides** (Raf.) Cory · E:Wild Hyacinth;
G:Östliche Prärielilie · ⹋ Z7 ∧ IV-V;
Can.: Ont.; USA: NE, NCE, Kans., SC, SE

Camelina Crantz -f- *Brassicaceae* ·
10 spp. · E:Gold of Pleasure; F:Caméline;
G:Leindotter
- **alyssum** (Mill.) Thell. · G:Gezähnter
Leindotter · ⊙ Z7 V-VIII; Eur.* exc. BrI
- **microcarpa** Andrz. · E:Small-seed False
Flax; G:Kleinfrüchtiger Leindotter · ⊙ Z7
V-VII; Eur.* exc. Ib; Cauc., W-Sib., E-Sib.,
C-As.
- **rumelica** Velen. · G:Balkanischer Leindotter · ⊙ Z7 V-VII; Eur.: Ba; TR, Cyprus,
Syr., Cauc., Iran, Afgh., C-As., Egypt, nat.
in Ib, Fr, Ital-P, C-Eur., EC-Eur.
- **sativa** (L.) Crantz
- var. **sativa** · E:Big-seed False Flax, Gold
of Pleasure; G:Saat-Leindotter · ⊙ Z7
V-VII ⓝ; Eur.*, TR
- var. **zingeri** Mirek · G:Behaarter Saat-
Leindotter · ⊙ Z7 V-VII; D +

Camellia L. -f- *Theaceae* · c. 200 spp. ·
E:Camellia; F:Camélia, Théier; G:Kame-
lie, Teestrauch
- **chrysantha** (Hu) Tuyama · ♄ e Z8 ⊕;
S-China
- **cuspidata** (Kochs) C.H. Wright ex H.J.
Veitch · ♄ e Z7 III-IV; China
- **granthamiana** Sealy · ♄ e Z8 ⊕; Hong
Kong
- **hongkongensis** Seem. · ♄ e Z8 ⊕ I-II;
China: Hong Kong
- **japonica** L.
- subsp. **japonica** · E:Common Camellia;
F:Camélia du Japon; G:Japanische
Kamelie · ♄ ♄ e Z8 ⊕ I-IV ⓝ; Jap., Korea,
Ryukyu-Is., Taiwan
- **many cultivars**
- × **maliflora** Lindl. · ♄ ♄ e ⊕ I-III; China

– **oleifera** C. Abel · E:Tea Oil Plant; G:Öl-Teestrauch · ♄ e Z8 Ⓚ X-XII Ⓝ; China: Sichuan, Hunan, Kiangsu
– **pitardii** Cohen-Stuart · ♄ ♄ e Z8 Ⓚ; W-China
– **reticulata** Lindl. · ♄ e Z8 Ⓚ II-III; China
– **rosiflora** Hook. · ♄ e Z8 Ⓚ; China
– **salicifolia** Champ. ex Benth. · ♄ e Z8 Ⓚ XI-II; China, Taiwan
– **saluenensis** Stapf ex Bean · ♄ e Z7 IX-III; Yunnan
– **sasanqua** Thunb. · E:Sasquana Camellia; G:Sasanqua-Kamelie · ♄ ♄ e D Z8 Ⓚ XI-III Ⓝ; China, Jap., Riukiu-Is., Vietn., Laos
– **some cultivars**
– **sinensis** (L.) Kuntze · G:Teestrauch; E:Tea Plant
– var. **assamica** (Mast.) Kitam. · E:Assam Tea; G:Assam-Teestrauch · ♄ ♄ e Z8 Ⓚ Ⓝ; Burma
– var. **sinensis** · E:China Tea; G:China-Teestrauch · ♄ ♄ e Z8 Ⓚ ⚕ Ⓝ; Ind.: Assam; Burma, China
– *thea* Link = Camellia sinensis var. sinensis
– *theifera* Griff. = Camellia sinensis var. sinensis
– × **williamsii** W.W. Sm. (*C. japonica* × *C. saluenensis*) · ♄ e Z8 Ⓚ; cult.
– **some cultivars**
– **Cultivars:**
– **many cultivars**

Campanula L. -f- *Campanulaceae* · c. 300 spp. · E:Bellflower; F:Campanule; G:Glockenblume
– **alliariifolia** Willd. · E:Ivory Bells; F:Campanule à feuilles d'ail; G:Knoblauchrauken-Glockenblume, Lauchblättrige Glockenblume · ♃ Z3 VI-VII; TR, Cauc.
– **alpestris** All. · E:Large-flowered Bellflower · ♃ △ Z5 VI-VII; Eur.: F, I; SW-Alp.
– **alpina** Jacq. · E:Alpine Bellflower; G:Alpen-Glockenblume · ⊙ ♃ △ Z4 VII-VIII; Eur.: C-Eur., EC-Eur., Ba, RO, W-Russ.; E-Alp., Carp., Balkan
– **arvatica** Lag. · ♃ Z7 Ⓐ VII; NW-Sp.
– **aucheri** A. DC. · ♃ △ Z5 VI; E-Cauc., Iran
– **barbata** L. · E:Bearded Bellflower; G:Bärtige Glockenblume · ⊙ ♃ △ Z6 VI-VII; Eur.: F, I, C-Eur., EC-Eur., Slove., Norw.; Alp., E-Sudeten, Norw.
– **baumgartenii** Becker · G:Lanzettblättrige Glockenblume · ♃ Z6 VIII; Eur.: E-F, SW-D
– **beckiana** Hayek · G:Becks Glockenblume · ♃ VI-IX; Eur.: A, Slove.; E-Alp.
– **bellidifolia** Adams · ♃ △ Z5 V-VI; Cauc.
– **bertolae** Colla · G:Bertols Glockenblume · ♃ VI-VIII; Eur.: I; SW-Alp., ? Apenn.
– **betulifolia** K. Koch · F:Campanule à feuilles de bouleau; G:Birkenblättrige Glockenblume · ♃; TR, Cauc.
– **bononiensis** L. · G:Bologneser Glockenblume · ♃ Z3 VII-IX ▽; Eur.: Fr, Ital-P, C-Eur., EC-Eur., Ba, E-Eur.; TR, Cauc., Iran, W-Sib., C-As.
– *carnica* Schiede ex Mert. & W.D.J. Koch = Campanula linifolia
– **carpatica** Jacq. · E:Carpathian Harebell, Tussock Bellflower; G:Karpaten-Glockenblume
– **some cultivars**
– var. **carpatica** · F:Campanule des Carpathes · ♃ △ Z3 VI-VII; Eur.: Slova., PL, RO, W-Russ.; Carp., nat. in H
– var. **turbinata** (Schott, Nyman & Kotschy) G. Nicholson · F:Campanule des Carpathes en toupie · ♃ △ Z3 V-VI; Carp.
– **many cultivars**
– **cenisia** L. · E:Mount Cenis Bellflower; G:Mont-Cenis-Glockenblume · ♃ △ Z5 VII-VIII; Eur.: F, I, Sw, A; Alp.
– **cervicaria** L. · G:Borstige Glockenblume · ⊙ Z6 VI-VIII ▽; Eur.* exc. BrI, ? Ib; W-Sib., E-Sib.
– **cespitosa** Scop. · G:Rasen-Glockenblume · ♃ △ VIII-IX; Eur.: I, A, Slove.; Alp.
– **cochleariifolia** Lam. · E:Fairies' Thimbles; F:Campanule élégante, Campanule fluette; G:Zwerg-Glockenblume · ♃ △ Z6 VI-VII; Eur.* exc. BrI, Sc
– **many cultivars**
– **collina** M. Bieb. · G:Kaukasus-Hügel-Glockenblume · ♃ △ Z5 VI-VII; TR, Cauc.
– **elatines** L. · E:Adriatic Bellflower; G:Adriatische Glockenblume · ♃ △ Z7 ∧ VI-VII; I (Piemont)
– **erinus** L. · ⊙; Eur.: Ib, F, Ital-P, Ba, Crim; TR, N-Iraq, Cauc., Iran, Moroc.
– **excisa** Schleich. ex Murith · E:Perforate Bellflower; G:Ausgeschnittene Glockenblume · ♃ ⇝ △ Ⓐ VII; Eur.: F, I, Sw; Alp.
– **fenestrellata** Feer
– subsp. **fenestrellata** · ♃ △ Z7 ∧ VI-VII;

Eur.: Croatia, AL
- subsp. **istriaca** (Feer) Fed. · ⟁ Z7; Croatia
- *finitima* Fomin = Campanula betulifolia
- **formanekiana** Degen & Dörfl. · ☉ Z7; GR, Maced.
- **fragilis** Cirillo · ⟁ ⚡ Z8 ⌂ VI-VII; Eur.: I
- **garganica** Ten. · F:Campanule du Gargano · ⟁ △ Z7 ∧ VI-VIII; Eur.: I (Monte Gargano), GR (Kephallinia) ? AL
- subsp. *fenestrellata* (Feer) Hayek = Campanula fenestrellata subsp. fenestrellata
- **gentilis** Kovanda · G:Fremde Glockenblume · ⟁ VI-VIII; Eur.: SE-G, CZ
- **glomerata** L. · E:Clustered Bellflower; F:Campanule agglomérée; G:Knäuel-Glockenblume · ⟁ Z2 VI-VIII; Eur.*, W-Sib., E-Sib., C-As.
- some cultivars
- *graminifolia* L. = Edraianthus graminifolius
- *grandiflora* Lam. = Campanula medium
- **grossekii** Heuff. · G:Serbische Glockenblume · ⟁ Z6; Serb., BG, RO
- × **haylodgensis** hort. (*C. carpatica* × *C. cochleariifolia*) · F:Campanule élégante · ⟁ Z5; cult.
- **isophylla** Moretti · E:Italian Bellflower, Star of Bethlehem; G:Stern-Glockenblume · ⟁ ⚡ Z8 ⌂ VII-IX; Eur.: I (Liguria: Savona)
- *jacquinii* (Sieber) A. DC. = Trachelium jacquinii subsp. jacquinii
- **kemulariae** Fomin · ⟁ Z4; Cauc.
- **kolenatiana** C.A. Mey. ex Rupr. · ☉ ⟁ △ Z5 VI-VII; Cauc.
- **laciniata** L. · ⟁ Z8 ⌂ VI; S-GR, Crete
- **lactiflora** M. Bieb. · E:Milky Bellflower; G:Riesen-Dolden-Glockenblume · ⟁ Z5 VI-VII; Cauc., TR, nat. in BrI
- **lanata** Friv. · ☉ △ Z7 VI-VII ▽; Eur.: S-Ba
- **latifolia** L. · G:Wald-Glockenblume
- var. **latifolia** · E:Greater Bellflower; G:Breitblättrige Wald-Glockenblume · ⟁ Z3 VI-VII ▽; Eur.*, Cauc., TR, W-Sib., C-As., W-Him.
- var. **macrantha** (Fisch. ex Hornem.) Erhardt, Götz & Seybold Z3
- *latiloba* A. DC. = Campanula persicifolia subsp. sessiliflora
- *liliifolia* L. = Adenophora liliifolia
- **linifolia** Scop. · E:Flax-leaved Bellflower; G:Karnische Glockenblume · ⟁ Z5 VI-VIII; Eur.: I, A, Slove., Croatia; S-Alp.

- **longestyla** Fomin · ☉ Z6 VI-VII; Cauc.
- *macrantha* Fisch. ex Hornem. = Campanula latifolia var. macrantha
- **macrostyla** Boiss. & Heldr. · ☉ Z7 VII; TR
- **medium** L. · E:Canterbury Bells, Cup and Saucer Plant; F:Campanule carillon; G:Marien-Glockenblume · ☉ ⋈ Z8 ∧ VI-VII; Eur.: SE-F, I, nat. in BrI, C-Eur., sp., H, RO
- some cultivars
- *michauxioides* Boiss. = Asyneuma michauxioides
- **mirabilis** Albov · ☉ Z5 VI-VII; W-Cauc.
- **moesiaca** Velen. · ☉ Z6 VI-VII; Eur.: Bosn., YU, AL, BG
- **moravica** (Spitzn.) Kovanda · G:Mährische Glockenblume · ⟁ VI-IX; Eur.: A, EC-Eur., W-Ba, RO
- **ochroleuca** (Kem.-Nath.) Kem.-Nath. · ⟁ Z6; Cauc.
- **orphanidea** Boiss. · ☉ △ Z7 ∧ VI-VII; NE-GR, S-BG
- **patula** L. · G:Wiesen-Glockenblume
- subsp. *abietina* (Griseb.) Simonk. · G:Späte Wiesen-Glockenblume · ⟁ △ Z6 VI-VIII; Carp., N-Balkan
- subsp. **patula** · E:Spreading Bellflower; G:Gewöhnliche Wiesen-Glockenblume · ☉ Z6 V-VII; Eur.*, W-Sib.
- **persicifolia** L. · E:Peach Leaved Bellflower, Peach-bells, Willow Bell; G:Pfirsichblättrige Glockenblume
- some cultivars
- subsp. **persicifolia** · F:Campanule à feuilles de pêcher; G:Gewöhnliche Pfirsichblättrige Glockenblume · ⟁ Z3 VI-IX; Eur.* exc. BrI; Cauc., W-Sib., nat. in BrI
- subsp. **sessiliflora** (K. Koch) Velen. · G:Große Pfirsichblättrige Glockenblume · ⟁ ⋈ Z3 VI-VII; Eur.: Ba
- some cultivars
- **piperi** Howell · ⟁ Z7; USA: Wash.
- **portenschlagiana** Schult. · E:Dalmatian Bellflower, Wall Harebell; F:Campanule de Dalmati; G:Dalmatiner Glockenblume e · ⟁ △ Z4 VI-VIII; Eur.: Croatia, Bosn.
- **poscharskyana** Degen · E:Trailing Bellflower; G:Hängepolster-Glockenblume · ⟁ △ Z3 VI-IX; Eur.: Croatia
- some cultivars
- **praesignis** Beck · G:Auffällige Glockenblume · ⟁ VI-IX; Eur.: A; NE-Alp.
- **primulifolia** Brot. · ⟁ Z8 VI-VII; P,

SW-Sp.

– × **pseudoraineri** hort. (*C. carpatica var. turbinata* × *C. raineri*) · ♃ Z4; cult.

– **pulla** L. · E:Solitary Harebell; G:Dunkle Glockenblume · ♃ △ Z6 VI-VIII; Eur.: A; NE-Alp.

– × **pulloides** hort. (*C. carpatica var. turbinata* × *C. pulla*) · ♃ Z6; cult.

– **punctata** Lam. · E:Spotted Bellflower; G:Gewöhnliche Punktierte Glockenblume · ♃ △ Z6 VI-VII; Jap., Korea, NW-China, E-Sib.

– *pusilla* Haenke = Campanula cochleari-ifolia

– **pyramidalis** L. · E:Chimney Bellflower; G:Pyramiden-Glockenblume · ♃ Z8 ⌂ ⌷ VI-VIII; Eur.: Slove., Croatia, Bosn., Montenegro

– **raddeana** Trautv. · ♃ △ Z6 VI-VII; Cauc.

– **raineri** Perp. · ♃ Z6; I; SE-Alp.

– **rapunculoides** L. · E:Creeping Bell-flower; F:Campanule fausse raiponce; G:Acker-Glockenblume · ♃ Z3 VI-IX; Eur.* exc. BrI; TR, Cauc., Iran, C-As., W-Sib., nat. in BrI, N-Am.

– **rapunculus** L. · E:Rampion, Rampion Bellflower; G:Rapunzel-Glockenblume · ⊙ VI Ⓝ; Eur.* exc. BrI, Sc; Cauc.; nat. in BrI, Sc

– **rhomboidalis** L. · E:Broad-leaved Hare-bell; G:Rautenblättrige Glockenblume · ♃ Z5 VI-VII; Eur.: F, I, Sw; Alp., Jura, nat. in B, NL, A, D

– **rotundifolia** L. · E:Harebell, Scottish Bluebell; F:Campanule à feuilles rondes; G:Rundblättrige Glockenblume · ♃ Z3 X; Eur.*, W-Sib., E-Sib.

– **rupestris** Sibth. & Sm. · ⊙ Z9 ⌂ VI-VII; C-GR

– **sarmatica** Ker-Gawl. · F:Campanule de Sarmatie · ♃ Z5 VI-VII; Cauc.

– **saxifraga** M. Bieb. · ♃ △ Z4 VI-VII; Cauc.

– **scheuchzeri** Vill. · G:Scheuchzers Glockenblume · ♃ Z5 VII-VIII; Eur.: Ib, Fr, Ital-P, C-Eur, .EC-Eur., Ba, RO.; mts.

– *sessiliflora* K. Koch = Campanula persicifolia subsp. sessiliflora

– **sibirica** L. · G:Sibirische Glockenblume · ⊙ Z6 VI-VIII; Eur.: I, C-Eur., EC-Eur., Ba, E-Eur.; W-Sib., E-Sib.

– **speciosa** Pourr. · E:Pyrenean Bellflower; G:Pyrenäen-Glockenblume · ♃ ⌂ VI-VII; Eur.: sp., F; Pyr., Corbières, Cevénnes

– **spicata** L. · E:Spiked Bellflower; G:Ährige Glockenblume · ⊙ △ V-VII;

Eur.: F, I, Sw, A, Slove., Croatia, Montenegro; mts.

– × **stansfieldii** hort. (*C. carpatica var. turbinata* × *C. waldsteiniana*) · ♃ △ Z5 VII-VIII; cult.

– **takesimana** Nakai · E:Korean Bellflower; G:Korea-Glockenblume · ♃ Z7; Korea

– **thyrsoides**

– subsp. **thyrsoides** · E:Yellow Bellflower; G:Gewöhnliche Strauße-Glockenblume · ⊙ △ Z5 VII-VIII ▽; Eur.: F, I, C-Eur., Ba; Alp., Jura, Balkan

– **tommasiniana** W.D.J. Koch ex F.W. Schultz · ♃ △ Z6 VI-VII; Eur.: Croatia (Mala Ucka)

– **trachelium** L. · E:Bats in the Belfry, Nettle-Leaved Bellflower; F:Campanule gantelée; G:Nesselblättrige Glocken-blume · ♃ Z3 VII-VIII; Eur.*, TR, Syr., N-Iran, W-Sib., NW-Afr.

– **tridentata** Schreb. · ♃ △ Z4 IV-V; TR, Cauc.

– *turbinata* Schott, Nyman & Kotschy = Campanula carpatica var. turbinata

– × **vanhouttei** Carrière (*C. latifolia* × *C. punctata* var. *punctata* × ?) · ♃ Z4 VI-VII; cult.

– **versicolor** Andrews · ♃ Z8 ∧ VII-IX; Eur.: S-I, Ba

– *vidalii* H.C. Watson = Azorina vidalii

– **waldsteiniana** Schult. · ♃ △ Z6 VI-VII; Croatia

– **witasekiana** Vierh. · E:Paniculate Bellflower; G:Witasek-Glockenblume · ♃ VII-IX; Eur.: A, I, Slove., Bosn., BG; E-Alp., Balkan

– × **wockei** Sünd. (*C. pulla* × *C. waldsteiniana*) · ♃ △ Z5 VII; cult.

– **zoysii** Wulfen · E:Crimped Bellflower; G:Nickende Glockenblume, Zois-Glockenblume · ♃ △ Z6 VII-VIII; Eur.: I, A, Slove.; SE-Alp.

– **Cultivars:**

– **some cultivars**

Campe Dulac = Barbarea

– *barbarea* (L.) W. Wight ex Piper = Barbarea vulgaris

Campelia Rich. = Tradescantia

– *zanonia* (L.) Humb., Bonpl. & Kunth = Tradescantia zanonia

Camphorosma L. -f- *Chenopodiaceae* · 11 sp. · F:Camphorine; G:Kampferkraut

– **annua** Pall. · G:Kampferkraut · ⊙ VIII-IX;
Eur.: A, EC-Eur., Ba, E-Eur.

Campomanesia Ruiz & Pav. -f- *Myrtaceae* ·
30 (-80) spp.
– **lineatifolia** Ruiz & Pav. · ♄ ⓜ Ⓝ; Col.,
Ecuad., Peru, Bol., NW-Braz.

Campsidium Seem. -n- *Bignoniaceae* · 1 sp.
– *chilense* Reissek & Seem. = Campsidium
valdivianum
– **filicifolium** Van Geert = Pandorea
pandorea
– **valdivianum** (Phil.) Skottsb. · ♄ e ⚥ Z10
ⓐ; Chile

Campsis Lour. -f- *Bignoniaceae* · 2 spp. ·
E:Trumpet Creeper; F:Bignone de Chine;
G:Trompetenblume, Trompetenwinde
– *chinensis* (Lam.) Voss = Campsis
grandiflora
– **grandiflora** (Thunb.) K. Schum. ·
E:Campsis, Chinese Trumpet Vine;
G:Chinesische Trompetenwinde · ♄ d ⚥
Z7-8 ⓐ VIII-IX; China
– × *hybrida* Zabel = Campsis × tagliabuana
– **radicans** (L.) Seem. ex Bureau ·
E:Trumpet Creeper, Trumpet Honeysuckle; F:Bignone de Virginie; G:Ameri-
kanische Trompetenwinde · ♄ d ⚥ Z6
VII-IX; USA: NE, NCE, SC, SE, Fla.
– × **tagliabuana** (Vis.) Rehder (*C.
grandiflora* × *C. radicans*) · G:Hybrid-
Trompetenwinde · ♄ d ⚥ Z7 ⋀ VII-VIII;
cult.

Camptosorus Link = Asplenium
– *rhizophyllus* (L.) Link = Asplenium
rhizophyllum

Camptotheca Decne. -f- *Nyssaceae* · 1 sp.
– **acuminata** Decne. · E:Happy Tree;
G:Glücksbaum · ♄ d ⓐ; China, Tibet

Campyloneurum C. Presl -f-
Polypodiaceae · 44 spp. · E:Strap Fern;
G:Riemenfarn
– **phyllitidis** (L.) C. Presl · E:Cow-tongue
Fern, Florida Strap Fern; G:Florida-
Riemenfarn · ⚄ Z10 ⓜ; USA: Fla.; trop.
S-Am.

Campylotropis Bunge -f- *Fabaceae* ·
65 spp.
– **macrocarpa** (Bunge) Rehder · ♄ d Z7

VIII-IX; N-China, C-China

Cananga (DC.) Hook. f. & Thomson -f-
Annonaceae · 2 spp. · G:Ylang-Ylangbaum;
E:Ylang Ylang
– **odorata** (Lam.) Hook. f. & Thomson ·
G:Ylang-Ylangbaum; E:Ylang Ylang ·
♄ e Z10 ⓜ ⚥ Ⓝ; Malay. Arch., Phil.,
N-Austr., Pacific Is.

Canarina L. -f- *Campanulaceae* · 3 spp. ·
E:Canary Island Bellflower; F:Campanule
des Canaries; G:Kanarenglockenblume
– **canariensis** (L.) Vatke · E:Canary Island
Bellflower; G:Kanarische Glockenblume ·
⚄ ⚥ Z9 ⓐ XI-III; Canar.

Canarium L. -n- *Burseraceae* · 77 spp. ·
E:Chinese Olive; F:Canarion, Elemi;
G:Kanaribaum, Kanarinuss
– **album** (Lour.) Raeusch. · E:Chinese
Olive; G:Weiße Kanarinuss · ♄ ⓜ Ⓝ;
S-China, Vietn.
– *commune* L. = Canarium indicum
– *edule* (G. Don) Hook. = Dacryodes edulis
– **indicum** L. · E:Java Olive; G:Galipnuss
· ♄ ⓜ Ⓝ; Molucca, N.Guinea, Solom.
Vanuatu
– **luzonicum** Miq. · E:Elemi Canary-tree;
G:Elemiharz, Manila-Elemi · ♄ ⓜ ⚥ Ⓝ;
Phil.
– **ovatum** Engl. · E:Pilinut; G:Pilinuss · ♄
ⓜ Ⓝ; Phil.: Luzon
– **pimela** K.D. Koenig · E:Wu Lan;
G:Schwarze Kanarinuss · ♄ ⓜ Ⓝ;
S-China, Hong Kong, Hainan, Laos,
Cambodia, Vietn.
– **strictum** Roxb. · E:Black Dammar;
G:Weißer Mahagonibaum · ♄ e ⓜ Ⓝ;
Ind., Burma

Canavalia DC. -f- *Fabaceae* · 51 sp. ·
E:Jack Bean; F:Pois-sabre; G:Jackbohne,
Schwertbohne
– **ensiformis** (L.) DC. · E:Gotani Bean,
Jack Bean; G:Jackbohne, Pferde-Schw-
ertbohne · ⚄ ⚥ Z10 ⓜ Ⓝ; trop. S-Am.
– **gladiata** (Jacq.) DC. · E:Chopper Bean;
G:Schwertbohne · ⚄ ⚥ Z10 ⓜ Ⓝ; trop.
Afr., trop. As.
– **plagiosperma** Piper · E:Oblique-seeded
Blackbean · Z10 ⓜ Ⓝ; trop. Am.
– **polystachya** (Forssk.) Schweinf. · ⚄ ⚥
Z10 ⓜ Ⓝ; Eth., Somalia, Madag., Arab.,
Ind., SW-China

Canella P. Browne -f- *Canellaceae* · 1 sp. · E:Wild Cinnamon; F:Cannelier; G:Kaneelbaum, Zimtrindenbaum
- *alba* Murray = Canella winterana
- **winterana** (L.) Gaertn. · E:White Cinnamon, Wilde Cinnamon; G:Weißer Zimtrindenbaum · ♄ e D Z10 Ⓦ ⚕ Ⓝ; S-Fla., W.Ind.

Canistropsis (Mez) Leme -f- *Bromeliaceae* · 10 spp.
- **billbergioides** (Schult. & Schult. f.) Leme Z10; E-Braz.
- **burchellii** (Baker) Leme · ♃ Z10; Braz.
- **seidelii** (L.B. Sm. & Reitz) Leme Z10; Braz.

Canistrum E. Morren -n- *Bromeliaceae* · 14 spp.
- *amazonicum* (Baker) Mez = Nidularium amazonicum
- **aurantiacum** E. Morren · ♃ Z10 Ⓦ; Braz.
- *eburneum* E. Morren = Canistrum fragrans
- **fosterianum** L.B. Sm. · ♃ Z10 Ⓦ; Braz.
- **fragrans** (Linden) Mabb. · ♃ Z10 Ⓦ; Braz.
- *lindenii* Mez = Canistrum fragrans
- *roseum* E. Morren = Canistrum fragrans

Canna L. -f- *Cannaceae* · 23 spp. · E:Canna Lily; F:Balisier; G:Blumenrohr
- **flaccida** Salisb. · E:Bandanna of the Everglades; F:Balisier, Canna · ♃ ~ Z8 Ⓦ Ⓚ; USA: SE, Fla.
- × **generalis** L.H. Bailey (*C. indica* × ?) · ♃ Ⓚ; cult.
- **glauca** L. · ♃ Z10 Ⓚ VI-IX; W.Ind., S-Am.
- **indica** L. · E:Indian Shot, Queensland Arrowroot; F:Balisier, Canna; G:Essbares Blumenrohr, Westindisches Blumenrohr · ♃ Z8 Ⓚ VII-IX Ⓝ; C-Am., W.Ind., S-Am., nat. in S-USA, trop. Afr., trop. As.
- **iridiflora** Ruiz & Pav. · G:Irisblütiges Blumenrohr · ♃ Z9 Ⓚ VI-IX; Peru
- *lutea* Mill. = Canna indica
- × **orchiodes** L.H. Bailey (*C. flaccida* × *C.* × *generalis*) Z8; cult.
- **Cultivars:**
- **many cultivars**

Cannabis L. -f- *Cannabaceae* · 1 sp. · E:Hemp, Marijuana; F:Chanvre; G:Hanf
- *indica* Lam. = Cannabis sativa subsp. indica
- *ruderalis* Janisch. = Cannabis sativa subsp. spontanea
- **sativa** L.
- subsp. **indica** (Lam.) Small & Cronquist · E:Marijuana, Pot; G:Haschischpflanze, Indischer Hanf · ⊙ Z9 Ⓦ Ⓚ ⚕ Ⓝ; Ind.
- subsp. **sativa** · G:Kultur-Hanf; E:Hemp · ⊙ Z8 VII-VIII; cult., nat. in Eur., N-Am.
- subsp. **spontanea** Serebr. · G:Wilder Hanf; E:Hemp · Z8 V-VII; ? C-As., ? W-As.

Cantua Juss. ex Lam. -f- *Polemoniaceae* · 6 spp. · F:Cantua; G:Cantue
- **buxifolia** Juss. ex Lam. · ♄ e Z9 Ⓚ IV; Peru, Bol., Chile

Capnoides Mill. -n- *Fumariaceae* · 1 sp.
- **sempervirens** (L.) Borkh. · E:Pink Corydalis, Rock Harlequin; G:Rosa Lerchensporn · ⊙ ⊙ △ VII; Alaska, Can., USA: NE, NCE, NC, Tenn., Mont., nat. in Norw.

Capparis L. -f- *Capparaceae* · 250 spp. · E:Caper; F:Câprier; G:Kapernstrauch
- **spinosa** L. · E:Caper Plant; G:Kapernstrauch
- subsp. **orientalis** (Duhamel) Jafri · G:Dornenloser Kapernstrauch · ♄ d Z8 Ⓚ Ⓝ; Eur.: Ib, F, Ital-P, Ba; TR, N-Afr, N-Ind.
- subsp. **spinosa** · E:Common Caper; G:Gewöhnlicher Kapernstrauch · ♄ d Z8 Ⓚ ⚕ Ⓝ; Eur.: Ib, Fr, Ital-P, Ba, Crim; TR, Levant, Cauc., Iran, C-As., Kashmir, N-Afr.
- var. *inermis* auct. = Capparis spinosa subsp. orientalis

Capsella Medik. -f- *Brassicaceae* · 5 spp. · E:Shepherd's Purses; F:Capselle; G:Hirtentäschel
- **bursa-pastoris** (L.) Medik. · E:Shepherd's Purse; G:Gewöhnliches Hirtentäschel · ⊙ ⊙ I-X ⚕ Ⓝ; Eur.*, cosmop. exc. Trop.
- **rubella** Reut. · E:Pink Shepherd's Purse; G:Rötliches Hirtentäschel · ⊙ VI-X; Eur.: Ib, Fr, Ital-P, Ba, BrI; TR, ? N-Afr., nat. in C-Eur.

Capsicum L. -n- *Solanaceae* · 10 spp. · E:Pepper, Sweet Pepper; F:Chili, Piment; G:Chili, Paprika
- **annuum** L. · E:Green Pepper, Red

Pepper, Sweet Pepper; G:Spanischer
Pfeffer, Paprika · ⊙ ⊙ ⁴ ♭ Z9 VI-IX ⚡ Ⓝ;
? Mex.
– **many cultivars**
– **Cerasiforme Group** · E:Cherry Pepper;
G:Zier-Paprika · ; cult.
– **Conioides Group** · E:Cone Pepper;
G:Spitz-Paprika · Ⓝ; cult.
– **Fasciculatum Group** · E:Red Cone
Pepper; G:Büschel-Paprika · Ⓝ; cult.
– **Grossum Group** · E:Bell Pepper,
Pimento, Sweet Pepper; G:Gemüse-
Paprika, Süßer Paprika · ⁴ Ⓝ; trop. Am.
– **Longum Group** · E:Cayenne Pepper,
Chilli Pepper; G:Cayennepfeffer,
Peperoni · Ⓝ; cult.
– var. *cerasiforme* (Mill.) Irish = Capsicum
annuum Cerasiforme-Group
– var. *longum* (DC.) Sendtn. = Capsicum
annuum Longum-Group
– **baccatum** L.
– var. **baccatum** · E:Locoto · ⊙ ♭ ♭ Z9 ⚡ ;
Peru, Bol., S-Braz. Parag., N-Arg.
– var. **pendulum** (Willd.) Eshbaugh ·
E:Brown's Pepper; G:Peruanischer Pfeffer
· ⊙ ⊙ ⁴ ♭ Z9 Ⓝ; Peru, Bol.
– **chinense** Jacq. · ⊙ ⊙ ⁴ ♭ Z9 ⚡ Ⓝ; ?
W-Amazon.; cult.
– **frutescens** L. · E:Hot Pepper, Tabasco
Pepper; G:Chili, Tabasco · ⊙ ⊙ ⁴ ♭ Z9 ⚡
Ⓝ; trop. Am.
– *minimum* Roxb. = Capsicum frutescens
– *pendulum* Willd. = Capsicum baccatum
var. baccatum
– **pubescens** Ruiz & Pav. · E:Apple Chile;
G:Baum-Chili, Filziger Paprika · ⊙ ♭ Z9
Ⓝ; S-Am, C-Am.

Caragana Fabr. -f- *Fabaceae* · c. 80 spp. ·
E:Pea Shrub, Pea Tree; F:Acacia jaune;
G:Erbsenstrauch
– **ambigua** Stocks ex Hook. · ♭ d; Pakistan
– **arborescens** Lam. · E:Siberian Pea Tree;
F:Caragan arborescent; G:Gewöhnlicher
Erbsenstrauch · ♭ d Z3 V ⚘ Ⓝ; W-Sib.,
E-Sib., C-As., Mong., nat. in F
– **aurantiaca** Koehne · E:Dwarf Peashrub;
G:Orangeblütiger Erbsenstrauch · ♭ d Z5
V-VI; C-As., China: Sinkiang
– **boisii** C.K. Schneid. · ♭ d; W-China
– **decorticans** Hemsl. · E:Afghan Pea
Shrub; G:Afghanischer Erbsenstrauch · ♭
d Z6 VI; Afgh.
– *frutescens* (L.) Medik. = Caragana frutex
– **frutex** (L.) K. Koch · E:Russian Pea

Shrub; G:Busch-Erbsenstrauch, Rus-
sischer Erbsenstrauch · ♭ d Z3 V; Eur.:
BG, RO, Russ.; Cauc., W-Sib., E-Sib.,
C-As.
– **gerardiana** (Royle) Benth. · ♭ d Z5 IV-V;
Him., Tibet
– **grandiflora** (M. Bieb.) DC. · ♭ d; Cauc.,
C-As.
– **jubata** (Pall.) Poir. · E:Shag-spine Pea
Shrub; G:Mähnen-Erbsenstrauch · ♭ d Z3
IV-V; E-Sib., Amur, C-As., Mong., Tibet.,
Him., China
– **laeta** Kom. · ♭ d; C-As., China: Sinkiang
– **maximowicziana** Kom. · G:Maximowicz
Erbsenstrauch · ♭ d Z2 V-VI; W-China
– **microphylla** Lam. · E:Littleleaf Peashrub;
G:Kleinblättriger Erbsenstrauch · ♭ d Z4
V-VI; Sib., N-China
– **pygmaea** (L.) DC. · F:Caragan nain;
G:Zwerg-Erbsenstrauch · ♭ d △ Z4 V-VI;
NW-China, Sib.
– **sinica** (Buc'hoz) Rehder · G:Chinesischer
Erbsenstrauch · ♭ d Z4 V-VI; N-China
– × **sophorifolia** Tausch (*C. arborescens* ×
C. microphylla) · ♭ d Z3; cult.
– **spinosa** (L.) DC. · G:Dorniger Erbsenstrauch · ♭ d Z3 IV-VI; Sib.
– **tangutica** Maxim. ex Kom. · ♭ d; China:
Kansu

Caralluma R. Br. -f- *Asclepiadaceae* ·
53 spp. · F:Caralluma; G:Fliegenblume
– *atrosanguinea* (N.E. Br.) N.E. Br. =
Huerniopsis atrosanguinea
– *brownii* Dinter & A. Berger = Orbea lutea
subsp. vaga
– **burchardii** N.E. Br. · ⁴ ¥ Z9 ㊛ ▽;
Canar., S-Moroc.
– *compta* (N.E. Br.) Schltr. = Piaranthus
comptus
– *crassa* N.E. Br. = Whitesloanea crassa
– **europaea** (Guss.) N.E. Br. · ⁴ ¥ Z9 ㊛;
Eur.: sp., Sic.; N-Afr.
– *grandidens* I. Verd. = Orbea maculata
– *leendertziae* N.E. Br. = Orbea melanantha
– *lugardii* N.E. Br. = Orbea lugardii
– *lutea* N.E. Br. = Orbea lutea subsp. lutea
– subsp. *vaga* (N.E. Br.) L.C. Leach = Orbea
lutea subsp. vaga
– *maculata* N.E. Br. = Orbea maculata
– *mammillaris* (L.) N.E. Br. = Quaqua
mammillaris
– *melanantha* (Schltr.) N.E. Br. = Orbea
melanantha
– **moniliformis** P.R.O. Bally · ⁴ ¥ Z10 ㊛;

Somalia
- *nebrownii* A. Berger = Orbea lutea subsp. vaga
- *pseudonebrownii* Dinter = Orbea lutea subsp. vaga
- *vansonii* Bremek. & Oberm. = Orbea lutea subsp. lutea

Carapa Aubl. -f- *Meliaceae* · 2 spp. · E:Crabwood; G:Läuseholz
- **guianensis** Aubl. · E:Crabwood; G:Läuseholz · ♄ e ⓦ Ⓝ; C-Am., Col., Venez., Guyan., Trinidad, Braz.
- **procera** DC. · E:Uganda Crabwood; G:Uganda-Läuseholz · ♄ e ⓦ Ⓝ; trop. Afr.

Cardamine L. -f- *Brassicaceae* · c. 150 spp. · E:Bitter Cress; F:Cardamine; G:Schaumkraut, Zahnwurz
- **alpina** Willd. · E:Alpine Bitter Cress; G:Alpen-Schaumkraut · ⠃ Z4 VII-VIII; Eur.: Pyr., Alp.
- **amara** L. · E:Large Bitter Cress; G:Bittere Kresse, Bitteres Schaumkraut · ⠃ IV-VI Ⓝ; Eur.*, TR, W-Sib.
- **bulbifera** (L.) Crantz · E:Coral Root Bittercress; G:Zwiebel-Zahnwurz · ⠃ Z6 V; Eur.* exc. Ib; TR, Cauc., N-Iran
- **dentata** Schult. · G:Sumpf-Schaumkraut · ⠃ IV-VI; Eur.
- **enneaphyllos** (L.) Crantz · E:Drooping Bittercress; G:Quirl-Zahnwurz, Quirlblättrige Zahnwurz · ⠃ Z7 IV-VI ⚥ ; Eur.: C-Eur., I, EC-Eur., Ba, RO
- **flexuosa** With. · E:Wavy Bitter Cress; G:Wald-Schaumkraut · ⊙ ⊚ IV-X; Eur.*, Moroc., Alger., nat. in N-Am., N-China, Jap.
- **heptaphylla** (Vill.) O.E. Schulz · E:Dentaria, Pinnate Coralroot; G:Fieder-Zahnwurz · ⠃ Z6 IV-V; Eur.: sp., F, I, Sw, D
- **hirsuta** L. · E:Hairy Bitter Cress; G:Viermänniges Schaumkraut · ⊙ III-VI; Eur.*, TR, Levant, Cauc., Iran, Him., NW-Afr., Libya, Cameroon, Eth., Kilimandsharo, nat. in cosmop.
- **impatiens** L. · E:Narrow-leaved Bitter Cress; G:Spring-Schaumkraut · ⊙ ⊚ V-VII; Eur.*, TR, Cauc., Iran, W-Sib., E-Sib., Amur, Sakhal., C-As., Him. Tibet
- **kitaibelii** Bech. · G:Kitaibels Zahnwurz, Vielblättrige Zahnwurz · ⠃ Z6 VII-IX; Eur.: I, Sw, Slove.; Alp., Apenn.
- **matthioli** Moretti · G:Weißes Wiesen-Schaumkraut · ⠃ IV-VI; Eur.: I, A, Slove., Slova., CZ, H, BG, RO
- *palustris* (L.) Kuntze = Cardamine dentata
- **parviflora** L. · E:Sand Bitter Cress; G:Kleinblütiges Schaumkraut · ⊙ V-VII; Eur.* exc. BrI; Alger.
- **pentaphyllos** (L.) Crantz · E:Five-leaflet Bitter Cress; G:Finger-Zahnwurz · ⠃ Z6 IV-VI; Eur.: sp., F, I, C-Eur., ? Croatia, Bosn.
- **pratensis** L. · E:Cuckoo Flower, Lady's Smock; F:Cardamine des prés; G:Wiesen-Schaumkraut · ⠃ Z4 IV-V ⚥ ; Eur.*, W-Sib., E-Sib., Amur, Sakhal., Kamchat., Korea, Mong., W-Tibet, Eth., Alaska, Can., USA: NE, SE; Greenl.
- **resedifolia** L. · G:Resedablättriges Schaumkraut · ⠃ V-VIII; Eur.* exc. BrI, Sc; mts.; Cauc., Iran, W-Sib., E-Sib., Amur, C-As., Mong., Tibet, E-As.
- **rivularis** Schur · G:Voralpen-Wiesen-Schaumkraut · ⠃ VI-VIII; Eur.: BG, RO
- **trifolia** L. · E:Trifoliate Bittercress; F:Cardamine à trois feuilles; G:Dreiblättrige Zahnwurz, Kleeblättriges Schaumkraut · ⠃ △ Z7 IV-VI; Eur.: Fr, I, G, A, EC-Eur., Slove., Croatia, Bosn.
- **udicola** Jord. · G:Morast-Schaumkraut · ⠃ IV-V; Eur.
- **waldsteinii** Dyer · G:Illyrische Zahnwurz · ⠃; Eur.: A, H, Slove.

Cardaminopsis (C.A. Mey.) Hayek -f- *Brassicaceae* · 13 spp. · F:Arabette des sables; G:Schaumkresse
- **arenosa** (L.) Hayek · E:Tall Rock Cress; G:Sand-Schaumkresse · ⊙ ⠃ Z7 IV-VIII; Eur.* exc. BrI, Ib
- **halleri** (L.) Hayek · G:Hallers Schaumkresse, Wiesen-Schaumkresse · ⠃ Z6 IV-VI; Eur.: Fr, Ital-P, C-Eur., EC-Eur., E-Eur.; mts.
- **petraea** (L.) Hiitonen · G:Felsen-Schaumkresse · ⠃ Z7 V-VII; Eur.* exc. Ib, Ba

Cardaria Desv. -f- *Brassicaceae* · 6 spp. · F:Cardaire, Passerage drave; G:Pfeilkresse
- **draba** (L.) Desv. · E:Hoary Cress, Whitetop; G:Pfeilkresse · ⠃ V-VII; Eur.* exc. BrI, Sc; TR, Levant, SW-As., Egypt, nat. in BrI, Sc

Cardiocrinum (Endl.) Lindl. -n- *Liliaceae* ·
3 spp. · E:Giant Lily; F:Lis géant;
G:Riesenlilie
- **cathayanum** (E.H. Wilson) Stearn ·
G:Chinesische Riesenlilie · ⌖ Z7;
C-China, E-China
- **cordatum** (Thunb.) Makino · G:Herz-
blättrige Japanische Riesenlilie · ⌖ Z7
VIII; China, S-Jap., S-Sakhal.
- **giganteum** (Wall.) Makino · G:Gewöhn-
liche Himalaya-Riesenlilie · ⌖ Z7 VII-VIII;
Him., SE-Tibet, NW-Burma

Cardiogyne Bureau = Maclura

Cardiospermum L. -n- *Sapindaceae* ·
14 spp. · E:Balloon Vine; F:Pois de cœur;
G:Ballonrebe, Ballonwein, Herzsame
- **grandiflorum** Sw. · E:Heartseed;
G:Großblütiger Herzsame · ♄ d ⚥ Z9 ⓦ;
trop. Am.
- **f. hirsutum** (Willd.) Radlk. · G:Rau-
haariger Herzsame · ⌇ d ⚥ Z9 ⓚ
- **halicacabum** L. · E:Balloon Vine, Heart
Pea; G:Ballonrebe, Ballonwein, Blasen-
Herzsame · ⊙ ⊙ ⚥ ⚭ Z9; USA.: Fla, SE,
SC; trop. Am., trop. Afr., Ind., nat. in
Trop.

Carduncellus Adans. -m- *Asteraceae* ·
30 spp. · F:Cardoncelle; G:Färberdistel
- **mitissimus** (L.) DC. · ⌖ Z7; F, NE-Sp.
- **rhaponticoides** Coss. & Durieu ex
Pomel · ⌖ Z7 ⋀ V-VI; Moroc., Alger.

Carduus L. -m- *Asteraceae* · 91 sp. ·
E:Thistle; F:Chardon; G:Distel
- **acanthoides** L. · E:Welted Thistle;
G:Weg-Distel · ⊙ Z7 VI-IX; Eur.* exc. Ib;
TR, Cauc.
- **acicularis** Bertol. · G:Benadelte Distel · ⊙
Z7; Eur.: Fr, Ital-P, Ba; TR, Iraq, Cyprus,
Syr., nat. in Sw
- **carduelis** Ten. · E:Southeastern Thistle;
G:Stieglitz-Distel · ⌖ Z7 VI-IX; Eur.: I, A,
Ba; mts.
- **collinus** Waldst. & Kit. · G:Hügel-Distel ·
⊙; Eur.: I, EC-Eur., Ba, RO
- *crassifolius* Willd. = Carduus defloratus
- **crispus** L. · G:Krause Distel · ⊙ VII-IX;
Eur.* exc. BrI; Cauc., nat. in N-Am., Jap.,
Arg.
- **defloratus** L.
- subsp. **carlinifolius** (Lam.) Ces. · N-Sp.,
F, Sw, I; mts. NE-Sp., Pyr., Alps, Apenn.

- subsp. **defloratus** · E:Alpine Thistle;
G:Berg-Distel · ⌖ VI-VIII; Eur.: C-Eur.,
EC-Eur., I, Slove., Croatia, RO; mts.
- subsp. **tridentatus** sensu Heitz · G:Eber-
wurzblättrige Distel, Rätische Distel · ⌖
VI-IX
- subsp. **tridentinus** (Evers) Murr · ; Eur.:
C-Alp, E-Alp.
- **hamulosus** Ehrh. · G:Hakige Distel ·
⊙; Eur.: EC-Eur., Ba, E-Eur.; TR, Cauc.,
NW-Iran, nat. in Sw, A
- **kerneri** Simonk. · ⌖ VII-VIII; Eur.: Ba,
Ro, W-Russ.
- **macrocephalus** Desf. · E:Giant Thistle ·
⊙; Eur.: Ital-P, Ba; TR, Moroc., Alger.,
Tun., nat. in Sw
- *medius* Gouan = Carduus defloratus
subsp. defloratus
- *mollis* L. = Jurinea mollis
- **nutans** L. · E:Musk Thistle · ⊙ VII-VIII ⓝ;
Eur.*
- **personata** (L.) Jacq. · E:Great Marsh
Thistle; G:Kletten-Distel · ⌖ VII-VIII;
Eur.: Fr, Ital-P, C-Eur., EC-Eur., Ba, RO,
W-Russ.; mts.
- **pycnocephalus** L. · E:Italian Thistle;
G:Knaulköpfige Distel · ⊙; Eur.: Ib, Fr,
Ital-P, Ba, E-Eur.; TR, Lebanon, Syr, Palest, Iraq, Cauc., Iran, Afgh., C-As., N-Afr.
- **tenuiflorus** Curtis · E:Shore Thistle;
G:Dünnköpfige Distel · ⊙ VI; Eur.: BrI,
Fr, Ib, Ital-P, Sw, nat. in Sc
- **thoermeri** Weinm. · ⊙; Eur.: H, Ba,
E-Eur., G, Sw; TR, Cauc., NW-Afr.
- *viridis* A. Kern. = Carduus defloratus
subsp. defloratus
- **vivariensis** Jord. · ⊙; Eur.: sp., F, I, nat.
in Sw

Carex L. -f- *Cyperaceae* · 1770 spp. ·
E:Sedge; F:Laîche; G:Segge
- **acuta** L. · E:Slender-tufted Sedge;
G:Schlank-Segge · ⌖ ∿ Z3 V-VI; Eur.*,
TR, Lebanon, Syr., Cauc. ., W-Sib.,
NW-Afr.
- **acutiformis** Ehrh. · E:Lesser Pond Sedge;
F:Laîche des marais; G:Sumpf-Segge
· ⌖ ∿ Z3 VI; Eur.*, Cauc., TR, Iran,
Iraq, Afgh., Pakist., W-Sib., E-Sib., C-As.,
Alger.
- **alba** Scop. · E:White Sedge; G:Weiße
Segge · ⌖ Z6 IV; Eur.* exc. BrI, Sc; Cauc.,
W-Sib., E-Sib.
- **appropinquata** Schumach. · E:Fibrous
Tussock Sedge; G:Schwarzschopf-Segge ·

♃ ⌣ V-VI; Eur.* exc. Ib; Cauc., W-Sib., E-Sib.

- **aquatilis** Wahlenb. · E:Water Sedge; G:Wasser-Segge · ♃ ⌣ VI-VII; Eur.: BrI, Sc, G, NL, Russ.; W-Sib., E-Sib.
- **arenaria** L. · E:Sand Sedge ; G:Sand-Segge · ♃ Z7 V-X ⚥ Ⓝ; Eur.: Ib, Fr, BrI, Sc, G, PL, Russ., nat. in N-Am.
- **atherodes** Spreng. · E:Wheat Sedge; G:Große Grannen-Segge · ♃ ⌣ V-VI; Eur.: FIN, G, PL, Russ.; TR, Cauc., Sib., China, N-Am.
- **atrata** L. · G:Trauer-Segge
- subsp. **aterrima** (Hoppe) Hartm. · G:Große Trauer-Segge, Rußgeschwärzte Segge · ♃ Z3 VI-VIII; Eur.: Alp., Sudeten, Ba, Ural, TR, Cauc.
- subsp. **atrata** · E:Black Alpine Sedge; G:Gewöhnliche Trauer-Segge, Schwarze Segge · ♃ Z3 VI-VIII; Eur.*
- **atrofusca** Schkuhr · E:Dark Brown Sedge; G:Schwarzrote Segge · ♃ VII-VIII; Eur.: BrI, Sc, Fr, Ital-P, C-Eur., EC-Eur., RO, N-Russ.; N-Alp., Carp., Ural, N-Am., Greenl.
- **austroalpina** Bech. · G:Südalpine Segge · ♃ V-VI; Eur.: I, Sw; S-Alp.
- **baccans** Nees · G:Beeren-Segge · ♃ ⚭ Z8 ⓚ; Ind.
- **baldensis** L. · G:Monte-Baldo-Segge · ♃ △ Z7 VI-VII ▽; Eur.: I, Sw, G, A; Alp.
- **bebbii** Olney ex Britton · E:Bebb's Sedge · ♃; Alaska, USA: NE, NEC, NC, Rocky Mts., NW
- × **beckmanniana** Figert (*C. riparia* × *C. rostrata*) · G:Beckmanns Bastard-Segge · ♃ ⌣ ; Eur.: Sw, G, PL
- **bicolor** All. · E:Twocolor Sedge; G:Zweifarbige Segge · ♃ ⌣ VII; Eur.* exc. BrI, Ib; W-Sib., E-Sib., Mong., Greenl.
- **bigelowii** Torr. ex Schwein. · E:Stiff Sedge; G:Starre Segge · ♃ ⌣ VI-VII; Alaska, Can., USA: NE, Rocky Mts.; Eur.: BrI, Sc, Fr, C-Eur., EC-Eur., E-Eur., ?Ba
- **binervis** Sm. · E:Green-ribbed Sedge; G:Zweinervige Segge · ♃ V-VI; Eur.: Sc, BrI, Fr, G, Ib; NW-Afr.
- **bohemica** Schreb. · E:Bohemian Sedge; G:Zypergras-Segge · ♃ ⌣ VI-IX; Eur.* exc. BrI; Cauc., W-Sib., E-Sib., C-As., Manch., Jap.
- **brachystachys** Schrank · E:Short-spiked Sedge; G:Kurzährige Segge · ♃ VI-VIII; Eur.: sp., F, I, C-Eur., EC-Eur., Croatia, Bosn., Serb., RO, mts.

- **brizoides** L. · E:Quaking Grass Sedge; G:Seegras-Segge, Zittergras-Segge · ♃ V-VI; Eur.* exc. BrI, Sc
- **brunnea** Thunb. · E:Greater Brown Sedge · ♃ Z8 ⓦ ⓚ ▢; Him., Ind., Sri Lanka, Malay. Arch., Mascarene Is., Austr.
- **brunnescens** (Pers.) Poir. · E:Brownish Sedge; G:Gewöhnliche Bräunliche Segge · ♃ VII; Eur.* exc. BrI, Ib; W-Sib., E-Sib., C-As., N-Jap., N-Am.
- **buchananii** Berggr. · E:Leatherleaf Sedge; F:Laîche de Buchanan; G:Fuchsrote Segge · ♃ △ Z7; NZ
- **buekii** Wimm. · G:Banater Segge · ♃ V; Eur.: C-Eur., EC-Eur., Ba, E-Eur., ? I; Cauc.
- **buxbaumii** Wahlenb. · E:Club Sedge; G:Buxbaums Segge · ♃ ⌣ V-VI; Eur.* exc. Ib; W-Sib., E-Sib., C-As.
- **canescens** L. · E:Silvery Sedge; F:Laîche blanchâtre; G:Graue Segge · ♃ ⌣ V-VI; Eur.*, TR, Cauc., W-Sib., E-Sib., Amur, Sakhal., Kamchat., C-As., Manch., Korea, Jap., N-Am.
- **capillaris** L. · E:Hair Sedge; G:Kleine Haarstielige Segge · ♃ V-VII; Eur.*, TR, C-As., E-Sib., N-Am.
- **capitata** L. · E:Capitate Sedge; G:Kopf-Segge · ♃ ⌣ V-VI; Eur.: Sc, Russ., A, I; N, E-Alp.; W-Sib., E-Sib., Amur, N-Am.
- **caryophyllea** Latourr. · E:Spring Sedge; G:Frühlings-Segge · ♃ Z7 IV; Eur.*, TR, Cauc., W-Sib., C-As.
- **cespitosa** L. · E:Lesser Tufted Sedge; G:Rasen-Segge · ♃ ⌣ V-VI; Eur.* exc. BrI, Ib; Cauc., W-Sib., E-Sib., C-As.
- **chordorrhiza** L. f. · E:String Sedge; G:Fadenwurzelige Segge, Strick-Segge · ♃ ⌣ V-VI; Eur.: BrI, Sc, Fr, C-Eur., EC-Eur., E-Eur.; W-Sib., E-Sib., Amur, Sakhal., Kamchat.
- **colchica** J. Gay · G:Französische Segge · ♃ IV-V; Eur.: Sc, Fr, G, EC-Eur., Ba, E-Eur.; TR, Cauc., W-Sib.
- **comans** Berggr. · ♃ Z7 △; NZ
- **conica** Boott · ♃ Z7 IV-VI; Jap.
- **crawfordii** Fernald · E:Crawford's Sedge; G:Crawfords Segge, Falsche Hasenfuß-Segge · ♃; N-Am., nat. in BrI, NL
- **cuprina** (I. Sándor ex Heuff.) Nendtv. ex A. Kern. · E:False Fox Sedge; G:Falsche Fuchs-Segge · ♃ V-VII
- *curta* Gooden. = Carex canescens
- **curvula** All. · G:Krumm-Segge · ♃ △

VII-VIII; Eur.: sp., F, I, Sw, A, Ba, RO, W-Russ.; mts.
- **davalliana** Sm. · E:Davall's Sedge; G:Davalls-Segge · ⚄ ⌒ V-VI; Eur.* exc. BrI, Sc; TR
- *demissa* Hornem. = Carex viridula subsp. oedocarpa
- **depauperata** Curtis ex With. · E:Starved Wood Sedge; G:Armblütige Segge · ⚄ IV-V; Eur.: Ib, Fr, Ital-P, Ba, BrI, Sw, RO, Crim; Cauc.
- **depressa** Link
- subsp. **transsilvanica** (Schur) T.V. Egorova · G:Siebenbürger Segge · ⚄ IV-V; Eur.: Carp., SE-Eur.; TR, Cauc., N-Iran
- **diandra** Schrank · E:Lesser Tussock Sedge; G:Draht-Segge · ⚄ ⌒ V-VI; Eur.* exc. Ib; TR, Cauc., W-Sib., E-Sib., C-As., N-Am.
- **digitata** L. · E:Fingered Sedge, Fringed Sedge; F:Laîche digitée; G:Finger-Segge · ⚄ Z6 V; Eur.*, Cauc., W-Sib.
- **dioica** L. · E:Dioecious Sedge; G:Zwei-häusige Segge · ⚄ ⌒ V-VI; Eur.*, W-Sib., E-Sib.
- **distans** L. · E:Distant Sedge; G:Entfern-tährige Segge · ⚄ ⌒ VI-VII; Eur.*, TR, Iraq, Cyprus, Syr., Arab., N-Afr.
- **disticha** Huds. · E:Brown Sedge; G:Zweizeilige Segge · ⚄ ⌒ V-VI; Eur.*, Cauc., W-Sib., E-Sib., C-As.
- **divisa** Huds. · E:Divided Sedge; G:Geteilte Segge · ⚄ ⌒ IV-VI; Eur.: BrI, Ib, Fr, Ital-P, C-Eur., EC-Eur., Ba, RO, Crim; TR, Cauc., N-Afr., nat. in N-Am., S-Afr., NZ
- **divulsa** Stokes · E:Grassland Sedge; G:Unterbrochenährige Segge · ⚄ V-VIII; Eur.*, TR, Lebanon, Syr., Cauc., N-Iran, C-As., N-Afr.
- **echinata** Murray · E:Star Sedge; G:Igel-Segge · ⚄ ⌒ V-VI; Az., Eur.* , Moroc., TR, W-As., Cauc., W-Sib., Kamchat., Sakhal., China, Korea, Jap., Malaysia, Austr., NZ, N-Am., Santo Domingo
- **elata** All. · E:Tufted Sedge; F:Laîche élevée; G:Steife Segge · ⚄ ⌒ Z6 IV-V; Eur.*, TR, Cauc., NW-Iran, Alger.
- **elongata** L. · E:Elongated Sedge; G:Langährige Segge, Walzen-Segge · ⚄ ⌒ V-VI; Eur.* exc. Ib; Cauc., W-Sib., E-Sib.
- × **elytroides** Fr. (*C. acuta* × *C. nigra* subsp. *nigra*) · G:Bastard-Segge · ⚄ ⌒ ; Eur.: BrI, Sc, G, N-Russ. +

- **ericetorum** Pollich · E:Heath Sedge; G:Heide-Segge · ⚄ ⤳ IV-V; Eur.*, Cauc., W-Sib., E-Sib., C-As.
- **extensa** Gooden. · E:Longbract Sedge; G:Strand-Segge · ⚄ ⌒ VII-VIII; Eur.*, TR, Cyprus, Cauc., Egypt
- **ferruginea** Scop. · G:Rost-Segge · ⚄ VI-IX; Eur.: sp., F, I, C-Eur., Ba, RO; mts.
- **filiformis** L. · E:Downy-fruited Sedge; G:Filz-Segge · ⚄ V-VI; Eur.*, Cauc., W-Sib., E-Sib., C-As.
- **fimbriata** Schkuhr · G:Gefranste Segge · ⚄ VII-VIII; Eur.: F, I, Sw, Alp.
- **firma** Host · E:Dwarf Pillow Sedge; G:Polster-Segge · ⚄ △ VI-VIII; Eur.: F, I, C-Eur., EC-Eur., Slove., Croatia, RO, W-Russ.; Alp., Apenn., Carp.
- **flacca** Schreb. · E:Blue-green Sedge; F:Laîche glauque; G:Blaugrüne Segge · ⚄ Z5 V-VII; Eur.*, TR, N-Iraq, Syr., Cyprus, Cauc., Iran, Pakist., N-Afr.
- **flava** L. · G:Gelb-Segge
- var. *alpina* Kneuck. = Carex flava var. nevadnesis
- var. **flava** · E:Yellow Sedge; G:Gewöhnliche Gelb-Segge · ⚄ ⌒ V-VII; Eur.*, TR, Cauc., Iran, Him.. NW-Afr., Alaska, Can., USA: NE, NCE, NC, Rocky Mts.
- var. **nevadensis** (Boiss. & Reut.) Briq. · G:Alpen-Gelb-Segge · ⚄ ⌒ VII; Eur.: sp., F, Cors, C-Eur., ? W-Ba; Sierra Nevada, Alp., Cors ; TR
- **foetida** All. · G:Schneetälchen-Segge · ⚄ VII-VIII; Eur.: sp., F, I, Sw, A; Pyr., Alp.
- *fraseri* Andrews = Cymophyllus fraserianus
- **frigida** All. · G:Eis-Segge · ⚄ VI-VIII; Eur.: sp., F, Ital-P, C-Eur., Slove.; mts.
- **fritschii** Waisb. · G:Fritschs Segge · ⚄ IV-VI; Eur.: F, I, C-Eur., EC-Eur., Slove.
- **fuliginosa** Schkuhr · E:Red-brown Sedge; G:Ruß-Segge · ⚄ VI-VIII; Eur.* exc. BrI, Sc; Cauc., W-Sib.. E-Sib., Greenl., N-Can.
- *fusca* All. = Carex nigra subsp. nigra
- *glauca* Scop. = Carex flacca
- *gracilis* Curtis = Carex acuta
- **grayi** Carey · E:Mace Sedge; G:Morgenstern-Segge · ⚄ ⌒ Z7 VI; Can.: E; USA; NE, NCE, SE
- *guestphalica* (Boenn. ex Rchb.) Boenn. ex O. Lang = Carex divulsa
- **hachijoensis** Akiyama · ⚄ ; Jap.
- **halleriana** Asso · G:Grundstielige Segge, Hallers Segge · ⚄ IV-V; Eur.: Ib, Fr, Ital-P,

C-Eur., EC-Eur., Ba, RO, Crim; TR, Cauc., Afgh., Him.

- **hartmanii** Cajander · G:Hartmans Segge · ⁌ ∿ V-VI; Eur.* exc. BrI, Ib; Cauc., W-Sib., E-Sib., C-As., e. N-Am.
- **heleonastes** L. f. · E:Peat Sedge; G:Torf-Segge · ⁌ ∿ V-VI; Eur.* exc. Ib, BrI; Cauc., W-Sib., E-Sib.
- **hirta** L. · E:Hairy Sedge; F:Laîche hérissée; G:Behaarte Segge · ⁌ ∿ V-VI; Eur.*, TR, Cauc., N-Am.
- **hordeistichos** Vill. · E:Barley Sedge; G:Gersten-Segge · ⁌ VI; Eur.: Ib, Fr, C-Eur., Ba, EC-Eur., ? Cors; TR, Cauc., Iran, ? Afgh., Pakist., NW-Afr.
- **hostiana** DC. · E:Tawny Sedge; G:Saum-Segge · ⁌ ∿ VI-VII; Eur.* , Cauc., Iran , Can.: E, Greenl.
- *hudsonii* A.W. Benn. = Carex elata
- **humilis** Leyss. · E:Dwarf Sedge; F:Laîche humble; G:Erd-Segge · ⁌ Z4 IV; Eur.* exc. Sc; TR, Cauc., W-Sib.
- × **involuta** (Bab.) Syme (*C. rostrata* × *C. vesicaria*) · G:Bastard-Blasen-Segge · ⁌ ∿
- *japonica* hort. = Carex morrowii
- *jemtlandica* (Palmgr.) Palmgr. = Carex viridula subsp. viridula var. jemtlandica
- *juncella* (Fr.) Th. Fr. = Carex nigra subsp. juncella
- **lachenalii** Schkuhr · E:Hare's-foot Sedge; G:Lachenals Segge · ⁌ VII-VIII; Eur.*, N-As., N-Am., NZ
- **laevigata** Sm. · E:Smooth-stalked Sedge; G:Glatte Segge · ⁌ IV-V; Eur.: Ib, Fr, Cors, BrI, D
- **lasiocarpa** Ehrh. · E:Slender Sedge; G:Faden-Segge · ⁌ ∿ VI-VII; Eur.*, Cauc., W-Sib., E-Sib., Amur, Sakhal., Kamchat., C-As., Mong.
- *leersiana* Rouy = Carex divulsa
- *lepidocarpa* Tausch = Carex viridula subsp. viridula var. elatior
- **leporina** L. · G:Hasenpfoten-Segge · ⁌ VI-VII
- *ligerica* J. Gay = Carex colchica
- **limosa** L. · E:Bog Sedge, Mud Sedge; G:Schlamm-Segge · ⁌ ∿ VI-VII; Eur.*, TR, Cauc., W-Sib., E-Sib., Amur, Sakhal., Kamchat., Mong., Manch., N-Am.
- **liparocarpos** Gaudin · E:Glossy-fruited Sedge; G:Glanz-Segge · ⁌ IV-V; Eur.* exc. BrI, Sc; TR, Cauc., N-Iran
- **loliacea** L. · E:Darnel Sedge, Ryegrass Sedge; G:Lolchartige Segge · ⁌ ∿ ; Eur.:

Sc, PL, E-Eur.; W-Sib., E-Sib., Amur, Sakhal., Kamchat., C-As., Manch., Korea, N-Jap.
- **magellanica** Lam. · E:Boreal Bog Sedge
- subsp. **irrigua** (Wahlenb.) Hultén · G:Riesel-Segge · ⁌ ∿ VI-VIII; Eur.* exc. Ib, Ba; TR, Cauc., Sib., Mong., E-As., N-Am.
- **maritima** Gunnerus · E:Curved Sedge; G:Binsenblättrige Segge · ⁌ VII-VIII; Eur.: BrI, Sc, Balt., F, I, Ch, A, ? sp.; N, Alp.; Sib., N-Am.
- *maxima* Scop. = Carex pendula
- **melanostachya** M. Bieb. ex Willd. · E:Nodding Pond Sedge; G:Schwarzäh-rige Segge · ⁌ ∿ V-VI; Eur.* exc. BrI, Sc; TR, Iraq, Cauc., Iran, Afgh., W-Sib., C-As.
- **michelii** Host · G:Michelis Segge · ⁌ IV-V; Eur.: I, A, EC-Eur., Ba, E-Eur.; Cauc., nat. in ? F
- **microglochin** Wahlenb. · E:Bristle Sedge; G:Kleingrannige Segge · ⁌ ∿ V-VII; Eur.: BrI, Sc, N-Russ., Fr, Ital-P, C-Eur., ? Balt.; TR, Cauc., W-Sib., E-Sib.
- × **microstachya** Ehrh. (*C. canescens* × *C. dioica*) · G:Kleinährige Bastard-Segge · ⁌ ∿ ; Eur.: G, PL, Alp.
- **montana** L. · E:Mountain Sedge; F:Laîche des montagnes; G:Berg-Segge · ⁌ △ Z6 III-V; Eur.*, Cauc., W-Sib.
- **morrowii** Boott · E:Japanese Sedge, Morrow Sedge; G:Japan-Segge · ⁌ Z7; Jap.
- some cultivars
- **mucronata** All. · G:Stachelspitzige Segge · ⁌ V-VIII; Eur.: F, Ital-P, C-Eur., Slove., Croatia., ? RO; Alp., Apenn.; ? Cauc.
- **muricata** L. · E:Rough Sedge; G:Sparrige Segge · ⁌ ; Eur.*, TR, Cauc., N-Am.
- **muskingumensis** Schwein. · E:Muskingum Sedge; G:Palmwedel-Segge · ⁌ Z7; Can.: E; USA: NE, NCE, NC
- **nigra** (L.) Reichard
- subsp. **juncella** (Fr.) Lemke · G:Binsenar-tige Segge · ⁌ V-VI; N-Eur.
- subsp. **nigra** · E:Smooth Black Sedge; F:Laîche sombre; G:Braun-Segge, Wiesen-Segge · ⁌ ∿ Z5 V-VI; Eur.*, TR, W-Sib.
- **norvegica** Retz. · E:Close-headed Alpine Sedge; G:Norwegische Segge · ⁌ VII-VIII; Eur.: BrI, Sc, Russ., C-Eur., I, ? F; Greenl.
- **obtusata** Lilj. · E:Obtuse Sedge; G:Stumpfe Segge · ⁌ IV-V; Eur.: G, Swed,

Russ.; Cauc., W-Sib., E-Sib., Amur, C-As.,
w N-Am.
- *oederi* Ehrh. = Carex viridula subsp.
viridula var. viridula
- × **oenensis** A. Neumann ex B. Walln. (*C.
acuta* × *C. randalpina*) · G:Bastard-Inn-
Segge · ⟁ V; C-Eur.
- **ornithopoda** Willd. · G:Vogelfuß-Segge
- subsp. **ornithopoda** · E:Birds Foot Sedge;
F:Laîche pied-d'oiseau; G:Gewöhnliche
Vogelfuß-Segge · ⟁ △ Z6 V-VI; Eur.*
- subsp. **ornithopodioides** (Hausm.)
Nyman · G:Vogelfußähnliche Segge · ⟁
VII-VIII; Eur.: Pyr., Alp., ? Ba mts.
- *ornithopodioides* Hausm. = Carex
ornithopoda subsp. ornithopodioides
- *otrubae* Podp. = Carex cuprina
- *ovalis* Gooden. = Carex leporina
- **pairae** F.W. Schultz · G:Pairas Segge · ⟁
V-VIII; Eur.*, TR, Cauc., W-Sib., E-Sib.,
N-Afr., Madeira, nat. in N-Am.
- **paleacea** Schreb. ex Wahlenb. · E:Chaffy
Sedge · ⟁ ; Eur.: Sc, N.Russ.; Can.,
Greenl.
- **pallescens** L. · E:Pale Sedge; G:Bleiche
Segge · ⟁ V-VII; Eur.*, TR, Syr., Cauc.,
N-Iran, W-Sib., E-Sib., Amur, C-As, w
N-Am.
- **panicea** L. · E:Grass-like Sedge; G:Hirse-
Segge · ⟁ ⌢ V-VI; Eur.*, TR, Iraq,
Cauc., Iran, W-Sib., E-Sib., Amur, C-As
- **paniculata** L. · E:Greater Tussock Sedge;
F:Laîche paniculée; G:Rispen-Segge · ⟁
⌢ Z6 V-VI; Eur.*, Cauc.
- **parviflora** Host · E:Small-flowered
Sedge; G:Kleinblütige Segge · ⟁ VII-VIII;
Eur.* exc. BrI, Sc +; mts.
- **pauciflora** Lightf. · E:Few-flowered
Sedge; G:Armblütige Segge · ⟁ ⌢
V-VII; Eur.* exc. Ib; W-Sib., E-Sib., Amur,
Sakhal., Kamchat., C-As, N-Am.
- *paupercula* Michx. = Carex magellanica
subsp. irrigua
- **pediformis** C.A. Mey. · G:Dickwurzel-
Segge · ⟁ V-VII; Eur.: Sc, EC-Eur., E-Eur.,
A
- **pendula** Huds. · E:Drooping Sedge, Pen-
dulous Sedge; F:Laîche géante, Laîche
pendante; G:Hänge-Segge, Riesen-Segge
· ⟁ ⌢ Z6 VI; Eur.*, Cauc., N-Iran
- × **peraffinis** Appel (*C. cespitosa* × *C. nigra
subsp. nigra*) · G:Bastard-Rasen-Segge · ⟁
⌢ ; Eur.: G, PL
- **petriei** Cheeseman · ⟁ ∧ VII-X; NZ
- **pilosa** Scop. · G:Wimper-Segge · ⟁ V-VI;

Eur.: Fr, Ital-P, C-Eur., EC-Eur., Ba,
E-Eur.
- **pilulifera** L. · G:Pillen-Segge · ⟁ V-VI;
Eur.*
- **plantaginea** Lam. · E:Plantain Leaved
Sedge; F:Laîche à feuilles de plantain · ⟁
Z7 V-VI; Can.: E; USA; NE, NCE, SE
- *praecox* Jacq. = Carex caryophyllea
- **praecox** Schreb. · E:Early Sedge;
G:Frühe Segge
- subsp. **intermedia** (Čelak.) W. Schultze-
Motel · G:Gekrümmte Segge, Gekrümmte
Frühe Segge · ⟁ V-VI; Eur.: B, F(Alsace),
G, PL, CZ, Slova., A, RO
- subsp. **praecox** · G:Gewöhnliche Frühe
Segge · ⟁ IV-VI; Eur.* exc. BrI, Sc; Cauc.,
W-Sib., E-Sib., C-As., nat. in FIN
- **pseudobrizoides** Chabaud · G:Reichen-
bachs Zittergras-Segge · ⟁ IV-VI; Eur.: Fr,
G, PL, CZ
- **pseudocyperus** L. · E:Cyperus Sedge;
F:Laîche faux-souchet; G:Scheinzyper-
gras-Segge · ⟁ ⌢ VI; Eur.*, TR, Syr.,
Cauc., N-Iran, W-Sib., E-Sib., C-As.,
Mong., NW-Afr., Can., USA: NE, NCE,
NC; NZ
- **pulicaris** L. · E:Flea Sedge; G:Floh-Segge
· ⟁ ⌢ V-VI; Eur.*
- **punctata** Gaudin · E:Dotted Sedge;
G:Punktierte Segge · ⟁ V-VII; Eur.* exc.
EC-Eur.; TR
- **randalpina** B. Walln. · G:Inn-Segge · ⟁ ;
Eur.: A, D
- **remota** L. · E:Remote Sedge; G:Winkel-
Segge · ⟁ ⌢ VI-VII; Eur.*, Cauc.,
N-Iran, Alger.
- **repens** Bellardi · G:Kriech-Segge · ⟁
V-VI; Eur.: I, G, A, EC-Eur., RO, ? F
- **riparia** Curtis · E:Pond Sedge; F:Laîche
des rives; G:Ufer-Segge · ⟁ ⌢ Z6 VI;
Eur.*, Cauc., TR, Iran, W-Sib., E-Sib.,
C-As.
- **rostrata** Stokes · E:Beaked Sedge;
G:Schnabel-Segge · ⟁ ⌢ VI; Eur.*,
TR, Cauc., N-Iran, W-Sib., E-Sib., Amur,
Sakhal., Kamchat., C-As., N-Am.
- **rupestris** All. · E:Rock Sedge; G:Felsen-
Segge · ⟁ VI-VII; Eur.*, Cauc., W-Sib.,
E-Sib., ? Amur, Mong., N-Am.
- *ruthenica* V.I. Krecz. = Carex caryophyllea
- *scabricuspis* V.I. Krecz. = Carex caryophyllea
- **scaposa** C.B. Clarke · ⟁ Z8 ⊛ IX-XI;
S-China, Indochina
- **secalina** Willd. ex Wahlenb. · E:Rye

Sedge; G:Roggen-Segge · ⚃ ⌣ VI; Eur.:
C-Eur., EC-Eur., E-Eur.; Cauc., W-Sib.,
E-Sib., C-As.
- **sempervirens** Vill. · E:Evergreen Sedge;
G:Horst-Segge, Immergrüne Segge · ⚃
VI-VIII; Eur.* exc. BrI, Sc
- *serotina* Mérat = Carex viridula subsp.
viridula var. viridula
- **siderosticta** Hance · ⚃ Z7 IV-V; Amur,
China, Manch., Korea, Jap.
- **spicata** Huds. · E:Prickly Sedge;
G:Dichtährige Segge · ⚃ V-VIII; Eur.*,
TR, Cauc., N-Iran, W-Sib., Canar., N-Afr.,
nat. in N-Am.
- **stenophylla** Wahlenb. · G:Schmalblatt-
Segge · ⚃ IV-VIII; Eur.: I, A, W-Ba,
EC-Eur., ? sp.; TR, Cauc., Iran, Afgh.,
C-As., Kashmir, Mong.
- *stricta* Gooden. = Carex elata
- **strigosa** Huds. · E:Thin-spiked Wood
Sedge; G:Dünnährige Segge · ⚃ VI-VII;
Eur.*, Cauc., N-Iran
- **supina** Willd. ex Wahlenb. · E:Small
Sedge; G:Steppen-Segge · ⚃ IV-V; Eur.:
I, C-Eur., EC-Eur., Croatia, E-Eur.; Cauc.,
W-Sib., C-As.
- **sylvatica** Huds. · E:Wood Sedge;
F:Laîche des bois; G:Wald-Segge · ⚃ Z6
VI; Eur.*, Cauc., W-Sib.
- *tomentosa* L. = Carex filiformis
- **trinervis** Degl. · E:Three-nerved Sedge;
G:Dreinervige Segge · ⚃ VI-VII; Eur.: Fr,
G, DK, PL, ? sp.; coasts
- × **turfosa** Fr. (*C. elata subsp. elata × C.
nigra subsp. nigra*) · G:Bastard-Steif-
Segge · ⚃ ⌣ ; Eur.
- **umbrosa** Host · E:Shady Sedge; F:Laîche
des ombrages; G:Schatten-Segge · ⚃ Z6
V; Eur.* exc. BrI, Sc; TR, Cauc.
- **vaginata** Tausch · E:Sheathed Sedge;
G:Scheiden-Segge · ⚃ VI-VII; Eur.* exc.
Ital-P, Ba; Cauc., W-Sib., E-Sib.
- **vesicaria** L. · E:Bladder Sedge; G:Blasen-
Segge · ⚃ ⌣ VI; Eur.*, Cauc., W-Sib.,
E-Sib., C-As., N-Afr., N-Am.
- **viridula** Michx. · E:Little Green Sedge;
G:Späte Gelb-Segge
- subsp. **oedocarpa** (Andersson) B.
Schmid · G:Grün-Segge, Grünliche
Gelb-Segge · ⚃ V-VII; Eur.* exc. Ital-P,
Ba; Can.: E; Tasm., NZ
- subsp. **viridula**
- var. **elatior** (Schltr.) Crins · G:Schup-
penfrüchtige Gelb-Segge · ⚃ ⌣ VI-VII;
Eur.* , Moroc., e. N-Am.

- var. **jemtlandica** (Palmgr.) Blackst. &
P.A. Ashton · ⚃ ; Eur.: Sc, N-Russ., Balt., ?
Sw
- var. **pulchella** (Lönnr.) B. Schmid ·
G:Küsten-Gelb-Segge, Skandinavische
Gelb-Segge · ⚃ ⌣ ; N-Am.
- subsp. **virudula** var. **viridula** ·
G:Gewöhnliche Späte Gelb-Segge, Oed-
ers Segge · ⚃ ⌣ V-IX; N-Am., Kamchat.,
Sakhal., Jap.
- **vulpina** L. · E:Fox Sedge; G:Fuchs-Segge
· ⚃ ⌣ Z7 V-VI; Eur.*, Cauc., W-Sib.,
E-Sib., C-As.
- **vulpinoidea** Michx. · E:American Fox
Sedge; G:Fuchsartige Segge · ⚃ ⌣ V-VI;
N-Am., nat. in Eur.: BrI, Fr, Sw, EC-Eur.;
TR

Carica L. -f- Caricaceae · 23 spp. ·
E:Pawpaw; F:Arbre-aux-melons, Papayer;
G:Melonenbaum, Papaya
- × *heilbornii* V.M. Badillo = Carica
pentagona
- *nothovar. pentagona* (Heilborn) V.M.
Badillo = Carica pentagona
- **papaya** L. · E:Papaya; G:Melonenbaum,
Papaya · ♄ e Z10 🌳 ⚘ Ⓝ; S-Am., nat. in
S-Fla., Mex., C-Am., W.Ind., trop. Afr.,
trop. As,
- **pentagona** Heilborn · E:Babaco;
G:Babaco · ♄ 🌳 Ⓝ; S-Am.; ? And.
- **pubescens** Lenné & K. Koch ·
E:Mountain Papaya; G:Berg-Papaya · ♄ e
🌳 Ⓝ; Panama, Col., Ecuad., Chile; And.

Carissa L. -f- Apocynaceae · 37 spp. ·
E:Natal Plum; F:Arbre-à-cire, Carisse;
G:Wachsbaum
- *acokanthera* Pichon = Acokanthera
oppositifolia
- *arduina* Lam. = Carissa bispinosa
- **bispinosa** (L.) Desf. ex Brenan ·
E:Hedgethorn; G:Dorniger Wachsbaum ·
♄ e Z10 🌳; S-Afr.
- **carandas** L. · E:Karanda; G:Karanda-
Wachsbaum · ♄ ♄ e Z10 🌳 Ⓝ; Ind.,
Malay. Arch.
- **edulis** Vahl · E:Carandas Plum;
G:Karanda-Pflaume · ♄ e Z10 🌳; trop.
Afr., Arab.
- *grandiflora* (E. Mayer) A. DC. = Carissa
macrocarpa
- **macrocarpa** (Eckl.) A. DC. · E:Natal
Plum; G:Natal-Pflaume · ♄ e Z10 🌳 Ⓝ;
S-Afr.

– *schimperi* A. DC. = Acokanthera
schimperi
– *spectabilis* (Sond.) Pichon = Acokanthera
oblongifolia

Carlina L. -f- *Asteraceae* · 28 spp. ·
E:Carline Thistle; F:Carline; G:Eberwurz,
Silberdistel, Wetterdistel
– **acanthifolia** All. · F:Carline à feuilles
d'acanthe, Chardon-soleil; G:Acanthus-
blättrige Eberwurz · ⳡ △ Z7 ⋀ VII-IX;
Eur.: Ib, Fr, Ital-P, Ba, PL, EC-Eur.
– acaulis L. · G:Silberdistel, Wetterdistel
– subsp. **acaulis** · E:Stemless Carline
Thistle; F:Carline à tige courte; G:Große
Eberwurz, Stängellose Silberdistel · ⳡ Z4
VII-IX ⚥ ▽; Eur.* exc. BrI, Sc
– subsp. *caulescens* (Lam.) Schübl. & G.
Martens = Carlina acaulis subsp. simplex
– subsp. **simplex** (Waldst. & Kit.) Nyman ·
F:Carline argentée; G:Krausblättrige
Silberdistel · ⳡ △ Z4 VII-IX ▽; Eur.* exc.
BrI, Sc
– var. *alpina* Jacq. = Carlina acaulis subsp.
simplex
– **biebersteinii** Bernh. ex Hornem.
– subsp. **biebersteinii** · G:Steife Golddistel · ⊙ VII-IX; Eur.: Sc, C-Eur., EC-Eur.,
E-Eur.; Sib., TR
– subsp. **brevibracteata** (Andrae) K.
Werner · G:Mittlere Golddistel · ⊙ VII-IX
– *caulescens* Lam. = Carlina acaulis subsp.
simplex
– *utzka* Hacq. = Carlina acanthifolia
– **vulgaris** L. · E:Common Carline Thistle;
G:Gewöhnliche Golddistel, Kleine
Eberwurz · ⊙ ⳡ VII-IX Ⓝ; Eur.*, TR,
Cauc., N-Iran

Carludovica Ruiz & Pav. -f- *Cyclanthaceae* ·
4 spp. · F:Palmier du Panama; G:Carludo-
vike, Panamapalme
– *atrovirens* H. Wendl. = Dicranopygium
atrovirens
– *humilis* Poepp. & Endl. = Asplundia
humilis
– *moritziana* Klotzsch = Asplundia
moritziana
– **palmata** Ruiz & Pav. · E:Panama Hat
Plant; G:Panamahutpalme, Panamapalme · ♄ e Z10 Ⓜ Ⓝ; trop. S-Am.,
nat. in W.Ind., E-Afr., Pacific Is.
– *plicata* Klotzsch = Asplundia moritziana

Carmichaelia R. Br. -f- *Fabaceae* · 40 spp. ·

F:Carmichaelia; G:Rutenblume
– **arborea** (G. Forst.) Druce · ♄ Z8 Ⓚ
VI-VII; NZ
– *australis* auct. non R. Br. ex Lindl. =
Carmichaelia arborea
– **enysii** Kirk · ♄ Z8 Ⓚ VI-VIII; NZ
– **flagelliformis** Colenso ex Hook. f. · ⳡ ♄
Z8 Ⓚ VI; NZ
– **monroi** Hook. f. · ♄ Z8 Ⓚ; NZ
– **orbiculata** Colenso · ♄ Z8 Ⓚ; NZ
– **petriei** Kirk · ♄ Z8 Ⓚ; NZ
– **rivulata** G. Simpson · ♄ Z8 Ⓚ; NZ
– **williamsii** Kirk · ♄ Z8 Ⓦ III-IV; NZ

Carmona Cav. -f- *Boraginaceae* · 1 sp.
– *heterophylla* Cav. = Carmona retusa
– *microphylla* (Lam.) G. Don = Carmona
retusa
– **retusa** (Vahl) Masam. · E:Scorpion Bush ·
♄ Ⓜ; Ind., Malay. Arch, Phil., Taiwan

Carnegiea Britton & Rose -f- *Cactaceae* ·
1 sp. · E:Saguaro; F:Sagaro; G:Riesenkak-
tus, Saguaro
– *euphorbioides* (Haw.) Backeb. = Neobuxbaumia euphorbioides
– **gigantea** (Engelm.) Britton & Rose ·
E:Giant Cactus, Saguaro; G:Riesenkak-
tus, Saguaro · ♄ ⳡ Z9 Ⓚ Ⓝ ▽ ❊; USA:
S-Calif., Ariz.; Mex.
– *polylopha* (DC.) D.R. Hunt = Neobuxbaumia polylopha

Carpanthea N.E. Br. -f- *Aizoaceae* · 1 sp.
– **pomeridiana** (L.) N.E. Br. · ⊙ ⳡ VI-IX;
Cape

Carpenteria Torr. -f- *Hydrangeaceae* · 1 sp. ·
E:Tree Anemone; G:Baumanemone
– **californica** Torr. · E:Tree Anemone;
G:Baumanemone · ♄ e Z8 Ⓚ VI-VII;
Calif.

Carpesium L. -n- *Asteraceae* · 20-25 spp. ·
F:Carpésium; G:Kragenblume
– **cernuum** L. · G:Nickende Kragenblume ·
⊙ VII-IX; Eur.* exc. BrI, Sc; TR, Cauc.,
N-Iran, Him., China, Jap.

Carpinus L. -f- *Betulaceae* · 41 sp. ·
E:Hornbeam; F:Charme; G:Hainbuche
– **betulus** L. · E:Common Hornbeam, Euro-
pean Hornbeam; F:Charme commun,
Charmille; G:Gewöhnliche Hainbuche,
Weißbuche · ♄ d ⚙ Z5 IV-VI Ⓝ; Eur.*,

Cauc., TR, Iran
- **some cultivars**
- **caroliniana** Walter · E:American
  Hornbeam; G:Amerikanische Hainbuche
  · ♄ ♄ d ⚭ Z5 Ⓝ; Can.: E; USA: NE, NCE,
  SE, SC; Mex., Guat., Belize
- *caucasica* Grossh. = Carpinus betulus
- **cordata** Blume · G:Herzblättrige
  Hainbuche · ♄ d ⚭ Z5; Jap., Korea, China
- **japonica** Blume · E:Japanese Hornbeam;
  G:Japanische Hainbuche · ♄ d Z5; Japan
- **laxiflora** (Siebold & Zucc.) Blume ·
  G:Lockerblütige Hainbuche · ♄ d Z5;
  Japan, Korea
- **orientalis** Mill. · E:Oriental Hornbeam;
  G:Orientalische Hainbuche · ♄ ♄ d ⚭ Z6;
  Eur.: Ital-P, Ba, H, RO, Crim; TR, Cauc.,
  N-Iran
- **polyneura** Franch. · ♄ d; W-China:
  Sichuan, Hupeh
- **tschonoskii** Maxim. · G:Tschonoskis
  Hainbuche · ♄ d ⚭ Z5; Jap., Korea,
  N-China
- *yedoensis* Maxim. = Carpinus tschonoskii

Carpobrotus N.E. Br. -m- *Aizoaceae* ·
13 spp. · E:Hottentot-Fig; F:Figue des
Hottentots; G:Hottentottenfeige
- **acinaciformis** (L.) L. Bolus · E:Sally-
  my-handsome · ♃ Ψ Z9 ⓐ VII-XI; S-Afr.:
  Cape, Natal; Austr., Tasman.
- **edulis** (L.) N.E. Br. · E:Hottentot Fig;
  G:Hottentottenfeige · ♃ Ψ Z8 ⓐ Ⓝ; Cape
- **muirii** (L. Bolus) L. Bolus · G:Magere
  Hottentottenfeige · ♃ Ψ Z9 ⓐ; Cape

Carpogymnia (H.P. Fuchs ex Janch.) Á.
Löve & D. Löve = Gymnocarpium
- *dryopteris* (L.) Á. Löve & D. Löve =
  Gymnocarpium dryopteris

Carruanthus (Schwantes) Schwantes -m-
Aizoaceae · 2 spp.
- *caninus* (Haw.) Schwantes = Carruanthus
  ringens
- **peersii** L. Bolus · ♃ Ψ Z9 ⓐ; Cape
- **ringens** (L.) Boom · ♃ Ψ Z9 ⓐ; Cape

Carthamus L. -m- *Asteraceae* · 17 spp. ·
E:Safflower; F:Carthame, Safran bâtard;
G:Saflor
- **lanatus** L. · E:Distaff Thistle, Downy
  Safflower; G:Wolliger Saflor · ⊙ VI-VII;
  Eur.: Ba, Ib, EC-Eur., Fr, Ital-P, E-Eur.,
  Ba, Sw; Iraq, Cauc., Iran, C-As., N-Afr.

- **tinctorius** L. · E:Dyer's Saffron, Fake
  Saffron, Safflower; G:Färber-Distel,
  Färber-Saflor · ⊙ VII ⚥ ⚒ Ⓝ; W-As.,
  cult. S-Eur., Ind., Calif, nat. in C-Eur.,
  S-Eur.

Carum L. -n- *Apiaceae* · c. 30 spp. ·
E:Caraway; F:Cumin; G:Kümmel
- **carvi** L. · E:Caraway; G:Wiesen-Kümmel ·
  ⊙ Z3 V-VI ⚥ Ⓝ; Eur.* exc. BrI; TR, Cauc.,
  N-Iran, W-Sib., E-Sib., Kamchat., C-As.,
  Mong., Afgh., Him. China, NW-Afr., nat.
  in N-Am., NZ
- *copticum* (L.) Benth. & Hook. f. =
  Trachyspermum ammi
- **verticillatum** (L.) W.D.J. Koch ·
  E:Whorled Caraway; G:Quirlblättriger
  Kümmel · ♃ VII-VIII; Eur.: BrI, Fr, Ib

Carya Nutt. -f- *Juglandaceae* · c. 20 spp. ·
E:Hickory, Pecan; F:Noyer d'Amérique;
G:Hickorynuss
- *alba* (L.) Nutt. = Carya ovata
- *amara* (F. Michx.) Nutt. = Carya
  cordiformis
- **cordiformis** (Wangenh.) K. Koch ·
  E:Bitternut Hickory, Swamp Hickory;
  G:Bittere Hickorynuss, Bitternuss · ♄ d Z6
  Ⓝ; Can.: E; USA: NE, NCE, NC, SC, SE,
  Fla.
- **glabra** (Mill.) Sweet · E:Pignut; G:Ferkel-
  nuss · ♄ d Z6 Ⓝ; Ont., USA: NE, NCE, SC,
  SE, Fla.
- **illinoinensis** (Wangenh.) K. Koch ·
  E:Pecan; G:Pekannuss · ♄ d Z6 Ⓝ; USA:
  NCE, Ky.
- **laciniosa** (F. Michx.) Loudon ·
  E:Shellbark Hickory; G:Königsnuss · ♄ d
  Z6 Ⓝ; Ont., USA: NE, NCE, NC, Okla., SE
- *microcarpa* Nutt. = Carya ovalis
- **myristiciformis** (F. Michx.) Nutt. ·
  E:Nutmeg Hickory; G:Muskat-Hickory-
  nuss · ♄ d Z9 ⓐ; USA: SE, SC.; Mex.:
  Nuevo Leon
- *olivaeformis* Nutt. = Carya illinoinensis
- **ovalis** (Wangenh.) Sarg. · E:Red Hickory;
  G:Rote Hickorynuss · ♄ d Z6 Ⓝ; Can.:
  Ont.; USA: NE, NCE, SE
- **ovata** (Mill.) K. Koch · E:Shagbark
  Hickory; G:Schuppenrinden-Hickorynuss
  · ♄ d Z6 Ⓝ; Can.: E; USA: NE, NCE, NC,
  SC, SE; Mex.
- *pecan* (Marshall) Engl. & Graebn. = Carya
  illinoinensis
- *porcina* (F. Michx.) Nutt. = Carya glabra

– *pubescens* (Willd.) Sweet = Carya
laciniosa
– *sulcata* Nutt. = Carya laciniosa
– **tomentosa** (Lam. ex Poir.) Nutt. · E:Big
Bud Hickory, Mockernut; G:Spottnuss · ♄
d Z6 Ⓝ; Ont., USA: NE, NCE, NC, SC, SE,
Fla.

Caryocar L. -n- *Caryocaraceae* · 15 spp. ·
E:Butternut; G:Souarinuss
– **Braziliense** Cambess. · ♄ Z10 ⓦ Ⓝ;
Braz., Parag., Bol.
– **nuciferum** L. · E:Butternut; G:Souarinuss
· ♄ Z10 ⓦ Ⓝ; Guyan., Braz., Peru

Caryophyllus L. = Syzygium
– *aromaticus* L. = Syzygium aromaticum

Caryopteris Bunge -f- *Verbenaceae* · 6 spp. ·
E:Bluebeard; F:Caryoptéris; G:Bartblume
– × **clandonensis** N.W. Simmonds ex Rehder (*C. incana* × *C. mongholica*) · E:Blue
Beard, Blue Spiraea; F:Caryoptéris;
G:Clandon-Bartblume · ♄ d Z6 IX; cult.
– **some cultivars**
– **incana** (Thunb. ex Houtt.) Miq. · F:Barbe
bleue; G:Graufilzige Bartblume · ♄ d Z7
∧ IX-X; China, Korea, Jap., Taiwan
– *mastacantha* Schauer = Caryopteris
incana
– **mongholica** Bunge · G:Mongolische
Bartblume · ♄ d Z7 ∧ VIII-IX; Mong.,
N-China
– *sinensis* (Lour.) Dippel = Caryopteris
incana
– *tangutica* Maxim. = Caryopteris incana

Caryota L. -f- *Arecaceae* · 13 spp. · E:Fishtail
Palm; F:Palmier queue-de-poisson;
G:Fischschwanzpalme
– **maxima** Blume · G:Indonesische
Fischschwanzpalme · ♄ e Z10 ⓦ; Java
– **mitis** Lour. · E:Burmese Fishtail Palm;
G:Buschige Fischschwanzpalme · ♄ e Z10
ⓦ; Burma, Malay. Pen., Java, Phil.
– *sobolifera* Wall. ex Mart. = Caryota mitis
– **urens** L. · E:Sago Palm, Wine Palm;
G:Brennpalme, Sagopalme · ♄ e Z10 ⓦ
Ⓝ; Ind., Sri Lanka, Malay. Pen.

Casimiroa La Llave & Lex. -f- *Rutaceae* ·
6 spp. · E:White Sapote; F:Sapote
blanche; G:Weiße Sapote
– **edulis** La Llave & Lex. · E:Mexican Apple,
White Sapote; G:Weiße Sapote · ♄ e Z9

ⓦ Ⓝ; Mex., Guat.

Cassandra D. Don = Chamaedaphne
– *calyculata* (L.) D. Don = Chamaedaphne
calyculata

Cassia L. -f- *Caesalpiniaceae* · c. 30 spp. ·
E:Shower Tree; F:Séné; G:Gewürzrinde,
Kassie, Senna
– *acutifolia* Delile = Senna alexandrina
– *angustifolia* Vahl = Senna alexandrina
– *artemisioides* Gaudich. ex A. DC. = Senna
artemisioides
– *corymbosa* Lam. = Senna corymbosa var.
corymbosa
– *cotinifolia* G. Don = Chamaecrista
cotinifolia
– *didymobotrya* Fresen. = Senna didymobotrya
– **fistula** L. · E:Golden Shower, Indian
Laburnum, Purging Cassia; G:Röhren-
Kassie · ♄ s Z10 ⓦ ☼ Ⓝ; Ind.
– *floribunda* Cav. = Senna × floribunda
– **grandis** L. f. · E:Appleblossom Cassia,
Pink Shower; G:Grobfrüchtige Kassie,
Rosen-Kassie · ♄ s Z10 ⓦ Ⓝ; Mex.,
C-Am., W.Ind., trop. S-Am.
– *hebecarpa* Fernald = Senna hebecarpa
– *italica* (Mill.) Lam. ex Steud. = Senna
italica
– **javanica** L. · E:Rainbow Shower; G:Rosa-
farbene Kassie · ♄ d Z10 ⓦ; Malay. Arch.
– *marilandica* hort. = Senna hebecarpa
– *marilandica* L. = Senna marilandica
– *nairobensis* L.H. Bailey = Senna didymobotrya
– *nodosa* Roxb. = Cassia javanica
– *obovata* Collad. = Senna italica
– **odorata** R. Morris · E:Sicklepod · ♄ Z9
☖; Austr.: N.S.Wales
– *senna* L. = Senna alexandrina
– *siamea* Lam. = Senna siamea
– *spectabilis* DC. = Senna spectabilis
– *tomentosa* L. f. = Senna multiglandulosa

Cassine L. -f- *Celastraceae* · c. 80 spp.
– **orientalis** (Jacq.) Kuntze · E:False Olive;
G:Falscher Olivenbaum · ♄ Z10 ⓦ;
Madag., Mauritius

Cassinia R. Br. -f- *Asteraceae* · 20 spp.
– **fulvida** Hook. f. · E:Golden Cottonwood,
Golden Heather; G:Goldpappel · ♄ Z9 ☖
VII-VIII; NZ
– **retorta** A. Cunn. ex DC. · ♄ Z8 ☖; NZ

– **vauvilliersii** (Hombr. & Jacquinot ex Decne.) Hook. f. · ♄ Z8 ⓚ VII-VIII; NZ

Cassiope D. Don -f- *Ericaceae* · 12 spp. · E:Mountain Heather; F:Cassiope; G:Schuppenheide
– **fastigiata** (Wall.) D. Don · G:Himalaya-Schuppenheide · ♄ e IV-V; Him., China
– **hypnoides** (L.) D. Don · G:Moosige Schuppenheide · ♄ e △ Z2 VI-VII; Eur.: Sc, N-Russ.; W-Sib., Greenl.
– **lycopodioides** (Pall.) D. Don · E:Clubmoss Mountain Heather; G:Bärlappähnliche Schuppenheide · ♄ e Z5 IV-V; Alaska, Kamchat., Jap.
– **mertensiana** (Bong.) D. Don · E:Western Moss Heather; G:Weiße Schuppenheide · ♄ e △ Z5 IV; Alaska, Can.: W; USA: NW, Calif., Nev.
– **tetragona** (L.) D. Don · E:White Arctic Mountain Heather; G:Vierkantige Schuppenheide · ♄ e △ Z5 V; Eur.: Sc, N-Russ; W-Sib., E-Sib., Amur, Kamchat., Alaska, N-Can., Greenl.
– **wardii** C. Marquand · E:Ward's Moss Heather; G:Wards Schuppenheide · ♄ e △ V; SE-Tibet

Cassytha L. -f- *Lauraceae* · 20 spp. · E:Dodder Laurel
– **pubescens** R. Br. · E:Downy Dodder Laurel · ♄ ⚥ ⓚ; Austr.

Castanea Mill. -f- *Fagaceae* · 8 spp. · E:Chestnut; F:Châtaignier; G:Kastanie
– *americana* (Michx.) Raf. = Castanea dentata
– **crenata** Siebold & Zucc. · E:Japanese Chestnut; G:Japanische Kastanie · ♄ ♄ d Z6 Ⓝ; Jap.
– **dentata** (Marshall) Borkh. · E:American Chestnut; G:Amerikanische Kastanie · ♄ d Z5 Ⓝ; Ont., USA: NE, NCE, SE
– *hystrix* Hook. f. & Thomson ex Miq. = Castanopsis purpurella
– *japonica* Blume = Castanea crenata
– **mollissima** Blume · E:Chinese Chestnut; G:Chinesische Kastanie · ♄ d Z4 Ⓝ; China, Korea, Taiwan
– **pumila** (L.) Mill. · E:Allegheny Chinkapin; G:Pennsylvanische Kastanie · ♄ ♄ d Z6 Ⓝ; USA: NE, SE, Fla., SC
– **purpurella** Miq. = Castanopsis purpurella
– **sativa** Mill. · E:Spanish Chestnut, Sweet Chestnut; F:Châtaignier commun;

G:Edel-Kastanie, Ess-Kastanie, Marone · ♄ d Z6 VI ⚥ Ⓝ; Eur.: Ital-P, A, EC-Eur., Ba; TR, Cauc., N-Iran, NW-Afr., nat. in BrI, Sc, Fr, BrI, E-Eur.
– some cultivars
– *vesca* Gaertn. = Castanea sativa
– *vulgaris* Lam. = Castanea sativa

Castanopsis (D. Don) Spach -f- *Fagaceae* · 134 spp. · E:Chinquapin; F:Faux-châtaignier; G:Scheinkastanie
– *chrysophylla* (Douglas ex Hook.) A. DC. = Chrysolepis chrysophylla
– **cuspidata** (Thunb.) Schottky · ♄ e Z7; S-Jap., SE-China
– *hystrix* A. DC. = Castanopsis purpurella
– **purpurella** (Miq.) N.P. Balakr. · E. Asia

Castanospermum A. Cunn. ex Hook. -n- *Fabaceae* · 1 sp. · E:Australia Chestnut; F:Châtaignier d'Australie; G:Australische Kastanie
– **australe** A. Cunn. & Fraser ex Hook. · E:Australia Chestnut, Black Bean Tree, Moreton Bay Chestnut; G:Australische Kastanie, Giftkastanie · ♄ e Z9 ⓚ ⚥ ; Austr.: N.S.Wales

Castilla Cerv. -f- *Moraceae* · 3 spp. · E:Rubber Tree; F:Arbre à caoutchouc du Panama; G:Kautschukbaum
– **elastica** Sessé ex Cerv. · E:Castilla Rubber Tree, Panama Rubber Tree; G:Panama-Kautschukbaum · ♄ Z10 ⓜ Ⓝ; S-Mex., C-Am., trop. S-Am.
– **ulei** Warb. · E:Caucho Rubber G:Schwarzer; Kautschukbaum · ♄ Z10 ⓜ Ⓝ; S-Am.

Casuarina L. -f- *Casuarinaceae* · c. 70 spp. · E:Australian Pine, Beefwood; F:Casuarina; G:Kängurubaum, Kasuarine, Keulenbaum
– **cunninghamiana** Miq. · E:River Oak; G:Fluss-Keulenbaum · ♄ e Z9 ⓚ Ⓝ; Austr.: Queensl., N.S.Wales
– **equisetifolia** J.R. Forst. & G. Forst. · E:Horsetail Tree, South Sea Ironwood; G:Eisenholz, Strand-Keulenbaum · ♄ e Z9 ⓚ Ⓝ; SE-As., NE-Austr., Polyn., nat. in S-Fla., Bermudas etc.
– **littoralis** Salisb. · E:Black Sheoak · ♄ e Z9 ⓚ; Austr.: Queensl., N.S.Wales, Victoria, Tasman.
– **nana** Sieber ex Spreng. · E:Dwarf She

Oak; G:Zwerg-Keulenbaum · ♄ e Z9 ⓚ; Austr.
- *quadrivalvis* Labill. = Casuarina stricta
- **stricta** Dryand. · E:Drooping Sheoak · ♄ e Z9 ⓚ Ⓝ; Austr., Tasman.
- **torulosa** Dryand. · E:Forest Oak · ♄ e Z9 ⓚ Ⓝ; Austr.: Queensl., N.S.Wales

Catabrosa P. Beauv. -f- *Poaceae* · 2-4 spp. · E:Whorl Grass; F:Catabrosa; G:Quellgras
- **aquatica** (L.) P. Beauv. · E:Whorl Grass; F:Glycérie panachée; G:Europäisches Quellgras · ⁒ ⌢ VI-X; Eur.*, TR, Iraq, Cauc., Iran, W-Sib., E-Sib., C-As., Afgh., Pakist., Mong., Tibet, Him., Alger., Libya, Can., USA: NCE, NC, SW, Rocky Mts.; Greenl., Arg.

Catalpa Scop. -f- *Bignoniaceae* · 11 sp. · E:Catalpa; F:Arbre-aux-trompettes, Catalpa; G:Trompetenbaum
- **bignonioides** Walter · E:Indian Bean Tree; F:Catalpa commun, Catalpa de la Caroline; G:Gewöhnlicher Trompetenbaum · ♄ d Z5 VI-VII ⚥ Ⓝ; USA: SE, Fla., nat. in USA
- **bungei** C.A. Mey.
- var. **bungei** · E:Manchurian Catalpa; G:Bunges Trompetenbaum · ♄ d Z6 VII-VIII Ⓝ; N-China
- var. **heterophylla** C.A. Mey. · ♄ d Z6; N-China
- × **erubescens** Carrière (*C. bignonioides* × *C. ovata*) · E:Hybrid Catalpa; G:Hybrid-Trompetenbaum · ♄ d Z6 VI-VII; cult.
- **fargesii** Bureau · E:Farges' Catalpa; G:Farges Trompetenbaum · ♄ d Z6 VII; W-China
- f. **duclouxii** (Dode) Gilmour · ♄ d Z6; C-China, W-China
- *henryi* Dode = Catalpa ovata
- × *hybrida* Späth = Catalpa × erubescens
- *kaempferi* (DC.) Siebold & Zucc. = Catalpa ovata
- **ovata** G. Don · E:Chinese Catalpa, Yellow Catalpa; F:Catalpa jaune; G:Kleinblütiger Trompetenbaum · ♄ d Z6 VII; China, nat. in USA: NE
- **speciosa** (Warder ex Barney) Engelm. · E:Northern Catalpa, Western Catalpa; G:Prächtiger Trompetenbaum · ♄ d Z6 VI Ⓝ; USA: NCE, Tenn., Ark., nat. in W.Va., Va.
- *vestita* Diels = Catalpa fargesii

Catananche L. -f- *Asteraceae* · 5 spp. · E:Blue Cupidone; F:Cupidone; G:Rasselblume
- **caerulea** L. · E:Blue Cupidone, Cupid's Dart; G:Amorpfeil, Blaue Rasselblume · ⁒ Z7 VII-IX; Eur.: sp., F, I; NW-Afr., Libya
- **lutea** L. · E:Yellow Cupidone; G:Gelbe Rasselblume · ⊙ Z7; Eur.: Ba, Ital-P, Ib; TR

Catapodium Link -n- *Poaceae* · 2 spp. · E:Fern Grass; G:Steifgras
- **marinum** (L.) C.E. Hubb. · E:Sea Fern Grass; G:Gewöhnlicher Lolchschwingel, Niederliegendes Steifgras · ⊙; Eur.: Ib, Fr, BrI, Ital-P, Ba; coasts
- **rigidum** (L.) C.E. Hubb. · E:Fern Grass; G:Gewöhnliches Steifgras · ⁒ ⋈ V-IX; Eur.: Ib, Fr, Ital-P, Ba, ? RO, Crim, C-Eur., BrI; TR, N-Iraq, Syr., Cauc., Iran

Catasetum Rich. ex Kunth -n- *Orchidaceae* · 163 spp.
- **atratum** Lindl. · ⁒ Z10 ⓜ V ▽ ✳; Braz.
- **barbatum** (Lindl.) Lindl. · ⁒ Z10 ⓜ V ▽ ✳; Guyan., Braz., Peru
- **callosum** Lindl. · ⁒ Z10 ⓜ XII ▽ ✳; Col., Venez.
- **cernuum** (Lindl.) Rchb. f. · ⁒ Z10 ⓜ V-VI ▽ ✳; Braz.
- **expansum** Rchb. · ⁒ Z10 ⓜ V-VI ▽ ✳; Col., Ecuad.
- **fimbriatum** (C. Morren) Lindl. · ⁒ Z10 ⓜ V-VI ▽ ✳; trop. S-Am.
- **integerrimum** Hook. · ⁒ Z10 ⓜ IX ▽ ✳; Guat., Col., Ecuad., Venez.
- **macrocarpum** Rich. ex Kunth · ⁒ Z10 ⓜ X-XII ▽ ✳; S-Am.
- **pileatum** Rchb. f. · ⁒ Z10 ⓜ X ▽ ✳; Venez., Trinidad, Braz.
- *platyglossum* Schltr. = Catasetum expansum
- **saccatum** Lindl. · ⁒ Z10 ⓜ ▽ ✳; Guyan., Braz., Peru
- **socco** (Vell.) Hoehne · ⁒ Z10 ⓜ IX ▽ ✳; Braz.

Catha Forssk. ex Schreb. -f- *Celastraceae* · 1 sp. · G:Kathstrauch; E:Khat
- **edulis** (Vahl) Forssk. ex Endl. · E:Bushman's Tea, Khat, Khat Tree; G:Arabischer Tee, Khat · ♄ e Z10 ⓚ ⚥ ⚘ Ⓝ; Eth., trop. Afr., S-Afr., Yemen

Catharanthus G. Don -m- *Apocynaceae* ·

8 spp. · E:Madagascar Periwinkle;
F:Pervenche de Madagascar; G:Catharan-
the, Zimmerimmergrün
- **roseus** (L.) G. Don · E:Madagascar
Periwinkle, Rosy Periwinkle; F:Pervenche
de Madagascar; G:Rosafarbenes Zimmerimmergrün · ♃ Z10 ⌂ ⓚ III-X ⚥ ⚘;
Madag., nat. in Trop.
- **some cultivars, see Section III**

Catopsis Griseb. -f- *Bromeliaceae* · 20 spp. ·
E:Strap Air Plant; G:Riementillandsie
- **berteroniana** (Schult. f.) Mez ·
E:Powdery Strap Airplant ; G:Pudrige
Riementillandsie · ♃ Z10 ⌂; S-Fla.,
C.-Am., W.Ind., Venez., Trinidad, E-Braz.
- *brevifolia* Mez & Wercklé = Catopsis
morreniana
- **floribunda** (Brongn.) L.B. Sm. · E:Florida
Strap Airplant; G:Reichblütige Riementillandsie · ♃ Z10 ⌂; S-Fla., W-Ind., C.-Am.,
trop. S-Am
- **hahnii** Baker · G:Hahns Riementillandsie · ♃ Z10 ⌂; S-Mex., Guat., Hond.,
Nicar.
- **morreniana** Mez · G:Kurzblättrige
Riementillandsie · ♃ Z10 ⌂; S-Mex.,
C-Am.
- **nutans** (Sw.) Griseb. · E:Nodding Strap
Airplant; G:Nickende Riementillandsie ·
♃ Z10 ⌂; C.-Am., W.Ind., trop. S-Am.
- *penduliflora* C.H. Wright = Fosterella
penduliflora
- **sessiliflora** (Ruiz & Pav.) Mez ·
G:Schlanke Riementillandsie · ♃ Z10 ⌂;
S-Mex., C.-Am., trop. S-Am.

Cattleya Lindl. -f- *Orchidaceae* · 46 spp.
- **aclandiae** Lindl. · ♃ Z10 ⌂ VI-VII ▽ ⚘;
Braz.: Bahia
- **amethystoglossa** Linden & Rchb. f. · ♃
Z10 ⌂ IV-V ▽ ⚘; Braz.: Bahia, Minas
Gerais
- **aurantiaca** (Bateman ex Lindl.) P.N.
Don · ♃ Z10 ⌂ VII-VIII ▽ ⚘; Mex.
- **bicolor** Lindl. · ♃ Z10 ⌂ IX-XI ▽ ⚘;
Braz.: Rio de Janeiro, Minas Gerais
- **bowringiana** O'Brien · ♃ Z10 ⌂ X-XI ▽
⚘; C.-Am.
- **dormaniana** (Rchb. f.) Rchb. f. · ♃ Z10
⌂ I-II ▽ ⚘; Braz.: Rio de Janeiro
- **dowiana** Bateman & Rchb. f. · E:Queen
Cattleya
- var. **aurea** (Linden) B.S. Williams &
Moore · ♃ Z10 ⌂ IX-X ▽ ⚘; Col.

- var. **dowiana** · ♃ Z10 ⌂ ▽ ⚘; C-Am.
- **elongata** Barb. Rodr. · ♃ Z10 ⌂ V ▽ ⚘;
Braz.: Bahia, Minas Gerais
- **forbesii** Lindl. · ♃ Z10 ⌂ VII-IX ▽ ⚘;
E-Braz., S-Braz.
- **gaskelliana** (N.E. Br.) Rchb. f. ·
E:Summer Cattleya · ♃ Z10 ⌂ VII-IX ▽
⚘; Venez., Braz.
- **granulosa** Lindl. · ♃ Z10 ⌂ VIII-IX ▽ ⚘;
Braz.: Espirito Santo
- **guttata** Lindl. · ♃ Z10 ⌂ X-XI ▽ ⚘; Braz.
- **harrisoniana** Bateman ex Lindl. · ♃ Z10
⌂ ▽ ⚘; Braz.
- **intermedia** Graham ex Hook. · ♃ Z10 ⌂
V-XI ▽ ⚘; NE-Braz.
- **labiata** Lindl. · E:Autumn Cattleya · ♃
Z10 ⌂ ▽ ⚘; NE-Braz.
- var. *autumnalis* hort. = Cattleya labiata
- var. *dowiana* (Bateman & Rchb.) J.H.
Veitch = Cattleya dowiana var. dowiana
- var. *gaskelliana* N.E. Br. = Cattleya
gaskelliana
- var. *mendelii* (O'Brien) H.J. Veitch =
Cattleya mendelii
- var. *schroederae* (Rchb.) hort. = Cattleya
schroederae
- var. *trianaei* (Linden & Rchb. f.) H.J.
Veitch = Cattleya trianae
- var. *vera* H.J. Veitch = Cattleya labiata
- var. *warneri* (T. Moore ex R. Warner)
H.J. Veitch = Cattleya warneri
- var. *warscewiczii* (Rchb. f.) H.J. Veitch =
Cattleya warscewiczii
- **lawrenceana** Warsz. ex Rchb. f. · ♃ Z10
⌂ III-IV ▽ ⚘; Venez., Guyan.
- **loddigesii** Lindl. · ♃ Z10 ⌂ VIII-IX ▽ ⚘;
Braz., Parag.
- **lueddemanniana** Rchb. f. · ♃ Z10 ⌂
VII-IX ▽ ⚘; Venez.
- **luteola** Lindl. · ♃ Z10 ⌂ XI-XII ▽ ⚘;
Ecuad., Peru, Braz.: Amazon.; Bol.
- **maxima** Lindl. · ♃ Z10 ⌂ X-I ▽ ⚘; Col.,
Ecuad., Peru
- **mendelii** L. Linden & Rodigas · E:Virgin's
Cattleya · ♃ Z10 ⌂ V-VI ▽ ⚘; Col.
- **mossiae** C.S.P. Parish ex Hook. · E:Easter
Cattleya · ♃ Z10 ⌂ V-VI ▽ ⚘; Venez.
- **nobilior** Rchb. f. · ♃ Z10 ⌂ V-VI ▽ ⚘;
SW-Braz.
- **percivaliana** (Rchb. f.) O'Brien ·
E:Christmas Cattleya · ♃ Z10 ⌂ I-III ▽
⚘; Venez.
- **rex** O'Brien · ♃ Z10 ⌂ VII-VIII ▽ ⚘; Col.,
Peru
- *sanderiana* hort. = Cattleya warscewiczii

- **schilleriana** Rchb. f. · ♃ Z10 ⓦ VII-IX ▽ *; Braz.: Bahia
- **schroederae** Rchb. f. · ♃ Z10 ⓦ III-V ▽ *; Col.
- **skinneri** Bateman · ♃ Z10 ⓦ III-IV ▽ *; Mex., C-Am.
- **trianae** Linden & Rchb. f. · E:Christmas Orchid · ♃ Z10 ⓦ XII-II ▽ *; Col.
- **velutina** Rchb. f. · ♃ Z10 ⓦ V-VII ▽ *; Braz. (Paraiba)
- **violacea** (Kunth) Rolfe · ♃ Z10 ⓦ VII-IX ▽ *; Col., Ecuad., Peru, Venez., Guyan.
- *violacea* hort. = Cattleya loddigesii
- **walkeriana** Gardner · ♃ Z10 ⓦ II-V ▽ *; Braz., Bol.
- **warneri** T. Moore ex R. Warner · ♃ Z10 ⓦ VI-VII ▽ *; Braz.: Minas Gerais, Espirito Santo
- **warscewiczii** Rchb. f. · ♃ Z10 ⓦ VII-VIII ▽ *; Col. (Medellin)
- **Cultivars:**
- **many cultivars**

× **Cattleytonia** hort. -f- *Orchidaceae* (*Broughtonia* × *Cattleya*)

Caucaea Schltr. -f- *Orchidaceae* · 18 spp.
- **nubigena** (Lindl.) M.W. Chase & N.H. Williams · ♃ Z10 ⓦ XII-I ▽ *; Col., Ecuad., Peru
- **phalaenopsis** (Linden & Rchb. f.) M.W. Chase & N.H. Williams · ♃ Z10 ⓚ XII-IV ▽ *; Ecuad.

Caucalis L. -f- *Apiaceae* · 1 sp. · G:Haftdolde; F:Caucalis
- **platycarpos** L. · E:Carrot Bur Parsley; G:Gewöhnliche Acker-Haftdolde · ⊙ V-VII; Eur.* exc. Sc, BrI; TR, Cauc., Iran

Caularthron Raf. -n- *Orchidaceae* · 4 spp.
- **bicornutum** (Hook.) Raf. · ♃ Z10 ⓦ IV ▽ *; trop. S-Am.

× **Caulocattleya** Dressler -f- *Orchidaceae* (*Cattleya* × *Caularthron*)

Caulophyllum Michx. -n- *Berberidaceae* · 2 spp. · E:Papoose Root; G:Indianerwiege
- **thalictroides** (L.) Michx. · E:Papoose Root, Squaw Root; G:Indianische Blaubeere, Indianerwiege · ♃ Z7 V ♱ ☠; Can.: E; USA; NE, NCE, SE

Cautleya (Benth.) Hook. f. -f- *Zingiberaceae* · 4 spp.
- **gracilis** (J.J. Sm.) Dandy · ♃ Z8 ⓚ VIII; Him.
- *lutea* (Royle) Royle ex Hook. f. = Cautleya gracilis

Cavendishia Lindl. -f- *Ericaceae* · c. 100 spp.
- **acuminata** (Hook.) Benth. ex Hemsl. · ♃ e ≹ Z10 ⓚ XI; Col., Ecuad.

Cayratia Juss. -f- *Vitaceae* · 45 spp.
- **japonica** (Thunb.) Gagnep. · E:Bushkiller, Lakum · ♃ ≹ Z8 VI-VII; Ind., China, Malay. Pen., Ryukyu Is., Jap.
- **thomsonii** (M.A. Lawson) Suess. · ♄ ≀ d ≹ Z8 ⓚ; W-China, C-China, Him.

Ceanothus L. -m- *Rhamnaceae* · 55 spp. · E:California Lilac; F:Céanothe; G:Säckelblume
- **americanus** L. · E:New Jersey Tea, Wild Snowball; G:Amerikanische Säckelblume · ♄ d Z6 VII-IX ♱; Can.: E; USA: NE, NCE, SC, SE, Fla.
- *arnouldii* Carr = Ceanothus × delilianus
- **coeruleus** Lag. · ♄ e ⓚ VII-X; Mex., Guat.
- × **delileanus** Spach (*C. americanus* × *C. coeruleus*) · E:French Hybrid Ceanothus; F:Céanothe d'été; G:Französische Hybrid-Säckelblume · ♄ e Z6; cult.
- **some cultivars**
- **fendleri** A. Gray · E:Buckbrush; G:Fendlers Säckelblume · ♄ e Z5 VI-VII; USA: NC, Rocky Mts, SW; N-Mex.
- **gloriosus** J.T. Howell · E:Point Reyes Creeper · ♄ e Z8 ⓚ; Calif.
- **griseus** (Trel.) McMinn · E:Carmel Ceanothus · ♄ e Z8 ⓚ; Calif.
- **impressus** Trel. · E:Santa Barbara Ceanothus; G:Sankt-Barbaras Säckelblume · ♄ e Z8 ⓚ; Calif.
- × **lobbianus** (Hook.) McMinn (*C. dentatus* × *C. griseus*) · ♄ e Z8 ⓚ; Calif.
- **ovatus** Desf. · E:New Jersey Tea; G:Ovalblättrige Säckelblume · ♄ d Z5 VI; Can.: E; USA: NE, NCE, SC, SE
- × **pallidus** Lindl. (*C.* × *delilianus* × *C. ovatus*) · G:Hybrid-Säckelblume · ♄ d Z6; cult.
- **some cultivars**
- **thyrsiflorus** Eschsch.
- var. *griseus* Trel. ex B.L. Rob. = Ceanothus griseus

– var. **repens** McMinn · E:Creeping Blue
Blossom; G:Kriechende Säckelblume · ⚘ e
⤳ Z8 🔂; N-Calif.; coast
– var. **thyrsiflorus** · E:Blue Blossom;
F:Céanothe à feuilles de thyrse; G:Blaue
Säckelblume · ♄ ♄ e Z8 🔂; Calif.,
S-Oregon
– × **veitchianus** Hook. (*C. griseus* × *C.
rigidus*) · G:Veitchs Säckelblume · ♄ e Z8
🔂; cult.
– **Cultivars:**
– **many cultivars**

Cecropia Loefl. -f- *Cecropiaceae* ·
75-100 spp. · E:Snake Wood; F:Parasolier;
G:Ameisenbaum
– **palmata** Willd. · E:Ambay, Snakewood
Tree; G:Mexikanischer Ameisenbaum · ♄
Z9 🔂; Mex., W.Ind., Braz.
– **peltata** L. · E:Trumpet Tree;
G:Karibischer Ameisenbaum · ♄ Z9 🔂 Ⓝ;
C-Am., W.Ind., trop. S-Am.

Cedrela P. Browne -f- *Meliaceae* · 8 spp. ·
F:Cèdre bâtard; G:Zedrele
– **odorata** L. · E:Spanish Cedar, Toona;
G:Westindische Zedrele · ♄ Z9 🔂 Ⓝ ✳;
Mex., C-Am., S-Am.
– *sinensis* A. Juss. = Toona sinensis
– *toona* Roxb. ex Rottler = Toona ciliata

Cedronella Moench -f- *Lamiaceae* · 1 sp. ·
F:Baume de Galaad; G:Balsamstrauch
– *cana* Hook. = Agastache cana
– **canariensis** (L.) Webb & Berthel. ·
E:Balm of Gilead; G:Balsamstrauch · ⚃
Z8 🔂 ⚘ ; Canar.,; Azor., Madeira
– *mexicana* (Kunth) Benth. = Agastache
mexicana
– *triphylla* Moench = Cedronella canariensis

Cedrostis Post & Kuntze = Kedrostis

Cedrus Trew -f- *Pinaceae* · 4 spp. · E:Cedar;
F:Cèdre; G:Zeder
– **atlantica** (Endl.) Manetti ex Carrière ·
E:Atlantic Cedar, Atlas Cedar; F:Cèdre
de l'Atlas; G:Atlas-Zeder · ♄ e Z7 ⚘ Ⓝ;
Moroc., Alger.; Atlas
– **some cultivars**
– **brevifolia** (Hook. f.) A. Henry · E:Cyprus
Cedar; G:Zypern-Zeder · ♄ Z7; Cyprus
– **deodara** (Roxb.) G. Don · E:Deodar,
Indian Cedar; F:Cèdre de l'Himalaya;

G:Himalaya-Zeder · ♄ e Z7 Ⓝ; Afgh.,
W-Him.
– **some cultivars**
– **libani** A. Rich. · E:Cedar of Lebanon;
G:Libanon-Zeder
– **some cultivars**
– subsp. *atlantica* (Endl.) O. Schwarz =
Cedrus atlantica
– subsp. *brevifolia* (Hook. f.) Meikle =
Cedrus brevifolia
– subsp. **libani** · G:Gewöhnliche Libanon-
Zeder · ♄ e Z7 Ⓝ; S-TR, Lebanon, Cyprus
– subsp. **stenocoma** (O. Schwarz) P.H.
Davis · G:Hohe Libanon-Zeder · ♄ e Z6;
SE-TR
– *libanotica* Link = Cedrus libani subsp.
libani
– subsp. *atlantica* (Endl.) O. Schwarz =
Cedrus atlantica

Ceiba Mill. -f- *Bombacaceae* · 10 spp. ·
E:Kapok Tree; F:Kapokier; G:Kapokbaum
– **pentandra** (L.) Gaertn. · E:Kapok Tree,
Silk Cotton Tree; G:Weißer Kapokbaum ·
♄ d Z10 🔂 ⚘ Ⓝ; orig. ?; cult. Trop.

Celastrus L. -m- *Celastraceae* · 32 spp. ·
E:Bittersweet; F:Bourreau des arbres;
G:Baumwürger
– **angulatus** Maxim. · G:Kantiger
Baumwürger · ♄ d ⚘ ⚘ Z5 VI; NW-China,
C-China
– *articulatus* Thunb. = Celastrus orbiculatus
var. orbiculatus
– *edulis* Vahl = Catha edulis
– **flagellaris** Rupr. · ♄ ⚘ ⚘ Z4 VI; Amur,
N-China, Manch., Korea, Jap.
– **hookeri** Prain · ♄ ⚘ ⚘ Z6; S-China, Him.
– **hypoleucus** (Oliv.) Warb. ex Loes. · ♄ ⚘ d
⚘ Z8 🔂 VI; C-China: Sichuan, Hupeh
– **loeseneri** Rehder & E.H. Wilson · ♄ ⚘
Z6; C-China
– **orbiculatus** Thunb.
– var. **orbiculatus** · E:Oriental Bittersweet,
Staff Vine; F:Bourreau des arbres;
G:Rundblättriger Baumwürger · ♄ d ⚘ ⚘
Z5 VI; China, Manch., Jap. Sakhal., nat.
in E-USA
– var. **punctatus** (Thunb.) Rehder · ♄ ⚘ d ⚘
Z4 VI; s E-As.
– **rosthornianus** Loes. · ♄ d ⚘ ⚘ Z5 VI;
W-China, C-China
– **scandens** L. · E:American Bittersweet, Waxwork; G:Amerikanischer
Baumwürger · ♄ d ⚘ ⚘ Z5 VI ✳; Can.: E;

USA: NE, NCE, Okla., SE

Celmisia Cass. -f- *Asteraceae* · 62 spp.
- **coriacea** (G. Forst.) Hook. f. · ♃ Z7 ⒶＮ; NZ
- **holosericea** (G. Forst.) Hook. f. · ♃ Z7 ⒶＮ; NZ

Celosia L. -f- *Amaranthaceae* · c. 50 spp. · E:Cockscomb, Woolflower; F:Célosie, Crête-de-coq; G:Brandschopf, Hahnenkamm
- **argentea** L.
- var. **argentea** · E:Red Spinach; G:Silber-Brandschopf · ⊙ Z9 VII-IX Ⓝ; Trop.
- var. **cristata** (L.) Kuntze · E:Cockscomb; F:Célosie crête de coq; G:Hahnenkamm · ⊙ Z9 VII-IX; cult.
- **many cultivars, see Section III**
- *cristata* L. = Celosia argentea var. cristata
- *plumosa* Burv. = Celosia argentea var. cristata

Celsia L. = Verbascum
- *rechingeri* Murb. = Verbascum phoeniceum

Celtis L. -f- *Ulmaceae* · c. 80-100 spp. · E:Hackberry, Nettle Tree; F:Micocoulier; G:Zürgelbaum
- **australis** L. · E:Nettle Tree; G:Südlicher Zürgelbaum · ♄ ♄ d Z6 III-IV ⚥ Ⓝ; Eur.: Ib, Fr, Ital-P, Ba, RO; TR, Levant, Cauc., Madeira, NW-Afr., Libya, nat. in Sw
- **biondii** Pamp. · ♄ d Z5; C-China
- **bungeana** Blume · ♄ d Z6; C-China, N-China, Manch., Korea
- **caucasica** Willd. · E:Caucasian Nettle Tree; G:Kaukasischer Zürgelbaum · ♄ ♄ d Z6; E-BG, TR, Cauk., C-As, Afgh.
- **glabrata** Planch. · G:Kahler Zürgelbaum · ♄ ♄ d Z5; Cauc., Crim, TR
- **integrifolia** Lam. · ♄ Z9 ⒶＮ; trop. Afr., Arab.
- *integrifolia* Nutt. = Celtis laevigata
- **julianae** C.K. Schneid. · ♄ d; C-China
- **koraiensis** Nakai · G:Koreanischer Zürgelbaum · ♄ Z6; Korea, Manch., N-China
- **labilis** C.K. Schneid. · ♄ d Z6; C-China
- **laevigata** Willd. · E:Sugarberry; G:Glattblättriger Zürgelbaum · ♄ Z6 Ⓝ; USA: Va., Mo., Kans., SE, SC, N.Mex.; Mex., W.Ind.
- *mississippiensis* Spach = Celtis laevigata

- **occidentalis** L.
- var. **cordata** Willd. · ♄ ♄ d Z5; S-USA
- var. **occidentalis** · E:Common Hackberry, Mississippi Hackberry; G:Amerikanischer Zürgelbaum · ♄ d Z5 Ⓝ; E-Can., USA: NE, NCE, NC, SC, SE
- var. *pumila* (Pursh) Dippel = Celtis occidentalis var. occidentalis
- **reticulata** Torr. · E:Netleaf Hackberry · ♄ ♄ d Z6; SW-USA
- **sinensis** Pers. · E:Chinese Hackberry; G:Chinesischer Zürgelbaum · ♄ d Z8 ⋀; Jap., Korea, E-China
- **tournefortii** Lam. · G:Tourneforts Zürgelbaum · ♄ ♄ d Z6; Eur.: Sic., Ba, Crim; TR, N-Iraq, N-Iran

Cenchrus L. -m- *Poaceae* · 25 spp. · E:Sandbur; G:Klebgras, Stachelgras
- **ciliaris** L. · E:African Foxtail Grass, Buffel Grass; G:Klebgras · ♃ Z8 Ⓝ; Afr., SW-As., Sic.
- **incertus** M.A. Curtis · E:Coast Sandbur, Spiny Burr Grass; G:Stachelgras · ⊙ Z9; Am., nat. in Cors, I, ? F, ? sp.

Centaurea L. -f- *Asteraceae* · c. 500 spp. · E:Knapweed, Star Thistle; F:Bleuet, Centaurée; G:Flockenblume, Kornblume
- **americana** Nutt. · E:American Star Thistle, Basket Flower; G:Amerikanische Flockenblume · ⊙ Z4 VII-VIII; USA: Mo. SE, SC, SW; Mex.
- **argentea** L. · ♃ Z8 Ⓐ; Eur.: Crete; mts.
- **babylonica** (L.) L. · E:Syrian Knapweed · ♃ Z6; S-TR, Lebanon
- **bella** Trautv. · F:Centaurée élégante; G:Zierliche Silber-Flockenblume · ♃ ⋀ Z6 VI-VII; Cauc.
- **bracteata** Scop. · G:Hellschuppige Flockenblume · ♃ VII-IX; Eur.: F, I, Sw, A, Slove.; Croatia; S-Alp.
- **calcitrapa** L. · E:Purple Star Thistle; G:Stern-Flockenblume · ⊙ ⊙ VII-X; Eur.*, NW-Afr., nat. in BrI, A, G, N-Am.
- **cana** Waldst. & Kit. · ♃ ; Eur.: Ba, Crim
- *candidissima* hort. = Centaurea ragusina
- *candidissima* Lam. = Centaurea cineraria
- **cineraria** L. · E:Dusty Miller · ♃ ♄ Z8 Ⓐ VII-VIII; Eur.: W-I, Sic.
- **clementei** Boiss. ex DC. · ♃ Z6; SW-Sp.
- **cyanus** L. · E:Bachelor's Button, Cornflower; G:Kornblume · ⊙ ⋈ VI-X ⚥ ; Eur.: Sic., Ba, nat. in Eur.*, Cauc., W-Sib., E-Sib., NW-Afr., N-Am.

- many cultivars
- **dealbata** Willd. · E:Whitewash Corn-
  flower; F:Centaurée blanchâtre · ⁴ Z3
  VI-VII; Cauc.
- **diffusa** Lam. · E:White Knapweed;
  G:Sparrige Flockenblume · ⊙ VII-VIII;
  Eur.: Ba, E-Eur.; TR, nat. in C-Eur.,
  EC-Eur., F, I
- **glastifolia** L. · ⁴ ∿ Z6 VI-IX; Eur.:
  Russ.; TR, Cauc.
- **hypoleuca** DC. · ⁴ Z5 VII-X; TR, Cauc.,
  NW-Iran
- **jacea** L. · E:Brown Knapweed; G:Wiesen-
  Flockenblume
- subsp. *gaudini* (Boiss. & Reut.) Gremli =
  Centaurea bracteata
- subsp. **jacea** · G:Gewöhnliche Wiesen-
  Flockenblume · ⁴ Z6 VI-X; Eur.* exc. BrI;
  TR, nat. in BrI, N-Am.
- **kosaninii** Hayek · ⁴ △ VI; AL
- **kotschyana** Heuff. ex W.D.J. Koch · ⁴ Z5
  VI-VII; Eur.: Ba, RO, W-Russ.; mts.
- **macrocephala** Muss. Puschk. ex Willd. ·
  E:Great Golden Knapweed; F:Centaurée
  à grosse tête; G:Großköpfige Flocken-
  blume · ⁴ Z3 VII-VIII; Cauc.
- **melitensis** L. · E:Maltese Star Thistle;
  G:Malteser Flockenblume · ⊙ X-VII;
  Eur.: Ib, F, Ital-P, Ba; Canar., Madeira,
  NW-Afr.
- **microptilon** (Godr.) Gren. & Godr. ·
  G:Kleinfederige Flockenblume · ⁴ ;
  Eur.: sp., F, B, NL
- **montana** L. · E:Mountain Knapweed,
  Perennial Cornflower; F:Centaurée des
  montagnes; G:Berg-Flockenblume · ⁴ Z3
  V-X; Eur.: Ib, Fr, Ital-P, C-Eur., EC-Eur.,
  Slove., Croatia ; mts., nat. in FIN
- *moschata* L. = Amberboa moschata
- **nigra** L.
- subsp. **debeauxii** (Gren. & Godr.)
  Malag. · ⁴ Z5; SW-F, N-Sp.
- subsp. **nemoralis** (Jord.) Gremli ·
  G:Hain-Flockenblume · ⁴ Z5 VII-IX; Eur.:
  C-Eur., F
- subsp. **nigra** · E:Black Knapweed,
  Common Knapweed; G:Schwarze
  Flockenblume · ⁴ Z5 VII-IX; Eur.: Fr, BrI,
  Ib, Ital-P, C-Eur., Ba, Sc, nat. in N-Am.,
  NZ
- **nigrescens** Willd. · E:Tyrol Knapweed,
  Vochin Knapweed; G:Schwärzliche
  Flockenblume · ⁴ VII-IX; Eur.: Fr, Ital-P,
  C-Eur., EC-Eur., Ba, RO, ? W-Russ.
- *odorata* hort. = Amberboa moschata

- **orientalis** L. · ⁴ Z7 ∧ VII-IX; Eur.: Ba,
  E-Eur.
- **paniculata** L. · E:Jersey Knapweed;
  G:Rispige Flockenblume · ⊙ VII-IX; Eur.:
  Ib, F, I
- **phrygia** L. · E:Wig Knapweed; G:Phry-
  gische Flockenblume · ⁴ Z6 VIII-IX; Eur.:
  Ital-P, C-Eur., EC-Eur., Sc, Ba, E-Eur., ;
  Cauc.
- × **psammogena** Gáyer (*C. diffusa* × *C.
  stoebe*) · G:Sandbürtige Flockenblume · ;
  Eur.: D (Mannheim)
- **pseudophrygia** C.A. Mey. · G:Perücken-
  Flockenblume · ⁴ VIII-IX; C-Eur., DK,
  Norw., S-Russl.
- **pulcherrima** Willd. · G:Silber-Flocken-
  blume · ⁴ Z6 VI-VII; Cauc., TR
- **ragusina** L. · E:Dusty Miller · ⁴ Z7
  VII-VIII; Eur.: Croatia
- **rhaetica** Moritzi · E:Rhaetian Knapweed;
  G:Rätische Flockenblume · ⁴ VII-VIII;
  Eur.: I, Sw; S-Alp.
- *rhapontica* L. = Stemmacantha rhapontica
- *rhenana* Boreau = Centaurea stoebe
  subsp. stoebe
- **ruthenica** Lam. · G:Gelbe Flockenblume ·
  ⁴ Z3 VII-VIII; Eur.: E-Eur.; Cauc., W-Sib.,
  C-As.
- **scabiosa** L. · G:Skabiosen-Flockenblume
- subsp. **alpestris** (Hegetschw.) Nyman ·
  G:Alpen-Flockenblume · ⁴ Z4 VII-VIII;
  Eur.: F, I, Sw, A, EC-Eur., ? sp.; Pyr., Alp.,
  Jura, W-Carp.
- subsp. **fritschii** Hayek · G:Fritschs Flockenblume · ⁴ Z4 VI-X; Eur.: A, Slove., H,
  BG, AL
- subsp. **grineensis** (Reut.) Nyman ·
  G:Schmalblättrige Flockenblume · ⁴ Z4
  VI-IX; Eur.: I, C-Eur., EC-Eur., Ba, RO
- subsp. **scabiosa** · E:Greater Knapweed;
  F:Centaurée scabieuse; G:Gewöhnliche
  Skabiosen-Flockenblume · ⁴ Z4 VII-VIII;
  Eur.*, W-Sib., E-Sib.
- **simplicicaulis** Boiss. & A. Huet · ⁴ △ Z4
  VI; Cauc. (Armen.)
- **solstitialis** L. · E:St Barnaby's Thistle,
  Yellow Star Thistle; G:Sonnwend-
  Flockenblume · ⊙ ⊙ VII-X; Eur.: Ib, Fr,
  Ital-P, Ba, E-Eur.; TR, Lebanon, Cauc.,
  Iran, nat. in BrI, C-Eur., EC-Eur., N-Am.
- **speciosa** Boiss. · ⁴ ♄ ⚘; TR, Palest.
- **splendens** L. · G:Glänzende Flocken-
  blume · ⊙ ⁴ VII-VIII; Eur.: I, Sw, Ba
- **stenolepis** A. Kern. · G:Schmalschuppige

Flockenblume · ♃ Z5 VIII-IX; Eur.: I, A, EC-Eur., Ba, E-Eur.
- **stoebe** L. · E:Spotted Knapweed; G:Rispen-Flockenblume
- subsp. *maculosa* (Lam.) Schinz & Thell. = Centaurea stoebe subsp. stoebe
- subsp. **micranthos** (Gugler) Hayek · G:Kleinköpfige Rispen-Flockenblume · ♃ VII-IX; Eur.: A, H
- subsp. **stoebe** · G:Gefleckte Flockenblume, Gewöhnliche Rispen-Flockenblume · ⊙ ♃ VII-IX; Eur.: F, C-Eur., N-I, nat. in N-Am.
- *suaveolens* Willd. = Amberboa moschata
- **transalpina** Schleich. ex DC. · E:Alpine Knapweed; G:Südliche Flockenblume · ♃; Eur.: F, Sw, A, I; Alp.
- **triumfettii** All.
- subsp. **cana** (Waldst. & Kit.) Dostál · ♃ Z5; Ba, Crim
- subsp. **triumfettii** · G:Bunte Flockenblume · ♃ Z5 V-VII; Eur.* exc. BrI, Sc; TR, Lebanon, Cauc., N-Iran, Moroc.
- **uniflora** Turra
- subsp. **nervosa** (Willd.) Bonnier & Layens · E:Plume Knapweed; G:Federige Flockenblume · ♃ Z4 VII; Eur.: F, I, C-Eur., Ba, RO; Alp., N-Apenn., S-Carp., Balkan mts.
- subsp. **uniflora** · ♃ Z4; Eur.: F, I, Sw; SW-Alp., Apenn.
- **vallesiaca** (DC.) Jord. · G:Walliser Flockenblume · ⊙ VII-IX; Eur.: F, Sw, I; SW-Alp.

Centaurium Hill -n- *Gentianaceae* · c. 30 spp. · E:Centaury; F:Gentianelle, Petite centaurée; G:Tausendgüldenkraut
- *chloodes* (Brot.) Samp. = Centaurium confertum
- **confertum** (Pers.) Druce · ⊙ ⊙ △ Z8 ⌂ VII-IX ▽; Eur.: Ib, F; costs
- **erythraea** Rafn · E:Centaury, Common Centaury; G:Echtes Tausendgüldenkraut, Kopfiges Tausendgüldenkraut · ⊙ ⊙ Z8 VII-X ⚕ ▽; Eur.*, TR, Levant, Cauc., N-Iraq, Iran, W-Sib., C-As., Afgh., Pakist., NW-Afr., Libya
- **littorale** (Turner) Gilmour · E:Seaside Centaury; G:Gewöhnliches Strand-Tausendgüldenkraut · ⊙ Z8 VII-IX ▽; Eur.: Sc, BrI, Fr, C-Eur., EC-Eur., E-Eur., ? I
- *minus* auct. non Moench = Centaurium erythraea

- **pulchellum** (Sw.) Druce · E:Lesser Centaury; G:Gewöhnliches Kleines Tausendgüldenkraut · ⊙ Z8 VII-IX ▽; Eur.*, TR, Levant, Cauc., C-As.
- **scilloides** (L. f.) Samp. · E:Perennial Centaury; G:Staudiges Tausendgüldenkraut · ⊙ ⊙ ♃ △ Z8 VII-IX ▽; Eur.: Ib, F, BrI
- **spicatum** (L.) Fritsch · G:Ähriges Tausendgüldenkraut · ⊙ ⊙ Z8 ▽; Eur.: Ib, Fr, Ital-P, Ba, E-Eur.; TR, Levant, Iraq, Cauc., Iran, Afgh., C-As., N-Afr.
- *umbellatum* Gilib. = Centaurium erythraea

Centella L. -f- *Apiaceae* · c. 40 spp. · E:Pennywort ; G:Sumpfpfennigkraut
- **asiatica** (L.) Urb. · E:Asiatic Pennywort, Indian Pennywort; G:Asiatisches Sumpfpfennigkraut · ♃ ~ ⌂ ⚕ ⚘ Ⓝ; ? Afr.

Centradenia G. Don -f- *Melastomataceae* · 4 spp.
- **floribunda** Planch. · ♄ Z9 ⌂ II-VI; Guat.
- **grandifolia** (Schltdl.) Endl. · ♄ Z9 ⌂ XI-XII; S-Mex., Guat.
- **inaequilateralis** (Schltdl. & Cham.) G. Don · ♄ Z9 ⌂ XI-I; Mex.
- *rosea* Lindl. = Centradenia inaequilateralis

Centranthus Lam. & DC. -m- *Valerianaceae* · 9 spp. · E:Red Valerian; F:Valériane des jardins; G:Spornblume
- **angustifolius** (Mill.) DC. · E:Narrow-leaved Valerian; G:Schmalblättrige Spornblume · ♃ ∧ VI-VII; Eur.: F, Sw, I
- **calcitrapae** (L.) Dufr. · E:Annual Valerian · ⊙ VII-VIII; Eur.: Ib, Fr, Ital-P, Ba, Crim; TR, Cyprus, Madeira, Canar., NW-Afr.
- **macrosiphon** Boiss. · E:Spanish Valerian · ⊙ V-VIII; Eur.: S-Sp.; Alger., nat. in I
- **ruber** (L.) DC. · E:Jupiter's Beard, Red Valerian; F:Lilas d'Espagne, Valériane rouge; G:Rote Spornblume · ♃ Z7 V-VII ⚕ ; Eur.: Ib, Fr, Ital-P, Ba; NW-TR, Syr., NW-Afr., nat. in BrI, C-Eur., Crim

Centropogon C. Presl -m- *Campanulaceae* · 230 spp. · G:Stachelbart
- **cornutus** (L.) Druce · ♄ ⚕ Z10 ⌂ XII-II; C-Am., trop. S-Am.

– **fastuosus** Scheidw. Z10 ⓦ
– × **lucyanus** Schönland (*C. fastuosus* ×
Siphocampylus betulifolius) · ♄ Z10 ⓦ
XII-II; NE-TR, Syr., Lebanon
– *surinamensis* C. Presl = Centropogon
cornutus

Centrosema (DC.) Benth. -n- *Fabaceae* · c.
40 spp. · E:Butterfly Pea; F:Pois bâtard,
Pois-rivière; G:Schmetterlingserbse
– **plumieri** (Turpin ex Pers.) Benth. ·
E:Feefee. · ♃ ⓦ Ⓝ; trop. Am., nat. in
trop. As., Afr.
– **pubescens** Benth. · ♃ ⓦ Ⓝ; trop. Am.
– **virginianum** (L.) Benth. · E:Butterfly
Pea, Conchita; G:Virginische Schmetterlingserbse · ♃ ⚥ Z6 VII-VIII; USA: NE, SE,
Fla., SC; trop. S-Am., nat. in trop. Afr.

Centrosolenia Benth. = Nautilocalyx
– *bullata* Lem. = Nautilocalyx bullatus
– *picta* Hook. = Nautilocalyx pictus

Cephaelis Sw. = Psychotria
– *acuminata* H. Karst. = Psychotria
cuspidata
– *ipecacuanha* (Brot.) A. Rich. = Psychotria
ipecacuanha

Cephalanthera Rich. -f- *Orchidaceae* ·
21 sp. · E:Helleborine; F:Céphalanthère;
G:Waldvögelein
– **damasonium** (Mill.) Druce · E:White
Helleborine; G:Bleiches Waldvögelein ·
♃ Z6 V-VI ▽ ✳; Eur.*, TR, Cauc., N-Iran,
N-As., Alger.
– *ensifolia* (Sw.) Rich. = Cephalanthera
longifolia
– *grandiflora* Gray = Cephalanthera
damasonium
– **longifolia** (L.) Fritsch · E:Sword-leaved
Helleborine, White Lady; G:Langblät-
triges Waldvögelein, Schwertblättriges
Waldvögelein · ♃ Z7 V-VI ▽ ✳; Eur.*,
TR, Lebanon, Cauc., Iran, Him., C-As.,
E-As.
– *pallens* Rich. = Cephalanthera longifolia
– **rubra** (L.) Rich. · E:Red Helleborine;
G:Rotes Waldvögelein · ♃ Z6 VI-VII ▽
✳; Eur.*, TR, Cyprus, Cauc., NW-Iran,
Moroc.

Cephalanthus L. -m- *Rubiaceae* · 6 spp. ·
E:Buttonbush; F:Pois-bouton; G:Knopf-
busch

– **occidentalis** L. · E:Button Bush, Button
Willow; G:Knopfbusch · ♄ d Z5 VII-VIII;
Can.: E; USA: NE, NCE, SE, Fla., SC, SW,
Calif.; Mex. W.Ind.

Cephalaria Schrad. ex Roem. & Schult.
-f- *Dipsacaceae* · c. 65 spp. · E:Giant Scabious; F:Céphalaire; G:Schuppenkopf
– **alpina** (L.) Schrad. ex Roem. & Schult. ·
E:Alpine Scabious; G:Alpen-Schup-
penkopf · ♃ VII-VIII; Eur.: I, C-Eur.; Alp.,
Jura, Apenn.
– **gigantea** (Ledeb.) Bobrov · E:Giant
Scabious, Yellow Scabious; G:Großer
Schuppenkopf · ♃ VII-VIII; Cauc.
– **leucantha** (L.) Schrad. ex Roem. &
Schult. · ♃ VII-VIII; Eur.: Ib, Fr, Ital-P,
Ba; Moroc., Alger.
– **radiata** Griseb. & Schenk · G:Strahlender
Schuppenkopf · ♃; Eur.: RO; mts.
– **syriaca** (L.) Schrad. ex Roem. & Schult. ·
E:Syrian Cephalaria; G:Orientalischer
Schuppenkopf · ⊙ Ⓝ; Cauc., Iran, Afgh.,
C-As., nat. in F, I
– *tatarica* hort. non (L.) Roem. & Schult. =
Cephalaria gigantea
– **transsylvanica** (L.) Roem. & Schult. ·
G:Siebenbürger Schuppenkopf · ⊙ VII-
VIII; Eur.: Fr, Ital-P, EC-Eur., Ba, E-Eur.;
TR, Cauc., Iran, nat. in A

Cephalipterum A. Gray -n- *Asteraceae* ·
1 sp. · E:Silver-flowered Everlasting;
F:Immortelle argentée; G:Silberne
Strohblume
– **drummondii** A. Gray · E:Silver-flowered
Everlasting; G:Silberne Strohblume · ⊙
⚻ Z8 ⓚ; W-Austr., S-Austr.

Cephalocereus Pfeiff. -m- *Cactaceae* · 1 sp.
– *blossfeldiorum* Werderm. = Espostoa
blossfeldiorum
– *dybowskii* (Rol.-Goss.) Britton & Rose =
Austrocephalocereus dybowskii
– *glaucescens* (Labour.) Borg = Pilosocereus
glaucescens
– *guentheri* Kupper = Espostoa guentheri
– *lehmannianus* Werderm. = Austrocephalocereus lehmannianus
– *leucostele* (Gürke) Britton & Rose =
Stephanocereus leucostele
– *melanostele* Vaupel = Espostoa melanostele
– *palmeri* Rose = Pilosocereus leucocephalus

– *pentaedrophorus* (Labour.) Britton & Rose = Pilosocereus pentaedrophorus
– *polyanthus* Werderm. = Micranthocereus polyanthus
– *purpureus* Gürke = Austrocephalocereus purpureus
– **senilis** (Haw.) Pfeiff. · G:Greisenhaupt; E:Old Man Cactus · ⴈ Z9 ⓜ ▽ ✳; C-Mex.

Cephalocleistocactus F. Ritter = Cleistocactus
– *ritteri* (Backeb.) Backeb. = Cleistocactus ritteri

Cephalophyllum (Haw.) N.E. Br. -n- *Aizoaceae* · 32 spp.
– *decipiens* (Haw.) L. Bolus = Cephalophyllum loreum
– **loreum** (L.) Schwantes · ⁴ ⴈ Z9 ⓚ; Cape
– **subulatoides** (Haw.) N.E. Br. · ⁴ ⴈ Z9 ⓚ; Cape
– **tricolorum** (Haw.) Schwantes · ⁴ ⴈ Z9 ⓚ; Cape

Cephalotaxus Siebold & Zucc. -f- *Cephalotaxaceae* · 10 spp. · E:Plum Yew; F:If-à-prunes; G:Kopfeibe
– *drupacea* Siebold & Zucc. = Cephalotaxus harringtonii var. drupacea
– **fortunei** Hook. · ♄ e Z7; C-China
– **harringtonii** (Knight ex J. Forbes) K. Koch · E:Japanese Plum Yew; G:Harringtons Kopfeibe, Japanische Kopfeibe
– var. **drupacea** (Siebold & Zucc.) Koidz. · E:Cow's Tail Pine, Plum Yew; G:Pflaumen-Kopfeibe · ♄ e Z7 Ⓝ; Jap., C-China
– var. **harringtonii** · E:Japanese Plum Yew; G:Gewöhnliche Japanische Kopfeibe · ♄ ♄ e Z6; China, Korea, Jap.
– *pedunculata* Siebold & Zucc. = Cephalotaxus harringtonii var. harringtonii

Cephalotus Labill. -m- *Cephalotaceae* · 1 sp. · E:Australian Pitcher Plant; F:Plante-outre; G:Drüsenköpfchen
– **follicularis** Labill. · E:Australian Flycatcher Plant; G:Drüsenköpfchen · ⁴ Z10 ⓜ ⓚ; W-Austr.

Cerastium L. -n- *Caryophyllaceae* · c. 100 spp. · E:Mouse Ear; F:Céraiste; G:Hornkraut
– **alpinum** L. · G:Alpen-Hornkraut
– subsp. **alpinum** · E:Alpine Mouse Ear;

G:Gewöhnliches Alpen-Hornkraut · ⁴ Z3 VII-VIII; Eur.*; N, mts.
– subsp. **lanatum** (Lam.) Asch. & Graebn. · G:Wolliges Alpen-Hornkraut · ⁴ △ Z3 VI-VIII; Eur.*; N, mts.; N-As., China, N-Am., Greenl.
– **arvense** L. · E:Field Mouse Ear; F:Céraiste des champs; G:Gewöhnliches Acker-Hornkraut · ⁴ △ Z3 IV-V; Eur.*, Cauc., W-Sib., E-Sib., Amur, C-As., Mong., N-China, Moroc., nat. in N-Am.
– **biebersteinii** DC. · ⁴ ⟿ V-VI; Crim
– **brachypetalum** N.H.F. Desp. ex Pers. · E:Grey Mouse Ear; G:Bärtiges Hornkraut, Kleinblütiges Hornkraut · ☉ IV-VI; Eur.*, TR, Levant, Moroc., Alger.
– **candidissimum** Correns · ⁴ ⟿ V-VI; GR
– **carinthiacum** Vest
– subsp. **austroalpinum** (Kunz) Kunz · G:Südalpines Hornkraut · ⁴ VI-IX; Eur.: Sw, A
– subsp. **carinthiacum** · G:Kärntner Hornkraut · ⁴ VI-IX; Eur.: Sw, I, A, Slove.; E-Alp.
– **cerastoides** (L.) Britton · E:Starwort Mouse Ear; G:Dreigriffeliges Hornkraut · ⁴ VII-VIII; Eur.*, TR, Levant, Cauc., Iran, W-Sib., E-Sib., C-As., Him., Mong., Moroc., N-Am., Greenl.
– **diffusum** Pers. · G:Viermänniges Hornkraut
– subsp. **diffusum** · E:Sea Mouse Ear; G:Gewöhnliches Viermänniges Hornkraut · ☉ III-VI; Eur.*, NW-TR, Moroc., Alger., Libya
– subsp. **subtetrandrum** (Lange) P.D. Sell & Whitehead · G:Fünfmänniges Hornkraut · III-V; Eur.: A, EC-Eur., S-Swed
– **dubium** (Bastard) Guépin · G:Klebriges Hornkraut · ☉ IV-VI; Eur.* exc. BrI, Sc; TR, Levant, Alger.
– **fontanum** Baumg. · E:Common Mouse Ear; G:Quellen-Hornkraut · ⁴ IV-VI; Eur.*, TR, Moroc., Tun.
– **glomeratum** Thuill. · E:Sticky Mouse Ear; G:Knäuel-Hornkraut · ☉ III-IX; Eur.*, TR, Levant, Cauc., C-As., NW-Afr., Libya, N-Am., S-Am., S-Afr., Austr.
– **glutinosum** Fr. · G:Bleiches Zwerg-Hornkraut · ☉ III-V; Eur.*, TR, Cauc., Moroc.
– **grandiflorum** Waldst. & Kit. · ⁴ △ VII-VIII; Eur.: Croatia, Bosn., Montenegro, YU, , AL

– **holosteoides** Fr. · G:Gewöhnliches Hornkraut · ⚄ III-VI; Eur.*, TR, Moroc., Tun., nat. in cosmop.
– **julicum** Schellm. · G:Julisches Hornkraut · ⚄ V-VII; Eur.: A, Slove.; SE-Alp.
– *lanatum* Lam. = Cerastium alpinum subsp. lanatum
– **latifolium** L. · G:Breitblättriges Hornkraut · ⚄ VII-VIII; Eur.: F, I, C-Eur., EC-Eur., RO; Alp., Apenn., Carp.
– **ligusticum** Viv. · G:Ligurisches Hornkraut · ⊙ IV-V; Eur.: Ital-P, Ba, ? F; TR
– **lucorum** (Schur) Möschl · G:Großfrüchtiges Hornkraut · ⚄ IV-VI; N-Sp. to C-Eur.
– **pedunculatum** Gaudin ex Ser. · G:Langstieliges Hornkraut · ⚄ VII-VIII; Eur.: F, I, G, A; Alp.
– **pumilum** Curtis · E:Dwarf Mouse Ear; G:Dunkles Zwerg-Hornkraut, Niedriges Hornkraut · ⊙ III-V; Eur.*, TR, Cauc., Iran, Moroc., Tun.
– *repens* M. Bieb. non L. = Cerastium biebersteinii
– **semidecandrum** L. · E:Little Mouse Ear; G:Sand-Hornkraut · ⊙ III-V; Eur.*, TR, Cyprus, Cauc., N-Iran
– **siculum** Guss. · G:Sizilianisches Hornkraut · ⊙; Eur.: Balear., F, I, ? sp.
– **sylvaticum** Waldst. & Kit. · G:Wald-Hornkraut · ⚄ VI-VII; Eur.: I, A, EC-Eur., Ba, E-Eur.
– **tenoreanum** Ser. · G:Tenores Hornkraut · ⊙ IV-V; Sw, A, I, Ba
– **tomentosum** L. · E:Snow-in-Summer; G:Filziges Hornkraut
– subsp. **columnae** (Ten.) Arcang. · F:Céraiste laineux · ⚄ ⤳ △ Z4 V-VI; S-I
– subsp. **tomentosum** · F:Céraiste feutré, Céraiste laineux · ⚄ Z4 V-VII; Eur.: I, Sic., Apenn., nat. in BrI, Sc, C-Eur., EC-Eur.
– **uniflorum** Clairv. · G:Einblütiges Hornkraut · ⚄ VII-VIII; Eur.: I, C-Eur., EC-Eur., Slove., Bosn., Serb.; Alp., Carp., Bosn., Serb.
– *villosum* Baumg. = Cerastium alpinum subsp. lanatum

Cerasus Mill. = Prunus
– *avium* = Prunus avium
– *fruticosa* Pall. = Prunus fruticosa
– *vulgaris* Mill. = Prunus cerasus

Ceratocapnos Durieu -f- *Fumariaceae* · 3 spp. · G:Lerchensporn

– **claviculata** (L.) Lidén · E:Climbing Corydalis; G:Rankender Lerchensporn · ⊙ VI-IX; Eur.: Sc, BrI, Fr, G, Ib

Ceratocephala Moench -f- *Ranunculaceae* · 3 spp. · F:Cératocéphale; G:Hornköpfchen
– **falcata** (L.) Pers. · G:Sichelfrüchtiges Hornköpfchen · ⊙ III-V; Eur.: Ib, Fr, Ital-P, Ba, E-Eur., ? H; TR, Cyprus, Cauc., Iran, C-As., Him., NW-Afr.
– **testiculata** (Crantz) Roth · E:Curveseed Butterwort; G:Geradfrüchtiges Hornköpfchen · ⊙ III-V; Eur.: A, EC-Eur., Ba, E-Eur.; TR, Cauc., Iran, Afgh., Pakist., Sib., Moroc., Alger.

Ceratonia L. -f- *Caesalpiniaceae* · 2 spp. · E:St John's Bread; F:Caroubier; G:Johannisbrotbaum
– **siliqua** L. · E:Carob, St John's Bread; G:Johannisbrotbaum · ♄ ♄ e Z8 ⬠ ⚥ Ⓝ; Eur.: Ib, Fr, Ital-P, Ba; TR, Levant, Arab., NW-Afr., Libya

Ceratopetalum Sm. -n- *Cunoniaceae* · 5 spp.
– **gummiferum** Sm. · E:New South Wales Christmas Rush · ♄ ♄ Z10 ⬠; Austr.: Queensl., N.S.Wales

Ceratophyllum L. -n- *Ceratophyllaceae* · 4 spp. · E:Hornwort; F:Cératophylle; G:Hornblatt
– **demersum** L. · E:Coon's Tail, Rigid Hornwort; F:Cératophylle émergé; G:Gewöhnliches Raues Hornblatt · ⚄ ≈ ⬠ VI-IX; Eur.*, TR, Cauc., W-Sib., E-Sib., N-Afr.
– **submersum** L. · E:Soft Hornwort; F:Cératophylle submergé; G:Zartes Hornblatt · ⚄ ≈ ⬠ VI-VIII; Eur.*, TR, Palest., Cauc., W-Sib., C-As., Alger., Tun., Libya

Ceratopteris Brongn. -f- *Parkeriaceae* · 5 spp. · E:Floating Fern, Water Fern; F:Fougère cornue; G:Hornfarn
– **thalictroides** (L.) Brongn. · E:Water Fern; G:Wasser-Hornfarn · ⚄ Z10 ⬠; trop. Afr., Ind., Sri Lanka, Malay. Arch., S-Jap., Polyn., nat. in Jamaica

Ceratostigma Bunge -n- *Plumbaginaceae* · 8 spp. · E:Plumbago; F:Dentelaire;

G:Hornnarbe
- **griffithii** C.B. Clarke · ♄ e Z7; Tibet, Bhutan; Him.
- **plumbaginoides** Bunge · E:Dwarf Plumbago, Leadwort; F:Dentelaire bleue; G:Kriechende Hornnarbe · ⁴ ♄ d Z6 IX-X; W-China, nat. in NW-F, NW-I
- **willmottianum** Stapf · E:Chinese Plumbago; G:Willmotts Hornnarbe · ♄ d Z7 ∧ IX-X; Tibet, W-China

Ceratotheca Endl. -f- *Pedaliaceae* · 5 spp.
- **sesamoides** Endl. · E:False Sesame; G:Falscher Sesam · ⊙ Z10 ⓜ Ⓝ; W-Sah, trop. Afr.
- **triloba** E. Mey. ex Bernh. · ⊙ D Z10 ⓚ; S-Afr.

Ceratozamia Brongn. -f- *Zamiaceae* · 10 spp.
- *longifolia* Miq. = Ceratozamia mexicana var. longifolia
- **mexicana** Brongn.
- var. **longifolia** (Miq.) Dyer Z10 ⓜ ▽ ✳; Mex.
- var. **mexicana** Brongn. · ♄ e Z10 ⓜ ▽ ✳; Mex.
- var. **miqueliana** (H. Wendl.) J. Schust. Z10 ⓜ ▽ ✳; Mex.
- *miqueliana* H. Wendl. = Ceratozamia mexicana var. miqueliana
- *robusta* Miq. = Ceratozamia mexicana var. longifolia

Cerbera L. -f- *Apocynaceae* · 6 spp.
- **manghas** L. · E:Bentan, Bintaru, Madagascar Ordeal Bean; G:Gottesurteilsbohne · ♄ ♄ e ✕ Z10 ⓜ ✖; Ind., Sri Lanka, China, Malay. Arch., Austr., Pacific Is., Madag.
- *odollam* Gaertn. = Cerbera manghas
- *tanghin* Hook. = Cerbera manghas
- *venenifera* (Poir.) Steud. = Cerbera manghas

Cercidiphyllum Siebold & Zucc. -n- *Cercidiphyllaceae* · 2 spp. · E:Katsura Tree; F:Cercidiphyllum; G:Katsurabaum, Kuchenbaum
- **japonicum** Siebold & Zucc. · E:Katsura Tree; G:Katsurabaum, Kuchenbaum · ♄ d Z5; W-China, C-China, Jap.
- var. *magnificum* Nakai = Cercidiphyllum magnificum
- var. *sinense* Rehder & E.H. Wilson =

Cercidiphyllum japonicum
- **magnificum** (Nakai) Nakai · G:Großer Katsurabaum · ♄ d Z5 IV-V; Jap.

Cercis L. -f- *Caesalpiniaceae* · 6 spp. · E:Redbud; F:Arbre de Judée, gainier; G:Judasbaum
- **canadensis** L. · E:Eastern Redbud, Redbud; G:Kanadischer Judasbaum · ♄ d Z6 IV-V; Ont., USA: NE, NCE, NC, SC, SE, Fla.; Mex.
- **chinensis** Bunge · E:Chinese Redbud; G:Chinesischer Judasbaum · ♄ ♄ d Z7 V; C-China
- **griffithii** Boiss. · ♄ ♄ d Z7; Iran, Afgh., C-As
- **siliquastrum** L. · E:Judas Tree, Love Tree; F:Arbre de Judée; G:Gewöhnlicher Judasbaum · ♄ d Z7 IV-V Ⓝ; Eur.: Fr, Ital-P, Ba; TR, Syr., Palest., nat. in Ib, Crim

Cercocarpus Kunth -m- *Rosaceae* · 8 spp. · E:Mountain Mahogany; F:Acajou de montagne; G:Bergmahagoni
- *betuloides* Nutt. ex Torr. & A. Gray = Cercocarpus montanus var. glaber
- *intricatus* S. Watson = Cercocarpus ledifolius var. intricatus
- **ledifolius** Nutt. ex Torr. & A. Gray
- var. **intricatus** (S. Watson) M.E. Jones · E:Little Mountain Mahogany; G:Kleiner Bergmahagoni · Z8 ⓚ; USA: Utah, Ariz.
- var. **ledifolius** · E:Mountain Mahogany; G:Porstblättriger Bergmahgoni · ♄ ♄ e Z8 ⓚ Ⓝ; USA: NW, Calif., Rocky Mts, SW; Mex.: Baja Calif.
- **montanus** Raf. · E:Mountain Mahogany; G:Bergmahagoni
- var. **glaber** (S. Watson) F.L. Martin · E:Birchleaf Mountain Mahogany; G:Glatter Bergmahagoni · ♄ ♄ e Z7 ∧; USA: NW, Calif., SW; Baja Calif.
- var. **montanus** · E:Alderleaf Mountain Mahogany; G:Gewöhnlicher Bergmahagoni · ♄ e Z7 ∧; USA: NW, Rocky Mts, Calif., SW; Baja Calif.; N-Mex.
- *parvifolius* Nutt. ex Hook. & Arn. = Cercocarpus montanus var. montanus

Cereus Mill. -m- *Cactaceae* · c. 20 spp.
- *acranthus* Vaupel = Haageocereus acranthus subsp. acranthus
- **aethiops** Haw. · ⁴ Z9 ⓚ ▽ ✳; Arg.
- *alacriportanus* Pfeiff. = Cereus

hildmannianus
- *anguinus* Gürke = Cleistocactus baumannii subsp. anguinus
- *areolatus* Muehlenpf. ex K. Schum. =
Cleistocactus parviflorus
- *aureus* Meyen non Salm-Dyck = Corryocactus aureus
- *azureus* J. Parm. ex Pfeiff. = Cereus
aethiops
- *baumannii* Lem. = Cleistocactus baumannii subsp. baumannii
- *beneckei* C. Ehrenb. = Stenocereus
beneckei
- *brachypetalus* Vaupel = Corryocactus
brachypetalus
- *brevistylus* K. Schum. ex Vaupel = Corryocactus brevistylus
- **caesius** Salm-Dyck ex Pfeiff. · ⅊ Z9 ⒶⒶ ▽
✳; ? Braz.
- *chalybaeus* Otto = Cereus aethiops
- *chichipe* Rol.-Goss. = Polaskia chichipe
- *chlorocarpus* (Humb., Bonpl. & Kunth)
DC. = Browningia chlorocarpa
- *chosicensis* Werderm. & Backeb. =
Haageocereus pseudomelanostele
- *cinnabarinus* Eichlam = Heliocereus
cinnabarinus
- *coerulescens* Salm-Dyck = Cereus aethiops
- *damazioi* K. Schum. ex Weing. =
Arthrocereus microsphaericus
- *dayamii* Speg. = Cereus stenogonus
- *decumbens* Vaupel = Haageocereus
decumbens
- *dumortieri* Scheidw. = Isolatocereus
dumortieri
- *dybowskii* Rol.-Goss. = Austrocephalocereus dybowskii
- *elegantissimus* (Britton & Rose) A. Berger
= Heliocereus coccineus
- *emoryi* Engelm. = Bergerocactus emoryi
- **fernambucensis** Lem. · ⅊ Z9 ⒶⒶ ▽ ✳;
Braz.
- *flagelliformis* (L.) Mill. = Aporocactus
flagelliformis
- *flagriformis* Pfeiff. = Aporocactus flagelliformis
- *fluminensis* Miq. = Coleocephalocereus
fluminensis
- *forbesii* Otto ex C.F. Först. = Cereus
validus
- *giganteus* Engelm. = Carnegiea gigantea
- *grandiflorus* (L.) Mill. = Selenicereus
grandiflorus
- *greggii* Engelm. = Peniocereus greggii
- **hexagonus** (L.) Mill. · ⅊ Z9 ⒶⒶ ▽ ✳;

Venez., Surinam
- **hildmannianus** K. Schum. · E:Hedge
Cactus · ⅊ Z9 ⒶⒶ ▽ ✳; S-Braz., Parag.,
Urug.
- **huntingtonianus** Weing. · ⅊ Z9 ⒶⒶ ▽ ✳;
? Arg.
- *ianthothele* Monv. = Pfeiffera ianthothele
- *jalapensis* Vaupel = Selenicereus
coniflorus
- **jamacaru** DC. · ⅊ Z9 ⒶⒶ ▽ ✳; Braz.
- *leptophis* DC. = Aporocactus flagelliformis
- *limensis* Salm-Dyck = Haageocereus
acranthus subsp. acranthus
- *macdonaldiae* Hook. = Selenicereus
macdonaldiae var. macdonaldiae
- *marginatus* DC. = Pachycereus marginatus
- *martianus* Zucc. = Aporocactus martianus
- *melanostele* (Vaupel) A. Berger =
Espostoa melanostele
- *melanotrichus* K. Schum. = Corryocactus
melanotrichus
- *microspermus* Werderm. & Backeb. =
Browningia microsperma
- *microsphaericus* K. Schum. = Arthrocereus microsphaericus
- *neotetragonus* Backeb. = Cereus fernambucensis
- *pernambucensis* Britton & Rose = Cereus
fernambucensis
- *peruvianus* (L.) Mill. = Cereus repandus
- *queretaroensis* F.A.C. Weber = Stenocereus queretaroensis
- **repandus** (L.) Mill. · E:Peruvian Cactus ·
⅊ Z9 ⒶⒶ ▽ ✳; ? S-Am., nat. in SE-F
- *schottii* Engelm. = Lophocereus schottii
- *sericatus* Backeb. = Espostoa lanata
- *silvestrii* Speg. = Lobivia silvestrii
- *spachianus* Lem. = Trichocereus
spachianus
- *speciosissimus* (Desf.) DC. = Heliocereus
speciosus var. speciosus
- *speciosus* (Cav.) K. Schum. = Heliocereus
speciosus var. speciosus
- **stenogonus** K. Schum. · ⅊ Z9 ⒶⒶ ▽ ✳;
E-Bol., Parag., N-Arg.
- *striatus* K. Brandegee = Peniocereus
striatus
- *thurberi* Engelm. = Stenocereus thurberi
- *triangularis* hort. non (L.) Haw. =
Hylocereus undatus
- **validus** Haw. · ⅊ Z9 ⒶⒶ ▽ ✳; E-Bol., Arg.
- *versicolor* Werderm. & Backeb. =
Haageocereus versicolor
- *viperinus* F.A.C. Weber = Peniocereus

viperinus
- *weberbaueri* Vaupel = Weberbauerocereus weberbaueri
- *xanthocarpus* K. Schum. = Cereus hildmannianus

Cerinthe L. -f- *Boraginaceae* · 10 spp. · E:Honeywort; F:Mélinet; G:Wachsblume
- **glabra** Mill. · E:Smooth Honeywort; G:Alpen-Wachsblume · ⌣ △ Z5 V-VII; Eur.: Fr, Ital-P, C-Eur., EC-Eur., Ba, RO; TR; mts.
- **major** L. · E:Greater Honeywort; G:Große Wachsblume · ☉ Z5 VI-VII; Eur.: Ib, Fr, Ital-P, Ba; TR, Syr., Palest., N-Afr.
- **minor** L. · E:Lesser Honeywort; G:Kleine Wachsblume · ☉ ⌣ Z5 V-VII; Eur.: C-Eur., EC-Eur., Fr, Ital-P, E-Eur., Ba; TR, Iraq, Cauc., Iran

Ceriops Arn. -f- *Rhizophoraceae* · 2-3 spp.
- **candolleana** Arn. · ♄ Ⓦ Ⓝ; Trop.

Ceropegia L. -f- *Asclepiadaceae* · 160 spp. · F:Céropégia; G:Leuchterblume
- **africana** R. Br.
- subsp. **africana** · ⌣ Ψ ⚡ Z10 Ⓚ; S-Afr.: Cape, Natal
- subsp. **barklyi** (Hook. f.) Bruyns · ⌣ Ψ ⚡ ⚡ Z10 Ⓚ; S-Afr.: Natal
- **albisepta** Jum. & H. Perrier · ⌣ Ψ ⚡ Z10 Ⓦ V-VIII; Zaire
- *barklyi* Hook. f. = Ceropegia africana subsp. barklyi
- **bulbosa** Roxb. · ⌣ Ψ Z10 Ⓦ; Ind.
- var. *esculenta* (Edgew.) Hook. f. = Ceropegia bulbosa
- var. *lushii* (Graham) Hook. f. = Ceropegia bulbosa
- **crassifolia** Schltr. · ⌣ Ψ ⚡ Z10 Ⓚ; Namibia, S-Afr.
- **cumingiana** Decne. · ⌣ Ψ ⚡ Z10 Ⓦ VI-VIII; Malay. Arch., Phil., N.Guinea, trop. Austr.
- *debilis* N.E. Br. = Ceropegia linearis subsp. debilis
- **dichotoma** Haw. · ⌣ Ψ Z10 Ⓚ VII-X; Canar. (La Palma, Tenerife, Hierro)
- **distincta** N.E. Br. · ♄ Ψ Z10 Ⓚ; Zanzibar
- subsp. *haygarthii* (Schltr.) H. Huber = Ceropegia haygarthii
- subsp. *lugardiae* (N.E. Br.) H. Huber = Ceropegia lugardiae
- **elegans** Wall.
- var. **elegans** · ♄ Ψ ⚡ Z10 Ⓦ; Sri Lanka,

nat. in Cambodia
- var. **gardneri** (Thwaites ex Hook.) H. Huber · ♄ Ψ ⚡ Z10 Ⓦ; Sri Lanka
- **fusca** Bolle · ♄ Ψ Z10 Ⓚ VII-X; Canar.
- *gardneri* Thwaites ex Hook. = Ceropegia elegans var. gardneri
- *hastata* N.E. Br. = Ceropegia linearis subsp. woodii
- **haygarthii** Schltr. · ♄ Ψ ⚡ Z10 Ⓚ; S-Afr.: Cape, Natal, Transvaal
- **linearis** E. Mey.
- subsp. **debilis** (N.E. Br.) H. Huber · ⌣ Ψ ⚡ Z10
- subsp. **linearis** · ⌣ Ψ ⚡ ⚡ Z10 Ⓦ Ⓚ I-XII; Mozamb., S-Afr.: Natal
- subsp. **tenuis** (N.E. Br.) Bruyns · ⌣ Ψ ⚡ Z10; S-Afr. (Cape Prov.)
- subsp. **woodii** (Schltr.) H. Huber · E:Hearts on a String, Rosary Vine; G:Hängende Leuchterblume · ⌣ Ψ ⚡ Z10; Cape, Zimbabwe
- **lugardiae** N.E. Br. · ♄ Ψ ⚡ Z10 Ⓚ VI-VIII; E-Afr., trop-Afr.
- *lushii* Graham = Ceropegia bulbosa
- **radicans** Schltr. · ⌣ Ψ ⟿ Z10 Ⓚ VI-VIII; Cape
- *robynsiana* Werderm. = Ceropegia albisepta
- **sandersonii** Decne. ex Hook. f. · E:Fountain Flower, Parachute Plant; G:Kletternde Leuchterblume · ⌣ Ψ ⚡ Z10 Ⓚ VII-XI; Mozamb., S-Afr.: Natal, Transvaal
- **stapeliiformis** Haw. · ⌣ Ψ ⚡ Z10 Ⓚ VII-X; S-Afr.: Cape, Transvaal
- *thorncroftii* N.E. Br. = Ceropegia crassifolia
- *woodii* Schltr. = Ceropegia linearis subsp. woodii

Ceroxylon Bonpl. ex DC. -n- *Arecaceae* · 11 sp. · E:Wax Palm; F:Céroxylon, Palmier; G:Wachspalme
- **alpinum**
- subsp. **alpinum** · G:Berg-Wachspalme · ♄ e Z9 Ⓦ Ⓝ; Col.

Cestrum L. -n- *Solanaceae* · c. 175 spp. · E:Jessamine; F:Cestrum; G:Hammerstrauch
- **aurantiacum** Lindl. · E:Orange Cestrum; G:Orangefarbener Hammerstrauch · ♄ e Z9 Ⓚ VII-XI; Guat.
- **diurnum** L. · E:Day Jessamine · ♄ e D Z9 Ⓦ VIII-X; W.Ind.

- **elegans** (Brongn. ex Neumann) Schltdl.
- var. **elegans** · E:Red Cestrum; G:Roter Hammerstrauch · ♄ e Z9 ⌂ IV-IX; Mex.
- var. **longiflorum** Francey · ♄ e Z9 ⌂; Mex.
- **fasciculatum** (Endl.) Miers · E:Early Jessamine; G:Büscheliger Hammerstrauch · ♄ e Z9 ⌂ IV-V; Mex.
- **nocturnum** L. · E:Lady of the Night, Night Jessamine; G:Nachtjasmin · ♄ e Z9 ⌂; W.Ind.
- **parqui** L'Hér. · E:Willow Leaf Jessamine; G:Weidenblättriger Hammerstrauch · ♄ d Z9 ⌂ VI-VII ✹; Chile, nat. in S-Eur.
- *purpureum* (Lindl.) Standl. = Cestrum elegans var. elegans

Ceterach Willd. = Asplenium
- *officinarum* DC. = Asplenium ceterach

Chaenactis DC. -f- *Asteraceae* · 40 spp.
- **artemisiifolia** (Harv. & A. Gray) A. Gray · E:White Pincushion · ⊙ Z7 VII-VIII; S-Calif.
- **glabriuscula** DC.
- var. **glabriuscula** · E:Yellow Pincushion · ⊙ Z7; Calif.
- var. **tenuifolia** (Nutt.) H.M. Hall · ⊙ Z7 VII-VIII; S-Calif.
- *tenuifolia* Nutt. = Chaenactis glabriuscula var. tenuifolia

Chaenomeles Lindl. -f- *Rosaceae* · 4 spp. · E:Flowering Quince; F:Cognassier du Japon; G:Scheinquitte, Zierquitte
- × **californica** J.G.C. Weber (*C. japonica*) · G:Kalifornische Scheinquitte · ♄ d; cult.
- **cathayensis** (Hemsl.) C.K. Schneid. · G:Cathaya-Scheinquitte · ♄ d III-IV; C-China
- **japonica** (Thunb.) Lindl. ex Spach
- var. **alpina** Maxim. · ♄ d Z5 III-IV; Jap.
- var. **japonica** (Thunb.) Lindl. ex Spach · E:Japanese Quince, Maule's Quince; F:Cognassier du Japon; G:Japanische Scheinquitte · ♄ d Z5 IV Ⓝ; Jap.
- *lagenaria* (Loisel.) Koidz. = Chaenomeles speciosa
- var. *wilsonii* Rehder = Chaenomeles cathayensis
- **speciosa** (Sweet) Nakai · E:Chinese Quince; G:Chinesische Scheinquitte · ♄ d Z5 V-VI ⚘ ; China, nat. in Jap.
- **many cultivars**
- × **superba** (Frahm) Rehder (*C. japonica*

× *C. speciosa*) · E:Flowering Quince; G:Zierquitte · ♄ d Z5 III-IV; cult.
- **many cultivars**
- × **vilmoriniana** J.G.C. Weber (*C. cathayensis* × *C. speciosa*) · E:Vilmorin's Quince; G:Vilmorins Scheinquitte · ♄ d Z6; cult.

Chaenorhinum (DC.) Rchb. -n- *Scrophulariaceae* · 21 sp. · E:Dwarf Snapdragon, Toadflax; F:Linaire; G:Klaffmund, Orant, Zwerglöwenmaul
- *crassifolium* (Cav.) Lange = Chaenorhinum origanifolium subsp. crassifolium
- **glareosum** (Boiss.) Willk. · ♃ Z8; S-Sp. (Sierra Nevada, Sierra Tejeda)
- **minus** (L.) Lange · G:Klaffmund · Z8
- subsp. **litorale** (Willd.) Hayek · G:Strand-Klaffmund · ⊙ V-IX; Eur.: Adria, nat. in A (Kärnten, Steiermark)
- subsp. **minus** · E:Small Toadflax; G:Gewöhnlicher Klaffmund, Kleiner Orant · ⊙ VI-X; Eur.*, TR, Lebanon, Cauc., C-As., NW-Afr.
- **origanifolium** (L.) Kostel.
- subsp. **crassifolium** (L.) Lange · ♃ Z7; Eur.: sp., Ba
- subsp. **origanifolium** · E:Malling Toadflax · ♃ Z7; Eur.: Ib, I, F; Moroc., Alger., Tun.
- **villosum** (L.) Lange · ♃ Z7; S-Sp., SW-F, NW-Afr.

Chaerophyllum L. -n- *Apiaceae* · c. 35 spp. · E:Chervil; F:cerfeuil sauvage, Chérophylle; G:Kälberkropf, Kerbelrübe
- **aromaticum** L. · G:Gewürz-Kälberkropf · ♃ Z6 VII-VIII; Eur.: Ital-P, C-Eur., EC-Eur., Ba, E-Eur.
- **aureum** L. · G:Gold-Kälberkropf · ♃ Z6 VI-VII; Eur.: Ib, Fr, Ital-P, C-Eur., E-Eur., Ba; TR, Cauc., N-Iran
- **bulbosum** L. · E:Bulbous Chervil, Garden Chervil, Parsnip Chervil; G:Kerbelrübe, Knolliger Kälberkropf · ⊙ Z6 VI-VII Ⓝ; Eur.* exc. Ib, BrI; Cauc., C-As., nat. in N-Am.
- **elegans** Gaudin · G:Zierlicher Kälberkropf · ♃ Z6 VI-VIII; Eur.: I, Sw, A; Alp.
- **hirsutum** L. · G:Rauhaariger Kälberkropf
- subsp. **hirsutum** · E:Hairy Chervil; G:Berg-Kerbelrübe, Gewöhnlicher Rauhaariger Kälberkropf · ♃ Z6 V-VIII; Eur.* exc. BrI, Sc, nat. in DK
- subsp. **villarsii** (W.D.J. Koch) Briq. ·

G:Alpen-Kälberkropf, Villars Kälberkropf · ⁴ Z6 V-VI; Eur.: I, F, C-Eur.,
Slove., Croatia, AL
- *sativum* Lam. = Anthriscus cerefolium
var. cerefolium
- **temulum** L. · E:Rough Chervil;
G:Hecken-Kälberkropf, Taumel-
Kälberkropf · ⊙ ⊝ Z6 V-VII �; Eur.*, TR,
Cauc., NW-Afr.
- *trichospermum* Schult. non Lam. =
Anthriscus cerefolium var. trichocarpa

Chamaebatia Benth. -f- *Rosaceae* · 2 spp. ·
E:Mountain Misery; G:Fiederspiere
- **foliolosa** Benth. · E:Sierran Mountain
Misery; G:Kalifornische Fiederspiere · ♄ e
Z8 ⊛ VII; Calif.

Chamaebatiaria (Porter) Maxim. -f-
Rosaceae · 1 sp. · G:Harzspiere, Schein-
fiederspiere
- **millefolium** (Torr.) Maxim. · E:Desert
Sweet, Fernbush; G:Harzspiere,
Scheinfiederspiere · ♄ d Z7 ∧ VII-VIII;
USA: NW, Rocky Mts, Calif., SW

Chamaebuxus DC. = Polygala
- *alpestris* Spach = Polygala chamaebuxus
var. chamaebuxus
- *vayredae* (Costa) Willk. = Polygala
vayredae

Chamaecereus Britton & Rose = Lobivia
- *silvestrii* (Speg.) Britton & Rose = Lobivia
silvestrii

Chamaecistus Regel = Loiseleuria
- *procumbens* (L.) Kuntze = Loiseleuria
procumbens

Chamaecrista Moench -f- *Caesalpiniaceae* ·
265 spp.
- **cotinifolia** (G. Don) H.S. Irwin &
Barneby · ♄ ⋈ ⊛; Braz.

Chamaecyparis Spach -f- *Cupressaceae* ·
6 spp. · E:False Cypress; F:Faux-cyprès;
G:Scheinzypresse
- *funebris* (Endl.) Franco = Cupressus
funebris
- **lawsoniana** (A. Murray bis) Parl. ·
E:Lawson's Cypress, Oregon Cedar;
F:Cyprès de Lawson; G:Lawsons
Scheinzypresse · ♄ ♄ e Z5 III-IV ✲ ℕ;
USA: S-Oreg., N-Calif., nat. in Eur.

- many cultivars
- *nutkaensis* Lindl. & Gordon = Xanthocyparis nootkatensis
- **obtusa** (Siebold & Zucc.) Endl.
- many cultivars
- var. **obtusa** · E:Hinoki Cypress; F:Cyprès
nain; G:Gewöhnliche Feuer-Scheinzy-
presse, Hinoki-Scheinzypresse · ♄ e Z4
III-IV ✲ ℕ; Jap., Taiwan
- **pisifera** (Siebold & Zucc.) Endl. ·
E:Sawara Cypress; F:Cyprès porte-pois;
G:Erbsenfrüchtige Scheinzypresse · ♄ ♄ e
Z4 III-IV ✲ ℕ; Jap.
- many cultivars
- **thyoides** (L.) Britton, Sterns &
Poggenb. · E:Atlantic White Cedar;
F:Cyprès blanc; G:Gewöhnliche Weiße
Scheinzypresse · ♄ e Z5 IV ✲ ℕ; USA:
NE, SE, Fla.

Chamaecytisus Link -m- *Fabaceae* · c.
30 spp. · G:Geißklee, Zwergginster
- **albus** (Hacq.) Rothm. · G:Weißer
Zwergginster; E:Portuguese Broom,
White Broom · ⁴ d △ Z6 VI-VIII ✲; Eur.:
EC-Eur., Ba, E-Eur.
- **austriacus** (L.) Link · G:Österreichischer
Zwergginster, Österreichischer Geißklee ·
♄ d △ Z6 VI-VIII ✲; Eur.: EC-Eur., Ba,
E-Eur.; Cauc.
- **ciliatus** (Wahlenb.) Rothm. · ♄ d Z6;
Eur.: A, EC-Eur., RO, BG
- **eriocarpus** (Boiss.) Rothm. · ♄ d; Ba
- **glaber** (L. f.) Rothm. · ♄ d Z6 V-VI; Eur.:
YU, BG, RO
- **hirsutus** (L.) Link · G:Rauhaariger
Zwergginster · ♄ d Z6 IV-VI ✲; Eur.: Fr,
Ital-P, C-Eur., EC-Eur., Ba, E-Eur.; TR
- **proliferus** (L. f.) Link · E:Escabon · ♄ Z9
⊛ IV-V ℕ; Canar.
- **purpureus** (Scop.) Link · E:Purple
Broom; F:Genêt pourpre; G:Purpur-
Zwergginster · ♄ △ Z5 IV-VII ✲; Eur.: I,
A, Slove., Croatia, AL, nat. in D
- **ratisbonensis** (Schaeff.) Rothm. ·
G:Regensburger Zwergginster · ♄ ♄ d Z5
V-VI ✲; Eur.: C-Eur., EC-Eur., Ba, E-Eur.
- **ruthenicus** (Fisch. ex Wol.) Klásk. · ♄ d;
PL, Russ.
- **supinus** (L.) Link · E:Clustered Broom;
G:Kopf-Zwergginster · ♄ d Z6 VI-VII ✲;
Eur.* exc. BrI, Sc; TR
- × **versicolor** (Dippel) Karlsson (*C.
hirsutus* × *C. purpureus*) · ♄ d Z6 VI-VI;
cult.

Chamaedaphne Moench -f- *Ericaceae* · 1 sp. · G:Lederblatt, Torfgränke; E:Leatherleaf
- **calyculata** (L.) Moench · E:Leatherleaf; G:Torfgränke · ♄ e △ Z7 IV-V ☠; Eur.: Sc, PL, Russ.; N-As., Jap., Alaska, Can., USA: NE, SE, NCE;

Chamaedorea Willd. -f- *Arecaceae* · 107 spp. · F:Palmier de montagne; G:Bergpalme
- **arenbergiana** H. Wendl. · ♄ e Z9 (w); C-Am.
- *desmoncoides* H. Wendl. = Chamaedorea elatior
- **elatior** Mart. · ⌇ e Z9 (w); Mex., Guat.
- **elegans** Mart. · E:Parlour Palm; G:Mexikanische Bergpalme, Zierliche Bergpalme · ♄ e Z9 (w); Mex., Guat.
- **ernesti-augustii** H. Wendl. · ♄ e Z9 (w); Mex., Guat., Hond.
- *erumpens* H.E. Moore = Chamaedorea seifrizii
- **geonomiformis** H. Wendl. · ♄ e Z9 (w); Belize, Hond.
- **glaucifolia** H. Wendl. · ♄ e Z9 (w); S-Mex.
- **graminifolia** H. Wendl. · ♄ e Z9 (w); Mex., Guat.
- **metallica** O.F. Cook ex H.E. Moore · E:Miniature Fish-tail Palm; G:Metallische Bergpalme · ♄ e Z9 (w); Mex.
- *nana* hort. = Chamaedorea metallica
- **oblongata** Mart. · ♄ e Z9 (w); E-Mex., C-Am.
- **pinnatifrons** (Jacq.) Oerst. · ♄ e Z9 (w); Mex.
- **pochutlensis** Liebm. · ♄ e Z9 (w); Mex.
- **pumila** H. Wendl. ex Dammer · ♄ e (w); Costa Rica
- *pumila* hort. = Chamaedorea metallica
- **sartorii** Liebm. · ♄ e Z9 (w); Mex., C-Am.
- **seifrizii** Burret · E:Reed Palm; G:Seifriz-Bergpalme · ♄ e Z9 (w); Mex. (Yucatan)
- **tenella** H. Wendl. · ♄ e Z9 (w); Mex.
- **tepejilote** Liebm. · ♄ e Z9 (w) (N); S-Mex., C-Am.
- *wendlandiana* (Oerst.) Hemsl. = Chamaedorea tepejilote

Chamaelirium Willd. -n- *Melanthiaceae* · 1 sp. · E:Blazing Star; G:Funkelstern
- **luteum** (L.) A. Gray · E:Fairywand · ♃ Z4 ⚕; Can.: Ont.; USA: NE, NCE, SE, Fla.

Chamaemelum Mill. -n- *Asteraceae* · 4 spp. · E:Chamomile; F:Camomille romaine; G:Römische Kamille
- *inodorum* (L.) Vis. = Tripleurospermum perforatum
- **nobile** (L.) All. · E:Camomile; G:Römische Kamille · ♃ Z4 VI-IX ⚕ (N); Eur.: BrI, Fr, Ib, Azor.; Moroc., Alger., nat. in C-Eur., Ital-P, EC-Eur., BG

Chamaepericlymenum Hill = Cornus
- *canadense* (L.) Asch. & Graebn. = Cornus canadensis
- *suecicum* (L.) Asch. & Graebn. = Cornus suecica

Chamaeranthemum Nees -n- *Acanthaceae* · 4 spp.
- **beyrichii** Nees · ♃ (w); S-Braz.
- **gaudichaudii** Nees · ♃ (w); Braz.
- *igneum* (Linden) Regel = Xantheranthemum igneum
- **venosum** M.B. Foster ex Wassh. & L.B. Sm. · ♃; Braz.

Chamaerops L. -f- *Arecaceae* · 1 sp. · F:Palmier nain; G:Zwergpalme
- *excelsa* Mart. = Trachycarpus fortunei
- *fortunei* Hook. = Trachycarpus fortunei
- **humilis** L. · E:Mediteranean Fan Palm, Palmito; G:Europäische Zwerg-palme · ♄ e Z9 (k) (N); Eur.: Ib, F, Ital-P; N-Afr.
- *hystrix* (Fraser ex Thouin) Pursh = Rhapidophyllum hystrix

Chamaespartium Adans. -n- *Fabaceae* · 2-4 spp. · E:Winged Broom; F:Genêt ailé; G:Flügelginster
- **sagittale** (L.) P.E. Gibbs · G:Flügelginster
- subsp. **delphinensis** (Verl.) O. Bolòs & Vigo · ♄ ⇝ Z4 V-VI ☠; S-F
- subsp. **sagittale** · E:Arrow Broom, Winged Broom; F:Genêt ailé, Génistelle; G:Gewöhnlicher Flügelginster · ♄ ⇝ Z6 V-VI ☠; Eur.* exc. BrI, Sc

Chamaesyce Gray -f- *Euphorbiaceae* · 275 spp. · E:Spurge; G:Wolfsmilch
- **humifusa** (Willd. ex Schltr.) Prokh. · G:Niederliegende Wolfsmilch · ⊙ VI-IX ☠; Eur.: Russ.; Cauc., W-Sib., E-Sib., Amur, C-As, Mong., China: Sinkiang, Jap., nat. in Fr, Ital-P, C-Eur., EC-Eur.RO
- **maculata** (L.) Small · E:Spotted Spurge; G:Gefleckte Wolfsmilch · ⊙ VI-IX ☠; N-Am., nat. in Eur: : Ib, Fr, Ital-P, C-Eur.,

Ba, RO
- **nutans** (Lag.) Small · E:Eyebane; G:Nickende Wolfsmilch · ⊙ VII-IX ☠; N-Am., nat. in Eur: : Fr, Ital-P, C-Eur., Ba, RO
- **prostrata** (Aiton) Small · E:Prostrate Sandmat; G:Hingestreckte Wolfsmilch · ⊙ VI-IX ☠; N-Am., nat. in Eur.: Ib, I, Sic., GR
- **serpens** (Kunth) Small · E:Matted Sandmat; G:Schlängelnde Wolfsmilch · ⊙ ☠; Am., nat. in sp., S-F

Chambeyronia Vieill. -f- *Arecaceae* · 2 spp.
- **macrocarpa** (Brongn.) Vieill. ex Becc. · ₺ e Z10 ⓦ; N. Caled.

Chamelaucium Desf. -n- *Myrtaceae* · c. 20 spp.
- **uncinatum** Schauer · E:Geraldton Waxflower · ♄ e ⓚ III-IV; W-Austr.

Chamerion (Raf.) Raf. ex Holub = Epilobium
- *angustifolium* (L.) Holub = Epilobium angustifolium
- *dodonaei* (Vill.) Holub = Epilobium dodonaei
- *fleischeri* (Hochst.) Holub = Epilobium fleischeri

Chamomilla Gray = Matricaria
- *recutita* (L.) Rauschert = Matricaria recutita
- *suaveolens* (Pursh) Rydb. = Matricaria discoidea

Chamorchis Rich. -f- *Orchidaceae* · 1 sp. · F:Chamorchis, Orchis; G:Zwergorchis, Zwergständel
- **alpina** (L.) Rich. · E:False Orchid; G:Zwergorchis, Zwergständel · ♃ VII-VIII ▽ ✻; Eur.: Fr, Ital-P, C-Eur., EC-Eur., Slove., RO, N-Russ.; N, Alp., Carp.

× **Charlesworthara** hort. -f- *Orchidaceae* (*Cochlioda* × *Miltonia* × *Oncidium*)

Chartolepis Cass. = Centaurea
- *glastifolia* (L.) Cass. = Centaurea glastifolia

Chasmanthe N.E. Br. -f- *Iridaceae* · 3 spp. · E:Cobra Lily; F:Chasmanthe; G:Rachenlilie
- **aethiopica** (L.) N.E. Br. · E:African Cornflag ; G:Niedere Rachenlilie · ♃ Z9 ⓚ; S-Cape

Chasmanthium Link -n- *Poaceae* · 6 spp. · E:Bamboo Grass; G:Plattährengras
- **latifolium** (Michx.) H.O. Yates · E:Bamboo Grass, Sea Oats; G:Plattährengras · ♃ ⋊ Z4 VIII; USA: NE, NCE, NC, SC, SE, Fla.

Chasmatophyllum (Schwantes) Dinter & Schwantes -n- *Aizoaceae* · 8 spp.
- **musculinum** (Haw.) Dinter & Schwantes · ♃ ♆ Z9 ⓚ; S-Afr.: Cape, Orange Free State; Namibia

Cheilanthes Sw. -f- *Adiantaceae* · 203 spp. · E:Lip Fern; F:Cheilanthès; G:Lippenfarn, Pelzfarn, Schuppenfarn
- **acrostica** (Balb.) Tod. · G:Schuppenfarn · ♃ ⓚ IV-VI; Eur.: Ib, Fr, Ital-P, Ba; TR, Levant, NW-Afr., Libya
- *fragrans* (L. f.) Sw. = Cheilanthes pteridioides
- **hirta** Sw. · E:Parsley Fern · ♃ Z10 ⓚ; S-Afr.
- *marantae* (L.) Domin = Notholaena marantae
- **microphylla** (Sw.) Sw. · E:Southern Lip Fern · ♃ ⓚ; Fla., Mex., C-Am., W.Ind., S-Am.
- **pteridioides** (Reichard) C. Chr. · ♃ Z8 ⓚ; Eur.: Ib, Fr, Ital-P, Ba; TR, Levant, Cauc., Iran, C-As., NW-Afr., Libya

Cheiranthus L. = Erysimum
- *cheiri* L. = Erysimum cheiri
- *scoparius* Brouss. ex Willd. = Erysimum scoparium

Cheiridopsis N.E. Br. -f- *Aizoaceae* · 31 sp.
- *candidissima* (Haw.) N.E. Br. = Cheiridopsis denticulata
- *cigarettifera* (A. Berger) N.E. Br. = Cheiridopsis namaquensis
- **denticulata** (Haw.) N.E. Br. · ♃ ♆ Z9 ⓚ; Cape
- *gibbosa* Schick & Tischer = Cheiridopsis pillansii
- *marlothii* N.E. Br. = Cheiridopsis namaquensis
- **namaquensis** (Sond.) H.E.K. Hartmann · ♃ ♆ Z9; Cape
- **pillansii** L. Bolus · E:Lobster Claws · ♃ ♆

Z9 ⓐ; Cape
- **purpurea** L. Bolus · ♃ Ⴘ Z9 ⓐ; Cape

Chelidonium L. -n- *Papaveraceae* · 1 sp. ·
E:Greater Celadine; F:Chélidoine, Herbe-
aux-verrues; G:Schöllkraut
- *japonicum* Thunb. = Hylomecon japonica
- **majus** L. · E:Greater Celandine; G:Schöl-
lkraut
- var. **laciniatum** (Mill.) Syme · G:Gefran-
stes Schöllkraut · ♃ Z6 ✖
- var. **majus** · G:Gewöhnliches Schöllkraut · ⊙ ♃ Z6 IV-X ⚡ ✖; Eur.*, TR,
Cauc., W-Sib., C-As., Mong., Moroc.,
Alger., nat. in N-Am.

Chelone L. -f- *Scrophulariaceae* · 6 spp. ·
E:Shellflower, Turtlehead; F:Chélone ;
G:Schildblume, Schlangenkopf
- *barbata* Cav. = Penstemon barbatus
subsp. barbatus
- *campanulata* Cav. = Penstemon
campanulatus
- **glabra** L. · E:Snakehead, Turtlehead;
F:Galane en épis; G:Kahler Schlangenkopf · ♃ Z3 VIII-X ⚡ ; Can.: E; USA;
NE, NCE, SE
- **lyonii** Pursh · E:Pink Turtlehead · ♃
VII-IX; USA: Tenn., N.C., S.C., nat. in
USA: NE
- **obliqua** L. · E:Red Turtlehead; F:Galane
oblique; G:Miesmäulchen · ♃ Z6 VII-IX;
USA: NE, NCE, SE, Fla.
- var. *alba* hort. = Chelone glabra

Chelyorchis Dressler & N.H. Williams
-f- *Orchidaceae* · 1 sp.
- **ampliata** (Lindl.) Dressler & N.H. Williams · ♃ Z10 ⓜ IV-V ▽ ✳; C-Am., Col.,
Ecuad., Peru, Venez., Trinidad

Chenopodium L. -n- *Chenopodiaceae* · c.
150 spp. · E:Goosefoot; F:Chénopode;
G:Gänsefuß
- **album** L. · E:Fat Hen; G:Gewöhnlicher
Weißer Gänsefuß · ⊙ Z5 VII-X Ⓝ; Eur.*,
cosmop.
- *amaranticolor* (H.J. Coste & A. Reyn.)
Coste & A. Reyn. = Chenopodium
giganteum
- **ambrosioides** L. · E:Mexican Tea
- var. **ambrosioides** · E:Wormseed;
G:Mexikanischer Tee, Wohlriechender
Gänsefuß · ♃ VI-IX; trop. Am., nat. in
C-Eur., S-Eur., Canar., N-Afr., Can.: E,

USA*
- var. **anthelminticum** (L.) A. Gray ·
♃ Z5 ✖; USA: NE, NEC, SC, SE, Fla.;
Bermudas, Puerto Rico, Dom.Rep., Costa
Rica, C-Am.
- *anthelminticum* L. = Chenopodium
ambrosioides var. anthelminticum
- **aristatum** L. · E:Wormseed · ⊙ ✖ Z5
VI-IX; W-Sib., E-Sib., Amur, C-As.,
Mong., China, Korea, Jap.
- **berlandieri** Moq.
- subsp. **berlandieri** · E:Pitseed Goosefoot;
G:Berlandiers Gänsefuß · ⊙ Z5 VII-IX;
USA, Mex., nat. in Eur.
- subsp. **nuttalliae** (Saff.) H. Dan. Wilson
& Heiser · E:Nuttall's Goosefoot; G:Nut-
talls Gänsefuß · ⊙ Z5 Ⓝ; Mex.
- **bonus-henricus** L. · E:Good King Henry;
G:Guter Heinrich, Wilder Mehlspinat · ⊙
♃ Z5 VI-VIII Ⓝ; Eur.*, nat. in N-Am.
- **botryodes** Sm. · G:Dickblättriger Gänsefuß, Dickblatt-Gänsefuß · ⊙ Z5 III-X;
Eur.*, As., Afr., N-Am.; coasts, saline
habitats
- **botrys** L. · E:Jerusalem Oak; G:Klebriger
Gänsefuß · ⊙ ✖ VII-VIII; Eur.: Ib, Fr, Ital-
P, Ba, Sw, EC-Eur., E-Eur.; TR, Cyprus,
Syr., Cauc., Iran, W-Sib., C-As., Him.,
nat. in A, G, N-Am.
- **capitatum** (L.) Asch. · E:Strawberry
Blite; G:Kopfiger Erdbeerspinat · ⊙ Z5
VI-VIII Ⓝ; cult. Eur.
- *chenopodioides* = Chenopodium botryo-
des
- *ficifolium* Sm. · E:Fig-leaved Goosefoot;
G:Feigenblättriger Gänsefuß · ⊙ Z5 VI-IX;
Eur.* exc. Sc; TR, Iran, W-Sib., E-Sib. ,
C-As., Him., Jap., Egypt, nat. in Sc
- **foliosum** Asch. · E:Strawberry Goose-
foot; G:Durchblätterter Gänsefuß, Echter
Erdbeerspinat · ⊙ Z5 VI-VIII Ⓝ; Eur.: Ib,
Fr, C-Eur., Ba; TR, Cyprus, Syr., Cauc.,
N-Iran, C-As., Him., nat. in EC-Eur.,
E-Eur., S-Afr., N-Am.
- **giganteum** D. Don · E:Tree Spinach;
G:Spinatbaum · ⊙ Z5 VII-VIII Ⓝ; N-Ind.
- **glaucum** L. · E:Oak Leaved Goosefoot;
G:Graugrüner Gänsefuß · ⊙ Z5 VII-X;
Eur.*, Cauc., Iran, W-Sib., E-Sib. Amur,
Sakhal., Kamchat., C-As.
- **hircinum** Schrad. · E:Foetid Goosefoot;
G:Bocks-Gänsefuß · ⊙ Z5 VIII-X; S-Am.,
nat. in Eur., S-Afr.
- **hybridum** L. · E:Maple-leaved Goose-
foot, Sowbane; G:Bastard-Gänsefuß,

Stechapfelblättriger Gänsefuß, Unechter Gänsefuß · ⊙ Z5 VI-IX; Eur.* exc. BrI; TR, Cauc., W-Sib., E-Sib., Amur, C-As., Mong., Tibet, Him., Manch., China, Korea, nat. in N-Am.

– **murale** L. · E:Australian Spinach; G:Mauer-Gänsefuß · ⊙ Z5 VII-IX Ⓝ; Eur.*, TR, Levant, Cauc., Iran, C-As., Ind., N-Afr., nat. in N-Am., S-Am., Austr., NZ

– *nuttalliae* Saff. = Chenopodium berlandieri subsp. nuttalliae

– **opulifolium** Schrad. ex W.D.J. Koch & Ziz · E:Grey Goosefoot; G:Schneeballblättriger Gänsefuß · ⊙ Z5 VII-IX; Eur.* exc. BrI, Sc; TR, Cauc., Iran, W-Sib. C-As., N-Afr., nat. in Sc

– **pallidicaule** Aellen · ⚃ Ⓝ; Peru, Bol., Chile

– **polyspermum** L. · E:Many-seed Goosefoot; G:Vielsamiger Gänsefuß · ⊙ Z5 VII-IX; Eur.*, N-Afr., As.

– **pratericola** Rydb. · E:Desert Goosefoot; G:Schmalblättriger Gänsefuß · ⊙ Z5 VIII-X; N-Am., nat. in Eur., S-Am.

– **probstii** Aellen · E:Probst's Goosefoot; G:Probst-Gänsefuß · VIII-IX; Austr.: Queensl., S-Austr., nat. in Eur.

– **pumilio** R. Br. · E:Clammy Goosefoot; G:Australischer Gänsefuß · ⊙ Z5 VI-IX; Austr., Tasman., nat. in Eur.: Ib, B, G, F, N-Am., S-Afr., NZ

– **purpurascens** B. Juss. ex Jacq. · E:Purple Goosefoot · ⊙ Z5 VII-VIII; China

– **quinoa** Willd. · E:Quinoa; G:Quinoa, Reis-Melde · ⊙ Z5 VI-VIII Ⓝ; Col, Ecuad., Peru, Chile, Arg.

– **rubrum** L. · E:Red Goosefoot; G:Roter Gänsefuß · ⊙ Z5 VII-IX; Eur.*, Levant, Cauc., W-Sib., E-Sib. , C-As., Mong., China: Sinkiang, ? Manch., N-Am.

– **schraderianum** Schult. · G:Schraders Gänsefuß · ⊙ Z5 VII-IX; E-Afr., nat. in Eur.: EC-Eur., EC-Eur.; Cauc., Trop., Subtrop.

– **strictum** Roth · E:Striped Goosefoot; G:Gewöhnlicher Gestreifter Gänsefuß · ⊙ Z5 VIII-X; Eur.: C-Eur., EC-Eur., E-Eur.; Cauc., Iran, W-Sib., Amur, C-As., Him., China, Canar., Eth.

– **suecicum** Murr · G:Grüner Gänsefuß · ⊙ Z5 VI-VIII; Eur.* exc. Ib; W-Sib., E-Sib. Amur, Sakhal., Kamchat., C-As.

– **urbicum** L. · E:Upright Goosefoot; G:Gewöhnlicher Straßen-Gänsefuß · ⊙

Z5 VII-VIII; Eur.* exc. BrI, Sc; TR, Cauc., Iran, W-Sib., E-Sib. Amur, C-As., Mong., China: Sinkiang, Manch., nat. in BrI

– *virgatum* (L.) Ambrosi = Chenopodium foliosum

– **vulvaria** L. · E:Stinking Goosefoot, Vulvaria; G:Stinkender Gänsefuß · ⊙ Z5 VI-IX; Eur.*, TR, Levant, W-Sib., C-As., N-Afr., nat. in N-Am., Austr.

Chevaliera Gaudich. ex Beer = Aechmea
– *ornata* Gaudich. = Aechmea ornata
– *sphaerocephala* Gaudich. = Aechmea sphaerocephala

Chiapasia Britton & Rose -f- Cactaceae · 1 sp.
– **nelsonii** (Britton & Rose) Britton & Rose · ♄ Ψ Z9 ⓐ ▽ ✳; Mex., Hond.

Chiastophyllum (Ledeb.) A. Berger -n- Crassulaceae · 1 sp. · F:Goutte d'or; G:Walddickblatt
– **oppositifolium** (Ledeb.) Stapf ex A. Berger · E:Lamb's Tail; F:Goutte d'or; G:Goldtröpfchen, Walddickblatt · ⚃ Ψ △ Z7 VI; W-Cauc.

Chileniopsis Backeb. = Neoporteria
– *villosa* (Monv.) Backeb. = Neoporteria villosa

Chiliotrichum Cass. -n- Asteraceae · 2 spp.
– *amelloides* DC. = Chiliotrichum diffusum
– **diffusum** (G. Forst.) Kuntze · ♄ Z8 ⓐ; Chile, Arg., Anden

Chiloschista Lindl. -f- Orchidaceae · 19 spp.
– **lunifera** (Rchb. f.) J.J. Sm. · ⚃ ⓐ IV-V ▽ ✳; N-Ind., Sikkim, Burma, Thail.

Chimaphila Pursh -f- Pyrolaceae · 4-8 spp. · E:Prince's Pine; F:Chimaphile; G:Winterlieb
– **umbellata** (L.) W.P.C. Barton · E:Prince's Pine; G:Doldiges Winterlieb · ⚃ ♄ e Z4 VI-VIII ⚥ ▽; Eur.: Fr, C-Eur., Sc, EC-Eur., W-Ba, E-Eur.; W-Sib., Sakhal., Amur, Korea, Jap., Alaska, Can., USA* exc. SC, SW

Chimonanthus Lindl. -m- Calycanthaceae · 6 spp. · E:Wintersweet; F:Chimonanthe odorant; G:Winterblüte
– *fragrans* Lindl. = Chimonanthus praecox

- **praecox** (L.) Link · E:Wintersweet;
F:Chimonanthe odorant; G:Chinesische
Winterblüte · ♄ d D Z7 ∧ I-III; China

Chimonobambusa Makino -f- *Poaceae* ·
10 spp.
- **marmorea** (Mitford) Makino · E:Marbled
Bamboo; G:Marmorierter Winterbambus
· ♄ e Z6; Jap.

Chiococca P. Browne -f- *Rubiaceae* · 21 sp. ·
E:Snowberry; G:Schneebeere
- **alba** (L.) Hitchc. · E:West Indian
Snowberry; G:Westindische Schneebeere
· ♄ e D Z10 ⊕ II; S-Fla., W.Ind.

Chiogenes Salisb. ex Torr. = Gaultheria
- *serpyllifolia* (Pursh) Salisb. = Gaultheria
hispida

Chionanthus L. -m- *Oleaceae* · c. 100 spp. ·
E:Fringe Tree; F:Arbre de neige;
G:Schneeflockenstrauch
- **retusus** Lindl. & Paxton · E:Chinese
Fringe Tree; G:Chinesischer Schneeflock-
enstrauch · ♄ d Z6 VI-VII; China, Korea,
Taiwan
- **virginicus** L. · E:American Fringe Tree;
F:Arbre à franges, Arbre de neige;
G:Virginischer Schneeflockenstrauch · ♄
♄ d Z5 VI ⚘ ; USA: NE, NCE, SC, SE, Fla.

Chionodoxa Boiss. -f- *Hyacinthaceae* ·
8 spp. · E:Glory of the Snow; F:Gloire
des neiges; G:Schneeglanz, Schneestolz,
Sternhyazinthe
- **forbesii** Baker · E:Glory of the Snow;
G:Blauer Schneeglanz · ⚍ Z4 IV; W-TR
- *gigantea* Whittall = Chionodoxa luciliae
- **lochiae** Meikle · G:Zyprischer Schneeglanz · ⚍ Z4 V; Cyprus
- *luciliae* auct. non Boiss = Chionodoxa
forbesii
- **luciliae** Boiss. · G:Großer Schneeglanz,
Schneestolz, Sternhyazinthe · ⚍ Z4 ▽;
TR
- **nana** (Schult. & Schult. f.) Boiss. &
Heldr. · E:Glory of the Snow; G:Kleiner
Schneeglanz · ⚍ Z4 IV; Crete
- **sardensis** Whittall · G:Dunkler Schneeglanz · ⚍ Z4 IV; W-TR
- **siehei** Stapf · G:Wuchernder Schneeglanz
- **tmoli** Whittall · G:Weißer Schneeglanz

× **Chionoscilla** J. Allen ex G. Nicholson
-f- *Hyacinthaceae* · 1 sp. (*Scilla* ×
Chionodoxa)
- **allenii** J. Allen ex G. Nicholson (*Scilla
bifolia* × *Chionodoxa forbesii*) · ⚍ Z4
III-IV; cult.

Chirita Buch.-Ham. ex D. Don -f-
Gesneriaceae · 100-130 spp.
- **barbata** Sprague · ⚍ Z10 ⊕ VII-VIII;
Ind., Malay. Arch.
- **hamosa** (Wall.) R. Br. · ⚍ Z10 ⊕ VII-
VIII; Ind., Burma
- **lavandulacea** Stapf · ⚍ Z10 ⊕ I-III;
Malay.Arch.
- **micromusa** B.L. Burtt · ⚍ Z10 ⊕ VI-VIII;
Thail.
- **pumila** D. Don · ⚍ Z10 ⊕ VII-IX; Him.
- **sinensis** Lindl. · ⚍ Z10 ⊕; China (Hong
Kong)

Chironia L. -f- *Gentianaceae* · c. 15 spp. ·
E:Christmas Berry; F:Chironia; G:Chiro-
nie, Weihnachtsbeere
- **linoides** L. · ♄ Z9 ⊕ VII-X; S-Afr.

Chlidanthus Herb. -m- *Amaryllidaceae* ·
4 spp. · E:Fairy Lily; F:Pancrais jaune;
G:Prunkblüte
- **fragrans** Herb. · E:Fairy Lily, Perfumed
Fairy Lily; G:Prunkblüte, Schönblüte ·
⚍ D Z9 ⊕ VII-VIII; Peru, Bol., NE-Arg.;
And.

Chloranthus Sw. -m- *Chloranthaceae* ·
-20 spp.
- **spicatus** (Thunb.) Makino · ♄ e ⊕ Ⓝ;
S-China, nat. in Jap.

Chloris Sw. -f- *Poaceae* · c. 55 (-80) spp. ·
E:Finger Grass; G:Gilbgras
- **argentina** (Hack.) Lillo & Parodi ·
G:Argentinisches Fingergras · ⊙ ⚍ Z9;
Arg.
- **barbata** (L.) Sw. · E:Giant Finger Grass,
Swollen Windmill Grass; G:Bärtiges
Gilbgras · ⊙ ⚍ Z9 ⊕ VIII-IX; Trop.
- **gayana** Kunth · E:Rhodes Grass;
G:Rhodasgras · ⊙ ⚍ Z9 Ⓝ; trop. Afr.,
S-Afr., Sahara, S-As., Austr.
- **radiata** (L.) Sw. · E:Radiate Fingergrass ·
⚍ Z9 VIII-IX; W.Ind.
- **truncata** R. Br. · E:Creeping Windmill
Grass, Star Grass; G:Gestutztes Finger-
gras · ⚍ Z9 ⊕ VIII-IX; Austr.: Queensl.,

N.S.Wales,
- **virgata** Sw. · E:Feather Windmill Grass; G:Feder-Fingergras · ☉ ⁴ Z10 VII-IX; Trop.

Chlorophora Gaudich. -f- *Moraceae* · 2 (-5) spp. · G:Färberholz; E:Fustic; F:Iroko
- *excelsa* (Welw.) Benth. & Hook. f. = Milicia excelsa
- **tinctoria** (L.) Gaudich. ex Benth. & Hook. f. · E:Fustic Tree; G:Amerikanisches Färberholz · ♄ d Z10 ⓜ Ⓝ; Mex., C-Am., W.Ind., S-Am.

Chlorophytum Ker-Gawl. -n- *Anthericaceae* · 191 sp. · E:Spider Ivy, Spider Plant; F:Phalangère; G:Grüner Heinrich, Grünlilie
- *amaniense* Engl. = Chlorophytum filipendulum subsp. amaniense
- *bichetii* Backer = Chlorophytum laxum
- **capense** (L.) Voss · E:Bracket Plant · ⁴ Z9 ⓜ Ⓚ; S-Afr.
- **comosum** (Thunb.) Jacques · E:Spider Plant; G:Grünlilie · ⁴ Z9 ⓜ Ⓚ; S-Afr.: Cape, Natal
- *elatum* (Aitch.) R. Br. ex Ker-Gawl. = Chlorophytum comosum
- **filipendulum** Baker
- subsp. **amaniense** (Engl.) Nordal & A.D. Poulsen · ⁴ Z10 ⓜ; Tanzania (Usambara)
- *heyneanum* Wall. ex Hook. f. = Chlorophytum heynei
- **heynei** Baker · ⁴ Z10 ⓜ; Ind., Sri Lanka
- *hoffmannii* Engl. = Chlorophytum holstii
- **holstii** Engl. · ⁴ Z10 ⓜ; Tanzania
- **inornatum** Ker-Gawl. · ⁴ Z10 ⓜ; W-Afr.
- **laxum** R. Br. · ⁴ Z10 ⓜ; Gabon
- **macrophyllum** (A. Rich.) Asch. · ⁴ Z10 ⓜ; Eth.
- **nepalense** (Lindl.) Baker · ⁴ Z10 ⓜ; Nepal, Sikkim
- **orchidastrum** Lindl. · ⁴ Z10 ⓜ; W-Afr.: Sierra Leone
- *sternbergianum* (Schult. & Schult. f.) Steud. = Chlorophytum comosum
- *undulatum* Wall. ex Hook. f. = Chlorophytum nepalense

Chloroxylon DC. -n- *Rutaceae* · 1 sp. · E:Satin Wood; F:Bois jaune, Bois-satin; G:Grünholz
- **swietenia** DC. · G:Grünholz; E:Satin Wood · ♄ d ⓜ Ⓝ; Ind.

Choisya Kunth -f- *Rutaceae* · 7 spp. · E:Orange Blossom; F:Oranger du Mexique; G:Orangenblume
- *grandiflora* Regel = Choisya ternata
- **ternata** (La Llave & Lex.) Kunth · E:Mexican Orange Blossom; G:Mexikanische Orangenblume · ♄ e D Z8 Ⓚ V-VI; Mex.

Chondrilla L. -f- *Asteraceae* · 25 spp. · E:Nakedweed; F:Chondrille; G:Knorpellattich
- **chondrilloides** (Ard.) H. Karst. · G:Alpen-Knorpellattich · ⁴ VII-VIII; Eur.: Fr, Ital-P, C-Eur., Slove., ? RO; mts.
- **juncea** L. · E:Nakedweed; G:Binsen-Knorpellattich, Großer Knorpellattich · ⁴ VII-IX; Eur.* exc. BrI, Sc; TR, Syr., Iraq, Cauc., N-Iran, Afgh., NW-Afr.

× **Chondrobollea** hort. -f- *Orchidaceae* (Bollea × Chondrorhyncha)

Chondrodendron Ruiz & Pav. -n- *Menispermaceae* · 3 spp.
- **microphyllum** (Eichler) Moldenke · ♄ ⚥ ⓜ ⚲; Braz.: Bahia
- **platyphyllum** (A. St.-Hil.) Miers · ♄ ⚥ ⓜ ⚲; SE-Braz.
- **tomentosum** Ruiz & Pav. · E:Pareira · ♄ ⚥ ⓜ ⚲; Panama, S-Am.

Chondrorhyncha Lindl. -f- *Orchidaceae* · 26 spp.
- *chestertonii* Rchb. f. = Chondroscaphe chestertonii
- *fimbriata* (Linden & Rchb. f.) Rchb. f. = Chondroscaphe fimbriata

Chondroscaphe (Dressler) Senghas & G. Gerlach -f- *Orchidaceae* · 13 spp.
- **chestertonii** (Rchb. f.) Senghas & G. Gerlach · ⁴ Z10 ⓜ VI-VIII ▽ ✳; Col.
- **fimbriata** (Linden & Rchb. f.) Dressler · ⁴ Z10 ⓜ VII-VIII ▽ ✳; Col.

Chorisia Kunth -f- *Bombacaceae* · 5 spp. · E:Floss Silktree; F:Chorisia, Fromager; G:Florettseidenbaum, Wollbaum
- **speciosa** A. St.-Hil. · E:Floss Silktree; G:Brazilianischer Florettseidenbaum · ♄ d Z10 ⓜ; Braz., Arg.

Chorispora R. Br. ex DC. -f- *Brassicaceae* · 12 spp. · E:Crossflower; G:Gliederschote

– **tenella** (Pall.) DC. · G:Gliederschote;
E:Crossflower · ⊙ Z7 V; Eur.: BG, RO,
Russ.; TR, Syr., Iran, W-Sib., Mong.

Chorizema Labill. -n- *Fabaceae* ·
18-25 spp. · E:Flame Pea; F:Chorizema;
G:Flammenerbse, Kreisfahne
– **cordatum** Lindl. · E:Heart-leaved Flame
Pea; G:Herzförmige Flammenerbse · ♄ e
Z9 ⌂; W-Austr.
– **ilicifolium** Labill. · E:Holly Flame Pea;
G:Heilige Flammenerbse · ♄ e Z9 ⌂ ⬭
IV-V; W-Austr.
– *varium* Benth. ex Lindl. = Chorizema
ilicifolium

Chortolirion A. Berger -n- *Aloaceae* · 1 sp. ·
G:Weidelilie

Chosenia Nakai -f- *Salicaceae* · 1 sp.
– **arbutifolia** (Pall.) A.K. Skvortsov · ♄ d Z5
V; E-Sib., Amur, Manch., Korea, Jap.
– *bracteosa* (Turcz.) Nakai = Chosenia
arbutifolia

Christella H. Lév. -f- *Thelypteridaceae* ·
176 spp.
– **dentata** (Forssk.) Brownsey & Jermy · ♃
Z10 ⌂; Eur.: Azor., S-Sp., I, Crete; trop.
Afr., trop. As.

Christia Moench -f- *Fabaceae* · 12 spp.
– **vespertilionis** (L. f.) Backh. f. · ⊙ ♃ ⌂
VII-IX; Cambodia, S-Vietn.

Chrozophora Neck. ex Juss. -f-
Euphorbiaceae · 9 spp. · E:Tournesol;
F:Croton, Tournesol; G:Lackmuskraut
– **tinctoria** (L.) A. Juss. · E:Giradol,
Tournesol; G:Lackmuskraut · ⊙ ⌂ ⓝ;
Eur.: Ib, Fr, Ital-P, Ba, Crim; TR, Levant,
Socotra, Iran, Afgh., Ind., C-As., N-Afr.

Chrysalidocarpus H. Wendl. -m-
Arecaceae · 23 spp. · E:Yellow Palm;
F:Aréquier, Palmier doré; G:Goldfrucht-
palme
– **lutescens** H. Wendl. · E:Areca Palm,
Butterfly Palm, Madagascar Palm;
G:Madagaskar-Goldfruchtpalme · ♄ ♄ e
Z10 ⌂; Madag.

Chrysanthemoides Fabr. -f- *Asteraceae* ·
2 spp.
– **monilifera** (L.) Norl. · E:Bush-tick Berry ·

♄ Z9 ⌂; S-Afr.

Chrysanthemum L. -n- *Asteraceae* ·
37 spp. · E:Florist's Chrysanthemum;
F:Chrysanthème; G:Chrysantheme,
Winteraster
– *alpinum* L. = Leucanthemopsis alpina
– *anethifolium* (Willd.) Steud. = Argyranthemum foeniculaceum
– *arcticum* L. = Arctanthemum arcticum
– *argenteum* (Willd.) Bornm. = Tanacetum
argenteum
– *balsamita* L. = Tanacetum balsamita
– *biebersteinianum* Adams = Anthemis
marschalliana
– *cinerariifolium* (Trevir.) Vis. = Tanacetum
cinerariifolium
– **coreanum** (H. Lév. & Vaniot) Nakai ex T.
Mori · ♃ Z7; Korea
– *coronarium* L. = Glebionis coronaria var.
coronaria
– *corymbosum* L. = Tanacetum corymbosum subsp. corymbosum
– *densum* (Labill.) Steud. = Tanacetum
densum
– *erubescens* Stapf = Chrysanthemum
zawadskii var. latilobum
– *foeniculaceum* (Willd.) Desf. = Argyranthemum foeniculaceum
– *frutescens* L. = Argyranthemum frutescens
– *gayanum* Ball = Rhodanthemum
gayanum
– *×* **grandiflorum** (Ramat.) Kitam. (? × C.
indicum) · E:Chrysanthemum; G:Garten-
Chrysantheme · ♃ Z7 ⚘ ; cult.
– **many cultivars, see Section III**
– *haradjanii* Rech. f. = Tanacetum
haradjanii
– *× hortorum* W.T. Mill. = Chrysanthemum
× grandiflorum
– *indicum* hort. = Chrysanthemum ×
grandiflorum
– **indicum** L. · ♃ Z6 ⚘ ⓝ; China
– *× koreanum* hort. = Chrysanthemum ×
grandiflorum
– *majus* (Desf.) Asch. = Tanacetum
balsamita
– *maritimum* (L.) Pers. = Tripleurospermum maritimum
– *subsp. inodorum* (K. Koch) Vis. =
Tripleurospermum perforatum
– *mawii* Hook. f. = Rhodanthemum
gayanum
– *maximum* hort. = Leucanthemum ×
superbum

– *millefolium* (L.) Willd. = Tanacetum millefolium
– × *morifolium* Ramat. = Chrysanthemum × grandiflorum
– *naktongense* Nakai = Chrysanthemum zawadskii var. latilobum
– *nivellei* hort. non Braun-Blanq. & Maire = Heteranthemis viscidihirta
– *pacificum* Nakai = Ajania pacifica
– *ptarmiciflorum* (Webb) Brenan = Tanacetum ptarmiciflorum
– *roseum* Adams = Tanacetum coccineum
– *rubellum* Sealy = Chrysanthemum zawadskii var. latilobum
– *segetum* L. = Glebionis segetum
– *serotinum* L. = Leucanthemella serotina
– *sinense* Sabine ex Sweet = Chrysanthemum × grandiflorum
– × *superbum* Bergmans ex J.W. Ingram = Leucanthemum × superbum
– *tricolor* Andrews = Ismelia carinata
– *uliginosum* Pers. = Leucanthemella serotina
– *viscidehirtum* (Schott) Thell. = Heteranthemis viscidihirta
– **weyrichii** (Maxim.) Miyabe · F:Chrysanthème nain d'Extrême-Orient · ⵗ △ Z4 VI-VII; Jap.
– **zawadskii** Herbich
– var. **latilobum** (Maxim.) Kitam. · G:Koreanische Garten-Chrysantheme · ⵗ ⋉ Z7 ∧ IX-X ▽; Jap., Korea, Manch., N-China
– var. **zawadskii** · E:Korean Chrysanthemum; G:Korea-Chrysantheme · ⵗ ⤳ △ Z6 VI-VII ▽; Russ., Slova; Carp., Ural

Chrysobalanus L. -m- *Chrysobalanaceae* · 2 spp. · E:Coco Plum; F:Icaquier; G:Goldpflaume, Icacopflaume
– **icaco** L. · E:Coco Plum; G:Goldpflaume, Icacopflaume · ♄ ♄ e Z10 ⓌⓃ; Fla., Mex., C-Am., W.Ind., Ecuad., N-Braz.

Chrysocoma L. -f- *Asteraceae* · 18 spp. · E:Goldilock; F:Chrysocome; G:Goldhaar
– **coma-aurea** L. · E:Yellow Edging Daisy; G:Schopf-Goldhaar · ⵗ Z9 ⓚ VII-VIII; S-Afr.

Chrysogonum L. -n- *Asteraceae* · 1 sp. · E:Golden Knee; F:Chrysogonum; G:Goldkörbchen
– **virginianum** L. · E:Golden Star, Green-and-Gold; G:Goldkörbchen · ⵗ V-VII;

USA: NE, SE, Fla.

Chrysolarix H.E. Moore = Pseudolarix
– *amabilis* (J. Nelson) H.E. Moore = Pseudolarix amabilis

Chrysolepis Hjelmq. -f- *Fagaceae* · 2 spp. · E:Golden Chinkapin; G:Goldschuppen-kastanie
– **chrysophylla** (Douglas ex Hook.) Hjelmq. · E:Golden Chinkapin; G:Gold-schuppenkastanie · ♄ e Z7 ⓚ Ⓝ; USA: Wash., Oreg., Calif.

Chrysophyllum L. -n- *Sapotaceae* · 87 spp. · E:Star Apple; F:Caïmitier; G:Sternapfel
– **cainito** L. · E:Star Apple; G:Sternapfel · ♄ ♄ e Z10 Ⓦ Ⓝ; C-Am., W.Ind.
– **imperiale** (Linden ex K. Koch & Fintelm.) Benth. & Hook. f. · ♄ e Z10 Ⓦ; Braz.
– **sanguinolentum** (Pierre) Baehni
– subsp. **balata** Ducke · G:Conquirama · ♄ Ⓦ Ⓝ; Amazon.

Chrysopogon Trin. -m- *Poaceae* · 26 spp. · E:Love Grass; F:Barbon, Chrysopogon; G:Goldbart
– **gryllus** (L.) Trin. · G:Goldbart · ⵗ VI Ⓝ; Eur.: Fr, Ital-P, C-Eur., EC-Eur., Ba, E-Eur.; TR, Syr., N-Iraq, Cauc., Iran, Nepal, Ind. (Assam.), nat. in Austr.
– *nutans* (L.) Benth. = Sorghastrum nutans

Chrysopsis (Nutt.) Elliott -f- *Asteraceae* · 10 spp. · E:Golden Aster; F:Aster doré; G:Goldaster

Chrysosplenium L. -n- *Saxifragaceae* · c. 60 spp. · E:Golden Saxifrage; F:Cresson doré, Dorine; G:Milzkraut
– **alternifolium** L. · E:Alternate-leaved Golden Saxifrage; G:Wechsel-blättriges Milzkraut · ⵗ ⤳ ⌢ Z4 IV-VI; Eur.*, Cauc., W-Sib., E-Sib., Amur, Kamchat., Him., Mong., Jap., Can., USA (Iowa), Greenl.
– **oppositifolium** L. · E:Opposite-leaved Golden Saxifrage; G:Gegenblättriges Milzkraut
– var. **oppositifolium** · ⵗ ⌢ Z5 IV-VI; Eur.* exc. EC-Eur.
– var. **rosulare** Schott · ⵗ ⤳ ⌢ Z5 IV-VI

Chrysothamnus Nutt. -m- *Asteraceae* ·

16 spp. · E:Rabbitbush; F:Chrysothamne;
G:Kaninchenstrauch
– **nauseosus** (Pursh) Britton & A. Br. ·
E:Rubber Rabbitbush · ♄; Can.: B.C.,
Sask.; USA.: NW, Calif., Rocky Mts., SW,
SC; N-Mex.

Chrysothemis Decne. -f- *Gesneriaceae* ·
7 spp.
– **friedrichsthaliana** (Hanst.) H.E. Moore ·
⁴ Z10 ⓦ VII-VIII; C-Am., W-Col.
– **pulchella** (Donn ex Sims) Decne. ·
E:Squarestem · ⁴ Z10 ⓦ VI-VIII; C-Am.,
S-Am.

Chrysurus Pers. = Lamarckia
– *cynosuroides* Pers. = Lamarckia aurea

Chusquea Kunth -f- *Poaceae* · c. 195 spp.
– **coronalis** Soderstr. & C.E. Calderón · ♄ e
Z9 ⓦ; Guat., Costa Rica

Chysis Lindl. -f- *Orchidaceae* · 9 spp.
– **aurea** Lindl. · ⁴ Z10 ⓦ ▽ ✳; Mex., trop.
S-Am.
– var. *bractescens* (Lindl.) P.H. Allen =
Chysis bractescens
– **bractescens** Lindl. Z10 ⓦ ▽ ✳; Mex.,
Belize, Guat., Nicaragua
– **limminghii** Linden & Rchb. f. · ⁴ Z10 ⓦ
▽ ✳; Mex.

Cibotium Kaulf. -n- *Dicksoniaceae* · 11 sp. ·
E:Tree Fern; F:Fougère arborescente;
G:Vegetabilisches Lamm, Schatullenfarn
– *assamicum* Hook. = Cibotium barometz
– **barometz** (L.) Sm. · E:Scythian Lamb;
G:Chinesischer Schatullenfarn · ♄ e Z9 ⓚ
▽ ✳; S-China, Taiwan, Malay. Arch.
– **glaucum** (Sm.) Hook. & Arn. ·
E:Hawaiian Tree Fern; G:Hawaianischer
Schatullenfarn · ⁴ Z9 ⓚ; Hawaii
– **regale** Verschaff. & Lem. · ♄ e Z9 ⓚ;
Mex.
– **schiedei** Schltdl. & Cham. · E:Mexican
Tree Fern; G:Mexikanischer Baumfarn ·
♄ e Z9 ⓚ; Mex., Guat.

Cicendia Adans. -f- *Gentianaceae* · 2 spp. ·
E:Yellow Centaury; G:Fadenenzian,
Zindelkraut
– **filiformis** (L.) Delarbre · G:Europäischer
Fadenenzian, Zindelkraut · ☉ VII-X;
Eur.: Ib, Fr, BrI, G, Ital-P, Ba; TR, Levant,
Azor., NW-Afr.

Cicer L. -n- *Fabaceae* · 40 spp. · E:Chick
Pea; F:Cicer, Pois-chiche; G:Kichererbse
– **arietinum** L. · E:Chick Pea, Egyptian Pea;
G:Kichererbse · ☉ Z8 ⓝ; orig. ?; cult.
S-Eur., N-Afr., As., nat. in F, I

Cicerbita Wallr. -f- *Asteraceae* · 18 spp. ·
E:Blue Sowthistle; F:Mulgédie;
G:Milchlattich
– **alpina** (L.) Wallr. · E:Mountain Sow
Thistle; G:Alpen-Milchlattich · ⁴ Z4 VII;
Eur.*; N, mts.
– **bourgaei** (Boiss.) Beauverd · E:Pontic
Blue Sow Thistle · ⁴ Z5 VI-VII; TR
– **macrophylla** (Willd.) Wallr. ·
G:Gewöhnlicher Großblättriger Milchlat-
tig; E:Blue Sow Thistle · ⁴ Z4 VII; Eur.:
E-Russ.; Cauc., nat. in BrI, Sc, EC-Eur., G,
F, I
– **plumieri** (L.) Kirschl. · E:Hairless Blue
Sow Thistle; G:Französischer Milchlat-
tich · ⁴ Z5 VII-VIII; Eur.: sp., F, Sw, G, ?
Montenegro, BG; mts., nat. in BrI

Cichorium L. -n- *Asteraceae* · 8 spp. ·
E:Chicory; F:Chicorée; G:Chicorée,
Endivie, Wegwarte
– **calvum** Sch. Bip. · E:Sugar Loof;
G:Glatzfrucht-Wegwarte · ☉ VII-IX; Eth.
– **endivia** L. · G:Endivie
– var. **crispum** Lam. · G:Frisée-Endivie,
Krause Endivie · ☉ ⓝ; cult.
– var. **endivia** · E:Endive; G:Schnitt-
Endivie, Winter-Endivie · ☉ ☉ VII-IX ⓝ;
Eur.: Ib, Fr, Ital-P, Ba; TR, Iraq, Arab.,
Iran, Canar., Madeira, N-Afr.
– var. **latifolium** Lam. · E:Escarole;
G:Breitblättrige Endivie, Escariol · ☉ ⓝ;
cult.
– **intybus** L. · G:Wegwarte
– var. **foliosum** Hegi · E:Chicory Radiccio,
French Endive; F:Chicorée; G:Chicorée,
Fleischkraut, Radicchio, Salat-Zichorie ·
Z3
– var. **intybus** · E:Chicory; G:Gewöhnliche
Wegwarte, Zichorie · ⁴ Z3 VII-X ⚥ ;
Eur.*, TR, Cyprus, Cauc., Iran, C-As.,
Pakist., Him., W-Sib., E-Sib., Amur,
Sakhal., Kamchat., China
– var. **sativum** DC. · E:Coffee Chicory;
G:Kaffee-Zichorie, Wurzel-Zichorie · ⁴
Z3 ⓝ; cult.
– var. *sylvestre* Vis. = Cichorium intybus
var. intybus

Cicuta L. -f- *Apiaceae* · 8 spp. · E:Cowbane; F:Cicutaire, Ciguë aquatique; G:Wasserschierling
- **virosa** L. · E:Cowbane, Water Hemlock; G:Giftiger Wasserschierling · ♃ VII-VIII ☠; Eur.*, N-As., Jap.

Cimicifuga Wernisch. -f- *Ranunculaceae* · 18 spp. · E:Bugbane; F:Cierge d'argent; G:Silberkerze, Wanzenkraut
- **americana** Michx. · E:American Bugbane; G:Amerikanische Silberkerze · ♃ Z5 VIII-IX; USA: NE, SE
- *cordifolia* Pursh = Cimicifuga racemosa var. cordifolia
- **dahurica** (Turcz.) Torr. & A. Gray ex Maxim. · E:Bugbane; G:August-Silberkerze · ♃ Z5 VIII-IX ⚕; E-Sib., Amur, Mong., China, Jap.
- **europaea** Schipcz. · G:Wanzenkraut · ♃ VII-VIII; Eur.: A, EC-Eur., E-Eur.
- **japonica** (Thunb.) Spreng.
- var. **acerina** (Siebold & Zucc.) Huth · ♃ Z5 VIII-IX; Jap.
- var. **japonica** · G:Spätherbst-Silberkerze · ♃ Z5 IX; Jap.
- **racemosa** (L.) Nutt.
- var. **cordifolia** (Pursh) A. Gray · E:Appalachian Bugbane; G:Lanzen-Silberkerze · ♃ Z4 VIII-IX ☠; USA: Va., SE
- var. **racemosa** · E:Black Bugbane, Black Snakeroot; F:Herbe aux punaises; G:Juli-Silberkerze · ♃ Z4 VII-VIII ⚕ ☠; Ont., USA: NE, NCE, SE
- **ramosa** Nakai · G:September-Silberkerze · ♃ Z5 IX; Kamchat.
- **simplex** Wormsk. ex DC. · E:Kamchatka Bugbane; G:Oktober-Silberkerze · ♃ Z5 IX-X; Jap., Sakhal., Kamchat., Manch.
- **some cultivars**

Cinchona L. -f- *Rubiaceae* · 23 spp. · E:Jesuit's Bark, Sacred Bark; F:Quinquina; G:Chinarindenbaum, Chininbaum, Fieberrindenbaum
- **officinalis** L. · E:Peruvian Bark, Quinine Tree; G:Chinarindenbaum, Chininbaum, Fieberrindenbaum · ♄ ♄ Z9 (W) ⚕ (N); Col., Ecuad., Peru
- **pitayensis** (Wedd.) Wedd. · ♄ Z9 (W) (N); Col., Ecuad.
- **pubescens** Vahl · E:Red Peruvian Bark, Redbark; G:Roter China-rindenbaum · ♄ Z9 (W) ⚕ ☠; C-Am., trop. S-Am.
- *succirubra* Pav. ex Klotzsch = Cinchona pubescens

Cineraria L. -f- *Asteraceae* · 30-50 spp. · E:Cineraria; F:Cinéraire; G:Zinerarie
- *alpina* (L.) L. = Senecio alpinus
- *bicolor* Willd. = Senecio cineraria
- *candidissima* hort. = Senecio viravira
- *cruenta* hort. = Pericallis × hybrida
- × *hybrida* hort. = Pericallis × hybrida
- *maritima* (L.) L. = Senecio cineraria
- var. *candidissima* hort. = Senecio viravira
- **saxifraga** DC. · ♄ Z9 (K) III-IX; S-Afr.

Cinna L. -f- *Poaceae* · 4 spp. · E:Woodreed
- **latifolia** (Trevir.) Griseb. · E:Drooping Woodweed · ♃ ▽; Eur.: Sc, Russ.; Sib., Jap., Alaska, Can., USA* exc. SC

Cinnamodendron Endl. -n- *Canellaceae* · 5-7 spp. · G:Winterrinde
- **corticosum** Miers · E:False Winter's Bark; G:Falsche Winterrinde · ♄ (W) (N); W.Ind.

Cinnamomum Schaeff. -n- *Lauraceae* · c. 250 (-350) spp. · E:Camphor Tree, Cinnamon; F:Camphrier, Cannelier; G:Kampferbaum, Zimtbaum, Zimtlorbeer
- **aromaticum** Nees · E:Cassia Bark, Chinese Cinnamon; G:China-Zimtbaum · ♄ e Z9 (W) ⚕ (N); China: Kwangsi
- **burmanii** (Nees) Blume · E:Padang Cassia · ♄ ♄ e Z9 (W) (N); Malay. Arch.
- **camphora** (L.) J. Presl · E:Camphor Tree; G:Kampferbaum · ♄ e Z9 (W) ⚕ (N); S-China, S-Jap., Riukiu-Is., Taiwan, nat. in Fla., Ga., La.
- *cassia* Blume = Cinnamomum aromaticum
- **loureiroi** Nees · E:Saigon Cinnamon; G:Saigon-Zimtbaum · ♄ e Z9 (N); Jap., China, Indochina, Java
- **micranthum** (Hayata) Hayata · ♄ e Z9 (W) (N); Taiwan
- **tamala** (Buch.-Ham.) Nees & C.H. Eberm. · E:Indian Bark · ♄ e Z9 (W) (N); Ind.
- *verum* J. Presl = Cinnamomum zeylanicum
- **zeylanicum** Blume · E:Ceylon Cinnamon; G:Ceylon-Zimtbaum · ♄ Z10 (W) ⚕ (N); SW-Ind., Sri Lanka

Cionura Griseb. -f- *Asclepiadaceae* · 1 sp.

– **erecta** (L.) Griseb. · ♃ ⚥ D ⓚ VI-VII;
Eur.: Ba; TR, Cyprus, Syr.; Iran, Afgh.

Circaea L. -f- *Onagraceae* · 7 spp. ·
E:Enchanter's Nightshade; F:Circée;
G:Hexenkraut
– **alpina** L. · E:Alpine Enchanter's
Nightshade; G:Alpen-Hexenkraut · ♃ Z5
VI-VII; Eur.*, TR, Cauc., W-Sib., E-Sib.,
Amur, Sakhal., Kamchat., C-As., China,
Jap., Alaska, Can., USA* exc. SC, Fla.
– **cordata** Royle · ♃ Z5; N-Ind., China,
Amur, Manch., Korea, Jap., Taiwan
– × **intermedia** Ehrh. (*C. alpina* × *C.
lutetiana*) · G:Mittleres Hexenkraut · ♃
Z5 VI-VII; Eur.*, Cauc.
– **lutetiana** L. · E:Enchanter's Nightshade,
Paris Nightshade; G:Gewöhnliches
Hexenkraut · ♃ Z5 VI-VII; Eur.*, Cauc.,
W-Sib., E-Sib., C-As.

Cirrhaea Lindl. -f- *Orchidaceae* · 7 spp.
– **dependens** (Lodd.) Loudon · ♃ Z10 ⓜ
VI-VII ▽ ✳; Braz.
– **fuscolutea** Lindl. · ♃ Z10 ⓜ V-VI ▽ ✳;
Braz.
– *saccata* Lindl. = Cirrhaea fuscolutea

Cirrhopetalum Lindl. = Bulbophyllum
– *campanulatum* (Rolfe) Rolfe = Bulbophyllum auratum
– *collettii* Hemsl. = Bulbophyllum wendlandianum
– *gracillimum* Rolfe = Bulbophyllum gracillimum
– *longissimum* (Ridl.) Ridl. = Bulbophyllum
longissimum
– *makoyanum* Rchb. f. = Bulbophyllum
makoyanum
– *mastersianum* Rolfe = Bulbophyllum
mastersianum
– *medusae* Lindl. = Bulbophyllum medusae
– *ornatissimum* Rchb. f. = Bulbophyllum
ornatissimum
– *picturatum* Lodd. = Bulbophyllum
picturatum
– *psittacoides* Ridl. = Bulbophyllum gracillimum
– *thouarsii* Lindl. = Bulbophyllum longiflorum
– *umbellatum* (G. Forst.) Reinw. ex Hook.
& Arn. = Bulbophyllum longiflorum

Cirsium Mill. -n- *Asteraceae* · c. 250 spp. ·
E:Thistle; F:Cirse; G:Kratzdistel

– **acaule** Scop. · E:Ground Thistle;
G:Stängellose Kratzdistel · ♃ △ VII-VIII;
Eur.*
– *acaulon* (L.) Scop. = Cirsium acaule
– *afrum* (Jacq.) Fisch. = Ptilostemon afer
– **altissimum** (L.) Spreng. · E:Big Thistle;
G:Hohe Kratzdistel · ♃ VII-X; USA: NE,
NCE, NC, SC, SE, Fla.
– **arvense** (L.) Scop. · E:Canada Thistle,
Creeping Thistle; G:Acker-Kratzdistel ·
♃ VII-VIII; Eur.*, TR, Cauc., Iran, Afgh.,
Pakist., Him., C-As., W-Sib., E-Sib.,
Amur, Sakhal., Kamchat., Mong., China,
Korea, N-Jap., nat. in N-Am., Chile
– **brachycephalum** Jur. · G:Kurzkopf-
Kratzdistel · ⊙ ♃ VI-IX; Eur.: A, EC-Eur.,
Serb., RO
– **canum** (L.) All. · E:Queen Anne's Thistle;
G:Graue Kratzdistel · ♃ VII-VIII; Eur.:
C-Eur., I, EC-Eur., Ba, E-Eur.; TR, Cauc.,
W-Iran, W-Sib.
– **carniolicum** Scop. · E:Carnic Thistle;
G:Krainer Kratzdistel · ♃ VII-VIII;
Eur.: sp., F, I, A, Slove.; Pyr., E-Alp.
– *casabonae* (L.) DC. = Ptilostemon
casabonae
– **diacanthum** DC. · ⊙; TR
– **dissectum** (L.) Hill · E:Meadow Thistle;
G:Englische Kratzdistel · ♃ Z7 VI-VII;
Eur.: BrI, Fr, Ib, G, nat. in H, Norw.
– **eriophorum** (L.) Scop. · E:Woolly
Thistle; G:Wollköpfige Kratzdistel · ⊙ Z6
VII-VIII; Eur.* exc. Sc
– **erisithales** (Jacq.) Scop. · E:Yellow Mel-
ancholy Thistle; G:Klebrige Kratzdistel ·
♃ VII-IX; Eur.: Fr, Ital-P, C-Eur., EC-Eur.,
Ba, E-Eur.; mts.
– **heterophyllum** (L.) Hill · E:Melancholy
Thistle; G:Verschiedenblättrige Kratzdistel · ♃ ⋈ Z5 VII-VIII; Eur.* exc. ? Ib; Sib.,
nat. in N-Am.
– **japonicum** DC. · E:Tiger Thistle; F:Cirse
du Japon; G:Japanische Kratzdistel · ♃ ⋈
Z6 VI-VIII; Jap.
– *lanceolatum* (L.) Scop. = Cirsium vulgare
– **montanum** (Waldst. & Kit. ex Willd.)
Spreng. · G:Berg-Kratzdistel · ♃ VII-VIII;
Eur.: F, I, Slove., Croatia., YU; mts.
– **oleraceum** (L.) Scop. · E:Cabbage Thistle, Siberian Thistle; G:Kohl-Kratzdistel ·
♃ ⌇ VI-VIII ⚥ ⓝ; Eur.* exc. BrI; W-Sib.
– **palustre** (L.) Scop. · E:Marsh Thistle;
G:Sumpf-Kratzdistel · ⊙ ⊙ ⌇ Z4 VII-IX;
Eur.*, W-Sib.
– **pannonicum** (L. f.) Link · G:Pannonische

Kratzdistel · ⁴ VI-VIII; Eur.: A, Ital-P, Ba, EC-Eur., E-Eur.
- × **rigens** (Aiton) Wallr. (*C. acaule* × *C. oleraceum*) · G:Kurzstängelige Hybrid-Kratzdistel · ⁴; Eur.
- **rivulare** (Jacq.) All. · E:Brook Thistle; G:Bach-Kratzdistel · ⁴ Z5 V-VII; Eur.* exc. BrI, Sc
- *salisburgense* (Willd.) G. Don = Cirsium rivulare
- *silvaticum* Tausch = Cirsium vulgare
- **spinosissimum** (L.) Scop. · E:Spiny Thistle; G:Alpen-Kratzdistel · ⁴ Z5 VII-VIII; Eur.: F, I, C-Eur., Slove.; Alp., Apenn., Alpi Apuane
- **tuberosum** (L.) All. · E:Tuberous Thistle; G:Knollige Kratzdistel · ⁴ VII-VIII; Eur.: BrI, Fr, Ib, C-Eur., Slove., nat. in CZ
- **vulgare** (Savi) Ten. · E:Bull Thistle, Thistle; G:Gewöhnliche Kratzdistel, Lanzett-Kratzdistel · ⊙ Z2 VI-IX Ⓝ; Eur.*, TR, Cauc., N-Iran, W-Sib., C-As., NW-Afr., nat. in N-Am., C-Am., Austr.
- **waldsteinii** Rouy · G:Armköpfige Kratzdistel · ⁴ VII-VIII; Eur.: A, EC-Eur., Slove., RO, W-Russ.; E-Alp., Carp.

Cissus L. -f- *Vitaceae* · c. 350 spp. · E:Grape Ivy, Treebine; F:Liane du voyageur, Vigne d'appartement; G:Klimme, Zimmerrebe
- **adenopoda** Sprague · ⁴ ⚥ Ⓜ; W-Afr., C-Afr., Uganda
- **amazonica** Linden · ⁴ ⚥ Z10 Ⓜ; Amazon.
- **antarctica** Vent. · E:Kangaroo Vine; G:Känguru-Klimme, Känguruwein · ♄ e ⚥ Z10 Ⓚ; Austr.: Queensl., N.S.Wales
- *bainesii* Hook. f. = Cyphostemma bainesii
- *brevipedunculata* Maxim. = Ampelopsis brevipedunculata var. brevipedunculata
- *cactiformis* Gilg = Cissus quadrangularis
- *capensis* Willd. = Rhoicissus capensis
- *crameriana* Schinz = Cyphostemma currori
- *currorii* Hook. f. = Cyphostemma currori
- *dinteri* Schinz = Cissus nymphaeifolia
- **discolor** Blume · E:Rex Begonia Vine; G:Begonien-Klimme · ♄ e ⚥ Z10 Ⓜ; Java
- *fleckii* Schinz = Cyphostemma fleckii
- **gongylodes** (Burch. ex Baker) Planch. · ♄ e ⚥ Z9 Ⓜ; Braz., Peru, Parag.
- *incisa* (Nutt.) Des Moul. = Cissus trifoliata
- *juttae* Dinter & Gilg = Cyphostemma juttae

- *macropus* Welw. = Cyphostemma macropus
- **njegerre** Gilg · ⁴ e ⚥ Ⓜ; Tanzania (Usambara)
- **nymphaeifolia** Planch. · ⁴ ⤳ Z10 Ⓚ; Namibia
- *orientalis* Lam. = Ampelopsis orientalis
- **quadrangularis** L. · E:Velot Grape · ♄ ⅄ d ⚥ Z10 Ⓜ; trop. Afr., S-Afr., Madag., Arab.
- **rhombifolia** Vahl · E:Grape Ivy; G:Zimmerrebe · ⁴ ⚥ Z10 Ⓜ Ⓚ; Mex., C-Am., W.Ind., trop. S-Am.
- **rotundifolia** (Forssk.) Vahl · E:Arabian Wax Cissus · ♄ e ⚥ Z10 Ⓜ; Tanzania, Mozamb.
- **sicyoides** L. · E:Princess Vine; G:Prinzessinnenwein · ♄ e ⚥ Z10 Ⓜ Ⓚ; S-Am.
- **striata** Ruiz & Pav. · E:Miniature Grape Ivy; G:Kleine Zimmerrebe · ♄ e ⚥ Z10 Ⓜ Ⓚ; Chile, S-Braz.
- **trifoliata** (L.) L. · E:Ivy Treebine, Marine Ivy · ♄ ⅄ s ⚥ Z8 Ⓚ; USA: Mo., Kans., SC, SE, Fla.
- **tuberosa** Moç. & Sessé ex DC. · ⚐ ⅄ Z10 Ⓜ; Mex.

Cistanthe Spach -f- *Portulacaceae* · 34 spp.
- *tweedyi* (A. Gray) Hershk. = Lewisia tweedyi

Cistus L. -m- *Cistaceae* · 18-20 spp. · E:Rock Rose, Sun Rose; F:Ciste; G:Zistrose
- × **aguilarii** O.E. Warb. (*C. ladanifer* × *C. populifolius*) · ♄ Z8 Ⓚ; SW-Eur., N-Afr.
- **albidus** L. · E:White-leaved Rock Rose; G:Weißliche Zistrose · ♄ e Z8 Ⓚ; Eur.: Ib, Fr, Ital-P; Moroc., Alger.
- × **canescens** Sweet (*C. albidus* × *C. incanus*) · G:Filzige Zistrose · ♄ e Z8 Ⓚ; cult.
- × **corbariensis** Pourr. (*C. populifolius* × *C. salviifolius*) · ♄ e Z8 Ⓚ; S-Eur.
- *corsicus* Loisel. = Cistus creticus subsp. corsicus
- **creticus** L.
- subsp. **corsicus** (Loisel.) Greuter & Burdet · ♄ e Z8 Ⓚ; Cors, Sard., Moroc.
- subsp. **creticus** · ♄ Z8 Ⓚ Ⓝ; Eur.: Ital-P, GR, Crim; Cypus, Levant, TR, Cauc., Alger., Libya
- *crispus* hort. = Cistus × purpureus
- **crispus** L. · ♄ Z8 Ⓚ; Eur.: Ib, Fr, Ital-P; NW-Afr.
- × **cyprius** Lam. (*C. ladanifer* × *C.*

laurifolius) · ♄ e Z8 ⊛ ∧; SW-Eur.
– × **florentinus** Lam. (*C. monspeliensis × C. salviifolius*) · ♄ e Z8 ⊛; S-Eur., N-Afr.
– × *hybridus* Pourr. = Cistus × corbariensis
– **incanus** L. · E:Hairy Rock Rose · ♄ e Z8 ⊛; Eur.: Ib, Ital-P, Ba, Crim; TR, Cyprus, Levant, N-Afr.
– subsp. *corsicus* (Loisel.) Heywood = Cistus creticus subsp. corsicus
– subsp. *creticus* (L.) Heywood = Cistus creticus subsp. creticus
– **ladanifer** L. · E:Common Gum Cistus, Ladanum; G:Lack-Zistrose · ♄ e Z8 ⊛ ∧ ⚘ ; Eur.: Ib, F; Moroc., Alger.
– **laurifolius** L. · G:Lorbeerblättrige Zistrose · ♄ e Z7 ⊛ ∧ VI-VIII; Eur.: Ib, Fr, Ital-P; Moroc.
– × *loretii* Rouy & Foucaud = Cistus × stenophyllus
– × **lusitanicus** Maund non Mill. (*C. ladanifer × C. psilosepalus*) · ♄ e Z8 ⊛; SW-Eur.
– **monspeliensis** L. · E:Montpelier Rock Rose; G:Montpellier-Zistrose · ♄ e Z8 ⊛; Eur.: Ib, Fr, Ital-P, Ba; TR, Cyprus, NW-Afr.
– *palhinhae* J.W. Ingram = Cistus ladanifer
– **parviflorus** Lam. · G:Kleinblütige Zistrose · ♄ e Z8 ⊛; Eur.: Sic., GR, Crete; TR, Libya
– *polymorphus* Willk. = Cistus incanus
– **populifolius** L. · ♄ e Z8 ⊛ ∧; P, sp., S-F
– × **pulverulentus** Lam. (*C. albidus × C. crispus*) · ♄ e Z8 ⊛; SW-Eur.
– × **purpureus** Lam. (*C. creticus subsp. creticus × C. ladanifer*) · E:Purple Cistus; G:Purpur-Zistrose · ♄ e Z8 ⊛; cult.
– **salviifolius** L. · E:Sage-leaved Rock Rose; G:Salbeiblättrige Zistrose · ♄ e Z8 ⊛ V; Eur.: Ib, Ital-P, F, Ba, Sw; TR, Levant, N-Afr., nat. in W-Sib., C-As.
– **sintensii** Litard. · ♄ e Z8 ⊛; Eur.: GR, AL
– × **skanbergii** Lojac. (*C. monspeliensis × C. parviflorus*) · ♄ e Z8 ⊛; GR
– × **stenophyllus** Link (*C. ladanifer × C. monspeliensis*) · ♄ e Z8 ⊛; S-Eur., N-Afr.
– **symphytifolius** Lam. · ♄ e Z8 ⊛; Canar.
– *villosus* L. = Cistus incanus
– **Cultivars:**
– **some cultivars**

Citriobatus A. Cunn. ex Putt. -m- *Pittosporaceae* · 5 spp. · G:Orangenbeere
– **multiflorus** A. Cunn. · G:Reichblütige Orangenbeere · ♄ ⚘ ⊛ III-IV; Austr.:

Queensl., N.S.Wales

× **Citrofortunella** J.W. Ingram & H.E. Moore -f- *Rutaceae* · 2 spp. · E:Limequat; G:Limequat (*Citrus × Fortunella*)
– **floridana** J.W. Ingram & H.E. Moore (*Citrus aurantiifolia × Fortunella japonica*) · E:Limequat; G:Limequat · ♄ e Z9 ⊛; cult.
– *microcarpa* (Bunge) Wijnands = Citrus madurensis
– *mitis* (Blanco) J.W. Ingram & H.E. Moore = Citrus madurensis
– **swinglei** J.W. Ingram & H.E. Moore (*Citrus aurantiifolia × Fortunella margarita*) · E:Limequat · ♄ e Z9 ⊛; cult.

× **Citroncirus** J.W. Ingram & H.E. Moore -m- *Rutaceae* · E:Citrange; G:Citrange (*Citrus × Poncirus*)
– **webberi** J.W. Ingram & H.E. Moore (*Citrus sinensis × Poncirus trifoliata*) · E:Citrange; G:Citrange · ♄ ♄ s Z8 ⊛; cult.

Citronella D. Don -f- *Icacinaceae* · 21 sp.
– **megaphylla** (Miers) R.A. Howard · ♄ ♄ e Z9 ⊛; Braz.

Citropsis (Engl.) Swingle & M. Kellerm. -f- *Rutaceae* · 8 spp. · E:African Cherry Orange; G:Kirschorange
– **gilletiana** Swingle & M. Kellerm. · E:Gillet's Cherry Orange; G:Gillets Kirschorange · ♄ Z10 ⊛ Ⓝ; trop. Afr.

Citrullus Schrad. ex Eckl. & Zeyh. -m- *Cucurbitaceae* · 3 spp. · E:Water Melon; F:Pastèque; G:Arbuse, Koloquinte, Wassermelone
– **colocynthis** (L.) Schrad. · E:Bitter Apple, Vine of Sodom; G:Bitter-Melone · ⚃ ⚘ ⚶ ⊛ ⚘ ⚘ Ⓝ; Eur.: sp., Sic., GR, Canar.; S-TR, Levant, Iran, Ind., C-As., N-Afr., nat. in I, H, RO
– **lanatus** (Thunb.) Matsum. & Nakai · G:Wassermelone
– var. *caffer* (Schrad.) Mansf. = Citrullus lanatus var. vulgaris
– var. **citroides** (L.H. Bailey) Mansf. · E:Citron Melon, Stock Melon; G:Futter-Wassermelone · ⊙ Z9 ⊛ Ⓝ; S-Afr.
– var. **lanatus** · E:Wild Melon; G:Wilde Wassermelone · ⊙ Z9 VII-VIII; Namibia
– var. **vulgaris** (Schrad.) Mansf. · E:Water

Melon; G:Gewöhnliche Wassermelone ·
⊙ Z9 Ⓝ; cult.
- *vulgaris* Schrad. = Citrullus lanatus var.
lanatus

Citrus L. -f- *Rutaceae* · 146 (91) spp. ·
E:Grapefruit, Lemon, Lime, Mandarin,
Orange; F:Citronnier, Limetier,
Mandarinnier, Oranger, Pamplemoussier;
G:Apfelsine, Grapefruit, Limette, Manda-
rine, Orange, Zitrone
- **aurantiifolia** (Christm. & Panz.) Swingle · E:Lime, Mexican Lime, Sour Lime;
G:Limone, Sauere Limette · ℏ ℏ e ⚬ Z9
⚲ ⚥ Ⓝ; Malay. Arch., nat. in Trop., Fla.
- **aurantium** L. · E:Bigarade, Bitter
Orange, Key Lime, Marmelade Orange,
Seville Orange; G:Bitterorange, Pomer-
anze · ℏ e ⚬ Z9 ⚲ Ⓝ; S-Vietn., nat. in
Fla., Ga.
- subsp. *amara* (L.) Engl. = Citrus
aurantium
- subsp. *bergamia* (Risso & Poit.) Wight &
Arn. ex Engl. = Citrus bergamia
- subsp. *khatta* (Bonavia) Engl. = Citrus
karna
- var. *grandis* L. = Citrus maxima
- var. *ichangensis* Guill. = Citrus ichangensis
- var. *myrtifolia* (Raf.) Ker-Gawl. = Citrus
myrtifolia
- var. *sinensis* L. = Citrus sinensis
- *australis* Planch. = Microcitrus australis
- **bergamia** Risso & Poit. · ℏ e ⚬ Z9 ⚲ ⚥ ;
orig. ?
- *decumana* (L.) L. = Citrus maxima
- var. *racemosa* (Risso & Poit.) Roem. =
Citrus paradisi
- **deliciosa** Ten. · E:Mediterranean
Mandarin, Willow Leaf Mandarin;
G:Mittelmeer-Mandarine · ℏ e Z9 ⚲ Ⓝ;
orig. ?
- **many cultivars**
- *grandis* (L.) Osbeck = Citrus maxima
- *hindsii* (Champ. ex Benth.) Govaerts =
Fortunella hindsii
- **hystrix** DC. · E:Combavas, Kaffir Lime,
Leech Lime, Mauritius Papada; G:Kafir-
Limette · ℏ e ⚬ Z9 ⚳ Ⓝ; Indochina,
Malay. Pen., Sumat., Phil.
- **ichangensis** (Guill.) Swingle · E:Ichang
Lemon, Ichant Papada; G:Ichang-Zitrone
· ℏ e ⚬ Z8 ⚲ Ⓝ; Ind.: Assam; SW-China,
C-China
- *japonica* Thunb. = Fortunella japonica

- **junos** Siebold ex Tanaka · G:Yuzu-
Orange; E:Yuzu · ℏ e ⚬ Z9 ⚲ Ⓝ; China
- **karna** Raf. · ℏ e ⚬ Z9 ⚲ Ⓝ; Ind.
- **latifolia** (Yu. Tanaka) Yu. Tanaka ·
E:Bearss Lime, Persian Lime, Tahiti Lime;
G:Persische Limette · ℏ e ⚬ Z9 ⚲ Ⓝ;
Tahiti
- *lima* Macfad. = Citrus aurantiifolia
- **limetta** Risso · E:Bitter Orange;
G:Römische Limette, Süße Zitrone · ℏ e
⚬ Z9 ⚲ Ⓝ; trop. As.
- **limon** (L.) Burm. f. · E:Lemon; G:Zitrone
· ℏ e ⚬ Z9 ⚲ ⚥ Ⓝ; ? N-Myamar,
S-China, nat. in Fla., trop. Am.
- **many cultivars**
- **limonia** Osbeck · E:Lemandarin,
Mandarin Lime, Rangpur; G:Lemandarin,
Mandarinen-Limette, Volkamer Zitrone ·
ℏ e ⚬ D Z9 ⚲ ⚥ Ⓝ; China
- var. *limetta* (Risso) Asch. & Graebn. =
Citrus limetta
- *limonum* Risso = Citrus limon
- **madurensis** Lour. · E:Calamondin,
Panama Orange; G:Calamondin,
Panama-Orange · ℏ e ⚬ D Z9 ⚲ ◻; cult.
- *margarita* Lour. = Fortunella margarita
- **maxima** (Burm.) Merr. · E:Pomelo,
Pummelo, Shaddock; G:Pampelmuse · ℏ
e ⚬ Z9 ⚲ Ⓝ; ? Thail., ? Malay. Pen.
- **medica** L. · E:Citron; G:Zitronat-Zitrone ·
ℏ ℏ e Z9 ⚲ ⚥ Ⓝ; Ind., nat. in Fla.
- subsp. *acida* (Roxb.) Engl. = Citrus
aurantiifolia
- var. *limon* L. = Citrus limon
- *um* (Risso) Wight & Arn. = Citrus limon
- **meyeri** Yu. Tanaka · E:Meyer's Lemon;
G:Meyers Zitrone · ℏ e Z9 ⚲ Ⓝ; cult.
- **myrtifolia** Raf. · E:Myrtle-leaf Orange;
G:Myrtenblättrige Orange · ℏ e ⚬ Z9 ⚲
Ⓝ; ? China
- **nobilis** Lour. · E:Florida Orange, King
Mandarin, King Orange, Tangor;
G:Königs-Mandarine · ℏ e ⚬ Z9 ⚲ Ⓝ;
Vietn.
- **paradisi** Macfad. · E:Grapefruit;
G:Grapefruit, Paradisapfel · ℏ e ⚬ Z9 ⚲
Ⓝ; cult. W.Ind.
- *racemosa* (Risso & Poit.) Marcow. ex
Tanaka = Citrus paradisi
- **reticulata** Blanco · E:Common Mandarin, Mandarin Orange, Tangerine;
G:Gewöhnliche Mandarine · ℏ ℏ e ⚬ ⚲
⚥ Ⓝ; SE-As., Phil.
- var. *deliciosa* (Ten.) Swingle = Citrus
deliciosa

– **sinensis** (L.) Osbeck · E:Orange, Sweet
Orange; G:Apfelsine, Orange · ♄ e ♂ Z9
🅐 ⚥ Ⓝ; ? China, nat. in Fla.
– **many cultivars**
– *taitensis* Risso = Citrus limonia
– × **tangelo** J.W. Ingram & H.E. Moore
(*C. paradisi × C. reticulata*) · E:Tangelo;
G:Tangelo · ♄ e ♂ Z9 🅐 Ⓝ; ? China;
cult. China, Jap., USA
– **tangerina** Hort. ex Tanaka
– *trifoliata* L. = Poncirus trifoliata
– **unshiu** (Swingle) Marcow. · E:Satsuma
Mandarin; G:Satsuma · ♄ ♄ Z9 🅐 Ⓝ;
cult. Jap.: Prov. Satsuma
– *vulgaris* Risso = Citrus aurantium

Cladanthus Cass. -m- *Asteraceae* · 1 sp. ·
E:Palm Springs Daisy; F:Anthémis
d'Arabie; G:Astblume
– **arabicus** (L.) Cass. · G:Nordafrikanische
Astblume · ⊙ Z7 VII-X; S-Sp., N-Afr.

Cladium P. Browne -n- *Cyperaceae* ·
3 spp. · E:Great Fen Sedge; F:Marisque;
G:Schneide
– **mariscus** (L.) Pohl · E:Elk Sedge,
Great Fen Sedge; F:Cladium marisque;
G:Binsen-Schneide · ⌁ ⌁ ≍ Z3 VI-VIII;
Eur.*, Cauc., TR, Iran, C-As., Him., E-As.,
SE-As., N-Afr., Afr., Madag., N-Am.,
S-Am., Austr.

Cladothamnus Bong. -m- *Ericaceae* · 1 sp.
– **pyroliflorus** Bong. · ♄ d Z5 V-VI; Alaska,
Can.: B.C.; USA: NW

Cladrastis Raf. -f- *Fabaceae* · 6 spp. ·
E:Yellow Wood; F:Virgilier; G:Gelbholz
– **amurensis** (Rupr. & Maxim.) K. Koch =
Maackia amurensis var. amurensis
– var. *floribunda* Maxim. ex Franch. & Sav.
= Maackia amurensis var. buergeri
– *kentukea* (Dum.-Cours.) Rudd =
Cladrastis lutea
– **lutea** (F. Michx.) K. Koch · E:Kentucky
Yellow Wood; F:Virgilier à bois jaune;
G:Kentucky-Gelbholz · ♄ d Z5 V-VI Ⓝ;
USA: Ky. NCE, SE, Okla.
– **platycarpa** (Maxim.) Makino ·
E:Japanese Yellow Wood; G:Japanisches
Gelbholz · ♄ d Z4 V; Jap.
– **sinensis** Hemsl. · E:Chinese Yellow
Wood; G:Chinesisches Gelbholz · ♄ d Z6
VII-VIII; W-China, C-China
– *tinctoria* Raf. = Cladrastis lutea

Clappertonia Meisn. -f- *Tiliaceae* · 3 spp.
– **ficifolia** (Willd.) Decne. · G:Bolobo-
lobaum; E:Bolo-bolo · ♄ 🅐; trop. Afr.

Clarkia Pursh -f- *Onagraceae* · 33 spp. ·
E:Farewell to Spring, Godetia, Satin
Flower; F:Clarkia; G:Atlasblume, Clarkie,
Godetie
– **amoena** (Lehm.) A. Nelson & J.F.
Macbr. · E:Satin Flower; G:Atlasblume
– **many cultivars**
– subsp. **amoena** · ⊙ VI-IX; Calif.
– subsp. **whitneyi** (A. Gray) F.H. Lewis &
M.R. Lewis · ⊙ VI-IX; NW-Calif.
– **breweri** (A. Gray) Greene · E:Fairy Fans;
G:Feenfächer · ⊙ VII-VIII; Calif.
– **concinna** (Fisch. & C.A. Mey.) Greene ·
E:Red Ribbons; G:Rotband-Godetie · ⊙
VII-VIII; Calif.
– **pulchella** Pursh · E:Large-flowered
Clarkia, Pink Fairies; G:Großblütige
Godetie · ⊙ VII-VIII; Can.: B.C.; USA:
NW., Calif., Idaho, Mont., S.Dak.
– **rhomboidea** Douglas ex Hook. ·
E:Diamond Fairyfan; G:Diamanten-
Godetie · ⊙ VII-VIII; B.C., USA: NW,
Rocky Mts., Calif., SW
– **unguiculata** Lindl. · E:Elegant Clarkia;
G:Mandelröschen · ⊙ VII-VIII; Calif.

Clausena Burm. f. -f- *Rutaceae* · 23 spp.
– **dentata** (Willd.) M. Roem. · ♄ e Z10 Ⓝ;
Ind.
– **lansium** (Lour.) Skeels · E:Wampee;
G:Wampi · ♄ e Z10 🅐 Ⓝ; S-China

Clavija Ruiz & Pav. -f- *Theophrastaceae* ·
55 spp.
– **longifolia** (Jacq.) Mez · ♄ e D Z10 🅐;
Venez.
– *ornata* D. Don = Clavija longifolia

Claytonia L. -f- *Portulacaceae* · c. 20 spp. ·
E:Purslane; F:Claytone; G:Tellerkraut
– **perfoliata** (Donn ex Willd.) J.T. Howell ·
E:Miner's Lettuce, Winter Purslane;
G:Gewöhnliches Tellerkraut, Winter-
Portulak, Winterpostelein · ⊙ IV-VI ⚥ Ⓝ;
Can.: B.C.; USA: NW, Rocky Mts., Calif.,
SW; Mex.: Baja Calif., nat. in W-Eur.,
C-Eur., Cuba
– **sibirica** L. · E:Siberian Purslane,
Spring Beauty; F:Montia de Sibérie;
G:Sibirisches Tellerkraut · ⊙ △ Z3 IV-V;
Alaska, B.C., USA: NW, Rocky Mts.,

Calif., nat. in NL, GB
- **virginica** L. · E:Spring Beauty; G:Virginische Claytonie · ⚂ △ Z6 III; Can.: E; USA: NE, NCE, SC, SE; Mex.

Cleisostoma Blume -n- *Orchidaceae* · 88 spp.
- **filiforme** (Lindl.) Garay · ♄ Z9 ⓜ VI-X ▽ ✳; Him., Ind.: Khasia Hills; Burma
- **racemiferum** (Lindl.) Garay · ♄ Z9 ⓜ V-VI ▽ ✳; Nepal, Ind., Burma, Thail.

Cleistocactus Lem. -m- *Cactaceae* · c. 30 spp. · G:Silberkerzenkaktus; F:Cierge
- *acanthurus* (Vaupel) D.R. Hunt = Borzicactus acanthurus
- *anguinus* (Gürke) Britton & Rose = Cleistocactus baumannii subsp. anguinus
- *areolatus* (Muehlenpf. ex K. Schum.) Riccob. = Cleistocactus parviflorus
- **baumannii** (Lem.) Lem.
- subsp. **anguinus** (Gürke) P.J. Braun & Esteves · ⵙ Z9 ⓐ ▽ ✳; Parag.
- subsp. **baumannii** · ⵙ Z9 ⓐ ▽ ✳; NE-Arg., Parag., Urug.
- subsp. **chacoanus** (F. Ritter) P.J. Braun & Esteves
- **brookei** Cárdenas · ⵙ Z9 ⓐ ▽ ✳; S-Bol.
- *chacoanus* F. Ritter = Cleistocactus baumannii subsp. chacoanus
- *fossulatus* Mottram = Oreocereus pseudofossulatus
- **icosagonus** (Kunth) F.A.C. Weber ex Rol.-Goss. · ♄ ⵙ Z9 ⓐ ▽ ✳; S-Ecuad., N-Peru
- **parviflorus** (K. Schum.) Rol.-Goss. · ⵙ Z9 ⓐ ▽ ✳; Bol.
- **ritteri** Backeb. · ♄ ⵙ Z9 ⓐ ▽ ✳; C-Bol.
- *roezlii* (Haage) Backeb. = Borzicactus roezlii
- *samaipatanus* (Cárdenas) D.R. Hunt = Borzicactus samaipatanus
- *sepium* (Kunth) Rol.-Goss. = Borzicactus sepium
- *wendlandiorum* Backeb. = Cleistocactus brookei
- *winteri* D.R. Hunt = Hildewintera aureispina

Cleistogenes Keng -f- *Poaceae* · 20 spp. · G:Steifhalm
- **serotina** (L.) Keng · G:Steifhalm · ⚂ VIII-IX; Eur.* exc. BrI, Sc; TR, Cauc., N-China

Clematis L. -f- *Ranunculaceae* · 295 spp. ·

E:Clematis; F:Clématite; G:Clematis, Waldrebe
- **aethusifolia** Turcz. · G:Petersilienblättrige Waldrebe · ♄ d ⚐ Z5 ✿; N-China, Korea
- **afoliata** Buchanan · ♄ d D Z8 ⓐ V; NZ
- **akebioides** (Maxim.) Veitch · ſ d Z5; Sib., W-China
- **alpina** (L.) Mill. · E:Alpine Clematis; F:Clématite des Alpes; G:Alpen-Waldrebe · ſ d ⚐ Z5 V-VII ✿ ▽; Eur.* exc. BrI, Ib
- subsp. *sibirica* (L.) Kuntze = Clematis sibirica
- **apiifolia** DC. · G:Sellerieblättrige Waldrebe · ſ d ⚐ Z7 IX-X; C-China, Japan, Korea
- **armandii** Franch. · E:Evergreen Clematis; F:Clématite d'Armand; G:Armands Waldrebe · ♄ e ⚐ Z8 ⓐ V; C-China, S-China
- × **aromatica** Lenné & K. Koch (*C. flammula* × *C. integrifolia*) · ♄ Z5 VII ✿; cult.
- **australis** Kirk · ♄ ſ e ⚐ Z8 ⓐ; NZ
- *balearica* Rich. = Clematis cirrhosa var. balearica
- **buchananiana** DC. · G:Buchanans Waldrebe · ſ d ⚐ Z6; Pakist., N-Ind., Burma, W-China
- *calycina* Sol. = Clematis cirrhosa var. cirrhosa
- **campaniflora** Brot. · G:Glockenblütige Waldrebe · ♄ d ⚐ Z6 VI-VII ✿; P, S-Sp.
- **chrysocoma** Franch. · G:Goldschopfige Waldrebe · ♄ ſ d Z7 ✿; SW-China
- var. *sericea* (Franch.) C.K. Schneid. = Clematis spooneri
- **cirrhosa** L. · E:Fern Leaved Clematis; G:Macchien-Waldrebe
- var. **balearica** (Rich.) Willk. & Lange · G:Balearen-Waldrebe · ♄ e ⚐ Z8 ⓐ IX-III ✿; Cors, Minorca
- var. **cirrhosa** · G:Gewöhnliche Macchien-Waldrebe · ♄ e Z8 ⓐ I-III ✿; Eur.: Ib.Ital-P, Ba; TR, Levant, NW-Afr., Libya
- *coccinea* Engelm. ex Gray = Clematis texensis
- **colensoi** Hook. f. · ♄ e ⚐ Z8 ⓐ V-VI; NZ
- **columbiana** (Nutt.) Torr. & A. Gray · E:Columbia Virgin's Bower; G:Columbia-Waldrebe · ♄ ſ d ⚐ Z4; N-Am.
- **connata** DC. · G:Verwachsenblütige Waldrebe · ♄ ſ d ⚐ Z6; Him., SW-China
- **crispa** L. · E:Leather Flower; G:Krause Waldrebe · ♄ d ⚐ Z6 VI-VIII ✿; USA: Va.,

Ill., Mo., SC, SE, Fla.
- *cylindrica* Sims = Clematis crispa
- **denticulata** Vell. · ♄ ⚥ ⚤ ; s S-Am, Arg.
- *dioscoreifolia* H. Lév. & Vaniot = Clematis terniflora
- × **durandii** Durand (*C. integrifolia* × *C. lanuginosa*) · G:Durands Waldrebe · ♄; cult.
- *fargesii* Franch. = Clematis potaninii var. fargesii
- var. *souliei* hort. = Clematis potaninii var. potaninii
- **flammula** L. · E:Fragrant Clematis, Virgin's Bower; F:Flammule; G:Mandel-Waldrebe · ♄ d ⚤ Z6 VII-X; Eur.: Ib, Fr, Ital-P, Ba; TR, Syr., Palest., Cauc., Iran, Afgh., NW-Afr., Libya, nat. in EC-Eur., Crim
- var. *robusta* Carrière = Clematis terniflora
- **florida** Thunb. · ♄ s ⚤ Z7 VI-VIII ✿; China, nat. in Jap.
- *forrestii* W.W. Sm. = Clematis napaulensis
- **forsteri** J.F. Gmel. · ⚃ e ⚤ Z8; E-Sib., Amur, Mong., China
- **fremontii** S. Watson · E:Fremont's Leather Flower · ⚃ ⚤ Z4 VII-VIII; USA: Kans., Mo., Nebr.
- **fusca** Turcz. · ♄ ⚤ Z5 VII-VIII; E-Sib., Kamchat., Sakhal., Jap.
- *glauca* Willd. = Clematis orientalis var. daurica
- **heracleifolia** DC. · F:Clématite à feuilles de berce; G:Großblättrige Waldrebe · ♄ d Z5 ✿; C-China, N-China
- var. *ichangensis* Rehder & E.H. Wilson = Clematis heracleifolia
- *hexapetala* Pall. = Clematis forsteri
- *hilarii* Spreng. = Clematis denticulata
- **hirsutissima** Pursh · E:Old Man's Whiskers, Sugarbowl; G:Becher-Waldrebe, Rauhaarige Waldrebe · ⚃ Z6; B.C., USA: NW, Rocky Mts, SW
- *indivisa* Willd. = Clematis paniculata
- **integrifolia** L. · G:Ganzblättrige Waldrebe · ♄ Z5 V-VIII ✿; Eur.: I, Ba, EC-Eur., E-Eur.; Cauc., W-Sib., E-Sib., C-As., China: Sinkiang
- × **jackmanii** T. Moore (*C. lanuginosa* × *C. viticella*) · ♄ d ⚤ Z6 VII-X ✿; cult.
- **japonica** Thunb. ex Murray · G:Japanische Waldrebe · ⚤ Z6; Japan: Honshu
- × **jouiniana** C.K. Schneid. (*C. heracleifolia var. davidiana* × *C. vitalba*) · F:Clématite herbacée; G:Stauden-Waldrebe · ⚤ d Z5 VIII-X ✿; Afgh., Him.,

China
- **koreana** Kom. · G:Koeanische Waldrebe · ♄ d ⤳ Z6 VI; Manch., N-Korea
- **lanuginosa** Lindl. · G:Wollige Waldrebe · ♄ d ⚤ Z6 VI-X; E-China
- **lasiandra** Maxim. · G:Zottige Waldrebe · ♄ d ⚤ Z6 VIII-X; C-China.
- **ligusticifolia** Nutt. · E:Western White Clematis; G:Zungenblättrige Waldrebe · ⚤ d ⚤ Z5 VIII-IX ✿; w N-Am.
- **macropetala** Ledeb. · E:Downy Clematis; G:Großblumige Waldrebe · ♄ d ⚤ Z6 V-VI ✿; E-Sib., N-China
- **marata** J.B. Armstr. · ♄ ⚤ e ⚤ Z8 ⓚ; NZ
- **marmoraria** Sneddon · ♄ e Z8 ⓚ; NZ
- *maximowicziana* Franch. & Sav. = Clematis terniflora
- **microphylla** DC. · G:Kleinblättrige Waldrebe · ⚤ e ⚤ Z9 ⓚ; Austr.: Queensl., N.S.Wales, Victoria, Tasman., S-Austr., W-Austr.
- **montana** Buch.-Ham. ex DC.
- var. **montana** · F:Clématite des montagnes ; G:Berg-Waldrebe · ♄ d ⚤ Z6 V-VI ✿; Him., China: Yunnan
- var. *sericea* Finet & Gagnep. = Clematis spooneri
- **napaulensis** DC. · G:Himalaya-Waldrebe · ♄ ⚤ e ⚤ Z8 ⓚ; SW-China, N-Ind.
- **ochotensis** (Pall.) Poir. · G:Japanische Alpen-Waldrebe · ♄ Z5; E-Sib., Sakhal., Kamchat., Korea, Jap.
- **ochroleuca** Aiton · E:Curlyheads; G:Gelblich-weiße Waldrebe · ⚃ ♄ Z6 V-VI; USA: NE, SE
- **orientalis** L. · E:Orange Peel Clematis; G:Orientalische Waldrebe
- var. **daurica** (Pers.) Kuntze · ♄ ⚤ Z6 IX-X ✿; W-China, Sib.
- var. **orientalis** · ♄ d ⚤ Z6 VII-IX ✿; Eur.: GR, Russ.; TR, Cauc., Iran, Pakist., C-As., Mong., Tibet, China, nat. in sp., I
- **paniculata** J.F. Gmel. · ♄ e ⚤ Z6 V-VI; NZ
- *paniculata* Thunb. = Clematis terniflora
- **patens** C. Morren & Decne. · G:Offenblütige Waldrebe · ♄ d ⚤ Z6 V-VII ✿; China, Jap.
- **pitcheri** Torr. & A. Gray · E:Bluebill · ♄ ⚤ d ⚤ Z4; SE-USA
- **potaninii** Maxim. · G:Anemonen-Waldrebe
- var. **fargesii** (Franch.) Hand.-Mazz. · G:Farges Waldrebe · ♄ d ⚤ Z6 VI-IX ✿; W-China

– var. **potaninii** · ♄ d ⚥ Z7 ✿; S-China
– **quadribracteolata** Colenso · ∫ e ⚥ ⊡; NZ
– **recta** L. · F:Clématite droite; G:Aufrechte Waldrebe · ⚁ D Z5 VI-VII ✿; Eur.* exc. BrI, Sc; Cauc.
– **rehderiana** Craib · G:Rehders Waldrebe · ♄ d ⚥ Z6 VII-X ✿; W-China
– **serratifolia** Rehder · G:Koreanische Waldrebe · ♄ d ⚥ Z6 VIII-IX ✿; Jap., N-Korea, Manch., Amur
– **sibirica** (L.) Mill. · G:Sibirische Waldrebe · ♄ d △ V-VII ▽; Eur.: Sc, N-Russ.; W-Sib., E--Sib., C-As.
– *simsii* Sweet = Clematis crispa
– **songarica** Bunge · G:Songarische Waldrebe · ♄ d Z6 VIII-IX ✿; C-As., S-Sib., Mong., Korea
– **spooneri** Rehder & E.H. Wilson · ♄ d ⚥ Z6 VII-IX; Yunnan
– **stans** Siebold & Zucc. · G:Japanische Strauch-Waldrebe · ♄ ♄ ∫ d Z5 VIII-IX ✿; Jap.
– **tangutica** (Maxim.) Korsh. · E:Orange-peel Clematis · ♄ d ⚥ Z5 VI ✿; Mong., NW-China
– *ternata* Makino = Clematis japonica
– **terniflora** DC. · G:Rispenblütige Waldrebe · ♄ d ⚥ Z6 IX-X ✿; China, Korea
– **texensis** Buckland · E:Scarlet Clematis; G:Texas-Waldrebe · ♄ d ⚥ Z6 VII-IX ✿; Tex.
– *thunbergii* Steud. = Clematis terniflora
– **tibetana** Kuntze · G:Blaugrüne Waldrebe
– subsp. **tibetana** · ♄ ∫ d ⚥ Z6 ✿; China
– subsp. **vernayi** (Fisch.) Grey-Wilson · ♄ d ⚥ Z6 ✿; Nepal, Tibet
– × **triternata** DC. (C. flammula × C. viticella) · ♄ ∫ d ⚥ Z6 ✿; cult.
– × **vedrariensis** R. Vilm. (C. chrysocoma × C. montana var. rubens) · ♄ ∫ e ⚥ Z6; cult.
– **veitchiana** Craib · G:Veitchs Waldrebe · ♄ d ⚥ Z6 IX-X; W-China
– *vernayi* Fisch. = Clematis tibetana subsp. vernayi
– **villosa** DC. · ♄ d ⊡ VIII-IX; S-Afr., trop-Afr.
– **viorna** L. · E:Leather Flower, Vasevine; G:Braunblütige Waldrebe · ♄ d ⚥ Z6 VII ✿; USA: NE, NCE, SC, SE
– **virginiana** L. · E:Devil's Darning Needles, Virgin's Bower; G:Virginische Waldrebe · ♄ d ⚥ Z5 VIII-IX ✿; Can.: E; USA: NE, NCE, NC, SE
– **vitalba** L. · E:Old Man's Beard, Traveller's Joy; F:Clématite des haies;

G:Gewöhnliche Waldrebe · ♄ ∫ d ⚥ Z5 VI-IX ⚘ ✿ ⓝ; Eur.* exc. Sc; TR, Cyprus, Lebanon, Cauc., N-Iran, Afgh., Alger., nat. in Sc
– **viticella** L. · E:Purple Clematis; F:Clématite bleue; G:Italienische Waldrebe · ♄ ∫ d ⚥ Z6 VI-IX ✿; Eur.: I, Ba; TR, Cyprus, Cauc., Iran, nat. in Fr, G, CZ
– **Cultivars:**
– **many cultivars, see Section III**
– *'Jackmanii'* = Clematis × jackmanii

Clematoclethra (Franch.) Maxim. -f- *Actinidiaceae* · 10 spp.
– **integrifolia** Maxim. · ♄ ∫ d ⚥ Z6; NW-China
– **lasioclada** Maxim. · ♄ ∫ d ⚥ Z6; W-China

Clematopsis Bojer ex Hutch. = Clematis
– *villosa* (DC.) Hutch. = Clematis villosa

Cleome L. -f- *Capparaceae* · c. 150 spp. · E:Spider Flower; F:Cléome; G:Spinnen-pflanze
– *gigantea* hort. = Cleome hassleriana
– *grandis* hort. = Cleome hassleriana
– **gynandra** L. · E:African Spider Flower; G:Afrikanische Spinnenpflanze · ⊙ ⚘ ⓡ ⓝ; trop. Afr., trop. As., nat. in trop. Am..
– **hassleriana** Chodat · E:Spider Plant; G:Spinnenpflanze · ⊙ VII-X; SE-Braz., Arg.
– **some cultivars**
– *pentaphylla* L. = Cleome gynandra
– *pungens* auct. = Cleome hassleriana
– *pungens* Willd. = Cleome spinosa
– *spinosa* hort. = Cleome hassleriana
– **spinosa** Jacq. · E:Spiny Spider Flower; G:Dornige Spinnenpflanze · ⊙ VII-X ✿; S-Am.
– **violacea** L. · ⊙; Ib, NW-Afr.

Cleretum N.E. Br. -n- *Aizoaceae* · 3 spp.
– **herrei** (Schwantes) Ihlenf. & Struck · ⊙ ⚁ Z9 ⊡; Cape

Clerodendrum L. -n- *Verbenaceae* · c. 400 spp. · E:Glorybower; F:Clérodendron; G:Losbaum, Losstrauch
– **bungei** Steud. · E:Glory Flower; G:Her-rlicher Losstrauch · ♄ d Z8 ⊡ VIII-IX; China, Sikkim, Riukiu-Is.
– *foetidum* Bunge = Clerodendrum bungei
– *fragrans* (Vent.) R. Br. = Clerodendrum

philippinum
- **paniculatum** L. · G:Rispenblütiger Losstrauch · ♄ e Z10 ⓦ; SE-As.
- **philippinum** Schauer · E:Glory Bower; G:Lauben-Losstrauch · ♄ e D Z10 ⓦ I-XII; China, Jap. Nat. Trop
- **speciosissimum** Van Geert ex Morren · E:Javanese Glorybower · ♄ s Z10 ⓦ VI-IX; Malay. Arch., N.Guinea, Polyn.
- × **speciosum** Dombrain (*C. splendens* × *C. thomsoniae*) · ♄ e Z10 ⓦ; cult.
- **splendens** G. Don · ♄ e ≹ Z10 ⓦ XII-IV; trop. Afr.
- **thomsoniae** Balf. · E:Bleeding Heart Vine; G:Kletternder Losstrauch · ♄ e ≹ Z10 ⓦ III-VII; W-Afr., Cameroon
- **trichotomum** Thunb.
- var. **fargesii** (Dode) Rehder · ♄ d ♧ Z7 ∧ IX; China, Taiwan
- var. **trichotomum** · E:Glory Tree; G:Japanischer Losbaum · ♄ ♄ d Z7 ∧ ⚕; Jap.
- **ugandense** Prain · G:Uganda-Losstrauch · ♄ s ≹ Z10 ⓦ IV-IX; E-Afr., Zimbabwe

Clethra L. -f- *Clethraceae* · 64-67 spp. · E:Summer-Sweet, White Alder; F:Cléthra; G:Scheineller, Zimterle
- **acuminata** Michx. · E:Summersweet, White Alder; G:Berg-Zimterle · ♄ d Z6 VII-VIII; USA: NE, SE
- **alnifolia** L. · E:Sweet Pepper Bush, White Alder; F:Cléthra à feuilles d'aulne; G:Erlenblättrige Zimterle · ♄ d Z6 VII-IX; USA: NE, SE, Fla., SC
- **many cultivars**
- **arborea** Aiton · E:Lily-of-the-Valley Tree; G:Madeira-Zimterle, Maiglöckchen-Zimterle · ♄ e Z9 ⓚ VIII-IX; Madeira
- **barbinervis** Siebold & Zucc. · F:Cléthra; G:Japanische Zimterle · ♄ ♄ d Z6 VII-IX; Jap., Korea
- **delavayi** Franch. · G:Delavays Zimterle · ♄ d Z5 VII-VIII; W-China
- **fargesii** Franch. · G:Farges Zimterle · ♄ d Z5 VII-VIII; C-China
- **tomentosa** Lam. · F:Cléthra; G:Filzige Zimterle · ♄ d Z7 VIII-IX; USA: SE, Fla.

Cleyera Thunb. -f- *Theaceae* · 17 spp. · E:Sakaki; G:Sakakistrauch
- *fortunei* Hook. f. = Cleyera japonica
- **japonica** Thunb. · E:Sakaki; G:Sakakistrauch · ♄ ♄ e Z8 ⓚ; Him., Jap.
- var. *tricolor* Kobuski = Cleyera japonica
- *ochnacea* DC. = Cleyera japonica

Clianthus Sol. ex Lindl. -m- *Fabaceae* · 2 spp. · E:Glory Pea; F:Bec-de-perroquet; G:Prunkblume, Ruhmesblume
- **formosus** (G. Don) Ford & Vickery · E:Glory Pea, Sturt's Desert Pea; G:Queensland-Ruhmesblume · ♃ ♄ e Z9 ⓚ VII-IX; Austr.
- **puniceus** (G. Don) Sol. ex Lindl. · E:Lobster's Claw, Parrot's Bill; G:Kakadu-Ruhmesblume · ♄ e Z8 ⓚ III-V; NZ
- *speciosus* (G. Don) Asch. & Graebn. = Clianthus formosus

Clidemia D. Don -f- *Melastomataceae* · 117 spp. · E:Soap Bush; G:Seifenstrauch
- **hirta** (L.) D. Don · E:Soapbush; G:Seifenstrauch · ♄ ⓦ; Mex., W.Ind., trop. S-Am., nat. in OW Trop.

Clinopodium L. -n- *Lamiaceae* · 107 spp. · E:Calamint; F:Calament commun, Clinopode; G:Wirbeldost
- **vulgare** L. · G:Wirbeldost
- subsp. **arundanum** (Boiss.) Nyman · G:Östlicher Wirbeldost · ♃ Z7; S-Eur., TR, Syr., N-Iraq, Cauc., Iran, Afgh.
- subsp. **vulgare** · E:Cushion Calamint, Wild Basil; G:Gewöhnlicher Wirbeldost · ♃ Z7 VII-IX; Eur.*, Cauc., W-Sib., E-Sib.

Clinostigma H. Wendl. -n- *Arecaceae* · 11 sp.
- *mooreanum* (F. Muell.) H. Wendl. & Drude = Lepidorrhachis mooreana

Clintonia Raf. -f- *Convallariaceae* · 5 spp. · G:Clintonie
- **borealis** (Aiton) Raf. · E:Bluebeard; G:Blaubart-Clintonie · ♃ ♧ Z3 V; Can.: E; USA; NE, NCE, SE
- **umbellulata** (Michx.) Morong · E:Speckled Clintonia; G:Schirm-Clintonie · ♃ ♧ Z4 V; USA: NE, SE
- **uniflora** (Menzies ex Schult. & Schult. f.) Kunth · E:Bride's Bonnet, Queen's Cup; G:Einblütige Clintonie · ♃ Z6 V; Alaska, Can.: W; USA: NW, Rocky Mts., Calif.

Clitoria L. -f- *Fabaceae* · 60-70 spp. · E:Butterfly Pea, Pigeonwings; F:Pois razier, Pois savane; G:Schamblume
- **laurifolia** Poir. · ♄ Z10 ⓦ Ⓝ; trop. Am.;

cult. Sri Lanka, Malay. Arch.
- **ternatea** L. · E:Butterfly Pea; G:Blaue Schamblume · ♃ ⌇ Z10 ⓦ VI-IX Ⓝ; ? S-Am., nat. in Trop.

Clivia Lindl. -f- *Amaryllidaceae* · 6 spp. · E:Kaffir Lily; F:Clivia; G:Clivie, Riemenblatt
- × **cyrtanthiflora** (Van Houtte) Wittm. (*C. miniata* × *C. nobilis*) · G:Hybrid-Clivie · ♃ Z9 ⓚ ☠; cult.
- **gardenii** Hook. · ♃ Z9 ⓚ XII-III ☠; S-Afr.: Natal, Transvaal
- **miniata** (Lindl.) Bosse · E:Kaffir Lily; G:Zimmer-Clivie · ♃ Z9 ⓚ II-V ☠; S-Afr.: Natal
- **nobilis** Lindl. · E:Greentip Kaffir Lily; G:Edle Clivie · ♃ Z9 ⓚ VIII-XI ☠; S-Afr.

Clowesia Lindl. -f- *Orchidaceae* · 7 spp.
- **russelliana** (Hook.) Dodson · ♃ Z10 ⓦ VIII-IX ▽ *; Mex., C-Am., Venez.

Clusia L. -f- *Clusiaceae* · c. 145 spp. · E:Balsam Apple; F:Pommier baumier; G:Balsamapfel
- **grandiflora** Splitg. · G:Großblütiger Balsamapfel · ♄ e Z9 ⓦ; Guyan.
- **major** L. · E:Autograph Tree, Balsam Apple, Scotch Attorney; G:Rosafarbener Balsamapfel · ♄ ♄ e Z9 ⓦ Ⓝ; S-Fla., Mex., W.Ind., C-Am., S-Am.
- *rosea* Jacq. = Clusia major

Clypeola L. -f- *Brassicaceae* · 9 spp. · F:Clypéole; G:Schildkraut
- **jonthlaspi** L. · E:Disk Cress · ⊙; Eur.; Ib, Ital-P, Fr, Sw, E-Eur., Ba; SW-As.

Clytostoma Miers ex Bureau -n- *Bignoniaceae* · 9 spp. · E:Love Charm; F:Bignone d'Argentine; G:Schönmund
- **binatum** (Thunb.) Sandwith · ♄ ⌇ e ⌇ Z10 ⓦ; Venez., Guyana, Braz., Parag., Urug.
- **callistegioides** (Cham.) Bureau · E:Love Charm, Violet Trumpet Vine; G:Argentinischer Schönmund · ♄ e ⌇ Z10 ⓦ III-IV; S-Braz., Arg.

Cneorum L. -n- *Cneoraceae* · 2 spp. · F:Camélée; G:Zeiland, Zwergölbaum
- **tricoccon** L. · ♄ e Z9 ⓚ; Eur.: sp., F, Sard., I

Cnicus L. -m- *Asteraceae* · 1 sp. · E:Blessed Thistle; F:Chardon bénit, Cnicaut; G:Benediktenkraut, Bitterdistel
- **benedictus** L. · E:Blessed Thistle; G:Benediktenkraut, Bitterdistel · ⊙ Z8 VI-VII ⚕ Ⓝ; Eur.: Ib, Fr, Ital-P, Ba; TR, Levant, Cauc., Iran, C-As., Afgh., Alger., nat. in RO, S-Russ.
- *oleraceus* L. = Cirsium oleraceum
- *spinosissimus* L. = Cirsium spinosissimum

Cnidium Cusson ex Juss. -n- *Apiaceae* · 4-5 spp. · F:Cnide; G:Brenndolde
- **dubium** (Schkuhr) Thell. · G:Sumpf-Brenndolde · ♃ VIII-IX; Eur.: Sc, C-Eur., EC-Eur., E-Eur.; W-Sib., E-Sib., C-As.
- **silaifolium** (Jacq.) Simonk. · G:Silgenblättrige Brenndolde · ♃ VII-VIII; Eur.: Fr, Ital-P, Ba; TR, Syr., Lebanon

Cnidoscolus Pohl -m- *Euphorbiaceae* · 83 spp. · E:Spurge Nettle; G:Weißnessel
- **urens** (L.) Arthur
- var. **stimulosus** (Michx.) Govaerts · E:Finger Rot · ♃ ♄ ⓦ; USA: Va., SE, Fla.
- var. **urens** · E:Spurge Nettle, White Nettle; G:Brennende Weißnessel · ♄ Z10 ⓦ VII-IX ☠; S-Mex., C-Am., Lesser Antilles, S-Am.

Cobaea Cav. -f- *Cobaeaceae* · 10-20 spp. · E:Cup and Saucer Vine; F:Cobée; G:Glockenrebe
- **scandens** Cav. · E:Cup and Saucer Vine, Mexican Ivy; F:Cobée; G:Glockenrebe · ⊙ ♄ e ⌇ Z9 ⓚ VII-X; Mex.

Coccinia Wight & Arn. -f- *Cucurbitaceae* · 30 spp. · E:Scarlet-fruited Gourd ; G:Scharlachranke
- **abyssinica** (Lam.) Cogn. Z9 Ⓝ; Eth.
- **grandis** (L.) Voigt · E:Ivy Gourd; G:Große Scharlachranke · ♃ ⌇ ♧ Z9 ⓦ VII-VIII Ⓝ; trop. Afr., trop. As., Austr.: N.Terr., nat. in trop. Am.

Coccoloba P. Browne -f- *Polygonaceae* · c. 120 spp. · E:Sea Grape; F:Raisin de mer, Raisinier; G:Meertraubenbaum, Seetraube
- *grandifolia* Jacq. = Coccoloba pubescens
- **pubescens** L. · E:Leather Coat Tree; G:Ledermantelbaum · ♄ e Z10 ⓦ; Mex., W.Ind., Guyan.
- **uvifera** (L.) L. · E:Sea Grape; G:Meertraubenbaum, Seetraube · ♄ ♄ e Z10

Ⓦ Ⓝ; Fla., Bahamas, Bermuda, Mex., W.Ind., trop. S-Am.

Coccothrinax Sarg. -f- *Arecaceae* · 50 spp. · E:Silver Palm; F:Palmier argenté; G:Silberpalme
- *alta* (O.F. Cook) Becc. = Coccothrinax barbadensis
- **argentea** (Lodd. ex Schult. & Schult. f.) Sarg. ex Becc. · E:Florida Silver Palm, Silver Thatch Palm; G:Florida-Silberpalme · ₺ e Z10 Ⓚ Ⓝ; Haiti
- **barbadensis** (Lodd. ex Mart.) Becc. · E:Puerto Rico Silver Palm · ₺ e Z10 Ⓦ; W.Ind. (Guadeloupe)

Cocculus DC. -m- *Menispermaceae* · 11 sp. · E:Moonseed; F:Cocculus; G:Kokkelstrauch
- **carolinus** (L.) DC. · E:Carolina Moonseed; G:Carolina-Kokkelstrauch · ₺ d ≩ Z7 ∧; USA: NE, NCE, Kans., SC, SE, Fla.
- **laurifolius** (Roxb.) DC. · E:Coralbead; G:Himalaya-Kokkelstrauch · ₺ e Z8 Ⓚ; Him., China, Taiwan, Ryukyu-Is., Jap.
- **orbiculatus** (L.) DC. · E:Queen Coralbead; G:Asiatischer Kokkelstrauch · ₺ d ≩ Z7 ∧; Him., China, Jap., Phil.
- *trilobus* (Thunb.) DC. = Cocculus orbiculatus

Cochleanthes Raf. -f- *Orchidaceae* · 13 spp.
- **amazonica** (Rchb. f. & Warsz.) R.E. Schult. & Garay · ♃ Z10 Ⓦ XII-III ▽ *; Amazon., Venez.
- **discolor** (Lindl.) R.E. Schult. & Garay · ♃ Z10 Ⓦ I-III ▽ *; Hond., Costa Rica, Panama, Cuba, Venez.
- **flabelliformis** (Sw.) R.E. Schult. & Garay · E:Fan-shaped Orchid · ♃ Z10 Ⓦ XII-III ▽ *; W.Ind.
- **wailesiana** (Lindl.) R.E. Schult. & Garay · ♃ Z10 Ⓦ V-VI ▽ *; Braz.

Cochlearia L. -f- *Brassicaceae* · 25 spp. · E:Scurvygrass; F:Cranson; G:Löffelkraut
- **anglica** L. · E:English Scurvy Grass; G:Englisches Löffelkraut · ⊙ ♃ Z6 V-VII ▽; Eur.: Sc, BrI, G, Fr, Ib; coasts
- *armoracia* L. = Armoracia rusticana
- **bavarica** Vogt · G:Bayerisches Löffelkraut · ⊙ ♃ Z6 ▽; Eur.: D
- **danica** L. · E:Danish Scurvy Grass; G:Dänisches Löffelkraut · ⊙ Z6 V-VI ▽; Eur.: Sc, BrI, G, Balt., Fr, Ib; coasts
- **macrorhiza** (Schur) Pobed. · ⊙ ♃ Z6 III-VI ▽; C-Eur. , W-Eur.
- **officinalis** L. · E:Common Scurvy Grass, Spoonwort; G:Echtes Löffelkraut · ⊙ ♃ Z6 V-VI ⚕ Ⓝ ▽; Eur.* exc. Ital-P, Ba; coasts; Canar., Sib., Kamchat., N-Jap., Greenl., nat. in Ital-P
- **pyrenaica** DC. · E:Pyrenean Scurvy Grass; G:Pyrenäen-Löffelkraut
- subsp. **excelsa** (J. Zahlbr.) O. Schwarz · G:Alpen-Löffelkraut · ⊙ ♃ Z6 VII-VIII ▽; Eur.: A
- subsp. **pyrenaica** · G:Gewöhnliches Pyrenäen-Löffelkraut · ♃ Z6 V-VI ▽; Eur.: sp., F, C-Eur., BrI, Norw.
- *saxatilis* L. = Kernera saxatilis

× **Cochlenia** hort. -f- *Orchidaceae* (*Cochleanthes* × *Stenia*)

Cochlioda Lindl. -f- *Orchidaceae* · 8 spp.
- **densiflora** Lindl. · ♃ Z10 Ⓚ VII-XI ▽ *; Peru, Bol.
- **rosea** (Lindl.) Benth. · ♃ Z10 Ⓚ XII-III ▽ *; Ecuad., Peru

Cocos L. -f- *Arecaceae* · 1 sp. · E:Coconut; F:Cocotier; G:Kokosnuss, Kokospalme
- *australis* hort. = Butia capitata
- var. *bonnetii* (Becc.) hort. = Butia capitata
- *australis* Mart. = Syagrus romanzoffiana
- *bonnetii* (Becc.) hort. = Butia capitata
- *eriospatha* Mart. ex Drude = Butia eriospatha
- **nucifera** L. · E:Coconut, Coconut Palm; G:Kokosnuss, Kokospalme · ₺ e Z10 Ⓦ ⚕ Ⓝ; orig. ? ; cult. Trop., nat. in pantrop.
- *plumosa* Hook. = Syagrus romanzoffiana
- *romanzoffiana* Cham. = Syagrus romanzoffiana
- *weddelliana* H. Wendl. = Lytocaryum weddellianum
- *yatay* Mart. = Butia yatay

Codiaeum A. Juss. -n- *Euphorbiaceae* · 17 spp. · E:Croton; F:Croton; G:Wunderstrauch
- **variegatum** (L.) Blume · E:Croton; G:Kroton, Wunderstrauch
- var. *pictum* (Lodd.) Müll. Arg. = Codiaeum variegatum var. variegatum
- var. **variegatum** · ♄ ₺ e Z10 Ⓦ ☠; Molucca

Codonanthe (Mart.) Hanst. -f-
Gesneriaceae · c. 15 spp.
– **crassifolia** (Focke) C.V. Morton · ⌃ ⚥
Z10 ⊛; Trinidad, Guyana, Braz., E-Peru
– **gracilis** (Mart.) Hanst. · ⌃ Z10 ⊛;
S-Braz.
– *ventricosa* (Vell.) Hoehne = Codonanthe
gracilis

× Codonatanthus W.R. Saylor
-m- Gesneriaceae (Codonanthe ×
Nematanthus)

Codonopsis Wall. -f- Campanulaceae ·
c. 30 spp. · E:Bonnet Bellflower;
F:Codonopsis ; G:Glockenwinde
– **bulleyana** Forrest ex Diels · ⌃ △ Z4 VI;
NW-Yunnan, SE-Tibet
– **clematidea** (Schrenk ex Fisch. & C.A.
Mey.) C.B. Clarke · G:Tigerglocke · ⌃ △
Z4 VII; C-As.
– **convolvulacea** Kurz · ⌃ ⚥ △ Z5 VII;
Him., Tibet
– **forrestii** Diels · ⌃ ⚥ △ Z7 VI-VII; Yunnan
– **lanceolata** (Siebold & Zucc.) Trautv. ·
⌃ ⚥ △ Z7 VI-VII; China, Amur, Manch.,
Korea, Jap.
– **meleagris** Diels · ⌃ △ Z4 VIII; Yunnan
– **ovata** Benth. · ⌃ △ Z4 VIII; W-Him.
– **rotundifolia** Royle · ⌃ ⚥ △ Z7 VI-VII;
Him., SE-Tib.
– **tangshen** Oliv. · ⌃ ⚥ △ Z4 VI-VII ⚥ ;
China: Hupeh
– **ussuriensis** (Rupr. & Maxim.) Hemsl. · ⌃
⚥ △ Z7 VI-VII; Amur, Manch., Korea, Jap.
– *vinciflora* Kom. = Codonopsis convolvulacea
– **viridiflora** Maxim. · ⌃ △ Z7 VII-VIII;
China: Sichuan, Kansu

Coelia Lindl. -f- Orchidaceae · 2 spp.
– **bella** (Lem.) Rchb. f. · ⌃ Z10 ⊛ X-XI ▽
✳; Guat.
– *macrostachya* Lindl. = Bothriochilus
macrostachyus
– **triptera** (Sm.) G. Don ex Steud. · ⌃ Z10
⊛ II-IV ▽ ✳; Mex., W.Ind.

Coeloglossum Hartm. -n- Orchidaceae ·
1 sp. · E:Frog Orchid; F:Cœloglosse,
Habénaire; G:Hohlzunge
– **viride** (L.) Hartm. · E:Frog Orchid;
G:Grüne Hohlzunge · ⌃ Z6 V-VI ▽ ✳;
Eur.*, TR, N-As., N-Am.

Coelogyne Lindl. -f- Orchidaceae · 188 spp.
– **asperata** Lindl. · ⌃ Z10 ⊛ IV-VII ▽ ✳;
Malay. Arch., N.Guinea
– **barbata** Griff. · ⌃ Z10 ⊛ X-XII ▽ ✳;
Bhutan, NE-Ind.
– **carinata** Rolfe · ⌃ Z10 ⊛ VI ▽ ✳;
N.Guinea
– *corrugata* Wight = Coelogyne nervosa
– **corymbosa** Lindl. · ⌃ Z10 ⊛ VII-IX ▽ ✳;
Him., SW-China
– **cristata** Lindl. · G:Engelsorchidee · ⌃ Z10
⊠ I-IV ▽ ✳; E-Him.
– f. **hololeuca** (Rchb. f.) M. Wolff & O.
Gruss · G:Weiße Engelsorchidee · ⌃ Z10
⊠ I-IV ▽ ✳; Nepal
– *dayana* Rchb. f. = Coelogyne pulverula
– **fimbriata** Lindl. · ⌃ Z10 ⊠ VIII-X ▽ ✳;
Ind. (Khasi Mts.), Indochina, China
– **flaccida** Lindl. · ⌃ Z10 ⊛ III-IV ▽ ✳;
Nepal
– **flexuosa** Rolfe · ⌃ Z10 ⊛ IV-VI ▽ ✳;
Java
– *fuliginosa* Lodd. ex Hook. = Coelogyne
fimbriata
– **fuscescens** Lindl. · ⌃ Z10 ⊛ I-II ▽ ✳;
NE-Ind.
– **huettneriana** Rchb. f. · ⌃ Z10 ⊛ IV-VI ▽
✳; Burma, Thail.
– **lawrenceana** Rolfe · ⌃ Z10 ⊛ III-IV ▽
✳; Vietn.
– *massangeana* Rchb. f. = Coelogyne
tomentosa
– **miniata** (Blume) Lindl. · ⌃ Z10 ⊛ VII-IX
▽ ✳; Sumat., Java, Bali
– **nervosa** A. Rich. · ⌃ Z10 ⊛ IX-X; Ind.
– **nitida** (Wall. ex Don) Lindl. · ⌃ Z10 ⊠
IV-VI ▽ ✳; Him., Burma, Yunnan, Thail.,
Laos
– *ochracea* Lindl. = Coelogyne nitida
– **ovalis** Lindl. · E:Jivanti · ⌃ Z10 ⊛ VI-VIII
▽ ✳; Him., Yunnan, Burma, Thail.
– **pandurata** Lindl. · E:Black Orchid;
G:Schwarze Engelsorchidee · ⌃ Z10 ⊛
VI-VIII ▽ ✳; Malay. Pen., Kalimantan
– **parishii** Hook. f. · ⌃ Z10 ⊛ V-VI ▽ ✳;
Burma
– **pulverula** Teijsm. & Binn. · ⌃ Z10 ⊛
IV-VI ▽ ✳; Thail., Sumat., Kalimantan
– **rochussenii** de Vries · ⌃ Z10 ⊛ ▽ ✳;
Malay. Arch.
– **speciosa** (Blume) Lindl. · ⌃ Z10 ⊛ I-XII
▽ ✳; Sumat., Java, Kalimantan
– **swaniana** Rolfe · ⌃ Z10 ⊛ VII-VIII ▽ ✳;
Malay. Pen., Sumat., Kalimantan
– **tomentosa** Lindl. · ⌃ Z10 ⊛ IV-V ▽ ✳;

Thail., Sumat, Kalimantan
- **trinervis** Lindl. · ⚇ Z10 ⓜ I; Burma, Thail., Cambodia, Vietn., Malay. Pen., Java
- **veitchii** Rolfe · ⚇ Z10 ⓜ VII-VIII ▽ ✳; N.Guinea
- **viscosa** Rchb. f. · ⚇ Z10 ⓜ I-II ▽ ✳; N-Ind., SW-China, Burma, Malay. Pen.

Coffea L. -f- *Rubiaceae* · c. 90 spp. · E:Coffee; F:Caféier; G:Kaffeestrauch
- **arabica** L.
- var. **arabica** · E:Arabian Coffee; G:Arabischer Kaffeestrauch · ♄ e Z10 ⓜ ⚘ Ⓝ; Eth., Sudan
- var. **mokka** Cramer · E:Mokka Coffee; G:Mokka-Kaffeestrauch · ♄ e Z10 Ⓝ; ? E-Afr.
- *bengalensis* Roxb. = Psilanthus bengalensis
- **canephora** Pierre ex A. Froehner · E:Robusta Coffee; G:Robusta-Kaffeestrauch · ♄ ♄ e Z10 ⓜ Ⓝ; W-Afr., C-Afr., Sudan, Uganda, Angola
- **congensis** A. Fröhner · E:Congo Coffee; G:Kongo-Kaffeestrauch · ♄ Z10 ⓜ Ⓝ; Congo
- *dewevrei* De Wild. & T. Durand = Coffea liberica var. dewevrei
- **eugenioides** S. Moore · E:Nandi Coffee · ♄ ♄ Z10 ⓜ Ⓝ; Uganda, Tanzania, E-Congo
- **liberica** W. Bull ex Hiern
- var. **dewevrei** (De Wild. & T. Durand) Lebrun · E:Excelsa Coffee; G:Excelsa-Kaffeestrauch · ♄ ♄ e Z10 ⓜ; W-Afr.
- var. **liberica** · E:Liberian Coffee; G:Liberia-Kaffeestrauch · ♄ ♄ e Z10 ⓜ ⚘ Ⓝ; trop. Afr.
- **racemosa** Lour. · E:Wild Coffee; G:Wilder Kaffeestrauch · ♄ ♄ d Z10 ⓜ Ⓝ; Tanzania, Mozamb., Zimbabwe
- *robusta* L. Linden = Coffea canephora
- **stenophylla** G. Don · E:Sierra Leone Coffee; G:Sierra-Leone-Kaffeestrauch · ♄ ♄ Z10 ⓜ Ⓝ; W-Afr.: Guinea, Sierra Leone, Ivory Coast

Coincya Rouy -f- *Brassicaceae* · 6 spp. · G:Lacksenf, Schnabelsenf
- **monensis** (L.) Greuter & Burdet · G:Schnabelsenf
- subsp. **cheiranthos** (Vill.) Aedo et al. · E:Wallflower Cabbage; G:Goldlack-Schnabelsenf · ⚇ VI-X; Eur.: Fr, BrI, IB,

Ital-P

Coix L. -f- *Poaceae* · 6 spp. · E:Job's Tears; F:Larme-de-Job, Larme-de-Jupiter; G:Hiobsträne, Jupitertränen, Tränengras
- **lacryma-jobi** L. · E:Job's Tears; F:Larme-de-Job; G:Hiobsträne, Jupitertränen, Tränengras · ⊙ ⊙ ⚇ ⚘ Z9 ⚘ Ⓝ; trop. As.

Cola Schott & Endl. -f- *Sterculiaceae* · c. 125 spp. · E:Cola; F:Colatier; G:Kola-baum, Kolanuss
- **acuminata** (P. Beauv.) Schott & Endl. · E:Goora Nut, Kola; G:Kolanuss · ♄ e Z10 ⓜ ⚘ Ⓝ; W-Afr., C-Afr., Angola
- **anomala** K. Schum. · E:Bamenda Cola · ♄ Z10 ⓜ Ⓝ; Cameroon
- **nitida** (Vent.) Schott & Endl. · E:Kola Nut; G:Bittere Kolanuss · ♄ Z10 ⓜ ⚘ Ⓝ; Liberia, Ivory Coast
- **quinqueloba** (K. Schum.) Garcke · ♄ ⋉ Z10 ⓜ; trop. Afr.
- *vera* K. Schum. = Cola nitida
- **verticillata** (Thonn.) Stapf ex A. Chev. · E:Owé Cola · ♄ Z10 ⓜ Ⓝ; W-Afr., C-Afr.

Colchicum L. -f- *Colchicaceae* · 89 spp. · E:Autumn Crocus, Naked Ladies; F:Colchique; G:Zeitlose
- × **agrippinum** hort. ex Baker (*C. autumnale* × *C. variegatum*) · ⚇ Z5 IX ⚘; GR, nat. in BrI
- **alpinum** DC. · G:Alpen-Zeitlose · ⚇ Z4 VII-VIII ⚘; Eur.: F, Ital-P, Sw
- **arenarium** Waldst. & Kit. · ⚇ Z6 IX-X ⚘; Eur.: H, Slova., Serb.
- **autumnale** L. · E:Naked Ladies; F:Colchique d'automne; G:Herbst-Zeitlose · ⚇ Z5 X-XI ⚘ ⚘ Ⓝ; Eur.* exc. Sc, nat. in Sc
- **bivonae** Guss. · ⚇ Z6 IX-X ⚘; Eur.: Sard., I, Sic., Ba
- *bornmuelleri* Freyn = Colchicum speciosum
- *bowlesianum* B.L. Burtt = Colchicum bivonae
- *bulbocodium* Ker-Gawl. = Bulbocodium vernum
- × **byzantinum** Ker-Gawl. (*C. cilicium* × ?) · ⚇ Z6 ⚘; TR: Taurus
- **cilicium** (Boiss.) Dammer · ⚇ Z6; TR, Syr., Lebanon
- **cupanii** Guss. · ⚇ Z8 ⌂ ∧ ⚘; Eur.: F, Sard, I, Sic., GR, , Crete; Alg., Tun.
- *decaisnei* Boiss. = Colchicum troodi

- *haussknechtii* Boiss. = Colchicum persicum
- **laetum** Steven · ♃ Z7 IX-X ☠; Cauc.
- *longifolium* Castagne = Colchicum neapolitanum
- **luteum** Baker · ♃ Z7; C-As., Afgh., N-Ind., SW-China
- **neapolitanum** (Ten.) Ten. · ♃ Z6 VIII-IX ☠; Eur.: sp., F, Ital-P, W-Ba; NW-Afr.
- *pannonicum* Griseb. & Schenk = Colchicum autumnale
- **persicum** Baker · ♃ X ☠; Iran
- *sibthorpii* Baker = Colchicum bivonae
- **speciosum** Steven · ♃ Z5 IX-X ☠; Cauc., TR
- **troodi** Kotschy · ♃ Z8 Ⓐ ☠; Cyprus, TR, W-Syr., Lebanon, Israel
- **variegatum** L. · ♃ Z8 Ⓐ VIII ☠; Eur.: GR; TR
- *vernum* (L.) Stef. = Bulbocodium vernum

Coleanthus Seidl -m- *Poaceae* · 1 sp. · G:Scheidenblütgras
- **subtilis** (Tratt.) Seidl · E:Sheath Grass: G:Scheidenblütgras · ⊙ V-X ▽; Eur.: F, G, A, EC-Eur., Slova.; W-Sib., Amur, nat. in USA: NW

Coleocephalocereus Backeb. -m- *Cactaceae* · 6 spp.
- **fluminensis** (Miq.) Backeb. · ♄ ψ Z9 Ⓦ ▽ *; Braz.

Coleonema Bartl. & H.L. Wendl. -n- *Rutaceae* · 8 spp.
- **album** (Thunb.) Bartl. & H.L. Wendl. · E:White Breath of Heaven · ♄ e D Z9 Ⓚ III-V; Cape
- **calycinum** (Steud.) I. Williams · ♄ e D Z9 Ⓚ III-V; Cape
- **pulchrum** Hook. · ♄ e Z9 Ⓚ; S-Afr.

Coleostephus Cass. -m- *Asteraceae* · 2 spp.
- **multicaulis** (Desf.) Durieu · ⊙ VII-VIII; Alger.

Coleotrype C.B. Clarke -f- *Commelinaceae* · 9 spp.
- **natalensis** C.B. Clarke · ♃ Z9 Ⓦ; S-Afr.: Natal

Coleus Lour. = Plectranthus
- *amboinicus* Lour. = Plectranthus amboinicus
- *barbatus* (Andrews) Benth. = Plectranthus barbatus
- *blumei* Benth. = Plectranthus scutellarioides
- *esculentus* (N.E. Br.) G. Taylor = Plectranthus esculentus
- *forskohlii* (Poir.) Briq. = Plectranthus barbatus
- *pumilus* Blanco = Plectranthus scutellarioides
- *rehneltianus* A. Berger = Plectranthus scutellarioides
- *rotundifolius* (Poir.) A. Chev. & Perrot = Plectranthus rotundifolius

Colletia Comm. ex Juss. -f- *Rhamnaceae* · 17 spp. · E:Anchor Plant; F:Colletia; G:Ankerpflanze, Colletie
- *armata* Miers = Colletia hystrix
- **hystrix** Clos · ♄ Z8 Ⓚ; Chile
- **paradoxa** (Spreng.) Escal. · G:Ankerpflanze; E:Anchor Plant · ♄ Z8 Ⓚ XI-XII; S-Braz., Urug., N-Arg.
- *spinosa* Lam. = Colletia hystrix

Collinia (Liebm.) Liebm. ex Oerst. = Chamaedorea
- *elegans* (Mart.) Liebm. ex Oerst. = Chamaedorea elegans

Collinsia Nutt. -f- *Scrophulariaceae* · c. 20 spp. · E:Blue-eyed Mary; F:Collinsia; G:Collinsie
- **bicolor** Benth. · E:Chinese Houses, Innocence; G:Pagoden-Collinsie · ⊙ Z9 VII-VIII; Calif.
- **grandiflora** Douglas ex Lindl. · E:Blue Lips; G:Großblütige Collinsie · ⊙ Z9 VI-VIII; B.C., USA: NW, Calif.
- *heterophylla* Buist ex Graham = Collinsia bicolor
- **tinctoria** Hartw. ex Benth. · E:Tincture Plant · ⊙ Z9 VII-VIII; Calif.
- **verna** Nutt. · G:Blauäugige Collinsie; E:Blue Eyed Mary · ⊙ Z9 V-VI; USA: NE, NCE, Kans., Ark.

Collinsonia L. -f- *Lamiaceae* · 11 sp. · E:Horse Balm; G:Pferdemelisse
- **canadensis** L. · E:Horseweed, Stone Root; G:Kanadische Pferdemelisse · ♃ VII-IX ⚕; Ont., USA: NE, NCE, SE, Fla.

Collomia Nutt. -f- *Polemoniaceae* · 15 spp. · E:Collomia; F:Collomia; G:Leimsaat
- **cavanillesii** Hook. & Arn. · ⊙ VII-VIII;

Bol., Chile, Arg.
- *coccinea* Lehm. = Collomia cavanillesii
- **grandiflora** Douglas ex Lindl. · E:Mountain Trumpet; G:Großblumige Leimsaat · ☉ Z6 VI-VIII; B.C., USA: NW, Rocky Mts., Calif., nat. in W-Eur., C-Eur.
- **linearis** Nutt. · E:Tiny Trumpet · ☉; Can., USA* exc. SE, Fla.

× **Colmanara** hort. -f- *Orchidaceae* (*Miltonia* × *Odontoglossum* × *Oncidium*)

Colocasia Schott -f- *Araceae* · 14 spp. · E:Taro; F:Chou-chine, Taro; G:Zehrwurz
- **affinis** Schott · ♃ Z10 (W); S-Him.
- **esculenta** (L.) Schott · E:Coco Yam, Dasheen, Taro; G:Taro, Zehrwurzel · ♃ Z10 (W); Him., Ind., Sri Lanka, nat. in Trop., Subtrop.
- **fallax** Schott · ♃ Z10 (W); S-Him.
- **gigantea** (Blume) Hook. f. · ♃ Z10 (W); Ind., Indochina, Malay. Arch.
- *indica* auct. non (Lour.) Kunth = Colocasia gigantea

Colocynthis Mill. = Citrullus
- *citrullus* (L.) Kuntze = Citrullus lanatus var. lanatus
- *vulgaris* Schrad. = Citrullus colocynthis

Columnea L. -f- *Gesneriaceae* · 75 spp. · F:Columnéa; G:Kolumnee, Rachenrebe
- *affinis* C.V. Morton = Dalbergaria aureonitens
- **allenii** C.V. Morton · ♄ e ≹ Z9 (W) VII-X; Panama
- **arguta** C.V. Morton · ♄ e ≹ Z9 (W) IX-X; Panama
- *aureonitens* Hook. = Dalbergaria aureonitens
- × **banksii** Lynch (*C. oerstediana* × *C. schiedeana*) · ♄ e ≹ Z9 (W); cult.
- **billbergiana** Beurl. · ♄ e Z9 (W); Panama
- **crassifolia** Brongn. · ♄ e Z9 (K) VI-VIII; Mex., Guat.
- **glabra** Oerst. · ♄ e Z9 (W) VIII-V; Costa Rica
- **gloriosa** Sprague · E:Goldfish Plant · ♄ e ≹ Z9 (W) IX-V; Costa Rica
- **hirta** Klotzsch & Hanst.
- var. **hirta** · ♄ e Z9 (W) III-IV; Costa Rica
- var. **pilosissima** (Standl.) Standl. · ♄ e ≹ Z9 (W) III-V; Hond.
- *illepida* H.E. Moore = Trichantha illepida
- **lepidocaula** Hanst. · ♄ e Z9 (W); Costa Rica
- **linearis** Oerst. · ♄ e Z9 (W); Costa Rica
- **magnifica** Klotzsch & Hanst. ex Oerst. · ♄ e ≹ Z9 (W); Costa Rica, Panama
- **microphylla** Klotzsch & Hanst. ex Oerst. · ♄ e ≹ Z9 (W) III-VIII; Costa Rica
- **nicaraguensis** Oerst. · ♄ e Z9 (W); C-Am.
- **oerstediana** Klotzsch ex Oerst. · ♄ e ≹ Z9 (W) II-III; Costa Rica
- *percrassa* C.V. Morton = Columnea billbergiana
- *pilosissima* Standl. = Columnea hirta var. pilosissima
- *sanguinea* (Pers.) Hanst. = Dalbergaria sanguinea
- **scandens** L.
- var. **scandens** · ♄ e Z9 (W); Hispaniola, Puerto Rico, Lesser Antilles, Venez.
- var. **tulae** (Urb.) Wiehler · ♃ e ♣ Z9 (W); Puerto Rico, Haiti, Nicar.
- **schiedeana** Schltdl. · ♄ e Z9 (W) III-V; E-Mex.
- *tigrina* Raymond = Columnea zebrina
- *tulae* Urb. = Columnea scandens var. tulae
- × **vedrariensis** R. Vilm. ex Mottet (*C. magnifica* × *C. schiedeana*) · ♃ ♄ e ≹ ♣ Z9 (W) II-V; cult.
- **verecunda** C.V. Morton · ♄ e Z9 (W); Costa Rica
- **zebrina** Raymond · ♄ e Z9 (W); Panama
- **Cultivars:**
- **some cultivars**

Coluria R. Br. -f- *Rosaceae* · 5 spp.
- **geoides** (Pall.) Ledeb. · ♃ IV-V; Altai
- *potentilloides* R. Br. = Coluria geoides

Colutea L. -f- *Fabaceae* · 26 spp. · E:Bladder Senna; F:Baguenaudier ; G:Blasenstrauch
- **arborescens** L. · E:Bladder Senna; F:Baguenaudier commun; G:Gewöhnlicher Blasenstrauch · ♄ d ♣ Z6 VI-VIII ☠ (N); Eur.* exc. BrI, Sc, nat. in BrI
- **buhsei** (Boiss.) Shap. · ♄ d Z7 VII ☠; Iran
- **cilicica** Boiss. & Balansa · ♄ d Z6 VI-VII ☠; Eur.: GR, Crim; TR, Cauc.
- *cruenta* Dryand. = Colutea orientalis
- **gracilis** Freyn & Sint. · ♄ d Z6 VII ☠; C-As.
- × **media** Willd. (*C. arborescens* × *C. orientalis*) · E:Hybrid Bladder Senna; F:Baguenaudier hybride; G:Bastard-Blasenstrauch · ♃ d ♣ Z6 VI-VIII ☠;

cult.
- **orientalis** Mill. · E:Oriental Bladder Senna; G:Orientalischer Blasenstrauch · ♄ d Z6 VI-IX ☠; Crim, Cauc., nat. in S-Eur.
- **persica** Boiss. · ♄ d Z7 ☠; S-Iran
- var. *bushei* Boiss. = Colutea buhsei

Coluteocarpus Boiss. -m- *Brassicaceae* · 1 sp.
- **vesicaria** (L.) Holmboe · ♃ △ ♣ Z8 ∧ IV-V; TR, Cauc. (Armen), Lebanon

Combretum Loefl. -n- *Combretaceae* · c. 250 spp. · F:Chigommier; G:Langfaden
- **bracteosum** (Hochst.) Brandis · E:Hiccup Nut · ♄ ♄ ≀ ≀ Z10 ⓦ; S-Afr.
- **coccineum** Lam. · ♄ ≀ Z10 ⓦ IX-X; Madag.
- **comosum** G. Don · ♄ ≀ Z10 ⓦ VII-VIII; W-Afr.: Sierra Leone
- **grandiflorum** G. Don · ♄ ≀ Z10 ⓦ VII; W-Afr.: Sierra Leone
- *purpureum* Vahl = Combretum coccineum

Commelina L. -f- *Commelinaceae* · 209 spp. · E:Dayflower; F:Comméline, Ephémère; G:Commeline, Tagblume
- **benghalensis** L. · E:Benghal Dayflower; G:Bengalische Tagblume · ♃ ≀ ~ Z9 ⓦ; trop. Afr., trop. As.
- **communis** L. · E:Asiatic Dayflower · ⊙ Z7 VII-X; China, nat. in Eur.: I, Sw, EC-Eur., Croatia, RO, Russ.; Cauc., W-Sib., E-Sib., Kamchat.,
- **diffusa** Burm. f. · E:Climbing Dayflower; G:Kletternde Tagblume · ♃ ≀ ≀ ⇝ Z7 ⓦ ⓚ; USA: NE, NCE, Kans., SE, Fla., SC; S-Am, Trop.
- **tuberosa** L. · E:Dayflower; G:Knollige Tagblume · ♃ Z8 ⓚ VI-IX; C-Am., S-Am.
- **virginica** L. · E:Virgina Dayflower · ♃ ⓚ VI-VIII; USA: NE, NCE, Kans., SC, SE, Fla.

Commiphora Jacq. -f- *Burseraceae* · c. 190 spp. · E:Myrrh; F:Myrrhe; G:Myrrhe
- **abyssinica** Engl. · E:Abyssinian Myrrh; G:Arabische Myrrhe · ♄ Ψ ⓚ ⚕ Ⓝ; N-Eth., S-Arab.
- *molmol* (Engl.) Engl. = Commiphora myrrha
- **myrrha** (Nees) Engl. · E:Myrrh; G:Echte Myrrhe · ♄ Ψ ⓚ ⚕; Somalia
- **opobalsamum** (L.) Engl. · E:Balm of Gilead; G:Balsam-Myrrhe · ♄ Ψ ⓚ Ⓝ; Sudan, Eth., Somalia, Arab.

Comparettia Poepp. & Endl. -f- *Orchidaceae* · 7 spp.
- **coccinea** Lindl. · ♃ Z10 ⓦ XI-XII ▽ *; Braz.
- **falcata** Poepp. & Endl. · E:Snail Orchid · ♃ Z10 ⓦ XI-I ▽ *; Mex., C-Am., W.Ind., trop. S-Am.
- **macroplectron** Rchb. f. · ♃ Z10 ⓦ IX-X ▽ *; Col.
- *rosea* Lindl. = Comparettia falcata

Comptonia L'Hér. ex Aiton -f- *Myricaceae* · 1 sp. · E:Sweet Fern; F:Comptonie; G:Farnmyrte
- **peregrina** (L.) Coult.
- var. **aspleniifolia** (L.) Fernald · ♄ d Z6 IV-V; USA: NE
- var. **peregrina** · E:Sweet Fern; G:Farnmyrte · ♄ d Z6 ⚕; USA: NE

Conandron Siebold & Zucc. -n- *Gesneriaceae* · 1 sp.
- **ramondioides** Siebold & Zucc. · ♃ Z9 ⓚ V-VI; Jap., Taiwan

Conicosia N.E. Br. -f- *Aizoaceae* · 2 spp.
- *capensis* (Haw.) N.E. Br. = Conicosia pugioniformis
- *communis* (Edwards) N.E. Br. = Conicosia pugioniformis
- **pugioniformis** (L.) N.E. Br. · E:Narrowleaf Ice Plant · ♃ Z9 ⓚ; S-Afr. (SW-Cape)

Coniogramme Fée -f- *Adiantaceae* · 45 spp. · E:Bamboo Fern; F:Fougère-bambou; G:Goldfarn, Silberfarn
- **japonica** (Thunb.) Diels · E:Bamboo Fern; G:Japanischer Silberfarn · ♃ Z10 ⓚ; China, Korea, Jap., Riukiu-Is., Taiwan

Conioselinum Fisch. ex Hoffm. -n- *Apiaceae* · 10 spp. · F:Coniosélinum; G:Schirlingssilge
- **tataricum** Hoffm. · G:Schirlingssilge · ♃ VII-IX; Eur.: A, EC-Eur., Sc, E-Eur.; W-Sib., E-Sib., C-As.

Conium L. -n- *Apiaceae* · 3 (-7) spp. · E:Hemlock; F:Ciguë; G:Schierling
- **maculatum** L. · E:Poison Hemlock; G:Gefleckter Schierling · ⊙ Z5 VI-VIII

⚥ ⚘ Ⓝ; Eur.*, TR, Cauc., Iran, W-Sib., C-As., China: Sinkiang; NW-Afr., Eth., S-Afr., nat. in Can., USA, Mex.

Conoclinium DC. -n- *Asteraceae* · 3 spp. · E:Mist Flower; G:Nebelblume
- **coelestinum** (L.) DC. · E:Ageratum, Mist Flower; G:Himmelblaue Nebelblume · ⹁ VII-X; USA: NE, NCE, Kans., SC, SE, Fla.

Conophyllum Schwantes = Mitrophyllum
- *dissitum* (N.E. Br.) Schwantes = Mitrophyllum dissitum
- *gracile* Schwantes = Mitrophyllum abbreviatum
- *grande* (N.E. Br.) L. Bolus = Mitrophyllum grande
- *mitratum* (Marloth) Schwantes = Mitrophyllum mitratum

Conophytum N.E. Br. -n- *Aizoaceae* · 90 spp.
- *altile* (N.E. Br.) N.E. Br. = Conophytum ficiforme
- *ampliatum* L. Bolus = Conophytum bilobum subsp. bilobum
- **angelicae** (Dinter & Schwantes) N.E. Br. · ⹁ ⸙ Z9 ⌂; Namibia
- *assimile* (N.E. Br.) N.E. Br. = Conophytum ficiforme
- **bilobum** (Marloth) N.E. Br.
- subsp. **bilobum** · ⹁ ⸙ Z9 ⌂; Cape
- subsp. **gracilistylum** (L. Bolus) S.A. Hammer · ⹁ ⸙ Z9 ⌂; Cape
- **breve** N.E. Br. · ⹁ ⸙ Z9 ⌂; Cape
- **calculus** (A. Berger) N.E. Br. · ⹁ ⸙ Z9 Ⓦ; Cape
- *caroli* Lavis = Ophthalmophyllum caroli
- **depressum** Lavis · ⹁ ⸙ Z9 ⌂; Cape
- **ectypum** N.E. Br.
- subsp. **ectypum** · ⹁ ⸙ Z9 ⌂; W-Cape
- var. *tischleri* (Schwantes) Tischer = Conophytum ectypum subsp. ectypum
- *elishae* (N.E. Br.) N.E. Br. = Conophytum bilobum subsp. bilobum
- **fibuliforme** (Haw.) N.E. Br. · ⹁ ⸙ Z9 ⌂; Cape
- **ficiforme** (Haw.) N.E. Br. · ⹁ ⸙ Z9 ⌂; Cape
- *friedrichiae* (Dinter) Schwantes = Ophthalmophyllum friedrichiae
- **fulleri** L. Bolus · ⹁ ⸙ Z9 ⌂; Cape
- *gracilistylum* (L. Bolus) N.E. Br. = Conophytum bilobum subsp. gracilistylum
- *grandiflorum* L. Bolus = Conophytum

bilobum subsp. bilobum
- *herrei* Schwantes = Conophytum minusculum
- *johannis-winkleri* (Dinter & Schwantes) N.E. Br. = Conophytum pageae
- *longum* N.E. Br. = Ophthalmophyllum longum
- *maughanii* N.E. Br. = Ophthalmophyllum maughanii
- *meyerae* Schwantes = Conophytum bilobum subsp. bilobum
- **meyeri** N.E. Br. · ⹁ ⸙ Z9 ⌂; S-Afr. (Cape Prov.)
- **minimum** (Haw.) N.E. Br. · ⹁ ⸙ Z9 ⌂; Cape
- **minusculum** (N.E. Br.) N.E. Br. · ⹁ ⸙ Z9 ⌂; Cape
- *minutiflorum* (Schwantes) N.E. Br. = Conophytum pageae
- **minutum** (Haw.) N.E. Br. · ⸙ Z9 ⌂; S-Afr. (Cape Prov.)
- *mundum* N.E. Br. = Conophytum obcordellum
- *obconellum* (Haw.) Schwantes = Conophytum obcordellum
- **obcordellum** (Haw.) N.E. Br. · ⹁ ⸙ Z9 ⌂; Cape
- *odoratum* (N.E. Br.) N.E. Br. = Conophytum ficiforme
- **pageae** (N.E. Br.) N.E. Br. · ⹁ ⸙ Z9 ⌂; Namibia
- **pellucidum** Schwantes · ⹁ ⸙ Z9 ⌂; Cape
- *pictum* (N.E. Br.) N.E. Br. = Conophytum minimum
- *pillansii* Lavis = Conophytum subfenestratum
- *pusillum* (N.E. Br.) N.E. Br. = Conophytum minimum
- **saxetanum** (N.E. Br.) N.E. Br. · ⹁ ⸙ Z9 ⌂; Namibia
- *scitulum* (N.E. Br.) N.E. Br. = Conophytum minimum
- **stephanii** Schwantes · ⹁ ⸙ Z9 ⌂; Cape
- **subfenestratum** Schwantes · ⹁ ⸙ Z9 ⌂; Cape
- *tischleri* Schwantes = Conophytum ectypum subsp. ectypum
- **truncatum** (Thunb.) N.E. Br. · ⸙ Z9 ⌂; S-Afr. (Cape Prov.)
- subsp. **truncatum**
- subsp. **viridicatum** (N.E. Br.) S.A. Hammer · ⹁ ⸙ Z9 ⌂; Cape
- **turrigerum** (N.E. Br.) N.E. Br. · ⹁ ⸙ Z9 ⌂; Cape
- *ursprungianum* Tischer = Conophytum

obcordellum
- **wettsteinii** (A. Berger) N.E. Br. · ♃ ⩕ Z9
  ⟨ᴍ⟩; Cape

Conopodium W.D.J. Koch -n- *Apiaceae* ·
  20 spp. · E:Pignut; F:Conopode;
  G:Erdkastanie, Knollenkümmel
- **majus** (Gouan) Loret · E:Pignut;
  G:Französische Erdkastanie · ♃ V-VI;
  Eur.: Norw., BrI, F, Ib, Ital-P

Conringia Heist. ex Fabr. -f- *Brassicaceae* ·
  6-8 spp. · E:Hare's Ear Mustard;
  F:Conringia; G:Ackerkohl
- **austriaca** (Jacq.) Sweet · G:Österreich-
  ischer Ackerkohl · ⊙ V-VIII; Eur.: Ital-P,
  A, H, Ba, RO, Crim; TR, Cauc.
- **orientalis** (L.) Dumort. · E:Hare's Ear
  Cabbage; G:Orientalischer Ackerkohl
  · ⊙ V-VII Ⓝ; Eur.: C-Eur., EC-Eur., Ba,
  E-Eur., Ital-P; TR, Cauc., Iran, Iraq,
  Afgh., Pakist., N-Afr., nat. in Sc, Fr, Ib

Consolida Gray -f- *Ranunculaceae* ·
  43 spp. · E:Larkspur; F:Dauphinelle;
  G:Rittersporn
- **ajacis** (L.) Schur · E:Rocket Larkspur;
  G:Garten-Rittersporn, Hyazinthenblüti-
  ger Sommer-Rittersporn · ⊙ ⋈ VI-VIII;
  Eur.: Ib, Fr, Ital-P, Ba, Crim; TR, Syr.,
  Cyprus, Cauc., C-As, nat. in C-Eur., Ind.,
  N-Am.
- *ambigua* (L.) P.W. Ball & Heywood =
  Consolida ajacis
- **hispanica** (Costa) Greuter · G:Iberischer
  Rittersporn · ⊙ VI-VIII; Eur.: Ib, H, Ba,
  E-Eur.; TR, Levant, Cauc., Iran, NW-Afr.,
  nat. in F, Ital-P, C-Eur., EC-Eur.
- **orientalis** (J. Gay) Schrödinger ·
  E:Oriental Larkspur; G:Orientalischer
  Rittersporn · ⊙ VI-VIII; Eur.: Ib, H, Ba,
  EC-Eur.; TR, Syr., Cauc., Iran, C-As,
  Him., NW-Afr., nat. in Fr, Ital-P, C-Eur.,
  CZ
- **regalis** A. Gray · E:Field Larkspur;
  G:Acker-Rittersporn
- **some cultivars**
- subsp. **regalis** · E:Common Field Lark-
  spur; G:Gewöhnlicher Acker-Rittersporn
  · ⊙ V-VIII ⚥ ⚘; Eur.* exc. BrI, Ib; TR,
  Cauc., Iran, W-Sib., nat. in Ib

Convallaria L. -f- *Convallariaceae* · 3 spp. ·
  E:Lily of the Valley; F:Muguet; G:Mai-
  glöckchen

- *japonica* L. f. = Ophiopogon japonicus
- **majalis** L.
- **some cultivars**
- subsp. **majalis** · E:Lily-of-the-
  Valley; F:Muguet; G:Gewöhnliches
  Maiglöckchen · ♃ ⋈ D Z3 V ⚥ ⚘; Eur.*,
  N-TR, Cauc., E-Sib., Amur, Sakhal.,
  China, Korea, Jap., nat. in N-Am.
- *polygonatum* Lour. = Polygonatum
  odoratum var. odoratum

Convolvulus L. -m- *Convolvulaceae* · c.
  250 spp. · E:Field Bindweed; F:Liseron ;
  G:Winde
- **althaeoides** L. · E:Mallow Bindweed · ♃
  ⚥ △ Z8 ⋀ VI-IX; Eur.: Ib, Fr, Ital-P, Ba,
  RO; TR, Levant, N-Afr.
- **arvensis** L. · E:Bindweed, Field
  Bindweed; G:Acker-Winde · ♃ ⚥ Z5 VI-X
  ⚥ ; Eur.*, TR, Levant, Cauc., Iran, W-Sib.,
  E-Sib., nat. in cosmop.
- **boissieri** Steud.
- subsp. **boissieri** · ♃ ⌒ △ Z8 ⟨ᴍ⟩ ⋀
  VI-VIII; S-Sp.
- subsp. **compactus** Stace · ♃ Z8 ⟨ᴍ⟩; Eur.:
  Ba; TR
- **cantabrica** L. · G:Kantabrische Winde ·
  ♃ △ Z8 ⋀ VI-VII; Eur.: Ib, Fr, Ital-P, Ba,
  A, E-Eur.; TR, Syr., Palest., Cauc., Iran,
  NW-Afr.
- **cneorum** L. · ♄ e Z8 ⟨ᴍ⟩ V-IX; Eur.: sp., I,
  Sic., Croatia, AL
- *dahuricus* Herb. = Calystegia dahurica
- *dissectus* Jacq. = Merremia dissecta
- **farinosus** L. · ♃ ⚥ ⟨ᴍ⟩; S-Afr., nat. in P
- **floridus** L. f. · ♄ e Z9 ⟨ᴍ⟩; Canar.
- **humilis** Jacq. · ⊙ ♃ Z8; Eur.: P, sp., I,
  Sic.; Levant, N-Afr.
- **lineatus** L. · ♄ △ Z7 ⟨ᴍ⟩ ⋀ VII-VIII; Eur.:
  Ib, Fr, Ital-P, Ba, E-Eur.; TR, Levant,
  Cauc., Iran, W-Sib., C-As., N-Afr.
- *macrocarpus* L. = Operculina macrocarpa
- **meonanthus** Hoffmanns. & Link · ⊙ ;
  Eur.: Ib, I, Sic.; ? Moroc., ? Alger.
- *muricatus* L. = Ipomoea muricata
- *nitidus* Boiss. non Desr. = Convolvulus
  boissieri subsp. boissieri
- **oleifolius** Desr. · ♄ ⟨ᴍ⟩ VII-VIII; Eur.:
  Malta, GR, Crete; TR, Levant, Egypt,
  Libya
- *pellitus* Ledeb. = Calystegia hederacea
- *pulcher* (Brummitt & Heywood) Oberd. =
  Calystegia pulchra
- **sabatius** Viv. · E:Ground Morning Glory;
  G:Kriechende Winde · ♃ ♄ Z8 ⟨ᴍ⟩ V-X;

Eur.: I; Moroc., Alger.
- **scammonia** L. · E:Scammony; G:Kleina-
siatische Winde · ⟁ ⚥ Z7 VI ⚥ ⚘; Eur.: ?
GR, Crim; TR, Syr., Palest., N-Iraq
- **scoparius** L. f. · ♄ d Z9 ⓐ Ⓝ; Canar.
- *sepium* L. = Calystegia sepium
- **siculus** L. · ⟁ ⚥; Eur.: Ib, F, Ital-P, Ba;
TR, Cyprus, Levant, N-Afr., Macaron.,
Sokotra
- *silvaticus* Kit. = Calystegia silvatica
- *soldanella* L. = Calystegia soldanella
- *speciosus* L. f. = Argyreia nervosa
- **tricolor** L. · E:Dwarf Morning Glory;
F:Belle de jour, Liseron d'été; G:Dreifar-
bige Winde · ☉ ⟁ Z8 VI-IX; Eur.: Ib, Fr,
Ital-P, Ba; NW-Afr., Libya
- **some cultivars**
- *turpethum* L. = Operculina turpethum
- *undulatus* Cav. = Convolvulus humilis

Conyza Less. -f- *Asteraceae* · c. 50 spp. ·
E:Fleabane; F:Erigeron; G:Berufkraut
- **albida** Willd. ex Spreng. · G:Weißes
Berufkraut · ☉ Z7; orig. ?, nat. in nat.
in sp., F
- **bonariensis** (L.) Cronquist ·
E:Asthmaweed; G:Südamerikanisches
Berufkraut · ☉ Z7 VII-X; S-Am., nat. in
Eur.*: Ib, Fr, Ital-P, Ba
- **canadensis** (L.) Cronquist · E:Canada
Fleabane, Horse Weed, Mule Tail;
G:Kanadisches Berufkraut · ☉ Z7 VII-X
⚥; Can., USA*, C-Am., W.Ind., S-Am.,
nat. in cosmop.

Copaifera L. -f- *Caesalpiniaceae* · -30 spp. ·
E:Cobaiba; F:Copalier; G:Kopaivabalsam,
Kopaivabaum
- *copallifera* (Benn.) Milne-Redh. =
Guibourtia copallifera
- **coriacea** Mart. · ♄ Z10 ⓦ Ⓝ; S-Am.
- *demeusii* Harms = Guibourtia demeusii
- **gorskiana** Benth. · ♄ Z10 ⓦ Ⓝ; E-Afr.
- **guyanensis** Desf. · ♄ Z10 ⓦ Ⓝ; S-Am.
- *jacquinii* Desf. = Copaifera officinalis
- **langsdorffii** Desf. · E:Copaifera;
G:Kopaivabaum · ♄ Z10 ⓦ ⚥ Ⓝ; Braz.,
Parag.
- **multijuga** Hayne · ♄ Z10 ⓦ Ⓝ; Braz.
- **officinalis** (Jacq.) L. · E:Kopal;
G:Kopaivabalsam · ♄ Z10 ⓦ ⚥ Ⓝ;
W.Ind., S-Am.
- **reticulata** Ducke · ♄ Z10 ⓦ ⚥ Ⓝ; Braz.,
Bol.

Copernicia Mart. ex Endl. -f- *Arecaceae* ·
21 sp. · E:Caranda Palm; F:Palmier à cire;
G:Karnaubapalme
- **prunifera** (Mill.) H.E. Moore · E:Wax
Palm; G:Karnaubapalme · ♄ e Z10 ⓦ ⚥
Ⓝ; Braz.

Copiapoa Britton & Rose -f- *Cactaceae* · c.
25 spp.
- **cinerascens** (Salm-Dyck) Britton & Rose
- var. **cinerascens** · ⚇ Z9 ⓐ ▽ ✳; Chile:
Atacama
- var. **grandiflora** (F. Ritter) A.E. Hoffm. ·
⚇ Z9 ⓐ ▽ ✳; N-Chile
- **cinerea** (Phil.) Britton & Rose
- var. **cinerea** · ⚇ Z9 ⓐ ▽ ✳; Chile
- var. **columna-alba** (F. Ritter) Backeb. · ⚇
Z9 ⓐ ▽ ✳; N-Chile
- var. **gigantea** (Backeb.) N.P. Taylor · ⚇
Z9 ⓐ ▽ ✳; N-Chile
- **coquimbana** (Rümpler) Britton & Rose
- var. **coquimbana** · ⚇ Z9 ⓐ ▽ ✳; Chile:
Coquimbo
- var. **fiedleriana** (K. Schum.) A.E.
Hoffm. · ⚇ Z9 ⓐ ▽ ✳; N-Chile
- **echinoides** (Lem. ex Salm-Dyck) Britton
& Rose · ⚇ Z9 ⓐ ▽ ✳; Chile: Antofagasta
- *fiedleriana* (K. Schum.) Backeb. =
Copiapoa coquimbana var. fiedleriana
- *gigantea* Backeb. = Copiapoa cinerea var.
gigantea
- *grandiflora* F. Ritter = Copiapoa cinerascens var. grandiflora
- *haseltoniana* Backeb. = Copiapoa cinerea
var. gigantea
- **humilis** (Phil.) Hutchison
- var. **humilis** · ⚇ Z9 ⓐ ▽ ✳; N-Chile
- var. **taltalensis** (Werderm.) A.E. Hoffm. ·
⚇ Z9 ⓐ ▽ ✳; Chile
- **krainziana** F. Ritter · ⚇ Z9 ⓐ ▽ ✳;
N-Chile
- **pepiniana** (K. Schum.) Backeb. · ⚇ Z9 ⓐ
▽ ✳; Chile
- *taltalensis* (Werderm.) Looser = Copiapoa
humilis var. taltalensis
- **tenuissima** F. Ritter · ⚇ Z9 ⓐ ▽ ✳;
N-Chile
- *totoralensis* F. Ritter = Copiapoa
coquimbana var. fiedleriana

Coprosma J.R. Forst. & G. Forst. -f-
Rubiaceae · 99 spp. · E:Mirror Plant
- **acerosa** A. Cunn. · E:Sand Coprosma · ♄
e Z8 ⓐ; NZ
- **baueri** Endl. · ♄ e Z9 ⓐ Ⓝ; NZ, Norfolk

Is.
- × **kirkii** Cheeseman (*C. acerosa* × *C. repens*) · ♄ e ⟿ Z9 Ⓚ; NZ
- **lucida** J.R. Forst. & G. Forst. · ♄ e Z8 Ⓚ; NZ
- **petriei** Cheeseman · ♄ e ⟿ △ Z7 Ⓐ ∧; NZ
- **repens** A. Rich. · E:Creeping Mirror Plant · ♄ ♄ e Z9 Ⓚ; NZ
- **some cultivars**

Coptis Salisb. -f- *Ranunculaceae* · 15 spp. · E:Gold Threat; F:Coptide; G:Goldmund
- **trifolia** (L.) Salisb. · E:Gold Thread; G:Goldmund · ♃ △ Z2 V-VI ⚕; Alaska, Can., USA: NE, NCE; Sib., Jap., Greenl.

Corallodiscus Batalin -m- *Gesneriaceae* · 18 spp.
- **kingianus** (Craib) B.L. Burtt · ♃ Z9 Ⓚ VI-VII; China: Sichuan
- **lanuginosus** (DC.) B.L. Burtt · ♃ Z9 Ⓚ VI-VII; E-Him., Tibet, SW-China

Corallorhiza Gagnebin -f- *Orchidaceae* · 11 sp. · E:Coralroot Orchid; F:Racine corail; G:Korallenwurz
- **trifida** Châtel. · E:Coralroot Orchid; G:Europäische Korallenwurz · ♃ V-VII ▽ ✻; Eur.*, TR, Cauc., W-Sib., E-Sib., Amur, Kamchat., C-As., Mong., China, N-Am.

Corbularia Salisb. = Narcissus
- *bulbocodium* (L.) Haw. = Narcissus bulbocodium subsp. bulbocodium var. bulbocodium

Corchorus L. -m- *Tiliaceae* · c. 40 (-100) spp. · E:Jute; F:Jute; G:Jute
- **capsularis** L. · E:White Jute; G:Rundkapsel-Jute · ⊙ Z10 Ⓚ Ⓝ; orig. ?; cult. Ind., China, Jap., Taiwan
- **olitorius** L. · E:Nalta Jute; G:Langkapsel-Jute · ⊙ Z10 Ⓚ Ⓝ; Ind., nat. in trop. As.
- **trilocularis** L. · ⊙ Z10 Ⓝ; Afr., Arab., Ind.

Cordia L. -f- *Boraginaceae* · c. 300 spp. · F:Cordia, Sebestier; G:Kordie
- **alliodora** (Ruiz & Pav.) Oken · E:Salmwood, Spanish Elm; G:Lauch-Kordie · ♄ s D Z10 Ⓦ Ⓝ; Mex., C-Am., W.Ind., trop. S-Am.
- **decandra** Hook. & Arn. · ♄ e Z10 Ⓚ IV-V; Chile
- **glabra** Cham. · ♄ Z10 Ⓦ IX-X; Braz.
- **greggii** Torr. · ♄ Z10 Ⓚ VII-VIII; N-Mex.
- *retusa* Vahl = Carmona retusa
- **superba** Cham. · ♄ e Z10 Ⓦ IX; Braz.

Cordyline Comm. ex R. Br. -f- *Draceanaceae* · 24 spp. · E:Cabbage Tree; F:Cordyline; G:Keulenlilie, Kolbenbaum, Kolbenlilie
- **australis** (G. Forst.) Endl. · E:Cabbage Tree · ♄ e Z10 Ⓚ; NZ
- **banksii** Hook. f. · ♄ e Z10 Ⓚ; NZ
- *baueri* Hook. f. = Cordyline obtecta
- **fruticosa** (L.) A. Chev. · ♄ e Z10 Ⓦ Ⓝ; Ind., Malay. Arch., N.Guinea, NE-Austr., NZ, Polyn., Hawaii
- *haageana* K. Koch = Cordyline murchisoniae
- **indivisa** (G. Forst.) Endl. · ♄ ♄ e Z10 Ⓦ Ⓚ; NZ
- **murchisoniae** F. Muell. · ♄ e Z10 Ⓦ; Austr.: Queensl.
- **obtecta** (Graham) Baker · ♄ e Z10 Ⓚ; Norfolk Is.
- **pumilio** Hook. f. · ♄ e Z10 Ⓚ; NZ
- **rubra** Otto & A. Dietr. · ♄ e Z10 Ⓚ; orig. ?
- **stricta** (Sims) Endl. · ♄ e Z10 Ⓚ; Austr.: Queensl., N.S.Wales
- *terminalis* (L.) Kunth = Cordyline fruticosa

Corema D. Don -n- *Empetraceae* · 2 spp. · E:Crowberry
- **album** (L.) D. Don · E:Portuguese Crowberry · ♄ e Z8 Ⓚ; Eur.: sp., P, Azor.

Coreopsis L. -f- *Asteraceae* · c. 80 spp. · E:Tickseed; F:Coréopsis, Œil de Jeune fille; G:Mädchenauge, Schöngesicht, Wanzenblume
- *atkinsoniana* Douglas ex Lindl. = Coreopsis tinctoria var. atkinsoniana
- **auriculata** L. · E:Lobed Tickweed · ♃ Z4 V-VIII; USA: Va., Ky., SE, Fla.
- **basalis** (Otto & A. Dietr.) S.F. Blake · E:Goldenmane Tickweed · ⊙ VII-IX; Tex.
- **bigelovii** (A. Gray) Voss · E:Bigelow's Tickseed; G:Bigelows Mädchenauge · ⊙ VII-IX; Calif.
- **californica** (Nutt.) H. Sharsm. · E:California Tickseed; G:Kalifornisches Mädchenauge · ⊙ VII-IX; S-Calif., S-Ariz.
- **calliopsidea** (DC.) A. Gray · E:Leaf Stem Tickseed · ⊙ VII-VIII; S-Calif.

– *cardaminifolia* (DC.) Torr. & A. Gray =
Coreopsis tinctoria var. atkinsoniana
– **delphiniifolia** Lam. · E:Larkspur-leaf
Tickseed · ⨁ Z7 VIII-IX; USA: SE
– *diversifolia* Hook. = Coreopsis basalis
– **douglasii** (DC.) H.M. Hall · E:Douglas
Tickseed; G:Douglas-Mädchenauge · ⊙
VII-VIII; C-Calif.
– *drummondii* (D. Don) Torr. & A. Gray =
Coreopsis basalis
– *ferulifolia* Jacq. = Bidens ferulifolia
– **grandiflora** T. Hogg ex Sweet ·
E:Largeflower Tickseed; F:Coréopsis
à grandes fleurs; G:Großblumiges
Mädchenauge · ⊙ ⨁ ⋉ Z7 VI-VIII; USA:
SE, Fla., Kans., Mo., SC; N-Mex.
– **some cultivars**
– **lanceolata** L. · E:Lance Leaf Tickseed;
F:Coréopsis lancéolé; G:Lanzettblättriges
Mädchenauge · ⨁ ⋉ Z3 VI-VIII; Can.:
Ont.; USA: NE, NCE, SC, SE, Fla.; N-Mex.
– **major** Walter · E:Greater Tickweed · ⨁
Z7 VII-VIII; USA: NE, Ohio, SE
– **maritima** (Nutt.) Hook. f. · E:Sea Dahlia;
G:Nacktstängliges Mädchenauge · ⊙ ⨁
Z8 VI-IX; SW-Calif.
– **nuecensis** A. Heller · E:Crown Tickseed ·
⊙ Z8 VII-IX; Tex.
– **palmata** Nutt. · E:Stiff Tickseed;
G:Palmblatt-Mädchenauge · ⨁ Z4 IV-IX;
Can.: E; USA: NCE, SE, SC
– **pubescens** Elliott · E:Star Tickseed · ⨁ Z7
VI-IX; USA: NE, NCE, Okla., SE, Fla.
– **rosea** Nutt. · E:Pink Tickseed; G:Rosa
Mädchenauge · ⨁ △ Z4 VIII-IX; Can.: E;
USA: NE
– *senifolia* Michx. = Coreopsis major
– **stillmanii** (A. Gray) S.F. Blake ·
E:Stillman's Tickseed; G:Stillmans
Mädchenauge · ⊙ VII-IX; C-Calif.
– **tinctoria** Nutt.
– var. **atkinsoniana** (Douglas ex Lindl.)
H.M. Parker ex E.B. Sm. · E:Columbia
Coreopsis; G:Columbia-Mädchenauge · ⊙
⊙ VIII-IX; USA: NC, SW, SC, La.; Mex.
– var. **tinctoria** · E:Annual Coreopsis,
Tickseed; G:Färber-Mädchenauge · ⊙
VII-IX; Can., USA*
– **tripteris** L. · E:Tall Tickseed; G:Hohes
Mädchenauge · ⨁ Z4 VII-IX; Can.: Ont.;
USA: NCE, NE, SC, SE, Kans.
– **verticillata** L. · E:Moonbeam Coreopsis;
F:Coréopsis à feuilles en aiguilles;
G:Netzblattstern, Quirlblättriges
Mödchenauge · ⨁ Z6 VI-VIII; USA: NE,

SE, Fla.

Coriandrum L. -n- *Apiaceae* · 2-3 spp. ·
E:Coriander; F:Coriandre; G:Koriander
– **sativum** L. · E:Chinese Parsley, Coriander; G:Koriander · ⊙ VI-VIII ⚤ Ⓝ; orig. ?,
cult. cosmop., nat. in S-Eur.

Coriaria L. -f- *Coriariaceae* · -30 spp. ·
F:Corroyère; G:Gerberstrauch
– **japonica** A. Gray · G:Japanischer
Gerberstrauch · ♄ d Z6 V; Jap.
– **myrtifolia** L. · E:Tanner's Sumach;
G:Europäischer Gerberstrauch · ♄ d Z7 ∧
IV-V ⚘ Ⓝ; Eur.: Ib, Fr, I, ? GR; Moroc.,
Alger., nat. in P
– **terminalis** Hemsl.
– var. **terminalis** Hemsl. · G:Rispenblütiger
Gerberstrauch · ♄ d Z8 ∧; Him., W-China
– f. **fructurubro** Hemsl. Z8 ∧; orig. ?
– var. **xanthocarpa** Rehder & E.H. Wilson ·
♄ d ⊛ Z8 ∧ VI; Sikkim

Coris L. -m- *Primulaceae* · 2 spp. · F:Coris;
G:Stachelträubchen
– **monspeliensis** L. · ♄ △ Z7 VI-VII; Eur.:
Ib, Fr, Ital-P, Ba; N-Afr.

Corispermum L. -n- *Chenopodiaceae* ·
60-70 spp. · E:Bugseed; F:Corispermum;
G:Wanzensame
– **filifolium** C.A. Mey. · ⊙; Eur.: E-Russ.
– **intermedium** Schweigg. · G:Dünen-
Wanzensame · ⊙ VIII-IX; Eur.: G, PL,
Balt.; costs
– **leptopterum** (Asch.) Iljin · G:Großblät-
triger Wanzensame, Schmalflügeliger
Wanzensame · ⊙ VIII-IX; Eur.: G, A, H
– **marschallii** Steven · G:Grauer Wanzensame · ⊙ VII-IX; Eur.: G, EC-Eur., Ba,
E-Eur., nat. in NL, I
– **nitidum** Kit. ex Schult. · E:Shiny Bugseed; G:Glanz-Wanzensame · ⊙ VIII-X;
Eur.: EC-Eur., Ba, E-Eur.; TR, ? Cauc.

Cornus L. -f- *Cornaceae* · c. 45 spp. ·
E:Cornel, Dogwood; F:Cornouiller;
G:Hartriegel, Kornelkirsche
– **alba** L. · E:Siberian Dogwood;
F:Cornouiller blanc; G:Tatarischer
Hartriegel · ♄ d Z3 V-VI; N-Russ., W-Sib.,
E-Sib., Amur, Sakhal., Mong., NE-China,
Manch., N-Korea, Jap., nat. in N-Eur.
– **alternifolia** L. f. · E:Pagoda Dogwood;
F:Cornouiller à feuilles alternes;

G:Wechselblättriger Hartriegel · ℏ ℏ d Z_6
V-VI; Can.: E; USA: NE, NCE, SE, Fla.
- **amomum** Mill. · E:Silky Dogwood;
G:Seidenhaariger Hartriegel · ℏ d Z_5
V-VI; Can.: E; USA; NE, NCE, SE
- × **arnoldiana** Rehder (*C. obliqua* × *C. racemosa*) · ℏ d Z_4 VI-VII; cult.
- **asperifolia** Michx.
- var. **asperifolia** · E:Tough Leaf Dogwood; G:Raublättriger Hartriegel · ℏ; USA: SE
- var. **dummondii** (C.A. Mey.) Coult. &
W.H. Evans · E:Drummond Dogwood;
F:Cornouiller de Drummond; G:Drummonds Hartriegel · ℏ d Z_5 VI-VII Ⓝ; Can.:
Ont.; USA: NE, NCE, NC, SE, SC
- *australis* C.A. Mey. = Cornus sanguinea
subsp. australis
- *baileyi* Coult. & W.H. Evans = Cornus
sericea
- *brachypoda* K. Koch = Cornus controversa
- **bretschneideri** L. Henry · G:Bretschneiders Hartriegel · ℏ d Z_5 VI; N-China
- **canadensis** L. · E:Bunch Berry, Creeping
Dogwood; F:Cornouiller du Canada;
G:Kanadischer Hartriegel · ⚃ △ ⊛ Z_2
VI; Alaska, Can., USA: NE, NCE, Rocky
Mts., SW, NW, Calif., Greenl., Kamchat.,
Sakhal., Amur, Korea, Jap.
- *candidissima* Mill. = Cornus florida
- **capitata** Wall. · E:Bentham's Cornel;
F:Cornouiller de Bentham; G:Benthams
Hartriegel · ℏ ℏ e Z_8 ⊡ VI-VII; Him.
- **controversa** Hemsl. ex Prain · E:Giant
Dogwood; F:Cornouiller discuté,
Cornouiller des pagodes ; G:Pagoden-
Hartriegel, Riesen-Hartriegel · ℏ ℏ d Z_7
VI-VII; China, Korea, Jap.
- *drummondii* C.A. Mey. = Cornus
asperifolia var. dummondii
- **florida** L. · E:Eastern Flowering Dogwood, White Dogwood; F:Cornouiller à
fleurs; G:Blumen-Hartriegel · ℏ ℏ d Z_6
V Ⓝ; Ont., USA: NE, NCE, Kans., SC, SE,
Fla.; NE-Mex.
- **some cultivars**
- f. **rubra** (Weston) Schelle Z_5; cult.
- *foemina* Mill. = Cornus stricta
- *foemina* Wangerin = Cornus racemosa
- **glabrata** Benth. · E:Brown Dogwood,
Western Cornel; G:Westlicher Hartriegel
· ℏ ℏ d Z_6 VI; USA: Oreg., Calif.
- **hemsleyi** C.K. Schneid. & Wangerin · ℏ ℏ
d Z_6 VII; C-China
- **hessei** Koehne · G:Zwerg-Hartriegel · ℏ d

△ Z_5 VI-VIII; ? NE-As.
- **kousa** Hance
- **some cultivars**
- var. **chinensis** Osborn · G:Chinesischer
Blumen-Hartriegel · ℏ ℏ d Z_5 VI; China
- var. **kousa** · E:Japanese Dogwood;
F:Cornouiller kousa; G:Japanischer
Blumen-Hartriegel · ℏ ℏ d Z_5 VI; Jap.,
Korea
- **macrophylla** Wall. · E:Chinese
Dogwood; G:Großblättriger Hartriegel ·
ℏ ℏ d Z_6 VII-VIII; Him., China, Jap.
- **mas** L. · E:Cornelian Cherry;
F:Cornouiller mâle; G:Kornelkirsche · ℏ d
⊛ Z_5 III-IV ⚥ Ⓝ; Eur.: Fr, Ital-P, C-Eur.,
EC-Eur., Ba, E-Eur.; TR, Syr., Cauc., Iran,
nat. in BrI
- **nuttallii** Audubon · E:Mountain Dogwood, Pacific Dogwood; F:Cornouiller de
Nutall; G:Nuttalls Blumen-Hartriegel · ℏ
ℏ d Z_7 V Ⓝ; Can.: B.C.; USA: NW, Calif.,
Idaho
- **obliqua** Raf. · E:Silky Dogwood;
G:Schiefer Hartriegel · ℏ d Z_4 VI-VII;
Can.: E; USA: NC, NCE, NE, Ark., Okla
- **officinalis** Siebold & Zucc. · E:Japanese
Cornelian Cherry; F:Cornouiller officinal;
G:Japanische Kornelkirsche · ℏ d Z_5 III-IV
⚥ ; China, Korea, Jap.
- *paniculata* L'Hér. = Cornus racemosa
- **paucinervis** Hance · ℏ d Z_5 VII-VIII;
C-China
- *pubescens* Nutt. = Cornus sericea subsp.
occidentalis
- *purpusii* Koehne = Cornus obliqua
- **racemosa** Lam. · E:Grey Dogwood,
Panicled Dogwood; G:Rispen-Hartriegel ·
ℏ d Z_5 VI-VII; Can.: E; USA: NE, SE
- **rugosa** Lam. · E:Roundleaf Dogwood;
G:Rundblättriger Hartriegel · ℏ d Z_4
V-VII; Can.: E; USA: NE, NCE
- **sanguinea** L. · G:Blutroter Hartriegel
- **some cultivars**
- subsp. **australis** (C.A. Mey.) Jáv. ·
G:Östlicher Blutroter Hartriegel · ℏ d Z_5;
Eur.: C-Eur., EC-Eur., Ba + ; TR, Lebanon,
Cauc., C-As.
- subsp. **sanguinea** · E:Common Dogwood,
Dogberry; F:Cornouiller sanguin;
G:Gewöhnlicher Blutroter Hartriegel · ℏ
d Z_4 V-VI ⚥ Ⓝ; Eur.*, TR, Cauc., C-As.
- **sericea** L. · G:Weißer Hartriegel
- subsp. **occidentalis** (Torr. & A. Gray)
Fosberg · E:Creek Dogwood; G:Weichhaariger Hartriegel · ℏ d ⊛ Z_2 VI-VIII;

Alaska, Can.: W; USA: NW, Rocky Mts., Calif.
– subsp. **sericea** · E:American Dogwood, Red Osier Dogwood; G:Gewöhnlicher Weißer Hartriegel · ♄ d Z2 VI-VII
– *sibirica* Lodd. ex G. Don = Cornus alba
– *stolonifera* F. Michx. = Cornus sericea subsp. sericea
– var. *occidentalis* (Torr. & A. Gray) C.L. Hitchc. = Cornus sericea subsp. occidentalis
– **stricta** Lam. · E:Stiff Dogwood; G:Steifer Hartriegel · ♄ d Z7 V-VI; USA: SC, SE, Fla.
– **suecica** L. · E:Dwarf Cornel; G:Schwedischer Hartriegel · ④ △ Z2 V-VII ▽; Eur.: BrI, Sc, NL, G, PL, Russ.; Amur, Sakhal., Kamchat., Alaska, Can., Greenl.
– *tatarica* Mill. = Cornus alba
– × **unalaschkensis** Ledeb. (*C. canadensis* × *C. suecica*) · ④ Z2; Alaska, Nfld., Greenl.
– **walteri** Wangerin · ♄ d Z6 VI; C-China, W-China, Korea
– **Cultivars:**
– some cultivars

Corokia A. Cunn. -f- *Escalloniaceae* · 3-6 spp.
– **cotoneaster** Raoul · E:Wire Netting Bush; G:Zickzackstrauch · ♄ e Z8 ⌂ VI-VII; NZ
– **macrocarpa** Kirk · ♄ e Z8 ⌂; NZ (Chatham Is.)
– × **virgata** Turrill (*C. cotoneaster*) · ♄ e Z8 ⌂; cult.
– some cultivars

Coronaria Guett. = Silene
– *coriacea* Schischk. ex Gorschk. = Silene coronaria
– *flos-cuculi* (L.) A. Braun = Silene flos-cuculi
– *flos-jovis* (L.) A. Braun = Silene flos-jovis
– *tomentosa* A. Braun = Silene coronaria

Coronilla L. -f- *Fabaceae* · 20 spp. · E:Scorpion Vetch; F:Coronille; G:Kronwicke
– **coronata** L. · E:Scorpion Vetch; G:Berg-Kronwicke · ④ △ Z6 V-VII; Eur.: Fr, Ital-P, C-Eur., EC-Eur., Ba, E-Eur.; Cauc., Iran
– **cretica** L. · G:Kretische Kronwicke · ⊙ Z8; Eur.: I, Ba, Russ.; TR, Syr., Palest., Cauc.

– *emerus* L. = Emerus major
– **minima** L. · G:Kleine Kronwicke · ♄ ⟿ △ D Z7 ⋀ VI-VII; Eur.: P, sp., F, I, Sw; NW-Afr.
– *montana* Scop. = Coronilla coronata
– **orientalis** Mill. · ④ △ Z8 V-VII; TR
– **repanda** (Poir.) Guss. · ⊙; Eur.: Ib, Ital-P; Cyprus, Palest., NW-Afr., Libya
– **rostrata** Boiss. & Spruner · ⊙; Eur: : AL, GR, Creta, Crim ; TR
– **scorpioides** (L.) W.D.J. Koch · E:Scorpion Senna; G:Skorpion-Kronwicke · ⊙ Z7 Z6-VI ⚘; Eur.: Ib, Fr, Ital-P, Ba, RO, Crim; TR, Levant, Cauc., Iran, NW-Afr., Libya
– **vaginalis** Lam. · G:Scheiden-Kronwicke · ♄ △ Z6 V-VII; Eur.: Fr, Ital-P, C-Eur., EC-Eur., Ba, ? RO; mts.
– **valentina** L.
– subsp. **glauca** (L.) Batt. · E:Scorpion Vetch; G:Blaugrüne Valencia-Kronwicke · ♄ e Z9 ⌂ IV-VII; Eur.: Ib, Fr, Ital-P, Ba; TR, NW-Afr., Libya, nat. in BrI
– subsp. **valentina** · G:Valencia-Kronwicke · ♄ e Z9 ⌂; Eur.: Ib, F, Ital-P, Ba; TR, N-Afr.

Coronopus Zinn -m- *Brassicaceae* · 10 spp. · E:Swine Cress; G:Krähenfuß
– **didymus** (L.) Sm. · G:Zweiknotiger Krähenfuß · ⊙ VI-VIII; S-Am., nat. in Eur.* exc. Sc; N-Am., Austr.
– **squamatus** (Forssk.) Asch. · E:Crowfoot; G:Gewöhnlicher Krähenfuß, Niederliegender Knotenfuß · ⊙ V-VIII; Eur.*, TR, Levant, Cauc., Iran, N-Afr.

Corozo Jacq. ex Giseke = Elaeis
– *oleifera* (Humb., Bonpl. & Kunth) L.H. Bailey = Elaeis oleifera

Correa Andrews -f- *Rutaceae* · 11 sp. · E:Tasmanian Fuchsia; F:Fuchsia d'Australie; G:Australische Fuchsie, Correa
– **alba** Andrews · E:Botany Bay Tea Tree; G:Weiße Correa · ♄ e Z8 ⌂ I-XII; Austr.: N.S. Wales, S-Austr., Tasman., Victoria
– **backhouseana** Hook. · E:Australian Fuchsia; G:Cremefarbene Correa · ♄ e Z8 ⌂ V-VI; Tasman.
– **baeurlenii** F. Muell. · E:Chef's Cap Correa · ♄ e Z8 ⌂; Austr.: N.S.Wales
– × **bicolor** Paxton (*C. alba* × *C. pulchella*) · ♄ e Z8 ⌂; cult.

– *cardinalis* F. Muell. ex Hook. = Correa
reflexa var. cardinalis
– × **harrisii** Paxton (*C. pulchella* × *C. reflexa
var. reflexa*) · ♄ e Z8 ⓚ); cult.
– **pulchella** J. Mackay ex Sweet · E:Correa;
G:Lachs-Correa · ♄ e Z8 ⓚ); Austr.:
S-Austr.
– **reflexa** (Labill.) Vent.
– var. **cardinalis** (F. Muell. ex Hook.)
Court Z8 ⓚ); Austr.: Victoria
– var. **reflexa** · E:Common Correa; G:Aus-
tralische Fuchsie, Gemeine Correa · ♄ e
Z8 ⓚ) III-V; Austr.: N.S.Wales, Victoria,
S-Austr., Tasman.
– *speciosa* Donn ex Andrews = Correa
reflexa var. reflexa
– **Cultivars:**
– **'Anglesea'**

Corrigiola L. -f- *Molluginaceae* · 11-13 spp. ·
E:Strapwort; F:Corrigiola; G:Hirsch-
sprung
– **litoralis** L. · G:Gewöhnlicher Hirschsprung · ☉ VII-X; Eur.: Ib, Fr, Ital-P, Ba,
E-Eur., D; TR, Palest., N-Afr, Trop. Afr.,
S-Afr.; coasts

Corryocactus Britton & Rose -m-
Cactaceae · 14-20 spp.
– **aureus** (Meyen) Hutchison · ♄ ⅄ Z9 ⓚ ▽
✳; S-Peru, N-Chile
– **brachypetalus** (Vaupel) Britton & Rose ·
♄ ⅄ Z9 ⓚ ▽ ✳; S-Peru
– **brevistylus** (K. Schum. ex Vaupel)
Britton & Rose · ♄ ⅄ Z9 ⓚ ▽ ✳; S-Peru
– **melanotrichus** (K. Schum.) Britton &
Rose · ⅄ Z9 ⓚ ▽ ✳; Bol.
– *spiniflorus* (Phil.) Hutchison = Austrocactus spiniflorus
– **squarrosus** (Vaupel) Hutchison · ⅄ Z9 ⓚ
▽ ✳; Peru: Junin

Cortaderia Stapf -f- *Poaceae* · 24 spp. ·
E:Pampas Grass; F:Herbe de la pampa;
G:Pampasgras
– **selloana** (Schult. & Schult. f.) Asch. &
Graebn. · E:Pampas Grass; F:Herbe de
la pampa; G:Pampasgras · ⅄ Z7 ∧ IX-X
ⓝ; S-Braz., Urug., Arg., nat. in Azor.,
NW-Sp. , F
– **some cultivars**

Cortusa L. -f- *Primulaceae* · 8 spp. ·
F:Cortuse; G:Heilglöckchen
– **matthioli** L. · E:Alpine Bells;

G:Alpen-Heilglöckchen · ⅄ △ Z5 VII-VIII
▽; Eur.: Fr, C-Eur., EC-Eur., Ital-P, Ba,
E-Eur.
– f. **pekinensis** V.A. Richt. Z5 ▽; Amur,
N-China, Korea, Sakhal.

Coryanthes Hook. -f- *Orchidaceae* ·
43 spp. · E:Helmet Orchid; F:Orchidée-
casque; G:Maskenorchidee
– **macrantha** (Hook.) Hook. · ⅄ Z10 ⓜ V
▽ ✳; Venez., Guyana, Trinidad
– **maculata** Hook. · ⅄ Z10 ⓜ VI-VII ▽ ✳;
Guyan.
– **speciosa** (Hook.) Hook. · ⅄ Z10 ⓜ VI-VII
▽ ✳; C-Am., W.Ind., trop. S-Am.

Corydalis DC. -f- *Fumariaceae* · c.
300 spp. · E:Corydalis; F:Corydale;
G:Lerchensporn
– **angustifolia** (M. Bieb.) DC. · ⅄ △ Z6 IV;
TR, Cauc., Iran
– **bracteata** (Stephan) Pers. · ⅄ △ Z7 V-VI;
Altai, Sib.
– **capnoides** (L.) Pers. · ☉ VI-VIII; Eur.: I, A,
EC-Eur., E-Eur.; W-Sib., E-Sib., C-As.,
Tibet, Mong., nat. in FIN
– **cashmeriana** Royle · G:Blauer Himalaya-
Lerchensporn · ⅄ Z5 ⓐ V-VIII; Kashmir,
Him., SE-Tibet
– **cava** (L.) Schweigg. & Körte · E:Bulbous
Corydalis, Hollowroot; F:Corydale creu-
se; G:Hohler Lerchensporn · ⅄ Z6 III-V ⚶
✺; Eur.* exc. BrI; TR, Cauc., N-Iran
– **cheilanthifolia** Hemsl. · ⅄ △ Z6 V;
W-China
– *claviculata* = Ceratocapnos claviculata
– **flexuosa** Franch. · ⅄ Z5 III-VI; China
(Sichuan)
– *glauca* (Curtis) Pursh = Capnoides
sempervirens
– **intermedia** (L.) Mérat · G:Mittlerer
Lerchensporn · ⅄ III-IV; Eur.* exc. BrI
– *lutea* (L.) DC. = Pseudofumaria lutea
– **nobilis** (L.) Pers. · ⅄ △ Z6 IV-VI; W-Sib.
(Altai), C-As., nat. in Sc
– **ophiocarpa** Hook. f. & Thomson · ☉ △
Z6 VI; Him., China, Jap., Taiwan
– **pumila** W.D.J. Koch · G:Zwerg-Lerch-
ensporn · ⅄ III-IV; Eur.: Ital-P, C-Eur.,
EC-Eur., Sc, Ba, RO
– **saxicola** G.S. Bunting · ⅄ △ Z7 ∧ V-VI;
China
– *sempervirens* (L.) Pers. = Capnoides
sempervirens

– **solida** (L.) Clairv. · E:Bird in a Bush,
Fumewort; G:Gewöhnlicher Gefingerter
Lerchensporn · ⁴ Z6 IV ⚥ ; Eur.* exc. BrI;
TR, Lebanon, nat. in BrI
– *thalictrifolia* Franch. = Corydalis saxicola
– *transsilvanica* Schur = Corydalis solida
– **wilsonii** N.E. Br. · ⁴ △ Z7 ∧ V-IX;
C-China

Corylopsis Siebold & Zucc. -f-
Hamamelidaceae · c. 30 spp. · E:Winter
Hazel; F:Faux-noisetier; G:Scheinhasel
– **glabrescens** Franch. & Sav. · G:Kahle
Scheinhasel · ♄ d Z6 VI; Jap.
– **pauciflora** Siebold & Zucc. · E:Buttercup
Winter Hazel; F:Corylopsis à petites
fleurs; G:Armblütige Scheinhasel,
Niedrige Scheinhasel · ♄ d Z7 III-IV; Jap.,
Taiwan
– **platypetala** Rehder & E.H. Wilson · ♄ d
Z7 IV; China: Hupeh
– **sinensis** Hemsl. · E:Chinese Winter
Hazel; G:Chinesische Scheinhasel · ♄ ♄ d
Z7 III-IV; W-China, C-China
– var. *calvescens* Rehder & E.H. Wilson =
Corylopsis platypetala
– f. *veitchiana* = Corylopsis veitchiana
– **spicata** Siebold & Zucc. · E:Spike Winter
Hazel; F:Corylopsis en épis; G:Ährige
Scheinhasel, Winter-Scheinhasel · ♄ d Z7
II-IV; Jap.
– **veitchiana** Bean · G:Veitchs Scheinhasel ·
♄ d Z7 IV; China: Hupeh
– **willmottiae** Rehder & E.H. Wilson ·
F:Corylopsis de Miss Willmontt; G:Will-
motts Scheinhasel · ♄ d Z7 IV; W-Sichuan

Corylus L. -f- *Betulaceae* · 18 spp. · E:Hazel;
F:Noisetier; G:Hasel, Haselnuss
– **americana** Marshall · E:American Hazel ·
♄ d Z5; Can., e USA
– **avellana** L. · E:Cob, Hazel; F:Coudrier,
Noisetier commun; G:Gewöhnliche Hasel
· ♄ ♄ d Z5 II-IV ⚥ Ⓝ; Eur.*, Cauc., TR,
N-Iran
– some cultivars
– **chinensis** Franch. · E:Chinese Hazel;
G:Chinesische Hasel · ♄ d Z6 II-III Ⓝ;
W-China, C-China
– **colurna** L. · E:Turkish Hazel; F:Noisetier
de Byzance; G:Baum-Hasel · ♄ d Z5 II-III
Ⓝ; Eur.: Ba, RO; TR, Cauc., Iran
– var. *chinensis* (Franch.) Burkill = Corylus
chinensis
– × **colurnoides** C.K. Schneid. (*C. avellana*

× *C. colurna*) · ♄ ♄ d Z5; cult.
– **cornuta** Marshall · E:Beaked Hazel;
G:Schnabelnuss · ♄ d Z5 II-III; Can., USA:
NE, NCE, NC, SE, NW, Calif., Rocky Mts.
– **heterophylla** Fisch. & Trautv. ·
E:Siberian Hazel; G:Mongolische
Haselnuss · ♄ ♄ d Z5; Korea, Jap., E-Sib.,
Manch., Amur, E-Mong.
– **maxima** Mill. · E:Filbert; F:Noisetier
franc; G:Große Hasel, Lamberts Hasel · ♄
d Z5 II-III Ⓝ; Eur.: Croatia, Maced., GR;
TR, Cauc., nat. in BrI, A
– some cultivars
– *rostrata* Aitch. = Corylus cornuta
– var. *sieboldiana* (L.) Maxim. = Corylus
sieboldiana var. sieboldiana
– **sieboldiana** Blume
– var. **mandshurica** (Maxim. & Rupr.) C.K.
Schneid. · ♄ d Z5; Korea, Jap., Manch.,
Amur
– var. **sieboldiana** · E:Japanese Hazel;
G:Japanische Hasel · ♄ d Z5 II-III; Jap.
– **tibetica** Batalin · ♄ d Z7; China
– *tubulosa* Willd. = Corylus maxima

Corynabutilon (K. Schum.) Kearney =
Abutilon
– *vitifolium* (Cav.) Kearney = Abutilon
vitifolium

Corynanthe Welw. -f- *Rubiaceae* · 3 spp.
– *johimbe* K. Schum. = Pausinystalia
johimbe
– **pachyceras** K. Schum. · ♄ Ⓜ; trop. Afr.

Corynephorus P. Beauv. -m- *Poaceae* ·
5 spp. · E:Grey Hair Grass; G:Silbergras
– **canescens** (L.) P. Beauv. · E:Grey Hair
Grass; G:Gewöhnliches Silbergras · ⁴
VI-VIII; Eur.* exc. Ba; Moroc., nat. in
USA

Corynocarpus J.R. Forst. & G. Forst.
-m- *Corynocarpaceae* · 5 spp. ·
F:Corynocarpus; G:Karakabaum
– **laevigatus** J.R. Forst. & G. Forst. · E:New
Zealand Laurel; G:Neuseeländischer
Karakabaum · ♄ e ⬚ ✄; NZ

Corypha L. -f- *Arecaceae* · 6 spp. ·
F:Palmier, Palmier talipot; G:Schopf-
palme, Talipotpalme
– *australis* R. Br. = Livistona australis
– *elata* Roxb. = Corypha utan
– *gebanga* Blume = Corypha utan

– *nana* Humb., Bonpl. & Kunth =
Cryosophila nana
– **umbraculifera** L. · E:Talipot Palm;
G:Talipotpalme · ♄ e Z10 ⓜ Ⓝ; S-Ind.,
Sri Lanka
– **utan** Lam. · E:Gebang; G:Buri-
Schopfpalme · ♄ e ⓜ Ⓝ; E-Ind., Burma,
Andaman Is., Malay. Arch., Phil.

Coryphantha (Engelm.) Lem. -f-
Cactaceae · 57 spp. · E:Beehive Cactus
– *alversonii* (J.M. Coult. ex Zeiss.) Orcutt =
Escobaria vivipara
– *bella* (Britton & Rose) Fosberg =
Escobaria emskoetteriana
– *ceratites* (Quehl) A. Berger = Neolloydia
conoidea
– **clavata** (Scheidw.) Backeb. · ♁ Z9 ⓐ ▽
✳; Mex.: Hidalgo, Queretaro, San Luis
Potosí, Zacatecas, Guanajuato
– *conoidea* (DC.) Orcutt ex A. Berger =
Neolloydia conoidea
– **cornifera** (DC.) Lem. · ♁ Z9 ⓐ ▽ ✳;
Mex.: Coahuila, Durango, San Luis
Potosí, Zacatecas
– *dasyacantha* (Engelm.) Orcutt =
Escobaria dasyacantha
– **elephantidens** (Lem.) Lem. · ♁ Z9 ⓐ ▽
✳; Mex. (Morelos, Michoacán)
– **erecta** (Lem. ex Pfeiff.) Lem. · ♁ Z9 ⓐ
▽ ✳; Mex.: Hidalgo, San Luis Potosí,
Guanajuato, Querétaro
– *grandiflora* (Pfeiff.) A. Berger = Neolloydia conoidea
– **macromeris** (Engelm.) Lem. · E:Donana,
Nipple Beehive Cactus · ♁ Z9 ⓐ ▽ ✳;
USA: Tex., N.Mex.; N-Mex.
– *marstonii* Clover = Escobaria missouriensis
– *missouriensis* (Sweet) Britton & Rose =
Escobaria missouriensis
– *muehlenpfordtii* (Poselg.) Britton & Rose
= Coryphantha scheeri
– *neoscheerii* Backeb. = Coryphantha
scheeri
– *odorata* Boed. = Cumarinia odorata
– **poselgeriana** (A. Dietr.) Britton & Rose ·
♁ Z9 ⓐ ▽ ✳; Mex.: Coahuila
– *radians* (DC.) Britton & Rose = Coryphantha cornifera
– *robertii* A. Berger = Escobaria emskoetteriana
– *roseana* (Boed.) Moran = Escobaria
roseana
– **scheeri** (Kuntze) L.D. Benson ·

E:Scheer's Beehive Cactus · ♁ Z9 ⓐ ▽ ✳;
USA: N.Mex.; Mex.: Hidalgo
– *varicolor* Tiegel = Escobaria tuberculosa
– *vivipara* (Nutt.) Britton & Rose =
Escobaria vivipara
– *wissmannii* (Hildm. ex K. Schum.) A.
Berger = Escobaria missouriensis
– *zilziana* Boed. = Escobaria zilziana

Cosmos Cav. -m- *Asteraceae* · 26 spp. ·
E:Mexican Aster; F:Cosmos; G:Kosmee,
Schmuckkörbchen
– **atrosanguineus** (Hook.) Voss · E:Black
Cosmos, Chocolate Cosmos; G:Schwarzes
Schmuckkörbchen · ☉ ⳾ Z8 VII-X; Mex.
– **bipinnatus** Cav. · E:Garden Cosmos,
Mexican Aster; F:Cosmos; G:Fiederblät-
triges Schmuckkörbchen · ☉ ✂ X; Mex.,
C-Am., trop. S-Am.
– **some cultivars**
– **diversifolius** Otto · ☉ ☉ ⳾ Z9 VIII-X;
Mex.
– **sulphureus** Cav. · E:Yellow Cosmos;
G:Gelbes Schmuckkörbchen · ☉ VIII-IX;
Mex., C-Am., trop. S-Am.
– **some cultivars**

Costus L. -m- *Costaceae* · 112 spp. · E:Spiral
Flag, Spiral Ginger; F:Costus; G:Kostwurz
– **afer** Ker-Gawl. · E:Spiral Ginger · ⳾ Z10
ⓜ; W-Afr.
– **cuspidatus** (Nees & Mart.) Maas · ⳾ Z10
ⓜ I-XII; Braz.
– *igneus* N.E. Br. = Costus cuspidatus
– **lucanusianus** Braun-Blanq. & K.
Schum. · ⳾ D Z10 ⓜ; C-Afr.
– **malortieanus** H. Wendl. · ⳾ Z10 ⓜ;
Costa Rica
– **speciosus** (J. König) Sm. · E:Crape Ginger, Malay Ginger; G:Prächtige Kostwurz
· ⳾ Z10 ⓜ; Him., Ind., Sri Lanka, Malay.
Arch., N.Guinea
– **spicatus** (Jacq.) Sw. · E:Cimarron;
G:Ährige Kostwurz · ⳾ Z10 ⓜ; Haiti

Cotinus Mill. -m- *Anacardiaceae* · 3 spp. ·
E:Smoke Bush, Smokewood; F:Arbre à
perruque; G:Perückenstrauch
– *americanus* Nutt. = Cotinus obovatus
– **coggygria** Scop. · E:Smoke Tree,
Sumach; F:Arbre à perruque, Fustet;
G:Europäischer Perückenstrauch · ♄ d ⚥
Z6 VI-VII ⚘ Ⓝ; Eur.: Fr, Ital-P, C-Eur.,
EC-Eur., Ba, E-Eur.; TR, Syr., Cauc., Iran,
Him., China, nat. in sp.

– **obovatus** Raf. · E:American Smoketree; G:Amerikanischer Perückenstrauch · ♄ ♄ d ⊗ Z5 VI-VII; USA: SE, Mo., Okla.

Cotoneaster Medik. -m- *Rosaceae* · 261 sp. · E:Cotoneaster; F:Cotonéaster; G:Zwergmispel
– **acuminatus** Lindl. · G:Spitzblättrige Zwergmispel · ♄ d Z6 V; Him., nat. in F, D
– **acutifolius** Turcz. · G:Peking-Zwergmispel · ♄ d Z5 V-VI; N-China
– **adpressus** Bois · E:Creeping Cotoneaster; F:Cotonéaster rampant; G:Kriechende Zwergmispel, Spalier-Zwergmispel · ♄ d ⤳ △ Z5 VI; W-China
– var. *praecox* Bois & Berthault = Cotoneaster nanshan
– **affinis** Lindl.
– var. **affinis** · ♄ d Z7 ∧ V; Him., W-China
– var. **bacillaris** (Wall. ex Lindl.) C.K. Schneid. · ♄ ♄ d Z7 V-VI; Him.
– **ambiguus** Rehder & E.H. Wilson · G:Zweifarbige Zwergmispel · ♄ d Z6 V-VI; W-China
– **amoenus** E.H. Wilson · G:Schöne Zwergmispel · ♄ e Z7 ∧ VI; SW-China
– **apiculatus** Rehder & E.H. Wilson · E:Cranberry Cotoneaster; G:Preiselbeer-Zwergmispel · ♄ d Z4 VI; W-China
– **ascendens** Flinck & B. Hylmö · G:Aufsteigende Zwergmispel · ♄ d Z4; orig ? ; cult. China: Hubei
– **bullatus** Bois · E:Hollyberry Cotoneaster; G:Runzelige Zwergmispel · ♄ d ⊗ Z5 V-VI; W-China
– **buxifolius** Wall. ex Lindl. · G:Buchsblättrige Zwergmispel · ♄ e Z7 ∧; Ind. (Nilgiri)
– **cashmiriensis** G. Klotz · G:Kaschmir-Zwergmispel · ♄ e Z7; Kashmir
– *cochleatus* hort. = Cotoneaster cashmiriensis
– **congestus** Baker · G:Gedrungene Zwergmispel · ♄ e △ Z6 VI; Him.
– **conspicuus** Comber ex C. Marquand · G:Bogen-Zwergmispel, Tibetanische Zwergmispel · ♄ d Z6 V; SE-Tibet
– **dammeri** C.K. Schneid. · E:Bearberry Cotoneaster; F:Cotonéaster de Dammer; G:Teppich-Zwergmispel · ♄ e Z5; China
– **dielsianus** E. Pritz. · G:Diels Zwergmispel
– var. **dielsianus** · ♄ d ⊗ Z5 VI; W-China, C-China

– var. **elegans** Rehder & E.H. Wilson · ♄ d Z5 V-VI; W-China: Sichuan
– **divaricatus** Rehder & E.H. Wilson · E:Spreading Cotoneaster; G:Sparrige Zwergmispel · ♄ d ⊗ Z5 VI; W-China, C-China, nat. in Eur.
– *floccosus* (Rehder & Wilson) Flinck & B. Hylmö = Cotoneaster salicifolius var. floccosus
– **foveolatus** Rehder & E.H. Wilson · ♄ d Z4 VI; C-China.
– **franchetii** Bois · E:Franchet's Cotoneaster; G:Franchets Zwergmispel · ♄ d ⊗ Z7 VI; W-China
– var. *sternianus* Turrill = Cotoneaster sternianus
– **frigidus** Wall. ex Lindl. · G:Baum-Zwergmispel · ♄ d ⊗ Z7 VI; Him.
– **glabratus** Rehder & E.H. Wilson · G:Kahlwerdende Zwergmispel · ♄ e Z7; W-China: Sichuan
– **harrovianus** E.H. Wilson · ♄ e ⊗ Z7 ∧ VI; W-China
– **hebephyllus** Diels · ♄ d Z6 V; SW-China
– **henryanus** (C.K. Schneid.) Rehder & E.H. Wilson · G:Henrys Zwergmispel · ♄ d ⊗ Z7 VI; C-China.
– **horizontalis** Decne. · E:Herring Bone Cotoneaster; F:Cotonéaster horizontal; G:Fächer-Zwergmispel · ♄ d Z4 V-VI; W-China
– var. *perpusillus* C.K. Schneid. = Cotoneaster perpusillus
– var. *wilsonii* Havemeyer ex E.H. Wilson = Cotoneaster ascendens
– *humifusus* Duthie ex J.H. Veitch = Cotoneaster dammeri
– **hupehensis** Rehder & E.H. Wilson · E:Hubei Cotoneaster; G:Hupeh-Zwergmispel · ♄ d ⊗ Z5 V; W-China, C-China
– × *hybridus* hort. = Cotoneaster × watereri
– **ignavus** E.L. Wolf · ♄ d Z6 V; C-As.
– **insignis** Pojark. · ♄ ♄ s Z6 V; C-As., Iran, Afgh., Him.
– **integerrimus** Medik. · G:Gewöhnliche Zwergmispel · ♄ d ⊗ Z6 IV-V ⚥ ▽; Eur.*, Cauc.
– **integrifolius** (Roxb.) G. Klotz · G:Ganzblättrige Zwergmispel · ♄ e; Him., SW-China
– **lacteus** W.W. Sm. · G:Späte Zwergmispel · ♄ e ⊗ Z7 ∧ VI-VII; W-China
– *laxiflorus* Jacq. ex Lindl. = Cotoneaster melanocarpus
– **lindleyi** Steud. · ♄ d Z6; Him.

- **linearifolius** (G. Klotz) G. Klotz · ♄ e; Nepal
- **lucidus** Schltdl. · E:Shiny Cotoneaster; G:Glänzende Zwergmispel, Sibirische Zwergmispel · ♄ d Z5 V-VI; Altai
- **melanocarpus** Lodd. · ♄ d Z7; C-As.
- **microphyllus** Wall. ex Lindl. · F:Cotonéaster à petites feuilles; G:Kleinblättrige Zwergmispel · ♄ e △ ♋ Z7 V-VI; Him.
- var. *glacialis* Hook. f. = Cotoneaster congestus
- var. *thymifolius* (Baker) Koehne = Cotoneaster integrifolius
- var. *vellaeus* (Franch.) Rehder & E.H. Wilson = Cotoneaster microphyllus
- **multiflorus** Bunge · G:Vielblütige Zwergmispel
- var. **calocarpus** Rehder & E.H. Wilson · ♄ d ♋ Z5 V; W-China
- var. **multiflorus** · ♄ d Z5; NW-China
- **nanshan** Mottet · G:Nanshan-Zwergmispel · ♄ d △ ♋ Z5 VI; W-China
- *nebrodensis* (Guss.) K. Koch = Cotoneaster nummularius
- **niger** (Thunb.) Fr. · G:Schwarze Zwergmispel · ♄ d Z5 V-VI; Eur.: Sc, EC-Eur., Ba, E-Eur.; TR, Cauc., W-Sib., E-Sib., Amur, C-As., Mong., China, Korea
- **nitens** Rehder & E.H. Wilson · ♄ d △ ♋ Z6 V-VI; Him., SW-China
- **nummularius** Fisch. & C.A. Mey. · ♄ Z5; Crete, Cyprus, TR, Syr., Lebanon, N-Iraq, Cauc., Iran
- **obscurus** Rehder & E.H. Wilson · ♄ d ♋ Z5 VI; W-China
- **pannosus** Franch. · E:Silverleaf Cotoneaster; G:Grobflockige Zwergmispel · ♄ d ♋ Z7 VI; SW-China
- **perpusillus** (C.K. Schneid.) Flinck & B. Hylmö · G:Kleine Zwergmispel · ♄ d Z6; China (Hubei)
- *praecox* (Bois & Berthault) M. Vilm. = Cotoneaster nanshan
- *pyrenaicus* Chanc. = Cotoneaster congestus
- **racemiflorus** (Desf.) K. Koch · G:Dichtblütige Zwergmispel
- var. *nummularius* (Fisch. & C.A. Mey.) Dippel = Cotoneaster nummularius
- var. **racemiflorus** · ♄ d Z5; Syr., Cauc., N-Iran, C-As., Him.
- var. *royleanus* Dippel · ♄ d Z5; Him.
- var. *soongoricus* (Regel & Herder) C.K. Schneid. Z5; W-China

- **radicans** (C.K. Schneid.) G. Klotz · G:Kriechende Zwergmispel · ♄ e ⟿ △ Z5 V; W-China
- **rhytidophyllus** Rehder & E.H. Wilson · ♄ e ♋ Z7 ∧ VI; W-China
- **roseus** Edgew. · G:Rosarote Zwergmispel · ♄ d ♋ Z6 VI; Afgh., Pakist., Kashmir, NW-Ind.
- **rotundifolius** Wall. ex Lindl. · G:Rundblättrige Zwergmispel
- var. **lanatus** (Jacques) C.K. Schneid. · ♄ e Z6; Him.
- var. **rotundifolius** · ♄ e ♋ Z7 ∧ VI; Him.
- **rugosus** E. Pritz. · G:Runzelblättrige Zwergmispel · ♄ e ♋ Z6 VI; C-China.
- **salicifolius** Franch.
- var. **floccosus** Rehder & E.H. Wilson · ♄ e ♋ Z6 VI-VII; W-China
- var. *rugosus* (E. Pritz.) Rehder & E.H. Wilson = Cotoneaster rugosus
- var. **salicifolius** · E:Willowleaf Cotoneaster; F:Cotonéaster à feuilles de saule; G:Weidenblättrige Zwergmispel · ♄ e Z6; China
- **sargentii** G. Klotz
- **serotinus** Hutch. · G:Späte Zwergmispel · ♄ e ♋ Z7 ∧ VII; W-China
- **simonsii** Baker · E:Himalayan Cotoneaster; G:Himalaya-Zwergmispel · ♄ e ♋ Z6 VI-VII; Ind.: Khasia Hills, nat. in NW-Eur.
- **splendens** Flinck & B. Hylmö · G:Glänzende Zwergmispel · ♄ d Z5; W-China
- **sternianus** (Turrill) Boom · G:Wintergrüne Zwergmispel · ♄ e ♋ Z7 ∧ V-VI; Tibet
- × **suecicus** G. Klotz (*C. conspicuus* × *C. dammeri*) · G:Schwedische Zwergmispel
- *thymifolius* Baker = Cotoneaster integrifolius
- **tomentosus** Lindl. · G:Filzige Zwergmispel · ♄ d ♋ Z5 IV-VI; Eur.: Ib, F, Ital-P, C-Eur., EC-Eur., Ba, RO, nat. in Sc
- **wardii** W.W. Sm. · G:Wards Zwergmispel · ♄ e ♋ Z7 ∧ VI; SE-Tibet
- × **watereri** Exell (*C. frigidus* × *C. rugosus* × *C. salicifolius*) · G:Waterers Zwergmispel · ♄ s Z6; cult.
- **some cultivars**
- *wheeleri* Exell = Cotoneaster × watereri
- *wheeleri* hort. = Cotoneaster buxifolius
- **zabelii** C.K. Schneid. · G:Zabels Zwergmispel · ♄ d Z5 V; C-China.

Cottendorfia Schult. f. -f- *Bromeliaceae* ·

1 sp.
- **florida** Schult. f. · ♃ Z10 ⊛; E-Braz.

Cotula L. -f- *Asteraceae* · c. 80 spp. ·
E:Buttonweed; F:Cotule; G:Laugenblume
- **barbata** DC. · ☉ Z8 VII-VIII; S-Afr.
- **coronopifolia** L. · E:Brass Buttons;
F:Cotule à feuilles de sénebière;
G:Krähenfuß-Laugenblume, Wasserknopf
· ♃ Z7 VII-VIII; Cape, Austr., NZ, S-Am.,
nat. in BrI, Fr, Sard., Ib, Sc
- *potentillina* (F. Muell.) Druce = Leptinella
potentillina
- *squalida* (Hook. f.) Hook. f. = Leptinella
squalida

Cotyledon L. -f- *Crassulaceae* · 10 spp.
- *arborescens* Mill. = Crassula arborescens
- **barbeyi** Schweinf. ex Baker · ♄ ⚊ Z10 ⚇;
Yemen, Eth., Somalia
- *breviflora* (Boiss.) Maire = Pistorinia
breviflora subsp. breviflora
- *cacalioides* L. f. = Tylecodon cacalioides
- *coruscans* Haw. = Cotyledon orbiculata
var. oblonga
- *flanaganii* Schönland & Baker f. =
Cotyledon orbiculata var. flanaganii
- *gracilis* Haw. = Cotyledon papillaris
- *hispanica* L. = Pistorinia hispanica var.
hispanica
- *horizontalis* Guss. = Umbilicus horizontalis
- *intermedia* (Boiss.) Bornm. = Umbilicus
horizontalis var. intermedius
- *jacobseniana* Poelln. = Cotyledon papill-
laris
- *libanotica* Labill. = Rosularia sempervivum subsp. libanotica
- *macrantha* Berger = Cotyledon orbiculata
var. orbiculata
- *oppositifolia* Ledeb. ex Nordm. =
Chiastophyllum oppositifolium
- **orbiculata** L.
- var. **flanaganii** (Schönland & Baker)
Toelken Z10 ⚇; Cape Prov.
- var. **oblonga** (Haw.) DC. · ⚊ Z10 ⚇;
S-Afr. (Cape Prov.)
- var. **orbiculata** · E:Pig's Ears; G:Sch-
weinsohr · ♄ ⚊ Z10 ⚇ VII-VIII ⚘; S-Afr.,
Namibia, Angola, nat. in F, sp.
- *pachyphytum* Baker = Pachyphytum
bracteosum
- **papillaris** L. f. · ♄ ♄ ⚊ e Z10 ⚇ VII-VIII;
Cape
- *pendulina* DC. = Umbilicus rupestris

- *pistorinia* Ortega = Pistorinia hispanica
var. hispanica
- *reticulata* L. f. = Tylecodon reticulatus
- *rupestris* Salisb. = Umbilicus rupestris
- *salzmannii* (Boiss. ex Emb.) H. Lindb. =
Pistorinia breviflora subsp. breviflora
- *simplicifolia* hort. = Chiastophyllum
oppositifolium
- *umbilicus-veneris* L. = Umbilicus erectus
- *undulata* Haw. = Cotyledon orbiculata
var. oblonga

Couma Aubl. -f- *Apocynaceae* · 5 spp. ·
E:Sorva Gum; G:Sorvagummi
- **macrocarpa** Barb. Rodr. · E:Sorva Gum;
G:Sorvagummi · ♄ ⚊ Ⓝ; Amazon.

Coumarouna Aubl. = Dipteryx
- *odorata* Aubl. = Dipteryx odorata

Coussapoa Aubl. -f- *Cecropiaceae* ·
46-50 spp.
- **dealbata** André · ♄ e Z9 ⊛; Braz.
- **microcarpa** (Schott) Rizzini · ♄ e Z9 ⊛;
Braz.
- *schottii* Miq. = Coussapoa microcarpa

Coutarea Aubl. -f- *Rubiaceae* · 7 spp.
- **latifolia** Moç. & Sessé · ♄ e Z10 ⊛; Mex.

Crambe L. -f- *Brassicaceae* · 20 spp. · E:Sea
Kale; F:Chou marin, Crambe; G:Meerkohl
- **abyssinica** Hochst. ex R.E. Fr. ·
E:Abyssinian Kale; G:Abessinischer
Meerkohl, Krambe · Ⓝ; ?TR, nat. in USA
- **cordifolia** Steven · G:Meerkohl · ♃ Z6 VI;
Cauc.
- **maritima** L. · E:Sea Kale; G:Küsten-
Meerkohl, Strandkohl · ♃ Z5 V-VI Ⓝ ▽;
Eur.* exc. Ital-P ; Cauc.; coasts, nat. in
EC-Eur.
- **tataria** Sebeók · E:Tatarian Breadplant;
G:Tatarischer Meerkohl · ♃ Z5 IV-VI;
Eur.: I, A, EC-Eur., Ba, E-Eur.; TR, Cauc.,
W-Sib.

Craniolaria L. -f- *Pedaliaceae* · 3 spp. ·
F:Martynia; G:Vogelkopf
- **annua** L. · G:Einjähriger Vogelkopf · ☉
VII-VIII; trop. S-Am.

Craspedia G. Forst. -f- *Asteraceae* · 8
(-15) spp. · E:Billy Buttons; F:Baguette
de tambour; G:Junggesellenknopf,
Trommelschlägel

- **alpina** Backh. ex Hook. f. · E:Alpine
  Billy Buttons · ⹃ Z8 ⌂; Austr.: Tasman.,
  Victoria
- **globosa** Benth. · E:Drumsticks; G:Trom-
  melschlägel · ⊙ ⹃ ✕ Z8 ⌂ VI-VIII; Austr.
- **incana** Allan · ⹃ Z8 ⌂; NZ
- *lanata* (Hook. f.) Allan = Craspedia
  alpina
- **minor** (Hook. f.) Allan · ⹃ Z8 ⌂; NZ
- **uniflora** G. Forst. · E:Bachelor's Button,
  Billy Buttons · ⊙ ⹃ ✕ Z8 ⌂ VI-VII;
  Austr.: S-Austr., Tasman.; NZ

Crassocephalum Moench -n- *Asteraceae* ·
24-30 spp.
- **biafrae** (Oliv. & Hiern) S. Moore · ⓦ Ⓝ;
  W-Afr.

Crassula L. -f- *Crassulaceae* · 195 spp. ·
E:Pigmyweed; F:Crassula; G:Dickblatt
- **alba** Forssk.
- **alstonii** Marloth · ⹃ ⵜ Z9 ⌂ X-XI; Cape
- **aquatica** (L.) Schönland · E:Pigmyweed;
  G:Wasser-Dickblatt · ⊙ ⌇ VII-IX; Eur.:
  Sc, BrI, C-Eur., EC-Eur., E-Eur.; Amur,
  Korea, Jap., Calif.
- **arborescens** (Mill.) Willd. · ⓗ ⓗ ⵜ e Z9
  ⌂; S-Afr.: Cape, Natal
- *arta* Schönland = Crassula deceptor
- **barbata** Thunb. · ⹃ ⵜ Z9 ⌂ I-V; Cape
- **barklyi** N.E. Br. · ⹃ ⵜ Z9 ⌂; Cape,
  Namibia
- **capitella** Thunb.
- subsp. **capitella** · ⊙ ⹃ ⓗ ⵜ e Z9 ⌂; Cape
- subsp. **thyrsiflora** (Thunb.) Toelken · ⊙
  ⹃ ⓗ ⵜ e Z9 ⌂; S-Afr.(Natal, Oranje Free
  State, Cape Prov.), SE-Namibia
- *cephalophora* Thunb. = Crassula nudicaulis
- **coccinea** L. · ⓗ ⓗ ⓗ ⵜ e Z9 ⌂ VII-VIII;
  S-Afr.
- **columnaris** Thunb. · ⊙ ⵜ Z9 ⌂ X-XI; Cape
- *conjuncta* N.E. Br. = Crassula perforata
- *cooperi* Regel = Crassula exilis subsp.
  cooperi
- **corallina** Thunb. · ⹃ Z9 ⌂ VII-VIII;
  Cape, Namibia
- **cordata** Thunb. · ⓗ e Z9 ⌂ VI-VIII;
  SE-Cape
- *corymbulosa* Link & Otto = Crassula
  capitella subsp. thyrsiflora
- **cultrata** L. · ⓗ e Z9 ⌂; Cape
- *curta* N.E. Br. = Crassula setulosa var.
  rubra
- *dasyphylla* Harv. = Crassula corallina

- **deceptor** Schönland & Baker f. · ⵜ Z8 ⌂
  X-XI; S-Afr. (Cape Prov.), Namibia
- *deceptrix* Schönland = Crassula deceptor
- *decipiens* N.E. Br. = Crassula tecta
- *deltoidea* auct. non Thunb. = Crassula
  plegmatoides
- **deltoidea** Thunb. · ⓗ e Z9 ⌂; S-Afr.
  (Cape Prov.), SE-Namibia
- **dichotoma** L. · ⊙ Z9 ⌂ VII-VIII; Cape
- **exilis** Harv.
- subsp. **cooperi** (Regel) Toelken · ⹃ ⵜ Z9
  ⌂ III-V; Namibia, S-Afr. (Transvaal)
- subsp. **exilis** · ⊙ ⹃ ⵜ Z9 ⌂; Cape
- subsp. **sedifolia** (N.E. Br.) Toelken · ⹃ ⵜ
  △ △ Z8 ⌂ ⋀ VII-VIII; Cape
- *falcata* J.C. Wendl. = Crassula perfoliata
  var. minor
- **helmsii** (Kirk) Cockayne · E:New
  Zealand Pigmyweed; F:Cockayne;
  G:Nadelkraut-Dickblatt, Nadelkraut · ⹃
  Z9 ⌂ VIII-IX; Austr., NZ, nat. in BrI
- **hemisphaerica** Thunb. · ⹃ ⵜ Z9 ⌂;
  Namibia
- *impressa* N.E. Br. = Crassula schmidtii
- × **justi-corderoyi** H. Jacobsen & Poelln.
  (*C. expansa subsp. fragilis × C. perfoliata
  var. minor*) · ⹃ Z9 ⌂; cult.
- **lactea** Sol. ex Aiton · ⓗ ⵜ e Z9 ⌂ XII-III;
  S-Afr.: E-Cape, Natal, Transvaal
- *marginalis* Aiton = Crassula pellucida
  subsp. marginalis
- *marnieriana* (H. Huber) H. Jacobsen =
  Crassula rupestris subsp. marnieriana
- **mesembryanthemopsis** Dinter · ⹃ ⵜ Z9
  ⌂; Namibia
- **mesembryanthoides** (Haw.) D. Dietr. ·
  ⓗ ⵜ ⵟ Z9 ⌂; SE-Cape
- *milfordiae* Byles = Crassula setulosa var.
  rubra
- **multicava** Lem. · ⓗ ⵜ e Z9 ⌂ IV-VII;
  S-Afr.: Natal, Transvaal
- **muscosa** L. · E:Toy Cypress · ⓗ ⵜ e Z9 ⌂
  II-III; Namibia
- **nudicaulis** L. · ⹃ ⵜ Z9 ⌂; S-Afr.: Cape,
  Orange Free State, Namibia
- *obliqua* Aiton = Crassula ovata
- *obvallata* L. = Crassula nudicaulis
- **orbicularis** L. · ⹃ ⵜ Z9 ⌂ II-III; S-Afr.:
  Cape, Natal
- **ovata** (Mill.) Druce · E:Baby Jade, Jade
  Plant; G:Jadestrauch · ⓗ ⵜ Z9 ⌂ IV-VII;
  S-Afr.: Cape, Natal
- **pellucida** L.
- subsp. **marginalis** (Aiton) Toelken · ⹃ ⵜ
  Z9 ⌂; S-Afr.

- subsp. **pellucida** · ♃ ♆ Z9 Ⓚ; Cape
- **perfoliata** L. · E:Propeller Plant; G:Propellerpflanze
- var. *falcata* (J.C. Wendl.) Toelken = Crassula perfoliata var. minor
- var. **minor** (Haw.) G.D. Rowley · ♄ ♆ Z9 Ⓚ; S-Afr. (Cape Prov.)
- var. **perfoliata** · ♄ ♆ Z9 Ⓚ; S-Afr.: Cape, Natal
- **perforata** Thunb. · ♃ ♆ Z9 Ⓚ; Cape
- *perfossa* Lam. = Crassula perforata
- **plegmatoides** H. Friedrich · ♃ Z9 Ⓚ; Cape, Namibia
- *portulacea* Lam. = Crassula ovata
- *pseudolycopodioides* Dinter & Schinz = Crassula muscosa
- **pyramidalis** Thunb. · ⊙ ♆ Z9 Ⓚ; Cape
- *quadrifida* Baker = Crassula multicava
- *recurva* (Hook. f.) Ostenf. = Crassula helmsii
- *recurva* N.E. Br. = Crassula alba
- *rosularis* Haw. = Crassula orbicularis
- **rupestris** Thunb.
- subsp. **marnieriana** (H. Huber & H. Jacobsen) Toelken · ♃ ♆ Z9 Ⓚ; S-Afr. (Cape Prov.)
- subsp. **rupestris** · ♃ ♆ Z9 Ⓚ IV-V; Cape
- **schmidtii** Regel · ♃ ♆ Z9 Ⓚ IV-VIII; Namibia, S-Afr.
- *sedifolia* N.E. Br. = Crassula exilis subsp. sedifolia
- *sedoides* Mill. = Crassula orbicularis
- **setulosa** Harv.
- var. *curta* (N.E. Br.) Schönland = Crassula setulosa var. rubra
- var. **rubra** (N.E. Br.) G.D. Rowley · ♃ ♆ △ Z8 Ⓚ ∧; S-Afr.: Cape, Natal; Lesotho
- var. **setulosa** · ♃ ♆ Z9 Ⓚ; S-Afr.: Cape, Natal; Lesotho
- **socialis** Schönland · ♃ ♆ Z9 Ⓚ; SE-Cape
- **spathulata** Thunb. · ♃ ♆ Z9 Ⓚ IV-V; S-Afr.: SE-Cape, Natal
- **tecta** Thunb. · ♃ ♆ Z9 Ⓚ; W-Cape
- *teres* Marloth = Crassula barklyi
- **tetragona** L. · ♄ ♆ Z9 Ⓚ; E-Cape
- *thyrsiflora* Thunb. = Crassula capitella subsp. thyrsiflora
- **tillaea** Lest.-Garl. · E:Mossy Stonecrop; G:Moos-Dickblatt · ⊙ ♆ ~ Z9 V-IX; Eur.: Ib, Fr, Ital-P, Ba, BrI, C-Eur.; TR, NW-Afr., Libya
- *torquata* Baker f. = Crassula cultrata
- *trachysantha* (Eckl. & Zeyh.) Harv. = Crassula mesembryanthoides
- *turrita* Thunb. = Crassula capitella subsp. thyrsiflora

\+ **Crataegomespilus** Simon-Louis ex Bellair -f- *Rosaceae* · G:Bronvauxmispel; E:Bronvaux Medlar; F:Néflier de Bronvaux

- **dardarii** Simon-Louis ex Bellair (*Crataegus monogyna* × *Mespilus germanica*) · ♄ d Z6 V; cult.
- **potsdamensis** Bergann (*Crataegus laevigata 'Paul's Scarlet'* × *Mespilus germanica*) · ♄ d Z6 V; cult.

Crataegus L. -f- *Rosaceae* · 264 spp. · E:Hawthorn; F:Aubépine, Epine; G:Weißdorn

- **altaica** (Loudon) Lange · G:Altai-Weißdorn · ♄ d Z4 V; W-Sib.: Altai, C-As., Afgh.
- **aprica** Beadle · ♄ ♄ d Z5; USA: Va., SE
- **arkansana** Sarg. · ♄ d Z5; USA: NE
- **arnoldiana** Sarg. · ♄ d Z5 V; USA: NE
- **azarolus** L.
- var. **azarolus** · E:Azarole, Mediterranean Medlar; G:Azaroldorn, Welsche Mispel · ♄ d Z6 VII ⚕ Ⓝ; Eur.: Crete, nat. in sp., F, I, Sic.
- var. **sinaica** (Boiss.) Lange Z6; Sinai
- **calpodendron** (Ehrh.) Medik. · E:Pear Thorn; G:Filziger Weißdorn · ♄ ♄ d Z5 VI; Can.: Ont.; USA: NE, NCE, SE, SC, Kans.
- × *carrierei* Vauvel ex Carrière = Crataegus × lavallei 'Carrierei'
- × **celsiana** (Dum.-Cours.) Bosc (*C. crus-galli* × *C. pentagyna*) · ♄ ♄ d; cult.
- **chlorosarca** Maxim. · ♄ d V; Jap., Sakhal.
- **chrysocarpa** Ashe
- var. **chrysocarpa** · E:Bicknell's Thorn; G:Rundblättriger Weißdorn · ♄ ♄ d Z4 V; Can.: E, Sask.; USA: NE, NCE, NC, Rocky Mts., N.Mex.
- var. **phoenicea** E.J. Palmer · ♄ d Z5; E-Can.; USA: NE, NEC
- **coccinioides** Ashe · E:Kansas Hawthorn · ♄ ♄ d ♧ Z5 V; USA: Ill., Mo., Kans., Okla., Okla.
- **collina** Chapm. · ♄ d Z4 V; USA: Ne, NCE, Kans., Okla., SE
- **crus-galli** L. · E:Cockspur Thorn; F:Aubépine ergot de coq; G:Hahnensporn-Weißdorn · ♄ ♄ d Z5 V-VI; Can.: E; USA: NE, NCE, SC, SE, Fla., nat. in CZ
- *curvisepala* Lindm. = Crataegus rhipidophylla var. rhipidophylla

– **dahurica** Koehne ex C.K. Schneid. · ♄ d Z5 IV-V; E-Sib.
– × **dippeliana** Lange (*C. punctata* × *C. tanacetifolia*) · ♄ ♄ d Z5 VI; cult.
– **douglasii** Lindl. · E:Black Hawthorn; G:Oregon-Weißdorn · ♄ ♄ d Z5 V; Alaska, Can., USA: NW, Calif., Rocky Mts., NC, NCE
– **dsungarica** Zabel ex Lange · ♄ d Z5 V; E-Sib., N-China
– × **durobrivensis** Sarg. (*C. pruinosa* × *C.* × *subsphaericea*) · ♄ d Z5 V; USA: N.Y.
– **ellwangeriana** Sarg. · ♄ d Z5; E-USA
– **flava** Aiton · E:Summer Haw, Yellow Haw; G:Gelbfrüchtiger Weißdorn · ♄ ♄ d Z5 VI; USA: NE, SE, Fla.
– **fontanesiana** (Spach) Steud. · ♄ d Z6; USA: Pa.
– × **grignonensis** Mouill. (*C. crus-galli* × *C. pubescens*) · ♄ d Z5 V-VI; cult.
– **holmesiana** Ashe · E:Holmes' Hawthorn · ♄ ♄ d Z5 V; Can.: E; USA: NE, NCE
– **intricata** Lange · E:Thicket Hawthorn; G:Verworrener Weißdorn · ♄ d Z5 V; USA: NE, NCE, SE, Okla., nat. in RO
– **laciniata** Ucria · E:Oriental Thorn; G:Orientalischer Weißdorn · ♄ ♄ d ⚭ VI; Eur.: Ib, Ba, E-Eur.; Moroc., Alger., nat. in F
– **laevigata** (Poir.) DC. · E:May, Midland Hawthorn; F:Aubépine à deux styles; G:Gewöhnlicher Zweigriffeliger Weißdorn · ♄ ♄ d Z5 V ⚥ Ⓝ; Eur.*
– × **lavallei** Hérincq ex Lavallée (*C. crus-galli* × *C. pubescens* f. *stipulacea*) · E:Lavell Hawthorn; G:Lederblättriger Weißdorn · ♄ ♄ d ⚭ Z5 VI; cult.
– **'Carrierei'**
– × **macrocarpa** Hegetschw. (*C. laevigata* subsp. *laevigata* × *C. rhipidophylla*) · G:Großfrüchtiger Weißdorn · ♄ d V-VI; Eur.: Fr, I, C-Eur., Sc, PL, RO
– **maximowiczii** C.K. Schneid. · ♄ ♄ d Z5; E-Sib., Amur, Sakhal., Korea
– × **media** Bechst. (*C. laevigata* subsp. *laevigata* × *C. monogyna*) · G:Bastard-Weißdorn, Mittlerer Weißdorn · ♄ d V-VI; NW-Eur., C-Eur.
– **mollis** (Torr. & A. Gray) Scheele · E:Red Haw; G:Weichhaariger Weißdorn · ♄ d ⚭ Z5 VI; Can.: Ont.; USA: NC, NCE, SE, Okla.
– **monogyna** Jacq. · E:English Hawthorn, May; F:Aubépine monogyne;

G:Gewöhnlicher Eingriffeliger Weißdorn · ♄ ♄ d Z5 V-VI ⚥ Ⓝ; Eur.*, TR, Levant, N-Iraq, Cauc., N-Iran, NW-Afr.
– × **mordenensis** Boom (*C. laevigata* subsp. *laevigata* × *C. succulenta*) · ♄ ♄ d ⚭ Z5 V; cult.
– **nigra** Waldst. & Kit. · E:Hungarian Thorn; G:Schwarzfrüchtiger Weißdorn · ♄ ♄ d Z5 V ⚥; Eur.: Slova., H, Croatia, Bosn., AL, ? RO
– × **nitida** (Engelm.) Sarg. (*C. crus-galli* × *C. viridis*) · ♄ d ⚭ Z5 V; USA: NCE, Ark.
– **oliveriana** (Dum.-Cours.) Bosc · ♄ d Z6; W-As., SE-Eur.
– *orientalis* Pall. ex M. Bieb. = Crataegus laciniata
– *oxyacantha* auct. non L. = Crataegus laevigata
– **pedicellata** Sarg. · E:Scarlet Hawthorn; G:Scharlach-Weißdorn · ♄ ♄ d ⚭ Z5 V; Can.: E; USA: NE, NCE
– **pentagyna** Waldst. & Kit. ex Willd. · G:Fünfgriffeliger Weißdorn · ♄ ♄ d Z5 V ⚥; Eur.: EC-Eur., Ba, E-Eur.; TR, Cauc., N-Iran
– × **persimilis** Sarg. (*C. crus-galli* × *C. succulenta* var. *macracantha*) · G:Pflaumenblättriger Weißdorn · ♄ d Z5; USA (N.Y.)
– **'MacLeod'**
– 'Prunifolia' = Crataegus × persimilis 'MacLeod'
– **phaenopyrum** (L. f.) Medik. · E:Washington Thorn; G:Washington-Weißdorn · ♄ ♄ d Z5 V-VI; USA: NE, NCE, SE, Fla.
– **pinnatifida** Bunge
– var. **major** N.E. Br. · ♄ d Z6 Ⓝ; N-China
– var. **pilosa** C.K. Schneid. · ♄ d Z6; C-As., Korea
– var. **pinnatifida** · E:Chinese Haw; G:Fiederblatt-Weißdorn · ♄ d ⚭ Z6 V Ⓝ; Amur, Manch., Korea
– *populifolia* Walter = Crataegus phaenopyrum
– **pruinosa** H.L. Wendl. · E:Frosted Hawthorn; G:Bereifter Weißdorn · ♄ ♄ d ⚭ Z5 V; Can.: E; USA: NE, NCE, SE, Okla.
– × *prunifolia* Pers. = Crataegus × persimilis 'MacLeod'
– **pubescens** (Kunth) Steud. · ♄ d Z7; Mex.
– f. **stipulacea** (Loudon) Stapf · ♄ ♄ d Z7 V-VI; Mex.
– **punctata** Jacq. · E:Dotted Haw;

G:Punktierter Weißdorn · ♄ ♄ d ⚭ Z5 VI;
Can.: E; USA: NE, NCE, SE, Okla.
– **rhipidophylla** Gand. · G:Großkelchiger
Weißdorn
– var. **lindmannii** (Hrabětová) K.I. Chr. ·
G:Langkelch-Weißdorn, Lindmans
Weißdorn · ♄ d V; Eur.: Fr, C-Eur., Sc,
EC-Eur., E-Eur., RO
– var. **rhipidophylla** · G:Gewöhnlicher
Großkelchiger Weißdorn, Krummkelch-
Weißdorn · ♄ d V; Eur., TR, Cauc.
– **rivularis** Nutt. ex Torr. & A. Gray ·
E:River Hawthorn; G:Bach-Weißdorn · ♄
♄ d Z5 VI; USA: Rocky Mts., SW
– *rotundifolia* Lam. = Amelanchier ovalis
– *rotundifolia* Moench = Crataegus
chrysocarpa var. chrysocarpa
– **sanguinea** Pall. · G:Blut-Weißdorn · ♄ ♄
d Z4 V; Eur.: Russ.; W-Sib., E-Sib., C-As,
Mong., nat. in A, ? F
– **schraderiana** Ledeb. · ♄ d; GR, Crim
– **submollis** Sarg. · E:Quebec Hawthorn;
G:Quebec-Weißdorn · ♄ d Z5 VI; Can.: E;
USA: NE
– × **subsphaericea** Gand. (*C. monogyna* ×
C. rhipidophylla) · G:Verschiedenzähni-
ger Weißdorn · ♄ d; F, D +
– **succulenta** (Link) Schrad.
– var. **macracantha** (Lodd.) Eggl. Z4 V-VI;
SE-Can., USA. NE, NCE
– var. **succulenta** · E:Fleshy Hawthorn;
G:Saft-Weißdorn · ♄ d ⚭ Z5 V; Can.: E;
USA: NE, NCE, NC, Rocky Mts., SE, SW
– **tanacetifolia** (Lam.) Pers. · E:Tansy
Leaved Thorn; G:Rainfarn-Weißdorn · ♄
♄ d Z6; TR
– *tanacetifolia* auct. non (Lam.) Pers. =
Crataegus laciniata
– *tomentosa* Du Roi = Crataegus calpodendron
– *trilobata* (Labill.) Labill. = Malus trilobata
– **uniflora** Münchh. · E:Dwarf Hawthorn;
G:Einblütiger Weißdorn · ♄ d Z5 V-VI;
USA: NE, NCE, SC, SE, Fla.
– **viridis** L. · E:Green Hawthorn; G:Grüner
Weißdorn · ♄ d Z5 V-VI; USA: NE, NCE,
Kans., SC, SE, Fla.
– **wattiana** Hemsl. & Lace · ♄ d ⚭ Z5
V-VIII; C-As., Pakist.
– **wilsonii** Sarg. · ♄ ♄ d ⚭ Z6 V; C-China.

× **Crataemespilus** E.G. Camus -f-
Rosaceae · E:Haw Medlar; G:Weißdorn-
mispel
– **gillotii** Beck (*Crataegus monogyna*

× *Mespilus germanica*) · G:Gelappte
Weißdornmispel · ♄ d Z6 V-VI; cult.
– **grandiflora** (Sm.) E.G. Camus
(*Crataegus laevigata* subsp. *laevigata*
× *Mespilus germanica*) · G:Großblütige
Weißdornmispel · ♄ d Z6 V-VI; cult.

Crateva L. -f- *Capparaceae* · 6-9 spp. ·
E:Temple Plant; G:Tempelbaum
– **adansonii** DC. · ♄ d Z10 ⚘; trop. Afr.,
Ind., Sri Lanka, Burma, Malay. Arch.
– *religiosa* auct. non G. Forst. = Crateva
adansonii
– **religiosa** G. Forst. · E:Temple Plant;
G:Tempelbaum · ♄ ♄ d Z10 ⚘ Ⓝ; trop.
Afr., Madag., Ind., China, Malay. Pen.,
Austr.: Queensl.; Polyn.

× **Cremneria** Moran -f- *Crassulaceae*
– **mutabilis** (Deleuil ex E. Morren) Moran
(*Cremnophila linguifolia* × *Echeveria
carnicolor*) · ⚘ Z9 ⌂; cult.

Cremnophila Rose -f- *Crassulaceae* · 2 spp.
– **linguifolia** (Lem.) Moran · ⚘ ⚘ Z9 ⌂
III-V; Mex.
– **nutans** (Rose) Rose · ⚘ ⚘ Z9 ⌂ III; Mex.

Crepis L. -f- *Asteraceae* · c. 200 spp. ·
E:Hawk's Beard; F:Crépide, Crépis ;
G:Pippau
– **alpestris** (Jacq.) Tausch · G:Alpen-
Pippau · ⚘ VI-VIII; Eur.: F, I, C-Eur.,
Slova., Ba, RO; mts.
– **aurea** (L.) Cass. · E:Golden Hawk's
Beard; G:Gold-Pippau · ⚘ △ Z6 VI-VII;
Eur.: F, I, C-Eur., Ba; mts.
– **biennis** L. · E:Rough Hawk's Beard;
G:Wiesen-Pippau · ☉ Z6 V-VIII; Eur.*
– **bocconi** P.D. Sell · G:Berg-Pippau · ⚘
VI-VIII; Eur.: F, J, C-Eur., Slove.; Alp.
– **capillaris** (L.) Wallr. · E:Smooth Hawk's
Beard; G:Kleinköpfiger Pippau · ☉ Z6
VI-X; Eur.*
– **conyzifolia** (Gouan) A. Kern. ·
G:Großköpfiger Pippau · ⚘ Z6 VII-IX;
Eur.: Ib, Fr, C-Eur., EC-Eur., Ba, RO,
W-Russ.; mts.; TR, Cauc.
– **foetida** L. · G:Stinkender Pippau
– subsp. **foetida** · E:Stinking Hawk's Beard;
G:Gewöhnlicher Stinkender Pippau · ☉
VI-VIII; Eur.* exc. Sc; TR, Syr., Cyprus,
Cauc., Iran, C-As., Him.
– subsp. **rhoeadifolia** (M. Bieb.) Čelak. ·
G:Mohn-Pippau · ☉ VI-IX; Eur.: A,

EC-Eur., Ba, E-Eur.; TR, Syr., Cauc.,
N-Iran
- **froelichiana** DC. · G:Froelichs Pippau · ⳡ
V; Eur.: N-I; Alp.
- **incana** Sibth. & Sm. · E:Pink Dandelion ·
ⳡ △ Z8 VIII; S-GR
- **jacquinii** Tausch · G:Felsen-Pippau
- subsp. **jacquinii** · G:Gewöhnlicher
Felsen-Pippau · ⳡ △ Z5 VII-VIII; Eur.: I,
C-Eur., EC-Eur., Ba, RO; E-Alp., Carp.,
Balkan
- subsp. **kerneri** (Rech. f.) Merxm. ·
G:Kerners Felsen-Pippau · ⳡ Z5 VII-VIII;
Eur.: SE-Alp., NW-Ba
- *kerneri* Rech. f. = Crepis jacquinii subsp.
kerneri
- **mollis** (Jacq.) Asch. · E:Northern Hawk's
Beard; G:Gewöhnlicher Weichhaariger
Pippau · ⳡ VI-VIII; Eur.* exc. Sc, Ib
- **nicaeensis** Balb. · E:French Hawk's
Beard; G:Nizza-Pippau · ⊙ V-VI; Eur.: Ib,
Fr, Ital-P, Ba; Cauc., nat. in BrI, Sc, G,
EC-Eur., RO
- **paludosa** (L.) Moench · E:Marsh Hawk's
Beard; G:Sumpf-Pippau · ⳡ Z6 VI-VIII;
Eur.*, TR, Cauc., Sib.
- **pannonica** (Jacq.) K. Koch · G:Pan-
nonischer Pippau · ⊙ Z6 VI-VIII; Eur.: A,
EC-Eur., Ba, E-Eur.; TR, Cauc., NW-Iran
- **praemorsa** (L.) Walther · E:Leafless
Hawk's Beard; G:Abgebissener Pippau ·
ⳡ V-VI; Eur.* exc. BrI, Ib; Cauc., Sib.
- **pulchra** L. · E:Small-flowered Hawk's
Beard; G:Schöner Pippau · ⊙ V-VII; Eur.:
Ib, F, I, G, EC-Eur., Ba, RO, Crim; Moroc.,
Alger.
- **pygmaea** L. · G:Zwerg-Pippau · ⳡ △ Z6
VII-VIII; Eur.: sp., F, I, Sw; mts.
- **pyrenaica** (L.) Greuter · G:Pyrenäen-
Pippau, Schabenkraut-Pippau · ⳡ Z6
VI-VIII; Eur.: sp., F, I, C-Eur., Slove.; mts.
- **rhaetica** Hegetschw. · G:Rätischer
Pippau · ⳡ VII-VIII; Eur.: F, I, Sw, A; Alp.
- **rubra** L. · E:Pink Hawk's Beard;
F:Crépide rouge; G:Roter Pippau · ⊙ Z6
VI-VII; Eur.: S-I, Ba; W-TR, nat. in F
- **sancta** (L.) Babc. · G:Belgischer Pippau ·
ⳡ IV-V; Eur.: Ba, RO, Russ., nat. in Ib, F,
Ital-P, Sw
- **setosa** Haller f. · E:Bristly Hawk's Beard;
G:Borsten-Pippau · ⊙ VI-IX; Eur.: Fr,
C-Eur., Ital-P, EC-Eur., BA, RO, Crim; TR,
Cauc.
- **tectorum** L. · E:Narrow-leaf Hawk's
Beard; G:Dach-Pippau · ⊙ V-X; Eur.* exc.

BrI; Cauc., Sib.
- **terglouensis** (Hacq.) A. Kern. ·
G:Triglav-Pippau · ⳡ △ Z5 VII-VIII; Eur.:
C-Eur., I; E-Alp.
- **vesicaria** L. · G:Blasen-Pippau
- subsp. **taraxacifolia** (Thuill.) Thell. ·
E:Beaked Hawk's Beard; G:Löwenzahn-
Pippau · ⊙ V-VI; Eur.: Ib, BrI, I, Sw, G, A,
Slove., Croatia, Madeira; NW-Afr.
- *virens* L. = Crepis capillaris
- **zacintha** (L.) Babc. · E:Striped Hawk's
Beard · ⊙; Eur.: Ib, F, G, Ital-P, Ba, Crim;
TR, Syr., nat. in Sw, A

Crescentia L. -f- *Bignoniaceae* · 6 spp. ·
E:Calabash Tree; F:Calebassier;
G:Kalebassenbaum
- **cujete** L. · E:Calabash Tree; G:Kalebas-
senbaum · ♄ Z10 Ⓦ Ⓝ; S-Fla., Mex.,
W.Ind.

Crinitaria Cass. = Aster
- *linosyris* (L.) Less. = Aster linosyris

Crinodendron Molina -n- *Elaeocarpaceae* ·
4 spp. · E:Lantern Tree; F:Crinodendron;
G:Laternenbaum
- **hookerianum** Gay · E:Lantern Tree;
F:Arbre aux lanternes; G:Laternenbaum ·
♄ e Ⓚ V; Chile
- *lanceolatum* Miq. = Crinodendron
hookerianum
- **patagua** Molina · E:Lily-of-the-Valley
Tree; G:Maiglöckchenbaum · ♄ ♄ e Ⓚ
XI-II; Chile

Crinum L. -n- *Amaryllidaceae* · 101 sp. ·
E:Cape Lily; F:Crinum; G:Hakenlilie
- **abyssinicum** Hochst. ex A. Rich. · ⳡ Z9
Ⓚ; Eth.
- *amabile* Donn = Crinum asiaticum var.
asiaticum
- **asiaticum** L.
- var. **asiaticum** · E:Asiatic Poison Bulb;
G:Asiatische Hakenlilie, Giftlilie · ⳡ Z8
Ⓦ III-X ☀; Ind., Sri Lanka, trop. SE-As.,
Polyn.
- var. **pedunculatum** (R. Br.) Fosberg &
Sachet · G:Strand-Hakenlilie, Sumpf-
Hakenlilie · ⳡ Ⓚ VII-VIII; Austr.:
Queensl., N.S.Wales
- *augustum* Roxb. ex Ker-Gawl. = Crinum
asiaticum var. asiaticum
- **bulbispermum** (Burm. f.) Milne-Redh.
& Schweick. · E:Hardy Swamp Lily;

G:Orangefarbene Hakenlilie · ⁴ Z8 ⓚ ⋀
VII-VIII; S-Afr.
- *caffrum* Herb. = Crinum campanulatum
- **campanulatum** Herb. · G:Wasser-
Hakenlilie · ⁴ Z9 ⓚ VII-VIII; S-Afr.
- **erubescens** L. f. ex Aiton · ⁴ Z9 ⓦ
VII-VIII; trop. S-Am.
- *giganteum* Andrews = Crinum jagus
- × **herbertii** Sweet (*C. bulbispermum* × *C.
zeylanicum*) · ⁴ Z10; cult.
- **jagus** (J. Thomps.) Dandy · ⁴ ⓦ VI-VIII;
W-Afr., C-Afr., Sudan, Angola
- **lorifolium** Roxb. ex Ker-Gawl. · ⁴ Z10 ⓚ
VII-VIII; Ind.
- **macowanii** Baker · E:Pyjama Lily · ⁴ Z9
ⓚ X-XI; S-Afr.
- **moorei** Hook. f. · G:Busch-Hakenlilie · ⁴
Z8 ⓚ VII-VIII; S-Afr.: Natal
- **natans** Baker · ⁴ ≈ ⓦ; W-Afr.,
Cameroon, Ind.
- *pedunculatum* R. Br. = Crinum asiaticum
var. pedunculatum
- × **powellii** Baker (*C. bulbispermum* ×
C. moorei) · E:Crinum; G:Hakenlilie,
Kaplilie · ⁴ Z8 ⓚ`⋀ VII-IX; cult.
- *pratense* Herb. = Crinum lorifolium
- **purpurascens** Herb. · ⁴ ⌒ Z10 ⓦ I-XII;
W.Sudan, Sudan, Cameroon, Angola
- *scabrum* Herb. = Crinum zeylanicum
- *schmidtii* Regel = Crinum moorei
- *speciosum* L. f. = Cyrtanthus elatus
- **virgineum** Mart. · ⁴ ⓦ VI-VIII; S-Braz.
- **zeylanicum** (L.) L. · E:Milk and Wine
Lily, Poison Bulb · ⁴ Z10 ⓦ IV-V; trop.
Afr., trop. As.

Crithmum L. -n- *Apiaceae* · 1 sp. ·
E:Samphire; F:Perce-pierre; G:Meerfen-
chel
- **maritimum** L. · E:Rock Samphire, Sea
Fennel; G:Meer-Fenchel · ⁴ ⚱ Z7 VI-VIII
⚘ ⓝ; Eur.: Ib, Fr, Ital-P, Ba, Crim; TR,
Cauc., N-Afr., Canar., Madeira

Crocosmia Planch. -f- *Iridaceae* · 9 spp. ·
E:Montbretia; F:Montbretia; G:Mont-
bretie
- **aurea** (Pappe ex Hook.) Planch. ·
G:Reichblütige Gold-Montbretie · ⁴ Z8
ⓚ IV-V; E-Afr., S-Afr. (Cape, Natal)
- × **crocosmiiflora** (Lemoine) N.E. Br.
(*C. aurea* × *C. pottsii*) · E:Montbretia;
G:Garten-Montbretie · ⁴ ≈ Z7 ⋀ VII-IX;
cult.
- **many cultivars**

- **masoniorum** (L. Bolus) N.E. Br. · E:Giant
Montbretia; G:Masons Montbretie · ⁴ ≈
Z8 ⋀ VII-VIII; S-Afr. (Transkei)
- **some cultivars**
- **paniculata** (Klatt) Goldblatt · E:Aunt
Eliza; G:Hohe Montbretie · ⁴ Z8 ⓚ
VIII-IX; S-Afr.
- **pottsii** (Baker) N.E. Br. · E:Potts'
Montbretia; G:Potts' Montbretie · ⁴ Z8 ⋀
VIII; S-Afr.
- **Cultivars:**
- **many cultivars**

Crocus L. -m- *Iridaceae* · 88 spp. · E:Crocus;
F:Crocus; G:Krokus
- *albiflorus* Kit. = Crocus vernus subsp.
albiflorus
- **ancyrensis** (Herb.) Maw · E:Ankara
Crocus · ⁴ Z6 II-III ▽; TR
- **angustifolius** Weston · E:Cloth-of-Gold
Crocus · ⁴ Z4 III ▽; Cauc., Crim
- *balansae* J. Gay ex Baker = Crocus olivieri
subsp. balansae
- **banaticus** J. Gay · ⁴ Z4 IX-X ▽; Eur.:
Serb., RO, W-Russ
- **biflorus** Mill.
- subsp. **biflorus** · E:Scotch Crocus · ⁴ Z4
II-III ▽; Eur.: Ital-P, Ba, Russ.; TR, Cauc.,
N-Iraq, N-Iran
- subsp. *parkinsonii* Sabine = Crocus
biflorus subsp. biflorus
- *byzantinus* Ker-Gawl. = Crocus serotinus
subsp. salzmannii
- **cambessedesii** J. Gay · ⁴ Z8 ⓚ XI-III ▽;
Balear.
- **cancellatus** Herb. · ⁴ Z5 IX-XI ▽; S-TR,
Lebanon, N-Israel
- **candidus** E.D. Clarke · ⁴ Z7 ▽; NW-TR
- **chrysanthus** (Herb.) Herb. · E:Golden
Crocus; G:Kleiner Krokus · ⁴ Z4 II-IV ▽;
Eur.: Ba, RO; TR, nat. in CZ
- **many cultivars**
- *cilicius* Kotschy ex Baker = Crocus cancellatus
- *clusii* J. Gay = Crocus serotinus subsp.
clusii
- **corsicus** Vanucchi ex Maw · ⁴ Z7 IV ▽;
Cors
- **dalmaticus** Vis. · ⁴ Z7 II-III ▽; Eur.:
Croatia, Montenegro, N-AL. mts.
- **etruscus** Parl. · ⁴ Z6 III ▽; I (Toscana)
- **flavus** Weston · E:Yellow Crocus;
G:Gold-Krokus · ⁴ Z4 II-III ▽; Eur.: Ba,
RO, Crim; TR
- **fleischeri** J. Gay · ⁴ Z6 III ▽; TR

– **goulimyi** Turrill · ⁴ Z7 ▽; S-GR
(Areopolis)
– **hadriaticus** Herb. · ⁴ Z8 ⓐ ▽; GR
– **hyemalis** Boiss. & C.I. Blanche · ⁴ Z8
XI-XII ▽; Israel, Lebanon, Syr.
– **imperati** Ten. · ⁴ Z7 II-III ▽; W-I
– *iridiflorus* Heuff. ex Rchb. = Crocus
banaticus
– **korolkowii** Maw ex Regel · E:Celandine
Crocus · ⁴ Z6 III ▽; C-As., Afgh.,
N-Pakist.
– **kotschyanus** K. Koch · ⁴ Z5 IX-X ▽;
S-TR, Lebanon, Syr.
– **laevigatus** Bory & Chaub. · ⁴ Z7 X-II ▽;
Eur.: GR, Crete
– **longiflorus** Raf. · E:Italian Crocus · ⁴ Z5
X-XI ▽; Eur.: S-I, Sic., Malta
– × **luteus** Lam. (*C. angustifolius* × *C.
flavus*) · ⁴ Z4 III; cult.
– **medius** Balb. · ⁴ Z6 X-XI ▽; Eur.: SE-F,
NW-I
– **minimus** DC. · ⁴ Z8 III ▽; Cors, Sard.
– **niveus** Bowles · ⁴ Z6 X-XI ▽; S-GR
– **nudiflorus** Sm. · E:Autumn Crocus · ⁴ Z5
IX ▽; Eur.: sp., SW-F, nat. in BrI
– **ochroleucus** Boiss. & Gaill. · ⁴ Z5 ▽;
Syr.
– *odorus* Biv. = Crocus longiflorus
– **olivieri** J. Gay
– subsp. **balansae** (J. Gay ex Baker) B.
Mathew · ⁴ Z7 ▽; W-TR
– subsp. **olivieri** · ⁴ Z7 III ▽; Eur.: Ba, RO;
TR
– **pulchellus** Herb. · E:Hairy Crocus · ⁴ Z6
IX-XI ▽; GR, TR
– **reticulatus** Steven ex Adams · ⁴ Z8 II-III
▽; Eur.: NE-I, H, Ba, EC-Eur.; TR, Cauc.
– *salzmannii* J. Gay = Crocus serotinus
subsp. salzmannii
– **sativus** L. · E:Autumn Crocus, Saffron
Crocus; G:Echter Safran · ⁴ Z6 XI ⚘ ⚘
Ⓝ ▽; cult.
– var. *cashmirianus* Royle = Crocus sativus
– **scepusiensis** (Rehmann & Wol.) Borbás ex
Kulcz. = Crocus vernus
– **serotinus** Salisb. · E:Late Crocus
– subsp. **clusii** (J. Gay) B. Mathew · ⁴ Z6 X
▽; P, W-Sp.
– subsp. **salzmannii** (J. Gay) B. Mathew ·
⁴ Z6 IX-X ▽; Eur.: sp.; N-Afr.
– subsp. **serotinus** · ⁴ Z6 ▽; P
– **sieberi** J. Gay
– subsp. **atticus** (Boiss. & Orph.) B.
Mathew Z7 ▽; GR
– subsp. **sieberi** · E:Sieber's Crocus;

G:Siebers Krokus · ⁴ Z7 III ▽; Crete
– subsp. **sublimis** (Herb.) B. Mathew Z7
▽; S-Ba
– **speciosus** M. Bieb. · ⁴ Z4 IX-X ▽; TR,
Iran, Crim
– *susianus* Ker-Gawl. = Crocus angustifolius
– *suterianus* Herb. = Crocus olivieri subsp.
olivieri
– **tommasinianus** Herb. · E:Early Crocus;
G:Dalmatiner Krokus · ⁴ Z5 II-III ▽;
Eur.: H, Croatia, Bosn., YU, BG, nat. in
BrI, NL
– **vernus** (L.) Hill · E:Spring Crocus;
G:Frühlings-Krokus
– **many cultivars**
– subsp. **albiflorus** (Kit.) Asch. & Graebn. ·
G:Weißer Krokus · ⁴ Z4 II-IV ▽;
Eur.: sp., F, Ital-P, C-Eur., CZ, W-Ba; mts.
– **versicolor** Ker-Gawl. · ⁴ Z5 III-IV ▽;
Eur.: SE-F, NW-I
– **vitellinus** Wahlenb. · ⁴ Z8 I-II ▽;
Lebanon, W-Syr.
– *zonatus* J. Gay = Crocus kotschyanus

Crossandra Salisb. -f- *Acanthaceae* · c.
50 spp.
– **flava** Hook. · ⁴ Z10 ⓐ XII-VI; W-Afr.
– **infundibuliformis** (L.) Nees ·
E:Firecracker Flower · ♭ e Z10 ⓐ V-VIII;
Pakist., Ind., Sri Lanka, SE-As.
– **nilotica** Oliv. · ♭ e Z10 ⓐ V-VIII; Kenya,
Mozamb.
– **pungens** Lindau · ⁴ e Z10 ⓐ; E-Afr.
– **subacaulis** C.B. Clarke · ⁴ Z10 ⓐ VII-
VIII; E-Afr.
– *undulifolia* Salisb. = Crossandra
infundibuliformis

Crotalaria L. -f- *Fabaceae* · c. 600 spp. ·
E:Rattlebox; F:Crotalaria; G:Klapperhülse
– **agatiflora** Schweinf. · E:Canarybird
Bush; G:Vogelblume · ♭ ♭ Z9 ⓐ; E-Afr.,
NE-Afr.
– *anagyroides* Kunth = Crotalaria micans
– **capensis** Jacq. · G:Kap-Goldregen · ♭ ♭ e
Z9 ⓐ; S-Afr., Mozamb.
– **intermedia** Kotschy · ♭ Z9 ⓐ Ⓝ; trop.
Afr., nat. in N-Am.
– **juncea** L. · E:Sunhemp · ☉ Z9 ⓐ VIII-IX
Ⓝ; cult.
– **micans** Link · E:Caracas Rattlebox · ☉ Z9
ⓐ Ⓝ; trop. S-Am.
– **mucronata** Desv. · ⁴ Z9 ⓐ Ⓝ; Trop.,
Subtrop., Old World
– **retusa** L. · E:Devil Bean, Rattlebox · ☉

Z9 ⓐ VIII-IX Ⓝ; trop. Afr., S-As., nat. in trop. Am.
- **zanzibarica** Benth. · E:Curara Pea · ♄ Z9 ⓦ Ⓝ; E-Afr.

Croton L. -m- *Euphorbiaceae* · 1214 spp. · E:Croton; F:Croton; G:Kroton
- **cascarilla** (L.) L. · E:Wild Rosemary · ♄ ⓦ Ⓝ; Bahamas
- **eluteria** (L.) W. Wright · E:Cascarilla; G:Kaskarillabaum · ♄ ⓦ Ⓝ; W.Ind.
- *pictum* Lodd. = Codiaeum variegatum var. variegatum
- **tiglium** L. · E:Purging Croton; G:Krotonölbaum · ♄ e ⓦ ⚥ ⚙ Ⓝ; Ind., Sri Lanka, S-China, Phil., Molucca
- *variegatus* L. = Codiaeum variegatum var. variegatum

Crowea Sm. -f- *Rutaceae* · 3 spp.
- **angustifolia** Turcz. · ♄ e ⓚ III; W-Austr.
- **exalata** F. Muell. · E:Waxflower · ♄ e ⓚ; Austr.
- **saligna** Andrews · E:Willow-leaved Crowea; G:Rote Wachsblume · ♄ e ⓚ VII; Austr.: N.S.Wales

Crucianella L. -f- *Rubiaceae* · 31 sp. · E:Crosswort; F:Crucianelle; G:Kreuzblatt
- **angustifolia** L. · E:Narrow-leaved Crosswort · ⊙ Z8; Eur.: Ib, F, Ital-P, Ba, E-Eur.; TR, SW-As., NW-Afr.

Cruciata Mill. -f- *Rubiaceae* · 8 spp. · F:Croisette, Gaillet croisette; G:Kreuzlabkraut
- **glabra** (L.) Ehrend. · E:Slender Crosswort; G:Kahles Kreuzlabkraut · ⅃ IV-VI; Eur.* exc. BrI, Sc; W-As., Him., N-Afr.
- **laevipes** Opiz · E:Crosswort; G:Gewöhnliches Kreuzlabkraut · ⅃ IV-VI; Eur.*, TR, Cauc., Iran, W-Him., nat. in N-Am.
- **pedemontana** (Bellardi) Ehrend. · E:Piedmont Bedstraw; G:Piemonteser Kreuzlabkraut · ⊙ IV-V; Eur.* exc. BrI, Sc; TR, Lebanon, Cauc., Iran, Afgh., Pakist., Moroc.

Crupina (Pers.) DC. -f- *Asteraceae* · 3 spp. · F:Crupina; G:Schlupfsame
- **vulgaris** Cass. · E:Common Crupina, False Saw Wort; G:Gewöhnlicher Schlupfsame · ⊙ Z8 V-VII; Eur.: Ib, Fr, Ital-P, Ba, Sw, EC-Eur., E-Eur.; TR, Cauc., NW-Iran, Moroc.

Cryosophila Blume -f- *Arecaceae* · 10 spp. · F:Palmier à racines épineuses; G:Stechwurzelpalme
- **nana** (Humb., Bonpl. & Kunth) Blume · ♄ e ⓦ; Mex.
- **warscewiczii** (H. Wendl.) Bartlett · ♄ ♄ e ⓦ; Nicar., Costa Rica, Panama

Crypsis Aiton -f- *Poaceae* · 8-10 spp. · F:Crypsis piquant; G:Dorngras
- **aculeata** (L.) Aiton · E:Sharp-leaved Grass; G:Starres Dorngras · ⊙ ∽ VII-IX; Eur.: Fr, Ital-P, A, EC-Eur., Ba, E-Eur.; Cyprus, Palest., Iraq, Cauc., Iran, W-Sib., C-As., Mong., China, N-Afr.
- **alopecuroides** (Piller & Mitterp.) Schrad. · E:Fairy Foxtail; G:Fuchsschwanz-Sumpfgras · ⊙ ∽ VI-IX; Eur.: P, F, Ital-P, A, EC-Eur., Ba, E-Eur.; TR, Cyprus, Syr., Iraq, Cauc., Iran, W-Sib., C-As., N-Afr.
- **schoenoides** (L.) Lam. · E:Swamp Pricklegrass; G:Knopfbinsen-Sumpfgras · ⊙ ∽ VII-IX; Eur.: Ib, F, Ital-P, A, EC-Eur., Ba, E-Eur.; TR, Cauc., Iran, Afgh., Pakist., NW-Ind., W-Sib., C-As., Tibet, Mong., China: Sinkiang; N-Afr., trop. Afr., Madag., nat. in N-Am.

Cryptanthus Otto & A. Dietr. -m- *Bromeliaceae* · 50 spp. · E:Earth Star; F:Cryptanthus; G:Erdstern, Versteckblume
- **acaulis** (Lindl.) Beer · E:Green Earthstar, Starfish Plant; G:Grüner Erdstern · ⅃ Z9 ⓦ; Braz.
- var. *bromelioides* (Otto & A. Dietr.) Mez = Cryptanthus bromelioides
- **bahianus** L.B. Sm. · ⅃ Z9 ⓦ; Braz.
- **beuckeri** E. Morren · ⅃ Z9 ⓦ; Braz.
- **bivittatus** (Hook.) Regel · G:Erdstern; E:Earth Star · ⅃ Z9 ⓦ; E-Braz.
- **bromelioides** Otto & A. Dietr. · ⅃ Z9 ⓦ; Braz.
- **fosterianus** L.B. Sm. · ⅃ Z9 ⓦ; NW-Braz.
- **lacerdae** Antoine · ⅃ Z9 ⓦ; ? E-Braz.
- *praetextus* E. Morren ex Baker = Cryptanthus acaulis
- *sinuosus* L.B. Sm. = Cryptanthus acaulis
- *undulatus* Otto & A. Dietr. = Cryptanthus acaulis
- **zonatus** (Vis.) Beer · E:Zebra Plant; G:Zebra-Erdstern · ⅃ Z9 ⓦ; Braz.

Cryptocarya R. Br. -f- *Lauraceae* · c.
200 spp.
- **moschata** Nees & Mart. · E:Brazilian
  Nutmeg; G:Amerikanische Muskatnuss ·
  ♄ Z10 🌢 Ⓝ; Braz.

Cryptochilus Wall. -m- *Orchidaceae* · 4 spp.
- **luteus** Lindl. · ⵜ Z10 🌢 V-VI ▽ ✳; Ind.:
  Sikkim
- **sanguineus** Wall. · ⵜ Z10 🌢 V-VI ▽ ✳;
  Nepal, Sikkim

Cryptocoryne Fisch. ex Wydler -f-
Araceae · 53 spp. · E:Water Trumpet;
F:Trompette d'eau; G:Wassertrompete
- **affinis** N.E. Br. ex Hook. f. · ⵜ ≈ Z10
  🌢; Malay. Pen.
- **albida** R. Parker · G:Weißlicher Wasserkelch · ⵜ ≈ Z10 🌢; Burma
- *balansae* Gagnep. = Cryptocoryne
  crispatula var. balansae
- **beckettii** Thwaites ex Trimen ·
  E:Beckett's Water Trumpet; G:Becketts
  Wasserkelch · ⵜ ≈ Z10 🌢; Sri Lanka
- *blassii* de Wit = Cryptocoryne cordata var.
  cordata
- **ciliata** (Roxb.) Fisch. ex Wydler ·
  G:Bewimperter Wasserkelch · ⵜ ≈ Z10
  🌢; Pakist., Ind., Thail., Malay. Arch.,
  N.Guinea
- **cordata** Griff. · E:Swamp Coleus;
  G:Herzblättriger Wasserkelch
- var. **cordata** · ⵜ ≈ Z10 🌢; Thail.
- var. **grabowskii** (Engl.) N. Jacobsen · ⵜ
  ≈ Z10 🌢; Thail., Malay. Pen.
- var. **zonata** (de Wit) N. Jacobsen · ⵜ ⌒
  ≈ Z10 🌢; N-Kalimantan
- **crispatula** Engl. · G:Grasblättriger
  Wasserkelch
- var. **balansae** (Gagnep.) N. Jacobsen ·
  G:Kalk-Wasserkelch · ⵜ ≈ Z10 🌢;
  N-Vietn., Thail.
- **fusca** de Wit · G:Rotbrauner Wassrkelch ·
  ⵜ ≈ Z10 🌢; Kalimantan
- *grabowskii* Engl. = Cryptocoryne cordata
  var. grabowskii
- *grandis* Ridl. = Cryptocoryne cordata var.
  grabowskii
- **griffithii** Schott · G:Griffiths Wasserkelch · ⵜ Z10 🌢; Malay. Pen.,
  Sumat.
- *haerteliana* H. Jacobsen ex Milkuhn =
  Cryptocoryne affinis
- ×*lucens* de Wit = Cryptocoryne × willisii
- *lutea* Alston = Cryptocoryne walkeri

- **nevillii** Trimen ex Hook. f. · G:Nevills
  Wasserkelch · ⵜ ⌒ Z10 🌢; Sri Lanka
- **parva** de Wit · G:Kleiner Wasserkelch · ⵜ
  ⌒ ≈ Z10 🌢; Sri Lanka
- ×**purpurea** Ridl. (*C. cordata* × *C.
  griffithii*) · G:Purpur-Wasserkelch · ⵜ ⌒
  ≈ Z10 🌢; Malay. Pen.
- **retrospiralis** (Roxb.) Kunth ·
  G:Gedrehter Wasserkelch · ⵜ ⌒ ≈
  Z10 🌢; Ind., Mynamar
- *siamensis* Gagnep. = Cryptocoryne
  cordata var. cordata
- *somphongsii* hort. = Cryptocoryne
  crispatula var. balansae
- **thwaitesii** Schott · G:Thwaites Wasserkelch · ⵜ ≈ Z10 🌢; Sri Lanka
- *tortilis* de Wit = Cryptocoryne fusca
- **undulata** A. Wendt · G:Gewellter
  Wasserkelch · ⵜ ⌒ ≈ Z10 🌢; Sri
  Lanka
- **versteegii** Engl. · G:Versteegs Wasserkelch · ⵜ ⌒ Z10 🌢; N.Guinea
- **walkeri** Schott · G:Walkers Wasserkelch ·
  ⵜ ≈ Z10 🌢; Sri Lanka
- **wendtii** de Wit · G:Wendts Wasserkelch ·
  ⵜ ⌒ ≈ Z10 🌢; Sri Lanka
- *willisii* Engl. ex Baum = Cryptocoryne
  undulata
- ×**willisii** Reitz (*C. parva* × *C. walkeri*) ·
  G:Willis Wasserkelch · ⵜ ≈ Z10 🌢; Sri
  Lanka
- *zonata* de Wit = Cryptocoryne cordata
  var. zonata

Cryptogramma R. Br. -f- *Adiantaceae* ·
9 spp. · E:Parsley Fern; F:Alosure crépue;
G:Rollfarn
- **acrostichoides** R. Br. ex Hook. ·
  E:American Rockbrake; G:Amerika-
  nischer Rollfarn · ⵜ Z4; Alaska, Can.;
  USA: NW, Rocky Mts., Calif., SW, Mich.;
  Mex. (Baja Calif.), Kamchat.
- **crispa** (L.) R. Br. ex Hook. · E:European
  Parsley Fern; G:Krauser Rollfarn · ⵜ △
  Z6 VIII-IX ▽; Eur.*, TR, Cauc., W-Sib.
- var. *acrostichioides* (R. Br. ex Hook.) C.B.
  Clarke = Cryptogramma acrostichoides
- **stelleri** (S.G. Gmel.) Prantl · E:Fragile
  Rockbrake; G:Zierlicher Rollfarn · ⵜ △
  Z3; Alaska, Can., USA: NE, NCE, Rocky
  Mts., NW; Sib., Him., Jap.

Cryptomeria D. Don -f- *Taxodiaceae* · 1 sp. ·
E:Japanese Cedar; F:Cèdre du Japon;
G:Sicheltanne

- *fortunei* Hooibr. = Cryptomeria japonica var. sinensis
- **japonica** (Thunb. ex L. f.) D. Don · E:Japanese Cedar; G:Japanische Sicheltanne
- **some cultivars**
- var. **japonica** · F:Cryptoméria du Japon; G:Gewöhnliche Japanische Sicheltanne · ♄ e Z6 Ⓝ; Jap.
- var. **sinensis** Siebold ex Siebold & Zucc. · G:Chinesische Sicheltanne · Z6; S-China
- *kawaii* Hayata = Cryptomeria japonica var. sinensis

Cryptophoranthus Barb. Rodr. = Acianthera
- *maculata* (N.E. Br.) Rolfe = Pleurothallis maculata

Cryptostegia R. Br. -f- *Asclepiadaceae* · 2 spp.
- **grandiflora** (Roxb.) R. Br. · E:Rubber Vine · ♃ e ⌇ Ⓦ VII; trop. Afr., Mascarene Is., cult. Ind.

Cryptotaenia DC. -f- *Apiaceae* · 4 spp. · E:Honewort
- **canadensis** (L.) DC. · E:Honewort, White Chervil · ♃; N-Am., Jap., nat. in A.

Ctenanthe Eichler -f- *Marantaceae* · 15 spp. · F:Ctenanthe; G:Kammmaranthe
- **amabilis** (E. Morren) H. Kenn. & Nicolson · ♃ Z10 Ⓦ; Braz.
- **compressa** (A. Dietr.) Eichler · G:Grüne Kammmarante · ♃ Z10 Ⓦ; Braz.
- var. *luschnathiana* (Regel & Körn.) K. Schum. = Ctenanthe compressa
- **kummeriana** (E. Morren) Eichler · G:Gestreifte Kammmarante · ♃ Z10 Ⓦ; Braz.
- **lubbersiana** (E. Morren) Eichler ex Petersen · G:Bamburanta, Marmorierte Kammmarante · ♃ Z10 Ⓦ; Braz.
- **oppenheimiana** (E. Morren) K. Schum. · E:Never Never Plant; G:Hohe Kammmarante · ♃ Z10 Ⓦ; Braz.
- **setosa** (Roscoe) Eichler · G:Borstige Kammmarante · ♃ Z10 Ⓦ; Braz.

Cucubalus L. -m- *Caryophyllaceae* · 1 sp. · E:Berry Catchfly; F:Cucubale; G:Taubenkropf
- **baccifer** L. · E:Berry Catchfly; G:Taubenkropf · ♃ Z7 VII-IX; Eur.* exc. Sc; TR, Levant, Cauc., Iran, W-Sib., Amur, C-As., Him., China, Jap.

Cucumeropsis Naudin -f- *Cucurbitaceae* · 1 sp.
- **mannii** Naudin Z10 Ⓦ Ⓝ; trop. Afr.

Cucumis L. -m- *Cucurbitaceae* · 32 spp. · E:Cucumber, Melon; F:Concombre, Melon; G:Gurke, Melone
- **anguria** L. · E:West Indian Gherkin; G:Anguria-Gurke · ⊙ ⌇ ⇝ ♣ Z10 Ⓚ Ⓝ; trop. Afr., nat. in trop. Am., Austr.: Queensl.
- *citrullus* L. = Citrullus lanatus var. lanatus
- *colocynthis* L. = Citrullus colocynthis
- **dipsaceus** Ehrenb. ex Spach · E:Hedgehog Gourd; G:Igel-Gurke · ⊙ ⇝ ♣ Z10 Ⓚ; Arab.
- **melo** L. · E:Melon; G:Melone
- **Cantalupensis Group** · E:Cantaloupe; G:Gewöhnliche Zucker-Melone, Kantalupe
- **Chito Group** · E:Mango Melon, Melon Apple, Orange Melon; G:Apfel-Melone, Orangen-Melone
- **Conomon Group** · E:Oriental Pickling Melon; G:Gemüse-Melone · Ⓚ ▭
- **Dudaim Group** · E:Queen Anne's Pocket Melon, Stink Melon; G:Zier-Melone · Ⓚ ▭
- **Flexuosus Group** · E:Serpent Melon, Snake Melon; G:Armenische Melone · Ⓚ ▭
- **Inodorus Group** · E:Honeydew Melon, Winter Melon; G:Honig-Melone · Ⓚ ▭
- **Reticulatus Group** · E:Musk Melon, Netted Melon; G:Netz-Melone
- subsp. **agrestis** (Naudin) Greb. Z10
- var. **momordica** (Roxb.) Duthie & J.B. Fuller · E:Phoot, Snap Melon; G:Schnapp-Melone · Z10
- subsp. **melo** · E:Musk Melon, Sweet Melon; G:Zucker-Melone · ⊙ ⇝ Z10 Ⓚ ▭ VI-VIII Ⓝ; ? trop. Afr., ? W-As.; cult.
- **metuliferus** E. Mey. ex Schrad. · E:Horny Cucumber; G:Horn-Gurke, Kiwano · ⊙ ⇝ Z10 Ⓚ Ⓝ; trop. Afr., S-Afr., cult. NZ
- **myriocarpus** Naudin · E:Gooseberry Gourd · ⊙ Z10; S-Afr.
- **sativus** L. · E:Cucumber, Gherkin; G:Gurke · ⊙ ⌇ ⇝ Z10 VI-IX ⚕ Ⓝ; Ind.
- **many cultivars**

Cucurbita L. -f- *Cucurbitaceae* · 27 (13) spp. · E:Marrow, Pumpkin; F:Courge;

G:Kürbis
- **argyrosperma** C. Huber · E:Cushaw, Silver-seed Gourd; G:Ayote · ⊙ ⤳ Z9 Ⓝ; Mex., Guat.; cult.
- *citrullus* L. = Citrullus lanatus var. lanatus
- **ficifolia** C.D. Bouché · E:Fig Leaved Gourd; G:Feigenblatt-Kürbis · ⊙ ⑂ ⤳ ⚭ Z10 Ⓝ; N-Am.; cult.
- *hispida* Thunb. ex Murray = Benincasa hispida
- **maxima** Duchesne ex Lam. · E:Pumpkin; G:Riesen-Kürbis, Speise-Kürbis · ⊙ ⤳ ⚭ Z9 VI-IX ⚥ Ⓝ; S-Am.; cult.
- *mixta* Pangalo = Cucurbita argyrosperma
- **moschata** (Duchesne ex Lam.) Duchesne ex Poir. · E:Cushaw, Squash; G:Bisam-Kürbis, Moschus-Kürbis · ⊙ ⤳ Z10 VI-IX Ⓝ; C-Am; cult.
- **pepo** L. · E:Courgette, Vegetable Marrow, Zucchini; G:Gemüse-Kürbis, Patisson, Zucchini · ⊙ ⤳ ⚭ Z10 VI-VIII ⚥ Ⓝ; ? C-Am., ?SE-USA; cult.
- *siceraria* Molina = Lagenaria siceraria

Cudrania Trécul -f- *Moraceae* · 5-8 spp. · E:Silkworm Thorn; F:Epine du ver à soie; G:Seidenwurmdorn
- **tricuspidata** (Carrière) Bureau ex Lavallée · E:Chinese Silkworm Thorn; G:Seidenwurmdorn · ♄ d Z7 Ⓝ; Korea, C-China

Cuitlauzina Lex. -f- *Orchidaceae* · 5 spp.
- **convallarioides** (Schltr.) Dressler & N.H. Williams · ⑂ Z10 ⑳ IX-XI ▽ ✳; Costa Rica
- **pulchella** (Bateman ex Lindl.) Dressler & N.H. Williams · E:Lily-of-the-Valley Orchid · ⑂ D Z10 ⑳ II-IV ▽ ✳; Guat.

Culcasia P. Beauv. -f- *Araceae* · 24 spp.
- **mannii** (Hook. f.) Engl. · ⑂ ⑳; Cameroon

Culcita C. Presl -f- *Dicksoniaceae* · 3 spp.
- **macrocarpa** C. Presl · ⑂ e Z9 ⑳ Ⓝ ▽; Ib., Azor., Madeira, Canar.

Cumarinia Buxb. -f- *Cactaceae* · 1 sp.
- **odorata** (Boed.) Buxb. · ⚘ Z9 ⑳ ▽ ✳; Mex.: Tamaulipas, San Luis Potosí

Cuminum L. -n- *Apiaceae* · 4 spp. · E:Cumin; F:Cumin; G:Kreuzkümmel
- **cyminum** L. · E:Cumin; G:Kreuzkümmel

· ⊙ ⚥ Ⓝ; C-As., N-Afr., Eth., cult., nat. in sp., F, Sic..

Cunninghamia R. Br. -f- *Taxodiaceae* · 2 spp. · E:China Fir; F:Sapin chinois; G:Spießtanne
- *kawakamii* Hayata = Cunninghamia konishii
- **konishii** Hayata · E:Formosan Cunninghamia; G:Taiwan-Spießtanne · ♄ e Z9 ⑳; Taiwan
- **lanceolata** (Lamb.) Hook. · E:China Fir; G:Chinesische Spießtanne · ♄ e Z7 ⑳ ∧ Ⓝ; C-China, SE-China
- *sinensis* R. Br. = Cunninghamia lanceolata

Cunonia L. -f- *Cunoniaceae* · 16 spp. · E:Red Alder; F:Arbre à cuiller; G:Löffelbaum
- **capensis** L. · E:African Red Alder; G:Kap-Löffelbaum · ♄ ♄ e ⑳; S-Afr.

Cuphea P. Browne -f- *Lythraceae* · 260 spp. · E:Waxweed; F:Cuphéa, Fleur-cigarette; G:Köcherblümchen
- **hyssopifolia** Kunth · E:False Heather; G:Falsches Heidekraut · ♄ Z10 ⑳ III-X; Mex., Guat.
- **ignea** A. DC. · E:Mexican Cigar Plant; G:Zigarettenblümchen · ♄ ♄ e Z9 ⑳ V-IX; Mex.
- **lanceolata** W.T. Aiton
- var. **lanceolata** · ⊙ Z10; C-Mex.
- var. **silenoides** (Nees) Regel · ⊙ Z10 VII-IX; C-Mex.
- **llavea** La Llave & Lex.
- var. **llavea** · ♄ e Z10 ⑳; Mex.
- var. **miniata** Brongn. & Koehne · ♄ e Z10 ⑳ VII-IX; Mex.
- **micropetala** Kunth · ♄ e Z10 ⑳ XI-III; Mex.
- *miniata* Brongn. = Cuphea llavea var. miniata
- *platycentra* Lem. = Cuphea ignea
- **procumbens** Cav. · ⊙ Z10 VI-X; Mex.

× *Cupressocyparis* Dallim. = × Cuprocyparis
- *leylandii* (Dallim. & A.B. Jacks.) Dallim. = × Cuprocyparis leylandii

Cupressus L. -f- *Cupressaceae* · 16 spp. · E:Cypress; F:Cyprès; G:Zypresse
- **arizonica** Greene · E:Arizona Cypress; G:Arizona-Zypresse
- var. **arizonica** · E:Rough Barked Arizona Cypress; G:Gewöhnliche

Arizona-Zypresse · ♄ e Z7 Ⓝ; USA: SC,
SW, Calif.; N-Mex., Baja Calif.
- var. **glabra** (Sudw.) Little · E:Smooth
Arizona Cypress; G:Glattrindige Arizona-
Zypresse · ♄ Z7; Ariz.
- **bakeri** Jeps. · E:Baker's Cypress, Modoc
Cypress; G:Modoc-Zypresse · ♄ e Z7;
N-Calif.
- subsp. *matthewsi* C.B. Wolf = Cupressus
bakeri
- **cashmeriana** Royle ex Carr · E:Kashmir
Cypress; G:Kaschmir-Zypresse · ♄ e Ⓖ; ?
Him.
- **duclouxiana** Hickel ex A. Camus ·
E:Ducloux Cypress; G:Yunnan-Zypresse ·
♄ e Z8 Ⓖ; W-China
- **funebris** Endl. · E:Chinese Weeping
Cypress, Mourning Cypress; G:Tränen-
Zypresse, Trauer-Zypresse · ♄ e Z8 Ⓖ
⚘ Ⓝ; China: Yunnan, Hupeh, Kiangsi,
Anwhei, Tschekiang
- *glabra* Sudw. = Cupressus arizonica var.
glabra
- *glandulosa* Hook. ex Gordon = Cupressus
macnabiana
- **goveniana** Gordon ex Lindl. · E:Gowen
Cypress; G:Kalifornische Zypresse
- var. **goveniana** · G:Gewöhnliche Kalifornische Zypresse, Mendocino-Zypresse · ♄
♄ e Z8 Ⓖ; Calif.
- var. *pygmaea* Lemmon = Cupressus
goveniana var. goveniana
- *horizontalis* Mill. = Cupressus sempervirens
- *lambertiana* Hort. ex Carrière = Cupressus macrocarpa
- *lawsoniana* A. Murray bis = Chamaecyparis lawsoniana
- **lusitanica**
- var. **lusitanica** · G:Gewöhnliche
Mexikanische Zypresse · ♄ e Z9 Ⓖ Ⓝ;
Mex., Guat.
- **macnabiana** A. Murray bis · E:Macnab
Cypress; G:Harzige Kalifornische
Zypresse · ♄ ♄ e Z8 Ⓖ; N-Calif.
- **macrocarpa** Hartw. ex Gordon ·
E:Monterey Cypress; G:Monterey-
Zypresse · ♄ e Z8 Ⓖ Ⓝ; Calif. (Monterey
County)
- *nootkatensis* D. Don = Xanthocyparis
nootkatensis
- *obtusa* (Siebold & Zucc.) F. Muell. =
Chamaecyparis obtusa var. obtusa
- *pisifera* (Siebold & Zucc.) F. Muell. =
Chamaecyparis pisifera

- **sempervirens** L. · E:Italian Cypress;
G:Echte Zypresse, Italienische Zypresse,
Mittelmeer-Zypresse · ♄ e Z8 Ⓖ II-IV
⚥ ; Eur.: GR, Crete; TR, Cyprus, Palest.,
N-Iran, NW-Afr., nat. in Eur.: Ib, F, Sw,
Ital-P, Ba, Crim
- var. *horizontalis* (Mill.) Gordon = Cupres-
sus sempervirens
- *thyoides* L. = Chamaecyparis thyoides
- **torulosa** D. Don ex Lamb. · E:Himalayan
Cypress, West Himalayan Cypress;
G:Bhutan-Zypresse, Himalaya-Zypresse ·
♄ e Z8 Ⓖ Ⓝ; W-Him., W-China
- var. *cashmeriana* (Carrière) A.H. Kent =
Cupressus cashmeriana

× **Cuprocyparis** Farjon -f- Cupressaceae ·
3 spp. · E:Leyland Cypress; F:Cyprès
bâtard, Cyprès de Leyland; G:Bastardzyp-
resse (Xanthocyparis × Cupressus)
- **leylandii** (Dallim. & A.B. Jacks.) Farjon
(Xanthocyparis nootkatensis × Cupressus
macrocarpa) · E:Leyland Cypress;
G:Bastardzypresse, Leylandzypresse · ♄ e
Z7; cult.
- **some cultivars**

Curculigo Gaertn. -f- Hypoxidaceae · c. 15
(-35) spp. · E:Palm Grass; G:Rüssellilie
- **capitulata** (Lour.) Kuntze · E:Palm
Grass · ♃ Z10 Ⓦ; trop. As., Austr.;
N.Terr., Queensl., N.S.Wales
- **latifolia** Dryand. · E:Palm Grass;
G:Palmgras · ♃ Z10 Ⓦ; Burma, Malay.
Arch.
- *recurvata* Dryand. = Curculigo capitulata

Curcuma L. -f- Zingiberaceae · 83 spp. ·
F:Curcuma, Turmeric; G:Safranwurz
- **amada** Roxb. · G:Mangoingwer · ♃ Z10
Ⓦ ⚥ Ⓝ; Ind. (Bengal., Konkan)
- **angustifolia** Roxb. · E:Bombay
Arrowroot, Indian Arrowroot; G:Indische
Safranwurz · ♃ Z10 Ⓦ Ⓝ; Him., Ind.
- **aromatica** Salisb. · E:Wild Turmeric;
G:Würzige Safranwurz · ♃ Z10 Ⓦ ⚥ Ⓝ; ?
Ind.
- **caesia** Roxb. · ♃ Z10 Ⓦ Ⓝ; Ind.:
Bengalen
- *domestica* Valeton = Curcuma longa
- **heyneana** Valeton & Zijp · E:Zedgary · ♃
Z10 Ⓦ Ⓝ; Java
- **longa** L. · E:Turmeric; G:Gelbwurzel,
Kurkuma · ♃ Z10 Ⓦ ⚥ Ⓝ; ? Ind., ? SE-As.
- *mangga* Valeton & Zijp = Curcuma

zedoaria
- *pallida* Lour. = Curcuma zedoaria
- *purpurascens* Blume = Curcuma longa
- **roscoeana** Wall. · ⁴ Z₁o ⓜ VIII-X;
  Burma
- *xanthorrhiza* Roxb. = Curcuma zedoaria
- **zedoaria** (Christm.) Roscoe · E:Zedoary;
  G:Zitwer · ⁴ Z₁o ⓜ ⚥ ⓝ; cult., nat. in
  SE-As.

Currania Copel. = Gymnocarpium
- *dryopteris* (L.) Wherry = Gymnocarpium
  dryopteris
- *robertiana* (Hoffm.) Wherry = Gymnocarpium robertianum

Curtisia Aiton -f- *Cornaceae* · 1 sp.
- **dentata** (Burm. f.) C.A. Sm. · E:Assegai ·
  ♄ e Z9 ⓚ ⓝ; S-Afr.

Curtonus N.E. Br. = Crocosmia
- *paniculatus* (Klatt) N.E. Br. = Crocosmia
  paniculata

Cuscuta L. -f- *Convolvulaceae* · c. 150 spp. ·
  E:Dodder; F:Cuscute; G:Seide
- **approximata** Bab. · E:Alfalfa Dodder · ⊙
  ⚥; Eur.: Ib, Fr, Me, Ital-P, Ba, E-Eur.; TR,
  Levant, , Iran, C-As., Him., China
- *australis* R. Br. = Cuscuta scandens
- **campestris** Yunck. · E:Field Dodder;
  G:Nordamerikanische Seide · ⊙ ⚥ VII-X;
  USA*, nat. in Eur.* exc. Sc; Cauc., C-As.
- **epilinum** Weihe · E:Flax Dodder;
  G:Flachs-Seide · ⊙ ⚥ VI-VIII; Palest.,
  SW-As., nat. in Eur., N-Afr.
- **epithymum** (L.) L. · G:Thymian-Seide
- subsp. **epithymum** · E:Clover Dodder;
  G:Gewöhnliche Thymian-Seide · ⊙ ⚥
  VII-VIII ⚥; Eur.*, TR, Syr., Palest., Cauc.,
  Iran, W-Sib., C-As., NW-Afr., Libya, nat.
  in N-Am.
- subsp. **trifolii** (Bab. & Gibson) Berher ·
  G:Klee-Seide · ⊙ ⚥ VII-VIII; Eur.: BrI, Sc,
  Fr, Ital-P, C-Eur., H; Cauc., nat. in N-Am.,
  Chile, Austr., NZ
- **europaea** L. · G:Europäische Seide,
  Nessel-Seide
- subsp. **europaea** · E:European Dodder;
  G:Gewöhnliche Nessel-Seide · ⊙ ⚥
  VI-VIII; Eur.*, TR, Syr., Palest., Cauc.,
  Iran, W-Sib., E-Sib., Amur, Sakhal. C-As.,
  Mong., Him., Alger., Libya
- subsp. **nefrens** (Fr.) O. Schwarz ·
  G:Hecken-Seide · ⊙ ⚥; G, PL +

- subsp. **viciae** (Engelm.) Ganesch. ·
  G:Wicken-Seide · ⚥; G, H, PL +
- **gronovii** Willd. ex Roem. & Schult. ·
  E:Swamp-Dodder; G:Weiden-Seide · ⊙ ⚥
  VIII-IX; N-Am., nat. in Fr, I, G, EC-Eur.,
  Ba, W-Russ.
- **lupuliformis** Krock. · E:Hop Dodder;
  G:Pappel-Seide · ⊙ ⚥ VII-IX; Eur.: NL,
  C-Eur., EC-Eur., Ba, E-Eur.; Cauc.,
  W-Sib., E-Sib., C-As., Mong, China
- **odorata** Ruiz & Pav. · ⁴ ⚥ ⓜ; Peru
- **reflexa** Roxb. · E:Giant Dodder · ⊙ ⚥
  X-XII; Him., Ind., Sri Lanka, Malay. Pen.
- **scandens** Brot. · G:Gewöhnliche
  Südliche Seide · ⊙ ⚥ VI-IX; Eur.: Ib, Fr,
  G, Ital-P, Ba, E-Eur.; TR
- **suaveolens** Ser. · E:Lucerne Dodder;
  G:Chilenische Seide · ⊙ ⚥ VIII-IX; S-Am.,
  nat. in Eur.: Ib, Fr, Ital-P, C-Eur., EC-Eur.,
  E-Eur.; USA, Afr., Austr.
- *trifolii* = Cuscuta epithymum subsp.
  trifolii

Cusparia Humb. ex R. Br. = Angostura
- *febrifuga* Humb. ex DC. = Angostura
  trifoliata

Cussonia Thunb. -f- *Araliaceae* · 20 spp. ·
  E:Cabbage Tree; F:Cussonia
- **paniculata** Eckl. & Zeyh. · E:Cabbage
  Tree; G:Kohlpalme · ♄ ᛲ e Z₁o ⓚ; S-Afr.
- **spicata** Thunb. · E:Common Cabbage
  Tree; G:Kipersolbaum · ♄ ᛲ e Z₁o ⓚ;
  S-Afr.: Cape, Natal, Transvaal; Komor.

Cyamopsis DC. -f- *Fabaceae* · 3 spp. ·
  E:Cluster Bean; G:Büschelbohne
- *psoraloides* DC. = Cyamopsis
  tetragonoloba
- **tetragonoloba** (L.) Taub. · E:Cluster
  Bean, Guar; G:Büschelbohne · ⊙ Z₁o ⓜ
  ⚥ ⓝ; cult.

Cyananthus Wall. ex Benth. -m-
  Campanulaceae · c. 25 spp. · E:Trailing
  Bellflower; F:Cyananthus; G:Blauröhre
- **delavayi** Franch. · G:Delavays Blauröhre · ⁴ Z₇ ⓚ ∧ VII-VIII; Yunnan
- **formosus** Diels · ⁴ Z₇ ⓚ ∧ VII-VIII;
  Yunnan
- **forrestii** Diels · G:Forrests Blauröhre · ⁴
  △ ⓚ ∧ IX; Yunnan
- **lobatus** Wall. ex Benth. · G:Gelappte
  Blauröhre · ⁴ △ Z₇ ∧ VII-X; NW-Him.
- **microphyllus** Edgew. · G:Kleinblättrige

Blauröhre · ⁴ △ Z7 ∧ VII-VIII; N-Ind.,
Nepal
– **sherriffii** Cowan · G:Sherriffs Blauröhre ·
⁴ △ Z8 ⓚ ∧ VII-VIII; Bhutan, S-Tibet

Cyanastrum Oliv. -n- *Cyanastraceae* ·
7 spp.
– **cordifolium** Oliv. · ⁴ Z10 ⓦ; Cameroon,
Gabon

Cyanopsis Cass. -f- *Asteraceae* · 1 sp.
– **muricata** Dostál · E:Morocco Knapweed ·
⊙; S-Sp. (Prov. Malaga)

Cyanotis D. Don -f- *Commelinaceae* ·
49 spp. · E:Teddy Bear Vine; G:Teddy-
bärpflanze
– **beddomei** (Hook. f.) Erhardt, Götz &
Seybold · E:Teddy Bear Plant; G:Ted-
dybärpflanze · ⁴ ⚥ ⤳ Z9 ⓦ ⓚ; Ind.
(Malabar Coast)
– *kewensis* C.B. Clarke = Cyanotis beddomei
– **somaliensis** C.B. Clarke · E:Pussy Ears;
G:Katzenohren · ⁴ ⚥ ⤳ Z9 ⓦ ⓚ;
Somalia

Cyanus Mill. = Centaurea
– *arvensis* Moench = Centaurea cyanus
– *montanus* (L.) Hill = Centaurea montana
– *triumfettii* (All.) Á. Löve & D. Löve =
Centaurea triumfettii subsp. triumfettii

Cyathea Sm. -f- *Cyatheaceae* · 643 spp. ·
E:Tree Fern; F:Fougère arborescente;
G:Becherfarn
– **arborea** (L.) Sm. · E:West Indian Tree
Fern · ♄ e Z9 ⓚ ▽ ✱; W.Ind., Venez.,
N-Col.
– **australis** (R. Br.) Domin · E:Rough Tree
Fern; G:Rauer Becherfarn · ♄ e Z9 ⓚ ▽
✱; Austr.: Queensl., N.S.Wales, Victoria,
Tasman.
– **capensis** (L. f.) Sm. · G:Kap-Becherfarn ·
♄ Z9 ⓦ ▽ ✱; S.Afr., S-Braz.
– **cooperi** (F. Muell.) Domin · E:Lacy Tree
Fern; G:Schuppen-Becherfarn · ♄ e Z9 ⓚ
▽ ✱; Austr.: Queensl., N.S.Wales
– **dealbata** G. Forst. · E:Silver King Fern;
G:Ponga, Silber-Becherfarn · ♄ e Z9 ⓚ ▽
✱; NZ, Norfolk Is.
– **insignis** D.C. Eaton · ♄ Z9 ⓚ ▽ ✱;
Jamaica
– **medullaris** (G. Forst.) Sw. · E:Sago Fern;
G:Schwarzer Becherfarn · ♄ e Z9 ⓚ ▽

✱; Austr.: Victoria, Tasman.; NZ, Pacific
Is.
– **spinulosa** Wall. · ♄ e Z9 ⓚ ▽ ✱; Ind.,
Burma
– *tricolor* Colenso = Cyathea dealbata

Cyathodes Labill. -f- *Epacridaceae* · c.
15 spp.
– *acerosa* (Gaertn.) R. Br. = Cyathodes
juniperina
– **colensoi** (Hook. f.) Hook. f. · ♄ e ⤳ ⓚ
ⓚ II-IV; NZ
– **juniperina** (J.R. Forst. & G. Forst.)
Druce · ♄ e ⓚ; Austr., Tasman., NZ

Cybistax Mart. ex Meisn. -f- *Bignoniaceae* ·
3 spp.
– **donnell-smithii** (Rose) Seibert · ♄ ⓦ;
Mex., Guat.

Cycas L. -f- *Cycadaceae* · 20 spp. · E:Cycad;
F:Cycas; G:Sagopalmfarn
– **cairnsiana** F. Muell. · E:Mount Surprise
Sago · ♄ e Z10 ⓚ ▽ ✱; Austr.
– **circinalis** L. · E:False Sago; G:Eingeroll-
ter Sagopalmfarn · ♄ e Z10 ⓦ ▽ ✱;
S-Ind., Sri Lanka, Malay. Pen., Phil.,
Taiwan
– **media** R. Br. · E:Australian Nut Palm · ♄
e Z10 ⓦ ▽ ✱; Austr.: Queensl.
– **revoluta** Thunb. · E:Sago Cycas;
G:Japanischer Sagopalmfarn · ♄ e Z10 ⓦ
⚘ ▽ ✱; S-Jap., Ryukyu Is.
– **rumphii** Miq. · ♄ e Z10 ⓦ ▽ ✱; Malay.
Pen., N.Guinea, Polyn.
– **siamensis** Miq. · E:Thai Sago;
G:Thailändischer Sagopalmfarn · ♄ e Z10
ⓦ ▽ ✱; Burma, Thail.

Cyclamen L. -n- *Primulaceae* · 19 spp. ·
E:Persian Violet, Sowbread; F:Cyclamen,
Pain de pourceau; G:Alpenveilchen
– *abchasicum* (Medw.) Kolak. = Cyclamen
coum subsp. coum
– **africanum** Boiss. & Reut. · ⁴ Z9 ⓚ
VIII-X ▽ ✱; Alger., Tun.
– × *atkinsii* T. Moore = Cyclamen coum
subsp. coum
– **balearicum** Willk. · E:Majorca Cyclamen;
G:Balearen-Alpenveilchen · ⁴ Z8 ⓚ ▽
✱; S-F, Balear.
– **cilicium** Boiss. & Heldr. · ⁴ Z7 ⓚ ∧ IX-X
▽ ✱; S-TR
– var. *intaminatum* Meikle = Cyclamen
intaminatum

- **coum** Mill.
- subsp. **caucasicum** (K. Koch) O. Schwarz
  Z6 ▽ ✳; Cauc., NE-TR, N-Iran
- subsp. **coum** · E:Eastern Sowbread;
  F:Cyclamen de Kos; G:Vorfrühlings-
  Alpenveilchen · ⁴ △ Z6 II-IV ▽ ✳; Eur.:
  BG, Crim; TR, Cauc.
- subsp. *hiemale* (Hildebr.) O. Schwarz =
  Cyclamen coum subsp. coum
- **creticum** (Dörfl.) Hildebr. · ⁴ Z8 ⓚ III-V
  ▽ ✳; Crete
- **cyprium** Kotschy · ⁴ Z9 ⓚ IX-X ▽ ✳;
  Cyprus
- *europaeum* Albov = Cyclamen purpurascens subsp. ponticum
- var. *caucasicum* (K. Koch) O. Schwarz =
  Cyclamen coum subsp. caucasicum
- *fatrense* Halda & Soják = Cyclamen
  purpurascens subsp. purpurascens
- **graecum** Link · E:Greek Cyclamen;
  G:Griechisches Alpenveilchen · ⁴ Z9 ⓚ
  IX-X ▽ ✳; Eur.: GR, Crete; TR, Cyprus
- **hederifolium** Aiton · E:Ivy-leaved Cyclamen; F:Cyclamen de Naples; G:Herbst-
  Alpenveilchen, Neapolitanisches
  Alpenveilchen · ⁴ Z6 IX-XI ▽ ✳; Eur.: Fr,
  Ital-P, Sw, Ba; TR, nat. in BrI
- subsp. *creticum* (Dörfl.) O. Schwarz =
  Cyclamen creticum
- *hiemale* Hildebr. = Cyclamen coum subsp.
  coum
- *ibericum* T. Moore = Cyclamen coum
  subsp. caucasicum
- **intaminatum** (Meikle) Grey-Wilson · ⁴
  Z8 ⓚ IX-X ▽ ✳; TR
- *latifolium* Sibth. & Sm. = Cyclamen
  persicum
- **libanoticum** Hildebr. · ⁴ Z9 ⓚ IX-XI ▽
  ✳; TR: Amanus; Lebanon
- *linearifolium* DC. = Cyclamen hederifolium
- **mirabile** Hildebr. · ⁴ Z7 △ IX-X ▽ ✳; TR
  (Prov. Avelin)
- *neapolitanum* Boiss. = Cyclamen cyprium
- *neapolitanum* Duby = Cyclamen
  africanum
- *neapolitanum* Ten. = Cyclamen hederifolium
- *orbiculatum* Mill. = Cyclamen coum
  subsp. coum
- **parviflorum** Pobed. · ⁴ Z7 II-IV ▽ ✳;
  NE-TR
- **persicum** Mill. · E:Florist's Cyclamen;
  G:Zimmer-Alpenveilchen · ⁴ Z9 ⓚ ⓓ
  VIII-IV ✹ ▽ ✳; Eur.: Crete; TR, Levant,

Tun., Alger.
- **many cultivars**
- *ponticum* (Albov) Pobed. = Cyclamen
  purpurascens subsp. ponticum
- **pseudibericum** Hildebr. · ⁴ Z7 ⓐ △ II
  ▽ ✳; TR: Taurus, Amanus
- *pseudograecum* Hildebr. = Cyclamen
  graecum
- **purpurascens** Mill.
- subsp. **ponticum** (Albov) Grey-Wilson ·
  ⁴ Z6 VII-IX ▽ ✳; Cauc.
- subsp. **purpurascens** · F:Cyclamen
  d'Europe; G:Sommer-Alpenveilchen,
  Wildes Alpenveilchen · ⁴ △ Z6 VII-IX ⚥
  ✹ ▽ ✳; Eur.: Fr, C-Eur., EC-Eur., Ital-P,
  Slove., Croatia, Bosn., Serb., nat. in
  E-Eur.
- **repandum** Sm.
- subsp. **peloponnesiacum** Grey-Wilson
  Z7 ▽ ✳; GR (Peloponnese)
- subsp. **repandum** · F:Cyclamen de
  Naples; G:Efeublättriges Alpenveilchen ·
  ⁴ Z7 ⓐ △ III-V ▽ ✳; Eur.: Fr, Ital-P, Ba
- subsp. **rhodense** (Meikle) Grey-Wilson
  Z7 ▽ ✳; GR (Rhodos)
- var. *creticum* Dörfl. = Cyclamen creticum
- **rohlfsianum** Asch. · ⁴ Z9 ⓚ IX-X ▽ ✳;
  Libya (Cyrenaica)
- **trochopteranthum** O. Schwarz · ⁴ Z7 ▽
  ✳; SW-TR
- *vernale* Mill. = Cyclamen persicum
- *vernale* O. Schwarz = Cyclamen repandum subsp. repandum
- × **wellensiekii** Ietsw. (*C. cyprium* × *C.
  libanoticum*) · ⁴ ⓚ; cult.

Cyclanthera Schrad. -f- *Cucurbitaceae* ·
15 spp.
- **brachybotrys** (Poepp. & Endl.) Cogn. · ☉
  ↝ Z10 Ⓝ; Ecuad., Peru
- **brachystachya** (Ser.) Cogn. · ☉ ⚥ ↝ ⚬
  Z10; S-Am.; And.
- *explodens* Naudin = Cyclanthera brachystachya
- **pedata** (L.) Schrad. · E:Stuffing Gourd;
  G:Korila · ☉ ⚥ ⚬ Z10 Ⓝ; cult.

Cyclanthus Poit. -m- *Cyclanthaceae* ·
2 spp. · F:Cyclanthus; G:Scheibenblume
- **bipartitus** Poit. · ⁴ Z10 ⓐ; C-Am., trop.
  S-Am.
- *cristatus* Klotzsch = Cyclanthus bipartitus

Cycloloma Moq. -f- *Chenopodiaceae* · 1 sp.
- **atriplicifolia** (Spreng.) Coult. · E:Winged

Pigweed · ☉; Can.: Man.; USA* exc. NE, NW, Calif., nat. in F, I, EC-Eur., AL

Cyclophorus Desv. = Pyrrosia
- *adnascens* (Sw.) Desv. = Pyrrosia lanceolata
- *hastatus* (Thunb.) C. Chr. = Pyrrosia hastata
- *lingua* (Thunb.) Desv. = Pyrrosia lingua

Cyclosorus Link -m- *Thelypteridaceae* · c. 775 spp.
- **arcuatus** (Poir.) Alston
- var. **arcuatus** · ♃ Z10 Ⓦ; trop. S-Am.
- var. **lepidus** (T. Moore) Alston · ♃ Z10 Ⓦ; trop. S-Am.
- *dentatus* (Forssk.) Ching = Christella dentata

Cycnoches Lindl. -n- *Orchidaceae* · 31 sp. · E:Swan Orchid; F:Cycnoches; G:Schwanenorchis
- **aureum** Lindl. & Paxton Z10 Ⓦ ▽ *; C-Am.
- **chlorochilon** Klotzsch · ♃ Z10 Ⓦ V-VI ▽ *; Col., Venez., Guyan.
- **egertonianum** Bateman · ♃ Z10 Ⓦ VIII-IX ▽ *; C-Am.
- **loddigesii** Lindl. · ♃ Z10 Ⓦ VIII-X ▽ *; Col., Venez., Surinam, Braz.
- **maculatum** Lindl. · ♃ Z10 Ⓦ VIII-IX ▽ *; Mex., Venez.
- **pentadactylon** Lindl. · ♃ Z10 Ⓦ III-VI ▽ *; Braz.
- **ventricosum** Bateman · ♃ Z10 Ⓦ ▽ *; Mex., C-Am.

× **Cycnodes** hort. -f- *Orchidaceae* (*Cycnoches* × *Mormodes*)

Cydonia Mill. -f- *Rosaceae* · 1 sp. · E:Quince; F:Cognassier; G:Quitte
- *japonica* (Thunb.) Pers. = Chaenomeles japonica var. japonica
- *japonica* Loisel. = Chaenomeles speciosa
- *maulei* T. Moore = Chaenomeles japonica var. japonica
- **oblonga** Mill. · E:Quince; G:Echte Quitte
- var. **maliformis** (Mill.) C.K. Schneid. · G:Apfel-Quitte · Z5
- var. **oblonga** · F:Cognassier commun; G:Birnen-Quitte · ♄ ♄ d ♣ Z5 V-VI ⚕ Ⓝ; Cauc., N-Iran, nat. in Eur.* exc. BrI; TR, Syr., Arab., C-As., Afgh., Pakist., N-Afr.
- *sinensis* (Dum.-Cours.) Thouin = Pseudocydonia sinensis
- *vulgaris* Pers. = Cydonia oblonga var. oblonga

Cylindrophyllum Schwantes -n- *Aizoaceae* · 5 spp. · G:Walzenblatt
- **calamiforme** (L.) Schwantes · G:Röhren-Walzenblatt · ♃ ♆ Z9 Ⓚ; Cape

Cylindropuntia (Engelm.) F.M. Knuth = Opuntia
- *cylindrica* (Lam.) F.M. Knuth = Opuntia cylindrica
- *leptocaulis* (DC.) F.M. Knuth = Opuntia leptocaulis
- *tunicata* (Lehm.) F.M. Knuth = Opuntia tunicata

Cymbalaria Hill -f- *Scrophulariaceae* · 10 spp. · E:Toadflax; F:Cymbalaire; G:Zimbelkraut
- **aequitriloba** (Viv.) A. Chev. · ♃ ⤳ △ Z7 ∧ VI-VIII; Eur.: Balear., Cors, Sard., I (Is. north to Giglio)
- **hepaticifolia** (Poir.) Wettst. · E:Corsican Toadflax · ♃ ⤳ △ Z8 ∧ V-IX; Cors
- **muralis** G. Gaertn., B. Mey. & Scherb. · E:Ivy-leaved Toadflax, Pennywort; F:Ruine de Rome; G:Mauer-Zimbelkraut · ♃ ⤳ △ Z3 VI-IX ⚕; Eur.: Sw, I, Sic., Slove., Croatia, Bosn., Montenegro, nat. in BrI, Sc, Fr, C-Eur., EC-Eur., EC-Eur., Ib
- **pallida** (Ten.) Wettst. · E:Italian Toadflax; G:Bleiches Zimbelkraut · ♃ ⤳ △ Z7 ∧ VI-IX; Eur.: C-I; mts., nat. in BrI
- **pilosa** (Jacq.) L.H. Bailey · G:Behaartes Zimbelkraut · ♃ ⤳ △ Z4 VI-IX; Eur.: Sard., I

Cymbidium Sw. -n- *Orchidaceae* · 59 spp. · F:Cymbidium; G:Kahnorchis
- **aloifolium** (L.) Sw. · ♃ Z9 Ⓚ VII-VIII ▽ *; Him., S-Ind., S-China, Burma, Sumat., Java
- **canaliculatum** R. Br. · ♃ Z9 Ⓚ IV-V ▽ *; Austr.: North Terr., Queensl., N.S.Wales
- **devonianum** Lindl. & Paxton · ♃ Z9 Ⓚ V-VI ▽ *; Sikkim
- **eburneum** Lindl. · ♃ Z9 Ⓚ IV-V ▽ *; N-Ind., Burma
- **elegans** Lindl. · ♃ Z9 Ⓚ ▽ *; Him., W-China
- **ensifolium** (L.) Sw. · ♃ Z9 Ⓦ V ▽ *; China, Ind.: Assam

- **floribundum** Lindl. · ⁴ Z9 ⓚ ▽ ✳;
China, SE-Tibet, Jap.
- *grandiflorum* Griff. = Cymbidium
hookerianum
- **hookerianum** Rchb. f. · ⁴ Z9 ⓚ I-II ▽
✳; Nepal, Bhutan, Tibet
- **insigne** Rolfe · ⁴ Z9 ⓚ III-V ▽ ✳;
Vietn.: Annam
- **iridioides** D. Don · ⁴ Z9 ⓚ IX-X ▽ ✳;
N-Ind., Him., W-China
- *longifolium* D. Don = Cymbidium elegans
- **lowianum** (Rchb. f.) Rchb. f. · ⁴ Z9 ⓚ
II-V ▽ ✳; NE-Ind.: Khasia; Burma
- **madidum** Lindl. · ⁴ Z9 ⓚ ▽ ✳; Austr.:
Queensl., N.S.Wales
- **mastersii** Griff. ex Lindl. · ⁴ Z9 ⓚ XI-XII
▽ ✳; InG: Assam
- *pumilum* Rolfe = Cymbidium floribundum
- *syringodorum* Griff. = Cymbidium
eburneum
- **tigrinum** C.S.P. Parish ex Hook. f. · ⁴ Z9
ⓚ VI-VII ▽ ✳; Burma
- **tracyanum** L. Castle · ⁴ Z9 ⓚ ▽ ✳;
SW-China, N-Thail.
- **Cultivars:**
- **many cultivars**

Cymbopetalum Benth. -n- *Annonaceae* · 12
(27) spp.
- **penduliflorum** Baill. · G:Xochinacatztli ·
♄ ♄ ⓦ Ⓝ; Mex., Guat.

Cymbopogon Spreng. -m- *Poaceae* ·
56 spp. · E:Lemongrass; F:Citronnelle,
Verveine de Ceylan; G:Zitronellagras,
Zitronengras
- **citratus** (DC. ex Nees) Stapf · E:West
Indian Lemongrass; G:Westindisches
Zitronengras · ⁴ Z9 ⓦ ⚇ Ⓝ; ? Ind., ?
Malay. Arch.
- *confertiflorus* (Steud.) Stapf = Cymbopo-
gon nardus var. confertiflorus
- **flexuosus** (Nees ex Steud.) Stapf. ·
E:East Indian Lemongrass · ⁴ Z9 ⓦ Ⓝ;
Ind.
- **iwarancusa** (Jones) Schult. · ⁴ Z9 ⓦ Ⓝ;
Afgh., Him.
- **martinii** (Roxb.) Will. Watson · E:Rosha
Grass; G:Palmarosagras · ⁴ Z9 ⓦ Ⓝ; Ind.
- **nardus** (L.) Rendle. · E:Citronella Grass
- var. **confertiflorus** (Steud.) Bor ·
G:Dichtblättriges Zitronellagras · ⁴ Z9
ⓦ; S-Ind., Sri Lanka
- var. **nardus** · ⁴ Z9 ⓦ ⚇ Ⓝ; Ind.

- **schoenanthus** (L.) Spreng. · E:Geranium
Grass; G:Kamelgras · ⁴ Z9 ⓦ Ⓝ; N-Afr.,
NW-Ind.
- **winterianus** Jowitt · E:Java Citronella;
G:Javazitronelle · ⁴ Z9 ⓦ ⚇ ; Sri Lanka

Cymophyllus Mack. ex Britton & A. Br. -m-
Cyperaceae · 1 sp. · G:Appalachengras
- **fraseri** (Andrews) Mack. = Cymophyllus
fraserianus
- **fraserianus** (Ker-Gawl.) Kartesz &
Gandhi· G:Appalachengras · ⁴ Z7 V-VII;
USA: NE, NCE

Cynanchum L. -n- *Asclepiadaceae* · 200-
300 spp. · F:Cynanque; G:Hundswürger
- *aphyllum* (Thunb.) Schltr. = Sarcostemma viminale
- *aphyllum* hort. = Cynanchum gerrardii
- **gerrardii** (Harv.) Liede · ⁴ ⚇ Z10 ⓦ;
E-Afr., Arab.
- **macrolobum** Jum. & H. Perrier · ♄ ♈ Z10
ⓦ; SW-Madag.
- **marnierianum** Rauh · ♄ ♈ Z10 ⓦ;
SW-Madag.
- *nigrum* (L.) Pers. non Cav. = Vincetoxicum nigrum
- *sarcostemmatoides* K. Schum. = Cynanchum gerrardii
- *tetrapterum* hort. = Cynanchum gerrardii

Cynara L. -f- *Asteraceae* · 8 spp. · E:Globe
Artichoke; F:Artichaut, Cardon;
G:Artischocke, Kardy
- **cardunculus** L. · E:Cardoon; G:Kardy,
Wilde Artischocke · ⁴ Z6 VIII-IX ⚇ Ⓝ;
Eur.: Ib, Fr, Ital-P, Ba; N-Afr., nat. in
Arg., Chile
- **Scolymus Group** · E:Globe Artichoke;
G:Gemüse-Artischocke · ⁴ Z7 ⚇ ; cult.
- *horrida* Aiton = Cynara cardunculus
- *scolymus* L. = Cynara cardunculus
Scolymus Group

Cynodon Rich. -m- *Poaceae* · 8 spp. ·
E:Bermuda Grass; F:Chiendent, Pied-de-
poule; G:Bermudagras, Hundszahngras
- **dactylon** (L.) Pers. · E:Bahama Grass,
Bermuda Grass, Star Grass; G:Gewöhnli-
ches Hundszahngras · ⁴ ⤳ Z7 VII-IX ⚇
Ⓝ; Eur.* ecx. Sc; cosmop.
- **plectostachyus** (K. Schum.) Pilg. ·
E:Stargrass · ⁴ ⓦ Ⓝ; Eth., C-Afr., E-Afr.,
trop-Afr.
- **transvaalensis** Burtt Davy. · E:African

Dogstooth Grass · ♃ Z8 ⓚ Ⓝ; S-Afr.

Cynoglossum L. -n- *Boraginaceae* ·
c. 60 spp. · E:Hound's Tongue;
F:Cynoglosse, Langue-de-chien;
G:Hundszunge
– **amabile** Stapf & J.R. Drumm. · E:Chinese
Forget-me-not; G:Chinesische Hunds-
zunge · ⊙ Z7 VII-IX; Tibet, W-China
– **cheirifolium** L. · ⊙ Z7 VII-VIII; Eur.: Ib,
Fr, Ital-P; NW-Afr., Libya
– **coelestinum** Lindl. · ⊙ ♃ Z8 VII-IX;
N-Ind.
– **creticum** Mill. · G:Geaderte Hunds-
zunge · ⊙ Z7; Eur.*: Ib, Fr, Ital-P, Ba,
Crim, ? RO; TR, Levant, Iraq, Cauc., Iran,
C-As., NW-Afr.
– **germanicum** Jacq. · E:Green Hound's
Tongue; G:Deutsche Hundszunge · ⊙
V-VII; Eur.: Fr, BrI, EC-Eur., Ital-P, Ba,
E-Eur., Ib, C-Eur.; NW-TR, Cauc.
– **grande** Douglas ex Lehm. · E:Hound's
Tongue; G:Vergissmeinnichtähnliche
Hundszunge · ⊙ ♃ Z7 V-VI; Can.: W;
USA: NW, Calif.
– **hungaricum** Simonk. · G:Ungarische
Hundszunge · ⊙ V-VII; Eur.: A, EC-Eur.,
Ba, E-Eur.; TR
– **nervosum** Benth. ex Hook. f. ·
E:Himalayan Hound's Tongue; G:Hima-
laya-Hundszunge · ⊙ ♃ Z5 VII; Him.
– **officinale** L. · E:Common Hound's
Tongue; G:Gewöhnliche Hundszunge · ⊙
Z6 V-VI 𝄞 ⚕; Eur.*, Cauc., TR, W-Sib.,
E-Sib., C-As.

Cynosurus L. -m- *Poaceae* · 7 spp. · E:Dog's
Tail; F:Crételle, Cynosure; G:Kammgras
– *aureus* L. = Lamarckia aurea
– **cristatus** L. · E:Crested Dog's Tail;
G:Wiesen-Kammgras · ♃ VI-VII Ⓝ; Eur.*,
TR, Cauc., N-Iran, nat. in N-Am., Austr.,
NZ
– **echinatus** L. · E:Rough Dog's Tail;
G:Stachliges Kammgras · ⊙ Z7 V; Eur: :
Ib, Fr, Sw, Ital-P, Ba, RO, W-Russ., Crim;
TR, Cyprus, Syr., Lebanon, Israel, Iraq,
Cauc., Iran, C-As., NW-Afr., Macaron.,
nat. in G, A, H, Cz
– **elegans** Desf. · ⊙ Z7; IB, F, Ital-P, GR;
NW-Afr., Canar.; N-China, Jap.
– **siculus** Jacq. · ♃ ⋉ Z7; Eur.: sp., Ital-P;
NW-Afr.

Cypella Herb. -f- *Iridaceae* · 20 spp. ·

F:Cypella; G:Becherschwertel
– **coelestis** (Lehm.) Diels · G:Blaues
Becherschwertel · ♃ Z9 ⓚ VIII-IX; Braz.,
Urug., Arg., ? Parag.
– **herbertii** (Lindl.) Herb. · G:Becherschw-
ertel · ♃ Z9 ⓚ VII; S-Braz., Urug., Arg.

Cyperus L. -m- *Cyperaceae* · 682 spp. ·
E:Galingale; F:Souchet; G:Zypergras
– *adenophorus* Schrad. ex Nees = Cyperus
haspan
– **albostriatus** Schrad. · ♃ ～ Z9 ⓦ ⓚ;
Trop., S-Afr.
– **alopecuroides** Rottb. · E:Foxtail
Flatsedge · ♃ Z10 ⓦ ⓚ Ⓝ; trop. Afr.,
Ind., Sri Lanka, trop. As., Austr.
– *alternifolius* hort. non L. = Cyperus
alternifolius subsp. flabelliformis
– **alternifolius** L. · ♃ Z10 ⓦ ⓚ; Madag.,
Reunion, Mauritius, nat. in P, Azor.
– subsp. **flabelliformis** Kük. · E:Umbrella
Grass · ♃ ～ Z9 ⓦ ⓚ; trop. Afr., S-Afr.
– **brevifolius** (Rottb.) Hassk. · ♃ ～ ⓦ
ⓚ; trop. Am., trop. As.
– **congestus** Vahl · E:Dense Flat Sedge · ⊙
Z9 VII-VIII; S-Afr., Austr.
– *diffusus* hort. non Vahl = Cyperus
albostriatus
– **diffusus** Vahl · ♃ ⓚ; S-Afr.
– **entrerianus** Boeck. · E:Woodrush Flat
Sedge · ♃ ⋉ ⓚ ∧; Urug.
– **eragrostis** Lam. · E:American Galingale, Tall Flat Sedge; G:Frischgrünes
Zypergras · ♃ ⋉ Z8 ⓚ VI-IX; W-USA,
trop. Am., nat. in Ib, F
– **esculentus** L. · E:Chufa, Tiger Nut;
G:Erdmandel · ⊙ ♃ Z8 ⓚ 𝄞 Ⓝ; Eur.: P,
F, Ital-P, Ba; TR, Cauc., Ind., Afr., Alaska,
Can.: W; USA*, Mex., Peru, nat. in sp., A,
Russ.
– **fertilis** Boeck. · ♃ Z10 ⓦ; W-Afr., C-Afr.,
Angola
– *flabelliformis* Rottb. = Cyperus alternifo-
lius subsp. flabelliformis
– *flavescens* L. = Pycreus flavescens
– **fuscus** L. · E:Brown Flat Sedge;
G:Braunes Zypergras · ⊙ ～ VI-IX;
Eur.*, TR, Cauc., Iran, W-Sib., E-Sib.,
C-As, Him., China, N-Afr., nat. in N-Am.
– **glaber** L. · ⊙; Eur.: Ital-P, A, Ba, E-Eur.;
TR, Cauc., Iran, Pakist., C-As.
– **glomeratus** L. · G:Knäueliges Zypergras ·
♃ VII-IX; Eur.: Fr, Ital-P, C-Eur., EC-Eur.,
Ba.; TR, Cauc., W-Sib., Amur, C-As, Him.,
N

– **gracilis** R. Br. · E:Flat Sedge; G:Zierliches Zypergras · ⁴ ⌢ 🐾 🏠; Austr., N.Caled.
– **haspan** L. · ⁴ ⌢ Z8 🏠; USA: NE, NCE, SC; Trop.
– *involucratus* Roxb. = Cyperus alternifolius subsp. flabelliformis
– *laxus* hort. = Cyperus albostriatus
– **longus** L. · G:Hohes Zypergras
– subsp. **badius** (Desf.) Murb. · G:Kastanienbraunes Zypergras · ⁴ ⌢ Z7 VII-IX; Eur. most
– subsp. **longus** · E:Galingale, Sweet Galingale; F:Souchet odorant; G:Gewöhnliches Hohes Zypergras, Langes Zypergras · ⁴ ⌢ Z7 VII-X; Eur.* exc. Sc; TR, Cauc., Iran, C-As., Afgh., Him., Ind., Java, Afr., W-Austr.
– **michelianus** (L.) Delile · G:Zwerg-Zypergras · ⊙ ⌢ VII-IX; Eur.: P, Fr, Ital-P, C-Eur., EC-Eur., Ba, E-Eur.; TR, Cauc., W-Sib., Amur, C-As., Him., Ind., Indochina, China, Jap., N-Afr.
– *natalensis* auct. non Hochst. ex C. Krauss = Cyperus owanii
– **owanii** Boeck. · E:Owan's Flat Sedge · ⁴ ✂ 🏠; S-Afr.
– **pannonicus** Jacq. · G:Salz-Zypergras · ⁴ ⌢ VII-IX; Eur.: A, EC-Eur., Ba, E-Eur.; Cauc., W-Sib., C-As.
– **papyrus** L. · E:Egyptian Paper Plant, Papyrus · ⁴ ⌢ Z9 🐾 Ⓝ; C-Afr., Sudan, nat. in Sic., Egypt
– **prolifer** Lam. · E:Miniature Papyrus · ⁴ ⌢ Z9 🏠; S-Afr.
– **rotundus** L. · E:Nutgrass; G:Knolliges Zypergras · ⁴ 🏠 VII-IX ⚥ Ⓝ; Eur.: Ib, Fr, Ital-P, Ba, Sw, A; TR, SW-As, C-As., Ind., E-As., trop. Afr., S.Afr., N-Am., S-Am., Austr., nat. in USA
– **serotinus** Rottb. · G:Spätes Zypergras · ⁴ ⌢ ; Eur.: Ib, Fr, Ital-P, Ba, A, H, E-Eur.; TR, Cauc., Amur, C-As, N-Ind., E-China
– *vegetus* Willd. = Cyperus eragrostis

Cyphomandra Mart. ex Sendtn. -f- Solanaceae · 32 spp. · E:Tree Tomato; F:Arbre-à-tomates; G:Baumtomate
– **betacea** (Cav.) Sendtn. · G:Baumtomate; E:Tree Tomato · ♄ ɘ Z9 🏠 Ⓝ; Peru, S-Braz., ? Peru; cult. Trop., Subtrop., nat. in Peru: Anden
– *crassifolia* (Ortega) J.F. Macbr. = Cyphomandra betacea

Cyphostemma (Planch.) Alston

-n- Vitaceae · c. 150 spp.
– **bainesii** (Hook. f.) Desc. · E:African Tree Grape, Gouty Vine · ↯ Z9 🏠; Namibia
– *cramerianum* (Schinz) Desc. = Cyphostemma currori
– **currori** (Hook. f.) Desc. · E:Cobas · ↯ Z9 🏠; Angola, Namibia, Cape
– **fleckii** (Schinz) Desc. Z9 🏠; Namibia
– **juttae** (Dinter & Gilg) Desc. · ↯ Z9 🏠; Namibia
– **macropus** (Welw.) Desc. · ↯ Z9 🏠; Namibia

Cypripedium L. -n- Orchidaceae · 54 spp. · E:Lady's Slipper; F:Sabot-de-Vénus; G:Frauenschuh
– **acaule** Aiton · E:Pink Lady's Slipper; G:Kurzstängeliger Frauenschuh · ⁴ Z5 V-VI ▽ ✳; Can., USA: NE, NCE, SE
– **arietinum** R. Br. · E:Ram's Head Lady's Slipper; G:Gehörnter Frauenschuh · ⁴ Z4 V-VI ▽ ✳; Can.: E; USA: NE, NCE
– **calceolus** L. · E:Lady's Slipper Orchid; F:Sabot de Vénus; G:Gelber Frauenschuh, Marien-Frauenschuh · ⁴ Z5 V-VI ▽ ✳; Eur.*, W-Sib., E-Sib., Amur, Sakhal., Mong., N-China
– var. *parviflorum* (Salisb.) Fernald = Cypripedium parviflorum var. parviflorum
– var. *pubescens* (Willd.) Correll = Cypripedium parviflorum var. pubescens
– **californicum** A. Gray · E:Californian Lady's Slipper · ⁴ Z7 V ▽ ✳; USA: Oreg., Calif.
– **candidum** Muhl. ex Willd. · E:White Lady's Slipper · ⁴ ⌢ ∧ V-VI ▽ ✳; USA: NE, NCE, NC
– **cordigerum** D. Don · G:Herztragender Frauenschuh · ⁴ ▭ ∧ V-VI ▽ ✳; Him., Kashmir, Nepal
– **fasciculatum** Kellogg ex S. Watson · E:Clustered Lady's Slipper · ⁴ Z8 ▭ V-VI ▽ ✳; Can.: B.C.; USA: NW, Calif., Rocky Mts.
– **fasciolatum** Franch. · ⁴ 🏠 ▭ VI ▽ ✳; W-China
– **formosanum** Hayata · ⁴ ▽ ✳; Taiwan
– **guttatum** Sw. · E:Spotted Lady's Slipper; G:Getüpfelter Frauenschuh · ⁴ Z4 IV-V ▽ ✳; Eur.: Russ.; Sib., Alaska, Can.: W
– var. *yatabeanum* (Makino) Pfitzer = Cypripedium yatabeanum
– **japonicum** Thunb. · E:Japanese Lady's Slipper; G:Japanischer Frauenschuh · ⁴

Z8 ▭ ∧ V-VI ▽ ✳; China, Jap.
- **macranthos** Sw. · G:Großblütiger
  Frauenschuh · ♃ Z6 V-VI ▽ ✳; Russ.,
  W-Sib., E-Sib., Amur, Sakhal., Kamchat.,
  Mong., N-China, Manch., Korea, Jap.
- **montanum** Douglas ex Lindl. ·
  E:Mountain Lady's Slipper; G:Berg-
  Frauenschuh · ♃ Z5 ▭ V-VI ▽ ✳; Alaska,
  Can.: W; USA: NW, Calif., Rocky Mts.
- **parviflorum** Salisb.
- var. **parviflorum** · E:Lesser Yellow Lady's
  Slipper; G:Kleinblütiger Frauenschuh ·
  ♃ Z5 V-VI ▽ ✳; Can., USA: NW, Rocky
  Mts., NC, NCE, NE, SE
- var. **pubescens** (Willd.) O.W. Knight ·
  E:Greater Yellow Lady's Slipper;
  G:Behaarter Frauenschuh · ♃ Z5 V-VI ⚥
  ▽ ✳; Can.: E; USA: NE, NCE, SE
- *planipetalum* (Fernald) F.J.A. Morris &
  E.A. Eames = Cypripedium parviflorum
  var. pubescens
- *pubescens* Willd. = Cypripedium parviflorum var. pubescens
- **reginae** Walter · E:Showy Lady's Slipper;
  G:Königin-Frauenschuh · ♃ Z4 V-VI ▽ ✳;
  Can.: E; USA; NE, NCE, SE
- *spectabile* Salisb. = Cypripedium reginae
- **yatabeanum** Makino · ♃ Z4 ▽ ✳; Jap.
- **Cultivars:**
- **many cultivars**

Cyrtandra J.R. Forst. & G. Forst. -f-
  Gesneriaceae · c. 350 spp.
- **coccinea** Blume · ♄ Z10 ⊗; Malay. Arch.

Cyrtanthera Nees = Justicia
- *pohliana* Nees = Justicia carnea

Cyrtanthus Aiton -m- *Amaryllidaceae* ·
  55 spp. · E:Fire Lily; F:Cyrtanthus;
  G:Feuerblüte
- **angustifolius** (L. f.) Aiton · ♃ ⊗ V-VI;
  Cape
- **elatus** (Jacq.) Traub · E:Scarborough
  Lily; G:Scarborough-Feuerblüte · ♃ e Z10
  ⊛ VII-VIII; S-Afr. (Cape)
- **mackenii** Hook. f.
- var. **cooperi** (Baker) R.A. Dyer · ⊗;
  S-Afr.
- var. **mackenii** Hook. f. · E:Ifafa Lily;
  G:Ifafa-Feuerblüte · ♃ ⊗ V-VI; S-Afr.:
  Natal
- **macowanii** Baker · ♃ ⊗ VI; Cape
- **obliquus** (L. f.) Aiton · ♃ ⊗ V-VI; Cape
- **ochroleucus** (Herb.) Burch. ex Steud. ·

♃ ⊗ II; Cape
- *purpureus* (Aiton) Herb. = Cyrtanthus
  elatus
- **sanguineus** (Lindl.) Walp. · ♃ ⊗ VIII;
  S-Afr.: Cape, Natal

Cyrtochilum Kunth -n- *Orchidaceae* ·
  125 spp.
- **aureum** (Lindl.) Senghas · ♃ Z10 ⊗ V-VI
  ▽ ✳; Peru
- **edwardii** (Rchb. f.) Kraenzl. · ♃ Z10 ⊗
  II-III ▽ ✳; Ecuad.
- **halteratum** (Lindl.) Kraenzl. · ♃ Z9 ⊗
  IV-V ▽ ✳; Col., Venez.
- **macranthum** (Lindl.) · ♃ Z10 ⊗ V-VII ▽
  ✳; Col., Ecuad., Peru
- **serratum** (Lindl.) Kraenzl. · ♃ Z10 ⊛
  VII-VIII ▽ ✳; Peru

Cyrtomium C. Presl = Polystichum
- *caryotideum* (Wall.) C. Presl = Polystichum falcatum var. caryotideum
- *falcatum* (L. f.) C. Presl = Polystichum
  falcatum var. falcatum
- *fortunei* J. Sm. = Polystichum falcatum
  var. fortunei
- *macrophyllum* (Makino) Tagawa =
  Polystichum macrophyllum

Cyrtopodium R. Br. -n- *Orchidaceae* ·
  43 spp. · F:Orchidée; G:Krummfuß
- **andersonii** (Lamb. ex Andrews) R. Br. ·
  ♃ Z10 ⊛ IV-V ▽ ✳; Fla., Venez., Braz.
- **punctatum** (L.) Lindl. · E:Cow Horn
  Orchid · ♃ Z10 ⊛ IV-VI ▽ ✳; S-Fla.,
  C-Am., W.Ind., S-Am.

Cyrtorchis Schltr. -f- *Orchidaceae* · 16 spp.
- **arcuata** (Lindl.) Schltr. · ♄ Z9 ⊛ IV-V ▽
  ✳; trop. Afr., S-Afr.

Cyrtosperma Griff. -n- *Araceae* · 12 spp.
- *chamissonis* (Schott) Merr. = Cyrtosperma merkusii
- **johnstonii** (N.E. Br.) N.E. Br. · ♃ Z10 ⊛;
  Solom.
- **merkusii** (Hassk.) Schott · ♃ Z10 ⊛ Ⓝ;
  Malay Arch., N.Guinea, Pacific Is.

Cyrtostachys Blume -f- *Arecaceae* · 11 sp.
- *lakka* Becc. = Cyrtostachys renda
- **renda** Blume · E:Sealing Wax Palm · ♄ e
  Z10 ⊛; Malay. Pen., Sumat., Kalimantan

Cystopteris Bernh. -f- *Woodsiaceae* ·

23 spp. · E:Bladder Fern; F:Cystoptéride; G:Blasenfarn
- **alpina** (Roth) Desv. · E:Alpine Bladder Fern; G:Alpen-Blasenfarn · ⚃ △ Z6 VII-IX; Eur.: Ib, Fr, Ital-P, G, ? EC-Eur., ? Sc, Ital-P, Ba, E-Eur.; TR, Moroc., Alger.
- **bulbifera** (L.) Bernh. · E:Berry Bladder Fern; F:Cystoptéris bulbifère; G:Brutknospen-Balsenfarn · ⚃ △ Z5; Can.: E; USA: NE, NCE, SE, SW, Tex., Utah
- *crispa* (Gouan) H.P. Fuchs = Cystopteris alpina
- **dickieana** R. Sim · E:Dickie's Bladder Fern; G:Runzelsporiger Blasenfarn · ⚃ △ Z6 VIII-IX; Eur.* exc. EC-Eur., Ba; W-Sib., E-Sib.
- **fragilis** (L.) Bernh. · E:Brittle Bladder Fern; G:Zerbrechlicher Blasenfarn · ⚃ △ Z2 VII-IX; Eur.*, Cauc., W-Sib., E-Sib., C-As., Amur
- subsp. *alpina* (Lam.) Briq. = Cystopteris alpina
- subsp. *dickieana* (R. Sim) Moore = Cystopteris dickieana
- var. *dickieana* (R. Sim) T. Moore = Cystopteris dickieana
- **montana** (Lam.) Desv. · E:Mountain Bladder Fern; G:Berg-Blasenfarn · ⚃ △ Z4 VII-VIII ▽; Eur.*, Cauc., W-Sib., E-Sib.
- *regia* (L.) Desv. = Cystopteris fragilis
- *regia* auct. non (L.) Desv. = Cystopteris alpina
- **sudetica** A. Braun & Milde · G:Sudeten-Blasenfarn · ⚃ △ Z6 VII-IX ▽; Eur.: G, A, EC-Eur., Norw.; Cauc, W-Sib., E-Sib., Amur

Cytisanthus O. Lang = Genista
- *radiatus* (L.) O. Lang = Genista radiata

Cytisophyllum O. Lang -n- Fabaceae · 1 sp. · F:Faux-cytise; G:Scheingeißklee
- **sessilifolium** (L.) O. Lang · G:Kahler Geißklee, Meergrüner Geißklee, Scheingeißklee · ♄ d V-VII ✿; Eur.: sp., F, I

Cytisus Desf. -m- Fabaceae · 33 spp. · E:Broom; F:Genêt à balai; G:Besenginster, Geißklee
- *albus* (Lam.) Link = Cytisus multiflorus
- *albus* Hacq. = Chamaecytisus albus
- **ardoinoi** E. Fourn. · G:Ardoines Geißklee · ♄ d ⤳ △ Z7 IV-V ✿; Eur.: F

(Alp. Maritime)
- *austriacus* L. = Chamaecytisus austriacus
- *battandieri* Maire = Argyrocytisus battandieri
- ×**beanii** G. Nicholson (*C. ardoinoi* × *C. purgans*) · ♄ ♄ △ Z6 V ✿; cult.
- *biflorus* L'Hér. = Chamaecytisus ratisbonensis
- *canariensis* (L.) Kuntze = Genista canariensis
- *candicans* (L.) Lam. = Genista canariensis
- **cantabricus** (Willk.) Rchb. f. & Beck · ♄ ⤳ V-VI; Eur.: N-Sp., SW-F
- *capitatus* Scop. = Chamaecytisus supinus
- ×**dallimorei** Rolfe (*C. multiflorus* × *C. scoparius* 'Andreanus') · ♄ d Z6 V; cult.
- **decumbens** (Durande) Spach · F:Cytise rampant; G:Niederliegender Geißklee · ♄ d △ Z5 V-VI ✿; Eur.: F, Sw, I, Croatia, Bosn., Montenegro, AL
- *demissus* Boiss. = Chamaecytisus hirsutus
- *elongatus* Waldst. & Kit. = Chamaecytisus glaber
- **emeriflorus** Rchb. · G:Strauchwicken-Geißklee · ♄ d Z6 V-VI; Eur.: Sw, I; S-Alp.
- **filipes** Webb & Berthel. · ♄ d Z9 🏠 IV-V; Canar.
- *glaber* L. f. = Chamaecytisus glaber
- *hirsutus* L. = Chamaecytisus hirsutus
- subsp. *ciliatus* (Wahlenb.) Asch. & Graebn. = Chamaecytisus ciliatus
- ×**kewensis** Bean (*C. ardoinoi* × *C. multiflorus*) · G:Zwerg-Elfenbein-Ginster · ♄ d ⤳ △ Z6 V ✿; cult.
- *leucanthus* Waldst. & Kit. = Chamaecytisus albus
- *maderensis* (Webb & Berthel.) Masf. = Genista maderensis
- *monspessulanus* L. = Genista monspessulana
- **multiflorus** (L'Hér. ex Aiton) Sweet · E:White Spanish Broom; G:Vielblütiger Geißklee · ♄ d Z7 ∧ V-VI ✿; Eur.: Ib
- **nigricans** L. · E:Black Broom; G:Schwarzwerdender Geißklee · ♄ d D Z5 VI-VII ✿; Eur.: Ital-P, C-Eur., EC-Eur., Ba, E-Eur.
- ×**praecox** Bean (*C. multiflorus* × *C. purgans*) · E:Warminster Broom; F:Genêt précoce; G:Elfenbein-Ginster · ♄ d Z6 IV-V ✿; cult.
- **some cultivars**
- **procumbens** (Waldst. & Kit. ex Willd.) Spreng. · G:Niederliegender Besen-Ginster · ♄ d ⤳ △ Z5 IV-VI; Eur.: A,

EC-Eur., Ba, E-Eur.
– *proliferus* L. f. = Chamaecytisus proliferus
– **pseudoprocumbens** Markgr. · G:Ausge-
breiteter Besen-Ginster · ♄ V-VI; Eur.: I,
Slove., AL
– **purgans** (L.) Spach · E:Broom;
G:Abführender Geißklee · ♄ d Z7 ∧ V-VII
⚘; Eur.: P, sp., F
– *purpureus* Scop. = Chamaecytisus
purpureus
– × *racemosus* Marnock ex G. Nicholson =
Genista × spachiana
– *ratisbonensis* Schaeff. = Chamaecytisus
ratisbonensis
– *sagittalis* (L.) W.D.J. Koch = Chamaespartium sagittale subsp. sagittale
– **scoparius** (L.) Link · G:Besenginster
– **some cultivars**
– subsp. *cantabricus* (Willk.) M. Laínz &
Rivas Mart. et al. = Cytisus cantabricus
– subsp. **maritimus** (Rouy) Heywood ·
E:Prostrate Broom; G:Küsten-Besengin-
ster · Z6 ⚘; Eur.: BrI, D +; coasts
– subsp. **scoparius** E:Broom, Common
Broom, Scotch Broom; F:Genêt à balais;
G:Besenpfriem, Gewöhnlicher Besenginster · ♄ d Z6 V-VI ⚘ Ⓝ; Eur.*
– var. *prostratus* (C. Bailey) A.B. Jacks. =
Cytisus scoparius subsp. maritimus
– *sessilifolius* L. = Cytisophyllum sessilifolium
– **striatus** (Hill) Rothm. · E:Portuguese
Broom; G:Gestreifter Geißklee · ♄ d ⓐ;
Eur.: P, sp., nat. in F
– *supinus* L. = Chamaecytisus supinus
– × *versicolor* (G. Kirchn.) Dippel =
Chamaecytisus × versicolor

Daboecia D. Don -f- *Ericaceae* · 2 spp. · E:St
Daboec's Heath; F:Bruyère des Açores;
G:Glanzheide
– **azorica** Tutin & E.F. Warb. · G:Azoren-
Glanzheide · ♄ e Z8 ⓐ VI-VII; Azor.
– **cantabrica** (Huds.) K. Koch ·
E:Connemara Heath, St Dabeoc's Heath;
F:Bruyère de saint Daboec; G:Irische
Glanzheide · ♄ e Z7 ⓐ ∧ VI-IX; Eur.: Ib,
F, IRL
– **many cultivars**
– subsp. *azorica* (Tutin & E.F. Warb.) D.C.
McClint. = Daboecia azorica
– *polifolia* D. Don = Daboecia cantabrica
– × **scotica** D.C. McClint. (*D. azorica × D.
cantabrica*) · G:Schottische Glanzheide ·
♄ e Z7; cult.

Dacrycarpus (Endl.) de Laub. -m-
Podocarpaceae · 9 spp. · E:Dacryberry;
F:If verruqueux; G:Warzeneibe
– **dacrydioides** (A. Rich.) de Laub. · E:New
Zealand Dacryberry; G:Neuseeländische
Warzeneibe · ♄ Z9 ⓐ; NZ

Dacrydium Sol. ex G. Forst. -n-
Podocarpaceae · 21 spp. · E:Rimu; F:Pin
Huon, Pin rouge; G:Harzeibe
– **cupressinum** Sol. ex G. Forst. · E:Red
Pine, Rimu; G:Maniu, Zypressenartige
Harzeibe · ♄ e Z9 ⓐ Ⓝ; NZ

Dacryodes Vahl -m- *Burseraceae* · 40 spp.
– **edulis** (G. Don) Lam. · ♄ ⓐ Ⓝ; W-Afr.,
Cameroon, Angola

Dactylis L. -f- *Poaceae* · ~5 spp. · E:Cock's
Foot; F:Dactyle; G:Knäuelgras
– **glomerata** L. · E:Cocksfoot, Orchard
Grass; G:Wiesen-Knäuelgras · ⏀ Z5 V-VII
Ⓝ; Eur.*, TR, Levant, Syr., Iraq, Cauc.,
Iran, W-Sib., E-Sib., Afgh, Pakist., Him.,
Mong., China, Korea, Jap., Taiwan,
Moroc., Alger., nat. in N-Am., Arg., Chile,
S-Afr.
– **polygama** Horv. · E:Slender Cock's Foot;
G:Wald-Knäuelgras · ⏀ Z5 VI-VII; Eur.:
BrI, Sc, C-Eur., EC-Eur., I, Ba, E-Eur.

Dactylorchis (Klinge) Verm. = Dactylorhiza
– *majalis* (Rchb.) Verm. = Dactylorhiza
majalis

Dactylorhiza Neck. ex Nevski -f-
Orchidaceae · 30 spp. · E:Marsh Orchid,
Spotted Orchid; F:Dactylorhize;
G:Fingerwurz, Knabenkraut
– × **aschersoniana** (Hausskn.) Borsos
& Soó (*D. incarnata × D. majalis*) ·
G:Aschersons Bastard-Fingerwurz · ⏀ ▽
✳
– × **carnea** (E.G. Camus) Soó (*D. incarnata
× D. maculata* subsp. *ericetorum*) ·
G:Fleischrosa Bastard-Fingerwurz · ⏀ ▽
✳
– × **dinglensis** (Wilmott) Soó (*D. maculata*
subsp. *ericetorum × D. majalis* subsp.
occidentalis) · G:Dingles Bastard-
Fingerwurz · ⏀ ▽ ✳; D +
– **elata** (Poir.) Soó · G:Hohe Fingerwurz ·
⏀ Z7 ⓐ ∧ V-VI ▽ ✳; Eur.: Ib, F, Sic.;
Moroc., Alger.
– **fuchsii** (Druce) Soó · E:Common Spotted

Orchid; G:Gewöhnliche Fuchs' Fingerwurz · ♃ Z6 VI-VII ▽ ✻; Eur. exc. Ib., Sib., ? N-Afr.
- **incarnata** (L.) Soó · G:Fleischfarbige Fingerwurz
- subsp. **cruenta** (O.F. Müll.) P.D. Sell · G:Blutrote Fingerwurz · ♃ VI-VII ▽ ✻; N-Eur., E-Eur., Alp, TR, W-Sib., E-Sib.
- subsp. **incarnata** · E:Early Marsh Orchid; G:Gewöhnliche Fleischfarbige Fingerwurz · ♃ Z7 V-VII ▽ ✻; Eur.*, N-TR, W-Sib., E-Sib.
- **lapponica** (Laest. ex Hartm.) Soó · G:Lappländische Fingerwurz · ♃ VI-VIII ▽ ✻; Eur.: Sc
- **maculata** (L.) Soó · G:Gefleckte Fingerwurz
- subsp. *fuchsii* (Druce) Hyl. = Dactylorhiza fuchsii
- subsp. **maculata** · E:Heath Spotted Orchid; F:Orchis tacheté; G:Gewöhnliche Gefleckte Fingerwurz · ♃ Z6 V-VIII ▽ ✻; Eur. exc. SE-Eur.
- **majalis** (Rchb.) P.F. Hunt & Summerh. · E:Broad Leaved Marsh Orchid; G:Gewöhnliche Breitblättrige Fingerwurz · ♃ Z6 V-VI ▽ ✻; Eur.*
- **praetermissa** (Druce) Soó · E:Southern Marsh Orchid; G:Übersehene Fingerwurz · ♃ Z6 VI ▽ ✻; NW-Eur.
- **purpurella** (T. Stephenson & T.A. Stephenson) Soó · E:Northern Marsh Orchid; G:Purpurrote Fingerwurz · ♃ Z6 VI ▽ ✻; NW-Eur.
- **ruthei** (M. Schulze & R. Ruthe) Soó · G:Ruthes Fingerwurz · ♃ ▽ ✻; Eur.: G, PL
- **sambucina** (L.) Soó · E:Elderflower Orchid; G:Holunder-Fingerwurz · ♃ Z7 IV-VI ▽ ✻; Eur.* exc. BrI; Cauc.
- **sphagnicola** (Höppner) Aver. · G:Gewöhnliche Torfmoos-Fingerwurz · ♃ VI ▽ ✻; Eur.: Fr, G, Sk
- *strictifolia* (Opiz) Rauschert = Dactylorhiza incarnata subsp. incarnata
- × **transiens** (Druce) Soó (*D. fuchsii* × *D. maculata* subsp. *ericetorum*) · G:Gefleckte Bastard-Fingerwurz · ♃ ▽ ✻
- **traunsteineri** (Saut. ex Rchb.) Soó · G:Traunsteiners Fingerwurz · ♃ Z6 VII-VIII ▽ ✻; Eur.: BrI, Sc, C-Eur., EC-Eur., Slove., E-Eur., Ital-P; W-Sib.
- subsp. **curvifolia** (F. Nyl.) Soó · G:Ostsee-Fingerwurz · ♃ VI ▽ ✻; Eur.: G, PL, DK
- subsp. **traunsteineri** · G:Gewöhnliche Traunsteiners Fingerwurz

Daemonorops Blume -f- *Arecaceae* · 102 spp. · E:Dragon's Blood Palm; F:Palmier sang-de-dragon; G:Drachenblutpalme
- **draco** Blume · E:Dragon's Blood Palm; G:Drachenblutpalme · ₺ e Ⓦ ⚕ Ⓝ; Ind.
- **lewisiana** (Griff.) Mart. · ₺ e ⚕ Ⓦ; Malay. Pen. (Penang)

Dahlia Cav. -f- *Asteraceae* · 29 spp. · E:Dahlia; F:Dahlia; G:Dahlie, Georgine
- **coccinea** Cav. · E:Red Dahlia · ♃ Ⓚ VIII-IX; Mex.
- **excelsa** Benth. · ₺ Ⓚ XI; Mex.
- × **hortensis** Guillaumin (*D. coccinea* × *D. pinnata*) · ♃ Ⓚ VIII-IX; ? Mex.
- **imperialis** Roezl ex J.G. Ortega · ₺ Ⓚ XI-II; Mex.
- *juarezii* hort. ex Sasaki = Dahlia × hortensis
- *juarezii* M.E. Berg ex Mast. = Dahlia coccinea
- **merckii** Lehm. · E:Bedding Dahlia · ♃ Ⓚ VII-IX; Mex.
- **pinnata** Cav. · ♃ Ⓚ VIII-X; Mex.
- *rosea* Cav. = Dahlia pinnata
- *variabilis* (Willd.) Desf. = Dahlia pinnata
- **Cultivars:**
- **many cultivars, see Section III**

Dalbergaria Tussac -f- *Gesneriaceae* · 90 spp.
- **aureonitens** (Hook.) Wiehler · ♃ e Z9 Ⓦ; trop. S-Am.
- **sanguinea** (Pers.) Steud. · ₺ e Z9 Ⓦ; W.Ind.

Dalbergia L. f. -f- *Fabaceae* · c. 100 spp. · E:Rosewood; F:Bois de rose, Palissandre; G:Dalbergie, Rosenholz
- **latifolia** Roxb. ex DC. · E:Black Rosewood, Black Wood; G:Schwarzes Rosenholz · ₺ d Z9 Ⓦ Ⓝ; Ind.
- **melanoxylon** Guill. & Perr. · E:African Blackwood, Senegal Ebony; G:Afrikanische Grenadilla, Senegal-Ebenholz · ₺ Z9 Ⓦ Ⓝ; trop. Afr., nat. in C-Am.
- **nigra** (Vell.) Allemão ex Benth. · E:Bahia Rosewood; G:Brazilianisches Rosenholz · ₺ Z9 Ⓦ Ⓝ ▽ ✻; Braz.
- **retusa** Hemsl. · E:Cocobolo; G:Coccobolo, Rosenholz · ₺ Z9 Ⓦ Ⓝ; C-Am.,

S-Am.
- **sissoo** Roxb. ex DC. · E:Indian Rosewood, sisu; G:Ostindisches Rosenholz · ♄
d Z9 ⓦ ⓝ; S-Him.

Dalechampia L. -f- *Euphorbiaceae* ·
120 spp. · F:Dalechampia; G:Dalechampie
- *roezliana* Müll. Arg. = Dalechampia
spathulata
- **spathulata** (Scheidw.) Baill. · E:Winged
Beauty Shrub · ♄ e Z10 ⓦ; Mex.
- var. *rosea* Müll. Arg. = Dalechampia
spathulata

Danae Medik. -f- *Ruscaceae* · 1 sp. ·
E:Alexandrian Laurel; F:Laurier
d'Alexandrie; G:Alexandrinischer
Lorbeer, Traubendorn
- **racemosa** (L.) Moench · E:Alexandrian
Laurel; G:Alexandrinischer Lorbeer,
Traubendorn · ♄ e Z8 ⓐ ∧; Cauc., Iran,
N-Syr.

Daniella Benn. -f- *Caesalpiniaceae* · 9 spp.
- **ogea** Rolfe · E:Gum Copal · ♄ Z10 ⓦ ⓝ;
W-Afr., Benin, Nigeria, Liberia

Danthonia DC. -f- *Poaceae* · 10-20 spp. ·
E:Heath Grass; F:Danthonia; G:Dreizahn,
Kelchgras, Traubenhafer
- **alpina** Vest · G:Kelch-Traubenhafer,
Kelchgras · ⚃ V-VI; Eur.* exc. BrI, Sc
- **decumbens** (L.) Lam. & DC. · E:Heath
Grass; G:Gewöhnlicher Dreizahn · ⚃
VI-VII; Eur.*, TR, Cauc.

Daphne L. -f- *Thymelaeaceae* · c. 50 spp. ·
E:Daphne; F:Bois-joli, Camélée, Daphné;
G:Heideröschen, Kellerhals, Königs-
blume, Seidelbast
- **acutiloba** Rehder · ♄ e Z6 VII ✹ ▽;
W-China
- **alpina** L. · E:Alpine Mezereon; G:Alpen-
Seidelbast · ♄ d △ D Z5 V-VI ✹ ▽; Eur.:
F, I, Sw, A, Slove., Croatia, Bosn., YU,
? sp.; mts.
- **altaica** Pall. · G:Altai-Seidelbast · ♄ d △
D Z5 V-VI ✹ ▽; W-Sib. (Altai), C-As.
- **arbuscula** Čelak. · ♄ e △ Z6 VI ✹ ▽;
Slova.
- **aurantiaca** Diels · ♄ e Z6 ✹ ▽; SW-
China
- **bholua** Buch.-Ham. ex D. Don · ♄ e
Z8 ⓐ ✹ ▽; E-Him.: E-Nepal, Bhutan,
Sikkim, NW-Assam

- **blagayana** Freyer · E:Balkan Daphne;
G:Königs-Seidelbast · ♄ e △ D Z6 IV-V ✹
▽; Eur.: Ba, RO
- × **burkwoodii** Turrill (*D. caucasica* ×
D. cneorum) · E:Burkwood's Daphne;
G:Burkwoods Seidelbast · ♄ d D Z6 V-VI
✹; cult.
- **some cultivars**
- **caucasica** Pall.
- var. **axilliflora** Keissl. · ♄ d Z6 V-VI ✹
▽; Cauc.
- var. **caucasica** · E:Caucasian Daphne;
G:Kaukasischer Seidelbast · ♄ d D Z6
V-VI ✹ ▽; Cauc., TR
- **cneorum** L. · G:Heideröschen, Rosmarin-
Seidelbast
- var. **cneorum** · E:Garland Flower, Rose
Daphne; F:petite Thymélée, Thymélée
des Alpes; G:Gewöhnlicher Rosmarin-
Seidelbast · ♄ e △ D Z5 V-VI ✹ ▽;
Eur.* exc. BrI, Sc
- var. **verlotii** (Gren. & Godr.) Meisn. · ♄ e
Z5 IV-V ✹ ▽; SE-F, D (Bayern)
- **genkwa** Siebold & Zucc. · E:Chinese
Daphne; G:Chinesischer Seidelbast · ♄ d
Z5 IV-V ⚥ ✹ ▽; China, Korea
- *glandulosa* Spreng. = Daphne oleoides
- **glomerata** Lam. · ♄ e Z6 ✹ ▽; NE-TR,
Cauc.
- **gnidium** L. · ♄ e Z8 ⓐ VII-IX ✹ ▽;
Eur.: Ib, Fr, Ital-P, Ba, Canar., Madeira;
NW-Afr.
- × **hendersonii** Hodgkin ex C.D. Brickell
& B. Mathew (*D. cneorum* × *D. petraea*) ·
♄ ✹
- × **houtteana** Lindl. & Paxton (*D. laureola*
× *D. mezereum*) · ♄ s D Z6 IV ✹; cult.
- × **hybrida** Colville ex Sweet (*D. oleoides* ×
D. sericea) · ♄ e Z6 ✹; cult.
- **laureola** L. · G:Lorbeer-Seidelbast
- subsp. **laureola** · E:Spurge Laurel;
G:Gewöhnlicher Lorbeer-Seidelbast · ♄
e Z7 II-IV ✹ ▽; Eur.: Ib, Fr, BrI, Ital-P,
C-Eur., EC-Eur., Ba, RO; N-TR, Moroc.,
Alger.
- subsp. **philippi** (Gren.) Rouy · ♄ e ⤳ Z7
IV-V ✹ ▽; sp., F; Pyr.
- × **mantensiana** Manten ex T.M.C.
Taylor & Vrugtman (*D.* × *burkwoodii* × *D.
retusa*) · ♄ e ✹; cult.
- **mezereum** L. · E:February Daphne,
Mezereon; F:Bois gentil, Bois joli;
G:Gewöhnlicher Seidelbast, Kellerhals ·
♄ d D Z4 III-IV ⚥ ✹ ▽; Eur.*, Cauc., TR,
N-Iran, W-Sib., E-Sib.

– × **napolitana** Lodd. (*D. cneorum* × *D. sericea*) · ♄ e D Z8 ⊛ V-VI ☀; cult.
– **odora** Thunb. ex Murray · E:Winter Daphne; G:Duftender Seidelbast · ♄ e D Z7 I-III ☀ ▽; China
– **oleoides** Schreb. · ♄ e D Z7 V-VI ☀ ▽; Eur.: Ib, Ital-P, Ba; TR, Lebanon, Cauc., W-Iran, Alger., Libya
– **petraea** Leyb. · E:Rock Mezereon; G:Felsen-Seidelbast · ♄ e D Z6 VI ☀ ▽; Eur.: I (Brescia)
– *philippi* Gren. & Godr. = Daphne laureola subsp. philippi
– **pontica** L. · E:Twin-flower Daphne; G:Pontischer Seidelbast · ♄ e D Z6 V ☀ ▽; Eur.: BG; N-TR, Cauc.
– *retusa* Hemsl. = Daphne tangutica Retusa Group
– **sericea** Vahl · G:Berg-Seidelbast · ♄ e Z8 ⊛ V-VI ☀ ▽; Eur.: I, Sic., GR, Crete; TR, Syr., Lebanon
– **striata** Tratt. · G:Gestreifter Seidelbast, Steinröschen · ♄ ♄ e ↝ △ Z7 V-VII ☀ ▽; Eur.: F, I, C-Eur., Slove.; Alp.
– **tangutica** Maxim. · ♄ e D Z6 III-IV ☀ ▽; China: Kansu
– **Retusa Group** · ♄ D V-VI ☀ ▽; W-Him.
– × **thauma** Farrer (*D. petraea* × *D. striata*) · ♄ e Z7 ☀ ▽; N-I (Cima Tombea)

Daphniphyllum Blume -n- *Daphniphyllaceae* · 10 (-15) spp. · F:Faux-laurier; G:Scheinlorbeer
– **humile** Maxim. ex Franch. & Sav. · ♄ e Z7; Jap., Korea
– **macropodum** Miq. · G:Chinesischer Scheinlorbeer · ♄ ♄ e Z7; Jap., Korea

Darlingtonia Torr. -f- *Sarraceniaceae* · 1 sp. · E:Cobra Lily; F:Lis-cobra, Plante-cobra; G:Kobralilie, KoBrazchlauchpflanze
– **californica** Torr. · E:Californian Pitcher Plant, Cobra Lily; G:Kobralilie, KoBrazchlauchpflanze · ⌗ Z7 V-VIII; USA: S-Oreg, N-Calif.

Darmera Voss -f- *Saxifragaceae* · 1 sp. · E:Indian Rhubarb; F:Darmera; G:Schildblatt
– **peltata** (Torr. ex Benth.) Voss · E:Indian Rhubarb, Umbrella Plant; F:Saxifrage pelté; G:Schildblatt · ⌗ ↝ Z6 IV-V; USA: Oreg., Calif.

Darwinia Rudge -f- *Myrtaceae* · -45 spp.
– **hookeriana** (Meisn.) Benth. · ♄ e Z9 ⊛ IV; S-Austr.
– **macrostegia** (Turcz.) Benth. · E:Mondurup Bell · ♄ e Z9 ⊛ IV; S-Austr.

Dasylirion Zucc. -n- *Dracaenaceae* · 20 spp. · E:Bear Grass; F:Dasylirion; G:Rauschopf
– **acrotrichum** (Schiede) Zucc. · ♄ e Z9 ⊛; C-Mex.
– **glaucophyllum** Hook. · ♄ e Z9 ⊛; E-Mex.
– *gracile* (Lem.) J.F. Macbr. = Beaucarnea gracilis
– **graminifolium** (Zucc.) Zucc. · ⌗ Z9 ⊛; SE-Mex.
– *laxiflorum* Baker = Dasylirion serratifolium
– *longifolium* (Karw. ex Schult. f.) Zucc. = Nolina longifolia
– **longissimum** Lem. · ♄ e Z9 ⊛; E-Mex.
– *quadrangulatum* S. Watson = Dasylirion longissimum
– **serratifolium** (Karw. ex Schult. & Schult. f.) Zucc. · ⌗ Z9 ⊛; E-Mex.

Dasypyrum (Coss. & Durieu) T. Durand -n- *Poaceae* · 2 spp.
– **villosum** (L.) Borbás · ☉; Eur.: Ib, Fr, Ital-P, Ba, RO, Crim; TR, Cauc.

Datisca L. -f- *Datiscaceae* · 2 spp. · E:Acalbir; F:Faux-chanvre; G:Scheinhanf, Streichkraut
– **cannabina** L. · E:False Hemp; G:Scheinhanf, Streichkraut · ⌗ Z7 ∧ VII-VIII; Eur.: Crete; TR, Cyprus, Lebanon, Cauc., Iran, C-As., Him.

Datura L. -f- *Solanaceae* · 8 spp. · E:Thorn Apple; F:Faux-metel, Pomme du diable; G:Stechapfel
– *alba* Nees = Datura metel
– *arborea* L. = Brugmansia arborea
– *aurea* (Lagerh.) Saff. = Brugmansia aurea
– *bertolonii* Parl. ex Guss. = Datura stramonium var. inermis
– × *candida* (Pers.) Saff. = Brugmansia × candida
– **ceratocaula** Ortega · ☉ ↝ D Z10 VIII ☀; Mex.
– *cornigera* Hook. = Brugmansia arborea
– *fastuosa* L. = Datura metel
– **ferox** L. · E:Longspine Thorn Apple;

G:Dorniger Stechapfel · ⊙ Z8 VII-VIII ✕;
China, nat. in S-Eur., N-Afr.
– *inermis* Juss. ex Jacq. = Datura stramonium var. inermis
– **innoxia** Mill. · E:Pricklybur · ⊙ Z9 VIII-X
✕ Ⓝ; USA: SE, Fla., ; Mex., W.Ind.,
C-Am., S-Am., nat. in Eur.: Ib, F, Ital-P
– **metel** L. · E:Downy Thorn Apple, Horn
of Plenty; G:Flaumiger Stechapfel · ⊙ Z9
VI-VII ✕ Ⓝ; trop. Afr., trop. As, nat. in
Trop., Subtrop.
– *meteloides* DC. ex Dunal = Datura innoxia
– *mollis* Saff. = Brugmansia versicolor
– *praecox* Godr. = Datura stramonium var.
tatula
– **quercifolia** Humb., Bonpl. & Kunth ·
E:Oakleaf Datura; G:Eichenblättriger
Stechapfel · ⊙ Z8 VII ✕; USA: SW;
N-Mex.
– *rosei* Saff. = Brugmansia sanguinea
subsp. sanguinea
– *sanguinea* Ruiz & Pav. = Brugmansia
sanguinea subsp. sanguinea
– **stramonium** L. · E:Jimson Weed;
G:Weißer Stechapfel
– var. **godronii** Danert
– var. **inermis** (Juss. ex Jacq.) Timm ·
E:Thornless Thorn Apple; G:Dornloser
Stechapfel
– var. **stramonium** · E:Thorn Apple;
G:Gewöhnlicher Weißer Stechapfel · ⊙
Z7 IX-X ⚥ ✕; ? N-AM, nat. in Eur.*
– var. **tatula** (L.) Torr. · ⊙ Z7
– *suaveolens* Humb. & Bonpl. ex Willd. =
Brugmansia suaveolens
– *tatula* L. = Datura stramonium var. tatula
– *versicolor* (Lagerh.) Saff. = Brugmansia
versicolor

Daubentonia DC. = Sesbania
– *tripetii* Poit. = Sesbania tripetii

Daucus L. -m- *Apiaceae* · 22 spp. · E:Carrot;
F:Carotte ; G:Möhre
– **carota** L. · G:Möhre
– subsp. **carota** · E:Wild Carrot; G:Wilde
Möhre · ⊙ VI-IX
– subsp. **sativus** (Hoffm.) Schübl. & G.
Martens · E:Carrot; G:Gelbe Rübe,
Karotte, Mohrrübe, Speise-Möhre · ⊙
VI-IX ⚥ ; cult.

Davallia Sm. -f- *Davalliaceae* · 29 spp. ·
E:Hare's Foot Fern; F:Davallia; G:Hasen-
pfotenfarn, Krugfarn

– **bullata** Wall. · E:Hare's Foot Fern;
G:Hasenpfotenfarn · ⑁ Z10 ⓦ; trop. As.,
Jap., China
– var. *mariesii* (T. Moore) Baker = Davallia
mariesii
– **canariensis** (L.) Sm. · E:Canary Island
Hare's Foot Fern; G:Kanarischer
Hasenpfotenfarn · ⑁ ⟿ Z9 ⓚ; Eur.: Ib,
Canar., Madeira, Cap Verde
– **decurrens** Hook. · ⑁ Z10; Phil.
– **denticulata** (Burm. f.) Mett. ex Kuhn · ⑁
Z10 ⓦ; W-Afr., Madag., Ind., Sri Lanka,
Indochina, Malay. Arch., Polyn., N-Austr.
– **divaricata** Blume · ⑁ ⟿ Z10 ⓦ; N-Ind.,
China, Phil., Java, Sulawesi
– *elegans* Sw. = Davallia denticulata
– **fejeensis** Hook. · E:Rabbit's Foot Fern;
G:Kaninchenpfotenfarn · ⑁ ⟿ Z10 ⓦ;
Fiji
– *griffithiana* Hook. = Humata griffithiana
– *heterophylla* Sm. = Humata heterophylla
– *lonchitidea* Wall. = Microlepia platyphylla
– **mariesii** T. Moore · E:Squirrel's Foot
Fern; G:Ballfarn · ⑁ ⟿ Z9 ⓦ; China,
Korea, Jap., Taiwan
– *pedata* Sm. = Humata repens
– *polyantha* Hook. = Davallia divaricata
– **pyxidata** Cav. · E:Australian Hare's Foot
Fern; G:Australischer Hasenpfotenfarn ·
⑁ ⟿ Z10 ⓦ; Austr.: N.S.Wales
– **solida** (G. Forst.) Sw. · ⑁ ⟿ Z10 ⓦ;
Malay. Arch., Austr.: Queensl.; Polyn.
– **trichomanoides** Blume · ⑁ ⚥ ⟿ Z10 ⓦ;
Sri Lanka, Indochina, Malay. Arch., Jap.
– *tyermannii* (T. Moore) Baker = Humata
tyermannii

Davidia Baill. -f- *Nyssaceae* · 1 sp. · E:Dove
Tree; F:Arbre aux pochettes, Davidia;
G:Taschentuchbaum, Taubenbaum
– **involucrata** Baill. · E:Dove Tree, Ghost
Tree, Handkerchief Tree; G:Taschentuch-
baum, Taubenbaum
– var. **involucrata** · G:Gewöhnlicher
Taubenbaum · ♄ d Z7; W-China
– var. *laeta* (Dode) Krüssm. = Davidia
involucrata var. vilminiana
– var. **vilmoriniana** (Dode) Wangerin ·
G:Sichuan-Taubenbaum · ♄ d Z7 V-VI;
China: Sichuan, Hupeh
– *vilmoriniana* Dode = Davidia involucrata
var. vilmoriniana

Daviesia Sm. -f- *Fabaceae* · c. 110 spp. ·
E:Bitter Peas ; G:Bittererbse

– **polyphylla** Benth. · ♄ e Z9 ⬙; W-Austr.

Deamia Britton & Rose -f- *Cactaceae* ·
2 spp.
– **testudo** (Karw.) Britton & Rose · ⵣ ⵤ Z9
⬙ ▽ ✳; C-Am., Col.

Debregeasia Gaudich. -f- *Urticaceae* ·
4 spp.
– **longifolia** (Burm. f.) Wedd. · ♄ e ⬙;
S-Him., Ind., Sri Lanka, Burma, Java

Decaisnea Hook. f. & Thomson -f-
Lardizabalaceae · 2 spp. · F:Decaisnea;
G:Blauschote, Gurkenstrauch
– **fargesii** Franch. · ♄ d ⚇ Z7 V-VI;
W-China

Decaryia Choux -f- *Didiereaceae* · 1 sp. ·
G:Zickzackpflanze
– **madagascariensis** Choux · G:Zickzackp-
flanze · ♄ ⵣ Z10 ⬙ ▽ ✳; SW-Madag.

Decumaria L. -f- *Hydrangeaceae* · 2 spp. ·
E:Climbing Hydrangea; G:Sternhortensie
– **barbara** L. · E:Climbing Hydrangea,
Wood Vamp; G:Amerikanische
Sternhortensie · ♄ d ⵤ Z7 ∧ V-VI; USA:
Va., SE, Fla.
– **sinensis** Oliv. · G:Chinesische Sternhort-
ensie · ♄ e Z8 ⬙; C-China

Degenia Hayek -f- *Brassicaceae* · 1 sp.
– **velebitica** (Degen) Hayek · ⵣ Z7;
Croatia: Velebit

Deherainia Decne. -f- *Theophrastaceae* ·
2 spp.
– **smaragdina** Decne. · ♄ e ⬙; Mex.

Deinanthe Maxim. -f- *Hydrangeaceae* ·
2 spp. · F:Deinanthe; G:Scheinhortensie
– **bifida** Maxim. · G:Weiße Scheinhortensie · ⵣ Z7 ∧ VII-VIII; Jap.
– **caerulea** Stapf · G:Blaue Scheinhortensie · ⵣ Z7 ∧ VII-VIII; China: Hupeh

× **Dekensara** hort. -f- *Orchidaceae* (*Cattleya
× Rhyncholaelia × Schomburgkia*)

Delairea Lem. -f- *Asteraceae* · 1 sp. ·
E:German Ivy; F:Delairea; G:Salonefeu
– **odorata** Lem. · E:German Ivy, Parlour
Ivy; G:Salonefeu · ⵣ ⵤ ⤳ Z9 ⬙; Cape,
nat. in S-Eur., W-Eur., NW-Afr.

Delonix Raf. -f- *Caesalpiniaceae* · 10 spp. ·
E:Flame Tree; F:Flamboyant; G:Flam-
boyant
– **regia** (Bojer ex Hook.) Raf. ·
E:Flamboyant, Flame Tree; G:Flamboy-
ant · ♄ d Z9 ⬙; Madag., nat. in Trop.,
Subtrop.

Delosperma N.E. Br. -n- *Aizoaceae* ·
154 spp. · F:Delosperma, Ficoide;
G:Mittagsblume
– **aberdeenense** (L. Bolus) L. Bolus · ♄ ⵣ
Z9 ⬙; S-Afr.
– **brunnthaleri** (A. Berger) Schwantes ex
H. Jacobsen · ⵣ Z9; S-Afr. (Natal)
– **cooperi** (Hook. f.) L. Bolus · E:Hardy Ice
Plant · ⵢ ♄ ⵣ e Z7 ⬙ ∧ VI-VIII; S-Afr.:
Orange Free State
– **echinatum** (Lam.) Schwantes · ⵢ ⵣ Z9
⬙; Cape
– **ecklonis** (Salm-Dyck) Schwantes · ⵢ ⵣ
Z9 ⬙; Cape
– **lineare** L. Bolus · ♄ ⵣ Z7 ⬙ ∧ VI-VIII;
Lesotho
– **nubigenum** (Schltr.) L. Bolus ·
G:Lesotho-Mittagsblume · ♄ ⵣ Z9 ⬙;
S-Afr. Orange Free State
– *pruinosum* (Thunb.) J.W. Ingram =
Delosperma echinatum

Delphinium L. -n- *Ranunculaceae* · 250-
320 spp. · E:Larkspur; F:Pied-d'alouette;
G:Rittersporn
– *ajacis* L. = Consolida ajacis
– *ajacis* L. emend. J. Willm. = Consolida
orientalis
– **bicolor** Nutt. · E:Flat Head Larkspur;
G:Niederer Rittersporn · ⵢ △ Z4 V-VIII;
W-Can., USA: Rocky Mts., NC
– **brunonianum** Royle · ⵢ △ D Z4 VI-VII;
C-As., Afgh., Pakist., Tibet, Him.
– **bulleyanum** Forrest ex Diels · ⵢ Z7;
W-China
– **cardinale** Hook. · E:Scarlet Larkspur;
G:Roter Rittersporn · ⵢ Z7 ⬭ ∧ VII-VIII;
S-Calif.
– **cashmerianum** Royle · ⵢ △ Z5 VI-X;
Him.
– **cheilanthum** Fisch. ex DC. · ⵢ Z4 VI-VII;
E-Sib.
– *consolida* L. = Consolida regalis subsp.
regalis
– **elatum** L. · E:Alpine Larkspur; G:Hoher
Rittersporn · ⵢ Z3 VI-VIII ⚘ ▽; Eur.: Fr,
Ital-P, C-Eur., EC-Eur., Ba; mts.; W-Sib.,

E-Sib., Mong., nat. in Sc
- **fissum** Waldst. & Kit. · ♃ Z7 VI-VII; Eur.:
  Ib, Fr, Ital-P, Ba, E-Eur.; TR, Levant
- **grandiflorum** L. · F:Dauphinelle à
  grandes fleurs · ♃ △ Z3 VI-VIII; E-Sib.,
  W-China
- var. *chinense* Fisch. ex DC. = Delphinium
  grandiflorum
- **huetianum** Meikle · ♃ VIII-IX; N-TR
- **maackianum** Regel · F:Pied d'alouette ·
  ♃ Z3 VI-VII; Sib.
- **muscosum** Exell & Hillc. · ♃ △ Z7 VI-VII;
  Bhutan
- **nudicaule** Torr. & A. Gray · E:Red Larkspur; G:Nacktstängliger Lerchensporn · ♃
  △ Z7 ∧ VI-VII; N-Calif.
- *orientale* J. Gay = Consolida orientalis
- × **ruysii** hort. ex L. Möller (*D. elatum* × *D.
  nudicaule*) · ♃ Z6; cult.
- **semibarbatum** Bien. ex Boiss. · E:Zalil;
  F:Pied d'alouette; G:Gelber Rittersporn ·
  ♃ ⋈ Z7 ∧ VI-VII; Iran, Afgh., N-Ind.
- **staphisagria** L. · ♃ Z8 ⊛ ⚥ ⚔; Eur.: Ib,
  Fr, Ital-P, Ba; TR, Cyprus, Syr., NW-Afr.
- *sulphureum* hort. = Delphinium semibarbatum
- **tatsienense** Franch. · F:Dauphinelle du
  Setchouan · ♃ Z6 VII; Sichuan
- **tricorne** Michx. · E:Dwarf Larkspur · ♃
  Z4 V-VI; USA: NE, NCE, NC, SC, SE
- **triste** Fisch. · ♃ Z3 VI-VII; Sib.
- *zalil* Aitch. & Hemsl. = Delphinium
  semibarbatum
- **Cultivars:**
- **many cultivars, see Section III**

Dendranthema (DC.) Des Moul. =
  Chrysanthemum
- *arcticum* (L.) Tzvelev = Arctanthemum
  arcticum
- *coreanum* (H. Lév. & Vaniot) Vorosch. =
  Chrysanthemum coreanum
- *indicum* (L.) Des Moul. = Chrysanthemum indicum
- *indicum* hort. = Chrysanthemum ×
  grandiflorum
- *pacificum* (Nakai) Kitam. = Ajania
  pacifica
- *weyrichii* (Maxim.) Tzvelev = Chrysanthemum weyrichii
- *zawadskii* (Herbich) Tzvelev = Chrysanthemum zawadskii var. zawadskii

Dendrobium Sw. -n- *Orchidaceae* ·
  1197 spp.

- **aduncum** Wall. ex Lindl. · ♃ Z10 ⊛ VI-IX
  ▽ ✳; Him., Indochina, China
- *aggregatum* Roxb. = Dendrobium lindleyi
- **anosmum** Lindl. · ♃ Z10 ⊛ II-IV ▽ ✳;
  Thail., Laos, Vietn., Malay. Arch., Phil.,
  N.Guinea
- **aphyllum** (Roxb.) C.E.C. Fisch. · ♃ Z10
  ⊛ III-V ▽ ✳; NE-Ind., Him., SW-China,
  Indochina, Malay. Pen.
- *arachnites* Rchb. f. = Dendrobium
  dickasonii
- **atroviolaceum** Rolfe · ♃ Z10 ⊛ IV-V ▽
  ✳; N.Guinea
- **bellatulum** Rolfe · ♃ Z10 ⊛ IV-V ▽ ✳;
  Vietn.: Annam
- **bicaudatum** Reinw. ex Lindl. · ♃ Z10 ⊛
  V-VII ▽ ✳; Molucca: Ambon
- **bigibbum** Lindl. · ♃ Z10 ⊛ II-III ▽ ✳;
  N.Guinea, Austr.: Queensl.
- **brymerianum** Rchb. f. · ♃ Z10 ⊛ II-III ▽
  ✳; Burma, Thail., Laos
- **bullenianum** Rchb. f. · ♃ Z10 ⊛ ▽ ✳;
  Phil.
- **chrysanthum** Wall. ex Lindl. · ♃ Z10 ⊛
  VIII-IX ▽ ✳; Nepal, Him., Burma, Thail.
- **chrysotoxum** Lindl. · ♃ Z10 ⊛ III-IV ▽
  ✳; Ind., China, Burma, Laos
- *ciliatum* C.S.P. Parish ex Hook. f. =
  Dendrobium venustum
- **crepidatum** Lindl. & Paxton · ♃ Z10 ⊛
  IV-V ▽ ✳; Ind.: Sikkim, Assam; Burma
- **crumenatum** Sw. · ♃ Z10 ⊛ I-XII ▽ ✳;
  Burma, Malay. Pen.
- **dearei** Rchb. f. · ♃ Z10 ⊛ IV-VI ▽ ✳;
  Phil.
- **densiflorum** Lindl. · ♃ Z10 ⊛ ▽ ✳;
  Him., Indochina
- **devonianum** Paxton · ♃ Z10 ⊛ V-VI ▽
  ✳; Him., Indochina
- **dickasonii** L.O. Williams · ♃ D Z10 ⊛ V
  ▽ ✳; Burma, Thail.
- **discolor** Lindl. · ♃ Z10 ⊛ I-V ▽ ✳;
  N.Guinea, Austr.: Queensl.
- **draconis** Rchb. f. · ♃ Z10 ⊛ ▽ ✳;
  Burma, Thail.
- **falconeri** Hook. · ♃ Z10 ⊛ V-VI ▽ ✳;
  Ind.: Assam; S-Burma
- **falcorostrum** Fitzg. · ♃ Z10 ⊛ ▽ ✳;
  Austr.
- **farmeri** Paxton · ♃ Z10 ⊛ IV-V ▽ ✳;
  Him., Burma, Thail., Malay. Pen.
- **fimbriatum** Hook.
- var. **fimbriatum** · ♃ Z10 ⊛ ▽ ✳; Him.,
  Burma
- var. **oculatum** Hook. · ♃ Z10 ⊛ III-V ▽

✳; Sikkim
- **findleyanum** C.S.P. Parish & Rchb. f. · ♃
  Z₁₀ ⓜ II-III ▽ ✳; Burma, Thail.
- **formosum** Roxb. ex Lindl. · ♃ Z₁₀ ⓜ
  II-V ▽ ✳; Nepal, Him., Burma, Thail.
- **gibsonii** Paxton · ♃ Z₁₀ ⓚ VIII-X ▽ ✳;
  Him., Burma, Yunnan
- **gratiosissimum** Rchb. f. · ♃ Z₁₀ ⓜ III-V
  ▽ ✳; Burma, Thail.
- **heterocarpum** Wall. ex Lindl. · ♃ Z₁₀ ⓜ
  I-III ▽ ✳; Him., Ind., Sri Lanka, Burma,
  Phil., Java
- **histrionicum** (Rchb. f.) Schltr. · ♃ Z₁₀
  ⓜ IV-V ▽ ✳; Burma, Thail.
- **hookerianum** Lindl. · ♃ Z₁₀ ⓜ VIII-IX ▽
  ✳; Him., Ind.: Assam
- **infundibulum** Lindl.
- var. **infundibulum** · ♃ Z₁₀ ⓜ ▽ ✳;
  Burma, Thail.
- var. **jamesianum** (Rchb. f.) Veitch · ♃
  Z₁₀ ⓜ III-V ▽ ✳; Burma
- *infundibulum* Rchb. f. = Dendrobium
  formosum
- *jamesianum* Rchb. f. = Dendrobium
  infundibulum var. jamesianum
- **jonesii** Rendle · ♃ Z₁₀ ⓜ III-V ▽ ✳;
  N.Guinea, Queensl.
- **kingianum** Bidwill ex Lindl. · ♃ ⸋ Z₁₀ ⓚ
  IV-V ▽ ✳; Austr.: Queensl., N.S.Wales
- **lindleyi** Steud. · ♃ Z₁₀ ⓜ III-V ▽ ✳;
  Him., S-China, Indochina, Malay. Pen.
- **lituiflorum** Lindl. · ♃ Z₁₀ ⓜ IV-V ▽ ✳;
  NE-Ind., Burma, Thail.
- **loddigesii** Rolfe · ♃ Z₁₀ ⓜ II-IV ▽ ✳;
  China: Yunnan, Honan; Laos
- **luteolum** Bateman · ♃ Z₁₀ ⓜ I-V ▽ ✳;
  Burma
- *lyonii* Ames = Epigeneium lyonii
- *minax* Rchb. f. = Dendrobium bicaudatum
- **mirbelianum** Gaudich. · ♃ Z₁₀ ⓜ ▽ ✳;
  Austr.: Queensl.
- **moniliforme** (L.) Sw. · ♃ Z₁₀ ⓚ IV-V ▽
  ✳; China, S-Korea, Jap.
- **moschatum** (Willd.) Sw. · ♃ Z₁₀ ⓜ
  V-VII ▽ ✳; Sikkim, Burma, Thail., Laos
- **nobile** Lindl. · ♃ Z₁₀ ⓜ III-VI ⸋ ▽ ✳;
  Him., W-China, Taiwan
- **ochreatum** Lindl. · ♃ Z₁₀ ⓜ III-IV ▽ ✳;
  Ind.: Khasia Hills
- **parishii** Rchb. f. · ♃ Z₁₀ ⓜ V-VI ▽ ✳;
  S-China, Indochina
- *paxtonii* Lindl. = Dendrobium chrysanthum
- **pendulum** Roxb. · ♃ Z₁₀ ⓜ VIII-XII ▽

✳; Burma
- *phalaenopsis* Fitzg. = Dendrobium bigibbum
- *pierardii* Roxb. ex Hook. = Dendrobium
  aphyllum
- **primulinum** Lindl. · ♃ Z₁₀ ⓜ IV-V ▽
  ✳; Nepal, Him., S-China, Burma, Thail.,
  Vietn., Malay. Pen.
- **pulchellum** Roxb. ex Lindl. · ♃ Z₁₀ ⓜ
  IV-V ▽ ✳; Him., Indochina
- *ruppianum* A.D. Hawkes = Dendrobium
  jonesii
- **senile** C.S.P. Parish & Rchb. f. · ♃ Z₁₀ ⓜ
  IV-VI ▽ ✳; Burma
- **speciosum** Sm. · E:King Orchid, Rock
  Orchid · ♃ Z₁₀ ⓚ III-V ▽ ✳; Austr.:
  Queensl., N.S.Wales, Victoria
- var. *fusiforme* F.M. Bailey = Dendrobium
  jonesii
- **stratiotes** Rchb. f. · ♃ Z₁₀ ⓜ VI-VII ▽ ✳;
  Sulawesi
- × **superbiens** Rchb. f. (*D. bigibbum* × *D.
  discolor*) · ♃ Z₁₀ ⓜ X-XII ▽ ✳; N-Austr.
- *superbum* Rchb. f. = Dendrobium
  anosmum
- **taurinum** Lindl. · ♃ Z₁₀ ⓜ IX-XII ▽ ✳;
  Phil.
- **tetragonum** A. Cunn. ex Lindl. · ♃
  Z₁₀ ⓚ X-XII ▽ ✳; Austr.: Queensl.,
  N.S.Wales
- **thyrsiflorum** Rchb. f. ex André · ♃ Z₁₀
  ⓜ ▽; Burma, Thail.
- *topaziacum* Ames = Dendrobium bullenianum
- *undulatum* R. Br. = Dendrobium discolor
- **venustum** Teijsm. & Binn. · ♃ Z₁₀ ⓜ
  X-XI ▽ ✳; Indochina
- **wardianum** R. Warner
- *wilkianum* Rupp = Dendrobium
  mirbelianum
- **williamsonii** J. Day & Rchb. f. · ♃ Z₁₀ ⓚ
  III ▽ ✳; Ind.: Assam; Burma, Thail.
- **Cultivars:**
- **many cultivars**

Dendrocalamus Nees -m- *Poaceae* · c.
30 spp.
- **asper** (Schult.) Backer ex K. Heyne ·
  E:Giant Bamboo · ♄ e Z₁₀ ⓜ Ⓝ; orig. ?,
  nat. in Malay. Arch.
- **giganteus** Munro · E:Giant Bamboo · ♄ e
  Z₁₀ ⓜ Ⓝ; N-Guinea, Burma, Thail., Ind.,
  China: Sichuan
- **hamiltonii** Nees & Arn. · ♄ e Z₁₀ ⓜ Ⓝ;
  Him.

– **strictus** (Roxb.) Nees · E:Calcutta
Bamboo; G:Kalkuttabambus · ♄ e Z10 ⊚
Ⓝ; Ind., Burma, Thail., Malay. Pen.

Dendrochilum Blume -n- *Orchidaceae* ·
268 spp.
– **cobbianum** Rchb. f. · ⚄ Z10 ⊚ IX-X ▽
✳; Phil.: Luzon
– **cornutum** Blume · ⚄ Z10 ⊚ VII-VIII ▽
✳; Sumat., Java
– **filiforme** Lindl. · ⚄ Z10 ⊚ VI-VII ▽ ✳;
Phil.
– **glumaceum** Lindl. · E:Silver Chain · ⚄
Z10 ⊚ I-II ▽ ✳; Phil.
– **latifolium** Lindl. · ⚄ Z10 ⊚ II-IV ▽ ✳;
Phil.

Dendrocnide Miq. -f- *Urticaceae* · 37 spp.
– *moroides* (Wedd.) Chew = Laportea
moroides

Dendromecon Benth. -f- *Papaveraceae* ·
1 sp. · E:Tree Poppy; F:Pavot en arbre;
G:Baummohn
– *harfordii* Kellogg = Dendromecon rigida
subsp. harfordii
– **rigida** Benth.
– subsp. **harfordii** (Kellogg) P.H. Raven ·
E:Harford's Tree Poppy; G:Harfords
Baummohn · ♄ Z8 ⓚ; Calif. (Santa Cruz,
Santa Rosa Is.)
– subsp. **rigida** · E:Bush Poppy, Tree
Poppy; G:Mexikanischer Baummohn · ♄ e
Z8 ⓚ III-VI; Calif.

Denmoza Britton & Rose -f- *Cactaceae* ·
2 spp.
– **erythrocephala** (K. Schum.) A. Berger ·
Ψ Z9 ⓚ ▽ ✳; Arg.
– **rhodacantha** (Salm-Dyck) Britton &
Rose · Ψ Z9 ⓚ ▽ ✳; NW-Arg.

Dennstaedtia Bernh. -f- *Dennstaedtiaceae* ·
59 spp. · E:Hay-scented Fern;
F:Dennstaedtia; G:Schüsselfarn
– **cicutaria** (Sw.) T. Moore · ⚄ Z10 ⊚;
Mex., W.-Ind., trop. S-Am.
– **davallioides** (R. Br.) T. Moore ·
E:Lacy Ground Fern · ⚄ Z10 ⊚; Austr.:
Queensl., N.S.Wales, Victoria
– **obtusifolia** (Willd.) T. Moore · ⚄ Z10 ⊚;
C-Am., W.Ind., trop. S-Am.
– **punctilobula** (Michx.) T. Moore · E:Hay
Scented Fern, Wild Fern; G:Heuduf-
tender Schüsselfarn · ⚄ Z6; Can.: E; USA;

NE, NCE, SE

Dentaria L. = Cardamine
– *bulbifera* L. = Cardamine bulbifera
– *digitata* Lam. = Cardamine pentaphyllos
– *enneaphyllos* L. = Cardamine enneaphyllos
– *heptaphylla* Vill. = Cardamine heptaphylla
– *pentaphyllos* L. = Cardamine pentaphyllos
– *pinnata* Lam. = Cardamine heptaphylla
– *polyphylla* Waldst. & Kit. = Cardamine
kitaibelii

Dermatobotrys Bolus -m-
Scrophulariaceae · 1 sp.
– **saundersii** Bolus · ♄ d Z10 ⓚ I-III;
S-Afr.: Natal

Derris Lour. -f- *Fabaceae* · c. 40 spp. ·
E:Tuba Root; F:Derris; G:Tubawurzel
– **elliptica** (Sweet) Benth. · E:Derris Root,
Tuba Root; G:Tubawurzel · ♄ e ⚡ Z9 ⊚
⚡ ⚘ Ⓝ; Burma, Thail., Malay. Arch.
– **malaccensis** (Benth.) Prain · E:Fish
Poison; G:Fischgift-Tubawurzel · ♄ e ⚡
Z9 ⊚ ⚡ ; Malay. Pen.

Deschampsia P. Beauv. -f- *Poaceae* ·
c. 40 spp. · E:Hair Grass; F:Canche;
G:Schmiele
– **cespitosa** (L.) P. Beauv. · G:Rasen-
Schmiele
– **some cultivars**
– subsp. **cespitosa** · E:Tufted Hairgrass;
F:Canche cespiteuse; G:Gewöhnliche
Rasen-Schmiele · ⚄ ∼ VI-IX Ⓝ; Eur.*,
TR, Iran, W-Sib., E-Sib., C-As., Mong.,
Him., N-Am.
– **flexuosa** (L.) Trin. · E:Wavy Hair Grass;
F:Canche flexueuse; G:Gewöhnliche
Draht-Schmiele · ⚄ VI-VII; Eur.*, TR,
Cauc., N-Iran, W-Sib., E-Sib., Amur,
Sakhal., Kamchat., Jap., Taiwan, Moroc.,
Alger., Alaska, Can., USA: NE, NCE, SE,
SC; Greenl., Arg., Chile, nat. in N.Guinea,
Phil., Kalimantan, NZ
– **littoralis** (Gaudin) Reut. · G:Bodensee-
Schmiele, Ufer-Schmiele · ⚄ VII-VIII;
Eur.: C-Alp.
– **media** (Gouan) Roem. & Schult. ·
G:Binsen-Schmiele · ⚄ VI-VII; Eur.: Ib, F,
I, G, Ba; TR, Cauc.
– *rhenana* Gremli = Deschampsia littoralis
– **setacea** (Huds.) Hack. · E:Bog Hair

Grass; G:Borst-Schmiele · ♃ VII-VIII; Eur.: Sc, BrI, Fr, G, PL, Ib
- **wibeliana** (Sond.) Parl. · G:Elbe-Schmiele, Wibels Schmiele · ♃ V-VI; Eur.: NW-D

Descurainia Webb & Berthel. -f- *Brassicaceae* · 40-50 spp. · E:Flixweed; F:Réséda à balai; G:Besenrauke
- **sophia** (L.) Prantl · E:Flixweed; G:Gewöhnliche Besenrauke · ☉ ☉ V-IX; Eur.*, TR, Levant; Cauc., W-Sib., E-Sib., Amur, Kamchat., C-As., Tibet, Mong., China, Moroc., Alger., Egypt, nat. in N-Am.

Desfontainia Ruiz & Pav. -f- *Loganiaceae* · 1 sp.
- **spinosa** Ruiz & Pav. · ♄ e Z8 ⓚ VII-VIII; Costa Rica, S-Am.; And.

Desmazeria Dumort. -f- *Poaceae* · 1 sp.
- *rigida* (L.) Tutin = Catapodium rigidum
- **sicula** (Jacq.) Dumort. · ☉; Eur.: S-I, Sic., Sard.; N-Afr.

Desmodium Desv. -n- *Fabaceae* · 300 (-450) spp. · E:Beggarweed, Tick Trefoil; F:Sainfoin oscillant; G:Bettlerkraut, Wandelklee
- **canadense** (L.) DC. · E:Canada Tick Trefoil; G:Kanadischer Wandelklee, Zeckenklee · ♄ d Z2 VII; Can.: E, Sask.; USA: NE, NCE, Okla.
- **elegans** DC. · G:Ähriger Wandelklee · ♄ d Z6 VIII-X; Him., China
- **intortum** (Mill.) Urb. · E:Beggarlice; G:Grüner Wandelklee · ♃ ⓦ Ⓝ; C-Am., Braz. (Austr.)
- **motorium** (Houtt.) Merr. · E:Telegraph Plant; G:Telegrafenpflanze · ☉ ♃ ♄ Z10 ⓦ VIII-IX; Ind., Sri Lanka, Phil.
- *penduliflorum* Oudem. = Lespedeza thunbergii
- *tiliifolium* (D. Don) G. Don = Desmodium elegans
- **tortuosum** (Sw.) DC. · E:Florida Beggarweed; G:Florida-Wandelklee · ♃ ⓦ Ⓝ; Fla., W.Ind.
- **uncinatum** (Jacq.) DC. · E:Spanish Tick Clover; G:Spanischer Wandelklee · ♃ ⓦ Ⓝ; S-Am, nat. in Austr.

Desmoncus Mart. -m- *Arecaceae* · 12 spp. · F:Palmier; G:Hakenpalme
- *horridus* Splitg. ex Mart. = Desmoncus orthacanthos
- **orthacanthos** Mart. · ♄ e ≹ ⓦ; Surinam

Deuterocohnia Mez -f- *Bromeliaceae* · 17 spp.
- **brevifolia** (Griseb.) M.A. Spencer & L.B. Sm. · ♃ ⌂ Z9 ⓚ; NW-Arg., S-Bol.
- **longipetala** (Baker) Mez · ♃ Z9 ⓚ; Peru, Braz., Arg.
- **lorentziana** (Mez) M.A. Spencer & L.B. Sm. · ♃ ⌂ Z9 ⓚ; NW-Arg.

Deutzia Thunb. -f- *Hydrangeaceae* · c. 60 spp. · E:Deutsia; F:Deutzia; G:Deutzie
- × **candelabrum** (Lemoine) Rehder (*D. gracilis* × *D. scabra*) · G:Armleuchter-Deutzie · ♄ d Z6 V-VI; cult.
- × **candida** (Lemoine) Rehder (*D. scabra* × *D.* × *lemoinei*) · G:Weiße Deutzie · ♄ d Z6 VI; cult.
- × **carnea** (Lemoine) Rehder (*D. scabra* × *D.* × *rosea*) · G:Fleischfarbige Deutzie · ♄ d Z6; cult.
- **coreana** H. Lév. · G:Koreanische Deutzie · ♄ d Z6; Korea
- **corymbosa** R. Br. · G:Doldige Deutzie · ♄ d Z8 ⓚ VI; W-Him.
- **crenata** Siebold & Zucc. · G:Gekerbtblättrige Deutzie · ♄ d Z6 V-VI; Jap.
- **discolor** Hemsl. · G:Zweifarbige Deutzie · ♄ d Z6 VI; C-China.
- × **elegantissima** (Lemoine) Rehder (*D. purpurascens* × *D. scabra*) · G:Elegante Deutzie · ♄ d Z6; cult.
- × **excellens** (Lemoine) Rehder (*D. vilmorinae* × *D.* × *rosea*) · G:Hervorragende Deutzie · ♄ d Z5; cult.
- **gracilis** Siebold & Zucc. · E:Japanese Snow Flower, Slender Deutsia; F:Petit deutzia; G:Zierliche Deutzie · ♄ d Z5 V-VI; Jap.
- × **hybrida** Lemoine (*D. discolor* × *D. mollis*) · G:Hybrid-Deutzie · ♄ d Z6; cult.
- **some cultivars**
- × **kalmiiflora** Lemoine (*D. parviflora* × *D. purpurascens*) · G:Kalmiablütige Deutzie · ♄ d Z6; cult.
- × **lemoinei** Lemoine ex Bois (*D. gracilis* × *D. parviflora*) · G:Lemoines Deutzie · ♄ d Z5; cult.
- **longifolia** Franch. · G:Langblättrige Deutzie · ♄ d Z6 VI; Yunnan, Sichuan
- × **magnifica** (Lemoine) Rehder (*D. scabra* × *D. vilmorinae*) · G:Großartige

Deutzie · ♄ d Z5; cult.
- × **maliflora** Rehder (*D. purpurascens* × *D.*
× *lemoinei*) · G:Apfelblüte Deutzie · ♄ d
Z6; cult.
- **mollis** Duthie · G:Flaumige Deutzie · ♄ d
Z6; C-China: W-Hubei
- **monbeigii** W.W. Sm. · ♄ d Z6; SW-China
- × **myriantha** Lemoine (*D. parviflora* × *D.*
setchuenensis) · G:Reichblütige Deutzie ·
♄ d Z5; cult.
- **ningpoensis** Rehder · G:Ningpo-
Deutzie · ♄ d Z5 VII; E-China
- **parviflora** Bunge · G:Kleinblütige
Deutzie · ♄ d Z6 VI; N-China, Manch.,
Korea
- **pulchra** S. Vidal · G:Schöne Deutzie · ♄ d
Z6 V-VI; Phil., Taiwan
- **purpurascens** (Franch. ex L. Henry)
Rehder · G:Purpur-Deutzie · ♄ d Z6 V-VI;
W-China
- × **rosea** (Lemoine) Rehder (*D. gracilis* ×
D. purpurascens) · G:Rosa Deutzie · ♄ d
Z6; cult.
- **rubens** Rehder · G:Rote Deutzie · ♄ d Z6
VI; C-China: Sichuan, Hubei, Shaanxi
- **scabra** Thunb. · E:Deutzia; G:Raue
Deutzie · ♄ d Z6 VI-VII; Jap., Riukiu-Is.
- **schneideriana** Rehder · G:Schneiders
Deutzie
- var. **laxiflora** Rehder · ♄ d Z6; C-China
- var. **schneideriana** · ♄ d Z6 VI-VII;
C-China.
- **setchuenensis** Franch. · G:Sichuan-
Deutzie
- var. **corymbiflora** (Lemoine) Rehder ·
G:Sternblütige Sichuan-Deutzie · ♄ d Z6;
W-China, C-China
- var. **setchuenensis** · G:Gewöhnliche
Sichuan-Deutzie · ♄ d Z6 VI-VII; W-China
- **sieboldiana** Maxim. = Deutzia scabra
- **staminea** R. Br. ex Wall. · ♄ d Z8 ⌂
VI-VII; Him.
- **vilmorinae** Lemoine & Bois · G:Vilmorins
Deutzie · ♄ d Z6 VI; C-China.
- × **wilsonii** Duthie (*D. discolor* × *D.*
parviflora) · G:Wilsons Deutzie · ♄ d Z6;
cult.

× **Diabroughtonia** hort. -f- *Orchidaceae*
(*Broughtonia* × *Caularthron*)

Diacrium Benth. = Caularthron
- **bicornutum** (Hook.) Benth. = Caularthron
bicornutum

× **Dialaelia** hort. -f- *Orchidaceae*
(*Caularthron* × *Laelia*)

× **Dialaeliocattleya** hort. -f- *Orchidaceae*
(*Cattleya* × *Caularthron* × *Laelia*)

× **Dialaeliopsis** hort. -f- *Orchidaceae*
(*Caularthron* × *Laeliopsis*)

Dianella Lam. -f- *Phormiaceae* · 38 spp. ·
E:Flax Lily; F:Dianella; G:Flachslilie
- **caerulea** Sims · E:Blue Flax Lily;
G:Blaue Flachslilie · ⳇ ♄ e Z9 ⌂; Austr.:
N.S.Wales, Victoria; N. Guinea, Fiji,
N.Caled.
- **ensifolia** (L.) DC. · E:New Zealand
Lily Plant, Umbrella Dracaena; G:Neu-
seeländische Flachslilie · ♄ e ⚤ Z9 ⌂;
Madag., Mascarene Is., Ind., Burma, Sri
Lanka, Malay. Arch., Jap., Ryukyu Is.,
Taiwan, Austr., Pacific Is.
- **intermedia** Endl. · G:Norfolk-Flachslilie ·
ⳇ e ⚤ Z9 ⌂; NZ, Norfolk Is., Fiji
- **laevis** R. Br. = Dianella longifolia
- **longifolia** R. Br. · E:Smooth Flax Lily;
G:Langblättrige Flachslilie · ⳇ e ⚤ Z9
⌂; Austr.: Queensl., N.S.Wales, Victoria,
Tasman.
- **revoluta** R. Br. · E:Blue Flax Lily · ⳇ e Z9
⌂; Austr.: N.S.Wales, Tasman.
- **strumosa** Lindl. = Dianella longifolia
- **tasmanica** Hook. f. · E:Tasman Flax Lily;
G:Tasmanische Flachslilie · ⳇ e ⚤ Z9 ⌂;
Austr.: N.S.Wales, Victoria, Tasman.

Dianthus L. -m- *Caryophyllaceae* · c.
300 spp. · E:Carnation, Pink; F:Œillet;
G:Nelke
- × **allwoodii** hort. (*D. caryophyllus* × *D.*
plumarius) · E:Allwood Pink; G:Allwoods
Nelke · ⳇ Z3; cult.
- **alpinus** All. = Dianthus pavonius
- **alpinus** L. · E:Alpine Pink · ⳇ △ Z3
VII-VIII ▽; Eur.: A; NE-Alp.
- **amurensis** Jacq. · ⳇ Z3 ▽; E-As., China
- **anatolicus** Boiss. · ⳇ ⤳ △ Z6 VI-VII ▽;
TR
- **arenarius** L. · E:Stone Pink; F:Oeillet des
sables; G:Gewöhnliche Sand-Nelke · ⳇ
△ Z3 VI-IX ▽; Eur.: Sc, C-Eur., EC-Eur.,
N-Ba, E-Eur.
- **armeria** L. · E:Deptford Pink; G:Büschel-
Nelke, Raue Nelke · ☉ Z6 VI-VIII ▽;
Eur.* , W-As.
- × **arvernensis** Rouy & Foucaud (*D.*

monspessulanus × *D. seguieri*) · ♃ ⤳ △ Z4 VII-VIII; cult.
- **barbatus** L. · E:Sweet William; F:Oeillet des poètes; G:Bart-Nelke · ⊙ ♃ ⋊ Z4 VI-VIII ▽; Eur.* exc. BrI, Sc; mts., nat. in FIN
- **many cultivars**
- *bebius* Vis. ex Rchb. = Dianthus petraeus subsp. petraeus
- *boydii* hort. = Dianthus callizonus
- **brevicaulis** Fenzl · ♃ △ Z7 VII ▽; TR: Taurus
- **callizonus** Schott & Kotschy · ♃ △ Z7 Ⓐ ∧ V ▽; RO; S-Carp.
- **campestris** M. Bieb. · ♃ △ Z3 VI ▽; Eur.: E-Eur.; W-Sib.
- **carthusianorum** L. · E:Carthusian Pink, Charterhouse Pink; F:Oeillet des Chartreux; G:Karthäuser-Nelke · ♃ Z3 VI-IX ▽; Eur.* exc. BrI, Sc, nat. in Sc
- **caryophyllus** L. · E:Carnation, Clove Pink, Gilly Flower; G:Garten-Nelke, Land-Nelke · ♃ ⋊ Z7 VII-VIII ⚕ ▽; Eur.: Sard., I, Sic., GR, nat. in sp., F
- **many cultivars**
- **chinensis** L. · E:Annual Pink; F:Oeillet de Chine; G:Chinenser-Nelke, Kaiser-Nelke · ⊙ ⊙ ♃ ⋊ Z7 VII-IX ⚕ ▽; China, Korea
- **collinus** Waldst. & Kit. · G:Hügel-Nelke · ♃ VI-VIII ▽; Eur.: A, RO, W-Russ.
- *creticus* Tausch = Dianthus fruticosus subsp. creticus
- *croaticus* Borbás = Dianthus giganteus
- **cruentus** Griseb. · F:Oeillet sanguin; G:Blut-Nelke · ♃ Z7 VI-VII ▽; Eur.: Ba; TR
- **deltoides** L. · E:Maiden Pink; F:Oeillet à delta; G:Heide-Nelke · ♃ Z3 VI-IX ▽; Eur.*, W-Sib.
- **many cultivars**
- **erinaceus** Boiss. · G:Igel-Nelke · ♃ △ Z7 VI-VII ▽; TR
- **freynii** Vandas · G:Freyn-Nelke · ♃ △ Z6 VIII ▽; Bosn., S-BG
- *friwaldskyanus* Boiss. = Dianthus gracilis subsp. friwaldskyanus
- **fruticosus** L.
- subsp. **creticus** (Tausch) Runemark · G:Kretische Strauch-Nelke · ♄ Z9 Ⓚ VII-IX ▽; Eur.: Crete
- subsp. **fruticosus** · G:Strauch-Nelke · ♄ e Z9 Ⓚ ▽; Eur.: GR, Aegeis
- **giganteus** d'Urv. · ♃ Z5 VII-VIII ▽; Eur.: Ba, RO; W-TR
- **glacialis** Haenke · E:Glacier Pink; G:Gletscher-Nelke · ♃ △ Z5 VII-VIII ▽; Eur.: I, Sw, A, EC-Eur., Ro; E-Alp., Carp.
- **gracilis** Sibth. & Sm.
- subsp. **friwaldskyanus** (Boiss.) Tutin Z7 ▽; N-Maced., AL
- subsp. **gracilis** · G:Mazedonische Nelke · ♃ Z7 ▽; Eur.: Maced., AL, BG
- **graniticus** Jord. · ♃ △ Z6 VI-VIII ▽; Eur.: C-F
- **gratianopolitanus** Vill. · E:Cheddar Pink; F:Oeillet bleuâtre, Oeillet de la Pentecôte; G:Pfingst-Nelke · ♃ △ Z3 V-VI ▽; Eur.: BrI, Fr, C-Eur., EC-Eur., W-Russ.
- **some cultivars**
- **haematocalyx** Boiss. & Heldr. · ♃ ⤳ Z7 VI-VII ▽; Eur.: Maced., AL, GR
- *kitaibelii* Janka = Dianthus petraeus subsp. petraeus
- **knappii** (Pant.) Asch. & Kanitz ex Borbás · G:Schwefel-Nelke · ♃ Z3 VI ▽; Eur.: Bosn., Montenegro
- **microlepis** Boiss. · G:Bulgarische Zwerg-Nelke · ♃ △ Z5 VI ▽; BG
- **monspessulanus** L.
- subsp. **monspessulanus** · E:Fringed Pink; G:Montpellier-Nelke · ♃ Z4 VII ▽; Eur.: C-F
- subsp. **sternbergii** (Sieber ex Capelli) Hegi · ♃ △ Z4 VII-VIII ▽; Eur.: I, A, Slove.; SE-Alp.
- **myrtinervius** Griseb. · ♃ △ Z7 VI ▽; Maced.
- **nardiformis** Janka · ♃ △ Z6 VI ▽; Eur.: GB, RO
- *neglectus* Loisel. = Dianthus pavonius
- **nitidus** Waldst. & Kit. · ♃ Z6 VII-VIII ▽; W-Carp.
- **pavonius** Tausch · E:Alpine Pink; G:Pfauen-Nelke · ♃ △ Z4 VI-VIII ▽; Eur.: F, I; Alp.
- **pelviformis** Heuff. · ♃ V-VII ▽; AL, BG
- **petraeus** Waldst. & Kit.
- subsp. **noeanus** (Boiss.) Tutin · ♃ △ Z4 VI-VIII ▽; BG
- subsp. **petraeus** · G:Geröll-Nelke · ♃ Z4 ▽; Eur.: Ba, RO
- **plumarius** L. · E:Common Pink; F:Oeillet mignardise; G:Feder-Nelke, Hainburger Nelke · ♃ Z3 IV-VI ▽; Eur.: A, Slove., Croatia, nat. in BrI, G, I
- **some cultivars**
- **pontederae** A. Kern. · E:Tall Pink; G:Pannonische Kartäuser-Nelke · ♃ V-VII ▽; Eur.: N-I, A, Slove., H, BG, RO
- **seguieri** Vill. · G:Busch-Nelke

- subsp. **glaber** Čelak. · G:Kahle Busch-Nelke · ♃ Z7 VI-VIII ▽; Eur.: F, G, CZ
- subsp. **seguieri** · G:Gewöhnliche Busch-Nelke · ♃ Z7 VI-VIII ▽; Eur.: F, I, Sw
- subsp. *sylvaticus* (Hoppe) Hegi = Dianthus seguieri subsp. glaber
- **serotinus** Waldst. & Kit. · G:Spätblühende Nelke · ♃ ⇝ △ VII-X ▽; Eur.: CZ, Slova., H, Serb., RO
- *sinensis* Link = Dianthus chinensis
- **spiculifolius** Schur · G:Fransen-Nelke · ♃ △ Z6 VI-VIII ▽; Eur.: RO, W-Russ.; E-Carp.
- *sternbergii* Sieber ex Capelli = Dianthus monspessulanus subsp. sternbergii
- **strictus** Banks & Sol. · ♃ △ Z4 VI-VII ▽; Eur.: Crete; TR, Syr.
- **subacaulis** Vill. · E:Short Pink; G:Kurzstängelige Nelke · ♃ △ Z5 VI-VIII ▽; Eur.: sp., F; Moroc.; mts.
- **suffruticosus** Willd. · ♄ Ⓚ VII-IX ▽; orig. ?
- **superbus** L. · E:Pink; F:Oeillet superbe; G:Gewöhnliche Pracht-Nelke · ♃ Z4 VI-VIII ⚕ ▽; Eur.* exc. BrI; W-Sib., E-Sib., Amur, Sakhal., Mong., China, Jap., Taiwan
- *sylvaticus* Hoppe ex Willd. = Dianthus seguieri subsp. glaber
- **sylvestris** Wulfen · G:Stein-Nelke
- subsp. **sylvestris** · E:Wood Pink; F:Oeillet des bois; G:Gewöhnliche Stein-Nelke · ♃ △ Z5 VI-VIII ▽; Eur.: Ib, Fr, Ital-P, Ba, C-Eur.; NW-Afr.
- subsp. **tergestinus** (Rchb.) Hayek · ♃ △ Z5 VI-VII ▽; Eur.: Croatia, Bosn., Montenegro, AL, I (Monte Gargano)
- *tergestinus* (Rchb.) A. Kern. = Dianthus sylvestris subsp. tergestinus
- **trifasciculatus** Kit. · ♃ ▽; Ba, RO, W-Russl.
- *webbianus* Vis. = Dianthus erinaceus
- **Cultivars:**
- **many cultivars, see Section III**

Diapensia L. -f- *Diapensiaceae* · 4 spp. · F:Diapensia; G:Trauerblume
- **lapponica** L. · E:Pincushion Plant · ♃ e Z2 IV-V; Sc, N-Russ., W-Sib, E-Can., Greenl.

Diaphananthe Schltr. -f- *Orchidaceae* · 24 spp.
- **bidens** (Afzel. ex Sw.) Schltr. · ♃ Z9 Ⓦ VI-VII ▽ ✱; W-Afr., C-Afr., Angola, Uganda
- **pellucida** (Lindl.) Schltr. · ♃ Z9 Ⓦ XI-I ▽ ✱; W-Afr., C-Afr., Uganda

Diarrhena P. Beauv. -f- *Poaceae* · 4 spp.
- **americana** P. Beauv. · E:American Beakgrain · ♃ VII-VIII; USA: NE, NCE, NC, SC, SE

Diascia Link & Otto -f- *Scrophulariaceae* · 38 spp. · E:Twinspur; F:Diascia; G:Doppelhörnchen
- **barberae** Hook. f. · E:Twinspur; F:Diascia · ⊙ Z8 VII-IX; S-Afr.
- *cordata* hort. = Diascia barberae
- **cordata** N.E. Br. · ♃ △ Z8 Ⓐ; S-Afr.: Natal
- *elegans* hort. = Diascia vigilis
- **rigescens** E. Mey. ex Benth. · ♄ Z8 Ⓐ ∧ VIII-IX; S-Afr.
- **vigilis** Hilliard & B.L. Burtt · ♃ Z8 Ⓚ; S-Afr.: Orange Free State
- **Cultivars:**
- **many cultivars**

Diastema Benth. -n- *Gesneriaceae* · 40 spp.
- **quinquevulnerum** Planch. & Linden · ♃ Z10 Ⓦ VII-VIII; Venez.

Dicentra Borkh. ex Bernh. -f- *Fumariaceae* · 19 spp. · E:Bleeding Heart; F:Cœur de Marie; G:Herzblume, Tränendes Herz
- **canadensis** (Goldie) Walp. · E:Squirrel Corn; G:Kanadische Herzblume · ♃ △ Z5 V; Can.: E; USA: NE, NCE, Tenn., N.C.
- **chrysantha** (Hook. & Arn.) Walp. · E:Golden Eardrops; G:Goldene Herzblume · ♃ Z8 ∧ VIII-IX; USA: S-Oreg., Calif.
- **cucullaria** (L.) Bernh. · E:Dutchman's Breeches; G:Kapuzen-Herzblume · ♃ Z5 V; Can.: E; USA: NE, NCE, NC, SE, NW, Idaho
- **eximia** (Ker-Gawl.) Torr. · E:Turkey Corn; G:Zwerg-Herzblume · ♃ Z5 V-VI; USA: NE, SE
- **formosa** (Andrews) Walp.
- subsp. **formosa** · E:Wild Bleeding Heart; G:Kleines Tränendes Herz · ♃ Z7 VI-X; Can.: B.C.; USA: NW, Calif.
- subsp. **oregana** (Eastw.) Munz · E:Oregon Bleeding Heart; G:Oregon-Herzblume · ♃ Z5 IV-IX; USA: Oreg., Calif.
- *oregana* Eastw. = Dicentra formosa subsp.

oregana
- **spectabilis** (L.) Lem. · E:Bleeding Heart;
F:Coeur de Marie; G:Tränendes Herz · ⑂
⚹ Z6 V ✿; China, Manch., Korea
- **Cultivars:**
- **many cultivars**

Dichaea Lindl. -f- *Orchidaceae* · 133 spp.
- **muricata** (Sw.) Lindl. · ⑂ ⚘ Z10 ⓦ ▽ ✳;
C-Am., W.Ind., trop. S-Am.

Dichanthium P. Willemet -n- *Poaceae* ·
20 spp. · E:Blue Stem; G:Blaustängel
- **annulatum** (Forssk.) Stapf · E:Diaz
Blue Stem, Kleberg Grass, Ringed Beard
Grass; G:Kleberg-Blaustängel · ⑂ Z10;
Ind., China: S
- **aristatum** (Poir.) C.E. Hubb. ·
E:Angleton Blue Stem; G:Angleton-
Blaustängel · ⑂ Z10; Ind., E-As.
- *ischaemum* (L.) Roberty = Bothriochloa
ischaemum

Dichelostemma Kunth -n- *Alliaceae* ·
5 spp. · E:Snake Lily
- **congestum** (Sm.) Kunth · E:Northern
Saitas · ⑂ Z8 ⓐ VI-VII; USA: Wash.,
Oreg., Calif.
- **multiflorum** (Benth.) A. Heller · E:Wild
Hyacinth · ⑂ Z7 ⓐ VI-VII; USA: Oreg.,
Calif., Rocky Mts., SW

Dichondra J.R. Forst. & G. Forst. -f-
Convolvulaceae · 5-10 spp. · E:Ponysfoot
- **micrantha** Urb. · E:Asian Ponysfoot · ⑂
⤳ Z10 ⓐ XII-VII; Korea, S-Jap., China,
Taiwan, Trop., nat. in Azor., BrI, I, S-USA
- **repens** J.R. Forst. & G. Forst. · ⑂ ⤳ ⓐ
VI-IX; USA: NE, SE, Fla., SW; Trop.
- **sericea** Sw. · E:Silverleaf Ponysfoot · ⑂
⤳ ⓐ XII-VII; C-Am., S-Am.

Dichorisandra J.C. Mikan -f-
Commelinaceae · 37 spp.
- **mosaica** Linden ex K. Koch · ⑂ Z9 ⓦ;
Braz.
- **reginae** (L. Linden & Rodigas) W.
Ludw. · E:Queen's Spiderwort · ⑂ Z9 ⓦ;
C-Peru
- **thyrsiflora** J.C. Mikan · E:Blue Ginger · ⑂
Z9 ⓦ IX-X; SE-Braz.
- *undata* Linden ex K. Koch = Geogenanthus poeppigii

Dichostylis P. Beauv. = Fimbristylis

- *micheliana* (L.) Ness = Cyperus michelianus

Dichroa Lour. -f- *Hydrangeaceae* · 12 spp.
- **febrifuga** Lour. · E:Feverfuge · ♄ e ⓦ
IV-VI; Him., China, Phil., Java

Dichroanthus Webb & Berthel. = Erysimum
- *scoparius* Webb & Berthel. = Erysimum
scoparium

Dichrostachys (A. DC.) Wight & Arn.
-f- *Mimosaceae* · 12 spp.
- **cinerea** (DC.) Wight & Arn. · ♄ ♄ d Z10
ⓦ; Afr., Ind.

Dicksonia L'Hér. -f- *Dicksoniaceae* ·
22 spp. · E:Tree Fern; F:Fougère arborescente; G:Beutelfarn, Taschenfarn
- **antarctica** Labill. · E:Soft Tree Fern;
G:Australischer Taschenfarn · ♄ e Z8
ⓦ ▽ ✳; Austr.: Queensl., N.S.Wales,
Victoria, S-Austr., Tasman.
- *culcita* L'Hér. = Culcita macrocarpa
- *davallioides* R. Br. = Dennstaedtia davallioides
- **fibrosa** Colenso · E:Golden Tree Fern;
G:Filziger Taschenfarn · ♄ e Z9 ⓐ ▽ ✳;
NZ
- *obtusifolia* Willd. = Dennstaedtia
obtusifolia
- *regalis* (Verschaff. & Lem.) Baker =
Cibotium regale
- *schiedei* (Schltdl. & Cham.) Baker =
Cibotium schiedei
- **squarrosa** (G. Forst.) Sw. · E:New
Zealand Tree Fern; G:Neuseeländischer
Taschenfarn · ♄ e Z9 ⓐ ▽ ✳; NZ

Dicliptera Juss. -f- *Acanthaceae* · c. 150 spp.
- **suberecta** (André) Bremek. · ♄ ⑂ Z10 ⓦ;
Urug.

Dicranopygium Harling -n- *Cyclanthaceae* ·
54 spp.
- **atrovirens** (H. Wendl.) Harling · ⓦ; ?
Col.

Dicranostigma Hook. f. & Thomson
-n- *Papaveraceae* · 3 spp. · E:Eastern
Horned Poppies; F:Pavot cornu d'Orient;
G:Östlicher Hornmohn
- **franchetianum** (Prain) Fedde · E:Annual
Dicranostigma; G:Asiatischer Hornmohn
· ☉ △ Z6 IV-V; Yunnan, Sichuan

– **lactucoides** Hook. f. & Thomson ·
E:Himalayan Horned Poppy; G:Hima-
laya-Hornmohn · ⑵ Z6; Him.
– **leptopodum** (Maxim.) Fedde ·
G:Feinstieliger Hornmohn · ⊙ △ Z6 IV-V;
China: Kansu

Dictamnus L. -m- *Rutaceae* · 1 sp. ·
E:Dittany; F:Fraxinelle; G:Diptam
– **albus** L.
– var. **albus** · E:Burning Bush, Dittany;
F:Herbe aux éclairs; G:Gewöhnlicher
Diptam · ⑵ Z7 V-VI ⚥ ▽; Eur.: Ib, Ital-P,
C-Eur., EC-Eur., Ba, E-Eur.
– var. **caucasicus** (Fisch. & C.A. Mey.)
Rouy · G:Kaukasischer Diptam · ⑵ Z7
V-VI ▽; Eur.: S-Russ.; TR, Cauc., NW-
Iran
– *caucasicus* (Fisch. & C.A. Mey.) Grossh. =
Dictamnus albus var. caucasicus
– *fraxinella* Pers. = Dictamnus albus var.
albus
– *gymnostylis* Steven = Dictamnus albus
var. albus

Dictyosperma H. Wendl. & Drude
-n- *Arecaceae* · 1 sp. · E:Princess Palm;
F:Aréquier, Palmier; G:Hurrikanpalme
– **album** (Bory) H. Wendl. & Drude ex
Scheff. · E:Common Princess Palm,
Hurricane Palm; G:Hurrikanpalme · ♄ e
Z10 ⓦ; Mauritius

Dicypellium Nees & Mart. -n- *Lauraceae* ·
2 spp. · G:Nelkenzimt
– **caryophyllatum** (Mart.) Nees · G:Nel-
kenzimt · ♄ ⓦ Ⓝ; trop. Am.

Dicyrta Regel = Achimenes
– *candida* (Lindl.) Hanst. = Achimenes
candida
– *warszewicziana* Regel = Achimenes
warszewicziana

Didierea Baill. -f- *Didiereaceae* · 2 spp.
– **madagascariensis** Baill. · ♄ ♄ d Z10 ⓦ
▽ ✳; Madag.
– *mirabilis* Baill. = Didierea madagascariensis

Didymocarpus Wall. -m- *Gesneriaceae* · c.
180 spp.
– *hamosus* Wall. = Chirita hamosa
– **obtusus** Wall. · ⑵; Nepal

Didymochlaena Desv. -f- *Dryopteridaceae* ·
1 sp.
– **truncatula** (Sw.) J. Sm. · ⑵ Z10 ⓦ;
Trop.

Didymosperma H. Wendl. & Drude ex
Hook. f. = Arenga
– *porphyrocarpum* (Blume) H. Wendl. &
Drude = Arenga porphyrocarpa

Dieffenbachia Schott -f- *Araceae* · 40 spp. ·
E:Dumb Cane, Mother-in-law's Tongue;
F:Dieffenbachia; G:Dieffenbachie
– × **bausei** Regel (*D. weirii* × *D. seguine*) · ⑵
Z10 ⓦ ✿; cult.
– **bowmannii** Carrière · ⑵ Z10 ⓦ; Col.,
Braz.
– **costata** Klotzsch ex Schott · ⑵ Z10 ⓦ;
Peru
– **humilis** Poepp. · ⑵ Z10 ⓦ; Braz., Peru
– **imperialis** Linden & André · ⑵ Z10 ⓦ;
Peru
– *latimaculata* Linden & André = Dieffenbachia bowmannii
– **leopoldii** W. Bull · ⑵ Z10 ⓦ; Costa Rica
– *macrophylla* Poepp. = Dieffenbachia
costata
– *maculata* (Lodd.) G.S. Bunting = Dieffenbachia seguine
– × **memoria-corsii** Fenai (*D. wallisii* × *D.
seguine*) · ⑵ Z10 ⓦ; cult.
– **parlatorei** Linden & André · ⑵ Z10 ⓦ;
Col.
– var. *marmorea* Linden & André = Dieffenbachia parlatorei
– *picta* Schott = Dieffenbachia seguine
– *reginae* hort. = Dieffenbachia bowmannii
– **rex** hort. ex L. Gentil · ⑵ Z10 ⓦ; S-Am.
– **seguine** (Jacq.) Schott · E:Dumb Cane,
Mother-in-Law Plant; G:Dieffenbachie,
Schweigrohrwurzel · ⑵ Z10 ⓦ ✿;
W.Ind.
– × **splendens** W. Bull (*D. leopoldii* × *D.
seguine*) · ⑵ Z10 ⓦ; cult.
– **weirii** Berk. · ⑵ Z10 ⓦ; cult.

Dierama K. Koch -n- *Iridaceae* · 44 spp. ·
E:African Hairbell, Wand Flower; F:Canne
à pêche des anges; G:Trichterschwertel
– **dracomontanum** Hilliard · ⑵ Z9 ⓚ;
S-Afr., Lesotho
– **pendulum** (L. f.) Baker · E:Angel's Fish-
ing Rods; F:Canne-à-pêche-des-anges · ⑵
Z7 ⊏ ∧ VII-VIII; E-Afr., S-Afr.
– var. *pumilum* (N.E. Br.) Baker = Dierama

pumilum
- **pulcherrimum** (Hook. f.) Baker · 4 Z7
  ⌐ ∧ IX-X; S-Afr.
- **pumilum** N.E. Br.
- **Cultivars:**
- **many cultivars**

Diervilla Mill. -f- *Caprifoliaceae* · 3 spp. ·
  E:Bush Honeysuckle; F:Diervilla;
  G:Buschgeißblatt
- *canadensis* Willd. = Diervilla lonicera
- **lonicera** Mill. · E:Northern Bush Honeysuckle; G:Kanadisches Buschgeißblatt · ♄
  d Z5 VI-VII; Can.: E; USA: NE, NCE, N.C.
- **rivularis** Gatt. · E:Mountain Bush
  Honeysuckle; G:Bach-Buschgeißblatt · ♄
  d Z5 VII-VIII; USA: SE; S-Alleghenies
- **sessilifolia** Buckland · E:Southern Bush
  Honeysuckle; G:Stielloses Buschgeißblatt
  · ♄ d Z5 VI-VIII; USA: Va., SE
- × **splendens** Carrière (*D. lonicera* × *D.
  sessilifolia*) · ♄ d Z5 VI-VIII; cult.

Dietes Salisb. ex Klatt -f- *Iridaceae* · 6 spp.
- **bicolor** (Steud.) Klatt · 4 Z9 ⓚ VI-VII;
  Cape
- **iridioides** (L.) Klatt · 4 Z9 ⓚ VI-VIII;
  E-Afr., S-Afr.
- **robinsoniana** (F. Muell.) Klatt · 4 Z9 ⓚ
  VII-VIII; Lord Howe Is.
- *vegeta* (L.) N.E. Br. = Dietes iridioides

Digitalis L. -f- *Scrophulariaceae* · c.
  20 spp. · E:Foxglove; F:Digitale;
  G:Fingerhut
- **ferruginea** L.
- subsp. **ferruginea** · E:Rusty Foxglove;
  G:Rostiger Fingerhut · ⊙ 4 VII-VIII ⚘;
  Eur.: H, Ba, RO; TR, Lebanon, Cauc.
- subsp. **schischkinii** (Ivanina) K. Werner ·
  4 ⚘; Cauc., TR
- var. *parviflora* Lindl. = Digitalis ferruginea subsp. schischkinii
- × **fucata** Ehrh. (*D. lutea* subsp. *lutea* × *D.
  purpurea*) · 4 VI-VII ⚘; cult.
- *gloxinioides* Carrière = Digitalis purpurea
- **grandiflora** Mill. · E:Large Yellow
  Foxglove; F:Digitale à grandes fleurs;
  G:Großblütiger Fingerhut, Großer Gelber
  Fingerhut · ⊙ 4 VI-VII ⚘ ▽; Eur.: Fr,
  Ital-P, C-Eur., EC-Eur., Ba, E-Eur.; W-Sib.
  (Altai)
- **laevigata** Waldst. & Kit. · 4 ⚘; Eur.: Ba
- **lanata** Ehrh. · E:Woolly Foxglove;
  G:Gewöhnlicher Wolliger Fingerhut · ⊙

4 VI-VIII ⚘ ⚘; Eur.: H, Ba, nat. in A
- **lutea** L. · E:Small Yellow Foxglove, Straw
  Foxglove; F:Digitale jaune; G:Gelber
  Fingerhut, Kleiner Gelber Fingerhut ·
  4 VI-VIII ⚘ ⚘ ▽; Eur.: Ib, Fr, Ital-P,
  C-Eur., nat. in PL
- × **mertonensis** Buxton & C.D. Darl. (*D.
  grandiflora* × *d. purpurea*) · 4 V-VI ⚘;
  cult.
- **obscura** L. · ♄ 4 ⓚ ⚘; sp., Moroc.
- **parviflora** Jacq. · 4 ⚘; N-Sp.; mts.
- × *purpurascens* Roth = Digitalis × fucata
- **purpurea** L. · G:Roter Fingerhut
- **many cultivars**
- subsp. **purpurea** · E:Foxglove; F:Digitale
  pourpre; G:Gewöhnlicher Roter
  Fingerhut · ⊙ 4 VI-VII ⚘ ⚘; Eur.* exc.
  Ba, EC-Eur.; Moroc., Madeira
- **thapsi** L. · 4 VI-IX ⚘; Eur.: Ib

Digitaria Haller -f- *Poaceae* · c. 220
  (-300) spp. · E:Finger Grass; F:Digitaire;
  G:Fingerhirse
- **cruciata** (Nees) A. Camus Z7 Ⓝ; Him.;
  Ind., China
- *decumbens* Stent = Digitaria eriantha
- **eriantha** Steud. · E:Common Finger
  Grass, Pangolagrass ; G:Pangolagras · 4
  Z7 Ⓝ; S-Afr., nat. in C-Am., W.Ind.
- **exilis** (Kippist) Stapf · E:Hungry Rice;
  G:Fonio-Hirse · ⊙ Z8 ⓜ Ⓝ; cult. W-Afr.
- **iburua** Stapf · ⊙ Z8 ⓜ Ⓝ; Nigeria
- **ischaemum** (Schreb.) Muhl. · E:Finger
  Grass, Smooth Crab Grass; G:Faden-
  Fingerhirse, Faden-Hirse · ⊙ Z7 X; Eur.:
  Ib, Fr, Ital-P, Ba, E-Eur.; TR, Cauc.,
  W-Sib., E-Sib., Amur, C-As., Him., Ind.,
  Tibet, China, Jap., Can., USA*, nat. in
  BrI, Sc, C-Eur.
- **sanguinalis** (L.) Scop. · G:Blut-Finger-
  hirse
- var. **esculenta** (Gaudin) Caldesi · ⊙ Z7
  VII-IX Ⓝ; cult.
- var. **pectiniformis** Henrard · G:Wimper-
  Fingerhirse · Z7
- var. **sanguinalis** · E:Hairy Crab Grass;
  G:Gewöhnliche Blut-Fingerhirse · ⊙ Z7
  VII-X; Eur.: Ib, Fr, Ital-P, Ba, E-Eur., H;
  TR, Cauc., C-As., Burma, China, Korea,
  Jap., Afr., N-Am., S-Am., Austr., NZ, nat.
  in Sc, C-Eur.

Dillenia L. -f- *Dilleniaceae* · c.60 spp. ·
  E:Elephant's Apple; F:Dillénie; G:Rosen-
  apfel

– **indica** L. · E:Chulta, Elephant's Apple;
G:Elefantenapfel, Indischer Rosenapfel
· ♄ e ⓜ Ⓝ; Ind., Sri Lanka, Indochina,
Malay. Arch.

× **Dillonara** hort. -f- *Orchidaceae*
(*Epidendrum* × *Laelia* × *Schomburgkia*)

Dillwynia Sm. -f- *Fabaceae* · 12 (-24) spp. ·
E:Parrot Pea
– **floribunda** Sm. · E:Showy Parrot Pea · ♄
e Z9 ⓚ III-IV; Austr., Tasman.
– **juniperina** Lodd. · E:Prickly Parrot Pea ·
♄ e Z9 ⓚ; Austr.

Dimocarpus Lour. -m- *Sapindaceae* ·
5 spp. · E:Longan Fruit; G:Longanbaum
– **longan** Lour. · E:Longan Fruit; G:Lon-
ganbaum · ♄ Z10 ⓜ Ⓝ; Ind., Sri Lanka,
S-China

Dimorphanthus Miq. = Aralia
– *elatus* Miq. = Aralia elata var. elata
– *mandshuricus* (Rupr. & Maxim.)Maxim. =
Aralia elata var. elata

Dimorphorchis Rolfe -f- *Orchidaceae* ·
2 spp.
– **lowii** (Lindl.) Rolfe · ⚃ Z10 ⓜ VII-X ▽
✱; Kalimantan

Dimorphotheca Moench -f- *Asteraceae* · 7
(-19) spp. · E:Sun Marigold; F:Souci de
Cap; G:Kapkörbchen
– *annua* Less. = Dimorphotheca pluvialis
– *barberiae* Harv. = Osteospermum
barberiae
– *calendulacea* Harv. = Dimorphotheca
sinuata
– **pluvialis** (L.) Moench · E:Rain Daisy,
Weather Prophet; F:Souci pluvial;
G:Regenzeigendes Kapkörbchen · ⊙ Z9
VII-VIII; S-Afr.
– **sinuata** DC. · E:Namaqualand Daisy;
G:Buschiges Kapkörbchen · ⊙ Z9 VII-VIII;
S-Afr.

Dinochloa Buse -f- *Poaceae* · c. 25 spp.
– **scandens** (Blume ex Nees) Kuntze · ♄ ⚥
ⓜ; Java

Dinteranthus Schwantes -m- *Aizoaceae* ·
6 spp.
– **vanzylii** (L. Bolus) Schwantes · ⚃ ⚘ Z9
ⓚ; Cape

Dionaea Sol. ex J. Ellis -f- *Droseraceae* ·
1 sp. · E:Venus' Fly Trap; F:Attrappe-
mouches, Dionée; G:Venusfliegenfalle
– **muscipula** J. Ellis · E:Venus' Fly Trap,
Venus' Mouse Trap; G:Venusfliegenfalle ·
⚃ Z8 ⓚ ▭ V-VII ▽ ✱; USA: N.C., S.C.

Dionysia Fenzl -f- *Primulaceae* · 41 sp.
– **aretioides** (Lehm.) Boiss. · ⚃ △ Ⓐ;
Iran: Elburs

Dioon Lindl. -n- *Zamiaceae* · 10 spp. ·
E:Fern Palm; F:Dioon, Palmier mexicain;
G:Doppelpalmfarn
– **edule** Lindl. · E:Mexican Fern Palm;
G:Mexikanischer Doppelpalmfarn · ♄ e
Z10 ⓜ ▽ ✱; Mex.
– **spinulosum** Dyer ex Eichler · E:Giant
Dioon · ♄ e Z10 ⓜ ▽ ✱; Mex.

Dioscorea L. -f- *Dioscoreaceae* · 606 spp. ·
E:Yam; F:Igname; G:Yamswurzel
– **abyssinica** Hochst. · ⚃ ⚥ Z10 ⓜ Ⓝ; Eth.,
E-Afr.
– **alata** L. · E:Water Yam, White Yam;
G:Wasser-Yamswurzel · ⚃ ⚥ Z10 ⓜ Ⓝ;
orig. ?, nat. in trop. As.
– **balcanica** Košanin · ⚃ ⚥ Z6; Eur.:
Montenegro, N-AL
– *batatas* Decne. = Dioscorea polystachya
– *Braziliensis* Willd. = Dioscorea trifida
– **bulbifera** L. · E:Air Potato; G:Brotwurzel,
Yamswurzel · ⚃ ⚥ Z10 ⓜ Ⓝ; trop. Afr.,
Indochina, Malay. Pen., Phil.
– **caucasica** Lipsky · ⚃ ⚥; Cauc.
– **cayenensis** Lam.
– subsp. **cayenensis** · E:Yellow Yam;
G:Gelbe Yamswurzel · ⚃ ⚥ Z10 ⓜ Ⓝ;
W-Afr.
– subsp. **rotundata** (Poir.) J. Miège ·
E:White Guinea Yam; G:Guinea-
Yamswurzel · ⚃ ⚥ Z10 ⓜ Ⓝ; Ind., Burma,
N-Thail., Laos, N-Vietn., S-China
– **deltoidea** Wall. ex Griseb. · ⚃ ⚥ Z10
Ⓝ ▽ ✱; Afgh., N-Ind., Nepal, Kashmir,
China
– *discolor* Kunth = Dioscorea dodecaneura
– **dodecaneura** Vell. · ⚃ ⚥ Z10 ⓜ; trop.
S-Am.
– **dumetorum** (Kunth) Pax · E:Bitter Yam ·
⚃ ⚥ Z10 ⓜ Ⓝ; trop. Afr.
– **elephantipes** (L'Hér.) Engl. ·
E:Elephant's Foot, Hottentot Bread;
G:Elefantenfuß · ♄ d ⚥ Z8 ⓚ; S-Afr.:
E-Cape, Natal, Transvaal

– **esculenta** (Lour.) Burkill · E:Lesser Yam ·
4 ⚥ Z10 ⓜ Ⓝ; orig. ?; cult. trop. Afr.
– *fargesii* Franch. = Dioscorea kamoonensis
– **floribunda** M. Martens & Galeotti ·
E:Yam · 4 ⚥ Z10 ⓜ Ⓝ; S-Mex., C-Am.
– **hispida** Dennst. · E:Asiatic Bitter Yam;
G:Bittere Yamswurzel · 4 ⚥ Z10 ⓜ Ⓝ;
Indochina, Malay. Pen., Honan, Phil.
– **japonica** Thunb. · E:Japanese Yam · 4 ⚥
Ⓝ; Jap., cult. Jap., China
– **kamoonensis** Kunth · 4 ⚥; W-China
– *macroura* Harms = Dioscorea sansibarensis
– **nummularia** Lam. · E:Yam · 4 ⚥ Ⓝ;
SE-As.
– **pentaphylla** L. · E:Fiveleaf Yam · 4 ⚥ ⓜ
Ⓝ; Ind., Burma, Sri Lanka, Malay. Pen.,
nat. in China, Taiwan, Pacific Is.
– **polystachya** Turcz. · E:Chinese Yam;
F:Igname; G:Chinesische Yamswurzel · 4
⚥ Z5 ⓜ ⓚ Ⓝ; China, Korea, Jap., nat. in
E-USA
– **prazeri** Prain & Burkill · 4 ⚥ ⓜ Ⓝ; Ind.
– *rotunda* Poir. = Dioscorea cayensis subsp.
rotunda
– **sansibarensis** Pax · E:Zanzibar Yam · 4
⚥ Z10 ⓜ; trop. Afr., Madag.
– *sativa* hort. non L. = Dioscorea bulbifera
– **sylvatica** Eckl. · ♄ ⚥ Z8 ⓚ; trop. Afr.,
S-Afr.
– **trifida** L. f. · E:Cush Cush, Yampee;
G:Kuschkusch-Yamswurzel · 4 ⚥ Z10
ⓜ Ⓝ; W.Ind., Guat., Col., Ecuad., Peru,
Braz., Guyan.
– **villosa** L. · E:China Root, Wild Yam;
G:Wilde Yamswurzel · 4 ⚥ ♀; USA: NE,
NCE, SC, SE

Dioscoreophyllum Engl. -m-
Menispermaceae · 3 (10) spp.
– **cumminsii** (Stapf) Diels · E:Serendipity
Berry · 4 ⚥ ⓜ Ⓝ; trop. Afr.

Diosma L. -f- *Rutaceae* · 28 spp. · F:Parfum
des dieux; G:Götterduft
– *alba* Thunb. = Coleonema album
– *fragrans* Sims = Adenandra fragrans
– **hirsuta** L. · E:Wild Buchu · ♄ e Z9 ⓚ
I-XII; Cape
– *tenuifolia* C. Presl non Willd. = Coleonema calycinum

Diosphaera Buser = Trachelium
– *jacquinii* (Sieber) Buser = Trachelium
jacquinii subsp. jacquinii

– *rumeliana* (Hampe) Bornm. = Trachelium
jacquinii subsp. jacquinii

Diospyros L. -f- *Ebenaceae* · 475 spp. ·
E:Ebony; F:Kaki, Plaqueminier; G:Dattel-
pflaume, Ebenholz, Lotuspflaume
– **celebica** Bakh. · ♄ ⓜ Ⓝ; Sulawesi
– **crassiflora** Hiern · E:Benin Ebony ;
G:Westafrikanisches Ebenholz · ♄ ⓜ Ⓝ;
W-Afr.
– **digyna** Jacq. · E:Black Sapote;
G:Schwarzes Ebenholz · ♄ ⓜ Ⓝ; Mex.;
cult. Trop.
– *ebenaster* auct. non Retz. = Diospyros
digyna
– **ebenum** J. König · E:Ebony; G:Echtes
Ebenholz · ♄ d ⓜ Ⓝ; Ind., Sri Lanka
– **kaki** L. f. · E:Kaki, Persimmon; G:Kak-
ipflaume · ♄ d ⚘ Z8 ⓚ VI ♀ Ⓝ; China,
S-Korea, Jap.
– **lotus** L. · E:Date Plum; G:Lotuspflaume
· ♄ ♄ d ⚘ Z5 V-VI Ⓝ; TR, Korea, China,
nat. in Eur.: Ba
– **melanoxylon** Roxb. · E:Coromandel
Ebony; G:Coromandel-Ebenholz · ♄ ♄ ⓜ
Ⓝ; Ind., Sri Lanka
– **virginiana** L. · E:American Persimmon,
Winter Plum; G:Persimone · ♄ d ⚘ Z7
V-VI Ⓝ; USA: NE, NCE, Kans., SC, SE,
Fla.

Diotis Desf. = Otanthus
– *maritima* (L.) Desf. ex Cass. = Otanthus
maritimus

Dipcadi Medik. -n- *Hyacinthaceae* · c.
55 spp.

Dipelta Maxim. -f- *Caprifoliaceae* · 4 spp. ·
F:Dipelta; G:Doppelschild
– **floribunda** Maxim. · G:Doppelschild · ♄ d
Z6 V-VI; C-China
– **ventricosa** Hemsl. · G:Ohr-Doppelschild ·
♄ d Z6 V-VI; W-China

Diphasiastrum Holub -n- *Lycopodiaceae* ·
16 spp. · E:Alpine Clubmoss; F:Lycopode;
G:Flachbärlapp
– **alpinum** (L.) Holub · E:Alpine Clubmoss;
G:Alpen-Flachbärlapp · 4 VIII-IX ▽;
Eur.*, TR, Cauc., W-Sib., E-Sib., Amur,
Kamchat., C-As., E-As., N-Am.
– **complanatum** (L.) Holub · E:Ground
Pine; G:Gewöhnlicher Flachbärlapp ·
4 ⌇ VIII-IX ⚘ ▽; Eur.* exc. BrI; TR,

Cauc., W-Sib., E-Sib., Amur, Sakhal.,
Kamchat., China, N-Jap., Ind, Sri Lanka,
Malay. Arch., Phil., Alaska, Can., USA:
NE, NCE, SE, Rocky Mts., Wash.
- **issleri** (Rouy) Holub · G:Isslers Flachbärlapp · ⚃ VIII-IX ▽; Eur.: C-Eur , F, BrI
- **oellgardii** A.M. Stoor et al. · G:Oell-
gards Flachbärlapp · ⚃ ▽; Eur.: F, D +
- **tristachyum** (Pursh) Holub · E:Deeproot
Clubmoss; G:Zypressen-Flachbärlapp · ⚃
VIII-IX ▽; Eur.* exc. BrI, Ib; TR, N-Am.
- **zeilleri** (Rouy) Holub · G:Zeillers
Flachbärlapp · ⚃ VIII-IX ▽; Eur.

Diphasium C. Presl ex Rothm. = Diphasiastrum
- *alpinum* = Diphasiastrum alpinum
- *complanatum* (L.) Rothm. = Diphasiastrum complanatum

Diphylleia Michx. -f- *Berberidaceae* ·
3 spp. · E:Umbrella Leaf; F:Diphylleia;
G:Schirmblatt
- **cymosa** Michx. · E:Umbrella Leaf;
G:Schirmblatt · ⚃ Z7 V-VI; USA: Va., SE

Dipladenia A. DC. = Mandevilla
- *atropurpurea* (Lindl.) A. DC. = Mandevilla atroviolacea
- *boliviensis* Hook. f. = Mandevilla
boliviensis
- *eximia* Hemsl. = Mandevilla eximia
- *sanderi* Hemsl. = Mandevilla sanderi

Diplarrhena Labill. -f- *Iridaceae* · 2 spp. ·
G:Tasmanische Iris
- **latifolia** Benth. · G:Breitblättrige Tasma-
nische Iris · ⚃ Z8 ⚘ VII-VIII; Tasman.
- **moraea** Labill. · E:Butterfly Flag;
G:Schmalblättrige Tasmanische Iris
· ⚃ Z8 ⚘ VII-VIII; Austr.: N.S.Wales,
Victoria, Tasman.

Diplazium Sw. -n- *Woodsiaceae* · 474 spp.
- **acrostichoides** (Sw.) Butters · E:Silver
False Spleenwort · ⚃ ; Can.: E; USA: NE,
NCE, SE
- **australe** (R. Br.) N.A. Wakef. · E:Austral
Lady Fern · ⚃ Z8 ⚘; Austr., NZ
- **celtidifolium** Kunze · ⚃ Z10 ⚘; Ind., Sri
Lanka, S-China, Taiwan, Jap., Indochina,
Malay. Pen., Polyn.
- **lanceum** (Thunb.) C. Presl · ⚃ ⚘; Ind.,
Sri Lanka, China, Jap., Taiwan
- *pycnocarpon* (Spreng.) M. Broun =

Athyrium pycnocarpon
- **sylvaticum** (Bory) Sw. · ⚃ ⚘; Trop.
- *thelypteroides* C. Presl = Diplazium
australe

Diplocyclos (Endl.) Post & Kuntze
-m- *Cucurbitaceae* · 4 spp. · F:Fausse-
couleuvrée; G:Scheinzaunrübe
- **palmatus** (L.) C. Jeffrey · E:Lollipop
Climber · ⚃ ⚥ ⚘ Z10 ⚘ VII-IX; trop.
Afr., trop. As., Austr.: N.Terr., Queensl.,
N.S.Wales

Diploknema Pierre -f- *Sapotaceae* · 10 spp.
- **butyracea** (Roxb.) H.J. Lam · E:Indian
Buttertree; G:Fulwafettbaum · ♄ e ⚘ Ⓝ;
Tibet, Nepal, Bhutan, Ind., Andaman. I.

Diplotaxis DC. -f- *Brassicaceae* · 27 spp. ·
E:Wall Rocket; F:Diplotaxis; G:Doppel-
same
- **muralis** (L.) DC. · E:Wall Rocket;
G:Mauer-Doppelsame · ⊙ Z7 VI-IX; Eur.*
exc. BrI, Sc; Cauc.
- **tenuifolia** (L.) DC. · E:Lincoln's Weed,
Sand Rocket; G:Schmalblättriger Dop-
pelsame · ⚃ Z7 V-X; Eur.* exc. BrI, Sc;
TR, Syr.
- **viminea** (L.) DC. · G:Ruten-Doppelsame ·
⊙ Z8 VI-IX; Eur.: Ib, Fr, Ital-P, Ba, Crim;
TR, Levant, Moroc., Alger., Egypt, nat. in
G, RO

Diplothemium Mart. = Polyandrococos
- *caudescens* Mart. = Polyandrococos
caudescens

Dipogon Liebm. -m- *Fabaceae* · 1 sp. ·
E:Australian Pea; G:Okiebohne
- **lignosus** (L.) Verdc. · E:Australian Pea,
Dolichos Pea; G:Okiebohne · ♄ Z9 ⚘;
S-Afr.

Dipsacus L. -m- *Dipsacaceae* · 15 spp. ·
E:Teasel; F:Cardère; G:Karde
- **ferox** Loisel. · ⊙; Eur.: I, Sard., Cors
- **fullonum** L. · E:Common Teasel, Wild
Teasel; G:Wilde Karde · ⊙ Z3 VII-VIII;
Eur.* exc. Sc; TR, Levant, Cauc., Iran,
NW-Afr., nat. in DK
- **laciniatus** L. · E:Cut Leaved Teasel;
G:Schlitzblättrige Karde · ⊙ Z3 VII-VIII;
Eur.: Fr, Ital-P, C-Eur., EC-Eur., Ba,
E-Eur., ? Ib; TR, Iraq, Syr., Cauc., Iran,
C-As.

– **pilosus** L. · E:Small Teasel; G:Behaarte
Karde · ⊙ VII-VIII; Eur.*, Cauc., Iran
– **sativus** (L.) Honck. · E:Card's Thistle,
Fuller's Teasel; G:Weber-Karde · ⊙ Z5
VII-VIII Ⓝ; orig.?, cult., nat. in Eur.
– **strigosus** Willd. ex Roem. & Schult. ·
E:Yellow-flowered Teasel; G:Schlanke
Karde · ⊙ VII-VIII; Eur.: Russ.; TR, Cauc.,
N-Iran, C-As., nat. in BrI, Sc, EC-Eur.
– *sylvestris* Huds. = Dipsacus fullonum

Dipteracanthus Nees = Ruellia
– *devosianus* (Jacob-Makoy) Boom =
Ruellia devosiana
– *portellae* (Hook. f.) Boom = Ruellia
portellae

Dipterocarpus C.F. Gaertn.
-m- *Dipterocarpaceae* · 69 spp. ·
F:Diptérocarpus, Keruing; G:Zweiflügel-
fruchtbaum
– **alatus** Roxb. ex G. Don · ♄ d ⓦ Ⓝ;
Burma
– **turbinatus** C.F. Gaertn. · E:Copaiba
Balsam, Gurjun Balsam; G:Ostindischer
Zweiflügelfruchtbaum · ♄ e ⓦ Ⓝ; Ind.,
Burma

Dipteronia Oliv. -f- *Aceraceae* · 2 spp.
– **sinensis** Oliv. · ♄ d ⊗ Z7 ∧ VI; C-China

Dipteryx Schreb. -f- *Fabaceae* · 10 spp. ·
E:Tonka Bean; F:Coumarouna, Tonka;
G:Tonkabohne
– **odorata** (Aubl.) Willd. · E:Tonka Bean;
G:Tonkabohne · ♄ ⓕ ⚶ ⚘ Ⓝ; Guyan.,
Surinam, N-Braz.

Dirca L. -f- *Thymelaeaceae* · 2 spp. ·
E:Leatherwood; F:Bois de plomb;
G:Bleiholz, Lederholz
– **palustris** L. · E:Leatherwood, Rope Bark;
G:Sumpf-Lederholz · ♄ d Z5 III-V ⚘;
Can.: E; USA: NE, NCE, SE, Fla.

Disa P.J. Bergius -f- *Orchidaceae* · 170 spp.
– **uniflora** P.J. Bergius · E:Pride-of-Table-
Mountain; G:Stolz des Tafelberges · ⚃ Z9
ⓚ VII-VIII ▽ ✳; SW-Cape

Disanthus Maxim. -m- *Hamamelidaceae* ·
1 sp. · G:Doppelblüte
– **cercidifolius** Maxim. · G:Doppelblüte · ♄
d Z7 ∧ X; Jap.

Dischidia R. Br. -f- *Asclepiadaceae* · c.
40 spp. · F:Dischidia; G:Urnenpflanze
– **albida** Griff. · ⚃ Ψ e ⚶ ⓦ; Malay. Pen.,
Sumat., Kalimantan, Sulawesi
– **major** (Vahl) Merr. · E:Rattle Skulls · ⚃ Ψ
e ⚶ ⓦ; Ind., SE-As., Austr.
– **merrillii** Becc. · ⚃ Ψ e ⚶ ⓦ; Phil.
– *pectenoides* H. Pearson = Dischidia vidalii
– *rafflesiana* Wall. = Dischidia major
– **sagittata** (Blume) Decne. · ⚃ Ψ e ⚶ ⓦ;
Java
– **vidalii** Becc. · ⚃ Ψ e ⚶ ⓦ; Phil.

Disocactus Lindl. -m- *Cactaceae* · 3 spp.
– **biformis** (Lindl.) Lindl. · Ψ Z9 ⓦ ▽ ✳;
Guat., Hond.
– **eichlamii** (Weing.) Britton & Rose · Ψ Z9
ⓦ ▽ ✳; Guat.
– *flagelliformis* (L.) Barthlott = Aporocactus
flagelliformis
– *martianus* (Zucc.) Barthlott = Aporocactus martianus
– *nelsonii* (Britton & Rose) Linding. =
Chiapasia nelsonii
– *ramulosus* (Salm-Dyck) Kimnach =
Pseudorhipsalis ramulosa
– *speciosus* (Cav.) Britton & Rose =
Heliocereus speciosus var. speciosus

× **Disophyllum** Innes -n- *Cactaceae*
(*Disocactus* × *Epiphyllum*)
– **Cultivars:**
– **many cultivars**

Disphyma N.E. Br. -n- *Aizoaceae* · 5 spp. ·
E:Purple Dewplant; G:Purpurtaupflanze
– **australe** (Sol.) J.M. Black · ⚃ Ψ Z9 ⓚ;
NZ
– **crassifolium** (L.) L. Bolus · ⚃ Ψ Z9 ⓚ;
S-Afr., nat. in Balear., P

Disporum Salisb. ex G. Don -n-
Convallariaceae · 20 spp. · E:Fairy Bells;
F:Clochette des fées; G:Feenglöckchen
– **sessile** (Thunb.) D. Don ex Schult. &
Schult. f. · ⚃ Z7; Jap., Korea, Sachalin

Dissotis Benth. -f- *Melastomataceae* · c.
100 spp.
– **eximia** Harv. · ⚃ Z10 ⓚ; S-Afr.
– **plumosa** (D. Don) Hook. f. · ⚃ ⚶ ↝ Z10
ⓦ VII-IX; W-Afr., C-Afr.
– *princeps* Triana = Dissotis eximia
– *rotundifolia* (Sm.) Triana = Dissotis
plumosa

Distemonanthus Benth. -m- *Caesalpiniaceae* · 1 sp.
- **benthamianus** Baill. · E:Nigerian Satinwood; G:Afrikanisches Zitronenholz, Movingui · ♄ Ⓦ Ⓝ; W-Afr., C-Afr.

Distictis Mart. ex Meisn. -f- *Bignoniaceae* · 9 spp. · F:Bignone; G:Klettertrompete
- **buccinatoria** (DC.) A.H. Gentry · E:Mexican Blood Flower; G:Mexikanische Klettertrompete · ♄ ≀ e ≹ Z9 Ⓚ VII-VIII; Mex.
- **laxiflora** (DC.) Greenm. · ♄ ≀ ≹ Z9 Ⓚ; Mex., Nicar.

Distylium Siebold & Zucc. -n- *Hamamelidaceae* · 12 spp.
- **racemosum** Siebold & Zucc. · E:Isu Tree; G:Isubaum · ♄ ♄ e Z8 Ⓚ III-IV; Jap., Riukiu-Is.

Dittrichia Greuter -f- *Asteraceae* · 2 spp. · G:Alant; E:Fleabane; F:Aunée
- **graveolens** (L.) Greuter · E:Camphor Inula, Stinkweed; G:Drüsiger Alant, Klebriger Alant · ⊙ VII-IX; Eur.: Ib, Fr, Ital-P, Ba; TR, Iraq, Iran, Afgh., NW-Ind.

Dizygotheca N.E. Br. = Schefflera
- *elegantissima* (Veitch ex Mast.) R. Vig. & Guillaumin = Schefflera elegantissima
- *kerchoveana* (Veitch ex P.W. Richards) N. Taylor = Schefflera kerchoveana

Dodecatheon L. -n- *Primulaceae* · c. 15 spp. · E:Shooting Star; F:Fleur des dieux, Gyroselle; G:Götterblume
- **clevelandii** Greene · E:Cleveland Shootingstar; G:Cleveland-Götterblume · ♃ △ Z6 V-VI; Calif.: Sierra Nevada
- *cusickii* Greene = Dodecatheon pulchellum subsp. cusickii
- **dentatum** Hook. · E:White Shooting Star; G:Gezähnte Götterblume · ♃ Z5; B.C., USA: Wash., N-Oreg., Idaho, Utah
- **frigidum** Cham. & Schltdl. · E:Arctic Shootingstar; G:Alaska-Götterblume · ♃ △ Z3 V-VI; Alaska, Can.: W; Sib.
- **hendersonii** A. Gray · E:Mosquito Bills; G:Hendersons Götterblume · ♃ △ Z6 V-VI; Calif.: Sierra Nevada
- **jeffreyi** Van Houtte · E:Tall Shooting Star; G:Hohe Götterblume · ♃ △ Z5 V-VI; Alaska, Can.: W; USA: NW, Calif., Rocky Mts.
- **meadia** L. · E:American Cowslip, Pride of Ohio, Shooting Star; G:Meads Götterblume · ♃ △ Z3 V-VI; USA: NE, NCE, SE, SC
- *pauciflorum* (Durand) Greene = Dodecatheon meadia
- **pulchellum** (Raf.) Merr.
- subsp. **cusickii** (Greene) Calder · E:Cusick's Shooting Star · Z5; Can. (B.C.); USA: NW, Mont., Idaho
- subsp. **pulchellum** · E:Darkthroat Shooting Star; F:Gyroselle élégant; G:Schöne Götterblume · ♃ △ Z5 V-VI; Alaska, Can.: W; USA: NW, Calif., Rocky Mts.; Mex.
- *radicatum* Greene = Dodecatheon pulchellum subsp. pulchellum
- *tetrandrum* Suksd. ex Greene = Dodecatheon jeffreyi

Dodonaea Mill. -f- *Sapindaceae* · 68 spp. · F:Dodonéa; G:Dodonaee
- **triquetra** J.C. Wendl. · ♄ e Z9 Ⓚ ☠; Trop.
- **viscosa** (L.) Jacq. · E:Hop Bush, Hopwood, Native Hops; G:Australischer Hopfen · ♄ e Z9 Ⓚ ⚕ ☠ Ⓝ; USA: Fla., Ariz.; W.Ind., Trop.

Dolichos L. -m- *Fabaceae* · c. 70 spp. · F:Dolique; G:Helmbohne
- *biflorus* auct. non L. = Macrotyloma uniflorum
- *biflorus* L. = Vigna unguiculata subsp. unguiculata
- **kilimandscharicus** Taub. · ♃; C.-Afr., E-Afr.
- *lablab* L. = Lablab purpureus
- *lobatus* Willd. = Pueraria lobata
- *soja* L. = Glycine max
- *uniflorus* Lam. = Macrotyloma uniflorum

Dolichothele (K. Schum.) Britton & Rose = Mammillaria
- *balsasoides* (R.T. Craig) Backeb. = Mammillaria beneckei
- *baumii* (Boed.) Werderm. & Buxb. = Mammillaria baumii
- *longimamma* (DC.) Britton & Rose = Mammillaria longimamma
- *nelsonii* (Britton & Rose) Backeb. = Mammillaria nelsonii
- *surculosa* (Boed.) Backeb. ex Buxb. = Mammillaria surculosa
- *uberiformis* (Zucc.) Britton & Rose = Mammillaria longimamma

Dombeya Cav. -f- *Sterculiaceae* · 225 spp. ·
F:Hortensia en arbre; G:Hortensienbaum
– **acutangula** Cav. · ♄ Z10 ⓦ; Maskarene
Is.
– **burgessiae** Gerrard ex Harv. · E:Pink
Dombeya; G:Ahornblättriger Hortensienbaum · ♄ e Z10 ⓦ; E-Afr., trop-Afr.,
S-Afr.
– *calantha* K. Schum. = Dombeya burgessiae
– × **cayeuxii** André (*D. burgessiae × D.
wallichii*) · E:Pink Snowball; G:Rispiger
Hortensienbaum · ♄ e Z10 ⓦ; cult.
– *mastersii* Hook. f. = Dombeya burgessiae
– *natalensis* Sond. = Dombeya tiliacea
– **tiliacea** (Endl.) Planch. · E:Forest
Dombeya · ♄ e Z10 ⓦ; S-Afr.
– **wallichii** (Lindl.) Benth. & Hook. f. ·
E:Pink Ball Tree; G:Hortensienbaum,
Wallichs Hortensienbaum · ♄ e Z10 ⓦ
II-III; Madag.

× **Domindesmia** hort. -f- *Orchidaceae*
(*Domingoa × Hexadesmia*)

× **Domliopsis** hort. -f- *Orchidaceae*
(*Domingoa × Laeliopsis*)

Donia G. Don = Clianthus
– *punicea* G. Don = Clianthus puniceus
– *speciosa* G. Don = Clianthus formosus

Doodia R. Br. -f- *Blechnaceae* · 17 spp. ·
E:Rasp-Fern; F:Doodia rude; G:Raspel-
farn
– **aspera** R. Br. · ⁴ Z9 ⓐ; Austr.: Queensl.,
N.S.Wales, Victoria
– **caudata** (Cav.) R. Br. · ⁴ Z9 ⓐ; Austr.:
Queensl., N.S.Wales, Victoria, Tasman.;
NZ, Polyn.
– **media** R. Br. · ⁴ Z9 ⓐ; Austr., NZ,
N.Caled.

Dorema D. Don -n- *Apiaceae* · 12 spp. ·
E:Gum Ammoniac; F:Doréma, Gomme-
ammniaque; G:Ammoniakpflanze
– **ammoniacum** D. Don · E:Gum Ammoniac; G:Ammoniakpflanze · ⁴ VI ☩ ; Iran,
C-As., Afgh., Sib.

× **Doriella** hort. -f- *Orchidaceae* (*Doritis ×
Kingiella*)

× **Doritaenopsis** hort. -f- *Orchidaceae*
(*Doritis × Phalaenopsis*)

Doritis Lindl. -f- *Orchidaceae* · 2 spp.
– **pulcherrima** Lindl. · ⁴ Z9 ⓦ VIII-XI ▽
✳; S-China, Burma, Thail., Cambodia,
Malay. Pen., N-Sumat.

Doronicum L. -n- *Asteraceae* · 35-40 spp. ·
E:Leopard's Bane; F:Doronic; G:Gäms-
wurz
– **austriacum** Jacq. · E:Austrian Leopard's
Bane; G:Österreichische Gämswurz · ⁴
Z5 VII-VIII; Eur.* exc. Sc, BrI; W-TR; mts.
– **cataractarum** Widder · G:Sturzbach-
Gämswurz · ⁴ VII-IX; Eur.: A (Koralpe)
– **clusii** (All.) Tausch
– var. **clusii** · G:Clusius' Gämswurz, Zottige
Gämswurz · ⁴ Z6 VI-VII; Eur.* exc. BrI,
Sc; Cordillera Cantábrica, Pyr., Alp.,
Carp.
– var. **villosum** Tausch · G:Steirische
Gämswurz · ⁴ Z6 VII-IX; Eur.: Sw, A, RO
+ ; Alp., Carp.
– **columnae** Ten. · E:Eastern Leopard's
Bane; G:Herzblättrige Gämswurz · ⁴ Z5
V-VI; Eur.: C-Eur., E-Eur., I, Ba; mts.
– *cordatum* auct. non Lam. = Doronicum
columnae
– *cordifolium* Sternb. = Doronicum
columnae
– × **excelsum** (N.E. Br.) Stace (*D. columnae
× D. pardalianches × D. plantagineum*) · ⁴
Z6; cult.
– **glaciale** (Wulfen) Nyman · G:Gletscher-
Gämswurz
– subsp. **calcareum** (Vierh.) Hegi ·
G:Kalkliebende Gämswurz · ⁴ Z6 VI-VIII;
Eur.: A; NE-Alp.
– subsp. **glaciale** · G:Gewöhnliche
Gletscher-Gemswurz · ⁴ Z6 VII-VIII; Eur.:
I, G, A, Slove.; E-Alp.
– **grandiflorum** Lam. · G:Großblütige
Gämswurz · ⁴ Z5 VII-VIII; Eur.: Ib, Fr,
Ital-P, C-Eur., Ba, ? RO
– **orientale** Hoffm. · F:Doronic du Caucase;
G:Kaukasus-Gämswurz · ⁴ ⋉ Z5 IV-V;
Eur.: Ital-P, H, Ba, RO, W-Russ.; TR,
Lebanon, Cauc.
– **some cultivars**
– **pardalianches** L. · E:Great Leopard's
Bane; G:Kriechende Gämswurz · ⁴ Z6
V-VII; Eur.: sp., Fr, I, Sw, D; mts., nat. in
BrI, A
– **plantagineum** L. · F:Doronic plantain;
G:Wegerich-Gämswurz · ⁴ ⋉ Z6 IV-V;
Eur.: Ib, F, I, nat. in BrI, NL

Dorotheanthus Schwantes -m- *Aizoaceae* ·
6 spp. · E:Iceplant; F:Ficoide, Mésembryanthème; G:Mittagsblume
– **apetalus** (L. f.) N.E. Br. · ⊙ Ψ VII-IX; Cape
– **bellidiformis** (Burm. f.) N.E. Br. ·
  E:Livingstone Daisy; G:Garten-Mittagsb-
  lume · ⊙ Ψ VII-IX; Cape
– *criniflorus* (L. f.) Schwantes = Dorotheanthus bellidiformis
– *gramineus* (Haw.) Schwantes =
  Dorotheanthus apetalus
– *oculatus* N.E. Br. = Dorotheanthus
  bellidiformis

Dorstenia L. -f- *Moraceae* · 105 spp. ·
F:Dorstenia; G:Dorstenie
– **arifolia** Lam. · ⁴ ⓜ; Braz.
– **barteri** Bureau · ⁴ ⓜ; Nigeria,
  Cameroon
– **contrajerva** L. · E:Contra Hierba, Torn's
  Herb · ⁴ ⓜ ⚥ Ⓝ; S-Mex., W.Ind., Braz.,
  Afr.
– **convexa** De Wild. · ⁴ ⓜ; Zaire
– *erecta* Vell. = Dorstenia hirta
– **hildebrandtii** Engl. · ⁴ ⓜ; Kenya,
  Tanzania
– **hirta** Desv. · ⁴ ⓜ; Braz.
– **psilurus** Welw. · ⁴ ⓜ; trop. Afr.
– **turnerifolia** Fisch. & C.A. Mey. · ⁴ ⓜ;
  Lat.-Am.
– **urceolata** Schott · ⁴ ⓜ; Braz.
– **yambuyaensis** De Wild. · ⁴ ⓜ; Zaire

Doryanthes Corrêa -f- *Doryanthaceae* ·
2 spp. · E:Spear Lily; F:Lis-javelot;
G:Speerblume
– **excelsa** Corrêa · E:Australian Giant Lily,
  Spear Lily; G:Hohe Speerblume · ⁴ Z10
  ⓒ; Austr.: Queensl., N.S.Wales
– **palmeri** W. Hill Ex Benth. · E:Giant
  Spear Lily; G:Palmers Speerblume · ⁴
  Z10 ⓒ; Austr.: Queensl., N.S.Wales

Dorycnium Mill. -n- *Fabaceae* · 10 spp. ·
F:Dorycnium; G:Backenklee
– **germanicum** (Gremli) Rikli · G:Deut-
  scher Backenklee · ♄ VII; Eur.: I, Sw, G,
  A, CZ, H, Slove.
– **graecum** (L.) Ser. · ♄ ⁴ · E-Ba, Crim,
  Cauc., TR
– **herbaceum** Vill. · G:Krautiger Backenklee · ♄ ⁴ Z8 VI-VII; Ba, Ital-P, Crim, TR,
  Cauc.
– **hirsutum** (L.) Ser. · E:Hairy Canary Clover; F:Dorycnium hérissé; G:Behaarter

Backenklee, Zottiger Backenklee · ♄ ⁴
Z8 ⓒ VI-IX; Eur.: Ib, F, Ital-P, Ba; TR,
Levant, Moroc., Tun.
– **pentaphyllum** Scop. · E:Badassi;
  G:Fünfblättriger Backenklee · ♄ Z8 V-VI;
  Eur.: Ib, F, I
– subsp. *germanicum* (Gremli) Gams =
  Dorycnium germanicum
– **rectum** (L.) Ser. · E:Greater Badassi · ♄
  ⁴ Z8; Eur.: Ib, Fr, Ital-P, Ba; TR

Doryopteris J. Sm. -f- *Adiantaceae* ·
56 spp. · F:Fougère; G:Speerfarn
– **ludens** (Wall.) J. Sm. · ⁴ Z10 ⓜ;
  Indochina, Phil.
– *palmata* (Willd.) J. Sm. = Doryopteris
  pedata var. palmata
– **pedata** (L.) Fée
– var. **palmata** (Willd.) Hicken · ⁴ Z10 ⓜ;
  Mex., C-Am., trop. S- Am.
– var. **pedata** · E:Hand Fern; G:Gestielter
  Speerfarn · ⁴ Z10 ⓜ; W.Ind., trop. S-Am.
– **sagittifolia** (Raddi) J. Sm. · ⁴ Z10 ⓜ;
  trop. S-Am.

Dossinia C. Morren -f- *Orchidaceae* · 1 sp.
– **marmorata** C. Morren · ⁴ ⓜ VII-X ▽ ✳;
  Kalimantan (Sarawak)

Douglasia Lindl. = Androsace
– *vitaliana* (L.) Hook. f. ex Pax = Vitaliana
  primuliflora subsp. primuliflora

Dovyalis E. Mey. ex Arn. -f- *Flacourtiaceae* ·
15 spp.
– **caffra** (Hook. f. & Harv.) Hook. f. · E:Kei
  Apple; G:Kei-Apfel · ♄ d Z9 ⓒ Ⓝ; S-Afr.
– **hebecarpa** (Gardner) Warb. · E:Ceylon
  Gooseberry; G:Ceylon-Stachelbeere · ♄ d
  Z10 ⓒ; Ind., Sri Lanka

Downingia Torr. -f- *Campanulaceae* ·
11 sp. · E:Californian Lobelia; F:Clintonia,
Fausse-lobélie; G:Scheinlobelie
– **elegans** (Douglas) Torr. · E:Blue Calico
  Flower; G:Scheinlobelie · ⊙ VII-VIII;
  USA: NW, Idaho, Nev., Calif.
– **pulchella** (Lindl.) Torr. · E:Flatface
  Calico Flower · ⊙ VII-VIII; Calif.

Doxantha Miers = Macfadyena
– *capreolata* (L.) Miers = Bignonia
  capreolata
– *unguis-cati* (L.) Rehder = Macfadyena
  unguis-cati

Draba L. -f- *Brassicaceae* · c. 300 spp. · E:Whitlow Grass; F:Drave; G:Felsenblümchen
- **aizoides** L. · E:Yellow Whitlow Grass; F:Drave faux-aizoon; G:Immergrünes Felsenblümchen · ♃ △ Z4 IV ▽; Eur.* exc. Sc; mts.
- **aspera** Bertol. · G:Raues Felsenblümchen · ♃ Z4 VI-VII ▽; Eur.: Ba, Ital-P, F; mts.
- **brachystemon** DC. · ♃ ▽; Eur.: E-Pyr., Alp. (Monte Rosa)
- **bruniifolia** Steven
- subsp. **bruniifolia** · ♃ △ Z7 IV-V ▽; TR, Iraq, Cauc., Iran
- subsp. **olympica** (Sibth. ex DC.) Coode & Cullen Z7 ▽; TR
- *bryoides* DC. = Draba rigida var. bryoides
- **cuspidata** M. Bieb. · ♃ △ Z6 IV-V ▽; Crim
- **dedeana** Boiss. & Reut. ex Boiss. · ♃ △ Z7 IV-V ▽; Eur.: sp.; mts.
- **densifolia** Nutt. · ♃ ▽; Can. (B.C.); USA: NW, Calif.
- *diversifolia* Boiss. & A. Huet = Draba bruniifolia subsp. bruniifolia
- **dolomitica** Buttler · G:Dolomiten-Felsenblümchen · ♃ VI-VIII ▽; Eur.: I, A; Dolomiten, Brenner
- **dubia** Suter · E:Austrian Whitlow Grass; G:Eis-Felsenblümchen · ♃ Z6 V-VII ▽; Eur.: Ib, Fr, Ital-P, C-Eur., EC-Eur., Ba; mts.
- **fladnizensis** Wulfen · E:Austrian Whitlow Grass; G:Fladnitzer Felsenblümchen · ♃ △ Z5 V-VI ▽; Eur.: Sc, C-Eur., EC-Eur., F, I, E-Eur.; N, mts.; Alaska, USA: NW, Calif., Rocky Mts.; C-As., Him.
- **haynaldii** Stur · ♃ Z7 ▽; RO; S-Carp.
- **hoppeana** Rchb. · G:Hoppes Felsenblümchen · ♃ Z7 VII-VIII ▽; Eur.: F, I, C-Eur.; Alp.
- **incana** L. · E:Hoary Whitlow Grass; G:Graues Felsenblümchen · ⊙ ♃ △ Z4 V-VI ▽; Eur.: BrI, Sc, Fr, C-Eur., Ib, E-Eur.; N, mts.
- **ladina** Braun-Blanq. · E:Engadine Whitlow Grass; G:Bündner Felsenblümchen · ♃ VII-VIII ▽; Eur.: E-Sw; mts.
- **lasiocarpa** Rochel ex M. Bieb. · E:Woolly-fruited Whitlow Grass; G:Karpaten-Felsenblümchen · ♃ △ Z5 III-V ▽; Eur.: A, Ba, RO; Carp., Balkan
- **loiseleurii** Boiss. · ♃ Z9 Ⓐ ▽; Cors
- **mollissima** Steven · ♃ Z7 ∧ III-IV ▽; Cauc.
- **muralis** L. · E:Wall Whitlow Grass; G:Mauer-Felsenblümchen · ⊙ V-VI ▽; Eur.*
- **nemorosa** L. · G:Hain-Felsenblümchen · ⊙ V-VI ▽; Eur.* exc. BrI; TR, Cauc., W-Sib., E-Sib., Amur, Sakhal., Kamchat
- **norvegica** Gunnerus · E:Rock Whitlow Grass; G:Norwegisches Felsenblümchen · ♃ Z6 VI-VII ▽; Eur.: BrI, Sc, N-Russ., A; Sib., N-Am
- *olympica* Sibth. ex DC. = Draba bruniifolia subsp. olympica
- **pacheri** Stur · G:Tauern-Felsenblümchen · ♃ VI-VIII ▽; Eur.: E-A, Slova.
- **polytricha** Ledeb. · ♃ Z7 ▽; TR, Cauc.
- **rigida** Willd.
- var. **bryoides** (DC.) Boiss. Z7 ▽; TR, Cauc.
- var. **rigida** · ♃ △ Z7 IV-V ▽; Cauc.
- **sauteri** Hoppe · G:Sauters Felsenblümchen · ♃ △ VI ▽; Eur.: G, A; NE-Alp.
- **sibirica** (Pall.) Thell. · F:Drave de Sibérie · ♃ ⇝ △ Z1 V-VI ▽; Eur.: Russ.; Cauc., W-Sib., E-Sib., C-As., Mong., China: Sinkiang, Greenl.
- **siliquosa** M. Bieb. · G:Kärntner Felsenblümchen · ♃ △ Z6 V-VII ▽; Eur.: Ib, Ital-P, C-Eur., EC-Eur., E-Eur., BG; TR, Cauc., Iran
- subsp. *carinthiaca* (Hoppe) O. Bolòs & Vigo = Draba siliquosa
- **stellata** Jacq. · E:Starry Whitlow Grass; G:Sternhaar-Felsenblümchen · ♃ VI-VII ▽; Eur.: A; NE-Alp.
- *stylaris* W.D.J. Koch = Draba incana
- × **suendermannii** Sünd. (*D. dedeana* × ?) · F:Drave de Sündermann; G:Sündermanns Felsenblümchen · ♃; cult.
- **tomentosa** Clairv. · G:Filziges Felsenblümchen · ♃ Z6 VI-VIII ▽; Eur.: Fr, C-Eur., EC-Eur., Ba; mts.
- *tomentosa* Hegetschw. = Draba dubia
- *wahlenbergii* Hartm. = Draba fladnizensis

Dracaena Vand. ex L. -f- *Dracaenaceae* · 108 spp. · E:Dragon Tree; F:Dragonnier, Pléomèle; G:Drachenbaum, Schlangenlilie
- **aletriformis** (Haw.) Bos · ♄ e Z9 Ⓦ; S-Afr.
- **arborea** (Willd.) Link · ♄ e Z9 Ⓚ Ⓝ; W-Afr., C-Afr., Angola
- **aubryana** Brongn. ex E. Morren · ♄ e Z9 Ⓦ; W-Afr.

– *australis* G. Forst. = Cordyline australis
– **braunii** Engl. · E:Ribbon Plant;
  G:Panaschierter Drachenbaum · ♄ e Z_9
  ⚘; Cameroon
– **cinnabari** Balf. f. · E:Socotra Dragon
  Tree · ♄ e Z_9 ⚘ Ⓝ; Socotra
– **concinna** Kunth · ♄ e Z_9 ⚘; Mauritius
– *deremensis* Engl. = Dracaena fragrans
– **draco** (L.) L. · E:Dragon Tree; G:Echter
  Drachenbaum · ♄ e Z_9 ⚘ Ⓚ ▽; Canar.,
  Cap Verd.
– **elliptica** Thunb. · ♄ e Z_9 ⚘; Ind.,
  Sumat., Java
– **fragrans** (L.) Ker-Gawl. · ♄ e Z_9 ⚘ Ⓚ
  Ⓝ; trop. Afr.
– *godseffiana* Sander ex Mast. = Dracaena
  surculosa
– **goldieana** W. Bull ex Mast. & Moore · ♄
  e Z_9 ⚘; Nigeria, C-Afr.
– *hookeriana* K. Koch = Dracaena
  aletriformis
– *indivisa* G. Forst. = Cordyline indivisa
– *marginata* Lam. = Dracaena reflexa var.
  angustifolia
– **phrynioides** Hook. · ♄ e Z_9 ⚘; W-Afr.,
  Cameroon
– **reflexa** Lam.
– var. **angustifolia** Baker · E:Dragon Tree;
  G:Gerandeter Drachenbaum · ♄ e Z_9 ⚘;
  Reunion
– var. **reflexa** · E:Song of India · ♄ e Z_9 ⚘;
  Mauritius
– *rumphii* (Hook.) Regel = Dracaena
  aletriformis
– *sanderiana* Sander = Dracaena braunii
– *stricta* Sims = Cordyline stricta
– **surculosa** Lindl. · ♄ e Z_9 ⚘ Ⓚ; W-Afr.
– *thalioides* Jacob-Makoy ex Regel =
  Dracaena aubryana
– **umbraculifera** Jacq. · ♄ e Z_9 ⚘; ?
  Mauritius

Dracocephalum L. -n- *Lamiaceae* · 74 spp. ·
E:Dragon's Head; F:Tête-de-dragon;
G:Drachenkopf
– **arguense** Fisch. ex Link · 4 Z_7; E-Sib.,
  N-China, Manch., Korea, Jap.
– **austriacum** L. · G:Österreichischer
  Drachenkopf · 4 Z_4 V-VIII ▽; Eur.: F, I,
  Sw, A, EC-Eur, E-Eur.; TR, Cauc.
– **bipinnatum** Rupr. · 4 ♄ Z_7 VII-VIII;
  C-As., Afgh, Him, W-Tibet, China:
  Sinkiang
– **botryoides** Steven · 4 △ Z_5 IV; Cauc.
– **bullatum** Forrest ex Diels · 4 △ Z_7

VI-VII; Yunnan
– **calophyllum** Hand.-Mazz. · 4 △ Z_7 ⚘
  △ IX-X; Yunnan, Sichuan
– **forrestii** W.W. Sm. · 4 △ Z_7 △ VIII-X;
  Yunnan
– **grandiflorum** L. · 4 △ Z_3 VII-VIII; Sib.
– *hemsleyanum* (Oliv. ex Prain) Prain ex C.
  Marquand = Nepeta hemsleyana
– **isabellae** Forrest ex W.W. Sm. · 4 △ Z_7
  VII-VIII; C-China
– **moldavicum** L. · G:Türkischer
  Drachenkopf · ⊙ Z_7 VII-VIII; W-Sib.,
  E-Sib., Him., nat. in Eur.: PL, RO, Russ.;
  China
– **nutans** L. · 4 Z_3; E-Russ., W-Sib., E-Sib.,
  Amur, C-As., Mong., Manch., China:
  Xinjiang, nat. in E-Eur.
– **peregrinum** L. · 4 △ Z_7 VII-VIII; Altai
– *prattii* (H. Lév.) Hand.-Mazz. = Nepeta
  prattii
– **renati** Emb. · 4 Z_7; Moroc.
– *ruprechtii* Regel = Dracocephalum bipinnatum
– **ruyschiana** L. · E:Dragonhead;
  F:Dracocéphale de Ruysch; G:Nordischer
  Drachenkopf · 4 Z_3 VII-VIII ▽; Eur.: Fr,
  C-Eur., EC-Eur., E-Eur., Ital-P, Sc; Cauc.,
  W-Sib., E-Sib., C-As., Mong., Manch.

Dracontium L. -n- *Araceae* · 23 spp.
– **gigas** (Seem.) Engl. · 4 Z_{10} ⚘; Nicar.

Dracontomelon Blume -n- *Anacardiaceae* ·
8 spp. · E:Argus Pheasant; Tree G:Dra-
chenapfel
– **mangiferum** Blume · E:Argus Pheasant
  Tree; G:Drachenapfel · ♄ ⚘ Ⓝ; Malay.
  Arch, Phil., Fiji

Dracophyllum Labill. -n- *Epacridaceae* ·
48 spp. · F:Dragonnier; G:Drachenblatt
– **secundum** (Poir.) R. Br. · ♄ e Z_8 Ⓚ IV-V;
  Austr.: N.S.Wales

Dracopsis Cass. -f- *Asteraceae* · 1 sp. ·
G:Sonnenhut
– **amplexicaulis** (Vahl) Cass. · G:Stänge-
  lumfassender Sonnenhut · ⊙ Z_8 VII-VIII;
  USA: Kans., Mo., SE, SC

Dracula Luer -f- *Orchidaceae* · 120 spp. ·
F:Dracula; G:Draculaorchidee
– **bella** (Rchb. f.) Luer · 4 Z_{10} Ⓚ XII-VI ▽
  ✳; Col.
– **chimaera** (Rchb. f.) Luer · 4 Z_{10} Ⓚ XI-II

▽ ✳; Col.
- **erythrochaete** (Rchb. f.) Luer · ⳼ Z10 ⓚ
  IX-XI ▽ ✳; C-Am., Col.
- **radiosa** (Rchb. f.) Luer · ⳼ Z10 ⓚ V-VIII
  ▽ ✳; Col.

Dracunculus Mill. -m- *Araceae* · 2 spp. ·
  E:Dragon Arum; F:Serpentaire;
  G:Drachenwurz
- **canariensis** Kunth · G:Kanarische
  Drachenwurz · ⳼ Z9 ⓚ; Canar.
- *muscivorus* (L. f.) Parl. = Helicodiceros
  muscivorus
- **vulgaris** Schott · E:Dragon Arum;
  G:Drachenwurz, Schlangenwurz · ⳼ Z9
  ⓚ V ⚘; Eur.: Ital-P, Ba; TR, nat. in Ib, F

Dregea E. Mey. -f- *Asclepiadaceae* · 3 spp.
- **sinensis** Hemsl. · ♄ e ⚇ Z9 ⓚ VI-VII;
  China

Drepanostachyum Keng f. -n- *Poaceae* ·
  11 sp.

Drimia Jacq. ex Willd. -f- *Hyacinthaceae* ·
  91 sp.
- **haworthioides** Baker · ⳼ Z9 XI-I; S.Afr.

Drimiopsis Lindl. & Paxton -f-
  Hyacinthaceae · 12 spp.
- **botryoides** Baker · ⳼ Z10 ⓦ III-IX;
  Tanzania: Sansibar
- *kirkii* Baker = Drimiopsis botryoides
- **maculata** Lindl. & Paxton · ⳼ Z9 ⓦ
  IV-VII; S.Afr.

Drimys J.R. Forst. & G. Forst. -f-
  Winteraceae · 30-70 spp. · E:Winter's
  Bark; G:Winterrinde
- *aromatica* F. Muell. = Tasmannia
  lanceolata
- *lanceolata* Poir. = Tasmannia lanceolata
- **winteri** J.R. Forst. & G. Forst. · E:Drimys,
  Winter's Bark; G:Beißrinde, Winterrinde
  · ♄ ♄ e Z8 ⓚ; Chile, S-Arg.

Drosanthemum Schwantes -n- *Aizoaceae* ·
  107 spp.
- **bellum** L. Bolus · ♄ ⳨ ⓚ; Cape
- **floribundum** (Haw.) Schwantes · ♄ ⳨ ⓚ
  VI-VII; Cape, Namibia
- **hispidum** (L.) Schwantes · ♄ ⳨ ⓚ
  VI-VIII; Namibia, Cape, nat. in Mallorca
- **speciosum** (Haw.) Schwantes · ♄ ⳨ ⓚ;
  Cape

Drosera L. -f- *Droseraceae* · 155 spp.
- **adelae** F. Muell. · E:Lanceleaf Sundew ·
  ⳼ Z10 ⓚ ▽; Austr.: Queensl.
- **affinis** Welw. ex Oliv. · G:Ähnlicher
  Sonnentau · ⳼ ⓚ ▽; W-Afr.
- **aliciae** Raym.-Hamet · ⳼ Z9 ⓚ V-VIII ▽;
  S-Afr.
- **anglica** Huds. · E:English Sundew,
  Great Sundew; F:Rossolis d'Angleterre;
  G:Englischer Sonnentau, Langblättriger
  Sonnentau · ⳼ Z5 VII-VIII
- **binata** Labill. · E:Forked Sundew;
  G:Gabelblättriger Sonnentau · ⳼ Z9 ⓚ
  V-VII ▽; Austr.: N.S.Wales, Victoria,
  S-Austr.; NZ
- **brevifolia** Pursh · E:Dwarf Sundew;
  G:Kurzblättriger Sonnentau · ☉ Z9 ⓚ ▽;
  USA: NE, SE, Fla.; Mex., S-Am.
- **burkeana** Planch. · ⳼ Z9 ⓚ ▽; Madag.,
  S-Afr.
- **burmannii** Vahl · G:Burmanns Son-
  nentau · ⳼ Z9 ⓚ ▽; Ind., China, Jap.,
  N-Austr.
- **capensis** L. · E:Cape Sundew; G:Kap-
  Sonnentau · ⳼ Z9 ⓚ V-VIII ▽; S-Afr.
- **capillaris** Poir. · E:Pink Sundew; G:Rosa
  Sonnentau · ⳼ Z9 ⓚ ▽; USA: NE, SE,
  SC, Fla.; Mex., W.Ind., trop. S-Am.
- **cistiflora** L. · G:Zistrosen-Sonnentau · ⳼
  Z9 ⓚ ▽; SW-Cape
- **cuneifolia** L. f. · G:Keilblättriger Sonnentau · ⳼ Z9 ⓚ ▽; S-Afr.
- *dichotoma* Banks & Sol. ex Sm. = Drosera
  binata
- **dichrosepala** Turcz. · G:Zweifarbiger
  Sonnentau · ⳼ Z9 ⓚ ▽; SW-Austr.
- **filiformis** Raf. · E:Thread-leaf Sundew;
  G:Fadenblättriger Sonnentau · ⳼ Z8 ▭
  ▽; USA: NE, SE, Fla.
- **intermedia** Hayne · E:Long Leaved
  Sundew, Love Nest Sundew; G:Mittlerer
  Sonnentau · ⳼ Z6 VII-VIII ▽; Eur.*, TR,
  Cauc., Can.: W; USA: Ne, NCE, SE, Fla.;
  Cuba
- *longifolia* auct. non L. = Drosera intermedia
- *longifolia* L. = Drosera anglica
- **macrantha** Endl. · G:Kletternder Sonnentau · ⳼ Z8 ⓚ; Austr. (W-Austr.)
- **montana** A. St.-Hil. · G:Berg-Sonnentau ·
  ⳼ ⓚ ▽; Bol., S-Braz.
- **× obovata** Mert. & W.D.J. Koch (*D.
  anglica × D. rotundifolia*) · G:Bastard-
  Sonnentau · ⳼ VII-VIII; Eur. , N-As., Jap.
- **paleacea** DC. · G:Schuppiger Sonnentau ·

⩜ Z9 ⓐ ▽; W-Austr.
- **pauciflora** Banks ex DC. · G:Armblütiger
  Sonnentau · ⩜ ⓐ ▽; SW-Cape
- *planchonii* Hook. f. ex Planch. = Drosera
  macrantha
- **pygmaea** DC. · E:Tiny Sundew;
  G:Zwerg-Sonnentau · ⩜ Z8 ⓐ ▽;
  E-Austr., S-Austr., NZ
- **ramentacea** Burch. ex DC. · ⩜ ⓐ ⚥ ▽;
  SW-Cape
- **regia** Stephens · E:Giant Sundew ;
  G:Königs-Sonnentau · ⩜ Z9 ⓐ ▽; Cape
- **rotundifolia** L. · E:Round Leaved
  Sundew; F:Rossolis à feuilles rondes;
  G:Rundblättriger Sonnentau · ⩜ Z6
  VII-VIII ⚥ ▽; Eur.*, TR, Syr., Cauc.,
  W-Sib., E-Sib., Amur, Sakhal., Kamchat.,
  Jap., Alaska, Can., USA: NE, NCE, NC,
  SE, Rocky Mts., NW, Calif.
- **spatulata** Labill. · E:Spoonleaf Sundew;
  G:Löffelblättriger Sonnentau · ⩜ Z8 ⓐ
  ▽; Jap., China, Taiwan, Malay. Arch.,
  E-Austr., Tasman., NZ
- **villosa** A. St.-Hil. · G:Zottiger Son-
  nentau · ⩜ ⓐ ▽; SE-Austr., S-Austr.,
  Tasman.

Drosophyllum Link -n- *Drosophyllaceae* ·
1 sp. · E:Dewy Pine
- **lusitanicum** (L.) Link · G:Taublatt · ♄ Z9
  ⓐ; SW-Sp., P, N-Moroc.

Dryadella Luer -f- *Orchidaceae* · 46 spp.
- **lilliputana** (Cogn.) Luer · ⩜ Z10 ⓐ ▽ ✲;
  Braz.: Sao Paulo

Dryandra R. Br. -f- *Proteaceae* · c. 60 spp.
- **carduacea** Lindl. · ♄ e Z9 ⓐ; W-Austr.
- **floribunda** R. Br. · ♄ e Z9 ⓐ; W-Austr.
- **formosa** R. Br. · E:Showy Dryandra;
  G:Prächtige Dryandra · ♄ e ⋇ Z9 ⓐ;
  W-Austr.
- **nivea** (Labill.) R. Br. · ♄ e Z9 ⓐ;
  W-Austr.
- **nobilis** Lindl. · ♄ e Z9 ⓐ; W-Austr.
- **polycephala** Benth. · E:Many-head
  Dryandra; G:Vielköpfige Dryandra · ♄ e
  ⋇ Z9 ⓐ; W-Austr.
- **quercifolia** Meisn. · E:Oak Leaved
  Dryandra; G:Eichenblättrige Dryandra ·
  ♄ e ⋇ Z9 ⓐ; W-Austr.
- **squarrosa** R. Br. · ♄ e ⋇ Z9 ⓐ; W-Austr.

Dryas L. -f- *Rosaceae* · 3 spp.
- **drummondii** Richardson ex Hook.

- var. **drummondii** · E:Yellow Mountain
  Avens; G:Gelbe Silberwurz · ♄ e Z1; Can.;
  USA: Mont.; Greenl.
- var. **tomentosa** (Farr) L.O. Williams ·
  E:Tomentose Mountain Avens; G:Filzige
  Silberwurz · ♄ Z3; Can.: Alta., B.C.
- *integrifolia* Vahl = Dryas octopetala
  subsp. octopetala var. integrifolia
- *lanata* Stein ex Correvon = Dryas
  octopetala subsp. octopetala f. argentea
- **octopetala** L. · G:Weiße Silberwurz
- subsp. *chamaedryfolia* (Crantz) Gams =
  Dryas octopetala subsp. octopetala
- subsp. **octopetala** · E:Mountain Avens;
  F:Dryade à huit pétales; G:Gewöhnliche
  Weiße Silberwurz · ♄ e Z1 VI-VIII; Eur.*;
  N, mts.; W-Sib., E-Sib., Kamchat.,
  Sakhal., Amur, NW-China, Jap., Alaska,
  E-Can., USA: NW, Rocky Mts.; Greenl.
- f. **argentea** (Blytt) Hultén Z2; E-Alps
- var. **integrifolia** (Vahl) Hartz · ♄ Z2;
  N-Eur., Alaska, Can., Greenl.
- var. *vestita* Beck = Dryas octopetala
  subsp. octopetala f. argentea
- × **suendermannii** Keller ex Sünd. (*D.
  drummondii × D. octopetala*) · G:Sünder-
  manns Silberwurz · ♄ e Z3; cult.
- *tenella* Pursh = Dryas octopetala subsp.
  octopetala var. integrifolia
- *tomentosa* Farr = Dryas drummondii var.
  tomentosa
- *vestita* (Beck) hort. = Dryas octopetala
  subsp. octopetala f. argentea

Drymoglossum C. Presl = Pyrrosia
- *carnosum* (Wall.) J. Sm. = Pyrrosia
  confluens
- *heterophyllum* (L.) C. Chr. = Pyrrosia
  heterophylla
- *niphoboloides* (Luerss.) Baker = Pyrrosia
  niphoboloides
- *piloselloides* (L.) C. Presl = Pyrrosia
  heterophylla

Drymonia Mart. -f- *Gesneriaceae* · c.
100 spp.
- *punctata* Lindl. = Alsobia punctata
- **serrulata** (Jacq.) Mart. · ♄ ⚥ ⤳ Z10 ⓦ;
  Mex., C-Am., W.Ind., trop. S-Am.
- *spectabilis* (Kunth) Mart. ex DC. = Drymonia serrulata
- **turrialvae** Hanst. · ♄ Z10 ⓦ; Costa Rica,
  Panama, Col., Ecuad.

Drynaria (Bory) J. Sm. -f- *Polypodiaceae* ·

19 spp.
- **quercifolia** (L.) J. Sm. · E:Squirrel Head; G:Eichenblättriger Korbfarn · ⧠ Z10 ⓜ; Malay. Arch., Austr., Polyn.
- **rigidula** (Sw.) Bedd. · E:Basket Fern; G:Korbfarn · ⧠ Z10 ⓜ; Ind., S-China, Malay. Pen., Austr.: Queensl.; Polyn.

Dryobalanops C.F. Gaertn. -f-
Dipterocarpaceae · 7 spp.
- **aromatica** C.F. Gaertn. · E:Baru Camphor; G:Borneokampfer · ♄ e ⓜ ⚥ ⓝ; Sumat., N-Kalimantan

Dryopteris Adans. -f- *Dryopteridaceae* · c. 250 spp.
- **affinis** (Lowe) Fraser-Jenk. · E:Golden Shield Fern; F:Fougère à écailles dorées; G:Spreuschuppiger Wurmfarn · ⧠ Z6 VII-IX; Eur.*
- **many cultivars**
- **atrata** (Wall.) Ching · F:Fougère trompe-d'éléphant · ⧠ Z7 ∧; N-Ind., China, Taiwan, Jap.
- × **bootii** (Tuck.) Underw. (*D. cristata* × *D. intermedia*) · ⧠ Z4; Can.: E; USA: NE, Tenn.
- **carthusiana** (Vill.) H.P. Fuchs · E:Charterhouse Shield Fern, Narrow Buckler Fern; F:Dryoptéris de la Chartreuse; G:Dorniger Wurmfarn, Gewöhnlicher Dornfarn · ⧠ Z5 VII-VIII; Eur.*, TR, W-As.
- × **complexa** Fraser-Jenk. (*D. affinis* × *D. filix-mas*) · ⧠ Z5; BrI +
- **cristata** (L.) A. Gray · E:Crested Wood Fern; G:Kamm-Wurmfarn, Kammfarn · ⧠ ⌣ Z4 VII-IX ▽; Eur.*, W-Sib., Can., USA: NE, NCE, NC, SE, Mont.
- *decursive-pinnata* (H.C. Hall) Kuntze = Phegopteris decursive-pinnata
- × **deweveri** (Jansen) Jansen & Wacht. (*D. carthusiana* × *D. dilatata*) · G:Dewevers Dornfarn · ⧠; Eur.: N-Sp., Fr, C-Eur., Sc, EC-Eur., E-Eur.; N-TR, Cauc.
- **dilatata** (Hoffm.) A. Gray · E:Broad Buckler Fern; F:Fougère dilatée; G:Breitblättriger Wurmfarn, Breitblättriger Dornfarn · ⧠ Z5 VII-IX; Eur.*, TR, Cyprus, Cauc., N-As., N-Am., Greenl.
- **erythrosora** (Eaton) Kuntze · E:Japanese Shield Fern; F:Fougère à indusies rouges; G:Rotschleier-Wurmfarn · ⧠ Z8 ∧; China, Korea, Jap., Taiwan, Phil.
- **expansa** (C. Presl) Fraser-Jenk. &

Jermy · E:Northern Buckler Fern; G:Gewöhnlicher Feingliedriger Dornfarn · ⧠ Z3 VII-VIII; Eur.*
- **filix-mas** (L.) Schott · E:Male Fern; F:Fougère; G:Gewöhnlicher Wurmfarn mâle · ⧠ Z2 VII-IX ⚥ ✂; Eur.*, TR, Cauc., W-Sib., E-Sib., C-As., Him., Ind., China, Korea, Jap., Taiwan, NW-Afr., N-Am., Mex., Jamaica, S-Am. (Anden), E-Braz.
- **many cultivars**
- **fragrans** (L.) Schott · E:Fragrant Buckler Fern; G:Duftender Wurmfarn · ⧠ △ Z3 ▽; Eur.: FIN; W-Sib., E-Sib., Amur, Sakhal., Kamchat., Korea, N-Jap., Alaska, Can., USA: NE, NCE; Greenl.
- **goldieana** (Hook.) A. Gray · E:Goldie's Wood Fern; F:Dryoptéris géant; G:Riesen-Wurmfarn · ⧠ Z3; Can.: E; USA: NE, NCE, SE
- *hexagonoptera* (Michx.) C. Chr. = Phegopteris hexagonoptera
- **hirtipes** (Blume) Kuntze · ⧠ Z8 ⓚ ∧; Him., Ind., Sri Lanka, S-China, Indochina., Malay. Pen., Polyn.
- *lepida* (T. Moore) C. Chr. = Cyclosorus arcuatus var. arcuatus
- *linnaeana* C. Chr. = Gymnocarpium dryopteris
- **marginalis** (L.) A. Gray · E:Marginal Shield Fern · ⧠ △ Z4; Can.: E; USA: NE, NCE, Mo., Okla., SE
- *montana* (J.A. Vogler) Kuntze = Oreopteris limbosperma
- *noveboracensis* (L.) A. Gray = Parathelypteris noveboracensis
- **odontoloma** C. Chr. · ⧠; Him.
- **oreades** Fomin · E:Mountain Male Fern; G:Geröll-Wurmfarn · ⧠ Z6 VII-VIII; Eur.: BrI, Fr, G, Ib., Ital-P; Cauc.
- *oreopteris* (Ehrh.) Maxon = Oreopteris limbosperma
- *paleacea* auct. = Dryopteris affinis
- *parasitica* (L.) Kuntze = Christella dentata
- *pseudomas* (Woll.) Holub & Pouzar = Dryopteris affinis
- **remota** (A. Braun ex Döll) Druce · E:Scaly Buckler Fern; G:Entferntfiedriger Dornfarn · ⧠ VII-VIII; Eur.* exc. BrI; TR
- *robertiana* (Hoffm.) C. Chr. = Gymnocarpium robertianum
- × **sarvelae** Fraser-Jenk. & Jermy (*D. carthusiana* × *D. expansa*) · G:Sarvelas Dornfarn · ⧠; GB, FIN +

– **sieboldii** (Van Houtte) Kuntze ·
E:Christmas Fern · ♃ Z8 ⊕ ∧; Jap.,
Taiwan
– *spinulosa* D. Watt = Dryopteris carthusiana
– var. *americana* (Fisch.) Fernald =
Dryopteris dilatata
– var. *dilatata* (Hoffm.) D. Watt =
Dryopteris dilatata
– *standishii* (Moore) C. Chr. = Arachniodes
standishii
– × *tavelii* auct. non Rothm. = Dryopteris ×
complexa
– × *tavelii* Rothm. = Dryopteris affinis
– *thelypteris* (L.) A. Gray = Thelypteris
palustris
– **villarii** (Bellardi) Woyn. ex Schinz &
Thell. · G:Starrer Wurmfarn · ♃ △ Z4
VII-VIII; Eur.: Fr, C-Eur., Ba, ? PL; mts.;
Cauc., Iran, Afgh., NW-Afr.
– **wallichiana** (Spreng.) Hyl. · E:Alpine
Wood Fern; G:Gebirgs-Wurmfarn · ♃ Z6;
Pakist., Nepal, Burma, China

Drypis L. -f- *Caryophyllaceae* · 1 sp.
– **spinosa** L. · G:Dornnelke, Kronentau · ♃
Z8; Ba, I

Duboisia R. Br. -f- *Solanaceae* · 3 spp.
– **hopwoodii** (F. Muell.) F. Muell. ·
E:Pituri; G:Pituri · ♄ ⊕ Ⓝ; Austr.:
W-Austr., S-Austr., N.S.Wales
– **leichhardtii** (F. Muell.) F. Muell. · ♄ ⊕
Ⓝ; Austr.
– **myoporoides** R. Br. · E:Corkwood;
G:Korkholz · ♄ ♄ ⊕ ⚑ ✿ Ⓝ; Austr.:
Queensl., N.S.Wales; N.Caled.

Duchesnea Sm. -f- *Rosaceae* · 2 spp. ·
E:Indian Strawberry; G:Scheinerdbeere
– **indica** (Andrews) Focke · E:Indian
Strawberry, Mock Strawberry; F:Faux-
fraisier; G:Indische Erdbeere, Scheinerdbeere · ♃ ⚑ ↝ ⚭ Z6 V-IX; Ind., China,
Jap., nat. in USA, S-Eur.

Dudleya Britton & Rose -f- *Crassulaceae* ·
47 spp. · G:Dudleya
– **caespitosa** (Haw.) Britton & Rose · E:Sea
Lettuce · ♃ ♌ Z8 ⊕ III-IV; C-Calif.
– **candida** Britton · ♃ ♌ Z8 ⊕; Mex.: Baja
Calif.
– *cotyledon* (Jacq.) Britton & Rose =
Dudleya caespitosa
– **cymosa** (Lem.) Britton & Rose ·

E:Canyon Live Forever; G:Canyon-
Dudleya · ♃ ♌ Z8 ⊕ VII-VIII; Calif.
– **densiflora** (Rose) Moran · E:San Gabriel
Mountains Live Forever · ♃ ♌ Z8 ⊕
VI-VIII; Calif.
– **edulis** (Nutt.) Moran · ♃ ♌ Z8 ⊕;
S-Calif., N-Baja Calif.
– **farinosa** (Lindl.) Britton & Rose ·
E:Powdery Live Forever; G:Gepuderte
Dudleya · ♃ ♌ Z8 ⊕ III-IV; Calif.
– **pulverulenta** (Nutt.) Britton & Rose ·
E:Chalk Dudleya · ♃ ♌ Z8 ⊕ IV-VI; Calif.,
Mex.
– *purpusii* (K. Schum.) Britton & Rose =
Dudleya cymosa
– **rigida** Rose · ♃ ♌ Z8 ⊕ VII-VIII; Mex.:
Baja Calif.
– **variegata** (S. Watson) Moran ·
E:Variegated Live Forever · ♃ ♌ Z8 ⊕;
S-Calif., Baja Calif.

Dulacia Vell. -f- *Olacaceae* · 14 spp.
– **inopiflora** (Miers) Kuntze · E:Potency
Wood · ♄ ⊕ ⚑ ; Col., Venez., Braz., Peru

Duranta L. -f- *Verbenaceae* · 17 spp. ·
G:Himmelsblüte
– **erecta** L. · E:Pigeon Berry, Skyflower;
G:Einzelstämmige Himmelsblüte · ♄ e Z9
⊕ VIII; USA: Calif., Tex.; Mex., W.Ind.,
S-Am.
– **lorentzii** Griseb. · ♄ e ⚭ Z9 ⊕; Arg.
– *plumieri* Jacq. = Duranta erecta
– *repens* L. = Duranta erecta

Durio Adans. -m- *Bombacaceae* · 27 spp. ·
G:Durianbaum
– **zibethinus** Murray · E:Durian; G:Durian-
baum, Zibetbaum · ♄ e Z10 ⊕ Ⓝ; Malay.
Arch.

Duvalia Haw. -f- *Asclepiadaceae* · 18 spp.
– **caespitosa** (Masson) Haw. · ♃ ♌ Z9 ⊕;
S-Afr.: Cape, Orange Free State
– **pillansii** N.E. Br. · ♃ ♌ Z10 ⊕; Cape
– **polita** N.E. Br. · ♃ ♌ Z10 ⊕; Mozamb.,
Namibia, S-Afr.: Transvaal
– *radiata* (Sims) Haw. = Duvalia caespitosa

Dyckia Schult. f. -f- *Bromeliaceae* · 129 spp.
– **altissima** Lindl. · ♃ Z9 ⊕; Braz.
– **brevifolia** Baker · ♃ Z9 ⊕; Braz. ·
E:Sawblade
– **encholirioides** (Gaudich.) Mez
– var. **encholirioides** · ♃ Z9 ⊕; S-Braz.;

coast
- var. **rubra** (Wittm.) Reitz · ⏀ Z9 ⓚ;
S-Braz.
- **fosteriana** L.B. Sm. · ⏀ Z9 ⓚ; Braz.
- **rariflora** Schult. & Schult. f. · ⏀ Z9 ⓚ;
Braz.
- **remotiflora** Otto & A. Dietr. · ⏀ Z9 ⓚ;
Urug.
- *rubra* Wittm. = Dyckia encholirioides var.
rubra
- **velascana** Mez · ⏀ Z9 ⓚ; Arg.

Dyera Hook. f. -f- *Apocynaceae* · 2 spp.
- **costulata** (Miq.) Hook. f. · ♄ ⓦ ⓝ;
Malay. Arch.

Dypsis Noronha ex Mart. -f- *Arecaceae* ·
140 spp.
- **decaryi** (Jum.) Beentje & J. Dransf. ·
E:Triangle Palm; G:Dreieckspalme · ♄ e
ⓦ ▽ ✳; Madag.
- *lutescens* (H. Wendl.) Beentje & J. Dransf.
= Chrysalidocarpus lutescens

Dyssodia Cav. -f- *Asteraceae* · 4 spp.
- **papposa** (Vent.) Hitchc. · E:Foetid
Marigold · ⊙; USA: Rocky Mts., Ariz.,
NC, SC, SE; Mex.

Eberlanzia Schwantes -f- *Aizoaceae* · 8 spp.
- **sedoides** (Dinter & A. Berger) Schwantes
- **spinosa** (L.) Schwantes

Ebnerella Buxb. = Mammillaria
- *aureilanata* (Backeb.) Buxb. = Mammillaria aureilanata
- *bocasana* (Poselg.) Buxb. = Mammillaria
bocasana
- *carretii* (Rebut ex K. Schum.) Buxb. =
Mammillaria carretii
- *fraileana* (Britton & Rose) Buxb. = Mammillaria fraileana
- *glochidiata* (Mart.) Buxb. = Mammillaria
wildii
- *plumosa* (F.A.C. Weber) Buxb. = Mammillaria plumosa
- *schiedeana* (C. Ehrenb.) Buxb. = Mammillaria schiedeana
- *seideliana* (Quehl) Buxb. = Mammillaria
seideliana
- *surculosa* (Boed.) Buxb. = Mammillaria
surculosa
- *wildii* (A. Dietr.) Buxb. = Mammillaria
wildii
- *zephyrantoides* (Scheidw.) Buxb. =

Mammillaria zephyranthoides

Ebracteola Dinter & Schwantes -f-
Aizoaceae · 4 spp.
- **montis-moltkei** (Dinter) Dinter &
Schwantes · ⏀ ♍ Z9 ⓚ; Namibia

Ecballium A. Rich. -n- *Cucurbitaceae* ·
1 sp. · E:Squirting Cucmber; F:Concombre
sauvage, Ecbalie; G:Spritzgurke
- **elaterium** (L.) A. Rich. · E:Squirting
Cucumber; G:Eselsgurke, Spritzgurke · ⊙
⤳ Z9 VI-VIII ♈ ✿; Eur.: Ib, Fr, Ital-P,
Ba, E-Eur.; TR, Levant, Cauc., C-As.,
NW-Afr., Libya, nat. in BrI, EC-Eur.

Ecclinusa Mart. -f- *Sapotaceae* · 11 sp.
- *balata* Ducke = Chrysophyllum sanguinolentum subsp. balata
- **guianensis** Eyma

Eccremocarpus Ruiz & Pav. -m-
Bignoniaceae · 5 spp. · E:Glory Flower;
F:Eccremocarpus; G:Schönranke
- **scaber** Ruiz & Pav. · E:Glory Flower;
F:Bignone du Chili; G:Schönranke · ⊙ ⏀
♄ ♄ e ♨ Z9 VI-X; Chile
- **many cultivars**

Echeveria DC. -f- *Crassulaceae* · 139 spp. ·
E:Echeveria; F:Artichaut, Echévéria;
G:Echeverie
- **affinis** E. Walther · ⏀ ♍ Z8 ⓚ IV-V; Mex.
- **agavoides** Lem. · ⏀ ♍ Z8 ⓚ; Mex.
- **amoena** De Smet · ⏀ ♍ Z8 ⓚ III-V; Mex.
- *argentea* Lem. = Dudleya pulverulenta
- **bracteosa** (Link, Klotzsch & Otto) Lindl.
ex Paxton = Pachyphytum bracteosum
- *caespitosa* (Haw.) DC. = Dudleya
caespitosa
- *candida* (Britton) A. Berger = Dudleya
candida
- **carnicolor** (Baker) E. Morren · ⏀ ♍ Z8 ⓚ
I-III; Mex.
- × *clavifolia* A. Berger = × Pachyveria
clavata
- **coccinea** (Cav.) DC. · ♄ ♍ e Z8 ⓚ VI-VIII;
Mex.
- *cotyledon* (Jacq.) A. Nelson & J.F. Macbr.
= Dudleya caespitosa
- **cuspidata** Rose · ⏀ ♍ Z8 ⓚ VI-VII; Mex.
- *cymosa* Lem. = Dudleya cymosa
- *densiflora* (Rose) A. Berger = Dudleya
densiflora
- **derenbergii** J.A. Purpus · E:Painted

Lady · ⍒ ⍦ Z8 ⍟ IV-VI; Mex.
– *edulis* (Nutt.) Purpus ex A. Berger =
Dudleya edulis
– **elegans** Rose · ♄ ⍦ Z8 ⍟ III-VII; Mex.
– *farinosa* Lindl. = Dudleya farinosa
– **fulgens** Lem. · ♄ ⍦ e Z8 ⍟ XI-IV; Mex.
– **gibbiflora** DC. · ♄ ⍦ e Z8 ⍟; Mex.
– **gigantea** Rose & Purpus · ♄ ⍦ e Z8 ⍟
IX-X; Mex.
– *glauca* (Baker) E. Morren = Echeveria
secunda
– **harmsii** J.F. Macbr. · ⍒ ⍦ Z8 ⍟ V-VII;
Mex.
– **laui** Moran & J. Meyrán · ⍒ ⍦ Z8 ⍟ X-III;
Mex.
– **leucotricha** J.A. Purpus · ♄ ⍦ e Z8 ⍟
III-V; Mex.
– *linguifolia* Lem. = Cremnophila linguifolia
– **longissima** E. Walther · ⍒ ⍦ Z8 ⍟; Mex.
– **lutea** Rose · ⍒ ⍦ Z8 ⍟; Mex.
– *microcalyx* Britton & Rose = Echeveria
amoena
– **multicaulis** Rose · ♄ ⍦ Z8 ⍟ IV-V; Mex.
– *mutabilis* Deleuil ex E. Morren = ×
Cremneria mutabilis
– **nodulosa** (Baker) Otto · ♄ ⍦ Z8 ⍟ III-IV;
Mex.
– *pachyphytum* (Baker) E. Morren =
Pachyphytum bracteosum
– **paniculata** A. Gray · ⍒ ⍦ Z8 ⍟; Mex.
– **peacockii** Croucher · ⍒ ⍦ Z8 ⍟ IV-VII;
Mex.
– *perelegans* A. Berger = Echeveria elegans
– **pilosa** J.A. Purpus · ♄ ⍦ e Z8 ⍟ VI; Mex.
– **pringlei** (S. Watson) Rose · ⍒ ⍦ Z8 ⍟
III-IV; Mex.
– *pubescens* Schltdl. = Echeveria coccinea
– × **pulchella** A. Berger · ⍒ ⍦ Z8 ⍟ IV-V;
Mex.
– **pulidonis** E. Walther · ⍒ ⍦ Z8 ⍟ II-IV;
E-Mex.
– *pulverulenta* Nutt. = Dudleya pulverulenta
– **pulvinata** Rose · ♄ ⍦ e Z8 ⍟ III-IV; Mex.
– *pumila* Van Houtte = Echeveria secunda
– *purpusii* (K. Schum.) K. Schum. =
Dudleya cymosa
– *purpusii* Britton = Echeveria amoena
– **purpusorum** A. Berger · ⍒ ⍦ Z8 ⍟ V-VI;
S-Mex.
– **quitensis** (Kunth) Lindl. · ♄ ⍦ e Z8 ⍟
VII-VIII; Col., Ecuad.
– *retusa* Lem. = Echeveria fulgens
– *rigida* (Rose) A. Berger = Dudleya rigida
– **secunda** Booth

– f. **secunda** · ⍒ ⍦ Z8 ⍟ III-IV; Mex.
– var. *glauca* (Baker) Otto = Echeveria
secunda
– var. *pumila* (Schltdl.) Otto = Echeveria
secunda
– **setosa** Rose & Purpus · ⍒ ⍦ Z8 ⍟ IV-VII;
Mex.
– **Cultivars:**
– **some cultivars**

Echidnopsis Hook. f. -f- *Asclepiadaceae* ·
32 spp. · F:Echidnopsis; G:Schlangensta-
pelie
– **cereiformis** Hook. f. · ⍒ ⍦ Z9 ⍟;
S-Arab., Eth., Somalia

Echinacea Moench -f- *Asteraceae* · 9 spp. ·
E:Cone Flower; F:Echinacéa; G:Igelkopf,
Scheinsonnenhut
– **angustifolia** DC. · E:Coneflower;
G:Schmalblättriger Scheinsonnenhut · ⍒
Z3 VII-IX ⚥ · Can.: Sask., Man.; USA: SC,
NC, Rocky Mts.
– **purpurea** (L.) Moench · E:Purple Cone
Flower; F:Echinacée pourpre; G:Roter
Scheinsonnenhut · ⍒ Z3 VII-IX ⚥ ; USA:
NE, NCE, SE
– **some cultivars**

Echinaria Desf. -f- *Poaceae* · 2 spp.
– **capitata** (L.) Desf. · ⊙ ; Eur.: Ib, Fr,
Ital-P, Ba, Crim; NW-Afr., Cyprus, Syr.,
C-As.

Echinocactus Link & Otto -m- *Cactaceae* ·
7 spp.
– *andreae* Boed. = Gymnocalycium andreae
– *anisitsii* K. Schum. = Gymnocalycium
anisitsii
– *baldianus* Speg. = Gymnocalycium
baldianum
– *bicolor* Pfeiff. = Thelocactus bicolor var.
bicolor
– *chilensis* Hildm. ex K. Schum. = Neoporteria chilensis
– *chrysacanthus* Orcutt = Ferocactus
chrysacanthus
– *conothelos* Regel & E. Klein = Thelocactus
conothelos
– *coptonogonus* Lem. = Stenocactus
coptonogonus
– *crassihamatus* F.A.C. Weber = Sclerocactus uncinatus var. crassihamatus
– *cylindraceus* (Engelm.) Engelm. =
Ferocactus cylindraceus

- *denudatus* Link & Otto = Gymnocalycium denudatum
- *echidne* DC. = Ferocactus echidne
- *emoryi* Engelm. = Ferocactus emoryi
- *erectocentrus* J.M. Coult. = Echinomastus erectocentrus
- *flavovirens* Scheidw. = Ferocactus flavovirens
- *fordii* Orcutt = Ferocactus fordii
- *fossulatus* Scheidw. = Thelocactus hexaedrophorus
- *gibbosus* (Haw.) DC. = Gymnocalycium gibbosum
- *gielsdorfianus* Werderm. = Turbinicarpus gielsdorfianus
- *glaucescens* DC. = Ferocactus glaucescens
- *glaucus* K. Schum. = Sclerocactus glaucus
- *grandis* Rose = Echinocactus platyacanthus f. grandis
- **grusonii** Hildm. · E:Barrel Cactus, Mother-in-law's Seat; G:Goldkugelkaktus, Schwiegermuttersessel · ⍦ Z9 ⌂ ▽ ✳; Mex.
- *hamatacanthus* Muehlenpf. = Ferocactus hamatacanthus
- *haynei* Otto ex Salm-Dyck = Matucana haynei subsp. haynei
- *heterochromus* F.A.C. Weber = Thelocactus heterochromus
- *hexaedrophorus* Lem. = Thelocactus hexaedrophorus
- *histrix* DC. = Ferocactus histrix
- **horizonthalonius** Lem. · E:Devilshead · ⍦ Z9 ⌂ ▽ ✳; USA: SC, SW; N-Mex.
- *ingens* Zucc. ex Pfeiff. = Echinocactus platyacanthus f. platyacanthus
- *intertextus* Engelm. = Echinomastus intertextus
- *johnsonii* Parry ex Engelm. = Echinomastus johnsonii
- *leucacanthus* Zucc. ex Pfeiff. = Thelocactus leucacanthus var. leucacanthus
- *macrodiscus* Mart. = Ferocactus macrodiscus
- *mandragora* A. Berger = Turbinicarpus mandragora
- *mihanovichii* Frič & Gürke = Gymnocalycium mihanovichii var. mihanovichii
- *monvillei* Lem. = Gymnocalycium monvillei subsp. monvillei
- *multicostatus* Hildm. ex K. Schum. = Stenocactus multicostatus
- *multiflorus* Hook. = Gymnocalycium monvillei subsp. monvillei
- *palmeri* Rose = Echinocactus platyacanthus f. platyacanthus
- *pectinatus* Scheidw. = Echinocereus pectinatus var. pectinatus
- *peninsulae* F.A.C. Weber = Ferocactus peninsulae
- *phyllacanthus* Mart. = Stenocactus phyllacanthus
- *pilosus* Galeotti ex Salm-Dyck = Ferocactus pilosus
- **platyacanthus** Link & Otto
- – f. **grandis** (Rose) Bravo · ⍦ Z9 ⌂ ▽ ✳
- – f. **platyacanthus** · ⍦ Z9 ⌂ ▽ ✳; Mex.
- *polyancistrus* Engelm. & Bigelow = Sclerocactus polyancistrus
- **polycephalus** Engelm. & Bigelow
- – var. **polycephalus** · E:Cottontop Cactus · ⍦ Z9 ⌂ ▽ ✳; USA: S-Nev., S-Utah, W-Ariz., Calif.; NW-Mex.
- – var. **xeranthemoides** J.M. Coult. · ⍦ Z9 ⌂ ▽ ✳; S-Utah, N-Ariz.
- *pottsii* Salm-Dyck = Ferocactus pottsii
- *quehlianus* Haage ex Quehl = Gymnocalycium quehlianum
- *rhodacanthus* Salm-Dyck = Denmoza rhodacantha
- *rinconensis* Poselg. = Thelocactus rinconensis
- *ritteri* Boed. = Aztekium ritteri
- *robustus* Pfeiff. = Ferocactus robustus
- *roseanus* Boed. = Escobaria roseana
- *saglionis* Cels = Gymnocalycium saglionis subsp. saglionis
- *saueri* Boed. = Turbinicarpus saueri
- *scheerii* Salm-Dyck = Sclerocactus scheerii
- *schickendantzii* F.A.C. Weber = Gymnocalycium schickendantzii
- *schmiedickeanus* Boed. = Turbinicarpus schmiedickeanus
- *setispinus* Engelm. = Thelocactus setispinus
- *simpsonii* Engelm. = Pediocactus simpsonii
- *smithii* Muehlenpf. = Neolloydia smithii
- *stainesii* Audot = Ferocactus pilosus
- **texensis** Hopffer · E:Horse Crippler · ⍦ Z9 ⌂ ▽ ✳; USA: Tex., N.Mex.; NE-Mex.
- *tulensis* Poselg. = Thelocactus tulensis
- *turbiniformis* Pfeiff. = Strombocactus disciformis
- *uncinatus* Galeotti = Sclerocactus uncinatus var. uncinatus
- *unguispinus* Engelm. = Echinomastus unguispinus
- *vaupelianus* Werderm. = Stenocactus vaupelianus

– *viereckii* Werderm. = Turbinicarpus viereckii
– *viridescens* Torr. & A. Gray = Ferocactus viridescens
– *visnaga* Hook. = Echinocactus platyacanthus f. platyacanthus
– *weberbaueri* Vaupel = Matucana haynei subsp. myriacantha
– *wislizeni* Engelm. = Ferocactus wislizenii

Echinocereus Engelm. -m- *Cactaceae* · 45 spp. · E:Hedgehog Cactus; F:Cierge-hérisson; G:Igelsäulenkaktus
– *aggregatus* (Engelm.) Rydb. = Echinocereus coccineus
– *armatus* (Poselg.) A. Berger = Echinocereus reichenbachii var. armatus
– *baileyi* Rose = Echinocereus reichenbachii var. baileyi
– **berlandieri** (Engelm.) Haage · E:Berlandier's Hedgehog Cactus · ☥ Z9 ⊕ ▽ ✳; S-Tex., NE-Mex.
– var. *poselgerianus* (Linke) Lodé = Echinocereus berlandieri
– *blanckii* hort. ex Palmer = Echinocereus berlandieri
– var. *berlandieri* (Engelm.) Backeb. = Echinocereus berlandieri
– *caespitosus* (Engelm.) Engelm. = Echinocereus reichenbachii var. reichenbachii
– *chloranthus* (Engelm.) Haage = Echinocereus viridiflorus var. chloranthus
– **cinerascens** (DC.) Lem. · ☥ Z9 ⊕ ▽ ✳; Mex.
– **coccineus** Engelm. · E:Scarlet Hedgehog Cactus · ☥ Z9 ⊕ ▽ ✳; USA: Ariz.
– *cucumis* Werderm. = Echinocereus scheeri var. gentryi
– **dasyacanthus** Engelm. · E:Texas Rainbow Cactus · ☥ Z9 ⊕ ▽ ✳; USA: E-Ariz., W-Tex.; N-Mex.
– *dubius* (Engelm.) Rümpler = Echinocereus enneacanthus
– **engelmannii** (Scheidw.) Engelm. · E:Saints Cactus · ☥ Z8 ⊕ ▽ ✳; USA: Ariz., Utah, Calif.; NE-Mex.
– **enneacanthus** Engelm. · E:Strawberry Cactus · ☥ Z9 ⊕ ▽ ✳; USA: N.Mex., Tex.; NE-Mex.
– **fendleri** (Engelm.) Rümpler · E:Hedgehog Cactus · ☥ Z9 ⊕ ▽ ✳; Mex. (Chihuahua)
– *fitchii* Britton & Rose = Echinocereus reichenbachii var. fitchii
– *gentryi* Clover = Echinocereus scheeri var. gentryi
– *hexaedrus* (Engelm.) Rümpler = Echinocereus coccineus
– **knippelianus** Liebner · ☥ Z9 ⊕ ▽ ✳; Mex. (Coahuila, Nuevo León)
– *leptacanthus* (DC.) K. Schum. = Echinocereus pentalophus var. pentalophus
– *leucanthus* N.P. Taylor = Wilcoxia albiflora
– *luteus* Britton & Rose = Echinocereus subinermis var. subinermis
– *melanocentrus* Lowry = Echinocereus reichenbachii var. fitchii
– *merkeri* Hildm. ex K. Schum. = Echinocereus enneacanthus
– *oklahomensis* Lahman = Echinocereus reichenbachii var. baileyi
– **papillosus** Linke ex Rümpler · E:Allicoche Hedgehog Cactus · ☥ Z9 ⊕ ▽ ✳; USA: S-Tex.; Mex. (Tamaulipas)
– **pectinatus** (Scheidw.) Engelm. · E:Yellow Alicoche
– var. *dasyacanthus* (Engelm.) N.P. Taylor = Echinocereus dasyacanthus
– var. **pectinatus** · E:Hedgehog Cactus, Rainbow Cactus · ☥ Z9 ⊕ ▽ ✳; USA: SC, SW; N-Mex.
– var. *reichenbachii* (Terscheck ex Walp.) Werderm. = Echinocereus reichenbachii
– var. *rigidissimus* (Engelm.) Rümpler = Echinocereus rigidissimus var. rigidissimus
– var. *rubispinus* G. Frank & A.B. Lau = Echinocereus rigidissimus var. rubispinus
– var. **wenigeri** L.D. Benson · E:Weniger's Hedgehog Cactus · ☥ Z9 ⊕ ▽ ✳; USA: Tex.
– **pentalophus** (DC.) Lem.
– var. **pentalophus** · E:Lady Finger Cactus · ☥ Z9 ⊕ ▽ ✳; S-Tex., E-Mex.
– var. **procumbens** (Engelm.) P. Fourn.
– *perbellus* Britton & Rose = Echinocereus reichenbachii var. perbellus
– *poselgeri* Lem. = Wilcoxia poselgeri
– *purpureus* Lahman = Echinocereus reichenbachii var. reichenbachii
– **reichenbachii** (Terscheck ex Walp.) Haage
– var. **armatus** (Poselg.) N.P. Taylor · ☥ Z8 ⊕ ▽ ✳; Mex. (Nuevo León)
– var. **baileyi** (Rose) N.P. Taylor · E:Bailey's Hedgehog Cactus · ☥ Z8 ⊕ ▽ ✳; USA: Okla., Tex.
– var. **fitchii** (Britton & Rose) L.D. Benson · E:Fitch's Hedgehog Cactus · ☥ Z8 ⊕ ▽

✳; S-Tex., Mex.: Nuevo León, Tamaulipas
- var. **perbellus** (Britton & Rose) L.D. Benson · E:Lace Hedgehog Cactus · ⸸ Z8 ⒶⒸ ▽ ✳; W-Tex., E-N.Mex., SE-Colo.
- var. **reichenbachii** · E:Lace Hedgehog Cactus · ⸸ Z8 ⒶⒸ ▽ ✳; SW-USA, NE-Mex.
- **rigidissimus** (Engelm.) Haage
- var. **rigidissimus** · E:Rainbow Hedgehog Cactus · ⸸ Z9 ⒶⒸ ▽ ✳; USA: SW; NW-Mex.
- var. **rubispinus** G. Frank & A.B. Lau · ⸸ Z8 ⒶⒸ ▽ ✳; Mex. (Chihuahua, Mexico)
- *roemeri* (Muehlenpf.) Rydb. = Echinocereus coccineus
- × **roetteri** (Engelm.) Rümpler (*E. coccineus* × *E. dasyacanthus*) · ⸸ Z9 ⒶⒸ; USA: Tex.
- *sarissophorus* Britton & Rose = Echinocereus enneacanthus
- **scheeri** (Salm-Dyck) Scheer
- var. **gentryi** (Clover) N.P. Taylor · ⸸ Z9 ⒶⒸ; Mex.: Sonora
- var. **scheeri** · ⸸ Z9 ⒶⒸ ▽ ✳; N-Mex.
- *schmollii* (Weing.) N.P. Taylor = Wilcoxia schmollii
- *spinosissimus* Walton = Echinocereus dasyacanthus
- **stramineus** (Engelm.) F. Seitz · E:Strawberry Hedgehog Cactus · ⸸ Z8 ⒶⒸ ▽ ✳; USA: Tex., N.Mex.; N-Mex.
- **subinermis** Salm-Dyck ex Scheer
- var. *luteus* Britton & Rose = Echinocereus subinermis var. subinermis
- var. **subinermis** · ⸸ Z9 ⒶⒸ ▽ ✳; NW-Mex.
- **triglochidiatus** Engelm. ex Haage · E:King Cup Cactus, Spineless Hedgehog · ⸸ Z8 ⒶⒸ ▽ ✳; USA: SC, SW, Rocky Mts.; N-Mex.
- **viridiflorus** Engelm. · E:Golden-spine Hedgehog, Green Hedgehog
- var. **chloranthus** (Engelm.) Backeb. · ⸸ Z8 ⒶⒸ ▽ ✳; USA: Tex., N.Mex.; N-Mex.
- var. **viridiflorus** · E:Nylon Hedgehog Cactus · ⸸ Z8 ⒶⒸ ▽ ✳; USA: S.Dak., Wyom., Kans., Colo., N.Mex., Okla., Tex.

Echinochloa P. Beauv. -f- *Poaceae* · c. 35 spp. · E:Cockspur; F:Panic; G:Hühnerhirse
- **colona** (L.) Link · E:Jungle Rice, Shama Millet; G:Schama-Hirse · ⊙ ⒼⒸ VII-IX Ⓝ; Trop., nat. in Ib, F, Ital-P, Crete, Cauc.
- **crus-galli** (L.) P. Beauv. · E:Barnyard Grass, Cockspur; G:Gewöhnliche

Hühnerhirse · ⊙ Z6 VII-X Ⓝ; Eur.: Ib, Fr, Ital-P, Ba, E-Eur.; Cauc., W-Sib., E-Sib., Amur, C-As., Ind., China, Jap., Afr., N-Am., S-Am., Austr., nat. in Eur.: Sc, C-Eur., EC-Eur.; cosmop.
- **crus-pavonis** (Kunth) Schult. · E:Gulf Cockspur Grass · ⊙ Ⓝ; USA: SE, SC; W.Ind., trop. Am., nat. in N-I
- **frumentacea** Link · E:Billion Dollar Grass; G:Sawa-Hirse · ⊙ Ⓝ; Ind., SE-As, nat. in China, Jap., USA
- **muricata** (P. Beauv.) Fernald · E:Rough Barnyard Grass; G:Stachelfrüchtige Hühnerhirse · ⊙ VII-X; USA: NE, NEC, NC, SC, SE, Fla., nat. in G, BrI
- **pyramidalis** (Lam.) Hitchc. & Chase · E:Antelope Grass; G:Antilopengras · Ⓗ ⒼⒶ Ⓝ; Afr.: Nil, Niger-Sudd
- **stagnina** (Retz.) P. Beauv. · E:Hippo Grass · Ⓗ ⒼⒶ Ⓝ; C-Afr., As.
- **utilis** Ohwi & Yabuno · E:Japanese Millet; G:Japanische Hühnerhirse · ⊙ Ⓝ; Jap., China

Echinocystis Torr. & A. Gray -f- *Cucurbitaceae* · 1 sp. · E:Mock Cucumber; F:Concombre-oursin; G:Igelgurke
- **lobata** (Michx.) Torr. & A. Gray · E:Prickly Cucumber, Wild Balsam Apple ; G:Igelgurke · ⊙ ⚥ VI-VIII; Can.: Sask.; USA* exc. Calif., nat. in C-Eur., EC-Eur., W-Ba, E-Eur.

Echinodorus Rich. ex Engelm. -m- *Alismataceae* · 30 spp. · G:Schwertpflanze
- *amazonicus* Rataj = Echinodorus grisebachii
- *argentinensis* Rataj = Echinodorus grandiflorus
- *aureobrunneus* hort. = Echinodorus uruguayensis
- **berteroi** (Spreng.) Fassett · E:Upright Burhead; G:Zellophan-Schwertpflanze · Ⓗ ∼ ≈ Z9 ⒼⒶ; USA: Tex., Fla.; Mex., W. Ind.
- *bleheri* Rataj = Echinodorus grisebachii
- **bolivianus** (Rusby) Holm-Niels. · E:Bolivian Burhead; G:Zwerg-Schwertpflanze · ∼ ≈ Z9 ⒼⒶ; trop. Am: Mex. - Braz.
- **cordifolius** (L.) Griseb. · E:Creeping Burhead; G:Herzblättrige Schwertpflanze · Ⓗ ∼ ≈ Z9 ⒼⒶ; USA: NE, NCE, NC, Kans., SE, Fla.; Mex.
- **grandiflorus** (Cham. & Schltdl.)

Micheli · 4 ~ ≈ Z9 ⓦ; S-Braz.,
Urug., Arg.
- **grisebachii** Small · G:Amazonas-Schwertpflanze · 4 ~ ≈ Z9 ⓦ; Amazon.
- **horizontalis** Rataj · G:Horizontale Schwertpflanze · 4 ~ ≈ Z9 ⓦ; Amazon.
- *humilis* (Rich. ex Kunth) Buchenau = Ranalisma humile
- **macrophyllus** (Kunth) Micheli · G:Großblättrige Schwertpflanze · 4 ~ ≈ Z9 ⓦ; S-Am.
- *major* (Micheli) Rataj = Echinodorus martii
- **martii** Micheli · G:Gewelltblättrige Schwertpflanze · 4 ~ ≈ Z9 ⓦ; Braz.
- **nymphaeifolius** (Griseb.) Buchenau · G:Seerosenblättrige Schwertpflanze · 4 ~ ≈ Z9 ⓦ; Mex., Hond., Cuba
- *osiris* Rataj = Echinodorus uruguayensis
- **paniculatus** Micheli · G:Rispige Schwertpflanze · 4 Z9 ⓦ; n S-Am.
- *parviflorus* Rataj = Echinodorus grisebachii
- *pellucidus* Rataj = Echinodorus uruguayensis
- *quadricostatus* Fassett = Echinodorus bolivianus
- var. *xinguensis* Rataj = Echinodorus bolivianus
- *radicans* (Nutt.) Engelm. = Echinodorus cordifolius
- *ranunculoides* (L.) Engelm. = Baldellia ranunculoides
- **tenellus** (Mart.) Buchenau · E:Mud Babies; G:Grasartige Schwertpflanze · 4 ~ ≈ ⓦ; USA, Mex., C-Am., W.Ind., trop. S-Am.
- **uruguayensis** Arechav. · G:Uruguay-Schwertpflanze · 4 ≈ Z9 ⓦ; Braz.

Echinofossulocactus Lawr. -m- *Cactaceae* · -10 spp.
- *albatus* (A. Dietr.) Britton & Rose = Stenocactus vaupelianus
- *coptonogonus* (Lem.) Lawr. = Stenocactus coptonogonus
- *crispatus* (DC.) Lawr. = Stenocactus crispatus
- **gladiatus** (Link & Otto) Lawr. · ⍦ Z9 ⓚ ▽ ✳; Mex.
- *lamellosus* (A. Dietr.) Britton & Rose = Stenocactus crispatus
- *multicostatus* (Hildm. ex K. Schum.) Britton & Rose = Stenocactus multicostatus
- *phyllacanthus* Mart. ex A. Dietr. & Otto =

Stenocactus phyllacanthus
- *vaupelianus* (Werderm.) Tiegel & Oehme = Stenocactus vaupelianus
- *violaciflorus* (Quehl) Britton & Rose = Stenocactus crispatus

Echinomastus Britton & Rose -m- *Cactaceae* · 7 spp. · E:Fishhook Cactus
- *durangensis* (Runge) Britton & Rose = Echinomastus unguispinus
- **erectocentrus** (J.M. Coult.) Britton & Rose · E:Redspine Fishhook Cactus · ⍦ Z9 ⓚ; SW-Ariz., Mex.: Sonora
- **intertextus** (Engelm.) Britton & Rose · E:White Fishhook Cactus · ⍦ Z9 ⓚ; USA: Tex., SW; Mex: Chihuahua, Coahuila, Sonora
- **johnsonii** (Parry ex Engelm.) E.M. Baxter · E:Johnson's Fishhook Cactus · ⍦ Z9 ⓚ; USA: Calif., Nev., Ariz.
- **mariposensis** Hester · E:Lloyd's Fishhook Cactus · ⍦ Z9 ⓚ ▽ ✳; S-Tex., Mex.: Coahuila
- **unguispinus** (Engelm.) Britton & Rose · ⍦ Z9 ⓚ ▽ ✳; Mex.: Chihuahua, Zacatecas

Echinopanax Decne. & Planch. = Oplopanax
- *horridus* (Sm.) Sm. ex J.G. Cooper = Oplopanax horridus

Echinopepon Naudin -m- *Cucurbitaceae* · 12 spp.
- **wrightii** (A. Gray) S. Watson · E:Wild Balsam Apple · ☉; W-Tex., Ariz., N-Mex.

Echinops L. -m- *Asteraceae* · c. 120 spp. · E:Globe Thistle; F:Boule azurée; G:Kugeldistel
- **bannaticus** Rochel ex Schrad. · E:Blue Globe Thistle; F:Boule azurée; G:Banater Kugeldistel, Ruthenische Kugeldistel · 4 Z3 VII-IX; Eur.: Ba, Ro, Crim
- **exaltatus** Schrad. · E:Globe Thistle; G:Drüsenlose Kugeldistel · 4 Z3 VI-VIII; Eur.: NE-I, Ba, EC-Eur., nat. in A, G, DK
- **gmelinii** Turcz. · ☉ Z5; C-As., Mong., China
- **humilis** M. Bieb. · 4 Z3 VIII-IX; W-As.
- **niveus** Wall. ex Royle · F:Boule bleue · 4 Z7 VII-VIII; Him.
- *ritro* hort. non L. = Echinops bannaticus
- **ritro** L.
- subsp. **ritro** · E:Southern Globe Thistle · 4 Z3 VII-IX; Eur.: Ib, Fr, Ital-P, Ba,

EC-Eur., E-Eur.; TR, Cauc., W-Sib., C-As.
- subsp. **ruthenicus** (M. Bieb.) Nyman · ⌙
Z3 VII-IX; Eur.: A, I, Slove., Croatia, BG,
Russ.
- *ruthenicus* M. Bieb. = Echinops ritro
subsp. ruthenicus
- **sphaerocephalus** L. · E:Great Globe
Thistle; G:Drüsige Kugeldistel · ⌙ Z3
VI-VIII; Eur.* exc. BrI, Sc; TR, Cauc.,
C-As., nat. in Sc

Echinopsis Zucc. -f- *Cactaceae* · c. 20 spp. ·
F:Cactus-hérisson; G:Seeigelkaktus
- *albispinosa* K. Schum. = Echinopsis
tubiflora
- **ancistrophora** Speg. · ⌿ Z9 ⌂ ▽ ✳;
W-Arg.
- var. *hamatacantha* (Backeb.) Rausch =
Echinopsis hamatacantha
- var. *polyancistra* (Backeb.) Rausch =
Echinopsis polyancistra
- **arachnacantha** (Buining & F. Ritter) H.
Friedrich · ⌿ Z9 ⌂ ▽ ✳; Arg.: Salta
- **aurea** Britton & Rose · ⌿ Z9 ⌂ ▽ ✳;
Arg.: Catamarca
- *backebergii* Werderm. = Lobivia backebergii
- *boyuibenensis* F. Ritter = Echinopsis
obrepanda var. obrepanda
- *bruchii* (Britton & Rose) A. Cast. & H.V.
Lelong = Trichocereus bruchii
- **calochlora** K. Schum. · ⌿ Z9 ⌂ ▽ ✳;
Braz.: Goias
- *candicans* (Gillies ex Salm-Dyck) F.A.C.
Weber ex D.R. Hunt = Trichocereus
candicans
- *chamaecereus* H. Friedrich & G.D. Rowley
= Lobivia silvestrii
- *chrysantha* Werderm. = Lobivia chrysantha
- *cinnabarina* (Hook.) Labour. = Lobivia
cinnabarina
- **ferox** (Britton & Rose) Backeb. · ⌿ Z9 ⌂
▽ ✳; Bol., N-Arg.
- *formosa* (Pfeiff.) Salm-Dyck = Trichocereus formosus
- **hamatacantha** Backeb. · ⌿ Z9 ⌂ ▽ ✳;
Arg.: Salta
- *hertrichiana* (Backeb.) D.R. Hunt =
Lobivia hertrichiana
- *huascha* (F.A.C. Weber) H. Friedrich &
G.D. Rowley = Trichocereus huascha
- *kermesina* (Krainz) Krainz = Echinopsis
mamillosa var. kermesina
- **kratochviliana** Backeb. · ⌿ Z9 ⌂; Arg.:

Salta
- *kuehnrichii* (Frič) H. Friedrich & Glaetzle
= Lobivia kuehnrichii
- **leucantha** (Gillies ex Salm-Dyck) Walp. ·
⌿ Z9 ⌂ ▽ ✳; Arg.
- *leucorhodantha* Backeb. = Echinopsis
ancistrophora
- **longispina** (Britton & Rose) Backeb. · ⌿
Z9 ⌂ ▽ ✳; Arg.: Rio Negro
- *macrogona* (Salm-Dyck) H. Friedrich &
G.D. Rowley = Trichocereus macrogonus
- **mamillosa** Gürke
- var. **kermesina** (Krainz) H. Friedrich · ⌿
Z9 ⌂ ▽ ✳; Arg.: Jujuy
- var. **mamillosa** · ⌿ Z9 ⌂ ▽ ✳; Bol.:
Tarija
- *maximiliana* Heyder = Lobivia maximiliana
- *melanopotamica* Speg. = Echinopsis
leucantha
- *mirabilis* Speg. = Setiechinopsis mirabilis
- *multiplex* (Pfeiff.) Zucc. = Echinopsis
oxygona
- **obrepanda** (Salm-Dyck) K. Schum.
- var. **fiebrigii** (Gürke) H. Friedrich · ⌿ Z9
⌂ ▽ ✳; Bol. (Cochabamba)
- var. **obrepanda** · ⌿ Z9 ⌂ ▽ ✳; Bol.:
Cochabamba
- **oxygona** (Link) Zucc. · ⌿ Z9 ⌂ ▽ ✳;
S-Braz., N-Arg.
- *pachanoi* (Britton & Rose) H. Friedrich &
G.D. Rowley = Trichocereus pachanoi
- *pasacana* H. Friedrich & G.D. Rowley =
Trichocereus pasacana
- *pecheretiana* (Backeb.) H. Friedrich &
G.D. Rowley = Trichocereus huascha
- *pelecyrhachis* Backeb. = Echinopsis
ancistrophora
- *pentlandii* (Hook.) Salm-Dyck = Lobivia
pentlandii
- **polyancistra** Backeb. · ⌿ D Z9 ⌂ ▽ ✳;
Arg.: Salta
- *purpureopilosa* (Weing.) H. Friedrich &
G.D. Rowley = Trichocereus purpureopilosus
- **rhodotricha** K. Schum. · ⌿ Z9 ⌂ ▽ ✳;
NE-Arg., Parag
- *rojasii* Cárdenas = Echinopsis obrepanda
var. obrepanda
- *roseolilacina* Cárdenas = Echinopsis
obrepanda var. obrepanda
- *schickendantzii* (F.A.C. Weber) H.
Friedrich & G.D. Rowley = Trichocereus
schickendantzii
- *shaferi* Britton & Rose = Echinopsis

leucantha
- *spachiana* (Lem.) H. Friedrich & G.D. Rowley = Trichocereus spachianus
- *spiniflora* (K. Schum.) A. Berger = Acanthocalycium spiniflorum var. spiniflorum
- *strigosa* (Salm-Dyck) H. Friedrich & G.D. Rowley = Trichocereus strigosus
- *tapecuana* F. Ritter = Echinopsis obrepanda var. obrepanda
- *tarijensis* (Vaupel) H. Friedrich & G.D. Rowley = Trichocereus tarijensis
- *terscheckii* (J. Parm. ex Pfeiff.) H. Friedrich & G.D. Rowley = Trichocereus terscheckii
- *thelegona* (K. Schum.) H. Friedrich & G.D. Rowley = Trichocereus thelegonus
- **tubiflora** (Pfeiff.) K. Schum. · ⩇ Z9 ⓐ ▽ ✱; Arg.: Tucuman, Catamarca, Salta
- *violacea* Werderm. = Acanthocalycium spiniflorum
- **Cultivars:**
- **many cultivars**

Echinospartum (Spach) Fourr. -n- *Fabaceae* · 3 spp.
- **horridum** (Vahl) Rothm. · G:Abschreckender Ginster · ℏ d Z8 ⓐ △ VI-VIII ✼; Eur.: sp., S-F

Echioides Ortega = Arnebia
- *longiflora* (K. Koch) I.M. Johnst. = Arnebia pulchra

Echites P. Browne -f- *Apocynaceae* · 6 spp.
- *nutans* G. Anderson = Prestonia quinquangularis
- *peltatus* Vell. = Peltastes peltatus
- *rubrovenosus* Linden = Prestonia quinquangularis

Echium L. -n- *Boraginaceae* · c. 40 spp. · E:Bugloss; F:Vipérine; G:Natternkopf
- **angustifolium** Mill. · ⩇ Z8 ⓐ VI-VIII; Eur.: GR, Crete; TR, Levant, NW-Afr.
- **callithyrsum** Webb ex Bolle · ℏ Z8 ⓐ; Canar.: ? Teneriffa
- **candicans** L. f. · E:Pride-of-Madeira; G:Stolz von Madeira · ℏ Z8 ⓐ IV-VII ▽; Canar.
- **creticum** L. · E:Cretan Viper's Bugloss · ☉ VII-VIII; Eur.: Ib, F, Cors, Sard.; NW-Afr.
- *fastuosum* Jacq. = Echium candicans
- **italicum** L. · E:Italian Bugloss; G:Hoher Natternkopf · ☉ VI-IX; Eur.: Ib, Fr, Ital-P,

Ba, A, EC-Eur., E-Eur.; TR, Syr., Cauc., C-As., Egypt, Libya
- **lusitanicum** L. · ⩇; P, W-Sp.
- **pininana** Webb & Berthel. · E:Giant Viper's Bugloss · ⩇ Z8 ⓐ VI-VIII; Canar.: La Palma
- **plantagineum** L. · E:Purple Bugloss; F:Vipérine faux-plantain; G:Wegerichblättriger Natternkopf · ☉ ☉ VI-VIII; Eur.: Ib, Fr, Ital-P, Ba, BrI, EC-Eur, E-Eur.; TR, Levant, N-Afr., nat. in Cauc.
- **russicum** J.F. Gmel. · ☉ VI-VII; Eur.: A, EC-Eur., Ba, E-Eur.; TR, Cauc.
- *sericeum* Vahl = Echium angustifolium
- **vulgare** L. · E:Viper's Bugloss; G:Gewöhnlicher Natternkopf · ☉ V-VIII 🜊 ✱; Eur.*, Cauc., TR, Cyprus, W-Sib., C-As.
- **webbii** Coincy · ℏ Z8 ⓐ; Canar.
- **wildpretii** H. Pearson ex Hook. f. · E:Tower-of-Jewels; G:Diamant-Natternkopf · ℏ Z8 ⓐ VI-VIII; Canar.: Gran Canaria, Teneriffa

Edgeworthia Meisn. -f- *Thymelaeaceae* · 3 spp.
- **chrysantha** Lindl. · E:Oriental Paperbush · China
- *papyrifera* Siebold & Zucc. = Edgeworthia chrysantha

Edmondia Cass. -f- *Asteraceae* · 3 spp.
- **sesamoides** (L.) Hilliard · ℏ ⩘ Z9 ⓐ; S-Afr.

Edraianthus (A. DC.) DC. -m- *Campanulaceae* · 24 spp. · E:Grassy Bells; G:Becherglocke, Büschelglocke
- *croaticus* (A. Kern.) A. Kern. = Edraianthus graminifolius
- **dalmaticus** (A. DC.) A. DC. · G:Dalmatinische Büschelglocke · ⩇ Z6 VI-VII; Eur.: Croatia, Bosn., ? Montenegro
- **dinaricus** (A. Kern.) Wettst. · ⩇ △ Z7 VII-VIII; Eur.: Croatia
- **graminifolius** (L.) A. DC. · F:Edraianthus à feuilles de graminée; G:Grasartige Büschelglocke · ⩇ △ Z7 VII-VIII; Eur.: I, Sic., Ba, RO
- *kitaibelii* (A. DC.) A. DC. = Edraianthus graminifolius
- **parnassicus** (Boiss. & Spruner) Halácsy · ⩇ △ Z8 VI-VII; GR
- **pumilio** (Port.) A. DC. · F:Campanille; G:Zwerg-Büschelglocke · ⩇ △ Z6 VI-VII;

Eur.: Croatia (Biokovo Planina)
- var. *major* Vis. = Edraianthus dinaricus
- **serpyllifolius** (Vis.) A. DC. · ♃ △ Z7 VI-VII; Eur.: Croatia, Bosn., Montenegro, AL
- **tenuifolius** (Waldst. & Kit.) A. DC. · ♃ △ Z7 VI-VII; Eur.: Slove., Croatia, Bosn., Montenegro, AL, GR

Edwardsia Salisb. = Sophora
- *microphylla* (Aiton) Salisb. = Sophora microphylla
- *tetraptera* (J.S. Muell.) Poir. = Sophora tetraptera

Egeria Planch. -f- *Hydrocharitaceae* · 2 spp. · E:Waterweed; F:Peste d'eau; G:Wasserpest
- **densa** Planch. · E:Dense Waterweed; G:Dichtblättrige Wasserpest · ♃ ≈ Z7 V-VIII; Braz. (Minas Gerais), Urug., N-Arg., nat. in Eur.: BrI, F, C-Eur., I; N-Am., C-Am., Austr., NZ

Ehretia P. Browne -f- *Boraginaceae* · 50 spp.
- **acuminata** R. Br. · E:Silky Ash · ♄ d Z7 VIII; China, Jap.
- **dicksonii** Hance · ♄ d Z7; China, Taiwan, Ryukyu-Is.
- *microphylla* Lam. = Carmona retusa
- *thyrsiflora* (Siebold & Zucc.) Nakai = Ehretia acuminata

Eichhornia Kunth -f- *Pontederiaceae* · 6 spp. · E:Water Hyacinth; F:Jacynthe d'eau; G:Wasserhyazinthe
- **azurea** (Sw.) Kunth · E:Anchored Water Hyacinth · ♃ ~ ≈ Z10 Ⓦ VI-X; subtrop. Am., trop. Am.
- **crassipes** (Mart.) Solms · E:Water Hyacinth; F:Jacinthe d'eau; G:Wasserhyazinthe · ♃ ~ ≈ Z10 Ⓦ VI-IX; Braz., nat. in Trop., Subtrop., P, Calif.
- **paniculata** (Spreng.) Solms · E:Brazilian Water Hyacinth · ♃ ~ Z10 Ⓦ VII-VIII; trop. S-Am.
- *speciosa* Kunth = Eichhornia crassipes

Elaeagnus L. -f- *Elaeagnaceae* · c. 50 spp. · E:Oleaster; F:Chalef; G:Ölweide
- **angustifolia** L.
- var. **angustifolia** · E:Oleaster, Russian Olive; F:Olivier de Bohême; G:Schmalblättrige Ölweide · ♄ ♄ d Z4 V-VI; TR, Syr., Cauc., Iran, Afgh., Pakist., W-Sib., C-As., Mong., Tibet, Him., nat. in Eur.* exc. BrI, Sc
- var. *orientalis* (L.) Kuntze = Elaeagnus angustifolia var. angustifolia
- var. **spinosa** (L.) Kuntze · ♄ Z4
- *argentea* Moench = Elaeagnus angustifolia var. angustifolia
- *argentea* Pursh = Elaeagnus commutata
- **commutata** Bernh. ex Rydb. · E:Silver Berry; F:Chalef argenté; G:Silber-Ölweide · ♄ d D Z3 V-VII; Alaska, Can.; USA: NCE, NC, Rocky Mts.
- *crispa* Thunb. = Elaeagnus umbellata var. umbellata
- × **ebbingei** Boom ex Door. (*E. macrophylla* × *E. pungens*) · G:Wintergrüne Ölweide · ♄ e Z7 X-XII; cult.
- **some cultivars**
- *edulis* Carrière = Elaeagnus multiflora
- **glabra** Thunb. · ♄ e Z8 Ⓚ X-XI; China, Jap.
- *longipes* A. Gray = Elaeagnus multiflora
- **macrophylla** Thunb. · E:Broad-leaved Oleaster; G:Großblättrige Ölweide · ♄ e D Z8 Ⓚ IX-XI; Jap., Korea, Riukiu-Is.
- **multiflora** Thunb. · E:Cherry Elaeagnus; F:Goumi; G:Reichblütige Ölweide · ♄ ♄ d Z5; China, Korea, Jap.
- *orientalis* L. = Elaeagnus angustifolia var. angustifolia
- *parvifolia* Wall. ex Royle = Elaeagnus umbellata var. parvifolia
- **pungens** Thunb. · E:Spiny Oleaster; G:Dornige Ölweide · ♄ e Z7; N-China, Jap.
- var. *reflexa* (C. Morren & Decne.) C.K. Schneid. = Elaeagnus × reflexa
- × **reflexa** C. Morren & Decne. (*E. glabra* × *E. pungens*) · ♄ d D Z7 X-XI Ⓝ; cult.
- *spinosa* L. = Elaeagnus angustifolia var. spinosa
- **umbellata** Thunb.
- var. **parvifolia** (Wall. ex Royle) C.K. Schneid. Z5; Him.
- var. **umbellata** · E:Autumn Elaeagnus, Autumn Olive; G:Doldige Ölweide · ♄ d Z5; Him., China, Korea, Jap.

Elaeis Jacq. -f- *Arecaceae* · 2 spp. · E:Oil Palm; F:Palmier à huile; G:Ölpalme
- **guineensis** Jacq. · E:African Oil Palm, Macaw Fat; G:Afrikanische Ölpalme · ♄ e Z10 Ⓦ Ⓝ; W-Afr., C-Afr., Angola, E-Afr.
- *melanococca* Gaertn. = Elaeis oleifera

– **oleifera** (Kunth) Cortés · E:American Oil Palm; G:Amerikanische Ölpalme · ♄ e Z10 ⓦ Ⓝ; C-Am., trop. S-Am.

Elaeocarpus L. -m- *Elaeocarpaceae* · 60 (-360) spp. · E:Quandong; G:Ganiterbaum, Ölfrucht
– **cyaneus** W.T. Aiton ex Sims · E:Blueberry Ash · ♄ Z9 ⓚ Ⓝ; Austr.: N.S.Wales
– **floribundus** Blume · E:Egg Laurel · ♄ e Z9 ⓦ Ⓝ; Him., Burma
– *reticulatus* Sm. = Elaeocarpus cyaneus

Elaeodendron Jacq. -n- *Celastraceae* · 15 spp. · E:False Olive
– *orientale* Jacq. = Cassine orientalis

Elaphoglossum Schott ex J. Sm. -n- *Lomariopsidaceae* · 651 sp. · E:Tonguefern; F:Fougère-langue; G:Zungenfarn
– **crinitum** (L.) H. Christ · E:West Indian Tonguefern · ⚃ Z10 ⓦ; Mex., Guat., Costa Rica
– **latifolium** (Sw.) J. Sm. · E:Broadleaf Tonguefern · ⚃ Z10 ⓦ; Mex., W-Ind., trop. S-Am.
– **villosum** (Sw.) J. Sm. · ⚃ Z10 ⓦ; C-Am., W.Ind.

Elatine L. -f- *Elatinaceae* · 10 (-50) spp. · E:Waterwort; F:Elatine; G:Tännel
– **alsinastrum** L. · G:Quirl-Tännel · ⊙ ⚃ ∿ VII-VIII; Eur.* exc. BrI; Cauc., W-Sib., C-As, Jap., NW-Afr.
– *gyrosperma* Düben ex Meinsh. = Elatine hydropiper
– **hexandra** (Lapierre) DC. · E:Six-stamened Waterwort; G:Sechsmänniger Tännel · ⊙ ∿ VI-VIII; Eur.*
– **hydropiper** L. · E:Eight-stamened Waterwort; G:Gewöhnlicher Wasserpfeffer-Tännel · ⊙ ∿ VI-IX; Eur.*, TR, Cauc., W-Sib.
– **macropoda** Guss. · G:Langstängeliger Tännel · ⊙ ∿ Z8 ⓦ ⓚ; Eur.: Ib, Fr, Ital-P; TR, Levant, N-Afr.
– **triandra** Schkuhr · G:Dreimänniger Tännel · ⊙ VI-IX; Eur.* exc. Ib, BrI; ? C-As., NE-As.

Elatostema J.R. Forst. & G. Forst. -f- *Urticaceae* · c. 300 spp. · G:Melonenbegonie
– *pulchrum* (N.E. Br.) Hallier f. = Pellionia pulchra
– *repens* (Lour.) Hallier f. = Pellionia repens

Elegia L. -f- *Restionaceae* · 35 spp.
– **capensis** (Burm. f.) Schelpe · ⚃ ⋉ Z8 ⓚ; S-Afr. (Cape)

Eleocharis R. Br. -f- *Cyperaceae* · 253 spp. · E:Spike Rush; F:Eleocharis; G:Sumpfbinse
– **acicularis** (L.) Roem. & Schult. · E:Needle Spike Rush; F:Scirpe épingle; G:Nadel-Sumpfsimse · ⚃ ∿ VI-X; Eur.*, Cauc., W-Sib., E-Sib., Amur, Kamchat., C-As., Mong., Manch., N-Afr., Austr., USA*, S-Am.
– **atropurpurea** (Retz.) Kunth · E:Purple Spikerush; G:Schwarzrote Sumpfbinse · ⊙ ∿ VIII-IX; Eur.: I, Sw; Trop., Subtrop.
– *austriaca* Hayek = Eleocharis mammilata subsp. austriaca
– *carniolica* W.D.J. Koch = Eleocharis uniglumis
– **dulcis** (Burm. f.) Trin. ex Hensch. · E:Chinese Waterchestnut, Water Chestnut; G:Chinesische Wassernuss, Wasserkarstanie · ⚃ ∿ Z9 ⓚ Ⓝ; trop. Afr., Madag., Ind., trop. E-As., Austr., Pacific Is.
– **mamillata** (H. Lindb.) H. Lindb. · E:Northern Spikerush
– subsp. **austriaca** (Hayek) Strandh. · G:Österreichische Sumpfsimse · ⚃ ∿ V-VIII; Eur.*, Cauc., W-Sib., E-Sib., Amur
– subsp. **mamillata** · G:Zitzen-Sumpfsimse · ⚃ ∿ V-VIII; Eur.: Fr, C-Eur., EC-Eur., Sc, Ba, E-Eur.; W-Sib., E-Sib., Amur
– **multicaulis** (Sm.) Desv. · E:Many-stalked Spikerush; G:Vielstängelige Sumpfsimse · ⚃ ∿ VI-VII; Eur.* , NW-Afr.
– **ovata** (Roth) Roem. & Schult. · E:Oval Spikerush; G:Eiförmige Sumpfsimse · ⊙ ∿ VII-IX; Eur.: Fr, Ital-P, C-Eur., EC-Eur., Ba, E-Eur.; Cauc., E-Sib., Amur, Him., Manch.
– **palustris** (L.) Roem. & Schult. · E:Common Spike Rush, Creeping Spike Rush; G:Gewöhnliche Sumpfsimse
– subsp. **palustris** · F:Eleocharis des marais; G:Kleinfrüchtige Gewöhnliche Sumpfbinse · ⚃ ∿ V-VIII; Eur.*, Cauc., Iran, Afgh., Him., W-Sib., E-Sib., C-As.,

Mong., China
- subsp. **vulgaris** Walters · G:Groß-
früchtige Gewöhnliche Sumpfsimse · ⠵
⌒ V-VIII; Eur., ? TR, Cauc., W-Sib.,
E-Sib., C-As, Mong., N-Am.
- **parvula** (Roem. & Schult.) Palla · E:Little
Head Spike Rush; G:Kleine Sumpfsimse
· ⠵ ⌒ ≈ Z8 ⓕ VI-IX; Eur.*, C-As.,
Amur, Jap., Indochina, Java, N-Afr.,
Can., USA*, S-Am.
- *pygmaea* Torr. = Eleocharis parvula
- **quinqueflora** (Hartmann) O. Schwarz ·
E:Few-flowered Spikerush; G:Armblütige
Sumpfsimse · ⠵ ⌒ V-VI; Eur.* exc. ? Ib;
TR, N-As., Moroc., N-Am.
- **uniglumis** (Link) Schult. · E:Slender
Spikerush; G:Einspelzige Sumpfsimse · ⠵
⌒ V-VIII; Eur.*, Cauc., W-Sib., E-Sib.,
Kamchat., C-As., Him., Mong.
- **vivipara** Link · E:Viviparous Spikerush ·
⠵ ⌒ ≈ Z9 ⓕ; USA: Va., SE, Fla.
- *vulgaris* (Walters) A. Löve & D. Löve =
Eleocharis palustris subsp. vulgaris

Eleogiton Link = Isolepis
- *fluitans* (L.) Link = Isolepis fluitans

Elettaria Maton -f- *Zingiberaceae* · II sp. ·
E:Cardamom; F:Cardamome; G:Karda-
mom
- **cardamomum** (L.) Maton · E:Chester
Cardamom; G:Malabar-Kardamom · ⠵
Z10 ⓦ ⚥ ⓝ; S-Ind., Sri Lanka, SE-As.
- var. *major* (Sm.) Thwaites = Elettaria
ensal
- **ensal** (Gaertn.) Abeyw. · G:Ceylon-
Kardamom · ⠵ Z10 ⓦ ⓝ; Sri Lanka
- *major* Sm. = Elettaria ensal

Eleusine Gaertn. -f- *Poaceae* · 9 spp. ·
E:Yard Grass; F:Eleusine, panic digité;
G:Fingerhirse
- **coracana** (L.) Gaertn. · E:Caracan Millet,
Finger Millet; G:Fingerhirse, Korakan · ☉
Z9 ⓝ; trop. Afr., trop. As.
- **indica** (L.) Gaertn. · E:Indian Goose
Grass; G:Wilder Korakan · ☉ ⠵ ⋉ Z9 VII-
VIII; trop. Afr., trop. As., nat. in S-Eur.,
N-Am.
- **tristachya** (Lam.) Lam. · E:American
Yard Grass · ☉ Z9; Trop. Old World

Eleutherococcus Maxim. -m- *Araliaceae* ·
40 spp. · F:Acanthopanax; G:Fingeraralie
- **divaricatus** (Siebold & Zucc.) S.Y. Hu · ♄

d Z6 IX; China: Hopei, Honan; Jap.
- **giraldii** (Harms) Nakai · ♄ d Z6 VIII;
C-China, N-China
- **henryi** Oliv. · G:Henrys Fingeraralie · ♄ d
Z6 VIII-IX; C-China
- **leucorrhizus** Oliv. · ♄ Z6 VII; China:
Sichuan, Yunnan, Hubei, Kansu
- **senticosus** (Rupr. & Maxim.) Maxim. ·
E:Siberian Ginseng; G:Borstige Fingeraralie, Stachelpanax · ♄ d Z5 VII ⚥ ; Amur,
N-China, Manch., Korea, Jap., Sakhal.
- **sessiliflorus** (Rupr. & Maxim.) S.Y. Hu ·
G:Amur-Fingeraralie · ♄ d Z5 VII-IX;
Manch., N-China, Korea
- **setchuenensis** (Harms) Nakai · ⠵ d Z6
VII; W-China
- **sieboldianus** (Makino) Koidz. · G:Sie-
bolds Fingeraralie · ♄ d Z6 VI-VII; China
- **simonii** (Simon-Louis ex Mouill.) Hesse ·
♄ d Z6 VI; C-China.

Eleutheropetalum H. Wendl. = Chamaedorea
- *ernesti-augusti* (H. Wendl.) H. Wendl. ex
Oerst. = Chamaedorea ernesti-augustii

Elisena Herb. = Hymenocallis
- *longipetala* Lindl. = Hymenocallis
longipetala

Elisma Buchenau = Luronium
- *natans* (L.) Buchenau = Luronium natans

× **Elleanthera** hort. -f- *Orchidaceae*
(*Renanthera* × *Renantherella*)

Elleanthus C. Presl -m- *Orchidaceae* ·
III sp.
- **capitatus** (Poepp. & Endl.) Rchb. f. · ⠵
Z10 ⓦ X-XI ▽ ✳; Mex., C-Am., W.Ind.,
S-Am.
- **caravata** (Aubl.) Rchb. f. · ⠵ Z10 ⓦ IX-X
▽ ✳; Guyan.

Elmerrillia Dandy -f- *Magnoliaceae* · 4 spp.
- **tsiampacca** (L.) Dandy · ♄; Sulawesi,
Moluccas, New Guinea, Bismarck Arch.

Elodea Michx. -f- *Hydrocharitaceae* ·
6 spp. · E:Waterweed; F:Elodée, Peste
d'eau; G:Wasserpest
- **callitrichoides** (Rich.) Casp. · E:Greater
Water Thyme; G:Argentinische Wasserpest · ⠵ ≈ ⓦ ⓕ VII-IX; Arg., nat. in F
(Alsace), D

- **canadensis** Michx. · E:Canadian
  Pondweed; F:Elodée du Canada;
  G:Kanadische Wasserpest · ⑉ ≈ Ⓚ
  V-VIII; Can., USA*, nat. in cosmop.
- *crispa* hort. = Lagarosiphon major
- *densa* (Planch.) Casp. = Egeria densa
- *ernstae* H. St. John = Elodea callitrichoides
- **nuttallii** (Planch.) H. St. John ·
  E:Western Waterweed; G:Nuttalls
  Wasserpest, Schmalblättrige Wasserpest ·
  ⑉ ≈ Ⓚ VI-VIII; Can.: E; USA: NE, NCE,
  NC, NW, Calif., nat. in W-Eur., G, Jap.
- *occidentalis* (Pursh) H. St. John = Elodea
  nuttallii

Elsholtzia Willd. -f- *Lamiaceae* · 41 sp. ·
  E:Elsholtzia; F:Elsholtzia; G:Elsholtzia
- **ciliata** (Thunb.) Hyl. · E:Crested Late
  Summer Mint; G:Echte Kammminze · ⊙
  Z5 VII-XI Ⓝ; C-As., Jap., Korea, China,
  Taiwan, nat. in Eur.: Sc, C-Eur., EC-Eur.,
  Ba, E-Eur.
- *cristata* Willd. = Elsholtzia ciliata
- **stauntonii** Benth. · E:Mint Bush;
  F:Elsholtzia; G:Chinesische Kamm-Minze
  · ♃ d D Z7 IX-X; N-China

Elymus L. -f- *Poaceae* · c. 150 spp. ·
  E:Couch; F:Blé d'azur, Chiendent des
  sables, Elyme; G:Haargerste, Quecke
- *arenarius* L. = Leymus arenarius
- **arenosus** (Spenn.) Conert · G:Sand-
  Quecke · ⑉ Z6; NW-Eur.; coasts
- **athericus** (Link) Kerguélen · E:Sea
  Couch; G:Dünen-Quecke · ⑉ V-VII; Eur.:
  BrI, Sc, Ib, Fr, C-Eur., Ital-P, Ba, RO;
  coasts; TR, NW-Iran, Afgh., nat. in N-Am.
- **canadensis** L. · E:Canada Wild Rye;
  G:Kanada-Quecke · ⑉ Z3 VII-IX; Alaska,
  Can., USA*
- **caninus** (L.) L. · E:Bearded Couch;
  G:Hunds-Quecke · ⑉ VI-VII; Eur.*, TR,
  Iraq, Cauc., Iran, Afgh., Pakist., NW-Ind.,
  W-Sib., E-Sib., C-As., NW-Ind., W-China,
  nat. in N-Am., Jap., NZ
- **elongatus** (Host) Runemark · ⑉ Z5; Eur.:
  Ib, Fr, Ital-P, Ba, E-Eur. +
- **farctus** (Viv.) Runemark ex Melderis ·
  G:Strand-Quecke
- subsp. **boreoatlanticus** (Simonet &
  Guin.) Melderis · G:Binsen-Quecke · ⑉ Z5
  Ⓝ; W-Eur., G, nat. in N-Am.
- subsp. **farctus** E:Sand Couch;
  G:Gewöhnliche Stand-Quecke · ⑉ Z5

VI-VIII Ⓝ; Eur.*, TR, N-Afr.; coasts, nat.
  in N-Am.
- *giganteus* Vahl = Leymus racemosus
- **hispidus** (Opiz) Melderis · G:Graugrüne
  Quecke
- subsp. **hispidulus** (Schur) Melderis · ⑉
  Z5; SE-Eur.
- subsp. **hispidus** · G:Gewöhnliche
  Graugrüne Quecke · ⑉ Z5 VI-VII Ⓝ; Eur.*
  exc. BrI, Sc; TR, N-Iraq, Cauc., Iran,
  Pakist., C-As.
- × **laxus** (Fr.) Melderis & D.C. McClint.
  (*E. farctus* × *E. repens* subsp. *repens*) ·
  G:Lockerblütige Bastard-Quecke · ⑉; D +
- **obtusiflorus** (DC.) Conert · G:Pontische
  Quecke, Stumpfblütige Quecke · ⑉
  VIII-IX; Eur.: NL, G, Dk+, nat. in Eur.: F,
  I, G, A
- × **obtusiusculus** (Lange) Melderis &
  D.C. McClint. (*E. athericus* × *E. farctus*) ·
  G:Bastard-Binsen-Quecke · ⑉; Eur.:
  Slove., Serb., BG, RO; TR, nat. in F, I, A,
  D
- × **oliveri** (Druce) Melderis & D.C.
  McClint. (*E. athericus* × *E. repens* subsp.
  repens) · ⑉; D +
- *pauciflorus* (Schwein.) Gould = Elymus
  trachycaulus
- *racemosus* Lam. = Leymus racemosus
- **repens** (L.) Gould · E:Couch Grass;
  G:Gewöhnliche Kriech-Quecke · ⑉ VI-VIII
  ♃ Ⓝ; Eur.*, Can.; E; USA: Maine; Sib.,
  N-Afr., nat. in USA, Mex.
- **trachycaulus** (Link) Gould ex Shinners ·
  E:Slender Wheat Grass · Alaska, Can.;
  USA*; N-Mex., E-Sib., E-As.
- **virginicus** L. · E:Virginia Wild Rye;
  G:Virginische Quecke · ⑉ Z3; Can.; USA*
  exc. Calif.

Elyna Schrad. = Kobresia
- *myosuroides* (Vill.) Fritsch ex Janch. =
  Kobresia myosuroides

Elytrigia Desv. = Elymus
- *atherica* (Link) M.A. Carreras ex
  Kerguélen = Elymus athericus
- *intermedia* (Host) Nevski = Elymus
  hispidus subsp. hispidus
- subsp. *barbulata* (Schur) Á. Löve =
  Elymus trachycaulus
- *juncea* (L.) Nevski = Elymus farctus
  subsp. farctus
- *junceiformis* Á. Löve & D. Löve = Elymus
  farctus subsp. boreoatlanticus

– *repens* (L.) Nevski = Elymus repens

Emblica Gaertn. = Phyllanthus
– *officinalis* Gaertn. = Phyllanthus emblica

Embothrium J.R. Forst. & G. Forst. -n-
Proteaceae · 8 spp. · E:Fire Bush; F:Arbre
de feu; G:Flammenbusch
– **coccineum** J.R. Forst. & G. Forst. ·
E:Chilean Fire Bush; G:Chilenischer
Flammenbusch · ♄ e Z8 ⌂; Chile, W-Arg.

Emerus Mill. -m- *Fabaceae* · 1 sp. ·
G:Strauchkronwicke
– **major** Mill. · E:Scorpion Senna;
G:Strauchkronwicke · ♄ e Z6 V-VII; Eur.*
exc. BrI; TR, Cyprus, Syr., Cauc., Tun.,
Libya

Emex Neck. ex Campd. -f- *Polygonaceae* ·
2 spp. · E:Devil's Thorn; G:Teufelsdorn
– **spinosa** (L.) Campd. · E:Devil's Thorn;
G:Teufelsdorn · ☉ Z3; Eur.: Ib, Ital-P, Ba;
TR

Emilia (Cass.) Cass. -f- *Asteraceae* · c.
100 spp. · E:Tassel Flower; F:Emilie;
G:Emilie
– **coccinea** (Sims) G. Don ex Sweet ·
E:Scarlet Tassel Flower · ☉ Z9; Afr.
– *flammea* Cass. = Emilia sonchifolia
– *flammea* hort. = Emilia coccinea
– *javanica* (Burm. f.) C.B. Rob. = Emilia
sonchifolia
– *javanica* auct. = Emilia coccinea
– *sagittata* DC. = Emilia sonchifolia
– **sonchifolia** (L.) DC. · E:Lilac Tassel
Flower · ☉ Z9; trop. Afr., Ind., S-China

Emmenopterys Oliv. -f- *Rubiaceae* · 2 spp.
– **henryi** Oliv. · ♄ d Z8 ⌂ VI-VII; China:
Hupeh; Burma, Thail.

Empetrum L. -n- *Empetraceae* · 2 spp. ·
E:Crowberry; F:Camarine; G:Krähen-
beere
– **atropurpureum** Fernald & Wiegand. ·
E:Purple Crowberry · ♄ e ⤳ Z3 V; Can.:
E; USA: NE
– **hermaphroditum** Hagerup · E:Mountain
Crowberry; G:Zwittrige Krähenbeere ·
♄ ⤳ Z2 IV-V; Eur.*, TR, Cauc., W-Sib.,
E-Sib., Kamchat., Jap., Greenl.
– **nigrum** L. · E:Black Crowberry;
F:Camarine noire; G:Schwarze

Krähenbeere · ♄ e ⤳ Z2 IV-V; Can.,
USA: NW, Calif., NE, NEC; Eur.*; N,
mts.; W-Sib., E-Sib., Kamchat., Amur,
Korea, Sakhal., Jap., Alaska, Greenl.
– subsp. *hermaphroditum* (Hagerup)
Böcher = Empetrum hermaphroditum

Encephalartos Lehm. -m- *Zamiaceae* ·
46 spp. · E:Cycad; F:Arbre à pain;
G:Brotpalmfarn
– **altensteinii** Lehm. · E:Bread Tree, Prickly
Cycad · ♄ e Z9 ⊞ ⚘ ▽ ✳; S-Afr.
– **caffer** (Thunb.) Lehm. · E:Kaffir Bread;
G:Kafir-Brotpalmfarn · ⌘ e Z9 ⊞ ⚘ ▽
✳; Cape
– **cycadifolius** (Jacq.) Lehm. · ♄ e Z9 ⊞
⚘ ▽ ✳; S-Afr.
– **hildebrandtii** A. Braun & C.D. Bouché ·
♄ e Z9 ⊞ ⚘ ▽ ✳; E-Afr.
– **horridus** (Jacq.) Lehm. · E:Ferocious
Blue Cycad · ⌘ e Z9 ⌂ ▽ ✳; Cape
– **lebomboensis** I. Verd. · E:Lebombo
Cycad; G:Lebombo-Brotpalmfarn · ♄ e Z9
⌂ ⚘ ▽ ✳; S-Afr.
– **lehmannii** (Eckl. & Zeyh. ex Eckl.)
Lehm. · E:Karoo Cycad; G:Karoo-
Brotpalmfarn · ♄ e Z9 ⊞ ⚘ ▽ ✳; Cape
– **longifolius** (Jacq.) Lehm. · E:Bread
Palm, Suurberg Cycad; G:Suurberg-
Brotpalmfarn · ♄ e Z9 ⊞ ⚘ ▽ ✳; Cape
– **transvenosus** Stapf & Burtt Davy ·
E:Modjadji Cycad; G:Modjadji-
Brotpalmfarn · ♄ e Z9 ⊞ ⚘ ▽ ✳; S-Afr.:
Transvaal
– **villosus** Lehm. · ⌘ Z9 ⊞ ⚘ ▽ ✳; S-Afr.:
SE-Cape, Natal

Encephalocarpus A. Berger -m- *Cactaceae* ·
1 sp.
– **strobiliformis** (Werderm.) A. Berger · ⍦
Z9 ⌂; Mex.: Nuevo León, Tamaulipas

Encyclia Hook. -f- *Orchidaceae* · 150 spp.
– **adenocaula** (La Llave & Lex.) Schltr. · ⌘
Z10 ⊞ VII ▽ ✳; Mex.
– **alata** (Bateman) Schltr. · ⌘ Z10 ⊞ V-X
▽ ✳; C-Am.
– *baculus* (Rchb. f.) Dressler & G.E. Pollard
= Prosthechea baculus
– *boothiana* (Lindl.) Dressler = Prosthechea
boothiana
– *Brassavolae* (Rchb. f.) Dressler =
Prosthechea Brassavolae
– *citrina* (La Llave & Lex.) Dressler =
Euchile citrina

- *cochleata* (L.) Dressler = Prosthechea cochleata
- **cordigera** (Humb., Bonpl. & Kunth) Dressler · ♃ Z10 ⚘ IV-VI ▽ ✳; Mex., C-Am., Col., Venez.
- *fragrans* (Sw.) Dressler = Prosthechea fragrans
- *glumacea* (Lindl.) Pabst = Prosthechea glumacea
- *michuacana* (La Llave & Lex.) Schltr. = Prosthechea michuacana
- *nemoralis* (Lindl.) Schltr. = Encyclia adenocaula
- *odoratissima* (Lindl.) Schltr. = Encyclia patens
- **oncidioides** (Lindl.) Schltr. · ♃ Z10 ⚘ V-VI ▽ ✳; Guyan., Braz.
- **patens** Hook. · ♃ Z10 ⚘ VI-VII ▽ ✳; Braz.
- *prismatocarpa* (Rchb. f.) Dressler = Prosthechea prismatocarpa
- *radiata* (Lindl.) Dressler = Prosthechea radiata
- **tampensis** (Lindl.) Schltr. · E:Tampa Butterfly Orchid · ♃ Z10 ⚘ VI-VII ▽ ✳; Fla.
- *vespa* (Vell.) Dressler = Prosthechea michuacana
- *virgata* (Lindl.) Schltr. = Prosthechea michuacana
- *vitellina* (Lindl.) Dressler = Prosthechea vitellina

Endymion Dumort. = Hyacinthoides
- *campanulatus* (Aiton) Willk. = Hyacinthoides hispanica subsp. hispanica
- *hispanicus* (Mill.) Chouard = Hyacinthoides hispanica subsp. hispanica
- *non-scriptus* (L.) Garcke = Hyacinthoides non-scripta
- *nutans* (Sm.) Dumort. = Hyacinthoides non-scripta
- *patulus* (DC.) Dumort. = Hyacinthoides hispanica subsp. hispanica

Enkianthus Lour. -m- *Ericaceae* · 13 spp. · F:Enkianthus; G:Prachtglocke
- **campanulatus** (Miq.) G. Nicholson · G:Glockige Prachtglocke
- **some cultivars**
- var. **campanulatus** · ♄ d Z5 V; Jap.
- **cernuus** (Siebold & Zucc.) Benth. & Hook. f. ex Makino · G:Nickende Prachtglocke
- var. **cernuus** · G:Weiße Nickende Prachtglocke · ♄ d Z6 V; Jap.
- var. **rubens** (Maxim.) Benth. & Hook. f. ex Makino · G:Rote Nickende Prachtglocke · ♄ d Z6 V-VI; Jap.
- **chinensis** Franch. · G:Chinesische Prachtglocke · ♄ d Z7 ∧ V; W-China, C-China
- **perulatus** (Miq.) C.K. Schneid. · G:Frühblühende Prachtglocke · ♄ d Z7 V; Jap.
- **serrulatus** (Willd.) C.K. Schneid. · ♄ ♄ d Z6; C-China, W-China
- **subsessilis** (Miq.) Makino · ♄ d Z6 V-VI; Jap.

Ensete Bruce ex Horan. -n- *Musaceae* · 8 spp. · F:Bananier d'Abyssinie; G:Zierbanane
- *edule* Bruce & Horan. = Ensete ventricosum
- **ventricosum** (Welw.) Cheesman · E:Abyssinian Banana; G:Ensete, Zierbanane · ♃ Z10 ⚘ Ⓝ; E-Afr., C-Afr., trop-Afr., S-Afr.

Entada Adans. -f- *Mimosaceae* · c. 30 spp. · E:Sea Bean; F:Haricot de mer; G:Meerbohne, Riesenhülse
- **phaseoloides** (L.) Merr. · E:Drinking Vine · ♄ ⚵ ⚘ ⚶ Ⓝ; trop. Afr., trop. As., Pacific Is.

Entandrophragma C. DC. -n- *Meliaceae* · 11 sp.
- **angolense** (Welw. ex C. DC.) C. DC. · ♄ Ⓝ; trop. Afr.
- **candollei** Harms · G:Kosipo · ♄ ⚘ Ⓝ; W-Afr., C-Afr.
- **cylindricum** (Sprague) Sprague · E:Sapele · ♄ ⚘ Ⓝ; W-Afr., C-Afr., Uganda
- **utile** (Dawe & Sprague) Sprague · ♄ ⚘ Ⓝ; W-Afr., C-Afr., Angola

Entelea R. Br. -f- *Tiliaceae* · 1 sp.
- **arborescens** R. Br. · ♄ ♄ e ⚑; NZ

Enterolobium Mart. -n- *Mimosaceae* · 5 spp. · E:Elephant's Ear; G:Affenseife
- **cyclocarpum** (Willd.) Griseb. · E:Elephant's Ear; G:Affenseife · ♄ Z9 ⚘ Ⓝ; Mex., C-Am., W.Ind., trop. S-Am.

Eomecon Hance -f- *Papaveraceae* · 1 sp. · E:Snow Poppy; F:Coquelicot du soleil levant; G:Schneemohn

– **chionantha** Hance · G:Schneemohn · ⚃
Z7 ∧ IV; E-China

Epacris Cav. -f- *Epacridaceae* · 35 spp. ·
E:Australian Heath; F:Bruyère australe;
G:Australheide
– **heteronema** Labill. · E:Tasmanian
Swamp Heath · ♄ e Z9 ⊛ II-IV; Austr.:
N.S.Wales, Victoria, Tasman.
– **impressa** Labill. · E:Australian Heath;
G:Tasmanische Australheide · ♄ e Z9
⊛ XII-IV; Austr.: N.S.Wales, Victoria,
S-Austr., Tasman.
– **longiflora** Cav. · E:Bush Fuchsia;
G:Reichblütige Australheide · ♄ e Z9 ⊛
III-V; Austr.: N.S.Wales
– **microphylla** R. Br. · E:Coral Heath;
G:Kleinblättrige Australheide · ♄ e D Z9
⊛ III-V; Austr.: Queensl., N.S.Wales,
Tasman.; NZ
– *miniata* Lindl. = Epacris longiflora
– **obtusifolia** Sm. · E:Blunt-leaf Heath,
Common Heath; G:Stumpfblättrige
Australheide · ♄ e D Z9 ⊛ III-IV; Austr.:
Queensl., N.S.Wales, Victoria, Tasman.
– **paludosa** R. Br. · E:Alpine Heath, Swamp
Heath; G:Sumpf-Australheide · ♄ e Z9
⊛ III-V; Austr.: N.S.Wales, Victoria,
Tasman.
– *pulchella* Cav. = Epacris microphylla
– **purpurascens** R. Br. · ♄ e Z9 ⊛ III-V;
Austr.: N.S.Wales

Ephedra L. -f- *Ephedraceae* · c. 40 spp. ·
E:Joint Fir; F:Ephèdre, Raisin de mer;
G:Meerträubel
– **altissima** Desf. · E:Climbing Joint Fir;
G:Hohes Meerträubel · ♄ e ⚣ ⊛); N-Afr.
– *campylopoda* C.A. Mey. = Ephedra
foeminea
– **distachya** L.
– subsp. **distachya** · E:Joint Pine;
G:Gewöhnliches Meerträubel · ♄ e Z6
⚣ ✖; Eur.* exc. BrI, Sc; Cauc., W-Sib.,
C-As.
– subsp. **helvetica** (C.A. Mey.) Asch. &
Graebn. · G:Schweizerisches Meerträubel · ♄ e ⤳ △ Z6 IV-V; Eur.: Sw,
S-F, I; SW-Alp., S-Alp.
– subsp. **monostachya** (L.) Riedl Z4; Eur.:
E-Eur.; TR +
– *equisetiformis* Webb & Berthel. = Ephedra
major subsp. major
– **equisetina** Bunge · E:Mongolian
Ephedra; G:Mongolisches Meerträubel ·

♄ e △ Z7; C-As., Mong., N-China
– **foeminea** Forssk. · ♄ e ⚣ ⤳ △ ⊛); Eur.:
I, Ba; TR, Levant, Libya
– **fragilis** Desf. · ♄ e Z8 ⊛); Eur.: Ib, I, Sic.;
NW-Afr., Libya
– subsp. *campylopoda* (C.A. Mey.) K. Richt.
= Ephedra foeminea
– **gerardiana** Wall. ex C.A. Mey.
– var. **gerardiana** · E:Pakistani Ephedra;
G:Kriechendes Meerträubel · ♄ e Z6;
Him., China
– var. **sikkimensis** Stapf · ♄ e △ Z6; N-Ind.
– *helvetica* C.A. Mey. = Ephedra distachya
subsp. helvetica
– **major** Host
– subsp. **major** · G:Großes Meerträubel ·
♄ e △ Z7; Eur.: Ib, Fr, Ital-P, Ba; TR,
Cyprus, Pakistan, W-Him., NW-Afr.
– subsp. **procera** (Fisch. & C.A. Mey.)
Bornm. · ♄ Z7; Eur.: S-Ba; TR, Cyprus,
Cauc., Iran, Him.; mts.
– *nebrodensis* Tineo ex Guss. = Ephedra
major subsp. major
– *procera* Fisch. & C.A. Mey. = Ephedra
major subsp. procera
– *scoparia* Lange = Ephedra major subsp.
major
– **shennungiana** T.H. Tang · ♄ e ⊛);
China: Fukien
– **sinica** Stapf · E:Chinese Ephedra, Joint
Fir; G:Chinesisches Meerträubel · ♄ e ⊛
⚣ ; N-China
– *vulgaris* Rich. = Ephedra distachya subsp.
distachya

× **Epibroughtonia** hort. (*Broughtonia* ×
Epidendrum)

× **Epicattleya** Rolfe (*Cattleya* ×
Epidendrum)

Epidendrum L. -n- *Orchidaceae* · 1137 spp.
– *adenocaulum* La Llave & Lex. = Encyclia
adenocaula
– *alatum* Bateman = Encyclia alata
– **anceps** Jacq. · E:Brownflower Butterfly
Orchid · ⚃ Z10 ⊛ ▽ ✳; USA: Fla.;
C-Am., W.Ind., trop. S-Am., coasts
– *baculus* Rchb. f. = Prosthechea baculus
– *beyrodtianum* Schltr. = Prosthechea
baculus
– *bicornutum* Hook. = Caularthron
bicornutum
– *boothianum* Lindl. = Prosthechea
boothiana

– *Brassavolae* Rchb. f. = Prosthechea Brassavolae
– **ciliare** L. · E:Fringed Star Orchid · ♃ Z10 ⓜ XI-I ▽ ✳; C.-Am., W.Ind., trop. S-Am.
– **cnemidophorum** Lindl. · ♃ Z10 ⓚ IV-V ▽ ✳; Guat., Costa Rica
– *cochleatum* L. = Prosthechea cochleata
– **coronatum** Ruiz & Pav. · ♃ Z10 ⓜ ▽ ✳; Mex., C.-Am., trop. S-Am.
– **difforme** Jacq. · E:Umbrella Star Orchid · ♃ Z10 ⓜ ▽ ✳; Fla.; Mex., C.-Am., W.Ind., S-Am.
– **diffusum** Sw. · ♃ Z10 ⓜ ▽ ✳; C.-Am., W.Ind.
– *elegans* (Knowles & Westc.) Rchb. f. = Barkeria uniflora
– *fragrans* Sw. = Prosthechea fragrans
– *glumaceum* Lindl. = Prosthechea glumacea
– *grandiflorum* Humb. & Bonpl. = Stanhopea jenischiana
– **ibaguense** Kunth · ♃ Z10 ⓜ XII-V ▽ ✳; C.-Am., W.Ind., trop. S-Am.
– *latiflium* (Lindl.) Garay & H.R. Sweet = Epidendrum tridens
– **medusae** (Rchb. f.) Pfitzer · ♃ Z10 ⓜ VII-VIII ▽ ✳; Ecuad.
– *nemorale* Lindl. = Encyclia adenocaula
– **neoporpax** Ames · ♃ Z10 ⓜ ▽ ✳; Mex., C.-Am., trop. S-Am.
– **nocturnum** L. · E:Night Scented Orchid · ♃ Z10 ⓜ VIII-X ▽ ✳; Fla., W.Ind., trop. S-Am.
– var. *latifolium* Lindl. = Epidendrum tridens
– *odoratissimum* Lindl. = Encyclia patens
– *oncidioides* Lindl. = Encyclia oncidioides
– **paniculatum** Ruiz & Pav. · ♃ Z10 ⓜ X-XII ▽ ✳; C.-Am., W.Ind., trop. S-Am.
– **parkinsonianum** Hook. · ♃ Z10 ⓜ VII-VIII ▽ ✳; Mex.
– *pentotis* Rchb. f. = Prosthechea baculus
– *porpax* Rchb. f. = Epidendrum neoporpax
– *prismatocarpum* Rchb. f. = Prosthechea prismatocarpa
– **purum** Lindl. · ♃ Z10 ⓜ ▽ ✳; n S-Am.
– *skinneri* Bateman ex Lindl. = Barkeria skinneri
– *spectabile* (Bateman ex Lindl.) Rchb. f. = Barkeria spectabilis
– **stamfordianum** Bateman · ♃ Z10 ⓜ III-IV ▽ ✳; Mex., C.-Am., Col., Venez.
– **stenopetalum** Hook. · ♃ Z10 ⓜ II-III ▽ ✳; Mex., C.-Am., W.Ind., trop. S-Am.
– *tampense* Lindl. = Encyclia tampensis
– **tridens** Poepp. & Endl. · ♃ Z10 ⓜ VIII-X ▽ ✳; W.-Ind., Venez., Trinidad, Braz.
– *varicosum* Bateman ex Lindl. = Prosthechea varicosa
– *variegatum* Hook. = Prosthechea vespa
– *verrucosum* Lindl. = Encyclia adenocaula
– *vespa* Vell. = Prosthechea vespa
– *virgatum* Lindl. = Prosthechea michuacana
– *vitellinum* Lindl. = Prosthechea vitellina
– **Cultivars:**
– **many cultivars**

× **Epidiacrium** hort. -n- *Orchidaceae* (*Caularthron* × *Epidendrum*)

× **Epidrobium** hort. -n- *Orchidaceae* (*Dendrobium* × *Epidendrum*)

Epigaea L. -f- *Ericaceae* · 3 spp. · F:Epigée; G:Bodenlorbeer
– **asiatica** Maxim. · G:Japanischer Bodenlorbeer · ♄ e ⤳ Z4 IV-V; Jap.
– **gaultherioides** (Boiss. & Balansa) Takht. · G:Türkischer Bodenlorbeer · ♄ e Z6 III-IV; NE-TR, Cauc.
– × **intertexta** Mulligan (*E. asiatica* × *E. repens*) · ♄ e Z3; cult.
– **repens** L. · E:Mayflower, Trailing Arbutus; G:Kriechender Bodenlorbeer · ♄ e ⤳ Z2 III-IV ⚥; Can.: E, Sask.; USA: NE, SE, Fla.

Epigeneium Gagnep. -n- *Orchidaceae* · 41 sp.
– **amplum** (Lindl.) Summerh. · ♃ Z10 ⓜ V-VI ▽ ✳; Ind.: Sikkim
– *coelogyne* (Rchb. f.) Summerh. = Epigeneium amplum
– **lyonii** (Ames) Summerh. · ♃ Z10 ⓜ ▽ ✳; Phil.

× **Epigoa** hort. -f- *Orchidaceae* (*Domingoa* × *Epidendrum*)

× **Epilaelia** hort. -f- *Orchidaceae* (*Epidendrum* × *Laelia*)

× **Epilaeliocattleya** hort. -f- *Orchidaceae* (*Cattleya* × *Epidendrum* × *Laelia*)

× **Epilaeliopsis** hort. -f- *Orchidaceae* (*Epidendrum* × *Laeliopsis*)

Epilobium L. -n- *Onagraceae* ·

165-200 spp. · E:Willowherb; F:Epilobe;
G:Kolibritrompete, Weidenröschen
- *adenocaulon* Hausskn. = Epilobium
ciliatum
- **alpestre** (Jacq.) Krock. · E:Whorled-
leaved Willowherb; G:Quirlblättriges
Weidenröschen · ⩎ VII-VIII; Eur.* exc.
BrI, Sc; Cauc.; mts.
- **alsinifolium** Vill. · E:Chickweed Willow-
herb; G:Mierenblättriges Weidenröschen
· ⩎ Z3 VII-VIII; Eur.*; N, mts.
- **anagallidifolium** Lam. · E:Pimpernel
Willowherb; G:Gauchheilblättriges
Weidenröschen · ⩎ Z6 VII-VIII; Eur.*, TR,
Cauc., N-As., C-As., N-Am.
- **angustifolium** L. · E:Fire Weed, Rosebay
Willowherb; G:Schmalblättriges Weiden-
röschen · ⩎ Z3 VII-VIII ⚘ ⓦ; Eur.*, TR,
Syr., Iran, W-Sib., E-Sib., Amur, Sakhal.,
Kamchat., Korea, Him., Mong., Jap.
China, Moroc., Alaska, Can., USA* exc.
SC
- **brachycarpum** C. Presl · E:Tall Annual
Willowherb; G:Kurzfrüchtiges Weiden-
röschen · ; N-Am., nat. in D
- **canum** (Greene) P.H. Raven
- subsp. **angustifolium** (D.D. Keck) P.H.
Raven · G:Schmalblättriges Weiden-
röschen · ⩎ ♭ Z8 ⓐ; Calif.
- subsp. **canum** · E:California Fuchsia,
Hummingbird Flower; G:Kalifornisches
Weidenröschen, Kolibritrompete · ⩎ ♭ △
Z8 ⓐ ⋀ X-XI; Calif.
- subsp. **latifolium** (Hook.) P.H. Raven · ⩎
♭ ♭ △ Z8 ⓐ ⋀ VII-X; USA: Oreg., Calif.,
Nev., Ariz., N.Mex.
- **ciliatum** Raf. · E:Fringed Willowherb;
G:Drüsiges Weidenröschen · ⩎ VI-IX;
Alaska, Can., USA: NE, NCE, NC, Rocky
Mts., NW, Calif., nat. in BrI, Sc, Fr, G,
EC-Eur., E-Eur.
- **collinum** C.C. Gmel. · G:Hügel-Weiden-
röschen · ⩎ VI-IX; Eur.* exc. BrI
- **dodonaei** Vill. · E:Alpine Willowherb;
G:Rosmarin-Weidenröschen · ⩎ Z6 VII;
Eur.: Fr, Ital-P, C-Eur., EC-Eur., Ba,
E-Eur.; TR, W-Iran
- **duriaei** J. Gay · G:Durieus Weiden-
röschen · ⩎ VII; Eur.: sp., F, Sw
- **fleischeri** Hochst. · E:Alpine Willowherb;
G:Fleischers Weidenröschen, Kies-
Weidenröschen · ⩎ △ Z5 VII-IX; Eur.: F, I,
C-Eur.; Alp.
- **glabellum** G. Forst. · ⩎ Z8 ⓐ VII-VIII;
NZ

- **hirsutum** L. · E:Codlins and Cream;
G:Zottiges Weidenröschen · ⩎ VI-IX;
Eur.*, N-Afr., nat. in N-Am.
- **komarovianum** H. Lév. · E:Bronzy
Willowherb · ⩎ ↝ △ Z8 ⓐ VI-VIII; NZ
- **lanceolatum** Sebast. & Mauri · E:Spear-
leaved Willowherb; G:Lanzettblättriges
Weidenröschen · ⩎ VI-VIII; Eur.* exc. Sc;
TR, Cyprus, Cauc., N-Iran, Alger.
- **montanum** L. · E:Mountain Willowherb;
G:Berg-Weidenröschen, Hartheu-Wei-
denröschen · ⩎ VI-IX; Eur.*, TR, Levant,
Cauc., N-Iran, W-Sib., E-Sib., ? Sakhal.
- **nummariifolium** R. Cunn. ex A.
Cunn. · G:Rundblättriges Weiden-
röschen · ⩎ ↝ △ VI-VIII; NZ
- **nutans** F.W. Schmidt · E:Nodding Wil-
lowherb; G:Nickendes Weidenröschen ·
⩎ VII-VIII; Eur.: sp., Fr, C-Eur., EC-Eur.,
Ba, E-Eur.; mts.
- **obscurum** Schreb. · E:Dwarf Willowherb;
G:Dunkelgrünes Weidenröschen · ⩎
VI-IX; Eur.*, TR, Cauc., Madeira, Moroc.,
Alger.
- **palustre** L. · E:Marsh Willowherb;
G:Sumpf-Weidenröschen · ⩎ VII-IX;
Eur.*, TR, Cauc., N-Iran, W-Sib., E-Sib.,
Amur, Sakhal., Kamchat., C-As., Him.,
Tibet, Mong., China, Jap., N-Am., Greenl.
- **parviflorum** Schreb. · E:Hoary Willow-
herb; G:Kleinblütiges Weidenröschen · ⩎
VI-IX ⚘ ; Eur.*, TR, Levant, Cauc., Iran,
Him., NW-Afr.
- **purpuratum** Hook. f. · G:Purpur-
Weidenröschen · ⩎ ↝ △ Z8 VI-VIII; NZ
- **roseum** Schreb. · E:Pale Willowherb;
G:Rosenrotes Weidenröschen · ⩎ VII-IX;
Eur.*, TR, Lebanon, Cauc., Iran, C-As.
- *rosmarinifolium* Haenke = Epilobium
dodonaei
- **tetragonum** L. · G:Vierkantiges Weidenröschen
- subsp. **lamyi** (F.W. Schultz) Nyman ·
G:Graugrünes Weidenröschen · ⩎ VII-IX;
Eur.*, TR, Madeira
- subsp. **tetragonum** · E:Square-stalked
Willowherb; G:Gewöhnliches Vierkan-
tiges Weidenröschen · ⩎ VII-VIII; Eur.*,
TR, Levant, Cauc., Iran, W-Sib., C-As.,
NW-Afr.

Epimedium L. -n- Berberidaceae · 22
(-44) spp. · E:Bishop's Head, Bishop's
Mitre; F:Fleur des elfes; G:Elfenblume,
Sockenblume

- **alpinum** L. · E:Barrenwort, Pink
  Epimedium; F:Fleur des elfes alpinum;
  G:Alpen-Sockenblume · ⅟ Z5 III-V; Eur.:
  I, A, Slove., Croatia, Bosn., YU, AL, nat.
  in BrI, Fr, G, DK
- × **cantabrigiense** Stearn (*E. alpinum × E.
  pubigerum*) · ⅟ Z5; cult.
- *colchicum* Boiss. = Epimedium pinnatum
  subsp. colchicum
- **diphyllum** Graham · ⅟ Z5 IV-V; Jap.
- **grandiflorum** C. Morren · E:Barrenwort;
  F:Fleur des elfes à grandes fleurs;
  G:Großblütige Sockenblume · ⅟ Z5 IV-V;
  Jap., N-China
- **some cultivars**
- *hexandrum* Hook. = Vancouveria
  hexandra
- *macranthum* C. Morren & Decne. =
  Epimedium grandiflorum
- *musschianum* C. Morren & Decne. =
  Epimedium × youngianum
- × **perralchicum** Stearn (*E.
  perralderianum × E. pinnatum* subsp.
  colchicum) · ⅟ Z7; cult.
- **perralderianum** Coss. · E:Algerian
  Barrenwort · ⅟ Z8 IV-V; Alger.
- **pinnatum** Fisch. · E:Caucasian Barrenwort; G:Gefiederte Sockenblume
- subsp. **colchicum** (Boiss.) N. Busch · ⅟
  Z6 IV-V; W-Cauc., NE-TR
- subsp. **pinnatum** · G:Gewöhnliche
  Gefiederte Sockenblume · ⅟ Z6; N-Iran,
  E-Cauc.
- var. *elegans* hort. = Epimedium pinnatum
  subsp. colchicum
- var. *perralderinaum* (Coss.) H.R. Wehrh.
  = Epimedium perralderianum
- **pubigerum** (DC.) C. Morren & Decne. ·
  ⅟ Z5 V; BG, TR, Cauc.
- *purpureum* Vilm. = Epimedium × rubrum
- × **rubrum** C. Morren (*E. alpinum × E.
  grandiflorum*) · ⅟ Z5 IV-V; cult.
- × **versicolor** C. Morren (*E. grandiflorum
  × E. pinnatum* subsp. *colchicum*) · ⅟ Z5
  IV-V; cult.
- × **warleyense** Stearn (*E. alpinum × E.
  pinnatum* subsp. *colchicum*) · ⅟ Z5 V-VII;
  cult.
- × **youngianum** Fisch. & C.A. Mey.
  (*E. diphyllum* subsp. *diphyllum × E.
  grandiflorum*) · ⅟ Z5 IV-V; cult.

Epipactis Zinn -f- *Orchidaceae* · 38 spp. ·
E:Helleborine; F:Epipactis; G:Ständel-
wurz, Stendelwurz, Sumpfwurz

- **albensis** H. Nováková & Rydlo · G:Elbe-
  Ständelwurz · ⅟ VIII-XI ▽ ✳; Eur.: CZ, A,
  D
- **atrorubens** (Bernh.) Besser · E:Dark Red
  Helleborine; G:Rotbraune Ständelwurz ·
  ⅟ Z6 VI-VIII ▽ ✳; Eur.*
- *confusa* D.P. Young = Epipactis phyllanthes subsp. confusa
- *distans* Arv.-Touv. = Epipactis helleborine
  subsp. distans
- **gigantea** Douglas ex Hook. · E:Stream
  Orchid; G:Amerikanische Ständelwurz ·
  ⅟ Z6 ▽ ✳; N-Am.
- **greuteri** H. Baumann & Künkele ·
  G:Greuters Ständelwurz · ⅟ ▽ ✳; Eur.:
  GR, G, A +
- **helleborine** (L.) Crantz · G:Breitblättrige
  Ständelwurz
- subsp. **distans** (Arv.-Touv.) R. Engel & P.
  Quentin · G:Kurzblättrige Ständelwurz ·
  ⅟ ▽ ✳; D +
- subsp. **helleborine** · E:Broad Leaved Helleborine; G:Gewöhnliche Breitblättrige
  Ständelwurz · ⅟ Z6 VI-IX ▽ ✳; Eur.*, TR,
  Cyprus, Syr., Cauc., N-Iraq, Iran, Afgh.,
  Pakist., NW-Afr., Can., USA: NE, NCE,
  NW
- subsp. **leutei** (Robatsch) Kreutz ·
  G:Leutes Ständelwurz · ⅟ VII-VIII ▽ ✳;
  Eur.: A, Slove. +
- subsp. **renzii** (Robatsch) Løjtnant ·
  G:Jutländische Ständelwurz · ⅟ ▽ ✳;
  Eur.: DK
- *latifolia* (L.) All. = Epipactis helleborine
  subsp. helleborine
- **leptochila** (Godfery) Godfery
- subsp. **leptochila** · E:Narrow-lipped Helleborine; G:Schmallippige Ständelwurz ·
  ⅟ VII ▽ ✳; Eur.: BrI, F, DK, PL, Slova.
- subsp. **peitzii** (H. Neumann &
  Wucherpf.) Kreutz · ⅟ ▽ ✳; D +
- *leutei* Robatsch = Epipactis helleborine
  subsp. leutei
- **microphylla** (Ehrh.) Sw. · G:Kleinblät-
  trige Ständelwurz · ⅟ VI-VIII ▽ ✳; Eur.*
  exc. BrI, Sc; TR, Cyprus, Cauc., N-Iran
- **muelleri** Godfery · G:Müllers Ständelwurz · ⅟ VII-VIII ▽ ✳; Eur.: Fr, C-Eur.,
  EC-Eur.
- **nordeniorum** Robatsch · G:Nordens
  Ständelwurz · ⅟ VIII-X ▽ ✳; Eur.: A +
- **palustris** (L.) Crantz · E:Marsh
  Helleborine; F:Epipactis des marais;
  G:Sumpf-Ständelwurz · ⅟ Z6 VI-VII ▽ ✳;
  Eur.*, TR, N-Iraq, Cauc., N-Iran, W-Sib.,

E-Sib., C-As.
- *peitzii* H. Neumann & Wucherpf. =
  Epipactis leptochila subsp. peitzii
- **phyllanthes** G.E. Sm.
- subsp. **confusa** (D.P. Young) Løjtnant ·
  G:Zierliche Ständelwurz · ⁤4 VII-VIII ▽
  ✳; Eur.: Swed, DK
- subsp. **phyllanthes** · E:Green-flowered
  Helleborine; G:Grüne Ständelwurz · 4 ▽
  ✳; Eur.: F, BrI, Sc, G
- **pontica** Taubenheim · G:Pontus-Stän-
  delwurz, Schwarzmeer-Ständelwurz · 4
  VII-IX ▽ ✳; TR, A +
- *renzii* Robatsch = Epipactis helleborine
  subsp. renzii
- **viridiflora** Hoffm. ex Krock. · G:Violette
  Ständelwurz · 4 VIII-IX ▽ ✳; Eur.: BrI,
  DK, Fr, C-Eur., EC-Eur., Ba, Ro, W-Russ.

× **Epiphronitis** A.D. Hawkes -f-
Orchidaceae (*Epidendrum* × *Sophronitis*)

Epiphyllanthus A. Berger = Schlumbergera
- *obovatus* (Engelm.) Britton & Rose =
  Schlumbergera opuntioides

Epiphyllopsis (A. Berger) Backeb. & F.M.
  Knuth = Rhipsalidopsis
- *gaertneri* (Regel) A. Berger = Rhipsalidopsis gaertneri

Epiphyllum Haw. -n- *Cactaceae* · 15 spp. ·
  E:Orchid Cactus; F:Cactus des savetiers;
  G:Blattkaktus, Schusterkaktus
- **anguliger** (Lem.) G. Don · ⑴ Z10 ⓦ ▽ ✳;
  S-Mex.
- **chrysocardium** Alexander · ♄ ⑴ ⚡ Z9 ⓦ
  ▽ ✳; Mex.: Chiapas
- **crenatum** (Lindl.) G. Don · ♄ ⑴ Z9 ⓦ ▽
  ✳; Guat., Hond.
- *crispatum* Haw. = Rhipsalis crispata
- *grande* (Lem.) Britton & Rose = Epiphyllum oxypetalum
- **hookeri** (Link & Otto) Haw. · ♄ ⑴ Z9 ⓦ
  ▽ ✳; S-Mex., C-Am., Venez., Guyan.
- *nelsonii* Britton & Rose = Chiapasia
  nelsonii
- **oxypetalum** (DC.) Haw. · E:Duchman's
  Pipe Cactus · ♄ ⑴ Z9 ⓦ ▽ ✳; Mex.,
  Guat., Venez., Braz.
- *phyllanthoides* (DC.) Sweet = Nopalxochia phyllanthoides
- **pittieri** (F.A.C. Weber) Britton & Rose · ♄
  ⑴ Z9 ⓦ ▽ ✳; Costa Rica
- *russellianum* Hook. = Schlumbergera

russelliana
- var. *gaertneri* Regel = Rhipsalidopsis
  gaertneri
- **stenopetalum** (C.F. Först.) Britton &
  Rose · ♄ ⑴ Z9 ⓦ ▽ ✳; Mex.
- *strictum* (Lem.) Britton & Rose = Epiphyllum hookeri
- **thomasianum** (K. Schum.) Britton &
  Rose · ♄ ⑴ Z9 ⓦ ▽ ✳; Mex., C-Am.
- **Cultivars:**
- **many cultivars**

Epipogium Borkh. -n- *Orchidaceae* ·
  2 spp. · E:Ghost Orchid; F:Epipogium;
  G:Widerbart
- **aphyllum** Sw. · E:Ghost Orchid; G:Blatt-
  loser Widerbart · 4 VII-VIII ▽ ✳; Eur.*
  exc. Ib; TR, Cauc., NW-Iran, W-Sib.,
  E-Sib., Amur, Sakhal., Kamchat., Him.,
  E-As.

Epipremnum Schott -n- *Araceae* · 15 spp. ·
  E:Devil's Ivy; F:Pothos; G:Efeutute,
  Tongapflanze
- **aureum** (Linden & André) G.S. Bunting ·
  E:Devil's Ivy, Golden Hunters Robe;
  G:Goldene Efeutute · ♄ ∫ e Z10 ⓦ;
  Salomon. Is.
- *mirabile* Schott = Epipremnum pinnatum
- **pinnatum** (L.) Engl. · E:Tongavine,
  Variegated Philodendron; G:Gefleckte
  Efeutute · ♄ ⚡ Z10 ⓦ; Malay. Arch.,
  N.Guinea, Pacific Is.

Episcia Mart. -f- *Gesneriaceae* · 7 spp. ·
  E:Basket Plant, Flame Violet; F:Episcie;
  G:Episcie, Schattenröhre
- **cupreata** (Hook.) Hanst. · 4 Z10 ⓦ
  VI-IX; Col.
- *dianthiflora* H.E. Moore & R.G. Wilson =
  Alsobia dianthiflora
- **lilacina** Hanst. · 4 Z10 ⓦ IX-XII; Nicar.,
  Costa Rica, Panama
- *punctata* (Lindl.) Hanst. = Alsobia
  punctata
- **reptans** Mart. · 4 Z10 ⓦ VI-IX; Col.,
  Surinam, Braz.
- *tessellata* Linden ex Lem. = Nautilocalyx
  bullatus

Epithelantha F.A.C. Weber ex Britton
  & Rose -f- *Cactaceae* · 2 spp. · E:Button
  Cactus; G:Knopfkaktus
- **micromeris** (Engelm.) F.A.C. Weber ex
  Britton & Rose · E:Pingpong Ball Cactus ·

♃ Z9 ⚘ ▽ ✳; USA: Tex., Ariz.; NE-Mex.

× **Epitonia** hort. -f- *Orchidaceae*
(*Broughtonia* × *Epidendrum*)

Equisetum L. -n- *Equisetaceae* · 16 spp. ·
E:Horsetail; F:Prêle; G:Schachtelhalm
– **arvense** L. · E:Common Horsetail;
G:Acker-Schachtelhalm, Zinnkraut · ♃
Z2 III-IV ⚥ ; Eur.*, TR, Cauc., N-Iran,
W-Sib., E-Sib., Amur, Sakhal., Kamchat.,
C-As., Him., China, Korea, Jap., Alaska,
Can., USA*, Greenl.
– × **dycei** C.N. Page (*E. fluviatile* × *E.
palustre*) · G:Dyces Schachtelhalm · ♃
∼ ; G, BrI +
– **fluviatile** L. · E:Water Horsetail; F:Prêle
des bourbiers; G:Teich-Schachtelhalm · ♃
∼ Z2 V-VI; Eur. *, As. N-Am.
– **giganteum** L. · E:Giant Horsetail;
G:Großer Schachtelhalm · ♃ ⓦ; trop.
S-Am.
– **hyemale** L. · G:Winter-Schachtelhalm
– var. **hyemale** · E:Dutch Rush, Rough
Horsetail; G:Gewöhnli-
cher Winter-Schachtelhalm · ♃ ∼ Z5
VI-VIII ⚥ ⚔; Eur.*, Cauc., TR, W-Sib.,
E-Sib., Amur, Sakhal., C-As., Him.,
Korea, Jap.
– var. **robustum** (A. Braun) Eaton · F:Prêle
d'hiver · ♃ ∼ Z5; Alaska, Can., USA*,
Mex., Guat.
– *limosum* L. = Equisetum fluviatile
– × **litorale** Kühlew. ex Rupr. (*E. arvense
× E. fluviatile*) · G:Ufer-Schachtelhalm ·
♃ ∼ VI-VII; Eur.: N, C-Eur.; W-Sib.,
E-Sib., N-Am.
– *maximum* auct. non Lam. = Equisetum
telmateia
– × **meridionale** (Milde) Chiov. (*E.
ramosissimum* × *E. variegatum*) ·
G:Südlicher Schachtelhalm · ♃; Eur.: Sw,
N-I, CZ, Slova.
– × **moorei** Newman (*E. hyemale* × *E.
ramosissimum*) · G:Moores Schachtel-
halm · ♃; BrI, C-Eur., Slove., CZ, Slova.
– **palustre** L. · E:Horsetail, Marsh
Horsetail; F:Prêle des marais; G:Duwok,
Sumpf-Schachtelhalm · ♃ ∼ VI-IX ⚔;
Eur.*, TR, Syr., Cauc., W-Sib., E-Sib.,
Amur, Sakhal., Kamchat., Mong., Jap,
China, Alaska, Can., USA: NE, NCE, NC,
NW, Calif.
– **pratense** Ehrh. · E:Meadow Horsetail;
G:Wiesen-Schachtelhalm · ♃ V-VI; Eur.*

exc. Ib, ? Fr; TR, Syr. Leb., Cauc., W-Sib.,
E-Sib., Amur, Sakhal., Kamchat., C-As.,
China: Sinkiang; Mong., Korea, Jap.,
N-Am.
– **ramosissimum** Desf. · E:Branched
Horsetail; G:Gewöhnlicher Ästiger
Schachtelhalm · ♃ V-VII; Eur.* exc. BrI,
Sc; TR, Levant, Cauc., Iran, W-Sib., C-As,
Him., Tibet, Mong., China, Jap., N-Afr.,
Afr., Am.
– *robustum* A. Braun = Equisetum hyemale
var. robustum
– **schaffneri** Milde · ♃ ∼ ⓦ; Mex., Peru,
Chile
– **scirpoides** Michx. · E:Sedge Horsetail;
G:Zwerg-Schachtelhalm · ♃ △ ∼ Z2;
Eur.: Sc, Russ.; W-Sib., E-Sib., Amur,
Kamchat., Alaska, Can., USA: NE, NCE,
NC, NW
– **sylvaticum** L. · E:Wood Horsetail;
G:Wald-Schachtelhalm · ♃ IV-V; Eur.*,
W-Sib., E-Sib., Amur, Sakhal., Kamchat.,
Manch., China, Korea, Jap., Alaska,
Greenl., Can.; USA: NE, NCE, NW, Idaho
– **telmateia** Ehrh. · E:Giant Horsetail;
G:Riesen-Schachtelhalm · ♃ ∼ Z6
IV-V; Eur.*, TR, Levant, Cauc., N-Iran,
NW-Afr., Libya, Alaska, Can.: W; USA:
NCE, NW, Calif.
– × **trachyodon** (A. Braun) W.D.J. Koch (*E.
hyemale* × *E. variegatum*) · G:Rauzähni-
ger Schachtelhalm · ♃ ∼ VII-VIII; Eur.
, Cauc., W-Sib., E-Sib., Amur, Kamchat.,
C-As., Mong., China
– **variegatum** Schleich. ex F. Weber &
D. Mohr · E:Scouring Rush, Variegated
Horsetail; F:Prêle panachée; G:Bunter
Schachtelhalm · ♃ △ ∼ Z2 IV-IX; Eur.*,
TR, Cauc., Amur, Kamchat., Mong.,
Alaska, Can., USA: NW, Calif., Rocky
Mts., NC; Greenl.

Eragrostis Wolf -f- *Poaceae* · 250-300 spp. ·
E:Love Grass; F:Amourette, Eragrostis;
G:Liebesgras, Teffgras
– *abessinica* Link = Eragrostis tef
– **albensis** H. Scholz · G:Elbe-Liebesgras ·
☉; D +
– **amabilis** (L.) Hook. & Arn. · E:Japanese
Love Grass, Love Grass; G:Japanisches
Liebesgras · ☉ ✄ Z9 VIII; Braz.
– **cilianensis** (All.) Vignolo ex Janch. ·
E:Gray Love Grass, Stink Grass;
G:Großes Liebesgras · ☉ Z9 VII-X; Eur.:
Ib, Fr, Ital-P, Ba, RO, Crim; TR, Cauc.,

SW-As., C-As., nat. in C-Eur., CE-Eur.
- **curvula** (Schrad.) Nees · E:Weeping Love
Grass; G:Schwachgekrümmtes Liebesgras
· ⁴ Z7 VI-IX; Eth., trop. Afr., S-Afr.
- **minor** Host · E:Little Love Grass;
G:Kleines Liebesgras · ☉ VII-VIII; Eur.*
exc. BrI, Sc; TR, Cauc., Iran, W-Sib.,
E-Sib., Amur, C-As. Him., China:
Sinkiang, Korea, Jap., trop. Afr., nat. in
Austr., Am.
- **multicaulis** Steud. · G:Japanisches
Liebesgras · ☉ ⓜ VII-X; Ind., China,
Taiwan, Korea, Amur, Sakhal., Jap.,
Malay. Pen.
- **pilosa** (L.) P. Beauv. · E:Soft Love Grass;
G:Behaartes Liebesgras · ☉ Z7 VII-VIII Ⓝ;
Eur.* ; TR, W-Sib., E-Sib., Amur, C-As.,
China, Korea, Jap., Nigeria, Eth., E-Afr.,
nat. in USA, C-Am., W.Ind., S-Am.
- **superba** Peyr. · ⓜ Ⓝ; E-Afr.
- **tef** (Zuccagni) Trotter · E:Love Grass,
Teff;G:Äthiopisches Liebesgras, Zwerg-
Hirse · ☉ Z9 VIII-X Ⓝ; Eth.
- *tenella* (L.) P. Beauv. ex Roem. & Schult.
= Eragrostis amabilis
- **trichodes** (Nutt.) A.W. Wood · E:Sand
Love Grass; G:Sand-Liebesgras · ⁴
VIII-IX; USA: NCE, NC, Colo., SC, SE
- **unioloides** (Retz.) Nees ex Steud. ·
E:Chinese Love Grass · ☉ ✕ Z9 ⓚ
VI-VIII; trop. As.

Eranthemum L. -n- *Acanthaceae* · 30 spp. ·
F:Eranthémum; G:Frühlingsblume
- *atropurpureum* W. Bull non Hook. f. =
Pseuderanthemum atropurpureum
- *beyrichii* (Nees) Regel = Chamaeranthemum beyrichii
- *gaudichaudii* (Nees) Van Houtte =
Chamaeranthemum gaudichaudii
- *igneum* Linden = Xantheranthemum
igneum
- *nervosum* (Vahl) R. Br. ex Roem. &
Schult. = Eranthemum pulchellum
- **pulchellum** Andrews · E:Blue Sage;
G:Blaue Frühlingsblume · ♄ e Z10 ⓜ
XII-II; Ind.
- *reticulatum* Hook. f. = Pseuderanthemum
reticulatum
- *schomburgkii* hort. = Pseuderanthemum
reticulatum
- *sinuatum* (Vahl) R. Br. = Pseuderanthemum sinuatum
- **wattii** (Bedd.) Stapf · G:Purpurne
Frühlingsblume · ♄ e Z10 ⓜ XI-I; N-Ind.

Eranthis Salisb. -f- *Ranunculaceae* · 8 spp. ·
E:Winter Aconite; F:Eranthe, Hellé-
borine; G:Winterling
- **cilicica** Schott & Kotschy · ⁴ Z4 III ✿;
TR, Syr.
- **hyemalis** (L.) Salisb. · E:Winter Aconite;
G:Kleiner Winterling, Südeuropäischer
Winterling · ⁴ Z5 II-III ✿; Eur.: F, I,
Slove., Croatia, Bosn., YU, BG, nat. in
BrI, C-Eur., EC-Eur., RO
- *var. cilicica* (Schott & Kotschy) Huth =
Eranthis cilicica
- × **tubergenii** Bowles (*E. cilicica × E.
hyemalis*) · G:Tubergens Winterling · ⁴
Z5 II-III ✿; cult.

Ercilla A. Juss. -f- *Phytolaccaceae* · 2 spp.
- **spicata** (Bertero) Moq. · ♄ e ⅔ Z8 ⓚ
III-IV; Chile
- *volubilis* Juss. = Ercilla spicata

Erdisia Britton & Rose = Corryocactus
- *melanotricha* (K. Schum.) Backeb. =
Corryocactus melanotrichus
- *meyenii* Britton & Rose = Corryocactus
aureus
- *squarrosa* (Vaupel) Britton & Rose =
Corryocactus squarrosus

Erechtites Raf. -f- *Asteraceae* · 5 (-15) spp. ·
E:Burnweed; G:Scheingreiskraut
- **hieraciifolia** (L.) Raf. ex DC. ·
E:American Burnweed; G:Amerika-
nisches Scheingreiskraut · ☉ VII-X;
N-Am., S-Am., nat. in A, EC-Eur., Slove.,
Croatia, RO

Eremocitrus Swingle -m- *Rutaceae* · 1 sp. ·
E:Desert Lime; F:Limettier du désert;
G:Wüstenlimette
- **glauca** (Lindl.) Swingle · E:Australian
Desert; G:Australische Wüstenlimette
Lime · ♄ e Z9 ⓚ Ⓝ; NE-Austr.

Eremostachys Bunge -f- *Lamiaceae* ·
97 spp.
- **laciniata** (L.) Bunge · ⁴ Z8 ⓚ ∧ VI-VIII;
TR, Syr., Iran, C-As.

Eremurus M. Bieb. -m- *Asphodelaceae* ·
58 spp. · E:Desert Candle, Foxtail Lily;
F:Aiguille de Cléopâtre; G:Kleopatra-
nadel, Lilienschweif, Steppenkerze
- **aitchinsonii** Baker · ⁴ Z7 ∧ VI-VII; orig.
?

– **bucharicus** Regel · ⏀ Z6 VI-VII; C-As., Afgh.
– *bungei* Baker = Eremurus stenophyllus subsp. stenophyllus
– *elwesii* Micheli = Eremurus aitchinsonii
– **himalaicus** Baker · G:Himalaya-Steppenkerze · ⏀ Z7 ∧ VI; Afgh., NW-Ind, C-As.
– × **himrob** hort. (*E. himalaicus* × *E. robustus*) · G:Hybrid-Steppenkerze · ⏀ Z7 ∧
– × **isabellinus** R. Vilm. (*E. olgae* × *E. stenophyllus*) · G:Isabellen-Steppenkerze · ⏀ Z7 ∧; cult.
– **olgae** Regel · ⏀ Z7 ∧ VI; Iran, Afgh., C-As.(Tajik.)
– **robustus** (Regel) Regel · F:Aiguille de Cléopâtre, Lis des steppes; G:Turkestan-Steppenkerze · ⏀ Z7 ∧ VI-VII; C-As.
– var. *elwesii* (Micheli) Leichtlin = Eremurus aitchinsonii
– **spectabilis** M. Bieb. · ⏀ Z7 ∧ VI-VII; TR, Iraq, Lebanon, Iran
– **stenophyllus** (Boiss. & Buhse) Baker
– subsp. **stenophyllus** · G:Afghanistan-Steppenkerze · ⏀ Z5 ∧ VI-VII; Iran
– var. *bungei* (Baker) O. Fedtsch. = Eremurus stenophyllus subsp. stenophyllus
– *tauricus* Weinm. = Eremurus spectabilis
– × **tubergenii** Tubergen (*E. himalaicus* × *E. stenophyllus*) · G:Tubergens Steppenkerze · ⏀ Z7; cult.
– **Cultivars**:
– **many cultivars**

Erepsia N.E. Br. -f- *Aizoaceae* · 30 spp. · E:Lesser Sea-Fig; F:Figuier de mer; G:Seefeige
– *haworthii* (Donn) Schwantes = Lampranthus haworthii
– **includens** (Haw.) Schwantes · ♄ ⵂ Z9 ⌂ VII-IX; Cape
– **pillansii** (Kensit) Liede · ♄ ⵂ Z9 ⌂; Cape

Eria Lindl. -f- *Orchidaceae* · 405 spp.
– **bractescens** Lindl. · ⏀ Z9 ⌂ VI ▽ ✳; Malay. Pen., Java
– **javanica** (Sw.) Blume · ⏀ Z9 ⌂ IV-VI ▽ ✳; Him., Burma, Thail., Malay. Arch., Phil.
– *stellata* Lindl. = Eria javanica

Eriastrum Wooton & Standl. -n- *Polemoniaceae* · 14 spp.
– **densifolium** (Benth.) H. Mason · E:Giant Woolstar, Starflower · ⏀ ♄ ♄ e Z8 ⌂; Calif., Baja Calif.

Erica L. -f- *Ericaceae* · 735 spp. · E:Heath; F:Bruyère, Bruyère d'hiver; G:Erika, Heide
– **abietina** L. · ♄ e ⌂; S-Afr.
– **albens** L. · ♄ e ⌂ III-IV; S-Afr.
– **arborea** L. · E:Briar, Tree Heath; G:Baum-Heide · ♄ ♄ e Z8 ⌂ II-IV Ⓝ; Eur.: Ib, Fr, Ital-P, Ba, Canar., Madeira; TR, Cauc., Yemen, NW-Afr., Tibesti, mts. E-Afr.
– **aristata** Andrews · ♄ e ⌂ V-IX; S-Afr.
– **australis** L. · E:Southern Heath, Spanish Heath; G:Spanische Heide · ♄ e Z8 ⌂ IV-VI; Eur.: Ib; Moroc.
– **baccans** L. · ♄ e Z10 ⌂ IV-VII; S-Afr.
– **bauera** Andrews · ♄ e Z10 ⌂ VII-IX; S-Afr.
– **bergiana** L. · ♄ e Z9 ⌂ V-VII; S-Afr.
– *bowieana* Lodd. = Erica bauera
– **bucciniiformis** Salisb. · ♄ e ⌂ IX-X; S-Afr.
– **caffra** L. · ♄ e Z10 ⌂ III-V; S-Afr.
– **canaliculata** Andrews · ♄ e Z8 ⌂ II-V; S-Afr.
– **carnea** L. · F:Bruyère couleur chair, Bruyère des neiges; G:Schnee-Heide; E:Winter Heath · ♄ ♄ e Z5 II-IV ⚥; Eur.: F, I, C-Eur., EC-Eur., Ba, ? RO
– **many cultivars**
– × **cavendishiana** Paxton (*E. abietina* × *E. discolor*) · ♄ e ⌂ V-VII; cult.
– **cerinthoides** L. · G:Scharlach-Heide · ♄ e Z10 ⌂ VII-VIII; S-Afr.
– **chamissonis** Klotzsch · ♄ e Z10 ⌂ IV; S-Afr.
– **ciliaris** L. · E:Dorset Heath; G:Wimper-Heide · ♄ e Z8 ∧ VI-VII; Eur.: BrI, Fr, Ib; Moroc.
– **cinerea** L. · E:Bell Heather; F:Bruyère cendrée; G:Graue Heide · ♄ ♄ e Z6 VI-VIII; Eur.: BrI, Sc, Fr, Ib, C-Eur., Ital-P; Alger.
– **many cultivars**
– *coccinea* P.J. Bergius non L. = Erica abietina
– **colorans** Andrews · ♄ e Z9 ⌂ IV-VI; S-Afr.
– **conspicua** Sol. · ♄ e ⌂ V-VIII; S-Afr.
– **cruenta** Sol. · ♄ e Z9 ⌂ VIII-X; S-Afr.
– **curviflora** L. · ♄ e Z9 ⌂ III-VI; S-Afr.
– **cyathiformis** Salisb. · ♄ e ⌂ III-IV; S-Afr.
– × **cylindrica** Andrews · ♄ e ⌂ V-VII; cult.

– × **darleyensis** Bean (*E. carnea* × *E. erigena*) · E:Margaret Porter Heath; F:Bruyère hybride de Darleyens; G:Englische Heide · ♄ e Z7 I-V; cult.
– **some cultivars**
– **doliiformis** Salisb. · ♄ e ⊕ VI-VII; S-Afr.
– **erigena** R. Ross · E:Irish Heath; G:Purpur-Heide · ⚄ e Z8 ⊕ III-V; Eur.: IRL, F, Ib
– **exsurgens** Andrews · ♄ e ⊕ VI-IX; S-Afr.
– **flammea** Andrews · ♄ e ⊕ X-XII; S-Afr.
– **floribunda** Lodd. · ♄ e ⊕ III-V; S-Afr.
– *frondosa* Salisb. = Erica abietina
– **gracilis** J.C. Wendl. · ♄ e Z10 ⊕ IX-XII; S-Afr.
– *herbacea* L. = Erica carnea
– subsp. *occidentalis* (Benth.) M. Laínz = Erica erigena
– × **hiemalis** hort. · ♄ e Z8 ⊕ II-III; S-Afr.
– *laevis* Andrews = Erica cyathiformis
– **lusitanica** Rudolphi · E:Portugal Heath; G:Portugiesische Heide · ♄ e Z8 ⊕ II-IV; Eur.: Ib, F, nat. in BrI
– **mackaiana** Bab. · E:Mackay's Heath; G:Moor-Heide · ♄ e Z5 VII-IX; NW-Sp., W-IRL
– **mammosa** L. · E:Red Signal Heath; G:Signal-Heide · ♄ e Z9 ⊕ IV-X; S-Afr.
– *maweana* Backh. f. = Erica ciliaris
– *mediterranea* L. = Erica erigena
– **multiflora** L. · G:Vielblütige Heide · ♄ e ⊕ XI-II; Eur.: Ib, Fr, Ital-P, Ba; NW-Afr., Libya
– **nigrita** L. · ♄ e ⊕ III-IV; S-Afr.
– *pelviformis* Salisb. = Erica viridipurpurea
– *persoluta* L. = Erica subdivaricata
– var. *laevis* (Andrews) Benth. = Erica cyathiformis
– **petiveri** L. · ♄ e ⊕ XI-III; S-Afr.
– *purpurascens* auct. non L. = Erica erigena
– **recurvata** Andrews · ♄ e ⊕ III-IV; S-Afr.
– *regerminans* Andrews = Erica viridipurpurea
– **scoparia** L. · E:Besom Heath; G:Spanische Besen-Heide · ♄ e Z9 ⊕ V-VI; Eur.: Fr, Ib, Ital-P, Azoren, Madeira, Canar.; NW-Afr.
– **speciosa** Andrews · ♄ e Z10 ⊕ X-I; S-Afr.
– *speciosa* Schneev. = Erica mammosa
– *stricta* Donn ex Willd. = Erica terminalis
– × **stuartii** E.F. Linton (*E. mackaiana* × *E. tetralix*) · G:Stuarts Heide · ♄ e Z9 ⊕; cult.
– **subdivaricata** P.J. Bergius · ♄ e ⊕ III-V; S-Afr.

– **taxifolia** F.A. Bauer · ♄ e Z9 ⊕ IX-X; S-Afr.
– **terminalis** Salisb. · E:Corsican Heath; G:Steife Heide · ♄ e Z8 ⊕ ∧ VII-IX; Eur.: sp., Cors, Sard., I; Moroc., nat. in IRL
– **tetralix** L. · E:Cross Leaved Heath; F:Bruyère à quatre angles, Caminet; G:Glocken-Heide · ⚄ ♄ e Z5 VI-IX; Eur.: BrI, Sc, Fr, Ib, Me, PL, Balt., nat. in CZ
– **many cultivars**
– **transparens** P.J. Bergius · ♄ e ⊕ III-IV; S-Afr.
– **vagans** L. · E:Cornish Heath; F:Bruyère vagabonde; G:Cornwall-Heide · ♄ e Z6 VII-IX; Eur.: BrI, F, sp., nat. in Sw
– **many cultivars**
– × **veitchii** Bean (*E. arborea* × *E. lusitanica*) · G:Veitchs Heide · ♄ e Z8 ⊕; cult.
– **ventricosa** Thunb. · ♄ e Z10 ⊕ V-IX; S-Afr.
– **versicolor** J.C. Wendl. · ♄ e Z10 ⊕ I-XII; S-Afr.
– **vestita** Thunb. · ♄ e Z10 ⊕ II-V; S-Afr.
– **viridiflora** Andrews · ♄ e ⊕ VI-VIII; S-Afr.
– **viridipurpurea** L. · ⚄ ⚄ ♄ e ⊕ III-V; S-Afr.
– × **watsonii** (Benth.) Bean (*E. ciliaris* × *E. tetralix*) · G:Watsons Heide · ♄ e Z7 ∧ VII; cult.
– × **williamsii** Druce (*E. tetralix* × *E. vagans*) · G:Lizard-Heide · ♄ e Z5 VII-VIII; cult.
– × **willmorei** Knowles & Westc. · ♄ e ⊕ IV-V; cult.

Erigeron L. -m- Asteraceae · c. 200 spp. · E:Fleabane; F:Erigeron, Vergerette; G:Berufkraut, Feinstrahl
– **acris** L. · E:Blue Fleabane; G:Gewöhnliches Scharfes Berufkraut · ⚄ ☉ VI-IX; Eur.*, TR, Cauc., Iran, Afgh., C-As., N-As., Moroc., N-Am.
– **alpinus** L. · E:Mountain Fleabane; G:Alpen-Berufkraut · ⚄ △ Z5 VII-IX; Eur.* exc. Sc, BrI; Cauc., N-Iran, Lebanon, ? Afgh.; mts.
– var. *uniflorus* (L.) Griseb. = Erigeron uniflorus
– **annuus** (L.) Pers. · G:Einjähriger Feinstrahl
– subsp. **annuus** · E:Annual Fleabane; G:Gewöhnlicher Einjähriger Feinstrahl

- · ⊙ Z3 VI-IX; Can., N-USA, nat. in Eur.*
exc. BrI, Ba
- subsp. **strigosus** (Willd.) Wagenitz ·
G:Striegelhaariger Einjähriger Feinstrahl · ⊙ Z3 VI-X; Can., USA, Panama, nat.
in Eur.
- **atticus** Vill. · E:Greek Fleabane;
G:Drüsiges Berufkraut · ♃ Z6 VII-IX;
Eur.: Fr, C-Eur., EC-Eur., Ba, RO; mts.
- **aurantiacus** Regel · E:Orange Daisy;
G:Orangefarbenes Berufkraut · ♃ △ Z6
VII-VIII; C-As.
- *canadensis* L. = Conyza canadensis
- **candidus** Widder · G:Voralpen-
Berufkraut · ♃ VII-VIII; Eur.: SE-A
(Koralpe)
- **compositus** Pursh · E:Cutleaf Daisy ·
♃ △ Z5 VI-VII; Alaska, Can., USA: NC,
Rocky Mts., NW, Calif., SW; Greenl.
- **coulteri** Porter · E:Large Mountain
Fleabane; G:Rocky-Mountain-Berufkraut
· ♃ △ Z5 VI-VII; USA: Rocky Mts., SW,
Calif.
- **gaudinii** Brügger · G:Gaudins
Berufkraut · ♃ VII-VIII; Eur.: F, I, Sw, G,
A; Alp., Schwarzwald
- **glabellus** Nutt. · E:Streamside Fleabane ·
⊙ ♃ Z2 VI; Alaska, Can.: W, Man.; USA:
NCE, NC, Rocky Mts.
- **glabratus** Bluff & Fingerh. · G:Kahles
Berufkraut · ♃ Z6 VII-IX; Eur.: Ib, Fr,
Ital-P, C-Eur., EC-Eur., Ba, RO; TR; mts.
- **glaucus** Ker-Gawl. · E:Beach Aster,
Seaside Daisy; G:Strand-Berufkraut · ♃
△ Z3 VII-IX; USA: Oreg., Calif.
- **karvinskianus** DC. · E:Mexican Daisy,
Santa Barbera Daisy; G:Karwinskis
Berufkraut · ♃ ⤳ △ Z7 ⌂ ∧ IX-XI;
Austr. (N.S.Wales, Victoria, S-Austr.,
Tasman., W-Austr.), nat. in BrI, Ib, F, Sw,
I, S-Am
- **leiomerus** A. Gray · E:Rockslide Yellow
Fleabane · ♃ ⤳ △ Z3 VII-VIII; USA:
Rocky Mts., N.Mex.
- *mesa-grande* hort. = Erigeron speciosus
var. macranthus
- *mucronatus* DC. = Erigeron karvinskianus
- **neglectus** A. Kern. · E:Neglected
Fleabane; G:Verkanntes Berufkraut · ♃
VII-VIII; Eur.: F, I, Sw, G, A; Alp.
- **philadelphicus** L. · E:Frost Root,
Philadelphia Fleabane; G:Philadelphia-
Feinstrahl · ⊙ ♃ ✕ Z2 VI-VII; Can., USA:
NE, NCE, NC, SE, Fla., SC, Rocky Mts.,
Calif., NW

- *polymorphus* auct. non Scop. = Erigeron
glabratus
- **pulchellus** Michx. · E:Robin's Plantain ·
⊙ ♃ Z4 VI-VII; Can.: E; USA: NE, NCE,
SC, SE, Fla.
- **speciosus** (Lindl.) DC.
- var. **macranthus** (Nutt.) Cronquist · ♃ ✕
Z3 VI-VII; Can.: Alta.; USA: Rocky Mts.,
SW
- var. **speciosus** · E:Aspen Daisy, Aspen
Fleabane; G:Aspen-Berufkraut · ♃ Z3;
Can.: W; USA: NW, Rocky Mts., SW
- **uniflorus** L. · E:One Flower Fleabane;
G:Einköpfiges Berufkraut · ♃ △ Z2 VII-
VIII; Eur.* exc. BrI, N, mts.; TR, Cauc.,
Lebanon
- **Cultivars:**
- **many cultivars**

Erinacea Adans. -f- *Fabaceae* · 1 sp. ·
E:Hedgehog Broom; F:Erinacée;
G:Igelginster
- **anthyllis** Link · E:Blue Broom; G:Igelgin-
ster · ♄ e △ Z8 ⌂ ∧ IV-V; Eur.: sp., F;
NW-Afr.

Erinus L. -m- *Scrophulariaceae* · 2 spp. ·
E:Fairy Foxglove; F:Erine; G:Alpenbalsam
- **alpinus** L. · E:Alpine Balsam, Fairy
Foxglove, Liver Balsam; G:Alpenbalsam ·
♃ △ Z6 V-VII; Eur.: Ib, Fr, Ital-P, C-Eur.;
mts., nat. in Br

Eriobotrya Lindl. -f- *Rosaceae* · 26 spp. ·
E:Loquat; F:Bibacier, Néflier du Japon;
G:Wollmispel
- **japonica** (Thunb.) Lindl. · E:Japanese
Medlar, Loquat, Nispero; G:Japanische
Wollmispel · ♄ e Z8 ⌂ IX-X ⚥ Ⓝ; China,
S-Jap.

Eriocactus Backeb. = Notocactus
- *leninghausii* (K. Schum.) Backeb. =
Notocactus leninghausii
- *schumannianus* (Nicolai) Backeb. =
Notocactus schumannianus

Eriocaulon L. -n- *Eriocaulaceae* · 478 spp. ·
E:Pipewort; F:Eriocaulon; G:Wollstängel
- *kunthii* Körn. = Eriocaulon ligulatum
- **ligulatum** (Vell.) L.B. Sm. · ♃ ✕ ⌂;
Austr.

Eriocephalus L. -m- *Asteraceae* · 27 spp. ·
F:Faux-kapokier; G:Wollkopf

– **africanus** L. · ♄ Z9 ⓚ I-II; S-Afr.

Eriocereus Riccob. -m- *Cactaceae* · c.
10 spp.
– **bonplandii** (J. Parm. ex Pfeiff.) Riccob. ·
Ψ Z9 ⓚ ▽ ✳; S-Braz., Parag., N-Arg.
– **guelichii** (Speg.) A. Berger · Ψ Z9 ⓚ ▽
✳; N-Arg.
– **jusbertii** (K. Schum.) Riccob. · Ψ Z9 ⓚ
▽ ✳; orig. ?
– **martinii** (Labour.) Riccob. · Ψ Z9 ⓚ ▽
✳; Arg.
– *pomanensis* (F.A.C. Weber) Riccob. =
Eriocereus bonplandii
– **tortuosus** (J. Forbes) Riccob. · Ψ Z9 ⓦ
▽ ✳; Arg., Bol, Parag., Urug.

Eriodendron DC. = Ceiba
– *anfractuosum* DC. = Ceiba pentandra

Eriodictyon Benth. -n- *Hydrophyllaceae* ·
8 spp.
– **californicum** (Hook. & Arn.) Torr. ·
E:Consumptive's Weed, Holy Herb · ⁂ ⓚ
⅀ ; Calif.

Erioglossum Blume = Lepisanthes
– *rubiginosum* (Roxb.) Blume = Lepisanthes rubiginosa

Eriogonum Michx. -n- *Polygonaceae* ·
c. 240 spp. · E:Umbrella Plant, Wild
Buckwheat; F:Renouée laineuse;
G:Wollampfer, Wollknöterich
– **compositum** Douglas ex Benth. ·
E:Arrowleaf Buckwheat · ⁂ Z5; USA:
Wash., Oreg., Idaho, N-Calif.
– **corymbosum** Benth. · E:Crisp Leaf
Wild Buckwheat; G:Trockenblättriger
Wollknöterich · ♄ △ Z3 VII-IX; Calif.
– **flavum** Nutt. · E:Alpine Golden Wild
Buckwheat; G:Goldener Wollknöterich ·
⁂ ⤳ △ Z5 VII-IX; Calif.
– **jamesii** Benth. · E:Antelope Sage,
Buckwheat; G:Colorado-Wollknöterich ·
♄ △ Z4 VII-VIII; USA: Colo., N.Mex.
– **racemosum** Nutt. · E:Redroot Eri-
ogonum; G:Rotwurzeliger Wollknöterich
· ⁂ △ Z5 VII-VIII; USA: Utah, Colo.,
N.Mex., Ariz., Tex.
– **umbellatum** Torr. · E:Sulphur Flower;
G:Flaumiger Wollknöterich · ♄ e ⤳ △
Z7 VI-IX; USA: NW, Calif., Rocky Mts.

Eriolobus (DC.) M. Roem. = Malus

– *tschonoskii* Rehder = Malus tschonoskii

Eriophorum L. -n- *Cyperaceae* · 18 spp. ·
E:Cotton Grass; F:Linaigrette; G:Wollgras
– **angustifolium** Honck. · E:Common
Cotton Grass; F:Linaigrette à feuilles
étroites; G:Schmalblättriges Wollgras · ⁂
⤳ Z4 IV-V; Eur.*, Cauc., E-TR, W-Sib.,
E-Sib., Amur, Sakhal., Kamchat., C-As.,
Mong., Manch., Korea, Alaska, Can.,
USA: NE, NCE, NC, Rocky Mts, NW;
Greenl.
– **gracile** W.D.J. Koch · E:Slender Cotton
Grass; G:Schlankes Wollgras · ⁂ ⤳
V-VI; Eur.* exc. Ib; W-Sib., E-Sib., N-Am.
– **latifolium** Hoppe · E:Broad Leaved Cot-
ton Grass; F:Linaigrtte à feuilles larges;
G:Breitblättriges Wollgras · ⁂ ⤳ IV-V;
Eur.*, Cauc., TR, W-Sib., E-Sib., Amur,
Sakhal., Mong., Manch., Korea
– *polystachion* L. = Eriophorum angustifo-
lium
– **scheuchzeri** Hoppe · E:White Cotton
Grass; G:Scheuchzers Wollgras · ⁂ △ ⤳
Z6 VI; Eur.* exc. BrI; N, mts.; W-Sib.,
E-Sib., Sakhal., Kamchat., C-As., Alaska,
Can., Greenl.
– *spissum* Fernald = Eriophorum vaginatum
– **vaginatum** L. · E:Tussock Cotton Grass;
F:Linaigrette gainée; G:Scheiden-
Wollgras · ⁂ ⤳ III-V; Eur.*, TR, Cauc.,
W-Sib., E-Sib., Amur, Sakhal., Kamchat.,
Mong., Manch., Jap., Alaska, Can.

Eriophyllum Lag. -n- *Asteraceae* ·
12-15 spp. · E:Wooly Sunflower;
F:Eriophylle; G:Wollblatt
– **lanatum** (Pursh) J. Forbes · G:Großköp-
figes Wollblatt
– var. **integrifolium** (Hook.) Smiley · ;
USA: NW, Calif., Rocky Mts.
– var. **lanatum** · E:Woolly Sunflower;
F:Aster doré du désert, Eriophylle gazonnant; G:Gewöhnliches Großköpfiges
Wollblatt · ⁂ Z5 VII-VIII; Can.: B.C.; USA:
Calif.
– var. *leucophyllum* (DC.) W.R. Carter =
Eriophyllum lanatum var. integrifolium

Eriopsis Lindl. -f- *Orchidaceae* · 5 spp.
– **biloba** Lindl. · ⁂ Z10 ⓦ VIII-IX ▽ ✳;
C-Am., trop. S-Am.

Eriostemon Sm. -m- *Rutaceae* ·
33 spp. · E:Waxflower; F:Eriostémon;

G:Wollfadenraute
- **myoporoides** DC. · E:Long-leaf Waxflower · ℏ e Z10 ⌂ III-IV; Austr.: Queensl., N.S.Wales, Victoria

Eriosyce Phil. -f- *Cactaceae* · 2 spp.
- **aurata** (Pfeiff.) Backeb. · ⴶ Z9 ⌂ ▽ ✳; Chile: Aconcagoa, Coquimba, Santiago; Arg.
- *ceratistes* (Otto) Britton & Rose = Eriosyce aurata
- *sandillon* (Gay) Phil. = Eriosyce aurata

Eritrichium Schrad. ex Gaudin -n- *Boraginaceae* · c. 30 spp. · E:Alpine Forget-me-not; F:Roi des Alpes; G:Himmelsherold
- **canum** (Benth.) Kitam. · ⴶ △ Z5 VI-VIII; W-Sib., E-Sib., Mong., NE-China
- **nanum** (L.) Schrad. ex Gaudin · E:Alpine Forget-me-not, King of the Alps; G:Gletscher-Vergissmeinnicht, Himmelsherold · ⴶ △ VII; Eur.: F, I, Ch, A, Slove, ? W-Russ.; Alp., Carp.
- *rupestre* (Pall.) Bunge = Eritrichium canum
- *strictum* Decne. = Eritrichium canum

Erodium L'Hér. ex Aiton -n- *Geraniaceae* · c. 60 spp. · E:Heron's Bill, Stork's Bill; F:Bec-de-héron; G:Reiherschnabel
- **absinthoides** Willd. · ⴶ Z6; TR: Amanus
- **ballii** Jord. · G:Dünen-Reiherschnabel · ☉ IV-IX; Eur.: D +
- **cheilanthifolium** Boiss. · ⴶ △ Z6 VI-VII; Eur.: sp., F
- **chrysanthum** L'Hér. ex DC. · ⴶ △ Z7 VI-VIII; GR
- **ciconium** (L.) L'Hér. · G:Langschnäbliger Reiherschnabel · ☉ ☉ IV-VIII; Eur.: Ib, Fr, Ital-P, Ba, RO, S-Russ.; TR, Levant, Iraq, Cauc., Iran, Afgh., C-As., N-Afr., nat. in N-Am.
- **cicutarium** (L.) L'Hér. ex Aiton · E:Heron's Bill, Stork's Bill; G:Gewöhnlicher Reiherschnabel · ☉ ☉ IV-X ⳩ Ⓝ; Eur.*, TR, Levant, Iran, Cauc., W-Sib., E-Sib., Amur, Kamchat., C-As., W-Him., China, nat. in N-Am., S-Am., E-Afr., Austr.
- **corsicum** Léman · ⴶ △ ∧ VI-VII; Cors, Sard.
- **danicum** K. Larsen · G:Dänischer Reiherschnabel · ☉; Eur.: G, DK +; coasts
- **foetidum** (L.) L'Hér. · E:Rock Stork's

Bill · ⴶ Z6; Eur.: S-F; Pyr.
- **glandulosum** (Cav.) Willd. · ⴶ Z6 VI-VII; Eur.: sp., F
- **gruinum** (L.) L'Hér. ex Aiton · E:Long Beaked Stork's Bill · ☉ ☉ Z8 VI-VIII; Eur.: Sic., GR, Crete; TR, Levant, Iraq, Iran, Egypt, Libya, nat. in Fr
- **guttatum** (Desf.) Willd. · ⴶ Z8 ⌂; sp., N-Afr., Palest.
- × **hybridum** Sünd. (*E. daucoides* × *E. manescavii*) · ⴶ Z7; cult.
- × **kolbianum** Sünd. ex R. Knuth (*E. glandulosum* × *E. rupestre*) · ⴶ Z6; cult.
- **lebelii** Jord. · G:Drüsiger Reiherschnabel · ☉ IV-X; Eur.: Ib., F, Ital-P, D + ; coasts
- *macradenum* L'Hér. = Erodium glandulosum
- **malacoides** (L.) L'Hér. · E:Soft Stork's Bill; G:Herzblatt-Reiherschnabel · ☉; Eur.: Ib, Fr, Ital-P, Ba, Crim; TR, Levant, Cauc., Iran, C-As., .N-Afr., nat. in N-Am., S-Am., S-Afr.
- **manescavii** Coss. · E:Garden Stork's Bill; G:Pyrenäen-Reiherschnabel · ⴶ △ Z6 VI-IX; Eur.: F; Pyr.
- **moschatum** (L.) L'Hér. ex Aiton · E:Common Heron's Bill, Musky Stork's Bill; G:Moschus-Reiherschnabel · ☉ Z6 V-VIII Ⓝ; Eur.: Ib, Fr, Ital-P, Ba, BrI; TR, Levant, N-Iraq, Iran, N-Afr., nat. in C-Eur., EC-Eur., N-Am., S-Am., E-Afr., S-Afr., Austr., NZ
- **pelargoniiflorum** Boiss. & Heldr. · ⴶ Z6 VII-VIII; TR
- *petraeum* (Gouan) Willd. = Erodium foetidum
- subsp. *crispum* (Lapeyr.) Rouy = Erodium cheilanthifolium
- subsp. *glandulosum* (Cav.) Bonnier = Erodium glandulosum
- **reichardii** (Murray) DC. · E:Alpine Geranium; G:Balearen-Reiherschnabel · ⴶ △ Z7 ⌂ ∧ VII-VIII; Balear.
- **rupestre** (Pourr. ex Cav.) Guitt. · E:Stork's Bill; G:Felsen-Reiherschnabel · ⴶ △ Z6 VI-VII; NE-Sp.
- *supracanum* L'Hér. = Erodium rupestre
- × **variabile** A.C. Leslie (*E. corsicum* × *E. reichardii*) · ⴶ Z7; cult.
- × **wilkommianum** Sünd. & Kunth (*E. cheilanthifolium* × *E. glandulosum*) · ⴶ Z6; cult.
- **Cultivars:**
- **some cultivars**

Erophila DC. -f- *Brassicaceae* · 10 spp. ·
E:Whitlow Grass; G:Hungerblümchen
- **verna** (L.) DC. · G:Frühlings-Hunger-
blümchen
- subsp. **praecox** (Steven) Walp. ·
G:Frühes Hungerblümchen · III-V; Eur.,
TR, Levant, SW-As., N-Afr.
- subsp. **spathulata** (Láng) Vollm. ·
G:Rundfrüchtiges Hungerblümchen ·
III-V; Eur., TR, Iran, C-As., Moroc.
- subsp. **verna** · E:Spring Whitlow Grass;
G:Gewöhnliches Frühlings-Hungerblüm-
chen · ⊙ III-V; Eur.*, TR, Levant, Cauc.,
Iran, Kashmir, C-As., N-Afr., nat. in
N-Am.

Eruca Mill. -f- *Brassicaceae* · 5 spp. ·
E:Rocket Salad; F:Roquette; G:Rauke
- **sativa** Mill. · E:Arugula, Italian Cress,
Rocket Salad; G:Öl-Rauke, Rukola · ⊙ Z7
V-VI; Eur.: Ib, Fr, Ital-P, Ba, Sw, H, EC-
Eur.; TR, Cauc., Afgh., Levant, NW-Afr.,
Libya
- **vesicaria** (L.) Cav. · E:Rocket; G:Wilde
Rauke · ⊙ Z7; Eur.: Ib, Fr, Sw, Ital-P, H,
Ba, E-Eur., nat. in G, A, Cz, PL, Norw.
- subsp. *sativa* (Mill.) Thell. = Eruca sativa

Erucastrum (DC.) C. Presl -n-
Brassicaceae · 20 spp. · E:Hairy Rocket;
F:Erucastre; G:Hundsrauke
- **gallicum** (Willd.) O.E. Schulz · E:Hairy
Rocket; G:Französische Hundsrauke · ⊙
⊙ V-X; Eur.: sp., Fr, I, C-Eur., EC-Eur.,
nat. in BrI, Sc, EC-Eur.
- **nasturtiifolium** (Poir.) O.E. Schulz ·
E:Watercress-leaved Rocket; G:Stumpf-
kantige Hundsrauke · ⊙ ⊙ V-VIII; Eur.:
Ib, Fr, Ital-P, Ba, C-Eur., H, nat. in RO

Ervatamia (A. DC.) Stapf = Tabernaemontana
- *coronaria* (Jacq.) Stapf = Tabernaemontana divaricata

Ervum L. = Vicia
- *ervilia* L. = Vicia ervilia

Erycina Lindl. -f- *Orchidaceae* · 7 spp.
- **echinata** (Kunth) Lindl. · ⊙ Z10 ⓜ ▽ ✻;
Mex.
- **pusilla** (L.) N.H. Williams & M.W.
Chase · ⊙ Z10 ⓜ VII-VIII ▽ ✻; C-Am.,
S-Am.

Eryngium L. -n- *Apiaceae* · 230-250 spp. ·
E:Sea Holly; F:Chardon, Panicaut;
G:Edeldistel, Mannstreu
- **agavifolium** Griseb. · ⊙ Z7 I-III; Arg.
- **alpinum** L. · E:Queen of the Alps;
F:Panicaut des Alpes; G:Alpen-
Mannstreu · ⊙ △ ✕ VII-VIII ▽; Eur.: F, I,
Sw, A, Slove., Croatia
- **amethystinum** L. · E:Amethyst
Eryngium; G:Amethyst-Mannstreu · ⊙ ✕
VII-VIII; Eur.: Ital-P, Ba
- **bourgatii** Gouan · E:Pyrenean eryngo;
F:Panicaut de Bourgat; G:Pyrenäendistel,
Spanischer Mannstreu · ⊙ △ Z5 VII-VIII;
Eur.: sp., F (Pyr.); Moroc.; mts.
- **bromeliifolium** F. Delaroche · ⊙ ⓐ
VIII-IX; Mex.
- **caeruleum** M. Bieb. · ⊙ VII-VIII; TR,
Cauc., Iran, C-As., Kashmir, Him., Tibet
- **campestre** L. · E:Field Eryngo; G:Feld-
Mannstreu · ⊙ VII-VIII ⚥ ▽; Eur.*
exc. Sc; TR, Cyprus, Cauc., Iran, Afgh.,
NW-Afr., Libya
- **giganteum** M. Bieb. · E:Giant Sea Holly,
Miss Willmott's Ghost; F:Panicaut géant;
G:Elfenbein-Mannstreu · ⊙ ✕ Z6 VII-VIII;
Cauc., Iran
- **maritimum** L. · E:Sea Holly; G:See-
Mannstreu, Stranddistel · ⊙ ⊙ VI-X ⚥ ▽;
Eur.*, TR, Levant, Cauc., NW-Afr.; coasts
- ✕ **oliverianum** F. Delaroche (*E. giganteum × E. planum*) · ⊙ ✕ Z5 VII-VIII; cult.
- **palmatum** Pančić & Vis. · ⊙ Z6; Eur.: Ba
- **pandanifolium** Cham. & Schltdl. · ⊙ Z8
ⓐ VII-VIII; S-Braz., Arg., nat. in C-P
- **planum** L. · E:Blue Eryngo; F:Panicaut
à feuilles mutiques; G:Flachblättriger
Mannstreu · ⊙ ✕ Z4 VII-VIII ⚥ ; Eur.:
C-Eur., EC-Eur., YU; Cauc., W-Sib., C-As.
- **serbicum** Pančić · ⊙ ✕ Z6 VII-VIII; Serb.
- **serra** Cham. & Schltdl. · ⊙ Z8 ∧ VIII-IX;
Braz., Arg.
- **tricuspidatum** L. · G:Dreispitz-
Mannstreu · ⊙ Z8 VIII-IX; Eur.: sp., Sard.,
Sic.; N-Afr.
- ✕ **tripartitum** Desf. · ⊙ Z5 VII-VIII; orig. ?
- **variifolium** Coss. · ⊙ Z7 ∧ VIII; Moroc.;
Atlas
- **yuccifolium** Michx. · E:Buttonsnake
Root, Rattlesnake Master; G:Yuccablät-
triger Mannstreu · ⊙ VII-IX; USA: NE,
NCE, Kans., SC, SE, Fla.
- ✕ **zabelii** H. Christ ex Bergmans (*E.
alpinum × E. bourgatii*) · ⊙ ✕ Z5 VII-VIII;
cult.

Erysimum L. -n- *Brassicaceae* · c. 100 spp. ·
E:Wallflower; F:Vélar; G:Goldlack,
Schöterich
– × **allionii** hort. (*E. perofskianum* × *?*) ·
E:Siberian Wallflower; G:Goldlack-
Schöterich · ⊙ Z7 IV-V; cult.
– some cultivars
– **andrzejowskianum** Besser · G:Andrze-
jowski-Schöterich · ⊙ V-VII; ? Crim,
Cauc., W-Sib., E-Sib., C-As., Mong.
– **aureum** M. Bieb. · G:Gold-Schöterich · ⊙
Z6 V-VII; Eur.: Russ.; Cauc.
– **cheiranthoides** L. · E:Wormseed
Mustard; G:Acker-Schöterich · ⊙ Z5 V-IX
⚤ ; Eur.* exc. Ib, Ital-P; W-Sib., E-Sib.,
Amur, Sakhal., Kamchat., C-As., nat. in
N-Am
– **cheiri** (L.) Crantz · E:Wallflower;
F:Vélard; G:Goldlack · ⚇ ♄ D Z7 ∧ V-VI
⚤ ✹; TR, W-Syr., nat. in Eur.* exc. Sc
– many cultivars
– **crepidifolium** Rchb. · G:Bleicher
Schöterich · ⊙ ⚇ IV-VII ✹; Eur.: G, CZ,
H, RO
– **diffusum** Ehrh. · G:Grauer Schöterich · ⊙
⚇ V-VII ✹; Eur.: A, EC-Eur., Ba, E-Eur.;
TR, Cauc., C-As.
– *dubium* (Suter) Thell. non DC. =
Erysimum ochroleucum
– **hieraciifolium** L. · E:Alpine Wallflower;
G:Ruten-Schöterich, Steifer Schöterich ·
⊙ Z7 VI-IX; Eur.: Fr, C-Eur., EC-Eur., Sc,
Ba, E-Eur.
– *humile* Pers. = Erysimum ochroleucum
– **hungaricum** Zapal. · G:Ungarischer
Schöterich · ⊙; Eur.: A, EC-Eur., RO, ?
W-Russ.; Carp.
– **kotschyanum** J. Gay · ⚇ △ Z6 VI-VII; TR
– **linifolium** (Pers.) J. Gay · ⚇ Z6; C-Sp.,
N-Port.
– **marschallianum** Andrz. ex DC. ·
G:Harter Schöterich · ⊙ Z6 VI-IX; Eur.:
C-Eur., EC-Eur., E-Eur.; W-Sib., E-Sib.,
C-As., Him., Mong.
– × *marshallii* hort. = Erysimum × allionii
– **ochroleucum** DC. · G:Blassgelber Schö-
terich · ⚇ D Z6 VI; Eur.: F, Sw; SW-Alp.
– **odoratum** Ehrh. · G:Wohlriechender
Schöterich · ⊙ VI-VII; Eur.: EC-Eur., Fr,
Ital-P, Ba, E-Eur., A, D
– **perofskianum** Fisch. & C.A. Mey. ·
G:Afghanischer Schöterich · ⊙ Z8 III-V;
Cauc., Afgh.
– **pulchellum** (Willd.) J. Gay · ⚇ △ Z6
IV-VII; Eur.: Ba; TR, Cauc.

– *pumilum* auct. non Gaudin = Erysimum
rhaeticum
– **repandum** L. · E:Bushy Wallflower;
G:Sparriger Schöterich · ⊙ Z6 V-VII;
Eur.: C-Eur., EC-Eur., Ba, E-Eur.; TR,
Levant, Cauc., Iran, Kashmir, C-As.
– **rhaeticum** (Schleich. ex Hornem.) DC. ·
G:Schweizer Schöterich · ⚇ △ VI; Eur.: F,
I, Sw, A; Alp.
– **scoparium** (Brouss. ex Willd.) Sno-
gerup · ⚇ Z8 ☂; Canar. Is.
– **sylvestre** (Crantz) Scop. · E:Wood
Treacle Mustard; G:Wald-Schöterich · ⚇
Z6 IV-VII; Eur.: I, A, Slove.; E-Alp.
– Cultivars:
– many cultivars

Erythea S. Watson = Brahea
– *armata* (S. Watson) S. Watson = Brahea
armata
– *brandegeei* Purpus = Brahea brandegeei
– *edulis* (H. Wendl. ex S. Watson) S.
Watson = Brahea edulis

Erythraea Borkh. = Centaurium
– *centaurium* auct. non (L.) Pers. =
Centaurium erythraea
– *diffusa* J. Woods = Centaurium scilloides
– *massonii* Sw. = Centaurium scilloides

Erythrina L. -f- *Fabaceae* · 112 spp. ·
E:Coral Tree; F:Arbre-à-corail, Erythrine;
G:Korallenbaum
– **abyssinica** Lam. ex DC. · ♄ d Z10 ☸;
Eth., trop. Afr., Mozamb., Him
– **americana** Mill. · ♄ ♄ d Z9 ☸; Ariz.,
Mex.
– **caffra** Thunb. · E:Cape Kaffirboom,
Lucky Beantree; G:Kap-Korallenbaum · ♄
s Z10 ☒; S-Afr.
– **corallodendron** L. · E:Coral Tree;
G:Echter Korallenbaum · ♄ d Z10 ☒ ✹;
? W.Ind.
– *coralloides* A. DC. = Erythrina americana
– **crista-galli** L. · E:Cockspur Coral Tree;
F:Erythrine crête-de-coq; G:Gewöhnli-
cher Korallenbaum · ♄ d Z8 ☒ VII-IX ✹;
Braz., Parag., Bol., Arg.
– **falcata** Benth. · ♄ ♄ d Z10 ☸; S-Peru,
Bol., E-Braz., Parag., N-Arg.
– **flabelliformis** Kearney · ♄ ♄ Z9 ☒;
SE-Ariz., SW- N.Mex., W-Mex.
– **fusca** Lour. · E:Purple Coral Tree;
G:Scharlach-Korallenbaum · ♄ d Z8 ☒
Ⓝ; S-Am., Guyana, Venez.

– *glauca* Willd. = Erythrina fusca
– **herbacea** L. · E:Deer's Peas, Red Cardi-
nal; G:Mexikanischer Korallenstrauch · ♄
d Z10 ⓚ VIII-IX; USA: SE, Fla., SC; Mex.
– **humeana** Spreng. · E:Natal Coral Tree;
G:Natal-Korallenbaum · ♄ d Z9 ⓦ VII-X;
trop. Afr.
– **latissima** E. Mey. · ♄ d Z10 ⓦ; S-Afr.,
Mozamb.
– **lysistemon** Hutch. · E:Common Coral
Tree · ♄ s Z9 ⓚ; S-Afr., Rhodes.
– *piscipula* L. = Piscidia piscipula
– **poeppigiana** (Walp.) O.F. Cook ·
E:Mountain Immortelle · ♄ d Z10 ⓦ Ⓝ;
trop. Am.
– *princeps* A. Dietr. = Erythrina humeana
– **senegalensis** DC. · G:Senegal-Korallen-
baum · ♄ Z9 ⓦ Ⓝ; W-Afr., W-Sah
– **subumbrans** (Hassk.) Merr. ·
E:December Tree · ♄ Z10 ⓦ Ⓝ; trop. As.
– **variegata** L. · E:Indian Coral Tree;
G:Indischer Korallenbaum · ♄ d Z10 ⓦ
♀ Ⓝ; Tanzania, Ind., Sri Lanka, Burma,
China, Taiwan, Malay. Arch., Phil.,
Polyn.
– **vespertilio** Benth. · ♄ d Z10 ⓚ; Austr.:
Queensl., N.S.Wales, W-Austr., N.Terr.

Erythrochiton Nees & Mart. -m- *Rutaceae* ·
5-7 spp. · F:Erythrochiton; G:Rotkelch
– **Braziliensis** Nees & Mart. · ♄ e ⓦ;
E-Bol., Peru, S-Braz.

Erythronium L. -n- *Liliaceae* · 27 spp. ·
E:Dog's Tooth Violet; F:Dent-de-chien,
Erythrone; G:Hundszahn, Zahnlilie
– **albidum** Nutt. · E:White Trout Lily;
G:Weißer Hundszahn · ⚄ Z4 IV-V; Can.:
Ont.; USA: NCE, NE, SE, Okla.
– **americanum** Ker-Gawl. · E:Trout Lily,
Yellow Adder's Tongue; G:Amerika-
nischer Hundszahn · ⚄ Z3 IV-V ♀ ; Can.:
E; USA: NE, NCE, Okla.
– **californicum** Purdy · E:Fawn Lily;
G:Kalifornischer Hundszahn · ⚄ Z5 IV-V;
USA: N-Calif.
– **citrinum** S. Watson · E:Fawn Lily;
G:Gelber Hundszahn · ⚄ Z4 IV-V; USA:
S-Oreg.
– **dens-canis** L. · E:Dog's Tooth
Violet; F:Erythrone dent-de-chien;
G:Europäischer Hundszahn · ⚄ Z5 III-V;
Eur.* exc. BrI, Sc
– **grandiflorum** Pursh · E:Avalanche Lily;
G:Großblütiger Hundszahn · ⚄ Z5 IV-V;

B.C., USA: NW
– **hendersonii** S. Watson · E:Henderson's
Fawnlily; G:Hendersons Hundszahn · ⚄
Z5 IV-V; USA: S-Oreg.
– **multiscapoideum** (Kellogg) A. Nelson
& P.B. Kenn. · E:Sierra Fawn Lily · ⚄ Z5
IV-V; Calif.: Sierra Nevada
– **oregonum** Applegate · E:Giant Fawn
Lily; G:Riesen-Hundszahn · ⚄ Z5 IV-V;
B.C., USA: NW
– *purdyi* hort. = Erythronium multiscapoi-
deum
– **revolutum** Sm. · E:Pink Fawn Lily;
G:Rosa Hundszahn · ⚄ Z5 IV-V; B.C.,
USA: NW, N-Calif.
– **tuolumnense** Applegate · E:Trout
Lily, Tuolomne Fawn Lily; G:Stern-
Hundszahn · ⚄ Z5 IV; Calif.
– Cultivars:
– **some cultivars**

Erythrophleum Afzel. ex G. Don -n-
Caesalpiniaceae · 9 spp. · E:Ordeal Tree;
G:Gottesurteilsbaum
– **suaveolens** (Guill. & Perr.) Brenan · ♄ ⓦ
⚘ Ⓝ; W-Afr.: Sierra Leone

Erythrorhipsalis A. Berger -f- *Cactaceae* ·
1 sp.
– **pilocarpa** (Loefgr.) A. Berger · ♄ ♈ Z9
ⓦ; Braz.: Sao Paulo

Erythrotis Hook. f. = Cyanotis
– *beddomei* Hook. f. = Cyanotis beddomei

Erythroxylum P. Browne -n-
Erythroxylaceae · 230-250 spp. · E:Coca;
F:Coca, Cocaïer; G:Kokastrauch, Rotholz
– **acuminatum** Ruiz & Pav. · E:Wild Coca;
G:Wilder Kokastrauch · ♄ ⓦ; Peru
– **coca** Lam.
– var. **coca** · E:Coca; G:Echter Kokastrauch
· ♄ e ⓦ ♀ ⚘; S-Peru, Bol.
– var. **ipadu** Plowman · E:Amazonian
Coca; G:Amazonas-Kokastrauch · ♄ ⓦ ♀
⚘; Amazon.
– **lucidum** Kunth · ♄ ⓦ; Col.
– **monogynum** Roxb. · E:Bastard Sandal ·
♄ ⓦ; Ind., China
– **novogranatense** (D. Morris) Hieron.
– var. **novogranatense** · E:Colombian
Coca; G:Kolumbianischer Kokastrauch ·
♄ e ⓦ ♀ ⚘; Col., Venez.
– var. **truxillense** (Rusby) Plowman ·
E:Truxillo Coca; G:Truxillo-Kokastrauch ·

♄ e ⓦ ⚥ ⚘; N-Peru
- *truxillense* Rusby = Erythroxylum novogranatense var. novogranatense

Escallonia Mutis ex L. f. -f- *Escalloniaceae* · 39 spp. · F:Escallonia; G:Andenstrauch, Escallonie
- **alpina** Poepp. ex DC. · ♄ e Z9 ⓐ; Chile
- **bifida** Link & Otto · E:White Escallonia; G:Weißer Andenstrauch · ♄ ♄ e Z9 ⓐ VII-VIII; Braz., Parag., Urug., Arg.
- × **exoniensis** hort. Veitch (*E. rosea* × *E. rubra*) · ♄ ♄ e Z8 ⓐ; cult.
- **floribunda** Kunth · ♄ e Z9 ⓐ VII-VIII; Col., Venez.
- **grahamiana** Gillies · ♄ e Z9 ⓐ; Chile
- **illinita** C. Presl · ♄ e Z8 ⓐ VII-VIII; Chile
- **laevis** (Vell.) Sleumer · E:Pink Escallonia; G:Rosa Andenstrauch · ♄ e Z9 ⓐ VII-VIII; Braz.
- × **langleyensis** Veitch ex Mast. (*E. rubra* × *E. virgata*) · ♄ e Z8 ⓐ ∧ VII-VIII; cult.
- *montevidensis* (Cham. & Schltdl.) DC. = Escallonia bifida
- *organensis* Gardner = Escallonia laevis
- *philippiana* (Engl.) Mast. = Escallonia virgata
- **pulverulenta** (Ruiz & Pav.) Pers. · ♄ e Z9 ⓐ VII-IX; Chile
- × **rigida** Phil. (*E. rubra* × *E. virgata*) · G:Bastard-Andenstrauch · ♄ e Z9 ⓐ; Chile
- **rosea** Griseb. · ♄ e Z9 ⓐ VII-VIII; Arg., Chile
- **rubra** (Ruiz & Pav.) Pers. · E:Red Claws
- var. **macrantha** (Hook. & Arn.) Reiche · ♄ e Z8 ⓐ VII-VIII; Arg., Chile
- var. **rubra** · G:Roter Andenstrauch · ♄ e Z9 ⓐ VII-VIII; Arg., Chile
- **virgata** (Ruiz & Pav.) Pers. · G:Rutenförmiger Andenstrauch · ♄ e Z8 ⓐ ∧ VII-VIII; Arg., Chile
- var. *philippiana* Engl. = Escallonia virgata
- **Cultivars:**
- **many cultivars**

Eschscholzia Cham. -f- *Papaveraceae* · 8-10 spp. · E:Californian Poppy; F:Eschscholzia; G:Goldmohn, Kappenmohn
- **caespitosa** Benth. · E:Slender California Poppy, Tufted Poppy; G:Polster-Kappenmohn · ⊙ Z7 VII-IX; Calif.: Sierra Nevada
- **californica** Cham. · E:California Poppy; F:Pavot jaune de Californie;

G:Kalifornischer Kappenmohn, Schlafmützchen · ⊙ ⊙ ⁴ Z6 VI-X ⚥ ⚘; USA: Oreg., Calif., nat. in C-Eur., W-Eur.
- **many cultivars**
- **lobbii** Greene · E:Fryingpans · ⊙ Z7; Calif.
- *tenuifolia* Benth. = Eschscholzia caespitosa

Escobaria Britton & Rose -f- *Cactaceae* · 16 spp. · E:Foxtail Cactus
- **chihuahuensis** Britton & Rose · ꙮ Z9 ⓐ ▽ ✳; Mex.: Chihuahua
- **dasyacantha** (Engelm.) Britton & Rose · E:Big Bend Foxtail Cactus · ꙮ Z9 ⓐ ▽ ✳; USA: N.Mex., Tex.; N-Mex.
- **emskoetteriana** (Quehl) Borg · E:Junior Tom Thumb Cactus · ꙮ Z9 ⓐ ▽ ✳; S-Tex., NE-Mex.
- **missouriensis** (Sweet) D.R. Hunt · E:Missouri Foxtail Cactus · ꙮ Z8 ⓐ ▽ ✳; Can.: Man.; USA: NC, Rocky Mts., SC, SW, Calif.; N- Mex.
- **roseana** (Boed.) Buxb. · ꙮ Z9 ⓐ ▽ ✳; Mex.: Coahuila
- *strobiliformis* hort. non Poselg. = Escobaria tuberculosa
- **tuberculosa** (Engelm.) Britton & Rose · E:Whitecolumn Foxtail Cactus · ꙮ Z9 ⓐ ▽ ✳; USA: N.Mex., Tex.; N-Mex.
- **vivipara** (Nutt.) Buxb. · E:Spinystar · ꙮ Z9 ⓐ ▽ ✳; Can.: W, Man.; USA: Rocky Mts., NC, Tex.; N-Mex.
- **zilziana** (Boed.) Backeb. · ꙮ Z9 ⓐ ▽ ✳; Mex.: Coahuila

Esmeralda Rchb. f. -f- *Orchidaceae* · 2 spp.
- **cathcartii** (Lindl.) Rchb. f. · ⁴ Z10 ⓦ V-VII ▽ ✳; E-Him.

× **Esmeranda** Vacherot -f- *Orchidaceae* (*Esmeralda* × *Vanda*)

Espostoa Britton & Rose -f- *Cactaceae* · 10 spp.
- **blossfeldiorum** (Werderm.) Buxb. · ꙮ Z9 ⓦ ▽ ✳; N-Peru
- **guentheri** (Kupper) Buxb. · ꙮ Z9 ⓦ ▽ ✳; Bol.
- *huanucoensis* F. Ritter = Espostoa lanata
- **lanata** (Humb., Bonpl. & Kunth) Britton & Rose · E:Cotton Ball Cactus · ꙮ Z9 ⓦ ▽ ✳; N-Peru
- *laticornua* Rauh & Backeb. = Espostoa lanata

– **melanostele** (Vaupel) Borg · ⵌ Z9 ⓜ ▽
✳; Peru
– *nana* F. Ritter = Espostoa melanostele
– **ritteri** Buining · ⵌ Z9 ⓜ ▽ ✳; N-Peru
– *sericata* (Backeb.) Backeb. = Espostoa
lanata

Espostoopsis Buxb. = Austrocephalocereus
– *dybowskii* (Rol.-Goss.) Buxb. = Austrocephalocereus dybowskii

Etlingera Giseke -f- *Zingiberaceae* · 81 sp. ·
E:Torch Ginger; F:Sceptre de l'Empereur;
G:Fackelingwer
– **elatior** (Jack) R.M. Sm. · E:Philippine
Waxflower, Torch Ginger; G:Malayischer
Fackelingwer · ⵜ Z10 ⓜ VII-VIII; Malay.
Pen.

Euanthe Schltr. -f- *Orchidaceae* · 1 sp.
– **sanderiana** (Rchb. f.) Schltr. · ⵜ Z10 ⓚ
IX-X ▽ ✳; Phil.: Mindanao

Eucalyptus L'Hér. -f- *Myrtaceae* ·
500+ spp. · E:Gum, Ironbark;
F:Eucalyptus; G:Blaugummibaum,
Eukalyptus
– **alba** Reinw. ex Blume · E:White Gum ·
ℏ e Z10 ⓚ ⓝ; Malay. Arch., N.Guinea,
N-Austr.
– **amplifolia** Naudin · E:Cabbage Gum · ℏ
e Z10 ⓚ; Austr.: Queensl., N.S.Wales
– **amygdalina** Labill. · E:Black Peppermint · ℏ e D Z9 ⓚ; Tasman.
– **archeri** Maiden & Blakely · E:Alpine
Cider Gum · ℏ ℏ e Z9 ⓚ; Tasman.
– **astringens** (Maiden) Maiden · E:Brown
Mallet · ℏ e Z10 ⓚ ⓝ; W-Austr., cult.
Moroc., S-Afr., Cyprus
– **botryoides** Sm. · E:Bangalay · ℏ e Z10
ⓚ; Austr.: N.S.Wales, Victoria
– **caesia** Benth. · ℏ ℏ e Z9 ⓚ; W-Austr.
– **calophylla** R. Br. ex Lindl. · G:Marri-
Eukalyptus; E:Marri · ℏ e ✕ Z10 ⓚ ⓝ;
W-Austr.
– **camaldulensis** Dehnh. · E:Red River
Gum, River Red Gum; G:Roter Eukalyp-
tus · ℏ e Z9 ⓚ ⚥ ⓝ; Austr.
– **cinerea** F. Muell. ex Benth. · E:Argyle
Apple, Ash Colored Eukalyptus · ℏ e ✕
Z10 ⓚ; Austr.: N.S.Wales, Victoria
– **citriodora** Hook. · E:Lemon Eucalyptus,
Lemon Scented Gum; G:Zitronen-
Eukalyptus · ℏ e D Z10 ⓚ ⚥ ⓝ; Austr.:
Queensl.

– **cladocalyx** F. Muell. · E:Sugar Gum · ℏ e
Z9 ⓚ ⓝ; S-Austr.
– **cneorifolia** DC. · ℏ ℏ e Z10 ⓚ; S-Austr.
– **coccifera** Hook. f. · G:Trichterfrucht-
Eukalyptus · ℏ ℏ e Z8 ⓚ; Tasman.
– **cordata** Labill. · E:Silver Dollar Eukalyptus; G:Silberdollar-Eukalyptus · ℏ ℏ e Z8
ⓚ; Tasman.
– **cornuta** Labill. · E:Yate · ℏ e Z9 ⓚ;
W-Austr.
– **crebra** F. Muell. · E:Iron bark · ℏ e Z10 ⓚ
ⓝ; Austr.: Queensl., N.S.Wales
– **crucis** Maiden · E:Silver Mallee · ℏ e Z10
ⓚ; W-Austr.
– **curtisii** Blakely & C.T. White · E:Plunkett
Mallee · ℏ e Z10 ⓚ; Austr.: Queensl.
– **dalrympleana** Maiden · E:Mountain
Gum; G:Breitblättriger Eukalyptus · ℏ
e Z8 ⓚ; Austr.: N.S.Wales, Victoria,
Tasman.
– **delegatensis** R.T. Baker · E:Alpine
Ash, Stringybark · ℏ e Z9 ⓚ; Austr.:
N.S.Wales, Victoria, Tasman.
– **diversicolor** F. Muell. · E:Karri; G:Karri-
Eukalyptus · ℏ e Z10 ⓚ ⓝ; W-Austr.
– **dives** Schauer · E:Broad Leaved Peppermint Gum · ℏ e Z10 ⓚ ⚥ ⓝ; Austr.:
N.S.Wales, nat. in Zaire
– **eugenioides** Sieber ex Spreng. · E:Thin-
leaved Stringy Bark · ℏ e Z10 ⓚ; Austr.:
Queensl., N.S.Wales, Victoria
– **eximia** Schauer · E:Yellow Bloodwood ·
ℏ e Z10 ⓚ; Austr.: N.S.Wales
– **fastigiata** H. Deane & Maiden · E:Brown
Barrel · ℏ e Z10 ⓚ; Austr.: N.S.Wales,
Victoria
– **ficifolia** F. Muell. · E:Red Flowering
Gum; G:Purpur-Eukalyptus · ℏ e Z9 ⓚ;
W-Austr.
– **fraxinoides** H. Deane & Maiden ·
E:White Ash · ℏ e Z9 ⓚ; Austr.:
N.S.Wales, Victoria
– **fruticetorum** F. Muell. ex Miq. · E:Blue
Mallee · ℏ e Z8 ⓚ ⚥ ; Austr.
– **globulus** Labill.
– subsp. **bicostata** (Maiden, Blakely &
Simmonds) J.B. Kirkp. · E:Victorian Blue
Gum · Z9 ⓚ
– subsp. **globulus** · E:Blue Gum, Tas-
manian Blue Gum; F:Eucalyptus bleu;
G:Blaugummibaum, Fieberbaum · ℏ e Z9
ⓚ ⚥ ⓝ; Austr.: Victoria, Tasman., nat. in
Calif.
– subsp. **maidenii** (F. Muell.) J.B. Kirkp. ·
E:Maiden's Gum · ℏ e Z9 ⓚ ⓝ; Austr.:

N.S.Wales, Victoria
- **gomphocephala** DC. · E:Tuart · ♄ e Z9 (K) (N); W-Austr.
- **gunnii** Hook. f. · E:Cider Gum; F:Eucalyptus commun; G:Mostgummi-Eukalyptus, Tasmanischer Eukalyptus · ♄ e Z8 (K) (N); Tasman.
- **johnstonii** Maiden · E:Tasmanian Yellow Gum · ♄ e Z8 (K); Tasman.
- **largiflorens** F. Muell. · E:Black Box · ♄ e Z10 (K); Austr.: Queensl., N.S.Wales, Victoria, S-Austr.
- **lehmannii** (L. Preiss ex Schauer) Benth. · E:Bushy Yate · ♄ e ✕ Z9 (K); W-Austr.
- **leucoxylon** F. Muell. · E:White Ironbark, Yellow Gum; G:Weißer Gummi-Eukalyptus · ♄ e Z9 (K) (N); Austr.: N.S.Wales, Victoria, S-Austr.
- **macarthurii** H. Deane & Maiden · E:Paddy's River Box · ♄ e Z8 (K); Austr.: N.S.Wales
- **maculata** Hook. · E:Spotted Gum; G:Gesprenkelter Eukalyptus · ♄ e Z10 (K) (N); Austr.: Queensl., N.S.Wales, Victoria
- var. *citriodora* (Hook.) F.M. Bailey = Eucalyptus citriodora
- *maideni* F. Muell. = Eucalyptus globulus subsp. maidenii
- **mannifera** Mudie · E:Brittle Gum · ♄ e Z9 (K); Austr.: N.S.Wales
- **marginata** Donn ex Sm. · E:Jarrah, West Australian Mahogany · ♄ e ✕ Z10 (K) (N); W-Austr.
- **microcorys** F. Muell. · E:Tallow Wood · ♄ e Z10 (K) (N); Austr.: Queensl., N.S.Wales
- **nicholii** Maiden & Blakely · E:Narrow-leaved Black Peppermint · ♄ e Z8 (K); Austr.: N.S.Wales
- *niphophila* Maiden & Blakely = Eucalyptus pauciflora subsp. niphophila
- **nutans** F. Muell. · E:Red-flowered Moort · ♄ ♄ e Z10 (K); W-Austr.
- **obliqua** L'Hér. · E:Messmate · ♄ e Z9 (K) (N); Austr.: Queensl., N.S.Wales, Victoria, S-Austr., Tasman.
- **occidentalis** Endl.
- var. **astringens** Endl. · E:Brown Mallet; G:Malettorinde · ♄ e Z10 (K) (N)
- var. **occidentalis** · E:Swamp Yate · ♄ e Z10 (K); W-Austr.
- **orbifolia** F. Muell. · E:Round-leaved Mallee · ♄ ♄ e Z10 (K); Austr.: W-Austr., N.Terr., S-Austr.
- **ovata** Labill. · E:Swamp Gum · ♄ e Z8 (K); Austr.: N.S.Wales, S-Austr., Victoria,

Tasman.
- **paniculata** Sm. · E:Grey Ironbark · ♄ e Z10 (K) (N); Austr.: N.S.Wales
- **parvifolia** Cambage · E:Small-leaved Gum · ♄ e Z8 (K); Austr.: N.S.Wales
- **pauciflora** Siebold ex Spreng.
- subsp. **niphophila** (Maiden & Blakely) L.A.S. Johnson & Blaxell · E:Snow Gum · ♄ ♄ e Z7 (K); Austr.: N.S.Wales (Mt. Kosciusco)
- subsp. **pauciflora** · E:Snow Gum, White Sally · ♄ e Z8 (K) (N); Austr.: Queensl., N.S.Wales, Victoria, S-Austr., Tasman.
- **perriniana** F. Muell. ex Rodway · E:Spinning Gum · ♄ e Z8 (K); Austr.: N.S.Wales, Victoria, Tasman.
- *phellandra* R.T. Baker & H.G. Sm. = Eucalyptus radiata
- **pilularis** Sm. · E:Black Butt · ♄ e Z10 (K) (N); Austr.: SE-Queensl., N.S.Wales
- **polyanthemos** Schauer · E:Red Box · ♄ e Z9 (K); Austr.: N.S.Wales, Victoria
- *polybractea* R.T. Baker = Eucalyptus fruticetorum
- **preissiana** Schauer · E:Bell-fruited Mallee · ♄ e Z10 (K); W-Austr.
- **pulchella** Desf. · E:White Peppermint · ♄ e Z10 (K); Tasman.
- **pulverulenta** Sims · E:Silver Leaf Mountain Gum · ♄ ♄ e Z9 (K); Austr.: N.S.Wales
- **pyriformis** Turcz. · E:Pear Shaped Mallee; G:Birnen-Eukalyptus · ♄ e ✕ Z9 (K); W-Austr.
- **radiata** Sieber ex DC. · E:Narrow-leaved Peppermint; G:Pfefferminz-Eukalyptus · ♄ e Z9 (K) (N); Austr.
- **regnans** F. Muell. · E:Giant Gum, Mountain Ash · ♄ e Z9 (K) (N); Austr.: Victoria, Tasman.
- **resinifera** Sm. · E:Red Mahogany · ♄ e Z10 (K) (N); Austr.: Queensl., N.S.Wales
- × **rhodantha** Blakely & H. Steedman (*E. macrocarpa* × *E. pyriformis*) · E:Kino Gum · ♄ e Z10 (K); W-Austr.
- **robusta** Sm. · E:Swamp Mahogany · ♄ e Z10 (K) (N); Austr.: Queensl., N.S.Wales
- *rostrata* Schltdl. non Cav. = Eucalyptus camaldulensis
- *salicifolia* Cav. = Eucalyptus amygdalina
- **saligna** Sm. · E:Sydney Blue Gum · ♄ e Z10 (K) (N); Austr.: SE-Queensl., N.S.Wales
- **sideroxylon** A. Cunn. ex Woolls · E:Mugga, Pink Ironbark; G:Mugga-Eukalyptus · ♄ e Z9 (K) (N); Austr.: Queensl.,

N.S.Wales, Victoria
- **smithii** R.T. Baker · E:Gully Ash · ♄ e Z10 ⌂ ⚥ ; Austr.: N.S.Wales, Victoria
- **staigeriana** F. Muell. ex F.M. Bailey · E:Lemon Ironbark · ♄ e Z10 ⌂ Ⓝ; Austr., nat. in Braz., Guat., Zaire
- **stellulata** Sieber ex DC. · E:Black Sally · ♄ e Z10 ⌂; Austr.: N.S.Wales, Victoria
- **tereticornis** Sm. · E:Forest Red Gum, Grey Gum · ♄ e Z10 ⌂ Ⓝ; Austr.: Queensl., N.S.Wales, Victoria
- **tetragona** (R. Br.) F. Muell. · E:Tallerack · ♄ e Z10 ⌂; W-Austr.
- **tetraptera** Turcz. · E:Four-winged Mallee · ♄ e Z10 ⌂; W-Austr.
- **torquata** Luehm. · E:Coral Gum · ♄ e Z10 ⌂; W-Austr.
- *umbellata* (Gaertn.) Domin = Eucalyptus tereticornis
- **urnigera** Hook. f. · E:Urn Gum · ♄ e Z8 ⌂; Tasman.
- **viminalis** Labill. · E:Manna Gum, Ribbon Gum; G:Rutenförmiger Eukalyptus, Zucker-Gummi-Eukalyptus · ♄ e Z8 ⌂ Ⓝ; Austr.: N.S. Wales, S-Austr., Tasman., Victoria
- **wandoo** Blakely · E:Wandoo; G:Wandoo-Eukalyptus · ♄ e Z10 ⌂ Ⓝ; Austr.
- **woodwardii** Maiden · E:Lemon-flavoured Mallee · ♄ e Z10 ⌂; W-Austr.

Eucharidium Fisch. & C.A. Mey. = Clarkia
- *breweri* A. Gray = Clarkia breweri
- *concinnum* Fisch. & C.A. Mey. = Clarkia concinna

Eucharis Planch. & Linden -f-
Amaryllidaceae · 17 spp. · E:Amazon Lily; F:Lis du Brésil; G:Amazonaslilie, Herzkelch
- **amazonica** Planch. · E:Amazon Lily; G:Amazonaslilie · ⁴ ⋉ Z10 ⒨ XII-VII; Ecuad., Peru
- **candida** Planch. & Linden · G:Kolumbianischer Herzkelch · ⁴ Z10 ⒨ III; Col.
- × **grandiflora** Planch. & Linden (*E. moorei × E. sanderi*) · G:Großblütiger Herzkelch · ⁴ Z10 ⒨
- × *mastersii* Baker = Eucharis × grandiflora
- **sanderi** Baker · G:Sanders Herzkelch · ⁴ Z10 ⒨ II-IV; Col.
- *subedentata* (Baker) Benth. & Hook. f. = Caliphruria subedentata

Euchile (Dressler & G.E. Pollard) Withner

-f- *Orchidaceae* · 2 spp.
- **citrina** (La Llave & Lex.) Withner · ⁴ D Z10 ⒨ IV-V ▽ ✳; Mex.

Euchlaena Schrad. = Zea
- *mexicana* Schrad. = Zea mexicana

Euclidium R. Br. -n- *Brassicaceae* · 2 spp. · G:Schnabelschötchen
- **syriacum** (L.) R. Br. · G:Schnabelschötchen · ⊙ VI; Eur.: A, EC-Eur., Ba, E-Eur.; TR, Levant, Cauc., Iran, W-Sib., C-As., Him.

Eucnide Zucc. -f- *Loasaceae* · 8 spp. · E:Stingbush; F:Eucnide, Mentzelia; G:Schönnessel
- **bartonioides** Zucc. · E:Yellow Stingbush · ⊙ ⌂ VII-VIII; USA: N.Mex., Tex.; Mex.

Eucodonia Hanst. -f- *Gesneriaceae* · 2 spp.
- **verticillata** (M. Martens & Galeotti) Wiehler · ⁴ Z10 ⒨; Mex.

Eucomis L'Hér. -f- *Hyacinthaceae* · 10 spp. · E:Pineapple Flower; F:Eucomis; G:Schopflilie
- **autumnalis** (Mill.) Chitt. · G:Herbst-Schopflilie · ⁴ Z8 ⌂ III-IV; Malawi, Zambia, S-Afr.
- **bicolor** Baker · F:Eucomis du Cap; G:Gerandete Schopflilie · ⁴ Z8 ⌂; S-Afr.: Natal
- **comosa** (Houtt.) H.R. Wehrh. · E:Pineapple Flower; G:Ananansblume, Gewöhnliche Schopflilie · ⁴ Z8 ⌂ VI-VII; S-Afr.
- *punctata* (Thunb.) L'Hér. = Eucomis comosa
- *undulata* Aiton = Eucomis autumnalis

Eucommia Oliv. -f- *Eucommiaceae* · 1 sp. · E:Gutta Percha Tree
- **ulmoides** Oliv. · E:Gutta Percha Tree, Hardy Rubber Tree; F:Arbre à Gutta-Percha · ♄ d Z6 ⚥ Ⓝ; W-China, C-China

Eucryphia Cav. -f- *Eucryphiaceae* · 6 spp. · E:Ulmo; F:Eucryphia; G:Eucryphie, Scheinulme
- **cordifolia** Cav. · E:Roble de Chile, Ulmo; G:Chilenische Scheinulme · ♄ ♄ e Z9 ⌂ VIII; S-Chile
- **glutinosa** (Poepp. & Endl.) Baill. ·

G:Klebrige Scheinulme · ♄ e D Z8 ⓚ
VII-VIII; S-Chile
- × **hillieri** Ivens (*E. lucida* × *E. moorei*) · ♄
e Z8 ⓚ; cult.
- × **intermedia** J. Bausch (*E. glutinosa* × *E.
lucida*) · ♄ e Z8 ⓚ; cult.
- × **nymansensis** J. Bausch (*E. cordifolia* ×
E. glutinosa) · ♄ e Z7; cult.
- *pinnatifolia* Gay = Eucryphia glutinosa

Eugenia L. -f- *Myrtaceae* · c. 1000 spp. ·
E:Stopper; F:Eugenia; G:Kirschmyrte
- *aromatica* (L.) Baill. = Syzygium
aromaticum
- *Braziliensis* Lam. = Eugenia dombeyi
- *caryophyllata* Thunb. = Syzygium
aromaticum
- *caryophyllus* (Spreng.) Bullock ex S.G.
Harrison = Syzygium aromaticum
- *cumini* (L.) Druce = Syzygium cumini
- **dombeyi** (Spreng.) Skeels · E:Brazil
Cherry; G:Brazilianische Kirschmyrte · ♄
e Z10 ⓚ ⓝ; Braz.
- *jambolana* Lam. = Syzygium cumini
- *jambos* L. = Syzygium jambos
- **klotzschiana** O. Berg · ♄ e Z10 ⓜ; Braz.
- *luma* (Molina) O. Berg = Luma apiculata
- *michelii* Lam. = Eugenia uniflora
- *myriophylla* Casar. = Myrciaria myriophylla
- *myrtifolia* Sims = Syzygium paniculatum
- *paniculata* (Banks ex Gaertn.) Britten =
Syzygium paniculatum
- *ugni* (Molina) Hook. & Arn. = Ugni
molinae
- **uniflora** L. · E:Surinam Cherry; G:Cayen-
nekirsche, Surinam-Kirchmyrte · ♄ ♄ e
Z10 ⓚ ⓝ; W.Ind., trop. S-Am.

Eulalia Kunth -f- *Poaceae* · c. 30 spp.
- *japonica* Trin. = Miscanthus sinensis

Eulophia R. Br. ex Lindl. -f- *Orchidaceae* ·
204 spp.
- **alta** (L.) Fawc. & Rendle · ♃ Z9 ⓜ IX-X
▽ ✳; trop. Am.
- **bouliawongo** (Rchb. f.) J. Raynal · ♃ Z9
ⓜ VI-VII ▽ ✳; Zaire, Angola
- *gigantea* (Welw. ex Rchb. f.) N.E. Br. =
Eulophia bouliawongo
- **guineensis** Lindl. · ♃ Z9 ⓜ VIII-IX ▽ ✳;
W-Afr., C-Afr., E-Afr., Angola
- *horsfallii* (Bateman) Summerh. =
Eulophia rosea
- *longifolia* (Kunth) Schltr. = Eulophia alta

- *porphyroglossa* (Rchb. f.) Bolus =
Eulophia rosea
- **rosea** (Lindl.) A.D. Hawkes · ♃ Z9 ⓜ X
▽ ✳; W-Afr., C-Afr., E-Afr., trop-Afr.

Eulophidium Pfitzer = Oeceoclades
- *maculatum* (Lindl.) Pfitzer = Oeceoclades
maculata

Eulophiella Rolfe -f- *Orchidaceae* · 5 spp.
- **elisabethae** Linden & Rolfe · ♃ Z10 ⓜ
IV-V ▽ ✳; Madag.
- *peetersiana* Kraenzl. = Eulophiella
roempleriana
- **roempleriana** (Rchb. f.) Schltr. · ♃ Z10
ⓜ IV-VI ▽ ✳; Madag.

Eulychnia Phil. -f- *Cactaceae* · 5 spp.
- **acida** Phil. · ♄ ♄ ⇂ Z9 ⓚ ▽ ✳; Chile
- **breviflora** Phil. · ♄ ♄ ⇂ Z9 ⓚ ▽ ✳; Chile
(Coquimbo)
- **castanea** Phil. · ♄ ⇂ Z9 ⓚ ▽ ✳; Chile
- *clavata* Phil. = Austrocactus spiniflorus
- **ritteri** Cullmann · ♄ ⇂ Z9 ⓚ ▽ ✳; Peru
- **saint-pieana** F. Ritter · ♄ ⇂ Z9 ⓚ ▽ ✳;
N-Chile

Euodia J.R. Forst. & G. Forst. -f- *Rutaceae* ·
6 spp.
- *daniellii* (Benn.) Hemsl. = Tetradium
daniellii
- **glauca** Miq. · ♄ d ⓚ VII; Jap., China,
Taiwan
- *henryi* Dode = Tetradium daniellii
- *hupehensis* Dode = Tetradium daniellii
- **officinalis** Dode · ♄ ♄ d Z6; C-China,
W-China

Euonymus L. -m- *Celastraceae* · 177 spp. ·
E:Spindle; F:Fusain; G:Pfaffenhütchen,
Spindelstrauch
- **alatus** (Thunb.) Siebold · E:Winged
Spindle; F:Fusain ailé; G:Flügel-Spindel-
strauch
- var. **alatus** · ♄ d Z4 V-VI ⚘; China,
Amur, Manch., Korea, Jap., Sakhal.
- var. **apterus** Regel · ♄ d Z3 ⚘
- **americanus** L.
- var. **americanus** · E:Strawberry Bush;
G:Amerikanischer Spindelstrauch · ♄ d
⚘ Z6 VI; USA: NE, NCE, SE, Fla., SC
- var. **angustifolius** (Pursh) A.W. Wood ·
♄ d Z6; USA: Ga.
- **atropurpureus** Jacq. · E:Bitter
Ash, Burning Bush, Wahoo;

G:Purpur-Spindelstrauch · ♄ ♄ d Z4 ⚕ ☠; Can.: Ont.; USA: NE, NCE, NC, Rocky Mts., SC, SE, Fla.
- **bungeanus** Maxim. · G:Bunges Spindelstrauch · ♄ d Z4 V ☠; Manch., N-China.
- **europaeus** L. · G:Pfaffenhütchen
- var. **europaeus** · E:Common Spindle; F:Bonnet de prêtre, Fusain d'Europe; G:Gewöhnliches Pfaffenhütchen · ♄ d ♣ Z4 V-VI ⚕ ☠ Ⓝ; Eur.*, Cauc., TR
- var. **intermedius** Gaudin · ♄ d Z3; SE-Eur.
- **fimbriatus** Wall. · ♄ d Z8 ⓚ; Him.
- **fortunei** (Turcz.) Hand.-Mazz.
- **many cultivars**
- var. **fortunei** · E:Dwarf Euonymus; F:Fusain du Japon; G:Kletternder Spindelstrauch · ♄ e Z6 ☠; W-China, C-China
- var. **radicans** (Siebold ex Miq.) Rehder · ♄ e ⌇ ⇝ Z6 ☠; Jap., Korea, Riukiu-Is.
- var. **vegetus** (Rehder) Rehder · ♄ e Z6 ☠; China
- **hamiltonianus** Wall.
- var. **hamiltonianus** · E:Hamilton's Spindle; G:Hamiltons Spindelstrauch · ♄ ♄ d Z4 ☠; Him.
- var. **hians** (Koehne) Blakelock Z4; China, Manch., Korea, Jap., Sakhal.
- var. **lanceifolius** (Loes.) Blakelock Z4; C-China, S-China
- var. **maackii** (Rupr.) Kom. · E:Maack's Spindle; G:Maacks Spindelstrauch · d Z4 ☠; N-China, Korea
- var. *nikoensis* (Nakai) Blakelock = Euonymus hamiltonianus var. sieboldianus
- var. **sieboldianus** (Blume) H. Hara · E:Siebold's Spindle; G:Siebolds Spindelstrauch · ♄ ♄ d Z4 V ☠; Korea, Jap.
- var. *yedoensis* (Koehne) Blakelock = Euonymus hamiltonianus var. sieboldianus
- **japonicus** Thunb. · E:Evergreen Euonymus, Japanese Euonymus; G:Japanischer Spindelstrauch · ♄ ♄ e Z8 ⓚ ∧ ☠ Ⓝ; Jap., Korea, Riukiu-Is.
- **many cultivars**
- **kiautschovicus** Loes. · ♄ e ⇝ Z6; C-China, E-China
- *lanceifolius* Loes. = Euonymus hamiltonianus var. lanceifolius
- **latifolius** (L.) Mill. · E:Broad Leaved Spindle; G:Breitblättriges Pfaffenhütchen · ♄ d Z6 V-VI ☠ Ⓝ; Eur.: Fr, Ital-P, C-Eur., ? EC-Eur., Ba, E-Eur.; TR, Cyprus, Syr., Cauc., N-Iran, Moroc., Alger., nat. in RO, Crim
- *maackii* Rupr. = Euonymus hamiltonianus var. maackii
- **myrianthus** Hemsl. · ♄ e Z9 ⓚ; W-China
- **nanus** M. Bieb.
- var. *koopmannii* (Lauche) Lauche ex Koehne = Euonymus nanus var. turcestanicus
- var. **nanus** · E:Dwarf Spindle; G:Zwerg-Spindelstrauch · ♄ e Z4 ☠; Eur.: RO, W-Russ; Cauc., C-As., W-China
- var. **turcestanicus** (Dieck) Krysht. · ♄ d Z4 V-VI ☠; C-As.; Altai, Tien-schan
- *nikoensis* Nakai = Euonymus hamiltonianus var. sieboldianus
- **obovatus** Nutt. · E:Running Strawberry Bush · ♄ d ⇝ Z3; Ont., USA: NE, NCE, Tenn.
- **oxyphyllus** Miq. · G:Spitzblättriger Spindelstrauch · ♄ d Z6 ☠; China, Korea, Jap.
- *patens* Rehder = Euonymus kiautschovicus
- **pauciflorus** Maxim. · ♄ d Z5 V-VI; Amur, Manch.
- **phellomanus** Loes. ex Diels · E:Cork Spindle Tree; G:Kork-Spindelstrauch · ♄ d Z6 ☠; W-China, N-China
- **planipes** (Koehne) Koehne · E:Dingle Dangle Tree; G:Flachstieliger Spindelstrauch · ♄ d ♣ Z5 V; Jap., Korea, Manch., Amur
- *radicans* Sieber ex Miq. = Euonymus fortunei var. fortunei
- *sachalinensis* auct. non (Schmidt) Maxim. = Euonymus planipes
- **sanguineus** Loes. ex Diels · G:Blut-Spindelstrauch · ♄ d ♣ Z6 V ☠; W-China, C-China
- *turcestanicus* Dieck = Euonymus nanus var. turcestanicus
- **verrucosus** Scop. · G:Warzen-Pfaffenhütchen · ♄ d Z5 V-VI ☠; Eur.: Ital-P, C-Eur., EC-Eur., Ba, E-Eur.; TR, Cauc.
- *yedoensis* Koehne = Euonymus hamiltonianus var. sieboldianus

Eupatorium L. -n- *Asteraceae* · 45 spp. · E:Hemp Agrimony, Thoroughwort; F:Eupatoire; G:Kunigundenkraut, Wasserdost
- *ageratoides* L. f. = Ageratina altissima
- **album** L. · E:White Thoroughwort · ♃ Z4 VIII-IX; USA: NE, SE, Fla.

– **altissimum** L. · E:Tall Thoroughwort;
G:Hoher Wasserdost · ⌃ Z4 IX-X; USA:
NE, NCE, NC, SC, SE
– *aromaticum* L. = Ageratina aromatica
– *atrorubens* (Lem.) G. Nicholson = Bartlettina sordida
– **cannabinum** L. · E:Hemp Agrimony;
F:Eupatoire chanvrine; G:Gewöhnlicher
Wasserdost, Wasserhanf · ⌃ Z5 VII-IX ⚥ ;
Eur.*, TR, Lebanon, Israel, Cauc., Iran, ?
Him., C-As., Moroc., Alger.
– *coelestinum* L. = Conoclinium coelestinum
– *glechonophyllum* Less. = Ageratina
glechonophylla
– *ianthinum* (Hook.) Hemsl. = Bartlettina
sordida
– *incarnatum* Walter = Fleischmannia
incarnata
– **indigoferum** D. Parodi · ♄ Ⓝ; S-Braz.,
Arg., Parag.
– *ligustrinum* DC. = Ageratina riparia
– **maculatum** L. · E:Joe Pye Weed;
F:Eupatoire maculée; G:Gefleckter
Wasserdost · ⌃ Z5 VII-IX; Can., USA: NE,
N.C., NCE, NC, Rocky Mts., SW
– **some cultivars**
– *megalophyllum* (Lem.) Hook. & Benth. ex
Klatt = Bartlettina sordida
– *micranthum* Less. = Ageratina riparia
– **perfoliatum** L. · E:Boneset, Common
Boneset, Thoroughwort; G:Durchwach-
sener Wasserdost · ⌃ Z3 VII-X ⚥ ; Can.: E;
USA: NE, NCE, SC, SE, Fla.
– **purpureum** L. · E:Joe Pye Weed;
G:Purpur-Wasserdost · ⌃ Z4 VII-IX ⚥ ;
USA: NE, NCE, NC, Okla., SE, Fla.
– *riparium* Regel = Ageratina riparia
– *rugosum* Houtt. = Ageratina altissima
– *scandens* L. = Mikania scandens
– **sessilifolium** L. · E:Upland Boneset · ⌃
Z5 VIII-IX; USA: NE, NCE, SE
– *sordidum* Less. = Bartlettina sordida
– *triplinerve* Vahl = Ayapana triplinervis
– *urticifolium* Reichard = Ageratina
altissima
– *vernale* Vatke & Kurtz = Ageratina
vernalis
– *weinmannianum* Regel & Körn. =
Ageratina riparia

Euphorbia L. -f- *Euphorbiaceae* · 1603 spp. ·
E:Spurge; F:Euphorbe; G:Wolfsmilch;
– **abyssinica** J.F. Gmel. · G:Abessinische
Wolfsmilch · ♄ ⌿ d Z10 ⓖ ⚘ ▽ ✳; Eth.
– **aggregata** A. Berger · E:Pincushion

Euphorbia; G:Nadelkissen-Wolfsmilch · ♄
⌿ Z8 ⓖ ▽ ✳; S-Afr.: Cape, Orange Free
State
– *alcicornis* hort. = Euphorbia ramipressa
– **alluaudi** Drake
– subsp. **alluaudi** · ♄ ♄ ⌿; ? Madag.
– subsp. **oncoclada** (Drake) F. Friedmann
& Cremers · ♄ ⌿ Z10 ⓖ ▽ ✳; Madag.
– **ammak** Schweinf. · ♄ ⌿ d Z10 ⓖ ▽ ✳;
S-Arab.
– **amygdaloides** L.
– subsp. **amygdaloides** · E:Wood Spurge;
F:Euphorbe faux-amandier; G:Man-
delblättrige Wolfsmilch · ⌃ Z7 IV-V ⚘;
Eur.* exc. Sc; TR, Cauc., N-Iran, Alger.,
Tun., nat. in N-Am.
– subsp. **robbiae** (Turrill) Stace · E:Mrs
Robb's Bonnet; G:Robb-Wolfsmilch · ⌃
Z7 V-VII; TR
– **angularis** Klotzsch · ♄ ⓖ ▽ ✳; E-Afr.
– **angulata** Jacq. · G:Kanten-Wolfsmilch ·
⌃ V-VI; Eur.: Ib, Fr, Ital-P, A, EC-Eur.,
E-Eur.
– **antiquorum** L. · E:Triangular Spurge · ♄
⌿ d Z10 ⓖ ▽ ✳; Ind., Sri Lanka
– **antisyphilitica** Zucc. · E:Candelilla;
G:Candelillawachs · ♄ ⌿ Z8 ⓖ Ⓝ ▽ ✳;
SW-USA, Mex., C-Am.
– **aphylla** Brouss. ex Willd. · ♄ ⌿ Z9 ⓖ ▽
✳; Canar.
– **atropurpurea** Brouss. · ♄ ⌿ Z9 ⓖ ▽ ✳;
Canar.: Tenerife
– *austriaca* A. Kern. = Euphorbia illirica
– **avasmontana** Dinter · ♄ ⌿ Z9 ⓖ ▽ ✳;
Cape, Namibia
– **balsamifera** Aiton · ♄ ⌿ Z9 ⓖ ▽ ✳;
Canar., W-Afr., Somalia, S-Arab.
– *barnhartii* Croizat = Euphorbia lacei
– *beaumieriana* Hook. f. & Coss. = Euphorbia officinarum subsp. officinarum
– **beharensis** Leandri · ♄ ⌿ Z10 ⓖ ▽ ✳;
SW-Madag.
– **bergeri** N.E. Br. · ⌃ ⌿ Z10 ⓖ ▽ ✳; ? Cape
– *bojeri* Hook. = Euphorbia milii var. milii
– **bubalina** Boiss. · E:Buffalo Euphorbia · ♄
⌿ Z9 ⓖ ▽ ✳; Cape
– **bupleurifolia** Jacq. · ♄ ⌿ Z8 ⓖ ▽ ✳;
S-Afr.: Cape, Natal
– **caerulescens** Haw. · E:Noors · ♄ ⌿ Z8 ⓖ
✳; Cape
– **canariensis** L. · ♄ ⌿ Z10 ⓖ ▽ ✳; Canar.
– **candelabrum** Kotschy · E:Candelabra
Tree; G:Kandelaber-Wolfsmilch · ♄ ⌿ Z9
ⓖ ▽ ✳; Mozam., Zimbabwe, Swasiland, S-Afr.: Transvaal. Natal

– var. *erythraeae* A. Berger = Euphorbia abyssinica
– **capitulata** Rchb. · G:Zierliche Rasen-Wolfsmilch · ⁴ △ Z7 VI-VII; Eur.: Croatia, Bosn., Montenegro, Maced., AL, GR
– **caput-medusae** L. · E:Medusa's Head; G:Medusenhaupt-Wolfsmilch · ⁴ ♄ Ψ Z8 ⊞ ▽ ✳; Cape
– var. *minor* Aiton = Euphorbia bergeri
– **carniolica** Jacq. · E:Carnian Spurge; G:Krainer Wolfsmilch · ⁴ Z6 VI; Eur.: I, Sw, Slove., Croatia, Bosn., YU, RO, W-Russ.
– **characias** L.
– subsp. **characias** · E:Large Mediterranean Spurge; G:Palisaden-Wolfsmilch · ⁴ Z7; Eur.: Ib, Fr, Ital-P; Moroc., Libya
– **some cultivars**
– subsp. **wulfenii** (Hoppe ex W.D.J. Koch) Radcl.-Sm. · F:Euphorbe characias · ⁴ Z7 V-VI; Eur.: F, I, Ba; TR
– **some cultivars**
– **clava** Jacq. · ♄ Ψ Z8 ⊞ ▽ ✳; Cape
– *commelinii* DC. = Euphorbia caput-medusae
– **cooperi** N.E. Br. ex A. Berger · E:Lesser Candelabra Tree · ♄ Ψ Z7 ▽ ✳; S-Afr.: Natal, Transvaal; Swasiland
– **corollata** L. · E:American Spurge, Flowering Spurge; G:Amerikanische Wolfsmilch · ⁴ Z5 VIII; Ont., USA: NE, NCE, NC, SC, SE, Fla.
– **cylindrifolia** Marn.-Lap. · ⁴ Ψ ⤳ Z10 ⊞ ▽ ✳; SE-Madag.
– **cyparissias** L. · E:Cypress Spurge; G:Zypressen-Wolfsmilch · ⁴ Z4 IV-V ✳; Eur.* exc. BrI, Sc, nat. in N-Am.
– **decaryi** Guillaumin
– var. **cap-saintemariensis** (Rauh) Cremers · ⁴ Ψ Z10 ⊞; Madag.
– var. **decaryi** · ⁴ Ψ Z10 ⊞ ▽ ✳; SE-Madag.
– **dendroides** L. · E:Tree Spurge, Woody Spurge · ♄ d Z8 ⊞ ▽ ✳; Eur.: Ib, Fr, Ital-P, Ba; TR, Palest., N-Afr.
– **dulcis** L. · E:Sweet Spurge; G:Haarfrüchtige Süße Wolfsmilch · ⁴ Z6 V; Eur.* exc. BrI, Sc, nat. in BrI
– *echinus* Hook. f. & Coss. = Euphorbia officinarum subsp. echinus
– **ephedroides** E. Mey. ex Boiss. · ♄ Ψ Z8 ⊞ ▽ ✳; Cape
– **epithymoides** L. · E:Cushion Spurge; F:Euphorbe dorée, Euphorbe polychrome; G:Bunte Wolfsmilch, Vielfarbige Wolfsmilch · ⁴ Z6 V-VI ✳; Eur.: C-Eur., EC-Eur., Ba, Ital-P, E-Eur.
– *erythraea* (A. Berger) N.E. Br. = Euphorbia abyssinica
– **esculenta** Marloth · ⁴ Ψ Z8 ⊞ ▽ ✳; Cape
– **esula** L.
– nothosubsp. **pseudovirgata** (Schur) Govaerts (*E. esula* subsp. *esula* × *E. esula* subsp. *tommasiniana*) · E:Twiggy Spurge; G:Schein-Ruten-Wolfsmilch · ⁴ Z6; Eur.:
– subsp. **esula** · E:Leafy Spurge, Wolf's Milk; G:Esels-Wolfsmilch · ⁴ Z5 V-VII ✳; Eur.*, nat. in Sib., Amur, Manch., Korea, Jap., N-Am.
– subsp. **tommasiniana** (Bertol.) Kuzmanov · G:Ruten-Wolfsmilch · ⁴ Z5 V-VII ✳; Eur.: I, Ba, Crim; TR
– **exigua** L. · E:Dwarf Spurge; G:Kleine Wolfsmilch · ⊙ VI-X ✳; Eur.*, TR, Levant, Canar., NW-Afr., nat. in Cauc., N-Iran
– **falcata** L. · E:Sickle Spurge; G:Sichel-Wolfsmilch · ⊙ VI-X ✳; Eur.* exc. BrI, Sc; TR, Levant, Cauc., SW-As., Pakist., N-Afr.
– var. *acuminata* (Lam.) St.-Amans = Euphorbia falcata
– **fasciculata** Thunb. · ⁴ Ψ Z8 ⊞ ▽ ✳; Cape
– **ferox** Marloth · ⁴ Ψ Z8 ⊞ ▽ ✳; Cape
– **fimbriata** Scop. · ⁴ Ψ Z8 ⊞ ▽ ✳; Cape
– **franckiana** A. Berger · ♄ Ψ Z8 ⊞ ▽ ✳; ? Cape
– *fructus-pini* Mill. = Euphorbia caput-medusae
– **fulgens** Karw. ex Klotzsch · E:Scarlet Plume; G:Korallenröschen, Leuchtende Wolfsmilch · ♄ ✕ Z10 ⊞ XII-I ✳; Mex.
– **globosa** (Haw.) Sims · ♄ Ψ Z8 ⊞ ▽ ✳; Cape
– **gorgonis** A. Berger · E:Gorgon's Head; G:Gorgonenhaupt-Wolfsmilch · ⁴ Ψ Z8 ⊞ ▽ ✳; Cape
– **grandicornis** Goebel · ♄ Ψ Z8 ⊞ ▽ ✳; E-Afr.: Kenya, Tanzania; S-Afr.: Natal
– **grandidens** Haw. · E:Large-toothed Euphorbia · ♄ ✕ d Z8 ⊞ ▽ ✳; Cape
– **griffithii** Hook. f. · E:Griffith's Spurge; F:Euphorbe de l'Himalaya; G:Griffiths Wolfsmilch · ⁴ Z5 V-VI; Bhutan, S-Tibet
– **helioscopia** L. · E:Sun Spurge, Wolf's Milk; G:Sonnwend-Wolfsmilch · ⊙ Z6 VI-X ✳; Eur.*, TR, Levant, Cauc., Iran, C-As., Him., W-Ind. (Nilgiris), N-Afr., nat. in Jap., China

– **heptagona** L. · ⍋ ⇈ Z8 ⬠ ▽ ✳; Cape
– *hermentiana* Lem. = Euphorbia trigona
– **heterophylla** L. · E:Japanese Poinsettia, Mexican Fire Plant; G:Poinsettien-Wolfsmilch · ☉ ☉ ⍋ ♄ Z7 VII-IX; USA: Ariz; trop. Am., nat. in USA: La., Tex.
– *hislopii* N.E. Br. = Euphorbia milii var. hislopii
– **horrida** Boiss. · ♄ ⇈ Z7 ⬠ ▽ ✳; S-Afr. (Cape)
– *humifusa* Willd. ex Schltr. = Chamaesyce humifusa
– *hystrix* Jacq. = Euphorbia loricata
– var. *viridis* hort. = Euphorbia pentagona
– **illirica** Lam. · G:Zottige Wolfsmilch · ⍋ V-VII; Eur.: A, D (Passau)
– **inconstantia** R.A. Dyer · ♄ ⇈ Z8 ⬠ ▽ ✳; Cape
– **ingens** E. Mey. ex Boiss. · E:Cactus Spurge; G:Kaktus-Wolfsmilch · ♄ ⇈ Z8 ⬠; S-Afr.: Natal, Transvaal, Swasiland, Mocamb., Zimbabwe
– *jacquiniiflora* Hook. = Euphorbia fulgens
– **jansenvillensis** Nel · ⍋ ⇈ Z8 ⬠ ▽ ✳; Cape
– *kalaharica* Marloth = Euphorbia avasmontana
– **lacei** Craib · ♄ ⇈ Z9 ⬠ ▽ ✳; Ind.
– **lactea** Haw. · E:Candelabra Spurge · ♄ ♄ ⇈ Z10 ⬟ ▽ ✳; Ind., Sri Lanka, Molucca
– *laro* Drake = Euphorbia tirucalli
– **lathyris** L. · E:Caper Spurge, Mole Plant; F:Euphorbe épurge; G:Kreuzblättrige Wolfsmilch · ☉ Z6 VI-VIII ⚉ ✖; Eur.: F, Ital-P, Ba; NW-Afr., nat. in Eur.: BrI, C-Eur., EC-Eur., RO, Ib, TR, Cauc., N-Am., C-Am., S-Am., China
– **ledienii** A. Berger · ♄ ⇈ Z8 ⬠ ▽ ✳; Cape
– **lignosa** Marloth · ♄ ⇈ d Z10 ⬠ ▽ ✳; Namibia
– × **lomi** Rauh (*E. lophogona* × *E. milii*) · ♄ ⇈ Z10 ⬟ ⬠); cult.
– **lophogona** Lam. · ♄ ⇈ Z10 ⬟ ⬠ ▽ ✳; Madag.
– **loricata** Lam. · ♄ ⇈ d Z7 ▽; S-Afr. (Cape Prov.)
– **lucida** Waldst. & Kit. · E:Shining Spurge; G:Glänzende Wolfsmilch · ⍋ V-VII ✖ ▽; Eur.: C-Eur., EC-Eur., Ba.; W-Sib., nat. in ne N-Am.
– *maculata* L. = Chamaesyce maculata
– **mammillaris** L. · E:Corncob Cactus; G:Mammilarien-Wolfsmilch · ♄ ⇈ Z8 ⬠ ▽ ✳; Cape
– **marginata** Pursh · E:Snow on the

Mountain; G:Schnee auf dem Berge, Weißrand-Wolfsmilch · ☉ ⟿ Z4 VII-X ✖; USA: Minn., NC, SC, Colo., N.Mex.
– *marlothii* Pax = Euphorbia monteiroi
– **mauritanica** L. · E:Jackal's Food, Yellow Milkbush; G:Milchbusch · ♄ ⇈ Z8 ⬠ ▽ ✳; Namibia, S-Afr.: Cape, Natal
– *medusae* Panz. = Euphorbia caput-medusae
– **meloformis** Aiton
– subsp. **meloformis** · E:Melon Spurge; G:Melonen-Wolfsmilch · ⍋ ⇈ Z8 ⬠ ▽ ✳; Cape
– subsp. **valida** (N.E. Br.) G.D. Rowley · ⍋ ⇈ Z8 ⬠ ▽ ✳; Cape
– **milii** Des Moul.
– var. **hislopii** (N.E. Br.) Ursch & Leandri · ♄ ⇈ Z10 ⬠ ✳; Madag.
– var. **milii** · E:Christ's Thorn, Crown of Thorns; G:Christusdorn · ♄ ⇈ △ Z10 ⬟ ⬠ ✖ ▽ ✳; Madag.
– **monteiroi** Hook. · ♄ ⇈ △ Z8 ⬠ ▽ ✳; Angola, Namibia, Botswana
– **myrsinites** L. · E:Blue Spurge; F:Euphorbe de Cors; G:Walzen-Wolfsmilch · ⍋ △ Z6 IV-VI; Eur.: Ib, Ital-P, Ba, RO, Crim; TR, Iran, C-As., nat. in CZ
– *neriifolia* hort. = Euphorbia undulatifolia
– **neriifolia** L. · E:Oleander Spurge; G:Oleander-Wolfsmilch · ♄ ♄ ⇈ e Z10 ⬟ ▽; Ind., Burma, Malay. Arch., N.Guinea, Pakistan
– **nicaeensis** All.
– subsp. **glareosa** (Pall. ex M. Bieb.) Radcl.-Sm. · G:Pannonische Wolfsmilch · ⍋ Z6 VI-VII; Eur.: EC-Eur., E-Eur., Crim; TR, Cauc
– subsp. **nicaeensis** · G:Nizza-Wolfsmilch · ⍋ Z6 V-VII; Eur.* exc. BrI, Sc; TR, Cauc., Moroc., Alger.
– *niciciana* Borbás ex Novák = Euphorbia seguieriana subsp. seguieriana
– **nivulia** Buch.-Ham. · E:Milkhedge · ♄ ♄ ⇈ e Z10 ⬟ ▽ ✳; Ind., Burma
– *nutans* Lag. = Chamaesyce nutans
– **obesa** Hook. f. · E:Baseball Cactus, Living Baseball; G:Lebender Baseball · ⍋ ⇈ Z8 ⬠ ▽ ✳; Cape
– **officinarum** L.
– subsp. **echinus** (Hook. f. & Coss.) Vindt · ♄ ⇈ Z8 ⬠ ▽ ✳; S-Moroc.
– subsp. **officinarum** · E:Official Spurge · ♄ ⇈ Z9 ⬠ ▭ ▽ ✳; Moroc.
– *oncoclada* Drake = Euphorbia alluaudii subsp. oncoclada

- **ornithopus** Jacq. · ♄ ⁀ d Z8 ☖ ⚘ ∇ ❋; Cape
- **palustris** L. · E:Marsh Spurge; F:Euphorbe des marais; G:Sumpf-Wolfsmilch · ⚃ Z5 V-VI ⚘ ∇; Eur.* exc. BrI; TR, Cauc., W-Sib.
- **paralias** L. · E:Sea Spurge; G:Strand-Wolfsmilch · ⚃ Z8 ☖; Eur.: Ib, Fr, Ital-P, Ba, RO, BrI; TR, Levant, Cauc., Macaron., N-Afr.
- *parvimamma* Boiss. = Euphorbia caput-medusae
- **patula** Mill. · ⚃ ⁀ Z8 ☖ ∇ ❋; Cape
- **pentagona** Haw. · ♄ ⁀ Z8 ☖ ∇ ❋; Cape
- **peplus** L.
- var. **minima** DC. · ⊙; S-Eur., TR
- var. **peplus** · E:Petty Spurge; G:Garten-Wolfsmilch · ⊙ VII-X ⚘; Eur.*, TR, Levant, Cauc., Iran, Canar., N-Afr., nat. in N-Am., Eth., Austr., NZ, Hawaii
- **platyphyllos** L. · E:Broad Spurge; G:Breitblättrige Wolfsmilch · ⊙ VII-VIII ⚘; Eur.: Ib, Fr, Ital-P., Ba, EC-Eur., E-Eur., C-Eur.; TR, Cauc.
- *polychroma* A. Kern. = Euphorbia epithymoides
- **polygona** Haw. · ♄ ⁀ Z8 ☖ ∇ ❋; Cape
- **procumbens** Mill. · ⚃ ⁀ Z7 ∇ ❋; Cape
- *prostrata* Aiton = Chamaesyce prostrata
- **pseudocactus** A. Berger · ♄ ⁀ Z8 ☖ ∇ ❋; S-Afr.: Natal
- *× pseudovirgata* (Schur) Soó = Euphorbia esula nothosubsp. pseudovirgata
- **pteroneura** A. Berger · ♄ ⁀ Z9 ⚑ ∇ ❋; Mex.
- *pugniformis* Boiss. = Euphorbia procumbens
- **pulcherrima** Willd. ex Klotzsch · E:Christmas Star, Lobster Plant, Mexican Flameleaf, Poinsettia; G:Poinsettie, Weihnachtsstern · ♄ e ⚶ Z9 ⚑ ⎕ XII ⚘; S-Mex., C-Am.
- **pulvinata** Maroth · ♄ ⁀ Z8 ☖ ∇ ❋; S-Afr.
- *quercifolia* hort. = Euphorbia undulatifolia
- **ramipressa** Croizat · ♄ ♄ ⁀ Z8 ☖ ∇ ❋; Madag.
- **resinifera** O. Berg · E:Resin Spurge; G:Harz-Wolfsmilch · ♄ ⁀ Z8 ☖ ✶ ∇ ❋; Moroc.
- *rhipsaloides* Lem. = Euphorbia tirucalli
- **rigida** M. Bieb. · G:Zweidrüsen-Wolfsmilch · ⚃ △ Z8 ∧ IV-VIII; Eur.: P, Ital-P, Ba, Crim; TR, Syr., Cauc., N-Iran, Moroc.
- *robbiae* Turrill = Euphorbia amygdaloides subsp. robbiae
- **royleana** Boiss. · ♄ ⁀ Z9 ☖ ∇ ❋; Him.
- **salicifolia** Host · G:Weidenblättrige Wolfsmilch · ⚃ V-VI ⚘; Eur.: C-Eur., EC-Eur., Ba, RO, W-Russ.
- *san-salvador* hort. = Euphorbia resinifera
- **saxatilis** Jacq. · E:Rock Spurge; G:Felsen-Wolfsmilch · ⚃ V-VI; Eur.: A, N-I, Slove., Croatia
- **schimperi** C. Presl · ⚃ ⁀ Z10 ☖ ∇ ❋; S-Arab.
- *schubei* Pax = Monadenium schubei
- **segetalis** L. · E:Corn Spurge; G:Saat-Wolfsmilch · ⊙ VI-VII ⚘; Eur.: Ib, Fr, Ital-P, ? Crete, Canar., nat. in C-Eur., EC-Eur., RO
- **seguieriana** Neck. · G:Steppen-Wolfsmilch
- subsp. **niciciana** (Borbás ex Novák) Rech. f. · F:Euphorbe de Gérard · ⚃ Z5 V-IX ⚘; Eur.: Ba; TR, Iran, Pakist.
- subsp. **seguieriana** · G:Gewöhnliche Steppen-Wolfsmilch · ⚃ Z5 VI-VIII ⚘; Eur.* exc. BrI, Sc; TR, Cauc., W-Sib., C-As.
- *serpens* Kunth = Chamaesyce serpens
- **sikkimensis** Boiss. · ⚃ Z6 VII-VIII; Bhutan, Sikkim
- **squarrosa** Haw. · ⚃ ⁀ Z9 ☖ ∇ ❋; Cape
- **stellata** Willd. · ⚃ ⁀ ☖ ∇ ❋; Cape
- **stellispina** Haw. · ⚃ ⁀ Z8 ☖ ∇ ❋; Cape
- **stenoclada** Baill. · ♄ ⁀ d Z10 ☖ ∇ ❋; Madag.
- **stricta** L. · E:Tintern Spurge, Upright Spurge; G:Steife Wolfsmilch · ⊙ Z6 VI-IX ⚘; Eur.* exc. Sc; TR, Cauc., Iran, C-As.
- **submammillaris** (A. Berger) A. Berger · ⚃ ⁀ Z8 ☖ ∇ ❋; Cape
- **susannae** Maroth · ⁀ Z7 ☖ ∇ ❋; S-Afr. (Cape Prov.)
- **taurinensis** All. · G:Turiner Wolfsmilch · ⊙ V-IX; Eur.: Ib, Fr, Ital-P, Ba, Crim; TR, Cauc., nat. in A, H
- **tetragona** Haw. · ♄ ⁀ d Z8 ☖ ∇ ❋; Cape
- **tirucalli** L. · E:Pencil Tree, Rubber Euphorbia; G:Latex-Wolfsmilch · ♄ ♄ ⁀ d Z8 ☖ Ⓝ ∇ ❋; E-Afr., S-Afr., Madag.
- **triangularis** Desf. · E:River Euphorbia · ♄ ⁀ d Z8 ☖ ∇ ❋; S-Afr.: Cape, Natal
- *tridentata* Lam. = Euphorbia patula
- **trigona** Mill. · E:Sudu · ♄ ♄ ⁀ s Z9 ☖ ∇ ❋; Namibia
- **tubiglans** Maroth ex R.A. Dyer · ⚃ ⁀ Z8 ☖ ∇ ❋; Cape

– *uncinata* DC. = Euphorbia stellata
– **undulatifolia** Janse · E:Wavy-leaved Spurge; G:Wachsblättrige Wolfsmilch · ♄ ♄ ⩋ e Z10 ⊕ ⊕ ▽ ✳; Ind.?
– *valida* N.E. Br. = Euphorbia meloformis subsp. valida
– *variegata* Sims = Euphorbia marginata
– **verrucosa** L. · G:Warzen-Wolfsmilch · ⁴ V-VI ✾; Eur.: Ib, Fr, Ital-P, C-Eur., EC-Eur., Ba, RO
– **viguieri** Denis · ♄ ⩋ Z10 ⊕ ▽ ✳; W-Madag.
– *villosa* Waldst. & Kit. ex Willd. = Euphorbia illirica
– *viminalis* L. = Sarcostemma viminale
– *virgata* Waldst. & Kit. = Euphorbia esula subsp. tommasiniana
– **virosa** Willd. · ♄ ⩋ Z9 ⊕ ▽ ✳; Cape, Namibia
– *waldsteinii* (Soják) Radcl.-Sm. = Euphorbia esula subsp. tommasiniana
– *wulfenii* Hoppe ex W.D.J. Koch = Euphorbia characias subsp. wulfenii
– **xylophylloides** Brongn. ex Lem. · ♄ ♄ ⩋ d Z10 ⊕ ▽ ✳; Madag.

Euphrasia L. -f- Scrophulariaceae · c. 450 spp. · E:Eyebright; F:casse-lunette, Euphraise; G:Augentrost
– **alpina** Lam. · E:Alpine Euphrasia · ☉; Eur.: sp., F, I, Sw; Pyr., Alp., Apenn.
– *arctica* Lange ex Rostr. = Euphrasia stricta
– **borealis** (F. Towns.) Wettst. · ☉; Eur.: BrI, Norw.
– **christii** Favrat · ☉; Eur.: N-I, S-Sw
– **cisalpina** Pugsley · ☉; Eur.: NW-I, S-Sw
– **dunensis** Wimm. · G:Dünen-Augentrost · ☉; Eur.: DK
– **frigida** Pugsley · G:Nordischer Augentrost · ☉; Eur.: Sc, Russ; Sib., Can.: E; Greenl.
– **hirtella** Jord. ex Reut. · G:Zottiger Augentrost · ☉ VI-IX; Eur.: Ib, Fr, Ital-P, C-Eur., Ba, EC-Eur. +; mts.
– **inopinata** Ehrend. & Vitek · ☉; Eur.: A (Salzburg, Tirol)
– *kerneri* Wettst. = Euphrasia officinalis subsp. kerneri
– **micrantha** Rchb. · E:Northern Euphrasia; G:Schlanker Augentrost · ☉ VI-IX; Eur.* exc. Ba
– **minima** Jacq. ex DC. · E:Dwarf Euphrasia; G:Drüsiger Augentrost, Niedlicher Augentrost, Zwerg-Augentrost · ☉ VII-IX;

Eur.* exc. BrI, Sc
– **nemorosa** (Pers.) Wallr. · G:Hain-Augentrost
– subsp. **coerulea** (Hoppe & Fürnr.) Wettst. · G:Blauer Augentrost, Blauer Hain-Augentrost · V-VIII; Eur.: EC-Eur., RO, W-Russ., ? D
– subsp. *curta* Hoppe & Fürnr. = Euphrasia nemorosa subsp. nemorosa
– subsp. **nemorosa** · G:Bläulicher Augentrost, Gewöhnlicher Hain-Augentrost · ☉ VI-X; Eur.* exc. Ital-P, Ba
– **officinalis** L. · G:Augentrost
– subsp. **kerneri** (Wettst.) Eb. Fisch. · G:Kerners Augentrost · Z6 V-X; C-Eur., SE-Eur. ; mts.
– subsp. **officinalis** · E:Eufragia, Eufrasia, Eyebright, Gozlukotu; G:Gewöhnlicher Augentrost · ☉ Z6 V-X 𝄃 Ⓝ; Eur.*
– subsp. **picta** (Wimm.) Oborný · G:Bunter Augentrost · Z6; Eur.: Vosges, Alp., Carp.
– subsp. **rostkoviana** (Hayne) F. Towns. · E:Common Euphrasia; G:Großblütiger Augentrost · Z6 V-X; Eur.*, TR, W-Sib.
– *pectinata* Ten. = Euphrasia stricta
– *rostkoviana* Hayne = Euphrasia officinalis subsp. rostkoviana
– **salisburgensis** Funck ex Hoppe · G:Salzburger Augentrost · ☉ VII-X; Eur.*, TR
– **sinuata** Vitek & Ehrend. · G:Buchten-Augentrost · ☉; Eur.: A
– **stricta** D. Wolff ex J.F. Lehm. · E:Glossy Euphrasia; G:Kamm-Augentrost, Niedriger Augentrost, Steifer Augentrost, Tatarischer Augentrost, Zarter Augentrost · ☉ VI-X; Eur.* exc. BrI
– **tricuspidata** L. · G:Gewöhnlicher Dreispitziger Augentrost · ☉ VII-IX; Eur.: I ; SE-Alp.

Eupritchardia Kuntze = Pritchardia
– *gaudichaudii* (Mart.) Kuntze = Pritchardia martii
– *pacifica* (Seem. & H. Wendl. ex H. Wendl.) Kuntze = Pritchardia pacifica

Euptelea Siebold & Zucc. -f- Eupteleaceae · 2 spp. · F:Euptéléa; G:Schönulme
– *franchetii* Tiegh. = Euptelea pleiosperma
– **pleiosperma** Hook. f. & Thomson · G:Franchets Schönulme · ♄ d Z7; Him., SE-Tibet, C-China
– **polyandra** Siebold & Zucc. · G:Vielmännige Schönulme · ♄ d Z7; Jap.

× **Eurachnis** hort. -f- *Orchidaceae* (*Arachnis* × *Euanthe*)

Eurya Thunb. -f- *Theaceae* · c.70 spp. · F:Eurya; G:Sperrstrauch
- **japonica** Thunb. · G:Japanischer Sperrstrauch · ħ ŧ e Z9 Ⓚ; Ind., Sri Lanka, China, Korea, Taiwan, Jap., Malay. Arch., Fiji
- *latifolia* hort. = Cleyera japonica
- *ochnacea* (DC.) Szyszyl. = Cleyera japonica

Euryale Salisb. -f- *Nymphaeaceae* · 1 sp. · E:Fox Nuts; F:Euryale, Nénuphar épineux; G:Stachelseerose
- **ferox** Salisb. ex K.D. Koenig & Sims · E:Foxnuts; G:Stachelseerose · ♃ ≈ Z8 Ⓦ VI-VIII ⚕ Ⓝ; N-Ind., China, Jap., Taiwan

Euryangium Kauffm. = Ferula
- *sumbul* Kauffm. = Ferula moschata

Euryops (Cass.) Cass. -m- *Asteraceae* · 97 spp. · F:Marguerite dorée; G:Goldmargerite
- **abrotanifolius** DC. · G:Eberrauten-Goldmargerite · ħ e Z9 Ⓚ; S-Afr.
- **acraeus** M.D. Hend. · ħ e Z8 Ⓐ V-VI; S-Afr.
- **athanasiae** (L. f.) Less. · ħ e Z9 Ⓚ III-IV; S-Afr.
- **chrysanthemoides** (DC.) B. Nord. · E:Bull's Eye · ħ e Z9 Ⓚ IV-IX; S-Afr.
- **evansii** Schltr. · G:Evans Kapmargerite · ħ e Z9 Ⓐ V-VI; S-Afr.
- **pectinatus** (L.) Cass. · ħ e Z8 Ⓚ V-VI; S-Afr.
- **tenuissimus** (L.) DC. · E:Resin Bush; G:Zarte Kapmargerite · ħ e Z9 Ⓚ V-IX; Cape
- **virgineus** (L. f.) DC. · ħ e Z9 Ⓚ III-IV; S-Afr.

Eusideroxylon Teijsm. & Binn. -f- *Lauraceae* · 2 spp. · E:Ironwood
- *laurifolia* (Blanco) J. Schultze-Motel = Eusideroxylon zwageri
- **zwageri** (Teijsm.) Binn. · ħ Ⓦ Ⓝ; S-Sumat., Kalimantan, Phil.

Eustoma Salisb. -n- *Gentianaceae* · 3 spp. · F:Gentiane de la Prairie; G:Prärieenzian
- **grandiflorum** (Raf.) Shinners · E:Texas Bluebell, Tulip Gentian; G:Bauchblume, Großblütiger Prärieenzian · ⊙ ✂ Z9 Ⓚ VII-VIII; USA: NC, SC, Colo., N-Mex.
- **some cultivars**

Eutaxia R. Br. -f- *Fabaceae* · 8 spp. · E:Bush Pea; F:Eutaxia; G:Eutaxie, Straucherbse
- **myrtifolia** R. Br. · ħ e Z9 Ⓚ III-IV; W-Austr.

Euterpe Mart. -f- *Arecaceae* · 7 spp.
- **edulis** Mart. · E:Assai Palm; G:Assaipalme · ħ e Z10 Ⓚ; Braz., Arg.
- **oleracea** Mart. · ħ e Z10 Ⓦ Ⓝ; Venez., Guyan., Braz.

Eutrema R. Br. -n- *Brassicaceae* · 15 spp.
- **edwardsii** R. Br. · ♃; N-As.
- *wasabi* (Siebold) Maxim. = Wasabia japonica

Evolvulus L. -m- *Convolvulaceae* · 98 spp. · E:Dwarf Morning Glory
- **arbusculus** Poir. · ħ ⌇ Ⓦ I-XII; Hispaniola (Dominican. Rep.)
- **glomeratus** Nees & Mart.
- subsp. **glomeratus** · ħ Z8 Ⓦ; Braz.
- subsp. **grandiflorus** (D. Parodi) Ooststr. · ħ ⌇ Z8 Ⓦ I-XII; S-Braz., Parag., Arg.
- **purpureocoeruleus** Hook. · ♃ ⇝ Ⓦ VI-VIII; Jamaica

Exacum L. -n- *Gentianaceae* · c. 60 spp. · F:Violette allemande; G:Bitterblatt
- **affine** Balf. f. ex Regel · E:German Violet, Tiddly Winks; G:Blaues Lieschen · ⊙ Z9 Ⓚ VII-IX; Socotra

Excoecaria L. -f- *Euphorbiaceae* · 38 spp.
- *bicolor* (Hassk.) Zoll. ex Hassk. = Excoecaria cochinchinensis
- **cochinchinensis** Lour. · ħ e Ⓦ ☠; S-Vietn.

Exochorda Lindl. -f- *Rosaceae* · 4 spp. · E:Pearlbush; F:Exochorda; G:Blumenspiere, Radspiere
- **giraldii** Hesse
- var. **giraldii** · E:Pearl Bush; F:Exochorde; G:Dahurische Radspiere · ħ d Z5; C-China
- var. **wilsonii** (Rehder) Rehder · F:Exochorde · ħ d Z5 IV-V; C-China
- *grandiflora* Lindl. = Exochorda racemosa

- **korolkowii** Lavallée · G:Turkestanische Radspiere · ♄ d Z6 V; C-As.
- × **macrantha** (Lemoine) C.K. Schneid. (*E. korolkowii* × *E. racemosa*) · E:Pearl Bush; G:Perlen-Radspiere · ♄ d Z5 V; cult.
- **racemosa** (Lindl.) Rehder · E:Common Pearl Bush; F:Exochorde à grandes fleurs; G:Chinesische Radspiere · ♄ d Z5 V; E-China

Exogonium Choisy = Ipomoea
- *purga* (Wender.) Benth. = Ipomoea purga

Faba Mill. = Vicia
- *vulgaris* Moench = Vicia faba var. faba

Fabiana Ruiz & Pav. -f- *Solanaceae* · 25 spp. · F:Fabiana; G:Fabiane
- **imbricata** Ruiz & Pav. · E:Pichi; G:Falsche Heide · ♄ e Z8 ⊠ ⌂ ❦ ✄; S-Peru, Chile, Arg.

Facheiroa Britton & Rose -f- *Cactaceae* · 3 spp.
- *blossfeldiorum* (Engelm.) W.T. Marshall = Espostoa blossfeldiorum
- **ulei** (Gürke) Werderm. · ♄ Z9; E-Braz.

Fadyenia Hook. -f- *Dryopteridaceae* · 1 sp.
- **prolifera** Hook. · ♃ ⤳ Z10 ⊛; W.Ind.

Fagopyrum Mill. -n- *Polygonaceae* · 8 spp. · E:Buckwheat; F:Blé noir, Sarrasin; G:Buchweizen
- *convolvulus* (L.) H. Gross = Fallopia convolvulus
- **esculentum** Moench · E:Buckwheat; G:Echter Buchweizen · ☉ VII-X ❦ ⊛; C-As., S-Sib., N-China, nat. in Eur.*
- *sagittatum* Gilib. = Fagopyrum esculentum
- **tataricum** (L.) G. Gaertn. · E:Tatary Buckwheat; G:Falscher Buchweizen, Tatarischer Buchweizen · ☉ VII-IX ⊛; Russ., Cauc., W-Sib., E-Sib., Amur, Pakist., Him., Tibet, China
- *vulgare* Delarbre = Fagopyrum esculentum

Fagraea Thunb. -f- *Loganiaceae* · 35 spp.
- **fragrans** Roxb. · ♄ e Z10 ⊛ ⊛; Malay. Arch.

Fagus L. -f- *Fagaceae* · 10 spp. · E:Beech; F:Hêtre; G:Buche

- *americana* Sweet = Fagus grandifolia
- **crenata** Blume · E:Japanese Beech; G:Gekerbte Buche · ♄ d Z6 ⊛; Jap.
- **engleriana** Seemen ex Diels · E:Engler's Beech; F:Hêtre de Chine; G:Englers Buche · ♄ d Z6; C-China
- *ferruginea* Aiton = Fagus grandifolia
- **grandifolia** Ehrh. · E:American Beech; F:Hêtre d'Amérique; G:Amerikanische Buche · ♄ d Z4 ⊛; Can.: E; USA: NE, NCE, SE, Fla., SC
- *japonica* Maxim. · E:Japanese Blue Beech; G:Japanische Buche · ♄ d Z5; Jap.
- *macrophylla* (Hohen. ex DC.) Koidz. = Fagus orientalis
- × *moesiaca* (K. Malý) Czeczott = Fagus × taurica
- **orientalis** Lipsky · E:Oriental Beech; F:Hêtre d'Orient; G:Orient-Buche · ♄ d Z6; Eur.: Ba, Ro, Crim; TR, Cauc., N-Iran
- *sieboldii* Endl. ex A. DC. = Fagus crenata
- **sylvatica** L. · E:Beech, Common Beech, European Beech; F:Fayard, Hêtre commun; G:Rot-Buche · ♄ d Z5 IV-V ❦ ⊛; Eur.*, TR
- **many cultivars**
- subsp. *orientalis* (Lipsky) Greuter & Burdet = Fagus orientalis
- × **taurica** Popl. (*F. orientalis* × *F. sylvatica*) · ♄ d Z5; Eur.: BG, GR, Crim

Faidherbia A. Chev. -f- *Mimosaceae* · 1 sp. · E:Winterthorn; G:Anabaum
- **albida** (Delile) A. Chev. · E:Anatree, Winterthorn; G:Anabaum · ♄ ⊛ ⊛; Senegal to Namibia

Falcaria Fabr. -f- *Apiaceae* · 1 sp. · E:Longleaf; F:Falcaire; G:Sichelmöhre
- **vulgaris** Bernh. · E:Sickleweed; G:Sichelmöhre · ☉ ♃ VII-IX; Eur.: Ib, Fr, EC-Eur., Ital-P, Ba, E-Eur., A, Sw ; TR, SW-As., C-As., nat. in BrI, Sc, N-Am., S-Am.

Falkia L. f. -f- *Convolvulaceae* · 3 spp.
- **repens** L. f. · ♃ ⤳ ⊠ V-VIII; S-Afr.

Fallopia Adans. -f- *Polygonaceae* · 12 spp. · E:Knotweed; F:Renouée grimpante; G:Flügelknöterich
- *aubertii* (L. Henry) Holub = Fallopia baldschuanica
- **baldschuanica** (Regel) Holub · E:Mile-a-Minute Plant, Russian Vine;

G:Schling-Flügelknöterich, Silberregen
· ♄ ʃ d ⚥ Z5 VIII-X; C-As.: Tajik., nat. in
BrI, sp., A, EC-Eur., RO
– × **bohemica** (Chrtek & Chrtková) J.P.
Bailey (*F. japonica × F. sachalinensis*) ·
G:Bastard-Flügelknöterich · ♃ ; C-Eur.+
– **convolvulus** (L.) Á. Löve · E:Black
Bindweed; G:Acker-Flügelknöterich ·
⊙ ♃ ⚥ VIII-X; Eur.*, TR, Levant, Cauc.,
Iran, W-Sib., E-Sib., Amur, Sakhal.,
Kamchat., C-As., Mong., N-Afr., nat. in
N-Am., S-Afr.
– **dumetorum** (L.) Holub · E:Desert
Knotgrass; G:Hecken-Flügelknöterich · ⊙
⚥ VII-IX; Eur.*, TR, Cauc., Iran, W-Sib.,
E-Sib., Amur, Sakhal., C-As., Afgh., Him.,
Mong., Manch., N-China, Korea
– **japonica** (Houtt.) Ronse Decr. ·
E:Japanese Knotweed; G:Japanischer
Flügelknöterich
– var. **compacta** (Hook. f.) J.P. Bailey ·
G:Kleiner Japanischer Flügelknöterich ·
♃ Z4 VIII-X ⚥
– var. **japonica** · G:Gewöhnlicher Japa-
nischer Flügelknöterich · ♃ Z4 VII-IX;
Jap., nat. in Eur.*
– **multiflora** (Thunb.) K. Haraldson ·
E:Chinese Fleeceflower; G:Chinesischer
Flügelknöterich · ♃ ⚥ Z7 ∧ IX-X ⚥ ;
China
– **sachalinensis** (F. Schmidt) Ronse Decr. ·
E:Giant Knotweed; F:Renouée des
Sakhalines; G:Sachalin-Flügelknöterich ·
♃ Z4 VII-X; Jap., Sakhal., nat. in Eur.

Fallugia Endl. -f- *Rosaceae* · 1 sp. ·
E:Apache Plume; F:Plume des Apaches;
G:Apachenpflaume
– **paradoxa** (D. Don) Endl. · E:Apache
Plume; G:Apachenpflaume · ♄ d ⚥ Z7 ∧
VI-VIII ⓝ; USA: Tex., Colo., Nev., Utah,
Calif.; N-Mex.

Farfugium Lindl. -n- *Asteraceae* · 2 spp.
– *grande* Lindl. = Farfugium japonicum
– **japonicum** (L.) Kitam. · E:Leopard Plant;
G:Leopardenpflanze · ♃ ⓚ IX-X; Jap.

Fargesia Franch. -f- *Poaceae* · 83 spp. ·
E:Fountain Bamboo; F:Bambou;
G:Schirmbambus
– **murielae** (Gamble) T.P. Yi · E:Muriel
Bamboo; G:Muriels Schirmbambus · ♄ e
Z6; W-Him.
– **nitida** (Mitford) Keng f. · E:Fountain

Bamboo; G:Fontänen-Schirmbambus · ♄
e Z6; W-China, C-China
– **spathacea** Franch. · E:Chinese Fountain
Bamboo

Farsetia Turra -f- *Brassicaceae* · 20 spp.
– **aegyptica** Turra · ♄ Z8; N-Sudan

Fascicularia Mez -f- *Bromeliaceae* · 2 spp.
– **bicolor** (Ruiz & Pav.) Mez · ♃ Z8 ⓚ;
Chile
– **kirchhoffiana** (Wittm.) Mez · ♃ Z8 ⓚ;
Chile
– *pitcairniifolia* (B. Verl.) Mez = Ochagavia
litoralis

× **Fatshedera** Guillaumin -f- *Araliaceae* ·
F:Fatshédéra; G:Efeuaralie (*Fatsia* ×
Hedera)
– **lizei** (Cochet) Guillaumin (*Fatsia
japonica* 'Moseri' × *Hedera hibernica*) ·
E:Aralia Ivy; G:Efeuaralie · ♄ e Z8 ⓚ;
cult.

Fatsia Decne. & Planch. -f- *Araliaceae* ·
3 spp. · E:Fatsi; F:Fatsia; G:Fatsie,
Zimmeraralie
– **japonica** (Thunb.) Decne. & Planch. ·
E:Glossy-leaved Paper Plant, Japanese
Fatsia; G:Zimmeraralie · ♄ e Z8 ⓦ ⚘;
Jap., Ryukyu-Is., S-Korea

Faucaria Schwantes -f- *Aizoaceae* ·
8 spp. · E:Tiger Jaws; F:Gueule-de-tigre;
G:Rachenblatt, Tigerschlund
– **bosscheana** (A. Berger) Schwantes · ♃ ⵜ
Z9 ⓚ; Cape
– **britteniae** L. Bolus · ⵜ Z9 ⓚ; S-Afr.
(Cape: Albany Distr.)
– **felina** (Weston) Schwantes ex H.
Jacobsen · ♃ ⵜ Z9 ⓚ; Cape
– *grandis* L. Bolus = Faucaria britteniae
– *lupina* (Haw.) Schwantes = Faucaria
felina
– **tigrina** (Haw.) Schwantes · E:Tiger Jaw;
G:Tiger-Rachenblatt, Tigerrachen · ♃ ⵜ
Z9 ⓚ; Cape
– **tuberculosa** (Rolfe) Schwantes · ♃ ⵜ Z9
ⓚ; Cape

Fedia Gaertn. -f- *Valerianaceae* · 3 spp. ·
E:African Valerian; F:Corne d'abondance,
Valériane africaine; G:Afrikanischer
Baldrian
– **cornucopiae** (L.) Gaertn. · E:Horn of

Plenty; G:Afrikanischer Baldrian · ⊙ VII-VIII; Eur.: Ib, F, Ital-P, GR, Crete; N-Afr.

Feijoa O. Berg = Acca
– *sellowiana* (O. Berg) O. Berg = Acca sellowiana

Felicia Cass. -f- *Asteraceae* · 83 spp. · E:Blue Daisy, Blue Margeruite; F:Aster du Cap; G:Kapaster
– **amelloides** (L.) Voss · E:Blue Marguerite; F:Marguerite du Cap; G:Blaue Kapaster · ⵁ ♄ Z9 ⌂ I-XII; S-Afr.
– **amoena** (Sch. Bip.) Levyns · G:Liebliche Klapaster · ⊙ ⊙ ⵁ Z9 VIII-IX; S-Afr.
– **bergeriana** (Spreng.) O. Hoffm. ex Zahlbr. · E:Kingfisher Daisy; G:Eisvogel-Kapaster · ⊙ Z9 VII-VIII; S-Afr.
– **fruticosa** (L.) G. Nicholson · E:Shrub Aster; G:Buschige Kapaster · ♄ e Z9 ⌂; S-Afr.: Cape, Transvaal
– **heterophylla** (Cass.) Grau · ⊙ Z9 ⌂ VI-VIII; W-Cape
– *pappei* (Harv.) Hutch. = Felicia amoena
– **tenella** (L.) Nees · ⊙ ⊙ ⵁ Z9 ⌂ VII-VIII; S-Afr.
– **uliginosa** (J.M. Wood & M.S. Evans) Grau · ⵁ Z9 ⌂; S-Afr.

Fendlera Engelm. & A. Gray -f- *Hydrangeaceae* · 2-3 spp.
– **rupicola** A. Gray · E:Cliff Fendlerbush · ♄ d △ Z7 ⌂ ∧ V; USA: Colo., SW
– **wrightii** (A. Gray) A. Heller · E:Wright's Fendlerbush · ♄ d Z7 ∧; SW-USA, Tex., NW-Mex.

Fenestraria N.E. Br. -f- *Aizoaceae* · 1 sp. · G:Fensterblatt
– *aurantiaca* N.E. Br. = Fenestraria rhopalophylla subsp. aurantiaca
– **rhopalophylla** (Schltr. & Diels) N.E. Br.
– subsp. **aurantiaca** (N.E. Br.) H.E.K. Hartmann · E:Baby's Toes · ⵁ ♀ Z10 ⌂; Cape
– subsp. **rhopalophylla** · ⵁ ♀ Z10 ⌂; Cape

Fenzlia Benth. = Linanthus
– *dianthiflora* Benth. = Linanthus dianthiflorus

Ferocactus Britton & Rose -m- *Cactaceae* · 23 spp.
– *acanthodes* (Lem.) Britton & Rose = Ferocactus cylindraceus

– **chrysacanthus** (Orcutt) Britton & Rose · ♀ Z10 ⌂ ▽ ✳; N-Mex.: Isla Cedros
– *covillei* Britton & Rose = Ferocactus emoryi
– **cylindraceus** (Engelm.) Orcutt · E:Compass Barrel Cactus · ♀ Z10 ⌂ ▽ ✳; Mex.: Baja Calif., Sonora
– **echidne** (DC.) Britton & Rose · ♀ Z10 ⌂ ▽ ✳; N-Mex.
– **emoryi** (Engelm.) Orcutt · E:Emory's Barrel Cactus
– **flavovirens** (Scheidw.) Britton & Rose · ♀ Z10 ⌂ ▽ ✳; S-Mex.
– **fordii** (Orcutt) Britton & Rose · ♀ Z10 ⌂ ▽ ✳; NW-Mex.
– **glaucescens** (DC.) Britton & Rose · ♀ Z10 ⌂ ▽ ✳; E-Mex.
– **gracilis** H.E. Gates · ♀ Z10 ⌂ ▽ ✳; NW-Mex.
– **hamatacanthus** (Muehlenpf.) Britton & Rose · E:Turk's Head · ♀ Z10 ⌂ ▽ ✳; USA: N.Mex., Tex.; NE-Mex.
– **histrix** (DC.) G.E. Linds. · ♀ Z10 ⌂ ▽ ✳; C-Mex.
– *horridus* Britton & Rose = Ferocactus peninsulae
– **latispinus** (Haw.) Britton & Rose · E:Devil's Tongue · ♀ Z10 ⌂ ▽ ✳; Mex.
– **macrodiscus** (Mart.) Britton & Rose · ♀ Z10 ⌂ ▽ ✳; Mex.: Guanajuato, Oaxaca
– *melocactiformis* DC. = Ferocactus histrix
– *orcuttii* (Engelm.) Britton & Rose = Ferocactus viridescens
– **peninsulae** (F.A.C. Weber) Britton & Rose · ♀ Z10 ⌂ ▽ ✳; Mex.: Baja Calif.
– **pilosus** (Salm-Dyck) Werderm. · ♀ Z10 ⌂ ▽ ✳; N-Mex.
– **pottsii** (Salm-Dyck) Backeb. · ♀ Z10 ⌂ ▽ ✳; Mex.: Sonora, Chihuahua, Sinaloa
– **robustus** (Pfeiff.) Britton & Rose · ♀ Z10 ⌂ ▽ ✳; Mex.: Puebla
– *setispinus* (Engelm.) L.D. Benson = Thelocactus setispinus
– *stainesii* (Salm-Dyck) Britton & Rose = Ferocactus pilosus
– *victoriensis* (Rose) Backeb. = Ferocactus echidne
– **viridescens** (Torr. & A. Gray) Britton & Rose · E:Small Barrel Cactus · ♀ Z10 ⌂ ▽ ✳; S-Calif., Baja Calif.
– **wislizeni** (Engelm.) Britton & Rose · E:Candy Barrel Cactus · ♀ Z10 ⌂ ▽ ✳; Mex.: Sonora, Chihuahua, Sinaloa, Durango

Feronia Corrêa = Limonia
– *elephantum* Corrêa = Limonia acidissima
– *limonia* (L.) Swingle = Limonia acidissima

Ferraria Burm. ex Mill. -f- *Iridaceae* · 11 sp.
– **crispa** Burm. · ⁴ Z9 ⓐ III-IV; Cape, nat. in Mallorca
– *undulata* L. = Ferraria crispa

Ferula L. -f- *Apiaceae* · 172 spp. · E:Giant Fennel; F:Férule ; G:Riesenfenchel, Steckenkraut
– **asafoetida** L. · ⁴ Z8 ⓐ ⋀ VII-VIII ⚥ ⚘ Ⓝ; C-As., Iran, Afgh.
– **communis** L. · E:Giant Fennel; G:Riesenfenchel, Steckenkraut · ⁴ Z8 ⓐ ⋀ VII-VIII Ⓝ; Eur.: Ib, Fr, Ital-P, Ba, Canar.; TR, Cyprus, Lebanon, N-Afr.
– **foetida** (Bunge) Regel · G:Stinkasant · ⁴ Z8 ⓐ Ⓝ; C-As.
– *galbaniflua* Boiss. & Buhse = Ferula gummosa
– **gummosa** Boiss. · ⁴ Z8 ⚥ Ⓝ; Iran, C-As. (Kopet Dagh)
– *hispanica* Rouy = Ferula tingitana
– **moschata** (Reinsch) Koso-Pol. · E:Musk Root · ⁴ ; C-As.
– **narthex** Boiss. · ⁴ Z8 ⓐ ⋀ VII-VIII ⚥ Ⓝ; NW-Him.
– **rubricaulis** Boiss. · ⁴ ; W-As.
– *sumbul* (Kauffm.) Hook. f. = Ferula moschata
– **tingitana** L. · ⁴ Z8 ⓐ ⋀ VII-VIII; Eur.: Ib; N-Afr.

Ferulago W.D.J. Koch -f- *Apiaceae* · c. 45 spp. · F:Férule bâtarde, Petite férule; G:Birkwurz
– **galbanifera** (Mill.) W.D.J. Koch · G:Knotenblütige Birkwurz · ⁴ Z6; Eur.: F, Ital-P, Ba, E-Eur.; Cauc.

Festuca L. -f- *Poaceae* · 300-500 spp. · E:Fescue; F:Fétuque; G:Schwingel
– *acerosa* K. Koch = Festuca punctoria
– **acuminata** Gaudin · G:Zugespitzter Schwingel · ⁴ VII-VIII; Eur.: F, I, SW; Alp.
– **airoides** Lam. · G:Kleiner Schaf-Schwingel · ⁴ VI-VII; Eur.* exc. BrI, Sc; mts.
– **alpestris** Roem. & Schult. · G:Südalpen-Buntschwingel · ⁴ △ VII-VIII; Eur.: I, Slove.; SE-Alp.
– **alpina** Suter · G:Alpen-Schwingel · ⁴ △

VI-VIII; Eur.: F, I, C-Eur., Ba; Pyr., Alp., Balkan
– **altissima** All. · E:Wood Fescue; G:Wald-Schwingel · ⁴ VI-VII; Eur.*, Cauc., W-Sib., E-Sib., C-As.
– **amethystina** L. · E:Tufted Fescue; G:Gewöhnlicher Amethyst-Schwingel · ⁴ △ VI; Eur.: Fr, Ital-P, C-Eur., EC-Eur., Ba, E-Eur.; TR, Cauc.
– *apennina* De Not. = Festuca pratensis subsp. apennina
– **arundinacea** Schreb. · E:Meadow Fescue, Tall Fescue; G:Gewöhnlicher Rohr-Schwingel · ⁴ VI-VII Ⓝ; Eur.*, TR
– **beckeri** (Hack.) Trautv. · G:Dünen-Schaf-Schwingel · ⁴ VI-VII; Eur.: Sc, G, PL, Russ., ? NL; coasts
– **brevipila** R. Tracey · E:Hard Fescue; G:Gewöhnlicher Raublättriger Schaf-Schwingel, Raublatt-Schwingel · ⁴ V-VII; Eur.: Fr, C-Eur., EC-Eur., Sc, nat. in BrI, Russ.
– **calva** (Hack.) K. Richt. · G:Glatter Bunt-Schwingel, Kahler Buntschwingel · ⁴ VII; Eur.: I, A, Slove.; E-Alp.
– *capillata* Lam. = Festuca amethystina
– **cinerea** Vill. · ⁴ △ V-VI; Eur.: SE-F; NW-I
– *crinum-ursi* hort. non Ramond = Festuca gautieri
– *crinum-ursi* Ramond = Festuca eskia
– **curvula** Gaudin
– *diffusa* J.J. Vassil. = Festuca ovina
– **drymeia** Mert. & W.D.J. Koch · G:Berg-Schwingel · ⁴ VI; Eur.: Ital-P, A, EC-Eur., Ba, E-Eur.; TR, Cauc., Iran
– **duvalii** (St.-Yves) Stohr · G:Duvals Schaf-Schwingel · ⁴ ; Eur.: F, B, G, PL
– **eggleri** R. Tracey · G:Egglers Schwingel · ⁴ V-VI; Eur.: A (Murtal)
– *elatior* L. = Festuca arundinacea
– subsp. *pratensis* (Huds.) Hack. = Festuca pratensis subsp. pratensis
– **eskia** Ramond ex DC. · ⁴ ⤳ VII-VIII; Eur.: sp., F, ? RO; Pyr.
– *fallax* Thuill. = Festuca rubra
– **filiformis** Pourr. · E:Hair Fescue; G:Haar-Schaf-Schwingel · ⁴ VI-VII; Eur.* exc. Sc; Cauc., nat. in Sc, N-Am., NZ
– **flavescens** Bellardi · G:Gelblicher Schwingel · ⁴ VII-VIII; Eur.: F, I; SW-Alp.
– **frigida** (Hack.) K. Richt. · ⁴ △ VI-VII; S-Sp.: Sierra Nevada
– **gautieri** (Hack.) K. Richt. · E:Bear Skin Fescue; F:Fétuque de Gautier, Fétuque en balai; G:Bärenfellgras · ⁴ △ VI-VII;

SW-F, NE-Sp.
- **gigantea** (L.) Vill. · E:Giant Fescue;
  F:Fétuque géante; G:Riesen-Schwingel
  · ⑂ VII-VIII; Eur.*, Cauc., W-Sib., E-Sib.,
  C-As.
- **glacialis** (Miègev. ex Hack.) K. Richt. · ⑂
  △ VI-VII; sp., F; Pyr.
- **glauca** Vill. · E:Blue Fescue, Grey Fescue;
  F:Fétuque bleue; G:Blau-Schwingel · ⑂ ;
  SE-Eur., S-Eur.
- **guestfalica** Boenn. ex Rchb. · G:Harter
  Schaf-Schwingel, Westfälischer
  Schwingel · ⑂ V-VII; Eur.: BrI, Fr, C-Eur.,
  EC-Eur., ? RO
- **halleri** All. · G:Hallers Schwingel · ⑂ △
  VI-VIII; Eur.: F, I, Sw, A, Bosn., Maced.;
  Alp., mts.
- *hervieri* (St.-Yves) Patzke = Festuca
  marginata
- **heteromalla** Pourr. · G:Ausgebreiteter
  Rot-Schwingel · ⑂ VI-VII; Eur.: Fr, Ital-P,
  C-Eur., EC-Eur., Sc, ? RO
- **heteropachys** (St.-Yves) Patzke ex
  Auquier · G:Derber Schaf-Schwingel · ⑂
  VI-VII; Eur.: F, B, G, Sw
- **heterophylla** Lam. · E:Shade Fescue,
  Various-leaved Fescue; G:Verschieden-
  blättriger Schwingel · ⑂ VI-IX; Cauc.
- **intercedens** (Hack.) Lüdi ex Bech. ·
  G:Dazwischenliegender Schwingel · ⑂
  VI-VII; Eur.: I, Sw, A; Alp.
- **juncifolia** St.-Amans · G:Binsenblättriger
  Schwingel · ⑂ ; Eur.: BrI, Fr, sp.
- *lachenalii* (C.C. Gmel.) Spenn. =
  Micropyrum tenellum
- **laevigata** Gaudin · G:Glatter Schaf-
  Schwingel, Krumm-Schwingel · ⑂ V-VII;
  Eur.: F, I, Sw, G, A; Pyr., Alp., Apenn.
- **laxa** Host · G:Schlaffer Schwingel · ⑂
  VII-VIII; Eur.: A, Slove., I; SE-Alp.
- **mairei** St.-Yves · G:Atlas-Schwingel · ⑂ ;
  Moroc., Alger.
- **makutrensis** Zapal. · G:Makutrenser
  Schaf-Schwingel · ⑂ VI; Eur.: PL, Russ., ?
  D
- **marginata** (Hack.) Richt. · ⑂ ; Eur.: sp.,
  F, B
- *maritima* L. = Vulpia unilateralis
- **nigrescens** Lam. · G:Herbst-Rot-Schwin-
  gel, Schwarzwerdender Schwingel · ⑂
  〰 VI Ⓝ; Eur.*
- *nigricans* (Hack.) K. Richt. = Festuca
  violacea
- **nitida** Kit. · G:Glanz-Schwingel · ⑂ VII-
  VIII; Eur.: I, A, Slove., RO; SE-Alp., Carp.

- **norica** (Hack.) K. Richt. · G:Norischer
  Schwingel · ⑂ VII-VIII; Eur.: I, Sw, G, A,
  Slove.; E-Alp.
- **ovina** L. · E:Blue Fescue, Sheep's Fescue;
  F:Fétuque ovine; G:Gewöhnlicher
  Schaf-Schwingel · ⑂ V-VII Ⓝ; Eur.* exc.
  Ib; Cauc., W-Sib.
- **pallens** Host · G:Bleicher Schaf-Schwingel · ⑂ V-VI; Eur.: Fr, C-Eur., EC-Eur., ?
  Bosn., RO, W-Russ.
- **paniculata** (L.) Schinz & Thell. · G:Gold-
  Schwingel · ⑂ VI-VII; Eur.: Ib, Fr, Ital-P,
  C-Eur., Ba, RO; Moroc.
- **patzkei** Markgr.-Dann. · G:Patzkes Schaf-
  Schwingel · ⑂ ; Eur.: E-F, D , Luxemburg
- *picta* Kit. = Festuca picturata
- **picturata** Pils · G:Bunter Violett-Schwin-
  gel · ⑂ VII-VIII; Eur.: N-I, A, Slova., PL,
  BG, RO; mts.
- *polonica* Zapal. = Festuca beckeri
- **pratensis** Huds. · G:Wiesen-Schwingel
- subsp. **apennina** (De Not.) Hack. ex
  Hegi · G:Apenninen-Wiesen-Schwingel ·
  ⑂ VI-VII; Eur.: Alp., Apenn., Sic. mts.,
  Slove., Croatia, Carp.
- subsp. **pratensis** · E:Meadow Fescue;
  G:Gewöhnlicher Wiesen-Schwingel ·
  ⑂ VI-VII Ⓝ; Eur.*, TR, Cauc., W-Sib.,
  E-Sib., C-As., nat. in Amur, Sakhal.
- **psammophila** (Hack. ex Čelak.) Fritsch ·
  G:Sand-Schaf-Schwingel · ⑂ VI-VII; Eur.:
  G, PL, CZ, Balt.
- **pseudodalmatica** Krajina ex Domin ·
  G:Falscher Dalmatiner Schwingel · ⑂
  V-VI; Eur.: A, EC-Eur.; Cauc., Iran, C-As.
- **pseudodura** Steud. · G:Harter Schwin-
  gel · ⑂ VII-VIII; Eur.: I, Sw, A; E-Alp.
- **pseudovina** Hack. ex Wiesb. · G:Falscher
  Schaf-Schwingel, Harter Felsen-Schwin-
  gel · ⑂ VI-VII; Eur.: C-Eur., EC-Eur.,
  BaE-Eur.; Cauc., W-Sib., E-Sib., C-As.
- *puccinellii* Parl. = Festuca violacea
- **pulchella** Schrad. · G:Gewöhnlicher
  Schöner Schwingel, Zierlicher Schwingel · ⑂ VII-VIII; Eur.: F, I, C-Eur., Slove.,
  ? RO; Alp., Jura, ? Carp.
- *pumila* Vill. = Festuca quadriflora
- **punctoria** Sibth. & Sm. · ⑂ △ VI-VII;
  N-TR
- **quadriflora** Honck. · G:Niedriger
  Schwingel · ⑂ △ VII-VIII; Eur.: sp., F, I,
  C-Eur., Slove.; Pyr., Alp., Jura
- **rubra** L. · G:Rot-Schwingel
- subsp. **arenaria** (Osbeck) F. Aresch. ·
  G:Dünen-Rot-Schwingel · ⑂ ; Eur.:

NW-Eur., Balt.; coasts
- subsp. **juncea** (Hack.) K. Richt. · G:Binsen-Rot-Schwingel · ♃; Eur.: most exc. Russ.
- subsp. **litoralis** (G. Mey.) Auquier · G:Salzwiesen-Rot-Schwingel · ♃; W-Eur., Balt.; coasts
- subsp. **rubra** · E:Creeping Fescue, Red Fescue; G:Gewöhnlicher Rot-Schwingel · ♃ ⇝ VI Ⓝ; Eur.*, TR, Cauc., Iran, W-Sib., E-Sib., C-As., N-Ind., Mong., China, Jap., Moroc., Alger., nat. in N-Am., S-Am., Austr., NZ
- **rupicaprina** (Hack.) A. Kern. · G:Gämsen-Schwingel · ♃ △ VI-VII; Eur.: C-Eur., Slove.; Alp.
- **rupicola** Heuff. · G:Furchen-Schaf-Schwingel · ♃ V-VII; Eur.: Fr, Ital-P, C-Eur., EC-Eur., Ba; Cauc., W-Sib., C-As.
- *salina* Natho & Stohr = Festuca rubra subsp. litoralis
- **scabriculmis** (Hack.) K. Richt. · G:Rauhalmiger Schwingel · ♃ VII-VIII; Eur.: F, I, Sw; S-Alp.
- *scoparia* A. Kern. ex Hook. = Festuca gautieri
- **stenantha** (Hack.) K. Richt. · G:Schmalblütiger Schwingel · ♃ VII-VIII; Eur.: F, I, Sw, A, Slove., Croatia, Bosn.; Alp., Croatia, Bosn.
- **stricta** Host · G:Steif-Schwingel · ♃ V-VII; Eur.: I, A, EC-Eur., RO
- *supina* Schur = Festuca airoides
- *tenuifolia* Sibth. = Festuca filiformis
- **ticinensis** (Markgr.-Dann.) Markgr.-Dann. · G:Tessiner Schwingel · ♃ V-VII; Eur.: I, Sw; S-Alp.
- **trichophylla** (Ducros ex Gaudin) K. Richt. · G:Gämsen-Schwingel, Haarblättriger Schwingel · ♃ VI-VII; Eur.: Ib, Fr, Ital-P, C-Eur., EC-Eur., RO
- *unifaria* Dumort. = Festuca rubra subsp. juncea
- **vaginata** Waldst. & Kit. ex Willd. · G:Sand-Schwingel · ♃ V-VI; Eur.: A, EC-Eur., Ba, E-Eur.
- **valesiaca** Schleich. ex Gaudin · G:Walliser Schaf-Schwingel
- subsp. **parviflora** (Hack.) R. Tracey · G:Falscher Walliser Schaf-Schwingel · ; Eur.: C-Eur., EC-Eur., Ba, E-Eur.; Cauc., W-Sib., C-As.
- subsp. **valesiaca** · F:Fétuque du Valais ; G:Gewöhnlicher Walliser Schaf-Schwingel · ♃ △ VI; Eur.: Fr, Ital-P, C-Eur., EC-Eur., Ba, E-Eur.; TR, Cauc., C-As., Mong.
- **varia** Haenke · G:Bunt-Schwingel · ♃ VII-VIII; Eur.: I, A, Slove.; E-Alp.
- *versicolor* Tausch = Festuca varia
- *villosa* Schweigg. = Festuca rubra subsp. arenaria
- **violacea** Ser. ex Gaudin · G:Dunkelvioletter Schwingel, Violetter Schwingel · ♃ VII-VIII; Eur.: C-Eur., F, I; Alp., Jura
- **vivipara** (L.) Sm. · E:Viviparous Sheep's Fescue; G:Brutknospen-Schwingel · ♃ △ VI-VII; Eur.: BrI, Sc, N-Russ.; Sib., N-Am., Greenl.

× **Festulolium** Asch. & Graebn. -n- *Poaceae* · G:Schwingellolch (*Festuca* × *Lolium*)
- **loliaceum** (Huds.) P. Fourn. (*Festuca pratensis* × *Lolium perenne*) · E:Hybrid Fescue; G:Schwingellolch · ♃ Z5; Eur.*

Fibigia Medik. -f- *Brassicaceae* · 14 spp. · G:Schildkresse
- **clypeata** (L.) Medik. · ♃ △ ✄ Z7 ∧ V-VI; Eur.: I, Ba, Crim; TR, Syr., Palest., Iraq, Cauc. Iran, Egypt

Ficinia Schrad. -f- *Cyperaceae* · 60-75 spp.
- *poiretii* Kunth = Isolepis cernua

Ficus L. -f- *Moraceae* · c. 750 spp. · E:Fig; F:Figuier; G:Feige, Gummibaum
- **altissima** Blume · E:Council Tree, False Banyan; G:Hohe Feige · ♄ e Z10 ⓦ; Him., Ind., Sri Lanka, Burma, Malay. Arch., Phil.
- **aspera** G. Forst. · ♄ e ✿ Z10 ⓦ; Vanuatu
- **auriculata** Lour. · E:Roxburgh Fig; G:Ohr-Feige, Roxburgh-Feige · ♄ ♄ e ✿ Z10 ⓦ; Him., S-China, Thail., Vietn.
- *australis* Willd. = Ficus rubiginosa
- *barbata* Miq. = Ficus villosa
- **barteri** Sprague · ♄ ♄ e Z10 ⓦ; W-Afr., C-Afr.
- **benghalensis** L. · E:Banyan Tree, Indian Banyan; G:Banyan-Feige · ♄ ♄ e Z10 ⓦ ⚕; Him., Ind.
- **benjamina** L. · E:Benjamin Fig, Tropic Laurel, Weeping Fig; G:Benjamin-Feige, Benjamin-Gummibaum · ♄ e Z10 ⓦ; Him., Ind., Burma, S-China, Malay. Arch., N-Austr.
- **binnendijkii** (Miq.) Miq. · ♄ e Z10 ⓦ; Java
- **callosa** Willd. · ♄ e Z10 ⓦ; Ind., Sri

Lanka, Burma, Java
- *canonii* W. Bull ex Van Houtte = Ficus aspera
- *capensis* Thunb. = Ficus sur
- **carica** L. · E:Fig; G:Echte Feige · ♄ ♄ d Z8 ⌂ ∧ V-X ⚥ Ⓝ; Eur.: Ib, Fr, Ital-P, Ba; TR, Levant, N-Iraq, Iran, C.-As., NW-Afr., nat. in BrI, C-Eur., EC-Eur., Crim
- **celebensis** Corner · ♄ e Z10 🐾; Sulawesi
- *cerasiformis* Desf. = Ficus parietalis
- **cyathistipula** Warb. · ♄ e ⊗ Z10 🐾; trop. Afr.
- **deltoidea** Jack
- var. **deltoidea** · E:Mistletoe Fig · ♄ e ⊗ Z10 🐾; Malay. Arch.
- var. **diversifolia** (Blume) Corner · ♄ Z10 🐾; Malay. Arch.
- *diversifolia* Blume = Ficus deltoidea var. diversifolia
- **dryepondtiana** Gentil ex De Wild. · ♄ e Z10 🐾; C- Afr.
- *edulis* Bureau = Ficus habrophylla
- **elastica** Roxb. · E:India Rubber Tree, Rubber Plant; G:Gummibaum · ♄ e Z10 🐾 Ⓝ; E-Him., Burma, Malay. Arch.
- *foveolata* Wall. ex Miq. = Ficus sarmentosa var. sarmentosa
- var. *nipponica* (Franch. & Sav.) King = Ficus sarmentosa var. nipponica
- *glabella* Blume = Ficus virens var. glabella
- *glomerata* Roxb. = Ficus racemosa
- **habrophylla** G. Benn. & Seem. · ♄ e ⊗ Z10 🐾; N.Caled.
- **hispida** L. f. · E:River Fig, Rough Leaved Fig, Soft Fig; G:Fluss-Feige · ♄ ♄ e Z10 🐾; Ind., Sri Lanka, China, Malay. Arch., N-Austr.
- *indica* L. = Ficus benghalensis
- *krishnae* C. DC. = Ficus benghalensis
- *leprieurii* Miq. = Ficus natalensis subsp. leprieurii
- **lyrata** Warb. · E:Fiddle-leaf Fig; G:Leier-Gummibaum · ♄ e Z10 🐾; W-Afr.
- **macrophylla** Desf. ex Pers. · E:Australian Banyan, Moreton Bay Fig; G:Großblättrige Feige · ♄ e Z10 🐾; Austr.: Queensl., N.S.Wales, Lord Howe Is.
- **microcarpa** L. f.
- var. **hillii** (F.M. Bailey) Corner · ♄ e Z10 🐾; S-As., N.Caled.
- var. **microcarpa** · E:Chinese Banyan, Curtain Fig, Indian Laurel Fig; G:Vorhang-Feige · ♄ e Z10 🐾; Him., Ind., Burma, China, Malay. Arch., Austr., N.Caled.

- **montana** Burm. f. · E:Oak Leaved Fig; G:Eichenblättrige Feige · ♄ e ⤳ Z10 🐾; ? Ind., ? SE-As.
- **natalensis** Hochst.
- subsp. **leprieurii** (Miq.) C.C. Berg · ♄ e Z10 🐾; trop. Afr.
- subsp. **natalensis** · E:Natal Fig; G:Natal-Feige · ♄ ♄ Z10 🐾; trop. Afr., S-Afr.
- **neriifolia** Sm. · ♄ e Z9 🐾; Him.
- *nipponica* Franch. & Sav. = Ficus sarmentosa var. nipponica
- *nitida* Thunb. = Ficus benjamina
- **nymphaeifolia** Mill. · ♄ e Z10 🐾; Panama, trop. S-Am.
- **palmeri** S. Watson · E:Desert Fig; G:Wüsten-Feige · ♄ e Z10 🐾; Mex.: Baja Calif.
- *parcellii* Veitch ex Cogn. & Marchal = Ficus aspera
- **parietalis** Blume · E:Sharp Fig · ♄ ♄ e Z10 🐾; W-Afr.
- *porteana* Regel = Ficus callosa
- **pumila** L. · E:Creeping Fig, Fig Vine; G:Kletter-Feige · ♄ e ⚥ ⤳ Z9 🐾 ⌂; China, Jap., Riukiu-Is., Taiwan, N-Vietn.
- *quercifolia* Roxb. = Ficus montana
- **racemosa** L. · E:Cluster Fig, Country Fig · ♄ e Z10 🐾; Ind., Sri Lanka, China, SE-As.
- *radicans* Desf. = Ficus sagittata
- **religiosa** L. · E:Peepul Tree, Sacred Fig; G:Bobaum, Indischer Pepulbaum · ♄ e Z10 🐾 ⚥; Ind., Sri Lanka
- *retusa* hort. non L. = Ficus microcarpa var. microcarpa
- var. *nitida* (Thunb.) Miq. = Ficus benjamina
- *roxburghii* Miq. = Ficus auriculata
- **rubiginosa** Desf. ex Vent. · E:Port Jackson Fig, Rusty Fig; G:Rost-Feige · ♄ e Z10 ⌂; Austr.: Queensl., N.S.Wales
- **rumphii** Blume · ♄ e Z9 🐾; Ind., Malay. Pen., Molucca. Is.
- **sagittata** Vahl · E:Trailing Fig · ♄ e Z10 🐾 ⌂; E-Him., SE-As., Phil., Pacific Is.
- **sarmentosa** Buch.-Ham. ex Sm.
- var. **nipponica** (Franch. & Sav.) Corner · ♄ e ⚥ Z10 🐾 ⌂; Jap., Korea, China, Taiwan, E-Him.
- var. **sarmentosa** · ♄ e Z10 ⌂; Him., China, Korea, Jap., Ryukyu Is., Taiwan
- *schlechteri* Warb. = Ficus microcarpa var. hillii
- *stipulata* Thunb. = Ficus pumila
- **stricta** (Miq.) Miq. · ♄ e Z10 🐾; SE-As., China: Yunnan

- **subulata** Blume · ♄ e Z10 ⓜ; NE-Ind.,
SE-As., S-China
- **sur** Forssk. · E:Bush Fig, Cape Fig;
G:Kap-Feige · ♄ d Z10 ⓜ; trop. Afr.,
S-Afr., Yemen
- **sycomorus** L. · E:Mulberry Fig, Pharoah
Fig; G:Esels-Feige, Sykomore · ♄ d Z10 ⓚ
ⓝ; Sudan, E-Afr., trop-Afr., S-Afr., Arab.
- *triangularis* Warb. = Ficus natalensis
subsp. leprieurii
- *vesca* Miq. = Ficus racemosa
- **villosa** Miq. · E:Villous Fig · ♄ e ⚥ Z10 ⓜ;
NE-Ind., Andaman Is.
- **virens** Aiton
- var. **glabella** (Blume) Corner · ♄ e Z10
ⓜ; Thail., Malay. Arch.
- **wildemaniana** Warb. ex De Wild. & T.
Durand · ♄ Z10 ⓜ; W-Afr., C-Afr.

Filago L. -f- *Asteraceae* · c. 40 spp. ·
E:Cudweed; F:Cotonnière, Filago;
G:Fadenkraut, Filzkraut
- **arvensis** L. · E:Field Cudweed; G:Acker-
Filzkraut · ⊙ VII-IX; Eur.* exc. BrI; TR,
SW-As., Sib., C-As., Him., NW-Afr.
- **gallica** L. · E:Narrow-leaved Cudweed;
G:Französisches Filzkraut · ⊙ VI-VIII;
Eur.: Ib, Fr, Ital-P, Ba, C-Eur., BrI; TR,
Cyprus, Syr., Macaron., NW-Afr., Libya
- **lutescens** Jord. · E:Red-tipped Cudweed;
G:Gelbliches Filzkraut · ⊙ VII-IX; Eur.*,
Macaron., ? N-Afr.
- **minima** (Sm.) Pers. · E:Small Cudweed;
G:Kleines Filzkraut · ⊙ VII-IX; Eur.*
- **neglecta** (Soy.-Will.) DC. · G:Überse-
henes Filzkraut · ⊙; Eur.: F, B, Cors
- **pyramidata** L. · E:Broad-leaved Cud-
weed; G:Spatelblättriges Filzkraut · ⊙
VII-IX; Eur.: BrI, Ib, Fr, Ital-P, C-Eur., Ba,
Crim; TR, Cauc., SW-As., C-As., NW-Afr.
- **vulgaris** Lam. · E:Common Cudweed;
G:Deutsches Filzkraut · ⊙ VII-IX; Eur.*,
TR, Cauc., N-Iran, NW-Afr.

Filicium Thwaites ex Benth. -n-
Sapindaceae · 3 spp. · F:Arbre-fougère;
G:Flügelblatt
- **decipiens** (Wight & Arn.) Thwaites · ♄ e
ⓜ; C-Afr., E-Afr., Ind., Sri Lanka, Fiji

Filipendula Mill. -f- *Rosaceae* ·
10+ spp. · E:Dropwort, Meadowsweet;
F:Filipendule; G:Mädesüß
- **camtschatica** (Pall.) Maxim. · E:Giant
Meadowsweet; F:Filipendule du

Kamtchatka; G:Kamtschatka-Mädesüß ·
⁴ Z3 VII-VIII; Jap., Manch., Kamchat.
- **palmata** (Pall.) Maxim. · F:Filipendule
à feuilles palmées · ⁴ Z2 VI-VIII; E-Sib.,
Amur, Sakhal., Kamchat., Mong., China,
Jap.
- **purpurea** Maxim. · E:Red Meadowsweet;
G:Japanisches Mädesüß · ⁴ Z6 VI-VIII;
Jap.
- **rubra** (Hill) B.L. Rob. · E:Queen of the
Prairie; G:Prärie-Mädesüß · ⁴ Z2 VI-VII;
USA: NE, NCE, SE
- **ulmaria** (L.) Maxim. · E:Meadow Sweet,
Queen of the Meadow; F:Reine des prés;
G:Echtes Mädesüß · ⁴ ∼ Z2 VI-IX ⚥ ⓝ;
Eur.*, TR, Cauc., W-Sib., E-Sib., C-As.,
Mong., nat. in N-Am.
- **vulgaris** Moench · E:Dropwort;
F:Filipendule vulgaire; G:Kleines
Mädesüß · ⁴ Z3 VI-VII; Eur.*, TR, Cauc.,
W-Sib., E-Sib., nat. in N-Am.

Fimbristylis Vahl -f- *Cyperaceae* · 250-
300 spp. · F:Fimbristylis; G:Fransenbinse
- **annua** (All.) Roem. & Schult. ·
G:Fransenried · ⊙ VII-IX; Eur.: F, I,
Slove; TR, Cauc., C-As., E-As., N-Am.,
Trop., nat. in Sw, S-Eur., Austr., Afr.
- **globulosa** (Retz.) Kunth · ⁴ ⓜ ⓝ; Ind.,
Sri Lanka, Malay. Pen., Micron.

Firmiana Marsili -f- *Sterculiaceae* · 12 spp. ·
E:Parasol Tree; F:Firmiana; G:Sonnen-
schirmbaum
- **simplex** (L.) W. Wight · E:Chinese
Parasol Tree; G:Chinesischer Sonnenschirmbaum · ♄ d Z9 ⓚ; China, Taiwan,
Ryukyu Is., Indochina

Fittonia Coëm. -f- *Acanthaceae* · 2 spp. ·
E:Nerve Plant; F:Fittonia; G:Fittonie,
Silbernetzblatt
- **albivenis** (Lindl. ex Veitch) Brummitt ·
E:Mosaic Plant, Silver Net Leaf; G:Silber-
netzblatt · ⁴ Z10 ⓜ; Col., Ecuad., Peru,
Bol., N-Braz.
- *argyroneura* Coëm. = Fittonia albivenis
- **gigantea** Linden ex André · ⁴ Z10 ⓜ;
Peru
- **verschaffeltii** (Lem.) Van Houtte
- var. *argyroneura* (Coëm.) G. Nicholson =
Fittonia albivenis
- var. **pearcei** G. Nicholson Z10
- var. **verschaffeltii** · ⁴ Z10 ⓜ; Col.,
Ecuad., Peru, Bol.

Fitzroya Hook. f. ex Lindl. -f-
Cupressaceae · 1 sp. · E:Patagonian
Cypress; F:Cyprès de Patagonie;
G:Patagonische Zypresse, Alerce
– **cupressoides** (Molina) I.M. Johnst. ·
E:Patagonian Cypress; G:Patagonische
Zypresse, Alerce · ♄ e Z8 ⌂ Ⓝ ▽ ✳;
S-Chile, N-Patag.

Flacourtia Comm. ex L'Hér. -f-
Flacourtiaceae · c. 15 spp. · E:Governor's
Plum, Rukam; F:Prunier de Madagascar;
G:Flacourtie, Madagaskarpflaume
– **indica** (Burm. f.) Merr. · E:Madagascar
Plum ; G:Ramontchi · ♄ ♄ d Z10 ⓦ Ⓝ;
trop. Afr., trop. As.
– **rukam** Zoll. & Moritzi · E:Rukam;
G:Madagaskarpflaume · ♄ Z10 ⓦ Ⓝ;
Malay. Arch., Phil.

Fleischmannia Sch. Bip. -f- *Asteraceae* ·
79 spp.
– **incarnata** (Walter) R.M. King & H. Rob. ·
E:Pink Thoroughwort · ⚄ Z10 ⌂ V-X;
USA: W.Va., NCE, SE, Fla, SC, SW; Mex.

Flemingia Roxb. ex W.T. Aiton -f-
Fabaceae · 30 spp.
– **macrophylla** (Willd.) Merr. · ♄ Ⓝ; SE-As.
– **vestita** Benth. ex Baker · Ⓝ; Him., N-Ind.

Flueckigera Kuntze = Ledenbergia
– *macrantha* (Standl.) P. Wilson =
Ledenbergia macrantha

Fockea Endl. -f- *Asclepiadaceae* · 6 spp.
– **capensis** Endl. · ♄ ⚘ ⚄ ⌂; Cape
– *crispa* (Jacq.) K. Schum. = Fockea
capensis
– **multiflora** K. Schum. · ♄ ⚘ ⌂; S-Angola,
Tanzania

Foeniculum Mill. -n- *Apiaceae* · 1 sp. ·
E:Fennel; F:Fenouil; G:Fenchel
– *dulce* Mill. = Foeniculum vulgare subsp.
vulgare
– *piperitum* (Ucria) Sweet = Foeniculum
vulgare subsp. piperitum
– **vulgare** Mill. · E:Fennel; G:Fenchel · ⚄
⚄ VII-IX ⚥; Eur.: Ib, Fr, Ital-P, Ba, BrI;
TR, Cauc., Iran, N-Afr., nat. in C-Eur.,
EC-Eur., E-Eur., N-Am., S-Am., Jap.,
China, NZ
– subsp. **piperitum** (Ucria) Bég. · E:Bitter
Fennel; G:Pfeffer-Fenchel · ⚄ Z5

– subsp. **vulgare** Mill. · E:Finnochio;
G:Garten-Fenchel · ; Eur.*
– var. **azoricum** (Mill.) Thell. · E:Florence
Fennel; G:Gemüse-Fenchel, Knollen-
Fenchel · ⊙ ⚄ Z5; cult.
– var. **dulce** (DC.) Batt. · E:Sweet Fennel;
G:Gewürz-Fenchel · ⊙ ⚄ Z5 VII-VIII ⚥
Ⓝ; cult.
– var. **vulgare** · G:Wilder Fenchel · ⊙ ⚄ Z5
VII-VIII

Fokienia A. Henry & H.H. Thomas -f-
Cupressaceae · 1 sp. · G:Pemouzypresse
– **hodginsii** A. Henry & H.H. Thomas ·
G:Pemouzypresse · ♄ e Z8 ⌂; China:
Fukien

Fontanesia Labill. -f- *Oleaceae* · 1 sp. ·
E:Fontanesia; F:Fontanesie; G:Fontanesie
– *angustifolia* Dippel = Fontanesia phill-
lyreoides subsp. phillyreoides
– *fortunei* Carrière = Fontanesia phillyreoides subsp. fortunei
– **phillyreoides** Labill.
– subsp. **fortunei** (Carrière) P.S. Green &
Yalt. · G:Glattrandige Fontanesie · ♄ d Z5
V-VI; E-China
– subsp. **phillyreoides** · G:Kleinasiatische
Fontanesie · ♄ d Z6 V-VI; Eur.: Sic.; TR,
Lebanon, Syr., nat. in I

Forestiera Poir. -f- *Oleaceae* · 15 spp. ·
G:Adelie
– **acuminata** (Michx.) Poir. · E:Alligator
Tree, Swamp Privet; G:Spitzblättrige
Adelie, Sumpfliguster · ♄ ♄ d ⌇ Z6
IV-V; USA: NCE, Kans., SC, SE, Fla.
– **ligustrina** (Michx.) Poir. · E:Upland
Swamp Privet; G:Ligusterähnliche Adelie
· ♄ d Z6 VIII; USA: NE, SE, Fla.
– **neomexicana** A. Gray · E:Desert Olive,
New Mexico Privet; F:Olivier du désert;
G:Neumexikanische Adelie, Wüstenolive
· ♄ ♄ d Z6 IV-V; USA: SC, Colo., SW,
Calif.

Forsythia Vahl -f- *Oleaceae* · 7 spp. ·
E:Forsythia; F:Forsythia; G:Forsythie,
Goldglöckchen
– **europaea** Degen & Bald. · G:Europäische
Forsythie · ♄ d Z6 IV-V; Eur.: S-YU, AL
– **giraldiana** Lingelsh. · E:Early Forsythia ·
♄ d Z6 IV-V; NW-China
– × **intermedia** Zabel (*F. suspensa × F.
viridissima*) · F:Forsythia de Paris;

G:Garten-Forsythie · ♄ d ⋉ Z5 III-V; cult.
- **many cultivars**
- **japonica** Makino · ♄ d Z6 IV; Jap.
- **ovata** Nakai · E:Korean Forsythia;
  G:Koreanische Forsythie · ♄ d Z5 IV;
  Korea
- **suspensa** (Thunb.) Vahl
- var. **fortunei** (Lindl.) Rehder · G:Bogige
  Forsythie · ♄ d Z5 IV; E-China
- var. **sieboldii** Zabel · G:Kletter-
  Forsythie · ♄ d Z5 IV; Jap.
- var. **suspensa** · E:Weeping Forsythia;
  G:Hänge-Forsythie · ♄ d Z5 IV-V ⚥ ;
  China
- **viridissima** Lindl. · E:Green Forsythia;
  G:Grüne Forsythie · ♄ d Z6 IV-V; China
- **Cultivars:**
- **some cultivars**

Fortunella Swingle -f- *Rutaceae* · 5 spp. ·
E:Kumquat; F:Kumquat; G:Kumquat,
Zwergorange
- **hindsii** (Champ. ex Benth.) Swingle ·
  G:Hongkong-Kumquat; E:Hong Kong
  Kumquat · ♄ e Z9 ⓐ Ⓝ; Hong Kong,
  China
- **japonica** (Thunb.) Swingle · E:Round
  Kumquat; G:Runde Kumquat · ♄ e ⊗ Z9
  ⓐ Ⓝ; S-China
- **margarita** (Lour.) Swingle · E:Oval
  Kumquat; G:Ovale Kumquat · ♄ e Z8 ⓐ
  Ⓝ; S-China

Fosterella L.B. Sm. -f- *Bromeliaceae* ·
30 spp.
- **penduliflora** (C.H. Wright) L.B. Sm. · ⌗
  Z9 ⓦ; Bol, W-Arg.

Fothergilla L. -f- *Hamamelidaceae* · 2 spp. ·
E:Witch Alder; F:Fothergilla; G:Feder-
buschstrauch
- *alnifolia* L. f. = Fothergilla gardenii
- var. *major* Sims = Fothergilla major
- *carolina* (L.) Britton = Fothergilla
  gardenii
- **gardenii** Murray · E:Dwarf Witch Alder;
  G:Erlenblättriger Federbuschstrauch · ♄
  d △ Z7 V; USA: Va., SE
- **major** (Sims) Lodd. · E:Witch Alder ;
  G:Großer Federbuschstrauch · ♄ d Z7 V;
  USA: SE
- *monticola* Ashe = Fothergilla major
- *parvifolia* Kearney = Fothergilla gardenii

Fouquieria Kunth -f- *Fouquieriaceae* ·

11 sp. · E:Ocotillo; F:Cierge, Cirio;
G:Kerzenstrauch, Ocotillostrauch
- **columnaris** (Kellogg) Kellogg ex Curran ·
  E:Boojum Tree · ♄ ⇃ d Z9 ⓐ ▽ ✳; Mex.:
  Baja Calif., Sonora
- **splendens** Engelm. · E:American Desert
  Candlewood, Ocotillo; G:Kalifornischer
  Kerzenstrauch · ♄ ⇃ Z9 ⓐ; S-Calif., Baja
  Calif.

Fragaria L. -f- *Rosaceae* · 12 spp. ·
E:Strawberry; F:Fraisier; G:Erdbeere
- × **ananassa** (Duchesne) Guédès (*F.
  chiloensis* × *F. virginiana*) · E:Garden
  Strawberry, Strawberry; G:Garten-
  Erdbeere, Kultur-Erdbeere · ⌗ V-VI Ⓝ;
  cult., nat. in Eur.
- **bucharica** Losinsk. · ⌗ Ⓝ; C-As.
- **chiloensis** (L.) Mill. · E:Beach Strawberry, Chiloe Strawberry; G:Chile-Erd-
  beere · ⌗ Z4 Ⓝ; Alaska, Can.: W; USA:
  NW, Calif.; S-Chile, nat. in Teneriffa
- *fortensis* (Weston) Duchesne ex Rozier =
  Fragaria vesca var. hortensis
- *grandiflora* Ehrh. non (L.) Crantz =
  Fragaria × ananassa
- × **hagenbachiana** K.H. Lang & W.D.J.
  Koch (*F. vesca* × *F. viridis*) · G:Bastard-
  Erdbeere · ⌗; D. +
- *indica* Andrews = Duchesnea indica
- **iturupensis** Staudt · ⌗ Ⓝ; Jap.
  (S-Kurilen)
- × *magna* Thuill. = Fragaria × ananassa
- **moschata** (Duchesne) Weston ·
  E:Hautbois Strawberry; G:Zimt-Erdbeere
  · ⌗ Z6 V-VI Ⓝ; Eur.* exc. BrI, Sc; Cauc.,
  nat. in BrI, Sc
- × **neglecta** Lindem. (*F. moschata* × *F.
  viridis*) · G:Übersehene Erdbeere · ⌗; G,
  Crim, Cauc., E-Sib.+
- **ovalis** (Lehm.) Rydb. · ⌗ Ⓝ; USA: Rocky
  Mts., SW
- **vesca** L. · G:Wald-Erdbeere
- var. **hortensis** (Duchesne) Staudt ·
  G:Kultur-Wald-Erdbeere, Monats-
  Erdbeere · ⌗ Z5; cult.
- var. **monophylla** (L.) Pers. · E:Single
  Leaf Strawberry ; G:Einblättrige Wald-
  Erdbeere · ⌗ Z5; cult.
- var. **vesca** · E:Alpine Strawberry,
  Wild Strawberry; F:Fraisier des bois;
  G:Gewöhnliche Wald-Erdbeere · ⌗ Z5
  V-VI ⚥ Ⓝ; Eur.*, Cauc., W-Sib., E-Sib.,
  C-As., N-Afr.
- **virginiana** Mill. · E:Virginia Strawberry;

G:Virginische Erdbeere · ♃ Z3 Ⓝ; Alaska, Can., USA: * exc. Fla., nat. in E-Eur.
– **viridis** Weston · G:Knack-Erdbeere · ♃ Z6 V-VI Ⓝ; Eur.* exc. BrI; Cauc., W-Sib., E-Sib., C-As.

Frailea Britton & Rose -f- *Cactaceae* · 15 spp.
– *alacriportana* Backeb. & Voll = Frailea gracillima
– *asterioides* Werderm. = Frailea castanea
– *aureispina* F. Ritter = Frailea pygmaea
– *bruchii* Speg. = Gymnocalycium bruchii
– *carminifilamentosa* Kilian ex Backeb. = Frailea pumila
– **castanea** Backeb. · ♈ Z9 ⓐ ▽ ✳; Braz.: Rio Grande do Sul; Urug., Arg.: Misiones
– **cataphracta** (Dams) Britton & Rose · ♈ Z8 ⓐ ▽ ✳; Braz.: Mato Grosso; Parag., E-Bol.
– *cataphractoides* Backeb. = Frailea cataphracta
– *chrysacantha* Hrabětová = Frailea pumila
– **colombiana** (Werderm.) Backeb. · ♈ Z9 ⓐ; S-Braz., Urug.
– **gracillima** (Monv. ex Lem.) Britton & Rose · ♈ Z9 ⓐ ▽ ✳; Braz.: Rio Grande do Sul; N-Urug.
– **grahliana** (F. Haage) Britton & Rose · ♈ Z9 ⓐ ▽ ✳; Parag., ? Arg. (Misiones)
– *itapuensis* nom. inval. = Frailea gracillima
– **knippeliana** (Quehl) Britton & Rose · ♈ Z9 ⓐ ▽ ✳; S-Parag.
– *matoana* Buining & Brederoo = Frailea cataphracta
– **pumila** (Lem.) Britton & Rose · ♈ Z9 ⓐ ▽ ✳; Braz.: Rio Grande do Sul; Urug., Parag.
– **pygmaea** (Speg.) Britton & Rose · ♈ Z9 ⓐ ▽ ✳; Braz.: Rio Grande do Sul; Urug.

Franciscea Pohl = Brunfelsia
– *calycina* (Benth.) Miers = Brunfelsia pauciflora var. calycina
– *hopeana* Hook. = Brunfelsia uniflora

Francoa Cav. -f- *Saxifragaceae* · 1 sp. · E:Bridal Wreath; F:Francoa; G:Brautkranz, Jungfernkranz
– *appendiculata* Cav. = Francoa sonchifolia var. appendiculata
– *ramosa* D. Don = Francoa sonchifolia var. ramosa
– **sonchifolia** Cav.
– var. **appendiculata** (Cav.) Reiche · ♃ Z7;

Chile
– var. **ramosa** (D. Don) Reiche · E:Maiden's Wreath ; G:Jungfernkranz · ♃ Z7 V-VII; Chile
– var. **sonchifolia** · E:Bridal Wreath; G:Brautkranz · ♃ Z7; Chile

Frangula Mill. -f- *Rhamnaceae* · c. 20 spp. · E:Alder Buckthorn; F:Nerprun; G:Faulbaum
– **alnus** Mill. · E:Alder Buckthorn, Common Buckthorn; F:Bourdaine; G:Gewöhnlicher Faulbaum · ♄ ♄ Z3 V-VI ❦ ⚶ Ⓝ; Eur.*, TR, Syr., Cauc., N-Iran, W-Sib., E-Sib., C-As., NW-Afr.
– **purshiana** (DC.) J.G. Cooper · E:Cascara Buckthorn; G:Purgier-Faulbaum, Sagrada-Faulbaum · ♄ ♄ Z5 VII ❦ ⚶; B.C., USA: NW, Calif., Rocky Mts.
– **rupestris** (Scop.) Schur · G:Felsen-Faulbaum · ♄ ⤳ △ Z6 VI-VII ⚶; Eur.: I, Ba

Frankenia L. -f- *Frankeniaceae* · 40 spp. · E:Sea Heath; F:Frankénie; G:Frankenie, Seeheide
– **hirsuta** L. · G:Haarige Seeheide · ♄ e △ ⓐ ∧ VI-VIII; Eur.: Ib, Fr, Ital-P, Ba, E-Eur.; TR, Levant, Cauc., W-Sib., C-As., N-Afr., S-Afr.
– **laevis** L. · E:Sea Heath; G:Glatte Seeheide · ♃ △ ⓐ ∧ VI-VIII; Eur.: BrI, Fr, Ib, Ital-P; NW-Afr., Libya
– **thymifolia** Desf. · G:Thymianblättrige Seeheide · ♄ e ⓐ; sp., N-Afr.

Franklinia W. Bartram ex Marshall -f- *Theaceae* · 1 sp. · E:Franklin Tree; F:Franklinia; G:Franklinie
– **alatamaha** Marshall · E:Franklin Tree; G:Franklinie · ♄ d Z8 VIII-X; USA: Ga.

Fraxinus L. -f- *Oleaceae* · 65 spp. · E:Ash; F:Frêne; G:Esche
– **americana** L.
– var. **americana** · E:American Ash; G:Weiß-Esche · ♄ d Z5 IV-V Ⓝ; Can.: E; USA: NE, NCE, NC, SC, SE, Fla.
– var. **microcarpa** A. Gray · ♄ Z3; USA: Va., SE
– **angustifolia** Vahl
– subsp. **angustifolia** · E:Narrow-leaved Ash; F:Frêne à feuilles étroites; G:Quirl-Esche, Schmalblättrige Esche · ♃ ♄ d Z6 III-V; Eur.: Ib, Fr, A, BG, EC-Eur., E-Eur.;

TR
- var. **australis** (Gay) C.K. Schneid. Z6; S-Eur., N-Afr.
- subsp. **oxycarpa** (M. Bieb. ex Willd.) Franco & Rocha Afonso · G:Spitzfrüchtige Esche · ♄ d Z6; Eur.: Ib, F, Ital-P, Ba; Crim; TR, Cauc.
- subsp. **syriaca** (Boiss.) Yalt. · G:Syrische Esche · ♄ ♄ d Z6 V; TR, Syr., Iraq, Iran, Afgh., W-Pakist.
- **anomala** Torr. ex S. Watson · E:Single Leaf Ash, Utah Ash; G:Einblättrige Esche, Utah-Esche · ♄ ♄ d Z5; USA: Rocky Mts, SW, Calif.
- **biltmoreana** Beadle · G:Biltmore-Esche · ♄ d Z6; SE-USA
- **bungeana** A. DC. · E:Northern Ash; G:Bunges Blumen-Esche · ♄ d Z7; N-China
- **chinensis** Roxb.
- var. **chinensis** · E:Chinese; Ash G:Chinesische Esche · ♄ d Z6; China
- var. **rhynchophylla** (Hance) Hemsl. · G:Schnabel-Esche · ♄ d Z6; Jap., Korea, N-China
- **cuspidata** Torr. · E:Fragrant Ash; G:Stachelspitzige Blumenesche · ♄ ♄ d Z7 IV-V; USA: Ariz., N.Mex., Tex.; N-Mex.
- **excelsior** L. · E:Common Ash, European Ash; F:Frêne commun; G:Gewöhnliche Esche · ♄ d Z4 IV-V ⚥ Ⓝ; Eur.*, TR, Syr., Cauc., N-Iran
- **some cultivars**
- **holotricha** Koehne · G:Behaarte Esche · ♄ Z6 IV-V; SE-Eur. +
- *lanceolata* Borkh. = Fraxinus pennsylvanica var. pennsylvanica
- **lanuginosa** Koidz. · G:Wollflaumige Esche · ♄ d Z6 IV-V; Jap., ? S-Korea
- **latifolia** Benth. · E:Oregon Ash; G:Oregon-Esche · ♄ d Z6 Ⓝ; B.C., USA: NW, Calif.
- **longicuspis** Siebold & Zucc. · E:Japanese Ash; G:Langspitzige Esche · ♄ d Z6; China: Sichuan; Jap.
- **mandshurica** Rupr. · G:Mandschurische Esche · ♄ d Z5 Ⓝ; Amur, Sakhal., Manch., N-China, Korea, Jap.
- *mariesii* Hook. f. = Fraxinus sieboldiana
- **nigra** Marshall · E:Black Ash; G:Schwarz-Esche · ♄ d Z4 Ⓝ; Can.: E; USA: NE, NCE
- *oregona* Nutt. = Fraxinus latifolia
- **ornus** L. · G:Blumen-Esche
- var. **ornus** · E:Flowering Ash, Manna Ash; F:Frêne à fleurs, Frêne à manne;

G:Gewöhnliche Blumen-Esche, Manna-Esche · ♄ d Z7 IV-VI ⚥ Ⓝ; Eur.: Ib, Ital-P, Ba, Me, EC-Eur., RO; TR, Syr., Cauc., nat. in Fr
- var. **rotundifolia** (Lam.) Ten. · G:Rundblättrige Blumen-Esche · ♄ Z6; S-Med.
- *oxycarpa* M. Bieb. ex Willd. = Fraxinus angustifolia subsp. oxycarpa
- *oxyphylla* M. Bieb. = Fraxinus angustifolia subsp. angustifolia
- **pallisiae** Wilmott ex Pallis · ♄ d Z6; Eur.: Ba, RO, W-Russ.; TR
- *parvifolia* Lam. = Fraxinus ornus var. rotundifolia
- **paxiana** Lingelsh. · G:Chinesische Blumen-Esche · ♄ ♄ d Z7; Him., China
- **pennsylvanica** Marshall · G:Pennsylvanische Esche, Rot-Esche
- var. *lanceolata* (Borkh.) Sarg. = Fraxinus pennsylvanica var. subintegerrima
- var. **pennsylvanica** · E:Red Ash; G:Rot-Esche · ♄ d ~ Z4 IV-V Ⓝ; Can.: E; USA; NE, NCE, SE
- var. **subintegerrima** (Vahl) Fernald · G:Grün-Esche · ♄ d Z4; Can., USA: NE, NEC, NC, SC, SE, Fla.
- **platypoda** Oliv. · G:Breitstielige Esche · ♄ d Z6; China: Sichuan, Yunnan, Hupeh, Kansu; Jap.
- **potamophila** Herder · G:Fluss-Esche · ♄ d Z6; C-As.
- *pubescens* Lam. = Fraxinus pennsylvanica var. pennsylvanica
- **quadrangulata** Michx. · E:Blue Ash; G:Blau-Esche · ♄ d Z5 Ⓝ; Can.: Ont.; USA: NE, NCE, Okla., SE
- *rhynchophylla* Hance = Fraxinus chinensis var. rhynchophylla
- *rotundifolia* Lam. = Fraxinus ornus var. rotundifolia
- *rotundifolia* Mill. = Fraxinus angustifolia subsp. angustifolia
- **sieboldiana** Blume · E:Chinese Flowering Ash, Siebold Ash; G:Siebolds Esche · ♄ ♄ d Z6; China: Kingsi; S-Korea, Jap.
- **tomentosa** Michx. · E:Pumpkin Ash · ♄ d Z6; USA: NE, NCE, SE, Fla.
- **velutina** Torr. · E:Velvet Ash
- var. **coriacea** (S. Watson) Rehder · ♄ Z7; Calif., Nev., Utah, Ariz.
- var. **velutina** · G:Arizona-Esche · ♄ ♄ d Z7 V; USA: S-Calif., Ariz., N.Mex.; Mex.: Baja Calif., Sonora
- **xanthoxyloides** (G. Don) A. DC.
- var. **xanthoxyloides** · E:Afghan Ash;

G:Afghanische Esche · ♄ d Z6 Ⓝ; Moroc.,
Alger., Afgh., Kashmir, Nepal
- var. **dimorpha** (Coss. & Durieu) Wenz. ·
♄ d Z8; N-Afr.
- var. **dumosa** (Carrière) Lingelsh. · ♄ d
Z8; cult.

Freesia Eckl. ex Klatt -f- *Iridaceae* · 16 spp. ·
E:Freesia; F:Freesia; G:Freesie
- **alba** (G.L. Mey.) Gumbl. · ⚃ Z9 ⓚ;
S-Afr.
- **corymbosa** (Burm. f.) N.E. Br. · ⚃ Z9 ⓚ
II-V; S-Afr.
- *odorata* (Lodd.) Klatt = Freesia corymbosa
- **refracta** (Jacq.) Eckl. ex Klatt · ⚃ Z9 ⓚ
II-V; S-Afr., nat. in Mallorca
- var. *alba* G.L. Mey. = Freesia alba
- **sparmannii** (Thunb.) N.E. Br. · ⚃ D Z9
ⓚ II-V; Cape
- **Cultivars:**
- **many cultivars**

Fremontia Torr. = Fremontodendron
- *californica* Torr. = Fremontodendron
californicum
- *mexicana* (Davidson) J.F. Macbr. =
Fremontodendron mexicanum

Fremontodendron Coville -n-
Sterculiaceae · 3 spp. · E:Flannel Bush;
F:Arbre-à-flanelle; G:Flanellstrauch
- **californicum** (Torr.) Coville ·
E:California Beauty, Flannelbush, Fremontia; G:Kalifornischer Flanellstrauch ·
♄ ♄ e Z9 ⓚ; USA: Calif., Ariz.; Baja Calif.
- **mexicanum** Davidson · E:California
Beauty, Fremontia, Mexican Flannelbush; G:Mexikanischer Flanellstrauch · ♄
♄ e Z9 ⓚ; S-Calif., Baja Calif.

Frenela Mirb. = Callitris
- *hugelii* Carrière = Callitris columellaris

Freycinetia Gaudich. -f- *Pandanaceae* ·
305 spp. · G:Kletterschraubenpalme
- **cumingiana** Gaudich. · ♄ e ⚸ Z10 Ⓦ;
Phil.
- **insignis** Blume · ♄ e ⚸ Z10 Ⓦ IV-VI; Java
- *luzonensis* C. Presl = Freycinetia cumingiana

Freylinia Colla -f- *Scrophulariaceae* · 4 spp.
- **lanceolata** G. Don · E:Honey Bells · ♄ e
Z9 ⓚ XI; S-Afr.

- **undulata** Benth. · ♄ e Z9 ⓚ VI; S-Afr.

Fritillaria L. -f- *Liliaceae* · 134 spp. ·
E:Fritillary; F:Couronne impériale, Fritillaire; G:Kaiserkrone, Schachblume
- **acmopetala** Boiss. · ⚃ Z7 IV-V ▽; TR,
Cyprus, Lebanon, ? Syr.
- **affinis** (Schult. & Schult. f.) Sealy ·
E:Riceroot · ⚃ Z5 ▭ V ▽; Can.: B.C.;
USA: NW, Calif., Idaho
- **assyriaca** Baker · ⚃ Z6 ▽; TR, N-Iraq,
W-Iran
- **aurea** Schott · ⚃ Z7 IV ▽; TR
- **bithynica** Baker · ⚃ Z6 ▽; W-TR
- **camschatcensis** (L.) Ker-Gawl. · E:Black
Sarana · ⚃ Z4 VI ▽; Alaska, Can.: W;
USA: NW; Kamchat., Sakhal., Amur, Jap.
- *caussolensis* Goaty & Pons ex Ardoino =
Fritillaria orientalis
- **crassifolia** Boiss. & A. Huet · ⚃ Z7 ▽;
TR, N-Iraq, Cauc., Iran
- **davisii** Turrill · ⚃ Z7 ▽; S-GR
- **graeca** Boiss. & Spruner · ⚃ Z7 IV-V ▽;
Eur.: Ba
- **imperialis** L. · E:Crown Imperial;
F:Couronne impériale; G:Kaiserkrone ·
⚃ Z4 IV-V ⚘ ▽; TR, N-Iraq, Iran, Afgh.,
Pakist., Kashmir
- **involucrata** All. · ⚃ Z7 ▽; SE-F, NW-I
- *lanceolata* Pursh = Fritillaria affinis
- **latifolia** Willd. · ⚃ Z6 IV ▽; Cauc.
- **meleagris** L. · E:Snake's Head Fritillary;
F:Oeuf de vanneau; G:Gewöhnliche
Schachblume, Kiebitzei · ⚃ Z4 IV-V ⚘
▽; Eur.* exc. Sc, Ib, nat. in Sc
- **michailovskyi** Fomin · ⚃ Z7 ▽; NE-TR
- *nigra* hort. = Fritillaria orientalis
- *ophioglossifolia* Freyn & Sint. = Fritillaria
crassifolia
- **orientalis** Adams · ⚃ Z7 ▽; Eur.: F, I, Ba,
RO, W-Russ; Cauc.
- **pallidiflora** Schrenk · F:Fritillaire à fleurs
pâles; G:Bleiche Kaiserkrone · ⚃ Z3 IV ▽;
NW-China, E-Sib.
- **persica** L. · F:Fritillaire de Perse;
G:Persische Kaiserkrone · ⚃ Z5 ▭ IV ▽;
Iran, Syr., Iraq
- **pinardii** Boiss. · ⚃ Z7 ▽; TR, Syr.,
Lebanon, Cauc. (Armen.), Iran
- **pluriflora** Torr. · E:Adobe Lily · ⚃ Z5 ▭
IV-V ▽; Calif.
- **pontica** Wahlenb. · ⚃ Z6 IV-V ▽; Eur.:
Ba; TR
- **pudica** (Pursh) Spreng. · E:Yellow
Fritillary · ⚃ Z3 IV ▽; Can.: W; USA: NW,

Rocky Mts., Calif.
- **pyrenaica** L. · E:Pyrenean Snake's Head · ♃ Z5 V ▽; Eur.: N-Sp., S-F; mts.
- **raddeana** Regel · ♃ Z4 ▽; NW-Iran, C-As.
- **recurva** Benth. · E:Scarlet Fritillary · ♃ Z7 ▭ IV-V ▽; USA: S-Oreg., Calif.
- **ruthenica** Wikstr. · ♃ Z4 IV-V ▽; Eur.: Russ.; Cauc., W-Sib., C-As.
- *schliemannii* Sint. = Fritillaria bithynica
- **sewerzowii** Regel · ♃ Z5 IV ▽; C-As., NW-China
- **sibthorpiana** (Sibth. & Sm.) Baker · ♃ Z8 ▽; SW-TR
- **verticillata** Willd. · ♃ Z5 ⚕ ▽; C-As., W-Sib.

Froelichia Moench -f- *Amaranthaceae* · c. 20 spp. · E:Cottonweed; G:Schneckenbaumwolle
- **floridana** (Nutt.) Moq. · E:Plains Snakecotton · ⊙ Z6; USA: NCE, NC, SE, SC

Fuchsia L. -f- *Onagraceae* · 105 spp. · E:Fuchsia; F:Fuchsia; G:Fuchsie
- **alpestris** Gardner · ♄ ⚘ Z10 Ⓚ; Braz.
- **ampliata** Benth. · ♄ Z10 Ⓚ; S-Col., Ecuad., Peru
- **arborescens** Sims · ♄ ♄ e D Z10 Ⓚ X-III; Mex., Guat., Costa Rica
- **austromontana** I.M. Johnst. · ♄ Ⓚ; Peru
- **ayavacensis** Kunth · ♄ Z10 Ⓚ; Peru
- × **bacillaris** Lindl. (*F. microphylla* × *F. thymifolia subsp. thymifolia*) · ♄ Z9 Ⓚ VI-IX; Mex.
- **boliviana** Carrière
- var. **boliviana** · ♄ e Z10 Ⓚ VI-IX; Ecuad., Peru, Bol., Arg.
- var. **luxurians** I.M. Johnst. · ♄ e Z10 Ⓚ; C-Am., trop. S-Am.
- **coccinea** Aiton · ♄ Z9 Ⓚ VI-IX; S-Braz.
- × **colensoi** Hook. f. (*F. excorticata* × ?) · ♄ d Z9 Ⓚ VII-IX; NZ
- *conica* Lindl. = Fuchsia magellanica var. conica
- **corymbiflora** Ruiz & Pav. · ♄ Z10 Ⓚ VII-IX
- **denticulata** Ruiz & Pav. · ♄ Z10 Ⓚ; Peru, Bol.
- *discolor* Lindl. = Fuchsia magellanica var. discolor
- **encliandra** Steud. · ♄ Z10 Ⓚ; Mex.
- **excorticata** (J.R. Forst. & G. Forst.) L. f. · E:Tree Fuchsia; G:Baum-Fuchsie · ♄ d Z9 Ⓚ; NZ
- × **exoniensis** Paxton (*F. cordifolia* × *F. magellanica var. conica*) · ♄ Ⓚ; cult.
- **fulgens** Moç. & Sessé ex DC. · ♄ Z10 Ⓚ VI-VIII; Mex.
- *globosa* Lindl. = Fuchsia magellanica var. conica
- *gracilis* Lindl. = Fuchsia magellanica var. gracilis
- **hemsleyana** Woodson & Seibert · ♄ Z10 Ⓚ V-IX; Costa Rica, Panama
- **lycioides** Andrews · ♄ s Z10 Ⓚ; Chile
- **macrantha** Hook. · ♄ ⇝ Ⓚ IV-VI; Peru
- *macrostemma* Ruiz & Pav. = Fuchsia magellanica var. magellanica
- **magellanica** Lam.
- var. **conica** (Lindl.) L.H. Bailey · ♄ Z7; cult.
- var. **discolor** (Lindl.) L.H. Bailey · ♄ Z7; Falkland
- var. *globosa* (Lindl.) L.H. Bailey = Fuchsia magellanica var. conica
- var. **gracilis** (Lindl.) L.H. Bailey · ♄ Z7; Mex.
- var. **magellanica** · E:Hardy Fuchsia; G:Scharlach-Fuchsie · ♄ Z7 V-IX; S-Chile
- var. **molinae** Espinosa · ♄ Z7; Chile (Chiloe)
- **microphylla** Kunth · ♄ Z10 Ⓚ IX-X; Mex.
- **minutiflora** Hemsl. · ♄ Z10 Ⓚ; Mex.
- **paniculata** Lindl. · ♄ ♄ Z10 Ⓚ; Mex, C-Am.
- *parviflora* hort. = Fuchsia × bacillaris
- *pendula* Salisb. = Fuchsia coccinea
- **perscandens** Cockayne & Allan · ♄ ≀ d ⚘ Ⓚ; NZ
- **procumbens** R. Cunn. ex A. Cunn. · E:Creeping Fuchsia; G:Kriechende Fuchsie · ♄ d ⚘ ⇝ Z9 Ⓚ III-V; NZ
- **regia** (Vand. ex Vell.) Munz
- subsp. **regia** · ♄ Z10 Ⓚ; Braz.
- subsp. **reitzii** P.E. Berry · ♄ Z10 Ⓚ; Braz.
- subsp. **serrae** P.E. Berry · ♄ Z10 Ⓚ; Braz.
- var. *alpestris* (Gardner) Munz = Fuchsia alpestris
- **sanctae-rosae** Kuntze · ♄ Ⓚ; Peru, Bol.
- *serratifolia* Ruiz & Pav. = Fuchsia denticulata
- **simplicicaulis** Ruiz & Pav. · ≀ ⚘ Z10 Ⓚ; C-Peru
- **splendens** Zucc. · ♄ Z9 Ⓚ VIII-XI; Mex., Guat., Costa Rica
- *syringiflora* Carrière = Fuchsia arborescens
- **thymifolia** Kunth · ♄ Z9 Ⓚ VI-IX; Mex.

– **triphylla** L. · ♄ e Z10 ⊚ V-XI; Hispaniola
– **tuberosa** K. Krause · ♄ ⊚; Peru
– **venusta** Kunth · ♄ Z10 ⊚; Col.
– **Cultivars:**
– **many cultivars**

× **Fujiwarara** hort. -f- Orchidaceae
(*Brassavola* × *Cattleya* × *Laeliopsis*)

Fumana (Dunal) Spach -f- *Cistaceae* · 9
(-15) spp. · F:Fumana; G:Nadelröschen
– **ericoides** (Cav.) Gand. · G:Aufrechtes
Nadelröschen, Felsen-Nadelröschen · ♄ e
Z8 ⊚ V-VII; Eur.: Ib, Fr, Sw, Ital-P, Ba;
NW-Afr,
– **procumbens** (Dunal) Gren. & Godr. ·
G:Gewöhnliches Nadelröschen · ♄ e △
Z7 ⋀ VIII-X; Eur.* exc. BrI, Sc; TR, Syr.,
Cauc., Iran

Fumaria L. -f- *Fumariaceae* · 50 spp. ·
E:Fumitory; F:Fumeterre; G:Erdrauch
– *bulbosa* auct. non L. (DC.) = Corydalis
cava
– *bulbosa* L. = Corydalis solida
– **capreolata** L. · E:White Ramping Fumitory; G:Rankender Erdrauch · ⊙ V-IX;
Eur.: Fr, Ib, Ital-P, BrI, Sw, Ba; TR, Cauc.,
nat. in G, EC-Eur.
– *cava* (L.) Mill. = Corydalis cava
– **densiflora** DC. · E:Dense-flowered
Fumitory; G:Dichtblütiger Erdrauch · ⊙
V-VI; Eur.: Ib, Fr, BrI, Ital-P, Ba, RO; TR,
Levant, C-As., N-Afr.
– *fungosa* Aiton = Adlumia fungosa
– **muralis** Sond. ex W.D.J. Koch ·
G:Mauer-Erdrauch; E:Common Ramping
Fumitory · ⊙ VI-IX; Eur.: Sc, BrI, Fr, G, Ib
– **officinalis** L.
– subsp. **officinalis** · E:Common Fumitory;
G:Gewöhnlicher Erdrauch · ⊙ V-X ⚥ ✖;
Eur.*, TR, Cyprus, Syr., Cauc., N-Afr.
– subsp. **wirtgenii** (W.D.J. Koch) Nyman ·
G:Wirtgens Erdrauch · ⊙ V-X; Eur.,
Moroc.
– **parviflora** Lam. · E:Fine-leaved Fumi-
tory; G:Kleinblütiger Erdrauch · ⊙ VI-IX;
Eur.: Ib, Fr, BrI, Ital-P, G, H, Ba, EC-Eur.;
TR, Levant, Cauc., Iran, C-As., N-Afr.
– **rostellata** Knaf · G:Geschnäbelter
Erdrauch · ⊙ VI-IX; Eur.: C-Eur., EC-Eur.,
Ba, E-Eur.; TR
– **schleicheri** Soy.-Will. · G:Dunkler
Erdrauch, Schleichers Erdrauch · ⊙ VI-IX;
Eur.: Fr, Ital-P, C-Eur., EC-Eur., Ba,

E-Eur.; TR
– *solida* (L.) Mill. = Corydalis solida
– **vaillantii** Loisel. · G:Blasser Erdrauch
– subsp. **schrammii** (Asch.) Nyman ·
G:Schramms Erdrauch · ⊙ VI-VIII; Eur.:
Ib, Fr, C-Eur., H, Ba, W-Russ. +
– subsp. **vaillantii** · E:Few-flowered Fumitory; G:Gewöhnlicher Blasser Erdrauch,
Vaillants Erdrauch · ⊙ V-X; Eur.*, TR,
Levant, Cauc., Iran, C-As., Him., NW-
Afr., Libya
– *wirtgenii* W.D.J. Koch = Fumaria
officinalis subsp. wirtgenii

Funkia Spreng. = Hosta
– *ovata* Spreng. = Hosta ventricosa
– *subcordata* Spreng. = Hosta plantaginea

Funtumia Stapf -f- *Apocynaceae* · 2 spp.
– **elastica** (P. Preuss) Stapf · ♄ ⊛ Ⓝ;
C-Afr., Uganda

Furcraea Vent. -f- *Agavaceae* · 23 spp.
– **bedinghausii** K. Koch = Furcraea parmentieri
– **cabuya** Trel. · ♈ Z9 ⊚ Ⓝ; Costa Rica to
Ecuad.
– *cubensis* (Jacq.) Haw. = Furcraea
hexapetala
– *elegans* Tod. = Furcraea stricta
– *flavoviridis* Hook. = Furcraea selloa
– **foetida** (L.) Haw. · E:Green Aloe,
Mauritius Hemp; G:Mauritiushanf · ♈ Z9
⊚ Ⓝ; Mex. (Yucatan), C-Am., S-Am.
– *gigantea* Vent. = Furcraea foetida
– **hexapetala** (Jacq.) Urb. · E:Bayonette;
G:Kubahanf · ♈ Z9 ⊚; Cuba, Haiti
– *lindenii* Jacobi = Furcraea selloa
– *macrophylla* Baker = Furcraea hexapetala
– **parmentieri** (Roezl) García-Mend. · ♈ Z9
⊚; C-Mex.
– *pubescens* Baker = Furcraea undulata
– *roezlii* André = Furcraea parmentieri
– **selloa** K. Koch · ♈ Z9 ⊚; Mex., Guat.,
Col.
– var. *marginata* Trel. = Furcraea selloa
– **stricta** Jacobi · ♈ Z9 ⊚; Mex.
– **undulata** Jacobi · ♈ Z9 ⊚; ? Mex.

Gagea Salisb. -f- *Liliaceae* · 162 spp. · E:Star
of Bethlehem; F:Gagéa; G:Gelbstern
– **bohemica** (Zauschn.) Schult. & Schult.
f. · G:Felsen-Gelbstern
– subsp. **bohemica** · G:Böhmischer Felsen-
Gelbstern · ♃ III-IV; Eur.: BrI, C-Eur.,

EC-Eur., Ital-P, Ba; TR, Palest., ? N-Afr.
- subsp. **saxatilis** (Mert. & W.D.J. Koch)
Asch. & Graebn. · G:Gewöhnlicher
Felsen-Gelbstern · ⧧ III-IV; Eur.: Fr,
Ital-P, C-Eur., Ba
- *fistulosa* auct. = Gagea fragifera
- **fragifera** (Vill.) Ehr. Bayer & G. López ·
G:Röhriger Gelbstern · ⧧ VI-VII; Eur.: Ib,
Fr, C-Eur., Ital-P, Ba, E-Eur.; mts.
- **lutea** (L.) Ker-Gawl. · E:Yellow Star-of-
Bethlehem; G:Wald-Gelbstern · ⧧ Z6 IV;
Eur.*, Cauc., Him., W-Sib., E-Sib., Amur,
Sakhal., Kamchat. N-China, Korea, Jap.
- **minima** (L.) Ker-Gawl. · G:Kleiner Gelb-
stern · ⧧ Z6 III-IV; Eur.: Ital-P, C-Eur.,
EC-Eur., Sc, Ba, E-Eur.; Cauc., W-Sib.
- **pomeranica** R. Ruthe · G:Pommerscher
Gelbstern · ⧧; Eur.: D +
- **pratensis** (Pers.) Dumort. · G:Wiesen-
Gelbstern · ⧧ Z7 III-V; Eur.* exc. BrI; TR
- **pusilla** (F.W. Schmidt) Schult. & Schult.
f. · G:Zwerg-Gelbstern · ⧧ III-IV; Eur.:
C-Eur., EC-Eur., Ba, E-Eur., ? I; TR,
Cauc., C-As., China: Sinkiang
- **spathacea** (Hayne) Salisb. · G:Scheiden-
Gelbstern · ⧧ IV-V; Eur.: Fr, C-Eur.,
EC-Eur., Ba, Sc, E-Eur., ? Ital-P
- *sylvatica* (Pers.) Loudon = Gagea lutea
- **villosa** (M. Bieb.) Sweet · G:Acker-
Gelbstern · ⧧ Z7 III-IV; Eur.* exc. BrI; TR,
Cauc., Iran, NW-Afr.

Gaillardia Foug. -f- *Asteraceae* · 28 spp. ·
E:Blanketflower; F:Gaillarde; G:Kokar-
denblume
- **amblyodon** J. Gay · E:Maroon Blanket
Flower · ⊙ Z8 VI-XI; Tex.
- **aristata** Pursh · E:Great Blanket Flower;
G:Prärie-Kokardenblume · ⧧ Z6 VI-IX;
Can.: E; USA: NW, Rocky Mts., SW, nat.
in Azor., S-Sp.
- *bicolor* Lam. = Gaillardia pulchella var.
pulchella
- × **grandiflora** Van Houtte (G. aristata ×
G. pulchella) · G:Großblumige Kokardenblume · ⧧ Z6
- **some cultivars**
- **lanceolata** Michx. · ⊙ ⊙ ⧧ Z7 VI-IX;
USA: SE, Fla., SW
- *picta* Sweet = Gaillardia pulchella var.
picta
- **pulchella** Foug.
- var. **picta** (Sweet) A. Gray · E:Firewheel ·
⊙ Z8; Tex., Mex.
- var. **pulchella** · E:Annual Gaillardia,

Firewheel; F:Gaillardie; G:Kurzlebige
Kokardenblume · ⊙ Z8; USA: SE, Fla.,
SC, SW, Colo.

Galactites Moench -f- *Asteraceae* · 3 spp. ·
F:Chardon-Marie; G:Milchfleckdistel
- **tomentosa** Moench · ⊙ ⊙; Eur.: Ib,
Ital-P, Ba., Fr ; Canar., Moroc., Alger.,
Tun.

Galanthus L. -m- *Amaryllidaceae* · 20 spp. ·
E:Snowdrop; F:Perce-neige; G:Schnee-
glöckchen
- **elwesii** Hook. f. · E:Giant Snowdrop;
G:Großblütiges Schneeglöckchen · ⧧ Z6
II ▽ ✳; Eur.: Ba, RO, W-Russ.; TR
- **ikariae** Baker · ⧧ Z6 II-III ▽ ✳; TR,
Cauc.
- **nivalis** L. · E:Common Snowdrop,
Snowdrop; F:Perce-neige; G:Kleines
Schneeglöckchen · ⧧ Z4 II-III ⚘ ▽ ✳;
Eur.* exc. BrI, Sc, nat. in BrI, Sc
- **plicatus** M. Bieb. · E:Pleated Snowdrop ·
⧧ Z6 III ▽ ✳; Eur.: RO, Crim, W-Russ.
- **reginae-olgae** Orph. · E:Queen Olga's
Snowdrop; G:Herbst-Schneeglöckchen ·
⧧ Z7 ▽ ✳; Sic., GR, SW-TR
- **Cultivars:**
- **many cultivars**

Galax Sims -f- *Diapensiaceae* · 1 sp. ·
E:Wandflower, Wandplant; F:Galax;
G:Bronzeblatt
- **urceolata** (Poir.) Brummitt ·
E:Beetleweed, Wand Plant; G:Bronze-
blatt · ⧧ Z5 VI-VII; USA: NE, SE

Galaxia Thunb. -f- *Iridaceae* · 12 spp.
- **ovata** Thunb. · ⧧ Z9 ⚑ VII-VIII; SW-Cape

Gale Adans. = Myrica
- *palustris* (Lam.) A. Chev. = Myrica gale

Galeandra Lindl. -f- *Orchidaceae* · 37 spp.
- **batemanii** Rolfe · ⧧ Z10 ⚑ VII-VIII ▽ ✳;
Mex., Guat.
- **devoniana** R.H. Schomb. ex Lindl. · ⧧
Z10 ⚑ VI-VIII ▽ ✳; Guyan., Braz., Peru

Galega L. -f- *Fabaceae* · 6 spp. · E:Goat's
Rue; F:Rue de chèvre; G:Geißraute
- × **hartlandii** Hartland (G. officinalis × G.
orientalis) · ⧧ ⋈ Z4 VII-VIII; cult.
- **some cultivars**
- **officinalis** L. · E:Galega, Goat's Rue;

G:Echte Geißraute · � ⚥ Z4 VI-VIII ⚥
⚘ Ⓝ; Eur.* exc. BrI, Sc; TR, Lebanon,
Cauc., Iran, Pakist.
- **orientalis** Lam. · ⑫ Z6; Cauc.
- *persica* Pers. = Galega officinalis
- *tricolor* Hook. = Galega officinalis

Galeobdolon Huds. -m- *Lamiaceae* · 1 sp. ·
G:Falsche Goldnessel
- **endtmannii** (G.H. Loos) Holub ·
G:Falsche Goldnessel · ⑫ ; Eur.: D +

Galeopsis L. -f- *Lamiaceae* · 10 spp. ·
E:Hemp Nettle; F:Galéopsis; G:Hohlzahn
- **angustifolia** Hoffm. · E:Red Hemp
Nettle; G:Schmalblättriger Hohlzahn · ⊙
VI-X; Eur.*
- **bifida** Boenn. · E:Bifid Hemp Nettle;
G:Zweispaltiger Hohlzahn · ⊙ VI-X; Eur.*
exc. Ib; Cauc., W-Sib., E-Sib., Amur,
Sakhal., C-As., Mong., nat. in N-Am.
- **ladanum** L. · E:Broad-leaved Hemp Net-
tle, Red Hemp Nettle; G:Breitblättriger
Hohlzahn · ⊙ VI-X; Eur.* exc. BrI; TR,
Cauc., W-Sib., E-Sib.
- *ochroleuca* Lam. = Galeopsis segetum
- **pubescens** Besser · E:Hairy Hemp
Nettle; G:Gewöhnlicher Weichhaariger
Hohlzahn · ⊙ VII-IX; Eur.: Fr, Ital-P,
C-Eur., EC-Eur., Ba, E-Eur.
- **segetum** Neck. · E:Downy Hemp Nettle;
G:Gelber Hohlzahn; · ⊙ VI-IX ⚥ ; Eur.:
BrI, Fr, Ib, C-Eur., DK, Ital-P, Slove., nat.
in Ba, RO
- **speciosa** Mill. · E:Large-flowered Hemp
Nettle; G:Bunter Hohlzahn · ⊙ VI-X;
Eur.* exc. Ib; W-Sib.
- **tetrahit** L. · E:Common Hemp Nettle,
Hemp Nettle; G:Gewöhnlicher Hohlzahn
· ⊙ VI-X ⚥ ; Eur.*

Galeottia A. Rich. -f- *Orchidaceae* · 12 spp.
- **fimbriata** (Linden & Rchb. f.) Schltr. · ⑫
Z10 ⓜ ▽ ✳; Col.

Galinsoga Ruiz & Pav. -f- *Asteraceae* · c.
15 spp. · E:Gallant Soldier; F:Scabieuse
des champs; G:Franzosenkraut,
Knopfkraut
- **ciliata** (Raf.) S.F. Blake · E:Shaggy
Soldier; G:Behaartes Knopfkraut · ⊙ V-X;
Mex., nat. in cosmop., Eur.*
- **parviflora** Cav. · E:Gallant Soldier;
G:Franzosenkraut, Kleinblütiges Knopfkraut · ⊙ V-X; Mex., nat. in cosmop. exc.

Sib.; Eur.*
- *quadriradiata* auct. non Ruiz & Pav. =
Galinsoga ciliata

Galipea Aubl. -f- *Rutaceae* · 8-14 spp. ·
E:Angostura; F:Galipéa; G:Angostura-
baum
- **officinalis** J. Hancock · E:Angostura;
G:Angosturabaum · ♄ e ⓜ ⚥ ; S-Am.

Galium L. -n- *Rubiaceae* · 622 spp. ·
E:Bedstraw; F:Gaillet; G:Klebkraut,
Labkraut
- **album** Mill. · G:Großblütiges Wiesen-
Labkraut
- subsp. **album** · G:Weißes Wiesen-
Labkraut · ⑫ VI-IX; Eur.*, TR, Lebanon, ?
Syr., Cauc., W-Sib., Madeira
- subsp. **pycnotrichum** (Heinr. Braun)
Krendl · G:Dichthaariges Wiesen-
Labkraut · ⑫ VI-IX; EC-Eur., SE-Eur., TR,
Lebanon, Cauc., W-Sib.
- **anisophyllon** Vill. · G:Ungleichblättriges
Labkraut · ⑫ VII-IX; Eur.: Fr, Ital-P,
C-Eur., EC-Eur., Ba, E-Eur.; mts.
- **aparine** L. · E:Cleavers, Goosegrass;
G:Kletten-Labkraut · ⊙ IX-X ⚥ ; Eur.*,
TR, Levant, Cauc., W-Sib., C-As., NW-
Afr., Libya, nat. in cosmop.
- **aristatum** L. · E:False Baby's Breath;
G:Grannen-Labkraut · ⑫ Z6 VI-VIII; Eur.:
F, I, G, A, Sw; Pyr., Alp.
- **austriacum** Jacq. · G:Österreichisches
Labkraut · ⑫ VI-VIII; Eur.: A, EC-Eur., Ba,
I; mts.
- **boreale** L. · E:Northern Bedstraw; G:Nor-
disches Labkraut · ⑫ Z2 VII-VIII; Eur.: Ba,
Fr, BrI, EC-Eur., Sc, Ital-P, E-Eur., A, G,
Ch., TR, Cauc., Sib., E-As. As., N-Am.
- × **carmineum** Beauverd (*G. anisophyllon*
× *G.* × *centroniae*) · ⑫ ; Eur.: F, I, Sw;
S-Alp.
- × **centroniae** Cariot (*G. pumilum* × *G.
rubrum*) · G:Savoyer Labkraut · ⑫ VI-VIII;
Eur.: F, I, Sw, A, Slove ; Alp.
- *cruciata* (L.) Scop. = Cruciata laevipes
- **divaricatum** Lam. · G:Sparriges
Labkraut · ⊙; Eur.: Ib, Fr, Ital-P, EC-Eur.,
Ba, RO; TR, Syr., Cyprus, Lebanon, nat.
in Sw
- **glaucum** L. · G:Blaugrünes Labkraut · ⑫
V-VII; Eur.: Ib, Fr, C-Eur., EC-Eur., Ba,
E-Eur.
- **laevigatum** L. · G:Glattes Labkraut · ⑫
VI-VIII; Eur.: F, I, Sw, A, Ba , ? Ib; mts.

– **lucidum** All. · G:Glänzendes Labkraut ·
4 VI-VIII; Eur.: Ib, Fr, Ital-P, C-Eur., Ba,
RO; Cauc., Syr.
– **megalospermum** All. · G:Schweizer
Labkraut · 4 VII-VIII; Eur.: F, I, Sw, G, A;
Alp.
– **meliodorum** (Beck) Fritsch · G:Honig-
Labkraut · 4 VI-VIII; Eur.: A; NE-Alp.
– **mollugo** L. · E:False Baby's Breath,
Hedge Bedstraw; G:Kleinblütiges
Wiesen-Labkraut · 4 ⤳ Z3 V-IX ⚥ ;
Eur.*
– **noricum** Ehrend. · G:Norisches
Labkraut · 4 VII-IX; Eur.: I, G, A, Slove.;
E-Alp.
– **odoratum** (L.) Scop. · E:Sweet Wood-
ruff, Woodruff; F:Aspérule odorante;
G:Waldmeister · 4 D Z5 V-VI ⚥ Ⓝ; Eur.*,
TR, Cauc., N-Iran, W-Sib., E-Sib., Amur,
Sakhal., Jap., C-As.
– **palustre** L. · G:Sumpf-Labkraut
– subsp. **elongatum** (C. Presl) Lange ·
E:Great Marsh Bedstraw; G:Hohes
Labkraut · 4 VI-VIII; Eur.*
– subsp. **palustre** · E:Marsh Bedstraw;
G:Gewöhnliches Sumpf-Labkraut · 4
V-IX; Eur.*, TR, Cauc., Sib., C-As., nat. in
N-Am.
– **parisiense** L. · E:Wall Bedstraw;
G:Pariser Labkraut · ⊙ VI-VIII; Eur.* exc.
Sc; N-Afr.
– × **pomeranicum** Retz. (*G. album* × *G.
verum*) · G:Weißgelbes Labkraut · 4
VI-IX; Eur.*
– **pumilum** Murray · E:Slender Bedstraw;
G:Heide-Labkraut, Triften-Labkraut · 4
VII-IX; Eur.* exc. BrI, Ib
– **rivale** (Sibth. & Sm.) Griseb. · G:Bach-
Labkraut · 4 VII-VIII; Eur.: A, EC-Eur.,
Ba, E-Eur.; TR, Cauc., Iran, W-Sib., C-As.
– **rotundifolium** L. · G:Rundblättriges
Labkraut · 4 VI-IX; Eur.* exc. BrI, Sc; TR,
Cauc., Iran, Afgh., nat. in Sc
– **rubioides** L. · G:Krapp-Labkraut · 4 VI-
VIII; Eur.: A, EC-Eur., Ba, E-Eur.; Cauc.,
W-Sib., nat. in Sw
– **rubrum** L. · G:Rotes Labkraut · 4 △ Z6
VII; Eur.: Ch, I; S-Alp., Apenn.
– **saxatile** L. · E:Heath Bedstraw; G:Harzer
Labkraut · 4 VI-VIII; Eur.*
– **schultesii** Vest · G:Schultes Labkraut · 4
VI-IX; Eur.: C-Eur., EC-Eur., Ba, E-Eur.
– **spurium** L. · E:False Cleavers; G:Acker-
Labkraut, Kahles Grünblütiges Labkraut
· ⊙ V-X; Eur.*, TR, Iraq, Iran, Afgh.,

Pakist., C-As., N-As., N-Afr.
– **sterneri** Ehrend. · E:Limestone Bedstraw;
G:Sterners Labkraut · 4 VI-VIII; Eur.: BrI,
Sc, D
– **sudeticum** Tausch · G:Sudeten-
Labkraut · 4 VII-IX; Eur.: G, CZ, PL; mts.
– **suecicum** (Sterner) Ehrend. · G:Schwed-
isches Labkraut · 4 VI-VIII; Eur.: Swed,
N-D
– **sylvaticum** L. · E:Scotch Mist; G:Wald-
Labkraut · 4 VII-VIII; Eur.: Fr, C-Eur.,
EC-Eur., Ital-P, Ba
– *triandrum* Hyl. = Asperula tinctoria
– **tricornutum** Dandy · E:Rough Corn
Bedstraw; G:Dreihörniges Labkraut · ⊙
VII-X; Eur.* exc. BrI; TR, Iraq, Cauc.,
Iran, C-As., Kashmir, Tibet, nat. in BrI
– **trifidum** L. · G:Dreispaltiges Labkraut ·
4 VI-VII; Eur.: Sc, PL, Russ., F (E-Pyr.),
A(E-Alp.); TR, W-Sib., E-Sib., Kamchat.,
Mong., Jap., N-Am.
– **triflorum** Michx. · E:Fragrant Bedstraw;
G:Dreiblütiges Labkraut · 4 VII-VIII;
Eur.: Sc, Russ., Sw; circumboreal,
Greenl.
– **truniacum** (Ronniger) Ronniger ·
G:Traunsee-Labkraut · 4 VI-VIII; Eur.: G,
A; NE-Alp.
– **uliginosum** L. · E:Fen Bedstraw;
G:Moor-Labkraut · 4 VI-IX; Eur.*, TR,
N-As., C-As.
– **valdepilosum** Heinr. Braun · G:Mähr-
isches Labkraut · 4 VI-VIII; Eur.: G, DK,
EC-Eur., W-Russ.
– **verrucosum** Huds. · G:Anis-Labkraut ·
⊙ VI-VII; Eur.: Ib, Fr, Ital-P, Ba, nat. in
C-Eur., EC-Eur.
– **verum** L. · E:Lady's Bedstraw, Yellow
Bedstraw; G:Echtes Labkraut · 4 Z3 VI-IX
⚥ ; Eur.*, TR, Syr., N-Iraq, Cauc., Iran,
W-Sib., E-Sib., Amur, Sakhal., Kamchat.,
C-As., Mong., Manch., Jap., NW-Afr., nat.
in N-Am.
– **wirtgenii** F.W. Schultz · G:Wirtgens
Labkraut · 4 V-VI; C-Eur.

Galphimia Cav. -f- *Malpighiaceae* · 10 spp.
– *glauca* (Poir.) Cav. = Thryallis glauca

Galtonia Decne. -f- *Hyacinthaceae* · 4 spp. ·
E:Summer Hyacinth; F:Galtonia, Jacinthe
du Cap; G:Galtonie, Sommerhyazinthe
– **candicans** (Baker) Decne. · E:Summer
Hyacinth; G:Sommerhyazinthe · 4 Z7
VII-VIII; S-Afr.

Garcia Vahl ex Rohr -f- *Euphorbiaceae* ·
  2 spp.
– **nutans** Vahl ex Rohr · E:False Tungoil
  Tree · ♄ ⓦ Ⓝ; Mex., C-Am., W.Ind., Col.

Garcinia L. -f- *Clusiaceae* · c. 200 spp. ·
  E:Mangosteen; F:Guttier, Mangoustanier;
  G:Mangostane
– **cochinchinensis** (Lour.) Choisy · ♄ e ⓦ
  Ⓝ; Cambodia, S-Vietn.
– **dulcis** (Roxb.) Kurz · E:Gourka · ♄ e ⓦ
  Ⓝ; Java, Timor, Molucca Is., Phil.
– **hanburyi** Hook. f. · E:Gamboge; G:Gum-
  migutti · ♄ e ⓦ ⚘ Ⓝ; Indochina
– **indica** (Thouars) Choisy · ♄ e ⓦ Ⓝ; Ind.
– **madruno** (Kunth) Hammel · G:Marien-
  balsam · ♄ e ⓦ Ⓝ; Col., Ecuad., Peru
– **mangostana** L. · E:Mangosteen;
  G:Mangostane · ♄ e ⓦ Ⓝ; Malay. Pen.
– **morella** Desr. · ♄ e ⓦ Ⓝ; Ind., Sri Lanka,
  Burma, Thail., Malay. Pen.

Gardenia J. Ellis -f- *Rubiaceae* · 144 spp. ·
  E:Gardenia; F:Gardénia, Jasmin du Cap;
  G:Gardenie
– **amoena** Sims · ♄ e ⓦ VI; China
– *augusta* Merr. = Gardenia jasminoides
– **cornuta** Hemsl. · E:Horned Gardenia;
  G:Horn-Gardenie · ♄ e ⓦ; S-Afr.
– *florida* L. = Gardenia jasminoides
– **jasminoides** J. Ellis · E:Cape Jasmine;
  G:Kap-Gardenie · ♄ e ✕ D ⓦ VII-X ♀ Ⓝ;
  Jap., Riukiu-Is., Taiwan, China
– **some cultivars**
– *lucida* Roxb. = Gardenia resinifera
– **resinifera** Roth · ♄ ♄ e ⓦ; Ind., Burma,
  Phil.
– *spatulifolia* Stapf & Hutch. = Gardenia
  volkensii subsp. spathulifolia
– *stanleyana* Hook. = Rothmannia
  longiflora
– **thunbergia** L. f. · E:White Gardenia;
  G:Thunbergs Gardenie · ♄ e ⓦ I-III;
  Mozamb., S-Afr.
– **volkensii** K. Schum.
– subsp. **spathulifolia** (Stapf & Hutch.)
  Verdc. · ♄ ♄ e ⓦ; S-Afr.

Garrya Douglas ex Lindl. -f- *Garryaceae* ·
  15 spp. · E:Silk Tassel, Tassel Tree;
  F:Garrya; G:Becherkätzchen
– **elliptica** Douglas ex Lindl. · E:Silk Tassel
  Bush ; G:Spalier-Becherkätzchen · ♄ ♄ e
  Z8 Ⓚ I-III Ⓝ; USA: Oreg., Calif.
– **fadyenii** Hook. · ♄ e Z9 Ⓚ I-III; Jamaica,

Cuba
– **fremontii** Torr. · E:Bearbrush · ♄ e Z7;
  Calif., Oreg., Wash.
– **wrightii** Torr. · E:Wright's Silk Tassel · ♄
  e Z8 Ⓚ; USA: SW, W-Tex.

Gasoul Adans. = Mesembryanthemum
– *crystallinum* (L.) Rothm. = Mesembryanthemum crystallinum

Gasteria Duval -f- *Aloaceae* · 17 spp. ·
  F:Gastérie, Langue-de-chevreuil;
  G:Gasterie
– **acinacifolia** (Jacq.) Haw. · ⌃ Ⴗ Z9 Ⓚ;
  S-Afr.
– *angulata* (Willd.) Haw. = Gasteria
  carinata var. carinata
– *angustifolia* (Aiton) Duval = Gasteria
  disticha
– *armstrongii* Schönland = Gasteria nitida
  var. armstrongii
– **bicolor** Haw.
– var. **bicolor** · ⌃ Ⴗ Z9 Ⓚ; Cape
– var. **liliputana** (Poelln.) Van Jaarsv. · ⌃ Ⴗ
  Z9 Ⓚ; S-Afr.
– *caespitosa* Poelln. = Gasteria bicolor var.
  bicolor
– *candicans* Haw. = Gasteria acinacifolia
– **carinata** (Mill.) Duval
– var. **carinata** · ⌃ Ⴗ Z9 Ⓚ; S-Cape.
– var. **verrucosa** (Mill.) Van Jaarsv. · ⌃ Ⴗ
  Z9 Ⓚ; Cape
– **disticha** (L.) Haw. · ⌃ Ⴗ Z9 Ⓚ; Cape
– var. *angustifolia* (Aiton) Baker = Gasteria
  disticha
– *excavata* (Willd.) Haw. = Gasteria
  carinata var. carinata
– *formosa* Haw. = Gasteria bicolor var.
  bicolor
– *humilis* Poelln. = Gasteria carinata var.
  carinata
– *liliputana* Poelln. = Gasteria bicolor var.
  liliputana
– *lingua* (Thunb.) A. Berger = Gasteria
  disticha
– *maculata* (Thunb.) Haw. = Gasteria
  bicolor var. bicolor
– *minima* hort. = Gasteria bicolor var.
  liliputana
– *neliana* Poelln. = Gasteria pillansii
– *nigricans* (Haw.) Duval = Gasteria
  disticha
– **nitida** (Salm-Dyck) Haw.
– var. **armstrongii** (Schönland) Van
  Jaarsv. · ⌃ Ⴗ Z9 Ⓚ; Cape

– var. **nitida** · ⌁ ⍦ Z9 ⌂; S-Afr.
– *obliqua* (DC.) Duval = Gasteria bicolor
var. bicolor
– *picta* Haw. · = Gasteria bicolor var. bicolor
– **pillansii** Kensit · ⌁ ⍦ Z9 ⌂; S-Afr.
– *planifolia* (Baker) Baker = Gasteria
bicolor var. bicolor
– **pulchra** (Aiton) Haw.
– **rawlinsonii** Oberm. · ⌁ ⍦ Z9 ⌂; SE-Cape
– *schweickerdtiana* Poelln. = Gasteria
carinata var. carinata
– *subcarinata* (Salm-Dyck) Haw. = Gasteria
carinata var. carinata
– *verrucosa* (Mill.) Duval = Gasteria
carinata var. verrucosa

Gastridium P. Beauv. -n- *Poaceae* · 3 spp. ·
E:Nit Grass; F:Gastridium; G:Nissegras
– **ventricosum** (Gouan) Schinz & Thell. ·
E:Nit Grass; G:Nissegras · ⊙; Eur.: Ib,
Fr, Ital-P, Ba, RO, BrI; TR, Syr., Iraq,
Lebanon, Israel, W-Iran, NW-Afr., Libya,
nat. in USA, S-Austr.

Gastrochilus D. Don -m- *Orchidaceae* ·
52 spp.
– **bellinus** (Rchb. f.) Kuntze · ⌁ Z10 ⌂
II-III ▽ ✳; Burma, Thail.

Gaudinia P. Beauv. -f- *Poaceae* · 4 spp. ·
E:French Oat Grass; F:Gaudinie;
G:Ährenhafer
– **fragilis** (L.) P. Beauv. · E:French Oat
Grass; G:Zerbrechlicher Ährenhafer ·
⊙ ⋈ VI-VIII; Eur.: Ib, Fr, Ital-P, Sw, Ba,
Crim; TR, Syr., Canar., NW-Afr., Libya,
nat. in BrI

× *Gaulnettya* Marchant = Gaultheria
– *wisleyensis* Marchant = Gaultheria ×
wisleyensis

Gaultheria Kalm ex L. -f- *Ericaceae* ·
134 spp. · E:Shallon; F:Gaultheria, Thé
des bois; G:Rebhuhnbeere, Scheinbeere
– **cuneata** (Rehder & E.H. Wilson) Bean ·
G:Chinesische Scheinbeere · ♄ e ⚭ Z6 VI;
W-China
– **forrestii** Diels · G:Forrests Scheinbeere ·
♄ e Z6 V-VI; W-China: Yunnan
– **hispida** R. Br. · E:Snow Berry, Tasmanian Waxberry; G:Tasmanische
Scheinbeere · ♄ e ⚭ Z9 ⌂ V-VI; Austr.:
Victoria, Tasman.
– **hookeri** C.B. Clarke · G:Hookers

Scheinbeere · ♄ e ⚭ Z6 III-IV; E-Him.
– **insana** (Molina) D.J. Middleton · ♄ e Z8
⌂ ✻; Chile, Arg.
– **itoana** Hayata · G:Taiwanesische
Scheinbeere · ♄ e ⚭ Z6; Taiwan
– **miqueliana** Takeda · G:Miquels
Scheinbeere · ♄ e ⚭ Z7 VI; Jap., Sakhal.,
Aleuten
– **mucronata** (L. f.) Hook. & Arn. ·
E:Prickly Heath; F:Pernettya mucronée;
G:Kahle Steife Scheinbeere · ♄ e ⚭ Z6
V-VI ✻; S-Chile
– **myrsinoides** Kunth
– var. **myrsinoides** · ♄ e Z9 ⌂; C-Am.,
S-Am.
– var. **pentlandii** (DC.) Kunth · ♄ e ⚭ Z9
⌂ V-VI; C-Am., S-Am.
– **nummarioides** D. Don · G:HImalaya-
Scheinbeere · ♄ e Z9 ⌂; Him., Ind.:
Khasia Hills; SW-China, Burma, Malay.
Arch.
– **procumbens** L. · E:Checkerberry;
F:Gaulthérie du Canada; G:Niedere Rebhuhnbeere, Niederliegende Scheinbeere
· ♄ e ⌇ ⚭ Z5 VII-VIII ☦; Can.: E; USA;
NE, NCE, SE
– **pyroloides** Hook. f. & Thomson ex Miq. ·
♄ e ⚭ Z6 V-VI; E-Him.
– **rupestris** (L. f.) D. Don ex G. Don · ♄ e
Z7 VI-VII; NZ
– **semi-infera** (C.B. Clarke) Airy Shaw · ♄
e ⚭ Z9 ⌂ V; Him., W-China
– **shallon** Pursh · E:Salal; F:Palommier;
G:Hohe Rebhuhnbeere, Shallon-
Scheinbeere · ♄ e Z6 V-VI; Alaska, Can.:
W; USA: NW, Calif.
– **tasmanica** (Hook. f.) D.J. Middleton · ♄
e ⌇ ⚭ Z7 V; Tasman.
– **trichophylla** Royle · ♄ e ⌇ ⚭ Z7 ∧ V;
Him., W-China
– **veitchiana** Craib · G:Veitchs Scheinbeere · ♄ e ⚭ ⌂ V; China: Hubei
– × **wisleyensis** Marchant ex D.J.
Middleton (*G. mucronata* × *G. shallon*) ·
G:Hybrid-Scheinbeere · ♄ e Z7 IV-VI; cult.
– **yunnanensis** (Franch.) Rehder ·
G:Yunnan-Scheinbeere · ♄ e Z6 V-VI;
China: Yunnan

× **Gauntlettara** hort. -f- *Orchidaceae*
(*Broughtonia* × *Cattleyopsis* × *Laeliopsis*)

Gaura L. -f- *Onagraceae* · 21 sp. · E:Bee
Blossom; F:Gaura; G:Prachtkerze
– **coccinea** (Nutt. ex Fraser) Pursh ·

E:Scarlet Beeblossom; G:Duftende
Prachtkerze · ⏀ Z4 VII-X; Can., USA:
NCE, NC, SC, SW, Rocky Mts., Calif.
- **lindheimeri** Engelm. & A. Gray ·
  E:Lindheimer's Bee Blossom · ⏀ ♄ d Z4
  VII-X; USA: La., Tex.
- **some cultivars**

Gaylussacia Kunth -f- *Ericaceae* · 48 spp. ·
  E:Huckleberry; F:Gaylussacia; G:Buckel-
  beere
- **baccata** (Wangenh.) K. Koch · E:Black
  Huckleberry, Huckleberry G:Schwarze;
  Buckelbeere · ♄ d V-VI; Can.: E, Sask.;
  USA: NE, NCE, SE
- **brachycera** (Michx.) A. Gray · E:Box
  Huckleberry; G:Buchs-Buckelbeere · ♄ e
  ∧ V-VI; USA: NE, Tenn.
- **dumosa** (Andrews) Torr. & A. Gray ex A.
  Gray · E:Dwarf Huckleberry; G:Zwerg-
  Buckelbeere · ♄ d ⤳ V-VI; Can.: E; USA:
  Ne, SE, Fla.
- **frondosa** (L.) Torr. & A. Gray ex Torr. ·
  E:Blue Huckleberry, Dangleberry;
  G:Blaue Buckelbeere · ♄ d V-VI; USA: NE,
  SE, Fla.
- *resinosa* (Aiton) Torr. & A. Gray =
  Gaylussacia baccata

Gazania Gaertn. -f- *Asteraceae* · 16 spp. ·
  E:Treasureflower; F:Gazanie; G:Gazanie
- *bracteata* N.E. Br. = Gazania krebsiana
  subsp. serrulata
- **krebsiana** Less.
- subsp. **krebsiana** · ⏀ Z9 ⍟; S-Afr.
- subsp. **serrulata** (DC.) Roessler · ⏀ Z9
  ⍟; S-Afr.
- **linearis** (Thunb.) Druce · ⊙ ⊙ ⏀ Z9 ⍟
  VII-IX; S-Afr.
- *longiscapa* DC. = Gazania linearis
- *nivea* auct. non Less. = Gazania krebsiana
  subsp. krebsiana
- **pavonia** (Andrews) R. Br. · E:Cape
  Treasure Flower; G:Kap-Gazanie · ⏀ Z9
  ⍟ VI-VIII; S-Afr.
- **pinnata** (Thunb.) Less. · ⏀ Z9 ⍟ VI-VIII;
  Cape
- *pygmaea* Sond. = Gazania krebsiana
  subsp. serrulata
- **rigens** (L.) Gaertn.
- var. **rigens** · E:Treasure Flower;
  G:Geäugte Gazanie · ♄ Z9 ⍟ VII-IX;
  S-Afr., nat. in P, Balear.
- var. **uniflora** (L. f.) Roessler · ♄ e Z9 ⍟
  V-IX; S-Afr.

- *splendens* hort. = Gazania rigens var.
  rigens
- *uniflora* (L. f.) Sims = Gazania rigens var.
  uniflora
- **Cultivars:**
- **many cultivars**

Geissorhiza Ker-Gawl. -f- *Iridaceae* ·
  85 spp.
- **aspera** Goldblatt · ⏀ Z8 ⍟ V; S-Afr.
- *excisa* (L. f.) Ker-Gawl. = Geissorhiza
  ovata
- *grandis* Hook. f. = Gladiolus grandiflorus
- **humilis** (Thunb.) Ker-Gawl. · ⏀ Z8 ⍟
  VI-VII; Cape
- **inflexa** (F. Delaroche) Ker-Gawl. · ⏀ Z8
  ⍟; SW-Cape
- var. **erosa** (Salisb.) Goldblatt = Geissorhiza inflexa
- **ovata** (Burm. f.) Asch. & Graebn. · ⏀ Z8
  ⍟ IV-V; S-Afr.
- *quinquangularis* Eckl. ex Klatt = Geissorhiza inflexa
- **radians** (Thunb.) Goldblatt · E:Wine
  Cup · ⏀ Z8 ⍟ V; S-Afr.
- *rochensis* (Ker-Gawl.) Ker-Gawl. = Geissorhiza radians
- *secunda* (P.J. Bergius) Ker-Gawl. =
  Geissorhiza aspera

Geitonoplesium A. Cunn. ex R. Br. -n-
  Philesiaceae · 1 sp.
- **cymosum** (R. Br.) A. Cunn. ex R. Br. ·
  ♄ e ⚥ ⍟; Phil., Kalimantan, N.Guinea,
  Solom., Austr.: Queensl., N.S.Wales,
  Victoria; Fiji

Gelsemium Juss. -n- *Loganiaceae* · 3 spp. ·
  E:Trumpet Flower, Yellow Jessamine;
  F:Jasmin de Virginie; G:Jasminwurzel
- **rankinii** Small · E:Rankin's Trumpet
  Flower · ♄ e Z8 ⍟; USA: SE, Fla.
- **sempervirens** (L.) J. St.-Hil. · E:Evening
  Trumpet Flower, False Jasmine, False
  Jessamine; G:Gelbe Jasminwurzel · ♄ e ⚥
  D Z9 ⍟ IV-VI ⚥ ⚔; USA: Va., SE, Fla.;
  Guat.

Gemmingia Heist. ex Fabr. = Belamcanda
- *chinensis* (L.) Kuntze = Belamcanda
  chinensis

Genipa L. -f- *Rubiaceae* · 3 spp. ·
  E:Genipap; F:Génipayer; G:Genipap
- **americana** L. · E:Genipap, Marmalade

Box; G:Genipap · ♄ e Z10 ⓚ Ⓝ; Mex.,
C-Am., W.Ind., trop. S-Am.

Genista L. -f- *Fabaceae* · 87 spp. ·
E:Greenweed, Woadwaxen; F:Genêt;
G:Ginster
- **aetnensis** (Raf. ex Biv.) DC. · E:Mount
Etna Broom; G:Ätna-Ginster · ♄ d Z8 ⓚ
VII ✴; Sard., Sic.
- **anglica** L. · E:Needle Furze, Petty Whin;
G:Englischer Ginster · ♄ d Z7 V-VII ✴;
Eur.: BrI, Sc, C-Eur., Fr, Ib, Ital-P; Moroc.
- **aspalathoides** Lam. · ♄ d Z8 ⓚ VI ✴;
Sic., Alger., Tun.
- **canariensis** L. · E:Florist's Genista,
Genista · ♄ e Z9 ⓚ ✴; Canar.
- *candicans* L. = Genista canariensis
- *cinerea* (Vill.) DC. · G:Grauer Ginster · ♄
d Z7 V-VI ✴; Eur.: sp., F, I; Alger., Tun.
- *dalmatica* Bartl. = Genista sylvestris var.
sylvestris
- *decumbens* (Durande) Willd. = Cytisus
decumbens
- *delphinensis* Verl. = Chamaespartium
sagittale subsp. delphinensis
- *depressa* M. Bieb. = Genista tinctoria
subsp. tinctoria
- **ephedroides** DC. · ♄ d D Z9 ⓚ V-VI ✴;
Eur.: Sard.
- **germanica** L. · E:German Greenweed;
G:Deutscher Ginster · ♄ d Z6-7 V-VII ✴;
Eur.* exc. BrI, Ib
- **hispanica** L. · E:Spanish Gorse;
G:Spanischer Ginster · ♄ d △ Z7 ∧ VI-VII
✴; S-F, sp.
- *horrida* (Vahl) DC. = Echinospartum
horridum
- *humifusa* Vill. non L. = Genista villarsii
- **januensis** Viv. · E:Genoa Broom;
G:Genua-Ginster · ♄ d Z8 ⓚ V-VI ✴;
Eur.: Ital-P, Ba, RO
- **linifolia** L. · E:Flax Broom; G:Leinblät-
triger Ginster · ♄ e Z9 ⓚ ✴; Eur.: sp.,
Canar.; N-Afr.
- **lydia** Boiss. · E:Lydia Broom; F:Genêt de
Lydie; G:Lydischer Ginster · ♄ d Z7 ∧
V-VI ✴; Eur.: Ba; TR, Syr.
- **maderensis** (Webb & Berthel.) Lowe ·
G:Madeira-Ginster · ♄ e Z9 ⓚ V-VI ✴;
Madeira
- **monspessulana** (L.) O. Bolòs & Vigo ·
E:Montpelier Broom; G:Montpellier-
Ginster · ♄ e D Z8 ⓚ V-VI ✴; Eur.: Ib,
Fr, Ital-P, Ba; Azor., Canar., TR, Syr.,
Cauc., NW-Afr.

- **nissana** Petrovic · ♄ d Z6 VI-VII ✴;
Serb., AL, Maced.
- **pilosa** L. · E:Hairy Greenweed, Prostrate
Broom; F:Genêt poilu; G:Behaarter
Ginster · ♄ d ⤳ Z6 V-VII ✴; Eur.*
- *purgans* L. = Cytisus purgans
- **radiata** (L.) Scop. · E:Southern Greenweed; F:Genêt rayonnant; G:Strahlen-
Ginster · ♄ d Z6 V-VI ✴; Eur.: F, C-Eur.,
I, Ba, RO
- *sagittalis* L. = Chamaespartium sagittale
subsp. sagittale
- *scoparius* (L.) DC. = Cytisus scoparius
subsp. scoparius
- **sericea** Wulfen · E:Silvery Broom · ♄ d Z7
∧ V-VI ✴; Eur.: I, Ba; mts.
- × **spachiana** Webb (*G. canariensis* × *G.
stenopetala*) · ♄ e Z9 ⓚ III-V ✴; Canar.
(Tenerife)
- **stenopetala** Webb & Berthel. · ♄ e Z9 ⓚ
✴; Canar. Is.
- **sylvestris** Scop.
- **var. pungens** (Vis.) Rehder · ♄ d ⤳ Z8
ⓚ ⓐ V-VII ✴; Eur.: I, Ba
- **var. sylvestris** · E:Dalmatian Broom;
G:Wald-Ginster · ♄ d Z7 ✴; Eur.: I,
Slove., Croatia, Bosn., YU, AL
- **tinctoria** L. · G:Färber-Ginster
- **subsp. tinctoria** · E:Dyer's Broom, Dyer's
Greenweed; F:Genêt des teinturiers;
G:Eiblatt-Ginster, Gewöhnlicher Färber-
Ginster · ♄ d Z5 VI-VIII ⚥ ✴; Eur.*,
W-Sib.
- **var. hirsuta** K. Koch · ♄ d Z5 ✴
- **var. humilior** (Willd.) C.K. Schneid. · ♄ d
Z3 ✴; N-I, Sw (Tessin)
- **villarsii** Clementi · ♄ ⤳ △ Z7 VI ✴;
Eur.: F, Croatia, AL

Genistella Ortega = Chamaespartium
- *sagittalis* (L.) Gams = Chamaespartium
sagittale subsp. sagittale

Gentiana L. -f- *Gentianaceae* · 361 sp. ·
E:Gentian; F:Gentiane; G:Enzian
- **acaulis** L. · E:Trumpet Gentian;
F:Gentiane acaule, Gentiane à tige
courte; G:Keulen-Enzian, Kochs Enzian,
Stängelloser Silikat-Enzian · ⁴ △ Z3
VI-VII ⚥ ▽; Eur.* exc. BrI, Sc
- var. *alpina* (Vill.) Griseb. = Gentiana
alpina
- **affinis** Griseb. ex Hook. · ⁴ Z5 ▽; Can.:
W; USA: NW, Rocky Mts.
- **alpina** Vill. · E:Southern Gentian;

G:Alpen-Glocken-Enzian, Südalpen-
Enzian · ♃ △ Z6 VI ▽; Eur.: sp., F, I, Sw;
Sierra Nevada, Pyr., Alp.
- **andrewsii** Griseb. · E:Closed Gentian;
G:Blinder Enzian, Geschlossener Enzian
· ♃ Z6 VIII ▽; Can.: E, Sask.; USA: NE,
NCE, NC, SE, Colo.
- **angustifolia** Vill. · F:Gentiane à feuilles
étroites; G:Schmalblättriger Enzian · ♃ △
Z7 V-VI ▽; Eur.: F, Sw, I; Pyr., SW-Alp.,
Jura
- **asclepiadea** L. · E:Willow Gentian;
F:Gentiane fausse asclépiade; G:Schwal-
benwurz-Enzian · ♃ Z6 VII-VIII ⚥ ▽;
Eur.: Fr, Ital-P, C-Eur., EC-Eur., Ba
- **bavarica** L. · E:Bavarian Gentian · ♃ Z5
VII-VIII ▽; Eur.: Fr, Ital-P, Ba, C-Eur.;
Alp., Carp., Apenn.
- **brachyphylla** Vill. · E:Short-leaved
Gentian; G:Kurzblättriger Enzian · ♃ Z4
VII-VIII ▽; Eur.: sp., F, I, C-Eur., W-Ba,
RO; Sierra Nevada, Pyr., Alp.
- **burseri** Lapeyr. · ♃ Z7 ▽; Eur.: F, sp., I;
Pyren., SW-Alp.
- **clusii** E.P. Perrier & Songeon · E:Trumpet
Gentian; G:Clusius' Enzian, Stängelloser
Kalk-Enzian · ♃ △ Z6 VI ⚥ ▽; Eur.: F, I,
C-Eur., EC-Eur., Slove., Croatia, RO; mts.
- **cruciata** L. · G:Kreuz-Enzian
- subsp. **cruciata** · E:Cross Gentian;
F:Gentiane croisette; G:Gewöhnlicher
Kreuz-Enzian · ♃ Z5 VII-VIII ▽; Eur.*
exc. BrI, Sc; TR, Cauc., Iran, W-Sib.,
C-As.
- subsp. **phlogifolia** (Schott & Kotschy)
Tutin · G:Großer Kreuz-Enzian · ♃ Z5
VI-VII ▽; E-Carp., S-Carp.
- **dahurica** Fisch. · F:Gentiane de Sibérie;
G:China-Enzian, Dahurischer Enzian
· ♃ Z4 VI-VII ▽; E-Sib., Mong., Tibet,
N-China
- **decumbens** L. f. · G:Sibirischer Enzian ·
♃ Z4 VII-VIII ▽; Eur.: E-Russ.; C-As.,
NE-As.
- **dinarica** Beck · F:Gentiane des Alpes
Dinariques; G:Dinarischer Glocken-
Enzian · ♃ △ Z6 V-VI ▽; Eur.: I, Croatia,
AL; mts.
- *excisa* C. Presl = Gentiana acaulis
- **farreri** Balf. f. · G:Wellensittich-Enzian ·
♃ △ Z5 VIII-IX ▽; China: Tibet, Gansu
- **fetisowii** Regel & C.G.A. Winkl. · ♃
Z4 VIII ▽; W-Sib., C-As., Tibet, China:
Sinkiang
- **freyniana** Bornm. ex Freyn ·

G:Kleinasiatischer Enzian · ♃ △ Z7 VIII
▽; TR
- **frigida** Haenke · E:Styrian Gentian;
G:Kälte-Enzian, Tauern-Enzian · ♃ Z5
VII-IX ▽; Eur.: A, EC-Eur., BG, RO,
W-Russ.; Alp., Carp., SW-BG
- **froelichii** Jan ex Rchb. · E:Karawanken
Gentian; G:Karawanken-Enzian · ♃ Z6
VII-IX ▽; Eur.: I, A, Slove.; SE-Alp.
- **gracilipes** Turrill · G:Rosetten-Enzian · ♃
Z6 VII-VIII ▽; China: Kansu
- × **hexafarreri** hort. (*G. farreri* × *G.
hexaphylla*) · ♃ Z6; cult.
- **hexaphylla** Maxim. · G:Sechszipfliger
Enzian · ♃ Z5 VII-VIII ▽; China: Kansu,
E-Tibet
- *kesselringii* Regel = Gentiana walujewii
- *kochiana* E.P. Perrier & Songeon =
Gentiana acaulis
- **kurroo** Royle · G:Kies-Enzian · ♃ △ Z7
IX-X ▽; Him.
- **lutea** L. · E:Great Yellow Gentian, Yellow
Gentian; F:Gentiane jaune; G:Gelber
Enzian · ♃ Z5 VI-VIII ⚥ Ⓝ ▽; Eur.: Ib, Fr,
Ital-P, Ba, C-Eur., EC-Eur.; TR; mts., nat.
in CZ
- × **macaulayi** hort. (*G. farreri* × *G. sino-
ornata*) · ♃ Z4 ▽; cult.
- **macrophylla** Pall. · G:Großblättriger
Enzian · ♃ ⚥ ▽; China
- **makinoi** Kusn. · G:Japanischer Enzian ·
♃ Z6 ▽; Jap.: Honshu
- **nivalis** L. · E:Alpine Gentian; G:Schnee-
Enzian · ☉ Z5 VII-VIII ▽; Eur.*, Cauc.
- **occidentalis** Jakow. · E:Pyrenean Gen-
tian; G:Westlicher Glocken-Enzian · ♃ ▽;
Eur.: F, sp.; Pyr., Cordillera Cantábrica
- **orbicularis** Schur · G:Rundblättriger
Enzian · ♃ VII-VIII ▽; Eur.: Alp., Carp.;
TR
- **ornata** (Wall. ex G. Don) Griseb. ·
G:Nepal-Enzian · ♃ △ Z6 VIII-IX ▽;
Nepal
- **pannonica** Scop. · E:Brown Gentian;
G:Ungarischer Enzian · ♃ Z5 VII-IX ⚥ ▽;
Eur.: C-Eur., CZ, I, Slove.
- **parryi** Engelm. · E:Parry's Gentian;
G:Colorado-Enzian · ♃ △ Z4 VIII ▽;
USA: Utah, Colo., N.Mex.
- *phlogifolia* Schott & Kotschy = Gentiana
cruciata subsp. phlogifolia
- **pneumonanthe** L. · E:Marsh Gentian;
F:Gentiane pneumonanthe; G:Lungen-
Enzian · ♃ Z4 VII-IX ▽; Eur.*, Cauc.,
W-Sib., E-Sib.

– **prostrata** Haenke · E:Prostrate Gentian;
G:Niederliegender Enzian · ⊙ VII-VIII ▽;
Eur.: I, Sw, A; E-Alp.; Cauc.
– **pumila** Jacq. · G:Niedriger Frühlings-
Enzian, Zwerg-Enzian · ⁎ Z6 VI-X ▽;
Eur.: F, I, A, Slove.; Alp.
– **punctata** L. · E:Spotted Gentian;
G:Tüpfel-Enzian · ⁎ Z5 VII-IX ⚥ ▽; Eur.:
Fr, Ital-P, C-Eur., EC-Eur., Ba; mts.
– *purdomii* C. Marquand = Gentiana
gracilipes
– **purpurea** L. · E:Purple Gentian;
G:Purpur-Enzian · ⁎ Z5 VII-IX ⚥ Ⓝ ▽;
Eur.: F, C-Eur., I, Norw.
– **saxosa** G. Forst. · G:Neuseeländer
Strand-Enzian · ⁎ Z8 ⚑ ▽; NZ
– *schleicheri* (Vacc.) Kunz = Gentiana
terglouensis subsp. schleicheri
– **septemfida** Pall.
– var. **lagodechiana** Kusn. · G:Kaukasus-
Enzian · ⁎ △ Z3 VIII-IX ▽; E-Cauc.
– var. **septemfida** · E:Summer Gentian;
F:Gentiane d'été; G:Sommer-Enzian · ⁎
Z3 ▽; TR, Cauc., Iran
– **sino-ornata** Balf. f. · G:Chinesischer
Herbst-Enzian, Oktober Enzian · ⁎ △
Z7 ∧ IX-X ▽; China: Sichuan, Xizang,
Yunnuan
– **many cultivars**
– **straminea** Maxim. · G:Stroh-Enzian · ⁎
△ Z5 VIII-IX ▽; NE-Tibet, NW-China
– **terglouensis** Hacq. · E:Triglav Gentian;
G:Julischer Enzian, Triglav-Frühlings-
Enzian · ⁎ VII-VIII ▽; Eur.: F, I, Sw, A,
Slove.; Alp.
– subsp. **schleicheri** (Vacc.) Tutin · G:Sch-
leichers Frühlings-Enzian · ⁎ VII-VIII ▽;
Eur.: sp., F, I, Sw
– **tianshanica** Rupr. ex Kusn. · ⁎ Z7 ▽;
C-As., Him., Pakist., W-Ind., China
– **tibetica** King ex Hook. f. · G:Tibet-
Enzian; F:Gentiane du Tibet · ⁎ VII-VIII
▽; Him., Tibet
– **triflora** Pall. · ⁎ Z5 VIII-IX ▽; E-Sib.,
Amur, Sakhal., Korea, Jap.
– **utriculosa** L. · E:Bladder Gentian;
G:Schlauch-Enzian · ⊙ Z6 V-VIII ▽; Eur.:
BrI, Sc, Fr, G, EC-Eur., Croatia, E-Eur.
– **veitchiorum** Hemsl. · G:Veitchs Enzian ·
⁎ △ Z6 IX-X ▽; E-Tibet, Sichuan
– **verna** L. · E:Spring Gentian · ⁎ △ Z5
III-V ▽; Eur.* exc. Sc; TR, Cauc., N-Iran,
Moroc.
– **walujewii** Regel & Schmalh. · ⁎ ▽;
C-As.

– var. *kesselringii* (Regel) Kusn. = Gentiana
walujewii
– **wutaiensis** C. Marquand · ⁎ Z7 ▽;
China
– **Cultivars:**
– **many cultivars**

Gentianella Moench -f- Gentianaceae ·
125 spp. · E:Felwort; F:Gentiane ciliée;
G:Fransenenzian
– **amarella** (L.) Börner · E:Felwort; G:Bit-
terer Fransenenzian · ⊙ VIII-X ▽; Eur.:
BrI, Sc, Fr, Ital-P, EC-Eur., E-Eur.
– subsp. *uliginosa* (Willd.) Tzvelev =
Gentianella uliginosa
– **anisodonta** (Borbás) Á. Löve & D. Löve ·
G:Ungleichzähniger Fransenenzian · ⊙
VI-IX ▽; Eur.: I, Sw, A, Slove., Croatia;
Alp., Apenn., Croatia
– **aspera** (Hegetschw.) Skalický, Chrtek &
J. Gill · G:Rauer Fransenenzian · ⊙ V-IX
▽; Eur.: Sw, G, A, CZ, Slove.
– **austriaca** (A. Kern. & J. Kern.) Holub ·
G:Österreichischer Fransenenzian
– *austriaca* auct. non (A. Kern. & J. Kern.)
Holub = Gentianella bohemica
– **bohemica** Skalický · G:Böhmischer
Fransen-Einzian · ⊙ VII-X ▽; Eur.: SE-G,
NE-A, EC-Eur.
– **campestris** (L.) Börner · G:Feld-
Fransenenzian
– subsp. **baltica** (Murb.) Á. Löve & D.
Löve · G:Baltischer Fransenenzian · VIII-X
▽; Eur.: Swed, NW-F, G, PL
– subsp. **campestris** · E:Field Gentian;
G:Gewöhnlicher Feld-Fransenenzian · ⊙
V-X ▽; Eur.* exc. Ba
– **ciliata** (L.) Borkh. · E:Fringed Gentian;
G:Gewöhnlicher Fransenenzian · ⊙ VIII-X
▽; Eur.* exc. BrI; TR, Cauc., Iran, ? Sib.,
Moroc.
– **engadinensis** (Wettst.) Holub ·
G:Engadiner Fransenenzian · ⊙ VII-VIII
▽; Eur.: I, Sw; Alp.
– **germanica** (Willd.) Börner · E:German
Gentian; G:Gewöhnlicher Deutscher
Fransenenzian · ⊙ IX ▽; Eur.: BrI, Fr,
Ital-P, C-Eur., EC-Eur., RO
– **insubrica** (Kunz) Holub · G:Insubrischer
Fransenenzian · ⊙ VI-IX ▽; Eur.: S-Sw
– **lutescens** (Velen.) Holub · G:Karpaten-
Fransenenzian · ⊙ V-IX ▽; Eur.: G, A,
EC-Eur., RO
– **nana** (Wulfen) N.M. Pritch. · G:Zwerg-
Fransenenzian · ⊙ VII-IX ▽; Eur.: I, A;

E-Alp.
- *praecox* (A. Kern. & Jos. Kern.) Dostál ex E. Mayer = Gentianella lutescens
- **ramosa** (Hegetschw.) Holub · G:Büschel-Fransenenzian · ⊙ VII-IX ▽; Eur.: I, Sw, ? F; Alp.
- **tenella** (Rottb.) Börner · E:Slender Gentian; G:Zarter Fransenenzian · ⊙ VIII ▽; Eur.* exc. BrI; W-Sib., E-Sib., Kamchat., C-As.
- **uliginosa** (Willd.) Börner · E:Dune Gentian; G:Sumpf-Fransenenzian · ⊙ VIII-X ▽; Eur.: BrI, Sc, NL, G, EC-Eur., E-Eur., ? F

Geogenanthus Ule -m- *Commelinaceae* · 3 spp.
- **poeppigii** (Miq.) Faden · ⁴ ⑭; Braz., Peru
- *undatus* (K. Koch & Linden) Mildbr. & Strauss = Geogenanthus poeppigii
- *wittianus* (Ule) Ule = Geogenanthus poeppigii

Geonoma Willd. -f- *Arecaceae* · 64 spp.
- *acaulis* Mart. = Geonoma macrostachys var. acaulis
- **cuneata** H. Wendl. ex Spruce
- var. **gracilis** (H. Wendl.) Skov ex Govaerts & J. Dransf. · ♄ e ⑭; Braz.
- *elegans* Mart. = Geonoma pauciflora
- *ghiesbreghtiana* Linden & H. Wendl. = Calyptrogyne ghiesbreghtiana
- *gracilis* H. Wendl. = Geonoma cuneata var. gracilis
- **macrostachys** Mart.
- var. **acaulis** (Mart.) A.J. Hend. · ♄ e ⑭; C-Braz.
- **maxima** (Poit.) Kunth
- var. **spixiana** (Mart.) A.J. Hend. · ♄ e ⑭; Braz.
- **pauciflora** Mart. · ♄ e ⑭; C-Braz.
- **pohliana** Mart. · ♄ e ⑭; trop. Braz.
- *spixiana* Mart. = Geonoma maxima var. spixiana

Geranium L. -n- *Geraniaceae* · c. 300 spp. · E:Crane's Bill; F:Bec-de-grue, Géranium; G:Storchschnabel
- **albanum** M. Bieb. · G:Ostkaukasus-Storchschnabel · ⁴ Z7; SE-Cauc., Iran
- **argenteum** L. · G:Silber-Storchschnabel · ⁴ △ Z6 VI-VIII; Eur.: F, I, Slove.; mts.
- **aristatum** Freyn & Sint. · G:Alpenveilchen-Storchschnabel · ⁴ Z7 VI-VII;

Eur.: Maced., AL, GR; mts.
- **balkanum** hort. ex N. Taylor · ⁴; cult.
- **bohemicum** L. · G:Böhmischer Storchschnabel · ⊙ VI-VII; Eur.* exc. BrI, Ib; Cauc.
- × **cantabrigiense** Yeo (*G. dalmaticum* × *G. macrorrhizum*) · G:Cambridge-Storchschnabel · ⁴ Z5; cult.
- **some cultivars**
- **cinereum** Cav. · G:Grauer Storchschnabel
- subsp. **cinereum** · E:Ashy Cranesbill; F:Géranium cendré · ⁴ △ Z5 VI-VII; Eur.: Ib, Fr; Pyr.
- subsp. **subcaulescens** (L'Hér. ex DC.) R. Knuth · ⁴ △ Z5 VI-VII; Eur.: I, Ba; TR, Syr.
- **clarkei** Traub · G:Clarkes Storchschnabel · ⁴ Z7; Kashmir
- **columbinum** L. · E:Dove's Foot Cranesbill; G:Tauben-Storchschnabel · ⊙ Z7 VI-IX; Eur.*, TR, Levant, Cauc., N-Iran, NW-Afr., Libya, nat. in N-Am.
- **dalmaticum** (Beck) Rech. f. · F:Géranium de Dalmatie; G:Dalmatiner Storchschnabel · ⁴ △ Z5 VI-VII; Eur.: W-Ba
- **dissectum** L. · E:Cut Leaved Cranesbill; G:Schlitzblättriger Storchschnabel · ⊙ Z7 V-IX; Eur.*, TR, Levant, Cauc., Iran, C-As., N-Afr., nat. in Am., Austr.
- **divaricatum** Ehrh. · E:Spreading Cranesbill; G:Spreizender Storchschnabel · ⊙ VI-VIII; Eur.* exc. BrI, Sc; TR, Iraq, Cauc., Iran, Afgh., W-Sib., C-As., China: Sinkiang
- **endressii** J. Gay · E:French Cranesbill; F:Géranium des Pyrénées, Géranium en coussinet; G:Pyrenäen-Storchschnabel, Rosa Storchschnabel · ⁴ Z5 V-VI; sp., F; W-Pyr.
- *eriostemon* Fisch. ex DC. = Geranium platyanthum
- **farreri** Stapf · G:Farrers Storchschnabel · ⁴ △ Z4 VI-VIII; China: Kansu, Sichuan
- **himalayense** Klotzsch · E:Dwarf Cranesbill, Hardy Geranium; F:Géranium de l'Himalaya; G:Himalaya-Storchschnabel · ⁴ △ Z4 VII-IX; Afgh., Kashmir, NW-Ind., Nepal
- **ibericum** Cav. · E:Caucasian Cranesbill · ⁴ △ Z6 VII-VIII; TR, Cauc., nat. in Fr
- *lancastriense* With. = Geranium sanguineum var. striatum
- **lucidum** L. · E:Shining Cranesbill;

G:Glänzender Storchschnabel · ☉ Z7
V-VIII; Eur.* exc. Sc; TR, Levant, C-As.,
NW-Afr., Libya
- **macrorrhizum** L. · E:Bulgarian Geranium, Rock Cranesbill; F:Géranium des
Balkans; G:Felsen-Storchschnabel · ⅃ △
Z4 V-VII; Eur.: Fr, I, A, Ba, RO, W-Russ.,
nat. in BrI, G, Crim
- **some cultivars**
- **maculatum** L. · E:Spotted Cranesbill;
G:Amerikanischer Storchschnabel · ⅃ Z4
VI-VII ⚘ ; Can.: E; USA: NE, NCE, Kans.,
SE
- × **magnificum** Hyl. (*G. ibericum subsp.
ibericum* × *G. platypetalum*) · G:Pracht-
Storchschnabel · ⅃ Z5 VI-VII; cult.
- *meeboldii* Briq. = Geranium himalayense
- **molle** L. · E:Dovesfoot Cranesbill, Soft
Cranesbill; G:Weicher Storchschnabel · ☉
☉ V-X; Eur.*, TR, Levant, Cauc., N-Iran,
Him., N-Afr., nat. in N-Am., Austr.
- × **monacense** Harz (*G. phaeum* × *G.
reflexum*) · G:Münchner Storchschnabel ·
⅃ Z5; cult.
- *napuligerum* hort. non Franch. =
Geranium farreri
- **nepalense** Sweet · E:Nepalese Cranesbill;
G:Nepal-Storchschnabel · ⅃ △ Z7 V-VII;
Afgh., Pakistan, W-China, Sri Lanka
- **nodosum** L. · E:Knotted Cranesbill;
F:Géranium noueux; G:Knotiger
Storchschnabel · ⅃ Z6 V-IX; Eur.: Ib, Fr,
Sw, Ital-P, Slove., Croatia, YU, nat. in
BrI, NL, D
- × **oxonianum** Yeo (*G. endressii* × *G.
versicolor*) · E:Druce's Cranesbill;
G:Oxford-Storchschnabel · ⅃ Z5; cult.
- **some cultivars**
- **palmatum** Cav. · G:Riesen-Storchschna-
bel · ⅃ Z9 ⌂ VII-IX; Canar., Madeira
- **palustre** L. · E:Marsh Cranesbill;
F:Géranium des marais; G:Sumpf-
Storchschnabel · ⅃ ∼ ≈ Z6 VI-VIII;
Eur.* exc. BrI; Cauc.
- **phaeum** L. · G:Brauner Storchschnabel
- **some cultivars**
- var. **phaeum** · E:Dusky Cranesbill;
F:Géranium brun; G:Gewöhnlicher
Brauner Storchschnabel · ⅃ Z5 V-VII;
Eur.* exc. BrI, Sc, nat. in BrI, Sc
- **platyanthum** Duthie · G:Großblütiger
Storchschnabel · ⅃ Z5 VI-VII; China
- **platypetalum** Fisch. & C.A. Mey. ·
E:Glandular Cranesbill; G:Horstiger
Storchschnabel · ⅃ Z5 VI-VIII; TR, Cauc.,

Iran
- **pratense** L. · E:Meadow Cranesbill;
F:Géranium des prés; G:Wiesen-
Storchschnabel
- subsp. **pratense** · ⅃ VI-VIII; Eur.*, TR,
W-Sib., E-Sib., C-As., Mong., China
- **procurrens** Yeo · G:Niederliegender
Storchschnabel · ⅃ Z7; Him.
- **psilostemon** Ledeb. · E:Armenian
Cranesbill; G:Armenischer Storchschna-
bel · ⅃ Z6 VI-VII; NE-TR, SW-Cauc.
- **purpureum** Vill. · E:Little Robin;
G:Purpurner Stink-Storchschnabel · ☉
V-IX; Eur.: Ib, Fr, BrI, Ital-P, Ba, Crim, ?
RO; TR, Levant, Cauc., N-Iran, NW-Afr.,
Libya, nat. in NZ
- **pusillum** Burm. f. ex L. · E:Small-flow-
ered Cranesbill; G:Zwerg-Storchschnabel
· ☉ V-X; Eur.*, TR, Levant, C-As., Moroc.,
Alger., nat. in N-Am.
- **pylzowianum** Maxim. · G:Knöllchen-
Storchschnabel · ⅃ Z5 VI-VIII; China:
Yunnan, Sichuan, Schansi, Kansu
- **pyrenaicum** Burm. f. · E:Hedgerow
Cranesbill; G:Pyrenäen-Storchschnabel ·
⅃ Z7 V-X; Eur.: Ib, Fr, Ital-P, BrI, C-Eur.,
H, Ba, RO; TR, Levant, Cauc., N-Iran,
NW-Afr., Libya, nat. in G, N-Am.
- **reflexum** L. · E:Reflexed Cranesbill;
G:Zurückgebogener Storchschnabel · ⅃
Z6 VI-VII; Eur.: I, Ba, nat. in D
- **renardii** Trautv. · F:Géranium à feuilles
de crêpe; G:Kaukasus-Storchschnabel · ⅃
VI; Cauc.
- **richardsonii** Fisch. & Trautv. · E:White
Cranesbill; G:Richardsons Storchschnabel · ⅃ ∼ V-VI; Alaska, Can.: W; USA:
NC, SW, Rocky Mts., NW, Calif.
- × **riversleaianum** Yeo (*G. endressii* × *G.
traversii*) · G:Riverslea-Storchschnabel ·
⅃ Z7; cult.
- **rivulare** Vill. · G:Blassblütiger Storchschnabel · ⅃ Z6 VII-VIII; Eur.: F, Sw, I;
Alp.
- **robertianum** L. · G:Stink-Storchschnabel
- subsp. *purpureum* = Geranium purpureum
- subsp. **robertianum** · E:Herb Robert;
G:Gewöhnlicher Stink-Storchschnabel,
Ruprechtskraut · ☉ Z6 V-X ⚘ ; Eur.*, TR,
Levant, Cauc., Iran, W-Sib., C-As., China,
Jap., NW-Afr., Libya, nat. in N-Am., NZ
- **rotundifolium** L. · E:Round-leaved
Cranesbill; G:Rundblättriger

Storchschnabel · ⊙ VI-X; Eur.* exc. Sc;
TR, N-Afr.
– **sanguineum** L. · G:Blutroter Storchschnabel
– **some cultivars**
– var. *lancastriense* (With.) G. Nicholson =
Geranium sanguineum var. striatum
– var. *prostratum* (Cav.) Pers. = Geranium
sanguineum var. striatum
– var. **sanguineum** · E:Bloody Cranesbill;
F:Géranium sanguin; G:Gewöhnlicher
Blutroter Storchschnabel · ⁂ Z5 VI-VIII;
Eur.*, TR, Cauc.
– var. **striatum** Weston · F:Géranium
sanguin · ⁂ ⤳ Z5; BrI
– **sessiliflorum** Cav. · ⁂ △ Z7 VI-VII;
S-Am., Austr., Tasman., NZ
– **sibiricum** L. · G:Sibirischer Storchschnabel · ⁂ Z6 VII-VIII; RO, Russ., China, nat.
in Eur.: C-Eur., EC-Eur.; N-Am.
– **stapfianum** Hand.-Mazz. · ⁂ △ V-VI;
Yunnan, Sichuan
– *subcaulescens* L'Hér. ex DC. = Geranium
cinereum subsp. subcaulescens
– **sylvaticum** L. · E:Wood Cranesbill;
G:Wald-Storchschnabel
– var. **sylvaticum** · F:Géranium des bois;
G:Gewöhnlicher Wald-Storchschnabel
· ⁂ Z4 V-VII; Eur.*, TR, Cauc., W-Sib.,
E-Sib., C-As., nat. in N-Am.
– f. **albiflorum** A. Blytt
– 'Album' = Geranium sylvaticum var.
sylvaticum f. albiflorum
– **traversii** Hook. f. · ⁂ Z8 ⌂ VII-IX; NZ
– **tuberosum** L. · E:Tuberous Wild
Geranium · ⁂ Z7 IV-V; Eur.: Fr, Ital-P,
Ba, Crim; TR, Levant, Iraq, Cauc., Iran,
Alger., Tun., Libya
– **wallichianum** D. Don · ⁂ △ Z7 ∧
VIII-IX; Him.: Afgh., Kashmir, NW-Ind.,
Nepal, Bhutan
– **wlassovianum** Link · ⁂ Z3 VI-X; E-Sib.,
Amur, Mong., Manch.
– **Cultivars:**
– **many cultivars**

Gerbera L. -f- *Asteraceae* · c. 30 spp. ·
E:Transvaal Daisy; F:Gerbéra; G:Gerbera
– **jamesonii** Bolus ex Hook. f. ·
E:Barberton Daisy; G:Barberton-Gerbera
· ⁂ ⋉ Z8 ⌂ IV-IX; S-Afr.
– **viridifolia** Sch. Bip. · ⁂ Z8 ⌂ IV-VIII;
S-Afr.
– **Cultivars:**
– **many cultivars**

Gesneria L. -f- *Gesneriaceae* · c. 50 spp. ·
E:Gesneria; F:Gesnéria; G:Gesnerie
– **cubensis** (Decne.) Baill. · ♄ Z10 ⓐ
VI-VII; Cuba, Haiti
– **cuneifolia** (Moç. & Sessé ex DC.)
Fritsch · ⁂ Z10 ⓐ; Puerto Rico
– **libanensis** Linden ex C. Morren · ♄ e Z10
ⓐ VII-VIII; E-Cuba
– *macrantha* hort. non Spreng. = Sinningia
cardinalis
– **pedunculosa** (DC.) Fritsch · E:Arbol de
Navidad · ⁂ Z10 ⓐ VII-VIII; Puerto Rico
– **ventricosa** Sw. · ♄ e Z10 ⓐ VI-VIII;
Lesser Antilles

Geum L. -n- *Rosaceae* · 40-70 spp. ·
E:Avens; F:Benoîte; G:Nelkenwurz
– × **borisii** Kellerer ex Sünd. (*G.
bulgaricum* × *G. reptans*) · G:Prinz-Boris-
Nelkenwurz · ⁂ Z4; cult.
– **bulgaricum** Pančić · F:Benoîte bulgare;
G:Bulgarische Nelkenwurz · ⁂ Z4; Bosn.,
Montenegro, Maced., AL, BG; mts.
– **chiloense** Balb. ex Ser. · G:Chile-
Nelkenwurz · ⁂ VI-VIII; Chile (Chiloe)
– **some cultivars**
– **coccineum** Sibth. & Sm. · E:Avens;
F:Benoîte rouge; G:Rote Nelkenwurz · ⁂
Z5 V-VII; Eur.: Ba; TR, Cauc.
– × **heldreichii** hort. ex Bergmans (*G.
coccineum* × *G. montanum*) · G:Heldre-
ichs Nelkenwurz · ⁂ Z5; cult.
– **japonicum** Thunb. · E:Japanese Avens;
G:Japanische Nelkenwurz · ⁂ Z7; E-As.,
Kamchat., N-Am., nat. in BrI, Norw.,
Russ., G, Cz
– **macrophyllum** Willd. · E:Large-leaved
Avens; G:Großblättrige Nelkenwurz · ⁂
Z4; E-As., N-Am., nat. in D
– **montanum** L. · E:Alpine Avens; G:Berg-
Nelkenwurz · ⁂ △ Z6 V-X; Eur.* exc. BrI,
Sc; mts.
– **pyrenaicum** Mill. · E:Pyrenean Avens;
G:Pyrenäen-Nelkenwurz · ⁂ Z6; Eur.:
F, sp. ; Pyren.
– **reptans** L. · E:Creeping Avens; F:Benoîte
rampante; G:Kriechende Nelkenwurz · ⁂
△ Z6 VI-VII; Eur.: F, I, C-Eur., EC-Eur.,
Ba, RO; Alp., Carp., Balkan
– × **rhaeticum** Brügger (*G. montanum* × *G.
reptans*) · G:Rhätische Nelkenwurz · ⁂ △
Z6 V-VI; G, Sw +
– **rivale** L. · E:Indian Chocolate Root,
Water Avens; G:Bach-Nelkenwurz · ⁂ Z3
IV-VI; Eur.*, TR, Cauc., W-Sib., E-Sib.,

C-As.
- *sibiricum* hort. = Geum chiloense
- **triflorum** Pursh · E:Old Man's Whiskers, Prairie Smoke; G:Prärie-Nelkenwurz · ⚁ Z1 V-VIII; Can., USA: NE, NCE, NC, Rocky Mts., SW, Calif., NW
- **urbanum** L. · E:Clove Root, Herb Bennet, Wood Avens; G:Echte Nelkenwurz · ⚁ Z6 V-X ⚥ ; Eur.*, TR, Syr., N-Iraq, Cauc., N-Iran, W-Sib., C-As., W-Him., NW-Afr.

Gevuina Molina -f- *Proteaceae* · 1 sp. · E:Chilean Nut; F:Noisetier du Chili; G:Chilenuss
- **avellana** Molina · E:Chilean Hazel, Chilean Nut; G:Chilenuss · ♄ e Z9 ⓚ Ⓝ; Arg., Chile

Gibasis Raf. -n- *Commelinaceae* · 14 spp.
- **geniculata** (Jacq.) Rohweder · E:Tahitian Bridalveil · ⚁ ⌇→ Z9 ⓜ; Mex., C-Am., W.Ind., S-Am.

Gibbaeum N.E. Br. -n- *Aizoaceae* · 26 spp.
- **album** N.E. Br. · ⚁ ⚇ Z9 ⓚ; Cape
- **gibbosum** (Haw.) N.E. Br. · ⚁ ⚇ Z9 ⓚ; Cape
- **heathii** (N.E. Br.) L. Bolus · ⚁ ⚇ Z9 ⓚ; Cape
- **muirii** N.E. Br.
- **pubescens** (Haw.) N.E. Br. · ⚁ ⚇ Z9 ⓚ; Cape
- **velutinum** (L. Bolus) Schwantes · ⚁ ⚇ Z9 ⓚ; Cape

Gigantochloa Kurz ex Munro -f- *Poaceae* · 18 spp. · G:Riesenbambus; F:Bambou géant
- **apus** (Schult. f.) Kurz ex Munro · ♄ e ⓜ Ⓝ; Burma
- *aspera* (Schult. f.) Kurz = Dendrocalamus asper
- **atter** (Hassk.) Kurz ex Munro · ♄ e ⓜ Ⓝ; S-China
- *kurzii* Gamble = Gigantochloa wrayi
- **levis** (Blanco) Merr. · ♄ e ⓜ Ⓝ; Malay. Arch.
- *verticillata* Ridl. = Gigantochloa levis
- **wrayi** Gamble · ♄ e ⓜ Ⓝ; Java

Gilia Ruiz & Pav. -f- *Polemoniaceae* · c. 25 spp. · E:Gily Flower; F:Gilia; G:Gilie
- **achilleifolia** Benth. · E:California Gily Flower; G:Kalifornische Gilie · ⊙ Z8 VIII; S-Calif., Baja Calif.

- *aggregata* (Pursh) Spreng. = Ipomopsis aggregata
- *androsacea* (Benth.) Steud. = Linanthus androsaceus subsp. androsaceus
- **capitata** Sims · E:Blue Head Gily Flower; G:Nadelkissen-Gilie · ⊙ Z8 VII-VIII; Can.: B.C.; USA: NW, Calif., Idaho; Mex.: Baja Calif.
- *densiflora* (Benth.) Benth. = Eriastrum densifolium
- *dianthoides* Endl. = Linanthus dianthiflorus
- *grandiflora* (Douglas ex Lindl.) A. Gray = Collomia grandiflora
- **laciniata** Ruiz & Pav. · ⊙ Z8 VII; Peru, Chile, Arg.
- *rubra* (L.) A. Heller = Ipomopsis rubra
- **tricolor** Benth. · E:Bird's Eyes; G:Dreifarbige Gilie · ⊙ Z7 VII; W-Calif.

Gillenia Moench -f- *Rosaceae* · 2 spp. · F:Glillenia; G:Dreiblattspiere, Gillenie
- **stipulata** (Muhl. ex Willd.) Nutt. · E:American Ipecac; G:Südliche Dreiblattspiere · ⚁ Z5 VII-VIII; USA: NE, NCE, NC, SE, SC
- **trifoliata** (L.) Moench · E:Bowman's Root, Gillenia, Indian Physic; F:Spirée à trois feuilles; G:Nördliche Dreiblattspiere · ⚁ Z4 VI-VIII ⚥ ; Ont., USA: NE, NCE, SE

Ginkgo L. -f- *Ginkgoaceae* · 1 sp. · E:Ginkgo, Maidenhair Tree; F:Arbre aux quarante écus; G:Fächertanne, Ginkgo, Mädchenhaarbaum
- **biloba** L. · E:Ginkgo, Maidenhair Tree; F:Arbre aux quarante écus; G:Fächertanne, Ginkgo, Mädchenhaarbaum · ♄ d ⚥ Z5 V-VI ⚥ Ⓝ; SE-China
- **some cultivars**

Gladiolus L. -m- *Iridaceae* · 268 spp. · E:Gladiolus; F:Glaïeul; G:Gladiole, Siegwurz
- *bicolor* Baker = Gladiolus murielae
- *byzantinus* Mill. = Gladiolus communis subsp. byzantinus
- *callianthus* Marais = Gladiolus murielae
- **cardinalis** Curtis · ⚁ Z9 ⓚ VI-VII ▽; SW-Cape
- × **colvillei** Sweet (*G. cardinalis × G. tristis*) · G:Zwerg-Gladiole · ⚁ Z8; cult.
- **communis** L.
- subsp. **byzantinus** (Mill.) A.P. Ham. · E:Byzantine Gladiolus; G:Byzantinische

Siegwurz · ♃ Z7 ∧ VI-VII ▽; Eur.: S-Sp., Sic.; NW-Afr.
- subsp. **communis** · E:Field Gladiolus; G:Gewöhnliche Siegwurz · ♃ Z6 VII-X ▽; Eur.: Ib, Fr, Ital-P, Ba, ? Crim; Cauc., Iran, NW-Afr.
- **cunonius** (L.) Gaertn. · ♃ Z9 Ⓚ V-VI ▽; S-Afr.
- **dalenii** Van Geel · E:Maid-of-the-Mist · ♃ Z9 Ⓚ VII-IX ▽; Eth., E-Afr., S-Afr., Arab.
- **grandiflorus** Andrews · ♃ Z8 Ⓚ IV-V; S-Afr.
- **illyricus** W.D.J. Koch · G:Illyrische Siegwurz · ♃ Z7 V ▽; Eur.: Ib, Fr, BrI, Ital-P, Ba, RO; TR, Cyprus, Cauc.
- **imbricatus** L. · G:Dachziegelartige Siegwurz, Wiesen-Siegwurz · ♃ ~ VII ▽; Eur.: C-Eur., EC-Eur., Ba, Ital-P; TR, Cauc., W-Sib., nat. in Fr, FIN
- **italicus** Mill. · E:Field Gladiolus; G:Saat-Siegwurz · ♃ Z7 V ▽; Eur.: Ib, Fr, Ital-P, Ba, RO, Crim, Sw; TR, Arab., SW-As., C-As.
- *laxus* Thunb. = Anomatheca laxa
- **murielae** Kelway & Langport · E:Acidanthera; G:Stern-Gladiole · ♃ D Z9 Ⓚ VII-VIII ▽; Eth., E-Afr., Malawi
- *natalensis* (Eckl.) Reinw. ex Hook. = Gladiolus dalenii
- **palustris** Gaudin · F:Glaîeul des marais; G:Sumpf-Siegwurz · ♃ ~ Z6 VI-VII ▽; Eur.: Fr, I, C-Eur., EC-Eur., Ba, E-Eur.
- **papilio** Hook. f. · ♃ Z8 Ⓚ VII-VIII ▽; S-Afr.
- *primulinus* Baker = Gladiolus dalenii
- *psittacinus* Hook. = Gladiolus dalenii
- *purpureoauratus* Hook. f. = Gladiolus papilio
- **saundersii** Hook. f. · ♃ Z8 Ⓚ VII-VIII ▽; S-Afr.
- *segetum* Ker-Gawl. = Gladiolus italicus
- *speciosus* Eckl. = Gladiolus cardinalis
- **tristis** L. · E:Yellow Marsh Afrikander; G:Eintönige Gladiole · ♃ Z8 Ⓚ V-VI ▽; Cape
- **Cultivars:**
- **many cultivars, see Section III**

Glaucidium Siebold & Zucc. -n- *Glaucidiaceae* · 1 sp.
- **palmatum** Siebold & Zucc. · ♃ Z7 ∧ IV-V; Jap.
- *paradoxum* Makino = Glaucidium palmatum

Glaucium Mill. -n- *Papaveraceae* · 25 spp. · E:Horned Poppy; F:Pavot cornu; G:Hornmohn
- **corniculatum** (L.) Rudolph · E:Horned Poppy, Red Horned Poppy, Sea Poppy; G:Roter Hornmohn · ⊙ ⊙ Z7 VI-VIII; Eur.* exc. BrI, Sc; TR, Levant, N-Iraq, Cauc., Iran, C-As., N-Afr.
- **flavum** Crantz · E:Yellow Horned Poppy; G:Gelber Hornmohn · ⊙ ⊙ ♃ Z7 VI-VII ☠; Eur.*, TR, Levant, Cauc., NW-Afr., Libya; coasts, nat. in CZ
- **grandiflorum** Boiss. & A. Huet · G:Großblütiger Hornmohn · ♃ Z7 VI-VIII; TR, Iran
- **squamigerum** Kar. & Kir. · G:Altai-Hornmohn · ⊙ Z7 VII-VIII; C-As.(Altai), China: Sinkiang
- *vitellinum* hort. non Boiss. & Buhse = Dicranostigma franchetianum

Glaux L. -f- *Primulaceae* · 1 sp. · E:Sea Milkwort; F:Glaux; G:Milchkraut
- **maritima** L. · E:Sea Milkwort; G:Milchkraut · ♃ V-VIII; Eur.* exc. Ital-P, Ba; TR, Cauc., Iran, W-Sib., E-Sib., Amur, Sakhal., C-As., Him., Mong., China, Jap., N-Am.

Glaziova Bureau -f- *Bignoniaceae* · 1 sp.
- **bauhinioides** Bureau ex Baill. · ♄ ≹ Ⓦ; Braz.

Glaziova Mart. ex Drude = Lytocaryum
- *martiana* Glaz. ex Drude = Lytocaryum weddellianum

Glebionis Cass. -f- *Asteraceae* · 2 spp. · E:Crown Daisy; G:Wucherblume
- *carinata* (Schousb.) Tzvelev = Ismelia carinata
- **coronaria**
- var. **coronaria** · E:Crown Daisy; G:Kronen-Wucherblume · ⊙ ✂ VI-IX; Eur.: Ib, Ital-P, Ba; TR, Levant, N-Iran, N-Afr., nat. in F, A, RO
- **segetum** (L.) Fourr. · E:Corn Marigold; F:Chrysanthème des moissons; G:Saat-Wucherblume · ⊙ ✂ VII-X; Eur.* exc. EC-Eur.; TR, Cyprus, Syr., NW-Afr., Libya
- × **spectabile** (Lilja) Karlsson (*G. coronaria var. coronaria* × *G. segetum*) · G:Hybrid-Wucherblume · ⊙ ✂ VII-IX; cult.

Glechoma L. -f- *Lamiaceae* · 7 spp. ·
E:Ground Ivy; F:Lierre terrestre; G:Erde-
feu, Gundelrebe, Gundermann
– **hederacea** L. · E:Alehoof, Ground Ivy;
F:Lierre terrestre; G:Gewöhnlicher
Gundermann · ⅄ ⚥ ⤳ IV-VI ⚘ ⚘;
Eur.*, Cauc., W-Sib., E-Sib., ? Amur,
C-As., nat. in N-Am.
– subsp. *hirsuta* (Waldst. & Kit.) F. Herm. =
Glechoma hirsuta
– **hirsuta** Waldst. & Kit. · G:Rauhaariger
Gundermann · ⅄ ⚥ ⤳ IV-VI ⚘; Eur.: A,
EC-Eur., Ba, E-Eur., Ital-P

Gleditsia L. -f- *Caesalpiniaceae* · 14 spp. ·
E:Honey Locust; F:Févier d'Amérique,
Gleditsia; G:Gleditschie, Lederhülsenbaum
– **amorphoides** (Griseb.) Taub. · ♄ d Z6;
N-Am., S-Am.
– **caspica** Desf. · G:Kaspische Gleditschie ·
♄ d Z6 VI-VII; N-Iran, Cauc.
– *horrida* Willd. = Gleditsia sinensis
– **japonica** Miq. · G:Japanische
Gleditschie · ♄ d Z6; Jap., Korea, China
– **macrantha** Desf. · G:Großblütige
Gleditschie · ♄ d Z6; C-China
– **sinensis** Lam. · E:Chinese Honey Locust;
G:Chinesische Gleditschie · ♄ d Z6;
China, Mong., Korea
– **triacanthos** L. · E:Honey Locust;
F:Epine-du-Christ, Févier d'Amérique;
G:Amerikanische Gleditschie, Falscher
Christusdorn · ♄ d Z6 VI-VII ⚘ Ⓦ; USA:
NE, NCE, NC, SC, SE, Fla., nat. in Eur.:
Ib, F, I, C-Eur., EC-Eur., Ba, RO
– f. **inermis** (L.) Zabel · ♄ d VI-VII; cult.

Gleichenia Sm. -f- *Gleicheniaceae* · 19 spp. ·
F:Fougère; G:Gabelfarn
– *flabellata* R. Br. = Sticherus flabellatus
– **microphylla** R. Br. · ⅄ Z10 ⓐ; Malay.
Pen., Austr., Tasman., NZ, N.Caled.

Gliricidia Kunth -f- *Fabaceae* · 6 spp.
– **sepium** (Jacq.) Kunth ex Walp. · E:Madre
de Cacao, Nicaraguan Cocao-shade,
Quickstick · ♄ ♄ d ⓦ Ⓦ; Mex., C-Am.,
Col.

Globba L. -f- *Zingiberaceae* · 99 spp.
– **atrosanguinea** Teijsm. & Binn. · ⅄ Z9
ⓦ; Kalimantan
– *bulbifera* Roxb. = Globba marantina
– **marantina** L. · ⅄ Z9 ⓦ VII-IX; Molucca:

Ambon; Pacific Is.
– **winitii** C.H. Wright · ⅄ Z9 ⓦ VII-IX;
Thail.

Globularia L. -f- *Globulariaceae* · 22 spp. ·
E:Globe Daisy; F:Globulaire; G:Kugel-
blume
– **alypum** L. · ♄ e ⓐ III-X ▽; Eur.: Ib, Fr,
Ital-P, Ba; Madeira, TR, NW-Afr., Libya
– *bisnagarica* L. = Globularia punctata
– **cordifolia** L. · E:Matted Globularia;
F:Globulaire à feuilles en coeur; G:Herz-
blättrige Kugelblume · ♄ ♄ e ⤳ △ Z6
V-VI ▽; Eur.: Ib, Fr, C-Eur., EC-Eur.,
Ital-P, Ba; mts.
– subsp. *bellidifolia* (Ten.) Wettst. =
Globularia meridionalis
– *elongata* Hegetschw. = Globularia
punctata
– **incanescens** Viv. · ⅄ Z7 ▽; N-I;
N-Apenn., Alpi Apuani
– **meridionalis** (Podp.) O. Schwarz ·
G:Südliche Kugelblume · ♄ e ⤳ △ Z5
V-VI ▽; Eur.: I, A, Ba; mts.
– **nudicaulis** L. · F:Globulaire à tige nue;
G:Nacktstängelige Kugelblume · ⅄ △ Z5
V-VII ▽; Eur.: sp., Fr, I, C-Eur., Slove.;
N-Sp., Pyr., Alp.
– **punctata** Lapeyr. · E:Common Globularia
F:Globulaire ponctuée; G:Gewöhnliche
Kugelblume · ⅄ △ Z5 V-VI ⚘ ▽; Eur.*
exc. Sc, BrI
– **repens** Lam. · G:Kriechende Kugelb-
lume · ♄ ⤳ △ V-VI ▽; Eur.: sp., F, I;
mts.
– **spinosa** L. · G:Dornige Kugelblume · ⅄
▽; SE-Sp.
– **stygia** Orph. ex Boiss. · G:Griechische
Kugelblume · ♄ e ⤳ △ Z8 ∧ V-VI ▽;
Eur.: GR (Peloponnes)
– **trichosantha** Fisch. & C.A. Mey. ·
G:Kaukasus-Kugelblume · ⅄ ⤳ △ Z6
V-VI ▽; Eur.: BG, Crim; TR, Syr., N-Iraq,
Cauc., N-Iran
– *willkommii* Nyman = Globularia punctata

Globulea Haw. = Crassula
– *canescens* Haw. = Crassula nudicaulis
– *cultrata* (L.) Haw. = Crassula cultrata
– *mesembryanthoides* Haw. = Crassula
mesembryanthoides

Gloriosa L. -f- *Colchicaceae* · 4 spp. ·
E:Climbing Lily, Glory Lily; F:Gloriosa,
Superbe de Malabar; G:Ruhmeskrone

– *carsonii* Baker = Gloriosa superba
– *rothschildiana* O'Brien = Gloriosa superba
– *simplex* L. = Gloriosa superba
– **superba** L. · E:Climbing Lily, Glory Lily;
G:Ruhmeskrone · ⁴ Z9 ⊛ VI-VIII ⚇ ✕;
trop. Afr., trop. As.
– *virescens* Lindl. = Gloriosa superba

Glottiphyllum N.E. Br. -n- *Aizoaceae* ·
16 spp. · G:Zungenblatt
– *apiculatum* N.E. Br. = Glottiphyllum
cruciatum
– **cruciatum** (Haw.) N.E. Br. · G:Oudt-
shoorn-Zungenblatt · ⁴ Ψ Z9 ⊛; Cape
– **depressum** (Haw.) N.E. Br. · G:Duf-
tendes Zungenblatt · ⁴ Ψ D Z9 ⊛; Cape
– *fragrans* (Salm-Dyck) Schwantes =
Glottiphyllum depressum
– *herrei* L. Bolus = Glottiphyllum suave
– **linguiforme** (L.) N.E. Br. · G:Wachs-
Zungenblatt · ⁴ Ψ Z9 ⊛; Cape
– **longum** (Haw.) N.E. Br. · G:Langes
Zungenblatt · ⁴ Ψ Z9 ⊛ VI; Cape
– **nelii** Schwantes · G:Prinz-Albert-
Zungenblatt · ⁴ Ψ Z9 ⊛; Cape
– *praepingue* (Haw.) N.E. Br. = Glottiphyllum cruciatum
– **suave** N.E. Br. · G:Graues Zungenblatt ·
⁴ Ψ D Z9 ⊛; Cape

Gloxinia L'Hér. -f- *Gesneriaceae* · 15 spp. ·
E:Gloxinia; F:Gloxinia; G:Gloxinie
– *fimbriata* Brongn. = Achimenes glabrata
– **perennis** (L.) Fritsch · E:Canterbury
Bells; G:Pfefferminz-Gloxinie · ⁴ D Z10
⊛ IX-XI; Col., Peru, Braz.
– **sylvatica** (Kunth) Wiehler · ⁴ Z10 ⊛
VII-X; Peru, Bol.
– *verticillata* M. Martens & Galeotti =
Eucodonia verticillata

Gluta L. -f- *Anacardiaceae* · 30 spp.
– **usitata** (Wall.) Ding Hou · ♄ ⊛ Ⓝ;
Malay. Arch., Burma, Thail.

Glyceria R. Br. -f- *Poaceae* · 40-50 spp. ·
E:Sweet Grass; F:Glycérie; G:Schwaden
– *aquatica* (L.) J. Presl & C. Presl =
Catabrosa aquatica
– *aquatica* (L.) Wahlenb. = Glyceria
maxima
– **declinata** Bréb. · G:Blaugrüner
Schwaden · ⁴ ⌇ VI-VIII; Eur.*,
Macaron., nat. in USA
– **fluitans** (L.) R. Br. · E:Sweet Grass,

Water Manna Grass; G:Flutender
Schwaden, Manna-Schwaden · ⁴ ⌇ ≈
V-IX Ⓝ; Eur.*, TR, Cauc., W-Sib., E-Sib.,
Madeira, Azor., Moroc., nat. in N-Am.,
Chile, Austr., NZ
– **maxima** (Hartm.) Holmb. · E:Reed
Sweet Grass; F:Glycérie panachée;
G:Großer Schwaden, Wasser-Schwaden ·
⁴ ≈ Z5 VII-VIII Ⓝ; Eur.* exc. Ib; TR
– **nemoralis** (R. Uechtr.) R. Uechtr. &
Körn. · G:Hain-Schwaden · ⁴ ⌇ VI-VII;
Eur.: EC-Eur., Ba, E-Eur.; TR
– **notata** Chevall. · E:Plicate Sweet
Grass; G:Falten-Schwaden, Gefalteter
Schwaden · ⁴ ⌇ VI-VII; Eur.*, TR, Syr.,
Iraq, Palest., Cauc., Iran, Afgh., Pakist.,
Him., W-Sib., NW-Afr.
– × **pedicellata** F. Towns. (*G. fluitans* ×
G. spectabilis) · E:Hybrid Sweet Grass;
G:Bastard-Schwaden · ⁴ ⌇ VI-VIII;
Eur.: BrI, Fr, C-Eur., EC-Eur., Ba, Sc, Balt.
– *plicata* Fr. = Glyceria notata
– *spectabilis* Mert. & W.D.J. Koch = Glyceria
maxima
– **striata** (Lam.) Hitchc. · E:Fowl Manna
Grass; G:Gestreifter Schwaden · ⁴ ⌇
VII-VIII; N-Am., nat. in F, Sw, A, Swed,
W-Russ.; nat. in D

Glycine Willd. -f- *Fabaceae* · 9 spp. · E:Soya
Bean; F:Soja; G:Sojabohne
– *hispida* (Moench) Maxim. = Glycine max
– **max** (L.) Merr. · E:Soya Bean; G:Soja-
bohne · ☉ Z8 VII-VIII ⚇ Ⓝ; E-Sib., China,
Manch., Korea, Jap., Taiwan
– *soja* Siebold & Zucc. = Glycine max
– *ussuriensis* Regel & Maack = Glycine max

Glycine L. = Apios
– *apios* L. = Apios americana
– *frutescens* L. = Wisteria frutescens
– *subterranea* L. = Vigna subterranea

Glycosmis Corrêa -f- *Rutaceae* · 43 spp.
– **arborea** (Roxb.) DC. · ♄ e D Z10 ⊛;
Him., Ind., Sri Lanka, Indochina, China,
Malay. Arch., Phil., Austr.

Glycyrrhiza L. -f- *Fabaceae* · 18 spp. ·
E:Sweetwood; F:Réglisse; G:Lakritze,
Süßholz
– **echinata** L. · E:Roman Liquorice;
G:Römisches Süßholz · ⁴ Z7 VI-IX Ⓝ;
Eur.: Ital-P, EC-Eur., Ba; TR, Syr., Palest.,
Cauc., Iran, E-As

– **glabra** L. · E:Liquorice; G:Lakritze,
Spanisches Süßholz · ⏀ Z8 ⓚ VI-IX ⚥ Ⓝ;
Eur.: Ib, Fr, Ital-P, Ba, E-Eur.; TR, Levant,
Cauc., Iran, W-Sib., C-As., China, Libya

Glyptostrobus Endl. -m- *Taxodiaceae* ·
I sp. · E:Chinese Swamp Cypress;
G:Wasserfichte
– *heterophyllus* (Brongn.) Endl. = Glyptostrobus pensilis
– *lineatus* (Poir.) Druce = Taxodium
distichum var. imbricatum
– **pensilis** (Staunton ex D. Don) K.
Koch · E:Chinese Swamp Cypress;
G:Wasserfichte · ♄ e Z8 ⓚ Ⓝ; SE-China

Gmelina L. -f- *Verbenaceae* · 35 spp.
– **arborea** Roxb. · ♄ d Z10 ⓦ Ⓝ; Ind., Sri
Lanka, Burma, Andaman Is.

Gnaphalium L. -n- *Asteraceae* · c. 150 spp. ·
E:Cudweed; F:Gnaphale; G:Ruhrkraut
– *dioicum* L. = Antennaria dioica var. dioica
– **hoppeanum** W.D.J. Koch · G:Hoppes
Ruhrkraut · ⏀ △ VII-VIII; Eur.: F, C-Eur.,
EC-Eur., Ba
– *luteoalbum* L. = Pseudognaphalium
luteoalbum
– *margaritaceum* L. = Anaphalis margarita-
cea var. margaritacea
– **norvegicum** Gunnerus · E:Highland
Cudweed; G:Norwegisches Ruhrkraut ·
⊙ ⏀ △ Z2 VII-IX; Eur.*, W-Sib., Greenl.,
E-Can.
– *orientale* L. = Helichrysum orientale
– **supinum** L. · E:Dwarf Cudweed;
G:Zwerg-Ruhrkraut · ⏀ △ Z2 VI-IX Ⓝ;
Eur.*, TR, Cauc., N-Iran, C-As., Greenl.,
E-Can.
– **sylvaticum** L. · E:Heath Cudweed;
G:Wald-Ruhrkraut · ⏀ Z4 VII-IX; Eur.*,
TR, Cauc., N-Iran, C-As., Sib.
– **uliginosum** L. · E:Low Cudweed, Marsh
Cudweed; G:Sumpf-Ruhrkraut · ⊙
VII-VIII ⚥ ; Eur.*, TR

Gnetum L. -n- *Gnetaceae* · 28 spp.
– **gnemon** L.
– var. **gnemon** · E:Spinach Joint Fir · ♄ Z10
ⓦ; Malay. Arch., Phil., N.Guinea, Fiji
– var. **ovalifolium** (Poir.) Blume · ♄ Z10 ⓦ
Ⓝ; Sulawesi , Fiji

Gnidia L. -f- *Thymelaeaceae* · 140-160 spp.
– **denudata** Lindl. · ♄ e Z9 ⓚ III-VI; S-Afr.

– **polystachya** P.J. Bergius · ♄ e Z9 ⓚ
IV-VI; S-Afr.

Godetia Spach = Clarkia
– *amoena* (Lehm.) G. Don = Clarkia
amoena subsp. amoena
– *grandiflora* Lindl. = Clarkia amoena
– *whitneyi* (A. Gray) T. Moore = Clarkia
amoena subsp. whitneyi

Goethea Nees -f- *Malvaceae* · 2 spp.
– **strictiflora** Hook. · ♄ e Z10 ⓦ VII-IX;
Braz.

Goldfussia Nees = Strobilanthes
– *anisophylla* (Wall. ex Lodd.) Nees =
Strobilanthes anisophyllus
– *isophylla* Nees = Strobilanthes isophyllus

Gomesa R. Br. -f- *Orchidaceae* · 12 spp.
– **crispa** (L.) Klotzsch & Rchb. f. · ⏀ Z10 ⓦ
V-VII ▽ ✳; Braz.

Gomphocarpus R. Br. = Asclepias
– *fruticosus* (L.) R. Br. = Asclepias fruticosa

Gompholobium Sm. -n- *Fabaceae* ·
25-30 spp.
– **huegelii** Benth. · ♄ e ⓚ; Austr.:
N.S.Wales
– **latifolium** Sm. · ♄ e ⓚ; Austr.: Queensl.,
N.S.Wales, Victoria

Gomphrena L. -f- *Amaranthaceae* ·
c. 100 spp. · E:Globe Amaranth;
F:Amarantine; G:Kugelamaranth
– **decumbens** Jacq. · ⊙ Z9; ? S-Braz., ?
Arg., Westindien, Mex., C-Am., nat. in
SE-USA
– **globosa** L. · E:Globe Amaranth;
F:Amarantine; G:Echter Kugelamaranth ·
⊙ ⋈ Z9 VII-X; Ind.; cult, trop. Am.
– **haageana** Klotzsch · E:Rio Grande Globe
Amaranth; G:Haage-Kugelamaranth · ⊙
Z9 VII-IX; Tex., Mex.

Gongora Ruiz & Pav. -f- *Orchidaceae* ·
66 spp.
– **galeata** (Lindl.) Rchb. f. · ⏀ Z10 ⓦ
VI-VIII ▽ ✳; Mex.
– **quinquenervis** Ruiz & Pav. · ⏀ Z10 ⓦ
IV-VI ▽ ✳; Mex., C-Am., trop. S-Am.
– **truncata** Lindl. · ⏀ Z10 ⓦ VI-VII ▽ ✳;
Mex.

Goniolimon Boiss. -n- *Plumbaginaceae* ·
20 spp.
– **elatum** (Fisch. ex Spreng.) Boiss. · ⚁ Z5
VII-IX; Eur.: SE-Russ.; C-As.
– **tataricum** (L.) Boiss. · E:Statice, Tatarian
Statice; F:Statice de Tartarie; G:Statice ·
⚁ ✂ Z4 VII-IX; Eur.: Ba, RO; Cauc., nat.
in H

Goniophlebium C. Presl -n- *Polypodiaceae* ·
17 spp.
– **glaucophyllum** Fée · ⚁ ⓦ; Antill. -
Ecuad.
– **subauriculatum** (Blume) C. Presl ·
E:Knight's Polypody · ⚁ ⚄ Z10 ⓦ; NE-
Ind., SW-China, SE-As., Austr.: Queensl.

Gonospermum Less. -n- *Asteraceae* · 4 spp.
– **canariense** Less. · ♄ e ⓚ; Canaren: La
Palma

Gonystylus Teijsm. & Binn. -m-
Thymelaeaceae · 20 spp.
– **bancanus** (Miq.) Kurz · ♄ ⓦ Ⓝ ✳;
Malay. Arch.

Goodenia Sm. -f- *Goodeniaceae* · 179 spp. ·
F:Goodenia; G:Goodenie
– **grandiflora** Sims · G:Großblütige
Goodenie · ♄ Z9 ⓚ VII; Austr.
– **ovata** Sm. · ♄ Z9 ⓚ VII-VIII; Austr.

Goodia Salisb. -f- *Fabaceae* · 1 (-3) spp.
– **lotifolia** Salisb. · E:Golden Tip · ♄ e ⓚ
IV-VII; Austr.

Goodyera R. Br. -f- *Orchidaceae* · 95 spp. ·
E:Creeping Lady's Tresses, Jewel Orchid;
F:Goodyera; G:Netzblatt
– **colorata** (Blume) Blume · G:Buntes
Netzblatt · ⚁ ⓦ ▽ ✳; Sumat., Java
– **hispida** Lindl. · G:Borstiges Netzblatt ·
⚁ ⓦ ▽ ✳; Bhutan, Ind.: Sikkim, Khasia
Hills
– **repens** (L.) R. Br. · E:Creeping
Lady's Tresses, Rattlesnake Plantain;
G:Kriechendes Netzblatt · ⚁ Z4 VII-VIII
▽ ✳; Eur.*, N-TR, Cauc., N-As., C-As.,
Alaska, Can., USA* exc. SC, Calif.
– **reticulata** (Blume) Blume · G:Java-
Netzblatt · ⚁ ⓦ ▽ ✳; Sumat., Java

Gordonia J. Ellis -f- *Theaceae* · 70 spp.
– *alatamaha* (Marshall) Sarg. = Franklinia
alatamaha

– **axillaris** (Roxb. ex Ker-Gawl.) Endl. · ♄ e
Z8 ⓚ XI-IV; S-China
– **lasianthus** (L.) J. Ellis · E:Loblolly Bay ·
♄ ♄ e Z8 ⓚ VII-VIII Ⓝ; USA: SE, Fla.

Gossweilerodendron Harms -n-
Caesalpiniaceae · 2 spp.
– **balsamiferum** (Vermoesen) Harms · ♄
ⓦ Ⓝ; Zaire

Gossypium L. -n- *Malvaceae* · 39 spp. ·
E:Cotton; F:Cotonnier; G:Baumwolle
– **arboreum** L. · E:Tree Cotton; G:Baum-
förmige Baumwolle · ⊙ ⊙ ⚁ ⓦ ⓚ Ⓝ;
Pakist.; cult.
– **barbadense** L.
– var. **barbadense** · E:Sea Island Cotton;
G:Westindische Baumwolle · ⊙; trop.
S-Am.
– var. *Braziliense* (Macfad.) Mauer =
Gossypium barbadense var. braziliense
– var. **braziliense** (Raf.) Fryxell · G:Brazil-
ianische Baumwolle · ♄ ⓦ ⓚ Ⓝ; e trop.
S-Am.
– *Braziliense* Macfad. = Gossypium
barbadense var. braziliense
– **herbaceum** L.
– var. **acerifolium** (Guill. & Perr.) A.
Chev. · G:Ahornblättrige Baumwolle · ⚁ e
Ⓝ; Eth., S-Arab.
– var. **herbaceum** · E:Common Cotton,
Levant Cotton; G:Gewöhnliche Baumwolle · ⊙ ⓦ ⓚ ⚄ Ⓝ; orig. ?; cult. Iran,
C-As., Afgh., Pakist., Ind., S-Afr., nat. in
Eur.: sp., Ital-P, Ba, RO; TR
– **hirsutum** L.
– var. **hirsutum** · E:Upland Cotton;
G:Amerikanische Baumwolle · ⊙; C-Am.,
nat. in S-Fla.
– var. **marie-galante** (G. Watt) J.B.
Hutch. · E:Marie-Galante Cotton · ♄ ♄ Ⓝ;
W.Ind., Panama, N-Braz.
– var. **punctatum** (Schumach. & Thonn.)
J.B. Hutch. · ⊙ ⓦ ⓚ Ⓝ; USA: SE, Fla.,
SC; Bahamas, C-Am., W.Ind.
– **klotzschianum** Andersson · G:Galapa-
gos-Baumwolle · Ⓝ; Galapagos
– *peruvianum* Cav. = Gossypium barbadense var. barbadense
– *punctatum* Schumach. & Thonn. =
Gossypium hirsutum var. punctatum
– *religiosum* L. = Gossypium hirsutum var.
punctatum
– *vitifolium* Lam. = Gossypium barbadense
var. barbadense

Grammatophyllum Blume -n-
Orchidaceae · 11 sp.
– **scriptum** (L.) Blume · ⁴ Z10 ⓜ VI ▽ ✳;
Molucca: Ambon
– **speciosum** Blume · ⁴ Z10 ⓜ ▽ ✳;
Malay. Arch., Phil.

Graptopetalum Rose -n- *Crassulaceae* ·
16 spp. · G:Felsenrose
– **amethystinum** (Rose) E. Walther ·
E:Jewel-leaf Plant; G:Rosablättrige
Felsenrose · ⁴ ⁴ Z9 ⓚ VII-VIII; Mex.
– **bellum** (Moran & J. Meyrán) D.R.
Hunt · E:Chihuahua Flower; G:Kolibri-
Felsenrose · ⁴ ⁴ Z9 ⓚ ▽ V-VI; Mex.:
Chihuahua
– **paraguayense** (N.E. Br.) E. Walther ·
E:Ghost Plant, Mother-of-Pearl Plant;
G:Punktierte Felsenrose · ⁴ ⁴ Z9 ⓚ; ?
Mex.
– *weinbergii* (Rose) E. Walther = Graptop-
etalum paraguayense

Graptophyllum Nees -n- *Acanthaceae* ·
10 spp.
– **pictum** (L.) Griff. · E:Caricature Plant · ♄
e Z10 ⓜ; ? N.Guinea

Gratiola L. -f- *Scrophulariaceae* · 25 spp. ·
E:Hedge Hyssop; F:Gratiole; G:Gnaden-
kraut
– **neglecta** Torr. · E:Clammy Hedge Hyssop; G:Übersehenes Gnadenkraut · ☉ Z6
V-IX; Can., USA*, nat. in F
– **officinalis** L. · E:Hedge Hyssop; F:Herbe
au pauvre homme; G:Gottes-Gnadenk-
raut · ⁴ ⌇ Z6 VI-VIII ⚷ ⚹ ▽; Eur.*
exc. BrI, Sc; TR, Cauc., W-Sib., C-As.

Gravesia Naudin -f- *Melastomataceae* ·
110 spp.
– **guttata** (Hook.) Triana · ⁴ ⓜ; Madag.

Gravisia Mez = Aechmea
– *aquilega* (Salisb.) Mez = Aechmea
aquilega
– *exsudans* (Lodd.) Mez = Aechmea
aquilega

Greenovia Webb & Berthel. -f-
Crassulaceae · 4 spp.
– **aizoon** Bolle · ⁴ ⁴ Z8 ⓚ V; Canar.
– **aurea** (C. Sm. ex Hornem.) Webb &
Berthel. · ⁴ ⁴ Z8 ⓚ III-IV; Canar.
– **dodrantalis** (Willd.) Webb & Berthel. · ⁴

⁴ Z8 ⓚ II-III; Canar.: Teneriffa
– *gracilis* Bolle = Greenovia dodrantalis

Greigia Regel -f- *Bromeliaceae* · 32 spp.
– **sphacelata** (Ruiz & Pav.) Regel · ⁴ ⓚ;
Peru, Chile

Grevillea R. Br. ex Knight -f- *Proteaceae* ·
261 sp. · E:Spider Flower; F:Grévillée;
G:Grevillee, Silbereiche
– **alpina** Lindl. · E:Mountain Grevillea · ♄ e
Z9 ⓚ IV-V; Austr.: N.S.Wales, Victoria
– **aspleniifolia** R. Br. ex Salisb. · ♄ ♄ e Z9
ⓚ III-V; Austr.: N.S.Wales
– **banksii** R. Br. · E:Red Silky Oak;
G:Rotblühende Silbereiche · ♄ ♄ e Z9 ⓚ;
Austr.: Queensl., N.S.Wales
– **crithmifolia** R. Br. · ♄ e Z9 ⓚ VI-VIII;
W-Austr.
– **glabrata** (Lindl.) Meisn. · G:Kahle
Silbereiche · ♄ e Z9 ⓚ; W-Austr.
– **hilliana** F. Muell. · E:White Silky Oak · ♄
♄ e Z9 ⓚ; Austr.: Queensl., N.S.Wales
– **juniperina** R. Br. · E:Juniper-leaf Grevillea · ♄ e Z9 ⓚ V; Austr.: N.S.Wales
– f. **sulphurea** (A. Cunn.) I.K. Ferguson ·
G:Schwefel-Silbereiche
– *manglesii* hort. = Grevillea glabrata
– **punicea** R. Br. · E:Red Spider Flower · ♄
e Z9 ⓚ III-VI; Austr.: N.S.Wales
– **robusta** A. Cunn. ex R. Br. · E:Silky Oak;
G:Australische Silbereiche · ♄ ♄ e Z9 ⓚ ▽
ⓝ; Austr.: Queensl., N.S.Wales, nat. in
C-Am, S-Am.
– **rosmarinifolia** A. Cunn. · E:Rosemary
Grevillea; G:Rosmarin-Silbereiche · ♄ e
Z8 ⓚ VII-VIII; Austr.: N.S.Wales, Victoria
– × **semperflorens** F.E. Briggs ex Mulligan
(*G. thelemanniana* × *G. juniperina* f.
sulphurea) · ♄ e Z8 ⓚ; cult.
– *speciosa* (Knight) McGill. = Grevillea
punicea
– *sulphurea* A. Cunn. = Grevillea juniperina
f. sulphurea
– **thelemanniana** Hügel ex Endl. ·
E:Hummingbird Bush, Spider Net
Grevillea; G:Spinnen-Silbereiche · ♄ e Z9
ⓚ III-V; W-Austr.

Grewia L. -f- *Tiliaceae* · 150 spp. · F:Grewia;
G:Grewie
– **asiatica** L. · E:Phalsa; G:Falsa · ♄ e Z10
ⓜ ⓝ; Ind.
– **biloba** G. Don · ♄ d Z7; Korea, China
– **occidentalis** L. · E:Crossberry, Lavender

Starflower; G:Kreuzbeere · ♄ ♄ e Z10 ⍟;
S-Afr.

Greyia Hook. & Harv. -f- *Greyiaceae* ·
3 spp. · E:Bottlebrush; F:Greya, Rince-
bouteille du Natal; G:Honigbaum
– **radlkoferi** Szyszyl. · E:Transvaal Bottlebrush ; G:Großer Honigbaum · ♄ s Z9
⍟; S-Afr.
– **sutherlandii** Hook. & Harv. · E:Natal
Bottlebrush; G:Natal-Honigbaum · ♄ s Z9
⍟ VII-X; S-Afr.: Natal

Griffinia Ker-Gawl. -f- *Amaryllidaceae* ·
19 spp.
– **hyacinthina** (Ker-Gawl.) Ker-Gawl. · ⚄
Z10 ⍟ VII-VIII; Braz.

Grindelia Willd. -f- *Asteraceae* · c. 60 spp. ·
E:Gumplant; F:Grindelia; G:Grindelie,
Gummikraut, Teerkraut
– **hirsutula** Hook. & Arn. · E:Hairy
Gumweed, Marsh Gumweed; G:Haariges
Gummikraut · ⚄ ; Calif.
– *humilis* Hook. & Arn. = Grindelia
hirsutula
– **lanceolata** Nutt. · E:Narrow-leaved
Gumweed; G:Schmalblättriges Gum-
mikraut · ⊙ Z5 VII-VIII; USA: SE, SC,
Mo., Kans.
– **robusta** Nutt. · E:Gumweed; G:Kalifor-
nisches Gummikraut · ⊙ ⚄ Z7 VI-IX ⍟;
Calif.
– **squarrosa** (Pursh) Dunal · E:Curly-cup
Gumweed; G:Sperriges Gummikraut · ⊙
⚄ Z3 VI-IX; Can.: W, Man.; USA: NCE,
NC, SE, SC, SW, Rocky Mts., SW

Griselinia J.R. Forst. & G. Forst. -f-
Griseliniaceae · 6 spp. · E:Broadleaf;
F:Griselinia; G:Griseline
– **littoralis** (Raoul) Raoul · E:Broadleaf;
G:Dichte Griseline, Kapuka · ♄ ♄ e Z8 ⍟;
NZ
– **lucida** (J.R. Forst. & G. Forst.) G. Forst. ·
G:Lockere Griseline, Puka · ♄ ♄ e Z8 ⍟;
NZ

Grobya Lindl. -f- *Orchidaceae* · 5 spp.
– **amherstiae** Lindl. · ⚄ Z10 ⍟ IX ▽ ✳;
Braz.
– **galeata** Lindl. · ⚄ Z10 ⍟ VIII-IX ▽ ✳;
Braz.

Groenlandia J. Gay -f- *Potamogetonaceae* ·

1 sp. · E:Frog's Lettuce; G:Fischkraut
– **densa** (L.) Fourr. · E:Frog's Lettuce;
G:Dichtblättriges Laichkraut, Fischkraut ·
⚄ ≈ Z7 VI-IX; Eur.*, TR, Levant, Cauc.,
NW-Iran, W-Him., NW-Afr.

Grossularia Mill. = Ribes
– *alpestris* (Wall. ex Decne.) A. Berger =
Ribes alpestre var. alpestre
– *oxyacanthoides* (L.) Mill. = Ribes
oxyacanthoides
– *uva-crispa* (L.) Mill. = Ribes uva-crispa
var. uva-crispa

Grusonia F. Rchb. ex Britton & Rose =
Opuntia
– *bradtiana* (J.M. Coult.) Britton & Rose =
Opuntia bradtiana

Guadua Kunth -f- *Poaceae* · c. 30 spp.
– **angustifolia** Kunth · e ⍟ ⍟; Col.,
Ecuad., nat. in USA, S-Am., C-Am.

Guaiacum L. -n- *Zygophyllaceae* · 6 spp. ·
E:Lignum Vitae; F:Bois de Gaïac, Gaïac;
G:Gujakbaum, Pockholz
– **officinale** L. · ♄ e Z10 ⍟ ⚘ ⚔ ⍟ ▽ ✳;
W.Ind., Panama, Col., Venez.
– **sanctum** L. · E:Holywood, Lignum Vitae;
G:Heiliges Pockholz · ♄ e Z10 ⍟ ⚘ ⍟ ▽
✳; Fla., S-Mex., W.Ind.

Guarea L. -f- *Meliaceae* · 40 spp.
– **cedrata** Pellegr. ex A. Chev. · ♄ ⍟ ⍟;
Ivory Coast
– **guidonia** (L.) Sleumer · E:American
Muskwood · ♄ e ⍟ ⚔ ⍟; Panama,
W.Ind., trop. S-Am.

Guibourtia Benn. -f- *Caesalpiniaceae* ·
16-17 spp.
– **copallifera** Benn. · ♄ ⍟ ⍟; W-Afr.
– **demeusii** (Harms) J. Léonard · ♄ ⍟ ⍟;
W-Afr.

Guilielma Mart. = Bactris
– *gasipaes* (Humb., Bonpl. & Kunth) L.H.
Bailey = Bactris gasipaes
– *speciosa* Mart. = Bactris gasipaes
– *utilis* Oerst. = Bactris gasipaes

Guillainia Ridl. = Alpinia

Guizotia Cass. -f- *Asteraceae* · 6 spp. ·
E:Niger; F:Guizotia; G:Nigersaat,

Ramtillkraut
- **abyssinica** (L. f.) Cass. · E:Niger Seed;
G:Nigersaat, Ramtillkraut · ☉ IX-X Ⓝ;
Eth., nat. in Calif.

Gunnera L. -f- *Gunneraceae* · c. 40 spp. ·
E:Giant Rhubarb; F:Rhubarbe géante;
G:Mammutblatt
- **hamiltonii** Kirk ex W. Ham. · ⹁ ⤳ Z8
Ⓚ Ⓐ; NZ
- **magellanica** Lam. · ⹁ Z8 ∧; S-Chile,
Falkland
- **manicata** Linden ex André · E:Chile
Rhubarb, Giant Rhubarb;G:Mammutblatt
· ⹁ Z8 ∧ VII-VIII; S-Braz.
- **microcarpa** Kirk · ⹁ ⤳ ⌢ Z8 Ⓚ Ⓐ;
NZ
- *mixta* Kirk = Gunnera microcarpa
- **prorepens** Hook. f. · ⹁ ⤳ ⌢ Z8 Ⓚ Ⓐ;
NZ
- *scabra* Ruiz & Pav. = Gunnera tinctoria
- **tinctoria** (Molina) Mirb. · F:Rhubarbe
géante · ⹁ Z8 ∧ VII-VIII; Chile

Gurania (Schltdl.) Cogn. -f- *Cucurbitaceae* ·
75 spp. · F:Gurania; G:Gurania
- **malacophylla** Barb. Rodr. · ♄ ⚥ Z10 Ⓦ
VIII-IX; Braz.

Guzmania Ruiz & Pav. -f- *Bromeliaceae* ·
202 spp. · E:Tufted Airplant; F:Guzmania;
G:Guzmanie
- **angustifolia** (Baker) Wittm. · ⹁ Z10 Ⓚ;
Costa Rica, Panama, Col., Ecuad.
- **berteroniana** (Schult. & Schult. f.) Mez ·
⹁ Z10 Ⓦ; Puerto Rico
- **conifera** (André) André ex Mez · ⹁ Z10
Ⓦ; Ecuad., Peru
- **dissitiflora** (André) L.B. Sm. · ⹁ Z10 Ⓦ;
Costa Rica, Panama, Col.
- **donnellsmithii** Mez ex Donn. Sm. · ⹁
Z10 Ⓦ; Costa Rica
- **erythrolepis** Brongn. ex Planch. · ⹁ Z10
Ⓦ; Costa Rica, W.Ind.
- **lindenii** (André) Mez · ⹁ Z10 Ⓦ; Peru
- **lingulata** (L.) Mez
- var. **concolor** Proctor & Cedeño-Mald. ·
Z10 Ⓦ; Costa Rica, Panama, Col., Ecuad.,
Braz.
- var. **lingulata** · ⹁ Z10 Ⓦ; C-Am., W.Ind.,
Col., Braz., Bol.
- var. *minor* (Mez) L.B. Sm. = Guzmania
lingulata var. concolor
- var. *splendens* (C.D. Bouché) Mez =
Guzmania lingulata var. lingulata

- **melinonis** Regel · ⹁ Z10 Ⓦ; Guyan., Col.
Ecuad. Peru, Bol.
- *minor* Mez = Guzmania lingulata var.
concolor
- **monostachia** (L.) Rusby ex Mez · E:West
Indian Tufted Airplant · ⹁ Z10 Ⓦ; Fla.,
C-Am., W.Ind., Venez., Col., Ecuad.,
Peru, Bol.
- **mucronata** (Griseb.) Mez · ⹁ Z10 Ⓦ;
Venez.
- **musaica** (Linden & André) Mez · ⹁ Z10
Ⓦ; Col., Panama
- **nicaraguensis** Mez & C.F. Baker ex Mez ·
⹁ Z10 Ⓦ; C-Am.
- **sanguinea** (André) André ex Mez · ⹁
Z10 Ⓦ; Costa Rica, Ecuad., Trinidad
- *tricolor* Ruiz & Pav. = Guzmania
monostachia
- **variegata** L.B. Sm. · ⹁ Z10 Ⓦ; Ecuad.,
N-Peru
- **vittata** (Mart. ex Schult. & Schult. f.)
Mez · ⹁ Z10 Ⓦ; Col., Braz.
- **wittmackii** (André) André ex Mez · ⹁
Z10 Ⓦ; Col.
- **zahnii** (Hook. f.) Mez · ⹁ Z10 Ⓦ; Costa
Rica, Panama

Gymnadenia R. Br. -f- *Orchidaceae* ·
10 spp. · E:Fragrant Orchid; F:Orchis
moucheron; G:Händelwurz
- **conopsea** (L.) R. Br. · E:Fragrant Orchid;
G:Gewöhnliche Mücken-Händelwurz ·
⹁ Z6 V-VIII ▽ ✳; Eur.*, TR, Cauc., Iran,
W-Sib., E-Sib., Amur, Sakhal., Mong.,
China, Korea, Jap.
- **odoratissima** (L.) Rich. · G:Gewöhnliche
Wohlriechende Händelwurz · ⹁ D Z6
VI-VIII ▽ ✳; Eur.* exc. BrI, Sc

Gymnandra Pall. = Lagotis
- *stolonifera* K. Koch = Lagotis stolonifera

Gymnanthocereus Backeb. = Browningia
- *chlorocarpus* (Kunth) Backeb. = Browningia chlorocarpa
- *microspermus* (Werderm. & Backeb.)
Backeb. = Browningia microsperma

Gymnocactus Backeb. = Turbinicarpus
- *conothelos* (Regel & E. Klein) Backeb. =
Thelocactus conothelos
- *gielsdorfianus* (Werderm.) Backeb. =
Turbinicarpus gielsdorfianus
- *horripilus* (Lem. ex C.F. Först.) Backeb. =
Turbinicarpus horripilus

- *mandragora* (Frič ex A. Berger) Backeb. =
Turbinicarpus mandragora
- *saueri* (Boed.) Backeb. = Turbinicarpus
saueri
- *viereckii* (Werderm.) Backeb. = Turbinicarpus viereckii

Gymnocalycium Pfeiff. -n- *Cactaceae* ·
50+ spp.
- **andreae** (Boed.) Backeb. · ¥ Z10 ⬠ ▽ ✳;
Arg.: Cordoba
- **anisitsii** (K. Schum.) Britton & Rose · ¥
Z9 ⬠ ▽ ✳; Parag.
- **baldianum** (Speg.) Speg. · ¥ Z10 ⬠
▽ ✳; Arg.: La Rioja, Catamarca, Salta,
Tucuman
- *brachypetalum* Speg. = Gymnocalycium
gibbosum
- **bruchii** (Speg.) Hosseus · ¥ Z10 ⬠ ▽ ✳;
Arg.: Cordoba
- **denudatum** (Link & Otto) Pfeiff. ex
Mittler · E:Spider Cactus · ¥ Z10 ⬠ ▽ ✳;
Braz.: Rio Grande do Sul, N-Urug.
- *fidaianum* (Backeb.) Hutchison =
Weingartia fidaiana
- **gibbosum** (Haw.) Pfeiff. ex Mittler · ¥ Z9
⬠ ▽ ✳; S-Arg.
- **hossei** (Haage) A. Berger · ¥ Z10 ⬠ ▽
✳; Arg.: La Rioja
- **hyptiacanthum** (Lem.) Britton & Rose ·
¥ ⬠
- *lafaldense* Vaupel = Gymnocalycium
bruchii
- *loricatum* Speg. = Gymnocalycium
spegazzinii subsp. spegazzinii
- *mazanense* (Backeb.) Backeb. = Gymnocalycium hossei
- **mihanovichii** (Frič & Gürke) Britton &
Rose
- var. **mihanovichii** · ¥ Z10 ⬠ ▽ ✳;
N-Parag.
- **monvillei** (Lem.) Britton & Rose
- subsp. **monvillei** · ¥ Z10 ⬠ ▽ ✳; Arg.:
Cordoba
- *multiflorum* (Hook.) Britton & Rose =
Gymnocalycium monvillei subsp. monvillei
- *neocumingii* (Backeb.) Hutchison =
Weingartia neocumingii
- *neumannianum* (Backeb.) Hutchison =
Weingartia neumanniana
- *occultum* Frič ex Schütz = Gymnocalycium stellatum subsp. occultum
- **ochoterenae** Backeb.
- **oenanthemum** Backeb. · ¥ Z10 ⬠ ▽ ✳;

Arg.: Cordoba, Mendoza
- **paraguayense** (K. Schum.) Hosseus · ¥
Z10 ⬠ ▽ ✳; N-Parag.
- *platense* (Speg.) Britton & Rose =
Gymnocalycium hyptiacanthum
- **quehlianum** (Haage ex Quehl) Hosseus ·
E:Chin Cactus · ¥ Z10 ⬠ ▽ ✳; Arg.:
Cordoba
- **saglionis** (Cels) Britton & Rose
- subsp. **saglionis** · ¥ Z10 ⬠ ▽ ✳; Arg.:
Catamarca, Salta, Tucuman
- subsp. **tilcarense** (Backeb.) H. Till & W.
Till · ¥ ⬠
- *sanguiniflorum* (Werderm.) Werderm. =
Gymnocalycium baldianum
- **schickendantzii** (F.A.C. Weber) Britton
& Rose · ¥ Z10 ⬠ ▽ ✳; Arg.: Catamarca,
Cordoba, Tucuman
- **spegazzinii** Britton & Rose
- subsp. **cardenasianum** (F. Ritter) R.
Kiesling & Metzing · ¥ Z10 ⬠ ▽ ✳;
S-Bol.
- subsp. **spegazzinii** · ¥ Z10 ⬠ ▽ ✳; Arg.:
Salta
- **stellatum** Speg. · ¥ Z9 ⬠; Arg.
(Cordoba)
- subsp. **occultum** Frič ex H. Till & W. Till
- subsp. **stellatum**
- *venturianum* (Frič) Backeb. = Gymnocalycium baldianum

Gymnocarpium Newman -n- *Woodsiaceae* ·
9 spp. · E:Oak Fern; F:Fougère du chêne;
G:Eichenfarn, Ruprechtsfarn
- **dryopteris** (L.) Newman · E:Oak Fern,
Western Oak Fern; G:Eichenfarn · ⳦ Z3
VII-VIII; Eur.*, TR, Cauc., Him., W-Sib.,
E-Sib., Amur, Sakhal., Kamchat., C-As.,
Mong., Manch., Korea, Jap., Alaska, Can,
USA: NE, NCE, NC, SW, Rocky Mts., NW;
Greenl.
- *phegopteris* (L.) Newman = Phegopteris
connectilis
- **robertianum** (Hoffm.) Newman ·
E:Limestone Oak Fern, Scented Oak
Fern; G:Ruprechtsfarn · ⳦ Z4 VII-VIII;
Eur.*, Cauc., Him., W-Sib., E-Sib., Amur,
N-China, Korea, Jap., Alger., Alaska,
Can., USA: NE, NCE

Gymnocereus Rauh & Backeb. = Browningia
- *microspermus* (Werderm. & Backeb.)
Backeb. = Browningia microsperma

Gymnocladus Lam. -m- *Caesalpiniaceae* ·

5 spp. · F:Chicot du Canada; G:Geweihbaum, Schusserbaum
- **dioica** (L.) K. Koch · E:Kentucky Coffeetree; G:Amerikanischer Geweihbaum · ♄ d Z6 V-VI ®; Ont., USA: NE, NCE, NC, SC, SE

Gymnospermium Spach -n- *Berberidaceae* · 8 spp.
- **albertii** (Regel) Takht. · ♃ Z4 ⓐ IV-V; C-As.

Gymnostachyum Nees -n- *Acanthaceae* · 30 spp.
- **ceylanicum** Arn. & Nees · ♃ ⓦ I-III; Sri Lanka
- **sanguinolentum** (Vahl) T. Anderson · ♃ ⓦ; Sri Lanka
- **venustum** (Wall.) T. Anderson · ♃ ⓦ X-XI; InG: S-Khasia

Gynandriris Parl. -f- *Iridaceae* · 9 spp.
- **sisyrinchium** (L.) Parl. · E:Barbary Nut · ♃ Z8 ▭ IV-V; Eur.: Ib, Ital-P, Ba; TR, SW-As, Pakist., Med.

Gynandropsis DC. = Cleome
- *gynandra* (L.) Briq. = Cleome gynandra

Gynerium Willd. ex P. Beauv. -n- *Poaceae* · 1 sp.
- *argenteum* Nees = Cortaderia selloana

Gynura Cass. -f- *Asteraceae* · c. 40 spp. · E:Velvet Plant; F:Gynure; G:Samtpflanze
- **aurantiaca** (Blume) DC. · E:Purple Velvet Plant; G:Purpur-Samtpflanze · ♄ ⓦ IX-X; Java, Sulawesi
- **procumbens** (Lour.) Merr. · E:Velvet Plant; G:Malayische Samtpflanze · ♃ ≹ ≹ ⓦ; W-Afr., China, Thail., Malay. Pen.
- *sarmentosa* (Blume) DC. = Gynura procumbens
- **scandens** O. Hoffm. · ♄ ≹ ≹ ⓦ IV-IX ☠; E-Afr.

Gypsophila L. -f- *Caryophyllaceae* · c. 150 spp. · E:Baby's Breath; F:Gypsophile; G:Gipskraut, Schleierkraut
- **acutifolia** Steven ex Spreng. · ♃ VII-IX; Eur.: W-Russ.; Cauc., nat. in RO
- **aretioides** Boiss. · ♃ △ Z5 VI-VII; N-Iran, Cauc.
- **cerastioides** D. Don · ♃ △ Z5 V-VI; Him.: Kashmir, NW-Ind., Nepal, Sikkim, Bhutan
- **curvifolia** Fenzl · ♃ △ ∧ VI; TR
- **elegans** M. Bieb. · E:Annual Baby's Breath; G:Sommer-Schleierkraut · ⊙ VII; S-Russ., TR, Cauc., Iran
- **fastigiata** L. · G:Büschel-Gipskraut · ♃ VI-IX ▽; Eur.: C-Eur., EC-Eur., Sc, E-Eur., ? W-Ba
- **libanotica** Boiss. · ♃ △ ∧ VI; TR, Lebanon, Syr.
- × **monstrosa** Gerbeaux (*G. repens* × *G. stevenii*) · ♃ △ V-VI; cult.
- **muralis** L. · E:Cushion Baby's Breath; G:Mauer-Gipskraut · ⊙ VI-X; Eur.* exc. BrI; TR, Cauc., W-Sib., E-Sib., Amur, C-As., Manch., nat. in N-Am.
- **pacifica** Kom. · G:Mandschurisches Gipskraut · ♃ ✂ Z3 VI-VIII; Amur, Manch.
- **paniculata** L. · E:Baby's Breath; F:Brouillard; G:Rispiges Gipskraut, Schleierkraut · ♃ ✂ Z4 VI-VIII; Eur.: C-Eur., EC-Eur., Ba, E-Eur.; Cauc., W-Sib., C-As., N-Mong., W-China, nat. in N-Am.
- **perfoliata** L. · G:Durchwachsenblättriges Gipskraut · ♃ VI-IX; Eur.: BG, RO, Russ.; TR, Levant, W-Sib., C-As., nat. in D
- **petraea** (Baumg.) Rchb. · ♃ △ Z7 VI-VIII; Eur.: RO; Carp.
- **repens** L. · E:Alpine Gypsophila; F:Gypsophile rampante; G:Kriechendes Gipskraut, Teppich-Schleierkraut · ♃ ⇝ △ Z4 V-VI; Eur.: Ib, Fr, Ital-P, C-Eur., EC-Eur.; mts.
- **scorzonerifolia** Ser. · G:Schwarzwurzel-Gipskraut · ♃ VI-IX; Eur.: E-Russ; Cauc., nat. in G, CZ
- **stevenii** Fisch. ex Schrank · ♃ △ VII; Cauc.
- × **suendermannii** Fritsch (*G. petraea* × *G. repens*) · ♃ △ V-VI; cult.
- **tenuifolia** M. Bieb. · ♃ ⌓ △ Z5 VI; Cauc., TR
- *transsylvanica* Spreng. = Gypsophila petraea

Haageocereus Backeb. -m- *Cactaceae* · 5-10 spp.
- **acranthus** (K. Schum. ex Vaupel) Backeb.
- subsp. **acranthus** · ♆ Z9 ⓚ ▽ *; C-Peru
- subsp. **olowinskianus** (Backeb.) Ostolaza
- **albispinus** (Akers) Backeb. · ♆ Z9 ⓚ ▽ *; C-Peru
- *aureispinus* Rauh & Backeb. =

Haageocereus pseudomelanostele subsp.
aureispinus
– **australis** Backeb.
– *chosicensis* (Werderm. & Backeb.)
Backeb. = Haageocereus pseudomelanostele
– **decumbens** (Vaupel) Backeb. · ♀ ⤳ Z9
⟨⟩ ▽ ✳; S-Peru, N-Chile
– **icosagonoides** Rauh & Backeb.
– **multangularis** (Willd.) F. Ritter · ♀ Z9 ⟨⟩
▽ ✳; C-Peru
– *olowinskianus* Backeb. = Haageocereus
acranthus subsp. olowinskianus
– **pseudomelanostele** (Werderm. &
Backeb.) Backeb.
– subsp. **aureispinus** (Rauh & Backeb.)
Ostolaza
– subsp. **pseudomelanostele**
– **versicolor** (Werderm. & Backeb.)
Backeb. · ♀ Z9 ⟨⟩ ▽ ✳; N-Peru
– *weberbaueri* (Vaupel) D.R. Hunt =
Weberbauerocereus weberbaueri

Habenaria Willd. -f- *Orchidaceae* ·
819 spp. · F:Habénaire; G:Riemenlippe,
Zügelständel
– *bonatea* L. f. = Bonatea speciosa
– **carnea** Weathers · G:Fleischfarbiger
Zügelständel · ⹁ Z9 ⟨⟩ IX-X ▽ ✳; Malay.
Pen.: Penang
– **radiata** (Thunb.) Spreng. · ⹁ Z10 ⟨⟩ VIII
▽ ✳; Jap., Korea
– **rhodocheila** Hance · G:Malayen-Zügel-
ständel · ⹁ Z9 ⟨⟩ IX-X ▽ ✳; S-China,
Indochina, Malay. Pen.
– *robusta* N.E. Br. = Bonatea speciosa

Haberlea Friv. -f- *Gesneriaceae* · 2 spp. ·
F:Haberléa; G:Haberlee
– **ferdinandi-coburgii** Urum. · ⹁ △ IV-V
▽; Eur.: C-BG
– **rhodopensis** Friv. · ⹁ △ IV-V ▽; Eur.:
BG, NE-GR; mts.

Habranthus Herb. -m- *Amaryllidaceae* ·
72 spp. · E:Copper Lily
– **brachyandrus** (Baker) Sealy · ⹁ Z9 ⟨⟩
VI-VIII; S-Braz., S-Chile
– **robustus** Herb. ex Sweet · E:Brazilian
Copper Lily · ⹁ Z9 ⟨⟩ VII-VIII; S-Braz., ?
Arg
– **tubispathus** (L'Hér.) Herb. · E:Rio
Grande Copper Lily · ⹁ Z9 ⟨⟩ VII-VIII;
E-Arg., S-Braz., S-Chile, Urug.
– *tubispathus* auct. non (L'Hér.) Herb. =

Habranthus robustus

Habrothamnus Endl. = Cestrum
– *elegans* Brongn. ex Neumann = Cestrum
elegans var. elegans
– *purpureus* Lindl. = Cestrum elegans var.
elegans

Hacquetia Neck. ex DC. -f- *Apiaceae* · 1 sp. ·
F:Hacquetia; G:Schaftdolde
– **epipactis** (Scop.) DC. · G:Goldteller,
Schaftdolde · ⹁ Z7 IV-V; Eur.: A, I, Slove.,
Croatia, PL, Slova., CZ

Hadrodemas H.E. Moore = Callisia
– *warszewiczianum* (Kunth & C.D. Bouché)
H.E. Moore = Callisia warszewicziana

Haemadictyon Steud. = Prestonia
– *venosum* Lindl. = Prestonia quinquangularis

Haemanthus L. -m- *Amaryllidaceae* ·
22 spp. · E:Blood Lily; F:Hémanthe;
G:Blutblume
– **albiflos** Jacq. · G:Elefantenohr, Weiß-
blütige Blutblume · ⹁ Z9 ⟨⟩ VII-X; S-Afr.
– var. *pubescens* auct. = Haemanthus
pubescens
– **coccineus** L. · E:Cape Tulip; G:Schar-
lachrote Blutblume · ⹁ Z9 ⟨⟩ VIII-IX;
Namibia, S-Afr.
– **humilis** Jacq.
– subsp. **hirsutus** (Baker) Snijman · ⹁ Z9
⟨⟩ VIII-IX; S-Afr.
– subsp. **humilis** · G:Niedere Blutblume · ⹁
Z9 ⟨⟩; S-Afr.
– *kalbreyeri* Baker = Scadoxus multiflorus
subsp. multiflorus
– *lindenii* N.E. Br. = Scadoxus cinnabarinus
– *multiflorus* Martyn = Scadoxus multiflorus subsp. multiflorus
– *natalensis* Hook. = Scadoxus puniceus
– **pubescens** L. · ⹁ Z9 ⟨⟩ VII-X; Namibia,
S-Afr.
– *puniceus* L. = Scadoxus puniceus
– *tigrinus* Jacq. = Haemanthus coccineus

Haemaria Lindl. = Ludisia
– *discolor* (Ker-Gawl.) Lindl. = Ludisia
discolor var. discolor

Haematoxylum L. -n- *Caesalpiniaceae* ·
3 spp. · E:Bloodwood Tree; F:Campêche,
Haematoxylon; G:Blutholzbaum,

Campecheholz
- **campechianum** L. · E:Bloodwood Tree, Logwood; G:Mexikanischer Blutholzbaum · ₶ e Z9 ⓦ ⚕ Ⓝ; Mex., C-Am., trop. S-Am.

Haemodorum Sm. -n- *Haemodoraceae* · 20 spp.
- **corymbosum** Vahl · ♃ ⓚ VIII; Austr.: Queensl., N.S.Wales
- **planifolium** R. Br. · ♃ ⓚ VIII; Austr.: Queensl., N.S.Wales
- *teretifolium* R. Br. = Haemodorum corymbosum

Hagenia J.F. Gmel. -f- *Rosaceae* · 1 sp. · G:Kosobaum
- **abyssinica** (Bruce) J.F. Gmel. · G:Kosobaum · ₶ e ⓚ ⚕ ☠ Ⓝ; Eth., E-Afr., top. S-Afr.

Hakea Schrad. -f- *Proteaceae* · c. 120 spp. · E:Pincushion Tree; F:Arbre-aux-oursins, Hakea; G:Hakea, Nadelkissen
- **bucculenta** C.A. Gardner · E:Red Pokers; G:Stachliges Nadelkissen · ♄ e Z9 ⓚ; W-Austr.
- **ceratophylla** R. Br. · E:Horn-leaf Hakea; G:Hornblättriges Nadelkissen · ♄ e Z9 ⓚ; W-Austr.
- **crassifolia** Meisn. · ♄ e Z9 ⓚ; W-Austr.
- **cyclocarpa** Lindl. · E:Curved Fruit Hakea; G:Hornfrüchtiges Nadelkissen · ♄ e Z9 ⓚ; W-Austr.
- **dactyloides** (Gaertn.) Cav. · E:Finger Hakea; G:Handförmiges Nadelkissen · ♄ e Z9 ⓚ; Austr.: Queensland, N.S.Wales, Victoria
- *eucalyptoides* Meisn. = Hakea laurina
- **ferruginea** Sweet · G:Rostfarbenes Nadelkissen · ♄ e Z9 ⓚ VII-VIII; W-Austr.
- **florida** R. Br. · E:Summer Snow · ♄ e Z9 ⓚ VII; W-Austr.
- **gibbosa** Cav. · E:Hairy Hakea · ♄ e Z9 ⓚ; Austr.: N.S.Wales
- **laurina** R. Br. · E:Pincushion Hakea, Sea Urchin; G:Ballförmiges Nadelkissen · ♄ ₶ e Z9 ⓚ Ⓝ; W-Austr.
- **leucoptera** R. Br. · E:Needlewood; G:Ausläufer-Nadelkissen · ₶ ♄ e Z9 ⓚ; Austr.: Queensl., N.S.Wales, Victoria, S-Austr., N. Terr.
- **multilineata** Meisn. · E:Grass-leaf Hakea · ♄ e Z9 ⓚ; W-Austr.
- **nitida** R. Br. · E:Shining Hakea; G:Knotiges Nadelkissen · ♄ e Z9 ⓚ; W-Austr.
- **nodosa** R. Br. · E:Yellow Hakea · ♄ e Z9 ⓚ; Austr.: S-Austr., Victoria
- **obtusa** Meisn. · G:Stumpfes Nadelkissen · ♄ e Z9 ⓚ; W-Austr.
- **oleifolia** R. Br. · E:Olive-leaved Hakea; G:Ölbaumblättriges Nadelkissen · ♄ ₶ e Z9 ⓚ; W-Austr.
- **orthorrhyncha** F. Muell. · E:Bird Hakea · ♄ e Z9 ⓚ; W-Austr.
- *pectinata* Colla = Hakea suaveolens
- **petiolaris** Meisn. · E:Sea Urchin Hakea · ♄ e Z9 ⓚ; W-Austr.
- **pugioniformis** Cav. · E:Dagger Hakea · ♄ e Z9 ⓚ V-VI; Austr.: S-Austr., Tasman., Victoria
- **salicifolia** (Vent.) B.L. Burtt · E:Willow-leaf Hakea; G:Weidenblättriges Nadelkissen · ♄ e Z9 ⓚ VII-VIII; Austr.: Queensl., N.S.Wales
- *saligna* (Andrews) Knight = Hakea salicifolia
- **sericea** Schrad. & J.C. Wendl. · E:Silky Hakea; G:Nadelblättriges Nadelkissen · ♄ e Z9 ⓚ V-VIII; Austr.: N.S.Wales, Victoria
- **suaveolens** R. Br. · E:Sweet Hakea; G:Duftendes Nadelkissen · ♄ e D Z9 ⓚ VII-VIII; W-Austr.
- **varia** R. Br. · E:Variable-leaved Hakea · ♄ e Z9 ⓚ; W-Austr.

Hakonechloa Makino ex Honda -f- *Poaceae* · 1 sp. · E:Hakone Grass; G:Japangras
- **macra** (Munro) Makino ex Honda · E:Hakone Grass, Japanese Reed Grass; G:Japangras · ♃ Z7 ∧ VII-X; Jap.

Haldina Ridsdale -f- *Rubiaceae* · 1 sp.
- **cordifolia** (Roxb.) Ridsdale · ₶ d ⓦ Ⓝ; Ind., Sri Lanka, Burma, Laos, Vietn.

Halenia Borkh. -f- *Gentianaceae* · c. 70 spp.
- **elliptica** D. Don · ⊙ Z5 VII-VIII; Him.
- **perrottetii** Griseb. · ⊙ Z5 VII-VIII; Ind.

Halesia J. Ellis ex L. -f- *Styracaceae* · 5 spp. · E:Silver Bell, Snowdrop Tree; F:Halésia; G:Schneeglöckchenbaum
- **carolina** L. · E:Carolina Silverbell, Snowdrop Tree; F:Arbre aux clochettes d'argent; G:Carolina-Schneeglöckchenbaum · ♄ ₶ d Z6 IV-V; USA: NE, NCE, SE,

Fla.
- **diptera** J. Ellis · E:Two-wing Silverbelt;
  G:Zweiflügeliger Schneeglöckchenbaum
  · ♄ ♄ d Z6 VI; USA: SE, SC, Fla.
- **monticola** (Rehder) Sarg. · E:Mountain
  Silverbell, Snowdrop Tree; G:Berg-
  Schneeglöckchenbaum · ♄ d Z5 IV Ⓝ;
  USA: SE, SC
- *tetraptera* J. Ellis = Halesia carolina

× **Halimiocistus** Janch. -m- *Cistaceae*
- **sahucii** (H.J. Coste & Soulié) Janch.
  (*Cistus salviifolius × Halimium
  umbellatum*) · ♄ e Z8 Ⓐ; S-F
- **wintonensis** O.E. Warb. & E.F. Warb.
  (*Cistus salviifolius × Halimium lasianthum
  subsp. lasianthum*) · ♄ e Z8 ⒶⒶ; cult.
- **Cultivars:**
- **some cultivars**

Halimium (Dunal) Spach -n- *Cistaceae* ·
  -12 spp.
- **lasianthum** (Lam.) Spach · ♄ e Z8 Ⓐ
  V-VI; Eur.: F, Ib
- **ocymoides** (Lam.) Willk. · ♄ e Z8 Ⓐ; sp.,
  P
- **umbellatum** (L.) Spach · ♄ e Z8 Ⓐ V-VI;
  Eur.: Ib, F, GR

Halimodendron Fisch. ex DC. -n-
  Fabaceae · 1 sp. · E:Salt Tree; F:Caragana
  argenté; G:Salzstrauch
- **halodendron** (Pall.) Voss · E:Salt Tree;
  G:Salzstrauch · ♄ d Z5 VI-VII Ⓝ; Eur.:
  Russ.; N-TR, Cauc., Iran, W-Sib., C-As.

Haloragis J.R. Forst. & G. Forst. -f-
  Haloragaceae · 27 spp. · E:Raspwort;
  G:Seebeere
- **erecta** (Banks ex Murray) Eichler · ♄ ♃
  Ⓐ; NZ

Haloxylon Bunge -n- *Chenopodiaceae* ·
  10 spp. · E:Saxaul; G:Salzbaum, Saxaul
- **ammodendron** (C.A. Mey.) Bunge · ♄ ♄
  Z5; Atlas, Ural, Iran, C-As., Mong., China:
  Sinkiang

Hamamelis L. -f- *Hamamelidaceae* ·
  5 spp. · E:Witch Hazel; F:Hamamélis;
  G:Zaubernuss
- × **intermedia** Rehder (*H. japonica ×
  H. mollis*) · E:Witch Hazel; G:Hybrid-
  Zaubernuss · ♄ d Z6 I-III; cult.
- **many cultivars**

- **japonica** Siebold & Zucc.
- var. **japonica** · E:Japanese Witch Hazel;
  F:Hamamélis du Japon; G:Japanische
  Zaubernuss · ♄ d Z6 I-IV; Jap.
- f. **flavopurpurascens** (Makino) Rehder ·
  ♄ d Z6 I-III; Jap.
- **mollis** Oliv. · E:Chinese Witch Hazel;
  F:Hamamélis de Chine; G:Chinesische
  Zaubernuss · ♄ d Z6 I-III; China: Hupeh
- **vernalis** Sarg. · E:Ozark Witch Hazel,
  Spring Witch Hazel; G:Frühlings-
  Zaubernuss · ♄ d Z6 I-III; USA: SE, SC
- **virginiana** L. · ♄ ♄ d Z5 IX-X ⚥ Ⓝ; Can.:
  E; USA: NE, NCE, SE, Fla.

Hamatocactus Britton & Rose = Thelocactus
- *crassihamatus* (F.A.C. Weber) Buxb. =
  Sclerocactus uncinatus var. crassihamatus
- *hamatacanthus* (Muehlenpf.) F.M. Knuth
  = Ferocactus hamatacanthus
- *setispinus* (Engelm.) Britton & Rose =
  Thelocactus setispinus
- *sinuatus* (A. Dietr.) Orcutt = Ferocactus
  hamatacanthus
- *uncinatus* (Galeotti) Buxb. = Sclerocactus
  uncinatus var. uncinatus

Hamelia Jacq. -f- *Rubiaceae* · 17 spp. ·
  E:Fire Bush; G:Feuerbusch
- **patens** Jacq. · E:Firebush, Scarlet Bush;
  G:Feuerbusch · ♄ e Z10 Ⓦ VI-IX; Fla.,
  Mex., Bahamas, W.Ind., trop. S-Am.

Hammarbya Kuntze -f- *Orchidaceae* · 1 sp. ·
  E:Bog Orchid; G:Weichwurz
- **paludosa** (L.) Kuntze · E:Bog Orchid;
  G:Weichwurz · ♃ VII-VIII ▽ ✳; Eur.*
  exc. Ital-P; W-Sib., E-Sib., Sakhal., Jap.,
  Alaska, NW-Can., C-USA

Hancornia Gomes -f- *Apocynaceae* · 1 sp. ·
  E:Mangabeira; G:Mangabeiragummi
- **speciosa** Gomes · E:Mangabeira;
  G:Mangabeiragummi · ♄ Ⓦ Ⓝ; E-Braz.

Haplopappus Cass. -m- *Asteraceae* · c.
  70 spp.
- *coronopifolius* (Less.) DC. = Haplopappus
  glutinosus
- *croceus* A. Gray = Pyrrocoma crocea
- **glutinosus** Cass. · ♃ △ Z8 △ VII-X;
  Chile. Arg.; And.

Haplophyllum A. Juss. -n- *Rutaceae* ·

66 spp.
- **patavinum** (L.) G. Don · ⁴ △ ⓚ VI-VIII; Eur.: I, Ba, RO

Hardenbergia Benth. -f- *Fabaceae* · 3 spp. · E:Coral Pea; F:Hardenbergia; G:Hardenbergie, Purpurerbse
- **comptoniana** (Andrews) Benth. · ♄ e ⚡ Z9 ⓚ I-IV; W-Austr.
- *monophylla* (Vent.) Benth. = Hardenbergia violacea
- **violacea** (Schneev.) Stearn · E:Coral Pea, Vine Lilac; G:Purpurerbse · ♄ e ⚡ ⇝ Z9 ⓚ III-IV; Austr.: Queensl., N.S.Wales, Victoria, Tasman.

Haronga Thouars = Harungana
- *madagascariensis* (Lam. ex Poir.) Choisy = Harungana madagascariensis

Harpagophytum DC. ex Meisn. -n- *Pedaliaceae* · 8 spp. · E:Grapple Plant; G:Afrikanische Teufelskralle
- **procumbens** (Burch.) DC. · E:Devil's Claw, Grapple Plant; G:Afrikanische Teufelskralle · ⁴ ⓚ ⚡ ; S-Afr.

Harpephyllum Bernh. ex C. Krauss -n- *Anacardiaceae* · 1 sp. · E:Kaffir Plum; F:Prunier des Cafres; G:Kafirpflaume
- **caffrum** Bernh. ex C. Krauss · E:Kaffir Plum; G:Kafirpflaume · ♄ e Z9 ⓚ; S-Afr.: Cape, Natal

Harpullia Roxb. -f- *Sapindaceae* · 26 spp.
- **pendula** Planch. & F. Muell. · E:Moreton Bay Tulipwood · ♄ e Z10 ⓦ; Malay. Arch., Phil., Austr.: Queensl., N.S.Wales

Harrimanella Coville = Cassiope
- *hypnoides* (L.) Coville = Cassiope hypnoides

Harrisia Britton -f- *Cactaceae* · c. 20 spp.
- *bonplandii* (J. Parm. ex Pfeiff.) Britton & Rose = Eriocereus bonplandii
- **gracilis** (Mill.) Britton · ♄ ⱡ Z9 ⓚ ▽ ✳; Fla., Jamaica
- *guelichii* (Speg.) Britton & Rose = Eriocereus guelichii
- *jusbertii* (K. Schum.) Borg = Eriocereus jusbertii
- *martinii* (Labour.) Britton & Rose = Eriocereus martinii
- *pomanensis* (F.A.C. Weber) Britton &

Rose = Eriocereus bonplandii
- **tetracantha** (Labour.) D.R. Hunt · ♄ ♄ ⱡ Z9 ⓚ ▽ ✳; Bol.
- *tortuosa* (J. Forbes) Britton & Rose = Eriocereus tortuosus

× **Hartara** hort. -f- *Orchidaceae* (*Broughtonia* × *Laelia* × *Sophronitis*)

Hartia Dunn = Stewartia
- *sinensis* Dunn = Stewartia pteropetiolata

Hartmannia Spach = Oenothera
- *rosea* (L'Hér. ex Aiton) G. Don = Oenothera rosea
- *speciosa* (Nutt.) Small = Oenothera speciosa

Harungana Lam. -f- *Clusiaceae* · 1 sp.
- **madagascariensis** Lam. ex Poir. · ♄ ⓦ ⚡ ⓝ; trop. Afr., Madag., Mauritius

Hasseanthus Rose = Dudleya
- *variegatus* (S. Watson) Rose = Dudleya variegata

Hatiora Britton & Rose -f- *Cactaceae* · 2 spp.
- *clavata* (F.A.C. Weber) Moran = Rhipsalis clavata
- *gaertneri* (Regel) Barthlott = Rhipsalidopsis gaertneri
- × *graeseri* (Werderm.) Barthlott = Rhipsalidopsis × graeseri
- *rosea* (Lagerh.) Barthlott = Rhipsalidopsis rosea
- **salicornioides** (Haw.) Britton & Rose · ♄ ⱡ Z9 ⓦ ▽ ✳; SE-Braz.

× **Hawaiiara** hort. -f- *Orchidaceae* (*Renanthera* × *Vanda* × *Vandopsis*)

Haworthia Duval -f- *Aloaceae* · 68 spp.
- **angustifolia** Haw. · ⁴ ⱡ Z9 ⓚ; S-Afr.
- **arachnoidea** (L.) Duval · ⁴ ⱡ Z9 ⓚ; S-Afr.
- *asperiuscula* Haw. = Haworthia viscosa
- **attenuata** (Haw.) Haw.
- var. **attenuata** · ⱡ Z9 ⓚ; S-Afr. (Cape Prov.)
- var. **radula** (Jacq.) M.B. Bayer · ⁴ ⱡ Z9 ⓚ; Cape
- **chloracantha** Haw. · ⁴ ⱡ Z9 ⓚ; Cape
- **coarctata** Haw. · ⱡ Z9 ⓚ; S-Afr. (Cape Prov.)

- **cooperi** Baker
- var. **cooperi** · ψ Z9 Ⓚ; S-Afr. (Cape Prov.)
- var. **pilifera** (Baker) M.B. Bayer
- × **cuspidata** Haw. (*H. cymbiformis var. cymbiformis × H. retusa*) · ♃ ψ Z9 Ⓚ; SE-Cape
- **cymbiformis** (Haw.) Duval
- var. **cymbiformis** · ♃ ψ Z9 Ⓚ; S-Afr.
- var. **obtusa** (Haw.) Baker · ψ Ⓚ; S-Afr. (Cape Prov.)
- *fasciata* hort. = Haworthia attenuata var. attenuata
- *foliolosa* (Haw.) Haw. = Astroloba foliolosa
- *fulva* G.G. Sm. = Haworthia coarctata
- **glabrata** (Salm-Dyck) Baker · ♃ ψ Z9 Ⓚ; S-Afr.
- **gracilis** Poelln.
- var. **tenera** (Poelln.) M.B. Bayer
- *guttata* Uitewaal = Haworthia reticulata
- **herbacea** (Mill.) Stearn · ♃ ψ Z9 Ⓚ; Cape
- *laetevirens* Haw. = Haworthia turgida
- **limifolia** Marloth
- var. **limifolia** · ♃ ψ Z9 Ⓚ; S-Afr.: Natal, Transvaal, Swasiland
- var. **ubomboensis** (I. Verd.) G.G. Sm.
- **longiana** Poelln. · ♃ ψ Z9 Ⓚ; Cape
- *margaritifera* Haw. = Haworthia pumila
- *maughanii* Poelln. = Haworthia truncata var. maughanii
- **mirabilis** (Haw.) Haw.
- var. **mirabilis** · ♃ ψ Z9 Ⓚ; ? Cape
- var. **triebneriana** (Poelln.) M.B. Bayer
- **mucronata** Haw. · ♃ ψ Z9 Ⓚ; Cape
- *nitidula* Poelln. = Haworthia mirabilis var. triebneriana
- *obtusa* Haw. = Haworthia cymbiformis var. obtusa
- var. *pilifera* (Baker) Uitewaal = Haworthia cooperi var. pilifera
- *papillosa* Haw. = Haworthia herbacea
- *pellucens* Haw. = Haworthia herbacea
- *pentagona* Haw. = Astroloba spiralis
- *pilifera* Baker = Haworthia cooperi var. pilifera
- **pumila** (L.) Duval · ♃ ψ Z9 Ⓚ; S-Afr.: Cape
- **pygmaea** Poelln. · ♃ ψ Z9 Ⓚ
- *radula* (Jacq.) Haw. = Haworthia attenuata var. radula
- *recurva* Haw. = Haworthia venosa subsp. venosa
- **reinwardtii** (Salm-Dyck) Haw. · ♃ ψ Z9 Ⓚ; Cape
- **reticulata** (Haw.) Haw. · ♃ ψ Z9 Ⓚ; E-Cape
- **retusa** (L.) Duval · ♃ ψ Z9 Ⓚ; Cape
- × **rigida** (Lam.) Haw. (*H. glabrata × H. × tortuosa*) · ♃ ψ Z9 Ⓚ; S-Afr.
- *rugosa* (Salm-Dyck) Baker = Haworthia attenuata var. radula
- *spiralis* (L.) Duval = Astroloba spiralis
- *subattenuata* (Salm-Dyck) Baker = Haworthia pumila
- *subrigida* (Schult. & Schult. f.) Baker = Haworthia viscosa
- *tenera* Poelln. = Haworthia gracilis var. tenera
- *tesselata* Haw. = Haworthia venosa subsp. tessellata
- × **tortuosa** (Haw.) Haw. (*H. nigra* ×) · ♃ ψ Z9 Ⓚ; orig. ?
- *translucens* (Willd.) Haw. = Haworthia herbacea
- subsp. *tenera* (Poelln.) M.B. Bayer = Haworthia gracilis var. tenera
- **truncata** Schönland
- var. **maughanii** (Poelln.) Halda
- var. **truncata** · ♃ ψ Z9 Ⓚ; Cape
- **turgida** Haw. · ♃ ψ Z9 Ⓚ; Cape
- **ubomboensis** I. Verd.
- **venosa** (Lam.) Haw.
- subsp. *recurva* (Haw.) M.B. Bayer = Haworthia venosa subsp. venosa
- subsp. **tessellata** (Haw.) M.B. Bayer Z9 Ⓚ; S-Afr.: Cape, Orange Free State; Namibia
- subsp. **venosa** · ♃ ψ Z9 Ⓚ; Cape, Namibia
- **viscosa** (L.) Haw. · ♃ ψ Z9 Ⓚ; Cape

Hebe Comm. ex Juss. -f- *Scrophulariaceae* · c. 75 spp. · E:Hedge Veronica; F:Hebe, Véronique arbustive; G:Strauchehrenpreis, Strauchveronika

- **albicans** (Petrie) Cockayne · ♄ e Z8 Ⓚ; NZ
- × **andersonii** (Lindl. & Paxton) Cockayne (*H. salicifolia × H. speciosa*) · ♄ e Z9 Ⓚ; cult.
- *anomala* (J.B. Armstr.) Cockayne = Hebe odora
- **armstrongii** (J.B. Armstr.) Cockayne & Allan · ♄ e Z7 V-VI; NZ
- **balfouriana** (Hook. f.) Cockayne · ♄ e Z7 Ⓐ ∧ VI-VII; NZ
- **benthamii** (Hook. f.) Cockayne & Allan · ♄ e Z8 Ⓚ; NZ
- **brachysiphon** Summerh. · ♄ e Z8 Ⓐ ∧; NZ

- **buchananii** (Hook. f.) Cockayne & Allan · F:Véronique arbustive · ♄ e Z8 ⊡ VI-VII; NZ
- **buxifolia** (Benth.) Cockayne & Allan · F:Véronique arbustive; G:Buchsblättriger Strauchehrenpreis · ♄ e Z8 ⊡ ∧ VI-VII; NZ
- **canterburiensis** (J.B. Armstr.) L.B. Moore · ♄ e Z9 ⊡; NZ
- **carnosula** (Hook. f.) Cockayne & Allan · ♄ e Z6 VI-VIII; NZ
- *catarractae* G. Forst. = Parahebe catarractae
- **cockayniana** (Cheeseman) Cockayne & Allan · ♄ e Z8 ⊡; NZ
- **colensoi** (Hook. f.) Cockayne · ♄ e Z8 ⊡; NZ
- **cupressoides** (Hook. f.) Andersen · G:Zypressen-Strauchehrenpreis · ♄ e Z8 ⊡ ∧ VI; NZ
- **diosmifolia** (R. Cunn. ex A. Cunn.) Cockayne & Allan · ♄ e Z8 ⊡ ▽ IV-V; NZ
- **elliptica** (G. Forst.) Pennell · ♄ e Z8 ⊡ VI-VII; NZ, S-Chile, Falkland
- **epacridea** (Hook. f.) Cockayne & Allan · ♄ e ⤳ Z7 ⊡ ∧ VII; NZ
- × **franciscana** (Eastw.) Souster (*H. elliptica* × *H. speciosa*) · ♄ e Z8 ⊡; cult.
- *glaucocaerulea* (J.B. Armstr.) Cockayne = Hebe pimeleoides var. glaucocaerulea
- **glaucophylla** (Cockayne) Cockayne · ♄ e Z7; NZ
- **haastii** (Hook. f.) Cockayne & Allan · ♄ e ⤳ Z7 ⊡ ∧; NZ
- **hectorii** (Hook. f.) Cockayne & Allan · G:Hektors Strauchehrenpreis · ♄ e Z8 ⊡ ∧ VII-VIII; NZ
- **hulkeana** (F. Muell.) Cockayne & Allan · E:New Zealand Lilac · ♄ e Z9 ⊡ V-VI; NZ
- **leiophylla** (Cheeseman) Cockayne & Allan · ♄ e Z7; NZ
- **lycopodioides** (Hook. f.) Cockayne & Allan · ♄ e Z7 ⊡ ∧ VI; NZ
- **ochracea** Ashwin · ♄ e △ Z7 V-VI; NZ
- **odora** (Hook. f.) Cockayne · ♄ e Z7; NZ
- **parviflora** (Vahl) Cockayne & Allan
- var. **parviflora** · E:Kokomura Taranga · Z7; NZ
- var. **angustifolia** (Hook. f.) L.B. Moore · ♄ e Z7; NZ
- **pauciflora** G. Simpson & J.S. Thomson · ♄ e Z7; NZ
- **pauciramosa** (Cockayne & Allan) L.B. Moore · ♄ e ⊡; NZ
- **pimeleoides** (Hook. f.) Cockayne & Allan
- var. **glaucocaerulea** (J.B. Armstr.) Cockayne & Allan · ♄ Z8 ⊡ ∧ VII-VIII; NZ
- var. **pimeleoides** · ♄ e ⤳ Z7 VII-VIII; NZ
- **pinguifolia** (Hook. f.) Cockayne & Allan · F:Véronique arbustive; G:Fettblättriger Strauchehrenpreis · ♄ e Z7 V-VII; NZ
- **poppelwellii** (Cockayne) Cockayne & Allan · ♄ e ⊡; NZ
- **propinqua** (Cheeseman) Cockayne & Allan · ♄ e Z7; NZ
- **rakaiensis** (J.B. Armstr.) Cockayne · ♄ e Z7; NZ
- **recurva** G. Simpson & J.S. Thomson · ♄ e ⊡; NZ
- **salicifolia** (G. Forst.) Pennell · ♄ e Z8 ⊡ VI-VII; NZ
- **salicornioides** (Hook. f.) Cockayne & Allan · ♄ e ⊡; NZ
- **speciosa** (A. Cunn.) Cockayne & Allan · ♄ e Z8 ⊡ IX-X; NZ
- **stricta** (Banks & Sol.) L.B. Moore
- var. **stricta** · ♄ Z9; NZ
- var. **macroura** (Benth.) L.B. Moore · ♄ e Z9 ⊡; NZ
- **subalpina** (Cockayne) Cockayne & Allan · ♄ e Z7 ⊡ ∧ VI; NZ
- **subsimilis** (Colenso) Ashwin · ♄ e ⊡; NZ
- **traversii** (Hook. f.) Cockayne & Allan · G:Travers Strauchehrenpreis · ♄ e Z8 ⊡ ∧ VI-VIII; NZ
- **tumida** (Kirk) Cockayne & Allan · ♄ e Z7; NZ
- **venustula** (Colenso) L.B. Moore · ♄ e Z9 ⊡; NZ
- **vernicosa** (Hook. f.) Cockayne & Allan · ♄ e Z7 ⊡ ∧ VII-VIII; NZ
- **Cultivars:**
- **many cultivars**

Hebeclinium DC. -n- *Asteraceae* · 20 spp.
- *atrorubens* Lem. = Bartlettina sordida
- *ianthinum* Hook. = Bartlettina sordida
- **macrophyllum** (L.) DC. · E:Large-leaf Thoroughwort · ⅔ Z10 III-V; Lat.-Am.
- *megalophyllum* Lem. = Bartlettina sordida

Hebenstretia L. -f- *Scrophulariaceae* · 25 spp.
- **comosa** Hochst. · ⊙ ⅔ Z10 VII-IX; Malawi, Zimbabwe, S-Afr.: Natal, Transvaal

– **dentata** L. · ⊙ Z10 VII-IX; Cape

Hechtia Klotzsch -f- *Bromeliaceae* · 49 spp.
– **argentea** Baker · ⁊ Z9 ⓚ; Mex.
– *desmetiana* (Baker) Mez = Hechtia rosea
– **glomerata** Zucc. · ⁊ Z9 ⓚ; Mex.
– **marnier-lapostollei** L.B. Sm. · ⁊ Z9 ⓚ;
   Mex.
– *pitcairniifolia* B. Verl. = Ochagavia
   litoralis
– **rosea** E. Morren ex Baker · ⁊ Z9 ⓚ;
   Mex.
– **schottii** Baker · ⁊ Z9 ⓚ; Mex.
– **texensis** S. Watson · E:Texas False
   Agave · ⁊ Z9 ⓚ; Tex.

Hedeoma Pers. -f- *Lamiaceae* · 43 spp.
– **pulegioides** (L.) Pers. · E:American
   Pennyroyal · ⊙ VII-VIII ⚥ ✹; Can.: E;
   USA: NE, NCE, NC, SE, Fla.

Hedera L. -f- *Araliaceae* · 16 spp. · G:Efeu;
   E:Ivy; F:Lierre
– **algeriensis** Hibberd · E:Algerian Ivy;
   G:Algerischer Efeu · ♄ e ⚥ Z8 ⓚ ✹
– *canariensis* hort. = Hedera algeriensis
– **canariensis** Willd. · E:Canary Island Ivy;
   G:Kanarischer Efeu · ♄ e ⚥ Z8 ⓚ VIII-X
   ✹; Eur.: P, Azor., Canar., Madeira;
   NW-Afr.
– **some cultivars**
– **colchica** (K. Koch) K. Koch · E:Colchis
   Ivy, Persian Ivy; F:Lierre de Perse, Lierre
   du Caucase; G:Kolchischer Efeu · ♄ e ⚥
   Z7 ∧ ✹; N-TR, Cauc., nat. in F, Crim
– **helix** L. · E:Common Ivy, English Ivy,
   Ivy; F:Lierre grimpant; G:Gewöhnlicher
   Efeu · ⌇ e ⚥ ⤳ Z5 IX-XI ⚥ ✹; Eur.*, TR,
   Levant, nat. in USA
– **many cultivars**
– f. **poetarum** (Nyman) McAllister & A.
   Rutherf. · ♄ e ⚥ ∧ IX-X ✹; Eur.: Gr; TR,
   Cauc., nat. in sp., F, I, NW-Afr., Egypt
– var. *hibernica* G. Kirchn. = Hedera
   hibernica
– **hibernica** (G. Kirchn.) Carrière ·
   E:Atlantic Ivy, Irish Ivy; F:Lierre d'Irlande
   G:Irischer Efeu;· ♄ e ⚥ Z7 IX-X ✹;
   SW-IRL
– *himalaica* Tobler = Hedera nepalensis
– *japonica* Paul = Hedera rhombea
– **nepalensis** K. Koch · E:Himalayan Ivy;
   G:Himalaya-Efeu · ♄ e ⚥ Z8 ∧ ✹; Him.
– **pastuchovii** Woronow · E:Persian Ivy;
   G:Persischer Efeu · ♄ e ⚥ Z7 ∧ ✹; Iran,

E-Cauc.
– **rhombea** Siebold & Zucc. ex Bean ·
   E:Japanese Ivy; G:Japanischer Efeu · ♄ e
   ⚥ Z7 ∧ ✹; Jap., Riukiu-Is.

Hedychium J. König -n- *Zingiberaceae* ·
   85 spp. · E:Garland Lily, Ginger Lily;
   F:Hédychium; G:Kranzblume, Schmetterlingsingwer
– *angustifolium* Roxb. = Hedychium
   coccineum var. angustifolium
– *aurantiacum* Wall. ex Roscoe = Hedychium coccineum var. aurantiacum
– *carneum* Roscoe = Hedychium coccineum
   var. coccineum
– *chrysoleucum* Hook. = Hedychium
   coronarium
– **coccineum** Buch.-Ham.
– var. **angustifolium** (Roxb.) Baker · ⁊ Z9
   ⓦ; Him.
– var. **aurantiacum** (Roxb.) Baker · ⁊ Z9
   ⓦ; Him.
– var. **coccineum** · E:Scarlet Ginger Lily;
   G:Roter Schmetterlingsingwer · ⁊ Z9 ⓦ;
   Him.
– **coronarium** J. König · ⁊ D Z9 ⓦ VIII;
   Ind.
– var. *chrysoleucum* (Hook. f.) Baker =
   Hedychium coronarium
– var. **coronarium** · E:Butterfly Lily, White
   Ginger Lily; G:Weißer Schmetterlingsingwer · ⁊ D Z9 ⓦ IV-V; Him., Ind., Sri
   Lanka, Malay. Arch.
– var. **maximum** (Roscoe) Baker · ⁊ D Z9
   ⓦ IV-V; Ind.
– **flavum** Roxb. · ⁊ Z9 ⓦ IV-V; Him.
– **gardnerianum** Sheppard ex Ker-Gawl. ·
   E:Kahila Ginger Lily; G:Himalaya-
   Schmetterlingsingwer · ⁊ D Z8 ⓦ ⓚ
   VIII-IX; Nepal, Sikkim, E-Him.
– **horsfieldii** R. Br. ex Wall. · ⁊ ⊗ Z10 ⓦ;
   Java
– *maximum* Roscoe = Hedychium
   coronarium var. maximum
– **speciosum** Wall. · ⁊ D Z9 ⓦ VIII; Him.
– **spicatum** Sm. · E:Ginger Lily; G:Ähriger
   Schmetterlingsingwer · ⁊ Z9 ⓦ X; Him.

Hedyotis L. -f- *Rubiaceae* · 109 spp. ·
   E:Bluets; F:Bleuet d'Amérique; G:Ohr-
   kraut
– *serpyllifolia* (Michx.) Torr. & A. Gray =
   Houstonia serpyllifolia

Hedysarum L. -n- *Fabaceae* · c. 100 spp. ·

F:Hédysarum; G:Hahnenkopf, Süßklee
- **coronarium** L. · E:French Honeysuckle;
  G:Hahnenkopf, Italienischer Süßklee · ⊙
  ⌇ Z8 ⌂ V-VII Ⓝ; Eur.: Ib, Ital-P, nat. in
  Fr, Ba
- **hedysaroides** (L.) Schinz & Thell. ·
  E:Alpine Sainfoin; G:Alpen-Süßklee · ⌇
  △ Z4 VII-VIII; Eur.: Fr, C-Eur., EC-Eur.,
  Ba, E-Eur., Ital-P; TR, Cauc.; mts.;
  W-Sib., E-Sib., Amur, Sakhal., Kamchat.,
  C-As., China, Alaska
- **multijugum** Maxim. · G:Mongolischer
  Süßklee · ♄ d Z6 VI-IX; Mong.
- *obscurum* L. = Hedysarum hedysaroides
- *striatum* Thunb. ex Murray = Kumme-
  rowia striata

Hedyscepe H. Wendl. & Drude -f-
Arecaceae · 1 sp. · E:Umbrella Palm;
G:Schirmpalme
- **canterburyana** (C. Moore & F. Muell.)
  H. Wendl. & Drude · E:Umbrella Palm;
  G:Schirmpalme · ♄ e Z9 ⓦ ⌂; Lord
  Howe Is.

Heeria Schltdl. = Heterocentron
- *elegans* Schltdl. = Heterocentron elegans
- *rosea* (A. Braun & C.D. Bouché) Triana =
  Heterocentron macrostachyum

Heimerliodendron Skottsb. = Pisonia
- *brunonianum* (Endl.) Skottsb. = Pisonia
  umbellifera

Helcia Lindl. -f- *Orchidaceae* · 4 spp.
- **sanguinolenta** Lindl. · ⌇ ⌂ I-II ▽ ✳;
  Col., Ecuad.

Helenium L. -f- *Asteraceae* · c. 40 spp. ·
E:Helen's Flower, Sneezeweed;
F:Hélénie; G:Sonnenbraut
- **amarum** (Raf.) H. Rock · E:Yellowdicks ·
  ⊙ Z3; USA: Va., SE, Fla, Mo., Kans., SC
- **autumnale** L. · E:Common Sneezeweed,
  Sneezeweed; G:Gewöhnliche Sonnenbraut · ⌇ ⋉ Z3 VIII-IX; Can., USA*
- **bigelovii** A. Gray · E:Bigelow's Sneezeweed; G:Bigelows Sonnenbraut · ⌇ Z7
  VI-VII; USA: Oreg., Calif.
- **bolanderi** A. Gray · ⌇ Z7 VI-VIII; NE-
  Calif.
- **flexuosum** Raf. · E:Purple Head
  Sneezeweed; G:Purpur-Sonnenbraut · ⌇
  Z4 VII-X; USA: SE, SC, Ky., Mo., Kans.
- *grandiflorum* Nutt. = Helenium

autumnale
- **hoopesii** A. Gray · E:Orange Sneezeweed; F:Hélénium de Hoopes; G:Hoopes
  Sonnenbraut · ⌇ Z3 V-VI; USA: Rocky
  Mts., Oreg., Calif., SW
- *nudiflorum* Nutt. = Helenium flexuosum
- **Cultivars:**
- **many cultivars**

Heliabravoa Backeb. -f- *Cactaceae* · 1 sp.
- **chende** (Rol.-Goss.) Backeb. · ♄ ⌇ Z9 ⌂
  ▽ ✳; S-Mex.

Heliamphora Benth. -f- *Sarraceniaceae* ·
8 spp. · E:Sun Pitcher; F:Héliamphora;
G:Sonnenkrug, Sumpfkrug
- **heterodoxa** Steyerm. · ⌇ Z9 ⓦ; Venez.
- **minor** Gleason · G:Kleiner Sonnenkrug ·
  ⌇ Z9 ⓦ; Venez.
- **nutans** Benth. · G:Nickender Sonnenkrug · ⌇ Z9 ⓦ; Guyana (Mt. Roraima)

Helianthella Torr. & A. Gray -f- *Asteraceae* ·
8 spp. · F:Hélianthelle, Petit soleil;
G:Zwergsonnenblume
- **quinquenervis** (Hook.) A. Gray ·
  E:Nodding Dwarf Sunflower; G:Nickende
  Zwergsonnenblume · ⌇ Z4 VI-IX; USA:
  NW, Rocky Mts., NC, SW

Helianthemum Mill. -n- *Cistaceae* ·
c. 110 spp. · E:Rock Rose, Sun Rose;
F:Hélianthème; G:Sonnenröschen
- *alpestre* (Jacq.) DC. = Helianthemum
  oelandicum subsp. alpestre
- **apenninum** (L.) Mill.
- **var. apenninum** · E:White Rock Rose;
  F:Hélianthème blanc; G:Apenninen-
  Sonnenröschen · ♄ e △ Z6 V-VII ▽; Eur.:
  Ib, Fr, Ital-P, Ba, BrI, C-Eur.
- **var. roseum** (Jacq.) C.K. Schneid. Z5 ▽;
  NW-I
- **canum** (L.) Baumg. · E:Hoary Rock Rose;
  G:Graues Sonnenröschen · ♄ △ Z6 V-VII
  ▽; Eur.*, TR, Cauc., Moroc., Alger.
- *chamaecistus* Mill. = Helianthemum
  nummularium subsp. nummularium
- *fumana* (L.) Mill. = Fumana procumbens
- *italicum* (L.) Pers. = Helianthemum
  oelandicum subsp. italicum
- subsp. *alpestre* (Jacq.) E.P. Perrier =
  Helianthemum oelandicum subsp.
  alpestre
- subsp. *rupifragum* (A. Kern.) Hayek
  = Helianthemum oelandicum subsp.

rupifragum
- *lasianthum* (Lam.) Pers. = Halimium lasianthum
- **lunulatum** (All.) DC. · E:Shrubby Rock Rose; F:Hélianthème à lunules · ♄ e △ ∧ VI-VII; Eur.: I (Alpes Maritimes)
- **macedonicum** hort. · ♄; cult.
- **nummularium** (L.) Mill. non Grosser · E:Rock Rose; G:Gewöhnliches Sonnenröschen
- subsp. **glabrum** (W.D.J. Koch) Wilczek · G:Kahles Sonnenröschen · ♄ e Z5 VI-IX; Eur.: Alp., Apenn., Carp., Balkan, Cauc.
- subsp. **grandiflorum** (Scop.) Schinz & Thell. · G:Großblütiges Sonnenröschen · ♄ e Z5 VI-IX; Eur., mts.
- subsp. **nummularium** · E:Rock Rose; F:Hélianthème nummulaire; G:Zweifarbiges Sonnenröschen · ♄ e △ Z5 VI-X; Eur.*, Cauc., TR, Syr.
- subsp. **obscurum** (Čelak.) Holub · G:Ovalblättriges Sonnenröschen · ♄ e Z5 V-IX; Eur. exc. BrI, TR
- subsp. **tomentosum** (Scop.) Schinz & Thell. · G:Filziges Sonnenröschen · ♄; Eur.: Pyr., S-Alp., Apenn., Carp., Balkan; TR, Cauc., Atlas
- **oelandicum** (L.) DC.
- subsp. **alpestre** (Jacq.) Breistr. · E:Alpine Rock Rose; G:Alpen-Sonnenröschen · ♄ e Z5 VI-VIII; Eur.: Pyr., Alp., Apenn., Carp., Balkan; TR (Bithyn. Olymp)
- subsp. **italicum** (L.) Font Quer & Rothm. · G:Italienisches Sonnenröschen · Z6; Eur.: sp., F, I, Croatia, Montenegro
- subsp. **oelandicum** · ♄ e △ Z6 V-VI; Eur.: Sc(Öland)
- subsp. **rupifragum** (A. Kern.) Breistr. Z6; Eur.: EC-Eur., Ba, RO, E-Eur.
- *polifolium* (L.) Mill. = Helianthemum apenninum var. apenninum
- *procumbens* Dunal = Fumana procumbens
- *rhodanthum* Dunal = Helianthemum apenninum var. roseum
- *rupifragum* A. Kern. = Helianthemum oelandicum subsp. rupifragum
- **salicifolium** (L.) Mill. · G:Weidenblättriges Sonnenröschen · ⊙ IV-V; Eur.: Ib, Fr, Sw, Ital-P, Ba, RO, Crim; TR, Levant, Arab., Cauc., Iran, N-Afr.
- **scardicum** hort. · ♄; cult.
- *tomentosum* (Scop.) Gray = Helianthemum nummularium subsp. tomentosum
- *umbellatum* (L.) Mill. = Halimium umbellatum
- *vulgare* Gaertn. = Helianthemum nummularium subsp. nummularium
- **Cultivars:**
- **many cultivars**

Helianthocereus Backeb. = Trichocereus
- *pasacanus* (F.A.C. Weber) Backeb. = Trichocereus pasacana

Helianthus L. -m- *Asteraceae* · 49 (-70) spp. · E:Sunflower; F:Soleil; G:Sonnenblume
- **angustifolius** L. · E:Native Sunflower, Swamp Sunflower; G:Sumpf-Sonnenblume · ⊙ ♃ VIII-X; USA: NE, NCE, SE, SC
- **annuus** L. · E:Common Sunflower ; G:Gewöhnliche Sonnenblume · ⊙ VIII-X ⚕ Ⓝ; USA: NCE, NC, Rocky Mts., NW, Calif.; N-Mex., nat. in Eur.
- **many cultivars**
- **argophyllus** Torr. & A. Gray · E:Silverleaf Sunflower · ⊙ VIII-X; Tex.
- **atrorubens** L. · E:Dark-eye Sunflower, Purple Disk Sunflower; F:Soleil vivace; G:Geäugte Sonnenblume · ♃ Z7 VII-X; USA: SE, Fla., Va
- **debilis** Nutt.
- subsp. **cucumerifolius** (Torr. & A. Gray) Heiser · E:Cucumber-leaf Sunflower; G:Gurkenblättrige Sonnenblume · ⊙ VII-IX; USA: SE, Fla., Tex.
- subsp. **debilis** · G:Texas-Sonnenblume · ⊙; USA: SE, Fla., Tex.
- **decapetalus** L. · E:Thin-leaved Sunflower; G:Stauden-Sonnenblume · ♃ Z5 VII-X; Can.: E; USA: NE, NCE, NC, SE
- **some cultivars**
- × **doronicoides** Lam. (*H. giganteus* × *H. mollis*) · ♃ Z4; USA: NEC, NE, SC
- **giganteus** L. · E:Giant Sunflower; G:Riesen-Sonnenblume · ♃ Z4 VIII-X; Can.; USA: NE, NCE, NC, Fla.
- × **laetiflorus** Pers. (*H. pauciflorus* × *H. tuberosus*) · E:Showy Sunflower; G:Schönblumige Sonnenblume · ♃ Z4 IX-X; Alaska, Can., USA* exc. Calif., nat. in F, G, DK, H, Russ.
- **microcephalus** Torr. & A. Gray · E:Small Woodland Sunflower · ♃ Z4 VIII-IX; USA: NE, NCE, SE, Fla.
- **mollis** Lam. · E:Ashy Sunflower · ♃ Z4 VII-IX; USA: NCE, SE, SC
- × **multiflorus** L. (*H. annuus* × *H. decapetalus*) · ♃ ⋉ Z5 VII-VIII; cult.

– **pauciflorus** Nutt. · E:Pauciflorus, Stiff
  Sunflower; G:Armblütige Sonnenblume
  · 4 Z4 VII-IX; Can.: Ont.; USA: NCE, NC,
  Rocky Mts., SC, SE, SW
– *rigidus* Rydb. = Helianthus pauciflorus
– **salicifolius** A. Dietr. · E:Sunflower, Wil-
  lowleaf Sunflower; F:Soleil à feuilles de
  saule; G:Weidenblättrige Sonnenblume ·
  4 Z4 IX-X; USA: NC, Mo., SC, Colo., Ark.
– *sparsifolius* Elliott = Helianthus atrorubens
– **strumosus** L.
– var. **strumosus** · E:Pale Leaved
  Sunflower; G:Kropfige Sonnenblume · 4
  Z4; Can.: W; USA: NE, NCE, NC, SC, SE
– var. **willdenowianus** Thell. · 4 Z4; cult.
– **tuberosus** L. · E:Jerusalem Artichoke;
  G:Erdbirne, Indianerknolle, Topinambur
  · 4 Z4 X ⓝ; Can.: Man.; USA: NE, NCE,
  Rocky Mts., nat. in Eur.* exc. BrI, Sc

Helichrysum Mill. -n- *Asteraceae* ·
  c. 500 spp. · E:Everlasting Flower;
  F:Immortelle; G:Strohblume
– **apiculatum** (Labill.) DC. · E:Yellow
  Buttons · ♄ e Z9 ⓚ; Austr.: N.S.Wales,
  Victoria, S-Austr.
– **arenarium** (L.) Moench · E:Yellow
  Everlasting Daisy; G:Sand-Strohblume ·
  4 ⤳ Z4 VII-IX ⚥ ▽; Eur.: Sc, Fr, C-Eur.,
  EC-Eur., Ba, E-Eur.; TR, Cauc. N-Iran,
  W-Sib., C-As., Mong.
– **bellidioides** (G. Forst.) Willd. · E:New
  Zealand Everlasting · 4 e ⤳ Z7; NZ
– **chionophilum** Boiss. & Balansa · ♄ 4 Z8
  ⓚ; TR, Iraq, Iran
– *coralloides* (Hook. f.) Benth. & Hook. f. =
  Ozothamnus coralloides
– **cordatum** DC. · E:Heart-leaved Everlasting; G:Herzblättrige Strohblume · ♄ e ✕
  Z10 ⓚ; W-Austr.
– **foetidum** (L.) Cass. · ⊙ Z9; S-Afr.
– **frigidum** (Labill.) Willd. · G:Korsisches
  Edelweiß · 4 e ⌓ Z8 ⓚ V-VII; Cors,
  Sard.
– **graveolens** (M. Bieb.) Sweet · ♄ Z7; Crim
– **harveyanum** Wild · 4 ✕ ⓚ; S-Afr.
– **italicum** (Roth) D. Don · 4 Z9 ⓚ
– subsp. **italicum** · ♄ e Z8 ⓚ ⚥ ; Eur.: Ib, F,
  Ital-P, Ba
– subsp. **microphyllum** (Willd.) Nyman · ♄
  Z8 ⓚ; Sard., Cors + ; coasts
– subsp. **serotinum** (Boiss.) P. Fourn. ·
  E:Curry Plant; G:Currystrauch · ♄ e Z8
  ⓚ; SW-Eur.

– *leontopodium* Hook. f. = Leucogenes
  leontopodium
– **milfordiae** Killick · 4 e ⌓ △ Z7 ⓚ ⋀
  VI-VIII; S-Afr., Lesotho
– **niveum** Boiss. & Heldr. · 4 Z7 VII; TR
– **orientale** (L.) Gaertn. · 4 ♄ e Z7 ⋀
  VIII-IX; Eur.: GR, Crete; TR, nat. in RO
– **petiolare** Hilliard & B.L. Burtt ·
  E:Liquorice Plant; G:Lakritz-Strohblume
  · ♄ e Z10 ⓚ VIII-IX; S-Afr. (Cape,
  Transkei). nat. in P
– **plicatum** DC. · 4 ⤳ Z7 VII-VIII; Eur.:
  Maced., AL, GR
– **plumeum** Allan · ♄ e Z8 ⓚ; NZ
– *ramosissimum* Hook. = Helichrysum
  apiculatum
– *scutellifolium* Benth. = Ozothamnus
  scutellifolius
– *selago* (Hook. f.) Benth. & Hook. f. ex
  Kirk = Ozothamnus selago
– *serotinum* Boiss. = Helichrysum italicum
  subsp. serotinum
– *sesamoides* (L.) Willd. = Edmondia
  sesamoides
– **sessile** DC. · ♄ Z9 ⓚ; S-Afr.
– **sibthorpii** Rouy · 4 Z7 VI-VII ▽; GR
  (Athos)
– *siculum* (Spreng.) Boiss. = Helichrysum
  stoechas subsp. barrelieri
– **splendidum** (Thunb.) Less. ·
  F:Immortelle · ♄ Z7; E-Afr., S-Afr.
– **stoechas** (L.) Moench
– subsp. **barrelieri** (Ten.) Nyman Z8 ⓚ;
  Eur.: I, Si, Ba; Cyprus, TR, Lebanon,
  NW-Afr.
– subsp. **stoechas** · E:Goldilocks · ♄ e ✕ Z8
  ⓚ; Eur.: Ib, Fr, Ital-P, Ba
– **subulifolium** F. Muell. · 4 ⓚ; W-Austr.
– *subulifolium* Harv. = Helichrysum
  harveyanum
– **thianschanicum** Regel · F:Immortelle du
  Tian-Shan · 4 ⤳ Z6 VII-VIII; C-As.
– **Cultivars:**
– **some cultivars**

Helicia Lour. -f- *Proteaceae* · c. 100 spp.
– **praealta** F. Muell. · E:Beefwood · ♄ e ✕
  ⓚ; Austr.

Helicodiceros Schott -m- *Araceae* · 1 sp. ·
  E:Dragon's Mouth; G:Drachenmaul
– **muscivorus** (L. f.) Engl. · E:Dragon's
  Mouth; G:Drachenmaul · 4 Z9 ⓚ III-IV;
  Cors, Sard., Balear.

Heliconia L. -f- *Heliconiaceae* · 197 spp. ·
E:Wild Plantain; F:Balisier; G:Falsche
Paradiesvogelblume, Heliconie, Hummerschere
– **angusta** Vell. · ♃ Z10 ⓜ; Braz.
– *angustifolia* Hook. = Heliconia angusta
– **aurantiaca** Ghiesbr. · ♃ ✄ Z10 ⓜ XII-I;
Guat.
– *bicolor* Benth. = Heliconia angusta
– **bihai** (L.) L. · E:Balisier, Firebird;
G:Scharlachrote Hummerschere · ♃ Z10
ⓜ; W.Ind.
– **caribaea** Lam. · E:Lobster Claw · ♃ ✄
Z10 ⓜ; W.Ind.
– *choconiana* S. Watson = Heliconia
aurantiaca
– *illustris* W. Bull = Heliconia indica
– **indica** Lam. · ♃ Z10 ⓜ; Ind., Java, Fiji
– **latispatha** Benth. · ♃ ✄ Z10 ⓜ; S-Mex.,
C-Am.
– **metallica** Planch. & Linden ex Hook. ·
E:Shining Bird of Paradise · ♃ Z10 ⓜ
I-XII; Panama, trop. S-Am.
– **psittacorum** L. f. · E:Parrot's Plantain;
G:Papageien-Hummerschere · ♃ ✄ Z10
ⓜ; W.Ind., Guyana, Braz., Parag.
– **rostrata** Ruiz & Pav. · E:Beaked
Heliconia; G:Hängende Hummerschere ·
♃ ✄ Z10 ⓜ; trop. S-Am.
– **stricta** Huber · G:Bananenblättrige
Hummerschere · ♃ Z10 ⓜ; trop. S-Am.
– *variegata* Loes. = Heliconia zebrina
– **wagneriana** Petersen · E:Wild Plantain;
G:Dreifarbige Hummerschere · ♃ ✄ Z10
ⓜ; Costa Rica, Panama
– **zebrina** Plowman, W.J. Kress & H.
Kenn. · ♃ Z10 ⓜ; Peru

Helictotrichon Besser -n- *Poaceae* ·
50-60 spp. · E:Oat Grass; F:Avoine des
prés; G:Flaumhafer, Wiesenhafer
– **adsurgens** (Schur ex Simonk.) Conert ·
G:Aufsteigender Wiesenhafer · ♃ VI-VII;
Eur.: A, H, N-I, Bosn., Maced., RO,
S-Russ.
– **desertorum** (Less.) Nevski ex Krasch. ·
G:Steppenhafer · ♃ V-VII; Eur.: A, CZ,
Russ.; W-Sib., E-Sib., C-As., Mong.
– **parlatorei** (J. Woods) Pilg. · G:Parlatores
Wiesenhafer · ♃ VII-VIII; Eur.: F, I, G, A,
Slove.; Alp.
– **petzense** H. Melzer · G:Petzen-Wiesen-
hafer · ♃ VII; Eur.: A, Slove.; SE-Alp.
(Karawanken)
– **planiculme** (Schrad.) Pilg. · ♃ Z5 VIII-IX;

Eur.: EC-Eur., Ba, E-Eur.; NE-TR
– **praeustum** (Rchb.) Tzvelev · G:Alpen-
Wiesenhafer · ♃ VI-VIII; Eur.: I, A,
EC-Eur., Ba, ? RO, W-Russ.
– **pratense** (L.) Besser · E:Meadow Oat
Grass; G:Echter Wiesenhafer, Gewöhnli-
cher Wiesenhafer · ♃ V-VII; Eur.* , Cauc.
– **pubescens** (Huds.) Pilg. · E:Downy Oat;
G:Flaumiger Wiesenhafer, Gewöhnlicher
Flaumhafer · ♃ V-VII ⓝ; Eur.*, TR, Cauc.,
W-Sib., E-Sib., C-As.
– **sempervirens** (Vill.) Pilg. · E:Oat Grass;
F:Avoine toujours verte; G:Blaustrahl-
Wiesenhafer · ♃ Z5 V-VI; Eur.: F, I;
SW-Alp.
– **versicolor** (Vill.) Pilg. · G:Bunter
Wiesenhafer · ♃ VII-VIII; Eur.: sp., Fr,
Ital-P, C-Eur., EC-Eur., Ba, RO, W-Russ.;
mts.

Heliocereus (A. Berger) Britton & Rose
-m- *Cactaceae* · 4 spp.
– **cinnabarinus** (Eichlam) Britton & Rose ·
⍦ Z9 ⓚ ▽ ✳; Guat.
– **coccineus** Britton & Rose · ⍦ Z9 ⓚ ▽ ✳;
C-Mex.
– *elegantissimus* Britton & Rose = Heliocereus coccineus
– **schrankii** (Zucc.) Britton & Rose · ⍦ Z9
ⓚ ▽ ✳; Mex.
– **speciosus** (Cav.) Britton & Rose
– var. *elegantissimus* (Britton & Rose)
Backeb. = Heliocereus coccineus
– var. **speciosus** · E:Sun Cactus · ⍦ Z9 ⓚ ▽
✳; Mex., Guat.

Heliophila Burm. f. ex L. -f- *Brassicaceae* ·
72 spp. · E:Cape Stock; F:Héliophila;
G:Sonnenfreund
– **integrifolia** L. · ⊙ Z9 VII-IX; Cape
– **longifolia** DC. · ⊙ Z9 VII-IX; S-Afr.
– *pilosa* Lam. = Heliophila integrifolia

Heliopsis Pers. -f- *Asteraceae* · 13 spp. ·
E:Ox Eye; F:Héliopsis; G:Sonnenauge
– **helianthoides** (L.) Sweet · G:Son-
nenauge
– var. **helianthoides** · E:Smooth Ox Eye;
G:Gewöhnliches Sonnenauge · ♃ Z4;
Can.: Ont.; USA: NE, NCE, SE
– var. **scabra** (Dunal) Fernald · G:Raues
Sonnenauge · ♃ ✄ Z4 VI-IX; Can.; USA:
NE, NCE, NC, Rocky Mts., SW, SC, SE
– **many cultivars**
– *scabra* Dunal = Heliopsis helianthoides

var. scabra

Heliotropium L. -n- *Boraginaceae* · c.
250 spp. · E:Heliotrope, Turnsole;
F:Héliotrope; G:Heliotrop, Sonnenwende
- **arborescens** L. · E:Cherry Pie,
Heliotrope; F:Héliotrope; G:Strauchige
Sonnenwende · ♭ e D ⬠ V-IX ✷; Peru
- *corymbosum* Ruiz & Pav. = Heliotropium
arborescens
- **europaeum** L. · E:Caterpillar Weed;
G:Europäische Sonnenwende · ☉ VII-IX
⚜ ; Eur.* exc. BrI, Sc; TR, Cyprus, Palest.,
Cauc., N-Iran, N-Afr.
- *peruvianum* L. = Heliotropium arborescens
- **Cultivars:**
- **some cultivars**

Helipterum DC. ex Lindl. -n- *Asteraceae* ·
c. 50 spp. · E:Strawflower; F:Acroclinium;
G:Sonnenflügel
- **canescens** (L.) DC. · ♭ ✕ Z9 ⬠; Cape
- **corymbiflorum** Schltdl. · ☉ Z9 VII-VIII;
Austr.
- **eximium** (L.) DC. · ♭ ✕ Z9 ⬠; Cape
- *manglesii* (Lindl.) F. Muell. = Rhodanthe
manglesii
- *roseum* (Hook.) Benth. = Acroclinium
roseum
- *sandfordii* Hook. = Rhodanthe humboldtianum

Helleborus L. -m- *Ranunculaceae* · 15 spp. ·
E:Hellebore; F:Hellébore, Rose de Noël;
G:Christrose, Nieswurz
- *abchasicus* A. Braun = Helleborus
orientalis subsp. abchasicus
- *antiquorum* A. Braun = Helleborus
orientalis subsp. abchasicus
- **argutifolius** Viv. · E:Corsican Hellebore;
F:Hellébore livide de Cors; G:Korsische
Nieswurz · ⚇ Z7 III-IV ✷; Cors, Sard.
- **atrorubens** Waldst. & Kit. · ⚇ Z6 IV-V
✷; Eur.: Slove., Bosn., YU
- *bocconei* Ten. = Helleborus multifidus
subsp. bocconei
- *caucasicus* A. Braun = Helleborus
orientalis subsp. orientalis
- *colchicus* Regel = Helleborus orientalis
subsp. abchasicus
- *corsicus* Willd. = Helleborus argutifolius
- **cyclophyllus** (A. Braun) Boiss. · ⚇ D Z7
IV-V ✷ ▽; Eur.: Ba
- **dumetorum** Waldst. & Kit. ex Willd. ·

G:Hecken-Nieswurz · ⚇ III-V ✷ ▽; Eur.:
A, H, PL, Slove., Croatia, RO
- subsp. *atrorubens* (Waldst. & Kit.)
Merxm. & Podlech = Helleborus
atrorubens
- **foetidus** L. · E:Bear's Foot, Stinking
Hellebore; F:Hellébore fétide, Pied-de-
griffon; G:Stinkende Nieswurz · ⚇ ♭ e Z6
III-IV ⚜ ✷ ▽; Eur.: Ib, Fr, Ital-P, C-Eur.,
BrI
- *guttatus* A. Braun & F.W.H. Sauer =
Helleborus orientalis subsp. guttatus
- *kochii* Schiffn. = Helleborus orientalis
subsp. orientalis
- **lividus** Aiton · E:Majorcan Hellebore;
G:Mallorquinische Nieswurz · ⚇ Z7 ∧
III-IV ✷ ▽; Balear.
- subsp. *corsicus* (Briq.) Tutin = Helleborus
argutifolius
- **multifidus** Vis.
- subsp. **bocconei** (Ten.) B. Mathew · ⚇
Z6 ✷ ▽; Eur.: I, Sic.
- subsp. **hercegovinus** (Martinis) B.
Mathew · ⚇ Z6 ✷ ▽; S-Ba
- subsp. **istriacus** (Schiffn.) Merxm. &
Podlech · ⚇ Z6 ✷ ▽; Eur.: ? Slove.,
Croatia, Bosn., Montenegro
- subsp. **multifidus** Vis. · ⚇ Z6 III-V ✷ ▽;
Eur.: Croat., Bosn., AL, ? RO
- subsp. *serbicus* (Adamović) Merxm. &
Podlech = Helleborus torquatus
- **niger** L.
- subsp. **macranthus** (Freyn) Schiffn. · ⚇
Z3 XII-III ✷ ▽; Eur.: I, Slove., Croatia
- subsp. **niger** · E:Christmas Rose;
F:Hellébore noire, Rose de Noël;
G:Christrose, Schwarze Nieswurz · ⚇ ✕
Z3 XII-III ⚜ ✷ ▽; Eur.: C-Eur., I, Slove.,
Croatia, nat. in F, CZ
- × **nigercors** J.T. Wall (*H. argutifolius* × *H.
niger*) · ⚇ ♭ e Z7 ✷; cult.
- **odorus** Waldst. & Kit. ex Willd. ·
E:Fragrant Hellebore; G:Duftende
Nieswurz · ⚇ D Z6 II-III ✷ ▽; Eur.: I, H,
Slove., Bosn., YU, Maced., AL, RO
- subsp. *laxus* (Host) Merxm. & Podlech =
Helleborus multifidus subsp. istriacus
- *olympicus* Lindl. = Helleborus orientalis
subsp. orientalis
- **orientalis** Lam.
- **some cultivars**
- subsp. **abchasicus** (A. Braun) B.
Mathew · ⚇ Z6 ✷ ▽; GR, TR, Cauc.
- subsp. **guttatus** (A. Braun & F.W.H.
Sauer) B. Mathew · ⚇ Z6 ✷ ▽; GR, TR,

Cauc.
- subsp. **orientalis** · E:Lenten Rose;
F:Hellébore d'Orient; G:Orientalische
Nieswurz · ⚄ Z6 II-IV ✹ ▽; Eur.: ? GR;
TR, Cauc.
- **purpurascens** Waldst. & Kit. · ⚄ Z6 III-IV
✹ ▽; Eur.: H, Slova., Bosn., Montenegro, RO, W-Russ., nat. in I
- × **sternii** Turrill (*H. argutifolius* × *H.
lividus*) · ⚄ Z7 ✹; cult.
- **torquatus** Archer-Hind · ⚄ Z6 ✹ ▽;
Eur.: Serb.
- **viridis** L. · G:Grüne Nieswurz
- subsp. **occidentalis** (Reut.) Schiffn. ·
G:Westliche Grüne Nieswurz · ⚄ Z6 II-III
✹ ▽; Eur.: sp., Fr, G, Sw, BrI
- subsp. **viridis** · E:Green Hellebore;
G:Gewöhnliche Grüne Nieswurz · ⚄ Z6
III-IV ⚥ ✹ ▽; Eur.: Fr, C-Eur.
- **Cultivars:**
- **many cultivars**

Helminthotheca Zinn -f- *Asteraceae* ·
4 spp. · E:Ox Tongue; F:Helminthie;
G:Wurmlattich
- **echioides** (L.) Holub · E:Bristly
Oxtongue; G:Natterkopf-Bitterkraut,
Wurmlattich · ☉ VII-IX; Eur.: Ib, Fr, Ital-
P, Ba, Crim; TR, Iran, N-Afr., Canar., nat.
in Eur.: BrI, C-Eur., EC-Eur., RO, N-Am.,
S-Am., , N-Am., ; Austr.

Helonias L. -f- *Melanthiaceae* · 1 sp. ·
E:Swamp Pink; G:Sumpfnelke
- **bullata** L. · E:Stud Flower, Swamp Pink;
G:Sterile Sumpfnelke · ⚄ ∿ Z7 V-VI;
USA: NE, SE
- *dioica* Pursh = Chamaelirium luteum

Heloniopsis A. Gray -f- *Melanthiaceae* ·
4 spp.
- *japonica* Maxim. = Heloniopsis orientalis
var. orientalis
- **orientalis** (Thunb.) Tanaka
- var. **breviscapa** (Maxim.) Ohwi · ⚄ ∧
IV; Jap.
- var. **orientalis** · ⚄; Jap., Korea, Sakhal.

Helwingia Willd. -f- *Helwingiaceae* · 3 spp. ·
F:Helwingie; G:Helwingie
- **japonica** (Thunb.) F. Dietr. · G:Japa-
nische Helwingie · ♄ d Z6-7 VI; Jap.,
Riukiu-Is.

Helxine Bubani = Soleirolia

- *soleirolii* Req. = Soleirolia soleirolii

Hemerocallis L. -f- *Hemerocallidaceae* ·
19 spp. · E:Day Lily; F:Hémérocalle, Lis
d'un jour; G:Taglilie
- **altissima** Stout · G:Hohe Taglilie · ⚄ Z6
VII-IX; China (Nanking)
- **citrina** Baroni · F:Lis d'un jour;
G:Zitronen-Taglilie · ⚄ D Z4 VII-VIII;
China: Schensi
- **dumortieri** C. Morren · G:Dumortiers
Taglilie · ⚄ Z4 V-VI; Jap., Korea, Manch.,
E-Sib.
- **esculenta** Koidz. · G:Essbare Taglilie · ⚄
Z4 V-VI; Jap., Sakhal.
- **forrestii** Diels · G:Forrests Taglilie · ⚄ Z5
VI; Yunnan
- **fulva** (L.) L.
- var. **aurantiaca** (Baker) M. Hotta ·
G:Orangefarbene Taglilie · ⚄ Z6 VII-VIII;
China
- var. **fulva** · E:Orange Daylily, Tawny
Daylily; G:Bahnwärter-Taglilie,
Braunrote Taglilie · ⚄ Z4 VII; ? Jap., nat.
in Eur., e N-Am.
- *graminea* Andrews = Hemerocallis minor
- *graminifolia* Schltdl. = Hemerocallis
minor
- **lilioasphodelus** L. · E:Lemon Daylily;
F:Hémérocalle jaune; G:Gelbe Taglilie,
Wiesen-Taglilie · ⚄ D Z4 VI; I, Slove.;
SE-Alp., nat. in Eur., W-Sib., E-Sib.,
Amur, China
- *lutea* L. = Hemerocallis lilioasphodelus
- **middendorffii** Trautv. & C.A. Mey. ·
E:Amur Day Lily; F:Hémérocalle de
Middendorff; G:Middendorffs Taglilie · ⚄
Z5 V-IX; Amur, N-China, Manch., Korea,
Jap., Sakhal.
- **minor** Mill. · E:Small Day Lily;
F:Hémérocalle naine; G:Kleine Taglilie,
Stern-Taglilie · ⚄ Z4 V-VI; E-Sib., Mong.,
N-China, Korea
- **multiflora** Stout · G:Vielblütige Taglilie ·
⚄ Z4 V-VI; China: Hunan
- **nana** W.W. Sm. & Forrest · G:Zwerg-
Taglilie · ⚄ D ⌂; W-Yunnan
- **thunbergii** Baker · F:Hémérocalle de
Thunberg; G:Thunbergs Taglilie · ⚄ D Z4
VII-VIII; Korea, N-China
- **Cultivars:**
- **many cultivars**

Hemigraphis Nees -f- *Acanthaceae* · c.
90 spp. · G:Efeuranke

- **alternata** (Burm. f.) T. Anderson · E:Red
  Ivy; G:Rotblättrige Efeuranke · ♃ e ⚥ Z10
  ⓦ; orig. ?, nat. in Malay. Arch., Phil.
- *colorata* (Blume) Hallier f. = Hemigraphis
  altèrnata
- **repanda** (L.) Hallier f. · ♃ e ⚥ Z10 ⓦ; ?
  Malay. Pen.

Hemionitis L. -f- *Adiantaceae* · 6 spp.
- **arifolia** (Burm.) T. Moore · ♃ Z10 ⓦ;
  Ind., Sri Lanka, Malay. Pen., Phil.
- *cordata* Hook. & Grev. = Hemionitis
  arifolia
- *japonica* Thunb. = Coniogramme japonica
- **palmata** L. · E:Star Fern · ♃ Z10 ⓦ;
  W.Ind., trop. S-Am.

Hemipappus K. Koch = Tanacetum
- *canus* K. Koch = Tanacetum argenteum

Hemiptelea Planch. -f- *Ulmaceae* · 1 sp. ·
  G:Dornulme
- **davidii** (Hance) Planch. · G:Dornulme · ♄
  d Z6; Manch., N-China.

Hepatica Mill. -f- *Ranunculaceae* · 10 spp. ·
  E:Liverleaf; F:Hépatique; G:Leberblüm-
  chen
- **acutiloba** DC. · E:Sharplobe Hepatica · ♃
  Z4 III-IV; USA: NE, NCE, SE
- *angulosa* auct. non Lam. = Hepatica
  transsilvanica
- × **media** Gürke (*H. nobilis* × *H.
  transsilvanica*) · ♃ Z5; RO
- **nobilis** Schreb.
- var. **japonica** Nakai · G:Japanisches
  Leberblümchen · Z5; Jap.
- var. **nobilis** · G:Gewöhnliches Leberblümchen · ♃ Z5 III-IV ⚥ ⚘ ▽; Eur.*
  exc. BrI; Amur, Manch., Korea
- **transsilvanica** Fuss · F:Hépatique de
  Transsylvanie; G:Siebenbürger Leberblümchen · ♃ Z5 II-IV; RO: Transsylvania
- *triloba* Chaix = Hepatica nobilis var.
  nobilis

× **Heppimenes** Batcheller -f- *Gesneriaceae*
  (*Heppiella* × *Achimenes*)

Heptacodium Rehder -n- *Caprifoliaceae* ·
  1 sp.
- *jasminoides* Airy Shaw = Heptacodium
  miconioides
- **miconioides** Rehder · E:Seven Son
  Flower · ♄ d D ∧ VIII-IX; China

Heptapleurum Gaertn. = Schefflera
- *arboricola* Hayata = Schefflera arboricola

Heracleum L. -n- *Apiaceae* · 65 spp. ·
  E:Hogweed; F:Berce, Berce géante;
  G:Bärenklau, Herkulesstaude
- **austriacum** L. · E:Austrian Hogweed;
  G:Österreichischer Bärenklau · ♃ VII-VIII;
  Eur.: I, C-Eur., Slove.; E-Alp.
- **lanatum** Michx. · E:Cow Parsnip,
  Masterwort; G:Wolliger Bärenklau · ♃
  VI-VII; W-Sib., E-Sib., Amur, Sakhal.,
  Kamchat., N-China, Korea, Jap., Alaska,
  Can., USA* exc. SW, Fla.
- **mantegazzianum** Sommier & Levier ·
  E:Giant Hogweed; F:Berce géante du
  Caucase; G:Herkulesstaude, Riesen-
  Bärenklau · ⊙ ♃ VII ⚘; Cauc., nat. in
  Eur.* exc. Ib., Ba
- *maximum* W. Bartram = Heracleum
  lanatum
- **pubescens** (Hoffm.) M. Bieb. · ⊙ ♃ VII;
  TR
- **sphondylium** L. · E:Hogweed;
  G:Gewöhnlicher Wiesen-Bärenklau · ⊙
  ♃ VI-X ⚥ Ⓝ; Eur.*, TR, Cauc., W-Sib.,
  Moroc., Alger.
- **stevenii** Manden. · E:Laciniate Hogweed;
  F:Berce de Steven; G:Stevens Bärenklau ·
  ⊙ ♃ VII; Cauc.
- *villosum* auct. = Heracleum stevenii

Herbertia Sweet -f- *Iridaceae* · 5 spp.
- **pulchella** Sweet · ♃ Z9 ⓐ VII-IX;
  S-Braz., S-Chile

Hereroa (Schwantes) Dinter & Schwantes
  -f- *Aizoaceae* · 26 spp.
- **hesperantha** (Dinter & A. Berger) Dinter
  & Schwantes · ♃ ♈ Z9 ⓐ; Namibia
- *karasbergense* L. Bolus = Hereroa
  hesperantha
- **nelii** Schwantes · ♃ ♈ Z9 ⓐ; Cape
- **puttkameriana** (A. Berger & Dinter)
  Dinter & Schwantes · ♃ ♈ Z9 ⓐ; Namibia

Hermannia L. -f- *Sterculiaceae* · 100+ spp. ·
  E:Honeybells; F:Hermannia; G:Herman-
  nie, Honigglöckchen
- **incana** Cav. · G:Kap-Honigglöckchen · ♃
  e ⓐ IV-VII; S-Afr.
- **verticillata** (L.) K. Schum. ·
  E:Honeybells; G:Duftendes Honigglöckchen · ♄ D ⓐ II-V; S-Afr.

Herminium L. -n- *Orchidaceae* ·
30-40 spp. · E:Musk Orchid;
F:Herminium; G:Honigorchis
– **monorchis** (L.) R. Br. · E:Musk Orchid;
G:Einknolle, Gewöhnliche Honigorchis
· ⚄ VI-VII ▽ ✳; Eur.* exc. Ib; W-Sib.,
E-Sib., Amur, C-As., Him., Tibet, Mong.,
China, Korea, Jap.

Hermodactylus Mill. -m- *Iridaceae* · 1 sp. ·
E:Snake's Head Iris; F:Iris tête-de-
serpent; G:Wolfsschwertel
– **tuberosus** (L.) Mill. · E:Snake's Head Iris,
Widow Iris; G:Wolfsschwertel · ⚄ 🏠 ∧
II-V; Eur.: F, Ital-P, Ba; Lebanon, Palest.,
nat. in BrI

Herniaria L. -f- *Illecebraceae* · 48 spp. ·
E:Rupturewort; F:Herniaire; G:Bruch-
kraut
– **alpina** Vill. · G:Alpen-Bruchkraut · ⚄
VII-VIII; Eur.: F, I, Sw, A, ? sp.; Pyr., Alp.
– **glabra** L. · E:Glabrous Rupturewort;
G:Kahles Bruchkraut · ⊙ ⊙ ⚄ ⤳ Z5 VI-X
⚣ ; Eur.*, TR, Syr., Palest., Cauc., N-Iran,
W-Sib., NW-Afr., Libya
– **hirsuta** L. · E:Hairy Rupturewort;
G:Behaartes Bruchkraut · ⊙ ⊙ ⚄ ⤳
VII-IX ⚣ ; Eur.* exc. BrI, Sc; TR, N-Afr.
– **incana** Lam. · G:Graues Bruchkraut · ⚄
VII-X; Eur.* exc. BrI, Sc; TR, Syr., Cauc.,
Iran, Afgh., Pakist., C-As., Alger.

Herpestis Gaertn. = Bacopa
– *amplexicaulis* (Michx.) Pursh = Bacopa
caroliniana
– *monnieri* (L.) Kunth = Bacopa monnieri

Hertia Neck. -f- · c. 10 spp.
– **cheirifolia** (L.) Kuntze · ♄ ♈ e △ Z8 🏠 🏠
V-VII; Alger., Tun.

Hertrichocereus Backeb. = Stenocereus
– *beneckei* (C. Ehrenb.) Backeb. = Stenocereus beneckei

Hesperaloe Engelm. -f- *Agavaceae* · 7 spp.
– **funifera** (Lem.) Trel. · E:New Mexico
False Yucca · ♈ Z7; N-Mex.
– **parviflora** (Torr.) Coult. · E:Red
Flowered Yucca · ♈ Z7; SW-Tex.

Hesperantha Ker-Gawl. -f- *Iridaceae* ·
81 sp. · F:Fleur du soir; G:Abendblüte
– **angusta** (Jacq.) Ker-Gawl. · ⚄ D Z9 🏠

IV-V; S-Afr.
– **falcata** (L. f.) Ker-Gawl. · ⚄ D Z9 🏠 IV;
S-Afr.
– *graminifolia* Sweet = Hesperantha spicata
subsp. graminifolia
– *inflexa* (D. Delaroche) R.C. Foster =
Hesperantha vaginata
– **spicata** N.E. Br.
– subsp. **graminifolia** (Sweet) Goldblatt ·
⚄ D Z9 🏠 IX-X; S-Afr.
– *stanfordiae* L. Bolus = Hesperantha
vaginata
– **vaginata** (Sweet) Goldblatt ·
E:Namaqualand Tulip; G:Kap-Abend-
blüte · ⚄ D Z9 🏠 IV-V; Cape

Hesperis L. -f- *Brassicaceae* · 30 (-60) spp. ·
E:Dame's Violet; F:Julienne; G:Nacht-
viole
– **bicuspidata** (Willd.) Poir. · ⚄ Z6 V-VI;
TR, Lebanon, Syr.
– **matronalis** L.
– subsp. **candida** (Kit.) Hegi & Em.
Schmid · G:Weiße Nachtviole · ⊙ ⚄ Z3
VI-VII; Eur.: sp., F, I, A, Slova.; Pyr., Alp.,
Carp.
– subsp. **matronalis** · E:Dame's Violet,
Sweet Rocket; F:Julienne des dames;
G:Gewöhnliche Nachtviole · ⊙ ⚄ Z3
V-VI; Eur.* exc. BrI, Sc; TR, Cauc., Iran,
W-Sib., C-As., nat. in BrI, Sc
– **sylvestris** Crantz · G:Wald-Nachtviole ·
⊙ ⚄ VI-VII; Eur.: A, EC-Eur., Ba, E-Eur.
– **tristis** L. · G:Trübe Nachtviole · ⚄ V-VI;
Eur.: A, EC-Eur., Ba, E-Eur.; Cauc.
– *violacea* Boiss. = Hesperis bicuspidata

Hesperomecon Greene -n- *Papaveraceae* ·
1 sp. · E:Narrowleaf Queen Poppy;
F:Pavot du soir; G:Abendmohn
– **lineare** (Benth.) Greene · G:Abend-
mohn · ⊙ VII-VIII; S-Calif.

Hesperoyucca (Engelm.) Baker -f-
Agavaceae · 1 sp.
– **whipplei** (Torr.) Baker · E:Our Lord's
Candle · ♈ Z8 🏠; Calif., Baja Calif.

Heteranthemis Schott -f- *Asteraceae* · 1 sp.
– **viscidihirta** Schott · ⊙ ✂ VII-IX; Eur.:
S-Sp., S-P; NW-Afr.

Heteranthera Ruiz & Pav. -f-
Pontederiaceae · 12 spp. · E:Mud Plantain;
F:Hétéranthère; G:Heteranthere,

Trugkölbchen
- **dubia** (Jacq.) MacMill. · E:Water Star
  Grass; G:Grasblättriges Trugkölbchen
  · ⳿4 ≈ Z8 ⓜ ⓚ; Can.: E; USA*; Mex.,
  Cuba, trop. S-Am.
- *graminea* Vahl = Heteranthera dubia
- **limosa** (Sw.) Willd. · E:Blue Mud
  Plantain · ⳿4 ⌇ Z8 ⓜ; USA: Ky., NCE,
  NC, Colo., N.Mex., SE, Fla.; Mex., trop.
  S-Am.
- **peduncularis** Benth. · ⳿4 ⌇ Z8 ⓜ;
  Mex., S-Am.
- **reniformis** Ruiz & Pav. · E:Mud Plantain;
  G:Nierenförmiges Trugkölbchen · ⳿4 ⌇
  Z8 ⓜ; USA: NE, NCE, NC, SE, SC, Fla.;
  trop. Am., nat. in N-I
- **zosterifolia** Mart. · G:Seegrasblättriges
  Trugkölbchen · ⳿4 ≈ Z10 ⓜ; Braz.

Heterocentron Hook. & Arn. -n-
Melastomataceae · 27 spp.
- **elegans** (Schltdl.) Kuntze · E:Spanish
  Shawl; G:Spanischer Schal · ⳿4 e ⤳ Z10
  ⓚ VI-VII; Mex.
- **macrostachyum** Naudin · ♄ e Z10 ⓜ
  IX-XII; Mex.
- **subtriplinervium** (Link & Otto) A. Braun
  & C.D. Bouché · E:Pearlflower · ♄ Z10 ⓜ
  IX-XI; Mex.

Heteromeles M. Roem. -f- *Rosaceae* ·
1 sp. · E:Christmas Berry; F:Hétéromelès;
G:Winterbeere
- **arbutifolia** (Aiton) M. Roem. ·
  E:Christmas Berry, Tollon, Toyon;
  G:Winterbeere · ♄ ♄ e Z9 ⓚ; Calif., Baja
  Calif.

Heteropogon Pers. -n- *Poaceae* · 6-8 spp. ·
E:Spear Grass
- **contortus** (L.) P. Beauv. ex Roem. &
  Schult. · E:Black Spear Grass · ⳿4 VIII-IX;
  Eur.: Ib, F, Ital-P, Sw, Croatia; Lebanon,
  Arab., Iraq, Iran, Afgh., Pakist., Ind.,
  Burma, China, S-As., Afr., N-Am., S-Am.,
  Austr.

Heterotheca Cass. -f- *Asteraceae* · c.
20 spp.
- **inuloides** Cass. · ⳿4 Z8 ⓚ VII-VIII; Mex.
- **villosa** (Pursh) Shinners · E:Hairy False
  Golden Aster; G:Goldauge · ⳿4 △ Z5
  VII-X; Can.: W; USA: NW, Calif. Rocky
  Mts., SW, SC, NC, NCE

Heterotrichum DC. -n- *Melastomataceae* ·
10-15 spp.
- **macrodon** Planch. · ♄ e ⓜ; Venez.

Heuchera L. -f- *Saxifragaceae* · 55 spp. ·
E:Alumroot, Coral Bell; F:Désespoir du
peintre, Heuchère; G:Purpurglöckchen
- **americana** L. · E:Rock Geranium;
  G:Hohes Purpurglöckchen · ⳿4 Z4 V-VIII
  ⚥ ; Can.: Ont.; USA: NE, NCE, SE, SC
- × **brizoides** hort. ex Lemoine (*H.
  americana* × *H. micrantha* × *H.
  sanguinea*) · ⳿4 Z4; cult.
- **many cultivars**
- **cylindrica** Douglas ex Hook. ·
  E:Roundleaf Alumroot; F:Heuchera
  cylindrique; G:Walzen-Purpurglöckchen
  · ⳿4 Z4 VI-VII; Can.: W; USA: NW, Rocky
  Mts., Calif.
- **micrantha** Douglas ex Lindl. · E:Crevice
  Alumroot; F:Heuchera à petites fleurs;
  G:Kleinblütiges Purpurglöckchen,
  Silbernes Purpurglöckchen · ⳿4 Z5 VI;
  B.C., USA: NW, Calif.
- **pubescens** Pursh · E:Downy Alumroot;
  G:Haariges Purpurglöckchen · ⳿4 Z5 V-VI;
  USA: NE, N.C.
- **sanguinea** Engelm. · E:Coralbells;
  F:Heuchera; G:Blut-Purpurglöckchen
  sanguin · ⳿4 Z3 V-VII; Ariz., N.Mex.;
  N-Mex.
- **Cultivars:**
- **many cultivars**

× **Heucherella** H.R. Wehrh. -f-
Saxifragaceae · F:Heuchèrelle; G:Bastard-
schaumblüte (*Tiarella* × *Heuchera*)
- **alba** (Lemoine) Stearn (*Tiarella wherryi*
  × *Heuchera* × *brizoides*) · G:Weiße
  Bastardschaumblüte · ⳿4 Z5 V-VI; cult.
- **tiarelloides** (Lemoine) H.R. Wehrh. ex
  Stearn (*Tiarella cordifolia* × *Heuchera*
  × *brizoides*) · G:Rosafarbene Bastardschaumblüte · ⳿4 Z5 V-VI; cult.

Hevea Aubl. -f- *Euphorbiaceae* · 9 spp. ·
E:Para Rubber; F:Arbre à caoutchouc;
G:Parakautschukbaum
- **benthamiana** Müll. Arg. · ♄ Z10 ⓜ ⓝ;
  Braz., Peru, Bol.
- **Braziliensis** (Willd. ex A. Juss.) Müll.
  Arg. · E:Para Rubber, Rubber Tree;
  G:Amazonas-Parakautschukbaum · ♄ e
  Z10 ⓜ ⓝ; Amazon.

Hexadesmia Brongn. = Scaphyglottis
– *crurigera* (Bateman ex Lindl.) Lindl. =
Scaphyglottis crurigera
– *fasciculata* Brongn. = Scaphyglottis
lindeniana
– *micrantha* Lindl. = Scaphyglottis
micrantha

Hexisea Lindl. -f- *Orchidaceae* · 6 spp.
– **bidentata** Lindl. · ⚄ Z10 ⚆ VI ▽ ✻;
Mex., C-Am., Col., Peru, Venez., Guyan.
– **imbricata** (Lindl.) Rchb. f. · ⚄ Z10 ⚆
V-VI ▽ ✻; Mex., C-Am., Col., Venez.

Heyderia K. Koch = Calocedrus
– *decurrens* (Torr.) K. Koch = Calocedrus
decurrens

Hibbertia Andrews -f- *Dilleniaceae* ·
123 spp. · E:Guinea Gold Vine;
F:Hibbertia; G:Hibbertie, Münzgold,
Südseegold
– **dentata** R. Br. ex DC. · E:Trailing Guinea
Flower · ♄ ⌇ e ⚌ ⚐; Austr.: Queensl.,
N.S.Wales, Victoria
– **lasiopus** Benth. · E:Large Hibbertia · ♄ e
Z10 ⚐; Austr.
– **scandens** (Willd.) Dryand. ex Hoogland ·
E:Guinea Gold Vine, Snake Vine; G:Klet-
terndes Münzgold · ♄ e ⚌ Z10 ⚐ VI-IX;
Austr.: Queensl., N.S.Wales
– *volubilis* (Vent.) Andrews = Hibbertia
scandens

Hibiscus L. -m- *Malvaceae* · c. 220 spp. ·
E:Giant Mallow, Rose Mallow; F:Ketmie,
Rose de Chine; G:Roseneibisch
– *abelmoschus* L. = Abelmoschus moschatus
– **acetosella** Welw. ex Hiern · ⊙ ⊙ ⚄ Z10
⚐ VII-VIII; W-Afr.
– *calycinus* Willd. = Hibiscus calyphyllus
– **calyphyllus** Cav. · ♄ ⚄ Z10 ⚐; trop.Afr.,
S-Afr., Madag., Mascaren. Is.
– **cannabinus** L. · E:Indian Hemp;
G:Dekanhanf, Gambohanf · ⊙ ⊙ ⚄ Z10
⚐ VII-VIII ⓝ; cult. trop. Afr., Ind.
– **diversifolius** Jacq. · E:Cape Hibiscus;
G:Kap-Roseneibisch · ⊙ ♄ ♄ Z10 ⚐; trop.
Afr.; Austr.: Queensl., N.S.Wales; Pacific
Is.
– *eetveldeanus* De Wild. & T. Durand =
Hibiscus acetosella
– *esculentus* L. = Abelmoschus esculentus
– **heterophyllus** Vent. · ♄ e Z10 ⚐; Austr.:
Queensl., N.S.Wales

– *huegelii* Endl. = Alyogyne huegelii
– *manihot* L. = Abelmoschus manihot
– **militaris** Cav. · ⚄ Z8 ⚆ VII-VIII; USA:
NE, NCE, NC, SC, SE, Fla.
– **moscheutos** L. · G:Sumpf-Roseneibisch
– subsp. **moscheutos** · E:Rose Mallow,
Swamp Rose Mallow; F:Ketmie des
marais; G:Bebänderter Sumpf-Roseneibisch · ⚄ ⌇ Z7 VIII-X; USA: NE, NCE,
SE, Fla.
– subsp. **palustris** (L.) R.T. Clausen ·
E:Marsh Mallow, Sea Hollyhook;
G:Gewöhnlicher Sumpf-Roseneibisch · ⚄
Z7; USA: NE, NCE, N.C., nat. in I, F, P
– **mutabilis** L. · E:Confederate Rose,
Cotton Rose; G:Filziger Roseneibisch · ♄
♄ s Z8 ⚆; S-China, Taiwan
– *palustris* L. = Hibiscus moscheutos subsp.
palustris
– **paramutabilis** L.H. Bailey · ♄ ♄ Z9 ⚐;
E-China
– **pedunculatus** L. f. · ♄ ⚄ Z10 ⚐;
Mozamb., S-Afr.
– *populneus* L. = Thespesia populnea
– **rosa-sinensis** L.
– **many cultivars**
– var. **calleri** L. Z9 ⚆ ⚐
– var. **rosa-sinensis** · E:China Hibiscus,
Rose of China; G:Chinesischer Roseneibisch · ♄ e Z9 ⚆ III-X ⚌ ; ? trop. As.
– **sabdariffa** L.
– var. **altissima** Wester Z10 ⚐ ⓝ; W-Afr.,
nat. in Ind., Java, Phil.
– var. **sabdariffa** · E:Roselle · ⊙ Z10 ⚐
VII-VIII ⚌ ⓝ; ? Angola, nat. in Trop.
– **schizopetalus** (Mast.) Hook. f.
– var. **schizopetalus** · E:Coral Hibiscus,
Japanese Hibiscus; G:Hängender
Roseneibisch · ♄ e Z10 ⚆ V-XI; E-Afr.
– var. **variegata** (Mast.) Hook. f. · ♄ Z10
⚐; cult.
– **syriacus** L. · E:Hibiscus; F:Hibiscus de
Syrie; G:Echter Roseneibisch · ♄ d Z7
VIII-IX; S-As., E-As., nat. in S-Eur.
– **many cultivars**
– **tiliaceus** L. · E:Mahaut, Sea Hibiscus;
G:Linden-Roseneibisch · ♄ ♄ e Z10 ⚐ ⓝ;
Ind., S-China, Taiwan, Malay. Pen., Jap.,
Austr., nat. in trop.Am., subtrop. Am.,
Fla.
– **trionum** L. · E:Flower-of-an-hour;
G:Stunden-Roseneibisch · ⊙ Z10 VII-X;
Eur.: Ital-P, EC-Eur., Ba, E-Eur.; TR,
Levant, Iran, Egypt, Tun., Alger., nat. in
Ib, Fr, C-Eur.

Hicoria Raf. = Carya
– *pecan* Britton = Carya illinoinensis

Hidalgoa La Llave -f- *Asteraceae* · 5 spp. ·
E:Climbing Dahlia; F:Dahlia grimpant;
G:Kletterdahlie, Klimmdahlie
– **wercklei** Hook. f. · ⁊ ⚥ Z10 ⓚ VIII-IX;
Costa Rica

Hieracium L. -n- *Asteraceae* · c. 100-
250 spp. · E:Hawkweed; F:Epervière;
G:Habichtskraut
– **alpicola** Schleich. ex Steud. & Hochst. ·
G:Seidenhaariges Habichtskraut · ⁊
VII-VIII; Eur.: Ital-P, C-Eur., EC-Eur., Ba,
RO
– **alpinum** L. · G:Alpen-Habichtskraut ·
⁊ △ Z3 VII-VIII; Eur.* exc. Ib; W-Sib.,
Greenl.
– **amplexicaule** L. · G:Stängelumfassendes
Habichtskraut · ⁊ VI-VIII; Eur.: Ib, Fr, I,
C-Eur., H; NW-Afr.
– **angustifolium** Hoppe · G:Gletscher-
Habichtskraut · ⁊ VII-VIII; Eur.: F, I, Sw,
G, A; Alp.
– **aurantiacum** L. · E:Devil's Paintbrush,
Orange Hawkweed; F:Epervière dorée;
G:Orangerotes Habichtskraut · ⁊ ⤳
VI-VIII; Eur.* exc. BrI, Ib, nat. in BrI
– **bauhini** Schult. · G:Ungarisches Habich-
tskraut · ⁊ V-VII; Eur.: Fr, I, C-Eur.,
EC-Eur., E-Eur.; Cauc., Lebanon, W-Sib.,
C-As.
– **bifidum** Kit. ex Hornem. · G:Gabeliges
Habichtskraut · ⁊ VI-VIII; Eur.*
– **bombycinum** Boiss. & Reut. ex Rchb. f. ·
⁊ △ V; Eur.: sp.
– **bornmuelleri** Freyn · ⁊ △ Z7 VI-VIII; TR
– **bupleuroides** C.C. Gmel. · G:Hasenohr-
Habichtskraut · ⁊ VII-VIII; Eur.: F, I, G,
A, EC-Eur.
– **caesium** (Fr.) Fr. · G:Blaugraues Habichtskraut · ⁊ VI-VIII; Eur.: Fr, C-Eur., Sc,
EC-Eur., Slove., E-Eur.
– **caespitosum** Dumort. · E:Yellow Fox
and Cubs, Yellow Hawkweed; G:Wiesen-
Habichtskraut · ⁊ V-VIII; Eur.: Fr, C-Eur.,
Sc, EC-Eur., Ba, E-Eur., nat. in BrI
– **cymosum** L. · G:Trugdoldiges Habich-
tskraut · ⁊ V-VII; Eur.* exc. BrI, Ib; TR,
W-Sib., E-Sib., ? Cauc.
– **dentatum** Hoppe · G:Gezähntes
Habichtskraut · ⁊ VII-VIII; Eur.: F, I,
Me, EC-Eur., Slove., Croatia, Bosn., RO,
W-Russ.; mts.

– **echioides** Lumn. · G:Natternkopf-
Habichtskraut · ⁊ VII-VIII; Eur.: C-Eur.,
EC-Eur., Ba, E-Eur.; TR, Lebanon,
W-Sib., Iran, Afgh., C-As., Mong., China:
Sinkiang
– × **floribundum** Wimm. & Grab. (*H.
caespitosum* × *H. lactucella*) · E:Yellow
Devil Hawkweed; G:Reichblütiges
Habichtskraut · ⁊ V-IX; Eur.: Sc, NL,
C-Eur., EC-Eur., E-Eur.
– **fuscocinereum** Norrl. · G:Pfeilblättriges
Habichtskraut · ⁊ V-VII; Eur.: BrI, Sc, F,
G, EC-Eur., Russ.
– *glaciale* Reyn. ex Lachen. = Hieracium
angustifolium
– **glaucinum** Jord. · G:Frühblühendes
Habichtskraut · ⁊ V-VII; Eur.*
– **glaucum** All. · G:Blaugrünes Habichtskraut · ⁊ Z6 VII-IX; Eur.: F, I, C-Eur., H,
Slove., Croatia, Bosn.; mts.
– **hoppeanum** Schult. · G:Hoppes
Habichtskraut · ⁊ V-VIII; Eur.: Ital-P, Me,
EC-Eur., Ba, Ro, Crim; TR, Syr., Cauc.,
Iran
– **humile** Jacq. · G:Niedriges Habichtskraut · ⁊ Z7 VI-VIII; Eur.: sp., F, Ital-P,
C-Eur., Slove., Croatia, Bosn., Montenegro
– **intybaceum** All. · G:Endivien-Habichtsk-
raut · ⁊ △ Z6 VII-VIII; Eur.: F, C-Eur., I,
Slove.; Alp.
– **jurassicum** Griseb. · G:Jurassisches
Habichtskraut · ⁊ VII-VIII; Eur.*, TR,
Cauc.
– **lachenalii** C.C. Gmel. · G:Gewöhnliches
Habichtskraut · ⁊ VI-VIII; Eur.*, W-As. +
– **lactucella** Wallr. · G:Öhrchen-Habichtsk-
raut · ⁊ V-VIII; Eur.* exc. BrI
– **laevigatum** Willd. · G:Glattes Habichtskraut · ⁊ Z6 VI-VIII; Eur.*, TR, Cauc.,
N-As., C-As.
– **lycopifolium** Froel. · G:Wolfstrappblät-
triges Habichtskraut · ⁊ VIII-IX; Eur.: F, I,
Sw, G, A; Alp.
– **macranthum** (Ten.) Ten. · G:Großköp-
figes Habichtskraut · ⁊ ; D +
– **murorum** L. · E:Golden Lungwort;
G:Wald-Habichtskraut · ⁊ Z6 V-VIII;
Eur.*, W-As.
– **pannosum** Boiss. · ⁊ △ Z6 VI-VII; Eur.:
Ba; TR, Cauc.; mts.
– **peleterianum** Mérat · G:Peletiers
Habichtskraut · ⁊ V-VI; Eur.: Sc, BrI, Fr,
Ib, C-Eur., Ital-P, N-Russ; Moroc.
– **picroides** Vill. · G:Bitterkrautartiges

Habichtskraut · ⁞ VIII-IX; Eur.: F, I, Sw, G, A; Alp.

– **pictum** Pers. · G:Geflecktes Habichtskraut · ⁞ VI-VII; Eur.: F, I, Sw; Alp., Apenn., Sard.

– **piliferum** Hoppe · G:Grauzottiges Habichtskraut · ⁞ VII-VIII; Eur.: sp., F, I, C-Eur., EC-Eur., Ju, RO; mts.

– **pilosella** L. · E:Mouse Ear Hawkweed; F:Epervière piloselle; G:Kleines Habichtskraut, Mäuseohr · ⁞ ⤳ Z5 V-X ⚥ ; Eur.*, Cauc., W-Sib.

– **piloselloides** Vill. · E:King Devil Hawkweed; G:Florentiner Habichtskraut · ⁞ V-VIII; Eur.: Fr, Ital-P, C-Eur., EC-Eur., Ba, E-Eur.; TR, Lebanon, Syr., Cauc., N-Iran, C-As.

– **pilosum** Schleich. ex Froel. · G:Wollköpfiges Habichtskraut · ⁞ VII-VIII; Eur.: Fr, I, C-Eur., Slova., Ba, RO; Alp., Jura, Apenn., Carp., Maced.

– **porrifolium** L. · G:Lauchblättriges Habichtskraut · ⁞ VII-IX; Eur.: I, A, Slove., Croatia; S-Alp., Croatia

– **prenanthoides** Vill. · G:Hasenlattich-Habichtskraut · ⁞ VII-IX; Eur.*, TR, Cauc.; mts.

– **racemosum** Waldst. & Kit. ex Kit. · G:Traubiges Habichtskraut · ⁞ VII-X; Eur.: Fr, Ital-P, C-Eur., EC-Eur., Ba, RO; TR

– × **rubrum** Peter (*H. aurantiacum* × *H.* × *floribundum*) · F:Epervière rouge ; G:Rotes Habichtskraut · ⁞ ⤳ VI-VII; Eur.: PL, CZ, RO

– **sabaudum** L. · G:Savoyer Habichtskraut · ⁞ VIII-X; Eur.*; TR, Cauc.

– **saussureoides** Arv.-Touv. · G:Spätblühendes Habichtskraut · ⁞ VI-VIII; Eur.: F, I; E-Pyr., W-Alp.

– **schmidtii** Tausch · G:Blasses Habichtskraut · ⁞ V-VII; Eur.*, TR, Lebanon

– **scorzonerifolium** Vill. · G:Schwarzwurzelblättriges Habichtskraut · ⁞ VII-VIII; Eur.: F, I, C-Eur., Slova., Slove., Croatia, Bosn., RO; Alp., Jura, Apenn.

– **sparsum** Friv. · G:Zerstreutköpfiges Habichtskraut · ⁞ VII-IX; Eur.: Ba, RO; TR

– *sylvaticum* (L.) L. = Hieracium murorum

– **tomentosum** (L.) L. · E:Woolly Hawkweed ; G:Wollfilziges Habichtskraut · ⁞ △ VI-VII; Eur.: Jura, Alp., Alpi Apuane

– **transsilvanicum** Heuff. · G:Siebenbürger Habichtskraut · ⁞ VI-VIII; Eur.: A,

EC-Eur., Ba, E-Eur.

– **umbellatum** L. · G:Doldiges Habichtskraut · ⁞ Z6 VII-X; Eur.*, TR, Cauc., Iran, W-Sib., E-Sib., Amur, Sakhal., Kamchat., C-As., Him., Mong., China, Jap., N-Am.

– **villosum** Jacq. · E:Shaggy Hawkweed; F:Epervière velue; G:Zottiges Habichtskraut · ⁞ △ Z6 VII; Eur.: F, I, C-Eur., EC-Eur., Ba, RO, W-Russ.; mts.

– **vogesiacum** (Kirschl.) Fr. · G:Vogesen-Habichtskraut · ⁞; Eur.: sp., F, I, Sw, BrI

– **waldsteinii** Tausch · ⁞ △ Z6 VI-VII; Eur.: Croatia, Bosn., YU, Maced., AL, GR

Hierochloe R. Br. -f- *Poaceae* · 20-30 spp. · E:Holy Grass; F:Hierochloa, Houque; G:Mariengras

– **australis** (Schrad.) Roem. & Schult. · E:Southern Holy Grass; G:Südliches Mariengras · ⁞ IV-V; Eur.: I, C-Eur., EC-Eur., Ba, E-Eur., FIN

– **hirta** (Schrank) Borbás · G:Gewöhnliches Raues Mariengras · ⁞ V-VI; Eur.: I, C-Eur., EC-Eur., Sc, Russ.; Cauc., W-Sib., E-Sib., Kamchat., China, N-Am.

– **odorata** (L.) P. Beauv. · E:Holy Grass, Sweet Grass; G:Duftendes Mariengras · ⁞ ⌢ D V-VI Ⓝ; Eur.* exc. Ib, Ba; Cauc., N-As., Alaska, Can., USA: NE, NCE, NC, Rocky Mts, SW, NW

– **repens** (Host) Simonk. · G:Kriechendes Mariengras · ⁞ V-VI; Eur.: A, EC-Eur., BG, E-Eur.; Cauc., W-Sib., C-As.

Higginsia Pers. = Hoffmannia

– *ghiesbreghtii* (Lem.) Hook. = Hoffmannia ghiesbreghtii

– **refulgens** Hook.

– var. *roezlii* Regel = Hoffmannia roezlii

Hildewintera F. Ritter -f- *Cactaceae* · 1 sp.

– **aureispina** (F. Ritter) F. Ritter · ⫯ ⚡ Z9 ⌂; Bol.

Hillebrandia Oliv. -f- *Begoniaceae* · 1 sp.

– **sandwicensis** Oliv. · ⁞ ⌂ V; Hawaii

Himantoglossum Spreng. -n- *Orchidaceae* · 7 spp. · E:Lizard Orchid; F:Orchis bouc; G:Riemenzunge

– **adriaticum** H. Baumann · G:Adriatische Riemenzunge · ⁞ Z7 ▽ ✳; I

– **hircinum** (L.) Spreng.

– var. **hircinum** · E:Lizard Orchid; G:Gewöhnliche Bocks-Riemenzunge · ⁞

Z7 V-VI ▽ ✳; Eur.* exc. Sc; Alger.

× **Hippeastrelia** hort. -f- *Amaryllidaceae*
(*Hippeastrum* × *Sprekelia*)

Hippeastrum Herb. -n- *Amaryllidaceae* ·
90 spp. · F:Amaryllis, Amaryllis de
Rouen; G:Amaryllis der Gärtner,
Ritterstern
– × **acramannii** hort. (*H. aulicum* × *H.
psittacinum*) · ⑴ ⑭ ✿; cult.
– **aulicum** (Ker-Gawl.) Herb. · ⑴ ⑭; Braz.,
Parag.
– f. *robustum* (A. Dietr. ex Walp.) Voss =
Hippeastrum aulicum
– **elegans** (Spreng.) H.E. Moore · ⑴ ⑭
I-VI; S-Am.
– **leopoldii** T. Moore · ⑴ ⑭; Bol.
– **pardinum** (Hook. f.) Dombrain · ⑴ ⑭
I-IV; Bol.
– **psittacinum** (Ker-Gawl.) Herb. · ⑴ ⑭
IV-V; S-Braz.
– **puniceum** (Lam.) Voss · E:Barbados Lily;
G:Barbados-Ritterstern · ⑴ ⑭ XII-IV;
Mex., W.Ind., S-Am.
– **reginae** (L.) Herb. · E:Mexican Lily;
G:Mexikanischer Ritterstern · ⑴ ⑭ I-IV;
Mex., C-Am., W.Ind., trop. S-Am.
– **reticulatum** (L'Hér.) Herb. · ⑴ D ⑭ IX;
S-Braz.
– *solandriflorum* (Lindl.) Herb. = Hippeastrum elegans
– **striatum** (Lam.) H.E. Moore · ⑴ ⑭
XI-III; Braz.
– **vittatum** (L'Hér.) Herb. · ⑴ ⑭ II-VI ✿;
Peru: And.
– **Cultivars:**
– **many cultivars**

Hippobroma G. Don = Isotoma
– *longiflora* (L.) G. Don = Isotoma
longiflora

Hippochaete Milde = Equisetum
– *hyemalis* (L.) Börner = Equisetum
hyemale var. hyemale
– *scirpoides* (Michx.) Farw. = Equisetum
scirpoides
– *variegata* (Schleich. ex F. Weber & D.
Mohr) Farw. = Equisetum variegatum

Hippocrepis L. -f- *Fabaceae* · 21 sp. ·
E:Horseshoe Vetch; F:Fer-à-cheval;
G:Hufeisenklee
– **comosa** L. · E:Horseshoe Vetch;

G:Gewöhnlicher Hufeisenklee · ⑴ △ V-X
Ⓝ; Eur.* exc. BrI, Sc

Hippomane L. -f- *Euphorbiaceae* · 5 spp.
– **mancinella** L. · E:Manchineel; G:Manza-
nilla · ♄ e ⑭ ✿; S-Fla., W.Ind., S-Am.

Hippophae L. -f- *Elaeagnaceae* · 3 spp. ·
E:Sea Buckthorn; F:Argousier; G:Sand-
dorn
– **rhamnoides** L. · G:Sanddorn
– subsp. **carpatica** Rousi · G:Karpaten-
Sanddorn · ♄ d ⚥ Z4 III-IV Ⓝ; G, A, H,
RO +
– subsp. **fluviatilis** Soest · G:Gebirgs-
Sanddorn · ♄ d ⚥ Z4 II-IV Ⓝ; sp., F, I
– subsp. *maritima* Soest = Hippophae
rhamnoides subsp. rhamnoides
– subsp. **rhamnoides** · E:Sea Buckthorn;
F:Argousier, Saule épineux; G:Küsten-
Sanddorn · ♄ d Z4 III-V ⚤; Eur.*, TR,
Cauc., Iran, W-Sib., E-Sib., C-As., Tibet,
Him., Mong.
– **salicifolia** D. Don · F:Argousier à feuilles
de saule ; G:Weidenblättriger Sanddorn ·
♄ d ⚥ Z6 III-IV; Him.

Hippuris L. -f- *Hippuridaceae* · 1 sp. ·
E:Mare's Tail; F:Pesse, Queue-de-cheval;
G:Tannenwedel
– **vulgaris** L. · E:Mare's Tail; F:Queue de
cheval; G:Tannenwedel · ⑴ ∼ ≈
V-VIII; Eur.*, TR, Cauc., Iran, W-Sib.,
E-Sib., Amur, Sakhal., Kamchat., C-As.,
Mong., Tibet, N-China, Jap., Alaska,
Can., USA: NE, NCE, NC, SW, Rocky
Mts., NW, Calif.

Hirschfeldia Moench -f- *Brassicaceae* ·
2 spp. · E:Hoary Mustard; F:Hirschfeldia;
G:Grausenf
– **incana** (L.) Lagr.-Foss. · E:Hairy Brassica;
G:Gewöhnlicher Grausenf · ☉ V-X; Eur.:
Ib, Fr, Ital-P, Ba; TR, Levant, SW-As.,
NW-Afr., Libya, nat. in BrI, DK, C-Eur.

Hoffmannia Sw. -f- *Rubiaceae* · 108 spp.
– *bullata* L.O. Williams = Hoffmannia
discolor
– **discolor** (Lem.) Hemsl. · ⑴ e Z10 ⑭;
Mex.
– **ghiesbreghtii** (Lem.) Hemsl. · ♄ e Z10
⑭; Mex., Guat.
– *refulgens* (Hook.) Hemsl. = Hoffmannia
discolor

– var. *roezlii* Regel = Hoffmannia roezlii
– **regalis** (Hook.) Hemsl. · ♄ e Z10 ⍟;
  Mex.
– **roezlii** (Regel) Regel · ⚁ e Z10 ⍟; Mex.

Hohenbergia Schult. & Schult. f. -f-
Bromeliaceae · 53 spp.
– **augusta** (Vell.) E. Morren · ⚁ Z9 ⍟;
  Braz.
– *exsudans* (Lodd.) Mez = Aechmea
  aquilega
– **stellata** Schult. & Schult. f. · ⚁ Z9 ⍟;
  Venez., Trinidad, Braz.
– *strobilacea* Schult. & Schult. f. =
  Acanthostachys strobilacea

Hoheria A. Cunn. -f- *Malvaceae* · 5 spp. ·
  E:Lacebark; F:Hohéria; G:Hoherie,
  Neuseelandeibisch
– **glabrata** Sprague & Summerh. ·
  E:Lacebark, Mountain Ribbon; G:Berg-
  Neuseelandeibisch · ♄ ♄ d Z8 ⍟ VI-VII;
  NZ
– **populnea** A. Cunn. · E:New Zealand
  Lacebark; G:Pappel-Neuseelandeibisch ·
  ♄ ♄ e Z8 ⍟ IX; NZ

Holboellia Wall. -f- *Lardizabalaceae* ·
  10-13 spp.
– **coriacea** Diels · ♄ ♪ e ⚄ Z9 ⍟; C-China
– **latifolia** Wall. · ♄ e ⚄ Z9 ⍟ VII-VIII;
  Him.

Holcus L. -m- *Poaceae* · 8 spp. · E:Soft
  Grass; F:Houque; G:Honiggras
– **lanatus** L. · E:Yorkshire Fog; G:Wolliges
  Honiggras · ⚁ Z5 VI-VIII ⍟; Eur.*, TR,
  Cauc.
– **mollis** L. · E:Creeping Soft Grass;
  G:Weiches Honiggras · ⚁ Z5 VI-VII;
  Eur.*, TR
– *odoratus* L. = Hierochloe odorata

Holmskioldia Retz. -f- *Verbenaceae* ·
  10 spp. · E:Chinese Hat Plant; G:Chine-
  senhut
– **sanguinea** Retz. · E:Chinese Hat Plant,
  Cup and Saucer Plant; G:Chinesenhut · ♄
  e Z10 ⍟; Him., Malay. Pen.

Holodiscus (K. Koch) Maxim. -m-
Rosaceae · 8 spp. · E:Oceanspray;
F:Holodiscus; G:Schaumspiere
– **discolor** (Pursh) Maxim. · E:Cream Bush,
  Ocean Spray; G:Wald-Schaumspiere · ♄

d Z5; Can.: B.C.; USA: NW, Calif., Mont.,
  Idaho
– var. *ariifolius* (Sm.) Asch. & Graebn. =
  Holodiscus discolor
– **dumosus** (Nutt. ex Hook.) A. Heller ·
  E:Rock Spiraea; G:Wüsten-Schaumspiere
  · ♄ d VII-VIII; USA: Rocky Mts., SW; Mex.

Holoschoenus Link = Scirpoides
– *vulgaris* Link = Scirpoides holoschoenus

Holosteum L. -n- *Caryophyllaceae* ·
  4-6 spp. · F:Holostée; G:Spurre
– **umbellatum** L. · E:Jagged Chickweed;
  G:Doldige Spurre · ⊙ III-V; Eur.* exc.
  BrI; TR, Levant, Cauc., Iran, Afgh., C-As.,
  Him., China

× **Holttumara** hort. -f- *Orchidaceae*
  (*Arachnis* × *Renanthera* × *Vanda*)

Homalanthus A. Juss. -m- *Euphorbiaceae* ·
  23 spp.
– **populifolius** Graham · E:Bleeding Heart
  Tree, Queensland Poplar; G:Blutendes
  Herz · ♄ e Z10 ⍟; N.Guinea, Austr.:
  Queensl., N.S.Wales, Victoria

Homalocephala Britton & Rose = Echinocactus
– *texensis* (Hopffer) Britton & Rose =
  Echinocactus texensis

Homalocladium (F. Muell.) L.H. Bailey -n-
Polygonaceae · 1 sp. · F:Homalocladium;
G:Bandbusch
– **platycladum** (F. Muell.) L.H. Bailey ·
  E:Centipede Plant, Ribbon Bush; G:Band-
  busch · ♄ e ⍟; Solom.

Homalomena Schott -f- *Araceae* · 106 spp.
– **lindenii** (Rodigas) Ridl. · ⚁ Z10 ⍟;
  N.Guinea
– **rubescens** (Roxb.) Kunth · ⚁ Z10 ⍟;
  Ind.: Sikkim, Assam; Burma
– **wallisii** Regel · ⚁ Z10 ⍟; Col., Venez.

Homeria Vent. = Moraea
– *collina* (Thunb.) Salisb. = Moraea collina

Homogyne Cass. -f- *Asteraceae* · 3 spp. ·
  E:Colt's Foot; F:Homogyne; G:Alpenlat-
  tich
– **alpina** (L.) Cass. · E:Alpine Coltsfoot;
  G:Alpen-Brandlattich, Grüner

Alpenlattich · ⳦ △ Z2 V-VI; Eur.* exc. BrI,
Sc; mts., nat. in BrI
- **discolor** (Jacq.) Cass. · G:Filziger
Alpenlattich · ⳦ △ Z2 VI-VII; Eur.: G, I, A,
Slove., Bosn.; E-Alp., mts. Bosn.
- **sylvestris** (Scop.) Cass. · G:Wald-
Alpenlattich · ⳦ △ Z2 V-VI; Eur.: I, A,
Sloven., Croatia, Montenegro; mts.

Honckenya Ehrh. -f- *Caryophyllaceae* ·
2-3 spp. · E:Sea Sandwort; F:Honckénéja;
G:Salzmiere
- **peploides** (L.) Ehrh. · E:Sea Sandwort;
G:Salzmiere · ⳦ VI-VII

Honckenya Willd. = Clappertonia
- *ficifolia* Willd. = Clappertonia ficifolia

Hoodia Sweet ex Decne. -f-
Asclepiadaceae · 14 spp.
- *bainii* Dyer = Hoodia gordonii
- var. *juttae* (Dinter) H. Huber = Hoodia
juttae
- **gordonii** (Masson) Sweet ex Decne. · ⳨
Z9 ⓚ; Cape, Namibia
- **juttae** Dinter · ⳨ Z9 ⓚ; Namibia

× **Hookerara** hort. -f- *Orchidaceae*
(*Cattleya* × *Caularthron* × *Rhyncholaelia*)

Hopea Roxb. -f- *Dipterocarpaceae* · 102 spp.
- **odorata** Roxb. · E:Chengal · ♄ e ⓜ Ⓝ;
Burma, Andaman I., Vietn., Kalimantan,
Phil.

Hoplophytum Beer = Aechmea
- *calyculatum* E. Morren = Aechmea calyculata

Hordelymus (Jess.) Jess. ex Harz -m-
Poaceae · 1 sp. · E:Wood Barley; F:Orge
des bois; G:Waldgerste
- **europaeus** (L.) Jess. ex Harz · E:Wood
Barley; G:Waldgerste · ⳦ VI-VIII; Eur.*,
TR, Cauc., NW-Afr.

Hordeum L. -n- *Poaceae* · c. 20 spp. ·
E:Barley; F:Orge; G:Gerste
- **bulbosum** L. · E:Bulbous Barley;
G:Knollen-Gerste · ⳦; Eur.: Ba, Ib,
EC-Eur., RO, Crim, Ital-P, nat. in F
- *distichon* L. = Hordeum vulgare Distichon
Group
- *hexastichon* L. = Hordeum vulgare
- **hystrix** Roth · G:Salz-Gerste · ☉ V-VII;

Eur.: Ib, Ital-P, A, EC-Eur., Ba, E-Eur.;
TR, Syr., Lebanon, Israel, Iraq, Cauc.,
Iran, Afgh., W-Sib., Egypt, nat. in N-Am.,
trop. Afr., Jap., Austr., NZ
- **jubatum** L. · E:Foxtail Barley, Squirrel
Tail; F:Orge à crinière; G:Mähnen-Gerste
· ☉ ⊙ ⳦ Z5 VI-VIII; Alaska, Can., USA*,
Mex., nat. in C-Eur.
- **marinum** L. · E: Sea Barley; G:Strand-
Gerste · ☉ V-VII; Eur.: Ib, BrI, Fr, Ital-P,
G, Ba, RO; TR, Cyprus, SW-As., Egypt +
- **murinum** L. · E:False Barley, Wall
Barley; G:Mäuse-Gerste · ☉ VI-X; Eur.*
exc. Sc; TR, Iraq, Arab., Syr., Lebanon,
Palest., Cyprus, Cauc., Iran, Iraq, Afgh.,
Pakist., NW-Ind., C-As., China, N-Afr.,
nat. in cosmop.
- *polystichon* Haller f. = Hordeum vulgare
- *sativum* Jess. = Hordeum vulgare
- **secalinum** Schreb. · E:Meadow Barley ·
⳦; Eur.*, Palest., Alger., nat. in N-Am.,
S-Am., S-Afr.
- **spontaneum** K. Koch · ☉; N-Afr., Crete,
TR, Syr., Cyprus, Iraq, Cauc., Iran, Afgh.,
Pakist., NW-Ind., C-As.
- **vulgare** L. · E:Barley; G:Mehrzeilige
Gerste, Saat-Gerste · ☉ V-VII ⚥ Ⓝ; cult.
- **Distichon Group** · E:Pearl Barley;
G:Zweizeilige Gerste · ☉ VI-VII ⚥ Ⓝ;
cult.

Hormathophylla Cullen & T.R. Dudley =
Alyssum
- *spinosa* (L.) P. Küpfer = Alyssum
spinosum

Hormidium Lindl. ex Heynh. = Prosthechea
- *tripterum* (Brongn.) Cogn. = Prosthechea
pygmaea

Horminum L. -n- *Lamiaceae* · 1 sp. ·
E:Dragon's Mouth; F:Horminelle, Sauge
hormin; G:Drachenmäulchen
- **pyrenaicum** L. · E:Dragon's Mouth,
Pyrenean Dead-nettle; F:Horminelle des
Pyrénées; G:Drachenmäulchen · ⳦ △ Z7
VI-VIII ▽; Eur.: sp., F, I, C-Eur., Slove.;
Pyr., Alp.

Hornungia Rchb. -f- *Brassicaceae* · 2 spp. ·
G:Felskresse
- **petraea** (L.) Rchb. · G:Kleine Felskresse ·
☉ III-V; Eur.*, TR, NW-Afr.

Horridocactus Backeb. = Neoporteria

– *curvispinus* (Bertero) Backeb. = Neoporteria curvispina
– *kesselringianus* Dölz = Neoporteria curvispina
– *nigricans* (A. Dietr.) Backeb. & Dölz = Neoporteria tuberisulcata
– *tuberisulcatus* (Jacobi) Y. Itô = Neoporteria tuberisulcata

Hosta Tratt. -f- *Hostaceae* · 48 spp. · E:Giboshi, Plantain Lily; F:Funkia; G:Funkie
– *albomarginata* (Hook.) Ohwi = Hosta sieboldii
– *caerulea* (Andrews) Tratt. = Hosta ventricosa
– **capitata** (Koidz.) Nakai · ⁎ ; Jap., Korea
– **'Crispula'** · G:Riesen-Weißrand-Funkie · VII
– *crispula* F. Maek. = Hosta 'Crispula'
– **decorata** L.H. Bailey · G:Zierliche Weißrand-Funkie · ⁎ VIII; cult.
– var. *marginata* Stearn = Hosta decorata
– **'Elata'** · G:Grüne Riesen-Funkie · VI-VII
– *elata* Hyl. = Hosta 'Elata'
– **'Fortunei'** · G:Graublatt-Funkie · VII
– *glauca* (Siebold ex Miq.) Stearn = Hosta sieboldiana
– **gracillima** F. Maek. · ⁎ VIII-X; Jap.
– **hypoleuca** Murata · ⁎ ; Jap.
– **lancifolia** (Thunb.) Engl. · G:Lanzenblatt-Funkie · ⁎ VII-IX; Jap.
– var. *albomarginata* (Hook.) L.H. Bailey = Hosta sieboldii
– var. **longifolia** (Honda) Honda
– var. *tardiflora* (W. Irving) L.H. Bailey = Hosta tardiflora
– *latifolia* (Miq.) Matsum. = Hosta ventricosa
– var. *albimarginata* H.R. Wehrh. = Hosta 'Crispula'
– *latifolia* H.R. Wehrh. = Hosta 'Elata'
– **longipes** (Franch. & Sav.) Matsum.
– var. *gracillima* (F. Maek.) N. Fujita = Hosta gracillima
– var. **latifolia** F. Maek. · ⁎ ; Jap., Korea
– var. **longipes** · ⁎ VIII-IX; Jap.
– **longissima** F. Maek. · ⁎ VII-VIII; Jap.
– var. *longifolia* (Honda) W.G. Schmid = Hosta longissima
– **minor** (Baker) Nakai · ⁎ ; Korea, ? Jap.
– *nakaiana* F. Maek. = Hosta capitata
– **plantaginea** (Lam.) Asch. · E:August Lily; G:Lilien-Funkie · ⁎ VIII-X; China
– f. *grandiflora* (Siebold & Zucc.) Asch. &
Graebn. = Hosta plantaginea
– var. *japonica* Kikuchi & F. Maek. = Hosta plantaginea
– **rectifolia** Nakai · ⁎ VII-VIII; Amur, Sakhal., Jap.
– **rupifraga** Nakai · ⁎ VIII; Jap., Korea
– **sieboldiana** (Hook.) Engl. · F:Hosta bleu; G:Blaublatt-Funkie · ⁎ ; Jap.
– **'Elegans'**
– var. *elegans* Hyl. = Hosta sieboldiana 'Elegans'
– var. *fortunei* (Baker) Asch. & Graebn. = Hosta 'Fortunei'
– var. *glauca* (Siebold ex Miq.) Makino = Hosta sieboldiana
– var. *longipes* (Franch. & Sav.) Matsum. = Hosta longipes var. longipes
– **sieboldii** (Paxton) J.W. Ingram · F:Hosta à feuilles étroites; G:Schmalblatt-Funkie · ⁎ VII-VIII; Jap.
– *subcordata* Spreng. = Hosta plantaginea
– × **tardiana** hort. (*H. sieboldiana* 'Elegans' × *H. tardiflora*) · ⁎ ; cult.
– **many cultivars**
– **tardiflora** (W. Irving) Stearn · G:Herbst-Funkie · ⁎ IX-XI; cult.
– **'Tokudama'** · G:Blaue Löffel-Funkie · VI-VII
– *tokudama* F. Maek. = Hosta 'Tokudama'
– **undulata** (Otto & A. Dietr.) L.H. Bailey · G:Schneefeder-Funkie · ⁎ VII-IX; cult.
– **'Erromena'**
– **'Mediovariegata'** = Hosta undulata
– **'Univittata'**
– var. *erromena* (Stearn) F. Maek. = Hosta undulata 'Erromena'
– var. *univittata* (Miq.) Hyl. = Hosta undulata 'Univittata'
– **ventricosa** Stearn · F:Hosta campanulée; G:Glocken-Funkie · ⁎ VIII; China, Jap., nat. in E-USA
– **venusta** F. Maek. · ⁎ VII-VIII; Jap.

Hottonia L. -f- *Primulaceae* · 2 spp. · E:Water Violet; F:Hottonie, Plume d'eau; G:Wasserfeder
– **palustris** L. · E:Featherfoil, Water Violet; F:Hottonie des marais; G:Europäische Wasserfeder, Wasserprimel · ⁎ ≈ Z6 V-VII ▽; Eur.* exc. Ib; N-TR

Houlletia Brongn. -f- *Orchidaceae* · 7 spp.
– **brocklehurstiana** Lindl. · ⁎ Z10 ⓦ XI ▽ ⁎; Braz.
– *landsbergi* Linden & Rchb. f. = Houlletia

tigrina
- **odoratissima** Linden ex Lindl. & Paxton ·
  ⌁ Z10 ⓜ VIII-IX ▽ ✳; Col., Peru, Bol.,
  Venez., Braz.
- **tigrina** Linden ex Lindl. · ⌁ Z10 ⓜ IX ▽
  ✳; Costa Rica

Houstonia L. -f- *Rubiaceae* · 30 spp. ·
E:Bluets; F:Bleuet d'Amérique; G:Engel-
sauge, Porzellansternchen
- **caerulea** L. · E:Bluets, Innocence, Quaker
  Ladies; G:Porzellansternchen · ⌁ △ Z6
  V-VI; Can.: E; USA; NE, NCE, SE
- **serpyllifolia** Michx. · E:Creeping Bluets;
  G:Kriechendes Porzellansternchen · ⌁ △
  Z6 V-VI; USA: NE, SE

Houttuynia Thunb. -f- *Saururaceae* · 1 sp. ·
E:Fishwort; F:Houttuynie; G:Houttuynie
- **cordata** Thunb. · E:Fishwort; G:Hout-
  tuynie · ⌁ ⌁ Z7 ∧ ⚥ ; Him., China,
  Jap., Ryukyu-Is., Taiwan, Java

Hovea R. Br. ex W.T. Aiton -f- *Fabaceae* ·
12 spp.
- **chorizemifolia** DC. · E:Holly-leaved
  Hovea · ♄ e Z9 ⓚ IV; W-Austr.
- **elliptica** DC. · E:Tree Hovea · ♄ e Z9 ⓚ;
  W-Austr.
- **pungens** Benth. · E:Devil's Pins · ♄ e Z9
  ⓚ IV-V; W-Austr.

Hovenia Thunb. -f- *Rhamnaceae* · 2 spp. ·
E:Raisin Tree; F:Raisin du Japon;
G:Rosinenbaum
- **dulcis** Thunb. · E:Japanese Raisin Tree;
  G:Japanischer Rosinenbaum, Quaffbirne
  · ♄ d Z6 VI-VII ⓝ; China, Korea, Jap.

Howea Becc. -f- *Arecaceae* · 2 spp. ·
E:Sentry Palm; F:Hovéa, Kentia;
G:Howeapalme, Kentiapalme
- **belmoreana** (C. Moore & F. Muell.)
  Becc. · E:Curly Palm, Sentry Palm;
  G:Bogige Kentiapalme · ♄ e Z10 ⓜ ⓚ;
  Lord Howe Is.
- **forsteriana** (C. Moore & F. Muell.)
  Becc. · E:Kentia, Paradise Palm;
  G:Kentiapalme · ♄ e Z10 ⓜ ⓚ; Lord
  Howe Is.

Hoya R. Br. -f- *Asclepiadaceae* · -200 spp. ·
E:Porcelaine Flower, Wax Flower; F:Fleur
de cire, Fleur de porcelaine); G:Porzellan-
blume, Wachsblume

- **australis** R. Br. ex Traill · E:Samoan
  Waxplant; G:Australische Porzellanblume · ♄ e ⚥ Z10 ⓚ IX-XI; Austr.:
  Queensl., N.S.Wales
- *bella* Hook. = Hoya lanceolata subsp.
  bella
- **carnosa** (L. f.) R. Br. · E:Waxplant;
  G:Porzellanblume · ♄ e ⚥ Z10 ⓚ V-IX;
  C-China, SE-As., Austr.: Queensl.
- **cinnamomifolia** Hook. · ♄ e ⚥ Z10 ⓜ
  VII; Java
- **imperialis** Lindl. · ♄ e ⚥ Z10 ⓜ VII-IX;
  Malay. Pen., Kalimantan, Molucca:
  Ambon
- **lacunosa** Blume · ♄ e ⚥ Z10 ⓜ III-VI;
  Malay. Pen., Sumat., Kalimantan, Java
- **lanceolata** Wall. ex D. Don
- subsp. **bella** (Hook.) D.H. Kent ·
  E:Miniature Waxplant; G:Zwerg-Porzel-
  lanblume · ♄ e ⚥ Z10 ⓜ V-IX; Burma
- subsp. **lanceolata**
- **linearis** Wall. ex D. Don · ♄ e ⚥ Z10 ⓜ;
  Him.
- **longifolia** Wall. ex Wight · E:String Bean
  Plant; G:Langblättrige Porzellanblume ·
  ♄ e ⚥ Z10 ⓜ VI; N-Ind.: Sikkim, Khasia
  Hills
- **multiflora** (Decne.) Blume · ♄ e ⚥ Z10 ⓜ
  VII-VIII; Malay.Arch., Phil.
- **purpureofusca** Hook. · ♄ e ⚥ Z10 ⓜ IX;
  Java

Huernia R. Br. -f- *Asclepiadaceae* · 67 spp. ·
E:Dragon Flower; F:Huernia; G:Aas-
blume
- **aspera** N.E. Br. · ♀ Z10 ⓚ; Tanzania:
  Zanzibar
- **barbata** (Masson) Haw. · ⌁ ♀ Z10 ⓚ;
  S-Afr.: Cape, Orange Free State
- *bicampanulata* I. Verd. = Huernia kirkii
- **brevirostris** N.E. Br. · ♀ Z10 ⓚ; Cape
- **campanulata** (Masson) Haw. · ⌁ ♀ Z10
  ⓚ; Cape
- **hystrix** (Hook. f.) N.E. Br. · ⌁ ♀ Z10
  ⓚ; Zimbabwe, Mozamb., S-Afr.: Natal,
  Transvaal
- **keniensis** R.E. Fr. · ♀ Z10 ⓚ; Kenya
- **kirkii** N.E. Br. · ♀ Z10 ⓚ; Mozamb.,
  S-Afr.: Transvaal
- **macrocarpa** (A. Rich.) Spreng. · ⌁ ♀ Z10
  ⓚ; Eth.
- **oculata** Hook. f. · ♀ Z10 ⓚ; Namibia
- *penzigii* N.E. Br. = Huernia macrocarpa
- *primulina* N.E. Br. = Huernia thuretii var.
  primulina

– **schneideriana** A. Berger · ⚑ Z10 ⍟;
Malawi, Mozamb.
– **thuretii** Cels
– var. **primulina** (N.E. Br.) L.C. Leach · ⚑
Z10 ⍟; Cape
– var. **thuretii** · ⚑ Z10 ⍟; S-Afr.:
SW-Namibia
– **transvaalensis** Stent · ⚑ Z10 ⍟; S-Afr.:
Transvaal
– **zebrina** N.E. Br. · E:Little Owl, Owl
Eyes; G:Gestreifte Aasblume · ⚑ Z10
⍟; Botswana, Namibia, S-Afr.: Natal,
Transvaal

Huerniopsis N.E. Br. -f- *Asclepiadaceae* ·
2 spp.
– **atrosanguinea** (N.E. Br.) A.C. White &
B. Sloane · ⌄ ⚑ Z10 ⍟; Botswana
– **decipiens** N.E. Br. · ⌄ ⚑ Z10 ⍟;
Botswana, Namibia, Cape
– *gibbosa* Nel = Huerniopsis atrosanguinea
– *papillata* Nel = Huerniopsis atrosanguinea

Hugueninia Rchb. -f- *Brassicaceae* · 1 sp. ·
E:Tansy-leaved Rocket; F:Hugueninia;
G:Farnrauke
– **tanacetifolia** (L.) Rchb. · E:Tansy-leaved
Rocket; G:Farnrauke · ⌄ ⚑ Z7 VII; Eur.:
Ib, F, I, Sw; mts. NE-Sp., Pyr., SW-Alp.

Humata Cav. -f- *Davalliaceae* · 50 spp.
– **falcinella** (C. Presl) Copel. · ⌄ Z10 ⍟;
Phil.
– **griffithiana** (Hook.) C. Chr. · ⌄ Z10 ⍟;
China, Taiwan, N-Ind.
– **heterophylla** (Sm.) Desv. · ⌄ ⌇ Z10 ⍟;
Malay. Arch., Polyn.
– **repens** (L. f.) Diels · ⌄ ⤳ Z10 ⍟; trop.
As., Austr.
– **tyermannii** T. Moore · E:Bear's Foot
Fern; G:Bärenfußfarn · ⌄ Z10 ⍟ ⍟;
China

Humea Sm. = Calomeria
– *elegans* Sm. = Calomeria amaranthoides

Humulus L. -m- *Cannabaceae* · 2 spp. ·
E:Hop; F:Houblon; G:Hopfen
– **japonicus** Siebold & Zucc. · E:Japanese
Hop; F:Houblon japonais; G:Japanischer
Hopfen · ☉ ⌇ Z5 VII-VIII; China, Jap.,
Taiwan, nat. in USA: NE
– **lupulus** L. · E:Common Hop, Hop;
G:Gewöhnlicher Hopfen · ⌄ ⌇ Z5 VII-VIII

⌇ ⍟; Eur.*, Cauc., W-Sib., C-As., TR,
nat. in N-Am.
– **some cultivars**
– *scandens* (Lour.) Merr. = Humulus japonicus

Hunnemannia Sweet -f- *Papaveraceae* ·
1 sp. · E:Mexican Tulip Poppy; F:Pavot
tulipe mexicain; G:Mexikomohn,
Tulpenmohn
– **fumariifolia** Sweet · E:Golden Cup,
Mexican Tulip Poppy; G:Mexikomohn,
Tulpenmohn · ☉ ⊙ ⌄ Z8 VI-X; Mex.

Hunteria Roxb. -f- *Apocynaceae* · 4-9 spp.
– **eburnea** Pichon · ♄ ⍟; W-Afr.

× **Huntleanthes** hort. -f- *Orchidaceae*
(*Cochleanthes* × *Huntleya*)

Huntleya Bateman ex Lindl. -f-
Orchidaceae · 14 spp.
– **meleagris** Lindl. · ⌄ Z10 ⍟ VI-VII ▽ ✳;
Guyana, Braz., Peru

Huperzia Bernh. -f- *Lycopodiaceae* ·
394 spp. · E:Fir Clubmoss; F:Lycopode;
G:Teufelsklaue
– **selago** (L.) Bernh. ex Schrank & Mart. ·
E:Fir Clubmoss; G:Europäische Teufel-
sklaue, Tannen-Bärlapp · ⌄ VII-X ⚘ ▽;
Eur.*, Cauc., N-As., Alaska, Can., USA:
NE, NCE; Greenl., SE-Austr., Tasman.,
NZ

Hura L. -f- *Euphorbiaceae* · 2 spp. ·
E:Sandbox Tree; G:Sandbüchsenbaum
– **crepitans** L. · E:Sandbox Tree; G:Sand-
büchsenbaum · ♄ Z10 ⍟ ⚘ ⍟; C-Am.,
W.Ind., S-Am.

Hutchinsia R. Br. = Pritzelago
– *alpina* (L.) R. Br. = Pritzelago alpina
subsp. alpina
– *auerswaldii* Willk. = Pritzelago alpina
subsp. auerswaldii
– *brevicaulis* (Hoppe) Hoppe ex W.D.J.
Koch = Pritzelago alpina subsp. brevicaulis

Huynhia Greuter = Arnebia
– *pulchra* (Willd. ex Roem. & Schult.)
Greuter & Burdet = Arnebia pulchra

Hyacinthella Schur -f- *Hyacinthaceae* ·

19 spp.
- *dalmatica* (Baker) Chouard = Hyacinthella leucophaea
- **leucophaea** (K. Koch) Schur · ♃ Z8; Eur.: PL, Ba, RO, Russ.; ? Cauc.
- *pallens* Schur = Hyacinthella leucophaea

Hyacinthoides Heist. ex Fabr. -f- *Hyacinthaceae* · 8 spp. · E:Bluebell; F:Jacinthe sauvage ; G:Hasenglöckchen
- **hispanica** (Mill.) Rothm.
- **some cultivars**
- subsp. **hispanica** · E:Spanish Bluebell; F:Scille d'Espagne; G:Spanisches Hasenglöckchen · ♃ ⚘ Z5 V ▽; Eur.: Ib, nat. in BrI, F, I, W-Ba
- **italica** (L.) Rothm. · E:Italian Bluebell · ♃ Z5 V ▽; Eur.: P, F, I, ? sp.
- **non-scripta** (L.) Chouard ex Rothm. · E:English Bluebell; G:Atlantisches Hasenglöckchen · ♃ Z5 IV-V ▽; Eur.: BrI, Fr, Ib, nat. in G, I, RO
- *racemosa* Medik. = Hyacinthoides hispanica subsp. hispanica

Hyacinthus L. -m- *Hyacinthaceae* · 1 sp. · E:Hyacinth; F:Jacinthe; G:Hyazinthe
- *amethystinus* (L.) = Brimeura amethystina
- *campanulatus* Mill. = Hyacinthoides non-scripta
- *candicans* Baker = Galtonia candicans
- *hispanicus* Lam. = Brimeura amethystina
- **orientalis** L.
- **many cultivars**
- subsp. **orientalis** · E:Hyacinth; F:Jacinthe; G:Hyazinthe · ♃ D IV-V Ⓝ; TR, Syr., nat. in F, Ital-P, Ba
- *romanus* L. = Bellevalia romana

Hydnocarpus Gaertn. -f- *Flacourtiaceae* · 40 spp.
- **anthelmintica** Pierre ex Laness. · E:Chaulmogra Tree · ♄ Z9 ⓦ Ⓝ; Indochina
- **kurzii** (King) Warb. · ♄ Z9 ⓦ ⚥ ⚘ Ⓝ; Burma, Ind.: Assam
- *laurifolia* (Dennst.) Sleumer = Hydnocarpus pentandra
- **pentandra** (Buch.-Ham.) Oken · ♄ Z9 ⓦ Ⓝ; SW-Ind.

Hydnophytum Jack -n- *Rubiaceae* · 95 spp.
- **formicarum** Jack · ♄ e ⓦ; Molucca, Sumat.

Hydrangea L. -f- *Hydrangeaceae* · 23 spp. · E:Hydrangea; F:Hortensia; G:Hortensie
- *altissima* Wall. = Hydrangea anomala subsp. anomala
- **anomala** D. Don
- subsp. **anomala** · E:Climbing Hydrangea; G:Kletter-Hortensie · ♄ ⎜ d ⚥ Z5; Him., China
- subsp. **petiolaris** (Siebold & Zucc.) E.M. McClint. · F:Hortensia grimpant · ♄ d ⚥ Z5 VII; S-Korea, Jap., Sakhal., Taiwan
- **arborescens** L.
- subsp. **arborescens** · E:Sevenbark, Tree Hydrangea; F:Hortensia de Virginie; G:Wald-Hortensie · ♄ d Z5 ⚥ ; USA: NE, SE
- subsp. **discolor** (Ser.) E.M. McClint. · ♄ d Z5 VI-VII; USA: NE, NCE, SE, Okla.
- subsp. **radiata** (Walter) E.M. McClint. · ♄ d Z7 ∧ VI-VII; USA: N.C., S.C.
- **aspera** D. Don · ♄ d
- subsp. **aspera** · E:Rough Leaved Hydrangea; F:Hortensia; G:Raue Hortensie · ♄ d Z6; Him., SW-China, Burma
- subsp. **robusta** (Hook. f. & Thomson) E.M. McClint. · ♄ Z7; E-As.
- subsp. **sargentiana** (Rehder) E.M. McClint. · F:Hortensia; G:Samt-Hortensie, Sargents Hortensie · ♄ d Z6 VII-VIII; China: Hupeh
- subsp. **strigosa** (Rehder) E.M. McClint. · F:Hortensia · ♄ d Z6 VIII; China
- var. *macrophylla* Hemsl. = Hydrangea aspera subsp. strigosa
- *chinensis* Maxim. = Hydrangea scandens subsp. chinensis
- var. *japonica* Maxim. = Hydrangea scandens subsp. chinensis f. macropetala
- *cinerea* Small = Hydrangea arborescens subsp. discolor
- **heteromalla** D. Don · G:Chinesische Hortensie · ♄ d Z5 VI-VII; Him., China
- *hortensia* Siebold = Hydrangea macrophylla
- **involucrata** Siebold & Zucc. · G:Hüllblatt-Hortensie · ♄ d Z7 VII-IX; Jap.
- **macrophylla** (Thunb. ex Murray) Ser. · E:Hortensia, Lace Cap Hydrangea; F:Hortensia à grandes feuilles; G:Garten-Hortensie · ♄ d Z6 VI-VII; Jap., Korea
- **many cultivars, see Section III**
- subsp. *serrata* (Thunb.) Makino = Hydrangea serrata
- var. *normalis* Wilson = Hydrangea macrophylla

- **paniculata** Siebold · E:Pee Gee Hydrangea; F:Hortensia paniculé; G:Rispen-Hortensie · ♄ d Z5 VII-VIII; Jap., Sakhal., SE-China
- **some cultivars**
- *petiolaris* Siebold & Zucc. = Hydrangea anomala subsp. petiolaris
- **quercifolia** W. Bartram · E:Oak Leaved Hydrangea; F:Hortensia à feuilles de chêne; G:Eichenblättrige Hortensie · ♄ d Z7 ∧ VI; USA: SE, Fla.
- *radiata* Walter = Hydrangea arborescens subsp. radiata
- *sargentiana* Rehder = Hydrangea aspera subsp. sargentiana
- **scandens** (L. f.) Ser.
- subsp. **chinensis** (Maxim.) E.M. McClint. · ♄ ♄ d Z9 ⌂; W-China
- f. **macropetala** Hayata
- subsp. **scandens** · E:Climbing Hydrangea; F:Hortensia grimpant; G:Hänge-Hortensie · ♄ ∫ d Z9 ⌂; Jap.
- **serrata** (Thunb.) Ser. · ♄ d Z6 VI-VIII; Jap.
- **many cultivars, see Section III**
- *strigosa* Rehder = Hydrangea aspera subsp. strigosa
- *villosa* Rehder = Hydrangea aspera
- *xanthoneura* Diels = Hydrangea heteromalla

Hydrastis L. -f- *Ranunculaceae* · 2 spp. · E:Golden Seal; F:Hydrastis; G:Orangenwurzel
- **canadensis** L. · E:Golden Seal, Indian Turmeric, Yellow Puccoon; G:Kanadische Orangenwurzel · ⚃ Z3 V ✿ ⚘ Ⓝ ▽ ✳; USA: NE, NCE, NC, SE

Hydrilla Rich. -f- *Hydrocharitaceae* · 1 sp. · E:Esthwaite Waterweed; G:Grundnessel, Wasserquirl
- **verticillata** (L. f.) Royle · E:Water Thyme; G:Grundnessel, Wasserquirl · ⚃ ≈ Z7 ⓦ ⌂ VII-VIII; Eur.: BrI, IRL, G, Russ.; W-Sib., Amur, China, Jap., Taiwan, Ind., Sri Lanka, Indochina, Phil., Malay. Arch., E-Afr., Mascarene Is., Austr.

Hydrocera Blume -f- *Balsaminaceae* · 1 sp. · F:Corne d'eau; G:Wasserhorn
- **triflora** (L.) Wight & Arn. · ⊙ ∿ ⓦ VII-IX; Ind., Sri Lanka, Indochina, Java

Hydrocharis L. -f- *Hydrocharitaceae* · 3 spp. · E:Frogbit; F:Morène, Mors-de-grenouille; G:Froschbiss
- **morsus-ranae** L. · E:Frogbit; F:Morène; G:Europäischer Froschbiss · ⚃ ∿ Z4 VI-VIII; Eur.*, Cauc., W-Sib., NW-Afr.

Hydrocleys Rich. -f- *Limnocharitaceae* · 5 spp. · E:Water Poppy; F:Pavot d'eau; G:Wassermohn
- **nymphoides** (Humb. & Bonpl. ex Willd.) Buchenau · E:Water Poppy; G:Wassermohn · ⚃ ≋ ⓦ VI-X; trop. S-Am.

Hydrocotyle L. -f- *Apiaceae* · c. 130 spp. · E:Pennywort; F:Ecuelle d'eau, Hydrocotyle; G:Wassernabel
- *asiatica* L. = Centella asiatica
- **dissecta** Hook. f. · ⚃ ∿ Z8 ⌂; NZ
- **moschata** G. Forst. · E:Hairy Pennywort · ⚃ ∿ Z8 ⌂; NZ, nat. in IRL
- **novae-zelandiae** DC. · E:New Zealand Pennywort · ⚃ ∿ Z8 ⌂ VII-VIII; NZ
- **vulgaris** L. · E:Marsh Pennywort, Pennywort;t G:Gewöhnlicher Wassernabel · ⚃ ∿ Z6 VII-VIII; Eur.*, Cauc., Moroc., Alger.

Hydrolea L. -f- *Hydrophyllaceae* · 11 (-20) spp. · G:Wasserbläuling
- **spinosa** L. · E:Espino; G:Amerikanischer Wasserbläuling · ♄ ∿ ⓦ VII-X; Guat., Ecuad., Peru, Venez.

Hydromystria G. Mey. = Limnobium
- *stolonifera* G. Mey. = Limnobium stoloniferum

Hydrophyllum L. -n- *Hydrophyllaceae* · 8 spp. · E:Waterleaf; F:Hydrophylle; G:Wasserblatt
- **canadense** L. · E:Waterleaf; G:Kanadisches Wasserblatt · ⚃ Z5 V-VI; Can.: Ont.; USA: NE, SE
- **macrophyllum** Nutt. · E:Largeleaf Waterleaf · ⚃ Z5 V-VI; USA: NE, NCE, SE
- **virginianum** L. · E:Shawnee Salad, Virginia Waterleaf; G:Virginisches Wasserblatt · ⚃ Z4 V-VI; Can.: E; USA: NE, NCE, NC, SE

Hydrosme Schott = Amorphophallus
- *rivieri* (Durand ex Carrière) Engl. = Amorphophallus konjac

Hygrophila R. Br. -f- *Acanthaceae* · c. 100 spp. · F:Hygrophile; G:Wasserfreund
- **angustifolia** R. Br. · E:Water Wisteria; G:Schmalblättriger Wasserfreund · ♃ ~ ≈ Z10 ⓦ; SE-As.
- **corymbosa** (Blume) Lindau · G:Riesen-Wasserfreund · ♃ ≈ Z10 ⓦ; Phil.
- **lacustris** (Schltdl. & Cham.) Nees · ♃ ≈ Z10 ⓦ; trop. Am.
- **polysperma** (Roxb.) T. Anderson · E:East Indian Swampweed; G:Indischer Wasserfreund · ⊙ ⊚ ♃ ~ ≈ Z10 ⓦ; Ind.
- *salicifolia* Nees = Hygrophila angustifolia
- **triflora** (Roxb.) Fosberg & Sachet · G:Dreiblütiger Wasserfreund · ♃ ~ ≈ ⓦ; trop. As.

Hylocereus (A. Berger) Britton & Rose -m- *Cactaceae* · 16 spp. · F:Cactus des bois; G:Waldkaktus
- **costaricensis** (F.A.C. Weber) Britton & Rose · ♄ Ψ ξ Z10 ⓦ ∇ ✻; Costa Rica
- **guatemalensis** (Eichlam) Britton & Rose · ♄ Ψ ξ Z10 ⓦ ∇ ✻; Guat.
- **monacanthus** (Lem.) Britton & Rose · ♄ Ψ ξ Z10 ⓦ ∇ ✻; Col., Panama
- **ocamponis** (Salm-Dyck) Britton & Rose · ♄ Ψ ξ Z10 ⓦ ∇ ✻; Mex.
- **polyrhizus** (F.A.C. Weber) Britton & Rose · ♄ Ψ ξ Z10 ⓦ ∇ ✻; Col., Panama
- **purpusii** (Weing.) Britton & Rose · ♄ Ψ ξ Z10 ⓦ ∇ ✻; Mex.
- **stenopterus** (F.A.C. Weber) Britton & Rose · ♄ Ψ ξ Z10 ⓦ ∇ ✻; Costa Rica
- *tricostatus* (Rol.-Goss.) Britton & Rose = Hylocereus undatus
- **trigonus** (Haw.) Saff. · E:Strawberry-pear · ♄ Ψ ξ Z10 ⓦ ∇ ✻; W.Ind.
- **undatus** (Haw.) Britton & Rose · E:Queen-of-the-Night, Strawberry Pear; G:Distelbirne · ♄ Ψ ξ Z10 ⓦ Ⓝ ∇ ✻; Haiti, Jamaica, Martinique

Hylomecon Maxim. -f- *Papaveraceae* · 1 (-3) spp. · E:Forest Poppy; F:Pavot des bois; G:Waldmohn
- **japonica** (Thunb.) Prantl & Kündig · E:Forest Poppy; F:Pavot jaune du Japon; G:Japanischer Waldmohn · ♃ Z7 V-VI; E-China, Korea, Jap.

Hylotelephium H. Ohba = Sedum
- *cauticola* (Praeger) H. Ohba = Sedum cauticola
- *pluricaule* (Kudô) H. Ohba = Sedum pluricaule

Hymenaea L. -f- *Caesalpiniaceae* · 15 spp. · E:Copal; F:Courbaril; G:Heuschreckenbaum
- **courbaril** L. · E:Brazilian Copal, Locust Tree; G:Brazilianischer Heuschreckenbaum · ♄ ⓦ Ⓝ; W.Ind., Venez., Guyana, Surinam, Braz.
- **verrucosa** Gaertn. · E:East African Copal; G:Ostafrikanischer Heuschreckenbaum · ♄ e ⓦ Ⓝ; Mozamb., Zanzibar, Madag., Mauritius

Hymenandra (DC.) Spach -f- *Myrsinaceae* · 3 -8 spp.
- **wallichii** DC. · ♄ ⓦ; Ind.: Bengalen, Assam

Hymenanthera R. Br. -f- *Violaceae* · 7-10 spp.
- **crassifolia** Hook. f. · ♄ e Z9 ⓚ Ⓐ IV-V; NZ

Hymenocallis Salisb. -f- *Amaryllidaceae* · 74 spp. · E:Spider Lily; F:Ismène, Lis-araignée; G:Schönhäutchen
- **amancaes** (Ruiz & Pav.) G. Nicholson · ♃ Z9 ⓚ VI-VII; Peru
- **caribaea** (L.) Herb. · E:Spider Lily; G:Westindisches Schönhäutchen · ♃ Z10 ⓦ VII-IX; W.Ind.
- **harrisiana** Herb. · ♃ Z10 ⓚ VI-VII; Mex.
- **longipetala** (Lindl.) J.F. Macbr. · ♃ Z9 ⓚ; Peru
- × **macrostephana** Baker (*H. narcissiflora* × *H. speciosa*) · ♃ Z9 ⓦ III-V; cult.
- **narcissiflora** (Jacq.) J.F. Macbr. · E:Peruvian Daffodil; G:Peruanisches Schönhäutchen · ♃ Z9 ⓚ VI-VII; Peru, Bol.
- **rotata** (Ker-Gawl.) Herb. · ♃ Z10 ⓦ III-V; USA: Fla.
- **speciosa** (L. f. ex Salisb.) Salisb. · E:Spider Lily; G:Prächtiges Schönhäutchen · ♃ Z10 ⓦ IX-XI; W.Ind.
- **tubiflora** Salisb. · ♃ Z10 ⓦ III-X; trop. S-Am.
- *undulata* (Kunth) Herb. = Hymenocallis tubiflora

Hymenogyne Haw. -f- *Aizoaceae* · 2 spp.
- **glabra** (Aiton) Haw. · ⊙ Ψ VII-VIII; Cape

Hymenolobus Nutt. -m- *Brassicaceae* ·
5 spp. · G:Salzkresse, Salztäschel,
Zartschötchen
– **procumbens** (L.) Nutt.
– subsp. **pauciflorus** (W.D.J. Koch) Schinz
& Thell. · G:Armblütige Salzkresse · ⊙
VI-VII; Eur.: sp., F, I, Sic., Sw, A; mts.
– subsp. **procumbens** · G:Niederliegende
Salzkresse, Salztäschel · ⊙ IV-V; Eur.: Ib,
Fr, Ital-P, Ba, C-Eur., E-Eur.; TR, Levant,
Cauc., Iran, W-Sib., C-As. Tibet, Mong.,
N-Afr., N-Am., nat. in Chile, Austr., NZ

Hymenophyllum Sm. -n-
Hymenophyllaceae · 349 spp. · E:Filmy
Fern; F:Fougère, Hyménophylle;
G:Hautfarn
– *ciliatum* (Sw.) Sw. = Hymenophyllum
hirsutum
– **demissum** (G. Forst.) Sw. & Schrad. · ⨌
Z8 ⓐ; NZ
– **hirsutum** (L.) Sw. · ⨌ Z10 ⓐ; Trop.
– **polyanthon** (Sw.) Sw. · ⨌ Z10 ⓐ; Trop.
– **tunbrigense** (L.) Sm. · E:Tunbridge
Filmy Fern; G:Englischer Hautfarn · ⨌ Z7
VIII ▽; Eur.: Azor., Canar., Madeira, sp.,
BrI, B, F, G, I; TR

Hymenosporum R. Br. ex F. Muell.
-n- *Pittosporaceae* · 1 sp. · E:Sweetshade;
G:Hautsamenbaum
– **flavum** (Hook.) F. Muell. · E:Native
Frangipani, Sweetshade; G:Hautsamen-
baum · ♄ ♄ e Z9 ⓐ; Austr.

Hymenostemma Kunze ex Willk. -n-
Asteraceae · 1 sp.
– **paludosum** (Poir.) Pomel · ⊙ VI-IX; Eur.:
P, sp., Balear.; N-Afr.

Hymenoxys Cass. -f- *Asteraceae* · 28 spp.
– **acaulis** (Pursh) K.L. Parker · ⨌ △ Z3
V-VI; Can., USA: NE, NCE, NC, SC, SW,
Rocky Mts., NW, Cailf.
– *californica* Hook. = Lasthenia coronaria
– **grandiflora** (Torr. & A. Gray ex A. Gray)
K.L. Parker · E:Pigmy Sunflower · ⨌ Z5
V-VI; USA: Rocky Mts.
– **linearifolia** Hook. · ⊙ Z5 VI-IX; USA: SC,
N.Mex.; Mex.
– **scaposa** (DC.) K.L. Parker · ⨌ Z4; USA:
Kans., Okla., Tex., Colo., N.Mex.; N-Mex.

Hyophorbe Gaertn. -f- *Arecaceae* ·
5 spp. · E:Bottle Palm, Pignut Palm;

F:Palmier-bouteille; G:Futterpalme
– **lagenicaulis** (L.H. Bailey) H.E. Moore · ♄
e Z10 ⓐ; Mauritius
– **verschaffeltii** H. Wendl. · E:Spindle
Palm; G:Spindel-Futterpalme · ♄ e Z10
ⓐ; Maskarene Is. (Rodriguez)

Hyoscyamus L. -m- *Solanaceae* · 15 spp. ·
E:Henbane; F:Jusquiame;G:Bilsenkraut
– **albus** L. · E:White Henbane; G:Weißes
Bilsenkraut · ⊙ ⊙ ⨌ Z7 ✳; Eur.: Ib,
Fr, Ital-P, Ba, E-Eur.; TR, Iraq, N-Afr.,
Macaron.
– **muticus** L. · E:Egyptian Henbane;
G:Ägyptisches Bilsenkraut · ⊙ ⊙ VII-IX
✳ Ⓝ; Alger., Sahara, Egypt, Sudan, Syr.,
Arab., Iran, Afgh., Pakist., N-Ind.
– **niger** L. · G:Schwarzes Bilsenkraut
– var. **niger** · E:Black Henbane, Henbane;
G:Gewöhnliches Schwarzes Bilsenkraut
· ⊙ ⊙ Z5 VI-X ⚥ ✳; Eur.*, TR, Cauc.,
Iran, W-Sib., E-Sib., C-As., Him., Ind.,
Mong., NW-Afr., nat. in E-As., N-Am.,
Austr.
– var. **pallidus** Waldst. & Kit. · ⊙ ⊙ Z5 ✳

Hyoseris L. -f- *Asteraceae* · 3-5 spp.
– *foetida* L. = Aposeris foetida
– **frutescens** Brullo & Pavone · ⨌; Sic.

Hyparrhenia E. Fourn. -f- *Poaceae* · c.
55 spp. · G:Kahngras
– **rufa** (Nees) Stapf · ⨌ Z9 Ⓝ; trop. Afr.,
nat. in Am.

Hypecoum L. -n- *Fumariaceae* · 20 spp. ·
F:Hypécoum; G:Lappenblume
– **imberbe** Sm. · ⊙ Z8 VII-IX; Eur.: Ib, Fr,
Ital-P, Ba; Cauc., Cyprus
– **pendulum** L. · G:Gelbäuglein · ⊙ Z8
VI-VII; Eur.: Ib, F, G, Ba; TR, SW-As.,
NW-Afr.
– **procumbens** L. · ⊙ Z8 VII-IX; Eur.: Ib,
Fr, Ital-P, Ba; TR, Cyprus, N-Iraq, N-Afr.

Hypericum L. -n- *Clusiaceae* · 400+ spp. ·
E:St John's Wort; F:Herbe de la St-Jean,
Millepertuis; G:Hartheu, Johanniskraut
– **aegypticum** L. · ♄ e ⓐ VIII; Eur.: Sard.,
Sic., GR, Crete; Alger., Tun., Libya
– **androsaemum** L. · E:Tutsan;
F:Androsème, Toute-saine; G:Mannsblut
· ♄ d Z6 VI-IX Ⓝ; Eur.: BrI, Fr, Ib, Ital-P,
Sw, BG; N-TR, Cauc., Iran, nat. in A
– **annulatum** Moris · ⨌ △ Z8 ∧ VI-VIII;

Eur.: Sard., Ba
- **ascyron** L. · E:Great St John's Wort · ♃ Z3 VII; W-Sib., E-Sib., Amur, Korea, China, Jap., Can.: E; USA: NE, NCE, NC
- *aureum* W. Bartram = Hypericum frondosum
- **balearicum** L. · ♄ e Z8 ⓚ; Balear.
- **barbatum** Jacq. · G:Bart-Johanniskraut · ♃ Z6 V-VI; Eur.: I, A, Ba
- **bellum** H.L. Li · ♄ d Z6; W-China: Yunnan, Sichuan, Xizang; , N-Burma, N-Ind.
- **calycinum** L. · E:Aaron's Beard, Rose of Sharon; F:Millepertuis à grandes fleurs; G:Großblütiges Johanniskraut · ♄ e △ Z6 VI-IX; Eur.: BG; N-TR, nat. in BrI, Fr, Sw, I, P, Russ., Cauc.
- **canariense** L. · ♄ ♄ d Z9 ⓚ; Canar., Madeira
- **cerastoides** (Spach) N. Robson · ♃ ⟿ △ Z7 ∧ VI-VIII; Eur.: GR, BG; TR
- **coris** L. · E:Yellow Coris; F:Millepertuis coris; G:Quirlblättriges Johanniskraut · ♄ e △ Z8 ⓚ ∧ VI-VIII; Eur.: S-F, Sw, I
- *cuneatum* Poir. = Hypericum pallens
- *degenii* Bornm. = Hypericum annulatum
- **densiflorum** Pursh · E:Bushy St. John's Wort; G:Dichtblütiges Johanniskraut · ♄ e Z6 VII-X; USA: NE, NCE, SC, SE, Fla.
- × **desetangsii** Lamotte (*H. maculatum* × *H. perforatum* var. *perforatum*) · G:Bastard-Flecken-Johanniskraut · ♃ VI-VIII; Eur.: sp., Fr, I, BrI, C-Eur.
- *elatum* Aiton = Hypericum × inodorum
- **elegans** Stephan ex Willd. · G:Zierliches Johanniskraut · ♃ Z5 VI-VII; Eur.: C-Eur., EC-Eur., Ba, E-Eur.; Cauc., W-Sib., E-Sib.
- **elodes** L. · G:Sumpf-Johanniskraut · ♃ Z7 VIII-IX ▽; Eur.: Ib, Fr, BrI, I, D
- **empetrifolium** Willd. · ♄ e Z9 ⓚ VII-VIII; Eur.: AL, GR, Crete; TR, Cyprus, Libya
- **ericoides** L. · ♄ ♄ e Z8 ⓚ; E-Sp., Moroc., Tun.
- **forrestii** (Chitt.) N. Robson · G:Forrests Johanniskraut · ♄ d Z6 VII-VIII; Him., W-China: Yunnan
- **fragile** Heldr. & Sart. ex Boiss. · ♃ △ Z8 ∧ VI-VIII; E-GR
- **frondosum** Michx. · E:Cedarglade St John's Wort; G:Gold-Johanniskraut · ♄ d Z6 VII-VIII; USA: SE, SC, Ky., Ind.
- **galioides** Lam. · E:Bedstraw St John's Wort · ♄ Z8 ⓚ; USA: SE, Fla.
- *grandiflorum* hort. = Hypericum olympicum
- **hircinum** L. · E:Stinking Tutsan; G:Stinkendes Johanniskraut · ♄ s Z7 V-VII; Eur.: Balear., Ital-P, Ba; TR, Levant, Arab., Moroc., nat. in Ib, Fr, BrI, Sw
- **hirsutum** L. · E:Hairy St John's Wort; G:Behaartes Johanniskraut · ♃ Z4 VII-VIII; Eur*., TR, Cauc., NW-Iran, Sib., Alger.
- **hookerianum** Wight & Arn. · G:Hookers Johanniskraut · ♄ s Z7 ∧ VII-IX; Ind.: Sikkim, Assam; W-China
- **humifusum** L. · E:Creeping St John's Wort; G:Niederliegendes Johanniskraut · ⊙ ♃ △ Z6 VI-X; Eur.*, Moroc., Alger.
- × **inodorum** Mill. (*H. androsaemum* × *H. hircinum*) · E:Tall Tutsan; G:Duftloses Johanniskraut · ♄ d Z6 VII-VIII; Cauc., Iran, Madeira
- **some cultivars**
- **japonicum** Thunb. · ⊙ ♃; Nepal, S-Ind., China, Korea, Jap., Java, SE-Austr., NZ
- **kalmianum** L. · E:Kalm's St John's Wort; G:Kalms Johanniskraut · ♄ e Z5 VIII; Can.: E; USA: NE, NCE
- **kouytchense** H. Lév. · ♄ d Z6 VI-X; W-China: Guizhou
- **leschenaultii** Choisy · ♄ e Z9 ⓚ; Sumat., Java, Lombok, SW-Sulawesi
- **lobocarpum** Gatt. · E:Five-lobe St John's Wort · ♄ e Z6; SE-USA
- **maculatum** Crantz · E:Imperforate St John's Wort; G:Geflecktes Johanniskraut
- subsp. **maculatum** · G:Gewöhnliches Geflecktes Johanniskraut · ♃ Z6 VII-VIII; Eur.* , W-Sib.
- subsp. **obtusiusculum** (Tourlet) Hayek · G:Stumpfblättriges Geflecktes Johanniskraut · ♃ Z6 VII-VIII; Eur.: BrI, NL, G, A, F, Sw +
- **majus** (A. Gray) Britton · E:Large St John's Wort: G:Großes Kanadisches Johanniskraut · ⊙ ♃ Z3; N-Am., nat. in F, D
- **monogynum** L. · ♄ Z9 ⓚ; SE-China, Taiwan, Jap.
- **montanum** L. · E:Pale St John's Wort; G:Berg-Johanniskraut · ♃ Z5 VI-VIII; Eur.*; TR, Cauc., Moroc., Alger.
- × **moserianum** André (*H. calycinum* × *H. patulum*) · F:Millepertuis; G:Bastard-Johanniskraut · ♄ s Z7 VI-VIII; cult.
- **mutilum** L. · E:Dwarf St John's Wort · ⊙ ♃ Z3; N-Am., nat. in Eur.: F, I, G, PL coasts
- **nummularium** L. · ♃ Z6; Pyr., Alp.

– **olympicum** L. · E:Polemonia; G:Olymp-Johanniskraut · ♄ △ Z7 ∧ VI-VII; Eur.: Ba; TR
– **orientale** L. · ⏀ Z7; TR, Cauc.
– **pallens** Banks & Soler. · ♄ Z8 ⌂; S-TR, W-Syr.
– **patulum** Thunb. · ♄ Z7 ∧ VII-IX; Jap.
– **perforatum** L. · E:St John's Wort; G:Gewöhnliches Tüpfel-Johanniskraut · ⏀ VII-VIII ⚥; Eur.*, TR, Cyprus, Syr., Cauc., Iraq, Iran, W-Sib., E-Sib., C-As., Mong., Him., NW-Afr.
– **polyphyllum** Boiss. & Balansa · G:Vielblättriges Johanniskraut · ♄ △ VI-VIII; TR
– **prolificum** L. · E:Shrubby St John's Wort; G:Sprossendes Johanniskraut · ♄ e Z6 VII-X; S-Ont., USA
– **pseudohenryi** N. Robson · ♄ d Z6; W-China: W-Hubei, W-Sichuan, Yunnan
– **pulchrum** L. · E:Slender St John's Wort; G:Schönes Johanniskraut · ⏀ Z5 VII-IX; Eur.* exc. EC-Eur.
– *pyramidatum* Aiton = Hypericum ascyron
– *quadrangulatum* auct. non L. = Hypericum maculatum subsp. maculatum
– **repens** L. · ⏀ ∿ △ VI; TR
– **reptans** Hook. f. & Thomson ex Dyer · ♄ ∿ △ Z7 ∧ IX-X; Sikkim
– *rhodopeum* Friv. = Hypericum cerastoides
– **richeri** Vill. · G:Richers Johanniskraut · ⏀ Z6 VII; Eur.: Ib, Fr, I, Ba, RO, W-Russ.; mts.
– **tetrapterum** Fr. · E:Square-stemmed St John's Wort, St Peter's Wort; F:Millepertuis à quatre ailes; G:Geflügeltes Johanniskraut · ⏀ Z5 VII-VIII; Eur.*; TR, N-Iraq, Syr., Cauc., Iran
– *webbii* Steud. = Hypericum aegypticum
– **xylosteifolium** (Spach) N. Robson · ♄ d Z5 V-VII; NE-TR, Cauc.
– **Cultivars:**
– **some cultivars**
– **yakusimense** Koidz. · ⊙ ⏀ Z8; Jap.

Hyphaene Gaertn. -f- *Arecaceae* · 8 spp. · E:Doum Plam; F:Palmier d'Egypte, Palmier doum; G:Dumpalme
– **thebaica** (L.) Mart. · E:Doum Palm; G:Dumpalme · ♄ e Z10 ⌼ ℕ; W.Sudan, Sudan, Egypt, Arab., Somalia

Hypochaeris L. -f- *Asteraceae* · c. 60 spp. · E:Cat's Ears; F:Porcelle; G:Ferkelkraut
– **glabra** L. · E:Smooth Cat's Ear; G:Kahles Ferkelkraut · ⊙ VI-X; Eur.*, TR, Lebanon, NW-Afr.
– **maculata** L. · E:Spotted Cat's Ear; G:Geflecktes Ferkelkraut · ⏀ V-VII; Eur.*, Cauc., W-Sib., E-Sib.
– **radicata** L. · E:Spotted Cat's Ear; G:Gewöhnliches Ferkelkraut · ⏀ VI-IX; Eur.*, TR, NW-Afr.
– **uniflora** Vill. · E:Giant Cat's Ear; G:Einköpfiges Ferkelkraut · ⏀ △ VII-VIII; Eur.: F, I, C-Eur., EC-Eur., E-Eur..; mts.

Hypocyrta Mart. = Nematanthus
– *nummularia* Hanst. = Nematanthus gregarius
– *radicans* Klotzsch & Hanst. ex Hanst. = Nematanthus gregarius

Hypoestes Sol. ex R. Br. -f- *Acanthaceae* · c. 40 spp. · E:Polka Dot Plant; F:Hypoestes; G:Hüllenklaue
– **phyllostachya** Baker · E:Baby's Tears · ♄ e Z9 ⌼; Madag.

Hypolepis Bernh. -f- *Dennstaedtiaceae* · 63 spp. · F:Hypolépis; G:Buchtenfarn
– **millefolia** Hook. · ⏀ Z10 ⌂; NZ
– **repens** (L.) C. Presl · E:Bramblefern · ⏀ Z10 ⌼; Fla., Mex., W-Ind., C-Am., S-Am.
– **tenuifolia** (G. Forst.) Bernh. ex C. Presl · ⏀ Z10 ⌼; Malay. Arch., Austr., NZ

Hypolytrum Rich. ex Pers. -n- *Cyperaceae* · 56 spp.
– **humile** (Hassk. ex Steud.) Boeck. · ⏀ ≈ ⌼; Ind.

Hypoxis L. -f- *Hypoxidaceae* · c. 150 spp. · E:Star Grass; G:Härtling, Sterngras
– **hirsuta** (L.) Coville · E:Stargrass; G:Filziges Sterngras · ⏀ Z7 IV-V; Can.: E; USA: NE, NCE, NC, SC, SE, Fla.

Hypsela C. Presl -f- *Campanulaceae* · 4 spp.
– **reniformis** (Kunth) C. Presl · ⏀ ∿ Z8 ⌂ VII-VIII; Chile

Hyptis Jacq. -f- *Lamiaceae* · 288 spp.
– **spicigera** Lam. · ♄ ⌼ ℕ; trop. Afr., Madag.

Hyssopus L. -m- *Lamiaceae* · 7 spp. · E:Hyssop; F:Ysope; G:Ysop
– *aristatus* Godr. = Hyssopus officinalis subsp. aristatus
– **officinalis** L. · G:Ysop

– subsp. **aristatus** (Godr.) Briq. ·
  G:Grannen-Ysop · ♄ △ Z7 VI-IX; Eur.: sp.,
  F, I, Ba; Moroc.
– subsp. **officinalis** · E:Hyssop; F:Hyssope;
  G:Gewöhnlicher Ysop · ♄ △ Z7 VII-X ⚥
  Ⓝ; Eur.* exc. BrI, Sc; TR, Cauc., Iran,
  W-Sib., Moroc., Alger.

Hystrix Moench -f- *Poaceae* · 6-10 spp. ·
  E:Bottle-Brush Grass; F:Hystrix;
  G:Flaschenbürstengras
– **patula** Moench · E:Bottle-Brush Grass;
  G:Flaschenbürstengras · ⚘ ⋊ VI-VIII;
  Can.: E; USA: NE, NCE, NC, SC, SE

Iberis L. -f- *Brassicaceae* · 30 spp. ·
  E:Candytuft; F:Thlaspi; G:Schleifen-
  blume
– **amara** L. · E:Wild Candytuft; G:Bittere
  Schleifenblume · ☉ Z7 V-VIII ⚥ ✿; Eur.:
  BrI, sp., F, I, C-Eur.; TR, Cauc., Alger.,
  nat. in EC-Eur., E-Eur., NZ
– *coronaria* hort. = Iberis amara
– **crenata** Lam. · ☉ Z7 VI-VIII; Eur.: sp.
– **gibraltarica** L. · ⚘ Z8 ⓐ IV-VI; Eur.: sp.
  (Gibraltar); Moroc.
– *intermedia* Guers. = Iberis linifolia subsp.
  linifolia
– **linifolia** (L.)
– subsp. **linifolia** · G:Gewöhnliche Mittlere
  Schleifenblume · ☉ ☉ Z7 VI-VII; Eur.: sp.,
  F, I, Sw, W-Ba, nat. in B
– **odorata** L. · ☉ Z7 V-VIII; Eur.: GR, Crete;
  Levant, SW-As, NW-Afr., Libya
– *pectinata* Boiss. = Iberis crenata
– **pinnata** L. · G:Fieder-Schleifenblume · ☉
  ☉ Z7 V-VIII; Eur.: Ib, Fr, Ital-P, Ba, Crim,
  Sw; N-TR, nat. in C-Eur., RO
– **pruitii** Tineo · ⚘ Z7 ⓐ ⋀ III-IV; Eur.: sp.,
  F, Ital-P, Ba; Tun.; mts.
– **saxatilis** L.
– var. **corifolia** Sims · ♄ e △ Z6 V-VI;
  S-Eur.
– var. **saxatilis** · F:Thlaspi des rochers;
  G:Felsen-Bauernsenf, Felsen-Schleifen-
  blume · ♄ ⚘ e Z6 IV-V; Eur.: sp., F, I, Sw,
  Ba, RO, Crim
– **semperflorens** L. · F:Thlaspi toujours
  vert; G:Immerblütige Schleifenblume · ♄
  ♄ e Z8 ⓐ IV-V; Eur.: Sic., I, nat. in RO
– **sempervirens** L. · E:Evergreen Candytuft; G:Immergrüne Schleifenblume · ♄
  e ⎸: △ Z6 V; Eur.: sp., F, I, Ba; TR, nat. in
  BrI, RO
– **some cultivars**

– *spruneri* Jord. = Iberis pruitii
– *stylosa* Ten. = Thlaspi stylosum
– **umbellata** L. · E:Annual Candytuft;
  G:Doldige Schleifenblume · ☉ ☉ ⋊ Z7
  VI-VIII; Eur.: F, I, Ba, nat. in BR, C-Eur.,
  EC-Eur., Ib, RO

Ibicella Van Eselt. -f- *Pedaliaceae* · 2 spp. ·
  E:Devil's Claw, Unicorn Plant; F:Ongle du
  diable; G:Einhornpflanze
– **lutea** (Lindl.) Van Eselt. · ☉ ⚭ VII-VIII;
  S-Braz., Parag., Urug., N-Arg.

Ida A. Ryan & Oakeley -f- *Orchidaceae* ·
  34 spp.
– **ciliata** (Ruiz & Pav.) A. Ryan & Oakeley ·
  ⚘ Z10 ⓜ III-V ▽ ✳; Col., Ecuad., Peru

Idesia Maxim. -f- *Flacourtiaceae* · 1 sp. ·
  F:Idésia; G:Orangenkirsche
– **polycarpa** Maxim.
– var. **polycarpa** · E:Igiri Tree; G:Oran-
  genkirsche · ♄ d Z7 ⋀ V-VI; Jap., Korea,
  China, Taiwan
– var. **vestita** Diels Z7; W-China:
  W-Sichuan

Idria Kellogg = Fouquieria
– *columnaris* Kellogg = Fouquieria
  columnaris

Ignatia L. f. = Strychnos
– *amara* L. = Strychnos ignatii

Ilex L. -f- *Aquifoliaceae* · c. 400 spp. ·
  E:Holly, Winterberry; F:Houx; G:Stech-
  palme, Winterbeere
– × **altaclerensis** (Loudon) Dallim. (*I.
  aquifolium × I. perado* subsp. *perado*) ·
  E:Highclere Holly; F:Houx de Highclere;
  G:Großblättrige Stechpalme · ♄ e Z7;
  cult.
– **some cultivars**
– **aquifolium** L. · E:Common Holly, English
  Holly; F:Houx commun; G:Gewöhnliche
  Stechpalme, Hülse · ♄ ♄ e ⚭ Z6-7 V-VI
  ⚥ ✿ Ⓝ ▽; Eur.* exc. Russ.; TR, Syr.,
  NW-Afr.
– **many cultivars**
– × **aquipernyi** Gable (*I. aquifolium × I.
  pernyi*) · ♄ e Z6; cult.
– × **attenuata** Ashe (*I. cassine × I. opaca*) ·
  E:Topal Holly · ♄ e Z7; USA: SE, Fla.
– **bioritsensis** Hayata · ♄ ♄ e Z7; China,
  Taiwan

- **cassine** L. · ♄ e Z7; Jap., China
- **centrochinensis** S.Y. Hu · ♄ ♄ e Z7; China
- **ciliospinosa** Loes. · E:September Gem Holly; G:Grannenborstige Stechpalme · ♄ e Z7 ∧; C-China, W-China
- **colchica** Pojark. · ♄ e Z7; BG, TR, Cauc.
- **corallina** Franch. · ♄ ♄ e Z8 ∧; C-China, W-China
- **cornuta** Lindl. & Paxton · E:Chinese Holly, Horned Holly; F:Houx; G:Chinesische Stechpalme · ♄ e Z7 VI-VII; E-China
- **crenata** Thunb.
- **many cultivars**
- var. **crenata** · E:Boxleaf Holly, Japanese Holly; F:Houx crénelé; G:Japanische Stechpalme · ♄ e Z7 V-VI; Jap.
- **decidua** Walter · E:Possumhaw Holly; G:Sommergrüne Winterbeere · ♄ ♄ d ⊗ Z6 V; USA: NE, NCE, Kans., SC, SE, Fla.; NE-Mex.
- **dimorphophylla** Koidz. · ♄ e Z7; Ryukyu Is.
- **fargesii** Franch. · G:Farges Stechpalme · ♄ e Z6 V-VI; W-China
- **georgei** Comber · ♄ e Z8 ⊞; N-Burma, China (Yunnan, Tibet)
- **glabra** (L.) A. Gray · E:Inkberry; G:Kahle Winterbeere, Tintenbeere · ♄ e Z3 VI; Can.: E; USA: NE, SC, SE, Fla.
- **integra** Thunb. · E:Elegance Female Holly, Mochitree · ♄ ♄ e Z7 III-IV; China, S-Korea, Jap., Taiwan
- **kingiana** Cockerell · ♄ e Z7; E-Him., Yunnan
- × **koehneana** Loes. (*I. aquifolium* × *I. latifolia*) · ♄ e Z7; cult.
- **laevigata** (Pursh) A. Gray · E:Smooth Winterberry; G:Glatte Stechpalme · ♄ d ⊗ Z5 VI-VII; USA: NE, SE
- **latifolia** Thunb. · E:Tarajo Holly; G:Tarajo-Stechpalme · ♄ ♄ e Z7 VI-VII; Jap., E-China
- **leucoclada** (Maxim.) Makino · ♄ e Z7 ∧; Jap.
- × **makinoi** H. Hara (*I. leucoclada* × *I. rugosa*) · ♄ e Z7; Jap.
- × **meserveae** S.Y. Hu (*I. aquifolium* × *I. rugosa*) · ♄ e Z6; cult.
- **opaca** Aiton · E:American Holly; G:Amerikanische Stechpalme · ♄ ♄ e Z6 VI; USA: NE, NCE, SC, SE, Fla.
- **some cultivars**
- **paraguariensis** A. St.-Hil. · E:Paraguay Tea; G:Mateteestrauch · ♄ e Z10 ⊞ ⚥ Ⓝ; Braz., Parag., Urug., Arg.
- **pedunculosa** Miq. · G:Langstielige Stechpalme · ♄ ♄ e Z6; C-China
- **perado** Aiton · E:Azorean Holly, Madeira Holly; F:Houx des Açores; G:Azoren-Stechpalme · ♄ e Z8 ⊞; Azor., Madeira, Canar.
- **pernyi** Franch. · E:Perny's Holly; F:Houx de Perny; G:Rautenblättrige Stechpalme · ♄ ♄ e Z7; C-China, W-China
- var. *manipurensis* Loes. = Ilex georgei
- var. *veitchii* (Veitch) Bean ex Rehder = Ilex bioritsensis
- **rotunda** Thunb. · ♄ e Z7; Jap., China, Korea, Ryukyu Is., Taiwan
- **rugosa** F. Schmidt · ♄ e Z3; Jap., Sakhal.
- **serrata** Thunb. · E:Japanese Winterberry; G:Japanische Winterbeere · ♄ d ⊗ Z7 VI; Jap.
- *sieboldii* Miq. = Ilex serrata
- **sugerokii** Maxim. · ♄ e Z7; Jap., Taiwan
- **verticillata** (L.) A. Gray · E:Virginia Winterberry; F:Houx; G:Amerikanische Winterbeere · ♄ d ⊗ Z4 VI-VII ⚥ ; Can.: E; USA: NE, NCE, SE, Fla.
- **vomitoria** Aiton · E:Winterberry, Yaupon · ♄ e Z7 ∧; USA: Va, SE, SC, Fla.
- **yunnanensis** Franch. · F:Houx du Yunnan; G:Yunnan-Stechpalme · ♄ e Z7 ∧; SW-China
- **Cultivars:**
- **some cultivars**

Iliamna Greene = Sphaeralcea
- *rivularis* (Hook.) Greene = Sphaeralcea rivularis

Illecebrum L. -n- Illecebraceae · 1 sp. · E:Coral Necklace; F:Illécèbre; G:Knorpelkraut
- **verticillatum** L. · E:Coral Necklace; G:Knorpelkraut · ⊙ VII-IX; Eur.: Fr, BrI, Ital-P, C-Eur., EC-Eur., Sc, Ba, Azor.; Moroc., Alger., Tun.

Illicium L. -n- Illiciaceae · 42 spp. · E:Anise Tree; F:Anis étoilé, Faux-anis; G:Sternanis
- **anisatum** L. · E:Aniseed Tree, Star Anise; G:Japanischer Sternanis · ♄ ♄ e Z8 ⊞ ⚘ Ⓝ; Jap., Korea
- **henryi** Diels · ♄ ♄ e Z8 ⊞; C-China, W-China
- *religiosum* Siebold & Zucc. = Illicium

anisatum
- **verum** Hook. f. · E:Chinese Anise;
G:Chinesischer Sternanis · ♄ e Z8 ⓚ ⚥
Ⓝ; cult.

Impatiens L. -f- *Balsaminaceae* · 850 spp. ·
E:Balsam, Busy Lizzie; F:Balsamine,
Impatiens; G:Fleißiges Lieschen, Rühr
mich nicht an, Balsamine, Springkraut
- **auricoma** Baill. · ⏀ Z10 ⓦ I-XII; Komor.
- **balfourii** Hook. f. · E:Kashmir Balsam;
G:Balfours Springkraut · ⏀ ⓚ VII-X;
W-Him., nat. in S-Eur., C-Eur.
- **balsamina** L. · E:Balsam; G:Garten-
Springkraut · ⊙ VII-IX; Ind., China,
Malay. Pen., nat. in F, EC-Eur.
- **some cultivars**
- *bicolor* Hook. f. = Impatiens niamniamen-
sis
- **capensis** Meerb. · E:Jewelweed, Orange
Balsam; G:Orangefarbenes Springkraut ·
⊙ Z2 VII-X; Alaska, Can., USA* exc. NW,
Rocky Mts., nat. in BrI, F
- **glandulifera** Royle · E:Himalayan
Balsam, Policeman's Helmet; G:Drüsiges
Springkraut, Indisches Springkraut ⊙ D
VII-X; Him., nat. in Eur., N-Am.: NE
- **hawkeri** W. Bull · ⏀ Z10 ⓦ ⓚ VIII-X;
N.Guinea
- *linearifolia* Warb. = Impatiens hawkeri
- **marianae** Rchb. f. ex Hook. f. · ⏀ ⤳
Z10 ⓦ VI-VII; InG: Assam
- **niamniamensis** Gilg · ⏀ Z10 ⓦ I-XII;
E-Afr.
- **noli-tangere** L. · E:Touch-me-not;
G:Rühr mich nicht an, Großes Spring-
kraut · ⊙ VII-VIII ⚥ ; Eur.*, TR, Cauc.,
W-Sib., E-Sib., Amur, Sakhal., Kamchat.,
C-As., China, Korea, Jap., nat. in N-Am.
- **parviflora** DC. · E:Small Balsam;
G:Kleinblütiges Springkraut · ⊙ VI-X;
C-As., Him., Mong., W-Sib., nat. in Eur.*
exc. Ib, Ba
- **platypetala** Lindl. · ⏀ Z10 ⓦ VII-VIII;
Java, Sulawesi
- **repens** Moon · ⏀ ⤳ Z10 ⓦ VI-VIII;
Ind., Sri Lanka
- *roylei* Walp. = Impatiens glandulifera
- **sodenii** Engl. & Warb. ex Engl. · ⏀ ⓚ
IV-VIII; Kenya, Tanzania
- *sultani* Hook. f. = Impatiens walleriana
- **walleriana** Hook. f. · E:Busy Lizzie;
F:Impatiens; G:Fleißiges Lieschen · ⏀ ⓚ
▽ I-XII; Tanzania, Mozamb.
- **many cultivars**

- **Cultivars:**
- **Neuguinea Group** · ; cult.

Imperata Cirillo -f- *Poaceae* · 8-10 spp. ·
E:Chigaya
- **cylindrica** (L.) P. Beauv. · E:Cogongrass ·
⏀ Z8 ⓚ Ⓝ; Eur.: Ib, Fr, Ital-P, Ba; TR,
Arab., C-As., NW-Ind., N-Afr., Macaron.,
nat. in N-Am., Chile
- *sacchariflora* Maxim. = Miscanthus
sacchariflorus

Incarvillea Juss. -f- *Bignoniaceae* · 14 spp. ·
F:Incarvillée; G:Freilandgloxinie
- **arguta** (Royle) Royle · ⏀ Z8 ⓚ ∧ VIII;
W-Him.
- *brevipes* (Sprague) hort. = Incarvillea
mairei var. mairei
- **compacta** Maxim. · ⏀ △ Z6 V-VII;
NW-China
- var. *grandiflora* H.R. Wehrh. = Incarvillea
mairei var. grandiflora
- **delavayi** Bureau & Franch. · E:Chinese
Trumpet Flower; F:Incarvillée de Delavay
G:Stängellose Freilandgloxinie; · ⏀ Z6
VI-VII; Yunnan
- **emodi** (Lindl.) Chatterjee · ⏀ Z8 ⓚ ∧
VIII; Him.
- *grandiflora* Bureau & Franch. = Incarvillea mairei var. grandiflora
- var. *brevipes* Sprague = Incarvillea mairei
var. mairei
- **lutea** Bureau & Franch. · ⏀ △ Z6 VI-VII;
SW-China
- **mairei** (H. Lév.) Grierson
- var. **grandiflora** (H.R. Wehrh.)
Grierson · F:Incarvillée à grandes fleurs ·
⏀ △ Z4 V-VI; Nepal, Bhutan, W-China,
SE-Tibet
- var. **mairei** · ⏀ Z4; SW-China
- **olgae** Regel · ⏀ Z7 VI-IX; C-As., Afgh.
- **sinensis** Lam.
- subsp. **sinensis** · E:Trumpet Flower;
G:Chinesische Freilandgloxinie · ⊙ ⏀ Z4;
Sib., Manch., China
- subsp. **variabilis** (Batalin) Grierson · ⊙
⏀ Z4 VI-VIII; W-China
- *variabilis* Batalin = Incarvillea sinensis
subsp. sinensis

Indigofera L. -f- *Fabaceae* · c. 700 spp. ·
E:Indigo; F:Indigo; G:Indigostrauch
- **amblyantha** Craib · ♄ d Z5 VII-X; China
- **arrecta** Hochst. ex A. Rich. · ♄ ⓦ Ⓝ;
W-Sah., W-Afr., E-Afr., S-Afr., Arab.

– **australis** Willd. · E:Australian Indigo; G:Australischer Indigostrauch · ♄ e Z9 🏠; Austr.: Queensl., N.S.Wales, Victoria
– **cylindrica** DC. · ♄ ♄ Z9 🏠; S-Afr.
– **decora** Lindl. · ♄ d Z7 ∧ VII-VIII; Jap., M-China
– **dielsiana** Craib · ♄ d Z6; SW-China
– **heterantha** Wall. ex Brandis · G:Himalaya-Indigostrauch · ♄ d Z7 ∧ VI-IX; Him.
– **hirsuta** L. · E:Hairy Indigo; G:Behaarter Indigostrauch · ⊙ 🐝 Ⓝ; Afr., S-As., N-Austr., nat. in Trop.
– *incarnata* Nakai = Indigofera decora
– **kirilowii** Maxim. ex Palib. · G:Kirilows Indigostrauch · ♄ d Z6 VI; Jap., Korea, Manch., N-China
– **potaninii** Craib · G:Potanins Indigostrauch · ♄ d Z7 VII-IX; NW-China
– **spicata** Forssk. · E:Creeping Indigo; G:Kriechender Indigostrauch · ♃ 🐝 Ⓝ; trop. Afr.
– **suffruticosa** Mill. · E:Anil Indigo; G:Mexikanischer Indigostrauch · ♄ 🐝 Ⓝ; trop. Am., nat. in Afr., S-As
– **tinctoria** L. · E:Common Indigo, Indigo, True Indigo; G:Indigostrauch · ♄ d Z10 🐝 VII Ⓝ; ? W-Afr.

Indocalamus Nakai -m- *Poaceae* · 35 spp.
– **tessellatus** (Munro) Keng f. · ♃ e Z6; Jap.

Inga Mill. -f- *Mimosaceae* · c. 350 spp. · E:Ice-Cream Bean; G:Ingabohne
– **edulis** Mart. · E:Ice Cream Bean; G:Ingabohne · ♄ e Z10 🏠 Ⓝ; C-Am., trop. S-Am.
– **feuillei** DC. · ♄ Z10 🏠 Ⓝ; Peru
– **laurina** (Sw.) Willd. · E:Sacky Sac Bean · ♄ Z10 🐝 Ⓝ; C-Am., W.Ind.

Inocarpus J.R. Forst. & G. Forst. -m- *Fabaceae* · 3 spp. · E:Tahitian Chestnut; G:Tahitikastanie
– **fagifer** (Parkinson ex Du Roi) Fosberg · E:Tahitian Chestnut; G:Tahitikastanie · ♄ e 🐝 Ⓝ; Malay. Arch., Polyn.

Intsia Thouars -f- *Caesalpiniaceae* · 3 spp.
– **bijuga** (Colebr.) Kuntze · E:Bajang; G:Borneo-Teakholz · ♄ 🐝 Ⓝ; E-Afr., S-As., Malay. Arch., N.Guinea, Austr.: Queensl.; Fiji, Pacific Is.

Inula L. -f- *Asteraceae* · c. 90 spp. ·

E:Fleabane; F:Aulnée, Inule; G:Alant
– **acaulis** Schott & Kotschy · ♃ △ Z6 VII-VIII; TR, Cauc.
– **britannica** L. · E:British Elecampane; G:Ufer-Alant · ♃ Z7 VII-IX; Eur.* exc. BrI; TR, Cauc., Iran, W-Sib., E-Sib., Amur, Sakhal., Kamchat.
– **conyzae** (Griess.) Meikle · E:Ploughman's Spikenard; G:Dürrwurz, Dürrwurz-Alant · ⊙ ♃ Z6 VI-X; Eur.*, TR, Cauc., Iran, Alger.
– **ensifolia** L. · E:Narrow-leaved Inula; F:Aunée à feuilles en épée; G:Schwertblättriger Alant · ♃ △ Z5 VII-VIII; Eur.* exc. BrI, Ib; N-TR, Cauc.
– **germanica** L. · E:German Elecampane; G:Deutscher Alant · ♃ VII-VIII ▽; Eur.: C-Eur., EC-Eur., Ba, E-Eur.; TR, Cauc., W-Sib., C-As.
– **helenium** L. · E:Elecampane, Scabwort; G:Echter Alant, Helenenkraut · ♃ Z5 VII-X ⚥ ; Eur.: Ital-P, Ba, E-Eur.; TR, Cauc., NW-Iran, W-Sib., C-As., nat. in Eur.: BrI, Sc, Fr, C-Eur., EC-Eur.; N-Am.
– **helvetica** Weber · E:Swiss Elecampane; G:Schweizer Alant · ♃ VII-IX; Eur.: sp., F, I, Sw, D
– **hirta** L. · F:Inule hérissée; G:Rauhaariger Alant · ♃ Z4 VI-IX; Eur.* exc. BrI, Sc; W-Sib.
– **hookeri** C.B. Clarke · ♃ Z6 VIII-IX; Sikkim
– **magnifica** Lipsky · E:Giant Inula; F:Grande aunée; G:Großer Alant · ♃ Z6 VII-VIII; Cauc.
– **oculus-christi** L. · E:Hairy Fleabane; G:Christusaugen-Alant · ♃ △ Z6 VI-VIII; Eur.: A, Ba, EC-Eur.; TR, Cauc., Iran
– **orientalis** Lam. · F:Inule d'Orient; G:Orientalischer Alant; · ♃ Z6 VI-VII; Cauc., TR
– **rhizocephala** Schrenk · ♃ △ Z7 ∧ VII-VIII; Afgh., Iran, Pakist., C-As.
– **royleana** DC. · ♃ Z6 VII-IX; Cauc., Him.
– *salicifolia* hort. = Inula salicina
– **salicina** L. · E:Irish Fleabane; G:Weidenblättriger Alant · ♃ Z6 VI-X; Eur.* exc. BrI; TR, Lebanon, Cauc., N-Iran, Sib., C-As., China, Korea, Jap.
– **spiraeifolia** L. · G:Sparriger Alant · ♃ Z6 VII-VIII; Eur.: Fr, Ital-P, Sw, Ba, ? RO

Iochroma Benth. -n- *Solanaceae* · 15 spp. · F:Arbre à violettes; G:Veilchenstrauch
– **australe** Griseb. · E:Argentine Pear · ♄ e

Z8 ⓚ VI; S-Bol., NW-Arg.
- **coccineum** Scheidw. · ♄ e Z9 ⓚ VII-VIII; C-Am.
- **cyaneum** (Lindl.) M.L. Green · ♄ Z9 ⓚ VII-VIII; Col.
- **fuchsioides** (Humb. & Bonpl.) Miers · ♄ e Z9 ⓚ VII-VIII; Col.
- **grandiflorum** Benth. · ♄ e Z9 ⓚ VII-VIII; Ecuad., Peru; And.
- *lanceolatum* (Miers) Miers = Iochroma cyaneum
- *tubulosum* Benth. = Iochroma cyaneum
- *warscewiczii* Regel = Iochroma grandiflorum

Ionopsidium Rchb. -n- *Brassicaceae* · 5 spp. · E:Violet Cress; F:Fausse-violette; G:Scheinveilchen
- **acaule** (Desf.) Rchb. · E:Diamond Flower, Violet Cress · ⊙ Z9 VI-VII ▽; P

Ionopsis Kunth -f- *Orchidaceae* · 6 spp. · E:Violet Orchid; F:Ionopsis; G:Veilchenständel
- *tenera* Lindl. = Ionopsis utricularioides
- **utricularioides** (Sw.) Lindl. · E:Delicate Violet Orchid; G:Rispen-Veilchenständel · ⌾ Z10 ⓦ XII-X ▽ ✳; Fla., Mex., W-Ind., C-Am., trop. S-Am.

Ipheion Raf. -n- *Alliaceae* · c. 20 spp. · E:Spring Starflower; F:Iphéion; G:Frühlingsstern
- **uniflorum** (Graham) Raf. · E:Spring Starflower; G:Frühlingsstern, Sternblume · ⌾ Z7 ∧ IV-V; S-Braz., Urug., Arg.
- **some cultivars**

Ipomoea L. -f- *Convolvulaceae* · c. 650 spp. · E:Morning Glory; F:Ipomée; G:Kaiserwinde, Prunkwinde, Purpurwinde
- **alba** L. · E:Moon Flower; G:Mondblüte, Weiße Prunkwinde · ⌾ ⚥ Z8 ⓦ VII-VIII; Trop.
- **aquatica** Forssk. · E:Water Convolvulus, Water Spinach; G:Sumpfkohl, Wasserspinat · ⊙ ⊙ ⌾ ∿ ⓦ XI-VI Ⓝ; Afr., Arab., Ind., Sri Lanka, trop. As., Austr., nat. in Trop.
- **arborescens** (Humb. & Bonpl. ex Willd.) G. Don · E:Morning Glory Tree, Tree Convolvulus · ♄ e ⓚ VI-VIII; Mex.
- **batatas** (L.) Lam. · G:Batate, Süßkartoffel; E:Sweet Potato · ⌾ ⚥ ∿ Z9 ⓦ Ⓝ;

cult.
- *biloba* Forssk. = Ipomoea pes-caprae
- *bona-nox* L. = Ipomoea alba
- **bonariensis** Hook. · ⌾ ⚥ ⓦ VIII-X; Arg.
- *Braziliensis* (L.) Sweet = Ipomoea pes-caprae
- **cairica** (L.) Sweet · E:Mile A Minute Vine · ⌾ ⚥ Z8 ⓦ II-VII; Trop.
- **carnea** Jacq.
- subsp. **carnea** · ♄ Z9 ⓦ; Fla., trop. Am., nat. in Trop.
- subsp. **fistulosa** (Mart. ex Choisy) D.F. Austin · E:Morning Glory Bush · ♄ Z9 ⓦ I-VI; C-Am., trop. S-Am.
- **coccinea** L. · E:Red Morning Glory, Star Ipomoea; G:Sternwinde · ⊙ ⚥ Z7 VII-X; Ariz., N.Mex.
- *crassicaulis* (Benth.) B.L. Rob. = Ipomoea carnea subsp. carnea
- *dissecta* (Jacq.) Pursh = Merremia dissecta
- **eriocarpa** R. Br. · ♄ Ⓝ; Afgh., Ind., Sri Lanka, Trop. Old World
- *fistulosa* Mart. ex Choisy = Ipomoea carnea subsp. fistulosa
- **hederacea** Jacq. · E:Ivy-leaved Morning Glory · ⊙ ⚥ Z8 VII-IX; trop. Am.
- **hederifolia** L. · E:Scarlet Creeper · ⊙ ⚥ Z8 VII-IX; USA: SC; S-Am., nat. in Trop.
- **horsfalliae** Hook. · ♄ ⚥ Z9 ⓚ X-I; W-Ind.
- **× imperialis** hort. (*I. nil* × ?) · ⌾ ⚥ Z9; cult.
- **indica** (Burm.) Merr. · E:Blue Dawn Flower, Ocean Blue Morning Glory; G:Indische Prunkwinde · ⌾ ⚥ Z9 ⓦ ⓚ VII-IX; Trop.
- *learii* Paxton = Ipomoea indica
- **lobata** (Cerv.) Thell. · G:Lappen-Prunkwinde · ⌾ ⚥ Z8 ⓚ VII-IX; S-Mex.
- **macrorhiza** Michx. · E:Large-root Morning Glory · ♄ e ⚥ ⓚ VIII-IX; USA: Calif., Fla., SW; Mex.
- **mauritiana** Jacq. · E:Mauritanian Convolvulus; G:Haiti-Prunkwinde · ⌾ ⚥ Z9 ⓦ VII-IX; Trop.
- *michauxii* Sweet = Ipomoea macrorhiza
- **× multifida** (Raf.) Shinners (*I. coccinea* × *I. quamoclit*) · ⊙ ⚥ Z9 VII-XI; cult.
- **muricata** (L.) Jacq. · ⌾ ⚥ ⓦ VII-VIII; Trop.
- **nil** (L.) Roth · E:Blue Morning Glory; G:Blaue Prunkwinde · ⌾ ⚥ Z9 ⓚ VII-IX; Trop.
- *palmata* Forssk. = Ipomoea cairica
- **pandurata** (L.) G. Mey. ·

E:Man-of-the-earth, Wild Potato Vine · ⌃ ⚳ Z7 ∧ VII-IX; Can.: Ont.; USA: NE, NCE, Kans., SC, SE, Fla.
- *paniculata* (L.) R. Br. = Ipomoea mauritiana
- **pes-caprae** (L.) R. Br. · E:Bayhops, Beach Morning Glory, Goat's Foot; G:Ziegenfuß-Prunkwinde · ⌃ ⚳ ↝ Z9 ⓦ I-VII Ⓝ; Trop.; coasts
- **purga** (Wender.) Hayne · E:Jalap; G:Herbst-Prunkwinde · ⌃ ⚳ ⓚ VII-X ⚘ ✿; Mex., Panama
- **purpurea** (L.) Roth · E:Common Morning Glory; G:Purpur-Prunkwinde · ⊙ ⚳ Z7 VI-IX; trop. Am., ? Mex., nat. in Trop.
- **quamoclit** L. · E:Cardinal Climber, Cypress Vine, Quamoclit; G:Zypressen-Prunkwinde · ⊙ ⚳ Z8 ⓚ VII-VIII; trop. Am.
- *reptans* auct. non (L.) Poir. = Ipomoea aquatica
- **setosa** Ker-Gawl. · E:Brazilian Morning Glory; G:Brasilianische Prunkwinde · ♄ ⚳ ⓦ VIII-X; Braz.
- *sibirica* (L.) Pers. = Merremia sibirica
- **stans** Cav. · ♄ ⓚ; Mex.
- **tricolor** Cav. · E:Flying Saucers, Heavenly Blue Morning Glory; F:Ipomée; G:Himmelblaue Prunkwinde · ⊙ ⌃ ⚳ Z8 ⓚ VIII-X ✿; Mex., C-Am., nat. in Trop.
- **some cultivars**
- *tuberosa* L. = Merremia tuberosa
- *turpethum* (L.) R. Br. = Operculina turpethum
- *violacea* auct. non L. = Ipomoea tricolor

Ipomopsis Michx. -f- *Polemoniaceae* · 24 spp.
- **aggregata** (Pursh) V.E. Grant · E:Scarlet Gilia, Skyrocket · ⊙ ⊙ Z7 VII-X; Can.: B.C.; USA: NW, Calif., Rocky Mts., SC, SW; Mex.
- *elegans* Michx. = Ipomopsis rubra
- **rubra** (L.) Wherry · E:Standing Cypress · ⌃ Z8 ⓚ VII-X; USA: SE, SC, Fla.

Iresine P. Browne -f- *Amaranthaceae* · 80 spp. · F:Irésine; G:Iresine
- **herbstii** Hook. f. · E:Beefsteak Plant, Blood Leaf; F:Irésine; G:Blutblatt · ⊙ ⥊ Z9 ⓦ; Braz.
- **lindenii** Van Houtte · E:Linden's Bloodleaf; F:Irésine · ⌃ ⥊ Z9 ⓦ; Ecuad.

Iridodictyum Rodion. = Iris

- *histrio* (Rchb. f.) Rodion. = Iris histrio
- *reticulatum* (M. Bieb.) Rodion. = Iris reticulata var. reticulata

Iris L. -f- *Iridaceae* · 239 spp. · E:Flag, Sword Lily; F:Iris; G:Iris, Schwertlilie
- **aphylla** L. · F:Iris sans feuille; G:Nacktstänglige Schwertlilie · ⌃ IV-V ▽; Eur.: F, I, G, EC-Eur., Ba, E-Eur..; Cauc.
- **atrofusca** Baker · ⌃ ⓚ ▽; Israel
- **atropurpurea** Baker · ⌃ ⓚ ▭ V ▽; Israel
- **aucheri** (Baker) Sealy · ⌃ △ ⓚ ∧ II-III ▽; TR, Syr., Iraq
- *bakeriana* Foster = Iris reticulata var. bakeriana
- **barnumae** Foster & Baker · ⌃ △ ▭ ∧ V-VI ▽; E-TR, NE-Iraq, Iran
- **bismarckiana** Regel · ⌃ △ ▭ ∧ V ▽; Lebanon
- **boissieri** Henriq. · ⌃ ∧ VI ▽; N-P, NW-Sp.
- *bosniaca* Beck = Iris reichenbachii
- **bracteata** S. Watson · E:Siskiyou Iris; G:Siskiyou-Iris · ⌃ V-VI ▽; USA: Oreg., Calif.
- **brevicaulis** Raf. · E:Louisiana Iris, Zigzag Iris; G:Louisiana-Iris · ⌃ VI ▽; USA: NCE, Kans., SC, SE
- **bucharica** Foster · G:Geweih-Iris · ⌃ △ ∧ III-IV ▽; NE-Afgh., C-As.: Tajik.
- **bulleyana** Dykes · ⌃ ∧ V-VI ▽; W-China, N-Burma
- **caucasica** Hoffm. · ⌃ △ III-IV ▽; TR, Cauc., Iran
- *chamaeiris* Bertol. = Iris lutescens
- **chrysographes** Dykes · ⌃ ∿ VI ▽; Yunnan, Sichuan
- **clarkei** Baker ex Hook. f. · ⌃ VI ▽; E-Him.
- **cristata** Sol. · E:Crested Iris; G:Kamm-Iris · ⌃ △ ∿ V-VI ▽; USA: NE, SE, SC
- **crocea** Jacquem. ex R.C. Foster · E:Golden Flag; G:Kaschmir-Iris · ⌃ VI ▽; Kashmir
- **danfordiae** (Baker) Boiss. · ⌃ △ D III-IV ▽; TR
- **delavayi** Micheli · ⌃ ∿ VII ▽; Yunnan
- *desertorum* Ker-Gawl. = Iris halophila
- **dichotoma** (Pall.) L.W. Lenz · ⊙ ⌃ Z7 VIII-IX; Sib., Mong., Manch.
- **douglasiana** Herb. · E:Douglas Iris, Mountain Iris; G:Douglas-Iris · ⌃ VI ▽; USA: Oreg., Calif.
- **ensata** Thunb. · E:Japanese Water Iris;

F:Iris du Japon; G:Japanische Sumpf-Schwertlilie · ⌃ VI Ⓝ ▽; C-As., China, Korea, Jap.
- **many cultivars**
- **filifolia** Boiss. · ⌃ ∧ VI ▽; SW-Sp., Moroc.
- **flavissima** Pall.
- *florentina* Kunze = Iris × germanica subsp. albicans
- **foetidissima** L. · E:Gladwyn, Roast Beef Plant, Stinking Iris; F:Iris gigot, Iris puant; G:Übelriechende Schwertlilie · ⌃ VI ▽; Eur.: Ib, Fr, Ital-P, Ba; N-Afr., nat. in Sw
- *foliosa* Mack. & Bush = Iris brevicaulis
- **forrestii** Dykes · F:Iris de Forrest · ⌃ V-VI ▽; Yunnan
- **fosteriana** Aitch. & Baker · ⌃ △ ∧ III ▽; Iran, NW-Afgh.
- **fulva** Ker-Gawl. · E:Louisiana Iris, Red Iris ; G:Terrakotta-Schwertlilie · ⌃ ⌢ VI ▽; USA: Ill., Mo., SE
- × **fulvala** Dykes (*I. brevicaulis* × *I. fulva*) · ⌃
- **gatesii** Foster · ⌃ ⌂ ⌐ V ▽; SE-TR, N-Iraq
- × **germanica** L. (*I. pallida* subsp. *pallida* × *I. variegata*)
- subsp. **albicans** (Lange) O. Bolòs & Vigo · ⌃; cult.
- subsp. **germanica** · E:Common Iris, German Iris, Orris; G:Deutsche Schwertlilie · ⌃ ⋉ V-VI Ⓝ ▽; Eur.: Ib, F, Ital-P, C-Eur., EC-Eur., Ba; TR, Palest., NW-Afr., nat. in Eur.*
- *gigantea* Carr = Iris orientalis
- **gracilipes** A. Gray · ⌃ △ VI ▽; Jap.
- **graeberiana** Sealy · ⌃ △ IV ▽; C-As.
- **graminea** L. · F:Iris à feuilles de graminée; G:Grasblättrige Schwertlilie, Pflaumenduft-Iris · ⌃ △ D V-VI ▽; Eur.* exc. BrI, Sc; Cauc.
- *gueldenstaedtiana* Lepech. = Iris halophila
- **halophila** Pall. · ⌃ V-VI ▽; S-Russ., Cauc., W-Sib., C-As., Mong., Him.
- **hexagona** Walter · E:Dixie Iris · ⌃ ∧ VI ▽; USA: Va., SE, Tex.
- **histrio** Rchb. f. · ⌃ △ ⌂ ∧ III ▽; TR, Syr.
- **histrioides** (G.F. Wilson) S. Arn. · ⌃ △ ⌂ III ▽; N-TR
- × **hollandica** hort. (*I. latifolia* × *I. tingitana* × *I. xiphium*) · E:Dutch Iris ; G:Holländische Iris · ⌃ ⌂; cult.
- **many cultivars**

- **hoogiana** Dykes · ⌃ ⌂ ∧ V ▽; C-As.
- **humilis** Georgi · G:Sand-Schwertlilie · ⌃ △ D IV-VI ▽; Eur.: A, H, ? W-Ba, RO, Russ.; Cauc., Altai
- *hyrcana* Woronow ex Grossh. = Iris reticulata var. reticulata
- **innominata** L.F. Hend. · E:Rainbow Iris · ⌃ △ ⋊ ∧ VI ▽; USA: Oreg., N-Calif.
- **japonica** Thunb. · E:Orchid Iris; G:Gefranste Schwertlilie · ⌃ ⌂ ∧ III-IV ▽; Jap., C-China
- **juncea** Poir. · ⌃ ⌂ ∧ V-VI ▽; Eur.: SW-Sp., Sic.; N-Afr., nat. in I
- *kaempferi* Siebold = Iris ensata
- **kochii** A. Kern. ex Stapf · ⌃ IV ▽; Eur.: N-I
- **korolkowii** Regel · ⌃ ∧ V-VI ▽; C-As., Afgh.
- **lacustris** Nutt. · E:Dwarf Lake Iris · ⌃ △ V ▽; Can.: Ont.; USA: Wisc.
- **laevigata** Fisch. · G:Asiatische Sumpf-Schwertlilie · ⌃ ⌢ VII-VIII ▽; China, Manch., Korea, Jap.
- **many cultivars**
- **latifolia** (Mill.) Voss · E:English Iris; F:Iris à bulbe des Pyrénées; G:Englische Schwertlilie · ⌃ ∧ VI ▽; Eur.: sp., F; Cordillera Cantábrica, Pyr.
- **longipetala** Herb. · ⌃ V-VI ▽; Calif.
- **lortetii** Barbey ex Boiss. · ⌃ ⌂ ∧ V-VI ▽; Lebanon
- **lutescens** Lam. · G:Grünliche Schwertlilie · ⌃ IV-V ▽; Eur.: NE-Ib, S-F, I, nat. in Sw, Sic.
- **magnifica** Vved. · ⌃ ⌂ ∧ IV ▽; C-As.
- **mandschurica** Maxim. · ⌃ V ▽; Korea, Manch.
- × *mesopotamica* Dykes = Iris × germanica subsp. germanica
- **milesii** Foster · ⌃ V-VII ▽; NW-Him.
- **missouriensis** Nutt. · E:Missouri Flag, Rocky Mountain Iris; G:Missouri-Schwertlilie · ⌃ V-VI ▽; Can.: B.C.; USA: NC, Rocky Mts., NW, Calif., SW; Mex.
- × *monnieri* DC. (*I. xanthospuria* × ?) · ⌃ VI-VII ▽; Crete
- *nudicaulis* Lam. = Iris aphylla
- *ochroleuca* L. = Iris orientalis
- **orchioides** Carrière · ⌃ △ ∧ IV ▽; C-As.
- **orientalis** Mill. · E:Butterfly Iris; G:Orientalische Schwertlilie · ⌃ ⋉ VI-VII ▽; NE-GR, W-TR
- *orientalis* Thunb. = Iris sanguinea
- **pallida** Lam. · E:Dalmatian Iris; G:Bleiche Schwertlilie · ⌃ D V-VI ⚡ Ⓝ

∇; Eur.: I, Slove., Croat., Montenegro, Maced., nat. in F, Sw, A, RO, Ba
- **paradoxa** Steven · ♃ ⌂ ∧ VI ∇; Cauc., N-Iran
- **persica** L. · ♃ △ ⌂ ∧ II-III ∇; S-TR, N-Syr., NE-Iraq, Egypt
- **planifolia** (Mill.) Fiori & Paol. · ♃ ⌂ XI-I ∇; Eur.: Ib, Sard., Sic., GR, Crete; N-Afr.
- **pseudacorus** L. · ♃; cult.
- var. **pseudacorus** · E:Flag Iris, Yellow Flag; F:Iris des marais; G:Sumpf-Schwertlilie · ♃ ∼ V-VI ⚘ ∇; Eur.*, TR, Syr., Cauc., Iran, W-Sib., Moroc.
- **pumila** L.
- subsp. **pumila** · E:Dwarf Flag; G:Zwerg-Schwertlilie · ♃ △ IV-V ∇; Eur.: A, EC-Eur.; Cauc.
- **reichenbachii** Heuff. · ♃ △ ⌂ IV ∇; Eur.: Ba, RO
- **reticulata** M. Bieb.
- **many cultivars**
- var. **bakeriana** (Foster) B. Mathew & Wendelbo · ♃ △ ∧ II-III ∇; E-TR, N-Iraq, W-Iran
- var. **reticulata** · E:Netted Iris, Winter Iris; G:Kleine Netzblatt-Iris · ♃ △ III ∇; TR, Iraq, Cauc., Iran
- × **robusta** E.S. Anderson (*I. versicolor* × *I. virginica*) · ♃; cult.
- **rosenbachiana** Regel · ♃ ⌂ I-III ∇; C-As., Afgh.
- *rudskyi* Horvat & M.D. Horvat = Iris variegata
- **ruthenica** Ker-Gawl. · ♃ △ V-VI ∇; Eur.: RO, ? E-Russ.; W-Sib., E-Sib., Amur, C-As., Mong., China, Korea
- × *sambucina* L. = Iris × squalens
- **sanguinea** Hornem. ex Donn · E:Siberian Iris; G:Frühe Sibirische Schwertlilie · ♃ V-VI ∇; Jap., Korea, Manch., E-Sib.
- **sari** Schott ex Baker · ♃ ⌂ ⌐ VII ∇; TR
- **setosa** Pall. ex Link · E:Beach Head Iris · ♃ VI ∇; Alaska, E-Sib., Sakhal., Jap.
- **sibirica** L. · E:Siberian Iris; F:Iris de Sibérie; G:Sibirische Schwertlilie, Wiesen-Schwertlilie · ♃ ∼ V-VI ∇; Eur.: Fr, Ital-P, C-Eur., EC-Eur., Ba, E-Eur.; TR, Cauc., W-Sib., E-Sib., nat. in Swed
- **many cultivars**
- *sicula* Tod. = Iris pallida
- *sindjarensis* Boiss. & Hausskn. = Iris aucheri
- **sintenisii** Janka · ♃ △ V-VI ∇; Eur.: I, Ba, E-Eur.; TR
- *sisyrinchium* L. = Gynandriris

sisyrinchium
- **songarica** Schrenk · ♃ V ∇; TR, Iran, C-As., Kashmir, China
- *spathacea* Thunb. = Moraea spathulata
- *spathulata* L. f. = Moraea spathulata
- **spuria** L.
- **many cultivars**
- subsp. *ochroleuca* (L.) Dykes = Iris orientalis
- subsp. **spuria** · E:Butterfly Iris; F:Iris des steppes; G:Steppen-Schwertlilie · ♃ ∼ V-VII ∇; Eur.: Ib, BrI, Fr, C-Eur., EC-Eur., GR, E Eur., Sc; Cauc., N-Iran, nat. in I
- × **squalens** L. (*I. pallida* × *I. variegata*) · G:Gelbliche Schwertlilie · ♃ VI; SE-Eur., SW-As.
- **stolonifera** Maxim. · ♃ ⋉ ∧ V-VI ∇; C-As.
- **suaveolens** Boiss. & Reut. · ♃ △ IV-V ∇; Eur.: Ba, RO; TR
- **susiana** L. · E:Mourning Iris; G:Dame in Trauer · ♃ ⌂ ⌐ ∧ V-VI ∇; ? Iran, ? Lebanon
- **tectorum** Maxim. · E:Roof Iris; G:Dach-Schwertlilie · ♃ △ ∧ VI ∇; China
- **tenax** Douglas ex Lindl. · E:Oregon Iris; G:Oregon-Iris · ♃ △ ∧ V ∇; USA: NW, Calif.; Baja Calif.
- **tingitana** Boiss. & Reut. · ♃ ⌂ IV-V ∇; Moroc., Alger.
- *tricuspis* Thunb. = Moraea tricuspidata
- *tuberosa* L. = Hermodactylus tuberosus
- **unguicularis** Poir. · E:Algerian Iris, Winter; Iris G:Winter-Iris · ♃ ⌂ XI-III ∇; Eur.: GR, Crete; TR, Syr., NW-Afr.
- **variegata** L. · G:Bunte Schwertlilie · ♃ V-VI ∇; Eur.: C-Eur., EC-Eur., Ba, E-Eur., nat. in I
- **vartanii** Foster · ♃ ⌂ XII-I ∇; Palest.
- **verna** L. · E:Dwarf Iris, Vernal Iris; G:Frühlings-Schwertlilie · ♃ △ ∧ IV ∇; USA: NE, SE
- **versicolor** L. · E:Blue Flag, Iris; F:Iris variable; G:Verschiedenfarbige Schwert-lilie · ♃ ∼ VI-VIII ⚥ ∇; Can.: E, nat. in BrI, D
- **many cultivars**
- **warleyensis** Foster · ♃ ⌂ ⌐ IV ∇; C-As.
- *watsoniana* Purdy = Iris douglasiana
- **willmottiana** Foster · ♃ ⌂ ⌐ III-IV ∇; C-As.
- **wilsonii** C.H. Wright · ♃ V-VI ∇; W-China
- **winogradowii** Fomin · ♃ △ ⌂ ∧ III-IV

▽; Cauc.
- *xiphioides* Ehrh. = Iris latifolia
- **xiphium** L. · E:Spanish Iris; G:Spanische Iris · ⨼ ∧ VI ▽; Eur.: S-F, P, sp.; N-Afr.
- **Cultivars:**
- **many cultivars, see Section III**

Isabelia Barb. Rodr. -f- *Orchidaceae* · 3 spp.
- **pulchella** (Kraenzl.) Van den Berg & M.W. Chase · ⨼ Z10 ⓜ X-XI ▽ ✳; S-Braz.
- **violacea** (Lindl.) Van den Berg & M.W. Chase · ⨼ Z10 ⓜ XI-II ▽ ✳; Braz.

Isatis L. -f- *Brassicaceae* · c. 30 spp. · E:Woad; F:Pastel; G:Färberwaid, Waid
- **tinctoria** L. · E:Common Dyer's Weed, Dyer's Woad; G:Färberwaid · ⊙ ⨼ Z7 V-VI ⚲ Ⓝ; Eur.*, TR, Cauc., C-As., W-Sib., E-Sib., nat. in N-Afr., Ind., E-As., Chile

Ischaemum L. -n- *Poaceae* · c. 65 spp.
- **indicum** (Houtt.) Merr. · ⨼ Ⓝ; SE-As.; cult. W-Afr., W.Ind., Fiji

Islaya Backeb. = Neoporteria
- *bicolor* Akers & Buining = Neoporteria islayensis
- *copiapoides* Rauh & Backeb. = Neoporteria islayensis
- *grandis* Rauh & Backeb. = Neoporteria islayensis
- *islayensis* (C.F. Först.) Backeb. = Neoporteria islayensis
- *minor* Backeb. = Neoporteria islayensis
- *molendensis* (Vaupel) Backeb. = Neoporteria islayensis
- *paucispinosa* (Monv.) F.A.C. Weber = Neoporteria islayensis

Ismelia Cass. -f- *Asteraceae* · 1 sp. · G:Bunte Wucherblume
- **carinata** (Schousb.) Sch. Bip. · E:Painted Daisy, Tricolor Chrysanthemum; G:Bunte Wucherblume, Kiel-Wucherblume · ⊙ ✂ VI-IX; NW-Afr.
- **many cultivars**

Ismene Salisb. ex Herb. = Hymenocallis
- *amancaes* (Ruiz & Pav.) Herb. = Hymenocallis amancaes
- *calathina* Herb. = Hymenocallis narcissiflora

Isnardia L. = Ludwigia

- *alternifolia* (L.) DC. = Ludwigia alternifolia
- *palustris* L. = Ludwigia palustris

Isoberlinia Craib & Stapf ex Holland -f- *Caesalpiniaceae* · 5 spp.
- **angolensis** (Welw. ex Benth.) Hoyle & Brenan · ♄ ✂ ⓜ; trop. Afr.

Isochilus R. Br. -m- *Orchidaceae* · 12 spp.
- **linearis** (Jacq.) R. Br. · ⨼ Z10 ⓜ VI-VII ▽ ✳; Mex., W.Ind., C-Am., trop. S-Am.

Isoetes L. -f- *Isoetaceae* · 143 spp. · E:Quillwort; F:Isoètes; G:Brachsenkraut
- **echinospora** Durieu · E:Spring Quillwort; G:Igelsporiges Brachsenkraut · ⨼ ≋ ⓐ ∧ VII-IX; Eur.*, Sakhal., Kamchat., Jap., Alaska, Can., USA: NE, NCE; Greenl., nat. in W-Sib., E-Sib.
- **lacustris** L. · E:Western Lake Quillwort; G:See-Brachsenkraut · ⨼ ≋ Z3 VII-IX ▽; Eur.* exc. Ba; W-Sib., Jap., Alaska, Can., USA: Rocky Mts., Calif.; Greenl.
- *leiospora* H. Klinggr. = Isoetes lacustris
- **malinverniana** Ces. & De Not. · ⨼ ≋ ⓜ ⓐ ▽; NW-I
- *setacea* auct. non Lam. = Isoetes echinospora
- *tenella* Léman ex Desv. = Isoetes echinospora

Isolatocereus (Backeb.) Backeb. -m- *Cactaceae* · 1 sp.
- **dumortieri** (Scheidw.) Backeb. · ♄ ♌ Z9 ⓐ ▽ ✳; Mex.

Isolepis R. Br. -f- *Cyperaceae* · 74 spp. · E:Club Rush; F:Scirpe; G:Moorbinse, Schuppensimse, Tauchsimse
- *acicularis* (L.) Schltdl. = Eleocharis acicularis
- **cernua** (Vahl) Roem. & Schult. · E:Low Bulrush, Slender Club Rush; G:Niedere Moorbinse · ⨼ ⌢ Z8 ⓜ; Eur.: Ib, Fr, BrI, Ital-P, Ba; N-Afr., E-Afr., S-Afr., Madag., Austr., NZ
- **fluitans** (L.) R. Br. · G:Flut-Moorbinse, Flutende Tauchsimse · ⨼ ≋ Z6 VII-IX; Eur.: Ib, Fr, I, BrI, G, W-Ba; Ind., Sri Lanka, Indochina, Malay. Arch., Jap., N.Guinea, E-Afr., Angola, S-Afr., Austr., NZ
- **prolifera** (Rottb.) R. Br. · ⨼ ⌢ Z8 ⓐ; Cape., Austr., NZ

– **setacea** (L.) R. Br. · E:Bristle Scirpus;
G:Borstige Moorbinse, Borstige Schup-
pensimse · ⌠4 ⁓ Z6 VII-X; Eur.*, W-Sib.,
E-Sib., C-As., Him., TR, Palest., Azor.,
Madeira, Moroc., Yemen, Eth., E-Afr.,
S-Afr., nat. in Tasman., NZ, N-Am.

Isoplexis (Lindl.) Loudon -f-
Scrophulariaceae · 3 spp.
– **canariensis** (L.) Loudon · ♭ e Z9 ⓐ V-VI;
Canar.

Isopogon R. Br. ex Knight -m- *Proteaceae* ·
35 spp. · E:Coneflower, Drum Sticks;
F:Isopogon; G:Paukenschlegel
– **baxteri** R. Br. · E:Stirling Range
Coneflower; G:Baxters Paukenschlegel ·
♭ e Z9 ⓐ III; W-Austr.
– **cuneatus** R. Br. · ♭ e Z9 ⓐ III-V;
W-Austr.
– **sphaerocephalus** Lindl. · E:Drumstick
Isopogon · ♭ e Z9 ⓐ IV-V; W-Austr.

Isopyrum L. -n- *Ranunculaceae* · 30 spp. ·
E:False Rue Anemone; F:Isopyre;
G:Muschelblümchen
– **thalictroides** L. · ⌠4 Z6 IV-V ✿; Eur.: Ib,
Fr, Ital-P, Ba, EC-Eur., E-Eur., A

Isotoma (R. Br.) Lindl. -f- · c. 8 spp.
– **axillaris** Lindl. · E:Rock Isotome · ☉ ⌠4
VII-IX; Austr.
– **fluviatilis** (R. Br.) F. Muell. · E:Bluestar
Creeper · ⌠4 ⤳ ⓐ; NZ, Austr.: S-Austr.,
Tasman.
– **longiflora** (L.) C. Presl · E:Star of
Bethlehem · ⌠4 ⓐ; USA: SE, Fla.; W.Ind.,
C-Am., trop. S-Am., nat. in trop. coasts
– *senecioides* A. DC. = Isotoma axillaris

Itea L. -f- *Escalloniaceae* · 15 spp. ·
E:Sweetspire; F:Itéa; G:Rosmarinweide
– **ilicifolia** Oliv. · E:Hollyleaf Sweetspire;
G:Stechpalmenblättrige Rosmarinweide ·
♭ e Z8 ⓐ VIII; W-China
– **virginica** L. · E:Sweetspire, Virginian
Willow; F:Itéa de Virginie; G:Amerika-
nische Rosmarinweide · ♭ d Z6 VII-VIII;
USA: NE, NCE, SC, SE, Fla.

Iva L. -f- *Asteraceae* · 15 spp. · E:Marsh
Elder; F:Iva; G:Schlagkraut
– **xanthiifolia** Nutt. · E:Marsh Elder;
G:Spitzklettenblättriges Schlagkraut · ☉
VIII-X; w N-Am., Amur, nat. in Fr, C-Eur.,

EC-Eur.

× **Iwanagara** hort. -f- *Orchidaceae* (*Cattleya*
× *Caularthron* × *Laelia* × *Rhyncholaelia*)

Ixia L. -f- *Iridaceae* · 51 sp. · E:Corn Lily;
F:Fleur du soir, Ixia; G:Klebschwertel
– **campanulata** Houtt. · E:Red Corn Lily ·
⌠4 ✕ Z9 ⓐ ▭ VI-VII; Cape
– *corymbosa* L. = Lapeirousia corymbosa
– *crateroides* Ker-Gawl. = Ixia speciosa
– **maculata** L. · E:African Corn Lily;
G:Geäugtes Klebschwertel · ⌠4 ✕ Z9 ⓐ
▭ V-VI; Cape
– **paniculata** D. Delaroche · E:Tubular
Corn Lily · ⌠4 ✕ Z9 ⓐ ▭ V-VI; Cape, nat.
in W-Eur.
– **speciosa** Andrews
– **viridiflora** Lam. · E:Green Ixia; G:Türk-
ises Klebschwertel · ⌠4 ✕ Z9 ⓐ ▭ V-VI;
Cape
– **Cultivars:**
– **many cultivars**

Ixiolirion Herb. -n- *Ixioliriaceae* · 4 spp. ·
F:Ixiolirion; G:Ixlilie
– *pallasii* Fisch. & C.A. Mey. = Ixiolirion
tataricum var. tataricum
– **tataricum** (Pall.) Schult. & Schult. f.
– var. **ixiolirioides** (Regel) X.H. Qian · ⌠4
Z7 ⋀ VI-VII; China: Sinkiang (Sairam
Nor)
– var. **tataricum** · ⌠4 △ V; W-Sib., C-As.,
Iran, Afgh., Iraq, Pakist.

Ixora L. -f- *Rubiaceae* · 536 spp.
– **acuminata** Roxb. · ♭ e D Z10 ⓐ; N-Ind.
– **borbonica** Cordem. · ♭ e Z10 ⓐ;
Reunion
– **chinensis** Lam. · E:Broken Pot, Red
Balance · ♭ e Z10 ⓐ VII-VIII; Ind.
– **coccinea** L. · E:Flame-of-the-Wood,
Ixora, Jungle Flame; G:Dschungelbrand ·
♭ e Z10 ⓐ IV-VIII; Ind.
– **congesta** Roxb. · ♭ e Z10 ⓐ VII-VIII;
Burma, Singapore
– **fulgens** Roxb. · ♭ e Z10 ⓐ VII-VIII;
Malay. Arch.
– *griffithii* Hook. = Ixora congesta

Jacaranda Juss. -f- *Bignoniaceae* · 34
(-49) spp. · E:Jacaranda; F:Faux-palis-
sandre, Jacaranda; G:Jacarandabaum,
Palisander
– **Braziliana** Pers. · ♭ ✕ Z9 ⓐ; Braz.

– **copaia** (Aubl.) D. Don · ♄ Z9 🐝; Guyan.
– **mimosifolia** D. Don · ♄ d Z9 🐝; Arg.
– *ovalifolia* R. Br. = Jacaranda mimosifolia
– *procera* Spreng. = Jacaranda copaia

Jacea Mill. = Centaurea
– *communis* Delarbre = Centaurea jacea
  subsp. jacea

Jacobinia Nees ex Moric. = Justicia
– *carnea* (Lindl.) G. Nicholson = Justicia
  carnea
– *ghiesbreghtiana* (Lem.) Hemsl. = Justicia
  ghiesbreghtiana
– *magnifica* (Nees) Lindau = Justicia carnea
– *pohliana* (Nees) Lindau = Justicia carnea
– *suberecta* André = Dicliptera suberecta

Jacobsenia L. Bolus & Schwantes -f-
  Aizoaceae · 3 spp.
– **kolbei** (L. Bolus) L. Bolus & Schwantes ·
  ⚃ Ѱ Z9 🐝; Cape

Jacquemontia Choisy -f- *Convolvulaceae* ·
  120 spp.
– **pentantha** (Jacq.) G. Don · E:Sky Blue
  Clustervine · ♄ ⚄ Z10 🌰 VII-IX; USA:
  Fla.; Mex., C-Am., W.Ind., trop. S-Am.

Jambosa Adans. = Syzygium
– *caryophyllus* (Spreng.) Nied. = Syzygium
  aromaticum
– *jambos* (L.) Millsp. = Syzygium jambos
– *vulgaris* DC. = Syzygium jambos

Jamesia Torr. & A. Gray -f- *Hydrangeaceae* ·
  1 sp. · E:Cliffbush; F:Jamesia; G:Jamesie
– **americana** Torr. & A. Gray · G:Jamesie ·
  ♄ d △ D Z7 ∧ V; USA: Nev., Ariz.,
  N.Mex.

Jancaea Boiss. -f- *Gesneriaceae* · 1 sp.
– **heldreichii** (Boiss.) Boiss. · ⚃ △ Z8 🌰
  VI-VII ▽; GR (Olymp)

Jasione L. -f- *Campanulaceae* · c. 20 spp. ·
  E:Sheep's Bit; F:Jasione; G:Sandglöck-
  chen, Sandrapunzel
– **crispa** (Pourr.) Samp. · E:Dwarf Sheep's
  Bit · ⊙ ⚃ Z7 VI-VIII; Eur.: IB, F; NW-Afr.
– *humilis* (Pers.) Loisel. = Jasione crispa
– **laevis** Lam. · E:Shepherd's Bit; F:Jasione
  lisse; G:Ausdauerndes Sandglöckchen · ⚃
  △ Z5 VII-VIII; Eur.: sp., Fr, Ital-P, G, Ba,
  RO, nat. in FIN

– **montana** L. · E:Sheep's Bit; G:Berg-
  Sandglöckchen · ⊙ ⚃ Z6 VI-VIII; Eur.*,
  NW-Afr.
– var. *littoralis* Fr. = Jasione montana
– *perennis* Vill. ex Lam. = Jasione laevis

Jasminum L. -n- *Oleaceae* · c. 200
  (-450) spp. · E:Jasmine, Jessamine;
  F:Jasmin; G:Jasmin
– *affine* Royle ex Lindl. = Jasminum
  officinale
– **azoricum** L. · G:Azoren-Jasmin · ♄ e ⚄ D
  Z9 🌰 VII-X ▽; Madeira
– **beesianum** Forrest & Diels · E:Red
  Jasmine; F:Jasmin rose · ♄ d ⚄ D Z8 🌰
  V; W-China
– **floridum** Bunge · ♄ e Z9 🌰 VII-IX;
  China, Jap.
– **fruticans** L. · G:Strauch-Jasmin · ♄ e Z8
  🌰 VII-IX; Eur.: Ib, Fr, I, Ba, RO, Crim;
  TR, Syr., Palest., Cauc., N-Iran, C-As.,
  NW-Afr., nat. in H, Sw
– *gracillimum* Hook. f. = Jasminum
  multiflorum
– **grandiflorum** L. · E:Royal Jasmine;
  G:Chinesischer Tee-Jasmin · ♄ D Z9 🐝
  VI-IX Ⓝ; SW-Arab.
– **humile** L. · E:Italian Yellow Jasmine;
  G:Niedriger Jasmin · ♄ e Z7; C-As., Afgh.,
  Him., Ind., SW-China, Burma
– f. **farreri** (Gilmour) P.S. Green · 🌰;
  N-Burma
– f. **wallichanum** (Lindl.) P.S. Green · 🌰;
  Nepal
– var. *glabrum* (DC.) Kobuski = Jasminum
  humile f. wallichanum
– var. *revolutum* (Sims) Stokes = Jasminum
  humile
– **mesnyi** Hance · E:Primrose Jasmine;
  G:Primel-Jasmin · ♄ e Z8 🌰 III-IV;
  W-China
– **multiflorum** (Burm. f.) Andrews · E:Star
  Jasmine; G:Sternblütiger Jasmin · ♄ e ⚄
  D 🐝 I-III; Ind.
– **nitidum** Skan · E:Angelwing Jasmine;
  G:Engelsflügel-Jasmin · ♄ e ⚄ D 🐝;
  N.Guinea (Admiralty Is.)
– **nobile** C.B. Clarke
– subsp. **rex** (Dunn) P.S. Green · ♄ e Z8 🐝;
  SW-Thail.
– **nudiflorum** Lindl. · E:Winter Jasmine;
  F:Jasmin d'hiver; G:Winter-Jasmin · ♄ d
  Z7 XII-III; W-China, nat. in F
– **odoratissimum** L. · E:Yellow Jasmine;
  G:Duftender Jasmin · ♄ e D 🌰 VI-IX Ⓝ;

Canar., Madeira
- **officinale** L. · E:Common Jasmine, Jessamine, White Jasmine; F:Jasmin officinal; G:Echter Jasmin, Weißer Jasmin · ♄ d Z8 ⊛ ⚥ ; Him., Kashmir, SW-China, nat. in Eur.: Ib, F, Ital-P, RO, ? Sw; Cauc., Iran
- **parkeri** Dunn · E:Dwarf Jasmine; G:Zwerg-Jasmin · ♄ e Z8 ⊛ ∧ VI; NW-Him.
- **polyanthum** Franch. · ♄ s ⚘ D Z8 ⊛ VI-IX; W-China
- *primulinum* Hemsl. = Jasminum mesnyi
- **pubigerum** D. Don · ♄ ⊛; Him.
- var. *glabrum* DC. = Jasminum humile f. wallichanum
- *rex* Dunn = Jasminum nobile subsp. rex
- **sambac** (L.) Aiton · E:Arabian Jasmine; G:Arabischer Jasmin · ♄ e ⚘ D Z9 ⊛ III-X Ⓝ; Ind., Sri Lanka
- × **stephanense** Lemoine (*J. beesianum* × *J. officinale*) · ♄ d ⚘ D Z7 ⊛ VI-VII; cult.
- **subhumile** W.W. Sm. · ♄ d Z8 ⊛; W-China; Him.
- **volubile** Jacq. · E:Wild Jasmine; G:Wilder Jasmin · ♄ e ⚘ ⊛ II-IV; Austr.
- *wallichianum* Lindl. = Jasminum humile f. wallichanum

Jateorhiza Miers -f- *Menispermaceae* · 2 spp.
- *columba* (Roxb.) Oliv. = Jateorhiza palmata
- **palmata** (Lam.) Miers · E:Calumba Root · ♄ ⚘ ⊛ ⚥ Ⓝ; E-Afr., Mozamb., Mauritius

Jatropha L. -f- *Euphorbiaceae* · 189 spp. · E:Physicnut; F:Jatropha; G:Purgiernuss
- *berlandieri* Torr. = Jatropha cathartica
- **cathartica** Terán & Berland. · G:Purgiernuss · ♄ ⚘ ⊛; Mex.
- **curcas** L. · E:Barbados Nut, Physic Nut; G:Termitenbaum · ⚘ ⚘ Z10 ⊛ ⚘ Ⓝ; Mex., Bermuda, S-Am.
- **macrocarpa** Griseb. · ♄ ⚘ Z10 ⊛; Arg.
- *manihot* L. = Manihot esculenta
- **multifida** L. · E:Coral Nut, St Vincent Physic Nut; G:Korallen-Pugiernuss · ♄ ⚘ Z10 ⊛ VII ⚘ Ⓝ; Mex., W.Ind., Venez., Braz.
- **podagrica** Hook. · E:Guatemalan Rhubarb; G:Guatemalarhabarber · ♄ ⚘ Z10 ⊛ V-VI ⚘; Guat., Nicar., Costa Rica, Panama
- *urens* L. = Cnidoscolus urens var. urens

Jeffersonia Barton -f- *Berberidaceae* · 2 spp. · E:Twin Leaf; F:Jeffersonia; G:Herzblattschale, Zwillingsblatt
- **diphylla** (L.) Pers. · E:Rheumatism Root; G:Zwillingsblatt · ⚘ △ Z5 V-VI; Can.: Ont.; USA: NE, NCE, SE
- **dubia** (Maxim.) Benth. & Hook. f. · E:Twin-Leaf; G:Herzblattschale · ⚘ △ Z5 IV-V; Manch.

Jensenobotrya A.G.J. Herre -f- *Aizoaceae* · 1 sp.
- **lossowiana** A.G.J. Herre · ⚘ ⚘ Z9 ⊛; Namibia

Jessenia H. Karst. = Oenocarpus
- *bataua* (Mart.) Burret = Oenocarpus bataua

Joannesia Vell. -f- *Euphorbiaceae* · 2 spp.
- **princeps** Vell. · ♄ Z8 ⊛ Ⓝ; Venez., N-Braz.

Jovellana Ruiz & Pav. -f- *Scrophulariaceae* · 6 spp.
- **punctata** Ruiz & Pav. · ♄ e Z9 ⊛ VI-VII; S-Chile
- **sinclairii** (Hook.) Kraenzl. · ♄ e Z9 ⊛ VI-VII; NZ
- **violacea** (Cav.) G. Don · ♄ e Z9 ⊛ VII-VIII; Chile

Jovibarba (DC.) Opiz -f- *Crassulaceae* · 4 spp. · E:Houseleek; F:Barbe-de-Jupiter; G:Donarsbart, Fransenhauswurz
- *allionii* (Jord. & Fourr.) D.A. Webb = Jovibarba globifera subsp. allionii
- *arenaria* (W.D.J. Koch) Opiz = Jovibarba globifera subsp. arenaria
- **globifera** (L.) J. Parn. · E:Hen and Chickens; G:Gewöhnlicher Fransenhauswurz
- subsp. **allionii** (Jord. & Fourr.) J. Parn. · G:Allionis Fransenhauswurz · ⚘ △ Z7 VII ▽; Eur.: I; SW-Alp.
- subsp. **arenaria** (W.D.J. Koch) J. Parn. · G:Sand-Fransenhauswurz · ⚘ △ Z7 VIII ▽; Eur.: A, I; E-Alp., nat. in D (Fichtelgebirge)
- subsp. **globifera** · G:Jupiterbart, Sprossende Fransenhauswurz · ⚘ △ Z5 VII ▽; Eur.: G, A, EC-Eur.
- subsp. **hirta** (L.) J. Parn. · G:Kurzhaar-Fransenhauswurz · ⚘ △ Z7 VII-VIII ▽; Eur.: I, A, H, W-Ba
- **heuffelii** (Schott) Á. Löve & D. Löve

- **many cultivars**
- var. **heuffelii** · G:Balkan-Fransen-hauswurz · ⟇ Ψ △ Z6 VIII ▽; Eur.: Ba, RO; mts.
- *hirta* (L.) Opiz = Jovibarba globifera subsp. hirta
- *sobolifera* (Sims) Opiz = Jovibarba globifera subsp. globifera

Juanulloa Ruiz & Pav. -f- Solanaceae · 6-10 spp.
- **mexicana** (Schltdl.) Miers · ♄ e Z8 ⓦ VI-X; Peru

Jubaea Kunth -f- Arecaceae · 1 sp. · E:Honey Palm, Wine Palm; F:Palmier à miel; G:Honigpalme, Mähnenpalme
- **chilensis** (Molina) Baill. · E:Chilean Wine Palm, Wine Palm; G:Honigpalme, Mähnenpalme · ♄ e Z8 ⓚ; Chile
- *spectabilis* Humb., Bonpl. & Kunth = Jubaea chilensis

Juglans L. -f- Juglandaceae · 21 sp. · E:Walnut; F:Noyer; G:Walnuss
- **ailantifolia** Carrière
- var. **ailantifolia** · E:Japanese Walnut; G:Japanische Walnuss · ♄ d Z6; Jap.
- var. **cordiformis** (Maxim.) Rehder · E:Heartnut; F:Noyer du Japon; G:Herzfrüchtige Walnuss · ♄ d Z6 Ⓝ; Jap.
- **californica** S. Watson · E:Southern California Walnut · ♄ ♄ d Z8 ⓚ; S-Calif.
- var. *hindsii* Jeps. = Juglans hindsii
- **cinerea** L. · E:Butternut, White Walnut; F:Noyer cendré; G:Butternuss · ♄ d Z5 ⚘ Ⓝ; Can.: E; USA: NE, NCE, NC, SE
- *cordiformis* Maxim. = Juglans ailantifolia var. cordiformis
- var. *ailantifolia* (Carrière) Rehder = Juglans ailantifolia var. ailantifolia
- *glabra* Mill. = Carya glabra
- **hindsii** (Jeps.) Jeps. ex R.E. Sm. · E:California Walnut; G:Kalifornische Walnuss · ♄ d Z8 ⓚ Ⓝ; C-Calif.
- *honorei* Dode = Juglans neotropica
- × **intermedia** Jacques (*J. nigra* × *J. regia*) · ♄ d Z5; cult.
- **mandshurica** Maxim. · E:Manchurian Walnut; F:Noyer de Mandchurie; G:Mandschurische Walnuss · ♄ d Z5 Ⓝ; Amur, Manch.
- **microcarpa** Berland. · E:Texas Walnut; G:Felsen-Walnuss · ♄ d Z5 Ⓝ; USA: Kans., SC, N.Mex; NE-Mex.

- **neotropica** Diels · E:Andean Walnut · ♄ d Z10 ⓚ Ⓝ; Venez., Col, Ecuad., Peru, Bol.; And.
- **nigra** L. · E:Black Walnut; F:Noyer noir d'Amérique; G:Schwarze Walnuss · ♄ d Z5 V Ⓝ; Can.: Ont.; USA: NE, NCE, NC, SC, SE, Fla.
- **regia** L.
- subsp. **fallax** (Dode) Popov · ♄ d Z6 Ⓝ; C-As.
- subsp. **kamaonica** (C. DC.) Mansf. · ♄ d Z6 Ⓝ; C-Him.
- subsp. **regia** · E:English Walnut, Persian Walnut; F:Noyer commun; G:Echte Walnuss · ♄ d Z6 V ⚘ Ⓝ; Eur.: A, I, Sic., Ba, RO; Cauc., Iran, C-As., nat. in BrI, Fr, Ib, EC-Eur., E-Eur.
- subsp. **turcomanica** Popov · ♄ d Z6 Ⓝ; C-As. (Kopet Dagh)
- *rupestris* Engelm. ex Torr. = Juglans microcarpa
- *sieboldiana* Maxim. = Juglans ailantifolia var. ailantifolia
- **stenocarpa** Maxim. · F:Noyer; G:Schmal-früchtige Walnuss · ♄ d; Manch.

Juncus L. -m- Juncaceae · 316 spp. · E:Rush; F:Jonc; G:Binse
- **acutiflorus** Ehrh. ex Hoffm. · E:Sharp-flowered Rush; G:Spitzblütige Binse · ⟇ ⌇ VII-IX; Eur.*, TR, Palest., Iran, Moroc.
- **alpinoarticulatus** Chaix · E:Alpine Rush; G:Alpen-Binse · ⟇ ⌇ VII-VIII; Eur.*, TR, Cauc., W-Sib., E-Sib., Kamchat., NW-Afr., N-Am.
- *alpinus* Vill. = Juncus alpinoarticulatus
- **anceps** Laharpe · G:Zweischneidige Binse · ⟇ ⌇ VII-VIII; Eur.: Ib, Fr, G, Sc, Ital-P, Ba; Alger., Tun.; coasts
- **arcticus** Willd. · E:Arctic Rush; G:Arktische Binse · ⟇ VII-VIII; Eur.: Sc, N-Russ., Fr, Ital-P, C-Eur., ? Ib; N, Alp., Apenn.; Sib., Greenl.
- **articulatus** L. · E:Joint Leaf Rush, Jointed Rush; G:Gewöhnliche Glieder-Binse · ⟇ ⌇ VII-X; Eur.*, TR, Cauc., Iran, C-As., E-Sib., N-Afr.
- **atratus** Krock. · G:Schwarze Binse · ⟇ ⌇ VII-IX; Eur.: Ital-P, C-Eur., EC-Eur., Ba, E-Eur.; Cauc., W-Sib., E-Sib., C-As., China
- **balticus** Willd. · E:Baltic Rush; F:Jonc de la Baltique; G:Baltische Binse · ⟇ ⌇ Z3 VII-VIII; Eur.: BrI, Sc, G, PL, E-Eur.; TR,

Alaska, Can., USA * exc. Fla
- **biglumis** L. · E:Two-flowered Rush;
G:Zweiblütige Binse · ⟁ ⁓ VII-VIII;
Eur.: BrI, Sc, N-Russ., A; W-Sib., E-Sib.,
Kamchat., N-Am.
- **bufonius** L. · E:Toad Rush; G:Kröten-
Binse · ⊙ ⁓ V-IX; Eur.*, cosmop.
- **bulbosus** L. · E:Bulbous Rush;
G:Gewöhnliche Rasen-Binse · ⟁ ⁓ Z5
VII-IX; Eur.*, Alger., Tun., Azor., Madeira
- **canadensis** J. Gay ex Laharpe ·
E:Canadian Rush; G:Kanadische Binse ·
⟁ ; Can: W; USA: NE, NCE, SE, nat. in B,
NL
- **capitatus** Weigel · E:Dwarf Rush;
G:Kopf-Binse · ⊙ VI-IX; Eur.*, TR,
SW-As., Afr., N-Afr.
- **castaneus** Sm. · E:Chestnut Rush;
G:Kastanienbraune Binse · ⟁ △ ⁓ Z3
VII; Eur.: BrI, Sc, C-Eur., I, EC-Eur.; Sib.,
Kamchat., Alaska, Can., USA: Rocky Mts.,
Calif., SW
- **compressus** Jacq. · E:Round-fruited
Rush; F:Jonc comprimé; G:Zusammenge-
drückte Binse · ⟁ ⁓ Z5 VII-IX; Eur.*,
Cauc., W-Sib., E-Sib., Mong.
- **conglomeratus** L. · E:Compact Rush;
G:Knäuel-Binse · ⟁ ⁓ V-VII; Eur.*, TR,
SW-As, NW-Afr., N-Am.
- *decipiens* (Buchenau) Nakai = Juncus
effusus
- **dudleyi** Wiegand · E:Dudley Rush;
G:Dudleys Binse · ⟁ VI-VIII; N-Am., nat.
in Scotland
- **effusus** L. · E:Common Rush, Soft Rush;
F:Jonc épars; G:Flatter-Binse · ⟁ ⁓ Z4
VI-VIII ⚡ ; Eur.*, TR
- **ensifolius** Wikstr. · E:Sword-leaved
Rush; G:Schwertblättrige Binse · ⟁ ⁓
Z3 VI-VIII; w N-Am., nat. in FIN
- **filiformis** L. · E:Thread Rush; G:Faden-
Binse · ⟁ ⁓ VI-VIII; Eur.*, TR, Cauc.,
W-Sib., E-Sib., N-Am.
- **gerardii** Loisel. · E:Saltmarsh Rush;
G:Bodden-Binse, Salz-Binse · ⟁ ⁓
VI-VII; Eur.*, TR, Levant, Iraq, Cauc.,
Iran, Afgh., W-Sib., C-As, N-Am.
- *glaucus* Sibth. = Juncus inflexus
- **hybridus** Brot. · ⟁ ⁓ ; Eur.: Ib, Fr,
Ital-P, Ba, ? RO; TR, SW-As.
- **inflexus** L. · E:Hard Rush; F:Jonc courbé;
G:Blaugrüne Binse · ⟁ ⁓ Z4 VI-VIII;
Eur.*, TR, Cauc., Iran, C-As.
- **jacquinii** L. · G:Gemsen-Binse, Jacquins
Binse · ⟁ VII-IX; Eur.: F, I, Sw, G, A,

Slove.; Alp., N-Apenn.
- *lampocarpus* Ehrh. ex Hoffm. = Juncus
articulatus
- **maritimus** Lam. · E:Sea Rush, Sparto;
F:Jonc maritime; G:Meerstrand-Binse,
Strand-Binse · ⟁ ⁓ VII-VIII; Eur.*, TR,
Cauc., Iran, C-As., NW-Ind., Macaron.,
Afr., N-Am., S-Am., Austr., NZ
- **minutulus** (Albert & Jahand.) Prain ·
E:Dwarf Toad Rush; G:Kleinste Binse · ⊙
VI-IX; Eur.* exc. Ba; W-Sib., C-As.
- **pygmaeus** Rich. & Thuill. · E:Pygmy
Rush; G:Zwerg-Binse · ⊙ ⁓ V-IX; Eur.:
Ib, Fr, BrI, Ital-P, G, DK, Croatia; TR,
NW-Afr.
- **ranarius** Perr. & Songeon · E:Frog Rush;
G:Frosch-Binse · ⊙ V-VIII; Eur.: BrI,
Sc, Fr, C-Eur., EC-Eur., E-Eur.; N-Am.,
Greenl.
- **sphaerocarpus** Nees · G:Kugelfrüchtige
Binse · ⊙ VI-VIII; Eur.: Ib, Fr, C-Eur.,
EC-Eur., Ba, E-Eur.; TR, Cauc., W-Sib.,
C-As.
- **squarrosus** L. · E:Heath Rush; G:Spar-
rige Binse · ⟁ VI-VIII; Eur.* exc. Ba;
Moroc., Greenl.
- **stygius** L. · E:Bog Rush; G:Moor-Binse
· ⟁ ⁓ VII-VIII ▽; Eur.: Sc, G, Sw, PL,
Russ.; W-Sib., Amur, Kamchat.
- **subnodulosus** Schrank · E:Blunt-
flowered Rush ; G:Stumpfblütige Binse
· ⟁ ⁓ Z6 VII-VIII; Eur.*, TR, Iraq, Syr.,
NW-Afr.
- **tenageia** Ehrh. ex L. f. · E:Sand Rush;
G:Sand-Binse · ⊙ ⁓ VI-VIII; Eur.* exc.
BrI, Sc; Cauc., W-Sib.
- **tenuis** Willd. · E:Slender Rush ; G:Zarte
Binse · ⟁ VI-IX; N-Am., nat. in Eur.*, TR,
Cauc.
- **trifidus** L. · G:Dreiblatt-Binse
- subsp. **monanthos** (Jacq.) Asch. &
Graebn. · G:Einblütige Binse, Wenig-
blütige Dreiblatt-Binse · ⟁ VII-VIII; Eur.:
Alp., Apenn.; N-Am.
- subsp. **trifidus** · E:Highland Rush;
G:Gewöhnliche Dreiblatt-Binse · ⟁ VII-
VIII; Eur.*, Cauc., Sib., N-Am., Greenl.
- **triglumis** L. · E:Three-flowered Rush;
G:Dreiblütige Binse · ⟁ ⁓ VII-VIII;
Eur.*, Cauc., W-Sib., E-Sib., C-As.

Juniperus L. -f- *Cupressaceae* · 53 spp. ·
E:Juniper; F:Genévrier; G:Wacholder
- **bermudiana** L. · E:Bermuda Juniper;
G:Bermuda-Wacholder · ♄ e Z9 🅰;

Bermuda
- *canadensis* Lodd. ex Burgsd. = Juniperus communis var. depressa
- **chinensis** L.
- **many cultivars**
- var. **chinensis** · E:Chinese Juniper; F:Genévrier de Chine; G:Gewöhnlicher Chinesischer Wacholder · ♄ ♄ e Z5 III-V; China, Mong., Jap.
- var. **sargentii** A. Henry · G:Sargents Chinesischer Wacholder · ♄ e Z4; NE-China, Jap.
- **communis** L. · E:Common Juniper, Juniper; G:Heide-Wacholder
- **many cultivars**
- subsp. *hemisphaerica* (J. Presl & C. Presl) Nyman = Juniperus communis var. communis
- var. **communis** · F:Genévrier commun; G:Gewöhnlicher Heide-Wacholder · ♄ ♄ e Z3 IV-V ⚥ ; Eur.*, TR, Cauc., Him., W-Sib., E-Sib., Amur, Sakhal., Kamchat., Manch., Korea, Jap., Moroc., Alger., Alaska, Can., USA* exc. Fla.
- var. **depressa** Pursh · G:Kanadischer Heide-Wacholder · ♄ Z3; Can.: E; USA: NE, NEC
- var. *erecta* Pursh = Juniperus communis var. communis
- var. *montana* Aiton = Juniperus communis var. saxatilis
- var. *nana* (Willd.) Baumg. = Juniperus communis var. saxatilis
- var. **saxatilis** Pall. · E:Mountain Juniper; G:Zwerg-Heide-Wacholder · ♄ Z3 VII-VIII; Eur. mts., Cauc., TR, C-As., Him., N-Sib., Amur, Sakhal., Kamchat., Mong., N-Korea, Jap., w N-Am., Greenl
- **convallium** Rehder & E.H. Wilson · G:Gewöhnlicher Mekong-Wacholder · ♄ e Z7; China
- *depressa* Steven = Juniperus communis var. communis
- **drupacea** Labill. · E:Syrian Juniper; G:Syrischer Wacholder · ♄ e Z8 ⌂; GR, TR, Syr.
- **excelsa** M. Bieb. · E:Greek Juniper; G:Griechischer Wacholder, Kleinasiatischer Wacholder
- subsp. **excelsa** · G:Gewöhnlicher Griechischer Wacholder · ♄ ♄ e Z8; Eur.: Ba, Crim; TR, W-Syr., Cyprus, Iran, Afgh.
- **foetidissima** Willd. · E:Stinking Juniper; G:Stinkender Baum-Wacholder · ♄ ♄ e Z8; Ba, Crim; TR, W-Syr., Cyprus, Cauc.

- *hemisphaerica* J. Presl & C. Presl = Juniperus communis var. communis
- **horizontalis** Moench · E:Creeping Juniper; F:Genévrier rampant; G:Kriech-Wacholder · ♄ e ⤳ △ Z4; Alaska, Can., USA: NE, NCE, Mont., Wyo.
- **many cultivars**
- *litoralis* Maxim. = Juniperus rigida subsp. conferta
- *macrocarpa* Sibth. & Sm. = Juniperus oxycedrus subsp. macrocarpa
- × *media* Melle = Juniperus × pfitzeriana
- *nana* Willd. = Juniperus communis var. saxatilis
- **occidentalis** Hook. · E:Western Juniper; G:Gewöhnlicher Westlicher Wacholder · ♄ e Z5; USA: Wash., Oreg., Idaho, Nev., Calif.
- **oxycedrus** L. · E:Prickly Juniper; G:Stech-Wacholder · Z8
- subsp. **macrocarpa** (Sibth. & Sm.) Ball · G:Großfrüchtiger Stech-Wacholder · ♄ e Z8; Eur.: Ib, F, Ital-P, Ba; NW-Afr., Libya; coasts
- subsp. **oxycedrus** · G:Rotbeeriger Stech-Wacholder · ♄ ♄ e Z7 ⚥ ; Eur.: Ib, Fr, Ital-P, Ba, Crim; TR, Levant, Cauc., N-Iran, N-Afr.
- × **pfitzeriana** (Späth) P.A. Schmidt (*J. chinensis* var. *chinensis* × *J. sabina* var. *sabina*) · G:Pfitzers Wacholder · ♄ e; cult.
- **many cultivars**
- **phoenicea** L. · E:Phoenician Juniper; G:Gewöhnlicher Phönizischer Wacholder · ♄ ♄ e Z9 ⌂ Ⓝ; Eur.: Ib, Fr, Ital-P, Ba; W-TR, Cyprus, Palest., NW-Afr., Libya
- **procera** Hochst. ex Endl. · E:East African Juniper; G:Ostafrikanischer Wacholder · ♄ e Z9 ⌂ Ⓝ; Eth., Kenya, Tanzania, Mozamb., Zimbabwe
- **procumbens** (Siebold ex Endl.) Miq. · E:Japanese Juniper; G:Japanischer Kriech-Wacholder · ♄ e Z6; S-Jap.
- *prostrata* Pers. = Juniperus horizontalis
- **recurva** Buch.-Ham. ex D. Don · E:Drooping Juniper, Himalayan Weeping Juniper; G:Hänge-Wacholder, Himalaya-Wacholder
- var. **coxii** (A.B. Jacks.) Melville · E:Coffin Juniper; G:Langnadliger Hänge-Wacholder · ♄ e Z7; E-Burma
- var. **recurva** · G:Gewöhnlicher Hänge-Wacholder · ♄ ♄ e Z8; Sikkim, Bhutan, SW-China
- **rigida** Siebold & Zucc. · E:Temple

Juniper; G:Nadel-Wacholder
- subsp. **conferta** (Parl.) Kitam. · E:Shore
Juniper; F:Genévrier des rivages;
G:Strand-Wacholder · ♄ e ∿ △ Z6; Jap.,
Sakhal.
- subsp. **rigida** · F:Genévrier à aiguilles;
G:Gewöhnlicher Nadel-Wacholder · ♄ ♄ e
Z6; Jap., Korea, N-China
- **sabina** L.
- var. **sabina** · E:Savin; F:Genévrier sabine;
G:Gewöhnlicher Stink-Wacholder · ♄ e
Z5 IV-V ⚘ ⚘; Eur.* exc. BrI, Sc; Cauc.,
Sib., C-As., Alger.; mts.
- **scopulorum** Sarg. · E:Colorado Juniper,
Rocky Mountain Juniper; F:Genévrier
des Montagnes Rocheuses; G:Felsenge-
birgs-Wacholder · ♄ e Z6 ⓝ; Can.: B.C.,
Alta.; USA: NW, Rocky Mts., NC, SW;
N-Mex.
- **semiglobosa** Regel · E:Russian Juniper;
G:Halbkugeliger Wacholder · ♄ ♄ e Z4;
C-As.
- *sibirica* Burgsd. = Juniperus communis
var. saxatilis
- **squamata** Buch.-Ham. ex D. Don · E:Blue
Star Juniper, Flaky Juniper; G:Schuppen-
Wacholder
- **many cultivars**
- var. **fargesii** Rehder & E.H. Wilson ·
G:Farges' Schuppen-Wacholder · ♄ e Z7;
SW-China
- var. **squamata** · F:Genévrier; G:Gewöhn-
licher Schuppen-Wacholder bleu · ♄ ♄ e
Z5; Him., W-China, C-China, Taiwan
- **taxifolia** Hook. & Arn. · E:Luchu Junipe;r
G:Luchu-Wacholder · ♄ ♄ e Z9 ⓐ; S-Jap.,
Ryukyu Is.
- **thurifera** L. · E:Spanish Juniper; G:Spa-
nischer Wacholder · ♄ e Z8 ⓐ; Eur.: sp.,
F, Cors; Moroc., Alger.
- **tibetica** Kom. · E:Tibetan Juniper;
G:Tibet-Wacholder · ♄ ♄ e Z6; E-Tibet,
W-China: Kansu
- **virginiana** L. · E:Eastern Red Cedar,
Pencil Cedar, Red Juniper; G:Rotzeder,
Virginischer Wacholder
- **some cultivars**
- var. *prostrata* (Pers.) Torr. = Juniperus
horizontalis
- var. **virginiana** · F:Bois à encens,
Genévrier de Virginie; G:Gewöhnlicher
Viriginischer Wacholder · ♄ ♄ e Z4 IV-V
⚘ ⓝ; Can.: E; USA: NE, NCE, SW, SC,
SE, Fla

Juno Tratt. = Iris
- *aucheri* (Baker) Klatt = Iris aucheri

Jurinea Cass. -f- *Asteraceae* · c. 250 spp. ·
F:Jurinée; G:Bisamdistel, Silberscharte
- **alata** (Desf.) Cass. · ⌗ Z6 VI-VII; Cauc.
- **cyanoides** (L.) Rchb. · G:Sand-Bisam-
distel, Sand-Silberscharte · ⌗ Z6 VII-VIII;
Eur.: G, CZ, Russ.; Cauc., W-Sib., C-As.
- *depressa* (Steven) C.A. Mey. = Jurinella
moschus
- **mollis** (L.) Rchb. · G:Silberscharte,
Spinnweben-Bisamdistel · ⌗ V-VII; Eur.:
Ital-P, A, EC-Eur., Ba, RO; TR

Jurinella Jaub. & Spach -f- *Asteraceae* ·
2 spp.
- **moschus** (Hablitz) Bobrov · ⌗ △ D Z6
VII-VIII; Cauc., TR

Justicia L. -f- *Acanthaceae* · c. 420 spp. ·
E:Water Willow; F:Bélopérone, Plante-
aux-crevettes ; G:Justizie, Purpurschopf,
Zimmerhopfen
- **adhatoda** L. · E:Malabar Nut · ♄ e Z10 ⓐ
⚘ ; S-Ind., Sri Lanka
- **brandegeeana** Wassh. & L.B. Sm. ·
E:Shrimp Plant; G:Garnelen-Justizie · ♄ e
ⓐ I-XII; NE-Mex., nat. in Fla.
- **carnea** Lindl. · E:Brazilian Plume Flower,
King's Crown, Pink Acanthus; G:Brazil-
ianische Justizie · ♄ e ⓐ ▽ VI-VIII; Braz.
- **carthaginensis** Jacq. · ♄ ⓐ IV-VII;
C-Am., W.Ind., trop. S-Am.
- **cydoniifolia** (Nees) Lindau · ♄ ⚘ ⓐ;
Braz.
- **ghiesbreghtiana** Lem. · ♄ ⓐ XI-II; Mex.
- **insularis** T. Anderson · ♄ e ⓐ ⓝ; W-Afr.,
C-Afr.
- *lanceolata* (Chapm.) Small = Justicia
ovata var. lanceolata
- **ovata** (Walter) Lindau · E:Looseflower
Water Willow
- var. **lanceolata** (Chapm.) R.W. Long · ⌗
ⓐ III; USA: Va., SE, Fla., Tex.
- var. **ovata** · ⌗; USA: Va., SE, Fla., Tex.
- *pauciflora* (Nees) Griseb. = Justicia
rizzinii
- × **penrhosiensis** (Carrière) L.H. Bailey
(*J. ghiesbreghtiana* × *J. pauciflora*) · ♄ ⓐ;
cult.
- *picta* L. = Graptophyllum pictum
- **plumbaginifolia** J. Jacq. · ♄ ⓐ XI-XII;
Braz.
- **rizzinii** Wassh. · ♄ ⓐ ▽ XII-II; Braz.

– *sanguinolenta* Vahl = Gymnostachyum
  sanguinolentum
– **spicigera** Schltdl. · ♄ e ⓦ; Mex., C-Am.
– *suberecta* André = Dicliptera suberecta
– *venusta* Wall. = Gymnostachyum
  venustum

Juttadinteria Schwantes -f- *Aizoaceae* ·
  5 spp.
– **deserticola** (Marloth) Schwantes · ⚁ ⅄
  Z9 ⓚ; Namibia

Kadsura Juss. -f- *Schisandraceae* · 22 spp. ·
  F:Kadsura; G:Kadsura, Kugelfaden
– **japonica** (L.) Dunal · ♄ e ⚸ ⚭ Z7 VII-XI;
  China, Jap., Taiwan

Kaempferia L. -f- *Zingiberaceae* · 29 spp. ·
  F:Kaempferia; G:Gewürzlilie
– **galanga** L. · E:Galanga; G:Indische
  Gewürzlilie · ⚁ D Z9 ⓦ VI-VIII ⚸ Ⓝ; Ind.
– **gilbertii** W. Bull · G:Gilberts Gewürzlilie ·
  ⚁ Z9 ⓦ VII-VIII; Ind.
– *ornata* N.E. Br. = Boesenbergia ornata
– *pandurata* Roxb. = Boesenbergia rotunda
– **roscoeana** Wall. · ⚁ Z9 ⓦ VII-IX; Burma
– **rotunda** L. · E:Resurrection Lily;
  G:Gefleckte Gewürzlilie · ⚁ D Z9 ⓦ
  VI-VIII Ⓝ; ? SE-As.
– **vittata** N.E. Br. · ⚁ Z9 ⓦ; Sumat.

Kalanchoe Adans. -f- *Crassulaceae* · c.
  110 spp. · F:Kalanchoe; G:Kalanchoe
– *beauverdii* Raym.-Hamet = Bryophyllum
  scandens
– **beharensis** Drake · E:Felt Bush, Felt
  Plant · ♄ ⅄ Z8 ⓚ; S-Madag.
– **bentii** C.H. Wright ex Hook. f. · ♄ ⅄ e Z8
  ⓚ IV-V; S-Arab.
– **blossfeldiana** Poelln. · E:Flaming Katy;
  G:Flammendes Käthchen · ♄ ⅄ e Z8 ⓚ ⬭
  II-V; Madag.
– **some cultivars**
– *carnea* N.E. Br. = Kalanchoe laciniata
– *coccinea* Welw. ex Britten = Kalanchoe
  crenata
– **crenata** (Andrews) Haw. · ♄ ⅄ e Z8 ⓚ
  V-VI; E-Afr., Ind. Thail.
– *crenata* (Baker) Raym.-Hamet =
  Bryophyllum laxiflorum
– *daigremontiana* Raym.-Hamet & H.
  Perrier = Bryophyllum daigremontianum
– *deficiens* Asch. & Schweinf.
– *flammea* Stapf = Kalanchoe glaucescens
– **glaucescens** Britten · ⚁ ⅄ Z8 ⓚ XII;

Somalia
– **globulifera** H. Perrier · ⚁ ⅄ Z8 ⓚ;
  Madag.
– **grandiflora** Wight & Arn. · ♄ ⅄ Z8 ⓚ V;
  E-Afr., Ind.
– *integra* (Medik.) Kuntze = Kalanchoe
  deficiens
– var. *crenata* (Andrews) Cufod. =
  Kalanchoe crenata
– × **kewensis** Dyer (*K. bentii* subsp. *bentii* ×
  K. glaucescens) · ♄ ⅄ e Z8 ⓚ; cult.
– **laciniata** (L.) DC. · E:Beach Bells · ♄ ⅄ e
  Z8 ⓚ V-VI; Braz., E-Afr., S-Afr., Yemen,
  Ind., Malay. Arch.
– *laxiflora* Baker = Bryophyllum laxiflorum
– **longiflora** Schltr. ex J.M. Wood ·
  E:Kalanchoe · ⚁ ⅄ Z8 ⓚ; S-Afr.: Natal
– *macrantha* Baker = Kalanchoe marmorata
– *manginii* Raym.-Hamet & H. Perrier =
  Bryophyllum manginii
– **marmorata** Baker · E:Pen Wiper Plant ·
  ⚁ ♄ ⅄ e Z8 ⓚ V-VI; Sudan, Eth., E-Afr.,
  C-Afr., Ind.
– *miniata* Hilsenb. & Bojer = Bryophyllum
  miniatum
– **peltata** (Baker) Baill. · ♄ ⅄ Z8 ⓚ; Eth.
– **petitiana** A. Rich. · ♄ ⅄ Z8 ⓚ; Eth.
– *pinnata* (Lam.) Pers. = Bryophyllum
  pinnatum
– *porphyrocalyx* (Baker) Baill. = Bryophyllum porphyrocalyx
– *prolifera* (Bowie) Raym.-Hamet =
  Bryophyllum proliferum
– **quartiniana** A. Rich. · ⚁ ⅄ Z8 ⓚ I-III;
  Eth., Malawi
– **rotundifolia** (Haw.) Haw. · ⚁ ⅄ Z8 ⓚ
  XII-IV; Cape, Socotra
– *schizophylla* (Baker) Baill. = Bryophyllum
  schizophyllum
– *somaliensis* Baker = Kalanchoe marmorata
– **spathulata** DC.
– *teretifolia* Deflers = Kalanchoe bentii
– **thyrsiflora** Harv. · ⚁ ⅄ Z8 ⓚ IV-V;
  S-Afr.: Cape, Transvaal
– *tomentosa* Baker · E:Panda Plant,
  Pussy Ears; G:Katzenohr · ♄ ⅄ e Z8 ⓚ;
  C-Madag.
– *tubiflora* (Harv.) Raym.-Hamet =
  Bryophyllum delagoense
– *uniflora* (Stapf) Raym.-Hamet =
  Bryophyllum uniflorum
– **velutina** Welw. ex Britten · ⚁ ⅄ Z8 ⓚ;
  C-Afr., Angola, Tanzania

Kalimeris (Cass.) Cass. -f- *Asteraceae* ·
10 spp. · F:Caliméris; G:Schönaster
– **incisa** (Fisch.) DC. · G:Schönaster · ⌱ Z4
VII-IX; N-Sib., N-China, Manch., Korea,
Jap.
– *integrifolia* hort. = Kalimeris incisa
– **mongolica** (Franch.) Kit. · E:Mongolia
Aster; G:Mongolische Schönaster · ⌱ Z6
VII-IX; China (Mongolia)

Kalmia L. -f- *Ericaceae* · 7 spp. · E:Sheep
Laurel; F:Kalmia; G:Berglorbeer,
Lorbeerrose
– **angustifolia** L. · E:Lambkill, Sheep
Laurel; F:Laurier des moutons;
G:Schmalblättrige Lorbeerrose · ♄ Z5
VI-VII ✿; Can.: E; USA; NE, NCE, SE,
nat. in G, NW-GB
– **hirsuta** Walter · E:Hairy Laurel;
G:Behaarte Lorbeerrose · ♄ e Z8 ⓚ VI-VII
✿; SE-USA
– **latifolia** L. · E:Calico Bush, Mountain
Laurel; F:Laurier des montagnes;
G:Berglorbeer, Breitblättrige Lorbeerrose
· ♄ e Z5 V-VI ✤ ✿; Can.: E; USA: NE,
NCE, SE, Fla.
– **some cultivars**
– **polifolia** Wangenh. · E:Bog Laurel,
Swamp Laurel; G:Östliche Sumpf-
Lorbeerrose, Poleiblättrige Lorbeerrose
· ♄ e Z2 V-VI ✿; Alaska, Can., USA: NE,
NCE, Rocky Mts., NW, nat. in BrI

Kalopanax Miq. -m- *Araliaceae* · 1 sp. ·
E:Tree Aralia; F:Aralia en arbre, Kalopanax; G:Baumaralie, Baumkraftwurz
– *pictus* (Thunb.) Nakai = Kalopanax
septemlobus
– *ricinifolius* (Siebold & Zucc.) Miq. =
Kalopanax septemlobus
– **septemlobus** (Thunb.) Koidz.
– var. **maximowiczii** (Van Houtte) Hand.-
Mazz. · ♄ d Z5 V; China, Jap.
– var. **septemlobus** · E:Castor Aralia,
Tree Aralia; F:Kalopanax du Japon;
G:Baumaralie, Baumkraftwurz · ♄ ♄ d
Z5 VII-VIII; China, Amur, Manch., Korea,
Jap., Sakhal.

Keckiella Straw -f- *Scrophulariaceae* ·
7 spp.
– **cordifolia** (Benth.) Straw · E:American
Wild Fuchsia; G:Kalifornischer Bartfaden
· ꜰ ⚥ Z8 ⓚ VI-VIII; S-Calif.

Kedrostis Medik. -f- *Cucurbitaceae* · 23 spp.
– **africana** (L.) Cogn. · ⌱ � ⚥ Z10 ⓦ;
Namibia, S-Afr.
– *punctulata* (Sond.) Cogn. = Kedrostis
africana

Kennedia Vent. -f- *Fabaceae* · 16 spp. ·
E:Coral Pea; F:Kennedia; G:Kennedie,
Purpurbohne
– **coccinea** Vent. · ♄ e ⚥ Z10 ⓚ IV-IX;
W-Austr.
– *comptoniana* (Andrews) Link = Harden-
bergia comptoniana
– **macrophylla** (Meisn.) Benth. · ♄ e ⚥ Z10
ⓚ; W-Austr.
– *monophylla* Vent. = Hardenbergia
violacea
– **nigricans** Lindl. · E:Black Bean;
G:Schwarze Purpurbohne · ♄ ⚥ Z10 ⓚ
V-VI; W-Austr.
– **prostrata** R. Br. · E:Running Postman,
Scarlet Coral Pea; G:Scharlach-
Purpurbohne · ♄ ↝ Z10 ⓚ IV-VI; Austr.,
Tasman.
– **rubicunda** (Schneev.) Vent. · E:Dusky
Coral Pea; G:Dunkle Purpurbohne · ♄
ꜰ e ⚥ Z10 ⓚ IV-VI; Austr.: N.S.Wales,
Victoria

Kensitia Fedde = Erepsia
– *pillansii* (Kensit) Fedde = Erepsia pillansii

Kentia Blume = Howea
– *baueri* (Hook. f. ex Lem.) Seem. =
Rhopalostylis baueri
– *belmoreana* C. Moore & F. Muell. =
Howea belmoreana
– *canterburyana* C. Moore & F. Muell. =
Hedyscepe canterburyana
– *forsteriana* C. Moore & F. Muell. = Howea
forsteriana
– *macarthurii* H. Wendl. ex H.J. Veitch =
Ptychosperma macarthurii
– *mooreana* F. Muell. = Lepidorrhachis
mooreana
– *sapida* (Sol. ex G. Forst.) Mart. =
Rhopalostylis sapida

Kentiopsis Brongn. -f- *Arecaceae* · 4 spp.
– *macrocarpa* Brongn. = Chambeyronia
macrocarpa
– **oliviformis** (Brongn. & Gris) Brongn. · ♄;
N.Caled.

Kernera Medik. -f- *Brassicaceae* · 2 spp. ·

F:Kernéra; G:Kugelschötchen
- **saxatilis** (L.) Sweet · G:Kugelschötchen · ♃ △ Z3 VI-VII; Eur.* exc. BrI, Sc

Kerria DC. -f- *Rosaceae* · 1 sp. · E:Kerria; F:Corète; G:Kerrie, Ranunkelstrauch
- **japonica** (L.) DC. · E:Japanese Rose, Jew's Mallow, Kerria; F:Corête du Japon; G:Japanisches Goldröschen, Kerrie, Ranunkelstrauch · ♄ d Z5 V; W-China, C-China, nat. in Sw, W-Russ.

Keteleeria Carrière -f- *Pinaceae* · 3 spp. · G:Goldtanne, Stechtanne
- **davidiana** (Bertrand) Beissn. · G:Gewöhnliche Sichuan-Stechtanne · ♄ e Z7 Ⓝ; W-China
- **fortunei** (A. Murray bis) Carrière · G:Hongkong-Stechtanne · ♄ e Z9 Ⓚ; SE-China

Khaya A. Juss. -f- *Meliaceae* · 7 spp. · E:Mahogany; F:Acajou d'Afrique; G:Mahagonibaum
- **anthotheca** (Welw.) C. DC. · E:White Mahogany; G:Weißer Mahagonibaum · ♄ Ⓦ Ⓝ; W-Afr., C-Afr., Uganda, Angola
- **grandifoliola** C. DC. · G:Benin-Mahagonibaum; E:Benin Mahogani · ♄ Ⓦ Ⓝ; W-Afr.
- **ivorensis** A. Chev. · E:African Mahogany; G:Afrikanischer Mahagonibaum · ♄ Ⓦ Ⓝ; W-Afr.
- **nyasica** Stapf ex Baker f. · ♄ Ⓦ Ⓝ; Cameroon, Zaire (Katanga), Zambia, Zimbabwe
- **senegalensis** (Desr.) A. Juss. · E:Dryzone Mahogany; G:Savannen-Mahgonibaum · ♄ Ⓦ Ⓝ; trop. Afr.

Kickxia Dumort. -f- *Scrophulariaceae* · 47 spp. · E:Fluellen; F:Kickxia; G:Tännelkraut
- **elatine** (L.) Dumort. · E:Sharp-leaved Fluellen; G:Spießblättriges Tännelkraut · ⊙ ♃ Z9 VII-X; Eur.*, TR, Iran, Madeira, Eth., nat. in USA
- **spuria** (L.) Dumort. · E:Round-leaved Fluellen; G:Eiblättriges Tännelkraut · ⊙ ♃ Z9 VII-X; Eur.* exc. Sc; TR, Syr., Cyprus, N-Afr., nat. in DK

Kigelia DC. -f- *Bignoniaceae* · 1 sp. · E:Sausage Tree; F:Arbre-à-saucisses; G:Götzenholz, Leberwurstbaum
- **africana** (Lam.) Benth. · E:Sausage Tree; G:Leberwurstbaum · ♄ Z10 Ⓦ; trop. Afr.
- *pinnata* (Jacq.) DC. = Kigelia africana

× **Kirchara** hort. -f- *Orchidaceae* (*Epidendrum* × *Laelia* × *Sophronitis* × *Cattleya*)

Kirengeshoma Yatabe -f- *Hydrangeaceae* · 1 sp. · F:Fleur de cire; G:Wachsglocke
- *koreana* Nakai = Kirengeshoma palmata Koreana Group
- **palmata** Yatabe · F:Fleur de cire; G:Wachsglocke · ♃ Z5 VIII-IX; Jap.
- **Koreana Group** · ♃; Korea

Kitaibela Willd. -f- *Malvaceae* · 2 spp. · G:Kitaibelie
- **vitifolia** Willd. · G:Kitaibelie · ♃ Z6 VII-VIII; Eur.: Bosn., YU, nat. in H, RO

Kitchingia Baker = Bryophyllum
- *porphyrocalyx* Baker = Bryophyllum porphyrocalyx
- *schizophylla* Baker = Bryophyllum schizophyllum
- *uniflora* Stapf = Bryophyllum uniflorum

Kleinia Mill. -f- *Asteraceae* · c. 40 spp. · F:Séneçon; G:Kleinie
- **amaniensis** (Engl.) A. Berger · ♃ ♆ Z10 Ⓚ; Tanzania
- **anteuphorbia** (L.) Haw. · E:Groundsel · ♄ ♆ Z9 Ⓚ; Cape, S-Moroc.
- *articulata* (L. f.) Haw. = Senecio articulatus
- **fulgens** Hook. f. · ♃ ♆ Z10 Ⓚ; S-Afr.: Natal
- **galpinii** A. Berger · ♄ ♄ ♆ e Z9 Ⓚ XII-I; S-Afr.: Transvaal
- *gonoclada* DC. = Senecio radicans
- *haworthii* (Sweet) DC. = Senecio haworthii
- *herreana* (Dinter) Merxm. = Senecio herreanus
- **longiflora** DC. · ♄ ♆ Z10 Ⓚ; Eth., trop. Afr., S-Afr.
- **neriifolia** Haw. · ♄ ♆ Z9 Ⓚ; Canar.
- **petraea** (R.E. Fr.) C. Jeffrey · ♄ ♆ ⟿ Z10 Ⓚ; Kenya, Tanzania
- *radicans* (L. f.) Haw. = Senecio radicans
- **semperviva** (Forssk.) DC. · ♃ ♆ Z9 Ⓚ; Eth., Tanzania
- **stapeliiformis** (E. Phillips) Stapf · ♃ ♆ Z9 Ⓚ; S-Afr.

tomentosa Haw. = Senecio haworthii

Knautia L. -f- *Dipsacaceae* · 60 spp. ·
E:Field Scabious; F:Knautia, Scabieuse;
G:Knautie, Witwenblume
– **arvensis** (L.) Coult. · E:Blue Buttons,
Field Scabious; G:Wiesen-Witwenblume
· ⚁ Z6 VII-IX; Eur.*, Cauc., Iran, W-Sib.,
C-As., nat. in Sakhal.
– **carinthiaca** Ehrend. · G:Kärntner Wit-
wenblume · ⚁ VI-VIII; Eur.: A (Kärnten)
– **dipsacifolia** Kreutzer · E:Wood Scabious;
G:Gewöhnliche Wald-Witwenblume · ⚁
VI-IX; Eur.: Fr, I, C-Eur., EC-Eur., E-Eur.,
Bosn., Serb.
– **drymeia** Heuff. · G:Ungarische Witwen-
blume
– subsp. **drymeia** · G:Gewöhnliche
Ungarische Witwenblume · ⚁ V-IX; Eur.:
I, C-Eur., EC-Eur., Ba, RO
– subsp. **intermedia** (Pernh. & Wettst.)
Ehrend. · G:Mittlere Ungarische Witwen-
blume · ⚁ V-VIII; Eur.: E-Alp., N-Apenn.
– **godetii** Reut. · G:Godets Witwenblume ·
⚁ VI-VIII; Eur.: F, Sw; mts.
– **integrifolia** (L.) Bertol. · G:Einjährige
Witwenblume · ☉; Eur.: Ib, Fr, Ital-P, Ba;
TR, Levant, nat. in Sw
– **kitaibelii** (Schult.) Borbás · G:Gelbe
Witwenblume · ⚁ VII-VIII; Eur.: G, A,
EC-Eur.
– **longifolia** (Waldst. & Kit.) W.D.J. Koch ·
G:Langblatt-Witwenblume · ⚁ VII-VIII;
Eur.: I, C-Eur., Ba, E-Eur.; Alp., Carp.,
Balkan
– **macedonica** Griseb. · F:Knautie de
Macédoine · ⚁ Z6 VII-VIII; Eur.: Ba, RO
– **magnifica** Boiss. & Orph. · ⚁ VII-VIII; GR
– × **norica** Ehrend. (*K. carinthiaca* × *K.
drymeia*) · G:Norische Witwenblume · ⚁
VI-VIII; Eur.: A (Kärnten, Steiermark)
– **purpurea** (Vill.) Borbás · G:Purpur-
Witwenblume · ⚁ VII-VIII; Eur.: sp., F, I,
Sw
– *sylvatica* (L.) Duby = Knautia dipsacifolia
– **transalpina** (H. Christ) Briq. · ⚁ VII-VIII;
Eur.: I, Sw; S-Alp.
– **velutina** Briq. · G:Samtige Witwenblume · ⚁ VII-VIII; Eur.: I; S-Alp.

Kniphofia Moench -f- *Asphodelaceae* ·
71 sp. · E:Red Hot Poker, Torch Lily;
F:Tritome; G:Fackellilie, Tritome
– *alooides* Moench = Kniphofia uvaria
– *burchellii* (Herb. ex Lindl.) Kunth =

Kniphofia uvaria
– **ensifolia** Baker · ⚁ Z8 ∧ VI-VII; S-Afr.
– **foliosa** Hochst. · ⚁ Z8 ⚑ VIII-IX; Eth.
– **galpinii** Baker · F:Faux aloès; G:Galpins
Fackellilie · ⚁ Z8 ▭ ∧ IX-X; S-Afr.:
Natal, Transvaal
– **gracilis** Harv. ex Baker · ⚁ Z8 ⚑ VI-VIII;
S-Afr.: Natal
– **laxiflora** Kunth · ⚁ Z8; S-Afr. (E-Cape
Prov., Natal)
– *nelsoni* Mast. = Kniphofia triangularis
– **praecox** Baker · G:Frühe Fackellilie · ⚁
Z7 ⚑; S-Afr. (S-Cape Prov.)
– **pumila** (Aiton) Kunth · G:Kleine
Fackellilie · ⚁ Z8 ⚑ ∧ VIII; Sudan, Eth.,
Uganda, Zaire
– *quartiniana* A. Rich. = Kniphofia foliosa
– × **rufa** Leichtlin ex Baker (*K. angustifolia*
× ?) · ⚁ Z8 ⚑ ∧ VI-VIII
– **triangularis** Kunth · E:Red Hot Poker;
G:Orangefarbene Fackellilie · ⚁ ⚘ Z8 ⚑
∧ VII-IX; S-Afr.
– *tuckii* Baker = Kniphofia ensifolia
– **uvaria** (L.) Oken · E:Red Hot Poker,
Torch Lily; G:Schopf-Fackellilie · ⚁ ⚘ Z8
▭ ∧ VIII-IX; S-Afr.
– **Cultivars:**
– **many cultivars**

Kobresia Willd. -f- *Cyperaceae* · 73 spp. ·
E:False Sedge; G:Nacktried, Schuppen-
ried
– **myosuroides** (Vill.) Fiori · E:Bellardi
Bog Sedge; G:Europäisches Nacktried · ⚁
VI-VIII; Eur.* exc. BrI; N, mts.; ? Cauc.,
W-Sib., E-Sib., Kamchat., Mong., C-As.,
China, Jap., Korea, Alaska, Can., Rocky
Mts., Greenl.
– **simpliciuscula** (Wahlenb.) Mack. ·
E:Simple Bog Sedge; G:Europäisches
Schuppenried · ⚁ VII-VIII; Eur.* exc. Ib;
N, mts.; TR, Cauc., W-Sib., E-Sib., C-As;
N-Am.

Kobus Kaempf. ex Salisb. = Magnolia
– *acuminata* (L.) Nieuwl. = Magnolia
acuminata

Kochia Roth = Bassia
– *scoparia* (L.) Schrad. = Bassia scoparia
subsp. scoparia

Koeleria Pers. -f- *Poaceae* · 25-30
(-60) spp. · E:Hair Grass; F:Keulérie;
G:Schillergras

– **arenaria** (Dumort.) Conert · G:Sand-
Schillergras · ⹁ V-VI; Eur.* exc. Ital-P, Ba
– **cenisia** P. Rev. · G:Mont-Cenis-Schiller-
gras · ⹁ VII-VIII; Eur.: F, I, Sw; S-Alp.
– **eriostachya** Pančić · G:Wolliges
Schillergras · ⹁ VII-VIII; Eur.: I, Sw, A,
Ba, RO; E-Alp., Carp., Balkan; TR, Cauc.,
W-Iran
– **glauca** (Schrad.) DC. · E:Glaucous Hair
Grass; F:Keulérie bleue; G:Blaugrünes
Schillergras · ⹁ △ Z4 V-VII; Eur.* exc.
Ital-P, Ba; W-Sib., E-Sib., C-As.
– *gracilis* Pers. = Koeleria macrantha
– **hirsuta** (DC.) Gaudin · G:Behaartes
Schillergras · ⹁ VII-VIII; Eur.: I, Sw, A;
Alp.
– **macrantha** (Ledeb.) Schult. · E:Crested
Hair Grass; F:Koelérie à crête; G:Zierli-
ches Schillergras · ⹁ Z2 VI; Eur.* exc. Sc;
TR, Cauc., Iran, C-As., Sib., Afgh., Pakist.
– **pyramidata** (Lam.) P. Beauv. ·
E:Pyramidal Hair Grass; G:Großes
Schillergras, Pyramiden-Schillergras · ⹁
Z2 VI-VII; Eur.: Fr, Ital-P, C-Eur., EC-Eur.,
Ba, Dk, E-Eur.; TR
– **splendens** C. Presl · G:Glänzendes
Schillergras · ⹁ V-VII; Eur.: Ib, Fr, Ital-P,
A, Ba, E-Eur.; Moroc., Alger.
– **vallesiana** (Honck.) Gaudin · E:Somerset
Hair Grass; F:Koelérie du Valais; G:Wal-
liser Schillergras · ⹁ V-VI; Eur.: Ib, F, I,
Sw, G, BrI; NW-Afr.

Koellikeria Regel -f- *Gesneriaceae* · 3 spp.
– **erinoides** (DC.) Mansf. · ⹁ Z10 ⓜ
VII-VIII; C-Am., S-Am.

Koelreuteria Laxm. -f- *Sapindaceae* ·
3 spp. · E:Golden Rain Tree;
F:Koelreuteria, Savonnier; G:Blasenbaum
– **paniculata** Laxm. · E:Golden Rain Tree;
F:Savonnier; G:Rispiger Blasenbaum
– var. **apiculata** (Rehder & E.H. Wilson)
Rehder · ♄ d Z7 VII-VIII; China: Sichuan
– var. **paniculata** · ♄ d ⊗ Z7 VII-VIII;
China, Korea, Jap.

Kohleria Regel -f- *Gesneriaceae* · 17 spp. ·
F:Kohléria; G:Gleichsaum, Kohlerie
– **amabilis** (Planch. & Linden) Fritsch ·
G:Liebliche Kohlerie · ⹁ Z10 ⓜ IV-X; Col.
– **bogotensis** (G. Nicholson) Fritsch ·
G:Bogota-Kohlerie · ⹁ Z10 ⓜ VII-IX; Col.
– **digitaliflora** (Linden & André) Fritsch ·
G:Fingerhut-Kohlerie · ⹁ Z10 ⓜ VIII-IX;

Col.
– **eriantha** (Benth.) Hanst. · G:Wollblütige
Kohlerie · ⹁ Z10 ⓜ VIII-X; Col.
– **hirsuta** (Kunth) Regel · G:Borstige
Kohlerie · ♄ e Z10 ⓜ VIII-X; Col., Venez.,
Trinidad, Guyan.
– **lindeniana** (Regel) H.E. Moore · ⹁ Z10
ⓜ IX-X; Ecuad.
– **ocellata** (Hook.) Fritsch · G:Geäugte
Kohlerie · ⹁ Z10 ⓜ VII-IX; Col.
– **spicata** (Kunth) Oerst. · G:Ährige
Kohlerie · ⹁ Z10 ⓜ VII-IX; Mex., C-Am.,
trop. S-Am.
– *wageneri* Regel = Kohleria spicata
– **warscewiczii** (Regel) Hanst. · ⹁ Z10 ⓜ
VII-IX; Col.

Kohlrauschia Kunth = Petrorhagia
– *prolifera* (L.) Kunth = Petrorhagia
prolifera

Kolkwitzia Graebn. -f- *Caprifoliaceae* ·
1 sp. · E:Beauty Bush; F:Kolkwitzia;
G:Kolkwitzie
– **amabilis** Graebn. · E:Beauty Bush, Cold
Whisky Plant; F:Buisson de beauté;
G:Kolkwitzie · ♄ d Z5 V-VI; China: Hupeh

Komaroffia Kuntze -f- *Ranunculaceae* ·
2 spp.
– **bucharica** Schipcz. · ⊙; C-As.

Korolkowia Regel = Fritillaria
– *sewerzowii* (Regel) Regel = Fritillaria
sewerzowii

Krainzia Backeb. = Mammillaria
– *guelzowiana* (Werderm.) Backeb. =
Mammillaria guelzowiana
– *longiflora* (Britton & Rose) Backeb. =
Mammillaria longiflora

Krameria L. ex Loefl. -f- *Krameriaceae* ·
15 spp. · E:Rhatany; F:Kraméria,
Rhatania; G:Ratanhia
– **lappacea** (Dombey) Burdet & B.B.
Simpson · E:Rhatany; G:Ratanhia · ♄ ⓜ
⚥ ; Peru, Bol., Chile
– *triandra* Ruiz & Pav. = Krameria lappacea

Krascheninnikovia Gueldenst. -f-
Chenopodiaceae · 8 spp. · E:Winterfat;
G:Hornmelde
– **cerastoides** (L.) Gueldenst. · E:Pamirian
Winterfat; G:Hornmelde · ♄ d VII-IX;

Eur.: sp., A, H, W-Ba, E-Eur.; TR, Cauc.,
Iran, Pakist., W-Sib., E-Sib., C-As.,
Mong., China

Kummerowia Schindl. -f- *Fabaceae* ·
2 spp. · E:Bush Clover; F:Lespédéza;
G:Buschklee
– **stipulacea** (Maxim.) Makino · E:Korean
Bush Clover, Korean Lespedeza; G:Kore-
anischer Buschklee · ⊙ Ⓝ; N-China,
Amur, Manch., Korea, Jap., nat. in E-USA
– **striata** (Thunb. ex Murray) Schindl. ·
E:Japanese Bush Clover, Japanese
Lespedeza; G:Japanischer Buschklee · ⊙
Ⓝ; Ind., China, E-Sib., Manch., Korea,
Jap., Taiwan, nat. in S-USA, E-USA

Kunzea Rchb. -f- *Myrtaceae* · 36 spp.
– **ambigua** (Sm.) Druce · E:Tick Bush · ♄ e
Z9 ⓜ VIII-II; Austr.: N.S.Wales, Victoria,
Tasman.
– **baxteri** (Klotzsch) Schauer · E:Scarlet
Kunzea · ♄ e Z9 ⓚ V; W-Austr.
– **parvifolia** Schauer · E:Small-leaved
Kunzea · ♄ e Z9 ⓚ; Austr.: N.S.Wales,
Victoria
– **pomifera** F. Muell. · E:Native Cranber-
ries · ♄ e Z9 ⓚ; Austr.: S-Austr., Victoria
– **pulchella** (Lindl.) A.S. George ·
E:Granite Kunzea · ♄ e Z9 ⓚ; W-Austr.

Labisia Lindl. -f- *Myrsinaceae* · 6-9 spp.
– *malouiana* Linden & Rodigas = Ardisia
malouiana

Lablab Adans. -f- *Fabaceae* · 1 sp. ·
E:Hyacinth Bean; F:Dolique lablab;
G:Faselbohne
– *niger* hort. = Lablab purpureus
– **purpureus** (L.) Sweet · E:Bonavist,
Hyacinth Bean, Lablab; G:Faselbohne,
Lablab-Bohne · ⊙ ⚥ Z9 ⓚ Ⓝ; Afr.
– *vulgaris* Savi = Lablab purpureus

+ **Laburnocytisus** C.K. Schneid.
-m- *Fabaceae* · E:Adam's Laburnum;
G:Geißkleegoldregen
– **adamii** (Poit.) C.K. Schneid.
(*Chamaecytisus purpureus* × *Laburnum
anagyroides*) · E:Adam's Laburnum;
F:Cytise d'Adam; G:Geißkleegoldregen ·
♄ d VI; cult.

Laburnum Fabr. -n- *Fabaceae* · 2 spp. ·
E:Bean Tree, Golden Rain; F:Aubour,

Cytise, Cytise aubour, Faux-ébénier;
G:Goldregen
– **alpinum** (Mill.) Bercht. & J. Presl ·
E:Scotch Laburnum; F:Cytise des Alpes;
G:Alpen-Goldregen · ♄ ♄ d Z5 V-VI ✿
Ⓝ; Eur.: Fr, Ital-P, C-Eur., EC-Eur., Ba,
E-Eur.
– **anagyroides** Medik. · E:Common
Laburnum, Golden Chain; F:Aubour,
Cytise faux ébénier; G:Gewöhnlicher
Goldregen · ♄ ♄ d Z5 V-VI ✿ Ⓝ; Eur.: Fr,
Ital-P, C-Eur., EC-Eur., Ba, E-Eur., nat. in
BrI
– *vulgare* Bercht. & J. Presl = Laburnum
anagyroides
– × **watereri** (G. Kirchn.) Dippel
(*L. alpinum* × *L. anagyroides*) ·
E:Goldenchain Tree; F:Cytise de Voss;
G:Hybrid-Goldregen · ♄ ♄ d Z6 V-VI ✿;
cult.

Lacaena Lindl. -f- *Orchidaceae* · 2 spp.
– **bicolor** Lindl. · ♃ ⓜ V-VI ▽ ✳; Mex.,
Guat.

Lachenalia J. Jacq. ex Murray -f-
Hyacinthaceae · 111 sp. · E:Cape Cowslip;
F:Jacinthe du Cap; G:Kaphyazinthe,
Lachenalie
– **aloides** (L. f.) Engl. · E:Cape Cowslip;
G:Echte Kaphyazinthe
– var. **aloides** · ♃ ⋉ Z9 ⓚ I-III; S-Afr.:
Cape, Natal
– var. **aurea** (Lindl.) Engl. Z9
– var. **quadricolor** (Jacq.) Engl. Z9
– **bulbifera** (Cirillo) Engl. · ♃ ⋉ Z9 ⓚ
I-III; S-Afr.
– **contaminata** Sol. ex Aiton · E:Wild
Hyacinth; G:Gefleckte Kaphyazinthe · ♃
Z9 ⓚ; S-Afr.
– *fragrans* Jacq. = Lachenalia unicolor
– **lilacina** Baker · ♃ Z9 ⓚ II-III; S-Afr.
– **liliiflora** Jacq. · ♃ Z9 ⓚ II-III; S-Afr.
– **mutabilis** Sweet · ♃ Z9 ⓚ II-III; S-Afr.:
Natal
– **orchioides** (L.) Sol. ex Aiton
– var. **glaucina** (Jacq.) W.F. Barker · ♃ Z9
ⓚ III-IV; Cape
– var. **orchioides** · ♃ Z9 ⓚ II-IV; Cape
– **orthopetala** Jacq. · ♃ Z9 ⓚ; S-Afr.
– **pallida** Sol. ex Aiton · ♃ Z9 ⓚ V; S-Afr.
– *pendula* Sol. ex Aiton = Lachenalia
bulbifera
– **purpureocaerulea** Jacq. · ♃ Z9 ⓚ III-IV;
S-Afr.

– **pustulata** Jacq. · � Z9 ⊙ II-III; S-Afr.
– **reflexa** Thunb. · � Z9 ⊙ II-III; S-Afr.
– **rubida** Jacq. · � Z9 ⊙ IX; Cape
– *tricolor* Thunb. = Lachenalia aloides var. aloides
– **unicolor** Jacq. · � Z9 ⊙ VIII; S-Afr.
– **unifolia** Jacq. · � Z9 ⊙ III; S-Afr.

Lactuca L. -f- *Asteraceae* · c. 100 spp. · E:Lettuce; F:Laitue; G:Lattich, Salat
– *alpina* (L.) Benth. & Hook. = Cicerbita alpina
– *bourgaei* (Boiss.) Irish & N. Taylor = Cicerbita bourgaei
– **indica** L. · E:Indian Lettuce; G:Chinesischer Salat · ⊙ ⊙ ⊛ Ⓝ; Ind., China, Jap., Phil., Malay. Arch.
– **perennis** L. · E:Mountain Lettuce; G:Blauer Lattich · � Z6 V-VI; Eur.: Ib, Fr, Ital-P, C-Eur., EC-Eur., Ba, RO
– *plumieri* (L.) Gren. & Godr. = Cicerbita plumieri
– **quercina** L. · E:Wild Lettuce; G:Eichen-Lattich · ⊙ VII-IX; Eur.: Fr, Ital-P, C-Eur., EC-Eur., Ba, E-Eur.
– **saligna** L. · E:Willow Leaf Lettuce, Willow Leaved Lettuce; G:Weidenblättriger Lattich · ⊙ VII-VIII; Eur.* exc. Sc; NW-Afr., Egypt
– **sativa** L. · E:Lettuce; G:Garten-Lattich, Grüner Salat · ⊙ VI-VIII; ? Egypt, ? W-As.
– var. **angustana** hort. ex L.H. Bailey · E:Asparagus Lettuce; G:Spargel-Salat · ⊙ Z6 Ⓝ; cult.
– var. **capitata** L. · E:Cabbage Lettuce, Head Lettuce; G:Kopf-Salat · ⊙ Z6 ⚇ Ⓝ; cult.
– var. **crispa** L. · E:Leaf Lettuce; G:Blatt-Salat, Pflück-Salat · ⊙ Z6 Ⓝ; cult.
– var. **longifolia** Lam. · E:Cos Lettuce; G:Binde-Salat, Römischer Salat · ⊙ Z6 Ⓝ; cult.
– **serriola** L. · E:Prickly Lettuce, Scarole; G:Kompass-Lattich · ⊙ Z7 VII-IX ⚇ ; Eur.*, TR, Levant, Iraq, Arab., Cauc., Iran, W-Sib., C-As., Afgh., NW-Afr., Egypt., Sudan
– f. **integrifolia** Bogenh.
– **tatarica** (L.) C.A. Mey. · E:Blue Lettuce; G:Tataren-Lattich · ⁴ VII-VIII; Eur.: BG, E-Eur.; TR, Cauc., Iran, Afgh., C-As., China, nat. in Sc, NL, C-Eur., EC-Eur.
– **viminea** (L.) J. Presl & C. Presl · E:Pliant Lettuce; G:Ruten-Lattich · ⊙ VII-VIII; Eur.* exc. BrI, Sc: TR, Iraq, Cauc.,

NW-Afr.
– **virosa** L. · E:Bitter Lettuce; G:Gift-Lattich · ⊙ ⊙ Z6 VII-IX ⚇ ⚘ Ⓝ; Eur.* exc. Sc; Alger.

Laelia Lindl. -f- *Orchidaceae* · 10 spp. · E:Laelia; F:Laelia; G:Laelie
– **albida** Bateman ex Lindl. · ⁴ Z10 ⚇ XII-I ▽ ✳; Mex.
– **anceps** Lindl. · ⁴ Z10 ⚇ XII-II ▽ ✳; Mex.
– **autumnalis** (Lex.) Lindl. · ⁴ Z10 ⚇ XI-I ▽ ✳; Mex.
– *crispa* (Lindl.) Rchb. f. = Sophronitis cinnabarina
– *crispata* (Thunb.) Garay = Sophronitis crispata
– *crispilabia* A. Rich. ex R. Warner = Sophronitis crispata
– *dayana* Rchb. f. = Sophronitis dayana
– *digbyana* (Lindl.) Benth. = Rhyncholaelia digbyana
– *flava* Lindl. = Sophronitis crispata
– **furfuracea** Lindl. · ⁴ Z10 ⚇ IX-XI ▽ ✳; Mex.
– *glauca* (Lindl.) Benth. = Rhyncholaelia glauca
– *grandis* Lindl. & Paxton = Sophronitis grandis
– *harpophylla* Rchb. f. = Sophronitis harpophylla
– *jongheana* Rchb. f. = Sophronitis jongheana
– *lobata* (Lindl.) H.J. Veitch = Sophronitis lobata
– *longipes* Rchb. f. = Sophronitis longipes
– *lundii* (Rchb. f. & Warm.) Rchb. f. & Warm. = Sophronitis lundii
– *milleri* Blumensch. ex Pabst = Sophronitis milleri
– *perrinii* (Lindl.) Bateman = Sophronitis perrinii
– *pumila* (Hook.) Rchb. f. = Sophronitis pumila
– *purpurata* Lindl. & Paxton = Sophronitis purpurata
– **rubescens** Lindl. · ⁴ Z10 ⚇ XI-I ▽ ✳; Mex., C-Am.
– *rupestris* Lindl. = Sophronitis crispata
– **speciosa** (Kunth) Schltr. · ⁴ Z10 ⚇ IV-V ▽ ✳; Mex.
– *tenebrosa* (Rolfe) Rolfe = Sophronitis tenebrosa

× **Laeliocattkeria** hort. -f- *Orchidaceae*

(*Barkeria* × *Cattleya* × *Laelia*)

× **Laeliocattleya** Rolfe -f- *Orchidaceae*
(*Cattleya* × *Laelia*)

× **Laeliopleya** hort. -f- *Orchidaceae*
(*Cattleya* × *Laeliopsis*)

Laeliopsis Lindl. = Broughtonia
– *domingensis* Lindl. = Broughtonia
domingensis

× **Laelonia** hort. -f- *Orchidaceae*
(*Broughtonia* × *Laelia*)

Lafoensia Vand. -f- *Lythraceae* · 11 sp.
– **punicifolia** DC. · ♄ ⒸⒶ Ⓝ; Mex., C-Am.,
trop. S-Am.

Lagarosiphon Harv. -m- *Hydrocharitaceae* ·
9 spp. · E:Curly Water Thyme; F:Fausse-
élodée; G:Scheinwasserpest, Wassergirlande
– **madagascariensis** Casp. · G:Madagas-
sische Wassergirlande · ⒉ ≈ ⒲; Madag.
– **major** (Ridl.) Moss · E:Oxygen Weed;
G:Große Wassergirlande, Scheinwasserpest · ⒉ ≈ ⒲ ⒸⒶ VII-VIII; S-Afr., nat. in
NZ, GB, N-I, NW-F
– **muscoides** Harv. · G:Moosähnliche
Wassergirlande · ⒉ ⒲ ⒸⒶ; trop. Afr.,
S-Afr.
– var. *major* Ridl. = Lagarosiphon major

Lagenandra Dalzell -f- *Araceae* · 15 spp.
– **ovata** (L.) Thwaites · ⒉ ⌒ Z10 ⒲ ⚘;
S-Ind., Sri Lanka

Lagenaria Ser. -f- *Cucurbitaceae* · 6 spp. ·
E:Bottle Gourd; F:Bouteille, Gourde;
G:Flaschenkürbis, Kalebasse
– **siceraria** (Molina) Standl. · E:Bottle
Gourd, Calabash Gourd; G:Flaschenkür-
bis, Kalebasse · ⊙ ⚥ ⊗ D Z10 ⒲ VI-IX Ⓝ;
trop. Afr., trop. As.
– var. *hispida* (Thunb. ex Murray) H. Hara
= Benincasa hispida

Lagenocarpus Nees -m- *Cyperaceae* · 31 sp.
– **rigidus** (Kunth) Nees · ⒉ ⋉ ⒲; Braz.

Lagerstroemia L. -f- *Lythraceae* · 53 spp. ·
E:Crape Myrtle; F:Lagerose, Lilas des
Indes; G:Kräuselmyrte, Lagerströmie
– *elegans* Wall. ex Paxton = Lagerstroemia
indica
– **floribunda** Jack · ♄; Ind., Malay. Pen.,
Thail., China
– *flos-reginae* Retz. = Lagerstroemia
speciosa
– **indica** L. · E:Crape Myrtle; G:Chinesische
Kräuselmyrte · ♄ ♄ d Z7 VIII-X; China,
Korea
– **speciosa** (L.) Pers. · E:Pride-of-India,
Queen's Crape Myrtle; G:Indische
Kräuselmyrte · ♄ Z9 ⒲ Ⓝ; trop. As.
– **Cultivars:**
– **many cultivars**

Lagoecia L. -m- *Apiaceae* · 1 sp. ·
G:Hasenkümmel
– **cuminoides** L. · E:Common Wild Cumin;
G:Hasenkümmel · ⊙; Eur.: Ib, Ital-P, Ba;
Syr., Iran, Iraq, TR

Lagotis Gaertn. -f- *Scrophulariaceae* ·
20 spp. · G:Rachenblüte
– **stolonifera** (K. Koch) Maxim. · G:Ährige
Rachenblüte · ⒉ ⌇ △ Z6 VI-VII; Cauc.

Lagunaria (DC.) Rchb. -f- *Malvaceae* ·
1 sp. · E:Norfolk Island Hibiscus;
F:Lagunaria; G:Norfolkeibisch
– **patersonia** (Andrews) G. Don · E:Cow
Itch Tree, Norfolk Island Hibiscus;
G:Norfolkeibisch · ♄ e Z9 ⒸⒶ; Austr.:
Queensl., Norfolk, Lord Howe Is.

Lagurus L. -m- *Poaceae* · 1 sp. · E:Hare's
Tail; F:Lagurier, Queue-de-lièvre;
G:Hasenschwanzgras, Samtgras
– **ovatus** L. · E:Hare's Tail; F:Queue de
lièvre; G:Hasenschwanzgras, Südliches
Samtgras · ⊙ ⊙ Z9 VI-VIII; Eur.: Ib,
Fr, Ital-P, Ba, Crim; TR, Levant, Cauc.,
Macaron., N-Afr., nat. in BrI, N-Am.,
S-Am., S-Afr., Austr.

Lallemantia Fisch. & C.A. Mey. -f-
Lamiaceae · 5 spp.
– **canescens** (L.) Fisch. & C.A. Mey. · ⊙ ⊙
Z7 VII-IX; TR, Cauc., Iran
– **iberica** (M. Bieb.) Fisch. & C.A. Mey. · ⊙
⊙ Z7 VII-VIII Ⓝ; TR, Syr., Palest., Iraq,
Iran
– **peltata** (L.) Fisch. & C.A. Mey. · ⊙ Z7
VII-VIII; TR, Cauc., Iran
– **royleana** (Benth.) Benth. · E:Rehana
Barry · ⊙ Z7 VII-VIII Ⓝ; Iran, Afgh.,
Pakist., C-As., W-China

Lamarckia Moench -f- *Poaceae* · 1 sp. ·
E:Golden Dog's Tail; F:Lamarckia;
G:Goldschwanzgras, Goldspitzengras,
Lamarkie
– **aurea** (L.) Moench · E:Golden Top Grass;
G:Goldschwanzgras, Goldspitzengras,
Lamarkie · ☉ Z7 VII-VIII; Eur.: Ib, Fr,
Ital-P, Ba; TR, Iran, Afgh., Pakist., N-Afr.,
Macaron., Eth.

Lamiastrum Heist. ex Fabr. = Lamium
– *flavidum* = Lamium galeobdolon subsp.
flavidum
– *galeobdolon* (L.) Ehrend. & Polatschek =
Lamium galeobdolon
– *montanum* = Lamium galeobdolon subsp.
montanum

Lamium L. -n- *Lamiaceae* · 28 spp. ·
E:Dead Nettles; F:Lamier; G:Goldnessel,
Taubnessel
– **album** L. · E:White Dead Nettle; G:Weiße
Taubnessel · ⁴ Z4 IV-X ⚥ ; Eur.*, TR,
Cauc., Iran, W-Sib., E-Sib., Amur, C-As.,
Him., Mong., Korea, Jap., Canar., nat. in
N-Am.
– **amplexicaule** L. · E:Henbit Dead Nettle;
G:Stängelumfassende Taubnessel · ☉
IV-VIII; Eur.*, TR, Levant, Iran, W-Sib.,
C-As., Him., N-Afr., Canar.
– **confertum** Fr. · E:Northern Dead Nettle;
G:Mittlere Taubnessel · ☉; Eur.: G, DK,
PL, BrI
– *endtmannii* G.H. Loos = Galeobdolon
endtmannii
– *flavidum* F. Herm. = Lamium galeobdolon
subsp. flavidum
– **galeobdolon** (L.) L. · E:Yellow Archangel; F:Lamier doré; G:Echte Goldnessel,
Gewöhnliche Goldnessel · ⁴ ⤳ Z6
V-VII; Eur.*, TR, Cauc.
– **some cultivars**
– subsp. **flavidum** (F. Herm.) Á. Löve & D.
Löve · G:Alpen-Goldnessel, Blassgelbe
Goldnessel · ⁴ VI-VII; Eur.: Alp., Apenn.
– subsp. **montanum** (Pers.) Hayek ·
G:Berg-Goldnessel · ⁴ V-VII; Eur., TR,
Cauc.
– **garganicum** L. · ⁴ ; Eur.: F, Ital-P, Ba, RO
– *luteum* Krock. = Lamium galeobdolon
– **maculatum** L. · E:Spotted Dead Nettle;
F:Lamier maculé; G:Gefleckte Taubnessel · ⁴ Z4 IV-VIII; Eur.* exc. BrI, Sc; TR,
Cauc., N-Iran, nat. in BrI, Sc
– **some cultivars**

– *moluccellifolium* = Lamium purpureum
var. moluccellifolium
– *montanum* (Pers.) Á. Löve & D. Löve =
Lamium galeobdolon subsp. montanum
– **orvala** L. · E:Giant Dead Nettle; F:Lamier
à grandes fleurs; G:Großblütige Taubnes-
sel · ⁴ Z6 IV-VI; Eur.: I, A, H, Slove.,
Croatia, Bosn., Montenegro, ? W-Russ.
– **purpureum** L. · G:Rote Taubnessel
– var. **incisum** (Willd.) Pers. · G:Bastard-
Taubnessel, Eingeschnittene Taubnessel ·
III-X; Eur.*
– var. **moluccellifolium** (Schumach.) Fr. ·
G:Entferntblättrige Taubnessel, Mittlere
Taubnessel · V-IX; Eur.: BrI, Sc, G,
N-Russ., nat. in P
– var. **purpureum** · E:Purple Archangel,
Red Dead Nettle; G:Gewöhnliche Rote
Taubnessel · ☉ III-X; Eur.*, TR, Syr.,
W-Sib., NW-Afr., nat. in N-Am.

Lampranthus N.E. Br. -m- *Aizoaceae* ·
241 sp. · E:Dewplant; F:Lampranthus;
G:Mittagsblume
– *aurantiacum* DC. = Lampranthus
glaucoides
– **aureus** (L.) N.E. Br. · ♄ ⁴ Z9 ⊕ VII-IX;
Cape
– **blandus** (Haw.) Schwantes · ♄ ⁴ Z9 ⊕
VII-IX; Cape
– **brownii** (Hook. f.) N.E. Br. · ♄ ⁴ Z9 ⊕
VII-IX; Cape
– **conspicuus** (Haw.) N.E. Br. · ♄ ⁴ Z9 ⊕
VII-IX; Cape
– *deltoides* (L.) Glen = Oscularia deltoides
– **falcatus** (L.) N.E. Br. · ♄ ⁴ D Z9 ⊕
VII-IX; Cape
– **glaucoides** (Haw.) N.E. Br. · ♄ ⁴ Z9 ⊕
VII-IX; Cape
– **glomeratus** (L.) N.E. Br. · ♄ ⁴ Z9 ⊕
VII-IX; Cape
– **haworthii** (Donn) N.E. Br. · ♄ ⁴ Z9 ⊕
VII-VIII; Cape
– **sociorum** (L. Bolus) N.E. Br. · ♄ ⁴ Z9 ⊕
VII-X; Cape
– **spectabilis** (Haw.) N.E. Br. · E:Trailing
Ice Plant; G:Kriechende Mittagsblume · ♄
⁴ Z9 ⊕ VII-IX; Cape
– **zeyheri** (Salm-Dyck) · ♄ ⁴ Z9 ⊕ VII-IX;
Cape

Landolphia P. Beauv. -f- *Apocynaceae* ·
64 spp.
– **heudelotii** A. DC. · ♄ ! ⚡ ⊛ Ⓝ; W-Afr.
– **kirkii** Dyer · ♄ ! ⚡ ⊛ Ⓝ; trop. E-Afr.

– **owariensis** P. Beauv. · ♄ ↯ ⚥ ⓦ ⓝ; trop.
Afr.

Lannea A. Rich. -f- *Anacardiaceae* · 40 spp.
– **coromandelica** (Houtt.) Merr. ·
G:Jhingangummi · ♄ ⓦ ⓝ; SE-As.

Lansium Corrêa -n- *Meliaceae* · 3 spp. ·
E:Langsat; F:Lansat; G:Lansibaum
– **domesticum** Corrêa · E:Langsat;
G:Lansibaum · ♄ ⓚ ⓝ; Malay. Pen., Phil.,
Sulawesi, N.Guinea, cult. Ind.

Lantana L. -f- *Verbenaceae* · 150 spp. ·
E:Lantana; F:Lantana, Lantanier;
G:Wandelröschen
– **camara** L. · E:Lantana; G:Wandelröschen
· ♄ e Z10 ⓚ VI-IX ⚘ ⓝ; Mex., trop. Am.,
nat. in Fla., Tex., Hawaii, Trop.
– **some cultivars**
– *crocea* Jacq. = Lantana camara
– *delicatissima* hort. = Lantana montevidensis
– **montevidensis** (Spreng.) Briq. ·
E:Creeping Lantana; G:Kriechendes
Wandelröschen · ♄ e Z10 ⓚ VI-IX ⚘;
Braz., Urug., nat. in USA: Tex., SE, Fla.
– *mutabilis* Salisb. = Lantana camara
– *nivea* Vent. = Lantana camara
– *sellowiana* Link & Otto = Lantana
montevidensis
– *urticifolia* Mill. = Lantana camara

Lapageria Ruiz & Pav. -f- *Philesiaceae* ·
1 sp. · E:Chile Bells; F:Lapageria; G:Chile-
glöckchen, Copihue, Lapagerie
– **rosea** Ruiz & Pav. · E:Chile Bells, Chilean
Bellflower; G:Chileglöckchen, Copihue,
Lapagerie · ♄ e ⚥ Z9 ⓚ VIII-XII; Chile

Lapeirousia Pourr. -f- *Iridaceae* · 39 spp. ·
F:Lapeirousia; G:Lapeirousie
– **corymbosa** (L.) Ker-Gawl. · ⚃ Z9 ⓚ V;
SW-Cape
– *cruenta* (Lindl.) Baker = Anomatheca laxa
– *grandiflora* (Baker) Baker = Anomatheca
grandiflora
– *juncea* (L. f.) Pourr. = Anomatheca
verrucosa
– *laxa* (Thunb.) N.E. Br. = Anomatheca
laxa

Laportea Gaudich. -f- *Urticaceae* · 21 sp. ·
E:Bush Nettle; F:Laportea; G:Brenn-
pflanze, Strauchnessel

– **canadensis** (L.) Wedd. · E:Bush Nettle,
Wood Nettle; G:Kanadische Strauchnes-
sel · ⚃ ⓝ; Can.: E; USA: NE, NCE, SE,
Fla., Okla.
– **moroides** Wedd. · E:Gympie Bush;
G:Australische Strauchnessel · ♄ ♄ ♂ ⓦ;
Austr.: Queensl.

Lappa Scop. = Arctium
– *major* Gaertn. = Arctium lappa
– *minor* Hill = Arctium minus
– *tomentosa* (Mill.) Lam. = Arctium
tomentosum

Lappula Moench -f- *Boraginaceae* ·
40-60 spp. · E:Bur Forget-me-not;
F:Echinosperme; G:Igelsame, Kletten-
kraut
– **deflexa** (Wahlenb.) Garcke · E:Nodding
Stick-seed; G:Wald-Igelsame · ⊙ VI-VII;
Eur.: Sc, Fr, C-Eur., EC-Eur., E-Eur., sp.;
N, mts.; Sib., Mong., Manch., N-Am.
– **heteracantha** (Ledeb.) Gürke · ⊙ VI-VII;
SC-Eur., S-Russ.; Cauc.
– **patula** (Lehm.) Gürke · ⊙; Eur.: sp., Sic.,
H, Ba, EC-Eur.; TR, Cauc., Iran, Afgh.,
W-Sib., C-As., China, : Sinkiang; NW-Afr.
– **squarrosa** (Retz.) Dumort. · E:Burr,
Stickweed; G:Kletten-Igelsame, Klet-
tenkraut · ⊙ VI-VII ⓝ; Eur.* exc. BrI, Sc;
TR, Cauc., Iran, C-As., W-Sib., E-Sib.,
nat. in Sc, N-Am.

Lapsana L. -f- *Asteraceae* · 9 spp. ·
E:Nipplewort; F:Lampsane, Poule grasse;
G:Rainkohl
– **communis** L. · E:Hawksbeard, Nip-
plewort; G:Gewöhnlicher Rainkohl · ⊙
⚃ VI-IX; Eur.*, TR, Lebanon, Syr., Cauc.,
N-Iraq, Iran, NW-Afr., nat. in N-Am.

Lardizabala Ruiz & Pav. -f-
Lardizabalaceae · 2 spp.
– **biternata** Ruiz & Pav. · ♄ e ♂ Z9 ⓚ XII;
Chile

Larix Mill. -f- *Pinaceae* · 11 sp. · E:Larch;
F:Mélèze; G:Lärche
– *amabilis* J. Nelson = Pseudolarix amabilis
– *dahurica* Turcz. & Trautv. = Larix
gmelinii var. gmelinii
– **decidua** Mill. · E:European Larch;
G:Europäische Lärche
– var. **decidua** · F:Mélèze commun;
G:Gewöhnliche Europäische Lärche · ♄

d Z4 III-IV ⚕ Ⓝ; Eur.: Fr, Ital-P, C-Eur., EC-Eur., Slove., Croatia, ? Bosn., E-Eur.; Alp., W-Carp., nat. in BrI, Sc
- var. **polonica** (Racib. ex Wóycicki) Ostenf. & Syrach · E:Polish Larch; G:Polnische Lärche · ♄ d Z4; W-Polen, NW-Ukraine
- × **eurokurilensis** Rohmeder & Dimpflm. (*L. decidua* × *L. gmelinii*) · G:Bayerische Hybrid-Lärche · ♄ d; cult.
- × **eurolepis** A. Henry (*L. decidua* × *L. kaempferi*) · E:Dunkeld Larch; G:Schottische Hybrid-Lärche · ♄ d; cult.
- *europaea* Lam. & DC. = Larix decidua var. decidua
- **gmelinii** (Rupr.) Kuzen.
- var. **olgensis** A. Henry · E:Olga Bay Larch; G:Olgabucht-Lärche · ♄ d Z1; Amur
- var. **principis-rupprechtii** (Mayr) Pilg. · E:Prince Rupprecht's Larch; G:Prinz-Rupprecht-Lärche · ♄ d; N-China, Manch., Korea
- **gmelinii** (Rupr.) Rupr. · E:Dahurian Larch; G:Dahurische Lärche
- var. **gmelinii** · G:Gewöhnliche Dahurische Lärche · ♄ d Z3; E-Sib., Amur, Sakhal., Kamchat., Manch., Korea
- var. **japonica** (Maxim. ex Regel) Pilg. · E:Kurile Larch; G:Kurilen-Lärche · ♄ Z1; Sakhal., Kurilen
- **kaempferi** (Lamb.) Carrière · E:Japanese Larch; F:Mélèze du Japon; G:Japanische Lärche · ♄ d Z5 IV Ⓝ; C-Jap.
- *kurilensis* Mayr = Larix gmelinii var. japonica
- **laricina** (Du Roi) K. Koch · E:American Larch, Tamarack; G:Amerikanische Lärche, Tamarack · ♄ d Z1 III Ⓝ; Alaska, Can., USA: NE, NCE
- *leptolepis* (Siebold & Zucc.) Siebold ex Gordon = Larix kaempferi
- *lubarskii* Sukaczev = Larix gmelinii var. olgensis
- **lyallii** Parl. · E:Alpine Larch, Subalpine Larch; G:Rocky-Mountain-Lärche · ♄ d Z3; USA: N-Idaho, W-Mont.
- × **marschlinsii** Coaz (*L. decidua* × *L. sibirica*) · G:Schweizer Hybrid-Lärche · ♄ d; cult.
- **occidentalis** Nutt. · E:Western Larch; G:Westamerikanische Lärche · ♄ d Z6 Ⓝ; B.C., USA: NW, Mont., Idaho
- × **pendula** (Sol.) Salisb. (*L. decidua* × *L. laricina*) · E:Weeping Larch; G:Hänge-Lärche · ♄ d Z4 III-IV; cult.
- **potaninii** Batalin · E:Chinese Larch; G:Gewöhnliche Chinesische Lärche · ♄ d Z6; W-China
- **sibirica** Ledeb. · E:Siberian Larch; G:Sibirische Lärche · ♄ d Z2 III-IV ⚕ Ⓝ; Eur.: Russ.; W-Sib., E-Sib., C-As
- *sukaczewii* Dylis = Larix sibirica

Laser G. Gaertn., B. Mey. & Scherb. -n- *Apiaceae* · 1 sp. · F:Cumin des chevaux, Laser; G:Rosskümmel
- **trilobum** (L.) Borkh. · G:Rosskümmel · ♃ V-VI ▽; Eur.: Fr, Ital-P, C-Eur., EC-Eur., Ba, E-Eur.; TR, Lebanon, Cauc., N-Iran

Laserpitium L. -n- *Apiaceae* · 25-35 spp. · F:Laser; G:Laserkraut
- **archangelica** Wulfen · E:Laserwort; G:Engelwurz-Laserkraut · ♃; Eur.: EC-Eur., Ba, RO; mts., nat. in A
- **halleri** Crantz · G:Hallers Laserkraut · ♃ VI-VIII; Eur.: F, Cors, I, Sw, A; Alp., Cors
- **krapfii** Crantz
- subsp. **gaudinii** (Moretti) Thell. · G:Schweizer Laserkraut · ♃ VII-VIII; Sw, N-I, A, Slove.
- **latifolium** L. · E:Broad-leaved Sermountain; G:Breitblättriges Laserkraut · ♃ VII-VIII; Eur.* exc. BrI; Iran
- **peucedanoides** L. · G:Haarstrang-Laserkraut · ♃ VI-VIII; Eur.: I, A, Slove., Croatia; SE-Alp., Croatia
- **prutenicum** L. · G:Preußisches Laserkraut · ⊙ VII-VIII; Eur.* exc. BrI, Sc
- **siler** L. · G:Berg-Laserkraut · ♃ VI-VIII; Eur.: Ba, Fr, Ib, Ital-P, C-Eur.; mts.

Lasia Lour. -f- *Araceae* · 2 spp.
- **spinosa** (L.) Thwaites · E:Sampi · ♄ ~ ⌂ VI-IX; Him., Ind., Sri Lanka, Malay. Arch., China

Lasiagrostis Link = Stipa
- *calamagrostis* (L.) Link = Stipa calamagrostis

Lasthenia Cass. -f- *Asteraceae* · 16 spp. · G:Lasthenie
- **californica** DC. ex Lindl. · E:California Goldfields · ⊙ VII-VIII; USA: Oreg., Calif., Ariz.; Baja Calif.
- *chrysostoma* (Fisch. & C.A. Mey.) Greene = Lasthenia californica
- **coronaria** (Nutt.) Ornduff · E:Royal

Goldfields · ⊙ VII-VIII; S-Calif., Baja Calif.

Lastrea Bory = Thelypteris
– *thelypteris* (L.) Bory = Thelypteris palustris

Latania Comm. ex Juss. -f- *Arecaceae* · 3 spp. · E:Latan; F:Latanier; G:Latanie
– *aurea* Duncan = Latania verschaffeltii
– *borbonica* hort. = Livistona chinensis
– *borbonica* Lam. = Latania lontaroides
– *commersonii* J.F. Gmel. = Latania lontaroides
– *glaucophylla* Devansaye = Latania loddigesii
– **loddigesii** Mart. · E:Blue Latan; G:Blaue Latanie · ♄ e Z10 ⌂; Mauritius
– **lontaroides** (Gaertn.) H.E. Moore · E:Red Latan; G:Rote Latanie · ♄ e Z10 ⌂; Maskarene Is.
– *rubra* Jacq. = Latania lontaroides
– **verschaffeltii** Lem. · E:Yellow Latan; G:Gelbe Latanie · ♄ e Z10 ⌂; Maskarene Is. (Rodriguez)

Lathraea L. -f- *Scrophulariaceae* · 7 spp. · E:Toothwort; F:Clandestine; G:Schuppenwurz
– **clandestina** L. · E:Purple Toothwort; G:Niedrige Schuppenwurz · ♃ IV-V; Eur.: sp., F, B, I, nat. in BrI
– **squamaria** L. · E:Toothwort; G:Laubholz-Schuppenwurz · ♃ III-V; Eur.*, TR, Cauc., Pakist., Him.

Lathyrus L. -m- *Fabaceae* · c. 150 spp. · E:Wild Pea; F:Pois de senteur, Pois vivace; G:Platterbse
– **annuus** L. · E:Fodder Pea; G:Einjährige Platterbse · ⊙ ≹; Eur.: Ib, Fr, Ital-P, Ba; TR, Levant, Iraq, Cauc., C-As., N-Iran, N-Afr.
– **aphaca** L. · E:Yellow Vetchling; G:Ranken-Platterbse · ⊙ ≹ VI-VII ☠ Ⓝ; Eur.* exc. BrI, Sc; TR, Levant; Cauc., Iran, C-As., Afgh., Him., N-Afr., Eth., nat. in Jap., China
– **bauhinii** P.A. Genty · G:Schwertblättrige Platterbse · ♃ V-VII ▽; Eur.: sp., F, Sw, G, Ba; Pyr., Alp., Jura, Balkan
– **cicera** L. · E:Red Vetchling; G:Kicher-Platterbse · ⊙ ≹ V-VIII ☠ Ⓝ; Eur.: Ib, Fr, Ital-P, Ba, E-Eur., Sw; TR, Levant, Iraq, Cauc., Iran, C-As., N-Afr.
– **clymenum** L. · ⊙ ≹ VII-VIII Ⓝ; Eur.: Ib, Fr, Ital-P, Ba; TR, NW-Afr., Libya
– **gmelinii** (Fisch. ex DC.) Fritsch · G:Gold-Platterbse · ♃ Z4 V-VII; Ural, C-As. mts.
– **grandiflorus** Sibth. & Sm. · E:Two-flowered Everlasting Pea; G:Großblütige Platterbse · ♃ ≹ Z7 ∧ VI-IX; Eur.: Ital-P, Ba
– **heterophyllus** L. · E:Norfolk Everlasting Pea; G:Verschiedenblättrige Platterbse · ♃ ≹ Z6 VII-VIII; Eur.: Ib, Fr, Ital-P, C-Eur., EC-Eur., Swed
– **hirsutus** L. · E:Caley Pea, Hairy Vetchling; G:Behhartfrüchtige Platterbse · ⊙ ≹ Z7 VI-VIII; Eur.* exc. BrI, Sc; TR, Lebanon, Cauc., N-Iran, C-As., NW-Afr., Egypt
– **inconspicuus** L. · ⊙; Eur.: Ib, Fr, Ital-P, Ba; TR, Levant, Cauc., Iran, C-As., Alger.
– *japonicus* Willd. = Lathyrus maritimus
– subsp. *maritimus* (L.) P.W. Ball = Lathyrus maritimus
– var. *glaber* (Ser.) Fernald = Lathyrus maritimus
– **laevigatus** (Waldst. & Kit.) Gren. · E:Yellow Pea; G:Gelbe Platterbse
– subsp. **laevigatus** · G:Westliche Gelbe Platterbse · ♃ Z5 V-VIII; Eur.* exc. BrI, Sc
– subsp. **occidentalis** (Fisch. & C.A. Mey.) Breistr. · G:Östliche Gelbe Platterbse · ♃ Z5 VI-VIII; C-Alp., SW-Alp., Pyr., N-Sp.
– **latifolius** L. · E:Everlasting Pea, Perennial Sweet Pea; F:Pois vivace; G:Breitblättrige Platterbse · ♃ ≹ Z5 VII-VIII; Eur.* exc. BrI, Sc; NW-Afr., nat. in BrI
– **linifolius** (Reichard) Bässler · E:Bitter Vetch; G:Berg-Platterbse · ♃ Z6 IV-VI; Eur.*
– *luteus* (L.) Peterm. = Lathyrus gmelinii
– **maritimus** (L.) Bigelow · E:Beach Pea; G:Strand-Platterbse · ♃ ≹ ⇝ VI-VIII; Eur.: BrI, Sc, G, N-Russ.; ; coasts; Sib., Amur, Sakhal., Kamchat., China, Jap., China, nat. in Eur.: BrI, Sc, C-Eur., EC-Eur., E-Eur.
– **niger** (L.) Bernh. · E:Black Pea; G:Schwarzwerdende Platterbse · ♃ Z6 VI; Eur.*, Cauc., TR, Syr., N-Iran, NW-Afr.
– **nissolia** L. · E:Grass Vetchling; G:Gras-Platterbse · ⊙ V-VII; Eur.* exc. Sc; Cauc., TR, N-Iraq, NW-Afr.
– **ochrus** (L.) DC. · E:Cyprus Vetch; G:Eselsohren, Scheidige Platterbse · ⊙ ≹ VI-VIII Ⓝ; Eur.: Ib, Fr, Ital-P, Ba; TR, Levant, NW-Afr., Libya

– **odoratus** L. · E:Sweet Pea; F:Pois de senteur; G:Duft-Wicke, Duftende Platterbse · ⊙ ⚥ ⋉ D VI-IX ✿; S-I, Sic.
– **many cultivars**
– **palustris** L. · E:Marsh Pea; G:Sumpf-Platterbse · ⌗ ⚥ Z5 VII-VIII ▽; Eur.*, TR, Cauc., W-Sib., E-Sib., C-As, China: Sinkiang
– **pannonicus** (Jacq.) Garcke · E:Felted Vetch; G:Kurzknollige Pannonische Platterbse · ⌗ V-VI ▽; Eur.* exc. BrI, Sc; Cauc., W-Sib.
– **pratensis** L. · E:Meadow Vetchling; G:Wiesen-Platterbse · ⌗ ⚥ Z4 VI-VII; Eur.*, TR, Syr., Cauc., Iran, W-Sib., E-Sib., C-As., W-Him., C-China, Moroc., Eth.
– **sativus** L. · E:Chickling Pea, Grass Pea; G:Saat-Platterbse · ⊙ ⚥ V-VIII ✿ Ⓝ; ? W-As., nat. in Eur., SW-As., N-Afr.
– **sphaericus** Retz. · G:Kugelsamige Platterbse · ⊙ ⚥ V; Eur.: Ib, Fr, Sw, Ital-P, Ba, Sc, RO, Crim; TR, Levant, Iraq, Cauc., Iran, C-As., Him., NW-Afr., Egypt
– **sylvestris** L. · E:Everlasting Pea; G:Gewöhnliche Wald-Platterbse · ⌗ ⚥ Z6 VII-IX Ⓝ; Eur.*, Cauc.
– **tingitanus** L. · E:Tangier Pea; G:Afrikanische Platterbse · ⌗ ⚥; Eur.: sp., P, Sard., Azor.; Moroc., Alger.
– **tuberosus** L. · E:Earthnut Pea, Tuberous Pea; G:Knollen-Platterbse · ⌗ ⚥ ⤳ Z6 VI-VII Ⓝ; Eur.* exc. BrI, Sc; TR, Cauc., Iran, W-Sib., C-As., nat. in BrI, Sc
– **venetus** (Mill.) Wohlf. · G:Venezianische Platterbse · ⌗ Z6 V-VI; Eur.: Ital-P, C-Eur., C-Eur., Ba, E-Eur.; TR
– **vernus** (L.) Bernh. · E:Spring Pea; F:Gesse du printemps, Pois printanier; G:Frühlings-Platterbse, Zarte Platterbse · ⌗ Z4 IV-V; Eur.* exc. BrI; TR, Cauc., W-Sib., E-Sib.

Launaea Cass. -f- *Asteraceae* · 30-40 spp. · G:Dornlattich
– **taraxacifolia** (Willd.) Amin ex C. Jeffrey · G:Löwenzahn-Dornlattich · Ⓜ Ⓝ; trop. Afr.

Laurentia Adans. = Solenopsis
– *axillaris* (Lindl.) E. Wimm. = Isotoma axillaris
– *canariensis* DC. = Solenopsis laurentia
– *fluviatilis* (R. Br.) E. Wimm. = Isotoma fluviatilis

– *gasparrinii* (Tineo) Strobl = Solenopsis laurentia
– *longiflora* (L.) Endl. = Isotoma longiflora
– *michelii* A. DC. = Solenopsis laurentia
– *minuta* (L.) A. DC. = Solenopsis minuta
– *tenella* (Biv.) A. DC. = Solenopsis minuta

Laurocerasus Duhamel = Prunus
– *lusitanica* (L.) M. Roem. = Prunus lusitanica
– *officinalis* M. Roem. = Prunus laurocerasus

Laurus L. -f- *Lauraceae* · 2 spp. · E:Bay, Laurel; F:Laurier; G:Lorbeerbaum
– **azorica** (Seub.) Franco · E:Canary Laurel; G:Kanarischer Lorbeerbaum · ♄ e Z9 ⓐ IV-V; Azor., Madeira, Canar.
– *canariensis* Webb & Berthel. = Laurus azorica
– **nobilis** L. · E:Bay, Bay Tree, Sweet Bay; G:Lorbeerbaum · ♄ e Z8 ⓐ IV-V ⚥ Ⓝ; Eur.: Ib, Fr, Ital-P, Ba; Cauc., nat. in Crim

Lavandula L. -f- *Lamiaceae* · 39 spp. · E:Lavender; F:Lavande; G:Lavendel
– **angustifolia** Mill.
– **some cultivars**
– subsp. **angustifolia** Chaix ex Vill. · E:English Lavender; F:Lavande vraie; G:Echter Lavendel · ♄ e △ D Z7 VII-VIII ⚥ Ⓝ; Eur.: Ib, Fr, Ital-P, ? Ba, nat. in Crim
– **canariensis** (L.) Mill. · ♄ e Z9 ⓐ; Canar.
– × **chaytorae** Upson & S. Andrews · G:Chaytor-Lavendel
– **dentata** L. · E:French Lavender; G:Französischer Lavendel, Zahn-Lavendel · ♄ e D Z9 ⓐ VI-VII; Eur.: sp., Balear.; NW-Afr., nat. in P, I, Sic.
– × **intermedia** Loisel. (*L. angustifolia* × *L. latifolia*) · E:Lavandin; G:Englischer Lavendel · ♄ e Z5; sp., F, I
– **some cultivars**
– **lanata** Boiss. · E:Woolly Lavender; G:Wolliger Lavendel · ♄ e D Z8 ⓐ VI-IX; Eur.: S-Sp.; mts.
– **latifolia** Medik. · E:Spike Lavender, Spikenard; G:Großer Lavendel, Speick-Lavendel · ♄ e △ D Z7 ⋏ VI-VII ⚥ Ⓝ; Eur.: Ib, Fr, Ital-P, Croatia
– *officinalis* Chaix = Lavandula angustifolia subsp. angustifolia
– **pedunculata** (Mill.) Cav. · ♄ e D Z8 ⓐ VII-IX; Eur.: P, sp.
– **pinnata** Lundmark · ♄ e D Z9 ⓐ VIII-IX;

Canar., Madeira
- *spica* L. = Lavandula angustifolia subsp.
  angustifolia
- **stoechas** L.
- **some cultivars**
- subsp. *pedunculata* (Mill.) Samp. ex
  Rozeira = Lavandula pedunculata
- subsp. **stoechas** · E:French Lavender,
  Italian Lavender; G:Schopf-Lavendel · ♄
  e D Z8 ⚘ VII-X ✿ ; Eur.: Ib, Fr, Ital-P, Ba;
  TR, NW-Afr.
- *vera* DC. = Lavandula angustifolia subsp.
  angustifolia

Lavatera L. -f- *Malvaceae* · 25 spp. · E:Tree
Mallow; F:Lavatère; G:Malve, Strauch-
pappel
- **arborea** L. · E:Malva, Tree Mallow;
  G:Baum-Malve · ⊙ Z8 ⚘ VII-IX; Eur.:
  Ib, F, BrI, Ital-P, Ba, Azor., Canar.; TR,
  Alger., Tun
- **cachemeriana** Cambess. · ⅔ ; Him.:
  Pakist., W-Ind.
- **olbia** L. · E:Bush Mallow; G:Strauch-
  Malve · ♄ ⚘ VII-X; Eur.: Ib, Fr, Ital-P;
  NW-Afr., Libya
- **punctata** All. · ⊙ ; Eur.: Ib, Ital-P, Fr, Ba;
  N-Iran, Cauc., Syr., C-As.
- **thuringiaca** L. · E:Tree Lavatera;
  F:Lavatère arbustive; G:Thüringer
  Strauchpappel · ⅔ VII-IX; Eur.: C-Eur.,
  EC-Eur., Ba, Ital-P, E-Eur.; TR, Cauc.,
  Iran, W-Sib., E-Sib., C-As., Him., nat. in
  Sc
- **some cultivars**
- **trimestris** L. · E:Rose Mallow; F:Lavatère
  d'un trimestre; G:Becher-Malve, Garten-
  Strauchpappel · ⊙ VII-X; Eur.: Ib, Fr,
  Ital-P, ? W-Ba; TR, Syr., Palest., NW-Afr.,
  nat. in E-Eur.

Lawrencia Hook. -f- *Malvaceae* · 12 spp.
- **helmsii** (F. Muell. & Tate) Lander ·
  E:Dunna-dunna · ♄ e ⤬ ⚘; Austr.

Lawsonia L. -f- *Lythraceae* · 1 sp. ·
E:Henna; F:Henné; G:Hennastrauch
- **inermis** L. · E:Henna; G:Hennastrauch ·
  ♄ s Z9 ⚘ ✿ Ⓝ; Arab., Iran, Afgh., Ind.,
  Sri Lanka, nat. in trop. Am.

⨯ **Laycockara** hort. -f- *Orchidaceae*
  (*Arachnis* ⨯ *Phalaenopsis* ⨯ *Vandopsis*)

Layia Hook. & Arn. -f- *Asteraceae* · c.

15 spp. · E:Tidytips
- **chrysanthemoides** (DC.) A. Gray ·
  E:Smooth Tidytips · ⊙ VII-VIII; Calif.
- **glandulosa** (Hook.) Fisch. & C.A. Mey. ·
  E:Whitedaisy Tidytips · ⊙ VII-VIII; Can.:
  B.C.; USA: NW, Calif., Idaho, SW; Mex.
- **platyglossa** (Fisch. & C.A. Mey.) A.
  Gray · E:Coastal Tidy Tips · ⊙ VII-VIII;
  Calif.

Lecythis Loefl. -f- *Lecythidaceae* · 26 spp. ·
E:Monkey Nut; F:Marmite de singe;
G:Krukenbaum, Paradiesnuss, Topffruchtbaum
- **pisonis** Cambess. · ♄ d Z9 ⚘ Ⓝ; Guyan.,
  Braz.
- *urnigera* Mart. ex O. Berg = Lecythis
  pisonis
- **zabucayo** Aubl. · E:Monkey Nut,
  Paradise Nut; G:Paradiesnuss · ♄ d Z9 ⚘
  Ⓝ; trop. Am., Guyan., Braz.

Ledebouria Roth -f- *Hyacinthaceae* · 41 sp.
- **cooperi** (Hook. f.) Jessop · ⹁ Z9 ⚘;
  S-Afr.
- **socialis** (Baker) Jessop · E:Silver Squill ·
  ⹁ Z9 ⚘ ⚘ IV-V; S-Afr.

Ledenbergia Klotzsch ex Moq. -f-
Phytolaccaceae · 2 spp.
- **macrantha** Standl.; El Salv., Nicar.

Ledum L. -n- *Ericaceae* · 4 spp. · E:Labrador
Tea; F:Romarin sauvage, Thé du
Labrador; G:Porst
- **groenlandicum** Oeder · E:Labrador Tea;
  F:Lédum du Labrador; G:Grönländischer
  Porst, Labrador-Porst · ♄ e Z1 V-VI ✿ ⚘;
  Greenl., Alaska, Can., USA: NE, NCE,
  Rocky Mts., NW, nat. in BrI, D
- **palustre** L. · E:Marsh Labrador Tea,
  Wild Rosemary; F:Lédum des marais;
  G:Sumpf-Porst · ♄ e Z1 V-VII ✿ ⚘ ▽;
  Eur.: Sc, C-Eur., EC-Eur., E-Eur.; W-Sib.,
  E-Sib., Amur, Sakhal., Kamchat., Manch.,
  nat. in BrI
- subsp. *groenlandicum* (Oeder) Hultén =
  Ledum groenlandicum

Leea D. Royen ex L. -f- *Leeaceae* · 34 spp.
- **amabilis** hort. Veitch ex Mast. · ♄ e Z10
  ⚘; W-Kalimantan
- **rubra** Blume ex Spreng. · E:West Indian
  Holly · ♄ e Z10 ⚘; Java
- **sambucina** (L.) Willd. · ♄ ♄ e Z10 ⚘;

Him., Ind., Sri Lanka, Indochina, China, Malay. Arch., Phil., Austr.

Leersia Sw. -f- *Poaceae* · 17 spp. · E:Cut Grass; F:Faux-riz, Léersia, Riz sauvage; G:Reisquecke
- **oryzoides** (L.) Sw. · E:Rice Cut Grass; F:Léerzia faux-riz; G:Europäische Reisquecke · ⁂ ⤳ ∿ VIII-X; Eur.*, As, , Can., USA*, W-Ind., S-Am.

Legousia Durande -f- *Campanulaceae* · 15 spp. · E:Venus' Looking Glass; F:Miroir-de-Vénus; G:Frauenspiegel, Venusspiegel
- **hybrida** (L.) Delarbre · E:Venus' Looking Glass; G:Kleiner Frauenspiegel · ⊙ VI-VII; Eur.* exc. Sc, EC-Eur.; TR, Cyprus, Palest., Cauc., Iran, Moroc., Tun.
- **pentagonia** (L.) Druce · ⊙ VI-IX; Eur.: Ba; TR, Syr., Palest., Cauc., Iraq, W-Iran, nat. in sp., F
- **speculum-veneris** (L.) Chaix · E:Venus' Looking Glass; G:Echter Frauenspiegel · ⊙ VI-IX; Eur.* exc. BrI, Sc; TR, Levant, N-Iraq, Cauc., Egypt

Leiophyllum (Pers.) R. Hedw. -n- *Ericaceae* · 1 sp. · E:Sand Myrtle; F:Myrtille des sables; G:Sandmyrte
- **buxifolium** (P.J. Bergius) Elliott · E:Sand Myrtle; G:Sandmyrte · ♄ e ⤳ ◠ Z6 V-VI; USA: NE
- var. **hugeri** (Small) C.K. Schneid. · ♄ e Z5; USA: NE, SE

Lemaireocereus Britton & Rose = Pachycereus
- *beneckei* (C. Ehrenb.) Britton & Rose = Stenocereus beneckei
- *chende* (Rol.-Goss.) Britton & Rose = Heliabravoa chende
- *chichipe* (Rol.-Goss.) Britton & Rose = Polaskia chichipe
- *dumortieri* (Scheidw.) Britton & Rose = Isolatocereus dumortieri
- *eruca* (Brandegee) Britton & Rose = Machaerocereus eruca
- *marginatus* (DC.) A. Berger = Pachycereus marginatus
- *pruinosus* (Otto) Britton & Rose = Stenocereus pruinosus
- *queretaroensis* (F.A.C. Weber) Saff. = Stenocereus queretaroensis
- *stellatus* (Pfeiff.) Britton & Rose = Stenocereus stellatus

- *thurberi* (Engelm.) Britton & Rose = Stenocereus thurberi
- *weberi* (J.M. Coult.) Britton & Rose = Pachycereus weberi

Lembotropis Griseb. = Cytisus
- *emeriflorus* (Rchb.) Skalická = Cytisus emeriflorus
- *nigricans* (L.) Griseb. = Cytisus nigricans

Lemmaphyllum C. Presl -n- *Polypodiaceae* · 13 spp. · F:Fougère; G:Schuppenblatt
- **carnosum** (Wall.) C. Presl Z10

Lemna L. -f- *Lemnaceae* · 7 (-13) spp. · E:Duckweed; F:Lenticule, Lentille d'eau; G:Entengrütze, Wasserlinse
- **aequinoctialis** Welw. · E:Lesser Duckweed; G:Schiefe Wasserlinse · ⁂ ≈ Z10; Am., Afr., As
- **gibba** L. · E:Fat Duckweed, Inflated Duckweed; F:Lentille d'eau bossue; G:Bucklige Wasserlinse · ⁂ ≈ Z4 IV-VI; Eur.*, Cauc., TR, Iran, C-As., Him., N-Afr., Eth., USA, Mex., C-Am., W.Ind., S-Am. (Anden)
- **minor** L. · E:Common Duckweed, Duckweed; G:Kleine Wasserlinse · ⁂ ≈ Z4 V-VI; Eur.*, Cauc., Him., W-Sib., E-Sib., Amur, Sakhal., Kamchat., C-As., Mong., China, Korea, Jap., Java, N-Afr., Eth., E-Afr., S-Afr., Can., USA*, Mex., S-Am. (Anden)
- *minuscula* = Lemna minuta
- **minuta** Humb., Bonpl. & Kunth · E:Least Duckweed; G:Winzige Wasserlinse · ⁂ ≈ V-IX; N-Am.
- **trisulca** L. · E:Ivy Duckweed, Star Duckweed; F:Lentille d'eau à trois lobes; G:Dreifurchige Wasserlinse · ⁂ ≈ VI; Eur.*, As., N-Afr., Alaska, Can.; USA* , Mex., Mauritius, S-Austr.
- **turionifera** Landolt · G:Rote Wasserlinse · ⁂ ≈ VI-VII; TR, Sib., C-As., Ind., E-As., N-Am.

Lenophyllum Rose -n- *Crassulaceae* · 7 spp. · G:Trogblatt
- **guttatum** (Rose) Rose · G:Geflecktes Trogblatt · ⁂ ⚇ ⤳ Z9 ⌂; Mex.
- *pusillum* Rose = Lenophyllum texanum
- **texanum** (J.G. Sm.) Rose · E:Coastal Stonecrop · ⁂ ⚇ ⤳ Z9 ⌂; Mex.

Lens Mill. -f- *Fabaceae* · 4-6 spp. · E:Lentil;

F:Lentille; G:Linse
- **culinaris** Medik. · E:Lentil; G:Gemüse-
Linse · ☉ Z8 VI-VIII Ⓝ; orig. ?; cult. Eur.,
As., nat. in Eur.* exc. BrI, Sc
- **ervoides** (Brign.) Grande · ☉ Z8; Eur.:
Ib, Ital-P, Ba, Crim; TR, Levant, Cauc.,
Moroc., Alger.

Leonotis (Pers.) R. Br. -f- *Lamiaceae* ·
9 spp. · E:Lion's Ear; F:Oreille-de-lion;
G:Löwenohr
- **leonurus** (L.) R. Br. · E:Lion's Ear;
G:Großblättriges Löwenohr · ♄ d Z9 Ⓚ
IX-XI; S-Afr.

Leontice L. -f- *Berberidaceae* · 3-5 spp. ·
G:Trapp; F:Léontice
- *chrysogonum* L. = Bongardia chrysogonum
- **leontopetalum** L. · ⚄ Z6 IV; Eur.: Ba;
TR, Levant, Iraq, Iran, Pakist., C-As.,
N-Afr.
- *thalictroides* L. = Caulophyllum thalictroides

Leontodon L. -n- *Asteraceae* · 40-50 spp. ·
E:Hawkbit; F:Dent-de-lion; G:Falscher
Löwenzahn, Milchkraut
- **autumnalis** L. · E:Autumn Hawkbit;
G:Gewöhnlicher Herbst-Löwenzahn · ⚄
VII-IX; Eur.*, W-Sib., NW-Afr., Greenl.
- **crispus** Vill. · G:Krauser Löwenzahn · ⚄
VI-VII; Eur.*: Ib, Fr, Ital-P, Ba, E-Eur.;
TR, Cauc.
- **croceus** Haenke · G:Safran-Löwenzahn ·
⚄ VII-VIII; Eur.: I, A, Ba, RO, W-Russ.;
E-Alp., Carp., BG
- **helveticus** Mérat · G:Schweizer Löwen-
zahn · ⚄ VII-IX; Eur.: F, C-Eur., I, Slove.,
Bosn.; Alp., Vosges, Schwarzwald
- **hispidus** L. · E:Rough Hawkbit ;
G:Gewöhnlicher Rauer Löwenzahn · ⚄
Z6 VI-X; Eur.*, TR, Cauc., N-Iran, N-Afr.,
nat. in N-Am.
- **incanus** (L.) Schrank · G:Grauer Löwenzahn · ⚄ V-VI; Eur.: F, I, C-Eur., EC-Eur.,
Slove., Croatia, Bosn., ? RO; mts.
- **montaniformis** Widder · G:Nord-
dostalpen-Löwenzahn · ⚄ VII-VIII; Eur.:
A, ; NE-Alp.
- **montanus** Lam.
- subsp. **montanus** · E:Mountain Hawbit;
G:Gewöhnlicher Berg-Löwenzahn · ⚄
VII-VIII; Eur.* exc. BrI, Sc; mts.
- **saxatilis** Lam. · E:Lesser Hawkbit;

G:Hundslattich, Nickender Löwenzahn ·
☉ ⚄ VII-VIII; Eur.* exc. Sc; NW-Afr., nat.
in Sc
- *taraxacum* L. = Taraxacum sect.
Ruderalia
- **tenuiflorus** (Gaudin) Rchb. · G:Schmal-
blättriger Löwenzahn · ⚄ IV-V; Eur.: I,
Sw

Leontopodium (Pers.) R. Br. ex Cass.
-n- *Asteraceae* · 35-58 spp. · E:Edelweiss;
F:Edelweiss; G:Edelweiß
- *alpinum* Cass. = Leontopodium nivale
subsp. alpinum
- subsp. *nivale* (Ten.) Tutin = Leontopodium nivale subsp. nivale
- var. *sibiricum* (Cass.) O. Fedtsch. =
Leontopodium leontopodioides
- var. *stracheyi* Hook. f. = Leontopodium
stracheyi
- **calocephalum** Diels · ⚄ △ Z5 VI-VII;
SW-China, Tibet
- **hayachinense** (Takeda) H. Hara &
Kitam. · ⚄ Z6; Jap. Honshu; mts.
- **himalayanum** DC. · ⚄ △ Z5 VI-VII; Him.,
China: Yunnan, Tibet
- **japonicum** Miq. · ⚄ Z5 VI-VII; China,
Jap.
- **leontopodioides** (Willd.) Beauverd · ⚄
△ Z5 VI-VII; Kashmir, Him., SW-China
- **nivale** (Ten.) A. Huet ex Hand.-Mazz. ·
G:Alpen-Edelweiß
- subsp. **alpinum** (Cass.) Greuter ·
G:Gewöhnliches Alpen-Edelweiß · ⚄ △
Z5 VI-VII ▽; I: Apenn.
- subsp. **nivale** · E:Edelweiss; F:Edelweiss
des Alpes; G:Weißes Alpen-Edelweiß ·
⚄ △ Z5 VII-IX ▽; Eur.* exc. Sc, BrI; mts.
Pyr., Alp., Carp., W-Ba
- *ochroleucum* Beauverd = Leontopodium
leontopodioides
- **palibinianum** Beauverd · ⚄ Z5 VI-VII;
Sib., Mong.
- *sibiricum* DC. = Leontopodium palibinianum
- **souliei** Beauverd · F:Edelweiss · ⚄ △ Z5
VI-VII; Yunnan, Sichuan
- **stracheyi** (Hook. f.) C.B. Clarke · ⚄ Z5
VI-VII; SW-China

Leonurus L. -m- *Lamiaceae* · 3-9 spp. ·
E:Motherwort; F:Agripaume, Léonure;
G:Herzgespann, Löwenschwanz
- **cardiaca** L. · E:Motherwort; G:Gewöhnli-
ches Echtes Herzgespann · ⚄ Z3 VI-IX ⚘ ;

Eur.* exc. BrI; TR, nat. in BrI, N-Am.
- **lanatus** (L.) Pers. · E:Woolly Mother-
wort; G:Wolliges Herzgespann · ⁴
VII-VIII ⚥ ; E-Sib., Mong.
- **marrubiastrum** L. · E:False Motherwort;
G:Filziges Herzgespann, Katzenschwanz
· ☉ VII-VIII; Eur.: Ital-P, C-Eur., EC-Eur.,
Ba, E-Eur.; Cauc., W-Sib., C-As., nat. in F,
N-Am.
- *villosus* d'Urv. = Leonurus cardiaca

Leopoldia Parl. = Muscari
- *comosa* (L.) Parl. = Muscari comosum

Leopoldinia Mart. -f- *Arecaceae* · 3 spp.
- **piassaba** Wallace · E:Para Piassava · ♄ e
🏠 Ⓝ; Venez., Braz.

Lepidium L. -n- *Brassicaceae* · c. 140 spp. ·
E:Peppergrass, Pepperwort; F:Cresson
alénois, Passerage; G:Kresse
- **bonariense** L. · E:Argentine Pepperwort ·
☉ ☉; S-Am., nat. in B, NL, G, H, sp.
- **campestre** (L.) R. Br. · E:Field Cress;
G:Feld-Kresse · ☉ V-VI; Eur.*, TR, Cauc.,
nat. in N-Am.
- **densiflorum** Schrad. · E:Prairie Peppergrass; G:Dichtblütige Kresse · ☉ V-VII;
N-Am., nat. in Sc, Fr, C-Eur., EC-Eur.,
Ital-P
- **graminifolium** L. · E:Tall Pepperwort ;
G:Grasblättrige Kresse · ⁴ VI-VIII; Eur.*
exc. BrI, Sc; TR, Levant., Moroc., Alger.,
nat. in BrI
- **heterophyllum** Benth. · G:Verschieden-
blättrige Kresse · ⁴ V-VI; Eur.: Sc, BrI, Fr,
Ib, EC-Eur., nat. in D
- **latifolium** L. · E:Perennial Peppergrass;
G:Breitblättrige Kresse · ⁴ V-VII; Eur.*,
TR, Levant, Cauc., Iran, W-Sib., C-As.,
Him., Tibet, Moroc., Egypt
- **meyenii** Walp. · ⁴ Ⓝ; Peru, Bol.
- *neglectum* Thell. = Lepidium densiflorum
- **perfoliatum** L. · E:Perfoliate Pepperwort;
G:Durchwachsene Kresse · ☉ V-VI; Eur.:
A, EC-Eur., Ba, E-Eur.; TR, Levant, Cauc.,
Iran, W-Sib., C-As., Him., nat. in DK, Fr,
Ib
- **ruderale** L. · E:Peppergrass; G:Schutt-
Kresse · ☉ V-X; Eur.*, TR, Palest., Iraq,
Cauc., W-Sib., E-Sib., C-As.
- **sativum** L. · E:Garden Cress, Pepperwort;
G:Garten-Kresse · ☉ ☉ V-VII Ⓝ; Egypt,
Sudan, Eth., Arabia, TR, Palest., Syr.,
Iran, Iraq, Pakist., W-Him., nat. in

cosmop.
- **virginicum** L. · E:Virginia Pepperweed;
G:Virginische Kresse · ☉ V-VIII ⚥ ;
N-Am., nat. in Eur.* exc. Br

Lepidocoryphantha Backeb. = Coryphantha
- *macromeris* (Engelm.) Backeb. =
Coryphantha macromeris

Lepidorrhachis (H. Wendl. & Drude) O.F.
Cook -f- *Arecaceae* · 1 sp.
- **mooreana** (F. Muell.) O.F. Cook · ♄ e 🏠
🏠; Lord Howe Is.

Lepidozamia Regel -f- *Zamiaceae* · 2 spp.
- **peroffskyana** Regel · ♄ e Z10 🏠 ⚘ ▽
✳; Austr.: Queensl., N.S.Wales

Lepironia Rich. -f- *Cyperaceae* · 1 sp.
- **articulata** (Retz.) Domin · ⁴ 🏠 Ⓝ; Sri
Lanka, Malaya, Queensl., Madag., Fiji

Lepisanthes Blume -f- *Sapindaceae* ·
24 spp.
- **rubiginosa** (Roxb.) Leenh. · E:Woodland
Rambutan · ♄ ♄ Z9 🏠 Ⓝ; Him., Ind.,
China, Burma, Malay. Arch., N-Austr.

Lepismium Pfeiff. -n- *Cactaceae* · 16 spp.
- *cavernosum* Lindb. = Lepismium
cruciforme
- *chrysocarpum* (Loefgr.) Backeb. =
Rhipsalis puniceodiscus var. chrysocarpa
- *commune* Pfeiff. = Lepismium cruciforme
- **cruciforme** (Vell.) Miq. · ♄ ⵋ ⵌ Z9 🏠
▽ ✳; Braz., Parag., Arg.
- *dissimile* G. Lindb. = Rhipsalis dissimilis
- *floccosum* (Salm-Dyck) Backeb. =
Rhipsalis floccosa
- *gibberulum* (F.A.C. Weber) Backeb. =
Rhipsalis floccosa
- *grandiflorum* (Haw.) Backeb. = Rhipsalis
hadrosoma
- **houlletianum** (Lem.) Barthlott ·
E:Snowdrop Cactus · ♄ ⵋ ⵌ Z9 🏠 ▽ ✳;
E-Braz.
- *ianthothele* (Monv.) Barthlott = Pfeiffera
ianthothele
- *marnierianum* Backeb. = Rhipsalis
dissimilis
- *megalanthum* (Loefgr.) Backeb. =
Rhipsalis neves-armondii
- *paradoxum* Salm-Dyck ex Pfeiff. =
Rhipsalis paradoxa
- *pulvinigerum* (G. Lindb.) Backeb. =

Rhipsalis pulvinigera
- *puniceodiscus* (G. Lindb.) Backeb. =
  Rhipsalis puniceodiscus var. puniceodiscus
- var. *chrysocarpum* (Loefgr.) Borg =
  Rhipsalis puniceodiscus var. chrysocarpa
- *trigonum* (Pfeiff.) Backeb. = Rhipsalis
  trigona

Leptarrhena R. Br. -f- *Saxifragaceae* · 1 sp.
- **pyrolifolia** (D. Don) R. Br. · E:Pearleaf ·
  ⚲ △ Z5 VI-VII; Kamchat., Aleuten,
  Alaska, W-Can., USA: Wash.

Leptinella Cass. -f- *Asteraceae* · 33 spp. ·
  F:Cotule; G:Fiederpolster
- **atrata** (Hook. f.) D.G. Lloyd & C.J.
  Webb · ⚲ ⤳ △ Z8 ⊕ VII-VIII; NZ
- **dioica** Hook. f. · F:Cotule dioïque;
  G:Salz-Fiederpolster · ⚲ ⤳ △ Z5 VII-
  VIII; NZ
- **potentillina** F. Muell. · ⚲ ⤳ Z8; NZ
- **squalida** Hook. f. · E:New Zealand Brass
  Buttons; G:Echtes Fiederpolster · ⚲ ⤳
  △ Z8 ∧ VI-VII; NZ

Leptocallisia (Benth.) Pichon = Callisia
- *monandra* (Sw.) W. Ludw. & Rohweder =
  Callisia monandra
- *multiflora* (M. Martens & Galeotti)
  Pichon = Callisia multiflora
- *umbellulata* (Lam.) Pichon = Callisia
  monandra

Leptocladodia Buxb. = Mammillaria
- *elongata* (DC.) Buxb. = Mammillaria
  elongata
- *leona* (Poselg.) Buxb. = Mammillaria
  pottsii
- *microhelia* (Werderm.) Buxb. = Mammillaria microhelia var. microhelia
- *sphacelata* (Mart.) Buxb. = Mammillaria
  sphacelata

Leptodermis Wall. -f- *Rubiaceae* · 48 spp.
- **lanceolata** Wall. · ♄ d Z9 ⊕ VI-X;
  NW-Him.
- **oblonga** Bunge · ♄ d Z7 ∧ VII-X;
  N-China

× **Leptolaelia** hort. -f- *Orchidaceae* (*Laelia*
  × *Leptotes*)

Leptopteris C. Presl -f- *Osmundaceae* ·
  7 spp.

- **hymenophylloides** (A. Rich.) C. Presl ·
  ⚲ Z10 ⊕; NZ
- **superba** (Colenso) C. Presl · E:Prince-of-
  Wales Feathers; G:Prinz-of-Wales-Farn ·
  ⚲ Z10 ⊕; NZ

Leptopyrum Rchb. -n- *Ranunculaceae* ·
  1 sp.
- **fumarioides** (L.) Rchb. · ⊙; W-Sib.,
  E-Sib., Amur, Mong, Tibet, China

Leptosiphon Benth. = Linanthus
- *grandiflorus* Benth. = Linanthus grandiflorus
- *luteus* Benth. = Linanthus androsaceus
  subsp. luteus

Leptospermum J.R. Forst. & G. Forst.
  -n- *Myrtaceae* · 79 spp. · E:Tea Tree;
  F:Leptospermum; G:Südseemyrte,
  Teebaum
- *ambiguum* Sm. = Kunzea ambigua
- **arachnoideum** Sm. · ♄ e Z9 ⊕ VII-VIII;
  Austr.: N.S.Wales
- *cunninghamii* S. Schauer = Leptospermum myrtifolium
- **grandiflorum** Lodd. · ♄ e Z9 ⊕ VIII;
  Tasman.
- *humifusum* A. Cunn. ex S. Schauer =
  Leptospermum rupestre
- **laevigatum** (Sol. ex Gaertn.) F. Muell. ·
  E:Australian Tea Tree; G:Australischer
  Teebaum · ♄ e Z9 ⊕ Ⓝ; Austr.: Queensl.,
  N.S.Wales, Victoria, Tasman.
- **lanigerum** (Aiton) Sm. · E:Woolly
  Tea Tree · ♄ e Z8 ⊕ VII-VIII; Austr.:
  N.S.Wales, Victoria, S-Austr., Tasman.
- **myrtifolium** Sieber ex DC. · E:Myrtle
  Tea Tree · ♄ e Z8 ⊕; Austr.: N.S.Wales,
  Victoria, Tasman.
- **petersonii** F.M. Bailey · E:Lemon-scented
  Tea Tree · ♄ ♄ e Z9 ⊕; Austr.: Queensl.,
  N.S.Wales
- **polygalifolium** Salisb. · E:Tantoon ·
  ♄ e Z9 ⊕ VII-VIII; Austr.: Queensl.,
  N.S.Wales, Victoria, Tasman.
- *pubescens* Lam. = Leptospermum
  lanigerum
- *rodwayanum* Summerh. & H.F. Comber =
  Leptospermum grandiflorum
- *roseum* hort. ex Otto & Dietr. = Leptospermum polygalifolium
- **rotundifolium** (Maiden & Betche)
  Domin · E:Round-leaf Tea Tree · ♄ e Z9
  ⊕; Austr.: N.S.Wales

– **rupestre** Hook. f. · ♄ Z9 ⌂; Tasman.
– **scoparium** J.R. Forst. & G. Forst. ·
  E:Broom Tea Tree, Manuka; G:Neusee-
  landmyrte · ♄ ♄ e ✕ Z8 ⌂ V-VI; Austr.:
  Victoria; NZ
– **some cultivars**
– **sericeum** Labill. · E:Swamp Tea Tree · ♄
  e Z9 ⌂; Austr.: W-Austr., Tasman.
– **squarrosum** Gaertn. · E:Peach Blossom
  Tea Tree · ♄ e Z9 ⌂; Austr.: N.S.Wales, ?
  Queensl.
– **trinervium** (Sm.) Joy Thomps. ·
  E:Slender Tea Tree · ♄ e Z9 ⌂ V; Austr.:
  Queensl., N.S.Wales

Leptotes Lindl. -f- *Orchidaceae* · 7 spp.
– **bicolor** Lindl. · ♃ Z10 ⌂ I-III ▽ ✳;
  E-Braz.
– **unicolor** Barb. Rodr. · ♃ Z10 ⌂ II ▽ ✳;
  S-Braz.

Lepyrodiclis Fenzl -f- *Caryophyllaceae* ·
  3 spp. · G:Blasenmiere
– **holosteoides** (C.A. Mey.) Fisch. & C.A.
  Mey. · G:Spurrenähnliche Blasenmiere ·
  ⊙ V-VI; TR, Cauc., Iran, C-As., Him.,
  W-China

Leschenaultia R. Br. -f- *Goodeniaceae* ·
  24 spp. · E:Leschenaultia;
  F:Leschenaultia; G:Leschenaultie
– **biloba** Lindl. · E:Blue Leschenaultia;
  G:Blaue Leschenaultie · ♄ e Z9 ⌂ VII-
  VIII; W-Austr.
– **formosa** R. Br. · E:Red Leschenaultia;
  G:Rote Leschenaultie · ♄ Z9 ⌂ VII-VIII;
  W-Austr.

Lespedeza Michx. -f- *Fabaceae* · 40 spp. ·
  E:Bush Clover; F:Lespédéza; G:Buschklee
– **bicolor** Turcz. · E:Bicolored Lespedeza;
  G:Zweifarbiger Buschklee · ♄ Z6 VIII-IX
  Ⓝ; Jap., Korea, Manch., N-China, Amur
– **cuneata** (Dum.-Cours.) G. Don ·
  E:Chinese Bush Clover; G:Chinesischer
  Buschklee · ♄ d VIII-IX Ⓝ; Afgh, Ind.,
  China, Korea, Jap., Taiwan, Phil., Austr.,
  nat. in S-USA, E-USA
– *formosa* Koehne = Lespedeza thunbergii
– **japonica** L.H. Bailey · ♄ d IX; Jap.,
  Korea, Manch.
– *macrocarpa* Bunge = Campylotropis
  macrocarpa
– **maximowiczii** C.K. Schneid. · ♄ d Z5
  VII-VIII; Jap., Korea

– *sericea* (Thunb.) Miq. non Benth. =
  Lespedeza cuneata
– *sieboldii* Miq. = Lespedeza thunbergii
– *stipulacea* Maxim. = Kummerowia
  stipulacea
– *striata* (Thunb. ex Murray) Hook. & Arn.
  = Kummerowia striata
– **thunbergii** (DC.) Nakai · F:Lespedeza de
  Thunberg; G:Thunbergs Buschklee · ♄ d
  Z7 ⋀ IX-X; Jap., N-China

Leucadendron R. Br. -n- *Proteaceae* ·
  79 spp. · E:Silver Tree; F:Arbre d'argent;
  G:Silberbaum
– **aemulum** R. Br. · ♄ e ✕ Z9 ⌂; S-Afr.
– **argenteum** (L.) R. Br. · E:Silver Tree;
  G:Echter Silberbaum · ♄ e Z9 ⌂; Cape
– **coniferum** (L.) Meisn. · ♄ e ✕ Z9 ⌂;
  Cape
– **corymbosum** P.J. Bergius · ♄ e Z9 ⌂;
  Cape
– **grandiflorum** (Salisb.) R. Br. · G:Groß-
  blütiger Silberbaum · ♄ e ✕ Z9 ⌂; Cape
– **levisianum** (L.) P.J. Bergius · ♄ e Z9 ⌂;
  Cape
– **muirii** E. Phillips · ♄ e ✕ Z9 ⌂; Cape
– **nervosum** E. Phillips & Hutch. · ♄ e ✕ Z9
  ⌂; Cape
– **platyspermum** R. Br. · ♄ e ✕ Z9 ⌂; Cape
– **plumosum** R. Br. · ♄ e Z9 ⌂; S-Afr.
– **pubescens** R. Br. · ♄ e ✕ Z9 ⌂; Cape
– **sabulosum** T.M. Salter · ♄ e ✕ Z9 ⌂;
  Cape
– **salignum** P.J. Bergius · ♄ e ✕ Z9 ⌂; Cape
– **tortum** R. Br. · ♄ e Z9 ⌂; S-Afr.

Leucaena Benth. -f- *Mimosaceae* · 22 spp. ·
  F:Tamarinier sauvage; G:Weißfaden
– *glauca* auct. = Leucaena leucocephala
– **leucocephala** (Lam.) de Wit · E:White
  Leadtree, Wild Tamarind; G:Pferdetama-
  rinde, Weißfaden · ♄ ♄ e Z9 ⌂ Ⓝ; Fla.,
  W.Ind., S-Am., nat. in Tex., Calif., Hawaii

Leucanthemella Tzvelev -f- *Asteraceae* ·
  2 spp. · E:Autumn Oxeye; F:Marguerite
  d'automne; G:Herbstmargerite
– **serotina** (L.) Tzvelev · E:Hungarian
  Daisy, Moon Daisy; F:Chrysanthème
  tardif; G:Herbstmargerite · ♃ Z7 X; Eur.:
  EC-Eur., Ba, E-Eur., nat. in Sw

Leucanthemopsis (Giroux) Heywood
  -f- *Asteraceae* · 6 spp. · E:Alpine Chrysanthemum; F:Marguerite des Alpes;

G:Alpenmargerite
- **alpina** (L.) Heywood · E:Alpine Moon Daisy; G:Alpenmargerite, Zwergmargerite · ⚥ △ Z6 VII-VIII; Eur.: sp., F, Ital-P, C-Eur., EC-Eur., Bosn., E-Eur.; mts.

Leucanthemum Mill. -n- *Asteraceae* · c. 25 spp. · E:Oxeye Daisy; F:Marguerite; G:Margerite
- **adustum** (W.D.J. Koch) Gremli · G:Berg-Margerite · ⚥ VII-VIII; Eur.: Sc, Fr, S-I, C-Eur., EC-Eur., Slove., RO
- **atratum** (Jacq.) DC.
- subsp. **atratum** · E:Saw-leaved Moon Daisy; F:Leucanthème noirâtre; G:Schwarzrandige Margerite · ⚥; Eur.: NE-Alp.
- subsp. **halleri** (Suter) Heywood · F:Leucanthème de Haller; G:Hallers Margerite · ⚥ VII-VIII; Eur.: Alp.
- *corymbosum* (L.) Gren. & Godr. = Tanacetum corymbosum subsp. corymbosum
- **gaudinii** Dalla Torre · G:Hügel-Margerite · ⚥ VI-VIII; Eur.: A, Sw +
- *gayanum* Maire = Rhodanthemum gayanum
- **halleri** (Suter) Polatschek
- **heterophyllum** (Willd.) DC. · G:Verschiedenblättrige Margerite · ⚥ VII-VIII; Eur.: S-Alp., C-Apenn.
- **ircutianum** DC. · G:Fettwiesen-Margerite · ⊙ ⚥ V-X; Eur.: most; N-As, nat. in N-Am.
- **lithopolitanicum** (E. Mey.) Polatschek · ⚥ VII-IX; Sloven.
- **maximum** (Ramond) DC. · E:Daisy Chrysanthemum; G:Pyrenäen-Margerite · ⚥ ✕ Z6 VI-VII; Eur.: Pyr.
- *maximum* hort. = Leucanthemum × superbum
- *paludosum* (Poir.) Bonnet & Barratte = Hymenostemma paludosum
- *parthenium* (L.) Gren. & Godr. = Tanacetum parthenium
- × **superbum** (Bergmans ex J.W. Ingram) D.H. Kent (*L. maximum × L. lacustre*) · E:Shasta Daisy; F:Marguerite d'été; G:Garten-Margerite · ⚥ Z5; cult.
- **many cultivars**
- **vulgare** Lam. · E:Moon Daisy, Ox-Eye Daisy; F:Grande marguerite; G:Magerwiesen-Margerite · ⚥ Z3 V-X ⚇ Ⓝ; Eur.*, TR, Cauc., W-Sib., E-Sib., Amur, Sakhal., Kamchat., nat. in N-Am
- **some cultivars**

Leuchtenbergia Hook. -f- *Cactaceae* · 1 sp.
- **principis** Hook. · ⚘ ⓐ ▽ ✳; N-Mex.

Leucocoryne Lindl. -f- *Alliaceae* · 45 spp.
- **ixioides** (Hook.) Lindl. · E:Glory of the Sun · ⚥ ✕ Z9 ⓐ III-IV; Chile

Leucogenes Beauverd -m- *Asteraceae* · 2 spp. · E:New Zealand Edelweiss; F:Leucogenes; G:Neuseelandedelweiß
- **leontopodium** (Hook. f.) Beauverd · ⚥ e Z8 ⓐ; NZ

Leucojum L. -n- *Amaryllidaceae* · 11 sp. · E:Snowflake; F:Nivéole; G:Knotenblume
- **aestivum** L. · E:Loddon Lily, Summer Snowflake; F:Nivéole d'été; G:Sommer-Knotenblume · ⚥ Z4 V-VI ⚇ ▽; Eur.* exc. Sc; TR, Cauc., Iran, nat. in DK
- **autumnale** L. · E:Autumn Snowflake, Snowflake; G:Herbst-Knotenblume · ⚥ Z8 ⓐ IX-X ⚇ ▽; Eur.: Ib, Sard., Sic.? Crete
- **vernum** L. · E:Spring Snowflake; F:Nivéole de printemps; G:Frühlings-Knotenblume, Märzenbecher · ⚥ Z5 II-IV ⚇ ▽; Eur.: I, C-Eur., EC-Eur., Slove., Croatia, Serb.

Leucophyllum Humb. & Bonpl. -n- *Scrophulariaceae* · 12 spp.
- **frutescens** (Berland.) I.M. Johnst. · E:Texas Ranger · ♄ e Z9 ⓐ IV-VII; Tex.
- *texanum* Benth. = Leucophyllum frutescens

Leucophyta R. Br. -f- *Asteraceae* · 1 sp. · E:Cushion Bush; G:Silberblatt
- **brownii** Cass.

Leucopogon R. Br. -m- *Epacridaceae* · c. 150 spp.
- **fraseri** A. Cunn. · ♄ e Z9 ⓐ VII-VIII; Austr.: N.S.Wales, Tasman.; NZ
- **virgatus** (Labill.) R. Br. · ♄ e Z9 ⓐ VII-VIII; Austr.: S-Austr., Tasman.

Leucospermum R. Br. -n- *Proteaceae* · 46 spp. · E:Pincushion; G:Gärtnerprotee, Nadelkissen
- **cordifolium** (Salisb. ex Knight) Fourc. · E:Nodding Pincushion, Pincushion; G:Herzblättriges Nadelkissen · ♄ e ✕ Z9 ⓐ; Cape
- **grandiflorum** (Salisb.) R. Br. ·

E:Fountain Pincushion; G:Großblütiges Nadelkissen · ♄ e Z9 ⓐ V-VII; Cape
- *nutans* R. Br. = Leucospermum cordifolium

Leucothoe D. Don -f- *Ericaceae* · 44 spp. · F:Andromède, Leucothoë; G:Traubenheide
- **axillaris** (Lam.) D. Don · E:Dog Hobble; G:Achsenblütige Traubenheide · ♄ e Z6 V-VI; USA: Va., SE, Fla.
- **catesbaei** (Walter) A. Gray · ♄ e Z6 IV-V; USA: SE
- *catesbaei* hort. = Leucothoe fontanesiana
- *editorum* Fernald & B.G. Schub. = Leucothoe fontanesiana
- **fontanesiana** (Steud.) Sleumer · E:Drooping Laurel, Fetter Bush, Switch Ivy; F:Leucothoë; G:Gebogene Traubenheide · ♄ Z6 IV-VI; USA: NE, SE
- **grayana** Maxim. · ♄ e Z6 V-VI; Jap.
- **keiskei** Miq. · G:Zwerg-Traubenheide · ♄ e Z5 VII; Jap.
- **racemosa** (L.) A. Gray · E:Fetter Bush, Swamp Sweetbells; G:Sommergrüne Traubenheide · ♄ d Z6 V-VI; USA: NE, SE, Fla.
- **recurva** (Buckland) A. Gray · E:Redtwig Dog Hobble · ♄ d Z7 ∧ IV-VI; USA: Va., SE
- *walteri* (Willd.) N.C. Melvin = Leucothoe fontanesiana

Leuzea DC. -f- *Asteraceae* · 3 spp. · F:Leuzée; G:Zapfenkopf
- **conifera** (L.) DC. · ♃ Z8 ⓐ; Eur.: Ib, Ital-P, F; Marok., Alger., Tun.
- *rhapontica* (L.) Holub = Stemmacantha rhapontica

Levisticum Hill -n- *Apiaceae* · 1 sp. · E:Lovage; F:Ache de montagne, Céleri vivace; G:Liebstöckel, Maggikraut
- **officinale** W.D.J. Koch · E:Lovage; G:Liebstöckel, Maggikraut · ♃ Z4 VII-VIII ⚥ Ⓝ; Iran, nat. in Eur.* exc. BrI, USA

Lewisia Pursh -f- *Portulacaceae* · 18 spp. · E:Bitterroot; F:Lewisia; G:Bitterwurzel, Lewisie
- **brachycalyx** Engelm. ex A. Gray · E:Shortsepal Lewisia · ♃ △ Z7 ⓐ ∧ V; USA: Calif., Rocky Mts, SW
- **columbiana** (Howell ex A. Gray) B.L. Rob. · E:Columbia Lewisia;

G:Columbia-Bitterwurz · ♃ △ Z7 ⓐ ∧ VI-VIII; Can.: W; USA: NW, Calif., Rocky Mts.
- **cotyledon** (S. Watson) B.L. Rob.
- var. **cotyledon** · E:Cliff Maids, Imperial Lewisia; G:Gewöhnliche Bitterwurz · ♃ Z7 ⓐ ∧; USA: Oreg.
- var. **heckneri** (C.V. Morton) Munz · ♃ △ Z7 ⓐ ∧ VI; Calif.
- var. **howellii** (S. Watson) Jeps. · ♃ △ Z7 ⓐ ∧ VI-VIII; USA: Oreg.
- *heckneri* (C.V. Morton) Gabrielson = Lewisia cotyledon var. heckneri
- **leeana** (Porter) B.L. Rob. · E:Quill-leaf Lewisia · ♃ △ Z7 ⓐ ∧ VI-VIII; USA: Oreg., Calif.
- **nevadensis** (A. Gray) B.L. Rob. · E:Nevada Bitter Root; G:Nevada-Bitterwurz · ♃ △ Z6 ⓐ VI-VII; USA: NW, Calif., Rocky Mts.
- **oppositifolia** (S. Watson) B.L. Rob. · ♃ △ Z7 ⓐ ∧ VI-VIII; USA: Oreg., Calif.
- **pygmaea** (A. Gray) B.L. Rob. · E:Alpine Lewisia · ♃ Z3; Alaska, Can.: W; USA: NW, Calif., Rocky Mts.
- var. *nevadensis* (A. Gray) Fosberg = Lewisia nevadensis
- **rediviva** Pursh · E:Bitter Root ; G:Auferstehende Bitterwurz · ♃ △ Z7 ⓐ ∧ VI-VIII; Can.: W; USA: NC, SW, Rocky Mts., NW, Calif.
- **tweedyi** (A. Gray) B.L. Rob. · ♃ △ Z7 ⓐ ∧ VI-VII; USA: NW, Rocky Mts.
- **Cultivars:**
- **many cultivars**

Leycesteria Wall. -f- *Caprifoliaceae* · 6 spp. · F:Herbe-aux-faisans, Leycesteria; G:Leycesterie
- **crocothyrsos** Airy Shaw · ♄ d Z9 ⓐ IV; InG: Assam
- **formosa** Wall. · E:Himalayan Honeysuckle, Pheasant Berry; F:Arbre à faisan; G:Schöne Leycesterie · ♄ d Z7 ⓐ ∧ VIII-IX; Him., SW-China

Leymus Hochst. -m- *Poaceae* · 40 spp. · E:Lyme Grass; F:Elyme; G:Strandroggen
- **arenarius** (L.) Hochst. · E:Lyme Grass; F:Seigle de mer; G:Gewöhnlicher Strandroggen · ♃ Z6 VI-VIII Ⓝ; Eur.: sp., Fr, BrI, , G, Sc, Russ..; N-As., Alaska, Can., USA: NE, SW, NW; Greenl., nat. in N-Am., Chile
- **racemosus** (Lam.) Tzvelev · ♃ VII-VIII;

Eur.: E-Sp., BG; N-TR, Cauc., C-As.
- **secalinus** (Georgi) Tzvelev · E:Wild Rye;
  G:Wilder Roggen · ⚂ Z5 VII-VIII; Alaska,
  Can., USA* exc. SC

× **Liaopsis** hort. -f- Orchidaceae (*Laelia* ×
Laeliopsis)

Liatris Gaertn. ex Schreb. -f- Asteraceae ·
33 (-43) spp. · E:Blazing Star, Button
Snake Root, Gay Feather; F:Liatride;
G:Prachtscharte
- **elegans** (Walter) Michx. · E:Pinkscale
  Blazing Star; G:Sand-Prachtscharte · ⚂
  Z7 VIII-IX; USA: Va., SE, Fla.
- **graminifolia** (Walter) Willd. · G:Gras-
  blättrige Prachtscharte · ⚂ VIII-X; USA:
  NE, SE, Fla.
- **punctata** Hook. · E:Snakeroot; G:Herbst-
  Prachtscharte · ⚂ Z3 VIII-X; Can.: W,
  Man.; USA NC, SC, SW, Rocky Mts, Ark.
- **pycnostachya** Michx. · E:Prairie Blazing
  Star; G:Prärie-Prachtscharte · ⚂ Z3
  VII-IX; USA: NCE, NC, Ky., SC, SE
- **scariosa** (L.) Willd. · E:Blazing Star,
  Devil's Bite; G:Kansas-Prachtscharte · ⚂
  Z3 VIII-IX; USA: NE, SE
- **spicata** (L.) Willd. · E:Button Snaker-
  oot, Gayfeather; F:Plume du Kansas;
  G:Ährige Prachtscharte · ⚂ Z3 VII-IX ⚥ ;
  Can.: Ont.; USA: NE, NCE, SE, Fla.
- **some cultivars**

Libanotis Haller ex Zinn = Seseli
- *transcaucasica* Schischk. = Seseli libanotis

Libertia Spreng. -f- Iridaceae · 11 sp. ·
E:Chilean Iris; F:Libertia; G:Andeniris,
Schwertelglocke
- **caerulescens** Kunth · ⚂ Z8 ⓚ V; Chile
- **formosa** Graham · E:Snowy Mermaid;
  G:Andeniris · ⚂ Z8 ⓚ V-VI; Chile
- **grandiflora** (R. Br.) Sw. · E:New Zealand
  Satin Flower; G:Neuseelandiris · ⚂ Z8 ⓚ
  VII-VIII; NZ
- **ixioides** (G. Forst.) Spreng. · ⚂ Z8 ⓚ
  IV-V; NZ
- **pulchella** (R. Br.) Spreng. · ⚂ Z8 ⓚ
  III-IV; Austr.: N.S.Wales, Victoria

Libidibia Schltr. = Caesalpinia
- *coriaria* (Jacq.) Schltr. = Caesalpinia
  coriaria

Libocedrus Endl. -f- Cupressaceae · 5 spp. ·

F:Libocèdre; G:Flusszeder
- **bidwillii** Hook. f. · E:Pahautea;
  G:Pahautea-Flusszeder · ♄ Z8; NZ
- *decurrens* Torr. = Calocedrus decurrens
- **plumosa** (D. Don) Sarg. · E:Kawaka;
  G:Kawaka-Flusszeder, Schuppen-
  Flusszeder · ♄ Z8; NZ

Libonia K. Koch = Justicia
- *floribunda* K. Koch = Justicia rizzinii
- × *penrhosiensis* Carrière = Justicia ×
  penrhosiensis

Licania Aubl. -f- Chrysobalanaceae ·
193 spp.
- **arborea** Seem. · ♄ ⓦ Ⓝ; Mex., C-Am.,
  Col., Ecuad., Peru
- *crassifolia* Benth. = Licania incana
- **incana** Aubl. · ♄ ♄ ⓦ; Col., Venez., Braz.
- **rigida** Benth. · ♄ ⓦ Ⓝ; Braz., French
  Guiana, Peru

Licuala Thunb. -f- Arecaceae · 135 spp. ·
E:Palas; F:Palmier-éventail; G:Palas-
palme, Strahlenpalme
- *elegans* Blume = Licuala pumila
- **grandis** H. Wendl. · ♄ e Z10 ⓦ; Vanuatu
- **peltata** Roxb. ex Buch.-Ham. · ♄ e Z10
  ⓦ; Ind., Burma
- **pumila** Blume · ♄ e Z10 ⓦ; Sumat., Java
- **spinosa** Thunb. · ♄ e Z10 ⓦ; Malay.
  Arch., Andam., Nicobar.

Ligularia Cass. -f- Asteraceae · c. 125 spp. ·
E:Leopard Plant; F:Ligulaire; G:Goldkol-
ben, Ligularie
- *clivorum* (Maxim.) Maxim. = Ligularia
  dentata
- **dentata** (A. Gray) H. Hara · E:Leopard
  Plant; G:Stern-Ligularie · ⚂ ⋉ Z4 VII-IX;
  China, Jap., nat. in BrI
- × **hessei** (Hesse) Bergmans (*L. dentata* ×
  L. wilsoniana) · G:Riesen-Ligularie · ⚂ ⋉
  Z5 VII; cult.
- **hodgsonii** Hook. f. · ⚂ Z5 VII-IX; Jap.,
  Sakhal.
- **japonica** Less. ex DC. · G:Japanische
  Ligularie · ⚂ Z5 VIII-IX; China, Korea,
  Jap., Taiwan
- *kaempferi* Siebold & Zucc. = Farfugium
  japonicum
- **macrophylla** (Ledeb.) DC. · G:Großblät-
  trige Ligularie · ⚂ Z4 VII-VIII; Cauc., Altai
- × **palmatiloba** hort. Hesse (*L. dentata* ×
  L. japonica) · G:Palmblatt-Ligularie · ⚂ ⋉

Z5 VI-VII; cult.
- **przewalskii** (Maxim.) Diels · ⧾ Z4
VIII-IX; China: Kansu
- **sibirica** (L.) Cass. · G:Sibirische Ligularie
- var. **sibirica** · ⧾ Z3 VII-VIII ▽; Eur.: F,
A, H, EC-Eur., BG, E-Eur.; Cauc., W-Sib.,
E-Sib., Amur, Mong., Him., Jap., China
- var. **speciosa** (Schrad. ex Link) DC. · ⧾
⌁ Z3 VII-VIII ▽; E-Sib., China, Manch.,
Korea, Jap., Sakhal.
- *speciosa* (Schrad. ex Link) Fisch. & C.A.
Mey. = Ligularia sibirica var. speciosa
- **stenocephala** (Maxim.) Matsum. &
Koidz. · ⧾ Z5 VI-VIII; Jap., N-China,
Taiwan
- *tussilaginea* (Burm. f.) Makino =
Farfugium japonicum
- **veitchiana** (Hemsl.) Greenm. · G:Veitchs
Ligularie · ⧾ ⌁ Z5 IX-X; W-China
- **wilsoniana** (Hemsl.) Greenm. ·
G:Wilsons Ligularie · ⧾ ⌁ Z5 IX-X;
C-China
- **Cultivars:**
- **some cultivars**

Ligusticum L. -n- *Apiaceae* · 25 (-50) spp. ·
E:Lovage; F:Ligustique; G:Mutterwurz
- **lucidum** Mill. · G:Glänzende Mutter-
wurz · ⧾ Z6 VII-VIII; Eur.: sp., Balear., F,
I, Sw, Ba; mts.
- **mutellina** (L.) Crantz · E:Alpine Lovage;
G:Alpen-Mutterwurz · ⧾ △ Z6 VI-VIII;
Eur.: Fr, C-Eur., EC-Eur., E-Eur., Ital-P,
Ba; mts.
- **mutellinoides** Vill. · E:Small Alpine
Lovage; G:Zwerg-Mutterwurz · ⧾ Z3 VII-
VIII; Eur.: F, I, C-Eur., EC-Eur., Croatia,
N-Russ.; Alp., Sudeten, Carp., N-Russ.
- *pyrenaeum* Gouan = Ligusticum lucidum
- **scoticum** L. · E:Scots Lovage; G:Schot-
tische Mutterwurz · ⧾ Z4 ⚥; Eur.: BrI, Sc,
Balt.; , Greenl., E-USA; coasts

Ligustrina Rupr. = Syringa
- *amurensis* Rupr. = Syringa reticulata
subsp. amurensis
- var. *japonica* (Maxim.) Franch. & Sav. =
Syringa reticulata subsp. reticulata
- *pekinensis* (Rupr.) hort. = Syringa
reticulata subsp. pekinensis

Ligustrum L. -n- *Oleaceae* · c. 50 spp. ·
E:Privet; F:Troène; G:Liguster, Rainweide
- **amurense** Carrière · E:Amur Privet;
G:Amur-Liguster · ♄ s Z5 VI-VII; N-China,

nat. in USA: SE
- *ciliatum* Siebold ex Blume = Ligustrum
ibota
- **compactum** Hook. f. & Thomson ex
Brandis · ♄ ♄ s Z8 ⌾ ∧ VI-VII; Him.,
SW-China
- **delavayanum** Har. · G:Delavays
Liguster · ♄ e Z7 ∧; Burma, Yunnan
- **henryi** Hemsl. · G:Henrys Liguster · ♄ e
Z7; C-China, SW-China
- × **ibolium** Coe ex Rehder (*L. obtusifolium*
× *L. ovalifolium*) · ♄ s Z4 VI-VII; cult.
- **ibota** Siebold & Zucc. · G:Bewimperter
Liguster · ♄ d Z5 VI; Jap.
- **indicum** (Lour.) Merr. · ♄ e Z8 ⌾; Him.,
Indochina
- *ionandrum* Diels = Ligustrum delavayanum
- **japonicum** Thunb. · E:Japanese Privet;
G:Japanischer Liguster · ♄ e Z8 ⌾ ∧
VI-VIII; Jap., Korea
- **lucidum** W.T. Aiton · E:Chinese Privet,
White Wax Tree; G:Glänzender Liguster ·
♄ ♄ e Z7 VIII-IX ⚥ Ⓝ; Him.
- **massalongianum** Vis. · ♄ e Z8 ⌾; Him.
- *medium* Franch. & Sav. = Ligustrum
ovalifolium
- *medium* hort. = Ligustrum tschonoskii
var. tschonoskii
- *nepalense* Wall. = Ligustrum indicum
- **obtusifolium** Siebold & Zucc. ·
G:Stumpfblättriger Liguster
- var. **obtusifolium** · ♄ d Z6; Jap.
- var. **regelianum** (Koehne) Rehder · ♄ d
⊗ Z6 VI; Jap.
- **ovalifolium** Hassk. · E:California Privet,
Garden Privet; F:Troène de Californie;
G:Wintergrüner Liguster · ♄ e D Z7 V-VII;
Jap., nat. in S-USA
- *prattii* Koehne = Ligustrum delavayanum
- *purpusii* Hoefker = Ligustrum quihoui
- **quihoui** Carrière · G:Quihois Liguster · ♄
d Z7 ∧ IX; China
- *regelianum* Koehne = Ligustrum obtusifolium var. regelianum
- **robustum** (Roxb.) Blume · ♄ ♄ e; China,
Burma, Malay. Arch.
- **sinense** Lour. · E:Chinese Privet;
G:Chinesischer Liguster
- var. **sinense** Lour. · ♄ d Z7; C-China
- var. **stauntonii** (A. DC.) Rehder · ♄ d Z7;
C-China
- *stauntonii* A. DC. = Ligustrum sinense
var. stauntonii
- **strongylophyllum** Hemsl. · ♄ e Z9 ⌾

VII; C-China
- **tschonoskii** Decne.
- var. **macrocarpum** (Koehne) Rehder · ♄ d Z6; Jap.
- var. **tschonoskii** · ♄ d ♻ Z6 VI; Jap.
- × **vicaryi** Rehder (*L. ovalifolium* × *L. vulgare*) · ♄ d Z5; cult.
- **vulgare** L. · E:Common Privet; F:Troène commun; G:Gewöhnlicher Liguster · ♄ d ♻ D Z5 VI-VII ⚘ ✿ Ⓦ; Eur.*, TR, Cauc., N-Iran, Moroc.
- *yunnanense* L. Henry = Ligustrum compactum

Lilaeopsis Greene -f- *Apiaceae* · c. 15 spp.
- **attenuata** (Hook. & Arn.) Fernald & Pérez-Mor. · E:Carolina Grasswort · ♃ ⤳ ∿ Ⓐ; USA: Va., SE, Fla., nat. in Ib

Lilium L. -n- *Liliaceae* · 103 spp. · E:Lily; F:Lis; G:Lilie
- **amabile** Palib. · ♃ Z5 VII ▽; Korea
- **auratum** Lindl. · E:Golden Rayed Lily; G:Goldband-Lilie · ♃ D Z6 ▭ VII-VIII ▽; Jap.
- **bolanderi** S. Watson · E:Thimble Lily; G:Fingerhut-Lilie · ♃ Z7 ▭ ∧ VII-VIII ▽; USA: S-Oreg., N-Calif.
- **brownii** F.E. Br. ex Miellez · E:Brown's Lily; G:Browns Lilie · ♃ Z7 ▭ ∧ VI-VII ▽; Burma, SE-China
- **bulbiferum** L. · G:Feuer-Lilie
- var. **bulbiferum** · E:Fire Lily, Orange Lily; F:Lis à bulbilles; G:Wiesen-Feuer-Lilie · ♃ Z7 VI-VII ▽; Eur.* exc. BrI, Sc, nat. in Sc
- var. **croceum** (Chaix) Pers. · G:Acker-Feuer-Lilie · ♃ Z7 VI-VII ▽; Eur.: F, Cors., Ital-P.
- **callosum** Siebold & Zucc. · ♃ Z6 VII-VIII ▽; China: Hupeh, Manch.; Jap., Taiwan
- **canadense** L. · E:Canada Lily, Meadow Lily; G:Kanadische Wiesen-Lilie · ♃ Z5 VII ▽; Can.: E; USA: NE, NCE, SE
- **candidum** L. · E:Madonna Lily, White Lily; G:Madonnen-Lilie, Weiße Lilie · ♃ ⋊ D Z6 VI-VII ⚘ ▽; Eur.: Maced., GR; Cauc., nat. in F, Ital-P
- **carniolicum** Bernh. ex W.D.J. Koch · G:Krainer Lilie · ♃ Z7 VI ▽; Eur.: I, A, Ba, RO; SE-Alp., Balkan, RO
- *carolinianum* Michx. = Lilium michauxii
- *cathayanum* Wilson = Cardiocrinum cathayanum
- **cernuum** Kom. · ♃ D Z3 VI-VII ▽;

Manch., Amur, Korea
- **chalcedonicum** L. · E:Red Martagon of Constantinople, Scarlet Martagon Lily; G:Rote Türkenbund-Lilie · ♃ Z5 VII-VIII ▽; GR
- **columbianum** Leichtlin ex Duch. · E:Columbia Lily; G:Columbia-Lilie · ♃ Z7 ▭ VII-VIII ▽; Can.: B.C.; USA: NW, Idaho, Nev., Calif.
- **concolor** Salisb. · E:Morning Star Lily; G:Morgenstern-Lilie · ♃ Z4 VI-VII ▽; China: Hunan, Hupeh, Yunnan
- *cordatum* (Thunb.) Koidz. = Cardiocrinum cordatum
- *croceum* Chaix = Lilium bulbiferum var. croceum
- *dahuricum* Reuthe = Lilium pensylvanicum
- *dauricum* Ker-Gawl. = Lilium pensylvanicum
- **davidii** Duch. ex Elwes
- var. **davidii** · E:Père David's Lily; G:Sichuan-Lilie · ♃ Z5 ▽; W-China
- var. **willmottiae** (E.H. Wilson) Raffill · ♃ Z5 VII-VIII ▽; China: Sichuan, Schansi, Hupeh
- *davuricum* E.H. Wilson = Lilium pensylvanicum
- **duchartrei** Franch. · ♃ D Z7 ∧ VI-VII ▽; China: Yunnan, Kansu, Sichuan
- *elegans* Thunb. = Lilium maculatum
- *farreri* Turrill = Lilium duchartrei
- **formosanum** Wallace · E:Formosa Lily; G:Formosa-Lilie · ♃ ⋊ D Z5 VII-VIII ▽; Taiwan (Mt. Morrison)
- *giganteum* Wall. = Cardiocrinum giganteum
- **grayi** S. Watson · ♃ Z7 VI-VII ▽; USA: Va., N.C., Tenn.
- **hansonii** Leichtlin ex D.D.T. Moore · G:Gold-Türkenbund-Lilie · ♃ Z5 VI ▽; Jap., Korea, Amur
- *harrisianum* Beane & Vollmer = Lilium pardalinum
- *heldreichii* Freyn = Lilium chalcedonicum
- **henryi** Baker · ♃ Z5 VIII-IX ▽; China: Hubei, Jiangxi, Gouzhou
- × **hollandicum** Bergmans (*L. bulbiferum* × *L. maculatum* var. *maculatum*) · ♃ Z5; cult.
- **humboldtii** Roezl & Leichtlin ex Duch. · E:Humboldt Lily; G:Humboldt-Lilie · ♃ Z8 ▭ VII-VIII ▽; C-Calif.
- **japonicum** Thunb. ex Houtt. · E:Bamboo Lily, Japanese Lily; G:Bambus-Lilie · ♃ D

Z5 VII-VIII ▽; Jap.
- **kesselringianum** Miscz. · ♃ D Z7 VII-VIII ▽; NE-TR, Cauc.
- *krameri* Hook. f. = Lilium japonicum
- **lancifolium** Thunb. · E:Devil Lily, Tiger Lily; G:Tiger-Lilie · ♃ Z4 VIII-IX Ⓝ ▽; Jap.
- **lankongense** Franch. · ♃ D Z5 VIII ▽; NW-Yunnan
- **ledebourii** (Baker) Boiss. · ♃ D Z5 V-VI ▽; Cauc. (Aserb.)
- **leichtlinii** Hook. f.
- var. **leichtlinii** · ♃ Z5 ▽; Jap., Korea, Manch.
- var. **maximowiczii** (Regel) Baker · ♃ Z5 ▽; Jap., Korea
- **leucanthum** (Baker) Baker
- var. **centifolium** (Stapf ex Elwes) Woodcock & Coutts · ♃ Z7 ▭ VII-VIII ▽; China: Kansu
- var. *chloraster* E.H. Wilson = Lilium leucanthum var. leucanthum
- var. **leucanthum** · ♃ Z7 ▽; W-China
- **longiflorum** Thunb. · E:Easter Lily; G:Oster-Lilie · ♃ ⋊ D Z6 VIII-IX ▽; Jap., Ryukyu-Is., Taiwan
- var. *formosanum* Baker = Lilium formosanum
- **mackliniae** Sealy · ♃ Z8 ▭ VI-VII ▽; NE-Ind. (Manipur)
- *macrophyllum* (D. Don) Voss = Notholirion macrophyllum
- **maculatum** Thunb. · ♃ Z4 ▽; Jap.
- *makinoi* Koidz. = Lilium japonicum
- × **marhan** Baker (*L. hansonii* × *L. martagon* var. *album*) · ♃ Z5; cult.
- **martagon** L. · G:Türkenbund-Lilie
- var. *albiflorum* Vuk. = Lilium martagon var. martagon
- var. *album* Weston = Lilium martagon var. martagon
- var. *cattaniae* Vis. = Lilium martagon var. martagon
- var. *dalmaticum* Elwes = Lilium martagon var. martagon
- var. **martagon** · E:Martagon, Martagon Lily, Turk's Cap; F:Lis martagon; G:Gewöhnliche Türkenbund-Lilie · ♃ Z4 VI-VII ▽; Eur.* exc. BrI, Sc; Cauc., W-Sib., E-Sib., N-Mong., nat. in BrI, Sc
- *maximowiczii* Regel = Lilium leichtlinii var. maximowiczii
- **medeoloides** A. Gray · ♃ Z5 VII ▽; China, Korea, Jap., Sakhal., Kamchat.
- **michauxii** Poir. · E:Carolina Lily;

G:Carolina-Lilie · ♃ D Z7 ▭ ∧ VIII ▽; USA: NE, SE, Fla.
- **monadelphum** M. Bieb.
- var. **armenum** (Miscz. ex Grossh.) P.H. Davis & D.M. Hend. Z5 ▽; NE-TR, Armen.
- var. **monadelphum** · G:Verwachsene Kaukasus-Lilie · ♃ Z5 VII ▽; NE-TR, N-Cauc.
- var. **szovitsianum** (Fisch. & Avé-Lall.) Elwes
- *myriophyllum* Franch. = Lilium sulphureum
- **nepalense** D. Don · ♃ D Z8 ⓚ VII-VIII ▽; Nepal, Bhutan; Him.
- **occidentale** Purdy · E:Eureka Lily, Western Lily; G:Heureka-Lilie · ♃ Z8 ▭ VII ▽; USA: S-Oreg., N-Calif.
- **papilliferum** Franch. · ♃ Z7 ▭ ∧ ▽; NW-Yunnan
- **pardalinum** Kellogg · E:Leopard Lily, Panther Lily; G:Panter-Lilie · ♃ Z8 VII ▽; S-Oreg.
- **parryi** S. Watson · E:Lemon Lily · ♃ D Z8 ▭ VII ▽; Calif., Ariz.
- **parvum** Kellogg · E:Sierran Lily; G:Sierra-Lilie · ♃ Z8 VII ▽; Calif.; mts.
- **pensylvanicum** Ker-Gawl. · ♃ Z5 VI ▽; Altai, Mong., Amur, Manch., N-Korea, Jap., Sakhal.
- **philadelphicum** L. · E:Wild Lily, Wood Lily; G:Schalen-Lilie · ♃ Z7 ∧ VI-VIII ▽; Can., USA: NE, N.C., NCE, NC, Rocky Mts., SW
- **philippinense** Baker · ♃ D Z9 ⓚ VIII ▽; Phil.: Luzon
- var. *formosanum* E.H. Wilson ex A. Grove = Lilium formosanum
- **pomponium** L. · E:Red Lily; G:Stinkende Lilie · ♃ △ Z7 VI-VII ▽; Eur.: F, I , ? sp.; Alp. Maritimes
- *pseudotigrinum* Carrière = Lilium leichtlinii var. maximowiczii
- **pumilum** Delile · E:Coral Lily; G:Lackrote Lilie · ♃ Z5 VII ▽; E-Sib., Mong., N-China, Manch., N-Korea
- **pyrenaicum** Gouan · E:Pyrenean Lily; G:Pyrenäen-Lilie · ♃ D Z7 V-VI ▽; Eur.: N-Sp., S-F, nat. in BrI
- subsp. *carniolicum* (Bernh. ex W.D.J. Koch) V.A. Matthews = Lilium carniolicum
- **regale** E.H. Wilson · E:Regal Lily; G:Königs-Lilie · ♃ ⋊ D Z5 VII ▽; China: Sichuan

– **rubellum** Baker · ⚥ D Z7 V-VI ▽; Jap.
– **rubescens** S. Watson · E:Chaparral Lily, Redwood Lily; G:Siskiyou-Lilie · ⚥ D Z7 ⌐ ∧ VI-VII ▽; USA: S-Oreg., N-Calif.
– **sargentiae** E.H. Wilson · ⚥ D Z6 VII ▽; Sichuan
– **speciosum** Thunb. · G:Prächtige Lilie · ⚥ ⋊ D Z8 IX ▽; China: Anhwei, Kiangsi; Jap., Taiwan
– **sulphureum** Baker ex Hook. f. · ⚥ l: D Z7 ⌐ ∧ IX ▽; N-Burma, Yunnan
– **superbum** L. · E:American Turkscap Lily, Turk's Cap; G:Prächtige Türkenbund-Lilie · ⚥ Z6 VII-VIII ▽; USA: NE, NCE, SE
– *szovitsianum* Fisch. & Avé-Lall. = Lilium monadelphum var. szovitsianum
– **taliense** Franch. · ⚥ D Z5 VII ▽; NE-Yunnan
– *tenuifolium* Fisch. ex Hook. f. = Lilium pumilum
– × **testaceum** Lindl. (*L. candidum* × *L. chalcedonicum*) · E:Nankeen Lily; G:Isabellen-Lilie · ⚥ Z6 VII-VIII; cult.
– *thunbergianum* Schult. & Schult. f. = Lilium maculatum
– *tigrinum* Ker-Gawl. = Lilium lancifolium
– × *umbellatum* hort. = Lilium × hollandi-cum
– **wallichianum** Schult. & Schult. f. · ⚥ Z8 ⚘ X-XI ▽; Him., S-Ind.
– **wardii** Stapf & Stern · ⚥ D Z7 VIII-IX ▽; SE-Tibet
– **washingtonianum** Kellogg · E:Cascade Lily, Washington; Lily G:Washington-Lilie · ⚥ Z7 ⌐ ∧ VI-VII ▽; USA: NW, Calif.
– *willmottiae* E.H. Wilson = Lilium davidii var. willmottiae
– **Cultivars:**
– **many cultivars, see Section III**

× **Limara** hort. -f- *Orchidaceae* (*Arachnis* × *Renanthera* × *Vandopsis*)

Limnanthes R. Br. -f- *Limnanthaceae* · 7 spp. · E:Meadow Foam; F:Limnanthes; G:Sumpfblume
– **douglasii** R. Br. · E:Meadow Foam, Poached Egg Plant; G:Spiegeleierpflanze, Sumpfblume · ☉ Z8 VI-VIII; USA: Oreg., Calif.

Limnobium Rich. -n- *Hydrocharitaceae* · 2 spp. · E:Spongeplant; F:Grenouillette d'Amérique; G:Amerikanischer

Froschlöffel
– **spongia** (Bosc) Steud. · E:American Spongeplant; G:Amerikanischer Froschlöffel · ⚥ ≈ Z5; USA: NE, NCE, SC, SE, Fla.
– **stoloniferum** (G. Mey.) Griseb. · ⚥ ≈ ⚘; Mex., C-Am., W.Ind., trop. S-Am.

Limnocharis Humb. & Bonpl. -f-*Limnocharitaceae* · 2 spp. · G:Sumpflieb
– **flava** (L.) Buchenau · E:Sawah Lettuce, Yellow Velvetleaf; G:Sumpflieb · ⚥ ⁓ ≈ Z10 ⚘ VII-VIII; Mex., C-Am., W.Ind., trop. S-Am.
– *humboldtii* Rich. = Hydrocleys nymphoides

Limnophila R. Br. -f- *Scrophulariaceae* · 37 spp. · F:Limnophile; G:Sumpffreund
– *gratioloides* R. Br. = Limnophila indica
– **heterophylla** (Roxb.) Benth. · ⚥ ≈ Z9 ⚘; Pakist., Ind., Sri Lanka, Malay. Arch., S-China, Taiwan, Jap.
– **indica** (L.) Druce · ⚥ ≈ Z9 ⚘; Afr., subtrop. As, trop. As., Austr.
– **sessiliflora** Blume · ⚥ ≈ Z9 ⚘; Pakist., Ind., Sri Lanka, China, Korea, Jap., Malay. Arch., Micron.

Limodorum Boehm. -n- *Orchidaceae* · 2 spp. · F:Limodore; G:Dingel
– **abortivum** (L.) Sw. · E:Violet Birdsnest Orchid; G:Violetter Dingel · ⚥ V-VII ▽ ✳; Eur.: Ib, Fr, Ital-P, C-Eur., EC-Eur., Ba, Crim; TR, Cyprus, Syr., Cauc., Iran

Limonia L. -f- *Rutaceae* · 1 sp. · E:Elephant's Apple, Wood Apple; F:Pomme d'éléphant; G:Elefantenapfel
– **acidissima** L. · E:Elephant's Apple, Wood Apple; G:Elefantenapfel · ♄ d Z10 ⚘ ⚡ Ⓝ; Ind., Sri Lanka
– *arborea* Roxb. = Glycosmis arborea
– *pentaphylla* Retz. = Glycosmis arborea
– *trifolia* Burm. f. = Triphasia trifolia

Limoniastrum Fabr. -n- *Plumbaginaceae* · 10 spp. · F:Limoniastrum; G:Strauch-strandflieder
– **monopetalum** (L.) Boiss. · ♄ e Z8 ⚘ VII-IX; Eur.: Ib, F, Ital-P, Crete; N-Afr., Sinai

Limonium Mill. -n- *Plumbaginaceae* · c. 150 spp. · E:Sea Lavender; F:Lavande de mer, Statice; G:Meerlavendel,

Strandflieder, Widerstoß
- **arborescens** (Brouss.) Kuntze · ♄ e Z9 ⌂
  VII-VIII ▽; Canar.: Las Palmas, Teneriffa
- **bellidifolium** (Gouan) Dumort. · ⌗ △
  Z8 ⌂ ∧ VIII-X ▽; Eur.: Ib, Fr, Ital-P, Ba,
  E-Eur.; TR, C.-As., Alger.
- **binervosum** (G.E. Sm.) C.E. Salmon · ⌗
  ∧ VIII-IX ▽; Eur.: BrI, F, Ib
- **bonduellei** (T. Lestib.) Kuntze · ⊙ ⌗ ✕
  VIII-X ▽; NW-Afr., Libya, nat. in I
- **bourgeaui** (Webb) Kuntze · ♄ e Z7
  VII-VIII ▽; Canar.
- *caspium* (Willd.) Gams = Limonium
  bellidifolium
- *elatum* (Fisch. ex Spreng.) Kuntze =
  Goniolimon elatum
- **ferulaceum** (L.) Chaz. · ⌗ Z7 ∧ VII-VIII
  ▽; Eur.: Ib, Fr, Sic., Croatia
- **gmelinii** (Willd.) Kuntze · G:Steppen-
  schleier · ⌗ Z4 VII-VIII ▽; Eur.: EC-Eur.,
  Ba, E-Eur.; W-Sib., E-Sib., C.-As., Mong.,
  Him.
- **gougetianum** (Girard) Kuntze · ⌗ △ Z9
  ⌂ ∧ VII-VIII ▽; Alger., Balear.
- **humile** Mill. · ⌗ ▽; Eur.: BrI, Sc, F, D
- **latifolium** (Sm.) Kuntze · F:Statice
  vivace; G:Breitblättriger Steppenschleier
  · ⌗ Z5 V-VII ▽; Eur.: RO, BG, SE-Russ.
- **macrophyllum** (Brouss.) Kuntze · ♄ e Z9
  ⌂ VII-VIII ▽; Canar.: Teneriffa
- **minutum** (L.) Fourr. · ⌗ ⤳ △ Z8 ⌂ ∧
  VII-VIII ▽; SE-F
- **perezii** (Stapf) F.T. Hubb. · ♄ e Z9 ⌂
  VIII-X ▽; Canar.
- **puberulum** (Webb) Kuntze · ♄ Z9 ⌂
  V-VII ▽; Canar.
- **ramosissimum** (Poir.) Maire · ⌗ Z8 ∧
  VI-IX ▽; Eur.: Ib, Fr, Ital-P, GR; Alger.
- *sinense* (Girard) Kuntze = Limonium
  tetragonum
- **sinuatum** (L.) Mill. · E:Statice, Winged
  Sea Lavender · ⊙ ⊙ ⌗ ✕ Z9 VII-IX ▽;
  Eur.: Ib, Fr, Ital-P, Ba; TR, Levant, Cauc.
  (Batumi), N-Afr.
- *tataricum* (L.) Mill. = Goniolimon
  tataricum
- **tetragonum** (Thunb.) Bullock · ⊙ ⊙ ⌗ ✕
  Z6 ▽; China
- **some cultivars**
- *transwallianum* (Pugsley) Pugsley =
  Limonium binervosum
- **vulgare** Mill. · E:Marsh Rosemary, Sea
  Lavender; G:Gewöhnlicher Strandflieder
  · ⌗ Z6 VIII-IX ▽; Eur.* exc. EC-Eur.;
  coasts

Limosella L. -f- *Scrophulariaceae* ·
  11-15 spp. · E:Mudwort; F:Limoselle;
  G:Schlammling
- **aquatica** L. · G:Gewöhnlicher
  Schlammling · ⊙ ⌗ ≈ VI-X; Eur.*,
  TR, Cauc., Iran, W-Sib., E-Sib., Amur,
  Kamchat., C.-As., Him., Mong., Tibet,
  Manch., Jap., Afr., N-Am., S-Am., Austr.

Linanthus Benth. -m- *Polemoniaceae* ·
  35 spp.
- **androsaceus** (Benth.) Greene
- subsp. **androsaceus** · E:False Babystars ·
  ⊙ Z7; USA: Calif.
- subsp. **luteus** (Benth.) H. Mason · ⊙ Z7
  VII-VIII; S-Calif.
- subsp. **micranthus** (Steud. ex Benth.) H.
  Mason · ⊙ Z7 VII-VIII; S-Calif.
- **dianthiflorus** (Benth.) Greene ·
  E:Fringed Linanthus · ⊙ Z7 IV-VI;
  S-Calif., Baja Calif.
- **grandiflorus** (Benth.) Greene · E:Desert
  Trumpets, Mountain Phlox · ⊙ Z7 V-IX;
  Calif.
- **liniflorus** (Benth.) Greene · E:Narrowleaf
  Flax Flower · ⊙ Z7 VII-VIII; Calif.

Linaria Mill. -f- *Scrophulariaceae* ·
  c. 100 spp. · E:Toadflax; F:Linaire;
  G:Leinkraut
- *aequitriloba* (Viv.) Spreng. = Cymbalaria
  aequitriloba
- **aeruginea** (Gouan) Cav. · ⊙ ⌗ V-VII; Ib.
- **alpina** (L.) Mill. · E:Alpine Toadflax;
  F:Linaire des Alpes; G:Alpen-Leinkraut,
  Stein-Leinkraut · ⊙ ⌗ ⤳ △ Z4 VI-VIII;
  Eur.: Ib, Fr, Ital-P, C-Eur., Slova., Ba, RO;
  mts.
- **amethystea** (Lam.) Hoffmanns. & Link ·
  ⊙ V-VIII; P, sp., N-Afr.
- **angustissima** (Loisel.) Borbás ·
  G:Italienisches Leinkraut · ⌗ Z6 VI-VIII;
  Eur.* exc. Sc, BrI; mts.
- **arvensis** (L.) Desf. · G:Acker-Leinkraut ·
  ⊙ VII-IX; Eur.: Ib, Fr, Ital-P, C-Eur.,
  EC-Eur., Ba, ? RO; Moroc., Alger.
- **bipartita** (Vent.) Willd. · E:Cloven Lip
  Toadflax; G:Zweiteiliges Leinkraut · ⊙
  VI-VII; Eur.: Ib; NW-Afr.
- **chalepensis** (L.) Mill. · G:Aleppisches
  Leinkraut · ⊙; Eur.: Balear., Fr, Ital-P, Ba;
  TR, SW-As., Egypt
- *cymbalaria* (L.) Mill. = Cymbalaria
  muralis
- **genistifolia** (L.) Mill. ·

G:Ginster-Leinkraut
- subsp. **dalmatica** (L.) Maire & Petitm. · E:Dalmatian Toadflax; G:Dalmatiner Leinkraut · ♃ Z5 VII-VIII; Eur.: I, Ba, nat. in C-Eur
- subsp. **genistifolia** · G:Gewöhnliches Ginster-Leinkraut · ♃ Z5 VI-X; Eur.: I, A, EC-Eur., Ba, E-Eur.; TR, Cauc., W-Sib., C-As., nat. in D
- *hepaticifolia* (Poir.) Steud. = Cymbalaria hepaticifolia
- *incarnata* (Vent.) Spreng. = Linaria bipartita
- **maroccana** Hook. f. · E:Baby Snapdragon; G:Marokko-Leinkraut · ⊙ VI-VII; Moroc.
- *origanifolia* (L.) Cav. = Chaenorhinum origanifolium subsp. origanifolium
- *pallida* Ten. = Cymbalaria pallida
- *pilosa* (Jacq.) DC. = Cymbalaria pilosa
- **purpurea** (L.) Mill. · E:Purple Toadflax; F:Linaire pourpre ; G:Purpur-Leinkraut · ♃ Z7 ∧ VII-X; I, Sic., nat. in BrI
- **some cultivars**
- **repens** (L.) Mill. · E:Striped Toadflax; G:Gestreiftes Leinkraut · ♃ Z6 VII-VIII; Eur.: sp., Fr, I, G, nat. in BrI, Sc, Balt., EC-Eur.
- *reticulata* (Sm.) Desf. = Linaria aeruginea
- **simplex** (Willd.) DC. · G:Einfaches Leinkraut · ⊙ VI-VIII; Eur.: Ib, Fr, Ital-P, Ba, Crim; TR, Cyprus, Syr., Cauc., Iran, NW-Afr., Canar., nat. in Sw
- **spartea** (L.) Willd. · G:Ruten-Leinkraut · ⊙ Z7; Eur.: Ib, Fr
- **supina** (L.) Chaz. · E:Prostrate Toadflax · ⊙ ⊙ ♃; Eur.: Ib, F, I, BrI, Swed; Moroc.
- **triornithophora** (L.) Willd. · E:Three-birds-flying · ♃ △ Z7 ∧ VI-IX; Eur.: Ib
- **triphylla** (L.) Mill. · ⊙ Z8; Eur.: Ib, Ital-P, Ba, Fr
- **tristis** (L.) Mill. · E:Dull-coloured Linaria; G:Trübes Leinkraut · ⊙ ⊙ ♃ △ Z9 VI-IX; Eur.: S-P, S-Sp.; Moroc., Alger.
- *villosa* (L.) DC. = Chaenorhinum villosum
- **vulgaris** Mill. · E:Butter-and-eggs, Common Toadflax, Yellow Toadflax; G:Frauenflachs, Gewöhnliches Leinkraut · ♃ Z4 IX-X ⚕; Eur.*, TR, Cauc., W-Sib., E-Sib., nat. in N-Am., Chile

Lindelofia Lehm. -f- *Boraginaceae* · 12 spp.
- **anchusoides** (Lindl.) Lehm. · ♃ △ Z7 VI-VII; Afgh., W-Him.
- **longiflora** (Benth.) Baill. · ♃ Z7 ∧ V-VI; W-Him.

Lindenbergia Lehm. -f- *Scrophulariaceae* · 15 spp.
- **grandiflora** (Buch.-Ham.) Benth. · ♄ Z9 ⓚ XI-II; S-Him.

Lindera Thunb. -f- *Lauraceae* · 80-100 spp. · G:Fieberstrauch; F:Lindera
- **benzoin** (L.) Blume · E:Benjamin Bush, Spicebush; G:Wohlriechender Fieberstrauch · ♄ d Z6 III-V ⚕ ; Ont.; USA: NE, NCE, Kans., SC, SE, Fla.
- **obtusiloba** Blume · G:Stumpflappiger Fieberstrauch · ♄ ♄ d Z6 IV; China, Korea, Jap.
- **praecox** (Siebold & Zucc.) Blume · G:Frühzeitiger Fieberstrauch · ♄ d Z7 ∧ IV; Jap.
- **sericea** (Siebold & Zucc.) Blume · ♄ d III-IV; Jap.

Lindernia All. -f- *Scrophulariaceae* · 50-80 spp. · E:False Pimpernel; F:Mazus; G:Büchsenkraut
- **dubia** (L.) Pennell · E:Yellowseed False Pimpernel; G:Großes Büchsenkraut · ⊙ VIII-IX; Can., USA*, Lat.-Am., nat. in Ib, F, I
- **procumbens** (Krock.) Borbás · E:Prostrate False Pimpernel; G:Liegendes Büchsenkraut · ⊙ VIII-IX ▽; Eur.* exc. BrI, Sc; TR, W-Sib., Amur, China, Jap., Iran, Ind., Malay. Arch., Polyn., nat. in USA

Lindheimera A. Gray & Engelm. -f- *Asteraceae* · 1 sp. · E:Star Daisy; F:Etoile du Texas, Lindheimera; G:Lindheimerie, Texasstern
- **texana** A. Gray & Engelm. · E:Star Daisy, Texas Star, Texas Yellowstar; G:Lindheimerie, Texasstern · ⊙ VII-IX; Tex., Mex.

Lindmania Mez -f- *Bromeliaceae* · 38 spp.
- **geniculata** L.B. Sm. · ♃; S. Venez.
- *penduliflora* (C.H. Wright) Stapf = Fosterella penduliflora

Linnaea L. -f- *Caprifoliaceae* · 1 sp. · E:Twinflower; F:Linnée; G:Moosglöckchen
- *americana* J. Forbes = Linnaea borealis var. americana
- **borealis** L. · G:Moosglöckchen

– var. **americana** (J. Forbes) Rehder ·
G:Amerikanisches Moosglöckchen · ♄ ♄
⟿ Z1; Alaska, Can., USA*, Greenl.
– var. **borealis** · E:Twinflower; G:Nördli-
ches Moosglöckchen · ♄ ♄ e ⟿ Z1 VI-VIII
▽; Eur.* exc. Ib; N, mts.; Cauc., W-Sib.,
E-Sib., Amur, Sakhal., Kamchat., Mong.,
Alaska, Greenl.
– *engleriana* Graebn. = Abelia engleriana
– *schumannii* Graebn. = Abelia schumannii
– *zanderi* Graebn. = Abelia zanderi

Linum L. -n- *Linaceae* · 180-200 spp. ·
E:Flax; F:Lin; G:Flachs, Lein
– **alpinum** Jacq. · E:Alpine Flax; G:Alpen-
Lein · ⅄ △ Z6 VI-VIII; Eur.: sp., F, I,
C-Eur., Ba; mts.
– subsp. *julicum* (Hayek) Hegi = Linum
alpinum
– **arboreum** L. · E:Tree Flax; G:Strauch-
Lein · ♄ e △ Z8 ⌂ V-VI ▽; Eur.: GR,
Crete; SW-TR, Rhodes
– **austriacum** L. · G:Österreichischer Lein ·
⅄ Z3 V-VII ▽; Eur.* exc. BrI, Sc; TR,
Iraq, Cauc., Iran, Afgh., W-Sib., Moroc.,
Alger.
– **bienne** Mill. · E:Pale Flax; G:Wild-Lein
· ⊙ ⅄ Z7 VI-VII ▽; Eur.: Ib, Fr, Ital-P,
Ba, Crim, BrI; TR, Levant, N-Iraq, Iran,
NW-Afr., Libya
– **campanulatum** L. · ♄ Z7 ⌂ ∧ VI-VII ▽;
Eur.: sp., F, I
– **capitatum** Kit. ex Schult. · ⅄ △ Z7 ∧
VI-VII ▽; Eur.: I, Ba
– **catharticum** L. · E:Purging Flax, White
Flax; G:Gewöhnlicher Purgier-Lein ·
⊙ VI-VIII ☫ ▽; Eur.*, TR, Cauc., Iran,
Moroc.
– *crepitans* (Boenn.) Dumort. = Linum
usitatissimum
– **elegans** Spruner ex Boiss. · ⅄ △ Z6 V-VI
▽; Eur.: Ba
– **flavum** L. · E:Golden Flax, Yellow Flax;
F:Lin jaune; G:Gelber Lein · ⅄ ♄ d △
Z5 VI-VIII ▽; Eur.: C-Eur., EC-Eur., Ba,
Ital-P, E-Eur.; TR, Cauc.
– **grandiflorum** Desf. · E:Red Flax, Scarlet
Flax; G:Roter Lein · ⊙ VI-IX ▽; Alger.
– **hirsutum** L. · G:Zotten-Lein · ⅄ Z6
VI-VIII ▽; Eur.: A, EC-Eur., Ba, E-Eur.;
TR
– **hypericifolium** C. Presl · G:Kaukasus-
Lein · ⅄ △ V-VI ▽; Cauc.
– *iberidifolium* Aucher ex Planch. = Linum
elegans

– **leonii** F.W. Schultz · G:Lothringer Lein ·
⅄ V-VII ▽; Eur.: F, W-D
– **maritimum** L. · G:Strand-Lein · ⅄ Z8
VI-X ▽; Sard.
– *montanum* Schleich. = Linum alpinum
– **narbonense** L. · F:Lin de Narbonne;
G:Südfranzösischer Lein · ⅄ Z7 ∧ VI-VII
▽; Eur.: Ib, Fr, Ital-P, Slove., Croatia,
nat. in Sw
– **ockendonii** Greuter & Burdet · G:Berg-
Lein · ⅄ ▽; Eur.: F, D +
– **perenne** L. · E:Blue Flax, Perennial Flax;
F:Lin vivace; G:Ausdauernder Lein · ⅄
Z7 VI-VIII ▽; Eur.* exc. Sc; TR, W-Sib.,
E-Sib., Amur, nat. in N-Am.
– some cultivars
– subsp. *alpinum* (Jacq.) Ockendon =
Linum alpinum
– *salsoloides* Lam. = Linum suffruticosum
subsp. salsoloides
– **suffruticosum** L.
– subsp. **salsoloides** (Lam.) Rouy ·
E:Pyrenean Flax · ⅄ △ Z7 ∧ V-VII ▽;
Eur.: sp.
– subsp. **suffruticosum** · ⅄ Z8 ▽;
Eur.: sp., F, I; NW-Afr.
– **tenuifolium** L. · G:Schmalblättriger
Lein · ⅄ d Z6 VI-VII ▽; Eur.* exc. BrI, Sc;
Cauc., N-Iran
– **usitatissimum** L. · E:Common Flax, Flax,
Linseed; G:Saat-Lein · ⊙ VI-VII ☫ ⓝ ▽;
orig. ?; cult., nat. in Ib, F
– **Crepitans-Group** · G:Kleng-Lein, Spring-
Lein · Z4; cult.
– **Mediterraneum-Group** · G:Öl-Lein · Z4;
cult.
– subsp. **angustifolium** (Huds.) Thell. =
Linum bienne
– **Usitassimum-Group** · G:Faser-Lein,
Flachs, Schließ-Lein · Z4; cult.
– **viscosum** L. · E:Sticky Flax; F:Lin
visqueux; G:Klebriger Lein · ⅄ Z7 ∧ V-VII
▽; Eur.: sp., F, I, C-Eur., Slove., Croatia

Liparis Rich. -f- *Orchidaceae* · 428 spp. ·
E:Fen Orchid; F:Liparis; G:Glanzständel
– **loeselii** (L.) Rich. · E:Fen Orchid;
G:Glanzkraut, Sumpf-Glanzständel · ⅄
VI-VII ▽ ✳; Eur.* exc. Ib; W-Sib., C-As.,
N-Am.
– **nervosa** (Thunb.) Lindl. · G:Geaderter
Glanzständel · ⅄ Z10 ⓦ VII-VIII ▽ ✳;
trop. Am., trop. Afr., Ind., China, Jap.,
Phil.
– **reflexa** Lindl. · ⅄ Z10 ⓦ IX-X ▽ ✳;

Austr.
- **viridiflora** (Blume) Lindl. · G:Grünblüti-
ger Glanzständel · ⁴ Z10 ⑩ XII-I ▽ ✻;
Him.: Sikkim; S-Ind., Sri Lanka, Java

Lippia L. -f- *Verbenaceae* · c. 200 spp. ·
G:Süßkraut
- *chamaedrifolia* (Cham.) Steud. = Aloysia
chamaedryfolia
- *citriodora* (Lam.) Kunth = Aloysia
citriodora
- **dulcis** Trevis. · E:Mexican Lippia, Yerba
Dulce; G:Aztekisches Süßkraut · ⁴ Z10;
Mex., C-Am., W.Ind., Col., Venez.
- **micromera** Schauer · E:Spanish Thyme;
G:Spanischer Thymian · ♄ Z10; W.Ind.,
Venez.
- *repens* Spreng. = Phyla nodiflora var.
nodiflora
- *triphylla* (L'Hér.) Kuntze = Aloysia
citriodora

Liquidambar L. -f- *Hamamelidaceae* ·
5 spp. · E:Sweet Gum; F:Copalme;
G:Amberbaum
- **orientalis** Mill. · E:Oriental Sweet Gum,
Storax; G:Orientalischer Amberbaum · ♄
d Z8 ∧ V ⚘ ⑩; S-TR, Syr.
- **styraciflua** L. · E:Red Gum, Sweet Gum;
F:Copalme d'Amérique; G:Amerika-
nischer Amberbaum · ♄ d Z5 V ⚘ ⑩;
USA: NE, NCE, SE, Fla., SC; Mex., Guat.
- **many cultivars**

Liriodendron L. -n- *Magnoliaceae* · 2 spp. ·
E:Tulip Tree; F:Tulipier; G:Tulpenbaum
- *fastigiatum* Dippel = Liriodendron
tulipifera
- *liliiferum* L. = Magnolia liliifera var.
liliifera
- *liliiflorum* Steud. = Magnolia obovata
- **tulipifera** L. · E:Canary Whitewood,
Tulip Polar, Tulip Tree; F:Tulipier de
Virginie; G:Amerikanischer Tulpenbaum
· ♄ d Z6 V-VII ⑩; Ont., USA: NE, NCE,
SE, Fla.

Liriope Lour. -f- *Convallariaceae* · 6 spp. ·
E:Lily Turf; F:Liriope; G:Liriope
- **graminifolia** (L.) Baker · E:Lily Turf;
G:Rasen-Liriope · ⁴ Z8 ⑳; Jap., China
- **muscari** (Decne.) L.H. Bailey · E:Big Blue
Lily Turf; F:Liriope; G:Horstbildende
Liriope · ⁴ Z7; China, Taiwan, Jap.
- **some cultivars**

- **spicata** Lour. · G:Lockerwüchsige
Liriope · ⁴ ⑳; Korea

Liriosma Poepp. & Endl. = Dulacia
- *ovata* Miers = Dulacia inopiflora

Lisianthius P. Browne -m- *Gentianaceae* ·
27 spp.
- **nigrescens** Cham. & Schltr. · E:Flor de
Muerto · ♄ Z9 VI-VIII; S-Mex., C-Am.
- *russellianus* Hook. = Eustoma grandiflorum

Lissochilus R. Br. = Eulophia
- *giganteus* Welw. = Eulophia bouliawongo
- *horsfallii* Bateman = Eulophia rosea

Listera R. Br. -f- *Orchidaceae* · c. 25 spp. ·
E:Twayblade; F:Listère; G:Zweiblatt
- **cordata** (L.) R. Br. · E:Lesser Twayblade;
G:Kleines Zweiblatt · ⁴ Z6 V-VIII ▽ ✻;
Eur.*, TR, Cauc., W-Sib., E-Sib., Amur,
Sakhal., Kamchat., Jap., Alaska, Can.,
USA*, Greenl.
- **ovata** (L.) R. Br. · E:Common Twayb-
lade; G:Großes Zweiblatt · ⁴ Z6 V-VII ▽
✻; Eur.*, TR, Cyprus, Syr., Cauc., Iran,
Afgh., Pakist., W-Sib., C-As.

Listrostachys Rchb. -f- *Orchidaceae* · 2 spp.
- *mystacidioides* Kraenzl. = Diaphananthe
bidens
- *pellucida* (Lindl.) Rchb. f. = Diaphananthe pellucida
- **pertusa** (Lindl.) Rchb. f. · ⁴ Z10; W-Afr.,
Zaire

Litchi Sonn. -f- *Sapindaceae* · 1 sp. ·
F:Cerisier de Chine, Litchi; G:Litschi;
E:Litchi
- **chinensis** Sonn. · E:Litchee, Lychee;
G:Litschi · ♄ e Z9 ⑩ V ⑩; S-China

Lithocarpus Blume -m- *Fagaceae* ·
338 spp. · E:Tanbark Oak; G:Steinfruch-
teiche, Südeiche
- **henryi** (Seemen) Rehder & E.H. Wilson ·
♄ e Z7; C-China

Lithodora Griseb. -f- *Boraginaceae* ·
7 spp. · E:Shrubby Gromwell; F:Grémil;
G:Steinsame
- **diffusa** (Lag.) I.M. Johnst. · F:Grémil
étalé · ♄ e △ Z7 ⑳ ∧ V-VII; Eur.: sp.
- **some cultivars**

– **fruticosa** (L.) Griseb. · ♄ e Z8 ⌂ V-VI; Eur.: sp., F; Moroc., Alger.
– **oleifolia** (Lapeyr.) Griseb. · ♄ e Z7 ⌂ VI; Eur.: sp. (E-Pyr.)
– **rosmarinifolia** (Ten.) I.M. Johnst. · ♄ e Z8 ⌂ I-II; S-I, Sic., Alger.
– **zahnii** (Heldr. ex Halácsy) I.M. Johnst. · ♄ e Z8 ⌂; S-GR

Lithops (N.E. Br.) N.E. Br. -f- *Aizoaceae* · 37 spp. · E:Flowering Stones, Living Stones; F:Caillou vivant, Plante-caillou; G:Lebender Stein
– *alpina* Dinter = Lithops pseudotruncatella subsp. pseudotruncatella
– **aucampiae** L. Bolus · ⁴ Z9 ⌂; S-Afr. (Cape Prov.)
– *aurantiaca* L. Bolus = Lithops hookeri
– *bella* N.E. Br. = Lithops karasmontana subsp. bella
– var. *eberlanzii* (Dinter & Schwantes) de Boer & Boom = Lithops karasmontana subsp. eberlanzii
– var. *lericheana* (Dinter & Schwantes) de Boer & Boom = Lithops karasmontana subsp. karasmontana
– *brevis* L. Bolus = Lithops dinteri subsp. dinteri
– **bromfieldii** L. Bolus · ⁴ Z9 ⌂; S-Afr. (Cape Prov.)
– var. *glaudinae* (de Boer) D.T. Cole = Lithops bromfieldii
– **comptonii** L. Bolus · ⁴ Z9 ⌂; Cape
– *deboeri* Schwantes = Lithops villetii subsp. deboerii
– *dendritica* Nel = Lithops pseudotruncatella subsp. dendritica
– **dinteri** Schwantes
– subsp. **dinteri** · ⁴ Z9 ⌂; Namibia
– var. *brevis* (L. Bolus) B. Fearn = Lithops dinteri subsp. dinteri
– *diutina* L. Bolus = Lithops marmorata
– **divergens** L. Bolus · ⁴ Z9 ⌂; Cape, Namibia
– **dorotheae** Nel · ⁴ Z9 ⌂; Cape
– *eberlanzii* (Dinter & Schwantes) N.E. Br. = Lithops karasmontana subsp. eberlanzii
– *elevata* L. Bolus = Lithops optica
– *elisae* de Boer = Lithops marmorata
– *erniana* Tischer & H. Jacobsen = Lithops karasmontana subsp. eberlanzii
– *framesii* L. Bolus = Lithops marmorata
– **francisci** (Dinter & Schwantes) N.E. Br. · ⁴ Z9 ⌂; Namibia
– *fulleri* N.E. Br. = Lithops julii subsp fulleri

– **fulviceps** (N.E. Br.) N.E. Br. · ⁴ Z9 ⌂; Namibia
– **geyeri** (Nel) · ⁴ Z9 ⌂; Cape
– *glaudinae* de Boer = Lithops bromfieldii
– **gracilidelineata** Dinter · ⁴ Z9 ⌂; Namibia
– **herrei** L. Bolus · ⁴ Z9 ⌂; Cape, Namibia
– var. *geyeri* (Nel) de Boer & Boom = Lithops geyeri
– **hookeri** (A. Berger) Schwantes · ⁴ Z9 ⌂; S-Afr. (NW-Cape)
– **julii** (Dinter & Schwantes) N.E. Br.
– **subsp fulleri** (N.E. Br.) B. Fearn · ⁴ Z9 ⌂; Cape
– subsp. **julii** · ⁴ Z9 ⌂; Namibia
– **karasmontana** (Dinter & Schwantes) N.E. Br.
– subsp. **bella** (N.E. Br.) D.T. Cole · ⁴ Z9 ⌂; Namibia
– subsp. **eberlanzii** (Dinter & Schwantes) D.T. Cole · ⁴ Z9 ⌂; Namibia
– subsp. **karasmontana** · ⁴ Z9 ⌂ ⌂; Namibia
– var. *mickbergensis* (Dinter) de Boer & Boom = Lithops karasmontana subsp. karasmontana
– var. *opalina* (Dinter) de Boer & Boom = Lithops karasmontana subsp. karasmontana
– var. *summitatum* (Dinter) de Boer & Boom = Lithops karasmontana subsp. karasmontana
– *lactea* Schick & Tischer = Lithops julii subsp. julii
– **lesliei** (N.E. Br.) N.E. Br. · ⁴ Z9 ⌂; S-Afr. (Cape Prov.)
– **localis** (N.E. Br.) Schwantes · ⁴ Z9 ⌂; Cape
– var. *peersii* (L. Bolus) de Boer & Boom = Lithops localis
– var. *terricolor* (N.E. Br.) de Boer & Boom = Lithops localis
– **marmorata** (N.E. Br.) N.E. Br. · ⁴ Z9 ⌂; Cape
– var. *elisae* (de Boer) D.T. Cole = Lithops marmorata
– **meyeri** L. Bolus · ⁴ Z9 ⌂; Cape
– *mickbergensis* Dinter = Lithops karasmontana subsp. karasmontana
– *nelii* Schwantes = Lithops ruschiorum
– **olivacea** L. Bolus · ⁴ Z9 ⌂; S-Afr. (Cape Prov.)
– *opalina* Dinter = Lithops karasmontana subsp. karasmontana
– **optica** (Marloth) N.E. Br. · ⁴ Z9 ⌂;

Namibia
- **pseudotruncatella** (A. Berger) N.E. Br.
- subsp. **dendritica** (Nel) D.T. Cole · ⌘ Ψ Z9 ⓚ; Namibia
- subsp. **groendrayensis** (H. Jacobsen) D.T. Cole · ⌘ Ψ Z9 ⓚ; Namibia
- subsp. **pseudotruncatella** · ⌘ Ψ Z9 ⓚ; Namibia
- var. *alpina* (Dinter) H. Jacobsen = Lithops pseudotruncatella subsp. pseudotruncatella
- **ruschiorum** (Dinter & Schwantes) N.E. Br. · ⌘ Ψ Z9 ⓚ; Namibia
- var. *nelii* (Schwantes) de Boer & Boom = Lithops ruschiorum
- **schwantesii** Dinter
- subsp. **schwantesii** · Ψ Z9 ⓚ; Namibia
- var. *triebneri* (L. Bolus) de Boer & Boom = Lithops schwantesii subsp. schwantesii
- **steineckeana** Tischer · ⌘ Ψ Z9 ⓚ; Namibia
- *summitatum* Dinter = Lithops karasmontana subsp. karasmontana
- *terricolor* N.E. Br. = Lithops localis
- *translucens* L. Bolus = Lithops herrei
- *triebneri* L. Bolus = Lithops schwantesii subsp. schwantesii
- **turbiniformis** (Haw.) N.E. Br. · ⌘ Ψ Z9 ⓚ; Cape
- *umdausensis* L. Bolus = Lithops marmorata
- **vallis-mariae** (Dinter & Schwantes) N.E. Br. · ⌘ Ψ Z9 ⓚ; Namibia
- var. *groendraaiensis* (H. Jacobsen) de Boer = Lithops pseudotruncatella subsp. groendrayensis
- **villetii** L. Bolus · Ψ Z9 ⓚ; S-Afr. (Cape Prov.)
- subsp. **deboerii** (Schwantes) D.T. Cole · ⌘ Ψ Z9 ⓚ; S-Afr.
- subsp. **villetii**

Lithospermum L. -n- *Boraginaceae* · 50-60 spp. · E:Gromwell; F:Grémil; G:Steinsame
- *angustifolium* Michx. = Lithospermum incisum
- **arvense** L. · E:Corn Gromwell; G:Gewöhnlicher Acker-Steinsame · ⊙ IV-VII; Eur.*, TR, Levant, Iran, W-Sib., E-Sib., C-As., Him., N-Afr., nat. in E-As., N-Am., S-Am., S-Afr., Austr.
- **canescens** (Michx.) Lehm. · E:Indian Plant, Puccoon; G:Grauer Steinsame · ⌘ △ Z3 IV-V; Can.: E, Sask.; USA: NE, NCE,

NC, SE, SC
- *diffusum* Lag. = Lithodora diffusa
- *fruticosum* L. = Lithodora fruticosa
- **gastonii** Benth. · ⌘ Z6 ⓚ VI-VII; F; W-Pyr.
- *graminifolium* Viv. = Moltkia suffruticosa
- **incisum** Lehm. · E:Gromwell, Puccoon; G:Eingeschnittener Steinsame · ⌘ Z3 V-VI; Can., USA: NCE, NC, SC, SW, Rocky Mts.; N-Mex.
- **officinale** L. · E:Gromwell; G:Echter Steinsame · ⌘ Z6 V-VII ⚥ ⓝ; Eur.*, Cauc., TR, Palest., Iran, W-Sib., E-Sib., C-As., Mong., China, nat. in N-Am.
- *oleifolium* Lapeyr. = Lithodora oleifolia
- *petraeum* (Tratt.) DC. = Moltkia petraea
- *prostratum* Loisel. non Buckland = Lithodora diffusa
- **purpurocaeruleum** L. · E:Blue Gromwell; F:Grémil; G:Blauroter Steinsame, Purpurblauer Steinsame · ⌘ Z6 IV-VI; Eur.* exc. Sc; TR, Syr., Cauc., N-Iran
- *rosmarinifolium* Ten. = Lithodora rosmarinifolia

Lithraea Miers ex Hook. & Arn. -f- *Anacardiaceae* · 3 spp.
- **molleoides** (Vell.) Engl. · ♄ e Z9 ⓚ; S-Braz., Arg, Bol.

Litsea Lam. -f- *Lauraceae* · c. 400 spp.
- **calophylla** (Miq.) Mansf. · ♄ d ⓦ ⓝ; Malay. Pen., Java, Kalimantan
- **japonica** (Thunb.) Juss. · ♄ e ⓚ IX-I; Jap., Ryukyu-Is., S-Korea
- *sebifera* Blume non Pers. = Litsea calophylla

Littonia Hook. -f- *Colchicaceae* · 7 spp. · E:Climbing Lily; G:Kletterlilie
- **modesta** Hook. f. · E:Climbing Lily; G:Kletterlilie · ⌘ ⚥ Z9 ⓦ VI-VII; S-Afr.

Littorella P.J. Bergius -f- *Plantaginaceae* · 3 spp. · F:Littorelle; G:Strandling
- **uniflora** (L.) Asch. · E:Shore Weed; G:Europäischer Strandling · ⌘ ⌇ ≈ V-IX; Eur.* exc. Ba

Livistona R. Br. -f- *Arecaceae* · 33 spp. · E:Fan Palm; F:Livistonia; G:Livingston-palme, Livistonie
- **australis** (R. Br.) Mart. · E:Australian Fan Palm, Cabbage Palm; G:Australische

Livingstonpalme · ₺ e Z10 ⓦ; Austr.: Queensl., N.S.Wales, Victoria
- **chinensis** (Jacq.) R. Br. ex Mart. · E:Chinese Fan Palm; G:Chinesische Livingstonpalme · ₺ e Z10 ⓦ; Japan (Shikoku, Kyushu, Ryukyu Is.), Taiwan
- **decipiens** Becc. · E:Ribbon Fan Palm, Weeping Cabbage Palm; G:Trauer-Livingstonpalme · ₺ e Z10 ⓚ; Austr.: Queensl.
- *hoogendorpii* Teijsm. & Binn. ex Miq. = Livistona saribus
- **rotundifolia** (Lam.) Mart. · G:Rundblättrige Livingstonpalme · ₺ e Z10 ⓦ; N-Kalimantan, Sulawesi, Molucca Is., Phil.
- **saribus** (Lour.) Merr. ex A. Chev. · G:Taraw-Livingstonpalme · ₺ e Z10 ⓦ; Malay. Arch., Phil.

Llavea Lag. -f- *Adiantaceae* · 1 sp.
- **cordifolia** Lag. · ♃ Z9 ⓚ; Mex.

Lloydia Salisb. ex Rchb. -f- *Liliaceae* · 12 spp. · E:Snowdon Lily; F:Loïdie; G:Faltenlilie
- **serotina** (L.) Rchb. · E:Snowdon Lily; G:Späte Faltenlilie · ♃ Z5 VII-VIII ▽; Eur.* exc. Ib, Sc; Cauc., W-Sib., E-Sib., Amur, Sakhal., Kamchat.

Loasa Adans. -f- *Loasaceae* · 105 spp. · F:Loasa; G:Loase
- **acanthifolia** Lam. · ⊙ ⊙ ♃ Z10 VII-IX; Chile
- *ambrosiifolia* Juss. = Loasa urens
- *aurantiaca* hort. = Caiophora lateritia
- *contorta* Lam. = Caiophora contorta
- *hispida* L. = Loasa urens
- *lateritia* (Hook.) Gillies ex Arn. = Caiophora lateritia
- *papaverifolia* Kunth = Loasa triphylla var. papaverifolia
- **tricolor** Ker-Gawl. · ⊙ Z10 VII-VIII; Chile
- **triphylla** Juss.
- var. **papaverifolia** (Kunth) Urb. & Gilg · ⊙ Z10; S-Am.
- var. **triphylla** · ⊙ Z10; n. S-Am.
- var. **volcanica** (André) Urb. & Gilg · ⊙ Z10 VII-IX; Col., Ecuad.
- **urens** Jacq. · E:Desert Stingbush · ⊙ Z10 VII-VIII; Peru
- *volcanica* André = Loasa triphylla var. volcanica
- *wallisii* Maxim. = Loasa triphylla var. volcanica

Lobelia L. -f- *Campanulaceae* · 365 spp. · E:Lobelia; F:Lobélie; G:Lobelie
- *angulata* G. Forst. = Pratia angulata
- **cardinalis** L. · E:Cardinal Flower, Scarlet Lobelia; F:Lobélie écarlate; G:Kardinals-Lobelie · ♃ ～ Z3 VII-IX; Can.: E, Sask.; USA: NE, NCE, SC, SE, Fla., Rocky Mts., Calif.; Mex., C-Am.
- **dortmanna** L. · E:Water Lobelia; F:Lobélie de Dortmann; G:Wasser-Lobelie · ♃ ≈ Z4 VII-VIII ☠ ▽; Eur.: Fr, BrI, Sc, G, PL, Russ.; N-Afr., TR, Can.: E, B.C.; USA: NE, NCE, NW
- **elongata** Small · E:Longleaf Lobelia · ♃ ～ ⓚ ∧ VIII-X; USA: NE, SE
- **erinus** L. · E:Edging Lobelia, Trailing Lobelia; F:Lobélie; G:Blaue Lobelie, Männertreu · ⊙ ⊙ ♃ V-X; Cape
- **many cultivars**
- **fenestralis** Cav. · E:Fringeleaf Lobelia · ⊙ ⊙ Z9 VII-VIII; USA: Tex., SW; Mex.
- **fulgens** Willd. · ⊙ ♃ Z8; Tex., Mex.
- × **gerardii** Chabanne & Goujon ex Sauv. (*L. cardinalis* × *L. siphilitica*) · F:Lobélie · ♃ Z7 ∧ VIII-IX; cult.
- **inflata** L. · E:Indian Tobacco; G:Indianer-Tabak · ⊙ VII-VIII ⚕ ☠; Can.: E, Sask.; USA: NE, NCE, NC, SE
- **laxiflora** Kunth · E:Sierra Madre Lobelia; G:Fackel-Lobelie · ♃ ♄ Z9 ⓚ VII-X; C-Am., Col.
- *longiflora* L. = Isotoma longiflora
- **sessilifolia** Lamb. · ♃ ～ Z5 VI-VII; Jap., Korea, Sakhal., E-Sib., Manch., Taiwan
- **siphilitica** L. · E:Great Lobelia; F:Lobélie géante; G:Blaue Kardinals-Lobelie · ♃ ～ Z5 VII-IX ⚕; Can.: E; USA: NE, NCE, NC, SE, SC
- × **speciosa** hort. (*L. cardinalis* × *L. siphilitica* × *L. splendens*) · G:Pracht-Lobelie · ♃ ⋈ Z7 VIII-IX; cult.
- **some cultivars**
- **splendens** Humb. & Bonpl. ex Willd. · E:Cardinal Flower · ♃ ～ ⓚ VII-X; USA: Mo., SC, NC, Rocky Mts., Calif.; Mex.
- **tenuior** R. Br. · ♃ Z9 ⓚ V-IX; W-Austr.
- **tupa** L. · E:Devil's Tobacco; G:Teufelstabak · ♃ Z8 ⓚ IX-X ☠; Chile
- **urens** L. · E:Heath Lobelia; G:Land-Lobelie · ♃; Eur.: Azor., BrI, Ib, Fr; Moroc., Madeira
- **valida** L. Bolus · ♄ ⓚ; Cape

Lobivia Britton & Rose -f- *Cactaceae* · c.
40 spp.
- *aculeata* Buining = Lobivia pentlandii
- *allegraiana* Backeb. = Lobivia hertrichiana
- *arachnacantha* Buining & F. Ritter =
Echinopsis arachnacantha
- *aurea* (Britton & Rose) Backeb. =
Echinopsis aurea
- **backebergii** (Werderm.) Backeb. · ⼁ Z9
ⓐ ▽ ✻; E-Bol., S-Peru
- *binghamiana* Backeb. = Lobivia hertrichiana
- *boliviensis* Britton & Rose = Lobivia
pentlandii
- *bruchii* Britton & Rose = Trichocereus
bruchii
- *caespitosa* J.A. Purpus = Lobivia maximiliana
- *charazanensis* Cárdenas = Lobivia
maximiliana
- *chorrillosensis* Rausch = Echinopsis
hamatacantha
- **chrysantha** (Werderm.) Backeb. · ⼁ Z9
ⓐ ▽ ✻; Arg.: Salta, Jujuy
- **cinnabarina** (Hook.) Britton & Rose · ⼁
Z9 ⓐ ▽ ✻; Bol.
- *claeysiana* Backeb. = Echinopsis ferox
- *corbula* Britton & Rose = Lobivia maximiliana
- *cylindrica* Backeb. = Echinopsis aurea
- *draxleriana* Rausch = Lobivia cinnabarina
- *drijveriana* Backeb. = Lobivia kuehnrichii
- *echinata* Rausch = Lobivia hertrichiana
- *euanthema* Backeb. = Rebutia aureiflora
- **famatinensis** (Speg.) Britton & Rose · ⼁
Z9 ⓐ ▽ ✻; Arg.: La Rioja, San Juan
- *ferox* Britton & Rose = Echinopsis ferox
- *hastifera* Werderm. = Echinopsis ferox
- **hertrichiana** Backeb. · ⼁ Z9 ⓐ ▽ ✻;
SE-Peru
- *higginsiana* Backeb. = Lobivia pentlandii
- *hualfinensis* Rausch = Echinopsis
hamatacantha
- *huascha* (F.A.C. Weber) W.T. Marshall =
Trichocereus huascha
- *huilcanota* Rauh & Backeb. = Lobivia
hertrichiana
- *incaica* Backeb. = Lobivia hertrichiana
- *kieslingii* Rausch = Trichocereus formosus
- *klusacekii* Frič = Lobivia kuehnrichii
- **kuehnrichii** Frič · ⼁ Z9 ⓐ ▽ ✻; Arg.:
Jujuy
- *larae* Cárdenas = Lobivia pentlandii
- *laui* Donald = Lobivia hertrichiana

- *lauramarca* Rauh & Backeb. = Lobivia
pentlandii
- *leucorhodon* Backeb. = Lobivia pentlandii
- *leucoviolacea* Backeb. = Lobivia pentlandii
- *longispina* Britton & Rose = Echinopsis
longispina
- **maximiliana** (Heyder) Backeb. · ⼁ Z9 ⓐ
▽ ✻; S-Peru, N-Bol.
- *minuta* F. Ritter = Lobivia hertrichiana
- **pentlandii** (Hook.) Britton & Rose · ⼁ Z9
ⓐ ▽ ✻; S-Peru, N-Bol.
- *planiceps* Backeb. = Lobivia hertrichiana
- *polaskiana* Backeb. = Lobivia chrysantha
- *prestoana* Cárdenas = Lobivia cinnabarina
- *purpureominiata* F. Ritter = Trichocereus
huascha
- *schneideriana* Backeb. = Lobivia pentlandii
- *shaferi* Britton & Rose = Echinopsis aurea
- **silvestrii** (Speg.) G.D. Rowley · ⼁ Z9 ⓐ
▽ ✻; Arg.: Tucuman
- *varians* Backeb. = Lobivia pentlandii
- *vilcabambae* F. Ritter = Lobivia hertrichiana
- *walterspielii* Boed. = Lobivia cinnabarina
- *weghaiana* Backeb. = Lobivia pentlandii

Lobostemon Lehm. -m- *Boraginaceae* ·
28 spp. · F:Fausse-vipérine; G:Schuppen-
faden
- **argenteus** (Lehm.) H. Buek · ♄ ⓐ VI;
S-Afr.
- **fruticosus** (L.) H. Buek · E:Eighty Day
Healing Bush · ♄ ⓐ V; S-Afr.
- **glaucophyllus** (Pers.) H. Buek · ♄ ⓐ V;
S-Afr.

Lobularia Desv. -f- *Brassicaceae* · 5 spp. ·
E:Sweet Alsion; F:Alysson; G:Duftstein-
rich, Silberkraut
- **maritima** (L.) Desv. · G:Strand-Silber-
kraut
- **many cultivars**
- var. **benthamii** (L.H. Bailey) · F:Alysse
odorant benthamii · ⊙ Z7; cult.
- var. **maritima** · E:Sweet Alison, Sweet
Alyssum; G:Gewöhnliches Strand-
Silberkaut · ⼁ Z7 VI-X; Eur.: Ib, Fr, Ital-P,
Ba; TR, N-Afr., Arab., nat. in BrI, Sc, A,
EC-Eur., RO, Crim

Lochnera Rchb. ex Endl. = Catharanthus
- *rosea* (L.) Rchb. ex Endl. = Catharanthus
roseus

Lockhartia Hook. -f- *Orchidaceae* · 26 spp.
- **lunifera** (Lindl.) Rchb. f. · ♃ Z10 ⓜ
  VII-VIII ∇ ✱; Braz.
- **oerstedii** Rchb. f. · ♃ Z10 ⓜ VI-VIII ∇
  ✱; Guat.
- *robusta* Schltr. = Lockhartia oerstedii
- *verrucosa* Rchb. f. = Lockhartia oerstedii

Lodoicea Comm. ex DC. -f- *Arecaceae* ·
  1 sp. · E:Double Coconut, Seychelles Nut;
  F:Cocotier de Seychelles; G:Seychellen-
  nuss
- **maldivica** (J.F. Gmel.) Pers. ex H.
  Wendl. · E:Coco de Mer, Double Coconut,
  Seychelles Nut; G:Seychellennuss · ♄ e
  Z10 ⓜ; Seych.

Logania R. Br. -f- *Loganiaceae* · 25 spp.
- **albiflora** (Andrews) Druce · E:Narrow-
  leaf Logania · ♄ Z9 ⓐ IV-V; Austr.:
  Queensl., N.S.Wales, Victoria

Loiseleuria Desv. -f- *Ericaceae* · 1 sp. ·
  E:Alpine Azalea, Trailing Azalea;
  F:Loiseleuria; G:Alpenazalee, Alpen-
  heide, Gämsheide
- **procumbens** (L.) Desv. · E:Alpine
  Azalea, Creeping Azalea, Moun-
  tain Azalea; F:Azalée des Alpes;
  G:Alpenazalee, Alpenheide, Gämsheide
  · ♄ e ⤳ △ Z1 VI-VII; Eur.* exc. EC-Eur.;
  E-Sib., Kamchat., Sakhal., Jap., Alaska,
  Greenl., Can., USA: Maine, N.H., Wash.

Lolium L. -n- *Poaceae* · 8-12 spp. · E:Rye
  Grass; F:Raygras; G:Lolch, Raigras,
  Raygras, Weidelgras
- × **boucheanum** Kunth (*L. multiflorum* ×
  L. perenne) · ♃ Ⓝ; cult.
- × *hybridum* Hausskn. = Lolium ×
  boucheanum
- *italicum* A. Braun = Lolium multiflorum
- **multiflorum** Lam. · E:Common Ryegrass,
  Italian Ryegrass; G:Italienisches
  Weidelgras, Vielblütiger Lolch · ⊙ ⊙ ♃
  VI-VIII Ⓝ; Eur.: Ib, Fr, Ital-P, Ba, RO; TR,
  Palest., Macaron., N-Afr., nat. in Eur. *,
  Iraq, Cauc., Iran, Ind., N-Am., S-Am.,
  S-Afr., Tasman., NZ
- **perenne** L. · E:Perennial Rye Grass;
  G:Deutsches Weidelgras, Englisches
  Weidelgras, Lolch · ♃ VI-X Ⓝ; Eur*, Cauc,
  TR, Cyprus, Syr., Lebanon, Palest., Iraq,
  Iran, N-Afr., Canar., Madeira, nat. in
  cosmop.

- var. *multiflorum* (Lam.) Parn. = Lolium
  multiflorum
- **remotum** Schrank · G:Lein-Lolch · ⊙
  VI-VIII; Eur.: E-Eur, EC-Eur.; Afgh.,
  Ind, Amur, nat. in N-Afr., Canar., Azor.,
  W-Austr.
- **rigidum** Gaudin · E:Stiff Darnel, Wim-
  mera Ryegrass; G:Steifer Lolch · ⊙ VI-IX;
  Eur.: Ib, Fr, Sw, Ital-P, Ba, Crim; TR, Syr.,
  Lebanon, Israel, Iraq, Cauc., Iran, Afgh.,
  Kashmir, Ind, N-Afr., Madeira, Canar.,
  nat. in S-Afr., N-Am., S-Am., Austr.
- **temulentum** L. · E:Bearded Ryegrass,
  Darnel; G:Taumel-Lolch · ⊙ VI-VIII ⚘;
  Eur.*, Levant, Iraq, Arab., Cauc., Iran,
  Afgh., Pakist., Sri Lanka, W-Sib., C-As,
  Ind., Amur, Sakhal., N-Afr., nat. in E-As.,
  Jap., Eth., trop. Afr., S-Afr., N-Am.,
  S-Am., Austr., NZ

Lomaria Willd. = Blechnum
- *ciliata* T. Moore = Blechnum moorei
- *gibba* Labill. = Blechnum gibba

Lomariopsis Fée -f- *Lomariopsidaceae* ·
  47 spp. · F:Fougère grimpante; G:Saum-
  farn
- **sorbifolia** (L.) J. Sm. emend. Underw. ·
  ♃ ⚭ ⓐ; trop. Afr., trop. As.

Lomatia R. Br. -f- *Proteaceae* · 12 spp.
- **ferruginea** (Cav.) R. Br. · ♄ e Z8 ⓐ VII;
  Chile
- **hirsuta** (Lam.) Diels ex J.F. Macbr. · ♄ ♄
  e Z8 ⓐ; Braz., Peru
- **myricoides** (C.F. Gaertn.) Domin ·
  E:Long-leaf Lomatia · ♄ e Z8 ⓐ VII;
  Austr.: N.S.Wales, Victoria
- *obliqua* (Ruiz & Pav.) R. Br. = Lomatia
  hirsuta

Lomatogonium A. Braun -n-
  Gentianaceae · 18 spp. · G:Saumnarbe,
  Tauernblümchen
- **carinthiacum** (Wulfen) Rchb. ·
  G:Kärntner Tauernblümchen · ⊙ VIII-IX
  ∇; Eur.: I, C-Eur., RO; Alp., S-Carp.;
  Cauc., W-Sib., E-Sib., Kamchat., C-As.,
  Him., China: Sinkiang

Lonas Adans. -f- *Asteraceae* · 1 sp. ·
  E:Yellow Ageratum; F:Agérate jaune;
  G:Gelber Leberbalsam
- **annua** (L.) Vines & Druce · E:African
  Daisy, Yellow Ageratum; G:Gelber

Leberbalsam · ⊙ VIII-X; Eur.: S-I, Sic.; N-Afr., nat. in F
- *inodora* (L.) Gaertn. = Lonas annua

Lonchitis L. -f- *Dennstaedtiaceae* · 6 spp. · F:Fougère, Ptéris; G:Lanzenfarn
- **hirsuta** L. · ♃ Z10 Ⓦ; Mex., C-Am., trop. S-Am.
- **pubescens** Willd. · ♃ Z10 Ⓦ; trop. Afr.

Lonchocarpus Kunth -m- *Fabaceae* · 130-150 spp. · E:Bitter Wood, Turtle Bone; G:Timboholz
- **nicou** (Aubl.) DC. · ♄ ≹ Z10 Ⓦ ☠ Ⓝ; ? Peru, ? W-Amazon.
- **urucu** Killip & A.C. Sm. · ♄ ≹ Z10 Ⓦ ☠ Ⓝ; Amazon.
- *utilis* A.C. Sm. = Lonchocarpus nicou

Lonicera L. -f- *Caprifoliaceae* · 180 spp. · E:Honeysuckle; F:Chèvrefeuille; G:Geißblatt, Heckenkirsche
- **acuminata** Wall. · G:Spitzblättriges Geißblatt · ⌇ e ≹ Z5; Him.: Nepal, Sikkim
- **albertii** Regel · F:Clématite d'Albert; G:Dornige Heckenkirsche · ♄ d ≹ D Z6 V ☠; C-As., Tibet
- **alpigena** L. · E:Alpine Honeysuckle; G:Alpen-Heckenkirsche · ♄ d ♧ Z6 V ☠; Eur.* exc. Sc, BrI; mts.
- **alseuosmoides** Graebn. · ♄ e ≹ Z6 VI-VII ☠; W-China
- **altmannii** Regel & Schmalh. · ♄ ⌇ d ≹ Z5 IV-V ☠; C-As.
- × **americana** (Mill.) K. Koch (*L. caprifolium* × *L. etrusca*) · G:Italienisches Geißblatt · ♄ d ≹ D Z7 VI-VIII ☠; S-F +
- × **amoena** Zabel (*L. korolkowii var. korolkowii* × *L. tatarica*) · ♄ d Z5 VI ☠; cult.
- **angustifolia** Wall. ex DC. · G:Schmalblättrige Heckenkirsche · ♄ d Z5 V-VI ☠; Kashmir, Him., SE-Tibet
- **arizonica** Rehder · E:Arizona Honeysuckle; G:Arizona-Heckenkirsche · ♄ d Z6 ☠; Ariz., N.Mex.
- × **bella** Zabel (*L. morrowii* × *L. tatarica*) · ♄ d Z4 ☠; cult.
- *brachypoda* DC. = Lonicera japonica var. repens
- × **brownii** (Regel) Carrière (*L. hirsuta* × *L. sempervirens*) · E:Scarlet Trumpet Honeysuckle · ♄ d ≹ Z6 V-VIII ☠; cult.
- **caerulea** L. · E:Blue Honeysuckle; F:Camérisier bleu; G:Gewöhnliche Blaue Heckenkirsche · ♄ d Z3 IV-V ☠; Eur.* exc. BrI; ? TR
- **canadensis** W. Bartram ex Marshall · E:American Fly Honeysuckle, Fly Honeysuckle; G:Kanadische Heckenkirsche · ♄ d Z3 V ☠; Can.: E, Sask.; USA: NE, NCE, NC
- **caprifolium** L. · E:Italian Honeysuckle; F:Clématite des jardins; G:Jelängerjelieber, Wohlriechendes Geißblatt · ♄ d ≹ D Z5 V-VI ⚕ ☠; Eur.: A, Ital-P, Ba, EC-Eur., RO; TR, Cauc., nat. in BrI, Sc, C-Eur., Fr, Ib
- **caucasica** Pall. · G:Kaukasische Heckenkirsche · ♄ d Z6 V-VII ☠; Cauc.
- **chaetocarpa** (Batalin ex Rehder) Rehder · G:Borstenfrüchtige Heckenkirsche · ♄ d ♧ Z5 V ☠; W-China
- *chinensis* P. Watson = Lonicera japonica var. japonica
- **chrysantha** Turcz. · G:Gelbblütige Heckenkirsche
- var. **chrysantha** · ♄ d Z4 V-VI ☠; Jap., Korea, Sakhal., E-Sib.
- var. **latifolia** Korsh. Z3 ☠; Korea +
- **ciliosa** (Pursh) Poir. ex DC. · E:Orange Honeysuckle; G:Bewimperte Heckenkirsche · ♄ ⌇ d ≹ Z4 VI ☠; B.C., USA: NW, Rocky Mts., Calif.
- **deflexicalyx** Batalin · G:Krummkelchige Heckenkirsche · ♄ d Z6 V-VI ☠; Tibet, W-China
- **demissa** Rehder · G:Graue Heckenkirsche · ♄ d Z6 V-VI ☠; Jap.
- **dioica** L. · E:Glaucous Honeysuckle; G:Blaugrüne Heckenkirsche · ♄ d ⁓ Z5 VI-VII ☠; Can.: E; USA: NE, NCE, SE
- var. *glaucescens* (Rydb.) Butters = Lonicera glaucescens
- **etrusca** Santi · E:Etruscan Honeysuckle; G:Toskanisches Geißblatt · ♄ ⌇ e ≹ Z7 Ⓚ ∧ V-VIII ☠; Eur.: Ib, Fr, Ital-P, Ba, Sw; TR, Levant, N-Afr., nat. in Crim
- **ferdinandii** Franch. · G:Ferdinands Heckenkirsche · ♄ d ♧ Z6 VI ☠; Mong., N-China
- **flava** Sims · E:Yellow Honeysuckle; G:Gelbblühendes Geißblatt · ♄ d ≹ D Z5 VI ☠; USA: SE, SC
- *flexuosa* Thunb. = Lonicera japonica var. repens
- **fragrantissima** Lindl. & Paxton · E:Fragrant Honeysuckle; F:Clématite d'hiver; G:Wohlriechende Heckenkirsche · ♄ d Z7 ∧ II-III; E-China

– *gibbiflora* Maxim. non Dippel = Lonicera chrysantha var. chrysantha
– **giraldii** Rehder · F:Clématite de Girald; G:Giralds Geißblatt · ♄ e ⚘ Z6 VI-VII; NW-China
– *glauca* Hill = Lonicera dioica
– **glaucescens** (Rydb.) Rydb. · G:Kahles Geißblatt · ♄ d ⚘ Z3 V-VI ✲; Can., USA: NE, N.C., NCE, NC, Okla.
– **gracilipes** Miq. · G:Feinstielige Heckenkirsche · ♄ d ⚙ Z6 IV-V ✲; Jap.
– × **heckrottii** Rehder (*L.* × *americana* × *L. sempervirens*) · E:Coral Honeysuckle, Gold Flame Honeysuckle · ♄ d ⚘ D Z6 VI-IX ✲; cult.
– **henryi** Hemsl. · F:Clématite de Henry; G:Henrys Geißblatt · ♄ e ⚘ ⤳ Z6 VI-VII ✲; W-China
– **hildebrandiana** Collett & Hemsl. · E:Giant Honeysuckle; G:Riesen-Geißblatt · ♄ e ⚘ D Z9 ⓦ ⓚ VI-VIII ✲; China, Burma, Thail.
– **hirsuta** Eaton · E:Hairy Honeysuckle; G:Rauhaariges Geißblatt · ♄ d ⚘ Z3 VI-VII ✲; Can.: E, Sask.; USA: NE, NCE, NC
– **hispida** (Stephan ex Fisch.) Pall. ex Roem. & Schult. · G:Steifhaarige Heckenkirsche · ♄ d Z5 V ✲; C-As., Pakist., Him., SW-China
– var. *chaetocarpa* Batalin ex Rehder = Lonicera chaetocarpa
– **iberica** M. Bieb. · G:Persische Heckenkirsche · ♄ d Z6 VI ✲; Cauc., Iran
– **implexa** Aiton · E:Minorca Honeysuckle; G:Macchien-Geißblatt · ♄ e ⚘ D Z9 ⓚ VI-VIII ✲; Eur.: Ib, Fr, Ital-P, Ba; TR, NW-Afr.
– **involucrata** (Richardson) Banks ex Spreng. · E:Black Twinberry; G:Behüllte Heckenkirsche
– var. **involucrata** · ♄ d ⚙ Z4 V-VI ✲; Alaska, Can.; USA: NW, Calif., Rocky Mts., SW, NCE; Mex.
– var. *ledebourii* (Eschsch.) Jeps. = Lonicera ledebourii
– var. **serotina** Koehne · ♄ d VII-VIII ✲; Colo.
– × *italica* Schmidt ex Tausch = Lonicera × americana
– **japonica** Thunb.
– **some cultivars**
– var. *chinensis* (P. Watson) Baker = Lonicera japonica var. repens
– var. **japonica** · E:Japanese Honeysuckle; F:Clématite du Japon; G:Japanisches

Geißblatt · ♄ e ⚘ ⤳ Z6 VI-IX ⚘ ✲; China, Manch., Korea, Jap., nat. in BrI, F, C-Eur., I, sp.
– var. **repens** (Siebold) Rehder · F:Clématite du Japon rampant · ♄ e ⚘ ⤳ D Z4 V-VII ✲; China, Jap.
– **kesselringii** Regel · ♄ d Z6 V-VII ✲; ? Kamchat.
– **korolkowii** Stapf · E:Blue-leaf Honeysuckle; G:Korolkows Heckenkirsche · ♄ d Z5 VI ✲; C-As., Afgh, Pakist.
– **ledebourii** Eschsch. · E:Twinberry Honeysuckle; G:Kalifornische Heckenkirsche, Ledebours Heckenkirsche · ♄ d ⚙ Z5 VI ✲; Calif.
– *ligustrina* Wall. = Lonicera nitida
– var. *pileata* (Oliv.) Franch. = Lonicera pileata
– var. *yunnanensis* Franch. = Lonicera nitida
– **maackii** (Rupr.) Maxim. · E:Amur Honeysuckle, Bush Honeysuckle; F:Clématite de Maack; G:Maacks Heckenkirsche · ♄ d Z3 ✲; Amur, N-China, Manch., Korea, Jap.
– f. **podocarpa** Franch. ex Rehder · ✲; China
– **maximowiczii** (Rupr.) Maxim. · G:Maximowiczs Heckenkirsche · ♄ d Z5 V-VI ✲; Korea, Manch.
– **microphylla** Willd. ex Roem. & Schult. · G:Kleinblättrige Heckenkirsche · ♄ d Z6 V ✲; C-As.
– × **minutiflora** Zabel (*L. morrowii* × *L.* × *xylosteoides*) · ♄ d Z6 V-VI ✲; cult.
– **morrowii** A. Gray · E:Morrow's Honeysuckle; F:Clématite de Morrow; G:Morrows Heckenkirsche · ♄ d ⚙ Z4 V-VI ✲; Jap.
– × **muendeniensis** Rehder (*L.* × *bella* × *L. ruprechtiana*) · ♄ d Z5 V ✲; cult.
– × **myrtilloides** J.A. Purpus (*L. angustifolia* × *L. myrtillus*) · G:Heidelbeerblättrige Heckenkirsche · ♄ d D Z6 V-VI ✲; cult.
– **myrtillus** Hook. f. & Thomson
– var. **depressa** (Royle) Rehder · ♄ d Z6 ✲; Him.: Nepal, Sikkim
– var. **myrtillus** · F:Clématite myrtille · ♄ d D Z6 V-VI ✲; Afgh., Pakist., Him., SW-China
– **nigra** L. · F:Camérisier noir; G:Schwarze Heckenkirsche · ♄ d Z5 V-VI ✲ ⓝ; Eur.* exc. BrI, Sc; mts.
– **nitida** E.H. Wilson ·

E:Black-berried Honeysuckle, Box
Honeysuckle; F:Clématite brillant;
G:Glänzende Heckenkirsche, Immergrüne Strauch-Heckenkirsche · ♄ e Z7 V
⚘; W-China
- **some cultivars** · ⚘
- **nummariifolia** Jaub. & Spach · ♄ d Z6
⚘; S-GR, Crete, C-As.
- **oblongifolia** (Goldie) Hook. · E:Swamp
Fly Honeysuckle · ♄ d Z3 V ⚘; Can.: E;
USA: NCE, NE
- **obovata** Royle ex Hook. f. & Thomson ·
♄ d Z5 V ⚘; Afgh., Kashmir, Him.,
SE-Tibet
- **orientalis** Lam. · G:Orientalische
Heckenkirsche · ♄ d Z5 ⚘; TR
- var. *caucasica* (Pall.) Rehder = Lonicera
caucasica
- var. *longifolia* Dippel = Lonicera kesselringii
- *parviflora* Lam. = Lonicera dioica
- **periclymenum** L. · E:Woodbine;
F:Clématite des bois; G:Wald-Geißblatt
· ♄ d ⚥ D Z5 VI ⚘; Eur.* exc. EC-Eur.;
Moroc.
- **some cultivars** · ⚘
- **pileata** Oliv. · E:Privet Honeysuckle;
F:Clématite à cupule; G:Immergrüne
Kriech-Heckenkirsche · ♄ e D Z6 V ⚘;
C-China, W-China
- f. *yunnanensis* (Franch.) Rehder =
Lonicera nitida
- **prolifera** (G. Kirchn.) Rehder · E:Grape
Honeysuckle; G:Sprossendes Geißblatt ·
♄ d Z5 VI-VII ⚘; Can.: E; USA: NE, NCE,
NC, SE
- **prostrata** Rehder · ♄ d ↝ Z5 VI ⚘;
W-China
- × **pseudochrysantha** A. Braun ex Rehder
(*L. chrysantha* × *L. xylosteum*) · ♄ d Z3
V-VI ⚘; cult.
- *pubescens* Sweet = Lonicera hirsuta
- × **purpusii** Rehder (*L. fragrantissima* × *L.
standishii*) · ♄ s D Z5 II-IV ⚘; cult.
- **pyrenaica** L. · E:Pyrenean Honeysuckle;
G:Pyrenäen-Heckenkirsche · ♄ d Z6 V ⚘;
Eur.: sp., F; Moroc.; mts.
- **quinquelocularis** Hardw. · G:Durch-
sichtige Heckenkirsche · ♄ d ⚭ Z6 VI ⚘;
Afgh., Pakist., Him., SW-China
- **rupicola** Hook. f. & Thomson · ♄ d Z7 ∧
V-VI ⚘; Him.
- **ruprechtiana** Regel · E:Manchurian
Honeysuckle; G:Ruprechts Heckenkirsche · ♄ d ⚭ Z4 V ⚘; Manch., China

- **sempervirens** L. · E:Everblooming
Honeysuckle, Trumpet Honeysuckle;
G:Trompeten-Geißblatt · ♄ e ⚥ Z7 ∧
V-VIII ⚘; USA: NE, NCE, NC, SC, SE,
Fla.
- **similis** Hemsl. · ⚘
- var. **delavayi** (Franch.) Rehder · ♄ e ⚥
Z9 ▣ VIII ⚘; W-China
- var. **similis** · ♄ e Z9 ▣ ⚘; SW-China
- **spinosa** Jacquem. ex Walp. · ♄ d Z5 ⚘;
Afgh., Him., Tibet
- var. *albertii* (Regel) Rehder = Lonicera
albertii
- **splendida** Boiss. · G:Glänzendes
Geißblatt · ♄ e ⚥ Z9 ▣ VI-VIII ⚘; S-Sp.
- **standishii** Jacques · E:Winter Honeysuckle; G:Immergrüne Heckenkirsche · ♄ e
D Z6 II-IV ⚘; China
- f. **lancifolia** Rehder · ♄ e Z6 III-IV ⚘;
China: Sichuan
- **syringantha** Maxim. · ♄ d; China
(Gansu, Ningxia, Qinghai, Sichuan,
Yunnan, Tibet)
- var. **syringantha** · F:Clématite à fleurs de
lilas; G:Fliederblütige Heckenkirsche · ♄
d Z5 ⚘; China, Tibet
- var. **wolfii** Rehder · ♄ d D Z4 V-VI ⚘;
NW-China
- **tangutica** Maxim. · G:Tangutische Heckenkirsche · ♄ d ⚭ Z6 V-VI ⚘; W-China
- **tatarica** L. · E:Tartarian Honeysuckle;
F:Clématite de Tartarie; G:Tataren-
Heckenkirsche · ♄ d Z3 V-VI ⚘ Ⓝ; Eur.:
Russ.; W-Sib., C-As., nat. in Ib, Fr, C-Eur.
EC-Eur.
- × **tellmanniana** P. Magyar ex Späth (*L.
sempervirens* × *L. tragophylla*) · ♄ d ⚥ Z7
∧ VI ⚘; cult.
- **thibetica** Bureau & Franch. · G:Tibet-
ische Heckenkirsche · ♄ d Z4 VI-VII ⚘;
W-China
- **tomentella** Hook. f. & Thomson ·
G:Flaum-Heckenkirsche · ♄ d Z5 VI ⚘;
Ind.: Sikkim
- **tragophylla** Hemsl. · E:Yellow Honey-
suckle; G:Bocksblatt-Heckenkirsche · ♄ d
⚥ Z6 VI ⚘; W-China
- **trichosantha** Bureau & Franch. ·
G:Behaartblütige Heckenkirsche · ♄ d Z6
VII ⚘; W-China, Tibet
- **webbiana** Wall. ex DC. · G:Webbs
Heckenkirsche · ♄ d Z8 ∧ IV-V ⚘; Afgh.,
Him.
- × **xylosteoides** Tausch (*L. tatarica* × *L.
xylosteum*) · ♄ d Z6 V ⚘; cult.

- **xylosteum** L. · E:Fly Honeysuckle; F:Camérisier à balais, Clématite des haies; G:Rote Heckenkirsche · ₺ d Z3 V-VI ☠ Ⓝ; Eur.*, N-TR, W-Sib.
- **yunnanensis** Franch. · G:Yunnan-Heckenkirsche · ₺ e ≹ Z8 Ⓚ ☠; SW-China
- *yunnanensis* hort. = Lonicera nitida

Lopezia Cav. -f- *Onagraceae* · 21 sp.
- *minuta* Lag. = Lopezia racemosa
- **racemosa** Cav. · ⊙ ⊙ ♃ Z10 IV-XI; Mex., C-Am.

Lophira Banks ex C.F. Gaertn. -f- *Ochnaceae* · 2 spp. · E:African Oak; G:Afrikanische Eiche
- **lanceolata** Tiegh. ex Keay · E:African Oak; G:Afrikanische Eiche · ₺ Ⓦ Ⓝ; W-Afr.

Lophocereus (A. Berger) Britton & Rose -m- *Cactaceae* · 2 spp.
- **schottii** (Engelm.) Britton & Rose · E:Cinita, Senita Cereus · ₺ ♆ Z9 Ⓚ ▽ *; Ariz., NW-Mex.

Lophomyrtus Burret -f- *Myrtaceae* · 2 spp. · F:Myrte; G:Schopfmyrte
- **bullata** (Sol. ex A. Cunn.) Burret · E:Rama Rama; G:Blasige Schopfmyrte · ₺ e Z9 Ⓚ; NZ
- **obcordata** (Raoul) Burret · ₺ e Z9 Ⓚ; NZ
- × **ralphii** (Hook. f.) Burret (*L. bullata* × *L. obcordata*) · ₺ ₺ e Z9 Ⓚ; NZ

Lophophora J.M. Coult. -f- *Cactaceae* · 2 spp. · E:Mescal, Peyote; F:Peyote, Peyoti; G:Mescalkaktus, Pejote, Pellote, Peyotl
- *fricii* Haberm. = Lophophora williamsii var. williamsii
- **williamsii** (Lem. ex Salm-Dyck) J.M. Coult.
- var. **lutea** (Rouhier) Soulaire · ♆ Z9 Ⓚ ▽ *; Mex.
- var. **williamsii** · E:Dumpling Cactus, Mescal; G:Peyotl, Schnapskopf · ♆ Z9 Ⓚ ⚕ ☠ ▽ *; USA: Tex., N.Mex.; Mex.

Lophospermum D. Don -n- *Scrophulariaceae* · 8 spp.
- *atrosanguineum* Zucc. = Rhodochiton atrosanguineus
- **erubescens** D. Don · E:Creeping Gloxinia, Mexican Twist; G:Kletter-gloxinie · ₺ ≹ Z9 Ⓚ VII-IX; Mex.
- **purpusii** (Brandegee) Rothm. · ♃ Z9 Ⓚ VII-VIII; SW-Mex.
- **scandens** D. Don · ₺ ≹ Z9 Ⓚ VII-IX; Mex.

Lophostemon Schott -m- *Myrtaceae* · 4-8 spp.
- **confertus** (R. Br.) Peter G. Wilson & J.T. Waterh. · E:Vinegar Tree · ₺ e Z10 Ⓚ; Austr. (Queensl., N.S.Wales)

Loranthus Jacq. -m- *Loranthaceae* · 1 sp. · G:Riemenblume
- **europaeus** Jacq. · E:Mistletoe; G:Eichenmistel, Riemenblume · ₺ d IV-VI; Eur.: C-Eur., EC-Eur., Ba, E-Eur., Ital-P: TR, Syr.

Loropetalum R. Br. ex Rchb. -n- *Hamamelidaceae* · 2 spp. · F:Loropetalum; G:Riemenblüte
- **chinense** (R. Br.) Oliv. · ₺ ₺ e Z8 Ⓚ XII-IV; Ind. (Assam, Khasi mts.) S-China, Jap.

Lotononis (DC.) Eckl. & Zeyh. -f- *Fabaceae* · 120-150 spp.
- **bainesii** Baker · ♃ Ⓝ; S-Afr. (N-Transvaal), Zimbabwe, nat. in Austr.: Queensl.

Lotus L. -m- *Fabaceae* · c. 100 spp. · E:Brid's Foot Trefoil; F:Lotier; G:Hornklee
- **alpinus** (DC.) Ramond · E:Alpine Bird's Foot Trefoil; G:Alpen-Hornklee · ♃ Z4 VI-VIII; Eur.: sp., F, I, C-Eur., Ba; Pyr., Apenn., Balkan; TR, Levant
- **berthelotii** Lowe ex Masf. · F:Lotier de Berthelot · ♃ ≹ ⟿ Ⓚ III-IV; Canar.: Teneriffa
- **borbasii** Ujhelyi · G:Slowakischer Hornklee · ♃ V-VII; Eur.: A, EC-Eur., Ba
- **corniculatus** L. · E:Bird's Foot Trefoil; F:Lotier corniculé; G:Gewöhnlicher Hornklee · ♃ ⟿ △ Z5 VI-IX ⚕ Ⓝ; Eur.*, TR, Cauc., Iran, C-As., Ind., NW-Afr.
- **edulis** L. · ⊙ Ⓝ; Eur.: Ib, Fr, Ital-P, Ba; TR, Levant, N-Afr.
- **jacobaeus** L. · ♃ Z9 Ⓚ IV-V; Cap Verde
- **maculatus** Breitf. · ₺ Ⓚ III-IV; Canar.
- **ornithopodioides** L. · G:Vogelfußartiger Hornklee · ⊙; Eur.: Ib, Fr, Ital-P, Ba, S-Russ.; TR, Levant, Cauc., N-Afr.
- *peliorhynchus* Hook. f. = Lotus berthelotii

– *siliquosus* L. = Tetragonolobus maritimus
– **tenuis** Waldst. & Kit. ex Willd. ·
   E:Narrow-leaf Trefoil; G:Salz-Hornklee,
   Schmalblättriger Hornklee · ⌇ Z4 VI-VIII;
   Eur.*, TR, Levant, Cauc., C-As., N-Afr.
– **uliginosus** Schkuhr · E:Greater Bird's
   Foot Trefoil; G:Sumpf-Hornklee · ⌇ ⁓
   Z6 VI-VII ⓝ; Eur.*, Cauc.

Lourea Neck. ex J. St.-Hil. = Christia
– *vespertilionis* (L. f.) Desv. = Christia
   vespertilionis

Lourya Baill. = Peliosanthes
– *campanulata* Baill. = Peliosanthes teta

× **Lowara** hort. -f- Orchidaceae (*Brassavola*
   × *Laelia* × *Sophronitis*)

Loxanthocereus Backeb. = Borzicactus
– *acanthurus* (Vaupel) Backeb. = Borzicactus acanthurus
– *aureispinus* (F. Ritter) Buxb. = Hildewintera aureispina

Luculia Sweet -f- *Rubiaceae* · 4 spp.
– **grandifolia** Ghose · ♄ e Z9 ⓜ; Bhutan
– **gratissima** (Wall.) Sw. · ♄ ♄ s D Z10 ⓜ
   XII-II; Him.
– **pinceana** Hook. · ♄ s Z9 ⓜ VII-VIII; Ind.:
   Khasia Hills

Lucuma Molina = Pouteria
– *caimito* (Ruiz & Pav.) Roem. & Schult. =
   Pouteria caimito
– *campechiana* Kunth = Pouteria campechiana
– *obovata* Kunth = Pouteria lucuma

Ludisia A. Rich. -f- *Orchidaceae* · 1 sp. ·
   F:Ludisia; G:Blutständel
– **discolor** (Ker-Gawl.) A. Rich. · G:Blut-
   ständel
– var. **dawsoniana** (S.H. Low ex Rchb. f.)
   Schltr. · ⌇ Z9 ⓜ IX-XII ▽ ✳; Malay. Pen.
– var. **discolor** · ⌇ Z9 ⓜ IX-XII ▽ ✳;
   S-China, Vietn., Malay. Pen.
– var. **rubrivenia** (Rchb. f.) Schltr. · ⌇ Z9
   ⓜ IX-XII ▽ ✳; Malay. Pen.

Ludovia Brongn. -f- *Cyclanthaceae* · 3 spp.
– **lancifolia** Brongn. · ♄ ! e ⌇̃ ⓜ; trop.
   S-Am.

Ludwigia L. -f- *Onagraceae* · 82 spp. ·

F:Jussie, Ludwigia, Œnothère aquatique;
   G:Heusenkraut
– **alternifolia** L. · E:Seedbox; G:Klapper-
   Heusenkraut · ⌇ ⁓ ≈ Z7 ⓜ ⓚ; Can.:
   Ont.; USA: NE, NCE, NC, SC, SE, Fla.;
   Mex., n S-Am., nat. in A (Kärnten)
– **arcuata** Walter · E:Piedmont Primrose
   Willow · ⌇ ⁓ ≈ ⓜ; USA: S.C., Ga.,
   Fla.
– **clavellina** M. Gómez & Molinet
– var. **clavellina** · ⌇ ≈ ⓜ; USA: SE, Fla.,
   nat. in USA: NE
– var. **grandiflora** (Michx.) M. Gómez ·
   E:Large-flower Primrose Willow · ⌇ ≈
   ⓜ VII-VIII; USA: SE, Fla.
– **helminthorrhiza** (Mart.) H. Hara · ⌇
   ≈ Z9 ⓜ; S-Mex. C-Am., S-Am.
– *macrocarpa* Michx. = Ludwigia alternifo-
   lia
– **natans** (L.) Elliott · E:Creeping Primrose
   Willow; G:Schwimm-Heusenkraut · ⌇
   ⁓ ≈ Z9 ⓜ VII-VIII; USA: NE, NCE,
   NC, SE, SC, NW, Calif.; Mex., W.Ind.
– **palustris** (L.) Elliott · E:Marsh Primrose
   Willow, Water Purslane; G:Sumpf-
   Heusenkraut · ⌇ ⁓ ≈ Z3 VII-VIII;
   Eur.* exc. Sc; TR, Syr., Palest., Cauc.,
   Iran, NW-Afr., S-Afr., Can., USA: NE,
   NCE, SE, SC, SW, Rocky Mts., NW, Calif.;
   Mex., W.Ind., nat. in NZ
– **peruviana** (L.) H. Hara · E:Peruvian
   Primrose Bush; G:Peruanisches
   Heusenkraut · ♄ ♄ ≈ Z9 ⓜ VII-VIII;
   USA: Fla.; C-Am., S-Am.
– **pulvinaris** Gilg · ⌇ ⁓ ≈ ⓜ; C-Afr.,
   S-Afr.
– *repens* Sw. = Ludwigia palustris
– **suffruticosa** (L.) M. Gómez · E:Shrubby
   Primrose Willow · ♄ ≈ ⓜ VII-VIII;
   Trop.

Lueddemannia Rchb. f. -f- *Orchidaceae* ·
   1 sp.
– **pescatorei** (Lindl.) Linden & Rchb. f. · ⌇
   Z10 ⓜ VII ▽ ✳; Col.

Luetkea Bong. -f- *Rosaceae* · 1 sp.
– **pectinata** (Pursh) Kuntze · E:Partridge
   Foot · ♄ e VII-IX; Alaska, W-Can., Calif.
   Rocky M.

Luffa Mill. -f- *Cucurbitaceae* · 7 spp. ·
   E:Loofah, Rag Gourd; F:Eponge végétale;
   G:Schwammgurke
– **acutangula** (L.) Roxb. · E:Angled

Loofah, Dishcloth Gourd, Strainer Vine;
G:Gerippte Schwammgurke · ⊙ ⚥ ⚯ Z9
ⓦ Ⓝ; trop. As.
– **aegyptiaca** Mill. · E:Loofah, Vegetable
Sponge; G:Schwammgurke · ⊙ ⚥ ⚯ Z9
ⓦ ⚥ Ⓝ; Afr., trop. As.
– *cylindrica* (L.) M. Roem. = Luffa aegyptiaca
– **operculata** (L.) Cogn. · ⊙ ⚥ ⚯ Z9 ⓦ Ⓝ;
Mex., C-Am., trop. S-Am.

× **Luisanda** hort. -f- *Orchidaceae* (*Luisia* ×
Vanda)

Luisia Gaudich. -f- *Orchidaceae* · 39 spp.
– **amesiana** Rolfe · ♃ Z9 ⓦ VI-VII ▽ ✳;
Burma
– *teretifolia* Gaudich. = Luisia tristis
– **tristis** (G. Forst.) Hook. f. · ♃ Z8 ⓦ VI-IX
▽ ✳; SE-As., Malay. Arch., N.Caled.

Luma A. Gray -f- *Myrtaceae* · 4 spp.
– **apiculata** (DC.) Burret · E:Orange Bark
Myrtle, Temu · ♄ e Z9 ⓚ Ⓝ; Arg., Chile
– **chequen** (Molina) A. Gray · ♄ ♄ e Z9 ⓚ;
Chile

Lunaria L. -f- *Brassicaceae* · 3 spp. ·
E:Honesty; F:Lunaire, Monaie du Pape;
G:Silberblatt
– **annua** L. · E:Annual Honesty; F:Monnaie
du pape; G:Einjähriges Silberblatt · ⊙ ⊙
⚯ ⋉ Z8 IV-VI; Eur.: I, Ba, Ro, nat. in BrI,
Sc, Fr, C-Eur., EC-Eur.
– *biennis* Moench = Lunaria annua
– **rediviva** L. · E:Perennial Honesty;
G:Ausdauerndes Silberblatt, Mondviole ·
♃ ⚯ D Z6 V-VII ⚘ ▽; Eur.* exc. BrI

Lupinus L. -m- *Fabaceae* · 200 spp. ·
E:Lupin; F:Lupin; G:Lupine, Wolfsbohne
– **albus** L. · E:White Lupin; G:Weiße
Lupine · ⊙ VI-VIII ⚘ Ⓝ; Eur.: Ba; TR,
nat. in Fr, C-Eur., Ital-P, Ib, EC-Eur., Alg.
– **angustifolius** L. · E:Blue Lupine;
G:Schmalblättrige Lupine · ⊙ VI-IX ⚘ Ⓝ;
Eur.: Ib, Fr, Ital-P, Ba; TR, Levant, N-Afr.,
nat. in C-Eur., EC-Eur., E-Eur.
– **arboreus** Sims · E:Tree Lupin; G:Baum-
Lupine · ♄ e Z8 ⓚ VII-VIII; Calif., nat. in
Wash., Br
– **densiflorus** Benth.
– var. **aureus** (Kellogg) Munz · ⊙ VI-IX;
Calif.
– var. **densiflorus** · E:White Whorl Lupin;

G:Quirl-Lupine · ⊙; Calif.
– var. *menziesii* (J. Agardh) C.P. Sm. =
Lupinus densiflorus var. aureus
– **hartwegii** Lindl. · ⊙ VII-X; Mex.
– **luteus** L. · E:Yellow Lupin; G:Gelbe
Lupine · ⊙ Z6 VI-IX ⚘ Ⓝ; Eur.: Ib; NW-
Afr., nat. in Fr, Ital-P, C-Eur., EC-Eur.,
Ba, EC-Eur.
– *menziesii* J. Agardh = Lupinus densiflorus
var. aureus
– **micranthus** Guss. · ⊙ Z8 VI-IX Ⓝ; Eur.:
Ib, Fr, Ital-P, Ba; TR, Levant, NW-Afr.,
Libya
– **mutabilis** Sweet
– var. **cruckshansii** (Hook.) Sweet · ⊙ Z9
VII-X Ⓝ; Peru; And.
– var. **mutabilis** · E:Andean Lupine;
G:Anden-Lupine · ⊙ Z9 VII-X Ⓝ; cult.
S-Am.
– **nanus** Douglas ex Benth. · E:Ocean Blue
Lupin; G:Zwerg-Lupine · ⊙ VI-VII; Calif.
– **nootkatensis** Donn ex Sims · E:Nootka
Lupin · ♃ Z4; nw N-Am., NE-As.
– **perennis** L. · E:Blue Bean, Sundial Lupin;
G:Ausdauernde Lupine · ♃ Z4 V-VIII Ⓝ;
Ont., USA: NE, NCE, SE, Fla., nat. in
C-Eur.
– **pilosus** Murray · ⊙ VI-VII Ⓝ; Eur.: GR;
TR, Syr., Palest., Egypt
– **polyphyllus** Lindl. · E:Garden Lupin;
G:Vielblättrige Lupine · ♃ Z3 VI-VIII ⚘
Ⓝ; Can.: W; USA: NW, Rocky Mts., Calif.,
nat. in ne N-Am., Eur.
– **pubescens** Benth. · ⊙; Mex., Guat.
– **subcarnosus** Hook. · E:Texas Bluebon-
net · ⊙; SW-USA
– *termis* Forssk. = Lupinus albus
– *varius* L. 1753 = Lupinus angustifolius
– *varius* L. 1763 = Lupinus pilosus
– **Cultivars**
– **many cultivars**

Luronium Raf. -n- *Alismataceae* ·
1 sp. · E:Floating Water Plantain;
F:Grenouillette; G:Froschkraut,
Schwimmlöffel
– **natans** (L.) Raf. · E:Floating Water
Plantain; F:Fluteau; G:Froschkraut,
Schwimmlöffel · ♃ ≈ Z7 V-VI ▽; Eur.*

Luzula DC. -f- *Juncaceae* · 117 spp. ·
E:Wood-Rush; F:Luzule; G:Hainsimse,
Marbel
– *albida* (Hoffm.) DC. = Luzula luzuloides
– **alpina** Hoppe · G:Alpen-Hainsimse · ♃

VI-VII; Eur.: G, A +
- **alpinopilosa** (Chaix) Breistr. ·
  G:Gewöhnliche Braune Hainsimse · ⑂
  VI-VIII; Eur.* exc. BrI, Sc, mts.
- **campestris** (L.) DC. · E:Field Wood
  Rush; G:Feld-Hainsimse, Hasenbrot · ⑂
  Z6 III-IV; Eur.*, TR, Cauc.
- **congesta** (Thuill.) Lej. · G:Kopfige
  Hainsimse · ⑂; Eur.: Sc, BrI, Fr, D +
- **desvauxii** Kunth · G:Pyrenäen-
  Hainsimse, Westliche Braune Hainsimse ·
  ⑂ VI-VII; Eur.: sp., F, G: mts.
- **divulgata** Kirschner · G:Schlanke
  Hainsimse · ⑂ IV-V; Eur.: A, D +
- **forsteri** (Sm.) DC. · E:Forster's Wood
  Rush; G:Forsters Hainsimse · ⑂ IV-V;
  Eur.* exc. Sc; TR, Cauc., Syr., Iran, Alger.
- **glabrata** (Hoppe) Desv. · G:Kahle
  Hainsimse · ⑂ VI-VII; Eur.: I, G, A; E-Alp.
- **lutea** (All.) DC. · G:Gelbe Hainsimse · ⑂
  Z6 VI-VIII; Eur.: sp., F, I, G, A; Pyr., Alp.,
  Apenn.
- **luzulina** (Vill.) Dalla Torre & Sarnth. ·
  G:Gelbliche Hainsimse · ⑂ Z6 VI-VII;
  Eur.* exc. BrI, Sc; mts.
- **luzuloides** (Lam.) Dandy & Wilmott ·
  E:Oak Forest Wood Rush; F:Luzule
  blanchâtre; G:Gewöhnliche Weißliche
  Hainsimse · ⑂ Z6 VI; Eur.: Fr, Ital-P,
  C-Eur., EC-Eur., Ba, E-Eur., ? sp., nat. in
  BrI, Sc
- *maxima* (Reichard) DC. = Luzula
  sylvatica subsp. sylvatica
- **multiflora** (Ehrh.) Lej. · E:Many-
  flowered Wood Rush; G:Vielblütige
  Hainsimse · ⑂ Z6 IV-V; Eur., As, N-Am.,
  Austr.
- *nemorosa* (Pollich) E. Mey. = Luzula
  luzuloides
- **nivea** (L.) DC. · E:Snowy Wood Rush;
  F:Luzule blanc de neige; G:Schneeweiße
  Hainsimse · ⑂ Z6 VI-VIII; Eur.: sp., F,
  C-Eur., I, Slove.
- **pallescens** Sw. · G:Bleiche Hainsimse · ⑂
  IV-V; Eur.: CZ, G, BrI+
- *pallidula* Kirschner = Luzula pallescens
- **pilosa** (L.) Willd. · E:Hairy Wood Rush;
  F:Luzule poilue; G:Behaarte Hainsimse ·
  ⑂ Z6 IV-V; Eur.*, Cauc., W-Sib., E-Sib.
- **spicata** (L.) DC. · E:Spiked Wood Rush;
  G:Ähren-Hainsimse · ⑂ VI-VIII; Eur.* exc.
  Ib; TR, Cauc., W-Sib., E-Sib., Amur, C-As,
  Him., N-Am.
- **sudetica** (Willd.) Schult. · G:Sudeten-
  Hainsimse · ⑂ VI-VIII; Eur.* exc. BrI; TR

- **sylvatica** (Huds.) Gaudin · G:Wald-
  Hainsimse
- **some cultivars**
- subsp. **sylvatica** · E:Great Wood Rush;
  F:Luzule des bois; G:Gewöhnliche Wald-
  Hainsimse · ⑂ Z6 V-VI; Eur.*, TR, Cauc.

Lycaste Lindl. -f- Orchidaceae · 31 sp.
- **aromatica** (Graham ex Hook.) Lindl. · ⑂
  D Z10 🌺 IV-V ▽ ✳; Mex., Guat., Hond.,
  Belize
- **brevispatha** (Klotzsch) Klotzsch ex Rchb.
  f. · ⑂ Z10 🌺 XII ▽ ✳; Nicar., Costa Rica,
  Panama
- **candida** Lindl.
- *costata* (Lindl.) Lindl. = Ida ciliata
- **cruenta** (Lindl.) Lindl. · ⑂ Z10 🌺 III-V ▽
  ✳; Mex., C-Am.
- **deppei** (Lodd.) Lindl. · ⑂ Z10 🌺 X-IV ▽
  ✳; Mex., Guat.
- **longipetala** (Ruiz & Pav.) Garay · ⑂
  Z10 🌺 VI-VIII ▽ ✳; Col., Ecuad., Peru,
  Venez.
- **macrophylla** (Poepp. & Endl.) Lindl. · ⑂
  Z10 🌺 XI-I ▽ ✳; C-Am., trop. S-Am.
- **skinneri** (Bateman ex Lindl.) Lindl. · ⑂
  Z10 🏵 XI-III ▽ ✳; Mex., Guat., Hond.
- **tricolor** (Klotzsch) Rchb. f. · ⑂ Z10 🌺 ▽
  ✳; Guat., Costa Rica, Panama
- *virginalis* (Scheidw.) Linden = Lycaste
  skinneri
- **Cultivars:**
- **many cultivars**

× **Lycastenaria** hort. -m- Orchidaceae
  (Bifrenaria × Lycaste)

Lychnis L. = Silene
- × *arkwrightii* hort. = Silene × arkwrightii
- *chalcedonica* L. = Silene chalcedonica
- *coronaria* (L.) Desr. = Silene coronaria
- *dioica* L. = Silene dioica
- *flos-cuculi* L. = Silene flos-cuculi
- *flos-jovis* (L.) Desr. = Silene flos-jovis
- *sartorii* Boiss. = Silene atropurpurea
- *vespertina* Sibth. = Silene latifolia subsp.
  alba

Lycianthes (Dunal) Hassl. -f- Solanaceae ·
  180-200 spp.
- **rantonnetii** (Carrière) Bitter · ♄ ⚭ Z10
  🏵 VII-X; Arg., Parag.

Lycium L. -n- Solanaceae · 100 spp. ·
  E:Teaplant; F:Lyciet; G:Bocksdorn,

Teufelszwirn
- **barbarum** L. · E:Box Thorn, Matrimony Vine; F:Lyciet commun; G:Gewöhnlicher Bocksdorn · ♄ d Z5-6 VI-IX ⚥ ⚘; C-China, nat. in Eur.*, TR, Cauc., C-As., N-Afr.
- **chinense** Mill.
- var. **chinense** · E:Chinese Wolfberry, Duke of Argyle's Tea Tree; F:Lyciet de Chine; G:Chinesischer Bocksdorn · ♄ d Z5-6 VI-IX ⚥ ⚘; China
- var. **ovatum** (Veill.) C.K. Schneid. · ⚄ d ⚬ Z6 VI-X ⚘; N-China, nat. in Eur.
- **europaeum** L. · E:European Wolfberry; G:Europäischer Bocksdorn · ♄ d ⤳ Z9 ⚑ ⚘; Eur.: Ib, Fr, Ital-P, Ba; TR, N-Afr.
- *halimifolium* Mill. = Lycium barbarum
- **pallidum** Miers · E:Desert Thorn, Pale Desert Thorn, Wolf Berry; G:Blasser Bocksdorn · ♄ d ⚬ Z7 ∧ V-VIII ⚘; USA: Calif., Utah, Colo., Ariz., N.Mex., Tex..; Mex.
- *rhombifolium* Dippel = Lycium chinense var. ovatum
- **ruthenicum** Murray · ♄ d Z7 VII-VIII ⚘; S-Russ., TR, Cauc., Iraq, Iran, Pakist., C-As., Tibet, Mong.
- **turcomannicum** Turcz. ex Miers · ♄ d Z5 VI-VIII ⚘; TR, Syr., Cauc., C-As., Pakist.
- *vulgare* Dunal = Lycium barbarum

Lycopersicon Mill. -n- *Solanaceae* · 7 spp. · E:Tomato; F:Tomate; G:Tomate
- **cheesmanii** L. Riley Z9 Ⓝ; Galapagos
- **esculentum** Mill. · G:Tomate
- var. **cerasiforme** Alef. · E:Cherry Tomato; G:Cocktail-Tomate, Kirsch-Tomate · ⊙ ⚄ Z9 ⚬ Ⓝ; Peru
- var. **esculentum** · E:Tomato; G:Kultur-Tomate · ⊙ ⚄ ♄ Z9 VII-X; Ecuad., Peru
- var. **pimpinellifolium** (Jusl.) Mill. · E:Currant Tomato; G:Johannisbeer-Tomate · ⊙ ⚄ ⚬ Z9 ⚑ Ⓝ; Ecuad., Galapagos, Peru
- var. **pyriforme** (Dunal) Alef. · E:Pear-shaped Tomato; G:Birnenförmige Tomate · ⊙ ⚄ Z9; cult.
- *lycopersicum* (L.) H. Karst. = Lycopersicon esculentum var. esculentum
- *pimpinellifolium* (L.) Mill. = Lycopersicon esculentum var. pimpinellifolium

Lycopodiella Holub -f- *Lycopodiaceae* · 38 spp. · E:Marsh Clubmoss; G:Sumpf-bärlapp

- **inundata** (L.) Holub · G:Gewöhnlicher Sumpfbärlapp · ⚄ VIII-X ▽; Eur.*, Cauc., N-Am.

Lycopodium L. -n- *Lycopodiaceae* · 38 spp. · E:Clubmoss; F:Lycopode; G:Bärlapp
- *alpinum* L. = Diphasiastrum alpinum
- **annotinum** L. · E:Stiff Clubmoss, Stiff Ground Pine; G:Sprossender Bärlapp · ⚄ Z2 VIII-IX ⚘ ▽; Eur.*, Cauc., W-Sib., E-Sib., Amur, Sakhal., Kamchat., Alaska, Can., USA: NE, NCE, NC, Rocky Mts., NW
- **clavatum** L. · E:Club Moss, Running Pine; G:Keulen-Bärlapp · ⚄ ⤳ Z2 VII-VIII ⚥ ⚘ ▽; Eur.*, TR, Cauc., W-Sib., E-Sib., Amur, Sakhal., Kamchat., China, Korea, Jap. Taiwan, Ind., Malaysia, Polyn., Afr., Alaska, Can., USA: NE, NCE, SE, Rocky Mts., NW; Mex. W-Ind., C-Am., S-Am., Greenl., Afr.
- *complanatum* L. = Diphasiastrum complanatum
- **dubium** Zoëga · G:Stechender Berg-Bärlapp · ⚄ VI-IX ▽; Eur.: Sw +
- *hippuris* Desv. ex Poir. = Lycopodium squarrosum
- *selago* L. = Huperzia selago
- **squarrosum** G. Forst. · ⚄ Z10 ⚑ ▽; Ind., Sri Lanka, Java

Lycopsis L. = Anchusa
- *arvensis* = Anchusa arvensis
- *echioides* L. = Arnebia pulchra

Lycopus L. -m- *Lamiaceae* · 18 spp. · E:Gypsywort; F:Lycope; G:Wolfstrapp
- **europaeus** L.
- subsp. **europaeus** · E:Gipsywort; F:Chanvre d'eau, Lycope d'Europe; G:Gewöhnlicher Ufer-Wolfstrapp · ⚄ ⌒ Z5 VII-IX ⚥ ; Eur.*, TR, Syr., Iran, C-As., NW-Afr.
- **exaltatus** Ehrh. · G:Hoher Wolfstrapp · ⚄ VII-IX; Eur.: Ital-P, C-Eur., EC-Eur., Ba, EC-Eur.; Cauc., W-Sib., E-Sib., C-As.
- **virginicus** L. · E:Bugleweed, Gipsyweed; G:Virginischer Wolfstrapp · ⚄ ⌒ Z5 VII-IX ⚥ ; USA: NE, NCE, NC, SC, SE

Lycoris Herb. -f- *Amaryllidaceae* · 23 spp. · E:Spider Lily; G:Spinnenlilie
- *africana* (Lam.) M. Roem. = Lycoris aurea
- **aurea** (L'Hér.) Herb. · E:Golden Lily, Golden Spider Lily · ⚄ Z7 V-VIII; China,

Jap., Ryukyu-Is., Taiwan
- **incarnata** Comes ex Spreng. · ⧠ Z7 ⌒ ∧ VII-VIII; C-China.
- **radiata** (L'Hér.) Herb. · E:Red Spider Lily; G:Rosarote Spinnenlilie · ⧠ Z8 ⊛ ⓚ VIII-IX; Jap., Ryukyu-Is.
- **sanguinea** Maxim. · E:Spider Lily; G:Schwarzrote Spinnenlilie · ⧠ Z8 ⓚ VII-VIII; China, Jap.
- **sprengeri** Comes ex Baker · ⧠ Z7 ⌒ ∧ VII-VIII; C-China
- **squamigera** Maxim. · E:Magic Lily, Resurrection Lily; G:Weiße Spinnenlilie · ⧠ Z7 ⌒ ∧ VII-VIII; Jap.

Lygeum L. -n- *Poaceae* · 1 sp.
- **spartum** Loefl. ex L. · ⧠ ⓚ Ⓝ; Eur.: Ib, Ital-P, Crete; NW-Afr.

Lygodium Sw. -n- *Schizaeaceae* · 34 spp. · F:Fougère grimpante; G:Kletterfarn, Schlingfarn
- **flexuosum** (L.) Sw. · E:Big Lygodium; G:Großer Kletterfarn · ⧠ ⚘ Z10 ⊛; Ind., Sri Lanka, S-China, Phil., Austr.: Queensl.
- **japonicum** (Thunb.) Sw. · E:Japanese Climbing Fern; G:Japanischer Kletterfarn · ⧠ ⚘ Z10 ⊛; China, Korea, Jap., Ryukyu-Is., Taiwan
- **palmatum** (Bernh.) Sw. · G:Handförmiger Kletterfarn · ⧠ ⚘ Z7 ⓚ ∧; USA: NE, Ohio, SE
- *pinnatifidum* Sw. = Lygodium flexuosum
- **scandens** (L.) Sw. · E:Snake Fern; G:Schlangen-Kletterfarn · ⧠ ⚘ Z10 ⊛; trop. Afr., trop. As., Austr., Polyn.
- **volubile** Sw. · ⧠ Z10 ⊛; C-Am., W.Ind., trop. S-Am.

Lygos Adans. = Retama
- *monosperma* (L.) Heywood = Retama monosperma

Lyonia Nutt. -f- *Ericaceae* · 35 spp. · E:Lyonia, Staggerbush; F:Lyonia; G:Lyonie
- *calyculata* (L.) Rchb. = Chamaedaphne calyculata
- **ferruginea** (Walter) Nutt. · E:Rusty Stagger Bush · ♄ ♄ e Z9 ⓚ II-III; USA: SE, Fla.
- **ligustrina** (L.) DC. · E:Maleberry; G:Rispige Lyonie · ♄ d ⌒ Z5 V-VI ✿; USA: NE, NCE, SC, SE, Fla.

- **lucida** (Lam.) K. Koch · E:Fetter Bush; G:Glänzende Lyonie · ♄ e Z7 IV-V; USA: Va., SE, Fla.
- **mariana** (L.) D. Don · E:Piedmont Stagger Bush; G:Marien-Lyonie · ♄ d ⌒ Z6 V-VI; USA: NE, SE, Fla., Tex.
- **ovalifolia** (Wall.) Drude · ♄ d Z6 V-VI; Pakist., Him., Burma, China, Jap., Taiwan
- *racemosa* (L.) D. Don = Leucothoe racemosa

Lysichiton Schott -m- *Araceae* · 2 spp. · E:Skunk Cabbage; F:Lysichiton; G:Scheinkalla
- **americanus** Hultén & H. St. John · E:Yellow Skunk Cabbage; F:Arum bananier; G:Gelbe Scheinkalla · ⧠ ⌒ Z6 IV-V; Kamchat., Alaska, Can., USA: NW, Calif., Rocky Mts.
- **camtschatcensis** (L.) Schott · E:White Skunk Cabbage; F:Faux-arum blanc; G:Weiße Scheinkalla · ⧠ ⌒ Z6 V-VI; Jap., Kuril., Sakhal., Kamchat., Amur
- *japonicus* (A. Gray) Schott ex Miq. = Lysichiton camtschatcensis

Lysimachia L. -f- *Primulaceae* · c. 150 spp. · E:Loosestrife; F:Lysimaque; G:Felberich, Gilbweiderich
- **barystachys** Bunge · ⧠ Z5 VII-VIII; Jap., Korea, Manch., N-China
- **ciliata** L. · E:Fringed Loosestrife; F:Lysimaque ciliée; G:Bewimperter Felberich · ⧠ ⌒ Z4 VII-VIII; Can., USA* exc. Calif., SC
- **clethroides** Duby · E:Gooseneck Loosestrife; F:Lysimaque à feuilles de cléthra; G:Entenschnabel-Felberich · ⧠ Z4 VI-VII; China, Jap., Indochina
- **congestiflora** Hemsl. · ⧠ ⚘ ⌇ ⓚ V-IX; China
- **ephemerum** L. · F:Lysimaque éphémère · ⧠ Z7 ∧ VI-IX; Eur.: Ib, F
- **fortunei** Maxim. · ⧠ ⋈ Z7 VII-VIII; China, Korea, Jap., Taiwan
- **japonica** Thunb. · G:Japan-Gilbweiderich · ⧠ Z6; Jap., China, Taiwan, Malay. Arch.
- *monnieri* L. = Bacopa monnieri
- **nemorum** L. · E:Wood Pimpernel, Yellow Pimpernel; F:Lysimaque des bois; G:Hain-Gilbweiderich · ⧠ ⌇ Z6 V-VII; Eur.*
- **nummularia** L. · E:Creeping Jenny;

F:Lysimaque nummulaire; G:Pfennig-
Gilbweiderich, Pfennigkraut · ⚄ ⤳ Z4
V-VII ⚥ ; Eur.*, TR, Cauc., nat. in N-Am.
- **punctata** L. · E:Dotted Loosestrife;
F:Lysimaque ponctuée; G:Punktierter
Gilbweiderich · ⚄ ⤳ Z5 VI-VIII; Eur.:
A, Ital-P, Ba, EC-Eur., E-Eur.; TR, Cauc.,
nat. in BrI, Sc, Fr, N-Am.
- **thyrsiflora** L. · E:Tufted Loosestrife;
F:Lysimaque à fleurs en thyrse;
G:Straußblütiger Gilbweiderich · ⚄ ⤳
Z6 V-VII; Eur.* exc. Ib, Ital-P; W-Sib.,
E-Sib., Amur, Sakhal., Kamchat., C-As.,
Mong., China, Alaska, Can., USA: NE,
NCE, NC, Rocky Mts., NW, Calif.
- **vulgaris** L. · G:Gewöhnlicher Gilbwei-
derich
- var. **davurica** (Ledeb.) R. Knuth · ⚄ Z5;
Jap., E-As.
- var. **vulgaris** · E:Loosestrife, Yellow
Loosestrife; F:Lysimaque commune;
G:Gewöhnlicher Gilbweiderich · ⚄ ⤳
Z5 VI-VIII ⚥ ; Eur.*, TR, Iraq, Cauc., Iran,
W-Sib., E-Sib., C-As., Him., China, Jap.,
NW-Afr., Can.: E; USA: NE, NCE

Lythrum L. -n- *Lythraceae* · 38 spp. ·
E:Loosestrife; F:Salicaire; G:Weiderich
- **alatum** Pursh · E:Winged Loosestrife;
G:Geflügelter Weiderich · ⚄ ⤳ Z3
VI-VIII; Can.; USA: NE, NCE, NC, SE, SC,
Rocky Mts.
- **hyssopifolia** L. · E:Hyssop Loosestrife;
G:Ysopblättriger Weiderich · ☉ VII-IX;
Eur.* exc. Sc; TR, Levant, Cauc., W-Sib.,
C-As., N-Afr, nat. in Sc, S-Afr., C-Am.,
Austr., NZ
- **salicaria** L. · E:Purple Loosestrife, Spiked
Loosestrife; F:Salicaire; G:Blut-Weiderich
· ⚄ Z3 VII-VIII ⚥ ; Eur.*, TR, Syr., Palest.,
Cauc., Iran, W-Sib., E-Sib., Amur,
Sakhal., Mong., Tibet, Him., Korea,
China, Korea, Jap., NW-Afr., Austr.,
Tasman., nat. in N-Am.
- **some cultivars**
- **virgatum** L. · E:Loosestrife; G:Ruten-
Weiderich · ⚄ ⤳ VI-VIII; Eur.: C-Eur.,
EC-Eur., Ba, Ital-P, E-Eur., nat. in Fr

Lytocaryum Toledo -n- *Arecaceae* · 2 spp.
- **weddellianum** (H. Wendl.) Toledo ·
E:Weddel Palm; G:Zimmer-Kokospalme ·
♄ e ⓦ; trop. Braz.

Maackia Rupr. -f- *Fabaceae* · 8 spp. ·

F:Maackia; G:Maackie
- **amurensis** Rupr. & Maxim.
- var. **amurensis** · E:Amur Maackia;
F:Maackia de l'Amour; G:Asiatische
Maackie · ♄ d Z5 VII-VIII; Amur, China,
Manch., Korea, Jap., Taiwan
- var. **buergeri** (Maxim.) C.K. Schneid. · ♄
d Z5 VII-VIII; Jap.
- **chinensis** Takeda · G:Chinesische
Maackie · ♄ d Z5 VII-VIII; C-China:
Hupeh

Macadamia F. Muell. -f- *Proteaceae* · c.
10 spp. · E:Queensland Nut; F:Noyer
du Queensland; G:Macadamianuss,
Queenslandnuss
- **integrifolia** Maiden & Betche ·
E:Macadamia Nut, Queensland Nut;
G:Echte Macadamianuss, Queenslandnuss · ♄ e Z10 ⓚ ⓝ; Austr.: Queensl.
- **ternifolia** F. Muell. · E:Gympie Nut;
G:Dreiblütige Macadamianuss · ♄ e Z10
ⓚ ⓝ; Austr.: Queensl., N.S.Wales
- **tetraphylla** L.A.S. Johnson ·
E:Queensland Nut, Rough Shell Macadamia; G:Rauschalige Macadamianuss · ♄ e
Z10 ⓚ ⓝ; Austr.: Queensl., N.S.Wales

Macfadyena A. DC. -f- *Bignoniaceae* ·
4 spp. · G:Krallentrompete
- **unguis-cati** (L.) A.H. Gentry · E:Cat's
Claw; G:Krallentrompete · ♄ e ⚑ Z8 ⓚ;
Mex.: Yucatan; Guat., Arg.

Machaeranthera Nees -f- *Asteraceae* ·
36 spp. · E:Tansyaster

Machaerocereus Britton & Rose -m-
Cactaceae · 2 spp.
- **eruca** (Brandegee) Britton & Rose · ♄ ⚘
⤳ Z9 ⓚ ▽ ❋; Mex.: Baja Calif.

Machairophyllum Schwantes -n-
Aizoaceae · 6 spp. · G:Säbelblatt
- **acuminatum** L. Bolus · G:Spitzes
Säbelblatt · ⚘ Z9 ⓚ; Cape

Mackaya Harv. -f- *Acanthaceae* · 1 sp.
- **bella** Harv. · ♄ e Z9 ⓦ VI-VIII; S-Afr.

Macleania Hook. -f- *Ericaceae* · c. 40 spp.
- **angulata** Hook. · ♄ e Z10 ⓚ VII-VIII;
Peru
- **cordifolia** Benth. · ♄ e Z10 ⓚ III-IV;
Ecuad., Peru

– **insignis** M. Martens & Galeotti · ♄ e Z10
Ⓚ VII-VIII; Mex., Guat., Hond.
– *longiflora* Lindl. = Macleania insignis
– **ovata** Klotzsch · ♄ e Z10 Ⓚ; Costa Rica,
Panama
– *pulchra* Hook. f. = Macleania insignis
– *punctata* Hook. = Macleania cordifolia

Macleaya R. Br. -f- *Papaveraceae* · 2 spp. ·
E:Plume Poppy; F:Pavot plumeux;
G:Federmohn
– **cordata** (Willd.) R. Br.
– var. **cordata** · E:Plume Poppy; F:Boconie
à feuilles en coeur; G:Weißer Federmohn
· ⚁ Z6 VII-VIII ⚘; Jap., China, Taiwan
– var. **thunbergii** (Miq.) Miq. · ⚁ Z6 ⚘;
China, Jap., Taiwan
– var. *yedoensis* (André) Fedde = Macleaya
cordata var. cordata
– × **kewensis** Turrill (*M. cordata × M.
microcarpa*) · ⚁ Z5; cult.
– **microcarpa** (Maxim.) Fedde · E:Plume
Poppy; F:Boconie à petits fruits; G:Ock-
erfarbiger Federmohn · ⚁ Z5 VII-VIII;
China: Kansu, Schansi

× **Macludrania** André -f- *Moraceae* ·
G:Macludranie (*Cudrania × Maclura*)
– **hybrida** André (*Cudrania tricuspidata ×
Maclura pomifera*) · G:Macludranie · ♄ d
Z7; cult.

Maclura Nutt. -f- *Moraceae* · 12 spp. ·
E:Osage Orange; F:Oranger des Osages;
G:Milchorange, Osagedorn
– **pomifera** (Raf.) C.K. Schneid. · E:Osage
Orange; F:Oranger des Osages; G:Osage-
dorn · ♄ d ⚥ Z7 Ⓝ; USA: Ark., SC, nat. in
e N-Am.
– *tinctoria* (L.) D. Don ex Steud. =
Chlorophora tinctoria

Macodes (Blume) Lindl. -f- *Orchidaceae* ·
11 sp. · F:Macodes; G:Goldblatt
– *marmorata* Blume = Dossinia marmorata
– **petola** (Blume) Lindl. · ⚁ Z10 ⓜ ▽ ❋;
Malay. Arch., Phil.

Macrodiervilla Nakai = Weigela
– *middendorffiana* (Trautv. & C.A. Mey.)
Nakai = Weigela middendorffiana

Macropidia J.L. Drumm. ex Harv. -f-
Haemodoraceae · 1 sp.
– **fumosa** J.L. Drumm. ex Harv. · ⚁ Ⓚ

V-VI; W-Austr.

Macroplectrum Pfitzer = Angraecum
– *sesquipedale* (Thouars) Pfitzer = Angraecum sesquipedale

Macroptilium (Benth.) Urb. -n- *Fabaceae* ·
8 spp.
– **atropurpureum** (DC.) Urb. · E:Purple
Bushbean · ⚁ Ⓝ; USA: Tex., N.Mex.;
Mex., C-Am., Col., Ecuad., Peru, Arg.

Macrotyloma (Wight & Arn.) Verdc.
-f- *Fabaceae* · 24 spp. · G:Erdbohne,
Pferdebohne
– **geocarpum** (Harms) Maréchal &
Baudet · E:Ground Bean; G:Erdbohne,
Kandelbohne · Z10 ⓜ Ⓝ; W-Afr.
– **uniflorum** (Lam.) Verdc. · E:Horse
Gram; G:Pferdebohne, Pferdekorn · ☉
Z10 ⓜ Ⓝ; Him., Ind., Sri Lanka, Burma +

Macrozamia Miq. -f- *Zamiaceae* · 12-15 spp.
– **communis** L.A.S. Johnson ·
E:Burrawang; G:Burrawang · ♄ d Z9 ⓜ
⚘ ▽ ❋; Austr.: N.S.Wales
– *denisonii* C. Moore & F. Muell. =
Lepidozamia peroffskyana
– **miquelii** (F. Muell.) A. DC. · ⚁ ♄ e Z9 ⓜ
⚘ ▽ ❋; Austr.: Queensl., N.S.Wales
– **moorei** F. Muell. · ♄ e Z9 ⓜ ⚘ ▽ ❋;
Austr.: Queensl., N.S.Wales
– **pauli-guilielmi** W. Hill & F. Muell. · ⚁ ♄
e Z9 ⓜ ⚘ ▽ ❋; Austr.: Queensl.
– *peroffskyana* (Regel) Miq. = Lepidozamia
peroffskyana
– **riedlei** (Fisch. ex Gaudich.) Gardner · ♄ e
Z9 ⚘ ▽ ❋; Austr.: W-Austr.
– **spiralis** (Salisb.) Miq. · e Z9 ⓜ ⚘ ▽ ❋;
Austr.: N.S.Wales
– *tridentata* (Willd.) Regel = Macrozamia
spiralis

Maddenia Hook. f. & Thomson -f-
Rosaceae · 4 spp.
– **hypoleuca** Koehne · ♄ ♄ d Z5; C-China,
W-China

Madhuca Buch.-Ham. ex J.F. Gmel.
-f- *Sapotaceae* · 116 spp. · E:Buttertree;
F:Arbre à beurre, Illipe; G:Butterbaum
– *butyracea* (Roxb.) J.F. Macbr. =
Diploknema butyracea
– **longifolia** (J. König) ex L. J.F.
Macbr. · E:Mowra Buttertree;

G:Mowra-Butterbaum · ♄ d ⓦ Ⓝ; Ind.,
Sri Lanka, Burma

Madia Molina -f- *Asteraceae* · 18 spp. ·
E:Tarweed; F:Madi; G:Madie
– *capitata* Nutt. = Madia sativa var.
congesta
– **elegans** D. Don ex Lindl. · E:Common
Tarweed; G:Gewöhnliche Madie · ☉
VII-VIII; USA: NW, Calif.; Baja Calif.
– **sativa** Molina · E:Chilean Oil Plant,
Chilean Tarweed, Tarplant; G:Öl-Madie ·
☉ VII-VIII Ⓝ; USA: NW, Calif.; Chile
– var. **congesta** Torr. & A. Gray · ☉; Can.
(B.C.); USA: NW, Calif.

Magnolia L. -f- *Magnoliaceae* · 130 spp. ·
E:Magnolia; F:Magnolia, Magnolier;
G:Magnolie
– **acuminata** (L.) L. · G:Gurken-Magnolie
– var. **acuminata** · E:Cucumber Tree;
F:Arbre aux concombres, Magnolia à
feuilles acuminées; G:Blaue Gurken-
Magnolie · ♄ d Z5 V-VI Ⓝ; Ont., USA: NE,
NCE, SE, Okla.
– f. *aurea* (Ashe) Hardin = Magnolia
acuminata var. acuminata
– var. *alabamensis* Ashe = Magnolia
acuminata var. subcordata
– var. *cordata* (Michx.) Sarg. = Magnolia
acuminata var. acuminata
– var. *decandollei* (Savi) DC. = Magnolia
acuminata var. acuminata
– var. *ludoviciana* Sarg. = Magnolia
acuminata var. acuminata
– var. **subcordata** (Spach) Dandy ·
E:Yellow Cucumber Tree; G:Gelbe
Gurken-Magnolie · ♄ d Z6 V-VI; USA:
N.C, Ga., Alab. +
– *alexandrina* Steud. = Magnolia denudata
– *andamanica* (King) D.C.S. Raju & M.P.
Nayar = Magnolia liliifera var. liliifera
– *annonifolia* Salisb. = Michelia figo
– *atropurpurea* Steud. = Magnolia liliiflora
– *aulacosperma* Rehder & E.H. Wilson =
Magnolia biondii
– *auriculata* Desr. = Magnolia fraseri
– *australis* (Sarg.) Ashe = Magnolia
virginiana
– *axilliflora* T.B. Chao et al. = Magnolia
biondii
– **biondii** Pamp. · ♄ d Z8 ⚘; C-China
– *borealis* (Sarg.) Kudô = Magnolia kobus
– × **brooklynensis** Kalmb. (*M. acuminata* ×
M. liliiflora) · ♄ d Z5; cult.

– *burchelliana* Steud. = Magnolia virginiana
– **campbellii** Hook f. & Thoms.
– var. **campbellii** · E:Campbell Magnolia,
Pink Tulip Tree; G:Campbells Himalaya-
Magnolie · ♄ d Z9 ⚘; Him.: Nepal;
Burma, SW-China
– *candollei* (Blume) H. Keng = Magnolia
liliifera var. liliifera
– *candollei* Link = Magnolia acuminata var.
acuminata
– *champaca* (L.) Baill. ex Pierre = Michelia
champaca
– *citriodora* Steud. = Magnolia denudata
– *conspicua* Salisb. = Magnolia denudata
– var. *emarginata* Desr. = Magnolia
sargentiana
– var. *fargesii* Finet & Gagnep. = Magnolia
biondii
– var. *purpurascens* Maxim. = Magnolia
sprengeri
– var. *purpurascens* Rehder & E.H. Wilson =
Magnolia denudata
– var. *rosea* Veitch = Magnolia denudata
– var. *soulangeana* (Soul.-Bod.) Loudon =
Magnolia × soulangeana
– *cordata* Michx. = Magnolia acuminata
var. subcordata
– *craibiana* Dandy = Magnolia liliifera
– *cyathiformis* Ruiz ex K. Koch = Magnolia
denudata
– **cylindrica** E.H. Wilson · ♄ d Z6 IV-V;
China: Anhwei
– **dawsoniana** Rehder & E.H. Wilson ·
G:Dawsons Magnolie · ♄ ♄ d Z9 ⚘;
W-China, Sinkiang
– *decandollei* Savi = Magnolia acuminata
var. acuminata
– **denudata** Desr. · E:Lily Tree, Yulan;
F:Magnolia dénudé; G:Lilien-Magnolie,
Yulan-Magnolie · ♄ ♄ d Z6 III-IV; C-China
– var. *emarginata* (Finet & Gagnep.) Pamp.
= Magnolia sargentiana
– var. *fargesii* (Finet & Gagnep.) Pamp. =
Magnolia biondii
– var. *purpurascens* (Maxim.) Rehder &
E.H. Wilson = Magnolia sprengeri
– *discolor* Vent. = Magnolia liliiflora
– *elliptica* Link = Magnolia grandiflora
– **emarginata** Urb. & Ekman
– *exoniensis* Millais = Magnolia grandiflora
– *famasiha* Paul Parm. = Magnolia
salicifolia
– *fargesii* (Finet & Gagnep.) W.C. Cheng =
Magnolia biondii
– *fasciata* Vent. = Michelia figo

– *ferruginea* W. Watson = Magnolia grandiflora
– *figo* (Lour.) DC. = Michelia figo
– *foetida* (L.) Sarg. = Magnolia grandiflora
– *forbesii* King = Magnolia liliifera
– *fragrans* Salisb. = Magnolia virginiana
– **fraseri** Walter · E:Ear Leaved Magnolia; G:Berg-Magnolie · ♄ d Z6 V-VI; USA: Va., Ky., SE
– *frondosa* Salisb. = Magnolia tripetala
– *funiushanensis* T.B. Chao et al. = Magnolia biondii
– *fuscata* Andrews = Michelia figo
– *galissoniensis* Millais = Magnolia grandiflora
– *glauca* (L.) L. = Magnolia virginiana
– *glauca* Thunb. = Magnolia obovata
– **globosa** Hook. f. & Thomson · G:Tsa-rong-Magnolie · ♄ ♄ d Z9 ⚘; E-Him. (E-Nepal, NE-Assam, SE-Tibet), Burma, W-China
– var. *sinensis* Rehder & E.H. Wilson = Magnolia sieboldii subsp. sinensis
– *gloriosa* Millais = Magnolia grandiflora
– *gordoniana* Steud. = Magnolia virginiana
– *gracilis* Salisb. = Magnolia liliiflora
– **grandiflora** L. · E:Bull Bay, Evergreen Magnolia, Southern Magnolia; F:Magnolia à grandes fleurs; G:Immergrüne Magnolie · ♄ d D Z7 VI-VIII Ⓝ; Jap.
– **some cultivars**
– *halleana* auct. = Magnolia stellata
– *hartwegii* G. Nicholson = Magnolia grandiflora
– *hartwicus* G. Nicholson = Magnolia grandiflora
– *heptapeta* (Buc'hoz) Dandy = Magnolia denudata
– f. *purpurascens* (Maxim.) Ohba = Magnolia sprengeri
– *honanensis* B.Y. Ding & T.B. Chao = Magnolia biondii
– *honogi* Paul Parm. = Magnolia obovata
– *hypoleuca* Siebold & Zucc. = Magnolia obovata
– 'Purpurea' = Magnolia liliiflora
– × **kewensis** Pearce (*M. kobus* × *M. salicifolia*) · ♄ d Z6; cult.
– **kobus** DC. · E:Kobus Magnolia; F:Magnolia de Kobé; G:Kobushi-Magnolie · ♄ d Z5 IV-V; Jap.
– var. *borealis* Sarg. = Magnolia kobus
– var. *loebneri* (Kache) Spongberg = Magnolia × loebneri
– var. *stellata* (Siebold & Zucc.) Blackburn

= Magnolia stellata
– *kunstleri* King = Magnolia liliifera
– *lacunosa* Raf. = Magnolia grandiflora
– *latifolia* Aiton ex Dippel = Magnolia virginiana
– **liliifera** (L.) Baill. · Sikkim, Assam, Tahiland, Cambodia, Vietnam, Hainan, Sumatra, New Guinea
– var. *taliensis* (W.W. Sm.) Pamp. = Magnolia wilsonii
– **liliiflora** Desr. · E:Purple Magnolia; F:Magnolia pourpre; G:Purpur-Magnolie · ♄ d Z6 V ⚘; C-China
– **'Gracilis'**
– 'Purpurea' = Magnolia liliiflora
– × **loebneri** Kache (*M. kobus* × *M. stellata*) · ♄ d Z6 IV; cult.
– **some cultivars**
– *longifolia* Sweet = Magnolia grandiflora
– **macrophylla** Michx. · E:Bigleaf Cucumber Tree; G:Großblättrige Magnolie · ♄ d D Z7 ∧ VI-VIII; USA: Ohio, W.Va., Ky., SE, Fla.
– *major* Millais = Magnolia virginiana
– *maxima* Lodd. ex G. Don = Magnolia grandiflora
– *meleagrioides* DC. = Michelia figo
– *membranacea* Paul Parm. = Michelia champaca var. champaca
– *michauxiana* DC. = Magnolia macrophylla
– *microphylla* Ser. = Magnolia grandiflora
– *mutabilis* (Blume) H.J. Chowdhery & P. Daniel = Magnolia liliifera
– *nicholsoniana* Rehder & E.H. Wilson = Magnolia wilsonii
– *obovata* Aiton ex Link = Magnolia grandiflora
– var. *denudata* (Desr.) DC. = Magnolia denudata
– var. *purpurea* (Curtis) Sweet = Magnolia liliiflora
– **obovata** Thunb. · G:Honoki-Magnolie · ♄ d Z6 V-VI; Jap., Kurilen
– *odoratissima* Reinw. ex Blume = Magnolia liliifera
– **officinalis** Rehder & E.H. Wilson
– var. **officinalis** · ♄ d Z8 ⚘ ⚘; W-China, C-China
– var. *pubescens* C.Y. Deng = Magnolia officinalis var. officinalis
– *oyama* Korth. = Magnolia sieboldii subsp. sieboldii
– *pachyphylla* Dandy = Magnolia liliifera
– *parviflora* Blume = Michelia figo

– *parviflora* Siebold & Zucc. = Magnolia
sieboldii subsp. sieboldii
– *parvifolia* DC. = Michelia figo
– *pensylvanica* DC. = Magnolia acuminata
var. acuminata
– *pilosissima* Paul Parm. = Magnolia
macrophylla
– *praecocossima* Koidz. = Magnolia kobus
– *pravertiana* Millais = Magnolia grandiflora
– *precia* Corrêa ex Vent. = Magnolia
denudata
– × **proctoriana** Rehder (*M. salicifolia* × *M.
stellata*) · ℏ d Z5; cult.
– *pseudokobus* S. Abe & Akasawa =
Magnolia kobus
– *pumila* Andrews = Magnolia liliifera
– *purpurascens* (Maxim.) Makino =
Magnolia sprengeri
– *purpurea* Curtis = Magnolia liliiflora
– var. *denudata* (Desr.) Loudon = Magnolia
denudata
– *quinquepeta* (Buc'hoz) Dandy = Magnolia
liliiflora
– *rabaniana* (Hook. f. & Thomson) D.C.S.
Raju & M.P. Nayar = Magnolia liliifera
– *rotundifolia* Millais = Magnolia grandiflora
– *rumphii* (Blume) Spreng. = Magnolia
liliifera
– *rustica* DC. = Magnolia acuminata var.
acuminata
– **salicifolia** (Siebold & Zucc.) Maxim. ·
E:Anise Magnolia, Willow Leaf Magnolia;
F:Magnolia à feuilles de saule; G:Wei-
denblättrige Magnolie · ℏ ℏ d D Z6 IV-V;
Jap.
– **sargentiana** Rehder & E.H. Wilson · ℏ d
Z8 ⌂ IV-V; W-China: Yunnan, Sichuan,
Sikiang
– *siamensis* (Dandy) H. Keng = Magnolia
liliifera
– **sieboldii** K. Koch
– subsp. **sieboldii** · E:Siebold Magnolia;
F:Magnolia de Siebold ; G:Siebolds
Magnolie · ℏ ℏ d D Z6 VI-VII; Jap., Korea
– subsp. **sinensis** (Rehder & E.H. Wilson)
Spongberg · ℏ d D Z7 ⋀ VI; Sichuan
– *simii* Siebold ex Miq. = Magnolia stellata
– *sinensis* (Rehder & E.H. Wilson)
Stapf = Magnolia sieboldii subsp. sinensis
– *sinostellata* P.L. Chiu & Z.H. Chen =
Magnolia stellata
– *slavinii* B.E. Harkn. = Magnolia salicifolia
– × **soulangeana** Soul.-Bod. (*M. denudata*

× *M. liliiflora*) · E:Lenne's Magnolia, Saucer Magnolia; F:Magnolia de Soulange;
G:Tulpen-Magnolie · ℏ d Z6 IV-V; cult.
– **some cultivars**
– *spectabilis* G. Nicholson = Magnolia
denudata
– *splendens* Reinw. ex Blume = Magnolia
liliifera
– **sprengeri** Pamp. · ℏ d Z9 ⌂; C-China
– **stellata** (Siebold & Zucc.) Maxim. ·
E:Star Magnolia; F:Magnolia étoilé;
G:Stern-Magnolie · ℏ ℏ d D Z6 III-IV; Jap.
– *stricta* G. Nicholson = Magnolia grandiflora
– *superba* G. Nicholson = Magnolia
denudata
– *taliensis* W.W. Sm. = Magnolia wilsonii
– *tardiflora* Ser. = Magnolia grandiflora
– *thamnodes* Dandy = Magnolia liliifera
– × **thompsoniana** (Loudon) de Vos (*M.
tripetala* × *M. virginiana*) · ℏ Z5 VI-VII;
cult.
– *thurberi* G. Nicholson = Magnolia kobus
– *tomentosa* Ser. = Magnolia grandiflora
– *tomentosa* Thunb. = Edgeworthia
chrysantha
– **tripetala** (L.) L. · E:Elkwood, Umbrella
Magnolia; F:Magnolia parasol; G:Schirm-
Magnolie · ℏ d Z6 VI-VII; USA: NE,
NCE, SE, Okla.
– *triumphans* G. Nicholson = Magnolia
denudata
– *tsarongensis* W.W. Sm. & Forrest =
Magnolia globosa
– *umbellata* Steud. = Magnolia tripetala
– *umbrella* Desr. = Magnolia tripetala
– × **veitchii** Bean (*M. campbellii* var.
campbellii × *M. denudata*) · E:Veitch
Magnolia; G:Veitchs Magnolie · ℏ d Z7;
cult.
– **'Peter Veitch'**
– *verecunda* Koidz. = Magnolia sieboldii
subsp. sieboldii
– *versicolor* Salisb. = Michelia figo
– **virginiana** L. · E:Laurel Magnolia, Sweet
Bay; G:Sumpf-Magnolie · ℏ ℏ d D Z6 VI
⚥ Ⓝ; USA: NE, SE, Fla., SC
– var. *acuminata* L. = Magnolia acuminata
– var. *australis* Sarg. = Magnolia virginiana
– var. *foetida* L. = Magnolia grandiflora
– var. *tripetala* L. = Magnolia tripetala
– × *watsonii* Hook. f. = Magnolia × wiesneri
– × **wiesneri** Carrière (*M. hypoleuca* × *M.
sieboldii* subsp. *sieboldii*) · E:Wiesner's
Magnolia; G:Wiesners Magnolie · ℏ d D

Z7 VI-VIII; cult.
- **wilsonii** (Finet & Gagnep.) Rehder ·
  E:Wilson Magnolia; F:Magnolia de
  Wilson; G:Wilsons Magnolie · ♄ ♄ d Z7
  VI; China: Sichuan, Yunnan, Kansu
- *xerophila* Paul Parm. = Mimusops elengi
- *yulan* Desf. = Magnolia denudata
- **Cultivars:**
- **many cultivars**

Magydaris W.D.J. Koch ex DC. -f-
Apiaceae · 2 spp.
- **pastinacea** (Lam.) Paol. · ⚁ ✂ ⌂; Eur.:
  S-I, Sard., Sic.

Mahernia L. = Hermannia
- *verticillata* L. = Hermannia verticillata

× **Mahoberberis** C.K. Schneid. -f-
Berberidaceae · G:Berberitzenmahonie,
Hybridmahonie (*Berberis* × *Mahonia*)
- **aquicandidula** Jensen (*Berberis
  candidula* × *Mahonia aquifolium*) · ♄ e;
  cult.
- **aquisargentii** Jensen (*Berberis
  sargentiana* × *Mahonia aquifolium*) · ♄ d;
  cult.
- **neubertii** (Baumann ex Lem.) C.K.
  Schneid. (*Berberis vulgaris* × *Mahonia
  aquifolium*) · ♄ s Z6; cult.

Mahonia Nutt. -f- *Berberidaceae* · c.
100 spp. · E:Holly Grape, Oregon Grape;
F:Mahonia; G:Mahonie
- **acanthifolia** Wall. ex G. Don · ♄ e Z8 ⌂
  IX-II; Him., SW-China
- **aquifolium** (Pursh) Nutt. · E:Oregon
  Grape; F:Mahonia faux-houx;
  G:Gewöhnliche Mahonie · ♄ e Z5 IV-V ⚘
  ⚘; B.C., USA: NW, nat. in F
- **some cultivars**
- **bealei** (Fortune) Carrière · E:Leatherleaf
  Mahonia; F:Mahonia de Beal; G:Beales
  Mahonie · ♄ e D Z7 ⋀ II-V; China: Hupeh
- **eutriphylla** Fedde · ♄ e Z9 ⌂; Mex.
- *fascicularis* DC. = Mahonia pinnata
- **fortunei** (Lindl.) Fedde · E:Fortune
  Mahonia; G:Kleine Mahonie · ♄ e Z7 V;
  China: Hupeh, Sichuan
- **fremontii** (Torr.) Fedde · E:Holly Grape,
  Oregon Grape; G:Fremonts Mahonie ·
  ♄ e D Z8 ⌂ VI; USA: Calif., Nev., Utah,
  Colo., SW
- × **heterophylla** (Zabel) C.K. Schneid.
  (*M. aquifolium* × *M. fortunei*) ·

G:Verschiedenblättrige Mahonie · ♄ e Z7;
orig. ?
- **japonica** (Thunb. ex Murray) DC. ·
  E:Japanese Mahonia; F:Mahonia du
  Japon; G:Japanische Mahonie · ♄ e D Z7
  ⋀ II-V; cult.
- **lomariifolia** Takeda · G:Lomariablät-
  trige Mahonie · ♄ e D Z7 XI-III; Burma,
  W-China
- × **media** C.D. Brickell (*M. japonica* × *M.
  lomariifolia*) · ♄ e Z7 IX-III; cult.
- **some cultivars**
- **napaulensis** DC. · G:Nepal-Mahonie · ♄ e
  Z8 ⌂ III-IV; Nepal
- **nervosa** (Pursh) Nutt. · E:Longleaf Hol-
  lygrape; F:Mahonia; G:Nervige Mahonie
  · ♄ e Z7 ⋀ IV-V; Can.: B.C.; USA: NW,
  Calif.
- **pinnata** (Lag.) Fedde · E:Cluster Holly-
  grape; G:Fiederblättrige Mahonie · ♄ e
  Z8 ⌂ ⋀ V; USA: Oreg., Calif.; Mex.: Baja
  Calif.
- **piperiana** Abrams · G:Kalifornische
  Mahonie · ♄ e ⌂ III-IV; N-Calif., Oreg.
- **pumila** (Greene) Fedde · G:Zwerg-
  Mahonie · ♄ e Z7; USA: Oreg., Calif.
- **repens** (Lindl.) G. Don · E:Creeping
  Mahonia; F:Mahonia rampant;
  G:Kriechende Mahonie · ♄ e Z6 V; Can.:
  W; USA: NW, Calif., Rocky Mts., SW, NC
- × **wagneri** (Jouin) Rehder (*M. aquifolium*
  × *M. pinnata*) · G:Wagners Mahonie · ♄ e
  Z7; cult.

Maianthemum Weber -n- *Convallariaceae* ·
3 spp. · E:May Lily; F:Maïanthème;
G:Schattenblümchen
- **bifolium** (L.) F.W. Schmidt · E:May Lily;
  F:Maîanthème à deux feuilles; G:Zwei-
  blättriges Schattenblümchen · ⚁ Z3 V
  ⚘; Eur.*, W-Sib., E-Sib., Amur, Sakhal.,
  Kamchat., Mong., N-Jap.
- *racemosum* (L.) Link = Smilacina
  racemosa
- *stellatum* (L.) Link = Smilacina stellata

Maihuenia (Phil. ex F.A.C. Weber) K.
Schum. -f- *Cactaceae* · 2 spp.
- **patagonica** (Phil.) Britton & Rose · ♄ ⚇
  Z5 ▽ ✳; Arg.: Patag.
- **poeppigii** (Otto ex Pfeiff.) Phil. ex K.
  Schum. · ♄ ⚇ Z5 ▽ ✳; S-Chile

Majorana Mill. = Origanum
- *hortensis* Moench = Origanum majorana

– onites (L.) Benth. = Origanum onites

Malachium Fr. ex Rchb. = Stellaria
– aquaticum (L.) Fr. = Stellaria aquatica

Malachra L. -f- *Malvaceae* · 6-8 spp.
– **capitata** L. · 4 Z10 ⓜ Ⓝ; C-Am., S-Am.,
 W-Afr., nat. in Trop.

Malacocarpus Salm-Dyck = Parodia
– erinaceus (Haw.) Lem. ex C.F. Först. =
 Notocactus erinaceus
– maassii (Heese) Britton & Rose = Parodia
 maassii
– vorwerkianus (Werderm.) Backeb. =
 Notocactus erinaceus

Malaxis Sol. ex Sw. -f- *Orchidaceae* ·
 415 spp. · F:Malaxis; G:Einblatt,
 Weichorchis
– **discolor** (Lindl.) Kuntze · 4 Z10 ⓜ VII
 ▽ ✳; Sri Lanka
– **metallica** (Rchb. f.) Kuntze · 4 Z10 ⓜ V
 ▽ ✳; Kalimantan
– **monophyllos** (L.) Sw. · G:Einblättrige
 Weichorchis, Kleinblütiges Einblatt · 4
 VI-VII ▽ ✳; Eur.: Ital-P, C-Eur., EC-Eur.,
 Ba, E-Eur., Sc; W-Sib., E-Sib., Amur,
 Sakhal., Kamchat., Mong., China, Jap.,
 N-Am.

Malcolmia R. Br. -f- *Brassicaceae* · c.
 30 spp. · E:Virgina Stock; F:Julienne de
 Mahon; G:Meerviole
– **africana** (L.) R. Br. · G:Afrikanische
 Meerviole · ☉ VI-VII; Eur.: sp., Sic., GR,
 Crete, Crim, W-Russ; TR, Levant, Cauc.,
 Iran, W-Sib., C-As., China: Sinkiang,
 NW-Afr., Libya, nat. in F, EC-Eur.
– **graeca** Boiss. & Spruner · G:Griechische
 Meerviole
– subsp. **bicolor** (Boiss. & Heldr.) Stork · ☉
 Z9 VI-IX; GR, S-AL
– subsp. **graeca** · ☉ Z9; Eur.: GR
– **maritima** (L.) R. Br. · E:Virginia Stock;
 G:Graue Meerviole · ☉ Z8 VI-IX; Eur.:
 S-AL, GR, nat. in Ib, Fr, Ital-P, Ba

Malephora N.E. Br. -f- *Aizoaceae* · 16 spp.
– **engleriana** (Dinter & A. Berger) Dinter &
 Schwantes · ♄ ⫿ Z9 ⓚ; Namibia

Mallotus Lour. -m- *Euphorbiaceae* · 141 sp.
– **philippensis** (Lam.) Müll. Arg. · ♄ ♄ e
 ⓚ ⚶ Ⓝ; Ind., Sri Lanka, Burma, China,

Malay. Arch., Austr.

Malope L. -f- *Malvaceae* · 4 spp. · E:Annual
 Mallow; F:Malope; G:Trichtermalve
– **trifida** Cav. · ☉ VII-X; S-P, SW-Sp.,
 Moroc.

Malpighia L. -f- *Malpighiaceae* · c. 40 spp. ·
 E:Barbados Cherry; F:Cerisier des
 Antilles; G:Barbadoskirsche
– **coccigera** L. · E:Singapore Holly · ♄ e
 Z10 ⓜ VI-VIII; W.Ind.
– **glabra** L. · E:Barbados Cherry; G:Bar-
 badoskirsche · ♄ e Z10 ⓜ III-IX Ⓝ; USA:
 Tex.; W-Ind., n S-Am.
– **mexicana** Juss. · ♄ e Z10 ⓜ Ⓝ; Mex.
– punicifolia L. = Malpighia glabra
– **urens** L. · E:Cow Itch Cherry; G:Bren-
 nende Barbadoskirsche · ♄ e Z10 ⓜ Ⓝ;
 W.Ind.

Malus Mill. -f- *Rosaceae* · 55 spp. · E:Apple;
 F:Pommier; G:Apfel
– × **adstringens** Zabel (*M. baccata* × *M.
 pumila*) · ♄ d Z6; cult.
– **angustifolia** (Aiton) Michx. · E:Southern
 Crabapple, Southern Crab; G:Schmal-
 blättriger Apfel · ♄ ♄ d D Z6 IV-V; USA:
 NE, NCE, SE, Fla.
– × **arnoldiana** (Rehder) Sarg. (*M. baccata*
 × *M. floribunda*) · ♄ d Z6 V; cult.
– × **atrosanguinea** (Späth) C.K. Schneid.
 (*M. halliana* × *M. sieboldii*) · G:Kar-
 mensinroter Holz-Apfel · ♄ ♄ d Z6 V; cult.
– **baccata** (L.) Borkh. · E:Siberian Crab,
 Siberian Crabapple; F:Pommier à petits
 fruits; G:Beeren-Apfel
– var. **baccata** · ♄ d ⊗ Z3 IV-V; N-China,
 Manch., Korea, Sakhal.
– var. **mandshurica** (Maxim.) C.K.
 Schneid. · ♄ ♄ d ⊗ D Z3 IV-V; Amur,
 China, Korea, Jap., Sakhal.
– communis Poir. = Malus sylvestris
– **coronaria** (L.) Mill. · E:Crabapple, Sweet
 Crab Apple; G:Kronen-Apfel · ♄ d D Z5 V;
 Can.: Ont.; USA: NE, NCE, NC, SE
– dasyphylla Borkh. = Malus pumila var.
 pumila
– **domestica** Borkh. · E:Apple; F:Pommier
 commun; G:Kultur-Apfel · ♄ ♄ d Z5 IV-V
 ⚶ Ⓝ; cult.
– **many cultivars**
– **florentina** (Zuccagni) C.K. Schneid. ·
 E:Hawthorn Leaved Crab Apple;
 G:Italienischer Apfel · ♄ d Z6 V-VI; Eur.:

I, Ba
- **floribunda** Siebold ex Van Houtte ·
  E:Japanese Crab; G:Vielblütiger Apfcl · ħ
  ħ d ⊛ Z5 V; cult. Jap.
- **fusca** (Raf.) C.K. Schneid. · G:Alaska-
  Apfel · ħ ħ d Z6 V; Alaska, Can.: W; USA:
  NW, Calif.
- **halliana** Koehne · E:Hall's Crabapple ;
  G:Halls Apfel · ħ d Z6 V-VI; cult. China,
  Jap.
- × **hartwigii** Koehne (*M. baccata* × *M.
  halliana*) · ħ ħ d Z4; cult.
- **hupehensis** (Pamp.) Rehder · E:Tea
  Crabapple; F:Pommier du Hou-Pei;
  G:Tee-Apfel · ħ ħ d D Z6 IV-V; China,
  N-Ind.
- **ioensis** (A.W. Wood) Britton · E:Prairie
  Crab, Wild Crabapple; G:Prärie-Apfel · ħ
  d D Z3 V-VI; USA: NCE, NC, SC, Ark.
- **kansuensis** (Batalin) C.K. Schneid. ·
  G:Kansu-Apfel · ħ ħ d Z6 V; NW-China
- f. **calva** Rehder · ħ ħ d; NW-China
- × **magdeburgensis** Hartwig (*M. pumila* ×
  M. spectabilis) · G:Magdeburger Apfel · ħ
  ħ d Z6 V; cult.
- × **micromalus** Makino (*M. baccata* ×
  M. spectabilis) · E:Kaido Crab Apple;
  G:Kleiner Apfel · d Z6 V
- × **moerlandsii** Door. (*M. sieboldii* × *M.* ×
  zumi) · ħ ħ d Z6 V; cult.
- **some cultivars**
- **prattii** (Hemsl.) C.K. Schneid. ·
  F:Pommier de Pratt · ħ ħ d Z6 V;
  W-China, C-China
- **prunifolia** (Willd.) Borkh.
- var. **prunifolia** · E:Chinese Apple;
  F:Pommier à feuilles de prunus;
  G:Kirsch-Apfel · ħ d Z4 IV ⓝ; cult. ?
  NE-As.
- var. **rinkii** (Koidz.) Rehder · ħ d Z4 IV ⓝ;
  cult. E-As.
- **pumila** (L.) Mill. · G:Filz-Apfel, Johannis-
  Apfel
- var. **paradisiaca** (L.) C.K. Schneid. ·
  E:Paradise Apple; G:Paradies-Apfel · ħ ħ
  d Z3 V ⓝ; Eur.: Ba; W-As.
- var. **pumila** · ħ d Z3; cult.
- × **purpurea** (Barbier) Rehder (*M.
  pumila* 'Niedzwetzkyana' × *M.* × *zumi*) ·
  G:Purpur-Apfel · ħ ħ d Z6 IV-V; cult.
- *ringo* Siebold ex Carrière = Malus
  prunifolia var. rinkii
- × **robusta** (Carrière) Rehder (*M. baccata*
  × *M. prunifolia*) · E:Crabapples, Siberian
  Crab; G:Sibirischer Holz-Apfel · ħ ħ d Z6

IV-V; cult.
- **sargentii** Rehder · E:Sargent Crabapple;
  G:Strauch-Apfel · ħ ⊛ Z5 V; N-Jap.
- × **scheideckeri** Späth ex Zabel (*M.
  floribunda* × *M. prunifolia*) · ħ d Z6 V;
  cult.
- *sempervirens* Desf. = Malus angustifolia
- *sieboldii* (Regel) Rehder = Malus toringo
- **sieboldii** (Rehder) Fiala · ħ ħ d Z5 V; Jap.
- **sieversii** (Ledeb.) M. Roem. · ħ ħ d V ⓝ;
  C-As.
- **spectabilis** (Aiton) Borkh. · E:Asiatic
  Apple, Chinese Crab; G:Pracht-Apfel · ħ
  ħ d Z5 IV-V; cult. China
- **sylvestris** (L.) Mill. · E:Apple, Wild Crab;
  F:Pommier sauvage; G:Holz-Apfel, Wild-
  Apfel · ħ ħ d Z5 V ⓝ; Eur.*, TR, Cauc.,
  N-Iran
- subsp. *mitis* (Wallr.) Mansf. = Malus
  pumila var. pumila
- var. *domestica* (Borkh.) Mansf. = Malus
  domestica
- var. *paradisiaca* (L.) L.H. Bailey = Malus
  pumila var. paradisiaca
- *theifera* Rehder = Malus hupehensis
- **toringo** (Siebold) K. Koch · E:Toringo
  Crab; G:Toringo-Apfel · ħ ħ d Z5; Korea,
  Jap.
- var. *sargentii* (Rehder) Ponomar. = Malus
  sargentii
- **toringoides** (Rehder) Hughes · E:Cutleaf
  Crabapple; G:Chinesischer Apfel · ħ ħ d
  ⊛ Z6 V; NW-China
- **transitoria** (Batalin) C.K. Schneid. · ħ ħ
  d ⊛ Z5 V; NW-China
- var. *toringoides* Rehder = Malus
  toringoides
- **trilobata** (Labill. ex Poir.) C.K. Schneid. ·
  G:Dreilappiger Apfel · ħ ħ d Z5; Eur.:
  N-GR; Lebanon, Syr., Israel, nat. in BG
- **tschonoskii** (Rehder) C.K. Schneid. ·
  E:Pillar Apple; F:Pommier de Sukawa,
  Pommier-colonne; G:Wolliger Apfel · ħ d
  Z6 V; Jap.
- **yunnanensis** (Franch.) C.K. Schneid.
- var. *veitchii* Rehder · ħ d Z6 V; C-China
- var. **yunnanensis** · E:Yunnan Crabapple;
  G:Yunnan-Apfel · ħ d Z5 V; W-China
- × **zumi** (Matsum.) Rehder (*M. baccata*
  var. *mandshurica* × *M. sieboldii*) · ħ d Z5;
  Jap.

Malva L. -f- *Malvaceae* · 30-40 spp. ·
  E:Mallow; F:Mauve; G:Malve
- **alcea** L. · E:Cut Leaved Mallow; F:Mauve

alcée; G:Rosen-Malve, Sigmarskraut · 4
Z4 VI-X ⚥ ; Eur.*
– *capensis* L. = Anisodontea capensis
– *involucrata* Torr. & A. Gray = Callirhoe
involucrata
– *mauritiana* L. = Malva sylvestris subsp.
mauritiana
– *meluca* Graebn. ex Medw. = Malva
verticillata
– **moschata** L. · E:Musk Mallow; F:Mauve
musquée; G:Moschus-Malve · 4 Z3
VII-IX; Eur.* exc. Sc; W-TR, nat. in Sc, ne
N-Am.
– *munroana* Douglas ex Lindl. = Sphaeralcea munroana
– **neglecta** Wallr. · E:Dwarf Mallow;
G:Käsepappel, Weg-Malve · ⊙ ⊙ VI-IX
⚥ ; Eur.*, TR, Levant, Cauc., Iran, C-As.,
Mong., Tibet, Him., W-China, N-China,
Moroc., Alger., nat. in N-Am., Chile,
Austr.
– **nicaeensis** All. · G:Nizzäische Käsepap-
pel · ⊙ ⊙ Z7; Eur.: Ib, Fr, Ital-P, Ba, Crim;
TR, Levant, Iran, N-Afr.
– *papaver* Cav. = Callirhoe papaver
– *pedata* Torr. & A. Gray = Callirhoe
leiocarpa
– **pusilla** Sm. · G:Kleinblütige Malve · ⊙
VI-IX; Eur.* exc. BrI, Ib; Cauc., NW-Iran,
nat. in BrI
– **sylvestris** L. · G:Wilde Malve
– **some cultivars**
– subsp. **mauritiana** (L.) Boiss. ex Cout. ·
G:Mauretanische Malve · Z5
– subsp. **sylvestris** · E:Blue Mallow, High
Mallow; G:Gewöhnliche Wilde Malve ·
⊙ ⊙ 4 Z5 VII-X ⚥ Ⓝ; Eur.*, TR, Levant,
Cauc., C-As, Him., N-Afr., nat. in N-Am.,
Austr., NZ, S-Am.
– **verticillata** L. · E:Curled Mallow;
G:Quirl-Malve · ⊙ Z6 VII-IX Ⓝ; Pakist.,
Him., Ind , China, nat. in Eur.* exc. Sc, Ib

Malvastrum A. Gray -n- *Malvaceae* ·
14 spp. · E:False Mallow, Malvastrum;
F:Fausse-mauve; G:Scheinmalve
– **americanum** (L.) Torr. · E:Spiked
Malvastrum; G:Dornige Schein-Malve
· ♄; USA: SC, SE; Mex., C-Am., Indian
Sub-C., Malay. Arch., Austr.
– *capense* (L.) Garcke = Anisodontea
capensis
– *munroanum* (Douglas ex Lindl.) A. Gray
= Sphaeralcea munroana

Malvaviscus Fabr. -m- *Malvaceae* · 3 spp. ·
E:Sleepy Mallow; F:Malvaviscus;
G:Beerenmalve
– **arboreus** Cav. · E:Wax Mallow;
G:Gewöhnliche Beerenmalve · ♄ e Z9 Ⓦ
XII-II; Mex., C-Am., trop. S-Am.
– *mollis* (Aiton) DC. = Malvaviscus
arboreus

Mamillopsis E. Morren ex Britton & Rose =
Mammillaria
– *senilis* (Salm-Dyck) Britton & Rose =
Mammillaria senilis

Mammea L. -f- *Clusiaceae* · c. 50 spp. ·
E:Mammee Apple; F:Abricot pays;
G:Mammiapfel
– **americana** L. · E:Mammee Apple;
G:Echter Mammiapfel · ♄ e Z10 Ⓦ Ⓝ;
C-Am., W.Ind., trop. S-Am.

Mammillaria Haw. -f- *Cactaceae* · c.
150 spp. · F:Mammillaire; G:Warzenkaktus
– *alamensis* R.T. Craig = Mammillaria
sheldonii
– **albicans** (Britton & Rose) A. Berger · Ѱ
Z10 ⌂ ▽ ✳; Mex.: Baja Calif.
– **albicoma** Boed. · Ѱ Z10 ⌂ ▽ ✳; C-Mex.
– **albilanata** Backeb. · Ѱ Z10 ⌂ ▽ ✳; Mex.:
Guerrero
– *applanata* Engelm. = Mammillaria
heyderi var. heyderi
– *atroflorens* Backeb. = Mammillaria
mystax
– *aureiceps* Lem. = Mammillaria rhodantha
subsp. aureiceps
– **aureilanata** Backeb. · Ѱ Z9 ⌂ ▽ ✳; Mex.
(San Luis Potosí)
– *aureoviridis* Heinrich = Mammillaria
aurihamata
– **aurihamata** Boed. · Ѱ Z10 ⌂ ▽ ✳;
C-Mex.
– **bachmannii** Boed. ex A. Berger · Ѱ Z10
⌂ ▽ ✳; Mex.
– *balsasoides* R.T. Craig = Mammillaria
beneckei
– **baumii** Boed. · Ѱ Z10 ⌂ ▽ ✳; NE-Mex.
– **beneckei** C. Ehrenb. · Ѱ Z10 ⌂ ▽ ✳;
W-Mex.
– **blossfeldiana** Boed. · Ѱ Z10 ⌂ ▽ ✳;
Mex.: Baja Calif.
– **bocasana** Poselg. · E:Powder Puff
Cactus · Ѱ Z9 ⌂ ▽ ✳; C-Mex.
– **bocensis** R.T. Craig · Ѱ Z10 ⌂ ▽ ✳; Mex.
– **bombycina** Quehl · G:Seidiger

Warzenkaktus · ψ Z10 ⌂K ▽ ✻; C-Mex.
- **brandegeei** (J.M. Coult.) K. Brandegee · ψ Z10 ⌂K ▽ ✻; Mex.: Baja Calif.
- **brauneana** Boed. · ψ Z10 ⌂K ▽ ✻; Mex.: Tamaulipas
- **bravoae** R.T. Craig · ψ Z10 ⌂K ▽ ✻; Mex.
- *bucareliensis* R.T. Craig = Mammillaria magnimamma
- *caerulea* R.T. Craig = Mammillaria chionocephala
- **calacantha** Tiegel · ψ Z10 ⌂K ▽ ✻; Mex.: Guanajuato, Queretaro
- **camptotricha** Dams · E:Bird's Nest Cactus · ψ Z10 ⌂K ▽ ✻; C-Mex.
- **candida** Scheidw. · E:Snowball Cactus · ψ Z10 ⌂K ▽ ✻; Mex.
- *caput-medusae* Otto = Mammillaria sempervivi
- **carnea** Zucc. ex Pfeiff. · ψ Z10 ⌂K ▽ ✻; S-Mex.
- **carretii** Rebut ex K. Schum. · ψ Z10 ⌂K ▽ ✻; Mex.: Coahuila
- *celsiana* auct. non Lem. = Mammillaria muehlenpfordtii
- *centricirrha* Lem. = Mammillaria magnimamma
- *cephalophora* Quehl = Mammillaria aureilanata
- **chionocephala** J.A. Purpus · ψ Z10 ⌂K ▽ ✻; NE-Mex.
- *collina* J.A. Purpus = Mammillaria haageana var. haageana
- **columbiana** Salm-Dyck · ψ Z10 ⌂K ▽ ✻; Mex.
- **compressa** DC. · ψ Z10 ⌂K ▽ ✻; Mex.
- *confusa* (Britton & Rose) Orcutt = Mammillaria karwinskiana
- *conoidea* DC. = Neolloydia conoidea
- *conzattii* (Britton & Rose) Orcutt = Mammillaria karwinskiana
- *crinita* DC. = Mammillaria wildii
- subsp. *wildii* = Mammillaria wildii
- *crispiseta* R.T. Craig = Mammillaria mystax
- *dasyacantha* Engelm. = Escobaria dasyacantha
- *dealbata* A. Dietr. = Mammillaria haageana var. haageana
- **densispina** (J.M. Coult.) K. Brandegee · ψ Z10 ⌂K ▽ ✻; C-Mex.
- **dioica** K. Brandegee · E:Strawberry Cactus · ψ Z10 ⌂K ▽ ✻; S-Calif., Baja Calif.
- *disciformis* DC. = Strombocactus disciformis
- **discolor** Haw. · ψ Z10 ⌂K ▽ ✻; Mex.: Puebla
- *dumetorum* J.A. Purpus = Mammillaria schiedeana
- *durispina* Boed. = Mammillaria kewensis
- **eichlamii** Quehl · ψ Z10 ⌂K ▽ ✻; Guat., Hond.
- *elegans* hort. = Mammillaria haageana var. haageana
- **elongata** DC. · E:Lace Cactus · ψ Z10 ⌂K ▽ ✻; C-Mex.
- *emskoetteriana* Quehl = Escobaria emskoetteriana
- *erectohamata* Boed. = Mammillaria aurihamata
- **eriacantha** (Link & Otto)Pfeiff. · ψ Z10 ⌂K ▽ ✻; Mex.: Veracruz
- **erythrosperma** Boed. · ψ Z10 ⌂K ▽ ✻; Mex.: San Luis Potosí
- *esperanzaensis* Boed. = Mammillaria discolor
- *essausieri* hort. = Mammillaria densispina
- *estanzuelensis* H. Möller ex A. Berger = Mammillaria candida
- *euthele* Backeb. = Mammillaria melanocentra
- *felicis* Schreier ex W. Haage = Mammillaria voburnensis
- *fischeri* Pfeiff. = Mammillaria karwinskiana
- *fissurata* Engelm. = Ariocarpus fissuratus var. fissuratus
- *flavescens* (DC.) Haw. = Mammillaria nivosa
- *flavovirens* Salm-Dyck = Mammillaria magnimamma
- **formosa** Galeotti ex Scheidw. · ψ Z9 ⌂K ▽ ✻; Mex. (San Luis Potosí, Tamaulipas)
- **fraileana** (Britton & Rose) Boed. · ψ Z10 ⌂K ▽ ✻; Mex.: Baja Calif.
- *fuauxiana* Backeb. = Mammillaria albilanata
- *fuscata* Link & Otto = Mammillaria rhodantha subsp. rhodantha
- **geminispina** Haw. · ψ Z10 ⌂K ▽ ✻; C-Mex.
- *gladiata* Mart. = Mammillaria magnimamma
- *glauca* A. Dietr. ex Linke = Mammillaria magnimamma
- *glochidiata* Mart. = Mammillaria wildii
- **gracilis** Pfeiff. · ψ Z10 ⌂K ▽ ✻; C-Mex.
- *graessneriana* Boed. = Mammillaria columbiana
- **guelzowiana** Werderm. · ψ Z10 ⌂K ▽ ✻;

N-Mex.: Durango
- *gummifera* Engelm. = Mammillaria heyderi var. heyderi
- **haageana** Pfeiff.
- var. **haageana** · ⚕ Z9 ⓚ ▽ ✳; S-Mex.
- var. **schmollii** (R.T. Craig) D.R. Hunt · ⚕ Z10 ⓚ ▽ ✳; C-Mex.
- **hahniana** Werderm. · E:Old Woman Cactus · ⚕ Z10 ⓚ ▽ ✳; Mex.: Guanajuato
- **halei** K. Brandegee · ⚕ Z10 ⓚ ▽ ✳; Mex.: Baja Calif.
- *hemisphaerica* Engelm. = Mammillaria heyderi var. heyderi
- **herrerae** Werderm. · ⚕ Z10 ⓚ ▽ ✳; Mex.: Queretaro, San Luis Potosí
- **heyderi** Muehlenpf.
- var. *applanata* hort. = Mammillaria heyderi var. heyderi
- var. *bullingtonia* Castetter = Mammillaria heyderi var. heyderi
- var. **heyderi** · E:Little Nipple Cactus · ⚕ Z10 ⓚ ▽ ✳; USA: SW, SC; N-Mex.
- *hidalgensis* J.A. Purpus = Mammillaria polythele
- *hoffmanniana* (Tiegel) Bravo = Mammillaria polythele
- *horripila* Lem. = Turbinicarpus horripilus
- *infernillensis* R.T. Craig = Mammillaria parkinsonii
- *ingens* Backeb. = Mammillaria polythele
- **karwinskiana** Mart. · E:Royal Cross · ⚕ Z10 ⓚ ▽ ✳; S-Mex: Puebla, Oaxaca
- **kewensis** Salm-Dyck · ⚕ Z10 ⓚ ▽ ✳; Mex.: Guanajuato, Hidalgo, Queretaro
- **klissingiana** Boed. · ⚕ Z10 ⓚ ▽ ✳; Mex.
- *kunthii* C. Ehrenb. = Mammillaria haageana var. haageana
- *lanata* (Britton & Rose) Orcutt = Mammillaria supertexta
- **lasiacantha** Engelm. · E:Lacepine Nipple Cactus · ⚕ Z10 ⓚ ▽ ✳; USA: Tex., N.Mex.; Mex.
- **lenta** K. Brandegee · ⚕ Z10 ⓚ ▽ ✳; Mex.: Coahuila
- *leona* Poselg. = Mammillaria pottsii
- **leucantha** Boed. · ⚕ Z10 ⓚ ▽ ✳; C-Mex.
- *leucotricha* Scheidw. = Mammillaria mystax
- **lloydii** (Britton & Rose) Orcutt · ⚕ Z10 ⓚ ▽ ✳; Mex.: Zacatecas
- **longiflora** (Britton & Rose) A. Berger · ⚕ Z10 ⓚ ▽ ✳; Mex.: Durango
- **longimamma** DC. · ⚕ Z10 ⓚ ▽ ✳; C-Mex.
- *macracantha* DC. = Mammillaria

magnimamma
- **magnimamma** Haw. · ⚕ Z10 ⓚ ▽ ✳; Mex.: Hidalgo, San Luis Potosí
- **mammillaris** (L.) H. Karst. · ⚕ ⚞ Z10 ⓚ ▽ ✳; N-Venez., Curaçao
- **marksiana** Krainz · ⚕ Z10 ⓚ ▽ ✳; Mex.: Sinaloa
- **mazatlanensis** K. Schum. ex Gürke
- var. **mazatlanensis** · ⚕ Z10 ⓚ ▽ ✳; Mex.: Sonora, Sinaloa, Nayarit
- var. **occidentalis** (Britton & Rose) Neutel. · ⚕ Z10 ⓚ ▽ ✳; Mex.: Colima
- *meissneri* C. Ehrenb. = Mammillaria haageana var. haageana
- **melaleuca** Karw. ex Salm-Dyck · ⚕ Z10 ⓚ ▽ ✳; Mex.
- **melanocentra** Poselg. · ⚕ Z10 ⓚ ▽ ✳; Mex.: Nuevo León
- *melispina* Werderm. = Mammillaria roseoalba
- **mendeliana** (Bravo) Werderm. · ⚕ Z10 ⓚ ▽ ✳; Mex.: Guanajuato
- **microhelia** Werderm.
- var. **microhelia** · ⚕ Z10 ⓚ ▽ ✳; Mex.: Queretaro
- var. **microheliopsis** (Werderm.) Backeb. · ⚕ △ Z10 ⓚ ▽ ✳; Mex.: Queretaro
- *microheliopsis* Werderm. = Mammillaria microhelia var. microheliopsis
- *micromeris* Engelm. = Epithelantha micromeris
- *missouriensis* Sweet = Escobaria missouriensis
- *mitlensis* Bravo = Mammillaria rekoi
- **moellendorffiana** Shurly · ⚕ Z9 ⓚ ▽ ✳; Mex. (Hidalgo)
- **muehlenpfordtii** C.F. Först. · ⚕ Z10 ⓚ ▽ ✳; C-Mex.
- *multiceps* Salm-Dyck = Mammillaria prolifera
- **mundtii** K. Schum. · ⚕ Z10 ⓚ ▽ ✳; C-Mex. (Toluca); mts.
- **mystax** Mart. · ⚕ Z10 ⓚ ▽ ✳; C-Mex., S-Mex.
- *nejapensis* R.T. Craig & E.Y. Dawson = Mammillaria karwinskiana
- **nelsonii** (Britton & Rose) Boed. · ⚕ Z10 ⓚ ▽ ✳; Mex.: Guerrero, Michoacan
- *neopotosina* R.T. Craig = Mammillaria muehlenpfordtii
- *neoschwarzeana* Backeb. = Mammillaria bocensis
- **neumanniana** Lem. · ⚕ Z10 ⓚ ▽ ✳; Mex.

– **nivosa** Link ex Pfeiff. · E:Woolly Nipple Cactus · Ψ Zio 🏵 ▽ ✳; W.Ind.
– **nunezii** (Britton & Rose) Orcutt · Ψ Zio 🏵 ▽ ✳; Mex.: Guerrero
– var. *solisii* (Britton & Rose) Backeb. = Mammillaria nunezii
– *occidentalis* (Britton & Rose) Boed. = Mammillaria mazatlanensis var. occidentalis
– *ochoterenae* (Bravo) Werderm. = Mammillaria discolor
– **orcuttii** Boed. · Ψ Zio 🏵 ▽ ✳; Mex.
– *ortizrubiana* (Bravo) Werderm. = Mammillaria candida
– *papyracantha* Engelm. = Sclerocactus papyracanthus
– **parkinsonii** C. Ehrenb. · Ψ Zio 🏵 ▽ ✳; C-Mex.
– **pectinifera** (Rümpler) F.A.C. Weber · Ψ Zio 🏵 Ⓝ ▽ ✳; C-Mex.
– **pennispinosa** Krainz · Ψ Zio 🏵 ▽ ✳; Mex.: Coahuila
– **perbella** Hildm. ex K. Schum. · Ψ Zio 🏵 ▽ ✳; Mex.: Hidalgo, Queretaro, Mexico
– **petterssonii** Hildm. · Ψ Zio 🏵 ▽ ✳; Mex.: Jalisco
– *pilensis* Shurly ex Eggli = Mammillaria petterssonii
– **plumosa** F.A.C. Weber · E:Feather Cactus; G:Gefiederter Warzenkaktus · Ψ Zio 🏵 ▽ ✳; Mex.: Coahuila
– **polyedra** Mart. · Ψ Zio 🏵 ▽ ✳; Mex.
– **polythele** Mart. · Ψ Zio 🏵 ▽ ✳; Mex.: Hidalgo
– **poselgeri** Hildm. · Ψ Zio 🏵 ▽ ✳; Mex.: Baja Calif.
– **pottsii** Scheer ex Salm-Dyck · E:Rat-tail Nipple Cactus · Ψ Zio 🏵 ▽ ✳; SW-Tex., N-Mex.
– **prolifera** (Mill.) Haw. · E:Texas Nipple Cactus · Ψ Zio 🏵 ▽ ✳; USA: Texas; NE-Mex., Cuba, Hispaniola
– *pseudocrucigera* R.T. Craig = Mammillaria sempervivi
– **pseudoperbella** Quehl · Ψ Zio 🏵 ▽ ✳; orig. ?
– **pugionacantha** C.F. Först. · Ψ Zio 🏵 ▽ ✳; Mex.
– *pyrrhocephala* Scheidw. = Mammillaria karwinskiana
– **rekoi** (Britton & Rose) Vaupel · Ψ Zio 🏵 ▽ ✳; Mex.: Oaxaca
– *rekoiana* R.T. Craig = Mammillaria rekoi
– **rettigiana** Boed. · Ψ Zio 🏵 ▽ ✳; Mex.
– **rhodantha** Link & Otto

– subsp. **aureiceps** (Lem.) D.R. Hunt
– subsp. **rhodantha** · Ψ Zio 🏵 ▽ ✳; N-Mex.: mts.
– *ritteriana* Boed. = Mammillaria chionocephala
– **roseoalba** Boed. · Ψ Zio 🏵 ▽ ✳; Mex.: Tamaulipas
– *rubida* F. Schwarz ex Backeb. = Mammillaria bocensis
– **ruestii** Quehl · Ψ Zio 🏵 ▽ ✳; Guat., Hond.
– *runyonii* (Britton & Rose) Boed. = Mammillaria melanocentra
– *saetigera* Boed. & Tiegel = Mammillaria brauneana
– *saffordii* (Britton & Rose) Bravo = Mammillaria carretii
– **sartorii** J.A. Purpus · Ψ Zio 🏵 ▽ ✳; Mex.: Veracruz
– *scheerii* Muehlenpf. 1847 non 1845 = Coryphantha scheeri
– *scheidweileriana* Otto ex A. Dietr. = Mammillaria erythrosperma
– **schiedeana** C. Ehrenb. · Ψ Zio 🏵 ▽ ✳; Mex.: Hidalgo
– *schmollii* (Bravo) Werderm. = Mammillaria discolor
– **schumannii** Hildm. · Ψ Zio 🏵 ▽ ✳; Mex.: Baja Calif.
– **seideliana** Quehl · Ψ Zio 🏵 ▽ ✳; Mex.: Zacatecas, Queretaro
– **sempervivi** DC. · Ψ Zio 🏵 ▽ ✳; C-Mex.
– var. *caput-medusae* (Otto) Backeb. = Mammillaria sempervivi
– **senilis** Salm-Dyck · Ψ Zio 🏵 ▽ ✳; NW-Mex.; mts.
– **sheldonii** (Britton & Rose) Boed. · Ψ Zio 🏵 ▽ ✳; N-Mex.: Sonora
– *simplex* Haw. = Mammillaria mammillaris
– *soehlemannii* W. Haage & Backeb. = Mammillaria columbiana
– *solisii* (Britton & Rose) Boed. = Mammillaria nunezii
– **sphacelata** Mart. · Ψ Zio 🏵 ▽ ✳; S-Mex.: Puebla, Oaxaca
– **sphaerica** A. Dietr. · E:Longmamma Nipple Cactus · Ψ Zio 🏵 ▽ ✳; SE-Tex., NE-Mex.
– **spinosissima** Lem. · Ψ Zio 🏵 ▽ ✳; C-Mex.
– *subdurispina* Backeb. = Mammillaria kewensis
– **supertexta** Mart. ex Pfeiff. · Ψ Zio 🏵 ▽ ✳; Mex.: Caxaca
– **surculosa** Boed. · Ψ Zio 🏵 ▽ ✳;

NE-Mex.
- *tenampensis* (Britton & Rose) A. Berger = Mammillaria sartorii
- *tetracantha* Pfeiff. = Mammillaria polythele
- **tetrancistra** Engelm. · E:Common Fishhook Cactus · ⫿ Z10 ⓐ ▽ ✳; USA: Calif., Nev., Utah, Ariz.; N-Mex.
- **tiegeliana** Backeb. · ⫿ Z10 ⓐ ▽ ✳; Mex.
- *tolimensis* R.T. Craig = Mammillaria compressa
- *tuberculosa* Engelm. = Escobaria tuberculosa
- *uberiformis* Zucc. = Mammillaria longimamma
- *vagaspina* R.T. Craig = Mammillaria magnimamma
- **viereckii** Boed. · ⫿ Z10 ⓐ ▽ ✳; Mex.: Tamaulipas
- *vivipara* (Nutt.) Haw. = Escobaria vivipara
- **voburnensis** Scheer · ⫿ Z9 ⓐ ▽ ✳; Mex. (Oaxaca)
- var. *eichlamii* (Quehl) Repp. = Mammillaria eichlamii
- *vonwyssiana* Krainz = Mammillaria parkinsonii
- **wildii** A. Dietr. · E:Fishhook Pincushion Cactus · ⫿ Z10 ⓐ ▽ ✳; Mex.: Hidalgo
- **woodsii** R.T. Craig · ⫿ ◠ Z10 ⓐ ▽ ✳; C-Mex.
- *wuthenauiana* Backeb. = Mammillaria nunezii
- *yucatanensis* (Britton & Rose) Orcutt = Mammillaria columbiana
- **zahniana** Boed. & F. Ritter · ⫿ Z10 ⓐ ▽ ✳; Mex.
- **zeilmanniana** Boed. · E:Rose Pincushion; G:Muttertags-Warzenkaktus · ⫿ Z10 ⓐ ▽ ✳; Mex.: Guanajuato
- **zephyranthoides** Scheidw. · ⫿ Z10 ⓐ ▽ ✳; C-Mex.
- **zeyeriana** Haage ex K. Schum. · ⫿ Z10 ⓐ ▽ ✳; Mex.: Coahuila, Durango
- *zuccariniana* Mart. = Mammillaria magnimamma

Mammilloydia Buxb. = Mammillaria
- *candida* (Scheidw.) Buxb. = Mammillaria candida

Mandevilla Lindl. -f- *Apocynaceae* · 150 spp. · E:Jasmine; F:Faux-jasmin, Jasmin du Chili; G:Falscher Jasmin
- × **amabilis** (Backh.) Dress (*M. splendens*

× ?) · ♄ ⌇ ⚜ Z10 ⓐ ✺; cult.
- **atroviolacea** (Stadelm.) Woodson · ♄ ⚜ Z10 ⓦ VII-VIII ✺; Braz.
- **boliviensis** (Hook. f.) Woodson · ♄ ⚜ Z10 ⓦ IV-X ✺; Bol.
- **eximia** (Hemsl.) Woodson · ♄ ⚜ Z10 ⓦ VI-VIII ✺; Braz.
- **laxa** (Ruiz & Pav.) Woodson · E:Chilean Jasmine; G:Chilejasmin · ♄ ⚜ Z9 ⓦ ⓐ VI-VIII ✺; Bol., Arg.
- **sanderi** (Hemsl.) Woodson · E:Brazilian Jasmine; G:Braziljasmin · ♄ ⚜ Z10 ⓦ VI-VIII ✺; Braz.
- **splendens** (Hook.) Woodson · ♄ ⚜ Z10 ⓦ VII-VIII ✺; Braz.
- *suaveolens* Lindl. = Mandevilla laxa

Mandirola Decne. = Eucodonia
- *lanata* Planch. & Linden ex Lem. = Eucodonia verticillata

Mandragora L. -f- *Solanaceae* · 6 spp. · E:Mandrake; F:Mandragore; G:Alraune, Alraunwurzel
- *acaulis* Gaertn. = Mandragora officinarum
- **autumnalis** Bertol. · E:Autumn Mandrake; G:Herbst-Alraune · ⟁ V ✺; Eur.: Ib, Ital-P, GR, Crete; TR, NW-Afr.
- **officinarum** L. · E:Devil's Apple, European Mandrake; G:Echte Alraune · ⟁ ⓐ ⚜ ✺ ▽; Eur.: N-I, W-Ba
- *vernalis* Bertol. = Mandragora officinarum

Manettia Mutis ex L. -f- *Rubiaceae* · 126 spp.
- **cordifolia** Mart. · ♄ e ⚜ Z10 ⓐ II-VI; Peru, Bol., Arg.
- *glabra* Cham. & Schltdl. = Manettia cordifolia
- **luteorubra** (Vell.) Benth. · ⟁ ♄ ⌇ e ⚜ Z10 ⓐ IV-IX; Braz., Parag., Urug.

Manfreda Salisb. = Agave
- *brachystachys* (Cav.) Rose = Agave scabra
- *maculosa* (Hook.) Rose = Agave maculosa
- *variegata* (Jacobi) Rose = Agave variegata
- *virginica* (L.) Salisb. = Agave virginica

Mangifera L. -f- *Anacardiaceae* · 40-60 spp. · E:Mango; F:Manguier ; G:Mango
- **caesia** Jack ex Wall. · ♄ e Z10 ⓦ ⓝ;

Malay. Arch., Phil.
- **foetida** Lour. · E:Gray Mango, Limus; G:Graue Mango · ♄ e Z10 ⓜ Ⓝ; Malay. Arch.
- **indica** J. König ex L. · E:Mango; G:Echte Mango · ♄ e Z10 ⓜ Ⓝ; NE-Ind., N-Burma; cult. Trop.
- × **odorata** Griff. (*M. foetida* × *M. indica*) · E:Kuwini, Saipan Mango; G:Saipan-Mango · ♄ e ⓜ Ⓝ; orig. ?
- *pinnata* L. f. = Spondias pinnata

Manglesia Lindl. = Grevillea
- *glabrata* Lindl. = Grevillea glabrata

Manglietia Blume -f- *Magnoliaceae* · 29 spp.
- *celebica* Miq. = Magnolia liliifera
- *sebassa* King = Magnolia liliifera *odes* (Dandy) Gagnep. = Magnolia liliifera

Manihot Mill. -f- *Euphorbiaceae* · 98 spp. · E:Cassava, Manioc; F:Maniok; G:Cassavastrauch, Maniok
- **carthagenensis** (Jacq.) Müll. Arg. · ♄ d Z10 ⓜ Ⓝ; Mex., C-Am., Col., Venez.
- **dichotoma** Ule · ♄ Z10 ⓜ Ⓝ; Braz.: Bahia
- **dulcis** (J.F. Gmel.) Pax
  - var. **dulcis** · E:Sweet Cassava; G:Süßer Maniok · ♄ Z10 ⓜ Ⓝ; S-Am.
  - var. **multifida** (Graham) Pax · ♄ Z10 ⓜ Ⓝ; Braz.: Parana
- **esculenta** Crantz · E:Bitter Cassava, Manioc, Tapioca; G:Echter Maniok · ♄ e Z10 ⓜ ⚥ Ⓝ; trop. Braz.
- **glaziovii** Müll. Arg. · E:Ceara Rubber; G:Cera-Kautschukbaum, Cera-Maniok · ♄ Z10 ⓜ Ⓝ; NE-Braz.
- *utilissima* Pohl = Manihot esculenta

Manilkara Adans. -f- *Sapotaceae* · 82 spp. · F:Sapotier; G:Breiapfelbaum, Chiclebaum
- **achras** (Mill.) Fosberg · ♄ e Z10 ⓜ Ⓝ; C-Am., Mex.
- *balata* Dubard = Manilkara bidentata
- **bidentata** (A. DC.) A. Chev. · E:Balata, Beef Wood · ♄ e Z10 ⓜ Ⓝ; Panama, W.Ind., trop. S-Am.
- **elata** (Allemão ex Miq.) Monach. · G:Massaranduba · ♄ e Z10 ⓜ Ⓝ; Amazon.
- **zapota** (L.) P. Royen · E:Marmalade Plum, Sapodilla; G:Breiapfelbaum · ♄ e

Z10 ⓜ Ⓝ; S-Mex., C-Am., nat. in Fla.

Manulea L. -f- *Scrophulariaceae* · 74 spp.
- *hispida* Thunb. = Sutera hispida
- **rubra** L. f. · ☉ ⌄ Z10 VI-VIII; S-Afr.

Maoutia Wedd. -f- *Urticaceae* · 15 spp.
- **puya** Wedd. · ⌄ ⓜ Ⓝ; Him., Ind.: Khasia Hills; Burma

Mapania Aubl. -f- *Cyperaceae* · 84 spp.
- *humilis* (Hassk. ex Steud.) Fern.-Vill. = Hypolytrum humile

Maranta L. -f- *Marantaceae* · 37 spp. · E:Maranta; F:Dictame barbade, Maranta; G:Pfeilwurz
- *amabilis* Linden = Ctenanthe amabilis
- *argyraea* Körn. = Calathea argyraea
- **arundinacea** L. · E:Arrowroot; G:Echte Pfeilwurz · ⌄ Z10 ⓜ ⚥ Ⓝ; trop. S-Am.
- **bachemiana** (E. Morren) Regel
- *bicolor* Ker-Gawl. = Maranta cristata
- **cristata** Nees & Mart. · G:Kamm-Pfeilwurz · ⌄ Z10 ⓜ; Guyan., Braz.
- **depressa** E. Morren · ⌄ ⤳ Z10 ⓜ; Braz.
- *fasciata* Linden ex K. Koch = Calathea fasciata
- *kegeliana* Regel = Calathea bachemiana
- *kummeriana* E. Morren = Ctenanthe kummeriana
- *leopardina* W. Bull = Calathea leopardina
- **leuconeura** E. Morren · E:Prayer Plant; G:Bunte Pfeilwurz, Gebetspflanze · ⌄ Z10 ⓜ VII-VIII; Braz.
- **lietzei** (E. Morren) C. Nelson · ⌄ Z9 ⓜ; Braz.
- *makoyana* (E. Morren) E. Morren = Calathea makoyana
- *mediopicta* E. Morren = Calathea mediopicta
- **noctiflora** Regel & Körn. · ⌄ Z10 ⓜ; ? Braz.
- *oppenheimiana* (E. Morren) Petersen = Ctenanthe oppenheimiana
- *ornata* Linden = Calathea majestica
- *roseopicta* Linden = Calathea roseopicta
- *warscewiczii* Matthieu ex Planch. = Calathea warscewiczii
- *wiotii* E. Morren = Calathea wiotii
- *zebrina* Sims = Calathea zebrina

Marattia Sw. -f- *Marattiaceae* · 57 spp.
- **alata** Sw. · ⌄ e Z10 ⓜ; W.Ind., trop. S-Am.

– **cicutifolia** Kaulf. · ♃ e Z10 ⬢; S-Braz.
– **fraxinea** J. Sm. · ♃ e Z10 ⬢; trop. Afr,
trop. As., Austr., NZ
– *kaulfussii* J. Sm. = Marattia alata
– *laevis* J. Sm. = Marattia alata
– *salicina* J. Sm. = Marattia fraxinea

Marcgravia L. -f- *Marcgraviaceae* · 45 spp.
– **umbellata** L. · ♄ ⚥ ⬢; W.Ind., trop.
S-Am.

Marginatocereus (Backeb.) Backeb. =
Stenocereus
– *marginatus* (DC.) Backeb. = Pachycereus
marginatus

Margyricarpus Ruiz & Pav. -m- *Rosaceae* ·
1 sp. · E:Pearl Fruit; G:Perlbeere
– **pinnatus** (Lam.) Kuntze · E:Pearl Berry,
Pearl Fruit; G:Perlbeere · ♄ e ⚬ Z9 ⬢
IV-VI; S-Am.; And.
– *setosus* Ruiz & Pav. = Margyricarpus
pinnatus

Marlea Roxb. = Alangium
– *begoniifolia* Roxb. = Alangium chinense
– *platanifolia* Siebold & Zucc. = Alangium
platanifolium var. platanifolium

Marniera Backeb. = Epiphyllum
– *chrysocardium* (Alexander) Backeb. =
Epiphyllum chrysocardium

Marrubium L. -n- *Lamiaceae* · 47 spp. ·
E:Horehound; F:Marrube; G:Andorn,
Mausohr
– **astracanicum** Jacq. · ♃ ⤳ △ Z8 ⬢ ⋀
VI-VII; TR
– **globosum** Montbret & Aucher ex Benth. ·
G:Kugel-Andorn
– subsp. **libanoticum** (Boiss.) P.H. Davis ·
G:Libanon-Kugel-Andorn · ♃ ⤳ △ Z8 ⋀
VI-VII; Lebanon
– **incanum** Desr. · G:Weißfilziger Andorn ·
♃ Z7 ⋀ VI-VII; Eur.: Sard., I, Sic, Ba
– *kotschyi* Boiss. & Hohen. = Marrubium
astracanicum
– *libanoticum* Boiss. = Marrubium
globosum subsp. libanoticum
– **peregrinum** L. · G:Ungarischer Andorn ·
♃ VII-VIII; Eur.: A, EC-Eur., Ba, E-Eur.;
TR, Cauc., nat. in F, I, D
– **supinum** L. · E:Spanish Horehound;
G:Spanischer Andorn · ♃ ⤳ △ Z7 ⋀
V-VII; Eur.: sp.; mts.

– **velutinum** Sibth. & Sm. · G:Gebirgs-
Andorn · ♃ △ Z8 ⋀ VI-VII; GR
– **vulgare** L. · E:Common Horehound,
White Horehound; G:Gewöhnlicher
Andorn · ♃ Z3 VI-VIII ⚥ ; Eur.*, TR,
Levant, Cauc. Iran, C-As., N-Afr., nat. in
N-Am.

Marsdenia R. Br. -f- *Asclepiadaceae* · c.
100 spp. · E:Condorvine; F:Vigne des
Andes; G:Andenwein
– **cundurango** Rchb. f. · E:Common Condorvine, Cundurango; G:Gewöhnlicher
Andenwein · ♄ e ⚥ ⬢ ⚥ ; Col., Ecuad.,
Peru (And.)
– *erecta* (L.) R. Br. = Cionura erecta
– *reichenbachii* Triana = Marsdenia
cundurango
– **tinctoria** R. Br. · E:Climbing Indigo;
G:Färber-Andenwein · ♄ e ⚥ ⬢ ⓝ; Him.,
China, Malay. Arch.

Marshallia Schreb. -f- *Asteraceae* · 7 spp.
– **caespitosa** Nutt. ex DC. · E:Puffballs · ♃
△ Z7 ⬢ ⋀ V-VI; USA: Mo., SC, SE

Marshallocereus Backeb. = Stenocereus
– *thurberi* (Engelm.) Backeb. = Stenocereus
thurberi

Marsilea L. -f- *Marsileaceae* · 60 spp. ·
E:Pepperwort, Water Clover; F:Marsilée;
G:Kleefarn
– **drummondii** A. Braun · E:Common
Nardoo; G:Essbarer Kleefarn · ♃ ⌇
Z9 ⬢; Austr.: North Terr., Queensl.,
N.S.Wales, Victoria, S-Austr., Tasman.,
W-Austr.
– **hirsuta** R. Br. · G:Rauhaariger Kleefarn ·
♃ ⌇ Z9 ⬢; Austr.: Queensl., N.S.Wales
– **quadrifolia** L. · E:Clover Fern, Pepper-
wort; F:Marsilia à quatre feuilles;
G:Vierblättriger Kleefarn · ♃ ⌇ Z5 IX-X
▽; Eur.* exc. BrI, Sc; Cauc., C-As., S-As.,
China, Jap., Can.: W; USA: NE, NCE

Martynia L. -f- *Pedaliaceae* · 1 sp. · E:Devil's
Claw, Unicorn Plant; F:Martynia;
G:Tigerklaue
– **annua** L. · E:Unicorn Plant; G:Tigerklaue
· ⊙ VII-VIII; Mex., C-Am., W.Ind.
– *craniolaria* Gloxin = Craniolaria annua
– *proboscidea* Gloxin = Proboscidea
louisianica
– *violacea* Engelm. = Proboscidea fragrans

Mascarena L.H. Bailey = Hyophorbe
– *lagenicaulis* L.H. Bailey = Hyophorbe
lagenicaulis
– *verschaffeltii* (H. Wendl.) L.H. Bailey =
Hyophorbe verschaffeltii

Masdevallia Ruiz & Pav. -f- *Orchidaceae* ·
552 spp.
– **amabilis** Rchb. f. & Warsz. · ♃ Z10 ⓚ
XII-II ▽ ✳; Peru
– *bella* Rchb. f. = Dracula bella
– **caloptera** Rchb. f. · ♃ Z10 ⓠ ▽ ✳;
S-Ecuad., N-Peru
– **caudata** Lindl. · ♃ Z10 ⓚ XI-III ▽ ✳;
Col., Ecuad., Peru, Venez.
– *chimaera* Rchb. f. = Dracula chimaera
– **coccinea** Linden ex Lindl. · ♃ Z10 ⓚ
III-VI ▽ ✳; Col., Peru
– **coriacea** Lindl. · ♃ Z10 ⓚ V-VII ▽ ✳;
Col.
– *erythrochaete* Rchb. f. = Dracula erythrochaete
– *harryana* Rchb. f. = Masdevallia coccinea
– **horrida** Teusch. & Garay · ♃ Z10 ⓚ ▽
✳; Costa Rica
– **infracta** Lindl. · ♃ Z10 ⓚ V-VII ▽ ✳;
Peru, S-Braz.
– *lilliputana* Cogn. = Dryadella lilliputana
– *lindenii* André = Masdevallia coccinea
– **macrura** Rchb. f. · ♃ Z10 ⓚ II-III ▽ ✳;
Col.
– *militaris* Rchb. f. & Warsz. = Masdevallia
coccinea
– *radiosa* Rchb. f. = Dracula radiosa
– **rolfeana** Kraenzl. · ♃ Z10 ⓚ IV-VII ▽ ✳;
Costa Rica
– **rosea** Lindl. · ♃ Z10 ⓚ V-VII ▽ ✳; Col.,
Ecuad.
– **schlimii** Linden ex Lindl. · ♃ Z10 ⓚ IV-V
▽ ✳; Col., Venez.
– **tovarensis** Rchb. f. · ♃ Z10 ⓚ XI-II ▽ ✳;
Venez.
– **veitchiana** Rchb. f. · ♃ Z10 ⓚ V-VI ▽ ✳;
Peru
– **velifera** Rchb. f. · ♃ Z10 ⓚ XI-I ▽ ✳;
Col.
– **Cultivars:**
– **many cultivars**

Matricaria L. -f- *Asteraceae* · 3 spp. ·
E:Mayweed; F:Camomille, Matricaire;
G:Kamille
– *capensis* hort. ex Vilm. = Tanacetum
parthenium
– *chamomilla* L. = Matricaria recutita

– **discoidea** DC. · E:False Chamomile;
G:Strahlenlose Kamille · ☉ VI-X; Eur.:
NE-As., ? w. N-Am., nat. in Eur.* exc. Ib
– *inodora* L. = Tripleurospermum perforatum
– *maritima* L. = Tripleurospermum
maritimum
– subsp. *inodora* (K. Koch) Soó = Tripleurospermum perforatum
– *parthenioides* (Desf.) hort. = Tanacetum
parthenium
– *parthenium* L. = Tanacetum parthenium
– *perforata* Mérat = Tripleurospermum
perforatum
– **recutita** L. · E:Chamomile, German
Chamomile; G:Echte Kamille · ☉ D V-VIII
⚥ Ⓝ; Eur.*, TR, Palest, Iraq, Cauc., Iran,
Afgh., NW-Ind., W-Sib., Canar., nat. in
N-Am., S-Am., Austr., NZ
– *suaveolens* (Pursh) Rydb. = Matricaria
discoidea
– *tchihatchewii* (Boiss.) Voss = Tripleurospermum oreades var. tchihatchewii

Matteuccia Tod. -f- *Woodsiaceae* · 4 spp. ·
E:Ostrich Fern; F:Fougère plume-
d'autruche; G:Straußenfarn, Straußfarn,
Trichterfarn
– **orientalis** (Hook.) Trevis. · F:Fougère
plume d'autruche; G:Flachwachsender
Straußenfarn · ♃ Z4; Him., China, Korea,
Jap.
– **pensylvanica** (Willd.) Raymond ·
E:Ostrich Fern; F:Fougère plume
d'autruche; G:Amerikanischer Straußen-
farn · ♃; Alaska, Can., USA: NE, NCE, NC
– **struthiopteris** (L.) Tod. · E:Ostrich Fern;
F:Fougère d'Allemagne; G:Europäischer
Straußenfarn · ♃ ∿ Z2 VII-VIII ▽; Eur.*
exc. BrI, Sc; TR, Sib., Sakhal., Kamchat.,
China, Manch., Korea, Jap., Alaska, Can.,
USA: NE, NCE, nat. in BrI
– var. *pensylvanica* (Willd.) C.V. Morton =
Matteuccia pensylvanica

Matthiola R. Br. -f- *Brassicaceae* · 55 spp. ·
E:Gillyflower, Stock; F:Giroflée, Violier;
G:Levkoje
– **fruticulosa** (L.) Maire · E:Sad Stock
– subsp. **fruticulosa** · ♃ e △ Z7 ⋀ V-VI;
Eur.: Ib, Fr, Ital-P, Ba; TR, Cyprus,
Lebanon, N-Afr.
– subsp. **valesiaca** (Boiss.) P.W. Ball ·
G:Trübe Levkoje · ♃ e Z6 V-VII; Eur.: F, I,
Sw; S-Alp.

- **incana** (L.) R. Br. · E:Brompton Stock,
  Stock, Ten Week Stock; G:Garten-
  Levkoje · ☉ ⊙ ⚤ ⚏ ⚥ D Z6 IV-X; Eur.: Ib,
  Fr, Ital-P, Ba, BrI; TR, Cyprus
- **many cultivars**
- **longipetala** (Vent.) DC.
- subsp. **bicornis** (Sibth. & Sm.) P.W.
  Ball · ☉ D Z6 V-VI; Eur.: GR; TR, Levant,
  Egypt, Libya
- subsp. **longipetala** · E:Night Scented
  Stock; G:Nacht-Levkoje · ☉ Z6; TR,
  Levant
- *tristis* R. Br. = Matthiola fruticulosa
  subsp. fruticulosa
- *varia* (Sibth. & Sm.) DC. = Matthiola
  fruticulosa subsp. fruticulosa

Matucana Britton & Rose -f- *Cactaceae* ·
  17 spp.
- **aurantiaca** (Vaupel) Buxb.
- subsp. **aurantiaca** · ⚥ Z9 ⚏ ▽ ✳; N-Peru
- subsp. **currundayensis** (F. Ritter)
  Mottram
- *blancii* Backeb. = Matucana haynei subsp.
  herzogiana
- *breviflora* Rauh & Backeb. = Matucana
  haynei subsp. hystrix
- *calocephala* Skarupke = Matucana haynei
  subsp. myriacantha
- **comacephala** F. Ritter
- *crinifera* F. Ritter = Matucana haynei
  subsp. herzogiana
- *currundayensis* F. Ritter = Matucana
  aurantiaca subsp. currundayensis
- *elongata* Rauh & Backeb. = Matucana
  haynei subsp. haynei
- **haynei** (Otto ex Salm-Dyck) Britton &
  Rose
- subsp. **haynei** · ⚥ Z9 ⚏ ▽ ✳; N-Peru
- subsp. **herzogiana** (Backeb.) Mottram
- subsp. **hystrix** (Rauh & Backeb.) Mottram
- subsp. **myriacantha** (Vaupel) Mottram ·
  ⚥ Z9 ⚏ ▽ ✳; Peru
- *herzogiana* Backeb. = Matucana haynei
  subsp. herzogiana
- *hystrix* Rauh & Backeb. = Matucana
  haynei subsp. hystrix
- var. *atrispina* Rauh & Backeb. =
  Matucana haynei subsp. hystrix
- *icosagona* (Kunth) Buxb. = Cleistocactus
  icosagonus
- *multicolor* Rauh & Backeb. = Matucana
  haynei subsp. hystrix
- *myriacantha* (Vaupel) Buxb. = Matucana

haynei subsp. myriacantha
- *purpureoalba* F. Ritter = Matucana haynei
  subsp. myriacantha
- **ritteri** Buining · ⚥ Z9 ⚏ ▽ ✳; Peru
- *variabilis* Rauh & Backeb. = Matucana
  haynei subsp. haynei
- **weberbaueri** (Vaupel) Backeb. · ⚥ Z9 ⚏
  ▽ ✳; NE-Peru
- *winteri* F. Ritter = Matucana haynei
  subsp. myriacantha
- *yanganucensis* Rauh & Backeb. =
  Matucana haynei subsp. herzogiana

Maurandella (A. Gray) Rothm. -f-
  Scrophulariaceae · 1 sp.
- **antirrhiniflora** (Willd.) Rothm. ·
  E:Roving Sailor, Violet Twining
  Snapdragon; G:Purpurnes Windendes
  Löwenmaul · ⚤ Z9 ⚏ ⚐ VI-IX; USA: Tex.
  Calif.; Mex.

Maurandya Ortega -f- *Scrophulariaceae* ·
  2 spp. · E:Twining Snapdragon; G:Win-
  dendes Löwenmaul
- *antirrhiniflora* Humb. & Bonpl. ex Willd.
  = Maurandella antirrhiniflora
- **barclaiana** Lindl. · E:Snapdragon Vine;
  G:Windendes Löwenmaul · ⚏ ⚥ Z9 ⚏
  VII-IX; Mex.
- *erubescens* (D. Don) A. Gray = Lophospermum erubescens
- *lophospermum* L.H. Bailey = Lophospermum scandens
- *purpusii* Brandegee = Lophospermum
  purpusii
- **scandens** (Cav.) Pers. · ☉ ⊙ ⚤ ⚏ ⚥ Z9 ⚏
  VI-X; Mex.

Mauritia L. f. -f- *Arecaceae* · 2 spp.
- **flexuosa** L. f. · ⚏ e ⚐ ⚐; S-Am.

Maxillaria Ruiz & Pav. -f- *Orchidaceae* ·
  559 spp.
- **coccinea** (Jacq.) L.O. Williams ex
  Hodge · E:Flame Orchid · ⚤ Z10 ⚐ VI-VII
  ▽ ✳; W.Ind.
- **densa** Lindl. Z10 ⚐ I-IV ▽ ✳; Mex.,
  Guat.
- **elatior** (Rchb. f.) Rchb. f. · ⚤ Z10 ⚐ ▽
  ✳; Mex., Guat., Hond., Costa Rica
- **fucata** Rchb. f. · ⚤ Z10 ⚐ V-VI ▽ ✳;
  Ecuad.
- **grandiflora** (Kunth) Lindl. · ⚤ Z10 ⚐
  V-VI ▽ ✳; trop. S-Am.
- *jugosa* Lindl. = Pabstia jugosa

– **lepidota** Lindl. · ⌄ Zıo 🌢 V-VII ▽ ✳;
Col., Ecuad., Peru, Venez.
– *longipetala* Ruiz & Pav. = Lycaste
longipetala
– **luteoalba** Lindl. · ⌄ Zıo 🌢 II-IV ▽ ✳;
Costa Rica, Panama, Col., Ecuad.
– *marginata* Fenzl = Maxillaria punctulata
– **nigrescens** Lindl. · ⌄ Zıo 🌢 VI-VII ▽ ✳;
Col., Venez.
– **ochroleuca** Lodd. · ⌄ Zıo 🌢 ▽ ✳; Braz.
– **picta** Hook. · ⌄ Zıo 🌢 I-IV ▽ ✳; E-Braz.
– **porphyrostele** Rchb. f. · ⌄ Zıo 🌢 II-IV
▽ ✳; Braz.
– **punctulata** Klotzsch · ⌄ Zıo 🌢 VII-X ▽
✳; Braz.
– **sanderiana** Rchb. f. ex Sander · ⌄ Zıo 🌢
VIII-X ▽ ✳; Ecuad., Peru
– **sanguinea** Rolfe · ⌄ Zıo 🌢 ▽ ✳; Costa
Rica, Panama
– **setigera** Lindl. · ⌄ Zıo 🌢 VI-VIII ▽ ✳;
Col.
– **sophronitis** (Rchb. f.) Garay · ⌄ Zıo 🌢
V-IX ▽ ✳; Venez.
– **striata** Rolfe · ⌄ Zıo 🌢 VII-IX ▽ ✳;
Ecuad., Peru
– **tenuifolia** Lindl. · ⌄ Zıo 🌢 VII-IX ▽ ✳;
Mex., C-Am.
– **variabilis** Bateman ex Lindl. · ⌄ Zıo 🌢
I-XII ▽ ✳; C-Am.
– **venusta** Linden & Rchb. f. · ⌄ Zıo 🌢
IX-XI ▽ ✳; Col., Venez.

Mayaca Aubl. -f- *Mayacaceae* · 5 spp.
– **fluviatilis** Aubl. · E:Stream Bogmoss · ⌄
⌇⌇ ≋ 🌢 VI-VIII; USA: SE, Fla., Tex.;
Mex., C-Am., S-Am.
– *madida* (Vell.) Stellfeld = Mayaca
sellowiana
– **sellowiana** Kunth
– *vandelii* (Roem.) Schott & Endl. =
Mayaca fluviatilis

Maytenus Molina -f- *Celastraceae* · 255 spp.
– **boaria** Molina · E:Mayten Tree · ♄ e Z8
🏵 V; Chile

Mazus Lour. -m- *Scrophulariaceae* · 15
(-50) spp. · F:Mazus; G:Lippenmäulchen
– **japonicus** (Thunb.) Kuntze · G:Japa-
nisches Lippenmäulchen · ☉ VI-VIII; Ind.,
China, Korea, Jap., Ryukyu-Is., nat. in
N-Am.
– **miquelii** Makino · ⌄ ⤳ △ V-VI; Jap.
– **pumilio** R. Br. · G:Sumpf-Lippen-
mäulchen · ⌄ △ ∧ V-VI; Austr., Tasman.,

NZ
– **radicans** (Hook. f.) Cheeseman ·
G:Rasen-Lippenmäulchen · ⌄ ⤳ △ Z7
∧ V-VI; NZ
– **reptans** N.E. Br. · ⌄; cult.
– *rugosus* Lour. = Mazus japonicus
– *stolonifer* (Maxim.) Makino = Mazus
miquelii

Mecodium C. Presl ex Copel. = Hymenophyllum
– *demissum* (G. Forst.) Copel. = Hymenophyllum demissum
– *polyanthon* (Sw.) Copel. = Hymenophyllum polyanthon

Meconopsis R. Vig. -f- *Papaveraceae* · c.
50 spp. · E:Asiatic Poppy; F:Méconopsis,
Pavot bleu; G:Keulenmohn, Scheinmohn
– **aculeata** Royle · ☉ △ Z7 VII-VIII;
W-Him.
– × **beamishii** Prain (*M. grandis* × *M.
integrifolia*) · ⌄; cult.
– **betonicifolia** Franch. · E:Blue Poppy;
Himalayan Poppy; F:Pavot bleu; G:Tibet-
Scheinmohn · ⌄ △ Z7 VI-VIII; China:
Tibet, Yunnan; N-Myamar
– **cambrica** (L.) Vig. · E:Welsh Poppy;
F:Pavot jaune des Pyrénées; G:Kambr-
ischer Scheinmohn, Pyrenäen-Schein-
mohn · ⌄ Z6 VI-X; Eur.: BrI, F, sp., nat. in
DK, Norw.
– var. *aurantiaca* hort. ex H.R. Wehrh. =
Meconopsis cambrica
– **chelidoniifolia** Bureau & Franch. ·
G:Wald-Scheinmohn · ⌄ Z7 VII-VIII;
W-Sichuan
– **dhwojii** G. Taylor ex Hay · ☉ Z7 VI-VIII;
Nepal
– **grandis** Prain · G:Großer Scheinmohn ·
⌄ Z5 VI-VII; Nepal, Sikkim, Tibet
– **horridula** Hook. f. & Thomson · E:Prickly
Blue Poppy; G:Stachliger Scheinmohn
· ☉ ⌄ Z6 VII-VIII; W-Nepal, Him., SW-
China
– **integrifolia** (Maxim.) Franch. ·
E:Lampshade Poppy; G:Gelbhaariger
Scheinmohn · ☉ △ Z7 VII-VIII; China:
Yunnan, Sichuan, Tibet, Kansu
– **napaulensis** DC. · E:Satin Poppy;
G:Nepal-Scheinmohn · ☉ Z7 VI; W-Nepal,
Him., SW-China
– **paniculata** (D. Don) Prain · G:Rispen-
Scheinmohn · ☉ Z7 VI-VII; Him., SE-Tibet
– *prattii* (Prain) Prain = Meconopsis

horridula
- **punicea** Maxim. · E:Red Poppywort; G:Roter Scheinmohn · ⊙ ┦ Z7 VII-VIII; China: Tibet, Sichuan, Kansu
- **quintuplinervia** Regel · E:Harebell Poppy; G:Teppich-Scheinmohn · ┦ △ Z7 VII-VIII; Tibet, W-China
- **regia** G. Taylor · G:Pracht-Scheinmohn · ⊙ Z7 VII-VIII ✳; Nepal
- × **sarsonsii** Sarsons (*M. betonicifolia* × *M. integrifolia*) · G:Sheldons Scheinmohn · ┦; cult.
- × **sheldonii** G. Taylor (*M. betonicifolia* × *M. grandis*) · ┦ Z6; cult.
- **some cultivars**
- **simplicifolia** (D. Don) Walp. · G:Schotter-Scheinmohn · ⊙ Z7 VII-VIII; Nepal, Tibet
- **sinuata** Prain · ⊙ Z7 VII-VIII; Nepal, Bhutan
- **superba** King ex Prain · G:Silber-Scheinmohn · ⊙ Z7 VII-VIII; Bhutan, Tibet
- **villosa** (Hook. f.) G. Taylor · G:Haariger Scheinmohn · ┦ △ Z7 ∧ VI; E-Nepal, Bhutan
- **violacea** Kingdon-Ward · ⊙ VII-VIII; Tibet, N-Burma
- *wallichii* Wall. = Meconopsis napaulensis

Medeola L. -f- *Convallariaceae* · 1 sp. · E:Cucumber Root; F:Fausse-asperge; G:Schlangenwurzel
- *asparagoides* L. = Asparagus asparagoides
- **virginiana** L. · E:Indian Cucumber Root; G:Indianer-Schlangenwurzel · ┦ Z3 VII-VIII; Can: E, USA: NE

Medicago L. -f- *Fabaceae* · 56 spp. · E:Bur Clover, Medick; F:Luzerne; G:Luzerne, Schneckenklee
- **arabica** (L.) Huds. · E:Spotted Bur Clover; G:Arabischer Schneckenklee · ⊙ IV-VI; Eur.* exc. Sc; N-Afr., S-Afr., SW-As, nat. in Sw, Swed
- **arborea** L. · E:Moon Trefoil; G:Baum-Schneckenklee · ♄ e Z8 ⌂; Eur.: Ib, Ital-P, Ba; TR, nat. in F
- **caerulea** Less. ex Ledeb. · ┦ VI-IX; Eur.: Crim, E-Russ.; TR, Cauc., Iran, C-As., Egypt
- **carstiensis** Jacq. · G:Karst-Schneckenklee · ┦ V-VI; Eur.: I, A, Ba
- **falcata** L. · E:Sickle Medick, Yellow Medick; G:Sichel-Luzerne, Sichelklee · ┦ Z6 VI; Eur.*, TR, Syr., Cauc., W-Sib.,

E-Sib., C-As., Moroc.
- **lupulina** L. · E:Black Medick, Shamrock; G:Hopfen-Schneckenklee, Hopfenklee · ⊙ ⊙ ┦ Z5 IV-X Ⓝ; Eur.*, TR, Levant, Cauc., Iran, W-Sib., E-Sib., Amur, C-As., Him., Mong., China, N-Afr., nat. in N-Am., Jap.
- **minima** (L.) L. · E:Little Bur Clover, Small Medick; G:Zwerg-Schneckenklee · ⊙ V-VI; Eur.*, TR, Levant, Cauc., Iran, Him., N-Afr., Eth.
- **orbicularis** (L.) Bartal. · E:Button Bur Clover; G:Kreisfrüchtiger Schneckenklee, Scheibenklee · ⊙; Eur.: Ba, Ib, Ital-P, Fr; TR, Syr., Iraq, Iran, C-As.
- **polymorpha** L. · E:California Bur Clover, Hairy Medick; G:Rauer Schneckenklee · ⊙ V-VII; Eur.: Ib, Fr, Ital-P, Ba, C-Eur., RO, Crim; TR, Levant, N-Afr., nat. in EC-Eur., Old World
- **prostrata** Jacq. · G:Niederliegender Schneckenklee · ┦ IV-VIII; Eur.: I, Ba, A
- **rigidula** (L.) All. · E:Tifton Bur Clover; G:Steifer Schneckenklee · ⊙; Eur.: Ib, Fr, Ital-P, Ba, RO, S-Russ., Crim; TR, Levant, Iraq, Cauc., Iran, Afgh., C-As., N-Afr., nat. in EC-Eur.
- **sativa** L. · E:Alfalfa, Lucerne; G:Luzerne · ┦ VI-IX ♃ Ⓝ; Eur.*, TR, Cauc., Iran, W-Sib., Amur, C-As., Ind., China, N-Afr., nat. in N-Am.
- subsp. *caerulea* (Less. ex Ledeb.) Schmalh. = Medicago caerulea
- subsp. *falcata* (L.) Arcang. = Medicago falcata
- subsp. *varia* (Martyn) Arcang. = Medicago × varia
- **scutellata** Mill. · ⊙; Eur.: Ib, Fr, Ital-P, Ba, S-Russ., Crim; TR, Levant, NW-Afr., nat. in A
- **truncatula** Gaertn. · ⊙; Eur.: Ib, Fr, Ital-P, Ba; TR, Levant, Cauc., ? N-Iran, N-Afr.
- × **varia** Martyn (*M. falcata* × *M. sativa*) · E:Bastard Medick, Sand Lucerne; G:Bastard-Luzerne, Sand-Luzerne · ┦ VI-VIII; cult.

Medinilla Gaudich. -f- *Melastomataceae* · 350-400 spp. · F:Médinilla; G:Medinille
- **curtisii** hort. Veitch · ♄ e Z10 ⌘; Sumat.
- **javanensis** Blume · ♄ e Z10 ⌘ XII-III; Java
- **magnifica** Lindl. · ♄ e Z10 ⌘ II-VIII; Phil.
- **sedifolia** Jum. & Perr. · ♄ e ⌇ Z10 ⌘;

Madag.
- **sieboldiana** Planch. · ♄ e Z10 ⓦ II-III;
Molucca
- **teysmannii** Miq. · ♄ e Z10 ⓦ III-V;
Sulawesi, N.Guinea
- **venosa** (Blume) Blume · ♄ e Z10 ⓦ I-XII;
Malay. Pen.

Meehania Britton -f- *Lamiaceae* · 1 sp. ·
E:Japanese Dead Nettle; F:Meehania;
G:Asiatische Taubnessel
- **urticifolia** (Miq.) Makino · E:Japanese
Dead Nettle; G:Asiatische Taubnessel · ⅃
⤳ Z5 V-VI; Jap., Korea, Manch.

Megaclinium Lindl. = Bulbophyllum
- *falcatum* Lindl. = Bulbophyllum falcatum
- *leucorhachis* Rolfe = Bulbophyllum
imbricatum

Meiracyllium Rchb. f. -n- *Orchidaceae* ·
2 spp.
- **trinasutum** Rchb. f. · ⅃ Z9 ⓦ ▽ ✳;
Mex., Guat.
- *wendlandii* Rchb. f. = Meiracyllium
trinasutum
- *wettstenii* Porsch = Isabelia pulchella

Melaleuca L. -f- *Myrtaceae* · 150-220 spp. ·
E:Honey Myrtle, Paperbark; F:Mélaleuca;
G:Myrtenheide
- **acuminata** F. Muell. · E:Mallee Honey
Myrtle · ♄ e Z9 ⓚ; Austr.: N.S.Wales,
Victoria, S-Austr., W-Austr.
- **armillaris** (Sol. ex Gaertn.) Sm. ·
E:Bracelet Honey Myrtle, Drooping
Melaleuca; G:Armring-Myrtenheide · ♄ e
Z9 ⓚ VI; Austr.: N.S.Wales, Victoria
- **citrina** Turcz. · ♄ e Z9 ⓚ; W-Austr.
- **coccinea** A.S. George · ♄ e Z9 ⓚ;
W-Austr.
- **decussata** R. Br. ex W.T. Aiton · E:Totem
Poles · ♄ e Z9 ⓚ VI; Austr.: S-Austr.,
Victoria
- **diosmifolia** R. Br. · E:Green Honey
Myrtle · ♄ e Z9 ⓚ; W-Austr.
- **ericifolia** Sm. · E:Heath Melaleuca,
Swamp Paperbark; G:Sumpf-Myrten-
heide · ♄ e Z9 ⓚ; Austr.: Queensl.,
N.S.Wales, Victoria, Tasman.
- *fimbriata* hort. = Melaleuca gibbosa
- *florida* G. Forst. = Metrosideros fulgens
- **fulgens** R. Br. · E:Scarlet Honey Myrtle ·
♄ e Z9 ⓚ VI; W-Austr.
- **gibbosa** Labill. · E:Slender Honey

Myrtle · ♄ e Z9 ⓚ; Austr.: Victoria,
S-Austr., Tasman.
- **huegelii** Endl. · E:Chenille Honey
Myrtle · ♄ e Z9 ⓚ; W-Austr.
- **hypericifolia** (Salisb.) Sm. · E:Dotted
Melaleuca; G:Johanniskrautblättrige
Myrtenheide · ♄ e Z9 ⓚ VI-VIII; Austr.:
Queensl., N.S.Wales
- **incana** R. Br. · E:Grey Honey Myrtle · ♄ e
Z9 ⓚ; W-Austr.
- **lanceolata** Otto · ♄ ♄ e Z9 ⓚ; W-Austr.
- **lateritia** A. Dietr. · E:Robin Red Breast;
G:Ziegelrote Myrtenheide · ♄ e Z9 ⓚ
VI-VIII; W-Austr.
- **leucadendra** (L.) L. · E:Broadleaf
Paperbark, Cajeput; G:Kajeputbaum · ♄ e
Z9 ⓚ ⚥ Ⓝ; Burma, Malay. Arch., Austr.
- **linariifolia** Sm. · E:Paperbark Tea Tree;
G:Leinkrautblättrige Myrtenheide · ♄ ♄ e
Z9 ⓚ ⚥ ; Austr.: Queensl., N.S.Wales
- **micromera** Schauer · E:Wattle Honey
Myrtle · ♄ e Z9 ⓚ; W-Austr.
- **nematophylla** F. Muell. · E:Wiry Honey
Myrtle · ♄ e Z9 ⓚ; W-Austr.
- **nesophila** F. Muell. · E:Pink Melaleuca;
G:Bunte Myrtenheide · ♄ ♄ e Z9 ⓚ;
W-Austr.
- **pulchella** R. Br. · E:Claw Honey Myrtle ·
♄ e Z9 ⓚ; W-Austr.
- **radula** Lindl. · E:Graceful Honey Myrtle ·
♄ e Z9 ⓚ IX-X; W-Austr.
- **spathulata** Schauer · E:Pompom Honey
Myrtle · ♄ e Z9 ⓚ; W-Austr.
- **squamea** Labill. · E:Swamp Honey
Myrtle · ♄ e Z9 ⓚ; Austr.: N.S.Wales,
Victoria, Tasman., S-Austr.
- **squarrosa** Sm. · E:Scented Paperbark ·
♄ e Z9 ⓚ; Austr.: N.S.Wales, Victoria,
Tasman., S-Austr.
- **styphelioides** Sm. · E:Prickly Paperbark ·
♄ e Z9 ⓚ V-VII; Austr.: N.S.Wales
- **thymifolia** Sm. · E:Thyme-leaf Honey
Myrtle · ♄ e Z9 ⓚ; Austr.: N.S.Wales,
Victoria
- **viridiflora** Sol. ex Gaertn. · E:Broad
Leaved Tea Tree; G:Grünblütige Myrtenheide · ♄ e Z9 ⓚ ⚥ Ⓝ; Austr.: W-Austr.,
N.Terr., Queensl.; N. Caled.
- **wilsonii** F. Muell. · E:Wilson's Honey
Myrtle · ♄ e Z9 ⓚ; Austr.: Victoria

Melampodium L. -n- *Asteraceae* · 37 spp.
- **paludosum** Kunth · G:Sterntaler · ⅃ ⓚ
VI-IX; S-Am.

Melampyrum L. -n- *Scrophulariaceae* ·
35 spp. · E:Cow Wheat; F:Mélampyre;
G:Wachtelweizen
– **arvense** L. · E:Field Cow Wheat;
G:Acker-Wachtelweizen · ⊙ VI-IX; Eur.*,
Cauc., W-Sib.
– **barbatum** Waldst. & Kit. ex Willd.
– subsp. **barbatum** · G:Bart-Wachtelwei-
zen · ⊙ V-VII; Eur.: A, EC-Eur., Ba, RO
– subsp. **carstiense** Ronniger · G:Karst-
Wachtelweizen · ⊙ VI-VII; Eur.: I, A, Ba
– **cristatum** L. · E:Crested Cow Wheat;
G:Kamm-Wachtelweizen · ⊙ VI-IX; Eur.*,
Cauc., W-Sib., E-Sib., C-As.
– **nemorosum** L. · G:Hain-Wachtelweizen ·
⊙ V-IX; Eur.: Ital-P, C-Eur., EC-Eur., Sc,
Ba, E-Eur.
– **polonicum** (Beauverd) Soó · G:Poln-
ischer Wachtelweizen · ⊙ VI-IX; Eur.: G,
PL, E-Eur.
– **pratense** L. · E:Common Cow Wheat,
Cow Wheat ; G:Gewöhnlicher Wiesen-
Wachtelweizen · ⊙ VI-VIII; Eur.*, W-Sib.,
E-Sib.
– **subalpinum** (Jur.) A. Kern. · G:Schmal-
blättriger Wachtelweizen · ⊙ VI-IX; Eur.:
A, ? CZ
– **sylvaticum** L. · E:Wood Cow Wheat;
G:Wald-Wachtelweizen · ⊙ VI-IX; Eur.*,
Cauc., W-Sib.

Melanorrhoea Wall. = Gluta
– *usitata* Wall. = Gluta usitata

Melanoselinum Hoffm. -n- *Apiaceae* ·
4 spp.
– **decipiens** (Schrad. & H.L. Wendl.)
Hoffm. · ⊙ ♄ Z9 ☖ IV-VI ▽; Azor.,
Madeira, Canar., Cap Verde

Melanthium L. -n- *Melanthiaceae* · 4 spp. ·
E:Bunchflower; G:Büschelgermer
– *hybridum* Walter = Melanthium virginicum
– **latifolium** Desr. · E:Crisped Bunchflower; G:Breitblättriger Büschelgermer ·
♃ Z6 VII-VIII; USA: NE, SE
– **virginicum** L. · E:Virginia Bunchflower;
G:Virginia-Büschelgermer · ♃ Z5 VII-
VIII; USA: NE, NCE, SC, SE, Fla.

Melastoma L. -n- *Melastomataceae* ·
c. 70 spp. · E:Indian Rhododendron;
F:Mélastome; G:Schwarzmund
– **candidum** D. Don · ♄ e Z10 ☖;

Ryukyu-Ins., Taiwan, Phil., SE-Austr.
– **malabathricum** L. · E:Indian Rhododendron; G:Indischer Schwarzmund · ♄ e
Z10 ☖ VII; Thail., Laos, Vietn., Malay.
Pen., N-Austr., Polyn.
– **sanguineum** Sims · G:Blut-Schwarz-
mund · ♄ e Z10 ☖ IX-X; S-China, Malay.
Arch.

Melia L. -f- *Meliaceae* · 3 spp. · E:China
Berry, Pagoda Tree; F:Lilas des Indes;
G:Paternosterbaum, Zederachbaum
– *azadirachta* L. = Azadirachta indica
subsp. indica
– **azedarach** L. · E:Bead Tree, China Berry,
Pride-of-India; G:Indischer Zederachbaum · ♄ d Z10 ☖ VI ⚡ ⚘ Ⓝ; Him.,
Ind., China, nat. in F, Ba, TR, Trop. Am.,
SE-USA
– *japonica* G. Don = Melia azedarach

Melianthus L. -m- *Melianthaceae* · 6 spp. ·
E:Honey Bush; F:Buisson-à-miel,
Mélianthe; G:Honigstrauch
– **comosus** Vahl · G:Schopfiger Honigstrauch · ♄ e Z9 ☖ VII-VIII; S-Afr.
– **major** L. · E:Honey Bush; G:Echter
Honigstrauch · ♄ e Z9 ☖ V-VII; S-Afr.,
nat. in Canar., Ind., Bol.
– **minor** L. · ♄ e Z9 ☖ V-VII; S-Afr.

Melica L. -f- *Poaceae* · 70-80 spp. ·
E:Melick; F:Mélique; G:Perlgras
– **altissima** L. · E:Siberian Melick; G:Hohes
Perlgras · ♃ Z5 VI; Eur.: A, EC-Eur., Ba,
E-Eur.; TR, Iran, nat. in Cauc., W-Sib.,
E-Sib., C-As.,
– **bauhinii** All. · ♃; Eur.: Balear., F, Cors, I,
? W-Ba
– **ciliata** L. · E:Eyelash Pearl Grass;
F:Mélique ciliée; G:Östliches Wimper-
Perlgras · ♃ VI; Eur.* exc. BrI; TR, N-Iraq,
Cauc., Iran, C-As.
– **mutica** Walter · E:Two Flower Melic
Grass; G:Zweiblütiges Perlgras · ♃ V-VI;
USA: NE, NCE, SC, SE, Fla.
– *nebrodensis* Parl. = Melica ciliata
– **nutans** L. · E:Mountain Melick; G:Nick-
endes Perlgras · ♃ Z6 V-VI; Eur.*, Cauc.,
Him., W-Sib., E-Sib., Amur, Sakhal.,
C-As., N-China, Korea, Jap.
– **picta** K. Koch · G:Buntes Perlgras · ♃
V-VI; Eur.: C-Eur., EC-Eur., Ba, E-Eur.,
FIN; TR, Cauc.
– × **thuringiaca** Rauschert (*M. ciliata*

subsp. *ciliata* × *M. transsilvanica*) ·
G:Thüringer Wimper-Perlgras · ⌗ ; D +
– **transsilvanica** Schur · F:Mélique de
Transsylvanie; G:Siebenbürger Wimper-
Perlgras · ⌗ Z6 VI; Eur.: Fr, C-Eur.,
EC-Eur., Ba, E-Eur., Ital-P; Cauc., W-Sib.,
E-Sib., C-As.
– **uniflora** Retz. · E:Wood Melick;
F:Mélique uniflore; G:Einblütiges
Perlgras · ⌗ Z7 V-VI; Eur.*, TR, Cauc.,
N-Iran, NW-Afr.

Melicoccus P. Browne -m- *Sapindaceae* ·
2 spp. · E:Honey Berry; F:Kénépier;
G:Honigbeere
– **bijugatus** Jacq. · E:Honey Berry, Spanish
Lime; G:Honigbeere · ♄ Z10 ⓐ Ⓝ; trop.
Am.

Melicope J.R. Forst. & G. Forst. -f-
Rutaceae · 150 spp.
– **ternata** J.R. Forst. & G. Forst. · ♄ e Z8 ⓐ
VI; NZ

Melicytus J.R. Forst. & G. Forst. -m-
Violaceae · 5 (-9) spp.
– **ramiflorus** J.R. Forst. & G. Forst. ·
E:Whitey Wood · ♄ e ⊛ Z9 ⓐ; NZ

Melilotus Mill. -m- *Fabaceae* · 20 spp. ·
E:Melilot, Sweet Clover; F:Mélilot;
G:Steinklee
– **albus** Medik. · E:White Sweet Clo-
ver; G:Weißer Steinklee · ⊙ VI-IX Ⓝ;
Eur.* exc. BrI, nat. in BrI
– **altissimus** Thuill. · E:Tall Melilot;
G:Hoher Steinklee · ⊙ VII-IX Ⓝ; Eur.*
exc. BrI; W-Sib. (Altai), nat. in BrI
– **dentatus** (Waldst. & Kit.) Pers. ·
G:Gezähnter Steinklee, Salz-Steinklee ·
⊙ VII-IX; Eur.: C-Eur., EC-Eur., W-Ba, Sc,
E-Eur.; Cauc., W-Sib., E-Sib., C-As.
– **indicus** (L.) All. · E:Indian Sweet Clover;
G:Kleinblütiger Steinklee · ⊙ VI-VII; Eur.:
Ib, Fr, Ital-P, Ba; TR, Levant, Cauc., Ind,
C-As., Canar., N-Afr., nat. in Eur.: BrI,
C-Eur., EC-Eur.; N-Am., Trop.
– **officinalis** (L.) Lam. · E:Sweet Clover,
Yellow Melilot; G:Echter Steinklee,
Gelber Steinklee · ⊙ VI-IX ⚥ Ⓝ; Eur.*
exc. BrI, Sc; TR, Cauc., Iran, W-Sib.,
E-Sib., C-As., Tibet, Him., nat. in N-Am.
– **sulcatus** Desf. · E:Grooved Melilot;
G:Gefurchter Honigklee · ⊙ VI-VIII; Eur.:
Ib, Fr, Ital-P, Ba; TR, Levant, N-Afr.

Melinis P. Beauv. -f- *Poaceae* · 22 spp.
– **repens** (Willd.) Zizka · E:Natal Grass,
Ruby Grass; G:Natal-Gras · ⊙ ⌗ ⋉ Z8
VII-VIII Ⓝ; trop. Afr., S-Afr., nat. in USA:
Fla.., Tex.., Ariz.

Meliosma Blume -f- *Sabiaceae* · c. 50 spp.
– *cuneifolia* Franch. = Meliosma dilleniifolia subsp. cuneifolia
– **dilleniifolia** (Wight & Arn.) Walp.
– subsp. **cuneifolia** (Franch.) Beusekom ·
♄ ♄ d Z7; W-China
– subsp. **tenuis** (Maxim.) Beusekom · ♄ d
Z9 ⓐ VII-VIII; Jap.
– **pinnata** (Roxb.) Maxim. · ♄ d Z9 ⓐ;
Korea, China
– *tenuis* Maxim. = Meliosma dilleniifolia
subsp. tenuis

Melissa L. -f- *Lamiaceae* · 4 spp. · E:Balm;
F:Citronnelle, Mélisse; G:Melisse
– **officinalis** L. · E:Bee Balm, Lemon Balm;
G:Zitronen-Melisse · ⌗ D Z4 VI-VIII ⚥ Ⓝ;
Eur.: Ib, Fr, Ital-P, Ba, RO; TR, Levant,
Cauc., N-Iraq, N-Iran, Moroc., Tun., nat.
in BrI, Sc, C-Eur., EC-Eur.

Melittis L. -f- *Lamiaceae* · 1 sp. · E:Bastard
Balm; F:Mélitte; G:Immenblatt
– **melissophyllum** L. · ⌗ Z6 V-VI ⚥ ▽;
Eur.* exc. Sc

Melocactus Link & Otto -m- *Cactaceae* ·
31 sp. · E:Turk's Cap Cactus; F:Cactus-
melon; G:Melonenkaktus
– *amoenus* Hoffmanns. = Melocactus
intortus
– **azureus** Buining & Brederoo · ⚘ Z10 ⓐ
▽ ✳; E-Braz.: Bahia
– *caesius* H.L. Wendl. = Melocactus
curvispinus subsp. caesius
– *communis* (Aiton) Link & Otto =
Melocactus intortus
– **curvispinus** Pfeiff.
– subsp. **caesius** (H.L. Wendl.) N.P.
Taylor · ⚘ Z10 ⓐ ▽ ✳; Trinidad
– subsp. **curvispinus** · ⚘ Z10 ⓐ ▽ ✳; Mex.,
Guat.
– *delessertianus* Lem. ex Labour. = Melocactus curvispinus subsp. curvispinus
– *depressus* Hook. = Melocactus violaceus
– **glaucescens** Buining & Brederoo · ⚘ Z10
ⓐ ▽ ✳; E-Braz.: Bahia
– *guitartii* León = Melocactus curvispinus
subsp. curvispinus

– **intortus** (Mill.) Urb. · E:Turk's Cap · ♛
Z10 ⍟ ▽ ✳; W.Ind.
– *jansenianus* Backeb. = Melocactus
peruvianus
– *loboguerreroi* Cárdenas = Melocactus
curvispinus subsp. curvispinus
– *maxonii* (Rose) Gürke = Melocactus
curvispinus subsp. curvispinus
– *melocactoides* (Hoffmanns.) DC. =
Melocactus violaceus
– *oaxacensis* (Britton & Rose) Backeb. =
Melocactus curvispinus subsp. curvispinus
– **oreas** Miq. · ♛ Z10 ⍟ ▽ ✳; E-Braz.
– **peruvianus** Vaupel · ♛ Z10 ⍟ ▽ ✳;
S-Ecuad., Peru
– **violaceus** Pfeiff. · ♛ Z10 ⍟ ▽ ✳; E-Braz.

Melocanna Trin. -f- *Poaceae* · 2 spp.
– **baccifera** (Roxb.) Kurz · ♄ ⍟ Ⓝ; Ind.,
Burma

Melothria L. -f- *Cucurbitaceae* · 10 spp. ·
E:Moccasin Grass; G:Haarblume
– *indica* (L.) Lour. = Zehneria indica
– *japonica* (Thunb.) Maxim. ex Cogn. =
Zehneria indica
– *maderaspatana* (L.) Cogn. = Mukia
maderaspatana
– **pendula** L. · E:Guadeloupe Cucumber,
Moccasin Grass; G:Haarblume · ⅄ ⚭ Z10
Ⓐ; USA: NE, NCE, SC, SE, Fla.; Mex.
– *punctata* (Thunb.) Cogn. = Zehneria
scabra
– *scabra* (L. f.) Naudin = Zehneria scabra

Mendoncella A.D. Hawkes = Galeottia
– *fimbriata* (Linden & Rchb. f.) Garay =
Galeottia fimbriata

Menispermum L. -n- *Menispermaceae* ·
2 spp. · E:Moonseed; G:Mondsame
– **canadense** L. · E:Moonseed, Yellow Sarsaparilla; G:Amerikanischer Mondsame ·
♄ d ⚥ Z5 VI-VII; Can.: E; USA: NE, NCE,
NC, SE, Fla., SC
– **dauricum** DC. · G:Dahurischer
Mondsame · ♄ d ⚥ Z5 VI-VII; Jap., Korea,
Manch., N-China, E-Sib.

Mentha L. -f- *Lamiaceae* · 23 spp. · E:Mints;
F:Menthe; G:Minze
– **aquatica** L. · E:Horsemint, Water Mint;
F:Menthe aquatique; G:Wasser-Minze · ⅄
⌢ D Z6 VII-X ⚥ Ⓝ; Eur.*, TR, Levant,

Cauc., Iran, NW-Afr., Libya
– **arvensis** L. · G:Acker-Minze · ⅄
– var. **arvensis** · E:Corn Mint, Wild Mint;
G:Gewöhnliche Acker-Minze · ⅄ D Z4
VI-X ⚥; Eur.*, TR, Cauc., W-Sib., E-Sib.,
Amur, Sakhal., Kamchat., C-As., Him.,
China, Alaska, Can., USA*, nat. in Java,
Phil., NZ
– var. **piperascens** Malinv. ex Holmes ·
G:Japanische Minze · ⅄ D Z4 VI-VIII ⚥
Ⓝ; W-Sib., E-Sib., Amur, N-China, Korea,
Jap.
– × **carinthiaca** Host (*M. arvensis* × *M.
suaveolens*) · G:Kärntner Minze · ⅄; Eur.:
G, A, Slove., Croatia, F, I (Alsace) +
– × *citrata* Ehrh. = Mentha × piperita
– × **dalmatica** Tausch (*M. arvensis* × *M.
longifolia*) · G:Dalmatiner Minze · ⅄;
Eur.: G, CZ, H, I, Slove., Croatia +
– × **dumetorum** Schult. (*M. aquatica* × *M.
longifolia*) · G:Gebüsch-Minze · ⅄ VII-IX;
G, F, I +
– × *gentilis* L. = Mentha × gracilis
– × **gracilis** Sole (*M. arvensis* × *M. spicata*
subsp. *spicata*) · E:Ginger Mint; G:Edel-
Minze; · ⅄ D Z6 Ⓝ; cult. Eur.
– **longifolia** (L.) L. · E:Biblical Mint, Horse
Mint; G:Ross-Minze · ⅄ D Z6 VII-IX ⚥
Ⓝ; Eur.* exc. Sc; TR, Levant, Cauc., Iraq,
Iran, NW-Afr.
– × **maximilianea** F.W. Schultz (*M.
aquatica* × *M. suaveolens*) · ⅄; C-Eur., BrI,
I +
– × *muelleriana* Sch. Bip. = Mentha ×
carinthiaca
– × *niliaca* Juss. ex Jacq. = Mentha ×
rotundifolia
– × **piperita** L. (*M. aquatica* × *M. spicata*
subsp. *spicata*) · E:Peppermint; F:Menthe
poivrée; G:Pfeffer-Minze, Pfefferminze ·
⅄ Z3 VI-VII ⚥; ? BrI; cult. nat. in Eur.*
– **some cultivars**
– *nothovar. citrata* (Ehrh.) B. Boivin =
Mentha × piperita
– **pulegium** L. · E:Pennyroyal; G:Polei-
Minze · ⅄ D Z7 VII-IX ⚥ ⚘ Ⓝ; Eur.*, TR,
Levant, Iran, N-Afr.
– **requienii** Benth. · E:Corsican Mint;
G:Korsische Minze · ⅄ ⤳ D Z7 Ⓐ ∧
VI-IX; Eur.: Cors, Sard., Montecristo, nat.
in BrI, P
– × **rotundifolia** (L.) Huds. (*M. longifolia* ×
M. suaveolens) · G:Apfel-Minze · ⅄ VI-IX;
Eur.: BrI, NL, G, Canar.; TR, NW-Afr.,
Macaron., nat. in W-Sib., C-As., N-Am.,

C-Am.
- × **smithiana** R.A. Graham (*M. aquatica ×
M. arvensis × M. spicata* subsp. *spicata*) ·
G:Rote Minze · ⊇4 Z6 ⚥ ; Eur.: Sc, C-Eur.,
I +, nat. in BrI, Fr, Ital-P, EC-Eur., RO
- **spicata** L. · G:Ährige Minze, Grüne
Minze
- **some cultivars**
- subsp. **spicata** · E:Spearmint; G:Gewöhn-
liche Grüne Minze · ⊇4 D Z3 VII-IX ⚥ Ⓝ;
orig. ?
- **suaveolens** Ehrh. · E:Apple Mint,
Pineapple Mint; G:Rundblättrige Minze ·
⊇4 Z6 VII-IX Ⓝ; Eur.: Ib, Fr, Ital-P, Ba, BrI;
TR, NW-Afr., nat. in Sc, C-Eur., EC-Eur.,
E-Eur.
- × *suavis* Guss. = Mentha × maximilianea
- *sylvestris* L. = Mentha longifolia
- × **verticillata** L. (*M. aquatica × M.
arvensis*) · G:Quirl-Minze · ⊇4 VII-VIII;
Eur.*
- × **villosa** Huds. (*M. spicata* subsp. *spicata
× M. suaveolens*) · G:Hain-Minze · ⊇4 Z5;
cult., nat. in W-Eur.
- × **villosonervata** Opiz (*M. longifolia ×
M. spicata* subsp. *spicata*) · G:Bastard-
Grünminze · ⊇4 ; D +, nat. in BrI
- *viridis* (L.) L. = Mentha spicata subsp.
spicata

Mentzelia L. -f- *Loasaceae* · 60 spp. ·
E:Blazing Star
- *aurea* (Lindl.) Baill. non Nutt. = Mentzelia lindleyi
- **decapetala** (Pursh) Urb. & Gilg ·
E:Gumbo Lily, Ten-petal Blazing Star · ☉
⊇4 � VIII-X; Can.: W; USA: Rocky Mts.,
NC, SC, Iowa
- **lindleyi** Torr. & A. Gray · E:Lindley's
Blazing Star · ☉ VII-VIII; Calif.

Menyanthes L. -f- *Menyanthaceae* · 1 sp. ·
E:Bogbean, Marsh Trefoil; F:Trèfle d'eau;
G:Bitterklee, Fieberklee
- **trifoliata** L. · E:Bogbean, Water Trefoil;
F:Trèfle d'eau; G:Bitterklee, Fieberklee
· ⊇4 ⌇ ≈ Z3 V-VI ⚥ ▽; Eur.*, TR,
Cauc., W-Sib., E-Sib., Amur, Sakhal.,
Kamchat., C-As., Mong., Manch., Jap.,
Moroc., Alaska, Can., USA: NE, NCE;
Greenl.

Menziesia Sm. -f- *Ericaceae* · 7 spp. ·
E:Menziesia; F:Menziesia; G:Menziesie
- **ciliicalyx** (Miq.) Maxim. · G:Bewimperte

Menziesie
- var. **ciliicalyx** · ♄ d Z6 V-VI; Jap.
- var. **purpurea** (Maxim.) Makino · ♄ d Z6
V-VI; Jap.
- **ferruginea** Sm. · E:False Azalea, Fool's
Huckleberry; G:Rostige Menziesie · ♄ d
Z6 VI; Alaska, B.C., USA: NW
- **pilosa** (Michx.) Juss. · E:Minniebush;
G:Borstige Menziesie · ♄ d Z6 V-VI; USA:
NE, SE
- **purpurea** Maxim. · G:Purpur-Menziesie ·
♄ d Z6 V-VI; Jap.

Mercurialis L. -f- *Euphorbiaceae* · 8 spp. ·
E:Mercury; F:Mercuriale; G:Bingelkraut
- **annua** L. · E:Annual Mercury, French
Mercury; G:Einjähriges Bingelkraut ·
☉ IV-X ⚥ ⚘; Eur.*, TR, Levant, Cauc.,
Canar., Azor., N-Afr.
- **ovata** Sternb. ex Hoppe · G:Eiblättriges
Bingelkraut · ⊇4 IV-V ⚘; Eur.: I, C-Eur.,
EC-Eur., Ba, E-Eur.; TR, Levant, Cauc.
- × **paxii** Graebn. (*M. ovata × M. perennis*) ·
⊇4 IV-V ⚘; G, I +
- **perennis** L. · E:Dog's Mercury;
F:Mercuriale pérenne; G:Ausdauerndes
Bingelkraut, Wald-Bingelkraut · ⊇4 IV-V
⚘; Eur.*, Cauc.

Merremia Dennst. ex Endl. -f-
Convolvulaceae · 70-80 spp.
- **dissecta** (Jacq.) Hallier f. · E:Alamo
Vine · ⊇4 ⚥ Z9 ⌂ VII-X; USA: SE, Fla.,
Tex.; S-Am.
- *macrocarpa* (L.) Roberty = Operculina
macrocarpa
- **sibirica** (L.) Hallier f. · ☉ ⚥ Z9 VII-IX;
E-Sib., Amur, Mong., Manch., N-China
- **tuberosa** (L.) Rendle · E:Wooden Rose,
Yellow Morning Glory · ⊇4 Z9 ⌂ Ⓝ;
W.Ind., Braz., trop. Afr., Ind.
- *turpethum* (L.) Rendle = Operculina
turpethum

Mertensia Roth -f- *Boraginaceae* ·
45-50 spp. · E:Bluebell, Oysterplant;
F:Mertensia; G:Blauglöckchen
- **ciliata** (James ex Torr.) G. Don ·
E:Chiming Bells, Mountain Bluebell;
G:Berg-Blauglöckchen · ⊇4 Z4 V-VII; Can.:
W; USA: NW, Calif., Rocky Mts., SW
- **echioides** Benth. ex C.B. Clarke · ⊇4 △ Z6
V-VI; Tibet, W-Him.
- **elongata** Benth. ex C.B. Clarke · ⊇4 △ Z6
V-VI; Kashmir

- **lanceolata** (Pursh) DC. ex A.
DC. · E:Prairie Bluebells; G:Prärie-
Blauglöckchen · ♃ △ Z4 IV-V; Can.: W;
USA: Rocky Mts., NC
- **maritima** (L.) Gray · E:Oyster Plant;
G:Austernpflanze, Mertensie · ♃ Z5; Jap.,
Korea
- **paniculata** (Aiton) G. Don · E:Tall Blue-
bells; F:Mertensia paniculé; G:Rispiges
Blauglöckchen · ♃ Z4 V-VI; Alaska, Can.;
USA: Wash., Idaho, Mont., NC, NCE
- **primuloides** C.B. Clarke · ♃ ⤳ △ Z5
V-VI; Him.
- **pterocarpa** (Turcz.) Tatew. & Ohwi · ♃
△ Z3 V-VIII; Jap
- *pulmonarioides* Roth = Mertensia
virginica
- **sibirica** (L.) G. Don · ♃ Z3 V-VI; E-Sib.
- **tibetica** C.B. Clarke · ♃ ⤳ ⊡ V-VI;
Tibet
- **virginica** (L.) Pers. ex Link ·
E:Virginia Bluebells, Virginia Cowslip;
F:Mertensia de Virginie; G:Virginisches
Blauglöckchen · ♃ △ Z3 IV-V; Ont., USA:
NE, NCE, Kans., SE

Meryta J.R. Forst. & G. Forst. -f-
Araliaceae · 27 spp.
- **denhamii** Seem. · ♄ e Z10 ⊕; N.Caled.

Mesembryanthemum L. -n- *Aizoaceae* ·
30 spp. · F:Ficoide; G:Eiskraut
- *acinaciforme* L. = Carpobrotus acinaciformis
- *cordifolium* L. f. = Aptenia cordifolia
- *criniflorum* L. f. = Dorotheanthus bellidiformis
- **crystallinum** L. · E:Ice Plant; G:Eiskraut ·
⊙ � Z9 ⊡ VIII-IX ⚘ ⦾; Eur.: Ib, F, Ital-P,
Ba; Palest., Sinai, NW-Afr., Libya, S-Afr.,
Namibia, nat. in Calif., Austr.
- *echinatum* Lam. = Delosperma echinatum
- *edule* L. = Carpobrotus edulis
- *muirii* L. Bolus = Carpobrotus muirii
- *pomeridianum* L. = Carpanthea pomeridiana
- *pruinosum* Thunb. = Delosperma
echinatum
- *velutinum* Dinter = Astridia velutina

Mesospinidium Rchb. f. -n- *Orchidaceae* ·
7 spp.
- **peruvianum** Garay Z10; Ecuad., Peru
- *roseum* (Lindl.) Rchb. f. = Cochlioda
rosea

- *sanguineum* Rchb. f. = Odontoglossum
sanguineum

Mespilus L. -f- *Rosaceae* · 1 sp. · E:Medlar;
F:Néflier; G:Mispel
- *arbutifolia* L. = Aronia arbutifolia var.
arbutifolia
- var. *melanocarpa* Michx. = Aronia
melanocarpa var. melanocarpa
- **germanica** L. · E:Medlar; F:Néflier
commun; G:Echte Mispel · ♄ ♄ d Z5 V-VI
⚥ ⦾; Eur.: Ital-P, Ba, Crim; TR, Cauc.,
N-Iran, C-As., nat. in BrI, Fr, Ital-P,
C-Eur., EC-Eur.
- *prunifolia* Marshall = Aronia × prunifolia
- *prunifolia* Poir. = Crataegus × persimilis

Mesua L. -f- *Clusiaceae* · 40-48 spp.
- **ferrea** L. · E:Gau-gau, Ironwood; G:Gau-
gauholz · ♄ e Z10 ⊛ ⦾; Ind., Andaman I.,
Thail., Malay. Arch.

Metapanax J. Wen & Frodin -m-
Araliaceae · 2 spp.
- **davidii** (Franch.) J. Wen & Frodin · ♄ e
Z8 ⊡ VII-VIII; W-China, C-China

Metaplexis R. Br. -f- *Asclepiadaceae* · 6 spp.
- **japonica** Makino · ♃ Z7; Jap., Korea,
Manch., China

Metasequoia Hu & W.C. Cheng
-f- *Taxodiaceae* · 1 sp. · E:Redwood;
F:Métaséquoia; G:Urweltmammutbaum
- **glyptostroboides** Hu & W.C. Cheng ·
E:Dawn Redwood; F:Métaséquoia;
G:Urweltmammutbaum · ♄ d Z6 V ⦾;
China: Sichuan, Hupeh

Metrosideros Banks ex Gaertn. -f-
Myrtaceae · 50 spp. · E:Rata, Rata Vine;
F:Bois-de-fer; G:Eisenholz
- **angustifolia** (L.) Sm. · ♄ ♄ e Z9 ⊡;
S-Afr.
- *citrina* Curtis = Callistemon citrinus
- **diffusa** (G. Forst.) Sm. · E:Small Rata
Vine; G:Kurzes Lianen-Eisenholz · ♄ e ⚵
⤳ Z9 ⊡ IV-V; NZ
- **excelsa** Sol. ex Gaertn. · E:New Zealand
Christmas Tree, Pohutukawa; G:Pohutu-
kawa-Eisenholz · ♄ ♄ e Z9 ⊡ II-III; NZ
- *florida* (G. Forst.) Sm. = Metrosideros
fulgens
- **fulgens** Sol. ex Gaertn. · E:Rata Vine;
G:Lianen-Eisenholz · ♄ e ⚵ Z9 ⊡ VIII; NZ

– *hypericifolia* A. Cunn. = Metrosideros diffusa
– **kermadecensis** W.R.B. Oliv. · ♄ e Z9 ⊛ VI-VIII; NZ
– *lanceolata* Sm. = Callistemon citrinus
– **perforata** (J.R. Forst. & G. Forst.) A. Rich. · ♄ e ⚡ Z9 ⊛ IV-V; NZ
– **robusta** A. Cunn. · E:North Island Rata, Rata; G:Nordinsel-Eisenholz · ♄ e Z9 ⊛ III-IV; NZ
– *saligna* Sm. = Callistemon salignus
– *scandens* (J.R. Forst. & G. Forst.) Druce = Metrosideros fulgens
– *scandens* Sol. ex Gaertn. = Metrosideros perforata
– *semperflorens* Lodd. = Callistemon citrinus
– *speciosa* Sims = Callistemon glaucus
– *tomentosa* A. Rich. = Metrosideros excelsa
– **umbellata** Cav. · E:Southern Rata; G:Südinsel-Eisenholz · ♄ ♄ e Z9 ⊛ II-III; NZ

Metroxylon Rottb. -n- *Arecaceae* · 7 spp. · E:Sago Palm; F:Sagoutier; G:Sagopalme
– *rumphii* (Willd.) Mart. = Metroxylon sagu
– **sagu** Rottb. · E:Sago, Sago Palm; G:Sagopalme · ♄ e Z10 ⊛ Ⓝ; Malay. Arch., N.Guinea

Meum Mill. -n- *Apiaceae* · 3 spp. · E:Spignel; F:Baudremoine, Méum; G:Bärwurz
– **athamanticum** Jacq. · E:Baldmoney, Bearwort, Spignel; F:Fenouil des Alpes; G:Gewöhnliche Bärwurz · ⌗ △ D Z7 V-VIII ⚥; Eur.* exc. Sc, EC-Eur.; mts.
– *mutellina* (L.) Gaertn. = Ligusticum mutellina

Meyenia Nees -f- *Acanthaceae* · 1 sp.
– **erecta** Benth. · ♄ ⊛ I-XII; W-Afr.

Meyerophytum Schwantes -n- *Aizoaceae* · 2 spp.
– **globosum** (L. Bolus) Ihlenf. · ⌗ ⚘ Z9 ⊛; Cape

Mibora Adans. -f- *Poaceae* · 2 spp. · E:Sand Grass; F:Mibora; G:Zwerggras
– **minima** (L.) Desv. · E:Sand Bent, Sand Grass; G:Sand-Zwerggras · ⊙ Z7 III-V; Eur.: BrI, Fr, G, Ib, Ba; Alger., nat. in NL, USA, Austr.

Michauxia L'Hér. -f- *Campanulaceae* · 7 spp. · F:Michauxia; G:Michauxie, Türkenglocke
– **campanuloides** L'Hér. · ⊙ Z7 ∧ VII-IX; TR
– **laevigata** Vent. · ⊙ △ Z7 ∧ VII-VIII; N-Iran
– **tchihatchewii** Fisch. & Heldr. · ⊙ Z7 ∧ VII-VIII; S-TR

Michelia L. -f- *Magnoliaceae* · 49 spp.
– *acris* Ruiz & Pav. = Drimys winteri
– *amoena* Q.F. Zheng & M.M. Lin = Michelia figo
– *arfakiana* A. Agostini = Elmerrillia tsiampacca
– *aurantiaca* Wall. = Michelia champaca var. champaca
– *blumei* Steud. = Michelia champaca var. champaca
– *brevipes* Y.K. Li & X.M. Wang = Michelia figo
– *celebica* Koord. = Elmerrillia tsiampacca
– **champaca** L.
– var. *blumei* Moritzi = Michelia champaca var. champaca
– var. **champaca** · E:Champac; G:Champaka · ♄ e Z9 ⊛ Ⓝ; Ind., Java
– *champava* Lour. ex B.A. Gomes = Michelia champaca var. champaca
– *chartacea* B.L. Chen & S.C. Yang = Michelia champaca var. champaca
– *euonymoides* Burm. f. = Michelia champaca var. champaca
– *fascicata* (Andrews) Vent. = Michelia figo
– **figo** (Lour.) Spreng. · E:Banana Shrub · ♄ e D Z8 ⊛ IV-VI; SE-China
– *forbesii* Baker f. = Elmerrillia tsiampacca
– *fuscata* (Andrews) Blume = Michelia figo
– *gracilis* Kostel. = Magnolia kobus
– *parviflora* Deless. = Michelia figo
– *parvifolia* (DC.) B.D. Jacks. = Michelia figo
– *rheedei* Wight = Michelia champaca var. champaca
– *rufinervis* DC. = Michelia champaca var. champaca
– *sericea* Pers. = Michelia champaca var. champaca
– *skinneriana* Dunn = Michelia figo
– *suaveolens* Pers. = Michelia champaca var. champaca
– *tsiampacca* L. = Elmerrillia tsiampacca
– var. *blumei* Moritzi = Michelia champaca var. champaca

– *yulan* (Desf.) Kostel. = Magnolia
denudata

Miconia Ruiz & Pav. -f- *Melastomataceae* ·
c. 1000 spp.
– **calvescens** DC. · ♄ e ⓦ; Mex.
– **hookeriana** Triana · ♄ e ⓦ; Ecuad., Peru

Micranthemum Michx. -n-
Scrophulariaceae · 4 spp. · E:Mudflower
– *orbiculatum* Michx. = Micranthemum
umbrosum
– **umbrosum** (J.F. Gmel.) S.F. Blake ·
E:Shade Mudflower · ⧄ ⁓ ≈ Z9 ⓦ;
USA: Tex., SE, Fla. Va.; Mex., C-Am.,
W-Ind., S-Am.

Micranthocereus Backeb. -m- *Cactaceae* ·
9 spp.
– *lehmannianus* (Werderm.) F. Ritter =
Austrocephalocereus lehmannianus
– **polyanthus** (Werderm.) Backeb. · ♄ ψ Z9
ⓚ ▽ ✳; E-Braz.: Bahia
– *purpureus* (Gürke) F. Ritter = Austrocephalocereus purpureus

Microbiota Kom. -f- *Cupressaceae* · 1 sp. ·
F:Thuya nain; G:Zwerglebensbaum
– **decussata** Kom. · G:Zwerglebensbaum ·
♄ e ⤳ △ Z3; E-Sib. (Prov. Primorskaja)

Microcachrys Hook. f. -f- *Podocarpaceae* ·
1 sp. · G:Maulbeereibe
– **tetragona** (Hook.) Hook. f. ·
G:Maulbeereibe · ♄ e Z8 ⓚ; W-Tasman.

Microcitrus Swingle -f- *Rutaceae* · 4 spp. ·
E:Finger Lime; G:Fingerlimette
– **australasica** (F. Muell.) Swingle ·
E:Australian Finger Lime, Native Finger
Lime; G:Australische Fingerlimette · ♄ e
Z10 ⓚ; Austr.: Queensl., N.S.Wales
– **australis** (Planch.) Swingle ·
E:Australian Round Lime; G:Australische
Limette, Runde Fingerlimette · ♄ e Z10
ⓚ; NE-Austr.

Microcoelum Burret & Potztal = Lytocaryum
– *martianum* (Glaz. ex Drude) Burret &
Potztal = Lytocaryum weddellianum
– *weddellianum* (H. Wendl.) H.E. Moore =
Lytocaryum weddellianum

Microcycas (Miq.) A. DC. -f- *Zamiaceae* ·
1 sp. · E:Palma Corcho; F:Petit cycas;

G:Zwergpalmfarn
– **calocoma** (Miq.) A. DC. · E:Palma
Corcho; G:Zwergpalmfarn · ♄ e Z10 ⓦ ▽
✳; W-Cuba

Microglossa DC. -f- *Asteraceae* · 10 spp. ·
F:Aster blanchâtre; G:Rutenaster
– **afzelii** O. Hoffm. · ♄ ⚥; trop-Afr.
– *albescens* (DC.) C.B. Clarke = Aster
albescens

Microgramma C. Presl -f- *Polypodiaceae* ·
21 sp.
– **vacciniifolia** (Langsd. & Fisch.) Copel. ·
⧄ ⚥ Z10 ⓦ; trop. Am.

Microlepia C. Presl -f- *Dennstaedtiaceae* ·
101 sp.
– **hirta** (Kaulf.) C. Presl · ⧄ Z10 ⓦ; Ind.,
SE-As., Polyn.
– **platyphylla** (D. Don) J. Sm. · ⧄ Z10 ⓦ;
Ind., Sri Lanka
– **speluncae** (L.) T. Moore · E:Limp Leaf
Fern · ⧄ Z10 ⓦ; trop. Afr., S-Afr.

Micromeria Benth. -f- *Lamiaceae* · 90 spp. ·
F:Micromérie; G:Felsenlippe
– **croatica** (Pers.) Schott · G:Kroatische
Felsenlippe · ♄ △ Z7 VI-VII; Eur.: Croatia,
Bosn., YU
– **douglasii** Benth. · E:Yerba Buena
– **thymifolia** (Scop.) Fritsch · G:Thymian-
blättrige Felsenlippe; E:Mountain Mint ·
⧄ ♄ △ Z6 VII-X; Eur.: N-I, H, Croatia,
Bosn., YU, AL

Micropus L. -m- *Asteraceae* · 1 sp. ·
G:Falzblume
– **erectus** L. · G:Falzblume · ☉ VI-VII; Eur.:
Ib, F, Ital-P, Sw, A, EC-Eur., Ba, E-Eur.;
TR, Cauc., Iran, NW-Afr.

Micropyrum (Gaudin) Link -n- *Poaceae* ·
3 spp. · F:Fétuque du gravier; G:Dünn-
schwingel
– **tenellum** (L.) Link · E:Gravel Fescue;
G:Kies-Dünnschwingel, Kies-
Dünnschwanz, Trauben-Schwingel · ☉
V-VII; Eur.: Ib, Fr, Ital-P, C-Eur., Ba; TR,
Moroc., Alger, Madeira

Miconia Link -n- *Polypodiaceae* · 95 spp.
– **musifolium** (Blume) Copel. · ⧄ Z10 ⓦ;
Malay. Arch., N.Guinea
– **pteropus** (Blume) Copel. · G:Javafarn;

E:Java Fern · ⊔ ≈ Z10 ⓦ; Ind., Sri
Lanka, Java
- **punctatum** (L.) Copel. · ⊔ Z10 ⓦ;
Austr., Pacific Is.
- **scandens** (G. Forst.) Tindale · ⊔ Z10 ⓦ;
Austr., NZ

Microstrobos J. Garden & L.A.S. Johnson
-m- *Podocarpaceae* · 2 spp. · E:Dwarf Pine;
G:Zwergstrobe
- **fitzgeraldii** (F. Muell.) J. Garden &
L.A.S. Johnson · E:Blue Mountain Pine;
G:Australische Zwergstrobe · ♄ e Z8 ⓚ;
Austr.: N.S.Wales

Microstylis (Nutt.) Eaton = Malaxis
- *discolor* Lindl. = Malaxis discolor
- *metallica* Rchb. f. = Malaxis metallica
- *monophyllos* (L.) Lindl. = Malaxis
monophyllos

Mikania Willd. -f- *Asteraceae* · c. 400 spp.
- *apiifolia* DC. = Mikania ternata
- **scandens** (L.) Willd. · E:Climbing
Hempvine, Louse Plaster · ⊔ ⚥ ⤳ Z4
VII-VIII ⓝ; Can.: Ont.; USA: NE, NCE,
SE, Fla., SC; trop. Am.
- **ternata** (Vell.) B.L. Rob. · ⊔ ⚥ ⚥ Z10 ⓦ;
W-Braz.

Mila Britton & Rose -f- *Cactaceae* · 1 sp.
- **caespitosa** Britton & Rose · ♅ Z9 ⓚ ▽
✳; Peru
- *cereoides* Rauh & Backeb. = Mila
caespitosa
- *fortalezensis* Rauh & Backeb. = Mila
caespitosa
- *nealeana* Backeb. = Mila caespitosa

Milicia Sim -f- *Moraceae* · 2 spp.
- **excelsa** (Welw.) C.C. Berg · E:African
Teak, Iroko; G:Afrikanisches Teakholz · ♄
Z10 ⓦ ⓝ; trop. Afr.

Milium L. -n- *Poaceae* · 4-7 spp. · E:Millet;
F:Millet; G:Flattergras
- **effusum** L. · E:Bowles' Golden Grass,
Wood Millet; G:Wald-Flattergras, Wal-
dhirse · ⊔ ⤳ Z6 V-VII; Eur.*, NW-TR,
Cyprus, Cauc., N-Iran, Afgh., Ind. (Him.)
W-Sib., E-Sib., Amur, Sakhal., Kamchat.,
C-As., Afgh., Pakist., China, Manch.,
Korea, Jap., Taiwan, Can.: E; USA: NE,
NCE, NC, nat. in NZ
- **vernale** M. Bieb. · E:Early Millet;

G:Raues Flattergras · ☉ Z5; Eur.: Ib,
Fr, Ital-P, Ba, RO, W-Russ., Crim; TR,
Cyprus, Syr., Iraq, Cauc., Iran, C-As.,
N-Afr.

Milla Cav. -f- *Alliaceae* · 10 spp. · F:Etoile du
Mexique, Milla; G:Mexikostern
- **biflora** Cav. · E:Mexican Star; G:Zwei-
blütiger Mexikostern · ⊔ ⚥ ⓚ VII-VIII;
Mex., Guat.
- *uniflora* Graham = Ipheion uniflorum

Miltonia Lindl. -f- *Orchidaceae* · 11 sp. ·
E:Pansy Orchid; F:Miltonia; G:Miltonie
- *anceps* (Klotzsch) Lindl. = Miltonia flava
- **candida** Lindl. · ⊔ Z10 ⓦ VIII-XI ▽ ✳;
Braz.
- **clowesii** (Lindl.) Lindl. · ⊔ Z10 ⓦ IX-X
▽ ✳; Braz.
- **cuneata** Lindl. · ⊔ Z10 ⓦ II-III ▽ ✳;
Braz.
- **flava** Lindl. · ⊔ Z10 ⓦ IV-V ▽ ✳; Braz.
- **flavescens** (Lindl.) Lindl. · ⊔ Z10 ⓦ VI-X
▽ ✳; Braz.
- **phymatochila** (Lindl.) M.W. Chase &
N.H. Williams · ⊔ Z10 ⓦ IV-VI ▽ ✳;
Mex., Guat., Braz.
- **regnellii** Rchb. f. · ⊔ Z10 ⓦ VII-IX ▽ ✳;
E-Braz.
- *roezlii* (Rchb. f.) G. Nicholson = Miltoniopsis roezlii
- *schroederiana* O'Brien = Miltonioides
schroederiana
- **spectabilis** Lindl. · ⊔ Z10 ⓦ VIII ▽ ✳;
Braz.
- *vexillaria* (Rchb. f.) G. Nicholson =
Miltoniopsis vexillaria
- *warszewiczii* Rchb. f. = Oncidium
fuscatum
- **Cultivars:**
- **many cultivars**

× **Miltonidium** hort. -n- *Orchidaceae*
(*Miltonia* × *Oncidium*)

× **Miltonioda** hort. -f- *Orchidaceae*
(*Cochlioda* × *Miltonia*)

Miltonioides Brieger & Lückel -f-
Orchidaceae · 7 spp.
- **carinifera** (Rchb. f.) Senghas & Lückel ·
⊔ Z10 ⓚ III-IV ▽ ✳; Costa Rica
- **reichenheimii** (Linden & Rchb. f.)
Brieger & Lückel · ⊔ Z10 ⓚ ▽ ✳; Mex.
- **schroederiana** (O'Brien) Lückel · ⊔ Z10

⊛ I-II ▽ ✳; C-Am.

Miltoniopsis God.-Leb. -f- *Orchidaceae* ·
5 spp. · E:Pansy Orchid; F:Miltoniopsis;
G:Stiefmütterchenorchidee
- **phalaenopsis** (Linden & Rchb. f.) Garay
& Dunst. · ⁴ Z10 ⊛ VIII-XI ▽ ✳; Col.
- **roezlii** (Rchb. f.) God.-Leb. · ⁴ Z10 ⊛
X-XI ▽ ✳; Col.
- **vexillaria** (Rchb. f.) God.-Leb. · ⁴ Z10 ⊛
V-VI ▽ ✳; Col., Ecuad.
- **warscewiczii** (Rchb. f.) Garay & Dunst. ·
⁴ Z10 ⊛ II ▽ ✳; Costa Rica, Panama

× **Miltonpasia** hort. -f- *Orchidaceae*
(*Aspasia* × *Miltonia*)

× **Miltonpilia** hort. -f- *Orchidaceae*
(*Miltonia* × *Trichopilia*)

Mimosa L. -f- *Mimosaceae* · 480 spp. ·
E:Sensitive Plant; F:Mimosa, Sensitive;
G:Mimose, Sinnpflanze
- **diplotricha** C. Wright · E:Giant Sensitive
Plant; G:Große Sinnpflanze · ♭ Z9 ⊛ Ⓝ;
C-Am., S-Am.
- *glauca* L. 1763 = Leucaena leucocephala
- *invisa* Mart. = Mimosa diplotricha
- *lebbeck* L. = Albizia lebbeck
- *leucocephala* Lam. = Leucaena leucocephala
- **polycarpa** Kunth
- var. **polycarpa** · ♭ ♭ Z9 ⊛; S-Am.
- var. **spegazzinii** (Pirotta) Burkart · ♭ Z9
⊛; Arg.
- **pudica** L. · E:Humble Plant, Sensitive
Plant, Shame Plant, Touch-me-not;
G:Sinnpflanze · ♭ Z9 ⊛ VII-VIII Ⓝ; Braz.,
nat. in Trop.
- **sensitiva** L. · E:Sensitive Plant; G:Klet-
ternde Sinnpflanze · ♭ e ⅔ Z9 ⊛; trop.
Am.
- *spegazzinii* Pirotta = Mimosa polycarpa
var. spegazzinii
- *ulicifolia* Salisb. = Acacia ulicifolia

Mimulus L. -m- *Scrophulariaceae* ·
150 spp. · E:Monkeyflower, Musk;
F:Mimulus; G:Affenblume, Gauklerblume
- **aurantiacus** Curtis · E:Bush Monkey
Flower, Shrubby Musk; G:Buschige
Gauklerblume · ♭ Z8 ⓐ V-VIII; Calif.
- ×**burnetii** hort. (*M. cupreus* × *M. luteus*) ·
⁴ Z7; cult.
- **cardinalis** Douglas ex Benth. · E:Scarlet

Monkey Flower, Scarlet Musk; G:Schar-
lachrote Gauklerblume · ♭ Z7 VI-IX; USA:
Rocky Mts., SW, Oreg., Calif.; Mex.: Baja
Calif.
- **cupreus** Hort. ex Dombrain · G:Kupfer-
rote Gauklerblume · ⁴ ⤳ △ ∧ VII-IX;
Chile
- *glutinosus* J.C. Wendl. = Mimulus
aurantiacus
- **guttatus** Fisch. ex DC. · E:Common
Monkey Flower, Monkey Flower, Musk;
G:Gefleckte Gauklerblume · ⁴ ⤳ ⌒
Z6 VI-X; Alaska, Can.: W; USA: NCE, NC,
SW, Rocky Mts., NW, Calif.; Mex., nat. in
Eur., USA: NE
- ×**hybridus** hort. ex Sieber & Voss (*M.
guttatus* × *M. luteus*) · ⊙ ⁴ Z6; cult.
- **many cultivars**
- *langsdorffii* Donn ex Greene = Mimulus
guttatus
- **lewisii** Pursh · E:Great Purple Monkey
Flower; G:Klebrige Gauklerblume · ⁴
⌒ Z7 ∧ VI-VIII; Can.: B.C.; USA: NW,
Calif., Rocky Mts.
- **luteus** L. · E:Monkey Musk, Yellow
Monkey Flower; F:Mimule jaune;
G:Gelbe Gauklerblume · ⁴ ⌒ Z7 V-VIII;
Chile, nat. in Scotland
- *luteus* auct. non L. = Mimulus guttatus
- **moschatus** Douglas ex Lindl. · E:Musk,
Musk Plant, Muskflower; G:Moschus-
Gauklerblume · ⁴ ⤳ ⌒ Z7 ∧ VI-VIII;
Can., USA: NW, Calif., Rocky Mts., NE,
NCE, NC, nat. in Eur.
- **primuloides** Benth. · E:Yellow Creeping
Monkey Flower; G:Primel-Gauklerblume
· ⁴ ⤳ △ Z7 ∧ VI-IX; USA: Wash., Oreg.,
Calif.
- **repens** R. Br. · ⁴ ⤳ ⓐ; Austr., Tas-
man., NZ
- **ringens** L. · E:Monkey Flower, Square
Stemmed Monkey Flower; F:Mimule;
G:Affenblume · ⁴ Z3 VI-VIII; Can.: E;
USA: NE, NCE, NC, SE, SC, Colo.
- ×*tigrinus* hort. = Mimulus × hybridus

Mimusops L. -f- *Sapotaceae* · 47 spp. ·
E:Spanish Cherry; F:Cerise espagnole;
G:Affengesicht, Kugelbaum
- *balata* Crueg. ex Griseb. = Manilkara
bidentata
- **elengi** L. · E:Brazilian Milktree, Spanish
Cherry, Tanjong Tree · ♭ e D Z10 ⊛ Ⓝ;
Ind., Sri Lanka, Burma, Malay. Arch.,
N.Guinea, Solom.

Mina Cerv. = Ipomoea
– *lobata* Cerv. = Ipomoea lobata

Minuartia L. -f- *Caryophyllaceae* · c.
100 spp. · E:Sandwort; F:Alsine; G:Miere
– **austriaca** (Jacq.) Hayek · G:Österreichische Miere · ⑴ VI-VIII; Eur.: I, G, A,
Slove.; E-Alp.
– **biflora** (L.) Schinz & Thell. · G:Zweiblütige Miere · ⑴ VII-VIII; Eur.: Sc,
N-Russ., C-Eur., I
– **capillacea** (All.) Graebn. · G:Feinblättrige Miere · ⑴ VII-VIII; Eur.: F, Sw, I, Ba;
mts.
– **cherlerioides** (Hoppe) Bech. · G:Polster-Miere · ⑴ Z5 VII-VIII; Eur.: I, C-Eur.,
Slove.; Alp.
– *gerardii* Hayek = Minuartia verna subsp.
gerardii
– **glaucina** Dvoráková · G:Hügel-Miere · ⑴
V-VIII; Eur.: A +
– **graminifolia** (Ard.) Jáv. · F:Minuartie à
feuilles de graminée; G:Gras-Miere · ⑴ ◠
△ VII-VIII; Eur.: Ital-P, Ba, RO; mts.
– **hybrida** (Vill.) Schischk. · E:Fine-leaved
Sandwort; G:Gewöhnliche Zarte Miere ·
⊙ V-VII; Eur.* exc. Sc; TR, Levant, Iraq,
N-Afr., nat. in DK
– **juniperina** (L.) Maire & Petitm. · ⑴ ⤳
△ VI; Eur.: GR; TR, Syr., N-Iraq
– **langii** (G. Reuss) Holub · G:Karpaten-Miere · ⑴ VI-VII; Eur.: A +
– **laricifolia** (L.) Schinz & Thell. ·
F:Minuartie à feuilles de mélèze;
G:Nadelblättrige Miere · ⑴ △ Z5 VII-VIII;
Eur.: Ib, Fr, Ital-P, C-Eur., EC-Eur., RO;
mts.
– **mutabilis** (Lapeyr.) Schinz & Thell. ·
G:Geschnäbelte Miere · ⑴ VII-VIII;
Eur.: sp., F, Cors, I, Sw
– **recurva** (All.) Schinz & Thell. · G:Krummblättrige Miere · ⑴ ◠ △ Z5 VII-VIII;
Eur.* exc. Sc, EC-Eur.; TR
– **rubra** (Scop.) McNeill · G:Büschel-Miere · ⊙ VII-VIII; Eur.: sp., F, I, C-Eur.,
EC-Eur., Slove., RO
– **rupestris** (Scop.) Schinz & Thell. ·
G:Felsen-Miere · ⑴ VII-VIII; Eur.: F, I,
C-Eur., Slove.; Alp.
– **sedoides** (L.) Hiern · E:Mossy Cyphel;
G:Zwerg-Miere · ⑴ Z5 VII-VIII; Eur.: Ib,
Fr, BrI, C-Eur., EC-Eur., Ba, RO; Pyr.,
Alp., Carp., Balkan, Scotland
– **setacea** (Thuill.) Hayek · G:Borsten-Miere · ⑴ V-VIII; Eur.: Fr, C-Eur.,

EC-Eur., Ba, E-Eur.
– **stellata** (E.D. Clarke) Maire & Petitm. ·
G:Stern-Miere · ⑴ △ VII-VIII; Eur.: AL,
GR; mts.
– **stricta** (Sw.) Hiern · E:Bog Sandwort;
G:Steife Miere · ⑴ VI-VIII; Eur.: BrI,
Sc, N-Russ., Sw; W-Sib., E-Sib., Amur,
N-Am., Greenl.
– **verna** (L.) Hiern · G:Frühlings-Miere
– subsp. **verna** · E:Spring Sandwort, Vernal
Sandwort; G:Gewöhnliche Frühlings-Miere · ⑴ ◠ △ Z2 V-VIII; Eur.* exc. Sc;
Cauc., W-Sib., E-Sib., Amur, Kamchat.,
C-As., Mong., China, Jap., Moroc., Alger.,
Greenl.
– subsp. **gerardii** (Sw.) Hiern · G:Alpen-Frühlings-Miere · ⑴ Z2 VI-VIII; Eur.: Pyr.,
Cors, Alp., Apenn., Carp., Ba mts.
– **viscosa** (Schreb.) Schinz & Thell. ·
G:Klebrige Miere · ⑴ V-VII; Eur.* exc.
BrI, Ib; Cauc.

Mirabilis L. -f- *Nyctaginaceae* · 54 spp. ·
E:Umbrellawort; F:Belle-de-nuit;
G:Wunderblume
– **jalapa** L. · E:Four O' Clock Plant, Marvel
of Peru; F:Belle de nuit; G:Wunderblume
· ⊙ ⑴ Z8 🄫 VI-X; Peru, nat. in N-Am.
– **longiflora** L. · E:Sweet Four O'Clock · ⑴
D Z8 🄫 VII-VIII; Ariz., Tex., Mex.
– **nyctaginea** (Michx.) MacMill. · ⊙ ⑴ Z8;
USA: NCE, NC, Rocky Mts., SC, SE; Mex.,
nat. in EC-Eur.
– **viscosa** Cav. · ⊙ Z8; Mex., Col., Ecuad.,
Peru

Mirbelia Sm. -f- *Fabaceae* · 20 spp.
– **dilatata** R. Br. · ♄ 🄫; W-Austr.

Miscanthus Andersson -m- *Poaceae* ·
15-20 spp. · E:Silver Grass; F:Roseau de
Chine; G:Chinaschilf
– **floridulus** (Labill.) Warb. ex K. Schum.
& Lauterb. · E:Pacific Island Silver Grass,
Silver Grass; G:Pazifikschilf · ⑴ Z6
VII-VIII; Jap., Taiwan, Polyn.
– *japonicus* Andersson = Miscanthus
floridulus
– **oligostachyus** Stapf · ⑴ VIII-X; Jap.
– **purpurascens** Andersson · G:Purpur-Chinaschilf · ⑴ IX-X; Amur, China
– **sacchariflorus** (Maxim.) Hack. · E:Amur
Silver Grass; G:Amurschilf, Silberfahnengras · ⑴ Z7 VIII Ⓝ; Jap., Korea, Manch.,
N-China, Amur

- **sinensis** (Thunb.) Andersson · E:Chinese
  Silver Grass, Tiger Grass; F:Eulalie;
  G:Silber-Chinaschilf · ⑴ Z6 IX-X; China,
  Korea, Jap., Thail., nat. in E-USA
- **many cultivars**
- **tinctorius** (Steud.) Hack. · ⑴ Z6 VIII-IX;
  Jap.
- **transmorrisonensis** Hayata · G:Taiwan-
  Chinaschilf · ⑴ Z6 IX-X; Taiwan

Misopates Raf. -n- *Scrophulariaceae* ·
6-8 spp. · E:Weasel's Snout; F:Muflier des
champs; G:Ackerlöwenmaul, Katzenmaul
- **orontium** (L.) Raf. · E:Lesser Snapdragon, Weasel's Snout; G:Gewöhnliches
  Ackerlöwenmaul, Katzenmaul · ⊙ Z6
  VII-X; Eur.: Ib, Fr, BrI, Ital-P, C-Eur., H,
  Ba, E-Eur.; TR, SW-As, N-Afr., Macaron.,
  Eth., nat. in Sc

Mitchella L. -f- *Rubiaceae* · 2 spp. ·
E:Partridge Berry; F:Mitchella; G:Reb-
huhnbeere
- **repens** L. · E:Partridgeberry, Squaw
  Vine, Twinberry; G:Amerikanische
  Rebhuhnbeere · ⑴ ⤳ △ Z3 IV-VII ⚥ ;
  Can.: E; USA: NE, NCE, SE, Fla., SC;
  Mex.
- **undulata** Siebold & Zucc. · G:Japanische
  Rebhuhnbeere · ⑴ e Z6; Jap., S-Korea

Mitella L. -f- *Saxifragaceae* · 20 spp. ·
E:Bishop's Cap; F:Bonnet d'évêque;
G:Bischofskappe
- **breweri** A. Gray · E:Brewer's Mitrewort;
  G:Immergrüne Bischofskappe · ⑴ Z5;
  Can.: : B.C., Alb.; USA: NW, Calif., Idaho
- **caulescens** Nutt. · E:Leafy Stemmed
  Mitrewort; G:Rauhaarige Bischofskappe
  · ⑴ Z5 V; Can.: B.C.; USA: NW, Rocky
  Mts., Calif.
- **diphylla** L. · E:Two-leaf Mitrewort;
  G:Horstbildende Bischofskappe · ⑴ Z3
  IV-V; Can.: E; USA: NE, NCE, SE
- **ovalis** Greene · E:Coastal Mitrewort;
  F:Bonnet d'évêque; G:Ovale Bischofs-
  kappe · ⑴ Z7; B.C., USA: NW, Calif.
- **pentandra** Hook. · E:Five Point
  Mitrewort · ⑴ Z3 IV-V; Alaska, Can.: E;
  USA: NW, Rocky Mts., Calif., NW

Mitraria Cav. -f- *Gesneriaceae* · 1 sp. ·
F:Mitraria; G:Mützenstrauch
- **coccinea** Cav. · E:Mitre Flower;
  G:Mützenstrauch · ♄ e ⚥ Z10 ⓚ V-IX;

S-Chile

Mitrophyllum Schwantes -n- *Aizoaceae* ·
6 spp.
- **abbreviatum** L. Bolus · ⑴ Ψ Z9 ⓚ; Cape
- **dissitum** (N.E. Br.) Schwantes · ⑴ Ψ Z9
  ⓚ; Cape
- *gracile* (Schwantes) de Boer ex H.
  Jacobsen = Mitrophyllum abbreviatum
- **grande** N.E. Br. · ⑴ Ψ Z9 ⓚ; Cape
- **mitratum** (Marloth) Schwantes · ⑴ Ψ Z9
  ⓚ; Cape

× **Mizutara** hort. -f- *Orchidaceae* (*Cattleya*
× *Caularthron* × *Schomburgkia*)

Moehringia L. -f- *Caryophyllaceae* ·
20 spp. · E:Sandwort; F:Moehringia;
G:Moosmiere, Nabelmiere
- **bavarica** (L.) Gren. · G:Steirische
  Nabelmiere · ⑴ VI-VIII; Eur.: I, A, Slove.,
  AL; mts.
- **ciliata** (Scop.) Dalla Torre · G:Bewim-
  perte Nabelmiere · ⑴ VI-VIII; Eur.: F, I,
  C-Eur., Ba; Alp., Balkan
- **diversifolia** Dolliner ex W.D.J. Koch ·
  G:Verschiedenblättrige Nabelmiere · ⊙
  V-VII; Eur.: SE-A
- **muscosa** L. · F:Moehringie mousse;
  G:Moos-Nabelmiere · ⑴ △ Z5 V-VIII;
  Eur.* exc. Sc, BrI; mts.
- **trinervia** (L.) Clairv. · E:Three-nerved
  Sandwort; G:Dreinervige Nabelmiere ·
  ⑴ V-VII; Eur.*, TR, Cauc., Iran, W-Sib.,
  E-Sib., C-As., China: Sinkiang; NW-Afr.

Moenchia Ehrh. -f- *Caryophyllaceae* ·
3 spp. · E:Chickweed; F:Moenchia;
G:Weißmiere
- **erecta** (L.) G. Gaertn., B. Mey. &
  Scherb. · E:Upright Chickweed;
  G:Aufrechte Weißmiere · ⊙ IV-V; Eur.:
  Ib, Fr, BrI, Ital-P, G, Ba; TR, Levant,
  NW-Afr., nat. in PL
- **mantica** (L.) Bartl. · G:Fünfzählige
  Weißmiere · ⊙ V-VI; Eur.: I, C-Eur.,
  EC-Eur., Ba, RO; TR

× **Moirara** hort. -f- *Orchidaceae*
(*Phalaenopsis* × *Renanthera* × *Vanda*)

Molinia Schrank -f- *Poaceae* · 2-4 spp. ·
E:Moor Grass; F:Herbe-aux-pipes,
Molinie; G:Besenried, Pfeifengras
- **arundinacea** Schrank · E:Tall Moor

Grass; G:Rohr-Pfeifengras · ♃ ~ Z5 VII-IX; Eur.* exc. Ib, BrI, ? Sc; Cauc.
- **some cultivars**
- **caerulea** (L.) Moench · E:Purple Moor Grass; F:Canche bleue, Molinie bleue; G:Benthalm, Blaues Pfeifengras · ♃ ~ Z5 VII-IX Ⓝ; Eur.*, TR, Lebanon, Syr., Israel, Cauc., W-Sib., C-As., Alger., Eth., N-Afr., Kenya (Mt. Kenya), nat. in USA
- **some cultivars**
- subsp. *altissima* (Link) Domin = Molinia arundinacea
- subsp. *arundinacea* (Schrank) H.K.G. Paul = Molinia arundinacea
- subsp. *litoralis* (Host) Braun-Blanq. = Molinia arundinacea

Mollugo L. -f- *Molluginaceae* · c. 35 spp. · E:Carpetweed; F:Mollugine, Mollugo; G:Weichkraut
- **verticillata** L. · E:Carpetweed; G:Quirlblättriges Weichkraut · ⊙; trop. Am., nat. in S-Eur.

Molopospermum W.D.J. Koch -n- *Apiaceae* · 1 sp. · F:Moloposperme, Séséli; G:Striemensame
- **peloponnesiacum** (L.) W.D.J. Koch · E:Striped Hemlock; G:Striemensame · ♃ VI; Eur.: sp., F, I, G, Sw; Pyr., SE-Alp.

Moltkia Lehm. -f- *Boraginaceae* · 3-6 spp. · F:Moltkia; G:Moltkie
- **coerulea** (Willd.) Lehm. · G:Türkische Moltkie · ♃ △ Ⓐ ∧ VI-VII; TR
- **doerfleri** Wettst. · G:Albanische Moltkie · ♃ △ VI-VII; NE-AL
- *graminifolia* (Viv.) Nyman = Moltkia suffruticosa
- × **intermedia** (Froebel) J.W. Ingram (*M. petraea* × *M. suffruticosa*) · G:Hybrid-Moltkie · ♄ △ Z6 V-VIII; cult.
- **petraea** (Tratt.) Griseb. · F:Moltkia des rochers; G:Felsen-Moltkie · ♄ s △ Z7 VI-VII; Eur.: Croatia, Bosn., Montenegro, AL, GR; mts.
- **suffruticosa** (L.) Brand · G:Italienische Moltkie · ♄ △ Z7 Ⓐ ∧ VI-VII; I: Alp.

Moluccella L. -f- *Lamiaceae* · 2 spp. · E:Shell Flower; F:Clochette d'Irlande, Molucelle; G:Muschelblume, Trichtermelisse
- **laevis** L. · E:Bells-of-Ireland; F:Clochette d'Irlande; G:Muschelblume · ⊙ ✂ Z7 VII-VIII; TR, Cyprus, Syr., Iraq, Cauc.

Momordica L. -f- *Cucurbitaceae* · 45 spp. · E:Bitter Cucumber; F:Balsamine, Margose; G:Balsamapfel, Bittergurke
- **balsamina** L. · E:Balsam Apple; G:Echter Balsamapfel · ⊙ ≩ ♣ Z9 Ⓚ VI-VIII Ⓝ; Afr., W-As., NW-Ind., Malay. Arch., Austr., nat. in trop. Am., Austr.
- **charantia** L. · E:Balsam Pear, Bitter Melon; G:Amerikanische Bittergurke, Balsambirne · ⊙ ≩ ♣ Z9 Ⓚ VI-VIII ⚕ Ⓝ; Trop., nat. in SE-USA
- **cochinchinensis** (Lour.) Spreng. · E:Spiny Bitter Cucumber; G:Indische Bittergurke · ♃ ≩ Z9 Ⓚ VI-VIII; Ind., Vietn., Phil., Taiwan
- *cylindrica* L. = Luffa aegyptiaca
- *elaterium* L. = Ecballium elaterium
- **involucrata** E. Mey. ex Sond. · ♃ ≩ ♣ Z9 Ⓚ VI-VIII; S-Afr.: Natal
- *lanata* Thunb. = Citrullus lanatus var. lanatus
- *luffa* L. = Luffa aegyptiaca
- *muricata* Willd. = Momordica charantia

Monadenium Pax -n- *Euphorbiaceae* · 73 spp.
- **lugardiae** N.E. Br. · ♄ ♆ Z10 Ⓚ; Namibia, Zimbabwe, S-Afr.: Transvaal
- **schubei** (Pax) N.E. Br. · ♄ ♆ Z10 Ⓚ; S-Afr.: Transvaal; Zimbabwe

Monanthes Haw. -f- *Crassulaceae* · 9 spp. · F:Monanthes; G:Felswurz
- **anagensis** Praeger · G:Anaga-Felswurz · ♃ ♆ Z8 Ⓚ V-VI; Canar.: Tenerife
- *atlantica* Ball = Sedum surculosum
- **brachycaulos** (Webb & Berthel.) Lowe · G:Kurzstängelige Felswurz · ♃ ♆ Z8 Ⓚ; Canar., Azor.
- **laxiflora** (DC.) Bolle ex Bornm. · G:Lockerblütige Felswurz · ♄ ♆ Z8 Ⓚ III-IV; Canar.
- **muralis** (Webb ex Bolle) Hook. f. · G:Mauer-Felswurz · ♃ ♄ ♄ ♆ Z8 Ⓚ V-VI; Canar.
- **pallens** (Webb) H. Christ · G:Bleiche Felswurz · ♃ ♆ Z8 Ⓚ V-VI; Canar.
- **polyphylla** Haw. · ♃ ♆ Z8 Ⓚ VI; Canar.
- *subcrassicaulis* (Kuntze) Praeger = Monanthes muralis

Monarda L. -f- *Lamiaceae* · 19 spp. · E:Beebalm, Wild Bergamot; F:Monarde,

Thé d'Oswego; G:Indianernessel
- **didyma** L. · E:Bergamot, Oswego Tea;
  G:Scharlach-Indianernessel · ⅄ Z4 VII-IX
  ⚥ ; USA: NE, NCE, SE
- **fistulosa** L. · E:Bee Balm; G:Späte
  Indianernessel · ⅄ D Z4 VII-IX ⚥ ; Can.,
  USA* exc. NW, Calif.; Mex.
- **punctata** L. · E:Bergamot, Spotted Bee
  Balm; G:Punktierte Indianernessel · ⅄
  Z6 VII-IX ⚥ ; USA: NE, NCE, SC, SE, Fla.;
  Mex.
- **russeliana** Nutt. ex Sims · E:Russel's
  Monarda; G:Russels Indianernessel · ⅄
  VII-VIII; USA: Ky., NCE, SE, SC
- **Cultivars:**
- **many cultivars**

Monardella Benth. -f- *Lamiaceae* · 33 spp. ·
- **macrantha** A. Gray · E:Red Monardella ·
  ⅄ △ Z9 ⊕ VIII-IX; S-Calif.

Moneses Salisb. ex Gray -f- *Pyrolaceae* ·
1 sp. · E:Wintergreen; F:Pyrole; G:Moos-
auge, Wintergrün
- **uniflora** (L.) A. Gray · E:One-flowered
  Wintergreen, Woodnymph; G:Einblütiges
  Wintergrün, Moosauge · ⅄ Z2 V-VII;
  Eur.*, TR, Cauc., W-Sib., E-Sib., Amur,
  Sakhal., Kamchat., C-As., Mong., Him.,
  Alaska, Can., USA: NE, NCE, NC, SW,
  Rocky Mts, NW, Calif., Greenl.

Moniera P. Browne = Bacopa
- *amplexicaulis* Michx. = Bacopa caroliniana
- *cuneifolia* Michx. = Bacopa monnieri

Monilaria (Schwantes) Schwantes -f-
Aizoaceae · 5 spp.
- **chrysoleuca** (Schltr.) Schwantes
- *globosum* (L. Bolus) L. Bolus = Meyerophytum globosum

Monochaetum (DC.) Naudin -n-
Melastomataceae · 45 spp.
- **alpestre** Naudin · ♄ ⊕ II-IV; Mex.
- **bonplandii** (Kunth) Naudin · ♄ Z9 ⊕ II;
  Col., Peru, Venez.
- *hirtum* (H. Karst.) Triana = Monochaetum humboldtianum
- **humboldtianum** (Kunth & C.D. Bouché)
  Walp. · ♄ ⊕; Venez.

Monodora Dunal -f- *Annonaceae* ·
  -20 spp. · E:Calabash Nutmeg;

G:Kalebassenmuskat
- **myristica** (Gaertn.) Dunal · E:Calabash
  Nutmeg, Jamaica Nutmeg; G:Kalebas-
  senmuskat · ♄ e Z10 ⊕ Ⓝ; W-Afr., C-Afr.,
  Angola, Uganda

Monolena Triana -f- *Melastomataceae* ·
15 spp.
- **primuliflora** Hook. f. · ⅄ Z10 ⊕; Col.

Monopsis Salisb. -f- *Campanulaceae* ·
18 spp. · F:Monopsis; G:Sonderkraut
- **unidentata** (W.T. Aiton) E. Wimm. · ⊙ ⚥
  ⤳ VI-IX; S-Afr.

Monotropa L. -f- *Ericaceae* · 2 spp. ·
E:Bird's Nest; F:Monotropa, Sucepin;
G:Fichtenspargel
- **hypophegea** Wallr. · G:Buchenspargel ·
  ⅄ VI-VII; Eur.: G, A, Sw, BrI +
- **hypopitys** L. · E:Yellow Birdsnest;
  G:Fichtenspargel · ⅄ VI-VII; Eur.*, TR,
  Cyprus, Cauc., W-Sib., E-Sib., Amur,
  Sakhal., C-As., Afgh., Him., Manch,
  S-Korea, Jap., Can., USA, Mex.

Monstera Adans. -f- *Araceae* · 33 spp. ·
E:Swiss-Cheese Plant, Windowleaf;
F:Cerima, Philodendron; G:Fensterblatt
- **acuminata** K. Koch · E:Shingle Plant;
  G:Spitzes Fensterblatt · ♄ e ⚥ Z10 ⊕;
  C-Am.
- **adansonii** Schott · G:Geschlitztes
  Fensterblatt · ♄ e ⚥ Z10 ⊕; C-Am., trop.
  S-Am.
- **deliciosa** Liebm. · E:Swiss Cheese Plant;
  G:Großes Fensterblatt · ♄ e ⚥ Z10 ⊕ Ⓚ
  ⚘ Ⓝ; Mex.
- **obliqua** (Miq.) Walp. · G:Löchriges
  Fensterblatt · ♄ e ⚥ Z10 ⊕; trop. S-Am.
- *pertusa* (L.) de Vriese = Monstera
  adansonii

Montanoa Cerv. -f- *Asteraceae* · 23 spp.
- **bipinnatifida** (Kunth) K. Koch · ♄ e Z10
  Ⓚ II-III; Mex.
- **mollissima** Brongn. & Groenland · ♄ e
  Z10 Ⓚ IX-X; Mex.

Montbretia DC. = Crocosmia
- *crocosmiiflora* Lemoine = Crocosmia ×
  crocosmiiflora
- *pottsii* Baker = Crocosmia pottsii

Montia L. -f- *Portulacaceae* · 10-15 spp. ·

E:Blink, Winter Purslane; F:Montia;
G:Quellkraut
- **fontana** L. · E:Blinks; F:Montia des fon-
taines; G:Glanzsamiges Bach-Quellkraut
· ☉ ≈≈ VI-VIII; Eur.*, TR, Sib., Amur,
Kamchat., Jap., NW-Afr., Eth., trop. Afr.,
N-Am., Austr., NZ
- *sibirica* (L.) J.T. Howell = Claytonia
sibirica

Monvillea Britton & Rose -f- *Cactaceae* ·
15 spp.
- **anisitsii** (K. Schum.) A. Berger · ♄ Ψ Z9
ⓐ ▽ ✳; Parag.
- **cavendishii** (Monv.) Britton & Rose · ♄ Ψ
Z9 ⓐ ▽ ✳; S-Braz., N-Arg.
- **diffusa** Britton & Rose · ♄ Ψ Z9 ⓐ ▽ ✳;
S-Ecuad., N-Peru
- **haageana** Backeb. · ♄ Ψ ⁀ Z9 ⓐ ▽ ✳;
Parag.
- **lindenzweigiana** (Gürke) Backeb. · ♄ Ψ
Z9 ⓐ ▽ ✳; Parag.
- **maritima** Britton & Rose · ♄ Ψ Z9 ⓐ ▽
✳; S-Ecuad., N-Peru
- **phatnosperma** (K. Schum.) Britton &
Rose · ♄ Ψ Z9 ⓐ ▽ ✳; Parag.
- **spegazzinii** (F.A.C. Weber) Britton &
Rose · ♄ Ψ ⁀ ⤳ Z9 ⓐ ▽ ✳; Arg.

Moraea Mill. -f- *Iridaceae* · 169 spp.
- **aristata** (D. Delaroche) Asch. & Graebn. ·
⁂ Z9 ⓐ VI-VII; Cape
- *bicolor* Steud. = Dietes bicolor
- **collina** Thunb. · ⁂ Z9 ⓦ VII-VIII; S-Afr.
- *galaxia* (L. f.) Goldblatt & J.C. Manning =
Galaxia ovata
- *glaucopis* (DC.) Drapiez = Moraea aristata
- *herbertii* Lindl. = Cypella herbertii
- *iridioides* L. = Dietes iridioides
- *neopavonia* R.C. Foster = Moraea
tulbahensis
- *pavonia* (L. f.) Ker-Gawl. = Moraea
tulbahensis
- **polyanthos** L. f. · ⁂ Z9 ⓐ VI-VII; Cape
- *robinsoniana* (F. Muell.) Benth. & F.
Muell. = Dietes robinsoniana
- *sisyrinchium* (L.) Ker-Gawl. = Gynandriris
sisyrinchium
- *spathacea* (Thunb.) Ker-Gawl. = Moraea
spathulata
- **spathulata** (L. f.) Klatt · ⁂ Z8 ⓐ III-IV;
S-Afr.: Cape, Natal, Orange Free State
- **tricuspidata** (L. f.) G.J. Lewis · ⁂ Z9 ⓐ
V-VI; Cape
- *tricuspis* (Thunb.) Ker-Gawl. = Moraea

tricuspidata
- **tulbahensis** L. Bolus · ⁂ Z9 ⓐ VI-VII;
Cape

Morawetzia Backeb. = Oreocereus
- *doelziana* Backeb. = Oreocereus
doelzianus

Moricandia DC. -f- *Brassicaceae* · 8 spp. ·
F:Moricandia; G:Morikandie
- **arvensis** (L.) DC. · E:Purple Mistress;
G:Acker-Morikandie · ☉ ⁂ Z8 VII-VIII;
Eur.: Ib, Ital-P, GR; NW-Afr.

Morina L. -f- *Morinaceae* · 4 spp. ·
F:Morina; G:Kardendistel, Steppendistel
- **bulleyana** Forrest & Diels · G:Bulleys
Kardendistel · ⁂ Z7 ⋀ VI-VII; W-China
- **kokanica** Regel · G:Borstige Kardendis-
tel · ⁂ Z7 ⋀ VI-VII; C-As.
- **longifolia** Wall. · E:Whorl Flower;
G:Nepal-Kardendistel · ⁂ Z7 ⋀ VI-VIII;
Nepal
- **persica** L. · G:Persische Kardenistel · ⁂
Z7 ⋀ VII-VIII; Eur.: Ba; TR, Lebanon,
Syr., Iran, C-As.

Morinda L. -f- *Rubiaceae* · 126 spp. ·
F:Mûrier des Indes; G:Indische Maulbeere, Nonibaum
- **citrifolia** L. · E:Indian Mulberry, Pain-
killer; G:Indische Maulbeere, Nonibaum
· ♄ e Z10 ⓦ ⚥ Ⓝ; Him., Ind., Sri Lanka,
China, Taiwan, Malay. Arch., Austr.,
Pacific Is.

Moringa Adans. -f- *Moringaceae* ·
12-14 spp. · E:Horseradish Tree;
F:Moringa; G:Bennussbaum, Meerrettichbaum
- *arabica* (Lam.) Pers. = Moringa peregrina
- **oleifera** Lam. · E:Ben Oil, Horseradish
Tree; G:Meerrettichbaum · ♄ d Z10 ⓦ ⚥
Ⓝ; Him., Ind., nat. in Trop.
- **peregrina** (Forssk.) Fiori · ♄ Ψ d Z10 ⓐ
Ⓝ; Israel, Egypt, Somalia
- *pterygosperma* Gaertn. = Moringa oleifera

Morisia J. Gay -f- *Brassicaceae* · 1 sp.
- **monanthos** (Viv.) Asch. · ⁂ △ Z7 ⓐ ⋀
V-VII; Cors, Sard.

Mormodes Lindl. -f- *Orchidaceae* · 76 spp. ·
F:Mormodes; G:Gespensterorchidee
- **aromatica** Lindl. · ⁂ Z9 ⓦ X ▽ ✳; Mex.

- **buccinator** Lindl. · ♃ Z9 ⓦ X-XI ▽ ✻; Mex., Guat., Panama, Col., Venez., Guyana
- **colossus** Rchb. f. · ♃ Z9 ⓦ III ▽ ✻; Costa Rica, Panama
- *macrantha* Lindl. & Paxton = Mormodes colossus
- **maculata** (Klotzsch) L.O. Williams · ♃ Z9 ⓦ IX-X ▽ ✻; Mex.
- *pardina* Bateman = Mormodes maculata
- **variabilis** Rchb. f. · ♃ Z9 ⓦ ▽ ✻; Ecuad.

Mormolyca Fenzl -f- *Orchidaceae* · 8 spp.
- **ringens** (Lindl.) Schltr. · ♃ Z10 ⓦ V-X ▽ ✻; Mex., C-Am.

Morus L. -f- *Moraceae* · 12 spp. · E:Mulberry; F:Mûrier; G:Maulbeerbaum
- **alba** L. · E:Silkworm Mulberry, White Mulberry; F:Mûrier blanc; G:Weißer Maulbeerbaum
- var. **alba** · ♄ ♄ d Z5 V ⚕ ⓝ; China, nat. in sp., A, Ba, EC-Eur., TR, E-USA
- var. **tatarica** (Pall.) Ser. · ♄ ♄ d Z5
- **australis** Poir. · G:Südlicher Maulbeerbaum · ♄ ♄ d Z6; China, Korea, Jap., Taiwan
- *bombycis* Koidz. = Morus alba var. alba
- **cathayana** Hemsl. · ♄ ♄ d Z6; C-China, E-China
- *kagayamae* Koidz. = Morus alba var. alba
- **mongolica** (Bureau) C.K. Schneid. · G:Mongolischer Maulbeerbaum · ♄ ♄ d Z5; China, Manch., Korea
- **nigra** L. · E:Black Mulberry, Common Mulberry, Mulberry; F:Mûrier noir; G:Schwarzer Maulbeerbaum · ♄ ♄ d Z6 V ⓝ; C-As., nat. in sp., I, Ba, RO, TR, Iran, se. USA
- **rubra** L. · E:Red Mulberry; G:Roter Maulbeerbaum · ♄ d Z6 V ⓝ; Can.: Ont.; USA: NE, NCE, NC, SC, SE, Fla., Bermudas

Moschosma Rchb. = Tetradenia
- *riparia* Hochst. = Tetradenia riparia

Moussonia Regel -f- *Gesneriaceae* · 11 sp.
- **elegans** Decne. ex Planch. · ♃ ⓦ VII-IX; S-Mex., C-Am.

Mucuna Adans. -f- *Fabaceae* · 100 spp. · E:Velvet Bean; F:Poil à gratter; G:Brennhülse, Juckbohne
- **capitata** (Roxb.) Wight & Arn. · E:Bengal Velvet Bean · ⊙ Z10 ⓦ ⓝ; Ind., Him., Java
- **pruriens** (L.) DC.
- subsp. *deeringiana* (Bort) Hanelt = Mucuna pruriens var. utilis
- var. **pruriens** · E:Velvetbean; G:Samtige Juckbohne · ⊙ Z10 ⓦ ⚕ ☠ ⓝ; ? trop. As.
- var. **utilis** (Wall. ex Wight) Baker ex Burck · ⊙ Z10 ⓦ ☠ ⓝ; cult.

Muehlenbeckia Meisn. -f- *Polygonaceae* · 22 spp. · E:Wireplant; F:Muehlenbeckia; G:Drahtstrauch, Mühlenbeckie
- **adpressa** (Labill.) Meisn. · E:Australian Ivy, Climbing Lignum; G:Tasmansicher Drahtstrauch · ♄ e ≩ ⟿ Z9 ⓚ; Austr.: N.S.Wales, Victoria, S-Austr., Tasman., W-Austr.
- **axillaris** (Hook. f.) Walp. · E:Creeping Wire Vine; F:Muehlenbeckia; G:Schwarzfrüchtiger Drahtstrauch · ♄ e △ Z7 ∧; NZ
- **complexa** (A. Cunn.) Meisn. · E:Maidenhair Vine, Mattress Vine, Wire Plant; G:Weißfrüchtiger Drahtstrauch · ♄ ≀ e ≩ ⟿ Z8 ⓚ; NZ
- *platyclada* (F. Muell.) Meisn. = Homalocladium platycladum

Muhlenbergia Schreb. -f- *Poaceae* · c. 160 spp. · E:Muhly
- **mexicana** (L.) Trin. · E:Mexican Muhly · ♃ VII-IX; Can.; USA: NE, N.C., NCE, NC, Rocky Mts., SW, Calif.
- **schreberi** J.F. Gmel. · E:Nimblewill; G:Tropfensame · ♃ IX-X; USA: NE, NCE, NC, SE, Fla., SC; E-Mex., nat. in S-Russ.

Mukdenia Koidz. -f- *Saxifragaceae* · 2 spp. · G:Ahornblatt
- **rossii** (Oliv.) Koidz. · G:Ahornblatt · ♃ Z7; N-China, Manch., Korea

Mukia Arn. -f- *Cucurbitaceae* · 4 spp.
- **maderaspatana** (L.) M. Roem. · ⊙ ≩ ♧ Z9 ⓚ; trop. Afr., trop. As., Austr.

Mundulea (DC.) Benth. -f- *Fabaceae* · 15 spp.
- **sericea** (Willd.) A. Chev. · E:Silver Bush, Supti; G:Silberbusch · ♄ Z10 ⓦ ☠ ⓝ; trop. Afr., Madag., S-Afr., Ind., Malay. Arch.

Muntingia L. -f- *Tiliaceae* · 1 sp. · E:Jamaica Cherry; F:Cerise de la Jamaïque; G:Jamaikakirsche
- **calabura** L. · E:Jamaica Cherry; G:Jamaikakirsche · ♄ ♄ e Z10 ⓦ Ⓝ; Mex., C-Am., trop. S-Am., nat. in Thail., Phil.

Murbeckiella Rothm. -f- *Brassicaceae* · 5 spp.
- **pinnatifida** (Lam.) Rothm. · G:Fieder-rauke · ⳡ VII-VIII; Eur.: sp., F, I, Sw; Pyr., W-Alp.

Murraya L. -f- *Rutaceae* · 4 (-11) spp. · E:Orange Jessamine; F:Murraya; G:Orangenraute
- *exotica* L. = Murraya paniculata
- **koenigii** (L.) Spreng. · E:Curry Leaf; G:Curry-Orangenraute · ♄ ♄ e Z10 ⓦ ⚉ Ⓝ; Ind., Sri Lanka, Burma, Thail., Laos, Cambodia
- **paniculata** (L.) Jack · E:Barktree, Orange Jessamine, Satinwood; G:Jasmin-Orangenraute · ♄ ♄ e D Z10 ⓦ Ⓝ; N-Ind., Sri Lanka, Sumat., Java, Phil., Austr., Pacific Is.

Musa L. -f- *Musaceae* · 68 spp. · E:Banana, Plantain; F:Bananier; G:Banane
- **acuminata** Colla · E:Banana, Plantain; G:Banane · ⳡ Z10 ⓦ Ⓝ; Ind. (Assam), Burma, Thail., Vietn., Malay. Arch., Phil., N.Guinea, Austr.
- *arnoldiana* De Wild. = Ensete ventrico-sum
- **balbisiana** Colla · ⳡ Z10 ⓦ Ⓝ; Ind., Burma, S-China, Phil., N.Guinea, New Britain
- **basjoo** Siebold & Zucc. · E:Japanese Banana; G:Japanische Faser-Banane · ⳡ Z9 ⓦ Ⓝ; Ryukyu-Is.
- **coccinea** Andrews
- *ensete* J.F. Gmel. = Ensete ventricosum
- *fehi* Bertero ex Vieill. = Musa troglody-tarum
- *japonica* H.J. Veitch = Musa basjoo
- **mannii** H. Wendl. ex Baker · ⳡ Z9 ⓦ; InG: Assam
- × **paradisiaca** L. (*M. acuminata* × *M. balbisiana*) · E:Edible Banana, Plantain; G:Ess-Banane · ⳡ Z9 ⓦ Ⓝ; cult. Trop.
- × *rosacea* Jacq. = Musa × paradisiaca
- **sanguinea** Hook. f. · ⳡ Z9 ⓦ; InG: Assam
- × *sapientum* L. = Musa × paradisiaca

- *seminifera* Lour. p.p. = Musa balbisiana
- **sumatrana** Becc. ex André · E:Blood Banana; G:Blut-Banane · ⳡ Z10 ⓦ; Sumat.
- **textilis** Née · E:Abaca, Manila Hemp; G:Faser-Banane, Manilahanf · ⳡ Z9 ⚉ Ⓝ; Phil., N-Kalimantan
- **troglodytarum** L. · ⳡ Z10 ⓦ Ⓝ; N.Caled., Fiji, Tahiti
- *uranoscopos* Seem. = Musa troglodytarum
- **velutina** H. Wendl. & Drude · G:Kenia-Banane · ⳡ Z9 ⓦ; NE-Ind.
- *ventricosa* Welw. = Ensete ventricosum
- *zebrina* Van Houtte ex Planch. = Musa acuminata

Musanga C. Sm. ex R. Br. -f- *Cecropiaceae* · 2 spp. · E:Umbrella Tree; G:Schirmbaum
- **smithii** R. Br. · E:Corkwood, Umbrella Tree; G:Bosenge, Schirmbaum · ♄ e ⓦ Ⓝ; trop. Afr.

Muscari Mill. -n- *Hyacinthaceae* · 55 spp. · E:Grape Hyacinth; F:Muscari; G:Träubel, Traubenhyazinthe
- **armeniacum** Leichtlin ex Baker · G:Armenische Traubenhyazinthe · ⳡ Z4 III-IV ▽; Eur.: Ba; TR, ? NW-Iran
- **some cultivars**
- **aucheri** (Boiss.) Baker · ⳡ Z6 III-IV ▽; N-TR
- **azureum** Fenzl · ⳡ Z8 III-IV ▽; TR
- **botryoides** (L.) Mill. · E:Grape Hyacinth; F:Muscari raisin; G:Kleine Trauben-hyazinthe · ⳡ Z3 IV-V ▽; Eur.: Fr, Ital-P, C-Eur., EC-Eur., Ba, E-Eur.
- **comosum** (L.) Mill. · E:Tassel Hyacinth; G:Schopfige Traubenhyazinthe · ⳡ Z7 V-VI ⚉ ▽; Eur.* exc. BrI, Sc; TR, Syr., Arab., Iran, N-Afr., nat. in BrI, DK
- *heldreichii* Boiss. = Muscari botryoides
- **latifolium** Kirk · G:Breitblättrige Traubenhyazinthe · ⳡ Z4 V-VI ▽; TR
- **macrocarpum** Sweet · G:Großfrüchtige Traubenhyazinthe · ⳡ Z7 IV-V ▽; Eur.: GR, Crete; W-TR
- **neglectum** Guss. ex Ten. · E:Common Grape Hyacinth; G:Weinbergs-Trauben-hyazinthe · ⳡ D Z4 IV ▽; Eur.* exc. BrI, Sc; TR, Cyprus, Syr., Cauc., Iran, C-As., N-Afr., nat. in BrI, USA
- *pinardii* (Boiss.) Boiss. = Muscari comosum
- *polyanthum* Boiss. = Muscari armeniacum
- **racemosum** (L.) Mill. · G:Traubige

Schopfhyazinthe · Z6; SW-TR
- **tenuiflorum** Tausch · G:Schmalblütige Traubenhyazinthe · Z5 V-VI ▽; Eur.: C-Eur., EC-Eur., Ba, E-Eur.; TR, Syr., Iraq, Cauc., Iran
- *tubergenianum* Hoog ex Turrill = Muscari aucheri

Mussaenda L. -f- *Rubiaceae* · 218 spp. · E:Red Flag Bush; G:Signalstrauch
- **erythrophylla** Schumach. & Thonn. · E:Red Flag Bush; G:Signalstrauch · ♄ Z10 ⓦ VI-VIII; W-Afr.

Musschia Dumort. -f- *Campanulaceae* · 2 spp.
- **aurea** (L. f.) Dumort. · ⓚ VII-IX ▽; Madeira
- **wollastonii** Lowe · ♄ ⓚ VI-IX ▽; Madeira

Mutisia L. f. -f- *Asteraceae* · 59 spp.
- **clematis** L. f. · ♄ e Z9 ⓦ VII-X; Col., Ecuad., Peru
- **coccinea** A. St.-Hil. · ♄ ∫ Z9 ⓚ; S-Braz., Parag., Urug., NE-Arg.
- **decurrens** Cav. · ♄ e Z8 ⓚ VII-VIII; Chile
- **ilicifolia** Cav. · ♄ e Z9 ⓚ; Chile
- *inflexa* Cav. = Mutisia subulata
- **linearifolia** Cav. · ♄ ⤳ Z9 ⓚ; Chile
- **sinuata** Cav. · ♄ ⤳ Z9 ⓚ; Chile
- **speciosa** Aiton · ♄ Z9 ⓦ VII-X; Braz.
- **subulata** Ruiz & Pav. · ♄ Z9 ⓚ; Chile

Myagrum L. -n- *Brassicaceae* · 1 sp. · E:Muskweed; F:Caméline, Myagrum; G:Hohldotter
- **perfoliatum** L. · E:Mite Cress, Muskweed; G:Hohldotter · ⊙ V-VII; Eur.: Fr, Ib, C-Eur., EC-Eur., Ital-P, Ba, E-Eur.; Syr., Cauc., Iran, N-Iraq, nat. in Sc
- *sativum* L. = Camelina sativa var. sativa

Mycelis Cass. -m- *Asteraceae* · 1 sp. · E:Wall Lettuce; G:Mauerlattich
- **muralis** (L.) Dumort. · E:Wall Lettuce; G:Mauerlattich · VII-VIII; Eur.*, TR, Cauc.

Myoporum Banks & Sol. ex G. Forst. -n- *Myoporaceae* · 32 spp.
- **acuminatum** R. Br. · E:Northern Boobialla · ♄ e Z9 ⓚ IV; Austr.
- **laetum** G. Forst. · ♄ e Z9 ⓚ IV-VII; NZ

- **parvifolium** R. Br. · E:Creeping Myoporum · ♄ e Z9 ⓚ VII-VIII; Austr., Tasman.
- **tetrandrum** (Labill.) Domin · ♄ ♄ e Z9 ⓚ V; Austr.

Myosotis L. -f- *Boraginaceae* · c. 50 (-100) spp. · E:Forget-me-not; F:Myosotis, Ne-m'oubliez-pas; G:Vergissmeinnicht
- **alpestris** F.W. Schmidt · E:Alpine Forget-me-not; G:Alpen-Vergissmeinnicht · Z4 VII-VIII; Eur.* exc. Sc; Cauc.
- *alpestris* hort. = Myosotis sylvatica
- **arvensis** (L.) Hill · E:Common Forget-me-not; G:Gewöhnliches Acker-Vergissmeinnicht · ⊙ ⊙ Z6 IV-VIII; Eur.*, TR, Cauc., W-Sib., E-Sib., C-As., NW-Afr., nat. in N-Am.
- **australis** R. Br. · Z8 ⓚ VI-VIII; Austr., Tasman., NZ
- **azorica** H.C. Watson · E:Azores Forget-me-not; G:Azoren-Vergissmeinnicht · Z9 ⓚ IV-X; Azor.
- *caespititia* (DC.) A. Kern. = Myosotis rehsteineri
- **cespitosa** Schultz · ⊙ Z6; Eur.*, Sib., Moroc., Alger., Tun., e. N-Am.
- subsp. *rehsteineri* (Wartm.) Nyman = Myosotis rehsteineri
- **decumbens** Host · G:Niederliegendes Vergissmeinnicht · VI-VIII; Eur.*, Moroc., Alger.
- **discolor** Pers. · G:Buntes Vergissmeinnicht · ⊙ ⊙ IV-VI; Eur.* exc. Ib; TR, Cyprus, NW-Afr.
- **explanata** Cheeseman · Z8 ⓚ III-V; NZ
- **laxa** Lehm. · G:Rasen-Vergissmeinnicht · ⊙ Z6 V-VII; Eur.*, TR, Palest., As., NW-Afr., N-Am.
- **nemorosa** Besser · G:Hain-Vergissmeinnicht, Scharfkantiges Sumpf-Vergissmeinnicht · ⊙ VI-VII; Eur.*
- *oblongata* Link = Myosotis sylvatica
- *palustris* (L.) Hill = Myosotis scorpioides
- subsp. *caespititia* (DC.) E. Baumann = Myosotis rehsteineri
- *praecox* = Myosotis scorpioides subsp. praecox
- **ramosissima** Rochel ex Schult. · G:Hügel-Vergissmeinnicht · ⊙ IV-VI; Eur.*, TR, Levant, Cauc., NW-Iran, NW-Afr.
- **rehsteineri** Wartm. · G:Bodensee-Vergißmeinnicht · ∼ Z6 IV-V ▽; Eur.: S-G, N-I, Sw, A

– **scorpioides** L. · E:Forget-me-not;
F:Myosotis des marais; G:Sumpf-
Vergissmeinnicht · ⅃ V-VIII; Eur.* exc. Ib;
TR, Cauc., W-Sib., E-Sib., Mong., nat. in
N-Am.
– **some cultivars**
– subsp. **praecox** (Hülph.) Dickoré ·
G:Großblütiges Vergissmeinnicht,
Großblütiges Sumpf-Vergissmeinnicht · ⅃
Z5 VI-VII; D; coast
– subsp. **scorpioides** · E:Water Forget-me-
not; F:Myosotis des marais; G:Gewöhn-
liches Sumpf-Vergissmeinnicht,
Lockerblütiges Vergissmeinnicht · ⅃ Z5
V-IX; Eur.* +
– **sparsiflora** J.C. Mikan ex Pohl ·
G:Zerstreutblütiges Vergissmeinnicht · ☉
IV-VI; Eur.: C-Eur., EC-Eur., Ba, E-Eur.;
TR, Cauc., Iran, C-As.
– **stenophylla** Knaf · G:Schmalblatt-
Vergissmeinnicht · ⅃ V-VIII; Eur.: A,
EC-Eur., E-Eur.; Cauc., W-Sib., E-Sib.,
Amur, Kamchat., C-As.
– **stricta** Link ex Roem. & Schult. · G:Sand-
Vergissmeinnicht · ☉ Z6 III-VI; Eur.*,
TR, Levant, Cauc., N-Iran, Him., W-Sib.,
E-Sib., C-As., N-Afr., nat. in N-Am.
– **sylvatica** Ehrh. ex Hoffm. · E:Wood
Forget-me-not; F:Myosotis des bois, Ne
m'oubliez-pas; G:Wald-Vergissmeinnicht
· ☉ ⅃ Z5 V-VII; Eur.* exc. Ib; TR, Cauc.,
Iran

Myosoton Moench = Stellaria
– *aquaticum* (L.) Moench = Stellaria
aquatica

Myosurus L. -m- *Ranunculaceae* ·
6-15 spp. · E:Mousetail; F:Myosure,
Queue-de-souris; G:Mäuseschwänzchen
– **minimus** L. · E:Mousetail, Tiny Mouse-
tail; G:Kleines Mäuseschwänzchen · ☉
IV-VI; Eur.*, Cyprus, Syr., Cauc., W-Sib.,
C-As., Moroc., Alger., Libya, Alaska, Can.,
USA*, Austr.

Myrciaria O. Berg -f- *Myrtaceae* · 40 spp.
– **cauliflora** (DC.) O. Berg · E:Jaboticaba;
G:Jaboticabababaum · ♄ e Z10 ⓚ ⓝ;
S-Braz.
– **myriophylla** (Casar.) O. Berg · ♄ Z10 ⓜ;
Braz.

Myrica L. -f- *Myricaceae* · c. 55 spp. ·
E:Bog Myrtle; F:Arbre-à-cire, Cirier;

G:Gagelstrauch
– *aspleniifolia* L. = Comptonia peregrina
var. aspleniifolia
– **californica** Cham. & Schltdl. ·
E:California Wax Myrtle; G:Kalifor-
nischer Gagelstrauch · ♄ ♄ e Z7; USA:
NW, Calif.
– *carolinensis* hort. = Myrica pensylvanica
– *caroliniensis* Mill. = Myrica cerifera
– **cerifera** L. · E:Wax Myrtle, Waxberry;
F:Cirier; G:Wachsmyrte · ♄ ♄ e ∼ Z8 ⓚ
IV-V ⚥; USA: NE, SE, Fla., Tex.
– **gale** L. · ♄ d ∼ D Z3 IV ⚘; Eur.* exc.
Ba, Ital-P
– **pensylvanica** Lam. · E:Bayberry,
Northern Bayberry; G:Amerikanischer
Gagelstrauch · ♄ d Z3 IV-V; Can.: E; USA:
NE, Ohio, N.C., nat. in NL, S-GB
– **rubra** (Lour.) Siebold & Zucc. · E:Red
Bayberry; G:Japanischer Gagelstrauch · ♄
♄ e Z10 ⓚ ⓝ; Jap., Taiwan, China
– **tomentosa** (C. DC.) Asch. & Graebn.
= Myrica gale · ♄ ♄ ⓜ; Panama, trop.
S-Am.

Myricaria Desv. -f- *Tamaricaceae* · c. 10
(-40) spp. · E:Myrtle; F:Faux-tamaris,
Miricaire; G:Rispelstrauch
– **germanica** (L.) Desv. · E:False Tamarisk;
F:Myricaire d'Allemagne; G:Deutsche
Tamariske, Rispelstrauch · ♄ d Z6 VI-VIII;
Eur.* exc. BrI; TR, Cauc., Iran, Afgh.,
Pakist.

Myriocarpa Benth. -f- *Urticaceae* · 18 spp. ·
F:Myriocarpe; G:Tausendfrucht
– **densiflora** Benth. · G:Dichtblütige
Tausendfrucht · ♄ e ⓜ; S-Am.
– **stipitata** Benth. · ♄ Z10 ⓜ; Braz.

Myriophyllum L. -n- *Haloragaceae* · c.
60 spp. · E:Water Milfoil; F:Myriophylle;
G:Tausendblatt
– **alterniflorum** DC. · E:Alternate-flowered
Water Milfoil; G:Wechselblütiges
Tausendblatt · ⅃ ≈ Z6 VI-VIII; Eur.*
exc. Ba; NW-Afr., Alaska, Can., USA: NE;
Greenl.
– **aquaticum** (Vell.) Verdc. · E:Diamond
Milfoil, Parrots Feather; F:Millefeuille
d'eau, Myriophylle du Brésil; G:Brazil-
ianisches Tausendblatt · ⅃ ≈ Z10 ⓚ;
S-Am., nat. in Ib, F
– *Braziliense* Cambess. = Myriophyllum
aquaticum

– **elatinoides** Gaudich. · G:Tännelähnliches Tausendblatt · ⟂ ≋ Z10 🄺; Mex., S-Am., Falkland, Chatham Is., Austr., Tasman., NZ
– **heterophyllum** Michx. · E:Broadleaf Water Milfoil; G:Verschiedenblättriges Tausendblatt · ⟂ ≋ Z6 VI-IX; Can.: E; USA: NE, NCE, NC, SC, SE, Fla., nat. in BrI, A
– **hippuroides** Nutt. ex Torr. & A. Gray · E:Western Water Milfoil; G:Tannenwedel-Tausendblatt · ⟂ ≋ Z7; Can.: W; USA: NW, Calif.; Mex.
– **pinnatum** (Walter) Britton, Sterns & Poggenb. · E:Cutleaf Water Milfoil; G:Rotstängeliges Tausendblatt · ⟂ ≋ Z6; USA: NE, NCE, NC, SC, SE, Fla.; W.Ind.
– *proserpinacoides* Gillies ex Hook. & Arn. = Myriophyllum aquaticum
– *scabratum* Cham. & Schltdl. = Myriophyllum hippuroides
– *scabratum* Michx. = Myriophyllum pinnatum
– **spicatum** L. · E:Millefolium, Spiked Water Milfoil; F:Myriophylle en épis; G:Ähriges Tausendblatt · ⟂ ≋ Z6 VII-VIII; Eur.*, cosmop. exc. S-Am., Austr.
– **verticillatum** L. · E:Water Milfoil, Whorled Water Milfoil; F:Myriophylle verticillé; G:Quirliges Tausendblatt · ⟂ ≋ Z3 VI-VIII; Eur.*, Cauc., Syr., W-Sib., E-Sib., Kamchat., C-As., Mong., China, Jap., Moroc., Alger., N-Am., S-Am.

Myristica Gronov. -f- *Myristicaceae* · 72 spp. · E:Nutmeg; F:Muscadier; G:Muskatnuss
– **argentea** Warb. · E:Silver Nutmeg; G:Silberne Muskatnuss · ♄ e Z10 🄰 Ⓝ; N.Guinea
– **fragrans** Houtt. · E:Nutmeg; G:Duftende Muskatnuss · ♄ e Z10 🄰 ⚥ Ⓝ; Molucca
– **malabarica** Lam. · ♄ e Z10 🄰 Ⓝ; Ind.
– *officinalis* L. f. = Myristica fragrans

Myrmecodia Jack -f- *Rubiaceae* · 27 spp. · F:Plante aux fourmis; G:Ameisenknolle
– *antoinii* Becc. = Myrmecodia platytyrea subsp. antoinii
– *echinata* F. Muell. = Myrmecodia tuberosa
– *inermis* DC. = Myrmecodia tuberosa
– **platytyrea** Becc.
– subsp. **antoinii** (Becc.) Huxley & Jebb · ♄ e 🄰; Austr.: Torres-Street

– subsp. **platytyrea** · ♄ e 🄰; N.Guinea
– **tuberosa** Jack · ♄ e 🄰; Malay. Pen.

Myroxylon L. f. -n- *Fabaceae* · 3 spp. · E:Balsam; F:Balsamier; G:Balsambaum
– **balsamum** (L.) Harms
– var. **balsamum** · E:Tolu Tree, Tolubalsam; G:Tolu-Balsambaum · ♄ e Z8 🄰 ⚥ Ⓝ; Guat., Col., Ecuad., Venez., Braz.
– var. **pereirae** (Royle) Harms · ♄ e Z8 🄰 ⚥ Ⓝ; S-Mex., C-Am.
– *pereirae* (Royle) Klotzsch = Myroxylon balsamum var. pereirae
– *toluiferum* A. Rich. = Myroxylon balsamum var. balsamum

Myrrhis Mill. -f- *Apiaceae* · 1 sp. · E:Sweet Cicely; F:Cerfeuil vivace; G:Süßdolde
– **odorata** (L.) Scop. · E:Garden Myrrh, Sweet Cicely; G:Süßdolde · ⟂ Z5 VI ⚥ Ⓝ; Eur.: Ib, Fr, Ital-P, Ba, C-Eur.; Cauc.

Myrrhoides Heist. ex Fabr. = Physocaulis
– *nodosa* (L.) Cannon = Physocaulis nodosus

Myrsine L. -f- *Myrsinaceae* · 5 spp. · F:Myrsine; G:Myrsine
– **africana** L.
– var. **africana** · E:African Boxwood, Cape Myrtle · ♄ e Z9 🄺; Azor., E-Afr.(mts.), S-Afr., Him., China
– var. **microphylla** Drège · ♄ e Z9 🄺 III-V; Azor., S-Afr., Afgh., Him.
– var. **retusa** Aiton · ♄ e Z9 🄺 III-V; Azor.

Myrsiphyllum Willd. = Asparagus
– *asparagoides* (L.) Willd. = Asparagus asparagoides

Myrtillocactus Console -m- *Cactaceae* · 4 spp. · F:Cactus à myrtilles; G:Heidelbeerkaktus
– **cochal** (Orcutt) Britton & Rose · ♄ ♈ Z9 🄰 ▽ ✳; Mex.: Baja Calif.
– **geometrizans** (Mart.) Console · E:Blue Candle · ♄ ♈ Z9 🄰 ▽ ✳; Mex., Baja Calif.
– **schenckii** (J.A. Purpus) Britton & Rose · ♄ ♈ Z9 🄰 ▽ ✳; Mex.

Myrtus L. -f- *Myrtaceae* · 2 spp. · F:Vrai myrte; G:Myrte
– *apiculata* DC. = Luma apiculata
– *bullata* Sol. ex A. Cunn. = Lophomyrtus bullata

– *chequen* (Molina) Spreng. = Luma chequen
– **communis** L. · E:Common Myrtle, Myrtle; G:Braut-Myrte, Gewöhnliche Myrte · ♄ e D Z8 ⊛ VI-X ⚥ ; Eur.: Ib, Fr, Ital-P, Ba; TR, Levant, Iran, C-As., Pakistan, NW-Afr., Libya
– *cumini* L. = Syzygium cumini
– *luma* Molina = Luma apiculata
– *obcordata* (Raoul) Hook. f. = Lophomyrtus obcordata
– *ugni* Molina = Ugni molinae

Nabalus Cass. -m- *Asteraceae* · 15 spp.
– **albus** (L.) Hook. · E:Rattlesnake Root, White Lettuce · ⁴ Z5 VII-IX; Can.: E, Sask.; USA: NE, NCE, NC, SE
– **serpentarius** (Pursh) Hook. · E:Cankerweed, Gall-of-the-Earth, Lion's Foot · ⁴ Z5 VIII-IX; USA: NE, Ohio, SE, Fla.

Naegelia Rabenh. = Smithiantha
– *multiflora* (M. Martens & Galeotti) Hook. = Smithiantha multiflora
– *zebrina* (Paxton) Regel = Smithiantha zebrina

Nageia Gaertn. -f- *Podocarpaceae* · 6 spp. · E:Nagi; G:Nagibaum
– **nagi** (Thunb.) Kuntze · E:Nagi; G:Echter Nagibaum · ♄ e Z8 ⊛ Ⓝ; S-Jap., Ryukyu-Is., Taiwan

Nageliella L.O. Williams -f- *Orchidaceae* · 2 spp.
– **purpurea** (Lindl.) L.O. Williams · ⁴ Z10 ⊛ VI-VIII ▽ ✳; Mex., Guat.

Najas L. -f- *Najadaceae* · c. 35 spp. · E:Naiad, Water Nymph; F:Naïade; G:Nixkraut
– **flexilis** (Willd.) Rostk. & W.L.E. Schmidt · E:Nodding Water Nymph; G:Biegsames Nixkraut · ⊙ ≈ Z5 VI-VIII ▽; Eur.: BrI, Sc, C-Eur., EC-Eur., E-Eur.; W-Sib., N-Am
– **graminea** Delile · E:Ricefield Water Nymph; G:Grasartiges Nixkraut · ⊙ ⊙ ⁴ ≈ Z8 ⊛ ⊛; C-Afr., NE-Afr., S-As., Austr., N.Caled., nat. in I, BG, RO
– **guadalupensis** (Spreng.) Morong · E:Southern Water Nymph: G:Guadalupe-Nixkraut · ⁴ ≈ Z9 ⊛; C-Am, S-Am.
– **indica** (Willd.) Cham. · G:Indisches

Nixkraut · ⁴ ≈ Z10 ⊛; trop. As.
– **malesiana** W.J. de Wilde · ⁴ ≈ Z10 ⊛; SE-As.
– **marina** L.
– subsp. **marina** · E:Marine Najad, Spiny Najad; G:Meer-Nixkraut · ⊙ ≈ VI-VIII; Eur.*, Cauc., W-Sib., E-Sib., Amur, C-As., S-As., E-As., N-Afr., N-Am., S-Am., Austr.
– *microdon* A. Braun = Najas guadalupensis
– **minor** All. · E:Brittle Water Nymph; G:Kleines Nixkraut · ⊙ ≈ Z6 VI-VIII; Eur.* exc. Sc, BrI; TR, Cauc., Iran, W-Sib., Amur, C-As., E-As., S-As., N-Afr., Afr.

× **Nakamotoara** hort. -f- *Orchidaceae* (*Ascocentrum* × *Neofinetia* × *Vanda*)

Nananthus N.E. Br. -m- *Aizoaceae* · 6 spp.
– *orpenii* N.E. Br. = Prepodesma orpenii
– **vittatus** (N.E. Br.) Schwantes · ⁴ ⚭ Z9 ⊛; S-Afr.

Nandina Thunb. -f- *Berberidaceae* · 1 sp. · E:Heavenly Bamboo; F:Bambou sacré; G:Himmelsbambus, Nandine
– **domestica** Thunb. ex Murray · E:Heavenly Bamboo, Sacred Bamboo; F:Bambou sacré; G:Himmelsbambus, Nandine · ♄ e Z8 ⊛ VI-VII ✷; Jap., C-China

Nannorrhops H. Wendl. -f- *Arecaceae* · 1 sp. · E:Marari Palm; G:Mazaripalme
– **ritchieana** (Griff.) Aitch. · E:Marari Palm; G:Mazaripalme · ♄ e ⌒ ⊛; Iran, Afgh., Pakistan

Nanodes Lindl. -n- *Orchidaceae* · 2 spp.
– *medusae* Rchb. f. = Epidendrum medusae
– *porpax* (Rchb. f.) Brieger = Epidendrum neoporpax

Napaea L. -f- *Malvaceae* · 1 sp.
– **dioica** L. · E:Glade Mallow; G:Zwei-häusige Malve · ⁴ Z4; USA: NCE

Narcissus L. -m- *Amaryllidaceae* · 54 spp. · E:Daffodil; F:Narcisse; G:Jonquille, Narzisse, Osterglocke, Tazette
– **assoanus** Dufr. ex Schult. & Schult. f. · E:Rush-Leaved Jonquil; G:Binsen-Narzisse · ⁴ △ Z7 ∧ III-IV ✷ ▽; Eur.: S-F, sp., ? Cors, nat. in TR
– **asturiensis** (Jord.) Pugsley · E:Dwarf

Daffodil; G:Zwerg-Narzisse · 4 △ Z7 ∧ III-IV ▽; N-P, N-Sp.

– **bulbocodium** L. · E:Bulbocodium, Hoop Petticoat Daffodil; G:Reifrock-Narzisse

– subsp. **bulbocodium** var. **bulbocodium** · 4 Z7 ∧ IV-V ▽; SW-F, Ib., Moroc., Alger.

– subsp. *bulbocodium* var. *citrinus* Baker = Narcissus gigas

– × **compressus** Haw. (*N. jonquilla* × *N. tazetta*) · 4 Z8 ∧; SW-F, NE-Sp., nat. in Ba, I

– **cyclamineus** DC. · E:Donkey's Ears; G:Alpenveilchen-Narzisse · 4 △ Z7 ∧ III-IV ▽; NW-P, NW-Sp.

– **elegans** (Haw.) Spach · G:Zierliche Tazette · 4 D Z8 🅐 ∧ IX-X ▽; Eur.: Balear., I, Sic.; NW-Afr.

– **gigas** (Haw.) Steud. · G:Zitronengelbe Reifrock-Narzisse · 4 Z7; sp.

– × *gracilis* Sabine = Narcissus × tenuior

– × *grenieri* K. Richt. = Narcissus × medioluteus

– **hispanicus** Gouan · 4 Z4 IV-V ▽; Eur.: sp., P, S-F

– × **incomparabilis** Mill. (*N. poeticus* × *N. pseudonarcissus*) · E:Nonesuch Daffodil; G:Unvergleichliche Narzisse · 4 Z4 III-IV; F, nat. in S-Eur., W-Eur.

– *intermedius* Loisel. = Narcissus × compressus

– × **johnstonii** (Baker) Pugsley (*N. pseudonarcissus* × *N. triandrus* subsp. *pallidulus*) · 4 IV; P

– **jonquilla** L. · E:Wild Jonquil; G:Echte Jonquille · 4 △ D Z7 ∧ IV Ⓝ ▽; Eur.: Ib, nat. in F, I, Croatia, Montenegro

– *juncifolius* Req. ex Lag. = Narcissus assoanus

– × **medioluteus** Mill. (*N. poeticus* × *N. tazetta*) · E:Primrose Peerless; G:Zweiblütige Narzisse · 4 D Z7 IV-V; F, nat. in S-Eur.

– *minimus* hort. = Narcissus asturiensis

– **minor** L. · G:Kleine Narzisse · 4 Z4 ▽; Eur.: F, N-Sp.; Pyr.

– var. *conspicuus* Haw. = Narcissus minor

– × **odorus** L. (*N. pseudonarcissus* × *N. jonquilla*) · E:Campernelle Jonquil; G:Duft-Narzisse · 4 D Z6 IV-V; cult.

– **papyraceus** Ker-Gawl. · 4 D Z8 🅐 I-III ▽; Eur.: Ib, Fr, Ital-P, Ba

– × *poetaz* hort. ex L.H. Bailey = Narcissus × medioluteus

– **poeticus** L. · G:Dichter-Narzisse

– subsp. **poeticus** · E:Pheasant Eye Narcissus, Poet's Narcissus; G:Gewöhnliche Dichter-Narzisse, Weiße Narzisse · 4 ⚥ Z4 IV-V ⚘ Ⓦ ▽; Eur.: Ib, Fr, Ital-P, C-Eur., Ba, E-Eur., nat. in BrI

– subsp. **verbanensis** (Herb.) P.D. Sell · G:Langensee-Narzisse · 4 Z4 IV-V ▽; Sw, N-I

– subsp. **radiiflorus** (Salisb.) Baker · G:Westalpen-Narzisse · 4 ⚥ Z4 IV-V ⚘ ▽; SC-Eur., W-Ba

– **pseudonarcissus** L. · G:Osterglocke

– subsp. *major* (Curtis) Baker = Narcissus hispanicus

– subsp. **pseudonarcissus** · E:Lent Lily, Tenby Daffodil, Wild Daffodil; G:Gelbe Narzisse, Gewöhnliche Osterglocke · 4 ⚥ Z4 III-IV ⚘ ▽; Eur.: BrI, Fr, Ib, Sw, G, nat. in A, I, Ba, RO

– var. *johnstonii* Baker = Narcissus × johnstonii

– var. *porrigens* (Jord.) Pugsley = Narcissus pseudonarcissus subsp. pseudonarcissus

– *radiiflorus* Salisb. = Narcissus poeticus subsp. radiiflorus

– var. *stellaris* (Haw.) A. Fern. = Narcissus poeticus subsp. radiiflorus

– *requienii* M. Roem. = Narcissus assoanus

– **rupicola** Dufour · G:Stängellose Jonquille

– subsp. **rupicola** · 4 Z8 🅐 ▽; C-Sp., N-P

– subsp. **watieri** (Maire) Maire & Weiller · 4 Z8 🅐 VI ▽; Moroc.

– **scaberulus** Henriq. · G:Raue Jonquille · 4 Z8 🅐 ▽; N-P (Mondego-Tal)

– *stellaris* Haw. = Narcissus poeticus subsp. radiiflorus

– **tazetta** L. · E:Bunch-Flowered Narcissus; G:Echte Tazette

– subsp. *papyraceus* (Ker-Gawl.) G. Nicholson = Narcissus papyraceus

– subsp. **tazetta** · 4 ⚥ D Z7 III-V ▽; Eur.: Ib, Fr, Ital-P, Ba

– × *tazettopoeticus* Gren. & Godr. = Narcissus × medioluteus

– × **tenuior** Curtis (*N. jonquilla* × *N. poeticus*) · 4 Z7; cult.

– **triandrus** L. · E:Angel's Tears; G:Engelstränen-Narzisse

– subsp. **pallidulus** (Graells) D.A. Webb · G:Bleiche Engelstränen-Narzisse · 4; Ib.

– subsp. **triandrus**

– var. **triandrus** · 4 Z4 IV-V ▽; Eur.: Ib, F

– var. *albus* (Haw.) Baker = Narcissus triandrus subsp. triandrus var. triandrus

– *verbanensis* (Herb.) Herb. = Narcissus

poeticus subsp. verbanensis
- *watieri* Maire = Narcissus rupicola subsp. watieri
- **Cultivars:**
- **many cultivars, see Section III**

Nardostachys DC. -f- *Valerianaceae* · 1 sp. · F:Nardostachyde de l'Inde; G:Nardenähre, Speichenähre
- **grandiflora** DC. · E:Nard, Spikenard; G:Nardenähre, Speichenähre · ⑂ △ ⚥ Ⓝ ▽ ✳; Him., SW-China
- *jatamansi* (D. Don) DC. = Nardostachys grandiflora

Nardus L. -f- *Poaceae* · 1 sp. · E:Mat Grass; F:Nard; G:Borstgras
- **stricta** L. · E:Mat Grass, Moor Mat Grass; G:Borstgras · ⑂ △ V-VIII; Eur.*, TR, Cauc., Moroc., nat. in E-Sib., N-Am., Greenl., Tasman., NZ

Narthecium Huds. -n- *Melanthiaceae* · 7 spp. · E:Bog Asphodel; F:Narthécie; G:Ährenlilie, Beinbrech
- **ossifragum** (L.) Huds. · E:Bog Asphodel; G:Beinbrech, Moor-Ährenlilie · ⑂ ⌢ Z6 VII-VIII ⚘ ▽; Eur.: BrI, Sc, G, Fr, Ib

Nasturtium R. Br. -n- *Brassicaceae* · 6 spp. · E:Watercress; F:Cresson de fontaine; G:Brunnenkresse
- **microphyllum** (Boenn.) Rchb. · E:Onerowed Watercress; G:Kleinblättrige Brunnenkresse · ⊙ ⑂ ≈ Z6 V-X Ⓝ; Eur.* exc. Ib, E-Eur.; Moroc.
- **officinale** R. Br. · E:Common Watercress; F:Cresson de fontaine; G:Echte Brunnenkresse · ≈ V-X ⚥ Ⓝ; Eur.*, TR, Cauc., cosmop., nat. in N-Am., Eth.
- var. *microphyllum* (Boenn. ex Rchb.) Boenn. = Nasturtium microphyllum
- × **sterile** (Airy Shaw) Oefelein (*N. microphyllum* × *N. officinale*) · G:Bastard-Brunnenkresse · ⑂ Z6; cult.

Naumburgia Moench = Lysimachia
- *thyrsiflora* (L.) Rchb. = Lysimachia thyrsiflora

Nauplius (Cass.) Cass. -m- *Asteraceae* · 8 spp.
- **sericeus** (L. f.) Cass. · ♄ Z9 ⌂; Canar. Is.

Nautilocalyx Linden ex Hanst.

-m- *Gesneriaceae* · 38 (-60) spp.
- **bullatus** (Lem.) Sprague · ⑂ Z10 ⑩; Amazon., Peru
- **forgetii** (Sprague) Sprague · ⑂ Z10 ⑩; Peru
- **lynchii** (Hook. f.) Sprague · ⑂ Z9 ⑩; ? Peru, ? Ecuad.
- **pallidus** (Sprague) Sprague · ⑂ Z10 ⑩; Peru
- **picturatus** L.E. Skog · ⑂ Z10 ⑩; Peru
- **pictus** (Hook.) Sprague · ⑂ Z10 ⑩; Amazon., Guyan.

Navarretia Ruiz & Pav. -f- *Polemoniaceae* · 30 spp.
- **squarrosa** (Eschsch.) Hook. & Arn. · E:Skunkbush · ⊙ Z7; B.C., USA: NW, Calif.

Neanthe O.F. Cook = Chamaedorea
- *bella* O.F. Cook = Chamaedorea elegans

Nectaroscordum Lindl. -n- *Alliaceae* · 2 spp. · E:Honey Garlic; F:Ail; G:Honiglauch
- *bulgaricum* Janka = Nectaroscordum siculum subsp. bulgaricum
- **siculum** (Ucria) Lindl. · G:Gewöhnlicher Honiglauch
- subsp. **bulgaricum** (Janka) Stearn · G:Bulgarischer Honiglauch · ⑂ Z6; Eur.: Ba, EC-Eur., E-RO, NW-TR, Crim
- subsp. **siculum** · E:Sicilian Honey Garlic; G:Sizilianischer Honiglauch · ⑂ ≋ Z6 V; Eur.: F, Ital-P

Negundo Boehm. ex Ludw. = Acer
- *aceroides* Moench = Acer negundo subsp. negundo
- *californicum* Torr. & A. Gray = Acer negundo subsp. californicum
- *fraxinifolium* (Raf.) de Vos = Acer negundo subsp. negundo

Neillia D. Don -f- *Rosaceae* · 11 sp. · E:Neillia; F:Neillia; G:Traubenspiere
- **affinis** Hemsl. · G:Rote Traubenspiere · ♄ d Z6 V-VI; W-China
- *longiracemosa* Hemsl. = Neillia thibetica
- **sinensis** Oliv. · G:Blasse Traubenspiere · ♄ d Z6 V-VI; C-China, W-China
- **thibetica** Franch. · G:Tibetische Traubenspiere · ♄ d Z7 V-VI; Him., W-China
- **thyrsiflora** D. Don · G:Himalaya-Traubenspiere · ♄ d Z7 VIII; Him.

Nelumbium Juss. = Nelumbo
– *luteum* Willd. = Nelumbo lutea
– *speciosum* Willd. = Nelumbo nucifera

Nelumbo Adans. -f- *Nelumbonaceae* ·
2 spp. · E:Lotus; F:Lotus, Lotus des Indes;
G:Lotosblume
– **lutea** (Willd.) Pers. · E:American Lotus,
Water Chinquapin; G:Amerikanische
Lotosblume · ⧎ ≈ Z7 ⓜ ⓚ VII-VIII;
Can.: Ont.; USA: NE, NCE, SE, Fla., SC;
Mex., C-Am, W.Ind., Col.
– **nucifera** Gaertn. · E:Lotus, Sacred Indian
Lotus; G:Indische Lotosblume · ⧎ ≈
Z8 ⓚ IV-VIII ⚥ ⓝ; Eur.: E-Russ.; Cauc.,
Amur, Him., China, Malay. Arch., Austr.,
nat. in I, RO, Jap.
– *pentapetala* (Walter) Fernald = Nelumbo
lutea
– *speciosa* Willd. = Nelumbo nucifera
– **Cultivars:**
– **some cultivars**

Nematanthus Schrad. -m- *Gesneriaceae* ·
26 spp. · E:Pouch Flower; G:Kussmäulchen
– **crassifolius** (Schott) Wiehler · ♄ e Z10
ⓜ XII-II; Braz.
– **gregarius** D.L. Denham · E:Clog Plant,
Goldfish Plant; G:Goldfischpflanze · ♄ ♄
e ⟿ Z10 ⓜ VII-VIII; Mex., Guat., Costa
Rica, Panama
– **hirtellus** (Schott) Wiehler · ⧎ ♄ ♄ e Z10
ⓜ; Braz.
– *longipes* DC. = Nematanthus crassifolius
– *perianthomegus* (Vell.) H.E. Moore =
Nematanthus hirtellus
– *radicans* (Klotzsch & Hanst.) H.E. Moore
= Nematanthus gregarius
– *radicans* C. Presl = Nematanthus strigillosus
– **strigillosus** (Mart.) H.E. Moore · ♄ e Z10
ⓜ III-V; Braz.
– **Cultivars:**
– **some cultivars**

Nemesia Vent. -f- *Scrophulariaceae* ·
65 spp. · F:Némésia; G:Nemesie
– **floribunda** Lehm. · ⊙ Z9 VII-VIII; S-Afr.
– **lilacina** N.E. Br. · ⊙ Z9 VII-VIII; SW-Cape
– **strumosa** Benth. · ⊙ Z9 VI-IX; S-Afr.
– **versicolor** E. Mey. ex Benth. · ⊙ Z9
VII-VIII; S-Afr.

Nemopanthus Raf. -m- *Aquifoliaceae* ·
2 spp. · E:Mountain Holly; F:Faux-houx,

Némopanthe; G:Berghülse
– **mucronatus** (L.) Trel. · E:Catberry;
G:Berghülse · ♄ d ⟿ Z5 V-VI; Can.: E;
USA: NE, NCE

Nemophila Nutt. -f- *Hydrophyllaceae* ·
11 sp. · E:Nemophila; F:Némophile;
G:Hainblume
– **maculata** Benth. ex Lindl. · E:Five Spot,
Five Spot Nemophila; G:Gefleckte Hainblume · ⊙ VI-VII; Calif.: Sierra Nevada
– **menziesii** Hook. & Arn. · E:Baby Blue
Eyes
– var. **atomaria** (Fisch. & C.A. Mey.) Voss ·
⊙; Calif., Oreg.
– var. **discoidalis** (Lam.) Voss · ⊙; cult.
– var. **menziesii** · E:Baby Blue Eyes,
California Bluebell; G:Blaue Hainblume ·
⊙ VI-VIII; Oreg., Calif.

Neoalsomitra Hutch. -f- *Cucurbitaceae* ·
12 spp.
– **sarcophylla** (Wall.) Hutch. · ♄ ⚡ Z10 ⓜ;
Burma, Thail., Timor

Neobesseya Britton & Rose = Escobaria
– *missouriensis* (Sweet) Britton & Rose =
Escobaria missouriensis
– *wissmannii* (Hildm.) Britton & Rose =
Escobaria missouriensis
– *zilziana* (Boed.) Boed. = Escobaria
zilziana

Neobuxbaumia Backeb. -f- *Cactaceae* ·
8 spp.
– **euphorbioides** (Haw.) Buxb. · ♄ ⚡ Z9 ⓚ
▽ ✳; Mex.
– **polylopha** (DC.) Backeb. · ♄ ⚡ Z9 ⓚ ▽
✳; C-Mex.

Neocardenasia Backeb. = Neoraimondia
– *herzogiana* Backeb. = Neoraimondia
herzogiana

Neochilenia Backeb. ex Dölz = Neoporteria
– *aerocarpa* (F. Ritter) Backeb. = Neoporteria odieri
– *chilensis* (Hildm. ex K. Schum.) Backeb. =
Neoporteria chilensis
– *napina* (Phil.) Backeb. = Neoporteria
napina
– *odieri* (Lem.) Backeb. = Neoporteria
odieri
– *taltalensis* (Hutchison) Backeb. =
Neoporteria taltalensis

Neodypsis Baill. = Dypsis
– *decaryi* Jum. = Dypsis decaryi

Neofinetia Hu -f- *Orchidaceae* · 3 spp.
– **falcata** (Thunb.) Hu · � Z9 ⓐ VI-VII ▽
✳; Jap., Korea, Ryukyu-Is.

Neoglaziovia Mez -f- *Bromeliaceae* · 3 spp.
– **concolor** C.H. Wright · ⁴ Z10 ⓜ Ⓝ;
Braz.: Bahia
– **variegata** (Arruda) Mez · ⁴ Z10 ⓜ Ⓝ;
Braz.

Neogomesia Castañeda = Ariocarpus
– *agavoides* A. Cast. = Ariocarpus agavoides

Neogyna Rchb. f. -f- *Orchidaceae* · 1 sp.
– **gardneriana** (Lindl.) Rchb. f. · ⁴ ⓜ XII
▽ ✳; Nepal, Yunnan

Neohenricia L. Bolus -f- *Aizoaceae* · 2 spp.
– **sibbettii** (L. Bolus) L. Bolus · ⁴ ᵞ Z9 ⓐ;
S-Afr.: Orange Free State

Neolauchea Kraenzl. = Isabelia
– *pulchella* Kraenzl. = Isabelia pulchella

Neolitsea (Benth.) Merr. -f- *Lauraceae* · c.
85 spp.
– *glauca* hort. = Neolitsea sericea
– **sericea** (Blume) Koidz. · ♄ e Z9 ⓐ
VII-VIII; China, Korea, Jap., Taiwan

Neolloydia Britton & Rose -f- *Cactaceae* ·
14 spp.
– *ceratites* (Quehl) Britton & Rose = Neolloydia conoidea
– **conoidea** (DC.) Britton & Rose ·
E:Chihuahuan Beehive · ᵞ Z9 ⓐ ▽ ✳;
Tex., E-Mex.
– *gielsdorfiana* (Werderm.) F.M. Knuth =
Turbinicarpus gielsdorfianus
– *grandiflora* (Pfeiff.) F.M. Knuth = Neolloydia conoidea
– *horripila* (Lem.) Britton & Rose =
Turbinicarpus horripilus
– *lophophoroides* (Werderm.) E.F. Anderson = Turbinicarpus lophophoroides
– *mandragora* (A. Berger) E.F. Anderson =
Turbinicarpus mandragora
– *odorata* (Boed.) Backeb. = Cumarinia
odorata
– *pseudomacrochele* (Backeb.) E.F. Anderson = Turbinicarpus pseudomacrochele
– *pseudopectinata* (Backeb.) E.F. Anderson

= Turbinicarpus pseudopectinatus
– *saueri* (Boed.) F.M. Knuth = Turbinicarpus saueri
– *schmiedickeana* (Boed.) E.F. Anderson =
Turbinicarpus schmiedickeanus
– **smithii** (Muehlenpf.) Kladiwa & Fittkau ·
ᵞ Z9 ⓐ ▽ ✳; Mex.: Coahuila, Nuevo
Leon, San Luis Potosí
– *valdeziana* (L. Möller) E.F. Anderson =
Turbinicarpus valdezianus
– *viereckii* (Werderm.) F.M. Knuth =
Turbinicarpus viereckii

Neomarica Sprague -f- *Iridaceae* · 16 spp.
– **caerulea** (Ker-Gawl.) Sprague · ⁴ Z10 ⓜ
IV-VII; Braz.
– **gracilis** (Herb. ex Hook.) Sprague · ⁴
Z10 ⓜ IV-VII; Braz.
– **northiana** (Schneev.) Sprague · ⁴ Z10
ⓜ IV-VII; Braz.

Neomortonia Wiehler -f- *Gesneriaceae* ·
1 sp.
– *nummularia* (Hanst.) Wiehler =
Nematanthus gregarius
– **rosea** Wiehler · ⁴ Z10 ⓜ; Costa Rica,
Panama, Col.

Neonotonia J.A. Lackey -f- *Fabaceae* ·
2 spp.
– **wightii** (Arn.) J.A. Lackey · ⁴ Ⓝ; Afr.,
trop. As., nat. in Austr.

Neopanax Allan = Pseudopanax
– *arboreus* (Murray) Allan = Pseudopanax
arboreus

Neoporteria Britton & Rose -f- *Cactaceae* ·
25 spp.
– *andicola* hort. = Neoporteria curvispina
– **aricensis** (F. Ritter) Donald & G.D.
Rowley · ᵞ Z9 ⓐ ▽ ✳; Chile: Arica
– *armata* (F. Ritter) Krainz = Neoporteria
tuberisulcata
– *atrispinosa* (Backeb.) Backeb. = Neoporteria villosa
– **bulbocalyx** (Werderm.) Donald & G.D.
Rowley · ᵞ Z9 ⓐ ▽ ✳; Arg.: La Rioja,
Catamarca
– *castanea* F. Ritter = Neoporteria subgibbosa
– **chilensis** (Hildm. ex K. Schum.) Britton
& Rose · ᵞ Z9 ⓐ ▽ ✳; Chile
– **curvispina** (Bertero) Donald & G.D.
Rowley · ᵞ Z9 ⓐ ▽ ✳; Chile (Santiago)

– var. *lissocarpa* (F. Ritter) Donald & G.D. Rowley = Neoporteria curvispina
– *horrida* (Gay) D.R. Hunt = Neoporteria tuberisulcata
– **islayensis** (C.F. Först.) Donald & G.D. Rowley · ⍦ Z9 Ⓐ ▽ ✳; S-Peru, N-Chile
– *laniceps* F. Ritter = Neoporteria villosa
– *mammillarioides* (Hook.) Backeb. = Neoporteria curvispina
– *mitis* nom. inval. = Neoporteria napina
– **napina** (Phil.) Backeb. · ⍦ Z9 Ⓐ ▽ ✳; Chile: Huasco
– **nidus** (Söhrens) Britton & Rose · ⍦ Z9 ⒶⒶ ▽ ✳; Chile
– *nigricans* (Werderm. & Backeb.) Backeb. = Neoporteria tuberisulcata
– **odieri** (Lem.) Backeb. · ⍦ Z9 ⒶⒶ ▽ ✳; Chile
– *polyraphis* (Pfeiff.) Backeb. = Neoporteria villosa
– *rupicola* (F. Ritter) Donald & G.D. Rowley = Neoporteria taltalensis
– *scoparia* (F. Ritter) Donald & G.D. Rowley = Neoporteria taltalensis
– **subgibbosa** (Haw.) Britton & Rose · ⍦ Z9 ⒶⒶ ▽ ✳; Chile
– **taltalensis** Hutchison · ⍦ Z9 ⒶⒶ ▽ ✳; Chile
– **tuberisulcata** (Jacobi) Donald ex G.D. Rowley · ⍦ Z9 ⒶⒶ ▽ ✳; Chile (Santiago)
– **villosa** (Monv.) A. Berger · ⍦ Z9 ⒶⒶ ▽ ✳; Chile: Huasco
– *woutersiana* (Backeb.) Donald & G.D. Rowley = Neoporteria taltalensis

Neoraimondia Britton & Rose -f-
Cactaceae · 2 spp.
– **arequipensis** (Meyen) Backeb. · ♄ ⍦ Z9 ⒶⒶ ▽ ✳; N-Peru
– **herzogiana** (Backeb.) Buxb. · ♄ ⍦ Z9 ⒶⒶ ▽ ✳; Bol.
– *macrostibas* (K. Schum.) Backeb. = Neoraimondia arequipensis
– *roseiflora* (Werderm. & Backeb.) Backeb. = Neoraimondia arequipensis

Neoregelia L.B. Sm. -f- *Bromeliaceae* · 113 spp.
– **ampullacea** (E. Morren) L.B. Sm. · ⌗ Z10 ⒶⒶ; Braz. (Rio de Janeiro)
– **binotii** (E. Morren) L.B. Sm. · ⌗ Z10 ⒶⒶ; S-Braz.
– **carolinae** (Beer) L.B. Sm. · E:Blushing Bromeliad · ⌗ Z10 ⒶⒶ; Braz.
– **chlorosticta** (Baker) L.B. Sm. · ⌗ Z10 ⒶⒶ; Braz.

– **concentrica** (Vell.) L.B. Sm. · ⌗ Z10 ⒶⒶ; Braz.
– **farinosa** (Ule) L.B. Sm. · ⌗ Z10 ⒶⒶ; Braz.
– **fosteriana** L.B. Sm. · ⌗ Z10 ⒶⒶ; Braz.
– *morreniana* (Antoine) L.B. Sm. = Neoregelia pineliana
– **pineliana** (Lem.) L.B. Sm. · ⌗ Z10 ⒶⒶ; Braz.
– **princeps** (Baker) L.B. Sm. · ⌗ Z10 ⒶⒶ; Braz.
– **sarmentosa** (Regel) L.B. Sm. · ⌗ Z10 ⒶⒶ; Braz.
– **spectabilis** (T. Moore) L.B. Sm. · E:Fingernail Plant, Painted Fingernail · ⌗ Z10 ⒶⒶ; Braz.
– **tristis** (Beer) L.B. Sm. · ⌗ Z10 ⒶⒶ; Braz.
– **zonata** L.B. Sm. · ⌗ Z10 ⒶⒶ; Braz.

× **Neostylis** hort. -f- *Orchidaceae* (*Neofinetia* × *Rhynchostylis*)

Neotinea Rchb. f. -f- *Orchidaceae* · 4 spp. · G:Keuschorchis, Waldwurz
– **tridentata** (Scop.) R.M. Bateman, Pridgeon & M.W. Chase · E:Toothed Orchid · ⌗ Z6 V-VI ▽ ✳; Eur.: Ib, Fr, C-Eur., Ital-P, EC-Eur., Ba, RO, Crim; TR, Iraq, Cauc., Iran, Moroc.
– **ustulata** (L.) R.M. Bateman, Pridgeon & M.W. Chase · E:Burnt Tip Orchid; G:Brand-Keuschorchis · ⌗ Z5 V-VII ▽ ✳; Eur.*, Cauc., W-Sib.

Neottia Guett. -f- *Orchidaceae* · 19 spp. · E:Bird's Nest Orchid; F:Néottie; G:Nestwurz
– **nidus-avis** (L.) Rich. · E:Bird's Nest Orchid; G:Vogel-Nestwurz · ⌗ V-VI ▽ ✳; Eur.*, TR, Cauc., Iran, W-Sib.

Nepenthes L. -f- *Nepenthaceae* · 72 spp. · E:Pitcher Plant; F:Nepenthes, Tasse-de-singe; G:Kannenstrauch
– **albomarginata** T. Lobb ex Lindl. · ♄ e Z10 ⒶⒶ ▽ ✳; Malay. Arch.
– **ampullaria** Jack · ♄ e ⌗ Z10 ⒶⒶ ▽ ✳; Malay. Arch., N.Guinea
– **bicalcarata** Hook. f. · ♄ e ⌗ Z10 ⒶⒶ ▽ ✳; Kalimantan
– **burkei** Mast. · ♄ e Z10 ⒶⒶ ▽ ✳; Phil.
– × **coccinea** F.N. Williams ex Mast. (*N. mirabilis* × *N.* × *dormanniana*) · ♄ e Z10 ⒶⒶ; cult.
– *curtisii* Mast. = Nepenthes maxima

– **distillatoria** L. · ♄ e ⚥ Z10 ⊕ ▽ ✳; Sri Lanka
– **gracilis** Korth. · ♄ e ⚥ Z10 ⊕ ▽ ✳; Malay. Pen., Sumat., Kalimantan
– × **hookeriana** Lindl. (*N. ampullaria* × *N. rafflesiana*) · ♄ e ⚥ Z10 ⊕ ▽ ✳; Kalimantan
– **khasiana** Hook. f. · ♄ e ⚥ Z10 ⊕ ▽ ✳; Ind.: Khasia Hills
– **madagascariensis** Poir. · ♄ e Z10 ⊕ ▽ ✳; Madag.
– **maxima** Reinw. ex Nees · ♄ e ⚥ Z10 ⊕ ▽ ✳; N.Guinea, Kalimantan, Sulawesi
– **mirabilis** (Lour.) Druce · E:Monkey Cup · ♄ e ⚥ Z10 ⊕ ▽ ✳; S-China, Indochina, Malay. Arch., N.Guinea, Austr.: Queensl.
– **northiana** Hook. f. · ♄ e ⚥ Z10 ⊕ ▽ ✳; Kalimantan
– **rafflesiana** Jack · ♄ e ⚥ Z10 ⊕ ▽ ✳; Malay. Pen., Sumat., Kalimantan
– **rajah** Hook. f. · ♄ e Z10 ⊕ ▽ ✳; Kalimantan
– **sanguinea** Lindl. · ♄ e ⚥ Z10 ⊕ ▽ ✳; Malay. Pen.
– **veitchii** Hook. f. · ♄ e ↝ Z10 ⊕ ▽ ✳; Kalimantan
– **ventricosa** Blanco · ♄ e Z10 ⊕ ▽ ✳; Phil.

Nepeta L. -f- *Lamiaceae* · 248 spp. · E:Cat Mint; F:Menthe-des-chats; G:Katzenminze
– **cataria** L. · E:Catmint, Catnip; G:Gewöhnliche Katzenminze · ⚣ D Z3 VII-IX ⚥ ; Eur.* exc. Sc, C-Eur.; TR, Syr., Cauc., W-Sib., Amur, C-As., Him., nat. in N-Am., Jap., S-Afr.
– × **faassenii** Bergmans ex Stearn (*N. nepetella* × *N. racemosa*) · E:Catmint; F:Chataire, Herbe aux chats; G:Blaue Katzenminze, Blauminze · ⚣ Z3 V-IX; cult.
– **govaniana** Benth. · G:Gelbe Katzenminze · ⚣ Z5; W-Him.
– **grandiflora** M. Bieb. · E:Caucasus Catmint; G:Großblütige Katzenminze · ⚣ Z3 VII-VIII; Cauc., nat. in E-Eur., EC-Eur.; Queb., N.Y.
– *hederacea* (L.) Trevis. = Glechoma hederacea
– **hemsleyana** Oliv. ex Prain · ⚣ △ Z7 VII-IX; SE-Tibet
– *macrantha* Fisch. ex Benth. = Nepeta sibirica
– *mussinii* hort. = Nepeta × faassenii

– **nepetella** L. · E:Lesser Catmint; G:Iberische Katzenminze · ⚣ Z6; Eur.: sp., F, I
– **nervosa** Royle ex Benth. · F:Menthe aux chats; G:Geaderte Katzenminze · ⚣ △ Z5 VII-IX; Kashmir
– **nuda** L. · G:Pannonische Katzenminze
– subsp. **albiflora** (Boiss.) Gams · G:Weißblütige Katzenminze · ⚣ Z6; GR, Maced., TR, N-Iraq, Lebanon, Cauc., Iran
– subsp. **nuda** · G:Kahle Katzenminze · ⚣ Z6 VII-VIII; Eur.* exc. BrI, Sc; Cauc., W-Sib., E-Sib., C-As.; Mong., China: Sichuan
– *pannonica* L. = Nepeta nuda subsp. nuda
– **prattii** H. Lév. · G:Pratts Katzenminze · ⚣ Z6; W-China
– **racemosa** Lam. · G:Traubige Katzenminze · ⚣ Z4 VI-VIII; Cauc., W-Iran
– **sibirica** L. · G:Sibirische Katzenminze · ⚣ Z3 VII-VIII; S-Sib., Mong., China: Kansu

Nephelium L. -n- *Sapindaceae* · 22 (-38) spp. · E:Rambutan; F:Longanier, Néphélium, Ramboutan; G:Rambutan
– **lappaceum** L. · E:Rambutan; G:Rambutan · ♄ e Z10 ⊕ ⓝ; Ind., S-Vietn., Malay. Arch., Phil.
– *litchi* Cambess. = Litchi chinensis
– **mutabile** Blume · E:Pulasan; G:Pulasan · ♄ Z10 ⊕ ⓝ; Malay. Arch., Phil.

Nephrolepis Schott -f- *Nephrolepidaceae* · 44 spp. · E:Ladder Fern, Swort Fern; F:Néphrolépis; G:Schwertfarn
– **acuminata** (Houtt.) Kuhn · ⚣ Z10 ⊕; Malay. Arch.
– *acuta* (Schkuhr) C. Presl = Nephrolepis biserrata
– **biserrata** (Sw.) Schott · E:Giant Sword Fern; G:Großer Schwertfarn · ⚣ Z10 ⊕; Trop.
– **cordifolia** (L.) C. Presl · E:Erect Sword Fern, Narrow Sword Fern, Southern Sword Fern; G:Schlanker Schwertfarn · ⚣ Z10 ⊕; Trop., Jap., NZ
– *davallioides* (Sw.) Kuntze = Nephrolepis acuminata
– **exaltata** (L.) Schott · E:Boston Fern, Boston Sword Fern; G:Aufrechter Schwertfarn · ⚣ Z10 ⊕; Trop.
– **pectinata** (Willd.) Schott · E:Basket Fern · ⚣ Z10 ⊕; S-Mex., W-Ind., C-Am., trop. S-Am.
– *tuberosa* Hook. = Nephrolepis cordifolia

Nephthytis Schott -f- *Araceae* · 6 spp.
– **afzelii** Schott · ⁴ Z10 ⓜ; W-Afr.: Sierra
Leone, Liberia
– *picturata* N.E. Br. = Rhektophyllum
mirabile

Neptunia Lour. -f- *Mimosaceae* · 12 spp.
– **oleracea** Lour. · ⁴ ⌒ Z9 ⓜ Ⓝ; Trop.
– **plena** (L.) Benth. · ♄ ≈ Z10 ⓜ VI-VIII;
Lat.Am., trop. As.

Nerine Herb. -f- *Amaryllidaceae* · 25 spp. ·
E:Nerine; F:Nérine; G:Nerine
– *aurea* (L'Hér.) Bury = Lycoris aurea
– **bowdenii** W. Watson · ⁴ Z8 ⓚ IX; S-Afr.
– **some cultivars**
– *curvifolia* (Jacq.) Herb. = Nerine
sarniensis var. curvifolia
– *flexuosa* (Jacq.) Herb. = Nerine undulata
– **humilis** (Jacq.) Herb. · ⁴ Z9 ⓚ VIII-IX;
Cape
– **pudica** Hook. f. · ⁴ Z9 ⓚ IX-X; S-Afr.
– **sarniensis** (L.) Herb.
– var. **corusca** (Herb.) Baker · ⁴ Z9 ⓚ
IX-X; S-Afr. (Table Mountain)
– var. **curvifolia** (Jacq.) Traub · ⁴ Z9 ⓚ
IX-X; S-Afr. (Cape Prov.)
– var. **sarniensis** · E:Guernsey Lily;
G:Guernseylilie, Rote Nerine · ⁴ Z9 ⓚ;
Cape
– var. **venusta** (Ker-Gawl.) Baker · ⁴ Z9 ⓚ
IX-X; S-Afr. (Cape Prov.)
– **undulata** (L.) Herb. · ⁴ Z9 ⓚ IX-X; Cape
– *venusta* (Ker-Gawl.) Herb. = Nerine
sarniensis var. venusta

Nerium L. -n- *Apocynaceae* · 1 sp. ·
E:Oleander, Rose Bay; F:Laurier rose;
G:Oleander
– *divaricatum* L. = Tabernaemontana
divaricata
– *obesum* Forssk. = Adenium obesum
– **oleander** L. · E:Oleander, Rosebay;
F:Laurier rose; G:Oleander · ♄ e Z9 ⓚ
VI-IX ☝ ☀; Eur.: Ib, Fr, Ital-P, Ba; TR,
Levant, Iran, NW-Afr., Libya, nat. in
Crim, Cauc.
– **many cultivars**

Nertera Banks & Sol. ex Gaertn.
-f- *Rubiaceae* · 15 spp. · E:Beadplant;
F:Plante-perle; G:Korallenmoos
– **granadensis** (Mutis ex L. f.) Druce ·
E:Bead Plant, Coral Moss; G:Koral-
lenmoos · ⁴ ⌇ ⊛ Z9 ⓚ V-VI; C-Am.,

S-Am., Austr.: N.S.Wales, Victoria,
Tasman.; NZ

Neslia Desv. -f- *Brassicaceae* · 2 spp. ·
F:Neslie; G:Finkensame
– **paniculata** (L.) Desv.
– subsp. **paniculata** · E:Ball Mustard;
G:Gewöhnlicher Finkensame · ⊙ V-VII;
Eur, N-Afr., Cauc., Tien-Shan, nat. in
Can.

Neviusia A. Gray -f- *Rosaceae* · 2 spp. ·
E:Snow Wreath; G:Schneelocke
– **alabamensis** A. Gray · E:Alabama Snow
Wreath; G:Schneelocke · ♄ d Z6 VI-VII;
USA: Ala.

Nicandra Adans. -f- *Solanaceae* · 1 sp. ·
E:Apple of Peru; F:Faux-coqueret;
G:Giftbeere
– **physalodes** (L.) G. Gaertn. · E:Apple-
of-Peru; G:Giftbeere · ⊙ Z8 VII-IX ☀ Ⓝ;
Peru, nat. in C-Eur., SE-Eur.

Nicodemia Ten. = Buddleja
– *diversifolia* Ten. = Buddleja indica

Nicolaia Horan. = Etlingera
– *elatior* (Jack) Horan. = Etlingera elatior

Nicotiana L. -f- *Solanaceae* · 67 spp. ·
E:Tobacco; F:Tabac; G:Tabak
– *affinis* T. Moore = Nicotiana alata
– **alata** Link & Otto · E:Flowering Tobacco,
Tobacco; Plant G:Flügel-Tabak · ⊙ ⊙ ⁴
D Z7 VII-IX; SE-Braz., Urug., Parag., Arg.,
nat. in E-Eur.
– **many cultivars**
– **glauca** Graham · E:Tree Tobacco;
G:Blaugrüner Tabak · ⊙ ⊙ ⁴ ♄ e D Z8
ⓚ VII-X ☀; Arg., Parag., Bol., nat. in
S-Eur., USA: SE, Fla.
– **langsdorffii** Weinm. · ⊙ Z9 VII-VIII;
Braz., Chile
– **latissima** Mill. · G:Maryland-Tabak · ⊙;
cult. USA
– **longiflora** Cav. · E:Longflower Tobacco ·
⊙ ⁴ D Z8 VIII; Arg., Chile
– **rustica** L. · E:Indian Tobacco, Wild
Tobacco; G:Bauern-Tabak · ⊙ ⊙ ⁴ Z8
VI-IX ☀ Ⓝ; ? N-Am., nat. in Eur., USA: E
– × **sanderae** hort. Sander ex W. Watson
(*N. alata × N. forgetiana*) · F:Tabac
d'ornement; G:Niederer Zier-Tabak,
Sander-Tabak · ⊙ Z7 VII-IX; cult.

– **some cultivars**
– **suaveolens** Lehm. · E:Australian Tobacco · ☉ ⊙ D Z8 VII-VIII; SE-Austr.
– **sylvestris** Speg. & Comes · E:Flowering Tobacco; F:Tabac sylvestre; G:Berg-Tabak · ☉ ⚄ D Z8 VII-IX; Arg.
– **tabacum** L. · E:Common Tobacco, Tobacco ; G:Virginischer Tabak · ☉ ⊙ ⚄ Z8 VI-IX ⚘ ⚔ Ⓝ; ? S-Am., cult.
– **tomentosa** Ruiz & Pav. · ☉ ♄ Z9 VII-VIII; Braz., Peru
– **wigandioides** K. Koch & Fintelm. · ♄ Z9 ⓚ VII-VIII; Col.

Nidularium Lem. -n- *Bromeliaceae* · 45 spp. · E:Bird's-Nest Bromeliad; F:Nidularium; G:Nestbromelie, Trichterbromelie
– *acanthocrater* E. Morren = Neoregelia concentrica
– **amazonicum** (Baker) Linden & E. Morren · ⚄ Z10; Braz.
– *ampullaceum* E. Morren = Neoregelia ampullacea
– *billbergioides* (Schult. f.) L.B. Sm. = Canistropsis billbergioides
– *binotii* E. Morren = Neoregelia binotii
– *burchellii* (Baker) Mez = Canistropsis burchellii
– *chlorostictum* (Baker) E. Morren = Neoregelia chlorosticta
– *citrinum* (Burch. ex Baker) Mez = Canistropsis billbergioides
– *farinosum* Ule = Neoregelia farinosa
– **fulgens** Lem. · E:Blushing Bromeliad · ⚄ Z10 ⚄; E-Braz.
– **innocentii** Lem. · ⚄ Z10 ⚄; E-Braz.
– var. *lineatum* (Mez) L.B. Sm. = Nidularium innocentii
– var. *paxianum* (Mez) L.B. Sm. = Nidularium innocentii
– var. *striatum* Wittm. = Nidularium innocentii
– var. *wittmackianum* (Harms) L.B. Sm. = Nidularium longiflorum
– *lindenii* Regel = Canistrum fragrans
– **lineatum** Mez
– **longiflorum** Ule · ⚄ Z10; E-Braz.
– *meyendorffii* (Regel) Regel = Neoregelia carolinae
– *morrenianum* (Antoine) Baker = Neoregelia pineliana
– *paxianum* Mez = Nidularium innocentii
– *princeps* (Baker) E. Morren = Neoregelia princeps

– **procerum** Lindm. · ⚄ Z10 ⚄; E-Braz.
– **purpureum** Beer · ⚄ Z10 ⚄; E-Braz.
– *regelioides* Ule = Nidularium rutilans
– **rutilans** E. Morren · ⚄ Z10 ⚄; Braz.
– *sarmentosum* Regel = Neoregelia sarmentosa
– **scheremetiewii** Regel · ⚄ Z10 ⚄; E-Braz.
– *seidelii* L.B. Sm. & Reitz = Canistropsis seidelii
– *striatum* W. Bull = Nidularium innocentii
– *triste* (Beer) Regel = Neoregelia tristis
– **utriculosum** Ule · ⚄ Z10 ⚄; E-Braz.
– *wittmackianum* Harms = Nidularium longiflorum

Nierembergia Ruiz & Pav. -f- *Solanaceae* · 23 spp. · E:Cupflower; F:Nierembergia; G:Nierembergie, Weißbecher, Becher-blüte
– *calycina* hort. ex Vilm. = Nierembergia gracilis
– **gracilis** Hook. · ⚄ Z7 VII-VIII; Arg.
– **hippomanica** Miers
– var. **hippomanica** · E:Cup Flower · ⚄ Z8 ⓚ; Arg.
– var. **violacea** Millán · F:Nirembergia · ⚄ Z8 ⓚ VI-IX; Arg.
– **repens** Ruiz & Pav. · E:White Cup; G:Weißbecher, Weiße Becherblüte · ⚄ ↝ Z7 VII-IX; Urug., Arg., Chile
– *rivularis* Miers = Nierembergia repens
– **scoparia** Sendtn. · ♄ Z8 ⓚ VII-IX; Arg., Urug.

Nigella L. -f- *Ranunculaceae* · 14-20 spp. · E:Fennel Flower, Love-in-a-Mist; F:Nigelle; G:Braut in Haaren, Gretel im Busch, Jungfer im Grünen, Schwarzküm-mel
– **arvensis** L. · E:Wild Fennel; G:Acker-Schwarzkümmel ☉ VII-IX; Eur.: Fr, Ital-P, C-Eur., EC-Eur., Ba, E-Eur.; TR, Iraq, Levant, Cauc., C-As., N-Afr.
– *bucharica* Schipcz. = Komaroffia bucharica
– **ciliaris** DC. · ☉; Syr.
– **damascena** L. · E:Love-in-a-mist · ☉ ⚅ VI-IX ⚘ ; Eur.: Ib, Fr, Ital-P, Ba, Crim; TR, Cyprus, Cauc., Iran, NW-Afr., Libya, nat. in C-Eur.
– **some cultivars**
– **hispanica** L. · ☉ VII-VIII; Eur.: Ib, F
– **nigellastrum** (L.) Willk. · ☉; Eur.: Fr, sp., GR, Crete, Crim; Cauc., N-Iraq,

Cyprus
- **orientalis** L. · ⊙; BG, Cauc, Crim, TR,
Iran, C-As.
- **sativa** L. · ⊙ VI-VIII ♀ Ⓝ; ? SW-As., nat.
in Eur.: Fr, Ital-P, Ba, EC-Eur.; Cauc.,
Iran, C-As. N-Afr., Eth.

Nigritella Rich. -f- *Orchidaceae* · 13 spp. ·
E:Vanilla Orchid; F:Nigritelle; G:Kohl-
röschen
- **archiducis-joannis** Teppner & E. Klein ·
G:Erzherzog-Johann-Kohlröschen · ⁂
VII-VIII ▽ ✳; Eur.: A (Steiermark)
- **nigra** (L.) Rchb. f. · E:Black Vanilla
Orchid; G:Schwarzes Kohlröschen · ⁂ △
V-VI ▽ ✳; Eur.: Ib, F, I, C-Eur., Sc, Ba,
RO
- **rhellicani** Teppner & E. Klein · ⁂ VI-VIII
▽ ✳; C-Eur., S-Eur.
- **rubra** (Wettst.) K. Richt. · G:Rotes
Kohlröschen · ⁂ VI-VIII ▽ ✳; Alp., mts.
RO
- **stiriaca** (Rech.) Teppner & E. Klein ·
G:Steirisches Kohlröschen · ⁂ VI-VIII ▽
✳; Eur.: A
- **widderi** Teppner & E. Klein · G:Widders
Kohlröschen · ⁂ VII ▽ ✳; Eur.: A, G, I;
Alp., Apenn.

Niphidium J. Sm. -n- *Polypodiaceae* ·
10 spp.
- **crassifolium** (L.) Lellinger · ⁂ Z10 Ⓜ;
C-Am., trop. S-Am.

Niphobolus Kaulf. = Pyrrosia
- *adnascens* (Sw.) Kaulf. = Pyrrosia
lanceolata
- *lingua* (Thunb.) J. Sm. = Pyrrosia lingua
- *tricuspis* J. Sm. = Pyrrosia hastata

Nipponanthemum (Kitam.) Kitam.
-n- *Asteraceae* · 1 sp. · E:Nippon Daisy;
G:Nipponchrysantheme
- **nipponicum** (Franch. ex Maxim.)
Kitam. · E:Nippon Daisy; G:Nipponchry-
santheme · ♄ Z8 Ⓚ; Jap.; coasts

Nitraria L. -f- *Zygophyllaceae* · 6 spp.
- **schoberi** L. · ♄ Z6; S-Russ., Cauc.,
W-Sib., C-As, Iran, Mong., China:
Sinkiang

Nivenia Vent. -f- *Iridaceae* · 5-9 spp.
- **corymbosa** (Ker-Gawl.) Baker · ♄ Z9 Ⓚ
II-IV; Cape

Noccaea Moench = Thlaspi
- *alpina* (L.) Rchb. = Pritzelago alpina
subsp. alpina
- *auerswaldii* (Willk.) Willk. & Lange =
Pritzelago alpina subsp. auerswaldii

Nolana L. f. -f- *Nolanaceae* · 18 spp. ·
F:Nolana; G:Glockenwinde
- *atriplicifolia* D. Don = Nolana paradoxa
subsp. atriplicifolia
- **coelestis** (Lindl.) Miers · ♄ Z8 Ⓚ VI-X;
Chile
- *grandiflora* Lehm. ex G. Don = Nolana
paradoxa subsp. atriplicifolia
- **humifusa** (Gouan) I.M. Johnst. · ⊙ ⚘ ⤳
VII-VIII; Peru
- *lanceolata* (Miers) Miers ex Dunal =
Nolana paradoxa subsp. atriplicifolia
- **napiformis** Phil. · ⊙ ⚘ ⤳ VII-VIII; Peru,
Chile
- **paradoxa** Lindl.
- subsp. **atriplicifolia** (D. Don) Mesa · ⊙
VI-IX; Chile
- subsp. **paradoxa** · ⊙ ⤳ VII-VIII; Chile
- *prostrata* L. f. = Nolana humifusa
- × **tenella** Lindl. (*N. humifusa* × *N.
paradoxa*) · ⊙; cult.

Nolina Michx. -f- *Dracaenaceae* · 27 spp.
- *gracilis* (Lem.) Cif. & Giacom. =
Beaucarnea gracilis
- **longifolia** (Karw. ex Schult. & Schult. f.)
Hemsl. · E:Mexican Grasstree; G:Mexika-
nischer Grasbaum · ♄ ♈ e Z10 Ⓚ; S-Mex.
- *recurvata* (Lem.) Hemsl. = Beaucarnea
recurvata
- *stricta* (Lem.) Cif. & Giacom. = Beaucarnea stricta
- *tuberculata* (Roezl) hort. = Beaucarnea
recurvata

Noltea Rchb. -f- *Rhamnaceae* · 1 sp.
- **africana** (L.) Rchb. · E:Soap Bush · ♄ e
Z9 Ⓜ V; S-Afr.

Nomocharis Franch. -f- *Liliaceae* · 9 spp. ·
F:Nomocharis; G:Prachtlilie
- **aperta** (Franch.) W.W. Sm. & W.E.
Evans · ⁂ Z7 VI-VII; China: Tibet, Yunnan; N-Burma
- **farreri** (W.E. Evans) Cox · ⁂ Z7 VI-VII;
NE-Burma
- *mairei* H. Lév. = Nomocharis pardanthina
- **pardanthina** Franch. · ⁂ Z7 VI-VII;
NW-Yunnan, Sichuan

– var. *farreri* W.E. Evans = Nomocharis
farreri

Nonea Medik. -f- *Boraginaceae* · 35 spp. ·
F:Nonnée; G:Mönchskraut
– **erecta** Bernh. · G:Braunes Mönchskraut ·
⁂ V-VIII; Eur.: C-Eur., EC-Eur., Ba,
E-Eur.; Cauc., W-Sib., E-Sib., C-As., nat.
in F, FIN
– **lutea** (Desr.) DC. · G:Gelbes Mönchskraut · ⊙ IV-VI; Russ., Cauc, N-Iran, nat. in
H, W-Ba, RO
– *pulla* DC. = Nonea erecta
– **rosea** (M. Bieb.) Link · G:Rosenrotes
Mönchskraut · ⁂ VI-IX; TR, N-Iraq, Cauc.,
N-Iran

Nopalea Salm-Dyck = Opuntia
– *cochenillifera* (L.) Salm-Dyck = Opuntia
cochenillifera

Nopalxochia Britton & Rose -f- *Cactaceae* ·
4 spp.
– **phyllanthoides** (DC.) Britton & Rose · ♄
Z10 ⓦ ▽ ✳; Mex.

Normanbokea Kladiwa & Buxb. =
Turbinicarpus
– *pseudopectinata* (Backeb.) Kladiwa &
Buxb. = Turbinicarpus pseudopectinatus
– *valdeziana* (L. Möller) Kladiwa & Buxb. =
Turbinicarpus valdezianus

Nothofagus Blume -f- *Fagaceae* · 36 spp. ·
E:Southern Beech; F:Hêtre austral;
G:Scheinbuche, Südbuche
– **alpina** (Poepp. & Endl.) Oerst. · ♄ d Z7
Ⓝ; Arg., Chile
– **antarctica** (G. Forst.) Oerst. · E:Antarctic
Beech; F:Hêtre austral, Hêtre de Magel-
lan; G:Scheinbuche, Südbuche · ♄ d Z7 V;
Chile
– **cunninghamii** (Hook. f.) Oerst. ·
E:Myrtle Beech; G:Tasmanische Schein-
buche · ♄ e Z9 ⚘; Austr.: Tasman.,
Victoria
– **dombeyi** (Mirb.) Oerst. · E:Coigue · ♄ e
Z8 ⚘ Ⓝ; Chile
– **menziesii** (Hook. f.) Oerst. · E:Silver
Beech; G:Silberne Scheinbuche · ♄ e Z9
⚘; NZ
– **obliqua** (Blume) Oerst. · E:Roble Beech;
F:Roble; G:Pellin-Scheinbuche · ♄ d Z7
Ⓝ; Chile, S-Arg.
– *procera* Oerst. = Nothofagus alpina

Notholaena R. Br. -f- *Adiantaceae* · 28 spp.
– **marantae** (L.) R. Br. · G:Pelzfarn · ⁂
Z7 ⚘ ⋀ V-VII; Eur.: Ib, F, Ital-P, Sw, A,
EC-Eur., Ba, RO, Crim, Canar., Madeira;
TR, Cauc., Him., Eth.

Notholirion Wall. ex Boiss. -n- *Liliaceae* ·
5 spp.
– **campanulatum** Cotton & Stearn · ⁂ Z7
⋀ V-VI; E-Him., W-China
– **macrophyllum** (D. Don) Boiss. · ⁂ Z7 ⋀
III-V; Nepal, Bhutan, Sikkim, W-China
– **thomsonianum** (Royle) Stapf · ⁂ Z7 ⋀
V-VI; Afgh., W-Him.

Nothopanax Miq. = Polyscias
– *arboreus* (Murray) Seem. = Pseudopanax
arboreus
– *davidii* (Franch.) Harms ex Diels =
Metapanax davidii
– *fruticosus* (L.) Miq. = Polyscias fruticosa
– *guilfoylei* (W. Bull) Merr. = Polyscias
guilfoylei

Nothoscordum Kunth -n- *Alliaceae* ·
86 spp. · E:False Garlic, Honeybells;
F:Ail; G:Bastardlauch
– **bivalve** (L.) Britton · E:Crow Poison · ⁂
Z5; USA: NE, NEC, NC, SE, Fla.
– *fragrans* (Vent.) Kunth = Nothoscordum
gracile
– **gracile** (Aiton) Stearn · ⁂ D Z7 V-VI;
Mex.
– *inodorum* (Aiton) G. Nicholson = Allium
neapolitanum
– *striatum* (Jacq.) Kunth = Nothoscordum
bivalve

Notocactus (K. Schum.) Frič -m-
Cactaceae · c. 25 spp. · E:Ball Cactus
– *acutus* F. Ritter = Notocactus ottonis
– *agnetae* Vliet = Notocactus concinnus
– *ampliocostatus* (F. Ritter) S. Theun. =
Notocactus schumannianus
– *apricus* (Arechav.) A. Berger = Notocactus concinnus
– *arechavaletae* (Speg.) Herter = Notocactus ottonis
– *bommeljei* Vliet = Notocactus concinnus
– **buenekeri** (Buining) Buxb. · � Z9 ⚘ ▽
✳; Braz.: Santa Catarina, Rio Grande do
Sul
– **buiningii** Buxb. · � Z9 ⚘ ▽ ✳; Braz.:
Rio Grande do Sul; N-Urug.
– **caespitosus** (Speg.) Backeb. · � Z9 ⚘ ▽

✳; Braz.: Rio Grande do Sul; Urug.
- *campestrensis* F. Ritter = Notocactus ottonis
- **concinnus** (Monv.) A. Berger · ⵣ Z9 ⓚ ▽ ✳; Braz.: Rio Grande do Sul; Urug.
- **erinaceus** (Haw.) Krainz · ⵣ Z9 ⓚ ▽ ✳; Braz.: Rio Grande do Sul; Urug., NE-Arg.
- *floricomus* (Arechav.) A. Berger = Notocactus mammulosus
- *glaucinus* F. Ritter = Notocactus ottonis
- *globularis* F. Ritter = Notocactus ottonis
- **graessneri** (K. Schum.) A. Berger · ⵣ Z9 ⓚ ▽ ✳; Braz.: Rio Grande do Sul
- *grossei* (K. Schum.) Frič = Notocactus schumannianus
- **haselbergii** (Haage) A. Berger · E:Scarlet Ball Cactus · ⵣ Z9 ⓚ ▽ ✳; Braz.: Rio Grande do Sul
- **herteri** (Werderm.) Buining & Kreuz. · ⵣ Z9 ⓚ ▽ ✳; Braz.: Rio Grande do Sul; Urug.
- *ibicuiensis* (Osten) Herter = Notocactus ottonis
- *incomptus* N. Gerloff = Notocactus ottonis
- *laetevirens* F. Ritter = Notocactus ottonis
- **leninghausii** (K. Schum.) A. Berger · E:Golden Ball Cactus · ⵣ Z9 ⓚ ▽ ✳; Braz.: Rio Grande do Sul
- *leucocarpus* (Arechav.) G. Schäf. = Notocactus erinaceus
- **mammulosus** (Lem.) A. Berger · E:Lemon Ball · ⵣ Z9 ⓚ ▽ ✳; Braz.: Rio Grande do Sul; Urug., NE-Arg.
- *megapotamicus* Osten ex Herter = Notocactus ottonis
- **mueller-melchersii** Frič ex Backeb. · ⵣ Z9 ⓚ; Urug.
- *mueller-moelleri* Z. Fleisch. & Schütz = Notocactus mammulosus
- *muricatus* (Pfeiff.) A. Berger = Notocactus concinnus
- **ottonis** (Lehm.) A. Berger · ⵣ Z9 ⓚ ▽ ✳; NE-Arg., S-Parag.
- *oxycostatus* Buining & Brederoo = Notocactus ottonis
- *roseoluteus* Vliet = Notocactus mammulosus
- **rutilans** Däniker & Krainz · ⵣ Z9 ⓚ ▽ ✳; N-Urug.
- **schumannianus** (Nicolai bis) A. Berger · ⵣ Z9 ⓚ ▽ ✳; NE-Arg., S-Parag.
- **scopa** (Spreng.) A. Berger · E:Silver Ball Cactus · ⵣ Z9 ⓚ ▽ ✳; Braz.: Rio Grande do Sul; Urug.
- *securituberculatus* F. Ritter = Notocactus

ottonis
- *sessiliflorus* (Pfeiff.) Krainz = Notocactus erinaceus
- *submammulosus* (Lem.) Backeb. = Notocactus mammulosus
- *tabularis* (Cels ex K. Schum.) A. Berger = Notocactus concinnus
- *vanvlietii* Rausch = Notocactus concinnus

Notospartium Hook. f. -n- *Fabaceae* · 3 spp. · E:Southern Broom; F:Genêt austral; G:Südginster
- **carmichaeliae** Hook. f. · ♄ Z8 ⓚ VII; NZ

Nuphar Sm. -f- *Nymphaeaceae* · 16 spp. · E:Yellow Pond Lily; F:Jaunet d'eau, Nénuphar jaune; G:Mummel, Teichrose
- **advena** (Aiton) W.T. Aiton · E:American Spatter Dock, Cow Lily, Yellow Water Lily; F:Nénuphar d'Amérique; G:Amerikanische Teichrose · ⵄ ≈ Z3 V-VIII; USA: NE, NCE, NC, SC, SE, Fla.; Mex., W.Ind.
- *intermedia* Ledeb. = Nuphar × spenneriana
- **japonica** DC. · F:Nénuphar du Japon; G:Japanische Teichrose · ⵄ ≈ Z6 VII-VIII; Jap.
- **lutea** (L.) Sibth. & Sm. · E:Brandy Bottle, Yellow Pond Lily, Yellow Water Lily; F:Nénuphar commun; G:Gelbe Teichrose, Mummel · ⵄ ≈ Z4 VI-VIII ⚘ ▽; Eur.*, TR, Cauc., W-Sib., E-Sib., C-As.
- **pumila** (Timm) DC. · F:Nénuphar nain; G:Kleine Teichrose · ⵄ ≈ Z4 VII-VIII ▽; Eur.* exc. Ital-P; W-Sib., E-Sib., Amur, Sakhal., Kamchat., Mong., China, Jap.
- × **spenneriana** Gaudin (*N. lutea* × *N. pumila*) · G:Bastard-Teichrose · ⵄ; C-Eur., Sc, Russ.; W-Sib.

Nuttallia Torr. & A. Gray = Oemleria
- *cerasiformis* Torr. & A. Gray ex Hook. & Arn. = Oemleria cerasiformis

Nyctanthes L. -f- *Verbenaceae* · 2 spp. · G:Trauerbaum; E:Tree of Sadness
- **arbor-tristis** L. · E:Tree of Sadness; G:Trauerbaum · ♄ d D Z10 Ⓦ VII Ⓝ; C-Ind.

Nycteranthus Neck. ex Rothm. = Aridaria
- *noctiflorus* (L.) Rothm. = Aridaria noctiflora

Nycterinia D. Don = Zaluzianskya
– *capensis* Benth. = Zaluzianskya capensis

Nyctocereus (A. Berger) Britton & Rose
-m- *Cactaceae* · 3 spp.
– **serpentinus** (Lag. & Rodr.) Britton &
Rose · ♉ Z9 ⌂ ▽ ✳; Mex.

Nymphaea L. -f- *Nymphaeaceae* · c.
50 spp. · E:Water Lily; F:Nénuphar;
G:Seerose
– **alba** L. · E:White Water Lily; F:Nymphéa
blanc; G:Weiße Seerose · ♃ ≈ Z5
VI-VIII ⚥ ⚘ ▽; Eur.*, TR, Cauc.
– **amazonum** Mart. & Zucc. · ♃ ≈ D Z10
⚘ V-VIII; Mex., C-Am., trop. S-Am.
– **caerulea** Savigny · E:Blue Egyptian
Lotus; G:Blaue Ägyptische Seerose,
Blauer Ägyptischer Lotus · ♃ ≈ Z10 ⚘
⌂ V-VIII; Palest., Egypt, trop. Afr.
– **candida** C. Presl · F:Nymphéa luisant;
G:Glänzende Seerose · ♃ ≈ Z4 VI-VIII
▽; Eur.: Sc, Fr, C-Eur., EC-Eur., E-Eur.;
Cauc., W-Sib., E-Sib., C-As.
– **capensis** Thunb. · E:Blue Water Lily,
Cape Blue Water Lily; G:Blaue Seerose
· ♃ ≈ Z10 ⚘ V-VIII; E-Afr., S-Afr.,
Madag.
– *citrina* Peter = Nymphaea stuhlmannii
– **colorata** Peter · ♃ ≈ Z10 ⚘ V-VIII;
Tanzania
– × **daubenyana** W.T. Baxter ex Daubeny
(*N. caerulea* × *N. micrantha*) · ♃ ≈ Z10
⚘ III-X; cult.
– **elegans** Hook. · E:Tropical Royal Blue
Water Lily · ♃ ≈ D Z9 ⚘ V-VIII; Tex.,
N.Mex., Mex., Guat.
– *flavovirens* Lehm. = Nymphaea gracilis
– **gigantea** Hook. · E:White Pond Lily;
G:Große Seerose · ♃ ≈ D Z10 ⚘ VII-IX;
N.Guinea, Austr.
– **gracilis** Zucc. · ♃ ≈ Z10 ⚘ VI-VIII;
Mex.
– × **helvola** Lat.-Marl. (*N. mexicana* × *N.
tetragona*) · ♃ Z6; cult.
– **lotus** L. · E:Egyptian Lotus, White Egyptian Lotus; G:Weiße Ägyptische Seerose,
Weißer Ägyptischer Lotus · ♃ ≈ D Z10
⚘ VI-IX ⚥; Egypt, trop. Afr., Ind., Malay.
Arch., Phil.,
– var. *dentata* (Schumach. & Thonn.) G.
Nicholson = Nymphaea lotus
– var. *thermalis* (DC.) Tuzson = Nymphaea
lotus
– **mexicana** Zucc. · E:Yellow Water Lily · ♃

≈ D Z9 ⚘ VI-VIII; Tex., Fla., Mex.
– **micrantha** Guill. & Perr. · ♃ ≈ D Z10
⚘ III-X; W-Afr.
– **nouchalii** Burm. f. · E:Blue Lotus;
G:Stern-Seerose · ♃ ≈ Z10 ⚘ VI-VIII;
Ind., SE-As., Malay. Pen., Afr.
– **odorata** Aiton
– subsp. **odorata** · E:Fragrant Water Lily;
F:Nymphéa odorant; G:Wohlriechende
Seerose · ♃ ≈ D Z3 VI-VIII ⚥ ; Can.:
E; USA: NE, NCE, SE, Fla., SC ; Mex.,
C-Am., W.Ind., nat. in W-Eur.
– subsp. **tuberosa** (Paine) Wiersema
& Hellq. · E:Tuberous Water Lily;
F:Nymphéa tubéreux · ♃ ≈ Z3 VI-VIII;
Can.: E; USA: NE, NCE, NC, Ark.
– var. *rosea* Pursh = Nymphaea odorata
subsp. odorata
– **pubescens** Willd. · ♃ ≈ Z10 ⚘ VI-VIII;
Ind., nat. in H
– *rubra* Roxb. ex Andrews = Nymphaea
pubescens
– *stellata* Willd. = Nymphaea nouchalii
– **stuhlmannii** (Engl.) Schweinf. & Gilg · ♃
≈ D Z10 ⚘ V-VIII; E-Afr. (Malongwe)
– **tetragona** Georgi · E:Pygmy Water Lily;
G:Zwerg-Seerose · ♃ ≈ D Z2 VI-VIII;
Eur.: FIN, N-Russ; N-As, China, Jap.
Him., Alaska, Can., USA: NE, NCE, Rocky
Mts., Wash.
– *thermalis* DC. = Nymphaea lotus
– *tuberosa* Paine = Nymphaea odorata
subsp. tuberosa
– **Cultivars:**
– **many cultivars, see Section III**

Nymphoides Ség. -f- *Menyanthaceae* ·
20 spp. · E:Floating Heart, Fringed Water
Lily; F:Petit nénuphar; G:Seekanne
– **aquatica** (Walter) Kuntze · E:Banana
Plant, Fairy Water Lily; G:Wasserbanane
· ♃ ≈ Z7 ⚘ ⌂; USA: NE, SE, Fla., SC
– **humboldtiana** (Kunth) Kuntze ·
G:Humboldts Seekanne · ♃ ≈ Z10 ⚘
VII-IX; trop. Am.
– **indica** (L.) Kuntze · E:Water Snowflake;
G:Indische Seekanne · ♃ ≈ Z10 ⚘
VII-IX; SW-China, Jap., SE-As., Austr.,
Fiji
– **peltata** (S.G. Gmel.) Kuntze · E:Water
Fringe, Yellow Floating Heart; F:Faux
nénuphar, Limnanthème; G:Gewöhnli-
che Seekanne · ♃ ≈ Z6 VI-IX ▽; Eur.*
exc. Sc; Cauc., Iran, W-Sib., E-Sib., Amur,
C-As., Him., Mong., China, Jap., nat. in Sc

Nypa Steck -f- *Arecaceae* · 1 sp. · E:Mangrove Palm; F:Nipa; G:Nipapalme
- **fruticans** Wurmb · ħ e ~ Z10 Ⓦ Ⓝ; Sri Lanka, Burma, Malay. Arch., Phil., trop. Austr.

Nyssa L. -f- *Nyssaceae* · 5-8 spp. · E:Tupelo; F:Tupélo; G:Tupelobaum
- **aquatica** L. · E:Cotton Gum, Water Tupelo; G:Wasser-Tupelobaum · ħ d ~ Z8 Ⓚ V Ⓝ; USA: Va., Ky., SE, Fla., SC
- **sylvatica** Marshall · E:Black Gum, Black Tupelo, Sour Gum; F:Tupélo; G:Wald-Tupelobaum · ħ d ~ Z3 VI Ⓝ; Ont., USA: NE, NCE, SC, SE, Fla.; Mex.

Obregonia Frič -f- *Cactaceae* · 1 sp.
- **denegrii** Frič · Ψ Z9 Ⓚ ∇ ✱; Mex.: Tamaulipas

Ochagavia Phil. -f- *Bromeliaceae* · 4 spp.
- **carnea** (Beer) L.B. Sm. & Looser · ♃ Z10 Ⓚ; Chile
- **litoralis** (Phil.) Zizka, Trumpler & Zöllner · ♃ Z8 Ⓚ; Chile

Ochna L. -f- *Ochnaceae* · 86 spp. · E:Bird's Eye Bush; F:Ochna ; G:Nagelbeere
- **kirkii** Oliv. · ħ e Z10 Ⓦ; Kenya, Tanzania, N-Mozamb.
- **serrulata** (Hochst.) Walp. · E:Bird's Eye Bush, Mickey Mouse Plant · ♄ e ♣ Z9 Ⓦ Ⓚ II-IV; trop. Afr.

Ochroma Sw. -n- *Bombacaceae* · 1 sp. · E:Balsa, Down-Tree; F:Balsa, Patte-de-lièvre; G:Balsabaum
- *lagopus* Sw. = Ochroma pyramidale
- **pyramidale** (Cav. ex Lam.) Urb. · E:Balsa Tree; G:Balsabaum · ħ e Z10 Ⓦ Ⓝ; Mex., C-Am., W.Ind., trop. S-Am.

Ocimum L. -n- *Lamiaceae* · 68 spp. · E:Basil; F:Basilic; G:Basilikum
- **americanum** L. · E:American Basil; G:Zitronen-Basilikum · ⊙ Z10 Ⓚ VII Ⓝ; trop. Afr., trop. As.
- **basilicum** L. · E:Basil; G:Basilienkraut, Basilikum · ⊙ ♃ D Z10 VI-VIII ⚕ Ⓝ; orig.?; cult. Trop., Subtrop.
- **some cultivars**
- *canum* Sims = Ocimum americanum
- *crispum* Thunb. = Perilla frutescens var. nankinensis
- *sanctum* L. = Ocimum tenuiflorum
- **tenuiflorum** L. · G:Kleines Basilikum · ♄ Z10 Ⓚ ⚕ Ⓝ; W-As., Arab., Ind., Sri Lanka, Malay. Arch., Austr., Pacific Is.

Ocotea Aubl. -f- *Lauraceae* · 350 spp.
- **bullata** E. Mey. · E:Black Stinkwood · ħ e Ⓚ Ⓝ; S-Afr.
- **puchury-major** Mart. · ħ e Ⓦ Ⓝ; Braz.
- **rodiaei** (R.H. Schomb.) Mez · ħ e Ⓦ Ⓝ; Guyan.
- **usambarensis** Engl. · ♄ Ⓦ Ⓝ; Kenya, Tanzania

Octomeria R. Br. -f- *Orchidaceae* · 149 spp.
- **crassifolia** Lindl. · ♃ Z10 Ⓦ ∇ ✱; Braz.
- **gracilis** Lodd. ex Lindl. · ♃ Z10 Ⓦ ∇ ✱; Braz.
- **graminifolia** (L.) R. Br. · ♃ Z10 Ⓦ IV ∇ ✱; W.Ind., trop. S-Am.
- **grandiflora** Lindl. · ♃ Z10 Ⓦ X ∇ ✱; Trinidad, Surinam, Braz., Parag., Bol.
- **juncifolia** Barb. Rodr. · ♃ Z10 Ⓦ X ∇ ✱; Braz.

× **Odontioda** hort. -f- *Orchidaceae* (*Cochlioda* × *Odontoglossum*)

Odontites Ludw. -m- *Scrophulariaceae* · c. 30 spp. · E:Bartsia; F:Odontitès; G:Zahntrost
- **litoralis** (M. Bieb.) Link · G:Salz-Zahntrost · ⊙ V-VI; Eur.: Sc, N-G, PL, Balt.
- **luteus** (L.) Clairv. · G:Gelber Zahntrost · ⊙ VII-X; Eur.* exc. BrI, Sc; TR, Cauc., C-As., NW-Afr.
- *ruber* Gilib. = Odontites vernus
- **vernus** (Bellardi) Dumort. · E:Red Bartsa; G:Acker-Zahntrost, Frühlings-Zahntrost · ⊙ Z6 V-IX; Eur.*
- **viscosus** (L.) Clairv. · G:Klebriger Zahntrost · ⊙; Eur.: Ib, F, I, Sw, NW-Afr.
- **vulgaris** Moench · G:Herbst-Zahntrost, Roter Zahntrost · ⊙ VII-IX; Eur.*, TR, Iran, N-As.

× **OdontoBrassia** hort. -f- *Orchidaceae* (*Brassia* × *Odontoglossum*)

× **Odontocidium** hort. -n- *Orchidaceae* (*Odontoglossum* × *Oncidium*)
- **Cultivars:**
- **many cultivars**

Odontoglossum Kunth -n- *Orchidaceae* · 67 spp.

– × **adrianum** L. Linden (*O. nobile* × *O. luteopurpureum*) · ⁴ Z₁₀ ⓚ X-IV ▽ ✳; Col.
– **astranthum** Linden & Rchb. f. · ⁴ Z₁₀ ⓚ ▽ ✳; Ecuad.
– *aureum* (Lindl.) Garay = Cyrtochilum aureum
– *bictoniense* (Bateman) Lindl. = Rhynchostele bictoniensis
– **blandum** Rchb. f. · ⁴ Z₁₀ ⓚ ▽ ✳; Col.
– *cariniferum* Rchb. f. = Miltonioides carinifera
– *cervantesii* Lex. = Rhynchostele cervantesii
– **cirrhosum** Lindl. · ⁴ Z₁₀ ⓚ IV-V ▽ ✳; Ecuad., Peru
– **constrictum** Lindl. · ⁴ Z₁₀ ⓚ X-XII ▽ ✳; Ecuad., Col., Venez.
– *convallarioides* (Schltr.) Ames & Correll = Cuitlauzina convallarioides
– *cordatum* Lindl. = Rhynchostele cordata
– **crispum** Lindl. · E:Lace Orchid · ⁴ Z₁₀ ⓚ II-IV ▽ ✳; Col.
– **cristatum** Lindl. · ⁴ Z₁₀ ⓚ IV-V ▽ ✳; Col., Ecuad.
– **cruentum** Rchb. f. · ⁴ Z₁₀ ⓚ ▽ ✳; Col., Ecuad.
– *edwardii* Rchb. f. = Cyrtochilum edwardii
– **hallii** Lindl. · ⁴ Z₁₀ ⓚ III-IV ▽ ✳; Col., Ecuad., Peru
– **harryanum** Rchb. f. · ⁴ Z₁₀ ⓚ VII-VIII ▽ ✳; Col., Ecuad., Peru
– × *hunnelwellianum* Rolfe = Odontoglossum × adrianum
– **lindleyanum** Rchb. f. & Warsz. · ⁴ Z₁₀ ⓚ V-VII ▽ ✳; Col.
– *loxense* F. Lehm. & Kraenzl. = Odontoglossum astranthum
– **luteopurpureum** Lindl. · ⁴ Z₁₀ ⓚ III-VI ▽ ✳; Col.
– *maculatum* Lex. = Rhynchostele maculata
– *majale* Rchb. f. = Rhynchostele majalis
– **nevadense** Rchb. f. · ⁴ Z₁₀ ⓚ ▽ ✳; Col.
– **nobile** Rchb. f. · ⁴ Z₁₀ ⓚ III-VI ▽ ✳; Col.
– **odoratum** Lindl. · ⁴ Z₁₀ ⓚ III-V ▽ ✳; Col., Venez.
– *pescatorei* Linden ex Lindl. = Odontoglossum nobile
– *phalaenopsis* Linden & Rchb. f. = Miltoniopsis phalaenopsis
– *platycheilum* Weathers = Rhynchostele majalis
– *pulchellum* Bateman ex Lindl. = Cuitlauzina pulchella
– *reichenheimii* Linden & Rchb. f. =

Miltonioides reichenheimii
– *roezlii* Rchb. f. = Miltoniopsis roezlii
– *roseum* Lindl. = Cochlioda rosea
– *rossii* Lindl. = Rhynchostele rossii
– *sanderianum* Rchb. f. = Odontoglossum constrictum
– **sanguineum** (Rchb. f.) Dalström · ⁴ Z₁₀ ⓚ X-XI ▽ ✳; Peru, Ecuad.
– **spectatissimum** Lindl. · ⁴ Z₁₀ ⓚ III-V ▽ ✳; Col.
– *stellatum* Lindl. = Rhynchostele stellata
– *triumphans* Rchb. f. = Odontoglossum spectatissimum
– *uroskinneri* Lindl. = Rhynchostele uroskinneri
– *vexillarium* Rchb. f. = Miltoniopsis vexillaria
– *warscewiczii* Rchb. f. = Miltoniopsis warscewiczii
– **Cultivars:**
– **many cultivars**

Odontonema Nees -n- *Acanthaceae* · 26 spp.
– **schomburgkianum** (Nees) Kuntze · ♄ e Z₁₀ ⓜ XII-I; Col.

× **Odontonia** Rolfe -f- *Orchidaceae* (*Miltonia* × *Odontoglossum*)
– **Cultivars:**
– **many cultivars**

Odontospermum Neck. ex Sch. Bip. = Asteriscus
– *maritimum* (L.) Sch. Bip. = Asteriscus maritimus
– *sericeum* (L. f.) Sch. Bip. = Nauplius sericeus

Oeceoclades Lindl. -f- *Orchidaceae* · 38 spp.
– **maculata** (Lindl.) Lindl. · E:Monk Orchid · ⁴ Z₁₀ ⓜ VIII-X ▽ ✳; Fla., W.Ind., trop. S-Am., trop. Afr.

Oehmea Buxb. = Mammillaria
– *nelsonii* (Britton & Rose) Buxb. = Mammillaria nelsonii

Oemleria Rchb. -f- *Rosaceae* · 1 sp. · E:Oregon Plum, Osoberry; F:Prunier de l'Orégon; G:Oregonpflaume
– **cerasiformis** (Torr. & A. Gray ex Hook. & Arn.) J.W. Landon · E:Indian Plum, Osoberry; G:Oregonpflaume · ♄ d Z6 V;

B.C., USA: NW, Calif.

Oenanthe L. -f- *Apiaceae* · 30-40 spp. · E:Water Dropwort; F:Œnanthe; G:Wasserfenchel

- **aquatica** (L.) Poir. · E:Fine Leaved Water Dropwort; F:Oenanthe aquatique; G:Großer Wasserfenchel, Pferdesaat · ⊙ ~ VI-VIII ⚕ ☠ Ⓝ; Eur.*, Cauc., W-Sib., E-Sib., C-As., nat. in N-Am.
- **conioides** Lange · G:Schierlings-Wasserfenchel, Tide-Wasserfenchel · ⊙ ~ VI-VII ▽; Eur.: D (untere Elbe), B
- **fistulosa** L. · E:Water Dropwort; G:Röhriger Wasserfenchel · ♃ ~ VI-VIII; Eur.*; NW-Afr., Lebanon, Palest., Cauc. (Azerbeidschan), N-Iran,
- **fluviatilis** (Bab.) Coleman · G:Flutender Wasserfenchel · ⊙ ⊙ ~ VI-VII; Eur.: BrI, Fr, G, DK
- **javanica** (Blume) DC. · E:Javan Water Dropwort; G:Java-Wasserfenchel · ⊙ ~ Z10 Ⓚ Ⓝ; Ind., Indochina, China, Korea, Jap., Malay. Arch., Phil., Austr.
- **lachenalii** C.C. Gmel. · G:Wiesen-Wasserfenchel · ♃ ~ VII-IX; Eur.* exc. EC-Eur.; Cauc., Alger.
- **peucedanifolia** Pollich · G:Haarstrang-Wasserfenchel · ♃ ~ VI-VII; Eur.: Ib, Fr, C-Eur., Ba, RO, EC-Eur.; Moroc., Alger.
- *phellandrium* Lam. = Oenanthe aquatica
- **pimpinelloides** L. · E:Corky Fruit Water Dropwort; G:Bibernell-Wasserfenchel · ♃ ~ Z8; Eur.: BrI, Ib, Fr, Ital-P, Ba, Crim; TR, Syr., Cauc.
- **silaifolia** M. Bieb. · E:Narrow Leaf Water Dropwort; G:Silaublättriger Wasserfenchel · ♃ ~ V-VII; Eur.* exc. Sc, Ib; TR, Cauc., N-Iran, NW-Afr.

Oenocarpus Mart. -m- *Arecaceae* · 9 spp.

- **bataua** Mart. · ₺ e Ⓦ Ⓝ; n S-Am.

Oenothera L. -f- *Onagraceae* · 124 spp. · E:Evening Primrose; F:Onagre, Œnothère; G:Nachtkerze

- **acaulis** Cav. · ⊙ ♃ △ D Z5 VI-X; Chile
- × **arendsii** Silva Tar. & C.K. Schneid. (*O. rosea* × *O. speciosa*) · ♃ △ ∧ VI-IX; cult.
- *berlandieri* (Spach) Walp. = Oenothera speciosa
- **biennis** L. · E:Common Evening Primrose, Evening Primrose; G:Gewöhnliche Nachtkerze · ⊙ Z4 VI-IX ⚕ Ⓝ; Can., USA*, Mex., nat. in Eur., TR, NZ
- × **braunii** Döll (*O. biennis* × *O. oakesiana*) · E:Braun's Evening Primrose; G:Brauns Nachtkerze · ⊙; C, Sw +
- **caespitosa** Nutt. · E:Large White Evening Primrose; G:Stängellose Nachtkerze · ⊙ ♃ △ Z4 VI-VIII; USA: NW, Rocky Mts., Calif., NC
- **drummondii** Hook. · E:Beach Evening Primrose; G:Küsten-Nachtkerze · ⊙ ⊙ Z6 VII-VIII; Tex., NE-Mex.
- × **fallax** Renner (*O. biennis* × *O. grandiflora*) · G:Täuschende Nachtkerze · ⊙; G, GB +
- **fruticosa** L.
- subsp. **fruticosa** · E:Sundrops; F:Onagre tétragone; G:Rotstängelige Nachtkerze · ♃ ♄ d Z4 VI-VIII; USA: NE, NCE, Okla., SE, Fla.
- subsp. **glauca** (Michx.) Straley · ♃ Z4 VI-VIII; USA: S-Appalachen
- *glauca* Michx. = Oenothera fruticosa subsp. glauca
- **glazioviana** Micheli · E:Large-leaved Evening Primrose; G:Rotkelchige Nachtkerze · ⊙ Z3 VI-IX; orig. ?, nat. in W-Eur, C-Eur., N-Am.
- **grandiflora** L'Hér. · G:Großblütige Nachtkerze · ⊙; cult.
- *linearis* Michx. = Oenothera fruticosa subsp. fruticosa
- **macrocarpa** Nutt. · E:Missouri Evening Primrose, Prairie Evening Primrose; F:Onagre du Missouri; G:Missouri-Nachtkerze · ♃ ⇝ △ Z5 VI-IX; USA: SC, Mo., Kans., Nebr.
- *missouriensis* Sims = Oenothera macrocarpa
- **oakesiana** (A. Gray) J.W. Robbins ex S. Watson & J.M. Coult. · E:Oakes' Evening Primrose; G:Oakes Nachtkerze · ⊙; N-Am., nat. in D +
- *odorata* hort. non Jacq. = Oenothera stricta
- **odorata** Jacq. · E:Fragrant Evening Primrose; F:Onagre odorant; G:Duftende Nachtkerze · ♃; S-Am, Calif.
- **parviflora** L. · G:Kleinblütige Nachtkerze · ⊙ VI-VIII; N-Am., nat. in Fr, I, G, EC-Eur., Norw.
- **perennis** L. · E:Sundrops; G:Stauden-Nachtkerze · ⊙ ♃ Z5 V-VIII; Can.: E; USA; NE, NCE, SE
- *pumila* L. = Oenothera perennis
- **rosea** L'Hér. ex Aiton · E:Pink Evening

Primrose; G:Rosafarbene Nachtkerze · ⊙ ♃ Z6 Ⓐ VI-VII; USA: Tex.; S-Am., nat. in S-Eur.
- **speciosa** Nutt. · E:White Evening Primrose; G:Weiße Nachtkerze · ⊙ ♃ Z5 VI-IX; USA: Mo., Kans., Tex.; Mex.
- **stricta** Ledeb. ex Link · ♃; Calif., nat. in Ib, Fr, Ital-P, C-Eur., Crim
- **suaveolens** Pers. · G:Duftende Nachtkerze
- *taraxacifolia* Sweet = Oenothera acaulis
- *tetragona* Roth = Oenothera fruticosa subsp. glauca
- var. *fraseri* (Pursh) Munz = Oenothera fruticosa subsp. glauca
- **villosa** Thunb. · E:Hairy Evening Primrose; G:Graublättrige Nachtkerzel · ⊙; N-Am., nat. in D
- **Cultivars:**
- **many cultivars**

Oftia Adans. -f- *Scrophulariaceae* · 3 spp.
- **africana** (L.) Bocq. · ♄ e Ⓚ IV-IX; S-Afr.

Oldenburgia Less. -f- *Asteraceae* · 4 spp.
- **arbuscula** DC. · ♄ e Z9 Ⓚ; S-Afr.

Olea L. -f- *Oleaceae* · 20-30 spp. · E:Olive; F:Olivier; G:Ölbaum, Olive
- *africana* Mill. = Olea europaea subsp. africana
- *aquifolium* Siebold & Zucc. = Osmanthus heterophyllus
- *chrysophylla* Lam. = Olea europaea subsp. africana
- **europaea** L.
- **some cultivars**
- subsp. **africana** (Mill.) P.S. Green · E:African Olive, Wild Olive; G:Afrikanischer Ölbaum · ♄ e Z8 Ⓚ; trop. Afr., S-Afr., SW-China
- subsp. **europaea** · E:Olive; G:Ölbaum, Olivenbaum · ♄ ♄ Z8 Ⓚ V ⚕ Ⓝ; cult.
- subsp. **sylvestris** (Mill.) Rouy · G:Oleaster, Wilder Ölbaum · ♄ e Z8 Ⓚ VII-VIII; Eur.: Ib, Fr, Ital-P, Ba, Crim; TR, Palest., NW-Afr., Libya, nat. in Sw
- var. *oleaster* (Hoffmanns. & Link) DC. = Olea europaea subsp. sylvestris
- *oleaster* Hoffmanns. & Link = Olea europaea subsp. sylvestris
- *sativa* Hoffmanns. & Link = Olea europaea subsp. europaea
- *yunnanensis* Franch. = Osmanthus yunnanensis

Oleandra Cav. -f- *Oleandraceae* · 49 spp.
- **articulata** (Sw.) C. Presl · ♃ ⟿ Z10 Ⓦ; S-Mex., C-Am., Col, Venez.

Olearia Moench -f- *Asteraceae* · c. 130 spp. · E:Daisy Bush; F:Oléaria; G:Gänseblümchenstrauch
- **albida** (Hook. f.) Hook. f. · ♄ ♄ e Z8 Ⓚ; NZ
- **angustifolia** Hook. f. · ♄ e Z8 Ⓚ VII-VIII; NZ
- **arborescens** (J.R. Forst. & G. Forst.) Cockayne & Laing · ♄ e Z8 Ⓚ; NZ
- **argophylla** (Labill.) F. Muell. · E:Muskwood; G:Silberblättriger Gänseblümchenstrauch · ♄ e Z8 Ⓚ VII-VIII; Austr.: Queensl., N.S.Wales, Victoria, S-Austr., Tasman., W-Austr.
- **avicenniifolia** (Raoul) Hook. f. · ♄ ♄ e Z8 Ⓚ; NZ
- **erubescens** (DC.) Dippel · ♄ e Z8 Ⓚ V-VI; Austr.: N.S.Wales, S-Austr., Tasman., Victoria
- *forsteri* (Hook. f.) Hook. f. = Olearia paniculata
- *gunniana* (DC.) Hook. = Olearia phlogopappa
- × **haastii** Hook. f. (*O. avicenniifolia* × *O. moschata*) · E:Daisy Bush; G:Gänseblümchenstrauch, Maßliebchenstrauch · ♄ e Z8 Ⓚ VII-VIII; cult.
- *insignis* Hook. f. = Pachystegia insignis
- **macrodonta** Baker · E:New Zealand Holly; G:Neuseeländischer Gänseblümchenstrauch · ♄ e Z8 Ⓚ VII-VIII; NZ
- **moschata** Hook. f. · ♄ e D Z8 Ⓚ VII-VIII; NZ
- **nummulariifolia** (Hook. f.) Hook. f. · ♄ e Z8 Ⓚ; NZ
- **odorata** Petrie · ♄ e Z8 Ⓚ VII-VIII; NZ
- **paniculata** (J.R. Forst. & G. Forst.) Druce · ♄ e Z8 Ⓚ; NZ
- **phlogopappa** (Labill.) DC. · E:Tasmanian Daisy Bush; G:Tasmanischer Gänseblümchenstrauch · ♄ e Z8 Ⓚ VI; Tasman.
- **ramulosa** (Labill.) Benth. · ♄ e Z8 Ⓚ I-III; Austr., Tasman.
- **semidentata** Decne. ex Hook. f. · ♄ e Z8 Ⓚ; NZ, Chatham Is.
- **solandri** (Hook. f.) Hook. f. · ♄ e Z8 Ⓚ VIII-X; NZ
- **speciosa** Hutch. · ♄ e Z8 Ⓚ IV-V; Austr.
- *stellulata* (Labill.) DC. = Olearia phlogopappa

– **traversii** F. Muell. ex Buchanan · ♄ ♄ e Z8 ⓚ; NZ
– **virgata** (Hook. f.) Hook. f.
– var. **virgata** · ♄ e Z8 ⓚ; NZ
– **Cultivars:**
– **some cultivars**

Olfersia Raddi -f- *Dryopteridaceae* · 1 sp.
– **cervina** (L.) Kuntze · ⒌ ⚥ Z10 ⓜ; Mex., C-Am., W.Ind., trop. S-Am.
– *corcovadensis* Raddi = Olfersia cervina

Oliveranthus Rose = Echeveria
– *elegans* Rose = Echeveria harmsii

Olmedia Ruiz & Pav. = Pseudolmedia
– *laevis* Ruiz & Pav. = Pseudolmedia laevis

Olsynium Raf. -n- *Iridaceae* · 8 spp. · E:Grass Widow; G:Purpuraugengras
– **douglasii** (A. Dietr.) E.P. Bicknell · E:Grass Widow, Spring Bell; G:Purpuraugengras · ⒌ Z9 ⓚ V-VI; B.C., USA: NW, N-Calif.
– **filifolium** (Gaudich.) Goldblatt · ⒌ Z9 ⓚ; Falkland

Omalotheca Cass. = Gnaphalium
– *hoppeana* (W.D.J. Koch) Sch. Bip. & F.W. Schultz = Gnaphalium hoppeanum
– *norvegica* (Gunnerus) Sch. Bip. & F.W. Schultz = Gnaphalium norvegicum
– *supina* (L.) DC. = Gnaphalium supinum
– *sylvatica* (L.) Sch. Bip. & F.W. Schultz = Gnaphalium sylvaticum

Omphalodes Mill. -f- *Boraginaceae* · 28 spp. · E:Navelseed, Navelwort; F:Nombril de Vénus, Petite bourrache; G:Gedenkemein, Nabelnüsschen
– **cappadocica** (Willd.) DC. · E:Navelwort; F:Nombril de Vénus; G:Kaukasus-Gedenkemein · ⒌ △ Z7 ∧ IV-V; TR, W-Cauc.
– **linifolia** (L.) Moench · E:Venus' Navelwort; G:Venus-Nabelnüsschen · ⊙ VI-IX; Eur.: Ib, F; W-Cauc., nat. in E-Eur.
– **luciliae** Boiss. · ⒌ △ Z7 V-VI; GR, TR
– **nitida** Hoffmanns. & Link · ⒌ △ Z7 ∧ V-VI; N-P, NW-Sp.
– **scorpioides** (Haenke) Schrank · G:Wald-Nabelnüsschen · ⊙ ⊙ IV-V; Eur.: C-Eur., EC-Eur., E-Eur.; Cauc.
– **verna** Moench · E:Blue Eyed Mary; F:Petite bourrache;

G:Frühlings-Nabelnüsschen, Gedenkemein · ⒌ Z6 IV-V; Eur.: I, A, Slove., Croatia, Montenegro, GR, RO, nat. in BrI, Fr, EC-Eur., E-Eur.

× **Oncidenia** hort. -f- *Orchidaceae* (*Macradenia* × *Oncidium*)

× **Oncidesa** hort. -f- *Orchidaceae* (*Gomozia* × *Oncidium*)

× **Oncidioda** hort. -f- *Orchidaceae* (*Cochlioda* × *Oncidium*)

Oncidium Sw. -n- *Orchidaceae* · 305 spp.
– **altissimum** (Jacq.) Sw. · E:Dancing Lady Orchid · ⒌ Z10 ⓜ IV-VII ▽ ✳; Lesser Antilles (Martinique, St. Vincent)
– *ampliatum* Lindl. = Chelyorchis ampliata
– **ansiferum** Rchb. f. · ⒌ Z10 ⓜ ⓚ XI-I ▽ ✳; Guat., Costa Rica, Panama
– *aureum* Lindl. = Cyrtochilum aureum
– **auricula** (Vell.) Pabst · ⒌ Z10 ⓜ V ▽ ✳; Braz.
– *bicallosum* Lindl. = Trichocentrum bicallosum
– **brachyandrum** Lindl. · ⒌ Z10 ⓜ V-VII ▽ ✳; Mex., Guat.
– **bracteatum** Rchb. f. & Warsz. · ⒌ Z10 ⓚ ▽ ✳; Costa Rica, Panama
– *carthagenense* (Jacq.) Sw. = Trichocentrum carthagenense
– *cavendishianum* Bateman = Trichocentrum cavendishianum
– *cebolleta* (Jacq.) Sw. = Trichocentrum cebolleta
– **cheirophorum** Rchb. f. · E:Colombia Buttercup · ⒌ Z10 ⓚ X-XII ▽ ✳; Col., Panama
– **concolor** Hook. · ⒌ Z10 ⓜ IV-V ▽ ✳; Braz.: Rio de Janeiro, Minas Gerais
– **cornigerum** Lindl. · ⒌ Z10 ⓜ VIII-IX ▽ ✳; Braz.
– **crispum** Lodd. ex Lindl. · ⒌ Z10 ⓜ IX-XII ▽ ✳; Braz.
– **dasystyle** Rchb. f. · ⒌ Z10 ⓜ V-VII ▽ ✳; Braz.
– **divaricatum** Lindl. · ⒌ Z10 ⓜ IX-X ▽ ✳; S-Braz.
– **excavatum** Lindl. · ⒌ Z10 ⓜ IX-X ▽ ✳; Ecuad., Peru
– **flexuosum** Lodd. · E:Dancing Doll Orchid · ⒌ Z10 ⓜ IX-XII ▽ ✳; Braz., Parag., Arg.
– **forbesii** Hook. · ⒌ Z10 ⓜ IX-XI ▽ ✳;

Braz.
- **fuscatum** Rchb. f. · ♃ Z₁₀ 🌢 III-IV ▽ ✳;
Costa Rica, Col., Peru
- **gardneri** Lindl. · ♃ Z₁₀ 🌢 VI-VII ▽ ✳;
Braz.
- **graminifolium** Lindl.
- *harrisonianum* Lindl. = Oncidium
auricula
- **hastilabium** (Lindl.) Beer · ♃ Z₁₀ 🌢
IV-VII ▽ ✳; Col.
- **heteranthum** Poepp. & Endl. · ♃ Z₁₀ 🌢
IV-VII ▽ ✳; Costa Rica, Panama, Col.
Venez., Ecuad., Peru, Bol.
- **hians** Lindl. · ♃ Z₁₀ 🌢 IX-X ▽ ✳; Braz.
- **incurvum** Barker ex Lindl. · ♃ Z₁₀ 🌢
IX-XI ▽ ✳; Mex.
- *jonesianum* Rchb. f. = Trichocentrum
jonesianum
- **kramerianum** Rchb. f. · E:Butterfly
Orchid · ♃ Z₁₀ 🌢 I-XII ▽ ✳; Costa Rica,
Panama, Ecuad., Peru
- *lanceanum* Lindl. = Trichocentrum
lanceanum
- **leucochilum** Bateman ex Lindl. · ♃ Z₁₀
🌢 I-V ▽ ✳; Mex., Guat., Hond.
- *liebmannii* Rchb. f. ex Kraenzl. =
Oncidium suave
- **longipes** Lindl. · ♃ Z₁₀ 🌢 III-V ▽ ✳;
Braz. (Serra dos Orgaos)
- *luridum* Lindl. = Trichocentrum luridum
- *macranthum* Lindl. = Cyrtochilum
macranthum
- **maculatum** (Lindl.) Lindl. · ♃ Z₁₀ 🌢
V-VII ▽ ✳; Mex., Guat., Hond.
- **maizifolium** Lindl. · ♃ Z₁₀ 🌢 IX-X ▽ ✳;
Venez.
- **marshallianum** Rchb. f. · ♃ Z₁₀ 🌢 V-VI
▽ ✳; Braz.
- *microchilum* Bateman ex Lindl. =
Trichocentrum microchilum
- *nanum* Lindl. = Trichocentrum nanum
- *nubigenum* Lindl. = Caucaea nubigena
- *oblongatum* Lindl. = Oncidium pelicanum
- *onustum* Lindl. = Zelenkoa onusta
- **ornithorhynchum** Kunth · ♃ Z₁₀ 🌢 X-XI
▽ ✳; Mex., Guat., El Salv., Costa Rica
- **papilio** Lindl. · E:Butterfly Orchid · ♃ Z₁₀
🌢 I-XII ▽ ✳; Col., Ecuad., Peru, Venez.,
Trinidad
- **pelicanum** Lindl. · ♃ Z₁₀ 🌢 VII-VIII ▽
✳; Mex., Guat.
- *phalaenopsis* Linden & Rchb. f. = Caucaea
phalaenopsis
- *phymatochilum* Lindl. = Miltonia
phymatochila

- **praetextum** Rchb. f. · ♃ Z₁₀ 🌢 VII ▽ ✳;
S-Braz.
- **pubes** Lindl. · ♃ Z₁₀ 🌢 VI-VIII ▽ ✳;
Braz.: Rio de Janeiro, Minas Gerais,
Parana
- *pulvinatum* Lindl. = Oncidium divaricatum
- *pumilum* Lindl. = Trichocentrum
pumilum
- **reflexum** Lindl. · ♃ Z₁₀ 🌢 IX-X ▽ ✳;
Mex., Guat.
- **sanderae** Rolfe · ♃ Z₁₀ 🌢 VII-VIII ▽ ✳;
Peru
- **sarcodes** Lindl. · ♃ Z₁₀ 🌢 IV-V ▽ ✳;
Braz.
- **schillerianum** Rchb. f. · ♃ Z₁₀ 🌢 VIII-X
▽ ✳; Braz.
- *serratum* Lindl. = Cyrtochilum serratum
- **sphacelatum** Lindl. · ♃ Z₁₀ 🌢 IV-VI ▽
✳; Mex., C-Am.
- *sphegiferum* Lindl. = Oncidium divaricatum
- *splendidum* A. Rich. ex Duch. = Trichocentrum splendidum
- *sprucei* Lindl. = Trichocentrum cebolleta
- **stenotis** Rchb. f. · ♃ Z₁₀ 🌢 XII-II ▽ ✳;
C-Am., Col., Ecuad.
- **stramineum** Bateman ex Lindl.
- **suave** Lindl. · ♃ Z₁₀ 🌢 ▽ ✳; Mex.
- *superbiens* Rchb. f. = Cyrtochilum
halteratum
- **tigrinum** Lex. · ♃ Z₁₀ 🌢 X-XII ▽ ✳;
Mex.
- *unguiculatum* Klotzsch = Oncidium
concolor
- **unguiculatum** Lindl. Z₁₀ 🌢 X-XII ▽ ✳;
Mex.
- **varicosum** Lindl.
- var. **rogersii** Rchb. f. · ⤳ Z₁₀ 🌢 X-I ▽
✳; Braz.
- var. **varicosum** · E:Dancing Lady · ♃ Z₁₀
🌢 ▽ ✳; Braz.
- *volvox* Rchb. f. = Oncidium maizifolium
- **wentworthianum** Bateman ex Lindl. · ♃
Z₁₀ 🌢 VI-VIII ▽ ✳; Mex., Guat.
- *zonatum* Cogn. = Oncidium heteranthum
- **Cultivars:**
- **many cultivars**

× **Oncidpilia** hort. -f- Orchidaceae
(*Oncidium* × *Trichopilia*)

Ongokea Pierre -f- Olacaceae · 1 sp.
- **gore** (Hua) Pierre · ♄ 🌢 Ⓝ; W-Afr.,
C-Afr., Angola

× **Onoara** hort. -f- *Orchidaceae*
(*Ascocentrum* × *Renanthera* × *Vanda* ×
Vandopsis)

Onobrychis Mill. -f- *Fabaceae* · 130 spp. ·
E:Sainforn; F:Esparcette;, Sainfoin
G:Esparsette
– **arenaria** (Kit.) DC. · E:Small Sainfoin;
G:Sand-Esparsette · ⁴ Z6 VI-VII; Eur.: Fr,
Ital-P, C-Eur., EC-Eur., Ba, E-Eur.; TR
– **crista-galli** (L.) Lam. · ⊙ Z7; S-Eur.,
N-Afr., TR, Cyprus, Syr., Iran
– **montana** DC. · E:Mountain Sainfoin;
G:Berg-Esparsette · ⁴ Z5 VII-VIII; Eur.:
Fr, Ital-P, C-Eur., EC-Eur., Ba, RO; TR,
Levant
– **viciifolia** Scop. · E:Sainfoin; G:Futter-
Esparsette · ⁴ Z6 V-VII Ⓝ; ? C-Eur., nat.
in Eur.*

Onoclea L. -f- *Woodsiaceae* · 2 spp. ·
E:Sensitive Fern; F:Onocléa sensitive;
G:Perlfarn
– *orientalis* (Hook.) Hook. = Matteuccia
orientalis
– **sensibilis** L. · E:Sensitive Fern; F:Fougère
sensitive; G:Perlfarn · ⁴ ⌒ Z7; Can.:
E; USA: NE, NCE, SE, Fla., SC ; E-Sib.,
Sakhal., Jap., Korea, Manch., nat. in BrI
– *struthiopteris* (L.) Hoffm. = Matteuccia
struthiopteris

Ononis L. -f- *Fabaceae* · 75 spp. ·
E:Restharrow; F:Arrête-bœuf, Bugrane;
G:Hauhechel
– **arvensis** L. · G:Bocks-Hauhechel · ⁴ Z6
VI-VII; Eur.: Ital-P, C-Eur., EC-Eur., Sc,
Ba, E-Eur.; Cauc., W-Sib.
– **cristata** Mill. · E:Mount Cenis Resthar-
row; G:Kamm-Hauhechel · ⁴ ⤳ △ Z7 ∧
VI-IX; Eur.: sp., F, I; Moroc., Alger.
– **fruticosa** L. · E:Shrubby Restharrow;
G:Strauchige Hauhechel · ♄ △ Z7 ∧
VI-VIII; SE-F, sp., Alger.
– **natrix** L. · E:Goat Root, Large Yellow
Restharrow; G:Gelbe Hauhechel · ⁴ △ Z7
V-VIII; Eur.: Ib, Fr, Ital-P, Ba, C-Eur.; TR,
Syr., Palest., N-Afr.
– **pusilla** L. · G:Zwerg-Hauhechel · ⁴ VI;
Eur.* exc. BrI, Sc; TR, Levant, Cauc.,
W-Iran, NW-Afr.
– **repens** L. · E:Restharrow; G:Dünen-
Hauhechel · ⁴ ♄ d ⤳ Z6 VI-VII; Eur.*,
TR, Moroc.
– **rotundifolia** L. · E:Round Leafed

Restharrow; G:Rundblättrige Hauhechel
· ⁴ ♄ △ Z7 ∧ V-IX; Eur.: sp., F, I, Sw, A
– **spinosa** L. · E:Restharrow, Spiny
Restharrow; G:Gewöhnliche Dornige
Hauhechel · ⁴ ♄ d ⤳ Z6 VI-IX ⚥ ; Eur.*,
TR, Levant, N-Iraq, Iran, C-As., Pakist.,
NW-Afr., Libya

Onopordum L. -n- *Asteraceae* · 40-60 spp. ·
E:CottonThistle; F:Chardon-des-ânes,
Pet-d'âne; G:Eselsdistel
– **acanthium** L. · E:Giant Thistle, Scotch
Thistle; F:Chardon aux ânes; G:Gewöhn-
liche Eselsdistel · ⊙ Z6 VII-IX ⚥ ; Eur.*,
TR, Levant, Arab., N-Iran, C-As., N-Afr.,
nat. in N-Am.
– **acaulon** L. · E:Horse Thistle; G:Stängel-
lose Eselsdistel · ⊙ Z8 ∧ VII-VIII;
Eur.: sp., F; mts.; NW-Afr.
– **bracteatum** Boiss. & Heldr. · ⊙ Z6
VII-VIII; Eur.: GR, Crete, BG; TR, Cyprus
– **illyricum** L. · E:Illyrian Thistle; G:Illyr-
ische Eselsdistel · ⊙ Z7 VII-VIII; Eur.: Ib,
Fr, Ital-P, Ba; TR, Cyprus
– **tauricum** Willd. · G:Taurische Eselsdistel · ⊙ VII-VIII; Eur.: Ba, RO, Crim; TR,
Cyprus, nat. in I, F
– *virens* DC. = Onopordum tauricum
– *viscosum* Hornem. ex Spreng. = Onopordum tauricum

Onoseris Willd. -f- *Asteraceae* · 32 spp.
– **onoseroides** (Kunth) B.L. Rob. · ♄ Z10
⊕ I-V; S-Mex., Guat., Hond., Panama,
Col., N-Venez.

Onosma L. -f- *Boraginaceae* · c. 150 spp. ·
E:Golden Drop; F:Onosma; G:Goldtrop-
fen, Lotwurz
– **alborosea** Fisch. & C.A. Mey. · ⁴ △ Z7 ∧
V-VI ▽; TR
– **arenaria** Waldst. & Kit. · G:Sand-
Lotwurz · ⁴ Z6 V-VI ▽; Eur.: C-Eur.,
EC-Eur., Ba
– **bourgaei** Boiss. · ⁴ △ Z7 ∧ V-VI ▽;
Cauc. (Armen.)
– **echioides** L. · E:Yellowdrop · ⁴ △ Z7 ∧
V-VI ▽; Eur.: I, Sic., Croatia, Bosn.Serb.,
AL
– **helvetica** (A. DC.) Boiss. · G:Schweizer
Lotwurz · ⊙ Z6 V-VI ▽; Eur.: A, ?H
– **pseudoarenaria** Schur · G:Zweifelhafte
Lotwurz · ⁴ V-VII ▽; Eur.: F, I, Sw,
W-Ba, RO
– **sericea** Willd. · ⁴ △ Z7 ∧ V-VI ▽; TR,

Iran
- **sieheana** Hayek · ⌁ △ Z8 ∧ V-VI ▽; C-TR
- **stellulata** Waldst. & Kit. · ⌁ △ Z6 V-VI ▽; Eur.: W-Ba
- **taurica** Pall. ex Willd. · G:Goldtropfen, Türkische Lotwurz · ⌁ Z6 V-VI ▽; Eur.: Ba, Crim., RO, TR, Cauc., Syr.
- **visianii** Clementi · G:Dalmatiner Lotwurz · ⊙ V-VI ▽; Eur.: A, EC-Eur., Ba, RO, Crim; Cauc., ? C-As.

Onychium Kaulf. -n- *Adiantaceae* · 10 spp. · E:Claw Fern; F:Fougère; G:Klauenfarn
- **japonicum** (Thunb.) Kunze · E:Carrot Fern; G:Japanischer Klauenfarn · ⌁ Z10 ⌂; Ind., China, Taiwan, S-Korea, Jap., Malay. Pen., nat. in Azor.

Oophytum N.E. Br. -n- *Aizoaceae* · 2 spp.
- **oviforme** (N.E. Br.) N.E. Br. · ⌁ Ψ Z9 ⌂; Cape

Operculina Silva Manso -f- *Convolvulaceae* · 18 spp.
- *dissecta* (Jacq.) House = Merremia dissecta
- **macrocarpa** (L.) Urb. · ⌁ ⌂ Ⓝ; W.Ind., Braz.
- *tuberosa* (L.) Meisn. = Merremia tuberosa
- **turpethum** (L.) Silva Manso · E:Indian Jalap · ♄ ⌂ ⚥ ⚘; E-Afr., trop. As., Austr., Polyn.

Ophioglossum L. -n- *Ophioglossaceae* · 52 spp. · E:Adder's-Tongue; F:Langue de serpent, Ophioglosse; G:Natternfarn, Natternzunge
- **pendulum** L. · E:Ribbon Fern; G:Hängende Natternzunge · ⌁ ⚥ Z10 ⌂; Madag., Seych., Ind., Sri Lanka, Indochina, Malay. Pen., Phil., Taiwan, Jap., Austr., Polyn.
- **vulgatum** L. · E:Adder's Tongue; G:Gewöhnliche Natternzunge · ⌁ VI-VII; Eur.*, Cauc., W-Sib., Kamchat., N-Afr.

Ophiopogon Ker-Gawl. -m- *Convallariaceae* · 65 spp. · E:Lilyturf; F:Barbe de serpent, Herbe aux turquoises; G:Schlangenbart
- **jaburan** (Siebold) Lodd. · E:White Lily Turf; G:Weißer Schlangenbart · ⌁ Z7 VII-VIII; Jap., Ryukyu-Is.,
- **japonicus** (Thunb.) Ker-Gawl. · E:Mondo

Grass; G:Japanischer Schlangenbart · ⌁ Z8 ⌂ ∧ VII-VIII ⚥ ; Jap., Korea, S-China, Phil.
- *muscari* Decne. = Liriope muscari
- **planiscapus** Nakai · E:Black Mondo; G:Schwarzer Schlangenbart · ⌁ ⊗ Z8 ⌂ ⌂ V-VI; Jap.
- **some cultivars**
- *spicatus* (Lour.) Ker-Gawl. = Liriope spicata

Ophrys L. -f- *Orchidaceae* · 25 spp. · E:Orchid; F:Ophrys, Orchidée; G:Ragwurz
- **apifera** Huds. · E:Bee Orchid; G:Gewöhnliche Bienen-Ragwurz · ⌁ Z7 V-VII ▽ ✳; Eur.* exc. Sc; TR, Lebanon., Palest., Cauc., N-Iran, NW-Afr.
- *arachnites* (Scop.) Reichard = Ophrys holoserica
- **araneola** Rchb.
- subsp. **araneola** · G:Kleine Spinnen-Ragwurz · ⌁ Z7 IV-VI ▽ ✳; Eur.: sp., F, I, Sw, G, Ba
- subsp. **tommasinii** (Vis.) Kreutz
- *aranifera* Huds. = Ophrys sphegodes
- **ciliata** Biv. · ⌁ Z8 ⌂ V ▽ ✳; Eur.: Ib, F, Ital-P, Ba; TR, Lebanon, Palest., Libya
- *fuciflora* Crantz = Ophrys holoserica
- **fusca** Link · E:Sombre Bee Orchid · ⌁ Z7 IV-V ✳; Eur.: Ib, Fr, Ital-P, Ba, RO; TR, Cyprus, N-Afr.
- **holoserica** (Burm. f.) Greuter · E:Late Spider Orchid; G:Hummel-Ragwurz · ⌁ Z6 V-VI ▽ ✳; Eur.* exc. Sc; TR, Syr.
- **insectifera** L. · E:Fly Orchid; G:Fliegen-Ragwurz · ⌁ Z6 V-VI ▽ ✳; Eur.*
- *muscifera* (Huds.) Salisb. = Ophrys insectifera
- **speculum** Link · E:Mirror Orchid
- **sphegodes** Mill. · E:Early Spider Orchid; G:Gewöhnliche Spinnen-Ragwurz · ⌁ Z7 IV-V ▽ ✳; Eur.* exc. Sc; TR, Palest., Cauc., Moroc., Alger.
- *tommasinii* Vis. = Ophrys araneola subsp. tommasinii

Ophthalmophyllum Dinter & Schwantes -n- *Aizoaceae* · 15 spp.
- **caroli** (Lavis) Tischer · Ψ Z9 ⌂; S-Afr. (Cape Prov.)
- **friedrichiae** (Dinter) Dinter & Schwantes · Ψ Z9 ⌂; Namibia
- *herrei* Lavis = Ophthalmophyllum longum
- **longum** (N.E. Br.) Tischer · ⌁ Ψ Z9 ⌂;

Cape
- **maughanii** (N.E. Br.) Tischer · ⚇ 🅐;
  Namibia
- *schuldtii* Schwantes ex H. Jacobsen =
  Ophthalmophyllum maughanii
- *triebneri* Schwantes ex H. Jacobsen =
  Ophthalmophyllum friedrichiae

Opithandra B.L. Burtt -f- *Gesneriaceae* ·
8+ spp.
- **primuloides** (Miq.) B.L. Burtt · ⚇ Z10 🅐
  V-VI; Jap.

Oplismenus P. Beauv. -m- *Poaceae* ·
8-10 spp. · E:Basket Gras; F:Herbe-à-
panier, Oplismène; G:Stachelspelze
- *crus-galli* (L.) Kunth = Echinochloa
  crus-galli
- *crus-pavonis* Kunth = Echinochloa crus-
  pavonis
- **hirtellus** (L.) P. Beauv. · E:Basket Grass;
  G:Ampel-Stachelspelze · ⚇ 🗲 ⤳ Z10 🅐;
  Mex., C-Am., W.Ind., S-Am., Afr., Polyn.
- *imbecillis* Roem. & Schult. = Oplismenus
  hirtellus
- **undulatifolius** (Ard.) Roem. & Schult. ·
  G:Grannenhirse, Stachelspelze · ⚇ Z10 🅦
  🅐 VII-IX; Eur.: I, Ba; TR, Cauc., N-Iran,
  N-Ind., China, Korea, Jap., Java, nat.
  in sp., Sw

Oplopanax (Torr. & A. Gray) Miq.
-m- *Araliaceae* · 3 spp. · E:Devil's Club;
F:Oplopanax; G:Igelkraftwurz
- **horridus** (Sm.) Miq. · E:Devil's Club,
  Devil's Walking Stick; G:Igelkraftwurz · ♄
  d ⌢ Z6 VII-VIII; Alaska, Can.: W; USA:
  NW, Rocky Mts., Calif., Mich.; Jap.

Opopanax W.D.J. Koch -m- *Apiaceae* ·
3 spp. · E:Hercules All Heal; F:Opopanax;
G:Heilwurz
- **chironium** (L.) W.D.J. Koch · E:Hercules
  All Heal; G:Heilwurz · ⚇ 🅐 VI-VII Ⓝ;
  Eur.: Ib, Fr, Ital-P, Ba, RO

× **Opsisanda** hort. -f- *Orchidaceae* (*Vanda*
  × *Vandopsis*)

× **Opsisanthe** hort. -f- *Orchidaceae*
  (*Euanthe* × *Vandopsis*)

Opuntia Neck. ex M. Gómez -f- *Cactaceae* ·
200+ spp. · E:Prickly Pear, Tuna; F:Figuier
de Barbarie, Nopal, Oponce, Raquette;

G:Feigenkaktus, Opuntie
- **acanthocarpa** Engelm. & Bigelow ·
  E:Buckthorn Cholla · ♄ ⑂ Z9 🅐 ▽ ✳;
  USA: Calif., Nev., Ariz.; Mex.
- **alexandri** Britton & Rose · ♄ ⑂ Z9 🅐 ▽
  ✳; Arg.
- **andicola** Pfeiff. · ♄ ⑂ Z9 🅐 ▽ ✳; Arg.
- **aoracantha** Lem. · ⑂ Z9 🅐 ▽ ✳; W-Arg.
- **aurantiaca** Gillies ex Lindl. · E:Tiger-
  pear · ♄ ⑂ ⤳ Z9 🅐 ▽ ✳; Urug., Arg.,
  nat. in E-Austr.
- **azurea** Rose · ♄ ⑂ Z9 🅐 ▽ ✳; Mex.
- **basilaris** Engelm. & Bigelow ·
  E:Beavertail Prickly Pear · ♄ ⑂ Z9 🅐 ▽
  ✳; USA: Rocky Mts, Calif., SW; Mex.:
  Sonora
- **beckeriana** K. Schum. · ♄ ⑂ Z9 🅐 ▽ ✳;
  orig. ?
- **bergeriana** F.A.C. Weber ex A. Berger · ♄
  ♄ ⑂ Z9 🅐 ▽ ✳; orig. ?
- **bigelovii** Engelm. · E:Teddybear Cholla ·
  ♄ ⑂ Z9 🅐 ▽ ✳; USA: Calif., Rocky Mts,
  SW; Baja Calif.
- **bradtiana** (J.M. Coult.) K. Brandegee · ♄
  ⑂ Z9 🅐 ▽ ✳; Mex.: Coahuila
- **Braziliensis** (Willd.) Haw. · ♄ ⑂ Z9 🅐 ▽
  ✳; S-Am.
- **bruchii** Speg. · ♄ ⑂ Z9 🅐 ▽ ✳; Arg.
- **brunnescens** Britton & Rose · ♄ ⑂ Z9 🅐
  ▽ ✳; N-Arg.
- *camanchica* Engelm. = Opuntia phaea-
  cantha var. camanchica
- **cholla** F.A.C. Weber · ♄ ⑂ Z9 🅐 ▽ ✳;
  Mex.: Baja Calif.
- **clavarioides** Pfeiff. · ♄ ⑂ Z9 🅐 ▽ ✳; Arg.
- **cochenillifera** (L.) Mill. · E:Cochineal
  Cactus; G:Cochenille-Feigenkaktus · ♄ ⑂
  Z9 🅐 Ⓝ ▽ ✳; orig. ?
- **compressa** (Salisb.) J.F. Macbr. ·
  E:Barbary Fig · F:Figuier de Barbarie · ♄ ⑂
  ⤳ Z8 🅐 VI ▽ ✳; Can.: Ont.; USA: NE,
  NCE, NC, Rocky Mts, SE, SC, nat. in sp.,
  F, Sard., I, Ba, Cyprus
- **corrugata** Salm-Dyck · ♄ ⑂ ⤳ Z9 🅐 ▽
  ✳; NW-Arg.
- **cylindrica** (Lam.) DC. · E:Cane Cactus · ♄
  ⑂ Z9 🅐 ▽ ✳; Peru, S-Ecuad.
- *decumana* (Willd.) Haw. = Opuntia
  maxima
- **decumbens** Salm-Dyck · ♄ ⑂ Z9 🅐 ▽ ✳;
  Mex., Guat.
- **diademata** Lem. · ♄ ⑂ Z9 🅐 ▽ ✳;
  W-Arg.
- *dillenii* (Ker-Gawl.) Haw. = Opuntia
  stricta

– **durangensis** Britton & Rose · ♄ Ψ Z9 ⌂ ▽ ✳; Mex.
– **elata** Link & Otto · ♄ ♄ Ψ Z9 ⌂ ▽ ✳; Braz., Parag.
– **engelmannii** Salm-Dyck · E:Cactus Apple · ♄ Ψ Z9 ⌂; USA: SE, SC, SW
– **erinacea** Engelm. & Bigelow
– var. **erinacea** · E:Grizzlybear Prickly Pear · ♄ Ψ ⤳ Z9 ⌂ ▽ ✳; USA: Colo.
– var. **utahensis** (Engelm.) L.D. Benson · E:Hairspine Prickly Pear · ♄ Ψ ⤳ Z9 ⌂ ▽ ✳; USA: NC, Rocky Mts., Calif., SW
– *exaltata* A. Berger = Opuntia subulata
– *extensa* Salm-Dyck = Opuntia aurantiaca
– **ficus-indica** (L.) Mill. · E:Barbary Fig, Indian Fig; G:Feigenkaktus · ♄ Ψ Z9 ⌂ ⚶ Ⓝ ▽ ✳; Mex.
– **floccosa** Salm-Dyck · ♄ Ψ Z9 ⌂ ▽ ✳; C-Peru, Bol.
– **fragilis** (Nutt.) Haw. · E:Brittle Prickly Pear · ♄ Ψ ⤳ Z8 ⌂ ▽ ✳; Can.: W, Man.; USA: NCE, NC, SC, SW, Rocky Mts., NW, Calif.
– **fulgida** Engelm. · ♄ Ψ Z9 ⌂ ▽ ✳; Ariz., Mex.
– **glomerata** Haw. · ♄ Ψ Z9 ⌂ ▽ ✳; N-Arg.
– *guerrana* Griffiths = Opuntia robusta
– *halophila* Speg. = Opuntia alexandri
– *herrfeldtii* Kupper = Opuntia rufida
– **hickenii** Britton & Rose · ♄ Ψ Z9 ⌂ ▽ ✳; S-Arg.
– *hossei* (Krainz & Gräser) G.D. Rowley = Opuntia paediophila
– *humifusa* (Raf.) Raf. = Opuntia compressa
– *hypogaea* Werderm. = Opuntia glomerata
– **hyptiacantha** F.A.C. Weber · ♄ Ψ Z9 ⌂ ▽ ✳; Mex.
– *hystricina* Engelm. & Bigelow = Opuntia erinacea var. erinacea
– **imbricata** (Haw.) DC. · E:Tree Cholla · ♄ Ψ Z9 ⌂ ▽ ✳; USA: Colo., N.Mex.; Mex.
– *inermis* DC. = Opuntia stricta
– **invicta** Brandegee · ♄ Ψ Z9 ⌂ ▽ ✳; Mex.: Baja Calif.
– **kleiniae** DC. · E:Candle Cholla · ♄ Ψ Z9 ⌂ ▽ ✳; USA: Tex., SW; Mex.
– **kuehnrichiana** Werderm. & Backeb. · Ψ Z9 ⌂ ▽ ✳; C-Peru
– *labouretiana* Console = Opuntia maxima
– **lagopus** K. Schum. · ♄ Ψ Z9 ⌂ ▽ ✳; Peru, Bol.
– **leptocaulis** DC. · E:Christmas Cactus, Prickly Pear · ♄ Ψ Z9 ⌂ ▽ ✳; USA: Tex., SW; N-Mex.

– **leucotricha** DC. · ♄ Ψ Z9 ⌂ ▽ ✳; C-Mex.
– **longispina** Haw.
– var. *corrugata* (Salm-Dyck) Backeb. = Opuntia corrugata
– var. **longispina** · Ψ Z9 ⌂ ▽ ✳; Chile
– **macracantha** Griseb. · ♄ Ψ Z9 ⌂ ▽ ✳; Cuba
– *macrocalyx* Griffiths = Opuntia microdasys var. microdasys
– **macrocentra** Engelm. · E:Purple Prickly Pear · ♄ Ψ Z9 ⌂ ▽ ✳; USA: Tex., SW; N-Mex.
– *mammillata* Schott ex Engelm. = Opuntia fulgida
– **marenae** S.H. Parsons · ♄ Ψ Z9 ⌂ ▽ ✳; N-Mex.: Sonora
– **marnieriana** Backeb. · ♄ Ψ Z9 ⌂ ▽ ✳; Mex.
– **maxima** Mill. · ♄ Ψ Z9 ⌂ ▽ ✳; orig. ?, nat. in S-Eur., N-Afr.
– *megacantha* Salm-Dyck = Opuntia ficus-indica
– **microdasys** (Lehm.) Pfeiff. · Ψ ⌂
– var. **microdasys** · E:Angel's Wings · ♄ Ψ Z8 ⌂ ▽ ✳; Mex.
– var. *rufida* (Engelm.) K. Schum. = Opuntia rufida
– *microdisca* F.A.C. Weber = Opuntia corrugata
– **mieckleyi** K. Schum. · ♄ Ψ Z9 ⌂ ▽ ✳; Parag.
– **miquelii** Monv. · ♄ Ψ Z9 ⌂ ▽ ✳; Chile
– *missouriensis* DC. = Opuntia polyacantha
– **monacantha** Haw. · E:Drooping Prickly Pear; G:Gewöhnliche Opuntie · ♄ Ψ Z9 ⌂ VI; Braz., Arg.
– **moniliformis** (L.) Haw. · ♄ Ψ Z9 ⌂ ▽ ✳; Haiti
– *occidentalis* Engelm. & Bigelow = Opuntia ficus-indica
– **pachypus** K. Schum. · ♄ Ψ Z9 ⌂ ▽ ✳; Peru
– **paediophila** A. Cast. · Ψ Z9 ⌂ ▽ ✳; W-Arg.
– **pailana** Weing. · ♄ Ψ Z9 ⌂ ▽ ✳; Mex.
– **pentlandii** Salm-Dyck · ♄ Ψ Z9 ⌂ ▽ ✳; Bol.
– **pestifer** Britton & Rose · ♄ Ψ Z9 ⌂ ▽ ✳; Ecuad., Peru
– **phaeacantha** Engelm. · E:Tulip Prickly Pear
– var. **camanchica** (Engelm.) L.D. Benson · F:Figuier de Barbarie à fruits violets · ♄ Ψ ⤳ Z9 ⌂ ▽ ✳; USA: Colo., SW, Tex.
– var. **phaeacantha** · F:Figuier de Barbarie

à fruits violets · ♄ ♍ Z9 ⓐ ▽ ✳; USA: Tex., SW; N-Mex.
- **platyacantha** Pfeiff. · ♄ ♍ Z9 ⓐ ▽ ✳; Arg.
- **polyacantha** Haw. · E:Plains Prickly Pear; F:Figuier de Barbarie · ♄ ♍ ⤳ Z3 ▽ ✳; Can.: Alta.; USA: NC, Rocky Mts., NW, SC, SW
- **pycnantha** Engelm. · ♄ ♍ Z9 ⓐ ▽ ✳; Mex.: Baja Calif.
- *rafinesquei* Engelm. = Opuntia compressa
- *rauppiana* K. Schum. = Opuntia sphaerica
- *rhodantha* K. Schum. = Opuntia erinacea var. utahensis
- **robusta** H.L. Wendl. & Pfeiff. · ♄ ♍ Z9 ⓐ ▽ ✳; C-Mex.
- **rubescens** Salm-Dyck · ♄ ♍ Z9 ⓐ ▽ ✳; W.Ind.
- **rufida** Engelm. · E:Blind Prickly Pear · ♄ ♍ Z9 ⓐ ▽ ✳; Tex., N-Mex.
- *rutila* Nutt. ex Torr. & A. Gray = Opuntia polyacantha
- **salmiana** Parm. ex Pfeiff.
- var. **salmiana** · ♄ ♍ Z9 ⓐ ▽ ✳; Bol, E-Arg., Braz., Parag.
- var. *spegazzinii* (F.A.C. Weber) G.D. Rowley = Opuntia spegazzinii
- **scheeri** F.A.C. Weber · ♄ ♍ Z9 ⓐ ▽ ✳; Mex.: Queretaro
- **spegazzinii** F.A.C. Weber · ♄ ♍ Z9 ⓐ ▽ ✳; N-Arg.
- **sphaerica** C.F. Först. · ♄ ♍ Z9 ⓐ ▽ ✳; Arg.
- **spinosissima** (Martyn) Mill. · E:Semaphore Prickly Pear · ♄ ♍ Z9 ⓐ ▽ ✳; Jamaica
- **stricta** (Haw.) Haw. · E:Erect Prickly Pear · ♄ ♍ Z9 ⓐ ▽ ✳; USA: SE; Bermudas, W.Ind., N-Venez., nat. in USA: SC
- **strobiliformis** A. Berger · ♄ ♍ Z9 ⓐ ▽ ✳; W-Arg.
- **subulata** (Muehlenpf.) Engelm. · ♄ ♍ Z9 ⓐ ▽ ✳; S-Peru
- **tomentosa** Salm-Dyck · E:Woollyjoint Prickly Pear · ♄ ♍ Z9 ⓐ ▽ ✳; Mex.
- **tunicata** (Lehm.) Link & Otto · E:Thistle Cholla · ♄ ♍ Z9 ⓐ ▽ ✳; Tex., Mex., nat. in Ecuad., Chile
- **verschaffeltii** Cels ex F.A.C. Weber · ♄ ♍ Z9 ⓐ ▽ ✳; Bol., N-Arg.
- **vestita** Salm-Dyck · ♄ ♍ Z9 ⓐ ▽ ✳; Bol.
- *violacea* Engelm. = Opuntia macrocentra
- var. *macrocentra* (Engelm.) L.D. Benson = Opuntia macrocentra
- *vulgaris* auct. non Mill. = Opuntia

compressa
- *vulgaris* Mill. = Opuntia monacantha
- *xanthostemma* K. Schum. = Opuntia erinacea var. erinacea

Orbea Haw. -f- *Asclepiadaceae* · 54 spp.
- **cooperi** (N.E. Br.) L.C. Leach · ⩜ ♍ Z9 ⓐ; SE-Cape
- **decaisneana** (Lem.) Bruyns · ⩜ ♍ Z10 ⓐ; Moroc., Alger., Maur., Seneg., Sudan
- **lugardii** (N.E. Br.) Bruyns · ⩜ ♍ Z9 ⓐ; Botswana, Namibia, Cape
- **lutea** (N.E. Br.) Bruyns
- subsp. **lutea** · ♍ Z9 ⓐ; S-Afr. (Cape)
- subsp. **vaga** (N.E. Br.) Bruyns · ⩜ ♍ Z9 ⓐ; Angola, Namibia, Cape
- **maculata** (N.E. Br.) L.C. Leach · ⩜ ♍ Z9 ⓐ; Botswana (N-Kalahari)
- **melanantha** (Schltr.) Bruyns · ⩜ ♍ Z9 ⓐ; Zimbabwe, S-Afr.: Transvaal
- **tapscottii** (I. Verd.) L.C. Leach · ⩜ ♍ Z9 ⓐ; Botswana, S-Afr.: Cape, Transvaal
- **variegata** (L.) Haw. · E:Carrion Flower, Toad Plant · ⩜ ♍ Z9 ⓐ; S-Afr. (Cape Prov.)
- **verrucosa** (Masson) L.C. Leach · ⩜ ♍ Z9 ⓐ; S-Afr.

Orbeopsis L.C. Leach = Orbea
- *lutea* (N.E. Br.) L.C. Leach = Orbea lutea
- *melanantha* (Schltr.) L.C. Leach = Orbea melanantha

Orbignya Mart. ex Endl. = Attalea
- *cohune* (Mart.) Dahlgren ex Standl. = Attalea cohune
- *martiana* Barb. Rodr. = Attalea speciosa
- *phalerata* Mart. = Attalea speciosa
- *spectabilis* (Mart.) Burret = Attalea spectabilis

Orchidantha N.E. Br. -f- *Lowiaceae* · 16 spp.
- **maxillarioides** (Ridl.) K. Schum. · ⩜ Z10 ⓦ; Malay. Pen. (Pulan Tawor)

Orchis L. -f- *Orchidaceae* · 35 spp. · E:Orchid; F:Orchidée, Orchis; G:Knabenkraut
- **anthropophora** (L.) All. · E:Man Orchid; G:Fratzenorchis, Ohnsporn, Puppenorchis · ⩜ Z5 V-VI ▽ ✳; Eur.: Ib, Fr, Ital-P, Ba, BrI
- *coriophora* L. = Anacamptis coriophora
- *elata* Poir. = Dactylorhiza elata

– *elegans* Heuff. = Anacamptis palustris
  subsp. elegans
– *fuchsii* Druce = Dactylorhiza fuchsii
– *fuciflora* Crantz = Ophrys holoserica
– *holoserica* Burm. f. = Ophrys holoserica
– *incarnata* L. = Dactylorhiza incarnata
  subsp. incarnata
– *latifolia* L. = Dactylorhiza incarnata
  subsp. incarnata
– *laxiflora* Lam. = Anacamptis laxiflora
– *maculata* L. = Dactylorhiza maculata
  subsp. maculata
– *majalis* Rchb. = Dactylorhiza majalis
– **mascula** (L.) L. · E:Early Purple Orchid;
  G:Stattliches Knabenkraut · ♃ Z5 V-VI ⚥
  ▽ ✳; Eur.*, TR, Lebanon, Cauc., N-Iran,
  NW-Afr.
– **militaris** L. · E:Military Orchid, Soldier
  Orchid; G:Helm-Knabenkraut · ♃ Z5 V-VI
  ℕ ▽ ✳; Eur.*, Cauc., Iran, W-Sib., E-Sib.,
  Mong.
– **pallens** L. · G:Blasses Knabenkraut · ♃
  Z5 IV-V ▽ ✳; Eur.: Ib, Fr, C-Eur., Ital-P,
  EC-Eur., Ba, E-Eur., RO, Crim; TR, Cauc.
– *palustris* Jacq. = Anacamptis palustris
– var. *elegans* (Heuff.) Beck = Anacamptis
  palustris subsp. elegans
– **provincialis** Balb. · E:Provence Orchid;
  G:Provenzialisches Knabenkraut · ♃ Z8
  ⌂ IV-V ▽ ✳; Eur.: Ib, Fr, Sw, Ital-P, Ba,
  Crim; TR, Cauc.
– **purpurea** Huds. · E:Lady Orchid;
  G:Purpur-Knabenkraut · ♃ Z5 V-VI ▽ ✳;
  Eur.*, TR, Cauc.
– *sambucina* L. = Dactylorhiza sambucina
– **simia** Lam. · E:Monkey Orchid; G:Affen-
  Knabenkraut · ♃ Z7 V-VI ▽ ✳; Eur.: Ib,
  Fr, BrI, C-Eur., Ital-P, H, Ba, RO, Crim;
  TR, Iraq, Cauc., Iran, C-As., NW-Afr.
– **spitzelii** W.D.J. Koch · G:Spitzels
  Knabenkraut · ♃ Z5 V-VII ▽ ✳; Eur.: sp.,
  F, I, A, Ba, Swed; TR, Cauc.
– *strictifolia* Opiz = Dactylorhiza incarnata
  subsp. incarnata
– *tridentata* Scop. = Neotinea tridentata
– *ustulata* L. = Neotinea ustulata

Oreocereus (A. Berger) Riccob. -m-
  Cactaceae · 6-7 spp.
– **celsianus** (Cels ex Salm-Dyck) Riccob.
– var. **celsianus** · ♉ Z9 ⌂ ▽ ✳; NW-Arg.,
  Bol.
– var. *hendriksenianus* (Backeb.) Krainz =
  Oreocereus hendriksenianus
– var. *trollii* (Kupper) Krainz = Oreocereus
  trollii
– **doelzianus** (Backeb.) Borg · ♉ Z9 ⌂ ▽
  ✳; C-Mex.
– *fossulatus* (Labour.) Backeb. = Oreocereus pseudofossulatus
– *hempelianus* (Gürke) D.R. Hunt =
  Arequipa hempeliana
– **hendriksenianus** Backeb. · ♉ Z9 ⌂ ▽ ✳;
  S-Peru, N-Chile
– *leucotrichus* (Phil.) Wagenkn. = Arequipa
  leucotricha
– *maximus* Backeb. = Oreocereus celsianus
  var. celsianus
– *neocelsianus* Backeb. = Oreocereus
  celsianus var. celsianus
– **pseudofossulatus** D.R. Hunt · ♄ ♉ Z9 ⌂
  ▽ ✳; Bol.
– *rettigii* (Quehl) Buxb. = Arequipa
  hempeliana
– **trollii** (Kupper) Backeb. · ♉ Z9 ⌂ ▽ ✳;
  S-Bol., N-Arg.

Oreochloa Link -f- *Poaceae* · 4 spp. ·
  F:Oréochloa; G:Kopfgras
– **disticha** (Wulfen) Link · G:Zweizeiliges
  Kopfgras · ♃ VII-VIII; Eur.: Fr, Ital-P,
  C-Eur., EC-Eur., RO, W-Russ.; Alp., Carp.

Oreodoxa Willd. = Roystonea
– *oleracea* (Jacq.) Mart. = Roystonea
  oleracea
– *regia* Humb., Bonpl. & Kunth = Roystonea regia

Oreopanax Decne. & Planch. -m-
  Araliaceae · 149 spp. · F:Oréopanax;
  G:Bergaralie
– **andreanus** Marchal · ♄ e Z9 ⌂; Ecuad.
– **capitatus** (Jacq.) Decne. & Planch. ·
  E:Caballero de Palo · ♄ ♄ e Z9 ⌂; C-Am.,
  S-Am.
– **nymphaeifolius** (Hibberd) Decne. &
  Planch. · ♄ ♄ e Z9 ⌂ I-III; Guat.
– *reticulatus* (Linden ex B.S. Williams) L.H.
  Bailey = Meryta denhamii

Oreopteris Holub -f- *Thelypteridaceae* ·
  3 spp. · E:Lemon-scented Fern; F:Fougère
  des montagnes; G:Bergfarn
– **limbosperma** (All.) Holub · E:Lemon
  Scented Fern, Mountain Buckler Fern;
  G:Gewöhnlicher Bergfarn · ♃ VII-VIII;
  Eur.*, TR, Palest., Cauc., E-Sib., Jap.,
  Moroc., Alger., w N-Am.

Origanum L. -n- *Lamiaceae* · 45 spp. ·
E:Majoram, Oregano; F:Marjolaine,
Origan; G:Dost, Majoran
- **amanum** Post · ⚁ △ Z8 ⓐ ∧ VII-VIII;
TR: Amanus
- **dictamnus** L. · E:Cretan Dittany;
G:Diptam-Dost, Kretischer Diptam · ♄ Z7
ⓐ ⌑ VII-VIII ⚘ ▽; Crete
- *heracleoticum* L. = Origanum vulgare
subsp. viridulum
- × **hybridum** Mill. (*O. dictamnus* × *O.
sipyleum*) · ⚁ △ Z8 ⓐ VII; W-As.
- **laevigatum** Boiss. · F:Marjolaine vivace ·
⚁ △ Z8 ∧ VIII-IX; Cyprus, TR: Amanus
- **majorana** L. · E:Marjoram, Sweet
Marjoram; G:Majoran · ☉ ☉ ⚁ Z7 VI-VII
⚘ Ⓝ; N-Afr., Cyprus, Arab., SW-As., Ind.,
nat. in sp., Cors, I, Sw, Ba
- × **majoricum** Cambess. (*O. majorana* ×
O. vulgare) Z7; Eur.: Ib
- **onites** L. · E:Pot Marjoram; G:Franzö-
sischer Majoran · ♄ Z8 ⓐ ⚘ Ⓝ; Eur.: Sic.,
Ba, ? sp.
- *pulchellum* Boiss. = Origanum × hybridum
- **rotundifolium** Boiss. · ⚁ Z8 ⓐ ∧
VII-VIII; Cauc. (Armen.)
- **scabrum** Boiss. & Heldr.
- subsp. **pulchrum** (Boiss. & Heldr.) P.H.
Davis · ⚁ △ Z8 ⓐ ∧ VII-VIII; S-GR
- subsp. **scabrum** · ⚁ △ Z8 ⓐ ∧ VII-VIII;
S-GR
- **vulgare** L. · G:Gewöhnlicher Dost · ⚁
- **some cultivars**
- subsp. **hirtum** (Link) Ietsw. · G:Borstiger
Gewöhnlicher Dorst · ♄ Z8 ⚘ ; Eur.:
Ital-P, Ba; TR
- subsp. *viride* (Boiss.) Hayek = Origanum
vulgare subsp. viridulum
- subsp. **viridulum** (Martrin-Donos)
Nyman
- subsp. **vulgare** · E:Oregano, Wild Marjoram; F:Marjolaine, Origan; G:Oregano,
Wilder Majoran · ⚁ Z5 VII-IX ⚘ Ⓝ;
Eur.*, TR, Cyprus, Iraq, Iran, W-Sib.,
E-Sib., C-As., Afgh., Pakist., Him., Mong.
NW-Afr., nat. in N-Am., China
- **Cultivars:**
- **some cultivars**

Orixa Thunb. -f- *Rutaceae* · 1 sp.
- **japonica** Thunb. · ♄ d Z6 V; China,
S-Korea, Jap.

Orlaya Hoffm. -f- *Apiaceae* · 3 spp. ·
F:Orlaya; G:Breitsame

- **daucoides** (L.) Greuter · ☉; Eur.: Ib, F,
Ital-P, Ba, Crim; TR, Syr., Iraq, Cauc.,
N-Iran, Moroc., Alger.
- **grandiflora** (L.) Hoffm. · G:Strahlen-
Breitsame · ☉ VI-VIII; Eur.* exc. BrI, Sc;
TR, Palest., Cauc., C-As., Alger.

Ormenis Cass. = Chamaemelum
- *nobilis* (L.) J. Gay ex Coss. & Germ. =
Chamaemelum nobile

Ornithidium R. Br. = Maxillaria
- *coccineum* (Jacq.) R. Br. = Maxillaria
coccinea
- *densum* (Lindl.) Rchb. f. = Maxillaria
densa
- *sophronitis* Rchb. f. = Maxillaria sophronitis

Ornithocephalus Hook. -m- *Orchidaceae* ·
47 spp.
- *grandiflorus* Lindl. = Zygostates grandiflora
- **iridifolius** Rchb. f. · ⚁ Z10 ⓦ ▽ ✻; Mex.

Ornithogalum L. -n- *Hyacinthaceae* ·
211 sp. · E:Star of Bethlehem; F:Etoile
de Bethléem, Ornithogale; G:Stern von
Bethlehem, Milchstern, Vogelmilch
- *angustifolium* Boreau = Ornithogalum
umbellatum
- **arabicum** L. · ⚁ ⋉ Z9 ⓐ; Eur.: Ib, Ital-P,
Ba; NW-Afr., nat. in F
- **boucheanum** (Kunth) Asch. · G:Bouchés
Milchstern · ⚁ IV-V; Eur.: I, C-Eur.,
EC-Eur., Ba, E-Eur. +
- *caudatum* Aiton = Ornithogalum
longibracteatum
- **conicum** Jacq. · E:Chincherinchee · ⚁ Z9
ⓐ VI-VII; Cape
- *corymbosum* Ruiz & Pav. = Ornithogalum
arabicum
- **gussonei** Guss. · ⚁; Eur.: Ib, Fr, Ital-P,
Ba; Cauc,
- *kochii* Parl. = Ornithogalum orthophyllum subsp. kochii
- *lacteum* Jacq. = Ornithogalum conicum
- *lacteum* Vill. = Ornithogalum narbonense
- *latifolium* L. = Ornithogalum arabicum
- **longibracteatum** Jacq. · E:Sea Onion · ⚁
Z9 ⓐ; S-Afr.
- **narbonense** L. · E:Bath Asparagus,
Star of Bethlehem · ⚁ Z7 V-VII; Eur.: Ib,
Fr, Ital-P, Ba, ? RO; TR, N-Iraq, Cauc.,
NW-Iran, NW-Afr.

– **nutans** L. · G:Nickender Milchstern · ♃
Z6 IV-V; Eur.: GR, BG; TR, nat. in BrI, Sc,
Fr, C-Eur., EC-Eur., Ib, Ital-P
– **orthophyllum** Ten.
– subsp. **kochii** (Parl.) Maire & Weiller ·
G:Kochs Milchstern · ♃ IV-V; Eur.: Ib,
Ital-P, C-Eur., EC-Eur., Ba, E-Eur., ? F;
TR, Cauc
– subsp. **orthophyllum**
– **pyramidale** L. · G:Pyramiden-Milch-
stern · ♃ Z6 VI-VII; Eur.: I, G, A, EC-Eur.,
Slove., Croatia, Bosn.Serb., RO, nat. in
NL
– subsp. *narbonense* (L.) Asch. & Graebn. =
Ornithogalum narbonense
– **pyrenaicum** L. · G:Pyrenäen-Milchstern ·
♃ Z6 VI-VII; Eur.* exc. BrI, Sc; TR, Cauc.,
Moroc.
– **saundersiae** Baker · E:Giant Chincher-
inchee; G:Saunders Milchstern · ♃ ⚹ Z9
⌂ I-V; S-Afr.
– **sigmoideum** Freyn & Sint. · ♃; Eur.: Ba,
RO; TR, Cauc., N-Iran
– **sphaerocarpum** A. Kern.
– *tenuifolium* Guss. = Ornithogalum
gussonei
– **thyrsoides** Jacq. · E:Chincherinchee · ♃
⚹ Z9 ⌂ VI-VIII; Cape
– **umbellatum** L. · E:Star of Bethlehem;
F:Dame de onze heures; G:Stern von
Bethlehem, Breitblättriger Dolden-
Milchstern · ♃ Z5 IV-V ⚔; Eur.* exc. Sc;
TR, Levant, nat. in Sc

Ornithopus L. -m- *Fabaceae* · 6 spp. ·
E:Bird's Foot; F:Pied-d'oiseau; G:Vogelfuß
– **perpusillus** L. · E:Bird's Foot; G:Kleiner
Vogelfuß, Mäusewicke · ⊙ V-VI; Eur.*
exc. Ib, Ba; Alger.
– **sativus** Brot. · E:Cultivated Bird's Foot;
G:Großer Vogelfuß, Serradella · ⊙ VI-VII
Ⓝ; Eur.: Ib, F; Moroc., Alger., nat. in
C-Eur., EC-Eur., E-Eur.

Orobanche L. -f- *Orobanchaceae* · c.
150 spp. · E:Broomrape; F:Orobanche;
G:Sommerwurz
– **alba** Stephan ex Willd. · E:Thyme
Broomrape; G:Thymian-Sommerwurz ·
♃ Z6 VI-IX; Eur.*, TR, Syr., Iran, Him.,
Moroc., Alger.
– **alsatica** Kirschl. · G:Elsässer Sommerwurz
– subsp. **alsatica** · E:Alsatian Broomrape;
G:Gewöhnliche Elsässer Sommerwurz ·

♃ Z6 VI-VII; Eur.: Fr, I, C-Eur., EC-Eur.,
Slove., Bosn., E-Eur.; Moroc.
– subsp. **libanotidis** (Rupr.) Pusch ·
G:Bartlings Sommerwurz · ♃ Z6 VI-VII;
Eur.: G, A, CZ, Slove.
– **amethystea** Thuill. · E:Amethyst
Broomrape; G:Amethyst-Sommerwurz
· ♃ Z6 VI; Eur.: Ib, Fr, Ital-P, Ba, BrI,
C-Eur.; NW-Afr.
– **artemisiae-campestris** Vaucher ex Gau-
din · E:Oxtongue Broomrape; G:Beifuß-
Sommerwurz, Panzer-Sommerwurz · ♃
Z6 VI-VII; Eur.*, Moroc.
– *caerulea* Vill. = Orobanche purpurea
– **caesia** Rchb. · E:Blue-gray Broomrape;
G:Blaugraue Sommerwurz, Weißwollige
Sommerwurz · ♃ Z6 VI-VII; Eur.: A,
EC-Eur., E-Eur.; TR, Cauc., Iran, Afgh.,
Sib., W-Him.
– **caryophyllacea** Sm. · E:Bedstraw
Broomrape, Clove-scented Broomrape;
G:Labkraut-Sommerwurz, Nelken-
Sommerwurz · ♃ Z6 VI-VII; Eur.* exc. Sc;
TR, SW-As., Pakist., Moroc., Alger.
– **coerulescens** Stephan · E:Bluish
Broomrape; G:Bläuliche Sommerwurz ·
♃ Z6 VI-VII; Eur.: C-Eur., EC-Eur., E-Eur.
– **crenata** Forssk. · E:Carnation-scented
Broomrape; G:Prächtige Sommerwurz ·
⊙ Z6 VI-VII; Eur.: Ib, Fr, Ital-P, Ba, Crim;
TR, Levant, Moroc., N-Iran, N-Afr.
– **elatior** Sutton · E:Tall Broomrape;
G:Große Sommerwurz · ♃ Z6 VI-VII;
Eur.*, TR, SW-As., C-As., E-As.
– *epithymum* DC. = Orobanche alba
– **flava** Mart. ex F.W. Schultz · E:Butterbur
Broomrape, Yellow Broomrape;
G:Hellgelbe Sommerwurz · ♃ Z6 VI-VII;
Eur.: Fr, Ital-P, C-Eur., EC-Eur., E-Eur.;
Moroc.; mts.
– **gracilis** Sm. · E:Slender Broomrape;
G:Blutrote Sommerwurz · ♃ Z6 V-VII;
Eur.* exc. BrI, Sc; TR, Cauc., Moroc.,
Alger.
– **hederae** Vaucher ex Duby · E:Ivy
Broomrape; G:Efeu-Sommerwurz · ♃ Z6
V-VIII; Eur.* exc. Sc, EC-Eur.; Crim; TR,
Cauc., N-Iran, Moroc., Alger.
– **laserpitii-sileris** Reut. ex Jord. ·
E:Laserpitium Broomrape; G:Laserkraut-
Sommerwurz · ♃ Z6 VII; Eur.: F, Sw, A,
Ba; Alp., Balkan
– **lucorum** F.W. Schultz · E:Barberry
Broomrape; G:Berberitzen-Sommerwurz
· ♃ Z6 VI-VIII; Eur.: C-Eur., I, ? RO;

E-Alp.
- *lutea* Baumg. · E:Yellow Broomrape;
  G:Gelbe Sommerwurz · ⁐ Z6 V-VI; Eur.*
  exc. Sc; TR, Cauc., Iran, C-As., China:
  Sinkiang
- **minor** Sm. · E:Lesser Broomrape;
  G:Kleewürger, Kleine Sommerwurz ·
  ⁐ Z6 VI-VII; Eur.* exc. Sc; TR, Levant,
  N-Afr., nat. in Sc
- **picridis** F.W. Schultz · E:Picris Broom-
  rape; G:Bitterkraut-Sommerwurz · ⁐
  Z6 VI-VII; Eur.: Ib, Fr, BrI, C-Eur., DK,
  EC-Eur., Ba; TR, Palest., Iraq, Cauc.,
  W-As., Moroc., Alger.
- **purpurea** Jacq. · E:Purple Broomrape;
  G:Gewöhnliche Violette Sommerwurz · ⁐
  Z6 VI-VII; Eur.*, TR, Syr., Cauc., N-Iran,
  Afgh, Ind., Moroc., Alger., Canar.
- **ramosa** L. · E:Hemp Broomrape;
  G:Ästige Sommerwurz · ⊙ ⁐ Z6 VII-VIII;
  Eur.* exc. BrI, Sc; TR, Levant, Cauc.,
  Iran, Ind., N-Afr., Eth., nat. in BrI, N-Am.
- **rapum-genistae** Thuill. · E:Greater
  Broomrape; G:Ginster-Sommerwurz · ⁐
  Z6 V-VI; Eur.: Ib, Fr, Ital-P, BrI, C-Eur.;
  Moroc., Alger.
- **reticulata** Wallr. · E:Thistle Broomrape;
  G:Netzige Distel-Sommerwurz · ⁐ Z6
  VI-VII; Eur.*, Moroc., Alger.
- **salviae** F.W. Schultz · E:Sage Broomrape;
  G:Salbei-Sommerwurz · ⁐ Z6 VII-VIII;
  Eur.: Fr, C-Eur., Ital-P, Slove., Croatia,
  RO
- *speciosa* DC. = Orobanche crenata
- **teucrii** Holandre · E:Germander
  Broomrape; G:Gamander-Sommerwurz ·
  ⁐ Z6 VI-VII; Eur.* exc. BrI, Sc; Alger.
- **variegata** Wallr. · E:Variegated Broom-
  rape; G:Bunte Sommerwurz · ⊙ Z6; Eur.:
  Fr, Ital-P, sp.; NW-Afr.

Orobus L. = Lathyrus
- *luteus* L. = Lathyrus gmelinii
- *niger* L. = Lathyrus niger
- *vernus* L. = Lathyrus vernus

Orontium L. -n- *Araceae* · 1 sp. · E:Golden
  Club; F:Orontium; G:Goldkeule
- **aquaticum** L. · E:Golden Club;
  F:Cryptocoryne américaine; G:Goldkeule
  · ⁐ ≋ Z7 V-VI; USA: NE, SE, Fla.

Orostachys Fisch. ex A. Berger
  -f- *Crassulaceae* · 12 spp. · F:Umbilic;
  G:Sternwurz

- *aggregata* (Makino) H. Hara = Orostachys
  malacophylla subsp. malacophylla var.
  aggregata
- **boehmeri** (Makino) H. Hara · ⊙ ⁐ Z7;
  Jap.
- *furusei* Ohwi = Orostachys boehmeri
- *iwarenge* (Makino) H. Hara = Orostachys
  malacophylla subsp. malacophylla var.
  iwarenge
- **malacophylla** (Pall.) Fisch. ex Sweet
- subsp. **malacophylla** · ⁐ ⁋ △ Z6 VI-VII;
  E-Sib., Amur, Sakhal., Mong., China, Jap.
- var. **aggregata** (Makino) H. Ohba · ⊙ ⁋
  Z7; Jap.: Hokkaido; coast
- var. **iwarenge** (Makino) H. Ohba · ⊙ ⁋
  Z6; ? China
- **spinosa** (L.) C.A. Mey. ex A. Berger · ⁐
  ⁋ △ Z4 VI-VII; Russ. (S-Ural), W-Sib.,
  E-Sib., Amur, China: Sinkiang, C-As.,
  Mong., Tibet

Oroxylum Vent. -n- *Bignoniaceae* · 1 sp. ·
  E:Midnight Horror, Tree of Damocles;
  G:Damoklesbaum
- **indicum** (L.) Kurz · E:Midnight Horror,
  Tree of Damocles; G:Damoklesbaum ·
  ♄ e ⋉ Z10 🅐 Ⓝ; Ind., Sri Lanka, China,
  Indochina, Malay. Arch.

Oroya Britton & Rose -f- *Cactaceae* · 2 spp.
- *gibbosa* F. Ritter = Oroya peruviana
- **peruviana** (K. Schum.) Britton & Rose ·
  ⁋ Z9 🅐 ▽ ✳; C-Peru

Orphium E. Mey. -n- *Gentianaceae* · 1 sp.
- **frutescens** (L.) E. Mey. · ♄ Z9 🅐 VII-
  VIII; Cape

Orthilia Raf. -f- *Pyrolaceae* · 1 sp. ·
  E:Wintergreen; F:Pyrole; G:Birngrün
- **secunda** (L.) House · E:Nodding
  Wintergreen; G:Birngrün, Nickendes
  Wintergrün · ⁐ e Z5 VI-VII; Eur.*, TR,
  Cauc., N-Iran, W-Sib., E-Sib., Amur,
  Sakhal., Kamchat.

Orthophytum Beer -n- *Bromeliaceae* ·
  38 spp.
- **foliosum** L.B. Sm. · ⁐ Z9 🅐; Braz.
- **navioides** (L.B. Sm.) L.B. Sm. · ⁐ Z9 🅐;
  E-Braz.
- **rubrum** L.B. Sm. · ⁐ Z9 🅐; E-Braz.
- **saxicola** (Ule) L.B. Sm. · ⁐ Z9 🅐;
  E-Braz.

Orthosiphon Benth. -m- *Lamiaceae* ·
33 spp.
– **aristatus** (Blume) Miq. · ⑵ Z10 ⓦ VII-
VIII ⚥ ; Ind., Indochina, China, Malay.
Arch., N.Guinea, N-Austr.

Orthostemon O. Berg = Acca
– *sellowianus* O. Berg = Acca sellowiana

Orthrosanthus Sweet -m- *Iridaceae* ·
9 spp. · E:Mornig Flag; G:Morgenblüte
– **chimboracensis** (Kunth) Baker ·
G:Mexikanische Morgenblüte · ⑵ Z9 ⓚ
VI; Mex., C-Am., Col., Ecuad., Peru; And.
– **multiflorus** Sweet · E:Morning Flag;
G:Australische Morgenblüte · ⑵ Z9 ⓚ VI-
VII; Austr.: Victoria, S-Austr., W-Austr.

Orychophragmus Bunge -m- *Brassicaceae* ·
2 spp.
– **violaceus** (L.) O.E. Schulz · ☉ ☺ Z7
VII-VIII; China

Oryza L. -f- *Poaceae* · c. 19 spp. · E:Rice;
F:Riz; G:Reis
– *clandestina* (Weber ex F.H. Wigg.) A.
Braun = Leersia oryzoides
– **glaberrima** Steud. · E:African Rice;
G:Afrikanischer Reis · ☉ ∼ Z10 ⓦ Ⓝ;
W-Afr., W-Sah
– **longistaminata** A. Chev. & Roehr. ·
E:Red Rice; G:Roter Reis · ☉ ∼ Z10 ⓦ
Ⓝ; trop. Afr., S-Afr.
– *oryzoides* (L.) Brand & W.D.J. Koch =
Leersia oryzoides
– **perennis** Moench emend. Sampath ·
G:Stauden-Reis · ☉ ⑵ ∼ Z10 ⓦ Ⓝ;
Trop.
– **rufipogon** Griff. · E:Red Rice; G:Salz-
Reis · ⑵ ∼ Z10 ⓦ Ⓝ; SE-As, Austr., Am.
– **sativa** L. · E:Rice; G:Reis · ☉ ∼ Z10 ⓦ
⚥ Ⓝ; SE-As., trop. Afr., N-Austr.

Oryzopsis Michx. -f- *Poaceae* · 1 sp. · E:Rice
Grass, Smilo Grass; F:Oryzopsis, Riz
barbu; G:Grannenhirse
– *miliacea* (L.) Asch. & Schweinf. =
Piptatherum miliaceum

Osbeckia L. -f- *Melastomataceae* · 50 spp.
– **stellata** Wall. · ⑵ Z9 ⓦ VII-VIII; Ind.,
China

Oscularia Schwantes -f- *Aizoaceae* · 23 spp.
– **caulescens** Mill.

– **deltoides** (L.) Schwantes · ⑵ ⚘ Z9 ⓚ
VII-IX; Cape
– *muricata* (Haw.) Schwantes ex H.
Jacobsen = Oscularia deltoides
– **pedunculata** N.E. Br.

Osmanthus Lour. -m- *Oleaceae* ·
30-40 spp. · E:Devil Wood, Sweet Olive;
F:Osmanthus; G:Duftblüte
– **americanus** (L.) A. Gray · E:Devilwood;
G:Amerikanische Duftblüte · ⚘ ⚘ e Z9 ⓚ
IV; SE-USA
– *aquifolium* (Siebold & Zucc.) Benth. &
Hook. f. = Osmanthus heterophyllus
– **armatus** Diels · ⚘ e D Z7 VII; W-China
– × **burkwoodii** (Burkwood & Skipwith)
P.S. Green (*O. decorus* × *O. delavayi*) ·
G:Burkwoods Duftblüte · ⚘ e D Z7 IV-V;
cult.
– **decorus** (Boiss. & Balansa) Kasapligil ·
F:Osmanthe; G:Stattliche Duftblüte · ⚘ e
Z6 V; NE-TR, Cauc.
– **delavayi** Franch. · E:Delavay Osmanthus;
G:Delavays Duftblüte · ⚘ e Z8 ⓚ IV;
W-China
– *forrestii* Rehder = Osmanthus yunnanensis
– × **fortunei** Carrière (*O. fragrans* × *O.
heterophyllus*) · ⚘ e D Z7; cult.
– **fragrans** (Thunb.) Lour. · E:Fragrant
Olive, Sweet Olive, Sweet Osmanthus;
G:Süße Duftblüte · ⚘ ⚘ e D Z9 ⓚ VI-VIII
Ⓝ; Jap., SW-China, E-Him.
– **heterophyllus** (G. Don) P.S. Green ·
E:Hollyleaf Osmanthus; F:Osmanthe
à feuilles de houx; G:Stachelblättrige
Duftblüte · ⚘ ⚘ e D Z7 IX-X; Jap., Taiwan
– *ilicifolius* (Hassk.) hort. ex Dippel =
Osmanthus heterophyllus
– **serrulatus** Rehder · G:Gesägtblättrige
Duftblüte · ⚘ e D Z8 ⓚ III-IV; Him.,
W-China
– **suavis** King ex C.B. Clarke · ⚘ ⚘ e Z8 ⓚ;
Him., Yunnan
– **yunnanensis** (Franch.) P.S. Green ·
G:Yunnan-Duftblüte · ⚘ e D Z7; W-China

× *Osmarea* Burkwood & Skipwith =
Osmanthus
– *burkwoodii* Burkwood & Skipwith =
Osmanthus × burkwoodii

Osmaronia Greene = Oemleria
– *cerasiformis* (Torr. & A. Gray) Greene =
Oemleria cerasiformis

× **Osmentara** hort. -f- *Orchidaceae*
(*Broughtonia* × *Cattleya* × *Laeliopsis*)

Osmunda L. -f- *Osmundaceae* · 15 spp. ·
E:Royal Fern; F:Fougère royale,
Osmonde; G:Königsfarn, Rispenfarn
– **cinnamomea** L. · E:Cinnamon Fern;
F:Fougère cannelle, Osmonde cinnamon;
G:Zimtfarn · 4 Z3; Can.: E; USA: NE,
NCE, SC, SE, Fla.; Mex., C-Am., W-Ind.,
trop. S-Am., E-As.
– **claytoniana** L. · E:Interrupted Fern;
F:Osmonde de Clayton; G:Dunkler
Münzrollenfarn, Kronenfarn, Teufelsfarn
· 4 Z3; Can.: E; USA: NE, NCE, SE; Amur,
Korea, Manch., SW-China, Taiwan
– *imbricata* Kunze = Osmunda cinnamomea
– *interrupta* Michx. = Osmunda claytoniana
– **regalis** L. · E:Royal Fern; F:Osmonde
royale; G:Gewöhnlicher Rispenfarn,
Königsfarn · 4 ∿ Z2 VI-VII ⚥ ▽; Eur.*
exc. E-Eur.; Can.: E; USA: NE, NCE, SC,
Fla.
– var. *gracilis* (Link) Hook. = Osmunda
regalis

Osteomeles Lindl. -f- *Rosaceae* · 3 spp. ·
F:Pomme de pierre; G:Steinapfel
– **schweriniae** C.K. Schneid. · G:Schwerins
Steinapfel
– var. **microphylla** Rehder & E.H. Wilson ·
♄ e Z8 ⓚ III-IV; W-China
– var. **schweriniae** · E:Hawaii Hawthorn;
G:Yunnan-Steinapfel · ♄ e Z8 ⓚ; Yunnan
– **subrotunda** K. Koch · G:Kleiner
Steinapfel · ♄ e Z8 ⓚ III-IV; SE-China

Osteospermum L. -n- *Asteraceae* · 67 spp. ·
F:Marguerite du Cap; G:Kapmargerite,
Paternosterstrauch
– **barberiae** (Harv.) Norl. · G:Bornholmer
Margerite · 4 ♄ e Z9 ⓚ; S-Afr.
– **ecklonis** (DC.) Norl. · E:African Daisy,
Vanstaden's River Daisy · ⊙ ♄ ♄ e Z9 ⓚ
VII-IX; S-Afr.
– *jucundum* hort. = Osteospermum
barberiae
– **Cultivars:**
– **many cultivars**

Ostrowskia Regel -f- *Campanulaceae* ·
1 sp. · E:Giant Bellflower; F:Campanule
géante; G:Riesenglocke
– **magnifica** Regel · E:Giant Bellflower;

G:Riesenglocke · 4 △ Z7 ⓚ VII-VIII;
C-As.

Ostrya Scop. -f- *Betulaceae* · 9 spp. · E:Hop
Hornbeam; F:Ostryer; G:Hopfenbuche
– **carpinifolia** Scop. · E:European Hop
Hornbeam; F:Charme houblon, Ostryer
commun; G:Gewöhnliche Hopfenbuche ·
♄ d Z6 IV-V Ⓝ; Eur.: Fr, Ital-P, Sw, A, H,
Ba; TR, Syr., Cauc.
– **japonica** Sarg. · E:Japanese Hop
Hornbeam; G:Japanische Hopfenbuche ·
♄ d Z6; China, Korea, Jap.
– **knowltonii** Coville · E:Knowlton's Hop
Hornbeam; G:Amerikanische Hopfenbuche · ♄ d Z5; Ariz., N.Mex., Utah, Tex.
– **virginiana** (Mill.) K. Koch · E:American
Hop Hornbeam; G:Virginische Hopfenbuche · ♄ d Z5; Can.: E; USA: NE, NCE,
SC, SE, Fla.; Mex. Guat.

Ostryopsis Decne. -f- *Betulaceae* · 2 spp. ·
F:Faux-ostryer; G:Scheinhopfenbuche
– **davidiana** (Baill.) Decne. · G:Hohe
Scheinhopfenbuche · ♄ d Z4; China:
Kansu, Schensi, Hopei

Otacanthus Lindl. -m- *Scrophulariaceae* ·
4 spp.
– **caeruleus** Lindl. · 4 Z10 ⓚ IV-VIII; Braz.

Otanthus Hoffmanns. & Link -m-
Asteraceae · 1 sp. · E:Cotton Weed;
F:Diotis; G:Filzblume, Ohrblume
– **maritimus** (L.) Hoffmanns. & Link ·
E:Cotton; G:Filzblume, Ohrblume Weed ·
4 ∿ Z8 ⓚ VIII-IX; Eur.: Ib, Fr, Ital-P,
Ba, BrI, Canar.; TR, Moroc.; coasts

Otatea (McClure & E.W. Sm.) C.E.
Calderón & Soderstr. -f- *Poaceae* ·
2 spp. · E:Weeping Bamboo; F:Bambou;
G:Trauerbambus
– **acuminata** (Munro) Calderón &
Soderstr. · E:Mexican Weeping Bamboo;
G:Mexikanischer Trauerbambus · ♄ e Z10
ⓚ; Mex.
– subsp. *aztecorum* (McClure & E.W. Sm.)
R. Guzmán et al. = Otatea acuminata

Othonna L. -f- *Asteraceae* · c. 120 spp.
– **capensis** L.H. Bailey · 4 Ψ ∿ Z9 ⓚ; Cape
– **carnosa** Less. · 4 Ψ Z9 ⓚ VII-VIII; Cape
– *cheirifolia* L. = Hertia cheirifolia
– *crassifolia* Harv. = Othonna capensis

- **euphorbioides** Hutch. · ♄ ♍ Z9 ⌂; Cape
- **retrorsa** DC. · ⌃ ♍ Z9 ⌂ I-X; Cape

Othonnopsis Jaub. & Spach = Othonna
– *cheirifolia* (L.) Benth. & Hook. = Hertia
  cheirifolia

Otoglossum (Schltr.) Garay & Dunst. -n-
Orchidaceae · 14 spp.
- **brevifolium** (Lindl.) Garay & Dunst. · ⌃
  Z10 ⌂ I-XII ▽ ✳; Col., Ecuad., Peru

Ottelia Pers. -f- *Hydrocharitaceae* · 20 spp.
- **alismoides** (L.) Pers. · ⌃ ≈ Z9 ⌂;
  Egypt, Ind., Sri Lanka, China, Jap.,
  Solom., N-Austr.
- *japonica* Miq. = Ottelia alismoides
- **ulvifolia** Walp. · ⌃ ≈ Z9 ⌂; W-Afr.,
  Zambia, Zimbabwe

Ourisia Comm. ex Juss. -f-
Scrophulariaceae · 27 spp.
- **coccinea** (Cav.) Pers. · ⌃ Z7 V-IX; Chile,
  Arg.
- *elegans* Phil. = Ourisia coccinea
- **macrophylla** Hook. · E:Mountain
  Foxglove · ⌃ Z7 VII; NZ

Oxalis L. -f- *Oxalidaceae* · 700-800 spp. ·
E:Shamrock, Sorrel; F:Faux-trèfle,
Oxalide, Surelle; G:Sauerklee
- **acetosella** L. · E:Common Wood Sorrel,
  Wood Sorrel; F:Oxalide petite oseille,
  Pain de coucou; G:Wald-Sauerklee · ⌃
  Z3 IV-V 🌼 ⚘; Eur.*, TR, Cauc., W-Sib.,
  E-Sib., Amur, Sakhal., Kamchat., Mong.,
  Him., China, Jap., Alaska, Can., USA: NE,
  NCE, SE
- **adenophylla** Gillies · E:Sauer Klee;
  G:Anden-Sauerklee · ⌃ △ Z7 ∧ IV; Chile,
  W-Arg.
- **articulata** Savigny
- subsp. **articulata** · E:Pink Oxalis;
  G:Raupen-Sauerklee · ⌃ Z8 ⌂; Parag.
- subsp. **rubra** (A. St.-Hil.) Lourteig · ⌃ Z8
  ⌂ IX-XI; Braz., Arg., Parag.
- *bowieana* Lodd. = Oxalis bowiei
- **bowiei** Lindl. · E:Redflower Wood
  Sorrel · ⌃ Z8 ⌂; Cape
- **Braziliensis** Lodd. ex Westc. & Knowles ·
  ⌃ Z9 ⌂ V; Braz.
- *cernua* Thunb. = Oxalis pes-caprae
- **corniculata** L. · E:Yellow Sorrel;
  G:Hornfrüchtiger Sauerklee · ☉ Z5 VI-X;
  Eur.* exc. BrI, Sc; TR, Levant, Cauc.,

Iran, C-As., Him., China, Jap., Amur,
Sakhal., N-Afr., nat. in cosmop. exc. Sib.
- **corymbosa** DC. · E:Sheep Sorrel;
  G:Brazilianischer Sauerklee · ⌃ Z9 ⌂;
  Braz., Arg.
- **decaphylla** Kunth · E:Ten-leaf Wood
  Sorrel; G:Zehnblättriger Sauerklee · ⌃ ;
  S-Am., nat. in D
- **depressa** Eckl. & Zeyh. · ⌃ Z7; S-Afr.
  (Cape Prov.)
- **dillenii** Jacq. · E:Slender Yellow Wood
  Sorrel; G:Dillenius' Sauerklee · ⌃ VII-X;
  Can., USA *, Mex., nat. in Eur.
- **enneaphylla** Cav. · E:Scurvy Grass;
  G:Schuppen-Sauerklee · ⌃ △ D Z6 IV;
  Patag., Falkland
- *esculenta* Otto ex A. Dietr. = Oxalis
  tetraphylla
- *europaea* Jord. = Oxalis stricta
- *floribunda* Lehm. = Oxalis articulata
  subsp. articulata
- *fontana* Bunge = Oxalis stricta
- **hedysaroides** Kunth · E:Fire Fern;
  G:Venezuela-Sauerklee · ♄ e Z9 ⌂ I-XII;
  Col., Venez.
- **herrerae** R. Knuth · ⌃ Z9 ⌂; Peru, Chile
- **hirta** L. · E:Sorrel; G:Kap-Sauerklee · ⌃
  Z9 ⌂ X-III; Cape
- *inops* Eckl. & Zeyh. = Oxalis depressa
- **lasiandra** Zucc. · ⌃ Z9 ⌂ VIII-X; Mex.
- **latifolia** Kunth · E:Broadleaf Wood
  Sorrel · ⌃ Z9 ⌂; Mex., C-Am., W.Ind.,
  trop. S-Am.
- **magellanica** G. Forst. · ⌃ Z6 IV-V;
  Austr., NZ, s S-Am.
- *martiana* Zucc. = Oxalis corymbosa
- **megalorrhiza** Jacq. · ♄ Z10 ⌂ I-XII;
  Galapagos, Peru, Bol., Chile
- **ortgiesii** Regel · ♄ Z8 ⌂; Peru: And.
- **pes-caprae** L. · E:Bermuda Buttercup;
  G:Nickender Sauerklee · ⌃ Z9 ⌂; S-Afr.,
  nat. in BrI, Ib, Fr, Ital-P, Ba, TR, Cauc.,
  Levant, N-Afr., Ind., C-Am.
- **purpurata** Jacq. · ⌃ Z9 ⌂; S-Afr. (Cape
  Prov.)
- var. *bowiei* (Lindl.) Sond. = Oxalis bowiei
- **purpurea** L. · E:Sorrel; G:Herbst-
  Sauerklee · ⌃ Z8 ⌂ X-XII; Cape, nat. in
  SW-Eur.
- **regnellii** Miq. · ⌃ Z8 ⌂; Peru. Bol.,
  Parag., Braz., Arg.
- **rosea** Jacq. · ☉ ⌂ VI-VIII; Chile
- *rubra* A. St.-Hil. = Oxalis articulata subsp.
  rubra
- **rusciformis** J.C. Mikan · ♄ Z10 ⌂; Braz.

- *speciosa* Jacq. = Oxalis purpurea
- **stricta** L. · E:Yellow Sheep Sorrel; G:Aufrechter Sauerklee · ♃ IX-X; Can.: E; USA: NE, NCE, NC, Rocky Mts., SW, SC, SE, Fla., NW, nat. in Eur., E-As.
- *succulenta* Barnéoud = Oxalis herrerae
- **tetraphylla** Cav. · E:Good Luck Leaf, Lucky Clover; G:Glücksklee · ♃ Z8 Ⓚ VII-VIII ☠; Mex., nat. in F, A, W-Ba
- **triangularis** A. St.-Hil. · ♃ Z8 Ⓚ; Braz.
- **tuberosa** Molina · E:Oca; G:Peruanischer Sauerklee · ♃ Z7 Ⓝ; cult. Col., Ecuad., Peru, Bol., Chile; And.
- **valdiviensis** Barnéoud · ⊙ Z9 VII-VIII; Chile
- *variabilis* Jacq. = Oxalis purpurea
- **versicolor** L. · ♃ Z9 Ⓚ II-III; Cape
- **vespertilionis** Zucc. · ♃ Z9 Ⓚ; Mex.
- **vulcanicola** Donn. Sm. · G:Buschiger Sauerklee

Oxandra A. Rich. -f- *Annonaceae* · 30 spp.
- **lanceolata** (Sw.) Baill. · E:Lancewood · ♄ Z9 Ⓦ Ⓝ; S-Afr.

Oxyanthus DC. -m- *Rubiaceae* · 34 spp.
- **formosus** Hook. f. · ♄ e D Z10 Ⓦ; trop. Afr.

Oxycoccus Hill = Vaccinium
- *microcarpus* = Vaccinium microcarpum
- *palustris* = Vaccinium oxycoccos

Oxydendrum DC. -n- *Ericaceae* · 1 sp. · E:Sorrel Tree, Sourwood; F:Oxydendron; G:Sauerbaum
- **arboreum** (L.) DC. · E:Sourwood; G:Sauerbaum · ♄ d Z6 VII-VIII Ⓝ; USA: NE, NCE, SE, Fla.

Oxylobium Andrews -n- *Fabaceae* · 15 spp. · G:Spitzhülse
- **linariifolium** (G. Don) Domin · ♄ e Z9 Ⓚ VII-VIII; W-Austr.

Oxypetalum R. Br. -n- *Asclepiadaceae* · 80-100 spp.
- *caeruleum* (D. Don) Decne. = Tweedia caerulea

Oxyria Hill -f- *Polygonaceae* · 2 spp. · E:Mountain Sorrel; F:Oxyria; G:Säuerling
- **digyna** (L.) Hill · E:Mountain Sorrel; G:Säuerling · ♃ △ Z2 VI-IX; Eur.*, TR, Syr., Cauc., N-Iran, W-Sib., E-Sib., Amur, Kamchat., C-As.

Oxytenanthera Munro -f- *Poaceae* · 1-2 spp.
- **abyssinica** (A. Rich.) Munro · ♄ Ⓦ Ⓝ; trop. Afr., Eth.

Oxytropis DC. -f- *Fabaceae* · 300-360 spp. · E:Crazy Weed, Locoweed, Point Vetch; F:Astragale, Oxytropis; G:Fahnenwicke, Spitzkiel
- **campestris** (L.) DC. · E:Yellow Oxytropis; G:Alpen-Spitzkiel · ♃ △ Z3 VII-VIII; Eur.*, Cauc., W-Sib., E-Sib., Sakhal., Alaska, Can., USA: NE, NCE, NC, Rocky Mts.
- × **carinthiaca** Fisch.-Oost. (*O. campestris* × *O. jacquinii*) · G:Kärntner Spitzkiel · ♃; A (Kärnten) +
- **foetida** (Vill.) DC. · E:Stinking Milk Vetch; G:Drüsiger Spitzkiel, Klebriger Spitzkiel · ♃ Z6 VII-VIII; Eur.: F, I, Sw; W-Alp.
- **halleri** Bunge ex W.D.J. Koch · E:Silky Milk Vetch; G:Hallers Spitzkiel · ♃ △ Z6 IV-VIII; Eur.* exc. Sc; Pyr., Alp, Carp., AL, Scotland
- **helvetica** Scheele · G:Schweizer Spitzkiel · ♃ VII-VIII; Eur.: F, I, Sw
- **jacquinii** Bunge · E:Mountain Milk Vetch; G:Berg-Spitzkiel · ♃ △ Z5 VII-VIII; Eur.: F, I, Sw, G, A; Alp., Jura
- **lapponica** (Wahlenb.) J. Gay · E:Northern Milk Vetch; G:Lappländer Spitzkiel · ♃ Z3 VII-VIII; Eur.: Fr, Ital-P, C-Eur., Sc, Ba; N, Pyr., Alp., AL; Cauc., W-Sib. (Altai), C-As., Tibet
- **neglecta** Ten. · G:Pyrenäen-Spitzkiel · ♃ VII-VIII; Eur.: sp., F, I, C-Eur., RO; mts.
- **pilosa** (L.) DC. · G:Zottiger Spitzkiel · ♃ Z6 VI-VII ▽; Eur.: Fr, Ital-P, C-Eur., EC-Eur., Ba, E-Eur.; TR, Cauc., W-Sib., E-Sib., Mong.
- **pyrenaica** Godr. & Gren. · ♃; Eur.: S, SC, Pyren., mts
- *sericea* (Lam.) Simonk. not Nutt.= Oxytropis halleri
- **triflora** Hoppe · G:Dreiblütiger Spitzkiel · ♃ VI-VIII; Eur.: A; E-Alp.

Ozothamnus R. Br. -m- *Asteraceae* · c. 50 spp.
- **coralloides** Hook. f. · ♄ e Z8 Ⓚ; NZ
- **hookeri** Sond. · ♄ Z9 Ⓚ; Austr.: N.S.Wales, Victoria, Tasman.; mts.

– **rosmarinifolius** (Labill.) DC. · ♄ ✂ Z8 ⬠
VI; Austr.: N.S.Wales, Victoria, Tasman.
– **scutellifolius** Hook. f. · ♄ Z9 ⬠; Tasman.
– **selaginoides** Sond. & F. Muell. · ♄ ⟁ e
Z9 ⬠; Tasman.
– **selago** Hook. f. · ♄ Z8 ⬠; NZ
– **thyrsoideus** DC. · ♄ e Z9 ⬠; Austr.
(N.S.Wales, Victoria, Tasman.)

Pabstia Garay -f- *Orchidaceae* · 5 spp.
– **jugosa** (Lindl.) Garay · ⟁ Z10 ⓜ V-VII ▽
❋; Braz.

Pachira Aubl. -f- *Bombacaceae* · 24 spp. ·
E:Shaving-Brush Tree; F:Châtaignier de
la Guyane; G:Rasierpinselbaum
– **aquatica** Aubl. · E:Guiana Chestnut, Pro-
vision Tree; G:Sumpf-Rasierpinselbaum ·
♄ e Z10 ⓜ VI; S-Mex., C-Am., trop. S-Am.
– *fastuosa* (Moç. & Sessé ex DC.) Decne. =
Pseudobombax ellipticum
– **insignis** (Sw.) Savigny · E:Wild Chestnut; G:Brazilianischer Rasierpinselbaum ·
♄ e Z10 ⓜ VII-VIII ⓝ; SW-Col., NW-Peru,
Braz., Guyana
– *macrocarpa* Cham. & Schltdl. = Pachira
aquatica

Pachycereus (A. Berger) Britton & Rose
-m- *Cactaceae* · 9-12 spp.
– **marginatus** (DC.) Britton & Rose ·
E:Organ Pipe Cactus; G:Orgelpfeifenkak-
tus · ♄ ⟊ Z9 ⬠; Mex.
– **pecten-aboriginum** (Engelm.) Britton &
Rose · E:Indian Comb · ♄ ⟊ Z9 ⬠ ▽ ❋;
W-Mex.
– **pringlei** (S. Watson) Britton & Rose · ♄ ⟊
Z9 ⬠ ▽ ❋; N-Mex., Baja Calif.
– *queretaroensis* (F.A.C. Weber) Britton &
Rose = Stenocereus queretaroensis
– *schottii* (Engelm.) D.R. Hunt = Lophocereus schottii
– **weberi** (J.M. Coult.) Backeb. · E:Mexican
Giant · ♄ ⟊ Z9 ⬠ ▽ ❋; S-Mex.

Pachycormus Coville ex Standl. -f-
Anacardiaceae · 1 sp.
– **discolor** (Benth.) Coville · ♄ Z10 ⓜ;
Mex.: Baja Calif.

Pachylophus Spach = Oenothera
– *caespitosus* (Nutt.) Spach = Oenothera
caespitosa

Pachyphragma (DC.) Rchb. -f-
Brassicaceae · 1 sp. · G:Scheinschaum-
kraut
– **macrophylla** (Hoffm.) N. Busch ·
G:Großblättriges Scheinschaumkraut · ⟁
Z7 V-VI; Cauc., C-As.

Pachyphytum Link, Klotzsch & Otto
-n- *Crassulaceae* · 15 spp. · G:Dickstamm;
F:Pachyphytum
– *amethystinum* Rose = Graptopetalum
amethystinum
– **bracteosum** Link, Klotzsch & Otto · ⟁ ⟊
Z9 ⬠ IV-VI; Mex.
– **brevifolium** Rose · ⟁ ⟊ Z9 ⬠; Mex.
– **compactum** Rose · ⟁ ⟊ Z9 ⬠ VI; Mex.
– **hookeri** (Salm-Dyck) A. Berger · ⟁ ♄ ⟊ e
Z9 ⬠ IV-V; Mex.
– **longifolium** Rose · ♄ ⟊ e Z9 ⬠ VII-VIII;
Mex.
– **oviferum** J.A. Purpus · E:Moonstones,
Sugared Almond Plum; G:Mondstein · ⟁
⟊ Z9 ⬠ V-VI; Mex.
– *uniflorum* Rose = Pachyphytum hookeri

Pachypodium Lindl. -n- *Apocynaceae* ·
20 spp. · F:Pachypodium, Palmier de
Madagascar; G:Madagaskarpalme
– **baronii** Costantin & Bois · ♄ ⟊ d Z9 ⬠
▽; C-Madag.
– var. **windsorii** (Poiss.) Pichon = Pachypodium windsori
– **brevicaule** Baker · ♄ ⟊ d Z9 ⓜ ▽ ❋;
Madag.
– **densiflorum** Baker · ♄ ⟊ d Z9 ⬠ ▽ ❋;
S-Madag.
– **geayi** Costantin & Bois · ♄ ⟊ d Z9 ⬠ ▽
❋; SW-Madag.
– **horombense** Poiss. · ♄ ⟊ Z9 ⓜ ▽ ❋;
Madag.
– **lamerei** Drake · E:Madagascar Palm;
G:Dickfuß, Madagaskarpalme · ♄ ⟊ d Z9
ⓜ ⚹ ▽ ❋; S-Madag.
– **namaquanum** (Wyley ex Harv.) Welw. ·
♄ ⟊ d Z9 ⓜ ▽ ❋; Cape, Namibia
– **rosulatum** Baker · ♄ ⟊ d Z9 ⓜ ▽ ❋;
Madag.
– **saundersii** N.E. Br. · ♄ ⟊ d Z9 ⓜ ▽ ❋;
Mozamb., Zimbabwe, S-Afr.
– **succulentum** (Thunb.) A. DC. · ♄ ⟊ d Z9
ⓜ VI-VIII ▽ ❋; Cape
– **windsori** Poiss. Z9 ⬠ ▽ ❋; N-Madag.

Pachyrhizus Rich. ex DC. -m- *Fabaceae* ·
5 spp. · E:Yam Bean; F:Pois-patate;

G:Yamsbohne
- **ahipa** (Wedd.) Parodi · 4 ⚥ Z10 ⓦ Ⓝ;
  orig. ?, cult. Bol, Arg.
- *angulatus* Rich. ex DC. = Pachyrhizus
  erosus
- **erosus** (L.) Urb. · E:Yam Bean;
  G:Yamsbohne · 4 ⚥ ⤳ Z10 ⓦ Ⓝ; Mex.,
  C-Am., nat. in S-Fla., Trop. OW
- **tuberosus** (Lam.) Spreng. · E:Potato
  Bean; G:Knollenbohne · 4 ⚥ Z10 ⓦ VII
  Ⓝ; Amazon. , Ecuad., Peru, Bol.

Pachysandra Michx. -f- *Buxaceae* · 4 spp. ·
  F:Euphorbe du Japon; G:Dickmännchen,
  Ysander
- **axillaris** Franch. · ♄ e Z6 IV; China
- **procumbens** Michx. · E:Allegheny
  Spurge, Mountain Spurge; G:Amerika-
  nischer Ysander · 4 ⤳ Z6 III-IV; USA:
  Ky., SE, Fla.
- **terminalis** Siebold & Zucc. · E:Japanese
  Spurge; G:Japanischer Ysander · ♄ ⤳
  Z5 IV ✿; China, Jap.

Pachystachys Nees -f- *Acanthaceae* ·
  12 spp. · F:Pachystachys; G:Dickähre
- **coccinea** (Aubl.) Nees · E:Cardinal's
  Guard; G:Rote Dickähre · ♄ e Z10 ⓦ;
  W.Ind., trop. S-Am.
- **lutea** Nees · E:Golden Candle, Lollipop
  Plant; G:Gelbe Dickähre, Gelber Zimmerhopfen · 4 Z10 ⓦ ▢ III-X; Peru

Pachystegia Cheeseman -f- · G:Baumaster
- **insignis** (Hook. f.) Cheeseman ·
  G:Baumaster · ♄ e Z8 ⓚ VI-VII; NZ

× **Pachyveria** Haage & E. Schmidt
  -f- *Crassulaceae* · G:Bastardecheverie
  (*Echeveria* × *Pachyphytum*)
- **clavata** E. Walther (*Echeveria affinis* ×
  Pachyphytum bracteosum) · ⵀ ⓚ; cult.
- **scheideckeri** (De Smet) E. Walther
  (*Echeveria secunda* × *Pachyphytum
  bracteosum*) · 4 ⵀ ⓚ; cult.

Packera Á. Löve & D. Löve -f- *Asteraceae* ·
  c. 65 spp.
- **aurea** (L.) Á. Löve & D. Löve · E:Golden
  Groundsel, Golden Ragwort, Squaw
  Weed · 4 Z3 V-VII ⚥ ; Can.: E; USA: NE,
  NCE, SE, Fla.

Paederia L. -f- *Rubiaceae* · 30 spp.
- **foetida** (Lour.) Merr. · E:Skunkvine · ⵃ d

⚥ Z6 VII-VIII; Jap., China, Korea
- *scandens* (Lour.) Merr. = Paederia foetida

Paederota L. -f- *Scrophulariaceae* · 2 spp. ·
  F:Véronique; G:Mänderle
- **bonarota** (L.) L. · G:Blaues Mänderle · 4
  △ Z7 ⋀ VII-VIII; Eur.: I, A, Slove; E-Alp.
- × **churchilli** Huter (*P. bonarota* × *P.
  lutea*) · 4 Z6; N-I +
- **lutea** Scop. · E:Yellow Veronica;
  G:Gelbes Mänderle · 4 △ Z6 VI-VIII;
  Eur.: I, A, Slove.; E-Alp.

Paeonia L. -f- *Paeoniaceae* · 33 spp. ·
  E:Peony; F:Pivoine; G:Päonie, Pfingstrose
- *albiflora* Pall. = Paeonia lactiflora
- **anomala** L.
- var. **anomala** · F:Pivoine de Chine · 4
  Z5; Russ., W-Sib., E-Sib., C-As., Mong.,
  China: Sinkiang
- var. **intermedia** (C.A. Mey. ex Ledeb.)
  B. Fedtsch. & O. Fedtsch. · 4 Z5 VI-VII;
  Eur.: Russ; C-As.
- *arietina* G. Anderson = Paeonia mascula
  subsp. arietina
- *banatica* Rochel = Paeonia officinalis
  subsp. banatica
- **broteroi** Boiss. & Reut. · 4 Z7 V; P, sp.
- **cambessedesii** (Willk.) Willk. ·
  G:Balearen-Pfingstrose · 4 Z8 ⓚ V-VI ▽;
  Balear.
- **caucasica** (Schipcz.) Schipcz. · 4 ; Cauc.
- *chinensis* hort. ex Vilm. = Paeonia
  lactiflora
- **clusii** Stern & Stearn · 4 Z7; Crete
- *corallina* Retz. = Paeonia mascula subsp.
  mascula
- **coriacea** Boiss. · 4 Z7 V-VI; S-Sp.,
  Moroc.
- *cretica* Tausch = Paeonia clusii
- *daurica* Andrews = Paeonia mascula
  subsp. triternata
- *decora* G. Anderson = Paeonia peregrina
  subsp. peregrina
- **delavayi** Franch. · E:Tree Peony;
  G:Delavays Strauch-Pfingstrose · ♄ d Z5
  VI; China: Yunnan, Sinkiang
- var. *angustiloba* Rehder & E.H. Wilson =
  Paeonia potaninii var. potaninii
- var. *lutea* (Franch.) Finet & Gagnep. =
  Paeonia lutea
- *edulis* Salisb. = Paeonia lactiflora
- *fragrans* (Sabine) Redouté = Paeonia
  lactiflora
- *humilis* Retz. = Paeonia officinalis subsp.

humilis
- *intermedia* C.A. Mey. ex Ledeb. = Paeonia anomala var. intermedia
- *kavachensis* Azn. = Paeonia mascula subsp. mascula
- *laciniata* Siev. = Paeonia anomala var. anomala
- **lactiflora** Pall. · E:Common Garden Peony, White Peony; G:Chinesische Pfingstrose · ⯝ Z6 VI-VII ⚥ ; E-Sib., China, Tibet, Manch., Korea
- **many cultivars**
- *lobata* Desf. = Paeonia peregrina subsp. peregrina
- **lutea** Franch. · E:Yellow Peony; G:Gelbe Pfingstrose · ♄ d Z7 ⋀ V-VI; China, Tibet
- **mascula** (L.) Mill.
- subsp. **arietina** (G. Anderson) Cullen & Heywood · ⯝ Z7 V-VI; Eur.: N-I, N-Ba; TR
- subsp. **mascula** · E:Coral Peony; G:Korallen-Pfingstrose · ⯝ Z7 V; Eur.: Ib, Fr, Ital-P, Ba, RO, Crim; TR, Levant, N-Iraq, Cauc., N-Iran, Moroc., Alger., nat. in BrI, A
- subsp. **triternata** (Boiss.) Stearn & P.H. Davis · ⯝ Z6 V-VI; Eur.: ? Slove., Crim; TR
- *microcarpa* Salm-Dyck = Paeonia officinalis subsp. villosa
- **mlokosewitschii** Lomakin · G:Gelbe Kaukasus-Pfingstrose · ⯝ Z6 IV-V; C-Cauc.
- **obovata** Maxim.
- var. **obovata** · ⯝ Z7; Amur, China, Manch., Korea, Jap., Sakhal.
- var. **willmottiae** (Stapf) Stern · ⯝ Z7 VI; China
- **officinalis** L.
- subsp. **banatica** (Rochel) Soó · ⯝ Z7; Eur.: H, RO, Maced.
- subsp. **humilis** (Retz.) Cullen & Heywood · G:Kleine Bauern-Pfingstrose · ⯝ Z7 V-VI; Eur.: sp., P, F
- subsp. **officinalis** · E:Common Peony, Cottage Peony; F:Pivoine officinale; G:Bauern-Pfingstrose, Gewöhnliche Pfingstrose · ⯝ Z7 V-VI ⚥ ⚘ Ⓝ; Eur.: Ib, Fr, Sw, H, Ba, RO; TR, Cauc., nat. in D
- subsp. **villosa** (Huth) Cullen & Heywood · G:Filzige Bauern-Pfingstrose · ⯝ Z7; S-F, I
- *paradoxa* G. Anderson = Paeonia officinalis subsp. humilis
- **peregrina** Mill.
- subsp. **peregrina** · E:Scarlet Peony; F:Pivoine voyageuse; G:Klebrige

Pfingstrose · ⯝ Z7 V-VI; Eur.: Ba, E-Eur., I; TR
- var. *humilis* (Retz.) Huth = Paeonia officinalis subsp. officinalis
- **potaninii** Kom.
- var. **potaninii** · ♄ d Z7; W-China
- var. **trollioides** (Stapf ex Stearn) Stearn · ♄ d Z7 VII-VIII; Tibet
- **rockii** (S.G. Haw & Lauener) T. Hong & J.J. Li
- subsp. **linyanshanii** T. Hong & Osti
- subsp. **rockii** · G:Gefleckte Strauch-Pfingstrose · ♄ Z7; China
- *sinensis* (Sims) hort. = Paeonia lactiflora
- × **smouthii** Van Houtte (*P. lactiflora* × *P. tenuifolia*) · ⯝ d; cult.
- × **suffruticosa** Andrews (*P. ostii* × *P. rockii* × *P. spontanea*) · E:Tree Peony; F:Pivoine en arbre; G:Strauch-Pfingstrose · ♄ d V-VI; cult. in NW-China, Tibet, Bhutan
- subsp. *rockii* S.G. Haw & Lauener = Paeonia × yananensis
- **tenuifolia** L. · F:Pivoine à feuilles menues; G:Netzblatt-Pfingstrose · ⯝ Z8 ⋀ V-VI; Eur.: Ba, RO, S-Russ.
- *triternata* Boiss. = Paeonia mascula subsp. triternata
- *trollioides* Stapf ex Stearn = Paeonia potaninii var. trollioides
- **veitchii** Lynch
- var. **veitchii** · E:Veitch's Peony; G:Veitchs Pfingstrose · ⯝ Z7; China
- var. **woodwardii** (Stapf & Cox) Stern · ⯝ △ Z7 VI-VII; China: Kansu
- *willmottiae* Stapf = Paeonia obovata var. obovata
- **wittmanniana** Hartwiss ex Lindl.
- var. **nudicarpa** Schipcz. · ⯝ Z7 V; W-Cauc.
- var. **wittmanniana** · G:Kaukasus-Pfingstrose · ⯝ Z7 V; NW-Cauc.
- *woodwardii* Stapf & Cox = Paeonia veitchii var. woodwardii
- × **yananensis** T. Hong & M.R. Li (*P. spontanea* × *P. rockii*) · ♄ d; cult. in China
- **Cultivars:**
- **many cultivars, see Section III**
- 'Rock's Variety' = Paeonia rockii subsp. rockii

Paepalanthus Kunth -m- *Eriocaulaceae* · 420 spp.
- **elongatus** (Bong.) Körn. · ⯝ ⋉ Z9 Ⓚ; Braz.

Palafoxia Lag. -f- *Asteraceae* · 12 spp. ·
E:Palafox
- **hookeriana** Torr. & A. Gray · E:Sand
Palafox · ⊙ VII-X; USA: NC, SC
- **texana** DC. · E:Texas Palafox · ⊙ VII-X;
Tex.

Palaquium Blanco -n- *Sapotaceae* · 121 sp. ·
E:Gutta Percha; F:Arbre à gutta, Gom-
mier; G:Guttaperchabaum
- **gutta** (Hook. f.) Baill. · E:Gutta Percha;
G:Guttaperchabaum · ♄ e Z10 ⓜ ⓝ;
Malay. Pen., Sumatra, Kalimantan

Palaua Cav. -f- *Malvaceae* · 15 spp.
- **dissecta** Benth. · ⊙ ⓐ VI-VIII; Peru,
Chile

Palisota Rchb. ex Endl. -f- *Commelinaceae* ·
25 spp.
- **albertii** Gentil · ♃ ⚭ Z10 ⓜ; trop. Afr.
- **barteri** Hook. f. · ♃ ⚭ Z10 ⓜ; trop. Afr.
- **bracteosa** C.B. Clarke · ♃ ⚭ Z9 ⓜ; trop.
Afr.
- *elizabethae* Gentil = Palisota pynaertii
- **pynaertii** De Wild. · ♃ Z10 ⓜ; trop. Afr.

Paliurus Mill. -m- *Rhamnaceae* · 8 spp. ·
E:Christ's Thorn; F:Epine du Christ;
G:Christdorn, Stechdorn
- **orientalis** Hemsl. · ♄ d Z9 ⓐ; W-China
- **ramosissimus** (Lour.) Poir. · ♄ d Z7;
China, Korea, Jap., Taiwan
- **spina-christi** Mill. · E:Crown of Thorns,
Jerusalem Thorn; G:Gewöhnlicher
Christdorn · ♄ d Z8 ⓐ ∧ VII; Eur.: Ib, Fr,
Ital-P, Ba; TR, Syr., N-Iraq, Cauc., Iran,
C-As., Alger.

Panax L. -m- *Araliaceae* · 11 sp. · E:Ginseng;
F:Ginseng; G:Ginseng, Kraftwurz
- *fruticosus* L. = Polyscias fruticosa
- **ginseng** C.A. Mey. · E:Ginseng; G:Kore-
anischer Ginseng · ♃ Z7 ∧ VI-VIII ⚥ ⓝ
▽ ✲; China, Amur, N-Korea
- **japonicus** (T. Nees) C.A. Mey. ·
E:Japanese Ginseng; G:Japanischer
Ginseng · ♃ ∧ VI-VIII ⓝ; Jap., China,
Vietn., Thail.
- **pseudoschinseng** Wall. · ♃ ∧ VI-VIII
⚥ ⓝ; N-Ind., Nepal, Burma, SW-China,
N-Vietn.
- **quinquefolius** L. · E:American Ginseng;
G:Kanadischer Ginseng · ♃ Z7 ∧ VII-VIII
⚥ ⓝ ▽ ✲; Can.: E; USA: NE, NCE, Okla.,
SE, Fla.
- *schinseng* T. Nees = Panax ginseng
- **trifolius** L. · E:Dwarf Ginseng; G:Drei-
blättriger Ginseng · ♃ Z3 V-VI; Can.: E;
USA: NE, NCE, NC, SE

Pancratium Dill. ex L. -n- *Amaryllidaceae* ·
20 spp. · E:Sea Daffodil; F:Lis-pancrais,
Pancrais; G:Pankrazlilie
- *calathinum* Ker-Gawl. = Hymenocallis
narcissiflora
- *caribaeum* L. = Hymenocallis caribaea
- **illyricum** L. · E:Illyrian Sea Daffodil;
G:Illyrische Pankrazlilie · ♃ D Z8 ⓐ ∧
V-VII; Eur.: Cors, Sard., I (Capraia)
- **maritimum** L. · E:Sea Daffodil; G:Dünen-
Pankrazlilie · ♃ D Z8 ⓐ VII-IX ✿; Eur.:
Ib, Fr, Ital-P, Ba; TR, Cauc., N-Afr.
- *narcissiflorum* Jacq. = Hymenocallis
narcissiflora
- *speciosum* L. f. ex Salisb. = Hymenocallis
speciosa
- *undulatum* Kunth = Hymenocallis
tubiflora

Pandanus Parkinson -m- *Pandanaceae* ·
791 sp. · E:Screw Pine; F:Arbre au
parasol, Pandanus; G:Schraubenbaum
- **amaryllifolius** Roxb. · ♄ e Z10 ⓜ ⓝ;
cult. Java, Molucca Is.
- *baptistii* Warb. = Pandanus tectorius
- **brosimos** Merr. & L.M. Perry · e Z10 ⓜ
ⓝ; N.Guinea
- **candelabrum** P. Beauv. · ♄ e Z10 ⓜ;
W-Afr.
- **caricosus** Spreng. · ♄ e Z10 ⓜ; Java
- **conglomeratus** Balf. f. · ♄ e Z10 ⓜ;
E-Afr. (islands)
- **dubius** Spreng. · ♄ e Z10 ⓜ; Molucca,
N.Guinea, Pacific Is,
- **furcatus** Roxb. · ♄ e Z10 ⓜ; Ind., Burma
- *horridus* Reinw. ex Blume = Pandanus
furcatus
- **houlletii** Carrière · ♄ e Z10 ⓜ; Malay.
Pen.: Singapore
- **labyrinthicus** Kurz ex Miq. · ♄ e Z10 ⓜ;
Sumat.
- *latifolius* Hassk. = Pandanus amaryllifolius
- **nitidus** Kurz ex Miq.
- *odoratissimus* L. f. = Pandanus odorifer
- **odorifer** (Forssk.) Kuntze; trop. and
subtrop. As.
- *odorus* Ridl. = Pandanus amaryllifolius
- *pacificus* Veitch ex Mast. = Pandanus

dubius
- **pygmaeus** Thouars · ♄ e Z10 ⓜ; Madag.
- *reflexus* (de Vriese) K. Koch = Pandanus conglomeratus
- *sanderi* Sander = Pandanus tectorius
- *spurius* Miq. = Pandanus utilis
- *stenophyllus* (Miq.) Kurz = Pandanus nitidus
- **tectorius** Parkinson ex Du Roi · E:Tahitian Screw Pine · ♄ e Z10 ⓜ ⚥ Ⓝ; Ind., Sri Lanka, Burma, Austr., Polyn., Mascarene Is.; coasts
- **utilis** Bory · E:Common Screw Pine · ♄ e Z10 ⓜ Ⓝ; Madag.
- **vandermeeschii** Balf. f. · ♄ e Z10 ⓜ; Mauritius
- *variegatus* Miq. = Pandanus tectorius
- *veitchii* Mast. = Pandanus tectorius

Pandorea (Endl.) Spach -f- Bignoniaceae · 6 spp. · E:Bower Plant; F:Bignone faux-jasmin; G:Pandoree
- **jasminoides** (Lindl.) K. Schum. · E:Bower Plant, Bower Vine; G:Rosa Pandoree · ♄ e ⚥ D Z9 ⚘ VII-IX; Austr.
- **pandorana** (Andrews) Steenis · E:Spear Wood, Wonga Wonga Vine; G:Holzige Pandoree · ♄ e ⚥ Z9 ⚘; Austr.

Pangium Reinw. -n- Flacourtiaceae · 1 sp.
- **edule** Reinw. · E:Pangium · ♄ Z10 ⓜ � Ⓝ; Malay.Arch.

Panicum L. -n- Poaceae · 500+ spp. · E:Crab Grass, Panic Grass; F:Panic; G:Hirse, Rispenhirse
- **antidotale** Retz. · ⚃ Ⓝ; Ind., Arab., nat. in Austr.
- **capillare** L. · E:Old Witch Grass, Witch Grass; G:Haarästige Rispenhirse · ⊙ ✂ Z5 VII-IX; Can., USA *, Bermuda, nat. in Sw, H
- **clandestinum** L. · E:Deertongue; G:Hirschzungen-Rispenhirse · ⚃ VII-VIII; Can.: E; USA: NE, NCE, Kans. SC, SE, Fla.
- *colonum* L. = Echinochloa colona
- **coloratum** L. · E:Kleingrass; G:Buntes Guineagras, Marikarigras · ⚃ ⚘ Ⓝ; S-Afr.
- *crus-galli* L. = Echinochloa crus-galli
- *crus-pavonis* (Kunth) Nees = Echinochloa crus-pavonis
- **dichotomiflorum** Michx. · E:Fall Panicgrass; G:Gabelästige Rispenhirse · ⊙ VII-IX; Arg., nat. in F, I, A, D

- *glaucum* L. = Pennisetum glaucum
- **hillmanii** Chase · E:Hillman's Panicgrass; G:Hillmans Hirse · ⊙ VII-VIII; USA, nat. in A
- *hirtellum* L. = Oplismenus hirtellus
- **laevifolium** Hack. · G:Südafrikanische Hirse · ⊙ VII-IX; S-Afr., nat. in C-Eur.
- *lineare* Krock. = Digitaria ischaemum
- **maximum** Jacq. · E:Guinea Grass; G:Gunineagras · ⊙ ⚃ Ⓝ; Eur.: Sic.; trop. Afr., S-Afr., Madag., Mascarene Is., nat. in Fla., trop. Am.
- **miliaceum** L. · E:Common Millet, Millet; G:Echte Hirse, Gewöhnliche Rispenhirse · ⊙ Z5 VI-VIII Ⓝ; SE-As.; cult.
- *miliare* auct. non Lam. = Panicum sumatrense
- *palmifolium* J. König = Setaria palmifolia
- *plicatum* Willd. non Lam. = Setaria palmifolia
- *sanguinale* L. = Digitaria sanguinalis var. sanguinalis
- *sulcatum* Bertol. non Aubl. = Setaria poiretiana
- **sumatrense** Roth ex Roem. & Schult. · E:Little Millet; G:Kutki-Hirse · ⊙ Ⓝ; cult., Ind., Sri Lanka
- **virgatum** L. · E:Switch Grass; G:Ruten-Hirse · ⚃ ✂ Z5 VII-IX; Can.: E, Sask.; USA* exc. NW, Calif.; Mex., C-Am., W-Ind., Bermuda
- **some cultivars**

Papaver L. -n- Papaveraceae · c. 80 spp. · E:Poppy; F:Pavot; G:Mohn
- **alboroseum** Hultén · ⚃ △ IV-VI; Alaska, Kamchat.
- **alpinum** L. · G:Alpen-Mohn
 - subsp. **alpinum** · E:Alpine Poppy; F:Pavot de Burser, Pavot des Alpes; G:Bursers Alpen-Mohn · ⚃ △ Z5 VI-VII ▽; Eur.: A
 - subsp. **ernesti-mayeri** Markgr. Z5 ▽; Slove., I (Venetia); mts.
 - subsp. **kerneri** (Hayek) Fedde · G:Illyrischer Alpen-Mohn · ⚃ △ Z5 VI-VII; Eur.: I, A, Slove., Bosn., Montenegro; mts.
 - subsp. **rhaeticum** (Leresche) Nyman · G:Gelber Alpen-Mohn · ⚃ △ Z5 VII; Eur.: F, I, A, Slove., Bosn., Montenegro; mts.
 - subsp. **sendtneri** (A. Kern. ex Hayek) Schinz & R. Keller · G:Weißer Alpen-Mohn · ⚃ △ Z5 VII; Eur.: Sw, G, A; Alp.
- **apulum** Ten. · G:Apulischer Mohn · ⊙ Z8 V-VI; Eur.: Ital-P, Ba

- **argemone** L. · E:Pale Poppy; G:Sand-Mohn · ☉ Z8 V-VII; Eur.*; N-Afr., SW-As
- **atlanticum** (Ball) Coss. · F:Pavot de l'Atlantique; G:Marokkanischer Mohn · ⳨ Z6 VI-VIII; Moroc., nat. in GB
- **aurantiacum** Loisel. · G:Gold-Mohn · ⳨ VII-VIII; Eur.: F, I, C-Eur., Ba, ? sp.
- *burseri* Crantz = Papaver alpinum subsp. alpinum
- **croceum** Ledeb. · G:Altai-Mohn · ⳨ Z2 VII-VIII; W-Sib., E-Sib., C-As., Mong., Him., NE-China
- **dubium** L. · G:Saat-Mohn
- subsp. **confine** (Jord.) Hörandl · G:Verkannter Saat-Mohn · ☉ Z7 IV-V ⚒; G, F+
- subsp. **dubium** · E:Long-head Poppy; G:Gewöhnlicher Saat-Mohn · ☉ Z7 V-VII ⚒; Eur.*, SW-As.
- subsp. **lecoqii** (Lamotte) Syme · G:Gelbmilchender Saat-Mohn, Lecoques Mohn · ☉ Z7 V-VII ⚒; Eur., TR, NW-Afr.
- **glaucum** Boiss. & Hausskn. · E:Tulip Poppy · ☉ Z8 VI-VIII; TR, Syr., N-Iraq, W-Iran
- **hybridum** L. · E:Rough Poppy; G:Bastard-Mohn, Krummborstiger Mohn, Ziegelroter Mohn · ☉ V-VII; Eur.: Ib, Ital-P, F, Ba; W-As., nat. in BrI
- *kerneri* Hayek = Papaver alpinum subsp. kerneri
- **lateritium** K. Koch · ⳨ △ Z7 VI-IX; Cauc. (Armen.), nat. in GB
- **miyabeanum** Tatew. · G:Kurilen-Mohn · ⳨ △ Z2 V; Kuril. Is.
- **monanthum** Trautv. · ⳨ △ Z7 VI-VIII; Cauc.
- **nudicaule** L. · E:Iceland Poppy, Icelandic Poppy; F:Pavot d'Islande; G:Island-Mohn · ⳨ △ Z2 IX-IX; E-Sib., Mong.
- **many cultivars**
- subsp. *xanthopetalum* Fedde = Papaver miyabeanum
- **occidentale** (Markgr.) H.E. Hess & Landolt · G:Westlicher Alpen-Mohn · ⳨ VII; Eur.: F, Sw
- **orientale** L. · E:Oriental Poppy; F:Pavot d'Orient; G:Türkischer Mohn · ⳨ ⤫ Z3 V-VI; TR, Cauc., N-Iran
- **many cultivars**
- **pavoninum** Fisch. & C.A. Mey. · E:Peacock Poppy; G:Pfauen-Mohn · ☉ Z8 VI-VII; Iran, C-As., China: Sinkiang
- **pilosum** Sibth. & Sm. · F:Pavot poilu; G:Bithynischer Mohn · ⳨ △ Z6 VI-VII;

NW-TR
- *pyrenaicum* A. Kern. = Papaver alpinum
- subsp. *rhaeticum* (Leresche) Fedde = Papaver alpinum subsp. rhaeticum
- subsp. *sendtneri* (A. Kern. ex Hayek) Fedde = Papaver alpinum subsp. sendtneri
- **radicatum** Rottb. · E:Arctic Poppy; G:Arktischer Mohn · ⳨ △ Z3 V-VI; Eur.: Sc, N-Russ.; E-Sib., Alaska, Can.: W, USA: Rocky Mts.; Greenl.
- *rhaeticum* Leresche = Papaver alpinum subsp. rhaeticum
- **rhoeas** L. · E:Corn Poppy, Field Poppy, Flanders Poppy; G:Klatsch-Mohn · ☉ Z5 V-VII ⚘ ⚒; Eur.*, TR, Cauc., Iran, Canar., N-Afr.
- **rupifragum** Boiss. & Reut. · E:Spanish Poppy; G:Spanischer Mohn · ⳨ Z7 VI-VIII; S-Sp.
- *sendtneri* A. Kern. ex Hayek = Papaver alpinum subsp. sendtneri
- *setigerum* DC. = Papaver somniferum subsp. setigerum
- **somniferum** L. · G:Schlaf-Mohn
- **some cultivars**
- subsp. **setigerum** (DC.) Corb. · ☉ Z7 ⚒; Eur.: Ib, F, Ital-P, GR; Cyprus, NW-Afr., Libya
- subsp. **somniferum** · E:Opium Poppy; G:Gewöhnlicher Schlaf-Mohn · ☉ Z7 VI-VIII ⚘ ⚒ ⓝ; cult., nat. in Eur., As.
- var. *glaucum* (Boiss. & Hausskn.) Kuntze = Papaver glaucum
- *strigosum* (Boenn.) Schur = Papaver rhoeas

Paphinia Lindl. -f- Orchidaceae · 16 spp.
- **cristata** (Lindl.) Lindl. · ⳨ Z10 ⓜ VIII-IX ▽ ✳; Col., Venez., Trinidad, Guyan.
- **grandiflora** Barb. Rodr. · ⳨ Z10 ⓜ IX-XI ▽ ✳; Braz.
- *grandis* Rchb. f. ex R. Warner = Paphinia grandiflora

Paphiopedilum Pfitzer -n- Orchidaceae · 77 spp. · E:Slipper Orchid, Venus' Slipper; F:Sabot de Vénus; G:Venusschuh
- **acmodontum** Schoser ex M.W. Wood · ⳨ Z10 ⓜ III-IV ▽ ✳; Phil.
- **appletonianum** (Gower) Rolfe · ⳨ Z10 ⓜ III-V ▽ ✳; Cambodia, Laos, Thail.
- **argus** (Rchb. f.) Stein · ⳨ Z10 ⓜ IV-V ▽ ✳; Phil.: Luzon
- **armeniacum** S.C. Chen & F.Y. Liu · ⳨

Z10 ⌂ ▽ ✳; Yunnan
- **barbatum** (Lindl.) Pfitzer · ♃ Z10 ⌂ IV-V ▽ ✳; Malay. Pen.
- **bellatulum** (Rchb. f.) Stein · ♃ Z10 ⌂ III-IV ▽ ✳; W-Burma, Thail.
- **bullenianum** (Rchb. f.) Pfitzer · ♃ Z10 ⌂ VI-VIII ▽ ✳; Malay. Pen., Sumat., Kalimantan
- **callosum** (Rchb. f.) Stein · ♃ Z10 ⌂ II-III ▽ ✳; Cambodia, Laos, Thail.
- **charlesworthii** (Rolfe) Pfitzer · ♃ Z10 ⌂ IX-X ▽ ✳; E-Burma
- **ciliolare** (Rchb. f.) Stein · ♃ Z10 ⌂ IV-VI ▽ ✳; Phil.
- **concolor** (Lindl. ex Bateman) Pfitzer · ♃ Z10 ⌂ XII-III ▽ ✳; China: Yunnan; Indochina
- **dayanum** (Lindl.) Stein · ♃ Z10 ⌂ V-VI ▽ ✳; Kalimantan (Sabah)
- **delenatii** Guill. · ♃ Z10 ⌂ ▽ ✳; Vietn.
- **druryi** (Bedd.) Stein · ♃ Z10 ⌂ V-VI ▽ ✳; S-Ind.
- **exul** (Ridl.) Rolfe · ♃ Z10 ⌂ V-VI ▽ ✳; Thail.
- **fairrieanum** (Lindl.) Stein · ♃ Z10 ⌂ IX-X ▽ ✳; Bhutan, Sikkim, NE-Ind.
- **glanduliferum** (Blume) Stein · ♃ Z10 ⌂ ▽ ✳; N.Guinea
- **glaucophyllum** J.J. Sm. · ♃ Z10 ⌂ I-XII ▽ ✳; Java
- **godefroyae** (God.-Leb.) Stein · ♃ Z10 ⌂ IV-VI ▽ ✳; Thail.
- **gratrixianum** (Mast.) Rolfe · ♃ Z10 ⌂ ▽ ✳; Laos
- **haynaldianum** (Rchb. f.) Stein · ♃ Z10 ⌂ I-III ▽ ✳; Phil. (Luzon, Negros)
- **hirsutissimum** (Lindl. ex Hook.) Stein · ♃ Z10 ⌂ III-V ▽ ✳; NE-Ind.
- **insigne** (Wall. ex Lindl.) Pfitzer · ♃ Z10 ⌂ XI-III ▽ ✳; NE-Ind.
- **javanicum** (Reinw. ex Lindl.) Pfitzer · ♃ Z10 ⌂ ▽ ✳; Java, Bali, Flores
- **lawrenceanum** (Rchb. f.) Pfitzer · ♃ Z10 ⌂ IV-V ▽ ✳; Kalimantan (Sarawak)
- **lowii** (Lindl.) Stein · ♃ Z10 ⌂ III-VII ▽ ✳; Malay. Pen., Sumat., Kalimantan, Java, Sulawesi
- **mastersianum** (Rchb. f.) Stein · ♃ Z10 ⌂ IV-VII ▽ ✳; Molucca
- **niveum** (Rchb. f.) Stein · ♃ Z10 ⌂ IV-VII ▽ ✳; S-Thail., Malay. Pen.
- **papuanum** (Ridl. ex Rendle) L.O. Williams · ♃ Z10 ⌂ ▽ ✳; N.Guinea; mts.
- **parishii** (Rchb. f.) Stein · ♃ Z10 ⌂ IV-VII ▽ ✳; SW-China, Burma, Thail.

- **philippinense** (Rchb. f.) Pfitzer · ♃ Z10 ⌂ V-VI ▽ ✳; Phil.
- *praestans* (Rchb. f.) Pfitzer = Paphiopedilum glanduliferum
- **primulinum** M.W. Wood & P. Taylor · ♃ Z10 ⌂ ▽ ✳; N-Sumat.
- **purpuratum** (Lindl.) Stein · ♃ Z10 ⌂ VI-IX ▽ ✳; China (Hong Kong)
- **rothschildianum** (Rchb. f.) Stein · ♃ Z10 ⌂ VII-IX ▽ ✳; Kalimantan
- **sanderianum** (Rchb. f.) Stein · ♃ Z10 ⌂ VII-IX ▽ ✳; Kalimantan (Sarawak)
- **spicerianum** (Rchb. f. ex Mast. & T. Moore) Pfitzer · ♃ Z10 ⌂ XI-I ▽ ✳; NE-Ind., NW-Burma
- **stonei** (Hook.) Stein · ♃ Z10 ⌂ V-VII ▽ ✳; Kalimantan (Sarawak)
- **sukhakulii** Schoser & Senghas · ♃ Z10 ⌂ IX-V ▽ ✳; NE-Thail.
- **superbiens** (Rchb. f.) Stein · ♃ Z10 ⌂ V-VII ▽ ✳; Sumat.
- **tonsum** (Rchb. f.) Stein · ♃ Z10 ⌂ III-VII ▽ ✳; Sumat.
- **venustum** (Wall. ex Sims) Pfitzer · ♃ Z10 ⌂ IX-I ▽ ✳; E-Nepal, Bhutan, NE-Ind.
- **victoria-regina** (Sander) M.W. Wood · ♃ Z10 ⌂ I-IX ▽ ✳; Sumat.
- **villosum** (Lindl.) Stein · ♃ Z10 ⌂ XII-IV ▽ ✳; NE-Ind., Burma, Thail.
- **violascens** Schltr. · ♃ Z10 ⌂ IX-X ▽ ✳; N.Guinea
- **wardii** Summerh. · ♃ Z10 ⌂ ▽ ✳; N-Burma, Thail.
- *wolterianum* (Kraenzl.) Pfitzer = Paphiopedilum appletonianum
- **Cultivars:**
- **many cultivars**

Papilionanthe Schltr. -n- *Orchidaceae* · II sp.
- **hookeriana** (Rchb. f.) Schltr. · E:Bone Plant · ♃ Z9 ⌂ VIII-IX ▽ ✳; Malay. Pen., Sumat., Kalimantan
- **teres** (Roxb.) Schltr. · ♃ Z9 ⌂ VI-VIII ▽ ✳; Burma, Thail., Laos
- **vandarum** (Rchb. f.) Garay · ♃ Z9 ⌂ II-VI ▽ ✳; Him.

Paradisea Mazzuc. -f- *Asphodelaceae* · 2 spp. · E:Paradise Lily; F:Lis de St-Bruno; G:Paradieslilie
- **liliastrum** (L.) Bertol. · E:St Bruno's Lily; F:Lis de Saint-Bruno; G:Echte Paradislilie · ♃ D Z7 VI; Eur.: sp., F, Sw, I, A, Slove.; Pyr., Alp., Jura, Apenn.

- **lusitanica** (Cout.) Samp. · G:Iberische
  Paradislilie · ⁴ Z7; N-P, W-Sp.

Parageum Nakai & H. Hara = Geum
- *montanum* (L.) H. Hara = Geum
  montanum
- *reptans* (L.) M. Král = Geum reptans

Parahebe W.R.B. Oliv. -f-
Scrophulariaceae · 30 spp.
- × **bidwillii** (Hook.) W.R.B. Oliv. (*P.
  decora* × *P. lyallii*) · ♄ e ⤳ Z8 ⒶⒸ ∧
  VI-VII; NZ
- **canescens** W.R.B. Oliv. · ♄ Z8 ⒶⒸ; NZ
- **catarractae** (G. Forst.) W.R.B. Oliv. · ♄ e
  Z8 ⒶⒸ; NZ
- **decora** Ashwin · ♄ Z8 ⒶⒸ; NZ
- **lyallii** (Hook. f.) W.R.B. Oliv. · ♄ e Z8 ⒶⒸ
  ∧ V-VI; NZ
- **perfoliata** (R. Br.) B.G. Briggs &
  Ehrend. · E:Digger's Speedwell · ⁴ Z8 ⒶⒸ;
  Austr. (N.S.Wales, Victoria)

Paraphalaenopsis A.D. Hawkes -f-
Orchidaceae · 4 spp.
- **denevei** (Sm.) A.D. Hawkes Z10 ⓦ;
  Kalimantan

Parapholis C.E. Hubb. -f- *Poaceae* · 6 spp. ·
E:Hard Grass; G:Dünnschwanz
- **strigosa** (Dumort.) C.E. Hubb. · E:Hard
  Grass; G:Gekrümmter Dünnschwanz · ⊙
  VI-VII; Eur.: Sc, BrI, Fr, G, Ib, Ital-P, Ba;
  coasts

Paraserianthes I.C. Nielsen -f-
Mimosaceae · 4 spp. · E:Plume Albizia;
G:Schirmakazie
- **falcataria** (L.) I.C. Nielsen
- subsp. **falcataria** · ♄ Z9 ⓦ Ⓝ; Malay.
  Arch.
- **lophantha** (Willd.) I.C. Nielsen
- subsp. **lophantha** · E:Plume Albizia;
  G:Schirmakazie · ♄ ♄ d Z9 ⒶⒸ III-IV;
  Austr.

Parathelypteris (H. Itô) Ching -f-
Thelypteridaceae · 25 spp.
- **noveboracensis** (L.) Ching · E:New York
  Fern · ⁴ ⌢ Z6; Can.: E; USA: NE, NCE,
  SE

× **Pardancanda** L.W. Lenz -f- *Iridaceae*
(*Belamcanda* × *Pardanthopsis*)
- **norrisii** L.W. Lenz · ⁴ ⒶⒸ; cult.

Pardanthopsis (Hance) L.W. Lenz = Iris
- *dichotoma* (Pall.) L.W. Lenz = Iris
  dichotoma

Pardanthus Ker-Gawl. = Belamcanda
- *chinensis* (L.) Ker-Gawl. = Belamcanda
  chinensis

Parentucellia Viv. -f- *Scrophulariaceae* ·
2-4 spp. · F:Parentucelle; G:Bartsie,
Parentucellie
- **viscosa** (L.) Caruel · E:Yellow Bartsia;
  G:Gelbe Bartsie · ⊙ V-VIII; Eur.: Ib, Fr,
  Br, Ital-P, Ba; TR, Cyprus, Cauc., Iran,
  Azor., Canar., NW-Afr., Egypt, nat. in DK,
  N-Am., Austr.

Parietaria L. -f- *Urticaceae* · 10-20 spp. ·
E:Pellitory of the Wall; F:Pariétaire;
G:Glaskraut
- *diffusa* Mert. & W.D.J. Koch = Parietaria
  judaica
- **judaica** L. · E:Pellitory of the Wall;
  G:Mauer-Glaskraut · ⁴ VI-X ♃ ; Eur.*
  exc. EC-Eur., Sc; TR; Cauc., Iran, C-As.,
  China: Sinkiang; N-Afr.
- **officinalis** L. · E:Upright Pellitory;
  G:Aufrechtes Glaskraut · ⁴ VI-X ♃ Ⓝ;
  Eur.: Fr, Ital-P, C-Eur., EC-Eur., Ba,
  E-Eur.; Canar., Madeira, Azor.; TR,
  Cauc., W-Iran, N-Afr., nat. in Sc
- **pensylvanica** Muhl. ex Willd. ·
  E:Pensylvania Pellitory; G:Pennsylva-
  nisches Glaskraut · ⊙ V-XI; N-Am., nat. in
  D

Parinari Aubl. -f- *Chrysobalanaceae* ·
44 spp.
- **campestris** Aubl. · ♄ e Z10 ⓦ Ⓝ; W.Ind.,
  Guyan., Braz.
- **corymbosa** (Blume) Miq. · ♄ e Z10 ⓦ Ⓝ;
  Java
- **excelsa** G. Don · E:Guinea Plum;
  G:Guineapflaume · ♄ e Z10 ⓦ Ⓝ; W-Afr.:
  Guinea
- **laurina** A. Gray · ♄ e Z10 ⓦ Ⓝ; Fiji
- **macrophylla** Sabine · E:Gingerbread
  Plum; G:Ingwerpflaume · ♄ e Z10 ⓦ Ⓝ;
  Seneg., W-Afr.: Sierra Leone, Ghana,
  Nigeria
- **scabra** Hassk. · ♄ e Z10 ⓦ Ⓝ; Java

Paris L. -f- *Trilliaceae* · 25 spp. · E:Herb
Paris; F:Parisette; G:Einbeere
- **quadrifolia** L. · E:Herb Paris;

G:Vierblättrige Einbeere · ⌃ Z6 V-VI ⚥ ⚘; Eur.*, Cauc., W-Sib., E-Sib., Mong.

Parkia R. Br. -f- *Mimosaceae* · 30-40 spp.
– **biglobosa** (Jacq.) Benth. · E:African Locust Bean; G:Sudan-Kaffee · ♄ Z10 ⓜ Ⓝ; W-Afr., W-Sah., nat. in W.Ind.
– **speciosa** Hassk. · ♄ Z10 ⓜ Ⓝ; Malay. Arch.

Parkinsonia L. -f- *Caesalpiniaceae* · 12-19 spp. · E:Jerusalem Thorn; F:Epine de Jérusalem; G:Jerusalemdorn, Parkinsonie
– **aculeata** L. · E:Jerusalem Thorn; G:Jerusalemdorn · ♄ ♄ e Z9 ⓜ Ⓝ; USA: Tex., SW; Mex., W.Ind., S-Am., nat. in Calif., Fla., W.Ind.

Parmentiera DC. -f- *Bignoniaceae* · 9 spp. · E:Candle Tree; F:Parmentiera; G:Kerzenbaum
– **aculeata** (Kunth) Seem. · G:Stachliger Kerzenbaum · ♄ e Z10 ⓜ Ⓝ; Mex., Guat., Hond., El Salv., Costa Rica
– **cereifera** Seem. · G:Echter Kerzenbaum · ♄ e Z10 ⓜ Ⓝ; C-Am., nat. in W.Ind., Trop.

Parnassia L. -f- *Parnassiaceae* · 15 spp. · E:Grass of Parnassus; F:Parnassie; G:Herzblatt, Studentenröschen
– **palustris** L. · E:Grass of Parnassus; F:Parnassie des marais; G:Sumpf-Herzblatt · ⌃ ∼ Z4 VII-IX ⚥ ▽; Eur.*, TR, Iraq, Cauc., N-Iran, Pakist., W-Sib., E-Sib., Amur, Sakhal., Kamchat., C-As., Mong., Tibet, China, Korea, Jap., Moroc., Alger., Tun., Alaska,

Parochetus Buch.-Ham. ex D. Don -m- *Fabaceae* · 1 sp. · E:Blue Oxalis; F:Fleur des dieux; G:Blauklee
– **communis** Buch.-Ham. · E:Blue Oxalis; G:Blauklee · ⌃ ⤳ △ Z9 ⓚ IX-II; E-Afr., trop. As.

Parodia Speg. -f- *Cactaceae* · ~50 spp.
– *aglaisma* F.H. Brandt = Parodia maassii
– **alacriportana** Backeb. & Voll · ♀ Z9 ⓚ ▽ ⚹; Braz.: Rio Grande do Sul
– *andreae* F.H. Brandt = Parodia maassii
– *aureicentra* Backeb. = Parodia microsperma
– *aureispina* Backeb. = Parodia mutabilis

– **ayopayana** Cárdenas · ♀ Z9 ⓚ ▽ ⚹; Bol.: Cochabamba
– *brevihamata* W. Haage = Parodia alacriportana
– *buenekeri* Buining = Notocactus buenekeri
– *buiningii* (Buxb.) N.P. Taylor = Notocactus buiningii
– *caespitosa* (Speg.) N.P. Taylor = Notocactus caespitosus
– *camargensis* F. Ritter = Parodia maassii
– *catamarcensis* Backeb. = Parodia microsperma
– **chrysacanthion** (K. Schum.) Backeb. · ♀ Z9 ⓚ ▽ ⚹; Arg.: Jujuy
– *concinna* (Monv.) N.P. Taylor = Notocactus concinnus
– *erinacea* (Haw.) N.P. Taylor = Notocactus erinaceus
– **erythrantha** (Speg.) Backeb. · ♀ Z9 ⓚ ▽ ⚹; Arg.: Salta
– *escayachensis* (Vaupel) Backeb. = Parodia maassii
– **faustiana** Backeb. · ♀ Z9 ⓚ ▽ ⚹; Arg.: Salta
– *fulvispina* F. Ritter = Parodia maassii
– *graessneri* (K. Schum.) F.H. Brandt = Notocactus graessneri
– *haselbergii* (Haage) F.H. Brandt = Notocactus haselbergii
– *herteri* (Werderm.) N.P. Taylor = Notocactus herteri
– *idiosa* F.H. Brandt = Parodia maassii
– *jujuyana* Frič & Subík = Parodia stuemeri
– *leninghausii* (K. Schum.) F.H. Brandt = Notocactus leninghausii
– *liliputana* (Werderm.) N.P. Taylor = Blossfeldia liliputana
– **maassii** (Heese) A. Berger · ♀ Z9 ⓚ ▽ ⚹; S-Bol., Arg.: Jujuy
– *malyana* Rausch = Parodia microsperma
– *mammulosa* (Lem.) N.P. Taylor = Notocactus mammulosus
– **microsperma** (F.A.C. Weber) Speg. · ♀ Z9 ⓚ ▽ ⚹; Arg.: Salta
– *minuscula* Rausch = Parodia microsperma
– *mueller-melchersii* (Frič ex Backeb.) N.P. Taylor = Notocactus mueller-melchersii
– *muhrii* F.H. Brandt = Parodia microsperma
– **mutabilis** Backeb. · ♀ Z9 ⓚ ▽ ⚹; Arg.: Salta
– **nivosa** Frič ex Backeb. · ♀ Z9 ⓚ ▽ ⚹; Arg.: Salta
– *obtusa* F. Ritter = Parodia maassii

- *ottonis* (Lehm.) N.P. Taylor = Notocactus ottonis
- *prestoensis* F.H. Brandt = Parodia maassii
- *pseudostuemeri* Backeb. = Parodia stuemeri
- *quechua* F.H. Brandt = Parodia maassii
- *ritteri* Buining = Parodia maassii
- *roseoalba* F. Ritter = Parodia maassii
- *rubellihamata* Backeb. = Parodia microsperma
- *rubristaminea* F. Ritter = Parodia microsperma
- *rutilans* (Däniker & Krainz) N.P. Taylor = Notocactus rutilans
- *schumanniana* (Nicolai bis) F.H. Brandt = Notocactus schumannianus
- **schwebsiana** (Werderm.) Backeb. · ⵜ Z9 ⊠ ▽ ✱; Bol.: Cochabamba
- *scopa* (Spreng.) N.P. Taylor = Notocactus scopa
- *setifera* Backeb. = Parodia microsperma
- *setosa* Backeb. = Parodia stuemeri
- **stuemeri** (Werderm.) Backeb. · ⵜ Z9 ⊠ ▽ ✱; Arg.: Jujuy
- *talaensis* F.H. Brandt = Parodia microsperma
- *tarabucina* Cárdenas = Parodia maassii
- *uhligiana* Backeb. = Parodia microsperma
- *varicolor* F. Ritter = Parodia microsperma
- *weberiana* F.H. Brandt = Parodia microsperma

Paronychia Mill. -f- *Illecebraceae* · c. 100 spp. · E:Nailwort, Whitlow-Wort; F:Paronyque; G:Mauermiere, Nagelkraut
- **argentea** Lam. · E:Silver Nailroot; G:Silbernes Nagelkraut · ⵁ ⤳ △ Z7 ∧ IV-VI; Eur.: Ib, Fr, Ital-P, Ba; TR, Levant, SW-As., N-Afr.
- **capitata** (L.) Lam. · ⵁ ⤳ △ Z5 IV-VI; Eur.: Ib, Fr, Ital-P, GR; Palest., N-Afr.
- **kapela** (Hacq.) A. Kern. · G:Nagelkraut
- subsp. **kapela** · F:Paronyque; G:Gewöhnliches Nagelkraut · ⵁ ⤳ △ Z7 ∧ V-VI; Eur.: Ib, Fr, Ital-P, Ba, RO; NW-Afr., Libya
- subsp. **serpyllifolia** (Chaix) Graebn. · F:Paronyque à feuilles de serpolet; G:Thymianblättriges Nagelkraut · ⵁ ⤳ △ Z7 ∧ V-VI; Eur.: sp., F, I; Pyr., SW-Alp.; Moroc., Alger.
- *serpyllifolia* (Chaix) DC. = Paronychia kapela subsp. serpyllifolia

Parrotia C.A. Mey. -f- *Hamamelidaceae* ·

1 sp. · E:Irontree, Ironwood; F:Parrotia; G:Parrotie
- **persica** (DC.) C.A. Mey. · E:Persian Ironwood, Parrotia; F:Parrotie de Perse; G:Parrotie · ℏ ℏ d Z5 III-IV; N-Iran

Parrotiopsis (Nied.) C.K. Schneid. -f- *Hamamelidaceae* · 1 sp. · F:Fausse-parrotia; G:Scheinparrotie
- **jacquemontiana** (Decne.) Rehder · F:Parrotia de Jacquemont; G:Scheinparrotie · ℏ ℏ d Z7 V; Him.

Parthenium L. -n- *Asteraceae* · 16 spp. · F:Guayule; G:Guayule, Prärieampfer
- **argentatum** A. Gray · E:Guayule; G:Guayule · ℏ Z8 ⊠ ℕ; Tex., N-Mex.
- **integrifolium** L. · E:American Feverfew, Prairie Dock, Wild Quinine; G:Prärieampfer · ⵁ Z3 VII-IX; USA: NE, NCE, SE, SC

Parthenocissus Planch. -f- *Vitaceae* · 10 spp. · E:Virginia Creeper; F:Vigne vierge; G:Jungfernrebe, Wilder Wein
- **henryana** (Hemsl.) Graebn. ex Diels & Gilg · G:Chinesische Jungfernrebe · ℏ d ⌇ Z7; C-China
- **himalayana** (Royle) Planch. · ∫ d ⌇ Z9 ⊠; Him.
- **inserta** (A. Kern.) Fritsch · E:Virginia Creeper; F:Vigne vierge commune; G:Fünfblättrige Jungfernrebe · ℏ ∫ d ⌇ Z3 VII-IX; Can.: E; USA: NE, NCE, NC, Rocky Mts., SW
- **quinquefolia** (L.) Planch. · E:Virginia Creeper
- var. **engelmannii** Rehder · ℏ ∫ d ⌇ Z5 VII-VIII; E-USA
- var. **hirsuta** (Pursh) Planch. · ℏ ∫ d ⌇ Z5 VII-VIII; E-USA, Mex.
- var. **quinquefolia** · E:Woodbine; F:Vigne vierge vraie; G:Gewöhnliche Jungfernrebe, Wilder Wein · ℏ ∫ d ⌇ Z5 VII-VIII; Can.: E; USA: NE, NCE, SC, SE, Fla.
- var. **saint-paulii** (Koehne & Graebn.) Rehder · ℏ ∫ d ⌇ Z5 VII-VIII; USA: NCE, SC
- var. **vitacea** (Knerr) L.H. Bailey = Parthenocissus inserta
- *thomsonii* (M.A. Lawson) Planch. = Cayratia thomsonii
- **tricuspidata** (Siebold & Zucc.) Planch. · E:Boston Ivy, Japanese Creeper, Japanese Ivy; F:Vigne vierge de Veitch;

G:Dreilappige Jungfernrebe · ♄ ≀ d ≹ Z6 VII-VIII; Jap., Korea, China
- **some cultivars**
- *veitchii* (Carrière) Graebn. = Parthenocissus tricuspidata
- *vitacea* (Knerr) Hitchc. = Parthenocissus inserta

Paspalum L. -n- *Poaceae* · c. 330 spp. · E:Finger Grass; F:Digitaire, Paspalum; G:Pfannengras
- **ceresia** (Kuntze) Chase · ♃ Z8 ⓦ VII-VIII; trop. S-Am.
- *commersonii* Lam. = Paspalum scrobiculatum
- **conjugatum** P.J. Bergius · E:Hilograss · ♃ Z8 ⓦ Ⓝ; trop. Am., Afr.
- **dilatatum** Poir. · E:Dallis Grass; G:Dallisgras · ♃ Z8 Ⓝ; C-Am., S-Am., nat. in S-Eur., USA
- **distichum** L. · E:Jointed Crown Grass, Knotgrass; G:Knotengras · ♃ Z8 Ⓝ; USA: Va., SE, SC, Fla., SW, Rocky Mts., NW, Calif.; Mex. C-Am., W.Ind., S-Am., coasts trop. Old World, N-Afr., nat. in S-Eur.
- *exile* Kippist = Digitaria exilis
- **notatum** Flüggé · E:Bahia Grass; G:Bahiagras · ♃ Z8 ⓚ Ⓝ; Mex., W.Ind., S-Am.
- *paspaloides* (Michx.) Scribn. = Paspalum distichum
- **scrobiculatum** L. · E:Indian Crown Grass, Kodo Millet; G:Kodo-Hirse · ♃ Z8 ⓦ Ⓝ; trop. Afr., trop. As., S-China, Jap., Austr.

Passerina L. -f- *Thymelaeaceae* · 18 spp. · F:Langue-de-moineau, Passerine; G:Spatzenzunge, Sperlingskopf
- **ericoides** L. · ♄ e Z9 ⓚ VII-VIII; S-Afr.
- **filiformis** L. · ♄ e Z9 ⓚ VII-VIII; S-Afr.

Passiflora L. -f- *Passifloraceae* · c. 430 spp. · E:Grandilla, Passion Flower; F:Fruit de la Passion, Passiflore; G:Eierfrucht, Grenadille, Passionsblume, Passionsfrucht
- **alata** Curtis · ♄ ≹ Z10 ⓦ IV-VIII Ⓝ; Braz., Peru
- × *alatocaerulea* hort. = Passiflora × belotii
- *alba* Link & Otto = Passiflora subpeltata
- × **albonigra** hort. (*P. alata* × *P. kermesina*) · ♄ ≀ ≹; cult.
- × **allardii** Lynch (*P. caerulea 'Constance Eliott'* × *P. quadrangularis*) · G:Cambridge-Passionsblume · ♄ ≀ ≹ Z9 ⓚ; cult.
- **amethystina** J.C. Mikan · ♄ ≀ ≹ Z10 ⓦ IX-IV; E-Braz., Parag., Bol.
- **antioquiensis** H. Karst. · E:Red Banana Passion Flower; G:Rote-Bananen-Passionsblume · ♄ ≹ Z9 ⓚ; Col.
- × **belotii** Pépin (*P. alata* × *P. caerulea*) · ♄ ≀ ≹ Z9 ⓚ; cult.
- **biflora** Lam. · E:Two-flowered Passion Flower; G:Zweiblütige Passionsblume · ≀ ≹ Z10 ⓦ; Mex, C-Am., Bahamas, Venez., Col., Ecuad.
- *Braziliana* Desf. = Passiflora alata
- *bryonioides* hort. = Passiflora morifolia
- **caerulea** L. · E:Blue Passion Flower; F:Passiflore; G:Blaue Passionsblume · ♄ ≹ Z7 ⓚ VI-IX ☠; S-Braz., Parag., Arg., nat. in Trop.
- × *caeruleoracemosa* hort. = Passiflora × violacea
- **capsularis** L. · ♄ ≹ D Z10 ⓦ VI-VII; C-Am., W.Ind., trop. S-Am.
- **cinnabarina** Lindl. · ♄ ≹ Z10 ⓚ III-VIII; Austr.
- **coccinea** Aubl. · E:Red Granadilla; G:Rote Granadilla · ♄ ≹ Z10 ⓦ; S-Venez., Guyana, Braz., Peru, Bol.
- × **colvillii** Sweet (*P. caerulea* × *P. incarnata*) · ♃ Z7; cult.
- **coriacea** Juss. · E:Bat-leafed Passion Flower; G:Fledermaus-Passionsblume · ♄ ≹ Z10 ⓦ; Mex., C-Am., trop. S-Am.
- × **decaisneana** Planch. (*P. alata* × *P. quadrangularis*) · ♄ ≹ Z10 ⓦ V-VI; cult.
- **edulis** Sims · E:Granadilla, Passion Fruit; G:Eierfrucht, Maracuja, Purpurgrenadille · ♃ ♄ ♄ e ≹ Z10 ⓦ VI-VIII Ⓝ; Braz., nat. in n S-Am., W.Ind.
- f. **flavicarpa** O. Deg. · ≀ e ≹ Z10
- × **exoniensis** Mast. (*P. antioquiensis* × *P. mollissima*) · ≀ ≹ Z10 ⓚ; cult.
- **foetida** L. · E:Stinking Granadilla, Wild Water Lemon; G:Stinkende Grenadille · ♃ ≹ Z10 ⓚ VII-IX Ⓝ; Puerto Rico, Jamaica, Lesser Antilles, S-Am., nat. in trop. Afr., trop. As.
- **gracilis** Jacq. ex Link · E:Annual Passion Flower; G:Einjährige Passionsblume · ⊙ ≹ ♧ Z10 ⓦ VII-VIII; Venez., nat. in trop. Am., subtrop. Am.
- **herbertiana** Ker-Gawl. · ≀ ≹ Z10 ⓚ; Austr.
- **holosericea** L. · ♄ ≹ D Z10 ⓦ; C-Am.
- **incarnata** L. · E:May Apple, May Pop, Wild Passion Flower; G:Winterharte Passionsblume · ♃ ≹ Z8 ⓚ ∧ V-VII ⚕ ☠;

USA: NE, NCE, SC, SE, Fla.; Bermudas
- **kermesina** Link & Otto · ♄ ⚥ Z10 ⚘
  V-IX; Braz.
- **laurifolia** L. · E:Jamaica Honeysuckle,
  Water Lemon; G:Gelbe Grenadille · ♄ ⚥
  Z10 ⚘ VI-VII ⚘; Venez., Braz., E-Peru,
  Arg.
- **ligularis** Juss. · E:Sweet Granadilla;
  G:Süße Grenadille · ♄ e ⚥ Z10 ⚘ IX-X ⚘;
  Guat., Ecuad., Peru, Venez.
- **lutea** L. · E:Yellow Passion Flower;
  G:Gelbe Passionsblume · ♄ ⚥ Z8 ⚘
  VI-VIII; USA: NE, NCE, NC, SC, SE, Fla.
- **maliformis** L. · E:Sweet Calabash, Sweet
  Cup; G:Apfel-Grenadille · ♄ ⚥ Z10 ⚘
  VII-XI ⚘; W.Ind., Col., Ecuad., Venez.
- *maliformis* Vell. = Passiflora alata
- **manicata** (Juss.) Pers. · ♄ Z9 ⚘; Venez.,
  Col., Ecuad., Peru, Bol.
- *mauritiana* Thouars = Passiflora alata
- **membranacea** Benth. · ♄ ⚥ Z10 ⚘ ⚘;
  Guat.
- *mollissima* (Kunth) L.H. Bailey = Passiflora tripartita var. mollissima
- **morifolia** Mast. · ♄ ⚭ ⚥ Z10 ⚘; Col. ,
  Braz., Parag.
- **organensis** Gardner · ♄ ⚥ Z10 ⚘ VII-
  VIII; Braz.
- **pinnatistipula** Cav. · ♄ Z10 ⚘ ⚘; Col.,
  Ecuad.
- *psilantha* (Sodiro) Killip = Passiflora
  tripartita var. tripartita
- **quadrangularis** L. · E:Granadilla,
  Grenadine; G:Königs-Grenadille,
  Riesen-Grenadille · ♄ ⚥ Z10 ⚘ V-VII ⚘
  ⚘; C-Am., W.Ind.
- **racemosa** Brot. · E:Red Passion Flower;
  G:Rote Passionsblume · ♄ ⚥ Z10 ⚘ V-IX;
  Braz.
- *raddiana* DC. = Passiflora kermesina
- **sanguinolenta** Mast. · ♄ ⚭ ⚥ Z9 ⚘;
  Ecuad.; mts.
- *sarcosepala* Barb.-Boiss. = Passiflora alata
- *sicyoides* hort. = Passiflora morifolia
- **suberosa** L. · ♄ ⚥ Z10 ⚘ VI-VIII; trop.
  S-Am.
- **subpeltata** Ortega · E:White Passion
  Flower; G:Weiße Passionsblume · ⚃ ⚭ ⚥
  Z10 ⚘; Mex., C-Am., Col., Venez.
- **trifasciata** Lem. · ♄ ⚥ D Z10 ⚘ VII-VIII;
  Peru
- **tripartita** (Juss.) Poir.
- var. **mollissima** (Kunth) Holm-Niels. ·
  E:Banana Passion Flower; G:Bananen-
  Passionsblume, Curuba · ♄ ⚥ Z9 ⚘ ⚘;

Venez., Col., Peru, Bol.
- var. **tripartita** · ♄ ⚭ ⚥ Z9; S-Am.
- *van-volxemii* Triana & Planch. = Passiflora antioquiensis
- × **violacea** Loisel. (*P. caerulea* × *P.*
  racemosa) · ♄ ⚥ Z10 ⚘ VIII-IX; cult.
- *violacea* Vell. = Passiflora amethystina
- *warmingii* Mast. = Passiflora morifolia
- **Cultivars:**
- **many cultivars**

Pastinaca L. -f- *Apiaceae* · 14 spp. ·
E:Parsnip; F:Panais; G:Pastinak
- **sativa** L. · E:Parsnip; G:Echter Pastinak,
  Hammelsmöhre · ☉ VII-VIII ⚘ ⚘; Eur.*
  exc. Sc; TR, Syr., Lebanon, Cauc., Iran,
  W-Sib., E-Sib, nat. in N-Am., S-Am.,
  Austr., NZ

Patrinia Juss. -f- *Valerianaceae* · 15 spp. ·
F:Valériane dorée; G:Goldbaldrian
- **gibbosa** Maxim. · ⚃ V-VI; Jap.
- **intermedia** (Hornem.) Roem. & Schult. ·
  ⚃; China
- *palmata* Maxim. = Patrinia triloba var.
  palmata
- **scabiosifolia** Fisch. · ⚃ V-VI; China,
  E-Sib., Manch., Korea, Jap., Sakhal.,
  Taiwan,
- **triloba** Miq.
- var. **palmata** (Maxim.) H. Hara · ⚃; Jap.
- var. **triloba** · F:Valériane jaune; G:Gold-
  Baldrian · ⚃ V-VI; Jap.
- **villosa** (Thunb.) Juss. · ⚃; Jap., Korea,
  Manch., China

Paullinia L. -f- *Sapindaceae* · 194 spp.
- **cupana** Kunth · E:Guarana; G:Guarana
  Shrub · ♄ e ⚥ Z10 ⚘ ⚘; trop. S-Am.
- **thalictrifolia** Juss. · ♄ e ⚥ Z10 ⚘; Braz.

Paulownia Siebold & Zucc. -f-
Scrophulariaceae · 17 (6) spp. · E:Foxglove
Tree; F:Paulownia; G:Blauglockenbaum,
Paulowine
- **elongata** Hu · ♄ d ⚘; China: Hubei,
  Honan, Schantung, Hopei
- **fortunei** (Seem.) Hemsl. · G:Fortunes
  Blauglockenbaum · ♄ d Z7; China,
  Taiwan, Jap.
- *imperialis* Siebold & Zucc. = Paulownia
  tomentosa
- **kawakamii** T. Itô · G:Taiwan-Blauglock-
  enbaum · ♄ d Z7; S-China, Taiwan
- **tomentosa** (Thunb. ex Murray)

Steud. · E:Empress Tree, Foxglove Tree;
F:Paulownia impérial; G:Chinesischer
Blauglockenbaum, Kaiser-Paulownie · ♄
d Z7 IV-V Ⓝ; China, nat. in E-USA, Sw, I

Paurotis O.F. Cook = Acoelorrhaphe
– *wrightii* (Griseb. & H. Wendl.) Britton =
Acoelorrhaphe wrightii

Pausinystalia Pierre ex Beille
-f- *Rubiaceae* · 5 spp. · E:Yohimbe;
F:Yohimbeh; G:Yohimbe
– **johimbe** (K. Schum.) Pierre ex Beille ·
E:Yohimbe; G:Yohimbe · ♄ Z10 Ⓜ ⚥ ⚔
Ⓝ; W-Afr.

Pavetta L. -f- *Rubiaceae* · 358 spp.
– **capensis** (Houtt.) Bremek. · ♄ Z10 Ⓜ
VI-VIII; S-Afr.
– **indica** L. · E:Jarum Jarum · ♄ e D Z10 Ⓜ;
Ind.

Pavonia Cav. -f- *Malvaceae* · 150 spp.
– × **gledhillii** Cheek (*P. multiflora × P.
mayokana*) · ♄ e Z10 Ⓜ; cult.
– **multiflora** Juss. · ♄ Z10 Ⓜ IX-V; Braz.
– **spinifex** (L.) Cav. · E:Gingerbush · ♄ d
Z10 Ⓜ; SE-USA, Bermuda, W.Ind., Mex.,
trop. S-Am.

Paxistima Raf. -f- *Celastraceae* · 2 spp. ·
F:Paxistima; G:Dicknarbe
– **canbyi** A. Gray · G:Zwerg-Dicknarbe · ♄ e
△ Z5 IV-V; USA: Va., W.Va., Ohio, Ky.
– **myrsinites** (Pursh) Raf. · E:Oregon
Boxwood; G:Gewöhnliche Dicknarbe · ♄
e △ Z6 IV; Can: B.C.; USA: NW, Calif.;
Mex.

Payena A. DC. -f- *Sapotaceae* · 21 sp.
– **leeri** (Teijsm. & Binn.) Kurz · ♄ Z10 Ⓜ
Ⓝ; Burma, W-Malaysia

Pecteilis Raf. -f- *Orchidaceae* · 5 spp.
– **gigantea** (Sm.) Raf. Z10; Him. - Burma
– *radiata* (Thunb.) Raf. = Habenaria
radiata

Pectinaria Haw. -f- *Asclepiadaceae* · 3 spp.
– **articulata** (Haw.) Haw. · ⚃ Z9 Ⓚ; Cape
– subsp. **asperiflora** (N.E. Br.) Bruyns · ⚃
⚇ Z9 Ⓚ; Cape
– *asperifolia* N.E. Br. = Pectinaria articulata
subsp. asperiflora
– *saxatilis* N.E. Br. = Stapeliopsis saxatilis

Pedicularis L. -f- *Scrophulariaceae* ·
350+ spp. · E:Lousewort, Wood Betony;
F:Pédiculaire; G:Läusekraut
– **ascendens** Schleich. ex Gaudin ·
E:Ascending Lousewort; G:Aufsteigendes
Läusekraut · ⚃ VII-VIII ▽; Eur.: F, I, Sw;
W-Alp.
– **aspleniifolia** Flörke ex Willd. · E:Fern-
leaved Lousewort; G:Farnblättriges
Läusekraut · ⚃ VII-VIII ▽; Eur.: I, Ch, A;
E-Alp.
– **elongata** A. Kern.
– subsp. **elongata** · G:Langähriges
Läusekraut · ⚃ VII-VIII ▽; Eur.: I, A,
Slove.; SE-Alp.
– subsp. **julica** (E. Mayer) Hartl ·
G:Julisches Läusekraut · ⚃ VII-VIII ▽;
Eur.: I, A, Slove.; SE-Alp.
– **foliosa** L. · E:Leafy Lousewort; G:Durch-
blättertes Läusekraut · ⚃ VI-VIII ▽;
Eur.: sp., F, I, CE-Eur.; mts.
– **gyroflexa** Vill. · G:Bogenblütiges
Läusekraut · ⚃ VI-VII ▽; Eur.: F, I, Sw;
Pyr., Alp.
– **hacquetii** Graf · G:Karst-Läusekraut · ⚃
VII-VIII ▽; Eur.: I, A, EC-Eur., Slove.,
RO, W-Russ.; SE-Alp., Apenn., Carp.
– **kerneri** Dalla Torre · G:Kerners
Läusekraut · ⚃ VII-VIII ▽; Eur.: sp., F, I,
Ch, A; Pyr., Alp.
– **oederi** Vahl · E:Crimson-tipped Lous-
ewort; G:Buntes Läusekraut · ⚃ VI-VIII
▽; Eur.* exc. BrI, Ib; W-Sib., E-Sib.,
Amur, Kamchat., C-As., China: Sinkiang;
Kashmir, Him., Tibet, Mong., N-Am.
– **palustris** L. · E:Marsh Lousewort,
Red Rattle; G:Gewöhnliches Sumpf-
Läusekraut · ⊙ V-VIII ▽; Eur.* exc. Ib;
TR
– **portenschlagii** Saut. ex Rchb. · E:Tavern
Lousewort; G:Zweiblütiges Läusekraut ·
⚃ VI-VIII ▽; Eur.: A; NE-Alp.
– **recutita** L. · E:Beakless Red Lousewort;
G:Gestutztes Läusekraut · ⚃ VII-VIII ▽;
Eur.: F, I, C-Eur., Slove.; Alp.
– **rosea** Wulfen · E:Pink Lousewort;
G:Rosarotes Läusekraut · ⚃ VII-VIII ▽;
Eur.: F, I, A, Slove., Croatia; Pyr., Alp.,
Croatia
– **rostratocapitata** Crantz · E:Beaked
Lousewort; G:Geschnäbeltes Läusekraut,
Kopfiges Läusekraut · ⚃ VI-VIII ▽; Eur.:
I, C-Eur., Slove., Croatia; SE-Alp., Croatia
– **rostratospicata** Crantz · E:Flesh-pink
Lousewort; G:Ähren-Läusekraut,

Fleischrotes Läusekraut · ♃ VII-VIII ▽; Eur.: F, I, C-Eur., Slove.; Pyr., Alp.
- **sceptrum-carolinum** L. · G:Karlszepter, Moorkönig · ♃ VI-VIII ▽; Eur.: Sc, G, EC-Eur., E-Eur.; W-Sib., E-Sib., Mong., Manch., Jap.
- **sylvatica** L. · E:Common Lousewort; G:Wald-Läusekraut · ⊙ V-VII ▽; Eur.* exc. Ib
- **tuberosa** L. · E:Long-beaked Yellow Lousewort; G:Knolliges Läusekraut · ♃ VI-VIII ▽; Eur.: sp., F, I, Sw, A; Pyr., Alp., Alpi Apuane, Apenn.
- **verticillata** L. · E:Whorled Lousewort; G:Quirlblättriges Läusekraut · ♃ VI-VIII ▽; Eur.* exc. BrI, Sc; N-Russ., mts.; W-Sib., E-Sib., Amur, Kamchat., Mong., Korea, Jap., Alaska, NW-Am.

Pedilanthus Neck. ex Poit. -m- *Euphorbiaceae* · 17 spp. · E:Slipper Spurge; F:Pédilanthe; G:Schuhblüte
- **bracteatus** (Jacq.) Boiss. · E:Slipper Spurge; G:Grüne Schuhblüte · ħ Ψ Z9 Ⓚ ☠ Ⓝ; Mex.
- *carinatus* Spreng. = Pedilanthus tithymaloides
- *pavonis* (Klotzsch & Garcke) Boiss. = Pedilanthus bracteatus
- **tithymaloides** (L.) Poit. · G:Rote Schuhblüte; E:Devil's Backbone, Jew Bush, Redbird Flower · ħ Ψ Z10 Ⓦ ☠; S-Mex., C-Am., Col.

Pediocactus Britton & Rose -m- *Cactaceae* · 6 spp.
- *papyracanthus* (Engelm.) L.D. Benson = Sclerocactus papyracanthus
- **peeblesianus** (Croizat) L.D. Benson · E:Navajo Pincushion Cactus · Ψ Z5 Ⓐ ▽ ✱; USA: Ariz.
- **simpsonii** (Engelm.) Britton & Rose · E:Mountain Ball Cactus, Plains Cactus · Ψ Z5 ▽ ✱; USA: NW, Rocky Mts., SW

Peganum L. -n- *Zygophyllaceae* · 6 spp. · E:Harmal, Harmel; F:Harmel, Péganion; G:Steppenraute
- **harmala** L. · E:Harmel, Wild Rue; G:Steppenraute · ♃ Z8 Ⓚ VII-VIII ⚕ ☠ Ⓝ; Eur.: Ib, Ital-P, Ba, EC-Eur.; TR, Cauc., Iran, C-As., Mong., Tibet, N-Afr.

Pelargonium L'Hér. ex Aiton -n- *Geraniaceae* · 250-280 spp. · E:Geranium; F:Géranium des balcons; G:Geranie der Gärtner, Pelargonie
- *acerifolium* hort. = Pelargonium vitifolium
- **acetosum** (L.) L'Hér. · ħ e Z9 Ⓚ; S-Afr.
- × **asperum** Willd. (*P. querceolatum* × *P. radula*)
- **betulinum** (L.) L'Hér. · ħ Z9 Ⓚ VII-VIII; Cape
- **capitatum** (L.) L'Hér. · E:Rose Scented Geranium; G:Rosenduft-Pelargonie · ħ e D Z9 Ⓚ VII-VIII ⚕ Ⓝ; S-Afr.
- **carnosum** (L.) L'Hér. ex Aiton · ħ Z9 Ⓚ V; Cape, Namibia
- × **citrosmum** (Andr.) Voigt (*P. crispum* × ?) · ħ D Z9 Ⓚ VII-VIII; cult.
- **cordifolium** (Cav.) Curtis · ħ Z9 Ⓚ V; Cape
- **crassicaule** L'Hér. · ħ Z9 Ⓚ VII; SW-Afr.
- **crispum** (P.J. Bergius) L'Hér. · E:Lemon Scented Geranium; G:Zitronenduft-Pelargonie · ħ e Z9 Ⓚ; S-Afr.
- *crispum* hort. = Pelargonium × citrosmum
- **crithmifolium** Sm. · ħ Z9 Ⓚ; Cape, Namibia
- **cucullatum** (L.) L'Hér. · ħ e Z9 Ⓚ VIII-IX; Cape
- **echinatum** (Thunb.) Curtis · ħ Z9 Ⓚ; S-Afr.
- **endlicherianum** Fenzl · ♃ △ Z7 Ⓐ ∧ VII; S-TR, N-Syr., Cauc. (Armen.)
- **exstipulatum** (Cav.) L'Hér. · ħ ħ D Z9 Ⓚ VI-IX; S-Afr.
- *ferulaceum* (Burm. f.) Willd. = Pelargonium carnosum
- × **fragrans** (Poir.) Willd. (*P. exstipulatum* × *P. odoratissimum*) · E:Scented Geranium; G:Duft-Pelargonie · ħ e D Z9 Ⓚ VII-VIII Ⓝ; S-Afr.
- **fulgidum** (L.) L'Hér. · ħ Z9 Ⓚ VIII-IX; Cape
- **gibbosum** (L.) L'Hér. · ħ Z9 Ⓚ VI; Cape
- **grandiflorum** (Andrews) Willd. · ħ e Z9 Ⓚ IV-VI; Cape, Namibia
- **graveolens** L'Hér. · E:Rose Geranium; G:Rosen-Pelargonie · ħ D Z9 Ⓚ VI-VIII ⚕ Ⓝ; cult.
- **some cultivars**
- **inquinans** (L.) L'Hér. · ħ e Z9 Ⓚ V-X; S-Afr.
- × **kewense** R.A. Dyer (*P. scandens* × *P. zonale*) · ♃ ħ Z9 Ⓚ; cult.
- **odoratissimum** (L.) L'Hér. · E:Apple Scented Geranium; G:Apfelduft-Pelargonie · ħ e D Z9 Ⓚ VII-VIII Ⓝ; S-Afr.

– **peltatum** (L.) L'Hér. · E:Ivy-leaved Geranium; F:Géranium lierre; G:Efeublättrige Pelargonie · ♄ e ⚥ ⟿ Z9 ⓚ IV-X; S-Afr.
– **polycephalum** E. Mey. · ♄ Z9 ⓚ; S-Afr.
– **quercifolium** (L. f.) L'Hér. · E:Oak Leaved Geranium; G:Eichblatt-Pelargonie · ♄ e D Z9 ⓚ VII-VIII; Cape
– **radens** H.E. Moore · E:Balsam Scented Geranium; G:Balsamduft-Pelargonie · ♄ e D Z9 ⓚ III-VIII ⚥ Ⓝ; Cape
– *radula* (Cav.) L'Hér. = Pelargonium radens
– **reniforme** (Andrews) Curtis · ♄ ⟊ Z10 ⓚ III-VIII ⚥ ; S-Afr. (E-Cape)
– **sidoides** DC. · ⩜ Z8 ⓚ III-VIII ⚥ ; S-Afr.
– **tetragonum** (L. f.) L'Hér. · ♄ e Z9 ⓚ VI; S-Afr.
– **tomentosum** Jacq. · E:Peppermint Scented Geranium; G:Pfefferminz-Pelargonie · ⩜ ♄ e D Z9 ⓚ ⚥ ; Cape
– **triste** (L.) L'Hér. · ⩜ ⟊ Z9 ⓚ VII-VIII; Cape
– **vitifolium** (L.) L'Hér. · ⩜ ♄ Z9 ⓚ; S-Afr.
– **zonale** (L.) L'Hér. · F:Pélargonium; Zonale G:Zonal-Pelargonie · ♄ ♄ e Z9 ⓚ V-X; Cape
– **Cultivars:**
– **many cultivars, see Section III**

Pelecyphora C. Ehrenb. -f- *Cactaceae* · 2 spp. · F:Cactus mille-pattes; G:Asselkaktus, Beilkaktus
– **aselliformis** C. Ehrenb. · E:Hatchet Cactus · ⟊ Z9 ⓚ ▽ ✳; Mex.: San Luis Potosí
– *pseudopectinata* Backeb. = Turbinicarpus pseudopectinatus
– *strobiliformis* (Werderm.) Frič & Schelle = Encephalocarpus strobiliformis
– *valdeziana* L. Möller = Turbinicarpus valdezianus

Peliosanthes Andrews -f- *Convallariaceae* · 16 spp.
– **teta** Andrews · ⩜ Z9 ⓦ; S-Vietn.

Pellaea Link -f- *Adiantaceae* · 67 spp. · E:Cliff Brake; F:Pelléa; G:Klippenfarn
– **atropurpurea** (L.) Link · E:Purple Cliff Brake; G:Purpur-Klippenfarn · ⩜ Z7 ⓚ; Can.: Ont.; USA: NE, NCE, NC, SE, Fla.
– *cordata* (Cav.) J. Sm. = Pellaea sagittata var. cordata
– **falcata** (R. Br.) Fée · E:Sickle Fern; G:Sichelförmiger Klippenfarn · ⩜ Z10 ⓚ; Ind., SE-As., E-Austr., Tasman., NZ

– *flexuosa* (Kaulf.) Link = Pellaea ovata
– *gracilis* Hook. = Cryptogramma stelleri
– *hastata* (L.) Link = Pellaea viridis
– **ovata** (Desv.) Weath. · E:One-leaf Cliff Brake · ⩜ Z10 ⓚ; USA: Tex., N.Mex.; Mex., C-Am., Haiti, S-Am.
– **rotundifolia** (G. Forst.) Hook. · ⩜ Z10 ⓚ; NZ, Norfolk Is.
– **sagittata** (Cav.) Link
– var. **cordata** (Cav.) A.F. Tryon · E:Heartleaf Cliff Brake · ⩜ Z10 ⓚ; Tex., Mex.
– var. **sagittata** · ⩜ Z10 ⓚ; C-Am., S-Am.
– *stelleri* (S.G. Gmel.) Baker = Cryptogramma stelleri
– **viridis** (Forssk.) Prantl · E:Green Cliff Brake; G:Grüner Klippenfarn · ⩜ Z10 ⓚ; S-Afr., Madag., Mascarene Is., nat. in Azor., Sri Lanka

Pellionia Gaudich. -f- *Urticaceae* · 50 spp. · F:Pellionia; G:Melonenbegonie, Pellionie
– *daveauana* (Carrière) N.E. Br. = Pellionia repens
– **pulchra** N.E. Br. · E:Rainbow Vine; G:Regenbogen-Melonenbegonie · ⩜ ⟿ Z10 ⓦ; S-Vietn.
– **repens** (Lour.) Merr. · E:Anteater Scales, Hill Dragon, Trailing Watermelon Begonia; G:Melonenbegonie · ⩜ ⟿ Z10 ⓦ; Burma, Malay. Pen., S-Vietn.

Peltandra Raf. -f- *Araceae* · 2 spp. · E:Arrow Arum; F:Peltandre; G:Pfeilaron
– **sagittifolia** (Michx.) Morong · E:White Arrow Arum; G:Weißer Pfeilaron · ⩜ ≈ Z7; USA: NE, SE, Fla.
– *undulata* Raf. = Peltandra virginica
– **virginica** (L.) Schott · E:Arrow Arum, Green Arrow Arum; G:Grüner Pfeilaron · ⩜ ≈ Z5; Can.: E; USA: NE, SE, Fla.

Peltaria Jacq. -f- *Brassicaceae* · 7 spp. · F:Peltaire; G:Scheibenschötchen
– **alliacea** Jacq. · G:Scheibenschötchen · ⩜ Z6 V-VII; Eur.: A, H, ? Slove., Croatia, Bosn., Montenegro, RO

Peltastes Woodson -m- *Apocynaceae* · 7 spp.
– **peltatus** (Vell.) Woodson · ♄ e ⚥ ⓦ; Braz.

Peltiphyllum Engl. = Darmera
– *peltatum* (Torr. ex Benth.) Engl. = Darmera peltata

Peltoboykinia (Engl.) H. Hara -f-
Saxifragaceae · 2 spp.
– **tellimoides** (Maxim.) H. Hara · ⅄ Z7
VI-VII; C-Jap.

Peltogyne Vogel -f- *Caesalpiniaceae* ·
23 spp.
– **paniculata** Benth. · ♄ Z10 ⓜ ⓝ; Guyan.,
Braz.

Peltophorum (Vogel) Benth.
-n- *Caesalpiniaceae* · 8 (-15) spp. ·
E:Flamboyant; G:Flammenbaum
– **africanum** Sond. · E:African Wattle;
G:Futter-Flammenblaum · ♄ e Z9 ⓚ;
S-Afr.

Peniocereus (A. Berger) Britton & Rose
-m- *Cactaceae* · 20 spp. · F:Cierge;
G:Spulenkaktus
– **greggii** (Engelm.) Britton & Rose ·
E:Night Blooming Cereus, Sweetpotato
Cactus · ⅄ Z9 ⓚ ▽ ✳; N-Mex.
– *serpentinus* (Lag. & Rodr.) N.P. Taylor =
Nyctocereus serpentinus
– **striatus** (K. Brandegee) Buxb. ·
E:Gearstem Cactus · ⅄ Z9 ⓚ ▽ ✳;
S-Ariz., NW-Mex.
– **viperinus** (F.A.C. Weber) Kreuz. · ⅄ Z9
ⓚ ▽ ✳; S-Mex.

Pennisetum Rich. -n- *Poaceae* · 130 spp. ·
E:Fountain Grass; F:Herbe-aux-
écouvillons; G:Federborstengras,
Lampenputzergras
– **alopecuroides** (L.) Spreng. · E:Chinese
Fountain Grass; F:Pennisétum; G:Japa-
nisches Federborstengras · ⅄ Z7 VIII-IX;
Korea, Jap., Phil.
– **some cultivars**
– *americanum* (L.) Leeke = Pennisetum
glaucum
– **clandestinum** Hochst. ex Chiov. ·
E:Kikuyu Grass; G:Kikuyugras · ⅄ ⓝ;
E-Afr., nat. in Col.
– *compressum* R. Br. = Pennisetum
alopecuroides
– **glaucum** (L.) R. Br. · E:Pearl Millet;
G:Negerhirse, Perlhirse · ☉ Z9 ⓝ; Trop.
– **incomptum** Nees ex Steud. · E:Kikuyu
Grass; G:Sibirisches Lampenputzergras ·
⅄ VII-IX; Him.
– *japonicum* Trin. = Pennisetum alopecuroides
– **latifolium** Spreng. · E:Uruguayan

Fountain Grass · ⅄ Z9 ⓚ VIII-X; Peru,
Braz., Urug., Arg.
– **macrostachyum** (Brongn.) Trin. · ⅄;
Ind.
– **macrourum** Trin. · E:African Feather-
grass; G:Afrikanisches Federborstengras ·
⅄ ⋉ Z7 ⋀ VIII-IX; S-Afr.
– **orientale** Rich. · ⅄ Z7 VIII-X; Egypt, TR,
Lebanon, Syr., Palest., Arab., Cauc.
– **purpureum** Schumach. · E:Elephant
Grass; G:Elefantengras · ⅄ ⓜ ⓝ; trop.
Afr., nat. in Trop.
– *rueppellii* Steud. = Pennisetum setaceum
– **setaceum** (Forssk.) Chiov. · E:Fountain
Grass; G:Afrikanisches Lampenputzergras, Einjähriges Lampenputzergras
· ☉ ⊙ ⅄ Z9 ⓚ VIII-X; Eur.: Sic., N-Afr.,
SW-As., Arab.
– *spicatum* (L.) Roem. & Schult. = Pennisetum glaucum
– *typhoides* (Burm. f.) Stapf & C.E. Hubb. =
Pennisetum glaucum
– *typhoideum* Rich. ex Pers. = Pennisetum
glaucum
– **villosum** R. Br. ex Fresen. · E:Feathertop;
G:Weißes Lampenputzergras · ☉ ⊙ ⅄ Z8
VIII-IX; NE-Afr., Arab., nat. in Balear.

Penstemon Schmidel -m-
Scrophulariaceae · 250 spp. · E:Beard-
tongue, Penstemon; F:Galane, Penstemon; G:Bartfaden
– **acuminatus** Douglas ex Lindl. · E:Sharp
Leaved Penstemon; G:Spitzblättriger
Bartfaden · ⅄ Z5 VII-VIII; USA: Oreg.,
Idaho, Nev.
– **alpinus** Torr. · E:Alpine Penstemon · ⅄ △
Z4 VII-VIII; USA: Rocky Mts., SW
– *arizonicus* A. Heller = Penstemon whippleanus
– **attenuatus** Douglas ex Lindl. · E:Taper
Leaved Penstemon · ⅄ Z4 V; USA: Wash.,
Oreg., Idaho
– **auriberbis** Pennell · E:Colorado
Beardtongue · ⅄ Z4; USA: Colo.
– **azureus** Benth. · E:Sky Blue Penstemon;
G:Blauer Bartfaden · ⅄ ♄ Z8 ⓚ ⋀ VII-
VIII; Calif.
– **barbatus** (Cav.) Roth
– subsp. **barbatus** · E:Beardtongue;
F:Penstemon; G:Roter Bartfaden · ⅄ Z3;
USA: Utah, Colo., SW; N-Mex.
– subsp. **torreyi** (Benth.) D.D. Keck · ⅄ Z3
VII-IX; USA: Colo., SW
– **barrettiae** A. Gray · ♄ Z7 ⓚ ⋀ V; USA:

Oreg.
- **bridgesii** A. Gray · E:Scarlet Penstemon; G:Scharlachroter Bartfaden · ♄ Z7 ∧ VII-IX; USA: SW, Colo., Calif.
- **caespitosus** Nutt. ex A. Gray · E:Mat Penstemon · ⚄ ⤳ △ Z3 VI-VII; USA: Colo., Utah
- **campanulatus** (Cav.) Willd. · E:Bellflower Beardtongue; F:Penstemon campanulé · ⚄ ♄ d Z8 ∧ VII-IX; Mex., Guat.
- **cardwellii** Howell · ⚄ Z8 ∧; USA: Wash., Oreg.
- **cobaea** Nutt. · E:Cobaea Penstemon ; G:Cobaea-Bartfaden · ⚄ Z4 VII-IX; USA: NC, SC, Ark.
- **confertus** Douglas · E:Yellow Penstemon; G:Gelber Bartfaden · ⚄ △ Z3 VI-VII; USA: Oreg., Calif., Rocky Mts.
- *cordifolius* Benth. = Keckiella cordifolia
- **cyananthus** Hook. · E:Wasatch Beardtongue · ⚄ Z4 ⓚ VI-IX; USA: Idaho, Wyo., Utah
- **davidsonii** Greene
- var. **davidsonii** · E:Davidson's Penstemon; G:Davidsons Bartfaden · ⚄ ⤳ △ Z6 VI-VIII; USA: Wash., Oreg., Calif.
- var. **menziesii** (D.D. Keck) Cronquist · E:Menzies' Penstemon · ♄ ⤳ △ Z7 ∧ VI-VII; Can.: W; USA: Wash.
- var. **praeteritus** Cronquist · E:Timberline Beardtongue
- *diffusus* Douglas ex Lindl. = Penstemon serrulatus
- **digitalis** Nutt. · E:Foxglove Penstemon; G:Fingerhut-Bartfaden · ⚄ Z3 VII-VIII; Can.: E; USA: NE, NCE, NC, SC, SE
- **eriantherus** Pursh · E:Crested Tongue; G:Kamm-Bartfaden · ♄ Z3 VI; Alaska, Can.: W; USA: Wash., Rocky Mts, NC
- **gentianoides** (Kunth) Poir. · E:Gentian Beardtongue; G:Enzian-Bartfaden · ⚄ Z9 ⓚ; S-Mex., Guat.
- *gentianoides* Lindl. = Penstemon hartwegii
- **glaber** Pursh · E:Smooth Penstemon; G:Glatter Bartfaden · ⚄ Z3 V-VI; USA: NC, Rocky Mts.
- var. *alpinus* (Torr.) A. Gray = Penstemon alpinus
- var. *cyananthus* (Hook.) A. Gray = Penstemon cyananthus
- *glaucus* Graham = Penstemon gracilis
- **gracilis** Nutt. · E:Slender Penstemon; G:Zierlicher Bartfaden · ⚄ Z3 VI-VII;

Can.; USA: NCE, NC, Rocky Mts, SW
- **hallii** A. Gray · E:Hall's Beardtongue · ⚄ △ Z3 VII-VIII; USA: Colo.
- **hartwegii** Benth. · ⚄ ♄ d Z8 ⓚ ∧ VI-VIII; Mex.
- **heterophyllus** Lindl. · E:Foothill Penstemon; G:Verschiedenblättriger Bartfaden · ⚄ ♄ d Z8 ⓚ VI-VIII; Calif.
- **hirsutus** (L.) Willd. · E:Hairy Penstemon; F:Penstemon hirsute; G:Haariger Bartfaden · ⚄ Z3 VI-VIII; Can.: E; USA: NE, NCE, Tenn.
- **humilis** Nutt. ex A. Gray · E:Low Beardtongue · ⚄ Z4 VI; USA: Calif., Rocky Mts.
- **laetus** A. Gray · E:Mountain Blue Penstemon
- var. **laetus**
- var. **roezlii** (Regel) Jeps. · E:Roezl's Penstemon · ♄ △ Z5 VI-VIII; USA: Oreg., Calif., Nev.
- **laevigatus** (L.) Aiton. · E:Eastern Smooth Beardtongue · ⚄ Z4 VI-VIII; USA: NE, SE, Fla.
- var. *digitalis* (Nutt.) A. Gray = Penstemon digitalis
- **linarioides** A. Gray · E:Toadflax Penstemon; G:Heideblättriger Bartfaden · ⚄ △ Z4 VI-VII; USA: Colo.
- **lyallii** (A. Gray) A. Gray · E:Lyall's Beardtongue · ♄ Z4 V-VI; USA: Mont., Idaho
- *menziesii* Hook. = Penstemon davidsonii var. menziesii
- var. *davidsonii* (Greene) Piper = Penstemon davidsonii var. davidsonii
- *micranthus* Nutt. = Penstemon procerus
- *micranthus* Torr. = Penstemon strictus
- **newberryi** A. Gray · E:Mountain Pride G:Immergrüner; Bartfaden · ♄ e △ Z8 ∧ VI-VII; Calif.
- **ovatus** Douglas · E:Broad Leaved Penstemon; G:Breitblättriger Bartfaden · ⚄ Z3 VII; B.C., USA: NW
- **pinifolius** Greene · E:Pineneedle Beardtongue; F:Penstemon à feuilles de pin · ⚄ △ Z8 ∧ VII-VIII; USA: Ariz., N.Mex.; Mex.
- **procerus** Douglas ex Graham · E:Short Flowered Penstemon; G:Matten-Bartfaden · ⚄ Z3 VI; Alaska, Can.: W; USA: NW, Calif., Rocky Mts., NC
- *pubescens* Sol. = Penstemon hirsutus
- **richardsonii** Douglas ex Lindl. · E:Cut Leaved Penstemon; G:Schönblättriger Bartfaden · ⚄ Z7 ∧ VII; B.C., USA: NW

– *roezlii* Regel = Penstemon laetus var.
roezlii
– **rupicola** (Piper) Howell · E:Rock
Penstemon; G:Felsen-Bartfaden · ♄ ⤳ △
Z7 ∧ VI-VII; USA: Wash., Oreg.
– **scouleri** Lindl. · E:Scouler's Penstemon;
G:Scoulers Bartfaden · ♄ △ Z5 VI-VII;
Can.: B.C.; USA: Wash., Idaho
– **secundiflorus** Benth. · E:Sidebells
Penstemon · ⵣ Z3 VI-VIII; USA: Colo.,
Wyo.
– **serrulatus** Menzies ex Sm. · E:Blue
Penstemon, Cascade Penstemon;
G:Eingeschnittener Bartfaden · ♄ Z5
VI-VII; B.C., USA: NW, Calif.
– **strictus** Benth. · E:Rocky Mountain Pen-
stemon; G:Rocky-Mountain-Bartfaden ·
ⵣ Z3; USA: Rocky Mts., SW
– **teucrioides** Greene · E:Germander
Beardtongue; G:Zwerg-Bartfaden · ♄ Z4
VI; USA: Colo.
– *torreyi* Benth. = Penstemon barbatus
subsp. torreyi
– **venustus** Douglas ex Lindl. · E:Blue
Mountain Penstemon; G:Anmutiger
Bartfaden · ♄ Z5 VI-IX; USA: NW, Idaho
– **whippleanus** A. Gray · E:Purple
Penstemon; G:Purpur-Bartfaden · ⵣ △ Z4
VII-VIII; Ariz.
– **wrightii** Hook. · E:Wright's Beardtongue · ♄ Z8 ∧ VI-VIII; USA: Tex., SW
– **Cultivars:**
– **many cultivars**

Pentace Hassk. -f- *Tiliaceae* · 25 spp.
– **burmanica** Kurz · ♄ e Z10 ⊛ Ⓝ; Burma

Pentacme A. DC. = Shorea
– *contorta* (S. Vidal) Merr. & Rolfe =
Shorea contorta

Pentactina Nakai -f- *Rosaceae* · 1 sp.
– **rupicola** Nakai · ♄ d Z5 VI; Korea

Pentaglottis Tausch -f- *Boraginaceae* ·
1 sp. · E:Green Alkanet; F:Buglosse
d'Espagne; G:Spanische Ochsenzunge
– *cespitosa* (Lam.) Tausch = Anchusa
cespitosa
– **sempervirens** (L.) Tausch ex L.H.
Bailey · E:Alkanet, Green Alkanet;
G:Spanische Ochsenzunge · ⵣ Z7 V-VI;
SW-F, P, sp., nat. in I, Br

Pentapterygium Klotzsch = Agapetes

– *rugosum* Hook. = Agapetes rugosa
– *serpens* (Wight) Klotzsch = Agapetes
serpens

Pentas Benth. -f- *Rubiaceae* · 39 spp.
– **lanceolata** (Forssk.) Deflers · E:Egyptian
Star Cluster, Star Cluster; G:Stern von
Ägypten · ♄ Z10 ⊛ IX-I; trop. Afr., Arab.

Penthorum L. -n- *Penthoraceae* · 1-3 spp. ·
E:Ditch Stonecrop
– **sedoides** L. · E:Ditch Stonecrop · ⵣ ⊛;
E-Can., USA: NE, NEC, SC, SE, Fla.

Peperomia Ruiz & Pav. -f- *Piperaceae* ·
c. 1000 spp. · E:Radiator Plant;
F:Pépéromia; G:Peperomie, Zwergpfeffer
– *angulata* Kunth = Peperomia quadrangularis
– **argyreia** (Miq.) E. Morren · E:Water
Melon Pepper; G:Silberblatt-Peperomie ·
ⵣ Z10 ⊛; trop. S-Am.
– **arifolia** Miq. · ⵣ Z10 ⊛; orig. ?
– var. *argyrea* (Miq.) Hook. f. = Peperomia
argyreia
– *bicolor* Sodiro = Peperomia velutina
– **blanda** (Jacq.) Kunth · ♄ Z10 ⊛; Fla.,
C-Am., W.Ind., trop. S-Am.
– **caperata** Yunck. · E:Emerald Ripple
Pepper, Little Fantasy Pepper;
G:Gerunzelte Peperomie, Smaragd-
Peperomie · ⵣ Z10 ⊛; ? Braz.
– **clusiifolia** (Jacq.) Hook. · ⵣ Z10 ⊛;
W.Ind.
– **columbiana** Miq. · ⵣ Z10 ⊛; Col.
– **dolabriformis** Kunth · ⵣ Z10 ⊛; Peru
– *eburnea* hort. = Peperomia maculosa
– **eburnea** Sodiro · ⵣ ⵦ Z10 ⊛; Ecuad.
– **fraseri** C. DC. · E:Flowering Pepper,
Mignonette Peperomia; G:Reseden-
Peperomie · ⵣ D Z10 ⊛ VI-VIII; Ecuad.
– **galioides** Kunth · ⵣ Z10 ⊛; C-Am.,
W.Ind., S-Am.
– **gardneriana** Miq. · ⵣ Z10 ⊛; Braz.
– **glabella** (Sw.) A. Dietr. · E:Cypress
Peperomia, Wax Privet; G:Zypressen-
Peperomie · ⵣ Z10 ⊛; C-Am., W.Ind.,
S-Am.
– **griseoargentea** Yunck. · E:Ivy Leaf
Peperomia; G:Efeublättrige Peperomie ·
ⵣ Z10 ⊛; orig. ?
– *hederifolia* hort. = Peperomia griseoargentea
– **incana** (Haw.) A. Dietr. · ⵣ Z10 ⊛;
SE-Braz.

– **maculosa** (L.) Hook. · E:Spotted
Peperomia · ♃ Z10 ⍟; trop. S-Am.
– **marmorata** Hook. · ♃ Z10 ⍟; S-Braz.
– **metallica** Linden & Rodigas · ♃ Z10 ⍟;
Peru
– **nivalis** Miq. · ♃ Z10 ⍝; Peru
– *nummularifolia* (Sw.) Kunth = Peperomia
rotundifolia var. rotundifolia
– **obtusifolia** (L.) A. Dietr. · E:Baby Rubber
Plant; G:Fleischige Peperomie · ♃ Z10 ⍟;
Mex., C-Am., trop. S-Am.
– var. *clusiifolia* (Jacq.) C. DC. = Peperomia
clusiifolia
– **orba** G.S. Bunting · ♃ Z10 ⍟; orig. ?
– **ornata** Yunck. · ♃ Z10 ⍟; Venez.,
N-Braz.
– **pereskiifolia** (Jacq.) Kunth · ♃ Z10 ⍟;
C-Am., trop. S-Am.
– **polybotrya** Kunth · ♃ Z10 ⍟; Col., Peru
– *prostrata* B.S. Williams = Peperomia
rotundifolia var. pilosior
– *pulchella* A. Dietr. = Peperomia verticillata
– **puteolata** Trel. · ♃ Z10 ⍟; Col.
– **quadrangularis** (J.V. Thomps.) A.
Dietr. · ♃ ⤳ Z10 ⍟; Panama, W.Ind.,
trop. S-Am.
– *resediflora* Lindl. & André = Peperomia
fraseri
– **rotundifolia** (L.) Humb., Bonpl. & Kunth
– var. **pilosior** (Miq.) C. DC. Z10 ⍟;
SE-Braz.
– var. **rotundifolia** · ♃ ⤳ Z10 ⍟; C-Am.,
S-Am.
– **rubella** (Haw.) Hook. · ♃ Z10 ⍟;
Jamaica
– *sandersii* C. DC. = Peperomia argyreia
– **scandens** Ruiz & Pav. · ♃ ⚘ ⤳ Z10 ⍟;
trop. S-Am.
– *serpens* hort. = Peperomia scandens
– **trichocarpa** Miq. · ♃ Z10 ⍟; Braz.
– **urocarpa** Fisch. & C.A. Mey. · ♃ Z10 ⍟;
trop. S-Am.
– **velutina** Linden & André · ♃ Z10 ⍟;
Ecuad.
– *verschaffeltii* Lem. = Peperomia marmorata
– **verticillata** (L.) A. Dietr. · ♃ Z10 ⍟;
Jamaica, Cuba

Peplis L. -f- *Lythraceae* · 3 spp. · F:Péplis;
G:Sumpfquendel
– **portula** L. · G:Gewöhnlicher Sumpfquendel · ⊙ VII-IX; Eur.*, TR, ? Cauc., W-Sib.,
NW-Afr., N-Am.

Peraphyllum Nutt. -n- *Rosaceae* · 1 sp. ·
F:Poire des sables; G:Sandbirne
– **ramosissimum** Nutt. · E:Wild Crab
Apple; G:Sandbirne · ♄ d △ Z5 IV-V;
USA: Oreg., Calif., Rocky Mts.

Pereskia Mill. -f- *Cactaceae* · 16 spp. ·
F:Cactus à feuilles; G:Pereskie, Rosenkaktus
– **aculeata** Mill. · E:Barbados Gooseberry;
G:Barbadosstachelbeere · ♄ ⚘ D Z9 ⍝ ⍟
▽ ✳; USA: Fla.; W.Ind., trop. S-Am.
– **bleo** (Kunth) DC. · ♄ Z9 ⍝ ▽ ✳; Col.,
Panama
– **grandifolia** Haw. · E:Rose Cactus · ♄ ♄
Z9 ⍝ VIII-IX ▽ ✳; Braz.
– **nemorosa** Rojas Acosta · ♄ ♄ Z9 ⍝ V-X
▽ ✳; Parag., Urug., Arg.
– *pereskia* (L.) H. Karst. = Pereskia aculeata
– **sacharosa** Griseb. · ♄ ♄ Z9 ⍝ VIII-X ▽
✳; Bol., Parag., Arg.

Pereskiopsis Britton & Rose -f- *Cactaceae* ·
9 spp.
– **diguetii** (F.A.C. Weber) Britton & Rose ·
♄ ⚘ Z9 ⍝ ▽ ✳; Mex.
– **rotundifolia** (DC.) Britton & Rose · ♄ ⚘
Z9 ⍝ ▽ ✳; Mex.
– **spathulata** (Otto ex Pfeiff.) Britton &
Rose · ♄ ⚘ Z9 ⍝ ▽ ✳; Mex.
– *velutina* Rose = Pereskiopsis diguetii

Perezia Lag. -f- *Asteraceae* · 32 spp.
– **multiflora** (Humb. & Bonpl.) Less.
– subsp. **multiflora** · ⊙ Z9 VII-VIII; Braz.
– subsp. **sonchifolia** (Baker) Vuilleum. · ⊙
Z9 VII-VIII; Urug.
– *sonchifolia* Baker = Perezia multiflora
subsp. sonchifolia
– **viscosa** Less. · ⊙ Z9 VI-VII; Chile

Pericallis D. Don -f- *Asteraceae* · 15 spp. ·
E:Cineraria, Florist's Cineraria;
F:Cinéraire; G:Aschenblume, Zinerarie
– **cruenta** (Masson ex L'Hér.) B. Nord. ·
E:Cineraria; G:Blutrote Zinerarie · ♃ Z9
⍝ III-IV; Canar.
– × **hybrida** B. Nord. (*P. cruenta* × *P.
lanata*) · E:Florist's Cineraria; G:Garten-
Zinerarie · ♃ Z9 ⍝ ✼; cult.
– **many cultivars**
– **lanata** (L'Hér.) B. Nord. · G:Wollige
Zinerarie · ♃ Z9 ⍝; Canar. Is. (Tenerifa)

Perilepta Bremek. = Strobilanthes

– *dyeriana* (Mast.) Bremek. = Strobilanthes dyerianus

Perilla L. -f- *Lamiaceae* · 6 spp. · E:Perilla
– **frutescens** (L.) Britton
– var. *crispa* (Thunb.) Decne. ex L.H. Bailey = Perilla frutescens var. nankinensis
– var. **frutescens** · E:Beefsteak Plant · ⊙ D Z8 IX-X ⚥ Ⓝ; Him., Burma, China, Jap.
– var. **nankinensis** (Lour.) Britton · ⊙ Z8; China
– *ocymoides* L. = Perilla frutescens var. frutescens

Periploca L. -f- *Asclepiadaceae* · 11 sp. · E:Silk Vine; F:Bourreau des arbres; G:Baumschlinge
– **graeca** L. · E:Silk Vine; F:Bourreau des arbres; G:Orientalische Baumschlinge · ⟊ d ⚥ Z6 VII-VIII ✼; Eur.: I, Ba, RO; TR, Syr., Palest., Cauc., N-Iraq, N-Iran, nat. in sp., F
– **sepium** Bunge · E:Chinese Silk Vine; G:Chinesische Baumschlinge · ♄ d ⚥ Z6 VI-VII ✼; N-China

Peristeria Hook. -f- *Orchidaceae* · 11 sp. · E:Dove Orchid; F:Peristeria; G:Taubenorchis
– *barkeri* Bateman = Acineta barkeri
– **cerina** Lindl. · ⌖ Z10 ⓜ VI-VII ▽ ✳; C-Am.
– **elata** Hook. · E:Holy Ghost Flower; G:Taubenorchis · ⌖ Z10 ⓜ VII-VIII ▽ ✳; Costa Rica, Panama, Col., Venez.
– *maculata* Loudon = Peristeria pendula
– **pendula** Hook. · ⌖ Z10 ⓜ I-III ▽ ✳; Venez., Guyana, Surinam, Peru

Peristrophe Nees -f- *Acanthaceae* · 15 spp. · F:Péristrophe; G:Gürtelklaue
– *angustifolia* Nees = Peristrophe hyssopifolia
– **hyssopifolia** (Burm. f.) Bremek. · ♄ e Z10 ⓜ; Java
– *salicifolia* (Blume) Hassk. = Peristrophe hyssopifolia
– **speciosa** (Roxb. ex Wall.) Nees · ♄ e Z10 ⓜ XII-III; Ind.: Bengalen

Pernettya Gaudich. = Gaultheria
– *furens* (Hook. & Arn.) Klotzsch = Gaultheria insana
– *mucronata* (L. f.) Gaudich. ex Spreng. =

Gaultheria mucronata
– *prostrata* (Cav.) Sleumer = Gaultheria myrsinoides var. myrsinoides
– var. *pentlandii* (DC.) Sleumer = Gaultheria myrsinoides var. pentlandii
– *tasmanica* Hook. f. = Gaultheria tasmanica

Perovskia Kar. -f- *Lamiaceae* · 9 spp. · E:Perovskia; F:Pérovskia; G:Perowskie
– **abrotanoides** Kar. · F:Pérovskia; G:Fiederschnittige Perowskie · ♄ d △ Z6 VIII-IX; Afgh., Him., C-As.
– **atriplicifolia** Benth. · E:Russian Sage; F:Pérovskia à feuilles d'arroche; G:Silber-Perowskie · ♄ d △ Z7 VIII-IX; Afgh., Him., Tibet
– **scrophulariifolia** Bunge · G:Runzelige Perowskie · ♄ d △ Z6 VIII-IX; C-As.
– **Cultivars:**
– **some cultivars**

Persea Mill. -f- *Lauraceae* · 150-200 spp. · E:Avocado; F:Avocatier; G:Avocado, Isabellenholz
– **americana** Mill. · E:Avocado; G:Avocado · ♄ e Z10 ⓜ ⓚ ⚥ Ⓝ; Mex., C-Am., trop. S-Am., nat. in Fla.
– *gratissima* C.F. Gaertn. = Persea americana
– **indica** (L.) Spreng. · ♄ e Z9 ⓚ; Canar., Azor.
– *leiogyna* S.F. Blake = Persea americana
– **lingue** (Ruiz & Pav.) Nees · ♄ e Z10 Ⓝ; S-Am., Chile, nat. in C-Afr.
– **schiedeana** Nees · E:Wild Avocado; G:Wilde Avocado · ♄ e Z10 ⓜ Ⓝ; Mex., C-Am.

Persica Mill. = Prunus
– *vulgaris* Mill. = Prunus persica var. persica

Persicaria (L.) Mill. -f- *Polygonaceae* · c. 100 spp. · E:Smartweed; F:Persicaire, Renouée; G:Knöterich
– *affinis* (D. Don) Ronse Decr. = Bistorta affinis
– *alata* (Buch.-Ham. ex D. Don) H. Gross = Persicaria nepalensis
– *alpina* (L.) H. Gross = Aconogonon alpinum
– **amphibia** (L.) Delarbre · E:Amphibious Bistort, Water Smartweed; F:Renouée amphibie; G:Wasser-Knöterich · ⌖ ≈ Z5

VI-IX; Eur.*, TR, Syr., Cauc., Iran, Him.,
W-Sib., E-Sib., Amur, Sakhal., Kamchat.,
C-As., Mong., China, Jap., Moroc., Alger.,
Alaska, Can., S-Afr.
– *amplexicualis* (D. Don) Ronse Decr. =
Bistorta amplexicaulis
– *bistorta* (L.) Samp. = Bistorta officinalis
subsp. officinalis
– *campanulata* (Hook. f.) Ronse Decr. =
Aconogonon campanulatum
– var. *lichiangense* (W.W. Sm.) Ronse Decr.
= Aconogonon lichiangense
– **capitata** (Buch.-Ham. ex D. Don) H.
Gross · ⵂ ⟿ Z8 ⍟ V-VIII; Pakist., Him.,
SW-China
– **dubia** (Stein) Fourr. · G:Milder
Knöterich · ☉ VII-X; Eur.* exc. Sc; TR
– **filiformis** (Thunb.) Nakai · ⵂ Z5 VII-VIII;
Jap.
– **hydropiper** (L.) Delarbre · E:Red
Knees, Water Pepper; G:Wasserpfeffer-
Knöterich · ☉ ⟿ VII-IX ⚥; Eur.*, TR,
Syr., Cauc., Iran, Him., W-Sib., E-Sib.,
Amur, C-As., China, Korea, Jap., Sri
Lanka, Indochina, Malay. Arch., Moroc.,
Alger., nat. in Alaska, Can., USA*
– **lapathifolia** (L.) Delarbre · G:Ampfer-
Knöterich
– subsp. **lapathifolia** · E:Pale Persicaria;
G:Gewöhnlicher Ampfer-Knöterich, Ufer-
Knöterich · ☉ VII-X; Eur.*, TR, Levant,
Cauc., W-Sib., E-Sib., Amur, Sakhal.,
Him., NW-Afr., Egypt, N-Am., nat. in Jap.
– subsp. **brittingeri** (Opiz) Soják ·
G:Donau-Knöterich, Fluss-Knöterich ·
VII-X; Eur.: Sw, D (obere Donau, Rhein)
– *maculata* (Raf.) Fourr. = Persicaria
maculosa
– **maculosa** Gray · E:Lady's Thumb;
G:Floh-Knöterich · ☉ VII-X; Eur.*, TR,
Cauc., W-Sib., E-Sib., Amur, C-As., Him.,
China, Jap.
– **minor** (Huds.) Opiz · G:Kleiner Knö-
terich · ☉ VII-X; Eur.*, TR, Cauc., W-Sib.,
E-Sib., Amur, C-As., Him., E-As., Java
– *mitis* (Schrank) Assenov = Persicaria
dubia
– **nepalensis** (Meisn.) H. Gross · ⵂ; Him.
– **odorata** (Lour.) Soják · ☉ D ⓝ;
Indochina
– **orientalis** (L.) Spach · E:Kiss-me-over-
the-Garden-Gate, Smartweed, Willow
Grass; G:Östlicher Knöterich · ☉ VII-X;
Iran, Ind., China, SE-As., nat. in I, G, Ba,
EC-Eur.

– **pensylvanica** (L.) M. Gómez ·
E:Pennsylvania Smartweed; G:Pennsyl-
vanischer Knöterich · ☉; Alaska, Can.: E;
USA* exc. NW, nat. in BrI
– *polystachya* (Wall. ex Meisn.) H. Gross =
Aconogonon polystachyum
– *sericea* (Pall.) H. Gross = Aconogonon
sericeum
– **tinctoria** (Aiton) Spach · G:Färber-
Knöterich · ⵂ ⓝ; China
– *vacciniifolia* (Wall. ex Meisn.) Ronse
Decr. = Bistorta vacciniifolia
– **virginiana** (L.) Gaertn. · E:Jumpseed · ⵂ
Z5; USA: NE, NEC, NC, SC, SE, Fla.
– *vivipara* (L.) Ronse Decr. = Bistorta
vivipara
– *wallichii* Greuter & Burdet = Aconogonon
polystachyum
– *weyrichii* (F. Schmidt ex Maxim.) Ronse
Decr. = Aconogonon polystachyum

Pertya Sch. Bip. -f- Asteraceae · 15 spp.
– **sinensis** Oliv. · ♄ Z5; C-China

Peruvocereus Akers = Haageocereus
– *albispinus* Akers = Haageocereus
albispinus

Pescatoria Rchb. f. -f- Orchidaceae · 16 spp.
– **cerina** (Lindl. & Paxton) Rchb. f. · ⵂ Z10
⍟ VI-VII ▽ ☀; Costa Rica, Panama
– **dayana** Rchb. f. · ⵂ Z10 ⍟ VI-IX ▽ ☀;
Col.
– **lamellosa** Rchb. f. · ⵂ Z10 ⍟ VII-VIII ▽
☀; Col.

× **Pescoranthes** hort. -f- Orchidaceae
(*Cochleanthes* × *Pescatoria*)

Petasites Mill. -m- Asteraceae · 15-19 spp. ·
E:Butterbur; F:Pétasites; G:Pestwurz
– **albus** (L.) Gaertn. · E:White Butterbur;
F:Pétasite blanc; G:Weiße Pestwurz · ⵂ
△ ⟿ Z5 IV; Eur.* exc. BrI, Ib; TR, Cauc.,
nat. in BrI
– **fragrans** (Vill.) C. Presl · E:Sweet Colts-
foot, Winter Heliotrope; F:Héliotrope
d'hiver; G:Vanillen-Pestwurz · ⵂ △ ⟿
D Z7 ∧ XII-III; Eur.: Sard., I, Sic.; Alger.,
Tun., Libya, nat. in Ib, Fr, BrI, Sw, DK
– **hybridus** (L.) G. Gaertn., B. Mey. &
Scherb. · E:Butterbur, Umbrella Plant;
G:Gewöhnliche Pestwurz · ⵂ ⟿ Z4 IV
♁; Eur.* exc. Sc; TR, Cauc., N-Iran, nat.
in Sc, N-Am.

– **japonicus** (Siebold & Zucc.) Maxim. ·
E:Butterbur; G:Gewöhnliche Japanische
Pestwurz · ⱱ ᔓ　D Z5 III-IV; China,
Korea, Jap., Sakhal., Ryukyu-Is.
– *officinalis* Moench = Petasites hybridus
– **paradoxus** (Retz.) Baumg. · E:Alpine
Butterbur; G:Alpen-Pestwurz · ⱱ △ ᔓ
Z5 IV-V; Eur.: sp., F, I, C-Eur., Bosn.,
Serbia, RO; mts.
– **spurius** (Retz.) Rchb. · G:Filzige Pest-
wurz · ⱱ Z5 IV; Eur.: Sc, G, PL, E-Eur.;
W-Sib., ? C-As.
– *tomentosus* DC. = Petasites spurius

Petrea L. -f- *Verbenaceae* · 30 spp. ·
E:Purple Wreath; F:Petrea; G:Purpur-
kranz
– **volubilis** L. · E:Purple Wreath; G:Pur-
purkranz · ♄ e ⚡ Z10 ⓦ III-IV; C-Am.,
W.Ind.

Petrocallis R. Br. -f- *Brassicaceae* · 1 sp. ·
F:Drave des Pyrénées, Pétrocallis;
G:Steinschmückel
– **pyrenaica** (L.) R. Br. · E:Rock Beauty;
G:Steinschmückel · ⱱ △ △ Z4 VI ▽;
Eur.: sp., F, I, C-Eur., Slova., Slove.,
Croatia, ? RO; Pyr., Alp., Carp.

Petrocoptis A. Braun ex Endl. -f-
Caryophyllaceae · 5-7 spp. · F:Lychnis des
Pyrénées, Pétrocoptis; G:Pyrenäennelke
– **glaucifolia** (Lag.) Boiss. · ⱱ △ Z7 VI-VIII;
N-Sp.; mts.
– *lagascae* (Willk.) Willk. = Petrocoptis
glaucifolia
– **pyrenaica** (Bergeret) A. Braun · ⱱ △ Z7
VI-VII; sp., F; Pyr., mts. N-Sp.

Petrocosmea Oliv. -f- *Gesneriaceae* · 27 spp.
– **kerrii** Craib · ⱱ Z10 ⓚ; Thail.
– **nervosa** Craib · ⱱ Z9 ⓚ; Yunnan
– **parryorum** C.E.C. Fisch. · ⱱ Z10 ⓚ;
N-Ind.: Assam

Petrophytum (Nutt. ex Torr. & A. Gray)
Rydb. -n- *Rosaceae* · 3 spp. · E:Rock
Spiraea; F:Spirée; G:Rasenspiere
– **caespitosum** (Nutt. ex Torr. & A. Gray)
Rydb. · E:Mat Rock Spiraea · ♄ e ⤳ △
Z3 VII-VIII; USA: NC, Rocky Mts., Calif.,
SW
– **cinerascens** (Piper) Rydb. · E:Olympic
Mountain Rockmat · ♄ e ⤳ △ Z5 IX;
USA: NW, Rocky Mts.

Petrorhagia (Ser.) Link -f-
Caryophyllaceae · 28 spp. · F:Tunique ;
G:Felsennelke
– **prolifera** (L.) P.W. Ball & Heywood ·
E:Proliferous Pink; G:Nelkenköpfchen,
Sprossende Felsennelke · ⊙ Z6 VI-X;
Eur.*, TR, Cauc., NW-Afr.
– **saxifraga** (L.) Link · E:Coat Flower,
Tunic Flower; F:Oeillet des rochers,
Tunique; G:Steinbrech-Felsennelke · ⱱ
△ Z6 VI-IX; Eur.* exc. BrI, Sc; TR, Cauc.,
N-Iran, Altai, nat. in BrI, Sc

Petroselinum Hill -n- *Apiaceae* · 2-3 spp. ·
E:Parsley; F:Persil; G:Petersilie
– **crispum** (Mill.) Nyman ex A.W. Hill ·
E:Parsley; G:Petersilie · ⊙ VI-VII ⚡ ; ?
SE-Eur., ? NW-Afr.; cult., nat. in Eur.*
– var. **crispum** · E:Double Curled Parsley;
G:Blatt-Petersilie, Krause Petersilie
– var. **neapolitanum** Danert · E:Italian
Parsley; G:Italienische Petersilie
– var. *radicosum* (Alef.) Danert =
Petroselinum crispum var. tuberosum
– var. **tuberosum** (Bernh.) Mart. Crov. ·
E:Hamburg Parsley, Turnip-rooted
Parsley; G:Knollen-Petersilie, Petersilien-
wurzel

Petteria C. Presl -f- *Fabaceae* · 1 sp. ·
F:Petteria; G:Petterie
– **ramentacea** (Sieber) C. Presl ·
E:Dalmatian Laburnum; G:Petterie · ♄ d
Z6 VI; Eur.: Croatia, Bosn., YU, AL

Petunia Juss. -f- *Solanaceae* · 35 spp. ·
E:Petunia; F:Pétunia; G:Petunie
– × **atkinsiana** D. Don (*P. axillaris × P.
integrifolia*) · E:Petunia; G:Garten-
Petunie · ⱱ Z7 VI-IX; cult.
– **axillaris** (Lam.) Britton, Sterns &
Poggenb. · E:Large White Petunia;
G:Weiße Petunie · ⊙ ⊙ ⱱ ♄ D Z7 VI-IX;
S-Braz., Urug., Arg.
– **integrifolia** (Hook.) Schinz & Thell. ·
E:Violet-flowered Petunia; G:Violette
Petunie · ⊙ ⊙ ⱱ ♄ Z7 VI-IX; Braz., Urug.,
Arg.
– *nyctaginiflora* Juss. = Petunia axillaris
– *violacea* Lindl. = Petunia integrifolia
– **Cultivars:**
– **many cultivars**

Peucedanum L. -n- *Apiaceae* ·
100 (-170) spp. · E:Hog's Fennel;

F:Impératoire, Peucédan; G:Haarstrang, Hirschwurz
- **alsaticum** L. · G:Elsässer Haarstrang · ⚄ VII-IX; Eur.: Fr, C-Eur., EC-Eur., Ba, E-Eur.
- *altissimum* (Mill.) Thell. = Peucedanum verticillare
- **austriacum** (Jacq.) Koch
- var. **rablense** (Wulfen) W.D.J. Koch · G:Raibler Haarstrang · ⚄ Z6 VII-VIII; Eur.: I, Sw, A, Slove.; SE-Alp.
- **austriacum** (Jacq.) W.D.J. Koch · G:Österreichischer Haarstrang · ⚄ Z6 VII-VIII; Eur.: Fr, Ital-P, C-Eur., Ba, E-Eur.
- **carvifolia** Vill. · G:Kümmel-Haarstrang · ⚄ VI-VIII; Eur.* exc. BrI, Sc; ? TR, Cauc.
- **cervaria** (L.) Lapeyr. · G:Hirschwurz · ⚄ Z6 VII-IX; Eur.* exc. BrI, Sc; Cauc., W-Sib., Alger.
- **officinale** L. · G:Arznei-Haarstrang, Echter Haarstrang · ⚄ VII-IX ⚥ ; Eur.* exc. Sc
- **oreoselinum** (L.) Moench · G:Berg-Haarstrang · ⚄ VII-VIII; Eur.* exc. BrI; ? Cauc.
- **ostruthium** (L.) W.D.J. Koch · E:Hogfennel, Masterwort ; G:Meister-wurz · ⚄ Z5 VII-VIII Ⓝ; Eur.: Fr, C-Eur., EC-Eur., Ib, Ital-P, Ba, ?RO, ? Crim, nat. in BrI, N-Am.
- **palustre** (L.) Moench · E:Milk Parsley; G:Sumpf-Haarstrang · ⚄ VII-VIII; Eur.* exc. Ib; W-Sib.
- **venetum** (Spreng.) W.D.J. Koch · E:Southern Masterwort ; G:Ven-ezianischer Haarstrang · ⚄ VII-VIII; Eur.: sp., F, I, Sw, Slove., Croatia; E-Pyr., S-Alp., Apenn., Croatia
- **verticillare** (L.) Spreng. · G:Riesen-Haarstrang · ⊙ ⚄ Z7 VII-VIII ✂ ; Eur.: Sw, I, A, H, Slove., Croatia

Peumus Molina -f- *Monimiaceae* · 1 sp. · E:Boldo; F:Boldo; G:Boldo
- **boldus** Molina · E:Boldo; G:Boldo · ♄ e Z9 ⚐ ⚥ ✂ ; Chile

Pfeiffera Salm-Dyck -f- *Cactaceae* · 2 spp.
- **ianthothele** (Monv.) F.A.C. Weber · ♄ Ψ Z9 ⚐; Bol., Arg.

Phacelia Juss. -f- *Hydrophyllaceae* · 150 spp. · E:Bluebell, Scorpion Weed; F:Phacélie; G:Büschelschön, Phazelie
- **campanularia** A. Gray · E:California

Bluebell, Desert Bluebells; G:Glockenblu-men-Büschelschön · ⊙ Z9 VII-IX; Can.: W; USA: Calif., Colo.
- **congesta** Hook. · E:Blue Curls, Caterpil-lars; G:Rainfarn-Büschelschön · ⊙ VII-X Ⓝ; USA: Calif., Ariz., N.Mex., Tex.; Baja Calif.
- **divaricata** (Benth.) A. Gray · ⊙ VII-VIII; Calif.
- **grandiflora** (Benth.) A. Gray · ⊙; S-Calif.
- **linearis** (Pursh) Holz. · E:Scorpion Weed; G:Schmalblättriges Büschelschön · ⊙ ⊙ ⚄ VII-IX; W-Can., USA: NW, Rocky Mts., Calif.
- *menziesii* Torr. = Phacelia linearis
- **minor** (Harv.) Thell. ex F. Zimm. · E:California Bluebell, Whitlavia; G:Kleines Büschelschön · ⊙ VII-VIII; S-Calif.
- **parryi** Torr. · ⊙ VI-IX; Calif., Mex.
- *tanacetifolia* A. DC. = Phacelia congesta
- **tanacetifolia** Benth. · E:Lacy Phacelia · ⊙; USA: Calif., Ariz.; Mex., nat. in Eur.* exc. Ital-P., BrI
- **viscida** (Benth. ex Lindl.) Torr. · E:Tacky Phacelia; G:Klebriges Büschelschön · ⊙ VI-VIII; Calif.
- *whitlavia* A. Gray = Phacelia minor

Phaedranassa Herb. -f- *Amaryllidaceae* · 9 spp. · E:Queen Lily; F:Reine des Andes; G:Andenkönigin
- **carmiolii** Baker · ⚄ Z8 ⚐; Costa Rica
- **lehmannii** Regel · ⚄ Z8 ⚐; Col.
- **schizantha** Baker · ⚄ Z8 ⚐; Ecuad., Peru

Phaedranthus Miers = Distictis
- *buccinatorius* (DC.) Miers = Distictis buccinatoria

Phaenocoma D. Don -f- *Asteraceae* · 1 sp.
- **prolifera** (L.) D. Don · ♄ ✕ Z9 ⚐; Cape

✕ **Phaiocalanthe** hort. -f- *Orchidaceae* (*Calanthe* × *Phaius*)

✕ **Phaiocymbidium** hort. -n- *Orchidaceae* (*Cymbidium* × *Phaius*)

Phaius Lour. -m- *Orchidaceae* · 48 spp.
- **flavus** (Blume) Lindl. · ⚄ ✕ Z10 ⚐ IV-V ▽ ✳; Ind., Malay. Arch.
- *grandifolius* Lour. = Phaius tankervilleae
- **humblotii** Rchb. f. · ⚄ ✕ Z10 ⚐ VI-VII ▽

✳; Madag.
- *maculatus* Lindl. = Phaius flavus
- **tankervilleae** (Banks ex L'Hér.) Blume ·
  ⧎ ⋊ Z10 🐝 II-VI ▽ ✳; Him., N-Ind.,
  Sri Lanka, Burma, China, Malay. Arch.,
  Austr.

Phalaenopsis Blume -f- *Orchidaceae* ·
62 spp. · E:Moth Orchid; F:Orchidée-
papillon; G:Malayenblume, Schmetterlingsorchidee
- **amabilis** (L.) Blume · ⧎ Z10 🐝 X-II ▽ ✳;
  Malay. Arch., N.Guinea, Austr.: Queensl.
- **amboinensis** J.J. Sm. · ⧎ Z10 🐝 XII-I ▽
  ✳; Molucca: Ambon
- **aphrodite** Rchb. f. · ⧎ Z10 🐝 XII-IV ▽
  ✳; Phil., Taiwan
- *buyssoniana* Rchb. f. = Doritis pulcherrima
- **cornu-cervi** (Breda) Blume & Rchb. f. · ⧎
  Z10 🐝 V-IX ▽ ✳; Burma, Thail., Nicobar.
  Is., Malay. Pen., Sumat., Kalimantan
- *denevei* J.J. Sm. = Paraphalaenopsis
  denevei
- **equestris** (Schauer) Rchb. f. · ⧎ Z10 🐝
  VIII-IX ▽ ✳; Phil., Taiwan
- *esmeralda* Rchb. f. = Doritis pulcherrima
- *grandiflora* Lindl. = Phalaenopsis
  amabilis
- **lueddemanniana** Rchb. f. · ⧎ Z10 🐝
  V-VI ▽ ✳; Phil.
- **mannii** Rchb. f. · ⧎ Z10 🐝 V-VIII ▽ ✳;
  Ind.: Sikkim, Assam; Vietn.
- **mariae** Burb. ex R. Warner & N.H.
  Williams · ⧎ Z10 🐝 VI-VIII ▽ ✳;
  Kalimantan, Phil.
- **parishii** Rchb. f. · ⧎ Z10 🐝 V-VI ▽ ✳;
  Burma
- *pulcherrima* (Lindl.) J.J. Sm. = Doritis
  pulcherrima
- *rimestadiana* (Linden) Rolfe = Phalaenopsis amabilis
- *rosea* Lindl. = Phalaenopsis equestris
- **schilleriana** Rchb. f. · ⧎ Z10 🐝 I-III ▽
  ✳; Phil.
- **stuartiana** Rchb. f. · ⧎ Z10 🐝 I-III ▽ ✳;
  Phil.
- **sumatrana** Korth. & Rchb. f. · ⧎ Z10 🐝
  V-VI ▽ ✳; Thail., Malay. Pen., Sumat.,
  Java, Kalimantan
- **violacea** Witte · ⧎ Z10 🐝 V-VII ▽ ✳;
  Malay. Pen., Sumat., Kalimantan
- **Cultivars:**
- **many cultivars**

× **Phalaerianda** hort. -f- *Orchidaceae*
  (*Aerides* × Phalaenopsis × *Vanda*)

× **Phalandopsis** hort. -f- *Orchidaceae*
  (*Phalaenopsis* × *Vandopsis*)

× **Phalanetia** hort. -f- *Orchidaceae*
  (*Neofinetia* × *Phalaenopsis*)

Phalaris L. -f- *Poaceae* · c. 20 spp. ·
E:Canary Grass; F:Alpiste, Baldingère;
G:Glanzgras
- **arundinacea** L. · E:Reed Canary Grass,
  Ribbon Grass; F:Baldingère, Phalaris-
  roseau; G:Rohr-Glanzgras · ⧎ ～ ⋊
  Z4 VI-VII Ⓝ; Eur.*, TR, Syr., Lebanon,
  Cauc., Iran, Him., N-Ind., Sri Lanka,
  W-Sib., E-Sib., Amur, Sakhal., Kamchat.,
  C-As., N-China, Korea, Jap., Taiwan,
  Java, Alger., Kenya (Mt. Kenya), Alaska,
  Can., USA*, Mex., nat. in S-Am., S-Afr.,
  Austr., NZ
- **brachystachys** Link · G:Gedrungen-
  blütiges Glanzgras · ☉; Eur.: Ib, Fr, Ital-P,
  Ba; Cauc.
- **canariensis** L. · E:Birdseed Grass, Canary
  Grass; G:Kanariengras · ☉ ⋊ Z6 VI-VIII
  Ⓝ; Eur.: Ib, Fr, Ital-P, Ba, E-Eur., Canar.
  Is., Azor.; Tun., TR, nat. in Eur.* exc. BrI,
  Sc; Cauc.
- **coerulescens** Desf. · E:Sunol Grass;
  G:Ausdauerndes Glanzgras · ⧎; Eur.: Ib,
  Fr, Ital-P, Ba; TR
- **minor** Retz. · E:Little Seed Canary Grass;
  G:Kleines Glanzgras · ☉ Z6; Eur.: Ib, Fr,
  Ital-P, Ba; TR, Cauc., Iran, C-As., Him.,
  Ind., N-Afr., Cape, nat. in Crim
- **paradoxa** L. · E:Hood Canary Grass;
  G:Sonderbares Glanzgras · ☉; Eur.: Ib,
  Fr, Ital-P, Ba; TR, Cauc., SW-As., N-Afr.

Phanerophlebia C. Presl = Polystichum
- *caryotidea* (Wall.) Copel. = Polystichum
  falcatum var. caryotideum
- *falcata* (L. f.) Copel. = Polystichum
  falcatum var. falcatum
- *fortunei* (J. Sm.) Copel. = Polystichum
  falcatum var. fortunei

Pharbitis Choisy = Ipomoea
- *acuminata* (Vahl) Choisy = Ipomoea
  indica
- *hederacea* (Jacq.) Choisy = Ipomoea
  hederacea
- *hispida* (Zucc.) Choisy = Ipomoea

purpurea
- *learii* (Paxton) Lindl. = Ipomoea indica
- *nil* (L.) Choisy = Ipomoea nil
- *purpurea* (Roth) Voigt = Ipomoea
  purpurea
- *rubrocaerulea* (Hook.) Planch. = Ipomoea
  tricolor

Pharus P. Browne -m- *Poaceae* · 5-8 spp.
- **latifolius** L. · E:Broad Stalkgrass · ⌅ Z9
  ⓦ; W.Ind.

Phaseolus L. -m- *Fabaceae* · 36 spp. ·
E:Bean; F:Haricot; G:Bohne
- *aconitifolius* Jacq. = Vigna aconitifolia
- **acutifolius** A. Gray · E:Tepary Bean
- var. **acutifolius** · E:Wild Bean; G:Tepary-
  Bohne · ⊙ ⌇ Z10 ⓦ ⓝ; USA: Ariz.,
  N.Mex., Tex.; Mex.
- var. **latifolius** G.F. Freeman · ⊙ ⌇ Z10 ⓦ
  ⓝ; N-Mex., Ariz., nat. in Afr.
- *angularis* (Willd.) W. Wight = Vigna
  angularis
- *aureus* Roxb. = Vigna radiata
- **coccineus** L. · E:Runner Bean, Scarlet
  Runner; G:Feuer-Bohne · ⊙ ⌇ Z10 VI-IX;
  ? Mex., ? C-Am.
- **lathyroides** L. · ⊙ ⌇ ⓝ; trop. Am.,
  Austr.: Queensl.; cult. E-Afr.
- *limensis* Macfad. = Phaseolus lunatus
- **lunatus** L. · E:Butter Bean, Lima Bean;
  G:Butter-Bohne, Lima-Bohne · ⊙ ⌇ Z10
  ⚘ ⓝ; S-Am.
- *max* L. = Glycine max
- *multiflorus* Lam. = Phaseolus coccineus
- *mungo* L. = Vigna mungo
- *retusus* Benth. = Phaseolus ritensis
- **ritensis** M.E. Jones · E:Santa Rita Mountain Bean · ⌅ ⓝ; USA: Ariz., N.Mex., Tex.
- **vulgaris** L.
- var. **nanus** (L.) G. Martens · E:Dwarf
  Bean; G:Busch-Bohne · ⊙ Z10 ⓝ; cult.
- var. **vulgaris** · E:Bean, Flageolet, French
  Bean, Green Bean, Haricot, Kidney Bean;
  G:Garten-Bohne, Stangen-Bohne · ⊙ ⌇
  Z10 VI-IX ⚘ ; cult.

Phegopteris Fée -f- *Thelypteridaceae* ·
4 spp. · E:Beech Fern; F:Fougère du
hêtre; G:Buchenfarn
- **connectilis** (Michx.) D. Watt · E:Long
  Beech Fern; F:Fougère des hêtres;
  G:Gewöhnlicher Buchenfarn · ⌅ Z5
  VII-VIII; Eur.*, TR, Cauc., W-Sib., E-Sib.,
  Amur, Sakhal., Kamchat., Manch., Korea,

Jap., Alaska, Can., USA: NE, NCE, SE;
Greenl.
- **decursive-pinnata** (H.C. Hall) Fée ·
  G:Tausendfüßlerfarn · ⌅ Z6; Ind.,
  Indochina, China, Taiwan, Jap.
- *dryopteris* (L.) Fée = Gymnocarpium
  dryopteris
- **hexagonoptera** (Michx.) Fée · E:Broad
  Beech Fern; F:Fougère des hêtres
  américaine; G:Breiter Buchenfarn · ⌅ Z5;
  Can.: E; USA: NE, NCE, Kans., SC, SE,
  Fla.
- *polypodioides* Fée = Phegopteris connectilis
- *robertiana* (Hoffm.) Asch. = Gymnocarpium robertianum
- *vulgaris* Mett. = Phegopteris connectilis

Phellandrium L. = Oenanthe
- *aquaticum* L. = Oenanthe aquatica

Phellodendron Rupr. -n- *Rutaceae* ·
10 spp. · E:Corktree; F:Arbre à liège;
G:Korkbaum
- **amurense** Rupr. · E:Amur Cork Tree;
  F:Phellodendron de l'Amour; G:Amur-
  Korkbaum · ♄ d Z5 VI ⚘ ⓝ; Amur,
  N-China, Manch., Korea, Jap.
- **chinense** C.K. Schneid. · E:Chinese Cork
  Tree; G:Chinesischer Korkbaum · ♄ d Z5
  VI; C-China
- **japonicum** Maxim. · E:Japanese Cork
  Tree; F:Phellodendron du Japon;
  G:Japanischer Korkbaum · ♄ d Z5 VI; Jap.
- **lavallei** Dode · E:Lavalle Cork Tree;
  G:Rostiger Korkbaum · ♄ d Z6 VI; Jap.
- **sachalinense** (F. Schmidt) Sarg. ·
  E:Sakhalin Cork Tree; G:Sachalin-
  Korkbaum · ♄ d Z4 VI; China, Korea,
  N-Jap., Sakhal.

Phellosperma Britton & Rose = Mammillaria
- *guelzowiana* (Werderm.) Buxb. = Mammillaria guelzowiana
- *longiflora* (Britton & Rose) Buxb. =
  Mammillaria longiflora
- *pennispinosa* (Krainz) Buxb. = Mammillaria pennispinosa
- *tetrancistra* (Engelm.) Britton & Rose =
  Mammillaria tetrancistra

Phelypaea L. = Orobanche
- *caerulea* (Vill.) C.A. Mey. = Orobanche
  purpurea
- *ramosa* (L.) C.A. Mey. = Orobanche

ramosa

Philadelphus L. -m- *Hydrangeaceae* ·
65 spp. · E:Mock Orange; F:Seringat;
G:Pfeifenstrauch, Sommerjasmin
- **argyrocalyx** Wooton · E:Silvercup Mock
Orange · ♄ d D Z7 VI-VIII; USA: N.Mex.
- **brachybotrys** (Koehne) Koehne · ♄ Z7
VI-VII; ? China
- **californicus** Benth. · E:California Mock
Orange; G:Kalifornischer Pfeifenstrauch ·
♄ d D Z7 VI-VII; Calif.
- **caucasicus** Koehne · E:Caucasian Mock
Orange; G:Kaukasischer Pfeifenstrauch ·
♄ d Z6 V-VI; Cauc.
- **coronarius** L. · E:Sweet Mock Orange;
F:Seringat des jardins; G:Falscher
Jasmin, Gewöhnlicher Pfeifenstrauch · ♄
d D Z5 V-VI; Eur.: A (Steiermark), I, nat.
in F, RO
- **delavayi** L. Henry · G:Delavays Pfeifenstrauch · ♄ d Z6 VI; Yunnan
- × **falconeri** Sarg. · G:Stern-Pfeifen-
strauch · ♄ d Z5; orig. ?
- **floridus** Beadle · E:Florida Mock
Orange · ♄ d Z7 VI; USA: Ga.
- *gloriosus* Beadle = Philadelphus inodorus
var. grandiflorus
- *grandiflorus* Willd. = Philadelphus
inodorus var. grandiflorus
- **hirsutus** Nutt. · E:Streambank Mock
Orange; G:Grauhaariger Pfeifenstrauch ·
♄ d Z7 VI; USA: Ky., SE
- **incanus** Koehne · G:Später Pfeifenstrauch · ♄ d D Z5 VII; China: Hubei,
Schansi
- **inodorus** L.
- var. **grandiflorus** (Willd.) A. Gray · ♄ d
Z7 VI; USA: Va., SE, Fla.
- var. **inodorus** · E:Scentless Mock
Orange; G:Duftloser Pfeifenstrauch · ♄ d
Z7; USA: Va., SE, Fla.
- var. **laxus** (Schrad. ex DC.) S.Y. Hu · ♄ d
Z7 VI; USA: Ga.
- var. **strigosus** Beadle · ♄ d Z7 VI; USA:
S.C.
- **insignis** Carrière · ♄ d D Z7 VI-VII; USA:
Oreg., Calif.
- **intectus** Beadle · ♄ d Z7 VI; USA: SE
- **kansuensis** (Rehder) S.Y. Hu · ♄ d D Z7
VII; NW-China
- *laxus* Schrad. ex DC. = Philadelphus
inodorus var. laxus
- × **lemoinei** Lemoine (*P. coronarius*
× *P. microphyllus*) · G:Lemoines

Pfeifenstrauch · ♄ d Z5; cult.
- **lewisii** Pursh
- var. **gordonianus** (Lindl.) Jeps. · ♄ d Z5
VI-VII; Can.: B.C.; USA: NW, Idaho, Calif.
- var. **lewisii** · E:Wild Mock Orange;
G:Oregon-Pfeifenstrauch · ♄ d Z5; Can.:
W; USA: NW, Calif., Rocky Mts.
- **microphyllus** A. Gray · E:Littleleaf Mock
Orange; G:Kleinblättriger Pfeifenstrauch
· ♄ d D Z6 VI; USA: Colo., SW
- **pekinensis** Rupr. · G:Peking-Pfeifen-
strauch · ♄ d D Z5 VI; N-China, Korea
- var. *brachybotrys* (Koehne) Koehne =
Philadelphus brachybotrys
- var. *kansuensis* Rehder = Philadelphus
kansuensis
- × **polyanthus** Rehder (*P. insignis* × *P.* ×
lemoinei) · ♄ d Z6; cult.
- **pubescens** Loisel. · E:Hoary Mock
Orange
- var. *intectus* (Beadle) A.H. Moore =
Philadelphus intectus
- var. **pubescens** · G:Weichhaariger
Pfeifenstrauch · ♄ d Z5; USA: NE, NCE,
SE
- var. **verrucosus** (Schrad. ex DC.) S.Y.
Hu · ♄ d Z5 VI; USA: NCE, SE
- **purpurascens** (Koehne) Rehder · ♄ d D
Z6 VI; W-China
- × **purpureomaculatus** Lemoine (*P.
coulteri* × *P.* × *lemoinei*) · ♄ d Z6; cult.
- **salicifolius** K. Koch · ♄ d D Z5 VI; orig. ?
- **satsumanus** Siebold ex Miq. · ♄ d Z6 VI;
Jap.
- **satsumi** (Siebold) S.Y. Hu · ♄ d D Z6 VI;
Jap.
- **schrenkii** Rupr. · G:Schrenks Pfeifenstrauch · ♄ d D Z5 V-VI; Manch., Korea
- **sericanthus** Koehne · ♄ d Z6 VI;
W-China, C-China
- *strigosus* (Beadle) Rydb. = Philadelphus
inodorus var. inodorus
- **subcanus** Koehne
- var. **magdalenae** (Koehne) S.Y. Hu · ♄ d
D Z6 VI; W-China
- var. **subcanus** · ♄ d Z6; W-China
- **tenuifolius** Rupr. & Maxim. · G:Mand-
schurischer Pfeifenstrauch · ♄ d Z5 VI;
Manch., Korea, E-Sib.
- **tomentosus** Wall. ex G. Don · G:Filziger
Pfeifenstrauch · ♄ d D Z6 VI; Him.
- *verrucosus* Schrad. ex DC. = Philadelphus
pubescens var. pubescens
- × **virginalis** Rehder · ♄ d Z5; cult.
- **Cultivars:**

– **many cultivars**

Philesia Comm. ex Juss. -f- *Philesiaceae* ·
1 sp. · F:Philésia; G:Kussblume
– **magellanica** J.F. Gmel. · ♄ e Z9 ⓚ;
Chile, S-Arg.

Philippicereus Backeb. = Eulychnia
– *castaneus* (Phil.) Backeb. = Eulychnia
castanea

Phillyrea L. -f- *Oleaceae* · 4 spp. · E:Mock
Privet; F:Filaria; G:Steinliguster,
Steinlinde
– **angustifolia** L. · G:Schmalblättrige
Steinlinde · ♄ e Z8 ⓚ V-VI; Eur.: Ib, Fr,
Ital-P, Ba; NW-Afr., nat. in Crim
– *decora* Boiss. & Balansa = Osmanthus
decorus
– **latifolia** L. · G:Breitblättrige Steinlinde ·
♄ ♄ e Z8 ⓚ V; Eur.: Ib, Fr, Ital-P, Ba; TR,
Levant, NW-Afr., Libya
– *media* L. = Phillyrea latifolia
– *vilmoriniana* Boiss. & Balansa = Osmanthus decorus

Philodendron Schott -n- *Araceae* ·
423 spp. · E:Philodendron;
F:Philodendron; G:Philodendron
– **adamantinum** Mart. ex Schott · ♄ e Z10
ⓦ; Parag.
– *andreanum* Devansaye = Philodendron
melanochrysum
– **angustisectum** Engl. · ∫ e ⚇ Z10 ⓦ;
W-Col.
– *asperatum* (K. Koch) K. Koch = Philodendron ornatum
– *augustinum* K. Koch = Philodendron
radiatum
– **bipennifolium** Schott · E:Fiddleleaf Philodendron; G:Geigenblatt-Philodendron ·
∫ e ⚇ Z10 ⓦ; S-Braz.
– **bipinnatifidum** Schott ex Endl. ·
G:Baum-Philodendron · ♄ e Z10 ⓦ;
SE-Braz.
– *cannifolium* Mart. ex Kunth = Philodendron martianum
– *cordatum* hort. = Philodendron hederaceum var. hederaceum
– **cordatum** Kunth · E:Heart Philodendron;
G:Herzblättriger Philodendron · ∫ e ⚇ Z10
ⓦ; SE-Braz.
– × **corsinianum** Senoner (*P. verrucosum* ×
?) · ∫ e ⚇ Z10 ⓦ; cult.
– **crassinervium** Lindl. · ∫ e ⚇ Z10 ⓦ;
Guyan.
– *daguense* Linden = Philodendron verrucosum
– **devansayeanum** L. Linden · ⚃ ∫ e ⚇ ⤳
Z10 ⓦ; Ecuad., Peru; And.
– **domesticum** G.S. Bunting · E:Spade
Leaf Philodendron; G:Spatenblatt-
Philodendron · ♄ e ⚇ Z10 ⓦ; ? Braz.
– *duisbergii* Epple ex G.S. Bunting =
Philodendron pedatum
– *eichleri* Engl. = Philodendron undulatum
– **elegans** K. Krause
– *elongatum* Engl. = Philodendron
hastatum
– **erubescens** K. Koch & Augustin ·
E:Blushing Philodendron, Redleaf Philodendron; G:Rotblättriger Philodendron
· ∫ e ⚇ Z10 ⓦ; Col.
– **eximium** Schott · e ⚇ Z10 ⓦ; Braz.
– **fendleri** K. Krause · ♄ e ⚇ Z10 ⓦ; Col.,
Venez., Trinidad
– **giganteum** Schott · ∫ e ⚇ Z10 ⓦ; W.Ind.
– **glaziovii** Hook. f. · e ⚇ Z10 ⓦ; Braz.
– **gloriosum** André · ⚃ e ⤳ Z10 ⓦ; Col.
– **grandifolium** (Jacq.) Schott · ∫ e ⚇ Z10
ⓦ; Guyan.
– *hastatum* hort. = Philodendron domesticum
– **hastatum** K. Koch & Sello · e ⚇ Z10 ⓦ;
Braz.
– **hederaceum** (Jacq.) Schott Z10
– var. **hederaceum** · E:Heart-leaf Philodendron; G:Kletternder Philodendron · ∫
e Z10; Mex., trop. Am.
– var. **oxycardium** (Schott) Croat · ⚇ Z10
ⓦ; E-Mex.
– **houlletianum** Engl. · ∫ e ⚇ Z10 ⓦ;
Guyan.
– *ilsemannii* hort. Saunders = Philodendron
ornatum
– **imbe** Schott ex Endl. · ∫ e ⚇ Z10 ⓦ;
S-Braz.
– *imperiale* Schott = Philodendron ornatum
– **lacerum** (Jacq.) Schott · ∫ e ⚇ Z10 ⓦ;
Cuba, Haiti, Jamaica
– *laciniatum* (Vell.) Engl. = Philodendron
pedatum
– *laciniosum* Schott = Philodendron
pedatum
– **latifolium** K. Koch · e Z10 ⓦ; Venez.
– *latilobum* Schott = Philodendron
panduriforme
– **longilaminatum** Schott · e ⚇ Z10 ⓦ;
S-Braz.
– **martianum** Engl. · ⚃ e ⤳ Z10 ⓦ;

SE-Braz.
- **melanochrysum** Linden & André ·
E:Black Gold Philodendron; G:Schwarz-
goldener Philodendron · ʃ e ⚲ Z10 ⓜ Ⓝ;
Col.
- **melinonii** Brongn. ex Regel · ⁴ e Z10 ⓜ;
trop. S-Am.
- **ornatum** Schott · ʃ e ⚲ Z10 ⓜ; trop.
S-Am.
- *oxycardium* Schott = Philodendron
hederaceum var. oxycardium
- **panduriforme** (Kunth) Kunth · ʃ e ⚲ Z10
ⓜ; Peru
- *panduriforme* hort. = Philodendron
bipennifolium
- **pedatum** (Hook.) Kunth · ʃ e ⚲ Z10 ⓜ;
Venez., Guyan., N-Braz
- *pertusum* (L.) Kunth & C.D. Bouché =
Monstera adansonii
- **pinnatifidum** (Jacq.) Schott · ⁴ e Z10
ⓜ; Venez., Trinidad
- **radiatum** Schott · ʃ e ⚲ Z10 ⓜ; SE-Mex.,
Guat.
- **rugosum** Bogner & G.S. Bunting · ʃ e ⚲
Z10 ⓜ; Ecuad.
- **sagittifolium** Liebm. · ʃ e ⚲ Z10 ⓜ;
S-Mex.
- *sanguineum* Regel = Philodendron sagittifolium
- *scandens* K. Koch & Sello = Philodendron
hederaceum
- *selloum* K. Koch = Philodendron bipinnatifidum
- *sellowianum* K. Koch = Philodendron
latifolium
- **simsii** (Hook.) Sweet ex Kunth · ⁴ e Z10
ⓜ; Venez.
- *sodiroi* hort. ex Bellair & St.-Lég. =
Philodendron ornatum
- **squamiferum** Poepp. · ʃ e ⚲ Z10 ⓜ;
Guyan., Braz.
- **tripartitum** (Jacq.) Schott · ʃ e ⚲ Z10 ⓜ;
C-Am., trop. S-Am.
- *triumphans* hort. = Philodendron verrucosum
- *tuxtlanum* G.S. Bunting = Philodendron
sagittifolium
- **undulatum** Engl. · ♄ e Z10 ⓜ; Braz.
- **verrucosum** L. Mathieu ex Schott · ʃ e ⚲
Z10 ⓜ; Costa Rica, Panama, Col., Ecuad.
- **wendlandii** Schott · ⁴ e Z10 ⓜ; C-Am.

Philydrum Banks ex Gaertn. -n-
Philydraceae · 1 sp.
- **lanuginosum** Banks ex Gaertn. · ⁴ ≈

Z10 ⓜ; Ind., Burma, China, Taiwan,
Jap., Thail., Malay. Pen., Austr.

Phlebodium (R. Br.) J. Sm. -n-
Polypodiaceae · 4 spp. · E:Golden
Polypody; G:Hasenfußfarn
- **aureum** (L.) J. Sm. · E:Golden Polypody,
Hare's Foot Fern; G:Goldener Hasenfuß-
farn · ⁴ ⌒ Z10 ⓜ; trop. S-Am., nat. in
Sri Lanka

Phleum L. -n- *Poaceae* · 15 spp. · E:Cat's
Tail, Timothy; F:Fléole; G:Lieschgras
- **alpinum** L. · E:Alpine Cat's Tail, Alpine
Timothy; G:Alpen-Lieschgras · ⁴
VII-VIII; Eur.*, TR, Cauc., W-Sib., E-Sib.,
Kamchat., C-As., Afgh., E-As., nat. in
N-Am., Mex., s S-Am.
- **arenarium** L. · E:Sand Cat's Tail;
G:Sand-Lieschgras · ⊙ V-VI; Eur.: Sc, BrI,
Fr, G, Ib, Ital-P, ? Crim; Syr., NW-Afr.,
Libya; coasts
- **bertolonii** DC. · E:Small Timothy;
G:Knolliges Lieschgras · ⁴ VI-VII; Eur.*,
TR, N-Iran, W-Sib., E-Sib., C-As., NW-
Afr., nat. in USA
- *commutatum* Gaudich. = Phleum alpinum
- **hirsutum** Honck. · G:Matten-Lieschgras,
Raues Lieschgras · ⁴ VII-VIII; Eur.: Fr,
Ital-P, C-Eur., EC-Eur., Ba, RO, W-Russ.;
mts.
- **paniculatum** Huds. · G:Rispiges
Lieschgras · ⊙ V-VII; Eur.: Ib, Fr, C-Eur.,
Ital-P, H, Ba, RO, ? Crim; TR, Cauc., Iran,
Afgh., C-As.
- **phleoides** (L.) H. Karst. · E:Boehmer's
Cat's Tail; G:Steppen-Lieschgras · ⁴ VI-
VII; Eur.*, TR, Iraq, Cauc., Iran, W-Sib.,
E-Sib., C-As., Mong., China: Sinkiang;
NW-Afr.
- **pratense** L. · E:Cat's Tail, Timothy;
G:Wiesen-Lieschgras · ⁴ VI-VII Ⓝ; Eur.*,
TR, Cauc., C-As., E-Sib., Amur, Sakhal.,
N-Afr., nat. in N-Am., Austr.
- **rhaeticum** (Humphries) Rauschert ·
G:Graubündener Lieschgras · ⁴ VII-VIII;
Eur.* exc. BrI, Sc; mts.
- **subulatum** (Savi) Asch. & Graebn. ·
G:Pfriemliches Lieschgras · ⊙; Eur.: Ib,
Fr, Ital-P, Ba, PL, RO, Crim; TR, Syr.,
Iraq, Arab., Pakist., Egypt

Phlomis L. -f- *Lamiaceae* · 152 spp. · E:Sage;
F:Phlomis; G:Brandkraut
- **bracteosa** Royle · ♄ Z8 ⓐ; Him.

– **cashmeriana** Royle ex Benth. · ♃ Z7 VI-VII; Afgh., Kashmir, W-Him.
– **chrysophylla** Boiss. · ♄ Z9 ⚘; Lebanon
– **fruticosa** L. · E:Jerusalem Sage; G:Strauchiges Brandkraut · ♄ ♄ e Z8 ⚘ VI-VII; Eur.: Ital-P, Ba; TR, Cyprus, nat. in BrI, Fr, Crim
– **herba-venti** L. · ♃ Z7 VII-VIII; Eur.: Ib, Fr, Ital-P, Ba, E-Eur.; Iran
– **italica** L. · G:Balearen-Brandkraut · ♄ e Z8 ⚘; Balear.
– *laciniata* L. = Eremostachys laciniata
– **russeliana** (Sims) Benth. · F:Sauge de Jérusalem · ♃ ♄ Z7 VI-VII; TR
– **samia** L. · ♃ Z7; Eur.: GR, Maced.; TR
– **tuberosa** L. · E:Jerusalem Artichoke, Jerusalem Sage; F:Sauge de Jérusalem; G:Knollen-Brandkraut · ♃ Z6 VI-VII; Eur.: C-Eur., EC-Eur., Ba, E-Eur.; TR, Cauc., N-Iran, W-Sib., E-Sib., Amur, Mong.
– *viscosa* hort. = Phlomis russeliana
– **viscosa** Poir. · ♄ Z8 ⚘; TR, Syr., Armen.

Phlox L. -f- *Polemoniaceae* · 67 spp. · E:Phlox; F:Phlox; G:Flammenblume, Phlox
– **adsurgens** Torr. · E:Woodland Phlox; G:Immergrüner Phlox · ♃ ⤳ △ Z6 V-VI; USA: Oreg., Calif.
– **amoena** Sims · E:Hairy Phlox; G:Kelch-Phlox · ♃ Z8; USA: Ky., SE, Fla.
– × **arendsii** hort. (*P. divaricata* × *P. paniculata*) · G:Arends' Phlox · ♃ Z3; cult.
– **bifida** Beck · E:Sand Phlox; G:Sand-Phlox · ♃ ⤳ △ Z6 IV-V; USA: NCE, Ky., Okla.
– **borealis** Wherry · E:Boreal Phlox; G:Alaska-Phlox · ♃ ⤳ △ Z2 IV-V; Alaska
– *canadensis* Sweet = Phlox divaricata subsp. divaricata
– **carolina** L. · E:Thick Leaf Phlox; G:Carolina-Phlox, Dickblatt-Phlox · ♃ Z5 VI-VII; USA: NE, Ind., SE
– **divaricata** L.
– **some cultivars**
– subsp. **divaricata** · E:Blue Phlox, Louisiana Phlox, Wild Sweet William; G:Blauer Phlox · ♃ △ Z4 V-VI; Can.: E; USA: NE, NCE, SE
– subsp. **laphamii** (A.W. Wood) Wherry · G:Wald-Phlox · ♃ △ Z4 V-VI; USA: NE, NCE, NC, SC, SE, Fla.
– var. *canadensis* hort. ex Wherry = Phlox divaricata subsp. divaricata
– **douglasii** Hook. · E:Alpine Phlox, Douglas Phlox; F:Phlox de Douglas; G:Polster-Phlox · ♃ ⤳ △ Z5 V-VI; USA: Wash., Mont., Calif.
– **some cultivars**
– **drummondii** Hook. · E:Annual Phlox; G:Sommer-Phlox · ☉ Z6 VIII-IX; Can.: E; USA: NE, NCE, SC, SE, Fla.
– **some cultivars**
– **glaberrima** L. · E:Smooth Phlox; G:Kahler Phlox · ♃ ⌣ Z4 VI-VIII; USA: NE, NCE, SE, Fla., SC
– **maculata** L. · E:Sweet William Phlox; F:Phlox maculé; G:Wiesen-Phlox · ♃ Z5 VI-VII; Can.: E; USA: NE, NCE, Tenn.
– **some cultivars**
– **nivalis** Lodd. ex Sweet · E:Trailing Phlox; G:Kiefern-Phlox, Schnee-Phlox · ♃ ⤳ △ Z6 III-V; USA: Va., SE, Fla, SC
– **ovata** L. · ♃ Z5 VII-VIII; USA: NE, NCE, SE
– **paniculata** L. · E:Garden Phlox, Phlox, Summer Phlox; G:Stauden-Phlox · ♃ Z4 VII-VIII; USA: NE, NCE, SE
– **many cultivars**
– **pilosa** L. · E:Downy Phlox; G:Prärie-Phlox · ♃ Z5 IV-V; Ont., USA: NE, NCE, Kans., SC, SE, Fla.
– × **procumbens** Lehm. (*P. stolonifera* × *P. subulata*) · G:Niederliegender Phlox · ♃ △ Z4 IV-V; USA: Ky., SE, Fla.
– *stellaria* A. Gray = Phlox bifida
– **stolonifera** Sims · E:Creeping Phlox; F:Phlox à stolons; G:Kriechender Phlox, Wander-Phlox · ♃ ⤳ △ Z4 IV-V; USA: NE, Ohio, SE
– **subulata** L. · G:Polster-Phlox
– **many cultivars**
– subsp. **brittonii** (Small) Wherry · G:Kleiner Polster-Phlox · ♃ ⤳ △ Z3 V-VI; USA: Va., N.C.
– subsp. **subulata** · E:Moss Phlox, Moss Pink; F:Phlox mousse; G:Gewöhnlicher Polster-Phlox, Moos-Phlox · ♃ ⤳ △ Z3 IV-V; USA: NE, N.C., Tenn.
– var. *nivalis* (Lodd. ex Sweet) Brand = Phlox nivalis
– *suffruticosa* Vent. = Phlox carolina

Phoebe Nees -f- *Lauraceae* · 94 spp.
– **formosana** (Hayata) Hayata · ♄ e Z10 ⚘; China, Taiwan

Phoenicaulis Nutt. -m- *Brassicaceae* · 1 sp. · E:Daggerpod; G:Purpurstängel
– **cheiranthoides** Nutt. · E:Daggerpod;

G:Purpurstängel · ⊔ △ Z5 IV-VI; USA:
NW, Idaho, Nev., N-Calif.

Phoenicophorium H. Wendl. -n-
Arecaceae · 1 sp.
– **borsigianum** (K. Koch) Stuntz · ♄ e Z9
ⓦ; Seych.

Phoenix L. -f- *Arecaceae* · 14 spp. · E:Date
Palm; F:Dattier, Palmier dattier;
G:Dattelpalme, Phönixpalme
– **acaulis** Buch.-Ham. · ♄ e Z9 ⓐ; Burma,
Ind.: Assam
– **canariensis** Chabaud · E:Canary Island
Date Palm; G:Kanarische Dattelpalme · ♄
e Z9 ⓐ; Canar.
– **dactylifera** L. · E:Date, Date Palm;
G:Dattelpalme · ♄ e Z9 ⓐ ⓝ; cult.
– *humilis* Royle = Phoenix loureirii
– *leonensis* Lodd. = Phoenix reclinata
– **loureirii** Kunth · ♄ e Z9 ⓐ; S-China,
Ind.: Assam
– **pusilla** Gaertn. · ♄ e Z9 ⓐ; S-Ind., Sri
Lanka
– **reclinata** Jacq. · E:Senegal Date Palm;
G:Senegal-Dattelpalme · ♄ e Z9 ⓐ; trop.
Afr., S-Afr., Madag.
– **roebelenii** O'Brien · E:Miniature Date
Palm, Pigmy Date Palm; G:Zwerg-
Dattelpalme · ♄ e Z10 ⓦ; Laos
– **rupicola** T. Anderson · E:Cliff Date Palm,
Cliff Date; G:Klippen-Dattelpalme · ♄ e
Z9 ⓐ; Him.
– *spinosa* Schumach. = Phoenix reclinata
– **sylvestris** (L.) Roxb. · E:Silver Date
Palm; G:Silber-Dattelpalme · ♄ e Z9 ⓐ
ⓝ; Ind.
– **theophrasti** Greuter · ♄ e ⓐ ▽; Crete

Pholidota Lindl. -f- *Orchidaceae* · 42 spp.
– **articulata** Lindl. · ⊔ Z9 ⓦ V-IX ▽ ✳;
Him., Indochina, Malay. Arch.
– **pallida** Lindl. · ⊔ Z9 ⓦ IV-VII ▽ ✳;
Him., Ind., Sri Lanka, Indochina, Malay.
Arch.
– **ventricosa** (Blume) Rchb. f. · ⊔ Z9 ⓦ
III-V ▽ ✳; Malay. Arch.

Pholistoma Lilja -f- *Hydrophyllaceae* ·
3 spp. · E:Fiesta Flower; F:Némophile;
G:Schuppenmund
– **auritum** (Lindl.) Lilja · E:Blue Fiesta
Flower; G:Blauer Schuppenmund · ⊙
VI-VII; Calif.

Pholiurus Trin. -m- *Poaceae* · 1 sp. ·
G:Schuppenschwanz
– **pannonicus** (Host) Trin. · G:Schup-
penschwanz, Ungarischer Schuppenschwanz · ⊙ VI-VII; Eur.: EC-Eur., Ba,
E-Eur., ? sp.; Cauc., W-Sib., C-As.

Phormium J.R. Forst. & G. Forst. -n-
Phormiaceae · 2 spp. · E:New Zealand
Flax; F:Lin de Nouvelle-Zélande;
G:Neuseelandflachs
– *aloides* L. f. = Lachenalia aloides var.
aloides
– **colensoi** Hook. f. · E:Mountain Flax;
G:Kleiner Neuseelandflachs · ⊔ e Z8 ⓐ;
NZ
– *cookianum* Le Jol. = Phormium colensoi
– **tenax** J.R. Forst. & G. Forst. · E:New
Zealand Flax; G:Neuseelandflachs · ⊔ e
Z8 ⓐ ⓝ; NZ
– **some cultivars**
– **Cultivars:**
– **some cultivars**

Photinia Lindl. -f- *Rosaceae* · 65 spp. ·
E:Christmas Berry; F:Photinia; G:Glanz-
mispel
– *arbutifolia* (Aiton) Lindl. = Heteromeles
arbutifolia
– **beauverdiana** C.K. Schneid.
– var. **beauverdiana** · ♄ ♄ d Z6 V;
W-China, C-China
– var. **notabilis** (C.K. Schneid.) Rehder &
E.H. Wilson · ♄ d Z6; China
– **davidiana** (Decne.) Cardot
– var. **davidiana** · F:Stranvaesia;
G:Lorbeer-Glanzmispel · ♄ ♄ e Z7;
W-China
– var. **salicifolia** (Hutch.) Cardot ·
G:Weiden-Glanzmispel · ♄ e ⊗ Z7 ∧ VI;
W-China
– var. **undulata** (Decne.) Cardot ·
G:Gewellte Glanzmispel · ♄ e ⊗ Z7 ∧ VI;
W-China, C-China
– × **fraseri** Dress (*P. glabra × P.
serratifolia*) · E:Fraser's Photinia; G:Fras-
ers Glanzmispel, Rotlaubige Glanzmispel
· ♄ e Z8 ⓐ; cult.
– **glabra** (Thunb.) Maxim. · E:Chinese
Photinia, Christmasberry; G:Japanische
Glanzmispel · ♄ e Z7 ∧ V-VI; Jap.
– **nussia** (D. Don) Kalkman · ♄ e Z9 ⓐ;
Him., NE-Ind.
– **parvifolia** (E. Pritz.) C.K. Schneid. · ♄ d
Z6 V-VI; China: Hubei

– **serratifolia** (Desf.) Kalkman · E:Japanese Photinia; G:Kahle Glanzmispel · ♄ e Z8 🏠 ⋀ V-VI ⒩; China
– *serrulata* Lindl. = Photinia serratifolia
– **villosa** (Thunb.) DC.
– var. **laevis** (Thunb.) Dippel · ♄ d Z6 V-VI; Japan, Korea, ? China
– var. **villosa** · E:Photinia; G:Warzen-Glanzmispel · ♄ d Z6 VI; China, Korea, Jap.

Phragmipedium Rolfe -n- Orchidaceae · 22 spp.
– **boissierianum** (Rchb. f.) Rolfe · ⚃ Z10 🏠 VIII-X ▽ ✳; Peru, Bol.
– **caricinum** (Lindl. & Paxton) Rolfe · ⚃ Z10 🏠 IV-VII ▽ ✳; Peru, Bol.
– **caudatum** (Lindl.) Rolfe · ⚃ Z10 🏠 II-V ▽ ✳; Panama, trop. S-Am.
– **lindleyanum** (M.R. Schomb. ex Lindl.) Rolfe · ⚃ Z10 🏠 XI ▽ ✳; Venez., Guyan.
– **longifolium** (Rchb. f. & Warsz.) Rolfe
– var. **longifolium** · ⚃ Z10 🏠 ▽ ✳; Costa Rica, Panama, Col., Ecuad.
– var. **roezlii** (Rchb. f. ex Regel) Pfitzer · ⚃ Z10 🏠 I-XII ▽ ✳; Col.
– **schlimii** (Lindl. & Rchb. f.) Rolfe · ⚃ Z10 🏠 I-XII ▽ ✳; Col.
– **Cultivars:**
– **many cultivars**

Phragmites Adans. -m- Poaceae · 4 spp. · E:Reed; F:Roseau; G:Rohr, Schilf
– **australis** (Cav.) Trin. ex Steud. · E:Common Reed, Reed, Reed Grass; F:Roseau; G:Gewöhnliches Schilf, Schilfrohr · ⚃ ≈ Z5 VII-IX ⚘ ⒩; Eur.*, cosmop.
– *communis* Trin. = Phragmites australis

Phryma L. -f- Phrymaceae · 1-2 spp.
– **leptostachya** L.
– var. **asiatica** H. Hara · ⚃ ; Him., E-Sib., China, Korea, Jap.
– var. **leptostachya** · E:American Lopseed· ⚃ ; Can.: E; USA: NE, NEC, NC, SC, SE, Fla.

Phrynella Pax & K. Hoffm. -f- Caryophyllaceae · 1 sp.
– **ortegioides** (Fisch. & C.A. Mey.) Pax & K. Hoffm. · ⚃ △ VIII-IX; TR

Phrynium Willd. -n- Marantaceae · 30 spp.
– *confertum* (Benth.) K. Schum. = Ataenidia conferta
– *cylindricum* Roscoe & K. Koch = Calathea cylindrica
– *lubbersianum* (E. Morren) hort. Jacob-Makoy = Ctenanthe lubbersiana
– *setosum* Roscoe = Ctenanthe setosa
– **villosulum** Miq. · ⚃ Z10; Malay. Pen.

Phuopsis (Griseb.) Hook. f. -f- Rubiaceae · 1 sp. · E:Caucasian Crosswort; F:Crucianelle; G:Baldriangesicht
– **stylosa** (Trin.) B.D. Jacks. · E:Caucasian Crosswort; F:Crucianelle rose, Lilas de terre; G:Baldriangesicht · ⚃ △ Z7 VI-VIII; Cauc., Iran

Phygelius E. Mey. ex Benth. -m- Scrophulariaceae · 2 spp. · E:Cape Figwort; F:Fuchsia du Cap; G:Kapfuchsie
– **aequalis** Harv. ex Hiern · ♄ e Z8 🏠 ⋀ VII-IX; S-Afr.
– **capensis** E. Mey. ex Benth. · E:Cape Figwort, Cape Fuchsia; G:Kapfuchsie · ♄ e Z8 🏠 ⋀ VII-X; S-Afr.
– × **rectus** Coombes (*P. aequalis × P. capensis*) · ♄ e Z8 🏠; cult.
– **some cultivars**

Phyla Lour. -f- Verbenaceae · 11-15 spp. · E:Frogfruit; G:Teppichverbene
– *canescens* (Kunth) Greene = Phyla nodiflora var. canescens
– **nodiflora** (L.) Greene
– var. **canescens** (Kunth) Moldenke · ⚃ ⤳ Z10 🏠 VII-VIII
– var. **nodiflora** · E:Turtle Grass; G:Teppichverbene · ⚃ Z10 🏠; Eur.: Ib, Ital-P, Ba, Canar.; TR, Cauc., Iran, C-As., Him., N-Afr., trop. Am.
– var. **rosea** (D. Don) Moldenke · ⚃ ⤳ Z10 🏠 VII-VIII

Phylica L. -f- Rhamnaceae · 150 spp. · E:Cape Myrtle; F:Myrte du Cap; G:Kapmyrte
– **ericoides** L. · ♄ e Z9 🏠 XI-III; Cape
– *myrtifolia* Poir. = Phylica paniculata
– **paniculata** Willd. · ♄ e Z9 🏠; S-Afr.: Cape, Natal, Transvaal; Zimbabwe
– **plumosa** L. · ♄ e Z10 🏠; Cape

Phyllagathis Blume -f- Melastomataceae · 47 spp.
– **rotundifolia** (Jack) Blume · ♄ e Z10 🏠; Sumat.

Phyllanthus L. -m- *Euphorbiaceae* ·
833 spp. · E:Foliage Flower; F:Cerisier de
Tahiti; G:Blattblüte
- **acidus** (L.) Skeels · E:Indian Gooseberry;
G:Stachelbeerbaum · ♄ e Z10 ⓜ Ⓝ;
Madag., Ind., Malay. Arch., nat. in Fla.,
W.Ind.
- **amarus** Schumach. & Thonn. · E:Carry-
me Seed; G:Bittere Blattblüte · ♄ e Z10
ⓜ; W-Afr., nat. in Trop.
- **angustifolius** (Sw.) Sw. · ♄ e Z10 ⓜ;
Jamaica, nat. in S-Fla.
- **arbuscula** (Sw.) J.F. Gmel. · E:Foliage
Flower · ♄ e Z10 ⓜ; Jamaica
- *distichus* (L.) Müll. Arg. = Phyllanthus
acidus
- **emblica** L. · E:Emblic, Emblic Myrobalan;
G:Amblabaum · ♄ e Z10 ⓜ ⓚ ⚥ Ⓝ; Ind.,
China, Malay. Arch., Mascarene Is.
- **grandifolius** L. · ♄ e Z10 ⓜ; S-Am.
- **mimosoides** Sw. · ♄ e Z10 ⓜ; W.Ind.
- *nivosus* W.G. Sm. = Breynia disticha
- **pulcher** (Baill.) Müll. Arg. · E:Dragon-of-
the-World; G:Schöne Blattblüte · ♄ e Z10
ⓜ; Thail., Malay. Pen., Sumat., Java
- *speciosus* Jacq. = Phyllanthus arbuscula

× **Phylliopsis** Cullen & Lancaster -f-
Ericaceae (*Kalmiopsis × Phyllodoce*)
- **hillieri** Cullen & Lancaster (*Kalmiopsis
leachiana × Phyllodoce breweri*) · ♄ e; cult.

Phyllitis Hill = Asplenium
- *scolopendrium* (L.) Newman = Asplenium
scolopendrium

Phyllobolus N.E. Br. -m- *Aizoaceae* ·
32 spp.
- **canaliculatus** (Haw.) Bittrich · ⚃ ♆ Z9
ⓚ; S-Afr.
- **melanospermus** (Dinter & Schwantes)
Gerbaulet · ♄ ♆ Z9 ⓚ; Namibia
- **oculatus** (N.E. Br.) Gerbaulet · ⚃ ♆ Z9 ⓚ
VII-VIII; Cape
- **resurgens** (Kensit) Schwantes · ⚃ ♆ Z9
ⓚ; Cape

Phyllocactus Link = Epiphyllum
- *anguliger* Lem. = Epiphyllum anguliger
- *biformis* (Lindl.) Hook. = Disocactus
biformis
- *chiapensis* J.A. Purpus = Chiapasia
nelsonii
- *crenatus* (Lindl.) Lem. = Epiphyllum
crenatum

- *darrahii* K. Schum. = Epiphyllum
anguliger
- *eichlamii* Weing. = Disocactus eichlamii
- *grandis* Lem. = Epiphyllum oxypetalum
- *hookeri* (Link & Otto) Salm-Dyck =
Epiphyllum hookeri
- *oxypetalus* (DC.) Link = Epiphyllum
oxypetalum
- *phyllanthoides* (DC.) Link = Nopalxochia
phyllanthoides
- *pittieri* F.A.C. Weber = Epiphyllum pittieri
- *stenopetalus* C.F. Först. = Epiphyllum
stenopetalum
- *thomasianus* K. Schum. = Epiphyllum
thomasianum

Phyllocladus Rich. ex Mirb. -m-
Phyllocladaceae · 4 spp. · E:Celery Pine;
G:Blatteibe
- **aspleniifolius** (Labill.) Hook. f. ·
E:Celery Top Pine; G:Tasmanische
Blatteibe · ♄ e Z9 ⓚ; Tasman.
- **trichomanoides** D. Don · G:Frauenhaar-
Blatteibe
- var. **alpinus** (Hook. f.) Parl. · E:Alpine
Celery Pine; G:Gebirgs-Blatteibe · ♄ ♄ Z8
ⓚ; NZ
- var. **trichomanoides** · E:Celery Pine,
Tanekaha; G:Gewöhnliche Frauenhaar-
Blatteibe · ♄ e Z9 ⓚ; NZ, Tasman.

Phyllodoce Salisb. -f- *Ericaceae* · 6-8 spp. ·
E:Blue Heath; F:Phyllodoce; G:Blau-
heide, Moosheide
- **aleutica** (Spreng.) A. Heller · E:Mountain
Heath; G:Arktische Moosheide · ♄ e ⟿
Z2 IV-V; Alaska, Kamchat., Sakhal., Jap.
- **breweri** (A. Gray) A. Heller · E:Purple
Heather, Red Mountain Heath;
F:Phyllodoce de Brewer; G:Purpur-
Moosheide · ♄ e Z3 VI-VII; USA: Calif.
- **caerulea** (L.) Bab. · E:Blue Mountain
Heath; G:Bläuliche Moosheide · ♄ e Z2
VI-VII; Eur.: BrI, Sc, F, N-Russ.; E-Sib.,
Amur, Sakhal., Mong., Korea, Jap.,
Alaska, Can., USA: NE; Greenl.
- **empetriformis** (Sm.) D. Don · E:Pink
Mountain Heath; G:Krähenbeerblättrige
Moosheide · ♄ e Z3 V-VII; B.C., USA: NW,
Rocky Mts., Calif.
- × **intermedia** (Hook.) Rydb. (*P.
empetriformis × P. glanduliflora*) · ♄ e Z3;
cult.
- **nipponica** Makino · ♄ e Z3 V-VII; Jap.

Phyllorachis Trimen -f- *Poaceae* · 1 sp.
- **sagittata** Trimen · ⌖ Z10 ⊕ X-II; Angola, Zambia, Malawi, Tanzania

Phyllostachys Siebold & Zucc. -f- *Poaceae* · 55 (-80) spp.
- **aurea** Carrière ex Rivière & C. Rivière · E:Fishpole Bamboo, Golden Bamboo; G:Goldrohrbambus · ♄ e Z8 ∧ ⓝ; S-China
- **aureosulcata** McClure · E:Yellow Groove Bamboo · ♄ e Z6; NE-China
- **bambusoides** Siebold & Zucc. · E:Giant Timber Bamboo, Japanese Timber Bamboo · ♄ e Z8 ⓚ ⓝ; C-China, S-China
- var. *aurea* (Carrière ex Rivière & C. Rivière) Makino = Phyllostachys aurea
- **bissetii** McClure · ♄ e Z5; orig. ?
- **decora** McClure · ♄ e; orig. ?
- **edulis** (Carrière) J. Houz. · E:Tortoiseshell Bamboo · ♄ e Z7 ⓝ; ?, nat. in SE-China, Taiwan
- *fastuosa* (Lat.-Marl. ex Mitford) G. Nicholson = Semiarundinaria fastuosa
- **flexuosa** (Carrière) Rivière & C. Rivière · E:Zigzag Bamboo · ♄ e Z7 ∧; China
- *heterocycla* (Carrière) Matsum. = Phyllostachys edulis
- *marmorea* (Mitford) Asch. & Graebn. = Chimonobambusa marmorea
- *mitis* Rivière & C. Rivière = Phyllostachys sulphurea
- **nidularia** Munro · E:Broom Bamboo · ♄ e Z8 ⓚ ⓝ; China
- **nigra** (Lodd. ex Lindl.) Munro · E:Black Bamboo; G:Schwarzrohrbambus · ♄ e Z8 ∧ ⚥; China
- f. **henonis** (Mitford) Muroi · ♄ e Z8 ∧; China
- **propinqua** McClure · ♄ e Z8; China
- *pubescens* Mazel ex Houz. = Phyllostachys edulis
- *quilioi* (Carrière) Rivière & C. Rivière = Phyllostachys bambusoides
- *reticulata* (Rupr.) K. Koch = Phyllostachys bambusoides
- **sulphurea** (Carrière) Rivière & C. Rivière · ♄ e Z7; China
- f. **viridis** (R.A. Young) Ohrnb. · ♄ e Z8; China
- **viridiglaucescens** (Carrière) Rivière & C. Rivière · ♄ e Z6 ⓝ; C-China, S-China
- *viridis* (R.A. Young) McClure = Phyllostachys sulphurea f. viridis

× **Phyllothamnus** C.K. Schneid. -m- *Ericaceae* · G:Bastardblauheide (*Phyllodoce* × *Rhodothamnus*)
- **erectus** (Lindl. & Paxton) C.K. Schneid. (*Phyllodoce empetriformis* × *Rhodothamnus chamaecistus*) · ♄ e Z6 VII-VIII; cult.

Phymatodes C. Presl = Microsorum
- *punctatum* (L.) C. Presl = Microsorum punctatum
- *scandens* (G. Forst.) C. Presl = Microsorum scandens

Phymosia Desv. -f- *Malvaceae* · 8 spp.
- *acerifolia* (Nutt. ex Torr. & A. Gray) Rydb. = Sphaeralcea rivularis
- **umbellata** (Cav.) Kearney · ♄ Z10 ⓚ X; S-Mex.

Phyodina Raf. = Callisia
- *navicularis* (Ortgies) Rohweder = Callisia navicularis

Physalis L. -f- *Solanaceae* · 80 spp. · E:Japanese Lanterns; F:Amour en cage, Lanterne chinoise; G:Blasenkirsche, Erdkirsche, Judenkirsche, Lampionblume
- **alkekengi** L. · G:Blasenkirsche
- var. **alkekengi** · E:Strawberry Tomato, Winter Cherry; G:Wilde Blasenkirsche · ⌖ ♁ ⋉ Z6 V-VIII ⚥ ⚘; Eur.* exc. BrI, Sc; TR, Cauc., Iran, C-As., China, Jap., nat. in BrI, N-Am.
- var. **franchetii** (Mast.) Makino · E:Chinese Lantern Plant; F:Amour en cage; G:Lampionpflanze, Laternen-Judenkirsche · ⌖ ♁ ⋉ Z6 VI-VII ⚘; Jap., Korea, N-China
- *bunyardii* hort. = Physalis alkekengi var. alkekengi
- *edulis* Sims = Physalis peruviana
- *franchetii* Mast. = Physalis alkekengi var. franchetii
- var. *bunyardii* (hort.) Makino = Physalis alkekengi var. alkekengi
- **ixocarpa** Brot. ex Hornem. · E:Jamberry, Mexican Husk Tomato, Tomatillo; G:Mexikanische Hülsentomate, Tomatillo · ☉ ♁ Z8 ⓝ; USA: Tex., N.Mex.; Mex., ? W.Ind., nat. in N-Am.
- **peruviana** L. · E:Cape Gooseberry; G:Andenkirsche, Kapstachelbeere, Peruanische Judenkirsche · ☉ ⌖ ♁ Z8 ⓝ; ? Peru, nat. in Eur.

– **philadelphica** Lam. · E:Tomatillo;
G:Mexikanische Blasenkirsche · ⊙ Z7 Ⓝ;
USA: N.Mex., S-Tex.; Mex., Guat., nat. in
e N-Am.
– **pruinosa** L. · E:Husk Tomato · ⊙ ⚭ Z5
Ⓝ; USA: NE, NCE, Kans., SE, Fla.
– **pubescens** L. · E:Groundcherry; G:Flau-
mige Blasenkirsche · ⊙ Z7 Ⓝ; Can., USA*
exc. NW; Mex., trop. Am., nat. in S-Russ.

Physocarpus (Cambess.) Maxim.
-m- *Rosaceae* · 10 spp. · E:Ninebark;
F:Physocarpe; G:Blasenspiere
– **amurensis** (Maxim.) Maxim. · E:Amur
Ninebark; F:Physocarpe de l'Amour;
G:Amur-Blasenspiere · ♄ d Z5 VI-VII;
Korea, Manch.
– **capitatus** (Pursh) Kuntze · E:Pacific
Ninebark; G:Pazifische Blasenspiere · ♄ d
Z6 VI; USA: Oreg., Calif., Utah
– *intermedius* (Rydb.) C.K. Schneid. =
Physocarpus opulifolius var. intermedius
– **malvaceus** (Greene) Kuntze · E:Mallow
Leaf Ninebark; G:Oregon-Blasenspiere ·
♄ d Z6 VI; B.C., USA: Oreg., Rocky Mts.
– **monogynus** (Torr.) Coult. · E:Mountain
Ninebark; F:Physocarpe monogyne;
G:Colorado-Blasenspiere · ♄ d △ Z6 V-VI;
USA: NC, Rocky Mts., SW, SC
– **opulifolius** (L.) Maxim. · G:Virginische
Blasenspiere
– var. **intermedius** (Rydb.) B.L. Rob. ·
E:Atlantic Ninebark · Z5; Can.: Ont.;
USA: NE, NCE, NC, SC, Ark., Colo.
– var. **opulifolius** · E:Common Ninebark;
G:Schneeball-Blasenspiere · ♄ d Z4 V-VII;
Can.: E; USA: NE, NCE, NC, Colo., SE
– var. **tomentellus** (Ser.) Boom · ♄ d Z2

Physocaulis (DC.) Tausch -m- *Apiaceae* ·
1 sp. · G:Knotendolde
– **nodosus** (L.) W.D.J. Koch ·
G:Europäische Knotendolde · ⊙; Eur.: Ib,
F, Ital-P, Ba, RO, Crim; NW-Afr.

Physochlaina G. Don -f- *Solanaceae* ·
6 spp.
– **orientalis** (M. Bieb.) G. Don · ⏉ Z8 △;
NE-TR, Cauc., NW-Iran

Physoplexis (Endl.) Schur -f-
Campanulaceae · 1 sp. · F:Griffe du diable;
G:Schopfteufelskralle
– **comosa** (L.) Schur · E:Devil's Claw;
G:Schopfteufelskralle · ⏉ △ VII-VIII ▽;

Eur.: I, A, Slove., ? Croatia; S-Alp.

Physosiphon Lindl. -m- *Orchidaceae* ·
6 spp.
– *loddigesii* Lindl. = Physosiphon tubatus
– **tubatus** (Lodd.) Rchb. f. · ⏉ Z9 ⓛ III-V
▽ ✱; Mex., Guat.

Physostegia Benth. -f- *Lamiaceae* · 12 spp. ·
E:False Dragon Head, Obedient Plant;
F:Cataleptique; G:Gelenkblume
– **virginiana** (L.) Benth. · E:Obedient
Plant; G:Gelenkblume · ⏉ ⋉ Z4 VII-IX;
Can.: E; USA: NE, NCE, N.C., Tenn.
– **many cultivars**

Physostigma Balf. -n- *Fabaceae* · 4 spp. ·
E:Calabar Bean; G:Gottesurteilsbohne
– **venenosum** Balf. · E:Calabar,
Calabar Bean; G:Calabarbohne,
Gottesurteilsbohne · ⏉ ⚥ Z10 ⓦ ⚡ ⚔ Ⓝ;
W-Afr.

Phytelephas Ruiz & Pav. -f- *Arecaceae* ·
6 spp. · F:Palmier ivoire; G:Elfenbein-
palme, Steinnusspalme
– **macrocarpa** Ruiz & Pav. · E:Ivory Nut
Palm; G:Elfenbeinpalme, Steinnusspalme
· ♄ e Z10 ⓦ Ⓝ; Panama, Col., Ecuad.,
Peru

Phyteuma L. -n- *Campanulaceae* · 40 spp. ·
E:Rampion; F:Griffe du diable; G:Teu-
felskralle
– **betonicifolium** Vill. · E:Betony-leaved
Rampion; G:Ziestblättrige Teufelskralle ·
⏉ △ VI-IX; Eur.: F, I, C-Eur.; Alp., N-I
– *canescens* Waldst. & Kit. = Asyneuma
canescens
– **charmelii** Vill. · E:Pyrenean Rampion;
G:Apenninen-Teufelskralle · ⏉ △ VI-VIII;
Eur.: sp., F, I; mts.
– *comosum* L. = Physoplexis comosa
– **globulariifolium** Sternb. & Hoppe ·
E:Rosette-leaved Rampion; G:Kugelblu-
menblättrige Teufelskralle · ⏉ VII-VIII;
Eur.: sp., F, I, Sw, A; Pyr., Alp.
– *halleri* All. = Phyteuma ovatum
– **hedraianthifolium** Rich. Schulz ·
E:Rhaetsan Rampion; G:Rätische
Rapunzel · ⏉ VII-VIII; Eur.: Sw, I; E-Alp.
– **hemisphaericum** L. · E:Globe-headed
Rampion; G:Halbkugelige Teufelskralle ·
⏉ VII-VIII; Eur.: sp., F, I, C-Eur.; mts.
– **humile** Schleich. ex Murith · E:Dwarf

Rampion; G:Niedrige Rapunzel · ♃ VII-VIII; Eur.: I, Sw, ? F; W-Alp.
- **michelii** All. · F:Raiponce à feuilles de bétoine · ♃; F, I; S-Alp.
- subsp. *betonicifolium* (Vill.) Arcang. = Phyteuma betonicifolium
- **nanum** Schur · G:Zungenblättrige Teufelskralle · ♃ VII-IX; Eur.: A, Ba, RO; mts.
- **nigrum** F.W. Schmidt · E:Black Rampion; G:Schwarze Teufelskralle · ♃ V-VII; Eur.: F, B, G, A, CZ
- **orbiculare** L. · G:Kugel-Teufelskralle
- subsp. **orbiculare** · E:Round-headed Rampion; G:Gewöhnliche Kugel-Teufelskralle · ♃ △ VI-IX; Eur.* exc. Sc
- subsp. **tenerum** (Rich. Schulz) Korneck · G:Zarte Teufelskralle · ♃; SW-Eur.
- **ovatum** Honck. · G:Eirunde Teufelskralle · ♃ △ V-VII; Eur.: F, I, C-Eur., Slove.
- **scheuchzeri** All. · E:Horned Rampion; F:Raiponce de scheuchzer; G:Scheuchzers Teufelskralle · ♃ △ V-VIII; Eur.: F, I, Sw, Slove., Croatia; S-Alp., Apenn.
- **scorzonerifolium** Vill. · G:Schwarzwurzelblättrige Rapunzel · ♃ VI-VII; Eur.: F, I, Sw; Alp., Apenn.
- **sieberi** Spreng. · G:Siebers Teufelskralle · ♃ △ V-VII; Eur.: I, A, Slove.; SE-Alp.
- **spicatum** L. · E:Spiked Rampion; F:Raiponce en épis; G:Ährige Teufelskralle · ♃ V-VII; Eur.*
- **zahlbruckneri** Vest · G:Steirische Teufelskralle · ♃ VII-VIII; Eur.: A, Slove., Croatia; E-Alp., Croatia

Phytolacca L. -f- *Phytolaccaceae* · 35 spp. · E:Pokeweed; F:Bel ombrage, Phytolaque, Raisin d'Amérique; G:Kermesbeere
- **acinosa** Roxb. · E:Indian Poke; G:Indische Kermesbeere · ♃ ♧ Z7 VI-X ⚕ Ⓝ; China, Jap., nat. in Ind., Eur.
- **americana** L. · E:American Pokeweed; F:Phytolaque américain; G:Amerikanische Kermesbeere · ♃ ♧ Z4 VI-VIII ⚕ ☠ Ⓝ; Can.: E; USA: NE, SE, SC; Mex., nat. in S-Eur., N-Afr.
- **chilensis** (Miers ex Moq.) H. Walter · ♃ Ⓝ; Chile
- *decandra* L. = Phytolacca americana
- **dioica** L. · E:Elephant Tree, Ombu; G:Bella Sombra, Zweihäusige Kermesbeere · ♄ e Z9 Ⓚ Ⓝ; Braz., Urug., Parag., Arg., Peru, nat. in S-Eur.
- **esculenta** Van Houtte · E:Pokeweed; G:Asiatische Kermesbeere, Essbare Kermesbeere · ♃ ♧ Z6 VII-X Ⓝ; China, Korea, Jap.
- **polyandra** Batalin · G:Chinesische Kermesbeere · ♃ ♧ Z6 VII-VIII; Yunnan

Piaranthus R. Br. -m- *Asclepiadaceae* · 16 spp.
- **comptus** N.E. Br. · ♃ ♆ Z9 Ⓚ; Cape
- *foetidus* N.E. Br. = Piaranthus geminatus var. foetidus
- **geminatus** (Masson) N.E. Br.
- var. **foetidus** (N.E. Br.) Meve · ♃ ♆ Z9 Ⓚ; Cape
- var. **geminatus** · ♃ ♆ Z9 Ⓚ; orig. ?
- *globosus* A.C. White & B. Sloane = Piaranthus geminatus var. geminatus
- **parvulus** N.E. Br. · ♃ ♆ Z9 Ⓚ; Cape
- *pillansii* N.E. Br. = Piaranthus geminatus var. geminatus

Picea A. Dietr. -f- *Pinaceae* · 34 spp. · E:Spruce; F:Epicéa; G:Fichte
- **abies** (L.) H. Karst. · E:Christmas Tree, Common Spruce, Norway Spruce; G:Gewöhnliche Fichte, Rot-Fichte
- subsp. *obovata* (Ledeb.) Hultén = Picea obovata
- var. *abies* f. *chlorocarpa* (Purk.) Th. Fr. = Picea abies var. abies
- f. *erythrocarpa* (Purk.) Rehder = Picea abies var. abies
- var. **abies** · F:Epicéa commun, Sapin de Norvège; G:Europäische Rot-Fichte · ♄ e Z2 IV-VI ⚕ Ⓝ; Eur.* exc. BrI, Ib, nat. in BrI, N-Sp. (Pyr.)
- *ajanensis* Fisch. ex Carrière = Picea jezoensis subsp. jezoensis var. jezoensis
- *alba* Link = Picea glauca var. glauca
- *albertiana* S. Br. = Picea glauca var. albertiana
- **alcoquiana** (Veitch ex Lindl.) Carrière · F:Epicéa d'Alcock; G:Zweifarbige Alcock-Fichte · ♄ e Z5 Ⓝ; C-Jap.
- **asperata** Mast. · E:Chinese Spruce, Dragon Spruce; G:Raue Fichte
- var. **asperata** · F:Epicéa de Chine; G:Gewöhnliche Raue Fichte · ♄ e Z5 Ⓝ; China: Hubei, Yunnan, Sichuan
- var. *heterolepis* (Rehder & E.H. Wilson) Rehder = Picea asperata var. notabilis
- var. **notabilis** Rehder & E.H. Wilson · G:Langnadlige Raue Fichte · ♄ e Z6; W-China
- **aurantiaca** Mast. · G:Orangefarbene

Fichte · ♄ e Z5; W-China
- *balfouriana* Rehder & E.H. Wilson = Picea likiangensis var. rubescens
- **brachytyla** (Franch.) E. Pritz. · E:Northern Sargent Spruce, Sargent Spruce; G:Silber-Fichte
- var. **brachytyla** · F:Epicéa de Sargent; G:Gewöhnliche Silber-Fichte · ♄ e Z6 ⓝ; NE-Ind., W-China
- var. **complanata** (Mast.) W.C. Cheng ex Rehder · G:Großfrüchtige Silber-Fichte · ♄ e Z6; China: W-Yunnan, W-Sichuan
- **breweriana** S. Watson · E:Brewer's Weeping Spruce; F:Epicéa de Brewer; G:Siskiyou-Fichte · ♄ e Z6; USA: S-Oreg., N-Calif.
- *canadensis* (Mill.) Britton, Sterns & Poggenb. = Picea glauca var. glauca
- **engelmannii** Parry ex Engelm. · E:Engelmann Spruce; F:Epicéa d'Engelmann; G:Gewöhnliche Engelmann-Fichte · ♄ e Z4 ⓝ; Can.; W; USA: NW, Rocky Mts., SW, Calif.
- *excelsa* (Lam.) Link = Picea abies var. abies
- × **fennica** (Regel) Kom. (*P. abies × P. obovata*) · G:Finnische Fichte · ♄ e Z3; Eur.: Sc, N-Russ.
- *gemmata* Rehder & E.H. Wilson = Picea retroflexa
- **glauca** (Moench) Voss · E:White Spruce; G:Kanadische Fichte, Schimmel-Fichte
- var. **albertiana** (S. Br.) Sarg. · E:Alberta Spruce, Alberta White Spruce; G:Alberta-Schimmel-Fichte · ♄ e Z4; NW-Can.: Rocky Mts., Alberta; USA: Mont.
- var. **glauca** · E:White Spruce; F:Epicéa blanc; G:Gewöhnliche Schimmel-Fichte · ♄ e Z4 ⓝ; Alaska, Can., USA: NE, NCE, Mont., Wyo., S.Dak.
- **glehnii** (F. Schmidt) Mast. · E:Sakhalin Spruce; G:Sachalin-Fichte · ♄ e Z4; Jap., Sakhal.
- *hondoensis* Mayr = Picea jezoensis subsp. hondoensis
- × **hurstii** De Hurst (*P. engelmannii × P. pungens*) · G:Hursts Fichte · ♄ e; cult.
- **jezoensis** (Siebold & Zucc.) Carrière · E:Yezo Spruce; G:Yedo-Fichte
- subsp. **hondoensis** (Mayr) P.A. Schmidt · E:Hondo Spruce; G:Hondo-Fichte · ♄ e Z5; C-Jap.
- subsp. **jezoensis** · G:Gewöhnliche Yedo-Fichte
- var. **jezoensis** · F:Epicéa du Japon;

G:Ajan-Fichte · ♄ e Z5 ⓝ; Jap., Manch., Sakhal.
- var. *microsperma* (Lindl.) W.C. Cheng & L.K. Fu = Picea jezoensis subsp. jezoensis var. jezoensis
- **koyamae** Shiras. · E:Koyama Spruce; G:Koyamai-Fichte · ♄ e Z6; Jap., Korea
- **likiangensis** (Franch.) E. Pritz. · E:Lijiang Spruce, Purple Spruce; G:Likiang-Fichte
- var. **likiangensis** · G:Gewöhnliche Likiang-Fichte · ♄ e Z6; Bhutan, W-China
- var. *balfouriana* (Rehder & E.H. Wilson) H.G. Hillier = Picea likiangensis var. rubescens
- var. *purpurea* (Mast.) Dallim. & A.B. Jacks. = Picea purpurea
- var. **rubescens** Rehder & E.H. Wilson · G:Rötliche Likiang-Fichte · ♄ e Z6; China: Sichuan
- **mariana** (Mill.) Britton, Sterns & Poggenb. · E:Black Spruce; F:Sapinette noire; G:Schwarz-Fichte · ♄ e Z3 ⓝ; Alaska, Can., USA: NE, NCE
- × **mariorika** Boom (*P. mariana × P. omorika*) · G:Hybrid-Schwarz-Fichte · ♄ e; cult.
- **maximowiczii** Regel ex Mast. · G:Maximowiczs Fichte · ♄ e Z5; Jap.
- *nigra* (Aiton) Link = Picea mariana
- **obovata** Ledeb. · E:Siberian Spruce; G:Altai-Fichte, Sibirische Fichte · ♄ Z1 ⓝ; Eur.: Sc, Russ.; W-Sib., E-Sib., Amur, Mong., Manch., Korea
- **omorika** (Pančić) Purk. · E:Serbian Spruce; F:Sapin de Serbie; G:Omorika-Fichte, Serbische Fichte · ♄ e Z5 V ⓝ; Eur.: Bosn., YU, nat. in BrI, Sc
- **orientalis** (L.) Link · E:Caucasian Spruce, Oriental Spruce; F:Sapin du Caucase; G:Kaukasus-Fichte, Sapindus-Fichte · ♄ e Z5 ⓝ; Cauc., TR
- *polita* (Siebold & Zucc.) Carrière = Picea torano
- **pungens** Engelm. · E:Blue Spruce, Colorado Spruce; F:Epicéa du Colorado; G:Blau-Fichte, Stech-Fichte · ♄ e Z4 IV-VI; USA: Rocky Mts., SW
- **purpurea** Mast. · E:Purple-coned Spruce; G:Purpur-Fichte · ♄ e Z6; W-China
- **retroflexa** Mast. · G:China-Fichte · ♄ e Z6; W-Sichuan
- **rubens** Sarg. · E:American Red Spruce, Red Spruce; G:Amerikanische Rot-Fichte · ♄ e Z3 ⓝ; Can.: E; USA: NE, Tenn., N.C.

– *rubra* (Du Roi) Link = Picea rubens
– *sargentiana* Rehder & E.H. Wilson = Picea brachytyla var. brachytyla
– **schrenkiana** Fisch. & C.A. Mey. · F:Epicéa de Schrenk; G:Schrenks Fichte · ♄ e Z6 Ⓝ; C-As.
– **sitchensis** (Bong.) Carrière · E:Sitka Spruce; F:Epicéa de Sitka; G:Sitka-Fichte · ♄ e Z5 V Ⓝ; Alaska, Can.: B.C., USA: NW, Calif.
– **smithiana** (Wall.) Boiss. · E:Himalayan Spruce, Morinda Spruce; F:Epicéa de l'Himalaya; G:Himalaya-Fichte · ♄ e Z7 Ⓝ; Him.: Afgh., Kashmir, NW-Ind., Nepal
– **torano** (Siebold ex K. Koch) Koehne · E:Japanese Spruce, Tiger Tail Spruce; F:Epicéa de tigre; G:Tiger-schwanz-Fichte · ♄ e Z6; Jap.
– *vulgaris* Link = Picea abies var. abies
– **wilsonii** Mast. · E:Wilson's Spruce; F:Epicéa de Wilson; G:Wilsons Fichte · ♄ e Z6; W-China, C-China

Picramnia Sw. -f- *Simaroubaceae* · 45 spp.
– **antidesma** Sw. · E:Cascara · ♄ Z10 Ⓜ; Mex., Hond., W.Ind.

Picrasma Blume -f- *Simaroubaceae* · 8 spp. · E:Quassia; F:Arbre amer; G:Bitterholz
– *ailanthoides* (Bunge) Planch. = Picrasma quassioides
– **excelsa** (Sw.) Planch. · E:Bitter Ash, Bitterwood, Quassia; G:Jamaika-Bitterholz · ♄ d Z10 Ⓚ ⚥ Ⓝ; W.Ind.
– **quassioides** (D. Don) Benn. · E:Nigaki; G:Bitterholz · ♄ d Z6 V-VI; Ind., N-China, Korea, Jap., Taiwan

Picris L. -f- *Asteraceae* · c. 40 spp. · E:Oxtongue; G:Bitterkraut
– *echioides* L. = Helminthotheca echioides
– **hieracioides** L. · G:Gewöhnliches Bitterkraut
– subsp. *crepioides* (Saut.) Nyman = Picris hieracioides subsp. villarsii
– subsp. **hieracioides** · E:Hawkweed Oxtongue; G:Gewöhnliches Bitterkraut · ⊙ ⑵ Z6 VIII-X; Eur.*, TR, W-Sib., E-Sib., Amur, Sakhal., Kamchat., C-As., Him., China, Korea, Jap., nat. in N-Am., S-Am., Austr.
– subsp. **villarsii** (Jord.) Nyman · G:Stängelumfassendes Bitterkraut · ⊙ ⑵ Z6 X-VII; W-Eur., C-Eur.

Picrorhiza Royle ex Benth. -f- *Scrophulariaceae* · 1 sp.
– **kurroa** Royle ex Benth. · ⑵ VIII ⚥ ▽ ✳; W-Him.

Pieris D. Don -f- *Ericaceae* · 7 spp. · E:Pieris; F:Andromède, Piéris; G:Lavendelheide
– **floribunda** (Pursh ex Sims) Benth. & Hook. f. · E:Fetterbush, Mountain Pieris; G:Vielblütige Lavendelheide · ♄ e Z5 IV-V; USA: Va., W.Va., SE
– **formosa** (Wall.) D. Don
– var. **formosa** · ♄ e Ⓚ IV-V; E-Him., N-Burma, China: Yunnan
– var. **forrestii** (R.L. Harrow) Airy Shaw · E:Chinese Pieris; G:Chinesische Lavendelheide · Ⓚ; SW-China, Burma
– *forrestii* R.L. Harrow = Pieris formosa var. forrestii
– **japonica** (Thunb.) D. Don ex G. Don · E:Japanese Pieris, Lily-of-the-Valley Bush; F:Piéride du Japon; G:Japanische Lavendelheide · ♄ e Z6 III-V ❀; Jap.
– **some cultivars**
– *lucida* (Lam.) Rehder = Lyonia lucida
– *mariana* (L.) Benth. & Hook. f. = Lyonia mariana
– **nana** (Maxim.) Makino · ♄ e △ III-V; Jap., Sakhal., Kamchat.
– **taiwanensis** Hayata · ♄ e ⋀ III-IV; Taiwan
– **Cultivars:**
– **many cultivars**

Pilea Lindl. -f- *Urticaceae* · 200+ (-600?) spp. · E:Artillery Plant; F:Piléa, Plante au feu d'artifice; G:Kanonenblume, Kanonierblume
– **cadierei** Gagnep. & Guillaumin · E:Aluminium Plant; G:Vietnamesische Kanonierblume · ⑵ e Z10 Ⓜ Ⓚ; N-Vietn.
– *callitrichoides* (Humb., Bonpl. & Kunth) Kunth = Pilea microphylla
– **crassifolia** (Willd.) Blume · ⑵ e Z10 Ⓜ III-V; Jamaica
– *globosa* Wedd. = Pilea serpyllacea
– **grandifolia** (L.) Blume · ♄ e Z10 Ⓜ; Jamaica
– *grandis* Wedd. = Pilea grandifolia
– **involucrata** (Sims) Urb. · E:Friendship Plant, Pan American Plant; G:Eingehüllte Kanonierblume · ⑵ e Z10 Ⓜ; W.Ind., C-Am., S-Am.
– **microphylla** (L.) Liebm. · E:Artillery

Plant, Gunpowder Plant; G:Artilleriep-
flanze, Kleinblättrige Kanonierblume · ⚁
e Z10 ⓦ ⓚ; Mex., C-Am., trop. S-Am.,
nat. in GR, TR
– *muscosa* Lindl. = Pilea microphylla
– **nummarifolia** (Sw.) Wedd. ·
E:Creeping Charlie; G:Münzenblät-
trige Kanonierblume · ⚁ e ↝ Z10 ⓦ;
Panama, W.Ind., trop. S-Am.
– **peperomioides** Diels · ⚁ e Z10 ⓦ ⓚ;
W-Yunnan
– *pubescens* hort. non Liebm. = Pilea
involucrata
– **repens** (Sw.) Wedd. · E:Black-leaf
Panamica; G:Dunkelblättrige Kanonierblume · ⚁ e Z10 ⓦ; W.Ind.
– **serpyllacea** (Kunth) Liebm. · ♄ e Z10 ⓚ;
Peru
– *spruceana* Wedd. = Pilea involucrata

Pileostegia Hook. f. & Thomson -f-
Hydrangeaceae · 4 spp.
– **viburnoides** Hook. f. & Thomson · ♄
e ⚲ Z8 ⓚ ∧ IX; N-Ind.: Khasia Hills;
S-China, Taiwan

Pilocarpus Vahl -m- *Rutaceae* · 22 spp. ·
E:Jaborandi; F:Jaborandi, Pilocarpe;
G:Jaborandistrauch
– **jaborandi** Holmes · E:Jaborandi;
G:Gewöhnlicher Jaborandistrauch · ♄ e
Z10 ⓦ ⚲ ✿; trop. S-Am.
– **microphyllus** Stapf · E:Maranhao
Jaborandi; G:Brasilianischer Jaborandistrauch · ♄ e Z10 ⓦ ⚲ ✿; NE-Braz.
– **pennatifolius** Lem. · ♄ e Z10 ⓦ ⚲ ✿;
Parag., S-Braz.
– **racemosus** Vahl · E:Guadalupe Jaborandi; G:Westindischer Jaborandistrauch
· ♄ ♄ e Z10 ⓦ ⚲ ✿; W.Ind.
– **spicatus** A. St.-Hil. · ♄ e Z10 ⓦ ✿; Braz.

Pilocereus K. Schum. = Pilosocereus
– *celsianus* Salm-Dyck = Oreocereus
celsianus var. celsianus
– *erythrocephalus* K. Schum. = Denmoza
rhodacantha
– *fossulatus* Labour. = Oreocereus pseudofossulatus
– *glaucescens* Labour. = Pilosocereus
glaucescens
– *lanatus* (Humb., Bonpl. & Kunth) F.A.C.
Weber = Espostoa lanata
– *leucostele* (Gürke) Werderm. = Stephanocereus leucostele

– *macrostibas* K. Schum. = Neoraimondia
arequipensis
– *palmeri* (Rose) F.M. Knuth = Pilosocereus
leucocephalus
– *pentaedrophorus* Labour. = Pilosocereus
pentaedrophorus
– *schottii* (Engelm.) Lem. = Lophocereus
schottii
– *senilis* (Haw.) Lem. = Cephalocereus
senilis

Pilosella Hill = Hieracium
– *aurantiaca* (L.) F.W. Schultz & Sch. Bip.
= Hieracium aurantiacum
– *caespitosa* (Dumort.) P.D. Sell & C. West
= Hieracium caespitosum
– *floribunda* (Wimm. & Grab.) Arv.-Touv. =
Hieracium × floribundum
– *officinarum* F.W. Schultz & Sch. Bip. =
Hieracium pilosella
– *piloselloides* (Vill.) Soják = Hieracium
piloselloides

Pilosocereus Byles & G.D. Rowley
-m- *Cactaceae* · 35 spp. · F:Cierge pileux;
G:Haarsäulenkaktus
– **glaucescens** (Labour.) Byles & G.D.
Rowley · ♄ ♈ Z9 ⓚ ▽ ✳; E-Braz.
– **leucocephalus** (Posegl.) Byles & G.D.
Rowley · ♄ ♈ Z9 ⓚ ▽ ✳; E-Mex.
– *maxonii* (Rose) Byles & G.D. Rowley =
Pilosocereus leucocephalus
– *palmeri* (Rose) Byles & G.D. Rowley =
Pilosocereus leucocephalus
– **pentaedrophorus** (Labour.) Byles &
G.D. Rowley · ♄ ♈ Z9 ⓚ ▽ ✳; E-Braz.:
Bahia
– **werdermannianus** (Buining & Brederoo) F. Ritter · ♄ ♈ Z9 ⓚ ▽ ✳; E-Braz.:
Minas Gerais

Pilularia L. -f- *Marsileaceae* · 5 spp. ·
E:Pillwort; F:Pilulaire; G:Pillenfarn
– **globulifera** L. · E:Pillwort; G:Gewöhnli-
cher Pillenfarn · ⚁ ≈ Z7 VII-IX; Eur.*
– **minuta** Durieu ex A. Braun · ⚁ ≈ Z8
ⓦ; Eur.: P, Balear., F, Cors, Sard., Sic.

Pimelea Banks & Sol. -f- *Thymelaeaceae* ·
108 spp. · E:Rice Flower; F:Pimelea;
G:Glanzstrauch
– **ferruginea** Labill. · E:Pink Rice Flower ·
♄ e Z9 ⓚ IV-V; W-Austr.
– **linifolia** Sm. · E:Slender Riceflower;
G:Leinblättriger Glanzstrauch · ♄ e Z9 ⓚ

V; Austr., Tasman.
- **prostrata** (J.R. Forst. & G. Forst.)
  Willd. · ♄ e Z9 ⓚ; NZ

Pimenta Lindl. -f- *Myrtaceae* · 15 spp. ·
  E:Allspice; F:Poivre de la Jamaïque,
  Quatre-épices; G:Nelkenpfeffer,
  Pimentbaum
- *acris* (Sw.) Kostel. = Pimenta racemosa
- **dioica** (L.) Merr. · E:Allspice, Jamaica
  Pepper; G:Nelkenpfeffer, Pimentbaum · ♄
  e Z10 � ⚥ Ⓝ; Mex., C-Am., W.Ind.
- *officinalis* Lindl. = Pimenta dioica
- **racemosa** (Mill.) J.W. Moore · E:Bayrum
  Tree; G:Bayarumbaum · ♄ e Z10 ⓚ ⚥ Ⓝ;
  W.Ind., Venez., Guyan.

Pimpinella L. -f- *Apiaceae* · c. 150 spp. ·
  E:Burnet Saxifrage; F:Anis vert, Boucage,
  Pimpinelle; G:Anis, Bibernelle, Pimpi-
  nelle
- **alpina** Vest ex Schult. · E:Alpine Anise;
  G:Alpen-Bibernelle · ⚃ VII-X; Eur.: A, Sw,
  N-I, Slov, ? Croat, Bosn., ? Serb., ? Maz.,
  RO
- **anisum** L. · E:Anise, Aniseed, Common
  Anise; G:Anis · ☉ VII-VIII ⚥ Ⓝ; ? W-As.,
  nat. in Eur.
- **major** (L.) Huds. · E:Greater Burnet
  Saxifrage; G:Große Bibernelle · ⚃ Z5 VI-X
  ⚥ Ⓝ; Eur.*, Cauc.
- **nigra** Mill. · G:Schwarze Bibernelle · ⚃
  VII-IX; Eur.: C-Eur., EC-Eur., S-Sc, Russ,
  Ba, N-I +
- **peregrina** L. · G:Fremde Bibernelle ·
  ☉ Z6 V-VII; Eur.: Ib, Fr, Ital-P, Ba, RO,
  Crim; TR, Syr., Cauc., C-As., Egypt
- **saxifraga** L. · E:Burnet Saxifrage, Lesser
  Burnet Saxifrage; G:Kleine Bibernelle · ⚃
  Z4 VII-X ⚥ Ⓝ; Eur.*, TR, Cauc., W-Iran,
  Him., W-Sib., E-Sib., C-As., nat. in
  N-Am., NZ

Pinanga Blume -f- *Arecaceae* · 131 sp. ·
  E:Bunga, Pinang; F:Palmier; G:Pinang-
  palme
- **coronata** (Blume ex Mart.) Blume · ♄ e
  Z10 �; Sumat., Java
- **decora** Linden & Rodigas · ♄ e Z10 �;
  Kalimantan
- *kuhlii* Blume = Pinanga coronata

Pinellia Ten. -f- *Araceae* · 6 spp. ·
  E:Pinellia; F:Pinellia; G:Pinellie
- **ternata** (Thunb.) Breitenb. · E:Pinellia;

G:Dreizählige Pinellie · ⚃ Z6 IV-VI ⚥ ;
China, Korea, Jap.

Pinguicula L. -f- *Lentibulariaceae* · 46 spp. ·
  E:Butterwort; F:Grassette; G:Fettkraut
- **alpina** L. · E:Alpine Butterwort; G:Alpen-
  Fettkraut · ⚃ △ ∿ Z3 V-VI ▽; Eur.*,
  E-Sib., Him., W-China; mts.
- *caudata* Schltdl. = Pinguicula moranensis
- **cyclosecta** Casper · ⚃ ∿ Z10 ⓚ; Mex.
- **grandiflora** Lam. · E:Butterwort, Greater
  Butterwort; G:Großblütiges Fettkraut
  · ⚃ △ ∿ Z7 VI; Eur.: sp.(Cordillera
  Cantábrica), F, Sw, IRL, nat. in BrI
- **gypsicola** Brandegee · ⚃ ∿ Z10 ⓚ ⌷
  VI-VIII; Mex.
- **leptoceras** Rchb. · E:Southern Butter-
  wort; G:Dünnsporniges Fettkraut · ⚃ ∿
  ⓚ VI-VIII; Eur.: F, I, Sw, A; Alp., Apenn.,
  Alpi Apuani
- **lusitanica** L. · E:Pale Butterwort · ⚃ ∿
  Z7; Eur.: BrI, F, Ib; Moroc., Alger.
- **moranensis** Kunth · ⚃ ∿ Z10 � ⓚ ⌷
  VI-IX; Mex.
- **villosa** L. · E:Hairy Butterwort;
  G:Haariges Fettkraut · ⚃ ∿ ; Eur.: Sc,
  N-Russ.
- **vulgaris** L. · E:Bog Violet, Butterwort,
  Common Butterwort; G:Gewöhnliches
  Fettkraut · ⚃ ∿ Z3 V-VI ⚥ ▽; Eur.*,
  W-Sib., Manch., Moroc., Greenl., Can.,
  USA: NE, NCE, NC, NW

Pinus L. -f- *Pinaceae* · 109 spp. · E:Pine;
  F:Pin; G:Föhre, Kiefer, Spirke
- *abies* L. = Picea abies var. abies
- **albicaulis** Engelm. · E:Whitebark Pine;
  G:Weißstämmige Zirbel-Kiefer · ♄ e Z6;
  Can.: B.C., Alta.; USA: NW, Calif., Rocky
  Mts.
- **aristata** Engelm. · E:Bristlecone Pine;
  F:Pin aristé; G:Grannen-Kiefer · ♄ ♄ e Z6
  Ⓝ; USA: Colo., SW
- **armandii** Franch. · E:Armand Pine; F:Pin
  d'Armand; G:Gewöhnliche Chinesische
  Weiß-Kiefer · ♄ e Z6 Ⓝ; W-China,
  C-China, Korea, Taiwan
- *australis* F. Michx. = Pinus palustris
- *austriaca* Höss = Pinus nigra subsp. nigra
- **ayacahuite** C. Ehrenb. ex Schltdl. ·
  E:Mexican White Pine; G:Gewöhnliche
  Mexikanische Weymouth-Kiefer · ♄ e ⋈
  Z8 ⓚ Ⓝ; Mex., Guat.
- **balfouriana** A. Murray bis · E:Foxtail
  Pine; G:Nördliche Fuchsschwanz-Kiefer ·

ħ e Z7; Calif.; mts.
- **banksiana** Lamb. · E:Jack Pine, Northern Scrub Pine; F:Pin de Banks; G:Banks' Kiefer, Strauch-Kiefer · ħ ħ e Z3 V Ⓝ; Can., USA: NE, NCE
- **brutia** Ten. · E:Calabrian Pine; G:Gewöhnliche Kalabrische Kiefer · ħ e Z8 Ⓐ; GR, Crim, TR, Cyprus, Lebanon
- **bungeana** Zucc. ex Endl. · E:Lacebark Pine; G:Bunges Kiefer, Tempel-Kiefer · ħ e Z6; NW-China
- **canariensis** C. Sm. · E:Canary Island Pine; G:Kanarische Kiefer · ħ e Z9 Ⓐ Ⓝ; Canar.
- **caribaea** Morelet · E:Caribbean Pine, Nicaraguan Pine; G:Gewöhnliche Karibische Kiefer, Nicaragua-Kiefer · ħ e Z10 Ⓦ Ⓝ; SE-USA, C-Am., Bahamas
- **cembra** L. · E:Arolla Pine, Swiss Stone Pine; F:Arolle, Pin cembro; G:Arve, Zirbel-Kiefer · ħ e Z4 VI-VII Ⓝ; Eur.: C-Eur., EC-Eur., I, E-Eur., nat. in Sc
- var. *sibirica* (Du Tour) G. Don = Pinus sibirica
- **cembroides** Zucc. · E:Mexican Nut Pine, Mexican Stone Pine, Pinyon Pine; G:Mexikanische Nuss-Kiefer · ħ e Z8 Ⓐ Ⓝ; SW-USA, Baja Calif., Mex.
- var. *monophylla* (Torr. & Frém.) Voss = Pinus monophylla
- *clusiana* Clemente = Pinus nigra subsp. salzmannii
- **contorta** Douglas ex Loudon · E:Lodgepole Pine, Shore Pine; G:Dreh-Kiefer, Küsten-Kiefer
- var. **contorta** · E:Beach Pine; F:Pin tordu; G:Gewöhnliche Dreh-Kiefer · ħ e Z5 IV-VI Ⓝ; Alaska, Can.: BC; USA: NW, Calif., Nev.
- var. **latifolia** Engelm. ex S. Watson · E:Rocky Mountain Lodgepole Pine; G:Rocky-Mountain-Dreh-Kiefer · ħ e Z5; Alaska, Can.: W; USA: NW, Rocky Mts., S.Dak.
- var. **murrayana** (Balf.) Engelm. · E:Sierra Lodgepole Pine; G:Sierra-Dreh-Kiefer · ħ e Z8 Ⓐ; Calif., Mex. (Baja Calif.)
- **coulteri** D. Don · E:Big Cone Pine, Coulter Pine; F:Pin à gros cônes; G:Coulters Kiefer · ħ e Z7 ∧; Calif., Baja Calif.
- **densiflora** Siebold & Zucc. · E:Japanese Red Pine; F:Pin rouge du Japon; G:Japanische Rot-Kiefer · ħ e Z6 Ⓝ; Jap., Korea

- *divaricata* (Aiton) Dum.-Cours. = Pinus banksiana
- *excelsa* Wall. ex D. Don = Pinus wallichiana
- **flexilis** E. James · E:Limber Pine; F:Pin des Rocheuses; G:Gewöhnliche Nevada-Zirbel-Kiefer · ħ e Z6 Ⓝ; Can.: B.C., Alta.; USA: NW, Rocky Mts., SW, NC
- **gerardiana** Wall. ex D. Don · E:Chilgoza Pine; G:Chilgoza-Kiefer, Gerards Kiefer · ħ e Z7 Ⓝ; Afgh., Pakist., Kashmir
- *griffithii* McClell. = Pinus wallichiana
- × **hakkodensis** Makino (*P. parviflora* var. *parviflora* × *P. pumila*) · G:Honshu-Kiefer · ħ e Z4; Jap.
- **halepensis** Mill. · E:Aleppo Pine; G:Aleppo-Kiefer, See-Kiefer · ħ e Z8 Ⓐ ♀ Ⓝ; Eur.: Ib, Fr, Ital-P, Ba, Crim; TR, Syr., Palest., NW-Afr., Libya
- var. *brutia* (Ten.) A. Henry = Pinus brutia
- **heldreichii** H. Christ · E:Bosnian Pine, Palebark Pine; F:Pin blanc de Bosnie; G:Panzer-Kiefer, Schlangenhaut-Kiefer · ħ e Z6 Ⓝ; Eur.: Ba, S-I; mts.
- var. *leucodermis* (Antoine) Markgr. & Fitschen = Pinus heldreichii
- *inops* Bong. = Pinus contorta var. contorta
- **jeffreyi** Balf. · E:Jeffrey's Pine; F:Pin de Jeffrey; G:Jeffreys Kiefer · ħ e Z6 Ⓝ; USA: S-Oreg., Calif.; Mex.: Baja Calif.
- **koraiensis** Siebold & Zucc. · E:Korean Pine; F:Pin de Corée; G:Korea-Kiefer · ħ e Z5 Ⓝ; Amur, Manch., Korea, Jap.
- **lambertiana** Douglas · E:Sugar Pine; G:Zucker-Kiefer · ħ e Z7 Ⓝ; USA: Oreg., Nev., Calif.; Baja Calif.
- *laricio* Poir. = Pinus nigra subsp. laricio
- **longaeva** D.K. Bailey · E:Ancient Pine; G:Langlebige Kiefer · ħ e Z6; USA: Calif., Utah, Nev.
- *longifolia* Roxb. ex Lamb. = Pinus roxburghii
- *maritima* Lam. = Pinus pinaster
- **merkusii** Jungh. & de Vriese · E:Merkus Pine, Sumatran Pine; G:Merkus' Kiefer, Sumatra-Kiefer · ħ e Z10 Ⓦ Ⓝ; Burma, Sumatra, Phil.
- **monophylla** Torr. & Frém. · E:One Leaf Pinyon, Single Leaf Pinyon; G:Einnadlige Weymouths-Kiefer · ħ e Z7 Ⓝ; USA: Rocky Mts, Calif., Ariz.; Mex.: Baja Calif.
- **montana** Mill. = Pinus mugo subsp. mugo
- subsp. *mughus* (Scop.) Willk. = Pinus

mugo subsp. mugo
- subsp. *pumilio* (Haenke) Willk. = Pinus mugo subsp. mugo
- var. *rostrata* (Antoine) Asch. & Graebn. = Pinus mugo subsp. uncinata
- var. *rotundata* (Link) Asch. & Graebn. = Pinus mugo subsp. rotundata
- **montezumae** Lamb. · E:Montezuma Pine; G:Gewöhnliche Montezuma-Kiefer · ♄ e Z9 ⒶⒹ; B:C., USA: NW, Calif; Mex.
- **monticola** Douglas ex D. Don · E:Californian Mountain Pine, Silver Pine, Western White Pine; G:Westliche Weymouths-Kiefer · ♄ e Z6 Ⓝ; Can.; W; USA: NW, Rocky Mts., Calif.
- *mughus* Scop. = Pinus mugo subsp. mugo
- **mugo** Turra · E:Mountain Pine; G:Berg-Kiefer, Krummholz-Kiefer, Latsche, Leg-Föhre
- subsp. **mugo** · F:Pin mugho; G:Gewöhnliche Berg-Kiefer, Gewöhnliche Leg-Föhre · ♄ e Z4 V-VII; Eur.: Fr, Ital-P, C-Eur., EC-Eur., Ba, E-Eur.
- subsp. *pumilio* (Haenke) Franco = Pinus mugo subsp. mugo
- subsp. **rotundata** (Link) Janch. & H. Neumayer · G:Moor-Kiefer, Moor-Spirke · ♄ ♄ e Z4; Eur.: G, A, PL, Slova.
- subsp. **uncinata** (Ramond ex DC.) Domin · E:Mountain Pine; G:Berg-Spirke, Haken-Kiefer · ♄ e Z4 VI-VII; Eur.: sp., F, I, C-Eur.; mts. C-Sp., Pyr., Alp.
- var. *mughus* (Scop.) Zenari = Pinus mugo subsp. mugo
- var. *pumilio* (Haenke) Zenari = Pinus mugo subsp. mugo
- var. *rostrata* (Antoine) Hoopes = Pinus mugo subsp. uncinata
- **nigra** J.F. Arnold · E:Black Pine; G:Schwarz-Kiefer
- subsp. **nigra** · E:Austrian Pine, Black Pine, Corsican Pine; F:Pin noir; G:Gewöhnliche Schwarz-Kiefer · ♄ e Z5 V-VI ⚥ Ⓝ; Eur.: A, I, Ba, nat. in BrI, Sc, EC-Eur.
- subsp. **pallasiana** (Lamb.) Holmboe · E:Crimean Pine; G:Taurische Schwarz-Kiefer · ♄ e Z5; Eur.: Ba, Crim; TR, Cyprus, Cauc.
- subsp. **salzmannii** (Dunal) Franco · E:Pyrenees Pine; G:Pyrenäen-Schwarz-Kiefer · ♄ e Z5; SW-F, sp., NW-Moroc.
- var. *austriaca* (Höss) Badoux = Pinus nigra subsp. nigra
- var. *caramanica* (Loudon) Rehder =

Pinus nigra subsp. pallasiana
- var. *cebennensis* (Godr.) Rehder = Pinus nigra subsp. salzmannii
- var. *poiretiana* (Loudon) C.K. Schneid. = Pinus nigra subsp. larico
- subsp. **larico** (Poir.) Maire · E:Corsican Pine; F:Pin larico; G:Korsische Schwarz-Kiefer · ♄ e Z5; Eur.: Cors, I (Calabria), Sic.
- var. *calabrica* (Loudon) C.K. Schneid. = Pinus nigra subsp. larico
- var. *corsicana* (Loudon) Hyl. = Pinus nigra subsp. larico
- var. *maritima* (Aiton) Melville = Pinus nigra subsp. larico
- *nigricans* Host = Pinus nigra subsp. nigra
- *omorika* Pančić = Picea omorika
- *pallasiana* Lamb. = Pinus nigra subsp. pallasiana
- **palustris** Mill. · E:Longleaf Pine, Southern Pine; G:Sumpf-Kiefer · ♄ e Z8 ⒶⒹ ⚥ Ⓝ; USA: Va., SE, Tex.
- **parviflora** Siebold & Zucc. · E:South Japanese White Pine; G:Südliche Mädchen-Kiefer · ♄ e Z6; Jap.
- **peuce** Griseb. · E:Macedonian Pine; F:Pin de Macédoine, Pin des Balkans; G:Mazedonische Kiefer, Rumelische Strobe · ♄ e Z5 Ⓝ; Eur.: Ba; mts.
- *picea* L. = Abies alba
- **pinaster** Aiton · E:Maritime Pine; G:Gewöhnliche Strand-Kiefer · ♄ e Z8 ⒶⒹ ⚥ Ⓝ; Eur.: Ib, Fr, Ital-P; NW-Afr, nat. in BrI, Ba
- **pinea** L. · E:Stone Pine, Umbrella Pine; G:Pinie, Schirm-Kiefer · ♄ e Z8 ⒶⒹ Ⓝ; Eur.: Ib, Fr, Ital-P, Ba; TR, Levant
- **ponderosa** Douglas ex C. Lawson · E:Ponderosa Pine, Western Yellow Pine; G:Gelb-Kiefer
- var. **ponderosa** · F:Pin jaune du Nouveau Monde; G:Großzapfige Gelb-Kiefer · ♄ e Z5 Ⓝ; Can.: B.C.; USA: NW, Calif., Nev.
- var. **scopulorum** Engelm. · E:Rocky Mountain Pine; G:Kleinzapfige Gelb-Kiefer · ♄ e Z5; Can.: B.C.; USA: Rocky Mts., NC, SC; Mex.
- **pumila** (Pall.) Regel · E:Dwarf Siberian Pine, Japanese Stone Pine; G:Ostasiatische Zwerg-Kiefer, Zwerg-Zirbel-Kiefer · ♄ e △ Z4 Ⓝ; Jap., Kamchat., NE-Sib.
- *pumilio* Haenke = Pinus mugo subsp. mugo
- **pungens** Lamb. · E:Hickory Pine, Prickly Pine, Table Mountain Pine;

G:Hickory-Kiefer, Stech-Kiefer · ♄ e Z6;
USA: NE, SE
- **radiata** D. Don · E:Monterey Pine;
G:Gewöhnliche Monterey-Kiefer · ♄ e Z8
⌂ Ⓝ; Calif., Baja Calif., nat. in NZ, Austr.
- **resinosa** Aiton · E:American Red Pine,
Red Pine; G:Amerikanische Rot-Kiefer,
Harzige Kiefer · ♄ e Z5 Ⓝ; Can.: E; USA:
NE, NCE, NCE
- **rigida** Mill. · E:Northern Pitch Pine;
G:Pech-Kiefer · ♄ e Z6 Ⓝ; Can.: E; USA:
NE, Ohio, SE
- *rotunda* Link = Pinus mugo subsp.
rotundata
- **roxburghii** Sarg. · E:Chir Pine, Indian
Longleaf Pine; G:Chir-Kiefer, Emodi-
Kiefer · ♄ e Z9 ⌂ Ⓝ; Him.: Afgh.,
Kashmir, NW-Ind., Nepal, Bhutan
- **sabineana** Douglas ex D. Don · E:Digger
Pine; G:Nuss-Kiefer, Weiß-Kiefer · ♄ e ✕
Z7 ⋀ Ⓝ; Calif.
- *salzmannii* Dunal = Pinus nigra subsp.
salzmannii
- × **schwerinii** Fitschen (*P. strobus* × *P.
wallichiana*) · G:Schwerins Kiefer · ♄ e
Z5; cult.
- **sibirica** Du Tour · E:Siberian Pine;
G:Sibirische Zirbel-Kiefer · ♄ e Z1 Ⓝ;
E-Russ., Sib.
- **strobus** L. · E:White Pine; F:Pin Wey-
mouth ; G:Gewöhnliche Weymouths-
Kiefer, Strobe · ♄ e Z5 IV-V Ⓝ; Can.: E;
USA; NE, NCE, SE
- **sylvestris** L. · E:Scots Pine; G:Föhre,
Wald-Kiefer
- var. **mongolica** Litv. · E:Mongolian Pine;
G:Mongolische Wald-Kiefer · Z2
- var. **sylvestris** · F:Pin sylvestre;
G:Gewöhnliche Wald-Kiefer · ♄ e Z1 V-VI
⚘ Ⓝ; Eur.*, TR, Cauc., W-Sib., E-Sib.,
Amur, Mong., Manch., nat. in N-Am.
- **tabuliformis** Carrière · E:Chinese Red
Pine; G:Gewöhnliche Chinesische
Rot-Kiefer · ♄ e Z5 Ⓝ; W-China, N-China,
Korea
- **taeda** L. · E:Loblolly Pine; G:Weihrauch-
Kiefer · ♄ e Z7 Ⓝ; USA: NE, SE, Fla., SC
- *thunbergiana* Franco = Pinus thunbergii
- **thunbergii** Parl. · E:Black Pine, Japanese
Black Pine; G:Japanische Schwarz-Kiefer,
Thunbergs Kiefer · ♄ e Z6 Ⓝ; Jap.
- *uncinata* Ramond ex DC. = Pinus mugo
subsp. uncinata
- subsp. *rotundata* (Link) Janch. & H. Neumayer = Pinus mugo subsp. rotundata

- **wallichiana** A.B. Jacks. · E:Blue Pine;
F:Pin pleureur de l'Himalaya; G:Gewöhn-
liche Tränen-Kiefer · ♄ e Z7 Ⓝ; Afgh.,
Him.

Piper L. -n- *Piperaceae* · c. 2000 spp. ·
E:Pepper; F:Poivrier; G:Pfeffer
- **aduncum** L. · E:Big Pepper; G:Geboge-
ner Pfeffer · ♄ ♄ e Z10 ⌂; Mex., C-Am.,
W.Ind., trop. S-Am.
- **angustifolium** Ruiz & Pav. · ♄ Z10 ⌂ ⚘
Ⓝ; Mex., C-Am., Westind., S-Am.
- **betle** L. · E:Betel, Betel Pepper; G:Betel-
Pfeffer, Kau-Pfeffer · ♄ e ⚘ Z10 ⌂ ⚘ Ⓝ;
Ind., Malay. Arch.
- *bicolor* Yunck. = Piper magnificum
- *celtidifolium* Desf. = Piper unguiculatum
- **clusii** (Miq.) C. DC. · ⚘ Z10 ⌂ Ⓝ; W-Afr.
- **crocatum** Ruiz & Pav. · ♄ e ⚘ Z10 ⌂;
Peru
- **cubeba** L. f. · E:Tailed Pepper; G:Kube-
ben-Pfeffer ♄ e ⚘ Z10 ⌂ ⚘ ⚘ Ⓝ; w
Malay. Arch.
- **guineense** Schumach. & Thonn. ·
E:Ashanti Pepper; G:Aschanti-Pfeffer · ♄
e ⚘ Z10 ⌂ Ⓝ; trop. Afr.
- **longum** L. · E:Indian Long Pepper, Long
Pepper; G:Langer Pfeffer · ♄ e ⚘ Z10 ⌂
⚘ Ⓝ; E-Him.
- **magnificum** Trel. · ♄ e Z10 ⌂; Peru
- **methysticum** G. Forst. · E:Kava Kava,
Kava Pepper; G:Kava Kava · ♄ e Z10 ⌂ ⚘
⚘ Ⓝ; Fiji, Pacific Is.
- **nigrum** L. · E:Brown's Pepper, Pepper
Plant; G:Echter Pfeffer, Schwarzer
Pfeffer, Weißer Pfeffer · ♄ e ⚘ Z10 ⌂ ⚘
Ⓝ; ? Ind. (Malabar Coast)
- **ornatum** N.E. Br. · E:Celebes Pepper · ♄
e ⚘ Z10 ⌂; Sulawesi
- **porphyrophyllum** (Lindl.) N.E. Br. ·
E:Malay Pepper; G:Malayischer Pfeffer ·
♄ e ⚘ Z10 ⌂; Malay. Pen., Kalimantan
- **retrofractum** Vahl · E:Java Longpepper;
G:Java-Pfeffer · ♄ e Z10 ⌂ Ⓝ; Malay.
Arch.
- **saigonense** C. DC. · ⚘ Z10 ⌂ Ⓝ; Vietn.
- **sylvaticum** Roxb. · E:Mountain Long
Pepper · ♄ e ⚘ ∿ Z10 ⌂; E-Him.
- **unguiculatum** Ruiz & Pav. · ♄ e Z10 ⌂;
Peru

Piptanthocereus (A. Berger) Riccob. =
Cereus
- *azureus* (Pfeiff.) Riccob. = Cereus
aethiops

– *chalybaeus* (Otto) Riccob. = Cereus
aethiops
– *jamacaru* (DC.) Riccob. = Cereus
jamacaru
– *peruvianus* (L.) Riccob. = Cereus
repandus
– *validus* (Haw.) Riccob. = Cereus validus

Piptanthus Sweet -m- *Fabaceae* · 2 spp. ·
E:Evergreen Laburnum; G:Nepalgold-
regen
– **nepalensis** (Hook.) Sweet · E:Evergreen
Laburnum, Nepal Laburnum; G:Nepal-
goldregen · ♄ e Z8 ⌂ V; Nepal, Sikkim,
Bhutan

Piptatherum P. Beauv. -n- · c. 50 spp. ·
G:Grannenreis
– **miliaceum** (L.) Coss. · E:Rice Millet,
Smilo Grass; G:Gewöhnlicher Gran-
nenreis, Südliche Grannenhirse · ⌗ Z8
V-X Ⓝ; Eur.: Ib, Fr, Ital-P, Ba; TR, Syr.,
N-Iraq, Sinai
– **virescens** (L.) Boiss. · G:Grünlicher
Grannenreis, Welligblättriger Grannen-
reis · ⌗ Z8 V-VII; Eur.: F, I, A, EC-Eur.,
Ba, E-Eur.; TR, Cauc., N-Iran

Piqueria Cav. -f- *Asteraceae* · 7 spp.
– **trinervia** (Jacq.) Cav. · ⌗ ⋉ Z10 ⌂
VII-II; Mex., Haiti

Piscidia L. -f- *Fabaceae* · 8 spp. ·
E:Dogwood
– **piscipula** (L.) Sarg. · E:Fish Fuddle,
Jamaica Dogwood · ♄ d Z10 ⌂ ⚘ ⚔ Ⓝ;
S-Fla., W.Ind., S-Mex.

Pisonia L. -f- *Nyctaginaceae* · 35 spp.
– *alba* Span. = Pisonia grandis
– *brunoniana* Endl. = Pisonia umbellifera
– **grandis** R. Br. · E:Brown Cabbage Tree,
Lettuce Tree · ♄ Z10 ⌂ Ⓝ; E-Afr., Sri
Lanka, Malay. Arch., N.Guinea, E-Austr.,
Polyn.
– **umbellifera** (J.R. Forst. & G. Forst.)
Seem. · E:Bird Catcher Tree, Para Para · ♄
♄ e Z10 ⌂; Austr.: Queensl., N.S.Wales,
Lord Howe Is., Norfolk; NZ, Mauritius

Pistacia L. -f- *Anacardiaceae* · 9 spp. ·
E:Pistachio; F:Pistachier; G:Pistazie
– **chinensis** Bunge · E:Chinese Pistachio;
G:Chinesische Pistazie · ♄ d Z8 ⌂; China,
Taiwan., Phil.

– **lentiscus** L. · E:Lentisc, Mastic; G:Mas-
tixbaum · ♄ ♄ e D Z9 ⌂ ⚘ ; Eur.: Ib, Fr,
Ital-P, Ba; TR, Levant, Canar., N-Afr.
– **terebinthus** L. · E:Terebinth, Turpentine
; G:Terpentin-Pistazie · ♄ ♄ d D Z8 ⌂
⚘ Ⓝ; Eur.: Ib, Fr, Ital-P, Ba; TR, Levant,
NW-Afr., Libya
– **vera** L. · E:Pistachio; G:Echte Pistazie · ♄
♄ e D Z9 ⌂ Ⓝ; Iran, C-As.

Pistia L. -f- *Araceae* · 1 sp. · E:Shell Flower,
Water Lettuce; F:Laitue d'eau; G:Was-
sersalat
– **stratiotes** L. · E:Water Lettuce; G:Wass-
ersalat · ⌗ ≈ Z10 ⌂ VII-X; Subtrop.,
Trop.

Pistorinia DC. -f- *Crassulaceae* · 3 spp.
– **breviflora** Boiss.
– subsp. **breviflora** · ⊙ ⍦ ⌂; S-Sp.
– subsp. **salzmannii** (Boiss.) H. Jacobsen ·
⊙ ⍦ ⌂ VII-VIII; Moroc., Alger.
– **hispanica** (L.) DC.
– var. **hispanica** · ⊙ ⍦ ⌂; Eur.: Ib
– var. **maculata** Maire · ⊙ ⍦ ⌂ VII-VIII;
Moroc.
– *salzmannii* Boiss. = Pistorinia breviflora
subsp. salzmannii

Pisum L. -n- *Fabaceae* · 2 spp. · E:Pea;
F:Pois; G:Erbse
– *arvense* L. = Pisum sativum subsp.
sativum Arvense-Group
– **sativum** L.
– subsp. **abyssinicum** (A. Braun)
Govorov · ⊙ ⚘ VI-IX Ⓝ; Yemen, Eth.
– subsp. **asiaticum** Govorov · ⊙ ⚘ VI-IX Ⓝ;
N-Afr., SW-As., C-As., Ind., Tibet
– subsp. **elatius** (Steven ex M. Bieb.) Asch.
& P. Graebn. · ⊙ ⚘ VI-IX Ⓝ; Eur.: Ib,
Ital-P, Ba, H, S-Russ.; TR, Levant, Iraq,
Cauc., Iran, Ind., Tibet, N-Afr.
– subsp. **sativum** · E:Garden Pea, Pea;
G:Erbse · ⊙ ⚘ V-VII Ⓝ; Eur.: Ib, Ital-P,
Ba, Ro, Crim, W-Russ.; TR, Levant, N-Afr.
– **Arvense-Group** · E:Field Pea; G:Futter-
Erbsen, Peluschken · ; cult.
– **Macrocarpon-Group** · E:Sugar Pea;
G:Zucker-Erbsen · ; cult.
– **Medullare-Group** · E:Wrinkled Pea;
G:Mark-Erbsen · ; cult.
– **Sativum-Group** · G:Pal-Erbsen, Schal-
Erbsen · ; cult.
– *convar. axiphium* Alef. = Pisum sativum
subsp. sativum Macrocarpon-Group

– *convar. medullare* Alef. = Pisum sativum subsp. sativum Medullare-Group
– *convar. sativum* = Pisum sativum subsp. sativum Sativum-Group
– *convar. speciosum* (Dierb.) Alef. = Pisum sativum subsp. sativum Arvense-Group
– subsp. **syriacum** A. Berger · E:Syrian Fodder Pea · ☉ ⚥ VI-IX Ⓝ; Cyprus, Lebanon, Syr., Israel, Jord., N-Iraq, NW-Iran
– subsp. **transcaucasicum** Govorov · ☉ ⚥ VI-IX Ⓝ; Eur.: SE-Russ., Cauc.

Pitcairnia L'Hér. -f- *Bromeliaceae* · 368 spp.
– **altensteinii** (Link, Klotzsch & Otto) Lem. · ⌗ Z9 ⓜ IV-V; Guat.
– **andreana** Linden · ⌗ Z9 ⓜ VI-VII; Col.
– **angustifolia** Sol. ex Aiton · ⌗ Z9 ⓜ IX; Puerto Rico
– **aphelandriflora** Lem. · ⌗ Z9 ⓜ VI-VII; Panama, Ecuad.
– **atrorubens** (Beer) Baker · ⌗ Z9 ⓜ VII-VIII; Mex., Costa Rica, Panama
– **corallina** Linden & André · ⌗ Z9 ⓜ III-V; Col., Peru
– **echinata** Hook. · ⌗ Z9 ⓜ VI-VII; Col.
– *exscapa* Hook. = Pitcairnia heterophylla
– **flammea** Lindl.
– var. **flammea** · ⌗ Z9 ⓜ; Braz.
– var. **roezlii** (E. Morren) L.B. Sm. · ⌗ Z9 ⓜ X-XI; S-Am.; And.
– **heterophylla** (Lindl.) Beer · ⌗ Z9 ⓜ II-III; S-Mex., C-Am., trop. S-Am.
– **integrifolia** Ker-Gawl. · ⌗ Z9 ⓜ VIII; Venez.
– **maidifolia** (C. Morren) Decne. ex Planch. · ⌗ Z9 ⓜ IV-V; Hond., Costa Rica, Col., Venez., Guyan., Surinam
– **paniculata** (Ruiz & Pav.) Ruiz & Pav. · ⌗ Z9 ⓜ XI-I; Peru, Bol.
– **punicea** Scheidw. · ⌗ Z9 ⓜ IV-V; Mex., Guat.
– **recurvata** (Scheidw.) K. Koch · ⌗ Z9 ⓜ III-V; Col.
– *roezlii* E. Morren = Pitcairnia flammea var. roezlii
– **spicata** (Lam.) Mez · ⌗ Z9 ⓜ III-VIII; W.Ind.
– **tabuliformis** Linden · ⌗ Z9 ⓜ; S-Mex.
– **undulata** Scheidw. · ⌗ Z9 ⓜ VII-VIII; Braz.
– *venusta* (Phil.) Baker = Puya venusta
– *violacea* Brongn. = Puya coerulea var. violacea
– **xanthocalyx** Mart. · ⌗ Z9 ⓜ VI-VIII; Mex.

Pithecellobium Mart. -n- *Mimosaceae* · 37 spp. · F:Ebène du Mexique, Ebène du Texas; G:Affenohrring
– **bigeminum** (L.) Mart. · ♄ Z10 ⓜ Ⓝ; E-Him., Sri Lanka, Malay. Arch., Phil.
– **dulce** (Roxb.) Benth. · E:Manila Tamarind; G:Camambilarinde, Mexikanischer Affenohrring · ♄ e Z10 ⓜ Ⓝ; Mex., C-Am., trop. S-Am.
– **jiringa** (Jack) Prain ex King · E:Jering Tamarind; G:Malayischer Affenohrring · ♄ Z10 ⓜ Ⓝ; S-Burma, Malay. Arch.
– *saman* (Jacq.) Benth. = Albizia saman

Pithecoctenium Mart. ex Meisn. -n- *Bignoniaceae* · 3 (-12) spp. · F:Liane à râpe, Peigne de singe; G:Affenkamm
– **crucigerum** (L.) A.H. Gentry · E:Monkey's Comb · ♄ e ⚥ ✕ Z10 ⓜ; Mex., Cuba, Jamaica, trop. S-Am.
– *echinatum* (Jacq.) K. Schum. = Pithecoctenium crucigerum
– *laxiflorum* DC. = Distictis laxiflora

Pittosporum Banks ex Sol. -n- *Pittosporaceae* · 150-200 spp. · E:Pittosporum; F:Pittosporum; G:Klebsame
– **bicolor** Hook. f. · ♄ ♄ e Z9 ⓚ; Austr.: N.S.Wales, Victoria, Tasman.
– **colensoi** Hook. f. · ♄ e Z9 ⓚ IV; NZ
– **coriaceum** Aiton · ♄ e D Z9 ⓚ V-VI ▽; Madeira, Canar.: Teneriffa
– **crassifolium** Banks & Sol. ex A. Cunn. · E:Karo, Stiff Leaf Cheesewood; G:Karo-Klebsame · ♄ ♄ e Z9 ⓚ VI-VIII; NZ
– **dallii** Cheeseman · ♄ e D Z9 ⓚ VI-VII; NZ
– **eugenioides** A. Cunn. · E:Lemonwood, Tarata; G:Zitronen-Klebsame · ♄ ♄ e D Z9 ⓚ VII-VIII; NZ
– **floribundum** Wight & Arn. · E:Golden Fragrance · ♄ e D Z9 ⓚ; S-Him.
– **glabratum** Lindl. · ♄ e D Z9 ⓚ V; S-China
– **heterophyllum** Franch. · ♄ e Z9 ⓚ V-VI; W-China
– **phillyreoides** DC. · E:Desert Willow, Willow Pittosporum; G:Weiden-Klebsame · ♄ e Z9 ⓚ; Austr.
– **ralphii** Kirk · ♄ e Z9 ⓚ; NZ
– **resiniferum** Hemsl. · ♄ e Z9 ⓚ Ⓝ; Phil.
– **revolutum** W.T. Aiton · ♄ e D Z9 ⓚ II-IV; Austr.: Queensl., N.S.Wales, Victoria

– **rhombifolium** A. Cunn. ex Hook. ·
E:Queensland Pittosporum; G:Queens-
land-Klebsame · ♄ e Z9 ⒶⒷ XI; Austr.:
Queensl., N.S.Wales
– **tenuifolium** Sol. ex Gaertn. · E:Kohuhu,
Tawiwhi; G:Schmalblättriger Klebsame ·
♄ ♄ e D Z9 ⒶⒷ IV-V; NZ
– **some cultivars**
– subsp. *colensoi* (Hook. f.) Kirk = Pittospo-
rum colensoi
– **tobira** (Thunb. ex Murray) W.T. Aiton ·
E:Australian Laurel, Mock Orange,
Tobira; G:Chinesischer Klebsame,
Pechsame · ♄ e D Z9 ⒶⒷ III-V; China,
S-Korea, Jap.
– **undulatum** Vent. · E:Australian
Cheesewood, Victoria Box; G:Orangen-
Klebsame · ♄ ♄ e D Z9 ⒶⒷ V-VII Ⓝ; Austr.:
Queensl., N.S.Wales, Victoria
– **viridiflorum** Sims · E:Cape Pittosporum;
G:Kap-Klebsame · ♄ ♄ e D Z9 ⒶⒷ V; S-Afr.

Pityrogramma Link -f- *Adiantaceae* ·
20 spp. · E:Gold Fern, Silver Fern;
F:Fougère argentée, Fougère dorée;
G:Goldfarn, Silberfarn
– **argentea** (Willd.) Domin · � Z10 ⓌⒺ;
trop. Afr., S-Afr.
– **calomelanos** (L.) Link · E:Silver Fern;
G:Silberfarn · � Z10 ⓌⒺ; W.Ind., S-Am.,
nat. in Trop.
– **chrysophylla** (Sw.) Link · E:Gold Fern ·
� Z10 ⓌⒺ; Puerto Rico, Lesser Antilles,
nat. in Azor.
– **dealbata** (C. Presl) R.M. Tryon · � Z10
ⓌⒺ; Mex., C-Am.
– *ebenea* (L.) Proctor = Pityrogramma
tartarea
– **pulchella** (T. Moore) Domin · � Z10 ⓌⒺ;
Venez.
– *schaffneri* (Fée) Weath. = Pityrogramma
dealbata
– **schizophylla** (Baker ex Jenman)
Maxon · � Z10 ⓌⒺ; Jamaica
– **sulphurea** (Sw.) Maxon · E:Jamaica
Gold Fern; G:Goldfarn · � Z10 ⓌⒺ;
W.Ind., nat. in Sri Lanka
– **tartarea** (Cav.) Maxon · � Z10 ⓌⒺ; Mex.,
C-Am., W.Ind., trop. S-Am.

Plagianthus J.R. Forst. & G. Forst.
-m- *Malvaceae* · 2 spp. · E:Ribbon Wood;
F:Plagianthe; G:Streifenrinde
– **divaricatus** J.R. Forst. & G. Forst. · ♄ e
Z8 ⒶⒷ VI; NZ

Plagiorhegma Maxim. = Jeffersonia
– *dubium* Maxim. = Jeffersonia dubia

Plagiospermum Oliv. = Prinsepia
– *sinense* Oliv. = Prinsepia sinensis

Plantago L. -f- *Plantaginaceae* · 193 spp. ·
E:Plantain; F:Plantain; G:Wegerich
– **alpina** L. · G:Alpen-Wegerich · � Z3
V-VII; Eur.: sp., F, I, C-Eur.; mts., nat. in
W-Russ.
– **altissima** L. · G:Hoher Wegerich · �
V-VII; Eur.: A, I, EC-Eur., Ba, E-Eur.;
Tun., Alger., nat. in F, Sw, D
– **argentea** Chaix · G:Silberhaariger
Wegerich · � Z6 VII-VIII; Eur.: Ib, Fr,
Ital-P, Ba, H, RO; N-TR; mts.
– **atrata** Hoppe · G:Berg-Wegerich · �
V-VIII; Eur.: Ib, Fr, C-Eur., EC-Eur., Ba,
RO, W-Russ.; TR, SW-As.; mts.
– **bellardii** All. · G:Haariger Wegerich · ⊙;
Eur.: Ib, Fr, Ital-P, Ba; TR, Levant, Iraq,
Iran, NW-Afr., Egypt
– **coronopus** L. · E:Buckshorn Plantain,
Cut Leaved Plantain; G:Krähenfuß-
Wegerich; · ⊙ � Z6 VI-IX; Eur.*, TR +
Afgh., N-Afr., Levant
– **holosteum** Scop. · G:Kiel-Wegerich · �
V-VII; Eur.: sp., F, I, Ba +; TR, Levant
– *indica* L. = Psyllium arenarium
– **lagopus** L. · G:Zottiger Wegerich · ⊙ �;
Eur.: Ib, Fr, Ital-P, Ba; TR, Levant, Cauc.,
Iran, N-Afr.
– **lanceolata** L. · E:English Plantain,
Ribwort; G:Spitz-Wegerich · � Z6 V-IX
⚥; Eur.*, TR, Levant, Iran, Him., C-As.,
W-Sib., N-Afr., nat. in N-Am.
– **major** L. · G:Breit-Wegerich
– subsp. **intermedia** (Gilib.) Lange ·
G:Kleiner Wegerich, Vielsamiger Breit-
Wegerich · � Z5 VI-X; Eur., TR, Levant,
Moroc., Alger., Egypt
– subsp. **major** · E:Common Plantain, Plan-
tain; G:Gewöhnlicher Breit-Wegerich,
Großer Wegerich · � Z5 X ⚥; Eur.*, TR,
N-Afr., nat. in cosmop.
– subsp. **winteri** (Wirtg. ex Geisenh.) W.
Ludw. · G:Salz-Wegerich, Salzwiesen-
Breit-Wegerich · � Z5 VI-VIII; C-Eur.,
NE-Eur.; saline habitats
– **maritima** L. · G:Strand-Wegerich
– subsp. **maritima** · E:Sea Plantain;
G:Gewöhnlicher Strand-Wegerich · � VII-
X; Eur.*, Cyprus, Palest., Cauc. (Armen.),
Iran, C-As, N-Am., S-Am; coasts, saline

habitats
- subsp. **serpentina** (All.) Arcang. ·
  G:Schlangen-Wegerich · ⹁ V-VIII; S-Eur.
- **media** L. · E:Hoary Plantain; G:Mittlerer
  Wegerich · ⹁ Z6 V-VI; Eur.*, TR, Cauc.,
  N-Iraq, Iran, C-As., W-Sib., E-Sib., Amur,
  China, nat. in Can., NZ
- **nivalis** Boiss. · ⹁ △ Z7 ⓐ ∧ VII-VIII; sp.:
  Sierra Nevada
- **ovata** Forssk. · E:Blond Psyllium;
  G:Indischer Flohsame · ⹁ ⚥ Ⓝ; sp.,
  C-As., Ind., nat. in China
- *psyllium* L. 1753 = Psyllium arenarium
- *psyllium* L. 1759 = Psyllium sempervirens
- *psyllium* L. 1762 = Psyllium afrum
- *sempervirens* Crantz = Psyllium sempervirens
- *serpentina* All. = Plantago maritima
  subsp. serpentina
- **subulata** L.
- subsp. **insularis** (Gren. & Godr.)
  Nyman · ⹁ △ △ Z6 V; Cors, Sard., Sic.
- subsp. **subulata** · ⹁ Z6; Eur.: Ib, Fr,
  Ital-P, Ba, A, RO; Moroc., Alger.
- *suffruticosa* Lam. = Psyllium sempervirens
- **tenuiflora** Waldst. & Kit. · G:Dünnähren-
  Wegerich · ☉ IV-VI; Eur.: A, EC-Eur.,
  E-Eur., Swed (Öland)
- *uniflora* L. = Littorella uniflora

Platanthera Rich. -f- *Orchidaceae* ·
  129 spp. · E:Butterfly Orchid;
  F:Platanthère; G:Waldhyazinthe
- **bifolia** (L.) Rich. · E:Lesser Butterfly
  Orchid; G:Gewöhnliche Weiße Waldhyazinthe · ⹁ Z6 V-VI ▽ ✳; Eur.*, TR,
  Cauc., N-Iran, W-Sib., E-Sib., Him.
- **chlorantha** (Custer) Rchb. · E:Greater
  Butterfly Orchid; G:Grünliche Waldhyazinthe · ⹁ Z7 V-VI ▽ ✳; Eur.*, TR,
  Cauc., N-Iran, N-As., N-China, NW-Afr.

Platanus L. -f- *Platanaceae* · c. 8 spp. ·
  E:Plane; F:Platane; G:Platane
- × *acerifolia* (Aiton) Willd. = Platanus ×
  hispanica
- × **hispanica** Münchh. (*P. occidentalis* ×
  P. orientalis) · E:London Plane, Plane;
  F:Platane à feuilles d'érable; G:Bastard-
  Platane, Gewöhnliche Platane · ♄ d Z6 V;
  orig. ?
- × *hybrida* Brot. = Platanus × hispanica
- **occidentalis** L. · E:American Plane,
  Button Tree, Sycamore; F:Platane
  d'Occident; G:Nordamerikanische

Platane · ♄ d Z6 V Ⓝ; Ont., USA: NE,
NCE, NC, SC, SE, Fla.
- **orientalis** L. · E:Chenar, Oriental Plane;
  F:Platane d'Orient; G:Morgenländische
  Platane · ♄ d Z6 V Ⓝ; Eur.: S-I, Sic., Ba;
  TR, Syr.

Platonia Mart. -f- *Clusiaceae* · 1-2 spp.
- **esculenta** (Arruda) Rickett & Stafleu · ♄
  Z10 ⓦ Ⓝ; trop. Braz.

Platycarya Siebold & Zucc. -f-
  Juglandaceae · 3 spp. · F:Platycaryer;
  G:Zapfennuss
- **strobilacea** Siebold & Zucc. · G:Zapfen-
  nuss · ♄ ♄ d Z6; China, Korea, Jap.,
  Taiwan

Platycerium Desv. -n- *Polypodiaceae* ·
  16 spp. · E:Elkhorn Fern, Staghorn Fern;
  F:Corne d'élan; G:Geweihfarn
- *alcicorne* (P. Willemet) Tardieu =
  Platycerium vassei
- *alcicorne* (Sw.) Desv. = Platycerium
  stemaria
- *alcicorne* hort. = Platycerium bifurcatum
  var. bifurcatum
- **andinum** Baker · ⹁ Z10 ⓦ; Peru, Bol.
- **angolense** Welw. ex Baker · ⹁ Z10 ⓦ;
  trop. Afr.
- *biforme* (Sw.) Blume = Platycerium
  coronarium
- **bifurcatum** (Cav.) C. Chr.
- var. **bifurcatum** · E:Elkhorn Fern, Staghorn Fern; G:Gewöhnlicher Geweihfarn ·
  ⹁ Z10 ⓦ; N.Guinea, Austr.: Queensl.
- var. *hillii* (T. Moore) Domin = Platycerium hillii
- var. **lanciferum** Domin Z10 ⓦ; Austr.:
  Queensl.
- var. *normale* Domin = Platycerium
  bifurcatum var. bifurcatum
- var. **subrhomboideum** Domin Z10 ⓦ;
  Austr.: Queensl.
- **coronarium** (J. König ex O.F. Müll.)
  Desv. · ⹁ Z10 ⓦ; Indochina, Malay. Pen.,
  Phil.
- *elephantotis* Schweinf. = Platycerium
  angolense
- **ellisii** Baker · ⹁ Z10 ⓦ; C-Madag.
- **grande** (J. Sm. ex Fée) C. Presl ·
  E:Staghorn Fern; G:Großer Geweihfarn ·
  ⹁ Z10 ⓦ; Phil.: Luzon (Mt. Christobal)
- *grande* auct. = Platycerium superbum
- **hillii** T. Moore · ⹁ Z10 ⓦ; Austr.:

Queensl.
- **madagascariense** Baker · ⍓ Z10 ⓦ; Madag.
- **stemaria** (P. Beauv.) Desv. · E:Triangular Staghorn Fern; G:Triangel-Geweihfarn · ⍓ Z10 ⓦ; trop. Afr.
- *sumbawense* H. Christ = Platycerium willinckii
- **superbum** de Jonch. & Hennipman · E:Staghorn Fern; G:Prächtiger Geweihfarn · ⍓ Z10 ⓦ; Java, Kalimantan, Austr.: Queensl., N.S.Wales
- **vassei** Poiss. · ⍓ Z10 ⓦ ⓚ; Mozamb., Madag., Komor., Seych., Mauritius
- **veitchii** (Underw.) C. Chr. · ⍓ Z10 ⓦ; Austr.: Queensl.
- **wallichii** Hook. · ⍓ Z10 ⓦ; Malay. Pen.
- **wandae** Racib. · ⍓ Z10 ⓦ; N.Guinea
- *wilhelminae-reginae* Alderw. = Platycerium wandae
- **willinckii** T. Moore. · E:Java Staghorn Fern · ⍓ Z10 ⓦ; Java, Sulawesi, Timor, ? Austr.

Platycladus Spach -m- *Cupressaceae* · 1 sp. · E:Chinese Arborvitae, Oriental Thuja; F:Thuya d'Orient; G:Morgenländischer Lebensbaum
- **orientalis** (L.) Franco · E:Chinese Arborvitae, Oriental Thuja; F:Thuya d'Orient, Thuya de Chine; G:Morgenländischer Lebensbaum · ♄ ♄ e Z6 IV-V ⚥ � ⓝ; China, Korea
- **some cultivars**
- *stricta* Spach = Platycladus orientalis

Platycodon A. DC. -m- *Campanulaceae* · 1 sp. · E:Balloon Flower, Chinese Bellflower; F:Fleur ballon; G:Ballonblume
- **grandiflorus** (Jacq.) A. DC. · E:Balloon Flower; F:Platycodon à grandes fleurs; G:Großblütige Ballonblume · ⍓ Z4 VII-VIII ⚥; Jap., N-Korea, Manch., Amur
- **many cultivars**

Platystele Schltr. -f- *Orchidaceae* · 94 spp.
- **repens** (Ames) Garay · ⍓ Z10 ⓦ ▽ ✳; Guat.

Platystemon Benth. -m- *Papaveraceae* · 1 sp. · E:Cream Cup; G:Breitfaden
- **californicus** Benth. · E:California Creamcups, Creamcups; G:Kalifornischer Breitfaden · ⊙ Z8 VII-VIII; Calif.

Platystigma Benth. = Hesperomecon
- *lineare* Benth. = Hesperomecon lineare

Plectranthus L'Hér. -m- *Lamiaceae* · 411 sp. · F:Germaine; G:Buntnessel, Harfenstrauch, Mottenkönig
- **amboinicus** (Lour.) Spreng. · E:Indian Mint; G:Jamaika-Thymian · ⍓ e Z10 ⓦ ⚥ ⓝ; Ind., Indochina, Malay. Arch.
- *australis* R. Br. = Plectranthus parviflorus
- **autranii** (Briq.) Erhardt, Götz & Seybold · ⍓ Z10 ⓚ XII-I; E-Afr.
- **barbatus** Andrews · ⍓ Z10 ⓦ ⚥ ⓝ; Ind., E-Afr.
- **ciliatus** E. Mey.
- *coleoides* hort. non Benth. = Plectranthus forsteri
- **edulis** (Vatke) Agnew · G:Gala-Kartoffel · Z10 ⓝ; Eth.
- **esculentus** N.E. Br. · E:Kaffir Potato; G:Dozo-Kartoffel; · ⍓ Z10 ⓚ ⓝ; W-Afr., C-Afr., S-Afr.
- **forsteri** Benth. · E:Swedish Ivy · ⍓ e Z10 ⓚ; SE-Ind.
- **fruticosus** L'Hér. · G:Mottenkönig · ♄ e Z10 ⓚ II-V; S-Afr.
- **oertendahlii** Th. Fr. · E:Candle Plant · ⍓ e ⚥ ∿ Z10 ⓦ IX-X; S-Afr.
- **parviflorus** (Poir.) Henckel · E:Little Spurflower · ⍓ e Z10 ⓦ ⓚ; Austr.: North Terr., Queensl., N.S.Wales, Victoria, S-Austr.
- **prostratus** Gürke · ⍓ e ⚥ ∿ Z10 ⓦ ⓚ; Tanzania: Kilimandscharo
- **purpuratus** Harv. · ⍓ ⚥ ∿ Z10 ⓦ ⓚ; S-Afr.: Natal
- **rotundifolius** (Poir.) Spreng. · E:Hausa Potato; G:Hauskartoffel · ⍓ Z10 ⓚ ⓝ; cult.
- **scutellarioides** (L.) R. Br. · E:Coleus, Painted Nettle; G:Buntnessel · ⊙ ⍓ ⚥ Z10 ⓚ XI-I; Phil.: Luzon; N-Kalimantan
- **many cultivars**
- **thyrsoideus** (Baker) B. Mathew · ♄ e Z10 ⓚ XII-II; trop. Afr.

Pleioblastus Nakai -m- *Poaceae* · c. 45 spp.
- **argenteostriatus** (Regel) Nakai · ♄ e Z7; cult. in Jap.
- f. **pumilus** (Mitford) Muroi · ⍓ ♄ ∧; Jap.
- **auricomus** (Mitford) D.C. McClint. · ♄ e Z7 ∧; cult. in Jap.
- f. **chrysophyllus** Makino Z7; cult. Jap.
- **chino** (Franch. & Sav.) Makino · ⍓ e Z6; Jap.

– var. *viridis* f. *humilis* (Mitford) S. Suzuki
= Pleioblastus humilis
– f. *pumilus* (Mitford) S. Suzuki =
Pleioblastus argenteostriatus f. pumilus
– *fortunei* (Van Houtte) Nakai = Pleioblastus variegatus
– **gramineus** (Bean) Nakai · ♃ e Z7 ∧;
Jap.
– **hindsii** (Munro) Nakai · ♃ e ∧; China
(Hong Kong)
– **humilis** (Mitford) Nakai · ♃ e Z7 ∧; Jap.
– var. *pumilus* (Mitford) D.C. McClint. =
Pleioblastus argenteostriatus f. pumilus
– **purpurascens** Nakai · ♃
– **pygmaeus** (Miq.) Nakai · F:Bambou
Pleioblastus nain · ♃ e ⤳ Z7; Jap.
– **simonii** (Carrière) Nakai · E:Simon
Bamboo · ♃ e Z6 Ⓝ; Jap.
– **variegatus** (Siebold ex Miq.) Makino ·
E:Whitestripe Bamboo · ♄ e Z7; Jap.
– **'Fortunei'**
– **viridistriatus** (Regel) Makino · ♄ e Z7;
Jap.

Pleione D. Don -f- *Orchidaceae* · 21 sp. ·
E:Indian Crocus; F:Orchidée du Tibet,
Pléione; G:Tibetorchidee
– **bulbocodioides** (Franch.) Rolfe · ♃ △
Z8 ⒶⒾ ∧ V ▽ ✳; China, Taiwan, Tibet
– **formosana** Hayata · ♃ Z8 ⒶⒾ IV-VI ▽ ✳;
Yunnan
– **hookeriana** (Lindl.) J. Moore · ♃ Z8 ⒶⒾ
V-VI ▽ ✳; Nepal, Ind.: Sikkim, Assam;
Laos, Thailand
– **humilis** (Sm.) D. Don · ♃ Z8 ⒶⒾ VIII-V ▽
✳; Nepal, Sikkim, Burma
– × **lagenaria** Lindl. & Paxton (*P. maculata*
× *P. praecox*) · ♃ Z8 ⒶⒾ VI-VI ▽ ✳;
Bhutan, Ind.: Sikkim, Assam; Myamar,
Thail.
– **maculata** (Lindl.) Lindl. & Paxton · ♃ Z8
ⒶⒾ VII-VIII ▽ ✳; Bhutan, Ind.: Sikkim,
Assam; Myamar, Thail.
– *pogonioides* (Rolfe) Rolfe = Pleione
bulbocodioides
– **praecox** (Sm.) D. Don · ♃ Z8 ⒶⒾ VI-XII ▽
✳; N-Ind.: Sikkim, Assam; Nepal, Burma,
China
– *reichenbachiana* (T. Moore & Veitch)
Kuntze = Pleione praecox
– *wallichiana* (Lindl.) Lindl. = Pleione
praecox
– **yunnanensis** (Rolfe) Rolfe
– **Cultivars:**
– **many cultivars**

Pleiospilos N.E. Br. -m- *Aizoaceae* · 4 spp. ·
E:Living Granite, Living Rock
– **bolusii** (Hook. f.) N.E. Br. · E:Living Rock,
Mimicry Plant · ♃ ⚘ Z9 ⒶⒾ X-XI; Cape
– **nelii** Schwantes · ♃ ⚘ Z9 ⒶⒾ X-XI; Cape
– *prismaticus* (Marloth) Schwantes =
Tanquana prismatica
– **simulans** (Marloth) N.E. Br. · ♃ ⚘ D Z9
ⒶⒾ X-XI; Cape

Pleopeltis Humb. & Bonpl. ex Willd. -f-
Polypodiaceae · 25 spp.
– *crassifolia* (L.) T. Moore = Niphidium
crassifolium
– **macrocarpa** (Bory ex Willd.) Kaulf. · ♃
Z10; trop. Lat.-Am.
– *musifolia* (Blume) T. Moore = Microsorum musifolium
– *phyllitidis* (L.) Alston = Campyloneurum
phyllitidis

Pleuropteropyrum H. Gross = Aconogonon
– *undulatum* (Murray) Á. Löve & D. Löve =
Aconogonon alpinum

Pleurospermum Hoffm. -n- *Apiaceae* ·
3 spp. · F:Pleurosperme; G:Rippensame
– **austriacum** (L.) Hoffm. · G:Österreichischer Rippensame · ♃ Z7 VI-VII; Eur.*
exc. BrI

Pleurothallis R. Br. -f- *Orchidaceae* ·
710 spp.
– *gelida* Lindl. = Stelis gelida
– *ghiesbreghtiana* A. Rich. & Galeotti =
Stelis quadrifida
– *granids* Rolfe = Stelis alta
– *grobyi* Bateman ex Lindl. = Specklinia
grobyi
– *immersa* Linden & Rchb. f. = Stelis
immersa
– **maculata** N.E. Br. · ♃ Z10 Ⓜ VI-VII ▽ ✳;
Braz.
– *pectinata* Lindl. = Acianthera pectinata
– *quadrifida* (Lex.) Lindl. = Stelis quadrifida
– *racemiflora* Lindl. ex Lodd. = Stelis
quadrifida
– *repens* Ames = Platystele repens
– **revoluta** (Ruiz & Pav.) Garay · ♃ Z10 Ⓜ
I-III ▽ ✳; S-Am.
– *saurocephala* Lodd. = Acianthera
saurocephala
– *tribuloides* (Sw.) Lindl. = Specklinia
tribuloides

Plukenetia L. -f- *Euphorbiaceae* · 13 spp.
- *conophora* Müll. Arg. = Tetracarpidium conophorum
- **volubilis** L. · ♄ ⌇ Z10 Ⓦ Ⓝ; W.Ind., trop. S-Am.

Plumbagella Spach -f- *Plumbaginaceae* · 1 sp. · F:Petit plombago; G:Zwergbleiwurz
- **micrantha** (Ledeb.) Spach · G:Zwergbleiwurz · ⊙; C-As.

Plumbago L. -f- *Plumbaginaceae* · 12-15 (-24) spp. · E:Leadwort; F:Dentelaire, Plombago; G:Bleiwurz
- **auriculata** Lam. · E:Cape Leadwort; G:Kap-Bleiwurz · ♄ e Z9 Ⓚ VI-IX; S-Afr.
- *capensis* Thunb. = Plumbago auriculata
- **europaea** L. · ♃ Z8 Ⓚ IX; Eur.: Ib, Fr, Ital-P, Ba, RO; TR, Syr., Palest., Cauc. Iran, C-As., NW-Afr., nat. in CZ
- **indica** L. · ♄ e ⌇ Z10 Ⓦ VI-XI; Ind., SE-As.
- *larpentiae* Lindl. = Ceratostigma plumbaginoides
- *rosea* L. = Plumbago indica
- **scandens** L. · ♄ e ⌇ Z10 Ⓚ; Ariz., Flor., W.Ind., Mex., C-Am., S-Am.
- **zeylanica** L. · ♄ ⌇ Z10 Ⓦ I-III ⚕; Ind., SE-As.

Plumeria Tourn. ex L. -f- *Apocynaceae* · 8 spp. · E:Frangipani, Temple Tree; F:Frangipanier; G:Frangipani
- *acutifolia* Poir. = Plumeria rubra f. acutifolia
- **alba** L. · E:West Indian Jasmine; G:Westindische Frangipani · ♄ d D Z10 Ⓦ VI-IX; Lesser Antilles, Puerto Rico
- *lutea* Ruiz & Pav. = Plumeria rubra f. lutea
- **rubra** L. · E:Frangipani, Temple Tree; G:Rote Frangipani · ♄ d D Z10 Ⓦ VI-IX; C-Am.
- f. **acutifolia** (Poir.) Woodson · G:Weiße Frangipani · Ⓦ; cult.
- f. **lutea** (Ruiz & Pav.) Woodson · G:Gelbe Frangipani · Ⓦ; cult.
- f. **tricolor** (Ruiz & Pav.) Woodson · G:Bunte Frangipani · Ⓦ; cult.
- *tricolor* Ruiz & Pav. = Plumeria rubra f. tricolor
- **Cultivars:**
- **many cultivars**

Pneumonanthe Gled. = Gentiana
- *vulgaris* F.W. Schmidt = Gentiana pneumonanthe

Poa L. -f- *Poaceae* · c. 500 spp. · E:Meadow Grass; F:Pâturin; G:Rispengras
- *abyssinica* Jacq. = Eragrostis tef
- **alpina** L. · E:Alpine Blue Grass, Alpine Meadow Grass; G:Alpen-Rispengras · ♃ △ VI-VII; Eur.*, TR, Cauc., NW-Iran, W-Sib., E-Sib., C-As., Afgh., Pakist., Ind., Tibet, China, Korea, Alger., Moroc., Alaska, Can., USA: NCE, NC, Rocky Mts., NW; Greenl.
- var. *vivipara* L. = Poa alpina
- *amabilis* hort. non L. = Eragrostis unioloides
- **angustifolia** L. · E:Narrow-leaved Meadow Grass; G:Schmalblättriges Wiesen-Rispengras · ♃ V-VI; Eur.*, Cauc., W-Sib., E-Sib., Amur, Sakhal., Kamchat., SW-As., N-Ind., NW-Afr.
- **annua** L. · E:Annual Blue Grass; G:Einjähriges Rispengras · ⊙ ♃ I-XII; Eur.*, TR, Levant, Iraq, Arab., Cauc., Iran, W-Sib., E-Sib., C-As., Afgh., Pakist, N-Ind., Tibet, Mong., China, Korea, Jap., N-Afr., nat. in Greenl., N-Am., C-Am., S-Am., Phil., Austr., NZ
- *aquatica* (L.) Wahlenb. = Glyceria maxima
- **badensis** Haenke ex Willd. · G:Badener Rispengras · ♃ ⁓→ △ V-VII; Eur.: F, C-Eur., EC-Eur., Ba, RO, ? N-I; Cauc.
- **bulbosa** L. · E:Bulbous Blue Grass; G:Knolliges Rispengras · ♃ V Ⓝ; Eur.*, TR, Levant, Cauc., Iran, Afgh., Pakist., W-Sib., C-As., NW-Afr., Libya, S-Afr., nat. in N-Am.
- var. *vivipara* (Koeler) Willd. = Poa bulbosa
- **cenisia** All. · G:Mont-Cenis-Rispengras · ♃ VI-VIII; Eur.: Ib, Fr, C-Eur., Ital-P, Ba, RO; TR
- **chaixii** Vill. · E:Broad-leaved Meadow Grass; G:Wald-Rispengras · ♃ Z5 VI-VII; Eur.* exc. BrI, Sc; NE-TR, ? Cauc., nat. in BrI, Sc
- **compressa** L. · E:Flat Stem Blue Grass; G:Flaches Rispengras · ♃ ⁓→ VI-VII; Eur.*, TR, Lebanon, Cauc., W-Sib., C-As., Him., Amur, Sakhal., Korea, Jap., Alaska, Can., USA*, nat. in N-Am.
- **concinna** Gaudin · G:Niedliches Rispengras · ♃ IV-V; Eur.: F, Ital-P, Sw

– **glauca** Vahl · E:Glaucous Blue Grass;
F:Pâturin glauque; G:Blaugrünes Rispen-
gras · ⵚ △ Z5 VI-VII; Eur.* exc. Ib; Cauc.,
N-Iran, Afgh., Pakist., Him., W-Sib.,
E-Sib., Amur, Sakhal., Kamchat., Mong.,
China, Korea, Jap., Moroc., Alger., nat. in
N-Am., Arg., Chile, S-Afr.
– **humilis** Ehrh. ex Hoffm. · G:Bläuliches
Wiesen-Rispengras, Salzwiesen-Rispen-
gras · ⵚ VI-VII; Eur.: Sc, BrI, Fr, C-Eur.,
EC-Eur., nat. in N-Am., Kamchat.
– **hybrida** Gaudin · G:Gebirgs-Rispengras,
Großes Rispengras · ⵚ VI-VII; Eur.:
C-Eur., Ba, RO, W-Russ.; Alp., Jura,
Carp., Balkan; Cauc.
– **infirma** Kunth · E:Early Meadow Grass;
G:Frühlings-Rispengras · ⵙ IV-VI; Eur.:
Ib, Fr, BrI, Ital-P, Ba; TR, Syr., Cauc.,
Iran, Ind., NW-Afr., Libya, nat. in S-Am.
– **jurassica** Chrtek & V. Jirásek · ⵚ ; Sw
– **laxa** Haenke · E:Tufted Meadow Grass;
G:Schlaffes Rispengras · ⵚ VII-VIII; Eur.:
Fr, Ital-P, C-Eur., EC-Eur., Ba, RO; mts.
– **minor** Gaudin · G:Kleines Rispengras ·
ⵚ VII-VIII; Eur.: sp., F, I, C-Eur., Slove.,
Bosn., Montenegro, RO; mts.
– **molinerii** Balb. · G:Trocken-Rispengras ·
ⵚ VII; Eur.: Ib, F, I, C-Eur., Slova., Ba,
RO; mts.
– **nemoralis** L. · E:Forest Blue Grass,
Wood Meadow Grass; F:Pâturin des
bois; G:Hain-Rispengras · ⵚ Z5 VI-VII Ⓝ;
Eur.*, TR, Cauc., N-Iran, W-Sib., E-Sib.,
Amur, Sakhal., Kamchat., C-As., China,
NW-Afr., Greenl., nat. in N-Am.
– **palustris** L. · E:Marsh Meadow Grass;
G:Sumpf-Rispengras · ⵚ VI-VII Ⓝ; Eur.*
exc. Ib; Cauc., C-As., Iran, Pakist., Him.,
W-Sib., E-Sib., Amur, Sakhal., Kamchat.,
Mong., Manch., Korea, Jap., Taiwan,
Alaska, Can., USA* exc. SC; Greenl., Arg.
– *pilosa* L. = Eragrostis pilosa
– **pratensis** L. · E:Kentucky Blue Grass,
Smooth Meadow Grass; G:Wiesen-Ris-
pengras · ⵚ Z3 V-VII Ⓝ; Eur.*, TR, Iraq,
Levant, Arab., Cauc., Iran, Afgh., Pakist.,
Him., W-Sib., E-Sib., Amur, Sakhal.,
Kamchat., C-As., Mong., China, Korea,
Jap., Moroc., Alger., nat. in Greenl.,
N-Am., S-Am., S-Afr., Austr., NZ
– **pumila** Host · G:Niedriges Rispengras · ⵚ
VI-VIII; Eur.: N-I, Ba, RO; E-Alp, Balkan
– **remota** Forselles · G:Lockerblütiges
Rispengras · ⵚ VI-VII; Eur.: C-Eur.,
EC-Eur., Sc, E-Eur.; Cauc., W-Sib., C-As.

– **stiriaca** Fritsch & Hayek ex Dörfl. ·
G:Steirisches Rispengras · ⵚ VI-VIII; Eur.:
A, EC-Eur., Slove., Montenegro, RO
– *sudetica* Haenke = Poa chaixii
– **supina** Schrad. · G:Läger-Rispengras · ⵚ
IV-VI; Eur.* exc. BrI, Ba; mts; Cauc.
– **trivialis** L. · G:Gewöhnliches Rispengras
– subsp. **sylvicola** (Guss.) H. Lindb. ·
G:Waldbewohnendes Rispengras · ⵚ
VI-VII; Eur.: Ib, Fr, Ital-P, Ba, BrI, C-Eur.;
TR, Cauc., C-As., Moroc., Alger., nat. in
N-Am., S-Am., Austr.
– subsp. **trivialis** · E:Rough Meadow Grass;
G:Gewöhnliches Rispengras · ⵚ VI-VII
Ⓝ; Eur.*, TR, Levant, Iraq, Cauc., Iran,
Afgh., Pakist., Him., W-Sib., E-Sib., C-As.,
nat. in China, Korea, Jap., N-Am., S-Am.,
S-Afr., Tasman., NZ
– **violacea** Bellardi · E:Violet Meadow
Grass; G:Violettes Rispengras · ⵚ VII-VIII;
Eur.* exc. Sc, BrI; TR; mts.

Podachaenium Benth. ex Oerst. -n-
Asteraceae · 2 spp.
– **eminens** (Lag.) Sch. Bip. · E:Tacote · ♄ D
Z10 ⓚ I-III; C-Am.

Podalyria Willd. -f- Fabaceae · 22 spp. ·
E:Sweetpea Bush; G:Wickenstrauch
– **argentea** Salisb. · ♄ e Z9 ⓚ VII-VIII;
S-Afr.
– **calyptrata** (Retz.) Willd. · E:Water Blossom Pea; G:Großblütiger Wickenstrauch
· ♄ e Z9 ⓚ III-V; S-Afr.
– **sericea** (Andrews) R. Br. · E:Silver
Sweetpea Bush; G:Silberner Wickenstrauch · ♄ e Z9 ⓚ I-III; S-Afr.

Podanthum Boiss. = Asyneuma
– *canescens* (Waldst. & Kit.) Boiss. =
Asyneuma canescens

Podocarpus L'Hér. ex Pers. -m-
Podocarpaceae · 108 spp. · E:Podocarp;
F:Podocarpus; G:Steineibe
– **alpinus** R. Br. ex Hook. f. · E:Tasmanian
Podocarp; G:Tasmanische Alpen-
Steineibe
– *andinus* Poepp. ex Endl. = Prumnopitys
andina
– *chilinus* Rich. = Podocarpus salignus
– **chinensis** Wall. ex Parl. · G:Chinesische
Steineibe
– *dacrydioides* A. Rich. = Dacrycarpus
dacrydioides

- **elongatus** (Aiton) L'Hér. ex Pers. · E:African Yellow Wood, Cape Yellowwood, Fern Pine; G:Kap-Steineibe · ₺ e Z10 ⓚ; W-Afr.
- *falcatus* (Thunb.) Endl. = Afrocarpus falcatus
- *ferrugineus* G. Benn. ex D. Don = Prumnopitys ferruginea
- **glaucus** Foxw. · G:Blaue Steineibe · ₺ e ⓦ; Phil.
- *gracilior* Pilg. = Afrocarpus gracilior
- **latifolius** (Thunb.) R. Br. ex Mirb. · E:True Yellowwood, Upright Yellowwood; G:Breitblättrige Steineibe · ₺ e Z10 ⓚ; S-Afr.
- **lawrencei** Hook. f. · E:Mountain Plum Pine; G:Alpen-Steineibe · ₺ e Z7; Austr.: Victoria, Tasman.
- *lawrencei* auct. non Hook. f. = Phyllocladus trichomanoides var. alpinus
- **macrophyllus** (Thunb.) Sweet · G:Gewöhnliche Tempel-Steineibe · ₺ e Z7; S-China, S-Jap., Ryukyu-Is.
- *nageia* R. Br. ex Mirb. = Nageia nagi
- *nagi* (Thunb.) Pilg. = Nageia nagi
- **neriifolius** D. Don · E:Chilean Podocarp, Oleander Podocarp; G:Oleanderblättrige Steineibe · ₺ e Z10 ⓚ ✻; Him., Kalimantan
- **nivalis** Hook. · E:Alpine Totara; G:Neuseeländische Alpen-Steineibe, Schnee-Steineibe · ₺ e Z7 ⓐ ∧; NZ
- **nubigenus** Lindl. · E:Chilean Podocarp, Cloud Podocarp; G:Chilenische Steineibe · ₺ e Z7; Chile, Patag.
- **salignus** D. Don · E:Willow Podocarp; G:Weidenähnliche Steineibe · ₺ e Z8 ⓚ; Chile
- **totara** G. Benn. ex D. Don · E:Totara; G:Totara-Steineibe · ₺ e Z9 ⓚ; NZ

Podolepis Labill. -f- *Asteraceae* · 18 spp.
- **canescens** A. Cunn. ex DC. · ⊙ Z9 ⓚ VII-IX; Austr.
- **gracilis** (Lehm.) Graham · ⊙ Z9 ⓚ VII-IX; Austr.

Podophyllum L. -n- *Berberidaceae* · 7 spp. · E:May Apple; F:Pomme de mai; G:Maiapfel
- *diphyllum* L. = Jeffersonia diphylla
- **hexandrum** Royle · E:Himalayan Mayapple; F:Pomme de mai; G:Himalaya-Maiapfel · ♃ Z6 V ☠ ▽ ✻; Him.
- **peltatum** L. · E:Common May Apple, May Apple, Wild Lemon; F:Podophylle pelté; G:Entenfuß, Gewöhnlicher Maiapfel · ♃ Z4 V ⚕ ☠; Can.: E; USA: NE, NCE, SC, SE, Fla.
- **pleianthum** Hance · E:Chinese Mayapple; G:Chinesische Maiapfel · ♃ Z7 ∧ V ☠; China, Taiwan

Podospermum DC. = Scorzonera
- *laciniatum* (L.) DC. = Scorzonera laciniata

Podranea Sprague -f- *Bignoniaceae* · 2 spp. · E:Trumpet Vine; F:Liane-orchidée; G:Trompetenwein
- **brycei** (N.E. Br.) Sprague · E:Queen of Sheba, Zimbawe Climber; G:Purpur-Trompetenwein · ₺ ⌇ e ⌇ Z9 ⓚ; Zimbabwe
- **ricasoliana** (Tanfani) Sprague · E:Pink Trumpet Vine; G:Rosa Trompetenwein · ₺ e ⌇ Z9 ⓚ VII-X; S-Afr.

Poellnitzia Uitewaal -f- *Aloaceae* · 1 sp.
- **rubriflora** (L. Bolus) Uitewaal · ♃ ψ Z9 ⓚ; S-Cape

Pogonatherum P. Beauv. -n- *Poaceae* · 3 spp.
- **paniceum** (P. Beauv.) Hack. · ♃ Z10 ⓦ ▽; S-China, Malay. Pen., NE-Austr.

Pogostemon Desf. -m- *Lamiaceae* · 89 spp. · E:Patchouly; F:Patchouli; G:Patschuli
- **cablin** (Blanco) Benth. · E:Patchouly; G:Patschuli · ♃ ₺ D Z10 ⓦ VII-IX ⚕ Ⓝ; Phil., Sri Lanka, Thail., Vietn., Malay Arch., N. Guinea, Fiji
- *patchouly* Pellet. = Pogostemon cablin

Poinciana L. = Caesalpinia
- *coriaria* Jacq. = Caesalpinia coriaria
- *gilliesii* Wall. ex Hook. = Caesalpinia gilliesii
- *pulcherrima* L. = Caesalpinia pulcherrima
- *regia* Bojer ex Hook. = Delonix regia

Poinsettia Graham = Euphorbia
- *pulcherrima* (Willd. ex Klotzsch) Graham = Euphorbia pulcherrima

Polanisia Raf. -f- *Capparaceae* · 6 spp.
- **trachysperma** Torr. & A. Gray · E:Sandyseed Clammyweed · ⊙; W-Can.; USA: NEC, SC, Ark.

Polaskia Backeb. -f- *Cactaceae* · 2 spp.
- **chichipe** (Rol.-Goss.) Backeb. · ♄ ♈ Z8 ⒦
  ▽ ✳; Mex.

Polemonium L. -n- *Polemoniaceae* ·
25 spp. · E:Jacob's Ladder; F:Bâton de
Jacob, Valériane grecque; G:Himmelslei-
ter, Jakobsleiter, Sperrkraut
- **caeruleum** L. · G:Blaue Himmelsleiter
- subsp. **caeruleum** · E:Jacob's Ladder;
  F:Valériane grecque; G:Gewöhnliche
  Blaue Himmelsleiter, Jakobsleiter · ⚘
  Z2 VI-VII ▽; Eur.* exc. Ib; TR, W-Sib.,
  E-Sib.
- subsp. **himalayanum** (Baker) H. Hara ·
  ⚘ Z2 VI-VIII; Him.
- **carneum** A. Gray · ⚘ Z6 ⒜ V-VI; USA:
  Oreg., Calif.
- *confertum* A. Gray = Polemonium
  viscosum
- **foliosissimum** A. Gray · E:Towering
  Jacob's Ladder; G:Hohe Himmelsleiter ·
  ⚘ Z7 ⋀ VII-VIII; USA: Rocky Mts., SW
- **pauciflorum** S. Watson · E:Few-flowered
  Jacob's Ladder · ⊙ ⚘ Z7 ⋀ VI-VII; USA:
  Tex., SW; Mex.
- **pulcherrimum** Hook. · ⚘ Z4; N-Am.:
  Aleuten, Alaska, Can: : Yucon, B.C.; USA:
  NW, Calif., Colo.
- **reptans** L. · E:Greek Valerian; G:Horst-
  bildende Himmelsleiter · ⚘ Z4 IV-V ⚥ ;
  USA: NE, NCE, SE, SC
- × **richardsonii** hort. (*P. caeruleum* × *P.
  reptans*) · ⚘ Z6 IV-VII; cult.
- **viscosum** Nutt. · E:Sticky Jacob's Ladder;
  G:Klebrige Himmelsleiter · ⚘ △ Z7 ⋀
  VII-VIII; Can.: B.C.; USA: Rocky Mts., SW
- **Cultivars:**
- **many cultivars**

Polianthes L. -f- *Agavaceae* · 15 spp. ·
E:Tuberose; F:Tubéreuse; G:Nachthya-
zinthe
- **geminiflora** (La Llave & Lex.) Rose ·
  E:Twin Flower; G:Nickende Nachthyazinthe · ⚘ d ⋈ D Z9 ⒦ VII-VIII; Mex.
- **tuberosa** L. · G:Nachthyazinthe,
  Tuberose; E:Tuberose · ⚘ d ⋈ D Z9 ⒦
  VII-X Ⓝ; ? N-Mex.

Poliothyrsis Oliv. -f- *Flacourtiaceae* · 1 sp.
- **sinensis** Oliv. · ♄ d Z7 VII; C-China

Polyandrococos Barb. Rodr. -f- *Arecaceae* ·
1 sp.

- **caudescens** (Mart.) Barb. Rodr. · ♄ e Z10
  ⓦ; Braz.

Polybotrya Humb. & Bonpl. ex Willd.
-f- *Dryopteridaceae* · ·35 spp.
- *cervina* (L.) Kaulf. = Olfersia cervina
- **osmundacea** Humb. & Bonpl. ex Willd. ·
  ⚘ ⚥ Z10 ⓦ; Mex., W.Ind., trop. S-Am.
- **serratifolia** (Fée) Klotzsch · ⚘ ⚥ Z10 ⓦ;
  Mex., C-Am., trop. S-Am.

Polycarpon L. -n- *Caryophyllaceae* ·
16 spp. · F:Polycarpon; G:Nagelkraut
- **tetraphyllum** (L.) L. · E:Four-leaved
  All-seed ; G:Vierblättriges Nagelkraut · ⚘
  ⊙ VII-IX; Eur.: Ib, BrI, Ital-P, C-Eur., Ba;
  TR, Levant, Arab., Cauc., N-Iran, N-Afr.,
  nat. in CZ, S-Am., Austr., E-As.

Polycnemum L. -n- *Chenopodiaceae* ·
7-8 spp. · F:Polycnème; G:Knorpelkraut
- **arvense** L. · E:Field Needleleaf; G:Acker-
  Knorpelkraut · ⊙ VII-X; Eur.* exc. BrI, Sc;
  TR, Cauc., W-Sib., E-Sib. , C-As.
- **heuffelii** Láng · G:Heuffels Knorpelkraut · ⊙ VII-IX; Eur.: A, EC-Eur., Ba,
  E-Eur.
- **majus** A. Braun · G:Großes Knorpelkraut · ⊙ VII-IX; Eur.* exc. BrI, Sc; TR,
  Cauc., C-As.
- **verrucosum** Láng · G:Warziges Knorpelkraut · ⊙ VII-X; Eur.: C-Eur., EC-Eur.,
  W-Ba, E-Eur.; TR

Polycycnis Rchb. f. -f- *Orchidaceae* ·
7-15 spp. · F:Orchidée; G:Schlankschwän-
chen
- **barbata** (Lindl.) Rchb. f. · ⚘ Z10 ⓦ V-VII
  ▽ ✳; Costa Rica, Panama, Col., Venez.,
  Braz.

Polygala L. -f- *Polygalaceae* · c. 500 spp. ·
E:Milkwort; F:Polygala; G:Kreuzblüm-
chen
- **alpestris** Rchb. · E:Mountain Milkwort;
  G:Voralpen-Kreuzblümchen · ⚘ Z6
  VI-VII; Eur.: Ib, Fr, Ital-P, C-Eur., Ba
- **alpina** (Poir.) Steud. · E:Alpine Milkwort;
  G:Alpen-Kreuzblümchen, Westalpen-
  Kreuzblümchen · ⚘ VII-VIII; Eur.: sp., F,
  I, Sw; Pyr., W-Alp.
- **amara** L. · E:Bitter Milkwort; G:Lang-
  flügeliges Bitteres Kreuzblümchen · ⚘
  ⌢ Z6 V-VI ⚥ ; Eur.: C-Eur., EC-Eur., Ba,
  E-Eur.

- **amarella** Crantz · G:Gewöhnliches Sumpf-Kreuzblümchen · ⚥ Z6 IV-VI; Eur.* exc. Ib
- **butyracea** Heckel · ♄ Z10 ⓦ Ⓝ; W-Afr.
- **calcarea** F.W. Schultz · E:Chalk Milkwort; G:Kalk-Kreuzblümchen · ⚥ Z7 ⓐ IV-VI; Eur.: BrI, Fr, Ib, C-Eur.
- **chamaebuxus** L.
- var. **chamaebuxus** · E:Shrubby Milkwort; G:Buchsblättriges Kreuzblümchen, Zwergbuchs · ♄ e △ Z5 IV-IX; Eur.: Fr, C-Eur., EC-Eur., Ital-P, Slove., Croatia, RO
- var. **grandiflora** Gaudin · ♄ e Z6 IV-V; Sw: Tessin, Graubünden
- **comosa** Schkuhr · E:Tufted Milkwort; G:Schopfiges Kreuzblümchen · ⚥ V-VII; Eur.* exc. BrI; Cauc.
- × **dalmaisiana** L.H. Bailey (*P. myrtifolia var. grandiflora × P. oppositifolia var. cordata*) · E:Sweet Pea Shrub · ♄ ⓚ III-VIII; cult.
- **major** Jacq. · G:Großes Kreuzblümchen · ⚥ VI-VII; Eur.: Ital-P, A, EC-Eur., Ba, E-Eur.; TR, Cauc., N-Iran
- **myrtifolia** L.
- var. **grandiflora** (Lodd.) Hook. · ♄ e Z9 ⓚ III-VII; Cape
- var. **myrtifolia** · ♄ e Z9 ⓚ; S-Afr.
- **nicaeensis** Risso ex W.D.J. Koch · E:Nice Milkwort; G:Nizza-Kreuzblume, Pannonisches Kreuzblümchen · ⚥ V-VII; Eur.: Fr, Ital-P, C-Eur., H, Ba, E-Eur.; Alger., Tun.
- **oppositifolia** L.
- var. **cordata** Harv. · ♄ Z9 ⓚ III-VII; S-Afr. (Cape Prov.)
- var. **latifolia** Ker-Gawl. · ♄ Z9 ⓚ III-VII; S-Afr. (Cape Prov.)
- var. **oppositifolia** · ♄ e Z9 ⓚ; Cape
- **senega** L. · E:Senga Root, Snakeroot · ⚥ Z2 V-VII ⚥; Can., USA: NE, NCE, NC, SE
- **serpyllifolia** Host · E:Thyme-leaved Milkwort; G:Thymianblättriges Kreuzblümchen · ⚥ V-IX; Eur.* exc. EC-Eur.; Greenl.
- **vayredae** Costa · E:Pyrenean Milkwort · ♄ e △ Z7 ⓐ ∧ IV-VIII; Eur.: sp.; E-Pyr.
- **virgata** Thunb.
- var. **speciosa** (Sims) Harv. · ♄ e Z9 ⓚ III-VII; Cape
- var. **virgata** · E:Purple Broom · ♄ ♄ e Z8 ⓚ; S-Afr.
- **vulgaris** L. · G:Gewöhnliches Kreuzblümchen

- subsp. **oxyptera** (Rchb.) Schübl. & G. Martens · G:Spitzflügeliges Kreuzblümchen · ⚥ Z6 V-VIII; A (Kärnten), D +
- subsp. **vulgaris** · E:Gand Flower, Milkwort ; G:Gewöhnliches Kreuzblümchen · ⚥ Z6 V-VIII ⚥; Eur.*, TR, Sib.

Polygaloides Haller = Polygala
- *chamaebuxus* (L.) O. Schwarz = Polygala chamaebuxus var. chamaebuxus

Polygonatum Mill. -n- *Convallariaceae* · 71 sp. · E:Solomon's Seal; F:Sceau de Salomon; G:Salomonssiegel, Weißwurz
- **biflorum** (Walter) Elliott · G:Zweiblütige Weißwurz; E:Giant Solomon's Seal · ⚥ Z3 V; Can.: E; USA: NE, NCE, Okla
- *canaliculatum* (Muhl.) Pursh = Polygonatum biflorum
- *commutatum* (Schult. & Schult. f.) A. Dietr. = Polygonatum biflorum
- **falcatum** A. Gray · ⚥ Z6 V; Jap., Korea
- *giganteum* A. Dietr. = Polygonatum biflorum
- **hirtum** (Bosc ex Poir.) Pursh · G:Auen-Weißwurz · ⚥ Z5 V-VI ⚘; Eur.: I, A, EC-Eur., Ba, Russ; NW-TR, Cauc.
- **hookeri** Baker · ⚥ △ Z6 V; Sikkim, China: Yunnan, Tibet
- **humile** Maxim. · ⚥ Z5; Jap., Sakhal., Korea, Manch., Sib.
- × **hybridum** Brügger (*P. multiflorum × P. odoratum*) · E:Garden Salomon's Seal; G:Garten-Salomonsiegel · ⚥ Z6; N-Eur., W-Eur.
- *latifolium* Desf. = Polygonatum hirtum
- **multiflorum** (L.) All. · E:Solomon's Seal; F:Sceau de Salomon; G:Vielblütige Weißwurz · ⚥ Z4 V-VI ⚥ ⚘; Eur.*, TR, Cauc., Him., Jap.
- **odoratum** (Mill.) Druce · G:Salomonssiegel
- var. **odoratum** · E:Lesser Solomon's Seal; G:Echtes Salomonssiegel, Wohlriechende Weißwurz · ⚥ D Z4 V-VI ⚘; Eur.*, Cauc., W-Sib., E-Sib., Amur, Mong., China, Korea, Moroc.
- var. **thunbergii** (C. Morren & Decne.) H. Hara · ⚥ Z4 IV-V; Jap.
- *officinale* All. = Polygonatum odoratum var. odoratum
- **roseum** (Ledeb.) Kunth · ⚥ Z3 V-VI; W-Sib., C-As., China: Sinkiang
- **stenanthum** Nakai · ⚥ Z7 V-VII; Jap., Korea

– *thunbergii* C. Morren & Decne. =
Polygonatum odoratum var. thunbergii
– **verticillatum** (L.) All. · E:Whorled Salo-
mon's Seal; G:Quirlblättrige Weißwurz
· ⹘ Z5 V-VI ☙; Eur.*, TR, Cauc., N-Iran,
Him.

Polygonum L. -n- *Polygonaceae* · c.
50 spp. · E:Knotgrass; F:Renouée;
G:Vogelknöterich
– *affine* D. Don = Bistorta affinis
– *alatum* Buch.-Ham. ex D. Don =
Persicaria nepalensis
– *alpinum* All. = Aconogonon alpinum
– *amphibium* L. = Persicaria amphibia
– *amplexicaule* D. Don = Bistorta amplexicaulis
– **arenarium** Waldst. & Kit. · G:Sand-
Vogelknöterich · ⊙ VII-IX; Eur.: Fr, Ital-P,
EC-Eur., Ba, E-Eur.; TR, Levant, Cauc., ?
Moroc.
– **arenastrum** Boreau · G:Gewöhnlicher
Vogelknöterich
– subsp. **arenastrum** · E:Small-leaved
Knotgrass; G:Gewöhnlicher Vogelknöterich · ⊙ VII-X; Eur.: most; TR, Levant, ?
NW-Afr.
– subsp. **calcatum** (Lindm.) Wissk. · G:Nie-
driger Gewöhnlicher Vogelknöterich · ⊙
VII-IX; Eur.: most; TR
– *aubertii* L. Henry = Fallopia baldschuanica
– **aviculare** L. · G:Acker-Vogelknöterich
– subsp. **aviculare** · E:Knotweed;
G:Aufrechter Vogelknöterich,
Breitblättriger Acker-Vogelknöterich,
Verschiedenblättriger Vogelknöterich · ⊙
V-XI ⚥ ; Eur.*, Cauc., W-Sib., E-Sib. C-As.
– subsp. **rectum** Chrtek · G:Schmalblät-
triger Acker-Vogelknöterich
– subsp. **rurivagum** (Jord. ex Boreau) Berher · G:Unbeständiger Acker-Vogelknöterich, Unbeständiger Vogelknöterich ·
V-IX; Eur.* exc. E-Eur.; NW-Afr.
– *baldschuanicum* Regel = Fallopia
baldschuanica
– **bellardii** All. · G:Ungarischer Vogelknöterich · ⊙ VI-X; Eur.* exc. BrI, Sc; TR,
Levant, SW-As., W-Sib., N-Afr.
– *bistorta* L. = Bistorta officinalis subsp.
officinalis
– *brittingeri* Opiz = Persicaria lapathifolia
subsp. brittingeri
– *calcatum* Lindm. = Polygonum arenastrum subsp. calcatum

– *campanulatum* Hook. f. = Aconogonon
campanulatum
– *capitatum* Buch.-Ham. ex D. Don =
Persicaria capitata
– *carneum* K. Koch = Bistorta officinalis
subsp. carnea
– *coccineum* Muhl. = Persicaria amphibia
– *compactum* Hook. f. = Fallopia japonica
var. compacta
– *complexum* A. Cunn. = Muehlenbeckia
complexa
– *convolvulus* L. = Fallopia convolvulus
– *cuspidatum* Siebold & Zucc. = Fallopia
japonica var. japonica
– *dshawachischwilii* Kharkev. =
Aconogonon alpinum
– *dubium* = Persicaria dubia
– *dumetorum* L. = Fallopia dumetorum
– **equisetiforme** Sibth. & Sm. · ♄ ⓩ IX-X;
Eur.: Ib, Sic, Ba; TR, Levant, N-Afr.
– *fagopyrum* L. = Fagopyrum esculentum
– *filiforme* Thunb. = Persicaria filiformis
– **graminifolium** Wierzb. ex Heuff. · ⊙ ;
Eur.: EC-Eur., Serb., RO
– *heterophyllum* Sol. ex Meisn. = Polygonum aviculare subsp. aviculare
– *hydropiper* L. = Persicaria hydropiper
– *japonicum* Meisn. = Fallopia japonica var.
japonica
– var. *compactum* (Hook. f.) J.P. Bailey =
Fallopia japonica var. compacta
– *lapathifolium* = Persicaria lapathifolia
subsp. lapathifolia
– *lichiangense* W.W. Sm. = Aconogonon
lichiangense
– *macrophyllum* D. Don = Bistorta
macrophylla
– *multiflorum* Thunb. = Fallopia multiflora
– *odoratum* Lour. = Persicaria odorata
– *orientale* L. = Persicaria orientalis
– **oxyspermum** C.A. Mey. & Bunge
ex Ledeb. · G:Hellbrauner Strand-
Vogelknöterich · ⊙ VII-IX; Eur.* , E-Can.
Nova Scotia)
– *paleaceum* Wall. = Bistorta officinalis
subsp. carnea
– **patulum** M. Bieb. · ⊙ ; Eur.: H, RO,
Russ.; Cauc., Iran, C-As., China: Sinkiang
– *persicaria* L. = Persicaria maculosa
– *polymorphum* Ledeb. = Aconogonon
alpinum
– *polystachyum* Wall. ex Meisn. =
Aconogonon polystachyum
– *reynoutria* Makino = Fallopia japonica
var. japonica

– *rurivagum* Jord. ex Boreau = Polygonum aviculare subsp. rurivagum
– *sachalinense* F. Schmidt = Fallopia sachalinensis
– **scoparium** Req. ex Loisel. · ⁴ ♭ Z7; Cors, Sard.
– *sericeum* Pall. = Aconogonon sericeum
– *sieboldii* Reinw. ex de Vries = Fallopia japonica var. japonica
– *sphaerostachyum* Meisn. = Bistorta macrophylla
– *tataricum* L. = Fagopyrum tataricum
– *tenuicaule* Bisset & S. Moore = Bistorta tenuicaulis
– *tinctorium* Aiton = Persicaria tinctoria
– *vacciniifolium* Wall. ex Meisn. = Bistorta vacciniifolia
– *virginianum* L. = Persicaria virginiana
– var. *filiforme* (Thunb.) Merr. = Persicaria filiformis
– *viviparum* L. = Bistorta vivipara
– *weyrichii* F. Schmidt ex Maxim. = Aconogonon weyrichii
– *zuccarinii* Small = Fallopia japonica var. japonica

Polymnia L. -f- Asteraceae · 2 spp.
– **sonchifolia** Poepp. & Endl. · ⁴ Z9 ⓚ Ⓝ; Col. (And. Bogota)

Polypodium L. -n- *Polypodiaceae* · 181 sp. · E:Polypody; F:Polypode; G:Tüpfelfarn
– **angustifolium** Sw. · E:Narrow Strap Fern · ⁴ Z10 ⓜ; USA: Fla.; Mex., W.Ind, trop. S-Am.
– *aureum* L. = Phlebodium aureum
– *bifrons* Hook. = Solanopteris bifrons
– **cambricum** L. · E:Welsh Polypody; G:Südlicher Tüpfelfarn · ⁴ Z6 V-VI; Eur.: Ib, Fr, BrI, Sw, Ital-P, Ba, Crim; TR, Levant, NW-Afr.
– *coronans* Wall. ex Mett. = Aglaomorpha coronans
– *crassifolium* L. = Niphidium crassifolium
– **decurrens** Raddi · ⁴ Z10 ⓜ; W.Ind., Peru, Braz.
– *filix-femina* L. = Athyrium filix-femina
– *heracleum* Kuntze = Aglaomorpha heraclea
– **interjectum** Shivas · E:Western Polypody; G:Gesägter Tüpfelfarn · ⁴ Z5 IX-X; Eur.*, TR, Iran
– *irioides* Poir. = Microsorum punctatum
– *juglandifolium* D. Don = Arthromeris wallichiana

– *leiorhizum* Wall. ex Mett. = Polypodium lucidum
– **longifolium** Mett. · ⁴ Z10 ⓜ; Malay. Pen., Phil.
– **lucidum** Roxb. · ⁴ Z10 ⓜ; Ind.
– **lycopodioides** L. · ⁴ Z10 ⓜ; trop. Am.
– × **mantoniae** Rothm. & U. Schneid. (*P. interjectum* × *P. vulgare*) · E:Manton's Polypody; G:Mantons Tüpfelfarn · ⁴; Eur.: BrI, C-Eur., I, Slova., H +
– *meyenianum* (Schott) Hook. = Aglaomorpha meyeniana
– *musifolium* Blume = Microsorum musifolium
– *phegopteris* L. = Phegopteris connectilis
– *phyllitidis* L. = Campyloneurum phyllitidis
– **polypodioides** (L.) D. Watt · E:Resurrection Fern; G:Auferstehungsfarn · ⁴ ⤳ Z7 ⓚ; USA: NE, NCE, SC, SE, Fla.; Mex., C-Am., S-Am., S-Afr.
– *pteropus* Blume = Microsorum pteropus
– *punctatum* (L.) Sw. = Microsorum punctatum
– *reinwardtii* Kuntze = Goniophlebium subauriculatum
– *rigidum* Hoffm. non Aubl. = Dryopteris villarii
– *scandens* G. Forst. = Microsorum scandens
– *subauriculatum* Blume = Goniophlebium subauriculatum
– *vacciniifolium* Langsd. & Fisch. = Micrograma vacciniifolia
– **vulgare** L. · E:Common Polypody; F:Polypode vulgaire; G:Engelsüß, Gewöhnlicher Tüpfelfarn · ⁴ ⤳ Z3 VIII-IX ♀; Eur.*, TR, Cyprus, Cauc., W-Sib., C-As., E-As., Moroc., N-Am.
– subsp. *prionodes* (Asch.) Rothm. = Polypodium interjectum
– *wallichianum* Spreng. = Arthromeris wallichiana

Polypogon Desf. -m- *Poaceae* · 18 spp. · E:Beard Grass; F:Polypogon; G:Bürstengras
– **monspeliensis** (L.) Desf. · E:Annual Beard Grass, Annual Rabbit's Foot Grass; G:Bürstengras · ☉ ✂ Z8 IV-VII; Eur.: Ib, F, Ital-P, Ba, RO, S-Russ., BrI; TR, Iraq, Cauc., Iran, C-As., Afgh., Pakist., Him., Ind., Sri Lanka, Tibet, Mong., China, Korea, Jap., Taiwan , Canar., nat. in Cz, W-Russ., N-Am., S-Afr., Austr., NZ

– **viridis** (Gouan) Breistr. · E:Water Bent ·
24 Z7; Eur.: Ib, Fr, Sw, Ital-P, Ba, Crim;
TR, Iran, Afgh., Pakist., Canar., Madeira,
nat. in N-Am., S-Am., Afr., Austr.

Polyscias J.R. Forst. & G. Forst. -f-
Araliaceae · 100-150 spp. · E:Fern-leaf
Aralia; F:Polyscias; G:Fiederaralie
– *balfouriana* (Sander ex André) L.H.
Bailey = Polyscias scutellaria 'Balfourii'
– **cumingiana** (C. Presl) Fern.-Vill. ·
E:Malaysian Aralia · ♄ e Z10 ⓜ; Malay.
Arch.
– **filicifolia** (C. Moore ex E. Fourn.) L.H.
Bailey · E:Fern-leaf Aralia; G:Farnblät-
trige Fiederaralie · ♄ Z10 ⓜ; Malay.
Arch., Pacific Is.
– **fruticosa** (L.) Harms · E:Ming Aralie, Tea
Tree; G:Rötliche Fiederaralie · ♄ e Z10 ⓜ
Ⓝ; Malay. Arch., Polyn.
– **guilfoylei** (W. Bull) L.H. Bailey · E:Wild
Coffee; G:Polynesische Fiederaralie · ♄ e
Z10 ⓜ Ⓝ; Malay. Arch., Pacific Is.
– *pinnata* J.R. Forst. & G. Forst. = Polyscias
scutellaria
– *rumphiana* Harms = Polyscias cumingiana
– **scutellaria** (Burm. f.) Fosberg · E:Dinner
Plate Aralia; G:Glänzende Fiederaralie ·
♄ ♄ e Z10 ⓜ; N.Caled.
– **'Balfourii'** · E:Balfour Aralia; G:Balfours
Fiederaralie · ⓜ

Polystachya Hook. -f- *Orchidaceae* ·
228 spp.
– **affinis** Lindl. · 24 Z10 ⓜ VII-VIII ▽ ✳;
W-Afr., C-Afr., Angola, Uganda

Polystichum Roth -n- *Dryopteridaceae* ·
409 spp. · E:Holly Fern, Shield Fern;
F:Polystic; G:Schildfarn
– **acrostichoides** (Michx.) Schott ·
E:Christmas Fern, Dagger Fern;
F:Fougère de Noël; G:Dolch-Farn,
Weihnachts-Farn · 24 ⋉ Z4 ▽; Can.: E;
USA: NE, NCE, Mo., SC, SE, Fla; Mex.
– **aculeatum** (L.) Roth · E:Hard Shield
Fern, Prickly Shield Fern; F:Aspidie
lobée, Polystic à aiguillons; G:Dorniger
Schildfarn, Gelappter Schildfarn · 24 Z5
VIII-IX ▽; Eur.*, TR, Syr., Cauc., N-Iran,
N-As., China, Jap., Moroc., Alger.
– *adiantiforme* (G. Forst.) J. Sm. =
Rumohra adiantiformis
– **andersonii** Hopkins · E:Anderson's

Shield Fern; G:Andersons Schildfarn ·
24 Z4 ▽; Alaska, Can.: B.C.; USA: NW,
Idaho, Mont.
– **auriculatum** (L.) C. Presl · 24 Z9 ⓚ ▽;
Ind., Sri Lanka
– **braunii** (Spenn.) Fée · E:Braun's Holly
Fern, Shield Fern; F:Aspidie de Braun;
G:Brauns Schildfarn, Zarter Schildfarn
· 24 Z5 VII-VIII ▽; Eur.* exc. BrI; Cauc.,
Amur, Alaska, Can.: E; USA: NE, NCE;
Hawai
– **falcatum** (L. f.) Diels
– var. **caryotideum** (Wall.) Baker ·
E:Dwarf Net Vein Holly Fern; G:Kleiner
Mondsichelfarn · 24 Z9 ⓚ ▽; Ind., China,
Jap., Hawaii
– var. **falcatum** · E:Japanese Holly Fern;
G:Mondsichelfarn · 24 Z9 ⓚ ▽; Ind.,
China, Korea, Jap., Ryukyu-Is., Taiwan,
Malay. Arch., Polyn., S-Afr., nat. in GB,
Azor.
– var. **fortunei** (J. Sm.) Baker · G:Ilexblät-
triger Mondsichelfarn · 24 Z8 ⓚ ⓐ ▽;
China, Korea, Jap.
– *laserpitiifolium* J. Sm. = Arachniodes
standishii
– **lepidocaulon** (Hook.) J. Sm. · 24 Z8 ⓚ
▽; China, Korea, Jap., Taiwan
– *lobatum* (Huds.) Bastard = Polystichum
aculeatum
– **lonchitis** (L.) Roth · E:Northern Holly
Fern; G:Lanzen-Schildfarn · 24 Z4 VII-IX
▽; Eur.*, TR, Cauc., W-Sib., E-Sib.,
Sakhal., Kamchat., Jap., C-As., Alaska,
Can., USA: NE, NCE, NC, SW, Rocky
Mts., NW, Calif.; Greenl.; mts.
– **macrophyllum** (Makino) Tagawa · 24 ⓚ
∧ ▽; Him., China, Jap., Taiwan
– **mohrioides** (Bory) C. Presl · 24 Z5 ▽;
Can.: B.C.; USA: NW, Calif.
– **munitum** (Kaulf.) C. Presl · E:Western
Sword Fern; G:Schwertfarn · 24 ⋉ Z4
▽; Can.: B.C., Yukon; USA: NW, Calif.,
Idaho, Mont., S.Dak.; Mex.: Guadelupe
Isl., nat. in Eur.
– *nipponicum* Rosenst. = Arachniodes
nipponica
– *oreopteris* (Ehrh.) Bernh. = Oreopteris
limbosperma
– **polyblepharum** (Roem.) C. Presl ·
E:Japanese Lace Fern; F:Aspidie du
Japon; G:Japanischer Schildfarn · 24 Z5
▽; Jap., S-Korea
– **rigens** Tagawa · F:Aspidie · 24 Z7 ▽; Jap.
– **setiferum** (Forssk.) T. Moore ex Woyn. ·

E:Alaska Fern, Hedge Fern, Soft Shield Fern; F:Polysticà cils raides; G:Borstiger Schildfarn, Weicher Schildfarn · ♃ Z7 VIII-IX ▽; Eur.* exc. Sc; TR, Cauc., Iran, Him., Moroc., Afr.
– some cultivars
– × **setigerum** (C. Presl) C. Presl (*P. braunii* × *P. munitum*) · E:Alaska Holly Fern · ♃ Z3; Alaska, B.C., Aleutian Is.
– *standishii* (T. Moore) C. Chr. = Arachniodes standishii
– *thelypteris* (L.) Roth = Thelypteris palustris
– **tripteron** (Kunze) C. Presl · ♃ Z6 ▽; E-Sib., China, Jap.
– **tsus-simense** (Hook.) J. Sm. · ♃ Z7 ⋀ ▽; China, Korea, Jap., Taiwan

Pomaderris Labill. -f- *Rhamnaceae* · 55 spp.
– **apetala** Labill. · E:Dogwood · ♄ ♄ e Z9 ⌂ VI; Austr.: Victoria, Tasman.; NZ

Pometia J.R. Forst. & G. Forst. -f- *Sapindaceae* · 2 spp.
– **pinnata** J.R. Forst. & G. Forst. · ♄ ⍟ Ⓝ; Malay. Arch., N.Guinea, Pazific Is.

Poncirus Raf. -f- *Rutaceae* · 1 sp. · E:Bitter Orange; F:Oranger amer, Poncir; G:Bitterorange
– **trifoliata** (L.) Raf. · E:Bitter Orange, Trifoliate Orange; F:Orange amère, Poncir; G:Bitterorange · ♄ ♄ d ⌀ Z7 ⋀ IV-V; Him., C-China, nat. in Jap.

Pontederia L. -f- *Pontederiaceae* · 6 spp. · E:Pickerel Weed; F:Herbe-à-brochet; G:Hechtkraut
– **cordata** L. · E:Pickerel Weed, Pickerelweed; F:Pontédérie; G:Herzförmiges Hechtkraut · ♃ ≈ Z7 VI-X; Can.: E; USA: NE, NCE, SE, Fla.
– var. **lancifolia** (Muhl.) Torr.
– *crassipes* Mart. = Eichhornia crassipes
– *lanceolata* Nutt. = Pontederia cordata

Populus L. -f- *Salicaceae* · 35 spp. · E:Aspen, Cottonwood, Poplar; F:Peuplier; G:Espe, Pappel
– **alba** L. · E:White Poplar; F:Peuplier blanc; G:Silber-Pappel · ♄ d Z4 III-IV ⚥ Ⓝ; Eur.* exc. BrI, Sc; TR, Palest., Cauc., W-Sib., C-As., Him., N-Afr., nat. in BrI, DK, N-Am.
– var. *pyramidalis* Bunge = Populus alba

– **angustifolia** James ex Torr. · E:Narrowleaf Cottonwood, Willow Leaved Poplar; G:Schmalblättrige Pappel · ♄ d Z3; Can.: W, Man.; USA: Rocky Mts., Calif., SW, SC, NC; N-Mex.
– **balsamifera** L.
– var. **balsamifera** · E:Balsam Poplar, Tacamahaca; F:Peuplier baumier; G:Balsam-Pappel · ♄ d D Z3 IV ⚥ Ⓝ; Alaska, Can., USA: NE, NCE, NC, Rocky Mts., NW
– var. *fernaldiana* Rouleau = Populus balsamifera var. subcordata
– var. **subcordata** Hyl. · ♄ d D Z2; Can.: E; USA: NE, NCE
– × **berolinensis** (K. Koch) Dippel (*P. laurifolia* × *P. nigra* 'Italica') · E:Berlin Poplar; F:Peuplier de Berlin; G:Berliner Pappel · ♄ d Z4 Ⓝ; cult.
– × **canadensis** Moench (*P. deltoides* × *P. nigra*) · E:Canadian Poplar; F:Peuplier grisard, Peuplier hybride euraméricain; G:Bastard-Schwarz-Pappel, Kanada-Pappel · ♄ d Z4 IV Ⓝ; cult.
– × **canescens** (Aiton) Sm. (*P. alba* × *P. tremula*) · E:Grey Poplar; F:Peuplier grisard; G:Grau-Pappel · ♄ d Z5 III-IV Ⓝ; Eur.* exc. Sc, Ib; TR, Cauc., nat. in Sc, Ib, USA
– **cathayana** Rehder · ♄ d Z4; NW-China, Manch., Korea
– **deltoides** W. Bartram ex Marshall · E:Eastern Cottonwood, Necklace Poplar; G:Karolina-Pappel, Virginische Pappel · ♄ d Z6 IV Ⓝ; Can.: E; USA: NE, NCE, NC, SC, SE, Fla., nat. in Eur.
– subsp. *monilifera* (Aiton) Eckenw. = Populus sargentii
– var. *occidentalis* Rydb. = Populus sargentii
– × *euroamericana* (Dode) Guinier = Populus × canadensis
– × **generosa** A. Henry (*P. deltoides* × *P. trichocarpa*) · ♄ d Z6 Ⓝ; cult.
– × *gileadensis* Rouleau = Populus × jackii
– **grandidentata** Michx. · E:Big Tooth Aspen; G:Großzähnige Pappel · ♄ d Z4 Ⓝ; Can.: E; USA: NE, NCE, NC, Tenn., N.C.
– *italica* (Münchh.) Moench = Populus nigra subsp. nigra
– × **jackii** Sarg. (*P. balsamifera* × *P. deltoides*) · E:Balm of Gilead · ♄ d Z2; Can.: Ont.; USA: NE, NEC
– **koreana** Rehder · G:Koreanische

Balsam-Pappel · ħ d Z6; Korea
- **lasiocarpa** Oliv. · E:Chinese Necklace Poplar; F:Peuplier à fruits velus; G:Großblatt-Pappel · ħ d Z5 Ⓝ; W-China, C-China
- **laurifolia** Ledeb. · E:Laurel Poplar; G:Lorbeerblättrige Pappel · ħ d Z5 Ⓝ; W-Sib., E-Sib., C-As., China: Sikiang; Mong., NW-Ind., Jap.
- **maximowiczii** A. Henry · E:Japanese Poplar; G:Maximowiczs Pappel · ħ d Z4 Ⓝ; Amur, Manch., Korea, Jap., Sakhal., Kamchat.
- **nigra** L.
- subsp. **betulifolia** (Pursh) W. Wettst. · G:Birkenblättrige Schwarz-Pappel · ħ d Z5; Eur.: BrI, F
- subsp. **nigra** · E:Black Poplar; F:Peuplier noir; G:Echte Schwarz-Pappel · ħ d Z5 IV ⚕ Ⓝ; Eur.* exc. Sc; TR, Cauc., W-Sib., E-Sib., C-As.: Him., NW-Afr., nat. in DK
- var. *italica* Münchh. = Populus nigra subsp. nigra
- var. *pyramidalis* (Rozier) Spach = Populus nigra subsp. nigra
- *pyramidalis* Rozier = Populus nigra subsp. nigra
- **sargentii** Dode · E:Great Plains Cottonwood, Sargent Cottonwood; G:Sargents Pappel · ħ d Z2 ⚕ Ⓝ; Can.: W, Man.; USA: Rocky Mts., SW, SC, NC
- **simonii** Carrière · E:Cottonwood; F:Peuplier de Simon; G:Simons Pappel · ħ d Z4 IV Ⓝ; N-China
- **suaveolens** Fisch. ex Loudon · E:Poplar; G:Sibirische Balsam-Pappel · ħ d Z3 Ⓝ; E-Sib., Amur, Kamchat., N-China, Korea, N-Jap.
- **szechuanica** C.K. Schneid. · E:Chinese Poplar; G:Chinesische Balsam-Pappel · ħ d Z6 Ⓝ; Sichuan
- *tacamahaca* Mill. = Populus balsamifera var. balsamifera
- **tremula** L. · E:Aspen; F:Peuplier tremble; G:Espe, Zitter-Pappel · ♄ ħ d Z1 III-IV Ⓝ; Eur.*, TR, Lebanon, Cauc., W-Sib., E-Sib., Amur, Sakhal., Kamchat., C-As., Mong., Korea, N-China, Alger.
- **tremuloides** Michx. · E:American Aspen, Aspen, Quaking Aspen; F:Peuplier faux-tremble; G:Amerikanische Espe · ħ d Z1 ⚕ Ⓝ; Alaska, Can., USA: NE, NCE, NC, Rocky Mts., SW, Calif., NW; N-Mex., Baja Calif.
- **trichocarpa** Torr. & A. Gray ex Hook. · E:Black Cottonwood, Western Balsam Poplar; F:Peuplier baumier; G:Haarfrüchtige Balsam-Pappel · ħ d Z5 IV Ⓝ; Alaska, Can.: W; USA: NW, Rocky Mts., Calif; Mex.: Baja Calif.
- **tristis** Fisch. · G:Dunkelblättrige Pappel · ħ d Z1 Ⓝ; C-As.
- **wilsonii** C.K. Schneid. · E:Wilson's Poplar; G:Wilsons Großblatt-Pappel · ħ d Z6 Ⓝ; China: Hupeh, Sichuan
- **yunnanensis** Dode · G:Yunnan-Pappel · ħ d Z5; SW-China: Yunnan

Porana Burm. f. -f- *Convolvulaceae* · 20 spp.
- **paniculata** Roxb. · E:Bridal Bouquet, Snow Creeper; G:Schnee im Dschungel · ♄ ⌇ Z10 Ⓦ VIII; Ind., Malay. Pen.
- **racemosa** Roxb. · ⊙ Z10 Ⓦ VII-XI; Ind., Burma

Porlieria Ruiz & Pav. -f- *Zygophyllaceae* · 6 spp. · E:Soap Bush; G:Seifenbusch
- **hygrometra** Ruiz & Pav. · E:Soap Bush; G:Seifenbusch · ♄ Z10 Ⓚ IV; Peru

Porphyrocoma Scheidw. ex Hook. = Justicia
- *lanceolata* Scheidw. = Justicia ovata var. lanceolata

Porroglossum Schltr. -n- *Orchidaceae* · 35 spp.
- **echidnum** (Rchb. f.) Garay · ♃ Z9 Ⓚ V-VIII ▽ ✻; Col., Ecuad.

Portea Brongn. ex K. Koch -f- *Bromeliaceae* · 9 spp.
- **kermesina** Brongn. ex K. Koch · ♃ Z10 Ⓦ; Braz.
- **petropolitana** (Wawra) Mez · ♃ Z10 Ⓦ; Braz.

Portulaca L. -f- *Portulacaceae* · 40 spp. · E:Purslane, Rose Moss; F:Pourpier; G:Portulak
- **grandiflora** Hook. · E:Common Portulaca, Moss Rose, Sum Plant; F:Pourpier à grandes fleurs; G:Portulakröschen · ⊙ ψ VI-VIII; Braz., Urug., Arg., nat. in C-Eur., SE-Eur.
- **some cultivars**
- **oleracea** L. · G:Portulak
- subsp. **oleracea** · E:Purslane; G:Europäischer Portulak · ⊙ ψ VI-IX; Eur.*, TR, Levant, Cauc., Iran, C-As., Mong., Subtrop., Trop., nat. in Eur.* exc. Sk

– subsp. **sativa** (Haw.) Čelak. · ⊙ ♃ ♁ ;
cult.
– **umbraticola** Kunth · ⊙ ♃ VI-VIII; Col.

Portulacaria Jacq. -f- *Portulacaceae* ·
1-2 spp. · E:Elephant Bush; F:Pourpier en
arbre; G:Speckbaum, Strauchportulak
– **afra** Jacq. · E:Elephant Bush, Elephant's
Food; G:Speckbaum, Strauchportulak · ♄
♃ e Z9 ⌂; S-Afr.

Posidonia K.D. Koenig -f- *Posidoniaceae* ·
c. 5 spp.
– **oceanica** (L.) Delile · E:Mediterranean
Tapeweed · ♃ ≈ Ⓝ; Eur.: Ib, F, Ital-P,
Ba; N-Afr., Levant; coasts

Potamogeton L. -m- *Potamogetonaceae* ·
c. 90 spp. · E:Pondweed; F:Potamot;
G:Laichkraut
– **acutifolius** Link · E:Sharp Leaved
Pondweed; G:Spitzblättriges Laichkraut ·
♃ ≈ VI-VIII; Eur.* exc. Ib
– **alpinus** Balb. · E:Alpine Pondweed, Red-
dish Pondweed; G:Alpen-Laichkraut · ♃
≈ VI-VIII; Eur.*, Cauc., W-Sib., E-Sib.,
C-As.
– × **angustifolius** J. Presl (*P. gramineus* ×
P. lucens) · G:Schmalblättriges Lai-
chkraut · ♃ ≈ VI-VII; D+
– **berchtoldii** Fieber · E:Small Pondweed;
F:Potamot de Berchtold; G:Berchtolds
Laichkraut · ♃ ≈ VI-IX; Eur.* exc. Ib;
TR, N-As., N-Am., ? NW-Afr.
– **coloratus** Hornem. · E:Fen Pondweed;
G:Gefärbtes Laichkraut · ♃ ≈ VI-VIII;
Eur.*
– **compressus** L. · E:Grass-wrack Pond-
weed; G:Flachstängeliges Laichkraut · ♃
≈ VII-VIII; Eur.* exc. Ital-P; Sib., Amur,
Kamchat.
– **crispus** L. · E:Curled Pondweed, Water
Caltrop; F:Potamot crépu; G:Krauses
Laichkraut · ♃ ≈ V-VIII; Eur.*, TR,
Cauc., W-Sib., E-Sib., Amur, C-As., Him.,
Manch., Korea, Jap., Taiwan, Egypt, Afr.,
Austr., nat. in N-Am., NZ
– *densus* L. = Groenlandia densa
– **filiformis** Pers. · E:Slender-leaved
Pondweed; G:Faden-Laichkraut · ♃ ≈
VI-VII; Eur.*, TR, Cauc., NW-Iran, Afgh.,
Pakist., E-Sib., Amur, Kamchat.
– × **fluitans** Roth (*P. lucens* × *P. natans*) ·
G:Flutendes Laichkraut · ♃ ≈ ; G, BrI+
– **friesii** Rupr. · E:Flat-stalked Pondweed;

G:Stachelspitziges Laichkraut · ♃ ≈
VI-VIII; Eur.* exc. Ib; W-Sib., E-Sib.,
Kamchat., Manch., N-Am., nat. in Arg.
– **gramineus** L. · E:Grass-leaf Pondweed;
G:Grasartiges Laichkraut · ♃ ≈ VI-VII;
Eur.*, TR, Cauc., NW-Iran, Pakist., Sib.,
N-Am.
– **helveticus** (G. Fisch.) W. Koch ·
G:Schweizer Laichkraut · ♃ ≈ VIII-XI;
Eur.: G, Sw, H, A
– **lucens** L. · E:Shining Pondweed;
F:Potamot luisant; G:Glänzendes
Laichkraut · ♃ ≈ VI-VIII; Eur.*, W-Afr.
– **natans** L. · E:Broad-leaved Pondweed,
Floating Pondweed; F:Potamot nageant;
G:Schwimmendes Laichkraut · ♃ ≈
VI-VIII; Eur.*, TR, Syr., Cauc., W-Sib.,
E-Sib., Amur, Sakhal., Kamchat., C-As.,
Afgh., Pakist., Manch., Korea, Jap.,
N-Afr., cosmop.
– × **nitens** Weber (*P. gramineus* × *P.
perfoliatus*) · G:Schimmerndes Lai-
chkraut · ♃ ≈ VI-VIII; G, BrI, F+
– **nodosus** Poir. · E:American Pondweed,
Loddon Pondweed; G:Knoten-Laichkraut
· ♃ ≈ VI-VIII; Eur.* exc. Sc; TR, Cauc.,
W-Sib., C-As., SE-As., N-Am., C-Am., Afr.
– **obtusifolius** Mert. & W.D.J. Koch ·
E:Grassy Pondweed; G:Stumpfblättriges
Laichkraut · ♃ ≈ VI-VIII; Eur.* exc. Ib;
Cauc., Iran, W-Sib., E-Sib., C-As., Mong.,
N-Am.
– *panormitanus* = Potamogeton pusillus
– **pectinatus** L. · E:Fennel Pondweed, Sago
Pondweed; F:Potamot pectiné; G:Kamm-
Laichkraut · ♃ ≈ VI-VIII; Eur.*, E-USA,
S-Am., Afr.
– **perfoliatus** L. · E:Perfoliate Pondweed;
G:Durchwachsenes Laichkraut · ♃ ≈
VI-VIII; Eur.*, TR, Cauc., W-Sib., E-Sib.,
Amur, Sakhal., Kamchat., C-As.,
– **polygonifolius** Pourr. · E:Bog Pondweed;
G:Knöterich-Laichkraut · ♃ ≈ VI-VIII;
Eur.* exc. E-Eur.
– **praelongus** Wulfen · E:Long-stalked
Pondweed; G:Langblättriges Laichkraut
· ♃ ≈ VI-VII; Eur.* exc. Ib; TR, Cauc.,
W-Sib., E-Sib., Amur, Kamchat., N-Am.
– **pusillus** Biv. · E:Small Pondweed;
G:Zwerg-Laichkraut · ♃ ≈ VI-IX; Eur.*;
cosmop. exc. Austr.
– **rutilus** Wolfg. · E:Shetland Pondweed;
G:Rötliches Laichkraut · ♃ ≈ VII-VIII;
Eur.: BrI, Sc, F, G, EC-Eur.
– × **salicifolius** Wolfg. (*P. lucens* × *P.*

perfoliatus) · G:Weidenblättriges
Laichkraut · ♃ ≈ ; BrI, D+
- × **sparganiifolius** Laest. ex Fr. (*P.
gramineus* × *P. natans*) · G:Rippennerv-
iges Laichkraut · ♃ ≈ ; BrI, D+
- × **spathulatus** Schrad. ex W.D.J. Koch
& Ziz (*P. alpinus* × *P. polygonifolius*) ·
G:Spateliges Laichkraut · ♃ ≈ ; D
- **trichoides** Cham. & Schltdl. · E:Hair-like
Pondweed; G:Haarblättriges Laichkraut
· ♃ ≈ VI-VII; Eur.*, TR, Cauc., W-Sib.,
E-Sib., C-As., Afr.
- × *zizii* = Potamogeton × angustifolius

Potentilla L. -f- *Rosaceae* · c. 500 spp. ·
E:Cinquefoil, Five Finger; F:Potentille;
G:Fingerkraut
- **alba** L. · E:White Cinquefoil; F:Potentille
blanche; G:Weißes Fingerkraut · ♃ ⤳
Z5 IV-VI; Eur.: F, Ital-P, C-Eur., EC-Eur.,
Ba, E-Eur.
- **alchemilloides** Lapeyr. · ♃ ⤳ △ Z6
V-VI; sp.; F; Pyr.
- **alpicola** De la Soie · G:Alpen-Finger-
kraut · ♃ V-VII; Eur.: I, Sw
- **anglica** Laichard. · G:Niederliegendes
Fingerkraut · ♃ Z5 VII-IX; Eur.*
- **anserina** L. · E:Goose Grass, Silverweed,
Wild Tansy; G:Gänse-Fingerkraut · ♃ ⤳
Z5 V-VIII ⚥ ; Eur.*, Cauc., W-Sib., E-Sib.,
Amur, Sakhal., Kamchat., C-As., Him.,
Alaska, Can., USA* exc. SE, Fla., SC,
Austr., NZ
- **argentea** L. · E:Hoary Cinquefoil, Silver
Leaf Cinquefoil; G:Silber-Fingerkraut ·
♃ △ Z4 VI-VII; Eur.*, TR, Cauc., N-Iran,
W-Sib., E-Sib., C-As., nat. in N-Am.
- *argyrophylla* Wall. ex Lehm. = Potentilla
atrosanguinea var. argyrophylla
- **atrosanguinea** Lodd. ex D. Don
- var. **argyrophylla** (Wall. ex Lehm.)
Grierson & D.G. Long · G:Silber-
Fingerkraut · ♃ △ Z5 VI-VII; W-Him.
- var. **atrosanguinea** · F:Potentille
sanguine; G:Blutrotes Fingerkraut · ♃ Z5
VI-IX; Nepal
- **aurea** L. · E:Golden Cinquefoil; G:Gold-
Fingerkraut
- subsp. **aurea** · F:Potentille dorée;
G:Gewöhnliches Gold-Fingerkraut · ♃ △
Z5 VI-IX; Eur.* exc. BrI, Sc; mts.
- subsp. **chrysocraspeda** (Lehm.) Nyman ·
♃ ⤳ △ Z5 VI-VII; Eur.: Ba, Carp.;
NW-TR
- **brauneana** Hoppe ex Nestl. · E:Dwarf

Cinquefoil; G:Zwerg-Fingerkraut · ♃ Z6
VII-VIII; Eur.: sp., F, I, C-Eur., Slove.;
Pyr., Alp., Jura
- **caulescens** L. · G:Stängel-Fingerkraut ·
♃ △ Z5 VII-VIII; Eur.: Ib, F, Ital-P, C-Eur.,
Ba; mts.; Moroc., Alger.
- *chrysocraspeda* Lehm. = Potentilla aurea
subsp. chrysocraspeda
- *cinerea* Chaix = Potentilla incana
- **clusiana** Jacq. · E:Eastern Cinquefoil;
G:Ostalpen-Fingerkraut · ♃ △ Z6 VI-VIII;
Eur.: I, C-Eur., W-Ba; mts.
- **collina** Wibel · G:Gewöhnliches Hügel-
Fingerkraut · ♃ IV-VIII; Eur.* exc. BrI, Ib
- **crantzii** (Crantz) Beck ex Fritsch ·
E:Alpine Cinquefoil; G:Zottiges Fingerkraut · ♃ △ Z5 V-VII; Eur.*, TR, Cauc.,
N-Iran, W-Sib., Can.: E; Greenl.
- **cuneata** Wall. ex Lehm. · ♃ ⤳ △ Z5
VII-VIII; Him.
- *davurica* Nestl. = Potentilla fruticosa var.
davurica
- **erecta** (L.) Raeusch. · E:Bloodroot,
Shepherd's Knot, Tormentil; G:Aufrech-
tes Fingerkraut, Blutwurz, Tormentill · ♃
Z5 V-VIII ⚥ ; Eur.*, TR, Cauc., W-Sib.
- **frigida** Vill. · G:Gletscher-Fingerkraut · ♃
VII-VIII; Eur.: sp., F, I, C-Eur.; Pyr., Alp.
- **fruticosa** L.
- **many cultivars**
- var. **arbuscula** (D. Don) Maxim. · ♄ d Z2;
Him.
- var. **davurica** (Nestl.) Ser. · ♄ d Z2
V-VIII; Sib., N-China
- var. **fruticosa** · E:Golden Hardhack,
Shrubby Cinquefoil; F:Potentille arbustive; G:Gewöhnlicher Fingerstrauch,
Strauch-Fingerkraut · ♄ d Z2 VI-VIII;
Eur.: sp., F, I, Ba, BrI, Swed, Russ.; Cauc.,
Him., N-As., Jap., Alaska, Can., USA: NE,
NCE, NC, Rocky Mts., SW, NW, Calif.;
Greenl.
- var. **mandshurica** (Maxim.) E.L. Wolf ·
F:Potentille arbustive de Mandchourie · ♄
d Z2; Jap., Manch., N-China
- var. **rigida** (Wall. ex Lehm.) E.L. Wolf · ♄
d Z2; Him., N-China
- var. **unifoliolata** Ludlow · ♄ d Z2; Him.
(Bhutan)
- *glabrata* Willd. ex Schltdl. = Potentilla
fruticosa var. davurica
- **grammopetala** Moretti · E:Creamy
Cinquefoil; G:Schmalkronblättriges
Fingerkraut · ♃ VII; Eur.: I, Sw; Alp.
- **grandiflora** L. · E:Large-flowered

Cinquefoil; G:Großblütiges Fingerkraut · ♃ Z6 VII-VIII; Eur.: Ib, Fr, Ital-P, C-Eur.; Pyr., Alp.

- **heptaphylla** L. · G:Rötliches Fingerkraut · ♃ Z6 IV-VI; Eur.* exc. BrI, Ib; TR
- **incana** G. Gaertn., B. Mey. & Scherb. · E:Grey Cinquefoil; G:Aschgraues Fingerkraut, Sand-Fingerkraut · ♃ ⤳ △ IV-V; D +
- **inclinata** Vill. · G:Graues Fingerkraut · ♃ V-VIII; Eur.* exc. BrI, Sc; TR, Cauc., Iran, N-As., C-As.
- *insignis* Royle = Potentilla atrosanguinea var. atrosanguinea
- **intermedia** L. · G:Mittleres Fingerkraut · ⊙ ♃ VI-IX; Eur.: Russ., nat. in BrI, Sc, Fr, Ital-P, C-Eur., EC-Eur.
- **leucopolitana** P.J. Müll. · G:Elsässer Fingerkraut, Weißenburger Hügel-Fingerkraut · ♃ IV-VIII; Eur.: F, C-Eur., DK, EC-Eur., E-Eur.
- **megalantha** Takeda · F:Potentille à grandes fleurs · ♃ △ Z5 VI-VIII; Jap.
- **micrantha** Ramond ex DC. · G:Kleinblütiges Fingerkraut · ♃ Z6 III-V; Eur.* exc. BrI, Ib; TR, Syr., Cauc., Iran, NW-Afr.
- × **mixta** Nolte ex W.D.J. Koch (*P. anglica* × *P. reptans*) · G:Bastard-Fingerkraut · ♃ VI-IX; BrI +
- **multifida** L. · G:Schlitzblättriges Fingerkraut · ♃ Z3 VII-VIII; Eur.: Sc, Russ., F, I, Sw; N, Ural, Alp., Pyr.; Cauc., Iran, Afgh., Him., Tibet, Mong., W-Sib., E-Sib., Amur, China, N-Am.
- **neglecta** Baumg. · G:Übersehenes Fingerkraut · ♃ VI-VII; Eur.: most +
- **nepalensis** Hook. · E:Nepal Cinquefoil · ♃ Z5 VII-IX; W-Him.
- *neumanniana* Rchb. = Potentilla tabernaemontani
- **nevadensis** Boiss. · ♃ △ Z7 V-VI; S-Sp.: Sierra Nevada
- **nitida** L. · E:Pink Cinquefoil; F:Potentille brillante, Potentille des Dolomites; G:Dolomiten-Fingerkraut · ♃ △ Z5 VI-VIII; Eur.: F, I, A, Slove.; Alp., Apenn.
- **nivea** L. · E:Snowy Cinquefoil; G:Schnee-Fingerkraut · ♃ Z2 VII-VIII; Eur.: Sc, Russ., F, I, C-Eur.; N, Alp., Apenn.; Cauc., W-Sib., E-Sib.,
- **norvegica** L. · E:Rough Cinquefoil; G:Norwegisches Fingerkraut · ⊙ ⊙ Z3 VI-X; Eur.: Ital-P, C-Eur., EC-Eur., Sc; W-Sib., E-Sib., Amur, Kamchat., Mong.,

Jap., N-Am., nat. in BrI, Fr, Ba
- **palustris** (L.) Scop. · E:Marsh Cinquefoil; F:Potentille des marais; G:Sumpf-Fingerkraut, Sumpfblutauge · ♃ ⌇ Z3 VI-VII; Eur.*, Cauc., W-Sib., E-Sib., Amur, Sakhal., Kamchat., Mong., China, Alaska, Can., USA: NE, NCE, NC, Rocky Mts., Calif.; Greenl.
- **patula** Waldst. & Kit. · G:Ausgebreitetes Fingerkraut · ♃ IV-V; Eur.: C-Eur., EC-Eur., Ba, RO, E-Eur.; W-Sib.
- **praecox** F.W. Schultz · G:Frühes Hügel-Fingerkraut · ♃ IV-V; Eur.: G, Sw
- **pusilla** Host · G:Flaum-Fingerkraut, Seidenhaariges Frühlings-Fingerkraut · ♃ III-V; Eur.: Fr, Ital-P, C-Eur., EC-Eur., RO
- **pyrenaica** Ramond ex DC. · E:Pyrenean Cinquefoil · ♃ △ VII-VIII; Eur.: sp., F; Pyr, NE-Sp.
- **recta** L. · E:Sulphur Cinquefoil; G:Hohes Fingerkraut · ♃ Z4 VI-VII; Eur.* exc. BrI, Sc; TR, Syr., Cauc. Iran, W-Sib., C-As., NW-Afr., nat. in N-Am., S-Am.
- **reptans** L. · E:Creeping Cinquefoil; G:Kriechendes Fingerkraut · ♃ Z5 VI-VIII ⚥; Eur.*, TR, Syr., Cauc., Iran, W-Sib., C-As., Afgh., Kashmir, N-Afr.
- **rhenana** Zimmeter · G:Rheinisches Hügel-Fingerkraut · ♃ IV-VIII; Eur.: D
- **rupestris** L. · E:Prairie Tea, Rock Cinquefoil, Siberian Tea; G:Felsen-Fingerkraut · ♃ Z5 V-VII; Eur.*, TR, Moroc.
- **salesoviana** Stephan · G:Asiatischer Fingerstrauch · ♄ △ Z4 VI-VIII; W-Sib., C-As., Mong., Tibet, Him.
- **silesiaca** R. Uechtr. · ♃ IV-VIII; Eur.: PL
- **sordida** Aspegren · G:Schmutziges Hügel-Fingerkraut · ♃; Eur.: F, G, EC-Eur., BG
- **speciosa** Willd. · ♃ △ Z6 VI-VII; Eur.: Ba; TR, Syr., N-Iraq
- **sterilis** (L.) Garcke · E:Barren Strawberry; G:Erdbeer-Fingerkraut · ♃ III-V; Eur.* exc. EC-Eur.
- **supina** L. · G:Niedriges Fingerkraut · ⊙ ♃ VI-X; Eur.: Fr, Ital-P, EC-Eur., Ba, E-Eur.; N-Afr.
- *sylvestris* Neck. = Potentilla erecta
- **tabernaemontani** Asch. · E:Spring Cinquefoil; F:Potentille printanière; G:Frühlings-Fingerkraut · ♃ ⤳ Z5 IV-V; Eur.*
- *ternata* K. Koch = Potentilla aurea subsp. chrysocraspeda
- **thuringiaca** Bernh. ex Link · G:Thüringer

Fingerkraut · ⁂ V-VII; Eur.: Fr, I, C-Eur.,
EC-Eur., RO; TR, Cauc., nat. in Sc
- **thyrsiflora** Zimmeter · G:Reichblütiges
Hügel-Fingerkraut · ⁂ VI-VIII; Eur.: I, G,
EC-Eur., E-Eur.
- × **tonguei** hort. ex Baxt. (*P. anglica* × *P.
nepalensis*) · ⁂ ⤳ △ Z5 VII-VIII; cult.
- *tormentilla* Neck. = Potentilla erecta
- × *tormentilla-formosa* Tonque ex Loudon
= Potentilla × tonguei
- **tridentata** Aiton · E:Shrubby Fivefin-
gers · ♄ VI-VII; Can., USA: NE, NCE, SE;
Greenl.
- *verna* auct. non L. = Potentilla tabernaemontani
- **villosa** Pall. ex Pursh · E:Northern
Cinquefoil; G:Filziges Fingerkraut · ⁂ △
V-IX; E-Sib., Alaska, Can.: W; USA: NW,
Rocky Mts.
- **wiemannii** Günther & Schummel ·
G:Wiemann-Fingerkraut · ⁂; Eur.: F, I,
C-Eur., EC-Eur., Sc, Ba, Russ.

Pothos L. -m- *Araceae* · 55 spp.
- *argyraeus* Engl. = Scindapsus pictus
- *aureus* Linden & André = Epipremnum
aureum
- **beccarianus** Engl. · ♄ e ⚥ Z10 ⓦ;
Kalimantan
- *celatocaulis* N.E. Br. = Rhaphidophora
korthalsii
- *decipiens* Schott = Pothos scandens
- *loureiroi* Hook. & Arn. = Pothos repens
- *microphyllus* Schott = Pothos repens
- **repens** (Lour.) Druce · ♄ e ⚥ Z10 ⓦ;
S-China
- **scandens** L. · ∫ e ⚥ Z10 ⓦ; Ind., Malay.
Pen.
- *terminalis* Haenke = Pothos repens

× **Potinara** hort. -f- *Orchidaceae*
(*Brassavola* × *Cattleya* × *Laelia* ×
Sophronitis)

Pouteria Aubl. -f- *Sapotaceae* · 343 spp. ·
E:Egg Fruit; F:Abiu, Canistelle lucume,
Sapotillier; G:Eierfrucht
- **caimito** (Ruiz & Pav.) Radlk. · E:Egg
Fruit; G:Caimito-Eierfrucht · ♄ e Z10 ⓦ
ⓝ; Ecuad., Peru, Braz.: Amazon.; Guyan.
- **campechiana** (Kunth) Baehni ·
E:Canistel; G:Canistel-Eierfrucht · ♄
e Z10 ⓦ ⓝ; Mex., C-Am., Cuba, trop.
S-Am., nat. in Fla.
- **lucuma** (Ruiz & Pav.) Kuntze · ♄ e Z10

ⓚ ⓝ; Peru, Chile
- **sapota** (Jacq.) H.E. Moore & Stearn ·
E:Maramalde Tree, Sapote; G:Marme-
laden-Eierfrucht · ♄ e Z10 ⓦ ⓝ; Mex.,
C-Am.

Praecereus Buxb. = Monvillea
- *maritimus* (Britton & Rose) Buxb. =
Monvillea maritima

Pratia Gaudich. -f- *Campanulaceae* ·
c. 20 spp. · E:Lawn Lobelia; F:Pratia;
G:Teppichlobelie
- **angulata** (G. Forst.) Hook. f. · ⁂ ⤳ △
⚘ Z7 ⓐ ∧ VI-VIII; NZ
- **macrodon** Hook. f. · ⁂ ⤳ Z8 ⓚ VII-
VIII; NZ
- **nummularia** (Lam.) A. Braun & Asch. ·
⁂ ⤳ Z9 ⓚ VII-VIII; Him., Ind., S-China,
C-China, Burma, Thail., Vietn., Taiwan,
Phil.
- **pedunculata** (R. Br.) F. Muell. ex
Benth. · ⁂ ⤳ Z7 ∧; Austr.
- **repens** Gaudich. · ⁂ ⤳ Z8 ⓚ VII-X;
Falkland

Premna L. -f- *Verbenaceae* · c. 50 spp.
- **japonica** Miq. · ♄ ♄; Jap., Ryukyu-Is.,
Taiwan

Prenanthes L. -f- *Asteraceae* · 15-30 spp. ·
F:Prénanthe; G:Hasenlattich
- *alba* L. = Nabalus albus
- **purpurea** L. · E:Purple Lettuce;
G:Gewöhnlicher Hasenlattich · ⁂ Z5
VII-VIII; Eur.* exc. BrI, Sc; TR, Cauc.,
nat. in DK
- *serpentaria* Pursh = Nabalus serpentarius

Prenia N.E. Br. -f- *Aizoaceae* · 6 spp.
- **pallens** (Aiton) N.E. Br. · ♄ ♈ ⤳ Z9 ⓚ;
Cape
- *relaxata* (Willd.) N.E. Br. = Prenia pallens

Prepodesma N.E. Br. -f- *Aizoaceae* · 1 sp.
- **orpenii** (N.E. Br.) N.E. Br. · ⁂ ♈ Z9 ⓚ;
Cape

Prestonia R. Br. -f- *Apocynaceae* · 70 spp.
- **quinquangularis** (Jacq.) Spreng. · ∫ e
⚥ Z10 ⓦ; Costa Rica, Panama, W.Ind.,
trop. S-Am.

Primula L. -f- *Primulaceae* · 400 spp. ·
E:Cowslip, Primrose; F:Primevère;

G:Aurikel, Primel, Schlüsselblume
- **acaulis**
- var. *iberica* Hoffm. = Primula vulgaris subsp. sibthorpii
- var. *rubra* (Sibth. & Sm.) Lüdi = Primula vulgaris subsp. sibthorpii
- **algida** Adams · ♃ △ Z5 V ▽; Cauc., N-Iran, W-Sib., C-As., Mong.
- **allionii** Loisel. · E:Allioni's Primrose · ♃ Z7 ⌂ III-IV ▽; Eur.: F, I; Alp. Maritimes
- **many cultivars**
- **alpicola** Stapf · E:Moonlight Primrose; G:Mondschein-Primel · ♃ ⤳ Z6 V-VI ▽; SE-Tibet (Tsangpo)
- **amoena** M. Bieb. · ♃ △ Z5 IV ▽; NE-TR, Cauc.
- **anisodora** Balf. f. & Forrest · ♃ Z6 VI-VII ▽; Yunnan, Sichuan
- **aurantiaca** W.W. Sm. & Forrest · F:Primevère à fleurs oranges · ♃ ⁓ Z6 VII ▽; Yunnan
- **auricula**
- subsp. **auricula** · E:Auricula, Dusty Miller, Garden Auricula; F:Auricule; G:Gewöhnliche Alpen-Aurikel · ♃ △ Z3 IV-VI ▽; Eur.: F, C-Eur., EC-Eur., Ital-P, Ba, E-Eur.; Alp., Apenn., Carp.
- **auriculata** Lam. · ♃ △ Z5 IV-V ▽; TR, Cauc.
- **beesiana** Forrest · F:Primevère à étages; G:Etagen-Primel · ♃ ⁓ VI-VII ▽; Yunnan, Sichuan
- × **berninae** A. Kern. (*P. hirsuta* × *P. latifolia*) · ♃ ▽; Ch + cult.
- × **bullesiana** Janson. (*P. beesiana* × *P. bulleyana*) · ♃; cult.
- **bulleyana** Forrest · F:Primevère de Bulley; G:Bulleys Etagen-Primel · ☉ ♃ Z6 VI-VII ▽; NW-Yunnan, S-Sichuan
- **burmanica** Balf. f. & Kingdon-Ward · ♃ ⁓ Z6 VI-VII ▽; N-Burma, Yunnan
- **capitata** Hook.
- subsp. **capitata** · ♃ Z5 ▽; Bhutan, S-Tibet
- subsp. **crispata** (Balf. f. & Forrest) W.W. Sm. & Forrest Z5 ▽; Bhutan, S-Tibet
- subsp. **mooreana** (Balf. f. & Forrest) W.W. Sm. & Forrest · ♃ Z5 VII-VIII ▽; E-Him.
- subsp. **sphaerocephala** (Balf. f. & Forrest) W.W. Sm. & Forrest · ♃ Z5 VII-VIII ▽; W-China
- **carniolica** Jacq. · ♃ △ Z6 IV-V ▽; Eur.: Slove.
- **chionantha** Balf. f. & Forrest · ♃ ⁓ Z6

V-VI ▽; NW-Yunnan
- **chungensis** Balf. f. & Kingdon-Ward · F:Primevère du Yunnan · ♃ ⁓ Z6 V-VI ▽; Bhutan, Ind.: Assam; China: Yunnan, Sichuan
- **clarkei** G. Watt · ♃ △ ⁓ Z7 IV ▽; Kashmir
- **clusiana** Tausch · F:Primevère de Clusius; G:Clusius' Schlüsselblume · ♃ △ Z6 IV-V ▽; Eur.: G, A; NE-Alp.
- **cockburniana** Hemsl. · ☉ ⁓ Z5 V-VI ▽; SW-Sichuan
- *commutata* Schott = Primula villosa var. commutata
- *cordifolia* Rupr. = Primula elatior subsp. cordifolia
- **cortusoides** L. · ♃ △ Z3 IV-V ▽; W-Sib.
- **daonensis** Leyb. · G:Inntaler Schlüsselblume, Rätische Schlüsselblume, Val Daone-Primel · ♃ △ Z5 IV-VI ▽; Eur.: I, Sw, A; E-Alp.
- **darialica** Rupr. · ♃ △ ▽; Cauc.
- **denticulata** Sm. · E:Drumstick Primula; F:Primevère sphérique; G:Kugel-Primel · ♃ △ Z5 III-IV ▽; Afgh., Him., W-China
- var. *cachemeriana* (Munro) Hook. = Primula denticulata
- **elatior** (L.) Hill · G:Hohe Schlüsselblume
- subsp. **cordifolia** (Rupr.) W.W. Sm. & Forrest Z5 ▽; Cauc.
- subsp. **elatior** · E:Oxlip, Paigles; F:Primevère élevée; G:Gewöhnliche Hohe Schlüsselblume · ♃ Z5 III-V ⚥ ▽; Eur.*
- subsp. **intricata** (Gren. & Godr.) Widmer · G:Pyrenäische Schlüsselblume · ♃ Z5 IV-V ▽; S-Eur., SC-Eur.
- subsp. **leucophylla** (Pax) Hesl.-Harr. ex W.W. Sm. & H.R. Fletcher · ♃ Z5 ▽; Eur.: E-Carp.
- subsp. **pallasii** (Lehm.) W.W. Sm. & Forrest · ♃ Z5 ▽; Cauc., Iran, Ural, Altai
- subsp. **pseudoelatior** (Kusn.) W.W. Sm. & Forrest Z5 ▽; NE-TR, Cauc.
- var. *amoena* (M. Bieb.) Duby = Primula amoena
- var. *carpatica* (Griseb. & Schenk) Nikolic = Primula elatior subsp. elatior
- **ellisiae** Pollard & Cockerell · ♃ ▽; USA: SW
- × **facchinii** Schott (*P. minima* × *P. spectabilis*) · ♃ Z6 ▽; A, N-I
- **farinosa** L. · E:Bird's Eye Primrose; F:Primevère farineuse; G:Mehl-Primel · ♃ △ ⁓ ⤫ Z4 V ▽; Eur.*, W-Sib., E-Sib.,

Amur, Kamchat., N-Mong.
- **flaccida** N.P. Balakr. · ⁤ △ Z5 IV-V ▽;
  SW-Sichuan, Yunnan
- **floribunda** Wall. · ⁤ Z7 II-III ▽; Him.:
  Afgh., Kashmir, NW-Ind., Nepal
- **florindae** Kingdon-Ward · E:Himalayan
  Cowslip; F:Primevère estivale du Tibet;
  G:Tibet-Primel · ⁤ ∿ Z6 VII-IX ▽;
  SE-Tibet (Tsangpo)
- **forbesii** Franch. · ⊙ ⒶⒸ ▽ I-V ▽;
  N-Burma, Yunnan
- × **forsteri** Stein (*P. hirsuta* × *P. minima*) ·
  ⁤ Z5 ▽; A
- **frondosa** Janka · ⁤ △ ∿ Z5 V ▽; BG
- **gemmifera** Batalin · ⁤ △ IV-V ▽; China:
  Sichuan, E-Tibet, Kansu
- **geraniifolia** Hook. f. · ⁤ Z5 ▽; E-Him.,
  Yunnan
- **glaucescens** Moretti
- subsp. **calycina** (Duby) Pax · ⁤ △ Z6
  III-IV ▽; I: Alp.
- subsp. **glaucescens** · E:Glaucous
  Primrose · ⁤ Z6 ▽; Eur.: I; S-Alp.
- **glutinosa** Wulfen · E:Sticky Primrose;
  G:Klebrige Primel · ⁤ △ Z4 V-VI ▽; Eur.:
  I, Sw, A, Bosn.; mts.
- *glycocosma* Petitm. = Primula wilsonii
- **grandis** Trautv. · ⁤ ∿ V-VI ▽; Cauc.
- **halleri** J.F. Gmel. · E:Long-flowered
  Primrose; F:Primevère de Haller;
  G:Hallers Primel · ⁤ △ Z5 V-VI ▽; Eur.:
  Fr, C-Eur., EC-Eur., Ital-P, Ba, E-Eur.;
  Alp., Carp., Balkan
- × **heerii** Brügger (*P. hirsuta* × *P.
  integrifolia*) · ⁤ Z5 ▽; Alp. (Sw,
  Vorarlberg), Pyr.
- *helodoxa* Balf. f. = Primula prolifera
- **heucherifolia** Franch. · ⁤ Z6 ▽; Tibet,
  China
- **hirsuta** Vill. · G:Behaarte Schlüsselblume · ⁤ △ Z5 IV ▽; Eur.: sp., F, I, Sw, A;
  Pyr., Alp.
- × **hortensis** Wettst. (*P. auricula subsp.
  auricula* × *?*) · G:Garten-Schlüsselblume ·
  ⁤; cult.
- *inflata* Lehm. = Primula veris subsp. veris
- **integrifolia** Scop. · E:Entire-leaved
  Primrose; G:Ganzblättrige Primel · ⁤ △
  Z5 IV-VI ▽; Eur.: F, I, Sw, A; E-Pyr., Alp.
- × **intermedia** Port. (*P. clusiana* × *P.
  minima*) · ⁤ Z5 ▽; A
- *intricata* Gren. & Godr. = Primula elatior
  subsp. intricata
- **involucrata** Wall. · ⁤ △ ∿ IV ▽;
  W-Him., Bhutan, Sikkim, SE-Tibet,

Sichuan
- **ioessa** W.W. Sm. · ⁤ Z6 ▽; SE-Tibet
- **japonica** A. Gray · F:Primevère du Japon;
  G:Japanische Etagen-Primel · ⁤ Z5 V-VI
  ▽; Jap., Taiwan
- **juliae** Kusn. · E:Purple Primrose;
  F:Primevère tapissante du Caucase;
  G:Teppich-Primel · ⁤ △ Z5 IV ▽; Cauc.
  (Georgia)
- × **kewensis** W. Watson (*P. floribunda* × *P.
  verticillata*) · ⁤ Z9 ⒶⒸ ▽ II-IV; cult.
- **kitaibeliana** Schott · ⁤ △ Z7 IV-V ▽;
  Eur.: Croatia, Bosn.
- **latifolia** Lapeyr. · E:Viscid Primrose;
  G:Breitblättrige Primel · ⁤ D Z5 VI ▽;
  Eur.: sp., F, I, Sw; E-Pyr., Alp.
- **laurentiana** Fernald · E:Birdseye
  Primrose · ⁤ ∿ Z3 IV-V ▽; Can.: E ;
  USA: Maine
- *leucophylla* Pax = Primula elatior subsp.
  leucophylla
- *lichiangensis* (Forrest) Forrest = Primula
  polyneura
- × **loiseleurii** Sünd. (*P. allionii* × *P.
  auricula* subsp. *auricula*) · ⁤; cult.
- *longiflora* All. = Primula halleri
- **luteola** Rupr. · G:Gelbe Kaukasus-
  Primel · ⁤ △ ∿ Z5 IV-V ▽; E-Cauc.
- *macrocalyx* Bunge = Primula veris subsp.
  macrocalyx
- **macrophylla** D. Don · ⁤ Z5 ▽; Afgh.,
  Him., SE-Tibet
- **malacoides** Franch. · E:Baby Primrose,
  Fairy Primrose; G:Braut-Primel, Flieder-
  Primel · ⊙ ⁤ Z8 ⒶⒸ ▽ I-III ▽; Yunnan
- **marginata** Curtis · F:Primevère
  marginée; G:Meeralpen-Primel · ⁤ △ Z7
  III-IV ▽; Eur.: F, I; SW-Alp.
- **megaseifolia** Boiss. · ⁤ Z7 III-IV ▽; TR
  (Pontus), Cauc.
- **melanops** W.W. Sm. · ⁤ Z4 ▽; China
- **minima** L. · E:Least Primrose; G:Zwerg-
  Schlüsselblume · ⁤ △ Z5 VI-VII ▽; Eur.:
  C-Eur., Ital-P, Ba, EC-Eur., E-Eur.; mts.
- **mollis** Nutt. ex Hook. · ⁤ Z7 VI-VII ▽;
  Him., Bhutan, N-Ind.: Assam; Burma,
  China: Yunnan
- × **muretiana** Moritzi (*P. integrifolia* × *P.
  latifolia*) · ⁤ Z5 ▽; Sw
- **muscarioides** Hemsl. · ⁤ △ ∿ Z5 VI ▽;
  China: Sichuan, SE-Tibet, Yunnan
- *nutans* Delavay ex Franch. = Primula
  flaccida
- **obconica** Hance · E:German Primrose;
  G:Becher-Primel · ⊙ ⁤ Z8 ⒶⒸ ▽ I-XII ⚔

▽; China: Sichuan, Yunnan, Hupeh, Kwantung, Kweitschou
- *oenensis* E. Thomas ex Gremli = Primula daonensis
- *officinalis* (L.) Hill = Primula veris subsp. veris
- **palinuri** Petagna · ⟁ D Z8 ⓚ ⓐ III-IV ▽; SW-I (Cap Palinuri)
- *pallasii* Lehm. = Primula elatior subsp. pallasii
- subsp. *intricata* Gren. & Godr. = Primula elatior subsp. intricata
- *pannonica* A. Kern. = Primula veris subsp. veris
- **parryi** A. Gray · E:Parry's Primrose · ⟁ Z6 ▽; W-USA
- **pedemontana** E. Thomas ex Gaudin · ⟁ Z6 IV ▽; Eur.: sp., F, I; Cordillera Catábrica, SW-Alp.
- **poissonii** Franch. · ⟁ ∼ Z6 VI-VII ▽; W-Sichuan, W-Yunnan
- **polyneura** Franch. · F:Primevère à nervures nombreuses · ⟁ Z5 V-VI ▽; China: Sichuan, Yunnan, SE-Tibet, Kansu
- **praenitens** Ker-Gawl. · E:Chinese Primrose; G:Chinesische Primel · ⟁ ∼ ⓚ ♡ XII-IV ▽; orig. ?
- **prolifera** Wall. · E:Glory of the Marsh · ⟁ ∼ VI-VII ▽; Him.
- *pseudoelatior* Kusn. = Primula elatior subsp. pseudoelatior
- × **pubescens** Jacq. (*P. auricula subsp. auricula* × *P. hirsuta*) · G:Bastard-Aurikel, Garten-Aurikel · ⟁ △ Z5 V-VI; cult.
- **many cultivars**
- **pulverulenta** Duthie · F:Primevère poudreuse; G:Sichuan-Primel · ⟁ Z6 V-VI ▽; W-Sichuan
- **reidii** Duthie · ⟁ Z6 ▽; Him.
- **rosea** Royle · F:Primevère rose; G:Rosen-Primel · ⟁ △ ∼ Z6 III-IV ▽; NW-Him.: Afgh., Kashmir
- *rubra* J.F. Gmel. = Primula hirsuta
- **saxatilis** Kom. · ⟁ Z4 IV-V ▽; Manch., N-Korea
- var. *pubescens* Pax & K. Hoffm. = Primula polyneura
- **scotica** Hook. · E:Scottish Primrose · ⟁ △ ∼ Z4 IV-V ▽; Eur.: BrI (Scotland)
- **secundiflora** Franch. · ⟁ ≈ Z6 V-VI ▽; NW-Yunnan, SW-Sichuan
- *sibthorpii* Hoffmanns. = Primula vulgaris subsp. sibthorpii
- **sieboldii** E. Morren · E:Japanese Primrose; F:Primevère de Siebold; G:Siebolds

Primel · ⟁ Z5 V-VI ▽; N-Mong., Amur, Manch., Korea, Jap.
- **sikkimensis** Hook.
- var. **pudibunda** (Balf. f. & R.E. Cooper) W.W. Sm. & H.R. Fletche · ⟁ △ Z6 VI-VII ▽; Nepal, Bhutan, Sikkim, Sichuan, Tibet
- var. **sikkimensis** · ⟁ ∼ Z6 VI-VII ▽; Him.: Nepal, Bhutan; China: Yunnan, Tibet, Sichuan
- *sinensis* Sabine ex Lindl. = Primula praenitens
- **sinolisteri** Balf. f. · ⟁ ⓚ III-V ▽; Yunnan
- **sinoplantaginea** Balf. f. & Forrest · ⟁ △ VI-VII ▽; China: Yunnan, Sichuan, Tibet
- **sinopurpurea** Balf. f. · ⟁ △ Z5 VI ▽; China
- **spectabilis** Tratt. · E:Spectacular Primrose; F:Primevère spectaculaire · ⟁ △ Z6 IV-V ▽; I: Alp.
- *tsarongensis* Balf. f. & Forrest = Primula muscarioides
- **tyrolensis** Schott · ⟁ △ Z5 IV ▽; Eur.: I (Dolomites)
- *uralensis* Fisch. = Primula veris subsp. macrocalyx
- × **variabilis** Goupil (*P. veris* × *P. vulgaris*) · F:Primevère élevée des jardins · ⟁; cult.
- *veitchii* Duthie = Primula polyneura
- × **venusta** Host (*P. auricula* subsp. *auricula* × *P. carniolica*) · ⟁ Z6 ▽; Slov.
- **veris** L. · G:Echte Schlüsselblume, Wiesen-Schlüsselblume
- subsp. *canescens* (Opiz) Hayek ex Lüdi = Primula veris subsp. veris
- subsp. **columnae** (Ten.) Lüdi · G:Trockenrasen-Schlüsselblume · ⟁ ⋊ Z5 IV-V ▽; S-Eur., NE-TR; mts.
- subsp. **macrocalyx** (Bunge) Lüdi · G:Hohe Wiesen-Schlüsselblume · ⟁ ⋊ Z5 V ▽; Eur.: SE-Russ., Crim; Cauc., N-Iran, W-Sib., E-Sib.
- subsp. **veris** · E:Cowslip; F:Primevère officinale; G:Gewöhnliche Wiesen-Schlüsselblume · ⟁ Z5 IV-V ⚡ ⚘ ▽; Eur.: N-Sp., S-F, C-Eur.
- **verticillata** Forssk. · ⟁ ⓚ ♡ II-IV ▽; Yemen
- **vialii** Delavay ex Franch. · F:Primevère du Père Vial, Primevère-orchidée; G:Orchideen-Primel · ⟁ Z7 ∧ VI-VII ▽; NW-Yunnan, SW-Sichuan
- **villosa** Wulfen
- var. **commutata** (Schott) Lüdi · ⟁ ▽; A

(Steiermark)
- var. **villosa** · G:Zottige Primel · ⹏ △ Z5 IV-VI ▽; Eur.: F, I, A, Slove.; Alp.
- *viscosa* All. = Primula latifolia
- *viscosa* Vill. = Primula hirsuta
- *vittata* Bureau & Franch. = Primula secundiflora
- × **vochinensis** Gusmus (*P. minima* × *P. wulfeniana*) · ⹏ Z6 ▽; I: E-Dolomites
- **vulgaris** Huds. · G:Stängellose Schlüs-selblume
- subsp. **heterochroma** (Stapf) W.W. Sm. & Forrest · ⹏ Z6 IV ▽; N-Iran
- subsp. **sibthorpii** (Hoffmanns.) W.W. Sm. & Forrest · G:Karnevals-Primel · ⹏ Z6 IV ▽; Eur.: Ba, Crim; TR, Cauc., nat. in C-Eur.
- subsp. **vulgaris** Huds. · E:Primrose; F:Primevère acaule; G:Gewöhnliche Stängellose Schlüsselblume, Kissen-Primel · ⹏ Z6 II-V ⚥ ▽; Eur.*, Cauc.
- var. *rubra* (Sibth. & Sm.) Lüdi = Primula vulgaris subsp. sibthorpii
- **waltonii** G. Watt ex Balf. f. · ⹏ Z6 VI-VII ▽; Bhutan, SE-Tibet
- **warshenewskiana** B. Fedtsch. · ⹏ ⋀ IV-V ▽; C-As., Him.
- **wilsonii** Dunn · ⹏ ⁓ VI-VII ▽; W-Sichuan, W-Yunnan
- **wulfeniana** Schott · E:Wulfen's Primrose; G:Wulfens Primel · ⹏ △ Z5 IV-V ▽; Eur.: I, A, Slove., RO; SE-Alp., S-Carp.
- **yargongensis** Petitm. · ⹏ △ ⁓ IV-V ▽; China: Sichuan, Yunnan, SE-Tibet
- **Cultivars:**
- **many cultivars, see Section III**

Prinsepia Royle -f- *Rosaceae* · 4 spp. · G:Dornkirsche
- **sinensis** (Oliv.) Oliv. ex Bean · G:Mand-schurische Dornkirsche · ♄ d Z5 IV; N-China
- **uniflora** Batalin · G:Chinesische Dornkirsche · ♄ d Z6 IV; N-China

Prionium E. Mey. -n- *Juncaceae* · 1 sp. · F:Jonc palmier; G:Palmenschilf
- **serratum** (L. f.) Drège · ♄ e ⁓ Z10 ⓦ; S-Afr.

Pritchardia Seem. & H. Wendl. -f- *Arecaceae* · 29 spp. · E:Loulu Palm; F:Palmier, Pritchardia; G:Loulupalme
- *filifera* Linden ex André = Washingtonia filifera

- *gaudichaudii* (Mart.) H. Wendl. = Pritchardia martii
- **martii** (Gaudich.) H. Wendl. · ♄ e Z10 ⓦ ⓝ; Hawaii
- **pacifica** Seem. & H. Wendl. · ♄ e Z10 ⓦ ⓝ; Fiji, Samoa

Pritzelago Kuntze -f- *Brassicaceae* · 1 sp. · E:Chamois Cress; F:Cresson des chamois; G:Gämskresse
- **alpina** (L.) Kuntze · G:Alpen-Gäm-skresse, Gämskresse
- subsp. **alpina** · E:Chamois Cress, Chamois Grass; G:Alpen-Gämskresse · ⹏ Z5 V-VIII; Eur.: sp., F, I, C-Eur., Ba; mts.
- subsp. **auerswaldii** (Willk.) Greuter & Burdet · G:Kantabrische Gämskresse · ⹏ △ Z5 V-VI; Eur.: N-Sp. (Cordillera Cantábrica)
- subsp. **brevicaulis** (Hoppe) Greuter & Burdet · G:Kurzstängelige Gämskresse · ⹏ △ Z5 VII-VIII; Eur.: F, I, A, Sw, Ba; mts.

Proboscidea Schmidel -f- *Pedaliaceae* · 9 spp. · E:Devil's Claw, Unicorn Plant; F:Cornaret, Martynia à trompe; G:Gämshorn
- **fragrans** (Lindl.) Decne. · E:Sweet Unicornplant; G:Duftendes Gämshorn · ⊙ ⚘ D Z10 VIII; Mex.
- *jussieui* Medik. = Proboscidea louisianica
- **louisianica** (Mill.) Thell. · E:Ram's Horn; G:Louisiana-Gämshorn · ⊙ ⚘ Z10 VII-VIII ⓝ; USA: NE, NCE, SE, SC, N.Mex.; N-Mex.
- *lutea* (Lindl.) Stapf = Ibicella lutea

Promenaea Lindl. -f- *Orchidaceae* · 18 spp.
- **lentiginosa** (Lindl.) Lindl. · ⹏ Z10 ⓦ VII-VIII ▽ ✳; Braz.
- **rollisonii** (Lindl.) Lindl. · ⹏ Z10 ⓦ VII-VIII ▽ ✳; Braz.
- **stapelioides** (Link & Otto) Lindl. · ⹏ Z10 ⓦ VII-IX ▽ ✳; Braz.
- **xanthina** (Lindl.) Lindl. · ⹏ Z10 ⓦ VII-VIII ▽ ✳; Braz.

Prosartes D. Don -f- *Convallariaceae* · 6 spp. · G:Elfenglöckchen
- **smithii** (Hook.) Utech, Shinwari & Kawano · E:Fairy Lantern; G:Groß-blütiges Elfenglöckchen · ⹏ Z6; B.C., USA: NW, Calif.

Proserpinaca L. -f- *Haloragaceae* · -5 spp. ·

E:Mermaidweed
- **palustris** L. · E:Marsh Mermaidweed · ⁴
  ∼ 🌐; Can.: E; USA: NE, NCE, SC, SE,
  Fla.; W.Ind.

Prosopis L. -f- *Mimosaceae* · 44 spp. ·
E:Mesquite; F:Prosopis; G:Mesquite-
baum, Schraubenbohne, Süßhülsenbaum
- **alba** Griseb. · E:Argentine Mesquite;
  G:Argentinische Schraubenbohne · ♄ s
  Z10 🏠 Ⓝ; Bol., Arg.
- **chilensis** (Molina) Stuntz · E:Chilean
  Mesquite; G:Chilenische Schrauben-
  bohne · ♄ s Z10 🏠 Ⓝ; W.Ind., Peru, Bol.,
  Chile, Arg.
- **cineraria** (L.) Druce · ♄ d Z10 🏠 Ⓝ; Iran,
  Afgh., N-Ind., N-Afr.
- **juliflora** (Sw.) DC. · E:Mesquite;
  G:Mesquitebaum · ♄ ♄ e Z10 🏠 Ⓝ; USA:
  Kans., SC, SW, Calif.; Mex., W.Ind., Col.,
  Venez.
- *spicigera* L. = Prosopis cineraria
- **tamarugo** F. Phil. · ♄ d Z10 🏠; Chile

Prostanthera Labill. -f- *Lamiaceae* ·
c. 50 spp. · E:Australian Mint Bush;
F:Menthe d'Australie, Prostanthère;
G:Australminze
- **cuneata** Benth. · E:Alpine Mint Bush ·
  ♄ e Z9 🏠; Austr.: N.S.Wales, Victoria,
  Tasman.
- **nivea** A. Cunn. ex Benth. · E:Snowy Mint
  Bush · ♄ e D Z9 🏠 V; Austr.: Queensl.,
  N.S.Wales, Victoria, Tasman.
- **ovalifolia** R. Br. · E:Common Mint
  Bush · ♄ e D Z9 🏠 I-III; Austr.: Queensl.,
  N.S.Wales
- **rotundifolia** R. Br. · E:Round-leaved
  Mint Bush; G:Australischer Minzestrauch
  · ♄ e D Z9 🏠 II-III ⚥ ; Austr.: N.S.Wales,
  Victoria, S-Austr., Tasman.
- **sieberi** Benth. · E:Cut-leaved Mint Bush ·
  ♄ e D Z9 🏠 III-IV; Austr.: N.S.Wales
- **violacea** R. Br. · E:Violet Mint Bush · ♄ e
  D Z9 🏠 IV; Austr.: N.S.Wales

Prosthechea Knowles & Westc. -f-
Orchidaceae · 104 spp.
- **baculus** (Rchb. f.) W.E. Higgins · ⁴ Z10
  🌐 VII-IX ▽ ✳; Mex., C-Am., trop. S-Am.
- **boothiana** (Lindl.) W.E. Higgins ·
  E:Dollar Orchid · ⁴ Z10 🌐 ▽ ✳; Cuba
- **Brassavolae** (Rchb. f.) W.E. Higgins · ⁴
  Z10 🌐 VII-IX ▽ ✳; Mex., C-Am.
- **cochleata** (L.) W.E. Higgins ·

E:Clamshell Orchid · ⁴ Z10 🌐 XI-II ▽ ✳;
Fla., W.Ind., C-Am., Col., Venez., Guyan.
- **fragrans** (Sw.) W.E. Higgins · ⁴ Z10 🌐
  II-V ▽ ✳; Mex., C-Am., W.Ind., trop.
  S-Am.
- **glumacea** (Lindl.) W.E. Higgins · ⁴ Z10
  🌐 IX ▽ ✳; Ecuad., E-Braz.
- **michuacana** (La Llave & Lex.) W.E.
  Higgins · ⁴ Z10 🏠 VII-VIII ▽ ✳; Mex.,
  Guat.
- **prismatocarpa** (Rchb. f.) W.E. Higgins ·
  ⁴ Z10 🌐 VII-VIII ▽ ✳; Costa Rica
- **pygmaea** (Hook.) W.E. Higgins · ⁴ 🌐 ▽
  ✳; trop. Am.
- **radiata** (Lindl.) W.E. Higgins · ⁴ Z10 🌐
  V-VII ▽ ✳; Mex., C-Am.
- **varicosa** (Bateman ex Lindl.) W.E.
  Higgins · ⁴ Z10 🌐 VII-VIII ▽ ✳; C-Am.
- **vespa** (Vell.) W.E. Higgins · ⁴ Z10 🌐
  IV-V ▽ ✳; C-Am., trop. S-Am.
- **vitellina** (Lindl.) W.E. Higgins · ⁴ Z10 🏠
  X-XII ▽ ✳; Mex., Guat.

Protea L. -f- *Proteaceae* · 115 spp. ·
E:Protea, Sugarbush; F:Protée; G:Protee,
Schimmerbaum, Silberbaum
- **barbigera** Meisn. · E:Woolly Protea;
  G:Wollige Protee · ♄ e Z9 🏠; S-Afr.
- **cynaroides** (L.) L. · E:Giant Protea, King
  Protea; G:Königs-Protee · ♄ e Z9 🏠; Cape
- **eximia** (Knight) Fourc. · E:Broad-leaved
  Sugarbush · ♄ e Z9 🏠; S-Afr.
- **grandiceps** Tratt. · E:Peach Protea;
  G:Pfirsich-Protee · ♄ e ✕ Z9 🏠; Cape
- *latifolia* R. Br. = Protea eximia
- **nana** (P.J. Bergius) Thunb. · E:Mountain-
  rose Sugarbush · ♄ e Z9 🏠; Cape
- **neriifolia** R. Br. · E:Oleander Leaf
  Protea; G:Oleander-Protee · ♄ e ✕ Z9 🏠;
  S-Afr.
- **repens** (L.) L. · E:Common Sugarbush,
  Sugar Protea; G:Honig-Silberbaum,
  Zucker-Protee · ♄ e Z9 🏠; Cape
- **speciosa** (L.) L. · E:Brown-beard
  Sugarbush · ♄ ♄ e Z9 🏠; Cape

Prumnopitys Phil. -f- *Podocarpaceae* ·
9 spp. · G:Kirscheibe
- **andina** (Poepp. ex Endl.) de Laub. ·
  E:Chilean Yew, Plum Fruited Yew;
  G:Chilenische Kirscheibe · ♄ e Z8 🏠;
  S-Chile, Arg. (And.)
- **ferruginea** (G. Benn. ex D. Don) de
  Laub. · E:Miro; G:Rotbraune Kirscheibe ·
  ♄ e Z9 🏠; NZ

Prunella L. -f- *Lamiaceae* · 8 spp. ·
E:Selfheal; F:Brunelle; G:Braunelle
- **grandiflora** (L.) Scholler · G:Großblütige
  Braunelle
- subsp. **grandiflora** · E:Large Self-heal;
  F:Prunelle à grandes fleurs; G:Gewöhnli-
  che Größblütige Braunelle · ⅄ Z5 VI-VIII;
  Eur.* exc. BrI; ? TR, Cauc.
- subsp. **pyrenaica** (Gren. & Godr.) A.
  Bolòs & O. Bolòs · G:Pyrenäen-Braunelle ·
  ⅄ Z5 VI-VIII; Eur.: P, sp., F
- *hastifolia* Brot. = Prunella grandiflora
  subsp. pyrenaica
- **laciniata** (L.) L. · E:Cut-leaved Selfheal;
  G:Weiße Braunelle · ⅄ Z6 VI-VIII; Eur.*
  exc. BrI, Sc; TR, Levant, Cauc., Iran,
  NW-Afr.
- × **pinnatifida** Pers. (*P. laciniata* × *P.
  vulgaris*) · ⅄ VI-VIII; cult.
- **vulgaris** L. · E:Self Heal; F:Prunelle commune; G:Gewöhnliche Braunelle · ⅄ Z3
  VI-IX ⚥ ; Eur.*, TR, Cyprus, Syr., Cauc.,
  Iran, W-Sib., E-Sib., Amur, Sakhal.,
  Kamchat., C-As., Him., Ind. (Nilgiris),
  NW-Afr., Alaska, Can., USA*
- × *webbiana* hort. ex N. Taylor = Prunella
  grandiflora

Prunus L. -f- *Rosaceae* · c. 430 spp. ·
E:Almond, Apricot, Cherry, Peach, Plum;
G:Aprikose, Kirsche, Lorbeer-Kirsche,
Mandel, Pfirsich, Pflaume, Schlehe,
Traubenkirsche, Weichsel, Zwetsche,
Zwetschge
- *acida* Dumort. = Prunus cerasus subsp.
  acida
- **americana** Marshall · E:American
  Plum, American Red Plum, Goose Plum;
  G:Amerikanische Pflaume · ♄ ♄ d Z4
  III-IV Ⓝ; Can.: E; USA: NE, NCE, NC,
  Rocky Mts., SW, SC, SE, Fla.; Mex.
- × **amygdalopersica** (Weston) Rehder (*P.
  dulcis* × *P. persica*) · F:Prunus; G:Mandel-
  Pfirsich · ♄ ♄ d Z6 III-IV; cult.
- **angustifolia** Marshall · E:Chickasaw
  Plum; G:Chickasa-Pflaume · ♄ ♄ d Z6 IV
  Ⓝ; USA: NE, NCE, NC, SC, SE, Fla.
- **argentea** (Lam.) Rehder · ♄ d Z7; TR
- **armeniaca** L. · E:Apricot; G:Aprikose,
  Marille · ♄ d Z7 III-IV ⚥ Ⓝ; N-China, nat.
  in Eur.
- **many cultivars**
- *austera* (L.) Ehrh. = Prunus cerasus
  subsp. cerasus var. austera
- **avium** (L.) L. · E:Gean, Mazzard, Wild

Cherry; F:Cerisier des oiseaux, Merisier;
G:Süß-Kirsche, Vogel-Kirsche · ♄ d Z5
IV-V ⚥ Ⓝ; Eur.*, TR, Cauc., Iran, nat. in
N-Am.
- **many cultivars**
- **besseyi** L.H. Bailey = Prunus pumila var.
  besseyi · ♄ d Z3 V; Ca.: Man.; USA: Rocky
  Mts., NCE
- × **blireana** André (*P. mume* 'Rosea Plena'
  × *P. cerasifera* var. *pissardii*) · F:Prunier
  double · ♄ ♄ d Z5; cult.
- **brigantina** Vill. · E:Briançon Apricot;
  G:Briançon-Aprikose · ♄ ♄ d Z7 V Ⓝ; SE-F
- **campanulata** Maxim. · E:Bell Flowered
  Cherry, Formosan Cherry, Taiwan
  Cherry; G:Glocken-Kirsche · ♄ d Z7 III-IV;
  Ryukyu-Is., Taiwan
- **canescens** Bois · E:Greyleaf Cherry;
  G:Graublättrige Kirsche · ♄ d Z6 IV-V;
  W-China, C-China
- *capuli* Spreng. = Prunus salicifolia
- **caroliniana** (Mill.) Aiton · E:Carolina
  Laurel Cherry · ♄ e Z7; USA: SE, Tex.,
  Fla.
- **cerasifera** Ehrh.
- subsp. **cerasifera** · E:Cherry Plum,
  Myrobalan Plum; F:Myrobolan, Prunier-
  cerise; G:Kirschpflaume · ♄ ♄ d Z4 III-IV
  Ⓝ; Eur.: Ba, Crim; TR, Cauc., Iran, C-As.,
  nat. in Eur.* exc. Ib
- subsp. **divaricata** (Ledeb.) C.K.
  Schneid. · ♄ ♄ d Z4; Eur.: Ba; TR, Cauc.,
  C-As. Iran
- **cerasus** L. · E:Sour Cherry; G:Sauer-
  Kirsche, Weichsel · Z3
- subsp. **acida** (Dumort.) Asch. & Graebn. ·
  E:Bush Sour Cherry; G:Schattenmorelle,
  Strauch-Weichsel · ♄ d Z3 IV-V; C-Eur.
- subsp. **cerasus** · E:Tree Sour Cherry;
  F:Cerisier aigre; G:Amarelle, Baum-
  Weichsel · ♄ d Z5 IV-V ⚥ Ⓝ; cult. Eur.,
  As., N-Am., nat. in Eur., N-Am.
- var. **austera** L. · E:Morello Cherry;
  G:Morelle, Süß-Weichsel · ♄ d Z5; cult.
- var. *frutescens* Neilr. = Prunus cerasus
  subsp. acida
- var. **marasca** (Host) Vis. · E:Maraschino
  Cherry; G:Maraschino-Kirsche · Z5; cult.
- **many cultivars**
- × **cistena** (Hansen) Koehne (*P. pumila* ×
  P. cerasifera var. *pissardii*) · E:Dwarf Red
  Leaf Plum; G:Rote Sand-Kirsche · ♄ d Z4
  V; cult.
- *claudiana* (Pers.) Poit. & Turpin = Prunus
  domestica subsp. italica

- **cocomilia** Ten. · ħ ħ d Z6 IV; S-Ba, S-I, Sic..; mts.
- *communis* (L.) Arcang. = Prunus dulcis var. dulcis
- **concinna** Koehne · ħ ħ d Z6 IV; China: Hupeh
- *conradinae* Koehne = Prunus hirtipes
- **cornuta** (Royle) Steud. · E:Himalayan Bird Cherry; G:Himalaya-Traubenkirsche · ħ d Z5 V; Him.
- **cyclamina** Koehne · ħ ħ d Z6 V; C-China.
- × **dasycarpa** Ehrh. (*P. armeniaca* × *P. cerasifera*) · E:Black Apricot · ħ d Z7 ∧ III; cult.
- **davidiana** (Carrière) Franch. · E:Chinese Peach, Père David's Peach; G:Davids Pfirsich · ħ ħ d Z4 III; N-China
- **dielsiana** C.K. Schneid. · ħ ħ d Z6 IV; C-China
- *divaricata* Ledeb. = Prunus cerasifera subsp. divaricata
- **domestica** L. · G:Pflaume
- – subsp. **domestica** · E:Plum; G:Gewöhnliche Pflaume, Zwetsche, Zwetschge · ħ d Z5 IV ⚥ Ⓝ; TR, Cauc.; cult. Eur., W-As., N-Afr.
- **many cultivars**
- – subsp. **insititia** (L.) C.K. Schneid. · E:Bullace Plum; G:Hafer-Pflaume, Kriechen-Pflaume · ħ d Z5 IV-V; cult. Eur., W-As., Ind., N-Afr., N-Am.
- – subsp. **italica** (Borkh.) Gams ex Hegi · G:Reineclaude, Reneklode · ħ ħ d Z5; cult. C-Eur., S-Eur., As.
- **some cultivars**
- – subsp. *oeconomica* (Borkh.) C.K. Schneid. = Prunus domestica subsp. domestica
- – subsp. **syriaca** (Borkh.) Janch. ex Mansf. · G:Mirabelle · ħ d Z5; cult. C-Eur., S-Eur., N-Afr.
- **dulcis** (Mill.) D.A. Webb · G:Mandel, Mandelbaum
- **many cultivars**
- – var. **amara** (DC.) Buchheim · E:Bitter Almond; G:Bitter-Mandel · ħ d Z7 III-IV ⚥; cult.
- – var. **dulcis** · E:Almond; F:Amandier; G:Süße Mandel · ħ ħ d Z7 III-IV ⚥ Ⓝ; TR, Cauc., Iran, C-As., Afgh.
- – var. **fragilis** (Borkh.) Buchheim · G:Knack-Mandel · ħ d Z7; cult.
- × **eminens** Beck (*P. cerasus* × *P. glandulosa*) · G:Mittlere Weichsel · ħ d Z4 IV-V; cult.
- **fenzliana** Fritsch · G:Kaukasische Mandel · ħ d Z7 ∧ III; Cauc.
- × **fontanesiana** (Spach) C.K. Schneid. (*P. avium* × *P. mahaleb*) · ħ d; cult.
- **fremontii** S. Watson · E:Desert Apricot · ħ ħ d Z7; S-Calif.
- × **fruticans** Weihe (*P. spinosa* × *P. domestica* subsp. *insititia*) · G:Hafer-Schlehe, Weihe · ħ d IV Ⓝ; cult. G, A, CZ
- **fruticosa** Pall. · E:Ground Cherry; F:Prunier nain; G:Steppen-Kirsche, Zwerg-Kirsche · ħ d Z6 IV-V; Eur.: Ital-P, C-Eur., EC-Eur., Ba, E-Eur.; Cauc., W-Sib., C-As.
- **glandulosa** Thunb. ex Murray · E:Chinese Bush Berry, Dwarf Flowering Almond; F:Amandier à fleurs du Japon; G:Drüsen-Kirsche · ħ d Z5 V; China
- × **gondouinii** (Poit. & Turpin) Rehder (*P. avium* × *P. cerasus*) · ħ d Z4; cult.
- **grayana** Maxim. · ħ d Z5 VI; Jap.
- × **hillieri** hort. (*P. incisa* × *P. sargentii*) · E:Hillier's Cherry; G:Hilliers Kirsche · ħ d Z6 IV-V; cult.
- **hirtipes** Hemsl. · G:Borstenstängelige Kirsche · ħ d Z7 ∧ III; C-China.
- **hortulana** L.H. Bailey · E:Hortulan Plum; G:Amerikanische Sauer-Kirsche · ħ d Z6 IV-V Ⓝ; USA: NCE, Okla., SE
- **ilicifolia** (Nutt. ex Hook. & Arn.) Walp. · E:Hollyleaf Cherry · ħ ħ e Z9 Ⓔ; Calif., Baja Calif.
- **incana** (Pall.) Batsch · E:Willow Cherry; G:Graue Kirsch-Mandel · ħ d Z6 IV; TR
- **incisa** Thunb. ex Murray · E:Fuji Cherry; G:Fuji-Kirsche, März-Kirsche · ħ d Z6 III-IV; Jap.
- *insititia* L. = Prunus domestica subsp. insititia
- *italica* Borkh. = Prunus domestica subsp. italica
- **jamasakura** Sieber ex Koidz. · G:Japanische Berg-Kirsche · ħ d Z5; Korea, ? Jap.
- **japonica** Thunb. ex Murray · E:Chinese Plum Tree, Oriental Bush Cherry; G:Japanische Kirsch-Mandel · ħ d Z4 V ⚥; China, Korea
- × **juddii** E.F. Anderson (*P. sargentii* × *P.* × *yedoensis*) · ħ d Z6; cult.
- **laurocerasus** L. · E:Cherry Laurel, Laurel; F:Laurier-amande, Laurier-cerise; G:Kirschlorbeer, Lorbeer-Kirsche · ħ e Z7 IV-V ⚥ ⚘ Ⓝ; Eur.: Ba; TR, Cauc., Iran, nat. in P, Fr, Cors., BrI
- **some cultivars**

- **lusitanica** L. · E:Portugal Laurel, Portuguese Laurel; F:Laurier du Portugal; G:Portugiesische Lorbeerkirsche · ♄ ♄ e Z8 ⌂ ∧ VI ✀; Ib, SW-F, Canar., Azor.
- **maackii** Rupr. · E:Amur Cherry, Manchurian Cherry; F:Cerisier de Mandchourie; G:Amur-Traubenkirsche · ♄ d Z4 IV; Korea, Manch.
- **mahaleb** L. · E:Mahaleb Cherry, St Lucie Cherry; F:Cerisier de Sainte Lucie; G:Felsen-Kirsche, Stein-Weichsel · ♄ ♄ d Z5 IV-V Ⓝ; Eur.* exc. BrI, Sc; TR, Iraq, Syr., Lebanon, Cauc., N-Iran, Afgh., C-As., Moroc., nat. in N-Am.
- **mandshurica** (Maxim.) Koehne · G:Mandschurische Aprikose · ♄ d Z6 V; China, Korea, Mong., Amur
- *marasca* (Host) Rchb. = Prunus cerasus subsp. cerasus var. marasca
- **maritima** Marshall · E:Beach Plum; G:Strand-Pflaume · ♄ d Z3 IV; USA: NE
- **mume** Siebold & Zucc. · E:Japanese Apricot; F:Abricotier du Japon; G:Japanische Aprikose · ♄ d Z6 III-IV ⚥ ; Japan
- **munsoniana** W. Wight & Hedrick · E:Wild Goose Plum; G:Gänse-Pflaume · ♄ d Z6 IV-V Ⓝ; USA: NCE, Kans., SC, SE
- *myrobalana* (L.) Loisel. = Prunus cerasifera subsp. cerasifera
- *nana* (L.) Stokes = Prunus tenella
- *nana* Du Roi = Prunus virginiana
- **nigra** Aiton · E:Canada Plum, Canadian Plum; G:Bitter-Kirsche · ♄ ♄ d Z4 V-IV Ⓝ; Can.: E; USA: NE, NCE, SE
- **nipponica** Matsum. · G:Japanische Alpen-Kirsche
- var. **kurilensis** (Miyabe) E.H. Wilson · F:Petit cerisier des Kouriles; G:Kurilen-Kirsche · ♄ d Z5 IV; Sakhal., Jap.: Hokkaido
- var. **nipponica** · E:Japanese Alpine Cherry; F:Cerisier alpin du Japon; G:Nippon-Kirsche · ♄ ♄ d Z6 V; Jap.
- **padus** L. · G:Traubenkirsche
- subsp. **padus** · E:European Bird Cherry; F:Merisier à grappes; G:Gewöhnliche Traubenkirsche · ♄ ♄ d Z3 IV-V Ⓝ; Eur.* ; TR, Cauc., W-Sib., E-Sib., Amur, Sakhal., Kamchat., C-As., Korea, Jap., Moroc.
- subsp. **petraea** (Tausch) Domin · G:Gebirgs-Traubenkirsche · ♄ d Z3; Sc, C-Eur. mts.
- **pensylvanica** L. f. · E:Bird Cherry, Pin Cherry, Red Cherry; G:Feuer-Kirsche · ♄ ♄ d Z4 IV-V; Can., USA: NE, N.C., NCE,

NC, Rocky Mts.
- **persica** (L.) Batsch
- var. *nectarina* (W.T. Aiton) Maxim. = Prunus persica var. nucipersica
- var. **nucipersica** (L.) C.K. Schneid. · E:Nectarine; G:Nektarine · ♄ ♄ Z6 Ⓝ; cult.
- **many cultivars**
- var. **persica** · E:Peach; F:Pêcher commun; G:Pfirsich · ♄ ♄ d Z6 IV ⚥ Ⓝ; N-China, C-China
- **many cultivars**
- **pilosiuscula** (C.K. Schneid.) Koehne · ♄ ♄ d Z5 IV; W-China, C-China
- **prostrata** Labill. · E:Mountain Cherry, Rock Cherry; G:Niedrige Kirsch-Mandel · ♄ d △ Z6 IV; Eur.: Ib, Cors, Sard., Ba; TR, Syr., Lebanon, NW-Afr.
- **pseudocerasus** Lindl. · E:False Cherry; G:Falsche Weichsel · ♄ d Z6 III Ⓝ; China: Hupeh
- **pumila** L. · E:Sand Cherry; G:Sand-Kirsche
- var. **besseyi** (L.H. Bailey) Gleason · E:Western Sand Cherry · ♄ d Z2; Can.: Man.; USA: Rocky Mts., NEC, SC
- var. **depressa** (Pursh) Bean · E:Eastern Sand Cherry; G:Kriechende Sand-Kirsche · ♄ d Z2; E-Can.; USA: NE
- var. **pumila** · E:Great Lakes Sand Cherry; G:Strauchige Sand-Kirsche · ♄ d △ Z5 V; Can.: E; USA: NE, NCE
- **rufa** Hook. f. · G:Himalaya-Kirsche · ♄ d Z8 ⌂; Him.
- *sachalinensis* Miyoshi = Prunus sargentii
- **salicifolia** Kunth · E:Capulin · ♄ s Z8 ⌂; Mex., C-Am., Col., Peru + ; mts.
- **salicina** Lindl. · E:Japanese Plum; G:Chinesische Pflaume · ♄ d Z6 IV Ⓝ; N-China, SE-China
- **sargentii** Rehder · E:Sargent's Cherry; F:Cerisier de Sargent; G:Berg-Kirsche, Sachalin-Kirsche · ♄ d Z6 V; Jap., Korea, Sakhal.
- f. **pubescens** Tatew. Z4 IV-V
- × **schmittii** Rehder (*P. avium* × *P. canescens*) · G:Schmitts Kirsche · ♄ d Z5; cult.
- **sericea** (Batalin) Koehne · ♄ d Z6; China: Sichuan
- **serotina** Ehrh. · E:American Bird Cherry, Black Cherry, Rum Cherry; F:Cerisier tardif; G:Späte Traubenkirsche · ♄ d Z4 V-VI ⚥ ✀ Ⓝ; Can.: E; USA: NE, NCE, NC, SW, SC, SE, Fla.; Mex., Guat., nat. in

Eur.
- **serrula** Franch. · E:Birch Bark Cherry; F:Cerisier du Tibet; G:Mahagoni-Kirsche, Tibetische Kirsche · ħ ħ d Z6 IV-V; W-China
- **serrulata** Lindl. · E:Oriental Cherry; F:Cerisier des collines; G:Grannen-Kirsche, Japanische Blüten-Kirsche · ħ ħ d Z6 IV-V Ⓝ; China, Korea, Jap.
- var. *sachalinensis* (F. Schmidt) E.H. Wilson = Prunus sargentii
- var. *spontanea* (Maxim.) E.H. Wilson = Prunus jamasakura
- **sibirica** L. · E:Siberian Apricot; G:Sibirische Aprikose · ħ ħ d Z5 IV; E-Sib., Manch., N-China, Korea, Amur, Mong.
- × **sieboldii** (B. Verl.) Wittm. (*P. apetala* × *P. speciosa*) · G:Siebolds Kirsche · ħ d Z6 IV; orig. ?, nat. in Jap.
- **simonii** Carrière · E:Apricot Plum; G:Simons Pflaume · ħ d Z6 IV-V Ⓝ; N-China
- × **skinneri** Rehder (*P. japonica* × *P. tenella*) · ħ d Z6; cult.
- **speciosa** (Koidz.) Ingram · E:Oshima Cherry; G:Oshima-Kirsche · ħ d Z6 IV; Jap.
- **spinosa** L. · E:Blackthorn, Sloe; F:Epine noire, Prunellier ; G:Gewöhnliche Schlehe, Schwarzdorn · ħ d Z5 IV-V ♇ Ⓝ; Eur.*, TR, Cauc., Iran, W-Sib., Alger., nat. in N-Am.
- **subhirtella** Miq. · E:Autumn Cherry, Winter Flowering Cherry; F:Cerisier d'hiver; G:Frühjahrs-Kirsche, Higan-Kirsche · ħ d Z6 IV-V; Jap.
- *syriaca* Borkh. = Prunus domestica subsp. syriaca
- **tenella** Batsch · E:Dwarf Russian Almond, Russian Almond; F:Amandier nain; G:Russische Zwerg-Mandel · ħ d Z5 III-V; Eur.: C-Eur., EC-Eur., Ba, E-Eur.; Cauc., W-Sib., C-As., nat. in F
- **tomentosa** Thunb. ex Murray · E:Downy Cherry, Nanking Cherry; G:Japanische Mandel-Kirsche · ħ d Z4 IV-V Ⓝ; Tibet, W-China, N-China, Korea
- **triloba** Lindl. · E:Flowering Almond; F:Amandier de Chine; G:Mandelbäumchen
- var. **simplex** (Bunge) Rehder · G:Einfachblühendes Mandelbäumchen · ħ d Z5; China
- var. **triloba** · G:Gefülltblühendes

Mandelbäumchen · ħ d Z5 III-IV; China
- **ussuriensis** Kovalev & Kostina · ħ; Amur, Manch.
- **virens** (Wooton & Standl.) Shreve ex Sarg. · E:Black Cherry · ħ ħ e; S-USA.; Mex.
- **virginiana** L. · E:Virginian Bird Cherry, Western Choke Cherry; G:Virginische Trauben-Kirsche · ħ ħ d Z4 V Ⓝ; Can., USA: NE, N.C., NCE, NC, SC, Rocky Mts., Calif., SW
- × **yedoensis** Matsum. (*P. speciosa* × *P. subhirtella*) · E:Tokyo Cherry; F:Cerisier Yoshino; G:Tokio-Kirsche, Yoshino-Kirsche · ħ d Z6 IV; Jap.
- **Cultivars:**
- **some cultivars**

Psammophora Dinter & Schwantes -f- *Aizoaceae* · 4 spp.
- **modesta** (Dinter & A. Berger) Dinter & Schwantes · Ψ Z10 Ⓚ; Namibia

Pseudananas Hassl. ex Harms -m- *Bromeliaceae* · 1 sp. · F:Faux-ananas; G:Scheinananas
- **sagenarius** (Arruda) Camargo · Ψ Z10 Ⓜ; Braz., Parag.

Pseuderanthemum Radlk. -n- *Acanthaceae* · 60 spp.
- **alatum** (Nees) Radlk. · ħ e Z10 Ⓜ VII-VIII; Mex.
- **albiflorum** (Hook.) Radlk. · ħ e Z10 Ⓜ VI-VIII; Braz.
- **atropurpureum** (W. Bull) L.H. Bailey · ħ e Z10 Ⓜ; Polyn.
- **reticulatum** (Hook. f.) Radlk. · ħ e Z10 Ⓜ; Polyn.
- *seticalyx* (C.B. Clarke) Stapf = Ruspolia seticalyx
- **sinuatum** (Vahl) Radlk. · ħ e Z10 Ⓜ VI-VIII; N.Caled.
- **tuberculatum** (Hook. f.) Radlk. · ħ Z10 Ⓜ Ⓚ VIII-IX; Polyn.

Pseudobombax Dugand -n- *Bombacaceae* · 20 spp.
- **ellipticum** (Kunth) Dugand · ħ Ψ e Z10 Ⓜ; Mex., Guat.

Pseudocinchona A. Chev. = Corynanthe
- *africana* A. Chev. ex Perrot = Corynanthe pachyceras

Pseudocydonia (C.K. Schneid.) C.K.
Schneid. -f- *Rosaceae* · 1 sp. · E:Chinese
Quince; G:Holzquitte
– **sinensis** (Dum.-Cours.) C.K. Schneid. ·
E:Chinese Quince; G:Holzquitte · ♄ s Z6
V Ⓝ; China

Pseudoespostoa Backeb. = Espostoa
– *melanostele* (Vaupel) Backeb. = Espostoa
melanostele

Pseudofumaria Medik. -f- *Fumariaceae* ·
2 spp. · F:Faux-fumeterre; G:Lerchen-
sporn, Scheinlerchensporn
– **alba** (Mill.) Lidén · G:Blassgelber
Scheinlerchensporn
– subsp. **acaulis** (Wulfen) Lidén · G:Dal-
matiner Blassgelber Scheinlerchensporn ·
⅃ Z5 VI-X; Eur.: Ba, nat. in Fr, D
– subsp. **alba** · G:Gewöhnlicher Blassgelber
Lerchensporn · ⅃ △ Z5 VI-IX; Eur.: I,
Slove., Croatia, Bosn., YU, Maced., AL, ?
GR, nat. in Fr, D
– **lutea** (L.) Borkh. · E:Yellow Fumitory;
F:Corydale jaune; G:Gelber Scheinlerchensporn · ⅃ △ Z6 V-X; Eur.: N-I, Sw, nat.
in BrI, Sc, Fr, C-Eur., EC-Eur., E-Eur.

Pseudognaphalium Kirp. -n- *Asteraceae* ·
10 spp. · E:Cudweed; F:Faux-gnaphale;
G:Scheinruhrkraut
– **luteoalbum** (L.) Hilliard & B.L. Burtt ·
E:Jersey Cudweed; G:Gelbliches Schein-
ruhrkraut · ⊙ VII-X; Eur.*, TR, Cauc.,
Iran, C-As., S-As., N.Guinea, Afr., Austr.,
NZ, Pacific Is., nat. in N-Am., S-Am.
– **obtusifolium** (L.) Hilliard & B.L.
Burtt · E:Everlasting, Rabbit Tobacco;
G:Stumpfblättriges Scheinruhrkraut · ⊙
VII-IX; Can.: E; USA: NE, NCE, SE, SC,
Fla.

Pseudolarix Gordon -f- *Pinaceae* · 1 sp. ·
E:Golden Larch; F:Faux-mélèze;
G:Goldlärche
– **amabilis** (J. Nelson) Rehder · E:Golden
Larch; F:Mélèze de la Chine; G:Gold-
lärche · ♄ d Z6; E-China
– *kaempferi* (Lamb.) Gordon = Pseudolarix
amabilis

Pseudolmedia Trécul -f- *Moraceae* · 9 spp.
– **laevis** (Ruiz & Pav.) J.F. Macbr. · ♄ e Z9
🅐; Parag., Peru

Pseudolobivia (Backeb.) Backeb. =
Echinopsis
– *ancistrophora* (Speg.) Backeb. = Echinopsis ancistrophora
– *aurea* (Britton & Rose) Backeb. =
Echinopsis aurea
– *ferox* (Britton & Rose) Backeb. =
Echinopsis ferox
– *fiebrigii* (Gürke) Backeb. = Echinopsis
obrepanda var. fiebrigii
– *kermesina* Krainz = Echinopsis mamillosa
var. kermesina
– *kratochviliana* (Backeb.) Backeb. =
Echinopsis kratochviliana
– *leucorhodantha* (Backeb.) Backeb. =
Echinopsis ancistrophora
– *longispina* (Britton & Rose) Backeb. =
Echinopsis longispina
– *obrepanda* (Salm-Dyck) Backeb. =
Echinopsis obrepanda var. obrepanda
– var. *fiebrigii* (Gürke) Backeb. = Echinopsis obrepanda var. fiebrigii

Pseudolysimachion (W.D.J. Koch) Opiz
-n- *Scrophulariaceae* · 19 spp. · F:Fausse-
lysimaque; G:Blauweiderich
– **longifolium** (L.) Opiz · G:Langblättriger
Blauweiderich
– **some cultivars**
– subsp. **longifolium** · E:Garden Speedwell; F:Véronique à longues feuilles;
G:Gewöhnlicher Langblättriger Blauweiderich · ⅃ ⌢ Z4 VI-IX; Eur.* exc. BrI, Ib;
TR, Cauc., W-Sib., E-Sib., Amur, Sakhal.,
C-As.
– **orchideum** (Crantz) Wraber · G:Kna-
benkrautartiger Ehrenpreis · ⅃ VII-X;
SE-Eur., N-I
– **spicatum** (L.) Opiz · G:Ähriger Blauweiderich
– **some cultivars**
– subsp. **incanum** (L.) Opiz · G:Graulau-
biger Ähriger Blauweiderich · ⅃ △ Z3
VI-VII ▽; Eur.: EC-Eur., E-Eur.; W-Sib.,
E-Sib., C-As.
– subsp. **spicatum** · E:Spiked Speedwell;
F:Véronique en épis; G:Gewöhnlicher
Ähriger Blauweiderich · ⅃ Z3 VI-VIII;
Eur.* +
– **spurium** (L.) Rauschert · G:Rispiger
Blauweiderich · ⅃ Z3 VI; Eur.: EC-Eur.,
Ba, E-Eur.; Cauc., W-Sib., C-As.
– **subsessile** (Miq.) Holub · ⅃ Z6 VII-VIII;
Jap.

Pseudomammillaria Buxb. = Mammillaria
– *camptotricha* (Dams) Buxb. = Mammillaria camptotricha

Pseudopanax K. Koch -m- *Araliaceae* · 12 spp. · F:Faux-gingseng; G:Scheinginseng
– **arboreus** (Murray) K. Koch · E:Five Fingers; G:Fünffingriger Scheinginseng · ♄ e Z10 ⓚ VII-VIII; NZ
– **crassifolius** (Sol. ex A. Cunn.) K. Koch · E:Lancewood; G:Dickblättriger Scheinginseng · ♄ e Z9 ⓚ; NZ
– *davidii* (Franch.) Philipson = Metapanax davidii
– **discolor** (Kirk) Harms · ♄ e Z10 ⓚ; NZ
– **ferox** (Kirk) Kirk · ♄ ♄ e Z9 ⓚ; NZ
– **lessonii** (DC.) K. Koch · ♄ ♄ e Z9 ⓚ; NZ

Pseudophegopteris Ching -f- *Thelypteridaceae* · 22 spp.
– **pyrrhorhachis** (Kunze) Ching

Pseudopilocereus Buxb. = Pilosocereus
– *glaucescens* (Labour.) Buxb. = Pilosocereus glaucescens
– *pentaedrophorus* (Labour.) Buxb. = Pilosocereus pentaedrophorus
– *werdermannianus* Buining & Brederoo = Pilosocereus werdermannianus

Pseudorchis Ség. -f- *Orchidaceae* · 3 spp. · F:Faux-orchis; G:Weißzüngel
– **albida** (L.) Á. Löve & D. Löve · G:Gewöhnliches Weißzüngel, Weißzunge · ⑵ V-VIII ▽ ✳; Eur.*

Pseudorhipsalis Britton & Rose -f- *Cactaceae* · 5 spp.
– **himantoclada** (Rol.-Goss.) Britton & Rose · ♄ ⵜ Z9 ⓜ ▽ ✳; Costa Rica
– **ramulosa** (Salm-Dyck) Barthlott · ♄ ⵜ Z9 ⓜ ▽ ✳; W.-Ind., trop. Am.

Pseudosasa Makino ex Nakai -f- *Poaceae* · 4 spp.
– **amabilis** (McClure) Keng f. · ♄ e ⓚ Ⓝ; cult. Vietn., S-China
– **japonica** (Siebold & Zucc. ex Steud.) Makino ex Nakai · E:Arrow Bamboo; G:Maketebambus · ♄ e Z7; Jap., S-Korea

Pseudostellaria Pax -f- *Caryophyllaceae* · 16 spp. · F:Fausse-stellaire; G:Knollenmiere

– **europaea** Schaeftl. · G:Knollenmiere · ⑵ IV-V; Eur.: N-I, A, Slove.

Pseudotsuga Carrière -f- *Pinaceae* · 4 spp. · G:Douglasfichte, Douglasie
– *douglasii* (Sabine ex D. Don) Carrière = Pseudotsuga menziesii var. menziesii
– *glauca* (Beissn.) Mayr = Pseudotsuga menziesii var. glauca
– **menziesii** (Mirb.) Franco · E:Douglas Fir; G:Douglasie
– var. **glauca** (Beissn.) Franco · E:Blue Douglas Fir; G:Blaue Douglasie · Z7; Can.: B.C., Alta.; USA: NW, Rocky Mts., SW, Tex.; Mex.
– var. **menziesii** · G:Gewöhnliche Douglasie, Grüne Douglasie · ♄ e Z5 IV-V; Can.: B.C.; USA: NW, Calif., Nev.
– *taxifolia* (Lamb.) Britton & Sudw. = Pseudotsuga menziesii var. menziesii

Psidium L. -n- *Myrtaceae* · 100 spp. · E:Guava; F:Goyavier; G:Guajave
– *araca* Raddi = Psidium guineense
– *cattleianum* Salisb. = Psidium littorale var. longipes
– **friedrichsthalianum** (O. Berg) Nied. · ♄ e Z10 ⓜ Ⓝ; Guat., Costa Rica
– **guajava** L. · E:Guava; G:Guave · ♄ ♄ e Z10 ⓜ IV-V ⚘ Ⓝ; Mex., C-Am., trop. S-Am., nat. in Trop., Subtrop.
– **guineense** Sw. · ♄ ♄ e Z10 ⓜ Ⓝ; C-Am., W.Ind., trop. S-Am.
– **littorale** Raddi
– var. **littorale** · E:Strawberry Guava; G:Erdbeer-Guave · ♄ e Z10 ⓜ Ⓝ; Braz., nat. in Fla., Calif., S-Am., Ind., China , Afr.
– var. **longipes** (O. Berg) Fosberg · E:Purple Strawberry Guava; G:Purpurne Erdbeer-Guave · ♄ e Z10 ⓜ; S-Fla., Bahamas
– *longipes* (O. Berg) McVaugh = Psidium littorale var. longipes
– *pomiferum* L. = Psidium guajava
– *pyriferum* L. = Psidium guajava
– **sartorianum** (O. Berg) Nied. · ♄ ♄ e Z10 ⓜ Ⓝ; Mex.

Psilanthus Hook. f. -m- *Rubiaceae* · 18 spp.
– **bengalensis** (Roem. & Schult.) J.-F. Leroy · E:Bengal Coffee · ♄ Z10 ⓜ; Bengalen, Burma, Thail., Sumat. Java

Psilocaulon N.E. Br. -n- *Aizoaceae* · 14 spp.

– **coriarium** (Burch. ex N.E. Br.) N.E. Br. ·
♄ ⚕ Z9 ⊛; Cape
– *mentiens* (A. Berger) N.E. Br. = Psilocaulon coriarium

Psilostemon DC. = Trachystemon
– *orientalis* (L.) DC. = Trachystemon
orientalis

Psilotum Sw. -n- *Psilotaceae* · 2 spp. ·
E:Fork Fern, Whisk Fern; G:Gabelblatt
– **nudum** (L.) P. Beauv. · E:Skeleton Fork
Fern, Whisk Fern; G:Bronze-Gabelblatt
· ⚁ e Z10 ⊛; Trop., USA: SE, Fla.; S-Sp.,
Austr.

Psilurus Trin. -m- *Poaceae* · 1 sp. ·
G:Borstenschwanzgras
– **incurvus** (Gouan) Schinz & Thell. ·
E:Bristle-tail Grass; G:Borsten-
schwanzgras · ⊙; Eur.: Ib, Fr, Ital-P, Ba,
Ro, Crim; TR, Syr., Iraq, Cauc., Afgh.,
C-As., Pakist.

Psophocarpus DC. -m- *Fabaceae* · 10 spp. ·
G:Flügelbohne
– **palustris** Desv. · G:Sumpf-Flügelbohne ·
⚁ Z9 ⊛ ⓝ; Sudan, W-Sah
– **tetragonolobus** (L.) DC. · E:Winged
Bean; G:Gewöhnliche Flügelbohne,
Goa-Bohne · ⚁ ⚥ Z9 ⊛ ⓝ; S-As.

Psoralea L. -f- *Fabaceae* · 34 spp. · E:Scurf
Pea; F:Psoralée, Psoralier; G:Drüsenklee,
Harzklee
– *bituminosa* L. = Bituminaria bituminosa
– **pinnata** L. · E:Blue Pea; G:Blauer
Harzklee · ♄ Z9 ⊛ VI-VIII; S-Afr.

Psychotria L. -f- *Rubiaceae* · 1825 spp. ·
E:Wild Coffee; F:Céphélis, Ipéca;
G:Brechwurzel
– *acuminata* Benth. = Psychotria cuspidata
– **cuspidata** Bredem. ex Schult. · E:Wild
Coffee; G:Kolumbianische Brechwurzel ·
⚁ Z10 ⊛ ⚥ ⚘; C-Am., N-Col.
– **ipecacuanha** (Brot.) Standl. · E:Ipecac,
Wild Coffee; G:Brasilianische Brechwur-
zel · ⚁ Z10 ⊛ ⚥ ⚘; Braz., Bol.

Psygmorchis Dodson & Dressler = Erycina
– *pusilla* (L.) Dodson & Dressler = Erycina
pusilla

Psylliostachys (Jaub. & Spach) Nevski

-f- *Plumbaginaceae* · 10 spp. · E:Statice
– **suworowii** (Regel) Roshkova · ⊙ ⚘
VII-IX; C-As., Afgh.

Psyllium Mill. -n- *Plantaginaceae* · 16 spp. ·
F:Herbe-aux-puces; G:Flohsame
– **afrum** (L.) Mirb. · E:African Plantain;
G:Scharzer Flohsame · ⊙ V-VII ⚥ ; Eur.:
Ib, Fr, Ital-P, Ba; TR, Syr., Palest., Iran,
Pakist., N-Afr.
– **arenarium** (Waldst. & Kit.) Mirb. ·
E:Sand Plantain; G:Sand-Flohsame · ⊙
VI-IX ⚥ ; Eur.* exc. BrI, Sc; TR, Cyprus,
Palest., W-Sib., C-As., Egypt, Libya,
Moroc., nat. in N-Am.
– **sempervirens** (Crantz) Soják ·
E:Evergreen Plantain; G:Halbstrauchiger
Flohsame · ♄ ♄ e △ VI-VII; Eur.: Ib, F, I,
TR, nat. in Sw, A

Ptelea L. -f- *Rutaceae* · 11 sp. · E:Hop Tree,
Shrubby Trefoil; F:Orme de Samarie;
G:Kleeulme, Lederstrauch
– **baldwinii** Torr. & A. Gray · ♄ d ♂ D Z6
VI; Calif.
– **polyadenia** Greene · E:Pallid Hop Tree ·
♄ d Z6; USA: Ariz., N.Mex., Okla., Tex.
– **trifoliata** L.
– var. **mollis** Torr. & A. Gray Z5; S-USA,
Tex.
– var. **trifoliata** · E:Hop Tree, Stinking Ash;
G:Dreiblättriger Lederstrauch · ♄ ♄ d ♂
D Z5 VI ⚥ ; Can.: E; USA: NE, NCE, NC,
SW, SC, SE, Fla.; Mex.

Pteretis Raf. = Matteuccia
– *pensylvanica* (Willd.) Fernald = Matteuccia pensylvanica
– *struthiopteris* (L.) Nieuwl. = Matteuccia
struthiopteris

Pteridium Gled. ex Scop. -n-
Dennstaedtiaceae · 11 sp. · E:Bracken,
Brake; F:Fougère aigle; G:Adlerfarn
– **aquilinum** (L.) Kuhn · E:Bracken;
G:Gewöhnlicher Adlerfarn · ⚁ Z4 VII-IX
⚘; Eur.*, cosmop.

Pteris L. -f- *Pteridaceae* · 330 spp. ·
E:Ribbon Fern; F:Ptéris; G:Saumfarn
– *arguta* Aiton = Pteris incompleta
– **argyraea** T. Moore · ⚁ Z10 ⊛; Ind., Sri
Lanka
– **biaurita** L. · ⚁ Z10 ⊛; Subtrop., Trop.
– *crenata* Sw. = Pteris ensiformis

- **cretica** L. · E:Cretan Brake; G:Kretischer
  Saumfarn · ⚃ Z10 🄯 VI-VIII; Eur.: Fr,
  Ital-P, Sw, S-GR; TR, Cauc., Iran, Alger.,
  trop. As, E-Afr., N-Am., Hawaii, nat. in
  BrI, sp., H
- **dentata** Forssk. · ⚃ Z10 🄯; trop. Afr.,
  S-Afr.
- **ensiformis** Burm. f. · E:Slender Brake,
  Sword Brake; G:Schwertblättriger
  Saumfarn · ⚃ Z10 🄯; trop. As., Austr.,
  Polyn.
- *flabellata* Thunb. = Pteris dentata
- **incompleta** Cav. · ⚃ Z10 🄯; Eur.: Ib.;
  Moroc., nat. in P
- *laciniata* Willd. = Lonchitis hirsuta
- **multifida** Poir. · E:Spider Fern;
  G:Spinnen-Saumfarn · ⚃ Z10 🄯; Jap.,
  China, Indochina, nat. in Sri Lanka
- *palustris* Poir. = Pteris incompleta
- **quadriaurita** Retz. · ⚃ Z10 🄯; S-Ind., Sri
  Lanka
- var. *argyrea* (T. Moore) hort. = Pteris
  argyraea
- var. *biaurita* (L.) hort. = Pteris biaurita
- var. *tricolor* (Linden) hort. = Pteris
  quadriaurita
- **semipinnata** L. · ⚃ Z10 🄯; trop. As.,
  China, Taiwan, Jap.
- *serrulata* Forssk. = Pteris incompleta
- *serrulata* L. f. = Pteris multifida
- **tremula** R. Br. · E:Australian Brake,
  Trembling Brake; G:Australischer
  Saumfarn · ⚃ Z10 🄯; Austr., NZ
- *tricolor* Linden = Pteris quadriaurita
- **umbrosa** R. Br. · ⚃ Z10 🄯; Austr.
- **vittata** L. · E:Ladder Brake; G:Leitern-
  Saumfarn · ⚃ Z10 🄯; Trop., Subtrop. Old
  World, sp.

Pterocactus K. Schum. -m- *Cactaceae* ·
9 spp. · F:Cactus ailé; G:Flügelkaktus
- **kuntzei** K. Schum. · ♄ ⚇ ⤳ Z8 🄯 ▽ ✳;
  W-Arg., Patag.
- *tuberosus* (Pfeiff.) Britton & Rose =
  Pterocactus kuntzei

Pterocarpus Jacq. -m- *Fabaceae* · 21 sp. ·
E:Rosewood; F:Bois de santal, Ptéro-
carpe; G:Flügelfrucht
- **angolensis** DC. · E:Bloodwood,
  Muninga; G:Ostafrikanischer Padouk,
  Ostafrikanische Flügelfrucht · ♄ d Z10 🄰
  🄽; C-Afr., E-Afr., S-Afr.
- **erinaceus** Poir. · E:African Kino, African
  Rosewood; G:Afrikanische Flügelfrucht,

Gambia-Kino · ♄ Z10 🄰 🄽; W-Sah,
W-Afr., C-Afr.
- **indicus** Willd. · E:Burmese Rosewood,
  Padouk; G:Burma-Flügelfrucht · ♄ e Z10
  🄰 🄽; trop. As.
- **marsupium** Roxb. · E:Bastard Teak,
  Indian Kino; G:Indische Flügelfrucht · ♄
  d Z10 🄰 ⚘ 🄽; Ind., Sri Lanka
- **santalinus** L. f. · E:Sandalwood Padauk;
  G:Rote Flügelfrucht · ♄ Z10 🄰 ⚘ 🄽 ▽ ✳;
  S-Ind.
- **soyauxii** Taub. · E:African Padouk;
  G:Afrikanisches Padouk · ♄ Z10 🄰 🄽;
  W-Afr.

Pterocarya Kunth -f- *Juglandaceae* ·
8-10 spp. · E:Wingnut; F:Ptérocaryer;
G:Flügelnuss
- *caucasica* C.A. Mey. = Pterocarya
  fraxinifolia
- **fraxinifolia** (Lam.) Spach · E:Caucasian
  Wingnut; F:Ptérocaryer du Caucase;
  G:Kaukasische Flügelnuss · ♄ d Z5 VI;
  Cauc., N-Iran
- × **rehderiana** C.K. Schneid. (*P.
  fraxinifolia* × *P. stenoptera*) · G:Rehders
  Flügelnuss · ♄ d Z6; cult.
- **rhoifolia** Siebold & Zucc. · E:Japanese
  Wingnut ; G:Japanische Flügelnuss · ♄ d
  Z6 VI; Jap.
- **stenoptera** C. DC. · E:Chinese Wingnut;
  G:Chinesische Flügelnuss · ♄ d Z7 VI;
  China

Pteroceltis Maxim. -f- *Ulmaceae* · 1 sp. ·
F:Micocoulier ailé; G:Flügelzürgel
- **tatarinowii** Maxim. · F:Micocoulier
  ailé; G:Flügelzürgel · ♄ d Z5; N-China,
  C-China

Pterocephalus Adans. -m- *Dipsacaceae* ·
25 spp. · F:Scabieuse du Parnasse;
G:Flügelkopf
- *parnassi* Spreng. = Pterocephalus perennis
- **perennis** Coult. · ⚃ ⤳ △ Z7 ∧ VII-VIII;
  GR
- subsp. *parnassi* (Spreng.) Vierh. =
  Pterocephalus perennis

Pteroceras Hasselt ex Hassk. -n-
Orchidaceae · 24 spp.
- **pallidum** (Blume) Holttum · ⚃ Z10 🄰
  I-XII ▽ ✳; Phil.

Pteronia L. -f- *Asteraceae* · 80 spp.
– **fasciculata** L. f. · ♄ ⚲ Z9 ⓚ; Cape

Pterostylis R. Br. -f- *Orchidaceae* · 157 spp. ·
E:Greenhood; F:Orchidée; G:Grünkappe
– **banksii** R. Br. ex A. Cunn. · ♃ Z9 ⓚ VI-II
▽ ✳; NZ
– **curta** R. Br. · E:Blunt Greenhood · ♃ Z9
ⓚ VI-XI ▽ ✳; Austr.

Pterostyrax Siebold & Zucc. -f-
Styracaceae · 3 spp. · E:Epaulette Tree;
F:Styrax ailé; G:Flügelstorax
– **corymbosa** Siebold & Zucc. · E:Epaulette
Tree; G:Doldiger Flügelstorax · ♄ ♄ d Z7
VI; China, Jap.
– **hispida** Siebold & Zucc. · E:Fragrant
Epaulette; G:Borstiger Flügelstorax Tree ·
♄ ♄ d Z6 VI; Jap.

Pterygota Schott & Endl. -f- *Sterculiaceae* ·
15 spp.
– **alata** (Roxb.) R. Br. · ♄ d ⚲ Z10 ⓦ; trop.
As.

Ptilostemon Cass. -m- *Asteraceae* · 14 spp. ·
E:Ivory Thistle; F:Chardon ivoire;
G:Elfenbeindistel
– **afer** (Jacq.) Greuter · E:Ivory Thistle;
G:Elfenbeindistel · ⊙ ♃ Z5 VII-VIII; Eur.:
Ba, RO; mts.; TR
– **casabonae** (L.) Greuter · ⊙ ⊙ ♃ Z5
VII-VIII; Eur.: F, Cors, Sard., I, nat. in P
– *diacanthus* hort. = Ptilostemon afer

Ptilotrichum C.A. Mey. = Alyssum
– *spinosum* (L.) Boiss. = Alyssum spinosum

Ptilotus R. Br. -m- *Amaranthaceae* · c.
100 spp. · G:Haarschöpfchen
– **manglesii** (Lindl.) F. Muell. · E:Rose-
tipped Mulla Mulla · ♃ Z9 ⓚ IV-VIII;
W-Austr.

Ptychopetalum Benth. -n- *Olacaceae* ·
4 spp. · E:Potency Wood; G:Potenzholz
– **olacoides** Benth. · ♄ e Z10 ⓦ ⚨ ; Braz.,
Guyan.
– **uncinatum** Anselmino · ♄ Z10 ⓦ;
Amazon.

Ptychosperma Labill. -n- *Arecaceae* ·
31 sp. · F:Ptychosperme; G:Faltensamen-
palme
– *alexandrae* F. Muell. = Archontophoenix

alexandrae
– *cunninghamianum* H. Wendl. = Archontophoenix cunninghamiana
– **elegans** (R. Br.) Blume · E:Alexander
Palm, Solitaire Palm; G:Alexanderpalme
· ♄ e Z9 ⓚ; Austr.: Queensl.
– **macarthurii** (H. Wendl. ex H.J. Veitch)
H. Wendl. ex Hook. f. · ♄ e Z10 ⓚ;
N.Guinea

Ptychotis W.D.J. Koch -f- *Apiaceae* ·
1-2 spp. · G:Faltenohr
– *ajowan* DC. = Trachyspermum ammi
– *coptica* (L.) DC. = Trachyspermum ammi
– **saxifraga** (L.) Loret & Barrandon ·
G:Bibernell-Faltenohr · ⊙ ; Eur.: Ib, Fr,
Ital-P

Puccinellia Parl. -f- *Poaceae* · 25 spp. ·
E:Alkali Grass, Saltmarsh Grass;
G:Salzschwaden
– **capillaris** (Lilj.) Jansen · G:Haar-
Salzschwaden · ♃ VI-VII; Eur.: BrI, Sc,
NL, G, Balt., Russ.; coasts
– **distans** (Jacq.) Parl. · E:European Alkali
Grass; G:Gewöhnlicher Salzschwaden · ♃
VIII-X; Eur.*, W-Sib.
– **fasciculata** (Torr.) E.P. Bicknell ·
E:Borrer's Saltmarsh Grass; G:Büsche-
liger Salzschwaden · ⊙ ♃ ; Eur.: Ib, Fr,
N-I, Slova., Croatia; coasts
– **limosa** (Schur) Holmb. · G:Sumpf-
Salzschwaden · ♃ VI; SE-Eur., C-Eur.
– **maritima** (Huds.) Parl. · E:Common
Saltmarsh Grass; G:Andel, Strand-
Salzschwaden · ♃ VI-IX; Eur.: Sc,
N-Russ., Balt., BrI, Fr, G, Ib, ? Ital-P;
coasts, nat. in N-Am., NZ
– **nuttalliana** (Schult.) Hitchc. · E:Nuttall's
Alkali; Grass G:Nuttalls Salzschwaden ·
♃ Ⓝ; w. N-Am.
– **rupestris** (With.) Fernald & Weath. ·
E:Stiff Saltmarsh Grass; G:Dichtblütiger
Salzschwaden · ⊙ ⊙ V-VI; Eur.: BrI,
Norw., Fr, sp.; coasts

Pueraria DC. -f- *Fabaceae* · 17 spp. ·
E:Kudzu; F:Kudzu, Puéraria; G:Kudzu-
bohne
– **lobata** (Willd.) Ohwi · E:Japanese
Arrowroot, Kudzu; G:Kudzubohne · ♄ ⌇ d
⚵ D Z7 ∧ ⚨ Ⓝ; China, Korea, Jap., nat.
in USA: SE
– **phaseoloides** (Roxb.) Benth. · E:Tropical
Kudzu; G:Puero, Tropischer Kudzu · ♃ ⓦ

Ⓝ; N-Ind., Burma, China, Malay. Arch., nat. in Trop.

Pulicaria Gaertn. -f- *Asteraceae* · 50-80 spp. · E:Fleabane; F:Pulicaire; G:Flohkraut
- **dysenterica** (L.) Bernh. · E:Fleabane; G:Großes Flohkraut, Ruhr-Flohkraut · ♃ Z5 VII-IX ⚥ ; Eur.*, N-Afr.
- **vulgaris** Gaertn. · E:Small Fleabane; G:Kleines Flohkraut · ☉ Z5 VII-VIII; Eur.*, TR, Cauc., Iran, NW-Ind., W-Sib., C-As., Mong., Amur, China: Sinkiang; N-Afr.

Pulmonaria L. -f- *Boraginaceae* · c. 15 spp. · E:Lungwort; F:Pulmonaire; G:Lungen-kraut
- **angustifolia** L. · E:Blue Lungwort; F:Pulmonaire à feuilles étroites; G:Schmalblättriges Lungenkraut · ♃ Z5 III-V ▽; Eur.* exc. BrI, Ib;
- **australis** (Murr) W. Sauer · G:Südalpen-Lungenkraut · ♃ IV-VI; Eur.: S-Alp.
- *azurea* Besser = Pulmonaria angustifolia
- **carnica** W. Sauer · G:Kärntner-Lungenk-raut · ♃ IV-V; Eur.: A, Slove.
- **collina** W. Sauer · G:Hügel-Lungenk-raut · ♃ III-V; Eur.: G, Sw +
- **dacica** Simonk.
- **some cultivars**
- **helvetica** Bolliger · G:Schweizerisches Lungenkraut · ♃ III-V; Eur.: Sw +
- **kerneri** Wettst. · G:Kerners Lungenk-raut · ♃ V-VII; Eur.: A; NE-Alp.
- **longifolia** (Bastard) Boreau · G:Lang-blättriges Lungenkraut
- **some cultivars**
- subsp. **longifolia** · G:Gewöhnliches Langblättriges Lungenkraut · ♃ Z6; Eur.: Fr, Ib, England
- **mollis** Wulfen ex Hornem. · G:Weiches Lungenkraut · ♃ IV-V ▽; Eur.: Fr, C-Eur., EC-Eur., Ba, E-Eur.
- **montana** Lej. · G:Berg-Lungenkraut, Knolliges-Lungenkraut · ♃ Z6 III-V; Eur.: Fr, Sw, D
- subsp. *mollis* (Wulfen ex Hornem.) Gams = Pulmonaria mollis
- **obscura** Dumort. · G:Dunkles Lungenk-raut, Ungeflecktes Lungenkraut · ♃ III-V; Eur.: Fr, C-Eur., EC-Eur., Sc, Ba, E-Eur., nat. in BrI
- **officinalis** L. · E:Lungwort, Soldiers-and-Sailors, Spotted Dog; F:Pulmoine officinale; G:Echtes Lungenkraut, Kleingeflecktes Lungenkraut · ♃ Z6 III-V ⚥ ; Eur.* exc. BrI, Ib
- *picta* Rouy = Pulmonaria saccharata
- **rubra** Schott · F:Pulmonaire rouge; G:Ziegelrotes Lungenkraut · ♃ Z6 IV-V; Eur.: Ba, RO, Russ.; mts.
- **saccharata** Mill. · E:Bethlehem Sage, Jerusalem Sage; F:Pulmonaire saup-oudrée; G:Großgeflecktes Lungenkraut · ♃ Z5 IV-V; Eur.: SE-F, I, nat. in B
- **many cultivars**
- **stiriaca** A. Kern. · G:Steirisches Lungenk-raut · ♃ Z5 IV-V; Eur.: A, Slove.; E-Alp.
- *virginica* L. = Mertensia virginica
- **Cultivars:**
- **many cultivars**

Pulsatilla Mill. -f- *Ranunculaceae* · 38-43 spp. · E:Pasqueflower; F:Pulsatille; G:Küchenschelle, Kuhschelle
- **albana** (Steven) Bercht. & J. Presl · ♃ △ Z5 IV ▽; TR, Cauc., Iran
- **alpina** (L.) Delarbre · E:Alpine Pasque Flower; G:Alpen-Küchenschelle
- subsp. **alba** Domin · E:White Pasque Flower; G:Brocken-Küchenschelle, Brock-enanemone, Kleine Alpen-Küchenschelle · ♃ Z5 V-VIII ▽; Eur.: sp., F, C-Eur., EC-Eur., Ba, RO, W-Russ.; mts
- subsp. **alpina** · G:Große Alpen-Küchen-schelle · ♃ △ Z5 V-VIII ▽; Eur.: Ib, Fr, Ital-P, Ba, C-Eur.; mts.; Cauc.
- subsp. **apiifolia** (Scop.) Nyman · G:Schwefel-Anemone, Schwefelgelbe Alpen-Küchenschelle · ♃ Z5 ▽; Eur.: sp., F, I, A, Ba ; C-Alp., S-Alp.
- subsp. *sulphurea* auct. = Pulsatilla alpina subsp. apiifolia
- *apiifolia* Scop. = Pulsatilla alpina subsp. apiifolia
- *grandis* Wender. = Pulsatilla vulgaris subsp. grandis
- **halleri** (All.) Willd.
- subsp. **grandis** (Wender.) Meikle · ♃ Z5 ▽; C-Eur., Ukraine
- subsp. **halleri** · F:Pulsatille de Haller; G:Hallers Küchenschelle · ♃ △ Z5 V-VII ▽; Eur.: Fr, Ital-P, C-Eur., Alp.
- subsp. **rhodopaea** K. Krause · ♃ Z5 ▽; Maced., BG
- subsp. **slavica** (G. Reuss) Zämelis · ♃ △ Z5 III-IV ▽; W-Cauc.
- subsp. **styriaca** (Pritz.) Zämelis · G:Steirische Küchenschelle · ♃ Z5 III-IV

▽; A (Steiermark)
- subsp. **taurica** (Juz.) K. Krause · ⁴ Z5 ▽;
  Crim
- **montana** (Hoppe) Rchb. · G:Berg-
  Küchenschelle · ⁴ △ Z6 III-V ▽; Eur.: Fr,
  I, Sw, Ba, RO
- **patens** (L.) Mill. · E:Eastern Pasque
  Flower; G:Gewöhnliche Finger-
  Küchenschelle · ⁴ △ Z4 IV ▽; Eur.: G,
  Sc, EC-Eur., E-Eur.; W-Sib.
- **pratensis** (L.) Mill. · G:Wiesen-Küchen-
  schelle
- subsp. **nigricans** (Störck) Zämelis ·
  G:Dunkle Wiesen-Küchenschelle · ⁴ Z5
  ⚘ ▽; Eur.: C-Eur., EC-Eur., Ba, E-Eur.
- subsp. **pratensis** · G:Gewöhnliche
  Wiesen-Küchenschelle · ⁴ △ Z5 IV-V ⚘
  ▽; Eur.: C-Eur., EC-Eur., Ba, Sc, E-Eur.
- *slavica* G. Reuss = Pulsatilla halleri subsp.
  slavica
- **vernalis** (L.) Mill. · E:Spring Pasque
  Flower; G:Frühlings-Küchenschelle,
  Kuhschelle · ⁴ △ Z4 IV ▽; Eur.* exc. BrI,
  EC-Eur.
- **vulgaris** Mill. · G:Gewöhnliche Küchen-
  schelle
- subsp. **grandis** (Wender.) Zämelis ·
  G:Große Küchenschelle · ⁴ Z5 IV-V ⚘
  ▽; C-Eur., Ba, Ukraine
- subsp. **vulgaris** · E:Pasque Flower;
  G:Gewöhnliche Küchenschelle · ⁴ △ Z5
  IV ⚘ ▽; Eur.* exc. BrI, Ital-P

Pultenaea Sm. -f- *Fabaceae* · -120 spp.
- **flexilis** Sm. · E:Graceful Bush Pea · ♄ e
  Z9 ⓚ V; Austr.: N.S.Wales
- **gunnii** Benth. · E:Golden Bush Pea · ♄ e
  Z9 ⓚ V; Austr.: Victoria, Tasman.
- **rosea** F. Muell. · ♄ e Z9 ⓚ IV; Austr.:
  Victoria

Punica L. -f- *Punicaceae* · 2 spp. ·
  E:Pomegranate; F:Grenadier; G:Granat-
  apfel
- **granatum** L. · E:Pomegranate; G:Gra-
  natapfel · ♄ ♄ d Z8 ⓚ VI-VIII ⚘ Ⓝ; TR,
  SW-As., C-As., nat. in Eur.: Ib, F, Ital-P,
  Sw, BA, RO

Pupalia Juss. -f- *Amaranthaceae* · 4 spp.
- **atropurpurea** Moq. · ⁴ Z10 ⓖ; trop.
  Afr., trop. As., nat. in S-Sp.

Purshia DC. ex Poir. -f- *Rosaceae* · 7 spp. ·
  E:Antelope Bush; G:Antilopenstrauch

- **tridentata** (Pursh) DC. · E:Antelope
  Brush, Bitterbrush; G:Antilopenstrauch ·
  ♄ d Z7 V; USA: Oreg., Calif., Rocky Mts.,
  SW

Puschkinia Adams -f- *Hyacinthaceae* ·
  1 sp. · E:Puschkinia; F:Puschkinia, Scille;
  G:Kegelblume, Puschkinie
- *libanotica* Zucc. = Puschkinia scilloides
  var. libanotica
- **scilloides** Adams
- var. **libanotica** (Zucc.) Boiss. · G:Liba-
  non-Puschkinie · ⁴ Z5 II-III; Lebanon
- var. **scilloides** · E:Striped Squill;
  G:Kegelblume, Puschkinie · ⁴ Z5 II-III;
  Cauc., TR

Putoria Pers. -f- *Rubiaceae* · 2 spp. ·
  F:Putoria; G:Putorie
- **calabrica** (L. f.) DC. · ♄ e Z8 ⓖ; Eur.: Ba,
  Ib, S-I, Sic.; TR, Cyprus, Levant, N-Afr.,
  Canar.

Puya Molina -f- *Bromeliaceae* · 206 spp.
- **alpestris** (Poepp.) Gay · ♄ Z8 ⓖ; C-Chile
- **chilensis** Molina · ♄ Z9 ⓖ; C-Chile
- *coarctata* (Ruiz & Pav.) Fisch. = Puya
  chilensis
- **coerulea** Lindl.
- var. **coerulea** · ⁴ Z8 ⓖ; Chile
- var. **violacea** (Brongn.) L.B. Sm. &
  Looser · ⁴ Z8 ⓖ; Chile
- **gigas** André · ♄ Z9 ⓖ; Col.
- **raimondii** Harms · ♄ e Z8 ⓖ; Peru, Bol.,
  N-Chile
- **spathacea** (Griseb.) Mez · ⁴ Z8 ⓖ;
  C-Arg.
- **venusta** Phil. · ⁴ Z8 ⓖ; Chile
- *violacea* (Brongn.) Mez = Puya coerulea
  var. violacea

Pycnanthus Warb. -f- *Myristicaceae* · 7 spp.
- **angolensis** (Welw.) Warb. · ♄ Z10 ⓦ Ⓝ;
  Angola

Pycnostachys Hook. -f- *Lamiaceae* · 37 spp.
- **dawei** N.E. Br. · ⁴ Z9 ⓖ XII-II; Uganda
- **urticifolia** Hook. · ⁴ ⋉ Z9 ⓖ VIII; trop.
  Afr., S-Afr.

Pycreus P. Beauv. -m- *Cyperaceae* · 118 spp.
- **flavescens** (L.) P. Beauv. ex Rchb. ·
  G:Gelbliches Zypergras · ⊙ ⌢ VII-X;
  Eur.* exc. BrI, Sc; Tr, Cauc., C-As,
  SW-As., Afr., N-Am., nat. in Austr.

Pyracantha M. Roem. -f- *Rosaceae* ·
9 spp. · E:Firethorn; F:Buisson ardent;
G:Feuerdorn
- **angustifolia** (Franch.) C.K. Schneid. ·
E:Narrow-leaved Firethorn; G:Schmal-
blättriger Feuerdorn · ♄ e ⊗ Z7 VI-VII;
SW-China
- **atalantioides** (Hance) Stapf · G:China-
Feuerdorn · ♄ e Z7 V-VI; China
- **coccinea** M. Roem. · E:Burning Bush,
Firethorn; F:Buisson ardant; G:Mit-
telmeer-Feuerdorn · ♄ e ⊗ Z6 V; Eur.: Ib,
Fr, Ital-P, AL, Crim; TR, Cauc., N-Iran
- **crenatoserrata** (Hance) Rehder · ♄ ⊗ Z7
∧ V-VII; W-China, C-China
- **crenulata** (D. Don) M. Roem. · E:Nepal
Firethorn, Nepalese White Thorn;
G:Nepal-Feuerdorn · ♄ ♄ e Z7; Him.,
NW-China
- *fortuneana* (Maxim.) H.L. Li = Pyracantha
crenatoserrata
- **rogersiana** (A.B. Jacks.) Bean · G:Gelb-
früchtiger Feuerdorn · ♄ e ⊗ Z8 ⌂ VI;
SW-China
- *yunnanensis* Chitt. = Pyracantha
crenatoserrata
- **Cultivars:**
- **many cultivars**

× **Pyracomeles** Rehder ex Guillaumin
-f- *Rosaceae* · G:Bastardfeuerdorn
(*Osteomeles × Pyracantha*)
- **vilmorinii** Rehder ex Guillaumin
(*Osteomeles subrotunda × Pyracantha
crenatoserrata*) · G:Bastardfeuerdorn · ♄ s
Z8 ⌂ V; cult.

Pyrethrum Zinn = Tanacetum
- *balsamita* (L.) Willd. = Tanacetum
balsamita
- *carneum* M. Bieb. = Tanacetum coccineum
- *cinerariifolium* Trevir. = Tanacetum
cinerariifolium
- *corymbosum* (L.) Scop. = Tanacetum
corymbosum subsp. corymbosum
- *densum* Labill. = Tanacetum densum
- *gayanum* Coss. & Durieu = Rhodanthemum gayanum
- *macrophyllum* (Waldst. & Kit.) Willd. =
Tanacetum macrophyllum
- *parthenium* (L.) Sm. = Tanacetum
parthenium
- *roseum* M. Bieb. = Tanacetum coccineum

Pyrola L. -f- *Pyrolaceae* · 35 spp. ·
E:Shinleaf, Wintergreen; F:Pyrole;
G:Wintergrün
- **chlorantha** Sw. · E:Green Flowered
Wintergreen; G:Grünliches Wintergrün
· ⌃ Z5 VI-VII; Eur.*, TR, Cauc., W-Sib.,
E-Sib., Kamchat., N-Am.
- **media** Sw. · E:Intermediate Wintergreen;
G:Mittleres Wintergrün · ⌃ Z5 VI-VIII;
Eur.* exc. Ib; Cauc., W-Sib., E-Sib.
- **minor** L. · E:Common Wintergreen;
G:Kleines Wintergrün · ⌃ Z5 VI-VIII;
Eur.*, TR, Cauc., W-Sib., E-Sib., Amur,
Sakhal., Kamchat., C-As., Alaska, Can.,
USA: NE, NCE, NC, Rocky Mts., NW,
Calif.; Greenl.
- **rotundifolia** L. · E:Round Leaved Winter-
green; G:Rundblättriges Wintergrün ·
⌃ Z4 VI-VIII; Eur.*, Cauc., TR, N-Iran,
W-Sib., E-Sib., C-As., Alaska, Can., USA*
exc. SE, Fla., SC; Greenl.
- *secunda* = Orthilia secunda
- *uniflora* L. = Moneses uniflora
- *urceolata* Poir. = Galax urceolata

Pyrolirion Herb. -n- *Amaryllidaceae* ·
6 spp. · E:Flame Lily; G:Flammenlilie
- **arvense** (F. Dietr.) Erhardt, Götz &
Seybold · E:Flame Lily; G:Flammenlilie ·
⌃ Z9 ⌂ XII-I; Peru
- *aureum* Herb. = Pyrolirion arvense

Pyrostegia C. Presl -f- *Bignoniaceae* ·
4 spp. · F:Liane de feu; G:Feuerranke
- **venusta** (Ker-Gawl.) Miers · E:Orange
Trumpet Vine; G:Feuer auf dem Dach,
Feuerranke · ♄ e ⌇ Z10 ⌂ X-I; Braz.,
Parag.

Pyrrheima Hassk. = Siderasis
- *loddigesii* Hassk. = Siderasis fuscata

Pyrrhocactus Backeb. & F.M. Knuth =
Neoporteria
- *aricensis* F. Ritter = Neoporteria aricensis
- *bulbocalyx* (Werderm.) Backeb. =
Neoporteria bulbocalyx
- *curvispinus* (Bertero) Backeb. & F.M.
Knuth = Neoporteria curvispina
- *nigricans* (Linke) F. Ritter = Neoporteria
tuberisulcata

Pyrrocoma Hook. -f- *Asteraceae* · 10 spp.
- **crocea** (A. Gray) Greene. · E:Curlyhead
Goldenweed · ⌃ △ Z7 ∧ VII-X; USA:

Rocky Mts., SW

Pyrrosia Mirb. -f- *Polypodiaceae* · 74 spp. ·
E:Felt Fern; F:Fougère; G:Schneefarn
– **confluens** (R. Br.) Ching · E:Robber
Fern; G:Himalaya-Schneefarn · ⊈ Z10 ⓦ;
Him.
– **hastata** (Thunb.) Ching · ⊈ Z10 ⓦ; Jap.,
Korea, Manch.
– **heterophylla** (L.) M.G. Price · E:Dragon
Scales; G:Ungleichblättriger Schneefarn ·
⊈ Z10 ⓦ; Ind., SE-As., N.Guinea
– **lanceolata** (L.) Farw. · ⊈ ⚌ Z10 ⓦ; trop.
Afr., trop. As.
– **lingua** (Thunb.) Farw. · E:Japanese Felt
Fern; G:Japanischer Schneefarn · ⊈ Z10
ⓦ; China, Indochina, Taiwan, Jap.
– **niphoboloides** (Luerss.) M.G. Price · ⊈
Z10 ⓦ; Madag.

Pyrularia Michx. -f- *Santalaceae* · 3-5 spp. ·
E:Buffalo Nut; G:Büffelnuss
– **pubera** Michx. · E:Buffalo Nut; G:Büf-
felnuss · ℏ d Z4 ⚘ ⓝ; USA: NE, SE

Pyrus L. -f- *Rosaceae* · 25-30 (76) spp. ·
E:Pear; F:Poirier; G:Birne
– *americana* (Marshall) DC. = Sorbus
americana
– *angustifolia* Aiton = Malus angustifolia
– *arbutifolia* (L.) L. f. = Aronia arbutifolia
var. arbutifolia
– *aucuparia* (L.) Gaertn. = Sorbus
aucuparia subsp. aucuparia
– **austriaca** A. Kern. · G:Österreichischer
Birnbaum · ℏ d Z6 V; Eur.: Sw, A, Slova.,
H, ? RO
– *baccata* L. = Malus baccata var. baccata
– var. *mandshurica* Maxim. = Malus
baccata var. mandshurica
– **betulifolia** Bunge · E:Birchleaf Pear · ℏ d
Z5 V; N-China
– **bourgaeana** Decne. · ℏ d; W-Sp., P,
Moroc.
– **bretschneideri** Rehder · ℏ d Z5 IV-V;
N-China
– **calleryana** Decne. · G:Chinesische Birne
– var. **calleryana** · E:Callery Pear · ℏ d Z6;
C-China, S-China
– var. **dimorphophylla** (Makino) Koidz. ·
ℏ d Z6 V; Jap.
– var. **fauriei** (C.K. Schneid.) Rehder · ℏ d
Z6 V; Korea
– × **canescens** Spach (*P. nivalis* × *P.
salicifolia*) · G:Graublättrige Birne · ℏ d

Z6; cult.
– *chamaemespilus* (L.) Ehrh. = Sorbus
chamaemespilus
– **communis** L. · E:Common Pear, Pear;
F:Poirier commun; G:Garten-Birnbaum,
Kultur-Birne · ℏ d Z5 IV-V ⓝ; cult.
– **many cultivars**
– subsp. *salviifolia* (DC.) Gams = Pyrus
salviifolia
– var. *pyraster* L. = Pyrus pyraster
– *coronaria* L. = Malus coronaria
– var. *ioensis* A.W. Wood = Malus ioensis
– *decora* (Sarg.) Hyl. = Sorbus decora
– *domestica* Medik. = Pyrus communis
– **elaeagnifolia** Pall.
– var. **elaeagnifolia** · G:Ölweiden-Birne · ℏ
d Z5; TR
– var. **kotschyana** (Decne.) Boiss. · ℏ d Z5
IV-V; TR
– *floribunda* Lindl. = Aronia × prunifolia
– *hupehensis* Pamp. = Malus hupehensis
– *ioensis* (A.W. Wood) L.H. Bailey = Malus
ioensis
– *japonica* Thunb. = Chaenomeles japonica
var. japonica
– *kansuensis* Batalin = Malus kansuensis
– *malus* L. = Malus sylvestris
– var. *paradisiaca* L. = Malus pumila var.
paradisiaca
– var. *sylvestris* L. = Malus sylvestris
– *maulei* (T. Moore) Mast. = Chaenomeles
japonica var. japonica
– *melanocarpa* (Michx.) Willd. = Aronia
melanocarpa var. melanocarpa
– **nivalis** Jacq. · E:Snow Pear; G:Schnee-
Birne · ℏ d Z6 V ⓝ; Eur.: Fr, Ital-P,
C-Eur., EC-Eur., Ba, RO
– **pashia** Buch.-Ham. ex D. Don · ℏ d Z5;
Afgh., Him., W-China, Burma
– **phaeocarpa** Rehder · ℏ d Z5 V; N-China
– *prattii* Hemsl. = Malus prattii
– *prunifolia* Willd. = Malus prunifolia var.
prunifolia
– **pyraster** (L.) Burgsd. · E:Wild Pear;
F:Poirier sauvage ; G:Wild-Birne, Wilder
Birnbaum · ℏ d Z6 IV-V; Eur.* exc. BrI,
Sc; TR, Cauc., Iran
– **pyrifolia** (Burm. f.) Nakai
– var. **culta** (Makino) Nakai · E:Nashi Pear;
G:Nashi-Birne · ℏ d Z6 IV ⓝ; cult.
– var. **pyrifolia** · E:Sand Pear; G:China-
Birne · ℏ d Z6; W-China, C-China
– **regelii** Rehder · F:Poirier de Regel · ℏ d
Z6 V-VI; C-As.
– **salicifolia** Pall. · E:Willow Leafed Pear;

F:Poirier à feuilles de saule; G:Weiden-
Birne · ♄ d Z4 IV-V; TR, Cauc., Iran
- **salviifolia** DC. (*P. communis* × *P. nivalis*) · G:Salbeiblatt-Birnbaum · ♄ ♄ d
Z5 V; Eur.: Fr, C-Eur., EC-Eur., Ba, E-Eur.
- *sargentii* (Rehder) Bean = Malus toringo
- *serotina* Rehder = Pyrus pyrifolia var.
pyrifolia
- *sieboldii* Regel = Malus toringo
- *sinensis* (Thouin) Spreng. = Pyrus
pyrifolia var. culta
- *spectabilis* Aiton = Malus spectabilis
- **spinosa** Forssk. · E:Almond Leaved Pear;
G:Pfirsichblättrige Birne · ♄ ♄ d Z6 V ✿;
Eur.: Ib, Fr, Ital-P, Ba; TR
- *sylvestris* Gray = Malus sylvestris
- *toringoides* (Rehder) Osborn = Malus
toringoides
- *transitoria* Batalin = Malus transitoria
- *trilobata* (Labill.) DC. = Malus trilobata
- *tschonoskii* Maxim. = Malus tschonoskii
- **ussuriensis** Maxim.
- var. **hondoensis** (Kikuchi & Nakai)
Rehder · ♄ d Z6 IV; C-Jap.
- var. **ovoidea** (Rehder) Rehder · ♄ d Z6
IV; Korea, N-China
- var. **ussuriensis** · E:Ussurian Pear;
G:Ussuri-Birne · ♄ d Z6; Amur, Manch.,
Korea

Quamoclit Mill. = Ipomoea
- *coccinea* (L.) Moench = Ipomoea coccinea
- *hederifolia* (L.) G. Don = Ipomoea
hederifolia
- *lobata* (Cerv.) House = Ipomoea lobata
- × *multifida* Raf. = Ipomoea × multifida
- *pennata* Bojer = Ipomoea quamoclit
- × *sloteri* House = Ipomoea × multifida
- *vulgaris* Choisy = Ipomoea quamoclit

Quaqua N.E. Br. -f- Asclepiadaceae · 13 spp.
- **mammillaris** (L.) Bruyns · ⳃ ⳇ Z9 ⌂;
Cape

Quassia L. -f- Simaroubaceae · 35-40 spp. ·
E:Bitterwood; F:Quassier, Quassier amer;
G:Bitterholz, Quassiabaum
- **amara** L. · E:Bitterwood, Jamaica Bark;
G:Bitterholz · ♄ ♄ e Z10 ⌂ ⚥ Ⓝ; Mex.,
W.Ind., Guyan., N-Braz.

Quercus L. -f- Fagaceae · 522 spp. · E:Oak;
F:Chêne; G:Eiche
- **acuta** Thunb. · ♄ ♄ e Z8 ⌂; Jap.,
N-Korea, China

- **acutissima** Carruth. · E:Sawtooth Oak;
F:Chêne à dents de scie; G:Seidenrau-
pen-Eiche · ♄ d Z7 Ⓝ; Him., China, Korea,
Jap.
- *aegilops* L. = Quercus ithaburensis subsp.
macrolepis
- **alba** L. · E:White Oak; F:Chêne blanc;
G:Weiß-Eiche · ♄ d Z5 Ⓝ; Can.: E; USA:
NE, NCE, SC, SE, Fla.
- **aliena** Blume
- var. **acutiserrata** Maxim. · ♄ d Z5; Jap.,
Korea, C-China
- var. **aliena** · ♄ d Z5 Ⓝ; Jap., Korea, China
- **alnifolia** Poech · E:Golden Oak; G:Erlen-
blättrige Eiche · ♄ ♄ e Z8 ⌂ ∧; Cyprus
- *aquatica* (Lam.) Walter = Quercus nigra
- **arkansana** Sarg. · E:Arkansas Oak;
G:Arkansas-Eiche · ♄ d Z7; USA: Ark.
- *banisteri* Michx. = Quercus ilicifolia
- **bicolor** Willd. · E:Swamp White Oak;
F:Chêne à gros glands; G:Zweifarbige
Eiche · ♄ d Z4 Ⓝ; Can.: E; USA: NE, NCE,
NC, SC, SE
- *borealis* F. Michx. = Quercus rubra
- var. *maxima* (Marshall) Sarg. = Quercus
rubra
- *bungeana* F.B. Forbes = Quercus variabilis
- × **bushii** Sarg. (*Q. marilandica* × *Q. velutina*) · ♄ d Z5; USA: Okla. +
- × *calvescens* Vuk. = Quercus × streimii
- **canariensis** Willd. · G:Algerische Eiche ·
♄ d Z7; Eur.: Ib; Moroc., Alger., Tun.
- **castaneifolia** C.A. Mey. · F:Chêne à
feuilles de châtaignier; G:Kastanienblät-
trige Eiche · ♄ d Z7 Ⓝ; Cauc., Iran
- **cerris** L. · E:Turkey Oak; F:Chêne
chevelu; G:Zerr-Eiche · ♄ d Z6 IV Ⓝ;
C-Eur., S-Eur., Liban., nat. in C-Span.
- var. *austriaca* (Willd.) Loudon = Quercus
cerris
- *chinensis* Bunge = Quercus variabilis
- **coccifera** L. · E:Kermes Oak; F:Chêne à
cochenilles; G:Kermes-Eiche · ♄ ♄ e Z8
Ⓝ; Eur.: Ib, Fr, Ital-P, Ba; TR, Levant,
NW-Afr., Libya
- **coccinea** Münchh. · E:Scarlet Oak;
F:Chêne écarlate; G:Scharlach-Eiche · ♄
d Z5 Ⓝ; Can.: E; USA: NE, NCE, SE, Okla.
- *conferta* Kit. = Quercus frainetto
- *daimio* hort. ex K. Koch = Quercus
dentata
- **dalechampii** Ten. · G:Gelbliche Eiche · ♄
d Z7 IV-V; Eur.: I, A, EC-Eur., Ba, RO, ?
Sic.
- **dentata** Thunb. · E:Daimio Oak,

Japanese Emperor Oak; F:Chêne Daimyo; G:Kaiser-Eiche · ħ d Z5 Ⓝ; Jap., Korea, N-China, W-China
– × **exacta** Trel. (*Q. imbricaria* × *Q. palustris*) · ħ; USA
– **fabri** Hance · ħ d Z5; China, Korea
– **faginea** Lam. · E:Portuguese Oak; G:Portugiesische Eiche · ħ ħ s Z7; sp., P
– **falcata** Michx. · E:Southern Red Oak; G:Sichelblättrige Eiche, Sumpf-Rot-Eiche · ħ d Z6; USA: NE, SE, Fla., SC
– *farnetto* Ten. = Quercus frainetto
– *fastigiata* Lam. = Quercus robur subsp. robur
– × **fernaldii** Trel. (*Q. ilicifolia* × *Q. rubra*) Z5; USA (Mass.) +
– *ferruginea* F. Michx. = Quercus marilandica
– **frainetto** Ten. · E:Hungarian Oak; F:Chêne de Hongrie; G:Ungarische Eiche · ħ d Z6; Eur.: I, EC-Eur., Ba, RO; TR, Levant
– **garryana** Douglas ex Hook. · E:Oregon White Oak; G:Oregon-Eiche · ħ d Z8 Ⓛ; B.C., USA: Wash., Oreg., Calif.
– *glandulifera* Blume = Quercus serrata
– **glauca** Thunb. · E:Ring-cup Oak; G:Japanische Blau-Eiche · ħ e Z8 Ⓛ; Him., China, Indochina, Korea, Jap., Taiwan
– **hartwissiana** Steven · G:Armenische Eiche · ħ d Z5; Eur.: BG; TR, Cauc.
– × **heterophylla** F. Michx. (*Q. phellos* × *Q. rubra*) · G:Verschiedenblättrige Eiche · ħ d Z6; E-USA
– × **hispanica** Lam. (*Q. cerris* × *Q. suber*) · E:Spanish Oak; F:Chêne de Lucombe; G:Spanische Eiche · ħ s Z7; Eur.: Ib, S-F, I, Ba
– **ilex** L. · E:Evergreen Oak, Holm Oak; F:Chêne vert, Yeuse; G:Stein-Eiche · ħ e Z8 Ⓛ IV-V Ⓝ; Eur.: Ib, Fr, Ital-P, Ba; TR, NW-Afr., nat. in Crim, Sw, Br
– var. *rotundifolia* (Lam.) Trab. = Quercus rotundifolia
– **ilicifolia** Wangenh. · E:Bear Oak, Scrub Oak; G:Busch-Eiche · ħ ħ d Z6; USA: NE, N.C.
– **imbricaria** Michx. · E:Shingle Oak; F:Chêne à feuilles de laurier; G:Schindel-Eiche · ħ d Z5; USA: NE, NCE, NC, SE
– **infectoria** Olivier · E:Aleppo Oak; G:Aleppo-Eiche · ħ s Z8 Ⓛ ♀; Eur.: GR; TR, Cyprus, Palest., Cauc., N-Iraq, Iran
– **ithaburensis** Decne.

– subsp. **ithaburensis** · G:Syrische Eiche · ħ s Z8 Ⓛ; TR, Syr., Palest.
– subsp. **macrolepis** (Kotschy) Hedge & Yalt. · E:Dyer's Oak, Vallonia Oak; G:Valonea-Eiche · ħ s Z7 Ⓝ; Eur.: SE-I, Ba, GR; TR
– *lanuginosa* Lam. = Quercus pubescens subsp. pubescens
– **laurifolia** Michx. · E:Laurel Oak; G:Lorbeerblättrige Eiche · ħ d Z7 ∧; USA: NE, SE, SC, Fla.
– × **leana** Nutt. (*Q. imbricaria* × *Q. velutina*) · ħ d Z6; USA
– × **libanerris** Boom (*Q. cerris* × *Q. libani*) · G:Libanon-Hybrid-Eiche · ħ d Z6; cult.
– **libani** Olivier · E:Lebanon Oak; F:Chêne du Liban; G:Libanon-Eiche · ħ ħ d Z6; TR, Syr.
– **lobata** Née · E:California White Oak, Valley Oak; G:Kalifornische Weiß-Eiche · ħ d Z7; Calif.
– **lusitanica** Lam. · ħ d Z8 Ⓛ; SW-Sp., S-P, Moroc.
– *lusitanica* Webb = Quercus faginea
– **lyrata** Walter · E:Overcup Oak, Water White Oak; G:Leierblättrige Eiche · ħ d Z5 Ⓝ; USA: NE, NCE, SC, SE, Fla.
– **macranthera** Fisch. & C.A. Mey. ex Hohen. · E:Caucasian Oak; F:Chêne du Caucase ; G:Persische Eiche · ħ d Z6; SE-Cauc., N-Iran
– **macrocarpa** Michx.
– var. **macrocarpa** · E:Burr Oak, Mossy Cup Oak; G:Großfrüchtige Eiche · ħ d Z4 Ⓝ; Can.: E, Sask.; USA: NE, SE, SC, NCE, NC
– var. *oliviformis* (F. Michx.) A. Gray = Quercus macrocarpa
– *macrolepis* Kotschy = Quercus ithaburensis subsp. macrolepis
– **marilandica** (L.) Münchh. · E:Blackjack Oak, Scrub Oak; F:Chêne du Maryland; G:Schwarz-Eiche · ħ d Z7; USA: NE, NCE, NC, SC, SE, Fla.
– **michauxii** Nutt. · G:Korb-Eiche; E:Swamp Chestnut Oak · ħ d Z7; N-Am.
– **mongolica** Fisch. ex Ledeb.
– subsp. **mongolica** · E:Mongolian Oak; G:Mongolische Eiche · ħ d Z5 Ⓝ; E-Sib., N-China, Korea, N-Jap.
– subsp. **crispula** (Blume) Menitsky · ħ d Z5; Jap., Sakhal.
– **montana** Willd. · E:Basket Oak, Chestnut Oak; G:Kastanien-Eiche · ħ d Z6 Ⓝ; Ont., USA: NE, NCE, SE

- **muehlenbergii** Engelm. · E:Yellow Chestnut Oak; G:Gelb-Eiche · ℏ d Z6; USA: NE, NEC, NC, SC, N.Mex.
- *nana* (Marshall) Sarg. non Willd. = Quercus ilicifolia
- **nigra** L. · E:Water Oak; G:Wasser-Eiche · ℏ d Z6; USA: NE, NCE, SC, SE, Fla.
- *nigra* Wangenh. non L. = Quercus ilicifolia
- *obovata* Bunge = Quercus dentata
- *obtusiloba* Michx. = Quercus stellata
- **palustris** Münchh. · E:Pin Oak; F:Chêne des marais; G:Sumpf-Eiche · ℏ d ⌣ Z5 V ⊛; Can.: E; USA: NE, NCE, Kans., SE
- *pedunculata* Hoffm. = Quercus robur subsp. robur
- **petraea** (Matt.) Liebl. · G:Trauben-Eiche
- subsp. **iberica** (Steven ex M. Bieb.) Krassiln. · G:Reichfrüchtige Trauben-Eiche · ℏ d Z5; Eur.: A, EC-Eur., Ba, RO; TR, Cauc., N-Iran
- subsp. **petraea** · E:Durmast Oak, Sessile Oak; F:Chêne rouvre, Chêne sessile; G:Gewöhnliche Trauben-Eiche · ℏ d Z5 V ⚥ ⊛; Eur.*, TR, Syr., Cauc., N-Iran
- **phellos** L. · E:Willow Oak; F:Chêne à feuilles de saule; G:Weiden-Eiche · ℏ ℏ d ⌣ Z6; USA: NE, NCE, SE, Fla., SC
- **phillyreoides** A. Gray · ℏ ℏ e Z7; C-China, E-China, Jap.
- *platanoides* (Castigl.) Sudw. = Quercus bicolor
- **pontica** K. Koch · E:Armenian Oak, Pontine Oak; F:Chêne d'Arménie; G:Pontische Eiche · ℏ d Z6; Cauc.
- **prinoides** Willd. · E:Chinquapin Oak, Dwarf Chinquapin Oak; G:Chinquapin-Eiche · ℏ d Z5; USA: NE, NCE, SE, SC
- *prinus* L. = Quercus montana
- × *pseudosuber* Santi = Quercus × hispanica
- × *pseudoturneri* C.K. Schneid. = Quercus × hispanica
- **pubescens** Willd. · G:Flaum-Eiche
- subsp. *lanuginosa* (Lam.) O. Schwarz = Quercus pubescens subsp. pubescens
- subsp. **pubescens** E:Downy Oak; F:Chêne pubescent; G:Adriatische Flaum-Eiche · ℏ d Z6 IV-V ⚥ ⊛; Eur.* exc. BrI, Sc; TR, Cauc.
- **pyrenaica** Willd. · E:Pyrenean Oak; G:Pyrenäen-Eiche · ℏ ℏ d Z6 ⊛; Eur.: Ib, F, I; Moroc.
- **robur** L. · G:Stiel-Eiche
- subsp. **pedunculiflora** (K. Koch)

Menitsky · ℏ d Z3; Eur.: Ba, Crim; TR, Cauc., NW-Iran
- subsp. **robur** · E:English Oak, Oak, Pedunculate Oak; F:Chêne commun, Chêne pédonculé; G:Gewöhnliche Stiel-Eiche · ℏ d Z5 V ⚥ ⊛; Eur.*, TR, Cauc.
- × **rosacea** Bechst. (*Q. petraea* × *Q. robur* subsp. *robur*) · G:Gewöhnliche Bastard-Eiche · ℏ d
- **rotundifolia** Lam. · G:Rundblättrige Eiche · ℏ e Z7; Ib.F, NW-Afr.
- **rubra** L. · E:American Red Oak; F:Chêne rouge d'Amérique; G:Rot-Eiche · ℏ d Z5 V ⊛; Can.: E; USA: NE, NCE, NC, Okla., SE
- × **saulii** C.K. Schneid. (*Q. alba* × *Q. montana*) · G:Sauls Eiche · ℏ d
- × **schochiana** Dieck (*Q. palustris* × *Q. phellos*) · ℏ d Z6; E-USA
- *serrata* Carruth. = Quercus variabilis
- *serrata* Siebold & Zucc. = Quercus acutissima
- **serrata** Thunb. · E:Konara Oak; G:Gesägte Eiche · ℏ d; Jap., Korea, China
- *sessiliflora* Salisb. = Quercus petraea subsp. petraea
- *sessilis* Schur = Quercus petraea subsp. petraea
- **shumardii** Buckley · E:Shumard Oak · ℏ d Z5; Can.: Ont.; USA: NE, NCE, Kans., SC, SE, Fla.
- **stellata** Wangenh. · E:Post Oak; G:Pfahl-Eiche · ℏ d Z5 ⊛; USA: NE, NCE, Kans., SC, SE, Fla.
- × **streimii** Heuff. (*Q. petraea* × *Q. pubescens* subsp. *pubescens*) · G:Flaum-blättrige Bastard-Eiche · ℏ d
- **suber** L. · E:Cork Oak; F:Chêne-liège; G:Kork-Eiche · ℏ e Z8 ⌾ ⊛; Eur.: Ib, Fr, Ital-P; NW-Afr.
- **texana** Buckley · E:Texas Red Oak; G:Texas-Eiche · ℏ d Z6; USA: SE, Tex., Ill., Ky., Mo.
- *tinctoria* W. Bartram ex Michx. = Quercus velutina
- *toza* Bastard = Quercus pyrenaica
- **trojana** Webb · E:Macedonian Oak; G:Mazedonische Eiche · ℏ ℏ s Z7; Eur.: SE-I, Ba; W-TR
- × *turneri* Willd. = Quercus × hispanica
- *uliginosa* Wangenh. = Quercus nigra
- **variabilis** Blume · E:Oriental Corkoak; G:Orientalische Kork-Eiche · ℏ d Z4 ⊛; Jap., Korea, N-China, Taiwan
- **velutina** Lam. · E:Black Oak; F:Chêne des teinturiers, Quercitron; G:Färber-Eiche ·

♄ d Z5; Can.: E; USA: NE, NCE, NC, SC, SE, Fla.

Quesnelia Gaudich. -f- *Bromeliaceae* · 17 spp.
- **arvensis** (Vell.) Mez · ♃ Z9 ⓦ; Braz.
- **humilis** Mez · ♃ Z9 ⓦ; Braz.
- **liboniana** (De Jonghe) Mez · ♃ Z9 ⓦ; Braz.
- **marmorata** (Lem.) Read · ♃ Z9 ⓦ; Braz.
- **quesneliana** (Brongn.) L.B. Sm. · ♃ Z9 ⓦ; Braz.
- *roseomarginata* Carrière = Quesnelia quesneliana

Quillaja Molina -f- *Rosaceae* · 3 spp. · E:Soap Bark Tree; F:Quillay; G:Seifenspiere
- **saponaria** Molina · E:Soap Bark Tree, Soap Bark; G:Seifenspiere · ♄ e Z10 ⓚ ⚣ Ⓝ; Peru, Bol., Chile

Quisqualis L. -f- *Combretaceae* · 17 spp. · F:Quisqualier; G:Fadenröhre, Sonderling
- **indica** L. · E:Rangoon Creeper; G:Indischer Sonderling · ♄ d ⚣ Z10 ⓦ VII-VIII; W-Afr., C-Afr., E-Afr., S-Afr., Ind., SE-As.

Rabiea N.E. Br. -f- *Aizoaceae* · 4-7 spp.
- **albinota** (Haw.) N.E. Br. · ♃ ⚥ Z9 ⓚ; Cape

Racosperma Mart. = Acacia
- *mearnsii* (De Wild.) Pedley = Acacia mearnsii
- *melanoxylon* (R. Br.) Pedley = Acacia melanoxylon
- *pulchellum* (R. Br.) Pedley = Acacia pulchella

Radermachera Zoll. & Moritzi -f- *Bignoniaceae* · 15 spp.
- **sinica** (Hance) Hemsl. · ♄ e Z10 ⓦ; SE-China

Radiola Hill -f- *Linaceae* · 1 sp. · F:Radiole faux-lin; G:Zwergflachs
- **linoides** Roth · G:Zwergflachs · ⊙ VII-VIII; Eur.*, Lebanon, N-As., NW-Afr., Madeira, trop. Afr.mts..

Raimannia Rose = Oenothera
- *drummondii* (Hook.) Rose ex Sprague & L. Riley = Oenothera drummondii

Ramonda Rich. -f- *Gesneriaceae* · 3 spp. · E:Pyrenean Violet; F:Ramonde; G:Felsenteller, Ramondie
- *heldreichii* (Boiss.) Benth. & Hook. = Jancaea heldreichii
- **myconi** (L.) Rchb. · G:Felsenteller, Ramondie · ♃ △ Z6 V-VI; Eur.: NE-Sp., F (Pyr.)
- **nathaliae** Pančić & Petrovic · ♃ △ Z6 V; Eur.: Serb., Maced., GR
- *pyrenaica* Pers. = Ramonda myconi
- × **regis-ferdinandi** Kellerer (*R. myconi* × *R. serbica*) · ♃ △ Z6 V; cult.
- **serbica** Pančić · G:Serbischer Felsenteller · ♃ △ Z6 V-VI ▽; Eur.: Serb., Maced., AL, NW-GR, BG
- var. *nathaliae* (Pančić & Petrovic) hort. = Ramonda nathaliae

Ranalisma Stapf -f- *Alismataceae* · 2 spp.
- **humile** (Rich. ex Kunth) Hutch. · ♃ ⁓ ≈ Z9 ⓦ; W-Afr., C-Afr., Sudan, Tanzania, Zambia

Randia L. -f- *Rubiaceae* · 200+ spp.
- **formosa** (Jacq.) K. Schum. · ♄ ♄ Z10; trop. Lat.-Am.
- *maculata* DC. = Rothmannia longiflora

Ranunculus L. -m- *Ranunculaceae* · c. 600 spp. · E:Buttercup, Crowfoot; F:Renoncule; G:Hahnenfuß, Ranunkel, Scharbockskraut, Wasserhahnenfuß
- *acer* auct. = Ranunculus acris
- **aconitifolius** L. · E:Aconite-leaved Buttercup, Batchelor's Buttons; F:Renoncule à feuilles d'aconit; G:Eisenhutblättriger Hahnenfuß · ♃ Z5 V-VII; Eur.: Ib, Fr, Ital-P, Ba, C-Eur., EC-Eur.
- **acris** L. · E:Buttercup, Meadow Buttercup; F:Bouton d'or, Renoncule âcre, Renoncule éleve; G:Gewöhnlicher Scharfer Hahnenfuß · ♃ V-IX ⚣ ✿; Eur.*, Cauc., W-Sib., ? C-As., nat. in N-Am.
- *africanus* hort. = Ranunculus asiaticus
- **alpestris** L. · E:Alpine Buttercup; G:Alpen-Hahnenfuß · ♃ △ Z5 VI-VII; Eur.: Ib, Fr, Ital-P, C-Eur., EC-Eur., Ba, RO; mts.
- **amplexicaulis** L. · E:White Buttercup; G:Weißer Hahnenfuß · ♃ △ Z6 V-VI; Eur.: sp., F; mts.
- **aquatilis** L. · E:Water Buttercup, Water Crowfoot; F:Renoncule aquatique;

G:Gewöhnlicher Wasserhahnenfuß · ⑅
≈ Z5 IV-VIII; Eur.*, Cauc., NW-Afr.,
nat. in NZ
– **arvensis** L. · E:Corn Buttercup;
G:Acker-Hahnenfuß · ⊙ V-VII ⚥; Eur.*,
TR, Levant, Cauc., Iran, C-As., Him.,
NW-Afr., Libya
– **asiaticus** L. · E:Turban Buttercup;
G:Ranunkel · ⑅ ⚮ Z9 ⬡ V-VI; TR,
Cyprus, Syr., Iran, Iraq, N-Afr.
– **auricomus** L. · E:Goldilocks; G:Gold-
Hahnenfuß · ⑅ IV-V ⚥; Eur.*, Cauc.,
W-Sib.
– *baudotii* Godr. = Ranunculus peltatus
subsp. baudotii
– **brevifolius** Ten. · ⑅ Z7 V-VII; Eur.: C-I,
Ba; TR
– **breynianus** Crantz · G:Gebirgs-Hahnen-
fuß · ⑅ Z6 V-VII; Eur.: Fr, Ital-P, C-Eur.,
EC-Eur., Ba, E-Eur.; TR; mts.
– **bulbosus** L. · E:Bulbous Buttercup,
Buttercup; F:Renoncule bulbeuse;
G:Knolliger Hahnenfuß · ⑅ Z6 V-VIII ⚥;
Eur.*, TR, Cyprus, Syr., Iraq, Cauc., Iran,
Egypt, Alger., Moroc., nat. in N-Am.
– **calandrinioides** Oliv. · ⑅ Z7; Moroc.
– **carinthiacus** Hoppe · E:Carinthian Buttercup; G:Kärntner Hahnenfuß · ⑅ IV-VII;
Eur.: sp., F, I, C-Eur., Ba; mts.
– **cassubicus** L. · G:Kaschubischer
Hahnenfuß, Wenden-Gold-Hahnenfuß ·
⑅ IV-VII; Eur.: C-Eur., Ital-P, EC-Eur., Ba,
Sc, E-Eur.; W-Sib. (Altai)
– **circinatus** Sibth. · G:Spreizender
Wasserhahnenfuß · ⑅ ≈ V-IX; Eur.*
exc. Ib; C-As., Sib.., Alger.
– **crenatus** Waldst. & Kit. · E:Crenate But-
tercup; G:Kerb-Hahnenfuß · ⑅ Z5 VI-VII;
Eur.: I, Ba, RO, W-Russ.; E-Alp., Apenn.,
Carp., Balkan
– **ficaria** L. · E:Lesser Celandine, Pilewort;
F:Ficaire; G:Gewöhnliches Scharbock-
skraut · ⑅ Z5 III-V ⚘ ⚥; Eur.*, Cauc.,
W-Sib., C-As.
– **flabellaris** Raf. · E:Yellow Water
Crowfoot; G:Gelber Wasser-Hahnenfuß
· ⑅ ≈ Z4 VI-VII; Can.; USA: NE, NCE,
NC, SC, SE, Rocky Mts., NW, Calif.
– **flammula** L. · E:Lesser Spearwort;
F:Petite douve, Renoncule flamette;
G:Brennender Hahnenfuß · ⑅ ⌣ Z5 V-X
⚥; Eur.*, W-Sib. (Altai)
– **fluitans** Lam. · G:Flutender Wasser-
Hahnenfuß · ⑅ ≈ VI-VIII; Eur.* exc. Ib
– **glacialis** L. · E:Glacier Crowfoot;

G:Gletscher-Hahnenfuß · ⑅ Z4 VII-VIII;
Eur.: Sc, Fr, Ib, Ital-P, EC-Eur., C-Eur.;
Alp., Pyren., Sierra Nevada, Arkt. Eur.,
Island, Greenl.
– **gramineus** L. · F:Renoncule à feuilles de
graminée; G:Grasblättriger Hahnenfuß
· ⑅ △ Z7 IV-VI; Eur.: Ib, Fr, Ital-P, Sw;
NW-Afr.
– **hederaceus** L. · E:Ivy-leaved Water
Crowfoot; G:Efeublättriger Wasserhah-
nenfuß · ⑅ ≈ VI-IX; Eur.: BrI, Sc, Balt.,
Ib, Fr, D; Can.: E
– *hortensis* Pers. = Ranunculus asiaticus
– **hybridus** Biria · E:Hybrid Buttercup;
G:Bastard-Hahnenfuß, Nierenblättriger
Hahnenfuß · ⑅ VI-VIII; Eur.: I, G, A,
Slove., Montenegro; ? RO; E-Alp.
– **illyricus** L. · G:Illyrischer Hahnenfuß · ⑅
Z6 V-VI; Eur.: Ital-P, C-Eur., EC-Eur., Ba,
Sc (Öland); TR, Cauc.
– **kuepferi** Greuter & Burdet · G:Küpfers
Hahnenfuß · ⑅ VI-VII; Eur.: F, Cors, I,
Sw, A; Alp., Cors
– **lanuginosus** L. · G:Wolliger Hahnenfuß ·
⑅ Z5 V-VI; Eur.: C-Eur., Ital-P, EC-Eur.,
Ba, Sc, E-Eur.
– **lateriflorus** DC. · G:Seitenblütiger
Hahnenfuß · ⊙; Eur.: Ib, Fr, Ital-P,
EC-Eur., Ba, E-Eur.; TR, Levant, Cauc.,
C-As., W-Sib., Moroc., Alger.
– **lingua** L. · E:Greater Spearwort;
F:Grande douve; G:Zungen-Hahnenfuß ·
⑅ ⌣ Z4 VI-VIII ⚥ ▽; Eur.*, TR, Cauc.,
W-Sib., E-Sib., C-As.
– **millefoliatus** Vahl · ⑅ △ Z7 ∧ V-VI;
Eur.: Fr, Ital-P, EC-Eur., Ba, RO; TR, Syr.,
NW-Afr., Libya
– **monspeliacus** L. · G:Montpellier-
Hahnenfuß · ⑅ Z8 ∧ IV-V; Eur.: Ib, Fr,
Ital-P, nat. in Swed
– **montanus** Willd. · E:Mountain Butter-
cup; G:Berg-Hahnenfuß · ⑅ △ Z6 IV-IX;
Eur.: F, I, C-Eur., Slove., Croatia, Bosn.,
YU, Maced.; mts.
– **nemorosus** DC. · E:Wood Buttercup;
G:Gewöhnlicher Hain-Hahnenfuß, Wald-
Hahnenfuß · ⑅ Z5 V-VII; Eur.* exc. BrI
– **ololeucos** J. Lloyd · G:Reinweißer
Wasserhahnenfuß · ⑅ ≈ III-VI; Eur.: Ib,
Fr, D
– **omiophyllus** Ten. · G:Lenormands
Wasser-Hahnenfuß · ⑅ ≈ ; Eur.: BrI, Fr,
Ital-P, Ib
– **parnassifolius** L. · E:Parnassus-leaved
Buttercup; G:Herzblatt-Hahnenfuß · ⑅

Z5 VII; Eur.: sp., F, I, C-Eur.; N-Sp., Pyr.,
Alp.
- **peltatus** Schrank · G:Schild-Wasserhah-
nenfuß
- subsp. **baudotii** (Godr.) C.D.K. Cook ·
G:Brackwasser-Hahnenfuß, Salz-Wasser-
hahnenfuß · ⨆ ≈ V-IX; Eur.: coasts, F
(Alsace), A (Burgenland); TR, Moroc.
- subsp. **peltatus** · G:Gewöhnlicher Schild-
Wasserhahnenfuß · ⨆ ≈ V-IX; Eur.*,
TR, Levant, N-Afr.
- **penicillatus** (Dumort.) Bab. · G:Pinsel-
Wasserhahnenfuß · ⨆ ≈ V-IX; Eur.*,
Moroc.
- **platanifolius** L. · G:Platanenblättriger
Hahnenfuß · ⨆ Z5 V-VI; Eur.* exc. BrI
- **polyanthemoides** Boreau · G:Falscher
Vielblütiger Hahnenfuß, Schmalblättriger
Hain-Hahnenfuß · ⨆ VI-VIII; Eur.: F, I,
C-Eur., Sc, EC-Eur., Ba
- **polyanthemophyllus** W. Koch & H.E.
Hess · G:Schlitzblättriger Hain-Hahnen-
fuß · ⨆ V-VII; Eur.: F, I, Sw, D
- **polyanthemos** L. · E:Multi-flavoured
Buttercup; G:Vielblütiger Hain-Hahnen-
fuß · ⨆ V-VII; Eur.* exc. BrI, Ib; W-Sib.,
E-Sib., C-As.
- **psilostachys** Griseb. · ⨆ △ Z7 ∧ V; Eur.:
H, Ba
- **pygmaeus** Wahlenb. · E:Pygmy Butter-
cup; G:Zwerg-Hahnenfuß · ⨆ Z6 VII-VIII;
Eur.: Sc, N-Russ., C-Eur., EC-Eur., I; N,
E-Alp., W-Carp.; W-Sib., E-Sib., Kamchat.
- **pyrenaeus** L. · E:Pyrenean Buttercup;
G:Pyrenäen-Hahnenfuß · ⨆ △ Z6 V-VII;
Eur.: sp., F; mts.
- subsp. *plantagineus* (All.) Rouy &
Foucaud = Ranunculus kuepferi
- *pyrenaicus* hort. = Ranunculus pyrenaeus
- **repens** L. · E:Creeping Buttercup;
G:Kriechender Hahnenfuß · ⨆ ⤳ Z3
V-VIII ⚘; Eur.*, TR, Cauc., Iran, W-Sib.,
E-Sib., Amur, Sakhal., Kamchat., Manch.,
Korea, Jap., Moroc., Alger.
- **reptans** L. · E:Slender Creeping Spear-
wort; G:Ufer-Hahnenfuß · ⨆ VI-VIII;
Eur.* exc. BrI, Ib, ? EC-Eur.; W-Sib.,
E-Sib., Amur, Kamchat., Mong., N-Am.
- **rionii** Lagger · G:Rions Wasserhahnen-
fuß · ⊙ ≈ VI-VIII; Eur.: Fr, C-Eur.,
EC-Eur., Ba, E-Eur.; TR, Levant, Cauc.,
Iran, W-Sib., C-As., Him., W-China, w
N-Am., S-Afr.
- **sardous** Crantz · E:Hairy Buttercup;
G:Sardischer Hahnenfuß · ⊙ ⌢ ⚘;

Eur.*; ? TR
- **sceleratus** L. · E:Blister Buttercup,
Celery-leaved Crowfoot; G:Giftiger
Hahnenfuß · ⨆ ⌣ VI-X ⚘ Ⓝ; Eur.*, TR,
Levant, Cauc., Iran, W-Sib., E-Sib., Amur,
Sakhal., Kamchat., C-As., Him., Mong.,
China, N-Am., S-Am., Egypt., Austr.
- **seguieri** Vill. · G:Séguiers Hahnenfuß ·
⨆ Z5 V-VII; Eur.: sp., F, I, C-Eur., Slove.,
Montenegro; Cordillera Cantábrica, Alp.,
Apenn., Montenegro
- **serpens** Schrank · G:Wurzelnder Hain-
Hahnenfuß · ⊙ V-VII; Eur.* exc. BrI
- **strigulosus** Schur · ⨆; Eur.: EC-Eur., Ba,
E-Eur.
- **thora** L. · E:Thore's Buttercup; G:Schild-
blättriger Hahnenfuß · ⨆ △ Z5 V-VII ⚘;
Eur.* exc. BrI, Sc; mts.
- **traunfellneri** Hoppe · G:Traunfellners
Hahnenfuß · ⨆ Z6 V-VIII; Eur.: A, Slove.;
SE-Alp.
- **trichophyllus** Chaix · G:Gewöhnlicher
Haarblättriger Wasserhahnenfuß · ⨆ ≈
V-IX; Eur.*, TR, Levant, N-As., N-Afr.,
SW-Austr., Tasman., NZ
- **tripartitus** DC. · E:Three-lobed Water
Crowfoot; G:Dreiteiliger Wasser-
Hahnenfuß · ⨆ ≈ III-V; Eur.: Ib, Fr, BrI,
G, GR; Moroc.
- **villarsii** DC. · G:Greniers Hahnenfuß,
Villars Hahnenfuß · ⨆ Z6 V-VIII; Eur.: F,
I, C-Eur.; Alp.

Ranzania T. Itô -f- *Berberidaceae* · 1 sp.
- **japonica** (T. Itô) T. Itô · ⨆ Z7 V-VI; Jap.

Raoulia Hook. f. ex Raoul -f- *Asteraceae* ·
c. 20 spp. · F:Mouton végétal; G:Schafs-
teppich
- **australis** Hook. f. · G:Schafsteppich · ⨆
Z7; NZ
- *australis* auct. = Raoulia hookeri
- **glabra** Hook. f. · ⨆ ⤳ △ Z7 ⌂ ∧; NZ
- **hookeri** Allan · ⨆ ⤳ △ Z7 ∧ VII-IX; NZ
- **subsericea** Hook. f. · ⨆ ⤳ △ Z7 ⌂ ∧;
NZ
- **tenuicaulis** Hook. f. · ⨆ ⤳ △ Z7 ⌂ ∧;
NZ

Raphanus L. -m- *Brassicaceae* · 8 spp. ·
E:Radish; F:Radis, Ravenelle; G:Hede-
rich, Radieschen, Rettich
- **caudatus** L. · ⊙ Z8 Ⓝ; Ind., E-As.
- *landra* Moretti ex DC. = Raphanus
raphanistrum subsp. landra

- **raphanistrum**
- subsp. **landra** (Moretti ex DC.) Bonnier & Layens · G:Kurzfrüchtiger Hederich · ⊙; Eur.: Ib, F, Ital-P, Ba; NW-Afr.
- subsp. **raphanistrum** · E:Sea Radish, Wild Radish; G:Acker-Hederich · ⊙ VI-X; Eur.*, TR, Levant, Cauc., C-As., N-Afr., nat. in Sib., E-As., N-Am.
- **sativus** L. · E:Radish; G:Rettich · ⊙ V-IX; orig. ?
- var. **gayanus** (Fisch. & C.A. Mey.) Webb · G:Verwilderter Rettich · ⊙ Z6 V Ⓝ; cult.
- var. **longipinnatus** L.H. Bailey · E:Summer Radish; G:China-Rettich · ⊙ Z6 V Ⓝ; cult.
- var. **mougri** Helm · G:Schlangen-Rettich · ⊙ Z6 V Ⓝ
- var. **niger** (Mill.) J. Kern. · E:Oriental Radish; G:Garten-Rettich, Radi · ⊙ Z6 V Ⓝ; cult.
- var. **oleiformis** Pers. · E:Oil Radish; G:Öl-Rettich · ⊙ Z6 V Ⓝ; cult.
- var. *radicula* Pers. = Raphanus sativus var. sativus
- var. **sativus** · E:Small Radish; G:Radieschen · ⊙ Z6 Ⓝ; cult.

Raphia P. Beauv. -f- *Arecaceae* · 20 spp. · E:Raffia; F:Raphia; G:Bastpalme, Raffiapalme, Weinpalme
- **farinifera** (Gaertn.) Hyl. · E:Raffia Palm; G:Bastpalme · ♄ e Z10 ⓜ Ⓝ; E-Afr., Madag.
- **hookeri** G. Mann & H. Wendl. · E:Wine Palm; G:Raffiapalme · ♄ e Z10 ⓜ Ⓝ; W-Afr.
- *pedunculata* P. Beauv. = Raphia farinifera
- *ruffia* (Jacq.) Mart. = Raphia farinifera
- **vinifera** P. Beauv. · E:Bamboo Palm; G:Weinpalme · ♄ e Z10 ⓜ Ⓝ; W-Afr.

Rapistrum Crantz -n- *Brassicaceae* · 2-3 spp. · F:Rapistre; G:Rapsdotter
- **perenne** (L.) All. · G:Ausdauernder Rapsdotter · ⌗ VI-VIII; Eur.: Ital-P, C-Eur., EC-Eur., Ba, E-Eur., nat. in BrI, Fr
- **rugosum** (L.) All. · E:Common Giant Mustard; G:Gewöhnlicher Runzliger Rapsdotter · ⊙ VI-X; Eur.: Ib, Fr, Ital-P, Ba, Crim; TR, Cauc., Iran, C-As., N-Afr., nat. in BrI, C-Eur., EC-Eur., E-Eur.

Ratibida Raf. -f- *Asteraceae* · 6 spp. · E:Mexican Hat, Prairie Cone Flower; G:Präriesonnenhut

- **pinnata** (Vent.) Barnhart · E:Grey-head Coneflower; G:Nickender Prärieson-nenhut · ⌗ Z3; Can.: Ont., USA: NE, NCE, NC, Okla., SE

Rauvolfia L. -f- *Apocynaceae* · 75 spp. · E:Devil Pepper; F:Rauvolfia, Serpentaire de l'Inde; G:Teufelspfeffer
- *canescens* L. = Rauvolfia tetraphylla
- **serpentina** (L.) Benth. ex Kurz · E:Java Devil Pepper; G:Java-Teufelspfeffer · ♄ e Z10 ⓜ ⚥ ⚘ Ⓝ ▽ ✳; Ind., Sri Lanka, Thail., Sumat., Java
- **tetraphylla** L. · E:Four Leaf Devilpepper; G:Vierblättriger Teufelspfeffer · ♄ e Z10 ⓜ; trop. Am., subtrop. Am.
- **vomitoria** Afzel. · E:Swizzlestick; G:Brech-Teufelspfeffer · ♄ e Z10 ⓜ ⚘; W-Afr., C-Afr., E-Afr., Sudan, Egypt

Ravenala Adans. -f- *Strelitziaceae* · 1 sp. · E:Traveller's Tree; F:Arbre du voyageur; G:Baum der Reisenden
- **madagascariensis** J.F. Gmel. · E:Traveller's Tree; G:Baum der Reisenden · ♄ e Z10 ⓜ; Madag.

Reaumuria L. -f- *Tamaricaceae* · 12 spp.
- **hypericoides** Willd. · ♄ d △ ⓐ ∧ V-VI; Syr., Iran

Rebutia K. Schum. -f- *Cactaceae* · 30+ spp.
- **albiflora** F. Ritter & Buining · ⍦ Z9 ⓑ; Bol. (Tarija)
- **albipilosa** F. Ritter · ⍦ Z9 ⓑ; Bol. (Tarija)
- *arenacea* Cárdenas = Sulcorebutia arenacea
- *auranitida* (Wessner) Buining & Donald = Rebutia einsteinii
- **aureiflora** Backeb. · ⍦ Z9 ⓑ ▽ ✳; NW-Arg.
- *brachyantha* (Wessner) Buining & Donald = Rebutia steinmannii
- *brunneoradicata* F. Ritter = Rebutia steinmannii
- *buiningiana* Rausch = Rebutia pseudo-deminuta
- *cajasensis* F. Ritter = Rebutia fiebrigii
- *calliantha* Bewer. = Rebutia wessneriana
- *carminea* Buining = Rebutia minuscula
- *chrysacantha* Backeb. = Rebutia senilis
- *cincinnata* Rausch = Rebutia steinmannii var. steinmannii
- *colorea* F. Ritter = Rebutia pygmaea var.

pygmaea
- *costata* Werderm. = Rebutia steinmannii
- *cylindrica* (Donald & A.B. Lau) Donald = Sulcorebutia cylindrica
- **deminuta** (F.A.C. Weber) A. Berger · ⸲ Z9 ⓚ ▽ ✳; NW-Arg.
- f. *pseudominuscula* (Speg.) Buining & Donald = Rebutia pseudodeminuta
- **diersiana** Rausch · ⸲ Z9 ⓚ ▽ ✳; Bol. (Cuquisaca)
- *digitiformis* Backeb. = Rebutia pygmaea var. pygmaea
- **einsteinii** Frič · ⸲ Z9 ⓚ ▽ ✳; NW-Arg. (Volcan Chani)
- var. *conoidea* (Wessner) Buining & Donald = Rebutia einsteinii
- var. *rubroviridis* (Frič ex Backeb.) Buining & Donald = Rebutia einsteinii
- **fabrisii** Rausch · ⸲ Z9 ⓚ; N-Arg.
- *famatinensis* (Speg.) Speg. = Lobivia famatinensis
- *fidaiana* (Backeb.) D.R. Hunt = Weingartia fidaiana
- **fiebrigii** (Gürke) Britton & Rose · ⸲ Z9 ⓚ ▽ ✳; Bol., NW-Arg.
- *fusca* F. Ritter = Rebutia spegazziniana
- *glomeriseta* Cárdenas = Sulcorebutia glomeriseta
- *graciliflora* Backeb. = Rebutia xanthocarpa
- *hyalacantha* (Backeb.) Backeb. = Rebutia wessneriana
- **krainziana** Kesselr. · ⸲ Z9 ⓚ ▽ ✳; ? Bol.
- var. *hyalacantha* (Backeb.) Buchheim = Rebutia wessneriana
- **kupperiana** Boed. · ⸲ Z9 ⓚ ▽ ✳; Bol.: Tarija
- var. *spiniflora* F. Ritter = Rebutia kupperiana
- **marsoneri** Werderm. · ⸲ Z9 ⓚ ▽ ✳; Arg.: Jujuy
- **minuscula** K. Schum. · ⸲ Z9 ⓚ ▽ ✳; Arg.: Salta, Tucuman
- *neocumingii* (Backeb.) D.R. Hunt = Weingartia neocumingii
- *neumanniana* (Backeb.) D.R. Hunt = Weingartia neumanniana
- *nidulans* Frič & Kreuz. = Rebutia aureiflora
- *potosina* F. Ritter = Rebutia steinmannii var. steinmannii
- **pseudodeminuta** Backeb. · ⸲ Z9 ⓚ ▽ ✳; Bol., NW-Arg.
- **pygmaea** (R.E. Fr.) Britton & Rose · ⸲ Z9 ⓚ; Arg.

- var. *longispina* Backeb. = Rebutia pygmaea var. pygmaea
- var. **pygmaea** · ⸲ Z9 ⓚ ▽ ✳; NW-Arg.
- *rauschii* (G. Frank) D.R. Hunt = Sulcorebutia rauschii
- *schmiedcheniana* (U. Köhler) W.T. Marshall = Rebutia einsteinii
- **senilis** Backeb. · ⸲ Z9 ⓚ ▽ ✳; Arg. (Salta)
- **spegazziniana** Backeb. · ⸲ Z9 ⓚ ▽ ✳; NW-Arg.
- *steinbachii* Werderm. = Sulcorebutia steinbachii
- **steinmannii** (Solms) Britton & Rose
- var. *rauschii* (G. Frank) F. Ritter = Sulcorebutia rauschii
- var. **steinmannii** · ⸲ Z9 ⓚ ▽ ✳; Bol.: Chuquisaca
- *tarijensis* Rausch = Rebutia spegazziniana
- **wessneriana** Bewer. · ⸲ Z9 ⓚ ▽ ✳; N-Bol.
- **xanthocarpa** Backeb. · ⸲ Z9 ⓚ ▽ ✳; Arg.: Salta

× **Recchara** hort. -f- Orchidaceae (*Brassavola* × *Cattleya* × *Laelia* × *Schomburgkia*)

Rechsteineria Regel = Sinningia
- *cardinalis* (Lehm.) Kuntze = Sinningia cardinalis
- *verticillata* (Vell.) L.B. Sm. = Sinningia verticillata
- *warszewiczii* (C.D. Bouché & Hanst.) Kuntze = Sinningia incarnata

Rectanthera O. Deg. = Callisia
- *fragrans* (Lindl.) O. Deg. = Callisia fragrans

Regelia Schauer -f- Myrtaceae · 5 spp.
- **ciliata** Schauer · ♄ e Z9 ⓚ VII-VIII; W-Austr.

Regnellidium Lindm. -n- Marsileaceae · 1 sp.
- **diphyllum** Lindm. · ⨊ ⁀ Z10 ⓦ ⓚ; S-Braz., N-Arg.

Rehmannia Libosch. ex Fisch. & C.A. Mey. -f- Scrophulariaceae · 9 spp. · E:Chinese Foxglove; F:Digitale de Chine, Rehmannia; G:Chinafingerhut, Rehmannie
- **angulata** (D. Don) Hemsl. · ⨊ Z9 ⓚ V-VII; China

– **elata** N.E. Br. · G:Hoher Chinafingerhut ·
⳨ Z9 ⓚ V-VI; China
– **glutinosa** (Gaertn.) Libosch. ex Fisch.
& C.A. Mey. · E:Chinese Foxglove;
G:Klebriger Chinafingerhut · ⳨ Z9 ⓚ
V-VI ⚥ ; China
– **henryi** N.E. Br. · ⳨ Z9 ⓚ VI-VIII; China

Reicheocactus Backeb. = Neoporteria
– *floribundus* Backeb. = Neoporteria
aricensis

Reineckea Kunth -f- *Convallariaceae* ·
1 sp. · E:Reineckea; F:Reineckéa;
G:Reineckie
– **carnea** (Andrews) Kunth · ⳨ ⤳ Z7;
China, Jap.

Reinhardtia Liebm. -f- *Arecaceae* · 6 spp. ·
E:Window Palm; F:Palmier; G:Fenster-
palme
– **gracilis** (H. Wendl.) Burret · E:Window
Palm; G:Fensterpalme · ♄ e Z10 ⓦ; Mex.,
Guat., Hond.

Reinwardtia Dumort. -f- *Linaceae* · 1 sp. ·
E:Yellow Flax; G:Gelber Flachs
– **indica** Dumort. · E:Yellow Flax; G:Gelber
Flachs · ♄ e Z9 ⓚ XI-III; N-Ind., mts.
– *tetragyna* Planch. = Reinwardtia indica
– *trigyna* (Roxb.) Planch. = Reinwardtia
indica

Relhania L'Hér. -f- *Asteraceae* · 13 spp.
– **quinquenervis** Thunb. · ♄ e D Z9 ⓚ
VI-VIII; Cape

Remijia DC. -f- *Rubiaceae* · 47 spp.
– **ferruginea** (A. St.-Hil.) DC. · ♄ Z10 ⓦ;
S-Braz.

Remusatia Schott -f- *Araceae* · 4 spp.
– **vivipara** (Roxb.) Schott · ⳨ Z10 ⓦ; Ind.
mts.; Java

× **Renades** hort. -f- *Orchidaceae* (*Aerides* ×
Renanthera)

× **Renancentrum** hort. -n- *Orchidaceae*
(*Ascocentrum* × *Renanthera*)

× **Renanetia** hort. -f- *Orchidaceae*
(*Neofinetia* × *Renanthera*)

× **Renanopsis** hort. -f- *Orchidaceae*

(*Renanthera* × *Vandopsis*)

× **Renanstylis** hort. -f- *Orchidaceae*
(*Renanthera* × *Rhynchostylis*)

× **Renantanda** hort. -f- *Orchidaceae*
(*Renanthera* × *Vanda*)

Renanthera Lour. -f- *Orchidaceae* · 21 sp.
– **coccinea** Lour. · ♄ Z10 ⓦ III-X ▽ ✳;
S-Vietn.
– **imschootiana** Rolfe · ♄ Z10 ⓦ V-VII ▽
✳; Ind. (Assam), Indochina
– *lowii* (Lindl.) Rchb. f. = Dimorphorchis
lowii
– **pulchella** Rolfe · ♄ Z10 ⓦ VII ▽ ✳; InG:
Assam
– **storiei** Rchb. f. · ♄ Z10 ⓦ VI-VII ▽ ✳;
Phil.

× **Renanthoglossum** hort. -n- *Orchidaceae*
(*Ascoglossum* × *Renanthera*)

× **Renanthopsis** hort. -f- *Orchidaceae*
(*Phalaenopsis* × *Renanthera*)

Reseda L. -f- *Resedaceae* · -60 spp. ·
E:Mignonette; F:Réséda; G:Resede, Wau
– **alba** L. · E:White Mignonette; G:Weiße
Resede · ☉ ⳨ Z7 VI-IX; Eur.: Ib, Fr, Ital-P,
Ba; W-TR, Levant, Arab., N-Afr., nat. in
BrI, G, CZ, RO
– **glauca** L. · ⳨ ; Eur.: F, sp.; Pyr., Cordillera
Cantábrica
– **lutea** L. · E:Cutleaf Mignonette, Wild
Mignonette; G:Gelbe Resede, Gelber
Wau · ⳨ V-IX ⚥ ; Eur.* exc. BrI, Sc; TR,
Levant, Cauc., Iran, W-Sib., C-As., N-Afr.,
nat. in BrI, Sc, N-Am.
– **luteola** L. · E:Dyer's Rocket, Wild
Mignonette, Woad; G:Färber-Resede,
Färber-Wau · ☉ Z6 VI-VIII ⚥ ⓝ; Eur.: Ib,
Fr, Ital-P, EC-Eur., Ba, RO, Crim, DK; TR,
Levant, Cauc., Iran, C-As, Afgh., N-Afr.,
nat. in C-Eur., BrI
– **odorata** L. · E:Common Mignonette;
G:Garten-Resede · ☉ ☉ ⳨ D VII-IX ⚥ ⓝ;
? Libya, nat. in Eur.: sp., Balear., F, I, A,
CZ, RO, Russ.
– **some cultivars**
– **phyteuma** L. · G:Rapunzel-Resede · ⳨
VI-IX; Eur.: Ib, Ital-P, Fr, EC-Eur., Ba,
E-Eur., Sw; TR, N-Afr., nat. in G, A

Restrepia Kunth -f- *Orchidaceae* · 49 spp.

– **antennifera** Kunth · ⚃ Z10 Ⓚ II-III ▽ ✳;
Ecuad., Col., Venez.
– **elegans** H. Karst. · ⚃ Z10 Ⓚ I-III ▽ ✳;
Venez.
– **guttulata** Lindl. · ⚃ Z10 Ⓚ I-II ▽ ✳;
Ecuad., Col., Venez.

Retama Raf. -f- *Fabaceae* · 4 spp. ·
E:Retam; F:Rétama; G:Retamastrauch
– **monosperma** (L.) Boiss. · E:White
Broom; G:Weißer Retamastrauch · ♄ d
Z9 Ⓚ II-III Ⓝ; Eur.: Ib; Moroc., Alger.,
Egypt

Retinispora Siebold & Zucc. = Chamaecyparis
– *obtusa* Siebold & Zucc. = Chamaecyparis
obtusa var. obtusa
– *pisifera* Siebold & Zucc. = Chamaecyparis
pisifera

Reutealis Airy Shaw -f- *Euphorbiaceae* ·
1 sp. · E:Javillo; G:Banucalagnuss
– **trisperma** (Blanco) Airy Shaw · E:Javillo,
Soft Lumbang; G:Banucalagnuss · ♄ Z10
Ⓦ ✿ Ⓝ; Phil.

Reynoutria Houtt. = Fallopia
– *aubertii* (L. Henry) Moldenke = Fallopia
baldschuanica
– *baldschuanica* (Regel) Moldenke =
Fallopia baldschuanica
– *japonica* Houtt. = Fallopia japonica var.
japonica
– *sachalinensis* (F. Schmidt) Nakai =
Fallopia sachalinensis

Rhabdothamnus A. Cunn. -m-
Gesneriaceae · 1 sp.
– **solandri** A. Cunn. · ♄ e Z8 Ⓚ IX-X; NZ

Rhagadiolus Scop. -m- *Asteraceae* · 2 spp. ·
F:Rhagadiole; G:Sichelsalat, Sternlattich
– **stellatus** (L.) Gaertn. · G:Sternfrüchtiger
Sichelsalat, Sternlattich · ⊙; Eur.: Ib, Fr,
Ital-P, Ba, Crim; TR, Iraq, Iran, N-Afr.,
Canar., Madeira

Rhamnella Miq. -f- *Rhamnaceae* · 10 spp.
– **franguloides** (Maxim.) Weberb. · ♄ d Z6
V-VI; Jap., S-Korea, E-China

Rhamnus L. -f- *Rhamnaceae* · 125 spp. ·
E:Buckthorn; F:Alaterne, Nerprun;
G:Kreuzdorn

– **alaternus** L. · E:Italian Buckthorn;
G:Immergrüner Kreuzdorn · ♄ e Z8 Ⓚ
III-IV ✿; Eur.: Ib, Fr, Ital-P, Ba, Crim;
TR, Levant, NW-Afr., Libya
– **alnifolia** L'Hér. · E:Alderleaf Buckthorn;
G:Erlenblättriger Kreuzdorn · ♄ d ⤳ △
Z3 V-VI ✿; Can.; USA: NE, NCE, Rocky
Mts., NW, Calif.
– **alpina** L. · G:Alpen-Kreuzdorn · ♄ d Z5
V-VI ✿; Eur.: sp., F, Ital-P; Alp.; Moroc.,
Alger.
– subsp. *fallax* (Boiss.) Maire & Petitm. =
Rhamnus fallax
– *carniolica* A. Kern. = Rhamnus alpina
– **cathartica** L. · E:Common Buckthorn,
European Buckthorn; F:Nerprun
purgatif; G:Echter Kreuzdorn, Purgier-
Kreuzdorn · ♄ d Z4 V-VI ⚥ ✿ Ⓝ; Eur.*,
TR, Cauc., Iran, W-Sib., C-As., Moroc.,
Alger., nat. in e N-Am.
– **costata** Maxim. · ♄ d Z6 V ✿; Jap.; mts.
– **crenata** Siebold & Zucc. · ♄ d Z4 VI ✿;
Jap., Korea, N-China
– **davurica** Pall. · G:Dahurischer Kreuzdorn · ♄ d Z4 V ✿; E-Sib., Amur, Mong.,
Manch., Korea
– *erythroxyloides* Hoffmanns. = Rhamnus
pallasii
– **fallax** Boiss. · G:Krainer Kreuzdorn · ♄ Z5
V-VI ✿; Eur.: I, A, Ba; TR, Syr.
– *frangula* L. = Frangula alnus
– **globosa** Bunge · ♄ d ✿ Ⓝ; W-China,
N-China
– **imeretina** J.R. Booth ex G. Kirchn. ·
G:Kaukasischer Kreuzdorn · ♄ d Z6 VI
✿; TR, Cauc.
– *infectoria* L. = Rhamnus saxatilis
– **japonica** Maxim. · G:Japanischer
Kreuzdorn · ♄ d Z5 V ✿; Jap.
– **koraiensis** C.K. Schneid. · G:Korea-
Kreuzdorn · ♄ ✿; Korea
– **pallasii** Fisch. & C.A. Mey. · ♄ Z6 ✿;
NE-TR, Cauc., NW-Iran, C-As.
– **pumila** Turra · E:Dwarf Buckthorn;
F:Nerprun nain; G:Zwerg-Kreuzdorn · ♄
d ⤳ △ Z6 VI-VII ✿; Eur.: Ib, Fr, Ital-P,
Ba, C-Eur.; mts.
– *purshiana* DC. = Frangula purshiana
– **rhodopea** Velen. · ♄ Ⓚ ✿; Eur.: BG,
GR, Eur.TR
– *rupestris* Scop. = Frangula rupestris
– **saxatilis** Jacq. · E:Stony Buckthorn;
F:Nerprun des rochers; G:Felsen-
Kreuzdorn · ♄ d ⤳ △ Z6 IV-V ✿; Eur.:
Ib, Fr, C-Eur., Ital-P, EC-Eur., Ba, RO

– **utilis** Decne. · E:Chinese Buckthorn;
G:Chinesischer Kreuzdorn · ♄ d Z6 IV-V
⚘ Ⓝ; W-China

Rhaphidophora Hassk. -f- *Araceae* ·
96 spp.
– *aurea* (Linden & André) Birdsey =
Epipremnum aureum
– *celatocaulis* (N.E. Br.) Alderw. =
Rhaphidophora korthalsii
– **decursiva** (Wall.) Schott · ♄ e ⚥ Z10 Ⓦ;
Him., Ind., Indochina
– **korthalsii** Schott · ♄ e ⚥ Z10 Ⓦ;
Kalimantan

Rhaphiolepis Lindl. -f- *Rosaceae* ·
9-15 spp. · E:Hawthorn; F:Raphiolépis;
G:Traubenapfel
– × **delacourii** André (*R. indica* × *R.
umbellata*) · ♄ e Z8 Ⓚ III-V; cult.
– **indica** (L.) Lindl. · E:India Hawthorn;
G:Chinesischer Traubenapfel · ♄ e Z8 Ⓚ
II-VIII; S-China
– *japonica* Siebold & Zucc. = Rhaphiolepis
umbellata
– *ovata* Briot = Rhaphiolepis umbellata
– **umbellata** (Thunb.) Makino · G:Japa-
nischer Traubenapfel · ♄ e D Z8 Ⓚ V-VI;
Jap., Korea, Ryukyu-Is.,

Rhaphithamnus Miers -m- *Verbenaceae* ·
2 spp.
– **spinosus** (Juss.) Moldenke · ♄ e Z9 Ⓚ
III-IV; Arg., Chile

Rhapidophyllum H. Wendl. & Drude
-n- *Arecaceae* · 1 sp. · E:Needle Palm;
F:Palmier-aiguille; G:Nadelpalme
– **hystrix** (Fraser ex Thouin) H. Wendl. &
Drude · G:Nadelpalme; E:Needle Palm ·
♄ e Z8 Ⓚ; USA: SE, Fla.

Rhapis L. f. ex Aiton -f- *Arecaceae* · 8 spp. ·
E:Lady Palm; F:Palmier des dames;
G:Rutenpalme, Steckenpalme
– **excelsa** (Thunb.) A. Henry ex Rehder ·
E:Bamboo Palm, Ground Rattan Cane,
Lady Palm; G:Hohe Steckenpalme · ♄ e
Z9 Ⓚ; ? S-China
– *flabelliformis* L'Hér. ex Aiton = Rhapis
excelsa
– **humilis** Blume · E:Rattan Palm, Reed
Rhapis, Slender Lady Palm; G:Niedere
Steckenpalme · ♄ e Z9 Ⓚ; S-China

Rhaponticum Ludw. = Stemmacantha
– *scariosum* Lam. = Stemmacantha
rhapontica

Rhazya Decne. -f- *Apocynaceae* · 2 spp.
– *orientalis* (Decne.) A. DC. = Amsonia
orientalis

Rheedia L. = Garcinia
– *acuminata* (Ruiz & Pav.) Planch. &
Triana = Garcinia madruno
– *madruno* (Humb., Bonpl. & Kunth)
Planch. & Triana = Garcinia madruno

Rhektophyllum N.E. Br. -n- *Araceae* · 1 sp.
– **mirabile** (N.E. Br.) Bogner · ♰ e ⚥ Z10 Ⓦ;
W-Afr., C-Afr.

Rheum L. -n- *Polygonaceae* · c. 60 spp. ·
E:Rhubarb; F:Rhubarbe; G:Rhabarber
– **acuminatum** Hook. f. & Thomson · ♃ Z6
V-VI; Sikkim
– **alexandrae** Batalin · ♃ Z5 VI-VII; Tibet,
W-China
– **australe** D. Don · E:Himalaya Rhubarb;
G:Himalaya-Rhabarber · ♃ Z6 VI-VII;
C-As., Him.
– × *cultorum* Thorsrud & Reisaeter =
Rheum rhabarbarum
– *emodi* Wall. = Rheum australe
– *hybridum* hort. = Rheum rhabarbarum
– **kialense** Franch. · ♃ △ V-VI; China
– **nobile** Hook. f. & Thomson · ♃ Z7 VI-VII;
Ind.: Sikkim
– **officinale** Baill. · E:Chinese Rhubarb;
G:Gebräuchlicher Rhabarber, Südchine-
sischer Rhabarber · ♃ Z7 V-VII ⚘ ; Burma,
SE-Tibet, SW-China
– **palmatum** L.
– var. **palmatum** · E:Chinese Rhubarb;
G:Handlappiger Rhabarber · ♃ Z6 V-VI
⚘ ; E-Tibet, W-China
– var. **tanguticum** Maxim. ex Regel ·
E:Turkey Rhubarb; F:Rhubarbe de
Chine; G:Kron-Rhabarber, Tangutischer
Rhabarber · Z6 ⚘ ; NW-China
– **rhabarbarum** L. · E:Garden Rhubarb,
Rhubarb; G:Krauser Rhabarber, Öster-
reichischer Rhabarber · ♃ Z3 V-VI Ⓝ ▽;
BG (Rhodope)
– **some cultivars**
– **rhaponticum** L. · G:Bulgarischer
Rhabarber, Rhapontik · ♃ V-VI Ⓝ
– **ribes** L. · E:Syrian Rhubarb; G:Syrischer
Rhabarber · ♃ Z6 V-VI; Iran, Lebanon

– *undulatum* L. = Rheum rhabarbarum

Rhexia L. -f- *Melastomataceae* · 10-13 spp. ·
E:Deer Grass, Meadow Beauty;
G:Bruchheil
– **virginica** L. · E:Handsome Harry,
Meadow Beauty ; G:Virginischer Bruch-
heil · ♃ ⁓ Z7 ∧ VII-VIII; Can.: E; USA:
NE, NCR, Okla., SE, Fla.

Rhigozum Burch. -n- *Bignoniaceae* ·
7-9 spp.
– **obovatum** Burch. · ♄ ♄ d Z9 ⊡; S-Afr.,
Madag., Zimbabwe, Namibia

Rhinanthus L. -m- *Scrophulariaceae* ·
45 spp. · E:Yellow Rattle; F:Cocriste,
Rhinanthe; G:Klappertopf
– **alectorolophus** (Scop.) Pollich ·
E:Greater Yellow Rattle; G:Zottiger
Klappertopf
– subsp. **alectorolophus** · G:Gewöhnlicher
Zottiger Klappertopf · ⊙ ✕ Z6 V-IX; Eur.:
Fr, I, C-Eur., EC-Eur., Slove., E-Eur.
– subsp. **aschersonianus** (M. Schulze)
Hartl · G:Drüsiger Klappertopf · ⊙ Z6
V-VIII; Eur.: D (Jena)
– subsp. **facchinii** (Chabert) Soó ·
G:Südtiroler Klappertopf · ⊙ Z6; Alp.
– subsp. **freynii** (Sterneck) Hartl · G:Freyns
Klappertopf · ⊙ Z6; Eur.: N-I, Slove.
– **alpinus** Baumg. · G:Alpen-Klappertopf ·
⊙ Z6 VI-VIII; Eur.: A, EC-Eur., BG, RO,
W-Russ.; mts.
– **angustifolius** C.C. Gmel. · E:Narrow-
leaved Rattle; G:Großer Klappertopf
– subsp. **angustifolius** · G:Gewöhnlicher
Großer Klappertopf · ⊙ Z6; Eur.* exc. Ib
– subsp. **halophilus** (U. Schneid.) Hartl ·
G:Salzwiesen-Klappertopf · Z6 V-IX; Eur.:
D (Mecklenburg)
– **antiquus** (Sterneck) Schinz & Thell. ·
G:Altertümlicher Klappertopf, Bergam-
asker Klappertopf · ⊙ Z6 VIII; Eur.: I, Sw;
S-Alp.
– **borbasii** (Dörfl.) Soó · G:Puszta-
Klappertopf · ⊙ Z6 V-IX; Eur.: A, EC-Eur.,
Ba, E-Eur.
– **carinthiacus** Widder · G:Kärntner Klappertopf · ⊙ Z6 V-VIII; Eur.: A (Kärnten)
– **glacialis** Personnat · G:Grannen-
Klappertopf · ⊙ Z6 VI-IX; Eur.: Alp.
– *halophilus* U. Schneid. = Rhinanthus
angustifolius subsp. halophilus
– **minor** L. · E:Hay Rattle, Yellow Rattle;

G:Kleiner Klappertopf · ⊙ Z6 V-IX; Eur.*,
Cauc., W-Sib.
– *pulcher* Schummel ex Opiz = Rhinanthus
alpinus
– *rumelicus* Velen. = Rhinanthus alectorolophus subsp. aschersonianus
– *serotinus* (Schönh.) Schinz & Thell.
= Rhinanthus angustifolius subsp.
angustifolius

Rhinephyllum N.E. Br. -n- *Aizoaceae* ·
12 spp. · F:Rhinephyllum; G:Feilenblatt
– **broomii** L. Bolus · ♃ ↯ Z9 ⊡; Cape

Rhipsalidopsis Britton & Rose -f-
Cactaceae · 3 spp. · G:Osterkaktus
– **gaertneri** (Regel) Moran · E:Easter
Cactus; G:Osterkaktus · ♄ ↯ Z9 ⊚ ▽ ✳;
E-Braz.: Minas Gerais
– ✕ **graeseri** (Werderm.) Moran (*R.
gaertneri* ✕ *R. rosea*) · ♄ ↯ Z9 ⊡; cult.
– **rosea** (Lagerh.) Britton & Rose · ♄ ↯ Z9
⊚ ▽ ✳; Braz.: Parana

Rhipsalis Gaertn. -f- *Cactaceae* · 50 spp. ·
F:cactus-gui, Cactus-jonc; G:Binsenkak-
tus, Korallenkaktus, Rutenkaktus
– **baccifera** (J.S. Muell.) Stearn ·
E:Mistletoe Cactus · ♄ ↯ ⹁ Z9 ⊚ ▽ ✳;
Trop.
– *capilliformis* F.A.C. Weber = Rhipsalis
teres f. capilliformis
– *cassutha* Gaertn. = Rhipsalis baccifera
– **cereuscula** Haw. · E:Coral Cactus · ♄ ↯
Z9 ⊚ ▽ ✳; Braz., Parag., Urug., Arg.
– *chrysocarpa* Loefgr. = Rhipsalis puniceodiscus var. chrysocarpa
– **clavata** F.A.C. Weber · ♄ ↯ Z9 ⊚ ▽ ✳;
Braz.
– *conferta* Salm-Dyck = Rhipsalis teres
– *coriacea* Pol. = Pseudorhipsalis ramulosa
– *cribrata* (Lem.) Rümpler = Rhipsalis teres
– **crispata** (Haw.) Pfeiff. · ♄ ↯ Z9 ⊚ ▽ ✳;
E-Braz.
– *crispimarginata* Loefgr. = Rhipsalis
crispata
– *cruciformis* (Vell.) A. Cast. = Lepismium
cruciforme
– **dissimilis** (G. Lindb.) K. Schum. · ♄ ↯ Z9
⊚ ▽ ✳; E-Braz.
– *fasciculata* (Willd.) Haw. = Rhipsalis
baccifera
– **floccosa** Salm-Dyck · ♄ ↯ ⹁ Z9 ⊚ ▽ ✳;
Braz., Bol.
– *funalis* (Spreng.) Salm-Dyck = Rhipsalis

grandiflora
- *gaertneri* (Regel) Moran = Rhipsalidopsis gaertneri
- *gibberula* F.A.C. Weber = Rhipsalis floccosa
- × *graeseri* (Werderm.) Moran = Rhipsalidopsis × graeseri
- **grandiflora** Haw. · ♄ � Z9 ⊕ ▽ ✳; Braz.: Rio de Janeiro
- **hadrosoma** G. Lindb. · ♄ ⊬ Z9 ⊕ ▽ ✳; Braz.
- *himantoclada* Rol.-Goss. = Pseudorhipsalis himantoclada
- *houlletiana* Lem. = Lepismium houlletianum
- *ianthothele* (Monv.) K. Brandegee = Pfeiffera ianthothele
- *lindbergiana* K. Schum. = Rhipsalis baccifera
- *megalantha* Loefgr. = Rhipsalis neves-armondii
- *mesembryanthemoides* Steud. = Rhipsalis mesembryanthoides
- **mesembryanthoides** Haw. · ♄ ⊬ Z9 ⊕ ▽ ✳; Braz.
- **neves-armondii** K. Schum. · ⊬ Z10 ⊕ ▽ ✳; Braz.
- **pachyptera** Pfeiff. · ♄ ⊬ Z9 ⊕ ▽ ✳; SE-Braz.
- **paradoxa** (Salm-Dyck ex Pfeiff.) Salm-Dyck · E:Chain Cactus · ♄ ⊬ Z9 ⊕ ▽ ✳; Braz.
- *penduliflora* N.E. Br. = Rhipsalis teres
- *pilocarpa* Loefgr. = Erythrorhipsalis pilocarpa
- *pittieri* Britton & Rose = Rhipsalis floccosa
- *prismatica* Rümpler = Rhipsalis teres
- **pulvinigera** G. Lindb. · ♄ ⊬ Z9 ⊕ ▽ ✳; Braz., NE-Parag.
- **puniceodiscus** G. Lindb.
- var. **chrysocarpa** (Loefgr.) Borg · ♄ ⊬ ⚡ Z9 ⊕ ▽ ✳; Braz.
- var. **puniceodiscus** · ♄ ⊬ Z9 ⊕ ▽ ✳; Braz.
- *purpusii* Weing. = Pseudorhipsalis ramulosa
- **rhombea** (Salm-Dyck) Pfeiff. · ♄ ⊬ ⚡ Z9 ⊕ ▽ ✳; Braz.
- *rosea* Lagerh. = Rhipsalidopsis rosea
- *saglionis* (Lem.) Otto ex Walp. = Rhipsalis cereuscula
- *salicornioides* Haw. = Hatiora salicornioides
- *shaferi* A. Berger = Rhipsalis baccifera

- *squamulosa* (Salm-Dyck) K. Schum. = Lepismium cruciforme
- **teres** (Vell.) Steud. · ♄ ⊬ ⚡ Z9 ⊕ ▽ ✳; Braz.
- f. **capilliformis** (F.A.C. Weber) Barthlott & N.P. Taylor · ♄ ⊬ ⚡ Z9 ⊕ ▽ ✳; E-Braz.
- **trigona** Pfeiff. · ♄ ⊬ Z9 ⊕ ▽ ✳; Braz.
- *virgata* F.A.C. Weber = Rhipsalis teres

Rhizophora L. -f- *Rhizophoraceae* · 8-9 spp. · F:Palétuvier; G:Manglebaum, Mangrovebaum
- **conjugata** L. · ♄ e ⌢ Z10 ⊕ Ⓝ; trop. As., trop. Afr.; mangrove
- **mangle** L. · E:Red Mangrove; G:Manglebaum, Mangrovebaum · ♄ e ⌢ Z10 ⊕ Ⓝ; S-Fla., trop. Am., W-Afr., C-Afr., Angola, Polyn.; mangrove
- **mucronata** Lam. · E:Upriver Stilt Mangrove · ♄ e ⌢ Z10 ⊕ Ⓝ; E-Afr., Ind., Sri Lanka, SE-As., Austr.: N.Terr., Queensl.; Jap.; mangrove

Rhodanthe Lindl. -n- *Asteraceae* · c. 45 spp. · E:Paper Daisy; F:Immortelle, Rhodanthe; G:Immortelle
- **humboldtianum** (Gaudich.) Paul G. Wilson · ☉ VII-VIII; W-Austr.
- **manglesii** Lindl. · E:Paper Daisy; G:Rosen-Immortelle · ☉ ✄ VII-VIII; W-Austr.

Rhodanthemum (Vogt) B.H. Wilcox, K. Bremer & Humphries -n- *Asteraceae* · 15 spp.
- **gayanum** (Coss. & Durieu) B.H. Wilcox et al. · ♄ Z8 ⊕ VII-VIII; Moroc., Alger.

Rhodiola L. -f- *Crassulaceae* · 58 spp. · E:Roseroot; F:Rhodiole; G:Rosenwurz
- *crassipes* (Wall. ex Hook. f. & Thomson) = Rhodiola wallichiana
- **heterodonta** (Hook. f. & Thomson) Boriss. · ⅘ ⊬ △ Z5; Afgh., W-Him., Tibet
- **hobsonii** (Prain ex Raym.-Hamet) S.H. Fu · ⅘ ⊬ △ Z5 VII-VIII; Tibet
- **kirilowii** (Regel) Regel ex Maxim. · ⅘ ⊬ △ Z5 VI; Him., Mong., NW-China
- **pachyclados** (Aitch. ex Hemsl.) H. Ohba · ⅘ ⊬; Afgh.
- *primuloides* (Franch.) S.H. Fu = Rhodiola pachyclados
- **rhodantha** (A. Gray) H. Jacobsen · ⅘ ⊬ △ Z4 VI-VII; USA: Rocky Mts., SW
- **rosea** L. · E:Roseroot; G:Rosenwurz · ⅘ ⊬

△ Z1 VI-VII; Eur.*, W-Sib., E-Sib., Amur,
Sakhal., Kamchat., Mong., Him., China
(Schansi), Can. (Labrador), Greenl.
- **semenovii** (Regel & Herder) Boriss. · ⹁ ⹁
△ Z6 VI-IX; C-As.
- **wallichiana** (Hook. f.) S.H. Hu · ⹁ ⹁ VI;
Him., W-China, Tibet
- **yunnanensis** (Franch.) S.H. Fu · ⹁ ⹁
△ Z6 VI-IX; China: Sichuan, Yunnan,
Hupeh, Schansi

Rhodocactus (A. Berger) F.M. Knuth =
Pereskia
- *bleo* (Kunth) F.M. Knuth = Pereskia bleo
- *grandifolius* (Haw.) F.M. Knuth =
Pereskia grandifolia
- *sacharosus* (Griseb.) Backeb. = Pereskia
sacharosa

Rhodochiton Zucc. ex Otto & A. Dietr. -m-
Scrophulariaceae · 3 spp. · E:Bell Vine;
G:Purpurglockenwein, Rosenkelch
- **atrosanguineus** (Zucc.) Rothm. ·
E:Purple Bell Vine; G:Windender
Purpurglockenwein · ⹁ ⹃ Z9 ⌂; Mex.
- *volubilis* Zucc. = Rhodochiton atrosan-
guineus

Rhododendron L. -n- *Ericaceae* · c.
800 spp. · E:Azalea, Rhododendron;
F:Azalée, Rhododendron; G:Alpenrose,
Azalee, Rhododendron
- **aberconwayi** Cowan · ⹁ e Z7 V-VI;
W-China, Yunnan
- *achroanthum* Balf. f. & W.W. Sm. =
Rhododendron rupicola var. rupicola
- **adenogynum** Diels · ⹁ e Z7 ⋀ IV; Yunnan
- *adoxum* Balf. f. & Forrest = Rhododendron vernicosum
- *aechmophyllum* Balf. f. & Forrest =
Rhododendron yunnanense
- **aganniphum** Balf. f. & Kingdon-Ward ·
⹁; W-China, SE-Tibet
- var. **aganniphum** · ⹁ Z7 ⋀ V; China:
Xizang, Yunnan, Sichuan
- **Glaucopeplum Group** · ; cult.
- **Schizopeplum Group** · ; cult.
- var. **flavorufum** (Balf. f. & Forrest) D.F.
Chamb. · ⹁ Z7 IV-V; SE-Tibet, China:
SE-Xizang
- *aiolopeplum* Balf. f. & Forrest = Rhododendron phaeochrysum var. levistratum
- **alabamense** Rehder & E.H. Wilson ·
E:Alabama Azalea; G:Alabama-Azalee · ⹁

d ⤳ Z7 V; USA: Ala.
- **albrechtii** Maxim. · E:Albrecht's Azalea;
F:Rhododendron d'Albrecht; G:Albrechts
Azalee · ⹁ d Z6 IV-V; Jap.
- *algarvense* Page = Rhododendron
ponticum
- *amaurophyllum* Balf. f. & Forrest =
Rhododendron saluenense
- **ambiguum** Hemsl. · ⹁ e Z6 IV-V; Sichuan
- *annamense* Rehder = Rhododendron
simsii
- *araliiforme* Balf. f. & Forrest = Rhododendron vernicosum
- **arborescens** (Pursh) Torr. · E:Smooth
Azalea, Sweet Azalea; F:Rhododendron
arborescent; G:Baumartige Azalee · ⹁ ⹁ d
D Z6 VI; USA: NE, SE
- **arboreum** Sm. · E:Tree Rhododendron;
G:Baum-Alpenrose · ⹁ ⹁ e Z8 ⌂ III-IV
�֍; Pakist., Him., SE-Tibet, Sri Lanka
- **argyrophyllum** Franch. · ⹁ e Z6 IV-V;
Tibet, W-Sichuan
- *artosquamatum* Balf. f. & Forrest =
Rhododendron oreotrephes
- *ashleyi* Coker = Rhododendron maximum
- *astrocalyx* Balf. f. & Forrest = Rhododendron wardii
- **atlanticum** (Ashe) Rehder & E.H.
Wilson · E:Dwarf Azalea; G:Atlantische
Azalee · ⹁ d D Z6 V; USA: NE, SE, Tex.
- *atroviride* Dunn = Rhododendron concinnum
- **augustinii** Hemsl. · E:Blue Rhododendron; G:Augustines Rhododendron · ⹁ e
Z6 IV-V; Yunnan, Sichuan, Hupeh
- **aureum** Georgi · ⹁ Z2 IV ✖; W-Sib.,
E-Sib., Amur, Sakhal., Kamchat., Mong.,
China, Korea, Jap.
- **auriculatum** Hemsl. · ⹁ e Z8 ⌂ VII-VIII;
China: Hupeh
- *baeticum* Boiss. & Reut. = Rhododendron
ponticum
- *balsaminiflorum* Carrière = Rhododendron indicum
- **barbatum** Wall. · ⹁ e Z8 ⌂ IV; Nepal,
Sikkim
- *benthamianum* Hemsl. = Rhododendron
concinnum Benthamianum Group
- *bicolor* P.C. Tam = Rhododendron simsii
- *blepharocalyx* Franch. = Rhododendron
intricatum
- *bodinieri* Franch. = Rhododendron
yunnanense
- **brachyanthum** Franch.
- subsp. **brachyanthum** · ⹁ e Z6 VI;

Yunnan
- subsp. **hypolepidotum** (Franch.) Cullen · ♄ e Z6; NE-Burma, China (NW-Yunnan, SE-Tibet)
- **brachycarpum** D. Don ex G. Don
- subsp. **brachycarpum** · ♄ e Z5 VI; Jap., Korea
- subsp. **fauriei** (Franch.) D.F. Chamb. Z6; Korea
- *brevitubum* Balf. f. & R.E. Cooper = Rhododendron maddenii
- **burmanicum** Hutch. · ♄ e Z9 ⓐ V; SW-Burma
- *caeruleoglaucum* Balf. f. & Forrest = Rhododendron campylogynum
- **calendulaceum** (Michx.) Torr. · E:Cumberland Azalea, Flame Azalea, Yellow Azalea; F:Rhododendron jaune; G:Gelbe Alpenrose · ♄ d Z6 V-VI; USA: NE, Ohio, SE
- **callimorphum** Balf. f. & W.W. Sm. · ♄ e Z7 ∧ VI; NE-Burma, Yunnan
- *calophyllum* Nutt. = Rhododendron maddenii
- **calophytum** Franch. · ♄ e Z7 ∧ IV; Tibet, W-Sichuan
- **calostrotum** Balf. f. & Kingdon-Ward
- subsp. **calostrotum** · ♄ e △ Z7 ∧ IV; Ind., NE-Burma
- subsp. **keleticum** (Balf. f. & Forrest) Cullen · ♄ e △ Z7 ∧ IV; SE-Tibet
- **Radicans Group** · ; NE-Burma, W-China
- **campanulatum** D. Don · G:Glocken-blütiger Rhododendron · ♄ e Z7 IV-V; Kashmir, Him., SE-Tibet
- **campylocarpum** Hook. f. · ♄ ♄ e Z6 ∧ IV-V ⚕; Him., China (Tibet)
- **campylogynum** Franch. · ♄ e Z7 V-VI; Burma, SE-Tibet, W-Yunnan
- **camtschaticum** Pall. · E:Kamchatka Rhododendron; F:Rhododendron du Kamtchatka; G:Kamtschatka-Azalee · ♄ d Z5 V; Kamchat., Sakhal., Jap., Alaska
- **canadense** (L.) Torr. · E:Rhodora; F:Rhododendron du Canada; G:Kanadische Azalee · ♄ d Z5 IV-V; Can.: E; USA: NE
- *cantabile* Hutch. = Rhododendron russatum
- **capitatum** Maxim. · ♄ e Z8 ⓐ V; China: Kansu
- *cardoeoides* Balf. f. & Forrest = Rhododendron oreotrephes
- **catawbiense** Michx. · E:Catawba Rho-dodendron, Catawba Rosebay, Mountain

Rose Bay; G:Catawba-Rhododendron · ♄ e Z5 V-VI ⚕; USA: Va., W.Va., SE
- **caucasicum** Pall. · F:Rhododendron du Caucase; G:Kaukasus-Rhododendron · ♄ e Z5 V; Cauc.
- **cephalanthum** Franch. · ♄ e △ Z8 ⓐ ∧ V; Yunnan, Sichuan
- *cerasiflorum* Kingdon-Ward = Rhododendron campylogynum
- *chamaetortum* Balf. f. & Kingdon-Ward = Rhododendron cephalanthum
- **charitopes** Balf. f. & Farrer
- subsp. **charitopes** · ♄ e ⓐ; N-Burma
- subsp. **tsangpoense** (Kingdon-Ward) Cullen · ♄ e; Tibet, Burma, Ind. (Assam)
- *charitostreptum* Balf. f. & Kingdon-Ward = Rhododendron brachyanthum subsp. hypolepidotum
- *chartophyllum* Franch. = Rhododendron yunnanense
- *chengshienianum* W.P. Fang = Rhododendron ambiguum
- *chrysanthum* Pall. = Rhododendron aureum
- *chryseum* Balf. f. & Kingdon-Ward = Rhododendron rupicola var. chryseum
- **ciliatum** Hook. f. · ♄ e Z8 ⓐ IV; Nepal, Bhutan, China
- **ciliicalyx** Franch. · ♄ e D Z7 III-IV; Yunnan
- *cinereum* Balf. f. & Forrest = Rhododendron cuneatum
- **cinnabarinum** Hook. f. · ♄ e Z7 ∧ V-VI; Sikkim
- **clementinae** Forrest · ♄ e Z6 V; NW-Yunnan, SW-Sichuan
- *compactum* Hutch. = Rhododendron polycladum
- **concinnum** Hemsl. · G:Reizender Rhododendron · ♄ d Z7 ∧ IV-V; Sichuan
- **Benthamianum Group**
- **Pseudoyanthinum Group** · ♄ e IV-V; SW-China
- *coombense* Hemsl. = Rhododendron concinnum
- *coreanum* Rehder = Rhododendron yedoense var. poukhanense
- *coryi* Shinners = Rhododendron viscosum
- *cosmetum* Balf. f. & Forrest = Rhododendron saluenense
- *crispiflorum* Planch. = Rhododendron indicum
- *croceum* Balf. f. & W.W. Sm. = Rhododendron wardii
- **cuneatum** W.W. Sm. · ♄ e △ Z5 IV;

Yunnan, Sichuan
- *cuprescens* Nitz. = Rhododendron phaeochrysum var. phaeochrysum
- *cuthbertii* Small = Rhododendron minus
- *cyclium* Balf. f. & Forrest = Rhododendron callimorphum
- **dalhousiae** Hook. f.
- var. **dalhousiae** · ♄ e D Z9 ⓚ V-VI; Ind., Nepal, Bhutan, China, Burma
- var. **rhabdotum** (Balf. f. & R.E. Cooper) Cullen · ♄ e Z9 VI; Bhutan
- *damascenum* Balf. f. & Forrest = Rhododendron campylogynum
- **dauricum** L. · ♄ d; W-Sib.(Altai, Sajan), N-Mong.
- var. **dauricum** · E:Chinese Alprose; F:Rhododendron nain de Sibérie; G:Dahurische Azalee · ♄ d Z5 II-III; E-Sib., Amur, Mong., Manch.
- var. **sempervirens** Sims · ♄ d Z5; W-Sib., Mong.
- **davidsonianum** Rehder & E.H. Wilson · ♄ e Z7 ∧ IV-V; Yunnan, Sichuan
- **decorum** Franch.
- subsp. **decorum** · ♄ e D Z7 ∧ IV-VI; Yunnan, Sichuan
- subsp. **diaprepes** (Balf. f. & W.W. Sm.) T.L. Ming · ♄ e Z7 V; NE-Burma, Yunnan
- *decumbens* D. Don ex G. Don = Rhododendron indicum
- **degronianum** Carrière
- subsp. **degronianum** · E:Metternich's Rhododendron; F:Rhododendron de Metternich; G:Japanischer Rhododendron · ♄ e Z5 IV ✿; Jap.
- var. *pentamerum* (Maxim.) Hutch. = Rhododendron degronianum subsp. degronianum
- subsp. **yakushimanum** (Nakai) H. Hara · E:Yak; F:Rhododendron de Yakushima; G:Yakushima-Rhododendron · ♄ e Z6 VI; Jap.
- *depile* Balf. f. & Forrest = Rhododendron oreotrephes
- *desquamatum* Balf. f. & Forrest = Rhododendron rubiginosum Desquamatum Group
- *diaprepes* Balf. f. & W.W. Sm. = Rhododendron decorum subsp. diaprepes
- **dichroanthum** Diels · ♄ e Z7 ∧ V-VI; Yunnan
- *dichropeplum* Balf. f. & Forrest = Rhododendron phaeochrysum var. levistratum
- *dilatatum* Miq. = Rhododendron reticulatum

- *discolor* Franch. = Rhododendron fortunei subsp. discolor
- *dryophyllum* Balf. f. & Forrest = Rhododendron phaeochrysum var. phaeochrysum
- *dryophyllum* hort. = Rhododendron phaeochrysum var. levistratum
- **edgeworthii** Hook. f. · ♄ e D Z9 ⓚ IV-V; Ind., Bhutan, China, Burma
- **falconeri** Hook. f. · ♄ e Z9 ⓚ IV-V; Him.: Nepal, Bhutan
- *fargesii* Franch. = Rhododendron oreodoxa var. fargesii
- **fastigiatum** Franch. · E:Azalea; G:Aufstrebender Rhododendron · ♄ e △ Z6 IV-V; Yunnan
- *fauriei* Franch. = Rhododendron brachycarpum subsp. fauriei
- **ferrugineum** L. · E:Alpine Rose, Rusty Leaved Alprose; F:Rhododendron ferrugineux, Rose des Alpes; G:Rostblättrige Alpenrose · ♄ e Z5 V-VI ❦ ✿; Eur.: sp., F, I, C-Eur., Slove., Croat.; Pyr., Alp., Jura
- *fictolacteum* Balf. f. = Rhododendron rex subsp. fictolacteum
- **flammeum** (Michx.) Sarg. · E:Piedmont Azalea · ♄ d; USA: S.C., Ga.
- *flavorufum* Balf. f. & Forrest = Rhododendron aganniphum var. flavorufum
- *flavum* G. Don = Rhododendron luteum
- **floribundum** Franch. · ♄ e Z8 ∧ IV; China: E-Yunnan, S-Sichuan
- **forrestii** Balf. f. ex Diels
- **many cultivars**
- **Repens Group** · ♄ e Z6; cult.
- subsp. **forrestii** · E:Forrest's Rhododendron; G:Forrests Rhododendron · ♄ e ⤳ △ Z8 ∧ IV; NW-Yunnan, SE-Tibet
- var. *repens* (Balf. f. & Forrest) Cowan & Davidian = Rhododendron forrestii
- **fortunei** Lindl.
- subsp. **discolor** (Franch.) D.F. Chamb. · G:Verschiedenfarbiger Rhododendron · ♄ ♄ e Z7 ∧ VI-VII; China: Hupeh, Sichuan
- **Houlstonii Group** · ♄ e V-VI; China: Sichuan, Hupeh
- subsp. **fortunei** · E:Fortune's Rhododendron; G:Fortunes Rhododendron · ♄ e D Z7 ∧ V-VII; China: Tschekiang
- *franchetianum* H. Lév. = Rhododendron decorum subsp. decorum
- **fraseri** W. Watson · ♄ d IV; cult.
- **fulgens** Hook. f. · ♄ e Z7 ∧ III; Him: Nepal, Bhutan
- **fulvum** Balf. f. & W.W. Sm. · ♄ e Z7 ∧

III-V; Sichuan, W-Yunnan
- *giraudiasii* H. Lév. = Rhododendron decorum subsp. decorum
- *glaucoaureum* Balf. f. & Forrest = Rhododendron campylogynum
- *glaucopeplum* Balf. f. & Forrest = Rhododendron aganniphum var. aganniphum Glaucopeplum Group
- **glaucophyllum** Rehder · ♄ e △ Z8 ⚐ ∧ V; Ind., Nepal, Bhutan, China
- *glaucum* Hook. f. non Sweet = Rhododendron glaucophyllum
- *gloeblastum* Balf. f. & Forrest = Rhododendron wardii
- *gnaphalocarpum* Hayata = Rhododendron mariesii
- **grande** Wight · ♄ ♄ e Z8 ⚐ II-III; Bhutan, Sikkim
- **griersonianum** Balf. f. & Forrest · ♄ e Z8 ⚐ V-VI; W-Yunnan
- **griffithianum** Wight · ♄ e D Z8 ⚐ V; Him.: Sikkim, Bhutan
- *haemaleum* Balf. f. & Forrest = Rhododendron sanguineum subsp. sanguineum var. haemaleum
- **haematodes** Franch. · G:Blutroter Rhododendron · ♄ e Z7 V; Yunnan
- *hallaisanense* H. Lév. = Rhododendron yedoense var. poukhanense
- **hanceanum** Hemsl. · ♄ e Z8 ⚐; SW-China: Sichuan
- *harrovianum* Hemsl. = Rhododendron polylepis
- *hedythamnum* Balf. f. & Forrest = Rhododendron callimorphum
- *heftii* Davidian = Rhododendron wallichii
- **heliolepis** Franch. · ♄ e Z8 ∧ V-VI; Burma, Yunnan
- *helvolum* Balf. f. & Forrest = Rhododendron phaeochrysum var. levistratum
- **hemitrichotum** Balf. f. & Forrest · ♄ e △ Z8 ⚐ ∧ IV; N-Yunnan, SW-Sichuan
- *hexamerum* Hand.-Mazz. = Rhododendron vernicosum
- **hippophaeoides** Balf. f. & W.W. Sm. · G:Grauer Rhododendron · ♄ e △ Z6 IV; Yunnan
- **hirsutum** L. · E:Hairy Alpen Rose; F:Rhododendron pubescent, Rhododendron cilié; G:Bewimperte Alpenrose · ♄ e △ Z5 VI; Eur.: F, I, C-Eur., Slove., Croatia, Bosn.; Alp., mts.
- *hispidum* (Pursh) Torr. = Rhododendron viscosum
- **hodgsonii** Hook. f. · ♄ e Z9 ⚐ IV; Him.:

Nepal, Bhutan
- *hormophorum* Balf. f. & Forrest = Rhododendron yunnanense
- *houlstonii* Hemsl. & E.H. Wilson = Rhododendron fortunei subsp. discolor Houlstonii Group
- **hunnewellianum** Rehder & E.H. Wilson · ♄ e Z9 ⚐ III-IV; W-Sichuan
- *hutchinsonianum* W.P. Fang = Rhododendron concinnum
- *hypolepidotum* (Franch.) Balf. f. & Forrest = Rhododendron brachyanthum subsp. hypolepidotum
- *hypotrichotum* Balf. f. & Forrest = Rhododendron oreotrephes
- *imberbe* Hutch. = Rhododendron barbatum
- **impeditum** Balf. f. & W.W. Sm. · F:Rhododendron en coussinet; G:Veilchenblauer Rhododendron · ♄ e Z7 IV; China (SW-Sichuan)
- **some cultivars**
- **indicum** (L.) Sweet · E:Japanese Azalea · ♄ e Z8 ⚐ ∧ VI; Jap.
- var. *japonicum* Makino = Rhododendron kiusianum
- **insigne** Hemsl. & E.H. Wilson · G:Ausgezeichneter Rhododendron · ♄ e Z6 V-VI; SW-Sichuan
- × **intermedium** Tausch (R. ferrugineum × R. hirsutum) · ♄ e; cult.
- *intortum* Balf. f. & Forrest = Rhododendron phaeochrysum var. levistratum
- **intricatum** Franch. · ♄ e Z7 ∧ IV; W-Sichuan
- **irroratum** Franch.
- subsp. **irroratum** · ♄ ♄ e Z8 ⚐ III-IV; Yunnan
- subsp. *ningyuenense* (Hand.-Mazz.) T.L. Ming = Rhododendron irroratum subsp. irroratum
- *jenkinsii* Nutt. = Rhododendron maddenii
- **kaempferi** Planch. · E:Kaempfer's Azalea; G:Kaempfers Azalee · ♄ d Z6 IV-V; Jap.
- var. *japonicum* Rehder = Rhododendron kiusianum
- **keiskei** Miq. · E:Keisuke's Rhododendron; G:Keisukes Rhododendron · ♄ e Z6 IV-V ⚘; Jap.
- *keleticum* Balf. f. & Forrest = Rhododendron calostrotum subsp. keleticum
- **keysii** Nutt. · ♄ e Z7 ∧ V; C-Jap.
- **kiusianum** Makino · G:Kyushu-Azalee · ♄ e Z6 IV-V; Jap.
- *kwangfuense* Chun & W.P. Fang =

Rhododendron fortunei subsp. discolor
- **kyawii** Lace & W.W. Sm. · ♄ ♄ e Z9 ⓦ ⓚ V; NE-Burma
- **lacteum** Franch. · ♄ ♄ e Z7; China (W-Yunnan)
- var. *macrophyllum* Franch. = Rhododendron rex subsp. fictolacteum
- × **laetevirens** Rehder (*R. carolinianum* × *R. ferrugineum*) · ♄ e ⓚ V-VI; cult.
- *lancifolium* Hook. f. = Rhododendron barbatum
- *lancifolium* Moench = Rhododendron ponticum
- **lapponicum** (L.) Wahlenb. · E:Lapland Rhododendron; G:Alaska-Rhododendron · ♄ e △ Z2 IV; Eur.: Sc, N-Russ.; E-Sib., Jap., Alaska, Can., USA: NE, NCE; Greenl.
- *laticostum* J.W. Ingram = Rhododendron keiskei
- *leclerei* H. Lév. = Rhododendron rubiginosum
- *ledebourii* Pojark. = Rhododendron dauricum
- *ledifolium* (Hook.) G. Don = Rhododendron mucronatum
- *ledoides* Balf. f. & W.W. Sm. = Rhododendron trichostomum Ledoides Group
- **lepidostylum** Balf. f. & Forrest · ♄ e Z6 IV-V; W-Yunnan
- **lepidotum** G. Don · ♄ e Z6 V-VI; Him., Burma, Sichuan, Yunnan, Tibet
- **leucaspis** Tagg · ♄ e Z7 △ II-III; Tibet
- *leucolasium* Diels = Rhododendron hunnewellianum
- *linearifolium* Siebold & Zucc. = Rhododendron stenopetalum 'Linearifolium'
- *litangense* Balf. f. ex Hutch. = Rhododendron impeditum
- × **loderi** hort. (*R. griffithianum* × *R. fortunei*) · ♄; cult.
- *longifolium* Nutt. = Rhododendron grande
- *lophogynum* Balf. f. & Forrest = Rhododendron trichocladum
- *lucidum* Franch. = Rhododendron vernicosum
- **lutescens** Franch. · ♄ e Z7 △ III-IV; Sichuan
- *luteum* (L.) C.K. Schneid. = Rhododendron calendulaceum
- **many cultivars**
- **luteum** Sweet · E:Common Yellow Azalea; F:Rhododendron jaune; G:Pontische Azalee · ♄ d D Z5 V ✿; Eur.:

? A, Slove., PL, Russ.; TR, Cauc., nat. in BrI
- *macrogemmum* Nakai = Rhododendron kaempferi
- **macrosepalum** Maxim. = Rhododendron stenopetalum
- var. *linearifolium* (Siebold & Zucc.) Makino = Rhododendron stenopetalum 'Linearifolium'
- **maddenii** Hook. f. · E:Maddenii; G:Vietnamesischer Rhododendron · ♄ e D Z9 ⓚ VI; Ind., Bhutan, China, Burma, Vietn.
- **makinoi** Tagg · ♄ e Z8 △; Jap.
- *mandarinorum* Diels = Rhododendron fortunei subsp. discolor
- **mariesii** Hemsl. & E.H. Wilson · ♄ e Z8 △ V; C-China, SE-China
- **maximum** L. · E:Great Laurel, Rosebay; G:Riesen-Rhododendron · ♄ ♄ d Z5 VI-VII ⓝ; Can.: E; USA: NE, SE
- **mekongense** Franch. · ♄ e Z9 ⓚ; Nepal, NE-Burma, China (Yunnan, Tibet)
- var. *longipilosum* Cullen = Rhododendron trichocladum
- **metternichii** Siebold & Zucc.
- var. *angustifolium* (Makino) Bean = Rhododendron makinoi
- var. *pentamerum* Maxim. = Rhododendron degronianum subsp. degronianum
- var. *yakushimanum* (Nakai) Ohwi = Rhododendron degronianum subsp. yakushimanum
- **micranthum** Turcz. · G:Kleinblütiger Rhododendron · ♄ e Z5 VI; N-China, N-Korea
- **microgynum** Balf. f. & Forrest · ♄ Z8 ⓚ; W-China, SE-Tibet
- **Gymnocarpum Group** · ♄ ⓚ V; SE-Tibet
- **minus** Michx. · E:Carolina Rhododendron; F:Petit rhododendron, Rhododendron de Caroline; G:Kleiner Rhododendron · ♄ e Z6 VI-VII; USA: SE
- *missionarium* H. Lév. = Rhododendron ciliicalyx
- *modestum* Hook. f. = Rhododendron ciliatum
- **molle** (Blume) G. Don
- **many cultivars**
- subsp. **japonicum** (A. Gray) Kron · E:Renge Tutuji; G:Japanische Azalee · ♄ d Z5 V ✿; Jap.
- subsp. **molle** · E:Chinese Azalea; G:Chinesische Azalee · ♄ d Z5 V-VI ✿; C-China, E-China

– × **mortieri** Sweet (*R. calendulaceum* × *R. periclymenoides*) · ♄; cult.
– *motsouense* H. Lév. = Rhododendron racemosum
– **moupinense** Franch. · ♄ e Z8 ⓚ I-II; E-Tibet, Sichuan
– **mucronatum** (Blume) G. Don · F:Rhododendron ; G:Porstblättriger Rhododendron · ♄ d D Z6 V; Jap.
– **mucronulatum** Turcz.
– var. *ciliatum* Nakai = Rhododendron mucronulatum var. mucronulatum
– var. **mucronulatum** · G:Stachelspitzige Azalee · ♄ e Z5 II-III; China, Amur, E-Sib., Mong., Korea, Jap.
– **myrtifolium** Schott & Kotschy · F:Rhododendron à feuilles de myrte · ♄ e △ Z5 V; Eur.: BG, RO, W-Russ.
– *nanum* H. Lév. = Rhododendron fastigiatum
– *neglectum* Ashe = Rhododendron atlanticum
– **neriiflorum** Franch. · ♄ e Z7 ∧ IV-V; Yunnan
– *nikoense* Nakai = Rhododendron pentaphyllum
– *ningyuenense* Hand.-Mazz. = Rhododendron irroratum subsp. irroratum
– **nipponicum** Matsum. · ♄ d Z7 V; Jap.
– *nitidum* (Pursh) Torr. = Rhododendron viscosum
– *nudiflorum* (L.) Torr. = Rhododendron periclymenoides
– **nuttallii** T.J. Booth · ♄ e D Z10 ⓚ IV-V; Ind., China
– *nwaiense* Balf. f. & Kingdon-Ward = Rhododendron cephalanthum
– *oblongum* Griff. = Rhododendron griffithianum
– × **obtusum** (Lindl.) Planch. (*R. kaempferi* × *R. kiusianum* var. *kiusianum*) · G:Stumpfblättrige Azalee · ♄ d Z6 IV-V; Jap.
– **many cultivars**
– **'Amoenum' (A-ev)**
– var. *japonicum* Kitam. = Rhododendron kiusianum
– var. *kaempferi* (Planch.) E.H. Wilson = Rhododendron kaempferi
– **occidentale** (Torr. & A. Gray) A. Gray · E:Western Azalea; G:Westliche Azalee · ♄ d Z6 VI; USA: Oreg., Calif.
– *oporinum* Balf. f. & Kingdon-Ward = Rhododendron heliolepis
– **orbiculare** Decne. · F:Rhododendron à feuilles rondes; G:Rundblättriger Rhododendron · ♄ e Z6 IV; W-Sichuan
– **oreodoxa** Franch.
– var. **fargesii** (Franch.) D.F. Chamb. · ♄ e Z6 IV; China: Hupeh, Sichuan
– var. **oreodoxa** · G:Bergruhm-Rhododendron · ♄ e Z6 III-IV; W-Sichuan
– **oreotrephes** W.W. Sm. · ♄ e Z6 V; Yunnan, SE-Tibet
– *oresterum* Balf. f. & Forrest = Rhododendron wardii
– **orthocladum** Balf. f. & Forrest · ♄ e △ Z6 IV; N-Yunnan, Sichuan
– *osmerum* Balf. f. & Forrest = Rhododendron russatum
– *oulotrichum* Balf. f. & Forrest = Rhododendron trichocladum
– *palustre* Turcz. = Rhododendron lapponicum
– *parviflorum* F. Schmidt = Rhododendron lapponicum
– **pemakoense** Kingdon-Ward · ♄ e △ Z6 III-IV; Ind., Tibet (Pemako-Mts.)
– **pentaphyllum** Maxim. · E:Fiveleaf Azalea; G:Nikko-Azalee · ♄ d Z7 IV-V; Jap.
– *peramabile* Hutch. = Rhododendron intricatum
– **peregrinum** Tagg · ♄ ♄ e Z7 IV-V; SW-Sichuan
– **periclymenoides** (Michx.) Shinners · E:Pink Azalea, Pinxterbloom; G:Nacktblütige Azalee · ♄ d Z3 V; USA: NE, Ohio, SE
– *perulatum* Balf. f. & Forrest = Rhododendron microgynum
– *phaeochlorum* Balf. f. & Forrest = Rhododendron oreotrephes
– **phaeochrysum** Balf. f. & W.W. Sm.
– var. **levistratum** (Balf. & Forrest) D.F. Chamb. · ♄ e Z8 ⓚ; W-China
– var. **phaeochrysum** · ♄ e Z8 ⓚ; W-China
– *plebeium* Balf. f. & W.W. Sm. = Rhododendron heliolepis
– **polycladum** Franch. · ♄ e Z8 ⓚ; W-China
– **Scintillans Group** · ♄ △ Z8 ⓚ IV-V; Yunnan (Likiang)
– **polylepis** Franch. · ♄ e Z8 ⓚ IV; W-Sichuan
– **ponticum** L. · E:Ponticum, Purple Rhododendron; G:Pontische Alpenrose, Pontischer Rhododendron · ♄ e Z6 V-VI; Eur.: Ib, BG; TR, Cauc., nat. in Fr, BrI
– *poukhanense* H. Lév. = Rhododendron

yedoense var. poukhanense
- × **praecox** Carrière (*R. ciliatum*
  × *R. dauricum* var. *dauricum*) ·
  F:Rhododendron précoce; G:Vorfrüh-
  lings-Rhododendron · ♄ d Z6 III-IV; cult.
- *prasinocalyx* Balf. f. & Forrest = Rhododendron wardii
- **prinophyllum** (Small) Millais · E:Early
  Azalea · ♄ d D V; Can.: E; USA: NE, NCE,
  Okla., SE
- *pritzelianum* Diels = Rhododendron
  micranthum
- *procerum* Salisb. = Rhododendron
  maximum
- *prophanthum* Balf. f. & Forrest =
  Rhododendron kyawii
- *propinquum* Tagg = Rhododendron
  rupicola var. rupicola
- **przewalskii** Maxim. · ♄ e Z6 VI; China:
  NW-China, Tibet, Sichuan
- *pseudociliicalyx* Hutch. = Rhododendron
  ciliicalyx
- *pseudoyanthinum* Balf. f. ex Hutch. =
  Rhododendron concinnum Pseudoyanthinum Group
- *pubigerum* Balf. f. & Forrest = Rhododendron oreotrephes
- *purpureum* (Pursh) G. Don = Rhododendron maximum
- **quinquefolium** Bisset & S. Moore ·
  E:Cork Azalea; G:Fünfblättrige Azalee · ♄
  d Z6 IV-V; Jap.
- **racemosum** Franch. · G:Traubiger
  Rhododendron · ♄ e △ Z5 IV; Yunnan
- *radicans* Balf. f. & Forrest = Rhododendron calostrotum subsp. keleticum
  Radicans Group
- *rasile* Balf. f. & W.W. Sm. = Rhododendron decorum subsp. diaprepes
- **recurvoides** Tagg & Kingdon-Ward · ♄ e
  Z9 ⓚ V; N-Burma
- *reginaldii* Balf. f. = Rhododendron
  oreodoxa var. oreodoxa
- *repens* Balf. f. & Forrest = Rhododendron
  forrestii
- **reticulatum** D. Don ex G. Don · G:Netza-
  derige Azalee · ♄ d Z6 IV-V; Jap.
- **rex** H. Lév.
- subsp. **fictolacteum** (Balf. f.) D.F.
  Chamb. · ♄ ♄ Z8 ⓚ IV-V; Yunnan,
  Sichuan
- subsp. **rex** · ♄ e Z7; W-China, NE-Burma
- *rhabdotum* Balf. f. & R.E. Cooper = Rhododendron dalhousiae var. rhabdotum
- *rhantum* Balf. f. & W.W. Sm. =

Rhododendron vernicosum
- *rhodora* S.G. Gmel. = Rhododendron
  canadense
- *rhombicum* Miq. = Rhododendron
  reticulatum
- *rosthornii* Diels = Rhododendron
  micranthum
- **rubiginosum** Franch. · ♄ e Z7 ∧ IV-V;
  Yunnan
- **Desquamatum Group** · ; cult.
- *rubriflorum* Kingdon-Ward = Rhododendron campylogynum
- **rupicola** W.W. Sm.
- var. **chryseum** (Balf. F. & Kingdon-
  Ward) Philipson & M.N. Philipson ·
  G:Goldener Rhododendron · ♄ e Z7 V;
  SW-China: SW-Sichuan, NW-Yunnan;
  N-Burma
- var. **rupicola** · ♄ e △ Z7 IV-V; Yunnan
- **russatum** Balf. f. & Forrest · G:Rötlicher
  Rhododendron · ♄ e △ Z6 IV-V; NW-
  Yunnan
- *sakawanum* Makino = Rhododendron
  reticulatum
- **saluenense** Franch. · ♄ e Z7 ∧ IV-V;
  NW-Yunnan
- **sanguineum** Franch.
- subsp. *mesaeum* (Balf. f.) Cowan =
  Rhododendron sanguineum subsp.
  sanguineum var. haemaleum
- subsp. **sanguineum** · ♄ e Z8 ⓚ ∧ V;
  W-China
- var. **haemaleum** (Balf. f. & Forrest) D.F.
  Chamb. Z8 ⓚ; Yunnan, SE-Tibet
- **sargentianum** Rehder & E.H. Wilson · ♄
  e Z8 ⓚ ∧ V; Sichuan
- **schlippenbachii** Maxim. ·
  E:Schlippenbach's Azalea;
  F:Rhododendron de Schlippenbach;
  G:Schlippenbachs Azalee · ♄ d Z5 IV-V;
  Jap., Korea, NE-Manch.
- *sciaphilum* Balf. f. & Kingdon-Ward =
  Rhododendron edgeworthii
- *scintillans* Balf. f. & W.W. Sm. = Rhododendron polycladum Scintillans Group
- *sclerocladum* Balf. f. & Forrest = Rhododendron cuneatum
- **searsiae** Rehder & E.H. Wilson · ♄ e Z7
  ∧ IV-V; W-Sichuan
- *semanteum* Balf. f. = Rhododendron
  impeditum
- *sericocalyx* Balf. f. & Forrest = Rhododendron saluenense
- *sheltonii* Hemsl. & E.H. Wilson =
  Rhododendron vernicosum

– *shojoense* Hayata = Rhododendron mariesii
– *sichotense* Pojark. = Rhododendron dauricum
– *siderophylloides* Hutch. = Rhododendron oreotrephes
– *sieboldii* Miq. = Rhododendron kaempferi
– *sigillatum* Balf. f. & Forrest = Rhododendron phaeochrysum var. levistratum
– **simsii** Planch. · E:Indian Azalea; G:Indica-Azalee · ♄ e Z7 V ✿; China, Taiwan
– *sinense* (Lodd.) Sweet = Rhododendron molle subsp. molle
– **sinogrande** Balf. f. & W.W. Sm. · ♄ ♄ e Z8 ⓚ IV; NE-Burma, Yunnan, SE-Tibet
– *sinolepidotum* Balf. f. = Rhododendron lepidotum
– *sinonuttallii* Balf. f. & Forrest = Rhododendron nuttallii
– **smirnowii** Trautv. · E:Smirnow's Rhododendron; F:Rhododendron de Smirnow; G:Smirnows Rhododendron · ♄ e Z5 V-VI; NE-TR, Cauc.
– *sonomense* Greene = Rhododendron occidentale
– *speciosum* (Willd.) Sweet = Rhododendron calendulaceum
– **sperabile** Balf. f. & Farrer · ♄ e Z8 ⓚ V; NE-Burma
– *spooneri* Hemsl. & E.H. Wilson = Rhododendron decorum subsp. decorum
– *squarrosum* Balf. f. = Rhododendron rubiginosum
– **stenopetalum** (R. Hogg) Mabb. · ♄ △ IV-V; Jap.
– **'Linearifolium'**
– *stenophyllum* Makino = Rhododendron makinoi
– *stenoplastum* Balf. f. & Forrest = Rhododendron rubiginosum
– *strictum* H. Lév. = Rhododendron yunnanense
– **strigillosum** Franch. · ♄ e Z8 ⓚ II-III; Sichuan
– **sutchuenense** Franch. · F:Rhododendron du Sichuan; G:Sichuan-Rhododendron · ♄ e Z6 III-IV; China: Hupeh, Sichuan
– **taliense** Franch. · ♄ e Z6 V; W-Yunnan
– **tapetiforme** Balf. f. & Kingdon-Ward · ♄ △ Z5 IV-V; Burma, China: Xizang, Yunnan
– *taquettii* H. Lév. = Rhododendron mucronulatum var. mucronulatum
– *theiophyllum* Balf. f. & Forrest = Rhododendron phaeochrysum var. levistratum
– **thomsonii** Hook. f.
– subsp. **thomsonii** · ♄ e Z7 △ IV; Sikkim, Bhutan, Tibet
– **traillianum** Forrest & W.W. Sm.
– var. **trailianum** · ♄ e Z7 IV-V; NW-Yunnan, SW-Sichuan
– *trichocalyx* J.W. Ingram = Rhododendron keiskei
– **trichocladum** Franch. · ♄ d Z6; W-China: Yunnan; NE-Burma, E-Nepal
– *trichopodum* Balf. f. & Forrest = Rhododendron oreotrephes
– **trichostomum** Franch. · ♄ e Z7; China (Yunnan, Sichuan)
– **Ledoides Group** · ♄ d ⓚ; SW-China: Yunnan, Sichuan
– **triflorum** Hook. f. · ♄ e Z7 △ IV-V; Ind., Nepal, Bhutan, Tibet, NE-Burma
– *tsangpoense* Kingdon-Ward = Rhododendron charitopes subsp. tsangpoense
– var. *curvistylum* Kingdon-Ward ex Cowan & Davidian = Rhododendron charitopes subsp. tsangpoense
– **tschonoskii** Maxim. · ♄ d Z6 V; Jap., S-Korea
– *umbelliferum* H. Lév. = Rhododendron mariesii
– **ungernii** Trautv. · E:Ungern's Rhododendron; G:Ungerns Rhododendron · ♄ e Z5 VI ✿; NE-TR, Cauc.
– **vaseyi** A. Gray · E:Pink Shell Azalea; F:Rhododendron de Vasey; G:Vaseys Azalee · ♄ d Z5 IV-V; USA: N.C.
– **vernicosum** Franch. · ♄ ♄ e Z7 △ V; W-Sichuan, W-Yunnan
– *viburnifolium* W.P. Fang = Rhododendron simsii
– *vicinum* Balf. f. & Forrest = Rhododendron phaeochrysum var. levistratum
– **viscosum** (L.) Torr. · E:Swamp Azalea; G:Sumpf-Rhododendron · ♄ d D Z5 IV; USA: NE, Ohio, SE
– **wallichii** Hook. f. · ♄ e Z7 △ IV; Sikkim
– **wardii** W.W. Sm. · E:Ward's Rhododendron; F:Rhododendron wardii; G:Wards Rhododendron · ♄ e Z7 △ V; SE-Tibet, Sichuan, W-Yunnan
– **wightii** Hook. f. · E:Wight's Rhododendron; G:Wights Rhododendron · ♄ e Z7 IV-V; Him.: Nepal, Sikkim, Buthan; N-Ind., SE-Tibet, W-China: Sinkiang
– **williamsianum** Rehder & E.H. Wilson · E:William's Rhododendron; G:Williams

Rhododendron · ♄ e Z6 IV; Sichuan
- **many cultivars**
- *xanthinum* Balf. f. & W.W. Sm. =
  Rhododendron trichocladum
- *yakushimanum* Nakai = Rhododendron
  degronianum subsp. yakushimanum
- subsp. *makinoi* D.F. Chamb. = Rhododendron makinoi
- **yedoense** Maxim. ex Regel
- var. **yedoense** · ♄ d Z6; Korea
- var. **poukhanense** (H. Lév.) Nakai · ♄ d
  Z6 V; C-Korea, Jap.
- **yunnanense** Franch. · F:Rhododendron
  du Yunnan; G:Yunnan-Rhododendron ·
  ♄ e Z7 ∧ V; NE-Burma, China: Sichuan,
  Yunnan, Tibet
- **Cultivars:**
- **many cultivars, see Section III**

Rhodohypoxis Nel -f- *Hypoxidaceae* ·
6 spp.
- **baurii** (Baker) Nel · ⚃ △ Z8 ⓐ ∧ VII-
  VIII; S-Afr.; mts.
- **Cultivars:**
- **many cultivars**

Rhodomyrtus (DC.) Rchb. -f- *Myrtaceae* ·
11 sp. · E:Rose Myrtle; F:Myrte; G:Rosenmyrte
- **tomentosa** (Aiton) Hassk. · E:Ceylon Hill
  Cherry, Rose Myrtle; G:Rosenmyrte · ♄ e
  ⚭ Z10 ⓦ VI; trop. As.

Rhodophiala C. Presl -f- *Amaryllidaceae* ·
12 spp.
- **pratensis** (Poepp.) Traub · ⚃ Z9 ⓦ III-V;
  Chile

Rhodospatha Poepp. -f- *Araceae* · 12 spp.
- **heliconiifolia** Schott · ♄ ⚑ Z10 ⓦ; trop.
  S-Am.

Rhodothamnus Rchb. -m- *Ericaceae* ·
2 spp. · F:Rhodothamnus; G:Zwergalpenrose
- *camtschaticus* (Pall.) Lindl. = Rhododendron camtschaticum
- **chamaecistus** (L.) Rchb. · E:Dwarf
  Alpenrose; G:Ostalpine Zwergalpenrose ·
  ♄ ♄ e △ Z5 VI; Eur.: I, G, A, Slove.; E-Alp.
- **sessiliflorus** P.H. Davis · ♄ e; NE-TR

Rhodotypos Siebold & Zucc. -m- *Rosaceae* ·
1 sp. · F:Faux-kerria; G:Jabukistrauch,
Kaimastrauch, Scheinkerrie

- *kerrioides* Siebold & Zucc. = Rhodotypos
  scandens
- **scandens** (Thunb.) Makino · F:Rhodotype à quatre pétales; G:Jabukistrauch,
  Kaimastrauch, Scheinkerrie · ♄ d Z6 V-VI;
  China, Korea, Jap.

Rhoeo Hance = Tradescantia
- *discolor* (L'Hér.) Hance = Tradescantia
  spathacea
- *spathacea* (Sw.) Stearn = Tradescantia
  spathacea

Rhoicissus Planch. -f- *Vitaceae* · 12 spp. ·
G:Kapwein
- **capensis** (Burm. f.) Planch. · E:Evergreen Grape, Monkey Rope; G:Kapwein,
  Königswein · ♄ e ⚑ Z9 ⓚ; S-Afr.: Natal
- **digitata** (L. f.) Gilg & M. Brandt · ♄ e ⚑
  Z9 ⓚ; trop. Afr., S-Afr.
- *rhomboidea* hort. = Cissus rhombifolia

Rhombophyllum (Schwantes) Schwantes
-n- *Aizoaceae* · 5 spp.
- **nelii** Schwantes · E:Elk's Horns · ⚃ ♆ Z9
  ⓚ; Cape
- **rhomboideum** (Salm-Dyck) Schwantes ·
  ⚃ ♆ Z9 ⓚ; Cape

Rhopalostylis H. Wendl. & Drude
-f- *Arecaceae* · 2 spp. · E:Nikau Palm;
F:Aréquier; G:Nikaupalme
- **baueri** (Hook. f. ex Lem.) H. Wendl.
  & Drude · G:Norfolkpalme · ♄ e Z9 ⓚ;
  Norfolk Is.
- **sapida** (Sol. ex G. Forst.) H. Wendl.
  & Drude · E:Feather Duster Palm;
  G:Nikaupalme · ♄ e Z9 ⓚ; NZ

Rhus L. -f- *Anacardiaceae* · c. 200 spp. ·
E:Sumac, Sumach; F:Sumac; G:Essigbaum, Sumach
- **aromatica** Aiton · E:Fragrant Sumach,
  Lemon Sumach, Skunkbush; G:Duftender Sumach, Gewürz-Sumach · ♄ d D
  Z4 III-IV ⚥ ; Can.: E; USA: NE, NCE, NC,
  SC, SE, Fla.
- *canadensis* Marshall non Mill. = Rhus
  aromatica
- **chinensis** Mill. · E:Chinese Nut Gall Tree,
  Chinese Sumach; G:Gallen-Sumach · ♄
  ♄ d Z7 VIII-IX; China, Taiwan, Manch.,
  Korea, Jap., Malay. Arch.
- **copallinum** L. · E:Dwarf Sumach,
  Shining Sumach, Winged Sumach;

G:Korall-Sumach · ♄ ♄ d Z5 VII-VIII;
USA: NE, NCE, SE, SC, Fla.
– **coriaria** L. · E:Tanner's Sumach;
G:Gerber-Sumach · ♄ d Z9 ⓐ ⚘ Ⓝ; Eur.:
Ib, Fr, Ital-P, Ba, Crim, Azor., Canar.,
Madeira; TR, Cyprus, Syr., Sinai, Cauc.,
Iran, C-As., Alger.
– *cotinoides* Nutt. = Cotinus obovatus
– *cotinus* L. = Cotinus coggygria
– **glabra** L. · E:Scarlet Sumach, Smooth
Sumach, Upland Sumach; F:Vinaigrier;
G:Scharlach-Sumach · ♄ ♄ d Z6 VII-VIII
⚘ Ⓝ; Can., USA*, Mex.
– *hirta* (L.) Sudw. = Rhus typhina
– × *hybrida* Rehder = Rhus × pulvinata
– *javanica* Thunb. non L. = Rhus chinensis
– *osbeckii* Decne. = Rhus chinensis
– **potaninii** Maxim. · ♄ d Z5 V-VI; C-China,
W-China
– × **pulvinata** Greene (*R. glabra × R.
typhina*) · ♄ d VII-VIII; Can.: E; USA: NE,
NCE, N.C.
– **radicans** L. · E:Poison Ivy; G:Kletternder
Gift-Sumach · ♄ d ⚘ ⤳ Z4 VI-VII ⚘;
Can.; USA* exc. NW, Calif. ; Mex., Guat.,
W.Ind.
– *semialata* Murray = Rhus chinensis
– **succedanea** L. · E:Wax Tree; G:Schar-
lach-Sumach · ♄ ♄ d Z8 ⓐ Ⓝ; Ind.,
Malay. Pen., China, Jap., Taiwan
– **sylvestris** Siebold & Zucc. · E:Wood
Sumach; G:Wald-Sumach · ♄ d Z6 VI;
China, Korea, Jap., Taiwan
– **toxicodendron** L.
– var. **eximia** (Greene) McNair · ♄ d Z7
VI-VII; USA: Rocky Mts., SC
– var. **toxicodendron** · E:Poison Ivy,
Poison Oak; G:Behaarter Gift-Sumach · ♄
d Z6 V-VI ⚘ ⚘; USA: NE, NCE, SC, SE,
Fla.
– **trichocarpa** Miq. · ♄ d Z5 VII; Jap.,
China, Korea
– **trilobata** Nutt. ex Torr. & A. Gray ·
E:Skunkbush, Squawberry; G:Stink-
Sumach · ♄ d Z6 III-IV Ⓝ; Can.: Alta.,
Sask.; USA: NCE, NC, NW, Calif., Rocky
Mts., SC; Mex.
– **typhina** L. · E:Stag's Horn Sumach;
F:Sumac amarante, Sumac de Virginie;
G:Essigbaum, Kolben-Sumach · ♄ ♄ d
Z6 VI-VII ⚘ Ⓝ; Can.: E, USA: NE, NCE,
Tenn., N.C., nat. in Eur.: F, I, Sw, CZ, Ba,
RO
– **verniciflua** Stokes · E:Varnish Tree;
G:Lack-Sumach · ♄ d Z6 IV ⚘ Ⓝ; Jap.,

C-China
– **vernix** L. · E:Poison Elder, Poison
Sumach; G:Kahler Gift-Sumach · ♄ ♄ d
Z6 VI-VII ⚘; Can.: E; USA: NE, NCE, SC,
SE, Fla.

× **Rhynchocentrum** hort. -n- *Orchidaceae*
(*Ascocentrum × Rhynchostylis*)

Rhynchoglossum Blume -n- *Gesneriaceae* ·
11-13 spp.
– **notonianum** (Wall.) B.L. Burtt · ⳋ Z10
ⓜ III-IX; E-Ind., Sri Lanka

Rhyncholaelia Schltr. -f- *Orchidaceae* ·
2 spp.
– **digbyana** (Lindl.) Schltr. · ⳋ Z10 ⓜ
VI-VIII ▽ ✳; Mex., Belize
– **glauca** (Lindl.) Schltr. · ⳋ Z10 ⓜ II-III ▽
✳; Mex., Guat., Hond.

× **Rhynchonopsis** hort. -f- *Orchidaceae*
(*Rhynchostylis × Phalaenopsis*)

Rhynchosia Lour. -f- *Fabaceae* · c. 300 spp.
– **phaseoloides** (Sw.) DC. · ♄ ⚭ Z10 ⓜ
⚘; Mex., trop. Am.

Rhynchospermum Lindl. = Trachelospermum
– *jasminoides* Lindl. = Trachelospermum
jasminoides

Rhynchospora Vahl -f- *Cyperaceae* ·
348 spp. · E:Beak Sedge; F:Rhynchospore;
G:Schnabelried
– **alba** (L.) Vahl · E:White-beak Sedge;
G:Weißes Schnabelried · ⳋ ⁓ VII-VIII;
Eur.*, TR, Cauc., W-Sib., E-Sib.,
Kamchat., E-As., N-Am.
– **fusca** (L.) W.T. Aiton · E:Brown-beak
Sedge; G:Braunes Schnabelried · ⳋ ⁓
VI-VII; Eur.* exc. Ib

Rhynchostele Rchb. f. -f- *Orchidaceae* ·
15 spp.
– **bictoniensis** (Bateman) Soto Arenas
& Salazar · ⳋ Z10 ⓐ IX-X ▽ ✳; Mex.,
C-Am.
– **cervantesii** (Lex.) Soto Arenas &
Salazar · ⳋ Z10 ⓐ XI-III ▽ ✳; Mex.,
Guat.
– **cordata** (Lindl.) Soto Arenas & Salazar ·
⳦ Z10 ⓐ VII-VIII ▽ ✳; Mex., Guat.,
Hond., El Salv., Costa Rica, Venez.

– **maculata** (Lex.) Soto Arenas & Salazar · ⌃ Z10 ⍟ III-IV ▽ ✳; Mex., Guat.
– **majalis** (Rchb. f.) Soto Arenas & Salazar · ⌃ Z10 ⍟ ▽ ✳; Guat.
– **rossii** (Lindl.) Soto Arenas & Salazar · ⌃ Z10 ⍟ II-IV ▽ ✳; Mex., Guat., Nicar.
– **stellata** (Lindl.) Soto Arenas & Salazar · ⌃ Z10 ⍟ ▽ ✳; Mex.
– **uroskinneri** (Lindl.) Soto Arenas & Salazar · ⌃ Z10 ⍟ VII-IX ▽ ✳; Guat., Hond.

Rhynchostylis Blume -f- *Orchidaceae* · 4 spp. · E:Foxtail Orchid; F:Rhynchostylis; G:Fuchsschwanzorchidee
– **coelestis** (Rchb. f.) Rchb. f. ex Veitch · ℏ Z10 ⍟ VII-VIII ▽ ✳; Thail.
– **gigantea** (Lindl.) Ridl. · ℏ Z10 ⍟ XI ▽ ✳; China, Indochina, Malay. Pen., Kalimantan, Phil.
– **retusa** (L.) Blume · ℏ Z10 ⍟ VI-VII ▽ ✳; Him., Ind., Sri Lanka, Indochina, Malay. Arch., Phil.
– *violacea* (Lindl.) Rchb. = Rhynchostylis retusa

× **Rhynchovanda** hort. -f- *Orchidaceae* (*Rhynchostylis* × *Vanda*)

× **Rhyndoropsis** hort. -f- *Orchidaceae* (*Doritis* × *Phalaenopsis* × *Rhynchostylis*)

Rhytidophyllum Mart. -n- *Gesneriaceae* · 21 sp.
– **tomentosum** (L.) Mart. · ℏ Z10 ⍟ VII-IX; Jamaica

Ribes L. -n- *Grossulariaceae* · 150 spp. · E:Currant, Gooseberry; F:Cassis, Groseillier; G:Johannisbeere, Stachelbeere
– **alpestre** Wall. ex Decne.
– var. **alpestre** · ℏ d Z6; Him., W-China
– var. **giganteum** Jancz. · ℏ d Z6 IV-V Ⓝ; W-China
– **alpinum** L. · E:Alpine Currant, Mountain Currant; F:Groseillier des Alpes; G:Alpen-Johannisbeere · ℏ d Z3 IV-V; Eur.*, Cauc.
– **americanum** Mill. · E:American Blackcurrant, Black Currant; F:Groseillier d'Amérique; G:Kanadische Johannisbeere · ℏ d Z5 IV-V; Can.; USA: NE, NCE, NC, Rocky Mts., SW
– **aureum** Pursh · E:Buffalo Currant, Golden Currant; G:Gold-Johannisbeere ·

ℏ d Z3 IV-V Ⓝ; Can.: W; USA: NW, Calif., Rocky Mts., NC, SW
– *biebersteinii* Berland. = Ribes petraeum var. biebersteinii
– **bracteosum** Douglas ex Hook. · E:Stink Currant · ℏ d Z7; Alaska, Can.: W; USA. NW, N-Calif.
– **cereum** Douglas · E:Squaw Currant, Wax Currant; G:Wüsten-Johannisbeere · ℏ d △ Z5 IV-V; B.C., USA: NW, Rocky Mts., NC, Calif., SW
– × **culverwellii** Macfarl. (*R. nigrum* × *R. uva-crispa*) · E:Jostaberry; G:Jostabeere · ℏ d Z6 Ⓝ; cult.
– **some cultivars**
– **cynosbati** L. · E:Dogberry, Dogbramble; G:Hunds-Stachelbeere · ℏ d Z3; Can.: E; USA: NE, NCE, SE, Okl.
– **diacanthum** Pall. · ℏ d Z3; E-Sib., Mong., Manch., N-Korea
– **divaricatum** Douglas · E:Coastal Black Gooseberry, Common Gooseberry; G:Oregon-Stachelbeere · ℏ d Z6 IV-V; B.C., USA: NW, Calif.
– **fasciculatum** Siebold & Zucc. · E:Gooseberry; G:Dolden-Johannisbeere · ℏ d Z5 IV-V; Jap., Korea, N-China
– *floridum* L'Hér. = Ribes americanum
– *fragrans* Lodd. non Pall. = Ribes odoratum
– × **fuscescens** (Jancz.) Jancz. (*R. bracteosum* × *R. nigrum*) · ℏ d Z6; cult.
– **gayanum** (Spach) Steud. · ℏ d Z8 ⍟ V; Chile
– **glaciale** Wall. · ℏ d Z5 IV-V; Afgh., Him., China: Yunnan, Hubei, Xizang, Tibet
– **glandulosum** Grauer ex Weber · E:Skunk Currant, Wild Currant; G:Stinktier-Johannisbeere · ℏ d ⤳ △ Z4 IV; Alaska, Can., USA: NE, N.C., NCE
– × **gordonianum** Beaton (*R. odoratum* × *R. sanguineum*) · E:Gordon's Currant; G:Gordons Johannisbeere · ℏ d Z6 IV-V; cult.
– *grossularia* L. = Ribes uva-crispa var. reclinatum
– **hirtellum** Michx. · E:Hairy Stem Gooseberry, Wedgeleaf Gooseberry; G:Amerikanische Stachelbeere · ℏ d Z4 IV-V Ⓝ; Can.: E; USA: NE, NCE, NC
– × **holosericum** Otto & A. Dietr. (*R. petraeum* × *R. rubrum* var. *rubrum*) · ℏ d Z4; cult.
– **irriguum** Douglas · E:Idaho Gooseberry · ℏ d Z4 V-VI; Can.: B.C.; USA: Oreg.,

N-Idaho, W-Mont.
- **lacustre** (Pers.) Poir. · E:Bristly Black Gooseberry, Swamp Gooseberry; G:Sumpf-Stachelbeere · ♄ d ⁓ Z4 V; Alaska, Can., USA: NE, Tenn., NCE, Rocky Mts., NW, Calif.
- **laurifolium** Jancz. · ♄ d Z9 ⊛ II-III; N-China
- **leptanthum** A. Gray · E:Trumpet Gooseberry; G:Colorado-Stachelbeere · ♄ d Z6 IV-V; USA: Utah, Colo., N.Mex.
- **lobbii** A. Gray · E:Gummy Gooseberry, Sticky Gooseberry; G:Klebrige Stachelbeere · ♄ d Z7 ∧ IV-V; Can.: B.C.; USA: NW, Calif.
- **maximowiczii** Batalin
- var. **floribundum** Jesson · ♄ d Z6; W-China
- var. **maximowiczii** · ♄ d Z6 V; Jap., Korea, Manch.
- **multiflorum** Kit. ex Roem. & Schult. · G:Troddel-Johannisbeere · ♄ d Z6 IV-V; Eur.: Sard., I, Croatia, YU, GR, BG
- × **nidigrolaria** Rud. Bauer & A. Bauer (*R. divaricatum* × *R. nigrum* × *R. uva-crispa* var. *sativum*) · G:Bastard-Johannisbeere, Jochelbeere · ♄ d Ⓝ; cult.
- **nigrum** L. · E:Blackcurrant; F:Cassis, Cassissier; G:Schwarze Johannisbeere · ♄ d D Z5 IV-V ⚥ Ⓝ; Eur.* exc. Ib; Cauc., W-Sib., E-Sib., C-As., Mong.
- **many cultivars**
- **niveum** Lindl. · E:Snake River Gooseberry, Snow Currant; G:Schnee-Stachelbeere · ♄ d Z6 IV-V; USA: NW, Idaho, Nev.
- **odoratum** H.L. Wendl. · E:Buffalo Currant, Golden Currant; F:Groseillier doré; G:Wohlriechende Johannisbeere · ♄ d Z5 IV-V Ⓝ; USA: NCE, NC, SC, Ark.
- **oxyacanthoides** L. · E:Northern Gooseberry; G:Manitoba-Stachelbeere · ♄ d ⁓ Z4 IV-V; Can., USA: NCE, N.Dak., Mont.
- **petraeum** Wulfen · G:Felsen-Johannisbeere
- var. **biebersteinii** (Berland.) C.K. Schneid. · G:Kaukasische Felsen-Johannisbeere · ♄ d Z6; Cauc.
- var. **petraeum** · E:Rock Redcurrant, Stone Gooseberry; F:Groseillier des rochers; G:Gewöhnliche Felsen-Johannisbeere · ♄ d Z6 IV-VI Ⓝ; Eur.* exc. BrI, Sc; mts.; Cauc., W-As, Sib., Amur, NW-Afr.
- **pinetorum** Greene · E:Orange Gooseberry; G:Arizona-Stachelbeere · ♄ d Z6; Ariz., N.Mex.
- **reclinatum** L. = Ribes uva-crispa var. reclinatum
- **roezlii** Regel
- var. **cruentum** (Greene) Rehder · E:Shinyleaf Currant · ♄ d Z7; USA: S-Oreg., Calif.
- var. **roezlii** · E:Sierra Gooseberry · ♄ d Z7 V; Calif.
- **rubrum** L. · G:Rote Johannisbeere
- var. **domesticum** Wallr. · E:Red Currant, White Currant; G:Rote Garten-Johannisbeere, Weiße Garten-Johannisbeere · Z4 ⚥ ; cult.
- **many cultivars**
- var. **rubrum** · E:Currant; F:Groseillier rouge; G:Wilde Rote Johannisbeere · ♄ d Z4 IV-V Ⓝ; Eur.: BrI, Fr, G, I, nat. in Eur.
- **sanguineum** Pursh · E:Flowering Currant; F:Groseillier sanguin; G:Blut-Johannisbeere · ♄ d Z5 IV-V; B.C., USA: NW, N-Calif.
- **some cultivars**
- *sativum* (Rchb.) Syme = Ribes rubrum var. domesticum
- **spicatum** E. Robson · E:Downy Currant; G:Ährige Johannisbeere · ♄ d Z4 IV-V Ⓝ; Eur.: BrI, Sc, C-Eur., EC-Eur., E-Eur.; Sib. Manch.
- *sylvestre* (Lam.) Hayek = Ribes rubrum var. rubrum
- **uva-crispa** L. · E:Gooseberry; G:Stachelbeere
- subsp. *pubescens* (W.D.J. Koch) O. Schwarz = Ribes uva-crispa var. uva-crispa
- var. **reclinatum** (L.) Berland. · ♄ d Z5 IV-V Ⓝ; cult.
- var. **sativum** DC. · G:Kultur-Stachelbeere · ♄ d Z5 IV-V Ⓝ; cult.
- **many cultivars**
- var. **uva-crispa** · F:Groseillier à maquereau; G:Gewöhnliche Stachelbeere · ♄ d Z5 IV-V Ⓝ; Eur.* exc. Sc; Cauc., Sib., Manch., Him., NW-Afr., nat. in Sc
- *vulgare* Lam. = Ribes rubrum var. rubrum

Ricinodendron Müll. Arg. -n-
Euphorbiaceae · 1 sp.
- **heudelotii** (Baill.) Pierre ex Pax · E:African Nut-Tree; G:Afrikanisches Mahagoni · ♄ d Z10 ⊛ Ⓝ; trop. Afr.

Ricinus L. -m- *Euphorbiaceae* · 1 sp. · E:Castor Oil Plant; F:Ricin; G:Palma Christi, Rizinus, Wunderbaum
- **communis** L. · E:Castor Oil Plant; F:Ricin; G:Palma Christi, Rizinus, Wunderbaum · ⊙ ♄ ♄ ♄ e Z9 Ⓦ Ⓚ VIII-X ⚕ ☠ Ⓝ; ? trop. Afr., nat. in Trop., Subtrop.

× **Ridleyara** hort. -f- *Orchidaceae* (*Arachis* × *Trichoglottis* × *Vanda*)

Ridolfia Moris -f- *Apiaceae* · 1 sp. · E:False Fennel; F:Ridolfia; G:Falscher Fenchel, Ridolfie
- **segetum** Moris · E:False Fennel; G:Falscher Fenchel, Ridolfie · ⊙; Eur.: Ib, Fr, Ital-P, Croat.; TR, Syr., Canar., N-Afr.

Rindera Pall. -f- *Boraginaceae* · c. 25 spp.
- **caespitosa** (DC.) Gürke · ♃ △ Ⓚ ∧ V-VIII; TR
- **umbellata** (Waldst. & Kit.) Bunge · ♃ △ ∧ V-VII; Eur.: Serb., BG, RO, W-Russ.

Ritterocereus Backeb. = Stenocereus
- *pruinosus* (Otto) Backeb. = Stenocereus pruinosus
- *queretaroensis* (F.A.C. Weber) Backeb. = Stenocereus queretaroensis

Rivina L. -f- *Phytolaccaceae* · 1 sp. · E:Blood Berry; F:Rivinia; G:Blutbeere, Rivinie
- **humilis** L. · E:Blood Berry, Rouge Plant; G:Blutbeere, Rivinie · ♃ ♄ Z9 Ⓦ; USA: SE, Fla., Tex.; Mex., W.Ind., trop. S-Am.

Robinia L. -f- *Fabaceae* · 10 spp. · E:False Acacia; F:Faux-acacia, Robinier; G:Robinie, Scheinakazie
- × **ambigua** Poir. (*R. pseudoacacia* × *R. viscosa*) · E:Pink Locust; G:Rosafarbene Robinie · ♄ d Z6; cult.
- **fertilis** Ashe · E:Bristly Locust ; G:Fruchtbare Robinie · ♄ d Z5; USA
- **hispida** L. · E:Bristly Locust, Rose Acacia; F:Acacia rose; G:Borstige Robinie · ♄ d Z6 VI-IX; USA: Va., Ky., SE
- × **holdtii** Beissn. (*R. luxurians* × *R. pseudoacacia*) · ♄ d Z6; cult.
- **kelseyi** H.P. Kelsey ex Hutch. · E:Kelsey's Locust; G:Kelseys Robinie · ♄ d Z6 V-VI; USA: N.C.
- **luxurians** (Dieck) C.K. Schneid. · G:Üppige Robinie · ♄ ♄ d Z6 VI Ⓝ; USA: Rocky Mts., SW, SC; Mex.
- **neomexicana** A. Gray · E:New Mexico Locust; F:Robinier; G:Neu-Mexiko-Robinie · ♄ d Z6 VI-VII; USA: N.Mex.
- var. *luxurians* Dieck = Robinia luxurians
- *neomexicana* auct. non A. Gray = Robinia luxurians
- **pseudoacacia** L. · E:Acacia, Black Locust, Robinia; F:Faux acacia; G:Gewöhnliche Scheinakazie, Robinie · ♄ d Z6 V-VI ☠ Ⓝ; USA: NE, NCE, SE, Okla., nat. in Eur.
- var. *angustifolia* Koehne = Robinia pseudoacacia
- × **slavinii** Rehder (*R. kelseyi* × *R. pseudoacacia*) · ♄ d Z6; cult.
- **viscosa** Vent. · E:Clammy Locust; G:Klebrige Robinie · ♄ ♄ d Z6 VI-VIII; USA: NE, SE

Rochea DC. = Crassula
- *coccinea* (L.) DC. = Crassula coccinea
- *falcata* DC. = Crassula perfoliata var. minor
- *perfoliata* (L.) DC. = Crassula perfoliata var. perfoliata
- *versicolor* (Burch. ex Ker-Gawl.) Link = Crassula coccinea

Rodgersia A. Gray -f- *Saxifragaceae* · 6 spp. · F:Rodgersia; G:Bronzeblatt, Rodgersie, Schaublatt
- **aesculifolia** Batalin · F:Rodgersia à feuilles de marronnier; G:Kastanien-Schaublatt · ♃ Z5 VI-VII; C-China
- **henrici** (Franch.) Franch. · G:Prinz-Henri-Schaublatt · ♃ Z6; China, N-Burma, SE-Tibet
- **pinnata** Franch. · G:Gefiedertes Schaublatt · ♃ Z6 VII; Yunnan
- **podophylla** A. Gray · G:Gezähntes Schaublatt · ♃ Z5 VII-VIII; Jap., Korea
- **purdomii** hort. · G:Purdoms Schaublatt · ♃ VI-VII; China
- **sambucifolia** Hemsl. · F:Rodgersia à feuilles de sureau; G:Hollunderblättriges Schaublatt · ♃ Z6 VII-VIII; Yunnan
- *tabularis* (Hemsl.) Kom. = Astilboides tabularis
- **Cultivars:**
- **many cultivars**

× **Rodrassia** hort. -f- *Orchidaceae* (*Brassia* × *Rodriguezia*)

× **Rodrettia** hort. -f- *Orchidaceae* (*Comparettia* × *Rodriguezia*)

× **Rodricidium** hort. -n- *Orchidaceae*
(*Oncidium* × *Rodriguezia*)

× **Rodridenia** hort. -f- *Orchidaceae*
(*Macradenia* × *Rodriguezia*)

Rodriguezia Ruiz & Pav. -f- *Orchidaceae* ·
48 spp.
– **decora** (Lem.) Rchb. f. · ⨀ Z10 ⊛ IX-X ▽
✳; Braz.
– **lanceolata** Ruiz & Pav. · ⨀ Z10 ⊛ V-VI
▽ ✳; Panama, trop. S-Am.
– *secunda* Kunth = Rodriguezia lanceolata
– **venusta** Rchb. f. · ⨀ Z10 ⊛ X ▽ ✳; Braz.

× **Rodritonia** hort. -f- *Orchidaceae*
(*Miltonia* × *Rodriguezia*)

Roegneria K. Koch = Elymus
– *canina* (L.) Nevski = Elymus caninus
– *pauciflora* (Schwein.) Hyl. = Elymus
trachycaulus

Roemeria Medik. -f- *Papaveraceae* ·
6-8 spp.
– **hybrida** (L.) DC. · ⊙ VII-VIII ✿; Eur.: Ib,
Fr, Ital-P, Ba; TR, Levant, Iran, N-Afr.
– **refracta** DC. · ⊙ VII-VIII; TR, Cauc., Iran,
C-As., China: Sinkiang

Rohdea Roth -f- *Convallariaceae* · 1 sp.
– **japonica** (Thunb.) Roth · E:Lily-of-
China · ⨀ Z8 ⊛; SW-China

× **Rolfeara** hort. -f- *Orchidaceae* (*Cattleya* ×
Rhyncholaelia × *Sophronitis*)

Romanzoffia Cham. -f- *Hydrophyllaceae* ·
4 spp. · E:Romanzoffia; F:Romanzoffia;
G:Romanzoffie
– **sitchensis** Bong. · E:Sitka Mistmaiden;
G:Sitka-Romanzoffie · ⨀ Z8 ⊛ ∧ V-VI;
Alaska, Can.: W; USA: NW, Calif.
– **unalaschcensis** Cham. · E:Alaska
Mistmaiden; G:Aleuten-Romanzoffie · ⨀
⊛ ∧ V-VI; E-Aleuten

Romneya Harv. -f- *Papaveraceae* · 1 sp. ·
E:California Tree Poppy; F:Pavot de
Californie; G:Strauchmohn
– **coulteri** Harv. · E:California Tree
Poppy, Matilija Poppy; G:Kalifornischer
Strauchmohn
– var. **coulteri** · ⨀ Z8 ⊛ VII-IX; SW-Calif.,
NW-Mex.

– var. **trichocalyx** (Eastw.) Jeps. · E:Bristly
Matilija Poppy · ⨀ Z8 ⊛; Calif.
– *trichocalyx* Eastw. = Romneya coulteri
var. trichocalyx

Romulea Maratti -f- *Iridaceae* · 101 sp. ·
E:Sand Crocus; F:Faux-crocus, Romulée;
G:Sandkrokus, Scheinkrokus
– *bulbocodioides* Eckl. = Romulea tabularis
– **bulbocodium** (L.) Sebast. & Mauri ·
⨀ Z8 ⊛ III-IV; Eur.: Ib, Fr, Ital-P, Ba;
Levant, N-Afr.
– **linaresii** Parl. · ⨀ Z8 ⊛; Sic., GR, W-TR
– **tabularis** Eckl. ex Bég.
– **tempskyana** Freyn · ⨀ Z8 ⊛; TR,
Cyprus, Palest.

Rondeletia L. -f- *Rubiaceae* · 260 spp.
– **amoena** (Planch.) Hemsl. · ♄ e Z10 ⊛
III-V; C-Am.
– **cordata** Benth. · ♄ e Z10 ⊛ VI-VII; Guat.
– **odorata** Jacq. · ♄ e D Z10 ⊛ XI-III;
Panama, Cuba
– *speciosa* Lodd. = Rondeletia odorata

Ronnbergia E. Morren & André -f-
Bromeliaceae · 12 spp.
– **columbiana** E. Morren · ⨀ Z10 ⊛; Col.
– **morreniana** Linden & André · ⨀ Z10 ⊛;
Col.

Roridula L. -f- *Roridulaceae* · 2 spp. ·
F:Roridule; G:Fliegenbusch, Wanzenpflanze
– **dentata** L. · G:Gezähnte Wanzenpflanze ·
♄ e Z9 ⊛; Cape
– **gorgonias** Planch. · G:Haarige Wanzenpflanze · ♄ e Z9 ⊛; Cape

Rorippa Scop. -f- *Brassicaceae* · 70-80 spp. ·
E:Water Cress; F:Faux-cresson, Roripe ;
G:Sumpfkresse
– **amphibia** (L.) Besser · E:Great Yel-
lowcress; G:Wasser-Sumpfkresse · ⨀ Z6
V-VIII; Eur.*, Cauc., W-Sib., E-Sib., C-As.
– **anceps** (Wahlenb.) Rchb. · G:Niederlie-
gende Sumpfkresse · ⨀ V-IX; Eur.*, TR,
Cauc., E-Sib.
– × **armoracioides** (Tausch) Fuss (*R.
austriaca* × *R. sylvestris*) · ⨀; Eur.* exc.
BrI, Sc +
– × **astylis** (Rchb.) Rchb. (*R. palustris* × *R.
sylvestris*) · ⨀; A +
– **austriaca** (Crantz) Besser · E:Austrian
Yellow Cress; G:Österreichische

Sumpfkresse · ⍋ VI-VIII; Eur.: C-Eur.,
EC-Eur., Ba, E-Eur.; TR, Cauc., C-As., nat.
in BrI, Sc, F, I
– islandica (Oeder) Borbás · E:Marsh
Yellow Cress; G:Ufer-Sumpfkresse · ☉;
Eur.* exc. EC-Eur.; cosmop.
– lippizensis (Wulfen) Rchb. · G:Karst-
Sumpfkresse · ⍋; Eur.: Ba, I
– microphylla (Boenn.) Hyl. = Nasturtium
microphyllum
– palustris (L.) Besser · E:Bog Yellow
Cress; G:Gewöhnliche Sumpfkresse · ⍋
VI-IX; Eur.*, TR, Cauc., W-Sib., E-Sib.,
Amur, Sakhal., Kamchat., C-As., Him.,
Mong., E-As., N-Am., S-Am., Egypt,
Austr.
– pyrenaica (L.) Rchb. · G:Pyrenäen-
Sumpfkresse · ⍋ V-VIII; Eur.: Fr, Ital-P,
C-Eur., EC-Eur., Ba, E-Eur.
– sylvestris (L.) Besser · E:Creeping Yellow
Cress; G:Wilde Sumpfkresse · ⍋ V-IX;
Eur.*, TR, Cauc., N-As., N-Afr.

Rosa L. -f- Rosaceae · 100-150 spp. · E:Rose;
F:Eglantier, Rosier; G:Hagebutte, Rose
– abietina Gren. ex H. Christ = Rosa
acicularis var. acicularis
– acicularis Lindl.
– var. acicularis · E:Needle Rose, Prickly
Rose; G:Nadel-Rose · ♄ d D Z2 VI; Can.,
USA: NE, NCE, NC, Rocky Mts.
– var. bourgeauana (Crép.) Crép. Z2;
Alaska, Can., USA: NE, NEC, NC, Rocky
Mts.
– agrestis Savi · E:Field Briar; G:Feld-Rose
· ♄ d Z6 VI; Eur.*, NW-TR, NW-Afr.
– × alba L. (R. arvensis × R. gallica × ?) ·
E:White Rose, White Rose of York;
G:Weiße Rose · ♄ d D Z5 VI Ⓝ; cult.
– alpina L. = Rosa pendulina var. pendulina
– andegavensis Bastard = Rosa canina
– anemoniflora Fortune ex Lindl. = Rosa ×
beanii
– arkansana Porter · E:Prairie Rose;
G:Prärie-Rose · ♄ d Z4 VI-VII; Can., USA:
NE, NCE, NC, SC, N.Mex.
– arvensis Huds. · E:Field Rose, Musk
Rose; F:Rosier des champs; G:Kriechende
Rose · ♄ d ⚥ ⤳ D Z5 VI-VII; Eur.* exc.
Sc; TR
– balearica Desf. = Rosa sempervirens
– banksiae W.T. Aiton · E:Banksian Rose ·
♄ e ⚥ D Z8 Ⓐ IV-VII; W-China, C-China
– × beanii Heath (R. banksiae var. banksiae
× ? × R. moschata) · ♄ d Z7; cult. E-China

– beggeriana Schrenk · ♄ d Z7 VI; Afgh.,
N-Iran, C-As., China: Sinkiang
– bella Rehder & E.H. Wilson · ♄ d D Z6
VI; N-China
– bengalensis Pers. = Rosa chinensis
– berberifolia Pall. = Rosa persica
– blanda Aiton · E:Smooth Rose;
G:Labrador-Rose · ♄ d Z4 V-VI; Can.: E;
USA: NE, NCE, NC.
– boissieri Crép. = Rosa britzensis
– × borboniana N.H.F. Desp. (R. chinensis
× R. × damascena) · E:Bourbon Rose;
G:Bourbon-Rose · ♄ d ⋀ VI-IX; cult.
– bracteata J.C. Wendl. · E:Macartney
Rose · ♄ e Z7 VII-VIII; S-China, Taiwan,
nat. in USA: SE
– britzensis Koehne · ♄ d Z6 V-VI; TR,
Iraq, Cauc., Iran
– × bruantii Rehder (R. × odorata × R.
rugosa) · ♄ d; cult.
– brunonii Lindl. · E:Himalayan Musk
Rose; G:Himalaya-Moschus-Rose · ♄ d ⚥
D Z8 Ⓐ VI-VII; Afgh., Pakist., Kashmir,
Nepal, Sichuan
– caesia Sm. · G:Lederblättrige Rose · ♄ d
Z5 VI; Eur.*, TR
– calendarum Borkh. = Rosa × damascena
– californica Cham. & Schltdl. ·
E:California Rose; G:Kalifornische Rose ·
♄ d D Z5 V-VIII; Oreg., Calif., Baja Calif.
– canina L. · E:Common Briar, Dog Rose;
F:Eglantier commun, Rosier des chiens;
G:Hunds-Rose · ♄ d ⚥ Z4 VI-VIII ⚥
Ⓝ; Eur.*, TR, Syr., Cauc., Iran, C-As.,
Canar., Madeira, NW-Afr.
– carelica Fr. = Rosa acicularis var.
acicularis
– carolina L. · E:Carolina Rose; F:Rosier;
G:Carolina-Rose · ♄ d Z5 VII-VIII; Can.:
E; USA: NE, NCE, NC, SC, SE, Fla.
– carolinensis Marshall = Rosa virginiana
– caryophyllacea Besser · G:Nelken-Rose ·
♄ d VI; Eur.: I, A, EC-Eur., Ba, E-Eur.; ?
Cauc.
– caudata Baker · ♄ d Z6 VI; W-China
– × centifolia L. (R. canina × R. gallica × R.
moschata) · E:Cabbage Rose, Provence
Rose; F:Rosier cent-feuilles; G:Hun-
dertblättrige Rose · ♄ d D Z5 VI-VII ⚥; ?
Cauc.
– × chavinii Rapin ex Reut. (R. canina × R.
montana) · E:Chavin's Rose; G:Chavins
Rose · ♄ d VI-VII; Eur.: Sw, F, I; Alp.
– chinensis Jacq. · E:China Rose; G:China-
Rose · ♄ d Z6 Ⓐ VI-X; China

– *cinnamomea* L. 1753 = Rosa pendulina
var. pendulina
– var. *plena* L. 1759 = Rosa majalis
– *cinnamomea* L. 1759 = Rosa majalis
– *coriifolia* Fr. = Rosa caesia
– **corymbifera** Borkh. · E:Rose;
G:Déséglise-Rose, Hecken-Rose · ħ d ⊗
Z6 VI; Eur.*, TR, Cauc., C-As., Afgh.,
N-Afr.
– **corymbulosa** Rolfe · ħ d Z6; W-China:
Hubei, Shensi
– × **damascena** Mill. (*R. gallica* × *R.
moschata*) · E:Damask Rose; G:Portland-
Rose · ħ d D Z4 VI-IX ⚥ Ⓝ; cult.
– **davidii** Crép. · ħ d ⊗ Z7 ∧ VI-VII;
W-China
– **dumalis** Bechst. · G:Graugrüne Rose,
Vogesen-Rose · ħ d Z4 VI-VII; Eur. exc.
BrI, TR
– *dumetorum* Thuill. = Rosa corymbifera
– × **dupontii** Déségl. (*R. gallica* × *R.
moschata*) · ħ d Z6 VI; cult.
– **ecae** Aitch. · ħ d Z7 ∧ V-VI; Afgh.,
NW-Pakist., C-As., N-China
– *eglanteria* L. = Rosa rubiginosa
– **elliptica** Tausch · G:Keilblättrige Rose · ħ
d VI-VII; Eur.* exc. Sc
– *ferruginea* auct. non Vill. = Rosa glauca
– **filipes** Rehder & E.H. Wilson · ∫ d ⚥ Z5;
China
– **foetida** Herrm. · E:Austrian Briar;
G:Gelbe Rose · ħ d D Z5 VI; Iran, Afgh.,
NW-Him.
– **foliolosa** Nutt. ex Torr. & A. Gray ·
E:White Prairie Rose; G:Weiße Prärie-
Rose · ħ d Z6 VII-VIII; USA: Ark., SC
– × **francofurtana** Münchh. (*R. gallica* × *R.
majalis* × *?*) · G:Frankfurter Rose · ħ d Z6;
cult.
– *fraxinifolia* C.C. Gmel. non Borkh. = Rosa
blanda
– **gallica** L. · E:French Rose, Provence
Rose; F:Rosier de France, Rosier de
Provins; G:Essig-Rose, Gallische Rose · ħ
d D Z5 VI ⚥ Ⓝ; Eur.* exc. BrI, Sc, Ib; TR,
N-Iraq, Cauc., nat. in Ib, USA
– var. *damascena* (Mill.) Voss = Rosa ×
damascena
– **glauca** Pourr. · E:Rubrifolia; F:Rosier
glauque; G:Bereifte Rose, Rotblättrige
Rose · ħ d Z3 VI-VII; Eur.* exc. BrI, Sc,
nat. in Sc
– **gymnocarpa** Nutt. ex Torr. & A. Gray ·
E:Dwarf Rose, Wood Rose; G:Holz-Rose ·
ħ d △ Z7 ∧ VI-VII; B.C., USA: NW, Calif.,

Rocky Mts.
– × **hardii** Paxton (*R. clinophylla* × *R.
persica*) · ħ d Z8 ⚘; cult.
– × **harisonii** Rivers (*R. foetida* × *R.
pimpinellifolia*) · E:Harison's Yellow;
Rose G:Harisons Rose · ħ d Z4 V; cult.
– **helenae** Rehder & E.H. Wilson ·
G:Helenes Rose · ħ d ⊗ D Z7 ∧ VI-VII;
C-China
– **hemisphaerica** Herrm. · E:Sulphur Rose;
G:Schwefelgelbe Rose · ħ d Z6 VI-VII;
cult.
– **hemsleyana** G. Täckh. · ħ d Z6 VI;
C-China
– × **highdownensis** H.G.K. Hillier (*R.
moyesii* × *R. sweginzowii*) · ħ d Z6; cult.
– **hirtula** (Regel) Nakai · ħ d Z6; Jap.
– *holodonta* Stapf = Rosa moyesii 'Rosea'
– *hugonis* Hemsl. = Rosa xanthina f.
hugonis
– *humilis* Marshall = Rosa carolina
– *indica* Lour. non L. = Rosa chinensis
– var. *fragrans* Thory = Rosa × odorata
– var. *odorata* Andrews = Rosa × odorata
– **inodora** Fr. · G:Geruchlose Rose · ħ d
VI-VII; Eur.: Sc, BrI, G, A +
– **jundzillii** Besser · G:Raublättrige Rose · ħ
d Z5 VI; Eur.: Fr, Ital-P, C-Eur., EC-Eur.,
Ba, E-Eur.; Cauc.
– × **kamtschatica** Vent. (*R. davurica* × *R.
rugosa* × *?*) · G:Kamtschatka-Rose · ħ Z4;
E-Sib., Kamcaht.
– **laevigata** Michx. · E:Cherokee Rose;
G:Cherokee-Rose · ħ e D Z7 V-VI ⚥ ;
China: Hupeh, Fukien; Taiwan, nat. in
USA: SE
– **laxa** Retz. · ħ d Z6 VII; Sib., NW-China
– *lucida* Ehrh. = Rosa virginiana
– *lutea* Mill. = Rosa foetida
– × **macrantha** hort. non N.H.F. Desp. (*R.
canina* × *R. gallica* × *?*) · ħ d Z6; cult.
– **macrophylla** Lindl. · E:Big Hip Rose · ħ d
⊗ Z7 VI; Afgh., Pakist., Him., SW-China
– **majalis** Herrm. · E:Cinnamon Rose,
May Rose; F:Rosier cannelle, Rosier de
mai; G:Mai-Rose, Zimt-Rose · ħ d D Z4
V-VI; Eur.: Ital-P, Fr, C-Eur., EC-Eur., Sc,
E-Eur.; ? Cauc., W-Sib., E-Sib.
– × **mariae-graebneriae** Asch. & Graebn.
(*R. palustris* × *R. virginiana*) · ħ d Z5;
cult.
– **micrantha** Borrer ex Sm. · G:Kleinblütige
Rose · ħ Z5 V-VI; Eur.* exc. Sc; TR,
Lebanon, Cauc., NW-Afr.
– *microphylla* Roxb. ex Lindl. = Rosa

roxburghii f. normalis
- × **micrugosa** Henkel (*R. roxburghii* × *R. rugosa*) · ♄ d Z5; cult.
- **mollis** Sm. · G:Weichblättrige Rose, Weiche Rose · ♄ d Z5 VI-VII; Eur.* exc. Ital-P; TR, W-As.
- **montana** Chaix · E:Mountain Rose; G:Berg-Rose · ♄ d VI-VII; S-Eur., SC-Eur., N-Afr. mts.
- **moschata** Herrm. · E:Musk Rose; G:Moschus-Rose · ♄ e ⚥ D Z7 IV-VII Ⓝ; Eth., Him., nat. in S-Eur., s USA
- **moyesii** Hemsl. & E.H. Wilson · G:Mandarin-Rose · ♄ d ⊛ Z6 VI; Sichuan
- × **'Rosea'** · d
- **multibracteata** Hemsl. & E.H. Wilson · G:Kragen-Rose · ♄ d ⊛ Z7 VII; Sichuan
- **multiflora** Thunb. ex Murray · E:Multiflora Rose; F:Rosier multiflore; G:Vielblütige Rose · ♄ d ⚥ ⊛ Z5 VI-VII; Jap., Korea
- **nitida** Willd. · E:Shining Rose; G:Glanzblättrige Rose · ♄ d ⊛ Z4 VI-VII; Can.: E; USA: NE
- *nitidula* Besser = Rosa canina
- **nutkana** C. Presl · E:Nootka Rose; G:Nutka-Rose · ♄ d ⊛ Z4 VI-VII; Alaska, Can.: W; USA: NW, Calif, Rocky Mts.
- *obtusifolia* auct. non Desv. = Rosa tomentella
- × **odorata** (Andrews) Sweet (*R. chinensis* × *R. gigantea*) · E:Tea Rose; G:Tee-Rose · ♄ e ⤳ Z7 ⒶⒷ VI-IX; China
- *omeiensis* Rolfe = Rosa sericea subsp. omeiensis
- **orientalis** A.E. Dupont ex DC. · ♄; Ba, W-As.
- **oxyodon** Boiss. · ♄ ⊛ Z6 V-VI; E-Cauc.
- **palustris** Marshall · E:Swamp Rose; G:Sumpf-Rose · ♄ d Z4 VII-VIII; Can.: E; USA: NE, NCE, SE, Fla.
- × **paulii** Rehder (*R. arvensis* × *R. rugosa*) · ♄ d ⚥ Z4; cult.
- **pendulina** L. · G:Alpen-Rose
- var. *oxyodon* (Boiss.) Rehder = Rosa oxyodon
- var. **pendulina** · E:Alpine Rose; F:Rosier des Alpes; G:Gewöhnliche Alpen-Rose, Hängefrucht-Rose · ♄ d ⊛ Z6 VI-VII ⚥ ; Eur.* exc. BrI, Sc
- var. **pyrenaica** (Gouan) R. Keller · G:Pyrenäen-Rose · ♄ d Z5; Pyr..
- *pensylvanica* Michx. = Rosa palustris
- **persica** Michx. ex J.F. Gmel. · G:Persische Rose · ♄ d Z8 ⒶⒷ VI-VIII; Iran,

C-As., Afgh., W-Sib.
- *pimpinellifolia* L. = Rosa spinosissima
- **pisocarpa** A. Gray · E:Cluster Rose, Pea Rose; G:Erbsenfrüchtige Rose · ♄ d ⊛ D Z6 VI-VIII; B.C., USA: NW, Idaho, Calif.
- × **polliniana** Spreng. (*R. arvensis* × *R. gallica*) · ♄ d Z7; C-Eur., I+
- *polyantha* Siebold & Zucc. = Rosa multiflora
- **prattii** Hemsl. · G:Pratts Rose · ♄ d Z6 VI-VII; W-China
- **primula** Boulenger · ♄ d Z5 V; C-As., N-China
- **pseudoscabriuscula** (R. Keller) Henker & G. Schulze · G:Falsche Filz-Rose, Kratz-Rose · ♄ d VI-VII; Eur.*, TR, Cauc.
- × **pteragonis** W. Krause ex Kordes (*R. hugonis* × *R. omeiensis*) · ♄ d; cult.
- **pulverulenta** M. Bieb. · ♄ d Z6; SE-Eur., I, W-As., TR, Lebanon, Cauc., Iran, Afgh.
- *regeliana* Linden & André = Rosa rugosa
- *repens* Scop. = Rosa arvensis
- **rhaetica** Gremli · G:Rätische Rose · ♄ d VI-VII; Eur.: A, Sw, I; Alp.
- × **richardii** Rehder (*R. gallica* × *R. phoenicia*) · ♄ d Z7 VI; Eth.
- **roxburghii** Tratt. · E:Chestnut Rose, Chinquapin Rose; G:Igel-Rose · ♄ d ⊛ Z6 VI; China, Jap.
- f. **normalis** Rehder & E.H. Wilson · ♄ d Z6 V-VI; W-China, Jap.
- **rubiginosa** L. · E:Eglantine, Sweet Briar; F:Rosier rouillé ; G:Wein-Rose · ♄ d ⊛ Z5 VI ⚥ Ⓝ; Eur.*, TR, Cauc., NW-Ind., nat. in N-Am.
- *rubrifolia* Vill. = Rosa glauca
- **rubus** H. Lév. & Vaniot · ♄ ⌇ d ⚥ Z8 ⒶⒷ; W-China, C-China
- **rugosa** Thunb. · E:Japanese Rose; F:Rosier du Japon; G:Kartoffel-Rose · ♄ d ⊛ D Z5 VI-IX ⚥ Ⓝ; E-Sib., Sakhal., Kamchat., N-China, Korea, Jap., nat. in Eur.: BrI, Sc, Fr, C-Eur., EC-Eur., E-Eur.
- **many cultivars**
- × **rugotida** Darthuis (*R. nitida* × *R. rugosa*) · F:Eglantier odorant · ♄ V-IX; cult.
- *sancta* Rich. non Andrews = Rosa × richardii
- **saturata** Baker · ♄; C-China
- *scabriuscula* auct. non Sm. = Rosa pseudoscabriuscula
- × **scharnkeana** Graebn. (*R. californica* × *R. nitida*) · ♄; cult.
- **sempervirens** L. · E:Evergreen Rose;

G:Immergrüne Rose · ʃ e ⚡ Z8 ⓐ VI-VII;
Eur.: Ib, F, Ital-P, Ba; TR, Syr., NW-Afr.
– *sepium* Thuill. non Lam. = Rosa agrestis
– **serafinii** Viv. · ♄ d △ ⊗ Z7 VI; Eur.:
Ital-P, Ba, ? RO; NW-Afr.
– **sericea** Lindl.
– subsp. **omeiensis** (Rolfe) A.V. Roberts ·
♄ Z6; China
– f. **pteracantha** Franch. · F:Rosier
barbelé · ♄ d ⊗ Z6 V-VI; W-Sichuan
– subsp. **sericea** · E:Mount Omei Rose;
G:Seiden-Rose · ♄ d Z6 V; W-Him.
– **setigera** Michx. · E:Prairie Rose;
G:Prärie-Rose · ♄ d ⚡ Z5 VII-VIII; Ont.,
USA: NE, NCE, NC, SC, SE, Fla.
– **setipoda** Hemsl. & E.H. Wilson ·
G:Borsten-Rose · ♄ d ⊗ Z6 VII; C-China
– **sherardii** Davies · G:Samt-Rose · ♄ d Z5
VI-VII; Eur.* exc. Ital-P
– **sicula** Tratt. · G:Sizilianische Rose · ♄ d
△ ⊗ D Z8 ∧ VI; Eur.: Ib, F, Fr, Ital-P, Ba;
W-TR, Syr., NW-Afr.
– *simplicifolia* Salisb. = Rosa persica
– *soongarica* Bunge = Rosa laxa
– **soulieana** Crép. · ♄ d ⚡ D Z7 ∧ VI-VII;
W-China
– **spinosissima** L. · E:Burnet Rose, Scotch
Briar, Scotch Rose; F:Rosier à feuilles de
pimprenelle, Rosier d'Ecosse; G:Biber-
nell-Rose · ♄ Z3 V-VI; Eur.* exc. Ib; TR,
Cauc., W-Sib., C-As., China, Korea, nat.
in N-Am.
– **stellata** Wooton · E:Desert Rose · ♄ d △
⊗ Z7 VI-VII; USA: N.Mex., Tex.
– **stylosa** Desv. · G:Griffel-Rose, Verwach-
sengrifflige Rose · ♄ d Z6 VI; Eur.: Ib, Fr,
I, C-Eur., BrI+; Alger.
– **subcanina** (H. Christ) Dalla Torre &
Sarnth. · G:Falsche Hunds-Rose · ♄ d;
Eur.* exc. Ib, W-As.
– **subcollina** (H. Christ) R. Keller · G:Fals-
che Hecken-Rose · ♄ d; Eur.*, W-As.
– **sweginzowii** Koehne · G:Sweginzows
Rose · ♄ d ⊗ Z6 VI; NW-China
– *thea* Savi = Rosa × odorata
– **tomentella** Léman · G:Stumpfblättrige
Rose · ♄ V-VI; Eur.: BrI, C-Eur., S-Eur.;
Alger.
– **tomentosa** Sm. · E:Downy Rose; G:Filz-
Rose · ♄ d ⊗ Z5 VI-VII; Eur.*, TR, Cauc.,
Lebanon, nat. in Prince Edward Isl.
– **turcica** Rouy · G:Türkische Rose · ♄;
Eur.: Ba, RO, S-Russ.; Cauc., TR
– **tuschetica** Boiss. · ♄ d D V-VI; Cauc.
– **villosa** L. · E:Apple Rose, Soft Leaved

Rose; G:Apfel-Rose · ♄ d ⊗ Z5 VI-VII
Ⓝ; Eur.: Ital-P, Fr, C-Eur., EC-Eur, Ba,
E-Eur.; TR, Cauc., Iran, C-As., nat. in Sc
– **virginiana** Mill. · E:Virginia Rose;
G:Virginische Rose · ♄ d ⊗ Z4 VI-VII;
Can.: E; USA; NE, NCE, SE
– *vosagiaca* Desp. = Rosa dumalis
– × **waitziana** Tratt. (*R. canina* × *R.
gallica*) · ♄ d; Eur.
– **watsoniana** Crép. · G:Watsons Rose · ♄ d
⚡ Z5 VI; cult. in Jap.
– **webbiana** Royle · ♄ d Z6; C-As., Afgh.,
Pakist., Him., China: Xizang
– **wichuraiana** Crép. · E:Memorial Rose;
G:Wichuras Rose · ♄ d ⚡ ⤳ Z6 VI-VIII;
Jap., Korea, E-China, Taiwan
– **willmottiae** Hemsl. · G:Willmotts Rose ·
♄ d D Z7 VI-VII; W-China
– **woodsii** Lindl. · ♄ d
– var. **fendleri** (Crép.) Rydb. · E:Fendler
Rose; G:Fendlers Rose · ♄ d Z4 VI-VII;
Can.; USA: NCE, NC, Rocky Mts., SW,
NW, Calif.; Mex.
– var. **woodsii** · E:Western Wild Rose,
Woods' Rose; G:Woods Rose · ♄ d Z5;
Alaska, Can., USA: NCE, NE, NC, SC,
Rocky Mts., NW, Calif.; N-Mex.
– **xanthina** Lindl. · G:Goldgelbe Rose · ♄ d
Z6 V-VI; N-China, Korea
– f. **hugonis** (Hemsl.) A.V. Roberts ·
E:Father Hugo's Rose; F:Rosier jaune de
Chine; G:Vater Hugos Rose · ♄ d Z6 V-VI;
C-China.
– **Cultivars:**
– **many cultivars, see Section III**

Roscoea Sm. -f- *Zingiberaceae* · 20 spp. ·
F:Fausse-orchidée; G:Ingwerorchidee,
Scheinorchis
– **alpina** Royle · ⚘ △ Z7 ∧ VI-VIII; Ind.,
Nepal, Bhutan, Sikkim, Tibet
– **cautleoides** Gagnep. · ⚘ △ Z7 ∧ VI-VIII;
NW-Yunnan, Sichuan
– **humeana** Balf. f. & W.W. Sm. · ⚘ △ Z7
∧ VI-VII; Sichuan, W-Yunnan
– **purpurea** Sm. · ⚘ △ Z7 ∧ VIII-IX; Him.,
Assam, Pakist.
– *yunnanensis* Loes. = Roscoea cautleoides
– **Cultivars:**
– **some cultivars**

Roseocactus A. Berger = Ariocarpus
– *fissuratus* (Engelm.) A. Berger = Ariocarpus fissuratus var. fissuratus
– *kotschoubeyanus* (Lem.) A. Berger =

Ariocarpus kotschoubeyanus
- *lloydii* (Rose) A. Berger = Ariocarpus fissuratus var. lloydii

Rosmarinus L. -m- *Lamiaceae* · 3 spp. · E:Rosemary; F:Romarin; G:Rosmarin
- **eriocalix** Jord. & Fourr. · G:Wollkelch-Rosamrin
- × **lavandulaceus** Noë (*R. eriocalix* × *R. officinalis*)
- **officinalis** L. · E:Rosemary; F:Romarin; G:Rosmarin · ♄ e D Z8 ⌂ V-VI ⚥ Ⓝ; Eur.: Ib, Fr, Ital-P, Ba; TR, Alger., Tun., nat. in Sw, Crim
- **some cultivars**

Rossioglossum (Schltr.) Garay & G.C. Kenn. -n- *Orchidaceae* · 6 spp.
- **grande** (Lindl.) Garay & G.C. Kenn. · E:Clown Orchid, Tiger Orchid; G:Tigerorchidee · ⌗ Z10 ⌂ IX-III ▽ ✳; Mex., Guat.
- **insleayi** (Barker ex Lindl.) Garay & G.C. Kenn. · ⌗ Z10 ⌂ X-XII ▽ ✳; Mex.
- **schlieperianum** (Rchb. f.) Garay & G.C. Kenn. · ⌗ Z10 ⌂ IX-III ▽ ✳; Costa Rica, Panama
- **williamsianum** (Rchb. f.) Garay & G.C. Kenn. · ⌗ Z10 ⌂ VII-IX ▽ ✳; Guat., Hond., Costa Rica

Rostraria Trin. -f- *Poaceae* · c. 10 spp. · E:Mediterranean Hair Grass; G:Büschelgras
- **cristata** (L.) Tzvelev · E:Mediterranean Hair Grass; G:Echtes Büschelgras · ☉ Z6 IV-VI; Eur.: Ib, Fr, Ital-P, Ba, Crim; TR, Levant, Iraq, Arab., Cauc., Iran, Afgh., Pakist., Ind., N-Afr., nat. in USA, W.Ind., S-Afr., Jap., Austr.

Rosularia (DC.) Stapf -f- *Crassulaceae* · 25 spp. · F:Rosulaire; G:Dickröschen
- **adenotrichum** (Wall. ex Edgew.) C.-A. Jansson · ⌗ ⩏ △ V-VI; Him.
- **aizoon** (Fenzl) A. Berger · ⌗ ⩏ △ Z7 ∧ VII; TR
- **chrysantha** (Boiss. & Heldr. ex Boiss.) Takht. · ⌗ ⩏ △ Z7 VI-VIII; TR
- *libanotica* (L.) Sam. = Rosularia serrata
- *libanotica* (Labill.) Muirhead = Rosularia sempervivum subsp. libanotica
- *pallida* (Schott & Kotschy) Stapf = Rosularia aizoon
- **platyphylla** (Schrank) A. Berger · ⌗ ⩏

Z7; China
- **rechingeri** C.-A. Jansson · ⌗ ⩏ Z7; TR, Iraq
- *sedoides* (Decne.) H. Ohba = Sedum sedoides
- **sempervivum** (M. Bieb.) A. Berger
- subsp. **amanensis** Eggli · ⌗ ⩏ Z7; E-Med.
- subsp. **glaucophylla** Eggli · ⌗ ⩏ Z7; S-TR; Taurus
- subsp. **libanotica** (Labill.) Eggli · ⌗ ⩏ Z7; TR, Lebanon, Syr., Palest.
- subsp. **sempervivum** · ⌗ ⩏ △ Z7 ∧ VI; TR, Cauc., Iran
- **serrata** (L.) A. Berger · ⌗ ⩏ Z8 ⌂; Crete, Aegaeis, SW-TR
- *spathulata* hort. = Rosularia sempervivum subsp. glaucophylla
- *turkestanica* hort. = Rosularia rechingeri

Rothmannia Thunb. -f- *Rubiaceae* · 41 sp.
- **capensis** Thunb. · E:Scented Cups · ♄ e Z10 ⌂ VII; S-Afr.
- **globosa** (Hochst.) Keay · ♄ ♄ e D Z10 ⌂ VI; S-Afr.: Natal
- **longiflora** Salisb. · ♄ e Z10 ⌂ VI-VII; W-Afr.: Sierra Leone

Roupala Aubl. -f- *Proteaceae* · 50-90+ spp.
- **Braziliensis** Klotzsch · ♄ e Z10 ⌂; Braz.
- *corcovadensis* hort. ex Meisn. = Roupala macrophylla
- **macrophylla** Pohl · ♄ e Z10 ⌂; Braz.
- *pohlii* Meisn. = Roupala Braziliensis

Roystonea O.F. Cook -f- *Arecaceae* · 10 spp. · E:Royal Palm; F:Palmier royal; G:Königspalme
- **oleracea** (Jacq.) O.F. Cook · E:South American Royal Palm; G:Barbados-Königspalme · ♄ e Z10 ⌂; Barbados, Trinidad, Venez., E-Col.
- **regia** (Kunth) O.F. Cook · E:Cuban Royal Palm; G:Kubanische Königspalme · ♄ e Z10 ⌂; Cuba

Rubia L. -f- *Rubiaceae* · 77 spp. · E:Madder; F:Garance; G:Krapp, Röte
- **cordifolia** L. · E:Indian Madder; G:Ostasiatischer Krapp · ⌗ Z7 ⚥ Ⓝ; NW-Him., Mong., China: Sinkiang; Ind., Sri Lanka, Indochina, Malay. Pen., Java, Jap., trop. Afr.
- **peregrina** L. · E:Wild Madder; G:Kletten-Krapp · ⌗ Z8 ⌂ Ⓝ; Eur.: Ib, Fr, Ital-P, Ba, BrI; TR, Palest., Canar., Madeira,

NW-Afr.
- **tinctorum** L. · E:Madder; G:Echte
Färberröte, Färber-Krapp · ♃ Z7 VI-VIII
⚥ Ⓝ; Eur.: Ital-P, Ba; TR, Iran, C-As.,
NW-Him., nat. in Ib, Fr, C-Eur., EC-Eur.

Rubus L. -m- *Rosaceae* · 250+ spp. ·
E:Bramble, Raspberry; F:Framboisier,
Mûrier sauvage, Ronce; G:Brombeere,
Himbeere, Steinbeere
- **sect. Rubus** · G:Echte Brombeere · ♄ d Z5
V-VII ⚥ Ⓝ; Eur.
- **many cultivars**
- **adenophorus** Rolfe · ♄ d Z6 VII;
C-China: W-Hupeh.
- **alleghiensis** Porter · E:Allegheny
Blackberry; G:Alleghni-Brombeere · ♄ d
⚭ Z3 Ⓝ; Can.: E; USA: NE, NCE, Tenn.,
N.C.
- **almus** L.H. Bailey · E:Garden Dewberry ·
♄ d ⚥ ⚭ Z8 Ⓚ Ⓝ; Tex.
- **amabilis** Focke · ♄ d Z6 VI-VII; W-China:
W-Sichuan
- **arcticus** L. · E:Arctic Bramble; G:Ark-
tische Himbeere · ♃ △ Z1 VI-IX; Eur.: Sc,
E-Eur.; W-Sib., E-Sib., Amur, Sakhal.,
Kamchat., Alaska, Can.: W; USA: Rocky
Mts.
- **armeniacus** Focke · G:Armenische
Brombeere, Garten-Brombeere · ♄ d Ⓝ;
Cauc., nat. in A, D
- **australis** G. Forst. · ♄ e ⚥ Z9 Ⓚ; NZ
- **bellobatus** L.H. Bailey · E:Kittatinny
Blackberry · ♄ d ⚭ Z6 Ⓝ; Can.: E; USA:
NE
- **biflorus** Buch.-Ham. ex Sm.
- var. **biflorus** · G:Gold-Himbeere · ♄ d ⚥ D
Z8 ∧ V; Him.
- var. **quinqueflorus** Focke · ♄ d ⚥ Z8 ∧;
W-China
- **bifrons** Vest ex Tratt. · G:Zweifarbige
Brombeere · ♄ d ⚭ Z6 Ⓝ; Eur.: BrI, Fr,
Ital-P, C-Eur., EC-Eur.
- **caesius** L. · E:European Dewberry;
F:Ronce bleuâtre; G:Acker-Brombeere,
Kratzbeere · ♄ d Z4 VI-VIII Ⓝ; Eur.*, TR,
Cauc., W-Sib., Altai
- *calycinoides* Hayata ex Koidz. = Rubus
pentalobus
- **chamaemorus** L. · E:Cloudberry;
G:Moltebeere · ♃ d △ Z2 V-VI Ⓝ ▽; Eur.:
Sc, BrI, EC-Eur., E-Eur.; W-Sib., E-Sib.,
Amur, Sakhal., Kamchat., Korea, Alaska,
Can., USA: NE; Greenl.
- **chroosepalus** Focke · ♄ s Z6 VIII;

C-China: Hupeh
- **cockburnianus** Hemsl. · G:Tangutische
Himbeere · ♄ d Z6 VI; N-China, C-China
- **corchorifolius** L. f. · ♄ d Z6 IV; C-China,
Jap., S-Korea
- **coreanus** Miq. · E:Korean Blackberry;
G:Korea-Himbeere · ♄ d Z6 V-VI ⚥ ;
China, Korea, Jap.
- **corylifolius** (Sm.) F. Aresch. · G:Hasel-
blatt-Brombeere · ♄; Eur.
- **crataegifolius** Bunge · ♄ d V-VI; Jap.,
Korea, N-China, Mong.
- **cuneifolius** Pursh · E:Sand Blackberry;
G:Keilblättrige Brombeere · ♄ d ⚭ Z6 Ⓝ;
USA: NE, SE, Fla.
- **deliciosus** Torr. · E:Rocky Mountain
Raspberry; G:Colorado-Himbeere · ♄ d
Z5 V; USA: Colo.
- **flagellaris** Willd. · E:American Dewberry,
Dewberry; G:Amerikanische Acker-
Brombeere · ♄ e ⤳ ⚭ Z3 V-VI Ⓝ; Can.:
E; USA; NE, NCE, SE
- **flagelliflorus** Focke · ♄ e ⚥ Z7; C-China,
W-China
- **flosculosus** Focke · ♄ d Z6 VI; China
- *fockeanus* hort. non Kurz = Rubus
pentalobus
- **frondosus** (Torr.) Bigelow ·
E:Blackberry, Yankee Blackberry · ♄ d ⚭
Z5 Ⓝ; Can.: Ont.; USA: NE, NCE
- *fruticosus agg.* = Rubus sect. Rubus
- *giraldianus* Focke = Rubus cockburnianus
- **glaucus** Benth. · E:Andes Berry;
G:Anden-Himbeere · ♄ d ⚭ Z8 Ⓚ Ⓝ;
Costa Rica, Panama, Col., Ecuad.
- **henryi** Hemsl. & Kuntze
- var. **bambusarum** (Focke) Rehder · ♄ d
⚥ Z7 VI; C-China
- var. **henryi** · F:Ronce de Henry;
G:Kletter-Himbeere · ♄ d ⚥ Z7; W-China,
C-China
- **idaeus** L. · E:Raspberry; F:Framboisier;
G:Himbeere · ♄ d Z3 V-VIII ⚥ Ⓝ; Eur.*,
TR, Cauc., W-Sib., E-Sib., Amur, Sakhal.,
Kamchat., C-As., Mong., Manch., Korea,
Jap., Alaska, Can., USA* exc. SC
- **many cultivars**
- subsp. *strigosus* (Michx.) Focke = Rubus
strigosus
- **illecebrosus** Focke · E:Strawberry
Raspberry; G:Japanische Himbeere · ♄ d
⚭ Z5 VII-X Ⓝ; Jap.
- *incisus* Thunb. = Rubus microphyllus
- *inermis* Pourr. = Rubus ulmifolius
- **laciniatus** Willd. · E:Cut Leaved Bramble;

G:Geschlitztblättrige Brombeere · ♄ d ⚥
⚥ Z6 V-VII Ⓝ; orig. ?, nat. in Eur., N-Am.
- **lasiostylus** Focke · G:Haar-Himbeere · ♄
d ⚥ Z6 VI; C-China
- **leucodermis** Douglas ex Torr. &
A. Gray · E:Whitebark Raspberry;
G:Oregon-Himbeere · ♄ d Z6 V-VI; B.C.,
USA: NW, Rocky Mts., Calif.
- **linkianus** Ser. · ⚄ ; orig. ?
- **loganobaccus** L.H. Bailey · E:Logan-
berry; G:Loganbeere · ♄ d ⚥ ⚥ Z8 Ⓝ;
cult. USA
- **macropetalus** Douglas ex Hook. ·
E:Blackberry · ♄ d ⚥ ⚥ Z7 Ⓝ; B.C., USA:
NW, N-Calif.
- *macrostemon* Focke = Rubus procerus
- **microphyllus** L. f. · ♄ d Z9 ⓚ VI-VII;
China, Jap.
- *moluccanus* hort. non L. = Rubus reflexus
- × **nobilis** Regel (*R. idaeus* × *R. odoratus*) ·
♄ d VI-VII; cult.
- *nutkanus* Moç. & Ser. = Rubus parviflorus
- **occidentalis** L. · E:Black Cap, Black
Raspberry; G:Schwarze Himbeere · ♄ d
⚥ Z3 V-VI Ⓝ; Can.: E; USA: NE, NCE,
NC, Rocky Mts., SE
- **odoratus** L. · E:Flowering Raspberry;
F:Framboisier du Canada, Ronce
odorante; G:Zimt-Himbeere · ♄ d Z4
V-VIII; Can.: E; USA; NE, NCE, SE
- **parviflorus** Nutt. · E:Thimbleberry;
G:Nutka-Himbeere · ♄ d Z4 VI-VIII;
Alaska, Can.; USA: NW, Calif., Rocky
Mts., SW, NCE
- **pentalobus** Hayata · F:Ronce; G:Kriech-
Himbeere · ♄ e ⤳ △ Z7 ⋀ V-VII; Taiwan
- **phoenicolasius** Maxim. · E:Wineberry;
G:Japanische Weinbeere, Rotborstige
Himbeere · ♄ d Z6 VI-VII Ⓝ; China,
Korea, Jap.
- *polytrichus* Franch. = Rubus tricolor
- **procerus** P.J. Müll. ex Boulay ·
E:Himalaya Blackberry; G:Himalaya-
Brombeere · ♄ d ⚥ Z6 Ⓝ; Eur.
- × **pseudoidaeus** (Weihe) Lej. (*R. caesius*
× *R. idaeus*) · G:Bastard-Himbeere · ♄ d;
Eur.+
- **reflexus** Ker-Gawl. · ♄ e ⚥ Z9 ⓚ; China
- **roribaccus** (L.H. Bailey) Rydb. ·
E:Lucretia Dewberry · ♄ d ⚥ ⚥ Z6; Can.:
E; USA: NE
- **rosa** L.H. Bailey · E:Rose Blackberry · ♄ d
⚥ Z7 Ⓝ; Can.: E; USA: NE, NCE
- **rosifolius** Sm. · ♄ ⚄ e Z9 ⓚ; Him., Malay.
Arch., Jap.

- **saxatilis** L. · E:Rock Bramble; G:Felsen-
Himbeere, Steinbeere · ⚄ d Z4 V-VII;
Eur.*, Cauc., W-Sib., E-Sib., Amur, Jap,
China, Him., Greenl.
- **spectabilis** Pursh · E:Salmonberry;
G:Pracht-Himbeere · ♄ d Z5; Alaska,
Can.: W; USA: NW, Calif., Idaho, nat. in
BrI, Fr, D
- **squarrosus** Fritsch · ♄ e ⚥ Z9 ⓚ; NZ
- **strigosus** Michx. · E:Wild Red Raspberry;
G:Amerikanische Himbeere · ♄ d ⚥ Z3
Ⓝ; Can.; USA: NE, NC, NCE, Rocky Mts.
- **thibetanus** Franch. · G:Tibet-Himbeere ·
♄ d Z6 VI; W-China
- **tricolor** Focke · F:Ronce; G:Dreifarbige
Himbeere · ♄ d Z6 VII-VIII; W-China
- **trifidus** Thunb. · ♄ e Z6 IV-V; Japan:
Honshu
- **trivialis** Michx. · E:Dewberry, Southern
Dewberry · ♄ d ⚥ Z6 Ⓝ; USA: NE,
NCE, SC, SE, Fla.
- **ulmifolius** Schott · E:Elm-leaf
Blackberry; G:Mittelmeer-Brombeere,
Sand-Brombeere · ♄ ⚥ Z7 VI-VII Ⓝ;
Eur.*, NW-Afr., Macaron.
- **ursinus** Cham. & Schltdl. · E:California
Dewberry, Pacific Dewberry; G:Kalifor-
nische Brombeere · ♄ ♄ e ⚥ Z7 Ⓝ; USA:
Oreg., Calif.; Baja Calif.
- var. *loganobaccus* (L.H. Bailey) L.H.
Bailey = Rubus loganobaccus
- **velox** L.H. Bailey · ♄ d ⚥ Z8 ⋀ Ⓝ; cult.
- *vitifolius* Cham. & Schltdl. = Rubus
ursinus

Rudbeckia L. -f- *Asteraceae* · 15 spp. ·
E:Coneflower; F:Rudbeckia; G:Sonnen-
hut
- *amplexicaulis* Vahl = Dracopsis amplexicaulis
- *angustifolia* (L.) L. = Helianthus angustifolius
- **fulgida** Aiton
- var. **deamii** (S.F. Blake) Perdue ·
E:Deam's Coneflower · ⚄ Z4 VIII-IX;
USA: Ind.
- var. **fulgida** · E:Coneflower; G:Gewöhn-
licher Sonnenhut · ⚄ Z4 VIII-X; USA: NE,
NCE, SE, Fla.
- var. **palustris** (Eggert ex F.E. Boynton &
Beadle) Perdue · E:Prairie Coneflower ·
Z4; USA: Tenn., Mo., Ky., Ind.
- var. **speciosa** (Wender.) Perdue ·
E:Orange Coneflower · ⚄ ⋉ Z4 VIII-X;
USA: NE, NCE, SE

– var. **sullivantii** (F.E. Boynton & Beadle) Cronquist · ⅄ VIII-X; USA: NCE, SE
– **hirta** L. · G:Rauer Sonnenhut
– some cultivars
– var. **hirta** · E:Black-Eyed Susan · ⊙ ⊙ Z4 VII-IX; USA: NE, NCE, SE, nat. in C-Eur.
– var. **pulcherrima** Farw. · ⊙ Z4 VIII-IX; USA: NCE, SE, SC, nat. in S-Can., USA , Mex.
– **laciniata** L. · G:Schlitzblättriger Sonnenhut
– var. **humilis** A. Gray · ⅄ Z3 VII-IX; USA: Va., Ky., SE
– var. **laciniata** · E:Cutleaf Coneflower · ⅄ Z3 VII-VIII; Can.: E; USA* exc. Calif., nat. in C-Eur.
– *laevigata* Pursh = Rudbeckia laciniata var. humilis
– **maxima** Nutt. · E:Great Coneflower; G:Riesen-Sonnenhut · ⅄ Z7 VII-IX; USA: Tex., Okla., Ark., La.
– *newmanii* F.E. Boynton & Beadle = Rudbeckia fulgida var. speciosa
– **nitida** Nutt. · E:Shiny Coneflower; G:Glänzender Sonnenhut · ⅄ Z3 VII-IX; USA: SE, Fla., Tex.
– **occidentalis** Nutt. · E:Western Coneflower; G:Westlicher Sonnenhut · ⅄ Z7; W-USA
– *palustris* Eggert ex F.E. Boynton & Beadle = Rudbeckia fulgida var. palustris
– *purpurea* L. = Echinacea purpurea
– *serotina* Nutt. = Rudbeckia hirta var. pulcherrima
– *speciosa* Wender. = Rudbeckia fulgida var. speciosa
– var. *sullivantii* (F.E. Boynton ex Beadle) B.L. Rob. = Rudbeckia fulgida var. sullivantii
– **subtomentosa** Pursh · E:Sweet Coneflower ; G:Schwachfilziger Sonnenhut · ⅄ Z5 VII-IX; USA: NCE, SC, SE
– *sullivantii* F.E. Boynton & Beadle = Rudbeckia fulgida var. sullivantii
– **triloba** L. · E:Brown-eyed Susan; G:Dreiblättrige Sonnenhut · ⊙ ⊙ Z5 VII-IX; USA: NE, NCE, SE, Okla.

Rudolfiella Hoehne -f- *Orchidaceae* · 6 spp.
– **aurantiaca** (Lindl.) Hoehne · ⅄ Z10 ⓜ IX-X ▽ ✳; Venez., Guyana, Trinidad

Ruellia L. -f- *Acanthaceae* · c. 150 spp. · E:Wild Petunia; F:Ruellia; G:Rudel, Ruellie

– **devosiana** Jacob-Makoy · ♄ e Z10 ⓜ IX-XII; Braz.
– **graecizans** Backer · ♄ e Z10 ⓜ V-X; S-Am.
– **humilis** Nutt. · E:Fringeleaf Wild Petunia · ⅄ Z5 VIII-IX; USA: NE, NCE, NC, SC, SE, Fla.
– *longifolia* (Pohl) Griseb. ex Lindau = Ruellia graecizans
– **macrantha** Mart. ex Nees · E:Christmas Pride · ♄ e Z10 ⓜ XII-V; Braz.
– *maculata* Wall. = Strobilanthes maculatus
– **makoyana** Closon · E:Trailing Velvet Plant · ♄ e Z10 ⓜ IX-XII; Braz.
– **portellae** Hook. f. · ♄ e ⓜ; Braz.
– *repanda* L. = Hemigraphis repanda
– **strepens** L. · E:Limestone Wild Petunia · ⅄ Z5 ⓐ VIII-IX; USA: NE, NCE, NC, SC, SE

Rumex L. -m- *Polygonaceae* · c. 200 spp. · E:Dock; F:Oseille, Oseille sauvage; G:Ampfer, Sauerampfer
– **acetosa** L. · E:Garden Sorrel, Sorrel, Sour Dock; G:Großer Sauerampfer · ⅄ Z3 V-VII ⚥̂ ; Eur.*, Cauc., W-Sib., E-Sib., Amur, Sakhal., C-As., Mong., Him., China, Jap., Moroc., N-Am., Greenl.
– **acetosella** L. · G:Kleiner Sauerampfer
– subsp. **acetosella**
– var. **acetosella** · E:Sheep Sorrel; G:Gewöhnlicher Kleiner Sauerampfer · ⅄ ⤳ V-VII ⚥̂ ; Eur.*, Cauc., W-Sib., E-Sib., Amur, Sakhal., Kamchat., nat. in N-Am.
– var. **tenuifolius** (Wallr.) · G:Schmalblättriger Kleiner Sauerampfer · ⅄ V-VII; Eur.: most; TR, Cauc., W-Sib., E-Sib., Greenl.
– subsp. **pyrenaicus** (Pourr. ex Lapeyr.) Akeroyd · G:Hüllfrüchtiger Ampfer, Verwachsenblättriger Kleiner Sauerampfer · ⅄ V-VII; W-Eur., Moroc., Alger.
– **alpinus** L. · E:Monk's Rhubarb, Mountain Rhubarb; G:Alpen-Ampfer, Mönchsrhabarber · ⅄ Z5 VI-VIII ⚥̂ ; Eur.* exc. BrI, Sc; TR, Cauc., W-Iran; mts., nat. in Engl.
– *angiocarpus* Murb. = Rumex acetosella subsp. pyrenaicus
– **aquaticus** L. · E:Western Dock; G:Wasser-Ampfer · ⅄ ⌢ VII-VIII; Eur.* exc. Ib; Cauc., W-Sib., E-Sib., Amur, Kamchat., C-As., Mong., China, Jap.
– **arifolius** All. · G:Berg-Sauerampfer, Gebirgs-Sauerampfer · ⅄ VI-VIII; Eur.*

exc. BrI; N, mts.; Cauc., W-Sib., Sakhal., Kamchat.
- **confertus** Willd. · G:Gedrungener Ampfer · 4 VII-VIII; Eur.: I, EC-Eur., E-Eur.; Cauc., W-Sib., E-Sib., Amur, C-As., nat. in BrI, FIN
- **conglomeratus** Murray · E:Sharp Dock; G:Knäuelblütiger Ampfer · 4 VII-VIII; Eur.*, TR, Levant, Cauc., C-As., NW-Afr., Libya
- **crispus** L. · E:Curly Dock; G:Krauser Ampfer · 4 VI-VIII ⚤ ⚘; Eur.*, TR, Cauc., Amur, Kamchat., C-As., Mong., China, nat. in cosmop.
- **cristatus** DC. · G:Griechischer Ampfer · 4 VII-VIII; Eur.: Ital-P, H, Ba, RO; TR, Cyprus, nat. in Ib, Br
- **flexuosus** Sol. ex G. Forst. · 4 Z7 ⋀ VI-VII; NZ
- × **heterophyllus** Schultz (*R. aquaticus* × *R. hydrolapathum*) · G:Verschiedenblättriger Ampfer · 4; Eur.: G, A, PL, CZ +
- **hydrolapathum** Huds. · E:Great Water Dock; F:Patience aquatique; G:Fluss-Ampfer · 4 Z6 VII-VIII; Eur.*, TR, Cauc.
- **hymenosepalus** Torr. · E:Canaigre, Red Dock, Sand Dock; G:Canaigrewurzel, Gerb-Ampfer · 4 Z6 VII-VIII Ⓝ; USA: NC, SC, SW, Rocky Mts., Calif.
- **kerneri** Borbás · G:Kerners Ampfer · 4 VII-VIII; Eur.: H, RO, BG, GR
- **longifolius** DC. · E:Dooryard Dock; G:Gemüse-Ampfer · 4 VII-VIII; Eur.: Sc, BrI, Fr, G, Ib, EC-Eur.; Cauc., W-Sib., E-Sib., N-Am.
- **maritimus** L. · E:Golden Dock; G:Ufer-Ampfer · ☉ ☉ ⌇ VII-IX; Eur.* exc. Ib; W-Sib., E-Sib., Amur, Sakhal., C-As., Ind., Mong., Manch., Jap., Alger., Am.
- **nivalis** Hegetschw. · G:Schnee-Sauerampfer · 4 VII-IX; Eur.: C-Eur., Slove., Montenegro, AL
- **obtusifolius** L. · E:Bitter Dock, Broad-leaved Dock; G:Gewöhnlicher Stumpfblättriger Ampfer · 4 VII-VIII ⚤; Eur.*, TR, Lebanon, Syr., Palest., Cauc., N-Iran, Canar., Alger., nat. in N-Am., S-Am., S-Afr., Austr.
- **palustris** Sm. · E:Marsh Dock; G:Sumpf-Ampfer · ☉ ⌇ VII-IX; Eur.* exc. Ib; TR, Levant, Moroc., Alger.
- **patientia** L. · E:Patience, Patience Dock, Spinach Dock; G:Englischer Spinat, Garten-Ampfer · 4 VII-VIII ⚤ Ⓝ; Eur.: Ital-P, EC-Eur., Ba., E-Eur.; TR, Syr.,

Cauc., Iran, W-Sib., Amur, Sakhal., nat. in BrI, C-Eur., USA
- **pseudoalpinus** Höfft · G:Alpen-Ampfer
- **pseudonatronatus** Borbás · G:Finnischer Ampfer · 4 VII-VIII; Eur.: A, H, E-Eur., Sc; W-Sib., E-Sib., C-As.
- **pulcher** L. · E:Fiddle Dock; G:Schöner Ampfer · 4 V-VII; Eur.* exc. Sc; TR, Arab., Levant, Cauc., Iran, N-Afr.
- **rugosus** Campd. · E:Garden Sorrel; G:Garten-Sauerampfer · 4 V-VIII Ⓝ; cult.
- **salicifolius** Weinm. · E:Willow Dock; G:Weidenblatt-Ampfer
- var. **salicifolius** · G:Gewöhnlicher Weidenblatt-Ampfer · 4; N-Am.
- var. **triangulivalvis** (Danser) J.C. Hickman · G:Dreieckiger Weidenblatt-Ampfer · 4 VI-IX; N-Am., nat. in BrI, Sc, G, EC-Eur.
- **sanguineus** L. · E:Red-veined Dock; G:Blut-Ampfer, Hain-Ampfer · 4 Z6 VI-VIII; Eur.*, Cauc., N-Iran, NW-Afr.
- **scutatus** L. · E:French Sorrel; G:Römischer Ampfer, Schild-Sauerampfer · 4 Z6 V-VIII ⚤ Ⓝ; Eur.* exc. BrI, Sc; TR, Cauc., Iran, nat. in BrI, Sc
- **stenophyllus** Ledeb. · E:Narrow-leaved Dock; G:Schmalblättriger Ampfer · 4 VII-VIII; Eur.: C-Eur., EC-Eur., Ba, E-Eur.; Cauc., W-Sib., E-Sib., C-As.
- *tenuifolius* (Wallr.) A. Löve = Rumex acetosella subsp. acetosella var. tenuifolius
- **thyrsiflorus** Fingerh. · G:Rispen-Sauerampfer, Straußblütiger Sauermapfer · 4 VII-VIII; Eur.* exc. BrI; W-Sib., E-Sib., Amur, C-As.
- *triangulivalvis* (Danser) Rech. f. = Rumex salicifolius var. triangulivalvis
- **vesicarius** L. · E:Bladder Dock; G:Indischer Sauerampfer · ☉ Ⓝ; Eur.: GR; W-As., Ind., Malay. Pen., N-Afr.

Rumohra Raddi -f- *Dryopteridaceae* · 7 spp.
- **adiantiformis** (G. Forst.) Ching · E:Leatherleaf Fern, Iron Fern; G:Lederfarn · 4 Z9 🏠; C-Am., S-Am., S-Afr., Austr., NZ, Polyn.

Rupicapnos Pomel -f- *Fumariaceae* · 7 spp.
- **africana** (Lam.) Pomel · ☉ 4 Z8 🏠 V-VI; Eur.: SW-Sp.; Moroc., Alger.

Ruppia L. -f- *Ruppiaceae* · 7+ spp. · E:Tasselweed; F:Ruppia; G:Salde

– **cirrhosa** (Petagna) Grande · G:Schrau-
bige Salde · ⟂ ≈ VI-X; Eur.*, cosmop.
coasts
– **maritima** L. · G:Strand-Salde · ⟂ ≈
VI-X; Eur.*, cosmop.

Ruschia Schwantes -f- *Aizoaceae* ·
220 spp. · E:Shrubby Dewplant; F:Ficoïde
arbustive; G:Straucheiskraut
– **odontocalyx** (Schltr. & Diels)
Schwantes · ♄ ⟂ Z10 ⌂; Cape, Namibia
– **perfoliata** (Mill.) Schwantes · ♄ ⟂ Z10
⌂; Cape
– **semidentata** (Salm-Dyck) Schwantes · ♄
⟂ e Z10 ⌂; Cape
– **spinosa** (L.) M. Dehn · ♄ ⟂ ⌂; Cape,
Namibia
– **tumidula** (Haw.) Schwantes · ♄ ⟂ Z10
⌂; Cape, Namibia
– **umbellata** (L.) Schwantes · ♄ ⟂ Z10 ⌂;
Cape
– **uncinata** (L.) Schwantes · ♄ ⟂ Z10 ⌂;
Cape, Namibia
– **vulvaria** (Dinter) Schwantes · ♄ ⟂ Z10
⌂; Namibia

Ruscus L. -m- *Ruscaceae* · 6 spp. ·
E:Butcher's Broom; F:Epine de rat,
Fragon, Petit houx; G:Mäusedorn
– **aculeatus** L. · E:Butcher's Broom;
G:Stachliger Mäusedorn · ♄ e Z8 ⌂ III-IV
⚥ ✷; Eur.: Ib, Fr, Ital-P, Ba, Crim, H,
Sw, BrI, Azor.; TR, Cyprus, Syr., NW-Afr.
– *androgynus* L. = Semele androgyna
– **hypoglossum** L. · E:Spineless Butcher's
Broom; G:Hadernblatt · ♄ e Z8 ⌂ IV-V;
Eur.: NW-I, A, EC-Eur., BA, RO, Crim; TR
– **hypophyllum** L. · ♄ e Z8 ⌂ V-VI; Eur.:
S-Sp., F (Iles d`Hyeres?), Sic; NW-Afr.
– **ponticus** Woronow · ♄ e ⌂; Crim.,
Cauc., TR
– *racemosus* L. = Danae racemosa

Ruspolia Lindau -f- *Acanthaceae* · 4 spp.
– **seticalyx** (C.B. Clarke) Milne-Redh. · ♄ e
Z10 ⌂; E-Afr.

Russelia Jacq. -f- *Scrophulariaceae* ·
52 spp. · F:Plante-corail, Russélia;
G:Russelie
– **equisetiformis** Schltdl. & Cham. ·
E:Coral Plant, Firecracker, Fountain
Plant; G:Springbrunnenpflanze · ♄ e ⚘ Z9
⌂ V-X; Mex., Col., Peru
– *juncea* Zucc. = Russelia equisetiformis

– **sarmentosa** Jacq. · ♄ e Z9 ⌂ V-X; Mex.,
Cuba

Ruta L. -f- *Rutaceae* · 7 spp. · G:Raute;
E:Rue; F:Rue
– **graveolens** L. · E:Rue; G:Wein-Raute ·
⟂ ♄ ♄ e D Z5 VI-VII ⚥ ✷ Ⓝ; Eur.: Ib, Fr,
Ital-P, Ba, Crim, nat. in C-Eur., EC-Eur.,
RO
– *patavina* L. = Haplophyllum patavinum

Ruttya Harv. -f- *Acanthaceae* · 3 spp.
– **fruticosa** Lindau · ♄ e Z10 ⌂; trop. e Afr.

Ryania Vahl -f- *Flacourtiaceae* · 8 spp.
– **pyrifera** (Rich.) Uittien & Sleumer · ♄ e
Z10 ⌂ Ⓝ; W.Ind.

Rydbergia Greene = Hymenoxys
– *grandiflora* (Torr. & A. Gray ex A. Gray)
Greene = Hymenoxys grandiflora

Sabadilla Brandt & Ratzeb. = Schoenocaulon
– *officinarum* (Cham. & Schltdl.) Brandt &
Ratzeb. = Schoenocaulon officinale

Sabal Adans. -f- *Arecaceae* · 15 spp. ·
E:Palmetto; F:Palmette, Sabal; G:Palmet-
topalme, Sabalpalme
– *adansonii* Guers. = Sabal minor
– *blackburniana* Glazebr. ex Schult. &
Schult. f. = Sabal palmetto
– **domingensis** Becc.
– **mauriitiiformis** (H. Karst.) Griseb. & H.
Wendl. · E:Trinidad Palm; G:Trinidad-
Palmettopalme · ♄ e Z10 ⌂; Mex., C-Am.,
Col, Venez., Trinidad
– **minor** (Jacq.) Pers. · E:Dwarf Palmetto;
G:Zwerg-Palmettopalme · ♄ e Z9 ⌂;
USA: SE, Fla., Tex.
– **palmetto** (Walter) Lodd. ex Schult.
& Schult. f. · E:Cabbage Palmetto,
Palmetto; G:Gewöhnliche Palmettopalme
· ♄ e Z8 ⌂; USA: SE, Fla.; Bahamas
– *umbraculifera* (Jacq.) Mart. = Sabal
palmetto

Sabatia Adans. -f- *Gentianaceae* · 17 spp.
– **angularis** (L.) Pursh · E:Rose Gentian,
Rose Pink · ☉ Z6 VII-IX; Can.: Ont.; USA:
NE, NCE, SE, Fla., Okla.
– **campestris** Nutt. · E:Texas Star · ☉ Z6
VII-IX; USA: NCE, SC, Ark.
– **chloroides** Pursh · E:Marsh Rose

Gentian · ⊙ Z6 VII-IX; USA: NE, N.C.

Saccharum L. -n- *Poaceae* · 35-40 spp. ·
E:Plume Grass; F:Canne à sucre;
G:Ravennagras, Zuckerrohr
- **arundinaceum** Retz. · ⁴ Z9 ⓦ ⓝ;
NE-Ind., Sri Lanka, SE-As.
- **barberi** Jeswiet · E:Indian Cane;
G:Indisches Zuckerrohr · ⁴ Z9 ⓦ ⓝ; cult.
N-Ind.
- **officinarum** L. · E:Sugar Cane; G:Zucker-
rohr · ⁴ Z9 ⓦ ⓝ; cult., trop. SE-As.,
Polyn.
- subsp. *barberi* (Jeswiet) Burkill = Saccharum barberi
- subsp. *sinense* (Roxb.) Burkill = Saccharum sinense
- *paniceum* P. Beauv. = Pogonatherum
paniceum
- **ravennae** (L.) Murray · E:Ravenna Grass;
G:Italienisches Zuckerrohr · ⁴ Z8 ⓚ ⋀
IX-X; Eur.: Ib, Fr, Ital-P, Ba; TR, SW-As.,
Afgh., C-As., N-Ind., Alger., Somalia, nat.
in RO, SE-USA
- **robustum** Brandis & Jeswiet ex Grassl ·
E:Robust Cane · ⁴ Z9 ⓦ ⓝ; N.Guinea
- *saccharoideum* P. Beauv. = Pogonatherum
paniceum
- **sinense** Roxb. · ⁴ Z9 ⓦ ⓝ; cult., nat. in
N-Ind., S-China, Jap.
- **spontaneum** L. · E:Wild Sugar Cane ·
⁴ Z9 ⓦ; Egypt, SW-As., C-As., Ind.,
S-China, Malay. Arch., Phil., N-Guinea,
E-Austr.

Saccolabium Blume -n- *Orchidaceae* ·
5 spp.
- *ampullaceum* Lindl. = Ascocentrum
ampullaceum
- *bellinum* Rchb. f. = Gastrochilus bellinus
- *coeleste* Rchb. f. = Rhynchostylis coelestis
- *giganteum* Lindl. = Rhynchostylis
gigantea
- *violaceum* (Lindl.) Rchb. f. = Rhynchostylis retusa

Sageretia Brongn. -f- *Rhamnaceae* · 35 spp.
- **thea** (Osbeck) M.C. Johnst. · E:Pauper's
Tea · ♭ d D Z9 ⓦ ⓚ; Ind., C-China,
E-China, Jap., Ryukyu-Is., Taiwan
- *theezans* (L.) Brongn. = Sageretia thea

Sagina L. -f- *Caryophyllaceae* · c. 20 spp. ·
E:Pearlwort; F:Sagine; G:Knebel,
Mastkraut
- **apetala** Ard. · G:Kronblattloses
Mastkraut
- subsp. **apetala** · E:Common Pearlwort;
G:Bewimpertes Mastkraut · ⊙ IV-VII;
Eur.*, TR, Levant, Cauc., Canar., NW-
Afr., Libya, N-Am.
- subsp. **erecta** F. Herm. · G:Kronloses
Mastkraut · ⊙ V-IX; Eur.: Ib, F, I , C-Eur.
- **boydii** F.B. White · E:Boyd's Pearlwort ·
⁴ Z5; ? Scotland +
- **glabra** (Willd.) Fenzl · G:Kahles
Mastkraut · ⁴ VII-VIII; Eur.: F, I, Sw;
Alp., Apenn., ? Pyr.
- **maritima** G. Don · E:Sea Pearlwort;
G:Strand-Mastkraut · ⊙ V-VIII; Eur.*, TR,
Levant, NW-Afr., Libya
- *micropetala* Rauschert = Sagina apetala
subsp. erecta
- **nivalis** (Lindblad) Fr. · E:Snow
Pearlwort · ⁴; Eur.: BrI, Sc, N-Russ.; Sib.
- **nodosa** (L.) Fenzl · E:Knotted Pearlwort;
G:Knotiges Mastkraut · ⁴ VI-VIII; Eur.*
exc. Ba, Ital-P; W-Sib., E-Sib., N-Am.,
Greenl.
- **normaniana** Lagerh. · G:Normans
Mastkraut · ⁴ VI-VIII; Eur.: BrI, Sc, A;
mts.
- **procumbens** L. · E:Procumbent Pearl-
wort; G:Gewöhnliches Niederliegendes
Salzkraut · ⁴ Z4 V-IX; Eur.*, TR, Cauc.,
W-Sib., Him., Tibet, NW-Afr., N-Am.
- **saginoides** (L.) H. Karst. · E:Alpine
Pearlwort; G:Alpen-Mastkraut · ⁴
VI-VIII; Eur.*, TR, Cauc., W-Sib., E-Sib.,
Kamchat., C-As., Him., China: Sinkiang;
NW-Afr., N-Am., Mex.; mts.

Sagittaria L. -f- *Alismataceae* · 20 spp. ·
E:Arrowhead; F:Flèche d'eau, Sagittaire;
G:Pfeilkraut
- *alpina* Willd. = Sagittaria sagittifolia
subsp. sagittifolia
- **chilensis** Cham. & Schltdl. · ⁴ ∼ ≈
ⓚ; Chile
- *chinensis* Pursh = Sagittaria latifolia
- **engelmanniana** J.G. Sm. ·
E:Engelmann's Arrowhead; G:Engel-
manns Pfeilkraut · ⁴ ∼ Z6; USA: NE,
SE
- *filiformis* J.G. Sm. = Sagittaria subulata
- *gracilis* Pursh = Sagittaria latifolia
- **graminea** Michx. · E:Grass Leaf Arrowhead; F:Sagittaire à feuilles de graminée;
G:Grasblättriges Pfeilkraut · ⁴ ∼ ≈
Z6 ⓝ; Ind., China, Korea, Jap., nat. in

Panama, Java, Austr.
- var. *platyphylla* Engelm. = Sagittaria
  platyphylla
- var. *teres* (S. Watson) Bogin = Sagittaria
  teres
- *hastata* Pursh = Sagittaria latifolia
- **lancifolia** L. · E:Lance Leaf Arrowhead;
  G:Lanzettblättriges Pfeilkraut · �2⁴ ⌢ Z9
  🌿 VII-IX; USA: NE, SE, Fla., SC; Mex.,
  C.-Am., W.Ind., n S-Am
- **latifolia** Willd. · E:Broad Leaf Arrowhead, Duck Potato, Wapato; F:Sagittaire
  à larges feuilles; G:Veränderliches
  Pfeilkraut · ⁴ ⌢ Z7 ⋀ VIII-IX; Can.,
  USA*; Mex., C-Am., nw S-Am., nat. in
  Eur.
- *leucopetala* (Miq.) Bergmans = Sagittaria
  sagittifolia subsp. leucopetala
- **longiloba** Engelm. ex Torr. · E:Longbarb
  Arrowhead · ⁴ ≋ Z8 🔒; USA: Calif.,
  Rocky Mts., SW, SC, NC; Mex., Nicar.
- *longirostra* (Michx.) J.G. Sm. = Sagittaria
  latifolia
- *lorata* (Chapm.) Small = Sagittaria
  subulata
- **macrophylla** Zucc. · ⁴ ⌢ ≋ Z9 🔒;
  Mex.
- **montevidensis** Cham. & Schltdl. ·
  E:Giant Arrowhead; G:Montevideo-
  Pfeilkraut · ⁴ ⌢ Z10 🌿 VI-VIII; Braz.,
  Urug., Arg.
- subsp. *chilensis* (Cham. & Schltdl.) Bogin
  = Sagittaria chilensis
- *natans* Pall. = Sagittaria sagittifolia
  subsp. sagittifolia
- *obtusa* Muhl. ex Willd. = Sagittaria
  latifolia
- **platyphylla** (Engelm.) J.G. Sm. · E:Delta
  Arrowhead; G:Breitblättriges Pfeilkraut
  · ⁴ ⌢ ≋ Z7; USA: Mo., Kans., SC, SE;
  C-Am.
- **sagittifolia** L.
- subsp. **leucopetala** (Miq.) Hartog ex
  Steenis · ⁴ ⌢ Z8 🔒 VI-VII ℕ; trop. As.,
  Arab., S-China
- subsp. **sagittifolia** · E:Arrowhead,
  Common Arrowhead; F:Sagittaire
  nageante, Sagittaire à feuilles en flèche;
  G:Gewöhnliches Pfeilkraut · ⁴ ♄ ⌢ ≋
  Z7 VI-VIII; Eur.*; Sib.
- *simplex* Pursh = Sagittaria latifolia
- *sinensis* Sims = Sagittaria graminea
- **subulata** (L.) Buchenau · E:Awl-leaf
  Arrowhead; G:Flutendes Pfeilkraut · ⁴
  ≋ Z7; USA: NE, SE, Fla.; Col., Venez.,

S-Braz., nat. in H, RO
- **teres** S. Watson · E:Slender Arrowhead;
  G:Zartes Pfeilkraut · ⁴ ≋ Z7; USA: NE

Saintpaulia H. Wendl. -f- *Gesneriaceae* ·
20 spp. · E:African Violet; F:Violette
d'Usambara; G:Usambaraveilchen
- **confusa** B.L. Burtt · ⁴ Z10 🌿; Tanzania
- **goetzeana** Engl. · ⁴ Z10 🌿 🔒; Tanzania
  (Uluguru)
- **grotei** Engl. · ⁴ Z10 🌿; Tanzania
- **ionantha** H. Wendl. · ⁴ Z10 🌿 I-XII;
  Tanzania
- *kewensis* C.B. Clarke = Saintpaulia
  ionantha
- *kewensis* hort. = Saintpaulia confusa
- **magungensis** E.P. Roberts · ⁴ Z10 🌿;
  Tanzania
- **tongwensis** B.L. Burtt · ⁴ Z10 🌿;
  NE-Tanzania
- **Cultivars:**
- **many cultivars**

Salacca Reinw. -f- *Arecaceae* · 20 spp. ·
E:Salak Palm; F:Salacca; G:Salakpalme
- **zalacca** (Gaertn.) Voss · E:Salak Palm;
  G:Salakpalme · ♄ e Z10 🌿 ℕ; Malay.
  Arch.

Salicornia L. -f- *Chenopodiaceae* ·
14-28 spp. · E:Glasswort, Marsh
Samphire; F:Salicorne; G:Glasschmalz,
Queller
- *dolichostachya* Moss = Salicornia
  procumbens
- **europaea** L. · G:Kurzähren-Queller
- subsp. **brachystachya** (G. Mey.) Dahmen
  & Wissk. · G:Ästiger Queller, Gewöhnlicher Kurzähren-Queller · ⊙ ⌢ VIII;
  Eur.: BrI, Fr, G, Sc, +; coasts
- subsp. **europaea** · E:Salicorn;
  G:Europäischer Queller, Zierlicher
  Kurzähren-Queller · ⊙ ⌢ VIII-X; Eur.*;
  coasts; TR, Levant, Iran, C-As., W-Sib.,
  E-Sib., Amur, Sakhal., China, Jap., N-Afr.
- *fragilis* P.W. Ball & Tutin = Salicornia
  procumbens
- **procumbens** Sm. · G:Aufrechter Queller,
  Sandwatt-Queller · ⊙ ⌢ VIII-X; Eur.: D
  + ; coasts
- *ramosissima* J. Woods = Salicornia
  europaea subsp. brachystachya
- **stricta** Dumort. · G:Schlickwatt-Queller ·
  ⊙ ⌢ ; Eur.: BrI, Fr, G, Sc + ; coasts

Salix L. -f- *Salicaceae* · 300-400 spp. ·
E:Sallow, Willow; F:Saule; G:Weide
– **acutifolia** Willd. · E:Caspian Willow,
Sharp Leaf Willow; G:Spitzblättrige
Weide · ♃ d Z5 III Ⓝ; Eur.: FIN, Russ.;
Cauc., W-Sib., E-Sib
– **aegyptiaca** L. · E:Musk Willow;
G:Persische Weide · ♃ ♃ d Z6 III-V Ⓝ;
Eur.: NE-GR; TR, Israel, C-As.
– **alba** L. · G:Silber-Weide
– 'Vitellina' = Salix alba var. vitellina
– var. **alba** · E:White Willow; F:Saule
blanc; G:Gewöhnliche Silber-Weide · ♃ d
Z4 IV-V ⚥ ; Eur.* exc. Sc; TR, Cauc., Iran,
W-Sib., C-As., W-Him., NW-Afr., nat. in
Sc
– var. *argentea* Wimm. = Salix alba var.
sericea
– var. **sericea** Gaudin · ♃ d Z4; cult.
– var. **vitellina** (L.) Stokes · E:Golden
Willow; G:Bunte Weide, Dotter-Weide ·
♃ d Z4; cult.
– var. *vitellina-pendula* Rehder = Salix ×
chrysocoma
– × **alopecuroides** Tausch (*S. fragilis* × *S.*
triandra) · G:Fuchsschwanz-Weide · ♃ d;
NL, G, S-Swed
– **alpina** Scop. · G:Alpen-Weide, Myrten-
Weide · ♃ d Z5 VI-VII; Eur.: I, C-Eur.,
EC-Eur., Slove., RO, W-Russ.; E-Alp.,
Carp.
– × **ambigua** Ehrh. (*S. aurita* × *S. repens*) ·
G:Bastard-Ohr-Weide · ♃ d Z7; Eur. +
cult.
– *amygdalina* L. = Salix triandra subsp.
triandra
– **amygdaloides** Andersson · E:Peach Leaf
Willow; G:Pfirsich-Weide · ♃ ♃ d Z5 IV-V;
Can., USA* exc. Fla., Calif.; N-Mex.
– **apennina** A.K. Skvortsov · G:Apenninen-
Weide · ♃ d IV-VII; Eur.: I, Sic.; Apenn.,
Sic.
– **apoda** Trautv. · ♃ d △ Z6 IV; Cauc.,
N-Iran
– **appendiculata** Vill. · F:Saule à grandes
feuilles; G:Großblättrige Weide · ♃ ♃ d Z5
V; mts. C-Eur., EC-Eur., Ba, Fr, I
– **arbuscula** L. · E:Mountain Willow · ♃
d Z4; Eur.: I, Ba, Sc, N-Russ.; Cauc.,
W-Sib., E-Sib., C-As.
– *arbutifolia* Pall. = Chosenia arbutifolia
– *atrocinerea* = Salix cinerea subsp.
oleifolia
– **aurita** L. · E:Eared Willow; F:Saule à
oreillettes; G:Ohr-Weide · ♃ d ⌒ Z5

IV-V Ⓝ; Eur.*, Cauc.
– **babylonica** L. · E:Babylon Weeping Willow; F:Saule pleureur; G:Trauer-Weide ·
♃ d Z5 IV-V Ⓝ; C-China, ? Cauc., ? Iran
– × **balfourii** E.F. Linton (*S. caprea* × *S.*
lanata) · ♃ d Z4; cult. Engl.
– **bockii** Seemen · G:Chinesische Myrten-
Weide · ♃ d Z7 ∧ VIII-IX; W-China
– × **boydii** E.F. Linton (*S. lapponum* × *S.*
reticulata) · E:Dwarf Willow; F:Saule
nain de Boyd; G:Zwerg-Weide · ♃ d Z5 V;
Scotland
– **breviserrata** Flod. · E:Finely-toothed
Willow; G:Matten-Weide · ♃ d Z5 VI-VII;
Eur.: sp., F, I, C-Eur.; N-Sp., Alp., I
– **caesia** Vill. · E:Blue Willow; G:Blaugrüne
Weide · ♃ d △ ⌒ Z5 V-VI; Eur.: I, F, Sw,
A; W-Sib., E-Sib., C-As., Mong.
– **calodendron** Wimm. · ♃ ♃ d Z6; Eur.:
BrI, Sc, D
– **candida** Flügge ex Willd. · E:Hoary
Willow, Sage Willow, Silvery Willow;
F:Saule drapé; G:Salbei-Weide · ♃ d
⌒ Z5 IV; Alaska, Can., USA: NE, NCE,
Rocky Mts.
– **caprea** L. · E:Goat Willow, Pussy Willow,
Sallow; F:Saule Marsault; G:Sal-Weide
· ♃ ♃ d Z3 III-IV Ⓝ; Eur.*, TR, Cauc.,
N-Iran, W-Sib., E-Sib., Amur, Sakhal.,
Kamchat., China, Korea, Jap.
– **caspica** Pall. · ♃ ♃ d Z6; SE-Russ., C-As.,
? W-As.
– × **chrysocoma** Dode (*S. alba* var. *vitellina*
× *S. babylonica*) · E:Golden Weeping
Willow; G:Goldene Trauer-Weide · ♃ Z4
IV
– **cinerea** L. · G:Grau-Weide
– subsp. **cinerea** · E:Grey Willow; F:Saule
cendré; G:Gewöhnliche Grau-Weide · ♃
d Z5 III-IV Ⓝ; Eur.*, TR, Cauc., W-Sib.,
C-As.
– subsp. **oleifolia** (Sm.) Macreight ·
E:Common Sallow; G:Rostrote Weide · ♃
d Z4; Eur.: Ib, BrI, Fr, Cors, Sard.
– **cordata** Michx. · E:Furry Willow, Heart-
leaf Willow; G:Pelzige Weide · ♃ Z2 V;
Can.: E; USA: NE, NCE
– × **cottetii** A. Kern. (*S. myrsinifolia* × *S.*
retusa) · ♃ d △ ⌒ Z5; Eur.: Sw, A(E-
Tirol)
– **daphnoides** Vill. · G:Reif-Weide
– subsp. *acutifolia* (Willd.) O.C. Dahl =
Salix acutifolia
– var. **daphnoides** · E:Violet Willow;
F:Saule faux-daphné; G:Gewöhnliche

Rispen-Flockenblume · ♄ ♄ d Z4 III-IV Ⓝ;
Eur.* exc. BrI
– var. **pomeranica** (Willd.) W.D.J. Koch ·
♄ d Z4 III-IV; Eur.: G, PL, Balt. + ; coast
– × **dasyclados** Wimm. (*S. caprea* × *S.
cinerea* × *S. viminalis* × ?) · G:Bandstock-
Weide, Filzast-Weide · ♄ d Z6 III-IV Ⓝ;
cult.
– × **dichroa** Döll (*S. aurita* × *S. purpurea*) ·
♄ d; cult.
– **discolor** Muhl. · E:Pussy Willow;
G:Verschiedenfarbige Weide · ♄ ♄ d Z2
IV; Can., USA: NE, NCE, NC, Rocky Mts.
– **elaeagnos** Scop. · E:Bitter Willow;
F:Saule drapé; G:Lavendel-Weide ·
♄ d Z5 IV-V; Eur.* exc. BrI, Sc; N-TR,
NW-Afr.
– × **erdingeri** A. Kern. (*S. caprea* × *S.
daphnoides*) · ♄ d Z5 VI; Eur.: C-Eur.
– **eriocephala** Michx. · E:Missouri River
Willow; G:Herzblättrige Weide · ♄ ♄ d Z6
IV-V Ⓝ; Can., USA*, nat. in C-Eur.
– **exigua** Nutt. · G: E:Coyote Willow;
Kojoten-Weide · ♄ ♄ d Z2 IV-V; Alaska,
Can.: E, Sask.; USA: SE, SCE, NC
– **fargesii** Burkill · E:Farges' Willow;
G:Farges Weide · ♄ d Z6 IV-V; W-China:
W-Hubei, E-Sichuan
– **foetida** Schleich. ex DC. · G:Stink-
Weide · ♄ d Z6 VI-VII; Eur.: I, Sw, G, A, ?
F; Alp., ? Pyr.
– *formosa* Willd. = Chosenia arbutifolia
– **fragilis** L. · E:Crack Willow; F:Saule
cassant; G:Bruch-Weide, Knack-Weide
· ♄ ♄ d Z4 III-V ⚥ Ⓝ; Eur.* exc. BrI, Sc;
TR, Cauc., Iran, W-Sib., nat. in BrI, Sc
– × **friesiana** Andersson (*S. repens* × *S.
viminalis*) · ♄ d Z5; Eur. + cult.
– **glabra** Scop. · E:Hairless Willow;
G:Kahle Weide · ♄ d Z4 V; Eur.: I, C-Eur.,
Slove., Croatia, Bosn.; E-Alp., mts.
– **glauca** L. · E:Arctic Grey Willow; G:Ark-
tische Grau-Weide · ♄ ♄ d Z3 VI-VII; Eur.:
SC, Russ., N-As.
– **glaucosericea** Flod. · E:Silky Willow;
G:Seiden-Weide · ♄ d Z3 VI-VII; Eur.: F, I,
Sw, A; Alp.
– **gracilistyla** Miq. · E:Japanese Pussy
Willow; G:Ostasiatische Weide · ♄ d Z6
III-IV; China, Manch., Korea, Jap.
– var. *melanostachys* (Makino) C.K.
Schneid. = Salix melanostachys
– × **grahamii** Borrer ex Baker (*S. aurita*
× *S. herbacea* × *S. repens*) · ♄ d Z4;
Scotland, IRL

– **hastata** L. · E:Halberd Willow; F:Saule
de l'Engadine, Saule hasté; G:Spieß-
Weide · ♄ d Z5 V-VI; Eur.* exc. BrI; TR,
Cauc., W-Sib., E-Sib., Amur, Sakhal.,
Kamchat., C-As., Mong., Him.
– 'Wehrhahnii'
– **hegetschweileri** Heer · E:Alpine Willow;
G:Hochtal-Weide · ♄ d Z6 V-VII; Eur.: F,
I, Sw, A; Alp.
– × *helix* L. = Salix × rubra
– **helvetica** Vill. · E:Swiss Sallow; F:Saule
de Suisse; G:Schweizer Weide · ♄ d △ Z4
VI-VII; Eur.: I, F, Sw, A, Slova., PL; Alp.,
W-Carp.
– **herbacea** L. · E:Dwarf Willow; F:Saule
herbacé; G:Kraut-Weide · ♄ ♄ d △ Z4 VI;
Eur.*; N, mts.; Alaska, Can., USA: NE;
Greenl.
– × **holosericea** Willd. (*S. cinerea* × *S.
viminalis*) · G:Seidenblatt-Weide · ♄ d;
Eur. + cult.
– **hookeriana** Barratt · E:Dune Willow · ♄
♄ d Z6; Vancouver I., Wash., Oreg., Calif.
– **humilis** Marshall · E:Prairie Willow;
G:Prärie-Weide · ♄ d Z4 V-VI; Can.: E;
USA: NE, NCE, NC, SC, SE, Fla.
– *incana* Michx. = Salix candida
– *incana* Schrank = Salix elaeagnos
– **integra** Thunb. · ♄ d Z6 IV; Jap., Korea
– *interior* Rowlee = Salix exigua
– **irrorata** Andersson · E:Blue Stem
Willow; G:Amerikanische Reif-Weide · ♄
d Z5 IV; USA: Rocky Mts, SW, SC
– **laggeri** Wimm. · E:Lagger's Willow;
G:Weißfilzige Weide · ♄ d Z6 VI; Eur.: F,
I, Sw, A; Alp.
– **lanata** L. · E:Woolly Willow; F:Saule
laineux; G:Woll-Weide · ♄ d △ Z4 V;
Eur.: BrI, Sc, N-Russ.; W-Sib., E-Sib.,
Alaska
– **lapponum** L. · E:Downy Willow, Lapland
Willow; G:Lappland-Weide · ♄ d Z4 V-VI;
Eur.* exc. BrI; W-Sib., E-Sib.
– **lasiandra** Benth. · E:Pacific Red Willow,
Pacific Willow; G:Zottige Weide · ♄ ♄ d Z5
V; Alaska, Can.: W; USA: NW, Calif., SW
– *longifolia* Muhl. = Salix exigua
– **lucida** Muhl. · E:Shining Willow Bush;
G:Glanz-Weide · ♄ ♄ d Z3 V; Can.: E,
Sask; USA: NE, NCE, NC
– **magnifica** Hemsl. · E:Magnolia Leafed
Willow; G:Pracht-Weide · ♄ d Z7 V;
W-China
– **matsudana** Koidz. · E:Peking Willow;
G:Peking-Weide · ♄ d Z5 IV-V Ⓝ; Korea,

Manch., N-China
- *medemii* Boiss. = Salix aegyptiaca
- **melanostachys** Makino · ℏ d Z6; Jap.
- × **meyeriana** Rostk. ex Willd. (*S. fragilis*
  × *S. pentandra*) · G:Zerbrechliche
  Lorbeer-Weide · ℏ ℏ d Z5; Eur.
- **mielichhoferi** Saut. · E:Austrian Willow;
  G:Tauern-Weide · ℏ d Z6 V-VII; Eur.: I,
  A; E-Alp.
- × **mollissima** Hoffm. ex Elwert (*S.
  triandra* × *S. viminalis*) · G:Busch-Weide ·
  ℏ ℏ d Z6 IV Ⓝ; C-Eur. + cult.
- **moupinensis** Franch. · ℏ ℏ d Z6;
  W-China: Sichuan
- × **multinervis** Döll (*S. aurita* × *S.
  cinerea*) · G:Vielnervige Weide · ℏ d Z6;
  Eur. + cult.
- **myrsinifolia** Salisb. · E:Dark Leaved
  Willow; F:Saule à feuilles de myrte;
  G:Schwarzwerdende Weide · ℏ d ⌇ Z4
  IV-V; Eur.* exc. Ib; W-Sib., E-Sib.
- **myrsinites** L. · E:Whortle Willow;
  G:Heidelbeerblättrige Weide · ℏ d △ Z5
  V; Eur.: BrI, Sc, N-Russ; W-Sib., E-Sib.,
  Amur, Kamchat., Jap.
- **myrtilloides** L. · G:Heidelbeer-Weide ·
  ℏ d ⤳ △ ⌇ Z4 IV-VI; Eur.: Sc, C-Eur.,
  EC-Eur., E-Eur.; W-Sib., E-Sib., Amur,
  Jap.
- **nigra** Marshall · E:Black Willow;
  G:Schwarze Weide · ℏ ℏ d Z4 IV-V ⚥ ;
  Can.; E USA: NE, NCE, NC, SC, SE, Fla.;
  NE-Mex.
- *nigricans* Sm. = Salix myrsinifolia
- × **pendulina** Wender. (*S. babylonica* × *S.
  fragilis*) · E:Wisconsin Weeping Willow;
  G:Wisconsin-Trauer-Weide · ℏ Z4; cult.
- '**Blanda**' · ℏ d IV-V
- '**Elegantissima**' · ℏ d IV-V
- **pentandra** L. · E:Bay Willow, Laurel
  Willow; F:Saule à cinq étamines, Saule
  laurier; G:Lorbeer-Weide · ℏ ℏ d ⌇ Z4
  V-VI ⚥ ; Eur.*, TR, Cauc., W-Sib., E-Sib.,
  Amur, Kamchat., Mong., W-China
- **petiolaris** Sm. · E:Meadow Willow;
  G:Stiel-Weide · ℏ ℏ d Z2 IV Ⓝ; Can.,
  USA: NE, NCE, NC, Rocky Mts.
- **phylicifolia** L. · E:Tea Leaf Willow;
  G:Teeblättrige Weide · ℏ d Z5 V Ⓝ; Eur.:
  BrI, Sc, Russ, ? BG; Cauc., W-Sib., E-Sib.
- subsp. **bicolor** (Ehrh. ex Willd.) O. Bolòs
  & Vigo = Salix phylicifolia
- **piperi** Bebb · ℏ d; NW-USA
- × *pontederiana* Willd. = Salix × sordida
- **purpurea** L. · G:Purpur-Weide

- subsp. **lambertiana** (Sm.) A. Neumann
  ex Rech. f. · G:Flachland-Purpur-Weide ·
  ℏ d Z5 III-IV; Eur.+
- subsp. **purpurea** · E:Purple Osier, Purple
  Willow; F:Osier rouge, Saule pourpre;
  G:Gewöhnliche Purpur-Weide · ℏ ℏ d
  Z5 III-IV ⚥ Ⓝ; Eur.* exc. Sc; TR, Palest.,
  Cauc., N-Iran, W-Sib., C-As., China, Jap.,
  NW-Afr., nat. in Sc
- **pyrifolia** Andersson · E:Balsam Willow;
  G:Balsam-Weide · ℏ ℏ d Z4 IV; Can.;
  USA: NE, NCE
- **rehderiana** C.K. Schneid. ex Sarg. ·
  E:Rehder's Willow; G:Rehders Weide · ℏ
  ℏ d Z6 IV Ⓝ; China: Sichuan, Kansu
- × **reichardtii** A. Kern. (*S. caprea* ×
  S. cinerea) · E:Reichhardt's Willow;
  G:Reichhardts Weide · d; G, A+
- **repens** L. · G:Kriech-Weide
- subsp. **dunensis** Rouy · E:Sand Willow;
  F:Saule rampant argenté; G:Dünen-
  Weide, Sand-Kriech-Weide · ℏ ℏ d Z5
  IV-V; Eur.: BrI, Sc, Fr, G, Balt.
- subsp. **repens** · E:Creeping Willow;
  F:Saule rampant; G:Gewöhnliche Kriech-
  Weide · ℏ d Z5 IV-VI Ⓝ; Eur.*, W-As.,
  C-As., Sib.
- subsp. *rosmarinifolia* (L.) Hartm. = Salix
  rosmarinifolia
- var. *argentea* (Sm.) Cariot ex St.-Lag. =
  Salix repens subsp. dunensis
- var. *nitida* Wender. = Salix repens subsp.
  dunensis
- **reticulata** L. · E:Net Leaved Willow;
  F:Saule à feuilles réticulées; G:Netz-
  Weide · ℏ ℏ d △ Z4 VII; Eur.*; N, mts.;
  W-Sib., E-Sib., Amur, Kamchat., Mong.,
  Alaska, Can.
- **retusa** L. · G:Stumpfblättrige Weide · ℏ
  ℏ d ⤳ △ Z4 VII-VIII; Eur.* exc. BrI, Sc;
  mts.
- *rigida* Muhl. = Salix eriocephala
- **rosmarinifolia** L. · F:Saule rampant à
  feuilles de romarin; G:Rosmarinblättrige
  Weide · ☉ ♃ ℏ ℏ Z5 IV-V; Eur.* exc. BrI,
  Ib; W-Sib., E-Sib., C-As.
- × **rubens** Schrank (*S. alba* × *S. fragilis*) ·
  E:Hybrid Crack Willow; G:Fahl-Weide,
  Hohe Weide · ℏ d Z4 III-V; Eur.: C-Eur. +
- × **rubra** Huds. (*S. purpurea* × *S.
  viminalis*) · E:Green-leaf Willow;
  G:Blend-Weide · ℏ ℏ d Z5; Eur.
- *sachalinensis* F. Schmidt = Salix udensis
- **schraderiana** Willd. · G:Zweifarbige
  Weide · ℏ d Z5 VI-VII; Eur.: IB, F, G,

EC-Eur., RO, W-Russ.; mts.
- × **sepulcralis** Simonk. (*S. babylonica* ×
  S. × *chrysocoma*) · E:Weeping Willow;
  G:Trauer-Weide · ♄ ♄ d Z5; cult. Eur.
- nothovar. *chrysocoma* (Dode) Meikle =
  Salix × chrysocoma
- × **sericans** Tausch ex A. Kern. (*S. caprea*
  × *S. viminalis*) · ♄ ♄ d Z5 III-IV; cult.
- **sericea** Marshall · E:Silky Willow;
  G:Seidige Weide · ♄ d; Can.: E; USA: NE,
  NCE, NC, SE
- **serpyllifolia** Scop. · E:Thyme-leaved
  Willow; G:Quendelblättrige Weide · ♄ ♄
  d ⤳ △ Z2 VII; Eur.: F, I, C-Eur., Slove.,
  Bosn.; Alp.
- **silesiaca** Willd. · E:Silesian Willow;
  G:Schlesische Weide · ♄ d Z6; Carp., Ba
- × **simulatrix** F.B. White (*S. arbuscula* × *S.
  herbacea*) · ♄ d ⤳ Z5; BrI: Scotland
- × **smithiana** Willd. (*S. cinerea* × *S.
  viminalis*) · G:Kübler-Weide · ♄ d Z5 IV-V;
  Eur.: Sw, G, A +
- × **sordida** A. Kern. (*S. cinerea* × *S.
  purpurea*) · ♄ d Z5; Eur. + cult.
- *speciosa* Nutt. = Salix lasiandra
- **starkeana** Willd. · G:Bleiche Weide · ♄ d
  Z5 IV-V; Eur.: Sc, G, EC-Eur., RO, Russ.
- × **stipularis** Sm. (*S. cinerea* × *S. viminalis*
  × ?*) · ♄ d Z6; cult.
- **subopposita** Miq. · G:Japanische Weide ·
  ♄ d Z6 IV-V; Jap., Korea
- **triandra** L. · G:Mandel-Weide
- subsp. **discolor** (W.D.J. Koch) Arcang. ·
  ♄ ♄ d Z5; S-Eur., E-Eur, Alp.
- subsp. **triandra** · E:Almond Leaved
  Willow; F:Saule à trois étamines, Saule
  amandier; G:Gewöhnliche Mandel-
  Weide · ♄ ♄ d Z4 IV-V Ⓝ; Eur.*, TR, Iraq,
  Cauc., Iran, W-Sib., E-Sib., Amur, C-As.,
  Afgh., Mong., China, Manch., Jap.
- **udensis** Trautv. & C.A. Mey. · E:Sakhalin
  Willow; G:Amur-Weide · ♄ d Z5; E-Sib.,
  Amur, Sakhal., Kamchat., Jap.
- **uva-ursi** Pursh · E:Bearberry Willow;
  G:Bärentrauben-Weide · ♄ d ⤳ △ Z1;
  Alaska, Can., USA: NE; Greenl.
- **viminalis** L. · E:Common Osier, Osier;
  F:Osier des vanniers, Osier vert; G:Hanf-
  Weide, Korb-Weide · ♄ ♄ d Z4 III-IV Ⓝ;
  Eur.: Fr, C-Eur., EC-Eur., Ba, E-Eur.;
  Cauc., Iran, Him., W-Sib., E-Sib., Mong.,
  China (Sinkiang), Jap., nat. in BrI, Sc, Ib,
  Ital-P
- **waldsteiniana** Willd. · G:Bäumchen-
  Weide · ♄ d VI-VII; Eur.: I, A, G, Sw, Ba;

Alp., Balkan
- × **wimmeriana** Gren. (*S. caprea* × *S.
  purpurea*) · ♄ ♄ d; C-Eur. +

Salmalia Schott & Endl. = Bombax
- *malabarica* (DC.) Schott & Endl. =
  Bombax ceiba

Salpichroa Miers -f- Solanaceae · 17 spp.
- **origanifolia** (Lam.) Baill. · E:Lily-of-the-
  Valley Vine; G:Maiglöckchenwein · ♄ d ⚥
  ⚭ D Z8 ⓛ; S-Braz., Urug., Arg., nat. in
  S-Eur., NW-Afr.

Salpiglossis Ruiz & Pav. -f- Solanaceae ·
  2 spp. · F:Salpiglossis; G:Trompetenzunge
- **sinuata** Ruiz & Pav. · E:Painted Tongue,
  Salpiglossis; G:Trompetenzunge · ⊙ Z8
  VI-VIII; Chile

Salsola L. -f- Chenopodiaceae · 150 spp. ·
  G:Salzkraut, Sodakraut; F:Soude
- **kali** L. · E:Russian Thistle, Saltwort;
  G:Gewöhnliches Kali-Salzkraut · ⊙ VII-IX
  ⚔; Eur.*, TR, Levant, As., N-Afr.
- **soda** L. · G:Soda-Salzkraut, Sodakraut ·
  ⊙; Eur.: Ib, Fr, Ital-P, Ba, H, E-Eur.; TR,
  Levant, Cauc., W-Sib., C-As., NW-Afr.
- **vermiculata** L. · ♄ e ⓛ; Eur.: Ib, Sard.,
  Sic.; Moroc., Alger.

Salvia L. -f- Lamiaceae · 956 spp. · E:Sage;
  F:Sauge; G:Salbei
- **aethiopis** L. · E:African Sage; G:Mohren-
  Salbei, Ungarischer Salbei · ⊙ ♃ Z7 VI-VII
  Ⓝ; Eur.* exc. BrI, Sc; TR, Cauc., Iran,
  nat. in N-Am.
- **africana-lutea** L. · ♄ Z9 ⓛ; S-Afr. (Cape)
- *amplexicaulis* Benth. = Salvia virgata
- **argentea** L. · E:Silver Sage; F:Sauge
  argentée; G:Silberblatt-Salbei · ⊙ ♃ Z5
  VII-VIII; Eur.: Ib, Ital-P, Ba; TR, NW-Afr.
- *aurea* L. = Salvia africana-lutea
- **austriaca** Jacq. · E:Austrian Sage;
  G:Österreichischer Salbei · ♃ Z6 V-IX;
  Eur.: A, EC-Eur., Ba, E-Eur.
- **azurea** Michx. ex Lam.
- subsp. *pitcheri* (Torr. ex Benth.) Epling =
  Salvia azurea var. grandiflora
- var. **azurea** · E:Blue Sage; G:Blauer
  Salbei · ♃ Z4; USA: NCE, NC, SC, SE
- var. **grandiflora** Benth. · E:Pitcher Sage;
  F:sauge azurée · ♃ Z4 VIII-X; USA: NE,
  NCE, NC, SC, Ark.
- **barrelieri** Etl. · ⊙ ♃ ∧ V-VIII; Eur.: sp.;

NW-Afr.
- *bicolor* Desf. = Salvia barrelieri
- *blancoana* Webb & Heldr. = Salvia lavandulifolia subsp. blancoana
- **broussonetii** Benth. · ♭ Z9 ⌂; Canar.
- **canariensis** L. · E:Canary Islands Sage · ♭ e Z9 ⌂; Canar.
- **candelabrum** Boiss. · ♃ Z7 VII-VIII; S-Sp.
- **candidissima** Vahl · ♃ Z6; Eur.: AL, GR; TR, N-Iraq
- **carduacea** Benth. · E:Thistle Sage; G:Distel-Salbei · ☉ Z8 ⌂ VII-IX; Calif.
- **coccinea** Buc'hoz ex Etl. · E:Blood Sage; F:Sauge écarlate; G:Blut-Salbei · ☉ ♃ ♭ ⌂ VI-X; USA: SE, SC, Fla.; Mex., W.Ind., trop. Am.
- **columbariae** Benth. · E:Chia · ♃ Z7; SW-USA
- **concolor** Lamb. ex Benth. · ♭ ⌂ IX-XII; Mex., C-Am.
- *cyanea* Benth. = Salvia concolor
- **discolor** Kunth · E:Andean Sage; G:Peruanischer Salbei · ♃ Z9 ⌂; Peru
- **divinorum** Epling & Játiva · E:Herb of the Virgin; G:Azteken-Salbei · ♃ ⚑ Ⓝ; ? Mex.: Oaxaca
- **elegans** Vahl · E:Pineapple Sage; G:Honigmelonen-Salbei · ♭ D Z8 ⌂ VII-VIII; Mex., Guat.
- **farinacea** Benth. · E:Blue Sage, Mealy Sage; F:Sauge farineuse; G:Mehliger Salbei · ☉ ♃ ♭ d Z9 ⌂ V-X; USA: N.Mex., Tex.
- **flava** Forrest ex Diels · ♃ VII; China
- **fruticosa** Mill. · E:Greek Sage · ♭ Z9 ⌂ V ⚑ ; Eur.: I, Sic.Ba; TR, Levant, Libya
- **fulgens** Cav. · E:Cardinal Sage, Mexican Red Sage; G:Kardinals-Salbei · ♭ Z9 ⌂ VIII-X; Mex.
- **glutinosa** L. · E:Jupiter's Distaff, Sticky Sage; F:Sauge glutineuse; G:Klebriger Salbei · ♃ Z5 VII-X; Eur.* exc. Sc; TR, Cauc., N-Iran
- *grandiflora* Etl. = Salvia tomentosa
- *grandiflora* Sessé & Moq. = Salvia fulgens
- **greggii** A. Gray · E:Autumn Sage; G:Herbst-Salbei · ♭ ♭ Z8 ⌂ IX-X; Tex., Mex.
- *haematodes* L. = Salvia pratensis subsp. haematodes
- **heeri** Regel · ♭ Z10 ⌂ I-XII; Peru
- **hians** Royle ex Benth. · ♃ Z6 VII-VIII; Kashmir
- *horminum* L. = Salvia viridis
- **involucrata** Cav. · E:Roseleaf Sage · ♭ ♭

Z9 ⌂ VII-IX; Mex., C-Am.
- **judaica** Boiss. · ♃ Z9 ⌂; Palest.
- **jurisicii** Košanin · G:Serbischer Salbei · ♃ △ Z6 VI-IX; Maced.
- *lanata* Stokes = Salvia aethiopis
- **lavandulifolia** Vahl
- subsp. **blancoana** (Webb & Heldr.) Rosua & Blanca · ♭ Z8 ⌂; S-Sp., Moroc.
- subsp. **lavandulifolia** · E:Spanish Sage; F:Sauge à feuilles de lavande; G:Spanischer Salbei · ♃ ♭ e D Z7 VI-VIII ⚑ ; Eur.: sp., S-F
- **lemmonii** A. Gray · E:Lemmon's Sage
- **leucantha** Cav. · E:Mexican Bush Sage; G:Strauchiger Salbei · ♭ d ✕ Z10 ⌂ VII-VIII; Mex.
- *libanotica* Boiss. & Gaill. = Salvia fruticosa
- **microphylla** Kunth · E:Baby Sage
- var. **microphylla** · ♭ e Z9 ⌂ VII-IX; Mex.
- var. **neurepia** (Fernald) Epling · ♭ Z9 ⌂; Mex.
- var. **wislizeni** A. Gray · ♭ Z9 ⌂; Mex.
- **multicaulis** Vahl · ♭ Z8 ⌂; TR, Palest., Syr., Sinai, N-Iraq, Iran
- **nemorosa** L. · E:Steppen-Salbei
- subsp. **nemorosa** · E:Wild Sage, Woodland Sage; G:Gewöhnlicher Steppen-Salbei · ♃ Z5 VI-VII; Eur.: C-Eur., EC-Eur., Ba, Ital-P, E-Eur.; TR, Cauc., Iran, Afgh., nat. in BrI, Sc
- subsp. **pseudosylvestris** (Stapf) Bornm. · G:Hoher Steppen-Salbei · ♃ Z5; BG., Russ.
- subsp. *tesquicola* (Klokov & Pobed.) Soó = Salvia nemorosa subsp. pseudosylvestris
- *neurepia* Fernald = Salvia microphylla var. neurepia
- **nutans** L. · ♃ Z5 VI-VIII; Eur.: H, Maced., BG, E-Eur.
- **officinalis** L. · E:Common Sage; F:Sauge officinale; G:Echter Salbei · ♭ e D Z7 ⋀ V-VII ⚑ Ⓝ; Eur.: Slove., Croatia, Bosn., YU, Maced., AL, ? GR, nat. in Sp, F, Ital-P, Sw, RO
- **some cultivars**
- **patens** Cav. · E:Blue Sage; G:Mexikanischer Salbei · ♃ Z8 ⌂ ⋀ VI-IX; Mex.
- *peleponnesiaca* Boiss. & Heldr. = Salvia verticillata
- *pitcheri* Torr. ex Benth. = Salvia azurea var. azurea
- **pratensis** L. · E:Meadow Clary; F:Sauge des prés; G:Wiesen-Salbei · ♃ V-VIII;

Eur.* exc. Sc; Cauc., nat. in Sc
- subsp. **haematodes** (L.) Briq. · F:Sauge des prés · ♃ Z3 VI-VIII; Eur.: I
- **przewalskii** Maxim. · ♃ Z7 VI; China
- **recognita** Fisch. & C.A. Mey. · ♃ Z6 VII-VIII; TR
- **ringens** Sibth. & Sm. · ♃ Z7 ∧ VI-VII; Eur.: Ba, RO; Cauc.
- *rutilans* Carrière = Salvia elegans
- **scabiosifolia** Lam. · ♃ △ Z6 VII-VIII; NE-BG, Crim
- **sclarea** L. · E:Clary; F:Toute-bonne; G:Muskateller-Salbei · ♃ D Z5 VI-VII ⚕ Ⓝ; C-As., nat. in A, Sw
- **splendens** Sellow ex Roem. & Schult. · E:Scarlet Sage; F:Sauge écarlate; G:Pracht-Salbei · ♃ ♄ Z10 Ⓚ V-IX; Braz.
- **some cultivars**
- × *superba* (Silva Tar. & C.K. Schneid.) Stapf = Salvia nemorosa
- **sylvesris** L.
- *sylvestris* hort. = Salvia nemorosa
- **tomentosa** Mill. · ♃ ∧ VI-VII; Eur.: Ba, Crim; TR, Syr.
- **uliginosa** Benth. · E:Bog Sage · ♃ Z7 ∧ VII-IX; S-Braz., Urug., Arg.
- **verbascifolia** M. Bieb. · ⊙ ♃ Z6 VII-VIII; TR, Cauc.
- **verbenaca** L. · E:Vervain, Wild Clary; G:Eisenkraut-Salbei · ♃ Z6; Eur.: Ib, Fr, BrI, Ital-P, Ba, Crim; TR, Levant, Cauc., N-Afr.
- **verticillata** L. · E:Whorled Clary; G:Quirlblütiger Salbei · ♃ Z6 VI-IX; Cauc., nat. in BrI, Sc, N-Am.
- **virgata** Jacq. · ♃ Z7; Eur.: I, Ba, Crim; TR, Cyprus, Cauc., N-Iraq, Iran, Afgh., C-As.
- **viridis** L. · E:Annual Clary, Bluebeard; F:Sauge verte; G:Schopf-Salbei · ⊙ ♃ Z8 Ⓚ VI-VIII ⚕; Eur.: Ib.Ital-P, Ba, Crim; TR, Levant, Cauc., N-Iraq, Iran, NW-Afr., nat. in A

Salvinia Ség. -f- *Salviniaceae* · 12 spp. · E:Floating Fern; F:Fougère flottante, Salvinie; G:Schwimmfarn
- **auriculata** Aubl. · E:Butterfly Fern; G:Westindischer Schwimmfarn · ♃ ≈ Z10 Ⓦ; USA: Fla.; Mex., Bermuda, W.Ind., S-Am.
- **minima** Baker · E:Water Spangles · ♃ ≈ Z10 Ⓦ; Mex., C-Am., S-Am.
- **natans** (L.) All. · E:Floating Fern; F:Salvinia nageante; G:Gewöhnlicher Schwimmfarn · ⊙ ≈ Ⓚ VIII-X ▽; Eur.: Ib, G, Ital-P, EC-Eur., Ba, E-Eur.; TR, Cauc., W-Sib., C-As., Him., Indochina., Amur, China, Korea, Jap., Alger.
- *rotundifolia* Willd. = Salvinia auriculata

Samanea (DC.) Merr. = Albizia
- *saman* (Jacq.) Merr. = Albizia saman

Sambucus L. -f- *Caprifoliaceae* · c. 25 spp. · E:Elder; F:Sureau; G:Attich, Holunder
- **caerulea** Raf. · E:Blue Elder, Blue Elderberry; G:Blauer Holunder · ♄ d ⚘ D Z5 VI-VII Ⓝ; Can.: B.C., USA: NW, Rocky Mts., Calif., SW, Tex.; N-Mex., Baja Calif.
- **callicarpa** Greene · E:Pacific Coast Red Elderberry; G:Pazifischer Hollunder · ♄ ♄ d ⚘ Z6 VI-VII; Alaska, Can.; USA: NW, Calif., SW, Rocky Mts.
- **canadensis** L. · E:American Elder; F:Sureau du Canada; G:Kanadischer Holunder · ♄ d ⚘ D Z5 VI-VII Ⓝ; Can.: E; USA: NE, NCE, SC, SE, Fla.; Mex., W.Ind.
- **ebulus** L. · E:Danewort, Dwarf Elder; G:Attich, Zwerg-Holunder · ♃ D Z5 VI-VIII ⚕ ☠; Eur.* exc. BrI, Sc; TR, Syr. Lebanon, N-Iraq, W-Iran, nat. in BrI, Sc
- *glauca* Nutt. ex Torr. & A. Gray = Sambucus caerulea
- **kamtschatica** E.L. Wolf · E:Red Elder · ♄ d Z2; Kamchat., E-Sib.
- **melanocarpa** A. Gray · E:Black Elderberry, Rocky Mountain Elder; G:Schwarzfrüchtiger Holunder · ♄ d ⚘ Z6 VII-VIII; Can.: B.C.; USA: NW, Idaho, Calif., SW
- **nigra** L. · E:Common Elder, Elderberry; F:Sureau commun, Sureau noir; G:Schwarzer Holunder · ♄ ♄ d ⚘ D Z5 VI-VII ⚕ Ⓝ; Eur.*, TR, N-Iraq, W-Iran
- **some cultivars**
- **pubens** Michx. · E:Red Berried Elder, Red Elder; G:Stinkender Hollunder · ♄ d ⚘ Z5 VI-VII; Alaska, Can., USA* exc. SW
- **racemosa** L. · ♄ d
- subsp. **racemosa** · E:Red Berried Elder, Red Elderberry; F:Sureau à grappes, Sureau rouge; G:Roter Holunder, Trauben-Holunder · ♄ d ⚘ Z4 IV-V ☠ Ⓝ; Eur.* exc. BrI, Sc, nat. in BrI, Sc
- var. *callicarpa* (Greene) Jeps. = Sambucus callicarpa
- **sieboldiana** Blume ex Miq. · G:Japanischer Trauben-Holunder · ♄ ♄ d Z6 IV-V; Jap., Korea, ? China

Samolus L. -m- *Primulaceae* · 15 spp. ·
E:Brookweed; F:Samole; G:Bunge
– *floribundus* Kunth = Samolus parviflorus
– **parviflorus** Raf. · E:Seaside Brookweed ·
♃ ⁓ ≈ Z6 ⓚ; Alaska, Can.: E, B.C.;
USA: NE, NCE, SE, Fla., Calif.; Mex.,
trop. Am.
– **valerandi** L. · E:Brookweed; G:Salz-
Bunge · ♃ Z6 VI-X; Eur.*, TR, Cauc., Iran,
C-As., Him., China, N-Afr., cosmop.

Sampacca Kuntze = Michelia
– *euonymoides* Kuntze = Michelia champaca var. champaca
– *parviflora* (Deless.) Kuntze = Michelia
figo
– *suaveolens* (Pers.) Kuntze = Michelia
champaca var. champaca
– *velutina* Kuntze = Michelia champaca var.
champaca

Samuela Trel. -f- *Agavaceae* · 2 spp. ·
E:Eve's Needle
– **carnerosana** Trel. · ♄ e Z9 ⓜ ⓝ; SW-
Tex., Mex.
– **faxoniana** Trel. · ♄ e Z9 ⓚ; SW-Tex.,
N-Mex.

Sanchezia Ruiz & Pav. -f- *Acanthaceae* ·
20 spp. · F:Sanchezia; G:Sanchezie
– **nobilis** Hook. f. · ♄ e Z10 ⓜ; Ecuad.
– **parvibracteata** Sprague & Hutch. · ♄ e
Z10 ⓜ; trop. Am.

× **Sanderara** hort. -f- *Orchidaceae* (*Brassaia*
× *Cochlioda* × *Odontoglossum*)

Sandersonia Hook. -f- *Colchicaceae* · 1 sp. ·
E:Chinese Lantern Lily; F:Cloche de Noël,
Lanterne chinoise; G:Laternenlilie
– **aurantiaca** Hook. · E:Chinese Lantern
Lily, Chinese Lanterns; G:Laternenlilie ·
♃ Z9 ⓜ VII; S-Afr.

Sandoricum Cav. -n- *Meliaceae* · 5 spp.
– **koetjape** (Burm. f.) Merr. · E:Kechapi · ♄
e ⊗ Z10 ⓜ ⓝ; Malay. Arch.

Sanguinaria L. -f- *Papaveraceae* · 1 sp. ·
E:Bloodroot, Red Pucoon; F:Sanguinaire;
G:Blutwurzel
– **canadensis** L. · E:Bloodroot; F:Sangui-
sorbe du Canada; G:Blutwurzel · ♃ Z3
IV-V ⚥ ⚘; Can.: E; USA: NE, NCE, SC,
SE, Fla.

Sanguisorba L. -f- *Rosaceae* · c. 20 spp. ·
E:Burnet; F:Sanguisorbe; G:Wiesenknopf
– **canadensis** L. · E:Canadian Burnet;
G:Kanadischer Wiesenknopf · ♃ Z4 VII-X;
Can.: E; USA; NE, NCE, SE
– **dodecandra** Moretti · E:Italian Burnet ·
♃ Z7; N-I (Prov. Sondrio)
– *maior* Gilib. = Sanguisorba officinalis
– **minor** Scop. · G:Kleiner Wiesenknopf
– subsp. **minor** · E:Salad Burnet, Small
Burnet; F:Pimprenelle sanguisorbe;
G:Gewöhnlicher Kleiner Wiesenknopf · ♃
Z5 V-VIII ⚥ ⓝ; Eur.*, TR, Cauc., N-Iran,
W-Him., W-Sib. (Altai), C-As., NW-Afr.,
Libya
– subsp. *muricata* (Spach) Briq. =
Sanguisorba minor subsp. polygama
– subsp. **polygama** (Waldst. & Kit.) Holub ·
G:Höckerfrüchtiger Wiesenknopf · ♃ Z5
VI-VII ⓝ; Eur.*, TR, Cauc., C-As., W-As.,
N-Afr.
– *muricata* (Spach) Gremli = Sanguisorba
minor subsp. polygama
– **obtusa** Maxim. · F:Sanguisorbe du
Japon · ♃ ⋊ Z5 VII-IX; Jap.
– **officinalis** L. · E:Great Burnet; G:Großer
Wiesenknopf · ♃ Z4 VI-VIII ⚥ ⓝ; Eur.*,
W-Sib., E-Sib., C-As.
– *polygama* (Waldst. & Kit.) Beck =
Sanguisorba minor subsp. minor
– *spinosa* (L.) Bertol. = Sarcopoterium
spinosum
– **tenuifolia** Fisch. ex Link · F:Sangui-
sorbe à feuilles fines · ♃ Z4 VIII; E-Sib.,
Kamchat., Sakhal., Manch., Korea, Jap.

Sanicula L. -f- *Apiaceae* · 37 spp. ·
E:Sanicle; F:Sanicle; G:Sanikel
– **europaea** L. · E:Butterwort, Sanicle;
G:Wald-Sanikel · ♃ Z6 V-VII ⚥ ; Eur.*,
TR, Cauc., N-Iran, W-Sib., Ind., Malay.
Arch., N-Afr., Afr. (mts.), S-Afr.

Sansevieria Thunb. -f- *Dracaenaceae* ·
70 spp. · E:Bowstring Hemp, Snake Plant;
F:Langue de Belle-mère, Sansévière;
G:Bogenhanf
– **arborescens** Cornu ex Gérôme &
Labroy · ♃ ⸸ Z10 ⓜ; E-Afr.
– **cylindrica** Bojer · ♃ ⸸ Z10 ⓜ ⓝ; Angola
– *dooneri* N.E. Br. = Sansevieria parva
– **ehrenbergii** Schweinf. ex Baker · ♃ ⸸
Z10 ⓜ; E-Afr.
– **gracilis** N.E. Br. · ♃ ⸸ Z10 ⓜ; E-Afr.
– *grandis* Hook. f. = Sansevieria

hyacinthoides
- *guineensis* (L.) Willd. = Sansevieria hyacinthoides
- *guineensis* Baker = Sansevieria metallica
- *guineensis* Gérôme & Labroy = Sansevieria trifasciata var. trifasciata
- **hyacinthoides** (L.) Druce · E:Iguanatail · ♃ ⚭ Z10 ⚘ Ⓝ; S-Afr.
- **kirkii** Baker · ♃ ⚭ Z10 ⚘; E-Afr.
- *laurentii* De Wild. = Sansevieria trifasciata var. laurentii
- **liberica** Gérôme & Labroy · ♃ ⚭ Z10 ⚘; Liberia
- **longiflora** Sims · ♃ ⚭ Z10 ⚘ Ⓝ; W-Afr., C-Afr., Angola
- **metallica** Gérôme & Labroy · ♃ ⚭ Z10 ⚘; trop. Afr.
- **parva** N.E. Br. · ♃ ⚭ Z10 ⚘; E-Afr.
- **roxburghiana** Schult. & Schult. f. · ♃ ⚭ Z10 ⚘ Ⓝ; E-Ind., Burma
- *spicata* (Cav.) Haw. = Sansevieria hyacinthoides
- *thyrsiflora* (Petagna) Thunb. = Sansevieria hyacinthoides
- **trifasciata** Prain
- var. **laurentii** (De Wild.) N.E. Br.
- var. **trifasciata** · E:Mother-in-law's Tongue; G:Schwiegermutterzunge · ♃ ⚭ Z10 ⚘ ⚘ Ⓝ; W-Afr.
- **zeylanica** (L.) Willd. · E:Devil's Tongue; G:Teufelszunge · ♃ ⚭ Z10 ⚘; Sri Lanka

Santalum L. -n- *Santalaceae* · 10-25 spp. · E:Sandalwood; F:Santal blanc; G:Sandelholz
- **album** L. · E:Sandalwood, White Sandalwood; G:Weißes Sandelholz · ♄ e D Z10 ⚘ ⚘ ⚘ Ⓝ; ? Malay Arch.; cult. trop. As.

Santolina L. -f- *Asteraceae* · 18 spp. · E:Lavender Cotton; F:Santoline; G:Heiligenkraut
- **chamaecyparissus** L. · E:Lavender Cotton; F:Santoline petit cyprès; G:Graues Heiligenkraut · ♄ △ D Z7 ∧ VII-VIII ⚘ ; Eur.: Ib, Fr, Ital-P, Ba; Moroc., Alger., Tun.
- subsp. *tomentosa* (Pers.) Arcang. = Santolina pinnata subsp. neapolitana
- **elegans** Boiss. ex DC. · ♄ e △ Z7 ∧ ▽; S-Sp.: Sierra Nevada
- *ericoides* hort. = Santolina pinnata subsp. pinnata
- *ericoides* Poir. = Santolina

chamaecyparissus
- *incana* Lam. = Santolina chamaecyparissus
- × **lindavica** Sünd. (*S. chamaecyparissus* × *S. pinnata* subsp. *neapolitana*) · ♄ Z7; cult.
- *neapolitana* Jord. & Fourr. = Santolina pinnata subsp. neapolitana
- **pinnata** Viv.
- subsp. **neapolitana** (Jord. & Fourr.) Guinea ex C. Jeffrey · ♄ e △ D Z7 ⚘ ∧ VII-VIII; S-I
- subsp. **pinnata** · G:Gefiedertes Heiligenkraut · ♄ e Z7 VI-VII; I
- **rosmarinifolia** L. · E:Green Santolina; G:Grünes Heiligenkraut · ♄ e D Z8 ⚘ ∧ VII-VIII; Eur.: Ib, S-F; Moroc.
- *tomentosa* Pers. = Santolina pinnata subsp. neapolitana
- *virens* Mill. = Santolina rosmarinifolia
- *viridis* Willd. = Santolina rosmarinifolia

Sanvitalia Lam. -f- *Asteraceae* · 7 spp. · E:Creeping Zinnia; F:Bouton de hussard; G:Husarenknopf
- **procumbens** Lam. · E:Creeping Zinnia; G:Husarenknopf · ⊙ VII-X; Mex., Guat.

Sapindus L. -m- *Sapindaceae* · 13 spp. · E:Soapberry; F:Arbre à savon, Savon indien; G:Seifenbaum
- **mukorossi** Gaertn. · E:Chinese Soapberry · ♄ e Z9 ⚘ ⚘ Ⓝ; Him., Burma, China, Jap.
- **rarak** DC. · ♄ e Z10 ⚘ ⚘ Ⓝ; Indochina, Malay. Arch.
- **saponaria** L. · E:Soapberry · ♄ e Z10 ⚘ ⚘ Ⓝ; USA: SE, Fla.; Mex., W.Ind., S-Am.
- **trifoliatus** L. · E:Three-leaf Soapberry · ♄ e Z10 ⚘ Ⓝ; Ind., Sri Lanka

Sapium P. Browne -n- *Euphorbiaceae* · 100+ spp. · E:Tallow Tree; F:Arbre à suif; G:Talgbaum
- **sebiferum** (L.) Roxb. · E:Chinese Tallow Tree; G:Chinesischer Talgbaum · ♄ e Z9 ⚘ ⚘ Ⓝ; C-China, S-China, Hainan, Taiwan, N-Vietn., nat. in SE-USA

Saponaria L. -f- *Caryophyllaceae* · 20-40 spp. · E:Soapwort; F:Saponaire; G:Seifenkraut
- **bellidifolia** Sm. · ♃ ⌒ △ Z7 V-VI; Eur.: Ib, Fr, Ital-P, Ba, RO
- × **boissieri** hort. (*S. caespitosa* × *S.*

ocymoides) · ⌁; cult.
- **caespitosa** DC. · E:Tufted Soapwort · ⌁
  ⌂ △ Z7 V-VI; Eur.: sp., F; Pyr.
- **calabrica** Guss. · E:Calabrian Soapwort;
  G:Kalabrisches Seifenkraut · ☉ VI-IX;
  Eur.: I, Ba
- **cypria** Boiss. · ⌁ ⌂ ∧ VIII-IX; Cyprus
- *graeca* Boiss. = Saponaria calabrica
- **haussknechtii** Simmler · ⌁ △ VIII-IX; GR
- × **lempergii** hort. (*S. cypria* × *S.
  haussknechtii*) · ⌁ △ VIII-IX; cult.
- **lutea** L. · E:Yellow Soapwort; G:Gelbes
  Seifenkraut · ⌁ △ Z6 VII-VIII; Eur.: F, I,
  Sw; Alp.
- **ocymoides** L. · E:Rock Soapwort,
  Tumbling Ted; F:Saponaire faux-basilic;
  G:Kleines Seifenkraut, Rotes Seifenkraut
  · ⌁ ⤳ △ Z4 VII-X; Eur.: Ib, Fr, Ital-P, Ba,
  C-Eur., nat. in CZ
- **officinalis** L. · E:Soapwort; F:Saponaire
  officinale; G:Echtes Seifenkraut · ⌁ Z4
  VI-IX ☖ Ⓝ; Eur.* exc. Sc, BrI; TR, Cauc.,
  W-Sib., nat. in Sc, BrI, Jap., N-Am.
- × **olivana** Wocke (*S. caespitosa* × *S.
  pumilio*) · F:Saponaire rose hybride · ⌁ △
  VI-VII; cult.
- *ortegioides* (Fisch. & C.A. Mey.) Boiss. &
  Balansa = Phrynella ortegioides
- *pumila* Janch. ex Hayek = Saponaria
  pumilio
- **pumilio** (L.) Fenzl ex A. Braun · E:Dwarf
  Soapwort; G:Zwerg-Seifenkraut · ⌁ ⌂ △
  VIII; Eur.: I, A, RO; E-Alp., S-Carp.
- **sicula** Raf. · ⌁ Z7; Eur.: Sic., Sard.;
  Alger.
- subsp. *intermedia* (Simmler) Chater =
  Saponaria haussknechtii
- × **wiemannii** Fritsch (*S. caespitosa* × *S.
  lutea*) · ⌁ △ V-VI; cult.

× **Sappanara** hort. -f- *Orchidaceae*
(*Arachnis* × *Phalaenopsis* × *Renanthera*)

Sarcanthus Lindl. = Cleisostoma
- *filiformis* Lindl. = Cleisostoma filiforme
- *racemifer* (Lindl.) Rchb. f. = Cleisostoma
  racemiferum

Sarcocapnos DC. -f- *Fumariaceae* · 4 spp.
- **enneaphylla** (L.) DC. · ⌁ △ Z8 ⌂ VI;
  Eur.: sp., F (Pyr.); Moroc

Sarcocaulon (DC.) Sweet -n- *Geraniaceae* ·
14 spp. · F:Sarcaucolon; G:Buschmanns-
kerze, Dickstängel

- *burmannii* (DC.) Sweet = Sarcocaulon
  crassicaule
- **crassicaule** S.E.A. Rehm · ♄ ⵂ Z9 ⌂;
  Namibia
- **flavescens** S.E.A. Rehm · ♄ ⵂ Z9 ⌂;
  Namibia, NW-Cape
- **inerme** S.E.A. Rehm · ♄ ⵂ Z9 ⌂;
  Namibia
- **multifidum** E. Mey. ex R. Knuth · ♄ ⵂ Z9
  ⌂; Namibia, NW-Cape
- **patersonii** (DC.) G. Don · ♄ ⵂ Z9 ⌂;
  Namibia, NW-Cape
- *rigidum* Schinz = Sarcocaulon patersonii
- **vanderietiae** L. Bolus · ♄ ⵂ Z9 ⌂; E-Cape

Sarcochilus R. Br. -m- *Orchidaceae* ·
25 spp.
- **falcatus** R. Br. · ⌁ Z10 ⌂ IV-V ▽ ✳;
  Austr.: Queensl., N.S.Wales
- **hartmannii** F. Muell. · ⌁ Z10 ⌂ III-IV ▽
  ✳; W-Austr.
- *luniferus* (Rchb. f.) Benth. ex Hook. f. =
  Chiloschista lunifera
- *pallidus* (Blume) Rchb. f. = Pteroceras
  pallidum
- *unguiculatus* Lindl. = Pteroceras pallidum

Sarcococca Lindl. -f- *Buxaceae* · 11 sp. ·
E:Christmas Box, Sweet Box; F:Buis
de Noël, Sarcococca; G:Fleischbeere,
Schleimbeere
- **confusa** Sealy · ♄ e D Z6 XII-III; orig. ?
- **hookeriana** Baill.
- var. **hookeriana** · E:Sweet Box;
  G:Himalaya-Schleimbeere · ♄ e D Z7
  IX-XI; Afgh., W-Him.
- var. **humilis** Rehder & E.H. Wilson ·
  F:Sarcococca; G:Niedere Himalaya-
  Schleimbeere · ♄ D Z7 I-III; N-China
- *humilis* (Rehder & E.H. Wilson) Stapf
  ex Sealy = Sarcococca hookeriana var.
  humilis
- **ruscifolia** Stapf · E:Fragrant Sweet Box;
  G:Mäusedornblättrige Fleischbeere · ♄ e
  D Z7 XII-III; W-China, C-China
- **saligna** (D. Don) Müll. Arg. · ♄ e Z9 ⌂
  XII-III ⵂ; Him.

Sarcopoterium Spach -n- *Rosaceae* · 1 sp.
- **spinosum** (L.) Spach · E:Thorny Burnet ·
  ♄ d Z8 ⌂ V-VIII; Eur.: Ital-P, Ba; TR,
  Lebanon, Syria, Palest.

× **Sarcorhiza** hort. -f- *Orchidaceae*
(*Rhinerrhiza* × *Sarcochilus*)

Sarcostemma R. Br. -n- *Asclepiadaceae* ·
15 spp.
– *aphylla* (Thunb.) R. Br. = Sarcostemma
viminale
– **viminale** (L.) R. Br. · E:Causticbush,
Sacred Soma · ♄ ⸙ ⚡ Z10 ⓦ; trop. Afr.,
S-Afr.

× **Sarcothera** hort. -f- *Orchidaceae*
(*Renanthera* × *Sarcochilus*)

Sarmienta Ruiz & Pav. -f- *Gesneriaceae* ·
1 sp.
– **scandens** (Brandis) Pers. · ♄ ⚡ ⤳ Z9 ⓚ
II-III; Chile

Sarothamnus Wimm. = Cytisus
– *scoparius* (L.) Wimm. ex W.D.J. Koch =
Cytisus scoparius subsp. scoparius

Sarracenia L. -f- *Sarraceniaceae* ·
8 spp. · E:Pitcher Plant; F:Sarracénnie;
G:Fensterfalle, Krugpflanze, Sarrazenie,
Schlauchpflanze
– **alata** (A.W. Wood) A.W. Wood ·
E:Pale Pitcher Plant, Yellow Trumpets;
G:Bleiche Schlauchpflanze · ⚃ ⌇ D Z8
ⓚ ⛁ ▽ ✳; USA: SE, Tex.
– *drummondii* H.B. Croom = Sarracenia
leucophylla
– **flava** L. · E:Yellow Pitcher Plant;
G:Gewöhnliche Gelbe Schlauchpflanze ·
⚃ ⌇ Z8 ⓚ ⛁ ▽ ✳; USA: NE, SE, Fla.
– **leucophylla** Raf. · E:Crimson Pitcher
Plant, White Trumpet; G:Weiße
Schlauchpflanze · ⚃ ⌇ Z8 ⓚ ⛁ ▽ ✳;
USA: SE, Fla.
– **minor** Walter · E:Hooded Pitcher Plant;
G:Gewöhnliche Fensterfalle · ⚃ ⌇ Z8
ⓚ ⛁ ▽ ✳; USA: SE, Fla.
– **oreophila** (Kearney) Wherry · E:Green
Pitcher Plant; G:Grüne Schlauchpflanze ·
⚃ ⌇ Z8 ⓚ ⛁ ▽ ✳; USA: SE
– **psittacina** Michx. · E:Parrot Pitcher
Plant; G:Papageien-Schlauchpflanze · ⚃
⌇ Z8 ⓚ ⛁ ▽ ✳; USA: SE, Fla.
– **purpurea** L.
– subsp. **purpurea** · E:Purple Pitcher Plant;
G:Schlanke Braunrote Schlauchpflanze ·
⚃ ⌇ Z7 ⛁ ∧ VII ▽ ✳; Can.: E, Sask.;
USA: NE, SE, Fla.
– **rubra** Walter.
– subsp. **rubra** · E:Sweet Pitcher Plant;
G:Gewöhnliche Kupferrote Schlauch-
pflanze · ⚃ ⌇ Z8 ⓚ ⛁ ▽ ✳; USA: SE,

Fla.
– *sledgei* Macfarl. = Sarracenia alata
– *variolaris* Michx. = Sarracenia minor

Sasa Makino & Shibata -f- *Poaceae* ·
40 spp. · F:Bambou nain; G:Zwergbambus
– *albomarginata* (Franch. & Sav.) Makino
& Shibata = Sasa veitchii
– **borealis** (Hack.) Makino & Shibata · ♄ e
Z7; Jap., Korea
– *humilis* (Mitford) E.G. Camus = Pleioblastus humilis
– *japonica* (Siebold & Zucc. ex Steud.)
Makino = Pseudosasa japonica
– **kagamiana** Makino & Uchida
– subsp. **kagamiana** · ♄ e; Jap.
– subsp. **yoshinoi** (Koidz.) S. Suzuki · ♄ e;
Jap.
– **kurilensis** (Rupr.) Makino & Shibata ·
G:Kurilen-Zwergbambus · ♄ e Z7; Jap.,
Korea
– **palmata** (Burb.) E.G. Camus · E:Palmate
Bamboo; G:Breitblättriger Zwergbambus
· ♄ e Z7 ∧; Jap., Sakhal.
– *pumila* (Mitford) E.G. Camus = Pleioblastus argenteostriatus f. pumilus
– *pygmaea* (Miq.) Rehder = Pleioblastus
pygmaeus
– *ramosa* (Makino) Makino & Shibata =
Sasaella ramosa
– *tessellata* (Munro) Makino & Shibata =
Indocalamus tessellatus
– **tsuboiana** Makino · ♄ e Z6; Jap.
– **vagans** Koidz. · ♄ e; Jap.
– *variegata* (Siebold ex Miq.) E.G. Camus =
Pleioblastus variegatus
– **veitchii** (Carrière) Rehder · E:Kuma
Bamboo Grass · ♄ e Z8 ∧; Jap.

Sasaella Makino -f- *Poaceae* · 12 spp.
– **ramosa** (Makino) Makino · ♄ e Z7; Jap.

Sasamorpha Nakai = Sasa
– *borealis* (Hack.) Nakai = Sasa borealis

Sassafras Nees -n- *Lauraceae* · 3 spp. ·
E:Sassafras; F:Sassafras; G:Fenchelholz-
baum, Sassafras
– **albidum** (Nutt.) Nees
– var. **albidum** · E:Sassafras, Silky Sassafras; F:Sassafras; G:Sassafras, Seidiger
Fenchelholzbaum · ♄ d Z6 IV-V ⚡ ⚘ ⓝ;
USA: NE, NCE, Ark.
– var. **molle** (Raf.) Fernald · ♄ d Z6 IV-V
⚘ ⓝ; USA: NE, NCE, Kans., SC, SE, Fla.

Satureja L. -f- *Lamiaceae* · 59 spp. ·
  E:Savory; F:Sarriette; G:Bohnenkraut,
  Pfefferkraut
– *acinos* (L.) Scheele = Acinos alpinus
– *alpina* (L.) Scheele = Acinos alpinus
– **alternipilosa** (K. Koch) K. Koch · ⏚ ;
  Cauc.
– *calamintha* (L.) Scheele = Calamintha
  nepeta subsp. nepeta
– *croatica* (Pers.) Briq. = Micromeria
  croatica
– *douglasii* (Benth.) Briq. = Micromeria
  douglasii
– *grandiflora* (L.) Scheele = Calamintha
  grandiflora
– **hortensis** L. · E:Savory, Summer Savory;
  G:Sommer-Bohnenkraut · ⊙ D Z8 VII-X
  ⚑ Ⓝ; Eur.: Ib, Fr, Ba; TR
– *illyrica* Host = Satureja subspicata
– **montana** L.
– subsp. *illyrica* (Host) Nyman = Satureja
  subspicata
– subsp. **montana** · E:Winter Savory;
  F:Sarriette vivace; G:Winter-Bohnenk-
  raut · ♄ s △ Z6 VIII-X ⚑ Ⓝ; Eur.: Ib, Fr,
  Ital-P, Ba, RO, Crim; TR, Syr.
– *pygmaea* Sieber ex Vis. = Satureja
  subspicata
– **rumelica** Velen. · ⏚ △ Z6 VIII-IX; Eur.:
  S-BG
– *rupestris* Wulfen = Micromeria thymifolia
– **spicigera** (K. Koch) Boiss. · ⏚ Z7 IX ⚑ Ⓝ;
  TR, Cauc., Iran
– **subspicata** Bartl. ex Vis. · F:Sarriette
  vivace · ♄ s △ Z6 IX Ⓝ; Eur.: I, Slove.,
  Croatia, AL
– *thymifolia* Scop. = Micromeria thymifolia
– *vulgaris* (L.) Fritsch = Clinopodium
  vulgare subsp. vulgare

Saurauia Willd. -f- *Actinidiaceae* · c.
  300 spp.
– **gigantea** DC. · ♄ e Z10 ⓜ; Nepal, Java
– **tomentosa** (Kunth) Spreng. · ♄ e Z10 ⓜ;
  S-Am.

Sauromatum Guinea & Gómez Mor.
  -n- *Araceae* · 2 spp. · E:Vodoo Lily;
  F:Sauromatum; G:Eidechsenwurz
– *guttatum* (Wall.) Schott = Sauromatum
  venosum
– **venosum** (Dryand. ex Aiton) Kunth ·
  E:Voodoo Lily; G:Eidechsenwurz · ⏚ Z8
  ⓚ ⚘; Sudan, trop. Afr., Him., S-Ind.

Sauropus Blume -m- *Euphorbiaceae* ·
  83 spp.
– **androgynus** (L.) Merr. · E:Star Gooseberry · ♄ e Z10 ⓜ Ⓝ; Ind., Sri Lanka,
  China, SE-As.

Saururus L. -m- *Saururaceae* · 2 spp. ·
  E:Lizard's Tail; F:Queue-de-lézard;
  G:Molchschwanz
– **cernuus** L. · E:American Swamp Lily,
  Lizard's Tail; F:Queue de lézard;
  G:Amerikanischer Molchschwanz · ⏚
  〰 Z7 ⋀ VI-VII; Can.: E; USA: NE, NCE,
  Kans., SC, SE, Fla., nat. in N-I
– *cernuus* Thunb. = Saururus chinensis
– **chinensis** (Lour.) Baill. · E:Swamp Lily;
  F:Queue de renard; G:Chinesischer
  Molchschwanz · ⏚ 〰 Z7 ⋀ VI-VII;
  N-China, Korea, Jap., Phil.
– *loureirii* Decne. = Saururus chinensis
– *lucidus* Donn = Saururus cernuus

Saussurea DC. -f- *Asteraceae* · c. 300 spp. ·
  E:Alpine Saw Wort; F:Saussurée;
  G:Alpenscharte
– **alpina** (L.) DC. · G:Gewöhnliche
  Alpenscharte · ⏚ Z2 VII-VIII; Eur.*; N,
  mts.; W-Sib., E-Sib., C-As., ? Him.
– **costus** (Falc.) Lipsch. · ⏚ VII-VIII ⚑ Ⓝ ▽
  ❊; Kashmir
– **depressa** Gren. · G:Niedere Alpenscharte · ⏚ VII-IX; Eur.: Sw, F, I; Alp.
– **discolor** (Willd.) DC. · G:Zweifarbige
  Alpenscharte · ⏚ Z4 VII-VIII; Eur.: F, I,
  C-Eur., Slova., Ba, RO, W-Russ.; Alp.,
  Apenn., Carp.
– *lappa* (Decne.) C.B. Clarke = Saussurea
  costus
– **pygmaea** (Jacq.) Spreng. · G:Zwerg-
  Alpenscharte · ⏚ Z3 VII-VIII; Eur.: G, I, A,
  Slove., EC-Eur.; E-Alp., W-Carp.

Saxegothaea Lindl. -f- *Podocarpaceae* ·
  1 sp. · E:Prince Albert's Yew; F:If de
  Patagonie, If du Prince Albert; G:Patago-
  nische Eibe
– **conspicua** Lindl. · E:Prince Albert's Yew;
  F:If de Patagonie, If du Prince Albert;
  G:Patagonische Eibe · ♄ ♄ e Z8 ⓜ; Chile,
  W-Patag.

Saxifraga L. -f- *Saxifragaceae* · 370-
  440 spp. · E:Saxifrage; F:Saxifrage;
  G:Steinbrech
– **adscendens** L. · E:Biennial Saxifrage;

G:Aufsteigender Steinbrech · ⊙ VII-VIII ▽; Eur.* exc. BrI; TR, Cauc., N-Am.

– **aizoides** L. · E:Evergreen Saxifrage; Yellow Mountain Saxifrage; G:Fetthennen-Steinbrech · ⁊ ⤳ △ ⌢ Z5 VI-IX ▽; Eur.*; N, mts.; W-Sib., Alaska, Can., USA: NE, NCE; Greenl.

– × **andrewsii** Harv. (*S. hirsuta* × *S. paniculata*) · F:Saxifrage d'Andrew · ⁊ Z3; orig. ?

– **androsacea** L. · G:Mannsschild-Steinbrech · ⁊ VI-VIII ▽; Eur.* exc. BrI, Sc; mts.; W-Sib., E-Sib.

– × **anglica** Horný, Soják & Webr (*S. aspera* × *S. lilacina* × *S. media*) · ⁊ Z6; cult.

– **aphylla** Sternb. · G:Blattloser Steinbrech · ⁊ VII-IX ▽; Eur.: I, Sw, G, A; Alp.

– × **apiculata** Engl. (*S. marginata* × *S. sancta*) · F:Saxifrage Kabschia · ⁊ Z6; cult.

– **aquatica** Lapeyr. · ⁊ △ Z6 V-VI ▽; Eur.: sp., F; Pyr.

– × **arco-valleyi** Sünd. (*S. lilacina* × *S. marginata*) · ⁊ Z6; cult.

– × **arendsii** Engl. & Irmsch. (*S. exarata* × *S. granulata* × *S. hypnoides* var. *hypnoides* × *S. rosacea*) · ⁊ Z6; cult.

– **aretioides** Lapeyr. · E:Yellow Saxifrage · ⁊ ⌂ △ Z6 IV ▽; Eur.: sp., F; Cordillera Cantábrica, Pyr.

– **aspera** L. · E:Rough Saxifrage, Stiff-haired Saxifrage; G:Rauer Steinbrech · ⁊ ⤳ ⌂ Z6 VII-VIII ▽; Eur.: sp., F, I, Sw, A; E-Pyr., Alp., Apenn., Alpi Apuane

– × **bertolonii** Sünd. (*S. sempervivum* × *S. stribrnyi*) · ⁊ Z6; cult.

– × **biasolettii** Sünd. (*S. federici-augusti* × *S. sempervivum*) · ⁊ Z6; cult.

– **biflora** All. · E:Two-flowered Saxifrage; G:Zweiblütiger Steinbrech · ⁊ Z6 VII-VIII ▽; Eur.: A, F, G, Sw, I; GR; Alp.

– × **borisii** Kellerer ex Sünd. (*S. ferdinandi-coburgii* × *S. marginata*) · ⁊ Z6; cult.

– **boryi** Boiss. & Heldr. = Saxifraga marginata

– × **boydii** Dewar (*S. aspera* × *S. burseriana*) · ⁊ Z6; cult.

– **bronchialis** L. · E:Matted Saxifrage; G:Matten-Steinbrech · ⁊ ⌂ △ VI-VII ▽; Ural, N-As., Alaska, Can.: W; USA: NW, Rocky Mts., SW

– **brunonis** Wall. ex Ser. · ⁊ ⤳ △ Z7 ⊡ △ VI-VII ▽; Him.

– **bryoides** L. · E:Mossy Saxifrage; G:Moos-Steinbrech · ⁊ ⤳ △ Z6 VII-VIII ▽; Eur.*

exc. BrI, Sc; mts.

– **bulbifera** L. · E:Bulbous Saxifrage; G:Zwiebel-Steinbrech · ⁊ V ▽; Eur.: Ital-P, C-Eur., EC-Eur., Ba, E-Eur.

– × **burnatii** Sünd. (*S. cochlearis* × *S. paniculata*) · ⁊ Z5; cult.

– **burseriana** L. · F:Saxifrage de Burser; G:Bursers Steinbrech · ⁊ ⌂ △ Z6 IV-VI ▽; Eur.: I, G, A, Slove.; E-Alp.

– **caesia** L. · E:Blue Saxifrage; G:Blaugrüner Steinbrech · ⁊ ⌂ △ Z5 VI-VII ▽; Eur.: sp., Fr, I, C-Eur., EC-Eur., Slove., Bosn., Montenegro; Pyr., Alp., Apenn., Carp., Crna Gora

– **callosa** Sm.

– subsp. **callosa** · E:Limestone Saxifrage; G:Kalk-Steinbrech · ⁊ ⌂ △ Z7 VI ▽; Eur.: sp., F, Sard., I, Sic.

– subsp. **catalaunica** (Boiss. & Reut.) D.A. Webb · F:Saxifrage calleux · ⁊ ⌂ △ Z7 VI ▽; SE-F, NE-Sp.

– **canaliculata** Boiss. & Reut. ex Engl. · ⁊ △ Z7 VI ▽; N-Sp.

– **cartilaginea** Willd. = Saxifraga paniculata subsp. paniculata

– **catalaunica** Boiss. & Reut. = Saxifraga callosa subsp. callosa

– **caucasica** Sommier & Levier · ⁊ Z5 ▽; Cauc.

– **cebennensis** Rouy & E.G. Camus · ⁊ ⌂ △ Z7 V ▽; Eur.: F (Cevennes)

– **cernua** L. · E:Drooping Saxifrage; G:Nickender Steinbrech · ⁊ VII ▽; Eur.: Sc, BrI, Ital-P, C-Eur., EC-Eur.; N, Alp., Carp.; W-Sib., E-Sib., Kamchat., C-As.

– **cespitosa** L. · E:Tufted Saxifrage; G:Polster-Steinbrech · ⁊ ⌂ △ V ▽; Eur.: BrI, Sc, N-Russ.; W-Sib., E-Sib., Alaska, Can., USA: NW, Rocky Mts, SW; Greenl.

– × **churchillii** Huter (*S. hostii* × *S. paniculata*) · ⁊; cult.

– × **clarkei** Sünd. (*S. media* × *S. vandellii*) · ⁊; cult.

– **cochlearis** Rchb. · F:Saxifrage à feuilles spatulées · ⁊ ⌂ △ Z6 V-VI ▽; Eur.: F, I; Alpes Maritimes, Liguria

– **conifera** Coss. & Durieu · ⁊ ⌂ Z6 ▽; N-Sp., Alger.

– **cortusifolia** Siebold & Zucc. · G:Oktober-Steinbrech · ⁊ Z7 ▽; Jap.

– var. *fortunei* (Hook. f.) Maxim. = Saxifraga fortunei

– **corymbosa** Boiss. · ⁊ ⌂ △ Z6 IV ▽; Eur.: N-GR, BG; TR

– **cotyledon** L. · E:Great Alpine Rockfoil,

Pyramidal Saxifrage; F:Saxifrage
cotylédon; G:Strauß-Steinbrech · ⅄ △
Z6 V-VI ▽; Eur.: ? sp., I, C-Eur., Sc; Pyr.,
S-Alp., Sc
– **crustata** Vest · E:Encrusted Saxifrage;
F:Saxifrage incrusté; G:Krusten-
Steinbrech · ⅄ ◠ △ Z6 VI ▽; Eur.: I, A,
Slove., Bosn., YU; E-Alp., mts.
– **cuneata** Willd. · ⅄ ◠ △ Z6 VI ▽;
Eur.: sp., F; W-Pyr., N-Sp.
– **cuneifolia** L. · E:Shield-leafed Saxifrage;
F:Saxifrage à feuilles en coin; G:Keilblät-
triger Steinbrech · ⅄ △ Z6 V-VIII ▽;
Eur.: sp., F, I, Sw, A, Slove., Croatia, RO;
mts.
– **cuscutiformis** Lodd. · ⅄ ⤳ Z5 ⒶE ▽;
China
– **cymbalaria** L. · G:Zymbelkraut-Stein-
brech · ⊙ ⊝ △ Z6 V-VIII ▽; Eur.: RO; TR,
Syr., Cauc., Iran
– *decipiens* Ehrh. = Saxifraga rosacea subsp.
rosacea
– **diapensioides** Bellardi · E:Columnar
Saxifrage; G:Diapensienartiger Steinbrech · ⅄ ◠ △ Z6 IV-VI ▽; Eur.: F, I, Sw;
SW-Alp.
– **diversifolia** Wall. · ⅄ △ Z7 ∧ VI-VIII ▽;
Him.
– × **edithae** Sünd. (*S. marginata* × *S.
stribrnyi*) · ⅄ Z6; cult.
– × **elisabethae** Sünd. (*S. burseriana* × *S.
sancta*) · ⅄ Z6; cult.
– **erioblasta** Boiss. & Reut. · ⅄ ◠ △ ∧ VI
▽; Eur.: S-Sp.
– × **eudoxiana** Kellerer & Sünd. (*S.
ferdinandi-coburgii* × *S. sancta*) · ⅄ Z3;
cult.
– **exarata** Vill. · E:Furrowed Saxifrage;
G:Gefurchter Steinbrech · ⅄ Z6 V-VIII ▽;
Eur.: Ib, Fr, Ital-P, C-Eur., EC-Eur., Ba,
RO; TR, Cauc., N-Iran
– subsp. *moschata* (Wulfen) Cav. =
Saxifraga moschata
– × **farreri** nom. inval. (*S. callosa* × *S.
cochlearis*) · ⅄; cult.
– **federici-augusti** Biasol.
– subsp. **federici-augusti** · ⅄ Z7 ▽; Eur.:
Montenegro, AL, GR
– subsp. **grisebachii** (Degen & Dörfl.) D.A.
Webb · ⅄ ◠ △ Z7 IV ▽; Eur.: Montenegro, Maced., N-GR
– **ferdinandi-coburgii** Kellerer & Sünd. · ⅄
Z6 ▽; Eur.: N-GR, BG; mts.
– × **fleischeri** Sünd. (*S. federici-augusti* × *S.
luteoviridis*) · ⅄; cult.

– **fortunei** Hook. f. · F:Saxifrage
d'automne, Saxifrage de Fortune · ⅄ Z7
IX-X; China, Amur, Manch., Korea, Jap.,
Sakhal.
– **geranioides** L. · ⅄ △ Z7 VI ▽; Eur.: sp.,
F; E-Pyr., NE-Sp.
– × **geuderi** Heinrich & Sünd. (*S.
ferdinandi-coburgii* × *S.* × *boydii*) · ⅄; cult.
– **geum** L. 1762 = Saxifraga hirsuta
– × **geum** L. 1753 (*S. hirsuta* × *S. umbrosa*) ·
⅄ Z3 VI-VII; Eur.: sp., F; Pyr., nat. in
Eur.: B, C-Eur., I, BrI
– **globulifera** Desf. · ⅄ ◠ △ Z7 Ⓐ VI ▽;
Eur.: S-Sp.; NW-Afr.
– var. *erioblasta* (Boiss. & Reut.) Engl. &
Irmsch. = Saxifraga erioblasta
– × **gloriana** hort. ex Horný, Soják & Webr
(*S. lilacina* × *S. scardica*) · ⅄; cult.
– *granatensis* Boiss. & Reut. = Saxifraga
globulifera
– **granulata** L. · E:Fair Maids Of France,
Meadow Saxifrage; G:Knöllchen-
Steinbrech · ⅄ V-VI ▽; Eur.*, Moroc.
– × **grata** Engl. & Irmsch. (*S. aspera* × *S.
ferdinandi-coburgii*) · ⅄; cult.
– *grisebachii* Degen & Dörfl. = Saxifraga
federici-augusti subsp. grisebachii
– × **hardingii** Horný, Soják & Webr (*S.
aspera* × *S. burseriana* × *S. media*) · ⅄;
cult.
– × **heinrichii** Sünd. (*S. aspera* × *S.
stribrnyi*) · ⅄; cult.
– **hieraciifolia** Waldst. & Kit. ex Willd. ·
E:Hawkweed Saxifrage; G:Habichtsk-
raut-Steinbrech · ⅄ VII-VIII ▽; Eur.: Sc,
F, A, EC-Eur., E-Eur.; W-Sib., E-Sib.,
Mong.
– **hirculus** L. · G:Moor-Steinbrech · ⅄
VII-IX ▽; Eur.* exc. Ba, Ib, ? Ital-P; TR,
Cauc., W-Sib., Amur, Kamchat., C-As.,
As., Afgh., Pakist., Him., N-Am.
– **hirsuta** L. · E:Kidney Saxifrage;
F:Saxifrage benoîte; G:Nieren-Stein-
brech, Schatten-Steinbrech · ⅄ Z6 VII ▽;
Eur.: sp., F, IRL, nat. in GB
– × **hoerhammeri** Sünd. ex Engl. & Irmsch.
(*S. federici-augusti* subsp. *grisebachii* × *S.
marginata*) · ⅄; cult.
– × **hofmannii** Sünd. (*S. burseriana* × *S.
sempervivum*) · ⅄; cult.
– × **hornibrookii** Horný, Soják & Webr (*S.
lilacina* × *S. stribrnyi*) · ⅄ Z6; cult.
– **hostii** Tausch
– subsp. **hostii** · G:Host-Steinbrech · ⅄ ◠
Z6 V-VII ▽; Eur.: I, A, Slove., Croatia, ?

H; E-Alp.
- subsp. **rhaetica** (A. Kern.) Braun-Blanq. · ♃ ⌒ △ Z6 V-VI ▽; I: Alp.
- var. *altissima* (A. Kern.) Engl. = Saxifraga hostii subsp. hostii
- **hypnoides** L.
- var. **hypnoides** · E:Dovedale Moss, Mossy Rockfoil; G:Astmoos-Steinbrech · ♃ △ Z6 V-VI ▽; Eur.: Ice., Norw., BrI, N-F
- **iranica** Bornm. · ♃ Z6 ▽; Cauc., Iran
- **irrigua** M. Bieb. · ♃ ⌒ △ Z6 V-VI ▽; Crim
- × **irvingii** hort. ex A.S. Thompson (*S. burseriana* × *S. lilacina*) · ♃ Z6; cult.
- **juniperifolia** Adams · F:Saxifrage à feuilles de genévrier · ♃ ⌒ △ Z6 IV-V ▽; BG, Cauc.
- *juniperina* M. Bieb. = Saxifraga juniperifolia
- × **kellereri** Sünd. (*S. burseriana* × *S. stribrnyi*) · ♃ Z6; cult.
- × **kochii** Hornung (*S. biflora* × *S. oppositifolia*) · G:Großblütiger Steinbrech, Kochs Steinbrech · ♃ Z6 VII-VIII ▽; D +
- *kolenatiana* Regel = Saxifraga paniculata subsp. paniculata
- **kotschyi** Boiss. · ♃ ♭ △ IV ▽; TR
- **laevis** M. Bieb. · ♃ ⌒ △ IV-V ▽; Cauc.
- *latina* (Terracino) Hayek = Saxifraga oppositifolia subsp. oppositifolia var. latina
- **lilacina** Duthie · ♃ ⌒ △ Z5 IV ▽; W-Him.
- *lingulata* Bellardi = Saxifraga callosa subsp. callosa
- **longifolia** Lapeyr. · E:Pyrenean Saxifrage; G:Pyrenäen-Steinbrech · ♃ △ Z6 VI ▽; Eur.: sp., F; Pyr., E-Sp.
- × **luteopurpurea** Lapeyr. (*S. aspera* × *S. media*) · ♃ ▽; C-Pyr.
- *luteoviridis* Schott & Kotschy = Saxifraga corymbosa
- *macedonica* Degen = Saxifraga juniperifolia
- *macropetala* A. Kern. = Saxifraga biflora
- **manschuriensis** Kom. · ♃ Z7 ∧ VI ▽; Korea, Manch.
- **marginata** Sternb. · ♃ ▽; Eur.: I, Ba, RO; mts.
- var. **coriophylla** (Griseb.) Engl. · ♃ ⌒ △ Z7 V ▽; Eur.: Ba
- var. *eumarginata* Engl. & Irmsch. = Saxifraga marginata

- var. **rocheliana** (Sternb.) Engl. & Irmsch. · ♃ ⌒ △ Z7 V ▽; Eur.: Ba, RO
- × **mariae-theresiae** Sünd. (*S. burseriana* × *S. federici-augusti* subsp. *grisebachii*) · ♃; cult.
- × **megaseiflora** hort. ex A.S. Thompson (*S. aspera* × *S. burseriana* × *S. lilacina* × *S. stribrnyi*) · ♃ Z6; cult.
- **moschata** Wulfen · E:Musky Saxifrage; G:Moschus-Steinbrech · ♃ ⌒ △ VI ▽; Eur.: Ib, Fr, Ital-P, C-Eur., E-Eur., Ba; mts.; TR, Cauc., W-Sib. (Altai)
- *murithiana* Tissière = Saxifraga oppositifolia
- *muscoides* All. = Saxifraga moschata
- **mutata** L. · E:Orange Saxifrage; G:Kies-Steinbrech · ⊙ ♃ △ Z6 VI-VII ▽; Eur.: F, I, Sw, A, Slova., RO; Alp., Carp.
- **oppositifolia** L. · G:Gegenblättriger Steinbrech
- subsp. **blepharophylla** (A. Kern. & Hayek) Engl. & Irmsch. · G:Wimper-Steinbrech · ♃ Z2 IV-VII ▽; E-Alp.
- subsp. **oppositifolia** · E:Purple Saxifrage; G:Gegenblättriger Steinbrech · ♃ ⤳ △ Z2 V-VI ▽; Eur.*, W-Sib., E-Sib., Kamchat., C-As., Mong., Him., China, Alaska, Can., USA: NE, NC, NW, Rocky Mts.; Greenl.
- var. **latina** Terracino · ♃ Z2 ▽; I (Apenn.)
- subsp. **rudolphiana** (Hornsch.) Engl. & Irmsch. · G:Rudolphs Steinbrech · ♃ Z2 IV-VII ▽; Eur.: I, A, RO; E-Alp., E-Carp.
- *oranensis* Munby = Saxifraga globulifera
- **paniculata** Mill.
- subsp. **cartilaginea** (Willd.) D.A. Webb · ♃ ⌒ △ Z2 V-VI ▽; TR, Cauc., Iran
- subsp. *kolenatiana* auct. = Saxifraga paniculata subsp. cartilaginea
- subsp. **paniculata** · E:Livelong Saxifrage; F:Saxifrage panicué; G:Rispen-Steinbrech, Trauben-Steinbrech · ♃ Z2 VI-VII ▽; Eur.* exc. BrI, Sc; TR, Cauc., N-Iran, Can., USA: NE, NCE; Greenl.
- **paradoxa** Sternb. · E:Fragile Saxifrage; G:Glimmer-Steinbrech · ♃ VI-VIII; Eur.: A (Kärnten, Steiermark), Slove.
- × **paulinae** Sünd. (*S. burseriana* × *S. ferdinandi-coburgii*) · ♃ Z6; cult.
- **pedemontana** All.
- subsp. **cervicornis** (Viv.) Engl. · ♃ △ Z6 VI ▽; Cors, Sard.
- subsp. **pedemontana** · E:Piedmont Saxifrage · ♃ △ Z6 VI ▽; Eur.: F, Ital-P,

Ba, E-Eur.; mts.
- *peltata* Torr. ex Benth. = Darmera peltata
- **pensylvanica** L. · E:Branch Lettuce, Swamp Saxifrage; G:Pennsylvanischer Steinbrech · ♃ V-VI ▽; USA: NE, NCE
- × **petraschii** Sünd. ex W. Irving (*S. burseriana* × *S. tombeanensis*) · ♃ Z6; cult.
- **porophylla** Bertol. · ♃ ⌓ △ Z6 IV-V ▽; Eur.: I
- var. *montenegrina* (Halácsy & Bald.) Engl. & Irmsch. = Saxifraga federici-augusti subsp. grisebachii
- × **pragensis** Horný, Soják & Webr (*S. ferdinandi-coburgii* × *S. marginata* × *S. stribrnyi*) · ♃; cult.
- × **prossenii** (Sünd.) Ingw. (*S. sancta* × *S. stribrnyi*) · ♃ Z6; cult.
- *pseudosancta* Janka = Saxifraga sancta
- **pubescens** Pourr. · E:Hairy Saxifrage · ♃ Z6 ▽; Eur.: F, sp.; Pyren.
- *purpurea* All. = Saxifraga retusa
- **retusa** Gouan
- subsp. **augustana** (Vacc.) E. Fourn. · ♃ Z6 ▽; Eur.: F, I; SW-Alp.
- subsp. **retusa** · G:Gestutzter Steinbrech · ♃ Z6 V-VI ▽; Eur.: F, I, C-Eur., EC-Eur., RO, BG; Pyr., Alp., Carp., BG
- **rosacea** Moench · G:Rasen-Steinbrech
- subsp. **rosacea** · G:Gewöhnlicher Rasen-Steinbrech · ♃ Z6 V-VII ▽; Eur.: Fr, BrI, Sc, C-Eur., EC-Eur.
- subsp. **sponhemica** (C.C. Gmel.) D.A. Webb · G:Rheinischer Steinbrech · ♃ Z6 ▽; Eur.: Fr, G, EC-Eur.
- × **rosinae** Sünd. ex Horný, Soják & Webr (*S. diapensioides* × *S. marginata*) · ♃; cult.
- **rotundifolia** L.
- subsp. **rotundifolia** var. **heucherifolia** (Griseb. & Schenk) Engl. · ♃ Z6 VI-VII ▽; Eur.: S-Ba, RO; mts.
- subsp. **rotundifolia** var. **rotundifolia** · E:Round Leafed Saxifrage; F:Saxifrage à feuilles rondes; G:Rundblättriger Steinbrech · ♃ Z6 VI-IX ▽; Eur.: Ib, Fr, Ital-P, Ba, C-Eur., Slova., RO; TR, Cauc., nat. in BrI
- × **salmonica** Jenkins (*S. burseriana* × *S. marginata*) · ♃ Z6; cult.
- **sancta** Griseb. · ♃ ⌓ △ Z7 IV-V ▽; GR, TR
- *sarmentosa* L. f. = Saxifraga stolonifera
- **scardica** Griseb. · ♃ ⌓ △ Z7 V ▽; Eur.: Maced., AL, GR; mts.
- **sedoides** L.
- subsp. **hohenwartii** (Vest & Sternb.) O. Schwarz · G:Hohenwart-Steinbrech · ♃ VI-IX ▽; Eur.: I, A, Slove.; E-Alp.
- subsp. **sedoides** · G:Mauerpfeffer-Steinbrech · ♃ VI-IX ▽; Eur.: I, A, Ba; E-Alp., Apenn., N-Ba
- **seguieri** Spreng. · G:Séguiers Steinbrech · ♃ VII-VIII ▽; Eur.: F, I, Sw, A; Alp.
- × **semmleri** Sünd. ex Horný, Soják & Webr (*S. ferdinandi-coburgii* × *S. pseudolaevis* × *S. sancta*) · ♃; cult.
- **sempervivum** K. Koch · ♃ ⌓ △ Z7 IV-V ▽; Eur.: Ba; NW-TR
- *sponhemica* C.C. Gmel. = Saxifraga rosacea subsp. sponhemica
- **spruneri** Boiss. · ♃ ⌓ Z8 (A) ▭ V ▽; Eur.: ? AL, GR, BG; mts.
- **squarrosa** Sieber · G:Sparriger Steinbrech · ♃ Z6 VII-VIII ▽; Eur.: I, A, Slove.; SE-Alp.
- **stellaris** L. · E:Starry Saxifrage; G:Gewöhnlicher Stern-Steinbrech · ♃ Z6 V-VIII ▽; Eur.* exc. EC-Eur.; W-Sib., Greenl.
- **stolonifera** Meerb. · E:Mother-of-Thousands, Strawberry Geranium; G:Judenbart · ♃ Z8 (K) ⊍ V-VIII ▽; China, Jap.
- × **stormonthii** Sünd. ex Horný, Soják & Webr (*S. desoulavyi* × *S. sancta*) · ♃; cult.
- **stribrnyi** (Velen.) Podp. · ♃ ⌓ △ Z6 V ▽; BG, N-GR
- × **stuartii** Sünd. (*S. aspera* × *S. media* × *S. stribrnyi*) · ♃; cult.
- **tenella** Wulfen · G:Zarter Steinbrech · ♃ ⇝ △ Z6 VI-VII ▽; Eur.: I, A, Slove.; SE-Alp.
- **tombeanensis** Boiss. ex Engl. · ♃ ⌓ △ Z6 ▭ V ▽; I: Alp.
- **tridactylites** L. · G:Dreifinger-Steinbrech · ☉ Z5 IV-VI ▽; Eur.*, TR, Iraq, Syr., Cauc., Iran, C-As., N-Afr.
- **trifurcata** Schrad. · ♃ △ Z6 V-VI ▽; N-Sp.
- **umbrosa** L. · E:Wood Saxifrage; F:Désespoir du peintre, Saxifrage des ombrages; G:Porzellanblümchen, Schattenliebender Steinbrech · ♃ Z7 VI-VII ▽; Eur.: sp., F; Pyr., nat. in BrI, DK
- × **urbium** D.A. Webb (*S. hirsuta* × *S. umbrosa*) · E:London Pride; F:Saxifrage panaché · ♃ Z7 V-VI; cult.
- × **urumoffii** Sünd. ex Horný, Soják

& Webr (*S. ferdinandi-coburgii* × *S. luteoviridis*) · ⁴; cult.
- **valdensis** DC. · ⁴ ⌒ △ Z6 VI ▽; Eur.: F, I; SW-Alp.
- **vandellii** Sternb. · ⁴ ⌒ △ Z6 ▭ V ▽; I: Alp.
- **veitchiana** Balf. f. · ⁴ ⤳ △ V-VI ▽; China: Hupeh
- × **wendelacina** Horný & Webr (*S. lilacina* × *S. wendelboi*) · ⁴; cult.
- **wendelboi** Schönb.-Tem. · ⁴ ▽; Iran
- × **zimmeteri** A. Kern. (*S. cuneifolia* × *S. paniculata*) · ⁴; A + cult.
- Cultivars:
- **many cultivars, see Section III**

Scabiosa L. -f- *Dipsacaceae* · c. 80 spp. · E:Pincushion Flower, Scabious; F:Scabieuse; G:Grindkraut, Skabiose
- *alpina* L. = Cephalaria alpina
- *arvensis* L. = Knautia arvensis
- **atropurpurea** L. · E:Mournful Widow, Sweet Scabious; G:Samt-Skabiose · ⊙ ⊙ ✹ D VIII-X; Eur.: Ib, Fr, Ital-P, Ba; TR, NW-Afr., Libya, nat. in BrI
- **some cultivars**
- **canescens** Waldst. & Kit. · G:Graue Skabiose · ⁴ VII-XI; Eur.: Fr, C-Eur., EC-Eur., Croatia, Bosn., Sc, ? RO
- **caucasica** M. Bieb. · F:Scabieuse du Caucase / G:Große Skabiose · ⁴ ✹ Z4 VII-IX; Cauc.
- **many cultivars**
- **cinerea** Lapeyr. ex Lam. · ⁴; Eur.: sp., F, Ba; Pyr., E-Alp.
- subsp. **cinerea** · E:Pyrenean Scabious · ⁴; Eur.: sp. (Pyr.), Ba (mts.)
- subsp. **hladnikiana** (Host) Jasiewicz · G:Hladnicks Grindkraut, Krainer Skabiose · ⁴; Eur.: Alp., Slove., Croatia, Bosn.
- **columbaria** L. · E:Small Scabious, Yellow Scabious; G:Gewöhnliche Tauben-Ska-biose · ⁴ Z6 VII; Eur.*, TR, Syr., ? Arab., Cauc., N-Iran, C-As., Moroc., Alger., Eth., C-Afr., S-Afr.
- **graminifolia** L. · E:Grass-leaved Scabi-ous; F:Scabieuse à feuilles de graminée; G:Grasblättrige Skabiose · ⁴ △ Z7 VI-VIII; Eur.: sp., F, I, Sw, Ba; Moroc.
- **japonica** Miq. · G:Japanische Skabiose
- var. **alpina** Takeda · F:Scabieuse du Japon · ⊙ △ Z7 VII-IX; Jap.
- var. **japonica** · E:Pincushion Flower · ⊙ Z7 VII-IX; Jap.

- *longifolia* Waldst. & Kit. = Knautia longifolia
- **lucida** Vill. · E:Shining Scabious; F:Scabieuse brillante; G:Glänzende Skabiose · ⁴ △ Z5 VII-IX; Eur.: Fr, Ital-P, C-Eur., EC-Eur., Ba.; mts.
- **ochroleuca** L. · F:Scabieuse jaune; G:Gelbe Skabiose · ⊙ ⁴ Z6 VII-IX; Eur.: Ital-P, C-Eur., EC-Eur., Ba, E-Eur.; TR, Cauc., W-Sib., E-Sib., C-As., nat. in F
- **portae** A. Kern. ex Huter · ⁴; Eur.: I, Ba
- **prolifera** L. · E:Carmel Daisy · ⊙ VI-VII; Syr.
- **reuteriana** Boiss. · ⊙ VII-VIII; TR
- *rumelica* hort. = Knautia macedonica
- **silenifolia** Waldst. & Kit. · ⁴ △ Z6 VII-IX; Eur.: I, Slove., Croatia, Bosn., Montene-gro, AL; Apenn., mts.
- **stellata** L. · ⊙ VI-VIII; Eur.: Ib, F, Sard., I; NW-Afr., Libya
- **triandra** L. · G:Südliche Skabiose · ⁴ VI-VIII; Eur.: Ib, Fr, Ital-P, Ba, C-Eur., EC-Eur.
- **vestina** Facchini ex W.D.J. Koch · E:Tyrolean Scabious · ⁴ △ Z7 VI-VIII; Eur.: I; S-Alp., N-Apenn.

Scadoxus Raf. -m- *Amaryllidaceae* · 9 spp. · E:Blood Flower; F:Ail rouge, Hémanthe; G:Blutblume
- **cinnabarinus** (Decne.) Friis & Nordal · ⁴ Z10 ⓦ IV-V; W-Afr., C-Afr., Angola, Uganda
- **multiflorus** (Martyn) Raf. · G:Frühe Blutblume
- subsp. **katherinae** (Baker) Friis & Nor-dal · G:Reichblühende Frühe Blutblume · ⁴ Z10 ⓐ IV-V; S-Afr.
- subsp. **multiflorus** · E:Blood Flower, Ox Tongue Lily; G:Gewöhnliche Frühe Blutblume · ⁴ Z10 ⓐ IV-V; trop. Afr., S-Afr., Yemen
- **puniceus** (L.) Friis & Nordal · E:Royal Paintbrush; G:Gefleckte Frühe Blutblume · ⁴ Z10 ⓐ III-IV; E-Afr., S-Afr.

Scaevola L. -f- *Goodeniaceae* · 96 spp. · E:Fan Flower; F:Scaevola; G:Fächer-blume, Spaltglocke
- **aemula** R. Br. · E:Fairy Fan-flower; G:Blauviolette Fächerblume
- **calendulacea** (Andrews) Druce · E:Scented Fan Flower · ⁴ ♄ ⓐ; Austr.
- **humilis** R. Br. · ♄ Z10 ⓐ; Austr.
- **saligna** G. Forst. · ⁴ ♄ Z10 ⓐ; N.Caled.

– *suaveolens* R. Br. = Scaevola calendulacea

Scandix L. -n- *Apiaceae* · 15-20 spp. ·
F:Scandix; G:Nadelkerbel, Venuskamm
– **pecten-veneris** L. · E:Shepherd's
Needle; G:Gewöhnlicher Venuskamm,
Nadelkerbel · ⊙ V-VII; Eur.*, TR, Cauc.,
Iran, Pakist., C-As., Him., N-Afr., Canar.,
Madeira, nat. in N-Am., S-Afr., Chile, NZ

Scaphosepalum Pfitzer -n- *Orchidaceae* ·
44 spp.
– *ochthodes* (Rchb. f.) Pfitzer = Scaphosepalum verrucosum
– **verrucosum** (Rchb. f.) Pfitzer · ♃ Z10 ⓜ
I-XII ▽ ✲; Col.

Scaphyglottis Poepp. & Endl. -f-
Orchidaceae · 63 spp.
– **behrii** Rchb. f. · ♃ Z10 ⓜ III-V ▽ ✲;
Guat.
– **crurigera** (Bateman ex Lindl.) Ames &
Correll · ♃ Z10 ⓜ IV-V ▽ ✲; Guat., Costa
Rica
– **lindeniana** (A. Rich. & Galeotti) L.O.
Williams · ♃ Z10 ⓜ I-V ▽ ✲; Mex.
– **micrantha** (Lindl.) Ames & Correll · ♃
Z10 ⓜ IV-V ▽ ✲; Guat., Costa Rica

Sceletium N.E. Br. -n- *Aizoaceae* · 8 spp.
– *namaquense* L. Bolus = Sceletium
tortuosum
– **tortuosum** (L.) N.E. Br. · Ψ Z9 ⓚ IX-X;
Cape

Schaueria Nees -f- *Acanthaceae* · 8 spp.
– *calycotricha* (Link & Otto) Nees =
Schaueria flavicoma
– **flavicoma** (Lindl.) N.E. Br. · ♄ e Z10 ⓜ
VII-VIII; Braz.

Scheelea H. Karst. = Attalea
– *martiana* Burret = Attalea phalerata

Schefflera J.R. Forst. & G. Forst.
-f- *Araliaceae* · 582 spp. · E:Ivy Tree,
Umbrella Tree; F:Schefflera; G:Lackblatt,
Schefflera, Strahlenaralie
– **actinophylla** (Endl.) Harms · E:Octopus
Tree, Queensland Umbrella Tree,
Umbrella Tree; G:Queensland-Strahle-
naralie · ♄ e Z10 ⓜ; N.Guinea, Austr.:
North Terr., Queensl.
– **arboricola** (Hayata) Merr. · E:Parasol
Plant; G:Kleine Strahlenaralie · ♄ e Z10

ⓜ; Taiwan
– *cunninghamii* Miq. = Schefflera digitata
– **digitata** J.R. Forst. & G. Forst. · ♄ e Z10
ⓚ; NZ
– **elegantissima** (Veitch ex Mast.) Lowry
& Frodin · E:False Aralia; G:Neukaledo-
nische Strahlenaralie · ♄ e Z10 ⓜ; N.
Caled.
– **heptaphylla** (L.) Frodin · ♄ ♄ Z9 ⓜ;
Jap., Ryukyu-Is., S-China, Taiwan, Vietn.
– **kerchoveana** (Veitch ex P.W. Richards)
Frodin & Lowry · ♄ e Z10 ⓜ; Vanuatu
– *octophylla* (Lour.) Harms = Schefflera
heptaphylla
– **pueckleri** (K. Koch) Frodin · ♄ ♄ e Z10
ⓚ; Ind., SW-China, Burma, N-Thail.,
Laos, N-Vietn.
– **veitchii** (Carrière) Frodin & Lowry · ♄ e
Z10 ⓜ; N.Caled.
– **venulosa** (Wight & Arn.) Harms · ♄ e Z10
ⓜ; Ind.

Scheuchzeria L. -f- *Scheuchzeriaceae* ·
1 sp. · E:Rannoch Rush; F:Scheuchzérie;
G:Blasenbinse, Blumenbinse
– **palustris** L. · G:Blasenbinse, Blumenbinse · ♃ ⌢ V-VI ▽; Eur.* exc. Ib;
Cauc., W-Sib., E-Sib., Amur, Sakhal.,
Kamchat., N-China, Jap., N-Am.

Schinopsis Engl. -f- *Anacardiaceae* · 7 spp.
– **balansae** Engl. · ♄ Z10 ⓜ ⓝ; Arg., Parag.
– *lorentzii* (Griseb.) Engl. = Schinopsis
quebracho-colorado
– **quebracho-colorado** (Schltdl.) F.A.
Barkley & T. Mey. · ♄ Z10 ⓜ ⓝ; Braz.,
Parag., Urug., Arg.

Schinus L. -m- *Anacardiaceae* · 27 spp. ·
E:Peppertree; F:Faux-poivrier; G:Pfef-
ferbaum
– **longifolius** (Lindl.) Speg. · E:Peru
Peppertree; G:Peruanischer Pfefferbaum
· ♄ Z9 ⓚ; S-Braz., Parag., Urug., Arg.
– **molle** L.
– var. **areira** L. · ♄ e Z9 ⓚ; S-Braz., Parag.,
Bol.
– var. **molle** · E:Pepper Tree; G:Gewöhn-
licher Pfefferbaum · ♄ ♄ e Z9 ⓚ V ⓝ;
Mex., C-Am., trop. S-Am., nat. in sp.,
N-Afr.
– **polygamus** (Cav.) Cabrera · ♄ ♄ e Z10 ⓚ
V; w S-Am.
– **terebinthifolius** Raddi · E:Brazilian Peppertree; G:Brasilianischer Pfefferbaum ·

ħ e Z9 Ⓚ IV ☠ Ⓝ; Braz., nat. in Ib

Schisandra Michx. -f- *Schisandraceae* · 25 spp. · F:Schisandra; G:Beerentraube, Spaltkölbchen
- **chinensis** (Turcz.) Baill. · E:Chinese Magnolia Vine; G:Chinesisches Spaltkölbchen · ħ d ≹ ♣ D Z6 V-VI ⚕ ; Amur. China, Korea, Jap., Sakhal.
- **grandiflora** Hook. f. & Thomson · G:Großblütiges Spaltkölbchen · ≀ d Z9 Ⓚ; Him. (Ind.: Himachal Pradesh - SW-China), Burma
- var. **grandiflora** · G:Großblütiges Spaltkölbchen · ħ ≀ d ≹ Z7; Him.
- var. **rubriflora** (Rehder & E.H. Wilson) C.K. Schneid. · G:Rotblühendes Spaltkölbchen · ħ ≀ d ≹ Z7 IV-V; W-China: Sichuan, Sikang; Ind.: Assam
- **repanda** (Siebold & Zucc.) A.C. Sm. · ħ ≀ d ≹; Jap. mts., S-Korea
- *rubriflora* Rehder & E.H. Wilson = Schisandra grandiflora var. rubriflora
- **sphenanthera** Rehder & E.H. Wilson · ≀ d ≹ Z7 IV-V ⚕ ; C-China, W-China

Schismatoglottis Zoll. & Moritzi -f- *Araceae* · 103 spp. · E:Drop Tongue
- **acuminatissima** Schott · ♃ Z10 Ⓦ; Sumat., Java, Kalimantan
- **asperata** Engl. · ♃ Z10 Ⓦ; Kalimantan
- **calyptrata** (Roxb.) Zoll. & Moritzi · ♃ Z10 Ⓦ; N.Guinea
- *concinna* Schott = Schismatoglottis acuminatissima
- *lavallei* Linden = Schismatoglottis acuminatissima
- **motleyana** (Schott) Engl. · ♃ Z9 Ⓦ; Kalimantan
- *neuguineensis* (Linden ex André) N.E. Br. = Schismatoglottis calyptrata
- *picta* Schott = Schismatoglottis calyptrata
- *pulchra* N.E. Br. = Schismatoglottis motleyana

Schivereckia Andrz. ex DC. -f- *Brassicaceae* · 2 spp. · F:Cresson des oies, Drave; G:Zwerggänsekresse
- *bornmuelleri* Prantl = Schivereckia doerfleri
- **doerfleri** (Wettst.) Bornm. · ♃ △ IV-V; Eur.: Maced., AL, BG; TR
- **podolica** (Besser) Andrz. · ♃ △ IV; Eur.: RO, Russ

Schizachyrium Nees -n- *Poaceae* · 60+ spp. · E:Blue Stem; G:Präriegras
- **scoparium** (Michx.) Nash · E:Blue Stem, Prairie Grass; G:Kleines Präriegras · ♃ Z5; Can., USA* exc. Calif, NW

Schizanthus Ruiz & Pav. -m- *Solanaceae* · 12 spp. · E:Butterfly Flower; F:Schizanthe; G:Orchidee des armen Mannes, Schlitzblume, Spaltblume
- **pinnatus** Ruiz & Pav. · ⊙ Z10 VII-IX; Chile
- **retusus** Hook. · ⊙ Z10 VII-IX; Chile
- × **wisetonensis** H. Low (*S. grahamii* × *S. pinnatus*) · ⊙ Z10; cult.

Schizobasopsis J.F. Macbr. = Bowiea
- *volubilis* (Harv. & Hook. f.) J.F. Macbr. = Bowiea volubilis

Schizocapsa Hance = Tacca
- *plantaginea* Hance = Tacca plantaginea

Schizocodon Siebold & Zucc. = Shortia
- *soldanelloides* Siebold & Zucc. = Shortia soldanelloides

Schizopetalon Sims -n- *Brassicaceae* · -10 spp.
- **walkeri** Sims · ⊙ Z8 VI-VIII; Chile

Schizophragma Siebold & Zucc. -n- *Hydrangeaceae* · 2-4 (-8) spp. · F:Hortensia grimpant; G:Spalthortensie
- **hydrangeoides** Siebold & Zucc. · E:Climbing Hydrangea; F:Schizophragma; G:Spalthortensie · ħ ≀ d ≹ Z6 VII; Jap.
- **integrifolium** (Franch.) Oliv.
- var. *molle* Rehder = Schizophragma molle
- **molle** (Rehder) Chun · ħ d ≹ Z7; W-China

Schizostylis Backh. & Harv. -f- *Iridaceae* · 1 sp. · E:Kaffir Lily; F:Lis des Cafres; G:Kaffernlilie, Spaltgriffel
- **coccinea** Backh. & Harv. · E:Kaffir Lily; G:Kaffernlilie, Spaltgriffel · ♃ Z6 X-XII; S-Afr.
- **some cultivars**

Schleichera Willd. -f- *Sapindaceae* · 1 sp. · E:Gum Lac, Lac Tree; F:Bois de Macassar; G:Macassaölbaum
- **oleosa** Merr. · ħ d Z10 Ⓦ Ⓝ; Ind., Malay. Arch.

Schlumbergera Lem. -f- *Cactaceae* ·
6 spp. · F:Cactus de Noël; G:Gliederkak-
tus, Weihnachtskaktus
– × **buckleyi** (T. Moore) Tjaden (*S.
russelliana* × *S. truncata*) · ♄ ⚊ Z9 ⓜ;
cult.
– **gaertneri** (Regel) Britton & Rose =
Rhipsalidopsis gaertneri
– **opuntioides** (Loefgr. & Dusén) D.R.
Hunt · ♄ ⚊ ⚊ Z9 ⓜ XII-III ▽ ✳; Braz.: Rio
de Janeiro
– **orssichiana** Barthlott & McMillan · ♄ ⚊
Z9 ⓜ VIII-III ▽ ✳; SE-Braz. (Serra do
Mar)
– **russelliana** (Hook.) Britton & Rose ·
♄ ⚊ ⚊ Z9 ⓜ ▽ ✳; SE-Braz. (Serra dos
Orgaes)
– **truncata** (Haw.) Moran · E:False
Christmas Cactus · ♄ ⚊ Z9 ⓜ XII-I ▽ ✳;
Braz.: Rio de Janeiro

Schoenia Steetz -f- *Asteraceae* · 5 spp.
– **cassiniana** (Gaudich.) Steetz · E:Pink
Everlasting · ⊙ ✄ VII-VIII; Austr.

Schoenocaulon A. Gray -n- *Melanthiaceae* ·
10 spp.
– **officinale** (Cham. & Schltdl.) A. Gray ex
Benth. · E:Sabadilla; G:Sabadillgermer
· ⚊ Z9 ⓚ ❧ ✿; Mex., Guat., W.Ind.,
Venez.

Schoenoplectus (Rchb.) Palla -m-
Cyperaceae · 39 spp. · E:Club Rush; F:Jonc
des tonneliers; G:Seebinse, Teichsimse
– × **carinatus** (Sm.) Palla (*S. lacustris* × *S.
triqueter*) · G:Gekielte Teichsimse · ⚊ ⚊
VII-VIII; W-Eur., C-Eur., I
– × *kalmussii* (Asch., Abrom. & Graebn.)
Palla = Schoenoplectus × carinatus
– × **kuekenthalianus** (Junge) D.H. Kent
(*S. tabernaemontani* × *S. triqueter*) ·
G:Gekielte Salz-Teichsimse · ⚊ ⚊ ; D +
– **lacustris** (L.) Palla · E:Bulrush;
G:Gewöhnliche Teichsimse, Seebinse · ⚊
⚊ ≈ Z4 V-VII ⓝ; Eur.*, cosmop.
– subsp. **tabernaemontani** (C.C. Gmel.)
Á. Löve & D. Löve = Schoenoplectus
tabernaemontani
– **litoralis** (Schrad.) Palla · G:Strand-
Teichsimse · ⚊ ⚊ VI-VII; Eur.: Ib,
Ital-P, Ba, RO, ? A; TR, Cauc., C-As., Ind.,
SE-As., S-Afr.,
– **mucronatus** (L.) Palla · E:Bog Bulrush;
F:Scirpe mucroné; G:Stachelspitzige

Teichsimse · ⚊ ⚊ VIII-X; Eur.* exc.
BrI, Sc; TR, Cauc., Iran, Him., Amur,
C-As., S-As., SE-As., Jap., China, Egypt,
Cameroon, Austr., Polyn.
– **pungens** (Vahl) Palla · E:Sharp Club
Rush; G:Amerikanische Teichsimse,
Kleine Dreikant-Teichsimse · ⚊ ⚊ VII-
VIII; Eur.: Ib, Fr, Ital-P, C-Eur., EC-Eur.;
Alaska, Can., USA*, C-Am., S-Am.,
Tasm., NZ, nat. in BrI
– **supinus** (L.) Palla · E:Dwarf Club Rush;
G:Niedrige Teichsimse · ⊙ ⚊ VII-IX;
Eur.* exc. BrI, Sc; TR, Cauc., W-Sib.,
E-Sib., C-As, Him., Ind., Sri Lanka,
Malay. Arch., Afr., N-Am., Austr.
– **tabernaemontani** (C.C. Gmel.) Palla ·
E:Zebra Rush; F:Jonc des tonneliers,
Scirpe des lacs; G:Salz-Teichsimse · ⚊
⚊ ≈ Z4 VI-VII; Eur.*, Cauc., W-Sib.,
E-Sib., N-Am.
– **triqueter** (L.) Palla · E:Triangular Club
Rush; F:Scirpe triquètre; G:Dreikantige
Teichsimse · ⚊ ⚊ VI-VII; Eur.* exc. Sc;
TR, Cauc., C-As., Amur, Egypt, N-Am.

Schoenorchis Blume -f- *Orchidaceae* ·
26 spp. · F:Orchidée-jonc; G:Binsenor-
chidee
– **juncifolia** Blume · ⚊ ❧ Z10 ⓜ V-VI ▽ ✳;
Sumat., Java

Schoenus L. -m- *Cyperaceae* · 108 spp. ·
E:Bog Rush; F:Choin; G:Kopfried
– **ferrugineus** L. · E:Brown Bog Rush;
G:Rostrotes Kopfried · ⚊ ⚊ V-VI; Eur.*
exc. BrI, Ib
– × *intermedius* Brügger = Schoenus ×
scheuchzeri
– **nigricans** L. · E:Black Bog Rush;
G:Schwarzes Kopfried · ⚊ ⚊ VI-VII;
Eur.*, Cauc., Iran, Afgh., C-As., N-Afr.,
Somalia, S-Afr., N-Am.
– × **scheuchzeri** Brügger (*S. ferrugineus*
× *S. nigricans*) · G:Bastard-Kopfried · ⚊
⚊ ; Eur.: Sw, G, A, CZ

× **SchomboBrassavola** hort.
-f- *Orchidaceae* (*Rhyncholaelia* ×
Schomburgkia)

× **Schombocattleya** hort. -f- *Orchidaceae*
(*Schomburgkia* × *Cattleya*)

× **Schombodiacrium** hort. -n- *Orchidaceae*
(*Caularthron* × *Schomburgkia*)

× **Schomboepidendrum** hort.
 -n- *Orchidaceae* (*Schomburgkia* ×
 Epidendrum)

× **Schombolaelia** hort. -f- *Orchidaceae*
 (*Laelia* × *Schomburgkia*)

× **Schombotonia** hort. -f- *Orchidaceae*
 (*Broughtonia* × *Schomburgkia*)

Schomburgkia Lindl. -f- *Orchidaceae* ·
 14 spp.
 – **gloriosa** Rchb. f. · ♃ Z10 ⊛ X-XII ▽ ✳;
 Col., Ecuad., Peru, Bol., Venez., Braz.
 – **superbiens** (Lindl.) Rolfe · ♃ Z10 ⊛ IV-V
 ▽ ✳; Mex., Hond.
 – **undulata** Lindl. · ♃ Z10 ⊛ V-VII ▽ ✳;
 Venez.

Schotia Jacq. -f- *Caesalpiniaceae* · 5 spp. ·
 E:Boerboon; F:Fuchsia en arbre;
 G:Bauernbohne
 – **afra** (L.) Bodin · ♄ ♄ Z9 ⊛ IX-X; S-Afr.
 – **brachypetala** Sond. · E:Tree Fuchsia;
 G:Borstige Bauernbohne · ♄ Z9 ⊛ VIII;
 S-Afr.
 – **latifolia** Jacq. · ♄ ♄ Z9 ⊛; e S-Afr.
 – *speciosa* Jacq. = Schotia afra

Schrebera Roxb. -f- *Oleaceae* · 8-10 spp.
 – **arborea** A. Chev. · ♄ e ✄ Z10 ⊛; W-Afr.:
 Guinea

Schubertia Mart. -f- *Asclepiadaceae* · 6 spp.
 – **grandiflora** Mart. & Zucc. · ♄ ⚥ D Z10 ⊛
 VII-VIII; Braz.

Schwantesia Dinter -f- *Aizoaceae* · 11 sp.
 – **triebneri** L. Bolus · ♃ ♈ Z9 ⊛; Cape

Schwantesia L. Bolus = Mitrophyllum
 – *dissita* (N.E. Br.) L. Bolus = Mitrophyllum
 dissitum

Sciadocalyx Regel = Kohleria
 – *digitaliflora* Linden & André = Kohleria
 digitaliflora

Sciadopitys Siebold & Zucc. -f-
 Sciadopityaceae · 1 sp. · E:Umbrella Pine;
 F:Pin parasol japonais; G:Schirmtanne
 – **verticillata** (Thunb.) Siebold & Zucc. ·
 E:Umbrella Pine; F:Pin parasol; G:Japa-
 nische Schirmtanne · ♄ e Z6; Jap.

Scilla L. -f- *Hyacinthaceae* · 87 spp. ·
 E:Squill; F:Scille; G:Blaustern, Scilla
 – *adlamii* Baker = Ledebouria cooperi
 – **amoena** L. · E:Star Hyacinth; G:Schöner
 Blaustern · ♃ Z7 IV-V ▽; orig. ?, nat. in F,
 Ba, RO
 – **autumnalis** L. · E:Autumn Squill;
 G:Herbst-Blaustern · ♃ Z7 ⋀ IX-X ▽;
 Eur.* exc. C-Eur., Sc; TR, N-Iraq, Syr.,
 Cauc., N-Iran, NW-Afr.
 – **bifolia** L. · E:Alpine Squill; G:Zweiblät-
 triger Blaustern · ♃ Z6 III ⚘ ▽; Eur.*
 exc. BrI, Sc; TR, Syr., Cauc.
 – **bithynica** Boiss. · ♃ IV ▽; E-BG, NW-TR
 – *campanulata* Aiton = Hyacinthoides
 hispanica subsp. hispanica
 – *drunensis* (Speta) Speta = Scilla bifolia
 – **furseorum** Meikle · ♃ IV ▽; NE-Afgh.
 – *hispanica* Mill. = Hyacinthoides hispanica
 subsp. hispanica
 – **hohenackeri** Fisch. & C.A. Mey. · ♃ Z6
 III ▽; Cauc. (Azerb.), S-Iran
 – **hyacinthoides** L. · ♃ ⋀ IV-V ▽; Eur.:
 Ib, Fr, Ital-P, Ba; TR, Syr., N-Iraq, nat. in
 Alger.
 – *italica* L. = Hyacinthoides italica
 – **litardierei** Breistr. · ♃ Z6 V-VI ▽; Eur.:
 Croatia, Bosn., Montenegro, Serb.
 – *maritima* L. = Urginea maritima
 – **mischtschenkoana** Grossh. · ♃ Z6 III-IV
 ▽; Cauc.
 – *nana* (Schult. & Schult. f.) Speta =
 Chionodoxa nana
 – *non-scripta* (L.) Hoffmanns. & Link =
 Hyacinthoides non-scripta
 – *nutans* Sm. = Hyacinthoides non-scripta
 – *paucifolia* Baker = Ledebouria socialis
 – **peruviana** L. · E:Peruvian Scilla; G:Stern
 der Peru · ♃ Z8 ⊛ V-VI ▽; Eur.: Ib,
 Ital-P; NW-Afr.
 – *pratensis* Waldst. & Kit. = Scilla litardierei
 – **puschkinioides** Regel · ♃ Z6 III-IV ▽;
 C-As.
 – **scilloides** (Lindl.) Druce · ♃ Z5 VIII-IX
 ▽; China, Amur, Manch, Korea, Jap.,
 Taiwan
 – **siberica** Haw. · E:Siberian Squill; F:Scille
 de Sibérie; G:Sibirischer Blaustern · ♃ Z5
 III-IV ▽; Eur.: Russ.; TR, N-Iraq, Cauc., ?
 Iran, nat. in NL, A, EC-Eur., Ba, RO
 – *sicula* Tineo = Scilla peruviana
 – *socialis* Baker = Ledebouria socialis
 – **spetana** Kereszty · G:Speta-Blaustern · ♃
 III-IV ▽; Eur.: A, H
 – *tubergeniana* Stearn = Scilla

mischtschenkoana
- *vindobonensis* Speta = Scilla bifolia
- *violacea* Hutch. = Ledebouria socialis

Scindapsus Schott -m- *Araceae* · 35 spp.
- **aureus** (Linden & André) Engl. =
Epipremnum aureum
- **pictus** Hassk. · ʃ e ⚲ Z10 ⓦ ☀; Malay.
Pen.

Scirpidiella Rauschert = Isolepis
- *fluitans* = Isolepis fluitans

Scirpodendron Zipp. ex Kurz -n-
Cyperaceae · 2 spp.
- **ghaeri** (Gaertn.) Merr. · ♃ Z10 ⓦ ⓝ; Sri
Lanka, Indochina, Malay. Pen., Austr.
(Queensl.), Samoa

Scirpoides Ség. -m- *Cyperaceae* · 3 spp. ·
E:Round-headed Club Rush; F:Faux-
scirpe; G:Glanzbinse, Kopfsimse,
Kugelbinse
- **holoschoenus** (L.) Soják · E:Round-
headed Clubrush; G:Immergrüne
Kugelbinse · ♃ ⌒ Z7 VI-VIII; Eur.* exc.
Sc; Arab., Palest., Cauc, Iran, Afgh.,
W-Sib., C-As., NW-Ind., N-Afr., Canar.

Scirpus L. -m- *Cyperaceae* · 66 spp. ·
E:Wood Club Rush; F:Jonc des tonneliers, Scirpe; G:Simse
- *acicularis* L. = Eleocharis acicularis
- *cernuus* Vahl = Isolepis cernua
- **cyperinus** (L.) Kunth · E:Wool Grass;
G:Zypergras-Simse · ♃ ⌒ Z7 VI-VII;
N-Am., Mex.
- **georgianus** R.M. Harper · E:Georgia
Bulrush; G:Dunkelgrüne Simse,
Schwarzgrüne Simse · ♃ ⌒ V-VII;
N-Am.
- *globulosus* Retz. = Fimbristylis globulosa
- *holoschoenus* L. = Scirpoides holoschoenus
- *lacustris* L. = Schoenoplectus lacustris
- subsp. *tabernaemontani* (C.C. Gmel.)
Syme = Schoenoplectus tabernaemontani
- *maritimus* L. = Bolboschoenus maritimus
- *mucronatus* L. = Schoenoplectus
mucronatus
- *palustris* L. = Eleocharis palustris subsp.
palustris
- *parvulus* Roem. & Schult. = Eleocharis
parvula
- *prolifer* Rottb. = Isolepis prolifera

- **radicans** Schkuhr · G:Wurzelnde Simse ·
♃ ⌒ VI-VII; Eur.: Fr, C-Eur., EC-Eur.,
Slove., Serb., BG, E-Eur., Sc; W-Sib.,
E-Sib., Amur, Sakhal., Korea, Jap.
- **sylvaticus** L. · E:Wood Club Rush;
F:Scirpe des bois; G:Wald-Simse · ♃ ⌒
Z6 V-VII; Eur.*, Cauc., TR, W-Sib., E-Sib.,
Amur, Sakhal., C-As., Mong., China, Jap.
- *tabernaemontani* C.C. Gmel. = Schoeno-
plectus tabernaemontani
- *triqueter* L. = Schoenoplectus triqueter

Scleranthus L. -m- *Illecebraceae* · 15 spp. ·
E:Knawel; F:Gnavelle, Scléranthe;
G:Knäuel
- **annuus** L. · E:Annual Knawel; G:Einjäh-
riger Knäuel · ⊙ IV-X; Eur.*, TR, Cauc.,
Moroc., Alger., nat. in N-Am.
- **perennis** L. · G:Ausdauernder Knäuel · ♃
V-IX; Eur.*, TR, Cauc., Moroc.
- **polycarpos** L. · G:Triften-Knäuel · ⊙
IV-VII; Eur.: most; TR, Cauc., Moroc.,
Alger.
- **uniflorus** P.A. Will. · ♃ ⓐ; NZ
- **verticillatus** Tausch · G:Hügel-Knäuel,
Quirl-Knäuel · ⊙ IV-V; Eur.: Ib, Fr, Ital-P,
C-Eur., Ba; TR

Sclerocactus Britton & Rose -m-
Cactaceae · 19 spp. · E:Fishhook Cactus
- *erectocentrus* (J.M. Coult.) N.P. Taylor =
Echinomastus erectocentrus
- **glaucus** (K. Schum.) L.D. Benson. ·
E:Uinta Basin Hookless Cactus · ♀ Z9 ⓐ
▽ ✳; USA: Utah, Colo.
- *intertextus* (Engelm.) N.P. Taylor =
Echinomastus intertextus
- var. *dasyacanthus* (Engelm.) N.P. Taylor
= Echinomastus intertextus
- *johnsonii* (Engelm.) N.P. Taylor =
Echinomastus johnsonii
- *mariposensis* (Hester) N.P. Taylor =
Echinomastus mariposensis
- **papyracanthus** (Engelm.) N.P. Taylor ·
E:Paperspine Fishhook Cactus · ♀ Z9 ⓐ
▽ ✳; USA: Ariz., N.Mex.
- **polyancistrus** (Engelm. & Bigelow)
Britton & Rose. · E:Redspined Fishhook
Cactus · ♀ Z9 ⓐ ▽ ✳; USA: SW-Nev.,
S-Calif.
- **scheeri** (Salm-Dyck) N.P. Taylor ·
E:Scheer's Fishhook Cactus · ♀ Z9 ⓐ ▽
✳; S-Tex., Mex.: Nuevo León, Tamauli-
pas
- **uncinatus** (Galeotti) N.P. Taylor

– var. **crassihamatus** (F.A.C. Weber) N.P.
Taylor · ⸎ Z9 ⌂ ▽ ✳; USA: N.Mex., Tex.
– var. **uncinatus** · E:Cat Claw Cactus · ⸎ Z9
⌂ ▽ ✳; Tex., N.Mex.
– *unguispinus* (Engelm.) N.P. Taylor =
Echinomastus unguispinus

Sclerochloa P. Beauv. -f- *Poaceae* · 1 sp. ·
F:Sclérochloa; G:Hartgras
– **dura** (L.) P. Beauv. · G:Hartgras · ⊙ IV-
VII; Eur.* exc. BrI, Sc; TR, Levant, Iraq,
Cauc., Iran, Afgh., Pakist., Him., C-As.,
NW-Afr.

Scolochloa Link -f- *Poaceae* · 1 sp. · F:Herbe
des marais; G:Schwingelschilf
– **festucacea** (Willd.) Link · E:Swamp
Grass; G:Schwingelschilf · ⹌ VI-VII; Eur.:
Sc, G, PL, Russ.; Cauc., W-Sib., E-Sib.,
Mong.

Scolopendrium Adans. = Asplenium
– *officinale* DC. = Asplenium scolopendrium
– *officinarum* Sw. = Asplenium scolopendrium
– *vulgare* Sm. = Asplenium scolopendrium

Scolymus L. -m- *Asteraceae* · 3 spp. ·
E:Golden Thistle; F:Scolyme; G:Gold-
distel
– **hispanicus** L. · E:Golden Thistle, Spanish
Oyster Plant; G:Goldwurzel, Spanische
Golddistel · ⊙ ⹌ Z7 VIII Ⓝ; Eur.: Ib, Fr,
Ital-P, Ba, E-Eur.; TR, Canar., N-Afr.

Scopolia Jacq. -f- *Solanaceae* · 5 spp. ·
F:Scopolia; G:Tollkraut
– **anomala** (Link & Otto) Airy Shaw · ⹌;
Nepal, Sikkim
– **carniolica** Jacq. · E:Russian Belladonna,
Scopolia; G:Krainer Tollkraut · ⹌ Z5
⌂ III-IV ⚥ ⚘; Eur.: Ital-P, A, EC-Eur.,
Slove., Croatia, EC-Eur., nat. in DK, D
– *lurida* Dunal = Scopolia anomala
– **stramonifolia** Link & Otto · ⹌; Kashmir,
Him., SW-China

Scorpiurus L. -m- *Fabaceae* · 4 spp. ·
E:Caterpillar Plant; F:Chenille, Scorpiure;
G:Skorpionswicke
– **muricatus** L. · G:Skorpionswicke · ⊙;
Eur.: Ib, Fr, Ital-P, Ba, Crim; TR, Levant,
Iraq, Iran, N-Afr., E-Afr.

Scorzonera L. -f- *Asteraceae* · 150+ spp. ·

E:Viper's Grass; F:Scorsonère;
G:Schwarzwurzel, Stielsamen
– **aristata** Ramond ex DC. · E:Bearded
Viper's Grass; G:Grannen-Schwarzwurzel
· ⹌ Z6 VI-VIII; Eur.: sp., F, I, A, Slove.;
Pyr., S-Alp., Apenn.
– **austriaca** Willd. · G:Österreichische
Schwarzwurzel · ⹌ IV-V ▽; Eur.: Fr,
Ital-P, C-Eur., Ital-P, Ba, E-Eur.; ? Sib.,
E-China
– **cana** (C.A. Mey.) O. Hoffm. · G:Ausdau-
erndes Stielsamenkraut · ⹌ V-VIII; Eur.:
A, Ital-P, EC-Eur., Ba, E-Eur.; TR, Syr.,
Iraq, Cauc., Iran
– **hispanica** L. · E:Black Salsify, Viper's
Grass; G:Garten-Schwarzwurzel,
Gemüse-Schwarzwurzel · ⹌ Z6 VI-VIII Ⓝ
▽; Eur.* exc. BrI, Sc; Cauc., W-Sib.
– **humilis** L. · G:Niedrige Schwarzwurzel ·
⹌ V-VI ▽; Eur.*
– **laciniata** L. · G:Schlitzblättrige
Schwarzwurzel, Stielsamen · ⊙ Z6
V-VII; Eur.* exc. BrI, Sc; TR, Iran, C-As.,
NW-Afr.
– **parviflora** Jacq. · G:Kleinblütige
Schwarzwurzel · ⊙ V-VII; Eur.: Ib., Fr,
C-Eur., EC-Eur., Ba, E-Eur.; TR, Iran, Sib.
– **purpurea** L. · G:Violette-Schwarzwurzel
– subsp. **purpurea** · E:Purple Viper's Grass;
G:GewöhnlicheViolette Schwarzwurzel ·
⹌ Z6 V-VIII ▽; Eur.: F, I, C-Eur., EC-Eur.,
Ba, E-Eur.; W-Sib., C-As.
– subsp. **rosea** (Waldst. & Kit.) Nyman ·
G:Rosenrote Schwarzwurzel · ⹌ Z6
VI-VIII ▽; Eur.: A, Slove., Ba, I, RO; mts.
– *rosea* Waldst. & Kit. = Scorzonera
purpurea subsp. rosea
– **tau-saghyz** Lipsch. & G.G. Bosse · Ⓝ;
Kara-tau-Plateau

Scrophularia L. -f- *Scrophulariaceae* ·
c. 200 spp. · E:Figwort; F:Scrofulaire;
G:Braunwurz
– **auriculata** L. · E:Water Betony, Water
Figwort; G:Wasser-Braunwurz · ⹌ Z5
VI-VIII; Eur.: Ib, Fr, BrI, Ital-P, C-Eur,
Azor.; NW-Afr.
– **canina** L. · G:Hunds-Braunwurz
– subsp. **canina** · E:Alpine Figwort;
G:Gewöhnliche Hunds-Braunwurz · ⹌ △
Z7 VI-VIII; Eur.: Ib, Fr, Ital-P, C-Eur., Ba,
Crim; Cauc., N-Afr.
– subsp. **hoppei** (W.D.J. Koch) P. Fourn. ·
G:Jurassische Braunwurz · Z7; Eur.: Jura,
S-Alp., Apenn.

– *hoppei* W.D.J. Koch = Scrophularia
canina subsp. hoppei
– *juratensis* Schleich. ex Wydler = Scrophularia canina subsp. hoppei
– **nodosa** L. · E:Figwort; G:Knotige Braunwurz · ⅃ VI-VIII ⚥ ; Eur.*, TR, Cauc.,
W-Sib., E-Sib., E-Him., nat. in N-Am.
– **scopolii** Hoppe ex Pers. · G:Drüsige
Braunwurz · ⅃ VI-IX; Eur.: Ital-P, A,
EC-Eur., Ba, E-Eur.; TR, Iraq, Syr., Cauc.,
Iran, Him.
– **umbrosa** Dumort. · G:Geflügelte
Braunwurz · ⅃ VI-IX; Eur.* exc. Ib; TR,
N-As.
– **vernalis** L. · G:Frühlings-Braunwurz · ⊙
⅃ V-VII; Eur.* exc. BrI, Sc, ? Ib; Cauc.

Scutellaria L. -f- *Lamiaceae* · 441 sp. ·
E:Helmet Flower, Skullcap; F:Scutellaire;
G:Helmkraut
– **alpina** L. · E:Alpine Skullcap; G:Alpen-
Helmkraut · ⅃ △ Z5 VI-VIII; Eur.: Ib, Fr,
Ital-P, Ba, C-Eur., E-Eur.; mts.; W-Sib.
– subsp. *supina* (L.) I. Richardson = Scutel-
laria supina
– **altissima** L. · G:Hohes Helmkraut · ⅃ Z5
VI-VII; Eur.: Ital-P, EC-Eur., Ba, E-Eur.;
TR, Cauc., nat. in Fr, BrI
– **aurata** Lem. · ⅃ Z9 ⌂; Braz., Peru
– **baicalensis** Georgi · E:Chinese Skullcap;
F:Scutellaire du lac Baîkal; G:Chine-
sisches Helmkraut · ⅃ △ Z5 VII-VIII ⚥ ;
E-Sib., Mong., N-China
– **costaricana** H. Wendl. · ⅃ ♄ Z9 ⌂ V-VII;
Costa Rica
– **galericulata** L. · F:Scutellaire casquée;
G:Sumpf-Helmkraut · ⅃ ⁓ Z5 VI-IX;
Eur.*, TR, Palest., N-As., N-Am.
– **hastifolia** L. · G:Spießblättriges
Helmkraut · ⅃ ⁓ Z5 VI-VIII; Eur.* exc.
BrI, Ib; TR, Cauc., W-Sib., nat. in BrI
– **incana** Spreng. · E:Skullcap; F:Scutellaire
blanchâtre; G:Blaues Herbst-Helmkraut ·
⅃ Z5 VIII-IX; USA: NE, NCE, NC, SE
– **indica** L. · ⅃ Z7; Jap., Korea, China
– *macrantha* Fisch. = Scutellaria baicalensis
– **minor** Huds. · E:Lesser Skullcap;
G:Kleines Helmkraut · ⅃ ⁓ VII-IX; Eur.:
Ib, Fr, BrI, I, G, Swed, nat. in A
– *mociniana* hort. non Benth. = Scutellaria
costaricana
– **orientalis** L.
– subsp. **orientalis** · F:Scutellaire jaune · ⅃
Z7; Eur.: Ib, Ba, RO, Crim; Cauc.
– subsp. **pinnatifida** J.R. Edm. · ⅃ △ Z7

VII-IX; Eur.: Ba; TR
– **scordiifolia** Fisch. ex Schrank · ⅃ △ Z5
VI-VIII; Sib.
– **supina** L. · ⅃ ♄ △ Z5 V-VII; Eur.: E-Eur.;
W-Sib.
– **ventenatii** Hook. · ⅃ Z9 ⌂ VII-VIII; Col.
– **violacea** B. Heyne ex Benth. · ⅃ Z9 ⌂
VI-IX; S-Ind., Sri Lanka

Scuticaria Lindl. -f- *Orchidaceae* · 9 spp. ·
F:Scuticaire; G:Peitschenorchidee
– **hadwenii** (Lindl.) Hook. · ⅃ ⚬ Z10 ⌂
V-VI ▽ ✳; Guyana, Braz.
– **steelii** (Hook.) Lindl. · ⅃ ⚬ Z10 ⌂ V-X ▽
✳; Venez., Guyana, Braz.
– **strictifolia** Hoehne · ⅃ Z10 ⌂ ▽ ✳;
Braz.

Scyphanthus Sweet -m- *Loasaceae* · 2 spp. ·
G:Becherblume
– **elegans** Sweet · ⅃ ⚬ Z9 ⌂ VII-VIII; Chile

Scyphularia Fée -f- *Davalliaceae* · 8 spp. ·
E:Caterpillar Fern; F:Fougère-chenille;
G:Raupenfarn
– **pentaphylla** (Blume) Fée · ⅃ ⤳ Z10 ⌂;
Java, N.Guinea, Polyn.

Seaforthia R. Br. = Ptychosperma
– *elegans* R. Br. = Ptychosperma elegans

Secale L. -n- *Poaceae* · 8 spp. · E:Rye;
F:Seigle; G:Roggen
– **cereale** L. · E:Rye; G:Roggen · ⊙ ⊙ V-VI
Ⓝ; cult.
– **montanum** Guss. · E:Wild Rye · ⅃ ; Eur.:
Ib, Ital-P, Ba, RO +; TR, Cauc., Syr.,
N-Iraq, Iran, W-Pakist., N-Afr.

Sechium P. Browne -n- *Cucurbitaceae* ·
8 spp. · E:Chaco, Chayote; F:Chayotte;
G:Chayote, Stachelgurke
– **edule** (Jacq.) Sw. · E:Chayote, Christo-
phine; G:Chayote, Stachelgurke · ⅃ ⚬ ⚭
Z10 ⌂ Ⓝ; C-Am., cult.

Securigera DC. -f- *Fabaceae* · 12 spp. ·
E:Crown Vetch; F:Sécurigéra; G:Beilwi-
cke, Kronwicke
– **securidaca** (L.) Degen & Dörfl. ·
G:Beilwicke · ⊙; Eur.: Ital-P, Fr, Ba,
Crim; Cauc., Syr., Iran
– **varia** (L.) Lassen · E:Trailing Crown
Vetch; G:Bunte Kronwicke · ⅃ VI-VIII ⚥
✶; Eur.* exc. BrI, Sc; TR, Cauc., Iran,

W-Sib., C-As., nat. in BrI, Sc

Securinega Comm. ex Juss. -f-
Euphorbiaceae · 20 spp. · G:Beilholz
– **suffruticosa** (Pall.) Rehder · G:Beilholz ·
ħ d Z6 VII-VIII Ⓝ; Mong., N-China

× **Sedadia** Moran -f- *Crassulaceae* (*Sedum*
× *Villadia*)
– **amecamecanum** (Praeger) Moran
(*Sedum dendroideum* × *Villadia batesii*) ·
ħ Ψ e ⓐ V; Mex.

Sedirea Garay & H.R. Sweet -f-
Orchidaceae · 2 spp.
– **japonica** (Linden & Rchb. f.) Garay &
H.R. Sweet · ⚄ Z10 ⓜ VI-VII ▽ ✳; Korea,
Jap., Ryukyu-Is.

Sedum L. -n- *Crassulaceae* · 473 spp. ·
E:Stonecrop; F:Orpin, Poivre de muraille;
G:Fetthenne, Mauerpfeffer
– **acre** L. · E:Stonecrop, Wall Pepper;
F:Orpin âcre, Poivre des murailles;
G:Scharfer Mauerpfeffer · ⚄ Ψ ⤳ △
Z5 VI-VII ⚟ ✿; Eur.*, TR, Cauc., Sib.,
N-Afr., nat. in N-Am.
– *adenotrichum* Wall. ex Edgew. =
Rosularia adenotrichum
– **adolphi** Raym.-Hamet · E:Golden
Sedum · ⚄ Ψ e Z8 △ III-IV; Mex.
– **aizoon** L. · G:Deckblatt-Fetthenne · ⚄ Ψ
Z7 VII-VIII; W-Sib., E-Sib., Amur, Sakhal.,
Kamchat., Mong., Jap.
– **alamosanum** S. Watson · ⚄ Ψ Z8 ⓐ
II-IV; NW-Mex.
– *alboroseum* Baker = Sedum erythrostic-
tum
– **album** L. · G:Weiße Fetthenne
– var. **album** · E:White Stonecrop;
G:Gewöhnliche Weiße Fetthenne · ⚄
Ψ ⤳ △ Z6 VI-IX; Eur.*, Cauc., TR,
Lebanon, Iran, NW-Afr., Libya
– var. **micranthum** (Bastard) DC. ·
G:Kleinblütige Weiße Fetthenne · ⚄ Ψ ⤳
△ Z6 VI-IX; Eur.: sp., F, I, Sw; Moroc.
– **allantoides** Rose · ħ Ψ e Z8 ⓐ VI-VII;
Mex.
– **alpestre** Vill. · G:Alpen-Fetthenne · ħ Ψ
⤳ △ Z6 VI-VIII; Eur.* exc. BrI, Sc; TR
– *amecamecanum* Praeger = × Sedadia
amecamecanum
– **amplexicaule** DC. · ⚄ Ψ △ Z7; Eur.: Ib,
Fr, Ital-P, Ba; TR, Lebanon, NW-Afr.
– **anacampseros** L. · F:Orpin courbé;

G:Rundblättrige Fetthenne · ⚄ Ψ ⤳
△ Z6 VII-VIII; Eur.: sp., F, I, Sw; Pyr.,
SW-Alp., Apenn., nat. in Norw.
– **anglicum** Huds. · E:English Stonecrop;
G:Englische Fetthenne · ⚄ Ψ ⤳ △ Z6
VI-VII; Eur.: Ib, F, BrI, Sc
– **annuum** L. · E:Annual Stonecrop;
G:Einjährige Fetthenne · ⊙ Ψ Z6 VI-VIII;
Eur.*, TR, Cauc., Iran, Greenl.
– *athoum* DC. = Sedum album var. album
– **atratum** L. · E:Dark Stonecrop;
G:Gewöhnliche SchwärzlicheFetthenne ·
⊙ Ψ Z7 VI-VIII; Eur.* exc. BrI, Sc
– **bellum** Rose ex Praeger · ħ Ψ Z8 ⓐ III-V;
Mex.
– *bithynicum* Boiss. = Sedum pallidum
– **caeruleum** L. · ⊙ Ψ Z8 VII-IX; Cors,
Sard., Sic., Alger.
– **cauticola** Praeger · F:Orpin · ⚄ Ψ ⤳
VI-VII; Jap.
– **cepaea** L. · E:Pink Stonecrop; G:Rispen-
Fetthenne · ⊙ Ψ Z7 VI-VII; Eur.: Ital-P, Fr,
Ba, E-Eur.; TR; Syr., Alger., Tun., Libya,
nat. in NL, D
– **compactum** Rose · ⚄ Ψ ⤳ Z9 ⓐ VI-VII;
Mex.
– **compressum** Rose · ⚄ Ψ Z9 ⓐ I-V; Mex.
– *corsicum* Duby ex DC. = Sedum dasyphyllum var. glanduliferum
– **craigii** R.T. Clausen · ħ Ψ e Z8 ⓐ; Mex.
– *crassipes* Wall. ex Hook. f. & Thomson =
Rhodiola wallichiana
– **cupressoides** Hemsl. · ⚄ Ψ Z9 ⓐ VII-
VIII; Mex.
– **cyaneum** Rudolph · ⚄ △ VII-VIII; E-Sib.,
Amur, Sakhal., Kamchat.
– **dasyphyllum** L.
– var. **dasyphyllum** · E:Thick Leaved
Stonecrop; F:Orpin à feuilles glandu-
leuses; G:Dickblättrige Fetthenne · ⚄ Ψ
⤳ △ Z7 VI-VIII; Eur.: Fr, Ib, Ital-P, Ba,
C-Eur., RO; TR, NW-Afr., nat. in BrI, DK
– var. **glanduliferum** (Guss.) Moris · ⚄ ⤳
△ Z8 ⓐ ∧ VI-VIII; Eur.: sp.
– var. *suendermannii* Praeger = Sedum
dasyphyllum var. glanduliferum
– **dendroideum** Moç. & Sessé ex DC. ·
E:Woody Stonecrop; G:Strauchige Fetthenne · ħ Ψ ⤳ Z8 ⓐ V-VI; Mex., Guat.
– subsp. **praealtum** (A. DC.) R.T. Clausen ·
ħ Ψ e Z7; Mex.
– **diffusum** S. Watson · ⚄ ⤳ Z9 ⓐ; Mex.
(San Luis Potosí)
– **divergens** S. Watson · E:Pacific
Stonecrop, Spreading Stonecrop;

G:Kriechende Fetthenne · ♃ ♆ ⇝ Z6; B.C., USA: NW
- **ebracteatum** Moç. & Sessé ex DC. · ♃ ♆ Z8 Ⓚ X; Mex.
- **erythrostictum** Miq. · ♃ ♆ VI; cult. E-As.
- **ewersii** Ledeb. · F:Orpin de l'Himalaya · ♃ ♆ △ VII-VIII; W-Sib., C-As., Afgh., Mong., Him., China: Sinkiang
- **floriferum** Praeger · ♃ ♆ ⇝ △ Z7 VII; NE-China
- **forsterianum** Sm.
- subsp. **elegans** (Lej.) E.F. Warb. · ♃ △ Z7 VI-VIII; W-Eur.; Moroc.
- subsp. **forsterianum** · F:Orpin de Forster; G:Zierliche Fetthenne · ♃ ♆ Z7 VI-VIII; Eur.: Ib, Fr, BrI, D; Moroc.
- *glaucum* Waldst. & Kit. = Sedum hispanicum
- **gracile** C.A. Mey. · F:Orpin blanc; G:Schneepolster-Fetthenne · ♃ ♆ △ Z7 VI-VII; Cauc., N-Iran
- **greggii** Hemsl. · ♃ ♆ Z8 Ⓚ II-V; Mex.
- **griseum** Praeger · ♄ ♆ e Z8 Ⓚ I-II; Mex.
- **hemsleyanum** Rose · ♃ ♆ Z8 Ⓚ; Mex.
- *henryi* Diels = Rhodiola yunnanensis
- *heterodontum* Hook. f. & Thomson = Rhodiola heterodonta
- **hirsutum** All. · E:Hairy Stonecrop; G:Filzige Fetthenne · ♃; Eur.: Ib, F, I, Moroc.
- **hispanicum** L. · G:Spanische Fetthenne · ⊙ ⊙ ♆ △ Z8 VI-VII; Eur.: Ital-P, C-Eur., E-Eur., H, Ba; TR, Lebanon, Palest., Cauc., N-Iran, nat. in Swed
- var. **minus** Praeger · ♃ ♆ ⇝ △ Z8
- *hobsonii* Prain ex Raym.-Hamet = Rhodiola hobsonii
- **hultenii** Fröd. · ♄ ♆ Z9 Ⓚ; Mex.
- **humifusum** Rose · ♃ ♆ ⇝ Z9 Ⓚ IV-VI; Mex.
- **hybridum** L. · G:Sibirische Fetthenne · ♃ ♆ ⇝ Z7 V-VIII; Russ. (Ural), W-Sib., E-Sib., C-As., Mong
- **kamtschaticum** Fisch. & C.A. Mey.
- var. **ellacombianum** (Praeger) R.T. Clausen · ♃ ♆ Z7 VII-VIII; Jap.
- var. **kamtschaticum** · F:Orpin du Kamtchatka · ♃ ♆ Z7 VII-VIII; Kuril Is.
- var. **middendorffianum** (Maxim.) R.T. Clausen · ♃ ♆ Z7 VII-VIII; E-Sib., Manch.
- *kirilowii* Regel = Rhodiola kirilowii
- *krajinae* Domin = Sedum acre
- *laxiflorum* DC. = Monanthes laxiflora
- *libanoticum* L. = Rosularia sempervivum subsp. sempervivum
- **liebmannianum** Hemsl. · ♃ ♆ Z8 Ⓚ VI-VIII; Mex.
- **lineare** Thunb. · ♃ ♆ ⇝ △ Z7 Ⓐ ∧ V-VI; Jap., Ryukyu-Is.
- **lydium** Boiss. · ♃ ♆ ⇝ △ Z7 VI-VII; W-TR
- *maximowiczii* Regel = Sedum aizoon
- *maximum* (L.) Hoffm. = Sedum telephium subsp. maximum
- **mexicanum** Britton · ♃ ♆ Z8 Ⓚ IV-VI; Mex., nat. in NW-Sp.
- *micranthum* Bastard = Sedum album var. micranthum
- *middendorffianum* Maxim. = Sedum kamtschaticum var. middendorffianum
- *mite* Gilib. = Sedum sexangulare
- **monregalense** Balb. · ♃ ♆ △ Z8 ∧ VII-VIII; Eur.: Cors, Sard., I; mts.
- **montanum** Perr. & Songeon
- subsp. **montanum** · G:Berg-Mauerpfeffer · ♆ VII-IX; Eur.: Ba, Ib, Ital-P, H, A, Sw; Pyr., Apenn., Alp.
- subsp. **orientale** 't Hart · G:Harts Felsen-Mauerpfeffer, Östlicher Felsen-Mauerpfeffer · ♄ ♆ VI-VIII; Eur.: A, ? D +
- **moranense** Kunth · E:Red Stonecrop · ♃ ♆ e Z9 Ⓚ VII; Mex.
- **morganianum** E. Walther · E:Beaver Tail, Donkey's Tail; G:Schlangen-Fetthenne · ♃ ♆ ⌇ ⇝ Z9 Ⓚ; cult. Mex.
- **multiceps** Coss. & Durieu · ♃ ♆ Z8 Ⓚ VII; Alger.
- **nevii** A. Gray · F:Orpin de l'Alabama · ♃ ♆ ⇝ △ Z7 VI; USA: Va, W-Va., SE
- *nicaeense* All. = Sedum sediforme
- **nussbaumerianum** Bitter · ♄ ♆ e Z9 Ⓚ; Mex.
- *nutans* Rose = Cremnophila nutans
- **oaxacanum** Rose · ♃ ♆ ⇝ Z9 Ⓚ; Mex.
- **obcordatum** R.T. Clausen · ♄ ♆ Z9 Ⓚ; Mex.
- **ochroleucum** Chaix · G:Blassgelbe Fetthenne · ♆ △ Z7 VI-VII; Eur.: F, I, Sw, H, Ba, RO, nat. in N-Am., nat. in Maine
- **oreganum** Nutt. · E:Oregon Sedum, Oregon Stonecrop; G:Oregon-Fetthenne · ♆ ⌓ △ Z6 VII-VIII; Alaska, Can.: W; USA: NW, Calif.
- **oxypetalum** Kunth · ♃ ♆ e Z8 Ⓚ VI-VII; Mex.
- *pachyclados* Aitch. & Hemsl. = Rhodiola pachyclados
- **pachyphyllum** Rose · G:Schnapsnase · ♄ ♆ e Z8 Ⓚ IV; Mex.
- **pallidum** M. Bieb. · ♃ ∧; Eur.: Ba, Crim;

TR, Levant +
- var. **bithynicum** (Boiss.) D.F. Chamb. · ⚂
  Z8; TR
- **palmeri** S. Watson · ⚂ ⚘ e 🄫 I-VI; Mex.
- **pilosum** M. Bieb. · ⊙ ⚘ △ Z7 ∧ V-VI; TR,
  Cauc., Iran
- **pluricaule** Kudô · ⚘ △ Z7 VII-VIII; Amur,
  Sakhal., Jap.
- **populifolium** Pall. · F:Orpin à feuilles de
  peuplier · ⚂ ♄ ⚘ e △ Z2 VI-VII; Sib.
- *praealtum* A. DC. = Sedum dendroideum
  subsp. praealtum
- *praegerianum* W.W. Sm. = Rhodiola
  hobsonii
- **pruinatum** Link ex Brot. · ⚂ ⚘ ⤳ △ Z8
  ∧ VII; Eur.: P
- **pulchellum** Michx. · E:Widow's Cross · ⊙
  ⚂ ⚘ △ Z7 VII-VIII; USA: NE, NCE, NC, SE,
  SC
- *purpureum* (L.) Link = Sedum telephium
  subsp. telephium
- *reflexum* L. = Sedum rupestre
- **retusum** Hemsl. · ♄ ⚘ Z8 🄫 VI-IX; Mex.
- *rhodiola* DC. = Rhodiola rosea
- **rhodocarpum** Rose · ⚂ ⚘ Z7; Mex.
- *roseum* (L.) Scop. = Rhodiola rosea
- **rubens** L. · G:Rötliche Fetthenne · ⊙ ⚘
  Z8 V-VI; Eur.: Ib, Fr, Ital-P, C-Eur., Ba,
  RO, Crim, Canar.; TR, Levant, N-Iran,
  NW-Afr., Libya
- **rubrotinctum** R.T. Clausen · E:Christmas
  Cheer, Pork-and-Beans; G:Ampel-
  Fetthenne · ♄ ⚘ e Z9 🄫; Mex.
- **rupestre** L. · E:Rock Stonecrop; F:Orpin
  à inflorescence réfléchie; G:Felsen-
  Fetthenne, Tripmadam · ⚂ ⚘ ⌒ △ Z7
  VI-VIII Ⓝ; Eur.* exc. BrI, nat. in BrI
- subsp. *reflexum* (L.) Hegi & Em. Schmid =
  Sedum rupestre
- **sarmentosum** Bunge · G:Ausläufer-
  Fetthenne · ⚂ ⚘ △ Z7 ∧ VII; Jap., Korea,
  Manch., N-China
- *sartorianum* Boiss. = Sedum urvillei
- subsp. *stribrnyi* (Velen.) D.A. Webb =
  Sedum urvillei
- **sediforme** (Jacq.) Pau · ⚘ △ Z8 🄫
  V-VII; Eur.: Ib, Fr, Ital-P, Ba; TR, Cyprus,
  Lebanon
- **sedoides** (Decne.) Pau ex Vidal y Lopez ·
  G:Himalaya-Mauerpfeffer · ⚂ ⚘ Z7 ∧
  III-IV; Kashmir
- **selskianum** Regel & Maack · ⚂ ⚘ Z6 ▭
  VII-VIII; Amur., Manch.
- *semenowii* (Regel & Herder) Mast. =
  Rhodiola semenovii

- **sempervivoides** Fisch. ex M. Bieb. · ⊙ ⚘
  △ Z7 ∧ VI-VIII; TR, Cauc., Iran
- *sempervivum* Ledeb. = Sedum sempervivoides
- **sexangulare** L. · F:Orpin de Boulogne;
  G:Milder Mauerpfeffer · ⚂ ⚘ ⤳ Z7
  VI-VII; Eur.* exc. Ib, BrI
- **sieboldii** Sweet ex Hook. · ⚂ ⚘ △ 🄫 🄫
  ∧ IX-X; Jap.
- **spathulifolium** Hook. · E:Broad Leaved
  Stonecrop; F:Orpin spatulé; G:Colorado-
  Fetthenne · ⚂ ⚘ ⤳ Z7 VI; B.C., USA:
  NW, Calif.
- **spectabile** Boreau · E:Ice Plant; F:Orpin
  remarquable; G:Schöne Fetthenne · ⚂ ⚘
  VIII-IX; Korea, Manch.
- **some cultivars**
- **spurium** M. Bieb. · E:Two Row
  Stonecrop; F:Orpin bâtard; G:Kaukasus-
  Fetthenne · ⚂ ⚘ ⤳ △ Z7 VII-VIII; Cauc.,
  TR, N-Iran, nat. in Eur.* exc. Ba
- **some cultivars**
- **stahlii** Solms · ⚂ ⚘ ⤳ Z9 🄫 VIII-IX;
  Mex.
- **stellatum** L. · ⊙ ⚘ Z8; Eur.: Ib, Ital-P, Fr,
  Ba; Alger.
- **stenopetalum** Pursh · E:Wormleaf
  Stonecrop · ⚘ △ Z7 ∧ VI-VII; USA: NW,
  N-Calif.
- **stevenianum** Rouy & E.G. Camus · ⚂ ⚘
  ⤳ △ Z7 VII-VIII; Cauc.
- **stoloniferum** S.G. Gmel. · ⚂ ⚘ ⤳ △ Z7
  VI-VII; TR, Cauc. N-Iran
- *stribrnyi* Velen. = Sedum urvillei
- **surculosum** Coss. · ⚂ ⚘ Z8 🄫 V-VI; Atlas
- **tatarinowii** Maxim. · ⚂ ⚘ △ VII-IX;
  Mong., N-China
- **telephium** L. · G:Purpur-Fetthenne
- subsp. **fabaria** (W.D.J. Koch) Kirschl. ·
  G:Berg-Fetthenne · ⚂ ⚘ VII-VIII; W-Eur.,
  C-Eur.
- subsp. **maximum** (L.) Ohba · G:Große
  Fetthenne · ⚂ ⚘ VII-VIII; Eur., TR, Cauc.,
  Sib.
- subsp. **telephium** · E:Orpine; G:Purpur-
  Fetthenne · ⚂ ⚘ VII-IX ⚥; Eur.*, TR, nat.
  in N-Am.
- **ternatum** Michx. · E:Woodland
  Stonecrop · ⚂ ⚘ △ Z6 VI; USA: NE, NCE,
  SE
- × *thartii* L.P. Hébert = Sedum montanum
  subsp. orientale
- **treleasei** Rose · ♄ ⚘ e Z8 🄫 IV; Mex.
- *ukrainae* hort. = Sedum acre
- **urvillei** DC. · G:Ungarischer

Mauerpfeffer · ⍗ ♃ △ Z7 ∧ V-VII; Eur.: A, EC-Eur., Ba, RO, Crim; TR, Levant
- **villosum** L. · E:Hairy Stonecrop; G:Behaarte Fetthenne, Sumpf-Fetthenne · ⊙ ♃ ⁓ Z5 VI-VII; Eur.*, Greenl.
- *vulgare* (Haw.) Link = Sedum telephium subsp. fabaria
- *weinbergii* (Rose) A. Berger = Graptopetalum paraguayense
- *yunnanense* Franch. = Rhodiola yunnanensis
- **Cultivars:**
- **some cultivars**

Seemannia Regel = Gloxinia
- *latifolia* Fritsch = Gloxinia sylvatica
- *sylvatica* (Kunth) Hanst. = Gloxinia sylvatica

Selaginella P. Beauv. -f- *Selaginellaceae* · 691 sp. · E:Lesser Clubmoss; F:Sélaginelle; G:Moosfarn, Mooskraut
- *africana* A. Braun = Selaginella vogelii
- *albonitens* Spring = Selaginella tenella
- *amoena* W. Bull = Selaginella pulcherrima
- **apoda** (L.) Spring · E:Meadow Spike Moss; G:Wiesen-Moosfarn · ⍗ ⁓ Z3; Can.: E; USA: NE, NCE, SC, SE, Fla., nat. in D (Berlin)
- *apus* (L.) Spring = Selaginella apoda
- *azorica* Baker = Selaginella kraussiana
- **biformis** A. Braun ex Kuhn · ⍗ ⁓ Z9 🐱; Ind., E-As., Malay. Arch., Phil.
- **braunii** Baker · ⍗ Z8 🐱; W-China
- *caesia* (hort.) hort. ex Kunze = Selaginella uncinata
- var. *arborea* (hort. ex Courtin) hort. = Selaginella willdenowii
- *canaliculata* hort. = Selaginella delicatula
- *caulescens* (Wall. ex Hook. & Grev.) Spring = Selaginella involvens
- **concinna** (Sw.) Spring · ⍗ Z9 🐱; Mascarene Is.
- *cuspidata* (Link) Link = Selaginella pallescens
- **delicatissima** Linden ex A. Braun · ⍗ 🐱; Col.
- **delicatula** (Desv. ex Poir.) Alston · ⍗ Z9 🐱; E-Him, S-China
- **denticulata** (L.) Spring · E:Spike Moss; G:Gezähnter Moosfarn · ⍗ ⁓ △ Z9 🐱; Eur.: Ib, Fr, Ital-P, Ba; TR, Cyprus, Syr., NW-Afr., Libya
- *denticulata* hort. = Selaginella kraussiana

- **douglasii** (Hook. & Grev.) Spring · E:Douglas Selaginella; G:Rocky-Mountain-Moosfarn · ⍗ ⁓ △ Z6; B.C., USA: NW, Rocky Mts., Calif.
- *emmeliana* Van Geert = Selaginella pallescens
- **erythropus** (Mart.) Spring · ⍗ Z10 🐱; W.Ind., S-Am.
- var. *major* Spring = Selaginella umbrosa
- **flabellata** (L.) Spring · ⍗ Z10 🐱; W.Ind.
- **galeottii** Spring · ⍗ Z10 🐱; Mex.
- **grandis** T. Moore · ⍗ Z10 🐱; Kalimantan
- **griffithii** Spring ex Veitch · ⍗ Z10 🐱; trop. As.
- **haematodes** (Kunze) Spring · ⍗ Z10 🐱; Panama, Col., Ecuad., Venez., Bol.
- **helvetica** (L.) Spring · E:Swiss Club Moss; F:Sélaginelle de Suisse; G:Schweizer Moosfarn · ⍗ ⁓ △ Z5 VI-VII; Eur.: Fr, Ital-P, C-Eur., EC-Eur., Ba, E-Eur.; TR, Cauc., Amur, Korea, N-China
- **inaequalifolia** (Hook. & Grev.) Spring · ⍗ 🐱; Ind., Java +
- var. *perelegans* (T. Moore) Baker = Selaginella plana
- **involvens** (Sw.) Spring · ⍗ Z9 🐱; Ind., Sri Lanka, China, Jap., Malay. Pen., Java
- *japonica* T. Moore ex W.R. McNab = Selaginella involvens
- **kraussiana** (Kunze) A. Braun · E:Krauss' Spike Moss, Mossy Club Moss; G:Feingliedriger Moosfarn · ⍗ Z9 🐱 🐱; trop. Afr., S-Afr., nat. in S-Eur., W-Eur., Azor.
- **lepidophylla** (Hook. & Grev.) Spring · E:Resurrection Plant, Rose-of-Jericho; G:Auferstehender Moosfarn · ⍗ Z9 🐱; USA: Tex., SW; Mex., C-Am.
- **martensii** Spring · ⍗ Z9 🐱 🐱; Mex.
- **pallescens** (C. Presl) Spring · E:Arborvitae Fern; G:Bleicher Moosfarn · ⍗ Z10 🐱; Mex., C-Am., Col., Venez.
- **pilifera** A. Braun · E:Resurrection Plant · ⍗ Z9 🐱; Tex., Mex.
- **plana** (Desv.) Hieron. · ⍗ Z9 🐱; E-Him.
- *plumosa* (L.) C. Presl = Selaginella biformis
- **pulcherrima** Liebm. & E. Fourn. · ⍗ Z9 🐱; Mex.
- **rotundifolia** Spring · ⍗ Z10 🐱 🐱; W.Ind.
- *rubella* T. Moore = Selaginella concinna
- **rupestris** (L.) Spring · E:Ledge Spike Moss; G:Felsen-Moosfarn · ⍗ ⁓ △ Z5; Can.: E; USA: NE, NCE, SE

- **selaginoides** (L.) P. Beauv. · E:Lesser Club Moss, Northern Spike Moss; G:Dorniger Moosfarn · ♃ ⁓→ △ VII-VIII; Eur.*, Cauc., W-Sib., E-Sib., Kamchat., Jap., Greenl., Alaska, Can., USA: NE, NCE, Rocky Mts.
- **serpens** (Desv. ex Poir.) Spring · ♃ ⁓→ Z10 ⓦ; W.Ind.
- **sibirica** (Milde) Hieron. · ♃ ⁓→ △ Z4; E-Sib., Alaska, Sakhal., N-Korea, Jap.
- *spinulosa* A. Braun ex Döll = Selaginella selaginoides
- **stenophylla** A. Braun · ♃ Z9 ⓚ; Mex.
- **tenella** (P. Beauv.) Spring · ♃ ⁓→ Z10 ⓦ; W.Ind.
- **umbrosa** Lem. ex Hieron. · ♃ Z10 ⓦ; Mex.: Yucatan; C-Am., Col., Braz.
- **uncinata** (Desv. ex Poir.) Spring · ♃ ⁓→ Z10 ⓦ; S-China
- **underwoodii** Hieron. · ♃ △ Z4; USA: Rocky Mts., SW, SC; Mex.
- **victoriae** T. Moore · ♃ Z10 ⓦ; Kalimantan, Fiji
- **viticulosa** Klotzsch · ♃ Z10 ⓦ; Costa Rica, Panama, Col., Venez.
- **vogelii** Spring · ♃ Z10 ⓦ; W-Afr.
- **wallichii** (Hook. & Grev.) Spring · E:Vigorous Fern; G:Wüchsiger Moosfarn · ♃ Z10 ⓦ; Ind.
- **willdenowii** (Desv. ex Poir.) Baker · E:Peacock Fern; G:Pfauen-Moosfarn · ♃ ⸾ Z10 ⓦ; Him., S-China, Malay. Arch.

Selenicereus (A. Berger) Britton & Rose -m- *Cactaceae* · c. 20 spp. · E:Moonlight Cactus; F:Cierge de la Lune; G:Königin der Nacht, Schlangenkaktus
- **boeckmannii** (Otto) Britton & Rose · ♄ Ψ ⸾ Z9 ⓚ ▽ *; E-Mex., Cuba, Haiti
- **brevispinus** Britton & Rose · ♄ Ψ ⸾ Z9 ⓚ ▽ *; Cuba
- *chrysocardium* (Alexander) Kimnach = Epiphyllum chrysocardium
- **coniflorus** (Weing.) Britton & Rose · ♄ Ψ ⸾ Z9 ⓚ ▽ *; Mex. (Vera Cruz)
- **grandiflorus** (L.) Britton & Rose · E:Night Blooming Cereus, Queen-of-the-Night; G:Königin der Nacht · ♄ Ψ ⸾ Z9 ⓚ ⸾ ☠ ▽ *; E-Mex., ? Hond., Cuba, Hispaniola, Jamaica
- **hamatus** (Scheidw.) Britton & Rose · ♄ Ψ ⸾ Z9 ⓚ VII ▽ *; Mex.
- **hondurensis** (K. Schum.) Britton & Rose · ♄ Ψ ⸾ Z9 ⓚ ▽ *; Guat., Hond.
- **inermis** (Otto) Britton & Rose · ♄ Ψ ⸾ Z9 ⓚ ▽ *; Col., Venez.
- *kunthianus* (Otto ex Salm-Dyck) Britton & Rose = Selenicereus grandiflorus
- **macdonaldiae** (Hook.) Britton & Rose
- var. **grusonianus** (Weing.) Backeb. · ♄ Ψ ⸾ D Z9 ⓚ VII ▽ *; orig. ?
- var. **macdonaldiae** · ♄ Ψ ⸾ Z9 ⓚ ▽ *; ? Hond.
- **nelsonii** (Weing.) Britton & Rose · ♄ Ψ ⸾ Z9 ⓚ ▽ *; S-Mex.
- *pringlei* Rose = Selenicereus coniflorus
- **pteranthus** (Link & Otto) Britton & Rose · E:Princess of the Night · ♄ Ψ ⸾ Z9 ⓚ VII-VIII ▽ *; E-Mex.
- **spinulosus** (DC.) Britton & Rose · ♄ Ψ ⸾ Z9 ⓚ ▽ *; SE-Tex., E-Mex.
- *testudo* (Karw.) Buxb. = Deamia testudo
- **urbanianus** (Gürke & Weing.) Britton & Rose · ♄ Ψ ⸾ Z9 ⓚ ▽ *; Cuba, Haiti
- **vagans** (K. Brandegee) Britton & Rose · ♄ Ψ ⸾ Z9 ⓚ ▽ *; W-Mex.
- **vaupelii** (Weing.) A. Berger · ♄ Ψ ⸾ Z9 ⓚ ▽ *; Haiti

Selinum L. -n- *Apiaceae* · 6-8 spp. · E:Milk Parsley; F:Sélin; G:Silge
- **carvifolium** (L.) L. · G:Kümmel-Silge · ♃ VII-VIII; Eur.*, W-Sib., nat. in N-Am.
- *virosum* (L.) E.H.L. Krause = Cicuta virosa

Selliera Cav. -f- *Goodeniaceae* · 1 sp.
- **radicans** Cav. · ♃ ⁓→ ∼ ⓚ VII-IX; Chile, Austr., Tasman., NZ

Semecarpus L. f. -f- *Anacardiaceae* · c. 60 spp. · G:Tintenbaum
- **anacardium** L. f. · E:Marking Nut; G:Ostinidischer Tintenbaum · ♄ e Z10 ⓦ ☠ Ⓝ; Ind., mts.

Semele Kunth -f- *Ruscaceae* · 1 sp. · E:Climbing Butcher's Broom; F:Epine des rats grimpante; G:Klettermäusedorn
- **androgyna** (L.) Kunth · E:Climbing Butcher's Broom; G:Klettermäusedorn · ♄ e ⸾ Z9 ⓚ; Canar.

Semiaquilegia Makino -f- *Ranunculaceae* · 7 spp. · F:Fausse-ancolie; G:Scheinakelei
- **ecalcarata** (Maxim.) Sprague & Hutch. · G:Spornlose Scheinakelei · ♃ △ Z6 VI-VII; W-China

Semiarundinaria Makino ex Nakai -f- *Poaceae* · 7 spp. · E:Narihira Bamboo;

F:Bambou; G:Narihirabambus
- **fastuosa** (Lat.-Marl. ex Mitford) Makino ex Nakai · E:Narihira Bamboo; F:Bambou Semiarundinaria; G:Narihirabambus · ♄ e Z7 ∧; Jap.
- var. *yashadake* Makino = Semiarundinaria yashadake
- **yashadake** (Makino) Makino · ♄ e Z8; Jap.

Sempervivella Stapf = Sedum
- *alba* (Edgew.) Stapf = Sedum sedoides
- *sedoides* (Decne.) Stapf = Sedum sedoides

Sempervivum L. -n- *Crassulaceae* · 59 spp. · E:House Leek; F:Joubarbe; G:Dachwurz, Hauswurz
- *aizoon* (Bolle) H. Christ = Greenovia aizoon
- *album* Edgew. = Sedum sedoides
- *allionii* (Jord. & Fourr.) Nyman = Jovibarba globifera subsp. allionii
- **altum** Turrill · ⽤ Ψ △ Z6 VI ▽; Cauc.
- *annuum* C. Sm. ex Link = Aichryson laxum
- *anomalum* hort. = Sempervivum montanum subsp. montanum
- **arachnoideum** L. · G:Spinnweben-Hauswurz
- subsp. **arachnoideum** · E:Cobweb House Leek; F:Joubarbe aranéeuse; G:Gewöhnliche Spinnweben-Hauswurz · Ψ Z5 VII-IX ▽; Eur.: sp., F, Cors, I, C-Eur.; mts.
- subsp. *doellianum* (C.B. Lehm.) Schinz & Keller = Sempervivum arachnoideum subsp. arachnoideum
- subsp. **tomentosum** (C.B. Lehm. & Schnittsp.) Schinz & Thell. · F:Joubarbe aranéeuse ssp. tomentosum; G:Filzige Spinnweben-Hauswurz · ⽤ Ψ △ Z5 VII-VIII ▽; Eur.: G, F, I, Sw; mts.
- *arboreum* L. = Aeonium arboreum
- *arenarium* W.D.J. Koch = Jovibarba globifera subsp. arenaria
- **armenum** Boiss. & A. Huet · ⽤ Ψ △ Z7 VII ▽; N-TR
- **atlanticum** (Ball) Ball · ⽤ Ψ Z7 ⓐ VI ▽; Moroc.; Atlas
- *aureum* C. Sm. ex Hornem. = Greenovia aurea
- *balcanicum* Stoj. = Sempervivum marmoreum subsp. marmoreum
- *ballsii* Wale = Sempervivum marmoreum subsp. ballsii
- *balsamiferum* (Webb & Berthel.) Webb ex

H. Christ = Aeonium balsamiferum
- × **barbulatum** Schott (*S. arachnoideum × S. montanum*) · G:Bärtige Hauswurz · ⽤ Ψ ▽; Alp., N-Sp.
- *borisii* Degen & Urum. = Sempervivum ciliosum
- *caespitosum* C. Sm. ex Otto = Aeonium simsii
- **calcareum** Jord. · E:Limestone House Leek; F:Joubarbe du calcaire · ⽤ Ψ △ Z5 VI-VIII ▽; Eur.: F, I; SW-Alp.
- *canariense* L. = Aeonium canariense
- **cantabricum** J.A. Huber · ⽤ Ψ Z7 ⓐ ▽; N-Sp.
- **caucasicum** Rupr. ex Boiss. · ⽤ Ψ Z6 ▽; Cauc.
- *ciliatum* Willd. = Aeonium ciliatum
- **ciliosum** Craib · F:Joubarbe ciliée · ⽤ Ψ △ Z6 VI-VII ▽; Eur.: Maced., BG, GR
- **'Borisii'**
- subsp. **octopodes** (Turrill) Zonn. · ⽤ Ψ Z6 ▽; SW-Maced.
- *cuneatum* (Webb & Berthel.) Webb ex H. Christ = Aeonium cuneatum
- *decorum* H. Christ = Aeonium decorum
- *degenianum* Domokos = Sempervivum marmoreum subsp. reginae-amaliae
- *dichotomum* DC. = Aichryson laxum
- *dodrantale* Willd. = Greenovia dodrantalis
- *doellianum* C.B. Lehm. = Sempervivum arachnoideum subsp. arachnoideum
- **dolomiticum** Facchini · E:Dolomitic House Leek · ⽤ Ψ △ Z5 VI-VII ▽; Eur.: I; SE-Alp.
- × *domesticum* (Praeger) A. Berger = Aichryson × aizoides
- *erythraeum* Velen. = Sempervivum marmoreum subsp. erythraeum
- × **fauconnettii** Reut. (*S. arachnoideum × S. tectorum*) · Ψ ▽; Eur.
- × **fimbriatum** Schnittsp. & C.B. Lehm. (*S. arachnoideum × S. wulfenii*)
- × **funckii** A. Braun ex W.D.J. Koch (*S. arachnoideum × S. montanum × S. tectorum*) · G:Funcks Hauswurz · ⽤ Ψ; cult.
- *glutinosum* Aiton = Aeonium glutinosum
- *goochiae* (Webb & Berthel.) Webb ex H. Christ = Aeonium goochiae
- **grandiflorum** Haw. · E:Large-flowered House Leek; F:Joubarbe à grandes fleurs; G:Gaudins Hauswurz · ⽤ Ψ Z6 VI-VIII ▽; Sw, I ; W-Alp. (Susa -Simplon)
- *haworthii* hort. ex Webb & Berthel. =

Aeonium haworthii
- *heuffelii* Schott = Jovibarba heuffelii var. heuffelii
- *hierrense* Murray = Aeonium hierrense
- *hirtum* L. = Jovibarba globifera subsp. hirta
- *holochrysum* (Webb & Berthel.) Webb ex H. Christ = Aeonium holochrysum
- *juratense* Jord. & Fourr. = Sempervivum tectorum var. tectorum
- *kindingeri* Adamović = Sempervivum leucanthum
- **kosaninii** Praeger · ⁴ ♆ △ Z6 VII ▽; Eur.: Maced.
- *laggeri* Schott ex Hallier = Sempervivum arachnoideum subsp. tomentosum
- **leucanthum** Pančić · ⁴ ♆ △ Z6 VII ▽; Eur.: BG; mts.
- *lindleyi* (Webb & Berthel.) Webb ex H. Christ = Aeonium lindleyi
- *macedonicum* Praeger = Sempervivum marmoreum subsp. reginae-amaliae
- *manriqueorum* H. Christ = Aeonium arboreum
- **marmoreum** Griseb. · ⁴ ♆; Eur.: Ba
- subsp. **ballsii** (Wale) Zonn.
- subsp. **erythraeum** (Velen.) Zonn. · ⁴ ♆ △ Z6 VII-VIII ▽; BG
- subsp. **marmoreum** · ♄ ♆ △ Z5 VII ▽; Eur.: H, Slova, Ba, RO, W-Russ.
- subsp. **reginae-amaliae** (Heldr. & Sartori ex Boiss.) Zonn. · ⁴ ♆ ▽; Eur.: S-AL, GR; mts.
- **minutum** (Kunze ex Willk.) Nyman ex Pau · ♆ Z7 ▽; sp.: Sierra Nevada
- *monanthes* Aiton = Monanthes polyphylla
- var. *subcrassicaule* Kuntze = Monanthes muralis
- **montanum** L.
- subsp. **burnatii** (Wettst. ex Burnat) Hayek · ⁴ ♆ △ Z5 VI-VIII ▽; Eur.: SW-Alp.
- subsp. **montanum** · E:Mountain House Leek; F:Joubarbe des montagnes; G:Berg-Hauswurz · ⁴ ♆ △ Z5 VII-VIII ▽; Eur.: sp., F, Ital-P, C-Eur., EC-Eur., RO, W-Russ.; mts., nat. in Norw.
- subsp. **stiriacum** (Wettst. ex Hayek) Hayek · ⁴ ♆ △ Z5 VI-VIII ▽; Eur.: E-A
- *murale* Bureau = Sempervivum tectorum var. tectorum
- *nevadense* Wale = Sempervivum minutum
- *octopodes* Turrill = Sempervivum ciliosum subsp. octopodes
- *patens* Griseb. & Schenk = Jovibarba

heuffelii var. heuffelii
- *percarneum* Murray = Aeonium percarneum
- **pittonii** Schott, Nyman & Kotschy · G:Serpentin-Hauswurz · ⁴ ♆ Z6 VII-VIII ▽; A (Steiermark)
- **pumilum** M. Bieb. · ⁴ ♆ △ Z6 VII ▽; Cauc.
- *reginae-amaliae* Heldr. & Guicc. ex Halácsy = Sempervivum marmoreum subsp. reginae-amaliae
- × *roseum* Huter & Sander = Sempervivum × fimbriatum
- *'Fimbriatum'* = Sempervivum × fimbriatum
- *schlehanii* Schott = Sempervivum marmoreum subsp. marmoreum
- *sedifolium* (Webb) H. Christ = Aeonium sedifolium
- *sedoides* Decne. = Sedum sedoides
- *simsii* Sweet = Aeonium simsii
- *soboliferum* Sims = Jovibarba globifera subsp. globifera
- *spathulatum* Hornem. = Aeonium spathulatum
- *strepsicladum* (Webb & Berthel.) Webb ex H. Christ = Aeonium spathulatum
- *tabuliforme* Haw. = Aeonium tabuliforme
- **tectorum** L. · G:Dach-Hauswurz, Dachwurz
- subsp. *alpinum* (Griseb. & Schenk) Wettst. = Sempervivum tectorum var. tectorum
- subsp. *calcareum* (Jord.) Cariot ex St.-Lag. = Sempervivum calcareum
- var. *atlanticum* (Ball) Hook. = Sempervivum atlanticum
- var. **tectorum** · E:Common House Leek, Houseleek; F:Joubarbe des toits; G:Gewöhnliche Hauswurz, Gewöhnliche Dachwurz · ⁴ ♆ △ Z4 VII-IX ⚇ ▽; Eur.: Ib, F, C-Eur.; mts.
- *tortuosum* (Aiton) Praeger = Aichryson tortuosum
- **transcaucasicum** Muirhead · ⁴ ♆ △ Z6 VI ▽; TR, Cauc.
- *undulatum* (Webb & Berthel.) Webb ex H. Christ = Aeonium undulatum
- *urbicum* C. Sm. ex Hornem. = Aeonium urbicum
- *vicentei* Pau = Sempervivum cantabricum
- subsp. *cantabricum* (J.A. Huber) Fern. Casas = Sempervivum cantabricum
- **wulfenii** Hoppe ex Mert. & W.D.J. Koch · G:Wulfens Hauswurz · ⁴ ♆ △ Z5 VII-VIII

▽; Eur.: I, Sw, A, Slove.; E-Alp.
- *youngianum* (Webb & Berthel.) Webb ex
  H. Christ = Aeonium undulatum
- **zeleborii** Schott · ⚄ Ψ △ Z6 VI-VII ▽;
  BG, RO
- **Cultivars:**
- **many cultivars**

Senecio L. -m- *Asteraceae* · 1000-1250 spp. ·
E:Ragwort; F:Cinéraire, Séneçon;
G:Greiskraut, Kreuzkraut
- **abrotanifolius** L. · G:Eberrauten-
  Greiskraut
- subsp. **abrotanifolius** · G:Gewöhnliches
  Eberrauten-Greiskraut · ⚄ △ Z6 VII-IX;
  Eur.: I, C-Eur., EC-Eur., Ba, RO, W-Russ.;
  Alp., Carp., Balkan
- subsp. **carpathicus** (Herbich) Nyman · ⚄
  △ Z6 VI-VII; Eur.: Carp., Balkan
- subsp. *tiroliensis* (A. Kern. ex Dalla
  Torre) Gams = Senecio abrotanifolius
  subsp. abrotanifolius
- **acaulis** (L. f.) Sch. Bip. · ⚄ Ψ Z9 ⓚ III-IV;
  Cape
- *adenocalyx* Dinter = Senecio radicans
- **adonidifolius** Loisel. · F:Séneçon à
  feuilles d'adonis · ⚄ Ψ △ Z7 VI; Eur.: sp.,
  F
- **aloides** DC. · ♄ Z9 ⓚ; Namibia
- **alpinus** (L.) Scop. · G:Alpen-Greiskraut ·
  ⚄ ⁓ VII; Eur.: F, I, C-Eur., Slove.; Alp.,
  Apenn.
- *amaniensis* (Engl.) H. Jacobsen = Kleinia
  amaniensis
- *anteuphorbium* (L.) Sch. Bip. = Kleinia
  anteuphorbia
- **aquaticus** Hill · F:Séneçon aquatique;
  G:Wasser-Greiskraut · ⊙ VII-VIII; Eur.*
- **archeri** (Compton) H. Jacobsen · ♄ Ψ Z9
  ⓚ; Cape
- **articulatus** (L. f.) Sch. Bip. · E:Candle
  Plant, Sausage Crassula; G:Hohles
  Greiskraut · ♄ Ψ Z9 ⓚ; Cape
- *aurantiacus* (Hoppe ex Willd.) Less. =
  Tephroseris integrifolia subsp. aurantiaca
- *aureus* L. = Packera aurea
- **barbertonicus** Klatt · ♄ Ψ Z9 ⓚ;
  Zimbabwe, Mozamb., S-Afr.
- *bicolor* (Willd.) Tod. = Senecio cineraria
- **cacaliaster** Lam. · G:Pestwurz-
  Greiskraut · ⚄ VII-VIII; Eur.: F, I, A, Ba,
  Ro, ? sp.
- *capitatus* (Wahlenb.) Steud. = Tephroseris integrifolia subsp. capitata
- *chrysanthemoides* DC. = Euryops

chrysanthemoides
- **cineraria** DC. · E:Dusty Miller, Silver
  Groundsel; F:Séneçon bicolore; G:Silber-
  Greiskraut · ♄ e Z8; Ind., nat. in BrI, Crim
- var. *candidissima* hort. = Senecio viravira
- **citriformis** G.D. Rowley · ⚄ Ψ ⁓ Z9 ⓚ;
  Cape
- *cordatus* W.D.J. Koch = Senecio alpinus
- *cruentus* (Masson ex L'Hér.) DC. =
  Pericallis cruenta
- *cruentus* hort. = Pericallis × hybrida
- *cylindricus* (A. Berger) H. Jacobsen =
  Senecio talinoides subsp. cylindricus
- **doria** L. · F:Séneçon doria; G:Hohes
  Greiskraut · ⚄ Z6 VII-VIII; Eur.: Ib, Fr,
  Ital-P, Ba, A, EC-Eur., E-Eur.; TR, W-Sib.,
  Moroc., nat. in BrI
- **doronicum** (L.) L. · G:Gämswurz-Greisk-
  raut · ⚄ △ Z5 VII; Eur.: Ib, Fr, C-Eur., Ba,
  RO; mts.
- **elegans** L. · E:Red Purple Ragwort · ⊙ ⊙
  Z9 VII-X; S-Afr.
- **erraticus** Bertol. · G:Gewöhnliches
  Spreizendes Greiskraut · ⊙ ⚄ VII-X; Eur.:
  ? Ib, Fr, BrI, I, C-Eur., EC-Eur., Ba; TR,
  Syr., N-Afr.
- **erucifolius** L. · E:Hoary Ragwort;
  G:Gewöhnliches Raukenblättriges
  Greiskraut · ⚄ VII-IX; Eur.*, TR, Cauc.,
  C-As.
- **ficoides** (L.) Sch. Bip. · ♄ ♄ Ψ e ⁓ Z9
  ⓚ; Cape
- *fluviatilis* Wallr. = Senecio sarracenicus
- *fuchsii* C.C. Gmel. = Senecio ovatus
- *fulgens* (Hook. f.) G. Nicholson = Kleinia
  fulgens
- *galpinii* (Hook. f.) H. Jacobsen = Kleinia
  galpinii
- **germanicus** Wallr. · G:Deutsches
  Greiskraut, Flaumiges Hain-Greiskraut ·
  ⚄ VII-IX; Eur.: C-Eur., E-Eur., N-I
- *gracilis* hort. = Senecio citriformis
- **grandifolius** Less. · ♄ ♄ e Z9 ⓚ I-III;
  Mex.
- *greyi* Hook. f. = Brachyglottis greyi
- **halleri** Dandy · G:Hallers Greiskraut · ⚄
  △ Z6 VII-VIII; Eur.: F, Ch, I; Alp.
- **haworthii** (Sweet) Sch. Bip. · ♄ Ψ Z9 ⓚ;
  Cape
- *hectoris* Buchanan = Brachyglottis
  hectoris
- *helenitis* (L.) Schinz & Thell. = Tephroseris helenitis
- **hercynicus** Herborg · G:Gewöhnliches
  Hain-Greiskraut · ⚄; Eur.: Fr, N-I, C-Eur.,

EC-Eur., Ba
- **heritieri** DC. · ⁴ Z8 ⓐ II-III; Canar.: Teneriffa
- **herreanus** Dinter · ⁴ ⱷ ⤳ Z9 ⓐ; Namibia
- *hookerianus* (Hook. f.) H. Jacobsen = Kleinia fulgens
- × *hybridus* (Willd.) Regel = Pericallis × hybrida
- **inaequidens** DC. · G:Schmalblättriges Greiskraut · ⁴ VII-XI; S-Afr., nat. in BrI, F, I, D
- **incanus** L. · G:Graues Greiskraut
- subsp. **carniolicus** (Willd.) Braun-Blanq. · G:Krainer Greiskraut · ⁴ Z5 VII-IX ▽; Eur.: Sw, A, G, Slove.; Alp., Carp.
- subsp. **incanus** · G:Weißgraues Greiskraut · ⁴ Z5 VII-IX; Eur.: F, I, Sw, EC-Eur., Slove., W-Russ.; W-Alp., Apenn.
- *integrifolius* (L.) Clairv. = Tephroseris integrifolia subsp. integrifolia
- subsp. *aurantiacus* (Hoppe ex Willd.) Briq. & Cavill. = Tephroseris integrifolia subsp. aurantiaca
- subsp. *capitatus* (Wahlenb.) Cufod. = Tephroseris integrifolia subsp. capitata
- *jacobaea* L. · E:Jacobea, Ragwort, Staggerwort; G:Gewöhnliches Jakobs-Greiskraut · ☉ ⁴ Z5 VII-X ⚘ ⚘; Eur.*, TR, Cauc., W-Sib., E-Sib., C-As., Moroc.
- *jacobsenii* G.D. Rowley = Kleinia petraea
- **kirkii** Hook. f. ex Kirk · ⁴ Z9 ⓐ VII-VIII; N-NZ
- *kleinia* (L.) Less. = Kleinia neriifolia
- **kleiniiformis** Suess. · ♄ ⱷ Z9 ⓐ; S-Afr.
- **klinghardtianus** Dinter · ⁴ ⱷ Z9 ⓐ; Cape, Namibia
- *laxifolius* Buchanan = Brachyglottis laxifolia
- *ledebourii* Sch. Bip. = Ligularia macrophylla
- *leucostachys* Baker = Senecio viravira
- *longiflorus* (DC.) Sch. Bip. = Kleinia longiflora
- **macroglossus** DC. · E:Natal Ivy, Wax Vine; G:Kap-Greiskraut, Kapefeu · ⁴ ⱷ ⚘ Z10 ⓐ XII-II; S-Afr.
- *mandraliscae* (Tineo) H. Jacobsen · ♄ ⱷ Z9 ⓐ; ? Cape
- *maritimus* Koidz. = Senecio cineraria
- **medley-woodii** Hutch. · ♄ ⱷ Z9 ⓐ; S-Afr.: Natal
- *mikanioides* Otto ex Walp. = Delairea odorata

- *monroi* Hook. f. = Brachyglottis monroi
- **nemorensis** L. · E:Wood Ragwort · ⁴ Z6 VII-IX; Eur.* exc. BrI, Sc; TR, Cauc., Sib.
- subsp. *fuchsii* (C.C. Gmel.) Čelak. = Senecio ovatus
- **ovatus** (G. Gaertn., B. Mey. & Scherb.) Willd. · E:Woundwort; F:Séneçon de Fuchs; G:Gewöhnliches Fuchs' Greiskraut · ⁴ VII-IX; Eur.* exc. BrI; Cauc., Sib.
- *palmatifidus* (Siebold & Zucc.) Wittr. & Juel = Ligularia japonica
- **paludosus** L. · E:Great Fen Ragwort; G:Sumpf-Greiskraut · ⁴ ∼ Z6 VII-VIII; Eur.*, TR, W-Sib.
- **pendulus** (Forssk.) Sch. Bip. · ⁴ ⱷ ⤳ Z9 ⓐ; Yemen, Eth., Somalia
- **petasitis** (Sims) DC. · E:Velvet Groundsel · ⁴ Z9 ⓐ I-III; S-Mex.
- *przewalskii* Maxim. = Ligularia przewalskii
- *pteroneurus* (DC.) Sch. Bip. = Kleinia anteuphorbia
- **pulcher** Hook. & Arn. · ⁴ Z8 ⓐ VII-X; Arg., Urug.
- **radicans** (L. f.) Sch. Bip. · ⁴ ⱷ ⤳ Z9 ⓐ; Cape, Namibia
- *reinoldii* Endl. = Brachyglottis rotundifolia
- *sagittatus* (Vahl) Hieron. = Emilia sonchifolia
- **sarracenicus** L. · G:Fluss-Greiskraut · ⁴ VIII-IX; Eur.: Fr, C-Eur., EC-Eur., Ba, E-Eur.; ? TR, Sib., nat. in DK, BrI
- **scandens** Buch.-Ham. · E:Climbing Groundsel · ♄ ⚘ Z9 ⓐ; Ind., China, Jap., Taiwan, Phil.
- **scaposus** DC.
- var. **caulescens** Harv. · ♄ ⱷ Z9 ⓐ; Cape
- var. **scaposus** · ⁴ ⱷ Z8 ⓐ; S-Afr.
- *sempervivus* (Forssk.) Sch. Bip. = Kleinia semperviva
- *serpens* G.D. Rowley · ☉ ☉ ⁴ Z9 ⓐ VII-VIII; Cape
- *sibiricus* (L.) C.B. Clarke = Ligularia sibirica var. sibirica
- *spiculosus* (Sheph.) G.D. Rowley = Senecio talinoides subsp. cylindricus
- **squalidus** L. · E:Oxford Ragwort; G:Felsen-Greiskraut · ☉ V-VIII; Eur.: C-Eur., EC-Eur., Slove., Ba, RO, nat. in BrI, DK, F
- *stapeliiformis* E. Phillips = Kleinia stapeliiformis
- *stenocephalus* Maxim. = Ligularia stenocephala

– **subalpinus** W.D.J. Koch · G:Berg-Gre-
iskraut · ⧣ Z6 VII-IX; Eur.: G, A, EC-Eur.,
RO, Russ., ? GR; E-Alp., Bayerischer
Wald, Carp., Balkan,
– *succulentus* Sch. Bip. = Senecio serpens
– **sylvaticus** L. · E:Wood Groundsel;
G:Wald-Greiskraut · ☉ Z6 VI-VIII; Eur.*,
W-As., E-As., nat. in N-Am.
– **talinoides** (DC.) Sch. Bip.
– subsp. **cylindricus** (A. Berger) G.D.
Rowley · ☉ ⧣ ♄ ♄ ᴪ e ⤳ Z9 ⓕ; Namibia
– *tanguticus* Maxim. = Sinacalia tangutica
– *tiroliensis* A. Kern. ex Dalla Torre = Senecio abrotanifolius subsp. abrotanifolius
– **tropaeolifolius** MacOwan ex F. Muell. ·
♄ ᴪ Z9 ⓕ; S-Afr.
– **umbrosus** Waldst. & Kit. · G:Schatten-
Greiskraut · ⧣ VII-IX; Eur.: A, CZ, Ba,
S-Russ.; TR
– *uniflorus* (All.) All. = Senecio halleri
– *veitchianus* Hemsl. = Ligularia veitchiana
– **vernalis** Waldst. & Kit. · G:Frühlings-
Greiskraut · ☉ V-XI; Eur.: A, EC-Eur., Ba,
E-Eur.; TR, SW-As., C-As., nat. in Fr, G,
Sw, Sc
– **viravira** Hieron. · G:Pelziges Geiskraut ·
⧣ ♄ ♄ e Z8 ⓕ; Arg.
– **viscosus** L. · E:Sticky Groundsel;
G:Klebriges Greiskraut · ☉ VI-X; Eur.*
exc. Sc; TR, Cauc., nat. in Sc
– **vulgaris** L. · E:Common Groundsel,
Groundsel; G:Gewöhnliches Greiskraut
· ☉ Z6 II-XI ⚥ ; Eur.*, TR, Levant, Cauc.,
Iran, W-Sib., E-Sib., Amur, Sakhal.,
Kamchat., China, Jap., Taiwan, Eth.,
Cape., Austr., NZ, nat. in N-Am., S-Am.
– *wilsonianus* Hemsl. = Ligularia wilsoniana

Senegalia Raf. = Acacia
– *senegal* (L.) Britton = Acacia senegal

Senna Mill. -f- *Caesalpiniaceae* · c.
260 spp. · E:Senna; F:Séné; G:Senna
– **alata** (L.) Roxb. · ♄ e Z8 ⓦ; trop. Am,
nat. in Afr., SE-As., Austr.
– **alexandrina** Mill. · E:Alexandrian Senna,
Senna; G:Alexandrinische Senna · ♄
♄ Z10 ⓦ ⚥ ; trop. Afr., Alger., Egypt,
Palest., Ind.
– **artemisioides** (Gaudich. ex DC.)
Randell · E:Silver Cassia; G:Dichte Senna
· ♄ e Z10 ⓕ; Austr.: Queensl., N.S.Wales,
Victoria, S-Austr.
– **auriculata** (L.) Roxb. · E:Matara Tea;

G:Avarom-Senna · ♄ e Z10 ⓦ ⓝ; Ind.,
nat. in E-Afr., S-Afr.
– **corymbosa** (Lam.) H.S. Irwin & Barneby
– var. **corymbosa** · ♄ d Z8 ⓕ; Arg., Urug.,
S-Braz.
– var. **plurijuga** Benth. · ♄ d Z8 ⓕ VII-X;
S-Braz., Urug., Arg.
– **didymobotrya** (Fresen.) H.S. Irwin
& Barneby · E:Candle Bush, Golden
Wonder; G:Geflügelte Senna · ♄ s Z10 ⓕ;
trop. Afr., nat. in Trop.
– × **floribunda** (Cav.) H.S. Irwin &
Barneby (*S. multiglandulosa × S.
septemtrionalis*) · ♄ d Z10 ⓕ; Austr.:
Queensl., N.S.Wales, S-Austr., nat. in
Mex., Trop.
– **hebecarpa** (Fernald) H.S. Irwin &
Barneby · E:Wild Senna; G:Wilde Senna
· ⧣ Z7 ∧ VII-IX; USA: NE, NCE, Tenn.,
N.C.
– **italica** Mill. · ♄ d Z10 ⓕ ⓝ; trop. Afr.,
Alger., Libya, Egypt, Palest., NW-Ind.
– **marilandica** (L.) Link · ⧣ Z7 ∧ ⚥ ; USA:
NE, NCE, NC, SE, SC, Fla.
– **multiglandulosa** (Jacq.) H.S. Irwin &
Barneby · ♄ Z8 ⓕ; Mex., C-Am., trop.
S-Am.
– **occidentalis** (L.) Link · E:Coffee Senna;
G:Kaffee-Senna · ☉ Z9 ⓕ IX-X ⓝ; Mex.,
W.Ind., S-Am., nat. in USA, trop. Afr.,
trop. As.
– **septemtrionalis** (Viv.) H.S. Irwin &
Barneby · E:Smooth Senna; G:Glatte
Senna · ♄ Z9 ⓕ VII-VIII; Mex., trop. Am.
– **siamea** (Lam.) H.S. Irwin & Barneby ·
E:Siamese Senna; G:Siamesische Senna
· ♄ Z10 ⓦ ⓝ; Ind., Sri Lanka, Thail.,
Malay. Arch., nat. in trop. Am.
– **spectabilis** (DC.) H.S. Irwin & Barneby ·
♄ d Z10 ⓦ; C-Am., trop. S-Am.
– **tora** (L.) Roxb. · E:Sickle Senna; G:Chi-
nesische Senna · ☉ ⓕ VII-IX ⓝ; USA: NE,
NCE, NC, SC, SE, Fla; trop. Am.

Sequoia Endl. -f- *Taxodiaceae* · 1 sp. ·
E:Coastal Redwood; F:Séquoia; G:Küs-
tenmammutbaum, Küstensequoie
– *gigantea* (Lindl.) Decne. = Sequoiadendron giganteum
– *glyptostroboides* (Hu & W.C. Cheng)
Weide = Metasequoia glyptostroboides
– **sempervirens** (D. Don) Endl. ·
E:California Redwood, Coast Redwood,
Redwood; G:Küstenmammutbaum,
Küstensequoie · ♄ e Z8 ⓕ ∧ ⓝ; USA:

S-Oreg., Calif.
- *wellingtonia* Seem. = Sequoiadendron giganteum

Sequoiadendron J. Buchholz -n- *Taxodiaceae* · 1 sp. · E:Wellingtonia; F:Wellingtonia; G:Bergmammutbaum, Wellingtonie
- **giganteum** (Lindl.) J. Buchholz · E:Giant Sequoia, Wellingtonia; F:Séquoia géant; G:Bergmammutbaum, Wellingtonie · ♄ e Z6 Ⓝ; USA: Calif.

Serapias L. -f- *Orchidaceae* · 12 spp. · E:Tongue Orchid; F:Sérapias ; G:Zungenständel
- **cordigera** L. · ♃ Z8 Ⓚ ▭ V ▽ ✱; Eur.: Ib, Fr, Ital-P, Ba; NW-TR, N-Afr.
- **lingua** L. · G:Echter Zungenständel · ♃ Z7 V ▽ ✱; Eur.: Ib, Fr, Ital-P, Ba; N-Afr.
- **vomeracea** (Burm. f.) Briq. · G:Pflugschar-Zungenständel, Stendelwurz · ♃ Z7 V-VI ▽ ✱; Eur.: Ib, Fr, Sw, Ital-P, Ba; TR, Cyprus, Cauc., Syr., Palest.

Serenoa Hook. f. -f- *Arecaceae* · 1 sp. · E:Shrub Palmetto; G:Strauchpalmettopalme
- **repens** (W. Bartram) Small · E:Saw Palmetto, Shrub Palmetto; G:Sägezahnpalme, Strauchpalmettopalme · ♄ e ⇝ Z8 Ⓚ ⚕; USA: SE, Fla.

Sericographis Nees = Justicia
- *pauciflora* Nees = Justicia rizzinii

Serissa Comm. ex Juss. -f- *Rubiaceae* · 1 sp.
- **foetida** (L. f.) Poir. ex Lam. · E:Snowrose · ♄ Z10 Ⓦ ⚕; Jap., China, SE-As.
- *japonica* Thunb. = Serissa foetida

Serjania Mill. -f- *Sapindaceae* · 215 spp.
- **curassavica** Radlk. · ♄ ≹ Z10 Ⓦ Ⓝ; Ind.
- **cuspidata** Cambess. · ♄ e ≹ Z10 Ⓦ; Braz.

Serratula L. -f- *Asteraceae* · c. 70 spp. · E:Saw Wort; F:Serratule; G:Scharte
- *depressa* Steven = Jurinella moschus
- **lycopifolia** (Vill.) A. Kern. · E:Single-flowered Saw Wort; G:Ungarn-Scharte · ♃ VI-VII; Eur.: F, A, EC-Eur., Slove., Croatia, Bosn., E-Eur.
- **nudicaulis** (L.) DC. · G:Nacktstänglige Scharte · ♃ Z6 VI-VII; Eur.: sp., F, I, Sw; Moroc.; mts.
- **radiata** (Waldst. & Kit.) M. Bieb. · ♃; Eur.: EC-Eur., Ba, E-Eur.; Cauc.
- **seoanei** Willk. · F:Serratule des teinturiers · ♃ △ Z7 ∧ IX-X; Eur.: Ib, S-F
- *shawii* hort. = Serratula seoanei
- **tinctoria** L. · G:Färber-Scharte
- subsp. **macrocephala** (Bertol.) Wilczek & Schinz · G:Großköpfige Scharte, Großköpfige Färber-Scharte · ♃ Z6 VII-IX; Eur.: N-Sp., F, I, Sw, A, Slove.; mts.
- subsp. *seoanei* (Willk.) M. Laínz = Serratula seoanei
- subsp. **tinctoria** · E:Alpine Saw Wort, Saw Wort; G:Gewöhnliche Färber-Scharte · ♃ Z6 VII-VIII; Eur.*, Alger., ? TR
- **wolffii** Andrae · ♃ VIII; Eur.: RO, Russ.

Sesamoides Ortega -f- *Resedaceae* · 4 spp.
- **canescens** (L.) Kuntze · ♃ Ⓚ; Eur.: Ib, F, Ital-P; NW-Afr.
- **clusii** (Spreng.) Greuter & Burdet · ♃ Ⓚ; Eur.: sp., F, Ital-P

Sesamum L. -n- *Pedaliaceae* · 15 spp. · E:Sesame; F:Sésame; G:Sesam
- **alatum** Thonn. · ⊙ Z10 Ⓦ Ⓝ; W-Sah, Eth., E-Afr., trop-Afr.
- **indicum** L. · E:Sesame; G:Sesam · ⊙ Z10 Ⓦ ⚕ Ⓝ; ? Eth., ? Ind.

Sesbania Scop. -f- *Fabaceae* · c. 50 spp. · G:Sesbanie
- **aculeata** (Pers.) Pers. · E:Prickly Sesban; G:Stachlige Sesbanie · ♃ Z10 Ⓦ Ⓝ; Ind., Sri Lanka, China, trop. Afr.
- **cannabina** (Retz.) Pers. · ♄ Z10 Ⓦ Ⓝ; trop. Afr., trop. As., Austr.
- *cochinchinensis* (Lour.) DC. = Sesbania cannabina
- **grandiflora** (L.) Pers. · E:Wisteria Tree; G:Großblütige Sesbanie · ♄ e Z9 Ⓦ VII-VIII Ⓝ; Ind., Sri Lanka, Mauritius, SE-As., N-Austr.
- *punicea* (Cav.) Benth. = Sesbania tripetii
- **sesban** (L.) Merr. · E:Egyptian Sesban; G:Ägyptische Sesbanie · ♄ ♄ d Z10 Ⓦ VII-VIII Ⓝ; trop. Afr., S-Afr.
- **speciosa** Taub. ex Engl. · Ⓝ; ? Ind., cult. Ind.
- **tripetii** (Poit.) hort. ex F.T. Hubb. · E:Scarlet Wisteria Tree; G:Scharlachrote Sesbanie · ♄ d Z9 Ⓚ V-X; Braz., N-Arg.

Seseli L. -n- *Apiaceae* · 100-120 spp. ·
E:Moon Carrot; F:Séséli; G:Bergfenchel,
Sesel
– **annuum** L. · G:Steppen-Bergfenchel,
Steppenfenchel · ⊙ VII-IX; Eur.* exc. BrI,
Sc
– **caespitosum** Sibth. & Sm. · ⵕ △ VII-VIII;
NW-TR
– **elatum** L.
– subsp. **austriacum** (Beck) P.W. Ball ·
G:Österreichischer Bergfenchel · ⵕ
VIII-IX; Eur.: A, ? N-I, Slove.
– subsp. **osseum** (Crantz) P.W. Ball ·
G:Meergrüner Bergfenchel · ⊙ ⵕ VII-VIII;
Eur.: Ib, Fr, A, EC-Eur., Ba, RO
– **hippomarathrum** Jacq. · G:Pferde-
Bergfenchel · ⵕ VII-IX; Eur.: C-Eur.,
EC-Eur., Serb., E-Eur.; W-Sib.
– **libanotis** (L.) W.D.J. Koch · G:Heilwurz ·
⊙ Z4 VII-VIII; Eur.*, W-Sib., E-Sib.,
Mong.
– **montanum** L. · G:Echter Bergfenchel · ⵕ
Z5 VII-IX; Eur.: sp., F, I, Sw, Ba; Cauc.,
Moroc.
– **pallasii** Besser · G:Bunter Bergfenchel ·
⊙ ⵕ Z6 VII-VIII; Eur.: I, A, EC-Eur., Ba,
RO, Crim, Russ; TR

Sesleria Scop. -f- *Poaceae* · 33 spp. · E:Moor
Grass; F:Sesléria; G:Blaugras, Kopfgras
– **albicans** Kit. ex Schult. · E:Blue Moor
Grass; F:Seslérie blanchâtre; G:Kalk-
Blaugras · ⵕ △ Z4 III-V; Eur.: sp., Fr, BrI,
I, C-Eur., EC-Eur., Slove., ? W-Russ.
– **argentea** (Savi) Savi · G:Silber-Blaugras ·
ⵕ △ VI-VII; Eur.: sp., F, I
– **autumnalis** (Scop.) F.W. Schultz ·
E:Autumn Moor Grass; G:Herbst-Blau-
gras · ⵕ Z6 IX-X; Eur.: I, Slove., Croatia,
Bosn., Montenegro, AL
– **caerulea** (L.) Ard. · G:Moor-Blaugras ·
ⵕ △ Z4 V; Eur.: Sc, EC-Eur., N-I, A, Ba,
E-Eur.
– subsp. *varia* (Jacq.) Hayek = Sesleria
albicans
– **heufleriana** Schur · E:Balkan Blue Grass,
Green Moor Grass; G:Grünes Kopfgras ·
ⵕ Z5 IV-V; Eur.: Slova., H, RO, W-Russ.
– **nitida** Ten. · ⵕ IV-V; Eur.: I, Sic.; mts.
– **ovata** (Hoppe) A. Kern. · G:Eiförmiges
Blaugras, Zwerg-Blaugras · ⵕ VII-VIII;
Eur.: F, I, G, A, Slove.; Alp.
– **rigida** Heuff. ex Rchb. · ⵕ; Eur.: Ba, RO;
mts.
– **sadleriana** Janka · G:Pannonisches

Blaugras · ⵕ III-V; Eur.: A, H, PL, Slove.
– *varia* (Jacq.) Wettst. = Sesleria albicans

Sesuvium L. -n- *Aizoaceae* · 22 spp.
– **portulacastrum** (L.) L. · E:Shoreline
Sea Purslane · ⵕ Ⓨ ⤳ Z9 Ⓖ VII-VIII Ⓝ;
Subtrop., Trop.; coasts

Setaria P. Beauv. -f- *Poaceae* · 100-150 spp. ·
E:Bristle Grass; F:Millet à grappes,
Sétaire; G:Borstenhirse, Kolbenhirse
– **faberi** F. Herm. · G:Fabers Borstenhirse ·
⊙ VII-IX; China, nat. in Eur.: Sw, G, CZ;
N-Am.
– *glauca* (L.) P. Beauv. = Pennisetum
glaucum
– *glauca* auct. = Setaria pumila
– *gussonei* Kerguélen = Setaria verticillata
var. ambigua
– **italica** (L.) P. Beauv.
– subsp. **italica** · E:Foxtail Bristle Grass,
Italian Millet; G:Kolbenhirse · ⊙ Z6 VI-X
Ⓝ; cult.
– subsp. **moharia** (Alef.) H. Scholz · ⊙ Z6
Ⓝ; cult.
– *lutescens* (Stuntz) F.T. Hubb. = Setaria
pumila
– **macrostachya** Kunth · E:Large-spike
Bristle Grass · ⵕ VII-VIII; USA: Colo., SW,
Tex.; Mex.
– **palmifolia** (J. König) Stapf · E:Palm
Grass; G:Palmblättrige Borstenhirse · ⵕ
Z9 Ⓖ; trop. As.
– **poiretiana** (Schult.) Kunth · ⵕ Z10 Ⓖ;
Mex., C-Am., W.Ind., trop. S-Am.
– **pumila** (Poir.) Schult. · E:Yellow Foxtail;
G:Fuchsrote Borstenhirse · ⊙ ⤫ Ⓖ VII-X
Ⓝ; Eur.* exc. BrI, Sc; TR, Levant, Cauc.,
Iran, Afgh., Pakist., Ind., Indochina,
China, Jap., Canar., Moroc., Libya, Egypt,
nat. in N-Am., S-Am., S-Afr., Austr.
– **sphacelata** (K. Schum.) Stapf & C.E.
Hubb. · ⵕ Ⓝ; S-Afr. trop-Afr., nat. in Afr.,
Austr.
– *sulcata* Raddi = Setaria poiretiana
– **verticillata** (L.) P. Beauv. · G:Quirlige
Borstenhirse
– var. **ambigua** (Guss.) Parl. · G:Kurz-
borstige Borstenhirse, Unbeständige
Borstenhirse · ⊙ Z6 VI-IX; Eur.: , S-Russ.;
TR, Syr., Israel, Iraq, Arab., Cauc., Iran,
N-Afr.
– var. **verticillata** · E:Bristly Foxtail;
G:Quirlige Borstenhirse · ⊙ Z6 VI-IX;
Eur.: Ib, Ital-P, Fr, Ba, E-Eur.; TR, Cauc.,

C-As., Him., E-As., N-Am., Subtrop., nat.
in C-Eur., E-Eur.
– **viridis** (L.) P. Beauv. · E:Green Bristle
Grass; G:Gewöhnliche Grüne Borsten-
hirse · ⊙ IX-X; Eur.*, TR, Iraq, Cyprus,
Lebanon, Arab., Cauc., Iran, C-As., Afgh.,
Ind., W-Sib., E-Sib., Amur, China, Jap.,
Indochina, N-Afr., nat. in N-Am., S-Am.,
Phil., Austr.

Setcreasea K. Schum. = Tradescantia
– *purpurea* Boom = Tradescantia pallida

Seticereus Backeb. = Borzicactus
– *icosagonus* (Kunth) Backeb. = Cleistocactus icosagonus
– *roezelii* (Haage) Backeb. = Borzicactus
roezlii

Setiechinopsis (Backeb.) de Haas -f-
Cactaceae · 1 sp.
– **mirabilis** (Speg.) Backeb. · ⫛ Z9 ⌂; Arg.

Severinia Ten. -f- *Rutaceae* · 6 spp.
– **buxifolia** (Poir.) Ten. · ♄ ♄ e Z10 ⌂;
S-China, Vietn.

Shepherdia Nutt. -f- *Elaeagnaceae* ·
3 spp. · E:Buffalo Berry; F:Baie de Bison;
G:Büffelbeere
– **argentea** (Pursh) Nutt. · E:Silver Buffalo
Berry; G:Silber-Büffelbeere · ♄ ♄ d Z5
III-IV ℕ; Can.: W, Man.; USA: NW, Calif.,
Rocky Mts., SW, NC, NCE
– **canadensis** (L.) Nutt. · E:Buffalo Berry,
Soapberry; G:Kanadische Büffelbeere · ♄
d Z5 IV-V; Alaska, Can.; USA: NE, NCE,
NC, SW, Rocky Mts.

Sherardia L. -f- *Rubiaceae* · 1 sp. · E:Field
Madder; F:Shérardia; G:Ackerröte
– **arvensis** L. · E:Field Madder; G:Acker-
röte · ⊙ VI-X; Eur.*, TR, N-Iraq, Levant,
Cauc., NW-Afr., Libya

Shibataea Makino ex Nakai -f- *Poaceae* ·
8 spp.
– **kumasasa** (Zoll. ex Steud.) Makino ex
Nakai · ♄ e Z7; Jap.

× **Shipmanara** hort. -f- *Orchidaceae*
(*Broughtonia* × *Caularthron* ×
Schomburgkia)

Shorea Roxb. ex C.F. Gaertn.

-f- *Dipterocarpaceae* · 357 spp.
– **contorta** S. Vidal · ♄ Z10 ⌂ ℕ; Phil.
– **laevis** Ridl. · G:Balau
– **robusta** C.F. Gaertn. · G:Salharzbaum;
E:Sal Tree · ♄ Z10 ⌂ ℕ; Ind.

Shortia Torr. & A. Gray -f- *Diapensiaceae* ·
6 spp. · F:Shortia; G:Winterblatt
– **galacifolia** Torr. & A. Gray · E:Oconee
Bells; G:Echtes Winterblatt · ⨆ Z5 V-VI ▽
✳; USA: N.C.
– **soldanelloides** (Siebold & Zucc.)
Makino · E:Fringe Bell, Fringed Galax;
G:Gefranstes Winterblatt · ⨆ Z7 ⌂ III-IV;
Jap.; mts.
– **uniflora** (Maxim.) Maxim. · E:Nippon
Bells; G:Einblütiges Winterblatt · ⨆ Z6
IV-V; Jap.

Sibbaldia L. -f- *Rosaceae* · 8 spp. ·
F:Sibbaldia; G:Gelbling
– **procumbens** L. · E:Creeping Glow Wort;
G:Alpen-Gelbling · ⨆ ⤳ △ Z1 VI; Eur.*,
W-Sib., E-Sib., Amur, Sakhal., Kamchat.,
C-As., Jap., Alaska, Can., USA: NE, SW,
Rocky Mts., NW, Calif.; Greenl.

Sibbaldiopsis Rydb. = Potentilla
– *tridentata* (Aiton) Rydb. = Potentilla
tridentata

Sibiraea Maxim. -f- *Rosaceae* · 2 spp. ·
F:Sibérienne; G:Blauspiere
– **altaiensis** (Laxm.) C.K. Schneid.
– var. **altaiensis** · ♄ d Z5 V-VI; W-Sib.
(Altai)
– var. **croatica** (Degen) G. Back. · ♄ d Z5;
Croatia: Velebit
– *laevigata* (L.) Maxim. = Sibiraea
altaiensis var. altaiensis
– **tomentosa** Diels · ♄ d Z6; SW-China

Sibthorpia L. -f- *Scrophulariaceae* · 5 spp. ·
E:Moneywort; F:Sibthorpia; G:Sibthorpie
– **europaea** L. · E:Cornish Moneywort;
G:Cornwall-Sibthorpie · ⨆ ⤳ Z8 ⌂
V-VIII; Eur.: BrI, Fr, Ib, GR, Crete, Azor.;
Afr. mts.

Sicana Naudin -f- *Cucurbitaceae* · 2 spp. ·
G:Moschusgurke; E:Musc Cucumber;
F:Mélocoton
– **odorifera** (Vell.) Naudin ·
E:Cassabanana, Musk Cucumber;
G:Moschusgurke, Zombiegurke · ⨆ ⌇ Z10

ⓦ VI-VII ⓃN; cult.

Sicyos L. -m- *Cucurbitaceae* · 25-50 spp. ·
E:Bur Cucumber; F:Concombre chevelu;
G:Haargurke
– **angulatus** L. · E:Bur Cucumber;
G:Haargurke · ☉ ⚥ VI-VII; Can.: E; USA:
NE, NCE, SC, SE, Fla.

Sida L. -f- *Malvaceae* · 150-200 spp. ·
E:Virginia Mallow; F:Mauve de Virginie;
G:Virginiamalve
– *abutilon* L. = Abutilon theophrasti
– **hermaphrodita** (L.) Rusby · E:Virginia
Fanpetals · ⁴ Z6; USA
– **rhombifolia** L. · E:Cuban Jute ; G:Kuba-
jute · ☉ ⁴ ♄ e Z10 ⓦ ⓝ; Subtrop., Trop.

Sidalcea A. Gray -f- *Malvaceae* · 20 spp. ·
E:False Mallow, Prairie Mallow; F:Mauve
de la Prairie; G:Doppelmalve, Präprie-
malve, Schmuckmalve
– **candida** A. Gray · E:White Prairie
Mallow; G:Weiße Schmuckmalve · ⁴ Z7
△ VII-VIII; USA: Rocky Mts., N.Mex.
– **malviflora** (DC.) A. Gray ex Benth. ·
E:Checker Mallow; G:Kalifornische
Schmuckmalve · ⁴ Z7 △ VI-VIII; Calif.
– **neomexicana** A. Gray · E:Rocky
Mountain Checker Mallow; G:Rocky-
Mountain-Schmuckmalve · ⁴ Z7 △
VII-IX; USA: NW, Rocky Mts., Calif., SW;
Mex.
– **oregana** (Nutt. ex Torr. & A. Gray)
A. Gray · E:Oregon Checker Mallow;
G:Oregon-Schmuckmalve · ⁴ Z7 △
VII-IX; USA: NW, Calif., Nev.
– **Cultivars:**
– **many cultivars**

Siderasis Raf. -f- *Commelinaceae* · 2 spp.
– **fuscata** (Lodd.) H.E. Moore · ⁴ Z9 ⓦ;
Braz.

Sideritis L. -f- *Lamiaceae* · 161 sp. ·
F:Crapaudine; G:Gliedkraut
– **glacialis** Boiss. · ⁴ △ VI-VII; S-Sp., N-Afr.
– **hyssopifolia** L. · G:Ysopblättriges
Gliedkraut · ⁴ △ Z7 VII; Eur.: Ib, F, I, Sw,
nat. in D
– **macrostachys** Poir. · ♄ e Z9 ⓦ; Canar.
– **montana** L. · G:Berg-Gliedkraut · ☉ VII-
VIII; Eur.: Ib, Fr, Ital-P, Ba, A, EC-Eur.,
E-Eur.; TR, Cauc., Iran, C-As., N-Afr., nat.
in D

– **romana** L. · G:Römisches Gliedkraut · ☉;
Eur.: Ib, Fr, Ital-P, Ba; TR, NW-Afr., Libya
– **scardica** Griseb. · G:Balkan-Gliedkraut ·
⁴ △ VI-VII; Eur.: Maced., AL, GR, BG
– **syriaca** L. · G:Syrisches Gliedkraut · ⁴ Z8
ⓦ; Eur.: Ba, Ital-P, Crim; TR

Sideroxylon L. *Sapotaceae*
– **lanuginosum** Michx. · E:Gum Bully · ♄
d Z6; USA: NE, NCE, SE, SC, Kans., Fla.;
Mex.

Sieglingia Bernh. = Danthonia
– *decumbens* (L.) Bernh. = Danthonia
decumbens

Sieversia Willd. = Geum
– *montana* (L.) R. Br. = Geum montanum
– *reptans* (L.) R. Br. = Geum reptans
– *triflora* (Pursh) R. Br. = Geum triflorum

Sigesbeckia L. -f- *Asteraceae* · 3 spp. · E:St
Paul's Wort; F:Sigesbeckia; G:Siegesbe-
ckie
– *orientalis* L. = Sigesbeckia serrata
– **serrata** DC. · G:Herzblättrige Siegesbeckie · ☉ VIII-IX; S-Chile, nat. in BrI, D

Silaum Mill. -n- *Apiaceae* · 1 sp. · E:Pepper
Saxifrage; F:Cumin des prés, Silaüs;
G:Wiesensilge
– **silaus** (L.) Schinz & Thell. · G:Wiesen-
silge · ⁴ VI-IX; Eur.*, W-Sib.

Silene L. -f- *Caryophyllaceae* · c. 700 spp. ·
E:Campion, Catchfly; F:Attrape-mouche,
Compagnon, Silène; G:Leimkraut,
Lichtnelke, Pechnelke, Strahlensame
– **acaulis** (L.) Jacq.
– subsp. **acaulis** · E:Cushion Pink, Moss
Campion; F:Silène acaule ; G:Stängel-
loses Leimkraut · ⁴ Z2 VI-IX; Eur.*,
W-Sib., E-Sib., Kamchat., Alaska, Can.,
USA: NE, NCE, NC, Rocky Mts., SW, NW,
Calif.; Greenl.
– subsp. **exscapa** (All.) Killias · F:Silène
acaule; G:Kiesel-Polsternelke, Stielloses
Leimkraut · ⁴ ⌂ △ Z2 VI-VIII; Eur.: Pyr.,
W-Alp.
– *alba* (Mill.) E.H.L. Krause = Silene
latifolia subsp. alba
– **alpestris** Jacq. · E:Alpine Catchfly;
F:Silène des Alpes; G:Alpen-Leimkraut,
Großer Strahlensame · ⁴ △ Z5 VI-VIII;
Eur.: I, A, Slove., Croat.; mts.

– **altaica** Pers. · ♃ VI-VII; Russ. (S-Ural),
W-Sib., E-Sib., C-As., China
– × **arkwrightii** hort. (*S. banksia* × *S.
chalcedonica*) · ♃ Z6; cult.
– **armeria** L. · E:Sweet William Catchfly;
G:Morgenröschen, Nelken-Leimkraut ·
⊙ VI-VIII; Eur.: Fr, Ital-P, Sw, PL, E-Eur.,
Ba; TR, nat. in Ib
– **asterias** Griseb. · ♃ △ VI; Eur.: ? Bosn.,
YU, Maced., AL, BG, N-GR
– **atropurpurea** (Griseb.) Greuter &
Burdet · ♃ △ VI-VII; Serb., Maced., AL,
BG, N-GR, RO
– **banksia** (Meerb.) Mabb. · ♃ Z6 VI-VIII;
China
– **some cultivars siehe Kapitel III**
– **bupleuroides** L. · G:Langblütiges
Leimkraut · ♃; Eur.: EC-Eur., Ba, E-Eur.;
TR, Cauc., N-Iran, C-As.
– **chalcedonica** (L.) E.H.L. Krause ·
E:Maltese Cross; G:Brennende Liebe · ♃
Z4 VI-VII; Eur.: Russ
– **some cultivars**
– **chlorantha** (Willd.) Ehrh. · G:Grünliches
Leimkraut · ♃ VI-VIII; Eur.: G, PL, Ba,
E-Eur.; Cauc., W-Sib., E-Sib., C-As.
– **coeli-rosa** (L.) Godr. · E:Rose-of-Heaven;
G:Himmelsröschen · ⊙ VI-VIII; Eur.: Ib,
Ital-P; NW-Afr., nat. in H
– **compacta** Fisch. ex Hornem. · · ⊙; Eur.:
Ba, EC-Eur.; TR, N-Iraq, Cauc., N-Iran
– **conica** L. · G:Kegelfrüchtiges Leimkraut ·
⊙ VI-VII; Eur.* exc. Sc; TR, Iraq, Arab.,
Cauc., N-Iran, C-As., Sib., NW-Afr., nat.
in Sc
– **conoidea** L. · G:Großkegelfrüchtiges
Leimkraut · ⊙ VI-VII; Eur.: sp., F, I; TR,
Levant, Cauc., Iran, C-As., Him., China:
Sinkiang; N-Afr., N-Am.
– **coronaria** (L.) Clairv. · E:Crown Pink;
F:Coquelourde; G:Kronen-Lichtnelke,
Vexiernelke · ⊙ ♃ Z4 VI-VIII; Eur.* exc.
BrI, Sc; TR, Cauc., N-Iran, C-As., Him.
– **cretica** L. · G:Kreta-Leimkraut · ⊙ VI-VII;
Eur.: Ba; TR, Cyprus, Palest., nat. in Ib
– **dichotoma** Ehrh. · E:Forked Catchfly;
G:Gabel-Leimkraut · ⊙ VI-VIII; Eur.: I, H,
Ba, E-Eur.; Cauc., W-Sib., nat. in Sc, Fr,
C-Eur., N-Am.
– **dioica** (L.) Clairv. · E:Red Campion;
G:Rote Lichtnelke · ⊙ ♃ ∼ Z6 IV-VII;
Eur.*, Cauc., W-Sib., C-As., Moroc.
– **elisabethae** Jan · ♃ △ Z7 ∧ VI; Eur.: I;
S-Alp.
– *exscapa* All. = Silene acaulis subsp.
exscapa
– **flos-cuculi** (L.) Clairv. · E:Ragged Robin;
G:Kuckucks-Lichtnelke · ♃ Z6 V-VIII;
Eur.*, Cauc., W-Sib., E-Sib., nat. in ne
N-Am.
– **flos-jovis** (L.) Greuter & Burdet ·
E:Flower-of-Jove; F:Lychnis fleur-de-
Jupiter; G:Jupiter-Lichtnelke · ♃ Z5
VI-VII; Eur.: I, Sw, D; Alp., nat. in A,
EC-Eur.
– **fulgens** (Fisch. ex Sims) E.H.L. Krause ·
♃ ∧ VI-VIII; Jap., N-Korea, Manch.,
Amur
– **gallica** L. · E:French Catchfly; G:Franzö-
sisches Leimkraut · ⊙ ⊙ VI-VIII; Eur.*
exc. Sc; TR, Levant, Cauc., Iran, N-Afr.,
nat. in cosmop.
– **hookeri** Nutt. ex Torr. & A. Gray ·
E:Hooker's Silene; G:Hookers Leimkraut
· ♃ △ Z7 V-VI; USA: SW-Oreg., NW-Calif.
– *inflata* Sm. = Silene vulgaris subsp.
vulgaris
– **insubrica** Gaudin · G:Insubrisches
Leimkraut · ♃ VI-VII; Eur.: Sw, I; Alp.
– **italica** (L.) Pers. · G:Italienisches
Leimkraut · ♃ V; Eur.* exc. BrI, Sc; TR,
Levant, Cauc., N-Iran, C-As., N-Afr., nat.
in BrI
– **keiskei** (Miq.) Ohwi · ♃ Z6; Jap.; mts.
– **latifolia** Poir. · G:Weiße Lichtnelke
– subsp. **alba** (Mill.) Greuter & Burdet ·
G:Gewöhnliche Weiße Lichtnelke · ⊙ ♃
Z6 VI-IX; Eur.*, TR, Syr., Moroc., Alger.,
nat. in N-Am.
– subsp. **latifolia** · E:White Campion;
G:Südliche Weiße Lichtnelke · ⊙ ♃ Z6;
S-Eur., TR, NW-Afr.
– **linicola** C.C. Gmel. · G:Flachs-Leim-
kraut · ⊙ VI-IX; Eur.: F, nat. in I, W-Ba
– **miqueliana** (Rohrb. ex Franch. & Sav.)
H. Ohashi & H. Nakai · ♃ Z6 VII-X; Jap.
– **multiflora** (Waldst. & Kit.) Pers. ·
G:Vielblütiges Leimkraut · ♃ VI-VII; Eur.:
A, EC-Eur., E-Eur.; W-Sib., C-As.
– **nemoralis** (Waldst. & Kit.) Nyman ·
G:Hain-Leimkraut · ⊙ V-VII; Eur.: F, G,
A, H, CZ, Slova., Slove.
– **noctiflora** L. · E:Night-flowering
Catchfly; G:Acker-Lichtnelke · ⊙ VI-IX;
Eur.* exc. Ib, Sc; TR, SW-As., N-Am., nat.
in Ib
– **nutans** L. · E:Nottingham Catchfly;
G:Nickendes Leimkraut · ♃ Z6 V-VIII;
Eur.*, Cauc., N-As., N-Afr.
– **otites** (L.) Wibel · E:Spanish Catchfly;

G:Ohrlöffel-Leimkraut · ⅎ V-VIII; Eur.*,
Cauc., N-Iran, Sib.
- **pendula** L. · E:Nodding Catchfly;
G:Nickendes Leimkraut · ☉ VI-VIII; Eur.:
I; ? TR, Cauc., nat. in sp.
- **polypetala** (Walter) Fernald & B.G.
Schub. · E:Eastern Fringed Catchfly · ⅎ
V-VI; USA: Ga., Fla
- *pratensis* (Rafn) Godr. & Gren. = Silene
latifolia subsp. alba
- **pudibunda** Hoffmanns. ex Rchb. ·
G:Rosafarbenes Kleines Leimkraut · ⅎ
VII-IX; Eur.: A
- **pusilla** Waldst. & Kit. · G:Kleiner
Strahlensame, Vierzähniges Leimkraut ·
ⅎ △ VI-VIII; Eur.* exc. BrI, Sc; mts.
- *quadridentata* hort. = Silene alpestris
- *quadrifida* auct. non (L.) Rchb. = Silene
pusilla
- **rupestris** L. · E:Rock Campion; G:Felsen-
Leimkraut · ⅎ VII-VIII; Eur.* exc. BrI;
mts.
- **saxifraga** L. · E:Tufted Catchfly; G:Karst-
Leimkraut, Steinbrech-Leimkraut · ⅎ △
V-VI; Eur.: Ib, Fr, Ital-P, Ba, C-Eur., RO
- **schafta** S.G. Gmel. ex Hohen. · ⅎ △
VIII-IX; Cauc.
- **suecica** (Lodd.) Greuter & Burdet ·
E:Alpine Campion; G:Alpen-Pechnelke
· ⅎ △ VII-VIII; Eur.* exc. Ba, EC-Eur.;
Can.: W; Greenl.
- **tatarica** (L.) Pers. · G:Tataren-Leim-
kraut · ⅎ VII-IX; Eur.: G, PL, Sc, E-Eur.;
Cauc.
- **uniflora** Roth · E:Catchfly, Sea Campion;
F:Silène enflé; G:Klippen-Leimkraut · ⅎ
Z3 VI-VIII; Eur., N-Afr.; coasts
- **vallesia** L. · E:Valais Catchfly; G:Walliser
Leimkraut · ⅎ △ Z6 VI-VIII; Eur.: F, I, Sw,
Croatia, Bosn., Montenegro, Al
- **veselskyi** (Janka) H. Neumayer ·
G:Wolliges Leimkraut · ⅎ V-VII; Eur.: I,
A, Slove.; SE-Alp.
- **virginica** L. · E:Fire Pink · ⅎ △ Z7 ∧ VII-
VIII; Can.: Ont.; USA: NE, NCE, Okla., SE
- **viridiflora** L. · G:Grünblütiges Leim-
kraut · ⅎ VII; Eur.: Ib, Fr, Ital-P, Ba,
EC-Eur., E-Eur.; TR
- **viscaria** (L.) Jess. · E:Sticky Catchfly;
G:Gewöhnliche Pechnelke · ⅎ Z4 V-VII;
Eur.* exc. Ib; Cauc., W-Sib., nat. in
N-Am.
- **viscosa** (L.) Čelak. · G:Klebrige
Lichtnelke, Klebriges Leimkraut · ⅎ V-VII;
Eur.: Sc, C-Eur., EC-Eur., Bosn.; Cauc.,

Iran, W-Sib., E-Sib., C-As., Mong.
- **vulgaris** (Moench) Garcke · G:Taubenk-
ropf-Leimkraut
- subsp. *maritima* (With.) Á. Löve & D.
Löve = Silene uniflora
- subsp. **vulgaris** · E:Bladder Campion;
G:Gewöhnliches Taubenkropf-Leimkraut
· ⅎ V-IX; Eur.*, Cauc., TR, Levant, Iran,
W-Sib., E-Sib., Amur, Sakhal., Kamchat.,
C-As., Him., N-Afr., nat. in N-Am.
- **waldsteinii** Griseb. · ⅎ ⤳ △ V-VI; Eur.:
Ba; mts
- × **walkeri** hort. (*S. coronaria* × *S. flos-
jovis*) · ⅎ Z6; cult.
- **wilfordii** (Regel ex Maxim.) H. Ohashi &
H. Nakai · ⅎ Z6; E-Russ., Amur, Manch.
Korea, Jap.
- **zawadzkii** Herbich · ⅎ △ Z5 VI-VIII;
Eur.: RO, W-Russ.; E-Carp.

Silphium L. -n- Asteraceae · 23 spp. ·
E:Prairie Dock, Rosin-Weed; F:Plante-
compas; G:Becherpflanze, Kompass-
pflanze
- **integrifolium** Michx. · E:Rosin Weed;
G:Ungeschlitzte Becherpflanze · ⅎ Z5
VIII-IX; USA: NCE, Kans., SE
- **laciniatum** L. · E:Compass Plant, Pilot
Weed, Polar Plant; G:Kompasspflanze · ⅎ
Z4 VII-VIII; USA: NCE, NC, SC, SE
- **perfoliatum** L. · E:Cup Plant, Indian Cup
Plant, Indian Gum; G:Verwachsenblät-
trige Becherpflanze · ⅎ Z4 VII-IX; Ont.,
USA: NE, NCE, NC, Okla., SE
- **terebinthinaceum** Jacq. · E:Prairie Dock;
G:Harzige Becherpflanze · ⅎ Z4 VII-IX;
Can.: Ont.; USA: NE, NCE, SE
- **trifoliatum** L. · E:Whorled Rosin-weed;
G:Dreiblättrige Becherpflanze · ⅎ Z5
VII-IX; USA: NE, NCE, SE

Silybum Adans. -n- Asteraceae · 2 spp. ·
E:Milk Thistle; F:Chardon-Marie, Lait de
Notre-Dame; G:Mariendistel
- **eburneum** Coss. & Durieu · ☉ Z7 VI-IX;
Eur.: sp.; NW-Afr.
- **marianum** (L.) Gaertn. · E:Milk Thistle,
Our Lady's Thistle; G:Gewöhnliche
Mariendistel · ☉ ☉ Z7 VII-IX ⚲ ; Eur.: Ib,
Fr, Ital-P, Ba; TR, Iraq, Cauc., Iran, Afgh.,
N-Afr., Canar., Madeira, nat. in Eur.:
BrI, Sw, EC-Eur., E-Eur.; N-Am., S-Am.,
Austr.

Simmondsia Nutt. -f- Simmondsiaceae ·

1 sp. · E:Goat Nut, Jojoba; F:Jojoba;
G:Jojobastrauch
- **chinensis** (Link) C.K. Schneid. ·
E:Bucknut, Goat Nut; G:Jojobastrauch · ♄
Z10 ⊙ ⚥ Ⓝ; USA: Calif., SW; N-Mex.

Sinacalia H. Rob. & Brettell -f- *Asteraceae* ·
2 spp. · E:Chinese Ragwort; F:Séneçon de
Sibérie; G:Chinagreiskraut
- **tangutica** (Maxim.) B. Nord. · G:China-
greiskraut, Tungusisches Greiskraut · ⁴
⏦ Z5 X; N-China

Sinapis L. -f- *Brassicaceae* · 10 spp. ·
E:Mustard; F:Moutarde; G:Senf
- **alba** L. · E:Mustard, White Mustard;
G:Weißer Senf · ⊙ Z6 VI-VII ⚥ ; Eur.*,
TR, Cyprus, Syr., Iraq, Cauc., Iran,
W-Sib., E-Sib., C-As., N-Afr.
- **arvensis** L. · E:Charlock, Field Mustard;
G:Acker-Senf · ⊙ VI-X; Eur.*, TR, Syr.,
Iraq, Cauc., Iran, W-Sib., E-Sib., C-As.,
N-Afr.

Sinarundinaria Nakai -f- *Poaceae* · 1? spp.
- *murielae* (Gamble) Nakai = Fargesia
murielae
- *nitida* (Mitford) Nakai = Fargesia nitida

Sinningia Nees -f- *Gesneriaceae* · 75+ spp. ·
E:Florist's Gloxinia; F:Gloxinia sauvage,
Sinningia; G:Gartengloxinie
- **barbata** (Nees & Mart.) G. Nicholson · ⁴
Z10 ⓦ I-XII; Braz.
- **canescens** (Mart.) Wiehler · E:Brazilian
Edelweiss · ⁴ Z10 ⓦ IV-VIII; Braz.:
Parana
- **cardinalis** (Lehm.) H.E. Moore ·
E:Cardinal Flower, Helmet Flower · ⁴
Z10 ⓦ III-VIII; Braz.
- **concinna** (Hook. f.) G. Nicholson · ⁴ Z10
ⓦ I-XII; Braz.
- **eumorpha** H.E. Moore · ⁴ Z10 ⓦ VI-VII;
S-Braz.
- **gesneriifolia** (Hanst.) Clayberg · ⁴ Z10
ⓦ VII-VIII; Braz.
- **hirsuta** (Lindl.) G. Nicholson · ⁴ Z10 ⓦ
VI-VII; Braz.
- **incarnata** (Aubl.) Denham · ⁴ Z10 ⓦ;
Mex.
- **macropoda** (Sprague) H.E. Moore · ⁴
Z10 ⓦ III-IV; S-Braz.
- **pusilla** (Mart.) Baill. · ⁴ Z10 ⓦ IV-VIII;
Braz.
- *regina* Sprague = Sinningia speciosa

- **richii** Clayberg · ⁴ Z10 ⓦ IX-X; Braz.
- **speciosa** (Lodd.) Hiern · E:Florist's
Gloxinia; G:Falsche Gloxinie, Gartengloxinie · ⁴ Z10 ⓦ VI-VIII; Braz.
- **tubiflora** (Hook.) Fritsch · ⁴ Z10 ⓦ;
Arg.: Buenos Aires
- **verticillata** (Vell.) H.E. Moore · ⁴ Z10
ⓦ; Braz.
- *warszewiczii* (Bouché & Hanst.) H.E.
Moore = Sinningia incarnata
- **Cultivars:**
- **many cultivars**

Sinocalycanthus (W.C. Cheng & S.Y.
Chang) W.C. Cheng & S.Y. Chan -m-
Calycanthaceae · 1 sp.
- **chinensis** (W.C. Cheng & S.Y. Chang)
W.C. Cheng & S.Y. Chan · ♄ d Z5;
E-China

Sinocrassula A. Berger -f- *Crassulaceae* ·
7 spp. · F:Crassula de Chine, Sinocrassula; G:Chinadickblatt
- **indica** (Decne.) A. Berger · G:Indisches
Chinadickblatt · ⁴ ♇ Z9 ⊙ IX-X; Ind.
- **yunnanensis** (Franch.) A. Berger ·
G:Yunnan-Chinadickblatt · ⁴ ♇ Z9 ⊙
IX-X; Yunnan

Sinofranchetia (Diels) Hemsl. -f-
Lardizabalaceae · 1 sp.
- **chinensis** (Franch.) Hemsl. · ♄ d ⚥ ⊛ Z7
V; W-China, C-China

Sinojackia Hu -f- *Styracaceae* · 2 spp.
- **rehderiana** Hu · ♄ d Z7; E-China
- **xylocarpa** Hu · ♄ s Z7; China (Jiangsu)

Sinomenium Diels -n- *Menispermaceae* ·
1 sp.
- **acutum** (Thunb.) Rehder & E.H. Wilson ·
♄ ⌇ d ⚥ Z7; Jap., C-China

Sinowilsonia Hemsl. -f- *Hamamelidaceae* ·
1 sp.
- **henryi** Hemsl. · ♄ d Z6 V; W-China,
C-China

Siphocampylus Pohl -m- *Campanulaceae* ·
215 spp.
- **manettiiflorus** Hook. · ♄ e Z10 ⓦ IV-X;
Cuba

Sison L. -n- *Apiaceae* · 2 spp. · E:Stone
Parsley; F:Sison; G:Gewürzdolde

– **amomum** L. · E:Stone Parsley;
G:Gewürzdolde · ⊙ VII-VIII; Eur.: BrI, G,
Ib, Ital-P, Ba, RO; TR, Cauc.

Sisymbrium L. -n- *Brassicaceae* ·
80-90 spp. · E:Rocket; F:Sisymbre,
Tortelle, Vélar; G:Rauke, Raukensenf,
Wegrauke
– *alliaria* (L.) Scop. = Alliaria petiolata
– **altissimum** L. · E:Tall Rocket; G:Hohe
Rauke, Ungarische Rauke · ⊙ V-VII; Eur.:
EC-Eur., Ba, E-Eur.; TR, Lebanon, Syr.,
Cauc., Iran, W-Sib., C-As., H, nat. in Eur.:
BrI, Sc, Fr, C-Eur., Ib, Ital-P; N-Am.
– **austriacum** Jacq. · E:Austrian Rocket;
G:Österreichische Rauke · ⊙ ⩊ V-VI;
Eur.: Ib, Fr, I, C-Eur., EC-Eur., nat. in
W-Russ.
– **irio** L. · E:London Rocket; G:Glanz-Rauke
· ⊙ V-VIII; Eur.: Ib, Fr, Ital-P, Ba C-Eur.,
RO; TR, Levant, Cauc., Iran, C-As.,
N-Afr., nat. in BrI, EC-Eur.
– **loeselii** L. · E:False London Rocket;
G:Loesels Rauke · ⊙ VI-VIII; Eur.: Ital-P,
C-Eur., EC-Eur., Ba, E-Eur.; TR, Iraq,
Cauc., Iran, Afgh., W-Sib., C-As., Him.,
Mong., Amur, nat. in BrI, Sc, Fr, Ib
– **officinale** (L.) Scop. · E:Hedge Mustard,
Tumble Mustard; G:Wegrauke · ⊙ ⊙ V-X
⚥ ⚘; Eur.*, TR, Levant, Iraq, Cauc.,
Iran, W-Sib., E-Sib., Amur, NW-Afr.,
Libya, nat. in N-Am., Austr.
– **orientale** L. · G:Orientalische Rauke · ⊙
VI-VII; Eur.: Ib, Fr, Ital-P, Ba, H, RO; TR,
Levant, Cauc., Iran, nat. in Eur.: BrI, Sc,
C-Eur.; Austr.
– **strictissimum** L. · G:Steife Rauke · ⩊
VI-VII; Eur.: Fr, Ital-P, C-Eur., EC-Eur.,
Ba, E-Eur., nat. in BrI, ? Ib
– **supinum** L. · G:Niedrige Rauke · ⊙
VII-VIII ▽; Eur.: sp., Fr, Sw, Swed, Russ.
– **volgense** M. Bieb. ex E. Fourn. ·
G:Wolga-Rauke · ⩊ V-VIII; Eur.: SE-
Russ., nat. in BrI, G, EC-Eur.

Sisyrinchium L. -n- *Iridaceae* · 138 spp. ·
E:Blue-eyed Grass; F:Bermudienne;
G:Grasschwertel
– *anceps* Cav. = Sisyrinchium angustifolium
– **angustifolium** Mill. · E:Narrowleaf
Blue-eyed Grass; F:Herbe veuve, Tonique
printanier; G:Grasschwertel · ⩊ △ Z3
V-VI; Alaska, Can., USA* exc. SE, Fla.
– *bellum* hort. = Sisyrinchium idahoense
var. idahoense

– **bellum** S. Watson · E:Western Blue-eyed
Grass · ⩊ Z8 🔁; Calif.
– **bermudiana** L. · E:Strict Blue-eyed
Grass; G:Schmalblättriges Grasschwertel
· ⩊ △ Z8 🔁 ⋀ V-VII; Can.; USA: NE,
NCE, NC, Rocky Mts.
– *boreale* (E.P. Bicknell) J.K. Henry =
Sisyrinchium californicum
– *brachypus* (E.P. Bicknell) J.K. Henry =
Sisyrinchium californicum
– **californicum** W.T. Aiton · E:Blue-eyed
Grass; F:Sisyrinchum de Californie;
G:Kalifornisches Grasschwertel · ⩊ Z8 🔁
⋀ VI-VIII; USA: Oreg., Calif.
– **convolutum** Nocca · ⩊ Z9 🔁; C-Am.
– *douglasii* A. Dietr. = Olsynium douglasii
– *filifolium* Gaudich. = Olsynium filifolium
– *gramineum* Lam. = Sisyrinchium
angustifolium
– **graminifolium** Lindl. · ⩊ Z8 🔁 IV-V;
Chile
– *grandiflorum* Douglas ex Lindl. =
Olsynium douglasii
– **idahoense** E.P. Bicknell · E:Idaho Blue-
eyed Grass; G:Idaho-Grasschwertel
– var. **idahoense** · ⩊ Z3 🔁 V-VI; Can.:
B.C.; w N-Am.
– var. **macounii** (E.P. Bicknell) D.M.
Hend. · E:Macoun's Blue-eyed Grass · ⩊
Z3 🔁 ⋀ V-VI
– *macounii* E.P. Bicknell = Sisyrinchium
idahoense var. macounii
– *majale* Link & Klotzsch = Sisyrinchium
graminifolium
– **micranthum** Cav. · ⩊ Z8 🔁 VI; C-Am.,
S-Am.
– **mucronatum** Michx. · E:Needletip
Blue-eyed Grass. · ⩊ △ Z7 🔁 V-VI; USA:
NE, NCE, N.C.
– **striatum** Sm. · F:Sisyrinchum;
G:Gestreiftes Grasschwertel · ⩊ Z8 🔁
VI-VII; Arg., Chile
– **Cultivars:**
– **some cultivars**

Sium L. -n- *Apiaceae* · 14 spp. · E:Water
Parsnip; F:Berle, Chervis; G:Merk
– *erectum* Huds. = Berula erecta
– **latifolium** L. · E:Water Parsnip;
G:Großer Merk · ⩊ ≈ Z6 VII-VIII ⚘;
Eur.*, Cauc., N-Iraq, W-Sib., C-As., nat.
in Austr.
– **sisarum** L. · E:Skirret; G:Süßwurzel,
Zucker-Merk · ⩊ Z6 VII-VIII Ⓝ; Eur.: H,
BG, E-Eur.; TR, Syr., Cauc., N-Iraq, Iran,

C-As., W-Sib., E-Sib., nat. in C-Eur., I

Skiatophytum L. Bolus -n- *Aizoaceae* · 1 sp.
- **tripolium** (L.) L. Bolus · ⊙ ⊙ ♆ Z9 Ⓚ; Cape

Skimmia Thunb. -f- *Rutaceae* · 4 spp. · E:Skimmia; F:Skimmia; G:Skimmie
- *fragrans* Carrière = Skimmia japonica subsp. japonica
- **japonica** Thunb.
- **some cultivars**
- subsp. **japonica** · E:Japanese Skimmia; F:Skimmia du Japon; G:Japanische Skimmie · ♄ e ☘ D Z7 V; Jap., Ryukyu-Is., Taiwan
- subsp. **reevesiana** (Fortune) N.P. Taylor & Airy Shaw · E:Reeves's Skimmia; G:Reeves Skimmie · ♄ e ☘ Z7 V-VI; China, Taiwan, Phil.: Luzon
- **laureola** (DC.) Siebold & Zucc. · ♄ ♄ e Z7 V-VI; Nepal, Him. Burma, China
- *oblata* T. Moore = Skimmia japonica subsp. japonica
- *reevesiana* Fortune = Skimmia japonica subsp. reevesiana

Smilacina Desf. -f- *Convallariaceae* · 25 spp. · E:False Salomon's Seal; F:Petit smilax; G:Duftsiegel
- *amplexicaulis* Nutt. = Smilacina racemosa
- **racemosa** (L.) Desf. · E:False Spikenard, Solomon's Plume; G:Duftsiegel · ♃ Z4 V-VI; Alaska, Can., USA* exc. Fla.
- *sessilifolia* Nutt. ex Baker = Smilacina stellata
- **stellata** (L.) Desf. · E:Starflower; G:Sternförmiges Duftsiegel · ♃ Z3 V; Alaska, Can., USA* exc. Fla.
- *tubifera* Batalin = Smilacina stellata

Smilax L. -f- *Smilacaceae* · 259 spp. · F:Liseron épineux, Salsepareille, Smilax; G:Stechwinde
- **argyraea** L. Linden & Rodigas · ♄ e ≹ Z9 Ⓦ; Peru, Bol.
- **aristolochiifolia** Mill. · G:Veracruz-Stechwinde · ≀ ⚕ Ⓝ; S-Mex.
- **aspera** L. · E:Rough Bindweed; G:Raue Stechwinde · ♄ e ≹ ⇝ Z8 Ⓚ VIII-IX; Eur.: Ib, Fr, Ital-P, Ba, Canar.; TR, Eth., Him., Sri Lanka, N-Afr.
- **china** L. · E:Chinaroot · ♄ d Z6 Ⓐ V ⚕; China, Korea, Jap.
- **excelsa** L. · G:Hohe Stechwinde · ≀ d ≹ Z6; Eur.: BG, GR, Russ.Azor.; Cauc., TR, Iran
- **glauca** Walter · E:Saw Brier · ♄ s Z4 Ⓐ; USA: NE, NCE, SC, SE, Fla.
- *hispida* Muhl. ex Torr. = Smilax tamnoides
- *mauritanica* Poir. = Smilax aspera
- *medica* Schltdl. & Cham. = Smilax aristolochiifolia
- **regelii** Killip & C.V. Morton · E:Honduras Sarsaparilla; G:Honduras-Stechwinde · ♄ ≹ Z9 Ⓦ ⚕ Ⓝ; C-Am.
- **rotundifolia** L. · E:Green Briar, Horse Briar; G:Rundblättrige Stechwinde · ♄ e ≹ ⇝ Z4 VI; Can.: E; USA: NE, NCE, SC, SE, Fla.
- *saluberrima* Gilg = Smilax regelii
- **tamnoides** L. · E:Bristly Greenbriar; G:Steifborstige Stechwinde · ≀ d ≹ Z5 VI; USA
- *utilis* Hemsl. = Smilax regelii

Smithiantha Kuntze -f- *Gesneriaceae* · 4 spp. · E:Temple Bells; F:Cloche du temple; G:Tempelglocke
- *amabilis* (Regel) Kuntze = Smithiantha multiflora
- **cinnabarina** (Linden) Kuntze · ♃ Z10 Ⓦ IV-VI; S-Mex.
- **multiflora** (M. Martens & Galeotti) Fritsch · ♃ Z10 Ⓦ VII-VIII; S-Mex.
- **zebrina** (Paxton) Kuntze · ♃ Z10 Ⓦ VIII-X; S-Mex.
- **Cultivars:**
- **some cultivars**

Smyrnium L. -n- *Apiaceae* · 7 spp. · E:Alexanders; F:Maceron; G:Gelbdolde
- **olusatrum** L. · E:Alexanders; G:Schwarze Gelbdolde, Schwarzer Liebstöckel · ⊙ Z9 Ⓚ V-VI Ⓝ; Eur.: Ib, Fr, Ital-P, Ba; TR, Alger., Canar., nat. in BrI
- **perfoliatum** L. · G:Stängelumfassende Gelbdolde · ⊙ Z7 VI-VII; Eur.: Ib, Fr, Ital-P, EC-Eur., Ba, RO, Crim; TR, Syr., ? Cauc., nat. in BrI, DK, C-Eur.

Sobralia Ruiz & Pav. -f- *Orchidaceae* · 121 sp.
- **decora** Bateman · ♃ △ Z10 Ⓦ VI-VIII ▽ *; Guyan., Braz., Peru
- **leucoxantha** Rchb. f. · ♃ Z10 Ⓦ VI-VIII ▽ *; Costa Rica, Panama
- **macrantha** Lindl. · ♃ Z10 Ⓦ V-VI ▽ *; Mex., C-Am.

– *sessilis* Lindl. = Sobralia decora
– **xantholeuca** B.S. Williams · ⌠⅟ Z10 Ⓜ
VI-VIII ▽ ✳; C-Am.

Soehrensia Backeb. = Trichocereus
– *bruchii* (Britton & Rose) Backeb. =
Trichocereus bruchii
– *formosa* (Pfeiff.) Backeb. = Trichocereus
formosus
– *grandis* (Britton & Rose) Backeb. =
Trichocereus bruchii
– *korethroides* (Werderm.) Backeb. =
Trichocereus bruchii

Soja Moench = Glycine
– *hispida* Moench = Glycine max
– *max* (L.) Piper = Glycine max

Solandra Sw. -f- *Solanaceae* · 10 spp. ·
E:Chalice Vine; F:Solandra; G:Goldkelch
– **grandiflora** Sw. · G:Großblütiger Goldkelch · ♄ e ⚡ D Z10 Ⓜ VII-VIII; Jamaica,
Mex.
– **guttata** D. Don ex Lindl. · G:Getüpfelter
Goldkelch · ♄ e ⚡ D Z10 Ⓜ VII-VIII; Mex.
– **longiflora** Tussac · G:Länglicher
Goldkelch · ♄ e ⚡ D Z10 Ⓜ IX-X; Jamaica
– **maxima** (Sessé & Moç.) P.S. Green ·
E:Chalice Vine; G:Üppiger Goldkelch · ♄ ⚡
e ⚡ D Z10 Ⓜ VII-VIII; Mex.

Solanopteris Copel. -f- *Polypodiaceae* ·
4 spp.
– **bifrons** (Hook.) Copel. · ⌠⅟ ⚡ Z10 Ⓜ;
Col., Ecuad., Peru

Solanum L. -n- *Solanaceae* · 1400-
1700 spp. · E:Eggplant, Nightshade,
Potato; F:Aubergine, Morelle, Pomme de
terre; G:Aubergine, Eierfrucht, Kartoffel,
Nachtschatten
– **aculeatissimum** Jacq. · E:Dutch Eggplant, Love Apple · ♄ ⚭ Z10 Ⓚ VII-VIII;
Trop.
– **aethiopicum** L. · ♄ Z10 Ⓜ Ⓝ; W-Afr.,
C-Afr., trop. As.
– **ajanhuiri** Juz. & Bukasov · ⌠⅟ Z10 Ⓝ;
cult. N-Bol.
– *alatum* Moench = Solanum villosum
subsp. alatum
– **atropurpureum** Schrank · ♄ Z10 Ⓚ VII-
VIII; Col., Braz., Parag., Urug., NE-Arg.
– **aviculare** G. Forst. · E:Kangaroo Apple;
G:Queensland-Känguruapfel · ♄ e Z9
Ⓚ VIII-IX; Austr.: Queensl., N.S.Wales,

Victoria, S-Austr., Tasman.; NZ
– **berthaultii** Hawkes · ⌠⅟ Z9 Ⓚ Ⓝ; Bol.
– **bonariense** L. · ♄ e; S-Braz., Urug.,
NE-Arg.
– **capsicastrum** Link ex Schauer · E:False
Jerusalem Cherry; G:Falsche Jerusale-
mkirsche · ♄ ⚭ Z10 Ⓚ VI-VII; S-Braz.,
Urug.
– **citrullifolium** A. Braun · E:Melon-leaf
Nightshade; G:Melonenblättriger
Nachtschatten · ☉ Z4 VI-IX; USA: N.Mex.,
Tex.; Mex.
– *cornutum* hort. = Solanum rostratum
– **crispum** Ruiz & Pav. · E:Chilean Potato
Tree; G:Chile-Kartoffel · ♄ ⚡ D Z8 Ⓚ
VI-IX; Chile
– **dasyphyllum** K. Schum. & Thonn. ·
E:Nightshade; G:Rauer Nachtschatten · ⌠⅟
Z10 Ⓚ Ⓝ; trop. Afr., S-Afr.
– *diflorum* Vell. = Solanum capsicastrum
– **dulcamara** L. · E:Bittersweet Nightshade,
Woody Nightshade; F:Douce-amère,
Morelle; G:Bittersüßer Nachtschatten ·
♄ d ⚡ ～ Z6 VI-IX ⚡ ⚘ Ⓝ; Eur.*, TR,
Cauc., N-Iran, W-Sib., E-Sib., C-As.,
Afgh., Pakist., Him., NW-Afr., nat. in
N-Am.
– *duplosinuatum* Klotzsch = Solanum
dasyphyllum
– **erianthum** D. Don · E:Big Eggplant,
China Flower Leaf · ♄ ♄ Z10 Ⓚ VII-VIII;
Ind., SE-As., N-Austr., trop. Am., cult.
Trop., Subtrop., nat. in Subtrop. , Trop.
– **giganteum** Jacq. · E:African Holly · ♄ d
Z9 Ⓚ VII-VIII; Ind., Sri Lanka, S-Afr.
– **gilo** Raddi · ♄ Ⓝ; W-Afr., nat. in Braz.
– *goniocalyx* Juz. & Bukasov = Solanum
tuberosum
– **hispidum** Pers. · ♄ Z10 Ⓚ VII-IX; Mex.,
C-Am., Peru
– **incanum** L. · E:Bitter Apple · ♄ Ⓚ Ⓝ;
W-Sah, W-Afr., E-Afr., Ind.
– **integrifolium** Poir. · E:Chinese Scarlet
Eggplant · ☉ ⚭ Z10 Ⓚ VII-VIII; E-Afr.
– **jasminoides** Paxton · E:Potato Vine;
G:Jasmin-Nachtschatten · ♄ s ⚡ Z9 Ⓚ
II-XI; Braz.
– **laciniatum** Aiton · E:Kangaroo Apple;
G:Großer Känguruapfel · ♄ Z9 Ⓚ VIII-IX;
Austr.: N.S.Wales, Victoria, Tasman.; NZ
– *luteum* Mill. = Solanum villosum subsp.
villosum
– *lycopersicum* L. = Lycopersicon esculentum var. esculentum
– **macrocarpon** L. · ⌠⅟ Z10 Ⓚ Ⓝ; Madag.,

Mauritius, E-Afr.
- **mammosum** L. · E:Love Apple, Nipplefruit; G:Euter-Nachtschatten · ⚃ Z10 ⟨🏠⟩; Col., Ecuad.
- **marginatum** L. f. · E:Purple African Nightshade; G:Weißrandiger Nachtschatten · ♄ Z10 ⟨🏠⟩ VII-VIII; Eth.
- **mauritianum** Scop. · ♄ ♄ Z10 ⟨🏠⟩ VII-VIII; C-Am., S-Am., nat. in Subtrop., Trop.
- **melanocerasum** All. · E:Garden Huckleberry · ⊙ Z10; orig. ?, nat. in B, BrI, G, Swed
- **melongena** L. · E:Aubergine, Eggplant; G:Aubergine, Eierfrucht · ⊙ ⚃ ⚘ Z10 ⟨🏠⟩ VI-VII ⚥ Ⓝ; trop. Afr., Egypt, Arab., NW-Ind.
- **muricatum** L'Hér. ex Aiton · E:Melon Pear, Pepino; G:Melonenbirne, Pepino · ⚃ ♄ ⚘ Z9 ⟨🏠⟩ Ⓝ; cult.
- **nigrum** L. · E:Black Nightshade, Common Nightshade; G:Gewöhnlicher Schwarzer Nachtschatten · ⊙ VI-X ⚥ ⚘; Eur.*; cosmop.
- *nitidibaccatum* Bitter = Solanum physalifolium var. nitidibaccatum
- **pensile** Sendtn. · ♄ ⚥ Z10 ⟨🏠⟩ V-X; Amazon., Guyan.
- **phureja** Juz. & Bukasov · ⚃ Z9 ⟨🏠⟩ Ⓝ; cult., nat. in Col. Ecuad., Peru, N-Bol., Venez.
- **physalifolium** Rusby · G:Argentinischer Nachtschatten
- var. **nitidibaccatum** (Bitter) Edmonds · G:Glanzfrüchtiger Argentinischer Nachtschatten · VI-X ⚘; Arg., nat. in G, A
- var. **physalifolium** · G:Gewöhnlicher Argentinischer Nachtschatten · ⊙ ⚘; Arg.
- **pseudocapsicum** L. · E:Jerusalem Cherry, Madeira Winter cherry; G:Jerusalemkirsche · ♄ e ⚘ Z9 ⟨🏠⟩ ⛉ ⚘; Madeira
- **pyracanthum** Jacq. · ♄ d Z10 ⟨🏠⟩ VII-IX; trop. Afr., Madag.
- **quitoense** Lam. · E:Quito Orange; G:Naranjilla, Quito-Nachtschatten · ♄ Z9 ⟨🏠⟩ Ⓝ; Col., Ecuad., And., cult. C-Am.
- *racemigerum* (Lange) Zodda = Lycopersicon esculentum var. pimpinellifolium
- *rantonnetii* Carrière = Lycianthes rantonnetii
- **robustum** H. Wendl. · E:Shrubby Nightshade · ⚃ Z10 ⟨🏠⟩ VIII-IX; Braz.
- **rostratum** Dunal · E:Buffalo Bur, Horned

Nightshade; G:Stachel-Nachtschatten · ⊙ VI-IX; Can., USA* exc. NE; Mex., nat. in e. N-Am.
- **sarrachoides** Sendtn. · E:Hairy Nightshade; G:Saracho-Nachtschatten · ⊙ VI-IX; Braz., nat. in BrI, F, D
- **seaforthianum** Andrews · E:Brazilian Nightshade, Potato Creeper; G:Brazilianischer Nachtschatten · ♄ e ⚥ Z10 ⟨🏠⟩ ⟨🏠⟩ II-XI; C-Am., W.Ind.
- **sessiliflorum** Dunal · E:Cocona · ⚃ ⟨🏠⟩ Ⓝ; Amazon., Venez., Col., Ecuad., Peru
- **sisymbriifolium** Lam. · E:Sticky Nightshade, Viscid Nightshade; G:Klebriger Nachtschatten · ⊙ ⟨🏠⟩ VII-VIII ⚘; S-Am., nat. in USA: SC, SW, Calif.
- **sodomeum** L. · E:Sodom Apple · ♄ Z9 ⟨🏠⟩ ⚘; S-Afr., nat. in Eur.: Ib, Ital-P, Ba +; coasts
- **stenotomum** Juz. & Bukasov · ⚃ ⟨🏠⟩ Ⓝ; cult., nat. in S-Peru, Bol.
- **sublobatum** Willd. ex Roem. & Schult. · G:Zierlicher Nachtschatten · ⚃ VI-IX; se S-Am., nat. in sp., F, Sw
- **torvum** Sw. · E:Devil's Fig, Pea Eggplant; G:Teufels-Nachtschatten · ♄ Ⓝ; Trop.
- **triflorum** Nutt. · E:Cutleaf Nightshade; G:Dreiblütiger Nachtschatten · ⊙; Can.: W; USA: NW, Rocky Mts., SW, NC, nat. in BrI, B
- **tuberosum** L. · E:Potato; G:Kartoffel · ⚃ ⟨🏠⟩ VII-X ⚥ Ⓝ; cult., nat. in S-Am.
- **valdiviense** Dunal · ♄ d D Z10 ⟨🏠⟩ VII-VIII; Chile
- *verbascifolium* L. = Solanum erianthum
- **viarum** Dunal · Ⓝ; S-Am.
- **villosum** Mill. · G:Gelbfrüchtiger Nachtschatten
- subsp. **alatum** (Moench) Edmonds · G:Rotfrüchtiger Nachtschatten · VI-X ⚘; Eur.: Sw, G, A, EC-Eur.; TR
- subsp. **villosum** · G:Gelbfrüchtiger Nachtschatten · ⊙ VI-X ⚘; Eur.* exc. Sc; TR, Cauc., SW-As., Pakist., C-As., nat. in Sc
- *warscewiczii* Weick ex Lambertye = Solanum hispidum
- **wendlandii** Hook. f. · E:Costa Rican Nightshade, Potato Vine; G:Costa-Rica-Nachtschatten · ♄ d ⚥ Z10 ⟨🏠⟩ VI-VIII; Costa Rica

Soldanella L. -f- *Primulaceae* · 16 spp. · E:Snowbell; F:Soldanelle; G:Alpenglöckchen, Troddelblume

– *alpicola* F.K. Mey. = Soldanella pusilla subsp. alpicola
– **alpina** L.
– subsp. **alpina** · E:Alpine Snowbell; F:Soldanelle des Alpes; G:Gewöhnliche Alpen-Troddelblume · ⑭ △ Z5 IV-V ▽; Eur.: sp., F, C-Eur., I, Slove., Croatia, Bosn., YU, AL
– **carpatica** Vierh. · G:Karpaten-Troddelblume · ⑭ △ Z5 IV-V ▽; W-Carp.
– *dimoniei* Vierh. = Soldanella pindicola
– **hungarica** Simonk. · E:Hungarian Snowbell; G:Ungarische Troddelblume · ⑭ △ Z6 V ▽; Eur.: I, A, EC-Eur., Ba, E-Eur.
– **minima** Hoppe · G:Kleinste Troddelblume
– subsp. **austriaca** (Vierh.) Lüdi · G:Österreichische Troddelblume · ⑭ Z5 V-VII ▽; Eur.: A; Alp.
– subsp. **minima** · G:Kleinste Troddelblume · ⑭ △ Z6 V ▽; Eur.: I, G, A, Slove.; E-Alp., Apenn.
– **montana** Willd. · E:Mountain Tassel; F:Soldanelle des montagnes; G:Berg-Troddelblume · ⑭ △ Z6 V ▽; Eur.: C-Eur., EC-Eur., I, BG, E-Eur., nat. in FIN
– **pindicola** Hausskn. · G:Griechische Troddelblume · ⑭ △ Z6 IV-V ▽; NW-GR
– **pusilla** Baumg. · G:Zwerg-Troddelblume
– subsp. **alpicola** (F.K. Mey.) Chrtek · E:Dwarf Snowbell; G:Italienische Alpen-Troddelblume · ⑭ Z5 ▽; Eur.: C-Eur., I, Slove., Croatia, Maced., BG, RO
– **villosa** Darracq · G:Pyrenäen-Troddelblume · ⑭ △ Z6 IV-V ▽; Eur.: sp., F; W-Pyr.

Soleirolia Gaudich. -f- *Urticaceae* · 1 sp. · E:Baby's Tears, Mind your own Business; F:Helxine; G:Bubiköpfchen, Helxine
– **soleirolii** (Req.) Dandy · E:Angel's Tears, Baby's Tears, Irish Moss, Mind your own Business; G:Bubiköpfchen, Helxine · ⑭ ⤳ Z9 ⑭ ⑭; Eur.: Balear., Cors, Sard., I (islands), nat. in P, BrI, Fr

Solenanthus Ledeb. -m- *Boraginaceae* · c. 15 spp. · F:Bourrache géante; G:Riesenborretsch
– **apenninus** (L.) Fisch. & C.A. Mey. · G:Apenninen-Riesenborretsch · ☉ Z7 V-VII; Eur.: I, Sic., ? AL, ? GR

Solenomelus Miers -m- *Iridaceae* · 2 spp.

– **pedunculatus** (Gillies ex Hook.) Hochr. · ⑭ Z9 ⑭ VI; Chile
– **segetii** (Phil.) Kuntze · ⑭ Z9 ⑭ VI; Chile
– *sisyrinchium* (Griseb.) Pax = Solenomelus segetii

Solenopsis C. Presl -f- *Campanulaceae* · 7 spp.
– **laurentia** (L.) C. Presl · ⑭ ⑭ IV-VI; Eur.: Ib, Fr, Ital-P, Ba; TR, Syr., NW-Afr., nat. in GR, Crete
– **minuta** (L.) C. Presl · ⑭ △ ⑭ IV-VI; Eur.: Balear., Ital-P., Crete; Levant

Solenostemon Thonn. = Plectranthus
– *blumei* (Benth.) M. Gómez = Plectranthus scutellarioides
– *rotundifolius* (Poir.) J.K. Morton = Plectranthus rotundifolius
– *scutellarioides* (L.) Codd = Plectranthus scutellarioides
– *shirensis* (Gürke) Codd = Plectranthus autranii

Solidago L. -f- *Asteraceae* · c. 100 spp. · E:Goldenrod; F:Verge-d'or; G:Goldrute
– **arguta** Aiton · E:Atlantic Goldenrod ; G:Spitzige Goldrute · ⑭ VII-IX; Can.: Ont.; USA: NE, NCE, SE
– **caesia** L. · E:Wreath Goldenrod; F:Verge d'or bleuâtre; G:Blaustänglige Goldrute, Goldbandrute · ⑭ Z4 VIII-IX; Can.: E; USA: NE, NCE, SC, SE, Fla.
– **canadensis** L. · G:Kanadische Goldrute
– var. **canadensis** · E:Canada Goldenrod; G:Gewöhnliche Kandische Goldrute · ⑭ Z3 VIII-X; Can.: E, Sask.; USA: NE, NCE, NC, Rocky Mts., SW, nat. in Eur.* exc. Ital-P, Ba
– var. **scabra** (Muhl. ex Willd.) Torr. & A. Gray · G:Raue Kanadische Goldrute · ⑭ Z3; Can.: E, USA: NE, NEC, NC, SC, SE, Fla.
– **cutleri** Fernald · E:Cutler's Alpine Goldenrod; G:Cutlers Goldrute · ⑭ △ Z4 VII-IX; USA: NE
– **drummondii** Torr. & A. Gray · G:Drummonds Goldrute · ⑭ Z6 VIII-IX; USA: Ill., Mo., Ark., La.
– **flexicaulis** L. · E:Broad Leaved Goldenrod; G:Bogige Goldrute, Breitblättrige Goldrute · ⑭ Z4 VII-IX; Can.: E; USA: NE, NCE, NC, SE
– **gigantea** Aiton · E:Giant Goldenrod;

G:Riesen-Goldrute, Späte Goldrute · ♃ Z6 VIII-IX; Can., USA* exc. Calif., nat. in Eur.*
- **graminifolia** (L.) Salisb. · E:Fragrant Goldenrod; G:Grasblättrige Goldrute · ♃ ~ Z3 VII-IX; Can., USA: NE, NC, N.C., NCE, SC, SW, nat. in C-Eur.
- *latifolia* A. Gray = Solidago flexicaulis
- **missouriensis** Nutt. · E:Missouri Goldenrod; G:Missouri-Goldrute · ♃ Z7 VII-IX; Can.: B.C.; USA: NW, Rocky Mts., Calif., Ariz., nat. in N.J.
- **multiradiata** Aiton · E:Northern Groundsel, Rocky Mountain Goldenrod; G:Rocky-Mountain-Goldrute · ♃ △ Z2 VII-VIII; Alaska, Can., USA: NW, Calif., Rocky Mts., SW
- **nemoralis** Aiton · E:Gray Goldenrod; G:Graue Goldrute · ♃ Z3 VIII-IX; Can., USA: NE, NCE, NC, SC, SE
- **odora** Aiton · E:Sweet Goldenrod; G:Anis-Goldrute · ♃ D Z3 VII; USA: NE, NCE, SC, SE, Fla.
- **riddellii** Frank · E:Riddell's Goldenrod; G:Riddells Goldrute · ♃ ~ Z4 VIII-IX; Can.: Ont.; USA: NE, NCE,
- **rigida** L. · E:Stiff Goldenrod; G:Steife Goldrute · ♃ Z4 VIII-IX; Can.; USA: NE, NCE, NC, SC, SE, SW, Rocky Mts.
- **rugosa** Mill. · E:Rough Goldenrod; G:Raue Goldrute · ♃ Z3 VIII-IX; Can.: E; USA: NE, NCE, SC, SE, Fla.
- **sempervirens** L. · E:Seaside Goldenrod; G:Langlebige Goldrute · ♃ Z4; NE-Am., nat. in Azor.
- **shortii** Torr. & A. Gray · E:Short's Goldenrod; G:Königs-Goldrute · ♃ Z6 VII-VIII; USA: Ky.
- **virgaurea** L. · G:Gewöhnliche Goldrute
- subsp. *alpestris* (Willd.) Hayek = Solidago virgaurea subsp. minuta
- subsp. **minuta** (L.) Arcang. · G:Alpen-Goldrute · ♃ △ Z5 VII-IX; Eur.: N, mts.
- subsp. **virgaurea** · E:European Goldenrod; G:Gewöhnliche Goldrute · ♃ Z5 VII-IX ⚕; Eur.*, TR, Cauc., W-Sib., E-Sib., Amur, Sakhal., Kamchat., C-As, Him., China, Korea, Jap., NW-Afr.
- var. *alpina* Bigelow = Solidago cutleri
- var. *minutissima* Makino = Solidago virgaurea
- **Cultivars:**
- **many cultivars**

× **Solidaster** H.R. Wehrh. -m- *Asteraceae* · G:Goldrutenaster (*Aster* × *Solidago*)
- **luteus** M.L. Green ex Dress (*Aster ptarmicoides* × *Solidago sp.*) · G:Goldrutenaster · ♃ ✂ Z6 VII-IX; cult.

Solisia Britton & Rose = Mammillaria
- *pectinata* (Stein) Britton & Rose = Mammillaria pectinifera

Sollya Lindl. -f- *Pittosporaceae* · 3 spp.
- **heterophylla** Lindl. · E:Bluebell Creeper · ♄ e ≹ Z9 ⓚ VII; W-Austr.

Sonchus L. -m- *Asteraceae* · 62 spp. · E:Milk Thistle, Sow Thistle; F:Laiteron; G:Gänsedistel, Saudistel
- *alpinus* L. = Cicerbita alpina
- **arboreus** DC. · ♄ Z9 ⓚ IV-V; Canar.
- **arvensis** L. · E:Sow Thistle; G:Gewöhnliche Acker-Gänsedistel · ♃ VII-VIII; Eur.*, TR, Cauc., W-Sib., E-Sib., Amur, Sakhal., C-As., Mong., China, Korea, nat. in N-Am., Afr., Austr.
- **asper** (L.) Hill · E:Prickly Sow Thistle; G:Raue Gänsedistel · ⊙ VI-X; Eur.*, TR, Cauc., Iran, W-Sib., E-Sib., Amur, Sakhal., C-As., Him., China, Korea, Jap., nat. in N-Am.
- *macrophyllus* Willd. = Cicerbita macrophylla
- **oleraceus** L. · E:Milk Thistle, Sow Thistle; G:Kohl-Gänsedistel · ⊙ VI-X; Eur.*, TR, Cauc., N-As., Arab., N-Afr., Canar., nat. in cosmop.
- **palustris** L. · E:Marsh Sow Thistle; G:Sumpf-Gänsedistel · ♃ ~ VII-IX; Eur.* exc. Ib; TR, Cauc.
- *plumieri* L. = Cicerbita plumieri

Sonerila Roxb. -f- *Melastomataceae* · c. 170 spp.
- **margaritacea** Lindl. · ♄ Z10 ⓦ X-XI; Java

Sonneratia L. f. -f- *Sonneratiaceae* · 6 spp. · F:Sonnératia; G:Sonneratie
- **caseolaris** (L.) Engl. · ♄ ~ ⓦ Ⓝ; Malay. Pen., Kalimantan; mangrove

Sophora L. -f- *Fabaceae* · 52 spp. · F:Sophora; G:Schnurbaum
- **davidii** (Franch.) Skeels · G:Wickenblättriger Schnurbaum · ♄ d Z6 VI; W-China
- **flavescens** Aiton · ♃ d Z6 ⚕; China, Sib., Korea, Jap.
- *japonica* L. = Styphnolobium japonicum

- **microphylla** Aiton · ♄ ♄ e Z8 Ⓐ II-III; NZ
- **mollis** (Royle) Graham ex Baker ·
  G:Weicher Schnurbaum · ♄ d Z8 Ⓐ;
  Him.
- **prostrata** Buchanan · G:Niederliegender
  Schnurbaum · ♄ e Z8 Ⓐ; NZ
- **secundiflora** (Ortega) Lag. ex DC. ·
  E:Mescal Bean; G:Texas-Schnurbaum · ♄
  e Z8 Ⓐ; Tex., N.Mex.; N-Mex.
- **tetraptera** J.S. Muell. · E:Kowhai;
  G:Neuseeländischer Schnurbaum,
  Vierflügeliger Schnurbaum · ♄ ♄ e Z8 Ⓐ
  IV; NZ, Lord Howe Is.
- var. *microphylla* (Aiton) Hook. f. =
  Sophora microphylla
- *viciifolia* Hance = Sophora davidii

× **Sophrocattleya** hort. -f- *Orchidaceae*
(*Cattleya* × *Sophronitis*)

× **Sophrolaelia** hort. -f- *Orchidaceae*
(*Laelia* × *Sophronitis*)

× **Sophrolaeliocattleya** hort.
-f- *Orchidaceae* (*Cattleya* × *Laelia* ×
Sophronitis)

Sophronitella Schltr. = Isabelia
- *violacea* (Lindl.) Schltr. = Isabelia
  violacea

Sophronitis Lindl. -f- *Orchidaceae* · 58 spp.
- **cernua** Lindl. · ⒉ Z10 Ⓐ XI-I ▽ ✳; Braz.
- **cinnabarina** (Bateman ex Lindl.) Van
  den Berg & M.W. Chase · ⒉ Z10 Ⓐ II-V
  ▽ ✳; Braz.
- **coccinea** (Lindl.) Rchb. f. · ⒉ Z10 Ⓐ XI-II
  ▽ ✳; Braz.
- **crispa** (Lindl.) Van den Berg & M.W.
  Chase · ⒉ Z10 Ⓐ VII-VIII ▽ ✳; Braz.: Rio
  de Janeiro, Minas Gerais
- **crispata** (Thunb.) Van den Berg & M.W.
  Chase · ⒉ Z10 Ⓐ ▽ ✳; Braz.
- **dayana** (Rchb. f.) Van den Berg & M.W.
  Chase
- *grandiflora* Lindl. = Sophronitis coccinea
- **grandis** (Lindl. & Paxton) Van den Berg
  & M.W. Chase · ⒉ Z10 Ⓐ ▽ ✳; Braz.
- **harpophylla** (Rchb. f.) Van den Berg &
  M.W. Chase · ⒉ Z10 Ⓐ II-III ▽ ✳; Braz.:
  Espirito Santo, Minas Gerais
- **jongheana** (Rchb. f.) Van den Berg &
  M.W. Chase · ⒉ Z10 Ⓐ II-IV ▽ ✳; Braz.:
  Minas Gerais
- **lobata** (Lindl.) Van den Berg & M.W.

Chase · ⒉ Z10 Ⓐ IV-V ▽ ✳; Braz.: Rio de
Janeiro, Sao Paulo
- **longipes** (Rchb. f.) Van den Berg & M.W.
  Chase · ⒉ Z10 Ⓐ VII ▽ ✳; SE-Braz.
- **lundii** (Rchb. f. & Warm.) Van den Berg
  & M.W. Chase · ⒉ Z10 Ⓐ ▽ ✳; Braz.
- **milleri** (Blumensch. ex Pabst) Van den
  Berg & M.W. Chase · ⒉ Z10 Ⓐ V-VI ▽ ✳;
  Braz.: Minas Gerais
- **perrinii** (Lindl.) Van den Berg & M.W.
  Chase · ⒉ Z10 Ⓐ IX-X ▽ ✳; Braz.
- **pumila** (Hook.) Van den Berg & M.W.
  Chase · ⒉ Z10 Ⓐ IX-X ▽ ✳; Braz.
- **purpurata** (Lindl. & Paxton) Van den
  Berg & M.W. Chase · ⒉ Z10 Ⓐ V-VI ▽ ✳;
  Braz.
- **tenebrosa** (Rolfe) Van den Berg & M.W.
  Chase · ⒉ Z10 Ⓐ V-VI ▽ ✳; Braz.: Bahia,
  Espirito Santo
- *violacea* Lindl. = Isabelia violacea

Sorbaria (Ser. ex DC.) A. Braun
-f- *Rosaceae* · 9 spp. · E:False Spiraea;
F:Sorbaria; G:Fiederspiere
- **arborea** C.K. Schneid. · G:Chinesische
  Fiederspiere · ♄ d Z6 VII; C-China
- **assurgens** M. Vilm. & Bois ·
  G:Afghanische Fiederspiere · ♄ d Z6
  VII-VIII; Afgh., Pakist., Kashmir
- **grandiflora** (Sweet) Maxim. · G:Groß-
  blütige Fiederspiere · ♄ d △ Z5 VII; E-Sib.
- **kirilowii** (Regel) Maxim. · G:Baum-
  Fiederspiere · ♄ d Z6 VII; C-China.
- **sorbifolia** (L.) A. Braun · E:False Spiraea;
  G:Sibirische Fiederspiere
- var. **sorbifolia** · ♄ d Z3 VI-VII; W-Sib.,
  E-Sib., Amur, Sakhal., Kamchat., Mong.,
  Manch., Korea, Jap., nat. in USA: NE
- var. **stellipila** Maxim. · ♄ d Z2; Jap.,
  Korea
- **tomentosa** (Lindl.) Rehder
- var. **angustifolia** (Wenz.) Rahn ·
  E:Kashmir False Spiraea; G:Afghanische
  Fiederspiere, Kaschmir-Fiederspiere · ♄ d
  Z6 VII-VIII; Afgh., Pakist., Kashmir
- var. **tomentosa** · E:Himalaya False
  Spiraea; G:Himalaya-Fiederspiere · ♄ d
  Z8 ∧ VI-VIII; C-As., Afgh., Pakist., Him.

× **Sorbaronia** C.K. Schneid. -f- *Rosaceae* ·
G:Strauchebeeresche (*Aronia* × *Sorbus*)
- **alpina** (Willd.) C.K. Schneid. (*Aronia
  arbutifolia* × *Sorbus aria*) · ♄ ♄ d Z5 V;
  cult.
- **dippelii** (Zabel) C.K. Schneid. (*Aronia*

melanocarpa × *Sorbus aria*) · ħ ħ d Z5; cult.
- **fallax** (C.K. Schneid.) C.K. Schneid. (*Aronia melanocarpa* × *Sorbus aucuparia*) · ħ ħ d Z5; cult.
- **hybrida** (Moench) C.K. Schneid. (*Aronia arbutifolia* × *Sorbus aucuparia*) · ħ ħ d Z5; cult.
- **sorbifolia** (Poir.) C.K. Schneid. (*Aronia melanocarpa* × *Sorbus americana*) · ħ ħ d Z5; cult.

× **Sorbocotoneaster** Pojark. -f- *Rosaceae* · G:Mispeleberesche (*Cotoneaster* × *Sorbus*)
- **pozdnjakovii** Pojark. (*Cotoneaster laxiflorus* × *Sorbus aria*) · ħ d Z3; cult.

× **Sorbopyrus** C.K. Schneid. -f- *Rosaceae* · G:Hagebuttenbirne (*Sorbus* × *Pyrus*)
- **auricularis** (Knoop) C.K. Schneid. (*Pyrus communis* × *Sorbus aria*) · E:Bollwyller Pear; G:Hagebuttenbirne · ħ d Z5 IV-V; cult.

Sorbus L. -f- *Rosaceae* · 193 spp. · E:Mountain Ash, Whitebeam; F:Alisier, Alouchier, Cormier, Sorbier; G:Eberesche, Elsbeere, Mehlbeere, Speierling, Vogelbeere
- **alnifolia** (Siebold & Zucc.) K. Koch
- var. **alnifolia** · E:Korean Mountain Ash; F:Alisier à feuilles d'aulne; G:Erlenblättrige Mehlbeere · ħ d ⊛ Z6 V-VI; China, Amur, Manch., Korea, Jap.
- var. **submollis** Rehder · ħ d Z6; Jap., Korea, Mandsch., China, Amur
- × **ambigua** Michalet (*S. aria* × *S. chamaemespilus*) · G:Filzige Zwerg-Mehlbeere · d; Eur.: F, I, Sw, G, A, Ba, RO
- **americana** Marshall · E:American Mountain Ash; F:Sorbier d'Amérique; G:Amerikanische Eberesche · ħ ħ d ⌒ ⊛ Z2 V-VI; Can.: E; USA; NE, NCE, SE
- *arbutifolia* (L.) Heynh. = Aronia arbutifolia var. arbutifolia
- **aria** (L.) Crantz · E:Whitebeam; F:Alisier blanc, Alouchier; G:Gewöhnliche Mehlbeere · ħ ħ d Z5 V Ⓝ; Eur.* exc. Sc; NW-Afr.
- × **arnoldiana** Rehder (*S. aucuparia* × *S. discolor*) · G:Arnolds Eberesche · ħ d Z6; cult.
- **arranensis** Hedl. · ħ d Z6; W-ScotlanG:

Arran
- **aucuparia** L. · G:Vogelbeere
- subsp. **aucuparia** · E:Mountain Ash, Rowan; F:Sorbier des oiseleurs; G:Gewöhnliche Eberesche, Gewöhnliche Vogelbeere · ħ ħ d ⊛ Z3 V-VI ☦ Ⓝ; Eur.*, TR, Cauc., W-Sib.
- subsp. **moravica** (Zengerl.) Á. Löve · F:Sorbier des oiseleurs; G:Süße Eberesche · ħ d ⊛ Z3 V Ⓝ; Eur.: CZ; cult.
- var. *edulis* Dieck = Sorbus aucuparia subsp. moravica
- **austriaca** (Beck) Hedl. · G:Österreichische Mehlbeere · ħ ħ d Z6 V-VI; Eur.: A, EC-Eur., Ba, RO, W-Russ.; E-Alp., Carp., Balkan
- × **carpatica** Borbás (*S. aria* × *S. austriaca*) · G:Karpaten-Mehlbeere · d; Eur.: A, Slova., Ba, RO
- **cashmiriana** Hedl. · E:Kashmir Rowan; F:Sorbier du Cachemire; G:Himalaya-Eberesche · ħ d ⊛ Z6 V; Afgh., Kashmir
- **chamaemespilus** (L.) Crantz · G:Zwerg-Mehlbeere; E:False Medlar; F:Alisier nain · ħ d Z5 VI-VII; Eur.: BrI, Sc
- **commixta** Hedl. · E:Chinese Scarlet Rowan; F:Sorbier du Japon; G:Japanische Eberesche · ħ d Z6 VI; Jap., Sakhal.
- **danubialis** (Jáv.) Kárpáti · G:Donau-Mehlbeere · ħ d V; Eur.: C-Eur., EC-Eur., RO, W-Russ., ? Ba
- **decora** (Sarg.) C.K. Schneid. · E:Northern Mountain Ash; G:Labrador-Eberesche · ħ ħ d ⊛ Z3 V; Can.: E; USA: NE, NCE; Greenl.
- **discolor** (Maxim.) Maxim. · E:Snowberry Mountain Ash; G:Verschiedenfarbige Eberesche · ħ d ⊛ Z6 V; N-China
- **domestica** L. · E:Service Tree; F:Cormier; G:Speierling · ħ d Z6 V-VI ☦ Ⓝ; Eur.* exc. BrI, Sc; TR, Cauc., Moroc., Alger.
- f. **pomifera** (Hayne) Rehder Z6; cult.
- f. **pyriformis** (Hayne) Rehder Z6; cult.
- **dubia** Hedl. · d; orig. ?
- **epidendron** Hand.-Mazz. · ħ ħ d Z6 V; W-China
- *erubescens* A. Kern. ex Dippel = Sorbus × ambigua
- **esserteauana** Koehne · G:Esserteaus Eberesche · ħ ħ d ⊛ Z6 V; W-China
- **folgneri** (C.K. Schneid.) Rehder · E:Folgner's Whitebeam; G:Chinesische Mehlbeere · ħ ħ d ⊛ Z6 V; C-China

- **gracilis** (Siebold & Zucc.) K. Koch ·
  G:Zierliche Mehlbeere · ♄ d Z6 V; Jap.
- **graeca** (Spach) Lodd. ex S. Schauer ·
  G:Griechische Mehlbeere · ♄ ♄ d Z6 V;
  Eur.: Ital-P, C-Eur., EC-Eur., Ba, RO,
  Crim; TR, Cauc.
- × **hostii** (J. Jacq. ex Host) Hedl. (*S.
  austriaca × S. chamaemespilus*) · ♄ d ⊛
  Z6 V; Eur.: A, Slova; Alp., N-Carp.
- **hupehensis** C.K. Schneid.
- var. **hupehensis** · G:Weißfrüchtige
  Hupeh-Eberesche · ♄ d ⊛ Z6 V; W-China,
  C-China
- var. **obtusa** C.K. Schneid. · G:Rosa-
  früchtige Hupeh-Eberesche · ♄ d Z6;
  China: Hupeh
- × **hybrida** L. (*S. aucuparia × S.
  intermedia*) · E:Hybrid Mountain Ash;
  F:Alisier de Finlande; G:Bastard-
  Mehlbeere · ♄ d ⊛ Z5 V-VI; Eur.: Sc
- **intermedia** (Ehrh.) Pers. · E:Swedish
  Whitebeam; F:Alisier de Suède;
  G:Schwedische Mehlbeere · ♄ ♄ d Z5 V
  Ⓝ; Eur.: Sc, G, PL, Balt.
- **japonica** (Decne.) Hedl. · ♄ d Z6 V; Jap.,
  Korea
- **javorkae** (Soó) Kárpáti · d; EC-Eur.
- **koehneana** C.K. Schneid. · G:Weiß-
  früchtige Eberesche · ♄ d ⊛ Z5 V;
  C-China
- **latifolia** (Lam.) Pers. · E:Service Tree
  of Fontainebleau; F:Alisier de Fontainebleau; G:Breitblättrige Mehlbeere · ♄ d
  ⊛ Z5 V-VI; Eur.: P, sp., F, G, nat. in Swed
- **megalocarpa** Rehder · ♄ d ⊛ Z6 V;
  N-China
- × **meinichii** (Lindeb.) Hedl. (*S. aria × S.
  aucuparia*) · ♄ d Z5; S-Norw.
- *melanocarpa* (Michx.) Heynh. = Aronia
  melanocarpa var. melanocarpa
- **minima** (H. Lév.) Hedl. · ♄ d Z6 V-VI;
  Engl., Wales
- **mougeotii** Soy.-Will. · E:Pyrenean
  Whitebeam; F:Alisier de Mougeot;
  G:Vogesen-Mehlbeere · ♄ ♄ d Z5 V;
  Eur.: sp., F, Sw, I; Pyr., Alp., Jura, Vosges
- *nepalensis* hort. = Sorbus vestita
- × **pannonica** Kárpáti (*S. aria × S.
  graeca*) · G:Pannonische Mehlbeere · ♄ ♄
  d; Eur.: G, A, EC-Eur., ? RO
- **pluripinnata** (C.K. Schneid.) Koehne · ♄
  ♄ d Z6 V; W-China
- **pohuashanensis** (Hance) Hedl. ·
  G:Pohuasha-Eberesche · ♄ d Z5 V;
  N-China

- **prattii** Koehne
- f. **subarachnoidea** (Koehne) Rehder Z6;
  China: W-Sichuan
- var. **prattii** · F:Alisier de Pratt; G:Pratts
  Eberesche · ♄ d ⊛ Z6 V; W-China
- **pseudothuringiaca** Düll · G:Hersbrucker
  Mehlbeere · ♄ d; Eur.: D
- **reducta** Diels · E:Creeping Mountain
  Ash, Pygmy Rowan; G:Zwerg-Eberesche ·
  ♄ d △ Z6; China: Burma, W-China
- **rufoferruginea** (C.K. Schneid.) C.K.
  Schneid. · ♄ ♄ d Z6 VI; Jap.
- **rupicola** (Syme) Hedl. · ♄ d Z6; BrI,
  S-Sc, Estland
- **sambucifolia** (Cham. & Schltdl.) M.
  Roem. · G:Hollunderblättrige Eberesche ·
  ♄ d ⊛ VI; Jap., Sakhal., Kamchat.
- **sargentiana** Koehne · F:Saule de
  Sargent; G:Sargents Eberesche · ♄ d ⊛
  Z6 V; W-China
- **scalaris** Koehne · F:Saule scalariforme;
  G:Leitern-Eberesche · ♄ ♄ d ⊛ Z5 V-VI;
  W-China
- × **schinzii** Düll (*S. chamaemespilus × S.
  mougeotii*) · G:Schinzs Mehlbeere · ♄ d;
  Eur.: Sw, G, A
- **simonkaiana** Kárpáti · ♄ d; H
- × **thuringiaca** (Ilse) Fritsch (*S. aria ×
  S. aucuparia*) · E:Bastard Service Tree,
  Checker Tree; G:Thüringer Mehlbeere · ♄
  d Z5 V; Eur.: F, Sw, G, A, CZ
- **tianschanica** Rupr. · ♄ d ⊛ Z6 VI; C-As.,
  China: Sinkiang
- *toringo* Siebold = Malus toringo
- **torminalis** (L.) Crantz · E:Wild Service
  Tree; F:Alisier torminal; G:Elsbeere · ♄ d
  ⊛ Z6 V Ⓝ; Eur.*, TR, Cyprus, Lebanon,
  Syr., Cauc., N-Iran, Moroc., Alger.
- *trilobata* (Poir.) Heynh. = Malus trilobata
- **umbellata** (Desf.) Fritsch · G:Schirm-
  Mehlbeere · ♄ ♄ d Z6; Eur.: Ba, RO, Crim;
  Cyprus, TR, Syr., Lebanon, Palest., Cauc.,
  Iran
- var. *cretica* C.K. Schneid. = Sorbus graeca
- × **vagensis** Wilmott (*S. aria × S.
  torminalis*) · ♄ d; GB
- **vestita** (G. Don) Lodd. · ♄ d V; Him.,
  N-Burma
- **vilmorinii** C.K. Schneid. · E:Vilmorin
  Mountain Ash; F:Saule de Vilmorin;
  G:Rosafrüchtige Eberesche, Vilmorins
  Eberesche · ♄ ♄ d ⊛ Z6 VI; W-China
- **zahlbruckneri** C.K. Schneid. · ♄ d ⊛ Z6
  V; China
- **Cultivars:**

– **many cultivars**

Sorghastrum Nash -n- *Poaceae* · 17 spp. ·
E:Indian Grass; F:Faux-sorgho;
G:Indianergras
– *avenaceum* (Michx.) Nash = Sorghastrum
nutans
– **nutans** (L.) Nash · E:Yellow Indian
Grass; G:Gelbes Indianergras · ⚄ Z5;
Can.: E; USA: NE, NCE, NC, Rocky Mts.,
SW, SC, SE, Fla.; Mex.

Sorghum Moench -n- *Poaceae* · 24 spp. ·
E:Millet; F:Gros millet, Sorgho; G:Moh-
renhirse, Sorghumhirse
– **almum** Parodi · E:Columbus Grass;
G:Kolumbusgras · ⚄ Ⓝ; Arg., nat. in
Austr.
– **bicolor** (L.) Moench
– var. **arduinii** (Körn.) Snowden · ⚇ Z8 Ⓝ;
cult.
– var. **bicolor** · E:Great Millet, Kafir Corn,
Sorghum; G:Gewöhnliche Mohrenhirse ·
⚇ Z8 VII-IX; ? Afr., ? S-As.
– **caffrorum** (Retz.) P. Beauv. · E:Kafir
Corn; G:Kaffern-Mohrenhirse · ⚇ Ⓝ; cult.
– **caudatum** (Hack.) Stapf · E:Feterita · Ⓝ;
Afr.
– **cernuum** (Ard.) Host · E:White Durra;
G:Nickende Mohrenhirse · ⚇ Ⓝ; cult.
– **dochna** (Forssk.) Snowden · G:Zucker-
hirse · ⚇ Ⓝ; cult.
– **durra** (Forssk.) Stapf · E:Brown Durra ·
⚇ Ⓝ; cult.
– **guineense** Stapf · Ⓝ; W-Afr., Sudan
– **halepense** (L.) Pers. · E:Aleppo Grass,
Great Millet, Johnson Grass, Means
Grass; G:Aleppohirse, Wilde Mohrenhirse · ⚄ Z7 VI-VII Ⓝ; TR, Cauc., Levant,
W-As., Ind., C-As., Malay. Arch., N-Afr.,
Austr., N-Am., Mex., W.Ind., S-Am., nat.
in Eur.: sp, F, Sw, Ital-P, EC-Eur., Ba,
RO; cosmop.
– **nervosum** Besser ex Schult. · ⚇ Ⓝ; orig.
?; cult E-As.
– **nigricans** (Ruiz & Pav.) Snowden · ⚇ Ⓝ;
cult.
– *vulgare* Pers. = Sorghum bicolor var.
bicolor
– var. *angolense* Rendle = Sorghum
nigricans
– var. *caffrorum* (Retz.) F.T. Hubb. &
Rehder = Sorghum caffrorum
– var. *durra* (Forssk.) F.T. Hubb. & Rehder
= Sorghum durra

– var. *saccharatum* (Moench) Boerl. =
Sorghum dochna

Sparaxis Ker-Gawl. -f- *Iridaceae* · 15 spp. ·
E:Harlequinflower; F:Fleur arlequin,
Sparaxis; G:Fransenschwertel
– **bulbifera** (L.) Ker-Gawl. · ⚄ ✂ Z9 ⓚ V;
SW-Cape
– **grandiflora** (F. Delaroche) Ker-Gawl. ·
E:Harlequin Flower; G:Großblütiges
Fransenschwertel · ⚄ ✂ Z9 ⓚ IV-V;
SW-Cape
– **tricolor** (Schneev.) Ker-Gawl. ·
E:Harlequin Flower; G:Dreifarbiges
Fransenschwertel · ⚄ ✂ Z9 ⓚ VI-VII;
SW-Cape

Sparganium L. -n- *Sparganiaceae* · 21 sp. ·
E:Burr Reed; F:Rubanier, Sparganier;
G:Igelkolben
– **angustifolium** Michx. · E:Narrowleaf
Burr Reed; G:Schmalblättriger Igelkol-
ben · ⚄ ≈ VI-VIII; Eur.*, Sib., Kamchat.,
N-Am.
– **emersum** Rehmann · E:Simple Stem Bur
Reed; F:Rubanier simple; G:Einfacher
Igelkolben · ⚄ ≈ Z5 VI-VII; Eur.*, TR,
As., Malay. Arch., N-Am.
– **erectum** L. · E:Bur Reed; F:Ruban d'eau;
G:Gewöhnlicher Ästiger Igelkolben · ⚄
⌢ Z6 VI-VIII; Eur.*, TR, Cauc., W-Iran,
Sib., N-Afr.
– *minimum* Wallr. = Sparganium natans
– **natans** L. · E:Small Burr Reed; G:Zwerg-
Igelkolben · ⚄ ≈ Z2 VII-VIII; Eur.*, TR,
N-As., N-Am.
– *ramosum* Huds. = Sparganium erectum
– *simplex* Huds. = Sparganium emersum

Sparrmannia L. f. -f- *Tiliaceae* · 3 spp. ·
E:African Hemp; F:Tilleul d'appartement;
G:Zimmerlinde
– **africana** L. f. · E:African Hemp; G:Echte
Zimmerlinde · ♄ e Z10 ⓚ I-III; S-Afr.
– **ricinicarpa** (Eckl. & Zeyh.) Kuntze ·
G:Rhizinusfrüchtige Zimmerlinde · ♄ e
Z10 ⓚ VI-VIII; S-Afr.

Spartina Schreb. -f- *Poaceae* · 17 spp. ·
E:Cord Grass, Marsh Grass; F:Spartina;
G:Schlickgras
– **anglica** C.E. Hubb. · E:Common Cord
Grass; G:Englisches Schlickgras · ⚄ ⌢
VII-VIII; Eur.: BrI, nat. in Fr, G, DK
– *aureomarginata* hort. = Spartina

pectinata
- **maritima** (Curtis) Fernald · E:Small Cord
Grass; G:Niederes Schlickgras · ⑭ ⁓ ;
Eur.: Fr, BrI, Ib, Slove.; N-Afr., S-Afr.,
N-Am.; coasts
- *michauxiana* Hitchc. = Spartina pectinata
- **pectinata** Bosc ex Link · E:Prairie Cord
Grass; G:Kamm-Schlickgras · ⑭ ⁓ Z5
IX-X; Can., USA* exc. Calif.
- × **townsendii** H. Groves & J. Groves (*S.
anglica × S. maritima*) · E:Townsend's
Cord Grass; G:Townsends Schlickgras · ⑭
⁓ VII-X; Eur.: BrI, Fr; coasts

Spartium L. -n- *Fabaceae* · 1 sp. · E:Spanish
Broom; F:Genêt d'Espagne, Sparte;
G:Binsenginster, Pfriemenginster
- **junceum** L. · E:Spanish Broom;
G:Binsenginster, Pfriemenginster · ♄ d Z8
ⓐ ∧ V-IX ✹; Eur.: Ib, Fr, Ital-P, Ba; TR,
Syr., Palest., Cauc., NW-Afr., Libya, nat.
in Crim

Spartocytisus Webb & Berthel. = Cytisus
- *filipes* Webb & Berthel. = Cytisus filipes

Spathicarpa Hook. -f- *Araceae* · 4 spp.
- **hastiifolia** Hook. · ⑭ Z10 ⓦ I-XII;
S-Braz., Parag., Arg.
- *sagittifolia* Schott = Spathicarpa hastiifolia

Spathiphyllum Schott -n- *Araceae* ·
45 spp. · E:Peace Lily, Spathe Flower;
F:Spathyphyllum; G:Blattfahne,
Scheidenblatt
- **blandum** Schott · ⑭ Z10 ⓦ; W.Ind.,
Surinam
- **cannifolium** (Dryand. ex Sims) Schott ·
E:Spatheflower; G:Canna-Blattfahne · ⑭
Z10 ⓦ; Col., Venez., Guyan.
- **cochlearispathum** (Liebm.) Engl. · ⑭
Z10 ⓦ; S-Mex., Guat.
- **commutatum** Schott · ⑭ Z10 ⓦ; Malay.
Arch., Phil.
- **floribundum** (Linden & André) N.E.
Br. · E:Snow Flower; G:Reichblühende
Blattfahne · ⑭ Z10 ⓦ ✹; Col.
- **ortgiesii** Regel · ⑭ Z10 ⓦ; Mex.
- **patinii** (R. Hogg) N.E. Br. · ⑭ Z10 ⓦ;
Col.
- **phryniifolium** Schott · ⑭ Z10 ⓦ; Costa
Rica, Panama
- **wallisii** Regel · E:Peace Lily; G:Zwerg-
Blattfahne · ⑭ Z10 ⓦ; Col., Venez.

Spathodea P. Beauv. -f- *Bignoniaceae* ·
1 sp. · E:African Tulip Tree; F:Tulipier
africain; G:Afrikanischer Tulpenbaum
- **campanulata** P. Beauv. · E:African Tulip
Tree; G:Afrikanischer Tulpenbaum · ♄ e
Z10 ⓦ; trop. Afr.
- *nilotica* Seem. = Spathodea campanulata

Spathoglottis Blume -f- *Orchidaceae* ·
46 spp.
- **aurea** Lindl. · ⑭ Z10 ⓦ V ▽ ✹; Malay.
Pen.
- *fortunei* Lindl. = Spathoglottis pubescens
- **kimballiana** Hook. f. · ⑭ Z10 ⓦ IV-V ▽
✹; Kalimantan
- **plicata** Blume · E:Philippine Ground
Orchid · ⑭ Z10 ⓦ IV-V ▽ ✹; Ind., SE-As.,
Malay. Arch., Phil., N.Guinea
- **pubescens** Lindl. · ⑭ Z10 ⓦ I ▽ ✹;
China (Hong Kong)
- *vieillardii* Rchb. f. = Spathoglottis plicata

Specklinia Lindl. -f- *Orchidaceae* · 81 sp.
- **grobyi** (Bateman ex Lindl.) F. Barros ·
⑭ Z10 ⓦ VII ▽ ✹; Mex., W.Ind., C-Am.,
S-Am.
- **tribuloides** (Sw.) Pridgeon & M.W.
Chase · ⑭ Z10 ⓦ ▽ ✹; Mex., C-Am.,
Cuba, Jamaica

Specularia Heist. ex A. DC. = Legousia
- *pentagonia* (L.) A. DC. = Legousia
pentagonia
- *speculum-veneris* (L.) A. DC. = Legousia
speculum-veneris

Speirantha Baker -f- *Convallariaceae* · 1 sp.
- *convallarioides* Baker = Speirantha
gardenii
- **gardenii** (Hook.) Baill. · ⑭ Z8 ∧ V-VI;
E-China

Spenceria Trimen -f- *Rosaceae* · 2 spp.
- **ramalana** Trimen · ⑭ Z6 VII-VIII;
W-China

Spergula L. -f- *Caryophyllaceae* · 6 spp. ·
E:Spurrey; F:Spergule; G:Spark, Spergel
- **arvensis** L. · G:Acker-Spark, Acker-
Spergel
  - subsp. **arvensis** · E:Corn Spurrey;
G:Gewöhnlicher Acker-Spark · ⊙ ☉ VI-X;
Eur.*; cosmop. exc. trop. Afr.
  - subsp. **sativa** Čelak. · G:Saat-Acker-
Spark · ⊙ VI-X ⓝ; cult.

– **morisonii** Boreau · G:Frühlings-Spergel, Frühlings-Spark · ☉ IV-VI; Eur.: Ib, Fr, C-Eur., Sc, EC-Eur., E-Eur.; Alger.
– **pentandra** L. · G:Fünfmänniger Spergel, Fünfmänniger Spark · ☉ IV-V; Eur.: Ib, Fr, Ital-P, Ba, C-Eur., EC-Eur., RO; TR, SW-As., N-Afr.

Spergularia (Pers.) J. Presl & C. Presl -f- Caryophyllaceae · 25-40 spp. · E:Sand Spurrey, Sea Spurrey; F:Spergulaire; G:Schuppenmiere
– **echinosperma** (Čelak.) Asch. & Graebn. · G:Igelsamige Schuppenmiere · ⚃ VI-X; Eur.: G, A, CZ, PL, Slove.
– **media** (L.) C. Presl · G:Flügel-Schuppenmiere, Flügelsamige Schuppenmiere · ⚃ VII-IX; Eur.*, TR, Levant, N-Afr.
– **rubra** (L.) J. Presl & C. Presl · E:Sand Spurrey; G:Rote Schuppenmiere · ☉ ☉ ⚃ V-IX; Eur.*, Cauc., W-Sib., E-Sib., Amur, Sakhal., Kamchat., C-As.
– **salina** J. Presl & C. Presl · G:Salz-Schuppenmiere · ☉ V-IX; Eur.*, Levant, Cauc., W-Sib., E-Sib. Amur, Sakhal., C-As., Mong, China: Sinkiang; E-As., N-Afr., N-Am., S-Am., NZ
– **segetalis** (L.) G. Don · G:Saat-Schuppenmiere, Saatmiere · ☉ VI-VII; Eur.: Ib, F, C-Eur., PL; Moroc.

Sphaeralcea A. St.-Hil. -f- Malvaceae · c. 60 spp. · E:False Mallow, Globe Mallow; F:Sphéralcée; G:Kugelmalve
– acerifolia Nutt. ex Torr. & A. Gray = Sphaeralcea rivularis
– **bonariensis** (Cav.) Griseb. · ♄ Z9 ⌂ VII-IX; S-Am.
– cisplatina A. St.-Hil. = Sphaeralcea bonariensis
– **fendleri** A. Gray · E:Fendler Globe Mallow; G:Fendlers Kugelmalve · ♄ e Z4; USA: Colo., SW, Tex..; N-Mex.
– **munroana** (Douglas ex Lindl.) Spach · E:Orange Globe Mallow; G:Monroes Kugelmalve · ⚃ ⌂ VI-IX; B.C., USA: NW, N-Calif.
– **rivularis** (Hook.) Torr. ex A. Gray · E:Mountain Hollyhock; G:Bach-Kugelmalve · ⚃ ⌂ VI-IX; Can.: B.C.; USA: Rocky Mts., N.Mex.
– umbellata (Cav.) G. Don = Phymosia umbellata

Sphaerocionium C. Presl

-n- Hymenophyllaceae · c. 80 spp.
– hirsutum (L.) C. Presl = Hymenophyllum hirsutum

Sphaerogyne Naudin = Tococa
– cinnamomea Linden = Tococa neocinnamomea

Sphaeropteris Bernh. = Cyathea
– cooperi (F. Muell.) R.M. Tryon = Cyathea cooperi
– insignis (D.C. Eaton) R.M. Tryon = Cyathea insignis
– medullaris (G. Forst.) Bernh. = Cyathea medullaris

Sphalmanthus N.E. Br. = Phyllobolus
– dinteri (L. Bolus) L. Bolus = Phyllobolus melanospermus
– oculatus (N.E. Br.) N.E. Br. = Phyllobolus oculatus
– resurgens (Kensit) L. Bolus = Phyllobolus resurgens
– salmoneus (Haw.) N.E. Br. = Phyllobolus canaliculatus

Sphenostylis E. Mey. -f- Fabaceae · 7 spp. · E:Yam Pea; G:Knollenbohne
– **stenocarpa** (Hochst.) Harms · E:African Yam Bean; G:Afrikanische Knollenbohne · ⚃ ⚇ Ⓝ; Afr.

Spigelia L. -f- Loganiaceae · c. 50 spp. · E:Pink Root, Worm Grass; F:Spigélia; G:Amerikanische Nelkenwurz, Spigelie
– **anthelmia** L. · E:Pink Rouge of Demarara, West Indian Spigelia; G:Westindische Nelkenwurz · ☉ Z10 ⌾ ✻; USA: Fla., Mex., C-Am., trop. S-Am.
– **marilandica** (L.) L. · E:Indian Pink, Maryland Pink, Worm Grass; G:Indianer-Nelkenwurz · ⚃ Z8 ⌂ VII-IX ⚇ ✻; USA: NE, NCE, SC, SE, Fla.
– **splendens** H. Wendl. ex Hook. · ⚃ Z10 ⌂ VII-VIII; Guat., Costa Rica

Spilanthes Jacq. -f- Asteraceae · 6 spp.
– oleracea L. = Acmella oleracea

Spinacia L. -f- Chenopodiaceae · 3 spp. · E:Spinach; F:Epinard; G:Spinat
– **oleracea** L. · E:Spinach; G:Spinat · ☉ Z5 VI Ⓝ; cult.
– **turkestanica** Iljin · ☉ Ⓝ; C-As., Iran

Spiraea L. -f- *Rosaceae* · 80-100 spp. ·
E:Bridewort; F:Spirée; G:Spierstrauch
- *aitchisonii* Hemsl. = Sorbaria tomentosa
var. angustifolia
- **alba** Du Roi · E:Meadow Sweet;
G:Weißer Spierstrauch · ♄ d Z5 VI-VIII;
Can.: E, Sask.; USA: NE, N.C., NCE,
N.Dak.
- **alpina** Pall. · G:Sibirischer Spierstrauch ·
♄ d V-VI; W.-Sib., E.-Sib., Mong.
- **amoena** Spae · G:Aufrechter Spierstrauch · ♄ d Z7 V-VI; NW-Him.
- **arcuata** Hook. f. · G:Himalaya-
Spierstrauch · ♄ d Z7 ∧ V; Him.
- × **arguta** Zabel (*S. thunbergii* × *S.*
'Snowwhite') · E:Garland Wreath;
G:Braut-Spierstrauch · ♄ d Z5 IV-V; cult.
- *aruncus* L. = Aruncus dioicus var. dioicus
- **bella** Sims · G:Schöner Spierstrauch · ♄ d
Z7 VI; Him.
- **betulifolia** Pall.
- var. **aemiliana** (C.K. Schneid.) Koidz. · ♄
d Z4; Jap.
- var. **betulifolia** · E:White Spiraea;
G:Birkenblättriger Spierstrauch · ♄ d △
Z4 VI; Jap., Sakhal., E-Sib.
- var. **corymbosa** (Raf.) Voss · E:Shinyleaf
Meadowsweet · ♄ d Z5; E-USA
- var. **lucida** (Douglas ex Greene) C.L.
Hitchc. · E:Shinyleaf Spiraea · ♄ d Z5;
B.C., USA: Wash., Oreg., Wyom., Mont.
- × **billardii** Hérincq (*S. douglasii* × *S.*
salicifolia) · E:Billard's Spiraea; G:Billards
Spierstrauch · ♄ d Z5 VI-VII; cult.
- × **blanda** Zabel (*S. cantoniensis* × *S.*
chinensis) · ♄ d Z6 V-VI; cult.
- × **brachybotrys** Lange (*S. douglasii* × *S.*
canescens) · ♄ d Z4 VI-VII; cult.
- *bumalda* Burv. = Spiraea japonica
- *caespitosa* Nutt. ex Torr. & A. Gray =
Petrophytum caespitosum
- **calcicola** W.W. Sm. · G:Kalk-
bewohnender Spierstrauch · ♄ d Z5 VI;
Yunnan
- *callosa* Thunb. = Spiraea japonica var.
japonica
- **cana** Waldst. & Kit. · G:Graufilziger
Spierstrauch · ♄ d Z6 V; Eur.: NE-I,
Croatia, Bosn., YU
- **canescens** D. Don · G:Grauer Spierstrauch · ♄ d Z7 VI; Him.
- **cantoniensis** Lour. · E:Reeves' Meadowsweet; G:Kanton-Spierstrauch · ♄ d Z7
V-VI; China, nat. in Ibiza
- **chamaedryfolia** L.

- var. **chamaedryfolia** · G:Gamander-
Spierstrauch · ♄ d Z5 V-VI; Eur.: Ital-P,
C-Eur., EC-Eur., Ba, E-Eur.; W-Sib, E-Sib.,
C-As., Mong., nat. in F
- var. **ulmifolia** (Scop.) Maxim. ·
G:Ulmenblättriger Spierstrauch · ♄ d Z5;
SE-Eur., N-As, Jap.
- **chinensis** Maxim. · G:Chinesischer
Spierstrauch · ♄ d Z6; NE-China
- *cinerascens* Piper = Petrophytum
cinerascens
- × **cinerea** Zabel (*S. cana* × *S.*
hypericifolia) · G:Aschgrauer Spierstrauch · ♄ d Z5 V; cult.
- × **concinna** Zabel (*S. albiflora* × *S.*
amoena) · ♄ d; cult.
- *corymbosa* Raf. = Spiraea betulifolia var.
corymbosa
- *crataegifolia* Link = Spiraea betulifolia
var. corymbosa
- **crenata** L. · G:Kerb-Spierstrauch · ♄ d
Z6 V; Eur.: EC-Eur., Ba, E-Eur.; Cauc.,
W-Sib., C-As., nat. in Ib, Fr, C-Eur.
- **decumbens** W.D.J. Koch
- subsp. **decumbens** · F:Spirée prostrée;
G:Kärntner Spierstrauch, Niederliegender Spierstrauch · ♄ d △ Z6 V-VI; Eur.: A
(Kärnten), N-I, Slove.; SE-Alp.
- subsp. **pumilionum** (Zabel) · ♄ d △ Z5
VII-VIII
- subsp. **tomentosa** (Poech) Dostál · ♄ d △
Z5 V; NE-I
- **densiflora** Nutt. ex Torr. & A. Gray · ♄ d
Z5; Can.: B.C.; USA: NW, Calif.
- *digitata* Willd. = Filipendula palmata
- *discolor* Pursh = Holodiscus discolor
- **douglasii** Hook. · G:Oregon-Spierstrauch
- var. **douglasii** · E:Douglas Spiraea, Rose
Spiraea; F:Spirée de Douglas; G:Douglas-
Spierstrauch · ♄ d Z4 VI-VIII; USA: Oreg.,
Calif.
- var. **menziesii** (Hook.) C. Presl ·
E:Menzies' Spiraea; G:Menzies
Spierstrauch · ♄ d Z4 VI-VIII; USA: NW,
Idaho
- var. *roseata* (Rydb.) Hitchc. = Spiraea
douglasii var. douglasii
- *dumosa* Nutt. ex Hook. = Holodiscus
dumosus
- *expansa* Wall. ex K. Koch = Spiraea
amoena
- *fastigiata* C.K. Schneid. = Spiraea amoena
- *filipendula* L. = Filipendula vulgaris
- *flexuosa* Fisch. = Spiraea chamaedryfolia
var. chamaedryfolia

– × **fontenaysii** Lebas (*S. latifolia* × *S. canescens*) · ♄ d Z5 VI-VII; cult.
– × **foxii** (Voss) Zabel (*S. corymbosa* × *S. japonica*) · ♄ d Z5 VII; cult.
– **gemmata** Zabel · G:Kahler Spierstrauch · ♄ d Z5 V; NW-China
– × **gieseleriana** Zabel (*S. cana* × *S. chamaedryfolia*) · ♄ d Z6; cult.
– *hacquetii* Fenzl & K. Koch = Spiraea decumbens subsp. tomentosa
– **henryi** Hemsl. · E:Henry's Spiraea; G:Henrys Spierstrauch · ♄ d Z6 VI; W-China, C-China
– **hypericifolia** L.
– subsp. **hypericifolia** · G:Hartheu-Spierstrauch · ♄ d Z5 V-VII; Eur.: Ib, Fr, Ba, E-Eur.; TR, Cauc., W-Sib., E-Sib., C-As., Mong., Him., nat. in Ital-P, EC-Eur.
– subsp. **obovata** (Waldst. & Kit. ex Willd.) H. Huber · ♄ d Z5; SW-Eur., S-F, ? SE-Eur.
– × **inflexa** hort. ex K. Koch (*S. cana* × *S. crenata*) · ♄ d; cult.
– **japonica** L. f. · E:Japanese Mead-owsweet; F:Spirée du Japon; G:Japanischer Spierstrauch
– **some cultivars**
– var. **fortunei** (Planch.) Rehder Z5; E-China, C-China
– var. **glabra** (Regel) Koidz. · ♄ d Z5 VII-X; Him., China, Korea, Jap.
– var. **japonica** · ♄ d Z4 VII-VIII; China, Jap.
– *kamtschatica* Pall. = Filipendula camtschatica
– *lancifolia* Hoffmanns. = Spiraea decumbens subsp. tomentosa
– **latifolia** (Aiton) Borkh. · E:White Mead-owsweet; G:Breitblättriger Spierstrauch · ♄ d Z3 VI-VIII; Can.: E; USA: NE, NCE, N.C.
– *lobata* Gronov. ex Jacq. = Filipendula rubra
– **longigemmis** Maxim. · ♄ d Z5 VII; NW-China
– × **macrothyrsa** Dippel (*S. douglasii* × *S. latifolia*) · ♄ d Z4; cult.
– × **margaritae** Zabel (*S. japonica* × *S. syringiflora*) · ♄ d Z5 VI-VIII; cult.
– **media** Schmidt · G:Karpaten-Spierstrauch · ♄ d Z4 IV-V; Eur.: C-Eur., EC-Eur., Ba, E-Eur.; W-Sib., E-Sib., Amur, Kamchat., Amur, C-As., Mong., Manch., N-Korea, Jap.
– *menziesii* Hook. = Spiraea douglasii var.

menziesii
– × **multiflora** Zabel (*S. crenata* × *S. hypericifolia*) · ♄ d Z4 V; cult.
– **myrtilloides** Rehder · ♄ d; W-China
– **nipponica** Maxim. · G:Breitwüchsiger Japanischer Spierstrauch
– var. **nipponica** · ♄ d Z5 VI; Jap.
– var. **tosaensis** (Yatabe) Makino · ♄ d Z4; Jap. (Shikoku)
– × **notha** Zabel (*S. betulifolia* × *S. latifolia*) · ♄ d; cult.
– *opulifolia* L. = Physocarpus opulifolius var. opulifolius
– × **oxyodon** Zabel (*S. chamaedryfolia* × *S. media*) · ♄ d; cult.
– × **pachystachys** Zabel (*S. betulifolia* × *S. japonica*) · ♄ d; cult.
– *palmata* Murray = Filipendula rubra
– *palmata* Pall. = Filipendula palmata
– *palmata* Thunb. = Filipendula purpurea
– × **pikoviensis** Besser (*S. crenata* × *S. media*) · ♄ d Z6 V; S-Russ.
– × *pruinosa* hort. = Spiraea × brachybotrys
– **prunifolia** Siebold & Zucc. · E:Bridal Wreath; F:Spirée; G:Pflaumenblättriger Spierstrauch · ♄ d Z6 V; Korea, C-China, Taiwan
– f. **simpliciflora** Nakai · ♄ d Z6 IV-V; C-China, Taiwan, Korea
– × *pseudosalicifolia* Silverside = Spiraea × billardii
– **pubescens** Turcz. · ♄ d Z6 V; N-China
– *pumilionum* Zabel = Spiraea decumbens subsp. pumilionum
– *reevesiana* Lindl. = Spiraea cantoniensis
– × **revirescens** Zabel (*S. amoena* × *S. japonica*) · ♄ d Z5 VI-VII; cult.
– **salicifolia** L. · E:Bridewort; F:Spirée à feuilles de saule; G:Weidenblättriger Spierstrauch · ♄ d Z4 VI-VII; Eur.: C-Eur., EC-Eur., Ba, E-Eur.; W-Sib., E-Sib., Amur, Sakhal., Kamchat., Mong., N-Korea, Jap., nat. in BrI, Sc, Fr, Ital-P
– × **sanssouciana** K. Koch (*S. douglasii* × *S. japonica*) · ♄ d Z6 VI-VIII; cult.
– **sargentiana** Rehder · E:Sargent's Spiraea; G:Sargents Spierstrauch · ♄ d Z6 VI; W-China
– × **schinabeckii** Zabel (*S. chamaedryfolia* × *S. trilobata*) · ♄ d Z6; cult.
– × **semperflorens** Zabel (*S. japonica* × *S. salicifolia*) · ♄ d Z4 VII-IX; cult.
– *sorbifolia* L. = Sorbaria sorbifolia var. sorbifolia
– *stipulata* Muhl. = Gillenia stipulata

– *syringiflora* hort. ex K. Koch = Spiraea ×
semperflorens
– **thunbergii** Siebold ex Blume · ♄ d Z5
IV-V; China
– **tomentosa** L. · E:Hardhack, Steeplebush;
G:Filziger Spierstrauch · ♄ d ⁓ Z3
VII-IX; Can.: E; USA; NE, NCE, SE
– **trichocarpa** Nakai · G:Koreanischer
Spierstrauch · ♄ d Z5 V-VI; Korea
– *trifoliata* L. = Gillenia trifoliata
– **trilobata** L. · G:Dreilappiger Spierstrauch · ♄ d Z5 V-VI; W-Sib., C-As.,
N-China, Korea
– *ulmaria* L. = Filipendula ulmaria
– *ulmifolia* Scop. = Spiraea chamaedryfolia
var. ulmifolia
– × **vanhouttei** (Briot) Zabel (*S.
cantoniensis* × *S. trilobata*) · G:Belgischer
Spierstrauch · ♄ d Z5 V-VI; cult.
– **veitchii** Hemsl. · E:Veitch's Spiraea;
G:Veitchs Spierstrauch · ♄ d Z6 VII;
W-China, C-China

Spiraeanthus (Fisch. & C.A. Mey.) Maxim.
-m- *Rosaceae* · 1 sp.
– **schrenkianus** (Fisch. & C.A. Mey.)
Maxim. · ♄ Z10; C-As.

Spiranthes Rich. -f- *Orchidaceae* · 30 spp. ·
E:Lady's Tresses; F:Spiranthe; G:Dreh-
wurz, Wendelähre
– **aestivalis** (Poir.) Rich. · E:Summer
Lady's Tresses; G:Sommer-Drehwurz,
Sommer-Wendelähre · ⅃ ⁓ VII ▽ ✳;
Eur.: Ib, Fr, Ital-P, Ba, C-Eur., EC-Eur.;
Alger.
– *autumnalis* Rich. = Spiranthes spiralis
– **sinensis** (Pers.) Ames · G:Chinesische
Drehwurz · ⅃ Z9 ⓜ ▽ ✳; Sib., Sakhal.,
China, Manch., Korea, Jap., Taiwan, Ind.,
Malay. Arch., Austr., NZ
– **spiralis** (L.) Chevall. · E:Autumn Lady's
Tresses; G:Herbst-Drehwurz, Herbst-
Wendelähre · ⅃ ⁓ D Z6 X ▽ ✳; Eur.*,
TR, Cyprus, Syr., Cauc., N-Iran, Alger.

Spirodela Schleid. -f- *Lemnaceae* · 3 spp. ·
E:Greater Duckweed; F:Spirodèle;
G:Teichlinse
– **polyrhiza** (L.) Schleid. · E:Duckweed,
Great Duckweed; G:Vielwurzelige Teich-
linse · ⅃ ≈ Z5 V-VI; Eur.*, cosmop.

Spironema Lindl. = Callisia
– *fragrans* Lindl. = Callisia fragrans

– *warscewiczianum* (Kunth & C.D. Bouché)
G. Brückn. = Callisia warszewicziana

Spodiopogon Trin. -m- *Poaceae* · 9 spp. ·
F:Spodiopogon; G:Graubartgras
– **sibiricus** Trin. · G:Sibirisches Graubartgras · ⅃ Z7 VIII-IX; E-Sib., Amur, Mong.,
China, Manch., Korea, Jap.

Spondias L. -f- *Anacardiaceae* · 10 spp. ·
E:Hog Plum; F:Monbin, Pomme d'or,
Prune d'Espagne; G:Balsampflaume,
Mombinpflaume
– *cytherea* Sonn. = Spondias dulcis
– **dulcis** Parkinson · E:Ambarella, Polyne-
sian Plum; G:Goldene Balsampflaume · ♄
s Z10 ⓜ Ⓝ; Madag., Fiji, Samoa
– **mombin** L. · E:Hog Plum; G:Gelbe
Mombinpflaume · ♄ Z10 ⓜ Ⓝ; Mex.,
trop. Am., nat. in W-Afr.
– **pinnata** (J. König ex L. f.) Kurz ·
E:Yellow Plum; G:Gelbe Balsampflaume ·
♄ Z10 ⓜ Ⓝ; Ind., SE-As., Phil.
– **purpurea** L. · E:Red Mombin, Spanish
Plum; G:Rote Mombinpflaume · ♄ s Z10
ⓜ Ⓝ; ? C-Am., ? W.Ind., cult. trop. Am.

Sporobolus R. Br. -m- *Poaceae* · 160 spp. ·
E:Dropseed; F:Sporobole; G:Fallsamen-
gras, Vilfagras
– **cryptandrus** (Torr.) A. Gray · E:Sand
Dropseed; G:Verstecktblütiges Fallsamengras · ⅃ Z5; N-Am., N-Mex.
– **indicus** (L.) R. Br. · ⅃ Z9; Trop.,
Subtrop., China, nat. in S-Eur.

Sprekelia Heist. -f- *Amaryllidaceae* ·
2 spp. · E:Jacobean Lily; F:Lis de
St-Jacques; G:Jakobslilie
– **formosissima** (L.) Herb. · E:Jacobean
Lily; G:Jakobslilie · ⅃ Z9 ⓐ IV-V ✱;
Mex., Guat.

Stachyphrynium K. Schum. -n-
Marantaceae · 16 spp.
– **jagorianum** (K. Koch) K. Schum. · ⅃ Z10
ⓜ; Malay. Pen.

Stachys L. -f- *Lamiaceae* · 362 spp. ·
E:Betony, Hedge Nettle, Woundwort;
F:Bétoine, Crosne, Epiaire; G:Ziest
– **affinis** Bunge · E:Chinese Artichoke;
G:Knollen-Ziest · ⅃ Z5 VII-VIII Ⓝ;
N-China, C-China
– **alopecuros** (L.) Benth. · E:Yellow

Betony; G:Fuchsschwanz-Ziest · ⑴ Z5;
Eur.: Fr, Ib, Ital-P, C-Eur., Ba
- **alpina** L. · E:Alpine Woundwort;
G:Alpen-Ziest · ⑴ Z5 VII-IX; Eur.* exc. Sc;
TR, Cauc., N-Iran
- × **ambigua** Sm. (*S. palustris* × *S.
sylvatica*) · G:Bastard-Ziest · ⑴ ; D +
- **annua** (L.) L. · G:Einjähriger Ziest · ☉ Z5
VI-X; Eur.* exc. BrI, Sc; Cauc., W-Sib.
- **arvensis** (L.) L. · E:Field Woundwort;
G:Acker-Ziest · ☉ VII-X; Eur.* exc.
EC-Eur.; TR, Lebanon, Palest., NW-Afr.,
Afr., S-Afr., Am.
- **byzantina** K. Koch · E:Lamb's Ears,
Lamb's Lugs, Lamb's Tails; F:Epiaire
laineuse; G:Woll-Ziest · ⑴ ⁞ Z5 VII-IX; TR,
Crim, Cauc., N-Iran, nat. in Ont.
- **citrina** Boiss. & Heldr. ex Benth. ·
G:Zitronen-Ziest · ⑴ △ Z5 VI-VIII; TR
- **coccinea** Ortega · G:Scharlach-Ziest · ⑴
Z8 ⓐ VII-VIII; USA: SW, Tex.
- **corsica** Pers. · G:Korsischer Ziest · ☉ ☉ ⑴
⤳ Z8 ⓐ VIII-IX; Cors, Sard.
- **discolor** Benth. · G:Kaukasus-Ziest · ⑴ △
Z5 VII-VIII; Cauc., Iran
- **germanica** L. · E:Downy Woundwort;
G:Deutscher Ziest · ⑴ Z5 VI-VIII; Eur.*
exc. Sc; TR, Cauc., Moroc.
- *grandiflora* (Steph. ex Willd.) Benth. =
Stachys macrantha
- *labiosa* Bertol. = Stachys recta subsp.
grandiflora
- *lanata* Jacq. non Crantz = Stachys
byzantina
- **lavandulifolia** Vahl · F:Epiaire à feuilles
de lavande; G:Lavendelblättriger Ziest ·
⑴ △ Z5 VII-VIII; TR
- **macrantha** (K. Koch) Stearn · G:Groß-
blütiger Ziest · ⑴ Z5 VII-VIII; TR, Cauc.,
Iran
- *monieri* (Gouan) P.W. Ball = Stachys
officinalis
- *nivea* (Steven) Benth. = Stachys discolor
- **officinalis** (L.) Franch. · E:Betony,
Bishop's Wort, Wood Betony; G:Echter
Ziest, Heil-Ziest · ⑴ Z5 VII-VIII; Eur.*, TR,
Cauc., N-Iran, C-As., NW-Afr.
- *olympica* Briq. ex Poir. = Stachys
byzantina
- **palustris** L. · E:Hedge Nettle, Marsh
Betony, Marsh Woundwort; F:Epiaire des
marais; G:Sumpf-Ziest · ⑴ VI-IX ⚥ ; Eur.*
, N-As., N-Am.
- **recta** L. · G:Aufrechter Ziest
- subsp. **grandiflora** (Caruel) Arcang. ·

G:Großlippiger Aufrechter Ziest · ⑴ VI-X;
Eur.: Alp., Apenn., W-Ba
- subsp. **recta** · E:Yellow Woundwort;
G:Gewöhnlicher Aufrechter Ziest · ⑴
VI-X; Eur.* exc. BrI, Sc; TR, Cauc.
- subsp. **subcrenata** Vis. · G:Karst-Ziest · ⑴
VI-IX; SE-Eur., TR
- *sieboldii* Miq. = Stachys affinis
- *spicata* hort. = Stachys macrantha
- **sylvatica** L. · E:Hedge Woundwort;
G:Wald-Ziest · ⑴ VI-IX; Eur.*, N-Am.
- *tubifera* Naudin = Stachys affinis

Stachytarpheta Vahl -f- *Verbenaceae* ·
65 spp. · E:False Vervain, Snakeweed;
G:Schneckenkraut
- **mutabilis** (Jacq.) Vahl · E:Pink Snakeweed; G:Rosa Schneckenkraut · ♭ Z10 ⓦ
II-XI; N-Am , n S-Am.

Stachyurus Siebold & Zucc. -m-
Stachyuraceae · 6-10 spp. · F:Stachyurus;
G:Perlschweif, Schweifähre
- **chinensis** Franch. · G:Chinesischer
Perlschweif · ♭ d Z7 IV; C-China
- **praecox** Siebold & Zucc. · G:Japanischer
Perlschweif · ♭ d Z7 III-IV; Jap., Ryukyu-Is.

Staehelina L. -f- *Asteraceae* · 8 spp. ·
F:Stéhéline; G:Strauchscharte
- **uniflosculosa** Sibth. & Sm. · G:Einköp-
fige Strauchscharte · ♭ ⓐ; AL, GR,
Maced.

Stangeria T. Moore -f- *Stangeriaceae* · 1 sp.
- **eriopus** (Kunze) Nash · ⑴ Z9 ⓦ ▽ ❋;
S-Afr.: Natal (Pondoland)

Stanhopea Frost ex Hook. -f- *Orchidaceae* ·
57 spp.
- *bucephalus* Lindl. = Stanhopea oculata
- **ecornuta** Lem. · ⑴ Z10 ⓐ VII-IX ▽ ❋;
Guat., Hond., Nicar., Costa Rica
- **grandiflora** (Lodd.) Lindl. · ♭ Z10 ⓐ
VIII-IX ▽ ❋; Venez., Trinidad, Guyana,
Braz.
- **graveolens** Lindl. · ⑴ Z10 ⓐ VII-VIII ▽
❋; Mex., Guat., Hond.
- **hernandezii** (Kunth) Schltr. · ⑴ Z10 ⓐ
VII-XI ▽ ❋; Mex., Guat.
- **insignis** Frost ex Hook. · ⑴ Z10 ⓐ VIII-X
▽ ❋; Braz., ? Peru
- **jenischiana** Kramer ex Rchb. f. · ⑴ Z10
ⓐ ▽ ❋; Col., Ecuad.
- **oculata** (Lodd.) Lindl. · ⑴ Z10 ⓐ VII-X

▽ ✳; Mex., Guat., Hond., Belize
- **saccata** Bateman · ⩊ Z10 ⚘ VII-VIII ▽
  ✳; Guat.
- **tigrina** Bateman · ⩊ Z10 ⚘ VIII-XI ▽ ✳;
  Mex., C-Am., trop. S-Am.
- **wardii** Lodd. ex Lindl. · ⩊ Z10 ⚘ VII-IX
  ▽ ✳; C-Am., trop. S-Am.

Stapelia L. -f- *Asclepiadaceae* · 44 spp. ·
E:Carrion Flower, Starfish Flower;
F:Etoile, Stapélia; G:Aasblume
- *asterias* Masson · ⩊ ❡ Z9 ⚘; Cape
- *barbata* Masson = Huernia barbata
- *campanulata* Masson = Huernia
  campanulata
- **concinna** Masson · ⩊ ❡ Z9 ⚘; Cape
- *cooperi* N.E. Br. = Orbea cooperi
- *desmetiana* N.E. Br. = Stapelia grandiflora
- *dinteri* A. Berger = Tridentea jucunda var.
  dinteri
- *europaea* Guss. = Caralluma europaea
- *flavopurpurea* Marloth
  - var. **flavopurpurea** · ⩊ ❡ Z9 ⚘; W-Cape
  - var. **fleckii** (A. Berger & Schltr.) A.C.
    White & B. Sloane · ⩊ ❡ Z9 ⚘; Namibia
- *fleckii* A. Berger & Schltr. = Stapelia
  flavopurpurea var. fleckii
- **gigantea** N.E. Br. · E:Giant Stapelia,
  Giant Toad Flower; G:Riesenblütige
  Aasblume · ⩊ ❡ Z9 ⚘; Zimbabwe,
  Zambia, S-Afr.: Transvaal, Natal
- **grandiflora** Masson · ⩊ ❡ Z9 ⚘; S-Afr.:
  SE-Cape, Transvaal
- **hirsuta** L. · E:Hairy Toad Plant · ⩊ ❡ Z9
  ⚘; SE-Cape
- *hystrix* Hook. f. = Huernia hystrix
- *macrocarpa* A. Rich. = Huernia macrocarpa
- *mammillaris* L. = Quaqua mammillaris
- *melanantha* Schltr. = Orbea melanantha
- **mutabilis** Jacq. · ⩊ ❡ Z9 ⚘; orig. ?
- **pillansii** N.E. Br. · ⩊ ❡ Z9 ⚘; Cape
- *radiata* Sims = Duvalia caespitosa
- *replicata* Jacq. = Duvalia caespitosa
- *revoluta* (Masson) Haw. = Tromotriche
  revoluta
- *senilis* N.E. Br. = Stapelia grandiflora
- *tapscottii* I. Verd. = Orbea tapscottii
- *variegata* L. = Orbea variegata
- *verrucosa* Masson = Orbea verrucosa

Stapeliopsis Pillans -f- *Asclepiadaceae* ·
6 spp.
- **saxatilis** (N.E. Br.) Bruyns · ⩊ ❡ Z9 ⚘;
  Cape

Staphylea L. -f- *Staphyleaceae* · 11 sp. ·
E:Bladdernut; F:Faux-pistachier,
Staphilier; G:Pimpernuss
- **bolanderi** A. Gray · E:Sierran Bladdernut; G:Kalifornische Pimpernuss · ♄ ♄ d
  Z7 ⋀ IV-V; Calif.
- **bumalda** DC. · G:Japanische Pimpernuss · ♄ d Z5 VI; China, Manch., Korea,
  Jap.
- **colchica** Steven · G:Kolchische Pimpernuss · ♄ d Z6 V; Cauc.
- × **elegans** Zabel (*S. colchica* × *S.
  pinnata*) · ♄ d Z6 V; cult.
- **emodi** Wall. · ♄ ♄ d Z9 ⚘; Him.
- **holocarpa** Hemsl. · E:Chinese Bladdernut; G:Chinesische Pimpernuss · ♄ d Z6
  IV-V; C-China
- **pinnata** L. · E:Bladdernut, European
  Bladdernut; G:Gewöhnliche Pimpernuss
  · ♄ d Z5 V-VI; Eur.: F, I, C-Eur., EC-Eur.,
  Ba, E-Eur.; TR, Cauc., nat. in BrI
- **trifolia** L. · E:American Bladdernut, Bladdernut; G:Amerikanische Pimpernuss · ♄
  d Z5 V; Can.: E; USA: NE, NCE, SE, Okla.

Statice L. = Limonium
- *bellidifolia* (Gouan) DC. = Limonium
  bellidifolium
- *globulariifolia* Desf. = Limonium ramosissimum
- *limonium* L. = Limonium vulgare
- *perezii* Stapf = Limonium perezii
- *plantaginea* All. = Armeria arenaria
- *sinuata* L. = Limonium sinuatum

Stauntonia DC. -f- *Lardizabalaceae* ·
24 spp.
- **hexaphylla** (Thunb.) Decne. ·
  E:Stauntonia · ♄ ∫ e ⚘ Z9 ⚘ IV; Jap.,
  Ryukyu-Is., S-Korea
- *latifolia* (Wall.) Wall. = Holboellia
  latifolia

Stauropsis Rchb. f. = Vandopsis
- *gigantea* (Lindl.) Benth. ex Pfitzer =
  Vandopsis gigantea
- *violacea* (Witte) Rchb. f. = Phalaenopsis
  violacea

Steirodiscus Less. -m- *Asteraceae* · 5 spp.
- **tagetes** (L.) Schltr. · ⊙ Z9 VI-VII; S-Afr.

Steironema Raf. = Lysimachia
- *ciliatum* (L.) Baudo = Lysimachia ciliata

Stelechocarpus Hook. f. & Thomson -m-
Annonaceae · 5 spp.
– **burahol** (Blume) Hook. f. & Thomson · ♄
ⓦ Ⓝ; Malay. Arch., cult Java

Stelis Sw. -f- *Orchidaceae* · 688 spp.
– **alta** Pridgeon & M.W. Chase · ⌗ Z10 ⓦ
VIII-IX ▽ ✳; Costa Rica
– **gelida** (Lindl.) Pridgeon & M.W. Chase ·
⌗ Z10 ⓦ ▽ ✳; Fla., Mex., C-Am., W-Ind.,
S-Am.
– **immersa** (Linden & Rchb. f.) Pridgeon
& M.W. Chase · ⌗ Z10 ⓦ I-II ▽ ✳; Mex.,
C-Am., Col., Venez.
– **quadrifida** (Lex.) Solano & Soto Arenas ·
⌗ Z10 ⓦ ▽ ✳; Mex., C-Am., Jamaica,
Col., Venez.

Stellaria L. -f- *Caryophyllaceae* · 150-
200 spp. · E:Chickweed, Stitchwort;
F:Langue-d'oiseau, Stellaire; G:Stern-
miere
– **alsine** Grimm · E:Bog Stitchwort;
G:Quell-Sternmiere · ⌗ ⏜ V-VII; Eur.*,
Cauc., Sib., China, Korea, Jap., Taiwan,
N-Afr., N-Am.
– **aquatica** (L.) Scop. · E:Chickweed;
G:Wasserdarm · ⌗ ⚥ ⏝⏜ VI-IX;
Eur.*, TR, Cauc., W-As., Ind., N-As.,
Korea, Jap., Taiwan, N-Afr.
– **crassifolia** Ehrh. · G:Dickblättrige
Sternmiere · ⌗ ⏜ VII-VIII; Eur.: Sc, G,
PL, Russ.; Cauc., W-Sib., E-Sib. Kamchat.,
C-As., Jap., N-Am.
– *glauca* = Stellaria palustris
– **graminea** L. · E:Common Stitchwort;
G:Gras-Sternmiere · ⌗ V-VII; Eur.*, TR,
Cauc., W-Sib., E-Sib. , C-As., Mong. ,
Tibet, China: Sinkiang
– **holostea** L. · E:Stitchwort; G:Große
Sternmiere · ⌗ Z5 IV-VI; Eur.*, TR, Cauc.,
N-Iran, W-Sib., NW-Afr.
– **longifolia** Muhl. ex Willd. · G:Langblät-
trige Sternmiere · ⌗ VI-VIII; Eur.:
Ital-P, C-Eur., EC-Eur., Sc, E-Eur.; Cauc.,
W-Sib., E-Sib. Amur, Sakhal., Kamch.,
C-As., Jap., N-Am.
– **media** (L.) Vill. · E:Common Chickweed;
G:Vogel-Sternmiere, Vogelmiere · ⊙ Z5
I-XI ⚥; Eur.*, TR, Levant, N-Afr., N-As.,
Greenl., nat. in Can., USA*, cosmop.
– *montana* Rose = Stellaria nemorum
subsp. montana
– **neglecta** Weihe · E:Greater Chickweed;
G:Auwald-Sternmiere, Großblütige

Vogelmiere · ⌗ IV-VII; Eur.*, TR,
Lebanon, Palest., Cauc., C-As., China,
Jap.., NW-Afr.
– **nemorum** L. · G:Hain-Sternmiere
– subsp. **montana** (M.D. Pierrat) Berher ·
G:Berg-Hainsternmiere, Berg-Stern-
miere · ⌗ VI-VIII; Eur.
– subsp. **nemorum** · E:Wound Stitchwort;
G:Gewöhnliche Hain-Sternmiere · ⌗
V-IX; Eur.*, TR, Cauc.
– **pallida** (Dumort.) Crép. · E:Lesser
Chickweed; G:Bleiche Sternmiere,
Bleiche Vogelmiere · ⊙ III-V; Eur.*, TR,
Levant, Cauc., C-As., N-Afr.
– **palustris** Ehrh. ex Hoffm. · E:Marsh
Stitchwort; G:Sumpf-Sternmiere · ⌗
⏜ V-VII; Eur.* exc. Ib; TR, Cauc.,
W-Sib., E-Sib. C-As., Him., Mong., China:
Sinkiang; Jap.

Stemmacantha Cass. -f- *Asteraceae* ·
20 spp. · G:Bergscharte
– **rhapontica** (L.) Dittrich · G:Gewöhnliche
Bergscharte · ⌗ Z6 VII-VIII; Eur.: F, I, Sw,
A; Alp.

Stenandrium Nees -n- *Acanthaceae* ·
25 spp.
– *igneum* (Linden) André = Xantheranthemum igneum
– **lindenii** N.E. Br. · ⌗ ⏝ Z10 ⓦ; Ecuad.,
Peru, Bol.

Stenocactus (K. Schum.) A.W. Hill -m-
Cactaceae · 10 spp.
– *albatus* (A. Dietr.) F.M. Knuth =
Stenocactus vaupelianus
– **coptonogonus** (Lem.) A. Berger · ♇ Z9
ⓐ ▽ ✳; C-Mex.
– **crispatus** (DC.) A. Berger · ♇ Z9 ⓐ ▽ ✳;
Mex.
– *gladiatus* (Link & Otto) A. Berger & F.M.
Knuth = Echinofossulocactus gladiatus
– *lamellosus* (A. Dietr.) Britton & Rose =
Stenocactus crispatus
– *lloydii* (Britton & Rose) A. Berger =
Stenocactus multicostatus
– **multicostatus** (Hildm. ex K. Schum.) A.
Berger · ♇ Z9 ⓐ Ⓝ ▽ ✳; NE-Mex.
– **phyllacanthus** (Mart. ex A. Dietr. &
Otto) A. Berger · ♇ Z9 ⓐ ▽ ✳; C-Mex.
– **vaupelianus** (Werderm.) Backeb. · ♇ Z9
ⓐ ▽ ✳; Mex.: Hidalgo
– *violaciflorus* (Quehl) A. Berger =
Stenocactus crispatus

Stenocarpus R. Br. -m- *Proteaceae* · c.
25 spp. · E:Wheeltree; F:Sténocarpe;
G:Feuerradbaum
– **salignus** R. Br. · G:Weidenähnlicher
Feuerradbaum · ♄ e Z10 ⓚ; Austr.:
Queensl., N.S.Wales
– **sinuatus** (A. Cunn.) Endl. · E:Firewheel
Tree; G:Gewöhnlicher Feuerradbaum
· ♄ e Z10 ⓚ VII-VIII; N.Guinea, Austr.:
Queensl., N.S.Wales

Stenocereus (A. Berger) Riccob. -m-
Cactaceae · 25 spp.
– **beneckei** (C. Ehrenb.) Buxb. · ♄ ♈ Z9 ⓚ
▽ ✳; W-Mex.
– *dumortieri* (Scheidw.) Buxb. = Isolatocereus dumortieri
– *eruca* (Brandegee) A.C. Gibson & K.E.
Horak = Machaerocereus eruca
– *marginatus* (DC.) Buxb. = Pachycereus
marginatus
– **pruinosus** (Otto ex Pfeiff.) Buxb. · ♄ ♄ ♈
Z9 ⓚ ▽ ✳; S-Mex.
– **queretaroensis** (F.A.C. Weber ex Mathsson) Buxb. · ♄ ♈ Z9 ⓚ ▽ ✳; C-Mex.
– **stellatus** (Pfeiff.) Riccob. · ♄ ♈ Z9 ⓚ ▽
✳; S-Mex.
– **thurberi** (Engelm.) Buxb. · E:Organ Pipe
Cactus · ♄ ♈ Z9 ⓚ ▽ ✳; USA: S-Calif.,
SW; Baja Calif.; N-Mex.
– *weberi* (J.M. Coult.) Buxb. = Pachycereus
weberi

Stenochlaena J. Sm. -f- *Blechnaceae* ·
8 spp.
– **palustris** (Burm. f.) Bedd. · ⚃ ⚄ Z10 ⓜ;
trop. As., Austr., Polyn.
– *sorbifolia* (L.) J. Sm. = Lomariopsis
sorbifolia
– **tenuifolia** (Desv.) T. Moore · ⚃ ⚄ Z9 ⓜ;
trop. Afr., Madag.

Stenoglottis Lindl. -f- *Orchidaceae* · 4 spp.
– **fimbriata** Lindl. · ⚃ Z9 ⓚ IX-X ▽ ✳;
S-Afr.
– **longifolia** Hook. f. · ⚃ Z9 ⓚ IX-XI ▽ ✳;
S-Afr.: Natal (Zululand)

Stenolobium D. Don = Tecoma
– *stans* (L.) Seem. = Tecoma stans

Stenorrhynchos Rich. ex Spreng. -m-
Orchidaceae · 2 spp.
– **speciosum** (Jacq.) Rich. · ⚃ Z10 ⓜ II-IV
▽ ✳; W.Ind., C-Am., trop. S-Am.

Stenospermation Schott -n- *Araceae* ·
35 spp.
– **popayanense** Schott · ♄ e Z10 ⓜ; Col.,
Ecuad.

Stenotaphrum Trin. -n- *Poaceae* · 7 spp. ·
E:Buffalo Grass; F:Herbe de St-Augustin;
G:Hohlspelze
– **secundatum** (Walter) Kuntze · E:Buffalo
Grass, Shore Grass, St Augustine Grass;
G:St.-Augustin-Gras · ⚃ ⤳ Z9 ⓜ ⓚ ▢
ⓝ; trop. Am. , W-Afr., Pacific Is.; coasts

Stephanandra Siebold & Zucc. -f-
Rosaceae · 4 spp. · F:Stephanandra;
G:Kranzspiere
– **incisa** (Thunb.) Zabel · G:Kleine
Kranzspiere · ♄ d Z5 VI; Jap., Korea
– **tanakae** (Franch. & Sav.) Franch. &
Sav. · G:Große Kranzspiere · ♄ d Z6
VI-VII; Jap.

Stephanocereus A. Berger -m- *Cactaceae* ·
2 spp.
– **leucostele** (Gürke) A. Berger · ♄ ♈ Z9 ⓚ
▽ ✳; Braz.

Stephanophysum Pohl = Ruellia
– *longifolium* Pohl = Ruellia graecizans

Stephanotis Thouars -f- *Asclepiadaceae* ·
5 spp. · E:Waxflower; F:Jasmin de
Madagascar; G:Kranzschlinge
– **floribunda** (R. Br.) Brongn. ·
E:Madagascar Jasmine, Wax Flower;
G:Madagaskar-Kranzschlinge · ♄ e ⚄ D
Z10 ⓚ VI-IX; Madag.

Sterculia L. -f- *Sterculiaceae* · 150-200 spp. ·
F:Pois puant, Sterculier; G:Sterkulie,
Stinkbaum
– *acerifolia* A. Cunn. = Brachychiton
acerifolius
– *alata* Roxb. = Pterygota alata
– **apetala** (Jacq.) H. Karst. · E:Panama
Tree; G:Panama-Stinkbaum · ♄ d Z10 ⓚ
ⓝ; Mex., C-Am., W.Ind., S-Am.
– *diversifolia* G. Don = Brachychiton
populneus
– **foetida** L. · E:Java Olive; G:Gewöhnli-
cher Stinkbaum · ♄ e ⋉ Z10 ⓜ; trop. Afr.,
trop. As.
– *platanifolia* L. f. = Firmiana simplex
– *quinqueloba* K. Schum. = Cola quinqueloba

– *rupestris* (Michx. ex Lindl.) Benth. = Brachychiton rupestris
– **tragacantha** Lindl. · ♄ Z10 ⓜ Ⓝ; trop. Afr.
– **urens** Roxb. · ♄ d Z10 ⓜ Ⓝ; Ind., Pakist.

Stereospermum Cham. -n- *Bignoniaceae* · 15 spp.
– **kunthianum** Cham. · E:Pink Jacaranda · ♄ Z10 IV-VII; Trop. Afr.
– *sinicum* Hance = Radermachera sinica

Sternbergia Waldst. & Kit. -f- *Amaryllidaceae* · 10 spp. · E:Autumn Daffodil, Winter Daffodil; F:Amaryllis doré; G:Goldkrokus, Sternbergie
– **colchiciflora** Waldst. & Kit. · G:Zeitlosenblütiger Goldkrokus · ⚃ Z5 ⓐ; Eur.: Ib, I, Ba, H, RO, S-Russ., Crim; TR, Cauc., Israel, Iran
– **lutea** (L.) Ker-Gawl. ex Spreng. · E:Autumn Yellow Crocus, Winter Daffodil; G:Gelber Goldkrokus · ⚃ △ Z7 ∧ IX-X ⚘ ▽ ❋; Eur.: Ib, Ital-P, Ba; TR, Iraq, Cauc., Iran, C-As, nat. in F

Stetsonia Britton & Rose -f- *Cactaceae* · 1 sp.
– **coryne** (Salm-Dyck) Britton & Rose · E:Toothpick Cactus · ♄ ⇞ Z9 ⓐ ▽ ❋; NW-Arg., S-Bol.

Steudnera K. Koch -f- *Araceae* · 9 spp.
– **colocasiifolia** K. Koch · ⚃ Z10 ⓜ; Burma
– **discolor** W. Bull · ⚃ Z10 ⓜ; Burma

Stevensonia Duncan ex Balf. f. = Phoenicophorium
– *borsigiana* (K. Koch) L.H. Bailey = Phoenicophorium borsigianum
– *grandifolia* Duncan ex Balf. f. = Phoenicophorium borsigianum

Stevia Cav. -f- *Asteraceae* · 235 spp. · E:Candyleaf; F:Stévie; G:Stevie
– **rebaudiana** (Bertoni) Hemsl. · E:Sweet Leaf Of Paraguay; G:Paraguay-Stevie · ☉ Z9 ⓐ Ⓝ; NE-Parag.
– **serrata** Cav. · E:Sawtooth Candyleaf; G:Gesägtblättrige Stevie · ⚃ Z9 ⓐ; USA: Tex., SW; C-Am., trop. S.-Am.

Stewartia L. -f- *Theaceae* · 9 spp. · E:False Camellia; F:Faux-camélia, Stuartia; G:Scheinkamelie

– *koreana* Nakai ex Rehder = Stewartia pseudocamellia var. koreana
– **monadelpha** Siebold & Zucc. · E:Tall Stewartia; G:Hohe Scheinkamelie · ♄ d Z7 VII-VIII; Jap.
– **ovata** (Cav.) Weath.
– var. **grandiflora** (Bean) Weath. · ♄ ♄ d Z5 VI-VII; USA: Ga.
– var. **ovata** · E:Mountain Camellia; G:Amerikanische Scheinkamelie · ♄ d Z5 VII; USA: Va., Ky., SE
– *pentagyna* L'Hér. = Stewartia ovata var. ovata
– **pseudocamellia** Maxim. · ♄ d; Jap.; mts.
– var. **koreana** (Nakai ex Rehder) Sealy · E:Korean Stewartia; G:Koreanische Scheinkamelie · ♄ ♄ d Z6 VII-VIII; Korea
– var. **pseudocamellia** · E:Japanese Stewartia; G:Japanische Scheinkamelie · ♄ d Z6; Jap.
– **pteropetiolata** W.C. Cheng · E:Chinese Stewartia; G:Chinesische Scheinkamelie · ♄ ♄ d D Z7 VII; C-China
– **serrata** Maxim. · ♄ d Z7 VI; Jap.
– *sinensis* Rehder & E.H. Wilson = Stewartia pteropetiolata

Sticherus C. Presl -m- *Gleicheniaceae* · 68 spp. · E:Fan Fern; F:Fougère, Gleichenia; G:Fächerfarn
– **flabellatus** (R. Br.) H. St. John · ⚃ Z10 ⓐ; Austr., Tasman., NZ, N.Caled.

Stictocardia Hallier f. -f- *Convolvulaceae* · 9-12 spp.
– **beraviensis** (Vatke) Hallier f. · E:Mile-a-Minute Climber · ♄ ⚵ Z9 ⓜ; W-Afr., E-Afr., Zambia, Madag.

Stillingia L. -f- *Euphorbiaceae* · 29 spp.
– **sylvatica** L. · E:Queen's Root, Yaw Root · ⚃ Z8 ⓐ V-VI ⚵ ⚘ Ⓝ; USA: Va., SE, Fla., Tex.

Stipa L. -f- *Poaceae* · c. 300 spp. · E:Feather Grass, Needle Grass, Spear Grass; F:Esparsette, Stipa; G:Espartogras, Federgras, Pfriemengras, Raugras
– **avenacea** L. · E:Blackseed Spear Grass · ⚃ V-VI ▽; USA: NE, NCE, SC, SE, Fla.
– **barbata** Desf. · F:Stipa barbu; G:Reiher-Federgras · ⚃ Z8 ∧ VII-VIII ▽; sp., S-I, Sic.
– **borysthenica** Klokov ex Prokudin · G:Gewöhnliches Sand-Federgras · ⚃ V-VI

∇; Eur.: C-Eur., EC-Eur., Ba, E-Eur.;
Cauc., W-Sib., E-Sib., C-As.
- **bromoides** (L.) Dörfl. · G:Kurzgranniges
Pfriemengras · ♃ ∇; Eur.: Ib, Fr, Ital-P,
H, Ba, RO, Crim; TR, Iraq, Syr., Lebanon,
Palest., Cauc., Iran, C-As., Moroc., Alger.
- **calamagrostis** (L.) Wahlenb. · E:Rough
Feather Grass; F:Calamagrostide
argentée; G:Alpen-Raugras, Silber-
Ährengras · ♃ Z7 ∧ VI-IX; Eur.: sp., F, I,
C-Eur., Ba, RO
- **capillata** L. · E:Hair-like Feather Grass;
F:Stipa chevelu; G:Haar-Federgras,
Haar-Pfriemengras · ♃ VII ∇; Eur.* exc.
BrI, Sc; TR, Cauc., N-Iran, W-Sib., E-Sib.,
C-As., Mong.
- **dasyphylla** (Czern. ex Lindem.) Trautv. ·
G:Weichhaariges Federgras · ♃ V-VI ∇;
Eur.: G, EC-Eur., E-Eur.; W-Sib.
- *effusa* (Maxim.) Nakai ex Honda = Stipa
pekinensis
- **elegantissima** Labill. · E:Australian
Feather Grass · ♃ Z8 ⊛ VI-VII ∇; Austr.
- **eriocaulis** Borbás · G:Gewöhnliches
Zierliches Federgras · ♃ V-VI ∇; Eur.:
Ib, F, Ital-P, C-Eur., EC-Eur., Ba, E-Eur.;
Alger.
- **gigantea** Link · E:Giant Feather Grass;
G:Riesen-Federgras · ♃ Z8 ∧ VI-VII ∇;
Eur.: Ib
- **grandis** P.A. Smirn. · ♃ VI-VII ∇; Mong.
- **pekinensis** Hance · G:Chinesisches
Federgras · ♃ VII-VIII ∇; E-Sib., N-China,
Jap., Sakhal.
- **pennata** L. · E:Feather Grass; F:Stipa
penné; G:Echtes Federgras, Mädchen-
haargras · ♃ ♄ V-VI ∇; Eur.: Fr, C-Eur.,
EC-Eur., Ba, Sc, E-Eur.; TR, N-Iraq,
Cauc., ? Iran, W-Sib., E-Sib., C-As.
- subsp. *eriocaulis* (Borbás) Martinovsky &
Skalicky = Stipa eriocaulis
- **pulcherrima** K. Koch · G:Gelbscheidiges
Federgras
- subsp. **bavarica** (Martinovský & H.
Scholz) Conert · G:Bayerisches Gelbsc-
heidiges Federgras · ♃ V-VII ∇; Eur.: D
(Neuburg a.D.)
- subsp. **pulcherrima** · E:Golden Feather
Grass; F:Plumet; G:Gewöhnliches Gelbsc-
heidiges Federgras, Großes Federgras · ♃
∧ V-VII ∇; Eur.: Ib, Fr, C-Eur., EC-Eur.,
Ba, E-Eur., Ital-P; TR, Cauc., N-Iran,
W-Sib., C-As., Moroc., Alger.
- *sabulosa* Sljuss. = Stipa borysthenica
- **splendens** Trin. · E:Chee Grass;

G:Glänzendes Raugras · ♃ Z7 ∇; W-Sib.,
E-Sib., C-As., Iran, Him., Tibet., Mong.,
China, Jap., S-As, nat. in Eur.
- *stenophylla* (Czern. ex Lindem.) Trautv. =
Stipa tirsa
- **styriaca** Martinovský · G:Steirisches
Federgras · ♃ V-VI ∇; Eur.: A (Steier-
mark, Kärnten); mts.
- **tenacissima** L. · E:Esparto Grass;
G:Espartogras · ♃ Z8 ∧ VII-VIII ∇;
China: Hupeh, Sichuan
- **tirsa** Steven · E:Bristle-leaved Feather
Grass; G:Rossschweif-Federgras · ♃ V-VI
∇; Eur.* exc. BrI, Sc; NE-TR, Cauc.,
C-As., W-Sib.
- **ucrainica** P.A. Smirn. · G:Ukraine-
Federgras · ♃ ∇; Eur.: E-Eur.
- **viridula** Trin. · E:Green Needlegrass · ♃
∇; Can.; USA* exc. Calif., Fla.

Stirlingia Endl. -f- *Proteaceae* · 3-6 spp.
- **latifolia** (R. Br.) Steud. · ♄ e ⋉ Z10 ⊛;
Austr.

Stizolobium P. Browne = Mucuna
- *deeringianum* Bort = Mucuna pruriens
var. utilis
- *pruriens* (L.) Medik. = Mucuna pruriens
var. pruriens

Stoebe L. -f- *Asteraceae* · 34 spp.
- **cinerea** Thunb. · ♄ Z9 ⊛; Cape

Stokesia L'Hér. -f- *Asteraceae* · 1 sp. ·
E:Stike's Aster; F:Aster-centaurée,
Stokésia; G:Kornblumenaster, Stokesie
- **laevis** (Hill) Greene · E:Stoke's Aster,
Stokesia; G:Kornblumenaster, Stokesie ·
♃ ∧ VIII-IX; USA: SE, Fla.
- **some cultivars**

Stomatium Schwantes -n- *Aizoaceae* ·
38 spp.
- **suaveolens** (Schwantes) Schwantes · ♃
Ѱ D Z10 ⊛; Cape

Stranvaesia Lindl. = Photinia
- *davidiana* Decne. = Photinia davidiana
var. davidiana
- *undulata* Decne. = Photinia davidiana
var. undulata

Stratiotes L. -m- *Hydrocharitaceae* · 1 sp. ·
E:Water Soldier; F:Aloès d'eau, Macle;
G:Krebsschere, Wasseraloe

- **aloides** L. · E:Water Aloe, Water Soldier; F:Aloès d'eau; G:Krebsschere, Wasseraloe · ⌃ ≈ Z5 V-VIII ▽; Eur.*, Cauc., W-Sib.

Strelitzia Aiton -f- *Strelitziaceae* · 5 spp. · E:Bird of Paradise; F:Oiseau de paradis; G:Paradiesvogelblume, Strelitzie
- **alba** (L. f.) Skeels · ♄ e Z9 ⓜ I-III; Cape
- *augusta* Thunb. = Strelitzia alba
- **caudata** R.A. Dyer · ♄ e Z9 ⓜ; S-Afr.: Transvaal
- **juncea** Ker-Gawl. (Link) · ♄ e Z9 ⓚ II-VIII; Cape
- **nicolai** Regel & K. Koch · E:Giant Bird-of-Paradise, Wild Banana; G:Natal-Strelitzie · ♄ e Z9 ⓜ I-VI; S-Afr.: Natal
- *ovata* W.T. Aiton = Strelitzia reginae
- **parvifolia** W.T. Aiton
- var. *juncea* Ker-Gawl. = Strelitzia juncea
- **reginae** Banks ex Aiton · E:Bird-of-Paradise, Crane Flower; G:Königs-Strelitzie, Paradiesvogelblume · ⌃ ⋉ Z9 ⓚ II-VIII; Cape
- subsp. *juncea* (Ker-Gawl.) Sm. = Strelitzia juncea

Streptocalyx Beer = Aechmea
- *longifolius* (Rudge) Baker = Aechmea longifolia
- *poeppigii* Beer = Aechmea vallerandii
- *vallerandii* (Carrière) E. Morren = Aechmea vallerandii

Streptocarpus Lindl. -m- *Gesneriaceae* · c. 125 spp. · E:Cape Primrose; F:Primevère du Cap; G:Drehfrucht
- **caulescens** Vatke · ⌃ Z10 ⓜ VI-VIII; trop. Afr.
- **cyaneus** S. Moore · ⌃ Z10 ⓜ VI-VIII; S-Afr.: Transvaal, Swasiland
- **dunnii** Mast. ex Hook. f. · ⌃ Z10 ⓜ VII-VIII; S-Afr.: Transvaal
- **galpinii** Hook. f. · ⌃ Z10 ⓜ IX-X; S-Afr.: Transvaal
- **grandis** N.E. Br. ex C.B. Clarke · ⌃ Z10 ⓜ VII-VIII; S-Afr.: Natal (Zululand)
- **haygarthii** N.E. Br. ex C.B. Clarke · ⌃ Z10 ⓜ; S-Afr.: Natal
- **holstii** Engl. · ⌃ Z10 ⓜ VI-VIII; E-Afr.
- **kirkii** Hook. f. · ♄ Z10 ⓜ VII-X; E-Afr.
- **parviflorus** E. Mey. · ⌃ Z10 ⓜ VI-VIII; S-Afr.
- **polyanthus** Hook. · ⌃ Z10 ⓜ; S-Afr.: Natal

- **rexii** (Bowie ex Hook.) Lindl. · ⌃ Z10 ⓜ V-VIII; Cape
- **saundersii** Hook. · ⌃ Z10 ⓜ IX; S-Afr.: Natal
- **saxorum** Engl. · E:False African Violet · ⌃ Z10 ⓜ VI-X; Tanzania
- **wendlandii** Sprenger ex Hort. Dammann · ⌃ Z10 ⓜ VIII-XI; S-Afr.: Natal
- **Cultivars:**
- **many cultivars**

Streptopus Michx. -m- *Convallariaceae* · 8 spp. · E:Twisted Stalk; F:Streptope; G:Knotenfuß
- **amplexifolius** (L.) DC.
- var. **amplexifolius** · E:Claspleaf Twistedstalk; G:Gewöhnlicher Stängelumfassender Knotenfuß · ⌃ ⊗ Z5 VI-VIII; Eur.* exc. BrI, Sc; Amur, Sakhal., Kamchat., Jap., W-China, Alaska, Can., USA* exc. SC; Greenl.
- **lanceolatus** (Aiton) Reveal · E:Rose Mandarin, Rosy Twisted Stalk; G:Rosa Knotenfuß · ⌃ Z3 VI-VII; Can.: E; USA; NE, NCE, SE

Streptosolen Miers -m- *Solanaceae* · 1 sp. · E:Firebush; F:Streptosolen; G:Drehkrone
- **jamesonii** (Benth.) Miers · E:Fire Bush, Marmalade Bush; G:Drehkrone · ♄ e Z9 ⓚ IV-VI; Col., Ecuad.

Strobilanthes Blume -m- *Acanthaceae* · 250 spp. · E:Mexican Petunia; F:Strobilanthe; G:Zapfenblume
- **anisophyllus** (Wall. ex Lodd.) T. Anderson · ♄ e Z10 ⓜ; Ind. (Assam)
- **cusia** (Nees) Imlay · ♄ Z10 ⓜ Ⓝ; Ind.: Assam, Bengalen; N-Burma, S-China
- **dyerianus** Mast. · E:Persian Shield · ♄ Z10 ⓜ; Burma
- **isophyllus** (Nees) T. Anderson · ♄ e Z10 ⓜ; ? Ind. (Assam)
- **maculatus** (Wall.) Nees · ♄ Z10 ⓜ; InG: Assam

Stromanthe Sond. -f- *Marantaceae* · 19 spp. · F:Stromanthe; G:Blumenmaranthe
- *amabilis* E. Morren = Ctenanthe amabilis
- **porteana** Griseb. · ⌃ Z10 ⓜ; Braz.
- *sanguinea* Sond. = Stromanthe thalia
- **thalia** (Vell.) J.M.A. Braga · ⌃ Z10 ⓜ; Braz.

Strombocactus Britton & Rose -m-
Cactaceae · 1 sp. · G:Kreiselkaktus
– *denegrii* (Frič) G.D. Rowley = Obregonia
denegrii
– **disciformis** (DC.) Britton & Rose · ⚘ Z9
⊛ ▽ ✳; Mex.: Hidalgo
– *lophophoroides* (Werderm.) F.M. Knuth =
Turbinicarpus lophophoroides
– *pseudomacrochele* Backeb. = Turbinicarpus pseudomacrochele
– *schmiedickeanus* (Boed.) A. Berger =
Turbinicarpus schmiedickeanus

Strongylodon Vogel -m- *Fabaceae* ·
12 spp. · E:Jade Vine; G:Jadewein
– **macrobotrys** A. Gray · E:Jade Vine;
G:Jadewein · ♄ e ⚡ Z10 ⓦ; Phil.

Strophanthus DC. -m- *Apocynaceae* ·
39 spp.
– **caudatus** (L.) Kurz · ♄ e ⚡ Z10 ⓦ ✺;
Thail., Malay. Arch., Phil.
– *dichotomus* DC. = Strophanthus caudatus
– **gratus** (Wall. & Hook. ex Benth.) Baill. ·
♄ e ⚡ ⊛ Z10 ⓦ ⚡ ✺; W-Afr., C-Afr.
– **hispidus** DC. · ♄ ♄ ⚡ Z10 ⓦ ⚡ ✺ Ⓝ;
W-Afr., Zaire, Angola, Uganda, Tanz.
– **kombe** Oliv. · ♄ e ⚡ Z10 ⓦ ⚡ ✺; C-Afr.,
N-Angola, SE-Afr.
– **sarmentosus** DC. · ♄ e ⚡ Z10 ⓦ ✺;
W-Afr.

Struthiopteris Willd. = Matteuccia
– *filicastrum* All. = Matteuccia struthiopteris
– *germanica* Willd. = Matteuccia struthiopteris
– *orientalis* Hook. = Matteuccia orientalis
– *pensylvanica* Willd. = Matteuccia
pensylvanica

Strychnos L. -f- *Loganiaceae* · c. 190 spp. ·
E:Strychnine Tree; F:Strychnos,
Vomiquier; G:Brechnuss
– **ignatii** P.J. Bergius · E:Ignatius Bean,
Poison Nut; G:Ignatius-Brechnuss · ♄ ⚡
Z10 ⓦ ✺; Malay. Arch., SE-Phil.
– **nux-vomica** L. · E:Nux Vomica, Strych-
nine; G:Gewöhnliche Brechnuss · ♄ e Z10
ⓦ ⚡ ✺ Ⓝ; Ind., Sri Lanka, Malay. Arch.,
N-Austr.
– **spinosa** Lam. · E:Spiny Monkey Orange ·
♄ Z10 ⓦ ✺ Ⓝ; trop. Afr., S-Afr., Madag.,
Seych.
– **toxifera** R.H. Schomb. ex Benth. ·

E:Strychnine; G:Gift-Brechnuss · ♄ ⚡
Z10 ⓦ ✺; Col., Ecuad., Peru, Venez.,
Guyan., Amazon.,

Stuartia L'Hér. = Stewartia
– *pentagyna* L'Hér. = Stewartia ovata var.
ovata

Stultitia E. Phillips = Orbea
– *cooperi* (N.E. Br.) E. Phillips = Orbea
cooperi
– *tapscottii* (I. Verd.) E. Phillips = Orbea
tapscottii

Stylidium Sw. ex Willd. -n- *Stylidiaceae* ·
126 spp. · G:Säulenblume
– **adnatum** R. Br. · ⚘ Z9 ⊛ VI-VII; Austr.
– **graminifolium** Sw. ex Willd. · E:Trigger
Plant · ⚘ Z9 ⊛ V-VI; Austr.
– *majus* (Sw.) Druce = Stylidium graminifolium

Stylophorum Nutt. -n- *Papaveraceae* ·
3 spp. · E:Celandine Poppy; F:Célandine;
G:Schöllkrautmohn
– **diphyllum** (Michx.) Nutt. · E:Celandine
Poppy, Wood Poppy; F:Célandine;
G:Amerikanischer Schöllkrautmohn · ⚘
Z7 VI-VII; USA: NE, NCE, Tenn.
– *japonicum* (Thunb.) Miq. = Hylomecon
japonica

Stylophyllum Britton & Rose = Dudleya
– *densiflorum* Rose = Dudleya densiflora
– *edule* (Nutt.) Britton & Rose = Dudleya
edulis

Stylosanthes Sw. -f- *Fabaceae* · 25 spp.
– **guianensis** (Aubl.) Sw. · ⊙ ⓦ Ⓝ; trop.
Am., nat. in Austr.
– **humilis** Kunth · ⊛ Ⓝ; S-Afr., nat. in
N-Austr.

Styphnolobium Schott -n- *Fabaceae* ·
9 spp. · G:Pagodenbaum
– **japonicum** (L.) Schott · E:Japanese
Pagoda Tree; F:Sophora du Japon;
G:Japanischer Pagodenbaum · ♄ d Z6
VIII ⚡ ✺; China, Korea

Styrax L. -m- *Styracaceae* · c. 120 spp. ·
E:Snowbell, Storax; F:Aliboufier, Styrax;
G:Storaxbaum
– **americanus** Lam. · E:American Snowbell · ♄ d Z8 ⊛; USA: Va., Mo., SE, Fla.

- **benzoides** Craib · ₺ e Z10 Ⓦ ⚕; Indochina
- **benzoin** Dryand. · E:Benzoin; G:Benzoinbaum · ₺ e Z10 Ⓦ ⚕ Ⓝ; Malay. Pen., Sumat., W-Java
- **hemsleyanus** Diels · ₺ d Z7; W-China, C-China
- **japonicus** Siebold & Zucc. · E:Japanese Snowbell; G:Japanischer Storaxbaum · ħ ₺ d Z6 VI-VII; China, Korea, Jap., Taiwan, Phil.
- **obassia** Siebold & Zucc. · E:Fragrant Snowbell; G:Obassia-Storaxbaum · ħ ₺ d Z6 V-VI; China, Manch., Korea, Jap.
- **officinalis** L. · E:Snowdrop Bush, Storax; G:Gewöhnlicher Storaxbaum · ₺ d Z9 Ⓚ V Ⓝ; Eur.: I, Ba; TR, Cyprus, Syr., Calif., nat. in F
- **shiraianus** Makino · ₺ ħ Z6; Jap.; mts.
- **tonkinensis** (Pierre) Craib ex Hartwich · ₺ d Z9 Ⓚ ⚕ Ⓝ; E-Thail., Laos, Vietnam
- **wilsonii** Rehder · ħ d Z7 V-VI; W-China

Suaeda Forssk. ex Scop. -f- *Chenopodiaceae* · 100 spp. · E:Sea Blite; F:Soude, Suéda; G:Salzmelde, Sode
- **maritima** (L.) Dumort.
- subsp. **maritima** · E:Annual Sea Blite; G:Strand-Sode · ☉ VII-IX; Eur.*, TR, Levant, NW-Afr., Egypt
- subsp. **pannonica** (Beck) Soó ex P.W. Ball · G:Pannonische Salzmelde · VIII-IX; Eur.: A, H, Ba, RO
- **vera** Forssk. ex J.F. Gmel. · E:Shrubby Sea Blite; G:Horn-Salzmelde · ħ e Ⓚ Ⓐ ∧ VII; Eur.: Ib, Fr, Ital-P, Ba, BrI; Cyprus, Syr., N-Afr.

Submatucana Backeb. = Matucana
- *aurantiaca* (Vaupel) Backeb. = Matucana aurantiaca subsp. aurantiaca
- *myriacantha* (Vaupel) Backeb. = Matucana haynei subsp. myriacantha
- *ritteri* (Buining) Backeb. = Matucana ritteri

Subularia L. -f- *Brassicaceae* · 1 sp. · E:Awlwort; F:Subulaire; G:Pfriemenkresse
- **aquatica** L. · E:Awlwort; G:Pfriemenkresse · ☉ ⊙ ≈ Z5 VI-VII; Eur.: Sc, BrI, Fr, Ib, G, Ba, EC-Eur.

Succisa Haller -f- *Dipsacaceae* · 1 sp. · E:Devil's Bit Scabious; F:Mors du diable; G:Teufelsabbiss
- **pratensis** Moench · E:Devil's Bit Scabious; G:Gewöhnlicher Teufelsabbiss · ♃ Z5 VII-IX ⚕; Eur.*, TR, Cauc., W-Sib., NW-Afr., Madeira, nat. in N-Am.

Succisella Beck -f- *Dipsacaceae* · 4 spp. · F:Succiselle; G:Moorabbiss
- **inflexa** Kluk · G:Östlicher Moorabbiss · ♃ VI-IX; Eur.: A, EC-Eur., Ba, E-Eur., nat. in F, D

Succowia Medik. -f- *Brassicaceae* · 1 sp. · F:Succowia; G:Suckowie
- **balearica** (L.) Medik. · G:Suckowie · ☉; Eur.: Ib, Ital-P; Moroc., Alger., Tun.

Sulcorebutia Backeb. -f- *Cactaceae* · c. 40 spp.
- **arenacea** (Cárdenas) F. Ritter · ♆ Z9 Ⓚ; Bol.: Cochabamba
- **cylindrica** Donald & A.B. Lau · ♆ Z9 Ⓚ; Bol.: Cochabamba
- **glomeriseta** (Cárdenas) F. Ritter · ♆ Z9 Ⓚ; Bol.: Cochabamba
- **rauschii** G. Frank · ♆ Z9 Ⓚ; Bol.: Chuquisaca
- **steinbachii** (Werderm.) Backeb. · ♆ Z9 Ⓚ; Bol.: Cochabamba

Sutera Roth -f- *Scrophulariaceae* · 49 spp. · G:Schneeflockenblume
- **cordata** (Thunb.) Kuntze · G:Herzblatt-Schneeflockenblume · ♃ Z8 Ⓚ; S-Afr. (Cape Prov.)
- **grandiflora** (Galpin) Hiern · G:Großblütige Schneeflockenblume · ħ Z9 Ⓚ VII-IX; S-Afr.
- **hispida** (Thunb.) Druce · G:Borstige Schneeflockenblume · ₺ Z9 Ⓚ VI-IX; S-Afr.
- **polyantha** (Benth.) Kuntze · G:Reichblütige Schneeflockenblume · ħ Z9 Ⓚ VI-IX; S-Afr.

Sutherlandia R. Br. ex W.T. Aiton -f- *Fabaceae* · 5 spp. · E:Balloon Pea; F:Sutherlandia; G:Ballonerbse, Sutherlandie
- **frutescens** (L.) R. Br. · E:Cancer Bush, Duck Plant; G:Korallenrote Ballonerbse, Krebsstrauch · ₺ e Z9 Ⓚ VII-IX Ⓝ; Cape

Swainsona Salisb. -f- *Fabaceae* · c. 50 spp. · E:Darling Pea; F:Swainsonia;

G:Augenwicke, Swainsonie
- **galegifolia** (Andrews) R. Br. · ♄ Z9 Ⓚ VII-IX; Austr.: Queensl., N.S.Wales

Swertia L. -f- *Gentianaceae* · c. 50 spp. · E:Felwort; F:Swertia; G:Sumpfstern, Tarant
- **chirata** Buch.-Ham. ex Wall. · ⊙ Z7 IX-X ⚕; Him.
- **kingii** Hook. f. · ♃ Z7; Him.
- **perennis** L. · E:Felwort, Marsh Felwort; G:Gewöhnlicher Blauer Sumpfstern · ♃ ~ Z5 VI-IX ▽; Eur.* exc. BrI, Sc
- **petiolata** D. Don · ♃ Z7; Afghan., Him., SE-Tibet

Swietenia Jacq. -f- *Meliaceae* · 3 spp. · E:Mahogany; F:Mahogany d'Amérique; G:Mahagonibaum
- *chloroxylon* Roxb. = Chloroxylon swietenia
- **macrophylla** King · E:Mahogany; G:Mexikanischer Mahagonibaum · ♄ e Z10 Ⓦ Ⓝ ✻; Mex., C-Am., Col., Peru, Venez., Braz.
- **mahagoni** (L.) Jacq. · E:West Indian Mahogany; G:Echter Mahagonibaum, Westindischer Mahagonibaum · ♄ e Z10 Ⓦ Ⓝ ▽ ✻; S-Fla., W.Ind., Mex., Hond., Col., Ecuad., Peru

Syagrus Mart. -m- *Arecaceae* · 33 spp.
- **coronata** (Mart.) Becc. · E:Licuri Palm; G:Uricuripalme · ♄ e Z10 Ⓦ Ⓝ; trop. S-Am.
- **romanzoffiana** (Cham.) Glassman · E:Queen Palm; G:Romanzoffianische Kokospalme · ♄ e Z10 Ⓦ; Braz.
- *weddelliana* (H. Wendl.) Becc. = Lytocaryum weddellianum

× **Sycoparrotia** P.K. Endress & Anliker -f- *Hamamelidaceae* (*Parrotia* × *Sycopsis*)
- **semidecidua** P.K. Endress & Anliker (*Parrotia persica* × *Sycopsis sinensis*) · ♄ s Z7; cult.

Sycopsis Oliv. -f- *Hamamelidaceae* · 3-9 spp.
- **sinensis** Oliv. · ♄ e Z8 Ⓚ II-III; W-China, C-China

Sympagis (Nees) Bremek. = Strobilanthes
- *maculata* (Wall.) Bremek. = Strobilanthes maculatus

Symphoricarpos Duhamel -m- *Caprifoliaceae* · 17 spp. · E:Snowberry; F:Symphorine; G:Knallerbsenstrauch, Korallenbeere, Wolfsbeere
- **albus** (L.) S.F. Blake · G:Gewöhnliche Schneebeere
- var. **albus** · E:Snowberry, Waxberry; G:Gewöhnliche Schneebeere, Knallerbsenstrauch · ♄ d ⁂ Z3 VII-VIII ☠; Alaska, Can., USA: NE, NCE, NC, SE, NW, Calif., Rocky Mts.
- var. **laevigatus** (Fernald) S.F. Blake · F:Symphorine blanche; G:Dickichtbildende Schneebeere · ♄ d ⁂ Z3 VII-VIII ☠; Alaska, Can.: W; USA: NW, Calif., Rocky Mts.
- × **chenaultii** Rehder (*S. microphyllus* × *S. orbiculatus*) · E:Chenault Coralberry; G:Bastard-Korallenbeere · ♄ d ⁂ Z4 VI-VII ☠; cult.
- × **doorenbosii** Krüssm. (*S. albus var. laevigatus* × *S.* × *chenaultii*) · G:Garten-Schneebeere · ♄ d Z4 ☠; cult.
- **some cultivars**
- **hesperius** G.N. Jones · E:Trailing Snowberry · ♄ d ⁂ Z6 VI-VII ☠; B.C., USA: NW
- **microphyllus** Kunth · E:Pink Snowberry; G:Mexikanische Schneebeere · ♄ d Z8 Ⓚ VIII-IX ☠; Mex.
- **occidentalis** Hook. · E:Wolfberry; G:Westamerikanische Schneebeere, Wolfsbeere · ♄ d Z4 VI-VII ☠; Can.; USA: NCE, NC, Rocky Mts., SW, NW
- **orbiculatus** Moench · E:Coralberry, Indian Currant; F:Symphorine à baies-de-corail; G:Korallenbeere · ♄ d ⁂ Z5 VII-VIII ☠; USA: NE, NCE, NC, Colo., SC, SE, Fla.; Mex.
- *racemosus* Michx. = Symphoricarpos albus var. albus
- *rivularis* Suksd. = Symphoricarpos albus var. laevigatus
- **sinensis** Rehder · G:Chinesische Schneebeere · ♄ d Z6 ☠; C-China, SW-China
- *vulgaris* Michx. = Symphoricarpos orbiculatus

Symphyandra A. DC. -f- *Campanulaceae* · 12 spp. · E:Ring Bellflower; F:Campanule des pierres; G:Steinglocke
- **armena** (Steven) A. DC. · ♃ Z7; E-TR, Cauc., N-Iran
- **hofmannii** Pant. · ⊙ △ Z7 VII-IX; Eur.: Bosn.

- **pendula** (M. Bieb.) A. DC. · ♃ △ Z6
  VI-VII; Cauc.
- **wanneri** (Rochel) Heuff. · ♃ △ Z7 V-VI;
  Eur.: Serb., BG, RO: mts.

Symphyglossum Schltr. -n- *Orchidaceae* ·
  2 spp.
- **strictum** (Cogn.) Schltr.

Symphytum L. -n- *Boraginaceae* · 35 spp. ·
  E:Comfrey; F:Consoude; G:Beinwell
- **asperum** Lepech. · E:Rough Comfrey;
  G:Rauer Beinwell · ♃ Z5 VI-VII Ⓝ; Cauc.,
  nat. in BrI, Sc, Fr, C-Eur., Russ.
- **bulbosum** K.F. Schimp. · G:Knotiger-
  Beinwell · ♃ Z5 IV-V; Eur.: Fr, Sw, Ital-P,
  Ba; TR, nat. in D
- **caucasicum** M. Bieb. · E:Blue Comfrey;
  F:Consoude du Caucase; G:Kaukasus-
  Beinwell, Kaukasus-Wallwurz · ♃ Z5
  VI-VIII; Cauc.
- **grandiflorum** A. DC. · E:Dwarf Comfrey;
  F:Consoude à grandes fleurs; G:Groß-
  blumiger Beinwell, Kleiner Kaukasus-
  Beinwell · ♃ Z5 V-VII; Cauc.
- *ibericum* Steven = Symphytum grandiflorum
- **officinale** L. · G:Gewöhnlicher Beinwell
- subsp. **bohemicum** (F.W. Schmidt)
  Čelak. · G:Weißgelber Beinwell · ♃ Z5; D +
- subsp. **officinale** · E:Comfrey, Common Comfrey; F:Consoude officinale;
  G:Arznei-Beinwell · ♃ Z5 V-VII ⚘ Ⓝ;
  Eur.* exc. Sc; Cauc., W-Sib., C-As., nat.
  in Sc
- subsp. **uliginosum** (A. Kern.) Nyman ·
  G:Sumpf-Beinwell · ♃ Z5 V-VII; G,
  EC-Eur. +
- **orientale** L. · E:White Comfrey;
  G:Weißer Beinwell · ♃ Z5 VI-VII; Eur.:
  W-Russ.; TR, nat. in BrI, F, I
- *tanaicense* = Symphytum officinale subsp.
  uliginosum
- *tauricum* auct. non Willd. = Symphytum
  orientale
- **tuberosum** L. · E:Tuberous Comfrey;
  G:Gewöhnlicher Knolliger Beinwell · ♃
  Z5 IV-VI; Eur.* exc. Sc; TR
- × **uplandicum** Nyman (*S. asperum*
  × *S. officinale*) · E:Russian Comfrey;
  F:Consoude panachée; G:Futter-
  Beinwell, Komfrey · ♃ Z5 VI-VIII ⚘ Ⓝ;
  Cauc., nat. in BrI, Sc, Fr, C-Eur.

Symplocarpus Salisb. ex Nutt.

-m- *Araceae* · 1 sp. · E:Skunk Cabbage;
  F:Chou puant, Symplocarpe; G:Stinkkohl
- **foetidus** (L.) Nutt. · E:Polecat Weed,
  Skunk Cabbage; G:Stinkkohl · ♃ ∼ Z7
  III-IV ⚘; Can.: E; USA: NE, NCE, SE;
  Amur, Jap.

Symplocos Jacq. -f- *Symplocaceae* · c.
  250 spp. · F:Symplocos; G:Rechenblume,
  Saphirbeere
- **paniculata** (Thunb.) Miq. · E:Asiatic
  Sweetleaf, Sapphine Berry; G:Saphir-
  beere · ♄ d ⚘ Z5 V-VI; Him., China, Jap.

Synadenium Boiss. -n- *Euphorbiaceae* ·
  14 spp. · F:Euphorbe arborescente;
  G:Milchbusch
- **grantii** Hook. f. · E:African Milkbush;
  G:Afrikanischer Milchbusch · ♄ � Z9 ⊛;
  Uganda, Tanzania, Mozamb.

- *Syndesmon* Hoffmanns. = Anemonella
- *thalictroides* (L.) Hoffmanns. = Anemonella thalictroides

Synechanthus H. Wendl. -m- *Arecaceae* ·
  2 spp.
- **fibrosus** (H. Wendl.) H. Wendl. · ♄ e Z10
  ⊛; C-Am.

Syngonanthus Ruhland -m- *Eriocaulaceae* ·
  200 spp.
- **elegans** (Bong.) Ruhland · ♃ ✕ Z9 ⊛;
  Braz.
- **niveus** (Kunth) Ruhland · ♃ ✕ Z9 ⊛;
  Braz.

Syngonium Schott -n- *Araceae* · 35 spp. ·
  F:Syngonium; G:Fußblatt, Purpurtüte
- **auritum** (L.) Schott · E:Five Fingers;
  G:Westindische Purpurtüte · ♄ e ⚇ Z10
  ⊛; Hond.
- **podophyllum** Schott · E:Arrowhead;
  G:Veränderliche Purpurtüte · ♄ e ⚇ Z10
  ⊛; Mex., Guat., El Salv., Costa Rica
- **standleyanum** G.S. Bunting · ♄ e ⚇ Z10
  ⊛; Hond., Costa Rica
- *triphyllum* hort. = Syngonium standleya-
  num
- **wendlandii** Schott · ♄ e ⚇ Z9 ⊛; Costa
  Rica

- *Synnema* Benth. = Hygrophila
- *triflorum* (Roxb.) Kuntze = Hygrophila
  triflora

Synsepalum (A. DC.) Daniell -n-
Sapotaceae · 35 spp. · E:Miracle Fruit;
G:Wunderbeere
– **dulcificum** (Schumach. & Thonn.)
Daniell · E:Miracle Fruit; G:Wunderbeere
· ♄ ♄ d Z10 ⓦ Ⓝ; trop. W-Afr.

Synthyris Benth. -f- *Scrophulariaceae* ·
9 spp. · F:Synthyris; G:Frühlingsschelle
– **stellata** Pennell · E:Snow Queen; G:Früh-
lingsschelle · ♃ Z7 IV; USA: Wash., Oreg.

Syringa L. -f- *Oleaceae* · 22 spp. · E:Lilac;
F:Lilas; G:Flieder
– **afghanica** C.K. Schneid. · E:Afghan Lilac,
Cutleaf Lilac; F:Lilas; G:Afghanischer
Flieder · ♄ d V; Afgh., Him., Tibet
– *amurensis* Rupr. = Syringa reticulata
subsp. amurensis
– var. *japonica* (Maxim.) Franch. & Sav. =
Syringa reticulata subsp. reticulata
– × **chinensis** Willd. (*S. protolaciniata* ×
S. vulgaris) · E:Chinese Lilac; F:Lilas de
Rouen; G:Chinesischer Flieder, Königs-
Flieder · ♄ d D Z5 V; cult.
– *dielsiana* C.K. Schneid. = Syringa
pubescens subsp. microphylla
– × **diversifolia** Rehder (*S. oblata* × *S.
pinnatifolia*) · E:Varileaf Lilac; G:Ver-
schiedenblättriger Flieder · ♄ d Z5; cult.
– **emodi** Wall. ex Royle · E:Himalayan
Lilac; G:Himalaya-Flieder · ♄ d D Z5
V-VI; Him.: Afgh., Kashmir, NW-Ind.,
Nepal
– × **henryi** C.K. Schneid. (*S. josikaea* × *S.
villosa*) · G:Henrys Flieder · ♄ d Z4 V-VI;
cult.
– × **hyacinthiflora** (Lemoine) Rehder (*S.
oblata* × *S. vulgaris*) · E:American Lilac;
G:Frühlings-Flieder · ♄ d Z4; cult.
– *japonica* (Maxim.) Decne. = Syringa
reticulata subsp. reticulata
– **josikaea** J. Jacq. ex Rchb. · E:Hungarian
Lilac; F:Lilas de Hongrie; G:Ungarischer
Flieder · ♄ d Z5 V-VI; Eur.: RO, W-Russ.;
mts., nat. in D
– **komarowii** C.K. Schneid. · G:Komarovs
Flieder
– subsp. **komarowii** · G:Komarows
Flieder · ♄ d Z6 VI; N-China
– subsp. **reflexa** (C.K. Schneid.) P.S.
Green & M.C. Chang · E:Pendulous Lilac;
G:Bogen-Flieder · ♄ d Z4 VI; C-China
– × **laciniata** Mill. (*S. protolaciniata* ×
?) · E:Cutleaf Lilac; G:Gelapptblättriger

Flieder · ♄ d Z5 V; China: NW-China,
Kansu
– **meyeri** C.K. Schneid. · ♄ d Z5 V-VI;
N-China
– **oblata** Lindl. · E:Broadleaf Lilac, Early
Lilac; G:Rundblättriger Flieder
– subsp. **oblata** · E:Purple Early Lilac;
G:Gewöhnlicher Rundblättriger Flieder ·
♄ d D Z5 IV-V; N-China
– var. *giraldii* (Lemoine) Rehder = Syringa
oblata subsp. oblata
– *palibiniana* hort. = Syringa meyeri
– *palibiniana* Nakai = Syringa pubescens
subsp. patula
– × **persica** L. (*S. protolaciniata* × ?) ·
E:Persian Lilac; F:Lilas de Perse;
G:Persischer Flieder · ♄ d D Z6 V; cult.
– '*Laciniata*' = Syringa × laciniata
– **pinnatifolia** Hemsl. · E:Pinnate Lilac;
G:Fiederblättriger Flieder · ♄ d Z5 V;
SW-China
– × **prestoniae** McKelvey (*S. reflexa* ×
S. villosa) · E:Canadian Hybrid Lilac;
G:Amerikanischer Flieder, Kanadischer
Flieder · ♄ d Z5; cult.
– **protolaciniata** P.S. Green & M.C.
Chang · G:Buxblättriger Flieder · ♄ d Z7;
W-China
– **pubescens** Turcz. · E:Hairy Lilac; G:Wol-
liger Flieder
– subsp. **julianae** (C.K. Schneid.) M.C.
Chang & X.L. Chen · G:Julianes Wolliger
Flieder · ♄ d D Z5 V-VI; W-China
– subsp. **microphylla** (Diels) M.C. Chang
& X.L. Chen · E:Daphne Lilac; G:Klein-
blättriger Wolliger Flieder · ♄ d △ Z6 VI;
N-China
– var. *potaninii* (C.K. Schneid.) P.S. Green
& M.C. Chang · ♄ d D Z6 VI; W-China
– subsp. **patula** (Palib.) M.C. Chang & X.L.
Chen · E:Korean Lilac; G:Ausladender
Wolliger Flieder, Koreanischer Flieder · ♄
d D Z5 V-VI; Korea, N-China
– subsp. **pubescens** · G:Gewöhnlicher
Wolliger Flieder · ♄ d D Z6 IV-V; N-China
– **reticulata** (Blume) H. Hara · G:Japa-
nischer Flieder
– subsp. **amurensis** (Rupr.) P.S. Green &
M.C. Chang · E:Amur Lilac, Manchurian
Lilac; G:Amur-Flieder · ♄ ♄ d Z4 VI-VII;
Manch.
– subsp. **pekinensis** (Rupr.) P.S. Green &
M.C. Chang · E:Peking Lilac; G:Peking-
Flieder · ♄ d D Z5 VI; N-China
– subsp. **reticulata** · G:Gewöhnlicher

Japanischer Flieder · ♄ ♄ d Z4 VI-VII; Jap.
– var. *mandschurica* (Maxim.) H. Hara = Syringa reticulata subsp. amurensis
– × **rothomagensis** hort. = Syringa × chinensis
– × **swegiflexa** Hesse ex J.S. Pringle (*S. reflexa* × *S. sweginzowii*) · E:Pink Pearl Lilac; G:Perlen-Flieder · ♄ d Z5 VI; cult.
– **sweginzowii** Koehne & Lingelsh. · F:Lilas de Sweginzow; G:Sweginzows Flieder · ♄ d Z5 VI; NW-China
– *tigerstedtii* Harry Sm. = Syringa sweginzowii
– **tomentella** Bureau & Franch. · E:Felty Lilac; G:Filziger Flieder, Juni-Flieder · ♄ d D Z6 VI; W-China
– *velutina* hort. = Syringa meyeri
– *velutina* Kom. = Syringa pubescens subsp. patula
– **villosa** Vahl · E:Hairy Lilac; G:Zottiger Flieder · ♄ d Z4 V-VI; N-China
– **vulgaris** L. · E:Common Lilac, French Lilac; F:Lilas commun; G:Garten-Flieder, Gewöhnlicher Flieder · ♄ ♄ d D Z4 IV-V ⚘ Ⓝ; Eur.: Ba, RO, nat. in BrI, Fr, C-Eur., EC-Eur., Ital-P, Crim, TR, Iran, Cauc.
– **many cultivars**
– *wilsonii* C.K. Schneid. = Syringa tomentella
– **wolfii** C.K. Schneid. · G:Wolfs Flieder · ♄ d Z5 VI; Korea, Manch.
– **yunnanensis** Franch. · E:Yunnan Lilac; G:Yunnan-Flieder · ♄ d D Z6 VI; Yunnan

Syzygium Gaertn. -n- *Myrtaceae* · 500-1000 spp. · E:Jambos; F:Giroflier, Jambosier, Jamerosier; G:Jambos, Jambuse, Kirschmyrte, Rosenapfel
– **aqueum** (Burm. f.) Alston · E:Watery Roseapple · G:Wasser-Jambuse · ♄ e Z10 ⓦ Ⓝ; Bangladesh, Burma, Sri Lanka, Sumat., Molucca
– **aromaticum** (L.) Merr. & L.M. Perry · E:Clove, Clove Tree; G:Gewürznelken-baum · ♄ e Z10 ⚘ Ⓝ; Molucca
– **cumini** (L.) Skeels · E:Jambolan, Java Plum; G:Wachs-Jambuse · ♄ e Z10 ⓦ ⚘ Ⓝ; Ind., Sri Lanka, S-China, Malay. Arch., E-Austr.
– *jambolana* (Lam.) DC. = Syzygium cumini
– **jambos** (L.) Alston · E:Malabar Plum, Rose Apple; G:Rosen-Jambuse, Rosenap-fel · ♄ e Z10 ⓦ Ⓝ; SE-As.
– **malaccense** (L.) Merr. & L.M. Perry ·

E:Malay Apple; G:Malayen-Jambuse, Malayenapfel · ♄ e Z10 ⓦ Ⓝ; orig. ?, nat. in Malay. Arch.
– **oleosum** (F. Muell.) B. Hyland · E:Blue Lilly Pilly · ♄ e Z10 ⓦ; Austr.: Queensl., N.S.Wales
– **paniculatum** Banks ex Gaertn. · E:Brush Cherry; G:Australische Kirschmyrte · ♄ ♄ e Z10 Ⓚ III-V; Austr.: Queensl., N.S.Wales
– **samarangense** (Blume) Merr. & L.M. Perry · E:Java Apple · ♄ e Z10 ⓦ Ⓝ; Ind., Malay. Arch., Phil.

Tabebuia M. Gómez ex DC. -f- *Bignoniaceae* · 100 spp.
– *donell-smithii* Rose = Cybistax donnell-smithii
– **serratifolia** (Vahl) G. Nicholson · E:Yellow Poui · ♄ ♄ d Z10 ⓦ; W.Ind., Trinidad, trop. S-Am.

Tabernaemontana L. -f- *Apocynaceae* · 100 spp.
– *amsonia* L. = Amsonia tabernaemontana
– *coronaria* (Jacq.) Willd. = Tabernaemontana divaricata
– **divaricata** (L.) R. Br. ex Roem. & Schult. · E:Adam's Apple, Crape Jasmine · ♄ ♄ e D Z10 ⓦ VII Ⓝ; orig. ?; cult. Trop.

Tacca J.R. Forst. & G. Forst. -f- *Taccaceae* · 10 spp. · E:Bat Flower; F:Tacca; G:Tacca, Teufelsblüte
– *aspera* Roxb. = Tacca integrifolia
– **chantrieri** André · E:Bat Flower, Cat's Whiskers, Devil Flower; G:Thailändische Teufelsblüte · ⩜ Z10 ⓦ; NE-Ind., SE-As.
– *cristata* Jack = Tacca integrifolia
– **integrifolia** Ker-Gawl. · E:Bat Plant; G:Borneo-Teufelsblüte · ⩜ Z10 ⓦ; NE-Ind., Thail., Malay. Pen., Sumat., Java, Kalimantan
– **leontopetaloides** (L.) Kuntze · E:Bat Flower, Indian Arrowroot; G:Ostinidische Teufelsblüte · ⩜ Z10 ⓦ; Malay. Pen., trop., Austr., Pacific Is.
– *pinnatifida* J.R. Forst. & G. Forst. = Tacca leontopetaloides
– **plantaginea** (Hance) Drenth · ⩜ Z10 ⓦ; S-China, N-Vietn., Laos, Thail.

Tacitus Moran = Graptopetalum
– *bellus* Moran & J. Meyrán = Graptopeta-lum bellum

Taeniatherum Nevski -n- *Poaceae* · 1 sp.
- **caput-medusae** (L.) Nevski · ⊙; Eur.: Fr, Ib, Ital-P, EC-Eur., Ba; TR, Syr., Cyprus, Cauc, Iran, Iraq, Afgh., Pakist., C-As.

Tagetes L. -f- *Asteraceae* · c. 50 spp. ·
E:Marigold; F:Oeillet d'Inde, Rose d'Inde, Tagète; G:Sammetblume, Studentenblume, Tagetes
- **erecta** L. · E:African Marigold; G:Hohe Studentenblume · ⊙ Z9 VII-IX; Mex.
- **many cultivars**
- **lucida** Cav. · E:Sweet Marigold; G:Glänzende Studentenblume · ⊙ ⟂ Z9 VIII-IX ⚥ ; Mex., Guat.
- **minuta** L. · E:Dwarf Marigold, Wild Marigold; G:Mexikanische Studentenblume · ⊙ Z9 X Ⓝ; C-Am., S-Am., nat. in Trop., S-Eur.
- *papposa* Vent. = Dyssodia papposa
- **patula** L. · E:French Marigold; G:Gewöhnliche Studentenblume · ⊙ Z9 VII-X ⚥ ; Mex., Guat.
- **many cultivars**
- **tenuifolia** Cav. · E:Signet Marigold; F:Tagète tachée; G:Feinblatt-Studentenblume, Schmalblatt-Studentenblume · ⊙ Z9 VII-X ⚥ ; Mex.
- **many cultivars**

Taiwania Hayata -f- *Taxodiaceae* · 1 sp. ·
G:Taiwanie
- **cryptomerioides**
- var. **cryptomerioides** · G:Gewöhnliche Taiwanie · ♄ e Z9 ⓚ Ⓝ; Yunnan, Taiwan

Takasagoya Y. Kimura = Hypericum

Talbotia Balf. -f- *Velloziaceae* · 1 sp.
- **elegans** Balf. · ♄ Z9 ⓚ VI-VIII; S-Afr.: Natal

Talinum Adans. -n- *Portulacaceae* · c. 40 spp. · E:Fameflower
- **calycinum** Engelm. · E:Largeflower Fameflower · ⟂ Ψ ⓚ; USA: NCE, NC, SC, Ark.
- **okanoganense** English · E:Okanogan Fameflower · ⟂ Ψ △ Z10 ⓚ VI-VII; Can.: B.C., USA: Wash.
- **paniculatum** (Jacq.) Gaertn. · E:Fameflower, Jewels-of-Opar · ♄ Ψ e Z10 ⓚ VI-VIII; Mex., Lesser Antilles
- **teretifolium** Pursh · E:Quill Fameflower · ⟂ Ψ Z10 ⓚ; USA: NE, SE

- **triangulare** (Jacq.) Willd. · G:Blatt-Ginseng, Ceylonspinat; E:Ceylon Spinach · ⟂ Ψ Z10 ⓜ Ⓝ; C-Am , W.Ind., S-Am., nat. in trop. Afr.

Tamarindus L. -f- *Caesalpiniaceae* · 1 sp. ·
E:Tamarind; F:Tamarinier; G:Tamarinde
- **indica** L. · E:Indian Date, Tamarind; G:Tamarinde · ♄ e Z10 ⓜ VI-VII ⚥ Ⓝ; trop. Afr., nat. in trop. Am.

Tamarix L. -f- *Tamaricaceae* · 54 spp. ·
E:Salt Cedar, Tamarisk; F:Tamaris; G:Tamariske
- *aestivalis* hort. = Tamarix ramosissima
- **africana** Poir. · G:Spanische Tamariske · ♄ ♄ d Z6 VIII-IX; Eur.: Ib, Ital-P, F; Canar. Is., NW-Afr., nat. in BrI
- **articulata** Vahl · G:Arabische Tamariske · ♄ d ⓚ Ⓝ; Sahara, Arab., Iran
- **chinensis** Lour. · E:Chinese Tamarisk; G:Chinesische Tamariske · ♄ ♄ d Z7 VI-VIII Ⓝ; C-As., China, nat. in Oreg. , Calif.
- **gallica** L. · E:French Tamarisk, Tamarisk; G:Französische Tamariske · ♄ d Z6 VI-VIII ⚥ Ⓝ; Eur.: Ib, Fr, Ital-P, Canar., Madeira; N-Afr., nat. in E-USA, Calif.
- *germanica* L. = Myricaria germanica
- *hispanica* Boiss. = Tamarix africana
- *japonica* Dippel = Tamarix chinensis
- *odessana* Steven ex Bunge = Tamarix ramosissima
- **parviflora** DC. · E:Small Flower Tamarisk; F:Tamaris à floraison printanière; G:Kleinblütige Tamariske · ♄ ♄ d Z6 V; Eur.: Ba, TR, N-Afr., nat. in sp., Cors, I
- *pentandra* Pall. = Tamarix ramosissima
- *plumosa* Carrière = Tamarix chinensis
- **ramosissima** Ledeb. · E:Salt Cedar; F:Tamaris à floraison estivale; G:Kaspische Tamariske · ♄ ♄ d Z5 VI-VIII; SE-Russ., Afgh., Iraq, Iran, Pakist., Mong., China, Korea
- **tetrandra** Pall. ex M. Bieb. · E:Erica Tamarisk; F:Tamaris à quatre étamines; G:Viermännige Tamariske · ♄ ♄ d Z6 IV-V; Eur.: Ba, Crim; N-TR, Syr., Cyprus, Cauc.

Tamus L. -m- *Dioscoreaceae* · 4-5 spp. ·
E:Black Bryony; F:Herbe aux femmes battues, Tamier; G:Schmerwurz
- **communis** L. · E:Black Bryony, Bryony; G:Gewöhnliche Schmerwurz · ⟂ ♂ ⓚ

∧ V ⚲ ♁; Eur.: Ib, Fr, Ital-P, Ba, Crim,
RO, H, BrI, C-Eur.; TR, Cyprus, Syr., Iraq,
Cauc., N-Iran, NW-Afr., Canar.

Tanacetum L. -n- *Asteraceae* · c. 70
(-150) spp. · E:Tansy; F:Menthe coq,
Pyrèthre, Tanaisie; G:Balsamkraut,
Insektenblume, Margerite, Mutterkraut,
Pyrethrum, Rainfarn, Wucherblume
– **achilleifolium** (M. Bieb.) Sch. Bip. ·
G:Schafgarbenblättriges Balsamkraut · ⚃
D Z7 VI-VII; Eur.: SE-Russ., ? RO, ? BG
– *alpinum* (L.) Sch. Bip. = Leucanthemopsis
alpina
– **argenteum** Willd. · G:Silber-Balsam-
kraut · ⚃ △ Z7 ∧ VII; TR
– **balsamita** L. · E:Alecost, Costmary;
G:Echtes Balsamkraut, Frauenminze,
Marienblatt · ⚃ D Z6 VII-VIII ⚲ Ⓝ; TR,
Cauc., N-Iran, C-As., nat. in sp., F, I,
EC-Eur., Russ.
– **cinerariifolium** (Trevir.) Sch. Bip. ·
E:Dalmatian Pyrethrum, Pyrethrum;
F:Pyrèthre; G:Dalmatiner Insektenblume,
Pyrethrum · ⚃ Z7 V-VII ⚲ Ⓝ; Eur.:
Croatia, Bosn., Montenegro, AL, nat.
in sp., I, A, H, Russ.
– *clusii* (Fisch. ex Rchb.) A. Kern. = Tanacetum corymbosum subsp. subcorymbosum
– **coccineum** (Willd.) Grierson · E:Painted
Daisy, Pyrethrum; F:Tanaisie rose;
G:Bunte Margerite, Bunte Wucherblume
· ⚃ ✖ Z5 V-VI Ⓝ; Cauc., Iran
– **many cultivars**
– **corymbosum** (L.) Sch. Bip.
– subsp. **corymbosum** · F:Chrysanthème
en corymbe; G:Straußblütige Wucherblume · ⚃ VI-VII; Eur.* exc. BrI, Sc; TR,
Cauc., nat. in Sc
– subsp. **subcorymbosum** (Schur) Pawl. ·
⚃ ; Eur.: E-Alp., S-Alp., Carp., Balkan
– **densum** (Labill.) Sch. Bip. · E:Prince-
of-Wales Feathers · ♄ △ Z7 VII-VIII; TR,
Lebanon
– **haradjanii** (Rech. f.) Grierson ·
F:Tanaisie; G:Silbergefieder · ⚃ △ Z8 ∧
VII-VIII; TR
– **macrophyllum** (Waldst. & Kit.) Sch.
Bip. · G:Großblättrige Wucherblume · ⚃
Z6 VI-VIII; Eur.: Ba, RO; TR, Cauc., nat.
in G, DK, EC-Eur., W-Russ.
– **millefolium** (L.) Tzvelev · G:Kalk-
Balsamkraut · ⚃ VI-VII; Eur.: BG, E-Eur.;
TR, Cauc.
– **partheniifolium** (Willd.) Sch. Bip. ·

G:Grauhaarige Wucherblume · ⚃ Z8 Ⓚ
VII-VIII; Eur.: TR, Cauc., N-Iran, Crim
– **parthenium** (L.) Sch. Bip. · E:Feverfew;
F:Grande camomille; G:Mutterkraut ·
☉ ⚃ ✖ Z6 VI-IX ⚲ ; Eur.: Ba; TR, nat. in
Eur.*; cosmop.
– **many cultivars**
– **ptarmiciflorum** (Webb & Berthel.) Sch.
Bip. · E:Silver Lace; G:Silber-Wucherb-
lume · ♄ Z9 Ⓚ ▽; Canar.
– *serotinum* (L.) Sch. Bip. = Leucanthe-
mella serotina
– **vulgare** L. · E:Tansy; F:Barbotine,
Tanaisie vulgaire; G:Rainfarn · ⚃ Z4
VII-IX ⚲ ♁ Ⓝ; Eur.*, TR, Cauc., W-Sib.,
E-Sib., Amur, Sakhal., Kamchat., C-As.,
Mong., Manch., nat. in N-Am., S-Am.,
Austr., NZ

Tanakaea Franch. & Sav. -f- *Saxifragaceae* ·
1 sp. · E:Japanese Foam Flower;
F:Tanakéa; G:Japanische Schaumblüte
– **radicans** Franch. & Sav. · E:Japanese
Foam Flower; G:Japanische Schaumblüte
· ⚃ ∿ Z8 ∧ VI-VII; Jap.

Tanquana H.E.K. Hartmann & Liede -f-
Aizoaceae · 3 spp.
– **prismatica** (Schwantes) H.E.K. Hartmann & Liede · ⚃ Ψ Z9 Ⓚ IX-XI; Cape

Tapeinochilos Miq. -m- *Costaceae* · 18 spp.
– **ananassae** (Hassk.) K. Schum. · ⚃ Z10
Ⓦ VII-VIII; Molucca: Ceram

Taraxacum Weber ex F.H. Wigg. -n-
Asteraceae · c. 60 spp. · E:Blowballs,
Dandelion; F:Dent de lion, Pissenlit;
G:Kuhblume, Löwenzahn, Pfaffenröhr-
lein, Pusteblume
– **sect. Alpestria** Soest · G:Gebirgs-
Löwenzähne · ⚃ V-VII; Eur.: Sudeten,
Carp., Balkan
– **sect. Alpina** G.E. Haglund · G:Alpen-
Löwenzähne · ⚃ VI-IX; Eur.: Ib, Fr,
C-Eur., EC-Eur., Ba, RO; mts.
– **sect. Celtica** A.J. Richards · G:Moor-
Löwenzähne · ⚃ V-VII; Eur.: Sc, BrI, sp.
– **sect. Cucullata** Soest · G:Strohblütige
Löwenzähne · ⚃ VI-VIII; Eur.: F, Ch, A
– **sect. Erythrosperma** (H. Lindb.)
Dahlst. · G:Schwielen-Löwenzähne ·
⚃ IV-VI; Eur.*, TR, Syr., Cauc., C-As.,
NW-Afr., nat. in N-Am., S-Am.
– **sect. Fontana** Soest ·

G:Quell-Löwenzähne · 4 VI-VIII; Eur.:
Ch, A
– **sect. Obliqua** Dahlst. · G:Dünen-
Löwenzähne · 4 ; Eur.: Sc, BrI, NL, D
– **sect. Palustria** Dahlst. · G:Sumpf-
Löwenzähne · 4 IV-VI; Eur.: BrI, Fr
– **sect. Ruderalia** Kirschner, H. Ollg. &
Stepánek · E:Dandelion; G:Wiesen-
Löwenzähne · 4 IV-VII ⚥ Ⓝ; Eur.*,
W-Sib., E-Sib., nat. in cosmop.
– *alpestre agg.* = Taraxacum sect. Alpestria
– *alpinum agg.* = Taraxacum sect. Alpina
– **aquilonare** Hand.-Mazz. · G:Nördliches
Pfaffenröhrlein · 4 VII-VIII; Eur.: F, N-I,
A, H +
– **bessarabicum** (Hornem.) Hand.-Mazz. ·
G:Kleinköpfiger Löwenzahn · 4 VIII-X;
Eur.: F, A, EC-Eur., BG, E-Eur.; TR, Syr.,
Iran, Afgh., Libya
– **ceratophorum** (Ledeb.) DC. · G:Gehörn-
tes Pfaffenröhrlein · 4 VI-VIII; Eur.: F,
Sw, A, Sc, N-Russ.
– **concucullatum** A.J. Richards · 4 VI-VIII;
Eur.: F, Ch, A
– *cucullatum agg.* = Taraxacum sect. Cucullata
– **dissectum** (Ledeb.) Ledeb. · G:Schlitz-
blättriges Pfaffenröhrlein · 4 VII-VIII;
Eur.: sp., F, Sw, I; Cauc., Iran, C-As, Sib.,
Tibet, Him., China
– *fontanum agg.* = Taraxacum sect. Fontana
– **handelii** Murr · G:Arktischer Löwenzahn · 4 VII-VIII; Eur.: Sw, A
– **hybernum** Steven · 4 Ⓝ; Eur.: I, Ba,
Crim; TR, Syr. N-As
– **kok-saghyz** L.E. Rodin · 4 Ⓝ; C-As.
(Kazakh.)
– *laevigatum agg.* = Taraxacum sect.
Erythrosperma
– **mazzettii** Soest · 4 VI-VIII; Eur.: A +
– **megalorhizum** (Forssk.) Hand.-Mazz. ·
4 Ⓝ; Eur.: Ib, Fr, Ital-P, Ba, W-Russ. +
– **melzerianum** Soest · 4 VI-VIII; Eur.: A +
– **nordstedtii** Dahlst. · G:Norsteds
Löwenzahn · 4 V-VII; Eur.: BrI, Sc, Fr, Ib,
G, EC-Eur.
– *officinale agg.* = Taraxacum sect.
Ruderalia
– **pacheri** Sch. Bip. · G:Pachers Pfaffenröhrlein · 4 VII-VIII; Eur.: I, Sw, A; E-Alp.
– *palustre agg.* = Taraxacum sect. Palustria
– **reichenbachii** Huter ex Dahlst. · 4
VII-VIII; Eur.: A
– **schroeterianum** Hand.-Mazz. ·
G:Schröters Pfaffenröhrlein · 4 VII-VIII;

Eur.: sp., F, I, Sw
– **serotinum** (Waldst. & Kit.) Poir. · 4
VIII-X; Eur.: sp., F, A, EC-Eur., Ba, E-Eur.;
TR, Syr., Lebanon, Cauc., Iran, W-Sib.
– *spectabile agg.* = Taraxacum sect. Celtica
– **tiroliense** Dahlst. · G:Tiroler Löwenzahn · 4 VI-VIII; Eur.: Sw, A, D +

Tarchonanthus L. -m- *Asteraceae* · 2 spp. ·
E:Hottentot Tobacco; F:Tarchonanthus;
G:Totenstrauch
– **camphoratus** L. · E:Hottentot Tobacco;
G:Totenstrauch · ♄ ♄ e D Z10 Ⓛ; Eth.,
trop. Afr., S-Afr.

Tasmannia R. Br. ex DC. -f- *Winteraceae* ·
5 spp.
– *aromatica* R. Br. ex DC. = Tasmannia
lanceolata
– **lanceolata** (Poir.) A.C. Sm. · E:Mountain
Pepper; G:Pfefferbaum · ♄ e Z8 Ⓛ ⚥ ;
Austr.: N.S.Wales, Victoria, Tasman.

Tavaresia Welw. ex N.E. Br. -f-
Asclepiadaceae · 3 spp.
– **barklyi** (Dyer) N.E. Br. · 4 ⚇ Z10 Ⓛ VII-
VIII; Botswana, Namibia, S-Afr.: Cape,
Transvaal
– *grandiflora* (K. Schum.) N.E. Br. =
Tavaresia barklyi

Taxodium Rich. -n- *Taxodiaceae* · 2 spp. ·
E:Swamp Cypress; F:Cyprès chauve;
G:Sumpfzypresse
– *ascendens* Brongn. = Taxodium distichum
var. imbricarium
– **distichum** (L.) Rich. · G:Sumpfzypresse
– var. **distichum** · E:Bald Cypress, Swamp
Cypress; F:Cyprès chauve; G:Zweizeilige
Sumpfzypresse · ♄ d ⌒ Z6 V Ⓝ; USA:
NE, NCE, SC, SE, Fla.
– var. **imbricarium** (Nutt.) H.B. Croom ·
E:Pond Cypress; G:Aufsteigende
Sumpfzypresse · Z6
– var. *nutans* (Aiton) Sweet = Taxodium
distichum var. imbricarium

Taxus L. -f- *Taxaceae* · 10 spp. · E:Yew; F:If;
G:Eibe
– **baccata** L. · E:Common Yew, English
Yew; F:If commun; G:Europäische Eibe,
Gewöhnliche Eibe · ♄ ♄ e Z6 III-IV ⚥ ⚘
▽; Eur.*, Cauc., N-Afr.
– **some cultivars**
– **brevifolia** Nutt. · E:Pacific Yew, Western

Yew; G:Pazifische Eibe · ♄ e Z6 ⚕ ☠ Ⓝ; Alaska, Can: B.C., Alta; USA: NW, Calif., Idaho, Mont.
- **canadensis** Marshall · E:Canadian Yew; G:Kanadische Eibe · ♄ e Z4 ☠; Can.: E; USA: NE, NCE
- **chinensis** (Pilg.) Rehder · E:Chinese Yew; G:Chinesische Eibe
- var. **chinensis** · G:Gewöhnliche Chinesische Eibe · ♄ ♄ e Z6 ☠; China
- var. **mairei** (Lemée ex H. Lév.) W.C. Cheng & L.K. Fu · E:Maire Yew; G:Yunnan-Eibe · Z6 ☠; S-China, Phil., Malay. Arch
- **cuspidata** Siebold & Zucc. · F:If du Japon; G:Gewöhnliche Japanische Eibe · ♄ ♄ e Z5 ☠; Jap., Korea, Manch.
- × **media** Rehder (*T. baccata* × *T. cuspidata var. cuspidata*) · E:Hybrid Yew, Wellesley Yew; G:Hybrid-Eibe · ♄ e Z5 ☠; cult.
- **sumatrana** (Miq.) de Laub. · E:Sumatran Yew; G:Sumatra-Eibe · ♄ ♄ e ☠; China

Tecoma Juss. -f- *Bignoniaceae* · 12 spp. · E:Trumpet Bush; F:Bignone; G:Trompetenstrauch
- *capensis* (Thunb.) Lindl. = Tecomaria capensis
- **castaneifolia** (D. Don) Melch. · G:Kastanienblättriger Trompetenstrauch · ♄ s Z10 Ⓚ I-XII; Ecuad.
- *grandiflora* (Thunb.) Loisel. = Campsis grandiflora
- *jasminoides* Lindl. = Pandorea jasminoides
- **leucoxylon** (L.) Mart. · G:Grünes Ebenholz · ♄ Z10 Ⓦ Ⓝ; W.Ind., S-Am.
- *radicans* (L.) Juss. = Campsis radicans
- **stans** (L.) Juss. ex Kunth · E:Yellow Bells, Yellow Trumpet Flower; G:Gelber Trompetenstrauch · ♄ ♄ e Z10 Ⓚ VI-VIII; USA: SC, SE, Fla.; Mex., S-Am.

Tecomaria (Endl.) Spach -f- *Bignoniaceae* · 1 sp. · E:Cape Honeysuckle; F:Chèvrefeuille du Cap; G:Kapgeißblatt
- **capensis** (Thunb.) Spach · E:Cape Honeysuckle; G:Kapgeißblatt · ♄ e Z9 Ⓚ VIII-X; S-Afr.

Tecophilaea Bertero ex Colla -f- *Tecophilaeaceae* · 2 spp. · E:Chilean Crocus; F:Crocus du Chili; G:Chilekrokus
- **cyanocrocus** Leyb. · E:Chilean Crocus; G:Echter Chilecrocus · ♃ Z9 Ⓚ ▭ III; Chile

Tectaria Cav. -f- *Dryopteridaceae* · 216 spp.
- **cicutaria** (L.) Copel. · E:Button Fern · ♃ Z10 Ⓦ; Trop.
- **decurrens** (C. Presl) Copel. · ♃ Z10 Ⓦ; Polyn.
- **incisa** Cav. · ♃ Z10 Ⓦ; Mex., W.Ind., C-Am., trop. S-Am.
- *martinicensis* (Spreng.) Copel. = Tectaria incisa
- **trifoliata** (L.) Cav. · ♃ Z10 Ⓦ; Mex., C-Am., W.Ind., trop. S-Am.

Tectona L. f. -f- *Verbenaceae* · 3 spp. · E:Teak; F:Teck; G:Teakholz
- **grandis** L. f. · E:Teak ; G:Teakholz · ♄ d Z10 Ⓦ Ⓝ; Ind., Burma, Thail., Laos

Teesdalia R. Br. -f- *Brassicaceae* · 2 spp. · E:Shepherd's Cress; F:Tesdalia; G:Bauernsenf, Rahle
- **nudicaulis** (L.) R. Br. · G:Kahler Bauernsenf · ⊙ IV-V; Eur.*, Moroc.

Telekia Baumg. -f- *Asteraceae* · 1 sp. · E:Oxeye; F:Œil-de-bœuf; G:Telekie
- **speciosa** (Schreb.) Baumg. · E:Large Yellow Oxeye; G:Große Telekie · ♃ Z6 VI-VIII; Eur.: EC-Eur., Ba, E-Eur.; TR, Cauc., nat. in BrI, Fr, C-Eur.
- **speciosissima** (L.) Less. · G:Kleine Telekie · ♃ △ Z6 VI-VII; Eur.: N-I (Alpi Orobie)

Telephium L. -n- *Molluginaceae* · 5 spp. · F:Grand orpin; G:Telephie, Zierspark
- **imperati** L. · G:Telephie, Zierspark · ♃ Z8 VI-VII; Eur.: Ba, Fr, Ital-P, Ib, Sw

Telesonix Raf. = Boykinia
- *jamesii* (Torr.) Raf. = Boykinia jamesii

Telfairia Hook. -f- *Cucurbitaceae* · 3 spp. · F:Kouémé; G:Oysternuss, Talerkürbis
- **occidentalis** Hook. f. · E:Oyster Nuts; G:Oysternuss · ♄ e ⚘ Z9 Ⓦ Ⓝ; W-Afr.
- **pedata** (Sm. ex Sims) Hook. · E:Zanzibar Oil ; G:Talerkürbis · ♄ ⚘ Z9 Ⓦ Ⓝ; E-Afr., Madag., Mascarene Is.

Teline Medik. = Genista
- *monspessulana* (L.) K. Koch = Genista monspessulana

Tellima R. Br. -f- *Saxifragaceae* · 1 sp. ·
E:Fringecup; F:Tellima; G:Falsche
Alraunenwurzel
- **grandiflora** (Pursh) Douglas ex Lindl. ·
E:Fringecups; G:Falsche Alraunenwurzel
· ⚃ Z6 V-VI; Alaska, Can.: W; USA: NW,
Calif.
- *odorata* Howell = Tellima grandiflora

Telopea R. Br. -f- *Proteaceae* · 5 spp. ·
E:Waratah; F:Télopéa; G:Waratahprotee
- **truncata** (Labill.) R. Br. · ♄ ♄ e Z9 ⍟;
Tasman.

Teloxys Moq. = Chenopodium
- *aristata* (L.) Moq. = Chenopodium
aristatum

Templetonia R. Br. ex W.T. Aiton
-f- *Fabaceae* · 11 sp. · F:Genêt du désert,
Templetonia; G:Wüsten-ginster
- **retusa** (Vent.) R. Br. · E:Bullock Bush,
Coral Bush; G:Flammender Wüstenginster · ♄ e Z10 ⍟ III-VI; Austr.: S-Austr.,
W-Austr.

Tephroseris (Rchb.) Rchb. -f- *Asteraceae* ·
c. 50 spp. · E:Fleawort; F:Cinéraire;
G:Greiskraut
- **crispa** (Jacq.) Rchb. · G:Bach-Greiskraut,
Krauses Greiskraut · ⚃ V-VI; Eur.: I, G, A,
EC-Eur., E-Eur.; mts.
- **helenitis** (L.) B. Nord. · G:Gewöhnliches
Spatelblättriges Greiskraut · ⚃ V-VI;
Eur.: sp., Fr, Sw, G, A
- **integrifolia** (L.) Holub · G:Steppen-
Greiskraut
- subsp. **aurantiaca** Hoppe ex Willd. ·
G:Orangerotes Greiskraut · ⚃ △ Z6
VI-VIII; Eur.* exc. Ib; ? N-As.
- subsp. **capitata** (Wahlenb.) B. Nord. ·
G:Kopf-Greiskraut · ⚃ △ Z6 VI-VII; Eur.:
F, I, Sw, A, RO; Alp., Carp.; Cauc., Sib.,
Kamchat., China, Alaska
- subsp. **integrifolia** · E:Field Fleawort;
G:Gewöhnliches Steppen-Greiskraut · ⚃
Z6 V-VI; Eur.* exc. Ib; N-Russ.; N-As.,
Jap., Taiwan
- subsp. **serpentini** (Gáyer) B. Nord. · ⚃
Z6 V-VI; Eur.: A (Burgenland)
- **longifolia** (Jacq.) Griseb. & Schenk ·
G:Obir-Aschenkraut, Obir-Greiskraut,
Voralpen-Kreuzkraut · ⚃ V-VII; Eur.: G,
A, Slove., Croatia; E-Alp., Croatia mts.
- **palustris** (L.) Fourr. ·

G:Moor-Greiskraut · ⊙ Z4 VI-VII; Eur.:
BrI, Sc, Fr, G, EC-Eur., Russ; Sib.
- **pseudocrispa** (Fiori) Holub · ⚃ VI-VIII;
Eur.: G, A, PL, CZ, Slove., RO
- **tenuifolia** (Gaudin) Holub · G:Läger-
Greiskraut, Schweizer Greiskraut · ⚃
V-VII; Eur.: I, A, Sw; Alp., Apenn.

Tephrosia Pers. -f- *Fabaceae* · 400 spp. ·
E:Hoary Pea; F:Téphrosie; G:Aschenwi-
cke, Giftbaum
- **candida** (Roxb.) A. DC. · ♄ ⍟ Ⓝ; Ind.,
Him., Burma, Malay. Arch.
- **purpurea** (L.) Pers. · E:Wild Indigo;
G:Surinam-Giftbaum · ⚃ Z10 ⍟ ⚔ Ⓝ;
Him., Sri Lanka, Thail, Java
- **sinapou** (Buc'hoz) A. Chev. · ⍟ ⚔ Ⓝ;
Mex., C.-Am., trop. S-Am.
- **virginiana** (L.) Pers. · E:Catgut, Goat's
Rue; G:Virginischer Giftbaum · ⚃ Z4
VI-VII ⚔; Can.: Ont.; USA: NE, NCE, NC,
SC, SE, Fla.
- **vogelii** Hook. f. · E:Fish Poison Bean;
G:Fisch-Giftbaum · ⚃ ⍟ ⚔ Ⓝ; W-Afr.;
Guinea, Sierra Leone; trop-Afr.: Mozamb.

Terebinthus Mill. = Pistacia
- *lentiscus* (L.) Moench = Pistacia lentiscus

Terminalia L. -f- *Combretaceae* · -200 spp. ·
E:Myrobalan; F:Amandier des Indes,
Badanier; G:Almend, Almond, Myroba-
lane
- **bellirica** (Gaertn.) Roxb. · E:Belleric
Myrobalan; G:Belerische Myrobalane ·
♄ d Z10 ⍟ ⚥ Ⓝ; Ind., Sri Lanka, Burma,
Thail., Malay. Pen.
- **catappa** L. · E:Indian Almond, Olive Bark
Tree; G:Indische Myrobalane, Indischer
Mandelbaum · ♄ d Z10 ⍟ Ⓝ; E-Afr.,
Madag., Pakist., Ind., Java, N.Guinea,
nat. in S-Fla.
- **chebula** (Gaertn.) Retz. · E:Indian
Myrobalan, Ink Nut; G:Chebulische
Myrobalane · ♄ d Z10 ⍟ ⚥ Ⓝ; Ind., Sri
Lanka, Burma
- **superba** Engl. & Diels · E:White Afara;
G:Weiße Myrobalane · ♄ Z10 ⍟ Ⓝ;
W-Afr.

Ternstroemia Mutis ex L. f. -f- *Theaceae* ·
85 spp. · G:Ternströmie
- **gymnanthera** (Wight & Arn.) Sprague ·
♄ ♄ e Z9 ⍟; Jap.

Testudinaria Salisb. = Dioscorea
– *sylvatica* Kunth = Dioscorea sylvatica

Tetracarpidium Pax -n- *Euphorbiaceae* ·
1 sp.
– **conophorum** (Müll. Arg.) Hutch. &
Dalziel · ♄ Z10 ⓦ Ⓝ; W-Afr., C-Afr.

Tetracentron Oliv. -n- *Tetracentraceae* ·
1 sp. · E:Spur Leaf; F:Tétracentron;
G:Vierspornbaum
– **sinense** Oliv. · E:Spur Leaf; G:Vierspornbaum · ♄ d Z7 ∧ VI ✳; Nepal, NE-Ind.,
Burma, SW-China

Tetraclinis Mast. -f- *Cupressaceae* · 1 sp. ·
E:Arar Tree; F:Thuya articulé, Thuya
d'Algérie; G:Gliederzypresse, Sandarakbaum
– **articulata** (Vahl) Mast. · E:Arar Tree;
F:Thuya articulé, Thuya d'Algérie;
G:Gliederzypresse, Sandarakbaum · ♄
e Z10 ⓚ ⚥ Ⓝ; Eur.: sp. (Cartagena),
Malta; NW-Afr., Libya

Tetradenia Benth. -f- *Lamiaceae* · 13 spp.
– **riparia** (Hochst.) Codd · ⌗ Z10 ⓚ XII-II;
S-Afr.

Tetradium Lour. -n- *Rutaceae* · 9 spp. ·
F:Frêne puant; G:Stinkesche
– **daniellii** (Benn.) T.G. Hartley ·
G:Samthaarige Stinkesche · ♄ d ⚮ Z7
VII; Korea, N-China

Tetragonia L. -f- *Aizoaceae* · 57 spp. ·
E:New Zealand Spinach; F:Epinard de
Nouvelle-Zélande, Tétragone; G:Neuseelandspinat
– **echinata** Aiton · ☉ Ⓨ; S-Afr.
– **tetragonioides** (Pall.) Kuntze · E:New
Zealand Spinach; G:Neuseeländer Spinat
· ☉ Ⓨ ⤳ VII-IX Ⓝ; Austr., NZ, nat. in Ib, I

Tetragonolobus Scop. -m- *Fabaceae* ·
5 spp. · E:Dragon's Teeth; F:Lotier,
Tétragonolobe; G:Schotenklee,
Spargelerbse
– *edulis* Link = Tetragonolobus purpureus
– **maritimus** (L.) Roth · E:Dragon's Teeth;
G:Gelbe Spargelerbse · ⌗ Z6 V-IX; Eur.:
W, C u. S-Eur., Ukraine, N-Afr.
– **purpureus** Moench · E:Asparagus Pea;
G:Echte Spargelerbse, Kaffee-Erbse · ☉
VII-VIII Ⓝ; Eur.: Ib, F, Ital-P, Ba, E-Eur.;

W-TR, Levant, Cauc., NW-Afr., Libya,
nat. in Cz
– *siliquosus* Roth = Tetragonolobus
maritimus

× **Tetraliopsis** hort. -f- *Orchidaceae*
(*Laeliopsis* × *Tetramicra*)

Tetranema Benth. -n- *Scrophulariaceae* ·
2 spp.
– **roseum** (M. Martens & Galeotti) Standl.
& Steyerm. · E:Mexican Violet · ⌗ Z9 ⓦ
II-X; Mex., C-Am.

Tetraneuris Greene = Hymenoxys
– *acaulis* (Pursh) Greene = Hymenoxys
acaulis
– *grandiflora* (Torr. & A. Gray ex A. Gray)
K.L. Parker = Hymenoxys grandiflora
– *linearifolia* (Hook.) Greene = Hymenoxys
linearifolia
– *scaposa* (DC.) Greene = Hymenoxys
scaposa

Tetrapanax (K. Koch) K. Koch -m-
Araliaceae · 1 sp. · E:Rice-Paper Plant;
F:Tétrapanax; G:Reispapierbaum
– **papyrifer** (Hook.) K. Koch · E:Rice-Paper
Plant; G:Reispapierbaum · ♄ e Z8 ⓦ Ⓝ;
S-China, Taiwan

Tetrastigma (Miq.) Planch. -n- *Vitaceae* ·
90 spp. · E:Javan Grape
– **voinierianum** (Baltet) Pierre ex
Gagnep. · E:Chestnut Vine · ♄ e ⚵ Z10 ⓦ;
N-Vietn. (Tongking)

× **Tetratonia** hort. -f- *Orchidaceae*
(*Tetramicra* × *Broughtonia*)

Teucrium L. -n- *Lamiaceae* · 243 spp. ·
E:Germander; F:Germandrée; G:Gamander
– **arduini** L. · ♄; Ba
– **aroanium** Orph. ex Boiss. · ♄ ♄ e Z8 ⓚ;
GR
– **aureum** Schreb. · G:Goldrand-Gamander · ♄ e ⤳ △ Z7 ∧ VII-VIII; Eur.: sp., F,
Sic.; NW-Afr.
– **botrys** L. · G:Trauben-Gamander · ☉
VII-IX; Eur.* exc. Sc
– **chamaedrys** L. · E:Wall Germander;
G:Breitblättriger Edel-Gamander · ♄ e △
Z6 VII-VIII ⚥ Ⓝ; Eur.* exc. BrI, Sc; TR,
Cauc.

– *chamaepitys* L. = Ajuga chamaepitys
– *cinereum* Boiss. = Teucrium rotundifolium
– **compactum** Clemente ex Lag. · ♄ ⬔; sp.,
Tun., Alger.
– **flavum** L. · ♄ e Z8 ⬔; Eur.: Ba, Ib, Ital-P,
Fr; NW-Afr., TR
– **fruticans** L. · E:Bush Germander;
G:Baum-Gamander · ♄ e Z8 ⬔ VII-VIII;
Eur.: Ib, Fr, Ital-P, Croatia
– **hircanicum** L. · E:Caucasian Germander;
G:Kaukasus-Gamander · ⑂ Z6; NE-TR,
N-Iran, Cauc.
– × **lucidrys** Boom (*T. chamaedrys* × *T.
lucidum*) · G:Bastard-Gamander · ♄ ♄ e
VII-VIII; cult.
– **lucidum** L. · ⑂ e Z6; F, I; SW-Alp.
– **marum** L. · E:Cat Thyme; G:Amberkraut,
Katzen-Gamander · ♄ e D Z9 ⬔ ⚥ ; Eur.:
Balear., F, Cors, Sard., I, Croatia
– **massiliense** L. · E:Sweet Scented
Germander; F:Germandrée de Marseille;
G:Duftender Gamander · ♄ e ⸬ Z6 VI-VIII;
Eur.: sp., F, Cors, Sard., Crete
– **montanum** L. · E:Alpine Pennyroyal,
Mountain Germander; G:Berg-Gamander
· ♄ e ⤳ △ Z6 VII-VIII ⚥ ; Eur.* exc. BrI,
Sc
– **musimonum** Humbert ex Maire · ⑂ ⤳
△ ⋀ VI-IX; Moroc.; Atlas
– **orientale** L. · ⑂ Z7 ⋀ VII-VIII; TR,
Lebanon, Cauc., Iran
– **polium** L.
– subsp. *aureum* (Schreb.) Arcang. =
Teucrium aureum
– subsp. **polium** · E:Golden Germander;
G:Goldener Gamander · ♄ e Z7; Eur.: sp.,
S-F; NW-Afr.
– **pyrenaicum** L. · E:Pyrenean Ger-
mander; F:Germandrée des Pyrénées;
G:Pyrenäen-Gamander · ⑂ ⤳ Z6
VII-VIII; SW-F, N-Sp.
– **rotundifolium** Schreb. · ⑂; sp.; mts.
– **scordium** L. · G:Lauch-Gamander · ⑂ ⌇
VII-VIII ⚥ ; Eur.*, W-Sib., C-As.
– **scorodonia** L. · E:Wood Germander,
Wood Sage; F:Germandrée scorodoine;
G:Salbei-Gamander · ⑂ ♄ Z6 VII-IX ⚥ ;
Eur.* exc. EC-Eur., Sc, nat. in Sc
– **subspinosum** Pourr. ex Willd. · ♄ e Z9
⬔; Balear.

Thalia L. -f- *Marantaceae* · 6 spp. ·
E:Alligator Flag
– **dealbata** Fraser · E:Powdery Alligator

Flag · ⑂ ≈ Z9 ⬓ VII-VIII; USA: Mo, SE,
SC., Fla.
– **geniculata** L. · E:Bent Alligator Flag · ⑂
≈ Z9 ⬓ VII-VIII; USA: SE, Fla.; W.Ind.,
S-Am., nat. in trop. Afr.

Thalictrum L. -n- *Ranunculaceae* · c.
330 spp. · E:Meadow Rue; F:Pigamon;
G:Wiesenraute
– **alpinum** L. · E:Alpine Meadow Rue;
G:Alpen-Wiesenraute · ⑂ △ Z5 VI-VIII;
Eur.* exc. Ib, EC-Eur.; N, mts.; Cauc.,
W-Sib., E-Sib., Sakhal., Kamchat., C-As.,
Him., Mong., China, Alaska, Can., USA:
NC, SW, Rocky Mts., Calif.; Greenl.
– *anemonoides* Michx. = Anemonella
thalictroides
– **aquilegiifolium** L. · E:Columbine
Meadow Rue; F:Pigamon à feuilles
d'ancolie; G:Akeleiblättrige Wiesenraute
· ⑂ Z6 V-VII; Eur.* exc. BrI; NW-TR
– **coreanum** H. Lév. · ⑂ V; E-China,
N-China
– **delavayi** Franch. · ⑂ Z7 VII-VIII; W-China
– **dipterocarpum** Franch. · E:Chinese
Meadow Rue; G:Chinesische Wiesenraute · ⑂ VII-VIII; W-China
– *dipterocarpum* hort. = Thalictrum
delavayi
– **flavum** L.
– subsp. **flavum** · E:Yellow Meadow Rue;
G:Gelbe Wiesenraute · ⑂ Z6 VI-VII;
Eur.*, Cauc., W-Sib., E-Sib., Amur, C-As.
– subsp. **glaucum** (Desf.) Batt. · F:Pigamon
jaune · ⑂ Z6 VII-VIII; Eur.: Ib; Moroc.,
Alger.
– **foetidum** L. · E:Stinking Meadow Rue;
G:Stinkende Wiesenraute · ⑂ Z6 VI-VIII;
Eur.* exc. BrI, Sc; TR, Cauc., Iran,
W-Sib., E-Sib., Amur, C-As., ? Afgh.,
Mong., Tibet
– *glaucum* Desf. = Thalictrum flavum
subsp. glaucum
– **isopyroides** C.A. Mey. · ⑂ ; TR, Syr.,
N-Iraq, Cauc. (Armen.), Iran, Afgh., Altai
– **kiusianum** Nakai · ⑂ △ VI-VIII; Jap.
– **lucidum** L. · G:Glänzende Wiesenraute ·
⑂ Z7 VI-VIII; Eur.: C-Eur., EC-Eur., I, Ba,
E-Eur.; TR, nat. in FIN, Crim
– **minus** L. · E:Lesser Meadow Rue;
G:Gewöhnliche Kleine Wiesenraute · ⑂ ⋈
Z6 V-VI; Eur.*; TR, Cauc., Iran, W-Sib.,
E-Sib., Amur, Sakhal., Kamchat., C-As.,
Pakist., Mong., China, Korea
– **morisonii** C.C. Gmel. · G:Hohe

Wiesenraute · ⅃ VII-VIII; Eur.: sp., F,
Cors, I, Sw
– **orientale** Boiss. · ⅃ Z7 V-VI; S-GR, S-TR,
N-Syr.
– **polygamum** Muhl. · E:Muskrat Weed;
G:Zwittrige Wiesenraute · ⅃; E-Can.,
USA: NE, NEC, SE
– **rochebruneanum** Franch. & Sav. · ⅃ Z7;
Jap.
– **simplex** L. · G:Einfache Wiesenraute
– subsp. **gallicum** (Rouy & Foucaud)
Tutin · ⅃ Z7; F
– subsp. **simplex** · E:Small Meadow Rue;
G:Gewöhnliche Einfache Wiesenraute ·
⅃ Z7 VI-VII; Eur.* exc. BrI, Ib; TR, Cauc.,
Iran, W-Sib., E-Sib., Amur, Kamchat.
– *speciosissimum* L. = Thalictrum flavum
subsp. glaucum
– **tuberosum** L. · ⅃ △ Z8 ∧ VI-VII;
Eur.: sp., F

Thamnocalamus Munro -m- *Poaceae* ·
6 spp.
– *spathaceus* (Franch.) Soderstr. = Fargesia
murieliae
– **tessellatus** (Nees) Soderstr. & R.P. Ellis ·
ђ e Z7; S-Afr.

Thapsia L. -f- *Apiaceae* · 3 spp. · G:Purgier-
dolde; F:Thapsia
– **garganica** L. · ⅃ Ⓐ VII-VIII ⚘; Eur.: Ib,
Ital-P, Ba; TR , NW-Afr., Libya

Thaumatococcus Benth. -m- *Marantaceae* ·
1 sp.
– **danielii** Benth. · ⅃ Ⓐ Ⓝ; W-Afr., C-Afr.

Thea L. = Camellia
– *bohea* L. = Camellia sinensis var. sinensis
– *sinensis* L. = Camellia sinensis var.
sinensis
– *viridis* L. = Camellia sinensis var. sinensis

Thelesperma Less. -n- *Asteraceae* ·
12-15 spp. · E:Greenthreads;
F:Thélésperme; G:Warzensame
– **burridgeanum** (Regel, Körn. & Rach)
S.F. Blake · E:Burridge's Greenthread · ☉
VII-IX; Tex.
– **trifidum** (Poir.) Britton · E:Stiff
Greenthread · ☉ ☉ VI-IX; USA: NC, SC,
Colo., N.Mex., Mo.

Theligonum L. -n- *Theligonaceae* · 3 spp. ·
F:Crambe des chiens, Théligone;

G:Hundskohl
– **cynocrambe** L. · ☉ Ⓐ; Eur.: Ib, Ital-P,
Fr, Ba, Crim

Thelocactus (K. Schum.) Britton & Rose
-m- *Cactaceae* · 11 sp.
– **bicolor** (Galeotti ex Pfeiff.) Britton &
Rose
– var. **bicolor** · E:Texas Pride · ♍ Z9 Ⓐ ▽
✳; Tex., N.-Mex.
– var. *bolaensis* (Runge) N.P. Taylor =
Thelocactus bicolor var. bicolor
– var. **pottsii** (Salm-Dyck) Backeb. · ♍ Z9
Ⓐ
– *buekii* (E. Klein) Britton & Rose =
Thelocactus tulensis
– **conothelos** (Regel & E. Klein) F.M.
Knuth · ♍ Z9 Ⓐ ▽ ✳; NE-Mex.
– *ehrenbergii* (Pfeiff.) F.M. Knuth = Thelocactus leucacanthus var. leucacanthus
– *fossulatus* (Scheidw.) Britton & Rose =
Thelocactus hexaedrophorus
– *gielsdorfianus* (Werderm.) Bravo =
Turbinicarpus gielsdorfianus
– **heterochromus** (F.A.C. Weber) Oosten ·
♍ Z9 Ⓐ ▽ ✳; Mex.: Chihuahua, Durango
– **hexaedrophorus** (Lem.) Britton & Rose ·
♍ Z9 Ⓐ ▽ ✳; N-Mex.
– *horripilus* (Lem.) Kladiwa & Fittkau =
Turbinicarpus horripilus
– **leucacanthus** (Zucc. ex Pfeiff.) Britton &
Rose
– var. **leucacanthus** · ♍ Z9 Ⓐ ▽ ✳; E-Mex.
– var. *schmollii* Werderm. = Thelocactus
leucacanthus var. leucacanthus
– *lloydii* Britton & Rose = Thelocactus
hexaedrophorus
– *lophophoroides* Werderm. = Turbinicarpus lophophoroides
– *lophothele* (Salm-Dyck) Britton & Rose =
Thelocactus rinconensis
– *matudae* Sánchez-Mej. & A.B. Lau =
Thelocactus tulensis
– *nidulans* (Quehl) Britton & Rose =
Thelocactus rinconensis
– *phymatothelos* (Poselg.) Britton & Rose =
Thelocactus rinconensis
– *pottsii* (Salm-Dyck) Britton & Rose =
Thelocactus bicolor var. pottsii
– *pottsii* hort. = Thelocactus heterochromus
– *pseudopectinatus* (Backeb.) E.F. Anderson
& Boke = Turbinicarpus pseudopectinatus
– **rinconensis** (Poselg.) Britton & Rose · ♍
Z9 Ⓐ ▽ ✳; NE-Mex.
– *saueri* (Boed.) A. Berger = Turbinicarpus

saueri
- *saussieri* (F.A.C. Weber) A. Berger = Thelocactus conothelos
- **setispinus** (Engelm.) E.F. Anderson · E:Strawberry Cactus · ⚭ Z9 ⓚ ▽ ❋; S-Tex., Mex.: Tamaulipas
- **tulensis** (Poselg.) Britton & Rose · ⚭ Z9 ⓚ ▽ ❋; NE-Mex.
- *valdezianus* (L. Möller) Bravo = Turbinicarpus valdezianus
- *viereckii* (Werderm.) Bravo = Turbinicarpus viereckii

Thelypteris Schmidel -f- *Thelypteridaceae* · c. 280 spp. · E:Marsh Fern; F:Fougère des marais; G:Sumpffarn
- *decursivepinnata* (H.C. Hall) Ching = Phegopteris decursive-pinnata
- *dentata* (Forssk.) E.P. St John = Christella dentata
- *hexagonoptera* (Michx.) Weath. = Phegopteris hexagonoptera
- **limbosperma** (All.) H.P. Fuchs · E:Mountain Fern; G:Bergfarn · ⑭; Eur.*, TR, NE-As, Jap., Kamchat., Alaska, Can.: W
- *noveboracensis* (L.) Nieuwl. = Parathelypteris noveboracensis
- *oreopteris* (Ehrh.) Sloss. = Oreopteris limbosperma
- **palustris** Schott · E:Eastern Marsh Fern, Marsh Fern; F:Agrostic, Thélypteris des marais; G:Gewöhnlicher Sumpffarn · ⑭ ⌒ Z4 VII-IX; Eur.*, TR, Palest., Cauc., W-Sib., E-Sib., Amur, Sakhal., Kamchat., C-As., Moroc., Alger., N-Am., W-Afr., S-Afr., NZ
- *phegopteris* (L.) Sloss. = Phegopteris connectilis
- *thelypteroides* (F. Michx.) Holub = Thelypteris palustris

Themeda Forssk. -f- *Poaceae* · 18 spp. · F:Herbe aux kangourous; G:Rotschopfgras
- **triandra** Forssk.
- subsp. **japonica** (Willd.) T. Koyama · ⑭ Z10; Jap., Korea, Manch., China, Ind.

Theobroma L. -n- *Sterculiaceae* · 20 spp. · E:Cacao; F:Cacaoyer, Théobrome; G:Kakaobaum
- **bicolor** Humb. & Bonpl. · ♄ Z10 ⓦ Ⓝ; Mex., C-Am., Col., Braz.
- **cacao** L.

- subsp. **cacao** · E:Cacao, Chocolate Nut Tree; G:Echter Kakaobaum · ♄ ♄ e Z10 ⓦ ⚥ Ⓝ; C-Am., trop. S-Am.
- subsp. **sphaerocarpum** (A. Chev.) Cuatrec. · ♄ e Z10 ⓦ Ⓝ; trop. S-Am.

Theophrasta L. -f- *Theophrastaceae* · 2 spp.
- *imperialis* Linden ex K. Koch & Fintelm. = Chrysophyllum imperiale
- **jussieui** Lindl. · ♄ e Z10 ⓦ; Hispaniola
- *longifolia* Jacq. = Clavija longifolia

Thermopsis R. Br. -f- *Fabaceae* · 13 spp. · E:False Lupin, Goldenbanner; F:Fauxlupin; G:Fuchsbohne
- **barbata** Benth. · ⑭ Z7 VI; Him.
- *caroliniana* M.A. Curtis = Thermopsis villosa
- **fabacea** (Pall.) DC. · G:Fuchsbohne · ⑭ Z5 VI-VII; Sib.
- **lanceolata** R. Br. · ⑭ Z3 VI-VIII; SE-Russ., C-As.
- *lupinoides* (L.) Link = Thermopsis lanceolata
- **mollis** (Michx.) M.A. Curtis ex Gray. · E:Allegheny Mountain Goldenbanner · ⑭ Z6; USA: Va., SE
- **rhombifolia** (Pursh) Richardson · E:Buffalo Pea, Prairie Thermopsis; G:Rocky-Mountain-Fuchsbohne · ⑭ Z4 V; USA: NW, Calif., Rocky Mts.
- **villosa** (Walter) Fernald & B.G. Schub. · E:Aaron's Rod, Carolina Lupin; G:Carolina-Fuchsbohne · ⑭ Z7 VI-VII; USA: SE

Thesium L. -n- *Santalaceae* · 325 spp. · F:Thésion, Thésium; G:Bergflachs, Leinblatt
- **alpinum** L. · G:Alpen-Leinblatt · ⑭ VI-VII; Eur.* exc. BrI; Cauc.
- **arvense** Horv. · G:Ästiges Leinblatt · ⑭ VI-VIII; Eur.: Ital-P, C-Eur., EC-Eur., Ba, E-Eur.; TR, Cauc., Iran, W-Sib., C-As.
- **bavarum** Schrank · G:Bayerisches Leinblatt · ⑭ VI-IX; Eur.: Fr, Ital-P, C-Eur., EC-Eur., Ba, RO
- **dollineri** Murb. · G:Niedriges Leinblatt · ⑭ IV-IX; Eur.: A, EC-Eur., Ba, E-Eur.
- **ebracteatum** Hayne · G:Schopf-Leinblatt, Vorblattloses Leinblatt · ⑭ V-VI ▽; Eur.: C-Eur., DK, EC-Eur., E-Eur.; W-Sib.
- **humifusum** DC. · G:Niederliegendes Leinblatt · ⑭; Eur.: sp., Fr, BrI, ? Cors
- **linophyllon** L. · G:Mittleres Leinblatt · ⑭

VI-VII; Eur.: Fr, Ital-P, C-Eur., EC-Eur., Ba, E-Eur.
- **pyrenaicum** Pourr. · G:Gewöhnliches Wiesen-Leinblatt · ♃ VI-VII; Eur.: Ib, Fr, Ital-P, C-Eur., EC-Eur., Ba
- **rostratum** Mert. & W.D.J. Koch · G:Schnabelfrüchtiges Leinblatt · ♃ V-VII; Eur.: I, C-Eur., EC-Eur., Slove.

Thespesia Sol. ex Corrêa -f- *Malvaceae* · 17 spp. · E:Portia Tree; F:Thespésia; G:Tropeneibisch
- **populnea** (L.) Sol. ex Corrêa · E:Portia Tree; G:Küsten-Tropeneibisch · ♄ e Z10 Ⓦ Ⓝ; Afr., trop. As., nat. in W.Ind., Fla.

Thevetia L. -f- *Apocynaceae* · 8 spp. · E:Luckynut; F:Bois-lait, Thévétia; G:Schellenbaum, Thevetie
- **peruviana** (Pers.) K. Schum. · E:Yellow Oleander; G:Gelber Schellenbaum · ♄ ♄ e Z10 Ⓦ VI-VIII ☠; USA: Fla.; Mex., C-Am., W.Ind., S-Am.

Thibaudia Ruiz & Pav. -f- *Ericaceae* · 60 spp.
- **floribunda** Kunth · ♄ e Z9 Ⓚ; Col.

Thladiantha Bunge -f- *Cucurbitaceae* · 23 spp. · F:Thladianthe; G:Quetschblume, Quetschgurke
- **dubia** Bunge · E:Red Hailstone; G:Quetschblume, Quetschgurke · ♃ ♧ Z7 Ⓐ V-VII; Amur, N-China

Thlaspi L. -n- *Brassicaceae* · 60 spp. · E:Penny Cress; F:Tabaret, Thlaspi; G:Hellerkraut, Täschelkraut
- **alliaceum** L. · G:Lauch-Hellerkraut · ⊙ IV-VI; Eur.* exc. BrI, Sc; TR, nat. in BrI
- *alpestre* L. = Thlaspi caerulescens
- subsp. **sylvium** (Gaudin) Kerguélen · G:Penninisches Hellerkraut · ♃ Z6 VI-VIII; Eur.: F, I, Sw; Alp.
- *alpinum* Crantz = Thlaspi caerulescens
- **arvense** L. · E:Pennycress; G:Acker-Hellerkraut · ⊙ IV-V; Eur.*, Cauc., TR, Syr., Palest., Iran, W-Sib., E-Sib., Amur, Sakhal., Kamchat., C-As., Him., Mong., China, Alger., Canar., Eth., nat. in N-Am.
- **brachypetalum** Jord. · E:Small-flowered Penny Cress; G:Voralpen-Hellerkraut · ⊙ V-VII; Eur.: sp., F, I, D; Pyr., SW-Alp., Apenn., nat. in Swed
- **caerulescens** J. Presl & C. Presl · G:Gebirgs-Hellerkraut · ⊙ ⊙ IV-VI; Eur.* exc. Sc, E-Eur., nat. in Sc
- **calaminare** (Lej.) Lej. & Courtois · G:Galmei-Hellerkraut · ♃ V-VI; Eur.: B, D
- **cepaeifolium** (Wulfen) W.D.J. Koch · G:Julisches Hellerkraut
- subsp. **cepaeifolium** · G:Gewöhnliches Julisches Hellerkraut · ♃ Z6; Eur.: I, Slove.; SE-Alp.
- subsp. **rotundifolium** (L.) Greuter & Burdet · E:Round Leaved Pennycress; G:Rundblättriges Hellerkraut · ♃ △ Z6 VI; Eur.: F, I, C-Eur., Slove.; mts.
- **goesingense** Halácsy · G:Gösing-Hellerkraut · ♃ Z6 V-VI; Eur.: A, H, Ba
- **kerneri** Huter · G:Kerners Hellerkraut · ♃ Z6; Eur.: Slove., A (Kärnten), N-I
- **montanum** L. · E:Mountain Penny Cress; G:Berg-Hellerkraut · ♃ △ Z5 IV-V; Eur.: F, C-Eur., CZ, Slove., Croatia, Bosn., Montenegro, Maced.
- **perfoliatum** L. · E:Perfoliate Pennycress; G:Stängelumfassendes Hellerkraut · ⊙ III-VI; Eur.*, TR, Levant, Cauc., Iran, W-Sib., C-As., NW-Afr., Libya
- **praecox** Wulfen · E:Early Penny Cress; G:Frühes Hellerkraut · ♃ Z6 III-VI; Eur.: F, Ital-P, A, Ba; TR, Cauc.
- *rotundifolium* (L.) Gaudin = Thlaspi cepaeifolium subsp. rotundifolium
- **salisii** Brügger · G:Tiroler Hellerkraut · ⊙; Eur.: I, Sw, A; Alp.
- **stylosum** (Ten.) Mutel · ♃ ⇝ △ Z6 IV-V; Eur.: I; Apenn.
- **virens** Jord. · G:Grünes Täschelkraut · ⊙ IV-VI; Eur.: F, I, Sw, BrI; SW-Alp., BrI

Thomasia J. Gay -f- *Sterculiaceae* · 32 spp.
- **purpurea** J. Gay · ♄ e Z9 Ⓚ VI-VII; W-Austr.
- **quercifolia** J. Gay · ♄ e Z9 Ⓚ VI; W-Austr.
- **solanacea** J. Gay · ♄ e Z9 Ⓚ V-VII; W-Austr.

Thrinax Sw. -f- *Arecaceae* · 5 spp. · E:Key Palm, Thatch Palm; F:Pamier nain royal, Thrinax; G:Schilfpalme
- *floridana* Sarg. = Thrinax radiata
- *microcarpa* Sarg. = Thrinax morrisii
- **morrisii** H. Wendl. · E:Key Thatch Palm; G:Westindische Schilfpalme · ♄ e Z10 Ⓦ; Fla., W.Ind.
- **parviflora** Sw. · ♄ e Z10 Ⓦ; W.Ind., Belize, Mex.: Yucatan

– **radiata** Lodd. ex Schult. & Schult.
f. · E:Florida Thatch Palm; G:Florida-
Schilfpalme · ♄ e Z10 ⓦ; Fla., W-Ind.,
Mex., C-Am.

Thrixanthocereus Backeb. = Espostoa
– *blossfeldiorum* (Werderm.) Backeb. =
Espostoa blossfeldiorum

Thryallis Mart. -f- *Malpighiaceae* · 3 spp.
– **glauca** (Poir.) Kuntze · ♄ e ⓦ; C-Am.

Thuja L. -f- *Cupressaceae* · 5 spp. · E:Red
Cedar; F:Arbre-de-vie, Biota, Thuya;
G:Lebensbaum, Thuja
– *articulata* Vahl = Tetraclinis articulata
– *gigantea* Nutt. = Thuja plicata
– **koraiensis** Nakai · E:Korean Thuja;
G:Koreanischer Lebensbaum · ♄ ♄ e Z5
⚘; Korea
– **occidentalis** L. · E:Arborvitae, Red
Cedar; F:Arbre de paradis, Thuya occi-
dental; G:Abendländischer Lebensbaum ·
♄ ♄ e Z5 III-V ⚥ ⚘ ⓝ; Can.: E; USA: NE,
NCE, Tenn., N.C.
– **many cultivars**
– *orientalis* L. = Platycladus orientalis
– **plicata** Donn ex D. Don · E:Western Red
Cedar; F:Thuya géant de Californie;
G:Riesen-Lebensbaum · ♄ ♄ e Z5 IV ⚘
ⓝ; Alaska, Can.: B.C., Alta.; USA: NW,
Calif., Idaho, Mont.
– **many cultivars**
– **standishii** (Gordon) Carrière ·
E:Japanese Thuja; G:Japanischer
Lebensbaum · ♄ ♄ e Z6 ⚘; Jap.
– **sutchuenensis** Franch. · E:Szechuan
Thuja; G:Sichuan-Lebensbaum · ♄ ♄ e Z6
⚘; China: NE-Sichuan

Thujopsis Siebold & Zucc. ex Endl.
-f- *Cupressaceae* · 1 sp. · E:Hiba; F:Thuya
jiba; G:Hibalebensbaum
– **dolabrata** (L. f.) Siebold & Zucc. ·
E:Southern Japanese Thujopsis;
G:Südlicher Hibalebensbaum · ♄ e Z6 ⓝ;
Jap.
– var. **hondae** Makino · E:Northern
Japanese Thujopsis; G:Nördlicher
Hibalebensbaum · ♄ e Z5; N-Jap.

Thunbergia Retz. -f- *Acanthaceae* ·
90-100 spp. · E:Thunbergia; F:Suzanne
aux yeux noirs, Thunbergie; G:Schwarz-
äugige Susanne, Thunbergie

– **affinis** S. Moore · ♄ ⚥ Z10 ⓦ IX-X; E-Afr.
– **alata** Bojer ex Sims · E:Black-Eyed Susan;
F:Suzanne aux yeux noirs; G:Schwarzäu-
gige Susanne · ☉ ☉ ⌶ ⚥ Z10 V-X; trop.
Afr.
– **battiscombei** Turrill · ⌶ ⚥ Z10 ⓦ VI-VIII;
trop. Afr.
– **coccinea** (Nees) Wall. · ♄ d ⚥ Z10 ⓚ
I-IV; Ind., Burma
– *erecta* (Benth.) T. Anderson = Meyenia
erecta
– **fragrans** Roxb. · ⌶ ⚥ D Z10 ⓚ VI-VIII;
Ind.
– **grandiflora** (Roxb. ex Rottler) Roxb. ·
E:Bengal Trumpet, Blue Trumpet Vine;
G:Bengalische Thunbergie · ♄ e ⚥ Z10 ⓦ
VIII-X; Ind.: Bengalen
– **gregorii** S. Moore · E:Orange Clock Vine;
G:Orangefarbene Thunbergie · ⌶ ⚥ Z10
ⓚ VI-VIII; E-Afr., S-Afr.
– **laurifolia** Lindl. · E:Babbler's Vine;
G:Malayische Thunbergie · ♄ e ⚥ Z10 ⓦ
IV-X; Malay. Pen.
– **mysorensis** (Wight) T. Anderson ex
Bedd. · G:Indische Thunbergie · ♄ e ⚥
Z10 ⓦ III-VIII; Ind.: Nilgiri
– **natalensis** Hook. · G:Natal-Thunbergie ·
♄ Z10 ⓦ VI-VIII; S-Afr.: Natal
– **vogeliana** Benth. · ♄ Z10 ⓦ VII-VIII;
C-Afr.: Fernando Póo

Thunia Rchb. f. -f- *Orchidaceae* · 5 spp.
– **alba** (Lindl.) Rchb. f.
– var. **alba** · ⌶ Z10 ⓦ ⓚ VI-VII ▽ ✳;
Burma, Thail., S-China
– var. **bracteata** (Roxb.) N. Pearce &
P.J. Cribb · ⌶ Z10 ⓦ ⓚ VI-VIII ▽ ✳;
Indochina
– **bensoniae** Hook. f. · ⌶ Z10 ⓦ ⓚ VI-VII
▽ ✳; Burma
– *bracteata* (Roxb.) Schltr. = Thunia alba
var. bracteata
– *marshalliana* Rchb. f. = Thunia alba var.
alba

Thymelaea Mill. -f- *Thymelaeaceae* ·
30 spp. · F:Passerine thymélée, Thymélée;
G:Purgierstrauch, Spatzenzunge
– **passerina** (L.) Coss. & Germ. · E:Annual
Thymelaea; G:Kleine Spatzenzunge ·
☉ Z7 VII-VIII; Eur.* exc. BrI, Sc; TR,
SW-As., C-As.

Thymophylla Lag. -f- *Asteraceae* · 17 spp.
– **tenuiloba** (DC.) Small · E:Dahlberg

Daisy, Golden Fleece; G:Gelbes
Gänseblümchen · ⊙ ✂ Z9 VII-IX; USA:
SC; Mex.

Thymus L. -m- *Lamiaceae* · 242 spp. ·
E:Thyme; F:Serpolet, Thym; G:Quendel,
Thymian
– *alpigenus* (A. Kern. ex Heinr. Braun)
Ronniger = Thymus praecox subsp.
polytrichus
– *austriacus* Bernh. ex Rchb. = Thymus
odoratissimus
– **caespititius** Brot. · G:Azoren-Thymian ·
♄ Z8 ⌂; P, NW-Sp., Azor.
– *ciliatus* (Desf.) Benth. = Thymus
munbyanus subsp. ciliatus
– × **citriodorus** (Pers.) Schreb. (*T.
pulegioides* × *T. vulgaris*) · E:Lemon
Thyme; F:Thym à odeur de citron;
G:Zitronen-Thymian · ⚁ △ D Z7 ∧ VI-VII
⚥ ; cult.
– **comosus** Heuff. ex Griseb. & Schenk · ♄
Z5; RO
– **doerfleri** Ronniger · ⚁ ⌒ △ Z5 V-VI;
NE-AL
– *glabrescens* Willd. = Thymus odoratissimus
– subsp. *urumovii* (Velen.) Jalas = Thymus
roegneri
– *hirsutus* M. Bieb. = Thymus roegneri
– var. *doerfleri* (Ronniger) Ronniger =
Thymus doerfleri
– *humifusus* Bernh. ex Link = Thymus
praecox subsp. praecox
– *lanuginosus* hort. = Thymus praecox
subsp. britannicus
– **longicaulis** C. Presl · G:Langstängeliger
Thymian · ♄ ♄ e IV-VIII; Eur.: F, Ital-P,
Ba, RO, ? A, ? Sw, ? H; TR, nat. in D
– **membranaceus** Boiss. · ♄ Z7; SE-Sp.
– *micans* Sol. ex Lowe = Thymus caespititius
– *montanus* Waldst. & Kit. = Thymus
pulegioides subsp. montanus
– **munbyanus** Boiss. & Reut.
– subsp. **ciliatus** (Desf.) Greuter & Burdet ·
♄ Z9 ⌂; NW-Afr.
– **odoratissimus** M. Bieb. · G:Kahlblatt-
Thymian, Österreichischer Thymian · Z6;
Eur.: I, A, H, CZ, N-Ba, Russ.; C-As.
– **oenipontanus** Heinr. Braun · G:Tiroler
Thymian · ⚁ V-VIII; Eur.: F, I, Sw, A;
S-Alp., E-Alp.
– **pallasianus** Heinr. Braun · ♄ Z7 VI-VIII;
S-Russ.

– **pannonicus** All. · G:Steppen-Thymian · ♄
e Z5 VI-VIII; Eur.: A, EC-Eur., Ba, E-Eur.,
nat. in D
– *polytrichus* A. Kern. ex Borbás = Thymus
praecox subsp. polytrichus
– **praecox** Opiz · G:Frühblühender
Thymian
– subsp. **britannicus** (Ronniger) Holub ·
E:Woolly Creeping Thyme; G:Filziger
Niedergestreckter Thymian · ⚁ e ⤳ △
Z7 ∧ V-VI; W-Eur.
– subsp. **polytrichus** (A. Kern. ex Borbás)
Jalas · G:Alpen-Thymian · ⚁ e Z5 VII-IX;
Eur.: mts. S-Eur., C-Eur.
– subsp. **praecox** · E:Alba Thyme, Hairy
Thyme; F:Thym précoce; G:Gewöhnli-
cher Frühblühender Thymian, Niedergestreckter Thymian · ♄ e Z5 V-VII; Eur.*,
TR, Cauc., N-Iran
– var. *pseudolanuginosus* Ronniger & Jalas
= Thymus praecox subsp. britannicus
– *pseudolanuginosus* Ronniger = Thymus
praecox subsp. britannicus
– **pulegioides** L. · G:Arznei-Thymian,
Feld-Thymian
– subsp. *carnilicus* (Borbás ex Déségl.) P.
Schmidt = Thymus pulegioides subsp.
pannonicus
– subsp. **montanus** (Benth.) Ronniger ·
G:Istrischer Thymian, Kahler Arznei-
Thymian · ⚁ e Z5; Eur.: Ba
– subsp. **pannonicus** (All.) Kerguélen ·
G:Krainer Thymian, Piemonteser
Thymian · ⚁ e Z5 VI-VII; Eur.: sp., F, I,
Sw, G, A, Slove.
– subsp. **pulegioides** · E:Lemon Thyme;
G:Gewöhnlicher Arznei-Thymian · ⚁ ♄ e
Z5 V-X ⚥ Ⓝ; Eur.*
– **roegneri** K. Koch · ⚁ △ Z6 V-VI; Eur.:
GR, BG, Crim; TR
– *rotundifolius* Schur = Thymus serpyllum
– **satureioides** Coss. · ♄ ⌂ Ⓝ; Moroc.
– **serpyllum** L. · G:Sand-Thymian
– **some cultivars**
– subsp. **serpyllum** · E:Wild Thyme;
F:Thym serpolet; G:Gewöhnlicher Sand-
Thymian · ⚁ ♄ e ⤳ △ Z5 VI-IX ⚥ ; Eur.:
BrI, Sc, Fr, C-Eur., EC-Eur., E-Eur., nat. in
e N-Am.
– **sibthorpii** Benth. · ⚁ ; Eur.: Ba ; TR +
– **thracicus** Velen. · G:Langzahn-Thymian ·
♄ Z8 ⌂; Eur.: Ba, I; TR
– **villosus** L. · ♄ ♄ △ Z7 ⌂ ∧ VII-IX ▽;
S-P, SW-Sp.
– **vulgaris** L. · E:Common Thyme; F:Thym

commun; G:Echter Thymian, Quendel · ♄
e D Z6-7 VI-IX ⚤ Ⓝ; Eur.: sp., Balear., Fr,
I; Moroc., nat. in Sw
– **zygis** L. · ♄ Z8 Ⓚ ∧ ⚤ ; P, sp., Moroc.
– **Cultivars:**
– **many cultivars**

Thyrsacanthus Nees = Odontonema
– *rutilans* Planch. = Odontonema schomburgkianum
– *schomburgkianus* Nees = Odontonema
schomburgkianum

Thysanolaena Nees -f- *Poaceae* · 1 sp. ·
E:Tiger Grass; F:Herbe du tigre;
G:Tigergras
– **maxima** (Roxb.) Kuntze · ♃ Z9 Ⓜ Ⓝ;
Ind., SE-As.

Thysanotus R. Br. -m- *Anthericaceae* ·
49 spp. · E:Fringe Flower, Fringe Lily;
F:Thysanothe; G:Fransenlilie
– **multiflorus** R. Br. · E:Fringe Lily;
G:Vielblütige Fransenlilie · ♃ Z10 Ⓚ VIII;
W-Austr.

Tiarella L. -f- *Saxifragaceae* · 3-7 spp. ·
E:False Mitrewort, Foam Flower;
F:Bonnet-d'Evêque, Tiarelle; G:Bischofs-
kappe, Schaumblüte
– **cordifolia** L. · E:Heartleaf Foamflower;
F:Tiarella à feuilles cordées; G:Herzblät-
trige Schaumblüte, Wald-Schaumblüte
· ♃ ⤳ Z3 V-VI; Can.: E; USA: NE, NCE,
N.C., Tenn.
– **polyphylla** D. Don · ♃ Z7; China,
Taiwan, Japan, Him.
– **trifoliata** L. · E:Three Leaf Foamflower;
G:Dreiblättrige Schaumblüte · ♃ Z5 V;
B.C., USA: NW
– **unifoliata** Hook. · E:One-leaf Foam-
flower · ♃ Z3 V; Alaska, Can.: W; USA:
NW, Calif.
– **wherryi** Lakela · ♃ D Z6 V-VI; USA: NE,
SE
– **Cultivars:**
– **many cultivars**

Tibouchina Aubl. -f- *Melastomataceae* ·
243 spp. · E:Glory Bush; F:Fleur des
princesses, Tibouchina; G:Tibouchine
– *alba* hort. non Cogn. = Melastoma
candidum
– **grandifolia** Cogn. · ♄ e Z10 Ⓜ; Braz.
– **heteromalla** Cogn. · ♄ e Z10 Ⓜ; Braz.

– **holosericea** (Sw.) Baill. · ♄ e Z10 Ⓚ VII;
Braz.
– *semidecandra* hort. non (Schrank & Mart.
ex DC.) Cogn. = Tibouchina urvilleana
– **urvilleana** (DC.) Cogn. · E:Glory
Bush, Purple Glory Tree; G:Glänzende
Tibouche · ♄ e Z10 Ⓚ V-VIII; Braz.

Tieghemella Pierre -f- *Sapotaceae* · 2 spp. ·
E:Cherry Mahogany; F:Macoré, Makoré;
G:Macoré
– **heckelii** (A. Chev.) Pierre ex Dubard ·
E:Cherry Mahogany; G:Afrikanischer
Birnbaum, Makoré · ♄ Ⓜ Ⓝ; trop. W-Afr.

Tigridia Juss. -f- *Iridaceae* · 40 spp. ·
E:Peacock Flower, Tiger Flower; F:Lis de
tigre; G:Pfauenblume, Tigerblume
– **pavonia** (L. f.) DC. · E:Mexican Shell
Flower, Tiger Flower; G:Pfauenblume,
Tigerblume · ♃ Z9 Ⓚ VII-IX; Mex.

Tilia L. -f- *Tiliaceae* · 45 spp. · E:Lime,
Linden; F:Tilleul; G:Linde
– *alba* Aiton = Tilia tomentosa
– **americana** L. · E:American Basswood,
American Lime; F:Tilleul d'Amérique ;
G:Amerikanische Linde · ♄ d Z5 VII Ⓝ;
Can.: E; USA: NE, NCE, SC, SE
– *argentea* DC. = Tilia tomentosa
– *carlsruhensis* Simonk. = Tilia × flaccida
– **cordata** Mill. · E:Little Leaf Linden;
F:Tilleul à petites feuilles, Tilleul des
bois; G:Winter-Linde · ♄ d D Z4 VI-VII ⚤
Ⓝ; Eur.*, Cauc., N-Iran, W-Sib.
– **dasystyla** Steven · E:Caucasian Lime;
G:Kaukasische Linde · ♄ d Z6 VI; Cauc.,
N-Iran
– × **euchlora** K. Koch (*T. cordata* × *T.
dasystyla*) · E:Crimean Lime; F:Tilleul
de Crimée; G:Krim-Linde · ♄ d D Z5 VII;
Crim
– × *europaea* auct. non L. = Tilia × vulgaris
– × **flaccida** Host ex Bayer (*T. americana* ×
T. platyphyllos) · ♄ d Z6 VI-VII; cult.
– × *flavescens* A. Braun ex Döll (*T.
americana* × *T. cordata*) · ♄ d Z3 VII; cult.
– *glabra* Vent. = Tilia americana
– *grandifolia* Ehrh. ex W.D.J. Koch = Tilia
platyphyllos
– **henryana** Szyszyl. · ♄ d Z6; C-China
– **heterophylla** Vent. · E:White Basswood;
G:Verschiedenblättrige Linde · ♄ d Z6 VII
Ⓝ; USA: NE, SE, Fla.
– ¬ × *intermedia* DC. = Tilia × vulgaris

- **japonica** (Miq.) Simonk. · G:Japanische Linde · ♄ d Z5 VII; Jap.; mts.
- **mandshurica** Rupr. & Maxim. · E:Manchurian Linden; G:Mandschurische Linde · ♄ d Z5 VII Ⓝ; Amur, NE-China, Manch, Korea
- **maximowicziana** Shiras. · ♄ d Z5 VII; Jap.
- **miqueliana** Maxim. · E:Lime, Linden; G:Miquels Linde · ♄ d Z6 VI; E-China
- × **moltkei** Späth (*T. americana* × *T. tomentosa* 'Petiolaris') · G:Moltkes Linde · ♄ d VII; cult.
- **mongolica** Maxim. · E:Mongolian Linden; G:Mongolische Linde · ♄ d Z5 VII; Mong., N-China
- *monticola* Sarg. = Tilia heterophylla
- *nigra* Borkh. = Tilia americana
- **oliveri** Szyszyl. · E:Oliver's Lime; G:Olivers Linde · ♄ d Z6 VI; C-China
- *parvifolia* Ehrh. = Tilia cordata
- *petiolaris* DC. = Tilia tomentosa
- **platyphyllos** Scop. · E:Large Leaved Lime; F:Tilleul à grandes feuilles, Tilleul de Hollande; G:Gewöhnliche Sommer-Linde · ♄ d D Z4 VI ⚥ Ⓝ; Eur.* exc. BrI; Cauc., nat. in BrI
- *rubra* Steven non DC. = Tilia dasystyla
- *spaethii* C.K. Schneid. ╤ Tilia × flavescens
- **tomentosa** Moench · E:Silver Lime; F:Tilleul argenté, Tilleul de Hongrie; G:Silber-Linde · ♄ d D Z5 VII Ⓝ; Eur.: Ba, EC-Eur.; TR, Syr.
- **tuan** Szyszyl. · G:Rundblättrige Linde · ♄ d D Z6 VII; C-China
- *ulmifolia* Scop. = Tilia cordata
- × **vulgaris** Hayne (*T. cordata* × *T. platyphyllos*) · E:Common Lime, European Linden; F:Tilleul commun; G:Holländische Linde · ♄ d D Z4 VI-VII; Eur.* exc. BrI, nat. in BrI

Tillandsia L. -f- *Bromeliaceae* · 556 spp. · E:Air Plant; F:Mousse espagnole, Tilландsia; G:Greisenbart, Luftnelke, Tillandsie
- **aeranthos** (Loisel.) L.B. Sm. · ♃ Z9 ⓦ; Braz., Parag., Urug., Arg.
- **albertiana** Verv. · ♃ Z9 ⓦ; Arg.
- *aloifolia* Hook. = Tillandsia flexuosa
- **anceps** Lodd. · ♃ Z10 ⓦ; trop. S-Am.
- **andicola** Gillies ex Baker · ♃ Z9 ⓦ; Arg.
- **araujei** Mez · ♃ Z10 ⓦ; E-Braz.
- **argentea** Griseb. · ♃ Z10 ⓦ; Mex., Guat., Cuba, Jamaica
- **atroviridipetala** Matuda · ♃ Z9 ⓦ; Mex.

- *augustae-regiae* Mez = Tillandsia biflora
- **baileyi** Rose ex Small · E:Reflexed Air Plant · ♃ Z9 ⓦ; USA: SC; N-Mex.
- **balbisiana** Schult. & Schult. f. · E:Northern Needleleaf · ♃ Z9 ⓦ; USA: Fla.; Mex., C-Am., W.Ind., Venez.
- **bandensis** Baker · ♃ Z10 ⓦ; Bol., Arg., Parag., Urug.
- **bergeri** Mez · ♃ Z9 ⓦ; Arg.
- **biflora** Ruiz & Pav. · ♃ Z10 ⓦ; Costa Rica, Venez., Col., Ecuad., Peru, Bol.
- **bourgaei** Baker · ♃ Z10 ⓦ; S-Mex., C-Am.
- **brachycaulos** Schltdl. · ♃ Z9 ⓦ; S-Mex., C-Am.
- **bryoides** Griseb. ex Baker · ♃ Z9 ⓦ; Peru, Bol., Arg.
- **bulbosa** Hook. · E:Bulbous Air Plant · ♃ Z10 ⓦ; S-Mex., C-Am., W.Ind., Col., Braz.
- **butzii** Mez · ♃ Z10 ⓦ; Mex., C-Am.
- **cacticola** L.B. Sm. · ♃ Z9 ⓦ; N-Peru
- **caerulea** Kunth · ♃ Z10 ⓦ; Ecuad., Peru
- *caldasina* Baker = Tillandsia geminiflora
- *candelifera* Rohweder = Tillandsia imperialis
- **capillaris** Ruiz & Pav. · ♃ Z9 ⓦ; Mex., C-Am., Col., Ecuad., Peru, Bol., Chile, Arg.
- **capitata** Griseb. · ♃ ⓦ; Mex., Guat., Hond., Cuba
- **caput-medusae** E. Morren · ♃ Z10 ⓦ; Mex., Guat., Hond., El Salv., Costa Rica
- *caricifolia* E. Morren ex Mez = Tillandsia festucoides
- **caulescens** Brongn. ex Baker · ♃ Z9 ⓦ; Peru, Bol.
- **circinnatoides** Matuda · ♃ Z10 ⓦ; Mex., Costa Rica
- *coarctata* Gillies ex Baker = Tillandsia bryoides
- *coccinea* Platzm. ex E. Morren = Tillandsia geminiflora
- **complanata** Benth. · ♃ Z10 ⓚ; C-Am., W.Ind., trop. S-Am.
- **concolor** L.B. Sm. · ♃ Z10 ⓦ; Mex.
- *confusa* Hassl. = Tillandsia duratii var. confusa
- *cordobensis* Hieron. = Tillandsia capillaris
- **crocata** (E. Morren) N.E. Br. · ♃ Z9 ⓦ; Braz., Arg.
- *cubensis* Gand. = Tillandsia balbisiana
- **cyanea** Linden ex K. Koch · ♃ Z9 ⓦ; Ecuad.
- *decomposita* Baker = Tillandsia duratii

var. saxatilis
- *dependens* Hieron. ex Mez = Tillandsia capillaris
- **diaguitensis** A. Cast. · ⌂ Z9 ⍟; Parag., N-Arg.
- *dianthoidea* Rossi = Tillandsia aeranthos
- **didisticha** (E. Morren) Baker · ⌂ Z9 ⍟; Bol., Parag., Braz., Arg.
- **disticha** Kunth · ⌂ Z9 ⍟; Col., Ecuad., Peru
- **dura** Baker · ⌂ Z10 ⍟; Braz.
- **duratii** Vis.
- var. **confusa** (Hassl.) L.B. Sm. Z9 ⍟; Parag.
- var. **duratii** Z9 ⍟; Bol., Arg., Urug.
- var. **saxatilis** (Hassl.) L.B. Sm. Z9 ⍟; Arg.
- *ehlersiana* Rauh = Tillandsia seleriana
- *erubescens* H. Wendl. non Schltdl. = Tillandsia ionantha
- **espinosae** L.B. Sm. · ⌂ Z10 ⍟; S-Ecuad., N-Peru
- **fasciculata** Sw. · E:Giant Airplant · ⌂ Z10 ⍟; Mex., C-Am., Col., Ecuad., Peru
- **festucoides** Brongn. ex Mez · ⌂ Z10 ⍟; S-Mex., C-Am.
- **filifolia** Cham. & Schltdl. · ⌂ Z10 ⍟; S-Mex., Guat., Hond., Costa Rica
- **flabellata** Baker · ⌂ Z10 ⍟; Mex., Guat., El Salv.
- **flexuosa** Sw. · E:Twisted Airplant · ⌂ Z9 ⍟; Fla., W.Ind., Panama, Col., Venez., Guyan.
- **floribunda** Kunth · ⌂ Z9 ⍟; Ecuad., Peru
- **funckiana** Baker · ⌂ Z10 ⍟; Venez.
- **funebris** A. Cast. · ⌂ Z9 ⍟; Bol., Parag., Arg.
- **gardneri** Lindl. · ⌂ Z10 ⍟; Col., Venez., Trinidad, Braz.
- **geminiflora** Brongn. · ⌂ Z9 ⍟; Braz., Parag., Urug., Arg.
- *glaucophylla* (Hook.) Baker = Tillandsia fasciculata
- **grandis** Schltdl. · ⌂ Z10 ⍟; C-Am., S-Am.
- *grisebachiana* Baker = Tillandsia biflora
- *havanensis* Jacq. ex Beer = Tillandsia fasciculata
- *hieronymi* Mez = Tillandsia capillaris
- **hildae** Rauh · ⌂ Z9 ⍟; N-Peru
- **imperialis** E. Morren ex Roezl · ⌂ Z9 ⍟; Mex.
- *incana* Gillies ex Baker = Tillandsia capillaris

- **ionantha** Planch. · ⌂ Z10 ⍟; Mex.
- **juncea** (Ruiz & Pav.) Poir. · ⌂ Z9 ⍟; USA: Fla.; Mex., C-Am. , W.Ind., trop. S-Am.
- *juncifolia* Regel = Tillandsia juncea
- **kalmbacheri** Matuda · ⌂ Z10 ⍟; Mex.
- *langlassei* Poiss. & Menet = Tillandsia caput-medusae
- *lanuginosa* Gillies ex Baker = Tillandsia capillaris
- *lindeniana* Regel = Tillandsia lindenii
- **lindenii** Regel · E:Blue Flowered Torch · ⌂ Z10 ⍟; S-Ecuad., N-Peru
- var. *regeliana* E. Morren = Tillandsia lindenii
- var. *vera* Dombrain = Tillandsia cyanea
- **linearis** Vell. · ⌂ Z10 ⍟; Braz.
- **loliacea** Mart. ex Schult. & Schult. f. · ⌂ Z9 ⍟; Peru. Bol., Parag., Braz., Arg.
- **lorentziana** Griseb. · ⌂ Z9 ⍟; Bol., Parag., Braz., Arg.
- **makoyana** Baker · ⌂ Z9 ⍟; Mex., Guat., Hond., Costa Rica
- *mandonii* E. Morren = Tillandsia crocata
- *meridionalis* Baker = Tillandsia recurvifolia
- *morreniana* Regel = Tillandsia cyanea
- **multicaulis** Steud. · ⌂ Z10 ⍟; C-Mex., Costa Rica, Panama
- **myosura** Griseb. ex Baker · ⌂ Z9 ⍟; Bol., Arg.
- **narthecioides** C. Presl · ⌂ D Z10 ⍟; Ecuad.
- **paleacea** C. Presl · ⌂ Z9 ⍟; Col., Peru, Bol., Chile
- *pauciflora* Sessé & Moç. = Tillandsia recurvata
- *pedicellata* (Mez) A. Cast. = Tillandsia bryoides
- *permutata* A. Cast. = Tillandsia capillaris
- *pilosa* L.B. Sm. = Tillandsia bandensis
- **plumosa** Baker · ⌂ Z10 ⍟; Mex., C-Am.
- **pohliana** Mez · ⌂ Z9 ⍟; Peru, Braz., Parag., Arg.
- **polystachya** (L.) L. · ⌂ Z10 ⍟; Mex., C-Am., trop. S-Am.
- *polytrichioides* E. Morren = Tillandsia tricholepis
- *propinqua* Gay = Tillandsia capillaris
- **pruinosa** Sw. · E:Fuzzy Wuzzy Airplant · ⌂ Z10 ⍟; Mex., C-Am., W.Ind., Braz. Ecuad.
- **pueblensis** L.B. Sm. · ⌂ Z10 ⍟; Mex.
- **punctulata** Schltdl. & Cham. · E:Mexican Black Torch · ⌂ Z10 ⍟; C-Am., Surinam

– *pungens* Mez = Tillandsia fasciculata
– *pusilla* Gillies ex Baker = Tillandsia capillaris
– *quadrangularis* Mart. & Galeotti = Tillandsia juncea
– *quadriflora* Baker = Tillandsia bandensis
– **rauhii** L.B. Sm. · ⟁ Z9 ⓜ; N-Peru
– **rectangula** Baker · ⟁ Z9 ⓜ; Arg.
– **recurvata** (L.) L. · ⟁ Z8 ⓜ; USA: SC, SW; S-Am.
– **recurvifolia** Hook. · E:Small Ballmoss · ⟁ Z9 ⓜ; Braz., Parag., Arg.
– *regnellii* Mez = Tillandsia gardneri
– **remota** Wittm. · ⟁ Z10 ⓜ; Guat., El Salv.
– *rubentifolia* Poiss. & Menet = Tillandsia ionantha
– **schatzlii** Rauh · ⟁ Z10 ⓚ; Mex.
– **schiedeana** Steud. · ⟁ Z10 ⓜ; Mex., W.Ind., Venez., Col.
– *scopus* Hook. f. = Tillandsia ionantha
– **seleriana** Mez · ⟁ Z10 ⓜ; Mex., Guat.
– **setacea** Sw. · E:Southern Needleleaf · ⟁ Z9 ⓜ; USA: SE, Fla., SC; Mex., C-Am., Venez., Braz.
– *stolpii* Phil. = Tillandsia capillaris
– **streptophylla** Scheidw. ex E. Morren · ⟁ Z10 ⓜ; Mex., Guat., Hond., Jamaica
– **stricta** Sol. ex Ker-Gawl. · ⟁ Z9 ⓜ; Venez., Trinidad, Guyan., Braz., Parag., Arg.
– **subulifera** Mez · ⟁ Z10 ⓜ; Panama, Trinidad, Ecuad.
– **tectorum** E. Morren · ⟁ Z9 ⓜ; Peru
– *tenuifolia* Jacq. non L. = Tillandsia flexuosa
– **tenuifolia** L. · E:Narrowleaf Air Plant · ⟁ Z10 ⓜ; W.Ind., trop. S-Am.
– *tephrophylla* Harms = Tillandsia capitata
– **tricholepis** Baker · ⟁ Z9 ⓜ; Bol., Parag., Braz., Arg.
– **tricolor** Schltdl. & Cham. · ⟁ Z9 ⓜ; Mex., Guat., Nicar., Costa Rica
– **umbellata** André · ⟁ Z10 ⓜ; S-Ecuad.
– *urbaniana* Wittm. = Tillandsia balbisiana
– **usneoides** (L.) L. · E:Spanish Moss ; G:Greisenbart · ⟁ ⚶ Z8 ⓜ; USA: Va., SE, Fla., SC; Mex. C-Am., W.Ind., S-Am.
– **utriculata** L. · E:Spreading Airplant · ⟁ Z8 ⓜ; USA: Fla., Ga.; Mex., C-Am., W.Ind., Venez.
– **valenzuelana** A. Rich. · ⟁ Z9 ⓜ; Fla., S-Mex., C-Am., Venez., Col. , Bol.
– *variegata* Schltdl. = Tillandsia butzii
– **vernicosa** Baker · ⟁ Z9 ⓜ; Bol., Parag., Arg.

– **violacea** Baker · ⟁ Z9 ⓚ; Mex.
– *virescens* Ruiz & Pav. = Tillandsia capillaris
– **viridiflora** (Beer) Baker · ⟁ Z10 ⓜ; C-Am.
– **wagneriana** L.B. Sm. · ⟁ Z10 ⓜ; Peru: Amazon.
– *williamsii* Rusby = Tillandsia capillaris
– **xerographica** Rohweder · ⟁ Z10 ⓜ ▽ ✳; Mex., Guat., El Salv.
– **xiphioides** Ker-Gawl. · ⟁ Z9 ⓜ; Bol., Parag., Arg.

Tinantia Scheidw. -f- *Commelinaceae* · 13 spp. · E:False Dayflower, Widow's Tears
– **erecta** (Jacq.) Schltdl. · ⊙ Z9 VI-VIII; C-Am., S-Am.
– *fugax* Scheidw. = Tinantia erecta

Tipuana (Benth.) Benth. -f- *Fabaceae* · 1 sp. · E:Tipu Tree; F:Bois de rose, Tipu; G:Tipubaum
– **tipu** (Benth.) Kuntze · E:Tiputree; G:Tipubaum · ♄ s Z10 ⓚ; Braz., Arg., Bol.

Tischleria Schwantes = Carruanthus
– *peersii* Schwantes = Carruanthus ringens

Titanopsis Schwantes -f- *Aizoaceae* · 3 spp. · F:Plante-caillou, Titanopsis; G:Kalkblatt
– **calcarea** (Marloth) Schwantes · E:Jewel Plant; G:Echtes Kalkblatt · ⳨ Z9 ⓚ; S-Afr. (Cape Prov.)
– **schwantesii** (Schwantes) Schwantes · E:White Jewel; G:Perlen-Kalkblatt · ⟁ ⳨ Z9 ⓚ; Namibia

Titanotrichum Soler. -n- *Gesneriaceae* · 1 sp.
– **oldhamii** (Hemsl.) Soler. · ⟁ Z9 ⓜ V-VIII; S-China, Taiwan

Tithonia Desf. ex Juss. -f- *Asteraceae* · 11 sp. · E:Mexican Sunflower; F:Soleil mexicain; G:Tithonie
– **diversifolia** (Hemsl.) A. Gray · G:Riesen-Tithonie · ⊙ ⟁ Z9 VIII-X; S-Mex., Guat.
– **rotundifolia** (Mill.) S.F. Blake · E:Mexican Sunflower; G:Mexikanische Sonnenblume, Mexikanische Tithonie · ⊙ Z9 VIII-X; Mex.
– *speciosa* (Hook.) Hook. & Griseb. = Tithonia rotundifolia

– *tagetiflora* Desf. = Tithonia rotundifolia

Tococa Aubl. -f- *Melastomataceae* · 54 spp.
 – **neocinnamomea** Buchheim & Potztal · ♄
 e Z10 ⓦ; Costa Rica

Todea Willd. ex Bernh. -f- *Osmundaceae* ·
 2 spp. · E:Crepe Fern; F:Fougère arborescente, Todéa; G:Elefantenfarn
 – **barbata** (L.) T. Moore · ♄ e Z10 ⓦ;
 Austr.: Queensl., N.S.Wales, Victoria,
 S-Austr., Tasman.; NZ, S-Afr.
 – *hymenophylloides* A. Rich. = Leptopteris
 hymenophylloides
 – *superba* Colenso = Leptopteris superba

Tofieldia Huds. -f- *Melanthiaceae* · 10 spp. ·
 E:False Asphodel; F:Tofieldia; G:Sim-
 senlilie
 – *borealis* (Wahlenb.) Wahlenb. = Tofieldia
 pusilla
 – **calyculata** (L.) Wahlenb. · E:Alpine
 Asphodel, German Asphodel; G:Gewöhn-
 liche Simsenlilie · ⌗ △ ∼ Z6 VI-VIII;
 Eur.* exc. BrI
 – *palustris* Huds. = Tofieldia calyculata
 – **pusilla** (Michx.) Pers. · E:Scotch False
 Asphodel, Scottish Asphodel; G:Kleine
 Simsenlilie · ⌗ △ ∼ Z6 VII-VIII; Eur.:
 BrI, Sc, Fr, C-Eur., Croat., EC-Eur.,
 E-Eur.; Sib, Alaska, Can., USA: NCE, NC

Tolmiea Torr. & A. Gray -f- *Saxifragaceae* ·
 1 sp. · E:Pick-a-back Plant; F:Tolmiée;
 G:Lebendblatt, Tolmie
 – **menziesii** (Pursh) Torr. & A. Gray ·
 E:Mother-of-Thousands, Piggy Back
 Plant; F:La poule & les poussins;
 G:Henne mit Küken, Lebendblatt · ⌗ Z7;
 Alaska, Can.: W; USA: NW, Calif.
 – f. **gemmifera** Engl.

Tolpis Adans. -f- *Asteraceae* · 20 spp. ·
 F:Oeil du Christ, Trépane; G:Bartpippau,
 Christusauge, Grasnelkenhabichtskraut
 – **barbata** (L.) Gaertn. · G:Bartpippau · ⊙
 VI-IX; Eur.: Ib, Fr, Ital-P, Ba, ? RO; TR,
 Syr., N-Afr.
 – **staticifolia** (All.) Sch. Bip. · G:Gewöhn-
 liches Grasnelkenhabichtskraut · ⌗ Z6
 VI-IX; Eur.: F, I, C-Eur., CZ, Slove., AL;
 Alp., Jura, AL

Toluifera L. = Myroxylon
 – *balsamum* L. = Myroxylon balsamum var.

balsamum
 – *pereirae* (Royle) Baill. = Myroxylon
 balsamum var. pereirae

Tommasinia Bertol. = Peucedanum
 – *altissima* (Mill.) Thell. = Peucedanum
 verticillare

Toona (Endl.) M. Roem. -f- *Meliaceae* ·
 6 spp. · E:Toon; F:Cèdre bâtard, Cèdrella;
 G:Surenbaum
 – **ciliata** M. Roem. · E:Cedrela, Toon;
 G:Australischer Surenbaum · ♄ s D ⓚ ⓝ;
 Him., Burma, Thail.
 – **sinensis** (A. Juss.) M. Roem. · E:Red
 Toon; G:Chinesischer Surenbaum · ♄ d
 Z6 ⓝ; China, Korea, Jap.

Tordylium L. -n- *Apiaceae* · 18 spp. ·
 E:Hartwort; F:Tordyle; G:Zirmet
 – **apulum** L. · G:Apulische Zirmet · ⊙; Eur.:
 Ib, Fr, Ba; TR, NW-Afr.
 – **maximum** L. · G:Große Zirmet · ⊙ ⊙
 VI-VIII; Eur.* exc. Sc; TR, Cauc., N-Iran

Torenia L. -f- *Scrophulariaceae* · 40 spp. ·
 E:Wishbone Flower; F:Torénia;
 G:Schnappmäulchen, Torenie
 – **asiatica** L. · ⌗ Z9 ⓦ VI-IX; S-Ind.
 – **atropurpurea** Ridl. · ⌗ Z9 ⓦ VII-IX;
 Malay. Pen.
 – **flava** Buch.-Ham. ex Benth. · ⊙ Z9 ⓚ
 VI-VIII; S-Vietn.
 – **fournieri** Linden ex E. Fourn. ·
 E:Bluewings, Wishbone Flower · ⊙ Z9 ⓚ
 VII-IX; S-Vietn.

Torilis Adans. -f- *Apiaceae* · 15 spp. ·
 E:Hedge Parsley; F:Petit toryle, Torilis;
 G:Borstendolde, Klettenkerbel
 – **arvensis** (Huds.) Link · E:Spreading
 Hedge Parsley; G:Acker-Klettenkerbel · ⊙
 VII-VIII; Eur.* exc. Sc; TR, Syr., Lebanon,
 Cauc., Iran, Afgh., C-As., E-As., N-Afr.,
 Macaron., trop. Afr., nat. in N-Am.,
 Austr.
 – **japonica** (Houtt.) DC. · E:Upright Hedge
 Parsley ; G:Gewöhnlicher Klettenkerbel
 · ⊙ ⊙ VI-VIII; Eur.*, Cauc., Him., Amur,
 China, Korea, Jap., Taiwan, Vietn.
 – **leptophylla** (L.) Rchb. f. · G:Feinblät-
 triger Klettenkerbel · ⊙ VI-VII; Eur.*:
 Ib, Fr, Ital-P, Ba, Crim; TR, Iraq, Palest.,
 Cauc., Iran, C-As., Him., Canar., nat. in
 C-Eur., EC-Eur., Russ.

– **nodosa** (L.) Gaertn. · E:Knotted Hedge
Parsley; G:Knotiger Klettenkerbel · ⊙
IV-V; Eur.: BrI, Ib, Fr, Ital-P, Ba, RO,
Crim; TR, Cauc., Iran, C-As., N-Afr.,
Canar., Madeira, nat. in C-Eur., EC-Eur.,
USA

Torreya Arn. -f- *Taxaceae* · 5 spp. ·
E:Nutmeg Yew; F:If puant, Muscadier de
Californie; G:Nusseibe, Stinkeibe
– **californica** Torr. · E:California Nutmeg
Yew; G:Kalifornische Nusseibe · ℏ ℏ e Z8
ⓚ ⋀; Calif.
– **grandis** Fortune ex Lindl. · G:Gewöhn-
liche Große Nusseibe · ℏ e Z8 ⓚ Ⓝ;
E-China
– **nucifera** (L.) Siebold & Zucc. ·
E:Japanese Nutmeg Yew; G:Japanische
Nusseibe · ℏ e Z7; Jap.
– **taxifolia** Arn. · E:Florida Nutmeg, Stink-
ing Cedar Leaved Torreya; G:Florida-
Nusseibe · ℏ e Z9 ⓚ; USA: Ga., Fla

Toumeya Britton & Rose = Sclerocactus
– *lophophoroides* (Werderm.) Bravo & W.T.
Marshall = Turbinicarpus lophophoroides
– *papyracantha* (Engelm.) Britton & Rose =
Sclerocactus papyracanthus
– *pseudomacrochele* (Backeb.) Bravo &
W.T. Marshall = Turbinicarpus pseudomacrochele
– *schmiedickeana* (Boed.) Bravo & W.T.
Marshall = Turbinicarpus schmiedickeanus

Townsendia Hook. -f- *Asteraceae* · 25 spp. ·
E:Townsend Daisy; F:Townsedia;
G:Townsendie
– **exscapa** (Richardson) Porter · E:Easter
Daisy, Stemless Townsend Daisy;
G:Niedere Townsendie · ⌗ ⋀ Z7 ⋀ V-VI;
Can.: W; USA: Rocky Mts., SW; Mex.
– **florifera** (Hook.) A. Gray · E:Showy
Townsend Daisy · ⊙ ⊙ ⋀ Z7 ⋀ V-VI;
USA: NW, Nev., Utah
– **grandiflora** Nutt. · E:Large-flowered
Townsend Daisy; G:Großblütige
Townsendie · ⊙ ⋀ Z7 ⋀ V; USA: NC, SW,
Rocky Mts.
– **hookeri** Beaman · E:Hooker's Townsend
Daisy; G:Hookers Townsendie · ⌗ ⋀ Z7
⋀ V-VI; Can.: W; USA: Rocky Mts.
– **parryi** D.C. Eaton · E:Parry's Townsend
Daisy; G:Parrys Townsendie · ⊙ ⌗ ⋀ Z7
⋀ V; Can.: Alta.; USA: Rocky Mts.

– **rothrockii** A. Gray ex Rothr. ·
E:Rothrock's Townsend Daisy · ⌗ ⋀ Z7
ⓚ ⋀ V-VI; USA: W-Colo.
– *sericea* Hook. = Townsendia exscapa
– *wilcoxiana* A.W. Wood = Townsendia
exscapa

Toxicodendron Mill. = Rhus
– *quercifolium* (Michx.) Greene = Rhus
toxicodendron var. toxicodendron
– *radicans* (L.) Kuntze = Rhus radicans
– *succedaneum* (L.) Kuntze = Rhus succedanea
– *vernicifluum* (Stokes) F.A. Barkley = Rhus
verniciflua
– *vernix* (L.) Kuntze = Rhus vernix

Tozzia L. -f- *Scrophulariaceae* · 1 sp. ·
F:Tozzia; G:Alpenrachen
– **alpina** L. · G:Alpenrachen · ⊙ VI-VIII;
Eur.* exc. BrI, Sc; mts.

Trachelium L. -n- *Campanulaceae* · 7 spp. ·
E:Throatwort; F:Trachélium; G:Halskraut
– **asperuloides** Boiss. & Orph. · ⌗ ⋀ Z8 ⓚ
⋀ VII; S-GR
– **caeruleum** L. · E:Blue Throatwort;
G:Blaues Halskraut · ⌗ Z9 ⓚ VII-IX ✲;
Eur.: Ib, I, Sic.; Moroc., Alger., nat. in F
– **jacquinii** (Sieber) Boiss.
– subsp. **jacquinii** · ⌗ Z8 ⓚ; Eur.: GR
– subsp. **rumelianum** (Hampe) Tutin · ⌗
⋀ Z8 ⓚ VII-VIII; Eur.: BG, GR
– *rumelianum* Hampe = Trachelium
jacquinii subsp. rumelianum

Trachelospermum Lem. -n- *Apocynaceae* ·
14 spp. · F:Jasmin étoilé; G:Sternjasmin
– **asiaticum** (Siebold & Zucc.) Nakai ·
E:Asian Jasmine; G:Japanischer
Sternjasmin · ∫ e ⌘ Z8 ⓚ; Jap., Korea
– **jasminoides** (Lindl.) Lem. ·
E:Confederate Jasmine, Star Jasmine;
G:Chinesischer Sternjasmin · ℏ e ⌘ D Z8
ⓚ; China, Korea, Jap.

Trachomitum Woodson = Apocynum
– *venetum* (L.) Woodson = Apocynum
venetum

Trachycarpus H. Wendl. -m- *Arecaceae* ·
8 spp. · E:Chinese Windmill Palm, Fan
Palm; F:Palmier-chanvre; G:Hanfpalme
– *excelsus* hort. = Trachycarpus fortunei
– **fortunei** (Hook.) H. Wendl. · E:Chusan

Palm; G:Chinesische Hanfpalme · ♄ e Z8 ⓚ Ⓝ; Burma, China, S-Jap.

Trachylobium Hayne = Hymenaea
– *verrucosum* (Gaertn.) Oliv. = Hymenaea verrucosa

Trachymene Rudge -f- *Apiaceae* · 45 spp. · E:Lace Flower; F:Trachymène; G:Blaudolde, Raudolde
– **coerulea** Graham · E:Blue Lace Flower; F:Trachymène bleu; G:Blaudolde, Blaue Raudolde · ⊙ Z9 ⓚ VII-IX; W-Austr.

Trachyspermum Link -n- *Apiaceae* · 15 spp. · G:Indischer Kümmel
– **ammi** (L.) Sprague · G:Indischer Kümmel; E:Kummel · ⌡ ⓚ ⚥ Ⓝ; cult.
– *copticum* (L.) Link = Trachyspermum ammi
– **roxburghianum** (DC.) Craib · ⌡ ⓜ Ⓝ; orig. ?; cult. Ind.

Trachystemon D. Don -m- *Boraginaceae* · 2 spp. · E:Abraham, Isaac and Jacob; F:Bourrache du Caucase; G:Rauling
– **orientalis** (L.) G. Don · E:Abraham, Isaac and Jacob; G:Rauhling · ⌡ Z6 IV-V; Eur.: BG; TR, Cauc.

Tradescantia L. -f- *Commelinaceae* · 73 spp. · E:Spiderwort; F:Ephémère; G:Dreimasterblume, Tradeskantie
– *albiflora* Kunth = Tradescantia fluminensis
– × **andersoniana** W. Ludw. & Rohweder (*T. ohiensis* × *T. subaspera* × *T. virginiana*) · E:White Spiderwort; F:Ephémère de Virginie; G:Garten-Dreimasterblume · ⌡; cult.
– **many cultivars**
– **bracteata** Small ex Britton · E:Longbract Spiderwort · ⌡; USA: NEC, NC, Okla., Mont.
– **cerinthoides** Kunth · ⌡ Z8 ⓜ; Arg.
– **crassula** Link & Otto · ⌡ Z9 ⓚ; Urug.
– *diuretica* Mart. = Tripogandra diuretica
– **fluminensis** Vell. · E:Wandering Sailor; G:Rio-Dreimasterblume · ⌡ ⤳ Z9 ⓜ ⓚ; SE-Braz., Arg., nat. in Ib, Cors
– *fuscata* Lodd. = Siderasis fuscata
– *geniculata* Jacq. = Gibasis geniculata
– *myrtifolia* hort. = Tradescantia fluminensis
– *navicularis* Ortgies = Callisia navicularis

– **occidentalis** (Britton) Smyth. · E:Prairie Spiderwort · ⌡; USA: NEC, NC, SW, SC, Rocky Mts.
– **ohiensis** Raf. · E:Bluejacket · ⌡ Z7 IV-VI; USA: NE, NCE, NC, SC, SE, Fla.
– **pallida** (Rose) D.R. Hunt · E:Purple Heart; G:Mexikanische Dreimasterblume · ⌡ Z8 ⓜ; Mex.
– *pexata* H.E. Moore = Tradescantia sillamontana
– *reflexa* Raf. = Tradescantia ohiensis
– *reginae* L. Linden & Rodigas = Dichorisandra reginae
– **sillamontana** Matuda · E:White Velvet; G:Haarige Dreimasterblume · ⌡ Z9 ⓚ; NE-Mex.
– **spathacea** Sw. · E:Boat Lily, Moses-in-the-Boat; G:Purpurblättrige Dreimasterblume · ⌡ Z9 ⓜ; S-Mex., Guat., Belize
– **subaspera** Ker-Gawl. · E:Zigzag Spiderwort · ⌡ Z7 VI-VII; USA: NE, NCE, SE, Fla.
– **virginiana** L. · E:Spiderwort, Virginia Spiderwort; G:Virginische Dreimasterblume · ⌡ Z7 IV-V; USA: NE, NCE, SE
– *virginica* L. = Tradescantia virginiana
– *warscewicziana* Kunth & C.D. Bouché = Callisia warszewicziana
– **zanonia** (L.) Sw. · ⌡ Z9 ⓚ; Mex., C-Am., W.Ind., trop. S-Am.
– **zebrina** Heynh.
– **'Purpusii'** · ⤳
– var. **flocculosa** (G. Brückn.) D.R. Hunt · ⌡ ⤳ Z9 ⓜ; ? Mex.
– var. **zebrina** · E:Wandering Jew; G:Silber-Dreimasterblume · ⌡ ⚥ ⤳ Z9 ⓜ; Mex.

Tragopogon L. -m- *Asteraceae* · 100-110 spp. · E:Goat's Beard; F:Salsifis; G:Bocksbart
– *australis* Jord. = Tragopogon porrifolius subsp. australis
– **crocifolius** L. · G:Safranblättriger Bocksbart · ⊙ Z5 V-VII; Eur.: Ib, Fr, Ital-P, Ba; Moroc., Alger., nat. in Swed
– **dubius** Scop. · E:Yellow Salsify; G:Großer Bocksbart · ⊙ Z5 V-VII; Eur.: Ib, Fr, C-Eur., EC-Eur., Ba, E-Eur.; TR, Cauc.
– **porrifolius** L. · G:Haferwurzel, Weißwurzel
– subsp. **australis** (Jord.) Nyman · ⊙ Z5 VI-VII; Eur.: Ib, Fr, Ital-P, Ba, RO; Canar., Alger., nat. in BrI, Sc, C-Eur., EC-Eur.

– subsp. **porrifolius** · E:Salsify, Vegetable Oyster · ⊙ Z5 VI-VII Ⓝ; Eur.: Ib, Fr, Ital-P, Ba, RO; TR, N-Afr., nat. in Eur.: C-Eur., BrI, EC-Eur., Sc; N-Am.
– subsp. *sativus* (Gaterau) Braun-Blanq. = Tragopogon porrifolius subsp. porrifolius
– **pratensis** L. · G:Wiesen-Bocksbart
– subsp. **minor** (Mill.) Wahlenb. · G:Kleinblütiger Bocksbart, Kleiner Wiesen-Bocksbart · ⊙ Z3 V-VII; Eur.: Sw, G, PL, W-Eur.
– subsp. **orientalis** (L.) Čelak. · G:Östlicher Wiesen-Bocksbart, Orientalischer Bocksbart · ⊙ Z3 V-VII; C-Eur., E-Eur.
– subsp. **pratensis** · E:Goat's Beard, Jack-Go-To-Bed-At-Noon; G:Gewöhnlicher Wiesen-Bocksbart · ⊙ ⥣ Z3 V-VII ⚥ ⚘; Eur.*, TR, Cauc., C-As., nat. in N-Am.
– *sinuatus* Avé-Lall. = Tragopogon porrifolius subsp. australis

Tragus Haller -m- *Poaceae* · 6 spp. · E:Bur Grass; F:Bardanette; G:Klettengras
– **racemosus** (L.) All. · E:Spike Burr Grass; G:Traubiges Klettengras · ⊙ VI-VII; Eur* exc. BrI, Sc; TR , Cauc., C-As., Trop. Subtrop. Old World, nat. in Am.

Trapa L. -f- *Trapaceae* · 15 spp. · E:Water Chestnut; F:Châtaigne d'eau; G:Wassernuss
– **natans** L.
– var. **bispinosa** (Roxb.) Makino · E:Singhara Nut; G:Singhara Wassernuss · ⊙ ≈ Z7 Ⓝ ▽; China, Korea, Jap.
– var. **natans** · E:Jesuits Nut, Water Chestnut; F:Châtaigne d'eau; G:Gewöhnliche Wassernuss · ⊙ ≈ Z5 VII-VIII ▽; Eur.* exc. BrI, Sc; TR, C-As., N-Afr., C-Afr.

Traunsteinera Rchb. -n- *Orchidaceae* · 2 spp. · F:Orchis globuleux ; G:Kugelknabenkraut, Kugelorchis
– **globosa** (L.) Rchb. · E:Round-headed Orchid · G:Europäische Kugelorchis · ⥣ VI-VII ▽ ✳; Eur.* exc. BrI, Sc; TR, Cauc.

Trautvetteria Fisch. & C.A. Mey. -f- *Ranunculaceae* · 2 spp.
– **caroliniensis** (Walter) Vail · ⥣ Z5; USA: NE, NCE, SE

Treculia Decne. ex Trécul -f- *Moraceae* · 3 spp. · E:Breadfruit; F:Tréculia; G:Afrikanischer Brotfruchtbaum, Okwabaum

– **africana** Decne. ex Trécul · E:African Breadfruit; G:Afrikanischer Brotfruchtbaum, Okwabaum · ♄ e ⓦ Ⓝ; trop. W-Afr.

Trema Lour. -f- *Ulmaceae* · 14 spp.
– **orientalis** (L.) Blume · E:Indian Charcoal Tree · ♄ e Z9 ⓚ; Ind., S-China, Taiwan, Jap., Malay. Arch., Austr.

Tretorhiza Adans. = Gentiana
– *cruciata* (L.) Opiz = Gentiana cruciata subsp. cruciata

Trevesia Vis. -f- *Araliaceae* · 10 spp.
– **burckii** Boerl. · ♄ e Z10 ⓚ; Sumat., Kalimantan
– **palmata** (Roxb. ex Lindl.) Vis. · E:Snowflake Tree; G:Schneeflockenbaum · ♄ e Z10 ⓦ; Ind.
– *sanderi* hort. = Trevesia burckii

× **Trevorara** hort. -f- *Orchidaceae* (*Arachnis* × *Phalaenopsis* × *Vanda*)

Tribulus L. -m- *Zygophyllaceae* · 25 spp. · E:Caltrops; F:Tribule; G:Burzeldorn
– **terrestris** L. · E:Cat's Head, Small Caltrops; G:Burzeldorn · ⊙ ⊙ V-X; Eur.: Ba, Ib, Ital-P, Fr, EC-Eur., E-Eur.; TR, Cauc., W-Sib., E-Sib., C-As., Ind., Mong., Tibet, China: Sinkiang, ; Jap., N-Afr., Canar., nat. in Am., Afr., Trop.

Trichantha Hook. -f- *Gesneriaceae* · c. 70 spp.
– **illepida** (H.E. Moore) C.V. Morton · ♄ Z10 ⓚ; Panama
– **minor** Hook. · ⥣ ⚥ Z10 ⓦ XII-I; Ecuad.
– *teuscheri* C.V. Morton = Trichantha minor

Trichinium R. Br. = Ptilotus
– *manglesii* (Lindl.) F. Muell. = Ptilotus manglesii

Trichocaulon N.E. Br. -n- *Asclepiadaceae* · 15-20 spp.
– *cactiforme* (Hook.) N.E. Br. = Trichocaulon clavatum
– **clavatum** (Willd.) H. Huber · ⥣ ⚇ Z9 ⓚ; Botswana, Namibia
– *meloforme* Marloth = Trichocaulon clavatum
– **pedicellatum** Schinz · ⥣ ⚇ Z9 ⓚ; Namibia

– **simile** N.E. Br. · ⚄ ⚘ Z9 ⌂; Cape

Trichocentrum Poepp. & Endl. -n-
Orchidaceae · 69 spp.
– **albococcineum** Linden · ⚄ Z10 ⌂ VII-IX
▽ ✳; Braz.
– *albopurpureum* Rchb. f. ex Barb. Rodr. =
Trichocentrum albococcineum
– **bicallosum** (Lindl.) M.W. Chase & N.H.
Williams · ⚄ Z10 ⌂ VIII-X ▽ ✳; Mex.,
Guat., El Salv.
– **carthagenense** (Jacq.) M.W. Chase &
N.H. Williams · ⚄ Z10 ⌂ V-VI ▽ ✳; USA:
Fla.; Mex., C-Am., W.Ind., Col., Venez.
– **cavendishianum** (Bateman) M.W. Chase
& N.H. Williams · ⚄ Z10 ⌂ IV-V ▽ ✳;
Mex., Guat., Hond.
– **cebolleta** (Jacq.) M.W. Chase & N.H.
Williams · ⚄ Z10 ⌂ XI-V ▽ ✳; Mex.,
W-Ind., trop. S-Am.
– **jonesianum** (Rchb. f.) M.W. Chase &
N.H. Williams · ⚄ Z10 ⌂ VIII-X ▽ ✳;
Braz., Parag.
– **lanceanum** (Lindl.) M.W. Chase & N.H.
Williams · ⚄ Z10 ⌂ VI-VIII ▽ ✳; Venez.,
Trinidad, Guyana, Braz.
– **luridum** (Lindl.) M.W. Chase & N.H.
Williams · ⚄ Z10 ⌂ V-VIII ▽ ✳; USA:
Fla.; Mex., C-Am., W.Ind., n S-Am
– **microchilum** (Bateman ex Lindl.) M.W.
Chase & N.H. Williams · ⚄ Z10 ⌂ VI-VII
▽ ✳; Guat.
– **nanum** (Lindl.) M.W. Chase & N.H.
Williams · ⚄ Z10 ⌂ IV-V ▽ ✳; Venez.,
Guyana, Braz., Peru
– **orthoplectron** Rchb. f. · ⚄ Z10 ⌂ X ▽
✳; Braz.
– **pumilum** (Lindl.) M.W. Chase & N.H.
Williams · ⚄ Z10 ⌂ IV-V ▽ ✳; S-Braz.
– **splendidum** (A. Rich. ex Duch.) M.W.
Chase & N.H. Williams · ⚄ Z10 ⌂ X-XII
▽ ✳; Mex.
– **stramineum** (Bateman ex Lindl.) M.W.
Chase & N.H. Williams · ⚄ Z10 ⌂ IV-VI
▽ ✳; Mex.

Trichocereus (A. Berger) Riccob. -m-
Cactaceae · c. 50 spp.
– **bruchii** (Britton & Rose) F. Ritter · ⚘ Z9
⌂ ▽ ✳; Arg.: Tucuman
– **candicans** (Gillies ex Salm-Dyck) Britton
& Rose · ⚘ Z9 ⌂; W-Arg.
– *courantii* K. Schum. = Trichocereus
candicans
– **formosus** (Pfeiff.) F. Ritter · ⚘ Z9 ⌂;

Arg.: Mendoza
– **huascha** (F.A.C. Weber) Britton & Rose ·
⚘ Z9 ⌂ ▽ ✳; Arg.: Catamarca, La Rioja
– **macrogonus** (Salm-Dyck) Riccob. · ⚘ Z9
⌂ ▽ ✳; orig. ?
– **pachanoi** Britton & Rose · ⚘ D Z9 ⌂ ▽
✳; Ecuad.
– **pasacana** (F.A.C. Weber) Britton &
Rose · ⚘ Z9 ⌂ ▽ ✳; N-Arg.
– **purpureopilosus** Weing. · ⚘ Z9 ⌂ ▽ ✳;
Bol.
– *santiaguensis* (Speg.) Backeb. =
Trichocereus spachianus
– **schickendantzii** (F.A.C. Weber) Britton
& Rose · ⚘ Z9 ⌂ ▽ ✳; Arg.: Tucuman
– **spachianus** (Lem.) Riccob. · E:Golden
Column, White Torch Cactus · ⚘ Z9 ⌂ ▽
✳; Arg.
– **strigosus** (Salm-Dyck) Britton & Rose · ⚘
Z9 ⌂ ▽ ✳; W-Arg.
– **tarijensis** (Vaupel) Werderm. · ⚘ Z9 ⌂
▽ ✳; S-Bol., Arg.: Jujuy
– **terscheckii** (J. Parm. ex Pfeiff.) Britton &
Rose · ⚘ Z9 ⌂ ▽ ✳; N-Arg.
– **thelegonus** (K. Schum.) Britton & Rose ·
⚘ Z9 ⌂ ▽ ✳; Arg.: Tucuman

× **Trichocidium** hort. -n- *Orchidaceae*
(*Oncidium* × *Trichocentrum*)

Trichocladus Pers. -m- *Hamamelidaceae* ·
4 spp.
– **crinitus** (Thunb.) Pers. · ♄ e Z9 ⌂
VII-IX; S-Afr.

Trichodiadema Schwantes -n- *Aizoaceae* ·
34 spp.
– **densum** (Haw.) Schwantes · E:Desert
Rose · ♄ ⚘ Z9 ⌂ I-III; Cape

Tricholaena Schrad. ex Schult. & Schult. f.
-f- *Poaceae* · 4 spp.
– *repens* (Willd.) Hitchc. = Melinis repens
– *rosea* Nees = Melinis repens
– **teneriffae** (L. f.) Link · ⚄ Z9 ⌂; Eur.:
S-I, Sic.; SW-As., N-Afr., Macaron.

Trichomanes L. -n- *Hymenophyllaceae* ·
183 spp. · E:Killearney-Fern;
F:Trichomanès; G:Dünnfarn, Haarfarn
– *radicans* Sw. = Trichomanes speciosum
– **reniforme** G. Forst. · ⚄ ⟿ Z10 ⌂; NZ
– **scandens** L. · ⚄ ⟿ Z10 ⌂; Mex., W.Ind.
– **speciosum** Willd. · E:Killarney Fern;
G:Prächtiger Dünnfarn · ⚄ Z9 ⌂;

Eur.: sp., F, I, BrI, Azor.; Trop., nat. in P

Trichophorum Pers. -n- *Cyperaceae* ·
10 spp. · E:Deergrass; F:Scirpe gazonnant; G:Haarbinse, Haarsimse, Rasenbinse
– **alpinum** (L.) Pers. · G:Alpen-Haarsimse,
Alpen-Rasenbinse · 4 ⁓ IV-V; Eur.*
exc. Br; W-Sib., E-Sib., Amur, N-Am.
– **cespitosum** (L.) Hartm.
– subsp. **cespitosum** · E:Deer Grass, Tufted
Bulrush; G:Gewöhnliche Rasenbinse,
Rasen-Haarsimse · 4 ⁓ V-VIII; Eur.*,
TR, W-Sib., E-Sib., Sakhal., Kamchat.,
Jap., N.Guinea, NW-Afr., N-Am.,
Jamaica, Greenl.
– subsp. **germanicum** (Palla) Hegi ·
G:Deutsche Rasenbinse · 4 ⁓ ; Eur.:
BrI, Sc, Fr, G, PL
– *germanicum* = Trichophorum cespitosum
subsp. germanicum
– **pumilum** (Vahl) Schinz & Thell. ·
G:Zwerg-Haarried, Zwerg-Rasenbinse ·
4 ⁓ VII; Eur.: F, I, Sw, EC-Eur., Norw.,
E-Russ.; mts. ; TR, W-Sib., E-Sib., Iran,
C-As., Mong., China, : Sinkiang; N-Am.

Trichopilia Lindl. -f- *Orchidaceae* · 32 spp. ·
F:Trichopilia; G:Haarhütchen
– *crispa* Lindl. = Trichopilia marginata
– **fragrans** (Lindl.) Rchb. f. · 4 D Z10 ⓚ
XII-I ▽ ✳; W.Ind., Venez., Col., Ecuad.,
Peru, Bol.
– **galeottiana** A. Rich. · 4 Z10 ⓦ VI-VII ▽
✳; Mex.
– **laxa** (Lindl.) Rchb. f. · 4 Z10 ⓦ IX-XI ▽
✳; Col., Peru, Venez.
– **marginata** Henfr. · 4 Z10 ⓦ IV-V ▽ ✳;
C-Am., Col.
– *sanguinolenta* (Lindl.) Rchb. f. = Helcia
sanguinolenta
– **suavis** Lindl. & Paxton · 4 Z10 ⓦ III-IV
▽ ✳; Costa Rica, Panama, Col.
– **tortilis** Lindl. · 4 Z10 ⓦ XII-II ▽ ✳;
Mex., Guat., Hond., El Salv.

Trichosanthes L. -f- *Cucurbitaceae* · 15 spp. ·
E:Snake Gourd; F:Serpent végétal;
G:Haarblume, Schlangenhaargurke
– **cucumerina** L. · G:Schlangenhaargurke
– var. **anguina** (L.) Haines · E:Serpent
Cucumber; G:Weiße Schlangenhaargurke · ⊙ ⚥ ♂♂ Z10 ⓚ VI-VIII Ⓝ; Ind.
– var. **cucumerina** · E:Long Tomato,
Viper Gourd; G:Gewöhnliche

Schlangenhaargurke · ⊙ ⚥ ♂♂ Z10 ⓚ Ⓝ;
Ind., Sri Lanka, Malay. Arch., N-Austr.
– *japonica* (Miq.) Regel = Trichosanthes
kirilowii var. japonica
– **kirilowii** Maxim.
– var. **japonica** (Miq.) Kitam. · G:Japa-
nische Schlangenhaargurke · 4 ⚥ Z9 ⓚ
VII-VIII; Jap., Korea, Ryukyu-Is.,
– var. **kirilowii** · E:Chinese Cucumber;
G:Chinesische Schlangenhaargurke · 4 ⚥
♂♂ Z9 ⓚ VII-VIII ⚥ ; Mong.
– **ovigera** Blume · E:Snake Gourd;
G:Eiertragende Schlangenhaargurke · 4
⚥ ♂♂ Z10 ⓚ VI-VIII; China, Jap., Taiwan
– **tricuspidata** Lour. · G:Indische Schlangenhaargurke · 4 ⚥ ♂♂ Z10 ⓚ VII-VIII Ⓝ;
SW-As., Ind.

Trichostigma A. Rich. -n- *Phytolaccaceae* ·
3 spp.
– **peruvianum** (Moq.) H. Walter · ℏ e Z10
ⓦ IV-X; Ecuad., Peru

× **Trichovanda** hort. -f- *Orchidaceae*
(*Trichoglottis* × *Vanda*)

Tricuspidaria Ruiz & Pav. = Crinodendron
– *dependens* Ruiz & Pav. = Crinodendron
patagua
– *lanceolata* Miq. = Crinodendron hookerianum

Tricyrtis Wall. -f- *Calochortaceae* ·
22 spp. · E:Toad Lily; F:Lis des crapauds;
G:Höckerblume, Krötenlilie
– **affinis** Makino · G:Gebirgs-Krötenlilie · 4
Z6; Jap.
– *bakeri* Koidz. = Tricyrtis latifolia
– **formosana** Baker · E:Formosa Toad Lily;
G:Gewöhnliche Formosa-Krötenlilie · 4
Z7 VIII-IX; Taiwan
– **hirta** (Thunb.) Hook. · E:Japanese Toad
Lily; G:Borstige Krötenlilie · 4 Z5 VIII-X;
Jap.
– **latifolia** Maxim. · G:Breitblättrige
Krötenlilie · 4 Z5 VI-VII; China, Jap.
– **macropoda** Miq. · G:Groß-rhizomige
Krötenlilie · 4 Z5 VII-VIII; China, Jap.
– **maculata** (D. Don) J.F. Macbr. ·
G:Weichhaarige Krötenlilie · 4 Z5;
W-China, E-Him., E-Nepal
– *pilosa* Wall. = Tricyrtis maculata
– **puberula** Nakai & Kitag. · G:Flaum-
haarige Krötenlilie · 4 Z5; Jap., China

Tridax L. -f- *Asteraceae* · 26-30 spp. ·
F:Laitue du Mexique, Tridax; G:Dreibiss,
Mexikolattich
- **coronopifolia** (Kunth) Hemsl. · ⊙ Z9
VII-VIII; Mex.
- **trilobata** (Cav.) Hemsl. · ⊙ Z9 VIII-X;
Mex.

Tridentea Haw. -f- *Asclepiadaceae* · 17 spp. ·
- **jucunda** (N.E. Br.) L.C. Leach
- var. **dinteri** (A. Berger) L.C. Leach · ⁴ ⁴
Z9 ⒧; Namibia
- var. **jucunda** · ⁴ ⁴ Z9 ⒧; S-Afr.

Trientalis L. -f- *Primulaceae* · 4 spp. ·
E:Chickweed; F:Trientale; G:Siebenstern
- **europaea** L. · E:Chickweed Wintergreen;
F:Trientalis d'Europe; G:Europäischer
Siebenstern · ⁴ Z4 V-VII; Eur.* exc.
Ib, Ba; W-Sib., E-Sib., Amur, Sakhal.,
Kamchat., Mong., Manch., Jap., Alaska,
Can.: W

Trifolium L. -n- *Fabaceae* · 238 spp. ·
E:Clover; F:Trèfle ; G:Klee
- **alexandrinum** L. · E:Berseem Clover,
Egyptian Clover; G:Alexandriner-Klee ·
⊙ VI-IX Ⓝ; orig. ?; cult. SE-Eur., W-As.,
N-Afr.
- **alpestre** L. · E:Purple Globe Clover;
G:Hügel-Klee · ⁴ VI-VIII; Eur.: Fr, Ital-P,
C-Eur., EC-Eur., Ba, E-Eur., DK, ? Ib; TR,
Cauc.
- **alpinum** L. · E:Alpine Clover; G:Alpen-
Klee · ⁴ △ Z3 VI-VIII; Eur.: sp., F, I, Sw,
A; mts.
- **angustifolium** L. · E:Narrow-leaved
Crimson Clover; G:Fuchsschwanz-Klee,
Schmalblättriger Klee · ⊙; Eur.: Ib, Fr,
Ital-P, Ba, EC-Eur., RO, Crim; TR, Levant,
Iraq, Cauc., N-Iran, N-Afr.
- **arvense** L. · E:Field Clover, Rabbit Foot
Clover; G:Hasen-Klee · ⊙ ⊙ VI-VIII ⚥ ;
Eur.*, TR, Levant, N-Iraq, Cauc., Iran,
W-Sib., C-As., NW-Afr., Libya
- **aureum** Pollich · E:Large Hop Clover;
G:Gold-Klee · ⊙ Z3 VI-VII; Eur.* exc. BrI;
TR, Levant, Cauc., N-Iran, nat. in BrI
- **badium** Schreb. · E:Brown Clover;
G:Braun-Klee · ⁴ Z4 VII-VIII; Eur.: Fr,
Ital-P, C-Eur., EC-Eur., Ba, RO; mts.
- **campestre** Schreb. · E:Hop Clover;
G:Feld-Klee · ⊙ VI-IX; Eur.*, TR, Levant,
Iraq, Cauc., Iran, C-As., N-Afr.
- **cherleri** L. · G:Cherlers Klee · ⊙; Eur.:

Ib, Fr, Ital-P, Ba; TR, Levant, Iraq, Iran,
N-Afr.
- **diffusum** Ehrh. · ⊙; Eur.: Ib, Fr, Ital-P,
Ba, EC-Eur., E-Eur.; TR, Cauc.
- **dubium** Sibth. · E:Small Hop Clover;
G:Kleiner Klee · ⊙ V-IX; Eur.*, TR,
Cyprus, Cauc., Moroc., Tun.
- **fragiferum** L. · E:Strawberry Clover;
G:Erdbeer-Klee · ⁴ ⤳ VI-IX Ⓝ; Eur.*,
Cauc., W-Sib., C-As., Him.; cult. USA,
Austr.
- **glomeratum** L. · E:Cluster Clover;
G:Knäuel-Klee · ⊙; Eur.: Ib, Fr, Ital-P, Ba,
BrI; TR, Levant, Cauc., N-Iran, NW-Afr.
- **hirtum** All. · ⊙; Eur.: Ib, Fr, Ital-P, Ba,
Crim, ? RO; Levant, Iraq, Cauc., Moroc.,
Alger.
- **hybridum** L. · E:Hybrid Clover;
G:Gewöhnlicher Schweden-Klee · ⊙ ⁴
V-IX Ⓝ; Eur.* exc. BrI, Sc; Cauc.; TR,
Moroc., nat. in Sc, BrI, Can., USA, C-As.
- **incarnatum** L. · E:Crimson Clover, Ital-
ian Clover; G:Inkarnat-Klee · ⊙ ⊙ VI-VII
Ⓝ; Eur.*, TR
- **lappaceum** L. · E:Lappa Clover;
G:Kletten-Klee · ⊙; Eur.: Ib, Fr, Ital-P,
Ba, Crim; TR, Levant, Iraq, Cauc., N-Iran,
C-As., Canar., NW-Afr., Libya, nat. in
EC-Eur.
- **lupinaster** L. · ⁴ △ VI-VII; Eur.: EC-Eur.,
E-Eur.; W-Sib., E-Sib., Amur, Sakhal.,
C-As., Mong., Manch., NE-China
- **medium** L. · E:Zigzag Clover; G:Mittlerer
Klee, Zickzack-Klee · ⁴ VI-VIII; Eur.*, TR,
Cauc., NW-Iran, W-Sib., E-Sib.
- **michelianum** Savi · E:Big Flower Clover;
G:Michels Klee · ⊙; Eur.: Ib, Fr, Ital-P,
Ba, Ro; TR, Alger., Moroc.
- **micranthum** Viv. · G:Kleinster Klee · ⊙
V-VII; Eur.: Sc, BrI, Fr, Ib, G, H, Ba; TR,
Levant, Cauc., N-Iran, Canar., NW-Afr.,
Libya
- **montanum** L. · E:Mountain Clover;
G:Berg-Klee · ⁴ V-VII; Eur.: Ba, Fr,
EC-Eur., Sc, Ib, Ital-P, E-Eur., C-Eur.; TR,
Cauc.
- **nigrescens** Viv. · E:Ball Clover;
G:Schwärzlicher Klee · ⊙; Eur.: Ib, Fr,
Ital-P, Ba; TR, Levant., N-Afr.
- **noricum** Wulfen · E:Cream Clover ;
G:Norischer Klee · ⁴ VII-VIII; Eur.: I, A,
Ba; E-Alp., Apenn., Balkan
- **ochroleucon** Huds. · E:Sulphur Clover;
G:Blassgelber Klee · ⁴ VI-VII; Eur.* exc.
Sc; TR, Iran, Moroc., Alger.

- **ornithopodioides** L. · G:Vogelfuß-Klee · ⊙ VI-VII; Eur.: Ib, Fr, Ital-P, BrI, G, H, RO, Croatia; Moroc., Alger.
- **pallescens** Schreb. · E:Pale Clover; G:Bleicher Klee · ♃ Z5 VII-VIII; Eur.: sp., F, I, C-Eur., Ba, RO; mts.
- **pannonicum** Jacq. · E:Hungarian Trefoil; G:Ungarischer Klee · ♃ Z5 VI-VII Ⓝ; Eur.: Fr, Ital-P, EC-Eur., Ba
- **patens** Schreb. · G:Spreiz-Klee · ⊙ VI-VII; Eur.: Ib, Fr, Ital-P, C-Eur., EC-Eur., Ba, RO; TR, Levant, Egypt
- **pratense** L. · E:Red Clover; G:Gewöhnlicher Wiesen-Klee, Rot-Klee · ♃ Z6 VI-VII ⚕ Ⓝ; Eur.*, TR, Iran, Cauc., W-Sib., E-Sib., C-As, Him., NW-Afr., Alaska, Can., USA*, Greenl.
- **repens** L. · E:Ladino Clover, White Clover; G:Weiß-Klee · ♃ ⇝ Z4 V-X Ⓝ; Eur.*, TR, Levant, Iran, W-Sib., E-Sib., Amur, Sakhal., Kamchat., C-As., Mong., Him., China, NW-Afr., Egypt, nat. in N-Am., S-Afr., Jap.
- **resupinatum** L.
- subsp. **majus** Boiss. · G:Duftender Persischer Klee · ⊙ VI-IX Ⓝ; cult. Ba, W-As.
- subsp. **resupinatum** · E:Persian Clover, Reversed Clover; G:Persischer Klee · ⊙ IV-VI Ⓝ; Eur.: Ib, Fr, Ital-P, Ba, E-Eur.; TR, Levant, N-Iraq, Iran, N-Afr., nat. in BrI, C-Eur., EC-Eur.
- **retusum** L. · G:Kleinblütiger Klee · ⊙ V-VI; Eur.: Ib, Fr, C-Eur., EC-Eur., Ba, E-Eur.; TR, Cauc., Alger., Moroc.
- **rubens** L. · E:Red Trefoil; G:Purpur-Klee · ♃ VI-VII; Eur.* exc. BrI, Sc
- **saxatile** All. · G:Felsen-Klee · ⊙ VII-VIII ▽; Eur.: F, I, Sw, A, Alp.
- **scabrum** L. · G:Rauer Klee · ⊙ V-VII; Eur.: Ib, Fr, BrI, Ital-P, C-Eur., Ba, RO, Crim; TR, Levant, Iraq, Cauc., Iran, N-Afr.
- **spadiceum** L. · E:Large Brown Clover; G:Moor-Klee · ♃ VII-VIII; Eur.* exc. BrI; TR, Cauc., Iran, W-Sib.
- **squamosum** L. · E:Sea Clover · ⊙; Eur.: Ib, Fr, Ital-P, Ba, BrI; TR, Lebanon, N-Iran, NW-Afr.
- **stellatum** L. · E:Star Clover; G:Stern-Klee · ⊙; Eur.: Ib, Fr, Ital-P, Ba; TR, Levant, Iraq, Cauc., W-Iran, N-Afr.
- **striatum** L. · E:Knotted Clover, Striate Clover; G:Gestreifter Klee · ⊙ ⊙ VI-VII; Eur.*, TR, Cyprus, Iraq, Cauc., Iran, NW-Afr.
- **strictum** L. · G:Steifer Klee · ⊙; Eur.: Ib, Fr, Ital-P, EC-Eur., Ba, RO; TR, Cauc., NW-Afr., Libya, nat. in D
- **subterraneum** L. · E:Burrowing Clover, Subterranean Clover; G:Erd-Klee · ⊙ Ⓝ; Eur.* exc. BrI, Sc; TR, Levant, Cauc., N-Iran, NW-Afr., Libya
- **thalii** Vill. · G:Rasiger Klee · ♃ Z5 VII-VIII; Eur.: sp., F, I, C-Eur.; mts. N-Sp., Pyr., Alp., Apenn.

Triglochin L. -n- *Juncaginaceae* · 17 spp. · E:Arrowgrass; F:Troscart; G:Dreizack
- **maritimum** L. · E:Sea Arrowgrass; G:Strand-Dreizack · ♃ ~ Z5 VI-VIII ☠; Eur.*, cosmop.; saline habitats
- **palustre** L. · E:Marsh Arrowgrass; G:Sumpf-Dreizack · ♃ ~ Z5 VI-VIII ☠; Eur.*, cosmop.

Trigonella L. -f- *Fabaceae* · 50-80 spp. · E:Fenugreek, Greek Clover; F:Trigonelle; G:Bockshornklee
- **caerulea** (L.) Ser. · ⊙ VI-VII Ⓝ; orig. ?; cult.
- subsp. *procumbens* (Besser) Vassilcz. = Trigonella procumbens
- **corniculata** (L.) L. · G:Traubiger Bockshorn-Klee · ⊙; Eur.: Ib, Fr, Ital-P, Ba; TR
- **foenum-graecum** L. · E:Fenugreek, Halva; G:Griechischer Bockshorn-Klee · ⊙ VI-VII ⚕ Ⓝ; TR, Syr., N-Iraq, Arab., Iran, Eth., nat. in Eur.* exc. BrI, Sc
- *melilotus-caerulea* Asch. & Graebn. = Trigonella caerulea
- **monspeliaca** L. · G:Französischer Bockshorn-Klee · ⊙ III-V; Eur.* exc. BrI, Sc; TR, Levant, Iraq, Cauc., Iran, C-As., N-Afr.
- **procumbens** (Besser) Rchb. · ⊙ VI-VII; Eur.: C-Eur., EC-Eur., Ba, E-Eur.; TR, Cauc.

Trigonidium Lindl. -n- *Orchidaceae* · 14 spp.
- *ringens* Lindl. = Mormolyca ringens
- **seemannii** Rchb. f. · ♃ Z10 Ⓦ ▽ *; Panama

Trillium L. -n- *Trilliaceae* · 45 spp. · E:Trinity Flower, Wake Robin, Wood Lily; F:Trillium; G:Dreiblatt, Dreizipfellilie
- **catesbaei** Elliott · E:Bashful Wake Robin,

Rose Trillium; G:Rosa Dreizipfellilie · ⁴
Z8 ∧ IV; USA: SE
- **cernuum** L. · E:Nodding Trillium;
G:Nickende Dreizipfellilie · ⁴ Z6; Can.:
E; Sask.; USA: NE, NCE, SE
- **chloropetalum** (Torr.) Howell
- var. **chloropetalum** · E:Giant Trillium,
Giant Wakerobin; G:Grünblütige Dreizip-
fellilie · ⁴ Z6 V; USA: Wash., Oreg., Calif.
- var. **giganteum** (Hook. & Arn.) Munz ·
G:Riesige Dreizipfellilie · ⁴ Z6; Calif.
- **erectum** L. · E:Purple Trillium, Stinking
Benjamin; G:Braunrote Dreizipfellilie · ⁴
Z4 IV-V ☫ ⚥; Can.: E; USA; NE, NCE, SE
- *giganteum* (Hook. & Arn.) A. Heller =
Trillium chloropetalum var. chloropeta-
lum
- **grandiflorum** (Michx.) Salisb. · E:Great
White Trillium, Large-flowered Trillium;
G:Große Dreizipfellilie · ⁴ Z5 V-VI; Can.:
E; USA; NE, NCE, SE
- **luteum** (Muhl.) Harb. · E:Yellow Wake
Robin; G:Gelbe Dreizipfellilie · ⁴ Z7;
USA: Ky., Tenn., S.C., Ga.
- **nivale** Riddell · E:Dwarf Trillium,
Snow Trillium; G:Kleine Dreizipfellilie,
Schnee-Dreipzipfellilie · ⁴ Z5 IV-V; USA:
NE, NCE
- **sessile** L. · E:Toadshade, White Trillium;
G:Braune Dreizipfellilie · ⁴ Z4 V; USA:
NE, NCE, SE
- var. *californicum* S. Watson = Trillium
chloropetalum var. giganteum
- *stylosum* Nutt. = Trillium catesbaei
- **undulatum** Willd. · E:Painted Trillium;
G:Gewellte Dreizipfellilie · ⁴ Z4 IV-V;
Can.: E; USA: NE, NCE

Trinia Hoffm. -f- *Apiaceae* · c. 10 spp. ·
E:Honewort; F:Trinia; G:Faserschirm
- **glauca** (L.) Dumort. · G:Blaugrüner
Faserschirm · ⁴ IV-V; Eur. : Ib, Fr, BrI,
Ital-P, C-Eur., EC-Eur., Ba, E-Eur.; TR,
N-Iran
- **ramosissima** (Fisch. ex Trevir.) W.D.J.
Koch · G:Großer Faserschirm · ☉ ⁴ V-VI;
Eur.: A, Ba, E-Eur.

Triodanis Raf. -f- *Campanulaceae* · 7 spp.
- **perfoliata** (L.) Nieuwl. · ☉; Can.: B.C.;
USA*, C-Am., Hispaniola, Jamaica,
S-Am.

Triolena Naudin -f- *Melastomataceae* ·
22 spp.

- **hirsuta** (Benth.) Triana · ⁴ Z10 ⓜ; trop.
Am.
- **pustulata** Triana · ⁴ Z10 ⓜ; Ecuad.
- **scorpioides** Naudin · ⁴ Z10 ⓜ; Mex.

Triosteum L. -n- *Caprifoliaceae* · 6 spp. ·
E:Feverwort, Horse Gentian; F:Trioste ;
G:Fieberwurz
- **aurantiacum** E.P. Bicknell ·
E:Orangefruit Horse Gentian · ⁴ Z4;
Can.: W; USA: NE, NCE, SE, Kans.
- **perfoliatum** L. · E:Feverwort, Tinker's
Weed, Wild Coffee ; G:Durchwachsene
Fieberwurz · ⁴ Z6 V-VII; USA: NE, NCE,
NC, SE
- **pinnatifidum** Maxim. · ⁴ Z4 V-VI;
NW-China
- **rosthornii** Diels & Graebn. · ⁴ Z4 VI-VII;
China

Tripetaleia Siebold & Zucc. -f- *Ericaceae* ·
2 spp.
- **bracteata** Maxim. · ♄ d Z6 VII-VIII; Jap.;
mts.
- **paniculata** Siebold & Zucc. · ♄ d Z6; Jap.

Triphasia Lour. -f- *Rutaceae* · 3 spp.
- **trifolia** (Burm. f.) P. Wilson · E:Lime
Berry · ♄ e D Z10 ⓚ ⓝ; trop. As.

Tripleurospermum Sch. Bip. -n-
Asteraceae · 38 spp. · E:Scentless False
Chamomile; F:Matricaire; G:Kamille
- **caucasicum** (Willd.) Hayek ·
F:Matricaire du Caucase · ⁴ ⤳ △ V-VII;
AL, BG, TR, Cauc.
- *inodorum* (L.) Sch. Bip. = Tripleurospermum perforatum
- **maritimum** (L.) W.D.J. Koch · E:False
Mayweed, Sea Mayweed; G:Küsten-
Kamille · ☉ ⁴; Eur.: Ib, Fr, BrI, C-Eur.,
Sc, PL, EC-Eur.; coasts
- **oreades** (Boiss.) Rech. f.
- var. **oreades** · ⁴ ⤳ △ IV-VII; TR, Syr.
- var. **tchihatchewii** (Boiss.) E. Hossain ·
⁴ ⤳ △ V-VII; TR
- **perforatum** (Mérat) M. Laínz · ☉ ⁴ VI-X;
Eur.*, TR, Cauc., W-Sib., E-Sib., Amur,
Sakhal., Kamchat., Manch., nat. in N-Am.
- *tchihatchewii* (Boiss.) Bornm. = Tripleurospermum oreades var. tchihatchewii
- **tenuifolium** (Kit.) Freyn ex Freyn & E.
Brandis · G:Feinblättrige Kamille · ☉ ⁴
VII-X; Eur.: A, H, Ba, RO; TR

Triplochiton K. Schum. -m- *Sterculiaceae* ·
3 spp.
– **scleroxylon** K. Schum. · ♄ d Z10 ⓦ Ⓝ;
W-Afr., C-Afr.

Tripogandra Raf. -f- *Commelinaceae* ·
22 spp.
– **diuretica** (Mart.) Handlos · ⌃ Z9 ⓦ;
trop. S-Am.
– *warscewicziana* (Kunth & C.D. Bouché)
Woodson = Callisia warscewicziana

Tripsacum L. -n- *Poaceae* · 13 spp. ·
G:Gamagras, Guatemalagras
– **andersonii** J.R. Gray · ⌃ ⓦ Ⓝ; ? Venez.,
? Col.
– **dactyloides** (L.) L. · E:Eastern Gamagras;
G:Gamagras · ⌃ Ⓝ; USA: NE, NCE, NC,
SC, SE, Fla.; Mex., W.Ind., trop. S-Am.
– **laxum** Nash · E:Guatamalan Grass;
G:Guatemalagras · ⌃ Ⓝ; Mex.: Veracruz,
Oaxaca, nat. in W.Ind., trop. Am.

Tripterygium Hook. f. -n- *Celastraceae* ·
2 spp. · G:Dreiflügelfrucht
– **regelii** Sprague & Takeda · G:Japanische
Dreiflügelfrucht · ♄ d ⚥ Z6; Manch.,
Korea, Jap.
– **wilfordii** Hook. f. · ♄ d ⚥ Z9 ⓚ X-XI ⚘
Ⓝ; S-China, Taiwan

Trisetaria Forssk. -f- *Poaceae* · 15 spp. ·
G:Grannenhafer; F:Avoine barbue
– **cavanillesii** (Trin.) Maire · G:Cavanilles
Grannenhafer · ☉ IV-V; Eur.: sp, Sw,
I; TR, Iraq, Cauc., Iran, Afgh., Pakist.,
C-As., N-Afr., nat. in E-Russ.
– **panicea** (Lam.) Paunero · ☉; Eur.: Ib, Fr,
Ital-P; N-Afr., Macaron.

Trisetum Pers. -n- *Poaceae* · c. 70 spp. ·
E:Yellow Oat Gras; F:Avoine jaunâtre,
Trisète; G:Goldhafer
– **alpestre** (Host) P. Beauv. · G:Alpen-
Goldhafer · ⌃ VI-VII; Eur.: C-Eur.,
EC-Eur., Slove., ? Bosn., Montenegro,
RO, W-Russ.; Alp., Carp.
– **argenteum** (Willd.) Roem. & Schult. ·
G:Silber-Goldhafer · ⌃ VI-VII; Eur.: I, ?
Sw, A, Slove.; E-Alp.
– **distichophyllum** (Vill.) P. Beauv. ·
G:Zweizeiliger Goldhafer · ⌃ ⤳ △
VII-VIII; Eur.: sp, F, I, C-Eur., Ba; Cauc.:
mts.
– **flavescens** (L.) P. Beauv. · E:Yellow

Oat Grass; G:Gewöhnlicher Wiesen-
Goldhafer · ⌃ V-VI Ⓝ; Eur.*, TR, Cauc.,
N-Iran, C-As., N-Ind., NW-Afr., nat. in
N-Am., NZ
– **spicatum** (L.) K. Richt. · E:Northern Oat
Grass · ⌃ VII-VIII; Eur.: Sc, N-Russ., sp.,
F, I, C-Eur.; N. Pyr., Alp.; Cauc., W-Sib.,
E-Sib., Amur, Sakhal. Kamchat., C-As.,
Mong., Tibet, China, Korea, Jap., N-Am.,
S-Am.

Tristania R. Br. -n- *Myrtaceae* · 1 sp.
– *conferta* R. Br. = Lophostemon confertus
– **neriifolia** (Sims) R. Br. · E:Water Gum;
G:Wasser-Gummibaum · ♄ ♄ Z9 ⓚ;
Austr.: N.S. Wales

Triteleia Douglas ex Lindl. -f- *Alliaceae* ·
15 spp. · F:Triteleia; G:Triteleie
– **bridgesii** (S. Watson) Greene · E:Bridge's
Brodiaea; G:Bridges Triteleie · ⌃ Z7 ⓚ ∧
VI; USA: Oreg., Calif.
– **ixioides** (W.T. Aiton) Greene · E:Pretty
Face; G:Gelbe Triteleie · ⌃ Z7 ⓚ ∧ VI;
USA: Oreg., Calif.
– **laxa** Benth. · E:Grass Nut, Ithuriel's
Spear, Triplet Lily; G:Blaue Triteleie · ⌃
Z7 ⓚ ∧ VI; USA: Oreg., Calif.
– **peduncularis** Lindl. · E:Long Rayed
Triteleia; G:Langstielige Triteleie · ⌃ Z7
ⓚ ∧ VI-VII; N-Calif.
– × **tubergenii** L.W. Lenz (*T. laxa × T.
peduncularis*) · ⌃ ⓚ ∧ VII; cult.
– *uniflora* Lindl. = Ipheion uniflorum

Trithrinax Mart. -f- *Arecaceae* · 3 spp.
– **Braziliensis** Mart. · ♄ e Z10 ⓚ; S-Braz.

× **Triticosecale** Wittm. ex A. Camus -n-
Poaceae · E:Triticale, Wheat-rye Hybrid;
F:Triticale; G:Triticale (*Secale × Triticum*)

Triticum L. -n- *Poaceae* · 4 (-20) spp. ·
E:Wheat; F:Blé; G:Weizen
– **aestivum** L. · E:Wheat; G:Saat-Weizen ·
☉ VI-VII ⚥ Ⓝ; cult.
– **baeoticum** Boiss. · E:Wild Einkorn · ☉;
Eur.: Ba, ? Crim +
– *caninum* L. = Elymus caninus
– **carthlicum** Nevski · ☉ Ⓝ; cult.
– *cereale* Schrank = Triticum aestivum
– **compactum** Host · E:Club Wheat;
G:Buckel-Weizen, Zwerg-Weizen · ☉ VII;
cult. S-Eur., SC-Eur.
– *cristatum* (L.) Schreb. = Agropyron

cristatum subsp. cristatum
- **dicoccoides** (Körn. ex Asch. & Graebn.)
Aarons. · E:Wild Emmer; G:Wilder
Emmer · ⊙ ; TR, Cauc., Syr., Palest., Iran
- **dicoccon** Schrank · E:Emmer; G:Emmer,
Zweikorn-Weizen · ⊙ VI-VII Ⓝ; cult.
- *dicoccum* Schübl. = Triticum dicoccon
- **durum** Desf. · E:Durum Wheat; G:Hart-
Weizen · ⊙ VI-VII Ⓝ; cult.
- **georgicum** Dekapr. · ⊙ VI-VII Ⓝ; cult.
- *hybernum* L. = Triticum aestivum
- *junceum* L. = Elymus farctus subsp.
farctus
- **macha** Dekapr. & Menabde · ⊙ Ⓝ; cult.
- **monococcum** L. · E:Einkorn Wheat;
G:Einkorn-Weizen · ⊙ VI-VII Ⓝ; cult.
- *ovatum* (L.) Raspail = Aegilops geniculata
- *pauciflorum* Schwein. = Elymus trachycaulus
- **polonicum** L. · E:Polish Wheat; G:Poln-
ischer Weizen · ⊙ VI-VII Ⓝ; cult.
- *repens* L. = Elymus repens
- *sativum* Lam. = Triticum aestivum
- **spelta** L. · E:Spelt ; G:Dinkel, Spelz · ⊙ VI
Ⓝ; cult.
- **sphaerococcum** Percival · ⊙ Ⓝ; cult.
- **timopheevii** (Zhuk.) Zhuk. · ⊙ ; Cauc.
- *trachycaulum* Schwein. = Elymus
trachycaulus
- *triunciale* (L.) Raspail = Aegilops
triuncialis
- **turanicum** Jakubz. · ⊙ Ⓝ; cult.
- **turgidum** L. · E:Branched Wheat;
G:Englischer Weizen · ⊙ VI-VII Ⓝ; cult.
- *vagans* (Jord. & Fourr.) Greuter =
Aegilops geniculata
- *ventricosum* (Tausch) Ces. = Aegilops
ventricosa
- *vulgare* Vill. = Triticum aestivum

× *Tritisecale* Lebedev = × Triticosecale

Tritonia Ker-Gawl. -f- *Iridaceae* · 25 spp. ·
E:Tritonia; F:Tritonia; G:Tritonie
- *aurea* (Pappe ex Hook.) Planch. = Crocosmia aurea
- **crocata** (L.) Ker-Gawl. · E:Flame Freesia,
Tritonia; G:Safranfarbige Tritonie · ⏚ Z9
⚘ V-VI; Cape
- *pottsii* (Baker) Baker = Crocosmia pottsii

Tritoniopsis L. Bolus -f- *Iridaceae* · 24 spp.
- **caffra** (Ker-Gawl. ex Baker) Goldblatt · ⏚
Z9 ⚘; S-Afr.: Cape, Natal

Triumfetta L. -f- *Tiliaceae* · c. 70 spp.
- **rhomboidea** Jacq. · ♄ ⚘ Ⓝ; W-Sah,
W-Afr., Trop.

Trochiscanthes W.D.J. Koch -f- *Apiaceae* ·
1 sp. · F:Trochiscanthe; G:Radblüte
- **nodiflorus** (All.) W.D.J. Koch · G:Rad-
blüte · ⏚ VI-VIII; Eur.: F, N-I, Sw; mts.

Trochocarpa R. Br. -f- *Epacridaceae* ·
12 spp. · F:Trochocarpe; G:Radfrucht
- **laurina** (Rudge) R. Br. · ♄ ♄ e Z9 ⚘ VI;
Austr.: Queensl., N.S.Wales

Trochodendron Siebold & Zucc.
-m- *Trochodendraceae* · 1 sp. ·
F:Trochodendron; G:Radbaum
- **aralioides** Siebold & Zucc. · G:Rad-
baum · ♄ e Z7 V-VI; Jap., Ryukyu-Is.,
Taiwan

Trollius L. -m- *Ranunculaceae* · 31 spp. ·
E:Globeflower; F:Boule d'or, Trolle;
G:Trollblume
- **asiaticus** L. · ⏚ Z4 V-VI; Eur.: NE-Russ.;
W-Sib., C-As.
- **chinensis** Bunge · E:Chinese Globe-
flower; F:Trolle de Chine; G:Chinesische
Trollblume · ⏚ Z5 VI-VIII; NE-China
- **europaeus** L. · E:European Globeflower,
Globe Flower; F:Trolle d'Europe;
G:Europäische Trollblume · ⏚ Z5 V-VI ⚘
▽; Eur.*, W-Sib.
- **laxus** Salisb. · E:American Globeflower;
G:Amerikanische Trollblume · ♄ △ ⁓
Z4 IV-V; USA: NE, Ohio
- *ledebourii* hort. non Rchb. = Trollius
chinensis
- **ledebourii** Rchb. · ⏚ Z6; E-Sib.,
N-Mong., N-Korea
- **pumilus** D. Don · F:Trolle de l'Himalaya;
G:Zwerg-Trollblume · ⏚ △ Z5 VI-VII;
Him.
- **ranunculinus** (Sm.) Stearn · ⏚ Z6 V-VI;
TR, Cauc., Iran
- **stenopetalus** (Regel) T.V. Egorova &
Sipliv. · G:Schmalblütige Trollblume · ⏚
Z7; NE-Burma, SW-China
- **yunnanensis** (Franch.) Ulbr. · E:Yunnan
Globeflower; G:Yunnan-Trollblume · ⏚
Z5 VI-VII; Yunnan
- **Cultivars:**
- **many cultivars**

Tromotriche Haw. -f- *Asclepiadaceae* ·

3 spp.
- **revoluta** (Masson) Haw. · ⌃ ⁴ Z9 ⓚ; Cape

Tropaeolum L. -n- *Tropaeolaceae* · 87 spp. ·
  E:Nasturtium; F:Capucine; G:Kapuziner-
  kresse
- **azureum** Miers · ⌃ ⁑ Z9 ⓚ IX-X; Chile
- **brachyceras** Hook. & Arn. · ⌃ ⁑ Z9 ⓚ
  VI; Chile
- *canariense* hort. ex Lindl. & T. Moore =
  Tropaeolum peregrinum
- **leptophyllum** G. Don · ⌃ ⁑ Z8 ⓚ VII-
  VIII Ⓝ; Bol., Chile
- **majus** L. · E:Nasturtium; G:Echte
  Kapuzinerkresse · ⊙ ⌃ VII-X ⚥ Ⓝ; Col.,
  Ecuad., Peru
- **many cultivars**
- **minus** L. · G:Kleine Kapuzinerkresse · ⊙
  ⌃ VII-X; Peru
- **peltophorum** Benth. · ⊙ ⊙ ⌃ ♄ Z9 ⓚ
  I-XII; Col., Ecuad.
- **pentaphyllum** Lam. · G:Fünfblättrige
  Kauzinerkresse · ⌃ ⁑ Z8 ⓚ VII-XI;
  C-Braz., Urug., Parag., Arg., E-Bol.
- **peregrinum** L. · E:Canary Creeper;
  G:Kanarien-Kapuzinerkresse · ⊙ ⁑ Z9
  VII-X; Peru, ? Ecuad.
- **polyphyllum** Cav. · G:Chile-Kapuziner-
  kresse · ⌃ Z8 ⓚ VI-X; Arg., Chile
- **speciosum** Poepp. & Endl. · E:Flame
  Flower, Scotch Creeper; G:Flammende
  Kapuzinerkresse · ⌃ ⁑ Z8 ⓚ VIII-X; Chile
- **tricolor** Sw. · G:Dreifarbige Kapuzinerkresse · ⌃ ⁑ Z8 ⓚ III-V; Bol., Chile
- **tuberosum** Ruiz & Pav. · E:Tropaeolum;
  G:Knollenkresse, Peruanische Kapuzinerkresse · ⌃ ⁑ Z8 ⓚ VIII-IX Ⓝ; Peru, Bol.
- *yarratii* Youel ex Paxton = Tropaeolum
  tricolor

Tsuga Carrière -f- *Pinaceae* · 9 spp. ·
  E:Hemlock, Hemlock Spruce; F:Pruche;
  G:Hemlocktanne, Schierlingstanne
- **canadensis** (L.) Carrière · E:Eastern
  Hemlock; F:Sapin ciguë, Sapin du
  Canada; G:Kanadische Hemlocktanne · ♄
  e Z5 IV-V ⚥ ; Can.: E; USA; NE, NCE, SE
- **caroliniana** Engelm. · E:Carolina
  Hemlock; G:Carolina-Hemlocktanne · ♄ e
  Z6; USA: Va., SE
- **chinensis** (Franch.) E. Pritz. ·
  G:Gewöhnliche Chinesische Hemlock-
  tanne · ♄ e Z6; W-China
- **diversifolia** (Maxim.) Mast. · E:Northern
  Japanese Hemlock; F:Tsuga du Japon;

G:Nordjapanische Hemlocktanne,
  Verschiedenblättrige Hemlocktanne · ♄ e
  Z6; Jap.
- **heterophylla** (Raf.) Sarg. · E:Western
  Hemlock; G:Westamerikanische
  Hemlocktanne, Westliche Hemlocktanne
  · ♄ e Z6 Ⓝ; Alaska, Can.: B.C., Alta.; USA:
  NW, Calif., Idaho, Mont.
- **mertensiana** (Bong.) Carrière ·
  E:Mountain Hemlock; G:Berg-Hemlock-
  tanne
- subsp. **mertensiana** var. **mertensiana** ·
  F:Tsuga des montagnes; G:Gewöhnliche
  Berg-Hemlocktanne · ♄ e Z6; Alaska,
  Can.: B.C.; USA: NW, Calif., Rocky Mts.
  (Idaho, Mont., Nev.)
- *pattoniana* (Balf.) Sénécl. = Tsuga
  mertensiana subsp. mertensiana var.
  mertensiana
- **sieboldii** Carrière · E:Southern Japanese
  Hemlock; G:Araragi-Hemlocktanne,
  Südjapanische Hemlocktanne · ♄ e Z6;
  Jap.
- var. **nana** (Endl.) Carrière = Tsuga
  diversifolia

Tuberaria (Dunal) Spach -f- *Cistaceae* ·
  12 spp. · E:Spotted Rock Rose;
  F:Tubéraire; G:Sandröschen
- **guttata** (L.) Fourr. · G:Geflecktes
  Sandröschen · ⊙ Z8 VI-IX; Eur.: Ib, Fr,
  BrI, G, Ital-P, Ba; TR, Levant, NW-Afr.,
  Libya

Tulbaghia L. -f- *Alliaceae* · 26 spp. ·
  E:Society Garlic, Wild Garlic; F:Tulbaghia
  ; G:Kaplilie, Tulbaghie
- **capensis** L. · ⌃ Z8 ⓚ VI-VII; Cape
- **violacea** Harv. · E:Society Garlic;
  G:Knoblauchs-Kaplilie · ⌃ Z8 ⓚ VII-VIII;
  S-Afr.

Tulipa L. -f- *Liliaceae* · 109 spp. · E:Tulip;
  F:Tulipe; G:Tulpe
- *acuminata* Vahl ex Hornem. = Tulipa
  gesneriana
- **agenensis** DC. · ⌃ Z6 IV-V ▽; NW-Iran,
  nat. in S-F u. I
- **albertii** Regel · ⌃ Z6 ▽; C-As.
- **armena** Boiss. · ⌃ Z5 IV-V ▽; cult. in TR
- *batalinii* Regel = Tulipa linifolia
- **biflora** Pall. · ⌃ △ Z5 V-VI ▽; Eur.:
  W-Ba, E-Russ., Crim; TR, Palest., Arab.,
  Cauc., Iran, W-Sib., C-As., Egypt
- *celsiana* DC. = Tulipa sylvestris subsp.

australis
- *chrysantha* Boiss. = Tulipa stellata
- **clusiana** DC. · E:Lady Tulip; G:Damen-Tulpe · ⏾ ∇; Iran, NW-Pakist., N-Ind., nat. in S-Eur., TR
- *var.* *chrysantha* (A.D. Hall) Sealy = Tulipa stellata
- *var.* *stellata* (Hook.) Regel = Tulipa stellata
- **dasystemon** (Regel) Regel · ⏾ Z5 IV ∇; C-As., China: Sinkiang
- *didieri* Jord. = Tulipa gesneriana
- **fosteriana** W. Irving · ⏾ Z5 IV ∇; C-As.
- **gesneriana** L. · E:Gesner's Tulip; G:Gesners Tulpe · ⏾ ⋉ Z7 IV-V ⚥ ⚘ ∇; Eur.: SE-F, nat. in sp., F, I, Sw, ? GR
- **greigii** Regel · ⏾ Z5 IV-V ∇; C-As.
- *grengiolensis* Thommen = Tulipa gesneriana
- **hoogiana** B. Fedtsch. · ⏾ Z7 ▭ ∧ IV-V ∇; C-As.
- **humilis** Herb. · ⏾ Z7 V ∇; Cauc., Iran, N-Iraq
- **ingens** Hoog · ⏾ Z6 IV ∇; C-As.
- **kaufmanniana** Regel · E:Waterlily Tulip; G:Kaufmanns Tulpe · ⏾ △ Z5 III ∇; C-As.
- **kolpakowskiana** Regel · ⏾ Z6 IV ∇; C-As., Afgh.
- **lanata** Regel · ⏾ Z7 IV ∇; C-As., Afgh., NE-Iran
- **linifolia** Regel · ⏾ △ Z5 V ∇; C-As., N-Iran
- *marjolettii* E.P. Perrier & Songeon = Tulipa praecox
- **montana** Lindl. · ⏾ Z6 V ∇; C-As., N-Iran
- *oculus-solis* St.-Amans = Tulipa agenensis
- **orphanidea** Boiss. ex Heldr. · ⏾ Z5 IV ∇; Eur.: GR, TR, SE-Ba, Crete
- **'Whittallii'** · ∇
- *polychroma* Stapf = Tulipa biflora
- **praecox** Ten. · ⏾ Z5 III-IV ∇; orig. ?, nat. in S-Eur., W-TR
- **praestans** Hoog · ⏾ Z5 IV ∇; C-As.
- *pulchella* (Fenzl ex Regel) Baker = Tulipa humilis
- *var.* *humilis* hort. = Tulipa humilis
- **saxatilis** Sieber ex Spreng. · E:Candia Tulip; G:Kretische Tulpe · ⏾ Z6 IV ∇; Crete, W-TR
- *schrenkii* Regel = Tulipa suaveolens
- **sprengeri** Baker · ⏾ Z5 V-VI ∇; TR
- **stellata** Hook. · IV ∇; N-Iran, Afgh, C-As., NW-Ind.
- **suaveolens** Roth · ⏾ Z7 ∇; SE-Russ.

- **sylvestris** L. · G:Wilde Tulpe
- subsp. **australis** (Link) Pamp. · G:Südalpine Tulpe · ⏾ Z5 V ∇; Eur.: Ib, F, I, Ba; NW-Afr.
- subsp. **sylvestris** · E:Wild Tulip ; G:Weinberg-Tulpe · ⏾ D Z5 IV-V ∇; Eur.: Ib, Fr, Ital-P, C-Eur., Ba, E-Eur., Sw; TR, Cauc., nat. in BrI, Sc, EC-Eur., N-Afr., Sib., Middle East
- **tarda** Stapf · ⏾ △ Z5 IV ∇; C-As.
- **tubergeniana** Hoog · ⏾ Z5 IV ∇; C-As.
- **turkestanica** (Regel) Regel · ⏾ △ Z5 III-IV ∇; C-As.
- **undulatifolia** Boiss. · ⏾ Z5 IV-V ∇; Eur.: S-Ba; W-TR, Iran, C-As.
- **urumiensis** Stapf · ⏾ △ Z5 IV ∇; NW-Iran
- *violacea* Boiss. & Buhse = Tulipa humilis
- *var.* *pallida* Bornm. = Tulipa humilis
- *vvedenskyi* Botschantz. = Tulipa albertii
- *whittallii* (Dykes) A.D. Hall = Tulipa orphanidea
- **wilsoniana** Hoog
- **Cultivars:**
- **many cultivars, see Section III**

Tulipastrum Spach = Magnolia
- *acuminatum* (L.) Small = Magnolia acuminata

Tulipifera Mill. = Liriodendron
- *liriodendrum* Mill. = Liriodendron tulipifera

Tunica Ludw. = Petrorhagia
- *prolifera* (L.) Scop. = Petrorhagia prolifera
- *saxifraga* (L.) Scop. = Petrorhagia saxifraga

Tupidanthus Hook. f. & Thomson = Schefflera
- *calyptratus* Hook. f. & Thomson = Schefflera pueckleri

Turbinicarpus (Backeb.) Buxb. & Backeb. -m- *Cactaceae* · 14 spp.
- **gielsdorfianus** (Werderm.) V. John & Ríha · ⏹ Z9 ⌂ ∇ ✳; Mex.: Tamaulipas
- **horripilus** (Lem. ex C.F. Först.) V. John & Ríha · ⏹ Z9 ⌂ ∇ ✳; Mex.: Hidalgo
- **lophophoroides** (Werderm.) Buxb. & Backeb. · ⏹ Z9 ⌂ ∇ ✳; Mex.: San Suis Potosí
- **mandragora** (A. Berger) Zimmerman · ⏹

Z9 ⓚ ▽ ✳; Mex.: Coahuila, Nuevo Leon
- **pseudomacrochele** (Backeb.) Buxb. & Backeb. · ⵂ Z9 ⓚ ▽ ✳; Mex.: Queretaro
- **pseudopectinatus** (Backeb.) Glass & R.A. Foster · ⵂ Z9 ⓚ ▽ ✳; Mex.: Tamaulipas, Nuevo Leon
- **saueri** (Boed.) V. John & Ríha · ⵂ Z9 ⓚ ▽ ✳; Mex.: Tamaulipas
- **schmiedickeanus** (Boed.) Buxb. ex Backeb. · ⵂ Z9 ⓚ ▽ ✳; Mex.: Nuevo León, San Luis Potosi, Tamaulipas
- **valdezianus** (L. Möller) Glass & R.A. Foster · ⵂ Z9 ⓚ ▽ ✳; Mex.: Coahuila, Nuevo Leon
- **viereckii** (Werderm.) V. John & Ríha · ⵂ Z9 ⓚ ▽ ✳; Mex.: Nuevo León, Tamaulipas

Turgenia Hoffm. -f- *Apiaceae* · 2 spp. · F:Turgénia; G:Haftdolde, Turgenie
- **latifolia** (L.) Hoffm. · G:Breitblättrige Haftdolde, Turgenie · ☉ VI-VIII; Eur.* exc.Sc, BrI; TR, Cauc., C-As., Pakist., Kashmir, NW-Afr., nat. in N-Am.

Turnera L. -f- *Turneraceae* · 50-60 spp. · F:Turnéra; G:Damiana
- *aphrodisiaca* Ward = Turnera diffusa var. aphrodisiaca
- **diffusa** Willd. ex Schult.
- var. **aphrodisiaca** (Ward) Urb. · ♄ Z10 ⓜ ⚥ ; Braz.
- var. **diffusa** · E:Mexican Holly ; G:Schmalblättrige Damiana · ♄ Z10 ⓜ; Braz.
- **ulmifolia** L. · E:Sage Rose, West Indian Holly; G:Großblättrige Damiana · ♄ Z9 ⓜ; Mex., C-Am., W.Ind., S-Am.

Turritis L. = Arabis
- *glabra* L. = Arabis glabra

Tussilago L. -f- *Asteraceae* · 1 sp. · E:Coltsfoot; F:Pas d'âne, Tussilage; G:Huflattich
- **farfara** L. · E:Coltsfoot; G:Huflattich · ⵂ Z5 III-IV ⚥ ; Eur.*, TR, Levant, Cauc., Iran, W-Sib., E-Sib., C-As., Him., China, Moroc., Alger., nat. in N-Am.
- *japonica* L. = Farfugium japonicum

Tweedia Hook. & Arn. -f- *Asclepiadaceae* · 1 sp.
- **caerulea** D. Don ex Sweet · ♄ e ⚥ Z10 ⓚ VI-IX; S-Braz., Urug.

Tylecodon Toelken -m- *Crassulaceae* · 28-31 sp.
- **cacalioides** (L. f.) Toelken · ♄ ⵂ Z9 ⓚ; Cape
- **reticulatus** (L. f.) Toelken · ♄ ⵂ Z9 ⓚ; Cape, Namibia

Typha L. -f- *Typhaceae* · 27 spp. · E:Bulrush, Reedmace; F:Massette; G:Rohrkolben
- **angustifolia** L. · E:Lesser Bulrush; F:Massette à feuilles étroites; G:Schmalblättriger Rohrkolben · ⵍ ⌇ Z3 VII-VIII; Eur.*, TR, Cauc., Iran, C-As., Mong., Can., USA* exc. SW, Austr.
- **latifolia** L. · E:Bulrush, Cat Tail; F:Massette à feuilles larges; G:Breitblättriger Rohrkolben · ⵍ ⌇ Z3 VII-VIII ⚥ ⓝ; Eur.*, Cauc., Iran, W-Sib., E-Sib., C-As., Mong., N-China, N-Am.
- subsp. *shuttleworthii* (W.D.J. Koch & Sond.) Stoj. & Stef. = Typha shuttleworthii
- **laxmannii** Lepech. · E:Laxmann's Bulrush; F:Massette de Laxmann; G:Laxmanns Rohrkolben · ⵍ ⌇ Z4 VII-VIII; Eur.: E-Eur., Ba; TR, Cauc., W-Sib., E-Sib., Amur, C-As., Mong., N-China, nat. in F, I, G, EC-Eur.
- **lugdunensis** P. Chabert · G:Französischer Rohrkolben · ⵍ ⌇ ; Eur.: F, Sw, D
- **minima** Funck ex Hoppe · E:Lesser Bulrush; F:Massette petite; G:Zwerg-Rohrkolben · ⵍ ⌇ Z6 V-IX ⓝ; Eur.: F, I, C-Eur., EC-Eur., Serb., RO; TR, Cauc., Iran, Afgh., Pakist., C-As., Mong., Jap.
- **shuttleworthii** W.D.J. Koch & Sond. · E:Shuttleworth's Bulrush; F:Massette de Shuttleworth; G:Shuttleworths Rohrkolben · ⵍ ⌇ Z5 VI-VIII; Eur.: F, N-I, C-Eur., EC-Eur., Ba, RO; TR

Typhoides Moench = Phalaris
- *arundinacea* (L.) Moench = Phalaris arundinacea

Typhonium Schott -n- *Araceae* · 71 sp.
- **giganteum** Engl.
- var. **giganteum** · ⵍ Z10 ⓜ; China
- var. **giraldii** (Engl.) Baroni · ⵍ Z10 ⓜ; China (Peking)

Typhonodorum Schott -n- *Araceae* · 1 sp.
- **lindleyanum** Schott · ⵍ e Z10 ⓜ; trop. Afr., Madag., Mauritius

Uebelmannia Buining -f- *Cactaceae* · 5 spp.

- **pectinifera** Buining · ⵞ Z9 ⓚ ▽ ✳;
  Braz.: Minas Gerais

Ugni Turcz. -f- *Myrtaceae* · 5-15 spp.
- **molinae** Turcz. · E:Strawberry Myrtle;
  G:Chilenische Guave · ♄ e Z9 ⓚ Ⓝ; Bol.,
  Chile

Ulex L. -m- *Fabaceae* · 20 spp. · E:Furze,
  Gorse; F:Ajonc; G:Stechginster
- **europaeus** L. · E:Furze, Gorse, Whin;
  G:Gewöhnlicher Stechginster · ♄ e Z7
  ⋀ V-VII ✺ Ⓝ; Eur.: BrI, Fr, Ib, , Ital-P,
  C-Eur., nat. in Sc, EC-Eur., USA
- **gallii** Planch. · E:Dwarf Furze; G:Franzö-
  sischer Stechginster · ♄ Z8 ⓚ ✺; sp., F
- *jussiaei* (D.A. Webb) D.A. Webb = Ulex
  parviflorus
- **minor** Roth · E:Dwarf Furze; G:Kleiner
  Stechginster · ♄ Z7 ✺; Ib, F
- **parviflorus** Pourr. · G:Kleinblütiger
  Stechginster · ♄ d Z8 ⓚ ✺; Ib, F,
  Moroc., Alger.

Ullucus Caldas -m- *Basellaceae* · 1 sp. ·
  E:Ulluco; F:Baselle, Ulluque; G:Ulluco
- **tuberosus** Lozano · E:Ulluco; G:Ulluco ·
  ⚃ ⚥ ⤳ Z9 ⓚ Ⓝ; Col., Peru, Bol.

Ulmaria Hill = Filipendula
- *filipendula* (L.) Hill = Filipendula vulgaris

Ulmus L. -f- *Ulmaceae* · c. 45 spp. · E:Elm;
  F:Orme; G:Rüster, Ulme
- **alata** Michx. · E:Winged Elm; G:Klein-
  blättrige Ulme · ♄ d Z4; USA: NCE, Va.,
  SE, Fla., Kans.
- *alba* Raf. = Ulmus americana
- **americana** L. · E:American Elm, Water
  Elm, White Elm; G:Amerikanische Ulme,
  Weiß-Ulme · ♄ d Z4 ⚥; Can.: E, Sask.;
  USA* exc. SW, Calif., NW
- **bergmanniana** C.K. Schneid. · G:Berg-
  manns Ulme · ♄ d Z6; C-China
- *foliacea* Gilib. = Ulmus minor
- *fulva* Michx. = Ulmus rubra
- **glabra** Huds. · E:Elm, Scotch Elm, Wych
  Elm; F:Orme blanc, Orme de montagne;
  G:Berg-Ulme, Weißrüster · ♄ d Z5 III-IV
  Ⓝ; Eur.*, TR, Syr., Cauc., N-Iran
- *glabra* Mill. = Ulmus minor
- × **hollandica** Mill. (*U. glabra* × *U.
  minor*) · E:Dutch Elm; F:Orme de
  Hollande; G:Bastard-Ulme · ♄ d Z5 III-IV;
  S-F, Sw, I

- **some cultivars**
- **japonica** (Rehder) Sarg. · G:Japanische
  Ulme · ♄ d Z5; Jap., NE-As
- **laciniata** (Trautv.) Mayr · G:Geschlitz-
  tblättrige Ulme · ♄ d Z5 III-IV Ⓝ; Jap.,
  Korea, N-China, Kamchat., E-Sib.
- **laevis** Pall. · E:Russian Elm; F:Orme
  diffus, Orme lisse; G:Flatter-Ulme · ♄ d
  Z5 III-IV; Eur.* exc. BrI, Ib; Cauc.
- **minor** Mill. · E:European Field Elm;
  F:Orme champêtre, Ormeau; G:Feld-
  Ulme · ♄ ♄ d Z5 III-IV ⚥ Ⓝ; Eur.*, TR,
  Cyprus, Syr., Libya
- *montana* With. = Ulmus glabra
- **parvifolia** Jacq. · E:Chinese Elm; G:Japa-
  nische Ulme, Kleinblättrige Japan-Ulme
  · ♄ d Z6 VIII-IX Ⓝ; Jap., Korea, China,
  Taiwan
- **procera** Salisb. · E:English Elm; G:Eng-
  lische Ulme, Haar-Ulme · ♄ d Z6 II-IV ⚥ ;
  Eur.: BrI, Ib, Fr, H, Ba
- **pumila** L.
- var. **arborea** Litv. · G:Turkestanische
  Ulme · ♄ d Z3 III; E-As
- var. **pumila** L. · E:Siberian Elm;
  G:Sibirische Ulme · ♄ d Z4; E-Sib., Amur,
  C-As., Mong., N-China
- **rubra** Muhl. · E:Red Elm, Slippery Elm;
  G:Rot-Ulme · ♄ d Z4 III-IV ⚥ Ⓝ; Can.: E;
  USA: NE, NCE, NC, SC, SE, Fla.
- *scabra* Mill. = Ulmus glabra
- **thomasii** Sarg. · E:Cork Elm, Rock Elm;
  G:Felsen-Ulme · ♄ d Z2 IV Ⓝ; Can.: E;
  USA: NE, NCE, NC, Ark., Tenn.
- *turkestanica* Regel = Ulmus pumila var.
  arborea
- **Cultivars:**
- **in (resistenten) Sorten**

Umbellularia (Nees) Nutt. -f- *Lauraceae* ·
  1 sp. · E:California Laurel, California Bay;
  F:Laurier; G:Berglorbeer
- **californica** (Hook. & Arn.) Nutt. ·
  E:California Laurel, California Bay, Head-
  ache Tree, Pepperwood; G:Berglorbeer ·
  ♄ e Z8 ⓚ I-VI ⚥ Ⓝ; USA: Oreg., Calif.

Umbilicus DC. -m- *Crassulaceae* · 14 spp. ·
  E:Navelwort; F:Gobelets, Nombril de
  Vénus; G:Nabelkraut, Venusnabel
- *aizoon* Fenzl = Rosularia aizoon
- *chrysanthus* Boiss. & Heldr. = Rosularia
  chrysantha
- **erectus** DC. · G:Aufrechter Venusnabel ·
  ⚃ ⵞ Z8 ⓚ; Eur.: S-I, Ba; TR, Lebanon, Syr.

- **horizontalis** (Guss.) DC. · G:Waagrechter Venusnabel · ♃ Ψ Z8 Ⓚ; Eur.: Ib, Ital-P, Ba; TR, Cyprus, Syr., W-Iran, N-Afr.
- var. **intermedius** (Boiss.) Chamb. · ♃ Ψ Z8 Ⓚ; TR, Syr., Palest., W-Iran, Egypt
- *intermedius* Boiss. = Umbilicus horizontalis var. intermedius
- *libanoticus* (Labill.) DC. = Rosularia sempervivum subsp. sempervivum
- *malacophyllus* (Pall.) DC. = Orostachys malacophylla subsp. malacophylla
- *pendulinus* (DC.) DC. = Umbilicus rupestris
- *pestalozzae* Boiss. = Rosularia sempervivum subsp. sempervivum
- **rupestris** (Salisb.) Dandy · E:Navelwort, Pennywort; G:Echter Venusnabel · ♃ Ψ Z8 Ⓚ; Eur.: Ib, Fr, Ital-P, Ba, BrI; TR, Cyprus, Syr., Madeira, NW-Afr., Libya
- *sempervivum* (M. Bieb.) DC. = Rosularia sempervivum subsp. sempervivum

Uncaria Schreb. -f- *Rubiaceae* · 39 spp.
- **gambir** (Hunter) Roxb. · E:Gambier, Pale Catechu; G:Gambir · ♄ ≹ Z10 Ⓦ Ⓝ; Malay. Arch.

Ungnadia Endl. -f- *Sapindaceae* · 1 sp.
- **speciosa** Endl. · E:Mexican Buckeye, Spanish Buckeye; G:Mexikanische Kastanie · ♄ ♄ d Z9 Ⓚ VI ☠; USA: Tex., N.Mex; N-Mex.

Uniola L. -f- *Poaceae* · 4 spp. · E:Spangle Grass, Spike Grass
- *latifolia* Michx. = Chasmanthium latifolium
- **paniculata** L. · E:North American Sea Oats · ♃ Z7 Ⓝ; USA: Va., SE, SC, Fla.; Mex., C-Am., W.Ind., S-Am.

Uragoga Baill. = Psychotria
- *ipecacuanha* (Brot.) Baill. = Psychotria ipecacuanha

Urbinia Rose = Echeveria
- *agavoides* (Lem.) Rose = Echeveria agavoides
- *purpusii* Rose = Echeveria purpusorum

Urena L. -f- *Malvaceae* · 6 spp.
- **lobata** L. · E:Caesarweed; G:Kongojute · ⊙ ♄ Z10 Ⓦ VII-VIII Ⓝ; Trop.

Urera Gaudich. -f- *Urticaceae* · 35 spp.
- **baccifera** (L.) Gaudich. ex Wedd. · E:Cow Itch · ♄ ♧ Z10 Ⓦ; C-Am., W.Ind., trop. S-Am.

Urginea Steinh. -f- *Hyacinthaceae* · c. 40 spp. · E:Sea Onion; F:Scille maritime; G:Meerzwiebel
- *anthericoides* (Poir.) Steinh. = Urginea maritima
- **maritima** (L.) Baker · E:Sea Squill; G:Meerzwiebel · ♃ Z9 Ⓚ VII-VIII ⚕ ☠ Ⓝ; Eur.: Ib, Fr, Ital-P, Ba; Canar., TR, S-Iran, N-Afr.
- *scilla* Steinh. = Urginea maritima

Urospermum Scop. -n- *Asteraceae* · 2 spp. · F:Urosperme; G:Schwefelkörbchen, Schwefelsame
- **dalechampii** (L.) Scop. ex F.W. Schmidt · G:Weichhaariger Schwefelsame · ♃ Z6 VII-IX; Eur.: Ib, F, Ital-P, Croat.
- **picroides** (L.) F.W. Schmidt · G:Bitterkrautartiger Schwefelsame · ⊙ Z6; Eur.: Ib, Fr, Ital-P, Ba; TR, Syr., Cauc., Iran, N-Afr.

Urostachys (E. Pritz.) Herter = Huperzia
- *selago* (L.) Herter ex Nessel = Huperzia selago

Ursinia Gaertn. -f- *Asteraceae* · c. 40 spp. · F:Camomille des ours; G:Bärenkamille
- **anethoides** (DC.) N.E. Br. · ⊙ Z9 Ⓚ VI-VIII; S-Afr.
- **anthemoides** (L.) Poir.
- subsp. **anthemoides** · ⊙ Z9 VII-IX; S-Afr.
- subsp. **versicolor** (DC.) Prassler · ⊙ Z9 VI-VIII; S-Afr.
- *pulchra* N.E. Br. = Ursinia anthemoides subsp. anthemoides
- **speciosa** DC. · ⊙ Z9 VII-IX; S-Afr.
- *versicolor* (DC.) N.E. Br. = Ursinia anthemoides subsp. versicolor

Urtica L. -f- *Urticaceae* · 80-100 spp. · E:Nettle; F:Ortie; G:Brennnessel
- **cannabina** L. · ♃ Ⓝ; Eur.: S-Russ.; C-As., N-As.
- **dioica** L. · G:Große Brennnessel
- subsp. **dioica** L. · E:Nettle, Stinging Nettle; G:Gewöhnliche Große Brennnessel · ♃ VII-X ⚕ Ⓝ; Eur.*, TR, Levant, Cauc., N-Iran, W-Sib., E-Sib., NW-Afr., Libya, Alaska, Can., USA: NE, NCE, NC, SC, SE,

Fla., nat. in Polyn., N-Am., S-Am.
- subsp. **galeopsifolia** (Wierzb. ex Opiz) Chrtek · G:Hohlzahn-Brennnessel · 4 ; Eur.: BrI, EC-Eur., Ba, E-Eur., ? C-Eur., ? Swed
- **kioviensis** Rogow. · G:Röhricht-Brennnessel, Sumpf-Brennnessel · 4 VII-VIII; Eur.: Russ. (Dnjeper region)
- **pilulifera** L. · E:Roman Nettle; G:Pillen-Brennnessel · ⊙ VI-X; Eur.: Ib, Fr, Ital-P, Ba, W-Russ., Crim; TR, SW-As., W-Sib., E-Sib., Amur, C-As., Mong., Him., E-As., N-Afr.
- **urens** L. · E:Dog Nettle, Small Nettle; G:Kleine Brennnessel · ⊙ VI-IX ⚥ Ⓝ; Eur.*, TR, Cauc., W-Sib., E-Sib., Amur, N-Afr., Alaska, Can., USA: NE, NCE, SC; Greenl., nat. in N-Am.

Utricularia L. -f- *Lentibulariaceae* · 214 spp. · E:Bladderwort; F:Utriculaire; G:Wasserschlauch
- **alpina** Jacq. · 4 Z10 Ⓦ V-VI; W.Ind., S-Am.
- **australis** R. Br. · G:Südlicher Wasserschlauch, Verkannter Wasserschlauch · 4 ≈ Z7 VI-VIII; Eur.*, TR, N-As., Ind., SE-As., C-Afr., S-Afr., Austr.
- **bremii** Heer ex Koell. · G:Bremis Wasserschlauch · 4 ≈ VII-IX ▽; Eur.: F, B, BrI, DK, C-Eur., EC-Eur., N-I, RO
- **caerulea** L. · 4 ⤳ ⌒ Z9 Ⓦ; Ind.
- **dichotoma** Labill. · 4 Z10 Ⓦ; Tasman.
- **endresii** Rchb. f. · 4 Z10 Ⓦ; Costa Rica
- **gibba** L.
- subsp. **exoleta** (R. Br.) P. Taylor · 4 ≈ Z4 XII-III; Eur.: Ib; Palest., N-Afr.
- subsp. **gibba** · E:Humped Bladderwort; G:Zwerg-Wasserschlauch · ⊙ 4 ≈ Z4; Eur.: Ib; N-Afr., Palest., S-As., Austr.
- *ianthina* Hook. f. = Utricularia reniformis
- **intermedia** Hayne · G:Mittlerer Wasserschlauch · 4 ≈ Z2 VII-VIII; Eur.* exc. Ib; W-Sib., E-Sib., Kamchat., Manch., Korea, Jap. N-Am., Greenl.
- *janthina* Hook. f. = Utricularia reniformis
- **lateriflora** R. Br. · 4 Z10 Ⓦ; Austr., Tasman.
- **longifolia** Gardner · 4 Z10 Ⓦ VI-VIII; Braz.
- **minor** L. · E:Lesser Bladderwort; F:Petite utriculaire; G:Kleiner Wasserschlauch · 4 ≈ Z2 VI-IX; Eur.*, Cauc., W-Sib., E-Sib., Amur, Sakhal., Kamchat., C-As., W-Him., Manch., Jap., Alaska, Can., Greenl., USA:

NE, NCE, NC, Rocky Mts., NW, Calif.
- *montana* Jacq. = Utricularia alpina
- *neglecta* Lehm. = Utricularia australis
- **nelumbifolia** Gardner · 4 ≈ Z10 Ⓦ; Braz.
- **ochroleuca** R.W. Hartm. · G:Blassgelber Wasserschlauch · 4 ≈ VII-VIII ▽; Eur.: BrI, Sc, F, G, A, EC-Eur., W-Russ.; Afgh, Can.: E.; USA: NW, Colo., Ill.; Greenl.
- *peltata* Spruce ex Oliv. = Utricularia pubescens
- **prehensilis** E. Mey. · ⊙ ⌒ Z10 Ⓦ VI-VIII; trop. Afr.
- **pubescens** Sm. · 4 Z10 Ⓦ; C-Am., S-Am., trop. Afr., Ind.
- **reniformis** A. St.-Hil. · 4 Z10 Ⓦ VII-IX; Braz.
- **stygia** G. Thor · G:Dunkelgelber Wasserschlauch · 4 ≈ ; Eur.: G, A, Sw, F +
- **tricolor** A. St.-Hil. · 4 Z10 Ⓦ; S-Am.
- *uliginoides* Wight = Utricularia caerulea
- **volubilis** R. Br. · 4 ≈ Z10 Ⓦ; W-Austr.
- **vulgaris** L. · E:Common Bladderwort, Greater Bladderwort; F:Utriculaire commune; G:Gewöhnlicher Wasserschlauch · 4 ≈ Z5 VI-VIII ⚥ ; Eur.*, TR, Syr.

Uvularia L. -f- *Convallariaceae* · 5 spp. · E:Bellwort, Merry-Bells, Wild Oats; F:Uvulaire; G:Goldglocke, Goldsiegel, Trauerglocke
- **grandiflora** Sm. · E:Bellwort; F:Uvulaire à grandes fleurs; G:Hänge-Goldglocke · 4 Z3 IV-VI; Can.: E; USA: NE, NCE, NC, SE
- **perfoliata** L. · E:Straw Bell; G:Kleine Goldglocke · 4 Z4 V; Can.: E; USA: NE, NCE, NC, SE, Fla.
- **sessilifolia** L. · E:Sessile Bellwort; G:Aufrechte Goldglocke · 4 Z4 V-VI; Can.: E; USA: NE, NCE, NC, SE

Vaccaria Wolf -f- *Caryophyllaceae* · 1 sp. · E:Cowherb; F:Herbe-aux-vaches, Vaccaire; G:Kuhkraut
- **hispanica** (Mill.) Rauschert · E:Cow Cockle, Cowherb; G:Kuhkraut · ⊙ ✂ VI-VIII; Eur.* exc. Sc; TR, Levant, Cauc., Iran, W-Sib., Amur, C-As., Mong., Him., China, N-Afr., nat. in N-Am., Austr.
- *pyramidata* Medik. = Vaccaria hispanica

Vaccinium L. -n- *Ericaceae* · c. 450 spp. · E:Bilberry, Blueberry, Cranberry;

F:Airelle, Canneberge, Myrtillier;
G:Blaubeere, Heidelbeere, Moorbeere,
Moosbeere, Preiselbeere, Rauschbeere
- **angustifolium** Aiton · E:Blueberry,
Lowbush Blueberry · ♄ d ⚭ Z2 IV-V Ⓝ;
Can.: E, Sask.; USA: NE, NCE
- **arctostaphylos** L. · ♄ d Z6 V-VI; Cauc, ?
TR
- **ashei** J.M. Reade · ♄ e Z8 Ⓚ Ⓝ; USA: SE
- **atrococcum** (A. Gray) A. Heller · ♄ d ⚭
Z4 V Ⓝ; Can.: Ont.; USA: NE, NCE, SE,
Fla.
- **australe** Small · E:Southern Blueberry ·
♄ d Z6 Ⓝ; USA: NE, SE, Fla.
- **bracteatum** Thunb. · ♄ ♄ e ⚭ D Z7
VII-VIII; China, S-Korea, Jap., Ryukyu-Is.,
- **cespitosum** Michx. · E:Dwarf Bilberry;
G:Zwerg-Heidelbeere · ♄ d ⚭ Z2 V-VII;
Alaska, Can., USA: NE, NCE, Rocky Mts.,
NW, Calif.
- **corymbosum** L. · E:Blueberry, High
Bush Blueberry; F:Myrtille en corymbe;
G:Amerikanische Heidelbeere · ♄ d ⌇
Z5 V Ⓝ; Can.: E; USA: NE, NCE, SE, Fla.
- **some cultivars**
- **erythrinum** Hook. · ♄ Z10; Java
- *gaultherioides* Bigelow = Vaccinium
uliginosum subsp. pubescens
- **hirsutum** Buckley · E:Hairy Huckleberry;
G:Behaarte Heidelbeere · ♄ d ⚭ Z6 V-VI;
USA: SE
- **× intermedium** Ruthe (*V. myrtillus* × *V.
vitis-idaea var. vitis-idaea*) · G:Bastard-
Heidelbeere · ♄ e Z6; Eur.: G, PL, BrI
- **lucidum** (Blume) Miq. · ♄ ♄ e Z9 Ⓚ
V-VI; Sumat., Java, Sulawesi
- **macrocarpon** Aiton · E:Cranberry;
F:Airelle à gros fruits; G:Großfrüchtige
Moosbeere · ♄ e ⌇ ⚭ Z2 VI-VIII Ⓝ;
Can.: E; USA; NE, NCE, SE
- **microcarpum** (Turcz. ex Rupr.)
Schmalh. · E:Small Cranberry; G:Klein-
früchtige Moosbeere · ♄ e Z1; Eur.* exc.
Fr, Ib +
- **myrtilloides** Michx. · E:Canada Blue-
berry; G:Kanadische Heidelbeere · ♄ d ⚭
Z2 VII-VIII; Can., USA: NE, NCE, Mont.
- **myrtillus** L. · E:Bilberry, Blueberry,
Whinberry, Whortleberry; G:Blaubeere,
Heidelbeere · ♄ ♄ d ⚭ Z1 IV-VI ⚥ Ⓝ;
Eur.*, TR, Cauc., W-Sib., E-Sib., Mong.,
nat. in N-Am.
- **nummularium** Hook. f. & Thomson ex
C.B. Clarke · ♄ e Z7 IV-V; Bhutan, Sikkim
- **oxycoccos** L. · E:Wild Cranberry;

G:Gewöhnliche Moosbeere · ♄ e ⌇ ⌇
⚭ Z1 VI-VII; Eur.* exc. Ib.; N-As., Alaska,
Can., USA: NE, NCE, NW, Rocky Mts.;
Greenl.
- **padifolium** Sm. · ♄ e ⚭ Z9 Ⓚ VI;
Madeira
- *rollisonii* Hook. = Vaccinium lucidum
- **stamineum** L. · E:Deerberry, Squaw
Huckleberry · ♄ e Z5 IV-VI; Can.: Ont.;
USA: NE, NCE, Kans., SE, Fla.
- **uliginosum** L. · G:Moorbeere, Rauschbeere, Trunkelbeere
- subsp. **pubescens** (Wormsk.) S.B.
Young · G:Gaultheriaähnliche Rauschbeere · ♄ d Z2 V-VII ⚘
- subsp. **uliginosum** · E:Bog Bilberry, Bog
Whortleberry; G:Gewöhnliche Rausch-
beere · ♄ d ⚭ Z1 V-VI ⚥ ⚘; Eur.*, TR,
Cauc., W-Sib., E-Sib., Amur, Sakhal.,
Kamchat., Mong., Manch., Korea, Jap.,
Alaska, Can., USA: NE, Rocky Mts., NW,
Calif.; Greenl.
- **varingiifolium** (Blume) Miq. · ♄ e Z10 Ⓚ
X; Sumat., Java, Bali
- **vitis-idaea** L.
- **some cultivars**
- var. **vitis-idaea** · E:Cowberry, Foxberry;
F:Airelle rouge; G:Kronsbeere, Preisel-
beere · ♄ ♄ e ⚭ Z1 V-VI ⚥ Ⓝ; Eur.* exc.
Ib; Cauc., E-TR, W-Sib., E-Sib., Amur,
Sakhal., Kamchat., Mong., Manch.,
Korea, Jap., Alaska, Can., USA: NE, NCE,
NW, Calif.; Greenl.

Valantia L. -f- *Rubiaceae* · 7 spp. · G:Vail-
lantie; F:Vaillantie
- **hispida** L. · ⊙; Eur.: Ib, Ital-P, Ba, F; TR,
Canar., Iraq, Iran

Valeriana L. -f- *Valerianaceae* · 150-
200 spp. · E:Valerian; F:Valériane;
G:Baldrian
- **alliariifolia** Vahl · ♃ VI-VII; E-GR, TR,
Cauc.
- **arizonica** A. Gray · E:Arizona Valerian ·
♃ △ Ⓚ ∧ VII-VIII; USA: Colo., Utah,
Ariz.; N-Mex.
- **celtica** L. · E:Celtic Valerian; G:Keltischer
Baldrian · ♃ △ D VII-VIII ⚥ Ⓝ; Eur.: F,
Sw, I, A; Alp.
- **dioica** L. · E:Marsh Valerian; G:Kleiner
Baldrian · ♃ ⌇ V-VI; Eur.*, W-TR, Him.,
Alaska, Can.; USA: NW
- **elongata** Jacq. · G:Ostalpen-Baldrian · ♃
VI-VIII; Eur.: I, A, Slove.; E-Alp.

- **globulariifolia** Ramond ex DC. · ♃ △ V-VI; Eur.: sp., F; Cordillera Cantábrica, Pyr.
- **montana** L. · E:Mountain Valerian; G:Berg-Baldrian · ♃ △ IV-VI; Eur.* exc. BrI, Sc
- **officinalis** L. · E:Common Valerian; F:Valériane officinale; G:Echter Arznei-Baldrian · ♃ V-IX ⚕ ; Eur.*, TR, Cauc., W-Sib., E-Sib., Amur, Sakhal., C-As., Mong, China
- **phu** L. · ♃ VII-VIII; ? TR
- **pratensis** Dierb. · G:Wiesen-Arznei-Baldrian · ♃ V-VI; Eur.: D (Oberrhein)
- **procurrens** Wallr. · G:Ausläufer-Baldrian, Kriechender Arznei-Baldrian · ♃ VI-VIII; W-Eur., WC-Eur.
- **pyrenaica** L. · E:Pyrenean Valerian; G:Pyrenäen-Baldrian · ♃ ⏜ VI-VIII; Eur.: sp., E; Cordillera Cantábrica, Pyr.
- **saliunca** All. · E:Entire-leaved Valerian; G:Weidenblättriger Baldrian · ♃ VII-VIII; Eur.: F, I, Sw, A; Alp., Apenn.
- **sambucifolia** J.C. Mikan ex Pohl · G:Holunderblättriger Arznei-Baldrian · ♃ V-VI; N-Eur., C-Eur.
- **saxatilis** L. · E:Rock Valerian; G:Felsen-Baldrian · ♃ △ VI-VIII; Eur.: I, C-Eur., Ba; Alp., Apenn., Balkan
- **simplicifolia** (Rchb.) Kabath · G:Ganzblättriger Baldrian · ♃; Eur.: A, Slova., CZ, PL, Russ, RO, nat. in C-Eur.
- × **suendermannii** Melch. (*V. montana* × *V. supina*) · ♃ △ D V-VI; cult.
- **supina** Ard. · E:Dwarf Valerian; F:Valériane naine; G:Zwerg-Baldrian · ♃ △ VII-VIII; Eur.: I, C-Eur., Slove.; Alp.
- **tripteris** L. · E:Three-leaved Valerian; G:Gewöhnlicher Dreiblättriger Baldrian · ♃ △ IV-VI; Eur.* exc. BrI, Sc
- **versifolia** Brügger · G:Verschiedenblättriger Arznei-Baldrian · ♃ V-VI; Eur.: Alp.
- **wallrothii** Kreyer · G:Hügel-Baldrian, Schmalblättriger Arznei-Baldrian · ♃ V-VI; C-Eur.

Valerianella Mill. -f- *Valerianaceae* · c. 50 spp. · E:Cornsalad, Lamb's Lettuce; F:Mâche, Salade de blé, Valérianelle; G:Ackersalat, Feldsalat, Rapünzchen, Rapunzel
- **carinata** Loisel. · G:Gekielter Feldsalat · ⊙ IV-V; Eur.* exc. Sc; TR, Syr., Iraq, Cauc., Iran, N-Afr.
- **coronata** (L.) DC. · G:Krönchen-Feldsalat · ⊙ V-VI; Eur.: Ib, Fr, Ital-P, EC-Eur., Ba, E-Eur.; TR, SW-As., N-Afr.
- **dentata** (L.) Pollich · G:Gezähnter Feldsalat · ⊙ VI-VIII; Eur.*, TR, Iraq, Cauc., Iran, C-As., N-Afr., Macaron.
- **eriocarpa** Desv. · E:Italian Cornsalad; G:Wollfrüchtiger Feldsalat · ⊙ IV-V; Eur.: Ib, Fr, BrI, Ital-P, Ba, Crim, ? RO; Tr, N-Afr., Canar.
- **locusta** (L.) Laterr. · E:Cornsalad · ⊙ IV-V Ⓝ; Eur.*, TR, Cauc., Macaron., N-Afr.
- **rimosa** Bastard · G:Gefurchter Feldsalat · ⊙ IV-V; Eur.*, TR, Cauc.

Vallisneria L. -f- *Hydrocharitaceae* · 9 spp. · E:Eel Grass, Vallis; F:Vallisnérie; G:Sumpfschraube, Vallisnerie, Wasserschraube
- **americana** Michx. · E:American Eel Grass; G:Amerikanische Wasserschraube · ♃ ≈ Z9 ⌂; SE-As., Phil., N.Guinea, E-Austr., Tasman.
- **spiralis** L. · E:Eel Grass, Tape Grass; G:Gewöhnliche Wasserschraube · ♃ ≈ Z8 ⌂ VI-IX; Eur.: Ib, Fr, Ital-P, Ba, E-Eur., Sw; Cauc., C-As., W-As., Alger., trop. Afr., S-Am., Austr.

Vallota Salisb. ex Herb. = Cyrtanthus
- *purpurea* (Aiton) Herb. = Cyrtanthus elatus
- *speciosa* (L. f.) T. Durand & Schinz = Cyrtanthus elatus

× **Vancampe** hort. -f- *Orchidaceae* (*Acampe* × *Vanda*)

Vancouveria C. Morren & Decne. -f- *Berberidaceae* · 3 spp. · E:Insideout Flower; F:Vancouvéria; G:Rüsselsternchen, Vancouverie
- **chrysantha** Greene · E:Golden Insideout Flower · ♃ Z7 ⌂ ∧ V; USA: Oreg.
- **hexandra** (Hook.) C. Morren & Decne. · E:American Barrenwort, White Inside Out Flower; G:Rüsselsternchen · ♃ Z7 ∧ VI; USA: NW, Calif.
- **planipetala** Calloni · E:Redwood Ivy · ♃ Z7 ⌂ ∧ V; USA: Oreg., Calif.

Vanda Jones ex R. Br. -f- *Orchidaceae* · 50 spp.
- **alpina** Lindl. · ♃ Z9 ⌂ V-VI ▽ *; Him., N-Ind.: Khasia Hills

– *batemanii* Lindl. = Vandopsis lissochiloides
– **bensonii** Bateman · ♃ Z9 ⊛ VIII-X ▽ ✳;
Burma, Thail.
– *cathcartii* Lindl. = Esmeralda cathcartii
– **coerulea** Griff. ex Lindl. · ♃ Z9 ⊛ IX-XI
▽ ✳; Ind.: Assam; Burma, Thail.
– **coerulescens** Griff. · ♃ Z9 ⊛ III-V ▽ ✳;
Burma, Thail.
– **concolor** Blume · ♃ Z9 ⊛ I-IV ▽ ✳;
Sumat., Java
– **cristata** (Wall.) Lindl. · ♃ Z9 ⊛ XII-II ▽
✳; Him: NW-Ind.
– **denisoniana** Benson & Rchb. f. · ♃ Z9 ⊛
IV-V ▽ ✳; Burma (Arakan)
– *densiflora* Lindl. = Rhynchostylis gigantea
– *gigantea* Lindl. = Vandopsis gigantea
– *hookeriana* Rchb. f. = Papilionanthe
hookeriana
– **insignis** Blume · ♃ Z9 ⊛ X ▽ ✳;
Molucca, Timor
– **lamellata** Lindl. · ♃ Z9 ⊛ XI-XII ▽ ✳;
Phil., N-Kalimantan
– *lowii* Lindl. = Dimorphorchis lowii
– *multiflora* Lindl. = Acampe rigida
– **pumila** Hook. f. · ♃ Z9 ⊛ VI-VII ▽ ✳;
Bhutan, Sikkim, Thail.
– *sanderiana* (Rchb. f.) Rchb. f. = Euanthe
sanderiana
– *storiei* Storie ex Rchb. f. = Renanthera
storiei
– *teres* (Roxb.) Lindl. = Papilionanthe teres
– **tesselata** (Roxb.) Hook. ex G. Don · ♃ Z9
⊛ XI ▽ ✳; Ind., Sri Lanka, Burma
– **tricolor** Lindl. · ♃ Z9 ⊛ XI-V ▽ ✳; Laos,
Java
– **Cultivars:**
– **many cultivars**

× **Vandachnis** hort. -f- *Orchidaceae*
(*Arachnis* × *Vandopsis*)

× **Vandaenopsis** hort. -f- *Orchidaceae*
(*Phalaenopsis* × *Vanda*)

× **Vandofinetia** hort. -f- *Orchidaceae*
(*Neofinetia* × *Vanda*)

× **Vandopsides** hort. -f- *Orchidaceae*
(*Aerides* × *Vandopsis*)

Vandopsis Pfitzer -f- *Orchidaceae* · 4 spp.
– **gigantea** (Lindl.) Pfitzer · ♃ Z10 ⊛ II-IV
▽ ✳; Burma, Thail.
– **lissochiloides** (Gaudich.) Pfitzer · ♃ Z10

⊛ VII-X ▽ ✳; Phil., Thail.
– *lowii* (Lindl.) Schltr. = Dimorphorchis
lowii

× **Vandoritis** hort. -f- *Orchidaceae* (*Doritis*
× *Vanda*)

Vangueria Comm. ex Juss. -f- *Rubiaceae* ·
18 spp.
– **madagascariensis** J.F. Gmel. · E:Spanish
Tamarind · ♄ ♄ Z9 ⊛ Ⓝ; Afr., Madag.,
Mascarene Is.

Vanheerdea L. Bolus ex H.E.K. Hartmann
-f- *Aizoaceae* · 2 spp.
– *angusta* (L. Bolus) L. Bolus = Vanheerdea
roodiae
– **roodiae** (N.E. Br.) L. Bolus ex H.E.K.
Hartmann · ♃ ⸕ Z9 ⓚ; S-Afr. (N-Cape)

Vanilla Plum. ex Mill. -f- *Orchidaceae* ·
110 spp. · E:Vanilla; F:Vanillier; G:Vanille
– **aphylla** Blume · ♃ ⸙ Z10 ⊛ VII-VIII ▽
✳; Burma, Malay. Pen., Java
– **planifolia** Jacks. ex Andrews · E:Bourbon
Vanilla; G:Echte Vanille · ♃ ⸙ Z10 ⊛
VII-VIII ⸙ Ⓝ ▽ ✳; C-Am., W.Ind., S-Am.
– **pompona** Schiede · E:West Indian
Vanilla · ♃ ⸙ Z10 ⊛ VI-VII Ⓝ ▽ ✳;
SE-Mex., C-Am., trop. S-Am.
– *tahitiensis* J.W. Moore = Vanilla planifolia

Vanzijlia L. Bolus -f- *Aizoaceae* · 1 sp.
– **annulata** (A. Berger) L. Bolus · ♄ ⸕ Z9
ⓚ; Cape

× **Vascostylis** hort. -f- *Orchidaceae*
(*Ascocentrum* × *Rhynchostylis* × *Vanda*)

Vateria L. -f- *Dipterocarpaceae* · 2 spp.
– **copallifera** (Retz.) Alston · ♄ Z10 ⊛ Ⓝ;
Sri Lanka
– **indica** L. · ♄ e Z10 ⊛ Ⓝ; Ind.

Vatricania Backeb. = Espostoa
– *guentheri* (Kupper) Backeb. = Espostoa
guentheri

Vauanthes Haw. = Crassula
– *dichotoma* (L.) Kuntze = Crassula
dichotoma

Veitchia H. Wendl. -f- *Arecaceae* · 8 spp. ·
E:Christmas Palm; F:Palmier de manille;
G:Manilapalme

– *merrillii* (Becc.) H.E. Moore = Adonidia merrillii

Vella DC. -f- *Brassicaceae* · 4 spp.
– **pseudocytisus** L. · ♄ e Z8 Ⓚ V-VI; Eur.: sp.; Moroc., Alger.
– **spinosa** Boiss. · ♄ s Z7 VI; S-Sp.

Vellozia Vand. -f- *Velloziaceae* · 144 spp.
– **aloifolia** Mart. · ♄ ⋊ Z10 Ⓦ; Braz.
– *elegans* (Balf.) Talbot ex Hook. f. = Talbotia elegans

Veltheimia Gled. -f- *Hyacinthaceae* · 2 spp. · E:Veltheimia; F:Veltheimia; G:Veltheimie
– **bracteata** Baker · ♃ Z9 Ⓚ I-III; S-Afr.
– **capensis** (L.) DC. · ♃ Z9 Ⓚ; SW-Cape
– *deasii* Coutts = Veltheimia capensis
– *edulis* (Vahl) Vahl = Veltheimia capensis
– *glauca* (Aiton) Jacq. = Veltheimia capensis
– *roodeae* E. Phillips = Veltheimia capensis
– *viridifolia* Jacq. = Veltheimia bracteata

Venidium Less. = Arctotis
– *decurrens* Less. = Arctotheca calendula
– *fastuosum* (Jacq.) Stapf = Arctotis fastuosa

Ventenata Koeler -f- *Poaceae* · 5 spp. · F:Fausse-avoine; G:Grannenhafer, Schmielenhafer
– **dubia** (Leers) Coss. · E:Soft Bearded Oat Grass; G:Zweifelhafter Schmielenhafer · ⊙ Z8 VI; Eur.* exc. BrI, Sc; TR, Cauc., Alger.

Veratrum L. -n- *Melanthiaceae* · 27 spp. · E:Bunchflower, False Helleborine; F:Vérâtre; G:Germer
– **album** L. · E:White Veratrum; G:Weißer Germer · ♃ Z5 VI-VIII ⚕ ☠; Eur.* exc. BrI; TR, Cauc., W-Sib., E-Sib., Amur, C-As., Jap.
– **californicum** Durand · E:California Veratrum; G:Kalifornischer Germer · ♃ Z5 VII-VIII ☠; USA: NW, Calif., Rocky Mts., SW; Mex.: Baja Calif.
– **nigrum** L. · E:Black Veratrum; F:Vérâtre noir; G:Schwarzer Germer · ♃ D Z6 VII-VIII ☠; Eur.: Fr, Ital-P, C-Eur., EC-Eur., Ba, E-Eur.; W-Sib., E-Sib., Amur, C-As.
– **viride** Aiton · E:Green Veratrum; G:Grüner Germer · ♃ Z3 VII ⚕ ☠ Ⓝ; Can.: E; USA; NE, NCE, SE

Verbascum L. -n- *Scrophulariaceae* · c. 360 spp. · E:Mullein; F:Molène; G:Königskerze, Wollkraut
– **acaule** (Bory & Chaub.) Kuntze · ♃ Ⓐ ∧ VI-VII; S-GR
– **alpinum** Turra · G:Wollige Königskerze · ♃ V-VII; Eur.: I, A, Ba, E-Eur.
– **arcturus** L. · E:Cretan Mullein; G:Kretische Königskerze · ⊙ ♃ Ⓚ ▭ V-VII; Crete
– **austriacum** Schott ex Roem. & Schult. · G:Österreichische Königskerze · ♃; EC-Eur., Ba, RO
– **blattaria** L. · E:Moth Mullein, White Moth Mullein ; G:Schaben-Königskerze · ⊙ VI-VIII; Eur.: Ib, Fr, Ital-P, Ba, C-Eur., EC-Eur.; TR, Cauc., Iran, Afgh., C-As., W-Sib., NW-Afr., nat. in N-Am.
– **bombyciferum** Boiss. · F:Molène soyeuse; G:Seidenhaar-Königskerze · ⊙ Z6 VII-VIII; W-TR
– **bugulifolium** Lam. · ♃ Ⓐ ∧ V-VII; N-GR
– **chaixii** Vill. · E:Nettle-leaved Mullein; F:Molène de Chaix; G:Chaix-Königskerze · ♃ Z5 VII-VIII; Eur.* exc. BrI, Sc
– **some cultivars**
– **creticum** (L. f.) Cav. · ⊙ Ⓚ ▭ VI-VII; Eur.: Ib, Ital-P, ? F; Alger., Tun.
– **densiflorum** Bertol. · E:Large-flowered Mullein; G:Großblütige Königskerze · ⊙ Z5 VII-VIII ⚕; Eur.* exc. BrI; Moroc.
– **dumulosum** P.H. Davis & Hub.-Mor. · ♄ e △ Z8 Ⓐ V-VI; TR
– **lagurus** Fisch. & C.A. Mey. · ⊙ VII-VIII; Eur.: BG; NW-TR
– *lagurus* hort. = Verbascum bombyciferum
– **leianthum** Benth. · ⊙ Z8 Ⓚ VII-VIII; TR
– **longifolium** Ten.
– var. **longifolium** · F:Molène de Pannonie · ⊙ ♃ Z7 VI-VIII; Eur.: I, Ba
– var. **pannosum** (Vis. & Pančić) Murb. Z7
– **lychnitis** L. · E:White Mullein; G:Mehlige Königskerze · ⊙ Z6 VI-VIII; Eur.*, W-Sib., Moroc.
– **nigrum** L. · E:Dark Mullein; F:Bouillon noir, Molène noire; G:Schwarze Königskerze · ⊙ ♃ Z5 VI-IX; Eur.*, ? Cauc., W-Sib., E-Sib.
– **olympicum** Boiss. · E:Olympic Mullein; F:Molène d'Olympe; G:Kandelaber-Königskerze · ⊙ Z6 VI-VIII; NW-TR (Ulu Dagh)
– *pannosum* Vis. & Pančić = Verbascum

longifolium var. pannosum
- **pestalozzae** Boiss. · ♄ e Z8 ⓚ V-VI;
  W-TR
- **phlomoides** L. · E:Orange Mullein;
  G:Windblumen-Königskerze · ⊙ VII-IX
  ⚥ ; Eur.* exc. BrI, Sc; TR, Cauc., nat. in
  BrI
- **phoeniceum** L. · E:Purple Mullein;
  F:Molène rouge-pourpre ; G:Purpur-
  Königskerze · ⊙ ⁴ Z6 V-VI; Eur.: Ital-P,
  C-Eur., EC-Eur., Ba, E-Eur.; TR, Cauc.,
  Iran, W-Sib., C-As., nat. in NL
- **pulverulentum** Vill. · E:Hoary Mullein;
  G:Flockige Königskerze · ⊙ Z6 VII-VIII;
  Eur.: Ib, Fr, BrI, Ital-P, C-Eur., H, Ba, RO
- **sinuatum** L. · G:Gebuchtete Königsk-
  erze · ⊙ Z8 ⓚ; Eur.: Ib, Fr, Ital-P, Ba,
  W-Russ., Crim; TR, Cauc., Iran, C-As.,
  N-Afr., Canar., Madeira
- **speciosum** Schrad. · G:Pracht-Königsk-
  erze · ⊙ Z6 VI-VII; Eur.: A, EC-Eur., Ba,
  E-Eur.; Cauc.
- **spinosum** L. · ♄ Z8 ⓚ; Crete
- *thapsiforme* Schrad. = Verbascum
  densiflorum
- **thapsus** L. · G:Kleinblütige Königskerze
- subsp. **crassifolium** (Lam.) Murb. ·
  G:Dickblättrige Königskerze · ⊙ Z3 VI-IX;
  Eur.: mts.
- subsp. **thapsus** · E:Aaron's Rod, White
  Mullein; G:Gewöhnliche Kleinblüte
  Königskerze · ⊙ Z3 VII-IX ⚥ ; Eur.*,
  TR, Cauc., N-Iran, W-Sib., C-As., Him.,
  W-China, nat. in Jap., Hawaii, N-Am.
- **wiedemannianum** Fisch. & C.A. Mey. ·
  ⊙ Z7 VI-VIII; TR
- **Cultivars:**
- **some cultivars**

Verbena L. -f- *Verbenaceae* · 200-250 spp. ·
E:Vervain; F:Verveine; G:Eisenkraut,
Verbene
- **bipinnatifida** Nutt. · E:Dakota Vervain ·
  ⁴ Z3; USA: NC, NCE, SE, SW, Colo.
- **bonariensis** L. · E:Purple-top Vervain ·
  ⊙ ⁴ Z8 VII-X; S-Braz., Arg., nat. in Calif.,
  S-USA, W.Ind., Austr.
- **canadensis** (L.) Britton · E:Rose Verbena; G:Rosen-Verbene · ⊙ ⁴ Z4 VII-X;
  USA: NE, NCE, Kans., Colo., SC, SE, Fla.;
  Mex.
- **elegans** Kunth
- var. **asperata** L.M. Perry · E:Mountain
  Vervain · ⊙ ⁴ VII-X; Tex., Mex.
- var. **elegans** · ⊙ ⁴ ; USA: Tex.; Mex.

- **hastata** L. · E:American Vervain, Wild
  Hyssop; G:Lanzen-Verbene · ⁴ Z3 VII-IX;
  Can., USA*
- **incisa** Hook. · ⊙ ⁴ Z10 VII-X; S-Braz.,
  Parag., N-Arg.
- **officinalis** L. · E:Simpler's Joy, Turkey
  Grass, Verbena; G:Echtes Eisenkraut ·
  ⁴ Z4 VII-VIII ⚥ ; Eur.*, TR, Cauc., Iran,
  C-As., Him., N-Afr., Sudan, Eth., nat. in
  cosmop. exc. Sib.
- *patagonica* auct. = Verbena bonariensis
- **peruviana** (L.) Britton · ⁴ ♄ s Z9 ⓚ
  VII-IX; Peru, Bol., Braz., Arg.
- **phlogiflora** Cham. · ⊙ ⁴ ♄ Z10 VII-IX;
  Braz., Parag., Urug., Arg.
- **rigida** Spreng. · E:Tuberous Vervain,
  Veined Verbena; F:Verveine rugueuse;
  G:Steife Verbene · ⊙ ⁴ Z8 VI-X; S-Braz.,
  Arg., nat. in USA: SE
- **tenera** Spreng. · E:Blue Verbena; G:Zarte
  Verbene · ⊙ ⁴ ♄ ♄ e ⇜ Z9 VI-IX;
  S-Braz., Arg.
- **tenuisecta** Briq. · E:Moss Verbena;
  G:Moos-Verbene · ⁴ ⚥ Z9 ⓚ VII-IX; s
  S-Am.
- **teucrioides** Gillies & Hook. · ⊙ ⁴ ♄ Z9
  VII-IX; Peru, Chile, Braz., Parag., Urug.,
  Arg.
- **urticifolia** L. · E:White Vervain · ⁴ Z5;
  E-Can., USA: NE, NEC, NC, SC, SE, Fla.
- *venosa* Gillies & Hook. = Verbena rigida
- **Cultivars:**
- **many cultivars**

Verbesina L. -f- *Asteraceae* · c. 250 spp. ·
E:Crown Beard; F:Verbésine; G:Kronbart,
Verbesine
- **alternifolia** (L.) Britton ex Kearney ·
  E:Wingstem, Yellow Ironweed; G:Gelber
  Kronbart · ⁴ Z5 VIII-IX; Ont., USA: NE,
  NCE, Okla., SE, Fla.
- **encelioides** (Cav.) Benth. & Hook. f.
  ex A. Gray · E:Golden Crownbeard;
  G:Goldener Kronbart · ⊙ Z10 X; USA:
  NC, SC, Rocky Mts, SW; Mex.
- **helianthoides** Michx. · E:Gravelweed · ⁴
  Z5 VI-VII; USA: NCE, NC, SE, SC
- **purpusii** Brandegee · ⁴ Z9 ⓚ VIII-IX;
  Mex.

Vernicia Lour. -f- *Euphorbiaceae* · 3 spp. ·
E:Tungoil Tree; G:Tungölbaum
- **cordata** (Thunb.) Airy Shaw · E:Japanese
  Tungoil Tree; G:Japanischer Tungölbaum · ♄ e Z9 ⓚ ✿ Ⓝ; China, Jap.

- **fordii** (Hemsl.) Airy Shaw · E:Tungoil
  Tree; G:Gewöhnlicher Tungölbaum · ♄ e
  Z10 ⓜ ☈ ⓝ; C-As., W-China, C-China
- **montana** Lour. · E:Chinese Tungoil Tree;
  G:Chinesischer Tungölbaum · ♄ e Z9 ⓚ
  ☈ ⓝ; SE-China, N-Burma

Vernonia Schreb. -f- *Asteraceae* ·
-1000 spp. · E:Ironweed; F:Vernonie;
G:Scheinaster, Vernonie
- **amygdalina** Delile · ♄ ⓜ ⓝ; trop. Afr.
- **anthelmintica** (L.) Willd. · E:Kinka Oil;
  G:Wurm-Scheinaster · ⌃ ⓚ ⓝ; Ind.
- **arkansana** DC. · E:Arkansas Ironweed;
  G:Arkansas-Scheinaster · ⌃ ⌁ Z5 VIII-X;
  USA: Mo., Kans., Okla., Ark.
- *crinita* Raf. = Vernonia arkansana
- **gigantea** (Walter) Trel. · E:Giant
  Ironweed; G:Hohe Scheinaster · ⌃ ⌁
  Z4 VIII-IX; USA: NE, NCE, SE
- **noveboracensis** (L.) Michx. ·
  E:Ironweed, New York Ironweed;
  G:New-York-Scheinaster · ⌃ Z5 VIII-IX;
  USA: NE, NCE, SE

Veronica L. -f- *Scrophulariaceae* · c.
180 spp. · E:Bird's Eye, Speedwell;
F:Véronique; G:Ehrenpreis
- **acinifolia** L. · G:Drüsiger Ehrenpreis,
  Kölme-Ehrenpreis, Steinquendel-Ehren-
  preis · ⊙ IV-VI; Eur.: Ib, Fr, Ital-P, C-Eur.,
  EC-Eur., Ba, RO, Crim; Cauc., Iran, Him..
- **agrestis** L. · E:Field Speedwell ; G:Acker-
  Ehrenpreis · ⊙ IV-X; Eur.*, TR, Palest.,
  NW-Afr., Macaron., nat. in USA
- **allionii** Vill. · ⌃ ⌁ △ Z4 VII-VIII; Eur.:
  F, I; SW-Alp.
- **alpina** L. · E:Alpine Speedwell;
  G:Gewöhnlicher Alpen-Ehrenpreis · ⌃
  VII-VIII; Eur.*; N, mts.; W-Sib., E-Sib.,
  Manch., Korea
- *amethystina* Willd. = Pseudolysimachion
  spurium
- **anagallis-aquatica** L. · E:Water-
  Speedwell; F:Mouron d'eau, Véronique
  mouron; G:Blauer Wasser-Ehrenpreis,
  Gauchheil-Ehrenpreis, Ufer-Ehrenpreis ·
  ⌃ ⌁ V-X; Eur.*, TR, Cauc., Iran, W-Sib.,
  E-Sib., C-As., Him., Mong., China, Jap.,
  N-Afr., Eth., Macaron., N-Am., S-Am., NZ
- **anagalloides** Guss. · G:Schlamm-
  Ehrenpreis · ⊙ ⌁ VI-X; Eur.* exc. BrI,
  Sc; TR, Cauc., Iran, Afgh., W-Sib., Amur,
  C-As., Him., N-Afr.
- **aphylla** L. · G:Blattloser Ehrenpreis,

Nacktstieliger Ehrenpreis · ⌃ Z5 VI-VIII;
Eur.* exc. BrI, Sc; mts.
- **argute-serrata** Regel & Schmalh. ·
  G:Spitzzähniger Ehrenpreis · ⊙ IV-VI;
  Cauc., Kashmir, Him., China: Sinkiang
- **armena** Boiss. & A. Huet · G:Arme-
  nischer Ehrenpreis · ⌃ ⌂ △ Z4 VI-VII;
  TR, Cauc.
- **arvensis** L. · E:Wall Speedwell; G:Feld-
  Ehrenpreis · ⊙ Z5 IX-X; Eur.*, TR, Cauc.,
  C-As., Him., NW-Afr., nat. in N-Am.,
  S-Am., Jap., Hawaii, Cape, Austr., NZ
- **austriaca** L. · G:Österreichischer
  Ehrenpreis
- subsp. **austriaca** · E:Large Speedwell;
  G:Gewöhnlicher Österreichischer
  Ehrenpreis · ⌃ Z6 V-VII; Eur.* exc. BrI,
  Sc; Cauc.
- subsp. *jacquinii* (Baumg.) Eb. Fisch. ·
  E:Jacquin's Speedwell; G:Jacquins
  Ehrenpreis · ⌃ Z6 V-VII; Eur.: PL, Russ.,
  H, Slove., Croatia, Serb.; TR, Cauc., Iran
- subsp. *teucrium* (L.) D.A. Webb =
  Veronica teucrium
- **beccabunga** L. · E:Brooklime, Water
  Pimpernel; F:Salade de chouette,
  Véronique beccabonga; G:Bachbungen-
  Ehrenpreis · ⌃ ⌁ Z5 V-VIII ⚥ ; Eur.*,
  TR, Cauc., Iran, W-Sib., C-As., Him.,
  NW-Afr., Eth.
- **bellidioides** L. · E:Violet Speedwell;
  G:Gänseblümchen-Ehrenpreis · ⌃ Z6
  VII-VIII; Eur.* exc. BrI, Sc; mts.
- **bombycina** Boiss. & Kotschy · ⌃ ⌁ △
  Z8 ⓚ VI-VIII; S-TR, Lebanon, Syr.
- *bonarota* L. = Paederota bonarota
- **caespitosa** Boiss. · ⌃ ⌂ △ ⓚ ⋀ V-VI;
  TR, Lebanon, Syr.
- **catenata** Pennell · G:Roter Wasser-
  Ehrenpreis · ⌃ ⌁ VI-X; Eur.*, Cauc.,
  W-Sib., E-Sib., C-As., Alger., N-Am.
- **chamaedrys** L. · G:Gamander-Ehrenpreis
- subsp. **chamaedrys** · E:Bird's Eye,
  Germander Speedwell; G:Gewöhnlicher
  Gamander-Ehrenpreis · ⌃ ⌁ Z3 V-VIII;
  Eur.*, TR, Cauc., W-Sib., E-Sib., C-As.,
  nat. in N-Am.
- subsp. *vindobonensis* M.A. Fisch. ·
  G:Drüsiger Gamander-Ehrenpreis · ⌃
  Z3 IV-V; Eur.: C-Eur., EC-Eur., Ba, RO,
  E-Eur.; Cauc.
- **cinerea** Boiss. & Balansa · ⌃ ⌁ △ Z5
  VI-VII; TR
- **dillenii** Crantz · G:Dillenius' Ehrenpreis ·
  ⊙ IV-V; Eur.* exc. BrI, Sc; TR, Cauc.,

Iran, W-Sib., C-As.,
- *exaltata* Maund = Pseudolysimachion longifolium subsp. longifolium
- **filiformis** Sm. · E:Round Leaved Speedwell; F:Véronique filiforme; G:Faden-Ehrenpreis · ⳨ ⤳ Z3 III-VI; Cauc., N-TR, N-Iran, nat. in BrI, Sc, Fr, C-Eur., EC-Eur., Crim
- **fruticans** Jacq. · E:Rock Speedwell; F:Véronique buissonnante; G:Felsen-Ehrenpreis · ⳨ ♄ △ Z5 VI-VII; Eur.*; N, mts.; Greenl.
- **fruticulosa** L. · G:Halbstrauch-Ehrenpreis · ⳨ ♄ △ Z3 VI-VII; Eur.: sp., F, I, C-Eur., Slove., Croatia; mts.
- **gentianoides** Vahl · F:Véronique fausse-gentiane; G:Enzian-Ehrenpreis · ⳨ Z4 V-VI; TR, Cauc., NW-Iran
- *hectorii* Hook. f. = Hebe hectorii
- **hederifolia** L. · G:Efeu-Ehrenpreis
- subsp. **hederifolia** · E:Ivy-leaved Speed-well; G:Gewöhnlicher Efeu-Ehrenpreis · ⊙ III-V; Eur.*, TR, Syr., Palest., Cauc., N-Iran, Him., C-As., NW-Afr., nat. in USA, Jap.
- subsp. **lucorum** (Klett & Richt.) Hartl · G:Hain-Efeu-Ehrenpreis · III-V; Eur.: BrI, Sc, C-Eur., EC-Eur., Ba
- subsp. **triloba** (Opiz) Čelak. · G:Dreilap-piger Efeu-Ehrenpreis · III-V; Eur., Cauc., Iran, C-As., Him., China, Jap., N-Afr.
- *hendersonii* hort. = Pseudolysimachion subsessile
- *incana* L. = Pseudolysimachion spicatum subsp. incanum
- **kelleri** Degen & Urum. · ⳨ Z7; Maced.
- *latifolia* L. = Veronica teucrium
- *longifolia* L. = Pseudolysimachion longifolium subsp. longifolium
- var. *subsessilis* Miq. = Pseudolysimachion subsessile
- *lutea* (Scop.) Wettst. = Paederota lutea
- **montana** L. · E:Wood Speedwell; G:Berg-Ehrenpreis · ⳨ V-VI; Eur.*, Cauc., TR, NW-Afr.
- **officinalis** L. · E:Common Speedwell; G:Echter Ehrenpreis, Wald-Ehrenpreis · ⳨ Z3 VI-IX ❦ ; Eur.*, TR, Cauc., NW-Iran, Azor.
- **opaca** Fr. · G:Glanzloser Ehrenpreis · ⊙ III-X; Eur.* exc. BrI, Ib
- **orientalis** Mill. · ⳨ △ △ Z7 VI-VIII; Eur.: Crim, ? RO; TR, Syr., Lebanon, N-Iraq, Cauc., N-Iran
- *paniculata* L. = Pseudolysimachion

spurium
- **pectinata** L. · ⳨ ⤳ △ Z7 △ V-VI; Eur.: BG; TR
- **peduncularis** M. Bieb. · ⳨ ⤳ △ Z7 △ V-VI; Eur.: Crim, E-Russ.; TR, Cauc.
- **peregrina** L. · E:American Speedwell; G:Fremder Ehrenpreis · ⊙ V-VI; E-Sib., Amur, Jap., China, nat. in Eur.* exc. Ba, Sc
- *perfoliata* R. Br. = Parahebe perfoliata
- **persica** Poir. · E:Persian Speedwell; G:Persischer Ehrenpreis · ⊙ ⊙ I-XII; TR, Cauc., nat. in Eur.*, N-Afr., C-As., Jap., Am., NZ
- **petraea** Steven · ⳨ △ Z6 V-VI; Cauc.
- **poliifolia** Benth. · ⳨ △ △ VI-VIII; TR, Iraq, Syr., Cauc. (Armen.)
- **polita** Fr. · E:Grey Speedwell; G:Glänzender Ehrenpreis · ⊙ III-X; Eur.*, TR, Cauc., Iran, C-As., Him., Mong., Tibet, Jap., N-Afr., nat. in cosmop.
- **praecox** All. · G:Früher Ehrenpreis · ⊙ III-V; Eur.* exc. BrI; TR, Cauc., NW-Afr., nat. in BrI
- **prostrata** L. · E:Rockery Speedwell; F:Véronique prostrée; G:Gewöhnlicher Liegender Ehrenpreis · ⳨ ⤳ △ Z5 IV-VI; Eur.* exc. BrI, Sc; Cauc., W-Sib.
- **repens** Clarion ex DC. · E:Corsican Speedwell · ⳨ ⤳ △ Z7 △ V-VI; Eur.: sp., Cors; mts.
- *rupestris* hort. = Veronica prostrata
- **saturejoides** Vis. · ⳨ △ Z7 ☙ △ V-VI; Eur.: Croatia, Bosn., Montenegro, Maced., AL, BG
- *saxatilis* Scop. = Veronica fruticans
- **scardica** Griseb. · G:Balkan-Ehrenpreis · ⳨ VI-X; Eur.: A, EC-Eur., Ba, E-Eur.; TR
- **schmidtiana** Regel · ⳨ △ Z5 VI-VIII; Jap., Sakhal.
- **scutellata** L. · E:Marsh Speedwell; G:Gewöhnlicher Schild-Ehrenpreis · ⳨ ⌒ Z6 VI-IX; Eur.*, Cauc., W-Sib., E-Sib., Sakhal., Kamchat., C-As., Jap.
- **serpyllifolia** L. · E:Thyme-leaf Speed-well; G:Thymian-Ehrenpreis · ⳨ Z3 V-IX; Eur.*, TR, Cauc., Iran, W-Sib., Amur, C-As., Him., China, Jap., N-Afr., Macaron., N-Am.
- *spicata* L. = Pseudolysimachion spicatum subsp. spicatum
- subsp. *incana* (L.) Walters = Pseudolysi-machion spicatum subsp. incanum
- *spuria* L. = Pseudolysimachion spurium
- *stelleri* Pall. ex Link = Veronica wormsk-joldii

– *sublobata* M. Fisch. = Veronica hederifolia subsp. lucorum
– **surculosa** Boiss. & Balansa · ⌗ ⤳ △ Z6
V-VII; TR
– **teucrium** L. · E:Heavenly Blue Speedwell; G:Großer Ehrenpreis · ⌗ Z6 V-VII;
Eur.* exc. BrI, Sc; Cauc., W-Sib.
– *triloba* Opiz = Veronica hederifolia subsp.
triloba
– **triphyllos** L. · G:Dreiteiliger Ehrenpreis ·
⊙ III-V; Eur.*, TR
– **turrilliana** Stoj. & Stef. · ⌗ △ Z6 V-VI;
Eur.: BG, TR (Strandsha-mts.)
– **urticifolia** Jacq. · G:Nesselblättriger
Ehrenpreis · ⌗ VI-VIII; Eur.* exc. BrI, Sc
– **verna** L. · E:Spring Speedwell;
G:Frühlings-Ehrenpreis · ⊙ IV-V; Eur.*,
TR, Cauc., W-Sib., C-As.
– *vindobonensis* (M. Fisch.) M. Fisch. =
Veronica chamaedrys subsp. vindobonensis
– *virginica* L. = Veronicastrum virginicum
– **wormskjoldii** Roem. & Schult. ·
E:American Alpine Speedwell; G:Ameri-
kanischer Ehrenpreis · ⌗ Z4; Alaska,
USA: NE, NCE, NC, SW, Rocky Mts., NW,
Calif.; Greenl.

Veronicastrum Heist. ex Fabr. -n-
Scrophulariaceae · 2 spp. · E:Blackroot;
F:Véronique de Virginie; G:Arzneiehren-
preis
– **virginicum** (L.) Farw. · E:Black Root,
Culver's Root, Physic Root; F:Véronique
de Virginie; G:Virginischer Arzneiehrenpreis · ⌗ Z3 VII-IX; Can.: E; USA: NE,
NCE, SC, SE, Fla.

Verschaffeltia H. Wendl. -f- *Arecaceae* ·
I sp.
– **splendida** H. Wendl. · ♄ e Z10 ⓦ; Seych.

Verticordia DC. -f- *Myrtaceae* · 97 spp.
– **grandis** J.L. Drumm. ex Meisn. · ♄ e Z10
ⓐ; W-Austr.
– **nitens** Schauer · ♄ e ✕ Z10 ⓐ; W-Austr.

Vestia Willd. -f- *Solanaceae* · I sp.
– **foetida** (Ruiz & Pav.) Hoffmanns. · ♄ e D
Z9 ⓐ IV-VI; Chile
– *lycioides* Willd. = Vestia foetida

Vetiveria Bory -f- *Poaceae* · 10 spp. ·
E:Vetiver; F:Vétiver; G:Vetivergras
– **zizanioides** (L.) Nash · E:Cus Cus,

Vetiver; G:Vetivergras · ⌗ Z9 ⓦ ⚥ ⓝ;
Ind., Sri Lanka, Burma

Viburnum L. -n- *Caprifoliaceae* · 150+ spp. ·
E:Arrow Wood, Wayfaring Tree; F:Boule
de neige, Viorne; G:Schneeball
– **acerifolium** L. · E:Dockmackie; G:Ahorn-
blättriger Schneeball · ♄ d Z5 V-VI ✿;
Can.: E; USA; NE, NCE, SE
– *americanum* auct. non Mill. = Viburnum
trilobum
– **atrocyaneum** C.B. Clarke · ♄ e Z9 ⓐ;
Him.
– **betulifolium** Batalin · G:Birkenblätt-
triger Schneeball · ♄ d ⚭ Z5 VI-VII ✿;
W-China, C-China
– **bitchiuense** Makino · ♄ d D Z6 V; Jap.,
Korea
– × **bodnantense** Aberc. (*V. farreri* × *V.
grandiflorum*) · E:Winter Viburnum;
G:Bodnant-Schneeball · ♄ d D Z7 XI-III
✿; cult.
– **buddleifolium** C.H. Wright · G:Buddle-
jablättriger Schneeball · ♄ d Z6 V-VI ✿;
C-China
– **burejaeticum** Regel & Herder ·
G:Mongolischer Schneeball · ♄ d Z5 V ✿;
Manch., N-China.
– × **burkwoodii** Burkwood & Skipwith (*V.
carlesii* × *V. utile*) · E:Dawn Viburnum;
F:Viorne de Burkwood; G:Burkwoods
Schneeball · ♄ d D Z6 III-IV ✿; cult.
– × **carlcephalum** Burkwood ex A.V.
Pike (*V. carlesii* × *V. macrocephalum*) ·
E:Fragrant Snowball; F:Viorne · ♄ d D
IV-V ✿; cult.
– **carlesii** Hemsl. · E:Sweet Viburnum;
F:Viorne de Carles; G:Koreanischer
Schneeball · ♄ d D Z5 IV-V ✿; Korea
– **cassinoides** L. · E:Withe Rod; G:Birnblät-
triger Schneeball · ♄ d Z5 VI-VII ✿; Can.:
E; USA: NCE, NE, SE
– **cinnamomifolium** Rehder · G:Zimtblät-
triger Schneeball · ♄ e Z8 ⓐ VI; W-China
– **corylifolium** Hook. f. & Thomson ·
G:Haselblättriger Schneeball · ♄ d Z6 VI;
E-Him., W-China, C-China
– **cotinifolium** D. Don · G:Cotinusblät-
triger Schneeball · ♄ d Z6 V-VI ⓝ; Him.
– **cylindricum** Buch.-Ham. ex D. Don · ♄ e
Z6 VI-IX; Him., W-China
– **dasyanthum** Rehder · ♄ d Z6 VI; C-China
– **davidii** Franch. · E:Evergreen Viburnum;
F:Viorne de David; G:Davids Schneeball ·
♄ e Z7 ⋀ VI ✿; W-China

– **dentatum** L.
– var. **dentatum** · E:Arrowwood, Southern Arrow Wood; G:Gezähnter Schneeball · ♄ d Z4 VI-VII ✷; USA: NE, NCE, SC, SE, Fla.
– var. **pubescens** Aiton Z2 ✷; E-USA
– **dilatatum** Thunb. · E:Linden Viburnum; G:Breitdoldiger Schneeball · ♄ d ⚭ Z6 V-VI ✷; Jap.
– **erubescens** Wall.
– var. **erubescens** · ♄ ♄ d D Z6 VI; Nepal, W-China
– var. **gracilipes** Rehder · ♄ d Z6; C-China
– **farreri** Stearn · E:Fragrant Viburnum; F:Viorne odorante; G:Duftender Schneeball · ♄ d D Z6 XI-IV ✷; N-China
– **foetidum** Wall. · ♄ e Z9 ⍓; Him., Burma, W-China
– *fragrans* Bunge = Viburnum farreri
– × **globosum** Coombes (*V. davidii* × *V. calvum*) · ♄ e Z7; cult.
– **grandiflorum** Wall. ex DC. · G:Großblütiger Schneeball · ♄ d Z7 I-III; Him.
– **harryanum** Rehder · ♄ e Z9 ⍓; W-China
– **henryi** Hemsl. · E:Henry's Viburnum; G:Henrys Schneeball · ♄ e Z8 ∧ VIII ✷; C-China
– *hessei* Koehne = Viburnum wrightii var. hessei
– × **hillieri** Stearn (*V. erubescens* × *V. henryi*) · G:Hilliers Schneeball · ♄ e Z6; cult.
– **hupehense** Rehder · G:Hupeh-Schneeball · ♄ d Z6 V-VI ✷; C-China
– **ichangense** (Hemsl.) Rehder · G:Ichang-Schneeball · ♄ d Z6 VI; W-China, C-China
– × **jackii** Rehder (*V. lentago* × *V. prunifolium*) · G:Jacks Schneeball · ♄ d Z5 V; cult.
– **japonicum** (Thunb.) Spreng. · E:Japanese Viburnum; G:Immergrüner Japanischer Schneeball · ♄ e D Z7 VI; Jap., Ryukyu-Is., Taiwan
– × **juddii** Rehder (*V. bitchiuense* × *V. carlesii*) · G:Judds Schneeball · ♄ d D Z6 IV-V ✷; cult.
– **lantana** L. · E:Wayfaring Tree; F:Mansienne, Viorne lantane; G:Wolliger Schneeball · ♄ d Z4 IV-VI ✷ ⍟; Eur.* exc. Sc; TR, Iran, Moroc., Alger., nat. in Sc
– **lantanoides** Michx. · E:Hobblebush; G:Erlenblättriger Schneeball · ♄ Z3 V-VI; Can.: E; USA: NE, SE
– **lentago** L. · E:Nannyberry, Sheepberry;

G:Kanadischer Schneeball · ♄ ♄ d Z5 V-VI ✷; Can.: E, Sask.; USA: NE, NCE, NC, SE, Rocky Mts.
– **lobophyllum** Graebn. · G:Gelapptblätt-riger Schneeball · ♄ d ⚭ Z6 VI-VII ✷; W-China, C-China
– **macrocephalum** Fortune · E:Chinese Snowball; G:Chinesischer Schneeball · ♄ d Z7 V; China
– *macrophyllum* Thunb. = Viburnum japonicum
– *maculatum* Pant. = Viburnum lantana
– **molle** Michx. · E:Softleaf Arrow Wood · ♄ d Z6 VI; USA: NE, NCE, Ark.
– **mongolicum** (Pall.) Rehder · ♄ d Z5 V; E-Sib., N-China
– **nudum** L. · E:Possumhaw, Smooth Withe Rod; G:Gelber Schneeball · ♄ d ∿ Z6 VI-VII; USA: NE, SE, Fla., SC
– **odoratissimum** Ker-Gawl. · E:Sweet Viburnum; G:Starkduftender Schneeball · ♄ e D Z9 ⍓ V; Him.
– **opulus** L. · E:European Cranberry-bush, Guelder Rose; F:Viorne obier; G:Gewöhnlicher Schneeball · ♄ d Z4 V-VI ♀ ✷ ⍟; Eur.*, TR, Cauc., W-Sib., E-Sib., C-As.
– var. *americanum* Aiton = Viburnum trilobum
– **orientale** Pall. · G:Orientalischer Schneeball · ♄ d Z6 VI; TR, W-Cauc.
– *oxycoccos* Pursh = Viburnum trilobum
– **phlebotrichum** Siebold & Zucc. · ♄ d Z6 V-VI; Jap.
– **plicatum** Thunb. · E:Lace Cup Viburnum; F:Viorne de Chine; G:Japanischer Schneeball · ♄ d Z5 ✷; China, Jap., Taiwan
– f. **tomentosum** (Thunb.) Rehder · F:Viorne de Chine · ♄ d; Jap., China
– × **pragense** Vikulova (*V. × rhytidocarpum* × *V. utile*) · G:Prager Schneeball · ♄ e Z6 V; cult.
– **propinquum** Hemsl. · ♄ e Z7; C-China, W-China, Taiwan, Phil.
– **prunifolium** L. · E:Black Haw; G:Kirsch-blättriger Schneeball · ♄ ♄ d Z4 V-VI ♀ ✷ ⍟; USA: NE, NCE, Kans., SC, SE, Fla.
– **rafinesqueanum** Schult. · E:Downy Arrow Wood
– var. **affine** (Bush) House · ♄ d Z2 V-VI; Can.: Ont.; USA: NE, NCE, Ark.
– var. **rafinesquianum** · G:Rafinesques Schneeball · ♄ d Z2; USA: NE, NCE
– × **rhytidocarpum** Lemoine (*V.*

buddleifolium × *V. rhytidophyllum*) · ♄ s
Z6 V-VI; cult.
- × **rhytidophylloides** J.V. Suringar (*V.
lantana* × *V.* × *rhytidocarpum*) · ♄ Z5
V-VI; cult.
- **rhytidophyllum** Hemsl. · E:Leatherleaf
Viburnum; F:Viorne à feuilles ridées;
G:Runzelblättriger Schneeball · ♄ e Z6
V-VI ✿; W-China, C-China
- **rufidulum** Raf. · E:Southern Black Haw;
G:Rostiger Schneeball · ♄ ♄ d Z5 V-VI;
USA: NE, NCE, Kans., SC, SE, Fla.
- *sandankwa* Hassk. = Viburnum suspensum
- **sargentii** Koehne · E:Cramp Bark;
G:Sargents Schneeball · ♄ d ⚭ Z4 V-VI;
China, Manch., Korea, Jap., Sakhal.
- **setigerum** Hance · E:Tea Viburnum;
G:Borstiger Schneeball · ♄ d Z5 V-VI;
W-China, C-China
- **sieboldii** Miq. · G:Stinkender Schneeball · ♄ d ⚭ Z4 V-VI; Jap.
- **suspensum** Lindl. · E:Sandankwa Viburnum · ♄ e D Z9 ⚑ III-V; Jap., Ryukyu-Is.,
Taiwan
- **tinus** L. · E:Laurustinus; G:Immergrüner
Schneeball, Lorbeer-Schneeball · ♄ e D Z7
⚑ V-VIII ✿; cult., nat. in BrI
- *tomentosum* Thunb. non Lam. =
Viburnum plicatum f. tomentosum
- **trilobum** Marshall · E:American Cranber-
rybush; G:Amerikanischer Schneeball · ♄
d ⌇ ⚭ Z4 V-VI ✿ Ⓝ; Can., USA: NE,
NCE, NC, Rocky Mts., Wash.
- **utile** Hemsl. · G:Nützlicher Schneeball ·
♄ d Z7 V ✿; C-China
- **wrightii** Miq. · G:Sachalin-Schneeball
- var. **hessei** (Koehne) Rehder · ♄ d ⚭ Z5
V-VI; Jap.
- var. **wrightii** · ♄ d ⚭ Z5 V-VI; Jap.,
Korea, Sakhal.

Vicia L. -f- *Fabaceae* · 140 spp. · E:Bean,
Vetch; F:Fève, Vesce; G:Bohne, Wicke
- **angustifolia** L. · G:Gewöhnliche
Schmalblättrige Wicke · ⊙; Eur.*, TR,
Levant, N-Afr., nat. in N-Am.
- **articulata** Hornem. · E:One-flower
Vetch; G:Einblütige Wicke · ⊙ VI-VIII Ⓝ;
Eur.: Ib, Ital-P, Ba; TR, Egypt, nat. in Fr,
C-Eur., EC-Eur., RO
- **benghalensis** L. · E:Purple Vetch,
Reddish Tufted Vetch; G:Purpur-Wicke ·
⊙ Ⓝ; Eur.: Ib, Fr, Ital-P, GR; NW-Afr.
- **bithynica** (L.) L. · G:Bithynische Wicke ·
⊙; Eur.: Ib, Fr, BrI, Ital-P, Ba, Crim; TR,

Levant, Cauc., NW-Afr.
- **cassubica** L. · G:Kassuben-Wicke · ⌗
VI-VII; Eur.* exc. BrI, Sc; TR, Lebanon,
Cauc., N-Iran
- **cordata** Wulfen ex Hoppe · G:Herzblät-
trige Wicke · ⊙ V-VII; S-Eur., TR, Levant,
Egypt, Libya, Alger., Moroc.
- **cracca** L. · E:Tufted Vetch; G:Vogel-
Wicke · ⌗ Z5 VI-VII; Eur.*, TR, Cauc.,
W-Sib., E-Sib., Amur, C-As., nat. in
N-Am.
- **dalmatica** A. Kern. · G:Dalmatiner Vogel-
Wicke · ⌗; Eur.: I, H, Ba, RO, Crim; TR,
Levant, ? Iraq, Cauc., Iran
- **dumetorum** L. · G:Hecken-Wicke · ⌗
VI-VII; Eur.* exc. Ib, BrI
- **ervilia** (L.) Willd. · E:Bitter Vetch;
G:Linsen-Wicke, Stein-Linse · ⊙ V-VI
Ⓝ; Eur.: Ib, Fr, Ital-P, Ba; TR, Cyprus,
Syr., Cauc., Iran, Moroc., Alger., nat. in
C-Eur., EC-Eur.
- **faba** L.
- var. **equina** Pers. · E:Field Bean, Horse
Bean; G:Pferdebohne · ⊙ Ⓝ; cilt.
- var. **faba** · E:Broad Bean; G:Puff-Bohne,
Sau-Bohne · ⊙ V-VII Ⓝ; cult.
- var. **minuta** (hort. ex Alef.) Mansf. ·
E:Tickbean; G:Acker-Bohne · ⊙ Ⓝ; cult.
- **grandiflora** Scop. · G:Großblütige Wicke ·
⊙ V-VI; Eur.: Ital-P, A, EC-Eur., Ba, E-Eur.;
TR, Cauc., Iran, Afgh., nat. in D
- **hirsuta** (L.) Gray · E:Hairy Tare;
G:Rauhaarige Wicke, Zitter-Wicke · ⊙
VI-VII Ⓝ; Eur.*, TR, Cyprus, Syr., Iran,
Cauc., W-Sib., E-Sib., Amur, C-As., Him.,
China, Jap., NW-Afr., Egypt, Eth., nat. in
N-Am.
- **hybrida** L. · E:Hairy Yellow Vetch;
G:Bastard-Wicke · ⊙ V; Eur.: Ib, Fr,
Ital-P, Ba, RO, Crim; TR, Levant, Iraq,
Cauc., Iran, C-As.
- **incana** Gouan · G:Graue Wicke · ⌗
VI-VII; Eur.: Ib, Fr, Ital-P, Ba, EC-Eur.,
C-Eur.; TR
- **johannis** Tamamsch. · G:Maus-Wicke · ⊙
V-VI; Eur.: Ib, Fr, Ital-P, Ba, H, RO, Crim;
TR, Levant, Cauc., C-As., N-Afr., nat. in
C-Eur., EC-Eur.
- **lathyroides** L. · E:Spring Vetch;
G:Platterbsen-Wicke · ⊙ IV-VI; Eur.*,
Levant, Cauc., ? N-Iran, Moroc., Alger.
- **lutea** L. · E:Yellow Vetch; G:Gelbe Wicke
· ⊙ VI-VII; Eur.: Ib, Fr, EC-Eur., Ital-P, Ba,
E-Eur.; TR, Cauc., N-Afr., N-Iran, nat. in
D

– **melanops** Sm. · G:Grünblütige Wicke ·
  ⊙; Eur.: F, Ital-P, Ba; TR, nat. in EC-Eur.
– *monanthos* (L.) Desf. = Vicia articulata
– *narbonensis* L. = Vicia johannis
– **onobrychioides** L. · G:Esparsetten-
  Wicke · ⅃ Z7 V-VII; Eur.: Fr, Ital-P, Sw,
  Ba; NW-Afr.
– **oreophila** Chrtková · ⅃; Eur.: EC-Eur. +
– **oroboides** Wulfen · E:Pale Vetch;
  G:Walderbsen-Wicke · ⅃ Z5 V-VII; Eur.: I,
  A, H, Slove., Croatia, Bosn.
– **orobus** DC. · E:Bitter Vetch; G:Heide-
  Wicke · ⅃ Z6 VII-VIII; Eur.: Sc, BrI, Fr,
  C-Eur., Ib
– **pannonica** Crantz · E:Hungarian Vetch;
  G:Gewöhnliche Ungarische Wicke · ⊙
  V-VI Ⓝ; Eur.* exc. BrI, Sc; TR, Cyprus,
  Cauc., Iran
– **parviflora** Cav. · G:Zierliche Wicke · ⊙
  VI-VII; Eur.: Ib, Fr, BrI, Sw, Ital-P, Ba,
  RO, Crim; TR, Levant, N-Afr.
– **peregrina** L. · E:Broad-pod Vetch;
  G:Fremde Wicke · ⊙ IV-VI; Eur.: Ib, Fr,
  Ital-P, Ba, E-Eur.; TR, Levant, Cauc., Iran,
  C-As., Him., Moroc., Libya, Egypt, nat. in
  Ch, H
– **pisiformis** L. · E:Pale-flower Vetch;
  G:Erbsen-Wicke · ⅃ VI-VIII; Eur.* exc. Ib,
  BrI; Cauc.
– **pliniana** (Trab.) Muratova · ⊙ Ⓝ;
  Moroc., Alger.
– **pyrenaica** Pourr. · E:Pyrenean Vetch;
  G:Pyrenäen-Wicke · ⅃ △ Z7 ∧ V-VI;
  Eur.: sp., F; mts.
– **sativa** L. · E:Common Vetch, Spring
  Vetch; G:Futter-Wicke, Saat-Wicke · ⊙
  V-VII; orig. ?, cult.
– subsp. *angustifolia* (L.) Asch. & Graebn. =
  Vicia angustifolia
– subsp. *nigra* (L.) Ehrh. = Vicia angustifo-
  lia
– **sepium** L. · E:Bush Vetch; G:Zaun-Wicke
  · ⅃ Z6 V-VIII; Eur.*, Cauc., W-Sib., E-Sib.,
  C-As., Mong., Kashmir, nat. in Can.: E,
  USA: NE
– **serratifolia** Jacq. · G:Gezähnte Wicke · ⊙
  V-VI; S-Eur. , TR, Levant, Cauc., N-Afr.
– **sylvatica** L. · E:Wood; G:Wald-Wicke
  Vetch · ⅃ VI-VIII; Eur.*
– **tenuifolia** Roth · E:Fine-leaved Vetch;
  G:Feinblättrige Vogel-Wicke · ⅃ Z6
  VI-VIII; Eur.* exc. BrI; TR, Levant, Iraq,
  Cauc., Iran, W-Sib., E-Sib., C-As., nat. in
  BrI
– *tenuissima* Schinz & Thell. = Vicia

parviflora
– **tetrasperma** (L.) Schreb. · E:Lentil
  Vetch, Smooth Tare; G:Viersamige Wicke
  · ⊙ VI-VII; Eur.*, TR, Palest., Cauc.,
  W-Sib., E-Sib., C-As., N-Afr.
– **unijuga** A. Braun · E:Two-leaf Vetch;
  G:Zweiblättrige Wicke · ⅃ Z7 V-VI; Sib.
– **villosa** Roth · G:Zottige Wicke
– subsp. **varia** (Host) Corb. · E:Woolypod
  Vetch; G:Bunte Wicke · VI-VIII; S-Eur.;
  TR, Levant, N-Afr.
– subsp. **villosa** · E:Fodder Vetch; G:Kahle
  Wicke, Zottel-Wicke · ⊙ VI-VII Ⓝ; Eur.*
  exc. BrI, Sc; TR, Levant, Iraq, Cauc., Iran,
  C-As., N-Afr., nat. in BrI, Sc, N-Am.

Victoria Lindl. -f- *Nymphaeaceae* · 2 spp. ·
  E:Giant Water Lily; F:Victoria; G:Riesen-
  seerose, Victoria
– **amazonica** (Poepp.) Sowerby · E:Giant
  Waterlily; G:Amazonas-Riesenseerose · ⅃
  ≈ Z10 Ⓜ VII-X; Amazon., Guyan.
– **cruziana** Orb. · E:Santa Cruz Water Lily;
  G:Santa-Cruz-Riesenseelilie · ⅃ ≈ Z10
  Ⓜ VII-X; Braz: Parana; Parag., N-Arg.
– *regia* Lindl. = Victoria amazonica
– *trickeri* H. Henkel = Victoria cruziana

Vigna Savi -f- *Fabaceae* · 150 spp. · E:Mug
  Bean; F:Dolique, Fleur-escargot;
  G:Kuhbohne, Spargelbohne
– **aconitifolia** (Jacq.) Maréchal · E:Mat
  Bean, Moth Bean; G:Mattenbohne · ⊙
  ⤳ Z10 Ⓝ; Arab., Ind.
– **angularis** (Willd.) Ohwi & H. Ohashi ·
  E:Adzuki Bean; G:Adzukibohne · ⊙ Z10
  Ⓝ; ? E-As.
– **caracalla** (L.) Verdc. · E:Snail Flower,
  Snail Vine; G:Schneckenbohne · ⅃ ⚥ D
  Z10 Ⓜ VII-IX Ⓝ; W.Ind., S-Am.
– *catjang* (Burm. f.) Walp. = Vigna
  unguiculata subsp. cylindrica
– *cylindrica* (L.) Skeels = Vigna unguiculata
  subsp. cylindrica
– **hosei** (Craib) Backer · Ⓜ Ⓝ; Kalimantan
  (Sarawak), nat. in SE-As., Austr.:
  Queensl.
– **mungo** (L.) Hepper · E:Black Gram;
  G:Urdbohne · ⊙ ⤳ Ⓝ; Ind. (Maharash-
  tra); cult. Ind.
– **radiata** (L.) R. Wilczek
– var. **radiata** · E:Mungbean; G:Jerusalem-
  bohne, Mungbohne · ⊙ Ⓝ; Jap.
– var. **sublobata** (Roxb.) Verdc. · ⊙;
  E-Afr., Madag., Ind., Sri Lanka, SE-As.,

Malay. Arch., Austr.: Queensl.
- *sesquipedalis* (L.) Fruwirth = Vigna unguiculata subsp. sesquipedalis
- *sinensis* (L.) Savi ex Hassk. = Vigna unguiculata subsp. unguiculata
- **subterranea** (L.) Verdc. · E:Groundbean; G:Bambaraerdnuss · ⊙ Ⓚ Ⓝ; Cameroon, N-Nigeria
- **trilobata** (L.) Verdc. · ⊙ ♃ Ⓝ; Afgh., Him., Ind., Sri Lanka, Burma, Malay. Arch., Eth.
- **umbellata** (Thunb.) Ohwi & H. Ohashi · E:Rice Bean; G:Reisbohne · ⊙ Ⓝ; Ind., China, SE-As.
- **unguiculata** (L.) Walp.
- subsp. **cylindrica** (L.) Verdc. · E:Catjang Bean, Jerusalem Pea; G:Katjangbohne · ⊙ ≹ ⇝ Z10 Ⓝ; ? trop. Afr., ? Ind.
- subsp. **sesquipedalis** (L.) Verdc. · E:Yardlong Bean; G:Spargelbohne · ⊙ ≹ ⇝ Z10 Ⓝ; cult.
- subsp. **unguiculata** · E:Asparagus Bean, Cow Pea; G:Augenbohne · ⊙ ≹ ⇝ Z10; trop. Afr.
- **vexillata** (L.) Rich. · ♃ Ⓦ Ⓝ; trop. As., Afr., Austr.

Viguiera Kunth -f- *Asteraceae* · c. 150 spp.

Villadia Rose -f- *Crassulaceae* · 21 sp.
- **guatemalensis** Rose · ♃ Ψ Z8 Ⓚ; Guat.
- **imbricata** Rose · ♃ Ψ Z8 Ⓚ; Mex.

Villarsia Vent. -f- *Menyanthaceae* · 16 spp. · F:Villarsia; G:Villarsie
- **exaltata** (Sims) F. Muell. · ♃ ～ Z10 Ⓚ VII; Austr., Tasman.
- **ovata** (L. f.) Vent. · ♃ ～ Z10 Ⓚ VI; Cape
- **parnassiifolia** R. Br. · ♃ ～ Z10 Ⓚ VIII; Austr. (W-Austr.)
- *reniformis* R. Br. = Villarsia exaltata

Vinca L. -f- *Apocynaceae* · 5 spp. · E:Periwinkle; F:Pervenche; G:Immergrün
- *acutiflora* Bertol. = Vinca difformis
- **difformis** Pourr. · ♄ e Z9 Ⓚ ☠; Eur.: Ib, Fr, I, Azor.; N-Afr.
- **herbacea** Waldst. & Kit. · E:Periwinkle; G:Krautiges Immergrün · ♃ ⇝ Z5 V-VI ☠; Eur.: A, EC-Eur., Ba, E-Eur.; TR, Syr., Palest., N-Iraq, Cauc., Iran
- **major** L. · E:Greater Periwinkle; F:Grande pervenche; G:Gewöhnliches Großes Immergrün · ♄ e Z7 Ⓚ ∧ IV-V ⚕ ☠; Eur.: sp., F, I, Sic., Croatia; TR, Cyprus, Syr., Cauc., nat. in BrI, C-Eur., EC-Eur.
- **minor** L. · E:Smaller Periwinkle; F:Petite pervenche; G:Kleines Immergrün · ♃ ♄ e ⇝ Z6 IV-V ⚕ ☠; Eur.* exc. BrI, Sc; W-TR, Levant, Cauc. Iran, nat. in BrI, Sc
- **some cultivars**
- *rosea* L. = Catharanthus roseus

Vincetoxicum Wolf -n- *Asclepiadaceae* · 15 spp. · E:Swallowwort; F:Dompte-venin; G:Schwalbenwurz
- **hirundinaria** Medik. · E:White Swallow-wort; G:Weiße Schwalbenwurz · ♃ V-VII ⚕ ☠; Eur.* exc. BrI; TR, Cauc., Moroc., Alger.
- **nigrum** (L.) Moench · E:Black Swallow-root; G:Schwarze Schwalbenwurz · ♃ ≹ Z7 ☠; Eur.: Ib, F, I, nat. in NL
- *officinale* Moench = Vincetoxicum hirundinaria
- **rossicum** (Kleopow) Barbar. · ♃ ≹ ☠; Eur.: Russ.

Viola L. -f- *Violaceae* · 400-500 spp. · E:Pansy, Violet; F:Pensée, Violette; G:Stiefmütterchen, Veilchen
- **adunca** Sm. · E:Hook Spur Violet, Western Blue Violet; G:Sporn-Veilchen · ♃; Alaska, USA* exc. SE, Fla, SC; Greenl.
- **alba** Besser · E:Parma Violet; G:Gewöhnliches Weißes Veilchen · ♃ Z6 III-V; Eur.* exc. BrI; TR, Cauc., ? Iran, NW-Afr.
- **alpina** Jacq. · E:Alpine Pansy; G:Alpen-Stiefmütterchen · ♃ △ Z7 VI-VII; Eur.: A, Slova., RO; NE-Alp., Carp.
- **altaica** Ker-Gawl. · G:Altai-Veilchen · ♃ V-VII; Altai, Sib.
- **ambigua** Waldst. & Kit. · E:Austrian Violet; G:Pontisches Veilchen, Steppen-Veilchen · ♃ IV-V; Eur.: A, EC-Eur., Ba, E-Eur., D; TR, Cauc.
- **arborescens** L. · ♄ Z9 Ⓚ; Eur.: Ib, F, Sard.; NW-Afr.
- **arvensis** Murray · E:European Field Pansy; G:Gewöhnliches Acker-Stiefmütterchen · ⊙ V-X; Eur.*, TR, Cauc., W-Sib., E-Sib., nat. in N-Am.
- × **bavarica** Schrank (*V. reichenbachiana* × *V. riviniana*) · G:Bastard-Wald-Veilchen · ♃; Eur. +
- **bertolonii** Pio · ♃ △ Z7 ∧ V-VI; Eur.: F, I, Sic.
- **biflora** L. · E:Yellow Wood Violet; G:Zweiblütiges Veilchen · ♃ △ ～ V-VII;

Eur.* exc. BrI; N, mts; Cauc., Him.,
W-Sib., E-Sib., Amur, Sakhal., Kamchat.,
C-As., Mong., China, Jap., Alaska, Can.:
W; USA: Rocky Mts., NW
– **calaminaria** (Ging.) Lej. · G:Gelbes
Galmei-Stiefmütterchen · ⅄ VI-VIII ▽;
Eur.: NL, B, D
– **calcarata** L.
– subsp. **calcarata** · E:Spurred Violet;
G:Langsporniges Stiefmütterchen · ⅄ △
Z5 VI-VII ▽; Eur.: F, I, C-Eur., Ba
– subsp. **zoysii** (Wulfen) Merxm. ·
G:Karawanken-Stiefmütterchen · ⅄ Z5
V-VI ▽; Eur.: Slove., Bosn., Montenegro,
AL, Maced.
– **canadensis** L. · G:Kanada-Veilchen
– var. **canadensis** · E:Canadian White
Violet
– var. **rugulosa** (Greene) C.L. Hitchc. ·
E:Creeping Root Violet · ⅄; Can., USA*
exc. NE, SC, Calif., Fla
– **canina** L. · G:Hunds-Veilchen
– subsp. **canina** · E:Dog Violet; G:Gewöhn-
liches Hunds-Veilchen · ⅄ Z6 V-VI; Eur.*,
TR, Cauc., C-As., W-Sib., Canar., Greenl.
– subsp. **montana** (L.) Hartm. · G:Berg-
Veilchen · ⅄ Z6 V-VI; Eur.: Sw, G, Sc, A
+; Sib.
– subsp. **schultzii** (Billot ex F.W. Schultz)
Kirschl. · G:Schultzes Hunds-Veilchen · ⅄
Z6 V-VI; Eur.: C-Eur, N-I, S-RO
– **cenisia** L. · E:Mt Cenis Pansy; G:Mont-
Cenis-Stiefmütterchen · ⅄ Z6 VII; Eur.: F,
I, Sw; Alp.
– **collina** Besser · G:Hügel-Veilchen ·
⅄ IV-V; Eur.* exc. BrI; Cauc., W-Sib.,
E-Sib., Amur, Sakhal., C-As., Manch.
– **cornuta** L. · E:Horned Pansy; F:Violette
cornue; G:Gehörntes Veilchen, Horn-
Veilchen, Pyrenäen-Stiefmütterchen · ⅄
△ Z7 VI-VIII; Eur.: sp., F; Pyr., Cordillera
Cantábrica, nat. in BrI, C-Eur., I, RO
– **many cultivars**
– **cucullata** Aiton · E:Marsh Blue Violet;
G:Amerikanisches Veilchen · ⅄ ⤳ V-VI;
Can.: E; USA: NE, NCE, NC, Tenn., Ark.
– *cyanea* Čelak. = Viola suavis
– **dissecta** Ledeb.
– var. **chaerophylloides** (Regel) Makino ·
⅄ D IV; Jap.
– var. **dissecta** · E:Dissected Viola · ⅄;
W-Sib., E-Sib., Amur, C-As., Mong.,
China: Sinkiang, Manch.; Korea, Jap.
– *eizanensis* (Makino) Makino = Viola
dissecta var. chaerophylloides

– **elatior** Fr. · G:Hohes Veilchen · ⅄ Z5
V-VII; Eur.* exc. BrI, Ib; Cauc., W-Sib.,
C-As.
– **elegantula** Schott · ⅄ △ Z6 VII-VIII;
Eur.: Croatia, Bosn., Montenegro, AL;
mts.
– **epipsila** Ledeb. · G:Torf-Veilchen · ⅄
⤳ Z5 V-VI; Eur.: Sc, G, EC-Eur., E-Eur.;
W-Sib.
– **eugeniae** Parl. · ⅄; I; Apenn.
– × **florariensis** Correvon (*V. cornuta* × *V.
tricolor subsp. tricolor*) · ⅄ △ VI-VIII; cult.
– **gracilis** Sibth. & Sm. · ⅄ V-VIII; Eur.: Ba;
mts.
– **guestphalica** Nauenb. · G:Violettes
Galmei-Stiefmütterchen, Westfälisches
Galmei-Stiefmütterchen · ⅄ V-X ▽; Eur.:
D
– **hederacea** Labill. · E:Australian Violet;
G:Australisches Veilchen · ⅄ ⚘ ⤳ ⓦ
ⓐ IV-XI; Austr.: Queensl., N.S.Wales,
Victoria, S-Austr., Tasman.
– **hirta** L. · E:Hairy Violet; G:Rauhaariges
Veilchen · ⅄ IV-V; Eur.*, Cauc., W-Sib.,
E-Sib., C-As.
– **hymettia** Boiss. & Heldr. · ⊙; Eur.: P, Fr,
Ital-P, Ba
– **jooi** Janka · ⅄ △ D Z5 IV-V; C-RO
– **kitaibeliana** Schult. · G:Kleines Stiefmüt-
terchen · ⊙ IV-VII; Eur.* exc. Sc; TR,
Cyprus, Syr., Cauc.
– **labradorica** Schrank · E:Labrador Violet;
G:Labrador-Veilchen · ⅄ Z2 IV-V; Alaska,
Can.; USA: NE, NCE, NC, Rocky Mts.,
Calif., NW; Greenl.
– **lactea** Sm. · G:Milch-Veilchen · ⅄ Z7;
Eur.: BrI, F, Ib
– **lanceolata** L. · E:Bog White Violet · ⅄;
Can.: E; USA: NE, NCE, SE, Fla., SC
– **lutea** Huds. · E:Mountain Pansy;
G:Gelbes Stiefmütterchen · ⅄ Z5 VI-VIII;
Eur.: Ib, Fr, BrI, C-Eur., EC-Eur.; mts.
– **mirabilis** L. · E:Wonder Violet;
G:Wunder-Veilchen · ⅄ Z5 IV-V; Eur.*
exc. BrI, Sc; Cauc., W-Sib., E-Sib., Amur,
C-As., Mong., Manch., Jap.
– *montana* L. = Viola canina subsp.
montana
– *obliqua* Hill = Viola cucullata
– **odorata** L. · E:Sweet Violet, Violet;
G:März-Veilchen, Wohlriechendes
Veilchen · ⅄ ⋈ D Z6 III-IV ⓝ; Eur.*,
TR, Cyprus, Syr., N-Iraq, Cauc., N-Iran,
NW-Afr., Canar.
– **some cultivars**

– **palmata** L. · E:Early Blue Violet · ⌉ Z4
IV-V; Ont., USA: NE, NCE, SE, Fla.
– **palustris** L. · E:Marsh Violet; G:Sumpf-
Veilchen · ⌉ ⌢ V-VI; Eur.*, As., N-Am.
– *papilionacea* Pursh = Viola sororia
– **pedata** L. · E:Birdfoot Violet · ⌉ Z6; USA:
NE, NEC, SC, SE, Fla.
– **persicifolia** Schreb. · G:Gräben-
Veilchen · ⌉ ⌢ Z5 VI-VII; Eur.*, W-Sib.,
E-Sib.
– **pinnata** L. · E:Pinnate Violet; G:Fieder-
blättriges Veilchen · ⌉ △ D Z5 VI; Eur.: F,
I, Sw, A, Slove.; Alp.
– *pontica* W. Becker = Viola suavis
– **pumila** Chaix · G:Niedriges Veilchen · ⌉
Z5 V-VI; Eur.* exc. BrI, Ib; W-Sib., E-Sib.,
C-As., China: Sinkiang
– **pyrenaica** Ramond ex DC. · E:Pyrenean
Violet; G:Pyrenäen-Veilchen · ⌉ IV-V;
Eur.: sp., Fr, I, C-Eur., Ba; Pyr., Alp.,
Jura, Apenn., Balkan; Cauc., Moroc.
– **reichenbachiana** Jord. ex Boreau ·
E:Early Dog Violet, Woodland Violet;
G:Wald-Veilchen · ⌉ Z6 III-VI; Eur.*, TR,
Cauc., Kashmir, Moroc.
– *rhodopeia* W. Becker = Viola stojanowii
– **riviniana** Rchb. · E:Wood Violet; G:Hain-
Veilchen · ⌉ Z5 IV-VI; Eur.*, Alger.,
Madeira
– *rugulosa* Greene = Viola canadensis var.
rugulosa
– **rupestris** F.W. Schmidt · E:Teesdale
Violet; G:Sand-Veilchen · ⌉ ⤳ △ V;
Eur.*, Cauc., NE-TR, W-Sib., E-Sib.,
Amur, Sakhal., C-As.
– × **scabra** DC. (*V. hirta* × *V. odorata*) ·
G:Raues Veilchen · ⌉
– *schultzii* Billot ex F.W. Schultz = Viola
canina subsp. schultzii
– *sepincola* Jord. = Viola suavis
– *silvatica* Fr. ex Hartm. = Viola reichenbachiana
– **sororia** Willd. · E:Confederate Violet,
Woolly Blue Violet; G:Pfingst-Veilchen ·
⌉ Z4 IV-V; Can.: E; USA: NE, NCE, NC,
Okla., SE
– **stojanowii** W. Becker · ⌉ △ Z6 V-VII;
NE-GR, S-BG
– **suavis** M. Bieb. · E:Downy Blue Violet;
G:Blaues Veilchen, Kornblumen-Veilchen
· ⌉ ⋈ Z5 III; Eur.* exc. BrI, Sc; Cauc.,
C-As.
– *sylvestris* Lam. = Viola reichenbachiana
– **thomasiana** Perr. & Songeon · G:Sch-
weizer Veilchen · ⌉ IV-VI; Eur.: F, I, Sw,

A; Alp.
– **tricolor** L. · E:Heartsease, Wild Pansy;
G:Gewöhnliches Wildes Stiefmütterchen
· ⌉ Z8 ⓚ IV-VIII ⚥ ; Eur.: SW-Ba; mts.
– **uliginosa** Besser · G:Moor-Veilchen · ⌉
⌢ D Z4 III-V; Eur.: Sc, G, PL, E-Eur.,
Slove.
– *variegata* Vuk. = Viola tricolor
– × **wittrockiana** Gams ex Kappert (*V.
altaica* × *V. lutea* × *V. tricolor* subsp.
tricolor) · E:Garden Pansy, Pansy;
G:Garten-Stiefmütterchen · ⊙ IV-X; cult.
– **many cultivars**
– *zoysii* Wulfen = Viola calcarata subsp.
zoysii
– **Cultivars:**
– **many cultivars, see Section III**

Virgilia Poir. -f- *Fabaceae* · 2 spp.
– *lutea* F. Michx. = Cladrastis lutea
– **oroboides** (P.J. Bergius) T.M. Salter · ♄
♄ Z9 ⓚ VII; S-Afr.

Virola Aubl. -f- *Myristicaceae* · 45 spp.
– **surinamensis** Warb. · E:Ukahuba Nut;
G:Baboen · ♄ ⓐ ⓝ; ne S-Am., Guyana,
Venez.

Viscaria (DC.) Röhl. = Silene
– *alpina* (L.) G. Don = Silene suecica
– *atropurpurea* Griseb. = Silene atropurpurea
– *oculata* Lindl. = Silene coeli-rosa
– *sartorii* Boiss. = Silene atropurpurea
– *viscosa* (Scop.) Asch. = Silene viscaria
– *vulgaris* Bernh. = Silene viscaria

Viscum L. -n- *Viscaceae* · 65-70 spp. ·
E:Mistletoe; F:Gui; G:Mistel
– **album** L. · E:Mistletoe; G:Mistel
– subsp. **abietis** (Wiesb.) Janch. ·
G:Tannen-Mistel · ♄ e Z5 III-V ⚘ ⓝ;
Eur.: sp., Cors, Fr, C-Eur., EC-Eur., Ba,
E-Eur.; TR, Cauc.
– subsp. **album** · E:Mistletoe; G:Laubholz-
Mistel · ♄ e ⊛ Z5 II-IV ⚥ ⚘; Eur.*, TR,
Cauc., N-Iran, Him., Amur, China, Korea,
Jap., Burma, Vietn., Alger.
– subsp. **austriacum** (Wiesb.) Vollm. ·
G:Kiefern-Mistel · ♄ e Z5 III-V ⚘;
Eur.: sp., F, Ital-P, C-Eur., EC-Eur., Ba,
EC-Eur.; TR, Moroc.

Visnea L. f. -f- *Theaceae* · 1 sp. · F:Visnéa;
G:Mocanbaum

– **mocanera** L. f. · G:Echter Mocanbaum ·
ℏ ℏ e D Z8 ⓚ III; Canar., Madeira

Vitaliana Sesl. -f- *Primulaceae* · 1 sp. ·
F:Androsace, Grégoria; G:Goldprimel
– **primuliflora** Bertol.
– subsp. **cinerea** (Sünd.) I.K. Ferguson · ⬝⎞
△ Z5 IV-V; Eur.: sp., F, I; mts.
– subsp. **praetutiana** (Buser ex Sünd.) I.K.
Ferguson · ⬝⎞ △ Z5 IV-V; Eur.: I; mts.
– subsp. **primuliflora** · G:Goldprimel · ⬝⎞
Z5 VI-VII; Eur.: I; mts.

Vitellaria C.F. Gaertn. -f- *Sapotaceae* ·
1 sp. · E:Shea Butter Tree; F:Vitellaire;
G:Schibutterbaum
– **paradoxa** C.F. Gaertn. · E:Shea Butter
Tree ; G:Schibutterbaum · ℏ Z10 ⓦ ⓝ;
trop. Afr.

Vitex L. -f- *Verbenaceae* · c. 250 spp. ·
E:Chastetree; F:Gattilier, Poivre sauvage;
G:Keuschbaum, Mönchspfeffer
– **agnus-castus** L. · E:Chaste Tree;
G:Mönchspfeffer · ℏ ℏ d Z7 ⓐ ∧ IX-X ⚥ ;
Eur.: Ib, Fr, Ital-P, Ba, Crim; TR, Cauc.,
Iran, C-As., NW-Afr.
– *cienkowskii* Kotschy ex Peyr. = Vitex
doniana
– *cuneata* Schumach. & Thonn. = Vitex
doniana
– **doniana** Sweet · ℏ d Z10 ⓦ ⓝ; trop. Afr.
– **negundo** L.
– var. *cannabifolia* (Siebold & Zucc.)
Hand.-Mazz. = Vitex negundo var.
heterophylla
– var. **heterophylla** (Franch.) Rehder · ℏ d
Z8 ⓚ VII-VIII; Mong., N-China, C-China
– var. *incisa* (Lam.) C.B. Clarke = Vitex
negundo var. heterophylla
– var. **negundo** · E:Chinese Chaste Tree;
G:Chinesischer Mönchspfeffer · ℏ ℏ d Z8
ⓚ VII-VIII ⚥ ; E-Afr., Madag., Ind., Sri
Lanka, Afgh., China, SE-As., Phil.
– **trifolia** L. · G:Dreiblatt-Keuschbaum

Vitis L. -f- *Vitaceae* · 60-70 spp. · E:Grape
Vine; F:Vigne; G:Rebe, Weinrebe,
Weintraube
– **aestivalis** Michx. · E:Summer Grape;
G:Sommer-Rebe · ℏ d ⚥ ⚬ Z6 VI ⓝ;
USA: NE, NCE, NC, SE
– **amurensis** Rupr. · E:Amur Grape;
G:Amur-Rebe · ℏ d ⚥ Z5 VI ⓝ; Amur,
N-China, Manch., Korea, Jap.

– **berlandieri** Planch. · E:Winter Grape · ℏ
d ⚥ ⚬ Z7 VI ⓝ; USA: N.Mex., Tex.
– **cinerea** Engelm. · E:Downy Grape;
G:Flaumige Rebe · ∫ d ⚥ Z5 VI; N-Am.
– **coignetiae** Pulliat ex Planch. · E:Crimson
Glory Vine; G:Rostrote Rebe · ℏ ∫ d ⚥ Z6
V-VII; Jap., Korea, Sakhal.
– **davidii** (Carrière) Foex · G:Davids Rebe ·
ℏ d ⚥ Z7 VI-VII; China
– *dissecta* Carrière = Ampelopsis aconitifolia
– **flexuosa** Thunb. · E:Creeping Grape · ℏ ∫
d ⚥ Z6 VI; China, Korea, Jap.
– *gongylodes* Burch. ex Baker = Cissus
gongylodes
– *heterophylla* Thunb. = Ampelopsis
brevipedunculata var. maximowiczii
– *japonica* Thunb. = Cayratia japonica
– *labrusca* auct. non L. = Vitis coignetiae
– **labrusca** L. · E:Fox Grape; G:Fuchs-Rebe
· ℏ d ⚥ ⚬ Z5 VI ⓝ; USA: NE, SE
– *orientalis* (Lam.) Boiss. = Ampelopsis
orientalis
– **palmata** Vahl · E:Catbird Grape;
G:Katzen-Rebe · ℏ d ⚥ Z5 VII-VIII; USA:
NCE, SC, SE
– *pterophora* Baker = Cissus gongylodes
– *quinquefolia* (L.) Lam. = Parthenocissus
quinquefolia var. quinquefolia
– **riparia** Michx. · E:Riverbank Grape;
G:Ufer-Rebe · ℏ ∫ d ⚥ D Z4 VI ⓝ; Can.: E;
USA: NE, NCE, NC, Rocky Mts., SW, SC,
SE
– **romanetii** Rom. Caill. · ∫ d ⚥ Z6; China
– **rotundifolia** Michx. · E:Muscadine
Grape; G:Muscadiner-Rebe · ℏ d ⚥ ⚬ Z5
VI ⓝ; USA: NE, NCE, SE, Fla., SC; Mex.
– **rupestris** Scheele · E:Bush Grape, Sand
Grape; G:Sand-Rebe · ℏ ∫ d ⚥ Z6 VI ⓝ;
USA: NE, NCE, SC, SE
– *sylvestris* C.C. Gmel. = Vitis vinifera
subsp. sylvestris
– **thunbergii** Siebold & Zucc. · G:Thun-
bergs Weinrebe · ℏ ∫ d ⚥ Z6 VI-VII; Jap.,
China, Korea, Taiwan
– *veitchii* Lynch = Parthenocissus tricuspidata
– **vinifera** L. · G:Weinrebe
– **many cultivars**
– subsp. **caucasica** Vavilov · ℏ d ⚥ Z7
VI-VII; C-As.
– subsp. **sylvestris** (C.C. Gmel.) Hegi ·
G:Wilde Weinrebe · ℏ d ⚥ Z7 VI-VII ▽;
Eur.: Ital-P, Ba, EC-Eur., E-Eur.; TR,
Cauc., N-Iran, C-As.

– subsp. **vinifera** · E:Common Grape
Vine, Grape, Vine; G:Kultur-Weinrebe,
Weintraube · ⚶ d ⚥ Z7 VI-VII ♀ ; cult., nat.
in Eur.
– *voinieriana* Baltet = Tetrastigma
voinierianum
– **vulpina** L. · E:Frost Grape; G:Winter-
Rebe · ♄ ⚶ d ⚥ ⚭ Z6 VI-VII Ⓝ; USA: NE,
NCE, Kans., SC, SE, Fla.

Vittadinia A. Rich. -f- *Asteraceae* · 29 spp.
– **australis** A. Rich. · E:Fuzzweed · ♄ Z9 ⓚ
VII-IX; Austr., Tasman., NZ
– *triloba* hort. non DC. = Erigeron karvinskianus

Vittaria Sm. -f- *Vittariaceae* · 62 spp. ·
F:Fougère rubannée; G:Bandfarn
– **lineata** (L.) J. Sm. · E:Appalachian
Shoestring Fern; G:Appalachen-Bandfarn
· ⚃ Z10 ⓜ; USA: Ga., Fla.; Mex., W.Ind.,
C-Am., S-Am.

Voandzeia Thouars = Vigna
– *subterranea* (L.) Thouars ex DC. = Vigna
subterranea

Volkameria L. = Clerodendrum
– *fragrans* Vent. = Clerodendrum philippinum

Vriesea Lindl. -f- *Bromeliaceae* · 262 spp.
– **atra** Mez · ⚃ Z10 ⓜ; Braz.
– **barilletii** E. Morren · ⚃ Z10 ⓜ; Braz.
– **bituminosa** Wawra · ⚃ Z10 ⓜ; Braz.
– *blokii* (Hemsl.) Mez = Vriesea regina
– **carinata** Wawra · ⚃ Z10 ⓜ; SE-Braz.
– **cereicola** (Mez) L.B. Sm. · ⚃ Z10 ⓜ;
N-Peru
– **chrysostachys** E. Morren · ⚃ Z10 ⓜ;
Col., Peru, Trinidad
– *conferta* Gaudich. = Vriesea ensiformis
– **corcovadensis** (Britten) Mez · ⚃ Z10 ⓜ;
Braz.
– **ensiformis** (Vell.) Beer · ⚃ Z10 ⓜ; Braz.
– **erythrodactylon** (E. Morren) E. Morren
ex Mez · ⚃ Z10 ⓜ; Braz.
– *espinosae* (L.B. Sm.) Gilmartin =
Tillandsia espinosae
– **fenestralis** Linden & André · ⚃ Z10 ⓜ;
Braz.
– **flammea** L.B. Sm. · ⚃ Z10 ⓜ; Braz.
– **fosteriana** L.B. Sm. · ⚃ Z10 ⓜ; Braz.
– **friburgensis** Mez · ⚃ Z10 ⓜ; Braz., Arg.
– **gigantea** Gaudich. · ⚃ Z10 ⓜ; Braz.

– **guttata** Linden & André · ⚃ Z10 ⓜ; Braz.
– **heliconioides** (Kunth) Hook. ex Walp. ·
⚃ Z10 ⓜ; C-Am., trop. S-Am.
– **hieroglyphica** (Carrière) E. Morren ·
E:King of Bromeliads · ⚃ Z10 ⓜ; Braz.
– **imperialis** E. Morren ex Baker · ⚃ Z10
ⓜ; Braz.
– **incurvata** Gaudich. · ⚃ Z10 ⓜ; Braz.
– var. *inflata* (Wawra) Mez = Vriesea
inflata
– **inflata** (Wawra) Wawra · ⚃ Z10 ⓜ;
Braz.
– **jonghei** (K. Koch) E. Morren · ⚃ Z10 ⓜ;
Braz.
– *longibracteata* (Baker) Mez = Vriesea
splendens
– **malzinei** E. Morren · ⚃ Z10 ⓜ; Mex.
– *musaica* (Linden & André) Cogn. &
Marchal = Guzmania musaica
– **olmosana** L.B. Sm. · ⚃ Z10 ⓜ IV; N-Peru
– **pardalina** Mez · ⚃ Z10 ⓜ; Braz.
– **platynema** Gaudich. · ⚃ Z10 ⓜ; Braz.
– **platzmannii** E. Morren · ⚃ Z10 ⓜ; Braz.
– **psittacina** (Hook.) Lindl. · ⚃ Z10 ⓜ;
Braz., Parag.
– **racinae** L.B. Sm. · ⚃ Z10 ⓜ; Braz.
– **regina** (Vell.) Beer · ⚃ Z10 ⓜ; Braz.
– **rodigasiana** E. Morren · ⚃ Z10 ⓜ; Braz.
– *rostrum-aquilae* Mez = Vriesea incurvata
– **saundersii** (Carrière) E. Morren · ⚃ Z10
ⓜ; Braz.
– **scalaris** E. Morren · ⚃ Z10 ⓜ; Braz.
– **sceptrum** Mez · ⚃ Z10 ⓜ; Braz.
– **simplex** (Vell.) Beer · ⚃ Z10 ⓜ; Col.,
Braz., Trinidad
– **splendens** (Brongn.) Lem. · E:Flaming
Sword; G:Flammendes Schwert · ⚃ Z10
ⓜ; Venez., Surinam
– var. *longibracteata* (Baker) L.B. Sm. =
Vriesea splendens
– *tesselata* (Linden & André) E. Morren =
Vriesea gigantea
– **zamorensis** (L.B. Sm.) L.B. Sm. · ⚃ Z10
ⓜ; Ecuad.

Vulpia C.C. Gmel. -f- *Poaceae* · 22 spp. ·
E:Fescue; F:Queue-de-renard, Vulpin;
G:Federschwingel, Fuchsschwingel
– **bromoides** (L.) Gray · E:Squirrel-tail
Fescue; G:Trespen-Federschwingel · ☉
VI-VIII; Eur.*, TR, Syr., Cauc. N-Afr.,
Macaron., nat. in Afr., N-As., S-Am.,
Austr., NZ
– **ciliata** Dumort. · E:Bearded Fescue;
G:Behaarter Federschwingel · ☉ IV-VI;

Eur.: Ib, Fr, BrI, Ital-P, Ba, RO, Crim; TR, Syr., Lebanon, Israel, Cauc., Iran, Afgh., Pakist., Him., C-As., N-Afr.
– **ligustica** (All.) Link · ☉; Eur.: Fr, Ital-P, Ba; TR, NW-Afr.
– **myuros** (L.) C.C. Gmel. · E:Rat's Tail Fescue; G:Mäuseschwanz-Federschwingel · ☉ VI-X; Eur.*, TR, Levant, Palest., Iraq, Cauc., Iran, Afgh., Pakist., C-As., Him., N-Afr.
– **unilateralis** (L.) Stace · E:Mat-grass Fescue; G:Strand-Dünnschwanz, Strand-Federschwingel · ☉ V-VI; Eur.: Fr, BrI, Ital-P, Sw, Ba, Crim; TR, Syr., Lebanon, Palest., Arab., Iraq, Cauc., Afgh., Pakist., Him., NW-Afr.

× **Vuylstekeara** hort. -f- *Orchidaceae* (*Cochlioda* × *Miltonia* × *Odontoglossum*)
– **Cultivars:**
– **many cultivars**

Wachendorfia Burm. -f- *Haemodoraceae* · 5 spp.
– *hirsuta* Thunb. = Wachendorfia paniculata
– **paniculata** Burm. · �4 Z9 🖾 IV; S-Afr.
– **thyrsiflora** Burm. · 4 Z9 🖾 V; S-Afr.

Wahlenbergia Schrad. ex Roth -f- *Campanulaceae* · 150-200 spp. · E:Rock Bell; F:Campanille; G:Moorglöckchen
– **capensis** (L.) A. DC. · E:Cape Bluebell; G:Kap-Moorglöckchen · ☉ Z9 VII-VIII; S-Afr.
– *elongata* (Willd.) Schrad. ex Roth = Wahlenbergia capensis
– *grandiflora* (Jacq.) Schrad. = Platycodon grandiflorus
– **hederacea** (L.) Rchb. · E:Ivy-leaved Bellflower; G:Efeu-Moorglöckchen · 4 ⁓ Z7 VI ▽; Eur.: BrI, G, Fr, Ib

Waitzia J.C. Wendl. -f- *Asteraceae* · 5 spp.
– **aurea** Steetz · ☉ 🖾 VII-VIII; Austr.
– **corymbosa** J.C. Wendl. · ☉ 🖾 VII-VIII; W-Austr.
– *grandiflora* J.V. Thomps. = Waitzia aurea
– **grandiflora** Naudin · ☉ 🖾 VII-VIII; Austr.
– *odontolepis* Turcz. = Waitzia suaveolens
– **suaveolens** (Benth.) Druce · ☉ 🖾 VII-VIII; Austr.

Waldsteinia Willd. -f- *Rosaceae* · 6 spp. ·

F:Fraisier doré; G:Golderdbeere, Waldsteinie
– **fragarioides** (Michx.) Tratt. · E:Barren Strawberry; G:Golderdbeere · 4 Z3 V-VI; Can.: E; USA: NE, NCE, SE
– **geoides** Willd. · 4 Z5 IV-V; Eur.: EC-Eur., Ba, E-Eur., nat. in D
– **ternata** (Stephan) Fritsch · G:Dreiblättrige Waldsteinie · 4 ⤳ Z3 IV-V; Eur.: C-Eur., EC-Eur., Ba, E-Eur.; E-Sib., Amur, Sakhal., N-Jap., nat. in FIN
– subsp. *trifolia* (Rochel ex W.D.J. Koch) Teppner = Waldsteinia ternata
– *trifolia* Rochel ex W.D.J. Koch = Waldsteinia ternata

Wallichia Roxb. -f- *Arecaceae* · 10 spp.
– **caryotoides** Roxb. · ℏ e Z9 🖾; Ind., Burma
– **densiflora** Mart. · ℏ e Z9 🖾; Ind., Assam
– **disticha** T. Anderson · ℏ e Z9 🖾; Him., Ind., Burma

× **Warneara** hort. -f- *Orchidaceae* (*Comparettia* × *Oncidium* × *Rodriguezia*)

Warrea Lindl. -f- *Orchidaceae* · 4 spp.
– **warreana** (Lodd. ex Lindl.) C. Schweinf. · 4 Z10 🖾 VII-VIII ▽ ✳; Col., Venez.

Warscewiczella Rchb. f. = Cochleanthes
– *amazonica* Rchb. f. & Warsz. = Cochleanthes amazonica
– *discolor* (Lindl.) Schult. & Garay = Cochleanthes discolor
– *flabelliformis* (Sw.) Schult. & Garay = Cochleanthes flabelliformis
– *wailesiana* (Lindl.) E. Morren = Cochleanthes wailesiana

Wasabia Matsum. -f- *Brassicaceae* · 2-4 spp. · E:Wasabi; F:Raifort vert, Wasabi; G:Japanischer Meerrettich
– **japonica** (Miq.) Matsum. · E:Japanese Horseradish; G:Japanischer Meerrettich · 4 Z8 🖾 ⚥ Ⓝ; Jap., E-Sib.

Washingtonia H. Wendl. -f- *Arecaceae* · 2 spp. · E:Washingtonia; F:Palmier éventail, Washingtonia; G:Priesterpalme, Washingtonpalme
– **filifera** (Linden ex André) H. Wendl. · E:California Fan Palm, California Washingtonia, Cotton Palm; G:Kalifornische

Washingtonpalme · ♄ e Z9 ⌂; USA: S-Calif., Ariz.; Baja Calif.
– var. *robusta* (H. Wendl.) Parish = Washingtonia robusta
– **robusta** H. Wendl. · E:Mexican Fan Palm, Mexican Washingtonia; G:Mexikanische Washingtonpalme · ♄ e Z9 ⌂; Mex.
– *sonorae* S. Watson = Washingtonia robusta

Watsonia Mill. -f- *Iridaceae* · 51 sp. · E:Bugle Iris; F:Watsonia; G:Watsonie
– *beatricis* J.W. Mathews & L. Bolus = Watsonia pillansii
– **borbonica** (Pourr.) Goldblatt · ⚄ Z9 ⌂; S-Afr. (Cape Prov.)
– *bulbillifera* J.W. Mathews & L. Bolus = Watsonia meriana
– **densiflora** Baker · ⚄ Z9 ⌂ VI-VII; S-Afr: Natal, Orange Free State, Transvaal
– **humilis** Mill. · ⚄ Z9 ⌂ VI; Cape
– **meriana** (L.) Mill. · ⚄ Z9 ⌂ V-VI; Cape
– **pillansii** L. Bolus · ⚄ Z7 ⌂; S-Afr. (Cape Prov., Natal)
– *rosea* Ker-Gawl. = Watsonia borbonica

Wattakaka Hassk. = Dregea
– *sinensis* (Hemsl.) Stapf = Dregea sinensis

Weberbauerocereus Backeb. -m- *Cactaceae* · 4-8 spp.
– **fascicularis** (Meyen) Backeb. · ♄ ⚇ Z9 ⌂ ▽ ✲; S-Peru, N-Chile
– *horridispinus* Rauh & Backeb. = Weberbauerocereus weberbaueri
– **weberbaueri** (Vaupel) Backeb. · ♄ ⚇ Z9 ⌂ ▽ ✲; Peru

Weberocereus Britton & Rose -m- *Cactaceae* · 9 spp.
– **tonduzii** (F.A.C. Weber) G.D. Rowley · ♄ ⚇ ⚶ ⚶ ⤳ Z9 ⌂ ▽ ✲; Costa Rica

Wedelia Jacq. -f- *Asteraceae* · c. 70 spp.
– **trilobata** (L.) Hitchc. · E:Goldcup · ⚄ ⚶ ⚶ ⤳ Z10 ⌂ VII-IX; USA: S-Fla., W.Ind., trop. Am.

Weigela Thunb. -f- *Caprifoliaceae* · 10 spp. · E:Weigela; F:Weigelia; G:Weigelie
– **coraeensis** Thunb. · G:Koreanische Weigelie · ♄ d Z6 V-VII; Jap.
– **decora** (Nakai) Nakai · G:Nikko-Weigelie · ♄ d Z6; Jap.
– **floribunda** (Siebold & Zucc.) K. Koch ·

G:Reichblütige Weigelie · ♄ d Z6 V-VI; Jap.
– **florida** (Bunge) A. DC. · G:Liebliche Weigelie · ♄ d Z5 V-VI; Korea, Manch., N-China
– **many cultivars**
– *grandiflora* (Siebold & Zucc.) Fortune = Weigela coraeensis
– **hortensis** (Siebold & Zucc.) C.A. Mey. · G:Garten-Weigelie · ♄ d Z7 V-VI; Jap.
– **japonica** Thunb. · G:Japanische Weigelie · ♄ d Z6 V-VI; China, Jap.
– **maximowiczii** (S. Moore) Rehder · ♄ d Z6 V-VI; Jap.
– **middendorffiana** (Trautv. & C.A. Mey.) K. Koch · G:Gelbblütige Weigelie · ♄ d Z5 V-VI; Amur, Sakhal. Kurilen, Jap.
– **praecox** (Lemoine) L.H. Bailey · G:Frühblühende Weigelie · ♄ d Z5 V; Korea, Manch.
– *rosea* Lindl. = Weigela florida
– **Cultivars:**
– **many cultivars**

Weingaertneria Bernh. = Corynephorus
– *canescens* (L.) Bernh. = Corynephorus canescens

Weingartia Werderm. -f- *Cactaceae* · 4-9 spp.
– *buiningiana* F. Ritter = Weingartia neocumingii
– *corroana* Cárdenas = Weingartia neocumingii
– *erinacea* F. Ritter = Weingartia neocumingii
– **fidaiana** (Backeb.) Werderm. · ⚇ Z9 ⌂; Bol.
– *knitzei* F.H. Brandt = Weingartia neocumingii
– *multispina* F. Ritter = Weingartia neocumingii
– **neocumingii** Backeb. · ⚇ Z9 ⌂ ▽ ✲; Bol.
– **neumanniana** (Backeb.) Werderm. · ⚇ Z9 ⌂; Arg.: Jujuy
– *pilcomayensis* Cárdenas = Weingartia neocumingii
– *pulquinensis* Cárdenas = Weingartia neocumingii
– *trollii* Oeser = Weingartia neocumingii

Weldenia Schult. f. -f- *Commelinaceae* · 1 sp. · G:Weldenie
– **candida** Schult. f. · G:Weldenie · ⚄ Z9 ⌂ IV-V; Mex., Guat.

Wellingtonia Lindl. = Sequoiadendron
– *gigantea* Lindl. = Sequoiadendron
  giganteum

Welwitschia Hook. f. -f- *Welwitschiaceae* ·
  1 sp. · F:Welwitschia; G:Welwitschie
– **mirabilis**
– subsp. **mirabilis** · G:Angola-Welwitschie ·
  ♄ e Z9 ⓦ ▽ ✳; Angola
– subsp. **namibiana** Leuenb. · G:Namibia-
  Welwitschie · ♄ e Z9 ▽ ✳; Namibia

Wercklea Pittier & Standl. -f- *Malvaceae* ·
  12 spp.
– **insignis** Pittier & Standl. · ♄ e Z10 ⓚ;
  Costa Rica

Westringia Sm. -f- *Lamiaceae* · 29 spp.
– **fruticosa** (Willd.) Druce · E:Australian
  Rosemary; G:Australischer Rosmarin
  · ♄ e Z10 ⓚ IV-VII; Austr.: Queensl.,
  N.S.Wales
– *rosmariniformis* Sm. = Westringia
  fruticosa

Whitesloanea Chiov. -f- *Asclepiadaceae* ·
  1 sp.
– **crassa** (N.E. Br.) Chiov. · ⁴ ⵜ Z10 ⓚ;
  Somalia

Whitfieldia Hook. -f- *Acanthaceae* · 10 spp.
– **elongata** C.B. Clarke · ⁴ e Z10 ⓦ VI-VIII;
  W-Afr.
– **lateritia** Hook. · ♄ e Z10 ⓦ I-V; Afr.:
  Sierra Leone

Whitlavia Harv. = Phacelia
– *grandiflora* Harv. = Phacelia minor

Widdringtonia Endl. -f- *Cupressaceae* ·
  4 spp. · E:African Cypress; F:Cyprès
  africain; G:Afrikazypresse
– **cedarbergensis** J. Marshall ·
  E:Clanwilliam Cedar; G:Clanwilliams
  Afrikazypresse · ♄ e Z9 ⓚ Ⓝ; S-Afr.
– *cupressoides* (L.) Endl. = Widdringtonia
  nodiflora
– *dracomontana* Stapf = Widdringtonia
  nodiflora
– *juniperoides* (L.) Endl. = Widdringtonia
  cedarbergensis
– **nodiflora** (L.) Powrie · E:Mountain
  Cedar; G:Milanji-Afrikazypresse · ♄ ♄
  e Z9 ⓚ Ⓝ; E-Afr., Zambia, Zimbabwe,
  S-Afr. (N-Transvaal)

– **schwarzii** (Marloth) Mast. ·
  E:Willowmore Cedar; G:Schwarz'
  Afrikazypresse · ♄ e Z10 ⓚ; S-Afr.
– **whytei** Rendle · E:Mulanje Cedar;
  G:Whytes Afrikazypresse

Wigandia Kunth -f- *Hydrophyllaceae* ·
  2-3 spp. · F:Wigandia; G:Wigandie
– **caracasana** Kunth · ♄ Z10 ⓚ; S-Mex.,
  C-Am., Col., Venez., nat. in SW-Eur.

Wigginsia D.M. Porter = Notocactus
– *arechavaletai* (Mackie) D.M. Porter =
  Notocactus erinaceus
– *corynodes* (Otto ex Pfeiff.) D.M. Porter =
  Notocactus erinaceus
– *erinacea* (Haw.) D.M. Porter = Notocactus erinaceus
– *fricii* (Arechav.) D.M. Porter = Notocactus
  erinaceus
– *leucocarpa* (Arechav.) D.M. Porter =
  Notocactus erinaceus
– *sellowii* (Link & Otto) D.M. Porter =
  Notocactus erinaceus
– *sessiliflora* (Mackie) D.M. Porter =
  Notocactus erinaceus
– *tephracantha* (Link & Otto) D.M. Porter =
  Notocactus erinaceus
– *vorwerkiana* (Backeb.) D.M. Porter =
  Notocactus erinaceus

Wikstroemia Endl. -f- *Thymelaeaceae* ·
  c.70 spp.
– **alberti** Regel · ♄ VI; C-As.; mts.

Wilcoxia Britton & Rose -f- *Cactaceae* ·
  3 spp.
– **albiflora** Backeb. · ♄ ⵜ Z9 ⓚ; Mex.
  (Sonora, Sinaloa)
– **poselgeri** (Lem.) Britton & Rose ·
  E:Dahlia Cactus, Pencil Cactus · ♄ ⵜ Z9
  ⓚ; S-Tex., NE-Mex.
– **schmollii** (Weing.) Backeb. · E:Lamb's
  Tail Cactus · ♄ ⵜ Z9 ⓚ; Mex. (Querétaro,
  Hidalgo)
– *striata* (K. Brandegee) Britton & Rose =
  Peniocereus striatus
– *viperina* (F.A.C. Weber) Britton & Rose =
  Peniocereus viperinus

Willemetia Neck. -f- *Asteraceae* · 2 spp. ·
  F:Willemétie; G:Kronenlattich
– **stipitata** (Jacq.) Dalla Torre · G:Gestiel-
  ter Kronenlattich · ⁴ VI-VIII; Eur.: F, I,
  C-Eur., Ba

Willughbeia Roxb. -f- *Apocynaceae* · 17 spp.
– **coriacea** Wall. · ♄ ⚥ Z10 ⓦ Ⓝ; Malay.
Pen.
– *firma* Blume = Willughbeia coriacea

× **Wilsonara** hort. -f- *Orchidaceae*
(*Cochlioda* × *Odontoglossum* × *Oncidium*)
– **Cultivars:**
– **many cultivars**

Winteria F. Ritter = Hildewintera
– *aureispina* F. Ritter = Hildewintera
aureispina

Wissadula Medik. -f- *Malvaceae* · 40 spp.
– **periplocifolia** (L.) Thwaites · ♄ Z10 ⓦ
Ⓝ; Trop.

Wisteria Nutt. -f- *Fabaceae* · 6 spp. ·
E:Wisteria; F:Glycine; G:Blauregen,
Glyzine, Wisterie
– *brachybotrys* Siebold & Zucc. = Wisteria
floribunda
– var. *alba* W.T. Mill. = Wisteria venusta
– *chinensis* DC. = Wisteria sinensis
– **floribunda** (Willd.) DC. · E:Japanese
Wisteria; G:Japanischer Blauregen · ∫ d ⚥
Z6 V-VI �££; Jap.
– **many cultivars**
– × **formosa** Rehder (*W. floribunda* × *W.
sinensis*) · G:Duft-Blauregen · ∫ d ⚥ Z5 �££;
cult.
– **frutescens** (L.) Poir. · E:American
Wisteria; G:Amerikanischer Blauregen ·
♄ d ⚥ Z5 VII-IX �££; USA: NE, SE, Fla., SC
– **macrostachya** (Torr. & A. Gray) Nutt. ·
E:Kentucky Wisteria; G:Kentucky-
Blauregen · ♄ d ⚥ Z6 VI-VII �££; USA:
NCE, SC, SE
– *multijuga* Van Houtte = Wisteria
floribunda
– **sinensis** (Sims) Sweet · E:Chinese
Wisteria; G:Chinesischer Blauregen · ♄ ∫
d ⚥ Z6 IV-V �££; China, nat. in USA: NE
– **many cultivars**
– *speciosa* Nutt. = Wisteria frutescens
– **venusta** Rehder & E.H. Wilson · E:Silky
Wisteria; G:Seidiger Blauregen · ♄ d ⚥ Z6
VI-VII �££; China

Withania Pauquy -f- *Solanaceae* · 10 spp.
– **somnifera** (L.) Dunal · ♄ e ⓚ ⚥ �££;
Eur.: Ib, I; Canar., Ind., Afr.

× **Withnerara** hort. -f- *Orchidaceae*

(*Aspasia* × *Miltonia* × *Odontoglossum* ×
Oncidium)

Witsenia Thunb. -f- *Iridaceae* · 1 sp.
– *corymbosa* Ker-Gawl. = Nivenia corymbosa
– **maura** Thunb. · ♄ Z9 ⓚ; S-Afr.

Wittia K. Schum. = Wittiocactus
– *amazonica* K. Schum. = Wittiocactus
amazonicus
– *costaricensis* Britton & Rose = Pseudorhipsalis himantoclada
– *panamensis* Britton & Rose = Wittiocactus
amazonicus

Wittiocactus Rauschert -m- *Cactaceae* ·
1 sp.
– **amazonicus** (K. Schum.) Rauschert · ⵑ
Z10 ⓦ ▽ ✳; Costa Rica, Panama, Col.,
Ecuad., Peru, Venez., Braz.
– *panamensis* (Britton & Rose) Rauschert =
Wittiocactus amazonicus

Wittmackia Mez = Aechmea
– *lingulata* (L.) Mez = Aechmea lingulata

Wittrockia Lindm. -f- *Bromeliaceae* · 6 spp.
– *amazonica* (Baker) L.B. Sm. = Nidularium
amazonicum
– **gigantea** (Baker) Leme; SE-Braz.

Wolffia Horkel ex Schleid. -f- *Lemnaceae* ·
11 sp. · E:Watermeal; F:Petite lentille,
Wolffia; G:Zwergwasserlinse
– **arrhiza** (L.) Horkel ex Wimm. ·
G:Wurzellose Zwergwasserlinse · ⵑ ≈
Z7; Eur.* exc. Sc; Cauc., Ind., Afr., Austr.

Wollemia W.G. Jones, K.D. Hill & J.M.
Allen -f- *Araucariaceae* · 1 sp. · E:Wollemi
Pine; G:Wollemikiefer
– **nobilis** W.G. Jones, K.D. Hill & J.M.
Allen · E:Wollemi Pine; G:Wollemikiefer

Woodsia R. Br. -f- *Woodsiaceae* · 40 spp. ·
E:Woodsia; F:Fougère ciliée, Woodsia;
G:Wimperfarn
– **alpina** (Bolton) Gray · E:Northern Cliff
Fern, Northern Woodsia; G:Alpen-
Wimperfarn · ⵑ △ Z5 VII-VIII ▽; Eur.*;
N, mts.; TR, Cauc., Him., W-Sib., E-Sib.,
Kamchat., N-Am., Greenl.
– *hyperborea* (Lilj.) R. Br. = Woodsia alpina
– **ilvensis** (L.) R. Br. · E:Rusty Cliff Fern,

Rusty Woodsia; G:Rostroter Wimperfarn, Südlicher Wimperfarn · ♃ △ Z1 VII-VIII ▽; Eur.* exc. Ib; W-Sib., E-Sib., Amur, Sakhal., Kamchat., C-As.
- subsp. *arvonica* (With.) Milde = Woodsia alpina
- **obtusa** (Spreng.) Torr. · E:Blunt Lobe Cliff Fern, Common Woodsia; G:Stumpfblättriger Wimperfarn · ♃ △ Z4 ▽; Can.: E; USA: NE, NCE, NC, SC, SE
- **polystichoides** Eaton · ♃ △ Z4 ▽; Amur, China, Manch., Korea, Jap., Sakhal., Taiwan
- **pulchella** Bertol. · G:Zierlicher Wimperfarn · ♃ △ Z5 VII-VIII ▽; Pyr., E-Alp., C-Alp.

Woodwardia Sm. -f- *Blechnaceae* · 14 spp. · E:Chain Fern; F:Woodwardia; G:Grübchenfarn, Kettenfarn
- **areolata** (L.) T. Moore · E:Netted Chain Fern; G:Netz-Kettenfarn · ♃ ~ Z7 ∧; Can.: E; USA: NE, NCE, SC, SE, Fla.
- **radicans** (L.) Sm. · E:European Chain Fern; G:Europäischer Kettenfarn · ♃ Z8 Ⓚ ▽; Eur.: Ib.Ital-P, Crete, Canar., Madeira; Alger.
- **virginica** (L.) Sm. · E:Virginia Chain Fern; G:Virginischer Kettenfarn · ♃ ~ Z7 ∧; Can.: E; USA: NE, NCE, SC, SE, Fla.; Bermuda

Worsleya (Traub) Traub -f- *Amaryllidaceae* · 1 sp. · E:Blue Amaryllis; F:Amaryllis bleu; G:Blaue Amaryllis
- **rayneri** (Hook.) Traub & Moldenke · E:Blue Amaryllis; G:Blaue Amaryllis · ♃ Z10 Ⓦ VII-IX; Braz. (Serra dos Orgaos)

Wulfenia Jacq. -f- *Scrophulariaceae* · 3 (-5) spp. · F:Wulfénia; G:Kuhtritt, Wulfenie
- **amherstiana** Benth. · G:Himalaya-Kuhtritt · ♃ △ Z5 VI-VII; Afgh., Him.
- **baldaccii** Degen · G:Albanischer Kuhtritt · ♃ △ Z7 V-VI; N-AL
- **carinthiaca** Jacq. · G:Kärntner Kuhtritt · ♃ △ Z5 VII; Eur.: I, A, Montenegro, ? AL; SE-Alp., Montenegro
- **orientalis** Boiss. · G:Türkischer Kuhtritt · ♃ △ Ⓐ ∧ V-VI; TR
- × **suendermannii** hort. (*W. baldaccii* × *W. carinthiaca*) · G:Sündermanns Kuhtritt · ♃ △ V-VI; cult.

Wurmbea Thunb. -f- *Colchicaceae* · 42 spp.
- **capensis** Thunb. · ♃ Z10 Ⓚ V-VI; S-Afr.

Wyethia Nutt. -f- *Asteraceae*
- **angustifolia** (DC.) Nutt. · E:California Compassplant · ♃ Z7 ∧ VII-VIII; USA: Wash., Oreg., Calif.
- **helenioides** (DC.) Nutt. · E:Mule's Ear Daisy · ♃ Z7 ∧ VII-VIII; C-Calif.
- **mollis** A. Gray · E:Woolly Mule's Ears · ♃ Z8 Ⓚ ∧ VII-VIII; USA: Calif., Nev.
- **ovata** Torr. & A. Gray ex Torr. · E:Southern Mule's Ears · ♃ △ Z8 Ⓐ ∧ V-VI; Calif.

Xantheranthemum Lindau -n- *Acanthaceae* · 1 sp.
- **igneum** (Linden) Lindau · ♃ ⇝ Z9 Ⓦ; Peru

Xanthium L. -n- *Asteraceae* · 3 spp. · E:Cocklebur; F:Lampourde; G:Spitzklette
- **albinum** (Widder) H. Scholz · G:Ufer-Spitzklette
- subsp. **albinum** · G:Elbe-Spitzklette · ⊙ VIII-X; Eur.: Fr, C-Eur., EC-Eur., Sc, E-Eur.
- subsp. **riparium** (Čelak.) Widder & Wagenitz · G:Östliche Ufer-Spitzklette · ⊙ Ⓝ; Eur.: G, PL, Balt.
- **Brazilicum** Vell. · ⊙; W-As.
- **italicum** Moretti · G:Italienische Spitzklette · ⊙ VII-X; Eur.: sp., F, I, Slove.; TR
- **orientale** L. · G:Großfrüchtige Spitzklette · ⊙ VIII-IX; Eur.: sp., F, N-I., Sw, G, A, Slov.
- *riparium* Lasch = Xanthium albinum subsp. riparium
- *rupicola* Holub = Xanthium albinum subsp. riparium
- **saccharatum** Wallr. · E:Canada Cocklebur · G:Zucker-Spitzklette · ⊙ VIII-X; N-Am., nat. in A, D
- **spinosum** L. · E:Clotweed, Cocklebur; G:Dornige Spitzklette · ⊙ VIII-IX; S-Am., nat. in Eur.* exc. Sc, BrI; cosmop. exc. trop. As.
- **strumarium** L. · E:California Burr; G:Gewöhnliche Spitzklette · ⊙ VII-X ⚕; Eur.* exc. BrI, Sc; TR, Cauc., Iran, W-Sib., C-As., N-Am., nat. in cosmop.

Xanthoceras Bunge -n- *Sapindaceae* · 1 sp. · F:Epine jaune; G:Gelbhorn
- **sorbifolium** Bunge · G:Gelbhorn · ♄ ♄ d

Z6 V-VI; N-China

Xanthocyparis Farjon & Hiepko -f-
Cupressaceae · 2 spp. · G:Goldzypresse
– **nootkatensis** (D. Don) Farjon · E:Alaska
Cedar, Nootka Cypress; F:Cyprès de
Nootka, Cyprès pleureur de l'Alaska;
G:Nutka-Goldzypresse · ♄ ♄ e Z5 III-VI ⚘
Ⓝ; Alaska, Can.: B.C.; USA: NW, Calif.

Xanthophthalmum Sch. Bip. = Glebionis
– *coronarium* (L.) Trehane ex Cullen =
Glebionis coronaria var. coronaria
– *segetum* (L.) Sch. Bip. = Glebionis
segetum

Xanthorhiza Marshall -f- *Ranunculaceae* ·
I sp. · F:Xanthorhiza; G:Gelbwurz
– **simplicissima** Marshall · E:Yellowroot;
G:Gelbwurz · ♄ d Z4 IV-V; USA: NE, SE,
Fla.

Xanthorrhoea Sm. -f- *Xanthorrhoeaceae* ·
28 spp. · E:Grass Tree; F:Black boy;
G:Grasbaum
– **australis** R. Br. · E:Austral Grass Tree,
Botany Bay Gum; G:Südlicher Grasbaum
· ♃ e Z10 ⓜ; Austr.: N.S. Wales, S-Austr.,
Tasman., Victoria
– **hastilis** R. Br. · G:Spießförmiger Grasbaum · ♃ e Z10 ⓜ Ⓝ; Austr.: N.S.Wales,
Victoria
– **quadrangulata** F. Muell. · G:Vierkantiger
Grasbaum · ♃ e Z10 ⓜ; S-Austr.

Xanthosoma Schott -n- *Araceae* · 65 spp. ·
E:Malanga, Tannia, Yautia; F:Tanier taro;
G:Goldnarbe
– *atrovirens* K. Koch & C.D. Bouché =
Xanthosoma sagittifolium
– **belophyllum** Kunth · G:Pfeilblättrige
Goldnarbe · ♃ Z10 ⓜ Ⓝ; Venez., nat. in
W.Ind., n S-Am.
– **Braziliense** (Desf.) Engl. · G:Brazil-
ianische Goldnarbe · ♃ Z10 ⓜ Ⓝ; W.Ind.,
trop. S-Am.
– **caracu** K. Koch & C.D. Bouché · ♃ Z10 ⓜ
Ⓝ; trop. Am., nat. in Afr.
– *jacquinii* Schott = Xanthosoma undipes
– *lindenii* (André) T. Moore = Caladium
lindenii
– *mafaffa* Schott = Xanthosoma sagittifolium
– **maximiliani** Schott · ♃ Z10 ⓜ; Braz.
– *nigrum* (Vell.) Mansf. = Xanthosoma

sagittifolium
– **robustum** Schott · E:Capote; G:Capote-
Goldnarbe · ♃ Z10 ⓜ; Mex., C-Am.
– **sagittifolium** (L.) Schott · E:Malanga;
G:Tania-Goldnarbe · ♃ Z10 ⓜ Ⓝ; orig. ?;
cult. trop. Am., trop. Afr.
– **undipes** (K. Koch & C.D. Bouché) K.
Koch · G:Mexikanische Goldnarbe · ♃
Z10 ⓜ Ⓝ; Mex., C-Am., trop. S-Am., cult.
W.Ind.
– *violaceum* Schott = Xanthosoma sagittifolium

Xeranthemum L. -n- *Asteraceae* · 6 spp. ·
F:Immortelle annuelle, Xéranthème;
G:Papierblume
– **annuum** L. · E:Common Immortelle;
G:Einjährige Papierblume · ⊙ ⚘ VI-IX;
Eur.: A, EC-Eur., Ba, E-Eur.; TR, Syr.,
Lebanon, Cauc., NW-Iran, nat. in sp., I
– **inapertum** (L.) Mill. · G:Felsenheide-
Papierblume · ⊙ VI-VIII; Eur.: Ib, Fr,
Ital-P, Ba, Sw; TR, Cyprus, Lebanon,
Cauc., NW-Afr.
– *sesamoides* L. = Edmondia sesamoides

Xerochrysum Tzvelev -n- *Asteraceae* ·
6 spp. · G:Strohblume
– **bracteatum** (Vent.) Tzvelev · E:Paper
Daisy, Straw Daisy; G:Garten-Strohb-
lume · ⊙ ⚘ Z8 ⓜ VII-IX; S-Austr., nat.
in sp.

Xerophyllum Michx. -n- *Melanthiaceae* ·
2-3 spp. · E:Bear Grass, Elk Grass;
F:Xérophylle; G:Bärengras, Truthahnbart
– **asphodeloides** (L.) Nutt. · E:Turkey
Beard; G:Truthahnbart · ♃ Z7 ∧ V-VII;
USA: NE, SE
– **tenax** (Pursh) Nutt. · E:Elkgrass, Western
Turkeybeard; G:Bärengras · ♃ ⚘ Z7 ∧
VI-VII; B.C., USA: NW, Rocky Mts., Calif.

Xerosicyos Humbert -m- *Cucurbitaceae* ·
4 spp.
– **danguyi** Humbert · ♄ ⚭ Z10 ⓐ; Madag.
– **perrieri** Humbert · ♃ ⚭ ⚶ Z10 ⓐ; Madag.

Ximenia L. -f- *Olacaceae* · 8 spp. · G:Fals-
ches Sandelholz
– **americana** L. · E:Hog Plum, Tallow
Wood; G:Falsches Sandelholz · ♄ Z8
ⓐ Ⓝ; USA: Fla.; Mex., W.Ind., C-Am.,
S-Am., Trop. Old World

Xiphidium Aubl. -n- *Haemodoraceae* · 1 sp.
– **coeruleum** Aubl. · 4 Z10 ⓦ V-VI; Mex.,
C-Am., W.Ind., S-Am.

Xylia Benth. -f- *Mimosaceae* · 13 spp.
– **xylocarpa** (Roxb.) Taub. · ♄ d Z10 ⓦ Ⓝ;
Ind., Burma, S-Vietn., Malay. Pen., Phil.

Xylobium Lindl. -n- *Orchidaceae* · 31 sp.
– **hyacinthinum** (Rchb. f.) Schltr. · 4 Z10
ⓦ VII-VIII ▽ ✳; Venez.
– **variegatum** (Ruiz & Pav.) Garay &
Dunst. · 4 Z10 ⓦ VIII-IX ▽ ✳; C-Am.,
trop. S-Am.

Xylomelum Sm. -n- *Proteaceae* · 2 spp. ·
E:Woody Pear; F:Xylomèle; G:Holzbirne
– **pyriforme** (Gaertn.) R. Br. · E:Woody
Pear; G:Gewöhnliche Holzbirne · ♄ ✕
Z10 ⓐ; Austr.: Queensl., N.S.Wales

Xylopia L. -f- *Annonaceae* · c. 160 spp. ·
F:Malaguette, Maniguette; G:Mohren-
pfeffer
– **aethiopica** (Dunal) A. Rich. · E:Guinea
Pepper; G:Mohrenpfeffer · ♄ e Z10 ⓦ Ⓝ;
W-Afr., C-Afr.
– **aromatica** Baill. · G:Guineapfeffer,
Malaguetapfeffer · e Z10 Ⓝ; Afr., nat. in
S-Am., Antill.
– **quintasii** Pierre ex Engl. & Diels ·
E:Negro Pepper · ♄ e Z10 ⓦ Ⓝ; W-Afr.
– *striata* Engl. = Xylopia quintasii

Xylopleurum Spach = Oenothera
– *speciosum* (Nutt.) Raim. = Oenothera
speciosa

Xylosma G. Forst. -f- *Flacourtiaceae* ·
85-100 spp.
– **japonicum** (Walp.) A. Gray · ♄ e; China,
Taiwan, Jap.

Xyris L. -f- *Xyridaceae* · 352 spp. · E:Yellow-
eyed Grass; F:Jonc-sabre; G:Degenbinse
– **capensis** Thunb. · 4 Z10 ⓦ; trop. Afr.,
S-Afr.
– **indica** L. · E:Yellow-eyed Grass;
G:Gelbaugengras, Indische Degenbinse ·
4 Z10 ⓦ; Ind.
– **operculata** Labill. · G:Australische
Degenbinse · 4 Z10 ⓦ; Austr.

Xysmalobium R. Br. -n- *Asclepiadaceae* ·
10 spp.

– **undulatum** (L.) R. Br. · 4 Z9 ⓐ ♀ ⚸;
S-Afr.

✕ **Yamadara** hort. -f- *Orchidaceae* (*Cattleya*
✕ *Epidendrum* ✕ *Laelia* ✕ *Rhyncholaelia*)

✕ **Yapara** hort. -f- *Orchidaceae*
(*Phalaenopsis* ✕ *Rhynchostylis* ✕ *Vanda*)

Yucca L. -f- *Agavaceae* · 47 spp. · E:Spanish
Dagger; F:Yucca; G:Palmlilie
– **aloifolia** L. · E:Dagger Plant, Spanish
Bayonet; G:Graue Palmlilie · ♈ Z8 ⓐ
VIII-IX; USA: SE, Fla.; E-Mex., W.Ind.
– *angustifolia* Pursh = Yucca glauca
– **angustissima** Engelm. ex Trel.
– var. **angustissima** E:Narrowleaf Yucca ·
♈ Z8 ⓐ; USA: Ariz., N.Mex., Utah, Nev.
– var. **kanabensis** (McKelvey) Reveal ·
E:Kanab Yucca · ♈
– *arborescens* (Torr.) Trel. = Yucca
brevifolia
– *arizonica* McKelvey = Yucca ✕ schottii
– *australis* (Engelm.) Trel. = Yucca filifera
– **baccata** Torr. · E:Banana Yucca, Blue
Yucca; G:Blaue Palmlilie · ♈ Z9 ⓐ; USA:
Rocky Mts., SW
– **brevifolia** Engelm. · E:Joshua Tree;
G:Josua-Palmlilie · ♈ Z8 ⓐ; USA: Calif.,
Rocky Mts, SW
– *bulbifera* hort. = Furcraea parmentieri
– **decipiens** Trel. · ♈; Mex.
– **desmetiana** Baker · ♈ Z9 ⓐ; Mex.
– **elata** Engelm. · E:Palmella, Soap Tree;
G:Seifen-Palmlilie · ♈ Z9 ⓐ; USA: Ariz.,
N.Mex., Tex.; Mex.
– **elephantipes** Regel · E:Elephant Yucca;
G:Riesen-Palmlilie · ♈ Z10 ⓐ VIII-IX;
Mex., Guat.
– **filamentosa** L. · E:Adam's Needle,
Spoonleaf Yucca; G:Fädige Palmlilie · 4
Z5 VIII-IX; USA: NE, SE, Fla.
– **some cultivars**
– **filifera** Chabaud · ♈ Z8 ⓐ VII-IX; Mex.
– **flaccida** Haw. · E:Weak-leaf Yucca;
G:Schlaffe Palmlilie · ♈ Z5 VIII-IX; USA:
SE
– *flexilis* Carrière = Yucca recurvifolia
– *funifera* Lem. = Hesperaloe funifera
– **glauca** Nutt. ex Fraser · E:Bear Grass,
Blue Yucca, Spanish Bayonet; G:Blau-
grüne Palmlilie · ♄ e Z7 ⋀ VIII-IX; USA:
NCE, NC, Rocky Mts, SW, SC, SE
– **gloriosa** L. · E:Roman Candle, Soft Tip
Yucca; G:Kerzen-Palmlilie · ♈ Z7 VII-IX;

USA: SE, Fla.
- *graminifolia* Zucc. = Dasylirion graminifolium
- *guatemalensis* Baker = Yucca elephantipes
- *kanabensis* McKelvey = Yucca angustissima var. kanabensis
- × **karlsruhensis** Graebn. (*Y. filamentosa*
  × *Y. glauca*) · ψ Z5; cult.
- *longifolia* Karw. ex Schult. & Schult. f. =
  Nolina longifolia
- **louisianensis** Trel. · E:Gulf Coast Yucca ·
  ψ Z7; S-USA: La.
- *macrocarpa* (Torr.) Coville = Yucca
  torreyi
- *macrocarpa* Engelm. = Yucca madrensis
- **madrensis** Gentry · ψ Z9 ⓐ; USA: SW;
  N-Mex.
- *parviflora* Torr. = Hesperaloe parviflora
- *puberula* Haw. = Yucca flaccida
- *radiosa* (Engelm.) Trel. = Yucca elata
- *recurva* Haw. = Yucca recurvifolia
- **recurvifolia** Salisb. · E:Curve-leaf Yucca ·
  ψ Z8 ⓐ; USA: SE
- **rostrata** Engelm. ex Trel. · ψ Z8 ⓐ; Tex.,
  N-Mex.
- *schottii* Engelm. = Yucca madrensis
- × **schottii** Engelm. · E:Schott's Yucca
  pro sp. · ψ Z9 ⓐ; Ariz., Mex: Sonora
- *serratifolia* Karw. ex Schult. & Schult. f. =
  Dasylirion serratifolium
- **torreyi** Shafer · E:Torrey Yucca;
  G:Torrey-Palmlilie · ψ Z9 ⓐ; USA: Tex.,
  N.Mex.; N-Mex.
- **treculeana** Carrière · E:Spanish Bayonet,
  Yucca; G:Bajonett-Palmlilie · ψ Z9 ⓐ;
  Tex., NE-Mex.
- **valida** Brandegee · ψ Z9 ⓐ; Mex.
- *whipplei* Torr. = Hesperoyucca whipplei

Yushania Keng f. -f- *Poaceae* · c. 80 spp. ·
E:Fountain Bamboo; F:Bambou;
G:Fontänenbambus
- **alpina** (K. Schum.) W.C. Lin · ♭ Z9 Ⓝ;
  Kenya, Tanzania, Uganda, Ruanda,
  Sudan, Eth.
- **anceps** (Mitford) W.C. Lin · E:Himalayan
  Bamboo; G:Himalaya-Fontänenbambus ·
  ♭ Z9 ⓐ; Him.
- *jaunsarensis* (Gamble) T.P. Yi = Yushania
  anceps

Zaluzianskya F.W. Schmidt
-f- *Scrophulariaceae* · 55 spp. ·
F:Zaluzianskya; G:Sternbalsam
- **capensis** (Benth.) Walp. · ☉ ⊙ ⚁ ♭ ♭ D

Z9 ⓐ VII-IX; S-Afr.
- *selaginoides* Walp. = Zaluzianskya villosa
- **villosa** F.W. Schmidt · ⊙ D Z9 VII-IX;
  S-Afr.

Zamia L. -f- *Zamiaceae* · 30-40 spp.
- *angustifolia* Jacq. = Zamia pumila subsp.
  pumila
- *debilis* Aiton = Zamia pumila subsp.
  pumila
- **fairchildiana** L.D. Gómez · ⚁ e Z10 ⓐ ▽
  ✳; Costa Rica
- **fischeri** Miq. · ⚁ e Z10 ⓐ ▽ ✳; Mex.
- *floridana* A. DC. = Zamia pumila subsp.
  pumila
- **furfuracea** L. f. · E:Cardboard Palm · ⚁ e
  Z9 ▽ ✳; Mex.
- **lindenii** Regel ex André · ⚁ e Z10 ⓐ ▽
  ✳; Ecuad.
- **loddigesii** Miq. · ⚁ e Z10 ⓐ ▽ ✳; Mex.
- *media* Jacq. = Zamia pumila subsp.
  pumila
- **muricata** Willd. · ⚁ e Z10 ⓐ ▽ ✳; Mex.,
  Col., Venez.
- **obliqua** A. Braun · ⚁ e Z10 ⓐ ▽ ✳; Col.
- **pseudoparasitica** J. Yates · ⚁ e Z10 ⓐ
  ▽ ✳; Col., Ecuad., Peru
- **pumila** L.
- subsp. **pumila** · E:Coontie · ⚁ e Z9 ⓐ ▽
  ✳; Fla., W.Ind.
- subsp. **pygmaea** (Sims) Eckenw. ·
  E:Coontie · Z9 ⓐ ▽ ✳; W-Cuba
- *pygmaea* Sims = Zamia pumila subsp.
  pygmaea
- *roezlii* Regel = Zamia pseudoparasitica
- **skinneri** Warsz. · ⚁ e Z10 ⓐ ▽ ✳; C-Am.
- **wallisii** A. Braun · ⚁ e Z10 ⓐ ▽ ✳; Col.

Zamioculcas Schott -f- *Araceae* · 1 sp.
- **zamiifolia** (Lodd.) Engl. · ⚁ ψ Z10 ⓐ;
  E-Afr.

Zannichellia L. -f- *Zannichelliaceae* ·
3-8 spp. · E:Horned Pondweed;
F:Zannichellia; G:Teichfaden
- **palustris** L. · E:Horned Pondweed;
  G:Sumpf-Teichfaden · ⚁ ≈ Z2 V-IX;
  Eur.*, Cauc., cosmop. exc. Austr.

Zantedeschia Spreng. -f- *Araceae* · 8 spp. ·
E:Altar Lily, Arum Lily; F:Calla; G:Kalla,
Zimmerkalla
- **aethiopica** (L.) Spreng. · E:Arum Lily,
  Calla Lily, Pig Lily; G:Kalla · ⚁ ⋉ Z8 ⓐ
  I-VI ✿; S-Afr.: Cape, Natal

– **albomaculata** (Hook.) Baill. · E:Spotted Arum; G:Gefleckte Kalla · ♃ Z9 ⓚ; S-Afr.: Cape, Natal
– **elliottiana** (W. Watson) Engl. · E:Golden Calla; G:Goldene Kalla · ♃ ✕ Z9 ⓚ VI-VIII; orig. ?
– **jucunda** Letty · ♃ ✕ Z9 ⓚ; S-Afr.: Transvaal
– **rehmannii** Engl. · E:Pink Arum, Pink Calla; G:Rosafarbene Kalla · ♃ Z9 ⓚ VIII; S-Afr.: Natal

Zanthoxylum L. -n- *Rutaceae* · c. 250 spp. · E:Prickly Ash; F:Clavalier; G:Stachelesche
– *alatum* Roxb. = Zanthoxylum armatum
– var. *planispinum* (Siebold & Zucc.) Rehder & E.H. Wilson = Zanthoxylum armatum
– **americanum** Mill. · E:Northern Prickly-Ash, Toothache Tree · ♄ ♄ d Z3 IV Ⓝ; Can.: E; USA: NE, NCE, NC, SC, SE, Fla.
– **armatum** DC. · E:Winged Prickly-Ash · ♄ d Z6; Pakist., Him., Ind., Malay. Arch., Phil.
– *bungei* Planch. = Zanthoxylum simulans
– *fraxineum* Willd. = Zanthoxylum americanum
– **piperitum** DC. · E:Japanese Pepper; G:Japanischer Pfeffer · ♄ ♄ d Z6 ⚥ Ⓝ; China, Manch., Korea, Jap.
– *planispinum* Siebold & Zucc. = Zanthoxylum armatum
– **schinifolium** Siebold & Zucc. · ♄ d Z5; Jap., Korea, E-China, Mandsch
– **simulans** Hance · G:Täuschende Stachelesche · ♄ d Z6 V-VI ⚥ Ⓝ; N-China, C-China

Zauschneria C. Presl = Epilobium
– *californica* C. Presl = Epilobium canum subsp. angustifolium
– subsp. *angustifolia* D.D. Keck = Epilobium canum subsp. angustifolium
– subsp. *latifolia* (Hook.) Keck = Epilobium canum subsp. latifolium
– *cana* Greene = Epilobium canum subsp. canum
– *latifolia* (Hook.) Greene = Epilobium canum subsp. latifolium
– var. *arizonica* (Davidson) Hilend = Epilobium canum subsp. latifolium

Zea L. -f- *Poaceae* · 4 spp. · E:Maize; F:Maïs; G:Mais

– **mays** L. · E:Corn, Maize; G:Mais · ⊙ Z7 VII-X ⚥ ; ? Mex., ? C-Am.
– **Amylaca-Group** · G:Stärke-Mais · ⊙ VI-VII Ⓝ; cult.
– **Ceratina-Group** · G:Wachs-Mais · ⊙ VII Ⓝ; cult.
– **Dentiformis-Group** · G:Zahn-Mais · ⊙ VI-VII Ⓝ; cult.
– **Microsperma-Group** · E:Popcorn; G:Perl-Mais, Popcorn · ⊙ VI-VII Ⓝ; cult.
– **Saccharata-Group** · E:Sweet Corn; G:Zucker-Mais · ⊙ VI-VII Ⓝ; cult.
– subsp. *mexicana* (Schrad.) Iltis = Zea mexicana
– **Vulgaris-Group** · G:Hart-Mais · ⊙ VI-VII Ⓝ; cult.
– **mexicana** (Schrad.) Reeves & Mangelsd. · E:Mexican Teosinte · ⊙ Z7 Ⓝ; Mex.

Zebrina Schnizl. = Tradescantia
– *flocculosa* G. Brückn. = Tradescantia zebrina var. flocculosa
– *pendula* Schnizl. = Tradescantia zebrina var. zebrina
– *purpusii* G. Brückn. = Tradescantia zebrina

Zehneria Endl. -f- *Cucurbitaceae* · 30 spp.
– **indica** (L.) Keraudren · ♃ ⚥ ♋ Z10 ⓚ; Jap.
– **scabra** (L. f.) Sond. · ⊙ ⊙ ♃ ⚥ ♋ D Z10 ⓚ V-VIII; Mex.
– *suavis* (Schrad.) Endl. ex Walp. = Zehneria scabra

Zelenkoa M.W. Chase & N.H. Williams
– **onusta** (Lindl.) M.W. Chase & N.H. Williams · ♃ Z10 ⓦ IV-V ▽ ✳; Panama

Zelkova Spach -f- *Ulmaceae* · 5 spp. · E:Zelkova; F:Faux-orme de Sibérie, Zelkova; G:Zelkove, Zelkowe
– **carpinifolia** (Pall.) K. Koch · E:Caucasian Elm; G:Kaukasische Zelkove · ♄ d Z5 V Ⓝ; Cauc.
– *crenata* Spach = Zelkova carpinifolia
– *keaki* (Siebold) Maxim. = Zelkova serrata
– **serrata** (Thunb. ex Murray) Makino · E:Japanese Zelkova, Sawleaf Zelkova; G:Japanische Zelkove · ♄ d Z6 V Ⓝ; China, Korea, Jap.
– **sinica** C.K. Schneid. · E:Chinese Zekova; G:Chinesische Zelkove · ♄ d Z6; C-China, E-China

– *ulmoides* C.K. Schneid. = Zelkova
carpinifolia
– × *verschaffeltii* (Dippel) G. Nicholson =
Zelkova carpinifolia

Zenobia D. Don -f- *Ericaceae* · 1 sp. ·
F:Zénobia; G:Zenobie
– **pulverulenta** (W..Bartram ex Willd.)
Pollard
– f. **nitida** (Michx.) Fernald
– var. **pulverulenta** · E:Honeycup;
G:Gewöhnliche Zenobie · ♄ s Z6 V-VI;
USA: Va., N.C., S.C.
– var. *viridis* (Veill.) Boom = Zenobia
pulverulenta f. nitida

Zephyranthes Herb. -f- *Amaryllidaceae* ·
86 spp. · E:Rain Flower, Zephyr Flower;
F:Lis zéphir; G:Windblume, Zephirblume
– **atamasco** (L.) Herb. · E:Atamasco Lily ·
⧜ Z8 ⓧ III-IV; USA: NE, SE, Fla.
– *aurea* (Herb.) Baker = Pyrolirion arvense
– *Braziliensis* (Traub) Traub = Zephyranthes drummondii
– **candida** (Lindl.) Herb. · E:Flower-of-the-
Western-Wind; G:Weiße Windblume · ⧜
Z9 ⓧ VII-X; Urug., Arg.
– **drummondii** D. Don · ⧜ Z8 ⓧ; Braz.
– *grandiflora* Lindl. = Zephyranthes minuta
– **minuta** (Kunth) D. Dietr. · G:Großblütige
Windblume · ⧜ Z9 ⓧ IV-VII; Mex., Guat.,
Cuba, Jamaica
– *robusta* (Herb. ex Sweet) Baker =
Habranthus robustus
– **rosea** (Spreng.) Lindl. · E:Fairy Lily;
G:Rosafarbene Windblume · ⧜ Z10 ⓧ X;
Guat., W.Ind.
– *tubiflora* (L'Hér.) Schinz = Pyrolirion
arvense
– *verecunda* Herb. = Zephyranthes minuta

Zigadenus Michx. -m- *Melanthiaceae* ·
21 sp. · E:Death Camas; F:Zigadénus;
G:Jochlilie
– **elegans** Pursh
– subsp. **elegans** · E:Mountain Death
Camas; G:Weiße Jochlilie · ⧜ ⌇ Z3
VI-VIII; Alaska, Can.: W, Man.; USA* exc.
Calif.
– subsp. **glaucus** (Nutt.) Hultén · ⧜ ⌇
Z3; Can.: E; USA: NE, NCE, N.C.
– **fremontii** (Torr.) Torr. ex S. Watson ·
E:Fremont's Deathcamas, Star Lily;
G:Fremonts Jochlilie · ⧜ ⌇ Z8 ∧ VI-
VIII; USA: Oreg., Calif.; Mex.: Baja Calif.

– *glaucus* Nutt. = Zigadenus elegans subsp.
glaucus
– **nuttallii** A. Gray · E:Merryhearts, Poison
Sego; G:Nuttals Jochlilie · ⧜ Z6 V-VI;
USA: Kans., Mo., SC, SE

Zingiber Boehm. -n- *Zingiberaceae* ·
145 spp. · E:Ginger; F:Gingembre;
G:Ingwer
– *cassumunar* Roxb. = Zingiber montanum
– **mioga** (Thunb.) Roscoe · E:Japanese
Ginger, Mioga Ginger; G:Japan-Ingwer ·
⧜ Z10 ⓦ ⓝ; Jap.
– **montanum** (J. König) Link ex A. Dietr. ·
E:Bengal Ginger, Cassumunar Ginger ;
G:Bengal-Ingwer, Blockzitwer · ⧜ Z10 ⓦ
ⓝ; ? Ind.; cult. trop. As.
– **officinale** Roscoe · E:Ginger; G:Gewöhn-
licher Ingwer · ⧜ Z10 ⓦ ⚥ ⓝ; ? Pacific.
Is.
– *purpureum* Roscoe = Zingiber montanum
– **spectabile** Griff. · E:Nodding Gingerwort
; G:Nickender Ingwer · ⧜ Z10 ⓦ ⓝ;
Malay.Arch.
– **zerumbet** (L.) Roscoe ex Sm. · E:Wild
Ginger; G:Wilder Ingwer · ⧜ Z10 ⓦ
VIII-IX ⓝ; cult.

Zinnia L. -f- *Asteraceae* · 11 (-33) spp. ·
F:Zinnia; G:Zinnie
– **angustifolia** Kunth · E:Narrowleaf Zinnia; G:Schmalblättrige Zinnie · ⊙ VII-X;
USA: Ariz.
– **elegans** Jacq. · E:Youth-and-Old-Age;
G:Garten-Zinnie, Pracht-Zinnie · ⊙
VII-IX; Mex.
– **many cultivars**
– *gracillima* hort. = Zinnia elegans
– **haageana** Regel · ⊙ VII-IX; Mex.
– *linearis* Benth. = Zinnia angustifolia
– *mexicana* hort. ex Vilm. = Zinnia
haageana
– **peruviana** (L.) L. · E:Peruvian Zinnia · ⊙
VII-IX; USA: Ariz.; Mex., W.Ind., S-Am.

Zizania L. -f- *Poaceae* · 3 spp. · E:Water
Oats, Wild Rice; F:Riz sauvage; G:Was-
serreis, Wildreis
– **aquatica** L. · E:Annual Wild Rice, Canadian Wild Rice; G:Kanadischer Wildreis ·
⊙ ≋ Z6 ⓝ; Can.: E; USA: NE, NEC, SE,
Fla., nat. in E-Eur.
– *caduciflora* (Turcz.) Hand.-Mazz. =
Zizania latifolia
– **latifolia** (Griseb.) Turcz. · E:Water Rice,

Wild Rice; G:Gewöhnlicher Wildreis, Wasserbambus, Wasserreis · ⚇ ≋ Z7 Ⓝ; Eur.: E-Russ.; Sib., China, Jap., Taiwan, Burma, NE-Ind.
– *palustris* L. = Zizania aquatica

Zizia W.D.J. Koch -f- *Apiaceae* · 4 spp. · G:Alexander
– **aurea** (L.) W.D.J. Koch · E:Golden Zizia; G:Goldener Alexander · ⚇ Z3; Can.: E, Sask.; USA: NE, NEC, SC, SE, Fla.

Ziziphora L. -f- *Lamiaceae* · 16 spp.
– **capitata** L. · ⊙; Eur.: Ba, E-Eur., ? sp.; Cauc., Cyprus, Syr., N-Iraq, Iran, TR, nat. in I

Ziziphus Mill. -f- *Rhamnaceae* · 86 spp. · E:Jujube; F:Jujubier, Lotus des Anciens; G:Brustbeere, Judendorn, Jujube
– **jujuba** Mill. · E:Jujube; G:Brustbeere, Chinesische Dattel · ♄ ♄ d Z8 ⓐ IV-V ⚘ Ⓝ; Cauc., Iran, C-As., Tibet, Him., Ind., Mong., China, Korea, Jap., nat. in Eur.: sp., F, Ital-P, Ba, RO; TR
– **lotus** (L.) Lam. · ♄ d ⓐ Ⓝ; Eur.: sp., Sic., GR; S-TR, Levant, N-Afr.
– **mauritiana** Lam. · E:Indian Jujube; G:Filziger Judendorn · ♄ ♄ s Z10 ⓐ IV-V Ⓝ; trop. Afr., Alger., SW-As., Afgh., Ind., China, Malay. Pen., Austr.
– *vulgaris* Lam. = Ziziphus jujuba

Zostera L. -f- *Zosteraceae* · 16 spp. · E:Eelgrass; F:Zostère ; G:Seegras
– **marina** L. · E:Eel Grass, Grass Wrack; G:Gewöhnliches Seegras, Schmalblättriges Seegras · ⚇ ≋ VI-IX Ⓝ; Eur.*, TR, Cauc., Amur, Sakhal., Kamchat., Manch., Korea, Jap., Moroc., Can.: E, B.C.; USA: NE, SE, NW, Calif.; coasts
– **noltii** Hornem. · E:Dwarf Eel Grass, Dwarf Grass Wrack; G:Zwerg-Seegras · ⚇ ≋ VI-VIII Ⓝ; Eur.*, TR, C-As., N-Iran, N-Afr., Canar., W-Afr.; coasts

Zosterella Small = Heteranthera
– *dubia* (Jacq.) Small = Heteranthera dubia

× **Zygobatemannia** hort. -f- *Orchidaceae* (*Batemannia* × *Zygopetalum*)

Zygocactus K. Schum. = Schlumbergera
– *truncatus* (Haw.) K. Schum. = Schlumbergera truncata

× **Zygocaste** hort. -f- *Orchidaceae* (*Zygopetalum* × *Lycaste*)

× **Zygocolax** hort. -m- *Orchidaceae* (*Colax* × *Zygopetalum*)

Zygopetalum Hook. -n- *Orchidaceae* · 15 spp.
– **brachypetalum** Lindl. · ⚇ Z10 ⓐ XI-XII ▽ ✳; Braz.
– *coeleste* Rchb. f. = Bollea coelestis
– **crinitum** Lodd. · ⚇ D Z10 ⓐ X-XII ▽ ✳; Braz.
– *jugosum* (Lindl.) Schltr. = Pabstia jugosa
– *lalindei* (Linden) Rchb. f. = Bollea lalindei
– *lamellosum* (Rchb. f.) Rchb. f. = Pescatoria lamellosa
– *mackayi* Hook. = Zygopetalum maculatum
– **maculatum** (Kunth) Garay · ⚇ D Z10 ⓐ X-II ▽ ✳; Peru, Bol., S-Braz.
– **maxillare** Lodd. · ⚇ Z10 ⓐ VI-VII ▽ ✳; Braz. (Serra dos Orgaos)

× **Zygorhyncha** hort. -f- *Orchidaceae* (*Chondrorhyncha* × *Zygopetalum*)

Zygostates Lindl. -f- *Orchidaceae* · 20 spp.
– **grandiflora** (Lindl.) Mansf. · ⚇ Z10 ⓐ VII-VIII ▽ ✳; Braz.

× **Zygostylis** hort. -f- *Orchidaceae* (*Otostylis* × *Zygopetalum*)

X English vernacular plant names

In addition to numerous monographs, the following works in particular have been used as sources for English plant names: BRICKELL, C. (ed.) (1996), GRIFFITHS, M. (1994), STACE, C. (1999), WIERSEMA, J. H. & LEÓN, B. (1999), and other English-language floras.

In the above-named sources, the respective written form of the English vernacular names is as follows: with an initial upper-case letter and without a hyphen between the word components; exclusively in upper case; with initial upper-case letter and with a hyphen between the word components; and with lower-case letters and hyphen between the word components of the generic name. Hence, how English vernacular names are applied is ultimately the user's preference.

Abelia = Abelia
Abraham = Trachystemon
Acalbir = Datisca
Adam's Laburnum = + Laburnocytisus
Adder's-Tongue = Ophioglossum
African Cherry Orange = Citropsis
African Cypress = Widdringtonia
African Daisy = Arctotis
African Hairbell = Dierama
African Hemp = Sparrmannia
African Lily = Agapanthus
African Oak = Lophira
African Tulip = Spathodea
African Valerian = Fedia
African Violet = Saintpaulia
Agrimony = Agrimonia
Air Plant = Tillandsia
Akee = Blighia
Alder = Alnus
Alder Buckthorn = Frangula
Alexanders = Smyrnium
Alexandrian Laurel = Danae
Alison = Alyssum
Alkali Grass = Puccinellia
Alkanet = Alkanna, Anchusa
Allamanda = Allamanda
Allspice = Pimenta
Almond = Prunus
Aloe = Aloe
Alpine Azalea = Loiseleuria
Alpine Chrysanthemum = Leucanthemopsis
Alpine Clubmoss = Diphasiastrum
Alpine Forget-me-not = Eritrichium
Alpine Saw Wort = Saussurea
Altar Lily = Zantedeschia
Amaranth = Amaranthus

Amazon Lily = Eucharis
Anacyclus = Anacyclus
Anchor Plant = Colletia
Andelmin = Andira
Anemone = Anemone
Angel Wings = Caladium
Angel's Trumpet = Brugmansia
Angelica Tree = Aralia
Angelim = Andira
Angostura = Galipea
Anise Tree = Illicium
Annatto = Bixa
Annual Mallow = Malope
Antelope Bush = Purshia
Apache Plume = Fallugia
Apple = Malus
Apple Berry = Billardiera
Apple of Peru = Nicandra
Apricot = Prunus
Arar Tree = Tetraclinis
Archangel = Angelica
Arctic Chrysanthemum = Arctanthemum
Argantree = Argania
Argus Pheasant Tree = Dracontomelon
Arrow Arum = Peltandra
Arrow Wood = Viburnum
Arrowgrass = Triglochin
Arrowhead = Sagittaria
Artillery Plant = Pilea
Arum Lily = Zantedeschia
Asarabacca = Asarum
Ashe = Fraxinus
Asiatic Poppy = Meconopsis
Asparagus = Asparagus
Aspen = Populus
Asphodel = Asphodelus

Aster = Aster
Athamanta = Athamanta
Aubrietia = Aubrieta
Australia Chestnut = Castanospermum
Australian Heath = Epacris
Australian Mint Bush = Prostanthera
Australian Pea = Dipogon
Australian Pine = Casuarina
Australian Pitcher Plant = Cephalotus
Autumn Crocus = Colchicum
Autumn Daffodil = Sternbergia
Autumn Oxeye = Leucanthemella
Avens = Geum
Avocado = Persea
Awlwort = Subularia
Azalea = Rhododendron
Babassu Palm = Orbignya
Baboon Flower = Babiana
Baby's Breath = Gypsophila
Baby's Tears = Soleirolia
Bael Tree = Aegle
Balloon Flower = Platycodon
Balloon Pea = Sutherlandia
Balloon Vine = Cardiospermum
Balm = Melissa
Balsa = Ochroma
Balsam = Impatiens, Myroxylon
Balsam Apple = Clusia
Bamboo = Bambusa
Bamboo Fern = Coniogramme
Bamboo Grass = Chasmanthium
Banana = Musa
Baneberry = Actaea
Banksia = Banksia
Bar-Room Plant = Aspidistra
Barbados Cherry = Malpighia
Barbara's Herb = Barbarea
Barbel Palm = Acanthophoenix
Barberry = Berberis
Barleria = Barleria
Barley = Hordeum
Bartsia = Bartsia, Odontites
Basil = Ocimum
Basket Gras = Oplismenus
Basket Plant = Aeschynanthus, Episcia
Bastard Agrimony = Aremonia
Bastard Balm = Melittis
Bat Flower = Tacca
Bay = Laurus
Beach Fern = Phegopteris
Beach Grass = Ammophila
Beadplant = Nertera
Beak Sedge = Rhynchospora
Bean = Phaseolus, Vicia
Bean Tree = Laburnum

Bear Grass = Dasylirion, Xerophyllum
Bear's Breeches = Acanthus
Bearberry = Arctostaphylos
Beard Grass = Andropogon, Bothriochloa, Polypogon
Beauty Bush = Kolkwitzia
Bedstraw = Galium
Beebalm = Monarda
Beech = Fagus
Beefwood = Casuarina
Beet = Beta
Beggarweed = Desmodium
Begonia = Begonia
Bell Vine = Rhodochiton
Belladonna Lily = Amaryllis
Bellflower = Campanula
Bellwort = Uvularia
Bent Grass = Agrostis
Bentinck's Palm = Bentinckia
Bermuda Grass = Cynodon
Berry Catchfly = Cucubalus
Betony = Stachys
Bilberry = Vaccinium
Billbergia = Billbergia
Billy Buttons = Craspedia
Bindweed = Calystegia
Birch = Betula
Bird of Paradise = Strelitzia
Bird's Eye = Veronica
Bird's Eye Bush = Ochna
Bird's Foot = Ornithopus
Bird's Nest = Monotropa
Bird's Nest Orchid = Neottia
Bird's-Nest Bromeliad = Nidularium
Birthwort = Aristolochia
Bishop's Cap = Mitella
Bishop's Head = Epimedium
Bishop's Mitre = Epimedium
Bissaba Palm = Attalea
Bitter Cress = Cardamine
Bitter Cucumber = Momordica
Bitter Orange = Poncirus
Bitter Peas = Daviesia
Bitter Wood = Lonchocarpus
Bitterroot = Lewisia
Bittersweet = Celastrus
Bitterwood = Quassia
Black Bryony = Tamus
Blackroot = Veronicastrum
Bladder Fern = Cystopteris
Bladder Senna = Colutea
Bladdernut = Staphylea
Bladderwort = Utricularia
Blanketflower = Gaillardia
Blazing Star = Chamaelirium

Bleeding Heart = Dicentra
Blessed Thistle = Cnicus
Blink = Montia
Blood Berry = Rivina
Blood Flower = Scadoxus
Blood Lily = Haemanthus
Bloodroot = Sanguinaria
Bloodwood Tree = Haematoxylum
Blowballs = Taraxacum
Blue Amaryllis = Worsleya
Blue Corn Lily = Aristea
Blue Cupidone = Catananche
Blue Daisy = Felicia
Blue Heath = Phyllodoce
Blue Margeruite = Felicia
Blue Oxalis = Parochetus
Blue Sowthistle = Cicerbita
Blue Star = Amsonia
Blue Stem = Andropogon, Dichanthium, Schizachyrium
Blue-eyed Grass = Sisyrinchium
Bluebeard = Caryopteris
Bluebell = Hyacinthoides, Mertensia, Phacelia
Blueberry = Vaccinium
Bluets = Hedyotis, Houstonia
Blush Wort = Aeschynanthus
Boerboon = Schotia
Bog Arum = Calla
Bog Asphodel = Narthecium
Bog Myrtle = Myrica
Bog Orchid = Hammarbya
Bog Rosemary = Andromeda
Bog Rush = Schoenus
Bogbean = Menyanthes
Boldo = Peumus
Bonnet Bellflower = Codonopsis
Borage = Borago
Boronia = Boronia
Botlebrush = Beaufortia
Bottle Gourd = Lagenaria
Bottle Palm = Hyophorbe
Bottle Tree = Brachychiton
Bottle-Brush Bush = Callistemon
Bottle-Brush Grass = Hystrix
Bottlebrush = Greyia
Bottlebrush Orchid = Arpophyllum
Bougainvillea = Bougainvillea
Bouvardia = Bouvardia
Bower Plant = Pandorea
Bowstring Hemp = Sansevieria
Box = Buxus
Bracken = Pteridium
Brake = Pteridium
Bramble = Rubus

Brazil Nut = Bertholletia
Breadfruit = Artocarpus, Treculia
Brid's Foot Trefoil = Lotus
Bridal Wreath = Francoa
Bridewort = Spiraea
Bristle Grass = Setaria
Broadleaf = Griselinia
Brome = Bromus
Bromelia = Bromelia
Bronvaux Medlar = + Crataegomespilus
Brookweed = Samolus
Broom = Cytisus
Broomrape = Orobanche
Brunsvigia = Brunsvigia
Bryony = Bryonia
Buck's Beard = Aruncus
Buckthorn = Rhamnus
Buckwheat = Fagopyrum
Buffalo Berry = Shepherdia
Buffalo Gras = Buchloe
Buffalo Grass = Stenotaphrum
Buffalo Nut = Pyrularia
Bugbane = Cimicifuga
Bugle = Ajuga
Bugle Iris = Watsonia
Bugloss = Echium
Bugseed = Corispermum
Bullwort = Ammi
Bulrush = Typha
Bunchflower = Melanthium
Bunga = Pinanga
Bur Clover = Medicago
Bur Cucumber = Sicyos
Bur Forget-me-not = Lappula
Bur Grass = Tragus
Bur Marigold = Bidens
Burdock = Arctium
Burnet = Sanguisorba
Burnet Saxifrage = Pimpinella
Burnweed = Erechtites
Burr Reed = Sparganium
Bush Clover = Kummerowia, Lespedeza
Bush Honeysuckle = Diervilla
Bush Nettle = Laportea
Bush Pea = Eutaxia
Bush Violet = Browallia
Busy Lizzie = Impatiens
Butcher's Broom = Ruscus
Butterbur = Petasites
Buttercup = Ranunculus
Butterfly Bush = Buddleja
Butterfly Flower = Schizanthus
Butterfly Orchid = Platanthera
Butterfly Pea = Centrosema, Clitoria
Butternut = Caryocar

Buttertree = Madhuca
Butterwort = Pinguicula
Button Cactus = Epithelantha
Button Snake Root = Liatris
Buttonbush = Cephalanthus
Buttonweed = Cotula
Byfield Fern = Bowenia
Cabbage = Brassica
Cabbage Tree = Cordyline, Cussonia
Cacao = Theobroma
Calabar Bean = Physostigma
Calabash Nutmeg = Monodora
Calabash Tree = Crescentia
Calamint = Acinos, Calamintha,
    Clinopodium
Calandrina = Calandrinia
California Bay = Umbellularia
California Laurel = Umbellularia
California Lilac = Ceanothus
California Tree Poppy = Romneya
Californian Lobelia = Downingia
Californian Poppy = Eschscholzia
Calypso = Calypso
Camass = Camassia
Camel Thorn = Alhagi
Camellia = Camellia
Camphor Tree = Cinnamomum
Campion = Silene
Camwood = Baphia
Canary Grass = Phalaris
Canary Island Bellflower = Canarina
Candle Tree = Parmentiera
Candlenut Tree = Aleurites
Candytuft = Iberis
Cane Reed = Arundinaria
Canna Lily = Canna
Cape Chestnut = Calodendrum
Cape Cowslip = Lachenalia
Cape Figwort = Phygelius
Cape Honeysuckle = Tecomaria
Cape Lily = Crinum
Cape Myrtle = Phylica
Cape Primerose = Streptocarpus
Cape Stock = Heliophila
Caper = Capparis
Caranda Palm = Copernicia
Caraway = Carum
Cardamom = Amomum, Elettaria
Carline Thistle = Carlina
Carnation = Dianthus
Carpetweed = Mollugo
Carrion Flower = Stapelia
Carrot = Daucus
Cashew = Anacardium
Cassava = Manihot

Castor Oil Plant = Ricinus
Cat Mint = Nepeta
Cat's Ears = Antennaria, Hypochaeris
Cat's Tail = Acalypha, Phleum
Catalpa = Catalpa
Catchfly = Silene
Caterpillar Fern = Scyphularia
Caterpillar Plant = Scorpiurus
Catjang Pea = Cajanus
Caucasian Crosswort = Phuopsis
Cedar = Cedrus
Celandine Poppy = Stylophorum
Celery Pine = Phyllocladus
Centaury = Centaurium
Century Plant = Agave
Chaco = Sechium
Chain Fern = Woodwardia
Chalice Vine = Solandra
Chamois Cress = Pritzelago
Chamomile = Anthemis, Chamaemelum
Chastetree = Vitex
Chayote = Sechium
Cherry = Prunus
Cherry Mahogany = Tieghemella
Chervil = Anthriscus, Chaerophyllum
Chestnut = Castanea
Chick Pea = Cicer
Chickweed = Moenchia, Stellaria,
    Trientalis
Chicory = Cichorium
Chigaya = Imperata
Chile Bells = Lapageria
Chilean Cedar = Austrocedrus
Chilean Crocus = Tecophilaea
Chilean Iris = Libertia
Chilean Nut = Gevuina
China Aster = Callistephus
China Berry = Melia
China Fir = Cunninghamia
Chinese Arborvitae = Platycladus
Chinese Bellflower = Platycodon
Chinese Foxglove = Rehmannia
Chinese Ground Orchid = Bletilla
Chinese Hat Plant = Holmskioldia
Chinese Lantern Lily = Sandersonia
Chinese Olive = Canarium
Chinese Quince = Pseudocydonia
Chinese Ragwort = Sinacalia
Chinese Swamp Cypress = Glyptostrobus
Chinese Windmill Palm = Trachycarpus
Chinquapin = Castanopsis
Chocolate Vine = Akebia
Chokeberry = Aronia
Christ's Thorn = Paliurus
Christmas Bells = Blandfordia

Christmas Berry = Chironia, Heteromeles, Photinia
Christmas Palm = Veitchia
Cineraria = Cineraria, Pericallis
Cinnamon = Cinnamomum
Cinquefoil = Potentilla
Citrange = × Citroncirus
Claw Fern = Onychium
Clematis = Clematis
Cliff Brake = Pellaea
Cliffbush = Jamesia
Climbing Butcher's Broom = Semele
Climbing Dahlia = Hidalgoa
Climbing Hydrangea = Decumaria
Climbing Lily = Gloriosa, Littonia
Climbing Onion = Bowiea
Clover = Trifolium
Club Rush = Isolepis, Schoenoplectus
Clubmoss = Lycopodium
Cluster Bean = Cyamopsis
Cluster Lily = Brodiaea
Coastal Redwood = Sequoia
Cobaiba = Copaifera
Cobra Lily = Arisaema, Chasmanthe, Darlingtonia
Coca = Erythroxylum
Cock's Foot = Dactylis
Cocklebur = Agrimonia, Xanthium
Cockscomb = Celosia
Cockspur = Echinochloa
Coco Plum = Chrysobalanus
Coconut = Cocos
Coffee = Coffea
Cola = Cola
Coleus = Solenostemon
Colic Root = Aletris
Collomia = Collomia
Colt's Foot = Homogyne
Coltsfoot = Tussilago
Columbine = Aquilegia
Comfrey = Symphytum
Condorvine = Marsdenia
Cone Flower = Echinacea
Coneflower = Rudbeckia
Copal = Hymenaea
Copperleaf = Acalypha, Alternanthera
Coral Bell = Heuchera
Coral Drops = Bessera
Coral Necklace = Illecebrum
Coral Pea = Hardenbergia, Kennedia
Coral Plant = Berberidopsis
Coral Tree = Erythrina
Coral Vine = Antigonon
Coral Wood = Adenanthera
Coralroot Orchid = Corallorhiza

Cord Grass = Spartina
Coriander = Coriandrum
Corktree = Phellodendron
Corn Lily = Ixia
Corncockle = Agrostemma
Cornel = Cornus
Cornsalad = Valerianella
Corydalis = Corydalis
Cotoneaster = Cotoneaster
Cotton = Gossypium
Cotton Grass = Eriophorum
Cotton Weed = Otanthus
CottonThistle = Onopordum
Cottonweed = Froelichia
Couch = Elymus
Cow Tree = Brosimum
Cow Wheat = Melampyrum
Cowbane = Cicuta
Cowherb = Vaccaria
Cowslip = Primula
Crab Grass = Panicum
Crabwood = Carapa
Cradle Orchid = Anguloa
Cranberry = Vaccinium
Crane's Bill = Geranium
Crape Myrtle = Lagerstroemia
Crazy Weed = Oxytropis
Cream Cup = Platystemon
Creeping Lady's Tresses = Goodyera
Creeping Snapdragon = Asarina
Creeping Zinnia = Sanvitalia
Crepe Fern = Todea
Crocus = Crocus
Crossflower = Chorispora
Crosswort = Crucianella
Croton = Codiaeum, Croton
Crowberry = Corema, Empetrum
Crowfoot = Ranunculus
Crown Beard = Verbesina
Crown Daisy = Glebionis, Xanthophthalmum
Crown Vetch = Securigera
Cucumber = Cucumis
Cucumber Tree = Averrhoa
Cucumer Root = Medeola
Cudweed = Filago, Gnaphalium
Cumin = Cuminum
Cup and Saucer Vine = Cobaea
Cupflower = Nierembergia
Curly Water Thyme = Lagarosiphon
Currant = Ribes
Cushion Bush = Leucophyta
Custard Apple = Annona
Cut Grass = Leersia
Cycad = Cycas, Encephalartos

Cypress = Cupressus
Cypress-Pine = Callitris
Dacryberry = Dacrycarpus
Daffodil = Narcissus
Daggerpod = Phoenicaulis
Dahlia = Dahlia
Daisy = Bellis
Daisy Bush = Olearia
Dame's Violet = Hesperis
Dandelion = Taraxacum
Daphne = Daphne
Darling Pea = Swainsona
Date Palm = Phoenix
Day Lily = Hemerocallis
Dayflower = Commelina
Dead Nettles = Lamium
Deadly Nightshade = Atropa
Death Camas = Zigadenus
Deer Grass = Rhexia
Deergrass = Trichophorum
Desert Candle = Eremurus
Desert Lime = Eremocitrus
Desert Rose = Adenium
Deutsia = Deutzia
Devil Pepper = Rauvolfia
Devil Wood = Osmanthus
Devil's Bit Scabious = Succisa
Devil's Claw = Ibicella, Martynia,
   Proboscidea
Devil's Club = Oplopanax
Devil's Ivy = Epipremnum
Devil's Thorn = Emex
Devil's Tongue = Amorphophallus
Dewplant = Lampranthus
Dill = Anethum
Ditch Stonecrop = Penthorum
Dittany = Dictamnus
Djave = Baillonella
Dock = Rumex
Dodder = Cuscuta
Dog Fennel = Anthemis
Dog Grass = Agropyron
Dog's Tail = Cynosurus
Dog's Tooth Violet = Erythronium
Dogbane = Apocynum
Dogwood = Cornus, Piscidia
Double Coconut = Lodoicea
Doum Plam = Hyphaene
Dove Orchid = Peristeria
Dove Tree = Davidia
Down-Tree = Ochroma
Dragon Arum = Dracunculus
Dragon Flower = Huernia
Dragon Tree = Dracaena
Dragon's Blood Palm = Daemonorops

Dragon's Head = Dracocephalum
Dragon's Mouth = Helicodiceros,
   Horminum
Dragon's Teeth = Tetragonolobus
Drop Tongue = Schismatoglottis
Dropseed = Sporobolus
Dropwort = Filipendula
Drum Sticks = Isopogon
Duckweed = Lemna
Dumb Cane = Dieffenbachia
Dwarf Pine = Microstrobos
Dwarf Snapdragon = Chaenorhinum
Earth Star = Cryptanthus
Eastern Horned Poppies = Dicranostigma
Ebony = Diospyros
Echeveria = Echeveria
Edelweiss = Leontopodium
Eel Grass = Vallisneria
Eelgrass = Zostera
Egg Fruit = Pouteria
Eggplant = Solanum
Elder = Sambucus
Elephant Bush = Portulacaria
Elephant Ears = Bergenia
Elephant's Apple = Dillenia, Limonia
Elephant's Ear = Caladium, Enterolobium
Elephant's-Ear Plant = Alocasia
Elephantwood = Bolusanthus
Elk Grass = Xerophyllum
Elkhorn Fern = Platycerium
Elm = Ulmus
Elsholtzia = Elsholtzia
Enchanter's Nightshade = Circaea
Epaulette Tree = Pterostyrax
Esthwaite Waterweed = Hydrilla
Evening Primrose = Oenothera
Everglades Palm = Acoelorrhaphe
Evergreen Laburnum = Piptanthus
Everlasting Flower = Helichrysum
Eyebright = Euphrasia
Fairy Bells = Disporum
Fairy Foxglove = Erinus
Fairy Lily = Chlidanthus
False Acacia = Robinia
False Anemone = Anemonopsis
False Asphodel = Tofieldia
False Brome = Brachypodium
False Buck's Beard = Astilbe
False Camellia = Stewartia
False Chamomile = Boltonia
False Cypress = Chamaecyparis
False Dayflower = Tinantia
False Dragon Head = Physostegia
False Fennel = Ridolfia
False Garlic = Nothoscordum

False Indigo = Baptisia
False Indogo = Amorpha
False Lupin = Thermopsis
False Mallow = Sidalcea, Sphaeralcea
False Mitrewort = Tiarella
False Myrtle = Anamirta
False Nettle = Boehmeria
False Oat Grass = Arrhenatherum
False Olive = Elaeodendron
False Rue Anemone = Isopyrum
False Salomon's Seal = Smilacina
False Sedge = Kobresia
False Spiraea = Sorbaria
False Vervain = Stachytarpheta
Fameflower = Talinum
Fan Fern = Sticherus
Fan Palm = Livistona, Trachycarpus
Farewell to Spring = Clarkia
Fatsi = Fatsia
Feather Grass = Stipa
Felt Fern = Pyrrosia
Felwort = Gentianella, Swertia
Fen Orchid = Liparis
Fennel = Foeniculum
Fennel Flower = Nigella
Fenugreek = Trigonella
Fern Grass = Catapodium
Fern Palm = Dioon
Fern-leaf Aralia = Polyscias
Fescue = Festuca, Vulpia
Feverwort = Triosteum
Fiddleneck = Amsinckia
Field Bindweed = Convolvulus
Field Madder = Sherardia
Field Scabious = Knautia
Fiesta Flower = Pholistoma
Fig = Ficus
Figwort = Scrophularia
Filmy Fern = Hymenophyllum
Finger Grass = Chloris, Digitaria, Paspalum
Finger Lime = Microcitrus
Fir = Abies
Fir Clubmoss = Huperzia
Fire Bush = Embothrium, Hamelia
Fire Lily = Cyrtanthus
Firebush = Streptosolen
Firethorn = Pyracantha
Fishtail Palm = Caryota
Fishwort = Houttuynia
Five Finger = Potentilla
Flag = Iris
Flamboyant = Peltophorum
Flame Lily = Pyrolirion
Flame Nettle = Solenostemon
Flame Pea = Chorizema

Flame Tree = Delonix
Flamingo Flower = Anthurium
Flannel Bush = Fremontodendron
Flat Sedge = Blysmus
Flax = Linum
Flax Lily = Dianella
Fleabane = Conyza, Dittrichia, Erigeron, Inula, Pulicaria
Fleawort = Tephroseris
Flixweed = Descurainia
Floating Fern = Ceratopteris, Salvinia
Floating Heart = Nymphoides
Floating Water Plantain = Luronium
Florist's Chrysanthemum = Chrysanthemum
Florist's Cineraria = Pericallis
Florist's Gloxinia = Sinningia
Floss Silktree = Chorisia
Flossflower = Ageratum
Flowering Fern = Anemia
Flowering Maple = Abutilon
Flowering Quince = Chaenomeles
Flowering Rush = Butomus
Flowering Stones = Lithops
Fluellen = Kickxia
Foam Flower = Tiarella
Foliage Flower = Phyllanthus
Foll's Parsley = Aethusa
Fontanesia = Fontanesia
Forest Poppy = Hylomecon
Forget-me-not = Myosotis
Fork Fern = Psilotum
Forsythia = Forsythia
Fountain Bamboo = Fargesia, Yushania
Fountain Grass = Pennisetum
Fox Nuts = Euryale
Foxglove = Digitalis
Foxglove Tree = Paulownia
Foxtail Grass = Alopecurus
Foxtail Lily = Eremurus
Foxtail Orchid = Rhynchostylis
Fragrant Orchid = Gymnadenia
Frangipani = Plumeria
Franklin Tree = Franklinia
Freesia = Freesia
French Oat Grass = Gaudinia
Fringe Flower = Thysanotus
Fringe Lily = Thysanotus
Fringe Tree = Chionanthus
Fringecup = Tellima
Fringed Water Lily = Nymphoides
Fritillary = Fritillaria
Frog Orchid = Coeloglossum
Frog's Lettuce = Groenlandia
Frogbit = Hydrocharis

Frogfruit = Phyla
Fuchsia = Fuchsia
Fumitory = Fumaria
Furze = Ulex
Fustic = Chlorophora
Galingale = Cyperus
Gallant Soldier = Galinsoga
Gardenia = Gardenia
Garland Lily = Hedychium
Garlic = Allium
Garlic Mustard = Alliaria
Gay Feather = Liatris
Genipap = Genipa
Gentian = Gentiana
Geranium = Pelargonium
German Ivy = Delairea
Germander = Teucrium
Gesneria = Gesneria
Ghost Orchid = Epipogium
Giant Bellflower = Ostrowskia
Giant Fennel = Ferula
Giant Lily = Cardiocrinum
Giant Mallow = Hibiscus
Giant Reed = Arundo
Giant Rhubarb = Gunnera
Giant Scabious = Cephalaria
Giant Water Lily = Victoria
Giboshi = Hosta
Gillyflower = Matthiola
Gily Flower = Gilia
Ginger = Zingiber
Ginger Lily = Alpinia, Hedychium
Ginkgo = Ginkgo
Ginseng = Panax
Gladiolus = Gladiolus
Glasswort = Salicornia
Globe Amaranth = Gomphrena
Globe Artichoke = Cynara
Globe Daisy = Globularia
Globe Mallow = Sphaeralcea
Globe Thistle = Echinops
Globe Tulip = Calochortus
Globeflower = Trollius
Glory Bush = Tibouchina
Glory Flower = Eccremocarpus
Glory Lily = Gloriosa
Glory of the Snow = Chionodoxa
Glory Pea = Clianthus
Gloxinia = Gloxinia
Goat Grass = Aegilops
Goat Nut = Simmondsia
Goat's Beard = Aruncus, Tragopogon
Goat's Rue = Galega
Godetia = Clarkia
Gold Farn = Pityrogramma

Gold of Pleasure = Camelina
Gold Thread = Coptis
Gold-and-Silver Chrysanthemum = Ajania
Golden Aster = Chrysopsis
Golden Chinkapin = Chrysolepis
Golden Club = Orontium
Golden Dog's Tail = Lamarckia
Golden Knee = Chrysogonum
Golden Larch = Pseudolarix
Golden Polypody = Phlebodium
Golden Rain = Laburnum
Golden Rain Tree = Koelreuteria
Golden Saxifrage = Chrysosplenium
Golden Seal = Hydrastis
Golden Thistle = Scolymus
Goldenrod = Solidago
Goldenstars = Bloomeria
Goldilock = Chrysocoma
Gooseberry = Ribes
Goosefoot = Chenopodium
Gorse = Ulex
Goutweed = Aegopodium
Governor's Plum = Flacourtia
Grama Grass = Bouteloua
Grandilla = Passiflora
Granny's Bonnet = Aquilegia
Grape Hyacinth = Muscari
Grape Ivy = Cissus
Grape Vine = Vitis
Grapefruit = Citrus
Grapple Plant = Harpagophytum
Grass of Parnassus = Parnassia
Grass Widow = Olsynium
Grassy Bells = Edraianthus
Great Fen Sedge = Cladium
Great Forget-me-not = Brunnera
Great Pignut = Bunium
Greater Celadine = Chelidonium
Greater Duckweed = Spirodela
Greek Clover = Trigonella
Green Alkanet = Pentaglottis
Greenhood = Pterostylis
Greenthreads = Thelesperma
Greenweed = Genista
Grey Hair Grass = Corynephorus
Gromwell = Lithospermum
Ground Elder = Aegopodium
Ground Ivy = Glechoma
Gru Gru Palm = Acrocomia
Guava = Psidium
Guinea Gold Vine = Hibbertia
Gum = Eucalyptus
Gum Ammoniac = Dorema
Gum Lac = Schleichera
Gum Myrtle = Angophora

Gumplant = Grindelia
Gutta Percha = Palaquium
Gutta Percha Tree = Eucommia
Gypsywort = Lycopus
Hair Grass = Aira, Deschampsia, Koeleria
Hairy Rocket = Erucastrum
Hakone Grass = Hakonechloa
Hard Fern = Blechnum
Hard Grass = Parapholis
Hare's Ear = Bupleurum
Hare's Ear Mustard = Conringia
Hare's Foot Fern = Davallia
Hare's Tail = Lagurus
Harlequinflower = Sparaxis
Harmal = Peganum
Harmel = Peganum
Hartwort = Tordylium
Haw Medlar = × Crataemespilus
Hawk's Beard = Crepis
Hawkbit = Leontodon
Hawkweed = Hieracium
Hawthorn = Crataegus, Rhaphiolepis
Hazel = Corylus
Heath = Erica
Heath Grass = Danthonia
Heather = Calluna
Heavenly Bamboo = Nandina
Hedge Hyssop = Gratiola
Hedge Nettle = Stachys
Hedge Parsley = Torilis
Hedge Veronica = Hebe
Hedgehog Broom = Erinacea
Hedgehog Cactus = Echinocereus
Helen's Flower = Helenium
Heliotrope = Heliotropium
Hellebore = Helleborus
Helleborine = Cephalanthera, Epipactis
Helmet Flower = Scutellaria
Helmet Orchid = Coryanthes
Hemlock = Conium, Tsuga
Hemlock Spruce = Tsuga
Hemp = Cannabis
Hemp Agrimony = Eupatorium
Hemp Nettle = Galeopsis
Henbane = Hyoscyamus
Henna = Lawsonia
Herald's Trumpet = Beaumontia
Herb Paris = Paris
Hercules All Heal = Opopanax
Heron's Bill = Erodium
Hesper Palm = Brahea
Hiba = Thujopsis
Hickory = Carya
Hoary Alison = Berteroa
Hoary Mustard = Hirschfeldia

Hoary Pea = Tephrosia
Hog Paenut = Amphicarpaea
Hog Plum = Spondias
Hog's Fennel = Peucedanum
Hogweed = Heracleum
Holly = Ilex
Holly Fern = Polystichum
Holly Grape = Mahonia
Hollyhook = Alcea
Holy Grass = Hierochloe
Honesty = Lunaria
Honewort = Cryptotaenia, Trinia
Honey Berry = Melicoccus
Honey Bush = Melianthus
Honey Garlic = Nectaroscordum
Honey Locust = Gleditsia
Honey Myrtle = Melaleuca
Honey Palm = Jubaea
Honeybells = Hermannia, Nothoscordum
Honeysuckle = Lonicera
Honeywort = Cerinthe
Hop = Humulus
Hop Hornbeam = Ostrya
Hop Tree = Ptelea
Horehound = Ballota, Marrubium
Hornbeam = Carpinus
Horned Pondweed = Zannichellia
Horned Poppy = Glaucium
Hornwort = Ceratophyllum
Horse Balm = Collinsonia
Horse Chestnut = Aesculus
Horse Gentian = Triosteum
Horse Radish = Armoracia
Horseradish Tree = Moringa
Horseshoe Vetch = Hippocrepis
Horsetail = Equisetum
Hot Water Plant = Achimenes
Hottentot Tobacco = Tarchonanthus
Hottentot-Fig = Carpobrotus
Hound's Tongue = Cynoglossum
House Leek = Sempervivum
Houseleek = Jovibarba
Huckleberry = Gaylussacia
Hyacinth = Hyacinthus
Hyacinth Bean = Lablab
Hydrangea = Hydrangea
Hyssop = Hyssopus
Ice-Cream Bean = Inga
Iceplant = Dorotheanthus
Indian Crocus = Pleione
Indian Grass = Sorghastrum
Indian Mallow = Abutilon
Indian Rhododendron = Melastoma
Indian Rhubarb = Darmera
Indian Strawberry = Duchesnea

Indigo = Indigofera
Ironbark = Eucalyptus
Irontree = Parrotia
Ironweed = Vernonia
Ironwood = Eusideroxylon, Parrotia
Isaac and Jacob = Trachystemon
Ivory Thistle = Ptilostemon
Ivy = Hedera
Ivy Tree = Schefflera
Jaborandi = Pilocarpus
Jacaranda = Jacaranda
Jack Bean = Canavalia
Jacob's Ladder = Polemonium
Jacob's Rod = Asphodeline
Jacobean Lily = Sprekelia
Jade Vine = Strongylodon
Jamaica Cherry = Muntingia
Jambos = Syzygium
Japanese Cedar = Cryptomeria
Japanese Dead Nettle = Meehania
Japanese Foam Flower = Tanakaea
Japanese Lanterns = Physalis
Jasmine = Jasminum, Mandevilla
Javan Grape = Tetrastigma
Javillo = Reutealis
Jelly Palm = Butia
Jersey Fern = Anogramma
Jersey Lily = Amaryllis
Jerusalem Thorn = Parkinsonia
Jessamine = Cestrum, Jasminum
Jesuit's Bark = Cinchona
Jewel Orchid = Goodyera
Job's Tears = Coix
Joint Fir = Ephedra
Joint Vetch = Aeschynomene
Jojoba = Simmondsia
Joseph's Coat = Alternanthera
Jujube = Ziziphus
Juneberry = Amelanchier
Juniper = Juniperus
Jute = Corchorus
Kaffir Lily = Clivia, Schizostylis
Kaffir Plum = Harpephyllum
Kangaroo Paw = Anigozanthos
Kapok Tree = Ceiba
Katsura Tree = Cercidiphyllum
Kauri Pine = Agathis
Kerria = Kerria
Key Palm = Thrinax
Khat = Catha
Kidney Vetch = Anthyllis
Killearney-Fern = Trichomanes
King Palm = Archontophoenix
Kiwi Fruit = Actinidia
Knapweed = Centaurea

Knawel = Scleranthus
Knotgrass = Polygonum
Knotweed = Fallopia
Kudzu = Pueraria
Kumquat = Fortunella
Labrador Tea = Ledum
Lac Tree = Schleichera
Lace Flower = Trachymene
Lacebark = Hoheria
Ladder Fern = Nephrolepis
Lady Fern = Athyrium
Lady Palm = Rhapis
Lady's Mantle = Alchemilla
Lady's Slipper = Cypripedium
Lady's Tresses = Spiranthes
Ladybells = Adenophora
Laelia = Laelia
Lamb's Succory = Arnoseris
Langsat = Lansium
Lantana = Lantana
Lantern Tree = Crinodendron
Larch = Larix
Larkspur = Consolida, Delphinium
Latan = Latania
Laurel = Laurus
Lavender = Lavandula
Lavender Cotton = Santolina
Lawn Lobelia = Pratia
Leadwort = Plumbago
Leather Farn = Acrostichum
Leatherleaf = Chamaedaphne
Leatherwood = Dirca
Lemon = Citrus
Lemon-scented Fern = Oreopteris
Lemongrass = Cymbopogon
Lentil = Lens
Leopard Lily = Belamcanda
Leopard Plant = Ligularia
Leopard's Bane = Doronicum
Leschenaultia = Leschenaultia
Lesser Clubmoss = Selaginella
Lesser Sea-Fig = Erepsia
Lesser Water Plantain = Baldellia
Lettuce = Lactuca
Leyland Cypress = × Cuprocyparis
Lignum Vitae = Guaiacum
Lilac = Syringa
Lilac Hibiscus = Alyogyne
Lily = Lilium
Lily of the Incas = Alstroemeria
Lily of the Valley = Convallaria
Lily Turf = Liriope
Lilyturf = Ophiopogon
Lime = Citrus, Tilia
Limequat = × Citrofortunella

Linden = Tilia
Lion's Ear = Leonotis
Lip Fern = Cheilanthes
Lipstick Tree = Bixa
Litchi = Litchi
Liverleaf = Hepatica
Living Granite = Pleiospilos
Living Rock = Ariocarpus, Pleiospilos
Living Stones = Lithops
Lizard Orchid = Himantoglossum
Lizard's Tail = Saururus
Lobelia = Lobelia
Longan Fruit = Dimocarpus
Longleaf = Falcaria
Loofah = Luffa
Loosestrife = Lysimachia, Lythrum
Loquat = Eriobotrya
Lords and Ladies = Arum
Lotus = Nelumbo
Loulu Palm = Pritchardia
Lousewort = Pedicularis
Lovage = Levisticum, Ligusticum
Love Charm = Clytostoma
Love Grass = Chrysopogon, Eragrostis
Love Plant = Anacampseros
Love-in-a-Mist = Nigella
Luckynut = Thevetia
Lungwort = Pulmonaria
Lupin = Lupinus
Lyme Grass = Leymus
Lyonia = Lyonia
Madagascar Periwinkle = Catharanthus
Madder = Rubia
Madeira Vine = Anredera
Madwort = Alyssum, Asperugo
Magnolia = Magnolia
Maguey = Agave
Mahogany = Khaya, Swietenia
Maidenhair Fern = Adiantum
Maidenhair Tree = Ginkgo
Maize = Zea
Majoram = Origanum
Makola = Afzelia
Malabar Nightshade = Basella
Malanga = Xanthosoma
Mallow = Malva
Malvastrum = Malvastrum
Mammee Apple = Mammea
Man Orchid = Aceras
Mandarin = Citrus
Mandrake = Mandragora
Mangabeira = Hancornia
Mango = Mangifera
Mangosteen = Garcinia
Mangrove Palm = Nypa

Manila Palm = Adonidia
Manioc = Manihot
Manzanita = Arbutus
Maple = Acer
Maranta = Maranta
Marari Palm = Nannorrhops
Mare's Tail = Hippuris
Marguerite = Argyranthemum
Marigold = Calendula, Tagetes
Marijuana = Cannabis
Mariposa Tulip = Calochortus
Marlberry = Ardisia
Marrow = Cucurbita
Marsh Clubmoss = Lycopodiella
Marsh Elder = Iva
Marsh Fern = Thelypteris
Marsh Grass = Spartina
Marsh Mallow = Althaea
Marsh Marigold = Caltha
Marsh Orchid = Dactylorhiza
Marsh Trefoil = Menyanthes
Marshwort = Apium
Mask Flower = Alonsoa
Masterwort = Astrantia
Mat Grass = Nardus
May Apple = Podophyllum
May Lily = Maianthemum
Mayweed = Matricaria
Meadow Beauty = Rhexia
Meadow Foam = Limnanthes
Meadow Grass = Poa
Meadow Rue = Thalictrum
Meadowsweet = Filipendula
Medick = Medicago
Mediterranean Hair Grass = Rostraria
Medlar = Mespilus
Melagueta Pepper = Aframomum
Melick = Melica
Melilot = Melilotus
Melon = Cucumis
Menziesia = Menziesia
Mercury = Mercurialis
Merry-Bells = Uvularia
Mescal = Lophophora
Mesquite = Prosopis
Mexican Aster = Cosmos
Mexican Hat = Ratibida
Mexican Hyssop = Agastache
Mexican Poppy = Argemone
Mexican Sunflower = Tithonia
Mexican Tulip Poppy = Hunnemannia
Michaelmas Daisy = Aster
Midnight Horror = Oroxylum
Mignonette = Reseda
Milfoil = Achillea

Milk Parsley = Selinum
Milk Thistle = Silybum, Sonchus
Milk Tree = Brosimum
Milk Vetch = Astragalus
Milkweed = Asclepias
Milkwort = Polygala
Millet = Milium, Sorghum
Mimosa = Acacia
Mind your own Business = Soleirolia
Mints = Mentha
Miracle Fruit = Synsepalum
Mist Flower = Conoclinium
Mistletoe = Viscum
Moccasin Grass = Melothria
Mock Azalea = Adenium
Mock Cucumber = Echinocystis
Mock Orange = Philadelphus
Mock Privet = Phillyrea
Moneywort = Sibthorpia
Monk's Hood = Aconitum
Monkey Nut = Lecythis
Monkey Puzzle = Araucaria
Monkey-bread Tree = Adansonia
Monkeyflower = Mimulus
Montbretia = Crocosmia
Moon Carrot = Seseli
Moonseed = Cocculus, Menispermum
Moonwort = Botrychium
Moor Grass = Molinia, Sesleria
Mornig Flag = Orthrosanthus
Morning = Brunfelsia
Morning Glory = Argyreia, Ipomoea
Moth Orchid = Phalaenopsis
Mother-in-law's Tongue = Dieffenbachia
Motherwort = Leonurus
Mountain Ash = Sorbus
Mountain Ebony = Bauhinia
Mountain Heather = Cassiope
Mountain Holly = Nemopanthus
Mountain Mahogany = Cercocarpus
Mountain Misery = Chamaebatia
Mountain Sorrel = Oxyria
Mouse Ear = Cerastium
Mousetail = Myosurus
Mousetailplant = Arisarum
Mud Plantain = Heteranthera
Mudwort = Limosella
Mug Bean = Vigna
Mugwort = Artemisia
Mulberry = Morus
Mullein = Verbascum
Musc Cucumber = Sicana
Musk = Mimulus
Musk Orchid = Herminium
Muskroot = Adoxa

Muskweed = Myagrum
Mustard = Sinapis
Myrobalan = Terminalia
Myrrh = Commiphora
Myrtle = Myricaria
Nagi = Nageia
Naiad = Najas
Naked Ladies = Colchicum
Nakedweed = Chondrilla
Narihira Bamboo = Semiarundinaria
Nasturtium = Tropaeolum
Natal Plum = Carissa
Navelseed = Omphalodes
Navelwort = Omphalodes, Umbilicus
Needle Grass = Stipa
Needle Palm = Rhapidophyllum
Neem Tree = Azadirachta
Neillia = Neillia
Nemophila = Nemophila
Nerine = Nerine
Nerve Plant = Fittonia
Nettle = Urtica
Nettle Tree = Celtis
New Zaeland Spinach = Tetragonia
New Zealand Bur = Acaena
New Zealand Edelweiss = Leucogenes
New Zealand Flax = Phormium
Niger = Guizotia
Nightshade = Solanum
Nikau Palm = Rhopalostylis
Ninebark = Physocarpus
Nipplewort = Lapsana
Nippon Daisy = Nipponanthemum
Nit Grass = Gastridium
Noon and Night = Brunfelsia
Norfolk Island Hibiscus = Lagunaria
Nutmeg = Myristica
Nutmeg Yew = Torreya
Oak = Quercus
Oak Fern = Gymnocarpium
Oat = Avena
Oat Grass = Helictotrichon
Obedient Plant = Physostegia
Oceanspray = Holodiscus
Ocotillo = Fouquieria
Oil Palm = Elaeis
Oleander = Nerium
Oleaster = Elaeagnus
Olive = Olea
Onion = Allium
Orache = Atriplex
Orange = Citrus
Orange Blossom = Choisya
Orange Jessamine = Murraya
Orchid = Ophrys, Orchis

Orchid Cactus = Epiphyllum
Ordeal Tree = Erythrophleum
Oregano = Origanum
Oregon Grape = Mahonia
Oregon Plum = Oemleria
Oriental Thuja = Platycladus
Osage Orange = Maclura
Osoberry = Oemleria
Ostrich Fern = Matteuccia
Ox Eye = Buphthalmum, Heliopsis
Ox Tongue = Helminthotheca
Oxeye = Telekia
Oxeye Daisy = Leucanthemum
Oxtongue = Picris
Oysterplant = Mertensia
Pagoda Tree = Melia
Painted Nettle = Solenostemon
Palas = Licuala
Palm Grass = Curculigo
Palm Springs Daisy = Cladanthus
Palma Corcho = Microcycas
Palmetto = Sabal
Pampas Grass = Cortaderia
Panic Grass = Panicum
Pansy = Viola
Pansy Orchid = Miltonia, Miltoniopsis
Paper Daisy = Acroclinium, Rhodanthe
Paper Mulberry = Broussonetia
Paperbark = Melaleuca
Papoose Root = Caulophyllum
Para Cress = Acmella
Para Rubber = Hevea
Paradise Lily = Paradisea
Parasol Tree = Firmiana
Parsley = Petroselinum
Parsley Fern = Cryptogramma
Parsley Piert = Aphanes
Parsnip = Pastinaca
Partridge Berry = Mitchella
Pasqueflower = Pulsatilla
Passion Flower = Passiflora
Patagonian Cypress = Fitzroya
Patchouly = Pogostemon
Paurotis Palm = Acoelorrhaphe
Pawpaw = Asimina, Carica
Pea = Pisum
Pea Shrub = Caragana
Pea Tree = Caragana
Peace Lily = Spathiphyllum
Peach = Prunus
Peacock Flower = Tigridia
Peanut = Arachis
Pear = Pyrus
Pearl Fruit = Margyricarpus
Pearlbush = Exochorda

Pearlwort = Sagina
Pearly Everlasting = Anaphalis
Pecan = Carya
Pellitoeries of the Wall = Parietaria
Penny Cress = Thlaspi
Pennywort = Centella, Hydrocotyle
Penstemon = Penstemon
Peony = Paeonia
Pepper = Capsicum, Piper
Pepper Saxifrage = Silaum
Peppergrass = Lepidium
Peppertree = Schinus
Pepperwort = Marsilea
Perilla = Perilla
Periwinkle = Vinca
Perovskia = Perovskia
Persian Violet = Cyclamen
Peruvian Lily = Alstroemeria
Petunia = Petunia
Peyote = Lophophora
Pheasant's Eye = Adonis
Philodendron = Philodendron
Phlox = Phlox
Physicnut = Jatropha
Pick-a-back Plant = Tolmiea
Pickerel Weed = Pontederia
Pieris = Pieris
Pigmyweed = Crassula
Pignut = Conopodium
Pignut Palm = Hyophorbe
Pigweed = Amaranthus
Pillwort = Pilularia
Pimpernel = Anagallis
Pinang = Pinanga
Pincushion = Leucospermum
Pincushion Flower = Scabiosa
Pincushion Tree = Hakea
Pine = Pinus
Pineapple = Ananas
Pineapple Flower = Eucomis
Pinellia = Pinellia
Pink = Dianthus
Pink Root = Spigelia
Pipewort = Eriocaulon
Pistachio = Pistacia
Pitcher Plant = Nepenthes, Sarracenia
Pittosporum = Pittosporum
Plain Treasureflower = Arctotheca
Plane = Platanus
Plantain = Musa, Plantago
Plantain Lily = Hosta
Plum = Prunus
Plum Yew = Cephalotaxus
Plumbago = Ceratostigma
Plume Albizia = Paraserianthes

E

Plume Grass = Saccharum
Plume Poppy = Macleaya
Podocarp = Podocarpus
Point Vetch = Oxytropis
Poison Bush = Acokanthera
Poison Tree = Acokanthera
Pokeweed = Phytolacca
Polka Dot Plant = Hypoestes
Polypody = Polypodium
Pomegranate = Punica
Pondweed = Aponogeton, Potamogeton
Poplar = Populus
Poppy = Papaver
Poppy Mallow = Callirhoe
Porcelaine Flower = Hoya
Portia Tree = Thespesia
Potato = Solanum
Potato Bean = Apios
Potency Wood = Ptychopetalum
Pouch Flower = Nematanthus
Powder Puff Tree = Calliandra
Prairie Cone Flower = Ratibida
Prairie Dock = Silphium
Prairie Mallow = Sidalcea
Prickly Ash = Zanthoxylum
Prickly Ear = Acanthostachys
Prickly Pear = Opuntia
Prickly Thrift = Acantholimon
Primrose = Primula
Prince Albert's Yew = Saxegothaea
Prince's Pine = Chimaphila
Princess Palm = Dictyosperma
Privet = Ligustrum
Protea = Protea
Pumpkin = Cucurbita
Purple Dewplant = Disphyma
Purple Wreath = Petrea
Purslane = Claytonia, Portulaca
Puschkinia = Puschkinia
Pussy-Toes = Antennaria
Pyramid Orchid = Anacamptis
Pyrenean Violet = Ramonda
Quaking Grass = Briza
Quamash = Camassia
Quandong = Elaeocarpus
Quassia = Picrasma
Quebracho = Aspidosperma
Queen Lily = Phaedranassa
Queensland Nut = Macadamia
Quillwort = Isoetes
Quince = Cydonia
Rabbitbush = Chrysothamnus
Radiator Plant = Peperomia
Radish = Raphanus
Raffia = Raphia

Rag Gourd = Luffa
Ragweed = Ambrosia
Ragwort = Brachyglottis, Senecio
Rain Flower = Zephyranthes
Rainbow Plant = Byblis
Raisin Tree = Hovenia
Rambutan = Nephelium
Rampion = Phyteuma
Rannoch Rush = Scheuchzeria
Rapturewort = Herniaria
Rasp-Fern = Doodia
Raspberry = Rubus
Raspwort = Haloragis
Rat's-Tail Cactus = Aporocactus
Rata = Metrosideros
Rata Vine = Metrosideros
Rattan Palm = Calamus
Rattlebox = Crotalaria
Red Alder = Cunonia
Red Cedar = Thuja
Red Flag Bush = Mussaenda
Red Hot Poker = Kniphofia
Red Pucoon = Sanguinaria
Red Valerian = Centranthus
Redbud = Cercis
Redwood = Adenanthera, Metasequoia
Reed = Phragmites
Reedmace = Typha
Reineckea = Reineckea
Restharrow = Ononis
Retam = Retama
Rhatany = Krameria
Rhododendron = Rhododendron
Rhubarb = Rheum
Ribbon Fern = Pteris
Ribbon Wood = Plagianthus
Ribbonwood = Adenostoma
Rice = Oryza
Rice Flower = Pimelea
Rice Grass = Oryzopsis
Rice-Paper Plant = Tetrapanax
Rimu = Dacrydium
Ring Bellflower = Symphyandra
River Rose = Bauera
Rock Bell = Wahlenbergia
Rock Jasmine = Androsace
Rock Lily = Arthropodium
Rock Madwort = Aurinia
Rock Rose = Cistus, Helianthemum
Rock Spiraea = Petrophytum
Rockcress = Arabis
Rocket = Sisymbrium
Rocket Salad = Eruca
Romanzoffia = Romanzoffia
Rooibos = Aspalathus

Rose = Rosa
Rose Bay = Nerium
Rose Mallow = Hibiscus
Rose Moss = Portulaca
Rose Myrtle = Rhodomyrtus
Rose of Jericho = Anastatica
Rosemary = Rosmarinus
Roseroot = Rhodiola
Rosewood = Dalbergia, Pterocarpus
Rosin-Weed = Silphium
Round-headed Club Rush = Scirpoides
Royal Fern = Osmunda
Royal Palm = Roystonea
Rubber Tree = Castilla
Rue = Ruta
Rue Anemone = Anemonella
Ruffle Palm = Aiphanes
Rukam = Flacourtia
Rush = Juncus
Russian Knapweed = Acroptilon
Rye = Secale
Rye Grass = Lolium
Sacred Bark = Cinchona
Safflower = Carthamus
Saffron Spike = Aphelandra
Sage = Phlomis, Salvia
Sage Brush = Artemisia
Sago Palm = Metroxylon
Saguaro = Carnegiea
Sainforn = Onobrychis
Sakaki = Cleyera
Salak Palm = Salacca
Sallow = Salix
Salt Cedar = Tamarix
Salt Tree = Halimodendron
Saltbush = Atriplex
Saltmarsh Grass = Puccinellia
Sand Crocus = Romulea
Sand Grass = Mibora
Sand Myrtle = Leiophyllum
Sand Spurrey = Spergularia
Sand Verbena = Abronia
Sandalwood = Santalum
Sandbox Tree = Hura
Sandbur = Cenchrus
Sandwort = Arenaria, Minuartia,
    Moehringia
Sanicle = Sanicula
Sassafras = Sassafras
Satin Flower = Clarkia
Satin Wood = Chloroxylon
Sausage Tree = Kigelia
Savory = Satureja
Saw Wort = Serratula
Saxaul = Haloxylon

Saxifrage = Saxifraga
Scabious = Scabiosa
Scarlet-fruited Gourd = Coccinia
Scentless False Chamomile =
    Tripleurospermum
Scorpion Orchid = Arachnis
Scorpion Vetch = Coronilla
Scorpion Weed = Phacelia
Screw Pine = Pandanus
Scurf Pea = Psoralea
Scurvygrass = Cochlearia
Sea Bean = Entada
Sea Blite = Suaeda
Sea Buckthorn = Hippophae
Sea Club Rush = Bolboschoenus
Sea Daffodil = Pancratium
Sea Grape = Coccoloba
Sea Heath = Frankenia
Sea Holly = Eryngium
Sea Kale = Crambe
Sea Lavender = Limonium
Sea Milkwort = Glaux
Sea Onion = Urginea
Sea Rocket = Cakile
Sea Sandwort = Honckenya
Sea Spurrey = Spergularia
Sedge = Carex
Selfheal = Prunella
Senna = Senna
Sensitive Fern = Onoclea
Sensitive Plant = Mimosa
Sentry Palm = Howea
Serviceberry = Amelanchier
Sesame = Sesamum
Seychelles Nut = Lodoicea
Shallon = Gaultheria
Shampire = Crithmum
Shamrock = Oxalis
Shaving-Brush Tree = Pachira
Shea Butter Tree = Vitellaria
Sheep Laurel = Kalmia
Sheep's Bit = Jasione
Shell Flower = Moluccella, Pistia
Shellflower = Chelone
Shepherd's Cress = Teesdalia
Shepherd's Purses = Capsella
Shield Fern = Polystichum
Shinleaf = Pyrola
Shittimwood = Bumelia
Shooting Star = Dodecatheon
Shower Tree = Cassia
Shrub Palmetto = Serenoa
Shrubby Dewplant = Ruschia
Shrubby Trefoil = Ptelea
Signal Grass = Brachiaria

E

Sildweed = Asclepias
Silk Tassel = Garrya
Silk Vine = Periploca
Silk-Cotton Tree = Bombax
Silkworm Thorn = Cudrania
Silky Bent = Apera
Silver Bell = Halesia
Silver Fern = Pityrogramma
Silver Fir = Abies
Silver Grass = Miscanthus
Silver Palm = Coccothrinax
Silver Saw Palm = Acoelorrhaphe
Silver Tree = Leucadendron
Silver-flowered Everlasting =
    Cephalipterum
Skimmia = Skimmia
Skullcap = Scutellaria
Skunk Cabbage = Lysichiton, Symplocarpus
Sleepy Mallow = Malvaviscus
Slipper Orchid = Paphiopedilum
Slipper Spurge = Pedilanthus
Slipperwort = Calceolaria
Slough Grass = Beckmannia
Small Reed = Calamagrostis
Smartweed = Persicaria
Smilo Grass = Oryzopsis
Smoke Bush = Cotinus
Smokewood = Cotinus
Snake Gourd = Trichosanthes
Snake Plant = Sansevieria
Snake Wood = Cecropia
Snake's Head Iris = Hermodactylus
Snakeweed = Stachytarpheta
Snapdragon = Antirrhinum
Sneezeweed = Helenium
Snow Poppy = Eomecon
Snow Wreath = Neviusia
Snowbell = Soldanella, Styrax
Snowberry = Chiococca, Symphoricarpos
Snowdon Lily = Lloydia
Snowdrop = Galanthus
Snowdrop Tree = Halesia
Snowflake = Leucojum
Soap Bark Tree = Quillaja
Soap Bush = Clidemia, Porlieria
Soapberry = Sapindus
Soapwort = Saponaria
Society Garlic = Tulbaghia
Soft Grass = Holcus
Solomon's Seal = Polygonatum
Sorrel = Oxalis
Sorrel Tree = Oxydendrum
Sorva Gum = Couma
Sourwood = Oxydendrum
Southern Beech = Nothofagus

Southern Broom = Notospartium
Sow Thistle = Sonchus
Sowbread = Cyclamen
Soya Bean = Glycine
Spangle Grass = Uniola
Spanish Broom = Spartium
Spanish Cherry = Mimusops
Spanish Dagger = Yucca
Spear Grass = Heteropogon, Stipa
Spear Lily = Doryanthes
Speargrass = Aciphylla
Speedwell = Veronica
Spicebush = Calycanthus
Spider Flower = Cleome, Grevillea
Spider Ivy = Chlorophytum
Spider Lily = Hymenocallis, Lycoris
Spider Plant = Anthericum, Chlorophytum
Spiderwort = Tradescantia
Spignel = Meum
Spike Grass = Uniola
Spike Heath = Bruckenthalia
Spike Rush = Eleocharis
Spinach = Spinacia
Spindle = Euonymus
Spiny-Club Palm = Bactris
Spiral Flag = Costus
Spiral Ginger = Costus
Spleenwort = Asplenium
Spotted Laurel = Aucuba
Spotted Orchid = Dactylorhiza
Spotted Rock Rose = Tuberaria
Spring Starflower = Ipheion
Spruce = Picea
Spur Leaf = Tetracentron
Spurge = Chamaesyce, Euphorbia
Spurge Nettle = Cnidoscolus
Spurrey = Spergula
Squill = Scilla
Squirting Cucmber = Ecballium
St Daboec's Heath = Daboecia
St John's Bread = Ceratonia
St John's Wort = Hypericum
St Paul's Wort = Sigesbeckia
Staghorn Fern = Platycerium
Star Apple = Chrysophyllum
Star Daisy = Lindheimera
Star Grass = Aletris, Hypoxis
Star of Bethlehem = Gagea, Ornithogalum
Star Thistle = Centaurea
Starfish Flower = Stapelia
Statice = Psylliostachys
Stike's Aster = Stokesia
Stinking Bean Trefoil = Anagyris
Stitchwort = Stellaria
Stock = Matthiola

Stone Cress = Aethionema
Stone Parsley = Sison
Stonecrop = Sedum
Stopper = Eugenia
Storax = Styrax
Stork's Bill = Erodium
Strap Air Plant = Catopsis
Strap Fern = Campyloneurum
Strapwort = Corrigiola
Strawberry = Fragaria
Strawberry Tree = Arbutus
Strawflower = Helipterum
Strychnine Tree = Strychnos
Sumac = Rhus
Sumach = Rhus
Summer Cypress = Bassia
Summer Hyacinth = Galtonia
Summer-Sweet = Clethra
Sun Marigold = Dimorphotheca
Sun Pitcher = Heliamphora
Sun Rose = Cistus, Helianthemum
Sunflower = Helianthus
Swallowwort = Vincetoxicum
Swamp Cypress = Taxodium
Swamp Pink = Helonias
Swan Orchid = Cycnoches
Swan River Daisy = Brachyscome
Swan River Pea = Brachysema
Sweet Alsion = Lobularia
Sweet Box = Sarcococca
Sweet Cicely = Myrrhis
Sweet Clover = Melilotus
Sweet Fern = Comptonia
Sweet Flags = Acorus
Sweet Grass = Glyceria
Sweet Gum = Liquidambar
Sweet Olive = Osmanthus
Sweet Pepper = Capsicum
Sweetpea Bush = Podalyria
Sweetshade = Hymenosporum
Sweetspire = Itea
Sweetwood = Glycyrrhiza
Swine Cress = Coronopus
Swiss-Cheese Plant = Monstera
Sword Lily = Iris
Swort Fern = Nephrolepis
Tahitian Chestnut = Inocarpus
Tail Flower = Anthurium
Tail Grape = Artabotrys
Tallow Tree = Sapium
Tamarind = Tamarindus
Tamarisk = Tamarix
Tanbark Oak = Lithocarpus
Tannia = Xanthosoma
Tansy = Tanacetum

Tansy-leaved Rocket = Hugueninia
Taro = Colocasia
Tarweed = Madia
Tasmanian Fuchsia = Correa
Tassel Tree = Garrya
Tasselweed = Ruppia
Tea Tree = Leptospermum
Teak = Tectona
Teaplant = Lycium
Teasel = Dipsacus
Teddy Bear Vine = Cyanotis
Temple Bells = Smithiantha
Temple Plant = Crateva
Temple Tree = Plumeria
Thale Cress = Arabidopsis
Thatch Plam = Thrinax
Thistle = Carduus, Cirsium
Thorn Apple = Datura
Thrift = Armeria
Throatwort = Trachelium
Thunbergia = Thunbergia
Thyme = Thymus
Tick Trefoil = Desmodium
Tickseed = Coreopsis
Tiger Flower = Tigridia
Tiger Grass = Thysanolaena
Tiger Jaws = Faucaria
Timothy = Phleum
Tipu Tree = Tipuana
Toad Lily = Tricyrtis
Toadflax = Chaenorhinum,
  Cymbalaria, Linaria
Tobacco = Nicotiana
Toddy Palm = Borassus
Tomato = Lycopersicon
Tongue Orchid = Serapias
Tonka Bean = Dipteryx
Toon = Toona
Toothwort = Lathraea
Torch Ginger = Etlingera
Torch Lily = Kniphofia
Torchwood = Amyris, Bursera
Tournesol = Chrozophora
Townsend Daisy = Townsendia
Trailing Azalea = Loiseleuria
Trailing Bellflower = Cyananthus
Transvaal Daisy = Gerbera
Traveller's Tree = Ravenala
Treasureflower = Gazania
Tree Anemone = Carpenteria
Tree Aralia = Kalopanax
Tree Celandine = Bocconia
Tree Fern = Cibotium, Cyathea, Dicksonia
Tree Groundsel = Baccharis
Tree Mallow = Lavatera

Tree of Damocles = Oroxylum
Tree of Heaven = Ailanthus
Tree of Sadness = Nyctanthes
Tree Poppy = Dendromecon
Tree Tomato = Cyphomandra
Treebine = Cissus
Trinity Flower = Trillium
Triphyllon = Bituminaria
Triticale = × Triticosecale
Tritonia = Tritonia
Trumpet Bush = Tecoma
Trumpet Creeper = Campsis
Trumpet Vine = Bignonia, Podranea
Tuba Root = Derris
Tuberose = Polianthes
Tulip = Tulipa
Tulip Orchid = Anguloa
Tulip Tree = Liriodendron
Tuna = Opuntia
Tungoil Tree = Vernicia
Tupelo = Nyssa
Turk's Cap Cactus = Melocactus
Turnip Fern = Angiopteris
Turnsole = Heliotropium
Turtle Bone = Lonchocarpus
Twayblade = Listera
Twin Leaf = Jeffersonia
Twin-flower = Linnaea
Twining Snapdragon = Maurandya
Twinspur = Diascia
Twisted Stalk = Streptopus
Ulluco = Ullucus
Ulmo = Eucryphia
Umbrella Leaf = Diphylleia
Umbrella Palm = Hedyscepe
Umbrella Pine = Sciadopitys
Umbrella Plant = Eriogonum
Umbrella Tree = Musanga, Schefflera
Umbrellawort = Mirabilis
Unicorn Plant = Ibicella, Martynia,
    Proboscidea
Upas Tree = Antiaris
Valerian = Valeriana
Vallis = Vallisneria
Vanilla = Vanilla
Vanilla Leaf = Achlys
Vanilla Orchid = Nigritella
Veltheimia = Veltheimia
Velvet Bean = Mucuna
Velvet Plant = Gynura
Venus' Fly Trap = Dionaea
Venus' Looking Glass = Legousia
Venus' Slipper = Paphiopedilum
Vernal Grass = Anthoxanthum
Vervain = Verbena

Vetch = Vicia
Vetiver = Vetiveria
Violet = Viola
Violet Cress = Ionopsidium
Violet Orchid = Ionopsis
Viper's Grass = Scorzonera
Virgina Stock = Malcolmia
Virginia Creeper = Parthenocissus
Virginia Mallow = Sida
Vodoo Lily = Sauromatum
Wake Robin = Trillium
Wall Lettuce = Mycelis
Wall Rocket = Diplotaxis
Wallflower = Erysimum
Walnut = Juglans
Wand Flower = Dierama
Wandflower = Galax
Wandplant = Galax
Waratah = Telopea
Warty Cabbage = Bunias
Wasabi = Wasabia
Washingtonia = Washingtonia
Water Arum = Calla
Water Bush = Bossiaea
Water Chestnut = Trapa
Water Clover = Marsilea
Water Cress = Rorippa
Water Dropwort = Oenanthe
Water Fern = Azolla, Ceratopteris
Water Hyacinth = Eichhornia
Water Hyssop = Bacopa
Water Lettuce = Pistia
Water Lily = Nymphaea
Water Melon = Citrullus
Water Milfoil = Myriophyllum
Water Nymph = Najas
Water Oats = Zizania
Water Parsnip = Sium
Water Plantain = Alisma
Water Poppy = Hydrocleys
Water Schield = Brasenia
Water Shield = Cabomba
Water Soldier = Stratiotes
Water Starwort = Callitriche
Water Trumpet = Cryptocoryne
Water Violet = Hottonia
Water Willow = Justicia
Watercress = Nasturtium
Waterleaf = Hydrophyllum
Watermeal = Wolffia
Waterweed = Egeria, Elodea
Waterwheel Plant = Aldrovanda
Waterwort = Elatine
Wax Flower = Hoya
Wax Gourd = Benincasa

Wax Palm = Ceroxylon
Waxflower = Eriostemon, Stephanotis
Wayfaring Tree = Viburnum
Weasel's Snout = Misopates
Weeping Bamboo = Otatea
Weigela = Weigela
Wellingtonia = Sequoiadendron
Whattle = Acacia
Wheat = Triticum
Wheat-rye Hybrid = × Triticosecale
Wheatgrass = Agropyron
Wheeltree = Stenocarpus
Whisk Fern = Psilotum
White Alder = Clethra
White Forsythia = Abeliophyllum
White Sapote = Casimiroa
Whitebeam = Sorbus
Whitlow Grass = Draba
Whitlow-Wort = Paronychia
Whorl Grass = Catabrosa
Widow's Tears = Tinantia
Wild Bergamot = Monarda
Wild Buckwheat = Eriogonum
Wild Cinnamon = Canella
Wild Coffee = Psychotria
Wild Garlic = Tulbaghia
Wild Ginger = Asarum
Wild Oats = Uvularia
Wild Pea = Lathyrus
Wild Plantain = Heliconia
Wild Rice = Zizania
Willow = Salix
Willow Myrtle = Agonis
Willowherb = Epilobium
Windflower = Anemone
Window Palm = Reinhardtia
Windowleaf = Monstera
Wine Palm = Jubaea
Wineberry = Aristotelia
Winged Broom = Chamaespartium
Winged Everlasting = Ammobium
Wingnut = Pterocarya
Winter Aconite = Eranthis
Winter Cress = Barbarea
Winter Daffodil = Sternbergia
Winter Hazel = Corylopsis
Winter Purslane = Montia
Winter's Bark = Drimys
Winterberry = Ilex
Winterfat = Krascheninnikovia

Wintergreen = Moneses, Orthilia, Pyrola
Wintersweet = Chimonanthus
Winterthorn = Faidherbia
Wireplant = Muehlenbeckia
Wisteria = Wisteria
Witch Alder = Fothergilla
Witch Hazel = Hamamelis
Woad = Isatis
Woadwaxen = Genista
Wollemi Pine = Wollemia
Wood Apple = Limonia
Wood Barley = Hordelymus
Wood Betony = Pedicularis
Wood Club Rush = Scirpus
Wood Lily = Trillium
Wood-Rush = Luzula
Woodruff = Asperula
Woodsia = Woodsia
Woody Pear = Xylomelum
Woolflower = Celosia
Wooly Sunflower = Eriophyllum
Worm Grass = Spigelia
Wormwood = Artemisia
Woundwort = Stachys
Yam = Dioscorea
Yam Bean = Pachyrhizus
Yam Pea = Sphenostylis
Yard Grass = Eleusine
Yarrow = Achillea
Yautia = Xanthosoma
Yellow Ageratum = Lonas
Yellow Centaury = Cicendia
Yellow Flax = Reinwardtia
Yellow Jessamine = Gelsemium
Yellow Oat Gras = Trisetum
Yellow Palm = Chrysalidocarpus
Yellow Pond Lily = Nuphar
Yellow Rattle = Rhinanthus
Yellow Wood = Cladrastis
Yellow Wort = Blackstonia
Yellow-eyed Grass = Xyris
Yellowwood = Afrocarpus
Yerba Mansa = Anemopsis
Yew = Taxus
Ylang Ylang = Cananga
Yohimbe = Pausinystalia
Youth-and-Old-Age = Aichryson
Zelkova = Zelkova
Zephyr Flower = Zephyranthes

XI French plant names

Abélia = Abelia
Abiu = Pouteria
Abricot pays = Mammea
Absinthe = Artemisia
Abutilon = Abutilon
Acacia = Acacia
Acacia jaune = Caragana
Acaena = Acaena
Acajou d'Afrique = Khaya
Acajou de montagne = Cercocarpus
Acanthe = Acanthus
Acantholimon = Acantholimon
Acanthopanax = Eleutherococcus
Acantostachys = Acanthostachys
Ache de montagne = Levisticum
Achillée = Achillea
Achimène = Achimenes
Achyranthes = Achyranthes
Aciphylla = Aciphylla
Acokanthéra = Acokanthera
Aconit = Aconitum
Acore = Acorus
Acroclinium = Acroclinium, Helipterum
Acrocomia = Acrocomia
Acrostic = Acrostichum
Actinidia = Actinidia
Actinioptéris = Actiniopteris
Adénanthéra = Adenanthera
Adénocarpe = Adenocarpus
Adénophore = Adenophora
Adénostome = Adenostoma
Adénostyle = Adenostyles
Adonide = Adonis
Adoxa = Adoxa
Adromischus = Adromischus
Aechméa = Aechmea, Streptocalyx
Aegopode = Aegopodium
Aeschynanthus = Aeschynanthus
Aethionema = Aethionema
Agapanthe = Agapanthus
Agastache = Agastache
Agathis = Agathis
Agave = Agave
Agérate jaune = Lonas
Agératum = Ageratum
Aglaonema = Aglaonema
Agonis = Agonis

Agripaume = Leonurus
Agrostis = Agrostis
Aigremoine = Agrimonia
Aiguille de Cléopâtre = Eremurus
Ail = Allium, Nectaroscordum, Nothoscordum
Ail rouge = Scadoxus
Ailanthe = Ailanthus
Aira = Aira
Airelle = Vaccinium
Ajonc = Ulex
Akébia = Akebia
Akee = Blighia
Alangium = Alangium
Alaterne = Rhamnus
Albizzia = Albizia
Alchémille = Alchemilla
Alchémille des champs = Aphanes
Aldrovandie = Aldrovanda
Aleurite = Aleurites
Aliboufier = Styrax
Alisier = Sorbus
Allamande = Allamanda
Alliaire = Alliaria
Alocasia = Alocasia
Aloe = Aloe
Aloès d'eau = Stratiotes
Alonsoa = Alonsoa
Alosure crépue = Cryptogramma
Alouchier = Sorbus
Alpinie = Alpinia
Alpiste = Phalaris
Alsine = Minuartia
Alstroemère = Alstroemeria
Alternanthère = Alternanthera
Alyogyne = Alyogyne
Alysson = Alyssum, Lobularia
Amandier des Indes = Terminalia
Amaranthe = Amaranthus
Amarantine = Gomphrena
Amaryllis = Amaryllis, Hippeastrum
Amaryllis bleu = Worsleya
Amaryllis de Rouen = Hippeastrum
Amaryllis doré = Sternbergia
Ambreuvade = Cajanus
Ambroisie = Ambrosia
Amélanchier = Amelanchier

Ammi = Ammi
Amorpha = Amorpha
Amour en cage = Physalis
Amourette = Briza, Eragrostis
Amsonia = Amsonia
Anacampseros = Anacampseros
Anacamptis = Anacamptis
Anacardier = Anacardium
Anagyre = Anagyris
Ananas = Ananas
Anarrhinum = Anarrhinum
Ancolie = Aquilegia
Andrachné = Andrachne
Andromède = Andromeda, Leucothoe,
   Pieris
Andropogon = Andropogon
Androsace = Androsace, Vitaliana
Anémone = Anemone
Anémonelle = Anemonella
Aneth = Anethum
Angélique = Angelica
Anguloa = Anguloa
Anis étoilé = Illicium
Anis vert = Pimpinella
Anogramma = Anogramma
Anone = Annona
Anthémis d'Arabie = Cladanthus
Anthurium = Anthurium
Anthyllis = Anthyllis
Aphélandra = Aphelandra
Aphyllanthe = Aphyllanthes
Apocyn = Apocynum
Aponogeton = Aponogeton
Aposéris = Aposeris
Arabette = Arabis
Arabette des sables = Cardaminopsis
Arachide = Arachis
Arachnanthe = Arachnis
Aralia = Aralia
Aralia en arbre = Kalopanax
Araucaria = Araucaria
Arbousier = Arbutus
Arbre à beurre = Madhuca
Arbre à caoutchouc = Hevea
Arbre à caoutchouc du Panama = Castilla
Arbre à concombres = Averrhoa
Arbre à cuiller = Cunonia
Arbre à gomme = Amyris
Arbre à gutta = Palaquium
Arbre à lait = Brosimum
Arbre à liège = Phellodendron
Arbre à pain = Artocarpus, Encephalartos
Arbre à perruque = Cotinus
Arbre à savon = Sapindus
Arbre à suif = Sapium

Arbre à térébenthine = Bursera
Arbre à upas = Antiaris
Arbre à violettes = Iochroma
Arbre amer = Picrasma
Arbre au parasol = Pandanus
Arbre aux pochettes = Davidia
Arbre aux quarante écus = Ginkgo
Arbre d'argent = Leucadendron
Arbre de feu = Embothrium
Arbre de Judée = Cercis
Arbre de neige = Chionanthus
Arbre du voyageur = Ravenala
Arbre-à-cire = Carissa, Myrica
Arbre-à-corail = Erythrina
Arbre-à-encens = Boswellia
Arbre-à-flanelle = Fremontodendron
Arbre-à-laque = Butea
Arbre-à-saucisses = Kigelia
Arbre-à-tomates = Cyphomandra
Arbre-aux-melons = Carica
Arbre-aux-oursins = Hakea
Arbre-aux-trompettes = Catalpa
Arbre-bouteille = Beaucarnea
Arbre-de-vie = Thuja
Arbre-fougère = Filicium
Arbres-aux-papillons = Buddleja
Arctotide = Arctotis
Ardisia = Ardisia
Arec = Areca
Arémonia = Aremonia
Arénaire = Arenaria
Aréquier = Areca, Chrysalidocarpus,
   Dictyosperma, Rhopalostylis
Argémone = Argemone
Argousier = Hippophae
Arisaema = Arisaema
Aristéa = Aristea
Aristoloche = Aristolochia
Aristotélia = Aristotelia
Armérie = Armeria
Armoise = Artemisia
Arnica = Arnica
Arnoséris = Arnoseris
Aronia = Aronia
Arrête-bouf = Ononis
Arroche = Atriplex
Artichaut = Cynara, Echeveria
Arum = Arum
Arum aquatique = Calla
Asaret = Asarum
Asclépiade = Asclepias
Asiminier = Asimina
Asperge = Asparagus
Aspérule = Asperula
Asphodèle = Asphodelus

Asphodéline = Asphodeline
Aspidistra = Aspidistra
Aster = Aster
Aster blanchâtre = Microglossa
Aster doré = Chrysopsis
Aster du Cap = Felicia
Aster-centaurée = Stokesia
Astérolide = Asteriscus
Astilbe = Astilbe
Astragale = Astragalus, Oxytropis
Astrance = Astrantia
Asyneuma = Asyneuma
Athamante = Athamanta
Atropa = Atropa
Attrape-mouche = Silene
Attrappe-mouches = Dionaea
Aubépine = Crataegus
Aubergine = Solanum
Aubour = Laburnum
Aubriète = Aubrieta
Aucuba = Aucuba
Aulne = Alnus
Aulnée = Inula
Aunée = Dittrichia
Avocatier = Persea
Avoine = Avena
Avoine barbue = Trisetaria
Avoine des prés = Helictotrichon
Avoine en chapelet = Arrhenatherum
Avoine jaunâtre = Trisetum
Azalée = Rhododendron
Baccharis = Baccharis
Bacopa = Bacopa
Badanier = Terminalia
Baguenaudier = Colutea
Baguette de tambour = Craspedia
Baie de Bison = Shepherdia
Balanites = Balanites
Baldingère = Phalaris
Balisier = Canna, Heliconia
Ballote = Ballota
Balsa = Ochroma
Balsamier = Myroxylon
Balsamine = Impatiens, Momordica
Bambou = Fargesia, Otatea,
   Semiarundinaria, Yushania
Bambou géant = Gigantochloa
Bambou nain = Sasa
Bambou sacré = Nandina
Bananier = Musa
Bananier d'Abyssinie = Ensete
Bancoulier = Aleurites
Banksia = Banksia
Baobab = Adansonia
Barbarée = Barbarea

Barbe de serpent = Ophiopogon
Barbe-de-bouc = Aruncus
Barbe-de-Jupiter = Jovibarba
Barbon = Andropogon, Chrysopogon
Bardane = Arctium
Bardanette = Tragus
Barléria = Barleria
Bartsie = Bartsia
Baselle = Basella, Ullucus
Basilic = Ocimum
Bassia = Bassia
Bâton de Jacob = Polemonium
Baudremoine = Meum
Bauhinia = Bauhinia
Baume de Galaad = Cedronella
Beaufortia = Beaufortia
Beaumontia = Beaumontia
Bec-de-grue = Geranium
Bec-de-héron = Erodium
Bec-de-perroquet = Clianthus
Beckmannia = Beckmannia
Bégonia = Begonia
Bel ombrage = Phytolacca
Belladonne = Atropa
Belle-de-nuit = Mirabilis
Bélopérone = Justicia
Benoîte = Geum
Berbéris = Berberis
Berce = Heracleum
Berce géante = Heracleum
Bergenia = Bergenia
Berle = Sium
Bermudienne = Sisyrinchium
Bertéroa = Berteroa
Bertolonia = Bertolonia
Bérula = Berula
Bessera = Bessera
Bétoine = Stachys
Betterave = Beta
Bibacier = Eriobotrya
Bident = Bidens
Bignone = Bignonia, Distictis, Tecoma
Bignone d'Argentine = Clytostoma
Bignone de Chine = Campsis
Bignone faux-jasmin = Pandorea
Billbergia = Billbergia
Biota = Thuja
Bistorte = Bistorta
Black boy = Xanthorrhoea
Blandfordia = Blandfordia
Blé = Triticum
Blé d'azur = Elymus
Blé noir = Fagopyrum
Blechnum = Blechnum
Bleuet = Centaurea

Bleuet d'Amérique = Hedyotis, Houstonia
Bloomeria = Bloomeria
Bocconia = Bocconia
Bois chandelle = Amyris
Bois de Gaïac = Guaiacum
Bois de Macassar = Schleichera
Bois de plomb = Dirca
Bois de rose = Dalbergia, Tipuana
Bois de santal = Pterocarpus
Bois jaune = Chloroxylon
Bois puant = Anagyris
Bois-de-fer = Metrosideros
Bois-joli = Daphne
Bois-lait = Thevetia
Bois-satin = Chloroxylon
Boldo = Peumus
Boltonia = Boltonia
Bonnet d'évêque = Astrophytum, Mitella
Bonnet-d'Evêque = Tiarella
Boronia = Boronia
Bossiaea = Bossiaea
Boucage = Pimpinella
Bougainvillée = Bougainvillea
Boule azurée = Echinops
Boule d'or = Trollius
Boule de neige = Viburnum
Bouleau = Betula
Bourrache = Borago
Bourrache du Caucase = Trachystemon
Bourrache géante = Solenanthus
Bourreau des arbres = Celastrus, Periploca
Bouteille = Lagenaria
Bouton de hussard = Sanvitalia
Bouvardie = Bouvardia
Bowénia = Bowenia
Brachyglottis = Brachyglottis
Brachypode = Brachypodium
Brasénie = Brasenia
Brésillet = Caesalpinia
Brimeura = Brimeura
Brodiaea = Brodiaea
Brome = Bromus
Browalia = Browallia
Brunelle = Prunella
Brunfelsia = Brunfelsia
Bruyère = Erica
Bruyère à balai = Calluna
Bruyère australe = Epacris
Bruyère d'hiver = Erica
Bruyère des Açores = Daboecia
Bryone = Bryonia
Bryophyllum = Bryophyllum
Buffonia = Bufonia
Bugle = Ajuga
Buglosse = Anchusa

Buglosse d'Espagne = Pentaglottis
Bugrane = Ononis
Buis = Buxus
Buis de Noël = Sarcococca
Buisson ardent = Pyracantha
Buisson-à-miel = Melianthus
Bulbocode = Bulbocodium
Bulbophyllum = Bulbophyllum
Bunias = Bunias
Buplèvre = Bupleurum
Busserole = Arctostaphylos
Butéa = Butea
Butome = Butomus
Byblis = Byblis
Cabomba = Cabomba
Cacahuète = Arachis
Cacaoyer = Theobroma
Cachiman = Annona
Cactus = Ariocarpus
Cactus à feuilles = Pereskia
Cactus à myrtilles = Myrtillocactus
Cactus ailé = Pterocactus
Cactus de Noël = Schlumbergera
Cactus des bois = Hylocereus
Cactus des savetiers = Epiphyllum
Cactus étoilé = Astrophytum
Cactus mille-pattes = Pelecyphora
cactus-gui = Rhipsalis
Cactus-hérisson = Echinopsis
Cactus-jonc = Rhipsalis
Cactus-melon = Melocactus
Cactus-serpent = Aporocactus
Caféier = Coffea
Caillou vivant = Lithops
Caïmitier = Chrysophyllum
Caladium = Caladium
Calamagrostis = Calamagrostis
Calament = Acinos, Calamintha
Calament commun = Clinopodium
Calandrinia = Calandrinia
Calanthe = Calanthe
Calcéolaire = Calceolaria
Caldesia = Caldesia
Calebassier = Crescentia
Caliméris = Kalimeris
Calla = Calla, Zantedeschia
Calliandra = Calliandra
Callianthème = Callianthemum
Callicarpa = Callicarpa
Callisia = Callisia
Callistemon = Callistemon
Callitriche = Callitriche
Callune = Calluna
Calotropis = Calotropis
Calycanthus = Calycanthus

F

Calypso = Calypso
Camarine = Empetrum
Camassia = Camassia
Camélée = Cneorum, Daphne
Camélia = Camellia
Caméline = Camelina, Myagrum
Camomille = Anthemis, Matricaria
Camomille des ours = Ursinia
Camomille du Maroc = Anacyclus
Camomille romaine = Chamaemelum
Campanille = Wahlenbergia
Campanule = Campanula
Campanule des Canaries = Canarina
Campanule des pierres = Symphyandra
Campanule géante = Ostrowskia
Campêche = Haematoxylum
Camphorine = Camphorosma
Camphrier = Cinnamomum
Canarion = Canarium
Canche = Deschampsia
Canistelle lucume = Pouteria
Canne à pêche des anges = Dierama
Canne à sucre = Saccharum
Canne de Provence = Arundo
Canneberge = Vaccinium
Cannelier = Canella, Cinnamomum
Cantua = Cantua
Capillaire = Adiantum
Câprier = Capparis
Capselle = Capsella
Capuchon de moine = Arisarum
Capucine = Tropaeolum
Caquilier = Cakile
Caragana argenté = Halimodendron
Caralluma = Caralluma
Carambolier = Averrhoa
Cardaire = Cardaria
Cardamine = Cardamine
Cardamome = Amomum, Elettaria
Cardère = Dipsacus
Cardon = Cynara
Cardoncelle = Carduncellus
Carisse = Carissa
Carline = Carlina
Carmichaelia = Carmichaelia
Carotte = Daucus
Caroubier = Ceratonia
Carpésium = Carpesium
Carthame = Carthamus
Caryoptéris = Caryopteris
casse-lunette = Euphrasia
Cassiope = Cassiope
Cassis = Ribes
Casuarina = Casuarina
Catabrosa = Catabrosa

Cataleptique = Physostegia
Catalpa = Catalpa
Caucalis = Caucalis
Céanothe = Ceanothus
Cèdre = Cedrus
Cèdre à encens = Calocedrus
Cèdre bâtard = Cedrela, Toona
Cèdre du Chili = Austrocedrus
Cèdre du Japon = Cryptomeria
Cèdrella = Toona
Célandine = Stylophorum
Céleri = Apium
Céleri vivace = Levisticum
Célosie = Celosia
Centaurée = Centaurea
Centaurée jaune = Blackstonia
Centaurée musquée = Amberboa
Céphalaire = Cephalaria
Céphalanthère = Cephalanthera
Céphélis = Psychotria
Céraiste = Cerastium
Cératocéphale = Ceratocephala
Cératophylle = Ceratophyllum
Cercidiphyllum = Cercidiphyllum
Cerfeuil = Anthriscus
cerfeuil sauvage = Chaerophyllum
Cerfeuil vivace = Myrrhis
Cerima = Monstera
Cerise de la Jamaïque = Muntingia
Cerise espagnole = Mimusops
Cerisier de Chine = Litchi
Cerisier de Tahiti = Phyllanthus
Cerisier des Antilles = Malpighia
Céropégia = Ceropegia
Céroxylon = Ceroxylon
Cestrum = Cestrum
Chalef = Elaeagnus
Chamorchis = Chamorchis
Chanvre = Cannabis
Chardon = Carduus, Eryngium
Chardon bénit = Cnicus
Chardon ivoire = Ptilostemon
Chardon-des-ânes = Onopordum
Chardon-Marie = Galactites, Silybum
Charme = Carpinus
Chasmanthe = Chasmanthe
Châtaigne d'eau = Trapa
Châtaignier = Castanea
Châtaignier d'Australie = Castanospermum
Châtaignier de la Guyane = Pachira
Châtaignier du Cap = Calodendrum
Chayotte = Sechium
Cheilanthès = Cheilanthes
Chélidoine = Chelidonium
Chélone = Chelone

Chêne = Quercus
Chenille = Scorpiurus
Chénopode = Chenopodium
Chérimolier = Annona
Chérophylle = Chaerophyllum
Chervis = Sium
Chèvrefeuille = Lonicera
Chèvrefeuille du Cap = Tecomaria
Chicorée = Cichorium
Chicot du Canada = Gymnocladus
Chiendent = Agropyron, Cynodon
Chiendent des sables = Elymus
Chigommier = Combretum
Chili = Capsicum
Chimaphile = Chimaphila
Chimonanthe odorant = Chimonanthus
Chironia = Chironia
Choin = Schoenus
Chondrille = Chondrilla
Chorisia = Chorisia
Chorizema = Chorizema
Chou = Brassica
Chou marin = Crambe
Chou puant = Symplocarpus
Chou-chine = Colocasia
Chouard = Brimeura
Chrysanthème = Chrysanthemum
Chrysocome = Chrysocoma
Chrysogonum = Chrysogonum
Chrysopogon = Chrysopogon
Chrysothamne = Chrysothamnus
Cicer = Cicer
Cicutaire = Cicuta
Cierge = Cleistocactus, Fouquieria,
   Peniocereus
Cierge d'argent = Cimicifuga
Cierge de la Lune = Selenicereus
Cierge pileux = Pilosocereus
Cierge-hérisson = Echinocereus
Ciguë = Conium
Ciguë aquatique = Cicuta
Cinéraire = Cineraria, Pericallis, Senecio,
   Tephroseris
Circée = Circaea
Cirier = Myrica
Cirio = Fouquieria
Cirse = Cirsium
Ciste = Cistus
Citronnelle = Aloysia, Cymbopogon,
   Melissa
Citronnier = Citrus
Clandestine = Lathraea
Clarkia = Clarkia
Clavalier = Zanthoxylum
Claytone = Claytonia

Clématite = Clematis
Cléome = Cleome
Clérodendron = Clerodendrum
Cléthra = Clethra
Clinopode = Clinopodium
Clintonia = Downingia
Clivia = Clivia
Cloche de Noël = Sandersonia
Cloche du temple = Smithiantha
Clochette d'Irlande = Moluccella
Clochette des fées = Disporum
Clypéole = Clypeola
Cnicaut = Cnicus
Cnide = Cnidium
Cobée = Cobaea
Coca = Erythroxylum
Cocaïer = Erythroxylum
Cocculus = Cocculus
Cocotier = Cocos
Cocotier de Seychelles = Lodoicea
Cocriste = Rhinanthus
Codonopsis = Codonopsis
Cognassier = Cydonia
Cognassier du Japon = Chaenomeles
Colatier = Cola
Colchique = Colchicum
Coléus = Solenostemon
Colletia = Colletia
Collinsia = Collinsia
Collomia = Collomia
Cologlosse = Coeloglossum
Columnéa = Columnea
Comméline = Commelina
Compagnon = Silene
Comptonie = Comptonia
Concombre = Cucumis
Concombre chevelu = Sicyos
Concombre sauvage = Ecballium
Concombre-oursin = Echinocystis
Coniosélinum = Conioselinum
Conopode = Conopodium
Conringia = Conringia
Consoude = Symphytum
Copalier = Copaifera
Copalme = Liquidambar
Coptide = Coptis
Coquelicot du soleil levant = Eomecon
Corbeille d'argent = Arabis
Corbeille d'or = Alyssum
Cordia = Cordia
Cordyline = Cordyline
Coréopsis = Coreopsis
Corète = Kerria
Coriandre = Coriandrum
Coris = Coris

Corispermum = Corispermum
Cormier = Sorbus
Cornaret = Proboscidea
Corne d'abondance = Fedia
Corne d'eau = Hydrocera
Corne d'élan = Platycerium
Cornouiller = Cornus
Coronille = Coronilla
Corossol = Annona
Corrigiola = Corrigiola
Corroyère = Coriaria
Cortuse = Cortusa
Corydale = Corydalis
Corynocarpus = Corynocarpus
Cosmos = Cosmos
Costus = Costus
Cotonéaster = Cotoneaster
Cotonnier = Gossypium
Cotonnière = Filago
Cotule = Cotula, Leptinella
Coumarouna = Dipteryx
Cour de Marie = Dicentra
Courbaril = Hymenaea
Courge = Cucurbita
Courge céreuse = Benincasa
Couronne impériale = Fritillaria
Crambe = Crambe
Crambe des chiens = Theligonum
Cran = Armoracia
Cranson = Armoracia, Cochlearia
Crapaudine = Sideritis
Crassula = Crassula
Crassula de Chine = Sinocrassula
Crépide = Crepis
Crépis = Crepis
Cresson alénois = Lepidium
Cresson de fontaine = Nasturtium
Cresson de Para = Acmella
Cresson des chamois = Pritzelago
Cresson des oies = Schivereckia
Cresson des pierres = Aurinia
Cresson doré = Chrysosplenium
Crête-de-coq = Celosia
Crételle = Cynosurus
Crinodendron = Crinodendron
Crinum = Crinum
Crocus = Crocus
Crocus du Chili = Tecophilaea
Croisette = Cruciata
Crosne = Stachys
Crotalaria = Crotalaria
Croton = Chrozophora, Codiaeum, Croton
Crucianelle = Crucianella, Phuopsis
Crupina = Crupina
Crypsis piquant = Crypsis

Cryptanthus = Cryptanthus
Ctenanthe = Ctenanthe
Cucubale = Cucubalus
Cumin = Carum, Cuminum
Cumin des chevaux = Laser
Cumin des prés = Silaum
Cumin tubéreux = Bunium
Cuphéa = Cuphea
Cupidone = Catananche
Curcuma = Curcuma
Cuscute = Cuscuta
Cussonia = Cussonia
Cyananthus = Cyananthus
Cycas = Cycas
Cyclamen = Cyclamen
Cyclanthus = Cyclanthus
Cycnoches = Cycnoches
Cymbalaire = Cymbalaria
Cymbidium = Cymbidium
Cynanque = Cynanchum
Cynoglosse = Cynoglossum
Cynosure = Cynosurus
Cypella = Cypella
Cyprès = Cupressus
Cyprès africain = Widdringtonia
Cyprès bâtard = × Cuprocyparis
Cyprès chauve = Taxodium
Cyprès de Leyland = × Cuprocyparis
Cyprès de Patagonie = Fitzroya
Cyrtanthus = Cyrtanthus
Cystoptéride = Cystopteris
Cytise = Laburnum
Cytise aubour = Laburnum
Dactyle = Dactylis
Dactylorhize = Dactylorhiza
Dahlia = Dahlia
Dahlia grimpant = Hidalgoa
Dalechampia = Dalechampia
Danthonia = Danthonia
Daphné = Daphne
Darmera = Darmera
Dasylirion = Dasylirion
Dattier = Phoenix
Dauphinelle = Consolida
Davallia = Davallia
Davidia = Davidia
Decaisnea = Decaisnea
Deinanthe = Deinanthe
Delairea = Delairea
Delosperma = Delosperma
Dennstaedtia = Dennstaedtia
Dent de lion = Taraxacum
Dent-de-chien = Erythronium
Dent-de-lion = Leontodon
Dentelaire = Ceratostigma, Plumbago

Derris = Derris
Désespoir du peintre = Heuchera
Deutzia = Deutzia
Dianella = Dianella
Diapensia = Diapensia
Diascia = Diascia
Dictame barbade = Maranta
Dieffenbachia = Dieffenbachia
Diervilla = Diervilla
Digitaire = Digitaria, Paspalum
Digitale = Digitalis
Digitale de Chine = Rehmannia
Dillénie = Dillenia
Dionée = Dionaea
Dioon = Dioon
Diotis = Otanthus
Dipelta = Dipelta
Diphylleia = Diphylleia
Diplotaxis = Diplotaxis
Diptérocarpus = Dipterocarpus
Dischidia = Dischidia
Dodonéa = Dodonaea
Dolique = Dolichos, Vigna
Dolique lablab = Lablab
Dompte-venin = Vincetoxicum
Doodia rude = Doodia
Doradille = Asplenium
Doréma = Dorema
Dorine = Chrysosplenium
Doronic = Doronicum
Dorstenia = Dorstenia
Dorycnium = Dorycnium
Dracula = Dracula
Dragonnier = Dracaena, Dracophyllum
Drave = Draba, Schivereckia
Drave des Pyrénées = Petrocallis
Ebène du Mexique = Pithecellobium
Ebène du Texas = Pithecellobium
Ecbalie = Ecballium
Eccremocarpus = Eccremocarpus
Echévéria = Echeveria
Echidnopsis = Echidnopsis
Echinacéa = Echinacea
Echinosperme = Lappula
Ecuelle d'eau = Hydrocotyle
Edelweiss = Leontopodium
Eglantier = Rosa
Egylops = Aegilops
Elatine = Elatine
Elemi = Canarium
Eleocharis = Eleocharis
Eleusine = Eleusine
Elodée = Elodea
Elsholtzia = Elsholtzia
Elyme = Elymus, Leymus

Emilie = Emilia
Enkianthus = Enkianthus
Epervière = Hieracium
Ephèdre = Ephedra
Ephémère = Commelina, Tradescantia
Epiaire = Stachys
Epicéa = Picea
Epigée = Epigaea
Epilobe = Epilobium
Epinard = Spinacia
Epinard de Malabar = Basella
Epinard de Nouvelle-Zélande = Tetragonia
Epine = Crataegus
Epine de chameau = Alhagi
Epine de Jérusalem = Parkinsonia
Epine de rat = Ruscus
Epine des rats grimpante = Semele
Epine du Christ = Paliurus
Epine du ver à soie = Cudrania
Epine jaune = Xanthoceras
Epine-vinette = Berberis
Epipactis = Epipactis
Epipogium = Epipogium
Episcie = Episcia
Eponge végétale = Luffa
Erable = Acer
Eragrostis = Eragrostis
Eranthe = Eranthis
Eranthémum = Eranthemum
Erigeron = Conyza, Erigeron
Erinacée = Erinacea
Erine = Erinus
Eriocaulon = Eriocaulon
Eriophylle = Eriophyllum
Eriostémon = Eriostemon
Erucastre = Erucastrum
Erythrine = Erythrina
Erythrochiton = Erythrochiton
Erythrone = Erythronium
Escallonia = Escallonia
Eschscholzia = Eschscholzia
Esparcette = Onobrychis
Esparsette = Stipa
Ethuse = Aethusa
Etoile = Stapelia
Etoile d'eau = Callitriche
Etoile de Bethléem = Ornithogalum
Etoile du Mexique = Milla
Etoile du Texas = Lindheimera
Eucalyptus = Eucalyptus
Eucnide = Eucnide
Eucomis = Eucomis
Eucryphia = Eucryphia
Eugenia = Eugenia
Eupatoire = Eupatorium

F

Euphorbe = Euphorbia
Euphorbe arborescente = Synadenium
Euphorbe du Japon = Pachysandra
Euphraise = Euphrasia
Euptéléa = Euptelea
Eurya = Eurya
Euryale = Euryale
Eutaxia = Eutaxia
Exochorda = Exochorda
Fabiana = Fabiana
Falcaire = Falcaria
Fatshédéra = × Fatshedera
Fatsia = Fatsia
Fausse-ancolie = Semiaquilegia
Fausse-anémone = Anemonopsis
Fausse-arabette = Arabidopsis
Fausse-asperge = Medeola
Fausse-avoine = Ventenata
Fausse-camomille = Boltonia
Fausse-couleuvrée = Diplocyclos
Fausse-élodée = Lagarosiphon
Fausse-lobélie = Downingia
Fausse-lysimaque = Pseudolysimachion
Fausse-mauve = Malvastrum
Fausse-orchidée = Roscoea
Fausse-pâquerette = Bellium
Fausse-parrotia = Parrotiopsis
fausse-roquette = Bunias
Fausse-stellaire = Pseudostellaria
Fausse-violette = Ionopsidium
Fausse-vipérine = Lobostemon
Faux vernis du Japon = Ailanthus
Faux-acacia = Robinia
Faux-alysson = Alyssoides
Faux-ananas = Pseudananas
Faux-anis = Illicium
Faux-camélia = Stewartia
Faux-chanvre = Datisca
Faux-châtaignier = Castanopsis
Faux-coqueret = Nicandra
Faux-cresson = Rorippa
Faux-crocus = Romulea
Faux-cyprès = Chamaecyparis
Faux-cytise = Cytisophyllum
Faux-ébénier = Laburnum
Faux-fumeterre = Pseudofumaria
Faux-gingseng = Pseudopanax
Faux-gnaphale = Pseudognaphalium
Faux-houx = Nemopanthus
Faux-indigo = Amorpha
Faux-jasmin = Mandevilla
Faux-kapokier = Eriocephalus
Faux-kerria = Rhodotypos
Faux-laurier = Daphniphyllum
Faux-lupin = Thermopsis

Faux-mélèze = Pseudolarix
Faux-metel = Datura
Faux-myrte = Anamirta
Faux-noisetier = Corylopsis
Faux-orchis = Pseudorchis
Faux-orme de Sibérie = Zelkova
Faux-ostryer = Ostryopsis
Faux-palissandre = Jacaranda
Faux-pistachier = Staphylea
Faux-poivrier = Schinus
Faux-riz = Leersia
Faux-scirpe = Scirpoides
Faux-sorgho = Sorghastrum
Faux-tamaris = Myricaria
Faux-trèfle = Oxalis
Fenouil = Foeniculum
Fer-à-cheval = Hippocrepis
Férule = Ferula
Férule bâtarde = Ferulago
Fétuque = Festuca
Fétuque du gravier = Micropyrum
Fève = Vicia
Févier d'Amérique = Gleditsia
Ficoide = Delosperma, Dorotheanthus, Mesembryanthemum
Ficoïde arbustive = Ruschia
Figue des Hottentots = Carpobrotus
Figuier = Ficus
Figuier de Barbarie = Opuntia
Figuier de mer = Erepsia
Filago = Filago
Filaria = Phillyrea
Filipendule = Filipendula
Fimbristylis = Fimbristylis
Firmiana = Firmiana
Fittonia = Fittonia
Flamboyant = Delonix
Flèche d'eau = Sagittaria
Fléole = Phleum
Fleur arlequin = Sparaxis
Fleur ballon = Platycodon
Fleur de cire = Hoya, Kirengeshoma
Fleur de porcelaine = Hoya
Fleur des babouins = Babiana
Fleur des dieux = Dodecatheon, Parochetus
Fleur des elfes = Epimedium
Fleur des princesses = Tibouchina
Fleur du prophète = Arnebia
Fleur du soir = Hesperantha, Ixia
Fleur-araignée = Arachnis
Fleur-cigarette = Cuphea
Fleur-de-kangourou = Anigozanthos
Fleur-escargot = Vigna
Fleur-léopard = Belamcanda
Flouve = Anthoxanthum

Fontanesie = Fontanesia
Forsythia = Forsythia
Forsythia blanc = Abeliophyllum
Fothergilla = Fothergilla
Fougère = Doryopteris, Gleichenia,
  Hymenophyllum, Lemmaphyllum,
  Lonchitis, Onychium, Pyrrosia, Sticherus
Fougère aigle = Pteridium
Fougère aquatique = Azolla, Bolbitis
Fougère arborescente = Angiopteris,
  Cibotium, Cyathea, Dicksonia, Todea
Fougère argentée = Pityrogramma
Fougère ciliée = Woodsia
Fougère cornue = Ceratopteris
Fougère des marais = Thelypteris
Fougère des montagnes = Oreopteris
Fougère dorée = Pityrogramma
Fougère du chène = Gymnocarpium
Fougère du hêtre = Phegopteris
Fougère femelle = Athyrium
Fougère flottante = Salvinia
Fougère grimpante = Lomariopsis,
  Lygodium
Fougère plume-d'autruche = Matteuccia
Fougère royale = Osmunda
Fougère rubannée = Vittaria
Fougère-bambou = Coniogramme
Fougère-chenille = Scyphularia
Fougère-langue = Elaphoglossum
Fougère-palmier = Bowenia
Fragon = Ruscus
Fraisier = Fragaria
Fraisier doré = Waldsteinia
Framboisier = Rubus
Francoa = Francoa
Frangipanier = Plumeria
Frankénie = Frankenia
Franklinia = Franklinia
Fraxinelle = Dictamnus
Freesia = Freesia
Frêne = Fraxinus
Frêne puant = Tetradium
Fritillaire = Fritillaria
Fromager = Bombax, Chorisia
Fruit de la Passion = Passiflora
Fuchsia = Fuchsia
Fuchsia d'Australie = Correa
Fuchsia du Cap = Phygelius
Fuchsia en arbre = Schotia
Fumana = Fumana
Fumeterre = Fumaria
Funkia = Hosta
Fusain = Euonymus
Gagéa = Gagea
Gaïac = Guaiacum

Gaillarde = Gaillardia
Gaillet = Galium
Gaillet croisette = Cruciata
gainier = Cercis
Galane = Penstemon
Galanga = Calathea
Galax = Galax
Galéopsis = Galeopsis
Galipéa = Galipea
Galtonia = Galtonia
Garance = Rubia
Gardénia = Gardenia
Garrya = Garrya
Gastérie = Gasteria
Gastridium = Gastridium
Gattilier = Vitex
Gaudinie = Gaudinia
Gaultheria = Gaultheria
Gaura = Gaura
Gaylussacia = Gaylussacia
Gazanie = Gazania
Gazon d'Espagne = Armeria
Genêt = Genista
Genêt à balai = Cytisus
Genêt ailé = Chamaespartium
Genêt argenté = Argyrocytisus
Genêt austral = Notospartium
Genêt d'Espagne = Spartium
Genêt du désert = Templetonia
Genévrier = Juniperus
Génipayer = Genipa
Gentiane = Gentiana
Gentiane ciliée = Gentianella
Gentiane de la Prairie = Eustoma
Gentianelle = Centaurium
Géranium = Geranium
Géranium des balcons = Pelargonium
Gerbéra = Gerbera
Germaine = Plectranthus
Germandrée = Teucrium
Gesnéria = Gesneria
Gilia = Gilia
Gingembre = Zingiber
Ginseng = Panax
Giroflée = Matthiola
Giroflier = Syzygium
Glaïeul = Gladiolus
Glaux = Glaux
Gleditsia = Gleditsia
Gleichenia = Sticherus
Glillenia = Gillenia
Globulaire = Globularia
Gloire de Birmanie = Amherstia
Gloire des neiges = Chionodoxa
Gloriosa = Gloriosa

F

Gloxinia = Gloxinia
Gloxinia sauvage = Sinningia
Glycérie = Glyceria
Glycine = Wisteria
Glycine en arbre = Bolusanthus
Glycine tubéreuse = Apios
Gnaphale = Gnaphalium
Gnavelle = Scleranthus
Gobelets = Umbilicus
Gombo = Abelmoschus
Gomme-ammniaque = Dorema
Gommier = Bursera, Palaquium
Goodenia = Goodenia
Goodyera = Goodyera
Gouet = Arum
Gourde = Lagenaria
Goutte d'or = Chiastophyllum
Goyavier = Psidium
Grand orpin = Telephium
Grassette = Pinguicula
Gratiole = Gratiola
Grégoria = Vitaliana
Grémil = Lithodora, Lithospermum
Grenadier = Punica
Grenouillette = Alisma, Luronium
Grenouillette d'Amérique = Limnobium
Grévillée = Grevillea
Grewia = Grewia
Greya = Greyia
Griffe du diable = Physoplexis, Phyteuma
Grindelia = Grindelia
Griselinia = Griselinia
Gros millet = Sorghum
Groseillier = Ribes
Guayule = Parthenium
Gueule-de-loup = Antirrhinum
Gueule-de-tigre = Faucaria
Gui = Viscum
Guimauve = Althaea
Guizotia = Guizotia
Gurania = Gurania
Guttier = Garcinia
Guzmania = Guzmania
Gynure = Gynura
Gypsophile = Gypsophila
Gyroselle = Dodecatheon
Habénaire = Coeloglossum, Habenaria
Haberléa = Haberlea
Hacquetia = Hacquetia
Haematoxylon = Haematoxylum
Hakea = Hakea
Halésia = Halesia
Hamamélis = Hamamelis
Hardenbergia = Hardenbergia
Haricot = Phaseolus

Haricot de mer = Entada
Harmel = Peganum
Haworthia = Haworthia
Hebe = Hebe
Hédychium = Hedychium
Hédysarum = Hedysarum
Hélénie = Helenium
Héliamphora = Heliamphora
Hélianthelle = Helianthella
Hélianthème = Helianthemum
Héliophila = Heliophila
Héliopsis = Heliopsis
Héliotrope = Heliotropium
Hellébore = Helleborus
Helléborine = Eranthis
Helminthie = Helminthotheca
Helwingie = Helwingia
Helxine = Soleirolia
Hémanthe = Haemanthus, Scadoxus
Hémérocalle = Hemerocallis
Henné = Lawsonia
Hépatique = Hepatica
Herbe aux femmes battues = Tamus
Herbe aux kangourous = Themeda
Herbe aux turquoises = Ophiopogon
Herbe de la pampa = Cortaderia
Herbe de la St-Jean = Hypericum
Herbe de St-Augustin = Stenotaphrum
Herbe de St-Christophe = Actaea
Herbe de Ste-Barbe = Barbarea
Herbe des marais = Scolochloa
Herbe du tigre = Thysanolaena
Herbe-à-brochet = Pontederia
Herbe-à-moustiques = Bouteloua
Herbe-à-panier = Oplismenus
Herbe-aux-bisons = Buchloe
Herbe-aux-écouvillons = Pennisetum
Herbe-aux-faisans = Leycesteria
Herbe-aux-goutteux = Aegopodium
Herbe-aux-pipes = Molinia
Herbe-aux-puces = Psyllium
Herbe-aux-vaches = Vaccaria
Herbe-aux-verrues = Chelidonium
Hermannia = Hermannia
Herminium = Herminium
Herniaire = Herniaria
Hétéranthère = Heteranthera
Hétéromelès = Heteromeles
Hêtre = Fagus
Hêtre austral = Nothofagus
Heuchère = Heuchera
Heuchèrelle = × Heucherella
Hibbertia = Hibbertia
Hibiscus bleu = Alyogyne
Hierochloa = Hierochloe

Hirschfeldia = Hirschfeldia
Hochet du vent = Briza
Hohéria = Hoheria
Holodiscus = Holodiscus
Holostée = Holosteum
Homalocladium = Homalocladium
Homogyne = Homogyne
Honckénéja = Honckenya
Horminelle = Horminum
Hortensia = Hydrangea
Hortensia en arbre = Dombeya
Hortensia grimpant = Schizophragma
Hottonie = Hottonia
Houblon = Humulus
Houque = Hierochloe, Holcus
Houttuynie = Houttuynia
Houx = Ilex
Hovéa = Howea
Huernia = Huernia
Hugueninia = Hugueninia
Hydrastis = Hydrastis
Hydrocotyle = Hydrocotyle
Hydrophylle = Hydrophyllum
Hygrophile = Hygrophila
Hyménophylle = Hymenophyllum
Hypécoum = Hypecoum
Hypoestes = Hypoestes
Hypolépis = Hypolepis
Hystrix = Hystrix
Icaquier = Chrysobalanus
Idésia = Idesia
If = Taxus
If de Patagonie = Saxegothaea
If du Prince Albert = Saxegothaea
If puant = Torreya
If verruqueux = Dacrycarpus
If-à-prunes = Cephalotaxus
Igname = Dioscorea
Illécèbre = Illecebrum
Illipe = Madhuca
Immortelle = Helichrysum, Rhodanthe
Immortelle annuelle = Xeranthemum
Immortelle argentée = Cephalipterum
Immortelle d'argent = Anaphalis
Immortelle de sables = Ammobium
Impatiens = Impatiens
Impératoire = Peucedanum
Incarvillée = Incarvillea
Indigo = Indigofera
Inule = Inula
Ionopsis = Ionopsis
Ipéca = Psychotria
Iphéion = Ipheion
Ipomée = Ipomoea
Irésine = Iresine

Iris = Iris
Iris tête-de-serpent = Hermodactylus
Iris tigré = Belamcanda
Iroko = Chlorophora
Ismène = Hymenocallis
Isoètes = Isoetes
Isopogon = Isopogon
Isopyre = Isopyrum
Itéa = Itea
Iva = Iva
Ixia = Ixia
Ixiolirion = Ixiolirion
Jaborandi = Pilocarpus
Jacaranda = Jacaranda
Jacinthe = Hyacinthus
Jacinthe blétille = Bletilla
Jacinthe du Cap = Galtonia, Lachenalia
Jacinthe sauvage = Hyacinthoides
Jacynthe d'eau = Eichhornia
Jambosier = Syzygium
Jamerosier = Syzygium
Jamesia = Jamesia
Jasione = Jasione
Jasmin = Jasminum
Jasmin de Madagascar = Stephanotis
Jasmin de Virginie = Gelsemium
Jasmin du Cap = Gardenia
Jasmin du Chili = Mandevilla
Jasmin étoilé = Trachelospermum
Jatropha = Jatropha
Jaunet d'eau = Nuphar
Jeffersonia = Jeffersonia
Jojoba = Simmondsia
Jonc = Juncus
Jonc des tonneliers = Schoenoplectus,
  Scirpus
Jonc fleuri = Butomus
Jonc palmier = Prionium
Jonc-sabre = Xyris
Joubarbe = Sempervivum
Jujubier = Ziziphus
Julienne = Hesperis
Julienne de Mahon = Malcolmia
Jurinée = Jurinea
Jusquiame = Hyoscyamus
Jussie = Ludwigia
Jute = Corchorus
Kadsura = Kadsura
Kaempferia = Kaempferia
Kaki = Diospyros
Kalanchoe = Bryophyllum, Kalanchoe
Kalmia = Kalmia
Kalopanax = Kalopanax
Kapokier = Bombax, Ceiba
Kénépier = Melicoccus

F

Kennedia = Kennedia
Kentia = Howea
Kernéra = Kernera
Keruing = Dipterocarpus
Ketmie = Hibiscus
Keulérie = Koeleria
Kickxia = Kickxia
Kiwi = Actinidia
Knautia = Knautia
Koelreuteria = Koelreuteria
Kohléria = Kohleria
Kolkwitzia = Kolkwitzia
Kouémé = Telfairia
Kraméria = Krameria
Kudzu = Pueraria
Kumquat = Fortunella
Laelia = Laelia
Lagerose = Lagerstroemia
Lagunaria = Lagunaria
Lagurier = Lagurus
Laîche = Carex
Lait de Notre-Dame = Silybum
Laiteron = Sonchus
Laitue = Lactuca
Laitue d'eau = Pistia
Laitue du Mexique = Tridax
Lamarckia = Lamarckia
Lamier = Lamium
Lampourde = Xanthium
Lampranthus = Lampranthus
Lampsane = Lapsana
Langue de Belle-mère = Sansevieria
Langue de serpent = Ophioglossum
Langue du diable = Amorphophallus
Langue-d'oiseau = Stellaria
Langue-de-chevreuil = Gasteria
Langue-de-chien = Cynoglossum
Langue-de-moineau = Passerina
Lansat = Lansium
Lantana = Lantana
Lantanier = Lantana
Lanterne chinoise = Abutilon, Physalis,
 Sandersonia
Lapageria = Lapageria
Lapeirousia = Lapeirousia
Laportea = Laportea
Larme-de-Job = Coix
Larme-de-Jupiter = Coix
Laser = Laser, Laserpitium
Latanier = Latania
Laurier = Laurus, Umbellularia
Laurier d'Alexandrie = Danae
Laurier rose = Nerium
Lavande = Lavandula
Lavande de mer = Limonium

Lavatère = Lavatera
Léersia = Leersia
Lenticule = Lemna
Lentille = Lens
Lentille d'eau = Lemna
Léontice = Leontice
Léonure = Leonurus
Leptospermum = Leptospermum
Leschenaultia = Leschenaultia
Lespédéza = Kummerowia, Lespedeza
Leucogenes = Leucogenes
Leucothoë = Leucothoe
Leuzée = Leuzea
Lewisia = Lewisia
Leycesteria = Leycesteria
Liane à râpe = Pithecoctenium
Liane corail = Antigonon
Liane de feu = Pyrostegia
Liane du voyageur = Cissus
Liane-orchidée = Podranea
Liatride = Liatris
Libertia = Libertia
Libocèdre = Libocedrus
Lierre = Hedera
Lierre terrestre = Glechoma
Ligulaire = Ligularia
Ligustique = Ligusticum
Lilas = Syringa
Lilas des Indes = Lagerstroemia, Melia
Limetier = Citrus
Limettier du désert = Eremocitrus
Limnanthes = Limnanthes
Limnophile = Limnophila
Limodore = Limodorum
Limoniastrum = Limoniastrum
Limoselle = Limosella
Lin = Linum
Lin de Nouvelle-Zélande = Phormium
Linaigrette = Eriophorum
Linaire = Chaenorhinum, Linaria
Lindera = Lindera
Lindheimera = Lindheimera
Linnée = Linnaea
Liparis = Liparis
Liriope = Liriope
Lis = Lilium
Lis d'un jour = Hemerocallis
Lis de Joséphine = Brunsvigia
Lis de la prairie = Camassia
Lis de St-Bruno = Paradisea
Lis de St-Jacques = Sprekelia
Lis de tigre = Tigridia
Lis des Cafres = Schizostylis
Lis des crapauds = Tricyrtis
Lis des impalas = Adenium

Lis des Incas = Alstroemeria
Lis des rochers = Arthropodium
Lis du Brésil = Eucharis
Lis géant = Cardiocrinum
Lis zéphir = Zephyranthes
Lis-araignée = Hymenocallis
Lis-cobra = Darlingtonia
Lis-javelot = Doryanthes
Lis-pancrais = Pancratium
Liseron = Convolvulus
Liseron arbustif = Argyreia
Liseron brûlant = Caiophora
Liseron des haies = Calystegia
Liseron épineux = Smilax
Listère = Listera
Litchi = Litchi
Littorelle = Littorella
Livistonia = Livistona
Loasa = Loasa
Lobélie = Lobelia
Loïdie = Lloydia
Loiseleuria = Loiseleuria
Longanier = Nephelium
Loropetalum = Loropetalum
Lotier = Lotus, Tetragonolobus
Lotus = Nelumbo
Lotus des Anciens = Ziziphus
Lotus des Indes = Nelumbo
Ludisia = Ludisia
Ludwigia = Ludwigia
Lunaire = Botrychium, Lunaria
Lunetière = Biscutella
Lupin = Lupinus
Lupin indigo = Baptisia
Luzerne = Medicago
Luzule = Luzula
Lychnis des Pyrénées = Petrocoptis
Lyciet = Lycium
Lycope = Lycopus
Lycopode = Diphasiastrum, Huperzia,
    Lycopodium
Lyonia = Lyonia
Lysichiton = Lysichiton
Lysimaque = Lysimachia
Maackia = Maackia
Maceron = Smyrnium
Mâche = Valerianella
Macle = Stratiotes
Macodes = Macodes
Macoré = Tieghemella
Madi = Madia
Magnolia = Magnolia
Magnolier = Magnolia
Mahogany d'Amérique = Swietenia
Mahonia = Mahonia

Maïanthème = Maianthemum
Maïs = Zea
Makoré = Tieghemella
Malaguette = Aframomum, Xylopia
Malaxis = Malaxis
Malope = Malope
Malvaviscus = Malvaviscus
Mammilaire = Mammillaria
Mandarinnier = Citrus
Mandragore = Mandragora
Mangoustanier = Garcinia
Manguier = Mangifera
Maniguette = Aframomum, Xylopia
Maniok = Manihot
Manteau de Notre-Dame = Alchemilla
Maranta = Maranta
Margose = Momordica
Marguerite = Leucanthemum
Marguerite d'automne = Leucanthemella
Marguerite des Alpes = Leucanthemopsis
Marguerite dorée = Euryops
Marguerite du Cap = Osteospermum
Marguerite en arbre = Argyranthemum
Marisque = Cladium
Marjolaine = Origanum
Marmite de singe = Lecythis
Marronnier = Aesculus
Marrube = Marrubium
Marsilée = Marsilea
Martynia = Craniolaria, Martynia
Martynia à trompe = Proboscidea
Massette = Typha
Matricaire = Matricaria, Tripleurospermum
Maurandie = Asarina
Mauve = Malva
Mauve de la Prairie = Sidalcea
Mauve de Virginie = Sida
Mauve-pavot = Callirhoe
Mazus = Lindernia, Mazus
Méconopsis = Meconopsis
Médinilla = Medinilla
Meehania = Meehania
Mélaleuca = Melaleuca
Mélampyre = Melampyrum
Mélastome = Melastoma
Mélèze = Larix
Mélianthe = Melianthus
Mélilot = Melilotus
Mélinet = Cerinthe
Mélique = Melica
Mélisse = Melissa
Mélitte = Melittis
Mélocoton = Sicana
Melon = Cucumis
Menthe = Mentha

Menthe coq = Tanacetum
Menthe d'Australie = Prostanthera
Menthe de montagne = Calamintha
Menthe-des-chats = Nepeta
Mentzelia = Eucnide
Menziesia = Menziesia
Mercuriale = Mercurialis
Mertensia = Mertensia
Mésembryanthème = Dorotheanthus
Métaséquoia = Metasequoia
Méum = Meum
Mibora = Mibora
Michauxia = Michauxia
Micocoulier = Celtis
Micocoulier ailé = Pteroceltis
Micromérie = Micromeria
Milla = Milla
Millepertuis = Hypericum
Millet = Milium
Millet à grappes = Setaria
Miltonia = Miltonia
Miltoniopsis = Miltoniopsis
Mimosa = Acacia, Mimosa
Mimulus = Mimulus
Miricaire = Myricaria
Miroir-de-Vénus = Legousia
Mitchella = Mitchella
Mitraria = Mitraria
Moehringia = Moehringia
Moenchia = Moenchia
Molène = Verbascum
Molinie = Molinia
Mollugine = Mollugo
Mollugo = Mollugo
Molosperme = Molopospermum
Moltkia = Moltkia
Molucelle = Moluccella
Monaie du Pape = Lunaria
Monanthes = Monanthes
Monarde = Monarda
Monbin = Spondias
Monopsis = Monopsis
Monotropa = Monotropa
Montbretia = Crocosmia
Montia = Montia
Morelle = Solanum
Morène = Hydrocharis
Moricandia = Moricandia
Morina = Morina
Moringa = Moringa
Mormodes = Mormodes
Mors du diable = Succisa
Mors-de-grenouille = Hydrocharis
Mouron = Anagallis
Mousse espagnole = Tillandsia

Moutarde = Sinapis
Mouton végétal = Raoulia
Muehlenbeckia = Muehlenbeckia
Muflier = Antirrhinum
Muflier des champs = Misopates
Muflier grimpant = Asarina
Muguet = Convallaria
Mulgédie = Cicerbita
Mûrier = Morus
Mûrier à papier = Broussonetia
Mûrier des Indes = Morinda
Mûrier sauvage = Rubus
Murraya = Murraya
Muscadier = Myristica
Muscadier de Californie = Torreya
Muscari = Muscari
Myagrum = Myagrum
Myosotis = Myosotis
Myosotis du Caucase = Brunnera
Myosure = Myosurus
Myriocarpe = Myriocarpa
Myriophylle = Myriophyllum
Myrrhe = Commiphora
Myrsine = Myrsine
Myrte = Lophomyrtus, Rhodomyrtus
Myrte du Cap = Phylica
Myrtille des sables = Leiophyllum
Myrtillier = Vaccinium
Naïade = Najas
Narcisse = Narcissus
Nard = Nardus
Nardostachyde de l'Inde = Nardostachys
Narthécie = Narthecium
Ne-m'oubliez-pas = Myosotis
Néflier = Mespilus
Néflier de Bronvaux = + Crataegomespilus
Néflier du Japon = Eriobotrya
Neillia = Neillia
Némésia = Nemesia
Némopanthe = Nemopanthus
Némophile = Nemophila, Pholistoma
Nénuphar = Nymphaea
Nénuphar épineux = Euryale
Nénuphar jaune = Nuphar
Néottie = Neottia
Nepenthes = Nepenthes
Néphélium = Nephelium
Néphrolépis = Nephrolepis
Nérine = Nerine
Nerprun = Frangula, Rhamnus
Neslie = Neslia
Nidularium = Nidularium
Nielle = Agrostemma
Nierembergia = Nierembergia
Nigelle = Nigella

Nigritelle = Nigritella
Nipa = Nypa
Nivéole = Leucojum
Noisetier = Corylus
Noisetier du Chili = Gevuina
Noix d'Arec = Areca
Noix de Para = Bertholletia
Nolana = Nolana
Nombril de Vénus = Omphalodes,
    Umbilicus
Nomocharis = Nomocharis
Nonnée = Nonea
Nopal = Opuntia
Noyer = Juglans
Noyer d'Amérique = Carya
Noyer du Queensland = Macadamia
Ochna = Ochna
Odontitès = Odontites
Oeil du Christ = Tolpis
Oeil-de-bouf = Buphthalmum
Oeillet d'Inde = Tagetes
Oil de Jeune fille = Coreopsis
Oil-de-bouf = Telekia
Oillet = Dianthus
Oiseau de paradis = Strelitzia
Okra = Abelmoschus
Oléaria = Olearia
Olivier = Olea
Onagre = Oenothera
Onanthe = Oenanthe
Ongle du diable = Ibicella
Onocléa sensitive = Onoclea
Onosma = Onosma
Onothère = Oenothera
Onothère aquatique = Ludwigia
Ophioglosse = Ophioglossum
Ophrys = Ophrys
Oplismène = Oplismenus
Oplopanax = Oplopanax
Oponce = Opuntia
Opopanax = Opopanax
Oranger = Citrus
Oranger amer = Poncirus
Oranger des Osages = Maclura
Oranger du Mexique = Choisya
Orcanette = Alkanna
Orchidée = Arpophyllum, Cyrtopodium,
    Ophrys, Orchis, Polycycnis, Pterostylis
Orchidée du Tibet = Pleione
Orchidée-casque = Coryanthes
Orchidée-jonc = Schoenorchis
Orchidée-papillon = Phalaenopsis
Orchidée-roseau = Arundina
Orchis = Anacamptis, Chamorchis, Orchis
Orchis bouc = Himantoglossum

Orchis globuleux = Traunsteinera
Orchis moucheron = Gymnadenia
Orchis-homme pendu = Aceras
Oreille d'éléphant = Alocasia
Oreille-de-lièvre = Bupleurum
Oreille-de-lion = Leonotis
Oréochloa = Oreochloa
Oréopanax = Oreopanax
Orge = Hordeum
Orge des bois = Hordelymus
Origan = Origanum
Orlaya = Orlaya
Orme = Ulmus
Orme de Samarie = Ptelea
Ornithogale = Ornithogalum
Orobanche = Orobanche
Orontium = Orontium
Orpin = Sedum
Ortie = Urtica
Ortie de Chine = Boehmeria
Oryzopsis = Oryzopsis
Oseille = Rumex
Oseille sauvage = Rumex
Osmanthus = Osmanthus
Osmonde = Osmunda
Ostryer = Ostrya
Oxalide = Oxalis
Oxydendron = Oxydendrum
Oxyria = Oxyria
Oxytropis = Oxytropis
Oyat = Ammophila
Oyat bâtard = × Calammophila
Pachyphytum = Pachyphytum
Pachypodium = Pachypodium
Pachystachys = Pachystachys
Pain de pourceau = Cyclamen
Palétuvier = Rhizophora
Palissandre = Dalbergia
Palmette = Sabal
Palmier = Aiphanes, Astrocaryum,
    Ceroxylon, Corypha, Desmoncus,
    Dictyosperma, Pinanga, Pritchardia,
    Reinhardtia
Palmier à cire = Copernicia
Palmier à huile = Elaeis
Palmier à miel = Jubaea
Palmier à racines épineuses = Cryosophila
Palmier à sucre = Arenga
Palmier à vin = Borassus
Palmier argenté = Coccothrinax
Palmier butia = Butia
Palmier cohune = Orbignya
Palmier d'Egypte = Hyphaene
Palmier dattier = Phoenix
Palmier de Madagascar = Pachypodium

Palmier de manille = Veitchia
Palmier de montagne = Chamaedorea
Palmier des dames = Rhapis
Palmier doré = Chrysalidocarpus
Palmier doum = Hyphaene
Palmier du Panama = Carludovica
Palmier épineux = Acanthophoenix
Palmier éventail = Washingtonia
Palmier ivoire = Phytelephas
Palmier mexicain = Dioon
Palmier nain = Chamaerops
Palmier piassaba = Attalea
Palmier queue-de-poisson = Caryota
Palmier royal = Archontophoenix,
  Roystonea
Palmier sang-de-dragon = Daemonorops
Palmier talipot = Corypha
Palmier-à-gelée = Butia
Palmier-aiguille = Rhapidophyllum
Palmier-bouteille = Hyophorbe
Palmier-chanvre = Trachycarpus
Palmier-éventail = Brahea, Licuala
Pamier nain royal = Thrinax
Pamplemoussier = Citrus
Panacée des montagnes = Arnica
Panais = Pastinaca
Pancrais = Pancratium
Pancrais jaune = Chlidanthus
Pandanus = Pandanus
Panic = Echinochloa, Panicum
panic digité = Eleusine
Panicaut = Eryngium
Papayer = Carica
Pâquerette = Bellis
Pâquerette bleue = Brachyscome
Parasolier = Cecropia
Parentucelle = Parentucellia
Parfum des dieux = Diosma
Pariétaire = Parietaria
Parisette = Paris
Parmentiera = Parmentiera
Parnassie = Parnassia
Paronyque = Paronychia
Parrotia = Parrotia
Pas d'âne = Tussilago
Paspalum = Paspalum
Passerage = Lepidium
Passerage drave = Cardaria
Passerine = Passerina
Passerine thymélée = Thymelaea
Passiflore = Passiflora
Pastel = Isatis
Pastèque = Citrullus
Patchouli = Pogostemon
Patte-de-lièvre = Ochroma

Pâturin = Poa
Paulownia = Paulownia
Pavot = Papaver
Pavot bleu = Meconopsis
Pavot cornu = Glaucium
Pavot cornu d'Orient = Dicranostigma
Pavot d'eau = Hydrocleys
Pavot de Californie = Romneya
Pavot des bois = Hylomecon
Pavot du soir = Hesperomecon
Pavot en arbre = Dendromecon
Pavot plumeux = Macleaya
Pavot tulipe mexicain = Hunnemannia
Paxistima = Paxistima
Pédiculaire = Pedicularis
Pédilanthe = Pedilanthus
Péganion = Peganum
Peigne de singe = Pithecoctenium
Péjibaie = Bactris
Pelléa = Pellaea
Pellionia = Pellionia
Peltaire = Peltaria
Peltandre = Peltandra
Pensée = Viola
Penstemon = Penstemon
Pépéromia = Peperomia
Péplis = Peplis
Perce-neige = Galanthus
Perce-pierre = Crithmum
Peristeria = Peristeria
Péristrophe = Peristrophe
Pérovskia = Perovskia
Persicaire = Persicaria
Persil = Petroselinum
Pervenche = Vinca
Pervenche de Madagascar = Catharanthus
Pesse = Hippuris
Peste d'eau = Egeria, Elodea
Pet-d'âne = Onopordum
Pétasites = Petasites
Petit cycas = Microcycas
Petit houx = Ruscus
Petit nénuphar = Nymphoides
Petit plombago = Plumbagella
Petit smilax = Smilacina
Petit soleil = Helianthella
Petit toryle = Torilis
Petite bourrache = Omphalodes
Petite centaurée = Centaurium
Petite ciguë = Aethusa
Petite férule = Ferulago
Petite lentille = Wolffia
Petrea = Petrea
Pétrocallis = Petrocallis
Pétrocoptis = Petrocoptis

Petteria = Petteria
Pétunia = Petunia
Peucédan = Peucedanum
Peuplier = Populus
Peyote = Lophophora
Peyoti = Lophophora
Phacélie = Phacelia
Phalangère = Anthericum, Chlorophytum
Philésia = Philesia
Philodendron = Monstera, Philodendron
Phlomis = Phlomis
Phlox = Phlox
Photinia = Photinia
Phyllodoce = Phyllodoce
Physocarpe = Physocarpus
Phytolaque = Phytolacca
Pied-d'alouette = Delphinium
Pied-d'éléphant = Beaucarnea
Pied-d'oiseau = Ornithopus
Pied-de-chat = Antennaria
Pied-de-poule = Cynodon
Piéris = Pieris
Pigamon = Thalictrum
Piléa = Pilea
Pilocarpe = Pilocarpus
Pilulaire = Pilularia
Pimelea = Pimelea
Piment = Capsicum
Pimpinelle = Pimpinella
Pin = Pinus
Pin Huon = Dacrydium
Pin parasol japonais = Sciadopitys
Pin rouge = Dacrydium
Pin-cyprès = Callitris
Pinellia = Pinellia
Pissenlit = Taraxacum
Pistachier = Pistacia
Pittosporum = Pittosporum
Pivoine = Paeonia
Plagianthe = Plagianthus
Plantain = Plantago
Plantain d'eau = Alisma
Plante au feu d'artifice = Pilea
Plante aux fourmis = Myrmecodia
Plante des concierges = Aspidistra
Plante-arc-en-ciel = Byblis
Plante-aux-crevettes = Justicia
Plante-caillou = Argyroderma, Lithops,
  Titanopsis
Plante-cobra = Darlingtonia
Plante-compas = Silphium
Plante-corail = Russelia
Plante-du-savetier = Bergenia
Plante-outre = Cephalotus
Plante-perle = Nertera

Plaqueminier = Diospyros
Platane = Platanus
Platanthère = Platanthera
Platycaryer = Platycarya
Pléione = Pleione
Pléomèle = Dracaena
Pleurosperme = Pleurospermum
Plombago = Plumbago
Plume d'eau = Hottonia
Plume des Apaches = Fallugia
Podalyre = Baptisia
Podocarpus = Podocarpus
Poil à gratter = Mucuna
Poire des sables = Peraphyllum
Poirée = Beta
Poirier = Pyrus
Pois = Pisum
Pois à chapelet = Abrus
Pois bâtard = Centrosema
Pois d'angol = Cajanus
Pois de cour = Cardiospermum
Pois de senteur = Lathyrus
Pois puant = Sterculia
Pois razier = Clitoria
Pois savane = Clitoria
Pois vivace = Lathyrus
Pois-bouton = Cephalanthus
Pois-chiche = Cicer
Pois-patate = Pachyrhizus
Pois-rivière = Centrosema
Pois-sabre = Canavalia
Poivre de la Jamaïque = Pimenta
Poivre de muraille = Sedum
Poivre sauvage = Vitex
Poivrier = Piper
Polycarpon = Polycarpon
Polycnème = Polycnemum
Polygala = Polygala
Polygonum bistorte = Bistorta
Polypode = Polypodium
Polypogon = Polypogon
Polyscias = Polyscias
Polystic = Polystichum
Pomme d'éléphant = Limonia
Pomme d'or = Spondias
Pomme de mai = Podophyllum
Pomme de pierre = Osteomeles
Pomme de Sodome = Calotropis
Pomme de terre = Solanum
Pomme du diable = Datura
Pommier = Malus
Pommier baumier = Clusia
Poncir = Poncirus
Populage = Caltha
Porcelle = Hypochaeris

Potamot = Potamogeton
Potentille = Potentilla
Pothos = Epipremnum
Poule grasse = Lapsana
Pourpier = Portulaca
Pourpier en arbre = Portulacaria
Pratia = Pratia
Prêle = Equisetum
Prénanthe = Prenanthes
Primevère = Primula
Primevère du Cap = Streptocarpus
Pritchardia = Pritchardia
Prosopis = Prosopis
Prostanthère = Prostanthera
Protée = Protea
Pruche = Tsuga
Prune d'Espagne = Spondias
Prunier de l'Orégon = Oemleria
Prunier de Madagascar = Flacourtia
Prunier des Cafres = Harpephyllum
Psoralée = Psoralea
Psoralier = Psoralea
Ptéris = Lonchitis, Pteris
Ptérocarpe = Pterocarpus
Ptérocaryer = Pterocarya
Ptychosperme = Ptychosperma
Puéraria = Pueraria
Pulicaire = Pulicaria
Pulmonaire = Pulmonaria
Pulsatille = Pulsatilla
Puschkinia = Puschkinia
Putoria = Putoria
Pyrèthre = Tanacetum
Pyrole = Moneses, Orthilia, Pyrola
Quassier = Quassia
Quassier amer = Quassia
Quatre-épices = Pimenta
Queue-de-chat = Acalypha
Queue-de-cheval = Hippuris
Queue-de-lézard = Anemopsis, Saururus
Queue-de-lièvre = Lagurus
Queue-de-rat = Aporocactus
Queue-de-renard = Alopecurus, Vulpia
Queue-de-souris = Myosurus
Quillay = Quillaja
Quinquina = Cinchona
Quisqualier = Quisqualis
Racine corail = Corallorhiza
radiaire = Astrantia
Radiole faux-lin = Radiola
Radis = Raphanus
Raifort = Armoracia
Raifort vert = Wasabia
Raisin d'Amérique = Phytolacca
Raisin de mer = Coccoloba, Ephedra

Raisin du Japon = Hovenia
Raisin-d'ours = Arctostaphylos
Raisinier = Coccoloba
Ramboutan = Nephelium
Ramonde = Ramonda
Rapette = Asperugo
Raphia = Raphia
Raphiolépis = Rhaphiolepis
Rapistre = Rapistrum
Raquette = Opuntia
Rauvolfia = Rauvolfia
Ravenelle = Raphanus
Raygras = Lolium
Réglisse = Glycyrrhiza
Réglisse sauvage = Astragalus
Rehmannia = Rehmannia
Reine des Andes = Phaedranassa
Reine-marguerite = Callistephus
Reineckéa = Reineckea
Renoncule = Ranunculus
Renouée = Persicaria, Polygonum
Renouée des montagnes = Aconogonon
Renouée grimpante = Fallopia
Renouée laineuse = Eriogonum
Réséda = Reseda
Réséda à balai = Descurainia
Rétama = Retama
Rhagadiole = Rhagadiolus
Rhatania = Krameria
Rhinanthe = Rhinanthus
Rhinephyllum = Rhinephyllum
Rhodanthe = Rhodanthe
Rhodiole = Rhodiola
Rhododendron = Rhododendron
Rhodothamnus = Rhodothamnus
Rhubarbe = Rheum
Rhubarbe géante = Gunnera
Rhynchospore = Rhynchospora
Rhynchostylis = Rhynchostylis
Ricin = Ricinus
Ridolfia = Ridolfia
Rince-bouteille = Callistemon
Rince-bouteille du Natal = Greyia
Rivinia = Rivina
Riz = Oryza
Riz barbu = Oryzopsis
Riz sauvage = Leersia, Zizania
Robinier = Robinia
Rocouyer = Bixa
Rodgersia = Rodgersia
Roi des Alpes = Eritrichium
Romanzoffia = Romanzoffia
Romarin = Rosmarinus
Romarin sauvage = Ledum
Romulée = Romulea

Ronce = Rubus
Rondier = Borassus
Roquette = Eruca
Roquette de mer = Cakile
Roridule = Roridula
Roripe = Rorippa
Rose d'Inde = Tagetes
Rose de Chine = Hibiscus
Rose de Jéricho = Anastatica
Rose de Noël = Helleborus
Rose des Andes = Bejaria
Rose du désert = Adenium
Rose trémière = Alcea
Roseau = Phragmites
Roseau de Chine = Miscanthus
Rosier = Rosa
Rosulaire = Rosularia
Rotin = Calamus
Rubanier = Sparganium
Rudbeckia = Rudbeckia
Rue = Ruta
Rue de chèvre = Galega
Ruellia = Ruellia
Ruppia = Ruppia
Russélia = Russelia
Sabal = Sabal
Sabline = Arenaria
Sabot de Vénus = Paphiopedilum
Sabot-de-Vénus = Cypripedium
Safran bâtard = Carthamus
Sagaro = Carnegiea
Sagine = Sagina
Sagittaire = Sagittaria
Sagoutier = Metroxylon
Sainfoin = Onobrychis
Sainfoin oscillant = Desmodium
Salacca = Salacca
Salade de blé = Valerianella
Salicaire = Lythrum
Salicorne = Salicornia
Salpiglossis = Salpiglossis
Salsepareille = Smilax
Salsifis = Tragopogon
Salvinie = Salvinia
Samole = Samolus
Sanchezia = Sanchezia
Sanguinaire = Sanguinaria
Sanguisorbe = Sanguisorba
Sanicle = Sanicula
Sansévière = Sansevieria
Santal blanc = Santalum
Santoline = Santolina
Sapin = Abies
Sapin chinois = Cunninghamia
Saponaire = Saponaria

Sapote blanche = Casimiroa
Sapotier = Manilkara
Sapotillier = Pouteria
Sarcaucolon = Sarcocaulon
Sarcococca = Sarcococca
Sarracénnie = Sarracenia
Sarrasin = Fagopyrum
Sarriette = Satureja
Sassafras = Sassafras
Sauge = Salvia
Sauge hormin = Horminum
Saule = Salix
Sauromatum = Sauromatum
Saussurée = Saussurea
Savon indien = Sapindus
Savonnier = Koelreuteria
Saxifrage = Saxifraga
Scabieuse = Knautia, Scabiosa
Scabieuse des champs = Galinsoga
Scabieuse du Parnasse = Pterocephalus
Scaevola = Scaevola
Scandix = Scandix
Sceau de Salomon = Polygonatum
Sceptre de l'Empereur = Etlingera
Schefflera = Schefflera
Scheuchzérie = Scheuchzeria
Schisandra = Schisandra
Schizanthe = Schizanthus
Scille = Puschkinia, Scilla
Scille maritime = Urginea
Scirpe = Isolepis, Scirpus
Scirpe gazonnant = Trichophorum
Scléranthe = Scleranthus
Sclérochloa = Sclerochloa
Scolyme = Scolymus
Scopolia = Scopolia
Scorpiure = Scorpiurus
Scorsonère = Scorzonera
Scrofulaire = Scrophularia
Scutellaire = Scutellaria
Scuticaire = Scuticaria
Sebestier = Cordia
Sécurigéra = Securigera
Seigle = Secale
Sélaginelle = Selaginella
Sélin = Selinum
Séné = Cassia, Senna
Séneçon = Kleinia, Senecio
Séneçon de Sibérie = Sinacalia
Sensitive = Biophytum, Mimosa
Séquoia = Sequoia
Sérapias = Serapias
Seringat = Philadelphus
Serpent végétal = Trichosanthes
Serpentaire = Dracunculus

F

Serpentaire de l'Inde = Rauvolfia
Serpolet = Thymus
Serratule = Serratula
Sésame = Sesamum
Séséli = Molopospermum, Seseli
Sesléria = Sesleria
Sétaire = Setaria
Shérardia = Sherardia
Shortia = Shortia
Sibbaldia = Sibbaldia
Sibérienne = Sibiraea
Sibthorpia = Sibthorpia
Sigesbeckia = Sigesbeckia
Silaüs = Silaum
Silène = Silene
Sinningia = Sinningia
Sinocrassula = Sinocrassula
Sison = Sison
Sisymbre = Sisymbrium
Skimmia = Skimmia
Smilax = Smilax
Soja = Glycine
Solandra = Solandra
Soldanelle = Soldanella
Soleil = Helianthus
Soleil mexicain = Tithonia
Sonnératia = Sonneratia
Sophora = Sophora
Sorbaria = Sorbaria
Sorbier = Sorbus
Sorgho = Sorghum
Souchet = Cyperus
Souci = Calendula
Souci de Cap = Dimorphotheca
Souci du Cap = Arctotheca
Soude = Salsola, Suaeda
Sparaxis = Sparaxis
Sparganier = Sparganium
Sparte = Spartium
Spartina = Spartina
Spathyphyllum = Spathiphyllum
Spergulaire = Spergularia
Spergule = Spergula
Sphéralcée = Sphaeralcea
Spigélia = Spigelia
Spiranthe = Spiranthes
Spirée = Petrophytum, Spiraea
Spirodèle = Spirodela
Spodiopogon = Spodiopogon
Sporobole = Sporobolus
Stachyurus = Stachyurus
Stapélia = Stapelia
Staphilier = Staphylea
Statice = Limonium
Stéhéline = Staehelina

Stellaire = Stellaria
Sténocarpe = Stenocarpus
Stephanandra = Stephanandra
Sterculier = Brachychiton, Sterculia
Stévie = Stevia
Stipa = Stipa
Stokésia = Stokesia
Streptocalyx = Streptocalyx
Streptope = Streptopus
Streptosolen = Streptosolen
Strobilanthe = Strobilanthes
Stromanthe = Stromanthe
Strychnos = Strychnos
Stuartia = Stewartia
Styrax = Styrax
Styrax ailé = Pterostyrax
Subulaire = Subularia
Succiselle = Succisella
Succowia = Succowia
Sucepin = Monotropa
Suéda = Suaeda
Sumac = Rhus
Superbe de Malabar = Gloriosa
Sureau = Sambucus
Surelle = Oxalis
Sutherlandia = Sutherlandia
Suzanne aux yeux noirs = Thunbergia
Swainsonia = Swainsona
Swertia = Swertia
Symphorine = Symphoricarpos
Symplocarpe = Symplocarpus
Symplocos = Symplocos
Syngonium = Syngonium
Synthyris = Synthyris
Tabac = Nicotiana
Tabaret = Thlaspi
Tacca = Tacca
Tagète = Tagetes
Tamarinier = Tamarindus
Tamarinier sauvage = Leucaena
Tamaris = Tamarix
Tamier = Tamus
Tanaisie = Tanacetum
Tanakéa = Tanakaea
Tanier taro = Xanthosoma
Tarchonanthus = Tarchonanthus
Taro = Colocasia
Tasse-de-singe = Nepenthes
Teck = Tectona
Tellima = Tellima
Télopée = Telopea
Templetonia = Templetonia
Téphrosie = Tephrosia
Tesdalia = Teesdalia
Tête-de-dragon = Dracocephalum

Tétracentron = Tetracentron
Tétragone = Tetragonia
Tétragonolobe = Tetragonolobus
Tétrapanax = Tetrapanax
Thapsia = Thapsia
Thé d'Oswego = Monarda
Thé des bois = Gaultheria
Thé du Labrador = Ledum
Théier = Camellia
Thélésperme = Thelesperma
Théligone = Theligonum
Théobrome = Theobroma
Thésion = Thesium
Thésium = Thesium
Thespésia = Thespesia
Thévétia = Thevetia
Thladianthe = Thladiantha
Thlaspi = Iberis, Thlaspi
Thrinax = Thrinax
Thunbergie = Thunbergia
Thuya = Thuja
Thuya articulé = Tetraclinis
Thuya d'Algérie = Tetraclinis
Thuya d'Orient = Platycladus
Thuya jiba = Thujopsis
Thuya nain = Microbiota
Thym = Thymus
Thymélée = Thymelaea
Thysanothe = Thysanotus
Tiarelle = Tiarella
Tibouchina = Tibouchina
Tillandsia = Tillandsia
Tilleul = Tilia
Tilleul d'appartement = Sparrmannia
Tipu = Tipuana
Titanopsis = Titanopsis
Todéa = Todea
Tofieldia = Tofieldia
Tolmiée = Tolmiea
Tomate = Lycopersicon
Tonka = Dipteryx
Tordyle = Tordylium
Torénia = Torenia
Torilis = Torilis
Tortelle = Sisymbrium
Tournesol = Chrozophora
Townsedia = Townsendia
Tozzia = Tozzia
Trachélium = Trachelium
Trachymène = Trachymene
Tréculia = Treculia
Trèfle = Trifolium
Trèfle d'eau = Menyanthes
Trépane = Tolpis
Tribule = Tribulus

Trichomanès = Trichomanes
Trichopilia = Trichopilia
Tridax = Tridax
Trientale = Trientalis
Trigonelle = Trigonella
Trillium = Trillium
Trinia = Trinia
Trioste = Triosteum
Trisète = Trisetum
Triteleia = Triteleia
Triticale = × Triticosecale
Tritome = Kniphofia
Tritonia = Tritonia
Trochiscanthe = Trochiscanthes
Trochocarpe = Trochocarpa
Trochodendron = Trochodendron
Troène = Ligustrum
Trolle = Trollius
Trompette d'eau = Cryptocoryne
Trompette des anges = Brugmansia
Troscart = Triglochin
Tubéraire = Tuberaria
Tubéreuse = Polianthes
Tulbaghia = Tulbaghia
Tulipe = Tulipa
Tulipe de la Prairie = Calochortus
Tulipier = Liriodendron
Tulipier africain = Spathodea
Tunique = Petrorhagia
Tupélo = Nyssa
Turgénia = Turgenia
Turmeric = Curcuma
Turnéra = Turnera
Tussilage = Tussilago
Ulluque = Ullucus
Umbilic = Orostachys
Urosperme = Urospermum
Utriculaire = Utricularia
Uvulaire = Uvularia
Vaccaire = Vaccaria
Vaillantie = Valantia
Valériane = Valeriana
Valériane africaine = Fedia
Valériane des jardins = Centranthus
Valériane dorée = Patrinia
Valériane grecque = Polemonium
Valérianelle = Valerianella
Vallisnérie = Vallisneria
Vancouvéria = Vancouveria
Vanillier = Vanilla
Vélar = Erysimum, Sisymbrium
Veltheimia = Veltheimia
Vérâtre = Veratrum
Verbésine = Verbesina
Verge-d'or = Solidago

Vergerette = Erigeron
Vernonie = Vernonia
Véronique = Paederota, Veronica
Véronique arbustive = Hebe
Véronique de Virginie = Veronicastrum
Verveine = Verbena
Verveine de Ceylan = Cymbopogon
Verveine des sables = Abronia
Vesce = Vicia
Vésicaire = Alyssoides
Vétiver = Vetiveria
Victoria = Victoria
Vigne = Vitis
Vigne d'appartement = Cissus
Vigne de Madeire = Anredera
Vigne des Andes = Marsdenia
Vigne vierge = Ampelopsis, Parthenocissus
Villarsia = Villarsia
Violette = Viola
Violette allemande = Exacum
Violette d'Usambara = Saintpaulia
Violier = Matthiola
Viorne = Viburnum
Vipérine = Echium
Virgilier = Cladrastis
Visnéa = Visnea
Vitellaire = Vitellaria
Vomiquier = Strychnos
Vrai myrte = Myrtus

Vulpin = Alopecurus, Vulpia
Wasabi = Wasabia
Washingtonia = Washingtonia
Watsonia = Watsonia
Weigelia = Weigela
Wellingtonia = Sequoiadendron
Welwitschia = Welwitschia
Wigandia = Wigandia
Willemétie = Willemetia
Wolffia = Wolffia
Woodsia = Woodsia
Woodwardia = Woodwardia
Wulfénia = Wulfenia
Xanthophthalmum = Xanthophthalmum
Xanthorhiza = Xanthorhiza
Xéranthème = Xeranthemum
Xérophylle = Xerophyllum
Xylomèle = Xylomelum
Yohimbeh = Pausinystalia
Ysope = Hyssopus
Yucca = Yucca
Zaluzianskya = Zaluzianskya
Zannichellia = Zannichellia
Zelkova = Zelkova
Zénobia = Zenobia
Zigadénus = Zigadenus
Zinnia = Zinnia
Zostère = Zostera

XII German plant names

Aasblume = Huernia, Stapelia
Abelie = Abelia
Abendblüte = Hesperantha
Abendmohn = Hesperomecon
Absinth = Artemisia
Acajubaum = Anacardium
Ackerfrauenmantel = Aphanes
Ackerkohl = Conringia
Ackerlöwenmaul = Misopates
Ackerröte = Sherardia
Ackersalat = Valerianella
Adelie = Forestiera
Adlerfarn = Pteridium
Adonisröschen = Adonis
Ährenhafer = Gaudinia
Ährenheide = Bruckenthalia
Ährenlilie = Narthecium
Affenblume = Mimulus
Affenbrotbaum = Adansonia
Affengesicht = Mimusops
Affenkamm = Pithecoctenium
Affenohrring = Pithecellobium
Affenseife = Enterolobium
Affodill = Asphodelus
Afrikanische Eiche = Lophira
Afrikanische Teufelskralle =
  Harpagophytum
Afrikanischer Baldrian = Fedia
Afrikanischer Brotfruchtbaum = Treculia
Afrikanischer Tulpenbaum = Spathodea
Afrikazypresse = Widdringtonia
Afrogelbholz = Afrocarpus
Agave = Agave
Ahorn = Acer
Ahornblatt = Mukdenia
Akanthus = Acanthus
Akazie = Acacia
Akebie = Akebia
Akee = Blighia
Akelei = Aquilegia
Akipflaume = Blighia
Alangie = Alangium
Alant = Dittrichia, Inula
Alerce = Fitzroya
Alexander = Zizia
Alexandrinischer Lorbeer = Danae
Algenfarn = Azolla

Alkannawurzel = Alkanna
Allamande = Allamanda
Almend = Terminalia
Almond = Terminalia
Aloe = Aloe
Alpenazalee = Loiseleuria
Alpenbalsam = Erinus
Alpendost = Adenostyles
Alpenglöckchen = Soldanella
Alpenheide = Loiseleuria
Alpenhelm = Bartsia
Alpenlattich = Homogyne
Alpenmargerite = Leucanthemopsis
Alpenrachen = Tozzia
Alpenrose = Rhododendron
Alpenscharte = Saussurea
Alpenveilchen = Cyclamen
Alpinie = Alpinia
Alraune = Mandragora
Alraunwurzel = Mandragora
Amaryllis der Gärtner = Hippeastrum
Amazonaslilie = Eucharis
Amberbaum = Liquidambar
Amberkörbchen = Amberboa
Ambrosie = Ambrosia
Ameisenbaum = Cecropia
Ameisenknolle = Myrmecodia
Amerikanische Nelkenwurz = Spigelia
Amerikanischer Balsambaum = Bursera
Amerikanischer Froschlöffel = Limnobium
Amethystblume = Amethystea
Ammoniakpflanze = Dorema
Ampfer = Rumex
Amsonie = Amsonia
Anabaum = Faidherbia
Ananas = Ananas
Anattostrauch = Bixa
Andeniris = Libertia
Andenkönigin = Phaedranassa
Andenpolster = Azorella
Andenrose = Bejaria
Andenstrauch = Escallonia
Andenwein = Marsdenia
Andorn = Marrubium
Andrachne = Andrachne
Anemone = Anemone
Angelikabaum = Aralia

G

Angosturabaum = Galipea
Anis = Pimpinella
Ankerpflanze = Colletia
Anone = Annona
Antilopenstrauch = Purshia
Apachenpflaume = Fallugia
Apfel = Malus
Apfelbeere = Aronia
Apfelsine = Citrus
Appalachengras = Cymophyllus
Aprikose = Prunus
Aralie = Aralia
Araukarie = Araucaria
Arbuse = Citrullus
Ardisie = Ardisia
Aremonie = Aremonia
Arganbaum = Argania
Arnika = Arnica
Aronstab = Arum
Artischocke = Cynara
Arzneiehrenpreis = Veronicastrum
Aschenblume = Pericallis
Aschenwicke = Tephrosia
Asiatische Taubnessel = Meehania
Asphaltklee = Bituminaria
Asselkaktus = Pelecyphora
Astblume = Cladanthus
Aster = Aster
Astilbe = Astilbe
Atlasblume = Clarkia
Attich = Sambucus
Aubergine = Solanum
Augentrost = Euphrasia
Augenwicke = Swainsona
Augenwurz = Athamanta
Aukube = Aucuba
Aurikel = Primula
Australheide = Epacris
Australische Fuchsie = Correa
Australische Kastanie = Castanospermum
Australminze = Prostanthera
Avocado = Persea
Azalee = Rhododendron
Azarabaum = Azara
Babassupalme = Orbignya
Backenklee = Dorycnium
Bärengras = Xerophyllum
Bärenkamille = Ursinia
Bärenklau = Acanthus, Heracleum
Bärenohr = Arctotis
Bärentraube = Arctostaphylos
Bärlapp = Lycopodium
Bärwurz = Meum
Baldrian = Valeriana
Baldriangesicht = Phuopsis

Ballonblume = Platycodon
Ballonerbse = Sutherlandia
Ballonrebe = Cardiospermum
Ballonwein = Cardiospermum
Balsabaum = Ochroma
Balsamapfel = Clusia, Momordica
Balsambaum = Myroxylon
Balsamine = Impatiens
Balsamkraut = Tanacetum
Balsampflaume = Spondias
Balsamstrauch = Amyris, Cedronella
Bambus = Bambusa
Banane = Musa
Bandbusch = Homalocladium
Bandfarn = Vittaria
Banksie = Banksia
Banucalagnuss = Reutealis
Baobab = Adansonia
Barbadoskirsche = Malpighia
Barbarakraut = Barbarea
Barbenkraut = Barbarea
Barlerie = Barleria
Bartblume = Caryopteris
Bartelpalme = Acanthophoenix
Bartfaden = Penstemon
Bartgras = Bothriochloa
Bartisie = Bartsia
Bartpippau = Tolpis
Bartsie = Parentucellia
Baselle = Basella
Basilikum = Ocimum
Bastardblauheide = × Phyllothamnus
Bastardecheverie = × Pachyveria
Bastardfeuerdorn = × Pyracomeles
Bastardindigo = Amorpha
Bastardlauch = Nothoscordum
Bastardschaumblüte = × Heucherella
Bastardstrandhafer = × Calammophila
Bastardzypresse = × Cuprocyparis
Bastpalme = Raphia
Bauernbohne = Schotia
Bauernsenf = Teesdalia
Bauhinie = Bauhinia
Baum der Reisenden = Ravenala
Baumanemone = Carpenteria
Baumaralie = Kalopanax
Baumaster = Pachystegia
Baumkraftwurz = Kalopanax
Baummohn = Bocconia, Dendromecon
Baumschlinge = Periploca
Baumstachelbeere = Averrhoa
Baumtomate = Cyphomandra
Baumwollbaum = Bombax
Baumwolle = Gossypium
Baumwürger = Celastrus

Becherblüte = Nierembergia
Becherblume = Scyphanthus
Becherfarn = Cyathea
Becherglocke = Edraianthus
Becherkätzchen = Garrya
Becherpflanze = Silphium
Becherschwertel = Cypella
Beerenmalve = Malvaviscus
Beerentraube = Schisandra
Begonie = Begonia
Beifuß = Artemisia
Beilholz = Securinega
Beilkaktus = Pelecyphora
Beilwicke = Securigera
Beinbrech = Narthecium
Beinwell = Symphytum
Belbaum = Aegle
Belladonna = Atropa
Belladonnenlilie = Amaryllis
Benediktenkraut = Cnicus
Bennussbaum = Moringa
Bensonie = Bensoniella
Bentinckpalme = Bentinckia
Berberitze = Berberis
Berberitzenmahonie = × Mahoberberis
Berchemie = Berchemia
Bergaralie = Oreopanax
Bergenie = Bergenia
Bergfarn = Oreopteris
Bergfenchel = Seseli
Bergflachs = Thesium
Berghülse = Nemopanthus
Bergknöterich = Aconogonon
Berglinse = Astragalus
Berglorbeer = Kalmia, Umbellularia
Bergmahagoni = Cercocarpus
Bergmammutbaum = Sequoiadendron
Bergminze = Calamintha
Bergpalme = Chamaedorea
Bergscharte = Stemmacantha
Berle = Berula
Bermudagras = Cynodon
Bertolonie = Bertolonia
Bertram = Anacyclus
Berufkraut = Conyza, Erigeron
Besenginster = Cytisus
Besenheide = Calluna
Besenkraut = Bassia
Besenrauke = Descurainia
Besenried = Molinia
Bete = Beta
Betelpalme = Areca
Bettlerkraut = Desmodium
Beutelfarn = Dicksonia
Bibernelle = Pimpinella

Bilsenkraut = Hyoscyamus
Bingelkraut = Mercurialis
Binse = Juncus
Binsenginster = Spartium
Binsenkaktus = Rhipsalis
Binsenlilie = Aphyllanthes
Binsenorchidee = Schoenorchis
Birke = Betula
Birkwurz = Ferulago
Birne = Pyrus
Birngrün = Orthilia
Bisamdistel = Jurinea
Bisameibisch = Abelmoschus
Bisampflanze = Amberboa
Bischofskappe = Mitella, Tiarella
Bischofsmütze = Astrophytum
Bitterblatt = Exacum
Bitterdistel = Cnicus
Bittererbse = Daviesia
Bittergurke = Momordica
Bitterholz = Picrasma, Quassia
Bitterklee = Menyanthes
Bitterkraut = Picris
Bitterling = Blackstonia
Bitterorange = Poncirus
Bitterwurzel = Lewisia
Blasenbaum = Koelreuteria
Blasenbinse = Scheuchzeria
Blasenfarn = Cystopteris
Blasenkirsche = Physalis
Blasenmiere = Lepyrodiclis
Blasenschötchen = Alyssoides
Blasenspiere = Physocarpus
Blasenstrauch = Colutea
Blattblüte = Phyllanthus
Blatteibe = Phyllocladus
Blattfahne = Spathiphyllum
Blattkaktus = Epiphyllum
Blaubeere = Vaccinium
Blaudolde = Trachymene
Blaue Amaryllis = Worsleya
Blauer Hibiscus = Alyogyne
Blaues Gänseblümchen = Brachyscome
Blauglockenbaum = Paulownia
Blauglöckchen = Mertensia
Blaugras = Sesleria
Blaugummibaum = Eucalyptus
Blauhalm = Andropogon
Blauheide = Phyllodoce
Blaukissen = Aubrieta
Blauklee = Parochetus
Blauregen = Wisteria
Blauröhre = Cyananthus
Blauschote = Decaisnea
Blauspiere = Sibiraea

G

Blaustängel = Dichanthium
Blaustern = Scilla
Blauweiderich = Pseudolysimachion
Bleibusch = Amorpha
Bleiholz = Dirca
Bleiwurz = Plumbago
Blütenfarn = Anemia
Blumenbinse = Butomus, Scheuchzeria
Blumenmaranthe = Stromanthe
Blumenrohr = Canna
Blumenspiere = Exochorda
Blutbeere = Rivina
Blutblume = Haemanthus, Scadoxus
Blutholzbaum = Haematoxylum
Blutständel = Ludisia
Blutwurzel = Sanguinaria
Bocksbart = Tragopogon
Bocksdorn = Lycium
Bockshornklee = Trigonella
Bocksknöterich = Atraphaxis
Bodenlorbeer = Epigaea
Bogenhanf = Sansevieria
Bohne = Phaseolus, Vicia
Bohnenkraut = Satureja
Boldo = Peumus
Boltonie = Boltonia
Bootfarn = Angiopteris
Borassuspalme = Borassus
Borretsch = Borago
Borstendolde = Torilis
Borstenhirse = Setaria
Borstenschwanzgras = Psilurus
Borstgras = Nardus
Bougainvillee = Bougainvillea
Bouvardie = Bouvardia
Brachsenkraut = Isoetes
Brandkraut = Phlomis
Brandschopf = Celosia
Braunelle = Prunella
Braunwurz = Scrophularia
Braut in Haaren = Nigella
Brautkranz = Francoa
Brechnuss = Strychnos
Brechwurzel = Psychotria
Breiapfelbaum = Manilkara
Breitfaden = Platystemon
Breitsame = Orlaya
Breitschötchen = Braya
Brenndolde = Cnidium
Brennhülse = Mucuna
Brennnessel = Urtica
Brennpflanze = Laportea
Brennwinde = Caiophora
Brillenschötchen = Biscutella
Brodiee = Brodiaea

Brombeere = Rubus
Bronvauxmispel = + Crataegomespilus
Bronzeblatt = Galax, Rodgersia
Brotfruchtbaum = Artocarpus
Brotpalmfarn = Encephalartos
Browallie = Browallia
Bruchheil = Rhexia
Bruchkraut = Herniaria
Brunfelsie = Brunfelsia
Brunnenkresse = Nasturtium
Brunsvigie = Brunsvigia
Brustbeere = Ziziphus
Brutblatt = Bryophyllum
Bubiköpfchen = Soleirolia
Buche = Fagus
Buchenfarn = Phegopteris
Buchsbaum = Buxus
Buchtenfarn = Hypolepis
Buchweizen = Fagopyrum
Buckelbeere = Gaylussacia
Büchsenkraut = Lindernia
Büffelbeere = Shepherdia
Büffelgras = Buchloe
Büffelnuss = Pyrularia
Bürstengras = Polypogon
Büschelbohne = Cyamopsis
Büschelgermer = Melanthium
Büschelglocke = Edraianthus
Büschelgras = Rostraria
Büschelschön = Phacelia
Buffonie = Bufonia
Bunge = Samolus
Bunte Wucherblume = Ismelia
Buntnessel = Plectranthus, Solenostemon
Burzeldorn = Tribulus
Buschgeißblatt = Diervilla
Buschklee = Kummerowia, Lespedeza
Buschmannskerze = Sarcocaulon
Butterbaum = Madhuca
Caesalpinie = Caesalpinia
Callisie = Callisia
Camassie = Camassia
Camholz = Baphia
Campecheholz = Haematoxylum
Cantue = Cantua
Carludovike = Carludovica
Cashewnuss = Anacardium
Cassavastrauch = Manihot
Catharanthe = Catharanthus
Chayote = Sechium
Chiclebaum = Manilkara
Chicorée = Cichorium
Chileglöckchen = Lapageria
Chilekrokus = Tecophilaea
Chilenuss = Gevuina

Chilezeder = Austrocedrus
Chili = Capsicum
Chinadickblatt = Sinocrassula
Chinafingerhut = Rehmannia
Chinagras = Boehmeria
Chinagreiskraut = Sinacalia
Chinaorchidee = Bletilla
Chinarindenbaum = Cinchona
Chinaschilf = Miscanthus
Chinesenhut = Holmskioldia
Chininbaum = Cinchona
Chironie = Chironia
Christdorn = Paliurus
Christophskraut = Actaea
Christrose = Helleborus
Christusauge = Tolpis
Chrysantheme = × Chrysanthemum
Citrange = × Citroncirus
Clarkie = Clarkia
Clematis = Clematis
Clintonie = Clintonia
Clivie = Clivia
Colletie = Colletia
Collinsie = Collinsia
Commeline = Commelina
Copihue = Lapageria
Correa = Correa
Dachwurz = Sempervivum
Dahlie = Dahlia
Dalbergie = Dalbergia
Dalechampie = Dalechampia
Damiana = Turnera
Dammarabaum = Agathis
Damoklesbaum = Oroxylum
Dattelpalme = Phoenix
Dattelpflaume = Diospyros
Degenbinse = Xyris
Deutzie = Deutzia
Dickähre = Pachystachys
Dickblatt = Crassula
Dickmännchen = Pachysandra
Dicknarbe = Paxistima
Dickröschen = Rosularia
Dickstängel = Sarcocaulon
Dickstamm = Pachyphytum
Dieffenbachie = Dieffenbachia
Dill = Anethum
Dingel = Limodorum
Diptam = Dictamnus
Distel = Carduus
Dodonaee = Dodonaea
Doldenrebe = Ampelopsis
Donarsbart = Jovibarba
Doppelährengras = Beckmannia
Doppelblüte = Disanthus

Doppelfrucht = Amphicarpaea
Doppelhörnchen = Diascia
Doppelkappe = Adlumia
Doppelmalve = Sidalcea
Doppelpalmfarn = Dioon
Doppelsame = Diplotaxis
Doppelschild = Dipelta
Dorngras = Crypsis
Dornkirsche = Prinsepia
Dornlattich = Launaea
Dornmelde = Bassia
Dornulme = Hemiptelea
Dorstenie = Dorstenia
Dost = Origanum
Dotterblume = Caltha
Douglasfichte = Pseudotsuga
Douglasie = Pseudotsuga
Drachenapfel = Dracontomelon
Drachenbaum = Dracaena
Drachenblatt = Dracophyllum
Drachenblutpalme = Daemonorops
Drachenkopf = Dracocephalum
Drachenmäulchen = Horminum
Drachenmaul = Helicodiceros
Drachenwurz = Dracunculus
Draculaorchidee = Dracula
Drahtstrauch = Muehlenbeckia
Drehfrucht = Streptocarpus
Drehkelch = Streptocalyx
Drehkrone = Streptosolen
Drehwurz = Spiranthes
Dreibiss = Tridax
Dreiblatt = Trillium
Dreiblattspiere = Gillenia
Dreiflügelfrucht = Tripterygium
Dreimasterblume = Tradescantia
Dreizack = Triglochin
Dreizahn = Danthonia
Dreizipfellilie = Trillium
Drüsenbaum = Adenanthera
Drüsenginster = Adenocarpus
Drüsenklee = Psoralea
Drüsenköpfchen = Cephalotus
Dudleya = Dudleya
Dünnfarn = Trichomanes
Dünnschwanz = Parapholis
Dünnschwingel = Micropyrum
Duftblüte = Osmanthus
Duftnessel = Agastache
Duftraute = Agathosma
Duftsiegel = Smilacina
Duftsteinrich = Lobularia
Dumpalme = Hyphaene
Durianbaum = Durio
Ebenholz = Diospyros

G

Eberesche = Sorbus
Eberraute = Artemisia
Eberwurz = Carlina
Echeverie = Echeveria
Edeldistel = Eryngium
Edelweiß = Leontopodium
Efeu = Hedera
Efeuaralie = × Fatshedera
Efeuranke = Hemigraphis
Efeutute = Epipremnum
Ehrenpreis = Veronica
Eibe = Taxus
Eibisch = Althaea
Eiche = Quercus
Eichenfarn = Gymnocarpium
Eidechsenschwanz = Anemopsis
Eidechsenwurz = Sauromatum
Eierfrucht = Passiflora, Pouteria, Solanum
Einbeere = Paris
Einblatt = Malaxis
Einhornpflanze = Ibicella
Eisenholz = Metrosideros
Eisenhut = Aconitum
Eisenkraut = Verbena
Eiskraut = Mesembryanthemum
Elefantenapfel = Limonia
Elefantenfarn = Todea
Elefantenholz = Bolusanthus
Elfenbeindistel = Ptilostemon
Elfenbeinpalme = Phytelephas
Elfenblume = Epimedium
Elfenglöckchen = Prosartes
Elsbeere = Sorbus
Emilie = Emilia
Endivie = Cichorium
Engelsauge = Houstonia
Engelstrompete = Brugmansia
Engelwurz = Angelica
Entengrütze = Lemna
Enzian = Gentiana
Episcie = Episcia
Erbse = Pisum
Erbsenstrauch = Caragana
Erdbeerbaum = Arbutus
Erdbeere = Fragaria
Erdbirne = Apios
Erdbohne = Macrotyloma
Erdefeu = Glechoma
Erdkastanie = Conopodium
Erdkirsche = Physalis
Erdknolle = Bunium
Erdnuss = Arachis
Erdrauch = Fumaria
Erdstern = Cryptanthus
Erika = Erica

Erle = Alnus
Erlenblatt = Alniphyllum
Escallonie = Escallonia
Esche = Fraxinus
Eselsdistel = Onopordum
Esparsette = Onobrychis
Espartogras = Stipa
Espe = Populus
Essigbaum = Rhus
Eucryphie = Eucryphia
Eukalyptus = Eucalyptus
Eutaxie = Eutaxia
Evergladespalme = Acoelorrhaphe
Fabiane = Fabiana
Fackelbrennkraut = Caiophora
Fackelholz = Amyris
Fackelingwer = Etlingera
Fackellilie = Kniphofia
Fadenenzian = Cicendia
Fadenkraut = Filago
Fadenröhre = Quisqualis
Fächerblume = Scaevola
Fächerfarn = Sticherus
Fächertanne = Ginkgo
Färberdistel = Carduncellus
Färberholz = Chlorophora
Färberhülse = Baptisia
Färberkamille = Anthemis
Färberwaid = Isatis
Fahnenwicke = Oxytropis
Fallsamengras = Sporobolus
Falsche Alraunenwurzel = Tellima
Falsche Goldnessel = Galeobdolon
Falsche Paradiesvogelblume = Heliconia
Falscher Fenchel = Ridolfia
Falscher Jasmin = Mandevilla
Falscher Löwenzahn = Leontodon
Falsches Sandelholz = Ximenia
Faltenlilie = Lloydia
Faltenohr = Ptychotis
Faltensamenpalme = Ptychosperma
Falzblume = Micropus
Farnmyrte = Comptonia
Farnrauke = Hugueninia
Faselbohne = Lablab
Faserschirm = Trinia
Fatsie = Fatsia
Faulbaum = Frangula
Federblume = Acroptilon
Federborstengras = Pennisetum
Federbuschstrauch = Fothergilla
Federgras = Stipa
Federmohn = Macleaya
Federschwingel = Vulpia
Feenglöckchen = Disporum

Feige = Ficus
Feigenkaktus = Opuntia
Feijoa = Acca
Feilenblatt = Rhinephyllum
Feinstrahl = Erigeron
Felberich = Lysimachia
Feldsalat = Valerianella
Felsenbirne = Amelanchier
Felsenblümchen = Draba
Felsenlilie = Arthropodium
Felsenlippe = Micromeria
Felsenlöwenmaul = Asarina
Felsennelke = Petrorhagia
Felsenrose = Graptopetalum
Felsenteller = Ramonda
Felskresse = Hornungia
Felswurz = Monanthes
Fenchel = Foeniculum
Fenchelholzbaum = Sassafras
Fensterblatt = Fenestraria, Monstera
Fensterfalle = Sarracenia
Fensterpalme = Reinhardtia
Ferkelkraut = Hypochaeris
Fettblatt = Bacopa
Fetthenne = Sedum
Fettkraut = Pinguicula
Feuerblüte = Cyrtanthus
Feuerbusch = Hamelia
Feuerdorn = Pyracantha
Feuerkolben = Arisaema
Feuerpalme = Archontophoenix
Feuerradbaum = Stenocarpus
Feuerranke = Pyrostegia
Fichte = Picea
Fichtenspargel = Monotropa
Fieberklee = Menyanthes
Fieberrindenbaum = Cinchona
Fieberstrauch = Lindera
Fieberwurz = Triosteum
Fiederaralie = Polyscias
Fiederpolster = Leptinella
Fiederspiere = Chamaebatia, Sorbaria
Filzblume = Otanthus
Filzkraut = Filago
Fingeraralie = Eleutherococcus
Fingerhirse = Digitaria, Eleusine
Fingerhut = Digitalis
Fingerkraut = Potentilla
Fingerlimette = Microcitrus
Fingerwurz = Dactylorhiza
Finkensame = Neslia
Fischgras = Beckmannia
Fischkraut = Groenlandia
Fischschwanzpalme = Caryota
Fittonie = Fittonia

Flachbärlapp = Diphasiastrum
Flachs = Linum
Flachslilie = Dianella
Flacourtie = Flacourtia
Flamboyant = Delonix
Flamingoblume = Anthurium
Flammenbaum = Peltophorum
Flammenblume = Phlox
Flammenbusch = Embothrium
Flammenerbse = Chorizema
Flammenlilie = Pyrolirion
Flanellstrauch = Fremontodendron
Flaschenbaum = Brachychiton
Flaschenbürste = Beaufortia
Flaschenbürstengras = Hystrix
Flaschenkürbis = Lagenaria
Flattergras = Milium
Flaumhafer = Helictotrichon
Fleischbeere = Sarcococca
Fleißiges Lieschen = Impatiens
Flieder = Syringa
Fliegenblume = Caralluma
Fliegenbusch = Roridula
Flockenblume = Centaurea
Flohkraut = Pulicaria
Flohsame = Psyllium
Florettseidenbaum = Chorisia
Flügelblatt = Filicium
Flügelbohne = Psophocarpus
Flügelfrucht = Pterocarpus
Flügelginster = Chamaespartium
Flügelkaktus = Pterocactus
Flügelknöterich = Fallopia
Flügelkopf = Pterocephalus
Flügelnuss = Pterocarya
Flügelstorax = Pterostyrax
Flügelzürgel = Pteroceltis
Flussrose = Bauera
Flusszeder = Calocedrus, Libocedrus
Föhre = Pinus
Fontänenbambus = Yushania
Fontanesie = Fontanesia
Forsythie = Forsythia
Frangipani = Plumeria
Frankenie = Frankenia
Franklinie = Franklinia
Fransenbinse = Fimbristylis
Fransenenzian = Gentianella
Fransenhauswurz = Jovibarba
Fransenlilie = Thysanotus
Fransenschwertel = Sparaxis
Franzosenkraut = Galinsoga
Frauenfarn = Athyrium
Frauenhaarfarn = Adiantum
Frauenmantel = Alchemilla

G

Frauenschuh = Cypripedium
Frauenspiegel = Legousia
Freesie = Freesia
Freilandgloxinie = Incarvillea
Froschbiss = Hydrocharis
Froschkraut = Luronium
Froschlöffel = Alisma
Frühlingsblume = Eranthemum
Frühlingsschelle = Synthyris
Frühlingsstern = Ipheion
Fuchsbohne = Thermopsis
Fuchsie = Fuchsia
Fuchsschwanz = Amaranthus
Fuchsschwanzgras = Alopecurus
Fuchsschwanzorchidee = Rhynchostylis
Fuchsschwingel = Vulpia
Funkelstern = Chamaelirium
Funkie = Hosta
Fußblatt = Syngonium
Futtererdnuss = Amphicarpaea
Futterpalme = Hyophorbe
Gabelblatt = Psilotum
Gabelfarn = Gleichenia
Gämsheide = Loiseleuria
Gämshorn = Proboscidea
Gämskresse = Pritzelago
Gämswurz = Doronicum
Gänseblümchen = Bellis
Gänseblümchenstrauch = Olearia
Gänsedistel = Sonchus
Gänsefuß = Chenopodium
Gänsekresse = Arabis
Gärtnerprotee = Leucospermum
Gagelstrauch = Myrica
Galtonie = Galtonia
Gamagras = Tripsacum
Gamander = Teucrium
Gambagras = Andropogon
Ganiterbaum = Elaeocarpus
Garbe = Achillea
Gardenie = Gardenia
Gartengloxinie = Sinningia
Gasterie = Gasteria
Gauchheil = Anagallis
Gauklerblume = Mimulus
Gazanie = Gazania
Gedenkemein = Omphalodes
Geißbart = Aruncus
Geißblatt = Lonicera
Geißfuß = Aegopodium
Geißklee = Chamaecytisus, Cytisus
Geißkleegoldregen = + Laburnocytisus
Geißraute = Galega
Gelbdolde = Smyrnium
Gelbe Klette = Amsinckia

Gelber Flachs = Reinwardtia
Gelber Leberbalsam = Lonas
Gelbholz = Cladrastis
Gelbhorn = Xanthoceras
Gelbling = Sibbaldia
Gelbstern = Gagea
Gelbwurz = Xanthorhiza
Geleepalme = Butia
Gelenkblume = Physostegia
Genipap = Genipa
Georgine = Dahlia
Geranie der Gärtner = Pelargonium
Gerbera = Gerbera
Gerberstrauch = Coriaria
Germer = Veratrum
Gerste = Hordeum
Gesnerie = Gesneria
Gespensterorchidee = Mormodes
Geweihbaum = Gymnocladus
Geweihfarn = Platycerium
Gewürzdolde = Sison
Gewürzlilie = Kaempferia
Gewürzrinde = Cassia
Gewürzstrauch = Calycanthus
Giersch = Aegopodium
Giftbaum = Tephrosia
Giftbeere = Nicandra
Gilbgras = Chloris
Gilbweiderich = Lysimachia
Gilie = Gilia
Gillenie = Gillenia
Ginkgo = Ginkgo
Ginseng = Panax
Ginster = Genista
Gipskraut = Gypsophila
Gladiole = Gladiolus
Glanzbaum = Aglaia
Glanzbinse = Scirpoides
Glanzgras = Phalaris
Glanzheide = Daboecia
Glanzkölbchen = Aphelandra
Glanzmispel = Photinia
Glanzständel = Liparis
Glanzstrauch = Pimelea
Glaskraut = Parietaria
Glasschmalz = Salicornia
Glatthafer = Arrhenatherum
Gleditschie = Gleditsia
Gleichsaum = Kohleria
Gliederkaktus = Schlumbergera
Gliederschote = Chorispora
Gliederzypresse = Tetraclinis
Gliedkraut = Sideritis
Glockenblume = Campanula
Glockenrebe = Cobaea

Glockenwinde = Codonopsis, Nolana
Gloxinie = Gloxinia
Glyzine = Wisteria
Gnadenkraut = Gratiola
Godetie = Clarkia
Götterbaum = Ailanthus
Götterblume = Dodecatheon
Götterduft = Diosma
Götzenholz = Kigelia
Gold-und-Silber-Chrysantheme = Ajania
Goldaster = Chrysopsis
Goldbaldrian = Patrinia
Goldbart = Chrysopogon
Goldblatt = Macodes
Golddistel = Scolymus
Golderdbeere = Waldsteinia
Goldfarn = Coniogramme, Pityrogramma
Goldfruchtpalme = Chrysalidocarpus
Goldglocke = Uvularia
Goldglöckchen = Forsythia
Goldhaar = Chrysocoma
Goldhafer = Trisetum
Goldkelch = Solandra
Goldkeule = Orontium
Goldkörbchen = Chrysogonum
Goldkolben = Ligularia
Goldkrokus = Sternbergia
Goldlack = Erysimum
Goldlärche = Pseudolarix
Goldmargerite = Euryops
Goldmohn = Eschscholzia
Goldmund = Coptis
Goldnarbe = Xanthosoma
Goldnessel = Lamium
Goldpflaume = Chrysobalanus
Goldprimel = Vitaliana
Goldregen = Laburnum
Goldrute = Solidago
Goldrutenaster = × Solidaster
Goldschuppenkastanie = Chrysolepis
Goldschwanzgras = Lamarckia
Goldsiegel = Uvularia
Goldspitzengras = Lamarckia
Goldstern = Bloomeria
Goldtanne = Keteleeria
Goldtropfen = Onosma
Goldzypresse = Xanthocyparis
Goodenie = Goodenia
Gottesurteilsbaum = Erythrophleum
Gottesurteilsbohne = Physostigma
Gottvergess = Ballota
Granatapfel = Punica
Grannenhafer = Trisetaria, Ventenata
Grannenhirse = Oryzopsis
Grannenlilie = Aristea

Grannenreis = Piptatherum
Grapefruit = Citrus
Grasbaum = Xanthorrhoea
Graslilie = Anthericum
Grasnelke = Armeria
Grasnelkenhabichtskraut = Tolpis
Grasschwertel = Sisyrinchium
Graubartgras = Spodiopogon
Graukresse = Berteroa
Grausenf = Hirschfeldia
Greisenbart = Tillandsia
Greiskraut = Senecio, Tephroseris
Grenadille = Passiflora
Gretel im Busch = Nigella
Grevillee = Grevillea
Grewie = Grewia
Grindelie = Grindelia
Grindkraut = Scabiosa
Griseline = Griselinia
Grönlandmargerite = Arctanthemum
Grübchenfarn = Woodwardia
Grüner Heinrich = Chlorophytum
Grünholz = Chloroxylon
Grünkappe = Pterostylis
Grünlilie = Chlorophytum
Grundnessel = Hydrilla
Guajave = Psidium
Guatemalagras = Tripsacum
Guayule = Parthenium
Günsel = Ajuga
Gürtelklaue = Peristrophe
Gujakbaum = Guaiacum
Gummibaum = Ficus
Gummikraut = Grindelia
Gummimyrte = Angophora
Gundelrebe = Glechoma
Gundermann = Glechoma
Gurania = Gurania
Gurke = Cucumis
Gurkenbaum = Averrhoa
Gurkenkraut = Borago
Gurkenstrauch = Decaisnea
Guttaperchabaum = Palaquium
Guzmanie = Guzmania
Haarbinse = Trichophorum
Haarblume = Melothria, Trichosanthes
Haarfarn = Trichomanes
Haargerste = Elymus
Haargurke = Sicyos
Haarhütchen = Trichopilia
Haarnixe = Cabomba
Haarsäulenkaktus = Pilosocereus
Haarschöpfchen = Ptilotus
Haarschotengras = Bouteloua
Haarsimse = Trichophorum

Haarstrang = Peucedanum
Haberlee = Haberlea
Habichtskraut = Hieracium
Händelwurz = Gymnadenia
Härtling = Hypoxis
Hafer = Avena
Haferschmiele = Aira
Haftdolde = Caucalis, Turgenia
Hagebutte = Rosa
Hagebuttenbirne = × Sorbopyrus
Hahnenfuß = Ranunculus
Hahnenkamm = Celosia
Hahnenkopf = Hedysarum
Hainblume = Nemophila
Hainbuche = Carpinus
Hainsimse = Luzula
Hakea = Hakea
Hakenlilie = Crinum
Hakenpalme = Desmoncus
Halskraut = Trachelium
Hammerstrauch = Cestrum
Hanf = Cannabis
Hanfpalme = Trachycarpus
Hardenbergie = Hardenbergia
Harfenstrauch = Plectranthus
Hartgras = Sclerochloa
Hartheu = Hypericum
Hartriegel = Cornus
Harzeibe = Dacrydium
Harzklee = Psoralea
Harzspiere = Chamaebatiaria
Hasel = Corylus
Haselnuss = Corylus
Haselwurz = Asarum
Hasenfußfarn = Phlebodium
Hasenglöckchen = Hyacinthoides
Hasenkümmel = Lagoecia
Hasenlattich = Prenanthes
Hasenohr = Bupleurum
Hasenpfotenfarn = Davallia
Hasenschwanzgras = Lagurus
Hauhechel = Ononis
Hauswurz = Sempervivum
Hautfarn = Hymenophyllum
Hautsamenbaum = Hymenosporum
Haworthie = Haworthia
Hechtkraut = Pontederia
Heckenkirsche = Lonicera
Hederich = Raphanus
Heide = Erica
Heidekraut = Calluna
Heidelbeere = Vaccinium
Heidelbeerkaktus = Myrtillocactus
Heideröschen = Daphne
Heilglöckchen = Cortusa

Heiligenkraut = Santolina
Heilwurz = Opopanax
Heliconie = Heliconia
Heliotrop = Heliotropium
Hellerkraut = Thlaspi
Helmbohne = Dolichos
Helmgras = Ammophila
Helmkraut = Scutellaria
Helwingie = Helwingia
Helxine = Soleirolia
Hemlocktanne = Tsuga
Hennastrauch = Lawsonia
Herbstmargerite = Leucanthemella
Herkulesstaude = Heracleum
Hermannie = Hermannia
Heroldstrompete = Beaumontia
Herrscherpalme = Archontophoenix
Herzblatt = Parnassia
Herzblattschale = Jeffersonia
Herzblume = Dicentra
Herzgespann = Leonurus
Herzkelch = Eucharis
Herzlöffel = Caldesia
Herznussbaum = Anacardium
Herzsame = Cardiospermum
Hesperidenpalme = Brahea
Heteranthere = Heteranthera
Heuschreckenbaum = Hymenaea
Heusenkraut = Ludwigia
Hexenkraut = Circaea
Hibalebensbaum = Thujopsis
Hibbertie = Hibbertia
Hickorynuss = Carya
Himbeere = Rubus
Himmelsbambus = Nandina
Himmelsblüte = Duranta
Himmelsherold = Eritrichium
Himmelsleiter = Polemonium
Hiobsträne = Coix
Hirschsprung = Corrigiola
Hirschwurz = Peucedanum
Hirse = Panicum
Hirtentäschel = Capsella
Höckerblume = Tricyrtis
Hoherie = Hoheria
Hohldotter = Myagrum
Hohlsame = Bifora
Hohlspelze = Stenotaphrum
Hohlzahn = Galeopsis
Hohlzunge = Coeloglossum
Holunder = Sambucus
Holzbirne = Xylomelum
Holzquitte = Pseudocydonia
Honigbaum = Greyia
Honigbeere = Melicoccus

Honigglöckchen = Hermannia
Honiggras = Holcus
Honiglauch = Nectaroscordum
Honigorchis = Herminium
Honigpalme = Jubaea
Honigstrauch = Melianthus
Hopfen = Humulus
Hopfenbuche = Ostrya
Hornblatt = Ceratophyllum
Hornfarn = Ceratopteris
Hornklee = Lotus
Hornköpfchen = Ceratocephala
Hornkraut = Cerastium
Hornmelde = Krascheninnikovia
Hornmohn = Glaucium
Hornnarbe = Ceratostigma
Hortensie = Hydrangea
Hortensienbaum = Dombeya
Hottentottenfeige = Carpobrotus
Houttuynie = Houttuynia
Howeapalme = Howea
Hühnerhirse = Echinochloa
Hüllenklaue = Hypoestes
Hufeisenklee = Hippocrepis
Huflattich = Tussilago
Hummerschere = Heliconia
Hundsgift = Apocynum
Hundskamille = Anthemis
Hundskohl = Theligonum
Hundspetersilie = Aethusa
Hundsrauke = Erucastrum
Hundswürger = Cynanchum
Hundswurz = Anacamptis
Hundszahn = Erythronium
Hundszahngras = Cynodon
Hundszunge = Cynoglossum
Hungerblümchen = Erophila
Hurrikanpalme = Dictyosperma
Husarenknopf = Sanvitalia
Hyazinthe = Hyacinthus
Hybridmahonie = × Mahoberberis
Icacopflaume = Chrysobalanus
Igelginster = Erinacea
Igelgurke = Echinocystis
Igelkolben = Sparganium
Igelkopf = Echinacea
Igelkraftwurz = Oplopanax
Igelpolster = Acantholimon
Igelsäulenkaktus = Echinocereus
Igelsame = Lappula
Igelschlauch = Baldellia
Immenblatt = Melittis
Immergold = Aichryson
Immergrün = Vinca
Immortelle = Rhodanthe

Indianergras = Sorghastrum
Indianernessel = Monarda
Indianerwiege = Caulophyllum
Indigolupine = Baptisia
Indigostrauch = Indigofera
Indische Maulbeere = Morinda
Indische Sommerwurz = Aeginetia
Indischer Kümmel = Trachyspermum
Indischer Spinat = Basella
Ingabohne = Inga
Ingwer = Zingiber
Ingwerlilie = Alpinia
Ingwerorchidee = Roscoea
Inkalilie = Alstroemeria
Insektenblume = Tanacetum
Iresine = Iresine
Iris = Iris
Isabellenholz = Persea
Ixlilie = Ixiolirion
Jaborandistrauch = Pilocarpus
Jabukistrauch = Rhodotypos
Jacarandabaum = Jacaranda
Jackbohne = Canavalia
Jadewein = Strongylodon
Jägerblume = Callianthemum
Jakobskraut = Brachyglottis
Jakobsleiter = Polemonium
Jakobslilie = Sprekelia
Jamaikakirsche = Muntingia
Jambos = Syzygium
Jambuse = Syzygium
Jamesie = Jamesia
Japangras = Hakonechloa
Japanische Schaumblüte = Tanakaea
Japanischer Meerrettich = Wasabia
Jasmin = Jasminum
Jasminwurzel = Gelsemium
Jerichorose = Anastatica
Jerusalemdorn = Parkinsonia
Jochlilie = Zigadenus
Johannisbeere = Ribes
Johannisbrotbaum = Ceratonia
Johanniskraut = Hypericum
Jojobastrauch = Simmondsia
Jonquille = Narcissus
Juckbohne = Mucuna
Judasbaum = Cercis
Judendorn = Ziziphus
Judenkirsche = Physalis
Jujube = Ziziphus
Jungfer im Grünen = Nigella
Jungfernkranz = Francoa
Jungfernrebe = Parthenocissus
Junggesellenknopf = Craspedia
Junkerlilie = Asphodeline

G

Jupitertränen = Coix
Justizie = Justicia
Jute = Corchorus
Kadsura = Kadsura
Kälberkropf = Chaerophyllum
Kängurubaum = Casuarina
Känguerublume = Anigozanthos
Kängurupfote = Anigozanthos
Kaffeestrauch = Coffea
Kaffernlilie = Schizostylis
Kafirpflaume = Harpephyllum
Kahngras = Hyparrhenia
Kahnorchis = Cymbidium
Kaimastrauch = Rhodotypos
Kaiserkrone = Fritillaria
Kaiserwinde = Ipomoea
Kakaobaum = Theobroma
Kaladie = Caladium
Kalanchoe = Kalanchoe
Kalandrine = Calandrinia
Kalebasse = Lagenaria
Kalebassenbaum = Crescentia
Kalebassenmuskat = Monodora
Kalkblatt = Titanopsis
Kalla = Zantedeschia
Kalmus = Acorus
Kameldorn = Alhagi
Kamelie = Camellia
Kamille = Matricaria, Tripleurospermum
Kammgras = Cynosurus
Kammmaranthe = Ctenanthe
Kammminze = Elsholtzia
Kammquecke = Agropyron
Kampferbaum = Cinnamomum
Kampferkraut = Camphorosma
Kanarenglockenblume = Canarina
Kanaribaum = Canarium
Kanarinuss = Canarium
Kaneelbaum = Canella
Kaninchenstrauch = Chrysothamnus
Kannenstrauch = Nepenthes
Kanonenblume = Pilea
Kanonierblume = Pilea
Kapaster = Felicia
Kapernstrauch = Capparis
Kapfuchsie = Phygelius
Kapgeißblatt = Tecomaria
Kaphyazinthe = Lachenalia
Kapkastanie = Calodendrum
Kapkörbchen = Dimorphotheca
Kaplilie = Tulbaghia
Kaplöwenzahn = Arctotheca
Kapmargerite = Osteospermum
Kapmyrte = Phylica
Kapokbaum = Ceiba

Kappenmohn = Eschscholzia
Kappenständel = Calypso
Kapuzinerkresse = Tropaeolum
Kapwein = Rhoicissus
Karakabaum = Corynocarpus
Kardamom = Amomum, Elettaria
Karde = Dipsacus
Kardendistel = Morina
Kardy = Cynara
Karnaubapalme = Copernicia
Kartoffel = Solanum
Kassie = Cassia
Kastanie = Castanea
Kasuarine = Casuarina
Kathstrauch = Catha
Katsurabaum = Cercidiphyllum
Katzenmaul = Misopates
Katzenminze = Nepeta
Katzenpfötchen = Antennaria
Katzenschwanz = Acalypha
Kaukasusvergissmeinnicht = Brunnera
Kaurifichte = Agathis
Kautschukbaum = Castilla
Kegelblume = Puschkinia
Kelchgras = Danthonia
Kellerhals = Daphne
Kennedie = Kennedia
Kentiapalme = Howea
Kerbel = Anthriscus
Kerbelrübe = Chaerophyllum
Kermesbeere = Phytolacca
Kerrie = Kerria
Kerzenbaum = Parmentiera
Kerzenstrauch = Fouquieria
Kettenfarn = Woodwardia
Keulenbaum = Casuarina
Keulenlilie = Cordyline
Keulenmohn = Meconopsis
Keuschbaum = Vitex
Keuschorchis = Neotinea
Kichererbse = Cicer
Kiefer = Pinus
Kielkrone = Calotropis
Kirsche = Prunus
Kirscheibe = Prumnopitys
Kirschmyrte = Eugenia, Syzygium
Kirschorange = Citropsis
Kitaibelie = Kitaibelia
Kiwipflanze = Actinidia
Klaffmund = Chaenorhinum
Klapperhülse = Crotalaria
Klappertopf = Rhinanthus
Klauenfarn = Onychium
Klebgras = Cenchrus
Klebkraut = Galium

Klebsame = Pittosporum
Klebschwertel = Ixia
Klee = Trifolium
Kleefarn = Marsilea
Kleeulme = Ptelea
Kleinie = Kleinia
Kleopatranadel = Eremurus
Klette = Arctium
Klettengras = Tragus
Klettenkerbel = Torilis
Klettenkraut = Lappula
Kletterdahlie = Hidalgoa
Kletterfarn = Lygodium
Kletterlilie = Littonia
Klettermäusedorn = Semele
Kletterschraubenpalme = Freycinetia
Klettertrompete = Distictis
Klimmdahlie = Hidalgoa
Klimme = Cissus
Klimmtraube = Artabotrys
Klippenfarn = Pellaea
Klumpstamm = Beaucarnea
Knabenkraut = Dactylorhiza, Orchis
Knäuel = Scleranthus
Knäuelgras = Dactylis
Knallerbsenstrauch = Symphoricarpos
Knautie = Knautia
Knebel = Sagina
Knoblauch = Allium
Knoblauchsrauke = Alliaria
Knöterich = Persicaria
Knollenbohne = Sphenostylis
Knollenkümmel = Bunium, Conopodium
Knollenmiere = Pseudostellaria
Knopfbusch = Cephalanthus
Knopfkaktus = Epithelantha
Knopfkraut = Galinsoga
Knorpelkraut = Illecebrum, Polycnemum
Knorpellattich = Chondrilla
Knorpelmöhre = Ammi
Knotenblume = Leucojum
Knotendolde = Physocaulis
Knotenfuß = Streptopus
Knotenschötchen = Braya
Kobralilie = Darlingtonia
Kobraschlauchpflanze = Darlingtonia
Köcherblümchen = Cuphea
Königin der Nacht = Selenicereus
Königsblume = Daphne
Königsfarn = Osmunda
Königskerze = Verbascum
Königspalme = Roystonea
Kohl = Brassica
Kohlbaum = Andira
Kohlerie = Kohleria

Kohlröschen = Nigritella
Kokardenblume = Gaillardia
Kokastrauch = Erythroxylum
Kokkelstrauch = Cocculus
Kokosnuss = Cocos
Kokospalme = Cocos
Kolabaum = Cola
Kolanuss = Cola
Kolbenbaum = Cordyline
Kolbenfaden = Aglaonema
Kolbenhirse = Setaria
Kolbenlilie = Cordyline
Kolibritrompete = Epilobium
Kolkwitzie = Kolkwitzia
Koloquinte = Citrullus
Kolumnee = Columnea
Kompasspflanze = Silphium
Kopaivabalsam = Copaifera
Kopaivabaum = Copaifera
Kopfeibe = Cephalotaxus
Kopfgras = Oreochloa, Sesleria
Kopfried = Schoenus
Kopfsimse = Scirpoides
Korallenbaum = Erythrina
Korallenbeere = Symphoricarpos
Korallenkaktus = Rhipsalis
Korallenmoos = Nertera
Korallenraute = Boronia
Korallenstrauch = Berberidopsis
Korallentröpfchen = Bessera
Korallenwein = Antigonon
Korallenwurz = Corallorhiza
Korbmaranthe = Calathea
Kordie = Cordia
Koriander = Coriandrum
Korkbaum = Phellodendron
Kornblume = Centaurea
Kornblumenaster = Stokesia
Kornelkirsche = Cornus
Kornrade = Agrostemma
Kosmee = Cosmos
Kosobaum = Hagenia
Kostwurz = Costus
Krähenbeere = Empetrum
Krähenfuß = Coronopus
Kräuselmyrte = Lagerstroemia
Kraftwurz = Panax
Kragenblume = Carpesium
Krallentrompete = Macfadyena
Kranzblume = Hedychium
Kranzschlinge = Stephanotis
Kranzspiere = Stephanandra
Krapp = Rubia
Kratzdistel = Cirsium
Krebsschere = Stratiotes

Kreisblume = Anacyclus
Kreiselkaktus = Strombocactus
Kreisfahne = Chorizema
Kresse = Lepidium
Kreuzblatt = Crucianella
Kreuzblümchen = Polygala
Kreuzdorn = Rhamnus
Kreuzkraut = Senecio
Kreuzkümmel = Cuminum
Kreuzlabkraut = Cruciata
Kreuzrebe = Bignonia
Kreuzstrauch = Baccharis
Krötenlilie = Tricyrtis
Krokus = Crocus
Kronbart = Verbesina
Kronenlattich = Willemetia
Kronwicke = Coronilla, Securigera
Kroton = Croton
Krugfarn = Davallia
Krugpflanze = Sarracenia
Krukenbaum = Lecythis
Krummfuß = Cyrtopodium
Kuchenbaum = Cercidiphyllum
Kudzubohne = Pueraria
Küchenschelle = Pulsatilla
Kümmel = Carum
Kürbis = Cucurbita
Küstenmammutbaum = Sequoia
Küstensequoie = Sequoia
Kugelamaranth = Gomphrena
Kugelbaum = Mimusops
Kugelbinse = Scirpoides
Kugelblume = Globularia
Kugeldistel = Echinops
Kugelfaden = Kadsura
Kugelknabenkraut = Traunsteinera
Kugelmalve = Sphaeralcea
Kugelorchis = Traunsteinera
Kugelschötchen = Kernera
Kuhbaum = Brosimum
Kuhblume = Taraxacum
Kuhbohne = Vigna
Kuhkraut = Vaccaria
Kuhschelle = Pulsatilla
Kuhtritt = Wulfenia
Kumquat = Fortunella
Kunigundenkraut = Eupatorium
Kurzfähnchen = Brachysema
Kurzstiel = Adromischus
Kussblume = Philesia
Kussmäulchen = Nematanthus
Labkraut = Galium
Lachenalie = Lachenalia
Lackbaum = Butea
Lackblatt = Schefflera

Lackmuskraut = Chrozophora
Lacksenf = Coincya
Laelie = Laelia
Lämmersalat = Arnoseris
Lärche = Larix
Läuseholz = Carapa
Läusekraut = Pedicularis
Lagerströmie = Lagerstroemia
Laichkraut = Potamogeton
Lakritze = Glycyrrhiza
Lamarkie = Lamarckia
Lampenputzergras = Pennisetum
Lampenputzerstrauch = Callistemon
Lampionblume = Physalis
Langfaden = Combretum
Lansibaum = Lansium
Lanzenfarn = Lonchitis
Lanzenrosette = Aechmea
Lapagerie = Lapageria
Lapeirousie = Lapeirousia
Lappenblume = Hypecoum
Laserkraut = Laserpitium
Lasthenie = Lasthenia
Latanie = Latania
Laternenbaum = Crinodendron
Laternenlilie = Sandersonia
Lattich = Lactuca
Lauch = Allium
Lauchkraut = Alliaria
Laugenblume = Cotula
Lavendel = Lavandula
Lavendelheide = Pieris
Lebendblatt = Tolmiea
Lebender Stein = Lithops
Lebensbaum = Thuja
Leberbalsam = Ageratum
Leberblümchen = Hepatica
Leberwurstbaum = Kigelia
Lederblatt = Chamaedaphne
Lederholz = Dirca
Lederhülsenbaum = Gleditsia
Lederstrauch = Ptelea
Leimkraut = Silene
Leimsaat = Collomia
Lein = Linum
Leinblatt = Thesium
Leindotter = Camelina
Leinkraut = Linaria
Leopardenblume = Belamcanda
Lerchensporn = Ceratocapnos, Corydalis,
  Pseudofumaria
Leschenaultie = Leschenaultia
Leuchterblume = Ceropegia
Levkoje = Matthiola
Lewisie = Lewisia

Leycesterie = Leycesteria
Lichtblume = Bulbocodium
Lichtnelke = Silene
Lichtnussbaum = Aleurites
Liebesblume = Agapanthus
Liebesgras = Eragrostis
Liebesperlenstrauch = Callicarpa
Liebesröschen = Anacampseros
Liebstöckel = Levisticum
Lieschgras = Phleum
Ligularie = Ligularia
Liguster = Ligustrum
Lilie = Lilium
Lilienschweif = Eremurus
Lilientrichter = Blandfordia
Limequat = × Citrofortunella
Limette = Citrus
Linde = Tilia
Lindheimerie = Lindheimera
Linse = Lens
Lippenfarn = Cheilanthes
Lippenmäulchen = Mazus
Liriope = Liriope
Litschi = Litchi
Livingstonpalme = Livistona
Livistonie = Livistona
Loase = Loasa
Lobelie = Lobelia
Lochschlund = Anarrhinum
Löffelbaum = Cunonia
Löffelkraut = Cochlearia
Löwenmaul = Antirrhinum
Löwenohr = Leonotis
Löwenschwanz = Leonurus
Löwenzahn = Taraxacum
Lolch = Lolium
Longanbaum = Dimocarpus
Lorbeer-Kirsche = Prunus
Lorbeerbaum = Laurus
Lorbeerrose = Kalmia
Losbaum = Clerodendrum
Losstrauch = Clerodendrum
Lotosblume = Nelumbo
Lotuspflaume = Diospyros
Lotwurz = Onosma
Loulupalme = Pritchardia
Luftnelke = Tillandsia
Lungenkraut = Pulmonaria
Lupine = Lupinus
Luzerne = Medicago
Lyonie = Lyonia
Maackie = Maackia
Macadamianuss = Macadamia
Macassaölbaum = Schleichera
Macludranie = × Macludrania

Macoré = Tieghemella
Madagaskarpalme = Pachypodium
Madagaskarpflaume = Flacourtia
Madie = Madia
Mädchenauge = Coreopsis
Mädchenhaarbaum = Ginkgo
Mädesüß = Filipendula
Mähnenpalme = Jubaea
Mänderle = Paederota
Mäusedorn = Ruscus
Mäuseschwänzchen = Myosurus
Mäuseschwanz = Arisarum
Maggikraut = Levisticum
Magnolie = Magnolia
Mahagonibaum = Khaya, Swietenia
Mahonie = Mahonia
Maiapfel = Podophyllum
Maiglöckchen = Convallaria
Mais = Zea
Majoran = Origanum
Makolabaum = Afzelia
Malaguetapfeffer = Aframomum
Malayenblume = Phalaenopsis
Malve = Lavatera, Malva
Mammiapfel = Mammea
Mammutblatt = Gunnera
Mandarine = Citrus
Mandel = Prunus
Mangabeiragummi = Hancornia
Manglebaum = Rhizophora
Mango = Mangifera
Mangostane = Garcinia
Mangrovebaum = Rhizophora
Mangrovefarn = Acrostichum
Manilapalme = Adonidia, Veitchia
Maniok = Manihot
Mannsschild = Androsace
Mannstreu = Eryngium
Marbel = Luzula
Margerite = Leucanthemum, Tanacetum
Mariendistel = Silybum
Mariengras = Hierochloe
Maskenblume = Alonsoa
Maskenorchidee = Coryanthes
Maßliebchen = Bellis
Mastkraut = Sagina
Mauerlattich = Mycelis
Mauermiere = Paronychia
Mauerpfeffer = Sedum
Maulbeerbaum = Morus
Maulbeereibe = Microcachrys
Mausohr = Marrubium
Mazaripalme = Nannorrhops
Medinille = Medinilla
Meerbohne = Entada

G

Meerfenchel = Crithmum
Meerkohl = Crambe
Meerlavendel = Limonium
Meerrettich = Armoracia
Meerrettichbaum = Moringa
Meersenf = Cakile
Meerträubel = Ephedra
Meertraubenbaum = Coccoloba
Meerviole = Malcolmia
Meerzwiebel = Urginea
Mehlbeere = Sorbus
Meier = Asperula
Meister = Asperula
Melde = Atriplex
Melisse = Melissa
Melone = Cucumis
Melonenbaum = Carica
Melonenbegonie = Elatostema, Pellionia
Melonenkaktus = Melocactus
Menziesie = Menziesia
Merk = Berula, Sium
Mescalkaktus = Lophophora
Mesquitebaum = Prosopis
Mexikanischer Knöterich = Antigonon
Mexikolattich = Tridax
Mexikomohn = Hunnemannia
Mexikostern = Milla
Michauxie = Michauxia
Miere = Minuartia
Milchbaum = Brosimum
Milchbusch = Synadenium
Milchfleckdistel = Galactites
Milchkraut = Glaux, Leontodon
Milchlattich = Cicerbita
Milchorange = Maclura
Milchstern = Ornithogalum
Miltonie = Miltonia
Milzkraut = Chrysosplenium
Mimose = Mimosa
Mimose der Gärtner = Acacia
Minze = Mentha
Mispel = Mespilus
Mispeleberesche = × Sorbocotoneaster
Mistel = Viscum
Mittagsblume = Delosperma,
 Dorotheanthus, Lampranthus
Mocanbaum = Visnea
Möhre = Daucus
Mönchskraut = Nonea
Mönchspfeffer = Vitex
Mohn = Papaver
Mohnmalve = Callirhoe
Mohrenhirse = Sorghum
Mohrenpfeffer = Xylopia
Molchschwanz = Saururus

Moltkie = Moltkia
Mombinpflaume = Spondias
Mondraute = Botrychium
Mondsame = Menispermum
Montbretie = Crocosmia
Moorabbiss = Succisella
Moorbeere = Vaccinium
Moorbinse = Isolepis
Moorglöckchen = Wahlenbergia
Moosauge = Moneses
Moosbeere = Vaccinium
Moosfarn = Selaginella
Moosglöckchen = Linnaea
Moosheide = Bryanthus, Phyllodoce
Mooskraut = Selaginella
Moosmiere = Moehringia
Morgenblüte = Orthrosanthus
Morgenländischer Lebensbaum =
 Platycladus
Morikandie = Moricandia
Mormonentulpe = Calochortus
Moschusgurke = Sicana
Moschuskraut = Adoxa
Moskitogras = Bouteloua
Mottenkönig = Plectranthus
Mühlenbeckie = Muehlenbeckia
Münzgold = Hibbertia
Mützenstrauch = Mitraria
Mummel = Nuphar
Muschelblümchen = Isopyrum
Muschelblume = Moluccella
Muskatnuss = Myristica
Mutterkraut = Tanacetum
Mutterwurz = Ligusticum
Myrobalane = Terminalia
Myrrhe = Commiphora
Myrsine = Myrsine
Myrte = Myrtus
Myrtenheide = Melaleuca
Myrtenkraut = Andrachne
Nabelkraut = Umbilicus
Nabelmiere = Moehringia
Nabelnüsschen = Omphalodes
Nachthyazinthe = Polianthes
Nachtkerze = Oenothera
Nachtschatten = Solanum
Nachtviole = Hesperis
Nacktfarn = Anogramma
Nacktried = Kobresia
Nadelkerbel = Scandix
Nadelkissen = Hakea, Leucospermum
Nadelpalme = Rhapidophyllum
Nadelröschen = Fumana
Nagelbeere = Ochna
Nagelkraut = Paronychia, Polycarpon

Nagibaum = Nageia
Nandine = Nandina
Naraspflanze = Acanthosicyos
Nardenähre = Nardostachys
Narihirabambus = Semiarundinaria
Narzisse = Narcissus
Natternfarn = Ophioglossum
Natternkopf = Echium
Natternzunge = Ophioglossum
Nebelblume = Conoclinium
Nelke = Dianthus
Nelkenpfeffer = Calycanthus, Pimenta
Nelkenwurz = Geum
Nelkenwurzodermennig = Aremonia
Nelkenzimt = Dicypellium
Nemesie = Nemesia
Nepalgoldregen = Piptanthus
Nerine = Nerine
Nesselblatt = Acalypha
Nestbromelie = Nidularium
Nestwurz = Neottia
Netzblatt = Goodyera
Neuseelandedelweiß = Leucogenes
Neuseelandeibisch = Hoheria
Neuseelandflachs = Phormium
Neuseelandspinat = Tetragonia
Nierembergie = Nierembergia
Nieswurz = Helleborus
Nigersaat = Guizotia
Nikaupalme = Rhopalostylis
Nimbaum = Azadirachta
Nipapalme = Nypa
Nipponchrysantheme =
    Nipponanthemum
Nissegras = Gastridium
Nixkraut = Najas
Njabi = Baillonella
Nonibaum = Morinda
Norfolkeibisch = Lagunaria
Nusseibe = Torreya
Nussmaul = Anguloa
Ochsenauge = Buphthalmum
Ochsenzunge = Anchusa
Ocotillostrauch = Fouquieria
Odermennig = Agrimonia
Ölbaum = Olea
Ölfrucht = Elaeocarpus
Ölpalme = Elaeis
Ölweide = Elaeagnus
Östlicher Hornmohn = Dicranostigma
Ohnsporn = Aceras
Ohrblume = Otanthus
Ohrkraut = Hedyotis
Okiebohne = Dipogon
Okwabaum = Treculia

Oleander = Nerium
Olive = Olea
Opuntie = Opuntia
Orange = Citrus
Orangenbeere = Citriobatus
Orangenblume = Choisya
Orangenkirsche = Idesia
Orangenraute = Murraya
Orangenwurzel = Hydrastis
Orant = Chaenorhinum
Orchidee des armen Mannes = Schizanthus
Oregonpflaume = Oemleria
Orleanstrauch = Bixa
Osagedorn = Maclura
Osterglocke = Narcissus
Osterkaktus = Rhipsalidopsis
Osterluzei = Aristolochia
Oysternuss = Telfairia
Päonie = Paeonia
Pagodenbaum = Styphnolobium
Palasabaum = Butia
Palaspalme = Licuala
Palisadengras = Brachiaria
Palisander = Jacaranda
Palma Christi = Ricinus
Palmenschilf = Prionium
Palmettopalme = Sabal
Palmlilie = Yucca
Pampasgras = Cortaderia
Panamapalme = Carludovica
Pandoree = Pandorea
Pankrazlilie = Pancratium
Pantherblume = Belamcanda
Pantoffelblume = Calceolaria
Papageienblatt = Alternanthera
Papau = Asimina
Papaya = Carica
Papierblümchen = Acroclinium
Papierblume = Xeranthemum
Papierknöpfchen = Ammobium
Papiermaulbeerbaum = Broussonetia
Pappel = Populus
Paprika = Capsicum
Paradieslilie = Paradisea
Paradiesnuss = Lecythis
Paradiesvogelblume = Strelitzia
Parakautschukbaum = Hevea
Parakresse = Acmella
Paranuss = Bertholletia
Parentucellie = Parentucellia
Parkinsonie = Parkinsonia
Parrotie = Parrotia
Passionsblume = Passiflora
Passionsfrucht = Passiflora
Pastinak = Pastinaca

Patagonische Eibe = Saxegothaea
Patagonische Zypresse = Fitzroya
Paternosterbaum = Melia
Paternostererbse = Abrus
Paternosterstrauch = Osteospermum
Patschuli = Pogostemon
Paukenschlegel = Isopogon
Paulownie = Paulownia
Pavianblume = Babiana
Pechnelke = Silene
Peitschenkaktus = Aporocactus
Peitschenorchidee = Scuticaria
Pejote = Lophophora
Pelargonie = Pelargonium
Pellionie = Pellionia
Pellote = Lophophora
Pelzfarn = Cheilanthes
Pemouzypresse = Fokienia
Peperomie = Peperomia
Pereskie = Pereskia
Perlbeere = Margyricarpus
Perlfarn = Onoclea
Perlgras = Melica
Perlkörbchen = Anaphalis
Perlschweif = Stachyurus
Perowskie = Perovskia
Perückenstrauch = Cotinus
Pestwurz = Petasites
Petersilie = Petroselinum
Petterie = Petteria
Petunie = Petunia
Peyotl = Lophophora
Pfaffenhütchen = Euonymus
Pfaffenröhrlein = Taraxacum
Pfahlrohr = Arundo
Pfannengras = Paspalum
Pfauenblume = Tigridia
Pfeffer = Piper
Pfefferbaum = Schinus
Pfefferkraut = Satureja
Pfeifengras = Molinia
Pfeifenstrauch = Philadelphus
Pfeifenwinde = Aristolochia
Pfeilaron = Peltandra
Pfeilblatt = Alocasia
Pfeilkraut = Sagittaria
Pfeilkresse = Cardaria
Pfeilwurz = Maranta
Pferdebohne = Macrotyloma
Pferdemelisse = Collinsonia
Pfingstrose = Paeonia
Pfirsich = Prunus
Pfirsichpalme = Bactris
Pflaume = Prunus
Pfriemenginster = Spartium

Pfriemengras = Stipa
Pfriemenkresse = Subularia
Phazelie = Phacelia
Philodendron = Philodendron
Phlox = Phlox
Phönixpalme = Phoenix
Pillenfarn = Pilularia
Pimentbaum = Pimenta
Pimpernuss = Staphylea
Pimpinelle = Pimpinella
Pinangpalme = Pinanga
Pindrowpalme = Attalea
Pinellie = Pinellia
Pippau = Crepis
Pissavepalme = Attalea
Pistazie = Pistacia
Platane = Platanus
Plattährengras = Chasmanthium
Platterbse = Lathyrus
Pockholz = Guaiacum
Porst = Ledum
Portulak = Portulaca
Porzellanblume = Hoya
Porzellansternchen = Houstonia
Potenzholz = Ptychopetalum
Prachtglocke = Enkianthus
Prachtkerze = Gaura
Prachtlilie = Nomocharis
Prachtscharte = Liatris
Prachtspiere = Astilbe
Prärieampfer = Parthenium
Prärieenzian = Eustoma
Präriegras = Schizachyrium
Prärielilie = Camassia
Präriemalve = Sidalcea
Präriesonnenhut = Ratibida
Preiselbeere = Vaccinium
Priesterpalme = Washingtonia
Primel = Primula
Prophetenblume = Arnebia
Protee = Protea
Prunkblüte = Chlidanthus
Prunkblume = Clianthus
Prunkwinde = Ipomoea
Puderquastenstrauch = Calliandra
Purgierdolde = Thapsia
Purgiernuss = Jatropha
Purgierstrauch = Thymelaea
Purpuraugengras = Olsynium
Purpurbohne = Kennedia
Purpurerbse = Hardenbergia
Purpurglockenwein = Rhodochiton
Purpurglöckchen = Heuchera
Purpurkranz = Petrea
Purpurschopf = Justicia

Purpurstängel = Phoenicaulis
Purpurtaupflanze = Disphyma
Purpurtüte = Syngonium
Purpurwinde = Ipomoea
Puschkinie = Puschkinia
Pusteblume = Taraxacum
Putorie = Putoria
Pyrenäennelke = Petrocoptis
Pyrethrum = Tanacetum
Quassiabaum = Quassia
Quebrachobaum = Aspidosperma
Quecke = Elymus
Queenslandnuss = Macadamia
Queenslandpalmfarn = Bowenia
Quellbinse = Blysmus
Queller = Salicornia
Quellgras = Catabrosa
Quellkraut = Montia
Quellried = Blysmus
Quendel = Thymus
Quetschblume = Thladiantha
Quetschgurke = Thladiantha
Quitte = Cydonia
Rachenblatt = Faucaria
Rachenblüte = Lagotis
Rachenlilie = Chasmanthe
Rachenrebe = Columnea
Radbaum = Trochodendron
Radblüte = Trochiscanthes
Rade = Agrostemma
Radfrucht = Trochocarpa
Radieschen = Raphanus
Radmelde = Bassia
Radspiere = Exochorda
Raffiapalme = Raphia
Ragwurz = Ophrys
Rahle = Teesdalia
Raigras = Lolium
Rainfarn = Tanacetum
Rainkohl = Lapsana
Rainweide = Ligustrum
Rambutan = Nephelium
Ramie = Boehmeria
Ramondie = Ramonda
Ramtillkraut = Guizotia
Ranunkel = Ranunculus
Ranunkelstrauch = Kerria
Rapsdotter = Rapistrum
Rapünzchen = Valerianella
Rapunzel = Valerianella
Rasenbinse = Trichophorum
Rasenspiere = Petrophytum
Rasierpinselbaum = Pachira
Raspelfarn = Doodia
Rasselblume = Catananche

Ratanhia = Krameria
Rauchzypresse = Calocedrus
Raudolde = Trachymene
Raugras = Stipa
Rauke = Eruca, Sisymbrium
Raukensenf = Sisymbrium
Rauling = Trachystemon
Raupenähre = Beckmannia
Raupenfarn = Scyphularia
Rauschbeere = Vaccinium
Rauschopf = Dasylirion
Raute = Ruta
Rautenanemone = Anemonella
Ravennagras = Saccharum
Raygras = Lolium
Rebe = Vitis
Rebhuhnbeere = Gaultheria, Mitchella
Rechenblume = Symplocos
Regenbogenpflanze = Byblis
Rehmannie = Rehmannia
Reiherschnabel = Erodium
Reineckie = Reineckea
Reis = Oryza
Reispapierbaum = Tetrapanax
Reisquecke = Leersia
Reitgras = Calamagrostis
Resede = Reseda
Resedenwein = Anredera
Retamastrauch = Retama
Rettich = Raphanus
Rhabarber = Rheum
Rhododendron = Rhododendron
Ridolfie = Ridolfia
Riemenblatt = Clivia
Riemenblüte = Loropetalum
Riemenblume = Loranthus
Riemenfarn = Campyloneurum
Riemenlippe = Habenaria
Riementillandsie = Catopsis
Riemenzunge = Himantoglossum
Riesenbambus = Gigantochloa
Riesenborretsch = Solenanthus
Riesenfenchel = Ferula
Riesenglocke = Ostrowskia
Riesenhülse = Entada
Riesenkaktus = Carnegiea
Riesenlilie = Cardiocrinum
Riesenseerose = Victoria
Ringblume = Anacyclus
Ringelblume = Calendula
Rippenfarn = Blechnum
Rippensame = Pleurospermum
Rispelstrauch = Myricaria
Rispenfarn = Osmunda
Rispengras = Poa

G

Rispenhirse = Panicum
Rittersporn = Consolida, Delphinium
Ritterstern = Hippeastrum
Rivinie = Rivina
Rizinus = Ricinus
Robinie = Robinia
Rodgersie = Rodgersia
Römische Kamille = Chamaemelum
Röte = Rubia
Roggen = Secale
Rohr = Phragmites
Rohrkolben = Typha
Rollfarn = Cryptogramma
Romanzoffie = Romanzoffia
Rose = Rosa
Rose von Jericho = Anastatica
Rosenapfel = Dillenia, Syzygium
Roseneibisch = Hibiscus
Rosenholz = Dalbergia
Rosenkaktus = Pereskia
Rosenkelch = Rhodochiton
Rosenmyrte = Rhodomyrtus
Rosenwurz = Rhodiola
Rosinenbaum = Hovenia
Rosmarin = Rosmarinus
Rosmarinheide = Andromeda
Rosmarinweide = Itea
Rosskastanie = Aesculus
Rosskümmel = Laser
Rotangpalme = Calamus
Rotbusch = Aspalathus
Rotholz = Erythroxylum
Rotkelch = Erythrochiton
Rotschopfgras = Themeda
Ruchgras = Anthoxanthum
Rudel = Ruellia
Rübe = Beta
Rühr mich nicht an = Impatiens
Ruellie = Ruellia
Rüssellilie = Curculigo
Rüsselsternchen = Vancouveria
Rüster = Ulmus
Ruhmesblume = Clianthus
Ruhmeskrone = Gloriosa
Ruhrkraut = Gnaphalium
Ruprechtsfarn = Gymnocarpium
Russelie = Russelia
Rutenaster = Microglossa
Rutenblume = Carmichaelia
Rutenkaktus = Rhipsalis
Rutenpalme = Rhapis
Sabalpalme = Sabal
Säbelblatt = Machairophyllum
Säckelblume = Ceanothus
Säuerling = Oxyria

Säulenblume = Stylidium
Saflor = Carthamus
Safranwurz = Curcuma
Sagopalme = Metroxylon
Sagopalmfarn = Cycas
Saguaro = Carnegiea
Sakakistrauch = Cleyera
Salakpalme = Salacca
Salat = Lactuca
Salbei = Salvia
Salde = Ruppia
Salomonssiegel = Polygonatum
Salonefeu = Delairea
Salzbaum = Haloxylon
Salzkraut = Salsola
Salzkresse = Hymenolobus
Salzmelde = Suaeda
Salzmiere = Honckenya
Salzschwaden = Puccinellia
Salzstrauch = Halimodendron
Salztäschel = Hymenolobus
Sammetblume = Tagetes
Sammetmalve = Abutilon
Samtgras = Lagurus
Samtpappel = Abutilon
Samtpflanze = Gynura
Sanchezie = Sanchezia
Sandarakbaum = Tetraclinis
Sandbirne = Peraphyllum
Sandbüchsenbaum = Hura
Sanddorn = Hippophae
Sandelholz = Santalum
Sandglöckchen = Jasione
Sandimmortelle = Ammobium
Sandkraut = Arenaria
Sandkrokus = Romulea
Sandmyrte = Leiophyllum
Sandrapunzel = Jasione
Sandröschen = Tuberaria
Sandverbene = Abronia
Sanikel = Sanicula
Saphirbeere = Symplocos
Sarrazenie = Sarracenia
Sassafras = Sassafras
Saudistel = Sonchus
Sauerampfer = Rumex
Sauerbaum = Oxydendrum
Sauerdorn = Berberis
Sauerklee = Oxalis
Saumfarn = Lomariopsis, Pteris
Saumnarbe = Lomatogonium
Saxaul = Haloxylon
Schachblume = Fritillaria
Schachtelhalm = Equisetum
Schafgarbe = Achillea

Schafsteppich = Raoulia
Schaftdolde = Hacquetia
Schamblume = Clitoria
Schampflanze = Aeschynomene
Scharbockskraut = Ranunculus
Scharfkraut = Asperugo
Scharlachranke = Coccinia
Scharte = Serratula
Schattenblümchen = Maianthemum
Schattenröhre = Episcia
Schatullenfarn = Cibotium
Schaublatt = Rodgersia
Schaumblüte = Tiarella
Schaumkraut = Cardamine
Schaumkresse = Cardaminopsis
Schaumspiere = Holodiscus
Schefflera = Schefflera
Scheibenblume = Cyclanthus
Scheibenschötchen = Peltaria
Scheidenblatt = Spathiphyllum
Scheidenblütgras = Coleanthus
Scheinakazie = Robinia
Scheinakelei = Semiaquilegia
Scheinananas = Pseudananas
Scheinanemone = Anemonopsis
Scheinaster = Vernonia
Scheinbeere = Gaultheria
Scheinbuche = Nothofagus
Scheineller = Clethra
Scheinerdbeere = Duchesnea
Scheinfiederspiere = Chamaebatiaria
Scheingänseblümchen = Bellium
Scheingeißklee = Cytisophyllum
Scheinginseng = Pseudopanax
Scheingreiskraut = Erechtites
Scheinhanf = Datisca
Scheinhasel = Corylopsis
Scheinheide = Adenostoma
Scheinhopfenbuche = Ostryopsis
Scheinhortensie = Deinanthe
Scheinhyazinthe = Brimeura
Scheinindigo = Amorpha
Scheinkalla = Lysichiton
Scheinkamelie = Stewartia
Scheinkamille = Boltonia
Scheinkastanie = Castanopsis
Scheinkerrie = Rhodotypos
Scheinkrokus = Romulea
Scheinlerchensporn = Pseudofumaria
Scheinlobelie = Downingia
Scheinlorbeer = Daphniphyllum
Scheinmalve = Malvastrum
Scheinmohn = Meconopsis
Scheinmyrte = Anamirta
Scheinorchis = Roscoea

Scheinparrotie = Parrotiopsis
Scheinquitte = Chaenomeles
Scheinrebe = Ampelopsis
Scheinruhrkraut = Pseudognaphalium
Scheinschaumkraut = Pachyphragma
Scheinsonnenhut = Echinacea
Scheinulme = Eucryphia
Scheinveilchen = Ionopsidium
Scheinwasserpest = Lagarosiphon
Scheinzaunrübe = Diplocyclos
Scheinzypresse = Chamaecyparis
Schellenbaum = Thevetia
Schellenblume = Adenophora
Schibutterbaum = Vitellaria
Schiefblatt = Begonia
Schiefteller = Achimenes
Schierling = Conium
Schierlingstanne = Tsuga
Schildblatt = Darmera
Schildblume = Chelone
Schildfarn = Polystichum
Schildkraut = Clypeola
Schildkresse = Fibigia
Schildnarbe = Aspidistra
Schilf = Phragmites
Schilforchidee = Arundina
Schilfpalme = Thrinax
Schillergras = Koeleria
Schimmerbaum = Protea
Schirlingssilge = Conioselinum
Schirmakazie = Paraserianthes
Schirmbambus = Fargesia
Schirmbaum = Musanga
Schirmblatt = Diphylleia
Schirmpalme = Hedyscepe
Schirmtanne = Sciadopitys
Schlagkraut = Iva
Schlammling = Limosella
Schlangenäuglein = Asperugo
Schlangenbart = Ophiopogon
Schlangenhaargurke = Trichosanthes
Schlangenkaktus = Aporocactus,
  Selenicereus
Schlangenkopf = Chelone
Schlangenlilie = Dracaena
Schlangenstapelie = Echidnopsis
Schlangenwurz = Calla
Schlangenwurzel = Medeola
Schlankschwänchen = Polycycnis
Schlauchpflanze = Sarracenia
Schlehe = Prunus
Schleierkraut = Gypsophila
Schleifenblume = Iberis
Schleimbeere = Sarcococca
Schleimkraut = Brasenia

Schlickgras = Spartina
Schlingfarn = Lygodium
Schlitzblume = Schizanthus
Schlüsselblume = Primula
Schlupfsame = Crupina
Schmalwand = Arabidopsis
Schmerwurz = Tamus
Schmetterlingserbse = Centrosema
Schmetterlingsingwer = Hedychium
Schmetterlingsorchidee = Phalaenopsis
Schmetterlingsstrauch = Buddleja
Schmiele = Deschampsia
Schmielenhafer = Aira, Ventenata
Schmuckblume = Callianthemum
Schmuckkörbchen = Cosmos
Schmucklilie = Agapanthus
Schmuckmalve = Sidalcea
Schmuckzypresse = Callitris
Schnabelried = Rhynchospora
Schnabelschötchen = Euclidium
Schnabelsenf = Coincya
Schnappmäulchen = Torenia
Schneckenbaumwolle = Froelichia
Schneckenklee = Medicago
Schneckenkraut = Stachytarpheta
Schneeball = Viburnum
Schneebeere = Chiococca
Schneefarn = Pyrrosia
Schneeflockenblume = Sutera
Schneeflockenstrauch = Chionanthus
Schneeforsythie = Abeliophyllum
Schneeglanz = Chionodoxa
Schneeglöckchen = Galanthus
Schneeglöckchenbaum = Halesia
Schneelocke = Neviusia
Schneemohn = Eomecon
Schneestolz = Chionodoxa
Schneide = Cladium
Schnurbaum = Sophora
Schöllkraut = Chelidonium
Schöllkrautmohn = Stylophorum
Schönaster = Kalimeris
Schönfaden = Callistemon
Schönfrucht = Callicarpa
Schöngesicht = Coreopsis
Schöngift = Acokanthera
Schönhäutchen = Hymenocallis
Schönhülse = Calophaca
Schönmalve = Abutilon
Schönmund = Clytostoma
Schönnessel = Eucnide
Schönorchis = Calanthe
Schönpolster = Callisia
Schönranke = Eccremocarpus
Schönulme = Euptelea

Schöterich = Erysimum
Schokoladenblume = Berlandiera
Schopflilie = Eucomis
Schopfmyrte = Lophomyrtus
Schopfpalme = Acrocomia, Corypha
Schopfteufelskralle = Physoplexis
Schotenklee = Tetragonolobus
Schraubenbaum = Pandanus
Schraubenbohne = Prosopis
Schüsselfarn = Dennstaedtia
Schuhblüte = Pedilanthus
Schuppenblatt = Lemmaphyllum
Schuppenfaden = Lobostemon
Schuppenfarn = Cheilanthes
Schuppenfichte = Athrotaxis
Schuppenheide = Cassiope
Schuppenkopf = Cephalaria
Schuppenmiere = Spergularia
Schuppenmund = Pholistoma
Schuppenried = Kobresia
Schuppenschwanz = Pholiurus
Schuppensimse = Isolepis
Schuppenwurz = Lathraea
Schusserbaum = Gymnocladus
Schusterkaktus = Epiphyllum
Schusterpalme = Aspidistra
Schwaden = Glyceria
Schwalbenwurz = Vincetoxicum
Schwammgurke = Luffa
Schwanenorchis = Cycnoches
Schwanzblume = Anthurium
Schwarzäugige Susanne = Thunbergia
Schwarzkümmel = Nigella
Schwarzmund = Melastoma
Schwarznessel = Ballota
Schwarzwurzel = Scorzonera
Schwefelkörbchen = Urospermum
Schwefelsame = Urospermum
Schweifähre = Stachyurus
Schweifblume = Anthurium
Schwertbohne = Canavalia
Schwertelglocke = Libertia
Schwertfarn = Nephrolepis
Schwertlilie = Iris
Schwertpflanze = Echinodorus
Schwimmfarn = Salvinia
Schwimmlöffel = Luronium
Schwingel = Festuca
Schwingellolch = × Festulolium
Schwingelschilf = Scolochloa
Scilla = Scilla
Seebeere = Haloragis
Seebinse = Schoenoplectus
Seefeige = Erepsia
Seegras = Zostera

Seeheide = Frankenia
Seeigelkaktus = Echinopsis
Seekanne = Nymphoides
Seerose = Nymphaea
Seetraube = Coccoloba
Segge = Carex
Seide = Cuscuta
Seidelbast = Daphne
Seidenakazie = Albizia
Seidenpflanze = Asclepias
Seidenwollbaum = Bombax
Seidenwurmdorn = Cudrania
Seifenbaum = Sapindus
Seifenbusch = Porlieria
Seifenkraut = Saponaria
Seifenspiere = Quillaja
Seifenstrauch = Clidemia
Sellerie = Apium
Senf = Sinapis
Senna = Cassia, Senna
Sesam = Sesamum
Sesbanie = Sesbania
Sesel = Seseli
Seychellennuss = Lodoicea
Sibthorpie = Sibthorpia
Sichelblattorchidee = Arpophyllum
Sichelmöhre = Falcaria
Sichelsalat = Rhagadiolus
Sicheltanne = Cryptomeria
Siebenstern = Trientalis
Siegesbeckie = Sigesbeckia
Siegwurz = Gladiolus
Signalgras = Brachiaria
Signalstrauch = Mussaenda
Silberbaum = Leucadendron, Protea
Silberblatt = Leucophyta, Lunaria
Silberdistel = Carlina
Silbereiche = Grevillea
Silberfarn = Coniogramme, Pityrogramma
Silberginster = Argyrocytisus
Silbergras = Corynephorus
Silberhaut = Argyroderma
Silberimmortelle = Anaphalis
Silberkerze = Cimicifuga
Silberkerzenkaktus = Cleistocactus
Silberkraut = Lobularia
Silberne Strohblume = Cephalipterum
Silbernetzblatt = Fittonia
Silberpalme = Coccothrinax
Silberscharte = Jurinea
Silberwinde = Argyreia
Silge = Selinum
Simse = Scirpus
Simsenlilie = Tofieldia
Sinau = Aphanes

Sinnblume = Aeschynanthus
Sinnklee = Biophytum
Sinnpflanze = Mimosa
Skabiose = Scabiosa
Skimmie = Skimmia
Skorpionswicke = Scorpiurus
Sockenblume = Epimedium
Sodakraut = Salsola
Sode = Suaeda
Sojabohne = Glycine
Sommeraster = Callistephus
Sommerflieder = Buddleja
Sommerhyazinthe = Galtonia
Sommerjasmin = Philadelphus
Sommerwurz = Orobanche
Sommerzypresse = Bassia
Sonderkraut = Monopsis
Sonderling = Quisqualis
Sonnenauge = Heliopsis
Sonnenblume = Helianthus
Sonnenbraut = Helenium
Sonnenflügel = Helipterum
Sonnenfreund = Heliophila
Sonnenhut = Dracopsis, Rudbeckia
Sonnenkrug = Heliamphora
Sonnenröschen = Helianthemum
Sonnenschirmbaum = Firmiana
Sonnenwende = Heliotropium
Sonneratie = Sonneratia
Sorghumhirse = Sorghum
Sorvagummi = Couma
Souarinuss = Caryocar
Spaltblume = Schizanthus
Spaltglocke = Scaevola
Spaltgriffel = Schizostylis
Spalthortensie = Schizophragma
Spaltkölbchen = Schisandra
Spaltlilie = Anigozanthos
Spanische Ochsenzunge = Pentaglottis
Spanisches Rohr = Calamus
Spargel = Asparagus
Spargelbohne = Vigna
Spargelerbse = Tetragonolobus
Spark = Spergula
Spatzenzunge = Passerina, Thymelaea
Speckbaum = Portulacaria
Speerblume = Doryanthes
Speerfarn = Doryopteris
Speergras = Aciphylla
Speichenähre = Nardostachys
Speierling = Sorbus
Spergel = Spergula
Sperlingskopf = Passerina
Sperrkraut = Polemonium
Sperrstrauch = Eurya

G

Spierstrauch = Spiraea
Spießtanne = Cunninghamia
Spigelie = Spigelia
Spinat = Spinacia
Spindelstrauch = Euonymus
Spinnenlilie = Lycoris
Spinnenorchidee = Arachnis
Spinnenpflanze = Cleome
Spirke = Pinus
Spitzenblume = Ardisia
Spitzhülse = Oxylobium
Spitzkiel = Oxytropis
Spitzklette = Xanthium
Spornblume = Centranthus
Spreublume = Achyranthes
Springkraut = Impatiens
Spritzgurke = Ecballium
Spulenkaktus = Peniocereus
Spurre = Holosteum
Stachelähre = Acanthostachys
Stachelbart = Centropogon
Stachelbeere = Ribes
Stachelesche = Zanthoxylum
Stachelgras = Cenchrus
Stachelgurke = Sechium
Stachelmohn = Argemone
Stachelnüsschen = Acaena
Stachelpalme = Aiphanes
Stachelseerose = Euryale
Stachelspelze = Oplismenus
Stacheltraubchen = Coris
Ständelwurz = Epipactis
Stechapfel = Datura
Stechdorn = Paliurus
Stechginster = Ulex
Stechpalme = Ilex
Stechtanne = Keteleeria
Stechwinde = Smilax
Stechwurzelpalme = Cryosophila
Steckenkraut = Ferula
Steckenpalme = Rhapis
Steifgras = Catapodium
Steifhalm = Cleistogenes
Steinapfel = Osteomeles
Steinbeere = Rubus
Steinbrech = Saxifraga
Steineibe = Podocarpus
Steinfruchteiche = Lithocarpus
Steinglocke = Symphyandra
Steinklee = Melilotus
Steinkraut = Alyssum
Steinkresse = Aurinia
Steinliguster = Phillyrea
Steinlinde = Phillyrea
Steinnusspalme = Phytelephas

Steinquendel = Acinos
Steinsame = Lithodora, Lithospermum
Steinschmückel = Petrocallis
Steintäschel = Aethionema
Stendelwurz = Epipactis
Steppendistel = Morina
Steppenkerze = Eremurus
Steppenraute = Peganum
Sterkulie = Sterculia
Stern von Bethlehem = Ornithogalum
Sternanis = Illicium
Sternapfel = Chrysophyllum
Sternauge = Asteriscus
Sternbalsam = Zaluzianskya
Sternbergie = Sternbergia
Sterndolde = Astrantia
Sterngras = Hypoxis
Sternhortensie = Decumaria
Sternhyazinthe = Chionodoxa
Sternjasmin = Trachelospermum
Sternkaktus = Astrophytum
Sternlattich = Rhagadiolus
Sternmiere = Stellaria
Sternnusspalme = Astrocaryum
Sternwurz = Orostachys
Sternwurzel = Aletris
Stevie = Stevia
Stiefmütterchen = Viola
Stiefmütterchenorchidee = Miltoniopsis
Stielsamen = Scorzonera
Stiftblume = Albuca
Stinkbaum = Sterculia
Stinkeibe = Torreya
Stinkesche = Tetradium
Stinkkohl = Symplocarpus
Stinksalat = Aposeris
Stinkstrauch = Anagyris
Stockmalve = Althaea
Stockrose = Alcea
Stokesie = Stokesia
Storaxbaum = Styrax
Storchschnabel = Geranium
Stragel = Astragalus
Strahlenaralie = Schefflera
Strahlenfarn = Actiniopteris
Strahlengriffel = Actinidia
Strahlenpalme = Licuala
Strahlensame = Silene
Strandflieder = Limonium
Strandhafer = Ammophila
Strandling = Littorella
Strandroggen = Leymus
Strandsimse = Bolboschoenus
Straucheberesche = × Sorbaronia
Strauchehrenpreis = Hebe

Straucheiskraut = Ruschia
Straucherbse = Eutaxia
Strauchkronwicke = Emerus
Strauchmargerite = Argyranthemum
Strauchmohn = Romneya
Strauchnessel = Laportea
Strauchpalmettopalme = Serenoa
Strauchpappel = Lavatera
Strauchportulak = Portulacaria
Strauchscharte = Staehelina
Strauchstrandflieder = Limoniastrum
Strauchveronika = Hebe
Straußenfarn = Matteuccia
Straußfarn = Matteuccia
Straußgras = Agrostis
Streichkraut = Datisca
Streifenfarn = Asplenium
Streifenrinde = Plagianthus
Strelitzie = Strelitzia
Striemensame = Molopospermum
Strohblume = Helichrysum, Xerochrysum
Studentenblume = Tagetes
Studentenröschen = Parnassia
Suckowie = Succowia
Südbuche = Nothofagus
Südeiche = Lithocarpus
Südginster = Notospartium
Südseegold = Hibbertia
Südseemyrte = Leptospermum
Süßdolde = Myrrhis
Süßholz = Glycyrrhiza
Süßhülsenbaum = Prosopis
Süßklee = Hedysarum
Süßkraut = Lippia
Sumach = Rhus
Sumpfbärlapp = Lycopodiella
Sumpfbinse = Eleocharis
Sumpfblume = Limnanthes
Sumpffarn = Thelypteris
Sumpffreund = Limnophila
Sumpfkalla = Calla
Sumpfkresse = Rorippa
Sumpfkrug = Heliamphora
Sumpflieb = Limnocharis
Sumpfnelke = Helonias
Sumpfpfennigkraut = Centella
Sumpfquendel = Peplis
Sumpfschraube = Vallisneria
Sumpfstern = Swertia
Sumpfwurz = Epipactis
Sumpfzypresse = Taxodium
Surenbaum = Toona
Sutherlandie = Sutherlandia
Swainsonie = Swainsona
Tabak = Nicotiana

Tacca = Tacca
Tännel = Elatine
Tännelkraut = Kickxia
Täschelkraut = Thlaspi
Tafelblatt = Astilboides
Tagblume = Commelina
Tagetes = Tagetes
Taglilie = Hemerocallis
Tahitikastanie = Inocarpus
Taiwanie = Taiwania
Talerkürbis = Telfairia
Talgbaum = Sapium
Talipotpalme = Corypha
Tamarinde = Tamarindus
Tamariske = Tamarix
Tanne = Abies
Tannenwedel = Hippuris
Tarant = Swertia
Taschenblume = Bursaria
Taschenfarn = Dicksonia
Taschentuchbaum = Davidia
Tasmanische Iris = Diplarrhena
Taubenbaum = Davidia
Taubenerbsenbaum = Cajanus
Taubenkropf = Cucubalus
Taubenorchis = Peristeria
Taubnessel = Lamium
Tauchsimse = Isolepis
Tauernblümchen = Lomatogonium
Tausendblatt = Myriophyllum
Tausendfrucht = Myriocarpa
Tausendgüldenkraut = Centaurium
Tazette = Narcissus
Teakholz = Tectona
Teddybärpflanze = Cyanotis
Teebaum = Leptospermum
Teerkraut = Grindelia
Teestrauch = Camellia
Teffgras = Eragrostis
Teichfaden = Zannichellia
Teichlinse = Spirodela
Teichrose = Nuphar
Teichsimse = Schoenoplectus
Telekie = Telekia
Telephie = Telephium
Tellerkraut = Claytonia
Tempelbaum = Crateva
Tempelglocke = Smithiantha
Teppichlobelie = Pratia
Teppichverbene = Phyla
Ternströmie = Ternstroemia
Teufelsabbiss = Succisa
Teufelsauge = Adonis
Teufelsblüte = Tacca
Teufelsdorn = Emex

G

Teufelsklaue = Huperzia
Teufelskralle = Phyteuma
Teufelspfeffer = Rauvolfia
Teufelszwirn = Lycium
Texasstern = Lindheimera
Thevetie = Thevetia
Thuja = Thuja
Thunbergie = Thunbergia
Thymian = Thymus
Tibetorchidee = Pleione
Tibouchine = Tibouchina
Tigerblume = Tigridia
Tigergras = Thysanolaena
Tigerklaue = Martynia
Tigerschlund = Faucaria
Tillandsie = Tillandsia
Timboholz = Lonchocarpus
Tintenbaum = Semecarpus
Tipubaum = Tipuana
Titanenwurz = Amorphophallus
Tithonie = Tithonia
Tohabaum = Amherstia
Tollkirsche = Atropa
Tollkraut = Scopolia
Tolmie = Tolmiea
Tomate = Lycopersicon
Tongapflanze = Epipremnum
Tonkabohne = Dipteryx
Topffruchtbaum = Lecythis
Torenie = Torenia
Torfgränke = Chamaedaphne
Totenstrauch = Tarchonanthus
Townsendie = Townsendia
Tradeskantie = Tradescantia
Tränendes Herz = Dicentra
Tränengras = Coix
Träubel = Muscari
Tragant = Astragalus
Trapp = Leontice
Traubenapfel = Rhaphiolepis
Traubendorn = Danae
Traubenhafer = Danthonia
Traubenheide = Leucothoe
Traubenhyazinthe = Muscari
Traubenkirsche = Prunus
Traubenkraut = Ambrosia
Traubenrapunzel = Asyneuma
Traubenspiere = Neillia
Trauerbambus = Otatea
Trauerbaum = Nyctanthes
Trauerblume = Diapensia
Trauerglocke = Uvularia
Trespe = Bromus
Trichterbromelie = Nidularium
Trichterfarn = Matteuccia

Trichtermalve = Malope
Trichtermelisse = Moluccella
Trichterschwertel = Dierama
Triteleie = Triteleia
Triticale = × Triticosecale
Tritome = Kniphofia
Tritonie = Tritonia
Troddelblume = Soldanella
Trogblatt = Lenophyllum
Trollblume = Trollius
Trommelschlägel = Craspedia
Trompetenbaum = Catalpa
Trompetenblume = Campsis
Trompetenstrauch = Tecoma
Trompetenwein = Bignonia, Podranea
Trompetenwinde = Campsis
Trompetenzunge = Salpiglossis
Tropeneibisch = Thespesia
Trugkölbchen = Heteranthera
Truthahnbart = Xerophyllum
Tubawurzel = Derris
Tüpfelfarn = Polypodium
Türkenglocke = Michauxia
Tulbaghie = Tulbaghia
Tulpe = Tulipa
Tulpenbaum = Liriodendron
Tulpenmohn = Hunnemannia
Tulpenorchidee = Anguloa
Tungölbaum = Vernicia
Tupelobaum = Nyssa
Turgenie = Turgenia
Ulluco = Ullucus
Ulme = Ulmus
Upasbaum = Antiaris
Urnenpflanze = Dischidia
Urundayholz = Astronium
Urweltmammutbaum = Metasequoia
Usambaraveilchen = Saintpaulia
Vaillantie = Valantia
Vallisnerie = Vallisneria
Vancouverie = Vancouveria
Vanille = Vanilla
Vanilleapfel = Annona
Vanilleblatt = Achlys
Vegetabilisches Lamm = Cibotium
Veilchen = Viola
Veilchenbusch = Browallia
Veilchenständel = Ionopsis
Veilchenstrauch = Iochroma
Veltheimie = Veltheimia
Venusfliegenfalle = Dionaea
Venuskamm = Scandix
Venusnabel = Umbilicus
Venusschuh = Paphiopedilum
Venusspiegel = Legousia

Verbene = Verbena
Verbesine = Verbesina
Vergissmeinnicht = Myosotis
Vernonie = Vernonia
Versteckblume = Cryptanthus
Vetivergras = Vetiveria
Victoria = Victoria
Vierspornbaum = Tetracentron
Vilfagras = Sporobolus
Villarsie = Villarsia
Virginiamalve = Sida
Vogelbeere = Sorbus
Vogelfuß = Ornithopus
Vogelknöterich = Polygonum
Vogelkopf = Craniolaria
Vogelmilch = Ornithogalum
Wacholder = Juniperus
Wachsbaum = Carissa
Wachsblume = Cerinthe, Hoya
Wachsglocke = Kirengeshoma
Wachskürbis = Benincasa
Wachspalme = Ceroxylon
Wachtelweizen = Melampyrum
Waid = Isatis
Walch = Aegilops
Walddickblatt = Chiastophyllum
Waldgerste = Hordelymus
Waldhyazinthe = Platanthera
Waldkaktus = Hylocereus
Waldmohn = Hylomecon
Waldrebe = Clematis
Waldsteinie = Waldsteinia
Waldvögelein = Cephalanthera
Waldwurz = Neotinea
Walnuss = Juglans
Walzenblatt = Cylindrophyllum
Wandelklee = Desmodium
Wandelröschen = Lantana
Wanzenblume = Coreopsis
Wanzenkraut = Cimicifuga
Wanzenpflanze = Roridula
Wanzensame = Corispermum
Waratahprotee = Telopea
Warzeneibe = Dacrycarpus
Warzenkaktus = Mammillaria
Warzensame = Thelesperma
Washingtonpalme = Washingtonia
Wasserähre = Aponogeton
Wasseraloe = Stratiotes
Wasserbläuling = Hydrolea
Wasserblatt = Hydrophyllum
Wasserbusch = Bossiaea
Wasserdost = Eupatorium
Wasserfalle = Aldrovanda
Wasserfarn = Bolbitis

Wasserfeder = Hottonia
Wasserfenchel = Oenanthe
Wasserfichte = Glyptostrobus
Wasserfreund = Hygrophila
Wassergirlande = Lagarosiphon
Wasserhahnenfuß = Ranunculus
Wasserhorn = Hydrocera
Wasserhyazinthe = Eichhornia
Wasserlinse = Lemna
Wassermelone = Citrullus
Wassermohn = Hydrocleys
Wassernabel = Hydrocotyle
Wassernuss = Trapa
Wasserpest = Egeria, Elodea
Wasserquirl = Hydrilla
Wasserreis = Zizania
Wassersalat = Pistia
Wasserschierling = Cicuta
Wasserschild = Brasenia
Wasserschlauch = Utricularia
Wasserschraube = Vallisneria
Wasserstern = Callitriche
Wassertrompete = Cryptocoryne
Wasserysop = Bacopa
Watsonie = Watsonia
Wau = Reseda
Wegerich = Plantago
Wegrauke = Sisymbrium
Wegwarte = Cichorium
Weichkraut = Mollugo
Weichorchis = Malaxis
Weichsel = Prunus
Weichwurz = Hammarbya
Weide = Salix
Weidelgras = Lolium
Weidelilie = Chortolirion
Weidenmyrte = Agonis
Weidenröschen = Epilobium
Weiderich = Lythrum
Weigelie = Weigela
Weihnachtsbeere = Chironia
Weihnachtsglöckchen = Blandfordia
Weihnachtskaktus = Schlumbergera
Weihrauchbaum = Boswellia
Weihrauchzeder = Calocedrus
Weinbeere = Aristotelia
Weinpalme = Raphia
Weinrebe = Vitis
Weintraube = Vitis
Weißbecher = Nierembergia
Weißdorn = Crataegus
Weißdornmispel = × Crataemespilus
Weiße Sapote = Casimiroa
Weißfaden = Leucaena
Weißgummibaum = Bursera

G

Weißmiere = Moenchia
Weißnessel = Cnidoscolus
Weißwurz = Polygonatum
Weißzüngel = Pseudorchis
Weizen = Triticum
Weldenie = Weldenia
Wellingtonie = Sequoiadendron
Welwitschie = Welwitschia
Wendelähre = Spiranthes
Wendich = Calepina
Wermut = Artemisia
Wetterdistel = Carlina
Wicke = Vicia
Wickenstrauch = Podalyria
Widerbart = Epipogium
Widerstoß = Limonium
Wiesenhafer = Helictotrichon
Wiesenknöterich = Bistorta
Wiesenknopf = Sanguisorba
Wiesenraute = Thalictrum
Wiesensilge = Silaum
Wigandie = Wigandia
Wilder Wein = Parthenocissus
Wildreis = Zizania
Wimperfarn = Woodsia
Windblume = Zephyranthes
Winde = Convolvulus
Windendes Löwenmaul = Maurandya
Windhalm = Apera
Windröschen = Anemone
Winteraster = Chrysanthemum
Winterbeere = Heteromeles, Ilex
Winterblatt = Shortia
Winterblüte = Chimonanthus
Wintergrün = Moneses, Pyrola
Winterlieb = Chimaphila
Winterling = Eranthis
Winterrinde = Cinnamodendron, Drimys
Wirbeldost = Clinopodium
Wisterie = Wisteria
Witwenblume = Knautia
Wohlverleih = Arnica
Wolfsauge = Anchusa
Wolfsbeere = Symphoricarpos
Wolfsbohne = Lupinus
Wolfshut = Aconitum
Wolfsmilch = Chamaesyce, Euphorbia
Wolfsschwertel = Hermodactylus
Wolfstrapp = Lycopus
Wollampfer = Eriogonum
Wollbaum = Chorisia
Wollblatt = Eriophyllum
Wollemikiefer = Wollemia
Wollfadenraute = Eriostemon
Wollfruchtkaktus = Ariocarpus

Wollgras = Eriophorum
Wollknöterich = Eriogonum
Wollkopf = Eriocephalus
Wollkraut = Verbascum
Wollmispel = Eriobotrya
Wollstängel = Eriocaulon
Wucherblume = Glebionis, Tanacetum, Xanthophthalmum
Wüstenginster = Templetonia
Wüstenlimette = Eremocitrus
Wüstenrose = Adenium
Wulfenie = Wulfenia
Wunderbaum = Ricinus
Wunderbeere = Synsepalum
Wunderblume = Mirabilis
Wunderstrauch = Codiaeum
Wundklee = Anthyllis
Wurmlattich = Helminthotheca
Yamsbohne = Pachyrhizus
Yamswurzel = Dioscorea
Ylang-Ylangbaum = Cananga
Yohimbe = Pausinystalia
Ysander = Pachysandra
Ysop = Hyssopus
Zachunbaum = Balanites
Zackenschötchen = Bunias
Zahnbaum = Balanites
Zahnlilie = Erythronium
Zahntrost = Odontites
Zahnwurz = Cardamine
Zapfenblume = Strobilanthes
Zapfenkopf = Leuzea
Zapfennuss = Platycarya
Zartschötchen = Hymenolobus
Zauberglöckchen = Calibrachoa
Zaubernuss = Hamamelis
Zaunlilie = Anthericum
Zaunrübe = Bryonia
Zaunwinde = Calystegia
Zeder = Cedrus
Zederachbaum = Melia
Zedrele = Cedrela
Zehrwurz = Colocasia
Zeiland = Cneorum
Zeitlose = Colchicum
Zelkove = Zelkova
Zelkowe = Zelkova
Zenobie = Zenobia
Zephirblume = Zephyranthes
Zickzackpflanze = Decaryia
Zierbanane = Ensete
Zierquitte = Chaenomeles
Zierspark = Telephium
Ziest = Stachys
Zimbelkraut = Cymbalaria

Zimmeraralie = Fatsia
Zimmerhafer = Billbergia
Zimmerhopfen = Justicia
Zimmerimmergrün = Catharanthus
Zimmerkalla = Zantedeschia
Zimmerlinde = Sparrmannia
Zimmerrebe = Cissus
Zimmertanne = Araucaria
Zimtapfel = Annona
Zimtbaum = Cinnamomum
Zimterle = Clethra
Zimtlorbeer = Cinnamomum
Zimtrindenbaum = Canella
Zindelkraut = Cicendia
Zinerarie = Cineraria, Pericallis
Zinnie = Zinnia
Zirmet = Tordylium
Zistrose = Cistus
Zitrone = Citrus
Zitronellagras = Cymbopogon
Zitronengras = Cymbopogon
Zitronenstrauch = Aloysia
Zittergras = Briza
Zuckerpalme = Arenga
Zuckerrohr = Saccharum
Zügelständel = Habenaria
Zürgelbaum = Celtis
Zulukartoffel = Bowiea
Zungenblatt = Glottiphyllum
Zungenfarn = Elaphoglossum
Zungenständel = Serapias
Zweiblatt = Listera
Zweiflügelfruchtbaum = Dipterocarpus

Zweizahn = Bidens
Zwenke = Brachypodium
Zwergalpenrose = Rhodothamnus
Zwergbambus = Sasa
Zwergbleiwurz = Plumbagella
Zwergflachs = Radiola
Zwerggänsekresse = Schivereckia
Zwergginster = Chamaecytisus
Zwerggras = Mibora
Zwerglebensbaum = Microbiota
Zwerglöwenmaul = Chaenorhinum
Zwergmaßliebchen = Bellium
Zwergmispel = Cotoneaster
Zwergölbaum = Cneorum
Zwergorange = Fortunella
Zwergorchis = Chamorchis
Zwergpalme = Chamaerops
Zwergpalmfarn = Microcycas
Zwergpfeffer = Peperomia
Zwergsonnenblume = Helianthella
Zwergständel = Chamorchis
Zwergstrobe = Microstrobos
Zwergwasserlinse = Wolffia
Zwetsche = Prunus
Zwetschge = Prunus
Zwiebel = Allium
Zwiebelblatt = Bulbophyllum
Zwillingsblatt = Jeffersonia
Zylinderputzer = Callistemon
Zypergras = Cyperus
Zypresse = Cupressus
Zypressenkiefer = Callitris

G

XIII   Authors of plant names

The abbreviations strictly follow the list by Brummitt & Powell (1992), "Authors of Plant Names". We have sorted according to the author's surname. The latter is followed by the author's years of birth and death in parentheses; if these are not known, the year of publication is given instead, denoted by the abbreviation "fl." for "floruit", meaning when the person concerned was active, or "publ." for "published", meaning published.

Aarons. = Aaron Aaronsohn, 1876–1919
S. Abe = S. Abe, fl. 1956–89
C. Abel = Clarke Abel, 1789–1826
Aberc. = Henry Duncan McLaren Aberconway, 1879–1953
Abeyw. = Bartholomeusz Aristides Abeywickrama, 1920–
Abrams = Le Roy Abrams, 1874–1956
Abrom. = Johannes Abromeit, 1857–1946
Adamović = Lujo (Lulji, Lucian) Adamovic, 1864–1935
Adams = Johannes Michael Friedrich Adams, 1780–1838
Adans. = Michel Adanson, 1727–1806
Adelb. = Albert George Ludwig Adelbert, 1914–1972
Aedo = Carlos Aedo, 1960–
Aellen = Paul Aellen, 1896–1973
Afzel. = Adam Afzelius, 1750–1837
J. Agardh = Jakob Georg Agardh, 1813–1901
Agnew = Andrew David Quentin Agnew, 1929–
A. Agostini = Angela Agostini, fl. 1926
Aguiar = Joaquim Macedo de Aguiar, 1854–1882
Ahrendt = Leslie Walter Allen Ahrendt, 1903–1969
Airy Shaw = Herbert Kenneth Airy Shaw, 1902–1985
Aitch. = James Edward Tierney Aitchison, 1836–1898
Aiton = William Aiton, 1731–1793
W.T. Aiton = William Townsend Aiton, 1766–1849
Akasawa = Yoshyuki Akasawa, 1915–
Akeroyd = John Robert Akeroyd, 1952–
Akers = John Frank Akers, 1906–
Akiyama = Shigeo Akiyama, 1906–
Albert = Abel Albert, 1836–1909

Albov = Nicolaj Mihajlovic (Nikolas Michailowitsch) Albov (Alboff), 1866–1897
Alderw. = Cornelis Rugier Willem Karel van Alderwerelt van Rosenburgh, 1863–1936
Alef. = Friedrich Georg Christoph Alefeld, 1820–1872
Alexander = Edward Johnston Alexander, 1901–1985
Allan = Harry Howard Barton Allan, 1882–1957
Allemao = Francisco Freire Allemao e Cysneiro, 1797–1874
J. Allen = James Allen, c.1830–1906
P.H. Allen = Paul Hamilton Allen, 1911–1963
All. = Carlo Ludovico Allioni, 1728–1804
Alston = Arthur Hugh Garfit Alston, 1902–1958
Ambrosi = Francesco Ambrosi, 1821–1897
L.M. Ames = Lawrence Marion Ames, 1900–1966
Ames = Oakes Ames, 1874–1950
Amin = Amal Amin, 1929–
Andersen = Johannes Carl Andersen, 1873–1962
E.S. Anderson = Edgar Shannon Anderson, 1897–1969
E.F. Anderson = Edward Frederick Anderson, 1932–2001
G. Anderson = George W. Anderson, fl. 1800–1817
T. Anderson = Thomas Anderson, 1832–1870
Andersson = Nils Johan Andersson, 1821–1880
Andrae = Carl Justus Andrae, 1816–1885
André = Édouard François André, 1840–1911

Andr. = Gábor (Gabriel) Andréanszky, 1895–1967
Andrews = Henry Charles Andrews, c. 1770–1830
S. Andrews = Susyn M. Andrews, 1953–
Andrz. = Antoni Lukianowicz Andrzejowski, 1785–1868
Ångstr. = Johan Ångström, 1813–1879
Anliker = Johann Anliker, 1901–
Anselmino = Elisabeth Bertha Petronella Anselmino, 1905–
Antoine = Franz Antoine, 1815–1886
Appel = Friedrich Carl Louis Otto Appel, 1867–1952
Applegate = Elmer Ivan Applegate, 1867–1949
Arcang. = Giovanni Arcangeli, 1840–1921
Archer-Hind = Thomas H. Archer-Hind, fl. 1880
Ardoino = Nicolas Honoré Jean Baptiste Ardoino, 1819–1874
Ard. = Pietro Arduino, 1728–1805
Arechav. = José Cosme Arechavaleta, 1838–1912
Arends = Georg Adalbert Arends, 1863–1952
F. Aresch. = Fredric Wilhelm Christian Areschoug, 1830–1908
J.B. Armstr. = Joseph Beattie Armstrong, 1850–1926
J.F. Arnold = Johann Franz Xaver Arnold, fl. 1785
S. Arn. = Samuel Arnott, 1852–1930
Arn. = George Arnott Walker Arnott, 1799–1868
Arruda = Manoel Arruda da Cámara, 1752–1810
Arthur = Joseph Charles Arthur, 1850–1942
Arv.-Touv. = Jean Maurice Casimir Arvet-Touvet, 1841–1913
Asch. = Paul Friedrich August Ascherson, 1834–1913
Ashe = William Willard Ashe, 1872–1932
Ashwin = Margot Bernice Ashwin, 1935–
Aspegren = Georg Casten Aspegren, 1791–1828
Assenov = Vulevi Ivan Assenov, 1932–2004
Asso = Ignacio Jordán de Asso Y del Rio, 1742–1814
Aubl. = Jean Baptiste Christophe Fusée Aublet, 1720–1778
Aucher = Pierre Martin Rémi Aucher-Éloy, 1792–1838
Audot = N. Audot, fl. 1845
Audubon = John James Audubon, 1785–1851
Augustin = K. Augustin, fl. 1854

Auquier = Paul Henri Auquier, 1939–1980
D.F. Austin = Daniel Frank Austin, 1943–
Avé-Lall. = Julius Leopold Eduard Avé-Lallemant, 1803–1867
Aver. = Leonid V. Averyanov, 1955–
Azn. = Georges Vincent Aznavour, 1861–1920
Babc. = Ernest Brown Babcock, 1877–1954
Bab. = Charles Cardale Babington, 1808–1895
Bacig. = Rimo Carlo Felice Bacigalupi, 1901–1996
Backeb. = Curt Backeberg, 1894–1966
Backer = Cornelis Andries B. Backer, 1874–1963
Backh. = James Backhouse, 1794–1869
Backh. f. = James Backhouse, 1825–1890
V.M. Badillo = Victor Manuel Badillo, 1920–
Badoux = Henri Badoux, 1871–1951
Baehni = Charles Baehni, 1906–1964
Baen. = Karl (Carl) Gabriel Baenitz, 1837–1913
Bässler = Manfred Bässler, 1935–
C. Bailey = Charles Bailey, 1838–1924
D.K. Bailey = Dana K. Bailey, 1916–
F.M. Bailey = Frederick Manson Bailey, 1827–1915
J.P. Bailey = John Paul Bailey, 1951–
L.H. Bailey = Liberty Hyde Bailey, 1858–1954
Baill. = Henri Ernest Baillon, 1827–1895
Bailly = Émile Bailly, 1829–1894
C.F. Baker = Charles Fuller Baker, 1872–1927
Baker f. = Edmund Gilbert Baker, 1864–1949
Baker = John Gilbert Baker, 1834–1920
R.T. Baker = Richard Thomas Baker, 1854–1941
Bakh. = Reinier Cornelis Bakhuizen van den Brink, 1881–1945
N.P. Balakr. = Nambiyath Puthansurayil Balakrishnan, 1935–
Balansa = Benedict (Benjamin) Balansa, 1825–1892
Balb. = Giovanni Batista Balbis, 1765–1831
Bald. = Antonio Baldacci, 1867–1950
Balf. f. = Isaac Bayley Balfour, 1853–1922
Balf. = John Hutton Balfour, 1808–1884
Ball = John Ball, 1818–1889
P.W. Ball = Peter William Ball, 1932–
P.R.O. Bally = Peter René Oscar Bally, 1895–1980
Baltet = Charles Baltet, 1830–1908

Bancr. = Edward Nathaniel Bancroft, 1772–1842
Banks = Joseph Banks, 1743–1820
Barbar. = Andrej Ivanovic Barbaric (Barbarich), 1903–
Barbey = William Barbey, 1842–1914
Barb.-Boiss. = Caroline Barbey-Boissier, 1847–1918
Barbier = M. Barbier, fl. 1904
Barb. Rodr. = Joao Barbosa Rodrigues, 1842–1909
A.S. Barclay = Arthur Stewart Barclay, 1932–2003
Barker = George Barker, 1776–1845
W.F. Barker = Winsome Fanny Barker, 1907–1994
F.A. Barkley = Fred Alexander Barkley, 1908–1989
Barneby = Rupert Charles Barneby, 1911–2000
Barnéoud = François Marius Barnéoud, 1821–
Barney = Eliam E. Barney, 1807–1880
Barnhart = John Hendley Barnhart, 1871–1949
Baroni = Eugenio Baroni, 1865–1943
Barrandon = Auguste Barrandon, 1814–1897
Barratt = Joseph Barratt, 1796–1882
Barratte = Jean François Gustave Barratte, 1857–1920
F. Barros = Fábio de Barros, 1956–
G.M. Barroso = Graziela Maciel Barroso, 1912–2003
Bartal. = Biagio Bartalini, 1746–1822
Barthlott = Wilhelm A. Barthlott, 1946–
Bartlett = Harley Harris Bartlett, 1886–1960
Bartl. = Friedrich Gottlieb Theophil Bartling, 1798–1875
Barton = Benjamin Smith Barton, 1766–1815
W.P.C. Barton = William Paul Crillon Barton, 1786–1856
W. Bartram = William Bartram, 1739–1823
Bassi = Ferdinando Bassi, 1710–1774
Bastard = Toussaint Bastard, 1784–1846
Batalin = Aleksandr Fedorovic Batalin, 1847–1896
Batcheller = Frances N. Batcheller, fl. 1978
Bateman = James Bateman, 1811–1897
R.M. Bateman = Richard M. Bateman, fl. 1983–2004
D.M. Bates = David Martin Bates, 1935–
Batsch = August Johann Georg Karl Batsch, 1761–1802

Batt. = Jules-Aimé Battandier, 1848–1922
Baudet = Jean C. Baudet, 1944–
Baudo = Firmin Baudo, fl. 1843
F.A. Bauer = Franz (Francis) Andreas Bauer, 1758–1840
Rud. Bauer = Rudolf Bauer, 1910–1982
A. Bauer = Annelise Bauer, publ. 1986
Baum = Hugo Baum, 1866–1950
Baumann = Constantin Auguste Napoléon Baumann, 1804–1884
E. Baumann = Eugen Baumann, 1868–1933
H. Baumann = Helmut Adolf Baumann, 1937–
Baumg. = Johann Christian Gottlob Baumgarten, 1765–1843
J. Bausch = Jan Bausch, 1917–
E.M. Baxter = Edgar Martin Baxter, 1903–1967
W.T. Baxter = W.T. Baxter, fl. 1864
Ehr. Bayer = Ehrentraud Bayer, 1953–
Bayer = Johann Nepomuk Bayer, 1802–1870
M.B. Bayer = Martin Bruce Bayer, 1935–
Beadle = Chauncey Delos Beadle, 1866–1950
Beaman = John Homer Beaman, 1929–
Bean = William Jackson Bean, 1863–1947
Beane = Lawrence Beane, 1901–
Beaton = Donald Beaton, 1802–1863
Beauverd = Gustave Beauverd, 1867–1942
Bebb = Michael Schuck Bebb, 1833–1895
Becc. = Odoardo Beccari, 1843–1920
Bech. = Alfred Becherer, 1897–1977
Bechst. = Johann Matthaeus Bechstein, 1757–1822
Beck = Günther Beck Ritter von Mannagetta und Lërchenau, 1856–1931
Becker = Johannes Becker, 1769–1833
W. Becker = Wilhelm Becker, 1874–1928
Bedd. = Richard Henry Beddome, 1830–1911
Beentje = Henk Jaap Beentje, 1951–
Beer = Johann Georg Beer, 1803–1873
Bég. = Augusto Béguinot, 1875–1940
Beille = Lucien Beille, 1862–1946
Beissn. = Ludwig Beissner, 1843–1927
Bellair = Georges Adolphe Bellair, 1860–1939
Bellardi = Carlo Antonio Lodovico Bellardi, 1741–1826
Benary = Ernst Benary, 1819–1893
A.W. Benn. = Alfred William Bennett, 1833–1902
G. Benn. = George Bennett, 1804–1893
Benn. = John (Johannes) Joseph Bennett, 1801–1876

L.D. Benson = Lyman David Benson, 1909–1993

Benson = Robson Benson, 1822–1894

Benth. = George Bentham, 1800–1884

Bercht. = Bedricha (Friedrich) Wssemjra von Berchtold, 1781–1876

C.C. Berg = Cornelis Christiaan Berg, 1934–

O. Berg = Otto Karl (Carl) Berg, 1815–1866

M.E. Berg = Maria Elizabeth van den Berg, fl. 1970

Bergann = Friedrich Bergann, 1904–

A. Berger = Alwin Berger, 1871–1931

Berger = Ernst Friedrich Berger, 1814–1853

Bergeret = Jean-Pierre Bergeret, 1752–1813

Berggr. = Sven Berggren, 1837–1917

P.J. Bergius = Peter Jonas Bergius, 1730–1790

Bergmans = Johannes (John) Baptista Bergmans, 1892–1980

Berher = Laurent Eugène Berher, 1822–1900

Berk. = Miles Joseph Berkeley, 1803–1889

Berland. = Jean Louis Berlandier, 1805–1851

Bernh. = Johann Jakob Bernhardi, 1774–1850

Berry = Andrew Berry, fl. 1780–c. 1810

P.E. Berry = Paul Edward Berry, 1952–

Bertero = Carlo Luigi Giuseppe Bertero, 1789–1831

Berthault = François Berthault, 1857–1916

Berthel. = Sabin Berthelot, 1794–1880

Bertol. = Antonio Bertoloni, 1775–1869

Bertoni = Moisés de Santiago Bertoni, 1857–1929

Bertrand = Marcel C. Bertrand, fl. 1873

Besser = Wilibald Swibert Joseph Gottlieb von Besser, 1784–1842

Betche = Ernst L. Betche, 1851–1913

Beurl. = Pehr Johan Beurling, 1800–1866

Beusekom = C. F. van Beusekom, 1940–

Bewer. = W. Bewerunge, fl. 1948

Bhandari = Madan Mal Bhandari, 1929–

Biasol. = Bartolomeo Amadeo Biasoletto, 1793–1859

E.P. Bicknell = Eugene Pintard Bicknell, 1859–1925

Bidwill = John Carne Bidwill, 1815–1853

Bien. = Theophil Bienert, –1873

Bigelow = Jacob Bigelow, 1787–1879

Billot = Paul Constant Billot, 1796–1863

Binn. = Simon Binnendijk, 1821–1883

Birdsey = Monroe Roberts Birdsey, 1922–2000

Biria = J A. J. Biria, 1789–

Bisset = James Bisset, 1843–1911

Bitter = Friedrich August Georg Bitter, 1873–1927

Bittrich = Volker Bittrich, 1954–

Biv. = Antonius de Bivona-Bernardi, 1774–1837

Bizzarri = Maria Paola Bizzarri, 1937–

J.M. Black = John McConnell Black, 1855–1951

Blackburn = Benjamin Coleman Blackburn, 1908–

S.F. Blake = Sidney Fay Blake, 1892–1959

Blakelock = Ralph Antony Blakelock, 1915–1963

Blakely = William Faris Blakely, 1875–1941

Blanca = Gabriel Blanca López, 1954–

Blanch. = William Henry Blanchard, 1850–1922

C.I. Blanche = Charles Isodore Blanche, 1823–1887

Blanco = Francisco Manuel Blanco, 1778–1845

Blaxell = Donald Frederick Blaxell, 1934–

Bluff = Mathias Joseph Bluff, 1805–1837

Blume = Carl (Karl) Ludwig von Blume, 1796–1862

Blumensch. = Almiro Blumenschein, 1931–

A. Blytt = Axel Gudbrand Blytt, 1843–1898

Blytt = Matthias Numsen Blytt, 1789–1862

Bobrov = Evgenij Grigorievicz Bobrov, 1902–1983

Bocq. = Henri Théophile Bocquillon, 1834–1883

Bodin = Nicolas Gustavus Bodin, fl. 1798

Böcher = Tyge Wittrock Böcher, 1909–1983

Boeck. = Johann Otto Boeckeler, 1803–1899

Boed. = Friedrich Boedeker, 1867–1937

Boehm. = Georg Rudolf Boehmer, 1723–1803

Boenn. = Clemens Maria Griedrich von Boenninghausen, 1785–1864

Boerl. = Jacob Gijsbert Boerlage, 1849–1900

Börner = Carl (Karl) Julius Bernhard Börner, 1880–1953

Bogenh. = Carl Bogenhard, 1811–?1853

Bogin = Clifford Bogin, 1920–

Bogner = Josef Bogner, 1939–

Bois = Désiré Georges Jean Marie Bois, 1856–1946

Boiss. = Pierre Édmond Boissier, 1810–1885

B. Boivin = Joseph Robert Bernard Boivin, 1916–1985

Boivin = Louis Hyacinthe Boivin, 1808–1852

Bojer = Wenceslaus (Wenzel) Bojer, 1797–1856
Boke = Norman Hill Boke, 1913–1996
Bolle = Carl (Karl) August Bolle, 1821–1909
Bolliger = Markus Bolliger, 1951–
O. Bolòs = Oriol de Bolòs i Capdevila, 1924–2007
A. Bolòs = Antonio de Bolòs y Vayreda, 1889–1975
Bolton = James Bolton, 1758–1799
L. Bolus = Harriet Margaret Louisa Bolus, 1877–1970
Bolus = Harry Bolus, 1834–1911
Bonavia = Emanuel Bonavia, 1826–1908
Bong. = August (Gustav) Heinrich von Bongard, 1786–1839
Bonnet = Jean Jacques Édmond Bonnet, 1848–1922
Bonnier = Gaston Eugène Marie Bonnier, 1853–1922
Bonpl. = Aimé Jacques Alexandre Bonpland, 1773–1858
Boom = Boudewijn Karel Boom, 1903–1980
J.R. Booth = John Godfrey Booth, 1800–1847
T.J. Booth = Thomas Jonas Booth, 1829–after 1878
Booth = William Beattie Booth, c.1804–1874
Boott = Francis M.B. Boott, 1792–1863
Bor = Norman Loftus Bor, 1893–1972
Borbás = Vinczé (Vincent von) tól Borbás de Deétér, 1844–1905
Boreau = Alexandre Boreau, 1803–1875
Borg = John Borg, 1873–1945
Boriss. = Antonina Georgievna Borissova, 1903–1970
Borkh. = Moritz Balthasar Borkhausen, 1760–1806
Bornm. = Joseph Friedrich Nicolaus Bornmüller, 1862–1948
Borrer = William J. Borrer, 1781–1862
Borsos = Olga Borsos, 1926–
Bort = Katherine Stephens Bort, 1870–
Bory = Jean Baptiste Georges Geneviève Marcellin Bory, 1778–1846
Borzì = Antonino Borzì, 1852–1921
Bos = Jan Justus Bos, 1939–2003
Bosc = Louis Augustin Guillaume Bosc, 1759–1828
G.G. Bosse = Georg G. Bosse, 1887–1972
Bosse = Julius Friedrich Wilhelm Bosse, 1788–1864
Botschantz. = Zinaida Petrovna Botschantzeva, 1907–1973

C.D. Bouché = Carl David Bouché, 1809–1881
Bouché = Peter Carl Bouché, 1783–1856
Boucher = Jules Armand Guillaume Boucher de Crèvecoeur, 1757–1844
Boulay = Nicolas-Jean Boulay, 1837–1905
Boulenger = George Albert Boulenger, 1858–1937
Boutelje = Julius B. Boutelje, fl. 1954
Bowie = James Bowie,c. 1789–1869
Bowles = Edward Augustus Bowles, 1865–1954
F.E. Boynton = Frank Ellis Boynton, 1859–
Brade = Alexander Curt Brade, 1881–1971
J.M.A. Braga = Joao Marcelo Alvarenga Braga, 1971–
Bramwell = David Bramwell, 1942–
Brand = August Brand, 1863–1930
K. Brandegee = Mary Katharine Brandegee, 1844–1920
Brandegee = Townshend Stith Brandegee, 1843–1925
Brandis = Dietrich Brandis, 1824–1907
E. Brandis = E. Brandis, 1834–1921
F.H. Brandt = Fred H. Brandt, 1908–
Brandt = Johann Friedrich (von) Brandt, 1802–1879
M. Brandt = Max Brandt, 1884–1914
A. Braun = Alexander Karl (Carl) Heinrich Braun, 1805–1877
Heinr. Braun = Heinrich Braun, 1851–1920
P.J. Braun = Pierre Josef Braun, 1959–
Braun-Blanq. = Josias Braun-Blanquet, 1884–1980
Bravo = Helia Bravo Hollis, 1901–2001
W.L. Bray = William L. Bray, 1865–1953
Bréb. = Louis Alphonse de Brébisson, 1798–1872
Breda = Jacob Gijsbert Samuel van Breda, 1788–1867
Bredem. = Franz Bredemeyer, 1758–1839
Brederoo = Arnold J. ('Nol') Brederoo, c.1917–
Breistr. = Maurice André Frantz Breistroffer, 1910–1986
Breitenb. = Wilhelm Breitenbach, 1856–1937
Breitf. = Charlotte Breitfeld, 1902–c.2003
Bremek. = Cornelis Eliza Bertus Bremekamp, 1888–1984
K. Bremer = Kåre (Kaare) Bremer, 1948–
Brenan = John Patrick Mickelthwait Brenan, 1917–1985
Bresler = Moritz Bresler, 1802–c.1851
Brettell = R.D. Brettell, fl. 1974

C.D. Brickell = Christopher David Brickell, 1932–

Brieger = Friedrich Gustav Brieger, 1900–1985

B.G. Briggs = Barbara Gillian Briggs, 1934–

F.E. Briggs = F.E. Briggs, fl. 1937

S.M. Briggs = Scott Munro Briggs, 1889–1917

Brign. = Giovanni de Brignoli di Brunnhoff, 1774–1857

Briot = Pierre Louis (Charles) Briot, 1804–1888

Briq. = John Isaac Briquet, 1870–1931

Britten = James Britten, 1846–1924

Britton = Nathaniel Lord Britton, 1859–1934

Bromf. = William Arnold Bromfield, 1801–1851

Brongn. = Adolphe Théodore (de) Brongniart, 1801–1876

Brot. = Felix de (Silva) Avellar Brotero, 1744–1828

M. Broun = Maurice Broun, 1906–

Brouss. = Pierre Marie Auguste Broussonet, 1761–1807

A. Br. = Addison Brown, 1830–1913

N.E. Br. = Nicholas Edward Brown, 1849–1934

R. Br. = Robert Brown, 1773–1858

S. Br. = Stewardson Brown, 1867–1921

F.E. Br. = F.E. Brown, fl. 1845

P. Browne = Patrick Browne, c.1720–1790

Brownsey = Patrick John Brownsey, 1948–

Bruant = François Georges Léon Bruant Bruant, 1842–1912

Bruce = James Bruce, 1730–1794

G. Brückn. = Gerhard Brückner, 1902–

Brügger = Christian Georg Brügger, 1833–1899

H. Bruggen = Heinrich Wilhelm Eduard van Bruggen, 1927–

Brullo = Salvatore Brullo, 1947–

Brummitt = Richard Kenneth Brummitt, 1937–

Bruyns = Peter Vincent Bruyns, 1957–

Bubani = Pietro Bubani, 1806–1888

Buc'hoz = Pierre Joseph Buc'hoz, 1731–1807

Buchanan = John Buchanan, 1819–1898

Buch.-Ham. = Francis Buchanan-Hamilton, 1762–1829

Buchenau = Franz Georg Philipp Buchenau, 1831–1906

Buchet = Samuel Buchet, 1875–1956

Buchheim = Arno Fritz Günther Buchheim, 1924–

J. Buchholz = John Theodore Buchholz, 1888–1951

Buckland = William Buckland, 1784–1856

Buckley = Samuel Botsford Buckley, 1809–1884

H. Buek = Heinrich Wilhelm Buek, 1796–1878

Buhse = Friedrich Alexander Buhse, 1821–1898

Buining = Albert Frederik Hendrik Buining, 1901–1976

Buist = Robert Buist, 1805–1880

Bukasov = Sergej (Sergei) Mikhailovich Bukasov, 1891–1983

W. Bull = William Bull, 1828–1902

Bull. = Jean Baptiste François ('Pierre') Bulliard, 1752–1793

Bullock = Arthur Allman Bullock, 1906–1980

Bunge = Alexander Andrejewitsch (Aleksandr Andreevic) Bunge, 1803–1890

G.S. Bunting = George Sydney Bunting, 1927–

Burb. = Frederick William Thomas Burbidge, 1847–1905

Burch. = William John Burchell, 1781–1863

Burck = William Burck, 1848–1910

Burdet = Hervé Maurice Burdet, 1939–

Bureau = Louis Édouard Bureau, 1830–1918

E.S. Burgess = Edward Sandford Burgess, 1855–1928

Burgsd. = Friedrich August Ludwig von Burgsdorff, 1747–1802

Burkart = Arturo Erhardo (Erardo) Burkart, 1906–1975

Burkill = Isaac Henry Burkill, 1870–1965

Burkwood = A. Burkwood, fl. 1929

Burm. = Johannes Burman, 1707–1779

Burm. f. = Nicolaas Laurens (Nicolaus Laurent) Burman, 1733–1793

Burnat = Émile Burnat, 1828–1920

Burret = (Maximilian) Karl Ewald Burret, 1883–1964

B.L. Burtt = Brian Laurence ('Bill') Burtt, 1913–

Burtt Davy = Joseph Burtt Davy, 1870–1940

= Frédéric Burvenich, 1857–1917

Bury = Priscilla Susan Bury, fl. 1831–1837

N. Busch = Nicolai Adolfowitsch (Nikolaj Adolfovich) Busch, 1869–1941

Buse = Lodewijk Hendrik Buse, 1819–1888

Buser = Robert Buser, 1857–1931

Bush = Benjamin Franklin Bush, 1858–1937

B.T. Butler = Bertram Theodore Butler, 1872–1958

Butters = Frederick King Butters, 1878-1945
Buttler = Karl Peter Buttler, 1942–
Buxb. = Franz Buxbaum, 1900-1979
Buxton = Richard Buxton, 1786-1865
Byles = Ronald Stewart Byles, fl. 1957
Cabrera = Angel Lulio Cabrera, 1908-1999
Cajander = Aimo Kaarlo Cajander, 1879-1943
Caldas = Francisco José de Caldas, 1771-1816
Calder = James (Jim) Alexander Calder, 1915-1990
C.E. Calderón = Cleofé E. Calderón, 1940?–
Calderón = Graciela Calderón de Rzedowski, 1931–
Caldesi = Lodovico (Luigi) Caldesi, 1821-1884
Callier = Alfons S. Callier, 1866-1927
Calloni = Silvio Calloni, 1851-1931
Camargo = Felisberto Cardoso de Camargo, 1896-1943
Cambage = Richard Hind Cambage, 1859-1928
Cambess. = Jacques Cambessèdes, 1799-1863
Campd. = Francisco (François) Campderá, 1793-1862
A. Camus = Aimée Antoinette Camus, 1879-1965
E.G. Camus = Edmond Gustave Camus, 1852-1915
A. DC. = Alphonse Louis Pierre Pyramus de Candolle, 1806-1893
C. DC. = Anne Casimir Pyramus de Candolle, 1836-1918
DC. = Augustin Pyramus de Candolle, 1778-1841
Cannon = John Francis Michael Cannon, 1930–
Capelli = Carlo Matteo Capelli, 1763-1831
Cárdenas = Martin Cárdenas Hermosa, 1899-1973
Cardot = Jules Cardot, 1860-1934
Carey = William Carey, 1761-1834
Cariot = Antoine Cariot, 1820-1883
Carr = Cedric Errol Carr, 1892-1936
Carretero = José Luis Carretero, 1941–
Carrière = Élie Abel Carrière, 1818-1896
Carruth. = William Carruthers, 1830-1922
W.R. Carter = William R. Carter, fl. 1921
Caruel = Théodore (Teodoro) Caruel, 1830-1898
Casar. = Giovanni Casaretto, 1812-1879

Casp. = Johann Xaver Robert Caspary, 1818-1887
Casper = Siegfried Jost Casper, 1929–
Cass. = Alexandre Henri Gabriel de Cassini, 1781-1832
Castagne = Jean Louis Martin Castagne, 1785-1858
Castañeda = Marcelino Castañeda y Nuñez de Caceres, fl. 1941-54
A. Cast. = Alberto Castellanos, 1896-1968
Castetter = Edward Franklin Castetter, 1896-1978
Castigl. = Luigi Gomes Castiglioni, 1757-1832
L. Castle = L. Castle, fl. 1890
Cav. = Antonio José(Joseph) Cavanilles, 1745-1804
Cavara = Fridiano Cavara, 1857-1929
Cavill. = François Georges Cavillier, 1868-1953
Cedeño-Mald. = José Arnaldo Cedeño-Maldonado, 1970–
Čelak. = Ladislav Josef Celakovsky, 1834-1902
Cels = Jacques Philippe Martin Cels, 1743-1806
Cerv. = Vicente (Vincente) de Cervantes, 1755-1829
Ces. = Vincenzo di Cesati, 1806-1883
Chabanne = Charles Gabriel Chabanne, 1862-1906
Chabaud = Benjamin Chabaud, 1833-1915
Chabert = Jean Baptiste Alfred Chabert, 1836-1916
P. Chabert = Pierre Chabert, 1796-1867
Chaix = Dominique, Chaix, 1730-1799
Chamb. = Charles Joseph Chamberlain, 1863-1943
D.F. Chamb. = David Franklin Chamberlain, 1941–
Cham. = Ludolf Karl Adelbert von (Louis Charles Adelaïde) Chamisso (Chamisseau de Boncourt), 1781-1838
Champ. = John George Champion, 1815-1854
Chanc. = Lucien Chancerel, 1858–
M.C. Chang = Mei Chen Chang, 1933–
S.Y. Chang = Shao Yao Chang, fl. 1963
T.B. Chao = Tien Bang (Bung) Chao, fl. 1981
Chapm. = Alvin (Alvan) Wentworth Chapman, 1809-1899
M.W. Chase = Mark Wayne Chase, 1951–
Chase = Mary Agnes Chase, 1869-1963
Châtel. = Jean Jacques Châtelain, 1736-1822

Chater = Arthur Oliver Chater, 1933–
Chatterjee = Debabarta Chatterjee, 1911–1960
Chaub. = Louis Athanase (Anastase) Chaubard, 1781–1854
Chav. = Édouard Louis Chavannes, 1805–1861
Chaz. = Laurent Marie Chazelles de Prizy, fl. 1790
Cheek = Martin Roy Cheek, 1960–
Cheel = Edwin Cheel, 1872–1951
Cheeseman = Thomas Frederic Cheeseman, 1845–1923
Cheesman = Ernest Entwisle Cheesman, 1888–
B.L. Chen = Bao Liang Chen, 1944–1991
S.J. Chen = Sen Jen Chen, 1933–
S.C. Chen = Sing Chi Chen, 1931–
X.L. Chen = Xin Lu Chen, fl. 1989
Z.H. Chen = Zheng Hai Chen, fl. 1989
W.C. Cheng = Wan Chun Cheng, 1903–1983
A. Chev. = Auguste Jean Baptiste Chevalier, 1873–1956
Chevall. = François Fulgis Chevallier, 1796–1840
Chew = Wee-Lek Chew, 1932–
Ching = Ren Chang Ching, 1899–1986
Chiov. = Emilio Chiovenda, 1871–1941
Chitt. = Frederick James Chittenden, 1873–1950
P.L. Chiu = Pao Ling Chiu, fl. 1974
Chmel. = H. Chmelitschek, 1948–
Chodat = Robert Hippolyte Chodat, 1865–1934
Choisy = Jacques Denys (Denis) Choisy, 1799–1859
Chouard = Pierre Chouard, 1903–1983
Choux = Pierre Choux, 1890–1983
H.J. Chowdhery = Harsh J. Chowdhery, 1949–
H. Christ = Hermann Konrad Heinrich Christ, 1833–1933
C. Chr. = Carl Frederik Albert Christensen, 1872–1942
K.I. Chr. = Knud Ib Christensen, 1955–
Christm. = Gottlieb Friedrich Christmann, 1752–1836
Chrtek = Jindrich Chrtek, 1930–
Chrtková = Anna Chrtková-...ertová, 1930–
Chun = Woon Young (Huan Yung) Chun (Ch'en), 1890–1971
T.H. Chung = Tai Hyun Chung, 1882–1971
Cif. = Raffaele Ciferri, 1897–1964
Cirillo = Domenico Maria Leone Cirillo, 1739–1799

Clairv. = Joseph Philippe de Clairville, 1742–1830
A.R. Clapham = Arthur Roy Clapham, 1904–1990
Clarion = Jacques, Clarion, 1776–1844
C.B. Clarke = Charles Baron Clarke, 1832–1906
E.D. Clarke = Edward Daniel Clarke, 1769–1822
Clausen = Pedro Cláudio Dinamarquez (Peter) Clausen, 1855–
R.T. Clausen = Robert Theodore Clausen, 1911–1981
Clayberg = Carl Dudley Clayberg, 1931–
Clemente = Simón de Roxas (Rojas) Clemente y Rubio, 1777–1827
Clementi = Giuseppe C. Clementi, 1812–1873
Clem. = Frederick Edward Clements, 1874–1945
Clokey = Ira Waddell Clokey, 1878–1950
Clos = Dominique Clos, 1821–1908
Closon = Jules Closon, fl. 1897
Clover = Elzada Urseba Clover, 1897–1980
Coaz = Johann Wilhelm Fortunat Coaz, 1822–1918
Cochet = Pierre Charles Marie Cochet, 1866–1936
Cockayne = Leonard C. Cockayne, 1855–1934
Cockerell = Theodore Dru Alison Cockerell, 1866–1948
Codd = Leslie Edward Wostall Codd, 1908–1999
Coe = Ernest F. Coe, 1866–1951
Coëm. = Henri Eugène Lucien Gaëtan Coëmans, 1825–1871
Cogn. = Célestin Alfred Cogniaux, 1841–1916
Cohen-Stuart = Combertus Pieter Cohen-Stuart, 1889–1945
Coincy = Auguste Henri Cornut de Coincy, 1837–1903
Coker = William Chambers Coker, 1872–1953
D.T. Cole = Desmond Thorne Cole, 1922–
Colebr. = Henry Thomas Colebrooke, 1765–1837
Coleman = William Higgins Coleman, 1816?–1863
Colenso = (John) William Colenso, 1811–1899
Colla = Luigi (Aloysius) Colla, 1766–1848
Collad. = Louis Théodore Frederic Colladon, 1792–1862

Collett = Henry Collett, 1836–1901
Coltm.- Rog. = Charles Coltman Rogers,
  1854–1929
Colville = Colville, fl. 1958
H.F. Comber = Harold Frederick Comber,
  1897–1969
Comber = Thomas Comber, 1837–1902
Comes = Orazio Comes, 1848–1923
Comm. = Philibert Commerson, 1727–1773
Compton = Robert Harold Compton,
  1886–1979
Conert = Hans Joachim Conert, 1929–
Console = Michelangelo Console,
  1812–1897
Constance = Lincoln Constance, 1909–2001
Coode = Mark James Elgar Coode, 1937–
C.D.K. Cook = Christopher David Kentish
  Cook, 1933–
O.F. Cook = Orator Fuller Cook, 1867–1949
Coombes = Allen J. Coombes, fl. 1980
Coombs = Frank Andrew Coombs,
  1877–1964
J.G. Cooper = James Graham Cooper,
  1830–1902
R.E. Cooper = Roland Edgar Cooper,
  1890–1962
Copel. = Edwin Bingham Copeland,
  1873–1964
Corb. = François Mathieu Louis Corbière,
  1850–1941
Corner = Edred John Henry Corner,
  1906–1996
Cornu = Marie Maxime Cornu, 1843–1901
Corrêa = José Francisco Corrêa da Serra,
  1751–1823
Correll = Donovan Stewart Correll,
  1908–1983
Correns = Carl Franz Joseph Erich Correns,
  1864–1933
Correvon = Louis Henri Correvon,
  1854–1939
Cortés = Santiago Cortés, 1854–1924
Cory = Victor Louis Cory, 1880–1964
Coss. = Ernest Saint-Charles Cosson,
  1819–1889
Costa = Antonio Cipriano Costa y Cuxart,
  1817–1886
Costantin = Julien Noël Costantin,
  1857–1936
H.J. Coste = Hippolyte Jacques Coste,
  1858–1924
Cotton = Arthur Disbrowe Cotton,
  1879–1962
J.M. Coult. = John Merle Coulter,
  1851–1928

Coult. = Thomas Coulter, 1793–1843
Court = Arthur Bertram Court, 1927–
Courtois = Richard Joseph Courtois,
  1806–1835
Cout. = António Xavier Pereira Coutinho,
  1851–1939
Coutts = John Coutts, 1872–1952
Covas = Guillermo Covas, 1915–1995
Coville = Frederick Vernon Coville,
  1867–1937
Cowan = John Macqueen Cowan,
  1892–1960
Cox = Euan Hillhouse Methven Cox,
  1893–1977
Craib = William Grant Craib, 1882–1933
R.T. Craig = Robert Theodore Craig,
  1902–1986
Cramer = Johann Christian Cramer,
  fl. 1803
Crantz = Heinrich Johann Nepomuk von
  Crantz, 1722–1799
Cremers = Georges Cremers, 1936–
Crép. = François Crépin, 1830–1903
P.J. Cribb = Phillip James Cribb, 1946–
Crins = William J. Crins, 1955–
Croat = Thomas Bernard Croat, 1938–
Croizat = Léon Camille Marius Croizat,
  1894–1982
Cronquist = Arthur John Cronquist,
  1919–1992
H.B. Croom = Hardy Bryan Croom,
  1797–1837
Croucher = George Croucher, 1833–1905
Crueg. = Hermann Crueger, 1818–1864
Crusio = Wim Crusio, fl. 1979
Cuatrec. = José Cuatrecasas Arumi,
  1903–1996
Cufod. = Georg Cufodontis, 1896–1974
Cullen = James Cullen, 1936–
Cullmann = Willy (Wilhelm) Cullmann,
  1905–1992
A. Cunn. = Allan Cunningham, 1791–1839
R. Cunn. = Richard Cunningham,
  1793–1835
Curran = Mary Katherine Curran,
  1844–1920
M.A. Curtis = Moses Ashley Curtis,
  1808–1872
Curtis = William Curtis, 1746–1799
Cusson = Pierre Cusson, 1727–1783
Custer = Jakob Gottlieb Custer, 1789–1850
Czeczott = Hanna Czeczott, 1888–1982
Czern. = Vassilii Matveievitch Czernajew,
  1796–1871
D'Arcy = William Gerald D'Arcy, 1931–1999

d'**Urv.** = Jules Sébastien César Dumont
d'Urville, 1790–1842
Däniker = Albert Ulrich Däniker, 1894–1957
O.C. Dahl = Ove Christian Dahl, 1862–1940
Dahlgren = Bror Eric Dahlgren, 1877–1961
R. Dahlgren = Rolf Martin Theodor
Dahlgren, 1932–1987
Dahlst. = Gustav Adolf Hugo Dahlstedt,
1856–1934
Dahmen = Ralf Dahmen, fl. 1998
Dalla Torre = Karl (Carl) Wilhelm Dalla
Torre von Thurnberg-Sternhoff,
1850–1928
Dallim. = William Dallimore, 1871–1959
Dalström = Stig Dalström, fl. 1983
Dalzell = Nicol (Nicolas) Alexander
Dalzell, 1817–1878
Dalziel = John McEwen Dalziel, 1872–1948
Damboldt = Jürgen Damboldt, 1937–1978
Dammann = Hildegard Dammann, 1900–
Dammer = Carl Lebrecht Udo Dammer,
1860–1920
Dams = Erich Dams, fl. 1905
Dandy = James Elgar Dandy, 1903–1976
Danert = Siegfried Danert, 1926–1973
P. Daniel = Pitchai Daniel, 1943–
Daniell = William Freeman Daniell,
1817–1865
Danser = Benedictus Hubertus Danser,
1891–1943
C.D. Darl. = Cyril Dean Darlington,
1903–1981
Darracq = Ulysse Darracq, 1798–1872
Darthuis = Darthuis
Daubeny = Charles Giles Bridle Daubeny,
1795–1867
Davidian = Hagop Haroutune Davidian,
1907–2003
Davidson = Anstruther Davidson, 1860–1932
Davies = Hugh Davies, 1739–1821
P.H. Davis = Peter Hadland Davis,
1918–1992
E.W. Davis = E. Wade Davis, fl. 1983
Dawe = Morley Thomas Dawe, 1880–1943
E.Y. Dawson = Elmer Yale Dawson,
1918–1966
J. Day = John Day, 1824–1888
de Boer = Hendrik Wijbrand de Boer,
1885–1970
de Haas = Th. de Haas, 1888–
De Hurst = De Hurst
de Jonch. = Gerardus Johannes de
Joncheere, 1910–1988
P.C. De Jong = Petrus (Piet) Cornelis De
Jong, 1938–

De Jonghe = Jean De Jonghe, 1804–1876
De la Soie = Gaspard Abdon De la Soie,
1818–1877
de Lannoy = De Lannoy, fl. 1863
de Laub. = David John de Laubenfels,
1925–
De Not. = Giuseppe(Josephus) De Notaris,
1805–1877
De Smet = Louis De Smet, 1813–1887
de Vos = Cornelis de Vos, 1806–1895
de Vries = Hugo de Vries, 1848–1935
de Vriese = Willem Hendrik de Vriese,
1806–1862
W.J. de Wilde = Willem Jan Jacobus
Oswald de Wilde, 1936–
De Wild. = Émile Auguste(e) Joseph De
Wildeman, 1866–1947
de Wit = Hendrik Cornelis Dirk de Wit,
1909–1999
H. Deane = Henry Deane, 1847–1924
Debeaux = Jean Odon Debeaux, 1826–1910
Decne. = Joseph Decaisne, 1807–1882
Deflers = M.A. Deflers, fl. 1894
Degen = Árpád von Degen, 1866–1934
O. Deg. = Otto Degener, 1899–1988
Degl. = Jean Vincent Yves Degland,
1773–1841
Dehnh. = Friedrich Dehnhardt, 1787–1870
Dekapr. = Leonard Leonardovicz
Dekaprelevicz, 1886–
Delarbre = Antoine Delarbre, 1724–1807
D. Delaroche = Daniel Delaroche,
1743–1813
F. Delaroche = François Delaroche,
1780–1813
Delavay = Pierre Jean Marie Delavay,
1834–1895
Deless. = Jules Paul Benjamin Delessert,
1773–1847
Deleuil = J.B.A. Deleuil, fl. 1874
Delile = Alire Raffeneau Delile, 1778–1850
C.Y. Deng = Chao Yi Deng, 1960–
D.L. Denham = Dale Lee Denham, 1922–
Denham = Dixon Denham, 1786–1828
Denis = Marcel Denis, 1897–1929
Dennst. = August Wilhelm Dennstedt,
1776–1826
Des Moul. = Charles Robert Alexandre de
Gaux Des Moulins, 1798–1875
Desc. = Bernard M. Descoings, 1931–
Déségl. = Pierre Alfred Déséglise,
1823–1883
Desf. = René Louiche Desfontaines,
1750–1833
Desmarais = Yves Desmarais, 1918–

Desp. = Jean Baptiste Réné Pouppé
  Desportes, 1704–1748
N.H.F. Desp. = Narcisse Henri François
  Desportes, 1776–1856
Desr. = Louis Auguste Joseph
  Desrousseaux, 1753–1838
Desv. = Auguste Niçaise Desvaux,
  1784–1856
Devansaye = Alphonse de la Devansaye,
  1845–1900
Dewar = Daniel Dewar,c. 1860–1905
Dickoré = Wolf Bernhard Dickoré, 1959–
G.F. Dicks. = George Frederick Dickson,
  fl. 1839
Didr. = Didrik Ferdinand Didrichsen,
  1814–1887
Dieck = Georg Dieck, 1847–1925
Diels = Friedrich Ludwig Emil Diels,
  1874–1945
Dierb. = Johann Heinrich Dierbach,
  1788–1845
A. Dietr. = Albert Gottfried Dietrich,
  1795–1856
D. Dietr. = David Nathaniel Friedrich
  Dietrich, 1799–1888
F. Dietr. = Friedrich Gottlieb Dietrich,
  1768–1850
Dill. = Johann Jacob Dillenius, 1684–1747
Dimpflm. = Dimpflmeier
B.Y. Ding = Bing Yang Ding, 1953–
Dinter = Moritz Kurt Dinter, 1868–1945
Dippel = Leopold Dippel, 1827–1914
Dittrich = Manfred Dittrich, 1934–
Dode = Louis-Albert Dode, 1875–1945
Dodson = Calaway H. Dodson, 1928–
Döll = Johann(es) Christoph (Christian)
  Döll, 1808–1885
Dölz = Bruno Doelz, 1906–1945
Dörfl. = Ignaz Dörfler, 1866–1950
Dolliner = Georg Dolliner, 1794–1872
Dombey = Joseph Dombey, 1742–1796
Dombrain = Henry Honeywood Dombrain,
  1818–1905
Domin = Karel Domin, 1882–1953
Domokos = János Domokos, 1904–1978
D. Don = David Don, 1799–1841
G. Don = George Don, 1798–1856
Don = George Don, 1764–1814
P.N. Don = Patrick Neill Don, 1806–1876
Donald = John Donald Donald, 1923–1996
Donn = James Donn, 1758–1813
Donn. Sm. = John Donnell Smith,
  1829–1928
Door. = Simon Godfried Albert Doorenbos,
  1891–1980

Dostál = Josef Dostál, 1903–1999
Douglas = David Douglas, 1799–1834
Drake = Emmanuel Drake del Castillo,
  1855–1904
J. Dransf. = John Dransfield, 1945–
Drapiez = Pierre Auguste Joseph Drapiez,
  1778–1856
Drège = Jean François (Johann Franz)
  Drège, 1794–1881
Drejer = Solomon(Salomon) Thomas
  Nicolai Drejer, 1813–1842
Drenth = Engbert Drenth, 1945–
Dress = William John Dress, 1918–
Dressler = Robert Louis Dressler, 1927–
Druce = George Claridge Druce, 1850–1932
Drude = Carl Georg Oscar Drude,
  1852–1933
J.L. Drumm. = James Lawson Drummond,
  1783–1853
J.R. Drumm. = James Ramsay Drummond,
  1851–1921
Dryand. = Jonas Carlsson Dryander,
  1748–1810
Du Roi = Johann Philipp Du Roi, 1741–1785
Du Tour = Du Tour de Salvert, fl. 1803–1815
Dubard = Marcel Marie Maurice Dubard,
  1873–1914
Dubois = François Noel Alexandre Dubois,
  1752–1824
Duby = Jean Étienne Duby (de Steiger),
  1798–1885
Duch. = Pierre-Étienne-Simon Duchartre,
  1811–1894
Duchesne = Antoine Nicolas Duchesne,
  1747–1827
Ducke = Walter Adolpho Ducke, 1876–1959
Ducros = Ducros de St. Germain, fl. 1828
T.R. Dudley = Theodore ('Ted') Robert
  Dudley, 1936–1994
Düben = Magnus Wilhelm von Düben,
  1814–1845
Düll = Ruprecht Peter Georg Düll, 1931
  (nicht 1939)-
Dufour = Jean-Marie Léon Dufour,
  1780–1865
Dufr. = Pierre Dufresne, 1786–1836
Dugand = Armando Dugand, 1906–1971
Duhamel = Henri Louis Duhamel du
  Monceau, 1700–1782
Dulac = Joseph Dulac, 1827–1897
Dum.-Cours. = George(s) Louis Marie
  Dumont de Courset, 1746–1824
Dumort. = Barthélemy Charles Joseph
  Dumortier, 1797–1878
Dunal = Michel Félix Dunal, 1789–1856

Duncan = James Duncan, 1802–1876
Dunn = Stephen Troyte Dunn, 1868–1938
Dunst. = Galfried Clement Keyworth
Dunsterville, 1905–1988
A.E. Dupont = A.E. Dupont
Durand = Elias (Elie) Magliore Durand,
1794–1873
T. Durand = Théophile Alexis Durand,
1855–1912
Durande = Jean François Durande,
1732–1794
Durazz. = Antonio Durazzini, fl. 1772
Durieu = Michel Charles Durieu de
Maisonneuve, 1796–1878
Dusén = Per Karl Hjalmar Dusén,
1855–1926
Duthie = John Firminger Duthie, 1845–1922
Duval = Henri Auguste Duval, 1777–1814
Dvoráková = Marie Dvoráková, 1940–
R.A. Dyer = Robert Allen Dyer, 1900–1987
Dyer = William Turner Thiselton
(Thistleton) Dyer, 1843–1928
Dykes = William Rickatson Dykes, 1877–
1925
Dylis = Nikolai Vladislavovich Dylis,
1915–1985
E.A. Eames = Edward Ashley Eames, 1872–
Eastw. = Alice Eastwood, 1859–1953
Eaton = Amos Eaton, 1776–1842
D.C. Eaton = Daniel Cady Eaton, 1834–1895
C.H. Eberm. = Carl Heinrich Ebermaier,
1802–1870
Eckenw. = James E. Eckenwalder, 1949–
Eckl. = Christian Friedrich (Frederik)
Ecklon, 1795–1868
Edgew. = Michael Pakenham Edgeworth,
1812–1881
Edmonds = Jennifer M. Edmonds, fl.
1971–86
J.R. Edm. = John Richard Edmondson,
1948–
Edmondston = Thomas Edmondston,
1825–1846
Edwards = Sydenham Teast Edwards,
1769–1819
Eggert = Heinrich Karl Daniel Eggert,
1841–1904
Eggl. = Willard Webster Eggleston,
1863–1935
Eggli = Urs Eggli, 1959–
T.V. Egorova = Tatjana V. Egorova, 1930–
C. Ehrenb. = Carl August Ehrenberg,
1801–1849
Ehrenb. = Christian Gottfried Ehrenberg,
1795–1876

Ehrend. = Friedrich Ehrendorfer, 1927–
Ehrh. = Jakob Friedrich Ehrhart, 1742–1795
Eichlam = Friedrich (Federico) Eichlam,
–1911
Eichler = August Wilhelm Eichler,
1839–1887
Eig = Alexander Eig, 1894–1938
Ekman = Erik Leonard Ekman, 1883–1931
T.S. Elias = Thomas Sam Elias, 1942–
Elliott = Stephen Elliott, 1771–1830
J. Ellis = John Ellis, 1710–1776
R.P. Ellis = Roger Pearson Ellis, 1944–
Elwert = Johann Caspar Philipp Elwert,
1760–1827
Elwes = Henry John Elwes, 1846–1922
Emb. = Louis Marie Emberger, 1897–1969
Endl. = Stephan Friedrich Ladislaus
Endlicher, 1804–1849
P.K. Endress = Peter Karl Endress, 1942–
R. Engel = Roger Engel, 1923–
Engelm. = Georg (George) Engelmann,
1809–1884
Engl. = Heinrich Gustav Adolf Engler,
1844–1930
English = Carl Schurz English, 1904–
Epling = Carl Clawson Epling, 1894–1968
Epple = Paul Epple, fl. 1951
Erhardt = Walter Erhardt, 1952–
Escal. = Manuel G. Escalante, fl. 1946
Eschsch. = Johann Friedrich Gustav von
Eschscholtz, 1793–1831
Eshbaugh = William Hardy Eshbaugh, 1936–
Espinosa = Marcial Ramón Espinosa
Bustos, 1874–1959
Esteves = Eddie Esteves Pereira, 1939–
et. al. = and others
Etl. = Andreas Ernst Etlinger, fl. 1777
M.S. Evans = Maurice Smethurst Evans,
1854–1920
W.H. Evans = Walter Harrison Evans,
1863–1941
W.E. Evans = William Edgar Evans,
1882–1963
Everett = Thomas Henry Everett, 1903–
Evers = Georg Evers, 1837–1916
C.M. Evrard = Charles Marie Evrard, 1926–
Exell = Arthur Wallis Exell, 1901–1993
Eyma = Pierre Joseph Eyma, 1903–1945
Fabr. = Philipp Conrad Fabricius, 1714–1774
Facchini = Francesco Facchini, 1788–1852
Faden = Robert Bruce Faden, 1942–
Falc. = Hugh Falconer, 1808–1865
Falkenb. = Paul Falkenberg, 1848–1925
W.P. Fang = Wen Pei Fang, 1899–1983
Farjon = Aljos K. Farjon, 1946–

Farr = Edith May Farr, 1864–1956
Farrer = Reginald John Farrer, 1880–1920
Farw. = Oliver Atkins Farwell, 1867–1944
Fassett = Norman Carter Fassett, 1900–1954
Favrat = Louis Favrat, 1827–1893
Fawc. = William Fawcett, 1851–1926
B. Fearn = Brian Fearn, 1937–
Fedde = Friedrich Karl Georg Fedde, 1873–1942
Fed. = Andrej Aleksandrovich Fedorov, 1909–1987
B. Fedtsch. = Boris Alekseevic (Alexeevich) Fedtschenko, 1872–1947
O. Fedtsch. = Olga Aleksandrovna Fedtschenko, 1845–1921
Fée = Antoine Laurent Apollinaire Fée, 1789–1874
Feer = Heinrich (Henri) Feer, 1857–1892
Fenai = Fenai, fl. 1880
Fenzl = Eduard Fenzl, 1808–1879
A.R. Ferguson = Allan Ross Ferguson, 1943–
I.K. Ferguson = Ian Keith Ferguson, 1938–
Fernald = Merritt Lyndon Fernald, 1873–1950
A. Fern. = Abílio Fernandes, 1906–1994
Fern. Casas = Francisco Javier Fernández Casas, 1945–
Fern.-Vill. = Celestino Fernández-Villar, 1838–1907
Fiala = Franz Fiala, 1861–1898
Fieber = Franz Xaver Fieber, 1807–1872
Fielding = Henry Borron Fielding, 1805–1851
Figert = Ernst Figert, 1848–1925
Finet = Achille Eugène Finet, 1863–1913
Fingerh. = Carl Anton Fingerhuth, 1802–1876
Fintelm. = Gustav Adolf Fintelmann, 1803–1871
Fiori = Adriano Fiori, 1865–1950
C.E.C. Fisch. = Cecil Ernest Claude Fischer, 1874–1950
Eb. Fisch. = Eberhard Fischer, 1961–
Fisch. = Friedrich Ernst Ludwig von (Fedor Bogdanovic) Fischer, 1782–1854
G. Fisch. = Georg Fischer, 1844–1941
M. Fisch. = M. Fischer, fl. 1986
M.A. Fisch. = Manfred Adalbert Fischer, 1942–
Fisch.-Oost. = Carl von Fischer-Ooster, 1807–1875
Fitschen = Jost Fitschen, 1869–1947
Fittkau = Hans W. Fittkau, fl. 1971

Fitzg. = Robert Desmond (David) Fitzgerald, 1830–1892
Fitzh. = Wyndham Fitzherbert, –1916
Z. Fleisch. = Zdenék Fleischer, 1905–1978
Fleming = John Fleming, 1747–1829
H.R. Fletcher = Harold Roy Fletcher, 1907–1978
Flinck = Karl Evert Flinck, 1915–
Flod. = Björn Gustaf Oscar Floderus, 1867–1941
Flörke = Heinrich Gustav Flörke, 1764–1835
Florin = Carl Rudolf Florin, 1894–1965
Flueck. = Friedrich August Flueckiger, 1828–1894
Flüggé = Johannes Flüggé, 1775–1816
Focke = Wilhelm Olbers Focke, 1834–1922
C.F. Först. = Carl Friedrich Förster, fl. 1846
Fomin = Aleksandr Vasilievich Fomin, 1869–1935
Font Quer = Pio(Pius) Font i Quer, 1888–1964
F.B. Forbes = Francis Blackwell Forbes, 1839–1908
J. Forbes = James Forbes, 1773–1861
Ford = Neridah Clifton Ford, 1926–
Forkel = Forkel, fl. from 1848
Formánek = Eduard Formánek, 1845–1900
Forrest = George Forrest, 1873–1932
Forselles = Jacob Henrik af Forselles, 1785–1855
Forssk. = Pehr (Peter) Forsskål, 1732–1763
G. Forst. = Johann Georg Adam Forster, 1754–1794
J.R. Forst. = Johann Reinhold Forster, 1729–1798
P.I. Forst. = Paul Irwin Forster, 1961–
Fortune = Robert Fortune, 1812–1880
Fosberg = Francis Raymond Fosberg, 1908–1993
Foster = Michael Foster, 1836–1907
M.B. Foster = Mulford Bateman Foster, 1888–1978
R.C. Foster = Robert Crichton Foster, 1904–1986
R.A. Foster = Robert A. Foster, publ. 1968
Fotsch = Karl Albert Fotsch, –1940?
Foucaud = Julien Foucaud, 1847–1904
Foug. = Auguste Denis Fougeroux de Bondaroy, 1732–1789
Fourc. = Georges Henri Fourcade, 1866–1948
E. Fourn. = Eugène Pierre Nicolas Fournier, 1834–1884
P. Fourn. = Paul Victor Fournier, 1877–1964
Fourr. = Jules Pierre Fourreau, 1844–1871

Foxw. = Frederick William Foxworthy,
1877–1950
Fraas = Carl Nikolaus Fraas, 1810–1875
Frahm = G. Frahm, fl. 1898
Francey = Pierre Francey, fl. 1933
Franch. = Adrien René Franchet,
1834–1900
Franco = Joao Manuel Antonio do Amaral
Franco, 1921–
G. Frank = Gerhard R.W. Frank,
fl. 1963–1990
Frank = Joseph C. Frank, 1782–1835
Fraser = John Fraser, 1750–1811
Fraser-Jenk. = Christopher Roy Fraser-
Jenkins, 1948–
G.F. Freeman = George Fouché Freeman,
1876–1930
Frém. = John Charles Frémont, 1813–1890
Fresen. = Johann Baptist Georg Wolfgang
Fresenius, 1808–1866
Freyer = Heinrich Freyer, 1802–1866
Freyn = Josef Franz Freyn, 1845–1903
Frič = Alberto Vojtech Fric, 1882–1944
Friedlein = Johann Jakob Gottlieb
Friedlein, 1784–1836
F. Friedmann = F. Friedmann, 1941–
H. Friedrich = Heimo Friedrich, 1911–1987
R.E. Fr. = (Klas) Robert Elias Fries,
1876–1966
Fr. = Elias Magnus Fries, 1794–1878
Th. Fr. = Theodor (Thore) Magnus Fries,
1832–1913
Friis = Ib Friis, 1945–
Fritsch = Karl Fritsch, 1864–1934
Friv. = Imre (Emmerich) Friváldszky von
Friváld, 1799–1870
Frodin = David Gamman Frodin, 1940–
Froebel = Karl Otto Froebel, 1844–1906
Fröd. = Harald August Fröderström,
1876–1944
A. Fröhner = Albrecht Fröhner, fl. 1897
Froel. = Joseph Aloys von Froelich,
1766–1841
Frost = Charles Christopher Frost,
1805–1880
Fruwirth = Karl (Carl) Fruwirth, 1862–1930
Fryxell = Paul Arnold Fryxell, 1927–
L.K. Fu = Li Kuo Fu, 1934–
S.H. Fu = Shu Hsia Fu, 1916–1986
H.P. Fuchs = Hans Peter Fuchs, 1928–1999
Fürnr. = August Emanuel Fürnrohr,
1804–1861
N. Fujita = Noboru Fujita, 1946–
Funck = Heinrich Christian Funck,
1771–1839

Furtado = Caetano Xavier dos Remedios
Furtado, 1897–1980
Fuss = Johann Mihály (Michael) Fuss,
1814–1883
Gable = Joseph Benson Gable, 1886–1972
Gabrielson = Ira Noel Gabrielson,
1889–1977
C.F. Gaertn. = Carl (Karl) Friedrich von
Gaertner, 1772–1850
Gaertn. = Joseph Gaertner, 1732–1791
G. Gaertn. = Gottfried Gaertner, 1754–1825
Gagnebin = Abraham Gagnebin, 1707–1800
Gagnep. = François Gagnepain, 1866–1952
Gaill. = Charles Gaillardot, 1814–1883
Galeotti = Henri Guillaume Galeotti,
1814–1858
Galpin = Ernest Edward Galpin, 1858–1941
Gamble = James Sykes Gamble, 1847–1925
Gams = Helmut Gams, 1893–1976
Gandhi = Kancheepuram N. Gandhi, 1948–
Gand. = Jean Michel Gandoger, 1850–1926
Ganesch. = Sergej Sergejewitsch
Ganeschin, 1879–1930
Garay = Leslie (László) Andrew Garay,
1924–
García-Mend. = Abisai García-Mendoza,
1955–
Garcke = Christian August Friedrich
Garcke, 1819–1904
J. Garden = Joy Garden, 1923–
C.A. Gardner = Charles Austin Gardner,
1896–1970
Gardner = George Gardner, 1812–1849
Garnier = Max Garnier, fl. 1895–1918
Gasp. = Guglielmo Gasparrini, 1804–1866
Gaterau = Jean-Pierre Gaterau, 1763–1794
H.E. Gates = Howard Elliott Gates,
1895–1957
Gatt. = Augustin Gattinger, 1825–1903
Gaudich. = Charles Gaudichaud-Beaupré,
1789–1854
Gaudin = Jean François Aimée Gottlieb
Philippe Gaudin, 1766–1833
Gaussen = Henri Marcel Gaussen,
1891–1981
Gay = Claude Gay, 1800–1873
J. Gay = Jacques Étienne Gay, 1786–1864
Gáyer = Gyula(Julius) Gáyer, 1883–1932
Geisenh. = Franz Adolf Ludwig (Louis)
Geisenheyner, 1841–1926
Gentil = Ambroise Gentil, 1842–1929
A.H. Gentry = Alwyn Howard Gentry,
1945–1993
Gentry = Howard Scott Gentry, 1903–1993
P.A. Genty = André Paul Genty, 1861–1955

A.S. George = Alexander Segger George, 1939–
Georgi = Johann Gottlieb Georgi, 1729–1802
Gerbaulet = Maike Gerbaulet, publ. um 1994
Gerbeaux = Gerbeaux
G. Gerlach = Günter Gerlach, fl. 1987
N. Gerloff = Norbert Gerloff, 1947–
Germ. = Jacques Nicolas Ernest Germain de Saint-Pierre, 1814–1882
Gérôme = Joseph Gérôme, 1863–1928
Gerrard = William Tyrer Gerrard, –1866
Gerstl. = Lorenz Gerstlauer, 1853–1949
Ghiesbr. = Auguste Boniface Ghiesbreght, 1810–1893
Ghose = Birendra Nath Ghose, 1885–1983
Giacom. = Valerio Giacomini, 1914–1981
P.E. Gibbs = Peter Edward Gibbs, 1938–
A.C. Gibson = Arthur Charles Gibson, 1947–
Gibson = George Stacey Gibson, 1818–1883
Gilg = Ernest Friedrich Gilg, 1867–1933
Gilib. = Jean Emmanuel Gilibert, 1741–1814
J. Gill = Jirí Gill, 1936–
Gillies = John Gillies, 1792–1834
Gilmartin = Amy Jean Gilmartin, 1932–1989
Gilmour = John Scott Lennox Gilmour, 1906–1986
Ging. = Frédéric Charles Jean Baron Gingins de la Sarraz, 1790–1863
Giord. = Ferdinando Giordano, fl. early 19th Cent.
Girard = Frédéric de Girard, 1810–1851
Giroux = Mathilde Giroux, 1898–
Giseke = Paul Dietrich Giseke, 1741–1796
Glaetzle = Wolfgang Glaetzle, 1951–
Glass = Charles Edward Glass, 1934–1998
Glassman = Sidney Frederick Glassman, 1919–
Glazebr. = Thomas Kirkland Glazebrook, 1780–1885
Glaz. = Auguste François Marie Glaziou, 1828–1906
Gleason = Henry Allan Gleason, 1882–1975
Gled. = Johann Gottlieb Gleditsch, 1714–1786
Glen = Hugh Francis Glen, 1950–
Gloxin = Benjamin Peter Gloxin, 1765–1794
C.C. Gmel. = Carl (Karl) Christian Gmelin, 1762–1837
J.F. Gmel. = Johann Friedrich Gmelin, 1748–1804
S.G. Gmel. = Samuel Gottlieb Gmelin, 1744–1774

Goaty = Etienne Louis Henri Goaty, 1830–1890
God.-Leb. = Alexandre Godefroy-Lebeuf, 1852–1903
Godfery = Masters John Godfery, 1856–1945
Godr. = Dominique Alexandre Godron, 1807–1880
Goebel = Karl Christian Traugott Friedemann Goebel, 1794–1851
Götz = Erich Götz, 1940–
Goldblatt = Peter Goldblatt, 1943–
Goldie – John Goldie, 1793–1886
B.A. Gomes = Bernardino António Gomes, 1806–1877
Gomes = Bernardino Antonio Gomes, 1769–1823
M. Gómez = Manuel Gómez de la Maza y Jiménez, 1867–1916
Gómez Mor. = Manuel Gómez Moreno, fl. 1946
L.D. Gómez = Luis Diego Gómez Pignataro, 1944–
Gooden. = Samuel Goodenough, 1743–1827
Gordon = George Gordon, 1806–1879
Gorschk. = Sofia (Sofiya) Gennadievna Gorschkova (Gorshkova), 1889–1972
Górski = Stanislaw Batys Górski, 1802–1864
Gouan = Antoine Gouan, 1733–1821
Goujon = Joseph Goujon, 1858–
Gould = Frank Walton Gould, 1913–1981
Goupil = Clément Jacques Goupil, 1784–1858
Govaerts = Rafael Herman Anna Govaerts, 1968–
Govorov = Leonid Ipatevich Govorov, 1885–1941
Gower = William Hugh Gower, 1835–1894
Grab. = Heinrich Emanuel Grabowski, 1792–1842
Graebn. = Karl Otto Robert Peter Paul Graebner, 1871–1933
P. Graebn. = Paul Graebner, 1900–1978
Graells = Mariano de la Paz Graells, 1809–1898
Gräser = Robert Gräser, 1893–1977
Graf = Siegmund (Sigismund) Graf, 1801–1838
R.A. Graham = Rex Alan Henry Graham, 1915–1958
Graham = Robert Graham, 1786–1845
Grande = Loreto Grande, 1878–1965
V.E. Grant = Verne Edwin Grant, 1917–2007
Grassl = Carl Otto Grassl, 1908–

Grau = Hans Rudolf Jürke Grau, 1937–
Grauer = Sebastian Grauer, 1758–1820
A. Gray = Asa Gray, 1810–1888
N.E. Gray = Netta Elizabeth Gray,
1913–1970
Gray = Samuel Frederick Gray, 1766–1828
J.R. Gray = J.R. Gray, fl. 1976
Grayum = Michael Howard Grayum, 1949–
Greb. = Igor Sergeevich Grebenscikov,
1912–1986
Grecescu = Dimitrie (Demetrius) Grecescu,
1841–1910
P.S. Green = Peter Shaw Green, 1920–
M.L. Green = Mary Letitia Green (Mrs.
Manna Sprague), 1886–1978
Greene = Edward Lee Greene, 1843–1915
Greenm. = Jesse More Greenman,
1867–1951
Gremli = August(e) Gremli, 1833–1899
Gren. = Jean Charles Marie Grenier,
1808–1875
Greuter = Werner Rodolfo Greuter, 1938–
Grev. = Robert Kaye Greville, 1794–1866
Grey-Wilson = Christopher Grey-Wilson,
1944–
Grierson = Andrew John Charles Grierson,
1929–1990
Griess. = Ludwig Griesselich, 1804–1848
Griff. = William Griffith, 1810–1845
Griffiths = David Griffiths, 1867–1935
Grimm = Johann Friedrich Carl Grimm,
1737–1821
Gris = Jean Antoine Arthur Gris, 1829–1872
Griseb. = August Heinrich Rudolf
Grisebach, 1814–1879
L.E. Groen = L. E. Groen, 1946–
Groenland = Johannes Groenland,
1824–1891
Gronov. = Johan Frederik (Jan Fredrik)
Gronovius, 1686–1762
H. Gross = Hugo Gross, 1888–
Grosser = Wilhelm Carl Heinrich Grosser,
1869–
Grossh. = Alexander Alphonsovic
(Aleksandr Alphonsovich) Grossheim,
1888–1948
A. Grove = Arthur Stanley Grove,
1865–1942
H. Groves = Henry Groves, 1855–1912
J. Groves = James Groves, 1858–1933
Guédès = Michel Guédès, 1942–1985
Gueldenst. = Anton Johann von
Gueldenstaedt, 1745–1781
Günther = Karl Christian Günther,
1769–1833

Guépin = Jean-Pierre Guépin, 1778–1858
Gürke = Robert Louis August Maximilian
Gürke, 1854–1911
Guers. = Louis Ben Guersent, 1776–1848
Guett. = Jean Étienne Guettard, 1715–1786
Gugler = Wilhelm Gugler, 1874–1909
Guicc. = Giacinto Guicciardi, fl. 1855
Guillaumin = André Guillaumin, 1885–1974
Guill. = Jean Baptiste Antoine Guillemin,
1796–1842
Guinea = Emilio Guinea López, 1907–1985
Guinier = Marie Joseph Jean Baptiste
Philibert Guinier, 1876–1962
Guin. = Jean-Étienne Marcel Guinochet,
1909–1997
Guitt. = Guy Georges Guittonneau, 1934–
Gumbl. = William Edward Gumbleton,
1830–1911
Gunnerus = Johan Ernst Gunnerus,
1718–1773
Gusmus = Hermann Gusmus, 1843–
Guss. = Giovanni Gussone, 1787–1866
R. Guzmán = Rafael Guzmán Mejía, 1950–
F. Haage = Friedrich Ferdinand Haage,
1859–1930
Haage = Friedrich Adolph Haage,
1796–1866
W. Haage = Walther Haage, 1899–1992
Haberm. = V. Habermann, fl. 1975
Hablitz = Carl Ludwig von Hablitz
(Hablizl), 1751/1752–1821
Hack. = Eduard Hackel, 1850–1926
Hackett bis = Hackett, fl. 1900
Hacq. = Belsazar (Balthasar) A. Hacquet,
1739–1815
Haenke = Thaddäus(Tadeás) Peregrinus
Xaverius Haenke, 1761–1817
Haens. = Felix Haenseler, 1766–1841
Hagerup = Olaf Hagerup, 1889–1961
G.E. Haglund = Gustaf (Gösta)Emanuel
Haglund, 1900–1955
Haines = Henry Haselfoot Haines,
1867–1945
Halácsy = Eugen (Jenö) von Halácsy,
1842–1913
Halb. = Federico Halbinger, 1925–
Halda = Josef J. Halda, 1943–
A.D. Hall = Alfred Daniel Hall, 1864–1942
H.M. Hall = Harvey Monroe Hall,
1874–1932
H.C. Hall = Herman (Hermanus)
Christiaan van Hall, 1801–1874
Haller f. = Albrecht von Haller, 1758–1823
Haller = Albrecht von Haller, 1708–1777
Hallier = Ernst Hans Hallier, 1831–1904

Hallier f. = Hans (Johannes) Gottfried Hallier, 1868–1932
Raym.-Hamet = Raymond Hamet, 1890–1972
A.P. Ham. = Anthony Parke Hamilton, 1939–
Hammel = Barry Edward Hammel, 1946–
S.A. Hammer = Steven A. Hammer, 1951–
Hampe = Ernst Georg Ludwig Hampe, 1795–1880
Hance = Henry Fletcher Hance, 1827–1886
Hand.-Mazz. = Heinrich Raphael Eduard Freiherr von Handel-Mazzetti, 1882–1940
Handlos = Wayne L. Handlos, fl. 1975
Hanelt = Hans Peter Fritz Hanelt, 1930–
Hansen = Lars Hansen, 1788–1876
Hanst. = Johannes Ludwig Emil Robert von Hanstein, 1822–1880
H. Hara = Hiroshi Hara, 1911–1986
K. Haraldson = Kerstin Haraldson, fl. 1978
Harb. = Thomas Grant Harbison, 1862–1936
Hardin = James Walker Hardin, 1929–
Hardouin = Louis Marie Hardouin, 1796–1858
Hardw. = Thomas Hardwicke, 1757–1835
Har. = Paul Auguste Joseph Valentin Hariot, 1854–1917
B.E. Harkn. = Bernard Emerson Harkness, 1907–1980
Harling = Gunnar Wilhelm Harling, 1920–
Harms = Hermann August Theodor Harms, 1870–1942
R.M. Harper = Roland McMillan Harper, 1878–1966
S.G. Harrison = Sydney Gerald Harrison, 1924–1988
R.L. Harrow = Robert Lewis Harrow, 1867–1954
't Hart = Henk 't Hart, 1944–2000
Hartl = Dimitri Hartl, 1926–
Hartland = William Baylor Hartland, fl. 1903
T.G. Hartley = Thomas Gordon Hartley, 1931–
Hartm. = Carl Johan(n) Hartman, 1790–1849
R.W. Hartm. = Robert Wilhelm Hartman, 1827–1891
Hartmann = Franz Xaver Ritter von Hartmann, 1737–1791
H.E.K. Hartmann = Heidrun Elsbeth Klara Hartmann geb. Osterwald, 1942–
Hartog = Cornelis den Hartog, 1931–
Hartw. = Karl Theodor Hartweg, 1812–1871

Hartwich = Carl Hartwich, 1851–1917
Hartwig = August Karl Julius Hartwig, 1823–1913
Hartwiss = Nicolai Anders von Hartwiss, 1791–1860
Hartz = Hartz, fl. 1895
Harv. = William Henry Harvey, 1811–1866
Harz = Carl (Karl) Otto Harz, 1842–1906
Hasselt = Johan Coenraad van Hasselt, 1797–1823
Hassk. = Justus Carl Hasskarl, 1811–1894
Hassl. = Émile Hassler, 1861–1937
Hauman = Lucien Leon Hauman, 1880–1965
Hausm. = Franz von Hausmann zu Stetten, 1810–1878
Hausskn. = Heinrich Carl Haussknecht, 1838–1903
Havemeyer = Havemeyer, fl. 1900
S.G. Haw = Stephen George Haw, 1951–
A.D. Hawkes = Alex Drum Hawkes, 1927–1977
Hawkes = John Gregory Hawkes, 1915–2007
Haw. = Adrian Hardy Haworth, 1768–1833
Hay = William Perry Hay, 1872–1947
Hayata = Bunzô Hayata, 1874–1934
Hayek = August Edler von Hayek, 1871–1928
Hayne = Friedrich Gottlob Hayne, 1763–1832
Hazsl. = Friedrich August (Frigyes Agost) Hazslinszky von Hazslin, 1818–1896
Heath = Fannie Mahood Heath, –1931
L.P. Hébert = Louis-Philippe Hébert, 1947–
Heckel = Édouard Marie Heckel, 1843–1916
Hedge = Ian Charleson Hedge, 1928–
Hedl. = Johan Teodor Hedlund, 1861–1953
Hedrick = Ulysses Prentiss Hedrick, 1870–1951
R. Hedw. = Romanus (Romanes) Adolf Hedwig, 1772–1806
Heer = Oswald von Heer, 1809–1883
Heese = Emil Heese, 1862–1914
Hegetschw. = Johannes Jacob Hegetschweiler, 1789–1839
Hegi = Gustav Hegi, 1876–1932
Heilborn = Otto Heilborn, 1892–1943
Heimerl = Anton Heimerl, 1857–1942
O.R. Heine = Otto Rudolf Heine, 1920–
Heinrich = Walter Heinrich, fl. 1925
Heiser = Charles Bixler Heiser, 1920–
Heist. = Lorenz Heister, 1683–1758
Heldr. = Theodor Heinrich Hermann von Heldreich, 1822–1902

A. Heller = Amos Arthur Heller, 1867–1944
Hellq. = C. Baare Hellquist, 1940–
Helm = Friedrich Gustav Helm,
fl. 1809–1828
Hemsl. = William Botting Hemsley,
1843–1924
Henckel = Leo Victor Felix Henckel von
Donnersmarck, 1785–1861
D.M. Hend. = Douglas Mackay Henderson,
1927–2007
L.F. Hend. = Louis Forniquet Henderson,
1853–1942
M.D. Hend. = Mayda Doris Henderson,
1928–
A.J. Hend. = Andrew James Henderson,
1950–
Henfr. = Arthur Henfrey, 1819–1859
H. Henkel = Heinrich Henkel, fl. 1897–1914
Henkel = Johann Baptist Henkel, 1815–1871
Henker = Heinz Siegfried Henker, 1930–
Henn. = Paul Christoph Hennings,
1841–1908
Hennipman = Elbert Hennipman, 1937–
Henrard = Johannes (Jan) Theodoor
Henrard, 1881–1974
Henriq. = Julio Augusto Henriques,
1838–1928
A. Henry = Augustine Henry, 1857–1930
J.K. Henry = Joseph Kaye Henry,
1866–1930
L. Henry = Louis Armand Henry, 1854–1913
Hensch. = August Wilhelm Eduard
Theodor Henschel, 1790–1856
Hensl. = John Stevens Henslow, 1796–1861
Hepper = Frank Nigel Hepper, 1929–
Herb. = William Herbert, 1778–1847
Herbich = Franz Herbich, 1791–1865
Herborg = Joachim Herborg, fl. 1987
Herder = Ferdinand Gottfried Maximilian
Theobald von Herder, 1828–1896
Hereman = Samuel Hereman, fl. 1868
Hérincq = François Hérincq, 1820–1891
F. Herm. = Friedrich Hermann, 1873–1967
A.G.J. Herre = Adolar Gottlieb Julius
(Hans) Herre, 1895–1979
Herrm. = Johann (Jean) Herrmann,
1738–1800
Hershk. = Mark Alan Hershkovitz, 1958–
Herter = Wilhelm (Guillermo) Gustav(o)
Franz (Francis) Herter, 1884–1958
Hesl.-Harr. = John William Heslop-
Harrison, 1881–1967
H.E. Hess = Hans E. Hess, 1920–
Hesse = Hermann Albrecht Hesse, 1852–1937
Hester = J. Pinckney Hester, fl. 1943

Heuff. = János(Johann) A. Heuffel,
1800–1857
Heyder = Eduard Heyder, 1808–1884
B. Heyne = Benjamin Heyne, 1770–1819
K. Heyne = Karel Heyne, 1877–1947
Heynh. = Gustav Heynhold, 1800–1860
Heywood = Vernon Hilton Heywood, 1927–
Hibberd = James Shirley Hibberd,
1825–1890
Hickel = Paul Robert Hickel, 1865–1935
Hicken = Cristóbal María Hicken,
1875–1933
J.C. Hickman = James Craig Hickman,
1941–1993
Hiepko = Paul Hubertus Hiepko, 1932–
Hiern = William Philip Hiern, 1839–1925
Hieron. = Georg Hans Emmo (Emo)
Wolfgang Hieronymus, 1846–1921
W.E. Higgins = Wesley E. Higgins, fl. 1998
Hiitonen = Henrik Ilmari Augustus
Hiitonen, 1898–1986
Hildebr. = Friedrich Hermann Gustav
Hildebrand, 1835–1915
Hildm. = H. Hildmann, –1895
Hilend = Martha Luella Hilend, 1902–
A.W. Hill = Arthur William Hill, 1875–1941
Hill = John Hill, 1714–1775
K.D. Hill = Kenneth D. Hill, 1948–
W. Hill = Walter Hill, 1820–1904
Hillc. = Jean Olive Dorothy Hillcoat,
1904–1990
Hilliard = Olive Mary Hilliard geb. Hillary,
1926–
H.G.K. Hillier = Harold George Knight
Hillier, 1905–1985
Hilsenb. = Richard A. Hilsenbeck, 1952–
Hitchc. = Albert Spear Hitchcock,
1865–1935
C.L. Hitchc. = Charles Leo Hitchcock,
1902–1986
E. Hitchc. = Edward Hitchcock, 1793–1864
Hjelmq. = Karl Jesper Hakon Hjelmquist,
1905–
Hochr. = Bénédict Pierre Georges
Hochreutiner, 1873–1959
Hochst. = Christian Ferdinand Friedrich
Hochstetter, 1787–1860
W. Hochst. = Wilhelm Christian
Hochstetter, 1825–1881
Hodge = Walter Hendricks Hodge, 1912–
Hodgkin = Hodgkin
Höfft = Franz M.S.V. Höfft, fl. 1826
Hoefker = Heinrich Hoefker, 1859–1945
Hoehne = Frederico Carlos Hoehne,
1882–1959

Höppner = Hans Höppner, 1873–1946
Hörandl = Elvira Hörandl, 1964–
Höss = Franz Höss, 1756–1840
Hoffm. = Georg Franz Hoffmann,
1760–1826
O. Hoffm. = Karl August Otto Hoffmann,
1853–1909
K. Hoffm. = Käthe (Kaethe) Hoffmann,
1883–ca.1931
A.E. Hoffm. = Adriana E. Hoffmann
Jacoby, publ. 1978–1991
Hoffmanns. = Johann Centurius von
Hoffmannsegg, 1766–1849
R. Hogg = Robert Hogg, 1818–1897
T. Hogg = Thomas Hogg, 1820–1892
Hohen. = Rudolph Friedrich Hohenacker,
1798–1874
Holandre = Jean Joseph Jacques Holandre,
1778–1857
Holland = John Henry Holland, 1869–1950
Holm-Niels. = Lauritz Broder Holm-
Nielsen, 1946–
Holmb. = Otto Rudolf Holmberg,
1874–1930
Holmboe = Jens Holmboe, 1880–1943
Holmes = Edward Morell Holmes,
1843–1930
Holttum = Richard Eric Holttum,
1895–1990
Holub = Josef Ludwig Holub, 1930–1999
Holz. = John Michael Holzinger, 1853–1929
Hombr. = Jacques Bernard Hombron,
1800–1852
Honck. = Gerhard August Honckeny,
1724–1805
Honda = Masaji (Masazi) Honda,
1897–1984
T. Hong = Tao Hong, 1923–
Hoog = Johannes Marius Cornelis (John)
Hoog, 1865–1950
Hoogland = Ruurd Dirk Hoogland,
1922–1994
Hooibr. = Danield Hooibrenk, fl. 1848–1861
Hook. f. = Joseph Dalton Hooker, 1817–1911
Hook. = William Jackson Hooker,
1785–1865
Hoopes = Josiah Hoopes, 1832–1904
Hope = John Hope, 1725–1786
Hopffer = Carl Hopffer, 1810–
Hopkins = Lewis Sylvester Hopkins,
1872–1945
Hoppe = David Heinrich Hoppe, 1760–1846
K.E. Horak = Karl E. Horak, fl. 1978
Horan. = Pavel (Paul, Paulus) Fedorovic
(Fedorowitsch) Horaninow, 1796–1865

Horkel = Johann Horkel, 1769–1846
Hornem. = Jens Wilken Hornemann,
1770–1841
Hornsch. = Christian Friedrich
Hornschuch, 1793–1850
Hornung = Ernst Gottfried Hornung,
1795–1862
Horny = Radvan Horny, fl. 1974
Horvat = Ivo Horvat, 1897–1963
M.D. Horvat = Marija Dvorák Horvat, 1909–
Horv. = Tsigmond (Zigmund, Sigismund)
Horvátovszky, 1746–?,fl. 1774
E. Hossain = A.B.M.Enayet Hossain, 1945–
Hosseus = Carl Curt Hosseus, 1878–1950
Host = Nicolaus Thomas Host, 1761–1834
M. Hotta = Mitsuru Hotta, 1935–
Ding Hou = Ding Hou, 1921–
Houllet = R.J.B. Houllet, 1811~15–1890
House = Homer Doliver House, 1878–1949
Houtt. = Maarten (Martin) Houttuyn,
1720–1798
J. Houz. = Jean Houzeau de Lehaie,
1867–1959
Houz. = Jean Charles Houzeau de Lehaie,
1820–1888
R.A. Howard = Richard Alden Howard,
1917–2003
J.T. Howell = John Thomas Howell,
1903–1994
Howell = Thomas Jefferson Howell,
1842–1912
Hoyle = Arthur Clague Hoyle, 1904–1986
Hrabětová = Anežka Hrabětová-Uhrová,
1900–1981
S.Y. Hu = Shiu Ying Hu, 1910–
Hu = Hsen Hsu Hu, 1894–1968
Hua = Henri Hua, 1861–1919
C.E. Hubb. = Charles Edward Hubbard,
1900–1980
F.T. Hubb. = Frederic Tracy Hubbard,
1875–1962
C. Huber = C. Huber, fl. 1874
H. Huber = Heribert Franz Josef Huber,
1931–
Huber = Jakob ('Jacques') E. Huber,
1867–1914
J.A. Huber = Josef Anton Huber, 1899–
Hub.-Mor. = Arthur Huber-Morath,
1901–1990
Huds. = William Hudson, 1734–1793
Hügel = Karl (Carl) Alexander Anselm
Freiherr von Hügel, 1794–1870
Hülph. = K. A. Hülphers, 1882–1948
A. Huet = Alfred Huet du Pavillon,
1829–1907

Hughes = Dorothy Kate Hughes, 1899–1932
Hull = John Hull, 1761–1843
Hultén = Oskar Eric Gunnar Hultén, 1894–1981
Humbert = Henri Jean Humbert, 1887–1967
Humb. = Friedrich Heinrich Alexander Freiherr von Humboldt, 1769–1859
Humphries = Christopher John Humphries, 1947–
D.R. Hunt = David Richard Hunt, 1938–
P.F. Hunt = Peter Francis Hunt, 1936–
Hunter = Alexander Hunter, 1729–1809
Hutch. = John Hutchinson, 1884–1972
J.B. Hutch. = Joseph Burtt Hutchinson, 1902–1988
Hutchison = Paul Clifford Hutchison, 1924–1997
Huter = Rupert Huter, 1834–1919
Huth = Ernst Huth, 1845–1897
Huxley = Anthony Julian Huxley, 1920–1993
B. Hyland = Bernard Patrick Matthew Hyland, 1937–
Hyl. = Nils Hylander, 1904–1970
B. Hylmö = Bertil Hylmö, 1915–2001
Ietsw. = Jan H. Ietswaart, 1940–
Ihlenf. = Hans-Dieter Ihlenfeldt, 1932–
Iljin = Modest Mikhailovich Iljin, 1889–1967
Ilse = Adolf Ferdinand Hugo Ilse, 1835–1900
Iltis = Hugo Iltis, 1882–1952
Imlay = George (Gilbert) Imlay, 1754–
Ingram = Collingwood Ingram, 1880–1981
J.W. Ingram = John William Ingram, 1924–
Ingw. = Walter Edward Theodore Ingwersen, 1885–1960
Innes = Clive Frederick Innes, 1909–1999
Irish = Henry Clay Irish, 1868–1960
Irmsch. = Edgar Irmscher, 1887–1968
W. Irving = Walter Irving, 1867–1934
H.S. Irwin = Howard Samuel Irwin, 1928–
Isely = Duane Isely, 1918–2000
H. Itô = Hiroshi Itô, 1909–
T. Itô = Tokutarô Itô, 1868–1941
Y. Itô = Yoshi Itô, 1907–
Ivanina = L.I. Ivanina, 1917–
Ivens = Arthur J. Ivens, 1897–1954
Jack = William Jack, 1795–1822
A.B. Jacks. = Albert Bruce Jackson, 1876–1947
Jacks. = George Jackson, c.1780–1811
B.D. Jacks. = Benjamin Daydon Jackson, 1846–1927
Cordem. = Eugène Jacob de Cordemoy, 1837–1911

Jacob-Makoy = Lambert Jacob-Makoy, 1790–1873
Jacobi = Georg Albano von Jacobi, 1805–1874
H. Jacobsen = Hermann Johannes Heinrich Jacobsen, 1898–1978
N. Jacobsen = Niels Henning Günther Jacobsen, 1941–
Jacquem. = Venceslas Victor Jacquemont, 1801–1832
Jacques = Henri Antoine Jacques, 1782–1866
J. Jacq. = Joseph Franz von Jacquin, 1766–1839
Jacq. = Nicolaus (Nicolaas) Joseph Freiherr von Jacquin, 1727–1817
Jacquinot = Honoré Jacquinot, 1814–1887
Jafri = Saiyad Masudal (Saiyid Masudul) Hasan Jafri, 1927–1986
Jahand. = Émile Lucien Jahandiez, 1876–1938
Jakow. = Anton Jakowatz, 1872–
Jakubz. = Moisej Markovic (Markovich) Jakubziner, 1898–
Jalas = Arvo Jaakko Juhani Jalas, 1920–1999
E. James = Edwin James, 1797–1861
James = Thomas Potts James, 1803–1882
Jan = Georg (Giorgio) Jan, 1791–1866
Janch. = Erwin Emil Alfred Janchen, 1882–1970
Jancz. = Eduard von Glinka Janczewski, 1846–1918
Janisch. = Dmitrii Erastovich Janischewsky (Yanishevskii), 1875–1944
Janka = Victor Janka von Bulcs, 1837–1900
Janse = Johannes Albertus Janse, 1911–1977
Jansen = Pieter Jansen, 1882–1955
R.K. Jansen = Robert K. Jansen, 1954–
Janson. = Jan Jansonius, 1928–
C.-A. Jansson = Carl-Axel Jansson, 1925–
Jasiewicz = Adam Jasiewicz, 1928–
Játiva = Carlos D. Játiva, fl. 1963
Jaub. = Hippolyte François Jaubert, 1798–1874
Jáv. = Sándor (Alexander) Jávorka, 1883–1961
Jebb = Matthew Jebb, 1958–
C. Jeffrey = Charles Jeffrey, 1934–
Jeffrey = John Frederick Jeffrey, 1866–1943
Jenkins = Anna Eliza Jenkins, 1886–1973
Jenman = George Samuel Jenman, 1845–1902
Jensen = Johan Georg Keller Jensen, 1818–1886

Jeps. = Willis Linn Jepson, 1867–1946
Jermy = Anthony Clive Jermy, 1932–
Jess. = Karl Friedrich Wilhelm Jessen, 1821–1889
Jesson = Enid Mary Jesson (verh. Cotton), 1889–1956
Jessop = John Peter Jessop, 1939–
Jeswiet = Jacob Jeswiet, 1879–1966
V. Jirásek = Václav Jirásek, 1906–1991
V. John = Volker John, 1952–
H. Johnson = Joseph Harry Johnson, 1894–1987
L.A.S. Johnson = Lawrence Alexander Sidney Johnson, 1925–1997
I.M. Johnst. = Ivan Murray Johnston, 1898–1960
M.C. Johnst. = Marshall Conring Johnston, 1930–
B.M.G. Jones = Brian Michael Glyn Jones, 1933–
G.N. Jones = George Neville Jones, 1903–1970
M.E. Jones = Marcus Eugene Jones, 1852–1934
Jones = William Jones, 1746–1794
Jord. = Claude Thomas Alexis Jordan, 1814–1897
Joriss. = G. Jorissenne, fl. 1882
Jouin = V. Jouin, fl. 1910
Jowitt = John Fort Jowitt, 1846–1915
Juel = Hans Oscar Juel, 1863–1931
Jum. = Henri Lucien Jumelle, 1866–1935
Junge = Paul Junge, 1881–1919
Jungh. = (Friedrich) Franz Wilhelm Junghuhn, 1809–1864
Jur. = Jakob (Jacob) Juratzka, 1821–1878
Jusl. = Abraham Danielis Juslenius, 1732–1803
A. Juss. = Adrien Henri Laurent de Jussieu, 1797–1853
Juss. = Antoine Laurent de Jussieu, 1748–1836
B. Juss. = Bernard de Jussieu, 1699–1777
Juz. = Sergei Vasilievich Juzepczuk, 1893–1959
Kabath = Hermann Kabath, 1816–1888
Kache = Paul Kache, 1882–1945
Kaempf. = Engelbert Kaempfer, 1651–1716
Kalkman = Cornelis Kalkman, 1928–1998
Kalm = Pehr Kalm, 1716–1779
Kalmb. = George Anthony Kalmbacher, 1897–1977
Kanitz = August (Agost, Augustus) Kanitz, 1843–1896
Kappert = Hans Kappert, 1890–1976

Kar. = Grigorij Silyc (Gregor Silitsch) Karelin, 1801–1872
Karlsson = Thomas Karlsson, 1945–
Kárpáti = Zoltan E. Kárpáti, 1909–1972
Karrer = Sigmund Karrer, 1881–1954
H. Karst. = Gustav Karl Wilhelm Hermann Karsten, 1817–1908
Kartesz = John T. Kartesz, fl. 1990
Karw. = Wilhelm Friedrich Freiherr von Karwinsky von Karwin, 1780–1855
Kasapligil = Baki Kasapligil, 1918–1992
Kauffm. = Nikolai Nikolajevic (Nikolajevich) Kauffmann, 1834–1870
Kaulf. = Georg Friedrich Kaulfuss, 1786–1830
Kawano = Shoichi Kawano, 1936–
Kearney = Thomas Henry Kearney, 1874–1956
Keay = Ronald William John Keay, 1920–1998
D.D. Keck = David Daniels Keck, 1903–1995
Keck = Karl Keck, 1825–1894
Keissl. = Karl (Carl) Ritter von Keissler, 1872–1965
B. Keller = Boris Aleksandrovich (Alexandrovic) Keller, 1874–1945
Keller = Johann Christoph Keller, 1737–1796
R. Keller = Robert Keller, 1854–1939
Kellerer = Johann Kellerer, 1859–
M. Kellerm. = Maude Kellerman, 1888–
Kellogg = Albert Kellogg, 1813–1887
H.P. Kelsey = Harlan Page Kelsey, 1872–1959
Kelway = James Kelway, 1815–1899
Kem.-Nath. = Liubov Manucharovna Kemularia-Nathadze, 1891–1985
H. Keng = Hsüan Keng, 1923–
Keng = Yi Li Keng, 1897–1975
Keng f. = Pai Chieh Keng, 1917–
G.C. Kenn. = George Clayton Kennedy, 1919–1980
H. Kenn. = Helen Kennedy, 1944–
P.B. Kenn. = Patrick Beveridge Kennedy, 1874–1930
Kensit = Harriet Margaret Louisa Kensit, 1877–1970
A.H. Kent = Adolphus Henry Kent, 1828–1913
D.H. Kent = Douglas Henry Kent, 1920–1995
Ker-Gawl. = John Bellenden Ker-Gawler, 1764–1842
Keraudren = Monique Keraudren, 1928–1981

Kerch. = Oswald Charles Eugène Marie Ghislain de Kerchove de Denterghem, 1844–1906
Kereszty = Zoltán Kereszty, 1937–
Kerguélen = Michel François Jacques Kerguélen, 1928–1999
J. Kern. = Johann Simon von Kerner, 1755–1830
Jos. Kern. = Joseph Kerner, 1829–1906
A. Kern. = Anton Joseph Kerner Ritter von Marilaun, 1831–1898
Kesselr. = Friedrich Wilhelm Kesselring, 1876–1966
Kharkev. = Sigizmund Semenovich Kharkevich, 1921–1998
R. Kiesling = Roberto Kiesling, 1941–
Kikuchi = Akio Kikuchi, 1883–1951
Kilian = Günter Kilian, 1960–
Killias = Eduard Killias, 1829–1891
Killick = Donald Joseph Boomer Killick, 1926–
Killip = Ellsworth Paine Killip, 1890–1968
Kimnach = Myron William Kimnach, 1922–
Y. Kimura = Yojiro Kimura, 1912–2006
King = George King, 1840–1909
R.M. King = Robert Merrill King, 1930–
Kingdon-Ward = Francis Kingdon-Ward, 1885–1958
Kippist = Richard Kippist, 1812–1882
G. Kirchn. = Georg Kirchner, 1837–1885
Kir. = Ivan Petrovich (Iwan Petrovic, 'Johann') Kirilov (Kirilow), 1821–1842
Kirk = Thomas Kirk, 1828–1898
J.B. Kirkp. = James Barrie Kirkpatrick, 1946–
Kirp. = Moisey Elevich Kirpicznikov, 1913–1995
Kirschl. = Frédéric Kirschleger, 1804–1869
Kirschner = Jan Kirschner, 1955–
Kitag. = Masao Kitagawa, 1910–1995
Kit. = Pál (Paul) Kitaibel, 1757–1817
Kitam. = Siro Kitamura, 1906–2002
Kladiwa = Leo Kladiwa, 1920–1987
Klásk. = Anna Klásková, 1932–
Klatt = Friedrich Wilhelm Klatt, 1825–1897
E. Klein = Erich Klein, 1931–
Kleopow = Jurij Dmitrievic Kleopow, 1902–1942
Klett = Gustav Theodor Klett, –1827
Klinge = Johannes Christoph Klinge, 1851–1902
H. Klinggr. = Hugo Erich Meyer von Klinggräff, 1820–1902
Klokov = Michail Vasiljevich (Mikhail Vasilevich) Klokov, 1896–1981

G. Klotz = Gerhard Franz Klotz, 1928–
Klotzsch = Johann Friedrich Klotzsch, 1805–1860
Kluk = Krzysztof (Christoph) Kluk, 1739–1796
Knaf = Josef (Joseph) Friedrich Knaf, 1801–1865
Knerr = Ellsworth Brownell Knerr, 1861–1942
Kneuck. = Johann Andreas ('Andrees') Kneucker, 1862–1946
Knight = Joseph Knight, 1777?–1855
O.W. Knight = Ora Willis Knight, 1874–1913
Knoop = Johann Hermann Knoop, c. 1700–1769
Knowles = George Beauchamp Knowles, fl. 1820–1852
R. Knuth = Reinhard Gustav Paul Knuth, 1874–1957
F.M. Knuth = Frederik Marcus Knuth, 1904–1970
Kobuski = Clarence Emmeren Kobuski, 1900–1963
K. Koch = Karl (Carl) Heinrich Emil (Ludwig) Koch, 1809–1879
W. Koch = Walo Koch, 1896–1956
W.D.J. Koch = Wilhelm Daniel Joseph Koch, 1771–1849
Kochs = Julius Kochs, fl. 1900
U. Köhler = Udo Köhler, 1911–1983
Köhler = Johann Christian Gottlieb Köhler, 1759–1833
Koehne = Bernhard Adalbert Emil Koehne, 1848–1918
Koeler = Georg Ludwig Koeler, 1765–1807
Koelle = Johann Ludwig Christian Koelle, 1763–1797
Koell. = Rudolf Albert von Koelliker, 1817–1905
K.D. Koenig = Carl (Charles) Dietrich Eberhard Koenig, 1774–1851
J. König = Johann Gerhard König, 1728–1785
Körn. = Friedrich August Körnicke, 1828–1908
Körte = Heinrich Friedrich Franz (Ernst) Körte, 1782–1845
Koidz. = Gen'ichi (Gen-Iti) Koidzumi, 1883–1953
Kolak. = Alfred (Aldored) Alekseevich (Alekseyevic) Kolakovsky, 1906–
Kom. = Vladimir Leontjevich (Leontievic) Komarov, 1869–1945
Koord. = Sijfert Hendrik Koorders, 1863–1919

Kordes = W. J. H. Kordes, publ. 1938
Korneck = Dieter Korneck, 1935–
Korsh. = Sergei Ivanovitsch Korshinsky, 1861–1900
Korth. = Pieter Willem Korthals, 1807–1892
Koso-Pol. = Boris Mikhailovic (Mikhailovich) Koso-Poljansky (Kozo-Poliansky), 1890–1957
Kostel. = Vincenz Franz Kosteletzky, 1801–1887
Kostina = Klaudia Fedorovna Kostina, 1900–
Kotschy = Carl(Karl) Georg Theodor Kotschy, 1813–1866
Kovalev = Nikolai Vasilevich Kovalev, 1888–
Kovanda = Miloslav Kovanda, 1936–
T. Koyama = Tetsuo Michael Koyama, 1933–
Kraenzl. = Friedrich (Fritz) Wilhelm Ludwig Kraenzlin (Kränzlin), 1847–1934
Krainz = Hans Krainz, 1906–1980
Krajina = Vladimir Joseph Krajina, 1905–1993
M. Král = Milos Král, 1932–
Kralik = Jean-Louis Kralik, 1813–1892
Kramer = Wilhelm Heinrich Kramer, –1765
Krasch. = Ippolit (Hippolit Mihajlovic) Mikhailovich Krascheninnikov (Krascheninnikow), 1884–1947
Krasn. = Andrej Nikolaevic (Nikolaevich) Krasnov (Krassnov), 1862–1914
Krassiln. = Nikolay Aleksandrovich Krassilnikov, 1896–
E.H.L. Krause = Ernst Hans Ludwig Krause, 1859–1942
K. Krause = Kurt Krause, 1883–1963
W. Krause = W. Krause, fl. 1938
C. Krauss = Christian Ferdinand Friedrich von Krauss, 1812–1890
V.I. Krecz. = Vladimir I. Kreczetovicz (Kreczetowicz), 1901–1942
Krendl = Franz Xaver Krendl, 1926–
W.J. Kress = Walter John Emil Kress, 1951–
Kreutz = C.A.J. (Karel) Kreutz, fl. 1989–2004
Kreutzer = Karl(Carl) Joseph Kreutzer, 1809–1866
Kreuz. = Kurt G. Kreuzinger, 1905–1989
Kreyer = Georgij Kalowic (Karlovic) Kreyer, 1887–1942
Krock. = Anton Johann Krocker, 1744–1823
Krüssm. = Johann Gerd Krüssmann, 1910–1980
Krysht. = African Nikolaevich (Nikolaevic) Kryshtofowicz (Kristofovic), 1885–1953

Kudô = Yûshun Kudô, 1887–1932
Kühlew. = Paul Eduard von Kühlewein, 1798–1870
Kük. = Georg Kükenthal, 1864–1955
Kündig = Jakob Kündig, 1863–1933
Künkele = Siegfried Heinrich Künkele, 1931–2004
P. Küpfer = Philippe Küpfer, 1942–
Kütz. = Friedrich Traugott Kützing (Kuetzing), 1807–1893
Kuhn = Friedrich Adalbert Maximilian ('Max') Kuhn, 1842–1894
Kulcz. = Stanislaw Kulczynski, 1895–1975
Kumm. = Ferdinand Kummer, 1820–1870
Kunth = Karl (Carl) Sigismund Kunth, 1788–1850
Kuntze = Carl (Karl) Ernst (Eduard) Otto Kuntze, 1843–1907
Kunz = Hans Kunz, 1904–1982
Kunze = Gustav Kunze, 1793–1851
Kupper = Walter Kupper, 1874–1953
Kurtz = Fritz (Friedrich, Federico) Kurtz, 1854–1920
Kurz = Wilhelm Sulpiz Kurz, 1834–1878
Kusn. = Nicolai Ivanowicz (Ivanovic) Kusnezow, 1864–1932
Kuzmanov = Bogdan Antonov Kuzmanov, 1934–1991
L'Hér. = Charles Louis L'Héritier de Brutelle, 1746–1800
La Llave = Pablo de La Llave, 1773–1833
Labill. = Jacques Julien Houttou (Houtton) de Labillardière, 1755–1834
Labour. = J. Labouret, fl. 1853–58
Labroy = Oscar Labroy, 1877–1953
Lace = John Henry Lace, 1857–1918
Lachen. = Werner de Lachenal, 1736–1800
J.A. Lackey = J.A. Lackey, fl. 1978
Länger = Reinhard Martin Länger, 1960–
Laest. = Lars Levi Laestadius, 1800–1861
Lag. = Mariano Lagasca y Segura, 1776–1839
Lagerh. = Nils Gustaf von Lagerheim, 1860–1926
Lagger = Franz Josef Lagger, 1799–1870
Lagr.-Foss. = Adrien Rose Arnaud Lagrèze-Fossat, 1814–1874
Laharpe = Jean Jacques Charles de Laharpe (La Harpe), 1802–1877
Lahman = Bertha Marion Lahman, 1872–
Laichard. = Johann Nepomuk von Laicharding, 1754–1797
Laing = Robert Malcolm Laing, 1865–1941
M. Laínz = P. Manuel Laínz Gallo, 1923–
Lakela = Olga Korhoven Lakela, 1890–1980

H.J. Lam = Herman Johannes Lam, 1892–1977

Lam. = Jean Baptiste Antoine Pierre Monnet de Lamarck, 1744–1829

Lamb. = Aylmer Bourke Lambert, 1761–1842

Lambertye = Léonce Auguste Marie Comte de Lambertye, 1810–1877

Lamotte = Simon Gilbert ("Martial") Lamotte, 1820–1883

Lancaster = Charles Roy Lancaster, 1937–

Lander = Nicholas Sèan Lander, 1948–

Landolt = Elias Landolt, 1926–

J.W. Landon = John W. Landon, fl. 1975

Laness. = Jean Marie Antoine de Belloguet ("Jean-Louis") Lanessan, 1843–1919

Láng = Franz Adolph (Adolf) Láng, 1795–1863

K.H. Lang = Karl Heinrich Lang, 1800–1843

O. Lang = Otto Friedrich Lang, 1817–1847

Lange = Johan Martin Christian Lange, 1818–1898

Langport = Langport

Langsd. = Georg Heinrich von Langsdorff, 1774–1852

Lapeyr. = Philippe Picot Baron de Lapeyrouse, 1744–1818

Lapierre = Jean Marie Lapierre, 1754–1834

Larisey = Mary Maxine Larisey, 1909–

K. Larsen = Kai Larsen, 1926–

Lasch = Wilhelm Gottlob Lasch, 1787–1863

Lassen = Per Lassen, 1942–

Laterr. = Jean-François Laterrade, 1784–1858

Lat.-Marl. = Joseph (Bory) Latour-Marliac, 1830–1911

Latourr. = Marc Antoine Louis Claret de Fleurieu de Latourrette, 1729–1793

A.B. Lau = Alfred B. Lau, fl. 1940–1980

Lauche = (Friedrich) Wilhelm (Georg) Lauche, 1827–1883

Lauener = Lucien André (Andrew) Lauener, 1918–1991

Lauterb. = Carl(Karl) Adolf Georg Lauterbach, 1864–1937

Lauth = Thomas Lauth, 1758–1826

Lavallée = Pierre Alphonse Martin Lavallée, 1836–1884

Lavis = Mary Gwendolene Lavis, 1902–

Lavrenko = Evgenii Mikhailovic Lavrenko, 1900–1987

Lawr. = George Lawrence, fl. 1841

C. Lawson = Charles Lawson, 1794–1873

M.A. Lawson = Marmaduke Alexander Lawson, 1840–1896

Laxm. = Erich (Erik) Gustavovic Laxmann (Laxman, Laksman), 1737–1796

Layens = Georges Clément Joseph Bonnier de Layens, 1834–1897

Le Gall = Nicolas Joseph Marie de Kerlinou Le Gall, 1787–1860

Le Jol. = Auguste François Le Jolis, 1823–1904

L.C. Leach = Leslie (Larry) Charles Leach, 1909–1996

Leandri = Jacques Désiré Leandri, 1903–1982

Lebas = E. Lebas, 1800s

Lebedev = E.L. Lebedev, fl. 1968

Lebrun = Jean-Paul Antoine Lebrun, 1906–1985

Ledeb. = Carl (Karl) Friedrich von Ledebour, 1785–1851

Leeke = Georg Gustav Paul Leeke, 1883–1933

Leenh. = Pieter Willem Leenhouts, 1926–2004

Leers = Johann Georg Daniel Leers, 1727–1774

Legrand = Antoine Legrand, 1839–1905

C.B. Lehm. = Carl Bernhard Lehmann, 1811–1875

F. Lehm. = Friedrich Carl Lehmann, 1850–1903

J.F. Lehm. = Johann Friedrich Lehmann, fl. 1809

Lehm. = Johann Georg Christian Lehmann, 1792–1860

Leichtlin = Maximilian Leichtlin, 1831–1910

F.M. Leight. = Frances Margaret Leighton, 1909–2006

Lej. = Alexandre Louis (Alexander Ludwig) Simon Lejeune, 1779–1858

Lellinger = David Bruce Lellinger, 1937–

H.V. Lelong = H.V. Lelong, publ. 1935–1944

Lem. = (Antoine) Charles Lemaire, 1801–1871

Léman = Dominique Sébastien Léman, 1781–1829

Leme = Elton M.C. Leme, 1960–

Lemée = Albert Marie Victor Lemée, 1872–1900

Lemke = Willi Lemke, 1893–1973

Lemmon = John Gill Lemmon, 1832–1908

Lemoine = (Pierre Louis) Victor Lemoine, 1823–1911

Lenné = Peter Joseph Lenné, 1789–1866

L.W. Lenz = Lee Wayne Lenz, 1915–

León = (Hermano) León, 1871–1955

J. Léonard = Jean Joseph Gustave Léonard, 1920–

Lepech. = Ivan Ivanovich Lepechin, 1737–1802

Leresche = Louis François Jules Rodolphe Leresche, 1808–1885

J.-F. Leroy = Jean-François Leroy, 1915–1999

Lesch. = Jean Baptiste Louis (Claude) Théodore Leschenault de la Tour, 1773–1826

A.C. Leslie = Alan Christopher Leslie, 1953–

Lesp. = Jean Martial ("Gustave") Lespinasse, 1807–1876

Less. = Christian Friedrich Lessing, 1809–1862

Lest.-Garl. = Lester Vallis Lester-Garland, 1860–1944

T. Lestib. = Thémistocle Gaspard Lestiboudois, 1797–1876

Letty = Cythna Lindenberg Letty, 1895–1985

Leuenb. = Beat Ernst Leuenberger, 1946–

H. Lév. = Augustin Abel Hector Léveillé, 1863–1918

Levier = Emile (Emilio) Levier, 1839–1911

Levyns = Margaret Rutherford Bryan Levyns (geb. Michell), 1890–1975

F.H. Lewis = Frank Harlan Lewis, 1919–

G.J. Lewis = Gwendoline Joyce Lewis, 1909–1967

H.F. Lewis = Harrison Flint Lewis, 1893–1974

M.R. Lewis = Margaret Ruth Ensign Lewis, 1919–

Lex. = Juan José Martinez de Lexarza, 1785–1824

Leyb. = Friedrich Leybold, 1827–1879

Leyss. = Friedrich Wilhelm von Leysser, 1731–1815

H.L. Li = Hui Lin Li, 1911–

Y.K. Li = Yong Kang Li, 1918–

J.J. Li = Jia Jue Li, 1938–

C.F. Liang = Chou Fen(g) Liang, 1921–

Libosch. = Joseph Liboschitz, 1783–1824

Lidén = Magnus Lidén, 1951–

Liebl. = Franz Kaspar(Caspar) Lieblein, 1744–1810

Liebm. = Frederik Michael Liebmann, 1813–1856

Liebner = C. Liebner, fl. 1895

Liede = Sigrid Liede, 1957–

Lightf. = John Lightfoot, 1735–1788

Lilja = Nils Lilja, 1808–1870

Lilj. = Samuel Liljeblad, 1761–1815

Lillo = Miguel Lillo, 1862–1931

M.M. Lin = Mu Mu Lin, fl. 1987

W.C. Lin = Wei Chih Lin, fl. 1970

Lindau = Gustav Lindau, 1866–1923

G. Lindb. = Gustaf Anders Lindberg, 1832–1900

H. Lindb. = Harald Lindberg, 1871–1963

Lindb. = Sextus Otto Lindberg, 1835–1889

Lindblad = Matts Adolf Lindblad, 1821–1899

Lindeb. = Carl Johan Lindeberg, 1815–1900

Lindem. = Eduard Emanuilovitch von Lindemann, 1825–1900

Linden = Jean Jules Linden, 1817–1898

L. Linden = Lucien Linden, 1851–1940

Linding. = Karl Hermann Leonhard Lindinger, 1879–

Lindl. = John Lindley, 1799–1865

Lindm. = Carl Axel Magnus Lindman, 1856–1928

G.E. Linds. = George Edmund Lindsay, 1916–2002

Lingelsh. = Alexander von Lingelsheim, 1874–1937

Link = Johann Heinrich Friedrich Link, 1767–1851

Linke = August Linke, fl. 1853–57

L. f. = Carl von Linné, 1741–1783

L. = Carl (Carolus) von Linné (Linnaeus), 1707–1778

Lint = Harold LeRoy Lint, 1917–1986

E.F. Linton = Edward Francis Linton, 1848–1928

W. Lippert = Wolfgang Lippert, 1937–

Lipsch. = Sergej Julievitsch (Yulevich) Lipschitz, 1905–1983

Lipsky = Vladimir Ippolitovich (Wladimir Hippolitowitsch) Lipsky, 1863–1937

Litard. = René Verriet de Litardière, 1888–1957

Little = Elbert Luther Little, 1907–2004

Litv. = Dimitri Ivanovich Litvinov (Litwinow), 1854–1929

F.Y. Liu = Fang Yuan Liu, fl. 1982

T.S. Liu = Tang (Tung) Shui Liu, 1911–

Lloyd = Curtis Gates Lloyd, 1859–1926

D.G. Lloyd = David G. Lloyd, 1937–2006

J. Lloyd = James Lloyd, 1810–1896

T. Lobb = Thomas Lobb, 1820–1894

Lockwood = Tom (Tommie) Earl Lockwood, 1941–1975

Lodd. = Conrad (L.) Loddiges, 1738–1826

Lodé = Joël Lodé, 1952–

Loefgr. = (Johan) Albert(o) (Constantin) Löfgren (Loefgren), 1854–1918

Loefl. = Pehr Löfling (Loefling), 1729–1756

Lönnr. = Knut Johan Lönnroth, 1826–1885

Loes. = Ludwig Eduard Theodor Loesener, 1865–1941

A. Löve = Askell Löve, 1916–1994
D. Löve = Doris Benta Maria Löve (geb.
Wahlen), 1918–2000
Loisel. = Jean Louis Auguste Loiseleur-
Deslongchamps, 1774–1849
Lojac. = Michele Lojacono-Pojero,
1853–1919
Lomakin = Aleksandr Aleksandrovich
Lomakin, 1863–1930
D.G. Long = David Geoffrey Long, 1948–
R.W. Long = Robert William Long,
1927–1976
G.H. Loos = Götz Heinrich Loos, 1970–
Looser = Gualterio Looser, 1898–1982
G. López = Ginés Alejandro López
González, 1950–
Loret = Henri Loret, 1811–1888
Losinsk. = A.S.Losina- Losinskaja,
1903–1958
Loudon = John Claudius Loudon,
1783–1843
Lour. = Joao de Loureiro, 1717–1791
Lourteig = Alicia Lourteig, 1913–
H. Low = Hugh Low, 1824–1905
S.H. Low = Stuart Henry Low, 1826–1890
Lowe = Richard Thomas Lowe, 1802–1874
Lowry = Porter Peter Lowry, 1956–
Lozano = Gustavo Lozano Contreras,
1938–2000
Ludlow = Frank Ludlow, 1885–1972
Ludw. = Christian Gottlieb Ludwig,
1709–1773
W. Ludw. = Wolfgang Ludwig, 1924–
Lückel = Emil Lückel, fl. 1978
Lueder = Franz Hermann Heinrich Lueder,
–1791
Lüdi = Werner Lüdi, 1888–1968
Luehm. = Johann George W. Luehmann,
1843–1904
Luer = Carlyle August Luer, 1922–
Luerss. = Christian Luerssen, 1843–1916
Lumn. = István (Stephan) Lumnitzer,
1747–1806
Lundmark = Johan Daniel Lundmark,
1755–1792
Lynch = Richard Irwin Lynch, 1850–1924
McClell. = John M'Clelland (McClelland),
1805–1883
Maack = Richard Karlovich Maack (Maak),
1825–1886
Maas = Paulus Johannes Maria Maas,
1939–
Mabb. = David John Mabberley, 1948–
Macarthur = William Macarthur,
1800–1882

J.F. Macbr. = James Francis Macbride,
1892–1976
Macfad. = James Macfadyen, 1800–1850
Macfarl. = John Muirhead Macfarlane,
1855–1943
J. Mackay = James Townsend Mackay,
1775–1862
Mack. = Kenneth Kent Mackenzie,
1877–1934
Mackie = William Wylie Mackie, 1873–
MacMill. = Conway MacMillan, 1867–1929
MacOwan = Peter MacOwan, 1830–1909
Macreight = Daniel Chambers Macreight,
1799–1857
Madison = Michael T. Madison, 1947–
F. Maek. = Fumio Maekawa, 1908–1984
Magnier = Charles Alfred Maurice
Magnier, 1853–after 1913
P. Magyar = Pál Magyar, fl. 1930
Maiden = Joseph Henry Maiden, 1859–1925
Maire = Réné Charles Joseph Ernest Maire,
1878–1949
Makino = Tomitarô Makino, 1862–1957
Malag. = Teodoro Luis Ramón Peñaflor
Malagarriga, 1904–
Malinv. = Louis Jules Ernst Malinvaud,
1836–1913
Malte = Malte Oscar Malte, 1880–1933
Maly = Joseph Karl (Carl) Maly, 1797–1866
K. Maly = Karl Franz Josef Maly, 1874–1951
Manda = W. Albert Manda, fl. 1892
Manden. = Ida P. Mandenova, 1907–1995
Manetti = Xaverio Manetti, 1723–1785
Mangelsd. = Paul Christoph Mangelsdorf,
1899–1989
G. Mann = Gustav Mann, 1836–1916
J.C. Manning = John C. Manning, 1962–
Mansf. = Rudolf Mansfeld, 1901–1960
Manten = Jacob(Jack) Manten Manten,
1898–1958
Marais = Wessel Marais, 1929–
Maratti = Giovanni Francesco Maratti,
1723–1777
Marchal = Élie Marchal, 1839–1923
Marchant = William James Marchant,
1886–1952
Marcow. = Vasil Vasilevicz Marcowicz,
1865–1942
Maréchal = Robert Joseph Jean-Marie
Maréchal, 1926–
Markgr. = Friedrich Markgraf, 1897–1987
Markgr.-Dann. = Ingeborg Markgraf-
Dannenberg, 1911–1996
Marloth = Hermann Wilhelm Rudolf
Marloth, 1855–1931

Marn.-Lap. = Julien Marnier-Lapostolle, 1902–1976
Marnock = Robert Marnock, 1800–1889
C. Marquand = Cecil Victor Boley Marquand, 1897–1943
M. Bieb. = Friedrich August Marschall von Bieberstein, 1768–1826
Marshall = Humphry Marshall, 1722–1801
J. Marshall = Joseph Jewison Marshall, 1860–1934
W.T. Marshall = W.Taylor Marshall, fl. 1952
Marsili = Giovanni M. Marsili, 1727–1794
G. Martens = George Matthias von Martens, 1788–1872
M. Martens = Martin Martens, 1797–1863
F.L. Martin = Floyd Leonard Martin, 1909–
R.F. Martin = Robert Franklin Martin, 1910–
Mart. Crov. = Raul Nereo Martínez Crovetto, 1921–1988
Martinis = Z. Martinis, fl. 1973
Martinovsky = Jan Otakar Martinovsky, 1903–1980
Mart. = Carl (Karl) Friedrich Philipp von Martius, 1794–1868
Martrin-Donos = Julien Victor Comte de Martrin-Donos, 1801–1870
Martyn = Thomas Martyn, 1736–1825
Masam. = Genkei Masamune, 1899–1993
Masf. = Ramón Masferrer y Arquimbau, 1850–1884
H. Mason = Herbert Louis Mason, 1896–1994
Masson = Francis Masson, 1741–1805
Mast. = Maxwell Tylden Masters, 1833–1907
B. Mathew = Brian Frederick Mathew, 1936–
J.W. Mathews = Joseph ('Jimmy') William Mathews, 1871–1949
Mathias = Mildred Esther Mathias (verh. Hasler), 1906–1995
L. Mathieu = Louis Mathieu, 1793–1867
Mathsson = Albert Mathsson, –1898
Maton = William George Maton, 1774–1835
Matsum. = Jinzô Matsumura, 1856–1928
Mattf. = Johannes Mattfeld, 1895–1951
V.A. Matthews = Victoria Ann Matthews, 1941–
Matthieu = C. Matthieu, fl. 1853
Matt. = Heinrich Gottfried von Mattuschka, 1734–1779
Matuda = Eizi Matuda, 1894–1978
Mauer = Fedor Mihajlovic Mauer, 1897–1963

Maund = Benjamin Maund, 1790–1864
Mauri = Ernesto Mauri, 1791–1836
Maw = George Maw, 1832–1912
Maxim. = Carl Johann (Ivanovic) Maximowicz, 1827–1891
Maxon = William Ralph Maxon, 1877–1948
E. Mayer = Ernest Mayer, 1920–
Mayr = Heinrich Mayr, 1856–1911
Mazel = Mazel
Mazzuc. = Giovanni Mazzucato, 1787–1814
McAllister = Hugh A. McAllister, 1944–
D.C. McClint. = David Charles McClintock, 1913–2001
E.M. McClint. = Elizabeth May McClintock, 1912–2004
McClure = Floyd Alonzo McClure, 1897–1970
McGill. = Donald John McGillivray, 1935–
McKelvey = Susan Adams McKelvey, 1888–1964
McMillan = A.J.S. McMillan, fl. 1990
McMinn = Howard Earnest McMinn, 1891–1963
W.R. McNab = William Ramsay McNab, 1844–1899
McNair = James Birtley McNair, 1889–
McNeill = John McNeill, 1933–
McVaugh = Rogers McVaugh, 1909–
Medik. = Friedrich Kasimir (Casimir) Medikus (Medicus), 1736–1808
Medw. = Jakob Sergejewitsch (Jakov Sergeevic) Medwedew (Medvedev), 1847–1923
Meerb. = Nicolaas Meerburgh, 1734–1814
Meikle = Robert Desmond Meikle, 1923–
Meinsh. = Karl Friedrich Meinshausen, 1819–1899
Meisn. = Carl Daniel Friedrich Meisner (Meissner), 1800–1874
Melch. = Hans Melchior, 1894–1984
Melderis = Alexander (Aleksandre) Melderis, 1909–1986
Melle = Peter Jacobus van Melle, 1891–1953
Melville = Ronald Melville, 1903–1985
N.C. Melvin = Norman C. Melvin III., 1950–
H. Melzer = Helmut Melzer, 1922–
Menabde = Vladimir Levanovich Menabde, 1898–
Menet = André Menet, fl. 1908
Menitsky = Jurij (Yuri) Leonardovich (G.) Menitsky (Menitskii), 1937–2001
Menzies = Archibald Menzies, 1754–1842
Mérat = François Victor Mérat de Vaumartoise, 1780–1851
Merr. = Elmer Drew Merrill, 1876–1956

Mert. = Franz Karl (Carl) Mertens,
1764–1831
Merxm. = Hermann Merxmüller,
1920–1988
Mesa = Aldo Mesa, fl. 1971
Mett. = Georg Heinrich Mettenius,
1823–1866
Metzg. = Johann Metzger, 1789–1852
Metzing = Detlev Karl Erich Metzing,
1960–
Meve = Ulrich Meve, 1958–
Meyen = Franz Julius Ferdinand Meyen,
1804–1840
B. Mey. = Bernhard Meyer, 1767–1836
C.A. Mey. = Carl Anton (Andreevic) von
Meyer, 1795–1855
E. Mey. = Ernst Heinrich Friedrich Meyer,
1791–1858
F.K. Mey. = Friedrich Karl Meyer, 1926–
G.L. Mey. = G.L. Meyer, fl. 1881
G. Mey. = Georg Friedrich Wilhelm Meyer,
1782–1856
T. Mey. = Teodoro Meyer, 1910–
N.L. Meyer = Nicole L. Meyer, fl. 1995
J. Meyrán = Jorge Meyrán Garcia, 1918–
Mez = Carl Christian Mez, 1866–1944
Michalet = Louis Eugène Michalet,
1829–1862
Michx. = André Michaux, 1746–1803
F. Michx. = François André Michaux,
1770–1855
Micheli = Marc Micheli, 1844–1902
D.J. Middleton = David John Middleton,
1963–
J. Miège = Jacques Miège, 1914–1993
Miègev. = Joseph Miègeville, 1819–1901
Miellez = Auguste Miellez, ?–1860
Miers = John Miers, 1789–1879
J.C. Mikan = Johann Christian Mikan,
1769–1844
Mildbr. = Gottfried Wilhelm Johannes
Mildbraed, 1879–1954
Milde = Carl August Julius Milde,
1824–1871
Milkuhn = F.G. Milkuhn, fl. 1949
R.R. Mill = Robert Reid Mill, 1950–
Millais = John Guille Millais, 1865–1931
Millán = Aníbal Roberto Millán, 1892–
Mill. = Philip Miller, 1691–1771
W.T. Mill. = Wilhelm (William Tyler)
Miller, 1869–1938
Millsp. = Charles Frederick Millspaugh,
1854–1923
Milne-Redh. = Edgar Wolston Bertram
Handsley Milne-Redhead, 1906–1996

T.L. Ming = Tien Lu Ming, 1937–
Miq. = Friedrich Anton Wilhelm Miquel,
1811–1871
Mirb. = Charles François Brisseau de
Mirbel, 1776–1854
Mirek = Zbigniew Mirek, 1951–
Miscz. = Pavel Ivanovich Misczenko
(Mischtschenko), 1869–1938
Mitford = Algernon Bertram Freeman
Mitford, 1837–1916
Mitterp. = Ludwig Mitterpacher von
Mitterburg, 1734–1814
Mittler = Mittler, fl. 1844
Miyabe = Kingo Miyabe, 1860–1951
Miyoshi = Manabu Miyoshi, 1861–1939
Moç. = José Mariano Moçiño Suarez de
Figueroa, 1757–1820
H. Möller = Hjalmar August Möller,
1866–1941
L. Möller = Ludwig Möller, 1847–1910
Moench = Conrad Moench (Mönch),
1744–1805
Möschl = Wilhelm Möschl, 1906–1981
D. Mohr = Daniel Matthias Heinrich Mohr,
1780–1808
Moldenke = Harold Norman Moldenke,
1909–1996
Molina = Giovanni Ignazio (Juan Ignacio)
Molina, 1737–1829
Molinet = Amorós Eugenio Molinet, fl.
1889
Monach. = Joseph Vincent Monachino,
1911–1962
Montbret = Gustave Coquebert de
Montbret, 1805–1837
Monv. = M.Chevalier (de) Monville, fl. 1838
Moon = Alexander Moon, ?–1825
A.H. Moore = Albert Hanford Moore, 1883–
C. Moore = Charles Moore, 1820–1905
D.D.T. Moore = Daniel David Tompkins
Moore, 1820–1892
H.E. Moore = Harold Emery Moore,
1917–1980
J.W. Moore = John William Moore, 1901–
L.B. Moore = Lucy Beatrice Moore,
1906–1987
S. Moore = Spencer Le Marchant Moore,
1850–1931
T. Moore = Thomas Moore, 1821–1887
T.V. Moore = Thomas Verner Moore,
1877–1969
Moore = David Moore, 1808–1879
J. Moore = J. Moore, fl. 1885
Moq. = Christian Horace Bénédict Alfred
Moquin-Tandon, 1804–1863

Moran = Reid Venable Moran, 1916–
Morel = Francisque Morel, c.1849–1925
Morelet = Pierre Marie Arthur Morelet, 1809–1892
Moretti = Giuseppe L. Moretti, 1782–1853
T. Mori = Tamezô Mori, 1885–1962
Moric. = Moïse Étienne ("Stefano") Moricand, 1779–1854
Moris = Giuseppe Giacinto (Joseph Hyacinthe) Moris, 1796–1869
Moritzi = Alexander Moritzi, 1806–1850
Morong = Thomas Morong, 1827–1894
C. Morren = Charles François Antoine Morren, 1807–1858
E. Morren = Charles Jacques Édouard Morren, 1833–1886
D. Morris = Daniel Morris, 1844–1933
F.J.A. Morris = Francis John A. Morris, 1869–1949
R. Morris = Richard Morris, fl. 1820–1830
C.V. Morton = Conrad Vernon Morton, 1905–1972
J.K. Morton = John Kenneth Morton, 1928–
Moss = Charles Edward Moss, 1870–1930
Mottet = Séraphin Joseph Mottet, 1861–1930
Mottram = Roy Mottram, 1940–
Mouill. = Pierre Mouillefert, 1845–1903
Mucher = Walter Mucher, 1962–
Mudie = Robert Mudie, 1777–1842
Muehlenpf. = Friedrich Muehlenpfordt, fl. 1849–1891
J.S. Muell. = Johann Sebastian Mueller, 1715–1780
O.F. Müll. = Otto Friedrich (Friderich) Müller, 1730–1784
Müll. Arg. = Johannes (Jean) Müller (Argoviensis), 1828–1896
F. Muell. = Ferdinand Jacob Heinrich von Mueller (Müller), 1825–1896
P.J. Müll. = Philipp Jakob (Philippe Jacques) Müller (Muller), 1832–1889
Münchh. = Otto von Münchhausen, 1716–1774
Muhl. = Gotthilf Heinrich Ernest Muhlenberg, 1753–1815
Muirhead = Clara Winsome Muirhead, 1915–1985
Mulligan = Brian Orson Mulligan, 1907–
Munby = Giles Munby, 1813–1876
Munro = William Munro, 1818–1889
Munz = Philip Alexander Munz, 1892–1974
Murata = Gen Murata, 1927–
Muratova = V.S. Muratova, 1890–1948

Murb. = Svante Samuel Murbeck, 1859–1946
Murith = Laurent Joseph Murith, 1742–1818
Muroi = Hiroshi Muroi, 1914–
Murr = Josef Murr, 1864–1932
A. Murray bis = Andrew Murray, 1812–1878
E. Murray = Albert Edward Murray, 1935–
Murray = Johan Andreas (Anders) Murray, 1740–1791
Musil = Albina Frances Musil, 1894–
Muss. Puschk. = Apollos Apollossowitsch Mussin-Puschkin, 1760–1805
Mutel = Pierre Auguste Victor Mutel, 1795–1847
Mutis = José Celestino Bruno Mutis, 1732–1808
Nakai = Takenoshin (Takenosin) Nakai, 1882–1952
H. Nakai = Hideki Nakai, fl. 1996
Nannf. = John (Johan) Axel Frithiof Nannfeldt, 1904–1985
Nash = George Valentine Nash, 1864–1921
Natho = Horst Wolfgang Günther Natho, 1930–
Naudin = Charles Victor Naudin, 1815–1899
Nauenb. = Johannes Dietrich Nauenburg, 1951–
M.P. Nayar = Madhavan Parameswarau Nayar, 1932–
Neck. = Noël Martin Joseph de Necker, 1730–1793
Née = Luis Née, fl. 1789–1794
Nees = Christian Gottfried Daniel Nees von Esenbeck, 1776–1858
T. Nees = Theodor Friedrich Ludwig Nees von Esenbeck, 1787–1837
Neilr. = August Neilreich, 1803–1871
Nekr. = Vera Leontievna Nekrassova, 1881–1979
Nel = Gert Cornelius Nel, 1885–1950
A. Nelson = Aven Nelson, 1859–1952
C. Nelson = Cirilo H. Nelson, 1938–
J. Nelson = John Nelson, fl. 1860
Nendtv. = Carl Maximilian (Károli Miksa) Nendtvich, 1811–1892
Ness = Helge Ness, 1861–1928
Nessel = Hermann Nessel, 1877–1949
Nestl. = Chrétien Géofroy (Christian Gottfried) Nestler, 1778–1832
A. Neumann = Alfred Neumann, 1916–1973
Neumann = Joseph Henri François Neumann, 1800–1858
H. Neumann = Heinrich Philipp (Heinz) Neumann, 1932–
H. Neumayer = Hans Neumayer, 1887–1945

Neutel. = T.M.W. Neutelings, fl. 1986
Nevski = Sergei Arsenjevic Nevski, 1908–1938
Newman = Edward Newman, 1801–1876
Nicholls = William Henry Nicholls, 1885–1951
G. Nicholson = George Nicholson, 1847–1908
Nicolai = Ernst August Nicolai, 1800–1874
Nicolai bis = Nicolai, publ. 1893
Nicolson = Dan Henry Nicolson, 1933–
Nied. = Franz Josef Niedenzu, 1857–1937
I.C. Nielsen = Ivan Christian Nielsen, 1946–
Nieuwl. = Julius (Aloysius) Arthur Nieuwland, 1878–1936
Nikolic = E. Nikolic, fl. 1904
Nimmo = Joseph Nimmo, –1854
Nitz. = Tor G. Nitzelius, 1914–1999
Nocca = Domenico Nocca, 1758–1841
Noë = Friedrich Wilhelm Noë, –1858
Nolte = Ernst Ferdinand Nolte, 1791–1875
Nordal = Inger Nordal, 1944–
B. Nord. = Rune Bertil Nordenstam, 1936–
Nordm. = Alexander (Davidovic) von Nordmann, 1803–1866
Norl. = Nils Tycho Norlindh, 1906–
Noronha = Francisco (François) Noroña, c.1748–1787
Norrl. = Johan Petter (Peter) Norrlin, 1842–1917
Nothdurft = Heinrich Wilhelm Christian Nothdurft, 1921–
Novák = Frantisek Antonín Novák, 1892–1964
H. Nováková = Helena Nováková, publ. 1978
Nutt. = Thomas Nuttall, 1786–1859
F. Nyl. = Fredrik (Frederick) Nylander, 1820–1880
Nyman = Carl Fredrik Nyman, 1820–1893
Nym. = Nyman
O'Brien = James O'Brien, 1842–1930
Oakeley = Henry Francis Oakeley, 1941–
Oakes = William Oakes, 1799–1848
Oberd. = Erich Oberdorfer, 1905–2002
Oberm. = Anna Amelia Obermeyer-Maive, 1907–2001
Oborny = Adolf Oborny, 1840–1924
Ockendon = David Jeffery Ockendon, 1940–
Oeder = George Christian Edler von Oldenburg Oeder, 1728–1791
Oefelein = Hans Oefelein, 1905–1970
Oehme = Hanns Oehme, ?–1944

Oerst. = Anders Sandö (Sandoe) Örsted (Orsted), 1816–1872
Oeser = Rudolf Oeser, fl. 1976–1984
H. Ohashi = Hiroyoshi Ohashi, 1936–
H. Ohba = Hideaki Ohba, 1943–
Ohba = Tatsuyuki Ohba, 1936–
Ohrnb. = Dieter Ohrnberger, fl. 1990
Ohwi = Jisaburo Ohwi, 1905–1977
Oken = Lorenz Oken (Okenfuß), 1779–1851
Oliv. = Daniel Oliver, 1830–1916
W.R.B. Oliv. = Walter Reginald Brook Oliver, 1883–1957
Olivier = Guillaume Antoine Olivier, 1756–1814
H. Ollg. = Hans Ollgaard, 1943–
Olney = Stephen Thayer Olney, 1812–1878
Onno = Max Onno, 1903–
Oosten = M.W.B van Oosten, fl. 1840
Ooststr. = Simon Jan van Ooststroom, 1906–1982
Opiz = Philipp (Filip) Maximilian Opiz, 1787–1858
Orb. = Alcide Charles Victor Dessalines d' Orbigny, 1806–1876
Orcutt = Charles Russell Orcutt, 1864–1929
Ornduff = Robert Ornduff, 1932–2000
Orph. = Theodhoros Georgios Orphanides, 1817–1886
Ortega = Casimiro Gómez de Ortega, 1740–1818
J.G. Ortega = Jesús González Ortega, 1876–1936
Ortgies = Karl Eduard Ortgies, 1829–1916
Osbeck = Pehr Osbeck, 1723–1805
Osborn = Arthur Osborn, 1878–1964
Osten = Cornelius Osten, 1863–1936
Ostenf. = Carl Emil Hansen Ostenfeld, 1873–1931
Osti = Gian Lupo Osti, publ. 1994
Ostolaza = Carlos Ostolaza Nano, fl. 1983
Oterdoom = Herman John Oterdoom, 1917–
Otto = Christoph Friedrich Otto, 1783–1856
Oudem. = Cornelius Antoon Jan Abraham (Corneille Antoine Jean Abram) Oudemans, 1825–1906
G.B. Ownbey = Gerald Bruce Ownbey, 1916–
Pabst = Guido Joao Frederico Pabst, 1914–1980
C.N. Page = Christopher Nigel Page, 1942–
Page = William Bridgewater Page, 1790–1871
Paine = John Alsop Paine, 1840–1912
Palau = Antonio Palau y Verdera, –1793

Palib. = Ivan Vladimirovic Palibin,
1872–1949
P. Beauv. = Ambroise Marie François
Joseph Palisot de Beauvois, 1752–1820
Palla = Eduard Palla, 1864–1922
Pall. = Peter (Pyotr) Simon von Pallas,
1741–1811
Pallis = M. Pallis, fl. 1938
E.J. Palmer = Ernest Jesse Palmer,
1875–1962
Palmgr. = Alvar Palmgren, 1880–1960
Pamp. = Renato Pampanini, 1875–1949
Pančić = Josef (Giuseppe, Josif) Pančić
(Pancio, Panchic), 1814–1888
Pangalo = Konstantin Ivanovic Pangalo,
1883–1965
Pantl. = Robert Pantling, 1856–1910
Pant. = Jószef (Joseph) Pantocsek,
1846–1916
Panz. = Georg Wolfgang Franz Panzer,
1755–1829
Paol. = Giulio Paoletti, 1865–1941
Pappe = Karl (Carl) Wilhelm Ludwig
Pappe, 1803–1862
Paris = Jean Édouard Gabriel Narcisse
Paris, 1827–1911
C.S.P. Parish = Charles Samuel Pollock
Parish, 1822–1897
Parish = Samuel Bonsall Parish, 1838–1928
H.M. Parker = H.M. Parker, fl. 1975
K.L. Parker = Kittie Lucille Fenley Parker,
1910–1994
R. Parker = Richard Neville Parker,
1884–1958
Parkinson = Sydney C. Parkinson,
1745–1771
Parl. = Filippo Parlatore, 1816–1877
Parm. = Antoine Auguste Parmentier,
1737–1813
J. Parm. = Joseph Julien Ghislain
Parmentier, 1755–1852
Paul Parm. = Paul Parmentier, fl. 1896
J. Parn. = John Adrian Naicker Parnell,
1954–
Parn. = Richard Parnell, 1810–1882
D. Parodi = Domingo Parodi, 1823–1890
Parodi = Lorenzo Raimundo Parodi,
1895–1966
Parry = Charles Christopher Parry,
1823–1890
S.H. Parsons = Sidney H. Parsons, publ.
1936
Pass. = Giovanni Passerini, 1816–1893
Patzke = Erwin Patzke, 1929–
Pau = Carlos Pau, 1857–1937

H.K.G. Paul = Hermann Karl Gustav Paul,
1876–1964
Paul = William Paul, 1822–1905
Paunero = Elena Paunero, 1906–
Pauquy = Charles Louis Constant Pauquy,
1800–1854
Pav. = José Antonio Pavón y Jiménez,
1754–1844
Pavone = Pietro Pavone, 1948–
Pawl. = Bogumil Pawlowski, 1898–1971
Pax = Ferdinand Albin Pax, 1858–1942
Paxton = Joseph Paxton, 1803–1865
Pearce = Sydney Albert Pearce, 1906–1972
H. Pearson = Henry Harold Welch
Pearson, 1870–1916
M. Peck = Morton Eaton Peck, 1871–1959
Pedley = Leslie Pedley, 1930–
C. Pei = Chien Pei (P'ei), 1903?–1969
Pellegr. = François Pellegrin, 1881–1965
Pellet. = Pierre Joseph Pelletier, 1788–1842
Pennell = Francis Whittier Pennell,
1886–1952
Pépin = Pierre Denis Pépin, c.1802–1876
Percival = John Percival, 1863–1949
Perdue = Robert Edward Perdue, 1924–
E. Pereira = Edmundo Pereira, 1914–1986
Pérez-Mor. = Román A. Pérez-Moreau,
1905–1971
Perkins = Janet Russell Perkins, 1853–1933
Pernh. = Gustav von Pernhoffer, 1831–1899
Perp. = Helena (Candida Lena) Perpenti,
1764–1846
E.P. Perrier = Eugène Pierre Baron de
Perrier de la Bâthie, 1825–1916
H. Perrier = Joseph Marie Henry Alfred
Perrier de la Bâthie, 1873–1958
Perrine = Henry Perrine, 1797–1840
Perrot = Émile Constant Perrot, 1867–1951
Perr. = George (Georges Guerrard) Samuel
Perrottet, 1793–1870
L.M. Perry = Lily May Perry, 1895–1992
R.H. Perry = Reginald H. Perry, 1903–
Personnat = Victor Personnat, 1829–1885
Pers. = Christiaan Hendrik Persoon,
1761–1836
Petagna = Vincenzo Petagna, 1734–1810
Peter = Gustav Albert Peter, 1853–1937
Peterm. = Wilhelm Ludwig Petermann,
1806–1855
Petersen = Otto Georg Petersen, 1847–1937
Thouars = Louis Marie Aubert du Petit-
Thouars, 1758–1831
Petitm. = Marcel Georges Charles
Petitmengin, 1881–1908
Petrie = Donald Petrie, 1846–1925

Petrov = Vsevolod Alexeevic Petrov,
1896–1955
Petrovic = Sava Petrovic, 1839–1889
Peyr. = Johann Joseph Peyritsch, 1835–1889
Pfeiff. = Louis (Ludwig) Karl Georg
Pfeiffer, 1805–1877
Pfitzer = Ernst Hugo Heinrich Pfitzer,
1846–1906
Phil. = Rudolph (Rudolf) Amandus
(Rodolfo Amando) Philippi, 1808–1904
F. Phil. = Federico (Friedrich Heinrich
Eunom) Philippi, 1838–1910
Philipson = William Raymond Philipson,
1911–1997
E. Phillips = Edwin Percy Phillips,
1884–1967
Pic.Serm. = Rodolfo Emilio Giuseppe Pichi
Sermolli, 1912–2005
Pichon = Marcel Pichon, 1921–1954
M.D. Pierrat = M.D. Pierrat, fl. 1880
Pierre = Jean Baptiste Louis Pierre,
1833–1905
A.V. Pike = A.V. Pike, fl. 1946
Pilg. = Robert Knuds Friedrich Pilger,
1876–1953
Pillans = Neville Stuart Pillans, 1884–1964
Piller = Mathias Piller, 1733–1788
Pils = Gerhard Pils, publ. 1980
Pio = Giovanni Battista Pio, fl. 1813
Piper = Charles Vancouver Piper,
1867–1926
Pirotta = Pietro Romualdo Pirotta,
1853–1936
Pit. = Charles-Joseph Marie Pitard (Pitard-
Briau), 1873–1927
R. Pitcher = R. Pitcher, fl. 1900
Pittier = Henri François Pittier de Fabrega,
1857–1950
Planch. = Jules Émile Planchon, 1823–1888
Platzm. = Karl Julius Platzmann,
1832–1902
Plenck = Joseph Jacob von Plenck (Plenk),
1738–1807
Plowman = Timothy Charles Plowman,
1944–1989
Plum. = Charles Plumier, 1646–1704
Pobed. = Evgeniia (Eugenia) Georgievna
Pobedimova, 1898–1973
Podlech = Dietrich Johannes Georg
Podlech, 1931–
Podp. = Josef Podpera, 1878–1954
Poech = Josef (Alois) Poech, 1816–1846
Poelln. = Karl von Poellnitz, 1896–1945
Poepp. = Eduard Friedrich Poeppig,
1798–1868

Poggenb. = Justus Ferdinand Poggenburg,
1840–1893
Pohl = Johann Baptist Emanuel Pohl,
1782–1834
Poir. = Jean Louis Marie Poiret, 1755–1834
Poiss. = Henri Louis Poisson, 1877–1963
A. Poit. = Alexandre Poiteau, 1776–1850
Poit. = Pierre Antoine Poiteau, 1766–1854
Pojark. = Antonina Ivanovna Pojarkova,
1897–1980
Pol. = Hellmuth Polakowsky, 1847–1917
Polatschek = Adolf Polatschek, 1932–
Poljakov = Petr Petrovich Poljakov,
1902–1974
Pollard = Charles Louis Pollard, 1872–1945
G.E. Pollard = Glenn E. Pollard, 1901–1976
Pollich = Johann Adam Pollich, 1740–1780
Pomel = Auguste Nicolas Pomel, 1821–1898
Ponomar. = V.V. Ponomarenko, 1938–
Pons = Alexandre Pons, 1838–1893
Popl. = Henrietta Ippolitovna Poplavskaja,
1885–1956
Popov = Mikhail Grigoríevic (Grigoríevich)
Popov, 1893–1955
Porsch = Otto Porsch, 1875–1959
Porta = Pietro Porta, 1832–1923
Port. = Franz von Portenschlag-
Ledermayer, 1772–1822
D.M. Porter = Duncan MacNair Porter,
1937–
Porter = Thomas Conrad Porter, 1822–1901
Poselg. = Heinrich Poselger, 1818–1883
Post = George Edward Post, 1838–1909
Pott = Johann Friedrich Pott, 1738–1805
Potztal = Eva Hedwig Ingeborg Potztal,
1924–2000
Pourr. = Pierre André Pourret de Figeac,
1753–1818
Pouzar = Zdenek Pouzar, 1932–
Powrie = Elizabeth Powrie, 1925–1977
Praeger = Robert Lloyd Praeger, 1865–1953
Prain = David Prain, 1857–1944
Prantl = Karl Anton Eugen Prantl,
1849–1893
Prassler = Maria Prassler, 1938–
L. Preiss = Johann August Ludwig Preiss,
1811–1883
C. Presl = Carel (Karel) Boriwog Presl,
1794–1852
J. Presl = Jan Svatopluk (Swatopluk) Presl,
1791–1849
P. Preuss = Paul Rudolf Preuss, 1861–1926
M.G. Price = Michael Greene Price, 1941–
Pridgeon = Alec M. Pridgeon, fl. 1997
J.S. Pringle = James Scott Pringle, 1937–

N.M. Pritch. = Noël Marshall Pritchard, 1933–
E. Pritz. = Ernst Georg Pritzel, 1875–1946
Pritz. = Georg August Pritzel, 1815–1874
Proctor = George Richardson Proctor, 1920–
Prodán = Iuliu (Julius) Prodán, 1875–1959
Prokh. = Jaroslav Ivanovic (Yaroslav Ivanovich) Prokhanoff (Prokhanov), 1902–1964
Prokudin = Juri Nikolajevi Prokudin, 1911–
Proust = Louis Proust, 1878–1959
Pugsley = Herbert William Pugsley, 1868–1947
Pulliat = Victor Pulliat, 1827–1866
Purdy = Carlton Elmer Purdy, 1861–1945
Purk. = Emanuel Ritter von Purkyne, 1832–1882
Purpus = Carl Albert Purpus, 1851–1941
J.A. Purpus = Joseph Anton Purpus, 1860–1932
Pursh = Frederick Traugott Pursh, 1774–1820
Pusch = Jürgen Pusch, 1962–
Putt. = Aloys Putterlick, 1810–1845
Putz. = Jules Antoine Adolph Henri Putzeys, 1809–1882
X.H. Qian = Xiao Hu Qian, fl. 1984
Quehl = Leopold Quehl, 1849–1922
P. Quentin = Pierre Jacques Jean Quentin, 1954–
Rabenh. = Gottlob Ludwig Rabenhorst, 1806–1881
Rach = Louis Theodor Rach, 1821–1859
Racib. = Marjan (Maryan) Raciborski, 1863–1917
Radcl.-Sm. = Alan Radcliffe-Smith, 1938–
Radde = Gustav Ferdinand Richard Johannes von Radde, 1831–1903
Raddi = Giuseppe Raddi, 1770–1829
Raderm. = Jacobus Cornelius Matthaeus Radermacher, 1741–1783
Radlk. = Ludwig Adolph Timotheus Radlkofer, 1829–1927
Raeusch. = Ernst Adolf Raeuschel, fl. 1772–1797
Raffill = Charles Percival Raffill, 1876–1951
Raf. = Constantine Samuel Rafinesque-Schmaltz, 1783–1840
Rafn = Carl Gottlob Rafn, 1769–1808
Ragion. = Attilio Ragionieri, 1856–1933
Rahn = Knud Rahn, 1928–
Raim. = Rudolf Raimann, 1863–1896
D.C.S. Raju = D.C.S. Raju, 1936–
Ramat. = Thomas Albin Joseph d'Audibert de Ramatuelle, 1750–1794

Ramond = Louis Louis François Élisabeth Baron Ramond de Carbonnières, 1755–1827
Randell = Barbara Rae Randell, 1942–
Raoul = Édouard Fiacre Louis Raoul, 1815–1852
Rapin = Daniel Rapin, 1799–1882
Raspail = François Vincent Raspail, 1794–1878
Rataj = Karel Rataj, 1925–
Ratzeb. = Julius Theodor Christian Ratzeburg, 1801–1871
Rauh = Werner Rauh, 1913–2000
Rausch = Walter Rausch, 1928–
Rauschert = Stephan Rauschert, 1931–1986
P.H. Raven = Peter Hamilton Raven, 1936–
Raymond = Louis-Florent-Marcel Raymond, 1915–1972
J. Raynal = Jean Raynal, 1933–1979
Raynaud = Christian Raynaud, 1939–1993
Read = Robert William Read, 1931–2003
J.M. Reade = John Moore Reade, 1876–1937
Rebut = P. Rebut, –1898
Rech. = Karl Rechinger, 1867–1952
Rech. f. = Karl Heinz Rechinger, 1906–1998
Redouté = Pierre Joseph Redouté, 1759–1840
Reeves = Robert Gatlin Reeves, 1898–
Regel = Eduard August von Regel, 1815–1892
Rehder = Alfred Rehder, 1863–1949
S.E.A. Rehm = Sigmund Eugen Adolf Rehm, 1911–
Rehmann = Anton Rehmann (Rehman), 1840–1917
Reichard = Johann Jacob (Jakob) Reichard, 1743–1782
Reiche = Karl Friedrich (Carlos Federico) Reiche, 1860–1929
Rchb. = (Heinrich Gottlieb) Ludwig Reichenbach, 1793–1879
F. Rchb. = Friedrich Reichenbach, fl. 1896
Rchb. f. = Heinrich Gustav Reichenbach, 1824–1889
Reinsch = Paul Friedrich Reinsch, 1836–1914
Reinw. = Caspar Georg Carl Reinwardt, 1773–1854
Reisaeter = Oddvin Reisaeter, 1913–1983
Reissek = Siegfried Reissek (Reisseck), 1819–1871
Reitz = Raulino Reitz, 1919–1990
Rendle = Alfred Barton Rendle, 1865–1938
Renner = Otto Renner, 1883–1960

Repp. = Werner Reppenhagen, 1911–1996
Req. = Esprit Requien, 1788–1851
Resv.-Holms. = Hanna Marie Resvoll-
Holmsen, 1873–1943
Retz. = Anders Jahan Retzius, 1742–1821
G. Reuss = Gustáv Reuss, 1818–1861
Reut. = George François Reuter, 1805–1872
Reuthe = G. Reuthe, fl. 1891
Reveal = James Lauritz Reveal, 1941–
P. Rev. = Paul Alphonse Reverchon,
1833–1907
A. Reyn. = Alfred Reynier, 1845–1932
Reyn. = Jean Louis Antoine Reynier,
1762–1824
Riccob. = Vincenzo Riccobono, 1861–1943
A. Rich. = Achille Richard, 1794–1852
Rich. = Louis Claude Marie Richard,
1754–1821
A.J. Richards = Adrian John Richards,
1943–
P.W. Richards = Paul Westmacott
Richards, 1908–1995
I. Richardson = Ian Bertram Kay
Richardson, 1940–
Richardson = John Richardson, 1787–1865
Richt. = Hermann Eberhard Friedrich
Richter, 1808–1876
K. Richt. = Karl (Carl) Richter, 1855–1891
V.A. Richt. = Vincenz Aladár Richter,
1868–1927
Rickett = Harold William Rickett,
1896–1989
Riddell = John Leonard Riddell, 1807–1865
Ridl. = Henry Nicholas Ridley, 1855–1956
Ridsdale = Colin Ernest Ridsdale, 1944–
Riedl = Harald (Harold) Udo von Riedl,
1936–
Ríha = Jan Ríha, 1947–
Rikli = Martin Albert Rikli, 1868–1951
L. Riley = Laurence Athelstan Molesworth
Riley, 1888–1928
Risso = Joseph Antoine Risso, 1777–1845
F. Ritter = Friedrich Ritter, 1898–1989
Rivas Mart. = Salvador Rivas Martínez,
1935–
Rivers = Thomas Rivers, 1798–1877
C. Rivière = Charles Marie Rivière, 1845–
Rivière = Marie Auguste Rivière, 1821–1877
Rizzini = Carlos Toledo Rizzini, 1921–1992
Robatsch = Karl Robatsch, 1929–2000
J.W. Robbins = James Watson Robbins,
1801–1879
E.P. Roberts = Evan Paul Roberts, 1914–
A.V. Roberts = Andrew Vaughan Roberts,
1940–

Roberty = Guy Édouard Roberty, 1907–1971
B.L. Rob. = Benjamin Lincoln Robinson,
1864–1935
C.B. Rob. = Charles Budd Robinson,
1871–1913
H. Rob. = Harold Ernest Robinson, 1932–
E. Robson = Edward Robson, 1763–1813
N. Robson = Norman Keith Bonner
Robson, 1928–
Robyns = Frans Hubert Edouard Arthur
Walter Robyns, 1901–1986
Rocha Afonso = Maria da Luz de Oliveira
Tavares Monteiro Rocha Afonso, 1925–
Rochel = Anton Rochel, 1770–1847
H. Rock = Howard Francis Leonard Rock,
1925–1964
Rodigas = Émile Rodigas, 1831–1902
L.E. Rodin = Leonid Efimovic Rodin,
1907–1990
Rodion = Georgi Ivanovich Rodionenko,
1913–
Rodr. = José Demetrio Rodríguez, 1780–1846
Rodway = Leonard Rodway, 1853–1936
Röhl. = Johann Christoph Röhling,
1757–1813
Roehr. = Olivier Roehrich, fl. 1914
Roem. = Johann Jakob Roemer, 1763–1819
M. Roem. = Max Joseph Roemer, 1791–1849
Roessler = Helmut Roessler, 1926–
Roezl = Benedikt (Benito) Roezl,
1824–1885
Rogow. = Athanasi Semenovic
(Semenovich) Rogowicz (Rogovitch),
1815–1878
Rohmeder = Ernst Rohmeder, 1903–1972
Rohr = Julius Philip Benjamin von Rohr,
1737–1793
Rohrb. = Paul Rohrbach, 1846–1871
Rohweder = Otto Rohweder, 1919–
Rojas Acosta = Nicolás Rojas Acosta,
1873–1947
Rol.-Goss. = Robert Roland-Gosselin,
1854–1925
Rolfe = Robert Allen Rolfe, 1855–1921
Rom. Caill. = Frédéric Romanet du
Caillaud, fl. 1881–1888
Ronniger = Karl (Carl) Ronniger, 1871–1954
Ronse Decr. = Louis Philippe Ronse De
Craene, 1962–
Roscoe = William Roscoe, 1753–1831
Rose = Joseph Nelson Rose, 1862–1928
Rosenst. = Eduard Rosenstock, 1856–1938
Roshkova = Olga Ivanovna Roshkova,
1909–1989
R. Ross = Robert Ross, 1912–2005

Rossi = Pietro Rossi, 1738–1804
Rostk. = Friedrich Wilhelm Gottlieb Rostkovius, 1770–1848
Rostr. = (Frederik Georg) Emil Rostrup, 1831–1907
Rosua = José Luis Rosua, 1954–
Roth = Albrecht Wilhelm Roth, 1757–1834
Rothm. = Werner Hugo Paul Rothmaler, 1908–1962
Rothr. = Joseph Trimble Rothrock, 1839–1922
Rottb. = Christen Friis Rottboll, 1727–1797
Rottler = Johan Peter Rottler, 1749–1836
Rouhier = Alexandre Rouhier, fl. 1926
Rouleau = Joseph Albert Ernest Rouleau, 1916–1991
Rousi = Arne Henrik Rousi, 1931–
Rouy = Georges Rouy, 1851–1924
Rovelli = Renato Rovelli, 1806–1880
Rowlee = Willard Winfield Rowlee, 1861–1923
G.D. Rowley = Gordon Douglas Rowley, 1921–
Roxb. = William Roxburgh, 1751–1815
D. Royen = David van Royen, 1727–1799
P. Royen = Pieter van Royen, 1923–2002
Royle = John Forbes Royle, 1798–1858
Rozeira = Arnaldo Deodato da Fonseca Rozeira, 1912–
Rozier = Jean-Baptiste François Rozier, 1734–1793
Rudd = Velva Elaine Rudd, 1910–1999
Rudge = Edward Rudge, 1763–1846
Rudolph = Johann Heinrich Rudolph, 1744–1809
Rudolphi = (Israel) Karl Asmund (Carl Asmunt, Asmus) Rudolphi, 1771–1832
Rümpler = Karl Theodor Rümpler, 1817–1891
Ruhland = Wilhelm (Willy) Otto Eugen Ruhland, 1878–1960
Ruiz = Hipólito Ruiz López, 1754–1815
Rumph. = Georg Eberhard Rumphius, 1628–1702
Runemark = Hans Runemark, 1927–
Runge = C. Runge, fl. 1889
Rupp = Herman Montague Rucker Rupp, 1872–1956
Rupr. = Franz Josef (Ivanovich) Ruprecht, 1814–1870
Rusby = Henry Hurd Rusby, 1855–1940
R. Ruthe = Johann Gustav Rudolf Ruthe, 1823–1905
Ruthe = Johannes Friedrich Ruthe, 1788–1859

A. Rutherf. = Alison Rutherford, fl. 1993
Rydb. = Pehr Axel Rydberg, 1860–1931
Rydlo = Jaroslav Rydlo, 1950–
Rylands = Thomas Glazebrook Rylands, 1818–1900
Sabine = Joseph Sabine, 1770–1837
Sachet = Marie-Hélène Sachet, 1922–1986
Sadler = Joseph (Jószef) Sadler, 1791–1849
Saff. = William Edwin ('Ned') Safford, 1859–1926
St.-Amans = Jean Florimond Boudon de Saint-Amans, 1748–1831
J. St.-Hil. = Jean Henri Jaume Saint-Hilaire, 1772–1845
A. St.-Hil. = Augustin François César Prouvençal de Saint-Hilaire, 1779–1853
St.-Lag. = Jean Baptiste Saint-Lager, 1825–1912
St.-Yves = Alfred (Marie Augustine) Saint-Yves, 1855–1933
Salazar = Gerardo A. Salazar, 1961–
Saldanha = José de Saldanha da Gama, 1839–1905
Salisb. = Richard Anthony Salisbury, 1761–1829
Salm-Dyck = Joseph Franz Maria Anton Hubert Ignaz Fürst und Altgraf zu Salm-Reifferscheid- Dyck, 1773–1861
C.E. Salmon = Charles Edgar Salmon, 1872–1930
T.M. Salter = Terence Macleane Salter, 1883–1969
Salzm. = Philipp Salzmann, 1781–1851
Samp. = Gonçalo António da Silva Ferreira Sampaio, 1865–1937
Sampath = V. Sampath, fl. 1981
Sam. = Gunnar Samuelsson, 1885–1944
Sánchez-Mej. = Hernando Sánchez-Mejorada R., 1926–1988
Sander = Henry Frederick (Heinrich Friedrich) Conrad Sander, 1847–1920
I. Sándor = I. Sándor, 1853–
Sandwith = Noel Yvri Sandwith, 1901–1965
Santi = Giorgio Santi, 1746–1822
Sarg. = Charles Sprague Sargent, 1841–1927
Sarnth. = Ludwig Graf von Sarnthein, 1861–1914
Sarsons = Thomas Dixon Sarsons, 1880–1951
Sart. = Giovanni Battista Sartorelli, 1780–1853
Sartori = Joseph Sartori, 1809–1880
F.W.H. Sauer = Friedrich Wilhelm Heinrich Sauer, 1803–1873
W. Sauer = Wilhelm Sauer, 1935–

Saukel = Johannes Rudolf Saukel, 1953–
Saunders = William Wilson Saunders, 1809–1879
Saut. = Anton Eleutherius Sauter, 1800–1881
Sauv. = Camille François Sauvageau, 1861–1936
Sav. = Paul Amédée Ludovic Savatier, 1830–1891
Savi = Gaetano Savi, 1769–1844
Savigny = Marie Jules César Lelorgne de Savigny, 1777–1851
Schaeff. = Jacob Christian Schaeffer, 1718–1790
Schaeftl. = Hans Schaeftlein, 1886–1973
Schauer = Johannes Conrad Schauer, 1813–1848
S. Schauer = Sebastian Schauer, fl. 1847
Scheele = George Heinrich Adolf Scheele, 1808–1864
Scheer = Friedrich (Frederick) Scheer, 1792–1868
Scheff. = Rudolph Herman Christiaan Carel Scheffer, 1844–1880
Scheidw. = Michael Joseph François Scheidweiler, 1799–1861
Schelle = Ernst Schelle, 1864–1945
Schellm. = Carl Schellmann, publ. 1938
Schelpe = Edmund André Charles Lois Eloi ('Ted') Schelpe, 1924–1985
Schenk = Joseph August Schenk, 1815–1891
Scherb. = Johannes Scherbius, 1769–1813
Scheygr. = Arie Scheygrond, 1905–
Schick = Carl Schick, 1881–1953
Schiede = Christian Julius Wilhelm Schiede, 1798–1836
Schiffn. = Victor Félix Schiffner, 1862–1944
K.F. Schimp. = Karl (Carl) Friedrich Jobst Wilhelm Franz Schimper, 1803–1867
Schindl. = Anton Karl Schindler, 1879–1964
Schinz = Hans Schinz, 1858–1941
Schipcz. = Nikolaj Valerianovich Schipczinski, 1886–1955
Schischk. = Boris Konstantinovich Schischkin, 1886–1963
Schkuhr = Christian Schkuhr, 1741–1811
Schkur. = V.A. Schkurenko, fl. 1971
Schltdl. = Diederich Franz Leonhard von Schlechtendal, 1794–1866
Schltr. = Friedrich Richard Rudolf Schlechter, 1872–1925
Schleich. = Johann Christoph Schleicher, 1768–1834
Schleid. = Matthias Jacob Schleiden, 1804–1881

Schmalh. = Johannes Theodor (Ivan Fedorovich) Schmalhausen, 1849–1894
B. Schmid = B. Schmid, fl. 1983
Em. Schmid = Emil Schmid, 1891–1982
W.G. Schmid = Wolfram George Schmid, fl. 1991
Schmidel = Casimir Christoph Schmidel (Schmiedel), 1718–1792
E. Schmidt = Ernst Schmidt, 1834–1902
Schmidt = Franz Schmidt, 1751–1834
F.W. Schmidt = Franz Wilibald Schmidt, 1764–1796
J.A. Schmidt = Johann Anton Schmidt, 1823–1905
P. Schmidt = Paul Schmidt, 1846–
P.A. Schmidt = Peter Adam Schmidt, 1946–
W.L.E. Schmidt = Wilhelm Ludwig Ewald Schmidt, 1804–1843
F. Schmidt = Friedrich Karl (Fedor Bogdanovich) Schmidt, 1832–1908
Schneev. = George Voorhelm Schneevoogt, 1775–1850
C.K. Schneid. = Camillo Karl Schneider, 1876–1951
U. Schneid. = Ulrike Schneider, 1936–
Schnittsp. = Georg Friedrich Schnittspahn, 1810–1865
Schnizl. = Adalbert Carl (Karl) Friedrich Hellwig Conrad Schnizlein, 1814–1868
Schönb.-Tem. = Eva Schönbeck-Temesy, 1930–
Schönh. = Friedrich Christian Heinrich Schönheit, 1789–1870
Schönland = Selmar Schönland (Schonland), 1860–1940
Scholler = Friedrich Adam Scholler, 1718–1785
H. Scholz = Hildemar Wolfgang Scholz, 1928–
M.R. Schomb. = Moritz Richard Schomburgk, 1811–1891
R.H. Schomb. = Robert Hermann Schomburgk, 1804–1865
Schoser = Gustav Schoser, 1924–
Schott = Heinrich Wilhelm Schott, 1794–1865
Schottky = Ernst Max Schottky, 1888–1915
Schousb. = Peder Kofod Anker Schousboe, 1766–1832
Schrad. = Heinrich Adolph Schrader, 1767–1836
Schrank = Franz von Paula Ritter von Schrank, 1747–1835
Schreb. = Johann Christian Daniel von Schreber, 1739–1810

Schreier = K. Schreier, fl. 1973
Schrenk = Alexander Gustav von Schrenk
(Schrenck), 1816–1876
F.G. Schroed. = Fred-Günter Schroeder,
1930–
Schrödinger = Rudolph Schrödinger,
1857–1919
B.G. Schub. = Bernice Giduz Schubert,
1913–2000
Schübl. = Gustav Schübler, 1787–1834
Schütz = Bohumil Schütz, 1903–1993
Schult. = Josef (Joseph) August Schultes,
1773–1831
Schult. f. = Julius Hermann Schultes,
1804–1840
R.E. Schult. = Richard Evans Schultes,
1915–2001
Schultz = Carl (Karl) Friedrich Schultz,
1766–1837
Sch. Bip. = Carl (Karl) Heinrich
'Bipontinus' Schultz, 1805–1867
F.W. Schultz = Friedrich Wilhelm Schultz,
1804–1876
J. Schultze-Motel = Jürgen Schultze-
Motel, 1930–
W. Schultze-Motel = Wolfram Schultze-
Motel, 1934–
O.E. Schulz = Otto Eugen Schulz,
1874–1936
Rich. Schulz = Richard Schulz, fl. 1904
M. Schulze = Carl Theodor Maximilian
Schulze, 1841–1915
G. Schulze = Gerhard Karl Friedrich
Schulze, 1924–
Schumach. = Heinrich Christian Friedrich
Schumacher, 1757–1830
K. Schum. = Karl Moritz Schumann,
1851–1904
Schummel = Theodor Emil Schummel,
1785–1848
Schur = Philipp Johann Ferdinand Schur,
1799–1878
J. Schust. = Julius Schuster, 1886–1949
Schwantes = Martin Heinrich Gustav
(Georg) Schwantes, 1881–1960
F. Schwarz = (Erich) Frank Schwarz,
1857–1928
O. Schwarz = Otto Karl Anton Schwarz,
1900–1983
Schweick. = Herold Georg Wilhelm
Johannes Schweickerdt, 1903–1977
Schweigg. = August Friedrich Schweigger,
1783–1821
C. Schweinf. = Charles Schweinfurth,
1890–1970

Schweinf. = Georg August Schweinfurth,
1836–1925
Schwein. = Lewis (Ludwig) David von (de)
Schweinitz, 1780–1834
Schwer. = Fritz Kurt Alexander Graf von
Schwerin, 1856–1934
Scop. = Joannes Antonius (Giovanni
Antonio) Scopoli, 1723–1788
A.J. Scott = Andrew John Scott, 1950–
Scribn. = Frank Lamson Scribner, 1851–1938
Sealy = Joseph Robert Sealy, 1907–
Sebast. = Francesco Antonio Sebastiani,
1782–1821
Sebeók = Alexander (Sándor) Sebeók de
Szent-Miklós, fl. 1780
Seem. = Berthold Carl Seemann, 1825–1871
Seemen = Karl Otto von Seemen, 1838–1910
Ség. = Jean François Séguier, 1703–1784
Seibert = Russell Jacob Seibert, 1914–
Seidl = Wenzel Benno Seidl, 1773–1842
P.D. Sell = Peter Derek Sell, 1929–
Sello = Hermann Ludwig Sello, 1800–1876
Sellow = Friedrich Sellow, 1789–1831
Sendtn. = Otto Sendtner, 1813–1859
Sénécl. = Adrien Sénéclauze, fl. 1867
Senghas = Karlheinz Senghas, 1928–
Senoner = Adolf Senoner, 1806–1895
Serebr. = T.J. Serebrjakova, 1893–
Ser. = Nicolas Charles Seringe, 1776–1858
Sesl. = Lionardo (Leonard) Sesler, –1785
Sessé = Martín Sessé y Lacasta, 1751–1808
Seub. = Moritz August Seubert, 1818–1878
Seybold = Siegmund Gerhard Seybold,
1939–
F. Seym. = Frank Conkling Seymour,
1895–1985
Shafer = John Adolph Shafer, 1863–1918
Shap. = K. K. Shaparenko, 1908–1941
H. Sharsm. = Helen Katherine Sharsmith,
1905–1982
Sheph. = John Shepherd, 1764–1836
Sheppard = (Mrs.) Sheppard, fl. 1783–1867
Sherff = Earl Edward Sherff, 1886–1966
Shibata = Keita Shibata, 1877–1949
Shinners = Lloyd Herbert Shinners,
1918–1971
Shinwari = Zabta Khan Shinwari, fl. 1992
Shiras. = Homi (Yasuyoshi) Shirasawa,
1868–1947
Shivas = Mary Grant Shivas, 1926–
Shreve = Forrest Shreve, 1878–1950
Shurly = Ernest William Shurly, 1888–1963
Sibth. = John Sibthorp, 1758–1796
Sieber = Franz(e) Wilhelm Sieber,
1789–1844

Siebold = Philipp Franz (Balthasar) von Siebold, 1796–1866

Siehe = Walter Siehe, 1859–1928

Siesm. = J. A. Siesmayer, fl. 1888

Siev. = Johann Erasmus Sievers, ?–1795

P. Silva = António Rodrigo Pinto da Silva, 1912–1992

Silva Manso = António Luiz Patricio da Silva Manso, 1788–1818

Silva Tar. = Ernst Emanuel Graf Silva Tarouca, 1860–1936

Silverside = Alan James Silverside, 1947–

R. Sim = Robert Sim, 1791–1878

Sim = Thomas Robertson Sim, 1856–1938

Simmler = Gudrun Simmler, 1884–

Simmonds = Joseph Henry Simmonds, 1845–1936

N.W. Simmonds = Norman Willison Simmonds, 1922–

Simon-Louis = Léon L. Simon-Louis, 1834–1913

Simonet = Marc Simonet, 1899–1965

Simonk. = Lájos tól (Ludwig Philipp) Simonkai (Simkovics), 1851–1910

B.B. Simpson = Beryl Brintnall Simpson, 1942–

G. Simpson = George Simpson, 1880–1952

Sims = John Sims, 1749–1831

Sinskaya = Eugeniya Nikolayevna Sinskaya, 1889–1965

Sint. = Paul Ernst Emil Sintenis, 1847–1907

Sipliv. = Vladimir N. Siplivinsky, 1937–

Skalická = Anna Skalická, 1932–

Skalicky = Vladimír Skalicky, 1930–1994

Skan = Sidney Alfred Skan, 1870–1939

Skarupke = E. Skarupke, fl. 1973

Skeels = Homer Collar Skeels, 1873–1934

Skipwith = G.R. Skipwith, fl. 1929

L.E. Skog = Laurence Edgar (Larry) Skog, 1943–

Skottsb. = Carl Johan Fredrik Skottsberg, 1880–1963

Skov = Flemming Skov, 1958–

A.K. Skvortsov = Alexei Konstantinovich Skvortsov (Skvortzow), 1920–2008

Sleumer = Hermann Otto Sleumer, 1906–1993

Sljuss. = L.P. Sljussarenko, 1931–

B. Sloane = Boyd Lincoln Sloane, 1885–

Sloss. = Margaret Slosson, 1872–

Small = John Kunkel Small, 1869–1938

Smiley = Frank Jason Smiley, 1880–1969

P.A. Smirn. = Pavel Aleksandrovich Smirnov, 1896–1980

A.C. Sm. = Albert Charles Smith, 1906–1999

C.P. Sm. = Charles Piper Smith, 1877–1955

C. Sm. = Christen (Christian) Smith, 1785–1816

C.A. Sm. = Christo Albertyn Smith, 1898–1956

E.B. Sm. = Edwin Burnell Smith, 1936–

E.W. Sm. = Elmer William Smith, 1920–1981

G.G. Sm. = Gerald Graham Smith, 1892–1976

G.E. Sm. = Gerard Edwards Smith, 1804–1881

H.G. Sm. = Henry George Smith, 1852–1924

Sm. = James Edward Smith, 1759–1828

J.G. Sm. = Jared Gage Smith, 1866–1925

J.J. Sm. = Johannes Jacobus Smith, 1867–1947

J. Sm. = John Smith, 1798–1888

L.B. Sm. = Lyman Bradford Smith, 1904–1997

P.M. Sm. = Philip Morgans Smith, 1941–2004

R.E. Sm. = Ralph Elliott (Eliot) Smith, 1874–1953

R.M. Sm. = Rosemary Margaret Smith, 1933–

W.W. Sm. = William Wright Smith, 1875–1956

W.G. Sm. = Worthington George Smith, 1835–1917

Harry Sm. = Karl August Harald ('Harry') Smith, 1889–1971

Gideon F. Sm. = Gideon François Smith, 1959–

Smyth = Bernard Bryan Smyth, 1843–1913

Sneddon = Barry Victor Sneddon, 1942–

Snijman = Dierdré Anne Snijman, 1949–

Snogerup = Sven E. Snogerup, 1929–

Snowden = Joseph Davenport Snowden, 1886–1973

Sobol. = Gregor Fedorowitsch (Grigoriy Fedorovich) Sobolewskiy, 1741–1807

Soderstr. = Thomas Robert Soderstrom, 1936–1987

Sodiro = Luigi (Aloysius, Luis) Sodiro, 1836–1909

Söhrens = Johannes Söhrens, ?–1934

Soest = Johannes Leendert van Soest, 1898–1983

Soják = Jirí Soják, 1936–

Sol. = Daniel Carlsson (Carl) Solander, 1733–1782

Solano = Solano

Sole = William Sole, 1741–1802

Soler. = Hans Solereder, 1860–1920

Solms = Hermann Maximilian Carl Ludwig Friedrich Solms, Graf von und zu Laubach, 1842–1915

Sommier = Carlo Pietro Stefano(Stephen) Sommier, 1848–1922

Sond. = Otto Wilhelm Sonder, 1812–1881

Songeon = André Songeon, 1826–1905

Sonn. = Pierre Sonnerat, 1748–1814

Soó = Károly Rezsö Soó von Bere, 1903–1980

Soto Arenas = Miquel Angel Soto Arenas, 1963–

Soulaire = Soulaire

Soul.-Bod. = Étienne Soulange-Bodin, 1774–1846

Soulié = Joseph Auguste Louis Soulié, 1868–1930

Souster = John Eustace Sirett Souster, 1912–

Sowerby = James Sowerby, 1757–1822

Soy.-Will. = Hubert Félix Soyer-Willemet, 1791–1867

Spach = Édouard Spach, 1801–1879

Spae = Dieudonné Spae, 1819–1858

Späth = Franz Ludwig Späth, 1839–1913

Span. = Johan Baptist Spanoghe, 1798–1838

Speg. = Carlo Luigi (Carlos Luis) Spegazzini, 1858–1926

M.A. Spencer = Michael A. Spencer, fl. 1992

Spenn. = Fridolin Carl Leopold Spenner, 1798–1841

Speta = Franz Speta, 1941–

Spitzn. = Wenzel (Václav) Spitzner, 1852–1907

Splitg. = Frederik Louis Splitgerber, 1801–1845

Spongberg = Stephen Alex Spongberg, 1942–

Sprague = Thomas Archibald Sprague, 1877–1958

Spreeth = A. D. Spreeth, 1940–

Spreng. = Kurt (Curt) Polykarp Joachim Sprengel, 1766–1833

Sprenger = Carl (Charles) Ludwig Sprenger, 1846–1917

Spring = Anton Friedrich (Antoine Frédéric) Spring, 1814–1872

Spruce = Richard Spruce, 1817–1893

Spruner = Wilhelm von Spruner, 1805–1874

E.P. St John = Edward Porter St. John, 1866–1952

H. St. John = Harold St. John, 1892–1991

Stace = Clive Anthony Stace, 1938–

Stadelm. = Ernst Stadelmeyer, ?–1840

Stafleu = Frans Antonie Stafleu, 1921–1997

Standl. = Paul Carpenter Standley, 1884–1963

Stapf = Otto Stapf, 1857–1933

Staudt = Johann Gustav Günter Staudt, 1926–

Staunton = George Leonard Staunton, 1737–1801

Stearn = William Thomas Stearn, 1911–2001

Stechm. = Johannes (Johann) Paul Stechmann, fl. 1775

Steck = Abraham Steck, fl. 1757

H. Steedman = Henry Steedman, c. 1866–1953

Steenis = Cornelis Gijsbert Gerrit Jan van Steenis, 1901–1986

Steetz = Joachim Steetz, 1804–1862

Stef. = Boris Stefanoff (Stefanov) Popov, 1894–1979

Stein = Berthold Stein, 1847–1899

Steinh. = Adolph(e) Louis Frédéric Steinheil, 1810–1839

Stellfeld = Carlos Stellfeld, 1900–1970

Stent = Sydney Margaret Stent, 1875–1942

Stephan = Christian Friedrich Stephan, 1757–1814

Steph. = Franz Stephani, 1842–1927

Stephens = Edith Layard Stephens, 1884–1966

T. Stephenson = Thomas Stephenson, 1855–1948

T.A. Stephenson = Thomas Alan Stephenson, 1898–1961

Stern = Frederick Claude Stern, 1884–1967

Sternb. = Caspar (Kaspar) Maria Graf von Sternberg, 1761–1838

Sterneck = Jakob (Daublebsky) von Sterneck, 1864–1941

Sterner = Karl Rikard Sterner, 1891–1956

Sterns = Emerson Ellick Sterns, 1846–1926

Steud. = Ernst Gottlieb von Steudel, 1783–1856

Steven = Christian von (Christian Christianowitsch) Steven, 1781–1863

Steyerm. = Julian Alfred Steyermark, 1909–1988

C.H. Stirt. = Charles Howard Stirton, 1946–

Stocks = John Ellerton Stocks, 1820–1854

Störck = Anton Freiherr von Störck, 1731–1803

Stohr = Gerrit Stohr, 1928–

Stoj. = Nikolai Andreev Stojanov (Stoyanoff), 1883–1968

Stokes = Jonathan Stokes, 1755–1831
A.M. Stoor = Anu Maarit Stoor, 1966–
Storie = James G. Storie, fl. 1880s
Stork = Adélaïde Louise Stork, 1937–
Stout = Arlow Burdette Stout, 1876–1957
Straley = Gerald Bane Straley, 1945–1997
Strandh. = Sven Olof Strandhede, 1930–
Strauss = Heinrich Christian Strauss,
 1850–1922
Straw = Richard Myron Straw, 1926–
Strobl = Gabriel Strobl, 1846–1925
Struck = Mike Struck, fl. 1986
Stuntz = Stephen Conrad Stuntz, 1875–1918
Stur = Dionys (Dionyz) Rudolf Josef Stur
 (Stur), 1827–1893
Subík = Rudolf Subík, fl. 1981
Sudw. = George Bishop Sudworth,
 1864–1927
Sünd. = Franz Sündermann, 1864–1946
Suess. = Karl Suessenguth, 1893–1955
Sukaczev = Vladimir Nikolaevich
 (Wladimir Nikolajewitsch) Sukachev
 (Sukatchew, Sukaczev, Sukatschow),
 1880–1967
Suksd. = Wilhelm (William) Nikolaus
 Suksdorf, 1850–1932
Summerh. = Victor Samuel Summerhayes,
 1897–1974
J.V. Suringar = Jan Valckenier Suringar,
 1864–1932
Suter = Johann Rudolf Suter, 1766–1827
Sutton = Charles Sutton, 1756–1846
S. Suzuki = Shizuo Suzuki, fl. 1962
Sw. = Olof Peter Swartz, 1760–1818
H.R. Sweet = Herman Royden Sweet,
 1911–1991
Sweet = Robert Sweet, 1782–1835
Swingle = Walter Tennyson Swingle,
 1871–1952
Syme = John Thomas Irvine Boswell Syme,
 1822–1888
Syrach = Carl Syrach-Larsen, 1898–
Szyszyl. = Ignaz (Ignacy) Ritter von
 Szyszylowicz, 1857–1910
G. Täckh. = Gunnar Vilhelm Täckholm,
 1891–1933
Tafalla = Juan José Tafalla, 1755–1811
Tagawa = Motozi Tagawa, 1908–1977
Tagg = Harry Frank Tagg, 1874–1933
Tagl. = Giuseppe Tagliabue, fl. 1816
Takeda = Hisayoshi Takeda, 1883–1972
Takht. = Armen Leonovich Takhtajan,
 1910–
Talbot = William Alexander Talbot,
 1847–1917

P.C. Tam = Pui Cheung Tam, 1921–
Tamamsch. = Sophia G. Tamamschjan,
 1900–1981
Tanaka = Tyôzaburô Tanaka, 1885–
Yu. Tanaka = Yuichiro Tanaka, 1900–
Tanfani = Enrico Tanfani, 1848–1892
Tardieu = Marie Laure Tardieu, 1902–1998
O. Targ. Tozz. = Ottaviano Targioni
 Tozzetti, 1755–1829
Tate = Ralph Tate, 1840–1901
Tatew. = Misao Tatewaki, 1899–
Taubenheim = Gerd Taubenheim, fl. 1975
Taub. = Paul Hermann Wilhelm Taubert,
 1862–1897
Tausch = Ignaz Friedrich Tausch,
 1793–1848
G. Taylor = George Taylor, 1904–1993
N.P. Taylor = Nigel Paul Taylor, 1956–
N. Taylor = Norman Taylor, 1883–1967
P. Taylor = Peter Geoffrey Taylor, 1926–
T.M.C. Taylor = Thomas Mayne
 Cunninghame Taylor, 1904–1983
F.W. Taylor = F.W. Taylor, fl. 1925
Tebbitt = Mark C. Tebbitt, fl. 2000
Teijsm. = Johannes Elias Teijsmann
 (Teysmann), 1808–1882
Ten. = Michele Tenore, 1780–1861
Teppner = Herwig Teppner, 1941–
Terán = Manuel de Mier y Terán, –1852
N. Terracc. = Nicola Terracciano, 1837–1921
Terracino = A. Terracino
Terscheck = Terscheck, fl. c.1840
Teusch. = Heinrich (Henry) Teuscher,
 1891–1984
Thell. = Albert Thellung, 1881–1928
S. Theun. = Joseph (Sjef) Clément Marie
 Theunissen, 1938–
Thévenau = Antonin Victor Thévenau,
 1815–1876
E. Thomas = Abraham Louis Emmanuel
 (Emanuel) Thomas, 1788–1859
H.H. Thomas = Hugh Hamshaw Thomas,
 1885–1962
Thommen = Édouard Thommen,
 1880–1961
C.H. Thomps. = Charles Henry Thompson,
 1870–1931
J. Thomps. = John Thompson, fl. 1798
J.V. Thomps. = John Vaughan Thompson,
 1779–1847
Joy Thomps. = Joy Thompson geborene
 Garden, 1923–
J.S. Thomson = John Scott Thomson,
 1882–1943
Thomson = Thomas Thomson, 1817–1878

Thonn. = Peter Thonning, 1775–1848
G. Thor = Hans Göran Thor, 1953–
Thore = Jean Thore, 1763–1823
Thorsrud = Arne Thorsrud, 1895–1964
Thory = Claude Antoine Thory, 1759–1827
Thouin = André Thouin, 1747–1824
Thuill. = Jean-Louis Thuillier, 1757–1822
Thunb. = Carl Peter Thunberg, 1743–1828
Thwaites = George Henry Kendrick
  Thwaites, 1812–1882
Tidestr. = Ivar (Frederick) Tidestrom,
  1864–1956
Tiegel = Ernst Tiegel, 1879–1936
Tiegh. = Phillippe Édouard Léon van
  Tieghem, 1839–1914
H. Till = Johann Anton ("Hans") Till, 1920–
W. Till = Walter Georg Till, 1956–
Timm = Joachim Christian Timm,
  1734–1805
Tindale = Mary Douglas Tindale, 1920–
Tineo = Vincenzo Tineo, 1791–1856
Tischer = Arthur Tischer, 1895–2000
Tissière = Pierre Germain Tissière, 1828–
  1868
Tjaden = William Louis Tjaden, 1913–
Tobler = Friedrich Tobler, 1879–1957
Tod. = Agostino Todaro, 1818–1892
Toelken = Hellmut Richard Tölken
  (Toelken), 1939–
Toledo = Joaquim Franco de Toledo,
  1905–1952
Torr. = John Torrey, 1796–1873
Tourlet = Ernest Henri Tourlet, 1843–1907
Tourn. = Joseph Pitton de Tournefort,
  1656–1708
F. Towns. = Frederick Townsend,
  1822–1905
Trab. = Louis Charles Trabut, 1853–1929
R. Tracey = Reinhild Tracey, 1951–
Traill = George William Traill, 1836–1897
Tratt. = Leopold Trattinnick (Trattinick),
  1764–1849
Traub = Hamilton Paul Traub, 1890–1983
Trautv. = Ernst Rudolf von Trautvetter,
  1809–1889
Trécul = Auguste Adolphe Lucien Trécul,
  1818–1896
Trehane = Piers Trehane, fl. 1989
Trel. = William Trelease, 1857–1945
Trevir. = Ludolph Christian Treviranus,
  1779–1864
Trevis. = Vittore Benedetto Antonio
  Trevisan de Saint-Léon, 1818–1897
Trew = Christoph Jakob Trew, 1695–1769
Triana = José Jéronimo Triana, 1834–1890

Trimen = Henry Trimen, 1843–1896
Trin. = Carl Bernhard von Trinius,
  1778–1844
Trotter = Alessandro Trotter, 1874–1967
A.F. Tryon = Alice Faber Tryon, 1920–
R.M. Tryon = Rolla Milton Tryon,
  1916–2001
Tubergen = Cornelis Gerrit van Tubergen,
  1844–1919
Tuck. = Edward Tuckerman, 1817–1886
Turcz. = Porphir Kiril Nicolai
  Stepanowitsch von Turczaninow,
  1796–1863
Turner = Dawson Turner, 1775–1858
Turpin = Pierre Jean François Turpin,
  1775–1840
Turra = Antonio Turra, 1730–1796
Turrill = William Bertram Turrill,
  1890–1961
Tussac = François Richard Chevalier de
  Tussac, 1751–1837
Tutin = Thomas Gaskell Tutin, 1908–1987
Tuyama = Takasi Tuyama, 1910–2000
Tuzson = János Tuzson, 1870–1943
Tzvelev = Nikolai Nikolaievich Tzvelev,
  1925–
Uchida = Shigetaro Uchida, 1885–
Ucria = Bernardino da Ucria, 1739–1796
R. Uechtr. = Rudolf Carl (Karl) Friedrich
  Freiherr von Uechtritz, 1838–1886
Uitewaal = Antonius Josephus Adrianus
  Uitewaal, 1899–1963
Uittien = Hendrik Uittien, 1898–1944
Ujhelyi = József Ujhelyi, 1910–1979
Ulbr. = Oskar Eberhard Ulbrich, 1879–1952
Ule = Ernst Heinrich Georg Ule, 1854–1915
Uline = Edwin Burton Uline, 1867–1933
B. Ullrich = Bernd Ullrich, fl. 1992
Underw. = Lucien Marcus Underwood,
  1853–1907
Upson = T.M. Upson, fl. 1996
Urb. = Ignatz Urban, 1848–1931
Ursch = Eugène Ursch, 1882–1962
Urum. = Ivan Kiroff (Kirov) Urumoff
  (Urumov), 1857–1937
Vacc. = Lino Vaccari, 1873–1951
Vacherot = M. Vacherot
Vahl = Martin Vahl, 1749–1804
Vail = Anna Murray Vail, 1863–1955
Valeton = Theodoric Valeton, 1855–1929
Van den Berg = Cássio Van den Berg, 1971–
Van Eselt. = Glen Parker Van Eseltine,
  1888–1938
Van Geel = Pierre Corneille (Petrus
  Cornelius) Van Geel, 1796–1838

Van Geert = August(e) Van Geert, 1888–1938

van Gelderen = Dirk Martinus Van Gelderen, 1932–

Van Houtte = Louis Benoît Van Houtte, 1810–1876

Van Jaarsv. = Ernst Jacobus Van Jaarsveld, 1953–

Zijp = Coenraad van Zijp, 1879–

Vandas = Karel (Karl) Vandas, 1861–1923

Vand. = Domingo (Domenico) Vandelli, 1735–1816

Vaniot = Eugène Vaniot, 1846/47–1913

Vanucchi = Vanucchi, fl. 1838

Vasc. = Joao de Carvalho e Vasconcellos, 1897–1972

Vassilcz. = Ivan Tikhonovich Vassilczenko, 1903–

J.J. Vassil. = Ja.Ja. Vassiljev (Vassiliev), fl. 1940

Vatke = Georg (George) Carl Wilhelm Vatke, 1849–1889

Vaucher = Jean Pierre Étienne Vaucher, 1763–1841

Vaupel = Friedrich Karl Johann Vaupel, 1876–1927

Vauvel = Léopold Eugène Vauvel, 1848–1915

Vavilov = Nikolaj Ivanovich (Nikolai Iwanowitsch) Vavilov (Wawilow), 1887–1943

Veill. = Veillard, fl. 1800

H.J. Veitch = Harry James Veitch, 1840–1924

J.H. Veitch = James Herbert Veitch, 1868–1907

Veitch = John Gould Veitch, 1839–1870

Velen. = Josef (Joseph) Velenovsky, 1858–1949

Vell. = José Mariano da Conceiçao Vellozo, 1742–1811

Vent. = Étienne Pierre Ventenat, 1757–1808

Verdc. = Bernard Verdcourt, 1925–

I. Verd. = Inez Clare Verdoorn, 1896–1989

B. Verl. = Pierre Bernard Lazare Verlot, 1836–1897

Verl. = Jean Baptiste Verlot, 1825–1891

Verm. = Pieter Vermeulen, 1899–1981

Vermoesen = François Marie Camille Vermoesen, 1882–1922

Verschaff. = Ambroise Colette Alexandre Verschaffelt, 1825–1886

Verv. = Frederico Bernardo Vervoorst, 1923–

Vest = Lorenz Chrysanth von Vest, 1776–1840

Vickery = Joyce Winifred Vickery, 1908–1979

Vict. = Joseph Louis Conrad Frère Marie-Victorin, 1885–1944

S. Vidal = Sebastian Vidal, 1842–1889

Viehoever = Arno Viehoever, fl. 1920

Vieill. = Eugène (Deplanche Émile) Vieillard, 1819–1896

Vierh. = Friedrich (Karl Max) Vierhapper, 1876–1932

Vignolo = Ferdinando Vignolo-Lutati, 1878–1965

Vigo = Josep Vigo i Bonada, 1937–

Viguié = M.-Th. Viguié, fl. 1960

Vig. = L. G. Alexandre Viguier, 1790–1867

R. Vig. = René Viguier, 1880–1931

Vikulova = N.V. Vikulova, fl. 1939

Vill. = Domínique Villars, 1745–1814

M. Vilm. = Auguste Louis Maurice Levêque de Vilmorin, 1849–1918

Vilm. = Pierre Louis François Levêque de Vilmorin, 1816–1860

R. Vilm. = Roger Marie Vincent Philippe Lévêque de Vilmorin, 1905–1980

Vindt = Jacques Vindt, 1915–

Vines = Sydney Howard Vines, 1849–1934

Vis. = Roberto de Visiani, 1800–1878

Vitek = Ernst Vitek, 1953–

Vitman = Fulgenzio Vitman, 1728–1806

Viv. = Domenico Viviani, 1772–1840

Vliet = Dirk Jan van Vliet, 1924–

Vogel = (Julius Rudolph) Theodor Vogel, 1812–1841

J.A. Vogler = Johann Andreas Vogler, fl. 1781

Vogt = Robert Manfred Vogt, 1957–

Voigt = Joachim Otto Voigt, 1798–1843

Volkart = Albert Volkart, 1873–1951

Voll = Otto Voll, 1884–1959

Vollm. = Franz Vollmann, 1858–1917

Vollmer = Albert Michael Vollmer, 1896–1977

Vorosch. = Vladimir Nikolaevich Voroschilov, 1908–1999

Voss = Andreas Voss, 1857–1924

Vrugtman = Freek Vrugtman, 1927–

Vuilleum. = Beryl Brintnall Vuilleumier, 1942–

Vuk. = Ludwig (Ljudevit) von Farkas Vukotinovic, 1813–1893

Vved. = Aleksei Ivanovich Vvedensky (Vvedenski), 1898–1972

Wacht. = Willem Hendrik Wachter, 1882–1946

Wagenitz = Gerhard Wagenitz, 1927–

Wagenkn. = Rodolfo Wagenknecht, 1939–
J. Wagner = János (Johannes) Wagner,
   1870–1955
Wahlenb. = Georg (Göran) Wahlenberg,
   1780–1851
Waisb. = Anton Waisbecker, 1835–1916
N.A. Wakef. = Norman Arthur Wakefield,
   1918–1972
Waldst. = Franz de Paula Adam Graf von
   Waldstein, 1759–1823
Wale = Royden Samuel Wale, ?–1952
J.T. Wall = J. T. Wall, fl. 1934
Wallace = Alfred Russel Wallace, 1823–1913
Wall. = Nathaniel Wallich, 1786–1854
Wallis = Gustav Wallis, 1830–1878
B. Walln. = Bruno Wallnöfer, 1960–
Wallr. = Carl (Karl) Friedrich Wilhelm
   Wallroth, 1792–1857
Walp. = Wilhelm Gerhard Walpers,
   1816–1853
H. Walter = Hans Paul Heinrich Walter,
   1882–
Walter = Thomas Walter, 1740–1789
Walters = Stuart Max Walters, 1920–2005
E. Walther = Edward Eric Walther, 1
   892–1959
Walther = Friedrich Ludwig Walther,
   1759–1824
Walton = Frederick Arthur Walton,
   1853–1922
F.T. Wang = Fa Tsuan Wang, 1899–1985
X.M. Wang = Xiao Ming Wang, fl. 1987
Wangenh. = Friedrich Adam Julius von
   Wangenheim, 1749–1800
Wangerin = Walther (Leonhard) Wangerin,
   1884–1938
E.F. Warb. = Edmund Frederic Warburg,
   1908–1966
O.E. Warb. = Oscar Emanuel Warburg,
   1876–1937
Warb. = Otto Warburg, 1859–1938
Ward = Lester Frank Ward, 1841–1913
Warder = John Aston Warder, 1812–1883
Warm. = Johannes Eugenius Bülow
   Warming, 1841–1924
R. Warner = Robert Warner, c.1815–1896
Warsz. = Joseph Ritter von Rawicz
   Warszewicz, 1812–1866
Wartm. = Friedrich Bernhard Wartmann,
   1830–1902
Wassh. = Dieter Carl Wasshausen, 1938–
J.T. Waterh. = John Teast Waterhouse,
   1924–1983
H.C. Watson = Hewett Cottrell Watson,
   1804–1881

P. Watson = Peter William Watson,
   1761–1830
S. Watson = Sereno Watson, 1826–1892
W. Watson = William Watson, 1858–1925
Will. Watson = William Watson, 1832–1912
D. Watt = David Allan Poe Watt, 1830–1917
G. Watt = George Watt, 1851–1930
Wawra = Heinrich Wawra, 1831–1887
Weath. = Charles Alfred Weatherby,
   1875–1949
Weathers = John Weathers, 1867–1928
C.J. Webb = Colin James Webb, 1949–
D.A. Webb = David Allardice Webb,
   1912–1994
Webb = Philip Barker Webb, 1793–1854
F.A.C. Weber = Frédéric Albert Constantin
   Weber, 1830–1903
F. Weber = Friedrich Weber, 1781–1823
Weber = Georg Heinrich Weber, 1752–1828
J.G.C. Weber = Jean-Germaine Claude
   Weber, 1922–
Weberb. = August (Augusto) Weberbauer,
   1871–1948
Webr = Karel Mirko Webr, fl. 1974
Wedd. = Hugh Algernon Weddell,
   1819–1877
H.R. Wehrh. = Heinrich Rudolf Wehrhahn,
   1887–1940
Weick = Alphonse Weick, fl. 1863
Weide = Heinz Weide, 1933–
Weidlich = E. Weidlich, fl. 1928
Weigel = Christian Ehrenfried (von)
   Weigel, 1748–1831
Weihe = Carl Ernst August Weihe,
   1779–1834
Weiller = Marc Weiller, 1880–1945
Weing. = Wilhelm Weingart, 1856–1936
Weinm. = Johann Anton Weinmann,
   1782–1858
Welw. = Friedrich Martin Josef Welwitsch,
   1806–1872
Wendelbo = Per Erland Berg Wendelbo,
   1927–1981
Wender. = Georg Wilhelm Franz
   Wenderoth, 1774–1861
H.L. Wendl. = Heinrich Ludolph
   Wendland, 1791–1869
J.C. Wendl. = Johann Christoph Wendland,
   1755–1828
H. Wendl. = Hermann Wendland, 1825–1903
A. Wendt = Albert Wendt, 1887–1958
Wenz. = (Johann) Theodor Wenzig,
   1824–1892
Wercklé = Karl (Carlos) Wercklé, 1860–1924
Werderm. = Erich Werdermann, 1892–1959

K. Werner = Klaus Werner, 1928–
Wernisch. = Johann Jakob (Jacob) Wernischeck, 1743–1804
Wesm. = Alfred Wesmael, 1832–1905
Wessner = Wilhelm ("Willi") Wessner, 1904–1983
C. West = Cyril West, 1887–1986
Westc. = Frederic Westcott, ?–1861
Wester = Peter Jansen Wester, 1877–1931
Weston = Richard Weston, 1733–1806
Wettst. = Richard Wettstein Ritter von Westersheim, 1863–1931
Weyer = W. van de Weyer, fl. 1920
L.C. Wheeler = Louis Cutter Wheeler, 1910–1980
Wherry = Edgar Theodore Wherry, 1885–1982
A.C. White = Alain Campbell White, 1880–1951
C.T. White = Cyril Tenison White, 1890–1950
F.B. White = Francis Buchanan White, 1842–1894
Whitehead = F. H. Whitehead, 1913–
Whittall = Edward Whittall, 1851–1917
Wibel = August Wilhelm Eberhard Christoph Wibel, 1775–1813
Widder = Felix Joseph Widder, 1892–1974
Widmer = Elisabeth Widmer, 1862–1952
Wiegand = Karl McKay Wiegand, 1873–1942
Wiehler = Hans Joachim Wiehler, 1930–2003
Wiersema = John H. Wiersema, 1950–
Wierzb. = Peter (Petrus Paulus, Piotr Pawlus) Wierzbicki, 1794–1847
Wiesb. = Johann Baptist Wiesbaur, 1836–1906
F.H. Wigg. = Friderich Hinrich (Friedrich Heinrich) Wiggers (Wichers), 1746–1811
Wight = Robert Wight, 1796–1872
W. Wight = William Franklin Wight, 1874–1954
Wijnands = Dirk Onno Wijnands, 1945–1993
Wijsman = H.J.W. Wijsman, fl. 1982
Wikstr. = Johan Emanuel Wikström, 1789–1856
B.H. Wilcox = Balafama Helen Wilcox, publ. 1977–93
Wilczek = Ernst Wilczek, 1867–1948
R. Wilczek = Rudolf Wilczek, 1903–1984
Wild = Hiram Wild, 1917–1982
Willd. = Carl Ludwig Willdenow, 1765–1812
Willemet = Pierre Rémi Willemet, 1735–1807

P. Willemet = Pierre Rémi François de Paule Willemet, 1762–1790
B.S. Williams = Benjamin Samuel Williams, 1824–1890
F.N. Williams = Frederic Newton Williams, 1862–1923
I. Williams = Ion James Muirhead Williams, 1912–2001
L.O. Williams = Louis Otho Williams, 1908–1991
N.H. Williams = Norris H. Williams, 1943–
P.A. Will. = Phyllis Alison Williamson, 1925–
Willk. = Heinrich Moritz Willkomm, 1821–1895
J. Willm. = John Willmott, 1775–1834
Wilmott = Alfred James Wilmott, 1888–1950
E.H. Wilson = Ernest Henry Wilson, 1876–1930
G.F. Wilson = George Fox Wilson, 1896–1951
Paul G. Wilson = Paul Graham Wilson, 1928–
P. Wilson = Percy Wilson, 1879–1944
Peter G. Wilson = Peter Gordon Wilson, 1950–
R.G. Wilson = Robert Gardner Wilson, 1911–
Wilson = William Wilson, 1799–1871
Wimm. = Christian Friedrich Heinrich Wimmer, 1803–1868
E. Wimm. = Franz Elfried Wimmer, 1881–1961
H.J.P. Winkl. = Hubert J.P. Winkler, 1875–1941
C.G.A. Winkl. = Constantin (Konstantin) Georg Alexander Winkler, 1848–1900
Wirtg. = Philipp Wilhelm Wirtgen, 1806–1870
Wissk. = Rolf Wisskirchen, 1950–
Witasek = Johanna A. Witasek, 1865–1910
With. = William Withering, 1741–1799
Withner = Carl Leslie Withner, 1918–
Witte = Heinrich Witte, 1829–1917
Wittm. = Marx Carl Ludwig (Ludewig) Wittmack, 1839–1929
Wittr. = Veit Brecher Wittrock, 1839–1914
Wocke = Erich Wocke, 1863–1941
Wohlf. = Rudolf Wohlfarth, 1830–1900
C.B. Wolf = Carl Brandt Wolf, 1905–1974
E.L. Wolf = Egbert Ludwigowitsch Wolf, 1860–1931
Wolf = Nathanael Matthaeus von Wolf, 1724–1784

D. Wolff = D. Wolff
M. Wolff = Manfred Wolff, fl. 1989
Wolfg. = Johann Friedrich Wolfgang,
  1776–1859
Woll. = George Buchanan Wollaston,
  1814–1899
Wol. = Eustach Woloszczak, 1835–1918
A.W. Wood = Alphonso W. Wood,
  1810–1881
J.M. Wood = John Medley Wood, 1827–1915
M.W. Wood = Mark W. Wood, fl. 1973
Woodcock = Hubert Bayley Drysdale
  Woodcock, 1867–1957
J. Woods = Joseph Woods, 1776–1864
Woodson = Robert Everard Woodson,
  1904–1963
Woolls = William Woolls, 1814–1893
Wooton = Elmer Ottis Wooton, 1865–1945
Wormsk. = Martin (Morten) Wormskjöld,
  1783–1845
Woronow = Georg Jurij Nikolaewitch
  Woronow (Voronov), 1874–1931
Wóycicki = Zygmunt Wóycicki, 1871–1941
Woyn. = Heinrich Karl Woynar, 1865–1917
Wraber = Anton Martin ("Tone") Wraber,
  1938–
C.H. Wright = Charles Henry Wright,
  1864–1941
C. Wright = Charles (Carlos) Wright,
  1811–1885
W. Wright = William Wright, 1735–1819
T.L. Wu = Te Lin(g) Wu, 1934–
Wucherpf. = Wolfgang Wucherpfennig,
  1936–
Wulfen = Franz Xavier Freiherr von
  Wulfen, 1728–1805
Wurmb = Friedrich von Wurmb, –1781
Wydler = Heinrich Wydler, 1800–1883
Wyley = Andrew Wyley, 1820–
Yabuno = Tomosaburo Yabuno, 1924–
Yalt. = Faik Yaltirik, 1930–
S.C. Yang = Shao Cheng Yang, fl. 1988
Yatabe = Ryôkichi (Ruôkichi) Yatabe,
  1851–1899
H.O. Yates = Harris Oliver Yates, 1934–
J. Yates = James Yates, 1789–1871
Yeo = Peter Frederick Yeo, 1929–
T.P. Yi = Tong Pei Yi, 1934–

Youel = Youel
D.P. Young = Donald Peter Young,
  1917–1972
R.A. Young = Robert Armstrong Young,
  1876–1963
S.B. Young = S.B. Young, fl. 1970
Yunck. = Truman George Yuncker,
  1891–1964
Zabel = Hermann Zabel, 1832–1912
Zämelis = Aleksandrs Zämelis, 1897–1943
Zahlbr. = Alexander Zahlbruckner,
  1860–1938
J. Zahlbr. = Johann Baptist Zahlbruckner,
  1782–1851
Zapal. = Hugo Zapalowicz, 1852–1917
Zauschn. = Johann Baptista Josef
  Zauschner, 1737–1799
Zeiss. = Hermann Zeissold, fl. 1895
Zenari = Silvia Zenari, 1896–1956
Zengerl. = Zengerling, fl. 1889
Zenker = Jonathan Carl (Karl) Zenker,
  1799–1837
Zeyh. = Carl Ludwig Philipp Zeyher,
  1799–1858
Q.F. Zheng = Qing Fang Zheng, 1934–
Zhuk. = Peter Mikhailovich Zhukovsky,
  1888–1975
Ziesenh. = Rudolf Christian Ziesenhenne,
  1911–2005
Zimmerman = Dale Allan Zimmerman,
  fl. 1972
F. Zimm. = Friedrich Zimmermann,
  1855–1928
Zimmeter = Albert Zimmeter, 1848–1897
Zinn = Johann Gottfried Zinn, 1727–1759
Zipp. = Alexander Zippelius, 1797–1828
Ziz = Johann Baptist Ziz, 1779–1829
Zizka = Georg Zizka, 1955–
Zodda = Giuseppe Zodda, 1877–1968
Zoëga = Johann Zoëga, 1742–1788
Zöllner = Otto Zöllner, fl. 2001
Zoll. = Heinrich Zollinger, 1818–1859
Zonn. = Bernardus Joannes Maria
  Zonneveld, 1940–
Zuccagni = Attilio Zuccagni, 1754–1807
Zucc. = Joseph Gerhard Zuccarini,
  1797–1848

XIII Bibliography

General botany and systematics, dictionaries

Aeschimann, D., Heitz, C. (1996): Synonymie-Index der Schweizer Flora. Géneve: Zentrum des Datenverbundnetzes der Schweizer Flora.

Backer, C. A. (1936): Verklarend Woordenboek der wetenschappelijke namen van de in Nederland en Nederlandsch-Indie in het wild groeiende en in tuinen en parken gekweekte varens en planten. Batavia: Noordhoff-Kolff, Visser & Co.

Bundesministerium der Justiz (2001): Bekanntmachung der besonders und streng geschützten Tier- und Pflanzenarten gemäß § 20a Abs. 5 des Bundesnaturschutzgesetzes vom 1. Februar 2001. Bundesanzeiger 53, Nummer 35a.

Bischoff, G. H. (1833–1844): Handbuch zur botanischen Terminologie und Systemkunde. 3 Bände. Nürnberg: Verlag J. L. Schrag.

Boerner, F. (1989): Taschenwörterbuch der botanischen Pflanzennamen (4. Aufl.). Berlin, Hamburg: Verlag Paul Parey.

Bremer, K. (1994): Asteraceae (Cladistics & Classification). Portland: Timber Press.

Der Brockhaus (2001): Tiere und Pflanzen von A– Z. Leipzig, Mannheim: F. A. Brockhaus.

Brummitt, R. K. (1992): Vascular Plant Families and Genera. Kew: Royal Botanic Gardens.

Brummitt, R. K. & Powell, C. E. (1992): Authors of Plant Names. Kew: Royal Botanic Gardens.

Cronquist, A. (1981): An Integrated System of Classificationof Flowering Plants. New York: Columbia Univerity Press.

Engler, A. (1900–1953): Das Pflanzenreich. 107 Hefte. Leipzig: Verlag W. Engelmann (zuletzt Berlin: Akademie Verlag).

– (1940–...): Die natürlichen Pflanzenfamilien (2. Aufl.). Berlin: Duncker und Humblot-Verlag.

– (1954/64): Syllabus der Pflanzenfamilien, Band 1 und 2 (12. Auflage, ed. H. Melchior et E. Werdermann). Berlin: Gebrüder Borntraeger-Verlag.

– Prantl, K. (1887–1915): Die natürlichen Pflanzenfamilien (1. Aufl.). Leipzig: W. Engelmann-Verlag.

Erhardt, A. & W. (2000): Pflanze gesucht? (4. Aufl.). Stuttgart: Verlag Eugen Ulmer.

Farr, E. R., Leussink, J. A., Stafleu F. A., (eds.) (1979): Index Nominum Genericorum (Plantarum). Regnum Veg. 100–102: 1–1896.

– – Zijlstra, G., (eds.) (1986): Index Nominum Genericorum (Plantarum) Supplementum I. Regnum Veg. 113: 1–126.

Genaust, H. (1996): Etymologisches Wörterbuch der botanischen Pflanzennamen (3. Aufl.). Basel, Stuttgart: Birkhäuser Verlag.

Georges, K. E. (1913): Ausführliches Lateinisch-Deutsches Handwörterbuch. 2 Bände. Hannover.

Glen, H.F. (2002): Cultivated Plants of Southern Africa. Johannesburg: Jacana Education Ltd.

GOVAERTS, R. (1995–1999): World Checklist of Seed Plants, Vol. 1–3. Antwerpen: Continental Publishing.

GREUTER, W. et al. (1993): Names in Current Use for Extant Plant Genera. Königstein: Koeltz Scientific Books.

– et al. (1994): International Code of Botanical Nomenclature (Tokyo Code). Königstein: Koeltz Scientific Books.

– et al. (1995): Internationaler Code der Botanischen Nomenklatur (Tokyo Code - deutsche Übersetzung von Greuter, W., Hiepko, P.). Königstein: Koeltz Scientific Books.

– BURDET, H. M., LONG, G. (1984): Med-Checklist, Vol. 1–3 (2nd/1st ed.). Genève: Conservatoire et jardin botaniques de la ville de Genève.

GUNN, C. R. et al. (1992): Families and Genera of Spermatophytes Recognized by the Agricultural Research Service. U. S. Department of Agriculture.

HANSEN, R., MÜSSEL, H., SIEBER, J. (1970): Namen der Stauden. Weihenstephan-Freising: Internationale Stauden Union.

HEYWOOD, V. H. (ed.) (1982): Blütenpflanzen der Welt. Basel, Stuttgart: Birkhäuser Verlag.

HUTCHINSON, J. (1964–67): The Genera of Flowering Plants, Vol 1 & 2. Oxford: Clarendon Press.

INDEX KEWENSIS (1895–1995): 22 Bände. Oxford 1895–1996. (Verzeichnis aller bis 1995 veröffentlichter Namen für Blütenpflanzen-Arten und -Gattungen).

ISAACSON, R.T. (ed.) (2004): Andersen Horticultural Library's Source List of Plants and Seeds. 6th ed. University of Minnesota

ISTA (International Seed Testing Association) (1988): List of stabilized plant names (3. Aufl. Zürich).

KUBITZKI, K. (ed.) (1990): The Families and Genera of Vascular Plants, Vol. I: Pteridophytes and Gymnosperms. Berlin, Heidelberg: Springer Verlag.

– (ed.) (1993): The Families and Genera of Vascular Plants, Vol. II: Magnoliid, Hamamelid and Caryophyllid Families. Berlin, Heidelberg: Springer Verlag.

– (ed.) (1998a): The Families and Genera of Vascular Plants, Vol. III: Lilianae (except Orchidaceae). Berlin, Heidelberg: Springer Verlag.

– (ed.) (1998b): The Families and Genera of Vascular Plants, Vol. IV: Alismatanae and Commelinanae (except Gramineae). Berlin, Heidelberg: Springer Verlag.

– (ed.) (2002): The Families and Genera of Vascular Plants, Vol. V: Malvales, Capparales and Non-betalain Caryophyllales. Berlin, Heidelberg: Springer Verlag.

– (ed.) (2004a): The Families and Genera of Vascular Plants, Vol. VI: Celastrales, Oxalidales, Rosales, Cornales, Ericales. Berlin, Heidelberg: Springer Verlag.

– (ed.) (2004b): The Families and Genera of Vascular Plants, Vol. VII: Lamiales (except Acanthaceae, including Avicenniaceae. Berlin, Heidelberg: Springer Verlag.

– (ed.) (2007a): The Families and Genera of Vascular Plants, Vol. VIII: Flowering Plants. Eudicots: Asterales. Berlin, Heidelberg: Springer Verlag.

– (ed.) (2007b): The Families and Genera of Vascular Plants, Vol. IX: Flowering Plants. Eudicots: Berberidopsidales, Buxales, Crossosomatales, Fabales p.p., Eraniales, Gunnerales, Myrtales p.p., Proteales, Saxifragales, Passofloraceae Alliance, Dillenuaceae, Huaceae, Picramniaceae, Sabiaceae. Berlin, Heidelberg: Springer Verlag.

LANGENSCHEIDTS TASCHENWÖRTERBUCH (1967): Lateinisch-Deutsch (6. Aufl.). Berlin, München, Zürich: Langenscheidt Verlag.

LAUNERT, E. (1998): Biologisches Wörterbuch Deutsch – Englisch / Englisch – Deutsch. Stuttgart: Verlag Eugen Ulmer.

LEUNIS, J., FRANK, A. B. (1883–1886) Synopsis der Pflanzenkunde. 3 Bände (3. Aufl.). Hannover: Hahnsche Hofbuchhandlung.

LORD, T. (ed.) (2001): The RHS Plant Finder 2001–2002 (15th ed.). London, New York: Dorling Kindersley.

MABBERLEY, D. J. (1997): The Plant Book (2nd ed.). Cambridge: University Press.

NATHO, G., MÜLLER, C., SCHMIDT, H. (1990): Morphologie und Systematik der Pflanzen (2 Bände). Stuttgart: Gustav Fischer Verlag.

NICOLOV, H. (1996): Dictionary of Plant Names. Berlin, Stuttgart: J. Cramer.

PRITZEL, G. A. (1871–1877): Thesaurus Literaturae Botanicae ... Nachdruck Milano 1950; weiterer Nachdruck Koenigstein-Ts. 1972.

SCHUBERT, R., WAGNER, G. (1979): Pflanzennamen und botanische Fachwörter. Melsungen, Berlin: Verlag J. Neumann-Neudamm.

– – (2000): Botanisches Wörterbuch. Stuttgart: Verlag Eugen Ulmer.

SMITH, A. W. (1963): A gardener's dictionary of plant names. A handbook on the origin and meaning of some plant names. New York: St. Martin's Press.

STAFLEU, F. A., COWAN, R. S. (1976–1989): Taxonomic Literature (7 Vols., 2nd ed.). Den Haag. + Suppl. 1-6 (1992-2000)

STEARN, W. T. (1983): Botanical Latin (3rd. ed.). Newton Abbot, London: David & Charles.

STRASBURGER, E. ET AL (eds: Sitte, P., Ziegler, H., Ehrendorfer, F., Bresinsky, A.) (2002): Lehrbuch der Botanik für Hochschulen (35. Aufl.). Jena, New York: Gustav Fischer.

TERRELL, E. E. et al. (1986): A checklist of names for 3000 vascular plants of economic importance. Washington, D. C.:United States Department of Agriculture.

TREHANE, P. et al. (1995): International Code of Nomenclature for Cultivated Plants. Wimbourne: Quarterjack Publishing.

URANIA-PFLANZENREICH (1991–1994): 4 Bde. Urania-Verlag.

WALTER, K. E., GILETT, H. J. (ed.) (1998): 1997 IUCN Red List of Threatened Plants. Gland, Cambridge: IUCN, The World Conservation Union.

WARBURG, O. (1913–1922): Die Pflanzenwelt (3 Bde.). Mannheim: Bibliographisches Institut.

WEBERLING, F., SCHWANTES, H. O. (1987): Pflanzensystematik. Stuttgart: Verlag Eugen Ulmer.

WIELGORSKAYA, T. (1995): Dictionary of Generic Names of Seed Plants. New York: Columbia University Press.

WILLIS, J. C. (1973): A Dictionary of the Flowering Plants and Ferns (8th ed., neu bearbeitet von Airy Shaw, K. H.) Cambridge: University Press.

Floras

ABRAMS, L., FERRIS, R. S. (1968–1975): Illustrated Flora of the Pacific States, Vol. 1-4 (2nd ed.) Stanford: Stanford University Press.

ADAMS, C. D. (1972): Flowering Plants of Jamaica. Mona Jamaica: University of the West Indies.

ADLER, W. et al. (2005): Exkursionsflora von Österreich. Linz: Land Oberösterreich, Landesmuseen.

AICHELE, D., SCHWEGLER, H.-W. (1994–1996): Die Blütenpflanzen Mitteleuropas, Vol. 1-5. Stuttgart: Franckh-Kosmos Verlag.

ALLAN, H. H. et al. (1961–1980): Flora of New Zealand (3 Vols.). Wellington: Verlag P. D. Hasselberg.

ASCHERSON, P. F. A., GRAEBNER, K. O. R. P. P. (1896–1939): Synopsis der mitteleuropäischen Flora. Leipzig: Verlag W. Engelmann (später: Gebr. Bornträger).

BACKER, C. A., BACKHUIZEN VAN DEN BRINK, R. C. (1963–1968): Flora of Java, Vol. 1-3. Groningen: N. V. P. Noordhoff.

BENKERT, D., FUKAREK, F., KORSCH, H. (1996): Verbreitungsatlas der Farn- und Blütenpflanzen Ostdeutschlands. Jena, Stuttgart, Lübeck, Ulm: Gustav Fischer Verlag Jena.

BINZ, A. (1990): Schul und Exkursionsflora für die Schweiz (19. Aufl.). Basel: Schwabe & Co.

BLUNDELL, M. (1982): The Wild Flowers of Kenya. London: Collins.

BOLÒS, O. et al. (1990): Flora Manual dels Paisos Catalans. Barcelona: Editorial Pórtic.

BOND, P. & GOLDBLATT, P. (1984): Plants of the Cape Flora. A descriptive catalogue. Kirstenbosch: Botanical Society of South Africa.

CABRERA, A. L., ZARDINI, E. M. (1978): Manual de la Flora de los Alrededores de Buenos Aires. Buenos Aires: Editorial Acme S. A. C. I.

CASTROVIEJO et al. (1986): Flora Iberica, Vol. 1–8, 10, 14, 21. Madrid.

CORELL, D. S., JOHNSTON, M. C. (1970): Manual of the Vascular Plants of Texas. Renner: Texas Research Foundation.

DAVIS, P. H. (1965–2001): Flora of Turkey and the East Aegean Islands, Vol. 1–11. Edinburgh: University Press.

EHRENDORFER, F. et al. (1973): Liste der Gefäßpflanzen Mitteleuropas (2. Aufl.). Stuttgart: Verlag Gustav Fischer.

ELIOVSON, S. (1984): Wild Flowers of Southern Africa. (7th. ed.). (ohne Ort und Verlag).

FERNALD, M. L. (1950): Gray's Manual of Botany. (8th ed.). New York: American Book Company.

FLORA OF NORTH AMERICA EDITORIAL COMMITTEE (1993–2000): Flora of North America, Vol. 1–3, 22. Oxford: University Press.

FOURNIER, P. (1977) Les quatre flores de la France, Corse comprise. (2. Aufl.). Paris: Paul Lechevallier.

GAMBLE, J. S. (1935): Flora of the Presidency of Madras, 3 Vol. Reprint 1957 Calcutta: Botanical Survey of India.

GARCKE, A. (1972): Illustrierte Flora, Deutschland und angrenzende Gebiete. Berlin, Hamburg: Verlag Paul Parey.

GENTRY, A. H. (1993): A Field Guide to the Families and Genera of Woody Plants of Northwest South America (Columbia, Ecuador, Peru). Washington, D. C.: Conservation International.

GIBBS RUSSEL, G. E. (1985): List of Species of South African Plants. (2nd ed.). Pretoria: Botanical Research Institute.

GLEASON, H. A. (1952): The New Britton and Brown Illustrated Flora of Northeastern United States and Adjacent Canada (3 Vols.). New York.

GOLDBLATT, P., MANNING, J. (2000): Cape Plants. St. Louis: Missouri Botanical Garden.

HAEUPLER, H., SCHÖNFELDER, P. (1989): Atlas der Farn- und Blütenpflanzen Deutschlands (2. Aufl.). Stuttgart: Verlag Eugen Ulmer.

HAYEK, A. VON (1927–1933): Prodromus Florae peninsulae Balcanicae, 1–3. Band. Nachdruck 1970 Koenigstein Taunus: Verlag Otto Koeltz.

HEGI, G. (1906–1931): Illustrierte Flora von Mitteleuropa. München: J. F. Lehmanns Verlag.

– (1936–*): Illustrierte Flora von Mitteleuropa (2. Aufl.). München: Carl Hanser Verlag, ab 1975: Berlin, Hamburg: Verlag Paul Parey.

– (eds.: Conert, H. J, Jäger, E. J., Kadereit, J. W. et al.) (1966–*): Illustrierte Flora von Mitteleuropa in 6 Bänden und 23 Teilbänden (3. Aufl., noch nicht vollständig erschienen). Berlin: Blackwell Verlag.

HESS, H. E., LANDOLD, E., HIRZEL, R. (1976–1980): Flora der Schweiz und angrenzender Gebiete, Band 1–3 (2. Aufl.). Basel, Stuttgart: Birkhäuser Verlag.

HILLARD, O. M. (1977): Compositae in Natal. Pietermaritzburg: University of Natal Press.

HOHENESTER, A., WEISS, W. (1993): Exkursionsflora für die Kanarischen Inseln. Stuttgart: Verlag Eugen Ulmer.

HITCHCOCK, C. L., CRONQUIST, A. (1973): Flora of the Pacific Northwest. Seattle and London: University of Washington Press.

HOOKER, J. D. (1872–1897): The Flora of British India, Vol. 1–7. Reprint 1973 Dehra Dun: Bishen Singh Mahendra Pal Singh.

HUTCHINSON, J., DALZIEL, J. M. (1963–1973): Flora of West Tropical Africa, Vol. 1–3 (2nd ed.). London: Crown Agents for Overseas Governments and Administration.

ICONOGRAPHIA CORMOPHYTORUM SINICORUM (1972–1976): Vol. 1–5. Peking (+ Supplementa 1 und 2. 1982–1983).

JAHN. R., SCHÖNFELDER, R. (1995): Exkursionsflora für Kreta. Stuttgart: Verlag Eugen Ulmer.

KARTESZ, J. T. (1994): A Synonymized Checklist of the Vascular Flora of the United States Canada, and Greenland (2 Vols., 2nd ed.). Portland: Timber Press.

KEARNY, T. H., PEEBLES, R. H. et al. (1973): Arizona Flora. Berkeley, Los Angeles, London: University of California Press.

KOMAROV, V. L. ed. (1968-): Flora of the U.S.S.R., translated from the Russian. Israel Programm for Scientific Translations, Jerusalem.

LAUBER, K., WAGNER, G. (1998): Flora Helvetica (2. Aufl.). Bern, Stuttgart, Wien: Verlag Paul Haupt.

LID, J. (1985): Norsk, svensk, finsk Flora. Oso: Det Norske Samlaget.

LÓPEZ LILLO, A. et al. (2000-2003): Flora Ornamental Espanola, tomo I-III. Sevilla, Madrid: Mundi Prensa

MEUSEL, H., JÄGER, E., RAUSCHERT, S., WEINERT, E. (1965-1992): Vergleichende Chorologie der zentraleuropäischen Flora, Bd. 1-3. Jena: VEB Gustav Fischer.

MOSSBERG, B., STENBERG, L. (1992): Den Nordiska Floran. Wahlström &Widstrand.

MUNOZ PIZARRO, C. (1966): Synopsis de la Flora Chilena. Valparaiso: Editiones de la Universidad de Chile.

OBERDORFER, E. (2001): Pflanzensoziologische Exkursionsflora (8. Aufl.). Stuttgart: Verlag Eugen Ulmer.

OHWI, J. (1965): Flora of Japan. Washington D. C.: Smithonion Institution.

PIGNATTI, S. (1982): Flora d'Italia (3 Vols.). Bologna: Edagricola.

POLUNIN, O. (1980): Flowers of Greece and the Balkans. Oxford: University Press.

– STAINTON, A. (1984): Flowers of the Himalaya. Oxford: University Press.

PORSILD, A. E., CODY, W. J. (1980): Vascular Plants of Continental Northwest Territories, Canada. Ottawa: National Museums of Canada.

PRESS, J. R., SHORT, M. J. (eds.) (1994): Flora of Madeira. London: The Natural History Museum, London.

QUEZEL, P., SANTA, S. (1962-1963): Nouvelle Flore de l'Algérie, Tome I, Tome II. Paris: Editions du Centre National de la Recherche Scientifique.

RADFORD, A. E., AHLES, H. E., BELL, C. R. (1968): Manual of the Vascular Flora of the Carolinas. Chapel Hill: The University of North Carolina Press.

ROTHMALER, W. et al. (2005-2007): Exkursionsflora von Deutschland Band 2-4 (19., 11. und 10. Aufl.). Heidelberg, Berlin: Spektrum Akademischer Verlag.

RYDBERG, A. (1932): Flora of the Prairies and Plains of Central North America. Reprint 1965, New York, London: Hafner Publishing Company.

RYDBERG, P. A. (1922): Flora of the Rocky Mountains and Adjacent Plains. Reprint 1969, New York and London: Hafner Publishing Company.

SCHMEIL-FITSCHEN (ed.: Seybold, S.) (2006): Flora von Deutschland. (93. Aufl.). Wiebelsheim: Quelle und Meyer.

SCOGGAN, H. J. (1978): Flora of Canada (4 Vols.). Ottawa: National Museum of Natural Sciences.

SEBALD, O., SEYBOLD, S., PHILIPPI, G. (eds.) (1992-1998): Die Farn- und Blütenpflanzen Baden-Württembergs, Band 1-8 (1./2. Aufl.). Stuttgart. Verlag Eugen Ulmer.

SELL. P., MURRELL, G. (1996): Flora of Great Britain and Irleand, Vol. 5. Cambridge: University Press.

SHETLER, S. G., SKOG, L. E. (1978): A provisional Checklist of Species for Flora North America. Missouri: Botanical Garden.

SMALL, J. K. (1933): Manual of the South Eastern Flora. University of North Carolina Press.

STACE, C. (1997): New Flora of the British Isles (2nd ed.). Cambridge: University Press.

– (1999): Field Flora of the British Isles. Cambridge: University Press.

STANDLEY, P. C. (1920-1926): Trees and Shrubs of Mexico. Contributions from the United States Herbarium, Vol. 23. Washington, D. C.: Smithsonian Press.

TURLAND, N. J., CHILTON, L., PRESS, J. R. (1993): Flora of the Cretan Area. London: HMSO.

Tutin, T. G. (1968–1993): Flora Europaea, Vol. 1–5. (2nd/1st ed.) Cambridge: University Press.

Valdés, B., Talavera, S., Fernández-Galiano, E. (1987): Flora Vascular de Andalucía Occidental. Barcelona: Ketres Editora.

Wisskirchen, R., Haeupler, H. (1998): Standardliste der Farn- und Blütenpflanzen Deutschlands. Stuttgart: Verlag Eugen Ulmer.

Zohary, M., N. Feinbrun-Dothan (1966–1986): Flora Palestina, 4 Doppelbände, Jerusalem: Israel Academy of Sciences and Humanities.

Please visit www.efloras.org for further information on the following floras:
- A Catalogue of the Vascular Plants of Madagascar
- Annotated Checklist of the Flowering Plants of Nepal
- Flora of Chile
- Flora of China
- Flora of Missouri
- Flora of North America
- Flora of Pakistan
- Moss Flora of China
- Trees and Shrubs of the Andes of Ecuador

Cultivated plants, general

Bailey, L. H. (1919): The Standard Cyclopedia of Horticulture (6 Vols.). New York, London: Macmillan Company.

– (1949): Manual of Cultivated Plants (2nd ed.). New York:The Macmillan Company.

– Bailey, E. Z. (1976): Hortus Third. Revised and expanded by The Staff of the Liberty Hyde Bailey Hortorium. New York: Macmillan Publishing Company.

Boom, B. K. (1970): Flora de gekweekte, kruidachtige Gewassen (2. Aufl.). Wageningen:Veenman & Zonen.

Brickell, C. (ed.) (1996): The RHS A-Z Encyclopedia of Garden Plants (2 Vols.). London, New York: Dorling Kindersley.

Cheers, G. (ed.) (1998): Botanica. Köln: Könemann Verlagsgesellschaft.

Encke, F. (ed.) (1958/60): Pareys Blumengärtnerei, Band 1 und 2. Berlin, Hamburg: Verlag Paul Parey.

Graf, A. B. (1992): Hortica, Color Cyclopedia of Garden Flora and Indoor Plants. East Rutherford, N. J, USA: Roehrs Company Publishers.

Griffiths, M. (1994): Index of Garden Plants. London, Basingstoke: The Macmillan Press.

Haberer, M. (1990): Farbatlas Zierpflanzen. Stuttgart: Verlag Eugen Ulmer.

Huxley, A. J. (ed.) (1992): New Royal Horticultural Society Dictionary of Gardening (4 Vols.). London: Macmillan.

Maatsch, R. (ed.) (1956): Pareys Illustriertes Gartenbaulexikon (5. Aufl.). Berlin, Hamburg: Verlag Paul Parey.

Pienaar, K. (1984): The South African What Flower is That? C. Struik Publishers.

Walters, S. M. et al. (1984–2000): The European Garden Flora, Vol. 1–6. Cambridge: University Press.

Cultivated plants, ferns and grasses

Aichele, D., Schwegler, H.-W. (1988): Unsere Gräser. Stuttgart: Franckh'sche Verlagshandlung.

Conert, H. J. (2000): Pareys Gräserbuch. Berlin: Verlag Paul Parey.

Denkewitz, L. (1995): Farngärten. Stuttgart: Verlag Eugen Ulmer.

Grounds, R. (1989): Ornamental Grasses. Bromley: Christopher Helm Ltd.

HITCHCOCK, A. S. (1971): Manual of the Grasses of the United States (2nd revised ed.), 2 Vols. New York: Dover Publications.

HUBBARD, C. E. (1985): Gräser (2 Aufl.). Stuttgart: Verlag Eugen Ulmer.

JONES, D. L. (1987): Encyclopaedia of Ferns. Portland: Timber Press.

MAATSCH, R. (1980): Das Buch der Freilandfarne. Berlin, Hamburg: Verlag Paul Parey.

OHRNBERGER, D. (1999): The Bamboos of the World. Amsterdam, Lousanne, New York: Elsevier.

SCHMICK, H. (1990): Farne und Natur und Garten. Glinde: Privatdruck.

Cultivated plants, woody plants

BÄRTELS, A. (1991): Gartengehölze (3. Aufl.). Stuttgart: Verlag Eugen Ulmer.

– (2001): Enzyklopädie der Gartengehölze. Stuttgart: Verlag Eugen Ulmer.

BERG, J., HEFT, L. (1979): Rhododendron und immergrüne Laubgehölze (2. Aufl.). Stuttgart: Verlag Eugen Ulmer.

BOOM, B. K. (1978): Nederlandsche Dendrologie (10. Aufl.). Wageningen: Verlag H. Veenman u. Zonen

BRANDIS, D. (1906): Indian Trees. Reprint 1971 Dehra Dun.

CALLAWAY, D. J. (1994): Magnolias. London: B. T. Batsford Ltd.

CHEERS, G. (ed.) (1999): Rosen. Köln: Könemann Verlagsgesellschaft.

CHMELAR, J., MEUSEL, W. (1986): Die Weiden Europas. Wittenberg: A. Ziemsen Verlag.

COX, P. A., COX, N. E. (1997): The Encyclopedia of Rhododendron Species. Perth: Glendoick Publishing.

DALLIMORE, W., JACKSON, A. B. (1966): A Handbok of Coniferae and Ginkgoaceae. London: Edward Arnold Publishers.

DEUTSCHE DENDROLOGISCHE GESELLSCHAFT (1981/82): Mitteilungen der Deutschen Dendrologischen Gesellschaft. 1981, 1982. Nr. 73, 74: Erhebung über das Vorkommen winterharter Freilandgehölze. Stuttgart: Verlag Eugen Ulmer.

DIRR, R. (1994): Hamamelis und andere Zaubernussgewächse. Stuttgart: Verlag Eugen Ulmer.

ELLISON, D. (1995): Cutivated Plants of the World: Trees, Shrubs, Climbers. Brisbane Queensland Australia: Flora Publications International.

FARJON, A. (1998): World Checklist and Bibliography of Conifers. Kew: The Royal Botanic Gardens.

FITSCHEN, J. (2002): Gehölzflora (11. Aufl.). Wiebelsheim: Quelle und Meyer.

FRODIN, D. G., GOVAERTS, R. (1996): World Checklist and Bibliography of Magnoliaceae. Kew: The Royal Botanic Gardens.

GALLE, F. C. (1987): Azaleas. Portland: Timber Press.

– (1997): Hollies, The Genus Ilex. Portland: Timber Press.

GELDEREN, D. M. VAN, JONG, P. C. DE, OTERDAM, H. J. (1994): Maples ot the World. Portland: Timber Press.

GOVAERTS, R., FRODIN, D. G. (1998): World Checklist and Bibliography of Fagales. Kew: The Royal Botanic Gardens.

GREY-WILSON, C. (2000): Clematis – The Genus. London: B. T. Batsford Ltd.

HARKNESS, P. (1992): Rosen. Augsburg: Weltbild Verlag.

HARRISON, R. E. (1974): Handbook of Trees and Shrubs. Wellington, Sydney, London: A. H & A. W. Reed.

HILLIER, J. K. & J. (ed.) (1997): The Hillier Bäume & Sträucher. Braunschweig: Thalacker Medien.

KOLOC, K. (1961): So heißen die Werkhölzer. Handelsnamen - Botanische Namen. Leipzig.

KRÜSSMANN, G. (1976-1978): Handbuch der Laubgehölze (3 Bände). Berlin, Hamburg: Verlag Paul Parey.

– (1983): Handbuch der Nadelgehölze (2. Aufl.). Berlin, Hamburg: Verlag Paul Parey.

Lewis, J. (ed.) (1987–1998): The International Conifer Register, Part 1–4. London: The Royal Horticultural Society.

Little, E. L. (1971–1978): Atlas of United States trees (5 Vols.). Washington.

– (1979): Checklist of United States trees (native and naturalized). Washington.

McNaughton, V. (2000): Lavender – the Grower's Guide. Woodbridge: Garden Art Press.

Newsholme, C. (1992): The Genus Salix. London: B. T. Batsford Ltd.

Osti, G. L. (1999): The Book of Tree Peonies. Turin: Umberto Allemandy & C.

Palgrave, K. C. (1983): Trees of Southern Africa. Cape Town: C. Struik Publishers.

Phillips, R., Rix, M. (1989): Sträucher. München: Droemersche Verlagsanstalt.

Rehder, A. (1940): Manual of Cultivated Trees and Shrubs (2nd ed.). New York: The Macmillan Company.

– (1949): Bibliography of Cultivated Trees and Shrubs. Jamaica Plain (Mass.) : The Arnold Arboretum of Harvard University.

Roloff, A., Bärtels, A. (2006): Flora der Gehölze. Stuttgart: Verlag Eugen Ulmer.

Rose, P. Q. (1996): The Gardener's Guide to Growing Ivies. Portland: Timber Press.

Salley, H. E., Greer, H. E. (1992): Rhododendron Hybrids (2nd ed.). Portland: Timber Press.

Savige, T. J. (ed.) (1993): The International Camellia Register (2 Vols.). Wirlinga: International Camellia Society.

Schmidt, W. (1999): Gehölze für mediterrane Gärten (Hortus Mediterranus Bd. 2). Stuttgart: Verlag Eugen Ulmer.

Schultheis, H., H. & K. Urban (2006) Rosenlexikon mit CD-ROM. Bad Nauheim-Steinfurth, Frankfurt/M.

Schultze-Motel, J. (1966): Verzeichnis forstlich kultivierter Pflanzenarten. Die Kulturpflanze, Beiheft 4. Berlin.

Silva Tarouca, E., Schneider, C. (1922): Unsere Freiland-Laubgehölze (2. Aufl.). Leipzig: Verlag G. Freytag.

– – (1923): Unsere Freiland-Nadelgehölze (2. Aufl.). Leipzig: Verlag G. Freytag.

Snoeijer, W. (1996): Checklist of Clematis grown in Holland. Fopma, Boskoop, Netherlands, Privatdruck.

Spuy, U. van der (1976): South African Shrubs and Trees for the Garden. Johannesburg: Hugh Keartland Publishers.

Valder, P. (1995): Wisterias. Portland: Timber Press.

Welch, H., Haddow, G. (1993): The World Checklist of Conifers. Combe Martin: Landman's Bookshop.

Wrigley, J. W., Fagg, M. (1979): Australian Native Plants. Sidney, London: Collins.

Cultivated plants, cacti and succulents

Albers, F., U. Meve (2002): Sukkulenten-Lexikon Band 3: Asclepiadaceae. Stuttgart: Verlag Eugen Ulmer.

Anderson, E. F. (2001): The Cactus Family. Portland: Timber Press.

– (2005): Das große Kakteen-Lexikon. Stuttgart. Verlag Eugen Ulmer.

Backeberg, C. (1958–1962): Die Cactaceae (6. Bände). Jena: Gustav Fischer Verlag.

– (1970): Das Kakteenlexikon (2. Aufl.). Jena: Gustav Fischer Verlag.

Dicht, R., Lüthy, A. (2003): Coryphantha. Stuttgart. Verlag Eugen Ulmer.

Eggli, U., Taylor, N. (eds.) (1991): List of Cactaceae Names. Edinburgh: University Press.

Eggli, U. (1994): Sukkulenten. Stuttgart: Verlag Eugen Ulmer.

– (ed.) (2001): Sukkulenten-Lexikon Band 1: Einkeimblättrige Pflanzen. Stuttgart: Verlag Eugen Ulmer.

– (ed.) (2002): Sukkulenten-Lexikon Band 2: Zweikeimblättrige Pflanzen. Stuttgart: Verlag Eugen Ulmer.

– (ed.) (2003): Sukkulenten-Lexikon Band 4: Crassulaceae. Stuttgart: Verlag Eugen Ulmer.

GÖTZ, E., GRÖNER, G. (2000): Kakteen (7. Aufl.). Stuttgart: Verlag Eugen Ulmer.

HARTMANN, H.E.K. (2001): Illustrated Handbook of Succulent Plants: Aizoaceae (2 Vols.). Berlin, Heidelberg, New York: Springer Verlag.

IRISH, M. & F. (2000): Agaves, Yuccas and related Plants. Portland: Timber Press.

JACOBSEN, H. (1981): Das Sukkulentenlexikon (2. Aufl.). Stuttgart, New York: Gustav Fischer Verlag.

PRESTON MAFHAM, R. & K. (1992): Kakteen-Atlas. Stuttgart. Verlag Eugen Ulmer.

RAUH, W. (1979): Die großartige Welt der Sukkulenten (2. Aufl.). Berlin, Hamburg: Verlag Paul Parey.

RASCHIG, W. (1971): Die botanischen Kakteennamen. Ingelheim/Rhein: Stachelpost.

ROWLEY, G.D. (1980): Name that Sukkulent. Cheltenham: Stanley Thornes Publishers.

SAJEVA, M., COSTANZO, M. (2000): Succulents II. Portland: Timber Press.

TAYLOR, N. P. (1985): The Genus Echinocereus. Portland: Timber Press.

Cultivated plants, useful plants

BECKER, K., JOHN, S. (2000): Farbatlas Nutzpflanzen in Europa. Stuttgart: Verlag Eugen Ulmer.

BLANCKE, R. (2000): Farbatlas Exotische Früchte. Stuttgart: Verlag Eugen Ulmer.

BOWN, D. (1996): Du Mont's große Kräuterenzyklopädie. Köln: DuMont Buchverlag.

CHEVALLIER, A. (1998): Die BLV Enzyklopädie der Heilpflanzen. München, Wien, Zürich: BLV.

FRANKE, W. (1997): Nutzpflanzenkunde. Stuttgart, New York: Thieme Verlag.

GEISLER, G. (1991): Farbatlas Landwirtschaftliche Kulturpflanzen. Stuttgart: Verlag Eugen Ulmer.

HEEGER, E. F. (1956): Handbuch des Arznei- und Gewürzpflanzenbaues. Drogengewinnung. Berlin: Verlag Harri Deutsch.

HILLER, K., BICKERICH, G. (1988): Giftpflanzen. Leipzig, Jena, Berlin: Urania Verlag.

HOHENBERGER, E., CHRISTOPH, H.-J. (1998): Pflanzenheilkunde. Bad Wörishofen: Kneipp-Verlag.

HOPPE, H. A. (1958): Drogenkunde. 7. Auflage. Hamburg: Walter De Gruyter.

MANSFELD, R. (1986): Verzeichnis landwirtschaftlicher und gärtnerischer Kulturpflanzen (2. Aufl. herausgegeben von Schultze-Motel, 4 Bände). Berlin: Springer-Verlag.

MOSIG, A. (1961): Kurze Systematik der Arzneipflanzen (5. Aufl.). Dresden, Leipzig.

PAHLOW, M. (2001): Das große Buch der Heilpflanzen. Augsburg: Weltbild Verlag.

PHILLIPS, R., RIX, M. (1993): Vegetables. London. Pan Macmillan Publishers Ltd.

PURSEGLOVE, J. W. (1968): Tropical Crops. Dicotyledons. London: Longman.

– (1975): Tropical Crops. Monocotyledons. London: Longman.

ROTH, L., DUNDERER, M., KORMANN, K. (1994): Giftpflanzen, Pflanzengifte, 4. Aufl. Landsberg: ecomed.

SCHNEIDER, W., FREY, A. (1970): Drogenkunde (4. Aufl.). Darmstadt: O. Hoffmann.

SILBEREISEN, R., GÖTZ, G., HARTMANN, W. (1996): Obstsorten-Atlas. Stuttgart: Verlag Eugen Ulmer.

UPHOF, J. C. T. (1968): Dictionary of economic Plants (2nd ed.). Lehre: Verlag von J. Cramer.

VERMEULEN, N. (ohne Jahr): Die Enzyklopädie der Kräuter. Frechen: Komet Verlagsgesellschaft.

VOGEL, G. (1996): Handbuch des speziellen Gemüsebaues. Stuttgart: Verlag Eugen Ulmer.

VOTTELER, W. (1993): Verzeichnis der Apfel- und Birnensorten. München: Obst- und Gartenbauverlag.

– (1996): Lexikon der Obstsorten. München: Obst- und Gartenbauverlag.

WIERSEMA, J. H., LEÓN, B. (1999): World Economic Plants. Boca Raton, London, New York: CRC Press.

Cultivated plants, orchids

BAKER, M. L. & C. O. (1991): Orchid Species Culture: Pescatoria – Pleione. Portland: Timber Press.

– (1996): Orchid Species Culture: Dendrobium. Portland: Timber Press.

BAUMANN, H., KÜNKELE, S. (1988): Die Orchideen Europas. Stuttgart: Franckh'sche Verlagshandlung.

BAUMANN, H., KÜNKELE, S., LORENZ, R. (2006): Die Orchideen Europas mit angrenzenden Gebieten. Stuttgart: Verlag Eugen Ulmer.

BECHTEL, H. et al. (1980): Orchideenatlas. Stuttgart: Verlag Eugen Ulmer.

BOCKEMÜHL, L. (1989): Odontoglossum. Hildesheim: Brücke Verlag.

CRIBB, P. (1987): The Genus Paphiopedilum. Twickenham: Collingridge Books.

– (1997): The Genus Cypripedium. Portland: Timber Press.

– BUTTERFIELD, J. (1998): The Genus Pleione. Portland: Timber Press.

CULLEN, J. (1992): The Orchid Book. Cambridge: University Press.

DELFORGE, P. (1995): Orchids of Britain and Europe. London: Harper Collins Publishers.

DRESSLER, R. L. (1993): Phylogeny and Classification of the Orchid Family. Cambridge: University Press.

GRUSS, O., WOLFF, M. (1995): Phalaenopsis. Stuttgart: Verlag Eugen Ulmer.

JONES, D. L. (1994): Native Orchids of Australia. Canberra: REED.

KRUETZ, C.A.J. (2004): Kompendium der Europäischen Orchideen. Landgraaf: Kreutz Publishers.

PRESSER, H. (2002): Orchideen – Die Orchideen Mitteleuropas und der Alpen (2. Aufl.). Hamburg: Nikol Verlagsgesellschaft.

PRIDGEON, A. M. et al. (eds.) (1999–2005): Genera Orchidacearum Vol. 1–4. Oxford: University Press.

PRIDGEON, A. M. (ed.) (1992): The Illustrated Encyclopedia of Orchids. Portland: Timber Press.

SCHLECHTER, R. (1971–*): Die Orchideen (3. Aufl.). Berlin, Hamburg. Verlag Paul Parey.

SHEEHAN, T. & M. (1994): An illustrated Survyey of the Orchid Genera. Cambridge: University Press.

Cultivated plants, perennial herbs and summer flowers

BECKETT, K. (ed.) (1993): AGS Encyclopaedia of Alpines (2 Vols.). Pershore: AGS Publications.

CASE, F. W. & R. B. (1997): Trilliums. Portland: Timber Press.

CLEBSCH, B. (1997): A Book of Salvias. Portland: Timber Press.

CLIFTON, R. T. F. (ed.) (1995): Geranium Family Species Check List Part 2: Geranium. Dover: The Geraniaceae Group.

COBB, J. L. S. (1989): Meconopsis. Portland: Timber Press.

ERHARDT, W. (1988): Hemerocallis - Taglilien. Stuttgart: Verlag Eugen Ulmer.

EVANS, R. L. (1983): Handbook of Cultivated Sedum. Northwood, Middlesex: Science Reviews Limited.

FUCHS, H. (1994): Phlox. Stuttgart: Verlag Eugen Ulmer.

GREY-WILSON, C. (1989): The Genus Dionysia. Woking: Alpine Garden Society.

– (1993): Poppies. London: B. T. Batsford Ltd.

HALDA, J. J. (1996): The Genus Gentiana. Dobré: SEN.

HANSEN, R., STAHL, F. (1997): Die Stauden und ihre Lebensbereiche in Gärten und Grünanlagen (5. Aufl.). Stuttgart: Verlag Eugen Ulmer.

HERBEL, D. (1992): Sommerblumen. Stuttgart: Verlag Eugen Ulmer.

HIELSCHER, A., (1986): Sommerblumen in Wort und Bild (3. Aufl.). Leipzig, Radebeul: Neumann Verlag.

KAISER, K. (1995): Anemonen. Stuttgart: Verlag Eugen Ulmer.

KÖHLEIN, F. (1984): Primeln. Stuttgart: Verlag Eugen Ulmer.

– (1990): Nelken. Stuttgart: Verlag Eugen Ulmer.

– Menzel, P. (1992): Das neue große Blumenbuch. Stuttgart: Verlag Eugen Ulmer.

– (1994): Das große Buch der Steingartenpflanzen. Stuttgart: Verlag Eugen Ulmer.

– (1995): Saxifragen (2. Aufl.). Stuttgart: Verlag Eugen Ulmer.

Lidén, M., Zetterlund, H. (1997): Corydalis. Pershore: AGS Publications.

Lodewick, R. & K. (1999): Key to the Genus Penstemon and its related Genera in the Tribe Cheloneae. Oregon: Privatdruck.

Mathew, B. (1989): The Genus Lewisia. Portland: Timber Press.

McGergor, M. (1995): Saxifrages – The Complete Cultivars and Hybrids. The Saxifrage Society.

McGergor, M., Harding, W. (1998): Saxifrages – The Complete List of Species. The Saxifrage Society.

Phillips, R., Rix, M. (1992): Stauden. München: Droemersche Verlagsanstalt.

Rice, G., Strangman, E. (1993): The Gardener's Guide to Growing Hellebores. Newton Abbot: David & Charles.

Riviere, M. (1996): Prachtvolle Päonien. Stuttgart: Verlag Eugen Ulmer.

Schacht, W., Fessler, A. (eds.) (1985): Die Freiland-Schmuckstauden (3. Aufl.). Stuttgart. Verlag Eugen Ulmer.

Schmid, W. G. (1991): The Genus Hosta. Portland: Timber Press.

Schöllkopf, W. (1995): Astern. Stuttgart: Verlag Eugen Ulmer.

Silva Tarouca, E., Schneider, C. (1934): Unsere Freilandstauden (5. Aufl.). Leipzig: Verlag G. Freytag.

Smith, G., Lowe, D. (1997): The Genus Androsace. Pershore: AGS Pubilcations Ltd.

Species Group of the British Iris Society (1997): A Guide to Species Irises. Cambridge: University Press.

Stephenson, R. (1999): Sedum. Portland: Timber Press.

Trehane, P. (1989): Index Hortensis, Vol. 1: Perennials. Wimborne: Quarterjack Publishing.

Webb, D. A., Gornall, R. J. (1989): Saxifrages of Europe. London: Christopher Helm.

Yeo, P. F. (1988): Geranium. Stuttgart: Verlag Eugen Ulmer.

Cultivated plants, tropical plants, tub and indoor plants

Baensch, U. & U. (1994): Blühende Bromelien. Nassau, Bahamas: Tropic beauty Publishers.

Bärtels, A. (2000): Farbatlas Tropenpflanzen (4. Aufl.). Stuttgart: Verlag Eugen Ulmer.

Barthlott, W. et al. (2004): Karnivoren. Stuttgart: Verlag Eugen Ulmer.

Bergen, M. van, Snoeijer, W. (1996): Catharanthus. Leiden: Backhuys Publishers.

Blancke, R. (1999): Farbatlas Pflanzen der Karibik und Mittelamerikas. Stuttgart: Verlag Eugen Ulmer.

Bloombery, A., T. Rodd (1982): Palms. London, Sidney, Melbourne: Angus & Robertson Publishers.

Boom. B. K. (1968): Flora von Kamer- en Kasplanten. Wageningen.

Boullemier, L. B. (ed.) (1985): The Checklist of Species, Hybrids and Cultivars of the Genus Fuchsia. Poole: Blandford Press.

Clifton, R. T. F. (ed.) (1999): Geranium Family Species Check List Part 4: Pelargonium. Dover: The Geraniaceae Group.

Courtright, G. (1988): Tropicals. Portland: Timber Press.

Elison, D.R. (1995): Cultivated Plants of the World. Trees, Shrubs and Climbers. Brisbane: Flora Publications International Pty. Ltd.

Encke, F. (1987): Kalt- und Warmhauspflanzen (2. Aufl.). Stuttgart: Verlag Eugen Ulmer.

Erhardt, W. & A. (1993): Schöne Usambaraveilchen und andere Gesnerien. Stuttgart: Verlag Eugen Ulmer.

Graf, A. B. (1963): Exotica III. Pictoral Cyclopedia of Indoor Plants. Rutherford.

– (1978): Tropica, Color Cyclopedia of Exotic Plants and Trees for the Tropics and Subtropics. East Rutherford, N. J, USA: Roehrs Company Publishers.

HILLIARD, O. M., BURTT, B. L. (1971): Streptocarpus. Pietermaritzburg: University of Natal Press.

JONES, D. L. (1965): Cycads of the World. Chatswood: REED.

– (2000): Palmen. Köln: Könemann Verlagsgesellschaft.

KAWOLLEK, W. (1995): Kübelpflanzen. Stuttgart: Verlag Eugen Ulmer.

KÖCHEL, C. (2000): Oleander. Stuttgart: Verlag Eugen Ulmer.

KÖHLEIN, F. (1997): Die Haus und Kübelpflanzen. Stuttgart: Verlag Eugen Ulmer.

LLAMAS, K.L. (2003): Tropical Flowering Plants. Portland, Cambridge: Timber Press.

MILLER, D. (1996): Pelargoniums. London: B. T. Batsford Ltd.

MOORE JR., H. E. (1957): African Violets, Gloxinias and their relatives. New York: Macmillan Company.

PHILLIPS, R., RIX, M. (1997): Conservatory and Indoor Plants (2 Vols.). London: Macmillan Publishers Ltd.

PREISSEL, U. & H.-G. (1997): Engelstrompeten - Brugmansia und Datura. Stuttgart: Verlag Eugen Ulmer.

RAUH, W. (1990): Bromelien (3. Aufl.). Stuttgart: Verlag Eugen Ulmer.

RÜCKER, K. (1998): Die Pflanzen im Haus (2. Aufl.). Stuttgart: Verlag Eugen Ulmer.

SLACK, A. (1995): Karnivoren. Stuttgart: Verlag Eugen Ulmer.

ULMER, B. & T. (1997): Passionsblumen – Eine faszinierende Gattung. Witten: Privatdruck.

Cultivated plants, aquatic plants

HORST, K. (1986): Pflanzen im Aquarium. Stuttgart: Verlag Eugen Ulmer.

KASSELMANN, C. (1995): Aquarienpflanzen. Stuttgart: Verlag Eugen Ulmer.

KRAUSCH, H.-D. (1996): Farbatlas Wasser- und Uferpflanzen. Stuttgart: Verlag Eugen Ulmer.

PASCHER, A. (1980–1981): Süßwasserflora von Mitteleuropa. Band 23–24. Stuttgart, New York: Verlag Gustav Fischer.

RIEHL, R., BAENSCH, H. A. (2001): Aquarien Atlas Band 1 (13. Aufl.) Melle: Mergus Verlag.

SLOCUM, P. D., ROBINSON, P. (1996): Water Gardening – Water Lilies and Lotuses. Portland: Timber Press.

WACHTER, K. (1993): Der Wassergarten. (7. Aufl.). Stuttgart: Verlag Eugen Ulmer.

– (1998): Seerosen. Stuttgart: Verlag Eugen Ulmer.

Cultivated plants, bulbous and tuberous plants

BOTSCHANTZEVA, Z. P. (1982) Tulips. Rotterdam: A. A. Balkema.

BOYCE, P. (1993): The Genus Arum. london: HMSO.

BRYAN, J. E. (1989):. Bulbs (2 Vols.). Portland: Timber Press.

COOKE, J. (2001): The Gardener's Guide to Growing Cannas. Newton Abbot: David & Charles.

DAVIS, D. (1992): Allium. Stuttgart: Verlag Eugen Ulmer.

DAVIS, P. A. (1999): The Genus Galanthus. Portland: Timber Press.

ERHARDT, W. (1993): Narzissen. Stuttgart: Verlag Eugen Ulmer.

FELDMEIAER, C., McRAE, J. (1982): Lilien (2. Aufl.). Stuttgart: Verlag Eugen Ulmer.

FRANK, R. (1986): Zwiebel- und Knollengewächse. Stuttgart: Verlag Eugen Ulmer.

GOLDBLATT, P. (1986): Gladiolus in Tropical Africa. Portland: Timber Press.

– (1989): The Genus Watsonia. Kirstenbosch: National Botanic Garden.

GREY-WILSON, C. (1988): The Genus Cyclamen. Portland: Timber Press.

GRUNERT, C. (1980): Das Blumenzwiebelbuch. Stuttgart: Verlag Eugen Ulmer.

JEFFERSON-BROWN, M., HOWLAND, H. (1995): The Gardener's Guide to Growing Lilies. Newton Abbot: David & Charles.

KINGTON, S. (ed.) (1998): The International Daffodil Register and Classified List 1998. London: The Royal Horticultural Society.

MATHEW, B. (1982): The Crocus. London: B. T. Batsford Ltd.

PHILLIPS, R., RIX, M. (1989): Bulbs. London: Pan Books.

PRATT, K., JEFFERSON-BROWN, M. (1997): The Gardener's Guide to Growing Fritillaries. Newton Abbot: David & Charles.

ROWLANDS, G. (1999): The Gardener's Guide to Growing Dahlias. Newton Abbot: David & Charles.

SCHEEPEN, J. VAN. (ed.) (1996): Classified List and International Register of Tulip Names. Hillegom: KAVB.

SNIJMAN, D. (1984): The Genus Haemanthus. Kirstenbosch: National Botanic Gardens.

SYNGE, P. M. (1973): Collin's Guide to Bulbs. London: Book Club Associates.

Journals

Gartenpraxis – Ulmers Pflanzenmagazin. Stuttgart: Verlag Eugen Ulmer.

TAXON – International Journal of Plant Taxonomy, Phylogeny and Evolution. Washington: Smithsonian Institution.

The Garden – Journal of the Royal Horicultural Society. London: Royal Horicultural Society

The New Plantsman. London: Royal Horticultural Society.

CD-ROMs

BÖDEKER, N., KIERMEIER, P. (1999): Plantus (2. Aufl.). Stuttgart: Verlag Eugen Ulmer.

BUDDENSIEK, V. (1999): The Succulent Euphorbias.

BURKHARD, I. (2000): Die Rosen-Datenbank (Vers. 4).

DIETZE, P., BEER, H. et al. (2000): Gehölze für Garten und Landschaft. Stuttgart: Verlag Eugen Ulmer.

– – et al. (2001): Sommerblumen und Stauden. Stuttgart: Verlag Eugen Ulmer.

ERHARDT, A. & W. (2000): PPP-Index – Pflanzeneinkaufsführer für Europa (4. Aufl.). Stuttgart: Verlag Eugen Ulmer.

GIESEL, O. (1999): Agaven 1.0 – Bromelia 1.0 – Stapelia 1.0.

GÖTZ, E. (2003): Pflanzen bestimmen mit dem PC. Stuttgart: Verlag Eugen Ulmer.

GÖTZ, H., HÄUSSERMANN, M., SIEBER, J. (2006.): Stauden-CD (4. Aufl.) Stuttgart: Verlag Eugen Ulmer.

SEYBOLD, S. et al. (eds.) (2001): Schmeil-Fitschen interaktiv. Die umfassende Bestimmungs- und Informationsdatenbank der Pflanzenwelt Deutschlands und angrenzender Länder. Wiebelsheim: Verlag Quelle u. Meyer.

STOCKDALE, J. (2000): RHS Plant Finder 1999–2000. Lewes: The Plant Finder.

Recommended internet sites

http://apps.kew.org/wcsp/home.do: World Checklist of Selected Plant Families

www.ars-grin.gov/cgi-bin/npgs/html/index.pl?language=de: GRIN Taxonomie der Pflanzen

www.efloras.org: Florenwerke

http://homepages.caverock.net.nz/~bj/fern/list.htm: Liste der Farne und Farnverwandten

www.ipni.org: The International Plant Names Index

www.kew.org/data/grasses-db.html: The Online World Grass Flora

http://mobot.mobot.org/W3T/Search/vast.html: The Missouri Botanical Gardener's Vascular Tropicos

www.paeon.de/name/index.html: Carsten Burkhardts Päonien-Datenbank (Web Project Paeonia)

http://plantnet.rbgsyd.nsw.gov.au/PlantNet/cycad/index.html: The Cycad Pages

www.rhs.org.uk/plants/index.asp: Verschiedene Datenbanken der Royal Horticultural Society

www.thater.net/cactaceae/db: Kakteen-Datenbank

www.watergardenersinternational.org/waterlilies/main.html: Water Gardeners International

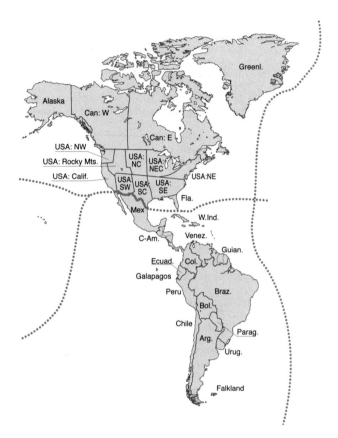

Alaska

Greenl.

Can: W

Can: E

USA: NW

USA: NC

USA: NEC

USA: Rocky Mts.

USA: Calif.

USA: SW

USA: SC

USA: SE

USA:NE

Fla.

Mex

W.Ind.

C-Am.

Venez.

Guian.

Ecuad.

Col.

Galapagos

Peru

Braz.

Bol.

Chile

Arg.

Parag.

Urug.

Falkland

Br. I

Sc

E-Eur.

W-Sib.

E-Sib.

Kamchat.

C-Eur.

EC-Eur.

Fr.

C-As.

Amur

Sakhal.

Ib.

Ital-P

Ba

Mong.

Macaron

Cauc.

TR

Jap.

Levant

Iraq

Afgh.

China

Korea

Iran

N-Afr.

Indian
Sub.-C

Taiwan

Cap
Verde

W-Sah.

Arab.

Sudan

Indo-
china

Phil.

Eth.

Malay.
Pen.

W-Afr.

C-Afr.

E-Afr.

Malay.
Arch.

N.Guinea

Solom.

trop.-Afr.

Mascarene Is.

N.
Terr.

Queensl.

Madag.

W-
Aust.

S-
Aust.

S-Afr.

N.S.Wales

Victoria

Tasman.

NZ